BERNARD SHAW

Collected Letters

1898–1910

(Photograph by Charlotte F. Shaw, 1910)

BERNARD SHAW

Collected Letters
1898-1910

EDITED BY DAN H. LAURENCE

MAX REINHARDT

LONDON SYDNEY

TORONTO

Printed and bound in Great Britain for
Max Reinhardt Ltd
9 Bow Street, Covent Garden, London WC2E 7AL
by William Clowes & Sons Ltd, Beccles
Set in Monotype Ehrhardt
First published 1972

For Doris and Jack
and for
Jo and Michael,
with the Editor's affection

Contents

Contents

Illustrations

PLATES

LINE ILLUSTRATIONS IN TEXT

Introduction

Bernard Shaw wrote to be understood. Clarity was a primary consideration, and the letters he produced contain some of the most lucid writing in the English language since Swift. His energetic prose is rhythmic, ardent, coruscating with wit. Its spontaneity seems to indicate that the author loved first thoughts best. And these thoughts most often are presented colloquially, for Shaw said he "came to seek idiom as being the most highly vitalised form of language." He made free use of Americanisms ("deadheads," "mugwump"); boxing terms ("ask the Chief Rabbi to weigh in"); wrestling terms ("the flying mare"). He coined a new word, "Superman," in preference to the literal "Overman" translation of Nietzsche's "Übermensch." In 1900, immediately following the hysterical joy that accompanied news of the relief of Mafeking from the Boer siege, Shaw converted the emotion into a verb, "mafficking." In 1904, in a letter to *The Times* on the subject of political electioneering by the Church, he argued that, although it was quite Protestant and independent and proper, still, regarded as electioneering, "it is not cricket."

He claimed never to have aimed consciously at style in his writing. Style, he said, is "a sort of melody that comes into my sentences by itself." The aim of a writer, he declared, is "to be able to write as a laborer digs or a carpenter planes, without any preoccupation with the technical process." To develop one's literary powers one has only to "write a thousand words a day for ten years . . . [and] keep on trying to express yourself as accurately as possible and to suggest the feeling as well as convey the facts." The result, as H. M. Tomlinson recognised in 1919, is a "rare and dynamic language, as straight as a ray of light, such as we get once or twice in a few centuries, as the result of passionate morality that happens to be gifted with the complete control of full expression."

And the range of Shaw's curiosities, John Mason Brown noted, "was so prodigious that the sun never set on his interests." He was interested in everything—because everything was interesting. With insatiable curiosity and tireless enthusiasm Shaw throughout his long life explored the myriad subjects reflected in his correspondence: penology, photography, architecture, psychic research, bee-keeping, calligraphy, oriental philosophy, archæology, cremation, puppetry, pugilism, anti-pollution, musical pitch, nitrogenous food diets, totalisators, tree nurseries, alphabet reform.

Jung charged that Shaw, far from being a sage, was yet a child, a Peter Pan who managed to evade real experience. Interestingly, Shaw had long since confessed to an extended adolescence, in a letter to Erica Cotterill in 1907: "I have never yet been able to feel grown up . . . the child remains there all the time." This perennial youthfulness was really symptomatic of the age, applying equally, I think, to such contemporaries as Kipling, Chesterton, Barrie, and Wells. The social and intellectual climate at the beginning of the new century inspirited imaginative men, and the resilient, ever-young Shaw delighted equally in the new ideas and the new toys. His writing abounded with ideas—and with impishness. "His knowledge of his subject is thorough," wrote an anonymous critic in the *New York Times* in 1894, "but he is fond of being at war with his fellow-men, especially those among them who are attached to traditions and conventions. He likes to shock his public. But his oddity is not mere affectation. Mr. Shaw has an extremely original mind, but it is a strong mind, too. His view of things may be as queer as Claude Monet's, to whom the grass is pink and the sky is purple, but like the great impressionist, he has that force of character which makes the thinking man, who believes in green grass and blue sky, pause and wonder if he has been wrong all his life."

Equally apparent is the childlike fascination with modern devices—both in Shaw's correspondence and in his use of gadgetry in the plays: a typewriter (*Candida*, 1895), a dentist's electric drill (*You Never Can Tell*, 1896), an open touring car (*Man and Superman*, 1903), a portable Turkish bath—and an offstage aeroplane crash (*Misalliance*, 1910), a television telephone (*Back to Methuselah*, 1921). He was drawn to the safety bicycle the instant it came into vogue in England in the mid-1890's; at the turn of the century he acquired a tandem and, in 1913, a Lea and Francis motor bike. He made a balloon ascent in 1906, and experienced his first plane flight a decade later. In 1909 he joined the Aeronautical Society of Great Britain; in 1947 he became the oldest member of the British Interplanetary Society.

Shaw's epistolary art, like his dramatic art, was essentially a comic one. "It is just as easy," he asserted, "to make a comedy of [a situation] as a tragedy." All genuinely intellectual work, he informed Florence Farr, is humorous. In his correspondence, as in his plays, Shaw took the measure of human nature, of social imperfection, and of human and social potentialities, as Swift had done, by employment of the devices of paradox, anti-climax, and exaggeration. "It is always necessary," he said, "to overstate a case startlingly to make people sit up and listen to it and to frighten them into acting on it." His letters, consequently, were crowded with "grim absurdities" which, in turn, were succeeded by "sane conclusions," for Shaw's comedy was a comedy of purpose. As G. K. Chesterton indicated in *Heretics*, "A man cannot be wise enough to be a great artist without being wise enough to wish to be a philosopher." To Shaw the great significance of art was that "it forms our ideas, and finally forms our ambitions and the human conscience."

The present volume contains 644 letters, two-thirds of which are hitherto unpublished, while a considerable number of the remainder have previously been published in extract only. In their preparation the same editorial procedures enumerated in the introduction to Volume 1 have been followed. In the second volume I have not infrequently performed drastic surgery on those letters which contained repetitive, trifling, or extraneous materials. The deletions are indicated conventionally, by ellipsis marks. In several instances I have also lopped off insignificant postscripts. I do not believe that any of these abridgments or truncations result in distortion, obfuscation, or concealment.

As the introduction to Volume 1 had included a comprehensive statement of my working methods, and of the rules which governed the editing of Shaw's letters, I was astonished to discover, when I read the critical notices (most of them favourable), that a number of the reviewers either had not troubled to peruse the introduction, or, worse, had declined to take my "first aid to critics" at face value. One London newspaper critic, for example, lamented that "the editor . . . makes poor Shaw lapse into errors that seem improbable . . . In a book apparently addressed to academic readers such little slips are unexpected." Improbable or not, the culprit was *not* the editor. Like his Elizabethan counterpart, Shaw was blithely unconcerned about orthographic consistencies and niceties. He doubled consonants or halved them, with impartial abandon, and incessantly omitted vowels, with the result that his correspondence is strewn with such exotic formations as "quarrell," "parrallel," "suddeness," "noticable," "withold," and "wheras." All of these, as explained in the earlier introduction, are reproduced in the text exactly as originally written. Doubtless I might have spared myself some criticism by peppering the text with square-bracketed *sics* to indicate every Shavian departure from the norm, but as I had also been accused by a few reviewers of the cardinal sin of pedantry, for one reason or another, without having resorted to this tactic, what might have been said if I had added this *sic*-ness to all my other faults? It should further be noted that Shaw managed to misspell virtually every proper name he encountered (to such a degree, in fact, that in the dedication to *The Intelligent Woman's Guide to Socialism* in 1928 he misspelled the name of his sister-in-law Mary Cholmondeley), and was quite capable of offering two variant spellings within a single sentence. The reviewers might have noted that, in such instances, the correct spelling always was supplied by the editor, unobtrusively, in the headnotes preceding the letters.

Admittedly, there *were* flaws in Volume I, though few of them were of a serious nature, only two textual misreadings and two genuine typographical errors having come to light in the six years since the volume first appeared. I am grateful to Mr Brian Best, Mr Hugh Brogan, Professor Martin Meisel, Professor Richard Nickson, and Mr Henry M. Pelling for calling these and a few significant factual errors to my attention. I have sought to make amends by incorporating a list of corrections and additions for Volume I at the end of the present volume. If a comparable list at the end of the next volume proves unnecessary, it will be due in large part to the patient, painstaking proofreading of the galleys of Volume II by Mr Raymond Mander and Mr Joe Mitchenson (who also provided several superb illustrations from their incomparable theatre collection), Professor Frederick McDowell, and Mr M. H. Mushlin. Mr Ernest Mehew, who kindly read a portion of the page proofs, also made some excellent suggestions.

My greatest indebtedness, however, and not for the first time, is to my dear friend Sir Rupert Hart-Davis, whose thorough scrutiny of the page proofs resulted in the elimination of several inexcusable gaffes. I am grateful also to Lady Hart-Davis for her generosity in providing neatly typed reports of Sir Rupert's criticisms and suggestions.

Other friends who have been equally magnanimous include Mrs Mary Hirth, the recently retired librarian of the Academic Center, University of Texas at Austin; Mr A. D. Holland, former Superintendent of the Reading Room, British Museum Newspaper Library at Colindale; and Mr Bernard Burgunder, whose Shaw collection at Cornell University (the second largest in the United States) has been an invaluable source of information.

Volume II was to have included a statement by Cyril Hogg, longtime managing director of Messrs Samuel French Ltd, London, as a rebuttal to Shaw's criticisms (published in Volume I) of the firm's rates of commission and methods of operation. Mr Hogg died, however, before he could complete his statement, and the present management has indicated that it "does not feel it has suffered in any way adversely from the comments made, and is very happy to release Professor Laurence from any obligation in the matter."

For permitting me to publish copyright material I should like to express my appreciation to Mrs Eva Reichmann for extracts from letters by Max Beerbohm; the late Mrs William Butler Yeats for extracts from a letter by Yeats; Miss Nancy Archer for extracts from letters by William Archer; Messrs Methuen & Co. for an extract from a letter from Methuen's; Messrs John Murray for an extract from a letter by John Murray; Messrs Allen & Unwin for extracts from letters by Gilbert Murray; Mr Alexander R. James for extracts from letters by Henry James, and Dr Leon Edel for permission to quote these passages from *The Complete Plays of Henry James*; Messrs Macmillan (New York) for extracts from letters by George P. Brett; Professor G. P. Wells for extracts from letters by H. G. Wells; Mr Arthur Leonard Ross for an extract from a letter by Frank Harris; Mr Bill Shine for an extract from a letter by J. L. Shine; Messrs Samuel French (London) for extracts from letters by Sir Arthur W. Pinero; and the Estate of Mrs Patrick Campbell for the letters of Shaw to Mrs Patrick Campbell.

I have previously acknowledged in Volume I the valuable aid of more than 150 individuals and institutions, many of whom have given me as much help with Volume II as with the earlier volume. To this roll I should like now to add the names of the following, with thanks for the loan or gift of letters, transcriptions, photocopies, books, newspaper cuttings, and associated papers, or for information or research assistance, and numerous other courtesies in the preparation of Volume II for publication:

Professor Sidney Albert; Miss Anna Brooke Allan, Curator of Manuscripts, University of North Carolina; Miss Maxine Audley; Mr R. F. Ayling; Miss Jennifer Aylmer of the British Theatre Museum; Miss Alixe Bartley; the late Edith Livia Beatty; Mr J. Terry Bender, Special Collections Librarian, Hofstra University; Mr Victor Bonham-Carter of the Society of Authors; Mr Albert Boni; Mrs Ursula Bridge; the late Lord Bridges; Mr Charles T. Butler; Mr William Cagle of the Lilly Library, Indiana University; Mr Herbert Cahoon of the J.P. Morgan Library; Mr Richard Cary of the Colby College Library; Mrs Mary Ceibert of the University of Illinois Library; Mr James Clifford;

Miss Dorothy E. Collins; Mr Eustace Cornelius, Librarian of the Royal College of Surgeons; Mr James C. Cox of the Cudahy Memorial Library, Loyola University (Chicago); Professor Louis Crompton; Mr Alan Denson; Mr Alan Dent; Miss Margaret Digby of the Sir Horace Plunkett Foundation; Dr R.B.Downs, Dean of Library Administration, University of Illinois; the late Philip C. Duschnes.

Professor Donald D.Eddy, Curator of the Bernard Burgunder Collection of Shaw and Rare Books Librarian, Cornell University Library; Docent Torsten Eklund; Mrs Lovelle Felt of the Missouri Historical Society; Mr Robert Flanders; Mr Eric Ford of the H. G. Wells Society; Miss Adele Freedman; Dr Tue Gard of the Royal Library, Copenhagen; Mr Richard Garnett; Mr Elmer Gertz; Major and Mrs Richard Gregory; Dr Theodore Grieder, Curator of the Fales Collection, New York University; Mr Miron Grindea, editor of *Adam*; Miss Christine D.Hathaway, Special Collections Librarian, Brown University; Mr Allen Hazen; Mr Frank Q.Helms, Director of Library Services, West Chester State College, Pa.; Professor James Hepburn; Mr Brian Hill; Mr Robert W.Hill, Keeper of Manuscripts, New York Public Library; Mr Michael Holroyd; Mr Michael Howard; the late Donald F.Hyde and Mrs Mary Hyde.

Mrs A.M.E.Jackson; Mr Thomas J.Jackson of Southern Illinois University Library; Mr Tom Jaine of the National Register of Archives; Mr A.Jeffcott, former Reference Librarian of Highgate Library; Professor Josephine Johnson; Mr Stanley J.Kauffmann; Professor Norman Kelvin; Miss Mary E.Klausner, Archivist, Grinnell College Library; the late Sir Allen Lane of Penguin Books Ltd; Mr Tony Latham of the Gabrielle Enthoven Collection, Victoria and Albert Museum; Miss Lesley Macdonald of the Society of Authors; Mr Roger Machell; Mr William R.Maidment, Borough of Camden (London) Librarian; Dr Ellsworth Mason, Director, Hofstra University Library; Mr Francis O.Mattson of the Berg Collection, New York Public Library; Miss Gwyneth McCleary, O.B.E.; Mr Ralph E. McCoy, Director, Southern Illinois University Library; Mr E.Merrett, Librarian of the *Daily Express*; Mr Michael Meyer; Mr James Michie of the Bodley Head; the late George Middleton; Mrs Maxine Miles; Mr Hugh Miller; Mr George Milne; Mrs Rietta Sturge Moore; Mr J.Morpurgo; the late Lily Mortlake; Mr Malcolm Muggeridge.

Dr Otto Nathan, Executor of the Albert Einstein Estate; Mr Beaumont Newhall, former Director of George Eastman House; Mrs J.M.Patterson, Secretary of the Royal Society of Literature; Mr B.Iden Payne; Mr Philip Phillips of *The Sun* (London); Mr David

Posner; the late C.B.Purdom; Mr Kenneth Rae, Secretary of the National Theatre (London); Mr David A.Randall, Director of the Lilly Library, Indiana University; Mr Michael Rhodes; Mr D.T. Richnell, Librarian, and Mr T.D.Rogers of the Goldsmiths' Library, University of London; Mr Arthur Leonard Ross; Mr H.F.Rubinstein. Mrs R.Schilling; Professor Charles H.Shattuck; Mr Paul G.Sifton of the Library of Congress; Mr Colin Smythe; Mr and Mrs Irwin Strasburger; Dr Felix F.Strauss; Dr Lola Szladits, Curator of the Henry W. and Albert A.Berg Collection, New York Public Library; Mrs Dorothy Thornycroft; the Editor of the *Times Literary Supplement*; Mr D.G.Vaisey, Department of Western Manuscripts, Bodleian Library; Mrs Margot Wade; Mrs Mary Manning Wale of Mills College Library (Oakland); Mr Lawrence Wallrich; Mr J.P.Wearing of University College, Swansea; the late Carl J.Weber; Mrs Lois P. Weisberg; Mrs M.Barbara Welch; Mr Victor Wittkowski; Mr Edward J.Wood.

I am indebted also to the staffs of the following institutions and organisations: Danish Information Office, New York; House of Lords Record Office; Kungliga Biblioteket, Stockholm; Manchester (England) Public Library; Mary Ward Settlement (formerly Passmore Edwards Settlement); Max-Reinhardt-Forschungs- und Gedenkstätte, Salzburg; National Register of Archives (London); New York Public Library Theatre Collection; Osgoode Hall Law Library; Public Records Office (London); St Louis Public Library; Salvation Army (London); San Antonio Public Library; University of California at Berkeley, General Library; University of California at Los Angeles, Research Library; University of Iowa Library; University of Kansas Library; University of Keele Library; University of Pennsylvania Library; University of Rochester Library; University of Victoria Library.

At the British Museum I have had the co-operation of the following past and present staff members: *Bloomsbury*—Mr John Mackenzie, Miss C.H.Olorenshaw, Dr Dennis Rhodes, Mr Derek Turner; *Colindale*—Mr George Goossens, Superintendent of the Reading Room, and Mr Bert Boyles, Mr George Evans, Mr Bernard Giusti, Mr Derek Shepherd.

At the Academic Center of the University of Texas I should like to thank the new librarian, Mrs June Moll, and the following past and present staff members: Mrs Dortha Collins, Dr David Farmer, Mr Morris Fry, Mrs Claire Hamilton, Mrs Lois Garcia, Mr John Kirkpatrick, Mr Eugene Lillard, Mrs Kate Macmillan, Mrs Betty Murphy,

Mr John R. Payne, Mrs Pat Wright. I am also indebted to the following student assistants and pages: Miss Suzette Calvillo, Miss Alice Lynch, Mr Mike Norman, Miss Ann Pickell, and Mr Paul Sullivan.

I have also had the enthusiastic assistance of several of my graduate and undergraduate students—Dr Jerald Bringle, Mr Roger Geyer (and his wife Mary), Miss Carol Gottuso, Mr Raymond Levites, Dr Howard Pechefsky, Mr Syd Smithline (and his wife Janet), and Mr Alan Weinblatt—who have performed such useful tasks as researching newspaper files, typing transcriptions of letters from photocopies, making paste-ups of previously published correspondence, and collating texts. Special acknowledgment must be made of the contribution of my student Peter Schuyten, who, while in Hong Kong, discovered and made copies of Shaw's letters to Sir Robert Ho Tung, which will appear in a subsequent volume.

This volume, like its predecessor, has benefited substantially from the award by the John Simon Guggenheim Foundation of a Guggenheim Fellowship in 1960–61, and by the gift of two grants-in-aid by New York University from the Arts and Science Research Fund. It has also been aided by two generous grants from the Estate of George Bernard Shaw.

Finally, I should like to thank those readers who responded to my appeal in Volume I for reports of any Shaw correspondence known to them which might not otherwise have come to my attention. I should be grateful for further reports, addressed to me in care of the Bodley Head, 9 Bow Street, London WC2E 7AL.

DAN H. LAURENCE

San Antonio, Texas.
November 1971

Code to description of correspondence

A Holograph letter
B Holograph letter-card
C Holograph postcard
D Holograph correspondence card
E Holograph note or "Compliments of Bernard Shaw" enclosure card
F Shorthand draft or copy
FF Shorthand draft in holograph of secretary
G Holograph draft or copy
H Typewritten letter
I Typewritten draft
J Typewritten letter-card
K Typewritten postcard
L Dictated letter, in holograph of Charlotte Shaw, signed by Shaw
M Dictated letter-card, in holograph of Charlotte Shaw, signed by Shaw
N Dictated postcard, in holograph of Charlotte Shaw, signed by Shaw
P Dictated letter, in holograph of secretary, signed by Shaw
Q Dictated letter-card, in holograph of secretary, signed by Shaw
R Dictated postcard, in holograph of secretary, signed by Shaw
S Transcription: original unlocated
T Transcription: original located but unavailable for examination
U Photographic reproduction: original unlocated
V Photographic reproduction: original located but unavailable for examination
W Facsimile publication
X Published text
Y Telegram
YY Cablegram or radiogram
c Carbon copy
f Fragment
ss Signed by secretary
t Typed signature
u Unsigned

Code to sources of
ownership of letters in this volume

NOTE

*The placement of an " e " after a code number in the
body of this work indicates that, in prior publication,
only an extract or abridged text of the letter
has appeared.*

1   Privately owned
2   British Museum
3   General Collections, Humanities Research Center, University of
    Texas at Austin
4   T.E. Hanley Collection, Humanities Research Center, University
    of Texas at Austin
5   Henry W. and Albert A. Berg Collection, New York Public
    Library, Astor, Lenox and Tilden Foundations
6   Houghton Library, Harvard University
7   Beinicke Library, Yale University
8   De Coursey Fales Collection, New York University Library
9   Bernard F. Burgunder Collection, Cornell University Library
10 Library of Congress
11 Princeton University Library
12 J. Harlin O'Connell Collection, Princeton University Library
13 British Library of Political and Economic Science
14 Passfield Trust Papers, British Library of Political and Economic
    Science
17 King's College Library, Cambridge University
18 National Library of Scotland
19 University of California Library, Los Angeles
21 Free Library of Philadelphia
22 Society of Authors Archive [now transferred to the British
    Museum]
23 Baker Library, Dartmouth College
24 Edward Laurence Doheny Memorial Library, St John's
    Seminary, California
26 University of Illinois Library
29 National Library of Wales
30 British Theatre Museum
34 Folger Library

Code to sources of prior publication

124 Doris Arthur Jones, *The Life and Letters of Henry Arthur Jones* (1930)

125 Bernard Shaw, *Advice to a Young Critic*, ed. E. J. West (1955)

126 Frank Harris, *Bernard Shaw* (1931)

129 *Yale University Library Gazette*, October 1937

130 Ashley Dukes, "A Doll's House and the Open Door," *Theatre Arts*, January 1928

135 Grant Richards, *Author Hunting* (1934)

141 Archibald Henderson, *George Bernard Shaw: Man of the Century* (1956)

147 Patrick J. Hogan Jr and J. O. Baylen, "G. Bernard Shaw and W. T. Stead," *Studies in English Literature 1500–1900*, Autumn 1961

151 Janet Dunbar, *Mrs G.B.S.: A Portrait* (1963)

152 Stephen Winsten, *Jesting Apostle* (1956)

154 F. E. Loewenstein, "The Copyrighting of Shaw's Early Dramatic Work," *Shaw Society* (London) *Bulletin*, Supplement No. 2, February 1952

155 *The Adult*, September 1898

156 *The Academy*, 24 December 1898

157 *The Flying Quill* (Goodspeed Book Store, Boston), July 1957

158 Pierre Nordon, *Sir Arthur Conan Doyle: L'Homme et l'œuvre* (1964)

159 Ancoats Recreation Brotherhood Programme, Spring 1907

160 Alan Dent (ed.), *Bernard Shaw and Mrs Patrick Campbell: Their Correspondence* (1952).

161 H. W. Nevinson, *Changes and Chances* (1923)

162 R. M. Gollin, "Beerbohm, Wilde, Shaw, and 'The Good-Natured Critic'," *New York Public Library Bulletin*, February 1964

163 *Labour Leader*, 6 January 1900

164 Stephen Winsten, *Salt and His Circle* (1951)

165 R. T. Hyndman, *The Last Years of H. M. Hyndman* (1923)

166 *Drama*, Autumn 1956

167 Hesketh Pearson, *Bernard Shaw: His Life and Personality* (1942)

168 C. B. Purdom (ed.), *Bernard Shaw's Letters to Granville Barker* (1957)

169 St John Ervine, "Bernard Shaw," *The Spectator*, 10 November 1950

170 Henry Festing Jones, *Samuel Butler* (1919)

171 "My Dear Walters," *British Weekly*, 24 July–7 August 1947

172 Mrs Clement Scott, *Old Days in Bohemian London* (1919)
173 *The Clarion*, 14 February 1902
174 *Daily Mail*, 28 March 1902
175 Ellen Terry, *The Story of My Life* (1908)
176 *Plain Talk*, February–March 1930
177 W.D.Orcutt, *Celebrities Off Parade* (1935)
178 *Metropolitan Magazine*, August 1904
179 *Review of Reviews*, August 1904
180 A.L.Coburn, *Photographer: An Autobiography*, eds. H. and A. Gernsheim (1966)
181 *New York Public Library Bulletin*, November 1927
182 Lillah McCarthy, *Myself and My Friends* (1933)
183 Sotheby & Company, Catalogue of sale, 13 November 1929
184 Margery Ross (ed.), *Robert Ross: Friend of Friends* (1952)
185 *Free Lance*, 25 January 1902
186 James Huneker, *Steeplejack* (1922)
187 Eleanor R. Belmont, *The Fabric of Memory* (1957)
188 Gilbert Murray, *An Unfinished Autobiography* (1960)
189 *New York Times*, 5 December 1915
190 *Vanity Fair*, February 1916
191 *Boston Evening Transcript*, 28 December 1929
192 *Literary Repository* (Catalogue of J.Stevens Cox), 2nd quarter 1954
193 *Success Magazine*, April 1905
194 Arnold T.Schwab, *James Gibbons Huneker* (1963)
195 *Tolstoy on Shakespeare*, ed. V.Tchertkoff (1906)
196 *New York Times*, 26 September 1905
197 Sidney Albert, "'In More Ways Than One': *Major Barbara*'s Debt to Gilbert Murray," *Educational Theatre Journal*, May 1968
198 *The World*, 7 July 1906
199 Robert Speaight, *William Rothenstein* (1962)
200 *The Tribune*, 15 February 1906
201 Printed letter distributed at meeting of the National Anti-Vaccination League, 27 February 1906
202 "Shaw's Letters to a Girl Who Loved Him," *Daily Herald*, 17–22 May 1951
203 Maisie Ward, *Gilbert Keith Chesterton* (1944)
204 Julian Park (ed.), "Some Unpublished Letters of George Bernard Shaw," *University of Buffalo Studies*, September 1939
205 *London Opinion*, 30 January 1909
206 *Charles Ricketts, R.A.*, introd. T.Sturge Moore (1933)

207   Charles Ricketts, *Self-Portrait*, ed. Cecil Lewis (1939)
208   *Collier's Weekly*, 25 April 1908
209   *The Flying Quill* (Goodspeed Book Store, Boston), October 1955
210   Barbara B. Watson, *The Shavian Guide to the Intelligent Woman* (1964)
211   *New York American*, 7 July 1906
212   Michael Hurd, *Immortal Hour* (1962)
213   American Art Association, Catalogue of Henderson sale, 16 January 1933
214   *Dublin Express*, 8 October 1908
215   *The Surplus* (International Emigration Office, Salvation Army, 1909)
216   Henry James, *Complete Plays*, ed. Leon Edel (1949)
217   Frank Bealey and Henry Pelling, *Labour and Politics 1900-1906* (1958)
218   Viscount Samuel, *Memoirs* (1945)
219   *Daily Telegraph*, 24 August 1909
220   Lady Gregory, *Our Irish Theatre* (1913)
221   *New York Sun*, 6 January 1910
222   Aylmer Maude, *Life of Tolstoy: Later Years* (1910)
223   *Evening Standard*, 6 February 1928
224   *The Times*, 10 June 1910
225   *Theatre Research*, Autumn 1967
226   Louis Marlow, *Swan's Milk* (1934)
227   Sidney Albert, "Shaw's Advice to the Players of *Major Barbara*," *Theatre Survey*, May 1969
228   Programme of *The Philanderer*, Mermaid Theatre, London, 27 January 1966
229   Mrs Patrick Campbell, *My Life and Some Letters* (1922)
230   *The Independent* (New York), 28 July 1910

PART I

1898-1903

I
(1898–1903)

TANNER [*explosively*] Ann: I will not marry you. Do you hear? I wont, wont, wont, wont, WONT marry you.

ANN [*placidly*] Well, nobody axed you sir she said sir she said sir she said. So thats settled.

TANNER. Yes, nobody has asked me; but everybody treats the thing as settled. It's in the air. When we meet, the others go away on absurd pretexts to leave us alone together. . . . I have a frightful feeling that I shall let myself be married because it is the world's will that you should have a husband.

This autobiographical echo in *Man and Superman* (1903) describes Shaw's situation precisely. The friends of Charlotte Payne-Townshend and Shaw had for the past two years assumed that they would ultimately marry, and had given them every encouragement. When Shaw seemed to take Charlotte's constant ministrations for granted, she was advised by Beatrice Webb to stop dancing attendance on him and to practise self-restraint. Lion Phillimore sagely incited her to make sudden disappearances to the Continent. When she lingered in Rome, Shaw conceded that he felt "detestably deserted," confessing "I want a woman and a sound sleep." During Easter the Phillimores bore him off to their home at Radlett where, as he subsequently reported to Sidney Webb, "they promptly proceeded to lecture me for my folly in not marrying Charlotte; to explain to me the delights of married life (chief among these being the escape from the pre-nuptial obligation to be constantly paying amorous attentions to one another); and to point out to me the numerous grave defects in my own character. I was totally incapable of self-defence . . ."

Although aware that he was now firmly in the grip of the Life Force (he confided to the Pakenham Beattys, in April, "I probably will marry the lady"), the bedevilled Shaw continued to the last to struggle Tanner-like "for my freedom, for my honour, for my self, one and indivisible." But Fate, kindred to Blanco Posnet's ruler of the universe, was a sly one. Shaw merely tied a boot lace too tight one morning and, presto, found himself lying "helpless and disabled . . . nailed by one foot to the floor like a doomed Strasburg goose . . ." Almost as

3

soon as Charlotte returned from abroad, he capitulated: "I proposed," he informed Mrs Richard Mansfield, "to make her my widow." On 1st June 1898 Miss Payne-Townshend became Mrs G. Bernard Shaw.

Once he had succumbed to marriage Shaw discovered leisure could be ineffably satisfying. Despite the pain and annoyance of his injury, and the extraordinary series of physical calamities which supervened in dizzying succession in ensuing months, he relished his emancipation, for the first time in some fifteen years, from the critical journalism which had demanded of him two thousand words a week for his bread and butter. He had been freed as well from the cruel grind of Fabian committees, the St Pancras Vestry, and all the related demands upon his time which had for so long been converting his "entire stock of energy . . . into pure genius." Charlotte transplanted him from "the mile radius of foul and sooty air which has its centre in the Strand" to an isolated corner of Surrey, where (except for a brief excursion to the Isle of Wight for a change of scene) they spent the remainder of 1898 and much of the following year.

Shaw had always savoured the countryside: the happiest hour of his life, he more than once confided, was in his childhood when his mother told him they were going to live on Dalkey Hill. Now his restlessness deserted him; his tension subsided; he slept more soundly than he had in years. Invigorated, he completed *Cæsar and Cleopatra* and *The Perfect Wagnerite*, and began a play for Ellen Terry, eventually to be called *Captain Brassbound's Conversion*. He dictated letters to Charlotte for friends, exhorting them to submit in like manner to what he called the "Goethe-Schiller illness," which attacks hardworking men in their middle years, after which one gets one's second wind, lives a long life, and rarely is troubled by illness again. As with the aid of crutches he became ambulatory, Shaw amused himself by accepting the post of critic-in-residence for the *Farnham, Haslemere, and Hindhead Herald*, reviewing a series of four Hindhead Hall concerts. He participated in meetings in favour of a Disarmament Conference. He lectured to the locals on Socialism, joined Grant Allen and other neighbours in a play-reading society, indulged a curiosity in meteorology (seeking out a sunshine recorder and an anemometer for determining the velocity of the wind), and assisted in the foundation of a model public house.

Charlotte, too, probably had never been more content. Aided by Shaw's fortuitous injuries she had succeeded in obtaining a marital arrangement that entirely excluded sex (they had agreed initially even

4

to maintain their separate domiciles in London), and she was free to indulge what she later described as a "managing, domineering strain" inherited from her mother. Since Shaw's professional earnings during the first twelve months of the marriage amounted only to £473 (by 1902 they dwindled to £90), the Shaws lived almost entirely on Charlotte's income. It afforded her joy to be needed and depended on, and she seemed impervious to the strain imposed upon her, even when obliged to entertain the steady stream of friends and business associates who came down from London at Shaw's invitation to spend a day with him—or a weekend.

By June 1899 Shaw had discarded the crutches completely, and was taking brisk three-mile walks. Inevitably the question of his future arose. Several of his Socialist friends sought to spur him into running for Parliament, in North Kensington. Theoretically Shaw was favourably disposed to such an action, for he saw the desirability of developing a Fabian party in the House of Commons. Eventually, however, he vetoed the idea of a political career for himself, opting instead to commence outlining in a small pocket diary the third-act "Hell" sequence for a new play provisionally titled *The Superman, or Don Juan's great grandson's grandson*. Charlotte, distressed by the renewed surge of activity and involvement, which she feared was premature, covered the dining-room table with travel folders and maps, and began to draw up an itinerary for their escape. It was the introduction into their lives of a pattern that would remain constant. "Charlotte is never happy," Shaw told a friend in 1903, "except when we are staying in some grubby public house out of reach of the servants and the two residences." The Shaws deserted Surrey for a month of sea bathing in Cornwall, returned to London just long enough to repack their bags, and sailed from Plymouth in the S.S. Lusitania on a Mediterranean cruise.

When they at last returned to London to re-establish residence, at the end of October 1899, Shaw made the decision to move into Charlotte's flat in Adelphi Terrace, exchanging his cluttered second-floor-front study in Fitzroy Square for a third-floor converted box-room opening off Charlotte's bedroom, overlooking the Thames. The Transvaal war had begun. The newly-founded Stage Society was clamouring for a play to produce, and for his committee participation. The St Pancras Vestry was undergoing a transformation into a Borough. There was a preface to write for *Three Plays for Puritans*, and textual revisions before the manuscript could be sent to the printer. The honeymoon was over.

To CHARLOTTE PAYNE-TOWNSHEND

[B/2]

29 Fitzroy Square W
4th January 1898

I forgot to say today that the [St Pancras] Vestry compels me to go to St Martin's Lane on Wednesdays before the midday crowd disperses. You will find it more comfortable to lunch at home at half past one as usual. You can have me or leave me at the [Orange Grove] restaurant, just as you please.

We must adopt some less heart-lacerating way of getting rid of one another than "Good afternoon: shant want you [for secretarial duties] till tomorrow." Besides, you dont play fair: you make a scene of it—as if *I* could help it!

GBS

To ELLEN TERRY

[U(A)/10; X/117]

29 Fitzroy Square W
5th January 1898

[Shaw's statement about Edward Aveling's depravity when women or money were in question is especially ironic in view of the fact that Aveling had just betrayed Eleanor Marx by marrying Eva Frye secretly in June 1897. The discovery of this fact was to lead to Eleanor's suicide on 31st March 1898 by poison. Aveling's theatrical pseudonym was Alec Nelson.

Teddy was Ellen's son Gordon Craig. St Aubyn Miller was a dramatist, several of whose plays were produced in the provinces between 1887 and 1897. *Peter the Great*, produced at the Lyceum on 1st January 1898, was a drama by Laurence Irving.]

Shut up your purse, tight, or else give me all your money to keep for you. No secrecy is necessary with regard to Edward Aveling. His exploits as a borrower have grown into a Homeric legend. He has his good points, has Alec: for instance, he does not deny his faiths, and will nail his atheism & socialism to the masthead incorruptibly enough. But he is incorrigible when women or money or the fulfilment of his engagements (especially prepaid ones) are in question. Better write to him as follows:—"Dear Dr Aveling: You must excuse me; but I know a great many people, among them some of your old friends of the National Secularist Society and the Socialist League, and some of your pupils. Dont ask me for any money. Yours sincerely, Ellen Terry." He will understand. If the application takes the form of a postdated cheque, dont cash it. If you would like to try a few references, consult Mrs Besant, John Robertson, George Standring, or the spirits of Bradlaugh & William Morris. Or come to see me, and I'll tell you all about him. Just walk into a room where we are all assembled, and say, in a cautious tentative way, "What sort of fellow is Dr Aveling?", and you will bring down the house with a shriek of laughter, and a shout of "How much have you lent him?"

Did you ever see him? He is always at the Lyceum on first nights, at the back of the dress circle. His [common-law] wife, Karl Marx's youngest daughter, is a clever woman. For some years past he has been behaving well, because Marx's friend Engels left Eleanor £9,000. But the other day he tried the old familiar postdated cheque on Sidney Webb—in vain. And then, I suppose, he tried you. Must I really not tell anyone? If you only knew how utterly your delicacy is wasted!

What has that rascal Teddy been doing? Remember: I'm a perfect mine of good advice as long as it is not applied to myself. Is Ted a scamp? I remember some time ago Charrington in my presence pitched into Janet because she had been unsympathetic to Ted. Janet at last confessed the awful truth. He had reminded her in some way of her former husband St Aubyn Miller. It flashed on me just then that Sally Fairchild had once looked bothered & uneasy when I asked her about Ted; and I said to myself: "Can this very agreeable young man be a petulant little villain, very prematurely married?"

The worry is all reaction after the parturition of Peter. The best thing for the knee is kissage; for the heart, careful wrapping round by the arms of a rather tall man, with, if possible, a red beard.

The book of plays [*Plays Pleasant and Unpleasant*] still creeps through the press. Oh those proofs, those proofs! Imagine going through a play again & again, scanning the commas, & sticking in words to make the printing look decent—to get the rivers of white out of it!

I never stop working now. I get no exercise. My digestion is beginning simply to stop. Oh, when you see me at last, you will be sorry that you did not bite me off and swallow me when I was young and beautiful.

GBS

8

To ELLEN TERRY

[U(A)/10; X/117.e]

29 Fitzroy Square W
18th January 1898

[Re Playgoers' Club dinner on 13th February, see I, 830. Louis F. Austin was Sir Henry Irving's secretary and adviser. Hugh Price Hughes (1847–1902) was a Methodist clergyman, who founded the West London Mission in 1886. Shaw's attack on Hughes and on Clement Scott appeared in the *Saturday Review* on 22nd January under the title "Church and Stage."]

For Heaven's sake, my dearest darling Ellen, dont tell me such frightful things about yourself. What new and horrible invention is "neuralgia in the palate"?—it goes right down into my entrails. Neuralgia means generally insufficient nourishment, except when it's constitutional, and is an alternative to gout or asthma or fits. Probably you dont take enough bodily exercise to sharpen your assimilative powers. You had better take my arm and let me walk you round the streets for a mile or two every day. Miss P.T. used to have neuralgia a good deal: she now hasnt much of it. When she walked with me she used to stop in five minutes & get palpitations and say I must not walk like an express train. Now she hooks on and steeplechases with me without turning a hair. The Webbs are going away in March for a tour round the world which I cant afford. They want her to go. If she does, she will be away for about a year, just time enough for a new love affair. Would you mind taking me on a short lease—my novelty would last very nearly all the time? You cant think what delightful agony it is to be in love with me: my genius for hurting women is extraordinary; and I always do it with the best intentions.

No, bless you, not next Sunday—not until the 13th February. I enclose you a cutting from a London letter which I attribute, at a guess, to L. F. Austin. Now L.F.A. is Henry's henchman; and he would dearly like to see a set-to between us. He was deputed to intervene in the Man of Destiny affray, and naturally found himself between my fire shovel and Henry's carpet bag, in the Pickwick manner. Do you suppose that Henry can be so gigantic an idiot as to let himself be drawn about the morality of actors? If so, gag him—sit on his head, if necessary. He doesnt live with his wife; and everyone knows it. You are a shocking character—two marriages, two affairs, two children; and everyone knows it. Now if Henry for one moment condescends to recognize the morality you have outraged, he gives you away, gives himself away, and disgusts everybody by his hypocrisy. On the other hand, if he rises to the occasion and says "If the morals of Mr [Clement]

9

Scott and Mr Hugh Price Hughes are not in harmony with the morals of my talented, my privately esteemed and courted, my publicly respected and admired friend and colleague Miss Ellen Terry, then so much the worse for the morals of Mr Scott and Mr Price Hughes [loud and enthusiastic cheering]"*—if, I say, he does this, he will go outside his role, which is not that of a Moral Crusader (that's *my* line), and will not be able to go through with it. In short, he'd better hold his tongue. I am running amuck again in next week's Saturday about it, with the express object of shutting up the virtuously indignant defenders of the profession.

So nothing will happen. I hate after-dinner speaking, and will not waste eloquence on a half drunk dinner party. I will simply fire off any half dozen sentences that occur to me at the moment. [John] Hare will burn the midnight oil for weeks preparing his reply. Henry will call in Austin, Stoker & all the rest of them to prepare an oration full of extensive classical learning & profound philosophy. And the whole speechifying business will be as dull & silly as it can be. Dont dream of coming: you'll be bored & headached to distraction. But if you like, I'll get them to invite you as a guest. I'm sure they'd be delighted. Now to bed—to my lonely Ellenless bed.

GBS

To CHARLES CHARRINGTON

[A/4]

29 Fitzroy Square W
22nd January 1898

[The Charringtons were in Manchester. Richard Flanagan (1849–1917), a Manchester theatrical manager, was known for very realistic productions of Shakespeare, in the style of Charles Kean. Louis Calvert had played Antony to Janet Achurch's Cleopatra in Manchester in 1897.]

Dear Charrington

Yes: I can advance Janet £10 until treasury day for her own use. What I cant, and, damn me, WONT, do, is to enable Janet to go to her creditors & say, "Out of this engagement I will repay you so much out of my salary and so much out of Shaw's" which is to all intents and purposes what will happen unless I insist on having the money back, which I accordingly do. Janet's view is that as I have no debts of my

* The square brackets are Shaw's.

own I can pay hers—an unspeakably exasperating one to me. If the money I advance on these ruinous engagements went down her throat or on her back or in any way added to her wellbeing, I should consider it as well spent in that as in any other fashion. Even if Flanagan had some of it in sausages, like Calvert, I should regard it as gone in the cause of humanity. But when it simply passes over to the creditors & stimulates them to worry her with redoubled vigor as they discover that the worrying draws blood, my brow gets blacker and my language worse with every cheque I draw. You know that she will not pay me: she never does. The American engagement left her poorer and more worried than ever, the Cleopatra one ditto; and that effect would have been less instead of more if I had resolutely refused to sink a farthing in either enterprise. She did not get a farthing of what she got from me —not even 10% on what she collected from me. I am now determined to make myself so hideously disagreeable that she will dread me more than all the rest of them put together. Tell her that I must have my pound of flesh next week. Tell her anything (immediately before your own flight to London) that will make her yell with rage and misery for at least half an hour afterwards.

GBS

To CHARLOTTE PAYNE-TOWNSHEND

[B/2]
29 Fitzroy Square W
4th March 1898

[Shaw was preparing for copyright performances of *You Never Can Tell* and *The Gadfly* (a dramatisation he had volunteered to make in January 1898 to protect the stage rights for the author, Mrs Ethel Voynich) on 23rd March, and *Mrs Warren's Profession* and *The Philanderer* on 30th March, all at the Victoria Hall, Bayswater. Shaw and Emery Walker were scheduled to visit Edward Burne-Jones on 13th March, but the appointment was cancelled due to the latter's sudden indisposition. He died later in the year.]

The plays for the copyrighting performance have arrived. They require endless cutting & folding and stapling into brown paper covers. If you can spare a little time tomorrow, come along & bring some long staples (5/8″ will do) with you—50, if you have them.

By the way the Burne Jones business is fixed for the 13th, not for the day after tomorrow.

My nerves are shattered by the scenes of which I have been made the innocent victim. I wonder are you at all ashamed of yourself. I have allied myself to a fountain of tears.

GBS

To CHARLES CHARRINGTON

29 Fitzroy Square W
[A/4]   7th March 1898

[The "son of an old pal" was Mazzini Beatty. Lucy Carr Shaw, now semi-invalided with consumption, received an allowance from Shaw regularly until her death in 1920. Charrington had run as a Progressive candidate for the London County Council in the Strand Division on 3rd March. Although defeated, he polled 1356 votes, reducing the margin between the parties by more than half. In the London Vestry Election in Chelsea in May 1899, he was again defeated, by 27 votes.]

Alas! the well is dry. The American remittances have simply stopped: I have had to write peremptorily threatening to withdraw "The Devil's Disciple" if they are not resumed. Meanwhile my expenditure is proceeding at a handsome rate. Just before your letter came I had to send off £10-10-0 to pay the term's schooling of the son of an old pal—also with men in possession. £21.0.0 to my sister, £18.18.0 for licensing & other expenses of copyrighting the plays, £35 to meet my I.T. [Independent Theatre] engagements: these are mere samples of the little extras which I have to meet out of the narrow ledge on which I am rallying after my investment. I had to refuse to lend £25 the other day under circumstances which made me feel quite dastardly. When you suggest £30, I simply laugh. You may tell your creditors that if they expect to intimidate *me* by selling *you* up, they have mistaken their man. The reputation of The Devil's Disciple has given me such practice in hardening my heart that I have lost all human sympathy.

If your blessed uncle knows anything about electioneering and Strand politics, he ought to endow you handsomely for your success at the polls, which was unexpectedly considerable. You did very well: your figures ought to smooth the way for another candidature. (By the way, why dont you make for the Chelsea Vestry?) They ought to be worth £30 to your uncle. . . .

GBS

29 Fitzroy Square W

[G/4; X/154]   12th March 1898

[The Acting Manager of the Victoria Hall (also known as the Bijou Theatre) had paid a reading fee to the Lord Chamberlain's office to obtain a licence for a copyright performance of *Mrs Warren's Profession*. The examiner of plays, G.A.Redford, informed the manager on 11th March that he was unable to recommend the play for licence.]

Dear Sir

I have just learned that you find yourself unable to recommend for license a play of mine entitled "Mrs Warren's Profession." This I of course anticipated, as I quite recognized the impossibility of anyone dividing with me the responsibility for such a play; and I took care that your attention should be specially called to the character of the piece by making a note on the copy sent you. But cannot the case be dealt with by the blue pencil? If the Lord Chamberlain licenses the first act, with the exception of the duologue between Praed and Crofts; the third act down to the beginning of the scene between Crofts and Vivie; and the last act from the entry of Praed onward, wholly omitting the 2nd act & leaving Mrs W's profession unspecified[,] the public will be as effectually protected against a performance of the whole play as if it had been entirely prohibited, whilst I shall be equally protected against the forfeiture of my stage rights, which may possibly prove valuable in America or elsewhere. I may point out that the forfeiture of the rights would multiply performances of the play outside your jurisdiction, since a piece with derelict rights, like "East Lynne," "A Doll's House" or Gounod's "Faust," is at everybody's disposal, whereas there is a considerable check on the number & character of the performances when the rights are appropriated. You are bound, I take it, to regard such a multiplication of performances as an evil; and since you can avert this, and at the same time relieve me from a loss of property as an indirect consequence of your veto, by recommending the Lord Chamberlain to license those portions of the play which, taken by themselves, have no significance, but without which no pirate could perform the unlicensed portions, I venture to suggest that a drastic expurgation such as I have suggested would be less objectionable both from the Lord Chamberlain's point of view and mine than an uncompromising veto.

The emergency in which I have sent in the play has arisen, not through any project for producing the piece in the ordinary course, but

13

because it will be published next month in a collected edition of my plays. In the present state of the law, performance prior to publication is necessary to secure dramatic copyright.

I believe this communication should be addressed to you by the lessee of the Victoria Hall; but you will perhaps excuse an informality which is altogether technical.

I am, dear Sir, your obedient servant

G. Bernard Shaw

[Redford, in a letter on 14th March, replied: "I beg to point out that as Examiner of Plays I have already issued 'an uncompromising Veto' to the *representation* of the Drama in 4 acts entitled *Mrs Warren's Profession*. You admit that you anticipated, and deliberately courted, this result, 'recognising the impossibility of anyone dividing with you the responsibility for such a play.' Most certainly it is not for me to attempt any 'dramatic expurgation' with the blue pencil, as you appear to suggest. It is for you to submit, or cause to be submitted, a licensable play, and if you do this I will endeavour to forget that I ever read the original" (Hanley, Texas).]

To CHARLOTTE PAYNE-TOWNSHEND

[E.u/2; X/151.e]

[29 Fitzroy Square W]

12th March 1898

[Miss Payne-Townshend departed for a visit to Rome that morning, accompanied by Lion Phillimore. Shaw resolved to keep an "almanack" of his activities for her. Actually, he made notes daily on the leaves of his desk calendar, and posted batches of these $3\frac{1}{2}'' \times 5''$ slips at intervals, with covering letters, to Rome.]

Charlotte deserts me at 11.
Divide the rest of the day between tears and answering letters.
Digestion wholly ceases.
Try to sing "Egypt was glad when they departed," by Handel. Failure.
No exercise today.

14th March 1898

[A. G. Markham, Richard Jefferson Dodd, and John Hunt were members of the St Pancras Vestry. Somers Town, a favourite residence of City clerks, was an area between the Euston, Pancras, and Hampstead Roads. Mary Penfield was an American freelance journalist; her interview is unknown.]

Renew the struggle with my letters. Censor writes refusing to expurgate Mrs Warren—says I can do it myself if I want to & offers to consider any licensable play submitted to him, obliterating the other from his mind. This means another two guineas—black mail. Thirst for his blood. Go to vestry after lunch—widows begging off their rates &c. Labor representative (Markham—tell Mrs P.) tells me he cannot support demand for 2 more sanitary inspectors in Somers Town. Knows there ought to be more inspection, but must respect strong feeling in Somers Town against sanitation & disturbance of the domestic hearth by measures against overcrowding. Ratepayers' Association in the evening. Compromise on Guardians & Vestry election upset by contumacy of one Dod, who refuses to withdraw from double candidature & leave seat on Guardians for West London Mission second candidate without contest. Dod present to speak for himself. Hunt, unaware of this (Dod being immediately behind him) cries out "Nous sommes trahis! Conspuez Dod!" Fracas averted by Dod's ignorance of French. I laugh. He laughs, pretending to understand. All laugh. I leave at 10 & before going to bed make a new version of "Mrs. Warren," omitting the second act & making Mrs W a pickpocket who trains young girls to steal. Despatch it with a cheque for £2.2.0 & my curse. Quite desperate for lack of exercise. Before retiring have to correct Miss Penfield's interview. A tissue of inaccuracies from end to end—the mildest a statement that Janet Achurch gave imitations of Mansfield, like Cissie Loftus. Relieve my feelings by abusive letter. Bed.

15th March 1898

[The *Saturday Review* article was a notice of William Archer's *The Theatrical "World" of 1897.* "Billy" was the nickname of Jenny Patterson, whom Shaw had not seen since the celebrated row over Florence Farr in February 1893.]

Article. Miserably inconvenient having to write it myself. Only accomplish five pages. Miss Penfield writes complaining that I have corrected her article more than Jones or Pinero did when she interviewed them. Reply in unmeasured terms. Lunch at 3.30. Get my hair cut—amazing rejuvenation in appearance as a result—look barely 55. At 5 go off on the bike. Go along West End Lane to Hampstead, then to Hendon. Between Hendon and Edgware darkness overtakes me & I get into a region of hills ending in watersplashes & have many perilous adventures. Come out safe at Edgware at last, and execrate Lion's whim of Italian travel, which prevents me getting my evening meal at Radlett. Ride home along the main road—total distance 25 miles, about

15

16 of it uphill. Enjoy unspeakable luxury of being physically tired. Do not get back until 8.30. Throw evening engagements to the winds. Read [Stendhal's] "Chartreuse de Parme" & amuse myself a little with "Götterdammerung." Despatch these in time for midnight post, your postcard having arrived with your address. . . .

Fearful contretemps omitted from yesterday's record. When I got back from Ratepayers' Association, I was walking into the next room when I saw—BILLY, audaciously sitting with my mother. I dived in here [the study, next to the parlour] like a rabbit; and she presently fled. . . .

16th March 1898

[Kate Salt performed secretarial duties for Shaw until Charlotte returned at the beginning of May. Susan was Lucinda Elizabeth Shaw's servant.]

Unexpected appearance during breakfast of Mrs Salt. Susan much perplexed as to how to class her. Mrs Salt comes to say that Olivier is going to America (with the Webbs) for a month on Colonial Office business and that Mrs Olivier wants me to go down to Limpsfield & take his place during that period. I receive this proposal with shouts of virtuous indignation, which Mrs S. thinks very stupid. She then wants to know what about the secretaryship. I am cross and incommoded to the last degree by having to adapt myself to changed circumstances; but finally I set her to finish the article from my dictation. She sits down on the floor in the window corner, and begins to write with the screen between her and the fire. For three sentences, I feel resentful, uncomfortable, and quite put out. At the fourth the switch operates and I am on to the new line as if I had never dictated to anybody else. Such is manly fidelity. In the absence of sentimental interruptions we get along famously; and when we part at the restaurant I enjoin her strictly to come tomorrow.

The Vestry is one long exasperation. Discussion about refreshments (which we abolish) to a crowded gallery. Talk about our dignity & respectability. Deputation arrives consisting of Yallop and three females. Yallop reads us a paper, ten minutes long, accusing us of every possible infamy. The Vestry shews itself void of courage & dignity & Yallop is left master of the situation. We get naughty & silly & refuse to pass necessary votes; so that there will evidently have to be a special vestry next Wednesday. Phillimore, exacerbated by celibacy, informs me wildly that he will resign, because "the Progressives" will not support the demand for two more sanitary inspectors, & it is useless to work with a party without discipline. I ridicule the notion that a party exists beyond our two selves. . . . I muddle away the rest of the evening over my letters & a brief bike.

18th March 1898

[Stratford St Andrew (Saxmundham) and Lotus (Dorking) were the country houses rented by Charlotte and the Webbs in 1896 and 1897, which Shaw had shared. The C.T.C. was the Cyclists' Touring Club, which had held its annual general meeting in the St Martin's Town Hall. W. Rees Jeffreys (1871–1954), a student of the London School of Economics, later became an authority on highway administration and transport.]

More letter writing. Immense progress. Lotus cleared off, and Stratford broken into. This is indeed a secretary. She does not come to the restaurant: she eats her bananas between the sentences, and sits here until five, copying out the letters fairly, so that they are ready for me to sign when I return. Haste to attack the Roman municipal problem; for there is clearly no future for you as a secretary. You must get your own work, your own, own, own work. Do you hear? As it is only a few minutes past seven when we adjourn the executive, I look in on my way home at the meeting of the C.T.C. But I should mention first that Olivier looks in at the Executive, and bids us farewell (Webb auch) before his journey to Washington. He also requests five minutes private conversation with me. In this we settle, as between man & man, that the romantic arrangements made by Mrs Salt & Mrs Olivier are not to be carried out, though appearances are to be kept up so as to secure us against all suspicion of being too conventional to be worthy of the New Age & the New Light. Thus are women deceived: thus do men stand by one another in the war of the sexes. I find a large audience at the C.T.C., and seize the opportunity to advertize myself in this new quarter by a speech. Beatty's brother [Octavius] is also eloquent, likewise Jeffries of the London school.

To WILLIAM S. DOUGLAS

[P/34]

29 Fitzroy Square W
18th March 1898

[Douglas, a resident of Glasgow, had written in response to Shaw's 12th February article in the *Saturday Review*, entitled "Manchester Still Expiating." In it Shaw had referred to "such splendid melodramas as 'Othello'. . .

or 'As you like it,' with its Adelphi hero, its prize-fight, its coquet in tights, its good father and wicked uncle ..." These two plays, said Shaw, are among "the half-dozen big popular melodramas which the Bard has sublimified by his tempests of grandiose verse ..."]

Dear Sir

I think you will find, on reflection, that the characteristic which differentiates a melodrama with a happy ending from true comedy consists in the substitution for genuine human characters of figures which are mere stalking-horses for our likes and dislikes. However exquisite may be the art with which such figures are made to resemble real people, they always betray themselves by the artificiality of the assortment of their qualities. The hero and heroine have no disagreeable qualities: the villain, no agreeable ones. If, from this point of view, you will make a careful comparison of, say, "Measure for Measure," or "All's Well that Ends Well," with "As You Like It," you will see that "As You Like It" is a melodrama. The fact that you may happen to prefer it is probably an additional proof of the truth of the distinction. Whenever you find that a play gives you unmixed delight, you may depend on it it is flattering you.

You understand, I hope, that a classification is not necessarily a disparagement. When I deny that a certain piece is a comedy, it is much as if I denied that a certain man is a Swede or an Italian: he might be all the better for being neither.

yrs faithfully
G. Bernard Shaw

To A. J. MARRIOTT

29 Fitzroy Square W
[S/1]   18th March 1898

[The Fabians were in favour of extending municipal control to include the sale of intoxicating liquors. Edward R. Pease drafted two tracts on the Drink Question in 1898, and Shaw found himself involved a year later in the management of a public house.]

Dear Mr Marriott

I agree about the absurdity of fining for acts of violence. A friend of mine who was a bit of a bruiser was once summoned at the Hammersmith Police Court for giving a man a black eye. While he was waiting for his case to be dealt with, he asked a policeman what would happen to him. The policeman replied, "£5 if he was a gentleman; £2 if he wasn't." My friend explained that the victim was a Board-school teacher. "£2," said the policeman promptly: and £2 it was. The worst of it is, however, that the wave of blackguardism which has somehow come over public opinion lately makes people imagine that greater severity means flogging or some other brutality of the kind.

The drink question is certainly a horribly difficult one. The old-fashioned public-house parlour was not half a bad institution.

yrs faithfully
G. Bernard Shaw

To CHARLOTTE PAYNE-TOWNSHEND

[E.u/2]

[29 Fitzroy Square W]
19th March 1898

[Shaw lectured on "Flagellomania" to the Humanitarian League in Essex Hall on 24th March. It was published in *Humanity*, May 1899 (and pirated by Charles Carrington in Paris, unknown to Shaw, as preface to a pornographic work, *Records of Personal Chastisement*, 1899). The pantomime at the Britannia, Hoxton, was *Will o' the Wisp*, which Shaw reviewed in the *Saturday Review* on 9th April. The Rev. A. W. Oxford was Charles Charrington's running mate, also defeated, in the L.C.C. election on 3rd March. Sergius Stepniak's play *The Convert* was staged by Charrington for a single matinée at the Avenue Theatre on 14th June 1898. Flanagan's production of *Macbeth*, in which Janet Achurch was appearing, had achieved the distinction of having the longest continuous run (by 14 performances) of that play in England.]

Have sent Felix Mansfield to Beatty to get Cyrano translated; now have to write B a long letter cautioning him how to protect himself. Miss Marbury, by the way, has cabled to say that she has collected all fees up to the 12th March. Mrs Salt announces that she is going to Limpsfield & wont be back until Tuesday. She complains of my temper & wants to know whether I would dare speak to you like that. I am desperately conscious of the urgency of getting ready for the Flagellomania lecture next Thursday, and yet I keep mechanically ploughing through the old letters. In the evening I go to the Britannia in Hoxton to see the last night of the pantomime. Find it very amusing. Oxford has his late opponent, [Major C.] Probyn, there.

By the way, Charrington called to get me to put my name on a committee to perform Stepniak's play. Refused on the old plea that a critic oughtnt to do this sort of thing. He is just off to Manchester for the last night of "Macbeth." He is furious about two things—(1) because Macbeth [William Mollison] has a limelight following him about the stage, leaving Janet in darkness; and (2) about the Ibsen testimonial, which has been restricted to the New Century clique & stupidly limited & mismanaged—the sum being only about £50 & the present a drinking cup(!) of George II design ! ! !

Miss Robins is in New York, Ibsenising there. She has told the interviewers that the American "leading men" are not gentlemen, whereas in every London theatre the leading man is a perfect gentleman!!!!!!

20th March 1898

Muddling over old letters, with some pecking at the flogging lecture. The Wallases are at Webbs', who start [for the United States] from Euston on Wednesday at 12.30. We agree to meet them & see them off. Usual political discussions . . . I outstay everybody until about 5. I mention Olivier incident, also your project for taking a house with the Phillimores. Beatrice highly approves, but urges strongly that the Phillimores cannot afford to go your pace in the way of money. She points out that even the Lotus arrangement will not do, because the housekeeping was half & half, which the Ph's ought not to undertake. She says they must simply contribute as much as they can afford per week, and that if you choose to insist on a style of living beyond what this runs to, there is no reason why you should not pay what your notions cost. This is good sense, except that clearly I must also contribute. I expect that if you do not present the arrangement on some such financial basis as this, you will find that Lion will have fifty conclusive reasons why she must absolutely stick to Radlett this spring.

Finally Beatrice got suddenly & violently alarmed lest people should all be supposing that the secret of my holidays with her & Webb was that she was in love with me & Webb & I had to soothe her with all our tact.

In the evening, responding to a telegram from Beatty, I rode out to Ealing & heard all about a long visit from Mansfield. He complained to them that when he introduced me to his brother, "one of the greatest living actors," I actually sat down and treated him as if I were his equal, to say no worse, thereby covering poor Felix with embarrassment. This was to illustrate the utter desperation of my character, & the danger of listening to my advice.

[The article was a report on the celebration by the British theatre of Ibsen's 70th birthday; it appeared in the *Saturday Review* on 26th March as "England's Delicate Compliment to Ibsen." Henry Salt had lent Shaw "an improper book" (as he noted on his calendar slip for 21st March), William M. Cooper's *History of the Rod* (1868), to be read as background material for his lecture on corporal punishment on the 24th.]

Dictated article—stupendous effort sustained for three hours without relief. Frightful not to be able to kiss your secretary occasionally. After lunch, recital—Irish parson [named Nesbitt, at Steinway Hall] with the makings of a reciter in him, but misled by rhetoric, after the national manner, and not cured of native uncouthness of diction. After ten devoted myself to study of History of the Rod. Perfectly disgusting except in the brutal historical parts. Finished it from a sense that nothing would induce me to give it another sitting. Biked round Regents Park to purify myself with the clear night air after it. Park not altogether free from improprieties, but quite frosty-pure after Cooper.

23rd March 1898

[Herbert Waring's projected production of *The Devil's Disciple* was later abandoned. Édouard Rod (1857–1910) was a Swiss novelist, formerly Professor of Comparative Literature at Geneva. The Webbs departed for a lengthy visit of America and Australasia; they did not return until the end of the year. Kate (Mrs Leonard) Courtney was one of Beatrice Webb's sisters. Sydney Olivier and C.P. Trevelyan accompanied the Webbs on their journey only as far as New York.]

Corrected article & dictated letters to Mrs S., who always begins by producing a comb & titivating herself at the glass in the sideboard. Waring ran me down in the restaurant—has taken the Lyric Theatre to produce the Devil's Disciple in the first week in May. Discussion about cast—nothing settled. He keeps me too late for the special Vestry; so I go on straight to Stafford House. Miles of carriages; aristocracy (female) in great force. August mansion in palace precinct: butler openly bullies policemen, who take it humbly. Frederic Harrison almost swears at the peeress-hostess because the seats are not numbered. Big audience. Rod lectures us from the landing. Intelligent, graceful, formal, arid French piffle, with pathetic reference to Dante's Francesca. Could have done it when I was five years old. Statement that France is more moral than her novels received with applause. As I leave, am captured by Bertha [Newcombe], who is waiting to find Miss [Nelly] Erichsen. Urge her to come with me & never mind Miss E. She says Miss E.

would not understand. I assure her she will. She says "goodbye." I fly to the Health Committee; then home, where I have a lot of business —Waring, money from America &c. Feel somewhat dissolute. Up until nearly 2, writing.

By the way, I forgot to describe the parting at Euston. Told Beatrice I had never come to see anyone off before. No tears; but Mrs Courtney's nose swelled with emotion. Present, Pease, R. C. Trevelyan, Mrs Courtney, two men, and the party: i.e., Webb, Beatrice, Olivier & C. P. Trevelyan.

24th March 1898

[Charlotte Granville had recently appeared as Gertrude to Forbes-Robertson's Hamlet. Shaw, in his *Saturday Review* article on 2nd October 1897, had questioned the casting: "It is like setting a fashionable modern mandolinist to play Haydn's sonatas." Shaw wanted Lena Ashwell to play Judith in *The Devil's Disciple*. Charles H. Hopwood (1829–1904) was a barrister and editor of the Middle Temple Records.]

Fearful day. Beginning of blizzard. Begin desperately tackling the lecture, dictating notes to Mrs Salt. In the middle of breakfast Miss Granville is announced. (Miss G. is the leading lady financing Waring, whom I have told him I wont have). Frightful, heart tearing scene, lasting about an hour—perhaps an hour and a half. It begins of course with her polite intimation that, as she is providing the money, she must have the part, or my play will not be produced. It is like a shrimp attacking Beachy Head. Then she plies on my iron intelligence and miserable nerves every argument, every plea, every wile. It is quite horrible. Once, something that I say catches her on the open wound of some bitter personal experience, and she flies to the window to hide a break down. I stand waiting, as it seems to me, for six hours, whilst she is struggling with her tears. I blow my nose to suggest that I am affected. When she goes, I am lacerated & shattered. She actually wants to come tomorrow; but she has not moved me an inch, and I *know* that she wont, though I *fear* that she will. The rest of the day is a wild struggle to get this fearful lecture & its illustrative documents into order. At five minutes to eight I rush out with a dozen sheets of Mrs Salt's notes & a sheaf of pamphlets & press cuttings. A hansom saves me from being more than 10 minutes late. The chairman (Hopwood) speaks for half an hour. The audience yell at him to stop. "I see you are anxious to hear our lecturer (frantic cheers); so I will only mention three more points," he says. We are all on tenterhooks. At 8.30 he stops at last. I rise, a frantic, muddled wreck, and for a mortal 100 minutes(!)

rivet the wretched audience to their chairs. I feel that it is a wild, incoherent mess. Discussion from 9.50 to 10.30. I reply. I get to bed at one, like a stamped-on beetle. But thank Heaven, it's over.

25th March 1898

. . . [Charrington] tells me that he was at the lecture last night with Janet (never saw them) and that it was one of my best performances. Much relieved to hear it. Walked [after Fabian Society meeting] to Temple Station with Bertha [Newcombe]. When we came within a few feet of it, she said "It seemed strange to hear you taking up such a subject last night." "Why," said I. "Because you are so horribly cruel," she said. And then went home happy. . . .

30th March 1898

More dictation of letters & drafting of agreement with Grant Richards. . . . Headache seems imminent; but I have ceased to notice that now: its getting chronic, although somehow my energy is not flagging—rather the contrary. Money from America—£486. This makes a total of more than £1980 from the play [*The Devil's Disciple*] already. My New Zealand bonds cost me £1124. Waring has the Chicago cuttings: I'll send them on when he returns them. Ellen says she gets dozens of Cyranos (translations) by every post. She says [W.S.] Gilbert ought to translate it. . . .

I must write a scrap of a letter with this & get a walk round the park before bed. There was an hour of sun today—warm sun; and the oceans of mud left by the blizzard & cherished by the shivery-livery wind since are drying up. I could bike tonight, in fact; but I won't.

To CHARLOTTE PAYNE-TOWNSHEND

29 Fitzroy Square W

[A/2; X/151.e]   30th March 1898

[Iken Heath is in Suffolk, near Saxmundham, where Shaw and Charlotte spent a summer with the Webbs in 1896. *Candida* was presented on 14th March in the Gentlemen's Concert Hall by the Manchester Branch of the Independent Theatre.]

Somehow, I am beginning to feel like my old self again. After all, it is magnificent to be alone, with the ivy stripped off. As I walk round the park at night, looking at the other stars, I no longer feel 42. The hopples are off; my soul is disentangled from Martha's parlormaid's uniform; I am natural once more. You count that I have lost only one Charlotte; but I have lost two; and one of the losses is a prodigious relief. I may miss "die schöne grünen Augen" occasionally, though the very privation throws me back, brutally great, to my natural dreamland; but then think of the other Charlotte, the terrible Charlotte, the lier-in-wait, the soul hypochondriac, always watching and dragging me into bondage, always planning nice sensible, comfortable, selfish destruction for me, wincing at every accent of freedom in my voice, so that at last I get the trick of hiding myself from her, hating me & longing for me with the absorbing passion of the spider for the fly. Now that she is gone, I realize for the first time the infernal tyranny of the past year, which left me the license of the rebel, not the freedom of the man who stands alone. I will have no more of it: if you hate women who pull flowers, what do you think of women who cut down trees? [See I, 92.] *That's* the Charlotte I want to see married. The Charlotte of Iken Heath is another matter; yet I have her in my dreamland, and sometimes doubt whether the other devil ever had anything to do with her.

I altogether disagree with you about Beatrice's advice. I never heard such vulgar Irish rubbish in my life as your meaning that the Phillimores should pay nothing, and Lion "divining" it, and Beatrice being too English to understand it, and all the rest of it. Good heavens! has a few weeks absence reduced you to this! Drivel—simple drivel. Why shouldnt they pay what they can afford? Why shouldnt I pay? Are we to be Lady Bountifulled across our heads in this fashion? And then, forsooth, after reproaching the poor Webbs in the loftiest fashion for not doing justice to your delicacy, you proceed, without the faintest misgiving, to accuse the Phillimores of the worldliest motives for avoiding you. Why not ask Lion whether that is the real reason? Perhaps she will be exasperated into suggesting that there is another reason staring you straight in the face, oh stupidest of created women. In what way would her loyalty to you "depend on Bobby"?

No: I didn't go to see "Candida." Janet says she got hold of the last scene for the first time: in fact, the whole play seems to have come off in an unprecedented manner. There is no hurry about the D's D. It will not be produced until May; and it *must* run, successful or not, for eight weeks; so if you are back in June it will do. If you come back before it is produced, you will find me in a ferocious and damnable temper, as indeed I am at present. I bully Mrs Salt brutally; and Charrington says that though my lecture was fine, I never relaxed a fierce frown from one end of it to the other. No matter: I am no longer unhappy, and no longer happy: I am myself. I am gathering myself up for the rehearsals.

It is close to midnight: I must stalk off into the path round the park, to embrace my true mistress the Night. I hope this letter will make the other Charlotte YELL with anguish—little enough to expiate my centuries of slavery & misery.

Wrrrrrrrrrrrrrrrrrrrrrrrrrrrrrrrrrrrrrrrrrrrrrrrrrrrrrrrrrrrrrrrrrrrrrrrrrrrrrrrr!

GBS

To CHARLOTTE PAYNE-TOWNSHEND

[29 Fitzroy Square W]
[E.u/2; X/151.e]   31st March 1898

[The "Nibelungen handbook" was published as *The Perfect Wagnerite*.]

Temper somewhat relieved by the extreme ferocity of yesterday's correspondence. Nevertheless Mrs Salt complains roundly of my irritability and savagery. At the restaurant my waitress informs me that this is the last time she will wait on me. I accuse her of contemplating marriage. She admits it. For $4\frac{1}{2}$ years this young woman has enjoyed the bliss of contemplating me for an hour a day; and yet she wants to go and get married & see no more of me. Feeling it impossible to leave a penny under my plate under such circumstances, I substitute a sovereign, not without misgiving as to the possibility of the rest of the staff following her example. I then get my bill from her, shake hands, make her a polite Irish speech, and pass out of her existence for ever. I call on Grant Richards with the final draft of the agreement, which he, young-manlike, loathes. He wants me to try joint luck with him in a Nibelungen handbook for the forthcoming Ring cyclus. He also proposes that I should write him a novel full of Socialism, revolution, anything that a workman could read, & sell it to him outright for seven years at any price I like to ask (within reason & conscience). Says he has a backer for such an enterprise. Not you, is it? After tea I bike over to Salts & play the Pastoral Symphony four handed with Mrs S. I spent part of the morning teaching her the typewriter. She exasperates me frightfully—"a dense divil" as my mother says.

1st April 1898

... I have almost made up my mind to give up the Saturday Review, if not now, certainly at the end of the season, unless the result of

25

publishing the plays should be altogether terrifying. Another long wrangle over the Drink Tract [Fabian Tract 86, *Municipal Drink Traffic*] at the Exec.: poor Pease very angry, but extraordinarily patient and self controlled over the destruction of his labors. When I get home your letter comes. My ferocity has subsided—want to hug you, not to batter you & stalk off to commune proudly with the stars. Some of your resolutely good passages are so hypocritical that they almost set me off again; but on the whole I am amiable. "The Irrational Knot" must have been a lacerating experience. But it was a magnificent thing to write that book at 24, out of apparent depths of ignorance & seedy indigence. Think of my circumstances & prospects getting worse & worse until they culminated in small pox next year (81) when I forced "Love Among the Artists" out of myself sentence by sentence! Have you yet read *that* masterpiece?

4th April 1898

[Although Shaw had received the news of Eleanor Marx Aveling's suicide, he was not yet aware of the complexity of the causes. Edward Aveling out-lived her by only four months.]

. . . At home, piles of letters—one from you—and the news of Eleanor Marx's suicide in consequence of Aveling having spent all her money. Massingham wants [me] to write about her. *I* want to write about Aveling; so conclude to hold my tongue. . . . Fatigue of two days continuous talking & one day's riding struggling hysterically & somewhat neuralgically with effect of change of air. Write innumerable letters, finishing with yours.

To CHARLOTTE PAYNE-TOWNSHEND

29 Fitzroy Square W

[A/2; X/151.e]   4th April 1898

I write this on a memorandum slip forming part of an imposing blotter, diary &c. with which the Victoria Stone Co bribes vestrymen.

Do you realize from "The Irrational Knot" how far I've come—eighteen years from that time, when I wrote five books like that, and, without turning a hair, listened in vain for the faintest response to them. When they first shewed me the last scene in "A Doll's House," I said: "Oh, I did that long ago." And they laughed. Do you wonder at my being as hard as nails, except in so far as I am old & breaking up.

26

£68 just in from America for four nights at St Louis. So I am not to be allowed to invest. I really cannot express my feelings at this absurdity. I am supposed, it appears, to be taunting you with my independence. Well, then, I *will* taunt you. It is too monstrous. I will invest another £500 tomorrow.

The municipal business is all nonsense: of course they'll tell you nothing. Try & find out about some particular job & then go to the Ratepayers' Gallery (if there is one) as you did at St Pancras, & watch the debate on it.

Curse this cycling & country air: it revives my brute strength & brings unrest. I want a woman & a sound sleep. I am never happy except when I am worked to desperation in London & can eat only a little. I may be frantic, desperate, piteous with arrears & burdens; but I am never unhappy. What people call health—appetite, weight, beefiness—is a mistake. Fragility is the only endurable condition.

GBS

To CHARLOTTE PAYNE-TOWNSHEND

[E.u/2; X/151.e]

[29 Fitzroy Square W]
5th April 1898

[The tone of this note probably reflects Shaw's awareness that Eleanor Marx was cremated that afternoon. He did not attend.]

Wrote article. No secretary. Weary at the end. Slamming the typewriter is furious nervous work. No exercise. No digestion. All my body in active preservation below the waistband and above the diaphragm; but the intermediate zone weak—wont digest, wont carry me about. Neuralgic still rather. Lonely—no, by God, never—*not* lonely, but detestably deserted.

7th April 1898

After breakfast call on [Dr W.J.] McDonald. . . . Anæsthetist—man named Silk, whom I seem to know—arrives. He achieves complete anæsthesia—my first experience of it—have on previous occasion dreamt something with incidents in dream obviously suggested by operations. Dreaming rather better fun, but have become too thorough a Realist to dream now. Curse it! I can't inhale: I shall be suffocated. Ah! now I've got it—the whole vast Atlantic into my lungs at one colossal heaving sniff. "Breathe quite naturally, Mr Shaw! you need make no effort to inspire." Ass! to say that to a man at the bottom of the sea: a public speaker, too, who breathes through his nose by instinct. Expiration—five minutes long. Second prodigious inspiration—half an hour long (seems only a few seconds to those two). Oh, that's all right, is it? Have the two broken ends of my consciousness joined on so perfectly. Feel the sharpness of the shapeless fang. Certainly—"needle point absorption," is it? Come back on Thursday the 21st for general repairs: all right. Good morning, Dr Silk: many thanks. Good morning. A lot of inflammation, you said. No doubt. And so into the open air. How very sympathetic those two men looked! Must have concluded from my appearance under gas that I am not long for this world. Ha! ha!

Laceration. Sense of violence done me. And must go to the theatre this evening. Oh Charlotte, Charlotte: is this a time to be gadding about in Rome!

8th April 1898

[Max Beerbohm was Shaw's own choice as his successor. "You are the only man to carry on the business," he told Beerbohm, who replied that it was a great compliment, but that he was worried about following Shaw in the post: "I should be always tripping up in your large and deep footsteps" (Beerbohm, *More Theatres*, 1969).

William Pember Reeves's *New Zealand* had just been published. The phrase "Some Italian doctor" was a sharp taunt, for it was in Rome that Charlotte had met Dr Axel Munthe in April 1894, which led to an emotional crisis for her.]

I *will* clear up those old letters & papers. For 12 hours I read & sort & endorse ancient histories. Then I write to Alma Murray excusing myself for not giving her the part in "The Devil's Disciple." And then, without any particular consideration, to Frank Harris to say that I must hand over the Saturday to Max Beerbohm at the end of the season. Then once round Regents Park on the bike & then to bed. A lovely day and a night with a moon bigger than Big Ben's dial (I have not heard B.B. for years); but no holiday for me. I am too much done up to face a holiday. Better dawdle over the letters & read Reeves's "New Zealand," which is Macaulayishly readable.

All this time, no letter from Rome. Some Italian doctor, no doubt, at the bottom of it. Well, I shall not be for ever snivelling to be petted. In this grim solitude I shall recuperate: the steel armor will harden again, with a fresh deposit of adamant all over it.

Hope you're not ill, by the way. But no: you would write to say it was my fault if you were.

I broke my head yesterday with a Shannon file accidentally. What with that and the feverish healing of my lacerated gum, I am in a most hypochondriacal state. Haven't spoken to a soul (except in vestry) all the week.

To SIDNEY WEBB

[A/14; X/151.e]

29 Fitzroy Square W
11th April 1898 (Easter Monday)

[Hardy's *Tess of the d'Urbervilles*, adapted for the stage by Lorimer Stoddard and starring Minnie Maddern Fiske, had been performed successfully in America for more than a year. Shaw had now received more than £2000 in royalties from Richard Mansfield (his statement of "well into the third thousand" should not be construed to mean that the royalties had gone *past* £3000).

Arthur Roberts was appearing at the Lyric Theatre in a musical comedy by Basil Hood and Walter Slaughter entitled *Dandy Dan, The Lifeguardsman*. Leonard Courtney (1832–1918), later 1st Baron Courtney, was Webb's brother-in-law, a journalist who became a university professor and statesman.

The Spanish–American war originated in February 1895 in the struggle of Cuba to gain independence from Spain. War was declared by Spain on 24th April 1898 and by the United States on the following day.]

I was considerably relieved by the arrival of the "Tess" playbill this morning. The day after you left, a fortnight of the most unprecedented hurricane and tempest set in here. Even in London, where the wind is so little felt, the town was almost torn up by the roots. What it must have been on the surface of the Atlantic baffled the imagination. I pictured the ship going to the bottom on purpose for safety.

There is no news. I live the life of a dog—have not spoken to a soul except my mother & the vestry since you left. The change to spring has struck me down with feverishness & weakness. I have had a huge grinder dragged out by McDonald, & now find that what was the matter was a general inflammatory & febrile disposition which produced mild toothache. I havent gone anywhere for Easter, the theatres being too active. Wallas is in Devonshire. Whilst the cold weather lasted, I so brutally exulted in my loneliness & freedom, not to mention my taking on Mrs Salt as amanuensis (she's gone off to [Edward] Carpenter's village for Easter) that Charlotte has given up writing to me. Ellen alone remains faithful: she showers endearments on me by post.

You will be relieved to hear that I have made investments. Wilson's firm got me £1000 N. Zealand stock for which I paid them £1174. £700 of the bonds are at 6% & £300 at 7%; but as they will all be paid off at par in 9 or 12 years, it is not so thickly gilt a transaction after all. When you get to N.Z., you might ask whether there is really such a place as the Borough of Timaru. New Plymouth Harbor & the City of Wellington sound plausible; but Timaru strikes me as a bit melodramatic, especially at 7%.

Meanwhile the Devil's Disciple royalties are now well into the third thousand, whilst the English rights are still untouched. In view of this, and of the fact that "Arms & The Man," though counting as a failure, brought me in 2½ yrs Saturday salary from first to last (£829-11-9), I have concluded that to hold on to £312 a year for criticism is cowardly, and a fraud on the younger generation. I have therefore given the Saturday notice that I shall drop them at the end of the season. The plunge was inevitable sooner or later.

Waring took the Lyric Theatre the other day to produce the D's D in London; but we find ourselves stopped by a clause enabling Arthur Roberts to hold on there through May & June as long as his business touches £700 a week. This week (Easter week) will decide his fate & ours.

The plays will be published on the 15th, before you get this. I have asked the American publishers—Stone & Co, Caxton Building, Chicago—to send you a copy to the White Star, also one to Trevelyan at his Chicago Bank.

"Mrs Warren," as expurgated by me, was duly licensed.

There was a most painful scene on the Euston platform after your departure. Wallas said "Webb's gone away perfectly confident that nothing will happen until he comes back." Thereupon I most unfortunately added, "Neither will it: nothing ever does happen unless he does it." The effect of this on Kate was frightful—at the moment, too, when she had been planning to be a mother to me in Beatrice's absence. She stopped dead and said "Oh, there I *really* cannot agree with you." I made a dash to retrieve the situation by picturing Leonard, no longer restrained by Webb's prudence, becoming a revolutionary leader; but I only confused her as to whether she ought to like it or not. At all events, her arrangements as to having me on Sundays (which filled me with terror) have not since been alluded to. [John] Burns says I shall have a chance now that your influence is removed.—We expect to hear tomorrow that America is at war with Spain.—Progressivism still booming at Guardian elections. No news.

GBS

To CHARLOTTE PAYNE-TOWNSHEND

[29 Fitzroy Square W]

[E.u/2; X/151.e]   12th April 1898

Gigantic recuperation. Attack Saturday article with violence. Attack everything. Plenty of business in view of approaching publication of Plays. Work like mad until midnight. Reach that hour in a parlous condition. No word yet from vindictive Irishwoman in Rome. Neuralgia warning me loudly. Nobody comforts me but my faithful Ellen. She writes me the tenderest letters; and when I write her savage & furious ones, blesses me with tears for softening her, making her feel, giving her the happiness of thinking & crying. Adorable Ellen!

13th April 1898

[Nora Fitzpatrick was Lion Phillimore's sister. Mrs Phillimore had just returned from Rome.]

... Long and tiresome Vestry meeting. Mrs Phillimore, seeing me on the verge of dissolution, brings me off to Radlett. In my prostration I can make no headway against the Phillimores, who bully me for hours about you & my character and my age & my foolishness & selfishness & devil knows what. I am so crushed that I go to bed with a volume of Kipling, and read The Phantom Rickshaw. I have a headache now, and am almost like what I was on the Jubilee day. Am told that there is no use my trying to impress Nora Fitzpatrick (who is in the house), and that I am never at ease with anybody, but always self conscious &c &c &c. Seems atrocious that I shall have to go to the theatre tomorrow night.

14th April 1898

[The play was Paul M. Potter's *The Conquerors*, with George Alexander and Julia Neilson, at the St James's Theatre. Shaw reviewed it in the *Saturday Review*, as "The Drama Purified," on 23rd April.]

Headache in full force. Lounge about, reading Kipling. Take the inevitable stroll to Wallas's cottage. Sit on stile talking to Lion. She coolly ascribes my prostration to years of debauchery. My ashes glow into mighty coals at the insult; but I lie low. In the afternoon I go back to town. The headache dwindles: my spirits rise: my strength returns. At the theatre I am in immense form. When I return, I triumph: the vindictive Irishwoman has written at last. Ha! ha! If only I had her here in these arms: all her ribs would crack.

19th April 1898

[The "girl" was Pakenham Beatty's older daughter, Edith ("Cissy Livia"), whose schooling Charlotte subsequently agreed to subsidise. Although Shaw doesn't mention it, this was the day of publication of *Plays Pleasant and Unpleasant*. The first copy had been sent to Ellen Terry, a week earlier, with the inscription:

> "From the Author to Ellen Ellen
> Ellen Ellen Ellen Ellen Ellen Ellen
> Ellen Terry. Easter 1898."

(The New Yorker, 16th January 1932)]

Saturday article. Exasperating condition of things as to Rome. Thoughtless woman there will not give me the faintest clue to her movements. Leaves me with a definite statement that she leaves to-morrow & yet evidently, from the tone of her letters, hasnt the slightest intention of doing anything of the sort.

In the evening I ride off to Ealing to the Beattys. Have told the girl that if she will take up something definitely I think I know somebody who will see her through.

When I get to Ealing I find my left foot unaccountably sore & have to take off my shoe. Not easy to get it on again. Ride home. On taking off the shoe again my foot expands to the size of a leg of mutton. Dont understand it, as there is nothing to account for it but the fact that a week or so ago I laced my shoe too tight & pinched my instep a little.

21st April 1898

[That evening Shaw attended a performance of R. C. Carton's *Lord and Lady Algy* at the Comedy Theatre. William Archer's review of *Plays Pleasant and Unpleasant* appeared in the *Daily Chronicle* in two parts, on 19th and 21st April.]

Locomotion now very excruciating. Can it be *gout*? Looks *awful*. Have to lunch at home & not stir until the theatre in the evening. Spite of cabs, the theatre makes it decidedly worse. Foot now as large as the Albert Hall. I spend most of the morning dictating a fatherly letter to Archer about his Chronicle criticisms. Am a fearful wreck.

To WILLIAM ARCHER

[29 Fitzroy Square W]
[H.f/2]   [Undated: assigned to 21st April 1898]

[The "fatherly letter" to Archer which Shaw had dictated was not sent. On 26th April he was informed by Shaw: "I see nothing in it that would interest you except the postscript, which contains simple information, and an explanation of the 'poet's secret' in 'Candida,' which will dry your tears" (BM). The two fragments were enclosed.

Laura Ormiston Chant (1848–1923) was a well-known social reformer. The original of Frank was R. C. Phillimore.]

When Eugene, with his apprehensive faculty raised to the highest sensitiveness by his emotional state, hears that long speech of Candida's about the household, he takes the whole thing in, grasps for the first time what it really means, what the conditions of such love are, and how it is essentially the creature of limitations which are far transcended in his own nature. He sees at once that no such life and no such love are possible for him, and instantly leaves them all far behind him. To put it another way, he jumps to the position from which the Master-builder saw that it was all over with the building of happy homes for human beings. He looks at the comfort and sweetness and happiness that has just been placed before him at its best, and turns away from it, exclaiming with absolute conviction, "Life is nobler than that." Thus Candida's sympathy with his supposed sorrow is entirely thrown away. If she were to alter her decision and offer herself to him he would be unspeakably embarrassed and terrified. When he says "Out into the night with me," he does not mean the night of despair and darkness, but the free air and holy starlight which is so much more natural an atmosphere to him than this stuffy fireside warmth of mothers and sisters and wives and so on. It may be that this exposition may seem to you to destroy all the pathos and sanity of the scene; but from no other point of view could it have been written. A perfect dramatic command, either of character or situation, can only be obtained from some point of view that transcends both. The absolute fitness which is the secret of the effectiveness of the ending of "Candida," would be a mere sham if it meant nothing more than a success for Morell at the cost of a privation for Eugene. Further, any such privation would take all the point from Candida's sub-consciousness of the real state of affairs; for you will observe that Candida knows all along perfectly well that she is no mate for Eugene, and instinctively relies on that solid fact to pull him through when he is going off, as she thinks, broken-hearted. The final touch of comedy is the femininely practical reason that she gives for their incompatibility.

. . . .

P.S. It may interest you to know some of the people who have, or might have, served me as models.

Candida—Ellen Terry, Mrs H.M. Stanley, Mrs Ormiston Chant.

Vivie—Mrs Sidney Webb (an absolutely new type in modern fiction).

Bluntschli v. Saranoff—Sidney Webb v. Cunningham Graham in the Socialist movement. Saranoff's "I never withdraw" is historical. It occurred in the House of Commons when Cunningham Graham said "Damn."

The Waiter standing between Crampton and his family—R.B. Haldane standing between Balfour and Asquith.

Raina—Mrs Besant.

Napoleon—Richard Mansfield and the historical Napoleon.

Cuthbertson—Clement Scott.

Crofts, Frank, Praed, Burgess, and Prossy were very definitely suggested to me by the outward aspect of certain individuals who are not necessarily at all like them in character: for instance, the original of Frank is now my colleague on the Vestry, a County Councillor, a devoted husband, a glutton for public work, and an exemplary citizen in all respects. Cokane is a real individual. Julia is a stormy reality from my own past. Of course all the characters are really composites; but some of them are types as well, the more vivid ones types of character, like Mrs Warren, the less vivid ones types of youth, like the twins in "You never can tell" (or Hilda Wangel), or of servitude, like Nicola. The only "work of art" is the Strange Lady in "The Man of Destiny," who is only a confection. The sub-lieutenant in that piece, by the way, is a little masterpiece of character; whilst your friend the inn-keeper is almost as nearly borrowed from Dickens as Bohun (see Cavaletto in "Little Dorrit" and Jaggers in "Great Expectations"). Mrs Clandon is a composite of the advanced woman of the George Eliot period, with certain personal traits of my mother.

[Archer replied on 30th April: "I ask for nothing better than to have it proved that my analysis of your limitations is wrong, imperfect, founded on insufficient or misread evidence. . . . But the evidence I want is good plays, not . . . assertions that such and such a character is taken from such & such a real person. That I don't doubt either; but the merit of a likeness depends not on whom it is meant for, but on whether it is like; and furthermore, a likeness may be very like & yet a shocking work of art, & especially out of place in a given dramatic picture." (Hol. draft, BM)]

To CHARLOTTE PAYNE-TOWNSHEND

[E.u/2; X/151.e]

[29 Fitzroy Square W]
22nd April 1898

[The Australian cousin was Greta Bergh Shaw of Hobart. The office of the Fabian Society was in a dank basement in Clifford's Inn, just off the Strand. Shaw had attended a Fabian business meeting that evening. Dr William Salisbury Sharpe was Alice Lockett's husband.]

No further difficulty about locomotion, as I now simply hop, my left foot being no longer of any use. Dictate a heap of letters. Do not suffer so much from want of exercise as might be expected, as the hopping up & down stairs is very arduous & violent, and shakes up my liver with salutary vehemence. Second visit from Australian cousin to see Lucy. Hop downstairs & into cab in the evening. Hop from cab along passage from Fleet St to Clifford's Inn, to the amazement of the populace. Long debate on Drink Resolutions. Hop back to Fleet St; cab; home; and hop upstairs. Hot water treatment repeated. Various theories by sympathetic friends—vegetarian gout popular because funny—Lucy insists that I have dislocated a toe. This being just possible, I make up my mind to get Salisbury Sharpe to look at it tomorrow on the chance of its being a bonesetter's business.

By the way, you have been elected to the Fabian Executive . . . I half expected to see you at the meeting tonight: you missed the insane spectacle of my entry on one leg.

23rd April 1898

[*Cæsar and Cleopatra*, begun on this date, was not completed until 9th December 1898, at Blen-Cathra. The play at the Globe Theatre was G. Stuart Ogilvie's *The Master*. Kate Perugini (1839-1929), a portrait painter, was the youngest daughter of Charles Dickens.]

Mrs Salt collapses with a sick headache & retires to bed after being dictated to. Snatch up my note book & make a start at last on "Cæsar

35

& Cleopatra." Lifelike scene in the courtyard of the palace at Alexandria among the bodyguard of Cleopatra. Screamingly amusing—will kill the seriousness of the whole play. This enforced inaction is going to save my life: I can actually be lighthearted again. After posthour the doctor comes. My medical skill is completely vindicated: I have been doing exactly the right thing. He opines that the long bicycle ride after the period of inaction & the tight shoe made the two toe joints slip over one another & inflame. Remedy, hot water and the minimum of use for the foot. He suggests 3 hours hot water in the morning & 1½ in the evening. Thank you—amputation sooner; but I will do my best. Also a mass of cottonwool swathes in an oiled silk mackintosh to sweat the foot heroically. He anticipates that I will have 10 days of it. He goes & I find that Alice has been in the next room all the time. Then I hop & cab to the Globe, & have a talk with Mrs Perugini.

24th April 1898

Hot water operations, & "Götterdämmerung" and Cleopatra. In the afternoon Janet comes. She has had £100 from her father's death & is clad in green & grey in a fashionable & distangay manner. I read her Cleopatra & make her shriek. She goes off, forgetting her book, and presently returns, stands in the middle of the street amid the Sunday crowds in the square & shouts "Bernard" in her most magnificent Drury Lane voice until I come to the window. Altogether, she is in great form, & only once verges on tears & a threat to pay you back your £25. . . .

You say you think of me skipping about at Radlett with the young lambs. Ha! ha! You should see me now, nailed to my chair, with my feet like this.

But the inaction is really resting me & helping Cleopatra.

GBS

25th April 1898

[The *Saturday Review* article on 30th April, entitled "Kate Terry," contained reviews of Ogilvie's *The Master* and Carton's *Lord and Lady Algy*.]

In the house all day. Began & finished Saturday article, with a bit of Cleopatra in. . . .

Neuralgia—ill in Italy!!! This is a knock down blow: I thought you were recuperating, and that the balmy Pincian airs were beating Adelphi Terrace all to fits & confuting all my theories. *Now* it appears that I was right about London. I always am. The cycle of Cathay is always a fraud: mud & fog are not so fatal as sciroccos & sibecchios & Reckitt's blue. Come back, then. *I* know what your nerves need.

26th April 1898

Still in the house all day. Finished whole scene of Cleopatra—Sc. 2 of the 1st act—quintessence of everything that has most revolted the chivalrous critics. Ha! ha! Julius Cæsar as the psychological woman tamer. Ho! ho!

The doctor came and I pumped him for half an hour about the Army medical staff & military-medical matters generally. We neither of us pretended to take the smallest interest in the foot, which is now simply an inconvenience. It is hardly noticeably bigger than the other one by this time; but it is far from being in working condition.

I add this on Wednesday [27 April] before going to the Vestry. Since you are to start on Friday morning, this is the last leaf I shall venture to send, as anything posted tomorrow would overshoot you, probably; and I cannot wait until midnight because the last post for me now is Susan's bedtime, not my own. I will try to find out when your train is due on Sunday night; and if the hour is not absolutely scandalous I shall present myself at the Terrace & crush in all your ribs with an embrace that has been accumulating for 2 months.

27th April 1898

[The St Pancras Vestry minutes for 27th April indicate that Shaw moved an amendment "That the free closet at the Women's Convenience, Pancras Road, be continued, and that the Highways, Sewers, and Public Works Committee be instructed to enquire into the alleged abuse of the closet, and to take such steps as may be necessary for the prevention of such abuse, and for the detection of offenders." The amendment was defeated, and a motion was passed to abolish "the free closet." The play that evening was Edward G. Knoblauch's *The Club Baby* at the Avenue Theatre.]

Odd jobs in the way of correspondence—I forget exactly what. Fearful trials at Vestry. Moved amendments to 3 Committee Reports. Defeated every time. Vestry getting afraid of me—men who supported me in Committee (decent elderly Conservatives) do not venture to support me in full vestry. I am found out, it appears. One particularly fearful business over a resolution to stop free accommodation for women in

sanitary conveniences. I move amendment. [J.W.] Dixon, a pillar of the
Church, rises in saintly majesty, and says my remarks are disgusting.
Then says Mrs Phillimore has behaved indecently in seconding me.
Chairman [W.H.Matthews], much ashamed, rebukes him & he collapses. Lion indifferent to the personality, but furious & frantic about
the resolution. I am too lame to take anything excitedly; so I sit
amiably & feel that I must soon unmask my guns & begin to fight the
vestry.

In the evening—theatre. Play with a baby in it. Might have been
written by one.

1st May 1898

At last. Charlotte due at 19½ at Victoria. Work at the Nibelungen
pamphlet after leafing through Sunday papers. After lunch I strike
work & take up a novel entitled Sunlight & Limelight, by one [Francis
Henry] Gribble, all about the love affairs of an actress. They are not at
all unlike mine. I finish the book at a sitting, as I dont want to be weary-
brained when Charlotte comes.

After 20, I limp down to Tottenham Court Road, my troubles all
over at last. I descend at Charing Cross, & limp slowly slowly, slowly,
to Adelphi Terrace. With a long gasp of relief, I lay my two-months
burden down & ring the bell. Martha's footstep on the stairs.

Well, I AM damned!

Wretch, devil, fiend!

The train has arrived; & you are not in it? Stopped in Paris, to see
Cyrano again, perhaps. No: Satan's own daughter would have telegraphed.

Let me be polite to Martha, at least. I suppose the train has missed
its connexion, and you will not arrive until midnight. 12.30, Martha
says, tacitly putting it to me whether, as a gentleman, I can wait.
Clearly I cannot. I limp back to my bus, & here I am.

[The following morning a letter from Charlotte was delivered: "Well, here I
am anyway now! Yes: I *might* have telegraphed: it was horrid of me. I am a
wreck, mental & physical. Such a journey as it was! . . . My dear—& your
foot? Shall I go up to you, or will you come here, & when? Only tell me what
you would prefer. Of course I am quite free—Charlotte" (BM).]

To BRAM STOKER

[G.u/2]   [Undated: assigned to 2nd May 1898]

[Stoker had invited Shaw to the first night of H.D.Traill and Robert S. Hichens's *The Medicine Man* at the Lyceum. Although he was no longer on Irving's critics' list, would he come "personally"? (BM) Hichens was Shaw's successor as music critic for *The World* (1894). Tregenna was a character in the play. Re the Irving–Richard III contretemps, see I, 747.]

Personally I have only one desire concerning the theatres of this accursed metropolis, and that is to see them, with their actors, managers, critics, and all complete, plunged into the blinding white hot heat of hell until everything theatrical is consumed out of them & nothing remains but a virgin art and a small heap of clinker representing the press. I have devoted four years of my life to them; and now I will enter into my well earned rest. I have duly notified to the Saturday Review that at the end of the present season my articles on the theatre will cease; and thereafter, by God, this foot shall never again cross the ungrateful threshold of a playhouse.

Whether I go or not on Wednesday, I shall have to criticize the play, I suppose, for the sake of Hichens & the British drama generally, just as I criticised Laurence's Peter. Now this would be a much less dull job for me if I saw the play. There's absolutely nothing in Tregenna; and I should like to see what notion of his own Irving will slip into his vacant dress suit. Further, it is not decent to have first nights at the Lyceum without me: it makes the front of the house ridiculous. Again, it produces an impression of a vendetta; and Irving & I are too eminent to indulge in such schoolboyishness in public. Yet again, the whole business of striking me off the list has been the most blasted nonsense from the beginning: Irving is firmly persuaded that he was drunk on the first night of Richard III, and that I betrayed him in my article, which, like all my articles, meant just exactly what it said, no less no more. Consequently, shall we put it as follows?—

Dear Mr Stoker

It would give me great pleasure personally to witness the performance of "The Medicine Man" on Wednesday, and thus to "assist" at what I feel sure will be a production worthy of the best traditions of the Lyceum.

yrs sincerely
[G.Bernard Shaw]

39

To SIDNEY WEBB

[H/14; X/141.e; 151.e]

29 Fitzroy Square W
7th May 1898

[R.Wherry Anderson was a Fabian who had been elected to the Executive Committee that week. William M.Thompson (1857–1907) was an Irish journalist and democrat, who edited *Reynolds's Newspaper*. Sir Charles W. Dilke (1843–1911), former M.P., was a radical statesman, who supported legislation involving trades-unions, hours of labour, minimum wage, and Redistribution of Income. The letter in the *Daily Chronicle* on 30th April was entitled "Mr. Shaw's Method and Secret." *The Grandissimes* (1884) was a novel by the southern American writer George Washington Cable (1844–1925).]

. . . Charlotte came back five days ago, with a gigantic collection of documents concerning the Roman municipality. She found her position as my secretary usurped by Mrs Salt, who suits me very well, as I can bully her unlimitedly, because she has no idea how effective she is. Charlotte demanded her post back again; I insisted on her setting to work at once on the Roman report. She declined. So Mrs Salt went off to Kew Gardens for a holiday; and Charlotte had one delirious day of being dictated to. Then, as usual, Reason resumed her sway. Mrs Salt came back; and the Roman book is supposed to be now under weigh. The only question is, what form it should take. Her lady-like instincts strongly urge her to a dry official report for the use of students at the school. I, on the other hand, insist on a thrilling memoir, giving the whole history of a lady of quality suffering from a broken heart (with full particulars) and being rescued from herself by the call of public work. The extent to which the call was reinforced by the renewed activity of the mended heart is to be described, and the whole is to conclude with the voyage to Italy, the adventures there among the old romantic associations, and, incidentally, a complete view, by glimpses, of the municipal humours of Rome. Charlotte sees dimly that the accomplishment of such a magnum opus would be indeed the conquest of a profession for herself, and consequent salvation; but she has got no further at present than arranging her materials.

By the way, she got in, at the Executive election, with 200 votes, which was handsome. Wherry Anderson also effected a lodgment. He and W.M.Thompson have organized a dinner to Hyndman at the Cafe Monaco on the 11th May, "in recognition of his 25 years of Public Labour on behalf of the People." I have magnanimously taken a ticket, but cannot go, as I am engaged to Dilke for that evening. The occasion of this dinner is H.M.H.'s notification to all and sundry that he cannot go on with his provincial campaigning any longer. . . . My confinement to the house is not altogether bad for work, and even the absolute cessation of gadding about except in cabs is turning out to be rather good physical economy. I am working at Cæsar and Cleopatra, which will throw a new light on history, and on an explanatory pamphlet, to be published by Grant Richards, on Der Ring des Nibelungen, jam full of Socialism in the manner of Ruskin.

The Chronicle is working up sympathy here with America at a great rate. It is catching on rather, because England's sentiment in the matter is based on a profound conviction that America is going to be the top dog in this conflict.

The reviewing of my Plays has been going on with immense vigour; but I am absorbed in struggles with the Vestry, which has become so recalcitrant that I have at last thrown off the mask and attacked it in print, to its collective indignation and individual exultation. The thing goes on like this. Cunningham Graham writes a letter to the Chronicle raising the question whether, as a dramatist, I am a pupil of Ibsen or De Maupassant. I reply with a long letter, shewing that the real force which influences me is the attitude of the St. Pancras Vestry on the question of providing free sanitary accommodation for women. This gives considerable piquancy to the correspondence, and has a most subduing effect on the Vestry.

I will hand round your letter as instructed. You might get me the photographs of the Devil's Disciple: I have received nothing but a portrait of Mrs Mansfield as Judith. I presume you have received the American edition of the Plays from Stone of Chicago. They were published technically on the 15th April; but I do not know whether the real publication has taken place yet. The usual thing is for the American publisher to sell a single copy as a matter of form on the day of publication in England, but not to let it really loose until the most favourable season for publishing.

I have not heard of Olivier yet. He may have come in the same ship as your letter.

Do not trouble to write me letters while you are busy. Just send me post-cards with your addresses; and I will send you whatever news is going. I have the addresses up to 7th July at San Francisco.

GBS

P.S. I had one dinner invitation from Kate [Courtney], but hopped out of it on my bad foot. Also one from Dolly Stanley, to meet Cable

[of] the Grandissimes. To this I succumbed; adding that she was the original of Candida and I adored her. With this exception my life since you left has been blameless.

PP.S Olivier has returned.

To JANET ACHURCH

29 Fitzroy Square W
[C.u/4]   9th May [1898] 8.20 p.m.

At 8.30 the operator & the chloroformer are due; so I must be brief. It is necessary to make a hole in my foot to let the matter out; & as it lies underneath arteries &c, it is necessary to make a regular operation of it. I dont suppose I shall be able to go to the Vestry on Wednesday afternoon; so you will probably find me if you look in. . . .

To JANET ACHURCH

29 Fitzroy Square W
[B/4; X/152.e]   11th May 1898

They didnt tell me not to see you: they knew better. They stopped you off their own bat; and I knew nothing about it until your letter arrived, to my great disappointment. Come tomorrow by all means.

They were all frightened out of their wits by the doctor, who wants to cure me of my vegetarian follies & says that I am in a critical condition—he says from undernourishment, *I* say from overwork. Anyhow, when he got down to the bone, it was *carious*, which certainly shews that I have been overdoing the superhuman, and turning everything that should have been shared with my bones into Saturday Reviewing energy.

GBS

To MAX BEERBOHM

29 Fitzroy Square W
[L/1]   17th May 1898

[Having dramatised his operation for *Saturday Review* readers in an article, "G.B.S. Vivisected," on 14th May, Shaw provided his "Valedictory" on the 21st, ending with the now famous words: "The younger generation is knocking at the door; and as I open it there steps spritely in the incomparable Max. . . . I am off duty for ever, and am going to sleep." Beerbohm did not review *Teresa* until it opened in the West End the following September. His first contribution as a drama critic (after reviewing Shaw's two volumes of plays on 14th and 21st May) was an article, "Why I ought not to have become a Dramatic Critic," on 28th May.]

My dear Max B.

As you will have seen by the Saturday, I am stranded here with a bad foot, & with no immediate prospect of getting back to my critical duties. This did not matter last week because there was nothing on at the theatres; but this week they are playing young George Bancroft's maiden effort "Teresa" at the Metropole in Camberwell. It is rather hard on him not to have a notice: besides, I have always made a strong point of backing up the suburban theatres whenever they produce an original play. Do you feel disposed to go to Camberwell and inaugurate your reign as dramatic critic of the Saturday this week?

On the whole I think it is better to change with the eyes of the season on us than for me to slip out & you to slip in before and after the holidays, with a pretence of unobtrusiveness. There is no doubt now that I must get away to the country to recuperate as soon as I can stand up; so that destiny has taken the matter out of my hands. You had better therefore settle matters with [Frank] Harris at once, & have the theatre tickets sent on to you in future as a matter of course.

By the way, they sent me a stall for the Metropole last night. I wired to them at the last moment to cancel it, having forgotten all about it til that moment. You will find that the acting managers have by this time got into tolerably decent training as to tickets for first nights.

I have read your article on my plays with some anxiety for your salvation. You must go on a vestry at the first opportunity. You have been badly brought up, & can only taste life when it is fried in fine art. Follow my glorious example, & go into the Park every Sunday morning with a kitchen chair & a red flag. That is all your genius needs to sun away the north light of the studio.

Farewell; and dont push the thing to the ridiculous extreme of getting an abscess in your foot.

yours ever
G. Bernard Shaw

To HENRY ARTHUR JONES

[B/4; X/124]

29 Fitzroy Square W
20th May 1898

[*Grace Mary* (1898) was a one-act play by Jones. Aylmer Maude's translation of Tolstoi's *What is Art?* had just been issued in three parts, as supplements to a journal *The New Order*. Shaw reviewed a new edition of the work in the *Daily Chronicle* on 10th September 1898. Jones's reply to Shaw's query was: "Yes, I would get married if I were you. But read the chapters in Rabelais and the advice that was given to Panurge on the subject" (*Life and Letters of Henry Arthur Jones*, 1930).]

One thing I quite forgot to say yesterday in writing about "Grace Mary." Have you read Tolstoi's "What is Art?" It is beyond all comparison the best treatise on art that has been done by a literary man (I bar Wagner) in these times. His theory is right all through, his examples the silliest obsolete nonsense. Among other things he is very strong on the Universality of good art, and the classiness of bad art—that good art is as intelligible to a peasant as to a gentleman &c. If there were any chance of his being able to wrestle with the Cornish lingo I should send him "Grace Mary" as a striking specimen of the universal play.

Miss Townshend is much fascinated by it.

By the way, would you advise me to get married?

yrs ever
G. Bernard Shaw

To MAX HECHT

[C/1]

29 Fitzroy Square W
23rd May 1898

[Max Hecht (*c*.1848–1908), a German Jew, was a City director with an interest in theatre and music. The "little bird" was Shaw himself: he had been giving out hints all over London. To Grant Richards he had confided, on the same day, "I am going to get married . . . Keep this dark until I have done it" (*Author Hunting*, 1934).]

Very Private [underlined 11 times]

If you can catch that little bird, tie his beak up tight. Some day I will give you my opinion of the report. Meanwhile, I shall do nothing but shake my head. If ever I get married, it will have to be done very secretly, because I have a great many friends who would make a fuss, and who would spend money which they cannot afford in giving me things which I don't want. I hate presents.

You may, however, tell Mrs Hecht not to be discouraged.

GBS

To GRAHAM WALLAS

[H/13]

29 Fitzroy Square W
26th May 1898

I found the votive pig skin on the floor after you left yesterday. I find it will come in handy for holding the sheets of literary masterpieces while in progress. Nevertheless it was an act of gross superstition. I don't believe you have ever realized what a thorough Protestant I am. Relics and symbols of all kinds excite iconoclastic fury in me. The average man is an idolator: he cannot get hold of a human relationship sufficiently closely and clearly to make it satisfactory to his own senses. Consequently he must attach some rite or symbol to it so as to get a material grip on it. Now I am not in this lowly predicament. My regard for you is perfectly safe and sensible to my grip without a pig skin handle; and the transubstantiation which makes a present sacred is a fraud against which my clear platonic vision of reality is proof. Hence my scoffs are the expression, not of cynical callousness, but of perfect intelligence of feeling.

My disabled condition has driven Miss Payne Townshend into the most humiliating experiences. I sent in for the man next door to marry us; but he said he only did births and deaths. Miss Payne Townshend then found a place in Henrietta Street, where she had to explain to a boy that she wanted to get married. The boy sent the news up a tube through which shrieks of merriment were exchanged, culminating in an order to shew the lady up. Upstairs she found a man who became greatly excited when he learnt the names of the parties, and offered to do the job any time after today (Thursday) for £2 17 11. She felt that it was extremely conscientious of him not to ask £2 18, and forked out. He implored her not to make it Friday unless she could come before 11 o'clock, as he would be off duty after that hour, and would lose the only chance of immortality his office had brought him. Miss Payne Townshend then had to suffer the final humiliation of buying a ring. The difficulty was to find a West End jeweller's in which she had never been before, but at last she succeeded, and returned with the symbol of slavery. We can now drop in at Henrietta Street any time and settle the job. The ring, by the way, is a modern article of such portentous weight and thickness, that it is impossible for anyone but a professional pianist to wear it; so my mother has presented her with my grandmother's wedding ring for general use.

The registrar offers to provide the necessary witnesses from his own official or domestic staff. I had thought of asking you and Mrs Salt, who violently objects to the whole proceeding, to see fair; but it doesnt seem necessary. If we should arrange it that way, I think I shall make Salt officiate instead of his wife, as she is quite capable of breaking out and forbidding the banns at the supreme moment.

GBS

To HENRY S. SALT

[Y/5]   31st May 1898

CAN YOU MEET US AT FIFTEEN HENRIETTA STREET COVENT GARDEN AT ELEVEN THIRTY TOMORROW WEDNESDAY TO WITNESS A CONTRACT

SHAW

[The wedding ceremony on 1st June, to judge by Shaw's subsequent account of it, contained all the ingredients for a successful West End farce: "I was ... altogether a wreck on crutches and in an old jacket which the crutches had worn to rags. I had asked my friends [Graham Wallas and Henry Salt] ... to act as witnesses, and, of course, in honour of the occasion they were dressed in their best clothes. The registrar never imagined I could possibly be the bridegroom; he took me for the inevitable beggar who completes all wedding processions. Wallas, who is considerably over six feet high, seemed to him to be the hero of the occasion, and he was proceeding to marry him calmly to my betrothed, when Wallas, thinking the formula rather strong for a mere witness, hesitated at the last moment and left the prize to me" (Henderson, *George Bernard Shaw: Man of the Century*, 1956).

The report in *The Star* on 2nd June was a journalistic scoop: Shaw had written it himself!

"As a lady and gentleman were out driving in Henrietta-st., Covent-garden yesterday, a heavy shower drove them to take shelter in the office of the Superintendant Registrar there, and in the confusion of the moment he

46

married them. The lady was an Irish lady named Miss Payne-Townshend, and the gentleman was George Bernard Shaw.

"Mr. Graham Wallas and Mr. H. S. Salt were also driven by stress of weather into the registrar's, and the latter being secretary of the Humanitarian League would naturally have remonstrated against the proceedings had there been time, but there wasn't. Mr. Bernard Shaw means to go off to the country next week to recuperate, and this is the second operation he has undergone lately, the first being conducted, not by a registrar, but by a surgeon.

"Startling as was the liberty undertaken by the Henrietta-st. official, it turns out well. Miss Payne-Townshend is an Irish lady with an income many times the volume of that which 'Corno di Bassetto' used to earn, but to that happy man, being a vegetarian, the circumstance is of no moment. The lady is deeply interested in the London School of Economics, and that is the common ground on which the brilliant couple met. Years of married bliss to them."

That the event was of more than local interest may be attested by its announcement in the staid *New York Times* on 22nd June, with the comment: "Mr. Shaw, having become the husband of a lady who possesses both wealth and amiability, will no longer be under the necessity of writing either slashing criticisms or plays in which he rails at human nature. He can now settle down and become a respectable, middle-class gentleman, devoted to charitable pursuits and his wife."]

To EDWARD R. PEASE

[S(A)/2]

29 Fitzroy Square W
5th June 1898

Dear Pease

Best thanks from both of us to both of you.

As to the Executive, I am quite impenitent. I have always repudiated the theory that man and wife on the Executive means two votes for the man (or woman). If I thought that Mrs. Shaw would vote against her view of the interest of the society out of duty to me, I should institute divorce proceedings forthwith. I often urged Mrs. Bland to come on the executive when she was an active member; and I am strongly of opinion that Mrs. Webb would, at a later period, have been extremely useful on the committee. I therefore flatly refuse to resign; and unless I offer myself along with my wife as a sacrifice to superstition the executive cannot in decency accept *her* resignation—should she fancy herself bound to resign. I am open to argument on the subject; but that is my view at present. Besides, I wish to create a precedent for Oakeshott, should he at any time follow my example.

We go to Hindhead next Friday for four months.

yrs ever
G. Bernard Shaw

To WILLIAM ARCHER

[C/2]

29 Fitzroy Square W
6th June 1898

[Shaw and Charlotte Payne-Townshend had attended a performance of H. V. Esmond's *One Summer's Day* at the Comedy Theatre on 8th or 9th October 1897.]

I introduced her to you at the Comedy Theatre. Ladylike woman with green eyes. So when you meet her remember that you know her already.

GBS

To GRANT RICHARDS

[C/4; X/135]

[Pitfold. Haslemere]
19th June 1898

[From 10th June to 12th November the Shaws resided in a rented house in Haslemere, Surrey.]

My wife has been having *such* a delightful honeymoon! First my foot had to be nursed and the day before yesterday, just as it was getting pretty well, I fell downstairs and broke my left arm close to the wrist. I am afraid this will make a hopeless mess of the Wagner book. I had got to work fiercely again when it occurred, and had actually carried the exposition to within one act of the end of the Ring; but in my present smashed condition I daren't attempt to work against time. I am very sorry, as I had hoped to complete the MS. next week.

G.B.S.

48

To CHARLES CHARRINGTON

[A/4]

Pitfold. Haslemere
20th June 1898

... The air here is very good & the country (little as I can see of it)
first rate. I should like to see you down here; BUT I rather suspect the
thing will require some stage management; for Mrs S has a way of
admitting that Mrs C. has "genius" which does not absolutely convince me of her intention of joining our confederacy, which, after all,
is a confederacy of three geniuses of a sort not largely represented in
my wife's previous state of existence. You see I am beginning already
to assimilate other people's ideas to the extent of admitting that marriage
creates a situation that cannot be rushed as I used to rush all personal
situations. Whether Charlotte finally makes up her mind to regard the
confederacy as an item in our joint account or not, she can at all events
be trusted to behave sensibly; and for the moment my instinct warns
me to avoid any appearance of being unable to exist without seeing
Janet. Not, observe, that she is jealous of Janet, but that she sees herself
on the verge of being hooked on to this confounded confederacy in
which she has naturally neither part nor lot, and being compelled to
act a theatrically effusive friendship with Janet, she acting badly and
with scruple, & Janet acting floridly and with the greatest relish, the
whole situation being quite revolting to her reserved habit.

I am not equal in my present condition to working this out to an
exact manual of conduct for all parties; but for the moment I shall go
slow in arranging a joyful meeting. I *must* coach Janet not to be magnanimous, not to be soulful, not to magnify the duty of being civil to
Shaw's wife into an obligation to take that wife to her bosom like a
radiant modern Mrs Crummles. If she does, there will be hell, Charles
Charrington—HELL.

This is as much as I can scribble with my other arm broken.

GBS

To BEATRICE WEBB

[A/14; X/141]

Pitfold. Haslemere
21st June 1898

[This letter recapitulates, with dramatic exaggeration and embroidery, all of
the principal events of the previous four months in Shaw's life. Miss Honnor
Morten (1861–1913) was a noted reformer and feminist, who for a brief time
was a Fabian. Sir Percy Ashley (1876–1945) was at this time a lecturer in

History and Public Administration at the London School of Economics; he joined the Board of Trade in 1906. Herbert S. Foxwell (1849–1936) was a lecturer at the L.S.E. who later became Professor of Political Economy at University College, London.]

All manner of extraordinary events have happened to me in consequence of your departure. After you left, there was nothing to take me out of town or away from my work. Adelphi Terrace was closed by the visit [of Charlotte] to Rome. I simply worked straight on end at all times & all hours, and gave up half my eating because I got no change or exercise to give me an appetite, & large meals disturbed my digestion without one. However, I got the book finally off my hands, gave the Saturday notice to quit, & generally prepared myself for a better life later on. If I had gone away at Easter, I should have saved the situation; but I had nowhere to go and nobody to go to; and the theatres were very exacting; so I ventured to let the opportunity slip. By this time I was in an almost superhuman condition—fleshless, bloodless, vaporous, ethereal, and stupendous in literary efficiency. Then the bolt fell. I rode out one night to Ealing & back on the bike; and when I returned, my left foot was like this . Even then I had it all but cured with simple hot water fomentation when the Vestry Election caught me & induced me to walk to a meeting & back. That settled it. The thing became an abscess, and after a few more days of fomenting, I had to deliver myself over to the knife & the ether bag. One of my ancient flames acted as nurse; & her husband operated. The anaesthetist was in the last agonies of influenza; but he managed to perform his function without inconveniencing me: I wasnt sick afterwards, only rather drunk, in which condition, when the anaesthetist had gone home to bed, & the surgeon had left the room to talk to my mother, I pretended to be delirious and raved all sorts of love to the nurse, who was deeply affected.

The surgeon did not trouble himself in the least about my etherized philanderings, but kicked up a tremendous row about my health. He said I was killing myself. When he cut into the foot he not only found no blood—"only some wretched sort of ichor" he said—but the bone was necrosed. He swore it was tubercular caries; drew up a dietary of the most butcherly kind; and told me flatly that I had to choose between it & death.

As it happened, somebody before the operation suggested the possibility of my dying under the anæsthetic, and I then found that the prospect was not in the least disagreeable to me—rather too tempting to be dwelt on, if anything. I backed vegetarianism to the extent of my life without a moment's hesitation. It did well enough too: I soon began to pull myself together. Sharpe (the doctor) no doubt took the case by the ordinary standard of breakdown deferred to the utmost point by the abuse of stimulants, whereas it was really a perfectly simple case of exhaustion & starvation (of fresh air & rest as much as food). But matters were left in a detestable way. Sharpe had not been prepared for a necrosis operation; and though he scraped away the bad bit of bone as well as he could, there is still a bit that will not heal & that must some day exfoliate and come away. Meanwhile the hole in my foot has to be packed afresh every day with iodoform gauze & treated constantly with boracic fomentations.

Meanwhile Charlotte had returned from Rome & was on the scene. It was now plain that I must go away to the country the moment I could be moved, & that somebody must seriously take in hand the job of looking after me. Equally plain, of course, that Charlotte was the inevitable & predestined agent appointed by Destiny. To have let her do this in any other character than that of my wife would (in the absence of your chaperonage) have involved our whole circle and its interests in a senseless scandal. You may wonder why I did not find that out long ago, instead of exploiting the chaperonage with complete selfishness. I can only say that I dont know—that the situation was changed by a change in my own consciousness. I found that my objection to my own marriage had ceased with my objection to my own death. This was the main change: there were of course many other considerations which we shall probably discuss at some future time. Possibly one of them was that the relation between us had never until then completely lost its inevitable preliminary character of a love affair. She had at last got beyond that corrupt personal interest in me, just as "The Devil's Disciple" had relieved me of the appearance of a pecuniary interest (more than was reasonable) in her. The thing being cleared thus of all such illusions as love interest, happiness interest, & all the rest of the vulgarities of marriage, I changed right about face on the subject and hopped down to the Registrar, who married me to her on one leg, after beginning the ceremony with Wallas, who had a new coat on[.]

The papers noticed the event as eagerly as the death of Gladstone. Mrs Chumly (I forget the full length spelling) wrote to Charlotte, "Do not ask me to meet This Man. And as a last kindness to me, & for my sake, I ask you to secure your money."

At last, after much nursing, we secured this house, on the south slope of Hindhead, until October. I came down on crutches. The air was so fine that our troubles seemed to be over; but they had only just begun. The moment I began to get strong, I recklessly returned to work on a Quintessence of Wagner which I had begun earlier; and in a few days I was at it as savagely as ever. Sharpe wrote vehemently commanding me not to tempt the gods. Before his letter arrived I found out, after dictating Wagner criticism one morning for half an hour, that I was myself conscious that all the strain was on again. I called a halt, and went upstairs on the crutches (a foolish feat) to get something from my bedroom. Coming down again, the crutches got planted behind my centre of gravity & shot me into the air. I snatched at a bannister on the landing above, and caught it in my right hand; but it snapped like an Argoed tree; and I was precipitated fifty fathom or thereabout into the hall, with my left arm doubled up in ruin under me—like this

WRIST · ALMIGHTY SMASH. ELBOW

Imagine poor Charlotte's feelings! She got a pair of butter pats & made splints of them. The local doctor, who did not come for half an hour, during which I lay in the hall with all the strain gone, perfectly relieved and happy, was fortunately a capable man; and the setting was a success. But fancy my condition *now* (this happened four days ago[)]. I am helpless—a nurse (disciple of Honnor Morten) has to wash and dress and all but feed me. I have a wheeled chair, which I cannot wheel, since when worked with one hand only, it simply spins round & round. Heaven knows what will happen to Charlotte when the anxiety about me is over. Last night a cat, shut up accidentally in the pantry, simulated a burglar so successfully that I sallied out, walking recklessly on the bad foot, at three in the morning, & thereby did myself as much harm as possible. I no longer feel any confidence in my ultimate recovery: it seems certain to me that I shall presently break all my other limbs as well.

I am sitting in my wheeled chair on the lawn, looking over the hills through a gap in the trees to a bit of heather which reminds me of the Argoed, and of all my previous honeymoons, with respect to which I may now, as a correctly married man, speak to you, dear Beatrice, with frank sentiment. Not until you left me a widower was I driven to be unfaithful to your fireside.

G. Bernard Shaw

The Honeymoon, 1898

Writing *Cæsar and Cleopatra*, on the downs at Freshwater, 1898
(*Photograph by Charlotte F. Shaw*)

"The Dying Vegetarian"
(*Photograph by Dorothy Kreyer*, 1898)

P.S. Tell Webb that I note his instructions about Ashley, & will keep "Miss Payne Townshend" (ha! ha!) in mind of them.

Also, unfortunately, that the London School is much the worse, evidently, for his absence. The City & Parochial has refused to fork out; and [W.A.S.] Hewins, almost in tears, declares that the attitude of the Technical Education Board can mean nothing else than a charge of downright malversation against him. None of them have the art of getting money or even of keeping it. In despair they are falling back on the Foxwell Library project (which seems to me a monstrous waste of money) as a possible bait for subsidies. Charlotte is of course cut off from all business now except my fractured limbs. However, it will have to be retrieved by your next book, which will probably prove that the London School is the palladium of British superiority to America.

I must break off here. The writing of this letter is against all orders.

By the way, the dates of the foregoing history are—the marriage, 1st June; the move to Hindhead, 10th June; the arm fracture, 17th June.

To CHARLES CHARRINGTON

[A/4]

Pitfold. Haslemere
23rd June 1898

[Although virtually every biographer of Shaw and Charlotte has spoken of a marriage settlement made by Charlotte in which Shaw's mother and (after her death) his sister received annuities, no such agreement actually existed, though it may have been spoken of. It was not until May 1899 that a settlement was drawn up by Charlotte's solicitors, and this merely guaranteed *to Shaw* the annual income from two trust funds, administered by Sidney Webb and Frederick Whelen. The settlement, dated 24th May 1899, contained no reference to Shaw's mother or sister; the funds were to revert to Charlotte in the event that Shaw should predecease her. The trust fund was not wound up until August 1938.]

How on earth can I lend you £50? What's the good of lending you £50? What have your creditors ever done for me that I should present them with £50? I will see them damned first.

Please observe my present position. I have married without a settlement, and have no more money than I had before, though I have the run of a house & servants, board &c. I have two ghastly & ruinous doctor's bills to meet. Furthermore, my wife loses some of her income

53

through her marriage, because her valuable founder's bank shares cannot be held by a married woman & must be sold out without the possibility of equivalent reinvestment. I am not bound to make up the difference; but I am not sure that I shall not try to do it. Anyhow, that would be a more sensible investment than encouraging the creditors (who have no doubt observed the newspaper pars about the wealth of the bride) to make the crisis in your affairs more chronic than it is at present.

I really wish there were any effective & possible way of extricating you; but you know well enough that there is no sort of sense in lending you £50 of Charlotte's money—for that is what it comes to.

I quite agree that Charlotte has got to find Janet's measure, and they will get on well enough then. But she must find it for herself. Clearly it would do no good for me to assure her that Janet is a child, even if it were altogether true, which it isnt. At least its not scientific enough to satisfy a woman. So far, Charlotte is a good deal more impressed by Janet's cleverness than by her childishness, and probably doesnt feel altogether safe with her. They must find out their natural relations for themselves: these jobs cannot be put up by third parties.

Coquelin & Sarah [Bernhardt] are quite right to have a fortnight here for a big advertisement. Janet might do worse than play for a fortnight in Paris if she were starting round the world. Damn your analogies: they are always wrong.

A worse evil than even broken bones & abscesses has overtaken me —nettle rash. Frightful! I scratch myself in torment all night & am half driven to tear off the splints & scratch *there*.

Here comes the nurse to foment & bandage & massage & put me to bed. Forgive me; and goodnight.

GBS

To HENRY S. SALT

Pitfold. Haslemere
[B/5; X/164]   8th July 1898

[Winfield Scott Schley (1839–1911), an American naval officer, who was second in command of the naval force blockading Santiago de Cuba, had directed action against the Spanish fleet upon its emergence on 3rd July, which resulted in the destruction of the fleet. Salt did not follow Shaw's suggestion to write to the *Daily Chronicle*.]

54

I find that it will be necessary in the Wagner pamphlet to point out that Shelley anticipated The Ring by Prometheus Unbound. I haven't the requisite dates; and I have no idea where my Shelley primer is stowed at Fitzroy Square. Could you lend me a copy, or, if you haven't one handy, give me the dates of Prometheus & of the birth & death of Shelley?

It seems to me that the H[umanitarian] League ought to make a howling protest against this war, especially after the impassioned confession of faith by Commander Schley after the roasting of the Spanish sailors (vide yesterday's Chronicle). Why not address a letter to the Chronicle protesting against our embracing America on the occasion of her deliberately declaring war without a clear case of necessity, and calling for a combination of the other powers in the name of civilization to force the combatants to cease these atrocities & submit their dispute to international arbitration. I think it might do some good, if only in reminding the papers that some cant of humanity would become them.

GBS

P.S. Why not take one of your Sunday excursions in this direction & lunch with us or dine & stay the night?

To ARNOLD DOLMETSCH

[A/24; X/169]

Pitfold. Haslemere
19th July 1898

My dear Dolmetsch

I have just heard that you are going into the hands of the surgeons. As I have been in those hands myself for a couple of months, I know what that means—among other things, a lot of expense. You will need two nurses at first; for if you try to do with one, Mrs Dolmetsch will break down; and then matters will be worse than ever.

Now as you are not an opera singer, but an artist the value of whose work is necessarily only understood by a very few people, I know, being an artist myself, that it is just as likely as not that all this expense is coming on you at just the most inconvenient moment. Consequently you may as well know that I am rather in luck myself, as my last play has been very successful in America, and I have more money lying unused at the bank than I shall want this year. I pledge you my word that it will make absolutely no difference to me if I transfer £50 to your credit until you sell a harpsichord or get in your next season's harvest.

55

The only person who will feel the loss will be my banker; and he can afford it better than either of us.

If by good luck you are rolling in wealth, you will excuse me for proposing this arrangement, as I hope we need not stand on ceremony with one another. If not, send me a wire with the address of your bank, and I will lodge the £50 (or more if necessary) by return of post.

As soon as you can be moved, get away into the country. It is the cheapest plan in the end, because you will mend so much faster in the fresh air.

An operation, as I have found, is not so bad for an overworked artist as it is for most people. It stops the overwork & keeps one in bed. Most of us, after 20 years work or so, want six weeks in bed; and anything that forces us to take it is a blessing in disguise. . . .

yrs sincerely
G. Bernard Shaw

To HENRY S. SALT

[C/5]

Pitfold. Haslemere
28th July 1898

[To this postcard Charlotte added a note: "He is doing very well—but must be kept absolutely quiet until the beginning of next week. Do come after that."]

Yesterday I inaugurated my 43rd year with a second operation on a grand scale. There were four doctors, including the eminent operator. There were two things to be done: one, to gouge a pound or two of bone out of my instep; the other to get the broken arm (now mended but stiffish) into working order. *They forgot the arm.* I am so unspeakably tickled by this triumph over the profession that I cannot resist the temptation to impart it to you. Dont publish it, though.

GBS

P.S. Are you coming down to see us soon?

To HENRY SEYMOUR

[X/155]

[Pitfold. Haslemere]
[Undated: August 1898]

[Henry Seymour was at this time the editor of *The Adult*. George Bedborough, Hon. Secretary of the Legitimation League, had been arrested for offering for sale a copy of Havelock Ellis's *The Psychology of Sex*. On 31st October he pleaded guilty to three counts of an indictment which charged him with publishing and selling "certain obscene literature." In return for his agreement to sever all connection with the Legitimation League he was "bound over in his own recognizances in £100 to come up for judgment if called upon" (*Times*, 1 November 1898).]

Dear Mr. Seymour

The prosecution of Mr Bedborough for selling Mr. Havelock Ellis's book is a masterpiece of police stupidity and magisterial ignorance. I have read the book carefully; and I have no hesitation in saying that its publication was more urgently needed in England than any other recent treatise with which I am acquainted. Until it appeared there was no authoritative scientific book on its subject within reach of Englishmen and Englishwomen who cannot read French or German. At the same time Englishmen and Englishwomen are paying rates and taxes for the enforcement of the most abominably superstitious penal laws directed against the morbid idiosyncrasy with which the book deals. It is almost invariably assumed by ignorant people that this idiosyncrasy is necessarily associated with the most atrocious depravity of character; and this notion, for which there appears to be absolutely no foundation, is held to justify the infliction of penalties compared to which the punishment of a man who batters his wife almost to death is a trifle.

My own attention was called to the subject many years ago by the passing of a sentence of twenty years' penal servitude on a harmless elderly gentleman who had been ill-advised enough to plead guilty to a piece of folly which involved no danger whatever to society. At that time I was as ignorant as most people are on the subject; but the sentence so shocked my common humanity that I made an attempt to get the press to protest. I then discovered that the fear of becoming suspected of personal reasons for desiring a change in the law in this matter, makes every Englishman an abject coward, truckling to the vilest vulgar superstitions, and professing in public and in print views which have not the slightest resemblance to those which he expresses in private conversation with educated and thoughtful men. This hypocrisy is much more degrading to the public than the subject of

57

Mr. Havelock Ellis's book can possibly be, because it is universal instead of being accidental and peculiar. In Germany and France the free circulation of such works as the one of Mr. Havelock Ellis's now in question has done a good deal to make the public in those countries understand that decency and sympathy are as necessary in dealing with sexual as with any other subjects. In England we still repudiate decency and sympathy, and make virtues of blackguardism and ferocity.

However, I am glad to see, by the names of your [Free Press Defence] committee, that a stand is going to be made at last for the right to speak and write truthfully and carefully on a subject which every rascal and hypocrite in the country is free to treat falsely and recklessly. It is fortunate that the police have been silly enough to select for their attack a writer whose character stands so high as that of Mr. Havelock Ellis; and I have no doubt that if we do our duty in the matter the prosecution, by ignominiously failing, will end by doing more good than harm.

yours faithfully
G. Bernard Shaw

To GRANT RICHARDS

Pitfold. Haslemere
[X/135]   20th August 1898

[*The Perfect Wagnerite* was published on 1st December 1898. Herbert S. Stone published the American edition in 1899.]

Dear G.R.

I send you herewith, by parcels post, the complete MS of the Wagner book. I compute it roughly at 35,000 words. This, in the type of the preface to the plays, would make 100 pages. I think, however, that it should be got up as a book of devotion for pocket use, and not bulked out as a treatise. I want to secure the American copyright: do you think Stone will venture upon it?

I have not made up my mind about the title. The Perfect Wagnerite seems to me the best. It might be *announced* as "The P.W.; or the New Protestantism." Quintessence won't do: it would be a weak repetition, and would suggest an explanation of all Wagner's works, whereas I have dealt with The Ring only. A sensible title would be "Wagner's Ring: What it Means"; but nobody would read a book with a sensible title; and quite right too.

We had better have a specimen page or two. If we decide on a biggish book like the plays, the type should be small pica Caslon set solid, like the prefaces to the plays, in which, however, three lines might be knocked off with advantage to the lower margin. If we carry out the idea of a pretty little book of devotion, the type should be as in the plays.

Get it into type as soon as possible, as I have no complete copy; and if the MS gets lost or burnt there is an end of it forever.

Shall I have to do a prospectus for you?

My foot seems to be filling up in a businesslike way at last; I hope to be able to walk in a few weeks.

yrs ever
G. Bernard Shaw

To LADY MARY MURRAY

[A/36]

Pitfold. Haslemere
1st September 1898

[Grayshott, a village near Hindhead, lacked a public house. To forestall the establishment of a pub by one of the major brewing interests, the local reformers, headed by the Rev. J. M. Jeakes, set out to guarantee "the absolute banishment of the private interest" by opening an inn which would be designed to discourage inebriety. The result in August 1899 was the Fox and Pelican, a public house for which the residents had bought shares in the amount of £2500, and which offered the workingman hot meals, social evenings, periodical smokers, a reading room, dominoes and draughts. Operated under the ægis of the Peoples' Refreshment House Association, its management was undertaken by local residents, supervised by Mrs Arnold Lyndon, the wife of a local doctor, and Mrs Jeakes, the Rector's wife. Charlotte had already bought shares in the enterprise; Shaw made an investment of his own at a slightly later date.]

Dear Lady Mary

I regard the allusions to me in your recent letter to my wife as a direct challenge to me on the Drink Question. Let me therefore scribble a word or two, as well as I can in a hammock.

The Drink Question is the question of supplying the people with drink in the best way. The ordinary workman requires a certain quantity of beer to keep him amiable and happy. If he does not get it, he sulks, mopes, beats his wife and children, envies his neighbor, and gets into a state in which it is impossible for him to say a civil word to anyone about him. It is a bad thing to be the wife of a drunkard; but it is ten

59

times worse to be the wife of a man who wants drink and cannot get it. A friend of mine [Pakenham Beatty] drank himself mad twice. In my innocence I wanted him to become a teetotaller. Finally I discovered that the chief obstacle was his unfortunate wife. The house was so miserable, and her children so wretched, when he was abstaining, that the evil of his periodically drinking too much was less than the continuous evil of his not drinking at all. If you dont understand this—if you imagine that everybody is strong enough to endure life without an anæsthetic, you dont understand the Drink Question a bit.

Lest you should suppose that I make too light of the other side of the case I may tell you that my father drank, and that it is not a year since my mother and I had to pension off and get rid of a relative of hers—a woman [Kate Gurly] who was an incorrigible drunkard, and who had for years been an unspeakable affliction to us. I know as much about drink as anybody outside a hospital of inebriates; and I am myself a teetotaller.

The misery of the working man's wife in this matter is that her husband cannot get his drink except in a public house, and that the publican's interest is to make him drink more than he ought and to give him adulterated liquor. It is *not* the publican's interest—at least in a village—to make him a drunkard and ruin him; for it is no man's interest to ruin his customers; but it is his interest to make him spend rather more on drink & less on other things than is sufficient to keep him in goodhumor. Therefore if you can replace the ordinary brewer's tied house with one which is conducted in the interest of the whole village, you will do a good thing for the villager's wife. The Grayshott affair is an attempt in that direction, and, as such, deserves a helping hand. There is only one thoroughly wrong article in its constitution. A profit is to be made by the manager on teetotal drinks (including that scourge of modern civilization, *tea*); but he is to be charged the full retail price for spirits and alcoholic beverages. This is not fair. He should have no motive whatever for influencing the customer's choice of beverages. Besides, to give a manager an inducement to substitute zoedone, or some pernicious decoction of kola, for good beer, is to sow the seeds of madness & despair in households.

The Teetotal question is quite another business. I happen to believe that the effect of alcohol on men is to lower their standard, and to enable them to put up with evils which, with their standard at full pitch, they could remove. The sensational part of the affair—the ruin, madness & crime & so on—I leave out of account, partly because drink probably averts more gross crime than it causes, and partly because it

60

is impossible to prevent the majority of moderate drinkers from drinking at all, merely because the minority drinks immoderately. If half the energy and social influence that is now directed to unjustifiably cutting off the drink supply of people who have not only no conviction that drink in moderation is a bad thing, but who are persuaded that it is a beneficial and even necessary thing, were only concentrated on releasing the husband or wife of the drunkard by making drunkeness a ground for divorce, we should begin to get ahead a little. But to return to the ordinary moderate drinker: am I, because I think the world would speedily become better if he sought his comfort in harder ways, justified in countenancing improved public houses? Well, let me put a parrallel case to you. I happen to consider that the worst public house in England is a paradise compared to a butcher's shop with its slaughter house in the yard. Yet I sit on a vestry committee which licenses slaughter houses; and I am an advocate of municipal abattoirs. I have an interest, as a member of the community, in seeing that the wants of the community are supplied in the best possible way. A great number of those wants I dont share: many of them I think pernicious and ridiculous. Horse traction, tall hats, furs and feathers, starched cotton shirts, and $\frac{99}{100}$ths of what people call art, I regard as more or less damnable. What would you think if I refused to help in any of the steps to improve the conditions under which the industries involved by these things are carried on, and limited myself to the advocacy of Local Option Bills to be applied separately to them? Clearly that would be Impossibilism; and the object of Fabianism is to destroy Impossibilism.

Now the object of this long discourse is not to induce you to take shares in the Grayshott public house. I have not done so myself, though my wife (who I grieve to say drinks whiskey at dinner) has. But I put it in as a plea for the relaxation of your moral attitude—moral attitudes being themselves more potent than alcohol as generators of madness, ruin & despair. By taking the position of my wife's better angel, you put me in the position of her worse one—and have indeed word-painted a sardonic, scoffing expression on my countenance, as of one who whispers satirical disparagements of your counsel. I throw myself on the Professor for support. Moral attitudes on your part will draw lines in *his* countenance—lines of care—just as they have drawn Mephistophelean ones in mine. I pledge you my word that Local Option is immoral, that Liberalism is immoral. For the last 20 years Liberalism has done nothing but make Liberals unhappy, whilst Fabianism has been spreading joy and insufferable self conceit on all its votaries. Don't be Liberal, I implore you. Ask Lady Carlisle whether, if she were beginning life like you, she could begin it with Liberalism. Never have an Ism: never be an Ist. Tout comprendre (especially on the subject of Drink) est tout pardonner.

Excuse this long letter. Like Pascal, I haven't enough energy in my present state of health to write a short one.

yrs sincerely
G. Bernard Shaw

To GILBERT MURRAY

Pitfold. Haslemere
[A/36]   19th September 1898

My dear Murray

I must say a word on your long letter in reply to mine, for which I am much indebted to you, as I want to get pulled over the subject by somebody. The point on which the facts strike me quite differently to you, is your estimate of the political force of Teetotalism—or let us say Local Optionism. At the last general election the Liberal party, which had survived Home Rule, was practically wiped out by Local Option. The result was quite unprecedented: nothing worse could have happened to a government which had lost a Sedan. Since then I have never dreamt of counting Local Option as a live political factor. It seemed obvious that the Liberals must drop Local Option, and that they must drop the Drink Question altogether unless they could hit on some acceptable form of Drink Legislation. I confess I am altogether taken aback by your contention that Local Option must be accepted because the voters are determined to have it, rightly or wrongly. My view of the situation is that it must be abandoned because the voters are determined to have none of it, wrongly or rightly, and have, in fact, already voted in that sense, with unparralleled (never could spell it) unanimity. This leaves us staring at one another, wondering which of us is politically blind. And there, for the present, I stick.

As to Grayshott, your handsome concession encourages me to sit on your head to the extent of urging that except in the few cases where a village is wholly owned by a teetotal despot, the case must always arise as a choice between a tied house and an untied one. The alternative of having no pub at all does not present itself.

We have just heard from Archer, who has returned from his travels, and will come to Pitfold with brother Charles on some day to be fixed hereafter.

I am sorry to hear that Tilford is not agreeing with you. Is country air, then, a fraud like all the other things? Why not try vegetarianism? It will amuse you for a while, anyhow.

> yrs sincerely
> G. Bernard Shaw

To GRANT RICHARDS

Pitfold. Haslemere
[A/4; X/156]   30th September 1898
[Having received Richards's statement of royalties for *Plays Pleasant and Unpleasant*, which included a deduction of charges for excessive proof corrections, Shaw responded by sending Richards a statement of account which he had drawn up "under that head, in the best Publishers Association style and spirit" (3rd October 1898, Hanley Texas).]

G. Bernard Shaw in a/c with Grant Richards.

Minimum customary allowance to Author for proof correction

Pleasant Plays	£10.0.0	
Unpleasant ,,	10.0.0	

Services rendered as Typographical Expert by Author to Publisher.

Choice of type	£5.5.0	
Design of page, margins &c	2.2.0	
Choice of paper	2.2.0	
Design of title page	10.10.0	
Inspection of proofs	52.10.0	
Choice of binding	2.2.0	
Consultations with publisher	105.0.0	
Letters of instruction	63.0.0	
Personal instruction (no charge)	– – –	
		242.11.0
Extra proof corrections in style of typesetting in the interest of the Publisher's reputation	21.0.0	
		283.11.0
Less amount charged in Publisher's a/c for "Author's Alterations & extra proofs"	10.6.0	
		273.5.0
Interest @ 6% for 6 months	8.3.9	
		£281.8.9

To CHARLES CHARRINGTON

[A/4]

Pitfold. Haslemere
13th October 1898

Now be praised, Heaven, that he did not leave you a million: you would have sent for £50,000 straight off.

My difficulty as to producing a hundred is a very simple one: I can't afford it. I have received nothing since my illness began, not even the money due me by the Saturday Review since February. The D's D had left off before that, and has not been played since. Meanwhile, my reserves have been flying. You are not the only man who has been left in a tight place by efforts to educate the B[ritish] P[ublic] in art: music has its desperadoes also; and one of them has had to be seen through a crisis lately. What with one thing & another, doctors, desperadoes, family, I am no more able to hand over £100 than you are.

Now, as to my wife's money. I can't get any of that for you, for this reason. She has been brought up in such a fashion that she has no notion of the real value of coin. She knows what I earned in my bachelor days; but she cannot conceive anyone living on so little except in the most extreme penury. She is firmly persuaded that everybody took advantage of my weakness of mind to make my little less by unheard-of borrowings, and that you, in particular, were a hardened offender in this way. It is of course no use arguing the point; if she chooses to look at the facts of the case that way, there is nothing more to be said. If I hand you £100, virtually at her expense, she will seriously set herself against your malignant influence over me (not to mention Janet's, as to which she is not disposed to be more than ominously [I scratch out a more terrifying word]* magnanimous). Further, it is not clear that I can do you any good. To refuse your creditors £100 does not cost me a pang: to take £25 a quarter from you in your present circumstances, or put you to the necessity of periodically explaining that you handnt got it, would be extremely unpleasant. If you owe a thousand, what is the use of letting the wolves taste blood (*my* blood) to the tune of £100? They will pass the word round fast enough that you can get the money if the screw is turned hard enough. Then you would want another £100; and I should have another row with my wife, who is of course in the cold-drawn right in objecting. Why borrow at all? Even if they make you bankrupt, that will probably save you from ruining yourself again, if it does not procure you engagements from managers who are now afraid of your starting against them on your own account.

* The square brackets are Shaw's.

I should have written sooner but for a fresh accident—a sprained ankle, which in point of anguish has beaten all the rest of the calamities. I tried to get up on a new bicycle & my long disused foot turned on the step with a brute of a twist & floored me.

We are at present looking about for winter quarters here. When I got back from Freshwater it turned out that the healing of the foot was a delusion, the bone being still bad; so that I am now just where I was 5 months ago. On the top of this pleasing discovery came the sprained ankle; so we have had a cheerful time of it. I am offered a fresh operation (with the results of the last to encourage me) as the best thing I can do. I am somewhat sceptical, naturally. At all events we must wait until we are established for the winter, either in this house or another, before taking any further steps.

I am working hard on The Perfect Wagnerite, which is passing energetically through the press.

Forbes Robertson is on the war path for plays again. I can make no headway with C & C. Can't get any drama out of the story—nothing but comedy & character.

GBS

To SIDNEY WEBB

[A/14; X/141.e]

Pitfold. Haslemere
18th October 1898

[Sir William Harcourt (1827–1904) was a statesman and M.P., described in the *Dictionary of National Biography* as the "last of the old school of parliamentarians." Louis De Rougement (actually a Swiss butler called Grin) had come to London with amazing tales of adventure in northern Australia. At first he lectured to large audiences, and his supposed exploits were reported graphically in the papers, but he was soon exposed as an impudent fraud.]

Since I can only catch you at Colombo, I have put off writing as long as possible, so that you might have the latest news. But there seems to be none, except that Mrs Wallas has borne G.W. a daughter, and both are doing as well as can be expected.

Your letter to Pease about New Zealand propaganda has just arrived. I agree; but I wish I was more on the spot (the Strand, not N.Z.) to push your proposals. They are so simple & definite that there ought to be no difficulty about them; but the Fabian is like everything else: it wants all the looking after it can get. They have just passed the Drink tract, which is rather better than it might have been; but I have failed (being absent from the meeting) to get them to cut certain sillinesses out of it that will seem brutal when Harcourt dies.

. . . It is clear that we shall have to winter here; and we are just now in extremity for a house, as we dont want to keep this on, and have not yet found another. However, that will settle itself in a few days. You will see by this that the chances of our meeting you on the way back are very slender. Another operation is out of the question until we are definitely housed: that is to say, until November. This will involve carving my foot up. Allow me six weeks to recover, and I shall be close upon your Naples date. But even this assumes an operation at the earliest possible moment, followed by a success in which I have no faith. You and I have been confronted often enough with the follies of current political science. May you never be confronted with the ten times deeper follies & ignorances of medical science! It is not that what they do they do badly—on the contrary; but their reasons for doing it—oh Lord!

The worst of it is that in my case there is a ready excuse for not thinking—the vegetarianism. That accounts for everything. If an operation fails, vegetarianism! If I have a bad night, vegetarianism! If I die, vegetarianism! There is only one advantage in this: it throws into the background the alcoholic people. It is clear that if I began to eat three beefsteaks a day, the ground would promptly be shifted to the want of stimulants; but as it is, heaven be praised, I am allowed to teetotallize in comparative peace.

Of course the real question is whether I have worn myself out or not. I am not at all convinced that I have; but I have been overdrawing my account for a long time; and it will take more than the digging out of a bone by a sporting specialist to make me quite solvent again. However it may turn out, I do not greatly care: I am satisfied that, on the whole, I have used myself economically and fired my whole broadside. I would not trust a chicken's neck to save the rest of my life, even if I were convinced that chicken broth would save it, which I am not. But the inconvenience of being married is that one's wife sets up an interest in one's life. As for me, I have always been a patient, obstinate beast; and the more they threaten me with death (which they all consider it their Christian duty to do at every turn) the more they clear my mind as to the worthlessness of living in obedience to such threats & terrors. But Charlotte has none of my convictions; and she is a worrier of the very first order, with an amazing power of mistrusting the wisdom of everything & everybody. This is hardly to be wondered at, considering the long course of shocks and alarms & medical contradictions to which she has been exposed; but it is none the less wearing for her. And as I have to oppose to her paroxysms of misgiving exactly the same apparently callous obstinacy I oppose to the outside anti-vegetarian world (though that is probably a very good thing for her) the strain on my doggedness is in some directions rather intensified than relieved by her solicitude. She has an instinctive sense that there is a certain way in which I do not care for myself, and that it follows that I do not care, *in* that way, for anybody else either; and she is quite right. It is a trying thing to be married to a Sprite, as Beatrice says, in any case; but a Sprite with necrosis is the devil. A woman thinks that the happier a man is, the more he should value his life. A Sprite knows that the happier he is, the less reason there is for waiting for life to bring him anything new.

The above is the sort of thing that my condition induces occasionally; but now it is wearing off as my strength accumulates. I am very glad that the Bo family has been out of the way of it all; and I hope it will be virtually over by the time we reassemble. It would no doubt have been better for me to have taken the trip with you, and averted the collapse; but then it might not have averted it; and that would have been a pretty business.

We have been amusing ourselves during the summer with a kodak. Charlotte is sending you some of the results. I have had one of them published [on 15th October] in "The Academy" (now an illustrated paper) with the inscription "The Dying Vegetarian." We live here with a nurse, one Dorothy Kreyer, who was induced by Honnor Morten (who has just resigned her Fabianship) to become a nurse & train in the City of London Hospital. She dresses me, washes me, massages me, and adores me, to the entire satisfaction of Charlotte, who gets all the manual labor of my accidents off her hands in this way. I am of course only helpless immediately after I break my limbs or dislocate them; but the massage goes on always, to keep the disused leg from withering. The Nursling, as Charlotte calls her, is a rather goodlooking young woman; and the success with which she has fitted herself into our domesticity without the least friction says much for her tact. She is fortunately not of an ardent temperament; and her devotion to me is of an irreproachable kind. . . .

Fabian Essays is very much on my conscience: I think we ought to bring it up to date to the extent at least of adding to any part of it in

67

which we now see errors an explanatory confession of them. My scruples are revived by the prospect of a New Zealand propaganda. Besides, it seems to me that it is more effective to first gain the sympathy of the natural born Socialist by making his mistakes & then shewing what is wrong with them, than to be right from the first with the certainty that the correctness will not attract him. However, I understand you to say that the Essays have had their turn in N.Z. and that it now [is] time to pour in the tracts.

Our visitors here are chiefly Hewins, who used to come every Tuesday until the L.S. began; Olivier, who is alone at Limpsfield, his family being at Lausanne; Standring and Pease, who run down occasionally, or at least intend to do so; and Massingham, who is just now full of De Rougemont, a Swiss courier who walked into the B[ritish] Ass[ociation] Geographical Section the other day and fired off a string of reminiscences of Robinson Crusoe & other cannibal romances, with the result that he was accepted as an explorer of the first importance; and his adventures for 30 years as chief of a tribe of bushmen began their course in the Wide World Magazine (one of Newnes's speculations) and are still proceeding. This simpleminded liar provoked all the genuine explorers to attack him in the most superior manner. They all contradicted one another, betrayed gross ignorance on the points they were most cocksure about, such as riding on turtleback and the like follies (which of course they had to confess, when challenged by De R., they had never tried), and were triumphantly confuted by the soi disant explorer. Massingham got excited about the business, & filled the Chronicle for weeks with columns headed Rougemont Day by Day, thereby hoping to compass the destruction of Newnes. This, & Fashoda, & the battle of Omdurman, where the whole British & Egyptian armies, firing all their magazine & machine guns as hard as they could for 20 minutes into a dense mass of dervishes in white blouses, killed exactly as many as *one* machine gun would have killed in the same time if everyone of its bullets had hit somebody, is all the papers have talked about. Rosebery made a spluttering attempt to resurrect himself by crowing Jingo over Fashoda; and Asquith followed, on the social question, by declaring that the Liberals would never rest until they had extended the Workmen's Compensation Act to the whole human race.

[John] Morley passed the autumn down here; but we saw nothing of him. Our local visitors are the doctor [Arnold Lyndon], whose wife is getting up a village public house which Charlotte is helping prodigally to endow, and Grant Allen.

68

The United Kingdom alliance says it never never will desert Local Veto.

I have a sty on my eye, and cannot write any more.

Charlotte will write to Beatrice by this or the next mail.

GBS

To CHARLES CHARRINGTON

[A/4]

Pitfold. Haslemere
23rd October 1898

Console yourself, Charrington: it is better to be still on the hill of Difficulty than in the Valley of the Shadow of Death. At certain phases of the foot process I look into that valley, and feel like Saul without David to play to him. So I have to play to myself on a piano we have put into the barn.

Your letter is an exasperating production. As usual, you begin cleverly enough; but you always end in the same way by flourishing your blessed Janet round, and calling on the world to accept appreciation of her lustrous qualities as the universal touchstone of human worth. Patriotism is bad enough: it is hard to be patient with the asses who dress up the Nelson column & demand the recognition of England as the first of nations because they were born in it. But a man who wants to make a Nelson column of his wife is beyond all toleration. Who on earth will trust you with a municipal theatre when you obviously only want it as a pedestal for your Galatea? Is there any villainy on earth that you would not perpetrate virtuously ad majoram gloriam Janetæ? The truth is, Spenlow & Jorkins [in Dickens's *David Copperfield*] is an innocent firm compared to C.C. & J.A. C.C., incorruptible on his own account, commits every crime that may serve the interests of J.A. J.A., the noblest of matrons as far as her own interests are concerned, sticks at nothing for the sake of C.C. The total result is precisely the same as if neither C.C. nor J.A. had a ray of conscience between them. And all because a woman is rather goodlooking & can act a bit in two or three parts!

If I were you, I should stick to literature. Janet cannot get into your MSS very well. You are, after all, a man of ideas chiefly; and books are the proper vehicles for ideas. Only, that requires application & perseverance; and you are a lazy old Alnaschar, always dreaming of vast enterprises between each smash of your basket of glass. After all,

69

the theatre is out of politics because nobody has written a big book about it. I shall have to do it myself someday.

Of course I talk to you like a family solicitor. That's how you need to be talked to occasionally. Bless my soul, you might do a lot with your income: Salt, with less than half of it, lives well and agitates England behind the mask of the Humanitarian League. On the 12th Nov. we move from this to Blen-cathra, Hindhead, which we have taken for 6 months at the modest rent of 12 guineas a week. It is an enormous house, containing four enormous rooms. We could get nothing else that would suit us. Our public spirit is concentrating itself on the building of a public house in Grayshott on the lines of the Bishop of Chester's Association. We are backing it up with noble openhandedness for the sake of Socialism. I fully expect to get 4 per cent out of it. Thus is the work of Terriss perpetuated.

I shall go in for another operation, I think, when we get into the new house. If the bone wont heal, they had better dig it out altogether. At this rate I shall write tragedies. I no longer sleep: I dream, dream, dream.

Cæsar & Cleopatra is no use. I can only spin out the same silly stuff: there is no drama in it. Hamlet in the second & third act, and Macbeth apostrophising sleep: that is me just at present. I picked up the book of Job today by chance & found my own history there, precisely.

Farewell. When I am in good spirits I neglect my correspondence & write fresh jokes for Cæsar & his British islander slave.

GBS

To MATTHEW EDWARD McNULTY

[C.u/4]

Blen-Cathra. Hindhead
[Undated: c. 12th November 1898]

Still invalided, and clamoring to have my toe taken off. Eminent specialist says try letting it alone a bit first. This experiment in Christian Science seems rather successful so far; but I still cherish the idea of amputation—an unnatural state of mind which speaks for itself as to the giving out of my patience.

To ELLEN TERRY

[D/1]

Blen-Cathra. Hindhead
30th December 1898

Call me a gentleman again, Ellen, and all is over between us. My wife, before her nerves got hardened, used to cry at the spots of soup on that tunic & the holes in the elbows & under the arms.

I perceive by the way you write (also the way you dont write) that you no longer care for me. Now that my health is returning, however, I love you as much as ever, in the ungentlemanliest, ungodliest manner. I am not to be held accountable for what I did when I was in the Valley of the Shadow. Turn over [the card].

I have finished "Cæsar & Cleopatra"; and Cæsar is a fine part, whilst Cleopatra will pass. I hope to have prompt copies ready in a week or two. I wish you'd read it & tell me whether it is improvable or not technically. Besides, you always read my plays; & I generally get something out of you that is useful.

The Webbs are here; and they are all clamoring at me to go play halma with them.

ever, dearest Ellen, yr
GBS

To HENRY ARTHUR JONES

[A/4; X/124]

Blen-Cathra. Hindhead
8th January 1899

. . . It is all very well to swim about in Wagner, without bothering as to his meaning; but the best established truth in the world is that no man produces a work of art of the very first order except under the pressure of strong conviction & definite meaning as to the constitution of the world. Dante, Goethe & Bunyan could not possibly have produced their masterpieces if they had been mere art-voluptuaries. It may be that the artistic by-product is more valuable than the doctrine; but there is no other way of getting the by-product than by the effort & penetrating force that doctrine braces a man to. Go straight for the by-product & you get Gounod instead of Wagner. Fricka is not Law: she is the dramatization of a woman with a legal mind, proceeding on the fundamental legal error. I have pointed out in the book that this is the only way in which an allegory can become a drama.

It is odd that you do not find in your own experience the clue to Wagner's way of working. What makes you the only considerable dramatist now in vogue in England is precisely because you are the only one who ever drives at any purpose with sufficient concern for extra theatrical concerns to make his art a by-product. In your plays you make the audience feel the world behind the scrap of it represented on the stage, just as Wagner does. Only, you are vaguer: you get stopped in the realization of your own drift by your amazing theology, which prevents you from seeing what Wagner saw: that is, the tragedy of God Almighty between Law on the one side and stupidity on the other. And when I point the way out of the muddle, you beg not to be rescued from it, and plead for mere swimming in the music. Well, swim away; but dont tell me that my "theory" is all wrong. It's not a theory: its a translation into intellectual terms of something that has been expressed by its author only in dramatic terms. Read the dramas through; and you will find that unless you accept my version of the scenes between Wotan & Brynhild, Fricka & Erda, you will be driven to the impossible conclusion that they are absolute nonsense, which by some accident has fallen into grammatical shape in the middle of an orchestral swimming bath.

You say "I cant grasp the technique of any art except playwriting— *if that has got a technique*.["] Precisely. The secret of musical technique is that there is no technique in the mysterious sense of the amateur critics. Wagner was no more governed by rules in the choice of notes to express what he wanted than you are in the choice of words. There is no difficulty except what lies on the surface. You have to know what notes a trombone can utter, and what they sound like. The same for a piccolo, a tenor, a soprano, or any other instrument, human or orchestral, you use. And you have to know how to write down the sounds so that the musician, reading his part (like the actor reading *his* part), may, as far as he is capable, make the sounds as and when you want them. What is there difficult to grasp in all that? It is odd that sounds should produce that magical effect; but there is nothing in that except the flat fact that they do.

I don't agree at all about the stage directions. They may bother *you*; but they make to the ordinary reader all the difference between an intelligible & readable drama and a mere dialogue which by itself can only be made self-explanatory by the obsolete devices of the Elizabethans, whose plays were recited, & not acted with business in our sense. Take the ordinary actor at a rehearsal. How often does he divine without a hint from you which way your lines are to be spoken in scenes which are neither conventional nor otherwise obvious? How many actors playing Shakespere can catch intentions in the speeches which are plain enough to you? I scrupulously avoid any direction that could not be conveyed by the action or make-up of the actor, as otherwise the play would no longer be a play. But I defy anybody to convey a complete impression of an acted play by dialogue alone. It is an attempt to do so that produces the literary play.

Excuse all this talky-talky. My accursed foot is discharging again; and I think I shall get another bit of the bone removed. The relapse is trifling; but it shews that there is still a scrap of bad bone there.

G. Bernard Shaw

To ARTHUR CONAN DOYLE

Blen-Cathra. Hindhead

[X/158] 24th January 1899

[Sir Arthur Conan Doyle (1859–1930), although best known as the creator of Sherlock Holmes, was a physician, zealous reformer, and crusader. He was one of Shaw's neighbours in Hindhead. William T. Stead was attempting to found a Pacifist League. A "Peace Crusade" meeting, in favour of the Disarmament Conference, was held in Hindhead Hall on 28th January, with Conan Doyle in the chair. Shaw and Grant Allen were the principal speakers.]

Dear Conan Doyle

Hadn't we better come to some agreement about the resolutions to be moved on Saturday? If we don't, we shall find ourselves landed with a string of rubbish about disarmament, truces of God, and the like, devised by Stead, and profoundly disbelieved in by all of us. I will move an amendment sooner than have all that stuff of the Tzar's (which he now repudiates, by the way—so Massingham tells me), rammed down our throats. I strongly object to making Queensberry rules for war: what I *do* believe in is a combination of the leading powers to police the world and put down international war just as private war is put down. The only thing that is not ridiculous in the Tzar's proposals is the international tribunal part. It is no use having the meeting at all unless it is sensible and unanimous. The speakers ought to meet and settle what they mean to support.

yours sincerely
G. Bernard Shaw

To JAMES WELCH

[A/5]

Blen-Cathra. Hindhead
30th January 1899

[The "classic Beetle" apparently was the actor Allan Aynesworth. *A Lady
of Quality*, dramatised by Frances Hodgson Burnett and Stephen Townes-
end from Mrs Burnett's novel, opened at the Comedy Theatre on 8th March
1899. J.B.Mulholland (1859–1925) was a theatre builder and owner who
had formerly been an actor. Winifred Arthur-Jones (1880–1950) appeared
in several of her father's plays, including *The Liars* (1897) and *The
Manoeuvres of Jane* (1898), touring the provinces for a number of years with
her husband Leslie Faber.]

My dear Welch

I am deeply touched by C[harrington]'s self sacrifice in proposing
to produce You Never Can Tell with your money, and giving you up
the important part of Phil, contenting himself with the humble waiter.
In such conduct I recognize that noble heart. But you would be much
better as the waiter; and he would give the requisite prominence to the
part of the cook—a light role, with a becoming costume.

Now hearken attentively, my son Jimmy. All that you say in praise
of that play falls short of its merits. It is not merely a good acting play:
it is absolutely actor proof except for about ten minutes, during which
it is the most difficult comedy in the Irish language. It has been
rehearsed up to an advanced stage by as good a company as you are
likely to pick up—Winifred Emery and Eva Moore, Cyril Maude and
Brandon Thomas, John Barnes Esquire and the classic Beetle. And the
end was that the author had to withdraw the piece as impossible under
the circumstances, and to concoct stories with the management to
conceal the disgraceful fact that the British drama had beaten the London stage. If you dismiss from your mind the harmless pleasantries of
the waiter & the children, and concentrate your attention on the final
scene of Act II, you will see the difficulty. If that scene fails, the play
fails. And nobody but a comedian of the very first forty-pound-a-week
order can touch that scene. It is not that a lesser man can only do it
badly: it is that *he can't do it at all*: the thing has to be seen to be
believed—seen as I saw it with a man who was quite able for most of
the rest of it, and rattling good in some of it. How are you going to get
over that difficulty? Can you get Hawtrey, or Wyndham, or John
Drew, or Bourchier?

Again, Mrs Clandon is a very difficult part to fill. At the Haymarket

Fanny Coleman tried it, and gave it up because the speeches were too long, and there were no laughs and no exits that she could discover. So you require a first rate woman even to know that the part is a good one. Can you get Mrs Kendal, or Kate Terry—for that is what it means, though an inferior artist is not so completely out of the question as in the case of Valentine?

So you see the job is a big one—no smaller even for your personal weight in the cast, because you would have to play the waiter, who could not fail anyhow, the only possible room for difference being between competence and genius. Dont be tempted to believe that the comic scenes could pull the play through: the better they are played, the more insufferable must the rest seem if ill played. If I were manager, and had to put it on with you and a dozen duffers, I should cast you for old Crampton (Brandon Thomas's part) and let the gasman play the waiter.

The only chance that occurs to me is this. A play called A Lady of Quality is going to be put on (or is it on already?) with Miss [Eleanor] Calhoun in the title part, & Mulholland running the show. It is a play so bad that it may very well succeed; but it is also so extra-sanguinarily bad that there is just a chance of its failing. Now it so happens that Miss Calhoun's appearance suits Gloria very well; and she knows her business better than most of our leading ladies. It also seems to me that Lord & Lady Algy must be nearly played out by this time. Hawtrey knows You Never Can Tell & is very sweet on Valentine. Well, if the Lady of Quality fails, you might suggest to Mulholland that a Calhoun-Hawtrey-Welch galaxy might save the situation. Or there are the Bourchiers—Violet Vanbrugh could play Gloria. There is a Miss Winifred Jones, daughter of the great Henry Arthur, who is very pretty & is playing Liars & Janes in the provinces: she is in her teens & would make an excellent Dolly. Kate Terry would be by far the best attainable Mrs Clandon, which reminds me that you might fall back on [John] Hare, who would have a nice amiable part as Crampton. And that exhausts all the suggestions I can think of.

My terms are easy; and my burden is light, especially now that I am a crippled invalid & cant attend rehearsals. A modest 10% will always satisfy my socialistic needs.

In my latest masterpiece "Cæsar & Cleopatra" (Forbes Robertson & Mrs Patrick Campbell) there is a brief but exquisite part for a Roman sentinel, with combat, to which you alone could do justice. Have you any promising disciple who would not disdain it?

The above details as to the Haymarket affair are confidential. You are bound to know them as a matter of business; but you will see that people's feelings might suffer if I gossipped about them.

yrs ever
G. Bernard Shaw

To ELIZABETH ROBINS

[S/8]

Blen-Cathra. Hindhead
13th February 1899

[Shaw had just discovered that "C.E.Raimond", the author of several novels, including *The Open Question* (1898) was actually Elizabeth Robins.]

Dear Miss Robins

Now that the murder is out, and that I have just read "An Open Question", I think you owe me an apology, though I do not think you will make it. For years, by a remorseless fraud, you have been discrediting my original estimate of you and discouraging the instinct on which that estimate was founded by pretending to be everything that I most deplore—an actress neglecting that everyday work at her profession which is the foundation of all real character and power, an American running after smart society, a woman jealously exacting the privileges which genius pays for with exhausting achievement, and for which you offered nothing apparently but a very occasional display of a visibly dwindling fancy for the stage. I tried to believe in you as long as possible; but I do not indulge myself largely in illusions (being very subject to them) when I can help it; and at last I gave you up; put down my original estimate of you to my own gullibility and your personal charm; and, what was perhaps worst, accepted your case as evidence in favour of the very widely held view that commercial honesty and self-respect in women (at least on the stage) are only part of such hold as conventionality may retain over them, and that when a woman is conventional enough to be both honest and continent, she is too conventional to be anything more than a lady. I dont mean that I gave the verdict in favor of this view; but I do mean that you manufactured evidence—false evidence—in favor of it. Therefore I say that you owe me an apology. But you owe it to everybody else who knows you and who was not your accomplice. Now you cannot apologize to everybody. But there may be among the dupes someone for whom you have some regard, and who is not as well able as I am to express the grievance. For the sake of such possible person or persons I take it on myself to inform you that you have committed a crime.

For my own part I am satisfied to find that I was right—that Miss Robins was a lie—that St Elizabeth was the truth—that, like myself, you can, and always could, make better people than real people to commune with. However, for that very reason, since I am to you a real person, I recognize my uncongeniality, and will say nothing more except a few words about the book.

All the criticism I have seen of the book as yet is mere copy-spinning. You are, as an authoress, more exactly like George Eliot than any two original novelists have hitherto been like another. Do not let the warning—for it is a warning as well as a recognition—be lost on you. You have the gift that enabled her to create Maggie Tulliver [in *The Mill on the Floss*] and to make her pictures of English life in the Midlands, just as she had the gift that has enabled you to create Val and make your pictures of American life. But she got her gift paralyzed by the fatalism which was the intellecually-&-morally-snobbishly-correct thing among advanced people in her day. None of her people have any power of moulding their own destiny: they drift along helpless in the clutch of heredity and environment—just like your Ganos. George Eliot was like the released Bastille prisoners: she was rescued from the chains of Evangelical religion & immediately became lost, numbed & hypnotized by "Science".

Again, Shakespear had the golden gift too. But he also lost his religion & his vulgar Jingo patriotism; and the result was that the moment he met with ill-health & disappointment, and realized death, he fell, nerveless & paralyzed, under its shadow, and spent the rest of his life cowering and demanding what was the use of it all since it must end in Alexander's clay & the rest of it. Consequently there is no hero in any one of his plays: he never trod the plains of heaven with Bunyan —never understood the mood in which George Herbert [in "The Church Porch"] said "All may have, if they dare try, a glorious life", or Mr. Valiant-for-Truth [in *The Pilgrim's Progress*], with his foot on the brink of the river, "Tho' with great difficulty I am got hither, yet now I do not repent me of all the trouble I have been at to arrive where I am". It is the grossest of mistakes to suppose that this mood is possible only to men who expect happiness in another world. No person worth a rap makes happiness, or love, or money, or anything but thoroughness of life itself, the criterion of life's value. Beware, beware, beware, beware, beware, BEWARE. All this undertaker's philosophy that you call "The Open Question" is nothing but fright. What has frightened you?

Another thing. Beware of your talent for sensationalism. I told you long ago . . . that anybody could do that. It was not quite true that anybody could do it so well; but it *is* true that anybody can produce an effect, and even a terrible effect, by vivisection. Don't do it. Art is much nobler than that. If you kill people in your books, do it in the high classic manner, or do it painlessly. Don't exploit the King of Terrors. And to compensate yourself, give greater scope to your humor, which is one of your divine gifts, not one of your infernal ones. The concluding chapters of The Open Question are very well done of their kind; but that kind, hunted down to the bottom quiddity of them, is hysterical bugaboo. . . .

Now one last word. Don't answer this letter. You write novels & plays very well; but the thing you can't write well is a letter to me. I am very sorry for it, and do not deny that it is my own fault. Forgive me as best you can, & believe me

yrs sincerely
G. Bernard Shaw

To MAX HECHT

Blen-Cathra. Hindhead
27th February 1899

[A/1]

["Lyceum Ltd.," in which Max Hecht was a principal investor, had had its capital oversubscribed on the first day it offered shares. Turning the Lyceum, over which Irving had ruled as sole monarch for so many years, into a limited liability company in 1898, was designed to ease the actor's financial burdens, but it "only precipitated the end," as Christopher St John noted in the Terry–Shaw Correspondence, "by making it more difficult for Irving to obtain credit."]

My dear Hecht

I see that you are a director of the Lyceum Limited, which I understand to be a benevolent society for the relief of distressed authors & actors. May I make an entirely interested suggestion to you in your new capacity. I have written a play—a magnificent, recklessly expensive play—for Forbes Robertson and Mrs Patrick Campbell: by name & subject "Cæsar & Cleopatra." But Forbes has no theatre and no money, Macbeth having cleaned him out. He is at present rallying his backers so as to astonish London as Julius Cæsar next winter. Now I think it extremely likely that Forbes isn't a good man of business, and that he will raise the money on unnecessarily hard terms unless he can persuade some able management to go into the affair with him. Why shouldn't the Lyceum Limited do this? On the whole, Forbes Robertson & Mrs Pat look more like the heir & heiress apparent to Irving & Ellen Terry than any other pair. When Irving goes to America, it would be much better to keep up the special character of the theatre by producing another spectacular historical play of the best literary class, with an actor of Shakespearean reputation in it, than to drop into pantomime & casual English opera, especially when the play, if not produced at the Lyceum, would be produced somewhere else. At all events it is worth considering.

I have said nothing to Robertson about this; the notion came into my head on seeing your name in the prospectus in the Sunday Special. What do you think of it?

I am unable to look after any business just now in person, or I would call on you & save you the trouble of writing. . . .

yrs sincerely
G. Bernard Shaw

To CHARLES CHARRINGTON

[D/4]

Blen-Cathra. Hindhead
10th March 1899

[Florence Grove (d. 1901) was a Fabian specialist on housing, and a member of the Board of Guardians. Christian S. MacTaggart, a Fabian, taught correspondence courses in Elementary Economics. A Shaw letter on "Socialism and Individualism" appeared on 11th March in the *Farnham, Haslemere and Hindhead Herald*. He and a Mrs G. V. Cox had undertaken to establish a local brass band. Charrington was preparing to address the Cambridge Fabians on "What a University Fabian Society Can Do." Sir Henry Campbell-Bannerman (1836–1908), a Liberal M.P. (1868–1908), former secretary for war and supporter of Gladstone's Irish home-rule policy, who became Prime Minister in 1905, was a Cambridge graduate.]

I see in Fabian News that somebody else has nominated you for the executive. I was waiting for some nomination to be made before I acted, because if no nominations are made except Pease's of the old executive, there is no contest: consequently it is not nice for a member of the executive to make the first outside nomination & so force a contest: one waits for some outsider to do it. I should have written to explain this; so that Miss Grove could have nominated Miss McTaggart & I could then have nominated you; but I am getting swallowed up in business & occupation of one sort or another almost as if I were in London. We stoked up the Parish Council Election here so successfully that we got all our people in at the head of the poll at an unprecedentedly full meeting. I have to write letters to the local papers, hold informal committees with everybody about drainage, a village band, and devil knows what not. Also I have to go into society & figure in Shakespear readings. My Benedick was a great success; but as Malvolio I got the sympathy for me instead of against me to such a tragic extent that I almost wrecked the play. I also sing "O rest in the Lord" to bereaved members of the aristocracy (with organ accompaniment) until they feel like Saul listening to David—not the time with the javelin. I could think of nothing for Cambridge except to point out what a chance there is now in the House to do what Bannerman has failed to do. Love to Janet.

GBS

P.S. The foot is just as it was last year.

To UNIDENTIFIED CORRESPONDENT

Blen-Cathra. Hindhead

[A/4] 15th March 1899

[The arguments set forth here for the benefit of a Socialist debater anticipate Shaw's preface to *Getting Married*, published in 1911. Dr John Clifford (1836–1923) was Pastor of the Praed Street Baptist Church and the most powerful individual in the Nonconformist churches. Frances Willard (1839–98) was an American educator and reformer, active in the temperance movement. Frank Smith (1854–1940), a Fabian, was for many years a member of the London County Council (at this time representing North Lambeth). Richard Whately (1787–1863), an English theologian and logician, was editor of Paley's *Moral Philosophy*. Henry Sidgwick (1838–1900), a philosopher who became a Cambridge professor, was the author of *Methods of Ethics* (1874).]

Dear Sir

Your line of argument is simple enough.

First, refuse to accept abusive descriptions of doctrines that have been put forward by men whose character stands quite as high as that of your opponent. If a controversialist is foolish enough to call Socialism Theft, there is nothing more to be said than that nobody advocates Theft or is likely to advocate it. If he calls Free Love Lust, the reply is the same. Nobody has advocated lust and nobody is likely to advocate it. If your opponent chooses to waste the time of the meeting in opposing what has never been advanced, you will not waste it by defending it.

Second: your opponent defends marriage. What does he mean by marriage? Is it legal marriage? If so, according to what law and what canon? In England marriage is regarded as indissoluble by Roman Catholics, who do not recognize divorce. The law grants divorce for adultery & cruelty, but not for crime, drink, madness, or incompatibility of temper. Does your opponent consider that those who think that divorce should be extended to rescue people from drunkards, criminals & lunatics, as you hope every humane man, Socialist or not, is, are advocates of Lust? In many of the American States divorce can be obtained practically if the pair become convinced that they made a mistake in choosing one another. In France, a blow entails divorce. In Turkey marriage includes polygamy. The Mormons mean polygamy when they speak of marriage; and among the advocates of polygamy we find so respectable a name as that of Martin Luther. Monogamic marriage, as established in England, places no restriction on what your opponent calls Lust. It rather encourages the very pernicious belief that when two people are once legally married they may behave without any sort of moderation; and the law permits a husband to commit a rape upon his wife with impunity. The parties can appeal to the courts to force each other to submit to intercourse. People who defend this state of things have no right to throw hard words at people who wish to reform it.

Nevertheless, your opponent has no ground whatever for assuming that all Socialists, or even many Socialists, are extreme reformers on the marriage question. The Fabian Society has refused to place marriage reform on its program. The S.D.F. is silent on the subject. The Socialist League, which denounced "the bourgeois property marriage," lapsed into Anarchism and soon became extinct. The members of the Fabian Society have each signed a declaration of Socialism. Dr Clifford is a member. Will your opponent venture to stigmatize Dr Clifford as an advocate of Lust? or Stopford Brooke? Or the late Miss Frances Willard? or Mr & Mrs Sidney Webb? or Graham Wallas, the chairman of the General Management Committee of the London Schoolboard? Or Mr H. W. Massingham, the editor of the Daily Chronicle? Or Mr

Clement Shorter, the editor of the Illustrated London News? Or Mr A E Fletcher, the editor of the New Age? Or Mr Walter Crane? Or Mr Sidney Olivier C.M.G? Or Mr Hubert Bland? Or Mrs Bland (Edith Nesbit the poetess)? All these are present or former members of the Fabian Society. Then take John Burns, Mr R.C.Phillimore (son of Sir W.Phill. the judge), Mrs Phillimore, Mr Frank Smith (who made his reputation in the Salvation Army), Mr Blatchford of the Clarion, Mr Keir Hardie, Mr H.M.Hyndman. All these are men of unimpeached domestic character—married, every man of them, as I am myself. Challenge your opponent to take that list and say, if he dares, that it consists of notorious evil livers & propagandists of lust. Ask him whether he proposes to apologize for having already done so by implication.

If he cites the case of the Oneida Creek Community and Grant Allen's "Woman who Did," point out that the Oneida C.C. objected to marriage because it was too licentious, & that [J.H.] Noyes, its head & founder, preached a doctrine of absolute continence except for the purpose of continuing the race. Also that Grant Allen, whose home is a model of domesticity, has advocated perfect freedom of marriage contract, but that so far from advocating licentiousness, his Woman Who Did has been laughed at as a mere piece of idealism, because her devotion to principle is superhuman. Robert Owen did not believe in our system of marriage: neither did Plato. Ask your opponent whether, because Plato advocated community of women & children in a work universally admired for its lofty wisdom (The Republic), he would accuse all philosophers, including Archbishop Whateley & Professor Sidgwick, of being Free Lovers. If not, why he accuses all Socialists of the same thing because one of them agreed with Plato. Ask him whether he has anything to allege against the family life of Karl Marx. Whether he is aware that Ferdinand Lassalle lost his life in a duel practically because he refused to elope with a young lady whose hand in marriage he was seeking. And, generally, whether he is not ashamed to resort to slander in order to destroy the characters of men whose arguments he is too lazy to study, and too thoughtless to deal with &c &c &c &c &c &c &c &c.

Altogether, you ought to be able to hold your own without much trouble on a point like this[.]

yrs faithfully
G.Bernard Shaw

82

To CHARLES CHARRINGTON

[D/4]

Blen-Cathra. Hindhead
23rd March 1899

[Percy Dearmer (1867-1936), a Fabian ecclesiastic who became Canon of Westminster at the end of his life, ran unsuccessfully for the Executive. Sir Thomas Smith (1833-1909) was an eminent London surgeon. Charrington was elected to the Fabian Executive in April, and served on the committee until his voluntary retirement in 1904.]

'Tis well: your high sense of personal honor is rewarded: Dearmer insists on a contest. And I may observe in passing that if you want a certificate as a man ostentatiously void of all the commercially valuable scruples, and indignantly full of all the idiotically sentimental ones, apply to me. As for me, I have at last been fed up to 11 stone (a gain of 5 lbs) and have now no scruples at all. My conscience is thoroughly robust; and I regret nothing except the honorable limits I set to my regard for Janet out of a puling regard for your conventional feelings. I feel like Richard III, and find that state exhilarating & happy. A fortnight ago I submitted my foot to Sir Thomas Smith. He said "Walk on it." I am walking on it. What the result will be I dont know yet. It is snowing like hell. The distant bells chime across the valley, melodiously singing "Turn again Charrington, Mayor of Chelsea." I enclose various documents of an interesting & improving character. The Ashton Jonsons were here the other day—said you both had the air of having come into several thousand a year.

GBS

To A. J. MARRIOTT

[S/1]

Blen-Cathra. Hindhead
10th April 1899

Dear Mr Marriott

Take the case of Ireland. You had there an Established Church and an unestablished and even to some extent persecuted Roman Catholic Church. What was the result? The Roman Catholic Church had a tight hold of the people; the priest made them confess, made them pay, and could ruin any contumacious individual by denunciation from the altar far more effectively than the government could by Coercion Acts.

The Established Church had no grip at all; but when it was disestablished it woke up and gained some real strength. The Church Sustentation Funds came out of the labor of the Catholic peasant just like the endowment. Disestablishment doesn't weaken a Church under modern conditions: it strengthens it.

As to persecution, all sects persecute when they have the power. Do you suppose the N.S.S. [National Secular Society] would allow any man to bring up his child a Baptist if it could prevent him? It seems to me that every Freethinker is bound to insist on the toleration of all opinions. When the Freethinker is a Socialist as well, he cannot very well be blind to the fact that this means the public endowment of all sects which are numerous enough to clearly supply a public need, and too poor to have decent places of meeting. I am aware that this cannot be done in the present intolerant state of opinion: but I think that when public opinion is educated to recognise the justice of the principle, a reform of the Church will become practicable. Such reform might bring the Church considerably in advance of the N.S.S. in point of real freethought, and get rid of the prayerbook, the articles, the worship of the Bible, and a good deal of obsolete nonsense, besides greatly modifying sectarian bitterness.

Anyhow, Disestablishment simply means handing over the property of the Church to the secular proprietors without any obligation on their part not to spend it at Monte Carlo. Atheism no longer means anything: the cleverest half of the congregationalists are by this time freer from superstition than Bradlaugh was. The belief of the Secularists in Reason and Science is just as old fashioned and seems to me just as dangerous on its bad side as the mysticism of the Guild of St Matthew. In fact, I am heterodox even in my Atheism; and that is the secret of the unexpectedness of my attitude.

yours faithfully
G. Bernard Shaw

To MRS PATRICK CAMPBELL

Blen-Cathra. Hindhead
[A/37; X/160]   12th April 1899

[Mrs Campbell had given a copyright performance of *Cæsar and Cleopatra* in Newcastle on 15th March, but she was not destined to recreate the rôle of Cleopatra on any subsequent occasion. "Cæsar" was Johnston Forbes-Robertson, to whom Shaw had sent a copy of the play in January.]

84

Dear Mrs Patrick Campbell

We have this house until the 14th May only; so come quickly. Mrs Shaw will be delighted to see you. But if the words are no plainer than the woman, they will be thrown away on me.

Why not play the first act of "C & C" as a curtain raiser? The public can have the rest of it when I publish it. Or get Pinero to write a sequel. *I* dont mind—and he can have all the fees.

The vegetables have triumphed over their traducers. I was told that my diet was so poor that I could not repair the bones that were broken & operated on. So I have just had an Xradiograph taken; and lo! perfectly mended solid bone so beautifully white that I have left instructions that, if I die, a glove stretcher is to be made out of them and sent to you as a souvenir.

We are having a spell of fine weather here. Why not bring Cæsar down to lunch: it would do him good, and dispel all remnants of your influenza.

yours sincerely
G. Bernard Shaw

To EMERY WALKER

[C/3]

Blen-Cathra. Hindhead
26th April 1899

[J.W.Mackail's *The Life of William Morris* was reviewed by Shaw in the *Daily Chronicle* on 27th April.]

I got Mackail's book yesterday afternoon, with a request for a review 4000 words long in time for tomorrow's paper, which means posting it this afternoon at one. Imagine having to read through two volumes of 350 & 375 pages in that time; to get a night's sleep and a couple of meals; and to write 2½ cols. for the Chronicle into the bargain! Of course it was impossible. I dipped into the book here and there with the help of the index, and sloshed down a heap of words to the general effect that Mackail has made a poor job of the Socialistic part. But it is a scandalously poor job of a review. Please explain to anybody who is disappointed that I had no chance of doing it decently, and that it was only by a *tour de force* that I succeeded in filling up the space at all.

GBS

To RICHARD MANSFIELD

Blen-Cathra. Hindhead

[A/21; X/116]   28th April 1899

[A.M.Palmer had been Mansfield's business manager and adviser since 1896.]

Oh, oh, oh ! ! !

Can't play Julius Cæsar, and want another twopenny melodrama.

I blush—I apologize to two continents for making people believe you a genius. My conscience cries "Dids't thou not share? hadst thou not fifteenpence?" [*The Merry Wives of Windsor*, II, iii, 14] I did: I had. Heaven forgive me!

Well, Forbes Robertson shall play it in New York under your Cyranian nose; and it shall be announced as "the play that beat Richard Mansfield."

Well, well, you shall have a nice easy play, suited to your capacity, as soon as I can think of something. Hitherto, when I have read "C & C" to people, and they have asked "Is Mansfield going to play it?" I have replied "I don't know. I suppose so." Henceforth I shall say "Mansfield!! Oh no: quite beyond him: I am writing a little melodrama for him." I disown you.

Hath he so long held out with me untired

And stops he now for breath? [*Richard III*, IV, ii, 44] Good: his next production will fail deservedly. He plays parts written for Terriss, not parts written for great actors.

So you dont want to act. You want your wires pulled for you. Well, you shall have them; but the whole world shall see my fingers at work. And Julius Cæsar will await you at Philippi.

Mr Palmer has just lunched with me. He gave me your messages. I told him I'd write mine. If only I had you here between my claws *I'd* teach you what is good for you. Farewell—*Pompey*.

GBS

To CHARLES A. BEARD

Blen-Cathra. Hindhead

[H/55]   1st May 1899

[Ruskin Hall, later known as Ruskin College, had been founded early in 1899 at Oxford for the purpose of providing a liberal education in a residential college for working men. The college owed its existence to two young

Americans: Walter Vrooman (1869–?) of St Louis, who had come to Oxford for graduate study in philosophy, and Charles A. Beard (1874–1948), one of F. York Powell's graduate students in English history, who was to become famous for a series of historical studies written in collaboration with his wife Mary.]

Dear Sir

I must apologize for having so long delayed my reply to the request which reached me in January as to lecturing in Ruskin Hall. I have been an invalid since last May; and my correspondents have had to suffer for it.

My first impulse on hearing of the Ruskin Hall project was to ask Mr Vrooman what on earth he wanted to send workmen to Oxford for. However, when one recollects that he is an American, and consequently sees the ideal and not the real Oxford, one understands the matter. No doubt an Oxford hall mark has a certain value as a commercial and social asset to men of a certain class—not the working class—whose standing might without it be open to question. Intellectually and morally it seems to me to cost more than it is worth to any other class of man. A workman ought to have a vulgar prejudice against Oxford. If he goes there he is likely to be cured of the vulgar prejudice without being taught the enlightened prejudice which led William Morris—an Oxonian likely to be much quoted at Ruskin Hall—to declare that the only money he had ever wantonly wasted was the fee he paid for his M.A. degree. He will learn nothing there that he cannot learn anywhere else, except the social tone, which will be as detrimental to him as a workman as it is useful to a gentleman, and the false perspective by which those dons who represent the survival at a university of the members least fit for the world, appear eminent to men too young to know what eminence at full pitch means. His danger will be all the greater, since it will be good form to be nice to him, and compliment him on mediocre academic performances. In short, if a workman asked me whether he should endeavor to put in a few terms at Ruskin Hall, I should strongly advise him not to unless he wanted to do exactly what you deplore—that is, change himself from a workman into a schoolman. The business of Oxford is to make a few scholars and a great many gentlemen; and that will remain its business until the latter half of the process loses its social importance sufficiently to make a sweeping measure of University Reform possible. In a few years Mr Vrooman will find this out; and I greatly doubt whether the success of the Hall in the meantime will be sufficient to attract an endowment or subscriptions sufficient to keep it in existence when he drops it.

I may be wrong: I hope I am; but whilst I take this view of the enterprise it is obviously inexpedient that I should accept your invitation to lecture.

yours faithfully
G. Bernard Shaw

To A. J. MARRIOTT

[Général Raoul F. C. Le Mouton de Boisdeffre (1839–1919), chief of staff of the French army, was one of the first to have doubts about the guilt of Alfred Dreyfus. As a result of the scandal which followed, he resigned from the army in 1898. Henri Rochefort (1830–1913) was a French politician, playwright, and journalist, who edited *L'Intransigeant* from 1880 to 1907. Archbishop William Laud (1573–1645) was an English prelate, beheaded after being impeached for high treason by the Long Parliament in 1641. Fabian lectures on Imperial politics were offered from October 1899 until March 1900, and included W. A. S. Hewins on "Foreign Trade and Foreign Politics," Frederick Whelen on "England and South Africa," Sydney Olivier on "The Psychology of Race," S. G. Hobson on "England and the Far East," and Shaw, on 23rd February 1900, on "Imperialism."]

Dear Mr Marriott

All sects, secular and supernaturalist, exist to do all the wicked things you impute to the Church. Take the case of the anti-Dreyfus people. What is it they do? Why, pick out all the general vices of humanity—all its greed and ambition and sensuality—and denounce the Jews for them, as if Christians were any less greedy, ambitious and sensual. You can see by Boisdeffre's face that he was born to be the gull of his priest; but did you never meet an evangelical English gull who was just as credulous as to the machinations of the Jesuits or the wickedness of the Atheists? If you make a single exception to the rule of toleration, you give away your own case against bigotry. When you speak of a party "whose every raison d'être is to destroy liberty, a party whose very virtues deprave a nation more than the vices of the vilest men &c" you are using the exact language in which Rochefort & Co denounce the Jews. I am amazed to find the free thinking A.J.M. talking about "accursed sacerdotalists"! When the antisacerdotalists had their turn after beheading Laud, were they any more tolerant than

88

he? Only by tolerating them all, and involving (by endowment) the toleration of each in the toleration of all, can you force them to tolerate each other.

You are right about Fabian Socialism being Collectivist rather than Democratic in the old sense. The old notion of Democracy, tried in its extremest form in the Trade Unions, with popular election of officials, referendum, initiative and all the rest of it, led straight to an official autocracy which the Tsar might admire. When the Cotton-spinners worked out the problem of getting some sort of control over their own officials, they arrived at the system of expert civil service and control by elected representatives, much as our parliamentary system is—bar, of course, the House of Lords and the obvious abuses of our electoral machinery. Webb has explained the position elaborately in his Industrial Democracy, which is a very remarkable book from this point of view.

What the deuce quarrel have you with Ruskin's honesty? That really is very cranky of you. Can a man do more than stick to his opinions; spend his fortune on them; and publish the balance sheet?

The difficulty about the Fabian paper, I imagine, is that you want to talk about the Empire, and we have already arranged a course of lectures on that subject and allotted the papers.

I have just sprained my ankle again (third time); so there is no chance of my escaping from quarantine just yet.

yours faithfully
G. Bernard Shaw

To MRS RICHARD MANSFIELD

Blen-Cathra. Hindhead
[A/21; X/116]   3rd May 1899

[George Gibbs Mansfield (1898–1918), the only child of Richard Mansfield, was killed in World War I. Victorien Sardou's *Robespierre*, in a translation by Laurence Irving, had been produced at the Lyceum Theatre on 15th April. Re Mrs Mansfield as Ibsen's Nora in *A Doll's House*, see I, 530.]

My dear Mrs Mansfield
The portraits have just arrived—G.G. much more like you than you are like yourself. He is a most terrifyingly clever looking baby.

I have cut off Richard without a shilling; and you may NOT say that you like the Devil's Disciple better than "C & C." The D's D is

89

a melodrama, made up of all the stale Adelphi tricks—the reading of the will, the heroic sacrifice, the court martial, the execution, the reprieve at the last moment. Anybody could make a play that way. But "C & C" is the first & only adequate dramatization of the greatest man that ever lived. I want to revive, in a modern way and with modern refinement, the sort of thing that Booth did the last of in America: the projection on the stage of the hero in the big sense of the word. Whoever plays Cæsar successfully will pass hors concours at once—get the sort of position Garrick, Kemble & Macready held, and that Irving holds here now without having ever quite achieved a heroic impersonation. Cleopatra is not a difficult part: Cæsar *is*: whoever can play the fourth act of it can play anything. Whoever can't, can play nothing. Hence my unappeasable wrath.

I haven't seen Robespierre; but nobody pretends that Sardou has become another & better man. Don't bother about it. Wyndham is going to play Cyrano, they say; but everybody here is always going to do something.

I haven't heard from Archer except through his articles. I am sure he is favorably disposed towards you as an early Nora.

I began the E. Terry play today—not quite sure what it will be like.

The gardener again reminds me that post hour is pressing. My best regards to you & G.G.M.: my unconquerable defiance to the Recreant.

yrs sincerely
G. Bernard Shaw

To GRANT RICHARDS

[Blen-Cathra. Hindhead]
[G.u/4] 29th May 1899
Dear G.R.

This is beyond all reason. You first write to me explicitly that you did not advertise the book [*The Perfect Wagnerite*]; and because I politely accepted that statement you reproach me for forgetting that you spent £14 on advertisements & that they attracted my own special attention by their misleading character. How am I to keep my head among these reckless contradictions?

I dont deny that it is your business to make your books look well: on the contrary, that is the exact ground of my complaint that instead of doing it you go about amusing yourself & leave the job to me. I still have the ghastly proofs you submitted to me before I took the matter in hand. To say, as you do, that "your [my]* superintendence of the production was entirely unnecessary" is to proclaim yourself void of moral and artistic sense. I blush for you.

It is quite true that I warned you repeatedly that my plays would probably ruin you. Since you admit this, why do you complain that they have not sold? I never expected them to sell beyond the circulation I told you had been achieved by Scott & other publishers. I dont expect them to sell. It is you who reproach me with their limited sale, not I you. I propose to take the responsibility on myself in future, not to add it to your burdens. Personally I find you, like all thoroughly un-businesslike people, a pleasant sort of ruffian, the kind of man I like to know. But why should I exhaust your capital & ruffle your temper by inflicting my books on you? If I take them in hand myself, the blame and loss will be mine. So long as you have them in hand, the blame & loss will be yours: that is what a publisher is for.

Any misunderstandings as to the arrangement with Stone are simply explained by the fact that you, not I, made it. I daresay they will send you particulars if you ask them. I never interfered in the business by a single word or line. If I had, it would have come out all right. Your plan, avowed by you from the first, of letting things slide, has its advantages; but you must not expect it to act exactly like the regular business plan of making explicit agreements. You admit that you did not carry out the arrangements; and as you know that *I* did not meddle, the conclusion is obvious there was no arrangement at all.

On the whole, it is not only certain now that you will be ruined, but that you will attribute your ruin to me. Why should I incur this responsibility? You had much better send me an exact account of the whole transaction, and let me readjust it on a commission basis as from the beginning. In this way I will make good all your loss; and you can sell the remainder of the edition for me on commission. Can I say fairer than that?

yrs sincerely
[G. Bernard Shaw]

* The square brackets are Shaw's.

To ELLEN TERRY

[U(A)/10; X/117]

Blen-Cathra. Hindhead
7th July 1899

[Shaw had drafted the scenario of the play for Ellen Terry, first called *The Witch of Atlas* but subsequently titled *Captain Brassbound's Conversion*, on 5th May. The dialogue of the play was begun on 14th May, and completed, as Shaw indicates, on 7th July. An amateur performance of the forest scenes from *As You Like It* was given in the Rectory Gardens, Hindhead, on 5th July. A letter from Shaw concerning the performance was published on 15th July in the *Farnham, Haslemere and Hindhead Herald* under the title "As You Don't Like It." Jacob Blumenthal (1829–1908), a well-known composer, was pianist to the Queen. The "journalism" included the Morris and Wagner reviews, a review of Nietzsche's works in the *Saturday Review* on 13th May, and "The Censorship of the Stage in England" in the *North American Review* in August.]

Finished, finished, dear Ellen, and on the whole not so bad as I feared. And yet, alas! not finished; for now I have to go over it to get the business right, which will take many grievous brainracking days. And then further delay whilst Charlotte deciphers my wretched note-books & makes a typewritten draft, with such unprofessional speed as her housekeeping & wifely cares allow. After that a final revision of the draft; and then Miss Dickens; and then, at last, you. But the main point is that the play now exists, though I died tomorrow, and cannot be unmade save by unlucky fire.

It is a shocking leading lady business, after all; but then, *such* a leading lady! All the other characters are the merest doormats for her. The wretched leading man has nothing in the last act but ignominious dumbness & ridicule until the final scene, in which he gets a consolation prize.

We had a real open air "As You Like It" in the woods yesterday. It nearly drove me mad. They had white soup plates full of roses to represent footlights (without which it would not have been real acting, of course); the foresters wore faded silk tights (also indispensable to true art); and there was a cottage piano to accompany Amiens in a new setting of Blow, blow, in the style of Blumenthal. I sang "Damn, damn" between my teeth all the time. Incarnadined fools!

I think you will have to christen the play yourself: I haven't yet invented a name for it.

Two months work, with some £60 worth of journalism stolen out of the middle of it.

And yet you think I do not love you: you do *not* believe each word I say.

GBS

To WILLIAM ARCHER

[A/2]

Blen-Cathra. Hindhead
27th July 1899

[William Pember Reeves had come down to Hindhead for a Saturday to Monday visit, developed diphtheria, and caused the quarantine of the household for three weeks. Mr Barlow is the pedantic tutor in Thomas Day's *Sandford and Merton* (1783–89).]

Will you send "C & C," when you are quite done with it, to Gilbert Murray, Barford, Churt, near Farnham. He has just moved in.

I think I will call the play "Captain Brassbound's Conversion." I can think of nothing else but "The Angel in the Atlas" (after Coventry Patmore), which is silly.

The bacillus has turned up in Charlotte's throat, which was a little sore & is now perfectly well. I cannot make the doctor see that this is checkmate to his bacteriological theories. He actually wants her to stay in her bedroom for three weeks, lest the insect should decimate Hindhead.—Oh, by the way, I forgot that you haven't heard the news. Reeves has diptheria! At least the bacillus turned up in *his* ulcerated throat; and we are all in a major state of siege, with nurses, carbolic sheets, & devil knows what not. Pints of antitoxin have been squirted into the whole household, excepting only my sceptical self. Perhaps its just as well that you didnt come into contact with him.

The defects of "C & C" seem to me to be inherent in the *genre* Chronicle Play. I tried cutting & compression; but when I came to read the play to people I found myself forced to restore the cuts— even the most apparently harmless ones. (Try this yourself if you doubt it). Finally I concluded that only one cut was possible—the omission of the third act chock-a-block. The first act could be played by itself almost: it is very effective; but, as in "Arms & The Man," one must pay the penalty of a good dramatic first act by a comparatively expository

93

second one. The chronicle ties you to the exposition of Cæsar's position at Alexandria; and there is no drama in it because Cæsar was so completely superior to his adversaries that there was virtually no *conflict*, only a few *adventures*, chiefly the hairbreadth escape when he jumped into the harbor. I was desperate about the business until, like Columbus with the egg, I solved the problem by making Cleopatra commit a murder. Of course the main feat to be performed was to do what Wully Shakspere didn't (his object being to heroify Brutus): that is, present Cæsar as a great man with a genuine differentiation of character & view in the greater direction, instead of merely sending on a leading man & saying "Let us assume that this is Cæsar, though he talks like a military Mr Barlow, with a touch of the modern wisdom of the Breakfast Table Autocrat." It is true that I have done this by making rather small beer of the protagonists; but I think he dwarfs them fairly and that his eminence is something more than an illusion produced by the flatness of the surrounding country. That achieved, I give up the rest as hopeless. The first act clearly cant go on through the play: it exhausts its theme. The chronicle must tell its historical story, which, I repeat, could only be made *melodramatic* in construction as a Relief of Lucknow business which would take all attention from the characters. Besides, if I attempted, with such a construction in view, to start with an exposition, as in "The Devil's Disciple" & "Brassbound," I should damn the play, because though an audience will take in a simple story of a family & a police case patiently & even eagerly before they see the people in it, they *wont* take in an exposition of the Eastern Question, whether Egyptian or Bulgarian, unless their curiosity & interest have been very strongly roused by a piquant adventure with some attractive Egyptian or Bulgarian. The fact is, when you come to do these things, you find out that the peculiar characteristics of the Shakespear chronicle play are not due to his neglect or failure to construct them like Othello, but are produced by the technical conditions of the feat. You say in the chronicle play "I will accept character and story from outside the drama—from History, not from my own dramatic invention & the needs of the dramatic appetite; and I will make the best play I can out of them. In the Othello–Devil's Disciple genre, you make the whole thing—character, story & everything else—out of the tree in your own garden.

This is the best explanation I can give of the scatteriness of the play. I cling rather to the hope that some of the bits that seem second rate or superfluous have their function. At least, as I said before, I found that I couldnt make the play fully intelligible & effective without them, bar always the third act, which, except as a bit of light, air, scenery & fun, might as well not exist, though the lighthouse & the carpet are "historical."

GBS

To ELLEN TERRY

Blen-Cathra. Hindhead

[U(A)/10; X/117]   1st August 1899

[*Three Plays for Puritans* was not published until January 1901. Fuller Mellish (1865–1936) had performed with Irving at the Lyceum in 1884 and again during the late 1890's; he performed in the United States for many years after the turn of the century. Dan Leno (1861–1904) was a celebrated music hall comedian and star of Drury Lane pantomime. Louie Freear (1872–1939) was a pintsized comedian who specialised in Cockney roles; she had one of her greatest successes in January 1900 when she appeared as Puck in Beerbohm Tree's production of *A Midsummer Night's Dream*. "Mrs Pat-Cat" was a Shavian epithet for Mrs Patrick Campbell.]

After much title-searching, I have resolved to give that play (which you seem to have thrown into your waste-paper basket with the other tragedies when it arrived last Friday morning) by the ugly but arresting name "Captain Brassbound's Conversion." I did my best to make Lady Cicely a "title part," but could find nothing better than "The Angel in the Atlas" or some such silliness. Besides, when I publish my next volume, which will contain The Devil's Disciple, Cæsar & Cleopatra, & Captain B, I will call it "Three Plays for Puritans." "Captain B's Conversion" has a blatant Puritan sound in it. . . .

Archer was down here last Sunday week. He says the critics wont like my damned ostentation of intellectual superiority, but begs me most earnestly to give the play a chance, by waiting at least two years for somebody to produce it before publishing it, and not infuriating all the managers by entering into personal negotiations with them. He vented his sense of years of suffering from your first-night imperfections by saying "She'll never learn it." He suggested H.B.Irving for Brassbound—not a bad idea if it could be managed. Drinkwater is a difficulty: he must be a genuine comedian, not merely an actor who can imitate cockney—(F*ll*r M*ll*sh for instance), but the real thing, a creature with tears in him. Dan Leno would probably undertake it for not more than twice your salary. Welch could do it if he could cocknify

95

himself enough. It requires a male Louie Freear. The other parts are easy enough, except that Sir Ahrd Allam [Howard Hallam] must be gentleman enough to be dignified when he is crusty.

However, there's your play—Ellen's play. My conscience was so burdened with the infamy of having written plays for Pat-Cats and other people about whom I dont care a straw (thank my stars they can't act them) and made no play for you, that it had to be done. Now it *is* done—the only thing on earth in my power to do for you. And now no more plays—at least no more practicable ones. None at all, indeed, for some time to come: it is time to do something more in Shaw-philosophy, in politics & sociology. Your author, dear Ellen, must be more than a common dramatist.

By the way, what are your wishes concerning the press? Shall I say nothing & leave everything of that sort to you; or shall I start an epidemic of paragraphs to the effect that I have written a play expressly for you? One way is to give a copyrighting performance (what about *that*, eh?) and send round copies of the program to the critics & paragraphists. That is what I generally do. But it is quite easy to let it alone, though the fact of the play being written is sure to leak out: the question is, do you want your name connected with it?

GBS

To ELLEN TERRY

[U(A)/10; X/117]

Blen-Cathra. Hindhead
4th August 1899

[Ellen Terry's first reaction to Shaw's play was a negative one. "I couldnt do this one," she wrote to Shaw on 3rd August, "and I believe it would never do for the stage. The two parts, the man and woman, are right; but that *bore* Drinkwater! Mrs Pat for Lady C! I couldnt do it ...[T]he expressions 'There's not a penny in it'—'More fitted for the closet than the stage,' occur to one when one has finished it." The legendary Frederick Robson (1821–64), an extraordinarily popular burlesque comedian of the 1850's, was noted for his ability to terrify audiences by his passionate intensity.]

Alas! dear Ellen, is it really so? Then I can do nothing for you. I honestly thought that Lady Cicely would fit you like a glove—that I had sacrificed everything to make the play go effectively from second to second—even that Drinkwater was a tragi-comic figure worthy of

Robson. And now you tell me that it is a play for the closet, and that Lady Cicely would suit Mrs P. C. All of which proves that either I am mad, or you are mad, or else there is an impassable gulf between my drama and your drama.

I wont suggest it to Mrs Pat, because I am now quite convinced that she would consider herself born to play it, just as you want to play Cleopatra. No: it is clear that I have nothing to do with the theatre of today: I must educate a new generation with my pen from childhood up—audience, actors & all, and leave them my plays to murder after I am cremated. Captain B. shall not be profaned by the stage: I will publish it presently with the D's D and Cæsar, and preach a nice sermon in the preface.

And so farewell our project—all fancy, like most projects. Send me back the script when you are done with it: I will send you the printed volume when it is ready.

Silly Ellen!

GBS

To ELLEN TERRY

Blen-Cathra. Hindhead
[U(A)/10; X/117]   8th August 1899

["Of course," Ellen replied on 6th August, "you never *really* meant Lady Cicely for me—but to be published along with other Plays." Charles A. Fechter (1824–79) was a well-known actor, whose Hamlet was the subject of much critical debate. Mary Henrietta Kingsley (1862–1900) was the author of *Travels in West Africa* (1897). Sir Henry Morton Stanley (1841–1904), the noted African explorer, was the author of *In Darkest Africa* (1890). "Dr Jim worship" refers to the popular reaction to the abortive *coup d'état*, against the Boers, of Sir Leander Starr Jameson (1853–1917), known as the Jameson Raid. John Singer Sargent's portrait of Ellen Terry as Lady Macbeth, painted in 1888, is now on display in the National Portrait Gallery, London.]

Oh you lie, Ellen, you lie: never was there a part so deeply written for a woman as this for you, silly, self-unconscious, will o' the wisp beglamored child actress as you still are. It is like offering the play to Kate [Terry]. "Sir, I do not do this sort of thing. Take it to some ordinary leading lady—I believe there is a person named Campbell, or is it Kendal?—whom it might suit. My line is romantic tragedy, supported

97

by Mr Fechter. Your offering it to me shews a complete misunderstanding of my rank as an artist. I expected something better from you —A classic language at least instead of this vulgar colloquialism; but—but no matter. Good morning."

Lyceum advantages! Haven't you had enough of them yet? You talk to me, ME, ME, of this ogre's den into which your talent has been thrown and eaten. Go then, wretch, and get Comyns Carr & Calmour to write you some nice new part with a name like the latest hairwash, and be as romantic and picturesque as you please, and bury what reality there is in Ellen under ten tons more of tomfoolery.

Listen to me, woman with no religion. Send to your library for two books of travel in Africa: one Miss Kingsley's (have you met her?) and the other H. M. Stanley's. Compare the brave woman, with her commonsense and good will, with the wild-beast man, with his elephant rifle, and his atmosphere of dread and murder, breaking his way by mad selfish assassination out of the difficulties created by his own cowardice. Think of all that has been rising up under your eyes in Europe for years past, Bismarck worship, Stanley worship, Dr Jim worship, and now at last Kitchener worship with dead enemies dug up and mutilated. Think also on the law—the gallows, penal servitude, hysterical clamoring for the lash, mere cowardice masquerading as "resolute government," "law and order" and the like. Well, how have you felt about these things? Have you had any real belief in the heroism of the filibuster? Have you had any sympathy with the punishments of the judge? Have you found in your own life and your own small affairs no better way, no more instructive heart wisdom, no warrant for trusting to the good side of people instead of terrorizing the bad side of them. I—poor idiot!—thought the distinction of Ellen Terry was that she had this heart wisdom, and managed her own little world as Tolstoy would have our Chamberlains & Balfours & German Emperors & Kitcheners & Lord Chief Justices and other slaves of false ideas & imaginary fears manage Europe. I accordingly give you a play in which you stand in the very place where Imperialism is most believed to be necessary, on the border line where the European meets the fanatical African, with judge on the one hand, and indomitable adventurer-filibuster on the other, said ind-adv-fil pushing forward "civilization" in the shape of rifles & pistols in the hands of Hooligans, aristocratic *mauvais sujets* and stupid drifters. I try to shew these men gaining a sense of courage and resolution from continual contact with & defiance of their own fears. I try to shew you fearing nobody and managing them all as Daniel managed the lions, not by cunning—above all, not by even a momentary appeal to Cleopatra's stand-by, their passions, but by simple moral superiority. It is a world-wide situation, and one totally incomprehensible to Cleopatras of all sorts and periods. (Cleopatra would have waited to guess which of the two men was going to beat the other, and then tried to seduce him, after which, as in the case of Antony & Cæsar, she would have found that she had guessed wrong.) Here then is your portrait painted on a map of the world—and you prefer Sargent's Lady Macbeth! Here you get far beyond Candida, with her boy & her parson, and her suspicion of trading a little on the softness of her contours—and you want to get back to Cleopatra! Here is a part which dominates a play because the character it represents dominates the world—and you think it might do for Mrs P.C.! The wretched Hooligan who gives the final touch by turning from the navy, the bench, and all the powers & principalities to Ellen in his extremity —"they dassent do it if you tell 'em not"—is dull to you. In every other play I have ever written—even in Candida—I have prostituted the actress more or less by making the interest in her partly a sexual interest: only the *man* in the Devil's Disciple draws clear of it. In Lady Cicely I have done without this, and gained a greater fascination by it. And you are disappointed.

Oh, wretch, wretch, wretch! It is true that the record of the play as a book written by me for you is worth a thousand Lyceum successes; but its publication with "Repudiated by Miss Ellen Terry as unworthy of her professional eminence" across it—do you think I intended that? And do you think I regard you as a person needing to be arranged with sphinxes & limelights to be relished by a luxurious public? Oh Ellen, Ellen, Ellen, Ellen, Ellen. This is the end of everything.

GBS

To GRAHAM WALLAS

Ruan Minor. Cornwall
[A/13]   24th August 1899

[The Shaws had rented a house at Ruan Minor for one month, from 15th August, for sea bathing. Frederick Jackson (1832–1915) was a London solicitor who had retired in 1890 to an estate on Hindhead. There he wrote political articles under the pseudonym "Vox Clamans," participated in public affairs (both local and national), played the organ, and indulged a genius for friendship. The Lizard is a promontory at the southern tip of Cornwall.]

We have no plans for the winter—or rather nothing more definite than a plan of taking a country dwelling within easy reach of London & making it our headquarters when I am not vestrying or Fabianing or the like. The question is, where is that particular pitch to be.

Reeves is all right; and we have at last got away to this place, where I swim twice a day, taking a turn on the surface on each occasion for my own amusement, and another underneath in the capacity of a life preserver for Charlotte, who is learning to swim with nothing between her and death but a firm grip of my neck. The sea being the only element I enjoy exercise in, I am putting up muscle & rather straightening myself up.

It is clear enough that if the practical result of our demonstration of the world's wrongness is to be a reconciliation with the world—which is a thoroughly English way of avoiding paradox—there will be an end of us for all useful purposes. However, I do not personally feel the reconciliation. My contempt for the status quo grows from year to year; and I do not despair of expressing it yet in a mind-changing manner.

All this committee work is nothing but being lazy by public machinery. A thoroughbred horse can work himself to sleep as effectually by pumping water as by steeplechasing; but he makes a donkey of himself in the process. What on earth is the use of spending 8 hours a day as a petty magistrate disposing of cases of drunken schoolmistresses, and perpetuating a system that ought to be abolished? Jackson the Sage said to me the other day when I said something about keeping in contact with life and experience by public work & the like, "Why, man, youre *bilious* with a surfeit of life & experience. Go and use your imagination whilst it's in its prime." I pass the admonition on to you, and heartily wish you a necrosed foot or something equally effectual to detach you from that foolish democratic mistake, the adhocious School Board. You'd much better write another book, without any preparation. Whelen wants books for his Fabian Series. Why not give him one?

There is an accursed fog today; and the Lizard sirens are exploding like tightly flatulent bullocks every two minutes. I should ask you down for a swim but for the fact that the journey is only tolerable by sleeping car; and our tickets (three of us) cost me twelve pound odd.

GBS

100

To ELLEN TERRY

[U(H)/10; X/117]

Ruan Minor. Cornwall
13th September 1899

[Walter John Gurly had died at Leyton on 30th August, at the age of 64, of diabetes and chronic convulsions. Shaw's solicitors had informed him that two sureties were required for the administration bond, and Shaw had asked Graham Wallas to supply the second. He gave the estate to the city of Carlow in 1944. The copyright performance of *Captain Brassbound's Conversion* took place at the Court Theatre, Liverpool, on 10th October, with Ellen Terry as Lady Cicely Waynflete and Laurence Irving as Brassbound.]

Thou dear Ellen

I return to London by tomorrow night's train, arriving on Friday morning. On the 21st I sail away and can do nothing for six weeks, nor can any effective business communication be kept up with me. In the meantime the play is not copyrighted; and as to America I have only a casual remark of yours that you might take the play there at some future time. Now you must give your inconstant mind more strenuously to this for a moment. Do you realize that these American rights are worth about £2,500 to me, argent comptant, and that if you ask me to keep them for you, and then dont use them, you may possibly deprive me of it altogether, and certainly deprive me of the interest on it for several years. Do you understand?—two thousand five hundred solid golden sovereigns. I shouldnt mind if the result of my losing them was that you would get them; but you wouldnt: they would be simply annihilated—wasted.

Ask your conscience in the small hours of the night whether there is any serious likelihood of your going to America next winter with a company of your own, and without Henry, who will then have to take somebody else if he also goes to America next year. If you can say to the conscience, "Yes: Henry isnt going next year; and I am; and I have fully made up my mind to book the dates or otherwise arrange the business this next tour," then I think you may commit yourself, always bearing in mind that if Henry is not in America he will be somewhere else and must replace you. If you cant say this, then cry off the American part of the plan, and leave half the globe to Ada Rehan.

I worry you about this purposely. It is important for yourself that you should get this business settled soon. The English production can wait as long as you like; but America is my lever to force you to action with. Besides, a horrible misfortune has happened to me—a money trouble. I have succeeded through the death of my uncle to a family estate in Ireland—a miserable relic of former county splendor, all mortgages and poor relations. I am not sure that I shall not repudiate it. What with this and a letter just received from America (proposing, among other things, a production of Mrs Warren's Profession) I feel for the moment quite avaricious. My blessed uncle had not paid even his servant's wages for ten years, and had borrowed every farthing he could. I shall have to pay his debts because I am inheriting the privileges of paying the interest on half a dozen Carlow mortgages. And this is the moment at which you propose to throw my thousands into the Atlantic!

Now as to the copyrighting. Will you do that for me, or shall I get it done at Bayswater by Florence Farr? If you will, you must arrange with the manager whose house you will be playing at a fortnight ahead, as he must send a copy of the play and a cheque for two guineas (both of which I will send you) to the Licenser, G. A. Redford, Lord Chamberlain's Office, St. James's Palace. Redford is not bound to license at less than a fortnight's notice. I have the parts all ready, and can send them to the theatre selected for the ceremony, addressed to you.

Dont do this unless it would be a piece of fun for you and your friends in the company. I can get it done without any trouble here. But one way or another it must be arranged for before I leave for the Bay of Biscay O.

I see an announcement that the Lyceum will reopen with a play on the Massacre of St Bartholomews. Are you to be Marguerite de Valois or Catherine de Medicis?

Now proceed to think, Ellen. Remember, it is a money question. Remember that I am a most mean man about money, and will throw it in your teeth for ever after if you dont make a heap of it for me. Breaking loose from the Lyceum means a great deal. And I dont think you can, without great generalship, elope with my play and keep your place at the Lyceum at the same time.

Forgive this confused letter: we are packing, or rather Charlotte is, bearing malice the while against me for writing letters instead of helping her.

GBS

To EDWARD ROSE

Just round Cape St Vincent,
entering the straits
25th September 1899

[The Shaws had sailed on 21st September aboard the S.S. "Lusitania" for a six weeks' Mediterranean cruise. The Garden City book was Ebenezer Howard's *Tomorrow: A Peaceful Path to Real Form* (1898).]

This is a godless cruise with godless people. We take our first look at the iron walls of these African coasts with a Hampton Court steamer band playing music hall tunes on a piano, two fiddles, a double bass & a cornet. The passengers gamble meanly by getting up sweeps on the daily run, with a third prize (1%) to God, represented by "the Marine charities" to secure indulgence from eternal justice. The more I see of the moneyed classes, the more I understand the guillotine. All excellent people, of course, not a *naturally* infamous person among them; but oh! what a ——

Well, enough of this. I got the Garden City book when it first appeared (the author sent it, I suppose); glanced at the maps; and said "the same old vision." It is of course possible that the threat of legislation against factories in London might drive a few big & philanthropic firms to combine & buy land with the object of placing their "hands" thereon in a model township. Factories are often built in the north as part of what is at bottom a land speculation. Join the Association by all means & follow its fortunes & discussions: they will be more convincing & instructive than anything I could write; but dont contribute a farthing more of that £240,000 than you are positively eager to lose. Of course an artificial city, so to speak, is no more impossible than a canal is: in fact Eastbourne & many other places are such cities; but the thing should be kept clear of philanthropy & utopian socialism because people (the tenants) will not stand being kept in a nursery.

Impossible to continue—an accursed place, this floating pleasure machine—I am dragged away—porpoises or something.

We return on the 31 October.

Our love to Mrs Rose

GBS

To ARNOLD DOLMETSCH

Off Cape St Vincent
[A/24]   25th September 1899

Dear Dolmetsch

. . . One of the attractions of this ship is a first class band. One double
bass, two violins, a piano (ad lib), and a cornet. The cornet is the star:
he plays The Lost Chord on Sundays. Nothing more horrible can be
imagined. When my fellow passengers are tired of listening to selections
from the Belle of New York and endless polkas to shew of [f] the
cornettist's double tonguing, they gamble, & give ten shillings out of
the sweep to the Marine Charities to sanctify the transaction.

They are playing a skirt dance (pizzicato) in my ear just now—I can
no more.

We return to London (if I am not hanged for murdering the band
first) on the 31 October.

yrs sincerely
G. Bernard Shaw

To BEATRICE WEBB

Off Malaga
[A/14; X/141.e]   29th September 1899

[Margaret Hobhouse (Beatrice Webb's sister) and her children Stephen and
Eleanor were travelling with the Shaws. Leonard Hobhouse (1864–1929), a
political theorist who became a professor of Sociology at the University of
London, was a cousin of Margaret's husband Henry. The reference to
Leonard may have been Shaw's error for Henry.]

We have just embarked after an expedition up country to Granada.
When the flying machine brings the Sierra Nevada within two hours of
London, land on Hindhead will be worth five shillings an acre; and the
ruins of Guildford will be one of the sights of Surrey. I should rather
like to work out the political situation that will arise then.

I write chiefly from an irresistible necessity to exercise my pen on
Maggie. Maggie is beyond everything I could have believed. Captain
Veale of this ship is a well conducted but tactless man. He commanded
the Ormuz in your time, and fell so abjectly into the net of your
fascination that both Maggie & Charlotte found themselves in the
strongest of positions here, Charlotte as the friend & Maggie as actually

the very sister of the most wonderful of women—one whose opinion on any subject, domestic or political, the infatuated Veale would take before that of the Privy Council. The fact that you sat at his table, and that he held his own with you in conversation on all topics, even to the deepest, hallmarks our captain as no common spirit: hence his readiness to gratify both ladies for the hour together with dithyrambs to Beatrice. Had they accepted the position, they might have commanded the ship.

Unfortunately, the creed that there is only one supreme Potter is not one which is either flattering or congenial to Maggie. And the sense of magnanimity with which Charlotte usually testifies to your virtues does not sustain her when Captain Veale takes the word from her. They have both come to the conclusion that the Captain is a most mediocre man. The long conversations of the first few days no longer take place.

This bond of sympathy between Maggie & Charlotte has not proved sufficient to completely lubricate their relations. Charlotte, brought up in a little household with a high opinion of itself has an exquisite sense of ceremonious privacy & personal dignity. Maggie, having suffered many sisters in a big house, has no such delicacies. On the first day in the channel Charlotte shrouded herself in the genteel seclusion of her bunk. Maggie went up on deck, and in the intervals of committing her contents to the deep under the open heavens, constituted herself commander of the ship, looked after her infants; looked after me, ordering the steward to bring me arrowroot when all other offers failed to tempt me; and, worst of all, bounced explosively from time to time into Charlotte's sacred cabin without knocking, asking her how she was, and then coming up on deck to tell me that Charlotte was so ill, poor creature, that she could only speak in the curtest fashion. The fact was, of course, that Charlotte, boiling with outraged privacy, was trying to snub Maggie—a hopeless task. Finally Maggie concluded that a little deck air would be good for Charlotte; so she made another brilliant charge into the citadel & told her that I was so bad that she must come up at once & look after me. Charlotte's fury on discovering that the alarm was false, and that Maggie had assumed the duties of a wife to me in the matter of the arrowroot, is not to be described.

Meanwhile, however, Maggie was campaigning in other directions. Being allotted a place at the purser's table, she roundly asserted that the conversation there was unfit for the ears of Eleanor; flourished special recommendations to the care of the company; and finally got transferred to the captain's table to console him for your absence. But this made the purser her bitter enemy; and when she proceeded to demand another cabin for Stephen, there was a fearful row, the purser declaring that it was not the captain's business, and finally, whilst perforce conceding the cabin, refusing her the particular one she wanted. Next came a lively breeze with the doctor. She declared that Stephen had influenza, caught from Charlotte. The doctor repudiated this diagnosis, and kept his temper in the scenes which ensued with a resolution that was rather worse than losing it. Under these circumstances the ship rapidly became conscious of a Reign of Terror, with Maggie as Robespierre.

Charlotte having now come to the verge of rudeness, Maggie consulted me as to whether her reason had not been dethroned by seasickness. I ingeniously explained that she got palpitations of the heart when startled by the unprepared presence of figures at her bunkside. "But," said Maggie, "I am not a stranger. She is my oldest & dearest friend—at least she is Beatrice's oldest & dearest friend; and it's all the same thing." Then, observing a lack of conviction in my manner, she added with a flash, "She *is* very fond of Beatrice, isnt she?" At last a gorgeous idea roused all her naughtiness. She concluded that Charlotte was jealous. Now she had also come to the conclusion that I was rather amusing to talk to occasionally, and that I might therefore be classed among those comforts of the ship of which it would be good business to get a good share. Also it had occurred to her that I might influence Stephen favorably: that is, against his notion of going into the Church, of which she greatly disapproves. Here policy and a delight in humorous mischief went hand in hand. On the second day of the new development Charlotte, who sternly refuses to gamble, was posted on the saloon stairs as having a stake in a sweep on the day's run. In her calling the offenders to account, they said I had been sitting with a lady & had paid for her, and they naturally concluded it was my wife. The lady, of course, was Maggie, who, shaking with internal laughter, gathers me like a flower at all hours (especially moonlit ones) from under Charlotte's very nose, and sometimes plucks me out of her very arms. The strain on Charlotte's good sense is fearful—all the worse because I am by no means a reluctant victim, there being between Maggie & myself a sort of rapscallionly freemasonry, as between a couple of tramps, of which Charlotte intensely disapproves.

Charlotte, however, has her revenge whenever there is a fog, or whenever she can get Maggie into a trap on a shore excursion behind a couple of lively Spanish mules, and a driver who treats human life as dross when there are four other traps to be raced to the railway station or landing place. Maggie is a prey to all the more primitive terrors. She lives in hourly dread of shipwreck; she screams when there is a smack of the whip & a wild lurch & rattle over the stones; she foresees Stephen ending his days a pauper. Charlotte's marble composure when her life hangs by a thread makes Maggie feel like a worm (as it is expressly meant to do); but the impression is never permanent: the next moment Maggie is laughing, pushing, and grabbing with a magnificent acquisitiveness which she is as ready to exercise for other people as for herself (after a certain degree of satiety), so buoyantly does she glory in it.

We finished up at Granada by a gipsy dance in the garden of a house (probably of ill fame). Charlotte & I were no sooner seated than Maggie, who had decorously sent Eleanor to bed, appeared & promptly sat on the other side of me, explaining that she wanted to hear my comments on the performance. I have always maintained that you are a gipsy; but about Maggie there was no possible mistake. Her dress became an absurdity: she looked like a gipsy who had fallen into the well & been rigged out by a respectable landlady whilst her own clothes were drying. She was recognized at once by the gipsy women as one of themselves; and she kissed her hand to them the moment they identified her. Her longing to dance was almost ungovernable; and I dared not encourage her, because I felt that the very gipsies themselves would be shocked if she once began. She declares that Leonard Hobhouse & her home & social position are a dream to her, & that this vagabondage is the only thing she feels to be real. We both recklessly urged our travelling agent to stimulate the gypsies to their most reckless exhibitions; but the agent looked at the two clergymen present and quailed. Finally Charlotte had to go back to the hotel alone whilst I helped Maggie to select photographs at a nocturnal shop. She selected 9 francs worth; put down 5 francs; and said to the man "That's all I've got: I know you'll give them to me for that; so roll them up, like a good man." He held up his hands to heaven; sighed; and succumbed. An amazing person, Maggie. The two children criticise her mercilessly, but on the whole stick to her loyally.

The captain has just requested me to give you rather more messages than I have room for.

GBS

To HERBERT S. STONE & CO.

[A/5]

Off Naples
4th October 1899

[Stone not only accepted Shaw's invitation to publish his non-copyright works by issuing an edition of *Love Among the Artists* in December 1900, but sent an agent to Shaw to ask for a copy of the work. Sheets of *Our Corner* were finally procured from the printer. The new copyright treaty with the United States had gone into effect in 1891. Brentano, which issued *Cashel Byron's Profession* in an unauthorised edition in New York in 1900, eventually succeeded Stone as Shaw's American publisher.]

Dear Sirs

Your letter has just reached me here . . . I see it stated that some American firm has issued an edition of an old novel of mine called "Cashel Byron's Profession," which is not copyrighted in the United States. As a matter of fact there is a mass of literary stuff by me which is in the same predicament. . . . Now I am aware that most authors regard the reprinting of their non-copyright works by American publishers as an act of piracy. You may therefore feel that your relations with me would be strained if you availed yourself on any occasion of the opportunity (such as it is) which is open to all American publishers. So I may as well tell you that I do not take the ordinary author's view. It may be hard on the English people that they have to bear the whole burden of supporting the English author whilst the American people read him as cheaply as they read Shakespear. I should substitute full international copyright to redress that injustice; but I should shorten its period, as the author may be presumed to get quite as much out of the right to levy on England alone as will pay him for his labor. Of course, like other authors, I will take what I can get; and since the new copyright treaty was made I have taken advantage of it; but I make no grievance of my old failure to secure American copyright, and see no reason why, because you now publish my copyright books, you should be cut off from the non-copyright ones which are open to your competitors in business. If ever you want to "pirate" them, go ahead: I shall be only too glad if you find it worth your while.

Harpers paid me £10 many years ago to ease their silly conscience when they published "Cashel Byron." Not having thought the question out then, I took it. My friend Tucker the Anarchist published "The Quintessence of Ibsenism" from a copy I sent him expressly for the purpose. A horrible fool trading under the name of Roycroft, expurgated & gentilified an essay of mine "On Going to Church" and printed it, as he thought, *artistically*. The brute did not know the ABC of good printing. As far as I know these are the only reprints yet made in the United States except the Cashel Byron just announced as issued by a firm with a name like Brentano—I forget its exact form.

yours faithfully
G. Bernard Shaw

To ELLEN TERRY

[U(A)/10; X/117]

In the Dardanelles
12th October 1899

[Marguerite de Valois (1553–1615) was the beautiful wife of Henry of Navarre, noted for her *Mémoires*, first published in 1628. W. Harrison Ainsworth (1805–82) wrote a number of historical novels, including *Rookwood* (1834), *Jack Sheppard* (1839), and *Guy Fawkes* (1841). *The Devil's Disciple* was produced during Shaw's absence by Murray Carson at the Princess of Wales Theatre, Kennington, on 26th September for thirteen performances. Lady Babbie is the heroine of J. M. Barrie's novel *The Little Minister* (1891), a dramatic version of which had been performed with great success at the Haymarket Theatre in 1897–8.]

Good God, Ellen, the Grecian Archipelago! Cant you see it in your mind's eye, a group of exquisite islands in a turquoise setting? Ugh! Cold, storm, sleety grey, pitching & rolling, misery, headaches, horrors of universal belchings! A moment's respite in the Dardanelles enables me to write to you: soon we shall be in the Sea of Marmora, reputed, as I learn for the first time, the coldest & windiest in the world.

However, I am at least quit of Athens, with its stupid classic Acropolis & smashed pillars. Charlotte, who *will* cultivate French acting & thinks the Comedie Française the most perfect thing on earth, insisted on my going to hear that bellowing donkey, Mounet Sully, as Othello. Good Lord! The 4th act ended at 12.30: the fifth began punctually at one. Poor Moony Silly grinned like a fairy queen in a fifth rate pantomime & howled like a newsboy. Shakespear won the third act triumphantly; and Moony got the credit of it. A horrible experience.

At Athens the best thing was your letter. Also a most aggravating telegram asking me what about the American rights—the very question I have been vainly asking you for a month past. However, there is no hurry about them now, since it is too late to do anything for this winter. So I will keep them for you until your return from your American tour, in the course of which you must try to arrange a Lady Cicely tour for 1900, on the understanding that the author's fees are to be the same as for England when *you* pay them. If Frohman or any other speculator pays them, they will be 10% all through, as for Mansfield.

Your offer of £500 for the entire rights of "Brassbound" shews a commendable wakening up on your part to your business responsibilities; but I wont take it, because it is far too little if the play succeeds, and far too much if it fails. Henry buys impossible plays from critics in that way, to bribe them. The fact is, if the play fails, I shall get nothing; but if it succeeds I fully intend you to make £5,000 for me before it is exhausted.

Marguerite de Valois was supposed some forty years ago to be a romantic person because she was a *femme galante*. As a matter of fact she was a beauty when she was a girl; but she ate too much & drank too much and soon became a ridiculous, fat, overrouged creature at whom everybody laughed. No really able dramatist could make a heroine of her. A play about her might appeal to Henry, who has never read anything since he read Ainsworth's novels in his boyhood (that is, if he ever read any books at all); but it wont appeal to the public unless it is a very strong & quite unhistorical play—which of course it quite possibly may be.

I am inundated with notices of The Devil's Disciple, but cannot make out whether it was anything more than a first night Shaw firework. You ought to get Edie or somebody to go on some off night (not Saturday) in the second week, to see whether there is anybody in the house. But bless me! it is too late: the fortnight will be over before this reaches you. It is very important for you to know the real state of affairs; for if The D's D. (third act) is not only tolerated but popular, the battle is won for Lady Cicely.

Do not be anxious about the rights of "Brassbound." I cannot do better than have you play it everywhere if you will. But I know the difficulties that will arise as to your getting free from the Lyceum; and I am not yet convinced that you will be able to do it at all. On the whole, if H. can induce you to postpone Lady C for Marguerite, there seems no reason why he should not repeat that exploit *ad infinitum*. He is a crafty scoundrel, and an expert in hanging up plays that he does not want to do or let anyone else do. If I think he is going to outwit you, I shall write you a letter stating that the play is going to the Haymarket to be Lady Babbied into popularity there with [Cyril]

Maude as the judge. And if that fails to rescue you I shall carry out the threat and devote the rest of my life to destroying H's prestige with my pen. So there! Ugh! Here's the Sea of Marmora! Farewell across the Atlantic.

GBS

To SYDNEY C. COCKERELL

[A/3]

Between Crete & Malta
17th October 1899

[Shaw had been reading *Satan Absolved* (1899), a work by Wilfrid Scawen Blunt (1840–1922), poet, traveller, and diarist, who served in some respects as the model for Hector Hushabye in *Heartbreak House*. Johann Tetzel (1465?–1519) was a German monk appointed by Archbishop Albert of Mainz in 1517 to sell indulgences. Shaw had undertaken to prepare an edition of Morris's manuscript lectures on Socialism. Only *Communism*, issued as Fabian Tract 113 in 1903, was published.]

Dear Cockerell

I have learnt one melancholy thing from the voyage: to wit, why Morris died. Life on board a pleasure steamer violates every moral & physical condition of healthy life except fresh air; and even that is cut off in this southern sea, where there is nothing to breathe but scirocco diluted with steam. It does not matter to the others, as they suck their pipes continually. It is a guzzling, lounging, gambling, dog's life. The only alternative to excitement is irritability. White stewards who never come to the surface, black firemen who only come up like goldfish to gasp occasionally, robust seamen who are truculent, civil seamen who are consumptive, a majority who would be decent enough if their lives were bearable, passengers who have nothing to do but enjoy themselves and are consequently only able to endure themselves and each other insofar as they have been brought up to do nothing else: it all makes a very vile life, which I advise you never to try. I started with a good stock of health, which has carried me through fairly well, though my balance dwindles from week to week. A mild combination of cholera and typhoid is chronic on board; my wife has had six days of it. In the Greek archipelago we had an Arctic tempest and were as sick as dogs, besides catching chills in all directions. Here further south over-whelming damp heat and poisonous chilly airs coexist at all hours. For

III

the first time in my life I put on an overcoat at sunset & shiver with the glass up to 75. And I wake up in the morning like one in prison, realizing where I am with a pang.

In return I have seen Athens—glorious Athens! If you pine to see glorious Athens, buy a few second hand classical columns & explode a pound or two of dynamite among them, and there you are. The senseless way in which these people leave broken lengths of perfectly uninteresting church portico pillar littering about in places that would look reasonably well if the rubbish were cleared away, gets more on one's nerves than any extremity of vandalism. Of course it is all a Godsend to English tourists, since they have heard about Socrates & Co, and can recognize a Corinthian capital as "artistic" at the first glance; but to the unsophisticated eye of the natural man the whole thing is simply exasperating. Take the prettiest seaside hill you know and dump down the tombstone makers' yards in the Euston Road upon it in a heap, smashing the stones as much as possible in the process, and you have Eleusis. The point of the thing is not the surviving remnants of the originals, but the dead ruins—ruins above all, and the more ruined the better. Ruin does not mean age or decay or weathering, but sheer smash. It is noteworthy that all this handsome-genteel pillar-pediment stuff could not gain sympathy enough to protect itself against mere brute mischief. But there is a beautiful little Byzantine church in the very middle of the town which was to have been removed because it obstructed the traffic. The people promptly began revoluting in its defence & it had to be let alone. The Parthenon is the best proportioned thing of its kind I ever saw; but as nothing but consummate propriety of proportion could give such childishly gentlemanly box-of-bricks "architecture" any merit, it leaves Phidias still dependent on his sculpture for his reputation.

Constantinople is better: St Sophia is easily the best *big* Byzantine church I ever saw—gigantic in actual measurement, yet comfortable as the tiniest Romanesque chapel you ever were in. St Marks nowhere by comparison except for mosaics. When the Turks came they tried to outdo it for the honor of the prophet. So they built an imitation (Sultan Ahmed mosque) with alterations to shew how big the place was—pillars as fat as Piccadilly Circus & so on. Very beastly, except for a sort of cloister round the *inside*, and a few pretty tiles. The supply of tiles ran short & they made up the deficiency with paint. However, half the ground is occupied with a cloistered court; and this is handsome. The champion Turkish mosque is the Sulieman, the 15th century stained glass windows in which do authentically bang all other windows in the universe of their kind. No figures or anything of that sort, only pure Persian looking decoration. If you saw a Goupil print of them you would say the round ones were jewelled snuffbox lids and the long oblong ones (no tracery, of course) Persian book covers. But in that style they are fit for the windows of heaven. The mosque itself is a successful attempt to take St Sophia and give it refined grandeur in the spirit of Brunelleschi and the early *dignified* Renaissancers. Highly artistic; but oh Lord! the superiority of dirty St Sophia itself, in which art is not only concealed (as the cant goes) but wholly eliminated and transcended—not a touch of anything so vulgar and self-conscious anywhere in it.

I have been to Granada and seen the Alhambra, which is undeniably a very neat specimen of the perforated card style of prettiness. The tile decoration is by far the best of it; but in spite of its elaboration, I would give the whole show in exchange for the palace in Tangier, which gives you the best of that sort of building & tiling, & just enough of it. But what a natural situation for a palace & summer town! Poor old Hindhead! The Moors certainly knew what they were about. The Spaniards themselves have two strong lines in cathedral work. Line No 1, a sort of superb peacock grandeur. Line No 2, a sort of naturalism (in the Zola sense) which enables them to carve wooden figures of saints & so forth with remarkable expression. On the whole, the wooden figures, which classical & Ruskinite tourists alike disdain, are the things best worth looking at—far superior to the figure heads at Vauxhall Bridge.

I found the Greek much less of a foreigner than the Spaniard or the Italian. Perhaps it is because he is a rascal that his brains work so very similarly to ours (or shall I politely say mine?); but I certainly felt more at home with the Athenians than I mostly do in English towns. But the life that appeals to me is the African. These people have learnt how to live. A few yards of cocoa matting furnishes their house for them. Our blundering beginnings with chairs & tables & all manner of absurd machinery for doing the simplest natural things clearly belong to the babyhood of human society. Tangier stinks less, and its inhabitants are cleaner than those of (here the literary construction compels me to put an impossible comma), any town I have visited on this tour except Canea. Crete, by the way, is a delightful place, full of handsome people. If you should set up a Mediterranean yacht, go to Suda Bay.

By the way, I expected to suffer from southern cruelty to animals. As a matter of fact I have seen no driver so cruel as a London driver. They drive two horses instead of one; and their flabby smacking whips do not cut as an English whip does. But then I have not seen very much of this side of southern life.

I brought W.S.B's poem on board to read. More power to his elbow. For some reason it is not natural to man (at least in England) to produce Alexandrines consecutively; so I am not surprised to find certain pages in which the poet's natural sense reels drunkenly and makes him hear an alexandrine in every phrase that has any sort of cadence in it. That sufficiently annoying criticism is the only one I have to make. Stop: there are two points to which I demur. One (p. 23) is the pronunciation of Apollyon as Apollion (like rapscallion) instead of as Bunyan pronounced it, Apoll Lion.

> "Hard by here was a battle fought
> Most strange and yet most true
> Christian and Apoll Lion sought
> Each other to subdue.

Not, observe

> Christeeyan and Apollion sought
> Each other to subdue.

The other is on p 29

> "None buy or sell
> Seats now at Thy right hand—(aside) grown quite unsaleable."

The truth is that Tetzel, if he were alive, would hold up his hands in horror at the present system of buying salvation by subscription to hospitals & the like.

The poem should have ended with the abdication of God in favor of Satan, who has clearly no right to abandon the universe to the care of so grossly credulous a gull. Indeed it is not clear why he should continue to respect an infatuated Almighty.

I must now break to you the frightful intelligence that the type-written copies of Morris's lectures went astray in the removal from Hindhead. The originals, which I did not trust even in my own hands, but sent about by registered post as I travelled, are safe; but they are in London, and of course they do not contain my notes & selections. Unless I can recover those copies when I get back to London, the delay will be disastrous, as I shall have to do a lot of the work over again. However, it cannot be helped, though I greatly regret it. All the same, I am not sure that the publication will add to Morris's reputation unless I can make the public believe that my impertinent meddling has led to the suppression of a great deal of matter which, as a matter of fact, is not valuable. We must have a talk over this when I return, at Walker's if possible. This ship is due at Tilbury on the 30th or 31st.

If you meet Walker, or are calling on him soon, you might let him read this to save me the trouble of writing another account of these my most accursed travels.

yours ever
G. Bernard Shaw

To EDWARD R. PEASE

Off the Nore
30th October 1899

[A/35; X/217.e]

[The war in the Transvaal had begun on 11th October after an ultimatum by President Paul Kruger (1825–1904) of the Transvaal, demanding the withdrawal of British troops from the frontiers of the two Boer Republics, followed by a surprise invasion of the Cape Colony by Boer forces.]

Dear Pease

I must have given back all the documents I took for that tract. If I had one, I should have all. In 97 I made a tremendous clearing out of old papers, and put together & kept all of any interest concerning the F.S. I should have found the minute book then if it had been in my possession. So I conclude I am not the delinquent this time.

All these documents about the Transvaal are rather alarming. Dont let us, after all these years, split the society by declaring ourselves on a non-socialist point of policy. To wreck ourselves on the Transvaal after weathering Home Rule would be too silly. Our sole business is to work out a practical scheme for securing the mines when we "resume" the Transvaal.

In a few hours we shall be back in London.

yours ever
GBS

To FREDERICK WHELEN

10 Adelphi Terrace WC
17th November 1899

[A/4]

[That the Fabian Society had been materially affected by the events in South Africa may be seen in the 17th annual report of the Society, published in

1900, which stated succinctly: "Notice of motion was given for a vote of urgency, with the object of expressing sympathy with the Boers, at the meeting of the Society on October 13th [1899]. The Executive Committee decided by a majority to advise the Society to reject the motion, and urgency was accordingly refused. Further action committing the Society to pronouncing against Imperialism was proposed by a minority of the Executive, and it was then decided to discuss the whole question at a meeting of the Society on December 8th. A resolution protesting against Imperialism and Capitalism in connection with the War was proposed by S.G.Hobson, and Bernard Shaw moved an amendment dealing mainly with the settlement to be made on the conclusion of peace. The amendment was defeated by a large majority, but a second amendment—'the previous question'—was carried by 58 to 50.

"The Executive Committee subsequently adopted a proposal to refer the matter to a vote of the whole Society, and, for the first time in its history, a plébiscite was taken. The members were asked to vote Yes or No to the question: 'Are you in favor of an official pronouncement being made now by the Fabian Society on Imperialism in relation to the War?' Circulars were issued by both sides [Shaw was draftsman for the one side, Walter Crane for the other], and in the end it was decided by 259 to 217 that no action should be taken."

Two members of the Executive Committee (J.Ramsay MacDonald and J.F.Green) resigned from the Society, as did some two dozen other members in March and April 1900, including Walter Crane, Henry S. Salt, Mrs Pankhurst, and Pete Curran. In the Executive election in March 1901 all the old members who had offered themselves for re-election were returned, and the places vacated by the two dissenters were filled by members who were opponents of Imperialism (F.W.Galton and S.G.Hobson), so that the composition of the Executive was unaltered, and there was no further proposal of a change of policy.

Shaw's letter to Whelen was written at the foot of a cyclostyled Fabian notice of "Transvaal War Meeting: Suggested Modification of Hobson's Resolution."]

Dear Whelen

The Executive instructed me on Friday to try to persuade Hobson to withdraw his resolutions in favor of something with regard to which there was some chance of unanimity. I have drafted the above accordingly & have sent it to Hobson. If he accepts it will you vote for it? Let me know in time for the Publishing Com^tee on Tuesday if you cannot attend it.

yrs
G.Bernard Shaw

To JANET ACHURCH

Hindhead Beacon Hotel. Haslemere
12th December 1899

[The relative of Shaw's mother was Georgina Gillmore (b. 1889), daughter of Mrs Shaw's half-sister Arabella, who resided with her in Fitzroy Square. Known to the family as "Judy," Miss Gillmore became Shaw's secretary in 1907. Her brother Walter (1888–1902) was killed at Chable sur Martigny, Switzerland, in a climbing accident while on a vacation paid for by the Shaws.]

My dear Janet

Your letter reached me here this morning: consequently I presume you are sold up by this time. And in my barbarous opinion, nothing better could possibly happen to you. That accursed furniture has been the source of all your embarrassments. Furniture means immobility, rent running during absence, above all, credit—the one thing utterly fatal to you. It is perfectly possible for you to live in furnished lodgings on 2 gns. a week without any dividend: it is *not* possible for you to live in a flat of your own, or half a flat, or quarter of a flat, or a mansion rent free, on ten guineas a week. If the sacrifice of your furniture will get you clear of that absurdly expensive flat, let it go with three times three.

As for me, what do you suppose my financial position is? I have practically earned no money since my illness: at least, if I have, my publishers have not sent it to me. I have settled on me by my wife about £750 a year more or less. Out of this I give my mother £300. I have undertaken to pay over £400 within the next few months to make Fitzroy Square decent and healthy. The rent of Fitzroy Square is £150. I am paying for the education of the daughter [Edith Beatty] of an old friend of mine at the rate of nearly £100 a year. I am supposed to pay half the expenses of our household, which of course I dont. There is another girl, a relative of my mother's, being educated by Charlotte (ought to be by me) for another £100 a year. There is her brother, to whom, in self defence against future draughts, we shall have to give a profession. There is that disastrously valueless and troublesome Irish property, the succession to which is running me up a solicitor's bill which I dare not think of. There is the Fabian, the London School, and other things of the same kind which swallowed up two thirds of our total income last year. There is my sister and my mother's half sister. All these are real items, not merely refused requests.

Now add this up as against my £750 for this year, and see in how

117

hopelessly insolvent a condition I am for the present. I shall get along by borrowing from Charlotte (who has an equally onerous budget of her own); but do you suppose I can ask her, in addition, for the £35 which you ask me for as cheerfully as if I were still the unembarrassed bachelor to whom a rush of royalties on a play meant a heap of money. Do you suppose she would lend it to me *willingly* for such a purpose? And there is a dozen at least of old friends and acquaintances without your 2 gns or your dividend, all clutching at the idea that I can get them out of their immediate squeeze with a ten pound note. You know enough of the world to know that this *must* be the case; and you know, or ought to know, enough of human nature to understand that if I were to make your difficulties a sore subject between myself and my wife I should finally do so much pure mischief, that it would be better for us all if I had allowed you to take to a street piano, with Charrington as a Christy Minstrel to help. Therefore I do solemnly declare that I wont lend you any money, no matter how heartrending your extremity may be—never again, whilst grass grows or water runs. I would throw a fistful of sovereigns into the Thames sooner. I could never look Charrington in the face again without shame if I were to allow him to hand me over to his creditors in such a way. So there!

GBS

To EDWARD ROSE

[H/1; X/162]

10 Adelphi Terrace WC
14th December 1899

[Ebenezer Howard (1850–1928), the Garden City projector, lectured at Hindhead on 11th December. Shaw spoke at length afterwards, noting that during the course of his political career a scheme of some kind similar to Howard's had been brought under his notice at least once in every seven years. The "affair the other night" was a Fabian business meeting on 8th December, which included a debate on the South African situation and on Shaw's amendment to Hobson's resolution. Speakers for the amendment included Robert E. Dell, Hubert Bland, and Frederick Whelen; those against it included Charles Charrington, H.T.Muggeridge, and F.Lawson Dodd. The amendment was defeated 27 to 58.]

...We went down to Hindhead from Saturday to yesterday. On Monday Ebenezer the Garden City Geyser lectured in Hindhead Hall, with a magic lantern giving views of that flourishing settlement in the manner of Mr Scadder in Martin Chuzzlewit. I had to make a speech, which had so fell an effect, in spite of my earnest endeavors to help him

118

over the stile, that the audience declined to hold up a single hand for his resolution. Finally the chairman put it again, coupling it with a vote of thanks, when, the situation becoming too poignant, I ostentatiously held up my paw, on which the others followed suit and Eb was saved. I pointed out that manufacturers were ready enough to go into the country; but that what they went there for was cheap labor. I suggested that half a dozen big manufacturers building a city could give good wages, and yet get so much of them back in rent and shop rent, or in direct butcher, baker, and dairy profits, that the enterprise might pay them all the same. At this the Hindhead proletariat grinned from ear to ear, and concluded that I was the man who really understood the manufacturing nature, the Geyser being a mere spring of benevolent mud.

You had better stick to the Fabian. You will find that there is no such thing in the world as a society that will or can entirely discharge your soul's message for you. At times, through the operation of Ibsen's Law of Change, you will get very tired of the Fabian and its old municipal tramway. At such moments you can subscribe without frequenting it or reading Fabian News. But just at present it looks as if we were at last being forced to a new birth pang with a foreign policy. The affair the other night shewed that in the absence of any alternative the Fabians fall back on Cobdenism, recruited by pure Humanitarianism, both based on a morality which, as the bold Haden Guest said, is obviously perfectly useless for the criticism of cosmic forces. Suppose the Boers lick us, which seems eminently possible at this moment. Well, the inevitable sequel will be the integration of South Africa in a great Afrikander Republican State, into which any recalcitrant colony will be forced by civil war if necessary, like the American Confederates. If this is to be, it will be; but the new state will inevitably become a great centre of capitalism like the United States, possibly with the spoils system, finally presenting the same contrast to America by its Manchesterism that America now does to us. The notion that it will be a more humane or just solution than a development under New Zealand conditions (for example) seems to me absurd—a notion only possible to a Gladstonian of the sixties, not to socialists educated by Marx. Anyhow, here is a tremendously interesting problem to be worked out in the Fabian, in the discussion of which, whatever may be the conclusion arrived at, we shall at all events blow Cobden to bits.

So dont resign just yet: the fun is only just going to begin.

GBS

119

To MAZZINI BEATTY

10 Adelphi Terrace WC
[S/2]   15th December 1899

[Mazzini Beatty (1881–1948), the eldest child of Pakenham Beatty (see I, 137) eventually became an engineer. The lecture at Aberystwyth on 16th December was announced as "Socialism and the Universities"; the *Welsh Gazette* reported on 21st December that Shaw had given "an address with that title in which not a single allusion was made to Socialism from beginning to end."]

Dear Bert

I have been away from London, and am off again tomorrow to Aberystwyth to lecture to the University Fabians there, and to stay over Christmas if I find the place tolerable. No chance therefore for the moment of seeing you, and only a hurried five minutes to answer your letter.

I understand quite well the difficulty you are in—I have been in it myself. When I was fifteen, I did what everybody will tell you was the manly, right, independent thing to do: that is, I went into an office to spare the family finances and support myself by my own exertions. Result, a waste of four or five years, a considerable assistance (I hope) to my employer, and failure to completely support myself at any moment of my manly industry. When at last I gave up this dutiful tomfoolery, and plunged into London, it took me *nine* years of preying on my mother and father and anybody else who, like your father, would stand me a dinner or a stall at a boxing competition, before I got on my legs as a journalist. Those nine years were my apprenticeship: I did a lot of work in them—wrote five novels and dozens of articles, lectured and ranted, and picked up all sorts of efficiencies; but I had no gleam of success and made not a rap except on a few casual opportunities not worth mentioning. I have no doubt whatever that I brought this on myself to a great extent by fooling away my time as a clerk for from £18 to £72 a year in a Dublin office when I should have been equipping myself for serious work, and that my mother had better have taken the worst of it then than later on. So don't you bother too much about Bradley Gardens. Both your mother & your father look enormously better and happier than they ever did when they were comparatively affluent; and after all there is money enough left to make it idiotically false economy to make a clerk of you. If it were a question of apprenticing you as a carpenter or mason, with a view to your becoming an architect and builder, I should heartily approve; but put the city and its dungeons out of your head.

That's all I have time to say just now. I shall be at the Queen's Hotel, Aberystwyth for the next week or so.

G. Bernard Shaw

To GEORGE SAMUEL

[X/163]

[30 Marine Terrace. Aberystwyth]
[Undated: c. 23rd–24th December 1899]

[George A. H. Samuel (1861– ?) was a Fabian who, under the pseudonym "Marxian," was a frequent contributor to the *Workman's Times* and the *Labour Leader*. On 13th January 1900 Samuel noted that "the Hogmanay printers did scanty justice" to Shaw's letters in the typesetting of the 6th January issue of the *Labour Leader*, in which Samuel had published them. John Seymour Keay (1839–1909), Anglo-Indian politician and Liberal M.P., was a writer of manifestos and pamphlets filled with "Radical Virtuous Indignation" (as Shaw noted elsewhere), including *Spoiling the Egyptians: A Tale of Shame Told from the Blue Books* (1882) and *The Great Imperial Danger* (1887).]

Marxian,

Cobdenite,

Disciple of Cremer,

Virtuous Indignation Merchant,

Have you reflected on the importance of the fact that our neglect, as Socialists, of foreign policy, has at last, in the hour of trial, left us nothing to fall back on but the most miserable 1880 Radicalism, to which we rally the anti-bloodshed humanitarians (mostly meat-eaters), and the members of the Peace Societies?

No; you have not reflected on this, because your mind has been enfeebled by years of abstinence from the Pierian spring of St. Bernard Shaw—that is to say, myself.

Now, have the goodness to get a stout kitchen-cloth, and clear your mind of cant about pencil bullets and lyddite shells. You have to deal with a war declared by a peasant-proprietor State after laying in a careful supply of the best they can afford in the pencil bullet and explosive line. The Boer and the Britisher are both fighting animals, like all animals who live in a chronic panic of death and defeat. They are also carnivorous animals and alcohol-drinking animals. You know my sentiments on all three subjects. Do you expect me solemnly to inform a listening nation that the solution of the South African problem

121

is that the lion shall lie down with the highly-armed lamb in mutual raptures of quakerism, vegetarianism, and teetotalism? No; hammer-headed as you are, you are not absurd enough for that. Now let us face the facts. Two hordes of predatory animals are fighting, after their manner, for the possession of South Africa, where neither of them has, or ever had, any business to be from the abstractly-moral, the virtuously indignant Radical, or (probably) the native point of view. Each of them, for party purposes, is trying to play-off this point of view against the other. "Parricides; ye desert the flag of your country in its hour of extensive ripping and tearing by the Boer bullets," cry the Conservatives. "Jingo betrayers of the Prince of Peace," cry the Liberals, "ye are shedding the blood of a people rightly struggling to be free, and on the miserable pretext that it has declared war on ye." Into the latter trap the Socialists [fall] by dozens, including Marxian who, from the bottom of the abyss, preaches at Shaw, who is smiling on the brink with the self-satisfaction of the fox who was too clever to be caught.

Now let me tell you some true things, Bishop Marxian. Number one: the moral position of the Boers and the British is precisely identical in every respect; that is, it does not exist. Two dogs are fighting for a bone thrown before them by Mrs Nature, an old-established butcher with a branch establishment in South Africa. The Socialist has only to consider which dog to back; that is, which dog will do most for Socialism if it wins.

Now—and here I am going to deliver a piece of exquisitely English wisdom—either the Boers will lick the British in this campaign, or the British will lick the Boers. You grant that, don't you? and admire its profundity.

Well, suppose the Boers beat the British. That takes South Africa out of our hands for ever as the United States were taken out. And what happens to South Africa? The Boers become a military power blazing with prestige, federate South Africa in a republic. If Rhodesia is recalcitrant or any colony loyal, 1861 will be repeated in a civil war to the death to consolidate Afrikanderdom. You are still Marxian enough to know that in such a republic the dreams of Rhodes will be realized more thoroughly than Chamberlain and Downing Street could ever realize them. All the throes of capitalism through which the United States have been dragged will be repeated as surely and as cruelly as if the martyrdoms of Lancashire and Pittsburgh had never been. This is what you are crying out for in the name of humanity, justice, Socialism, and all the other isms. As for me, if it is to be, it will be; but I am not enthusiastic. I prefer, on the whole, the history of New Zealand to the history of the United States. I prefer Downing Street, with all its faults, to American Freedom of Contract. I prefer civil servants like Webb and Olivier to the nominees of bosses. I prefer integration when the nucleus represents factory legislation and an efficient civil service, to disintegration, with an anarchistic, free-capitalistic nucleus substituted in the broken-off chunk. And I have a lot of ideas besides, which I will not trouble you with yet, because your brain is out of practice.

However, here's another fragment. I object to stray little states lying about in the way of great powers. I did not object to America assimilating Honolulu, nor to Germany assimilating Samoa. It is to me as if a trust had annexed a small shopkeeper: a capitalistic trans-action, no doubt, but one making, like all advanced capitalism, for Socialism.

Yet another thing. Do you remember our early days, when Seymour Keay wrote Spoiling the Egyptians, and we all followed this foolish Radical lead in denouncing the "Bondholder's War," and lavishing on Araby the sympathy we are now squandering on the pious but able Kruger? Why, this war was a hymn of Christianity compared to that. Well, Marxian, the good, were we right or were we shortsighted fools? What would you have said of me then if I had scorned Keay and all his pamphlets, and urged the miserable Little England Government to follow up their blow and make Gordon master of the Soudan? Just what you are saying of me now. And yet I would have been right. Alas! I was wrong; for even I can err, but not twice on the same subject, not twice, my boy.

And now eat your Christmas dinner—the slaughtered turkey, the eviscerated pig—in peace, and when they tell you that G.B.S. has gone soft with domesticity and luxury, lay your finger gently along your Roman nose, and wink. And write a nice little Christmas hymn entitled, "He is all there."

G.B.S.

To GEORGE SAMUEL

[30 Marine Terrace. Aberystwyth]
[X/163]   [Undated: c. 26th–30th December 1899]

Come; you are not going to get into bed again now that I have dragged you out of your humanely indignant blankets.

"The war," says you, "is a more-than-usually-disagreeable criminal-lunatic carnival of blundering and greed."

Now that is the sort of thing that I decline to have my mouth stopped with. Do you suppose that any war ever was, or ever will be, to those behind the scenes, anything else than that? How much further does it get us to blow off that pious statement? Have the goodness to stop moralizing. It is that sort of spiritual dram-drinking that rotted the lives of the old Radicals whom we superseded, and into whose vices we are lapsing in our old age.

You say, "we are at 1899–1900, not 1775." Yes, we in England may be (meaning about a half per cent. of us); but South Africa is not. South Africa is still plus [minus?] the electric light and photography and railways. Away with these silly illusions of time and space: the world does not set all its clocks by your watch. The history of America will repeat itself in South Africa if the European powers are driven out, as surely as the process following the sowing of an acorn repeats itself, Monroe doctrine and all.

You may say, very well, why not? Let us have another great republic, with all its faults, instead of another province of Downing Street. (I do not feel sure that the fates have not decreed this, myself). Take that line and stick to it if you will. Declare yourself on the side of the Boers as Pitt declared himself on the side of the Americans. But don't forget that the triumph of Afrikanderdom is the triumph of Rhodes. Rhodes began as an Afrikander out-and-out. But of course nobody would fight for an idea, when not personally uncomfortable. He tried an insurrection to get rid of the 17th century in the Rand; but as he is no statesman, he made a mess of it, selecting for his leader Jameson, a man even stupider than himself for Bismarckian purposes. All the same, the conflict that was inevitable from the moment that gold was discovered in the Rand—the conflict between a turnip-producing social organization and a gold-producing one—had to come; but it was England who took the field against the turnips, and not united Afrikanderdom. Now England victorious, and Downing Street interfering, and we agitating, will not give Rhodes the freedom of contract he wants. But Afrikanderdom united in a rally to Kruger's standard as soon as that standard is apparently certain to win, and Afrikanderdom victorious, with England and the powers kicked out; that will end in a South African Federation that will suit Rhodes as perfectly as the American Constitution suits Rockefeller—that will, in fact, exactly fulfil his original scheme.

In 1775 this solution was inevitable, because both England and

America were of the same date—in fact England was behind America if anything, being closer to George III. But today England is ahead—far ahead—miles nearer Socialism. America is suffering frightfully today because she has not an English Government and an English civil service. We have one Chamberlain, "not so black as he is painted"; America is governed by hosts of Chamberlains, much blacker than they are painted.

Now tell me on what ground you take the Afrikander side in this war. Mind: I do not say that a case cannot be made out for that side. But it cannot be made out on these rubbishly Radical moralizing lines. And it must recognize the fact that Krugerism must succumb anyhow, and that the true alternative is between an Afrikander policy and a Colonial policy. "Marxist fatalism" can clearly be claimed for both—more convincingly, perhaps, for the Afrikander policy than for the other. Only by embracing such fatalism to the extent of declaring that a Whig free-contract stage of development is inevitable in South Africa, and cannot be mitigated by English "palliatives" can Socialists pretend that the Afrikander side is naturally their side. And since they have evidently not considered this, and are merely shouting with the Harcourt-Morley section under the influence of a horror of war, coupled with a ridiculous oversight of the fact that the Boers declared this war after a formidable preparation for it, I positively decline to shout with them. I insist on an intelligent foreign policy for Socialists instead of a hysterical relapse into Seymour Keayism.

Just at present, prospects seem nicely balanced. If England is beaten, so much the worse for South Africa, but so much the better for herself, since her responsibilities will be lightened, and the infamous bragging and blackguardism of the last ten years will be shamed out of her. Only, if the result of that were only to drive her back into the arms of Harcourt & Co., the lesson would soon be wasted. Consequently I again urge you to make that Marxian column of yours an intelligently Socialist (that is, Shawist) one, and to clear the situation from Liberal cant no matter which side you declare for.

I have just been to Crete—delightful place, delightful people, all colours, all good-looking, "independence" guaranteed by six European flags on every government building, and six ships of war in Suda Bay, with six military bands playing "Her Golden Hair was Hanging Down Her Back," and "Now We Shan't be Long." Quite possible that the Transvaal may attain that sort of independence presently. Ha! Ha! Ha!!!

Farewell, G.A.H.S. Compliments of the season. Hark, the herald angels sing glory to our new-born king. Peace on earth and mercy mild to Louise who killed her child, and Kruger and the rest.

G.B.S.

To HUBERT BLAND

[A/39]

30 Marine Terrace. Aberystwyth
30th December 1899

[The Executive Committee of the Fabian Society for 1899–1900 consisted of: R.Wherry Anderson, Hubert Bland, Charles Charrington, J.Frederick Green, J.Ramsay MacDonald, H.W.Macrosty, J.F.Oakeshott, Miss Mary O'Brien, Sydney Olivier, Edward R. Pease, Shaw and Charlotte Shaw, George Standring, Sidney Webb, and Frederick Whelen.]

What we really want on that Exec. is *Fabians*. Apart from considerations of temperament and ability, Macdonald and Anderson are simply Chartist Radicals. Charrington's an Impossibilist; but his vote at the election is only the inevitable harvest of an effective speaker, with a wife who is also an effective speaker. Green is a Radical too, when it comes to foreign policy. The reason Macrosty, Pease, Webb, and Standring are firm is that they are Fabian & not Radical—Whelen also, though he has less of the old gang tradition. As to Olivier, the difficulty is that he is not expressed in the least by the Radicals. He has sent me a most fascinating and able memorandum, with a letter from Kropotkin and another document (old mem. of his own) which are quite irresistible from the point of view of an able official who for years has been watching imbecile cabinets and class-prejudiced bureaucrats being swindled and bounced by [Cecil] Rhodes & Co. But his position amounts to these two points. First—now past praying for—that war might quite easily have been avoided by simply sliding along until Kruger's death or defeat by the Reform party. Second—and this is the issue I should like to force upon Macdonald & Co—that the power of the Empire to assimilate and govern S.A. is an illusion, and that S.A. will develop better without our interference. This means of course that the Fabian side should be the Boer side, and its policy the expulsion of the Empire from S.A. I am by no means sure that this may not be the Way of Destiny; but clearly that is not what Hobson expressed the other night. And it would clearly suit Rhodes and the capitalists uncommonly well. However that may be, no such position

126

should be granted without a tremendous debate in which the advantages of Imperial development are defended to the death.

Suppose we do run a ticket, how is it to be done? The Society would not vote a ticket except as between two rival tails to the Exec. Why should Webb & Pease, for instance, go on a ticket when they would be quite safe and comfortable without one? Why should *you*, for that matter, unless you could contrive to force the Society to choose between you and Macdonald, or Green, or Anderson or Charrington? Of course the case is almost as good the other way: that is, the safe people have nothing to lose by a ticket as well as nothing to gain; and if the Opposition issued a Seymour-Keayite manifesto, with their signatures above those of the outside candidates whom they wished to get in, we could do the same, with the probable result that though the old favorites would get in on both sides, there would be a real contest between the outsiders and tailers.

But again, we should stand to lose our outsiders &c, unless we had campaigned a bit for our ideas. I dont see how we are to do that unless we lecture to the groups, and put down resolutions to be fought out at Clifford's Inn meetings in lieu of the customary lectures. The latter course would wake up the society and be good every way; and it seems to me that it is the immediately important thing for us to consider, the time being so short. . . .

This doesnt call for an answer. I suppose we shall have an Exec. before the dinner next Friday.

I have destroyed your letter: it is my general rule. Never keep a letter, and never write one that is fit for publication.

GBS

To MARY CHOLMONDELEY

[T(A)/1]

30 Marine Terrace. Aberystwyth
30th December 1899

[Charlotte's brother-in-law, Col. Hugh Cholmondeley, had recently been posted to the Transvaal in command of the City Imperial Volunteers Mounted Infantry. He was mentioned twice in despatches and, in addition to winning other decorations, was made Companion of the Bath.]

My dear Mrs Cholmondeley

Charlotte has caught a troublesome influenza cold, and asks me to write you a line to say that she has got your letter, and is too ill for the moment to answer it herself.

Before it came we had already learnt from the papers that Colonel Cholmondeley has got the branch of the Brigade on which public attention is so eagerly fixed, and from which all the new developments in tactics are expected. I suppose we must congratulate him professionally, and condole with poor Vincent, who is rather lefthandedly complimented with the routine command.

So here's success to the Mounted Infantry!

But personally our patriotism covers a natural anxiety to see him safely back again, which Charlotte feels doubly—on your account as well as on his own. However, that is all in the day's work.

Charlotte will write herself presently.

yours sincerely
G. Bernard Shaw

To J. S. STUART-GLENNIE

[G.u/2]

[10 Adelphi Terrace WC]
[Undated: c. January 1900]

[J. S. Stuart-Glennie, who had travelled with and written about his friendship with the historian H. T. Buckle in *Pilgrim-Memories* (1875), corresponded frequently with Shaw during this period. Massingham was dismissed from the editorship of the *Daily Chronicle* in December 1899. As Beatrice Webb wrote in her diary: "The dismissal . . . reflects the strong patriotic sentiment of its readers; any criticism of the war at present is hopelessly unpopular. The cleavage of opinion about the war separates persons hitherto united and unites those who by temperament and training have hitherto been divorced. No one knows who is friend and who is enemy" (*Our Partnership*, 1948).]

Dear Stuart-Glennie

The right to live is a Natural Right: that is to say it must be dogmatically postulated before any political constitution is possible. All argument on the matter leads irresistibly to Nowana—to universal suicide; and this must be rejected as a reductio-ad-absurdum, and a purely dogmatic Will to Live accepted as the basis from which all social order must start. It need not, however, be accepted quite unconditionally, though I think it should as against all such survivals of the expiation superstition as our criminal law presents. I should make each citizen appear before a Board once in seven years, and defend his claim to live. If he could not, then he should be put into a lethal chamber.

He could, of course, be represented by counsel; and Death would be represented by an Attorney General.

Massingham's successor on the Chronicle was W. J. Fisher. . . . [W]e are free to congratulate our friend on having refused to shout with the mob when the mob was shouting its loudest, and on maintaining his own personal independence as stoutly as he advocated that of the Transvaal.

yours sincerely
[G. Bernard Shaw]

To MRS RICHARD MANSFIELD

[H/21]
10 Adelphi Terrace WC
7th January 1900

[For Shaw's letter to Elbert Hubbard concerning permission to publish a Roycroft edition of the essay "On Going to Church," see I, 633. Mansfield did not venture another London appearance. William Archer, who had re-visited the United States for eight weeks in the Spring of 1899, published three articles on "The American Stage" in the *Pall Mall Magazine*, November 1899–January 1900, and a book in 1901 entitled *America Today*. Ibsen's new play was *When We Dead Awaken*, produced by the Stage Society in Archer's translation in January 1903. *You Never Can Tell* had been performed by the Stage Society at the Royalty Theatre on 26th November, with Yorke Stephens as Dr Valentine, Margaret Halstan as Gloria, Charles Charrington as Bohun, and James Welch, who staged the performance, as the Waiter. The book Shaw was contemplating may have been the book on religion he had been threatening to write for several years, or it may have been *Man and Superman*, which took shape in his mind in 1899 and in outline in 1901 before he actually began to write it.]

My dear Mrs Mansfield

What is this?—a Roycroft book! Have I lived—I, who was let run in and out of the Kelmscott Press by William Morris—to be presented by you with the most ignorant imposture that America has yet produced? Nice of me to say this, isnt it, in return for your kindness; but I must educate you if you are to play my plays.

Listen. A few years ago, the wretch Hubbard (the Roycroft fiend) asked my permission to reprint an article of mine. I told him that as the article was not copyright, it was at his disposal or at that of any other printer in America; and that the only interest I had in the matter was that it should be honestly used—that is, printed exactly as I wrote it. On this the scoundrel proceeded to rewrite my article in his own feeble patent-medicine-advertisement English, and issued it as an "authorized edition." He then sent me two copies, with the most perfect confidence in my being pleased with his "art printing," and told me I could have some more if I wanted them. My epistolary eloquence has seldom soared so high as it did in my reply to him.

The fact is, the creature does not know the ABC of good printing. I gave him so precise an account of his ignorance in that letter that he has made some attempt to correct those which admitted of correction by mechanical instruction. For instance, he now aims at having his margins right instead of not knowing anything about them. He no longer sticks two or three fly leaves of dirty brown felt at the end, under the impression that they are "esthetic" because they are ugly and silly. He has discarded his sham "Kelmscott Capitals," the design of which would have disgraced a learned pig, and substituted colored sham Chinese ones which are much less offensive. But in the essentials of printing he is as hopeless as ever. His type is set in the stupidest commercial way. Look at a page of a Morris book, and you see the block of letterpress constituting the printed page, as a piece of rich black on white. There are no bars of white across between the lines—no rivers of white trickling down between irregularly spaced words like drops of rain down a window pane on a wet day. You dont find half a dozen lines set sparsely and looking like a bald head, and the next half dozen squeezed into a smudge of black. The distribution of color is as beautifully even as it is in the best old manuscripts or the early printed books which followed the rules arrived at by the manuscript scribes. The little pictures of leaves which you see occasionally in the line, which Hubbard imitates under the impression that they are mere freaks of ornament, are put in always to fill up a space which would otherwise have made a white patch on the page. Hubbard gets his type set just as an advertisement of a lost dog, or a grocer's catalogue might be set, leaving white streaks and spots all over the place, and then pops in a leaf here and there out of pure idiocy—which is what art means to him. Again, look at his title page. Three different sizes of type on it! He would have got in six if he could. This is the essence of the commonest "display" work of the jobbing printer: a true artistic printer never uses two sorts of type on a page if one will do.

If you doubt this simple science of printing, take a Roycroft book in one hand and a Morris book in the other. You will throw the Roycroft book out of the window into its proper place, the gutter.

130

All this may sound needlessly fierce; but the fact is, America, having read a great deal about art, and not knowing anything about it, is being duped most frightfully by intense young people who are resolved to make Chicago flower with a fifteenth century luxuriance, and who will find one day that, as Wagner put it, they have grasped at art and let their lives slip by them.

So, no more Roycroft books.

As to Richard's coming to London, I have talked to him over and over again most parentally; but you know what a baby he is: he wont face the reality of the situation: he wants to be invited as a conqueror to invade a great metropolis, and shew how much better he can act than Irving and Tree and all the rest. That is all nonsense: London is, for theatrical purposes, an advertisement and nothing else: a thing to be paid for and used for what it is worth. You make me tear my hair when you speak of my arranging for a London Mansfield season. Where is the difficulty? Rejane does it. Sarah Bernhardt does it. Coquelin does it. Irving does it. Wilson Barrett does it. I dont arrange it for them. Nobody engages them. Nobody—in a sense—wants them. But it is their business to come, because all the great people are supposed to act in London, and because the provinces will not look at anything that doesnt come from London. Of course it doesnt pay directly. It pays the theatre proprietor, and the printer, and the wigmaker, and the author, and the callboy, and so on. And the money comes out of the star's pocket. But he gets it back—sometimes—in the provinces and in America. You have the same thing in New York: Dick has played there often enough to much worse business than in the other towns; but the other towns want something from New York. Well, it is a question, first, of having the money the advertisement will cost, and second, whether it is worth that money. That's all—positively all. The mistake about the previous visit was that it was too long. He should have played for a fortnight only, and come back next year and done the same. Richard III was nonsense—utterly premature. And then he was robbed no doubt by everybody. That is necessary, up to a certain point; but it is not necessary to carry that part of the business to an unremunerative extreme. The only respect in which the situation has changed since then is that the Londoners have found out that the theatre is not the best place to spend the hot summer evenings in, and that the suburbs are now covered with theatres which make, on the whole, for the good of superior business at the West End theatres, but spoil commonplace business there.

I explain this thus tediously for your information, not because it will do any good. Tomorrow I shall probably meet Felix in despair, with either of two pieces of news: number one, that Richard has cut off his income and that his orphans are perishing, or, number two, that Richard has sent him to inform London that he will not come here unless he is guaranteed £1,000 a week for three months. As if London wanted him or wanted anybody or anything! If London was told tomorrow that Christ was waiting at Putney for an invitation to make his second coming, London would stare helplessly and ask who he was. Irving now confesses in desperation and bitterness that he has bought his position with infinite toil and a net expenditure of £100,000. Does Richard think he is going to get that position for nothing? How much does he suppose Tree owes? I asked an eminent critic the other day—he having been in America lately—what Mansfield was like. He said he was the nearest thing in America to Tree (I am now speaking of his business position, not his artistic one). As an artist he cannot hope to make very much impression on a town which is frightfully demoralized and stupid, and takes years to realize the value of anything out of the commonest run. Probably by this time he has built up a mannerism which American audiences have been trained to, but which will puzzle English audiences until they, too, are trained to it. In fine, then, if Richard can afford to take a theatre for a fortnight in May or even June (if he can get one) and play a round of his parts to houses cleverly papered by a good acting manager, spending lavishly on advertisements, he will drop two or three thousand pounds and get a bundle of notices in the London papers and the prestige of a distinguished star who has shewn us the color of his money. Anything more than that takes ten years to build up.

As to You Never Can Tell, nothing would please me better than to have it produced successfully by you. But think of the reasons you give me. You say that the popular plays of the day are so intolerably different to it. Exactly; but they are popular: ergo, mine wouldnt be popular. Where is your man to come from? Will you import York Stephens, who played Valentine here at the private performance by the Stage Society the other night here? Of course you wont: it would be an absurd thing to do. But then where is your Valentine? And if you get him, there you are with a first rate leading man—Richard supplanted in his own theatre. Surely it is not practicable—not possible. You must not suppose I am merely trying to put you off in the ordinary sense. The fact is, I am quite accustomed to receive proposals just like yours, very flattering, and absolutely insane, to anybody who can see the inevitable ten yards ahead.

Forgive this hasty, grumpy, prolix letter: I will have more to say when I get Archer's second article (which I missed) and when I have read Ibsen's new play. I am in despair at the backwardness of my literary work—one book to write, another to edit [the Morris lectures], and a third to write prefaces to & see through the press before I can begin another play. But it doesnt matter: I shall write no more practicable plays—no more Devil's Disciples & Cæsars & Captain Brassbounds. The contemporary playgoer doesnt want me, and I dont want him (or her); and there are terrible things still to be said. My next play will be a horror—and a masterpiece.

yrs ever sincerely
G. Bernard Shaw

To EDITH LIVIA BEATTY

[H/6]   10 Adelphi Terrace WC
                                           7th January 1900

[Edith Beatty (1883–1966), who preferred to call herself Cecilia, or Cissy, was the second of Pakenham Beatty's three children. Charlotte had been paying for her schooling since September 1898. Mrs Agnes Hunter was headmistress of the training school in Holland Park which Miss Beatty was attending. The textbook in use was *General Elementary Science*, edited by William Briggs, Principal of the University Correspondence College.]

My dear Edith
    I have just been studying your school report, and find it a most disheartening document. 35 in "Literature"! What on earth does that mean? Mrs Hunter has just got from me one and elevenpence for "The Faery Queen." I suppose they call that literature. State the chief points of resemblance between Britomart and the institution which she is intended to typify. Mention those faults in the character of the Blatant Beast which might, in your opinion, have been corrected by greater care in his early education. Thank you: thirty-five marks.
    Again Mrs Hunter and her books! Brigg's Science, two and ninepence. In Heaven's name, who is Briggs? Newton I know, and Young and Tyndall and Darwin; but Briggs—! What is the date of his epoch making treatise? Is that "Natural Science"?
    Latin, 53. Greek, 55. Languages which you are taught to teach by people who can't write or speak them. French, 46:—if you had learnt it from an Englishwoman who did not know it instead of from your

133

mother, you would have got 100. German, oooo—you dont learn it apparently, Briggs and the Blatant Beast being more important. History (an improper subject for young ladies if true, and a misleading one if false) 68. Who writes the history? Is it Briggs?

And this is Education!

Now what I want you to consider is this. It is plain to me that this High School is teaching you nothing except how to become a High School mistress when you are too big to be a High School pupil. That is a miserable business unless you become a head mistress, and not a very delightful one even then. It is difficult to become a head mistress because the limit of age is now very foolishly fixed at 35; and most mistresses are past that before there is an opening for them. It is wiser to marry; but marriage is impossible to a woman with a countenance on which Briggs has left his mark. On the other hand, everything is possible to a woman who has been variously and energetically educated—mostly by herself.

You may ask me how you are to educate yourself. Well, chiefly by beginning to choose how and where you shall be taught what you want to know, instead of letting yourself be sent to school like a little lamb. You have at your disposal at present £100 a year (round numbers) to educate yourself with. I want you to grasp that fact firmly, and not allow yourself to regard yourself as a helpless infant who is being sent to school at somebody's expense. If you cling to Briggs, it is your own doing. If you stay at Mrs Hunter's, it is because, with the world before you, you choose Mrs Hunter's. You are under no limit as to the disposal of the £100 except that you must spend it on yourself: you are not at liberty to practise virtue with it in the way of generosity or benevolence: the money for *that* you must earn yourself. The burthen of absolute selfishness being thus laid on you, it behoves you to consider how to get the best value for that money.

For instance, you are trying to learn Greek. Well, you can't learn Greek at Notting Hill: you can only waste your time on a wretched sham taught by the ignorant to the unconscious. In Greece you can learn it. In Athens the other day I asked the excellent Cassimatis, my guide (also my philosopher and friend), whether he could read ancient Greek. He was quite indignant at the question. He declared that all educated Greeks could, and promptly said "You know the famous passage from So and So"—quoting it to me. I didnt; but, like Mr Wegg in Our Mutual Friend, I pretended I did. He then pointed out to me that most of the words in it were still in use. Now compare this with the case of William Morris. He translated the Odyssey (although

134

at Oxford or Notting Hill they would not have given him decent marks for *their* Greek); but he could not read modern Greek, as I know, having once seen him try to read a Greek Socialist newspaper.

Well, why dont you spend your hundred pounds on a visit to Greece to learn the language? I was once offered a trip to Athens with a party from Owen's College, Manchester, for £25, there and back, and a lot of other places thrown in. Call the two journeys £30, and you have £70 left, which would give you nearly three months at £1 a day, on which you could do yourself like a princess. Like a student, you could get six months easily. You could present yourself as the daughter of the modern Byron, whose poems during the war had earned the applause of the throne. You could represent your desire to learn Greek as the outcome of national enthusiasm. You could attend lectures by scientific men quite as eminent as Briggs. You would see the Parthenon every day: it is an overrated building, but better than Uxbridge Road station. After such a trip, you would have done enough educational work for the year; you would have done the equivalent of twenty years Notting Hill work at the language; and the girls at Mrs Hunter's would be the most abject little parochial grubs compared to you.

You could have the next year in Russia, the next in Germany, the next in an American College or where you pleased. You would become governess to a Russian Grand Duke and marry his son clandestinely, and starve with him when his father found it out, and finally succeed to millions on the father's death. There are a thousand things in the world better than Briggs, if one has a hundred a year for a while.

Think it over: keep always thinking it over. The High School teacher business is only Irish snobbery: dont let your life be sacrificed on the ridiculous altar of the respectability of your father's aunt, or of Uncle Jupiter [Charles Dowling] in Merrion Square. Remember that all the advice given by grown up people to young people has interested motives, and that the world belongs to the rebellious.

Get this letter framed, and hang it up in your room at Mrs Hunter's to keep you up to the mark.

yours sincerely—*really*
G. Bernard Shaw

135

To WILLIAM ARCHER

10 Adelphi Terrace WC
[H/3]   24th January 1900

[Archer had written on 22nd January: "The New Century Theatre ought to give its fourth production this spring—why shouldn't it be one of your plays?—either 'Candida' or 'Captain Brassbound.'... My one condition is that Miss [Elizabeth] Robins shall have the leading part in whatever we do.... Of course I can't tell whether she would care for the part in 'Captain Brassbound'; but I know she would be delighted to play Candida. Failing either of these, haven't you another play in hand that we could do?... Why didn't you give us the 'Devil's Disciple' rather than Murray Carson? We'd have given it a much better show." A postscript warned Shaw "N.B. NO PHILANDERERS NEED APPLY!" (Fales Collection, New York University Library.)

Sydney Olivier's play, performed by the Stage Society on 21st January 1900, was *Mrs Maxwell's Marriage*. *The Only Way* was F. Wills's romantic adaptation of Dickens's *A Tale of Two Cities*, which Martin Harvey had presented with success at the Lyceum Theatre in February 1899. Zola's *La Fécondité* was published in Paris in 1899, and in London by Vizetelly in 1900. Millicent Garrett Fawcett (1847-1929) and Lydia E. Becker (1827-90) were leaders of the women's suffrage movement.]

As luck will have it I have just consented to allow the Stage Society to do Candida. By the way, they told me you had joined that body (which has boomed into intense life with 300 odd members in a most unexpected way); but I havent seen you there. I put it down to influenza when You Never Can Tell was done; but you werent there last Sunday either—at least I didnt see you; and Olivier's play turned out a masterpiece, positively as good as Ibsen, with a very fine native style to boot. I should have sent you invitations both times but for their telling me that you and three or four other critics had come in.

I gave The D's D to Murray Carson for the trite reason that he had the cheek to ask me for it. You might have obtained it by the same subtle ruse. I dont know what to do for you now. Cleopatra would hardly do for Miss Robins; and Captain Brassbound could only be done by arrangement with Ellen Terry, who would certainly not let anyone else play Lady Cicely. Of course I could write another play for you; but I couldnt possibly begin it until the middle of the year or later. And besides, you probably wouldnt play it. Not that that would matter, as I could probably bring you to your senses; but unfortunately Miss Robins's judgment is disabled in precisely the same way as yours; and I cant make an American George Eliot understand the twentieth century. With you she gets on reasonably, because her American scheme of ethics exactly fits your Sir Walter Scottish social consciousness, and your stupendous ignorance of English life and character. But with me she is a perverse devil, because it is quite impossible to her to conceive my anti-gentlemanly, anti-literary, anti-ethical, anti-virtuous view of life as anything else but mere blackguardism. When one is young, one thinks that these things can be got over: later on, that illusion vanishes. She is quite right about me from her point of view. It so happens accidentally that a single play of mine, Candida, presents to her three people who have read all the books she has read, who speak touchingly in her dialect, and conduct a moving drama the relationship of which to, say, The Philanderer, is no more forced upon her than the implications of the Master Builder, which she plays without understanding, by poetic infection. But even if Candida were available, I am not sure that her enthusiasm for it would stand any revelation at rehearsal of the fact that Candida's nice domestic speech at the end suddenly leads the poet to the Master Builder's discovery that it is all over with the happy home ideal, and that he flies out into the night as a bird flies out of a cage or a trap. And there is not the least likelihood of my writing any more plays which will be not only acceptable to you both, but will also be uncommercial enough to be the business of the N.C.T. And what is the use of entering into friction-creating relations when we know quite well that we shall not be happy in them. As I said before, *you* dont matter: your dunderheadedness will only give rise to your national sport of argument; but with a woman such maladjustments create hatred. On the whole, it will be far better for you to arrange an appearance for her in some correctly Ethical play (why not ask Mrs Humphry Ward to write it?) and reserve me for some later occasion when it can be managed that we shall not meet.

My difficulty is, of course, to convince you that there is anything in all this solid and real enough to obstruct a concrete proposal to perform a play. But there is. You are becoming such a disgraceful old ruffian now that years of wallowing in theatrical love and murder have wiped all the intellectual passion out of you, and even extinguished your sense of humor, that unless I stimulate your jaded appetite with the brutalities of Mrs Warren, or soften you with the blandishments of a nice fat amiable ladylike Candida, who is a mother first, a wife twentyseventh, and nothing else, you outdo Clement Scott in your protests. It is positively indecent, the way you go on about that play. You are worse than Ian Robertson, who has just spent half an hour trying to persuade me to rewrite the third act of the D's D for Forbes in the spirit of a gentleman, with Richard in love with Judith, and a general flavor of the Only Way about it. I refuse to pander to these Renaissance sensualities. I will not create Haymarket heroes whose blood goes into their erotics (do you remember the disgraceful phrase "bloodless erotics"?) instead of into their metaphysics and politics. I will write no more glorifications of marriage, the only one of our institutions that is rooted in its avowed and utter licentiousness. If marrying Candida is to be accepted as the one noble and complete fulfilment of the human will, then you will get two sorts of drama: one, the Adelphi drama of lies; and two, the realistic drama of Zola and Maupassant (have you read Fecondite? if not, do), or the romance of Casanova glorified by Mozart or Byron into Don Juan. In the Philanderer I have shewn you the real Don Juan, the man whose blood has gone to his head, and left him with nothing but an appetite which entangles him ridiculously with a woman who is still very violently in the "flesh and blood" stage. You are just like all the managers: you want my talent and even my subjects with the ungentlemanly consequences left out. You will take Mrs Warren on condition that I leave in the prostitution, hot and strong, but leave out the inevitable complication that the prostitute's child never knows its brothers and sisters, and is dramatically certain to find them turning up unexpectedly in the third act. You attribute my insistence on this to the sensual attraction of the subject for me. And all the rest of my work is accounted for by the fact that all the characters are a projection of myself. I put on the stage for the first time a dramatization of those three generations which we have both seen arise: the old fashioned pious people, the generation of Mrs Fawcett, Lydia Becker, Stuart Mill &c, and the new Socialist-Nietzsche generation. I contrive with such labor and skill that not only does this history of the three generations come out as the most striking part of the performance, but that it presents itself in the guise of a perfect comedy, full of fun and character. But the subject is not an erotic one, and consequently does not exist for you, scandalous debauchee that you are. "A tedious farce" is your verdict, with a rider to the effect that it is a bad acting play—the most completely asinine piece of technical incompetence that has ever disgraced a once promising critic. I ask you, what do you mean by it? Where is your sense of shame? How have you the cheek to come to me for plays for your ridiculous Sixteenth Century Theatre, where I am to be treated as a Philanderer reformed by Candida? Do you suppose, because I am patient with the rest of the world, that I am bound to be patient with

138

you, who have some brains if you were not too lazy a voluptuary to use them. Every day I expect to meet you in an overcoat with an astrachan collar, and your hair dyed purple, talking literature, and living in a world of worn out shadows that still has its misty modes set by Hamlet and Falstaff. I am to devote my few remaining days to writing plays for your amusement and Miss Robins's, am I? Bother Miss Robins! To the dusty shades with the New Century Theatre—even the Euston Road is ashamed any longer to call itself the New Road. Get out.

The right thing for the N.C.T. to do now is to specialize in the George Eliot direction. I am quite serious in this. The Stage Society has altered the situation for you completely. It has caught on to the modern side of things by simply doing two plays which were lying ready to your hand if you had wanted them. The fact that you didnt want them really settles the question of your function in the movement. You must embrace your fate and set to work seriously to provide a theatre for the party of Secular Morality—the party of Matthew Arnold, George Eliot and Mrs Humphrey Ward, of the Ethical Societies of America, of South Place, Leslie Stephen and so on, with what you call a seamy side of Zola-Maupassant realism, all brought up to date. Now nobody can catch up all those threads better than the authoress of An Open Question. And nobody can help her better than Norman Britton [Archer's early pseudonym]. There's your line—an excellent and honorable one. It is not new; but by attacking it resolutely it will lead you somewhere, perhaps to the real new drama which my Irish eighteenth centuriness and rhetoric and obsolete laugh catching may miss. Anyhow there is nothing to be done by ridiculously sitting on your funds and doing nothing but asking me for work which you two may admire, but which you dont respect. When we found long ago that there was no new drama in existence, I turned my hand to the stage and supplied my own demand. You must do the same thing. What I supplied is not what you want: well, follow up Alan's Wife: even if you fail, it will freshen you for other successes. There: that's my advice to you and to Miss Elizabeth.

Can you come to lunch tomorrow (Friday) at half past one? Or on Friday next week if you are engaged tomorrow? If I don't hear from you we shall expect you.

GBS

139

To WILLIAM ARCHER

Beacon Hotel. Hindhead
[A.u/2]   27th January 1900

[Archer replied on 25th January: "As for your diatribe in which an a priori you, an a priori me, & an a priori Miss Robins play a number of fantastic tricks before high heaven, it is so utterly aloof from all reality that it simply leaves me dumb. There is only one thing I want to say, & that is that you are utterly and unaccountably wrong when you say that I attribute your insistence on the Vivie-&-Frank business to 'the sensual attraction of the subject for you.' I never dreamt of such a thing. I attribute it partly to the wrong-headed logic by which you here defend it, partly to the sheer pleasure it gives you to *épater le bourgeois*—a pleasure which I believe quite genuinely translates itself in your consciousness into a duty. Having logically convinced yourself that this question of uncertain paternity is an essential part of your theme & must be brought out, you wouldn't for untold gold flinch from doing it. Morally I admire your attitude, bating always the fact that, where there is any shocking to be done, duty & pleasure largely coincide; but artistically I protest. I don't think your logic in the least cogent; & if it were, there are ways & ways of doing a thing, & I don't like the Vivie-&-Frank way. But heavens above! I never dreamt of its having any 'sensual attraction' for you. As for the play in general I don't care a brass farthing whether it's about prostitution or what it's about; I call it a masterpiece because many of its scenes are intensely dramatic, & some of its 'repliques' are dramatic 'Trouvailles'—I can't be bothered translating into English.

"No, I have not joined the Stage Society because I am too old & too busy to take much interest in that sort of thing. The history of the N.C.T. sufficiently shows that I am a bad hand at coterie-theatre work. I haven't the faculty of persuading myself that a play is a good play merely because it is unconventional. It seems to be that my one gift as a critic is that of distinguishing 'live' work from dead work; anyway, rightly or wrongly, I have strong prejudices on the point, & my recollection of Olivier's play is that, whatever cleverness there may have been in it, it was dead as a doornail—therefore precisely fitted for a Sunday evening performance. I don't mean to say that 'You never can tell' was in the same case, but it never interested me much & was not a type of play that the N.C.T. could advantageously tackle. But believe me the N.C.T. is not & never has been guided by any of the superb moral or literary theories you manufacture for it. Give it a play as *is* a play— a play that is not merely commonplace or merely épatant—& that comes within its pecuniary means, & we will do it like a shot" (Fales Collection, New York University Library).

Re Pionians, see I, 400. *Secret Service* was a popular American melodrama by William Gillette, which had first been produced at Terry's Theatre in May 1895. Ibsen's *League of Youth* was produced by the Stage Society at the Vaudeville Theatre on 25th February, directed by Charles Charrington.]

You really are an utterly impossible chap. However, let us work out the position your way. Let it be granted that we three, Elizabeth, William & George Bernard, are three angelic and infinite cuttle fish; that we are not what you call Apry Ory beings, meaning that we have no temperaments and belong to no categories, biological, psychological, dramatic, literary or political; that we are unconditioned and universal; and that, consequently, the differences and destinies which lead other friends into divergent paths do not exist for us. True Pionians, all three.

Very well.

Now let us waive my previous remarks, based on a mistaken estimate of us as human beings. The parole is to you.

A voice as from an astrakan collar suddenly claims as its one critical gift, that of distinguishing "live" work from dead. It doesnt care a rap what theories or principles are behind a play. It has no prejudices: it means business. Give it a good play, "a play as *is* a play—a play that is not merely commonplace or merely épatant"—and it will do it "like a shot." It has "swallowed all the formulae," has this voice, and knows only two sorts of play, good ones and bad ones.

Alas, it needs no New Century Theatre to tell me this. For this, in letter and spirit, without word, thought or attitude altered by the shadow of a shade, is the voice of Tree, Alexander et hoc genus omne. Why should I give *you*, New Century Theatre manager, with your few paltry hundreds, a play that Her Majestys, the St James's, the Haymarket & all the rest, are clamoring for? *That* is what I mean by the astrakan collar. You have in process of time dropped into the practical attitude—the attitude into which experience drives all men who aim at *success*, whether pecuniary or simply artistic—and you say spontaneously and unconsciously exactly what all the other practical men say.

But you do not stick to it. The moment you are taken at your word and confronted with Mrs Warren & You Never Can Tell, you suddenly cease to be infinite and unconditioned and admit that there are things in those plays that you "don't like" and that "never interested you much." Is this much more infinite or less conditioned than John Hare, who will say if you ask him, "Give me a *good* play by Ibsen, and I'll do it tomorrow." You suggest the Wild Duck. Immediately he assures you that the Wild Duck is not a good play. By which he means that he doesn't like it. You didnt like You Never Can Tell, which happens to be an almost diabolically good play technically, and you solemnly assured the public that it is tedious farce, and doubted

141

whether even the most skilful acting could make it tolerable. And very likely if you had seen the performance at the Royalty, you would have felt thoroughly confirmed in your judgment, & slept as soundly as [Augustus] Harris did during the Wild Duck. And your case is worse than Harris's. He slept because the thing was above and beyond him. You see things—the same things—differently; and that is fatal. The difference is so biassing that the Shawish quality of my characters produces the same effect on you as the blackness of a negro does on a white man in a white country, to whom all negroes are alike, no distinction of age, complexion, good or bad looks being apparent to him. For example, to me the snubnosed Swiss soldier in Arms & The Man is a simple & unaffected man. Napoleon is exactly the opposite, an incorrigible actor, self conscious to his finger nails. The contrast (to me) is emphasized by the fact that they are both, as professional soldiers, alike in their freedom from vulgar illusions about war, though Bluntschli's experience stops short of Napoleon's generalized observation & reflection. Now to you these two opposites are alike. They are not even real men: they are only projections of a disagreeable affectation of my own. This is not the same thing as your disbelief in Vivie Warren & the Widowers' Houses people. *That* is pure Arcadian innocence: Sir Walter Scott would have said the same thing about them. But Bluntschli & Napoleon are within your scope: they belong to the world which the literary man explores imaginatively, whereas Miss Blanche Sartorius, Vivie & Co, belong to the vast English anti-literary majority of whose existence & characteristics I myself had not the faintest conception 20 years ago, and whom you have not discovered yet.

This being so, it's not possible for you to like my plays. Napoleon the Subtle duped easily by a woman, Bluntschli the Simple absolutely invulnerable—all these strokes & turns of comedy have no interest—no existence for you. You simply feel "I wish Shaw wouldnt go on like that." And you convince yourself that when I do really good work you can appreciate it, because you like Candida. But everybody likes Candida. Wyndham drops a tear over Candida; Alexander wants the poet made blind so that he can play him with a guarantee of "sympathy"; Mrs Pat wants to play Candida; Ellen Terry knows she *is* Candida; Candida is everybody's play except the utter groundlings'. Candida vindicates every wife & mother and every suburban home to her and itself. To me it does nothing of the kind: it shews how important the woman's part in the arrangement is; but it does not justify the arrangement itself; and indeed the original of Vivie Warren, who is not susceptible to the sexual sentimentality which gives the Candida household its false charm, heads a party which denounces the play as disgusting.

Now you may say that all this is idle, because you like my last three plays. No doubt you do. The first was written for Terriss, and is a melodrama. The second was written for Forbes Robertson & Mrs Pat, and is literary. The third was written for Ellen Terry, round a part which is about as realistic as Rosalind. All three have strong & moving situations which appeal to you and to me exactly as they appeal to every man in the pit. For that reason, they have nothing to do with the New Century Theatre.

And now, to what end all this insistence on the fact that my plays are antipathetic to you? Have I spent all this black lead and excellent valuable time on mere amertumous recritication? Not a bit of it. I am hammering at my old point: you must write the plays you want yourself, or at worst make others write them. You will tell me, with the modesty of ingrained laziness, that you are not a playwright. Unfortunately for your credit on such points, you formed an equally strong opinion that *I* was not a playwright, and did what a sincere wellwisher could to prevent my exposing my obvious incapacity to the whole world. As a matter of fact I am by a very great deal the best English-language playwright since Shakespear, and considerably *his* superior on a good many points. If you made that colossal blunder about me, how can you feel any confidence in your judgment of yourself? You have immense confidence in yourself as a critic, though you are in many ways the worst critic now alive, declaring Olivier's play a dead thing, and Secret Service a masterpiece and deuce knows what not. How do you know that playwriting, if you could once get on your destined plane, is not your forte after all. At all events, you have failed to get the plays you want from other people. Even Ibsen doesnt convince you: you always want to cut his plays; and you have left the League of Youth to the Stage Society. In me you have hatched a cockatrice. Olivier is equally a failure. "Alan's Wife" is the only seed that has come up as you wanted it. Well, here you are with a New Century Theatre and funds for a performance or two. It has plenty of talent on hand—yourself, Mrs Clifford & Miss Robins. Why dont you meet and say "The land is barren: we must make a play." There is more where "Alan's Wife" came from, and more where "Clive" came from. What is more, you three are not amateurs of an effete period: your vein has never been worked dramatically. It's a regular Rand.

143

This is all I have to say; and I am absolutely and perfectly right about it. And it is time for you to look to it; for we are both over 40, and your astrakan collar is growing rather alarmingly. The sooner you become as a little child again, the better. After all, it does not take so long to write a play; and it will be some expiation for flattering the Americans, and informing a stupended public that the verb "to scrap" is unknown in England. Cashel Byron could have told you that it is as hackneyed in the London streets as "copper" for policeman.

If you WONT, then hand over your NCT funds to the Stage Society, and it will do something with them.

We shall expect you on Friday, as arranged.

[The last word was Archer's, on 1st February: "As the man says in Stevenson, 'Golly, what a letter!' [R.L.Stevenson and Lloyd Osbourne, *The Wrong Box*, 1889.]

"I write to you suggesting that the N.C.T. might do one of your plays; you haven't a play that we want free for us to do; one would think nothing could be simpler. But somehow a 'position' is set up, which has got to be 'worked out' laboriously, with tons of black lead lavished upon it. There is no 'position' whatever. We have never agreed about plays, & we never will. There is not the least reason why we should. I have never given a red cent for the ideas in plays. You & other people have had to point out to me the ideas in Ibsen's plays. Some of them I see, some of them I don't (nor, I believe, does Ibsen). But the play has always been the first thing to me; it is the last thing to you.

"Never was black lead more hopelessly wasted than in this letter. You haven't even persuaded me that I ought to be ashamed of myself for admiring your later plays. As for the other plays, a few minutes after I read your letter I read a manuscript preface by Gilbert Murray to one of his own plays in which he says: 'I see that I am approaching the common pitfall of playwrights who venture upon prefaces, & am beginning to prove how good my play ought to be!' For 'prefaces' read 'letters.' I think I have solved the mystery of your friend Shakespeare's premature end: he no doubt broke a bloodvessel in trying to prove to Ben Jonson that *Titus Andronicus* was a good play & *Hamlet* a bad one" (C. Archer, *William Archer*, 1931).]

To AUGUSTIN HAMON

10 Adelphi Terrace WC
[S/1]   1 Fevrier 1900

[Mlle Henriette Rynenbroeck became Mrs Augustin Hamon in February 1901. It is not clear which work Shaw was correcting. Hamon's article "Le Congrès général des organisations socialistes françaises" had appeared in the January issue of *L'Humanité Nouvelle*, of which he was the editor. Jules Guesde (1845–1922) was a French Socialist and editor, who advocated the rejection of any compromise with capitalistic government.]

Mon cher Hamon

Voici enfin l'épreuve! Voulez vous avoir la bonté de corriger mes corrections: j'ai cherché d'éclaircir les phrases dont Mademoiselle Rynenbroeck n'a pas pu saisir le vrai sens; mais je n'ai aucune prétention de poser comme styliste français. Peut être vous croyez qu'une langue s'enrichit par des locutions étrangères: en ce cas, mes efforts sont à votre service. Seulement, excusez du peu les genres et la syntaxe. Mes heresies ont un peu epaté Mademoiselle Rynenbroeck, je crois: elle a cherché de les détremper. Elle a même omis les plus rudes. Mais il faut me laisser "epater le socialiste": c'est mon metier. D'ailleurs, il le mérite.

Il y a longtemps que je me suis rendu chez une dame de ma connaissance pour la prier de s'abonner à l'Humanité Nouvelle. Elle donna l'ordre à Hachette sur le Champ. J'etais si vivement touché que je la fis ma femme. Me voici donc abonné par mariage!

Combien pour une série complète de l'Humanité Nouvelle, de son commencement jusqu'à l'heure qu'il est? Je voudrais la présenter à la bibliothèque de la London School of Economics and Political Science.

Cordiale poignée de main.

G. Bernard Shaw

P.S. Votre compte rendu du Congrès est excellent. On peut voir et entendre Guesde et Jaurès. Guesde est honnête, n'est ce pas, comme tous les doctrinaires impossibilistes?

To R. ELLIS ROBERTS

10 Adelphi Terrace WC
[A/1]   7th February 1900

[Richard Ellis Roberts (1879–1953) was a young writer, who later published a critical study of Ibsen and translated *Peer Gynt* (1912). He frequently wrote on religious subjects.]

Dear Sir

I remember once recommending a friend of mine, who was very full of the Socialism of the early eighties, to set to work & qualify himself in medicine & surgery. He replied that he had thought of it, but as the period of qualification was four years, and he was convinced that "the revolution" would come within eighteen months, he had given up the idea as impracticable. When I pointed out to him that even under Socialism we should still need surgeons, he was taken aback, post-revolutionary Socialism having presented itself to his imagination as a condition in which no more needs or difficulties would exist—in short, a *heavenly* condition.

Are you sure you are not making the same mistake with regard to Tolstoyism? Even if we all embrace it, we cannot live for ever afterwards on one another's charity. We may simplify our lives and become vegetarians; but even the minimum of material life will involve the industrial problem of its production & distribution, and will defy Anarchism. On the latter point you will find among the Fabian tracts one entitled The Impossibilities of Anarchism, by myself, which will, I think, convince you that Anarchism in industry, as far as it is practicable, produces exactly the civilization that we have today, and that the first thing a Tolstoyan community would have to do would be to get rid of it. The Joint Stock Companies & the Trusts may not have come to stay; but their departure will be caused by an extension of their system of collectively owned capital to the whole community, and of the social insistence on the citizen becoming the servant of that community instead of the Anarchist adventurer fighting for his own hand against every other citizen.

Further, I submit to you that public questions cannot be shirked by the easy method of declaring that if people were something which they are not, the questions would not exist. For example, I am both a vegetarian and a teetotaller. But if I am asked how the meat supply & the spirit supply should be organized, I do not answer that they should not be organized at all because people would be better without them: I advocate municipal slaughterhouses, municipal public houses &c. I actually hold shares in the Fox & Pelican at Grayshott—an experiment in reforming the public house.

Man may have his opinion as to the relative importance of feeding his body and nourishing his soul, but he is allowed by Nature to have no opinion whatever as to the need for feeding the body before the soul can think of anything but the body's hunger. That need is a fact beyond all opinion. Nothing is less Tolstoyan than to refuse to deal with facts. Tolstoy has just described Ibsen as a delirious dreamer, mainly because Ibsen has got too far away from the realities of bread and butter.

yours faithfully
G. Bernard Shaw

146

To ELLEN TERRY

10 Adelphi Terrace WC

[U(H)/10; X/117]   9th February 1900

[For an explanation of the references to Minnie Maddern Fiske, see
Shaw's letter of 12th June 1900 to Mrs Richard Mansfield.]

Very well, dear Ellen: we cry off Brassbound. I have always foreseen, and foretold to you, that when it came to the point, you would
find it practically impossible to detach yourself from the Lyceum. And
apart from the business reasons, the breaking up of an old partnership
like yours and H.I's is not a thing to be done except on extreme
occasion. It was my feeling concerning this that made me so very
determined not to let you interfere in the Man of Destiny squabble. I
wrote Brassbound for you merely for the sake of writing it for you,
without any faith in your ever being able to produce it, knowing that
the existence of the play would strengthen your hold of H.I. (by
making you independent of him if you chose to abandon his ship) and
thereby make it doubly certain that he would not let you go for want
of asking you to stay—and obviously if he really wants you to stay,
stay you must. Consequently I am in no way disappointed or surprised:
destiny has fulfilled itself exactly as I foresaw it would if affairs took
their normal course.

You are quite right to return to America for the winter tour. I never
go into a theatre now; but the gossip is that business is very bad, the
war being apparently unfavorable to it. To throw away a certain
£2,400 for the chance of losing that sum and worrying your life out
with a new part and a new theatre would be madness. No sane friend,
as *was* a friend, could advise you to act otherwise than you are acting.

Only, I want you to face the fact that this means that you are not
going to do Brassbound at all—never, world without end. The reasons
which prevent you doing it now will be stronger in 1901. I told you
that if you accepted the St Bartholomew part, that would virtually cast
the die, as the same position would inevitably recur at the beginning of
every fresh season, and at each recurrence you would make the same
choice. So now for one of my celebrated *volte faces*. I hold on pretty
hard until the stars declare themselves against me, and then I always
give up and try something else with a promptitude which seems cynical
and unfeeling to the slow witted Englishman who only tells himself
his misfortunes by degrees. And now I recognize that you and I can
never be associated as author and player—that you will remain Olivia,
and that Lady Cicely is some young creature in short skirts at a High

147

School at this moment. I have pitched so many dreams out of the window that one more or less makes little difference—in fact, by this time I take a certain Satanic delight in doing it and noting how little it hurts me. So out of the window you go, my dear Ellen; and off goes the play to my agents as in the market for the highest bidder. Mrs Maddie Minnern Frisk shall have it unless somebody else offers sixpence more.

At least that is what I will do when I have time. But I am so full of serious work just now that I have hardly any time for bothering about these plays.

The agitation against the syndicate is all nonsense: it is just the same as the wail of the small shopkeeper when you go to the Stores or to Shoolbred's. It is quite true that the syndicate deals mostly in machine made melodramas and farcical comedies that are not even machine made; but that is because the public (meaning the shopgirls mostly) want them. The reason Mrs Maddie couldnt get any plays was that she wanted the same plays as the syndicate. If she had wanted better ones, she could have got them just as you did.

The Stage Society, a sort of Sunday night Independent theatre started by an energetic Fabian, did You Never Can Tell the other day. Performance might have been worse—at any rate we shall hear no more now about its being a bad stage play. I was ashamed of its tricks and laughs and popularities. It would make a great hit at the Lyceum with Henry as the Waiter.

This Stage Society, by the way, is catching on in its little coterie-theatre way. The announcement of You Never Can Tell brought in three hundred members at two guineas each like a shot. What do you think of that? Edie seems to be a member: she was at the last performance. Met her also at a Dolmetsch concert, immediately after a report had appeared in the papers here describing you as having harangued a crowd in your nightdress from the windows of a burning hotel, exhorting them to be calm, and being finally carried down the fire escape by Henry (in pyjamas) amid tremendous cheering. . . .

Do not excite yourself about the war: it is quite the usual thing. Charlotte's brother-in-law (Colonel Hugh Cholmondely) has gone out with the City Volunteers. They are all supposed to be young country gentlemen, hard riders and crack shots. Cholmondely took them out on Wimbledon Common to see them ride; and presently the common was strewn in all directions with the Dismounted Infantry. They had mostly learnt their manège at Mawgit or on Empstead Eath. Poor devils! . . .

148

Oh my dear Ellen, now that I have thrown you out of the window, I am fain to go and sweep you up gently and put you together again. But that would be weakness.

GBS

PS. You don't give me any address; so I must send this to the next theatre on your itinerary. Chicago is a comparatively enlightened town: my plays get good houses there. Mansfield revived Arms & The Man for a night in New York last month. It was still alive enough to draw $1000.

To CHARLES CHARRINGTON

Hindhead Beacon Hotel. Haslemere

[A/4] 4th March 1900

[Charrington had lectured on Imperialism and the Transvaal War at the first meeting of the new Fabian Hammersmith Group on 16th October 1899 and to the Kensington Group on 29th January. Henry Thomas Muggeridge (1864–1942), a City businessman, lecturer, and Fabian, was active in Croydon local politics, and later was Labour M.P. for Romford (1929–31). He was the father of Malcolm Muggeridge. George Odger (1820–77), a cobbler by trade, became a trades unionist and was made president of the International in 1864. Shaw is quoting Hamlet's Act I speech to the Ghost: "What may this mean, That thou, dead corse, again, in complete steel, Revisit'st thus the glimpses of the moon, Making night hideous."]

Dear Charrington

Now that the Fabian Executive election is at hand, I paternally suggest that you avoid the subject of Imperialism in your next few speeches at Clifford's Inn, and that you stump the groups & provinces as far as opportunity offers on some subject which admits of sensible treatment. If you had an original *Socialist* view of the war, you would be all right; but this eruption of original Martinesque family sin—a horrible compound of Redcliffe Square & Passmore Edwards Echoism—is no sort of good. At present the Fabian is troubled in its soul, because it knows that both the vulgar party sides about the war are wrong, and yet cannot find the right line, being unable to unravel the confusion between the social destiny of the world and the blunders & bad blood of the statesmen. Consequently it will cling to personal highmindedness and capacity rather than to a party ticket in voting.

149

Therefore be careful to turn on that particular blend of gas for the moment, and leave the Liberal drum to the Morning Leader & Muggeridge.

Of course, if there is no contest, this will not matter. I have heard nothing about any nominations from either side; but in excited times nominations are apt to be made freely; and what happens then is that though the old gang is pretty safe, the other seats go anyhow. Hobson ought to come on; and if he does, someone will have to go off. I dont think your risk is great, because any man who speaks a good deal and makes himself known to the provincial Fabians by lecturing is safer than the oldest old-ganger who does neither; but this cuts two ways if the speaking is on a subject on which feeling runs high. That is why I suggest that until the election is over you should either take subjects on which you can be sympathetic to all Fabians, or else strike a loftier note than that idiocy about the window & the usual rubbish about the infamous capitalist. By God, you talk like George Odger revisiting the glimpses of the moon.

I further suggest that the Stage Society should do Peer Gynt in two pieces—the first three acts one night & the last two the other. I think the S.S. is good business for you. Whelen comes to me amazed, and assures me that as a stage manager you have conscience, tact, ability, all the qualities in which in every other capacity you seem totally lacking. This is good for me too, as I am able to say "I told you so." But the Fabian is spoiling you as an actor. You are getting rhetorical; and you expound and illustrate your parts like the Ghost in Hamlet. Another thing: you should vary your make-up so as to lend an element of curiosity to your necessarily frequent appearances in the S.S. plays. In your unadorned condition, under-rouged, you look like a printer with a pianist's wig. It is all very well for Herman Vezin to play Crampton without any paint; but you should look as if you had some blood in you—not blue blood and bile, but red, sanguine gore. The notion that the liver is the seat of love is a medieval one. Try a curled Austrian beard & moustache, blond, the next time. . . .

I vainly tried to find Janet after exchanging a nod with her at the Vaudeville—a nod by which she distinctly conveyed her opinion that I am overacting the part of a respectable married man. But I am only rehearsing for my old age: my guiltiest passions are still glowing beneath the surface.

GBS

To CHARLES CHARRINGTON

10 Adelphi Terrace WC
[A/4]   8th March 1900

[George Edwardes (1852–1915), a theatrical manager, was best known as the managing director of the Gaiety Theatre, the principal home in London of musical comedy and other popular entertainments. Re Fabian Tract 70, see I, 674. Aslaksen was the rôle played by Charrington in *The League of Youth* in the Stage Society production at the Vaudeville Theatre on 25th February.]

You have caught party politics badly: now we shall have division between parent & child, husband & wife, brother & sister.

No: the purpose of my letter was exactly its explicit purport. Knowing that you are just in the mood to go about orating against the infamies of Imperialism, and knowing also that you *may* thereby lose half the votes which you hold, and which you can continue to hold by simply making yourself agreeable for the moment, I thought it best to give you a hint to that effect. It is all the more important as, if you are defeated, you will certainly attribute it to diabolical machinations on the part of the Imperialist conspirators.

I am not very anxious about defections. Hobson is obviously an out & out Imperialist; and most of you are the same if you only knew it. If you could once get that clear in your heads, you might begin a really effective campaign against the melodramatic methods in vogue. You yourself would not stop to listen to Labouchere talking virtuous indignation about the Transvaal, because you know that his whole position is obsolete and impracticable. Then what is the good of falling back on Laboucherism and hoping to make way with Socialists from *his* broken springboard? True, all these brainless howling patriots will next year or so be equally brainless howling reactionists, sending in a big Liberal majority at a General Election. But you dont want, I presume, to go into Parliament as a Local Optionist Little Englander. In the meantime dont be moved to ecstasies of horror by the poor devils who are at this moment marching up and down the Embankment waving Union Jacks & blowing toy trumpets, waiting for the Queen to pass. *That* wont last.

Above all, dont talk of "strengthening" the Fabian. You might as well talk of strengthening the Stage Society by making it agreeable to George Edwards. We have never been in line with the body of Socialists in the provinces & Europe with whom Anderson longs to mingle us; and we never shall as long as we have the brains to keep two or three streets ahead of them. Of course it will be a job to pull the Fabian through this excitement and bring it up to the advanced line, just as it was over Tract 70; but we shall do it.

I dont advise you to resign. *Never resign*. And I dont want you to be chucked at the election, a fate which you can easily avoid by doing a little non-contentious speaking & lecturing, whether the I.L.P. backs you or not, or at least by keeping quiet & relaxing your sense of a great crisis & a Machiavellian treachery. It is, from the S.S. point of view alone, convenient to have you & Whelen on the Exec., & to be able to see you regularly. You can indignate about your blessed Boers as much as you like, provided you dont spoil business; and it seems to me, on the whole, that keeping together is good business.

I quite appreciated Aslaksen's make-up. I do not see any very grave falling-off in your histrionics as yet; but once or twice I thought I detected a sort of impulse to *describe* the character rhetorically— quite a different thing from identifying it with yourself; and I thought I'd terrify you in time.

GBS

PS. The Queen has just passed. A street full of rampant Fenians would have cheered her more heartily, if only out of son-sentiment towards an old woman. These patriots have no guts in their bawling.

To HENRY S. SALT

10 Adelphi Terrace WC
[A/1; X/164.e]   12th March 1900

[Salt was editor of the *Humane Review*, in which Shaw's essay "The Conflict between Science and Common Sense" appeared in April 1900, and his "Civilization and the Soldier" in January 1901. Shaw used the title "Cannon Fodder" for an article in *The Clarion* on 21st November 1902.]

I called at Holbein House on Saturday evening, but could not get in. The Humane Review is rather on my conscience just at present because of our Imperialism controversy. I am afraid of your putting in some article not only against war as a method of settling international disputes, but against *the* war as a stroke of Government policy. This, believe me, will destroy the Review by making it at once a political organ—a Liberal one. On the other hand, if you avoid the subject altogether, it will be such bad journalism that nobody will buy the Review. I therefore adjure you *to write the article yourself*, stripping

152

the bunkum off both sides impartially without betraying the least political sympathy. Call it "Cannon Fodder" (Kanonen futter), and spare not the Boer with his Bible nor Thomas Atkins with his patent inoculation against enteric fever. The whole weight of the Review will depend on its not *taking sides* about war, but going for it with perfect integrity, and declining to admit that the most perfect justification of the policy of either party could justify the Boer attack or the British provocation. You cannot, & ought not to, entrust this job to any other hand: it must be done by the editor.

As for me, I delight in the war more & more. It has waked the country up out of its filthy wallowing in money (blood is a far superior bath); and it has put a fourpence on the Income Tax which will never come off if the Fabian can help it; so that Old Age Pensions will be within reach at the end of the ten years repayment period, if not sooner. And it has put a stop to the Chartered Company game, and the sort of hanging back that made a hell of New Zealand before the descent of the French forced us to take it on. Kruger as Joshua will also be exploded; and British military prestige of the schoolboy kind has been handsomely "reversed." The object lesson of our 30,000 men with unlimited Lyddite taking ten days to make 4000 poor wretches of all ages, with 6 cannons, come out of a ditch and surrender (mainly to stink and starvation) will have an extremely cooling effect on the military ardor of the Powers: in fact, until some new Napoleon devises new tactics, Bloch's thesis that war is impossible stands pretty well proved. On the whole *our* position is immensely fortified by the logic of burning facts. So you can afford to be goodhumored in your article.

Mind, do nothing *party*, either in the Fabian or out of it. Humanity must be neither Liberal nor Conservative; and you may see from my case how impossible it is to take any step in the matter without being interpreted at once as having taken one of the political sides. Charrington calls me a Tory because I declare for Imperialism as our social theory. Similarly, if you declare for Stop the War without the most scrupulous denunciation of *both* combatants, you will be set down as a Liberal; and then the whole force of your protest will be broken: you will make no more impression than Morley, & you will get no Conservatives to subscribe to the Review.

GBS

To EDWARD ROSE

[A/1]

10 Adelphi Terrace WC
13th March 1900

[Shaw was working desperately to mend fences, but to little avail. Rose resigned in April. A similar letter to Walter Crane, written on the same day, had no better result. S.G.Hobson (1864–1940), as Shaw predicted, was elected to the Executive, on which he served until 1909, when he resigned from the Fabian Society because he was no longer in agreement with its policy. Sir Alfred Lyall (1835–1911), long a British administrator in India, had since 1887 been a member of the India Council in London. George Curzon (1859–1925), later 1st Baron and 1st Marquess Curzon of Kedleston, became Viceroy and Governor-General of India in 1899.]

My dear Rose

You really must not resign your Fabianship now. Politics cannot be worked on this principle. You must stand to your guns. At the forthcoming Executive election Hobson will probably get on (I shall vote for him, anyhow). You will then have on the Exec. on your side Hobson, Lawson Dodd, Anderson, Charrington, and (if he will be persuaded not to resign) Green. Possibly also Macdonald; but I should not dissuade him from leaving us, because he is genuinely disaffected to the Society in a way which I could only describe by going into psychology—at all events, a way which does not resemble your case in the very remotest manner.

Besides these six or seven men who are open and strong partisans on your side, you have Standring, Macrosty, Pease and Webb who are beyond all suspicion of common Toryism. Whelen is Radical even in theatrical affairs. Miss O'Brien is equally free from Rhodesism. Assume now that Bland, Oakeshott & myself are dangerous Imperialists, and that my wife's vote goes with mine (a rash assumption, as she is intensely Irish & anti-English), and you will see that if you count us as the extreme Right, your people as the extreme Left, and Webb & Co the Centre upon which the extremes depend when it comes to voting, you have six votes and the sympathies & traditions of the Centre, whereas we have only four votes and the Centre's critical ear. Add to this the vote you got in the recent Referendum, and you will see, I think, that any sense of isolation you may feel is wholly imaginary. Of course there is the inevitable isolation of your individuality: no man can find a Society 800 strong which is an extension of his own self— even the society of 2 called marriage is a failure from that point of view—but you are no worse off that way than I am.

You could get on the Executive yourself quite easily if you would make speeches at Clifford's Inn as you did last night at Hampstead, and give a few lectures in the provinces. Charrington got on that way. However, I take it that you dont want to be bothered.

I thought [J.M.]Robertson put the anti-Empire case as well as it need be put. I quite agree with him that Empire is the disease that kills civilization, and that, as Morris put it "no man is good enough to be another man's master." But, all the same, Robertson's answer as to what we are to do with India is exactly Sir Alfred Lyall's answer or Curzon's. History certainly proves that you, as an East Anglian dumpling, are an incapable ruler and thinker, an oppressor and a hypocrite. I, as an Irishman, and Robertson, as a Scotchman, can perceive that with exquisite clearness. But you can't act on that assumption; and if you could and did, you would do ten times more harm than if you boldly disregarded the conclusion as a *reductio ad absurdum* of History. Besides, it puts not only your Imperial instincts out of court, but *all* your instincts, Imperial & Anti-Imperial. Therefore, *don't* resign.

GBS

P.S. You ought to have a look at Voysey's wall papers. The Law of Change (see "Little Eyolf") demands that we should not spend our lives within Morris walls.

To EDWARD ROSE

10 Adelphi Terrace WC
[A/1]   14th March 1900

[Pumblechook is a character in Dickens's *Great Expectations*.]

Just one word more, to steer you out of a no-thoroughfare. You are completely mistaken about Bland. His manners, like Pumblechook's, are "given to blusterous"; and he positively likes taking the chair. We take advantage of these points to shirk the chair ourselves; and I have no doubt the effect on those in front is that which he produces on you. But consider two other facts about him. 1. He has a household of nine persons to keep going. 2. Like all men of great muscle, he is very lazy. He comes to the Executive regularly because he is Treasurer: that is to say, he takes up the cheque book, signs half a dozen blank cheques, & leaves Pease to do the rest. He is not on the Publishing

Committee; he never writes a tract; he never drafts a scheme; he doesnt sit on any public body. If you think what this means for a moment, you will see that it is impossible that he could influence the Society except by impromptu criticisms sensible enough to convince fourteen other people who are not his partisans (rather the contrary, in fact) and who include at least five rather keen opponents of his at present.

The truth is that Bland is the only man on the Executive besides Webb (and Whelen, who is a little too modest) whose cleverness is backed by unfailing good sense. He is always against a foolish proposal, and never against a humane one. He knows the suburban Tory through and through; and the suburban Tory is a tremendous factor in English society. If you got him out of the Society, you would not diminish its activity much; but you would perceptibly unsteady its steering. In the old days I was always standing between Bland and the rustinesses that used to come from his Tory imperviousness to the Radical notions with which Socialism was adulterated—also his Catholic-philosophic aversion to materialistic Atheism. But I am quite sure I was right. He is legitimately on the Executive not only because he was one of the founders of the Fabian, but because he is and has always been one of the best fifteen (formerly best half dozen) members for the purpose. Like most men who affect a ferocious militarism of bearing, he is really an affectionate, imaginative sort of person. You may always vote for Bland without hesitation; and you need never bother about him. All his bads are in the shop window.

The definite intention to clear out of India as soon as the natives are capable of self rule is the most pious of superfluities—I mean the most superfluous of pieties. Count the population, and you will see that we are not likely to have much choice when that ever receding horizon is reached. If Robertson & Curzon are agreed as to the next twenty years, that is sufficient for the day.

The immorality, or unmorality, is fundamental. But be patient with us. Socialism is full of seductive cul-de-sacs and mirror-made halls of a million pillars. We have been down them all and in them all. They look most businesslike & sensible; but we pretty well found them out in 1885 or thereabouts. It was much jollier then, in a way: Fabian Socialism is, alas, Disillusioned Socialism; and you must take it at that. But why not supplement it by a Holland Park Socialist Society with Crane as Boss Joss, like Morris's Hammersmith one?

GBS

156

To MEMBERS OF THE FABIAN SOCIETY

89 Adelphi Terrace WC
[H/2]   11th April 1900

[Dr Frederick Lawson Dodd (1868–1962) was a dental surgeon, who served as treasurer of the Fabian Society from 1911 to 1936. On 12th April Shaw informed Edward Pease that he had mailed about seventy copies of this cyclostyled letter, addressed alternatively to "Dear Sir" or "Dear Madam."]

Dear Sir

Forgive me for reminding you, but you have not yet, I think, recorded your vote as a member of the Fabian Society for the election, now in progress, of the Executive Committee; and the poll closes on the 20th. The circumstances of the election are quite exceptional. You will see from the following brief statement of them how important it is that everybody should vote.

On the outbreak of the South African War, it was assumed by some very active and earnest members of the Society, including Mr. Walter Crane and Dr. Clifford, that there could be only one opinion on the subject among Socialists. You will remember that a majority of the Executive, consisting of Messrs. Pease, Bland, Webb, Oakeshott, Standring, Macrosty, Whelen, Miss O'Brien, my wife and myself, were convinced that no such unanimity existed. A vote of all the members was accordingly taken as to whether the Society should be committed to a pronouncement; and the result shewed that we were right: there was a wide division of opinion on the subject, the balance of votes being in our favor. Almost immediately after this, Dr Clifford, who had prepared an anti-Imperialist resolution for the Conference of Free Churches with the same confidence in a unanimous vote, had to withdraw it to avoid a counter-resolution and a scene of discord. I think you will admit, whichever side you may take on the war question, that we were justified in our estimate of the situation, and that we steered the Society safely through a rapid in which it might have been wrecked by a party pronouncement on the war.

Unfortunately, the feelings of those who opposed us have been so strongly worked on by current political events that they have nominated for the Fabian Executive, as the representatives of their views, five candidates, Messrs. S. G. Hobson, [J. E.] Matthews, Muggeridge, [Edward] Norton, and Mrs [Fenton] Macpherson, who, with their present representatives Messrs. Charrington, Lawson Dodd, and Wherry Anderson, make up the eight candidates necessary to make a majority possible for them in an Executive of fifteen. And they have

157

appealed to a considerable number of members to vote for these eight candidates *only*. Since we have made no counter nominations (Mr Dell's candidature is a matter of old standing) this advice on their part compels me to make an appeal to you not to adopt these tactics unless you really wish the contest to proceed on the ordinary lines of party electioneering. If you do so wish, then no doubt the scientific method is to vote either for the eight representatives of the present minority and nobody else, or for myself, my nine friends, our supporter Mr Dell, and for nobody else. Those of us whose seats are probably safe under any circumstances are placed in a very disagreeable dilemma by our personal relations with our opponents. If we ask you to take the usual straightforward Fabian course of voting for the fifteen candidates you think best, whilst our opponents vote their "ticket" on scientific electioneering principles, it is possible that the three or four of our number whose work, though of great value to the Society, is least in the public eye, may be defeated, and we ourselves, though elected, placed in a minority. On the other hand, if we ask you to vote for our eleven *only*, we are inviting you to withhold votes from the best four of our opponents, of whose claims we cannot speak too highly, though they have compelled us to resist them on this question of Fabian neutrality in the war. All I can do is to place the situation clearly before you, and leave it to your judgment.

But at all events, I beg you not to let an incomplete result occur through your abstention from voting. Last year hundreds of members did not take the trouble to fill their voting papers and send them in. It did not matter then, as there was nothing at stake. It matters very much now—so much, that I, for the first time at any Executive election, go so far as to canvass you. Not, believe me, that I want to sway you to one side or the other. But I *do* want you to vote somehow; so that we may know how we stand.

Excuse this long letter from

yours faithfully
G. Bernard Shaw

To CHARLES CHARRINGTON

Piccard's Cottage. St Catherine's. Guildford
[A/4]   15th April 1900

[Charrington produced a performance of *Widowers' Houses* at the Crystal Palace Theatre on May Day for the International Labour Festival. He lectured to the Fabian Society on 27th April on "Communal Recreation."]

You dont say where the rehearsal is to be. However, no matter, as I cant go.

I have no fear as to Welch letting anybody get a turn at Lickcheese. He will be only too glad to repeat his best show, so far. . . .

Dont thunder on your vowels. Your voice is much bigger than any of the other voices naturally. Knock them over by the sharpness of your consonants, and dont throw away any of the natural refinement of your tone. The ring of that is the real note of superiority: the artificial woolly boom is all nonsense, and sounds as if it would be bad in other parts and so prevent you getting engagements. What is wanted in the part is authority. Get it in your own way; and never mind my literary effects in the stage directions. Be not too tame neither &c &c &c.

I shall be here until the middle of May except Wednesdays to Saturday mornings, when I shall be in town. Not next week, though— indeed not until after your Fabian Lecture, as the Vestry has a three weeks' recess. . . .

GBS

To YORKE STEPHENS

Piccard's Cottage. Guildford
[H/40]   24th April 1900

[Yorke Stephens and James Welch presented *You Never Can Tell* for a series of six matinées at the Strand Theatre commencing 2nd May, in which Stephens appeared as Valentine and Welch as the Waiter.]

Dear Yorke Stephens

All right: let it stand at that for the present. If there is any prospect of further business at the end of the first week or fortnight we can make a more studied agreement. Meanwhile, I hereby license you to give a dozen matinees of You Never Can Tell at the Strand theatre before the 15th May 1900. . . .

As I have not received any calls, I conclude that I am not wanted at the rehearsals. I shall purposely keep away from the first performance, because if I go, there will probably be a call for a speech from me. Now my speeches are all very well in their way; but they have the effect of obliterating the manager and preventing him from saying a word or two about his experiment in matinees. It is important that you should do this. Tell them if they want me that you are very sorry, but that I have flatly refused to sit out one of my own plays twice. Then say that the matinees are a little experiment by you and your friends and colleagues to play a few plays that you think *ought* to be played to a special audience (meaning the talented and delightful assemblage you are now addressing) who *ought* to see them. Say that dramatic art is not a thing that can live by great popular successes alone, but by an occasional word of appreciation and encouragement for efforts like the present. You can conclude by an apology for Jimmy's bad acting.

Seriously, you must make a speech of some sort, to emphasize your lead, as I have received a heap of paragraphs mentioning Lewis Waller and a lot of other people as the leaders of the undertaking.

yours faithfully
G. Bernard Shaw

To H. M. HYNDMAN

[G.u/2; X/165]

10 Adelphi Terrace WC
28th April 1900

[Hyndman had written to Shaw on 12th April: "The truth is, my dear Shaw, that as all the men in this country who have any wide scientific or literary reputation outside England (with one or two exceptions) are on our side in this matter, as well as all the distinguished foreigners, with scarcely a single exception, you must necessarily take up the championship of the capitalist gang & their agents. These eccentricities give you pleasure & as they amuse other people nothing is hurt but your reputation for having any principles at all" (BM). John Thomas North (1841–96), known as the Nitrate King, and Barnett Barnato (1852–97) were well-known speculators. When Barnato's bubble burst, he committed suicide. Henry ("Harry") Quelch (1858–1913) was a leader in the Social Democratic Federation, active in the I.L.P. and in the new Labour Representation Committee, founded in 1899. Alfred Milner (1854–1925), created a Baron in 1901, was an administrator in South Africa who in 1899 was Governor of Cape of Good Hope. Auguste Maquet (1813–88) was the collaborator of Dumas *père* in many plays and novels.]

Dear Hyndman

The main objection to your letters is that there is so much life in them that they seduce one into answering them—uselessly, as you are quite irreclaimable.

However, you must not think that I disagree with you merely because disagreement is my pose. I am not a mere intellectual anti-gravitation man. Even if I were, you will admit that Jingo Imperialism at the present moment hardly satisfies the craving for an eccentric attitude—would it did! The real root of our differences is that you are a moralist: you see the world in terms of guilt and innocence, virtue and vice, with feelings of indignant abhorrence or enthusiastic championship, leading to a treatment of every case by expiation and retaliation or honor & glory. Now I am a pure natural-history student, and feel no more indignation against [John D.] Rockefeller or Rhodes than I do against a dog following a fox. I know the capitalist—a poor devil who follows the slot of money without the faintest consciousness of himself either as a beast of prey, or as a captain of industry. Ask him to give you an *idea* of himself; and he will stutter out something about the golden rule and our Lord Jesus Christ, with perfect sincerity. He preys on the proletariat as a cat preys on mice, through his instinct for gain. Even though you would restrain him from such predaciousness, that is no reason why you shouldnt take him up & stroke him and pet him if he is a pleasant animal (which he sometimes is) instead of allowing your instinct for righteousness to transform you into a talented terrier, and worrying him? It is out of that sort of worrying that the whole evil comes. You *will* resist moral evil. So, please observe, will Rockefeller. But, you will say, Rockefeller is robbing the poor all the time. So are you. So am I. Society leaves us no personal alternative except death, and no social alternative at all. But it in no way compels us to call for sacrifices to expiate the evil. If Rockefeller *deserves* hanging (an expression which belongs to your moral system) so does every man who would do the same as Rockefeller if he got the chance—say $99\frac{99}{100}\%$ of his indignant fellowmen. You cannot hang everybody, including yourself; and yet moralism leads to that or nothing.

Now Kruger is more than a moralist: he is a prophet of Jehovah, who is morality deified. The tide in the affairs of men came to Kruger after the Raid, when he had a respite sufficient to found his Republic to all eternity by playing the statesman. But he had no statesmanship. He saw that the Outlander was morally the inferior of the Boer. He proceeded to assert the supremacy of the moral man, and to arm himself for its defence by military force. To this day he has no word to say except that God, who implanted that instinct in him, will make it victorious in battle.

At such a point, you rally to Kruger. At the same point I perceive that Jehovah and Mammon must fight it out. And as Mammon can be developed into a Socialist power in proportion as men become Socialistically minded, whereas Jehovah makes any such change of mind impossible, and stands for the false categories of moral good and evil in nature, and consequently for implacable war, punishment, enmity, aggression & repression between men, my sympathies are with Mammon, his instinctive greed for gold & diamonds being far less dangerous than the reason and virtue which, on the moralist system, makes Man, as Mephistopheles says, beastlier than any beast. Jehovah is mighty; for he has his chain on men's minds. Your wretched Norths & Barnatos & Rothschilds have nothing but the cash nexus, by the utmost tightening of which they cannot get ten hours real good work out of the British workman in a week.

But the inconveniences of your moral system do not lame you on the South African question. They do nearer home. Once you start your system of reprobation & damnation, you are forced to recognize that the Socialists themselves are as bad as the capitalists. You teach our excellent old Quelch to divide his fellow creatures into sheep & goats, and to put Milner & Chamberlain among the goats. Instantly Quelch says simply & logically, Behold all their goatish qualities in Keir Hardie and J.R.Macdonald, & Jeremiahs them accordingly, with the usual harmonious results. What is to me a Scotch peculiarity to be reckoned with & suffered like the east wind is to Quelch an iniquity to be denounced & cast out.

You see, I really have a point of view, which will appear criminal to you if you take [it] seriously, and only amusing if you don't, but which will at least, if you once fairly catch it, explain me as a consistent, persistent doctrinaire and born preacher. You question the political and economic side of our institutions, never the moral side. In fact, [it is] the moralist side of our institutions that is never questioned: it is reaffirmed in every attack on the hypocrisy of Capital. Now the moralist side being the very one which I attack, I have the air of attacking everything for the sake of singularity. I find Marx as old as Amos—Das Kapital a wrathful Old Testament with new Blue Books and nothing else. I campaign against Shakespear, who is as old as Ecclesiastes. I dwell on the fact that Nietzsche's Tran[s]valuation of Moral Values & On t'other side of Good & Evil were anticipated by Blake, who boldly called the powers of mischief God & his Angels and the powers of well

162

being Satan & his devils. To you this has seemed the same old trick of affected singularity; but to that I reply as old Dumas used to reply to Maquet & the people who said his novels were manufactured by his apprentices: "Very good, friend Maquet," said Alick: "you have found out my trick: all you have to do is to produce your Musketeers & your Monte Cristo." Just so I said to the people who declared that my plays were mere topsyturvyisms, "Try the formula yourself, and see whether you can produce anything like a Shaw play by it." The fact is, when a man keeps up a joke for so long as you have known me, either he is mad or there is some kernel of earnestness in it. Your sense of humor may tempt you to embrace the former alternative; but I assure you I am only mad nor' nor' west: otherwise my views could not be so annoying as they sometimes are.

I write all this because if I were in conflict with you always without any discoverable conflict of social theory, you would simply put me down as personally unfriendly. The truth is that you are an economic revolutionary on a medieval moral basis of pure chivalry—Bayard educated by Marx. I am a moral revolutionary, interested, not in the class war, but in the struggle between human vitality and the artificial system of morality, and distinguishing, not between capitalist & proletarian, but between moralist and natural historian.

Your spirit is sufficiently choice to have glimpses of what I mean occasionally: otherwise I shouldn't waste this apologia pro mia vita on you[.]

yrs ever
[G. Bernard Shaw]

To GRANT RICHARDS

10 Adelphi Terrace WC
[X/135]   8th May 1900

My dear G.R.

... And now, what about *Three Plays for Puritans*? It is going to involve a lot of composition, and at least three plates, at the old price. You have not done so amazingly well with *Plays P. and Unpl.* (an edition of 1200 in two years) as to feel certain that this book is going to be a treasure. I offer to pay for it (instead of Clark), and hold you harmless. The public and the press won't know. The honor and glory of the thing will be the same. You do not deign to reply on the point, possibly because your feelings are hurt. I don't care about your feelings, except in so far as they seem likely to ruin you, which would be extremely inconvenient to me. I want to know definitely and at once, because if it is to be commission, I must set about the printing at once; and if it is to be as before, I must draw up an agreement, which, this time, must be properly considered and executed in spite of your shrieks. If you won't be businesslike with other people, you *shall* with me: I'll make you, if only for the sake of your education. *Do* wake up.

G.B.S.

To CHARLES CHARRINGTON

[A/12]

10 Adelphi Terrace WC
11th May 1900

If I can induce Ellen Terry & Forbes Robertson to play "Captain Brassbound's Conversion" for the Stage Society this season, will there be room & funds for it? Of course it would be better to hold it for the opening of next season; but we shant be able to get it then, whereas there is just a chance that it might be feasible now; and it would be a good advertisement for all parties. You could play the judge and Welch the Hooligan.

Do not run away at the Fabian with the notion that my chatter about having no principles is a sort of worn out red waistcoat belonging to the youth of the movement. I am more than ever convinced that the source of our confusion about the war is the pouring of our new political ideas into the old moral bottles. I urge this on you more particularly because it concerns you personally. The other fellows are not prevented from doing their day's work by their American ethics. You are. If you could get your mind free, you could write and write easily. At present you are lamed by judging everybody and everything by a standard which not only keeps you drugged with virtuous indignation, but which, applied to your own career, reduces it to infamy. Convert me to your opinion of Milner & Chamberlain, for instance (the Redcliffe Square opinion) and I shall decline to continue your acquaintance. You have got to get this straight, somehow: either live up to your opinions or find the justification of your life. So dont indignate at the executive: there is more method in my frivolity than you think.

GBS

164

To YORKE STEPHENS

Blackdown Cottage. Haslemere
[H/40]   21st May 1900

[Frank Curzon (1868–1927), former actor and partner of Charles Hawtrey, was at this time the manager of several West End theatres, including the Strand. *Facing the Music*, a farce by J.H.Darnley, had been running at the Strand since 1st February. Mabel Terry-Lewis (1872–1957), the daughter of Ellen Terry's sister Kate, retired from the stage on her marriage in 1904, but returned to the theatre in the 1930's.]

Dear Yorke Stephens

What the Strand proposal means is that the summer is emptying the theatres, and Mr Curzon, having clung to Facing the Music to the last—even to the extent of refusing you the Saturday matinee for You Never Can Tell—now proposes to save Jimmy's salary and the author's fees, and get a leading man for nothing, by putting up You Never Can Tell during the hot weather to pay his rent and electric lighting bill with. Our profits are easily computed: there wont be any. But there will be a larger contribution toward the expenses of the management than Facing the Music would bring with Father James at a salary.

Tell Mr Curzon that no play of mine is going into an evening bill at the end of May, under any circumstances whatever, short of an advance of £2,500 to the author. The 25th March is my latest date for a summer production, and the 1st of September my earliest for a winter one.

If he cares to make a serious proposal for a regular production in September, with certain comparatively expensive changes in the cast, new scenery, and everything firstrate, I am open to that or anything else in the regular way of business, though I shouldnt advise him to do anything of the sort, because nothing but a very stylish production at a very stylish theatre, with handsome advertising, will give the play a chance. But in any case no fresh move can be made at the West End before September.

Why do you not make Curzon keep up the matinée business? There is Stevenson and Henley's Robert Macaire, which would fit you and James to perfection. You could not lose much by it; and it would get you and J.W. a fresh batch of interesting notices (Stevenson is still booming in the literary world), which would confirm the impression made by the Y.N.C.T. notices, and fix the combination in the public mind as ripe for management. Even Widowers' Houses would keep a

165

few afternoons filled now that the Housing Question is in the air (tracts on it are selling like hot cakes); but the objection is that there is no part for you in it: you would be perfectly ghastly as the leading chump: besides, the Crystal Palace cast have the first call on the parts. They did it *very* well. Still, this generation of critics has not seen James as Lickcheese; and I should like them to before he has learnt the part and spoiled the unexpectedness of it.

Valentine has been a classic success this time; Miss [Mabel] Terry Lewis was the right Gloria for you. You are such a confoundedly impressionable character that you take a lot of casting and mounting. Two doors in a scene hurl you into farce; a leading lady with her eyes too much made up precipitates you into melodrama; and you get attacks of the Prisoner of Zenda (mostly in the knees) without any provocation at all. The Terry infant somehow drove away all these adulterations, and revived the original Yorke Stephens, who was a much better actor than you think. He seems to have been in great force at the recent matinées. But he'll never be seen again in the part without a complete Clandon family to support him, if I have any say in the selection. Casting a play is a perfectly different matter to finding people who will be good in the separate parts. Miss [Audrey] Ford was good, in her way, as Dolly; but was she Gloria's sister or Mrs Clandon's daughter? Miss [Elsie] Chester was good, in her way, as Mrs Clandon; but was she the woman who was too intellectual to live with Herman Vezin? [George] Raiemond is not a worse actor of elderly solicitors in Strand farces than [Sydney] Warden—rather better, in fact—but oh Lord! what a disastrous change it was!

Now they were all excellent people; but I will be boiled alive sooner than let the play go on again with them.

yrs ever
G. Bernard Shaw

P.S. I return to 10 Adelphi Terrace on Tuesday afternoon, coming back here Saturday morning. This place is miles away from a post-office: hence the delay in receiving and answering your letter.

To IAN ROBERTSON

[10 Adelphi Terrace WC]
[G.u/4]   [Undated: *c.* 23rd May 1900]

[Ian Robertson (1859–1936) was an actor who frequently served as stage manager for his brother Johnston Forbes-Robertson (1853–1937). The latter had appeared in *The Moonlight Blossom*, a Japanese romance by G. Chester-Bailey Fernald, which he produced at the Prince of Wales Theatre on 21st September 1899. He had earlier produced *Nelson's Enchantress* by Risden Home at the Avenue Theatre on 11th February 1897. Johnston Forbes-Robertson's most recent production of *Macbeth* had been offered at the Lyceum Theatre on 17th September 1898. *The Devil's Disciple* was first performed by Forbes-Robertson on 3rd September 1900 at Leeds; the tour ended on 14th December at Peckham.]

Dear Ian Robertson

The Devil's Disciple is still available; but the question is, how to nail up J.F.R. in such a manner as to create some sort of certainty that he will produce it. A play of mine is to him only a *pis aller*: if he can find any alternatives, however unpromising, from Moonlight Blossoms and Nelsons to Macbeths, he will embrace them with a sigh of relief and leave me with my market spoiled. Now it will always be possible to find such alternatives: in fact, I can find him a few myself, all congenial, gentlemanly, and certain to fail. He will never be in a better position to venture on a play of mine than he has been for the last two or three years; so I take his present reluctant resolution to swallow the horrors of the Devil's Disciple as a mere act of desperation, the result of ill health and discouragement. Presently he will get well; the world will smile on him; backers will produce money; authors will rain Moonlight Blossoms; he will fall in love with somebody who won't or can't play Judith; and then where shall I be? Shelved until he has withered all the Blossoms, lost all the money, tired of the leading lady, and is again lying exhausted under the maccaroni tree at Palermo. Then he will languidly ask me whether I could not alter the last act of the D's D so as to make it like a Delaroche picture. I dont blame him any more than I blame a baby for objecting to take physic; but can you seriously ask me, after my experience of him, to tie the play up for him in any way?

Let us wait until autumn; and then, if I have not disposed of the play otherwise, and if he has not got another play after his own heart, I daresay we can settle the matter without any difficulty. In the meantime he will be all the happier, and consequently the more thoroughly & rapidly convalescent, for feeling that there is still a chance of escape.

Do you think, by the way, that he would, for Ellen Terry's sake, play the leading part in my last play one Sunday evening for the Stage Society, she playing the lady, if I could bring such a thing about? It seems to me to be her only chance of "creating" a part which I wrote for her, and which she dearly loves (or pretends to), since she is, as far as her regular professional work is concerned, tied to the Lyceum.

yrs ever
[G.Bernard Shaw]

To G.F.McCLEARY

[H/1]

10 Adelphi Terrace WC
24th May 1900

[Dr George F.McCleary (1867–1962), Medical Officer of Health for Battersea, was one of the pioneers in England of the maternity and child welfare services. He was preparing Fabian Tract 95, *Municipal Bakeries*. His assistant may have been Miss G.Rose Armstrong, a Fabian. The *Clarion* article was "Shaw on South Africa," published on 26th May.]

Dear McCleary

I have been for some time in possession of a mass of literature by you and Miss Armstrong on the subject of Bakehouses, about which I know nothing. No vestryman ever does. The Fabian Publishing Committee, however, handed it over to me to read. Later on it came to the conclusion that it wanted only a leaflet on the subject, money for tracts being a bit short just now. . . .

Now as to your letter of the 15th April. You will presently see an article of mine in the Clarion which will perhaps make my position clearer. I have always said that the name Imperialism is a piece of theatrical claptrap, and that the slightest show of imperiousness on the part of England would be like shaking a tree loaded with ripe apples. But we have to take names as they catch on; and they generally catch on wrongly, from the etymological point of view, when the right handling of them requires classical scholarship. My one offence in the matter has been that I am an old Socialist, inveterately anti-Liberal, anti-Individualistic, anti-Jehovistic, anti-Independence-Liberty-Nationality and all the rest of it, and above all, boilingly contemptuous of the common English plan of dealing with social evils by catching a scapegoat, overwhelming him with virtuous indignation, and calling that politics. When you are a Medical Officer of Health (by the way, did I hear that you are one already?), you will not, I trust, propose to extirpate diphtheria by catching all the doctors who make money out of the epidemics, and denouncing them in the press and from the platform as murderers. That would be about as sensible as the Socialist plan

168

of denouncing the capitalists as the makers of this war, and implying that all will be well when Chamberlain is thrown out of office and Rhodes ruined. I have no patience with such rubbish.

Furthermore I regard war as wasteful, demoralizing, unnecessary, and ludicrously and sordidly inglorious in its reality. This is my unconditional opinion. I *dont* mean war in a bad cause, or war against liberty, or war with any other qualification whatever: I mean war. I recognize no right of the good man to kill the bad man or to govern the bad man. The Boers have gone to war in defence of these rights. We have gone to war from pugnacity, greed and overfeeding. If the Boers had had any able statesmen, there would have been no war. If we had any statesmen, instead of the parcel of grown-up schoolboys of whom Milner is a type, there would be no war. What of that? If the sky had fallen we should all have caught larks: that is all. If both parties regard the sword as the final arbiter, they must accept the consequences when the sword is drawn. If there were no such institution as war, no Socialist would be on the side of the Boers in this question any more than he would be on the side of Rhodes. I do not see then why we should take sides now that there is war. I am sorry they fight just as I am sorry they course hares and shoot pheasants and eat meat and believe in witch-inoculations as a charm against enteric fever. But why that should make me a pro-Boer when the Boer is just as bloodguilty as the Briton, and when I dont believe anything that the Boer believes, and dont believe that his pet institutions can ever produce anything but sordid misery for the mass of mankind, is a question which I leave you to answer. The fact is, every Englishman makes a fool of himself over this war on one side or the other. I, not being an Englishman, have kept my head; and there is the head and front of my offending. For the rest, see the Clarion of this week or next, and remember me to Mrs McCleary, and retain as much as you can of your former well deserved esteem for

yours ever
G. Bernard Shaw

To CHARLES CHARRINGTON

Blackdown Cottage. Haslemere
[A/4]   6th June 1900

[In an obituary of Granville-Barker (1877-1946), Shaw noted that, "in looking about for an actor suitable for the part of the poet in Candida . . .

I had found my man in a very remarkable person named Harley Granville-Barker. He was at that time 23 years of age . . . I saw him play in Hauptmann's Friedensfest and immediately jumped at him for the poet in Candida. His performance of this part—a very difficult one to cast—was, humanly speaking, perfect." Shaw did not mention, however, that Barker was Charrington's choice, not his. *Candida* was performed for the first time in London, by the Stage Society, on 1st July.]

I have often seen Granville Barker act, and as I cannot remember him in the least, and *can* remember [Henry V.] Esmond, I conclude that Esmond is the better man. I am prepared for a struggle on your part and Janet's to induce me to consent to everything most ruinous to both of us. But I WONT. Unless I can get a Eugene of Esmond's standing, the play shall not be done. You can put up Widowers' Houses instead. . . .

Yes: the Strand was a pretty poor business; and it *could* have been done decently if they had had the brains to want to do it. Kate Terry was quite available, for one thing.

Forbes Robertson is so utterly play-bankrupt that he is going on tour with the Devil's Disciple.

I am losing the power as well as the will to be either civil or reasonable when a performance of my plays is proposed. Wish they'd let me alone.

GBS

To CHARLES CHARRINGTON

Blackdown Cottage. Haslemere
[D/4]   7th June 1900

[Esmond was 31 years old. J.H.Atkinson had played Burgess in the Manchester performance. Lionel Brough (1837–1909) and George William Anson (1847–1920) were well-known, reliable character actors.]

Esmond *will* play Eugene: I have it on Janet's own authority. And he *shall* play it. No doubt he's too old. So is Janet. So are you. It will be a sere and yellow, bouncing and matronly business. But it will help the S.S. and help you and help me to have an actor of Esmond's standing in the cast: others will follow his lead who would certainly not follow G.B's. You will be jealous, of course, on J's account; but I dont care: if Eugene plays Morell & Candida off the stage, he will exactly fulfil my intention.

What about Burgess? Is your Manchester man available? If not, you had better ask Lionel Brough or Anson or somebody like that (though he'll ruin the play).

GBS

To CHARLES CHARRINGTON

Blackdown Cottage. Haslemere

[A/4]   9th June 1900

[Lionel Belmore had created the rôle of Burgess in the Charringtons' 1897 tour. He performed the rôle again in the London production on 1st July. Audrey Ford, who had played Dolly Clandon in the recent production of *You Never Can Tell*, was the wife of James Welch.]

Do you suppose, now that I am money-independent, that I am not going to have its value in all sorts of check? Will nothing teach you the arts of life? The first of them is never to deny an accusation: *embrace it* and make a merit of it.

If Belmore is available and you are satisfied with him, let him have the first call on the part by all means. When I saw him rehearse he had not realized that Burgess was not a conventional joskin; but I dare say he got over that.

As to Eugene, he was not created with the charitable purpose of helping novices to make reputations. Once the play is launched, you can cast Marcellus for Hamlet in it as much as you like; but for the trial trip I prefer a captain who has earned his certificates. On your plan, I might let Miss Audrie Ford play Candida, just to shew that my millions have not spoiled me.

Charles Charrington: you are—when I am not at your elbow—an Ass. But you have other qualities which will pull you through with the help of a little brutality from

yrs

GBS

To CHARLES CHARRINGTON

10 Adelphi Terrace WC

[D/4]   11th June 1900

[Gerhart Hauptmann's *Friedensfest*, in a translation by Janet Achurch and Dr C. E. Wheeler under the title *The Coming of Peace*, was presented by the

171

Stage Society on 10th June. Barker had appeared as Richard II in William Poel's production on 11th November 1899 in the Lecture Theatre, Burlington Gardens. The Stage Society programme announced a forthcoming performance of "Candida: A Pleasant Play."]

I withdraw my observations concerning G.B., whom I certainly never saw before. He is too clever to be so really boyish as E; but if E. fails us, he will be an excellent and rather more interesting substitute. I came up yesterday alone for the performance, with a horrible headache, which the roasting journey made worse. H.A. Jones sat out the show with me: he says G.B. played Richard II very well on some recent occasion. Your Lear was quite Homeric: when you *do* take advice (as to make-up variety) you do not take it by halves. Dorothy Hammond is a remarkably docile person: she gave Janet at second hand amazingly well. The whole thing was very well managed: no cast was ever made more of. Augusta [Gertrude Lovel] stuck it on a little too much, I thought. Graham Brown seems equal to all occasions.

By the way, Candida is announced as a Pleasant Play. I haven't a copy at hand just now; but if I am not mistaken all the plays are described in the table of contents by their proper class-names: Pleasant & Unpleasant is a book title.

Friedensfest was so foreign in many ways that it occasionally produced the impression of a spoof tragedy. As a whole, it was clear and forcible. In detail, I found myself utterly unable to explain it to H.A.J., who was quite addled by it, as he came in late for the exposition.

GBS

PS I am off to Blackdown again until Wednesday.

To MRS RICHARD MANSFIELD

Blackdown Cottage. Haslemere
[H/21]   12th June 1900

[Mrs Mansfield had been negotiating with Shaw for the American rights of *You Never Can Tell*. Alice Kauser (1872–1945) was a prominent dramatic agent and playbroker in New York. Harrison Grey Fiske (1861–1942) was a theatrical manager, playwright, and director. His wife, Minnie Maddern Fiske (1865–1932), starred under her husband's management for many years. Her performances in *A Doll's House*, *Rosmersholm*, and *Ghosts* did much to

172

make Ibsen's work known in America. Langdon Mitchell (1862–1935) was a popular adaptor of literary works for the stage. In addition to Hardy's *Tess*, he adapted *Vanity Fair* and *The Kreutzer Sonata*. Norman Hapgood (1868–1937), American journalist and critic, had published an article "The Theatrical Syndicate" in the *International Quarterly* in January 1900.]

Dear Mrs Mansfield

Your letter has just arrived. I thought you would find the play difficult to cast. Not that the parts are hard to fit separately. But when you have got a capital Dolly and an excellent Mrs Clandon, you find that they are not a bit like mother and daughter. The Clandon family is the difficulty. Half a dozen cheap, scratch performances of it have just been given here at the Strand Theatre, with great commotion in the press, and immense apparent success (really two hundred dollar houses and the like). But I didn't go to see it: the rehearsals lacerated my very soul—Crampton (Hermann Vezin) the most intellectual person in the cast, Mrs Clandon impressively melodramatic, Dolly very clever as a cockney Belle of New York, and so on: the items all right, the total damnable. Yorke Stephens was so good as Valentine at the private Sunday performance by the Stage Society that I had to consent to these public ones so as to let him get his press notices; but I altogether refused to let the thing go beyond the six matinees.

Charles Frohman saw it, and saw, too, how HE could make a great play of it. Fortunately Miss Marbury stood between him and the first results of this audacity. Finally I said I should be delighted to see his version if he would submit it. He then said he only wished to communicate his ideas. On this I communicated *my* ideas, which were of a high and mighty nature. But the vigilant Elisabeth intercepted them, and said we two great men should meet. The meeting has not come yet. And so the matter is hung up for the present. Elisabeth, thirsting for percentages, naturally wants Frohman to take up the play; but she heroically admitted that you would understand it and handle it better than anybody.

Another story. Ellen Terry shewed my last play "Captain Brass-bound's Conversion" to Mrs Fiske. Mrs Fiske told Mr Fiske to get it for her. Mr Fiske instructed Miss Alice Kauser to negotiate with me. Alice went to Langdon Mitchell for an introduction to me. Then began a comedy of errors. Miss Kauser mistook my address and her first letters miscarried. The others were consequently unintelligible. I was bewildered, Mrs Minnie Maddern grew impatient, Mitchell wrote, Alice cabled, Fiske cabled; and I could not make out who was who nor which was what. In desperation I referred them all to Miss Marbury.

Fiske cabled that he would not negotiate with an emissary of the accursed Trust. I thought this was from Alice, and exploded with the most destructive violence. Alarums and excursions ensued; and finally Fiske wrote to say that my proposals and terms were perfectly satisfactory, but that he would die sooner than enter into a contract with a truculent scoundrel (ME) whose evil reputation in America was only too well deserved. With reference to a remark made by me to Miss Kauser that it didnt matter about the Trust, as Mrs Fiske would probably presently make terms with it, he said that I got such dastardly ideas from the conduct of persons whose characters were as atrocious as my own. I suspect the initials of one of the atrocious persons here alluded to must be R.M., for Fiske evidently has Trust on the brain at present. He then sent me a copy of Norman Hapgood's article (which I of course knew all about); and so the matter dropped. I rather like Fiske: he is not afraid to pour out his indignant soul.

As likely as not he will have the satisfaction of seeing Klaw and Erlanger break with Frohman, and Frohman ruin himself by a Napoleonic campaign single handed; but though the men may fall, the Trust, as a development in organization, will last. With all its faults, it is better than the wretched anarchy and waste of our system.

In the end I believe *you* will have to play Brassbound, in which the hero is a mere doormat for the heroine. Richard will be simply your leading man.

My next play will be a Don Juan—an immense play, but not for the stage of this generation.

yours sincerely
G. Bernard Shaw

P.S. We have taken a cottage in Surrey for the summer, in a very pretty place, four miles from the railway. Why not pawn the boy for a month, put Richard on board-wages, and run over to see us, leaving all your worries behind?

To GERTRUDE KNIGHT

[A/4]

10 Adelphi Terrace WC
20th June 1900

[Gertrude Knight was Mrs Ian Robertson. Anderson was played by a distinguished character actor named H. Assheton Tonge (d.1927). The "leading lady" was Gertrude Elliott (1874–1950), who became Mrs Johnston Forbes-Robertson on 22nd December 1900.]

My dear Mrs Ian

They must wait: I begin to think the final text of The Devil's Disciple will arrive about fifteen hours before the curtain goes up. I am working at it like an exhausted man finishing a race against time. The existing copies are scrawled to pieces; and my wife is trying to decipher my corrections & produce fair copies which I must again correct for the printer. Forbes will get, not a prompt copy, but a six shilling novel to read. A frightful business, but worth doing. I know the delay means worry; but worry, misgiving, regret for having ever touched the hateful thing, are only the preliminary stages of the final Shaw fever in which the performances will consummate themselves. When people do my plays, their skins come off on the twelfth night, as if they had had scarlet fever.

I am very anxious about the casting of the part of Anderson: he must be a *very* good man. Tell Ian to look up Hogarth's portrait of Captain Coram, and get me a man like that, only a few years younger and a few pounds stronger.

Who is to be the leading lady?

In haste
yours sincerely
G. Bernard Shaw

To WILLIAM ARCHER

[A/2]

Blackdown Cottage. Haslemere
8th July 1900

. . . I am very sorry the Stage Society gave you up just when they had a chance of getting you to a performance. There has been a box always reserved for you hitherto; but I suppose your persistent neglect, the demands for seats for Candida, and the growing grumblings of the members at reservations of seats for anybody (since they have to scramble), broke down their hopes that you would come. I took it for granted that they would ask you, and so took no steps, worse luck.

Yes: the poet—Granville Barker—was the success of the piece. It was an astonishing piece of luck to hit on him. He is a very clever fellow—very young, but very expert—began with his mother (elocutionizing) at six, and has been on the stage 9 years. Charrington

175

began well as Morell; but he soon became so deeply affected by the part that his powers of speech departed; he wallowed in it internally; and if there had been 5 acts instead of 3, he would have been speechless in the 4th & motionless in the 5th. And as emotion takes a bilious form with him, he became uglier as he felt more deeply, and ended as a clerical Caliban, putting "Prossy's complaint" beyond all credibility. Janet has now lost all power of doing anything but her own particular *io son io*, which is not Candida's by any means; but her ancient flame of genius finally kindled, and she won at the post, so to speak.

. . . I have had to *conduct* the rehearsals for Forbes Robertson; and this for my credit's sake I had to do well—a matter involving elaborate study beforehand.

GBS

To WILLIAM ARCHER

Blackdown Cottage. Haslemere
[A/2]   9th July 1900

[The *Humane Review* article was "A Conflict Between Science and Common Sense" in April. Joseph H. Levy, the editor of *Personal Rights*, had written in the 16th April issue: "It is a distinct disservice to the humanitarian cause to make the inhumane conduct of some scientific men a reason for running amock at science generally, and to associate care for the lower animals with the statement that the moon is 87 miles distant from the earth. We do not deny that Mr. Bernard Shaw does this clowning with more than Grimaldian drollery; but it is quite out of place."

Henry Perigal (1801–98) was a fellow of the Royal Astronomical Society. Shaw retold the story of this meeting with Perigal in a "Foundation Oration" before the Union Society of University College, London, on 18th March 1920 (see *Platform and Pulpit*, 1962). H. G. Wells's *Love and Mr Lewisham* had been published in June. Alfred Sutro's *Cave of Illusion*, published by Samuel French, had not been produced professionally. Archer's article in the *Morning Leader* on 7th July was "The Dukes of the Drama," a witty contrast between the "parochial" Ibsen, as British critics had labelled him, and the snobbish "Playwright-Princes" of London.]

To resume—the object of the Humane Review article was to call attention to the fact that we have slipped into a doctrine of Omniscience & Infallibility as regards Science, of precisely the same kind as the old doctrine as to Religion.

176

Also to shew that the parrallel (or rather the identity) is so complete, that even the people who imagine themselves in a critical attitude towards Science, are shocked when anybody jokes about it, just as Deists used to be shocked at the jokes of Voltaire.

I have succeeded with ludicrous exactness. Even "Personal Rights," which has been denouncing "the medical priesthood" for years, and is edited by a man who poked fun at the Bible every week in the National Reformer, protests with horror against my "clowning" in the presence of this ineffably serious & sacred subject.

And I observe, with a chuckle, that even you, in the matter of the fireproof floor, are so absolutely convinced of the validity of the strain calculating system that you assume that the engineer made "a mistake in his calculation," of which there is not the smallest evidence, the plain fact being that the moment a floor was introduced which was heavier than the old floors, the house came down and proved, as the bicycle and a hundred other things have proved, that in mechanics as in art, theory comes after practice, and is mostly a pure figment. Yet when people are told by a guide that Beauvais cathedral fell because it was top heavy, they ascribe that to the ignorance of the Middle Ages; but when the Forth Bridge collapses, they think there must have been a mistake in the calculation. Mind: I do not profess to be an expert in these matters: I simply point out the conclusions that would be drawn as a matter of common sense, if there were no superstition to be deferred to.

Even my joke about the moon is not altogether a joke, although it is jocular enough for the test abovementioned. The story about Broadstairs pier and old Perigal is perfectly true. He was an FRS; and I had exactly the same warrant for the validity of his geometric chuck calculation as for the Newtonian one: that is, none at all. As to the millions & billions of miles, they are of course as possible as millions & billions of inches or millionths of inches. But that the astronomic talk about them, and the popularity of that talk, is pure miracle-gaping megalomania, I have not the smallest doubt. The agreement among the physicists as to the measurements is as imaginary as the agreement about nitrogen, oxygen & carbon dioxide accounting for the atmosphere.

I rejoice to see that Wells, in his last book "Mr Lewisham" blows the gaff on the system of proving theories to students by shewing them faked experiments. He introduces a spirit medium [James Chaffery] (who professes himself a pupil of mine!) who defends his impostures on the ground that they are the easiest way of teaching the truths of spiritualism, exactly as the professors who fake their experiments in

177

the St Januarius manner contend that it is the easiest way of teaching students the truths of science.

I see by your article that you cannot get science on to a purely secular plane; but that will come later on.

Your article on Ibsen & the Pinero-Jones dukes has given unqualified delight to all & sundry.

I have been reading Sutro's Cave of Illusion. *When* will people realize that [of all] undramatic and stupid no-thoroughfares of subjects adultery is quite the worst? Sutro could write quite a decent play if he could only get away from it.

I pant to redress the moral balance by beginning my Don Juan.

GBS

To ELLEN TERRY

[Blackdown Cottage. Haslemere]
[U(A)/10; X/117]   10th July 1900

[Edith Craig played Miss Proserpine Garnett in the performance of *Candida* on 1st July. In the production of *The Devil's Disciple*, E.W.Garden (1845–1939), a veteran of 36 years on the stage, was rehearsing as the Sergeant, but the part was soon taken over by a young actor named Leon Quartermaine (1876–1967). The silly brother, Christy, was played by W.Graham Browne (1870–1937).]

In my haste I left your last letter only half answered.

Edy pulled off the typist successfully—how, I dont exactly know. I believe she actually worked at it when it came to the point. The first impression she produces (professionally) on an author is that she is incapable of application, and lends a hand on the stage out of sheer good nature, to help a lame dog over a stile. At the rehearsals, she so utterly failed to express any indignation or surprise when she was called a liar by the poet, that we concluded that she had no moral sense, and had heard the same remark from you every day of her life since her birth.

All she had to say was "Oh!"; but she could only say "O," without any note of exclamation. "I'm saying it as loud as I can," she would observe, in reply to the agonized remonstrances of the author. She came to Adelphi Terrace for private instruction, and made a most agreeable impression on Charlotte, but received none whatever concerning the part from Charlotte's unfortunate husband. However, when

178

the night came, nervousness, or something that produced grip, seized her; and the audience was delighted. So was I, as she was pleasanter than the real Prossy, and kept the scene with the poet far nicer than she (the real one) could have done. . . .

I am nearly dead with work because of the wiliness of Forbes Robertson. I usually rely on my bad character to get me kept away from rehearsals; but Forbes politely begged me to *conduct* the first rehearsals & settle the business, besides reading the play. Of course the result is that everything goes on castors: at each rehearsal we take one act, and go through it twice. It goes without a hitch, and we are off in two hours to lunch, remarking, if you please, that the play is *quite easy*. And they think that since I only have to prepare an act at a time, it is holiday work for me, whereas with the Vestry, the Fabian, the printers (American & English) and a thousand other things, I am working like mad sixteen hours a day. Such is life—*my* life.

The only dreadful thing is that as far as I can ascertain there are only two men in the company who can act. Of course I have had to give them the two little parts (the sergeant & the silly brother) because these are comic & character parts; and you *must* have acting for comedy & character, whereas the big serious sympathetic parts take care of themselves with a little coaching. But imagine the feelings of a competent old professional, longing to play the big part & able to do it, when the author gives it to a goodhearted young duffer & puts him (the c. o. p.) into a mere bit of clowning. I experience agonies of remorse every time I meet E.W.Garden's eye: I long to atone by writing him a curtain raiser all to himself. Will you come & see us some day? I enclose a portrait of my latest love meeting me by moonlight alone.

GBS

To GILBERT MURRAY

Blackdown Cottage. Haslemere
28th July 1900

[A/36; X/166]

[Shaw attended a two days' conference on the housing of the working classes, held on 30th and 31st July, sponsored by the Sanitary Institute. He participated in the discussion on the second day. Mr Podsnap is a character in Dickens's *Our Mutual Friend*.]

Dear Murray

Where are you at present? I shall soon submit to you a few notes which I propose to append to Cæsar & Cleopatra.

My vestry is in recess; and I shall have a clean run down here for a few weeks now, though I have to go up for a Housing Conference on Monday & Tuesday.

I have carefully considered your comments on my history, and have modified accordingly. I am not quite convinced that I have overdone Cleopatra's ferocity. If she had been an educated lady of the time I should have made her quite respectable & civilized; but what I was able to gather about her father, the convivial Flute Blower, and other members of the household, joined with considerations of the petulance of royalty, led me to draw her as I did. I submit to you that if a dramatist, 2000 years hence, were to portray George IV as an ideal First Gentleman of Europe, with all the culture of his age upon him, he would miss his mark very considerably.

I also demur to your dictum that we have enough information about the ancient Britons to shew that they were not like Britannicus. In every line that I have come across concerning them I see Mr Podsnap. Surely, if they are like Britannicus now, after such romantic adulterations as the Roman & Norman invasions & conquests, how much more like him must they have been then, when they were the pure products of the climate? I am quite serious.

Further, I suggest that in the Gallic Wars, the style is not the man— at least, not the whole man. As a writer, Cæsar was an amateur, and could not have achieved complete self expression in letters even if he had lived now, when literature is no longer the game of style it was to Cicero's pals. If the dramatic stories about him are true, such as the burning of the letters after the final defeat of Cato, & the encounter with the mutinous legion—"Comrades: what do you want?" "Our discharge." "*Citizens:* you have it. Sorry you will not be able to share my triumph &c" & so on, not to mention his personal address in getting round people of all sorts & sizes, he *must* have been an adroit comedian. Now the style-man of the Gallic Wars is not a comedian; but neither is he a dandy; and Cæsar *was* a dandy. And I cannot conceive a great man as a grave man: to lack humor is to lack the universal solvent. If my Cæsar *can* be guyed, he is a failure. But I believe him to be authentic to the last comma.

yrs ever
G. Bernard Shaw

180

[Murray replied, on 30th July: "... I should like much to see the historical notes. You make a good defence at all points of my attack, especially about Cæsar. I own I dont understand him; and your reading may be the right one. Still the impression he made on a very clever and sensitive man like Cicero goes for a good deal. Cicero, if I remember right, does not say anything about his wit, but is amazed at his 'inhuman' power of work and attention to business, and at the inferiority of his followers. He did not invent the sarcasm of calling the soldiers 'Citizens.' It was vieux jeu. If I thought great men were like your Cæsar, I should like them better. I do not know if any Great Man has ever been generous or frank; Napoleon, Frederic, Cromwell & Co seem to me to be essentially mean and untruthful—like Chamberlain only vastly more so.

"As to Cleopatra, do not you think you ought at any rate to represent a highly civilised court and society surrounding her, even if she personally was a savage? I dont think, however, that she could conceivably have thought that Romans had trunks and many arms. Roman merchants and sailors were very common in Alexandria and elsewhere in Egypt; her dancing masters and tutors and many of her slaves would probably have been in Rome. However——.

"As to Britannicus, he is a sweet creature, and I would not have made him different" (BM).]

To EDWARD R. PEASE

[S/2]

Blackdown Cottage. Haslemere
23rd August 1900

[Webb's prediction about the general election was accurate. Parliament was dissolved on 25th September, and the election which followed, known as the "Khaki Election," gave a strong victory to the Right with the new parliament consisting of 402 Unionists, 186 Liberals, and 82 Nationalists. The Manifesto was *Fabianism and the Empire*, drafted by Shaw, which was published in an edition of 4000 copies on 2nd October.]

Dear Pease

Webb is strong in his faith that the election will be in October. I am working at the Manifesto, and hope to have it finished in a day or two. How are we to circulate it through the Executive? There isnt time to pass one copy from hand to hand: I am half inclined to get Standring to set it up and make myself personally responsible for the printing bill if it doesnt come off. However I shall send it round in MS to Webb and Hobson at all events as they will have to fill it in to some extent

181

with their specialities; and then I will send it to you and we will consider the next step.

I must come up to Town on Monday for the last rehearsals of the Devil's Disciple, and shall go to the office to confer with you.

yours ever
G. Bernard Shaw

To H. T. MUGGERIDGE

[A/1; X/167]
29 Fitzroy Square W
31st August 1900

[The Tichborne case was a fraudulent legal action brought in 1871–72 by Arthur Orton, who claimed to be the presumptive heir to the Tichborne family fortune. He was committed for perjury, and later confessed his guilt.]

Dear Muggeridge

You are in a devil of a hurry for an answer. I only got your letter six weeks ago, and now you set Pease on me like a bulldog. Six years is my usual time for answering letters—especially letters for lectures. . . . I have just finished drafting an Election Manifesto for the Fabian. It is a masterpiece, enormously long (a regular volume), and so extra-ultra-hyper-imperialist that you will turn the color of this paper [green] and fall down in convulsions when you read it. Nevertheless I hope for your vote for it. I am convinced that the Liberal agitation against the Government is greatly strengthening it, because nobody will dare to vote for a merely negative and impossibilist policy in the middle of a war. The Labor Leader's "white list" is the final stroke—the white flag held up to Liberalism at the moment when we are on the verge of victory over it. And all over this Kruger case which is only a second edition of the Tichborne case—a poor man being done out of his rights. We have got to teach both Kruger & Chamberlain that countries are not bits of private property to be fought for by dynasties, or races, or nations. You must have some International Socialism hammered into that obstinate walnut head of yours: that's MY imperialism.

yrs ever
G. Bernard Shaw

To J. M. STRUDWICK

10 Adelphi Terrace WC
[H/5]   4th September 1900

[Martinus Steyn (1857–1916) was a South African lawyer, who became president of the Orange Free State in 1896. In 1899 he negotiated the union of the Orange Free State and the Transvaal in the war against Great Britain. Dr Leslie Haden-Guest (later Baron Haden-Guest) (1877–1960) was a physician and Fabian who turned politician and became a Labour M.P.]

My dear Strudwick

So far, the Manifesto prospers, as both Webb and S.G.Hobson approve of it. Hobson thinks that even Hyndman might sign it! You will find your point that we are not going to nationalize the mines, and have gone to war, so far, simply to make them the private property of the cosmopolitan capitalists who have hitherto had to pay royalties to Kruger, abundantly and vigorously expressed. But I go a step further. I dont think gold reefs should be nationalized. Imagine Ireland with a gold reef, or Poland with a gold reef, or "gallant little Wales" with a gold reef, that is, with unlimited Mausers, Long Toms and Lyddite! We should have ten years of fierce patriotic, heroic, melodramatic wars. Such formidable agencies should be internationalized; and by far the nearest thing we have to an international organization is now the Great Power—British Commonwealth for choice, because England means a good deal of Europe, Asia, Africa, America and Australia. But America, France (with Algeria and the Western Soudan), Germany, and Russia are all big enough to have a mortal dread of war and a great deal to lose by it; whereas a tiny little oligarchy of pious frontiersmen like the Boers, once flooded with gold, will instantly start building itself up as a military power merely for self-defence, a policy which will finally force it to conquer territory and make itself as much of an "Empire" as it can. That is the view—the International Socialist view—that I could not get the Fabians to take last November; and it is from that point of view only that we can influence the course of events, or expose the utter lack of statesmanship in vulgar Imperialism. Mere virtuous indignation against Rhodes and Chamberlain is worth no more than it is against Kruger and Steyn; and Boer patriotic nationalism is just the same article as British patriotic nationalism. Both are as remote from Socialism as Transubstantiation is.

Do not too hastily condemn Haden Guest, the auburn haired youth (now down with enteric at the Cape—in a civilian capacity) and his

183

encouragers, of whom I am one. Remember, the objection to all progress is that it is immoral. And of the value of enthusiasm (alias "mafficking") you have seen enough lately, I should imagine, to make you suspect that there is something to be said for Guest's opinion of it. Dont get into a mere verbal quarrel about true and false morality and the rest of it: Guest has to use words as everybody else has to, subject to a reasonable interpretation. The change from Spencer's Data of Ethics to Nietzsche's Beyond Good and Evil is as inevitable as the change from Adam Smith's Wealth of Nations to Marx and Webb. You will find that Guest believes his Nietzschean anti-morality as intensely as Dr [Isaac] Watts believed *his* particular kind of principle. And remember that what you say of him and his heartless philosophy and his admiring young ladies is exactly what was said of the Fabian in its young days. We were "dilletantists," because we wouldnt stand enthusiasm. Thus do grown-up people forget what they were like when they were young. Perpend, therefore, my dear Strudwick, and let youth have its fling.

Of course Bland started as a Tory; and devilish useful it made him as a colleague of men who started as Whigs—an equally disgraceful origin. But it is not the original Toryism or Whiggery of the old gang that is making trouble now, but the confounded obsolete Reynold's Newspaper Radicalism of the younger men and of the S.D.F.

Dont bother to answer this; it is much more socialistic to paint (as you paint) than to worry about this wretched war.

yours ever
G. Bernard Shaw

To GRANT RICHARDS

[A/4; X/135]

10 Adelphi Terrace WC
21st September 1900

[Richards, at Shaw's request, printed 800 sets of galleys labelled "Strictly private and confidential" for distribution to Fabian members. This injunction was so scrupulously observed that not a single copy of the proofs appears to have survived. 200 proofs of the Shaw preface were distributed at the meeting on 25th September, informing members: "As the word editor is not a term of precision, it is necessary to explain that it means, in this instance, only the draughtsman employed by the eight hundred members of the Fabian Society to produce their Election Manifesto." In his *History of*

184

the Fabian Society (1916), Edward Pease commented: "Shaw has accomplished many difficult feats, but none of them . . . excels that of drafting for the Society and carrying through the manifesto . . ." R.B.Haldane, on 15th October 1900, wrote to tell Shaw that he and Lord Rosebery, both Imperialist Liberals, were delighted with the manifesto: "It is one of the most brilliant & incisive analyses of the existing situation that I have seen. If I were not a politician I would be a Fabian!" (BM)]

Dear G.R.

Will you get the enclosed corrections made. The Society may not pass them all; but I think it will pass so many of them (if the thing gets through at all) that it would be folly to leave them until after the meeting. They include an additional bit of MS for page 5.

I also enclose a preface, which will, I hope, help to get over some of the objections which are pouring in, to my utter and distracting confusion & overwork. Of this preface a couple of hundred proofs will be wanted for distribution at the meeting. Send 'em to Pease; but let me have a few—say half a dozen. I go down to Blackdown tomorrow evening, but shall come up on Tuesday; so post everything to Adelphi Terrace.

Tell the Chiswick people to be very careful to return my corrected proof with the revise, as I shall have to move all the corrections as amendments, and I have no other record of them.

I cant tell you how sick & brainblasted I am with the accursed thing.

GBS

To GRANT RICHARDS

[A/4; X/135]

10 Adelphi Terrace WC
26th September 1900. 3 a.m.

[Shaw had made requested revisions in the manifesto immediately following the long members' meeting of the previous evening.]

Grant Richards

Observe the hour: the early village cock hath thrice done salutation to the morn. Shakespear. [Misquotation of *Richard III*, V, iii, 209–210.]

The Manifesto has passed: all is well save its shattered author.

I enclose proofs which, though not absolutely final, are nearly so enough to justify you in paging & preparing for press. If you divide

185

into chapters as I have directed, it will not only make the book thicker & please the printer in search of fat, but it will prevent serious running over in case Webb & I at our final survey of it tomorrow should have to make alterations extensive enough to upset the lines much.

I shall drop this into your letterbox & then to bed.

yrs ever
G. Bernard Shaw

To GILBERT MURRAY

[A/36]
Blackdown Cottage. Haslemere
5th October 1900

[With the Fabian manifesto out of the way, Shaw had returned to work on *Three Plays for Puritans*. The assistance concerns passages in the "Notes to Cæsar and Cleopatra." At approximately the same time Shaw was bombarding R.B.Cunninghame Grahame with questions for *Captain Brassbound's Conversion*: "What flowers could the missionary grow?... how would the missionary be dressed on a hot afternoon?... May I safely cull flowers of Eastern speech from Captain Burton's Arabian Nights?" (Hanley, Texas)]

Dear Murray

If you are at Barford, will you fill in on p 206 of the enclosed proof suitable names from the 1st book (I think it is) of Plato's Republic. Also, if you have Darwin's works, will you correct the title of the Beagle book on p. 208 if I have got it inaccurately.

I am bookless here; and the neighbors have nothing but sermons & novels.

GBS

To CHARLES DILKE

[A/2]
10 Adelphi Terrace WC
18th October 1900

Dear Sir Charles Dilke

My delay in answering has been caused by the Fabian habit of making statements first & verifying them afterwards. Statements that are true to human nature always can be verified, if you take trouble enough.

As I had forgotten the details of the information on which the attack on the L.G.B. [Local Government Board] in Fabianism & The Empire was based, I wrote to Webb, who has the memory of an American filing cabinet, for refreshment. His reply is (naturally) marked Private; but I have his permission to shew it to you. I hope it is not too late for your purpose.

yours faithfully
G. Bernard Shaw

To H. T. MUGGERIDGE

[C/1]

29 Fitzroy Square W
27th October 1900

[Shaw was running as a Progressive candidate for election to the South Division of the newly created Borough Council, which had supplanted the St Pancras Vestry. In the election on 1st November, he was one of six successful candidates in a field of ten. The Fitzroy Square address was frequently used for convenience when Shaw was involved in local politics. In a letter of 5th November to Edward Pease, Shaw reported that, of the nearly 200 postcard appeals he had sent out, only three elicited any response. "Either my marriage or Fabianism & The Empire has ruined my popularity" (BM).]

To ELLEN TERRY

[U(A)/10; X/117]

[Blackdown Cottage. Haslemere]
28th October 1900

[The royalties from Forbes-Robertson's tour from September to December totalled £482.]

Dear Miss Terry

May I presume on a correspondence which passed between us several years ago so far as to ask your advice in the following matter.

A play of mine entitled Captain Brassbound's Conversion is to be performed privately by the Stage Society, probably under the new title "Ellen Brassheart's Obduracy." It was written for a deserving actress employed in a subordinate capacity by an Ogre at one of our leading theatres. Neither my personal advances nor my play, however, made any impression on this insensible female; and now the question is, who is to play the part? The matter is urgent; and I shall have to appeal in desperation to Mrs Kendal, as the only alternative supplying the requisite technical accomplishment, unless you will be good enough to suggest another way out of the difficulty.

You will be glad to hear that Mr Forbes Robertson's tour with The Devil's Disciple, Hamlet & Othello, has been—at least as far as the first named play is concerned (naturally I have not seen the returns from the others) a success. When Cæsar & Cleopatra is produced with the millions thus acquired, Mr Forbes Robertson will take the position that belongs to him on the English stage; but he will be generous to old employers: the part of second gravedigger will ever be at the disposal of the Ogre.

On the occasion of my last visit to Mr F.R's study, I observed that a certain laurel crowned portrait of Mrs Tanqueray had disappeared, and that the place of honor was again occupied by the woman who jilted *me*.

I have the honor to be, dear Miss Terry,

> your obedient servant
> George Bernard Shaw

To RATEPAYERS OF ST PANCRAS

[H/19]

29 Fitzroy Square W
31st October 1900

[This cyclostyled letter was posted to registered ratepayers of the new South Division (made up of the old Wards 7 and 8). A similar letter had been posted on 27th October to women voters, appealing to them to vote for Shaw and his five Progressive running-mates to protect women's rights in the Borough. (Texas)]

Dear Sir

There is a point in connexion with the election tomorrow (Thursday) to which I should like to call your attention. As you will see by the addresses already published, all parties and sections in the Borough,

Conservative and Liberal alike, have practically adopted what used to be called the Progressive programme: that is, they have pledged themselves to more of it than there is any reasonable likelihood of the first Council being able to carry out. Not one of them, however, has said a word on the very important question of how to secure properly qualified men for the official staff, and to make it impossible for the Council to job the appointments. The Vestry at present pays upwards of £14,000 a year to forty-eight departmental officers, without counting the rate collectors and their poundages, or the labour staff. There is nothing to prevent the Council from giving nearly all these forty-eight valuable appointments to relatives and friends of the councillors, or to their political supporters, without any special qualifications for the work. Such appointments have taken place, still do take place, and most assuredly will continue to take place in spite of the change from Vestry to Borough Council unless something is done.

I need not say that mere speechmaking in denunciation of each job as it comes to light is of no use. There has been plenty of that on the Vestry: our orators have lashed the abuse to their heart's content without altering it in the least. The effective remedy is to place the appointments on the same footing as those in the Civil Service, the banks and insurance offices, and the leading houses of business. Candidates for appointments should be examined by some public educational body entirely independent of the Borough Council. There are several such bodies. For subordinate clerkships, the City of London College and the Society of Arts examine candidates as part of their regular business. For technical departments like the Electric Lighting, there is the City and Guilds Technical Institute. Finally, and most important of all, there are the diplomas in Constitutional Government, Statistics, and Taxation just established by the London University through its School of Economics and Political Science for the express purpose of providing a modern standard qualification for the superior posts in municipal and parochial departments.

I have done my best to urge this reform on the Vestry; but so far, I have only succeeded in persuading them to make a rule (which the Council may rescind) that boy clerks shall not be promoted to regular clerkships until they have been examined by the City of London College and obtained at least fifty marks out of a hundred. This is a small beginning; but it has at least established the principle of examination by an outside, independent body.

I need hardly tell you that this is not a *popular* reform. Uneducated men do not understand it. Many vestrymen are afraid that it will introduce officials who will know too much for them, and make them feel it. If I am returned to the Council I shall have the hearty support of only the abler and better instructed members when I try to push the matter a step farther. I have always claimed that the more thoughtful ratepayers of the Ward are on my side in this matter, and that the quality of my support makes up for any shortcoming in quantity. But I cannot prove this claim, since the ballot shows nothing but the number of my supporters and says nothing about their quality. Therefore I want all the votes I can get; and I want to be able to say that those who vote for me are fully aware of my action on this particular question, and of the importance I attach to it.

As you are on the register, and will therefore have no trouble or delay at the polling station, will you, if you can spare five minutes on Thursday, be so good as to vote for me and for the five gentlemen who are standing with me: Messrs McGregor, May, Pettit, Suttle and Walters—the last six names on the ballot paper.

yours faithfully
G. Bernard Shaw

To R. GOLDING BRIGHT

[A/1; X/125]

10 Adelphi Terrace WC
2nd November 1900

[In succeeding months Shaw actively campaigned for fellow Fabians in the London School Board and London County Council (February 1901) contests, assisting in the election of the Rev. Stewart Headlam and Graham Wallas to the former and the return of Sidney Webb and R. C. Phillimore to the latter. *The Devil's Disciple* was performed in Dublin at the Theatre Royal on 18th and 20th October. The critic of the *Freeman's Journal* called it "a wonderful play," but added: "It is not easy by any more definite adjective to describe the piece which Mr. Bernard Shaw's vivid imagination and sardonic humour, in ill-assorted collaboration, has given to the stage." He concluded, however, that the play was "one of the greatest dramatic treats ever offered to a Dublin audience."]

Dear Golding Bright
Now that the Borough Council election is over, I can snatch a moment to answer your letter. "Three Plays for Puritans" is passed for press at last, though the effort has almost slain me; for you will observe that I have had not only to fight the municipal election, but to

190

write "Fabianism & the Empire" in the throes of the General Election before that. I have had, I need hardly say, no holiday. But the elections are over at last (though demands for speeches in connexion with the School Board & County Council elections are dropping in already); and the book is only waiting for the printing of the American edition and the reproduction of an Italian photograph of the mosaic in St Marks representing the lighthouse of Alexandria. That is, of course, for Cæsar & Cleopatra. There will also be a portrait of Cæsar from the Berlin bust (our famous British Museum one has been given up at last as unconnected with Cæsar), and a portrait of General Burgoyne (for the Devil's Disciple). Just observe, if you please, what these volumes mean. A play costs two or three times as much real work as a novel, which involves nothing but inkslinging. Yet I give an ungrateful public *three* plays in a volume, besides prefaces, notes & sermons without end. When I say *give* I mean give; for the book will not yield me dock laborer's wages for the mere manual toil it costs. This one has really three prefaces entitled respectively "Why for Puritans?", a criticism of the contemporary theatre, "On Diabolonian Ethics" explaining the foundation of "The Devil's Disciple," and "Better than Shakespear?" in which I clear up all that confusion to which you allude about Greek methods & Shakespear's epoch & so on.

Captain Brassbound's Conversion will be produced privately by the Stage Society in December if it can be cast—an open question at present. The Devil's Disciple is coining money in the provinces in the hands of Forbes Robertson: its production in Dublin the other day seems to have been furorious.

No more news at present: I do not even know yet whether I am elected for the Borough Council or not. If not, the relief will be enormous, and the dramatic output of next year a good deal bigger.

yrs sincerely
G. Bernard Shaw

To ELLEN TERRY

[U(A)/10; X/117]

10 Adelphi Terrace WC
3rd November 1900

[Ellen Terry had suggested, on 2nd November, a division of labour on Saturdays, with Ellen having the matinée to herself for *Captain Brassbound*, and Irving having the evening bill. Cora Urquhart Potter (1858–1936), known in the theatre as Mrs Brown Potter, was an American society woman who had made her professional theatre début in London in 1887. She had recently appeared in Henry Arthur Jones's *Carnac Sahib* at Her Majesty's Theatre.]

O Ellen, Ellen, you have given me no address. "A poor Manchester lodging" only oppresses me (I know those Manchester lodgings): it does not enable me to reach you through the post in time for H.I. on Sunday. The cough, too—but no matter: everybody has a cough now. It is the weather, I suppose. My mother has had to go to Margate; and as for me, I get fresh colds & sneezings every five minutes, and my gums ache, and my soul despairs, and my election to the Borough Council seems a sentence of hard labor (as it actually is). . . .

The Saturday arrangement as to Brassbound would not work, even if it were a reasonable proposal in other respects. The play, treated that way, would fail, probably. I dont care whether Henry likes the play or not: the quality of the play is my business, not his. If it is produced on his tour, he must play in it himself; and he must bind himself to produce it in London the next time he plays there. It must become the most important work he has in hand. I confer an enormous and undeserved favor on him by letting "the concern" have it for your sake.

But all this is hopeless and useless. I told you you would have to choose between Lady Cicely and Henry; and I foresaw that when it came to the point you would have no real choice in the matter. Only, when it comes to writing to Mrs Madge [Kendal], it seems a pity that you cannot at least create the part, and shew a select few what they will lose when you go back to your Amber Hearts & Nance Oldfields and the like.

How could we two be such fools as to avoid meeting each other lest we should rub the bloom off our relations, and then enter into that most accursed of all relations, the professional relation? Why did I not rather spring on that foolish Lyceum stage, drag you bodily away, and ravish you a thousand times rather than write a play for you? For it has now become a mere money business and nothing else. Charlotte is entitled to half profits; and I am no longer free to give the play away, save on honorable conditions; and these stolen Saturday conditions are silly.

Oh, let us have done with it & never mention it again. I am for the highest bidder now—did you mention a sum, Mrs Brown Potter, Mrs Anybody—

But never shall the Ogre be forgiven.

GBS

192

To FRANK HARRIS

Piccard's Cottage. Guildford

[H/6]   4th November 1900

[Frank Harris's play *Mr and Mrs Daventry*, with Mrs Patrick Campbell
and Frederick Kerr, had opened at the Royalty Theatre on 25th October.
The play's history was a curious and complicated one. Oscar Wilde had
outlined a play for George Alexander in 1894. At various times he apparently sold options on it to at least five different people, including Ada
Rehan. In 1900 he arranged to write the play in collaboration with Frank
Harris, but Harris eventually wrote the play entirely by himself and Wilde
sold Harris all his rights in it for a one-fourth share of the profits. Harris
was obliged thereafter to buy off some of the people who turned up with
prior options and claims.

Max Beerbohm had given the play a generally favourable notice in the
Saturday Review on 3rd November, but most of the criticisms were negative.
Pedro Calderón de la Barca (1600–81), the Spanish dramatist, was the
author of more than two hundred plays.]

Dear Harris

The moment the Borough Council Election was over, I went to the
Royalty. The play is good, and successful (which is not always the
same thing) in exact proportion as it is Frank Harris. Before the curtain
went up George Moore informed me that I should see at a glance that
the whole play was by Oscar Wilde. What I did see was that this was
George's honest opinion, because you have undoubtedly amused yourself by writing some imaginary conversations on Wilde's lines; and
George, who has no sense of humor, cannot see the underlying difference. Here I think you should not encourage yourself, because it is
not natural to you to play with an idea in Wilde's way, and make
people laugh by showing *its* absurdity: your notion of gambolling is
to unexpectedly fix your teeth in the calf of some sinner and hold on.
And you cannot help yourself out by observation in this instance,
because English society is not in the least witty, and always runs
curiously to see a wit like Wilde's exactly as it sits down eagerly to
look at a man playing the piano. The fact is, life does not *amuse* you
as it amuses the humorist. You perceive its ironies with a mordant
sensation about the corners of your mouth that may feel like laughter;
but when your teeth snap, they close, not on the irony, not even on the
unfortunate mortal who is the subject of it, but on the spectator whom
you are getting at. Please observe that this is a perfectly legitimate
comedic operation when it is done in your own manner. But when it is

193

done by one of the impossible drawingroom epigrammatists of the Wilde theatre, one feels at once that the fun is not real fun—it hurts; and that the epigrammarian ladies are figments. Wilde was careful to provide an ideal husband to keep them in countenance: the whole force of your play comes from the reality of the husband. This is what sets Max Beerbohm trying to express his feeling by the bull in the china shop. The prattling ladies are very like china shepherdesses trying to play up to a real shepherd. I speak feelingly on this point because we all make the same mistake at first: the more connoisseurship we start with, the more certain we are to begin with a mixture of genres—of those which have struck our fancy with that which is our original own. In the first version of my first play I introduced a lot of funny trifling of the Robertson-to-Pinero comic relief kind. The effect was perfectly frightful—like patching a suit of armor with a cheap chintz. Now Wilde's manner is immeasurably nearer akin to the new manner than the old comic relief was: consequently your drawingroom conversations produce no such disastrously hideous effect as my japes did; and you have saved the situation further by pure style; but still the incongruity is there, and it will come through and shew on the surface in a few years time, through the difference in wear between the two genres.

Fortunately for you, the play is a real beginning. You have hardly dug a foot into the vein as yet. The husband's suicide is all my eye. What you must do now is to begin a sequel to the play as follows:—

The shot does not kill Daventry (I have known a man recover and live for a long time after shooting himself straight between the eyes and lodging the bullet in the back of his skull). He sends a hurried note to the pair apologizing for the failure and warning them not to marry until he has divorced the lady, as he has, on reflection, become too curious to see how their marriage will turn out to reshoot himself more efficiently. His point is, that the lady's claim, carefully examined, is only a claim to a fool's paradise, and that her charge against him is simply that he has confronted her with a view of life which prevailed over her's, in spite of her prejudice against it, because the facts supported it and contradicted hers. Her feeling that the millionaire has restored her ideals means that she has met a young fool like herself, with money enough to make love's young dream seem for a moment like a real paradise even in such a sink as Monte Carlo. Therefore, says Daventry, I am going to wait until you are forty and see how a woman of your sort comes out when her imaginative illusions are gone. Already I have shattered—with my pistol—your fundamental illusion that the vileness of the world is only the vileness of my view of it. Further, I have shattered your notion that I am a mere animal because I am intelligent enough to keep the animal in me separate from the rudimentary poet and philosopher, and that you have attained a higher place than I because you scrupulously confuse your consciousness of the impulses which led you to hunt down and capture your millionaire. As you admit, I am a better man than you thought. It seems a simple thing to say *now*; but when you are my present age you will perceive that this is no mere sentimental-magnanimous admission, but a sinking away of the entire moral continent from under your feet into the depths of the sea, leaving you buffeting the waves for a moral foothold. Your millionaire has shewn himself so far the perfect dupe of the morality which can only justify itself by my proving a villain because I have kissed a coarser woman than my wife. The hole in my head goes straight through that morality; and whenever you return to it I shall point to the scar as the saints in the pictures point to their stigmata. And so on.

On this basis you get your drama, ending either in redivorce and re-marriage (which would be *my* ending) or a *ménage a trois* like the Nelson-Hamilton one, but on a fleshless basis. Moral: the one woman who should be sacred to a man is his wife. That is the true reductio ad absurdum of marriage.

If you go and sit out the play again you will find that the husband is the interesting person in it, and that it is strong whilst he is on a positive basis and weak whilst he is on an apologetic basis. As a rascal redeemed by an act of self-sacrifice he is not worth halfprice at nine o'clock. As a moralist claiming a real basis for morals, he is worth all the money and more. It is his instructive clutches at the positive position that give the play its drive. It is the lapses from this that land it among epigrams and duels and reverence for the pretty lady's ideals and the like anachronisms. Only make good your footing on the new moral ground and you will spout enthralling plays as profusely as Calderon for the next twenty years. You have swallowed more life than a thousand ordinary playwrights: what you want is a new philo-sophic digestion that will make bone and muscle of the realities which the old drama excreted, and excrete the sentimentalities which the old drama assimilated. This could be more briefly expressed, but not more elegantly.

I have seen you twice since I collapsed in '98. The first time you were in such a transport of laughter, apparently at some anecdote you were telling to the man with you, that I had not the heart to interrupt

195

the conversation. The second time you were in a hansom. I send this to the Royalty, not knowing your address. Somebody told me you had left Roehampton for Kingston.

yours ever
G.Bernard Shaw

P.S. An observation which I have not been able to work in above is that adultery is the worst of themes for shewing an author's range; and your range is what is most astonishing to people accustomed to the dramatists of commerce.

Also that your supremacy over all Macbeth commentators does not justify you in making Mrs Daventry express herself in the style of Duncan. I think I heard Mrs Pat say something about "measureless content."

[In his reply on 27th November, Harris argued: "All you say about the difference between Wilde's beautiful kindly humour and my sardonic bitterness is absolutely true—or at least seems so to me. You think I imitated him in the first act, and perhaps I did—at any rate it is certain that the first act is the weakest of the lot. The second act I think is spoiled by bad stage management; but then all we novices have to suffer at the hands of the actor or actress who knows that a part is greater than the whole.

"You think the shooting of Daventry all wrong; you dismiss it as contemptuously as Archer does. Well, here is my idea of it. The decay of Christianity and the belief in a future life has had for chief consequences first the demand on the part of the people for a better life on this earth—socialism—and 2nd the demand by the other oppressed class, woman, for a larger satisfaction of her instincts in this world. This new woman wants nothing but love, whatever form she may individually affect, affection or passion. I have taken her to demand affection in this case. But this new woman has been done before. Quite true; and it remains to be seen whether Mrs Daventry is 5% better or 5% worse than the new woman that other dramatists in our time have created. But I am the first to put opposite this new woman the old conventional view of sexual morality which is the husband's view and which I have here incorporated in the husband Mr Daventry.

"Now I have been more than fair to this old convention. So far from making him brutal I have allowed him to repent on the stage, promise reformation, &c in order to win your sympathies. Now how should he end? I maintain the old convention dies of its own falseness, kills itself, in fact, and that is what Daventry does. If you tell me that the individual man of this sort, Daventry, would not kill himself, I say you are mistaken. He is a man of forty who has had all the best of life. Almost for the first time he has failed. He has got himself into an impasse. It is your disappointed realist

who does blow out his brains—not your idealist whose soul is wide enough
to have sympathy for others.

"But there I could discuss the matter for ever. The truth is that naked
intelligence is no good in judging a work of art. A verdict of the public is—
I mean the best public; and the opinion of the half dozen who do count is
that Mrs Daventry is a creation and Daventry about as good.

"I am glad to be able to tell you that this view of the matter is borne out
by the box office. I am measureably content—which is not an imitation of
Duncan. . . .

"P.S. . . . I hardly venture to show myself a critic to so good a critic; but
why do you not give us another Candida—a piece I think worthy of Gold-
smith (a fact which shows how little use intellect is in creative work)"
(BM).]

To PAKENHAM BEATTY

[C/4]

Piccard's Cottage. Guildford
5th November 1900

[Stephen Phillips's verse play *Herod* had opened at Her Majesty's Theatre
on 31st October.]

Yes: I got the blackthorn; but it was not by it that I won the election: I wrote to all the electors & told them that I depended on the
support of the thoughtful few. As every man in St Pancras believes
that he is the centre of that charmed circle I came in triumphantly at
the heels of the two parsons & at the head of the three tradesmen. It
amounts to a sentence of two years hard labour, and a serious falling
off in the dramatic output.

I have not seen Herod, but see by the notices that it is the same old
game, only in decent verse.

GBS

To ELLEN TERRY

[U(A)/10; X/117]

10 Adelphi Terrace WC
8th November 1900

News this morning that the incontinent youth Johnston Forbes
Robertson is going to be led to the altar by his leading lady, Miss

197

Gertrude Elliott. I foresaw it, and wanted to put a clause in our agreement against it. However, he might do worse. She is a nice American woman, and will mend his extensively broken heart for him.

No reply as yet from Mrs Madge. Let us hope that she will indignantly refuse to act on Sunday. My feeling about it is that I should like everybody to refuse, leaving me to beat you with a poker for your infamous desertion of me. Duse herself can be nothing to me in the part but your supplanter. You wretch, you! You faithless, lazy, trifling good-for-nothing! Were your gifts entrusted to you to endow you as Matron of The Concern? Damn the Concern!

Of course he hates you when you talk to him about me. Talk to him about himself: then he will love you—to your great alarm. I know what it is to be loved. Good Heavens! You are a thousand times right to keep me out of reach of your petticoats: what people call love is impossible except as a joke (and even then one of the two is sure to turn serious) between two strangers meeting accidentally at an inn or in a forest path. Why, I dare not for my life's happiness make love to my own wife. A delusion, Ellen, all this love romance: that way madness lies.

You need not pay for detaining Brassbound. My allusion to Charlotte's interests was one of those brutalities which are useful in forcing people to attend to business. I get mischievous impulses of that sort occasionally. And I love the sordid side of business: the play of economc motive fascinates me.

I had a most tragic scene yesterday with the Charringtons, not having seen them since they played Candida at the Stage Society. They wanted to do matinees of it at the Comedy; and I said that Janet only pulled it through—wasnt the right woman for it at all—and that Charrington was grotesquely damnable as the parson, and should never play it again. Then the tempest raged round this heartless Eddystone. It was the more cruel because my marriage has cut me off a good deal from them, Charlotte being most rampagiously anti-Charringtonian. Janet said everything she could lay her tongue to: Charrington was cut to the soul: the Eddystone shone without a flicker until the exhausted ocean calmed itself & the sky shone again. But they sternly renounced their moral rights in the play, observing that now they had made it a success, no doubt other people would make money out of it. And so forth, the Eddystone, being a revolving light, merely winking. So you can now play Candida since you wont play Lady Cicely.

This is all the news, so far.

GBS

To CHARLES CHARRINGTON

Piccard's Cottage. Guildford
[A/4]   15th November 1900

[Miss Jeff. was Maud Jeffries (1874–1946), an actress who had been Wilson Barrett's leading lady for many years and who retired from the stage in 1906. Mrs H.(Tril)B.I. was Dorothea Baird, wife of H.B.Irving, who had created the rôle of Trilby in 1895. Mrs Winifred was Cyril Maude's wife, Winifred Emery. *Captain Brassbound's Conversion* suffered from endless casting problems. As late as 7th December Shaw was still experiencing difficulties, as a letter of that date to Barker indicates. It was only in the final days that Shaw was able to deal with a full cast in a complete rehearsal. Elizabeth Kennedy (d. 1962), a member of the Stage Society, noted in her diary after the 16th December performance: "At the end GBS made a speech in which he told us they had only begun to rehearse the play the Thursday before, this being Sunday, and related how they had scraped odds of scenery together from various managers out of various plays, the result being Morocco!" (Unpublished; courtesy Raymond Mander and Joe Mitchenson Theatre Collection.)]

... M[arion] T[erry] is out of the question. Whether she cant or wont learn her parts, the result is the same. Lady C. by the prompter would damn the play. If Miss Jeff. takes the same view as Welch & the rest, there is nothing for it but to write to the members telling them the state of the case & announcing for December, not Lady C, but the Lady from the C. This imbecile pun denotes my state of mind. I am taking it easy here for a day or two after the election.

I expect to hear from you in the morning. Perhaps H.B.I. will suggest Mrs H(Tril)B.I. for the part. I have a mind to ask Alma Murray, but a still greater mind to get out of the job if I can. Have you asked Hermann Vezin yet? If not, offer the part to Maude on condition that Mrs Winifred plays Lady C. If she wont, get Mary Moore—a nice business after asking Lena Ashwell first.

We shall have to wait for Mrs Kendal after all.

GBS

To CHARLES CHARRINGTON

Piccard's Cottage. Guildford
[A/4]   17th November 1900

[Margaret Halstan (1879–1967) was the daughter of H.A.Hertz, a founder of the German Theatre in London who was later a member of the Stage

Society's executive committee. Miss Halstan had played Gloria in the 1899 production of *You Never Can Tell.*]

There's nothing to be done but drop the play & turn on The Lady from the Sea, (or When We Dead Awaken) without any further hesitation. I wouldnt accept your three people if they were rolled into one and repainted expressly for the occasion. It cant be helped: I said from the first that it was a mere chance whether we could cast it or not. We can't; and there's an end of it for the present. If I were prepared to take anyone I could get, I should go to the young people—the Halstans, Terry-Lewises &c sooner than to these impossibles. Janet "pulling it through with her head" would be worth the three multiplied by 10.

If you like to try Mary Moore & Winifred Emery, you can; but they'll both refuse; and you will only cut short the little time left for Ibsen rehearsals. That makes a list of seven people whom I have offered to accept. Beyond that I positively wont go, unless you can get Ada Rehan, who has already seen the play & expressed Welch's opinion of it.

Give it up without further waste of time. Five refusals are enough to decide the matter with Xmas only four weeks off, and a performance due before it.

GBS

To CHARLES CHARRINGTON

[A/4]

10 Adelphi Terrace WC
30th November 1900

[The three "young" men on the Stage Society Executive Committee were Frederick Whelen, James Welch, and either W.H.Thomson or Ernest E. Williams.]

I interviewed the S.S. committee this evening. It seems to me that you dont make enough use of them. The result is that they remain in the dark as to what is going on, which makes them discontented, and convinces them that all the hitches are due to their being kept out of the negotiations. You should have made them make all the applications to the people to play. This would have kept them busy and *au courant* with the progress of the affair; and the refusals would have convinced them that their diplomacy is no more almighty than yours. The letter which arrived from you during the proceedings filled Whelen with remorse; but it was clear that *you* had hurt *their* feelings considerably by not being "frank" with them: that is, by not telling them all the difficulties and making them at least imagine that they were helping you.

The fact is, you dont realize how intolerable it is to humanity to be kept in the dark, especially when humanity wants to come behind the scenes of a theatre. As to the difficulty of time, you must *lose* time by writing all these letters yourself. Even if it were not so, you are mistaken in thinking time more valuable than support. This committee ought to be your bodyguard and soulguard. Instead of that, it is three young men whom you have kept at a distance, in your ancient proud, stiffnecked, Irish, *gentlemanly* way. All they wanted was to be told what was doing: all you told them was that it would be all right and that they might go on. Too proud to tell them your difficulties, you see: the old Adam! Good Lord, it is the difficulties that make the romance of the Stage Society; and these chaps joined it for the romance. You should have three meetings a week for no other purpose than to talk to them about the Society and convince each one of them that he is the central pillar of the whole institution. But you are a moralist: you think that because a man is an ass he has no human rights. Augustin Daly, who forbad his company to speak to him or claim his acquaintance outside the theatre, was an ardent republican compared to you.

However, I squared it with them for the moment, and made it clear to them that what could be done has been done, & that Janet was insisted on by me. They said, pathetically enough, that they only wanted to know—that if you'd only taken them into your [bloody]* confidence they would have been as lambs. I told them that whether I had asked the people or you asked them, the result was the same— refusal, and begged them to try their hands next time at asking, as it was quite possible that you and I might meet with refusals on personal grounds which they, as nobodies (though I did not put it in that way, exactly) had not to fear.

I saw the Devil's Disciple last night [at the Coronet Theatre, Notting Hill Gate] from the gallery. Oh Lord! Underdone opera bouffe! Just writing to F.R. to drop the notion of a West End production. Writing to you first to take the edge off.

GBS

* The square brackets are Shaw's.

To GRANT RICHARDS

[A/4]

10 Adelphi Terrace WC
30th November 1900

[Wentworth Hogg (1854–1940) was the managing director of Samuel French in London. He had been licensing a few of Shaw's plays for amateur performances. Shaw later balked at the 20% commission.]

Dear G.R.

I want your immediate attention to the following bit of business, as it may lead to the selling of some plays.

Hogg (Samuel French, 89 Strand) the theatrical publisher & amateur's guide & philosopher, says that he sells a hundred of Pinero's plays whilst Heinemann is not selling five. He says the traditional price of a play is sixpence; but he has got the price of really first class works up to eighteenpence, as witness the enclosed *édition de luxe* of [Madeleine L. Ryley's] "Jedbury Junior." Pinero's plays, as you know, are eighteenpence. Heinemann supplies Hogg with as many as he can absorb at ninepence—half price net—; Hogg puts them in his list, which the amateurs devour; he collects the fees for each performance for the author and at the same time sells as many copies as there are parts in the play plus a couple for stage manager & prompter; and off they go in batches like hot cakes. He estimates generously that as you have the plates, you can supply the millions he will require at two-pence per copy or thereabouts and retire presently on a competence. He is absolutely sceptical as to the possibility of selling a single copy of a six shilling volume of plays—knows all about it—can't be done. And he is issuing a new catalogue in six weeks & wants to have the eighteen-penny edition ready for it.

I have no doubt at all that this is good business. The notion of charging half a crown for single plays is absurd: it's like charging three halfpence for a newspaper. Hogg has a violent incentive to sell, because he not only gets eighteenpence in full for the book (at least so I presume, though perhaps the amateurs are sharp enough to demand discount) but he also gets a huge commission (20% he demands) on the fees, he having a practical monopoly of this huge & very specialized market which you can reach through him only. He keeps standing advertisements in a lot of big papers. Now these eighteenpenny editions could all bear an advertisement of the six shilling edition, with the prefaces, and would not interfere with the literary market, which is quite separate. Hogg will be enriched beyond the dreams of avarice; but you will get a hatful of the crumbs from his table. Make a better bargain for yourself if you can by claiming that half net is only business when a large number of copies are taken; but as a matter of fact it isnt so bad; you would send copies to America at that rate, or do a deal with Stoneham at it.

Besides, I shall want only twopence, which is a ridiculously nominal royalty.

Hogg says the cover must be *limp* & the book pocketable.

yrs
G. Bernard Shaw

To EVA CHRISTY

[G.u/2]
[10 Adelphi Terrace WC]
[Undated: December 1900]

[Miss Christy's name appears in an index-card list of "disciples" maintained by Shaw until 1904 (Hanley, Texas). She was a sportswoman who taught riding.]

Dear Madam

When Candida describes to the poet what her life and Morell's really is, he sees at once that it is no life for him. When he says "Out, then, into the night with me," Morell thinks that "the night" means darkness, despair & suicide—an essentially prosaic notion. To the poet the night means the transfiguration of the sordid noonday world by veiling shadows & magical starlight into a poet's world, in which Victoria Park sentimentality & domesticity have no part.

On the whole, you have made a fairly close guess; only Eugene has realized, not, as you put it, that there is "another kind of happiness" but that life at its noblest leaves mere happiness far behind; and indeed cannot endure it. And you must never say that "the knowledge of how to live without happiness *is* happiness." A teetotaller might as well preach that the knowledge of how to practise total abstinence is the truest drunkenness. Happiness is not the object of life: life has no object: it is an end in itself; and courage consists in the readiness to sacrifice happiness for an intenser quality of life.

yours faithfully
[G. Bernard Shaw]

To HARLEY GRANVILLE BARKER

[A/3; X/168]

10 Adelphi Terrace WC
6th December 1900

[Barker was rehearsing the part of the American naval officer, Captain Hamlin Kearney, in *Captain Brassbound's Conversion*.]

Dear G.B.

Unless you can make the acquaintance of a real American & live with him night & day for the next week, that part will ruin you. It's not a question of acting: its a question of intonation. Where are we to get a captain if you give it up Heaven only knows; but I had rather have the play postponed than let you, unwarned, miss fire after your previous bullseyes. Its most extraordinarily wrong—reminds me of a performance of the Soldiers' Chorus from Faust by a Siamese native orchestra under the title of The Celestial Glory. You have the intonation of an English gentleman, and rather smart & snappy at that; and the lines wont go to it: they are pure Chicagoan, not Piccadilly. For Redbrook it would be perfection; and you are much more likely to get bread & butter engagements in the Redbrook tone than in the captain's tone, which any old actor who is a good mimic & has heard enough of Chicagoan could hit off. There is no use my demonstrating what I want; for I am not a particularly good mimic; & an imitation of an imitation is a poor business. Couldnt you join an American club for a week? It's really serious; for that last act as it goes now is ruinous.

Excuse these candors; but Charrington would sacrifice you like a paschal lamb to get his cast complete. Or else he wants to create an emergency & play the captain himself—unconsciously, you understand, for consciously he is the soul of honor.

Why dont you play Drinkwater?—if you scorn Redbrook.

yr ever
G. Bernard Shaw

To FRANK HARRIS

[A/4]

10 Adelphi Terrace WC
16th December 1900

[Harris had just published *Montes the Matador and Other Stories*. "Sonia" was one of the "other stories." The paper Harris was "coming into" was

204

The Candid Friend, which was published from 1st May 1901 to 9th August 1902. Justin M'Carthy (1830–1912) was an Irish politician, historian, and novelist.]

My dear Harris

I am for the moment a done-up man: I must fly to the country for Xmas and rest. They are doing a play of mine tonight at the Stage Society; and the rehearsing (a month's work compressed into one wild week) has demoralized and destroyed me—that and unlimited Borough Council and Fabian Society together. So we must either put off the lunch, or you must take it at Piccards Cottage, St Catherine's, Guildford.

Thank you for the autographed copy of Montes. When I wrote last I had only read half of it: otherwise I should of course have been full of Sonia, which is a very fine shot at a star, and a bullseye at that. In Sonia and Mrs Daventry you are shewing the top end of your range. Why you want to plunge back into the journalistic mudbath again, Lord knows! You are the most extraordinary chap, with your genius and your shiny hats and Cafe Royal lunches and Hooleyisms and all sorts of incongruities! And now you want to give your struggling soul a final good chance of damnation by "coming into a paper," with sixteen pages by Beauchamp, one by me, no advertisements, and a note by you every two months or so. All pure waste of time: even parliament would be better. We're too old for it: journalism is not for men over forty, unless they are Justin McCarthys. What you have to do now is to make your will, so to speak, in a series of dramas, tales or what you will.

Piccard's Cottage is attainable by the main Portsmouth Road south from Guildford. A short mile from the town is St Catherine's post office. Turn to the right round the corner of that post office; go up the hill; and the last cottage on the right at the top is Piccard's. My wife, who turned up her nose at Montes, and said it was only a superior style of penny dreadful, capitulated before Sonia and is curious to see what sort of monster you may be.

yrs ever
G. Bernard Shaw

205

To JANET ACHURCH

[A/4; X/130]

Piccard's Cottage. Guildford
Xmas day 1900

[This criticism is of the first performance of *Captain Brassbound's Conversion* presented by the Stage Society at the Strand Theatre on 16th December. A second performance, on the 20th, was presented at the Criterion Theatre. "Jolly" John Nash (1828–1901) was a music-hall entertainer noted for the exuberance of his performance. Lottie Venne (1852–1928) was a popular character actress who had made her reputation in comedy acting. She had recently appeared at the Haymarket Theatre as Mrs Candour in *The School for Scandal*. The fourth leaf of this letter was reproduced in facsimile in *Theatre Arts*, New York, January 1928.]

My dear Janet

I saw the performance at the greatest possible disadvantage from the back of the worst box in the house. However, perhaps I am none the worse able to tell you about it for having seen the thing too close.

There is no doubt that you did, in a sort, begin to act for the first time in your life in the sense of painting a picture instead of merely looking into a mirror in a volcanic manner, and saying: There! there's your Nora, Candida &c. And you were so excited at finding the thing coming off, that each laugh produced the effect of a tablespoonful of brandy & soda; so that if the graver touches had not brought you back to your seriousness, dignity & power, you would finally have made Lady Cicely an exceptionally obstreperous mænad. You made points, rammed them home, rollicked and clowned in a way that would have scandalized Jolly John Nash. Of course the audience liked it; but they knew no better: their delight was the measure of your condescension. A well trained French audience—say an aristocratic Gluck & Molière XVIII century audience—would have been shocked. There were moments which you enjoyed amazingly, at which Sir Howard & Lady Cicely quite vanished, and what remained was "a Christian dorg an 'is woman."

The fact is, you tumbled to the trick of comedy acting suddenly and luckily; but the mere trick of it will carry you no further than Lottie Venne. You can save the situation by falling back, in *my* plays, where the opportunities are mixed & the comedy tissue is shot with reality & tragedy, on the great Janet; but in a St James's fashionable comedy you wouldnt get the chance. And that is why you would not suit the St James's, because your comedy is not delicate enough; your parts not studied enough for it; and your heavy qualities are not wanted.

Before you can play Lady Cicely perfectly, you will have to do what the author did, and do it much more minutely and personally than he: that is, make a careful study of the English lady. Mind: I dont mean the English bourgeoise, nor the English artist-Bohemian: I mean the great lady. It is very difficult to say a thing like this to a charwoman, because she immediately flushes indignantly and says "I ham a lidy." And as every human being has something of the charwoman's vanity & folly left, especially in their haughty youth, it is probable that the real reason why you have never dispassionately studied the great lady as an Icelander might study an elephant is that you have concluded that one lady is like another, and that since your father kept a gig (so to speak) you had nothing to learn. As a matter of fact there are no two animals in the whole human fauna more completely different in every trick & touch than a great lady & Janet Achurch.

I am like Molière in point of always consulting my cook about my plays. She is an excellent critic; goes to my lectures & plays; and esteems actors & actresses as filthy rags in comparison to the great author they interpret. Consulted as to Lady Cicely, she at once said: "No: she wasnt right: when she sat down she got her dress tucked in between her knees: no high lady would do that." Now that's an excellent criticism. You played the whole part, as far as the comedy went, with your dress tucked between your knees. Of the dress itself I say nothing; for we must do what we can afford in that way, not what we like; but although you solved the difficulty of looking well on *artistic* lines—on Liberty lines—on simple, sensible lines, such lines are quite wrong lines for Lady Cicely, who would associate that sort of dressing with Fitzjohn's Avenue and professional people who dont go to church. The directions in the play, to the effect that Lady C does not wear a tailor made tourists suit, and that she dresses as she would in summer in Surrey, mean that she is too conventional to regard dress as a wholly adaptable-to-circumstances matter. She would wear petticoats & drawers, just as she would say her prayers, for half a century after all the working women in the country would have taken to knickerbockers & agnosticism.

She would hardly ever shew real excitement, or lose her distinction and immense self conceit & habit of patronage. She wouldnt, for instance, if a fly bit her, go for it with a cat-o'-nine-tails as an Australian drover goes for a fly on the flank of the furthest off bullock with his stockwhip. She might have plenty of tricks, and silly tricks too; she might be childish, and make little jokes & puns that only courtiers laugh at; she might even go on with men in a way which in a shopgirl

207

would lead to overtures & be understood to have that intention; she might do forty thousand things that no woman who was not either above or below suspicion would do (the coincidences between the tramp & the aristocrat are very interesting); but in everything external she would be distinguished from the middle-class woman, who lives her whole life under suspicion & shortness of cash. Until you have mastered all these marks of caste, and can imitate them as easily as you can change a number five stick of grease paint for a number ten, you will not be able to do Lady Cicely as finely as a very obvious house-maid at the Theatre Français can do the Queen in [Victor Hugo's] Ruy Blas. It is not that ladylikeness is difficult, but it is antipathetic: the essence of it is flunkeyism, upper servantism; and you will have to become as heartless as I am before you can study it quite dispassion-ately and put it on quite cynically. But it is worth doing, as it involves a good deal of technical refinement along with its moral repulsiveness.

Meanwhile, to be able to do Eyolf's mother & not a commonplace comedy is to have something of Laurence Irving's fault of never being able to strike less than twelve, which means being out of an engagement for 22 hours out of the 24. Lady Cicely is the first sign you have given of reaching the wise age of comedy and being able to play the fiddle as well as the trombones and drums.

I went out of town dead beat, immediately after the Sunday per-formance, and did not see the Thursday one, nor get your letter in time to act on it. Was the Thursday performance worse than the Sunday one?—I expected it would be. You may have observed that the critics have shaken down at last into something like a firm opinion about me, the favorable ones playing up strongly & the unfavorable ones saying boldly out that the thing is a failure. That's a great advance on the help-a-lame-dog-over-a-stile business.

Barker was *very* good. We must stick to Barker. Charrington must tolerate his conceit & Whelen's.

yrs, dear Janet
GBS

To LAURENCE IRVING

Piccard's Cottage. Guildford
[A/3; postscript, A/30]   26th December 1900

[Irving had appeared as Brassbound in the Stage Society production. Silas Wegg is an old, one-legged ballad monger in Dickens's *Our Mutual Friend*.

Tallien was the character Irving had played in his translation of Sardou's *Robespierre* at the Lyceum in 1899. Owing to his father's illness, Laurence Irving had assumed the rôle of Peter in his own play *Peter the Great* at the Lyceum in January 1898.]

Dear Irving

Thanks for your pleasant letter: you are the nicest chap I have met for a long time, and so says Mrs G.B.S.

I did not see the Thursday performance; and what I saw of the Sunday one was very much out of focus, as I was in the worst box in the house, with the float right under my nose and only half the stage visible.

However, the critic in me still works automatically from long habit; and I can tell you lots of unpleasant things about yourself. You are at present like a soldier who can do nothing but win the Victoria Cross, an astronomer who can do nothing but observe the transit of Venus, or the fabled American doctor who could not cure measles, but was death on fits. You began the first act in the middle of the second, to the intense astonishment of the spectators. I am far from grudging Brassbound a certain sense of injury even in the first act; but you were a volcano smouldering with unutterable wrongs from your first step on the stage. When the right moment for the eruption came, the audience had acquired a Neapolitan indifference to lava, because there was such a lot of it about from the commencement that they had become used to it. Further, the captain became entirely one-sided, like the Flying Dutchman, who is so full of his doom that he is never allowed to talk or think about anything else. Now it is better to be able to make this mistake than not to be able to make it; but it is a mistake, all the same; and the real reason you make it is that you are weak in your normal register, so to speak.

Captain Brassbound's profession is one which gives a man a considerable concentration of will on entirely prosaic ends. If you were a "fighting mate" promoted to the command of a schooner, you would have a highly developed power of making yourself listened to when you only wanted a deck swabbed, and a comparatively limited power of expressing poetic emotion—probably none at all. And you would be equally at a loss in comedic expression.

But if Captain Brassbound were *you* (and please remember that your acting must always depend on the success of the pretence that the character is you, not on the pretence that you are the character—the amateur's notion—) he would find himself with a considerable power of expressing poetic or comedic feeling, and hardly any purely prosaic energy. Under which circumstances, he couldnt command the schooner.

209

Thus we have:—

	Brassbound	Irving
Prosaic energy	100	0
Poetic energy	0	100

This is their *normal* condition, not their mid-second-act condition. But Brassbound's normal is much more favorable to a good performance than Irving's. For Brassbound's prosaic energy may be intensified by passion at the crises of the play until it becomes poetic, just as a stubborn bit of non-conductor in an electric circuit becomes incandescent if you only put current enough on to it. But Irving, being helpless in the normal state, has to turn on his poetic feeling in the normal situation with frank inappropriateness; and so destroy the naturalness of his normal moments and discount the force of his abnormal ones at one blow.

What's the remedy? *I* should say, get elected to a Borough Council, and learn the sort of energy that moves assemblies on the subject of dust collecting, and feels a penny on the rates as the weightiest of human issues.

But I think the difficulty can be got over with your present resources if you can induce yourself to take sufficient interest in life as a whole to seek the power of artistic expression for *all* its phases as you have already sought it for its romantic & poetic phases. It is very easy to be a tragedian or a comedian, if you have a turn either or both ways: the difficulty is to be a man, dropping into poetry, like Mr Wegg, only on occasion. For this reason you will find Iago a much easier part than Othello, just as Lady Cicely is a much easier part than Brassbound. Iago is always *acting*, always posing, always scoring; so is Lady Cicely. Othello and Brassbound never act, never score, never pose: they both *are* (I feel: therefore I *am*); and they describe themselves in the last act as heroic simpletons.

You see, Brassbound is really a very difficult part—or rather a part requiring a talent which is very rare on the stage, since the men who have prosaic energy enough for it seldom adopt so romantic a profession. The typical part of the kind is Coriolanus, which everybody threatens and nobody dares execute. My father saw Macready play Coriolanus. I asked him what it was like. He said "It was like a mad bull." Macready, I suppose, roared his way through it. Now the first thing you did with Brassbound was to shout your way through it. Janet, or anybody else who plays with you, will entreat you to cultivate your "middle tones," your normal voice & so on. But it is useless to try to become an actor from the outside, *technically*. If you get at the right point of view, you will immediately *need* the proper technique, and then you will find it without having it pointed out to you, as a bird finds worms.

At the same time, I rather think that Tallien may have got you into a habit of shouting. And now that I think of it, you shouted like the very devil in Peter. I remember, in the General Election of 1892, when I was desperately overworked, I made an election speech in the open air in London, and quite unconsciously, through mere nervous weakness, shouted. As I have naturally no voice at all—what I do is mere fake—the shouting suddenly broke like a rotten stick & left me noiseless. I had to stop, and was desperately frightened, as I had to go off to Bradford next day and address three big open air meetings. In my dread of a second fiasco, I spoke very cautiously and quietly, and realized before I had uttered three sentences that this was exactly the right thing to do for sonority and effect. Now you have learnt this lesson to the extent of *shouting cautiously*, which has a funny effect, since men only shout naturally in transports of excitement, whereas you are most conscientious when you shout loudest. For instance if you shouted the line in Richard III

"Lo! here I lend thee this sharp pointed sword"

you wouldnt shout, as a man naturally would,

Lohee rilenthee thishar pointedsoard

you would outdo your father in insistence on the German detached attack on the vowel I, on the end | thee | this | sharp | pointedd &c.

Now I'll tell you some of the nasty things that have been said of you. On the Sunday night, after the first act, I went into the box of Lewis Hind, Archer & George Moore. The following ensued:—

Hind—May I ask does Irving realize your notion of Captain Brassbound?

Shaw—Realize it! Oh yes: ten times over. (Laughter)

It is true that the laughter of fools is like the crackling of thorns under a pot; but my reply would not have been even understood if your playing had not struck them as overcharged.

Again, a friend who violently abuses the whole affair, writes—"In spite of Irvings shocking, shocking result [? I think this is the word, though I dont quite understand it]*—and by the way are you

* The square brackets are Shaw's.

responsible for the change of clothes: I dont think its forgivable—one couldnt help seeing that he had in his mind a really sensible idea. It may have been yours, but it is evidently defensible. Why in the world he produced it in that ridiculous way I cannot understand. It was sheer farce. Yet for all that you could see he meant a real thing though he never shewed it but once—the last sentence of the second act."

This is an instructive example of what I call "the dram of eale" in acting: that is, the way in which a very small error will get imputed to a whole performance. If this correspondent of mine had missed the first act, he would not have read the overcharging of it into all the rest. In the seventies, when your father first tried the Macready—Barry Sullivan—Edwin Booth line, he raised a storm of hostile criticism by a few inexperienced attempts to make certain startling effects *by force* —effects that cannot be made in that way, and indeed always make themselves whilst the actor, having led up to them, carefully does *nothing*, as I discovered by watching Ristori & Salvini. If, in playing Hamlet, you do *one* ridiculous thing, your Hamlet will be called ridiculous. When I saw your father play Hamlet, he did one ridiculous thing—he was proud at that time and hurt Salvini's feelings very much by refusing to go and learn by seeing him play—and he had to struggle against the effect produced by this single inept stroke & a few others like it until he learnt what *not* to do by himself.

Of course the moral of this is to go ahead in your own way and worry through. But a clever man learns in all sorts of ways, and though he never takes advice (or regrets it afterwards if he does) nevertheless profits by it. The strongest part of your position is this: that though I, the author, know perfectly well that several London leading men whom I need not name would pass quite unchallenged in Brassbound, and play many of its strokes better than you did, yet I should never go to see them play it, the result being as foregone as the result of striking a safety match on the box. Now I should go to see you play it from time to time with some interest & curiosity; and that is the main thing.

This is too long; but as Madame de Sévigny said, I havent time to write a short one. I hope, by the way, you are not too sensitive to be talked to in this way. The fact is, I have so exhausted every conceivable error and ineptitude in my own attempts to learn to do something that I have become callous to such humiliations, and generally assume that other people are callous too. And, as I have so often said, a man can (and should) forgive another man everything EXCEPT an attempt to spare his feelings—the worst of disloyalties. And then, there is plenty to fall back on on the other side of the account[.]

yrs ever
G. Bernard Shaw

PS—Charlotte says you'll *never* act—that you should be an author or something nice. Perhaps she's right: the longer I live the more I lean to the time honored theory that all we theatrical people are rogues & vagabonds.

To MAX BEERBOHM

[A/1]
Piccard's Cottage. Guildford
30th December 1900

[Max Beerbohm's article on *Captain Brassbound's Conversion* appeared in the *Saturday Review* on 29th December. Edmund Gurney's book presumably was *The Power of Sound* (1880). Isidore de Lara (1858–1935) was an English pianist who became a composer of operas.]

My dear Max

This article of yours about Brassbound in the Saturday is not good enough for *me*. You are falling off in quality—getting careless, like Napoleon. Your blarney is in vain: I insist on a sound intellectual basis. It is bad enough to have Walkley becoming a bellygod, writing articles on toast, and clamoring for "passion": you must not take to that yet: it means fatty degeneration—liver served up with clever sauce as brain.

Here is the rotten spot in your article. "He does quite honestly believe that logic, not passion, is the pivot on which the world goes round." Now I will spare you a recital of the names of the donkeys who have said that before you; for the consciousness of such company would die your cheeks a permanent beet. It is—to take the most flattering example—what Buchanan has said about Goethe. It is what every man with a pound of brain says of a man with a pound and a half. I allow you a pound and a quarter at least; so you must not say it again, of anybody, under any circumstances, unless you join the Playgoers Club & make speeches there about Archer.

If you read Plato carefully (to suggest the most tolerable author for the purpose) you will find that he now and then does very oddly lose his grip of reality and assume that a thing must be true if it can be stated as the final term in a syllogism. And when you have by practice on Plato made your *flair* for this sort of *naïveté* perfect, you will find that it has innumerable vulgar forms as well as academic ones. The difference is that in the academic one, the logician insists on the validity of his conclusion because he was ingenious and scholarly enough to make the syllogism, and is jealous of his privilege of truthmaking as against the mother wit of the common people. In the vulgar form, the passionate man, ashamed to avow his naked appetite, and conscious that it will not influence other people, desperately casts round for a *reason* for the gratification of his passion, and snatches up the first excuse that presents itself, which excuse presents itself to himself & those who share his passion as an argument of overwhelming conclusiveness.

Here you have the real distinction between the pedant and the man of passion. But please observe that *both* proceed on the assumption that "logic, not passion, is the pivot on which the world goes round." And the passionate man is the incorrigible one of the two in this respect; for whereas you can tempt your professional logician to destroy his own science by refining it to impossible conclusions (such as the infinite possibility of halving a substance without ever coming to the end of it) your passionate man will never admit that he has no reason for wanting to kill the Boers, or that Ibsen's plays are not *wrong* instead of simply disagreeable to him.

Now all comedy consists in the deft exposure of this logic by the ironic contrast between its conclusions and reality. Molière was specially tickled by the academic logician, and observed correctly that the extreme instance of him is not the philosopher but the fencing master. Ibsen is more concerned with the bourgeois moralist of the XIX century, Sheridan with the virtuous sentimentalist of the XVIII. The comedian, however, (or comedist) does not arrive at his reductio-ad-absurdum by the Euclidian method: he has, as his specific gift, a sense of human nature, or "sense of character" which provides him with the permanent background of reality in his own mind against which the "reasonings" of men shew up as artificial at once, without any logical testing. *Anybody* can see the artificiality against this background. Therefore your Molière's task as a comedist is simply to present this background to the audience (who haven't got it by nature as he has) and make the conventional, factitious, ratiocinated motives & conclusions of his characters play against it, when their factitiousness instantly becomes ludicrously obvious to people who, when they leave the theatre, and lose the background, are completely taken in by them.

Now if you have followed this, you will see that any dramatist who

214

has ever entertained you in the comedic way, cannot possibly be one who believes "that logic, not passion, is the pivot on which the world goes round." Nay, if you are agile enough for a bit of a jump, you will suddenly see that what produces the impression of want of humanity in the high comedist, is precisely his freedom from this all but universal, and therefore ultra-human illusion. It is the Drury Lane—Adelphi melodrama that is logical from beginning to end, the terms natural & unnatural as used by the spectators meaning really conventional & unconventional: that is, logical & illogical.

You see why I give you this wigging, then. I do not say that there are not two sides to the case of Brassbound: I *do* say that you have come into court and mistaken your client. Briefed by Reasonable Emotion, you have addressed the jury on behalf of Unreasonable Passion. Retained to plead for a little coherence, a little logic, a sequence of action *thinkable* by the common man, you have actually pleaded for the moral anarchy which revolts you in my plays, as the absence of versified tunes once did in Wagner's music.

And, not liking the tuneless play, you do what the late Edmund Gurney did when he disliked the staveless free melody of Wagner. Gurney wrote a huge & futile book to prove logically that Wagner's music was *wrong* & Beethoven's right. Your article is an attempt to prove that my play is wrong. That is what has switched you off the track of what you dislike in it.

Finally, let me recommend you to join the Stage Society. Those second performances are hopeless failures. The plays are rehearsed for about three days, the casts seldom complete until a few hours before the curtain goes up. On the eventful Sunday, the play goes well from mere hysteria & the excitement of the first attempt, the author's presence & his speech (when the author is G.B.S.) and so on. The second performance has all the flatness of a second night plus the effects of under rehearsal. Besides, we want your two guineas.

I will try to rake out a copy of an old article of mine on Science & Common Sense & enclose it to you with this.

yrs ever
G. Bernard Shaw

P.S. Stick to my plays long enough, and you will get used to their changes of key & mode. I learnt my flexibility & catholicity from Beethoven; but it is to be learnt from Shakespear to a certain extent. My education has really been more a musical than a literary one as far

215

as dramatic art is concerned. Nobody nursed on letters alone will ever get the true Mozartian joyousness into comedy.

PPS I have been reading [Stephen Phillips's] "Herod" (I never go to the theatre now); and although I appreciate the real power over words, I see nothing in the way of character or passion that would excite the least surprise if it were done in music by Isidor de Lara.

To THE EDITOR OF THE *MORNING LEADER*

[G/1]

[10 Adelphi Terrace WC]
[Undated: assigned to 27th January 1901]

[Queen Victoria died on 22nd January. Her body lay in state in a *chapelle ardente* at Osborne until 1st February, when it was conveyed to London. Burial was at Frogmore on 4th February. Shaw's letter was not published. In rejecting it, the editor Ernest Parke replied to Shaw on 28th January: "I do not mind fighting the war policy of the nation, quorum pars magna fuisti, but I am not anxious to run counter to its loyalty in its most solemn expression. (Cheers)" (BM).]

Sir

I am loth to interrupt the rapture of mourning in which the nation is now enjoying its favorite festival—a funeral. But in a country like ours a total suspension of common sense and sincere human feeling for a whole fortnight is an impossibility. There are certain points in connection with the obsequies of Queen Victoria which call for vigorous remonstrance.

Why, may I ask, should the procedure in the case of a deceased sovereign be that which has long been condemned and discarded by all intelligent and educated persons as insanitary and superstitious? To delay a burial for a fortnight, to hermetically seal up the remains in a leaden coffin (and those who are behind the scenes at our cemeteries know well what will happen to that leaden coffin), is to exhibit a spectacle, not of reverent mourning, but of intolerable ignorance perpetuated by court tradition long after it has been swept away in more enlightened quarters. The remains of the Queen should have been either cremated or buried at once in a perishable coffin in a very shallow grave. The example set by such a course would have been socially invaluable. The example set by the present procedure is socially deplorable.

216

If at such a moment the royal family, instead of making each other Field Marshals, and emphasizing every foolish unreality and insincerity that makes court life contemptible, were to seize the opportunity to bring its customs into some sort of decent harmony with modern civilization, they would make loyalty much easier for twentieth century Englishmen.

yours truly
G. Bernard Shaw

To WILLIAM ARCHER

[A/2]   10 Adelphi Terrace WC
                                                    18th February 1901

[The new edition of *Cashel Byron's Profession*, including *The Admirable Bashville*, was published in October 1901. Archer's review of *Three Plays for Puritans* appeared in the *Morning Leader* on 16th February. In response to Shaw's "Why for Puritans?" preface, Archer had argued: "[W]hen he passes . . . to 'sensuality' and makes out that the serious drama, poetic and realistic, lives, or seeks to live, by stimulating the erotic instincts, his contention is monstrously and fantastically wide of the truth. . . . [I]f he will name a single serious play, from 'The Second Mrs. Tanqueray' to 'Mrs. Dane's Defence,' which owed its success to any sort of 'voluptuous' appeal, to any titillation of sensuality in any sane spectator, I will admit that the orbit of his asteroid is a million miles nearer the earth than I take it to be." *Trelawny of the "Wells"* (1898) was a romantic comedy by Pinero.]

Have you got that letter of Stevenson's about Cashel Byron's Profession which was mutilated by Colvin for the second volume of the Letters, p 96? I want to print the omitted uncomplimentary part in the preface to a new edition of the book, which will consist of a Preface (as usual), the novel, an essay on prizefighting, another preface, and a play in blank verse in the style of Marlow, entitled The Admirable Bashville, or Constancy Unrewarded. This latter masterpiece has been forced on me by the necessity for keeping the American adaptations off the English stage. I had to make an adaptation of my own in a hurry; and as I, or any fool, can write blank verse as fast as the pen will travel (this is the real secret of Shakespear's big output) I plunged into that medium, which proved very effective in bringing out the dramatic qualities of the tale.

Unless you dislike the publication of the suppressed passages of the

217

letter, will you lend it to me, or let me have a copy, which would perhaps be safer.

I gather from The Morning Leader that my Three Plays preface has turned your brain. You forget that the appeal to Puritans is a flat plagiarism from yourself in The Morning Leader as ever was. You raised the same cry, used the same "profaneness & immorality" quotation, and so moved Massingham that he lifted up his voice beside you. I am only the third Anabaptist in the trio: you are the first. I can't meet your mad challenge to name the plays in which the heroes & heroines do "all for love," because Parke would not give me space enough; but I can hardly think offhand of any plays I should exclude (barring Wilde's, Shakespear's & my own) except [Henry Arthur Jones's] The Triumph of The Philistines & Trelawney. There is only one instance in my plays of a couple meeting for the first time before lunch & being engaged after dinner; and that is a dread example of the fate of "the duellist of sex," who is swept into the family which is the real subject of this really great comedic sociological study like a butterfly. Read all the plays again, six times over.

By the way, if you want to understand why Brassbound was written at such a moment, read Stanley's African expeditions & then Miss Kingsley's. You will then begin to see dimly how I get my Brassbounds & Cicelys and why they appear so unnatural & unreal in that blessed old pays de Cocagne in which you have sat (in a stall) for 20 years. You really are

LOSING

YOUR

FACULTIES

GBS

To WILLIAM ARCHER

[A/2]

10 Adelphi Terrace WC
22nd February 1901

... Of course I meant plays in which love is the sole motive. But all that I meant, with its limitations, exceptions, & various modes, is set out most elaborately & completely in the preface.

The typical poetically voluptuous play—love the sole motive, and lovers in gorgeous robes & spectacular setting the sole personages, is

Herod. Now the whole history of the Lyceum is the history of Herodifying Shakespear—getting the brains & realism out & the Belsize Park suburban Jewish glamor in. Ellen Terry & Forbes Robertson as Guinevere & Lancelot in Comyns Carr's King Arthur was Lyceum ritual in excelsis. Herod is the same game; only Phillips can write verse & is a bit of a poet—much as Leighton was a bit of a painter—and Carr was a duffer.

On the grosser plane you have [Paul M. Potter's] The Conquerors, with the rape on the stage, and the woman, when she recovers from the faint which saves public decency at the last moment, falling in love with the hero because she believes that the rape was consummated during her swoon. Then you have Carton's Tree of Knowledge, with the strangling match (same two performers) substituted for the rape. Leading up to this you have Mrs Ebbsmith, with the (to A.W.P.) unreal, imaginary Trafalgar Square life suddenly changed into a glorious reality when the woman puts on a fashionable dress, & the man, at sight of her naked shoulders, knows what life & love are at last, & so does she. Then came [Henry Arthur Jones's] Michael & His Lost Angel, still under the influence of the overpowering *odor di femmina* from Mrs P[atrick] C[ampbell]. The same moral: the parson's social & religious work an unreal thing: love sweeping it away as the only real thing in the world. Then Pinero again [*The Princess and the Butterfly*] with the old Maupassant tragedy: the horror of passing 40 & being shelved sexually. Next variation: redemption for the roué by a Shunamite woman. Good Lord! & you ask me to name a single play &c.

However, you probably dont notice these things after quarter of a century in the theatre, just as water has no taste for us because it's always in our mouths. And yet from time to time youve howled, called for the Puritans, protested against the odor di femmina, tried to champion the unvoluptuous against Lily Hanbury & Mrs Fred Terry. But in the main you are a lost man, and, with that other disgraceful old father of a family A.B.W., have complained that my erotics are "bloodless" and clamored at me for reality, flesh & blood &c, meaning the aforesaid lovely Lily and the *odor*.

I blush for you.

In haste
GBS

To CHARLES CHARRINGTON

10 Adelphi Terrace WC
3rd March 1901

[A/4]

[Mary O'Brien, a member of the Fabian Executive, had just married a fellow Fabian, J. Theodore Harris. Mrs Fenton Macpherson was another of many enthusiastic women whose energies were never successfully harnessed and channelled by the Fabians. Webb's vote count in the recent London County Council election was 5496 as against the 2865 votes of the leading Moderate challenger.]

I forgot to say when I called the other evening that you ought to think twice about resigning from the Fabian Executive. Of course half the members of the committee are no use on it as far as the routine work is concerned. There are 15 wheels to a coach that runs quite well on 6. That's the reason we have lost so many people—Mrs Stanton Blatch, Honnor Morten &c &c &c and several others who finally declined to waste their time in sitting watching the old gang & Pease doing the needful. That is all the amusement that you & Dodd & Mrs MacPh. & Miss O B (as was) & my wife get out of it. Whelen never comes, & his staying away makes no difference except to the Stage Society, as it prevents him from meeting you. Consequently, if the matter were one of work merely, you would be perfectly justified in moving that the number be reduced to 10.

Why dont you do this? Why dont we do it ourselves? Because there is not only work but policy to be considered. An Opposition is needed to balance the old gang. In the war squabble you saw how important this was.

Considering, then, that even if you find everything that you think can be done by the Society getting done by the old uns there is yet a use for the contemplative deadhead, you ought not, I think, to resign unless you definitely cannot spare the time to attend, because whereas it is easy to hold on, it is difficult to get back after cutting loose.

It is a pity you were not on the register: you would have got on the L.C.C. The result of the election is like praying for rain & getting our windows promptly broken by a hailstorm. The votes that won the victory were probably Conservative Collectivist ones. Webb's huge majority was probably a villa vote. As far as one could guess he did little more than hold his own in the working class quarters. I feel pretty sure that my support in St Pancras is more square than slum.

I still think that the S.S. wants a lot more nursing before it can afford a fight. If a row is inevitable, attack *the system of management*, not the men. Do it by proposing a new constitution. This will enable you to heap up a case against the existing arrangements whilst protesting that the committee are the best fellows going, and have as much reason to complain as you have. But a row is the last resource. I still think you ought to make an adherent of Whelen. Janet is a greedy & pugnacious wretch: couldnt you agree that it's all her fault & that the authors (Shaw, Murray &c) *will* force her on the society because nobody else can act?

GBS

To GILBERT MURRAY

[A/36; X/166]

10 Adelphi Terrace WC
15th March 1901

[Murray's *Andromache* was performed by the Stage Society at the Strand Theatre on 24th February and at the Garrick Theatre the following evening. Constance Collier (1878–1955) had been making a name for herself in ingénue rôles since 1895. George R. Foss was stage manager and assistant to Shaw in the Avenue Theatre production of *Arms and the Man* in 1894. His wife Winifred Fraser had appeared briefly in *Arms and the Man*. Mr Guppy is the young clerk in *Bleak House* who discovered Lady Dedlock's secret. *The Man of Destiny* was presented at a matinée organised by J.T.Grein, at the Comedy Theatre on 29th March, with Margaret Halstan and Granville Barker.]

Dear Murray

Certain wars and rumors of wars at the Stage Society move me to warn you to waterproof yourself against all tales of intrigue & villainy which may reach you. The great object of the contending forces is to get an author as King's Evidence: the wise author preserves a bland neutrality. Do not allow yourself to be affected by the professional infamy, the treachery, the scoundrelism of Charrington, or the self-seeking intrigue, the hypocrisy, vanity, and mean envy of Whelen. It is all pure romance; but it always goes on, like schoolboy war & brigandage.

The fact is, the Stage Society is not a very eligible opening for professional ambition. It cant afford to pay its performers or to have scenic rehearsals. It begins rehearsing after a fortnight of applications & refusals, with an incomplete cast, and with performers of whom some, as the old hands pretty surely guess, wont go through with it

221

when they find what a rough & tumble affair it is going to be. I rather suspect that Miss Collier was a case in point. In the end the manager calls in his wife or some of his old allies on whom he can depend; and then, for the first time, he gets to work on the assumption that the thing is really going to happen. Of course the Opposition immediately denounce this course of nature as an intrigue of the manager in the interests of his own gang & his own wife. Equally of course, the manager and his wife are stung by the infamous conspiracy to oust them. And so they wrangle & fight, occasionally changing the Government when the press pitches into a performance hard enough to give the Opposition a victory, but never changing the system, as the new manager finds himself exactly in the same fix. "Andromache" has unseated Charrington & put in Foss; but the chances are about 10 to 1 that Foss will presently, after vainly trying to cast a play, fall back on Miss Winifred Fraser (Mrs Foss), and the recrimination will begin all over again. It may not happen the first time (Charrington got through The League of Youth, The Coming of Peace & Macaire without calling in Janet); but to that complexion it will come at last.

In the case of Brassbound I, anticipating all this, condescended to ask Mrs Kendal and Miss Lena Ashwell myself to play Lady Cicely. The committee tried; I tried; everybody tried, refusals coming in until there was no time left for anybody to rehearse, when I turned Janet on. But there was just the same faction afterwards: Charrington & Janet had intrigued to secure the part for her & so on. Every performance is followed by the same silly storm in a teacup & will be to the end of time. So sit tight; and dont believe a word that reaches you from either side. I am deep in the unwilling confidence of both parties.

"Andromache," which I saw twice (an unprecedented honor) was necessarily a failure in point of execution—a failure that illustrated our difficulties very perspicuously. The play requires an artistic form for its representation—a convention of fastidious beauty & dignity delicately impressed with sincere & natural acting. You want people trained to speak & move handsomely, and to strike the chords of the human heart feelingly enough to touch Mr Guppy. Instead of which you get your milk & water in separate cans. You get two artist's models who look feebly graceful in the manner of a Leighton picture, and who are unintelligible & (in one case) inarticulate. And you get two realistic Ibsen people who drive the meaning of their parts home with instruments of torture. The boy [Robert Bottomley] was the sole success: his youth was classic, his feeling was touching.

I blame you to some extent for not forcing Janet to contract herself into the limits of her duty. I grant you it would have required either a serpent's tongue or a kitchen poker; but it could have been done. Two things you should have said & stuck to. 1. Miss Achurch: you will please be content to see the Furies, not to act them. 2. Miss Achurch: you will please avoid using that part of your voice (the upper register) which was intended by Nature for use in a saw mill. Janet is magnificent when she is bullied into reason & moderation; but when she is not brutally tamed she smashes everything to pieces. Even then there is something momentous in the fact that the audience *dares* not laugh—that line about her beauty would have evoked a titter if Mrs Pat or Cleopatra herself had played it; but Janet's unerring laugh-if-you-dare pause & the stroke after it that shoots the ship clear of the rock are really wonderful. Of course she should have played Andromache; and you should have hammered at her with an extra large poker until she was right; but she could have been made much less destructive as Hermione. An actress of genius is an incarnation of all the devils in hell: that is why it is such a fearful & perilous joy to have one to rehearse. Charrington couldnt have been made better: nothing could make him classically beautiful. He hates classicism and romance, and hadnt the least notion what a good play Andromache is & what a genius you are until I reviled him into waking up a little about it.—Here I am interrupted by a rehearsal of "The Man of Destiny."

yrs ever
G. Bernard Shaw

P.S. We return to Piccard's Cottage, St Catherines, Guildford, this evening until Wednesday, bar a run up on Sunday afternoon to lecture at St George's Hall on the Problem Play or some such rot.

To SAMUEL BUTLER

[Piccard's Cottage.] Guildford
[A/42; X/170]   24th March 1901

[On 22nd March, Samuel Butler had sent Shaw his manuscript of *Erewhon Revisited*, at the suggestion of Emery Walker (who had first introduced Shaw to Butler on 15th November 1889). In the accompanying letter Butler informed Shaw: "Longmans . . . will not publish it even at my expense; they say it will give offence to their connection among the High Anglican party—which I should think not improbable, for it is far more wicked than Erewhon" (Texas).]

223

My dear Butler

It is almost incredible that Longmans should be such a stupendous ass. But I should think you could have any of the younger publishers for the asking, or without it if they knew that you were open to an offer.

My own publisher is a young villain named Grant Richards, who has no scruples of any kind. You had better let me shew him to you on approval. If you will come to lunch with us at 1.30, say on Wednesday or Thursday, I will invite Grant Richards too. If you can persuade Walker or Cockerell or both to come along with you, do. We shall then feel at home and independent, as Richards will be in a hopeless minority. My wife is a good Erewhonian and likes Handel: you wont find her in any way disagreeable. And 10 Adelphi Terrace is within easy reach.

I shall of course say nothing to Richards except that he will meet an eminent author; so that he will come as a palpitating fisherman. Publishing a sequel to Erewhon is an absolutely safe financial operation, as a sale sufficient to cover expenditure is certain. And as a young publisher would be glad to take you on at a loss for the sake of getting you on his list of authors, I shall be extremely surprised if you find the slightest difficulty so long as you avoid your own contemporaries, who are naturally all Buononcinists, so to speak.

Let me have a line to Adelphi Terrace to say which day you'll come, so that I may write to Richards.

I have started reading your MS instead of doing my work. So far I am surprised to find that so confounded a rascal as your original hero did not become a pious millionaire: otherwise he is as interesting as ever. More of this when I finish him.

yrs faithfully
G. Bernard Shaw

To GRANT RICHARDS

10 Adelphi Terrace WC
[A/4]   28th March 1901

[Grant Richards had been introduced to Butler earlier that day at lunch at Adelphi Terrace. He eventually published both *Erewhon Revisited* and a new, revised edition of *Erewhon*. In 1903, with Shaw's assistance, he published *The Way of All Flesh* posthumously.]

Dear G.R.

I return the title page proof [of the new edition of *Cashel Byron's Profession*], with a hideous error corrected.

Samuel Butler's address is 15 Clifford's Inn E.C. As he is far too polite & delicate an old bird to presume upon the friendly effusiveness of meal times, you had better write to him for the MS of Erewhon Revisited (which I have got, by the way).

He has taken a fancy to you; so you will get on excellently with him.

yrs ever
G.Bernard Shaw

To PAKENHAM BEATTY

[A/4]

10 Adelphi Terrace WC
6th April 1901

[Shaw had written "A Note on Modern Prizefighting" for the new edition of *Cashel Byron's Profession*. Edward Blair Michell was the author of *Boxing and Sparring* (1889). The new handbook, published in March, was Sir Walter Edgeworth Johnstone's *Boxing: The Modern System of Glove Fighting*.]

I should have acknowledged your letter about the verse in The Admirable Bashville, which was just what I wanted. Glad you found only one Irish trysyllable: there were several in my first draft, the best of them being forearm (four are um). I mentioned this & your discovery of fighersides to Cockerell; but he poured forth such a flood of precedents from Morris & other eminent poets that I came to the conclusion that Poe's fire-higher rhyme [in "The Bells"] is classical.

I will read Michell & send you a proof of what I have written about the noble art when I come back from Provence, whither I fly, more dead beat than words can express, tomorrow morning. I haven't had a day off for 17 months; and, what is worst, nothing seems to have got done in all that time.

Have you seen a new red shilling handbook of boxing (Championship Series) on the bookstalls. The Daily Mail wanted me to review it. I declined; but offered to give practical explanations of the pictures if required.

Dont address letters to London School of Economics. 10 Adelphi Terrace is enough & prevents the people downstairs from mistaking them for their own correspondence.

GBS

To J. E. LYONS

Piccard's Cottage. Guildford
[A/5]   [Undated: *c.* 4th May 1901]

[J. E. Lyons was Grant Richards' manager. The volume was the separate edition of *The Devil's Disciple*, which R. & R. Clark had printed on 19th April, during Shaw's absence abroad. The Shaws had been touring in France for a month, leaving for Marseilles on 7th April and visiting Arles, St Remy, Avignon, Nîmes, Toulouse, Bordeaux, Tours, Chartres, and Paris.]

Dear Mr Lyons

I return the copy of the D's D. You will see on examining it that it has been made up with utter carelessness. The cutting off of the imprint at the foot of the 4th page of the cover is only part of the neglect of the proper margins all through. On the front page of the cover there is a margin of 3/4″ at the top and 1/4″ at the bottom instead of vice versa. A printer capable of doing that should be boiled down into tallow forthwith & sold for what he will fetch. The inside is not quite so bad; but still the top margins are far too wide & the bottom ones too narrow; and some of the sheets have not even been folded or printed straight. Look at signature D, p 37, for instance. The letterpress slopes to the left like a shower of rain. These little things make all the difference between a respectable John Murray looking volume and a "book of the words" at a charity concert; and it costs no more to have them right than wrong. All that is necessary is to call the printer names: when he learns that you know the difference and care about it, he will do his duty and dump his slovenliness on to somebody who knows no better. Kindly transmit to him the author's curse, with my compliments.

yrs
G. Bernard Shaw

To CHARLES CHARRINGTON

10 Adelphi Terrace WC
[A/4]   27th June 1901

[Ibsen's *Pillars of Society*, translated by William Archer, was presented by the Stage Society at the Strand Theatre on 12th May and at the Garrick on the 13th. It was staged by Oscar Asche, who also played Consul Bernick.]

I shall perhaps look in on you tomorrow after 4.30, as I am going to spend the early afternoon being photographed by [Frederick H.] Evans,

Granville Barker and Charlotte Shaw, Guildford, 1901
(*Photograph by Bernard Shaw; Burgunder Collection,
Cornell University Library*)

Near Studland Bay, Dorset, 1901
(*Photograph by Granville Barker ; Frognal Bookshop*)

possibly with the marvellous boy Barker (I dont mean that I'll call with him, but that he may be at Evans's). . . . I have ceased to believe that we can do anything against the younger generation. When Barker observed to me at one of the rehearsals of The Man of Destiny that I was just his father's age, I realized how completely we have taken the place of the generation we helped to kick out of the way. We are old, Father William: they can do without us. Barker regards me as a vulgar old buffer, devilish clever, and with a sympathetic wife. I saw when they did Pillars, that they could do it *well enough to pass*. By the Lord, they laugh at us, except when we play Nestor or Dr Johnson or something suitably *old* off on them.

GBS

To CHARLES CHARRINGTON

[A/4]

10 Adelphi Terrace WC
28th June 1901

[Shaw had just chaired a stormy general meeting of the Stage Society. His "sermon" to the South Place Ethical Society on 30th June was on "Twentieth Century Freethinking."]

Just got your telegram. As I shall not have time to write tomorrow (I have to prepare a sermon for South Place on Sunday morning) I will write a scrawl now without waiting for your letter.

Part of my astuteness in the chair was due to the happy accident that something distracted my attention whilst Hobson was blurting out his question about you; and I knew nothing of it until I got home & heard of it from my wife.

Anyhow, that was the wrong line for Hobson to take. And the spectacle of Janet refusing to accept his defeat, and speaking with intense moderation whilst nervously hammering with her fists on an imaginary Speaker's table which was really the crown of poor Charlotte's hat, was most appalling.

I think we may take it that the financial question has crowded out the artistic one quite hopelessly this year. On the financial one, you can support the Committee. The more you are identified with them the better. Hobson's victimization line is one that you ought to disclaim in the largest manner. Say that in any matter on which you differ from your colleagues, they will, if you are in the right, find that out from

227

experience, as they have in the matter of the impossibility of giving 12 stalls for 2 guineas. Magnanimity is your line: the people say "Can this noble creature with the fine lines of countenance be the ruffianly Pyrrhus—the slimy Morell—the unwholesome Aslaksen?"

As to the artistic policy, I am quite convinced that an art manager is all my eye. They wouldnt appoint one; and if they did it would be only to make him the scapegoat for all the inevitable shortcomings. If you support such a proposal later on, you can only do it effectively by saying that nothing would induce you to resume that unfortunate position yourself. But you had better back the committee. The only possible line of attack—that against the series of actor-managers who succeeded you—is closed to you by the fact that you had to play yourself in the pieces you managed.

However, all this is mere argument: I'll tell you now the real cause of all the trouble.

You are a very tolerable manager, even to the extent of a bit of a genius, when you are doing work that you like. But with regard to people and plays that you dont like, you are a rogue-elephant of the most impossible kind. When you read a play and like it and see it and want it—the Wild Duck or the Weavers or something of that sort—then you go down to rehearsal helpful, authoritative, all there. But when revolutionary realism is not on hand, when literary elegance, wit, fancy, classicism turns up, then you wont even read the play. You postpone the disagreeable ordeal to the last moment; you go down to the rehearsals without having made up your mind about a single entrance; you exasperate the author, infuriate the actors, and hurl at *my* devoted head a crowd of people asking me where your vaunted ability as a manager comes in. When the performance comes off, as a consequence partly of the struggles of the disconcerted and disparaged company, and partly of your getting appalled by the consequences of your own neglect at the eleventh hour, it is no better than anybody else's performance & sometimes a good deal worse. And the worse it is the better you are pleased, because the failure proves the soundness of your judgment of the play. But there is the devil to pay for this satisfaction. The actors, having had their time wasted & been magnetically thwarted at the earlier rehearsals on top of all the inevitable annoyances of our scratch arrangements, swear they will never play under you again. The author repays your ill will with interest. The committee, which you have carefully alienated because government through committees is immoral & Fabian (meaning that talking over unsympathetic people is troublesome), are only too glad to have overwhelming evidence that you are a Jonah; and then overboard you go. And because you immediately put on a fine expression of countenance and look noble, they explain your confounded laziness and mulish malice against Macaires & Andromaches & pretty Bedford Park young ladies as the result of the devilish plots of your wicked wife. You really are the most disgraceful old ruffian in the whole blessed movement, taking jobs that you dont intend to do and dont want to do and would dearly like to see fail.

Now the moral of this is perfectly clear and irresistible. A stage manager is an artist like all the other artists concerned; and to have the same stage manager for every class of play is just as absurd as to have the same actor for every class of part. The committee have been driven by mere force of circumstances to the right conclusion—different managers for different plays. Of course, as they have reached this by drifting to it and not intelligently, they do not really attempt any selection, and the selection that occurs is natural selection—that is, actor-management. But that is better than Stevenson & Murray managed by you on the principles of Kemble managing Godwin. Only, when we presently put up a play of Bjornsen's (if we do) which you ought to manage & would manage better than anybody else, the whole establishment will go on strike at the mere mention of your name; and this will last until you pull off a success or two & the S.S. pulls off a failure or two, and there is a reaction.

And that's the whole law & the prophets on the subject.

Meanwhile, you had better magnanimously support the committee on the finance matter, since the other is past praying for for the moment, and smile & smile & be a villain.

My hearty curse on you for giving me the trouble of scribbling all this when I ought to be at work on my sermon.

GBS

To SIDNEY WEBB

[L/14]

Studland Rectory. Corfe Castle
26th July 1901

[The Shaws were vacationing in Dorsetshire, from 19th July to 28th August. Archibald Philip Primrose (1847–1929), 5th Earl Rosebery, had been foreign secretary under Gladstone (1886, 1892–94), Liberal Prime Minister (1894–95), and leader of the opposition (1895–96). He advocated an imperialist policy during the Boer War, leading the imperialist school in a split from the insular school of the Liberal party. Rosebery had an inherent fear of Socialism.

Shaw had written to Beatrice Webb on 24th July: "I think it was a stroke almost of genius on Rosebery's part to queer Asquith's pitch by cutting in with a really rattling speech at afternoon tea before the great dinner. *Our* policy is clearly to back him for all we are worth: I think Webb might do worse than write a magazine article about it. I would in his place: now is the psychological moment to commit himself, especially as it will commit him to nothing. I would do it myself if my reputation were of a nature to help R. But it isnt; and Webb's is" [A/14]. Webb accepted the suggestion; his article: "Lord Rosebery's Escape from Houndsditch" appeared in the *Nineteenth Century* in September. Beatrice Webb noted in her diary: "Sidney's article . . . has been a brilliant success," adding that "G.B.S. corrected the proof and inserted some of the brilliance" (*Our Partnership*, 1948).]

(dictated—this is G.B.S.—not me C.F.S.).

Your remark about Rosebery is a most alarming one: it shews middle aged dry rot of the most horrible English kind. If it goes on, I shall have to go & live with you for 3 months to correct your perspective & restore your tone.

The situation is exactly the reverse of your putting of it. Your advantage is that you are the free-est man in England. I should be equally free if it were not for the division of my energies & the destruction of my singleness of purpose by my accursed talent for pure literature. If Beatrice had sat out Ibsen's play the other day instead of allowing Mrs [Alice] Green to take her off for a drink, she would have discovered that Ibsen had something to tell her of more importance to you at present than the old fashioned stuff about Truth & Freedom & Emancipation of Women which she very defensibly snorted at. That something was the exclamation of the cornered hero "We pillars of society are only the tools of society." Now Rosebery, being a peer & a political pillar, is necessarily a political tool. He is at present screaming for somebody to come & handle him, exactly like the madman in Peer Gynt who thinks he is a pen, & implores people to write with him, finally cutting his throat by way of mending his nib. (There is really a lot to be learned from Ibsen if Beatrice would only read him in the proper spirit). Your strength has always lain in your willingness & your capacity to be the tool-wielder, just as the official people's weakness has lain in their coveting the pomp & glory of prominent tooldom. You are married to the only woman in England who dare ask Rosebery to dinner & ask him whether he will take beer or whiskey. That is a tremendously strong position, but only so long as your own sense & grip of it remain unclouded & firm. If you once succumb to the fatal English weakness of worshiping the idol you have yourself fashioned, with the marks of the potter's thumb all over its still moist clay, you are lost. Handel did not attain his summit as a musician by effacing himself in his admiration of the majestic sounds produced by the bellows blower who supplied his organ with wind. Rosebery is at present blowing the bellows very hard. So is Asquith; so is Campbell Bannerman; so is Chamberlain; so are the whole boodle of them—all like so many Pied Pipers of Hamelin; but the children (meaning the British Public) wont follow because there is no tune. And there wont be any tune—bar "Rule Britannia" & "God save the King," of which people are getting tired—until you put your fingers on the key board.

I suggested a magazine article because there is a rather complex situation to be analyzed; & this can only be done by somebody who knows the real political history of the Newcastle Program period. Rosebery missed his chance when he was Prime Minister not only because, as he alleges, the time was not ripe for his Imperialism, but also because he himself was not ripe for the Collectivism which was the true economic substance of that Imperialism. And the thing to be rubbed into him now is that his speeches convey no sort of assurance that he has matured on this side. To be imaginative & up to date on the Imperialist side without being also imaginative & up to date on the Industrial side, is to be simply a second hand Bismarck; & this popular leading part is already filled by Chamberlain. As long as Rosebery gets no further than this, he will set people talking; but nothing will happen except that the necessity for keeping up the talk will drive him more & more out of politics & into literature, in which he is too old to become a genuine expert. What he is avowedly aiming at is something quite different from this: to wit, a sudden party reconstruction in which the Liberalism of the future will crystallize on his epigrams. But the real party reconstruction is the one with the economic basis, the replacement of Tory & Whig by Collectivist & Individualist; & the reason the crystallization hangs fire is that no leader has yet made himself the spokesman of collectivism. If Rosebery did that, he would instantly differentiate himself from Chamberlain, & the rush to his standard might begin. But—& this is the note of interrogation on which an article should end—is he really converted to Collectivism, or does he still think that the Newcastle Program was a mistake, & that the business of the next Heaven-born steersman of the Liberal party is to complete the backing out of it.

I think that if anybody were to say this at the present time, he would be listened to, & would score a point, besides intimidating Rosebery most frightfully. What Rosebery himself has proved is that this is not a time for holding one's tongue. All the people who are not talking are listening; & you ought to take the opportunity to cross the stage effectively for a moment, lest the heap of work you do behind the scenes should bring you less than its desirable value in personal influence. At all events I offer the suggestion. Want of time or lazyness or genuine disagreement with my view of the situation may be valid excuses; but modest coughs about humble persons & peers I simply decline to entertain. We have not got to our present point on modest principles; & we are not likely to get any further in the same direction by turning right about face now.

GBS

To BEATRICE WEBB

[L/14]

Studland Rectory. Corfe Castle
30th July 1901

[Maeterlinck's *The Life of the Bee* had recently been published in Paris. Alfred Sutro's translation was published in London in the same year. John Athelstan Lawrie Riley (1858–1945) was a churchman who specialised in Eastern Christianity. Active in politics, he was a member of the London School Board from 1891 to 1897. Charles Lindley Wood (1839–1934), 2nd Viscount Halifax, was a church leader. Frederick S. Roberts (1832–1914), 1st Earl Roberts of Kandahar, Pretoria, and Waterford, was supreme commander of British forces in South Africa through most of the Boer War.]

(G.B.S. per C.F.S.)

My dear Beatrice

If Webb has started the article, I think I shall turn lazy & look on at him working. However, your letter suggests one thing to me. We shall have to be extremely careful to avoid any appearance of going back on our Socialism. Nothing is more unpopular in England than hauling down a flag, even if it has become a flagrantly impossible flag. If General [William] Booth were to declare tomorrow that he had given up the Bible & adopted the views of Huxley, he would obliterate himself from public life, because the Huxleyites would give him no credit for merely coming to his senses, & would never attach the least importance to a man who had compromised himself by salvationism; the pious people would be horrified; & everybody would regard him as an apostate. Politically, therefore, we are committed for life to Socialism; & any appearance of backing out of it would leave us less influence than Hyndman or Keir Hardie. This is always true; but it is extra-specially true at the present moment, when the public imagination is full of the running up of flags & the nailing of them to the top-gallant.

Personally, the same thing holds good. A certain number of clever people of the Haldane calibre will no doubt read the article to learn what Sidney Webb has to say; but a good many less definitely instructed people will want to know what the reasonable Socialist has to say, having ascertained that the more conventional politicians have nothing to say. He must therefore speak ostentatiously from the Socialist platform: in fact, that is the only way in which he can force the press to discuss what he says instead of merely letting it alone with a few timid complimentary phrases.

The substance of the article is quite another matter. I suggest that an effective line to take would be to hold up Socialism to Rosebery & the Imperialists as a lesson & a warning, as follows.

Take, roughly speaking, Socialism as the political boom of the decade 1885–95. Take Imperialism as the political boom of 95–05. Point out that both began with the most complete conviction on the part of their disciples that they constituted a new party which marked them off definitely, decisively, & irrevocably from the old Whig & Tory divisions. Then show how completely this conviction was exploded in the case of Socialism by subsequent events. Show that at no moment during the whole boom of Socialism was it possible to infer from the fact of a man being a Socialist how he would vote in any Parliamentary division; that when Socialists got into Parliament, as in the case of Cunninghame-Graham, John Burns & Keir Hardie, not only was there no concert between them, but they entirely failed to impress the public with the slightest consciousness that they had any unusual Parliamentary creed, or that any new element had been introduced into the House. Point out, in short, that the description of a man as a Socialist, conveys just as much Parliamentary information about him, no less & no more, than the statement that he is a Christian. And add, that a minute's consideration will convince any cool person that precisely the same thing is true today of Imperialism. Just as the most careful study of the Manifestoes to the Social Democratic Federation throws no light on the question of how Mr Hyndman would have voted in the last Parliament if he had been returned for Bromley, instead of staying outside to keep up a determined political feud with John Burns & the Fabian Society; just so do Lord Rosebery's Liberal Manifestoes & City Liberal speeches throw no light on the Parliamentary Program of the Party & the Government which he avowedly hopes someday to lead.

You can then point out, without the slightest air of apostasy, that the war has been fatal to the Socialistic boom because it has produced exactly the same dissensions among the Socialists as among the Gentiles. That the political solidarity of Socialism is an illusion had long been known to the inner rings of the Socialists themselves; but the public did not care twopence about these rings & their affairs: it was the war that dragged the dissensions into prominence, as it dragged so many other things.

It remains for the domestic policy of the next ten years to explode the imaginary solidarity of Imperialism as the foreign policy of the last five years has exploded the imaginary solidarity of Socialism. Imperialism is, like all the other isms, a mere shibboleth; & Webb should at this point of the argument flatly declare that he will rally to no leader who has nothing more than a shibboleth to offer, especially when it is offered by a politician who has declared that programs are a mistake. They may be mistakes; & they are certainly nuisances from the point of view of statesmen who wish to shirk thought, trouble & responsibility; but they are quite inevitable. The Liberal & Conservative parties exist today only because they have become associated with certain measures & with the opposition to certain other measures. If Lord Rosebery wishes to become a political entity he must become a personified program. I should instance here the case of [William Jennings] Bryan in America. It was as a personified program that he became a political personality. What Rosebery wants is some Free Silver to make him current. At present his Imperialism cannot compete even with Socialism, because Socialism has managed to produce a section which in its turn has managed to produce the term Fabianism, which, though as senseless a word as the vaguest politician could desire, got associated with a definite program and actually succeeded in producing the only real new party in the country: that is, the Municipal Progressive party, wheras, once the excitement of the war is over, Roseberyite Imperialism will not even seem to mean anything; and the Roseberyites will be at one another's throats on the first Stock Exchange, Trade Union or fiscal question that arises.

Having thus demonstrated the necessity for a program, you can pro-

234

ceed to criticise the existing programs & demonstrate their obsolescence to your heart's content. I should not spare the Newcastle Program by any means.

The Maximum Efficiency of the Nation is a good phrase for a treatise, but for a political article it is hardly succulent enough. And it is tremendously open to the sort of criticism that Bentham's formulae encountered. It may be that the Maximum Efficiency is only to be attained as the bees attain it; & unfortunately Maeterlinck has just described that method with a fullness that is hardly calculated to popularize it. The truth is that efficiency is obviously not a final term & cannot be held up as an end. So dont commit yourself. I'm too lazy to dictate any more.

GBS

P.S. In touching Home Rule & the old Radical Program of the reform of Political Machinery, I should dwell heavily on the fact that though the machinery has now been reformed enough for the moment, there is not enough of it. The other day this government, with its enormous majority, had to make an infamous capitulation to the Irish Catholics, to get their Factory Bill through. Government without sufficient machinery means the supremacy of the minorities who are absolutely indifferent to the public welfare—that is, to religious fanatics, Athelstane Rileys, Halifaxes, Irish Papists &c &c &c &c.

You should also be pretty definite as to the explodedness of the old Radical conception of Democracy. Mention that if the Prime Minister were popularly elected, the betting would be about even on Chamberlain, Lord Roberts and Sir Henry Irving.

To HENRY S. SALT

Studland Rectory. Corfe Castle
[A/5; X/164.e]   9th August 1901

["Count Somebody" was Leo Tolstoy. L. T. (Mrs Charles) Mallet (d. 1904), a member of the Fabian Executive 1890–92, was a popular lecturer, active with the Women's Liberal Federation and the Humanitarian League. Sir Robert Anderson (1841–1918), Assistant Commissioner of Police for London, had published an article (one of a series), "An Absurd System of Punishing Crime," in the February issue of *Nineteenth Century*. The Rev. William Douglas Morrison (1852–1943), Chaplain in H.M. Prison Service

1883–98, and author of *Crime and Its Causes* (1891), had replied to Anderson in an article "Spurious Remedies for Crime" in the April issue of the *Humane Review*.]

I mislaid your letter, and consequently your address, the day after we arrived here. Hence my delay in answering.

I dont think Wagner would be a good subject for a Humanitarian lecture, partly because the artistic interest of his life overwhelms all the other interests, but chiefly because he was one of those annoying people, a vegetarian in theory. Late in life he came across an impassioned humanitarian pamphlet by a Count Somebody; and it affected him so deeply that he wept like the carpenter in "Through the Looking Glass" over the animals he was eating, and wrote an essay of his own on the subject. Also he had a series of pets—dogs mostly, but including one adored parrot—to which he was extravagantly attached. There is a legend about his seeing a calf slaughtered in his boyhood and going almost out of his senses at it; but he did not abstain from veal on that account. Also he was horrified at the cruelty with which chickens were carried about on Swiss lake steamers; but he ate them all the same. On the whole, I think Mrs Mallett might do a moving paper on the subject: it does not seem to me to be worth more than a 10 minutes speech.

The man I want to lecture on is Anderson, with whose view of criminals & the law I enthusiastically agree. He is the first practical man who has really succeeded in shaking the idea of punishment in his own mind; and as the humanitarians, whose notions of mercy & forgiveness are only vengeance and expiation turned inside out, are just as likely to attack him (Morrison, for instance) as to hail him as a deliverer, I should enjoy developing his thesis & clearing it from its Andersonian crust of police prejudice.

We return to Guildford next month, but must give up the cottage in April next year. Can you suggest a country seat for us within an hour of Charing † ?

GBS

To REV. ENSOR WALTERS

[A/43; X/171]

10 Adelphi Terrace WC
14th September 1901

[The Rev. Charles Ensor Walters (1872–1938), who had recently been appointed assistant to Hugh Price Hughes at the West London Mission, had met Shaw on the St Pancras Vestry in 1898. Walters was chairman of the Health Committee of the Vestry, on which Shaw served. Dr John F. Sykes (d. 1913), author of *Public Health and Housing* (1901), was Medical Officer of Housing for St Pancras and the source for many of Shaw's accurate statistics on health conditions in the St Pancras parish. Shaw's letter to *The Times*, "Smallpox in St. Pancras," on 21st September, was the first in a two-year battle to awaken Londoners to the truth about health conditions in their midst. His letter "Vaccination Statistics" appeared in *The Times* on 8th October, and another on "Small-pox Prevention" in the *British Medical Journal* on 26th October. In a debate by the United Law Society, Shaw proposed a resolution "That it is desirable, with a view to ascertain how much (if anything) is really left of the pretensions of vaccination as a prophylactic, that a careful re-examination of the evidence should be made by a body of statistical and actuarial experts, from which body medical men should be rigorously excluded" (*Vaccination Inquirer*, 2nd December 1901). He published a dozen more letters on the subject in 1902.]

Dear Walters

I see 8 more cases of smallpox today. This means that we must act. You must demand what will amount to a credit of £1000 from the Council to meet the emergency by at once jamming on 4 temporary* inspectors for house to house inspection & measuring up of registered tenements exclusively. Sykes must declare that the situation demands this—that everything points to a devastating epidemic next spring if things are left as they are. It is better to frighten London now than to bury it next year.

A resolution should be put down for next Council meeting, even if it involves an emergency meeting of the Health Com^tee. Of course I can put it down myself as an outsider; but clearly it should come from you. If the Health refuses to support you you might quite well do it as a private member on your own responsibility. But we must do something striking and vigorous at all hazards. If we dont, an epidemic will leave us open to the reproach that we saw it coming and did nothing, though we knew that house-to-house inspection had ceased, that the registered houses had never been inspected, and that the L.C.C. had

---

* I am not sure that it would not be better to boldly ask for 6 inspectors for 6 months. That would break the back of the work for the moment; and we could probably either reappoint them in spring if things looked dangerous, or at all events retain the 2 best of them as permanent additions to the staff. The cost of the 6 for 6 months would be inside £1000.

warned us again & again of our insanitary condition. On the other hand, if we act & spend money, then, if there be no epidemic, our foresight and energy will have prevented it, and if there be one, we shall have done all in our power, and can affirm confidently that the death rate would be twice as high but for our exertions.

Probably I am only anticipating your own conclusions.

I am off now to Guildford until Wednesday—address Piccard's Cottage, St Catherines, Guildford.

yrs ever

G. Bernard Shaw

PS I am trying to find some precedent for an inclusive salary for the Town Clerk.

To REV. ENSOR WALTERS

[A/43; X/171]

Piccard's Cottage. Guildford
16th September 1901

Dear Walters

It is utterly totally completely entirely absolutely positively emphatically and finally stark staring smash bang impossible for this business to come from anybody but the Chairman of the Health Committee. To have the initiative taken & your hand forced by an outsider would be the end of all things for you. An epidemic is for you what a war is for a general—your chance in life. Besides, the year is nearly out; and all the strong chairmen will try, like the Mayor, for a second year. If your motion succeeds, you will be re-elected on the strength of it. If not, and you are not elected, you will fall a victim to your public spirit and have the glory of martyrdom without the work of chairman. In any case, let nobody take the word of the Lord out of the minister's mouth. Ride for a fall and you will get credit whether you land safely with your four inspectors or not.

Sykes is in a strong position. The old gang cannot be made more hostile to him than they already are; and he could blow them sky high by an alarmist letter to the Times.

As to the illegally occupied rooms, they must be cleared. We should have done it long ago. Nothing will be done until we put the screw on. If we dont the smallpox will relieve the pressure in an unpleasantly decisive way, mostly at the expense of the guardians.

238

I shall see you at the Parliamentary on Wednesday.

To cure the fag, make a rule to do nothing after lunch, and give up answering letters. As Napoleon said, they answer themselves if you leave them long enough.

GBS

To MRS PATRICK CAMPBELL

[A/37; X/229, 160]

10 Adelphi Terrace WC
7th November 1901

[Mrs Campbell had presented Jessie Muir's translation of Björnstjerne Björnson's *Beyond Human Power* at the Royalty Theatre that afternoon for a series of matinées. The "Hallelujah Chorus" was a hymn of praise sung by a chorus of peasants in the second act. Rachael [Rakel] was Lucy Milner, who played Mrs Campbell's daughter. George S. Titheradge (1848–1916) had performed in Australia for some twenty years, then returned to London to join the company of Robert Brough and Dion Boucicault, for whom he performed comedy leads for ten years.]

My dear Mrs Patrick Campbell

That was a really great managerial achievement. In future, when people ask me whether I go to the theatre I shall say "To the Royalty, not to any other."

I think the Hallelujah Chorus might be improved by steeping in boiling water for ten minutes or so before the next matinée. And if Rachael must have a scream at the end, it might be well to give her, at rehearsal, something to scream for. Titheradge was so remarkable a parson that you really ought to play Candida* for his benefit: he would cover himself with glory as Candida's husband; but he is wrong to gurgle like Othello cutting his throat. That scene gets far beyond the screaming & gurgling kind of realism. These physical obstructions and inconveniences have no business among the spiritual agonies. May I suggest, too, that Titheradge's determination to die parrallel to the float with his heels O.P. and his head P, whilst you occupy the corresponding position P & O.P. rather spoils the picture. After all, it is not natural that he should die unassisted, especially after gurgling; and it would be a great improvement if he would breathe his last in the arms of Horatio

---

* *Candida* is an old play of my own, with a most parsonic parson in it.

239

—say the sceptical parson who wants the miracle. That would compose the picture much better. It is one of the drawbacks to your power of rousing people's sense of beauty, that even trifles jar on it if they are unbecoming.

However, all that is nothing. The impression was overwhelming.

yours enthusiastically
G. Bernard Shaw

PS. I was greatly touched when Mrs Theodore Wright, who was a friend of Karl Marx and has been in all sorts of revolutionary circles, got so indignant at the conduct of Pastor Sang, that she clenched her fists and glared at the wickedness of religion instead of giving you your cue—the "My dear" cue. Forgive her: it was a generous slip.

To MRS PATRICK CAMPBELL

10 Adelphi Terrace WC
[I/37; X/229.e, 160]   22nd November 1901

[The photograph showed Mrs Campbell in *Beyond Human Power* at the miraculous moment when the bedridden wife of the pastor rises, walks, and stands with outstretched arms in the doorway. Ten years later, Shaw *did* photograph Mrs Campbell in bed! *Mrs Warren's Profession* was scheduled for production by the Stage Society on 8th December, but had to be postponed due to the inability to secure a theatre. The Society was turned down by more than a dozen theatres, two music halls, and a picture gallery, partly because *Mrs Warren* was an unlicensed play, but also because it was to be a Sunday performance. Finally, in desperation, the management settled for the small stage of the New Lyric Club. H. W. Massingham had been working for the *Manchester Guardian* since his dismissal from the *Daily Chronicle*.]

My dear Mrs Patrick Campbell
Thank you for the beautiful photograph; but *I* should have photographed you in bed, saying "It's tempting Providence." That was the finest passage in the play. After all, there are lots of beautiful people about; and some of them can perhaps even thread needles with their toes; but they cant take a filament of grey matter from their brains and thread it infallibly through that most elusive of eyelet holes in the top of a dramatist's needle. Besides, that produces a new sort of beauty, compared to which natural beauty is a mere reach-me-down from Nature's patterns. Long ago, when everybody was maudlin about your

240

loveliness, I snapped my fingers—admired nothing but your deft fingers & toes. Now I admire you ENORMOUSLY. You have picked the work of Nature to pieces & remade it whole heavens finer. It is the power to do that that is the real gift.

I am in hideous straits about the Stage Society's performance of a play of mine called "Mrs Warren's Profession," which Mr Redford wouldnt license. We had it all arranged beautifully—Fanny Brough for Mrs Warren—when the theatre was withdrawn lest the Reader of Plays should revenge himself by suspending its license. I wish you had a theatre of your very own; for if the Lord Chamberlain suspended you, I could make a revolution within half an hour of the announcement.

The enclosed letter is from one of my reverend Nonconformist constituents [C. Silvester Horne]. He wrote to me in great excitement about Beyond Human Power. I wrote back urging him to write to the Times and to get a lot of other divines to sign with him. Unluckily Massingham took the word of the Lord out of the minister's mouth.

yours sincerely
G. Bernard Shaw

To R. GOLDING BRIGHT

[H/1; X/125]

10 Adelphi Terrace WC
30th November 1901

[Lily Langtry (1852–1929), an almost legendary actress-manager, known as the Jersey Lily, had recently assumed the management of the newly rebuilt Imperial Theatre. Fanny Brough (1854–1914), a member of a well-known acting family, had had a long career in the theatre, mostly in comedy. She had appeared in Pinero's farce *The Times* (1891), in Wilde's *An Ideal Husband* (1895) and in F. Anstey's *The Man from Blankley's* (1901). *La Dame aux camélias* was by Alexandre Dumas *fils*. *Zaza* by David Belasco (from the French) had been produced at the Garrick Theatre on 16th April 1900. Pinero's *Iris* was presented at the Garrick on 21st September 1901. Golding Bright published Shaw's information in the *Daily Express* on 3rd December.]

Dear Golding Bright

The story of Mrs Warren may as well be advanced a stage further, now that Mrs Langtry has repudiated so indignantly the statement (which nobody made) that the performance was going to take place at the Imperial Theatre.

It is quite true that Miss Fanny Brough, on learning the nature of Mrs Warren's Profession, revoked her consent to play. But it is also true that on Miss Fanny Brough's proceeding to read the so-called wicked play, she energetically and enthusiastically withdrew her objection, resumed the part, and will, I guarantee, very considerably astonish two classes of people in it: namely, those who are now scribbling about the play without having read it, and those (mostly managers) who are under the impression that Miss Brough is only a comic actress.

The truth is, there has been a rally round the play which has astonished me. I opposed its production by the Stage Society on the ground that it might expose the manager of the theatre to the resentment of the Censor, who has unhappily committed himself to the old censorial position that illicit sexual relations must not be mentioned on stage unless, as in the case of the Dame aux Camellias, Zaza, and Iris, the heroines of them are made extremely attractive, so as to offer the largest possible inducements to poor girls in the gallery to follow their example. As it is clear that Mrs Warren will not make a single convert to the cause of Polyandry, the King's Reader of Plays will not tolerate her; but even his department has gone so far as to disclaim any cognizance of a performance which will be open to the public for payment at the doors. Still, I urged the Society to let it alone, and suggested the substitution of my fully authorised and licensed play, The Philanderer. But the Society strongly objected to the morals and tone of the Philanderer, and overbore me as to Mrs Warren. They would have it; and the cast would have it; and, in short, I had to withdraw my prudent objections in some disgrace, which served me right.

There has been no difficulty whatever with anyone, save only the Censor and Mrs Langtry, on the score of the play's character: quite the contrary. I had no suspicion that the play had made such an impression, though I of course knew from its reception by the reviewers on the publication of Plays, Pleasant and Unpleasant (to the horror of the then young and innocent R.G.B.), that there was danger of its being misunderstood as a mere impropriety. You will see by the letter from the National Vigilance Society in the Times today, that Mrs Warren is as busy and prosperous as ever in real life, in spite of all the committees that have been formed throughout Europe to suppress her. Alfred Place and its neighborhood is as crowded as ever with knots of women; and it is still not possible to say truthfully to one of them that she will be better treated and better paid by Society if she turns "honest" and takes to charwoman's work at the St Pancras standard of five shillings a week.

242

The cast is—Mrs Warren—Fanny Brough: Vivie Warren—Madge McIntosh: the Reverend Samuel Gardner—Charles Goodhart: Frank Gardner—Granville Barker: Praed—Julius Knight; and Crofts—tell you later on, as we are changing. [Goodhart eventually appeared as Crofts, and Cosmo Stuart as the Rev. Samuel Gardner.]

You will observe that none of these people have any inducement to play except the purely artistic inducement. They wont be paid; and they are not nobodies or novices. Their names and positions, and those of the Committee of the Stage Society are sufficient cards to play against the view to which the Censor has lent his countenance.

The sole obstacle to the performance is the intimidation of the Censor, and his absolutely autocratic power—to ruin any West End manager who offends him, without reason given or remedy available. But though he cannot divest himself of his powers, he has, to do him justice, disclaimed, as far as he officially can, any concern with private performances. And the disclaimer has been made in reply to an inquiry in connection with this performance and this play. It is still probable, however, that the performance will take place out of his jurisdiction.

All of which information I recommend to your best discretion in case you should be dealing with the subject in the Daily Express or elsewhere. It must figure as your own information, because I am not justified in making any official communication to the press without consulting the others; so this must be matter come to your private knowledge.

yrs
G. Bernard Shaw

_To_ H. G. WELLS

[H/26]

10 Adelphi Terrace WC
12th December 1901

[Herbert George Wells (1866–1946) appears to have been introduced to Shaw for the first time at the opening night of Henry James's _Guy Domville_ (St James's Theatre, 5th January 1895). They met frequently thereafter at first nights in the theatre, and sometimes walked home together after the performance, as Wells had to pass Fitzroy Square to get to his home in North London. They began to exchange books, and Shaw had received a copy of _Anticipations_, which was published in November.

Robert Owen (1771–1858) was a Welsh socialist and philanthropist. Shaw refers here to Owen's *The Book of the New Moral World* (1836). Laputa, in Book III of Swift's *Gulliver's Travels*, was a flying island peopled with scientific quacks and dreamy philosophers. *The Academy* had published on 7th December a series of lists by public figures of their two or three "Favourite Books of 1901." Sidney Webb had listed *Anticipations*. Wells had chosen *Three Plays for Puritans*, along with W. E. Henley's *Hawthorn and Lavender* and G. Archdall Reid's *Alcoholism*. Sir Victor Horsley (1857–1916) was a distinguished physiologist and surgeon.]

Wells, my boy

On the threshold of all new Republics lies a fell beast called the Currency Crank, whose object it is to prove that as the Guernsey Market was built for nothing on a basis of inconvertible paper, which the Channel Islanders took in with one another's washing, so can we take short cuts to the Millenium by a suitable modification of our standard of value. I have myself conversed with a man who came to a colony in America in the course of an afternoon's walk; did twenty minutes work; got a banknote for twenty minutes; and bought a dinner with the banknote. I have by me old volumes of Owen's journals of his New Moral World, with records of the Labor Exchanges in the Grays Inn Road and other places, where you exposed for sale the product of your labor marked in minutes and hours: that is, in Energy measured by Time. I grieve to say that these anticipations of Dobbsism have left so violent a prejudice against Currency projects in the minds of all experienced New Republicans that they dare not touch the best considered scheme of the kind for fear of being branded with Laputanism.

The letters sent me by Guest refer to previous correspondence, and leave me in the dark as to what Arthur C. Dobbs is exactly driving at. Guest himself calls it a token coinage representing units of energy. Now if, as appears to be the case, he means potential energy, every tramp can say, "Fill me with a shilling's worth of food and I will sell you half a crown's worth of potential energy; and you can stop the shilling out of the price." One foresees an attractive chapter on The Tramp as The Kinetic Man. But that sort of Kinetic Man, being a tramp, would not wash. On the other hand, if the energy is expended energy, it must take the form of a manufactured product. If it is stored energy, it must take the form of an accumulator, or a cylinder of compressed gas, or a connection with a generating station. In the three last cases, there is no special currency problem involved: the products or accumulators or connection can be paid for in money of the present type; and the problem of the New Republic need not be complicated

244

by the technical question of establishing new media of currency or standards of value.

You may reply, however, that the New Republic is not a problem, but simply the totality of a series of technical reforms of just this currency type. But that be blowed! Your business is the preaching of the synthesis, not the execution of its constituents. What can be done for Dobbs is to put him off the track of currency reform, and make him take up the question of energy straightforwardly. Ruskin long ago rubbed in the fallacy of measuring national wealth by exchangeable products: you may remember his illustration of the immoveable Tintoretto ceiling and the two-francs-fifty obscene Parisian lithograph. What needs rubbing in now is that English prosperity has hitherto depended on her contiguous heaps of coal and iron: that is, of her early exploitation of these stores of energy. We are now getting cut out because other nations are developing not only their coal and iron stores, but their waterfalls. Now we dont develop anything. Nature has given us tides which exist hardly anywhere else in the world, and has provided a current in the Pentland Firth which would, if used, mop up Niagara. But we sit staring at the tides and sketching them in water colors. If Dobbs will only hammer away at that, using his currency suggestion merely as an illustration to bring out how poorer we shall be than the energy-exploiting nations even when the country is covered with American millionaires paying us a vast Income Tax, he will do some good. Let him work out, if he can, a tabular index founded on our output of energy, for that founded on staple commodities in The Economist; but keep him off the notion that currency reform is any use by itself, or that the exploitation of Pentland Firth will be of no use without currency reform. That way madness lies, and exasperation on the part of the readers, and a premature end in bathostic ridicule for the New Republic.

This is what occurs to me at the first glance. I purposely shoot it down before there is time to reflect, because what my first impression is will be that of others also. I shall not exactly *mention* the matter to Webb; but I shall break it to him and see how he takes it. I dont think the London School would be quite so eager to harbor a new currency scheme as they would be to set up a smallpox ward—for the memories of Bimetallism are recent and bitter—but still the London School pulse can be felt in a casual manner. I see by the Academy that Webb has placed Anticipations among his books of the year. As it was I who shoved it on to him, I consider that I have rolled your log in return for your noble recognitions of the profundity of Plays for Puritans.

245

As it happens, I had been reading Reid on Alcoholism. But though he thinks with a certain vigour, science has induced in him an abject credulity which makes one despair of any good coming out of it all. The step from a mild belief in the efficacy of baptism to a frantic and persecuting conviction of the absolute necessity of Vaccination is so appallingly retrograde, and so characteristic of the whole scientific movement, that it indicates a decay of the human intellect. Besides, this turning from the simple truth of Lamarckism to the mechanical rationalism of Natural Selection is very unpromising. A man who cannot see that the fundamental way for a camelopard to lengthen his neck is to want it longer, and to want it hard enough, and who explains the camelopard by a farfetched fiction of an accidentally long necked Romeo of the herd meeting an accidentally longnecked Juliet, and browsing on foliage which the other Montagues and Capulets could not reach, ought really to be locked up! Tell Reid to read Samuel Butler's Luck or Cunning, and to bear in mind that the difference, so far, between the Pentateuch and the scriptures of the scientific materialism of the sixties, is the difference between shrewd nonsense and DAMNED nonsense. I am accustomed to hear all that side of things from the Anarchists, who shew the necessity of dynamite exactly as the Horsley sort of idiot shews the necessity of vivisection and all the other modern means of bringing "research" within the means of the lowest capacity.

Some of what Reid says needs saying; but this dream of a community rendered Immune from everything by giving up preventive and defensive measures and substituting Temptation in the Wilderness would scandalize the Inquisition, and revolt the builders of the tower of Jezreel. These doctors all think that science is knowledge, instead of being the very opposite of knowledge: to wit, speculation.

In haste, ever
G. Bernard Shaw

To CHARLES CHARRINGTON

[A/4]

Piccard's Cottage. Guildford
14th December 1901

[A. B. Walkley had lectured to the Fabians the previous evening on "The Modern French Drama," one of a series of lectures by Archer, Gilbert Murray, Shaw, and Alfred Sutro on "The Social Tendencies of the Drama." Alfred W. Gattie (1856–1925), playwright, inventor and promoter, provided the inspiration for Breakages, Ltd., in Shaw's *The Apple Cart* (1929). Samuel K. Ratcliffe (1868–1958) was a Fabian who enjoyed a reputation as a journalist and lecturer.]

. . . Walkley's paper was a very clever one, though it put out the debaters in a very odd way: nobody except Gatty succeeded in saying anything he meant, or even anything intelligible to me. I dont even know what you mean by my shutting up Ratcliffe. Did I? Nobody was clear or at ease. Mrs Walkley remarked to Charlotte when you spoke: "That man hates my husband." She gathered this from your agonized manner.

The fact is, Walkley's trick was so simple, that the extraordinary botheration it produced hid it. He was comparing a water consisting exclusively of oxygen with a water consisting exclusively of hydrogen, the reply being that though water consists of O_2H, and the O & H can be considered & discussed & analysed separately, water is O *and* H, and water consisting of O alone or H alone doesnt exist. His amazing bit of obtuseness about the scene of the parsons in Beyond Human Power was the most vulnerable bit of his address; but the address was so smart & so confusing that nobody took notes, and he escaped being brought to book. He also did not give an opening for an attack on the ground of his turning up his nose at the theatre, though that is really both the fault and the quality of the criticism. He had taken a great deal of pains; was horribly nervous (I had to rescue him from the questions); and really did his blood best right up to his limitations. The whole address had a special artistic character & individuality of its own: it was a piece of art, successfully acted out at the first trial. It was a strain to be in the chair; and somehow the meeting seemed to share the strain and get sore, perhaps because he held their attention so hard & peppered his points so neatly; but I think he made a distinct success. I must go to bed now: my very soul is fatigued.

GBS

To MAX BEERBOHM

[A/1]

10 Adelphi Terrace WC
17th December 1901

[Max Beerbohm's first one-man show had opened at the Carfax Gallery on 14th December. The drawing Shaw describes (reproduced in *The Candid*

247

Friend on 14th December) is "A Touching Coronation Scene—Mr W. Archer and Mr A.W.Pinero." It shows Archer standing behind Pinero and rather ineffectively crowning him with a laurel wreath. (See also Shaw's letter of 27th August 1903 to Archer.) Edward Tennyson Reed (1860–1933) and Sir Francis Carruthers Gould (1844–1925) were popular English caricaturists. The Salvation caricature (offered at five guineas) shows Shaw in Salvation Army uniform, and sticking out of his pocket a periodical called "The Shaw Cry." With one hand he is pointing to heaven; the other hand is on the shoulder of a disagreeable looking tart with "Drama" written on her hat. The drawing is labelled: "Frontispiece to *Three Plays for Puritans* (second edition). *Miss Tolty Drama*: 'Garn! 'Ow should I earn my livin'?'" The "treasonable" drawings probably were cruel caricatures of King Edward VII.

Beerbohm's drawings stimulated much controversy and heated reaction. John Hollingshead, a noted author, journalist, and manager of the Gaiety Theatre 1868–86, was referred to as "good old trenchant John" in Clement Scott's *Free Lance* on 21st December 1901 for his statement that Beerbohm's drawings "are as grotesque as the infant efforts of *some unlicked cub of nature* struggling to make a new race with distorted fancy and humour and black and grey putty."

The man Shaw calls "Carfax" probably was a member of the firm, Robert Ross or More Adey.]

My dear Max

I went to Carfax yesterday, and, to my horror, found my wife there in triumphant possession of the Archer–Pinero picture (which common decency forbids me, as a rival dramatist, to see the point of), and on the point of buying the capitalist G.B.S., with the object of concealing or destroying it as a libel on her husband's charms. And this suggests to me that if you desire immortality you should refuse to sell a caricature to the original, whilst if you desire money you should sell it to nobody else.

The only drawing I object to is the Sir W.Harcourt, because it offends that sense of beauty which you will not give me credit for. It's not merely worse than Reed at his worst in this respect, but positively as bad as Gould at his best—a hideous composition. If you were a realist, a perfect representation of Harcourt, however wooden, would justify itself. But from the moment you touch the grotesque, you stand bound, without one plea, to fill up your sheet of paper fascinatingly. If you draw real lions, you need not make a picture of them; but if you draw heraldic lions you must fill the quarter of the shield with a fine design of lions Ⓠ ! That is more grotesque than any heraldic lion; but it is more sordid than the vilest butter print. Try filling a

248

heraldic shield with three such Harcourts, but with the heads & legs duly twisted and turned to make a fine fantastic decoration. That is the sole expiation possible.

I was somewhat amazed at your political savagery, though I applaud it highly. What pleased me most, however, was the lot of fine drawing & design you show. Several of the caricatures whose originals I have never seen interested me as much, as drawings, as the others did. Why dont you swear an oath to caricature women only for six months. There *must* be a way of caricaturing women without insulting them as well as a way of caricaturing men. If you can preserve the charm of Dolmetsch, why not of Mrs Pat as well?

William Morris used to say of me that it was a mercy I couldnt draw caricatures. You are the body of his fear.

The Salvation caricature had come out of its box & was flaunting itself unashamed on the walls. The treasonable ones will be out next.

When my wife demurred to the Capitalist, Carfax suggested, with dealerlike urbanity, that he was sure Mr Beerbohm would accept a commission from her for a special caricature if she would explain the style of thing she preferred. He was profoundly serious.

yrs ever
G. Bernard Shaw

To HARLEY GRANVILLE BARKER

[H/3; X/168]

10 Adelphi Terrace WC
31st December 1901

[Barker's *The Marrying of Ann Leete*, which he himself directed, was performed by the Stage Society at the Royalty Theatre on 26th and 27th January 1902. Presumably a rehearsal of *Mrs Warren* had been scheduled in the Hotel Cecil, due to the continued lack of a theatre.]

Dear G.B.

You are losing sight in the last act of the new attitude of Vivie, hard as nails, and fiercely intolerant of any approach to poetry. Being of a poetic turn yourself, you have a constant tendency to modulate into E flat minor (which is short for Eugene flat minor) which is steadily lowering the tone of Frank, until he seems fairly likely to end as Hamlet. Instead of being incorrigibly good-for-nothing, you are incorrigibly the other thing. I have serious thoughts of having you to dinner on Sunday and making you very drunk; only I fear that you would become pious in your cups instead of gay. Instead of getting boundless amusement out of everything disastrous, you become the man of sorrows at every exhibition of human frailty, and seem to be bitterly reproaching me all through for the flippancy of my dialogue. Two rehearsals more, and you will draw tears even in the third act.

There is one passage which is particularly dreadful because it has absolutely no sense unless its mood is perfectly conveyed. "What do YOU say, govnor, eh?" You express neither curiosity nor amusement here; and far from singing "good old Crofts" like a lark in the heavens, you convey the impression that you know the man well and habitually talk of him and to him in that way.

In short, you need not be afraid of overdoing the part: the real danger is underdoing it. You have a frightful air of a youth in love—with Ann Leete probably.

It is a question of feeding, perhaps: you must come to lunch oftener.

When I was unable today to conceal the shock with which I saw you suddenly hit on the idea of playing that scene with Vivie exactly like the scene with Prossy in Candida, you sank into despair like a man whose loftiest inspiration had been quenched and whose noblest motives brutally misunderstood.

IT was really the fault of your cold, not mine. You nearly made Miss Brough cry.

It only wants lifting the least bit in the world. You should soar, not gravitate. If you let the part weigh on your mind much more, you will find yourself breaking into the Seven Ages of Man on the night.

You got my card about the Hotel Cecil, I presume.

We begin tomorrow with the fourth act—Vivie and Frank.

GBS

To CLEMENT SCOTT

[A/1; X/172]

10 Adelphi Terrace WC
4th January 1902

[*Mrs Warren's Profession* was finally to be produced by the Stage Society on 5th and 6th January. Clement Scott, Shaw's erstwhile enemy on the *Daily Telegraph*, had become editor in October 1900 of a weekly journal, *The Free Lance*. He published no review of the play.]

Fanny Brough as Kitty Warren in *Mrs Warren's Profession*, 1902
(*Photograph by Frederick H. Evans; Hanley Collection, University of Texas*)

My dear Scott

I am so afraid of your sending one of your young lions to my play at the Lyric Club on Monday instead of going yourself that I write this to make sure of your attention. I want you to see Fanny Brough's Mrs Warren. To the dunderheads Fanny means simply comic relief, whilst the clever brigade is sometimes not too clever about acting, and is given to writing rot about Bernard Shaw when it should be giving due credit to his cast. And so I am afraid that between the two sections she may not get all that she deserves. Of course you know as well as I do that the comic relief stuff is all rubbish; and that Mrs Warren, which is comedy & tragedy & character all in one, is just the chance she wants. But the Stage Society & its guests means 8 or 9 hundred people at most to see her; but if you *describe* her performance that means a huge extension of her range.

She has been extraordinarily good about it. Of course she refused the part when she heard what Mrs Warren's Profession was; but the moment she read the play she revoked her refusal & said it ought to be done & should be done. I promise you that even if the play horrifies you (it's really an AWFUL play; but the things it says need saying) her playing will bring you out at your best—nobody else is so susceptible to the real thing in acting. You are the man to give her her due & more. Take the change out of me if you like: I'll forgive you anything except sparing an ounce of your gunpowder in any direction.

Forgive this attempt to corrupt you; but I know that Miss Brough would be disappointed if she did not know your opinion.

yrs sincerely
G. Bernard Shaw

To T. H. S. ESCOTT

[G.u/2]

[10 Adelphi Terrace W C]
[Undated: January 1902]

[Thomas Hay Sweet Escott (1844–1924) was a political writer and social historian, who had just written *Gentlemen of the House of Commons* (1902). Lord Rosebery had spoken at Chesterfield on 15th December and at Swansea on 21st December 1901, the latter speech having dealt with the importance of municipal government and the duty of the citizen to take part in that government. Rosebery's adherents founded the Liberal League in 1902, following his split with Sir Henry Campbell-Bannerman. Shaw provided fuller accounts of the "Newcastle Program" history in Fabian Tract No. 41 (*The Fabian Society: What It Has Done and How It Has Done It*) and in Edward Pease's *The History of the Fabian Society* (1916). The Liberal "parliamentary candidate" was Edward J. Beale (d. 1901).

Francis Place (1771–1854), a workingman who became a trade-unionist and reformer, was instrumental in the passage of the 1832 Reform Bill. François Fourier (1772–1837), French reformer and social scientist, advocated a utopian, co-operative organisation of society, known as Fourierism. A notable experiment was Brook Farm in the United States. The Cobden Club, founded in 1870 in Manchester and London, was still active in 1902.

"Tooley St" is a metonym for the three tailors of that Southwark address who submitted a petition of grievance to Parliament, beginning, "We, the people of England." The phrase, says Brewer, "is used of any petifogging coterie that fancies it represents the nation."

This letter is one of a series of five undated letters drafted by Shaw early in 1902 in a school exercise book, which then presumably were transcribed by Charlotte Shaw.]

PRIVATE

Dear Sir

A couple of months ago Mr Edward Pease, the secretary of the Fabian Society, sent me a letter of yours in which you asked "whether the opinions lately expressed by Mr Sidney Webb in his article in the XIX Century are yet embodied in any political organization likely to influence votes in the House of Commons." Mr Pease suggested that I should write to you on the subject.

I had, however, to wait for the practical answer, which is Lord Rosebery's speech at Chesterfield. The object of Mr Webb's article was to induce Lord Rosebery to play that card. He has played it; and now it remains to be seen whether it will win the next general election for a Liberalism brought up to date by the acceptance of modern "world politics" and of Collectivism in industry.

The main difficulty is that Rosebery is not really a Collectivist. His life of Pitt is his Hamlet: the Pitt of his book is himself. He still believes in Adam Smith; and his later speech at Swansea shews that he is not a municipal socialist of the Webb type, but a sound old fashioned Ratepayer. It is quite possible that he made that speech expressly to clear himself from the suspicion of Fabian prompting.

However, the point that will interest you is the way in which the incident exemplifies the Fabian method. Every other Socialist Society has been conceived as a political organization which should finally enlist in its own ranks a majority of voters (or, formerly, barricade

252

combatants) and then proceed to reform the world, its own executive superseding the Cabinet or Chancellery or Throne, as the case might be. The Fabians, consisting of middle class people represented by a committee of upper division civil servants, political journalists, and people who know society a little, made a clean sweep of this traditional action, and, having first, by some years of private study & discussion, translated socialism into a practical English political program, set to work to graft the items of this program on to the programs of the existing parties, and to prompt the political figure heads much as a magistrate's clerk prompts a magistrate. Instead of asking Liberals and Conservatives to become Fabians, the Fabians joined the Liberal & Conservative organizations. For example, I joined a local London Liberal & Radical Association, and presently induced our parliamentary candidate to move, at an insignificant little meeting, a string of apparently innocent resolutions drafted by Sidney Webb for the purpose. Next morning, to the candidate's amazement, his resolutions were prominently noticed & commented on by certain papers (accessible to us) as the beginning of a revolt in the Liberal party against the old gang of Whigs on the front bench. These resolutions finally became the Newcastle Program. We worked our stage army so well that we forced the Liberals to fight the 1892 election on that program, which subsequently proved their ruin; for though by taking it up & dropping Home Rule they escaped defeat at the polls, they could do nothing with their slender majority, which, by bolting over their Employers' Liability Bill, shewed them that if they touched the Program they would be defeated at once. The Fabians had foreseen this, and even before the election were working up to their Manifesto in the Fortnightly Review in 1894 or thereabouts, entitled "To Your Tents, O Israel." This manifesto is now forgotten; but it made a very sufficient nine days pother at the time, & enabled the Fabian Society to pose later on (whenever advisable) as the hand that struck down the Government. Rosebery was furious, and acquired a sense of the danger of meddling with us and with programs which obsesses him to this day. But with Webb's article, the final stroke of some fifteen years work at the reconstitution of the Liberal Party as a Collectivist opposition, we seem[,] for the moment at least, to have landed him again.

A much more solid stroke of business done by us was the invention of the Municipal Progressive Party. When the County Councils were established about 1887, nobody had the least idea of what they were going to do. The Fabian Society, in the nick of time, shot out a leaflet entitled "Questions for County Councillors." It rushed into the vacuum, and was safely established as a political institution by the time the Times suddenly woke up to the fact that the Fabians were attempting to influence the County Council, a discovery which, very characteristically, took it about nine years to make.

You will understand that this sort of work depends for its success on the discretion of the people who do it. The Reform Bill of 1832 would never have been carried as a Bill of Francis Place, the Charing †️ tailor, though we now know that Place had more to do with it than any other single man. You may not, perhaps, have remarked that the biographer of Francis Place is Graham Wallas, formerly a very active member of the Fabian Executive, and now Chairman of the General Management Com^tee of the London School Board, just as Webb is a County Councillor & I a Borough Councillor. We took a great deal of trouble to find out how things were really done before we began trying to do them; and the biography of Francis Place was a much later & riper product of that trouble than Fabian Essays. I mark this letter private as a matter of Fabian etiquette; but what happened in the eighties & nineties (especially now that Chesterfield is pulled off) is of little consequence except to the curious historian. Our ideas are no longer our exclusive property; and, as we shall never see forty again, our revolutionary bolts are shot personally. The young men are reading Wells's "Anticipations" instead of attending to us; and unless we succeed in drawing fresh blood with a practicable & constitutional foreign policy which shall be to the old Internationalism of the Communist Manifesto what the Progressive program is to the Utopias of Fourier, we shall go on the shelf like the Cobden Club.

I trouble you with all this because your question, simple as it is, cannot be fully answered on shorter terms, and because, by your activity & influence as a writer, you have made it important that you should know what the Fabians have been thinking about. No doubt our absorption in our own work has warped our consciousness both of public events & our own share in them in the usual Tooley St manner; but you will be able to allow for that only too easily.

yrs faithfully
[G. Bernard Shaw]

254

To MRS ARNOLD LYNDON

[G.u/2]

[10 Adelphi Terrace W C]
[Undated: January 1902]

[The Annual Meeting of the Grayshott and District Refreshment Association
had been held on 14th December 1901 at the Fox and Pelican Hotel, the
shareholders present including Sir Frederick Pollock, the Shaws, Rev. and
Mrs J. M. Jeakes, Dr Arnold Lyndon, H. J. Craufurd, E. Nettleship, and Mrs
Charlotte Lyndon, Hon. Secretary. The meeting was concerned primarily
with the difficulties that had arisen from disagreements between the managers of the pub, one of whom had been dismissed (involving costly litiga-
tion), and several of the customers, who were either employed by or tenants
of Frederick Jackson. The principal troublemaker appears to have been
Thomas Madgwick, a workingman active in the Grayshott Men's Club.]

Dear Mrs Lyndon

I have not had time to write to you since the meeting at the Fox &
Pelican, where I hope I did not do any harm.

As far as I can judge from my interviews with two managers & a
manageress of the poor Fox on the one hand, and what I can ascertain
through Mr Jackson's lambs on the other, the position is an impossible
one. The managers are unanimous in denouncing the customers as
"savages," and proceeding on the assumption that they are not good
enough for so respectable a house, and that to give books to "the like
of them," or the best room to smoke & swear & expectorate in, would
be an act of indecent Vandalism.

On the other hand, the intelligent and independent young workman
is always on the alert to resent any such attitude towards him. He wants
the best room & the books. He knows that the place was built for him,
and that the manager is no real landlord, but only a hireling put in to
minister to him. If he is a teetotaller he is certain to be also opinionative,
atheistic, socialistic, probably pro-Boer.

The upshot of this is inevitable. The manager, as principal of a high
class refreshment house, with an aristocratic coffee room, books, pictures, a baronet in the chair & a bishop on the signboard, takes a high
tone with the savages; and affects to be shocked by strong language.
The free & independent working man instantly asks him who he is,
whether he thinks the place belongs to him &c &c. The manager refuses
to serve him—inevitably, because the manager is lost if he lets his
customers get the upper hand. Result: a public house from which the
thoughtful, energetic, teetotal working man is excluded, and the abject

255

sot or dullard welcomed because he gives the manager no trouble and doesnt care what room he is in provided he gets drink. A state of things which naturally revolts Mrs Jeakes, and is infinitely worse than an ordinary public house with a real publican.

I confess I see no remedy for this. Cut off the spirits altogether & the manager will quarrel with Madgwick & Co more than ever. Turn on Major Craufurd with his military notions and his determination to fight over the froth, and you will have the only thing that seems to be worse than a reformed public house: that is, a canteen. Turn it over to the Hampshire Trust; and they will make their philanthropy an excuse for not giving us the value of our property, and then proceed to repeat all the blunders of our inexperience at the expense of the morals of Grayshott.

It seems to me that the proper thing to do is to sell or lease the Fox to the Alton brewers or anyone else who is prepared to run it on the usual lines, thereby relieving the village of our managers whilst leaving them a much pleasanter public house than the brewers would have built, and release your own personal energy, and as much of the capital as you can coax us to give you, for the Institute. I am convinced that no practicable change in the system of management will be of the least use. I know what people are; and I know that we shant get anybody who will succeed where you have failed. The causes of the failure are social: they are quite beyond our control. If you could sit in the bar yourself and be the landlady, I would back you to conduct the house quite successfully. Mrs Jeakes could relieve you occasionally. But short of that, you *cannot* manage the house. You cannot put any subordinate on the footing with Madgwick & Co that Chandler is on with them; and no other footing will work. I believe if we leased the house to Budd, he would get on better than we do.

What do you say? Shall we sell out boldly, instead of throwing away your time and demoralizing the village and teaching its police to steal ducks? The thing was worth trying; but now that we know what it means, there is no use in throwing good time after bad & locking up money in a public house that is wanted for other things. I feel sure we have only to propose it & the others will let themselves be persuaded with secret relief. The moral infamy of the retreat can be laid on me.

At all events let me know what you think. There would be some difficulty about Nettleship's land; but it could be got over. There is also the question of your own services, which, if we suddenly abandon our philanthropic lines & clear out on purely commercial ones, should be considered. You can at least use them as a lever to get some of the capital for the [Grayshott] Institute [opened in May 1902].

yrs sincerely
[G. Bernard Shaw]

To F. T. DEL MARMOL

[G.u/2]

[10 Adelphi Terrace W C]
[Undated: January 1902]

[F. Tarrida del Marmol was London correspondent for *El Heraldo*, the leading daily newspaper of Madrid, and an occasional correspondent for the *Labour Leader* and other British Socialist papers. There is no record of *Le Petit Sou* having ever been published.]

Dear Sir

I greatly regret that I have been prevented from replying to your letter in time for the first number of Le Petit Sou by the rehearsals of one of my plays.

My advice to Mr Edwards is to study most carefully all the suggestions he receives from the English Socialist leaders, and do exactly the contrary of what they recommend. Why should a gentleman who has been conspicuously successful as a founder of newspapers seek the advice of us who have been so conspicuously unsuccessful in that capacity. The only way to be independent of advertisement is to have so large a circulation that the advertisers become dependent on the paper. The only way to remain independent of party ties is to maintain so high a standard of political criticism that whenever a measure is introduced in the Chamber, all parties will turn to Le Petit Sou to see what it has to say.

If the paper is to be a Socialist paper, it must have a Socialist policy. In England at present the South African war has disclosed the fact that in question[s] of foreign policy, English Socialists are simply Mazzinist Liberals and Nationalists. In my opinion the time has come for International Socialism to affirm that the age of the Powers has come, and that the traditional association of revolutionary nationalism, Irish, Polish, Boer &c, with Socialism must be dissolved. France is no longer France, but a vast Empire with provinces in Europe, Asia & Africa. The business of Socialism is not to defend petty States against inclusion in that or any other great Empire, but to turn the Empires into true Commonwealths.

257

Again, in dealing with the question of Militarism, a Socialist paper should boldly declare that the day of the soldier is past. To make a Frenchman a soldier is to make him a slave and an outlaw. His officers need not commend him; they have only to coerce him; and the brutality and stupidity with which they do it is proved by the high rate of desertion in your army. The remedy is to abolish the soldier altogether, and defend your country by

(a) a militia consisting of the entire male population between 18 & 21, not living in barracks, but being drilled just as English volunteers are, without any loss of freedom or self respect.

(b) a professional army recruited by voluntary enlistment, consisting of men with full civil rights, who choose arms as a permanent profession, serving up to the age of 60, but of course as free to leave the ranks and change their occupation as an English policeman is. Such a force of free Frenchmen skilled in arms, and commanded by officers who would gain and keep their authority by their personal ability solely, just as the manager of a railway does, would annihilate an English or German army of ordinary soldiers. In fact all the other Powers would be compelled to follow the example of France, not for the first time. With such a program as this, a Socialist paper can fight Militarism & destroy it. Without it, Militarism will destroy French Socialism. A year ago it would have seemed absurd; but the extraordinary resistance maintained by the Boer militia to the British against overwhelming odds has now proved that free citizens are far superior to soldiers for purposes of national defence.

To avoid unduly prolonging my letter I confine myself to these two suggestions, & remain

yrs faithfully
[G. Bernard Shaw]

To OSCAR HANSEN

[G.u/2]

[10 Adelphi Terrace W C]
[Undated: January 1902]

[Oscar Hansen (1856-1938) was a Danish philosopher and educator.]

Dear Sir

As Denmark has no copyright treaty with England, I have no consent to give and no rights to sell. I quite appreciate the sense of honor

258

which leads you to offer me the privileges of a Danish author; but I also am bound in honor not to accept payment for rights that do not exist. If Denmark, as a matter of public policy, thinks well to place all her literature freely at the disposal of other countries in return for her having all their literature freely at her own disposal, it is not for the authors of the large countries to complain. I have my rights in the British Empire and the United States, two vast markets, and my rights of translation in the countries within the Berne Convention. That is quite enough for me. It is the Danish author, with his limited market—and, let me add, his generally higher class of work—who suffers by the arrangement. At all events, as far as I am concerned, Denmark is heartily welcome to my works; and you need have no hesitation in taking the fullest advantage of the existing state of the law.

yours faithfully
[G. Bernard Shaw]

To CLEMENT SCOTT

[G.u/2; X/185]

[10 Adelphi Terrace W C]
[Undated: January 1902]

[Scott had asked Shaw for his views on an article, "Can Women Put Down War?" signed "An Islander," in the *Free Lance* on 18th January. Shaw's reply, under the heading "Should Women Stop War?" was published on 25th January. Emily Hobhouse (1860–1926) had published a *Report of a Visit to the Camps of Women and Children in the Cape and Orange River Colonies* (1901). Christina Lady Sykes had written *Side Lights on the War in South Africa* (1900). William Ashmead-Bartlett Burdett-Coutts (1851–1921) was a Conservative M.P. and philanthropist, who assisted his wife, Baroness Angela Burdett-Coutts (1814–1906), in her numerous benefactions.]

My dear Scott

Your Islander correspondent thinks that because women can be counted separately from men in the matter of sex, they can be counted separately in every other matter too. Now as a matter of fact there are dozens of subjects on which women think and feel exactly as men do; and as far as my experience goes, war is one of them. There are plenty of women who have made their views of the present war known; but none of these can be distinguished from the ordinary male Imperialist or Pro-Boer, as the case may be. Like most of the men, most of the women echo their leaders and their party newspapers. When they go and see for themselves, as Miss Hobhouse and Lady Sykes have done, their views are not distinguishable from those of male observers like Mr Burdett Coutts and Mr Frank Harris. I do not mean that Miss Hobhouse says exactly what Mr Burdett Coutts says & Lady Sykes exactly what Mr Frank Harris says: what I do mean is that the differences between the two men and the two women are just those which would arise between four men under the same circumstances. In short, there is no feminine view of war; and if a referendum were made to the whole adult population tomorrow on the alternatives of Stop the War and Fight it Out, the proportion of war votes to peace votes would be much the same among the women as among the men.

To say that women at home in England suffer more from our wars than men, is as much as to say that mothers love sons and fathers love daughters most. This may be true, but its bearing on war is discounted by the well known fact that the effect of deterrents depends much less on their severity than on their certainty. There is no certainty that a woman will lose her son if he goes to the front: in fact, the coalmine and the shunting yard are more dangerous places than the camps.

Your own suggestion that the more women are enslaved the greater their influence is, goes much deeper than the sentimental appeal of Islander, who writes as if the women of England were represented by the people who flutter between the Savoy Hotel and whatever theatres happen to be working their free lists hard. The truth is that a slave State is always ruled by those who can get round the masters: that is, by the more cunning of the slaves themselves. Thus fashionable London, like its outposts on the coast and on the Riviera, is bound, body & soul, under an organized tyranny of servants and tradesmen which no spirited coolie would endure without rebellion. That is why Liberal dukes and Radical earls excite no surprise, whereas a Radical valet or a Liberal west end jeweller has never yet been heard of. In exactly the same way the slavery of women means the tyranny of women. No fascinating woman ever wants to emancipate her sex: her object is to gather power into the hands of Man, because she knows that she can govern him. She is no more jealous of his nominal supremacy than he himself is jealous of the strength and speed of his horse. Women are supposed to have no political power; but clever women put stupid husbands into parliament and into ministerial offices quite easily; and every clever husband knows that in public life a captivating wife is one of the strongest cards he can have in his hand. The cunning & attractive slave women disguise their strength as womanly weakness, their audacity as womanly timidity, their unscrupulousness as womanly innocence, their impunities as womanly defencelessness: simple men are duped by them, and subtle ones disarmed and intimidated. They can be beaten only by brutal selfishness or by their own weapons, which many men learn to use with more than feminine skill. It is only the proud, straightforward women, who wish, not to govern, but to be free, that object to slavery and give a lead to the unattractive, drudging women, who cannot get round anybody.

Islander may take it, then, that if women wanted to put an end to war, they would have done it long ago.

[G. Bernard Shaw]

To GILBERT MURRAY

[C/36]

10 Adelphi Terrace W C
22nd January 1902

[Shaw's lecture to the Fabian Society on 24th January was "The English Drama" (in the series "The Social Tendencies of the Drama"). The preface Shaw was writing, "The Author's Apology," was intended for a separate edition of *Mrs Warren's Profession*, published by Grant Richards late in March 1902, with photographs of the Stage Society production taken by Frederick Evans.]

I have serious thoughts of beginning my lecture: "Ladies & Gentlemen: I need hardly say that the English Drama to which the title of my lecture refers is the sensational tragedy now being enacted on the veldt &c &c."

I have not had time to think about it, as I have been writing a terrific preface to Mrs Warren's Profession for its republication separately from the other plays.

On the whole, I am glad you are not coming, as I have nothing new to say; & you & Archer & Walkley have exhausted the interest of the series.

GBS

Pithecanthropangelus was probably Tennyson.

To ALEXANDER M. THOMPSON

[X/173]

[10 Adelphi Terrace W C]
[Undated: c. 7th–10th February 1902]

[Thompson's suggestion was "One Socialist Party," in his "Echoes of the Week" column in *The Clarion* on 7th December 1901, in which he stressed

261

"the urgent need for Socialist unity" after the Dewsbury election: "On every question likely to enter into the practical politics within the next 20 years the Socialists of Great Britain are in complete accord. What, then, hinders them from working together for the attainment of their common objects?" The Dewsbury (Yorkshire) election was a three-cornered by-election in January 1902, in which the S.D.F. had split with the I.L.P. and the Labour Representation Committee, running Harry Quelch as a rival candidate to the Liberal candidate, Walter Runciman. Although Runciman defeated both the Conservative candidate and Quelch, the S.D.F. showing was twice that which had been anticipated. Robert Blatchford, editor of *The Clarion*, was at this time fulminating against Keir Hardie and the I.L.P. in the pages of his paper.]

Dear Thompson

Your suggestion is magnificent. A great Socialist convention with no leaders and no officials only needs one thing to make it quite perfect, and that is no proceedings. For you will at once see, with that clear grasp of the situation which endears you to us all, that if any man is allowed to open his mouth for even the briefest space he will at once become a leader unless somebody contradicts him—and if he is contradicted, goodbye to Socialist unity.

This is not the first time that my voice has been raised to celebrate a fraternal reunion of all the jarring sections of our great cause. More than once the overwhelming sentiment of fellowship and brotherhood in the ranks has lifted Hyndman, Morris, Keir Hardie, and other good men off their feet and fairly hurled them into my aching arms. Our embarrassment on these touching occasions has been very fearful, but we have always been rescued from it by the powerful centrifugal force of our personal characters. Our last experience of this kind was a combination of the S.D.F., I.L.P., and Fabian into a band of brothers, one and indivisible. After a meeting or two the native shrewdness of Keir Hardie divined that the one chance of keeping the combination together was to place me on the wrong side of the door. The feeling on this point being quite unanimous, the Fabian Society could not resist it, and I was ignominiously cashiered. Keir Hardie breathed so much more freely in consequence that it presently occurred to him that if the Fabian Society could be got rid of altogether the warm-hearted I.L.P. and the enthusiastic S.D.F. would melt into one another in perfect bliss. This resolution was carried by acclamation in the office which the Fabian Society had lent for the occasion, and the Fabians were forthwith shown to the door of their own apartment. After this all was harmony until the question arose whether the S.D.F. had absorbed

262

the I.L.P. or the I.L.P. the S.D.F.; and on this issue feeling and language rose steadily as the years elapsed, to the point reached at the Dewsbury election, with its rapturous outburst of brotherly sentiment between Keir Hardie and his trusty comrades, Quelch, Hyndman, and Blatchford.

There seems to be a general feeling that the moment is a peculiarly auspicious one for reunion. As usual, *I* think, not what the other Socialists think, but what they will think 10 years hence. There has never been a moment at which union has been so difficult to maintain, even within the societies themselves, much more between one society and another. Summon a convention tomorrow, with all the leaders and notables of the movement safely stowed away in the cellar, bound hand and foot and gagged, and the two words "South Africa" will produce scenes compared to which the most exciting days at an International Socialist Congress will be as prayer meetings. Quelch's vote at Dewsbury, though I congratulate both him and the movement on it, may for all we know be as much an anti-Imperialist vote as a Socialist one, for Quelch was the only anti-Imperialist who went to the poll. Why anybody should suppose that three societies which could not unite on a home policy should now, without having settled a single one of their old difficulties, be able to unite because they have got foreign policy to quarrel about as well is quite beyond me. However, let us have the convention by all means. The result will not be the result you look for; but it will bring our imaginary unity to the test of that hand-to-hand conflict of personalities and programmes which must always rise—leaders or no leaders, officials or no officials—when Smith of Bolton and Jones of Bradford, Brown of Battersea and Robinson of Camberwell, who love each other because they have never seen each other, and who so earnestly deprecate the bickerings of those wicked leaders, are suddenly brought face to face for the first time and compelled to vote on the same motion. The Socialist policy, like all the great policies of history, will grow into a recognisable political shape in its own good time if not in ours. The one thing that may be quite safely predicted of it is that it will not be a policy of sentimental novices sending Christmas cards to one another.

How do you feel after that, Thompson? Cheer up!

G. Bernard Shaw

263

To WILLIAM ARCHER

[A/2]   1st & 2nd March 1902

[Edwin O. Sachs (1870–1919) was a distinguished architect and expert in theatre construction. In 1898 he had applied electrical power to the working of the stage for the first time in England, at the Drury Lane Theatre. Although Sachs may have assisted Archer in preparing his book, *A National Theatre: Scheme and Estimates* (privately printed, 1904), the work was finally a collaboration between Archer and Harley Granville Barker. Shaw had broached to George Alexander in February 1900 the idea of a school of dramatic arts at London University. John Coleman (1830–1904) was a former actor-manager and dramatic author, who ran a drama studio, as did Henry Neville (1837–1910), also a former actor. Eugene Sandow (1867–1925), the physical culture exponent who had been exhibited by Florenz Ziegfeld at the Chicago Fair (1893), had opened a health institute in London.]

Dear W.A.

I write in the train: hence joggling. Hope you can decipher.

I am game to back the Sachs–Archer book as you may direct. But I implore you to get rid of that superstition—the Dramatic School. In fact, I will contribute that section myself & present you with the copyright, and get Alexander to sign it, or sign it myself or impose the authorship on you, as you please, if you like.

My idea is this. Acting cannot be taught, as Tree, Irving &c are fond of telling us. But men can be physically trained for public life. Politicians, barristers, clergymen, lecturers, naval & military officers all depend greatly for their success on the style in which they can stand before an audience and address them or order them about. Toastmasters, servants, shopmen, auctioneers, bookmakers, and beadles also require deportment and oratory. Now what I want to agitate for is the addition of a Physical School of the Arts of Public Life to the schools of the London University, giving courses of instruction and training in platform accomplishments; so that a man or woman holding a certificate or diploma or degree from such a school could be depended on to deliver a lecture at the Royal Institution, preach a sermon, open a case in court, give an order in the field or from the quarterdeck & so on without making him- or herself ridiculous by the ineptness of the novice & the amateur. A National Theatre could demand such a degree from all its novices, just as a bishop demands a minimum of Greek before ordaining a curate. If the bishop demanded the physical degree too, and the same qualification was imposed for the bar and the services (including certain civil services), the School would become important, and its students would rub shoulders & criticisms with men of all classes, social & intellectual. The would-be actor would go there & have his horizon enlarged. He would not learn to act any more than the wouldbe barristers would learn to plead & cross-examine, or the clergyman to save souls, or the general to win battles; but he would go on the stage, as the others would go into court & pulpit & camp, *personally* qualified to begin. This plan would not only avoid the Puritan objection to subsidizing a theatrical school out of the rates, but place the theatrical profession on the level of the learned professions in the only possible way. And the school, supported by all the professions, could be on a scale impossible to any mere dramatic academy. It could get endowments from people & grants from public bodies who would not leave or give a penny to a National Theatre.

I do not mean that the apprenticeship of the future societaire should be wholly haphazard. The National Theatre would want supers. These supers should be for the most part young people "walking on"; but a teacher of dancing, pantomime &c should be kept for them; and the wardrobe master should be a bit of an artist, like Teddy Craig. They should do all the curtain raising, and the special performances for children at holiday times (and all times) not by performing inane little novelettes, but masques, pantomimes, Planché extravaganzas, harlequinades & so on—things requiring dancing & dressing & tomfooling and high spirits. In this way they could pick up "plastique," costume &c, and such acrobatism as may be good for them—enough to jump through a trap, at all events. (And this reminds me that one of the needs of a National Theatre would be an extra stage to enable two rehearsals to proceed simultaneously, and even a second theatre for the intimate performance of Ibsen plays & the like to small & superior audiences). There should be a strict age limit for this sort of thing; so that the apprentice-super who wished to devote his life to tomfooling & knockabout, or who was not graduated into the stock company of fully fledged actors, should be driven off to the music halls & commercial theatres at 24, say.

And this brings me to the necessity (later on) for a larger collectivism in the theatre than can be achieved by a single central house. The main artistic objection to stock companies is that they finally destroy dramatic illusion. Portia, Juliet, Imogen & Ophelia are different women: to make them all Ellen Terry ends in people going to the theatre to see Ellen Terry & accepting all sorts of conventions & absurdities in their forgetfulness of the play. This difficulty can be overcome only by circulation of companies; and this means that all the great centres of population should have national theatres, and that their artists should have an indefeasible right to play all their roles once a year (or two or three years) in London. This development would be useful commercially too. At present London is becoming more & more a place for advertisement, whilst the provinces bring in the money. The provinces should feed London, if necessary, in the same way under a scheme of national theatres; and the profits should be used to finance incursions to small and growing towns to set up a standard of taste there and lay the foundations of additional national theatres.

Provision should be made for long runs in the constitution of the theatre; not only for the sake of the theatre, but for the sake of attracting authors. For instance, there are plays of mine which I could not recommend any commercial manager to produce for a run, which yet might conceivably hit the public fancy either on their own account or through the fascination of somebody in the cast. Under such circumstances the national theatre should either hire another theatre and run the play for all it was worth or sublet it to one of the regular managers if he was ready & willing. At any rate they should either leave the author free to do this or else guarantee him a minimum number of performances of the play as a box office piece for two or three seasons. Mind, I am not suggesting that such proceedings should be obligatory, only that the powers of the N.T. should extend so far. I regard power to lease supplementary theatres on occasion as very important.

It is worth considering whether a public dramatic library should not be established, with an obligation on dramatic authors to deposit a copy of every published play as a condition of copyright (though a clause ought to attach to *all* public library copies of books to enable the author or publisher to recover the cost price of very expensive books).

However, all these are stray considerations. My main point is that the Dramatic School notion, intended to secure a stock company of the pupils of John Coleman and Henry Neville—even with voice production by Hermann Vezin, assisted by Mrs & Miss Behnke—is in every way a disastrous mistake, and that its functions should be undertaken by a University School of, say, Rhetoric (with a touch of Sandow). You have a precedent in the London School of Economics & Political Science, which grew out of the need of technical training for voters, which led to the need of technical training for town clerks & other municipal experts, which led again to the discovery that the staffs of railway companies, banks &c &c &c were in need of much the same training, and which is now a school of the London University with students

266

using it as the spring board to jump off into scores of different careers. In this way only will you ever get the actor out of his cabotinage and give him the University stamp as distinguished from the professional stamp. For please remember that the present anarchy has the advantage of destroying the old Crummles professionalism; and that the return to order by way of a National Theatre will revive it if the dramatic student is to be educationally segregated from the other professions.

In haste
GBS

P.S. Charlotte is in bed with influenza.

PPS In one of my prefaces to Plays Pleasant & Unpleasant I sketch a plan for developing a repertory theatre out of an opera subsidy to an established manager.

To MILLICENT MURBY

[Piccards Cottage. Guildford]
[A/1; X/228.e]   3rd March 1902

[Millicent B. Murby (1873–1951), a civil servant employed in the post office, who joined the Fabian Society in 1901, had obtained permission from Shaw to produce an amateur performance of *Candida* at the Cripplegate Institute on 15th February 1902. It was the first public performance of the play in London, under the auspices of the New Stage Club (consisting mainly of young Fabian women). Miss Murby played the rôle of Candida.]

Dear Madam

Mr Pease has handed me your letter to him about Candida. It was not at all a bad performance, considering that Morell was totally disabled. Burgess's part bears being treated in that way quite well: in fact, the difficulty is to get a Burgess who will play boldly enough for the laughs. If you repeat the performance, all you need say to him is that there is no reason why he should dress absurdly. He should wear a black frock coat and trousers and a solid looking watch chain, with a very clean shirt and a black tie. A double breasted waistcoat, with enough opening to shew the shirt down to a gold stud, would be all right. To dress like a knockabout grotesque at a music hall is simply foolish, & damages the effect of his acting, which is not at all bad. Morell wore a ratcatcher's wig, apparently because all amateurs think

267

that false hair & spears with tin tops are *de rigueur* on the stage. His own hair will do very well. I cannot, of course, tell what he can do when he has not got influenza; but an irresponsive Morell makes matters very difficult for Candida. Indeed the part needs a brilliant actor. The other parts, if played with sincerity, rather gain than lose by lack of stage accomplishment; but Morell is supposed to be himself a pulpit orator with all the tricks of an actor at his fingers' ends. He should at least make "Prossy's complaint" intelligible. When next you try the play, make Morell, if you can, take particular care of the line "Do you mean ME, Candida?" in the last act. The effect should be to take off the whole strain of the scene with a quite ludicrous awakening. It cannot possibly be overdone; and if it makes the audience laugh, so much the better. If it is underdone—if it does not make a sufficient break to rearrange the whole situation on a new footing—Candida's invitation to the others to sit down and begin talking all over again just at the moment when the audience is expecting to be released by the curtain will inevitably produce an unhappy effect.

Prossy was quite good enough; but her last exit suggested that she really was drunk, and that the curate was quite justified in his fear lest she should sing. The poet was astonishingly good, in spite of—or because of—his technical innocence of stagecraft. He must be naturally something of a poet: no mere actor could have done it that way. Mill was—Mill. I should like to see you play Candida to a Morell who would play back to you: you were quite successful; but certain things in the part depend absolutely on Morell. I enjoyed the performance; and this is saying a good deal for me.

yrs sincerely
G. Bernard Shaw

To WILLIAM ARCHER

Piccards Cottage. Guildford
[A/36]   4th March 1902

[The actress Isabella Glyn (1823–89) had told the story of Gladstone to Shaw at one of Lady Wilde's at homes.]

No: I dont agree about voice production as part of the business of the National Theatre staff. It belongs to the University School; and even there it would probably be a piece of quackery if it were specially

268

taught. All that is needed in the theatre is somebody in the gallery at rehearsal, to say (as Mrs Charles Kean used to say to Ellen Terry) "I can't hear you," and somebody in the stalls to say "Dont bawl like that." You must be frightfully careful to limit your proposals for a staff of instructors to the differentia of the theatre. Voice production is needed by the whole human race: the theatre might as well teach reading and writing. Stage dancing, pantomime, costume and make-up are the specialities of the theatre. And there should be a salle d'armes where stage combats & wrestlings could be practised—a gymnasium, in fact; but this ought not to attempt to supply the place of general physical schools. Above all, do not call these things a "Dramatic School." It is all-important that people should *think* rightly about the subject: at present their ideas are confused. The theatre must not have any taint of the school about it: the stage manager and ballet master should be taken as a matter of course like the carpenter and not promoted to a Chair.

Dont get hold of the idea that a University School of the Arts of Public Life is necessarily a longer way off than a National Theatre. It is probably much closer, as it appeals to a far larger public, and is commercially urgent. And as it is only emerging as a distinct idea, it has the enormous advantage of being new and setting people talking. The fact is, the intelligent, managing, initiative people wont stand the theatre: they will yawn in the face of a Théâtre Anglais; but they will prick up their ears at a big educational scheme. Gladstone did not trouble himself about the theatre; but he studied Charles Kean carefully in training himself as an orator (at least so Miss Glynn told me).

In any case, you must understand that as you will only get a tenth at most of what you ask for, you cannot possibly ask for too much provided your demands are interesting. We got 24/- a week for County Council laborers by strenuously demanding the socialization of land, capital & all the instruments of production & exchange. The only thing your book can do is to make people think & shew precedents to the politician.

Once more, be careful about voice-production. . . . As to your damned elocution professors they might be shunted; but on their ruins comes the phonetician, whose case is strongest of all. So beware.

GBS

To SIDNEY DARK

10 Adelphi Terrace W C

[C/34; X/174]   20th March 1902

[Sidney Dark (1874–1947) was a dramatic critic and journalist, employed at this time by the *Daily Mail*.]

All fiction should be founded on real characters. All good fiction is. The rottenness of most books is due to the fact that the authors are too lazy to observe & describe the people they meet: hence romantic invention, ending in hideous monotony, because every man makes an ass of himself in exactly the same way, whereas no two real persons are quite alike. All Shakespear's best people must have had models.

GBS

To WILLIAM ARCHER

Piccards Cottage. Guildford

[H/2]   27th March 1902

[Archer's "advice" was in reply to Shaw's request for an opinion as to Lily Langtry's competence to play Lady Cicely. Harold V. Neilson (1874–1956) was a young actor-manager who produced *Captain Brassbound's Conversion* at the Queen's Theatre, Manchester, on 12th May 1902, for six performances, with Janet Achurch and Charles Charrington in the cast. The programme, however, listed Richard Flanagan as the manager and Neilson merely as a featured member of Miss Achurch's Company.]

Dear W.A.

For this advice, much thanks. I quite agree with its principles; but in applying them to my case you must bear in mind that I am not suffering from lack of production. Eight of my ten plays have been produced and noticed and so forth; and there is now no question as to my competence and vocation. What remains undecided is the point you have so nobly championed: namely that my "Pleasant" plays would be commercially and fashionably successful on ordinary West End conditions. Now the decision on this point will turn on what happens the first time such an experiment is tried. If Mrs Langtry made a mess of it, the public might be taken in by a forced run; but the managers would not. They know me well enough now, and are sufficiently tempted by my parts, to be very curious as to how *their*

270

public would take me: in fact, some of them shiver on the brink from time to time until I persuade them to put on their clothes again and wait a bit. That is what I meant by saying that a failure at the Imperial would put me out of court.

I should not countenance the proposal at all without [Lewis] Waller. I gather from what you say that the reputation which I have so carefully cultivated for being an impossibilist at rehearsals has reached and impressed you; but you need not bother about that. I now conduct my own rehearsals; and I never have any trouble. On the contrary, my difficulty is to prevent the performance coming as an anti-climax to the rehearsals. It is possible, of course, that in this matter I may be the dupe of a consummate hypocrisy on the part of my companies: if so, I can only say that I wish they could act as well on the stage as off.

As to Thorpe, the quality you mention is by no means lost on my nerves; but he is a clever character actor. As the Judge in Brassbound, which he rehearsed hastily for me when nobody else would touch it, he took me aback by an unrehearsed makeup which was ludicrously wrong, and which shewed that he had not really got hold of the character at all. But it is he who has made Mrs Langtry read the play. Now suppose she is willing to give him the part. Vezin would be the right man for it; but Vezin was one of those who refused to play it originally. Under these circumstances, as I can correct Thorpe's make-up, and as he is quite clever enough to get hold of the part by the right end when I talk to him about it, I am bound to stand by him. Of course what he would like would be to play Brassbound; and there, if you like, his curious effeminacy would be appalling.

You will see that things are pretty complicated for an author who has to form a party, as it were, to get his plays into action. However, this business may come to nothing; for I have replied to Mrs Langtry not only with strong dissuasion, but with a warning that I cannot promise her exclusive provincial rights, as a provincial actor-manager named Harold Nielson has offered to try the play in Manchester for a fortnight with Janet Achurch as Lady Cicely; and this, again, I of course cannot refuse to sanction.

GBS

271

To ELLEN TERRY

[U(A)/10; X/175]

Piccards Cottage. Guildford
3rd April 1902

Mr Bernard Shaw's compliments to Miss Ellen Terry.

Mr Bernard Shaw has been approached by Mrs Langtry with a view to the immediate and splendid production of "Captain Brassbound's Conversion" at the Imperial Theatre.

Mr Bernard Shaw, with the last flash of a trampled out love, has repulsed Mrs Langtry with a petulance bordering on brutality.

Mr Bernard Shaw has been actuated in this ungentlemanly and un-businesslike course by an angry desire to seize Miss Ellen Terry by the hair and make her play Lady Cicely.

Mr Bernard Shaw would be glad to know whether Miss Ellen Terry wishes to play Martha at the Lyceum instead.

Mr Bernard Shaw will go to the length of keeping a minor part open for Sir Henry Irving when Faust fails, if Miss Ellen Terry desires it.

Mr Bernard Shaw lives in daily fear of Mrs Langtry recovering sufficiently from her natural resentment of his ill manners to reopen the subject.

Mr Bernard Shaw begs Miss Ellen Terry to answer this letter.

Mr Bernard Shaw is looking for a new cottage or house in the country and wants advice on the subject.

Mr Bernard Shaw craves for the sight of Miss Ellen Terry's once familiar handwriting.

GBS

To CHARLES CHARRINGTON

[A/4]

Royal Kent Hotel. Sandgate
20th May 1902

[Charles Frederick Kenyon (1879–1926) later wrote somewhat maliciously about Shaw and other literary figures under the pseudonym of Gerald Cumberland. Bernard Langdon-Davies (1876–1952), a member of the I.L.P. for many years, eventually became a publisher and bookseller. Shaw's letter to the *Manchester Guardian*, published on 17th May, commented that London playgoers know nothing about Janet Achurch and Marie Brema (both of Manchester) and the great modern dramatists "because they know nothing about the artistic and intellectual plane on which such artists move."

Janet Achurch had appeared for the Stage Society in Ibsen's *The Lady from the Sea* at the Royalty Theatre on 4th and 5th May. Kate Santley (1836–1923), an actress who had retired from the stage in 1894, was the lessee of the Royalty Theatre.]

Dear Charrington

Kenyon is a young man with a social conscience: rather a decent type of the viewy provincial. I had him for a day at Guildford, and promised to do what I could to help his book through. If you cant stop a biography it is as well to make the best of it. Besides, I rather liked the chap.

The interview was done by a young journalist who represents the Manchester Guardian for such occasions in London—by name Bernard Langdon-Davies, decidedly a clever fellow. I buried him under a mountain of talk; & his effort to collect some fragments was heroic. But he did not shew me a proof; and I was appalled when I saw what he said about Janet. However, as it drew that letter from me (I have not yet seen it) perhaps the net effect may be to the good from the advertisement point of view.

The Guardian certainly boomed us handsomely. All the notices agreed as to Nielson being transpontine (perhaps he modelled himself on Laurence the Pirate King), and on you being very first rate [as Sir Howard Hallam], besides, of course, the inevitable compliments to Janet.

Can you get me two or three playbills to keep as memoranda —programs, I mean, not posters? I am quite in the dark as to future plans. Why not have a go at the Devil's Disciple or some of the other plays, if the theatre dates are open? £25 a week is a thing to keep going if possible. You could play Anderson & Nielson Dick Dudgeon; but I dont see Janet playing a silly second moral violin like Judith. Still, nobody else has ever even attempted the trial scene.

Janet seems to be having a streak of genius just now. The Lady from the Sea was immense. I was terrified at first when she began to prattle like an artless young thing & seemed resolved to make that comb the chief feature in the production; but the moment she got to business she left everybody miles behind. The lucidity of her acting in difficult plays is extraordinary: I have serious thoughts of refusing to let anybody else touch my plays, although she is too fat for Cleopatra. (When she jumped down from that cliff the theatre rocked to its foundations: Kate Santley turned pale & clutched the front of her box until the oscillation ceased). The Stage Society Committee is howling over the expenses as usual.

Let me know what your movements are. I suppose Brassbound is over by this time; so I need not think any more of running down to see it.

I am at Sandgate (Folkestone) for the sake of H. G. Wells's company. Reply to Adelphi Terrace, as I return thither tomorrow.

G. Bernard Shaw

To FLORENCE FARR

10 Adelphi Terrace W C

[A/3; X/115]   6th June 1902

[William Butler Yeats (1865–1939), the Irish poet and dramatist, had first encountered Shaw in London in the early 1890's. They met frequently at Miss Farr's home in Dalling Road, where on more than one occasion they read their plays to each other and to guests invited by Miss Farr. Florence Farr Emery, as Shaw noted in a reminiscence of her published in 1941, was a woman who "set no bounds to her relations with men whom she liked," and Yeats had long since been added to her "Leporello list." Cantilating was a technique of chanting accompanied by a psaltery, which Miss Farr had developed under the influence of Yeats. Shaw's term "atalantilate" refers to a recitation by Miss Farr of a chorus from Swinburne's *Atalanta in Caly-don.*]

No: I should do no good by entering into cantilationary polemics. I was thinking of writing to you in a cautionary manner before your letter came. The fact is, there is no new art in the business at all: Yeats thinks so only because he does not go to church. Half the curates in the kingdom cantilate like mad all the time. Toastmasters cantilate. Public speakers who have nothing to say cantilate. And it is intolerable except in the one obvious & complete instance—the street cry. Sarah Bernhardt's abominable "golden voice," which has always made me sick, is cantilation, or, to use the customary word, intoning. It is no use for Yeats to try to make a distinction: there is no distinction, no novelty, no nothing but nonsense.

However, you might get some teaching out of all this advertisement. The psaltery amuses people; and there is no reason why they should not use a string or a pipe to remind them of the normal pitch of their voices. But for practical teaching the old rule remains: take care of the consonants and the vowels will take care of themselves. You want to get, first, an athletic articulation. With that you can give effect to the real thing, which is, your sense of the meaning of the words, your

274

emotional and intellectual conviction. That is the only thing that makes speech tolerable. Without it cantilation can do nothing except intensify ordinary twaddling into a nerve destroying crooning like the maunderings of an idiot-banshee. Remember that even in singing, it is an Irish defect to lose grip and interest by neglecting the words & thinking only of the music. Cats do the same thing when they are serenading one another; but the genuineness of their emotion gives them poignancy.

Moral: keep your head; and dont let your nieces cantilate or atalantalate anything in public until they can first *say* the piece interestingly and articulate it delicately and penetratingly. I have never been able to knock enough articulation into you, though you are much better than you were. You still think of how you are doing your recitations instead of what you are saying. The final consonant withers, and the light of the meaning goes out every now and then as you attend to your psaltery instead of to your business. At which moments I feel moved to throw things at you. And Yeats is heaping fresh artificialities & irrelevances & distractions & impertinences on you instead of sternly nailing you to the simple point of conveying the meaning & feeling of the author.

In haste
GBS

To WILLIAM ARCHER

10 Adelphi Terrace W C
20th June 1902

[A/2]

[The "Don Juan dream" was the just completed third-act Hell scene of *Man and Superman*, upon which Shaw had been working since May 1900. In the new preface to *Mrs Warren's Profession* Shaw quoted Archer as having "disowned" him on the ground that he "cannot touch pitch without wallowing in it." Archer replied in his *Morning Leader* article, "'Mrs Warren' Once More," on 21st June (he had apparently sent Shaw an advance proof) that the phrase, taken out of context, distorted his meaning, which was not intended to be a moral reproach but a purely artistic one. The case of Frank and Vivie, he argued later in the article, "cannot possibly be said to present a typical incident in the history of a polyandrous group, and has the air of being dragged in simply for the sake of its unpleasantness. This is a piece of clumsy construction which Mr Shaw probably realises by this time, and classes among the 'relapses into staginess' which 'betray the young playwright and the old playgoer in this early work of mine.' But does he realise how fatally such a fault of technique, or rather of logic, may mar the general impression produced by a play? Show us that a horror is inevitable, and we admire while we shudder; leave us with the feeling that it is gratuitous, and it is only too probable that weak human nature may 'wallow' a little in metaphors of reprobation."

Edward Westermarck (1862–1939), a Finnish philosopher and anthropologist, had published his *History of Human Marriage* in 1891.]

Thanks for the Don Juan dream. I am greatly afraid that the process of pulling it straight will lengthen it instead of shortening it; but the rest of the business will be so outrageous that this will be the merest trifle.

I dont approve of your Morning Leader article: you should push your attack home & see what comes of it. The wallowing in pitch phrase was a capital one: I seized on it because it exactly & forcibly expressed the effect produced by the play. What is more, it is justifiable in all the implications from which you shrink out of your reluctance to say anything that sounds personally nasty. A dramatist *must* wallow: the moment he ceases to wallow he ceases to be dramatic. You can see this plainly if you think of him as refusing to wallow in things that are congenial to you. When a conventional author introduces a character supposed to represent one of your own heterodoxies, and makes comic relief of him, or holds him up as a warning (like the Woman's Rights young lady in [The Case of] Rebellious Susan, for instance) you feel at once that the character is unreal—that the dramatist must take a character from its own point of view, and must actually wallow in that point of view, if he is to make that character live. You cannot absolve Shakespear from all complicity with Falstaff: he wallowed in Falstaff, and in Thersites. The elegant remark of Lucio [in *Measure for Measure*] when he meets the lady of the pavement:—"How now. Which of your hips has the most profound sciatica?" must have amused Shakespear or he couldnt have written it: he was Lucio when he wrote it. I believe that to people with no sense of humor & strong & refined conscientiousness, there must be something hideous in the derision of "the comic spirit." When I wallow in that serious point of view I feel that horror myself. So stick to your guns as to the wallowing: it may be the biggest part of your critical function to challenge the lawfulness of the ecstasy of derisory blackguardism which makes comedy so enormously amusing.

The paragraph about "inevitable" is all topsy-turvy. The customary thing in the polyandrous group is for the Franks & Vivies to be playmates from childhood, or at least acquaintances. My long arm of coincidence, instead of forcing in the dilemma artificially, actually sacrificed its normal inevitability for the sake of the main situation, which made it necessary that by hook or crook Mrs Warren & Vivie should be practically strangers to one another.

But the odd thing to me is that you should so dislike the Frank & Vivie courtship (which does not shock me in the least) and overlook the episode between Mrs Warren & Frank, which is to me the most exquisitely atrocious passage in the play. I know of a real case in which a young man, having very gallantly seduced a lady a good deal his senior, was taken aback by being told contemptuously that he was not half the man his father was. The Dilke case gives you the same thing with the man as the senior of the woman. It is, I believe, quite common in circles of the Mrs Warren type for this two-generation complication to arise. If you study the housing question & Westermarck & so on, you will see that the way in which Mrs Warren is enveloped in a web of possibilities of incest, Mrs Warren narrowly escaping an affair with the son of her old associate, Crofts wanting to have the daughter as her mother's successor even with a possibility of the daughter being his own, & Frank & Vivie making love to one another, is part of the situation. You really have not sounded the depths of the pitch or appreciated its blackness or you would not dwell on the comparatively rose-watery part of it.

Your final conclusion is right from your comparatively innocent point of view. But if you ever get to mine, you will laugh at many things that now seem very solemn to you; and you will also take some things very seriously that now seem to you to be mere paradoxes. You may observe that though I walk through hell with my bells jingling, I lose my temper a good deal when I walk through heaven. My moral perspective is not wrong from my own standpoint. My discords will not annoy you so much when you catch my way of resolving them. Damn it, you cant have my plays *all* your own way.

GBS

To SIEGFRIED TREBITSCH

[A/5; X/176]

Maybury Knoll. Woking
26th June 1902

[Siegfried Trebitsch (1869–1956), a young Austrian writer and journalist, on a visit to London in November 1900 had called on William Archer, whom he considered to be the best literary critic in London. Archer had drawn his attention to Shaw, giving him a copy of *Plays Pleasant and Unpleasant*. Trebitsch, fired by the plays, had instantly entered into negotiations with Shaw, who recalled later (in a programme note to *Jitta's Atonement* in 1925), "He was quite unknown to me when he appeared one day at my house and asked to see me with a view to his becoming my interpreter and apostle in Central Europe. . . . I did what I could to dissuade him from what seemed a desperate undertaking; but his faith in my destiny was invincible. I surrendered at discretion; and the result was that I presently found myself a successful and respected playwright in the German language whilst the English critics were still explaining laboriously that my plays were not plays, and urging me, in the kindest spirit, to cease my vain efforts to enter a profession for which Nature had utterly unfitted me." Trebitsch eventually wrote several plays of his own, one of which, *Frau Gittas Sühne* (1919), was translated freely by Shaw in 1922 as *Jitta's Atonement*.]

My dear Trebitsch

I am amazed at your industry. But why dont you write plays of your own?

You must tell the Volkstheater people that you quite agree with all their suggestions, and that you regret greatly that I am so unreasonable a man. But you must assure them that unless they will perform the play [*The Devil's Disciple*] exactly as it is written, the negotiation must drop at once. If they know how plays should be written let them write plays for themselves. If they dont, they had better leave the business to those who do. I wont have the two last acts run into one. I wont have a line omitted or a comma altered. I am quite familiar with the fact that every fool who is connected with a theatre, from the callboy to the manager, thinks he knows better than an author how to make a play popular and successful. Tell them with my compliments that I know all about that; that I am fortysix years old; that I know my business and theirs as well; that I am quite independent of tantièmes and do not care a snap of my fingers whether they produce my plays or not; that I shall give my plays titles thirtyfive words long if I like: in short, that I am a pigheaded, arrogant, obstinate, domineering man of genius, deaf to reason, and invincibly determined to have my own way about my own works.

Say the same thing to all the managers the moment they begin to sing that old song about alterations & modifications. Tell them it is no use: if my plays are too advanced for them, they can let them alone: they need not add stupidity & vandalism to Dichtersbeleidigung. But say how delighted you would be to meet their wishes if only I would let you. Let all the agreeable things come from you, and the disagreeable things from me.

278

I write in great haste on the eve of a journey. Next week I will answer the other points in your letter.

Once more, dont neglect your own work. Translation will not teach you half so much as original composition.

yrs sincerely
G. Bernard Shaw

To SIEGFRIED TREBITSCH

Maybury Knoll. Woking
[A/5]   7th July 1902

[Dr Paul Schlenther (1854–1916) was the theatre director of the Vienna Burgtheater and an important literary critic. The "latest" play presumably was *Man and Superman*, which Shaw had read to a few friends in its unpolished "draft" state the previous week, but the preface was not completed until 1903.]

My dear Trebitsch

"Das Capital" has been translated into English since I read it—at least the first volume has; but nobody ever read the second & third volumes, either in England or Germany. In 1882 there was nothing but the French version and the original, which I could not read.

Excuse my asking you a personal question? Are you dependent on your pen; or have you an independent income? My reason for asking is this: There are more ways than one of sharing half & half. We may say that we shall divide the royalties of every performance. Or we may agree that you shall take the first £50 and I the second, and, after that, share in the ordinary way for each performance. In that case if the play only produced £50 I should get nothing; if it produced £75 you would get £50 and I £25; if it produced £100 we should get £50 each; but you would get your £50 first. You would thus get some sort of payment for your trouble if the play were not successful; and I should not get my half unless there was enough to prevent you from being absolutely out-of-pocket by the time spent in translating. My wife says you must be a millionaire because you stayed at one of the most expensive hotels in London; but I tell her that you are perhaps only a man of genius, in which case you had better protect yourself by some such arrangement as I suggest.

Candida is too sentimental for the Burgtheater. Tell Dr Schlenther

279

to produce "Cæsar & Cleopatra," with Britannus changed into an echt Wiener bourgeois, and a splendid *mise en scène*. Candida would do better in Berlin, would it not?

Make them give you 10%, as it has to be shared. Sardou gets £30 (600m.) per performance for plays from the principal theatre here, though the mounting is enormously expensive and the translator has to be paid also. Making all possible allowance for lower prices of admission, the Burgtheater should not insult us by offering us less than half what Sardou gets.

My latest play is *very* unlike Candida. You must not translate it, as you would get six years in a fortress for the preface alone.

yrs ever
G. Bernard Shaw

To LUCINDA ELIZABETH SHAW

[C/4]

Victoria Hotel. Holkham
25th July 1902

[It had become the custom for the Shaws to spend a portion of each summer at a coastal resort for the sea bathing. They went to Norfolk in July and remained there until 14th September.

Shaw's mother had long been interested in the occult, and her son later insisted she had introduced the first planchette into Ireland. For years she held weekly séances, on Friday afternoons, in her home in London, conducted by Miss Violet Burton, a spiritualist medium from Blackheath, whose "control" was Father John, a spiritual leader in the other world so honest that he candidly admitted "any amount of fraud" among spiritualists. Mrs Shaw also went in for spirit drawings, which frequently resembled designs for wallpaper, and, later, for spirit photos (popularised by Conan Doyle).]

My address for the present is as above. Do not spend too much on interviews with Oscar Wilde; and do not ask any question that you know the answer to, as a reply would have no weight, unless indeed it were a wrong reply. And do not tell anybody else about the questions until you get them finally answered and hear from me as to what they mean.

GBS

To SIEGFRIED TREBITSCH

Victoria Hotel. Holkham

[C/5; X/176]   9th August 1902

[Carl Wiené, celebrated performer of the Dresden Hoftheater, was imported to Vienna for *Ein Teufelskerl* (*The Devil's Disciple*), his availability being one of the terms of the agreement with Trebitsch insisted upon by Ernst Geffke, the managing director of the Raimund Theater. The play was presented on 25th February 1903. Burgoyne was played by Willy Thaller, a popular Viennese comedian.]

Ausgezeichnet! Ganz vorzuglich! Furchtbar nett! Famos! Colossale! Wiené ist—wie heisst es?—Gastspieler, nicht wahr? Well, it does not much matter whether he can act or not: *anybody* can play the title part in the D's D. The most important part to cast well is Burgoyne, who must be both a fine comedian and a distinguished "père noble."

It is also very important to get the last scene well stage managered, with a big surging crowd. Unless both Burgoyne and the crowd are well handled the last act will collapse as mere opera bouffe. However, time enough to think about all that in October.

I suppose Wiené will try to get other theatres to take up the play if he makes a success in it.

We look forward to seeing you next month; but do not come to London too early in September or you will find everybody away at the seaside.

GBS

To EMERY WALKER

Victoria Hotel. Holkham

[C/3]   11th August 1902

[Although Shaw's interest in photography dated back to the 1880's, it was not until after his marriage and the retreat to Surrey that he found an opportunity to indulge in photography as a serious hobby. He had by now acquired a large inventory of cameras, photographic plates, and equipment. Shaw had reviewed the photographic exhibition for the *Amateur Photographer* in 1901 (11th and 18th October), and did so again in 1902 (9th and 16th October).]

I send you by parcel post a Watkins' Exposure Meter. I have two, and dont want this one. You may depend on it for outdoor work (it is rather slow for indoor, especially in winter) & save yourself a lot of time, besides using your largest stop instead of your smallest. I am gaily giving exposures of $\frac{1}{75}''$ $\frac{1}{100}''$ & $\frac{1}{150}''$ here without the slightest misgiving on a very fast film. You get the plate number from the card; but if you use a fast plate & it is not fresh, it is perhaps wise to conclude that it has slowed down a bit. Otherwise you need not make allowances to be on the safe side, as Watkins has taken care to do that. The real difficulty is to get a shutter that really gives the speeds marked. If you havnt such a thing, a slow plate and a suitably small stop will prolong the exposure sufficiently to make it manageable by hand with a cap.

G. Bernard Shaw

To SIEGFRIED TREBITSCH

[C/5; X/176]

Victoria Hotel. Holkham
29th August 1902

[The Burgtheater did not produce *Candida*. It was presented eventually by the Deutsches Volkstheater, Vienna, on 8th October 1904. The amateur production described by Shaw is that of the New Stage Club in February 1902, which was produced not *by* nurses, but in aid of a nursing institution. Millicent Murby, as noted earlier, played Candida. Prossy was performed by another young Fabian, Louise Salom, and the "idiot" who played Marchbanks was Charles Dalmon.]

Here I am still, enjoying the primeval simplicity & inaccessibility of this unerhörtes place (that adjective is not Viennese but Wagnerese). When I heard about Candida I was too disgusted to reply: the Burgtheater ought to be ashamed of itself for such a sentimental choice. Why dont they do Cæsar & Cleopatra & leave little Candida to the amateurs? However, since you are pleased, I shall not positively forbid the performance; but you may tell Dr Schenther that a man in his position ought to have a more robust mind. You are young and a poet, so I forgive you; but as for Schenther, he is wasting his subvention in producing a play that has been successfully performed in London for a charity by a couple of hospital nurses, a doctor, an idiot (who played Eugene) and an actor (who played the old man). It is mere child's play.

I hope to get back to London before the 20th Sep^r; but my movements are not yet decided on.

G.B.S.

To REV. ENSOR WALTERS

[D/43]

10 Adelphi Terrace W C
19th September 1902

[Shaw had offered to nominate Walters for an aldermanship of the St Pancras Borough and to get Alderman Donald McGregor to second the nomination, but the news that both the Progressives and the Moderates were unanimously backing Sir William Heaton Hamer (d. 1936), who later became Medical Officer of Health for the County of London, led Shaw to suggest that he and Walters must yield gracefully. Dr J. A. Angus was a fellow Borough Councillor, as was the Rev. G. A. Suttle of Westfield Tabernacle. The Bruges trip apparently was a very brief one, which Shaw made alone.]

I am off tomorrow morning to Bruges to see the collection of Flemish art there: it is a sort of thing that I must see as a matter of business as the chance may never occur again during my lifetime as a critic. I shall not be back until Tuesday evening or Wednesday morning. I called on you this evening; but you were out; and so was Mac., to whom I am writing. If unanimity on both sides can be obtained concerning Hamer, there is nothing more to be said: we must accept him. But if the Moderates refuse to accept him & say they will run Angus (whom they could certainly carry) then I think Angus, who is of the chivalrous Highland type, might possibly offer to withdraw in your favor but not in Hamer's, in which case the Progressives would have to choose between you & losing the robe.

It is perhaps just as well that I cannot attend the Prog. Com^tee, as I had no success last time. But Suttle behaved very handsomely on that occasion. I wonder would he propose you this time!

GBS

To GRANT RICHARDS

[A/44]

10 Adelphi Terrace W C
22nd October 1902

[Shaw had just received a royalty statement for *Three Plays for Puritans*. Re Simpkin, see I, 543. James Brand Pinker (1863–1922) was a very successful London literary agent.]

Dear G.R.

I rejoice at getting in a post ahead of you. Ha ha! Ha ha!

First, hand me over another pound and elevenpence. I have not had time to go carefully through the a/cs yet; but on the face of them they

283

knock 25% off my royalty on the eighteenpenny books. The royalty agreed on was twopence, not three halfpence.

The general criticism of these a/cs is obvious: you dont advertize. I have never yet had my attention called to the existence of my own works except by a review. The sale is the old sale to my disciples: I could almost name all the purchasers. I have never seen an advertisement, never met any human being who had ever seen one, never expect to meet one. Cashel Byron is a dead failure in consequence, because all the disciples have cherished it for years; and there has been nothing to tell them that the new edition adds anything to the old. But for the pleasure of talking to you occasionally I might as well publish with Simpkin. You dont even put me in your own lists.

Observe, I dont complain. I am aware that when an author has got far enough to make a book of his secure against actual out-of-pocket loss, his only chance of getting it pushed up to the hilt is to exact an advance which the publisher can recover only by pushing as hard as he can. You are not really free to push without this pressure: you are forced to fight at the dangerous places, not at the safe ones. So dont understand me as reproaching you.

On the other hand dont you reproach me if I take my next book to Pinker and say, "Get me what you can for that; and let me have no bother about it." At present I dont know what I am worth in the literary market; and as I like bargaining more than a Jew does, I rather want to find that out.

Are you available for lunch one of these days?

yrs ever
G. Bernard Shaw

To GRANT RICHARDS

[S/3]

10 Adelphi Terrace W C
7th November 1902

Dear G.R.

I wrote to Lyons at his request about the royalty. As the eighteen-pence was supposed to be net, he naturally thought the royalty was at least fivepence. I regarded my consent to twopence as a Quixotic sacrifice. . . .

I am at work revising the Superman. It will be a longish job. I seriously think I will, by way of experiment, simply sell it to whoever will give me the biggest advance. You will still have me on your list of authors, which is all you require, as you do not push the books past the point at which they replace their cost to you. *I* dont get the wages of a head clerk out of them; and I never will, and never can (such is the nature of business, though you dont understand it) unless I put the publisher in such a position that he will be ruined unless he makes the book a success. Now I dont want to ruin you, or keep you awake at nights; consequently if I make a hard bargain I had much rather make it with somebody else, and be guiltless of the bread of your infants.

However, sufficient unto the day is the evil thereof. Send me that extra halfpenny; and let us put off the Superman until he is ready for birth. I may publish him myself on commission & do my own advertizing, especially if I can induce my wife to take charge of the details.

yrs ever
G. Bernard Shaw

To EMILY GUEST

[G&I.u/2]

Maybury Knoll. Woking
11th November 1902

[Miss Guest was a resident of West Hampstead. Mr Hennesey apparently was a member of the local Board of Guardians. Mr Russell very likely was John Russell (2nd Earl Russell), a Fabian who was on the London County Council.]

Dear Madam

I had already sent on your letter to Mr Hennesey before your note came. No harm will come of it, and possibly some good.

You must, however, understand that the policy of all Guardians towards paupers who are ablebodied is one of persecution pure and simple. As the law stands the guardians must, whether they like it or not, relieve everyone who claims relief as a destitute person. A certain number of men and women, knowing this, systematically take advantage of it to live at the expense of the ratepayers. The problem always before the Guardians is how to make the workhouse intolerable for these people without making it also intolerable for those who are fairly past work or incapable of it. Disagreeable food, disagreeable work, disagreeable regulations, contemptuous and unsympathetic treatment, are all tried to the utmost; and yet, so miserable is the lot of the laborer

285

outside that there are always plenty of ablebodied paupers to be dealt with. Skilly is given precisely because it is loathed; and most guardians would discharge a cook who made skilly appetizing. As for tea, you might as well suggest diamond necklaces as a part of the workhouse uniform.

Please remember that these are not my *opinions*. You appealed to me through Mr Russell, and I simply tell you the facts—facts which you must bear in mind and reckon with if you wish to do any good to the paupers in whom you are intereste[d]. If you call tea a necessity and its denial cruelty to people under 55, the Guardians will give you up as a sentimental innocent; and the matron will mark your protegées as the pets of a lady visitor, possibly to their advantage, possibly not. On the other hand, if you are what the Guardians call reasonable, you may gain a good deal of influence with them, & perhaps succeed in reducing the tea age to 55 or even 50.

Personally I regard tea as an unmitigated curse to humanity, especially to poor women. However, that is a separate question. I do not consider that superannuated workers should be put into workhouses at all, or that their treatment should be in any way mixed up with that of ablebodied paupers. But whilst we have workhouses for them you may depend on it that it will never be possible to raise the standard of humanity within them until it is first raised without them. The workhouse is the merest symptom of the social disease that produces proletariats.

Excuse me for troubling you with all this; but your note, though I can take no exception to any word in it, somehow gives me a sensation of having my head snapped off as if I myself were a hardhearted Guardian. I assure you I am simply giving you the best information in my power; and though I certainly live by robbing the poor I have done what I could (without the least success) to persuade people that this is not a satisfactory state of things.

yours sincerely
[G. Bernard Shaw]

To MAX BEERBOHM

[A/1]

Maybury Knoll. Woking
12th November 1902

[Beerbohm had written on 11th November: "This is a begging letter, written by the President of the Playgoers' Club (myself!) Could you, would you, read or speak a lecture ... I don't approve of this kind of begging, in the ordinary way. But ... I know that self-expression is a natural instinct in you, and that you have so much to express that your one serious difficulty is in finding a sufficient number [of] vantage-places" (BM).]

Max Beerbohm
The bonds of friendship are now bursten. The cord is loosed, the bowl is broken, the grasshopper is become a burden. Damn the Playgoers! To the blackest pit with their lectures: they have too long profaned the Sabbath. Their laughter is as the crackling of thorns under a pot; and it generally comes in the wrong place. I have found some ray of grace in even the most degraded of other societies; but in this none —absolutely none. The club is, and always has been, an eighth circle of hell, in which the male and female damned sit in rows and make one long for even devils from the higher seventh circle to bring into the stale atmosphere some breathable ether, were it only brimstone fumes. I have never been lured among them without longing to spring up and say "Do you know what is the matter with the theatre? YOU!" and stalk out. I do not believe that you are the President. I deny it, contradict it, repudiate it. The thing is eternally impossible. It may be that some fiend sits there in your semblance and invites me to lecture in your handwriting. But the lures of Satan are vain. Vade retro.

You must come to lunch some day and be exorcised. I'll fix a date for the ceremony presently.

Don Juan is struggling through revision towards publication.

yrs ever
G. Bernard Shaw

To SIEGFRIED TREBITSCH

[A/5; X/176]

Maybury Knoll. Woking
18th November 1902

[Trebitsch was something of a hypochondriac, and throughout their correspondence he and Shaw discussed unconventional treatments, diets, and "cures." *Genesung* was Trebitsch's new novel, just published by S. Fischer in Berlin. Cotta was a Stuttgart publisher, who had just printed separate acting editions of Trebitsch's translations of *Candida*, *The Devil's Disciple*, and *Arms and the Man* (under the title *Helden*), which he subsequently issued in a single volume as *Drei Dramen* (1903).]

My dear Trebitsch

If your nerves are overtaxed, go to bed for a fortnight, and read nothing but the silliest stories you can find. Never eat meat or drink tea, coffee, or wine again as long as you live. Dont take any exercise; and do exactly the opposite of what the doctor advises. If you are very bad, hire yourself out as a laborer and live on your wages for a month or so. If you are very very very bad, become religious, and go every day three times to the nearest Roman Catholic Church. Go round all the Stations of the Cross on your knees, and pray incessantly. When you begin to feel sceptical you will be getting well.

I read 10 pages of Genesung three times a week with a Fräulein who acts as my dictionary. It must be a most scandalous book; for she refuses to translate most of it. I read a sentence and ask her what it means. She blushes and says it is nur dumme Zeug; and my wife tells me to go on to the next paragraph. I am much more interested now that Böhlau is getting tired of Lea and beginning to take a serious view of his profession. You should give up literature and take to politics. I owe all my originality, such as it is, to my determination not to be a literary man. Instead of belonging to a literary club I belong to a municipal council. Instead of drinking and discussing authors and reviews, I sit on committees with capable practical greengrocers and bootmakers (including a builder who actually reads Carlyle) and administer the collection of dust, the electric lighting of the streets, and the enforcement of the sanitary laws. You must do the same. Keep away from books and from men who get their ideas from books; and your own books will always be fresh. I notice in Genesung that you are genuinely concerned about the political and philosophical bearing of people's lives, and are much more than a mere romancer. . . .

I was much alarmed when I read in your letter of the 6th that Cotta had "behaved against us." To do anything *against* one means in English to do something hostile. "Towards" is the right word. Your English has only two faults. One is "against" for "towards": the other is "included" for "enclosed." Otherwise you write better English than most Englishmen. However, as to Cotta, you see what a good effect it has on a publisher to tell him that the author totally disapproves of his proposals and proceedings. It is very noble of him to advance the 900 books (send me 3—one of each); but bless you! it is the printer who will really advance them: Cotta wont pay him until the book is on the market; and when your half-profits account comes in you will find that it shews a huge loss on the edition, and we shall have to pay half the loss as well as the 320 marks. *Timeo dona ferentes.* I shall be quite

288

disappointed now if Cotta behaves well; but perhaps he will for your sake.

Do not bother about business until you are well. You carry Cæsar and his fortunes, not to mention your own as well.

Who is Doctor Buzzi? Is it starvation cure, or overfeeding cure, or water cure, or grape cure, or faith healing, or what?

yrs ever
G. Bernard Shaw

To FREDERICK H. EVANS

[C/4]

10 Adelphi Terrace W C
28th November 1902

Have you seen that a conscientious objector has got his certificate and floored the magistrate by simply sticking to it that V. [Vaccination] is "contrary to Nature and against the will of God"? I am not sure that this is not the fundamental position. Anyhow the bench collapsed & the objector triumphed.

The Kodak machine is all very well when you snap off a dozen exposures at the same time and in the same light. But I am a real scientific timing developist. If I develop with pyrocatechin, for instance, I develop for ten times the period between the pouring on of the developer and the appearance of the sky on the plate. This period may be half a minute or a minute and a quarter according to circumstances: that is, I may want to leave one plate in for five minutes & the next one for thirteen minutes. A five minute film would get terrific density & contrast in 13 minutes; and a 13 minutes one would be hopelessly underdone in 5.

However, I confess that I generally develop the whole roll without separating the exposures, & put up with the resultant variations for the sake of the simplicity of the operation.

GBS

To AGNES F. JENNINGS

[H/3]
10 Adelphi Terrace W C
4th December 1902

[Miss Jennings was a professional photographer, with a studio in Charles Street, who had exhibited in the London photographic shows in 1896 and 1897.]

Dear Miss Jennings

I have just discovered, to my dismay, that the packet of proofs which you sent me last July, and which I brought down to Norfolk to be dealt with during my holiday, somehow never got unpacked or acknowledged. Quite unpardonable of me, I confess. I hope you have not borne *much* malice.

The photographs seem to me just diabolical. It is no use: you can do nothing better with that lens and with the sitter staring meaninglessly at the corner of the camera in front of your left shoulder. I knew how it would be when you told me to look at that fatal spot; but you wouldnt have believed me if I had remonstrated; so I let you do your worst. The definition of the large heads is frightful: the skin is seen as under a microscope, whilst the size of the head is reduced greatly from life. There is no suggestion that I am anywhere: I am stuck flat on a background. It is all horrible, studioesque, photographic in the most injurious sense.

Now up to a certain point this is not your fault. The photographs are technically all right; and I suppose that villainous portrait lens cannot have its back cell unscrewed into soft definition. There is nothing wrong with the exposure or the development. But the total result is hideous. No woman will fall in love with any of those portraits: most people will mistrust and loathe the original of so unnatural an image. I am sure you cannot look at them yourself without detestation. You have betrayed this feeling by turning one of the negatives upside down and trying to soften the effect by printing glass-to-film instead of film-to-film. Quite useless: the thing only looks drunk, in spite of the nice lighting.

To shew you what can be done when one is not plagued with a studio and a background, I send you some hasty proofs of plates taken by myself. One of them is almost featureless because the face was denser than I allowed for in the lantern; and all of them are as rough as possible. But I submit to you that they look human, and that they convey an impression that I am somewhere. Also that I am not staring at a camera. I am at my ease for a very good reason—the exposure was

290

(Photograph by Agnes F. Jennings, 1902)

three mortal minutes. No matter: il faut souffrir pour etre belle. Lens, a Dallmeyer Stigmatic at full aperture (you *would* put stops into that thing of yours); time, 10 p.m.; light, electric; place, the drawingroom; size, quarter plate. The negatives are as sharp as can be; but the use of the full aperture, and the enlargement to whole plate, get rid of all harshness. I took no pains, but just slopped the prints into water with a dash of Rodinal in it and fixed them. With an enlarged negative and a careful carbon or gum print, quite nice pictures could be got out of them. Of course you couldnt shew such things as these proofs to regular customers; but with your skill you could easily get the qualities without the faults. The success of Hollyer, who has never used a background, shews that people think a photograph much more "natural" when an ordinary room is taken just as it comes.

I also think that people are too much afraid of long exposures. The best photograph I ever took of myself (by two candles and a reading lamp, with a slow spectacle glass of about 18 inch focus) came just right with an exposure of twelve minutes. Under such circumstances, you MUST make your sitters comfortable. It is the short exposures that make it possible to take people in attitudes that Nature rebels against.

In my opinion the best lens for portraits is the telephoto. Dallmeyer's new sort, the Adon, is much faster than the older ones; but I get decent telephoto portraits in my drawingroom at Woking in this weather in ten or fifteen seconds, with the old sort. You could get a telephoto attachment that would Christianize your portrait lens for Salon work without a very extravagant outlay.

However, I dont know much about the subject; but I maintain that I am more beautiful than those pictures of me which your lens has perpetrated.

yours sincerely—perhaps quite outrageously sincerely
G. Bernard Shaw

To SIEGFRIED TREBITSCH

[A/5]

10 Adelphi Terrace W C
10th December 1902

[*The Man of Destiny* was first called *Der Schlachtenlenker*, but Trebitsch altered this in the 1911 edition of Shaw's collected plays to *Der Mann des Schicksals*. A. Entsch was a Berlin play agent.]

My dear Trebitsch

Your letter has just reached me. As to the Man of Destiny, you must by no means say that you do not want anything for the performances [in German] in London. On the contrary, when London is concerned *you* must be stern and inflexible and I conciliatory and regretful. Entsch must conduct the business just as if it were a German transaction.

As to the title, is there no well known phrase attached to Napoleon corresponding to our Man of Destiny? Der Schichsalskerl would hardly do, I am afraid.

Now as to your translations. You are thinking about nothing but the artistic side of the business. About that I never concern myself: it is in the hands of Providence. As a work of art, your translations seem to me better than the originals in several ways, and to have a certain charm of style and character that cannot be purchased for money or contrived by corrections & the like. But all this we may leave to the critics & the public. There is a mechanical side to the business that can be mastered only by experience and by drudgery. Now there is no need for doing that drudgery twice over. I know ten times as much about all those *dramatis personae* as you do, or as you ever will. I could write you the whole history of Richard Dudgeon from his boyhood. I know all about Burgoyne, all about the war, all about Anderson's position & salary and religion. I remember every word they say, and keep alluding to these sayings pages after you have forgotten them. My stage effects are based on that. Let me give you an example. Look at page 94. Swindon says "Die englischen Soldaten (it should be in the singular) werden dann schon zeigen, was sie Können." On page 131, Burgoyne says to Swindon "Ihr Freund, der britische Beamte &c. &c. There is no sense in this: Swindon has never said a word about the britische Beamte. Burgoyne's exit speech, which brings down the house in England, is made quite pointless. Now in England the audience first hear Swindon utter his conventional brag about "the British soldier" (not soldier*s*). Attention is specially called to it by Burgoyne's retort, and by its value as shewing the man's character. Consequently when Burgoyne afterwards says "Your friend the British soldier &c," the audience takes it at once. But suppose Swindon first said unrhetorically "the English soldiers," and Burgoyne afterwards said, "your friend the British official," there would be no point, no sense, no fun in it. You see, I have the whole thing in my head: you have only read it and made a version of it; and though you remember the poetic connexion and course of the feelings and the more touching ideas of the characters, you cannot remember the mechanical connexions nor the comic incongruities. You are like my wife, who thinks that making people laugh is an unworthy and vulgar practice; but laughter is my sword and shield and spear.

Now you must make up your mind to undergo a most tedious and miserable apprenticeship to the stage over my plays. You are a sensitive & fastidious young poet: I am a sordid and disillusioned old charlatan. But I have built up these plays out of atoms of dust bit by bit, and planned them for the stage and corrected them for the press and rehearsed them for performance; and the result is that I can see at a glance these little oversights that seem trifles to you. Siegfried Trebitsch: I tell you it is the trifles that matter when you are a man of genius. You go right by instinct when you are on the top of the mountain; the avalanches that scare smaller men away have no terrors for you; but when you get back safe and triumphant to your hotel you trip over the umbrella stand and break your nose. And remember, the "heavy minded public," as you call it, can always be depended on to know when you break your nose, and to laugh at you, but you cannot go far up a mountain before they lose sight of you. The moment you are off the mountain you think nothing matters. You talk of "a few little things" (48 appalling errors & ruinous oversights in the D's D alone—I'll send you a marked copy tomorrow or next day)! You tell me not to be anxious about my stage directions (Good God!) because your directors & actors are much cleverer than English ones. Madman: all actors are idiots: all "directors" are impostors. Even if they were not, would you copy out Wagner's orchestral parts carelessly & omit a bar here and there because Austrian players have such virtuosity in fingering? Do not be deceived by reputations: unless you tell people exactly what to do, as if they were little children, and persuade them at the same time that they have thought of it all themselves, you will never get anything done properly. You and I have to teach all Europe; and you must learn how to do it in my plays so that you may know how to do it in your own. You must never trust anybody, never leave to chance anything you can arrange beforehand, no matter how distasteful & prosaic it may be. Cæsar's rule must be our rule: provide for every contingency you can foresee & then remember that Fate will decide. I have no room for more; but this is only the beginning of your troubles. When you are my age, you will have acquired a taste for trouble as other men acquire a taste for brandy. And now one question more. How often have you read your versions aloud to a circle of friends? You should do that 10 times before going to press. Even I, who cannot speak German, have read your version aloud to a German [H.A.Hertz] before writing you about it. How is your neuralgia? Immer Muth!

GBS

To SIEGFRIED TREBITSCH

[H/5]

10 Adelphi Terrace W C
18th December 1902

My dear Trebitsch

Good: we can do no more now as to the text.

Now as to the general philosophy of the thing. I know that the transfer of any work to the professional stage means desecration, prostitution, sacrilege and damnation. It means this *at best*. At worst it means mere ignorant rascality, lies, cheating, evasion, and interpolation of obscenities and idiocies. But you must never admit this, or make any truce with it, or allow anybody to tell you that it is the custom. When old actors grumble at my stage directions, I point out to them that an actor is not a mechanic to be ordered to cross right or left, sit, stand, or exit left upper entrance, without understanding why, but an artist who is entitled to demand that an author shall address himself to his taste, fancy, intellect, imagination, wit &c &c &c &c. This crushes him utterly: his self-respect compels him to agree with you; and when he returns to the greenroom he says to the first actor he meets there, in a loud voice, "You know, my dear Kainz-Barnay-Schulz, I dont agree with you about these stage directions of Shaw's. In my opinion he is quite right, because an actor is not a mechanic to be ordered to cross left and right, but an artist &c&c&c&c&c&c&c&c." In a theatre you must always assume that the noblest aims, the highest artistic integrity, the most scrupulous respect for artistic considerations, the most strenuous fidelity to the poet's text, are the law in that particular house, and that it is only in third rate places and among the lowest class of actors that malpractices occur and liberties are taken. Never let them put you in the position of a novice who does not know what theatres are really like: put *them* in the position of having to act up to your high estimate of their conscience and respectability. It is quite possible to do this pleasantly and familiarly if you have the requ[i]site social tact; but you will find that even the people who are not in that fortunate position are forced to do the same thing pompously and arbitrarily. The pompous author or manager is disliked and laughed at behind his

294

back; and the author who has social charm gets liked and respected; but both get the work done in the same way, by insisting on a high standard of artistic scrupulousness and intellectual character. The actors are not scrupulous and probably have no character at all: no matter: they cannot come to you and tell you that: they must pretend to be as good as you take them for; and the few good ones know [the] value of your respect and support you. Even opera singers, the most demoralized class of artists in existence, accustomed to perform under conditions which absolutely forbid honest and thorough work, were persuaded by Wagner to take unheard-of pains with his works at a time when they could hardly recognize them as music at all. The truth is, theatrical people, with all their insane vanity and lack of any positive element of character, are for that very reason easy to manage by any-one who thoroughly learns the business of the theatre. They are so susceptible that you can put anything you like into their heads, and finally work them up to believing that the production of the piece they are rehearsing is the most important event in the history of the world. The first thing is to read the piece over and over again to all your friends until you have learnt to do it effectively. Then read it to the cast and make a good impression to begin with. Then work out all the stage management and mark a copy to work from. This is very troublesome; but it is indispensable; for it makes you master of the situation at the first rehearsal. The stage manager never prepares his work as he should: he trusts to chance, and tries to invent the positions as he goes along, stopping and altering and disputing and wasting time. If you are ready to do his work for him, he will not dare to interfere with you. I always come to the first rehearsal with the whole stage business cut and dried. If the scenery is not ready (it never is in England) I seize chairs, forms &c with my own hands and arrange them to mark doors and objects of furniture. (The stage manager waits until he can order a carpenter to do it, as such manual work would compromise his dignity). I open the promptbook; seize the actor or actress who begins; lead them to their entrance in my pleasantest and busiest and friendliest manner, and say, "Here you are: this is your entrance—now down here and across to here" letting them read the words just as they please, and simply piloting them through the movements. At the end of the first act, I say "Now we'll go through that act again"; and the repetition of the act ends the rehearsal. Next day I go twice through the second act in the same way. Next day twice through the third act. I take care, of course, that Burgoyne (zum Beispiel) is not called for the first two days. On the fourth day I go straight through the whole play. By that

295

time the movements are settled. I then apologize for interfering and pretend that I am withdrawing to allow the stage manager to stage manage the play. Of course he does nothing, as the whole thing is virtually settled by that time. I then do not interfere for a day or two, because the actors are all trying to "swallow" their words, and until they have done that it is useless to try to get any expression out of them. When they get familiar with the play, then I take notes during the scenes—never actually interrupting if I can help it—and at the end explain the point and get the passage repeated. The great difficulty to a beginner is to refrain from saying too much. For instance, you will note, say, twelve points that the leading lady misunderstands or misses or spoils. If you tell her all the twelve on one day, you will worry her out of all loyalty to you. Tell her two at most, and save up the rest for the following rehearsals. You will find that she will correct some of them herself before you come to them.

At first you will have to depend on careful preparation and fore-thought to gain authority, as nothing but experience will teach you all that the actors themselves know; so that at first they will know better than you on certain points. But when you have rehearsed half a dozen plays you will have mastered the artistic business as well as the mechanical business; and then you will be able to double the value of every actor (except the *very* best) by coaching him in points that he would never think of himself. Then your authority behind the curtain will be as undisputed as that of Sardou. Remember: the actor is very jealous, and trusts neither the professional stage manager (who is generally an old actor) nor any of the other actors. But he knows that the author really wants to make the best of everybody; and consequently the author has only to take trouble enough to become an expert (and if he doesnt he will become a nuisance) to be more powerful on the stage than any other person in the theatre. . . . . . .* Who is to translate my new volume—a masterpiece? It contains, among other things, a most wonderful play, and a set of aphorisms ["Maxims for Revolutionists"] which eclipse Larochefoucauld's.

yrs ever
G. Bernard Shaw

PS My wife screamed with laughter at your telling me to "be quiet." It is what one says in England to a naughty child or a dog that barks too much!!!

---

* The ellipsis is Shaw's.

To SIEGFRIED TREBITSCH

Maybury Knoll. Woking
[A/5]   26th December 1902

My dear Trebitsch

I send you a corrected copy of "Helden." It is full of hideous and devastating errors, but not so full as Candida, which I will send you as soon as I have gone completely through it.

No doubt some of the passages I have marked cannot be done in my way without spoiling their effect in German; but some of them are the crimes—the unashamed, intentional crimes—of a classically educated Viennese litterateur. If you took to painting & made a portrait of me, you would give me the leg of Apollo and the torso of the Farnese Hercules, and if I complained you would think me an ignorant Philistine. Now all that—everything romantic, everything classical, everything that is academically de rigueur or romantically artistic, is just what I have come into the world to trample on, laugh out of countenance, and finally slay. However, I will say more of this when I send Candida.

In Arms & The Man the chief errors are due to your not acting the play over and over again until you know it by heart & then retiring for six months to the mountains to realize it right through to the bone. The way in which you translate every word just as it comes and then forget it and translate it some other way when it begins (or should begin) to make the audience laugh, is enough to whiten the hair on an author's head. Have you ever read Shakespear's Much Ado About Nothing? In it a man calls a constable an ass; and throughout the rest of the play the constable can think of nothing but this insult and keeps on saying "But forget not, masters, that I am an ass." Now if you translated Much Ado, you would make the man call the constable a Schaffkopf. On the next page he would be a Narr, then a Maul, then a Thier, and perhaps the very last time an Esel. And if Shakespear's ghost came to you to remonstrate, you would smile a superior smile and tell him that all accomplished litterateurs made it a point of style to vary their expressions and never repeat a word if they could help it. Whereupon Shakespear would place the pillow over your mouth and sit on it, and serve you right too!

But now I have something serious to say. What about my new book. Who is to translate *that*? This translating of old plays is all very well; but it is baby's work. I want my new book translated & published by Cotta simultaneously with the English edition. It will be a frightfully difficult task; and the publisher & printer will probably be sent to prison for it. But I want the Germans to know me as a philosopher, as an English (or Irish) Nietzsche (only ten times cleverer), and not as a mere carpenter of farces like Helden and nursery plays like Candida. Besides, I want to complete *your* education. You must begin where I leave off & surpass me as far as I surpass Goethe & Schiller & Shakespear and Strindberg & Ibsen & Hauptmann & Sudermann & Tolstoy *et hoc genus omne.* Genesung is not bad; but all that book will only make a sentence in your future work. And it is not lighthearted enough: you must learn to laugh, or, by Heavens, you will commit suicide when you realize all the infamy of the world as it is. You must avoid literary people & go into public life. I avoid literary and artistic people like the devil: the greengrocers and bootmakers and builders and publicans (Gasthauswirths) with whom I sit on committees in the Borough Council are far better company. What is the use of people whose hands are full of the very same books you have read yourself? Keep with people who never read anything. Wagner said that to devote yourself to Art is to make it certain that you will at last wake up and find that you have let life slip by you. The people at Buzzi's now—are they amusing?

I am glad your Hamburg man has promised to do Helden. Probably he wont (no play is ever done until the curtain falls on the last act— NEVER count on a promise or even an agreement by a theatre); but it rejoices me when you are pleased. As for me, Helden has no charms for me: it is past & done & gone & over. Wait until you see my new play: the third act alone will send you back to Buzzi's raving & struggling.

My wife sends you her hochachtful regards. The people in the foreign bookshops run to her with your translations in great excitement whenever she goes into them.

yrs ever
G. Bernard Shaw

To SIEGFRIED TREBITSCH

Overstrand Hotel. Cromer. Norfolk
[A/5]   10th January 1903

[The Shaws were spending a week at the seaside with the Webbs and the Graham Wallases, to whom Shaw had been reading *Man and Superman.*

My dear Trebitsch

Thanks for the Man of Destiny. I am writing by this post to H.A. Hertz, the financier of the German Theatre here, to tell him that you have finished & sent over the translation, and that any delay that may occur will be my fault & not yours. At the same time I will read & return it as soon as possible. Already some little delay has been caused by my absence from London. I am down here by the sea until the morning of Wednesday the 14th.

Der Schlachtenlenker is a perfect title for the Man of Destiny. So *that's* settled. The Strange Lady would not do at all. You will find some difficulty in getting the play performed unless the German playgoer tolerates a longer program than the London playgoer. Here it is too long for a "curtain raiser" or for an afterpiece, and not long enough for a principal piece.

As to Wiené, take the part away from him at once & tell him he can take the money at the doors on Shaw nights, and play Schiller & Shakespear on the other nights. I know exactly & precisely what he wants to do; and if he does it our ruin is certain. Good God! imagine the idiot whispering & crying out and "springing about," with the sergeant & the soldiers & the woman standing round admiring him like a Donizettian opera chorus! Tell him with my compliments that he is a Schufkopf. Also that the principal people in the scene are the woman & the sergeant, upon whom he is to play, and that all he has to do is just what he is told. I wrote it for a good but quite brainless actor [William Terriss] who was assassinated shortly afterwards. Tell him, in particular, that from the moment the sergeant arrests Richard a deadly suspense and silence must fall on that *little* room (I dont care how big the stage is: it is a little room). On that silence Richard's words must fall with frightful *quiet* distinctness: everyone of them must strike on Judith's heart with a pang of terror. The sergeant stands with his back turned & his head bent down as if at church; and at a certain point he must raise his head; at another point later on he must turn his head; and when Richard turns away, he must find himself confronted with a face full of suspicion. And then must come the great effect of Richard getting the quaint notion of removing the sergeant's suspicion by making Judith kiss him. All that will be utterly ruined if the damned scoundrel *acts*. He will want to act—to agonize, to make convulsive movements & play tricks with his voice. Dont let him. Tell him I say

299

that he shall not act. He may pray and fast and weep and go to confession; but *act*, by God, he shall not. I will have no monkey tricks in my play.

I write in great haste: a party is waiting for me to read my new play to them.

yrs ever
G. Bernard Shaw

To WILLIAM ARCHER

Overstrand Hotel. Cromer
[A/2]   12th January 1903

[Archer's article "The Two Georges" in the *Morning Leader* on 10th January was a discussion of an article by George Brandes, "Bernard Shaw's Teater," in the Copenhagen newspaper *Politikken* on 29th December 1902. Dr George Brandes (1842–1927) was a Danish critic and philosopher, whose writings were well-known in Britain and America. His principal work was the six-volume *Main Currents of Nineteenth Century Literature* (1872–90). "[I]t remains," wrote Archer, "a monstrous and almost incredible anomaly that a writer whom such a critic as Dr. Brandes can call 'the most original dramatist of the British Empire of to-day' should never have had a single play produced by an established management in the West-end of London." Josef Kainz (1858–1910) was a celebrated German actor, noted for his performances of Romeo, Tartuffe, Oswald (in Ibsen's *Ghosts*), Cyrano, and the heroes of Franz Grillparzer. *Mice and Men*, a play by Madeleine L. Ryley, had been presented by Forbes Robertson at the Lyric Theatre on 27th January 1902.]

I think you might draw the moral of your Two Georges article more definitely in favor of an endowed theatre. At present Trebitsch (whose translations, apart from the mere mistakes, which are mighty ones and millions, are so good that I prefer them in many respects to the originals) has a contract with money down for The Devil's Disciple at the Raiemund Theater in Vienna, and is negotiating with the Hamburg theatre & the Deutsches (Berlin) for "Helden" (alias Arms & The Man). The Burg Theater also flatters him with hopes for Candida, with Kainz as the rolypoly poet. That august institution the German Theatre in London (meaning Grein & Miss Halstan's father) is presently to produce Der Schlachtenlenker, ci devant Man of Destiny. All this, thin as it is, intoxicates Trebitsch with dreams of glory, and enables him to survive my unbounded comments on his translations without any worse consequences than six weeks in a Nerven Anstalt. You should see the metaphysics he has elaborated for Burgess in Candida because the poor old man exclaims "Blame me if it didnt come into my head once or twyst that he must be off his chump." "Tadeln Sie mich &c &c &c."

However, though it may all come to nothing, it is worth pointing out that our London system does cut off masterpieces which are eagerly sought after from Aberdeen to Cracow (my present limits) in the old world. Given theatres of the German type in England and my difficulties would be over at once. The managers are not hostile: they cant afford to be hostile. The interests at stake are too pressing to allow of much indulgence of personal feeling. If I would play their game tomorrow thoroughly they would jump at me, just as they have to put up with the autocracy of Pinero & Sardou & the empfindlichkeit of H.A.J[ones], all of whom treat them in an unspeakable manner.

But the difficulties are very great. The only play I have myself blocked is Candida. I wrote that long ago as a sort of consolation prize for Janet Achurch for the Doll's House; and under the circumstances it would have been rather mean to hand it over to anybody else. But for that it would have been played. Mrs Pat Campbell & others inquired about it; but I held out so that Janet should create the part in London. By that time, though she played certain bits of it—for instance, the scene with Morell in the second act—as nobody else could have done, yet she had grown out of the part. She has plenty of strength, and is beyond all the others in lucidity when there is intellectual tissue to be dissected; but Candida wants patience, tenderness & sweetness of a much more mawkish brand than Janet can supply, clever as she is. When she played it I considered the bargain off; and now Candida is free as air.

I have stopped two productions of The Devil's Disciple—or rather three, because it was impossible to cast it successfully. I refused to let Miss Granville produce it with Waring. Waring would have done it on his own account if he had been able to finance it himself; but Miss G. naturally would not pay without playing, and I told her that she would not succeed in it & that she must not throw her money away on it. I have stopped Forbes Robertson twice. The first time the conditions (at his short, late season at the Comedy) were positively exclusive of success or of its complete exploitation if, by a miracle, it occurred. The second time was the other day, as a stopgap before Othello. I told him he would have to put Lena Ashwell into the part his wife took in the provinces, because Lena has an unrivalled power of appealing to *pity*, which is exactly what Judith must do ("Mitleid"—patented by Parsifal—being the key to Richard) whereas Gertrude Elliott is absolutely incapable of arousing pity: she is indignant when she should be horrified, and playful when she should be childishly helpless. Her character is too positive. Well, I put it to Forbes whether he had not better follow up Mice & Men with a play which had a good part for her, instead of changing his leading lady in the face of the public. I suggested Much Ado as good business for both of them, as it would come in on tour as a Shakespearean repertory play even if it was not a great success on the spot. You Never Can Tell broke down purely over the cast: I did not withdraw it until I made Frederick Harrison attend a rehearsal & admit that the end of the second act was impossible for Aynesworth. So that as the superficial facts stand, it is the regular theatres that are unable to cast my plays, whereas the Independent Theatres can always make some sort of shift with them.

Of course these difficulties are really created partly by the illiterateness of the managers. The proposals they make are proposals to fool with my plays: there is generally an idea at the back of their minds that if they could get complete control of one of my plays they could adapt it as Daly adapted Shakespear. Frohman actually sounded me as to rewriting You Never Can Tell under his direction; but the ecstatic delight with which I embraced the suggestion struck terror into his soul, and the proposed interviews never came off. Still, the fact remains that when it comes to the point of a concrete proposal, neither you nor I could conscientiously recommend the manager to go on with it. For example, Alexander wanted to play Brassbound. Well, what could I say to him? I told him that it was a woman's play, and that he would have to get somebody like Ada Rehan or Ellen Terry, who would reap all the personal success. I also told him that Brassbound was a part that half a dozen melodramatic young Terrises in the provinces could play as well or better than he could, wheras his own special qualities would not shew at all, or if they did so much the worse. Naturally he did not pursue the project. I also refused to let him have the Man of Destiny unless he played Napoleon himself, unless of course he gave me H.B.Irving, in which case I pointed out that he would be definitely relinquishing the lead at his own theatre. This system of telling our actor-managers the exact truth is not always delightful to them; but it has the advantage that the proposals they make are dealt with on their merits and do not fall through because of irrelevant personal squabbles. They would much rather, perhaps, be promised gold mines by an eager and infatuated poetaster; and it spreads unspeakable terror; but still it is the

302

only possible course for me or for any author who writes at a certain level and is serious about it.

I note that you are still fundamentally amazed at the fact that a man whom you know, and whose voice you can hear in every line of his books, can appear to any sane person as a real author. This is really an enfantillage. That intense peculiarity which you cannot get away from, and which you are amazed to find not affecting Brandes as it affects you, is simply my style. I have to have a style like anybody else: I cant help it. Ben Jonson never could quite get over the absurdity of the Shakespearisms which he knew so well at the Mermaid passing off in cold ink as literature; and—though Lord forbid I should compare you to so dull a dog as Ben!—to the end of your life you will remonstrate with Europe for not distinguishing between mere Shawisms & real serious proper impersonal judicial drama.

Brandes is of course quite right about my genius for differentiating nations. You do not appreciate my extraordinarily happy command of classes & grades of civilization. You think Brandes has been taken in by a mirage. You are wrong: no doubt the thing is a mirage in the sense in which every picture, play or statue is a mirage; but if you consider that the one overwhelming characteristic of my plays is the friction between people on different planes of thought, of character, of civilization & of class prejudice (the overwhelming characteristic of the ordinary Pinero–Jones–Grundy play being that all the characters are on exactly the same planes in these respects, and the friction is purely external & artificial) you will see—or you would if you would take the trouble to criticize literature instead of amusing yourself with it—that these contrasts of which Brandes speaks are just the ones that interest me and are handled by me with the greatest care. My Bulgarians are wonderfully well done considering how restricted my sources of information were; and there is an American [Mr Malone] in my new play who is a masterpiece.

GBS

To SIEGFRIED TREBITSCH

10 Adelphi Terrace W C
[A/5]   15th January 1903

Dear Trebitsch

... Die Schacht bei Tavazzano will not do, because it is absolutely essential that the name of the play should proclaim it a Napoleon piece.

303

It would be better to call it simply "Bonaparte" than to give it the very wittiest title that did not mention him. The Schlachtenlenker is just what you want: why not let it stand?

How can you possibly conclude that "in some things I am wrong." My dear Trebitsch, *I am never wrong*. Other people are sometimes— often—nearly always wrong, especially when they disagree with me; but I am omniscient and infallible. The friends with whom you have deliberated simply dont understand the art of writing for the stage. I tell you again and again, most earnestly and seriously, that unless you repeat the words that I have repeated, you will throw away all the best stage effects and make the play unpopular with the actors. When you study my corrections in the Man of Destiny, you will understand this better. Half the art of dialogue consists in the *echoing* of words—the tossing back & forwards of phrases from one actor to another like a cricket ball. I have never objected to your varying a word or phrase when it doesnt matter. You will find that I have passed over dozens of variations without comment because I considered them either improvements or indifferences. But when you make Burgess forget the word that Morell has branded into his astonished brain as with a red hot iron, and then tell me that one can do that in German (as if it were a question of language) then I tear my hair & ask God why he has forsaken me. And when you spoil Candida's retort "Oh, the worse places arnt open on Sundays"—when you make it sound like this: Morell— "Why dont they go to worse places on Sundays?" Candida—"Oh, the less desirable places of entertainment are not available," and then tell me that a council of your friends has decided that this is permissible in Germany (Good God: as if we were arranging the conditions of a duel!), then my feelings go beyond all expression.

And now you tell me that "weisse Hand" is "Sprachgebranch" out of Goethe, Schiller, Heine &c. Of course it is. That's what I meant by calling it a "décrochez-moi-cela." That's just why I object to it. I never write Sprachgebranch; and neither must you. And remember that though we may be no bigger men than Goethe and Schiller, we are standing on their shoulders, and should therefore be able to see farther & do better. And after all, Schiller is only Shaw at the age of 8, and Goethe Shaw at the age of 32. This, by the way, is the highest compliment ever paid to Goethe.

All your business news is excellent. Go on and prosper.

Later on I will say a word about your preface. The new play is too bulky to send you in typescript. I will send you proofs as soon as I have arranged for its publication here. Meanwhile, do you think Cotta would care to publish it in Germany simultaneously with its appearance in England? He would be imprisoned for Majestatsbeleidigung for six months or so; but I shouldnt mind that in the least: it would be an excellent advertisement.

yrs ever
G. Bernard Shaw

To SIEGFRIED TREBITSCH

[A/5]

10 Adelphi Terrace W C
26th January 1903

[Dr Leon Kellner (1859–1928), a friend of Archer, was a Viennese literary scholar and philologist, who had attacked, in the *Neues Wiener Tageblatt*, the quality of Trebitsch's translations of Shaw as published by Cotta. After the first performance of *The Devil's Disciple* in Vienna on 25th February he returned to the attack, in the *Frankfurter Zeitung*. Kellner's was the first of a series of German criticisms of Trebitsch's translations, which continued all through the decade.]

Dear Trebitsch

Do not think me unfeeling—but I have laughed myself almost into hysterics over Kellner's onslaught. I quite expected that this would happen, though, oddly enough, I never thought of Kellner. He spent a day with me in 1898, and was one of the first German Shawites. As he wrote about me in the German press long ago, he is probably indignant at your entry on the scene as my discoverer.

And now, what is to be done? Well, first, let this experience cure you of your excessive sensitiveness to reviews. When you were so pleased at the favorable ones, you were preparing yourself for the penalty of being kept awake at night by the unfavorable ones. If I bothered about such things I should go mad three times a week, and die on the alternate days.

A reply to Kellner is impossible, because he is perfectly right on the points which admit of argument. You cannot *prove* that your translation is artistically good, any more than you can prove that Rembrandt was a great painter. Artistic qualities are matters of taste. Now Kellner, on the other hand, *can* prove that you dont know County Council English, and dont know what the Hackney Road is like, whereas he knows both. A letter to the paper will give him just what he wants: that is, an excuse for writing a second article in which he will pour out all the mistakes

305

that he had not room for in the first one. Besides, a letter from the author would be alluded to and quoted in other papers; and the result would be a big advertisement of a literary controversy instead of a simple review passed by in silence. The truth is, you are very lucky to get off so easily. Suppose he had read The Devil's Disciple as carefully as he has read his pet Candida, and had gone on to make fun of your translation of civilian as civilized person, and all your other slips! And he will do that if you give him the smallest excuse for writing another article on the same subject. There is nothing to be done but turn over and go to sleep like a philosopher, saying "Serve me right."

Now shall I tell you what I should do myself in your place? I should write straight away to Dr Kellner, hochundwohlgeboren, offering him ten guineas for a copy of the plays with all the blunders noted and corrected in the margin, and promising him to add to the preface in the second edition a paragraph like this: "I am indebted to Dr Leon Kellner, who was the first to draw the attention of the German readers to the works of Bernard Shaw, and whose knowledge of contemporary English local life and political organization is unrivalled, for several important corrections in this edition, especially in those technical references to the political structure of English suburban life which are intelligible only to one, who, like Dr Kellner, is an expert in English sociology as well as in English literature."

This is the grand style of fighting. It is just what any ordinary writer wouldnt do, and therefore it is what you should do at once. Remember, it is perfectly true and perfectly becoming and handsome for you to acknowledge as true. You made the mistakes, and you made an enemy at the same time. To remedy this you must not lie awake and get neuralgia: you must correct the mistakes and disarm the enemy. That will instantly cure your neuralgia and give you a sense of having compelled Kellner to respect you, as well as pleasing him. You must not bluntly offer him the ten guineas, as he might resent it as a bribe; but you may quite well ask him to correct the whole volume and ask him to allow you to negotiate with Messrs Cotta for a fee for the literary work involved.

One thing that comes out of it all is the uselessness of depending on me for technical corrections. If you call a Zunft a Vogel or a Steuerzahler a Pferd, I can correct that; but when you call them Gewerbeverein and Ratenzahler, naturally I am satisfied. That is where Kellner's special knowledge comes in; and since he has got it, there is no use rebelling against fate: the man who knows is master of the situation.

I will go shares in any fee that Kellner may be paid for corrections.

Of course he will offer artistic corrections as well; but these you need not bother about: it will be easy enough to pay him the compliment of adopting a word or two here and there (when it makes no real difference) to spare his feelings. He will be delighted at being consulted; for as he is the editor of a paper he could not possibly find time to make a translation himself: otherwise he would no doubt have offered to do so long ago. . . .

Meanwhile dont worry; be magnanimous with Kellner; sleep well; and do not neglect your work to grieve over your mistakes. Even I—I, Bernard Shaw—make mistakes sometimes.

> yrs ever
> G.Bernard Shaw

To J. B. PINKER

[S/1]

10 Adelphi Terrace W C
2nd February 1903

[Shaw had authorised Pinker to act for him in placing *Man and Superman* with British and American publishers. In December 1902 Pinker offered the play to Methuen, reporting to Shaw on 18th December: "He would be very pleased indeed to have a book by you, but . . . he asks me to try and give him more detailed particulars than I was in a position to furnish at this interview" (Texas).]

Dear Mr Pinker

The MS of my book is very nearly ready for the printer; and as I am always in a hurry to get a book into type so as to run as little risk as possible of losing it through the loss or destruction of the MS, I shall not wait long for the publishers to make up their minds. Unless I hear soon to the contrary I shall send it off to Clark of Edinburgh, who knows my ways as to printing; and then the publisher, whoever he may be, will have to employ Clark whether he likes it or not. Failing any offers I shall take the matter into my own hands and publish on commission.

You might mention this to Methuen or anybody else with whom you are negotiating, so as to stir them up a bit.

It occurs to me that they may want to see the MS before they make any proposal. If so, their reasonable curiosity will not be gratified, as I have not the smallest intention of letting anybody except the printer read the book until it is corrected for press.

> yours faithfully
> G.Bernard Shaw

To HAROLD V. NEILSON

10 Adelphi Terrace W C
[H/4]   5th February 1903

[Shaw had received only £11. 7. o in royalties for the six performances of *Captain Brassbound's Conversion* in May 1902. Neilson did not tour with the play at this time. There was no "difficulty" between Neilson and the Charringtons. The latter had indicated to Neilson that they did not wish to accept another engagement because they didn't believe there was any money to be made from the play.]

Dear Sir

Do you think it is wise to risk anything on Brassbound? Your experiment in Manchester was not very encouraging: in a week you did as much business as a successful play would have done in one night. No doubt you would have done much better had the play been produced beforehand in London; but matters are not mended in that respect; and it seems to me rather rash to let yourself in for ten weeks with Miss Marion Terry on your salary list for a play which has decisively failed on its trial trip under similar conditions.

Would you mind telling me exactly where your difficulty with Mr and Mrs Charrington arises. I shall of course make no use of the information in any way that would be embarrassing to you; and I shall return your letter so that you may be secured against its being mislaid or left about. As Mrs Charrington played the part for me in London under circumstances which placed me under a considerable obligation to her I cannot fairly take the part away from her (for that is what it comes to) without knowing why. Besides, from the point of view of the author of a modern play—a *really* modern play—the Charringtons have one quality which counterbalances a good many faults; and that is that they play an Ibsen play as an Ibsen play and a Shaw play as a Shaw play, instead of trying to cut it about and sentimentalize it into something between Caste and East Lynne. Not to mention that Miss Achurch, with all her faults, is a woman of genius, whilst the others, with all their perfections, are only women of charm. This makes them better than Miss Achurch in inane or conventional plays, in which Miss Achurch is much worse than useless; but when power and thought is required the tables are turned, and Miss Achurch holds a play which slips through the fingers of the charming people. Of course she is very difficult to manage, because she is very clever, and quite ungovernable by anyone who does not know as much as she does and a little to spare; and yet she has certain faults which are serious from the business point of view: for instance, she is contemptuous and careless of the little snobberies of the public in small matters. She has a way of behaving and dressing like a duchess (which is the public's idea of not behaving or dressing at all) instead of like an actress whose first business it is to dress and behave herself with extreme care. Consequently she wants just the opposite sort of management to an ordinary actress. Miss Marion Terry will dress and behave most charmingly, leaving you nothing to take care of but the dramatic part of the business. Miss Achurch will do all the dramatic part of the business so well that you may safely leave the whole planning and coaching of the acting to her; but you must dress her and brush her hair and polish her furniture as if she were a little girl and you her governess. All this means a great deal of trouble and taste in millinery; but any manager who possessed it could make as great a success of Miss Achurch as Augustin Daly made of Ada Rehan. Miss Terry would be much less trouble; but she would be with you today and gone tomorrow, wheras a combination with Miss Achurch might be permanent enough to be the making of a young manager. The thing can be done; but like most other important things, it will take a good deal of doing. It is ridiculous that an actress of such extraordinary talent should be wasted for want of a manager. Charrington is a character in his way, and very full of ideas; but he is no use to manage her, as he has all her faults, and is even more reckless than she is about the small change of stage snobbery.

yours faithfully
G. Bernard Shaw

To METHUEN & CO.

[G.u/2]

[10 Adelphi Terrace W C]
[Undated: assigned to 17th February 1903]

[As Pinker was not making sufficient progress, Shaw informed him that he was planning to proceed on his own with Methuen. "I am sorry," wrote Pinker on 16th February, "that I should have shattered your faith in literary agents, but of course it is quite possible for you to do things which could not be done by a literary agent, who has to treat these things seriously" (Texas).]

Dear Sirs
    Some time ago, being very hard pressed for time, I asked Mr James Pinker to undertake the negotiations for the publication of a book which

is at present ready for press. Mr Pinker informed me that you were willing to consider the matter; but he now tells me that you decline on the ground that my terms are unreasonable, an opinion in which he concurs.

As I have never had any difficulty of the kind before—perhaps because I never employed an agent before—it seems possible that there may be some misunderstanding. I should therefore like, before I dismiss the matter as finally closed, to put before you exactly what I would like a publisher to do for me.

In the first place, you will want to know why I am changing publishers. I am doing so solely because I am not satisfied that my present publisher is getting as much as can be got out of my books. Strictly speaking, he does not sell any copies at all; he is content with the number of copies which the public buy spontaneously on the appearance of the reviews—say from 1500 to 2000 copies. This sees him through without any expenditure (the printer no doubt advancing the printing); and under these circumstances he naturally concentrates his advertising powers on the books which will not sell at all without pushing, and leaves mine unaided. I believe that a sale of at least 5000 copies could be obtained by ordinarily energetic handling; and accordingly I want to find a publisher who will advance me £250, not because I am in need of ready money, but because I do not know how else to give my books a fair chance in competition with those which force the publishers to nurse them carefully. I am aware that 5000 copies would not be a large circulation for a popular novel; but I am assuming that you, like all leading publishers, are willing to deal to a certain extent with work of the higher literary class which appeals to a comparatively select circle of readers; and I am also assuming that you recognize me as an author of established reputation for the production of work of that class. Otherwise it would be absurd to touch my books at all.

The terms which I am accustomed to ask & to receive in London are a royalty of 20%, 13 copies being reckoned as 13 & not as 12. The ordinary covenants about remainders are unnecessary, because there never are any remainders. My books do not die after the first demand drops: they dribble away slowly but steadily. I expect the publisher to bear the entire cost of printing. I am willing to correct the printer's errors & to put in as much work on the proofsheets as may be needed to make the book as good as I know how to make it; but I will not pay the printer's bill for corrections or any part of it. I always send in a practically finished—and highly finished—typewritten MS (the present book [will] be printed from the *third* typed fair copy of my actual draft); so you need not fear a Balzac or Carlyle bill for corrections. Further, as

310

I occasionally contest elections, any contract that I make must contain a "fair wages" clause. This does not in practice lead to any difficulty, as it is unfortunately rather a political formula for the defence of parliamentary authors against hostile electioneering agents than an effective restriction. It would debar you from employing some three or four houses which you can quite easily do without, and a number of small printing shops to which you would never dream of resorting. Probably, however, you are familiar with "fair wages" clauses by this time. To the political author they are an absolute necessity: seats have been lost by the imprint on a poster; and I myself was much inconvenienced many years ago by the fact that my first book was printed by Hazell Watson & Viney at a time when they were a "closed house" to the London Compositors (they are no longer so).

My license to publish (I never assign copyright or stageright) is for the United Kingdom & the Colonies only, and should, after the expiration of 5 years, be terminable at any time on six months notice. But simultaneous publication in America is indispensable. The book must be copyrighted in America, because it contains a play with valuable stage rights; consequently the common plan of exporting copies is out of the question.

These are practically all the conditions I have to make. There is really nothing in them except the question of terms: nothing ever arises on them. No doubt they are not the conditions you make with everybody; but I am not everybody and you are not everybody: if I were everybody, you would not deal with me at all, and if you were everybody, I should not publish with you. At all events I should be glad to have your decision direct from yourself, if you will oblige me so far, as Mr Pinker probably never heard of a fair wages clause in his life, and is too much shocked by it to conduct my business with his usual self possession.

yrs faithfully
[G. Bernard Shaw]

[Methuen's replied on 23rd February: "We quite understand your views and wishes, but we are sorry to say that we do not feel disposed to make an agreement on the terms which you suggest. We hope that you will believe that we perfectly appreciate the brilliant reputation which you have achieved, but in carrying on our business we always endeavour to avoid any occasion for friction and controversy and we feel pretty sure that we should never, as author and publisher, see with the same eyes" (Texas).]

To SIEGFRIED TREBITSCH

Maybury Knoll. Woking
[C/5]   17th February 1903

[The Freie Volksbühne was a theatre for Berlin Socialist working people, founded in 1889 by Otto Brahm and a few young members of the intelligentsia. Paul Lindau (1839–1919) was a German novelist and playwright, who managed the Königliches Schauspielhaus, Berlin. The article in *Die Zeit* was "Ein Teufelskerl: Selbkritik," in Trebitsch's translation, on 22nd February. It was a typical Shavian puff, full of irrepressible fun and egotism, with some well-aimed thrusts at Kellner. It appeared three days before the opening performance of *The Devil's Disciple* in Vienna.]

I shall get into a nice mess over the Freie Volksbühne. As I knew nothing about Lindau's contract I wrote to [J.] Bloch that I had much rather be introduced to Germany by the F.V. than by any other theatre in the world. Now my plays will be denounced by the court papers because I am a Socialist, and by the Socialist papers because I have betrayed them for Lindau's sake.

However, it cannot be helped. But I assure you it is enormously important not to offend the Social Democrats, because all the clever journalists who become influential later on begin by being enthusiastic Socialists.

I wrote the Zeit article with a view to its being published at once. It is full of Kellner. Let the affair be forgotten when we have had the last word, but not until then. There is no harm in letting him know that my arm is long enough to reach Vienna if there is to be a newspaper war. The more we are written about the better. In such matters there is always the consolation that your enemy must either let you alone or advertize you.

GBS

To WILLIAM ARCHER

10 Adelphi Terrace W C
[C/2]   23rd February 1903

I have to inform you triumphantly that in view of the political disturbances in the Balkan states, the Austrian Censorship forbids the Burg Theater to produce Arms & The Man at present.

312

This tribute to the political actuality and ethnographical verisimilitude of my play will, I hope, be a warning to you not to disparage my historical researches in future.

GBS

To SIEGFRIED TREBITSCH

Maybury Knoll. Woking
[A/5]   1st March 1903

[The "enclosed cuttings" probably consisted of a reported interview in the *Westminster Gazette* on 26th February, headed "Mr. G.B.Shaw and His Plays: Why They are 'Booming' in Germany," and a letter from Shaw, in the same paper on 28th February, correcting a mis-statement. Hermann Bahr (1863–1934), a dramatist and critic, was the founder of the Viennese newspaper *Die Zeit*. Bahr's notice of the performance of *Ein Teufelskerl* was published in his book *Rezensionen: Wiener Theater 1901 bis 1903* (1903). Hermann Sudermann's *Es Lebe das Leben* had been produced at the Burgtheater in February 1902.]

Dear Trebitsch

I had no idea that there was any secrecy about the action of the Censorship. When you first told me of it I mentioned it to Archer and to another journalist. This other man promptly published it (I meant him to); and the enclosed cuttings are the result. I hope no harm will come of my indiscretion.

Reuter's telegram about the production appeared in nearly all the papers except the Daily Chronicle, which came out with a paragraph which I suspect was sent by Kellner himself.

I have not had time to read the notices from Vienna yet. I have, however, got through Bahr's feuilleton. Has he written any plays? He knows more about the business than most critics do. I guess from it that he is disgusted with Es lebe das Leben, which seems to me like a play written by Sardou in the style of Sudermann.

It is very dangerous to judge by newspaper notices; but it seems clear that Wiené was a complete failure, and that the play would have collapsed altogether but for Thaller. The Raimund people should try again with another Dick, another Judith, another Anderson & another Essie, since none of these seem to have made any impression. However, you may tell them that in England a play is rehearsed every day for

313

three weeks, and that every rehearsal is a general rehearsal. In my boyhood I saw the results of the "stock company & star" plan at the Dublin theatre; and it was quite hopeless. If they had played the D's D, Dick would have been a convention called "the juvenile lead," Anderson would have been "the heavy father" complicated with the stage clergyman, Essie would have been "the singing chambermaid," Christie "the joskin," Judith "the leading lady," Swindon "the utility," and so on and so forth, all playing exactly as they would play in every other piece from Shakespear to the latest melodrama, and all personally known by every tone of their voice & every trick of their gait to an audience deadly weary of the whole lot.

——A visitor has just interrupted me. I must break off.

GBS

To J. B. PINKER

[S/1; X/157.e]

10 Adelphi Terrace W C
5th March 1903

[Pinker had reported on 3rd March that he had approached an American firm, which seemed inclined to come to terms, and that he would, with Shaw's permission, negotiate with the firm. Shaw finally sent the manuscript to R. & R. Clark on 23rd March with instructions to print *Man and Superman* at his own expense.]

Dear Mr Pinker

I have settled nothing in America as yet, and am wide open to an offer. If you can plant the book there for me, do so by all means. Only, do not ask me to hold my own hand in the meantime. I am in a corner about this book; and the name of the man who has put me there is James B. Pinker. When I put the matter in your hands before Christmas, I expected that you would submit to me the best out of about a hundred and fifty proposals in three weeks. You were too polite to tell me that the affair was not worth your while; and so I got landed at the end of February with nothing except a refusal from Methuen to give me as good terms as my present publisher, and a refusal from you to do anything better for me. I have no time now to go round the market looking for a publisher; so there is nothing for it but to take the book into my own hands and publish on commission. The firm with which I am negotiating (Longmans) has an American house; and it may be that they will propose some arrangement which I shall accept for the

314

convenience of making one bargain instead of two. But nothing is settled yet; and I have nothing else in hand. I shall be very glad indeed if you can get the American business done for me; but this time you must allow me to pursue any other negotiations that may turn up in the meantime instead of referring all inquirers to you as I did before. I do not ask you to climb any trees for me on this understanding; but if the apple drops into your mouth you may as well help me out with it.

I had it out with Methuen since I last heard from you. The whole thing was nonsense; he simply wanted more than I was prepared to give him. I proposed no condition that is not to be found in thousands of contracts today.

yours faithfully
G. Bernard Shaw

To SIEGFRIED TREBITSCH

10 Adelphi Terrace W C
6th March 1903

[H/5]

Dear Trebitsch

I am very sorry you have had neuralgia over this business. Dismiss it from your mind now: there is no use bothering about a commercial failure. You have done everything that the oldest hand could have done: the interest was worked up to the utmost; and you contrived to send all the impressionable critics to the theatre quite determined to see something very remarkable, and to imagine they appreciated and enjoyed the play. All this is excellent so far as it gives the failure the air of being like the failure of Tannhäuser in the forties at Dresden: we can say that it is the public that has failed. But still a failure is a failure; so instead of getting neuralgia over it, let us laugh and try again.

I have a heap of press notices; but I have not had time to read more than two or three of the long ones. By far the best was a Viennese one—I forget the name of the paper just now, and I have left the cutting at Woking—in which the writer said that listening to the play was like eating oysters and pretending to like them because it was fashionable. The play, he said, was clever; but it was not kunstlerich, and did not convince you that the author really had any consistent intention. Now

315

that is the truth. That is what a capable theatregoer ought to feel when confronted with my work and my style for the first time, without having read the play beforehand, as Hermann Bahr no doubt did. It is what I think I should say myself of my own plays if I suddenly came across a performance of them for the first time. You cant feel at home with anything that is strange, no matter how openminded you may be. Until the critics get used to me, they will feel exactly as this writer felt. As to the public, we cannot even guess whether I shall ever hit their fancy.

You must be charitable to poor Kellner and people like him. When a man has had ardent literary ambitions, and has worked very hard to equip himself with plenty of information, it always seems to him unjust when the younger men, in whose work he can see nothing but a handful of mistakes, should suddenly get in front of him, and take from him the place he has aimed at as an original writer. Your contemporaries will never forgive you for being a genius until they are old and broken enough to accept the verdict of the world and to forget the time when you were to them only a damned young fool with whom they went to school. Your elders will never be able to understand it at all, unless they have themselves achieved so high a position that they can afford to make much of you as Haydn made much of Mozart. There is no use in resenting this. Be inexhaustibly patient; and things will gradually change. The older men will die out; the contemporaries will surrender; and the generations of boys to whom you are a literary hero will grow up and fight for you as enthusiastically as they will abuse their own contemporaries and poohpooh those who come after them. Meanwhile say all the nice things about Kellner you can; and never let the world see you angry.

If Schlenther hears about the English papers, tell him that the Fabian Society knows everything that happens in Europe. I am still in difficulties as to the publication of the new book; but I am afraid it must not wait until October. It is important that when people go away for their holiday in August & September they should take my book with them. I will send you an early set of proofsheets. The translation will be a fearful job: the plays are child's play in comparison.

yrs ever
G. Bernard Shaw

To STAGE SOCIETY CASTING COMMITTEE

[Maybury Knoll. Woking]
[L.u/2]   [Undated: c. 16th March 1903]

[The Stage Society's casting committee, which included Edith Craig,
Granville Barker, and H.A. Hertz, was in process of selecting a cast to be
invited to appear in the Society's production of Herman Heijerman's *The
Good Hope*, translated by Christopher St John. It was presented at the Im-
perial Theatre on 26th and 27th April 1903, with Margaret Halstan, Miss
Craig, and Barker in the cast.]

Mr Chair[man], Miss Craig & Gentlemen

I am sorry that I am unable to attend the Casting committee,
especially as the letters I have received suggest that the meeting is
likely to be an exceptionally interesting one—in fact quite like what the
Sal[vation] A[rmy] calls an Experience Meeting.

I find that a strong Self Denial movement has sprung up in the
Committee. It is felt that no member of it should be so self-indulgent
as to act for the Society or indeed to do anything whatever for it except
object strenuously to anybody else doing anything either. It is said
that we should think of the S[ociety] & not of our personal acquaintances. Now as we have been selected for a casting committee chiefly
because our personal acquaintance covers the whole theatrical profession, it seems to me that the result of our self denial will be either
that our cast must consist of amateurs who are too obscure to have any
personal acquaintances at all, even in the S[tage] S[ociety], or else that
the Society shall elect another committee of less exquisite moral
sensitiveness.

As matters stand at present Mr G. Barker & Miss Craig cannot
possibly be in the cast because it would be wrong for them to take
advantage of their position on the Committee to cast themselves for
parts in the S[ociety]'s plays. Miss Halstan is out of the question because her father [Hertz] is on the C[ommittee]; & the spectacle of the
father voting in favor of his own daughter would be so shocking that
the whole C[ommittee] would probably resign. Miss Suzanne Sheldon
is equally out of the question, because members of the C[ommittee]
have both spoken & written to me in her behalf & I cannot be a party
to any such favoritism. Similar objections apply to all the other proposals that have been made. All the artists mentioned must have been
known to some of us, or else they could not have been thought of. We
are therefore not free from prejudice with regard to them; so it is our
clear duty to strike all their names out at once.

On thinking the matter over very carefully I have come to the conclusion that the only course consistent with our moral principles is to
cut all the professional cards [actors' advertisements] out of the first
page of the Era, and put the women's names into one hat & the men's
names into another. The name of the part should be called out by the
Chairman; & a name should then be drawn from the hat by the youngest
& most innocent member of the Committee, who should be carefully
blindfolded & should prepare himself for the ordeal by prayer & fast-
ing. A cast arrived at in this way could not fail to produce a most curious
& interesting performance; & the most censorious critic could not
accuse us of prejudice, favoritism or jobbery.

Before my eyes were opened to the moral gravity of the situation I
was in favor of Miss Halstan, Miss Craig & Mr Granville Barker. The
highminded refusal of Mr Barker to take advantage of my low moral
tone has put me out of court as far as he is concerned; but I am still in
favor of Miss Craig & Miss Halstan unless my proposal about the hats
is adopted. I feel that the hats are the only thorough solution of the
moral difficulty & if they are not used it seems useless to waste time in
disputing about mere degrees of moral guilt.

[G. Bernard Shaw]

To SIEGFRIED TREBITSCH

[A/5]

[Maybury Knoll. Woking]
31st March 1903

Dear Trebitsch

You are the most ungrateful man alive. Kellner's article [in the
Frankfurter Zeitung] is ausgezeichnetissimus. That is what has got us the
offer from Frankfurt to do the Sch[l]achtenlenker (which will be a worse
failure than the Teufelskerl, as it requires Virtuosen of the first order
to act it). It is true that he calls you a Sekundaner; but then he tells the
Frankfurt managers that all the literary people in Vienna took the Shaw
boom up and swore that your translations were masterpieces and that
he was only a Philologer; and he also tells them that you organized the
réclame to perfection, which will impress them more than if he said
that I was Goethe & Shakespere & you Tieck & Sch[l]egel rolled into
one. He flatters me to the skies just as I flattered him: all that description of me is calculated to make people far more curious to see the plays
than any ordinary favorable criticism.

318

Your article is totally, utterly, completely, ausserordentlicherly, insanely out of the question. To begin with, it is a defence of yourself; and you must NEVER defend yourself. Worse than that, you reply to a thrust clean through the body with a pin prick. He says the piece ran for two nights only. You reply that he is a liar: it ran *three*!!! Good Heavens! does that matter? Everybody will forget the two nights until they hear about your triumphant three; and then they will laugh so much that it will be remembered forever. As to the spelling of my name, he is quite right to Germanise it. In England I do not write Michelagnolo or Händel, but Michael Angelo & Handel. You mustnt pick up *little* stones to throw at your adversaries: they dont hurt & they always get thrown back. Besides, you are wrong about my references to Kellner in Die Zeit. I meant to praise him: it would be in my eyes the most horrible crime against "altirischer Gastfreundlichkeit" to say that my guest had bored me with his billiards & his conversation. In fact you are all wrong, because you are not accustomed to be shot at in the newspapers. As for me, I am all over bullet marks; and I have come to enjoy the noise of the fusillade: it advertises me.

Bahr ought to be much obliged to Kellner, who does not disparage him, or say he is unknown, or that I am a libertine. On the contrary, it was Bahr who disparaged Kellner as an old pedant.

I must take poor Kellner under my protection, I see. I think his abuse of your slips in translation is wildly exaggerated; but there is no effective reply to that except perfect goodhumor & imperturbability. If you want me to see the depth of his villainy, you must induce him to abuse *me*.

Shall I put your letter in the fire? I want you to forget Kellner & go to Provence & cure your neuralgia. Dont bother about Frankfurt: they will cut the Schlachtenlenker & spoil it and worry you out of your life. Go straight to the Rhone & forget all about Drei Dramen von

yrs ever
G. Bernard Shaw

To JANET ACHURCH

[A/4]

Maybury Knoll. Woking
4th April 1903

[Janet Achurch had appeared as Queen Katharine in Shakespeare's *Henry VIII* at the Queen's Theatre, Manchester, in January 1903.]

Dear Janet

As to the first of May [annual Labour production], **NO**, by all that's holy. Quite unsuitable. You *must* find some labor play like The Weavers. Or else An Enemy of The People. Anyhow, Candida shant be used to block the way.

. . . I have for some time begun to see that I myself am one of your pieces of ill luck—that my plays, tempting as they seem, are not the right vehicles for your genius. Of course you can act: my parts will always *occupy* you; and you will do them better than anybody else in the difficult bits. But they wont *do you* as well as they would do a much sillier woman. You are not Candida and you are not Lady Cicely. You want much more powerful parts—parts which scarcely exist except in the old rhetorical repertory, which you cannot touch because it is not real enough. You are getting too old for Nora: the squirrel's jumps make the house shake. Why not face your destiny and tour with Little Eyolf and Rosmersholm? Remember, you have tried Brassbound & Candida with no results. The Doll's House is stale & you have outgrown it. You have no time to lose in cobbling these jobs: throw them away & try something that will carry your weight. Strindberg, who is a great man, is still unexploited in this country. Think over this seriously. The loss of all your Henry VIII savings over this tour is absolutely certain if you have nothing new & well up to your weight. Little Eyolf is a terror; but a terror is just what you want.

GBS

To FREDERICK H. EVANS

10 Adelphi Terrace W C
[H/4]   6th May 1903

[The Shaws were in Italy from 10th April to 4th May, where they visited Parma, Perugia, Assisi, Orvieto, Siena, Genoa, and Milan. When Evans, a pianola enthusiast, lectured on the subject to the Camera Club on 23rd February 1911, Shaw took the chair, and the two provided an evening of wit and music. In response to Shaw's inquiry in this letter about publishers, Evans suggested the firm of Constable.]

Dear Evans,

Just back from three weeks in Italy. Your letter waiting for me. Walker and Cockerell finally rather owned up that there isn't any really

320

safe way of sending negatives; and Cockerell evidently believed in his soul that if he kept Walker's promise the negatives would arrive in smithereens.

I think my collection of prints is more than complete. Was the Christmas parcel not acknowledged? I take your prints as callously as I take my breakfast, as part of the course of nature; but I am astonished at my wife. However, if I remonstrate, she will say that I said I should write to you. Very likely I did, as I am always more or less on the point of writing to you about something or other.

I took to Italy a pocket Kodak, an Absolutus screen, orthochromatic films and an Adon. The results are not yet developed. Most of the exposures were on Italian landscapes through the screen for half a second with an f. 6.3 lens. Or else a tenth of a second through a Burchett screen.

Yes; I have been pianoling. Of course it is indispensable to anybody who wants to range over piano literature. I started modestly with Liszt's Don Juan fantasia. Also Chopin's sonatas, as to which I at once discovered that the traditional disparagement of them was due to the fact that nobody could play them. However, this is a thing we must talk about. In some ways it is an abominably stupid machine, especially in the springs of the accent and pedal levers. I did not know of the Goldberg variations. The poverty of the Bach repertory disgusted me: I could get nothing but the chromatic fantasia and fugue. I find it very difficult to play things in perfectly steady time. The first movement of the moonlight sonata is very unmanageable; and as to Raff's march from the Lenore symphony, which I got in order to test the alleged mechanical rigidity of the thing, it is quite impossible: every extra note in the chord alters the wind pressure and (consequently) the time. Rushing and gushing is quite easy. At the first attempt I played Chopin's A flat polonaise a la Rubinstein-cum-Sapellnikoff to perfection, knocking some thirty guineas off the value of the piano in the process. I'll get Diabelli: I used to fumble over those variations 25 years ago—havnt seen them since.

The P & Ola is at Woking or I would ask you to come and perform on it straight away, as I hear your virtuosity is prodigious. As it is, I suppose I shall have to go to you. *Is* Woking out of the question for you?

The new play, which I think I shall publish in June if I can get the proofs corrected in time, is STUPENDOUS. Really and truly. Ask Barker if it isnt. By the way, I am printing it on my own account, and will publish on commission, abandoning Richards this time, because he sells no more than we could sell if we publish it at Takeleys. Can you suggest anything? I think of Longmans; but nothing is settled.

yours ever
G. Bernard Shaw

To JANET ACHURCH

[H/4]
10 Adelphi Terrace W C
8th May 1903

[Ibsen's *The Vikings* (also known as *The Warriors of Helgeland*), produced by Gordon Craig (who had designed the sets) with his mother Ellen Terry, had been running at the Imperial Theatre since 15th April. Re Barry Sullivan, see I, 778.]

What you say about A Doll's House is no doubt sound enough: I have no doubt that you will be playing it when you are eighty. But that does not really alter the fact that one squirrel does not make a repertory. Your difficulty in London has been that London wants a fleet of penny steamers and not a Great Eastern. You being a Great Eastern, and the west end theatres having no cables to lay, they have had no use for you. The only thing to do, then, is to go into the cable business. There is no use in going back to the old rhetorical plays: Adrienne is dead and Forget-me-not never was alive. Mary Stuart and Camille and all the rest of them have had their day. What you want is a repertory of plays which you can carry on your own shoulders, and in which you cannot come into competition with the young odalisques of the west end. After all, your plight is no worse than that of all the other big ships. Bernhardt and Duse have to wander about and batter the provinces with champion feats of strength instead of being leading ladies with flats in Sloane St. The mischief of it is that a big bowwowy modern repertory has not yet been produced. There is Magda, of course; but that is appropriated. I see nothing for it but Ibsen—Little Eyolf, Rosmersholm, and so on. There is also the Viking play, which has had a good advertisement from Ellen Terry. Why not try Hiordis? My plays are not heavy enough. You might use Candida or Lady Cicely as resting parts on a tour, just as Barry Sullivan used to play Don Felix and Benedict and Charles Surface to relieve the strain of Richard and Richelieu and so on; but your *pièces de resistance* must be more formidable. Of course the best thing would be to find some young genius who could write what you want; but such people dont grow on the bushes.

All of which is very wise and very useless.

I objected to Candida for Mayday because it was the wrong play for it. Doll's House is much better, though no doubt a Gorki would have been better still.

The reason I lapse into such conventionalities as Dear Janet is that I am getting old and demoralized. I have been in Italy for three weeks and at the Ring at Covent Garden for three nights; but I have left these games far behind me: the more I try professional art, the greater becomes my horror and weariness of it. That is partly why I have made the new play impossible in point of length and subject.

You do not understand the nature of Charlotte's objection to you. It is not a question of like and dislike in the ordinary sense: she has exactly the same objection to my mother, my sister, and everybody who forms part of that past in which she has no part. The moment you walk into the room where I am you create a world in which you and I are at home and she is a stranger. That is the real difficulty of marrying at forty; and it must be faced until in the lapse of time the new world so grows up and supersedes the old that it need no longer be jealous of it. It is just the same with me: the moment her old friends call I become a mere chance acquaintance. I dont mind (indeed I generally plead business and bolt after coruscating enough to satisfy curiosity); but Charlotte *does* mind; and so would any woman. These situations require very considerate handling. If you were to divorce Charlie and marry a man whom you had never seen before, you would find for many years that almost every woman he was at all intimate with knew him better than you, and had a larger stock of common experiences with him. And I think you will admit that unless he knew that better than you did, and took particular care not to make it intolerable for you, you would probably elope with Charlie again at the first opportunity.

I must break off hastily: I am wanted downstairs.

GBS

To ELLEN TERRY

10 Adelphi Terrace W C

[U(H)/10]   15th May 1903

[Miss Louisa Vining was a well-known nineteenth-century provincial actress, who had early in her career been billed as "the infant Sappho." Norman Forbes, younger brother of Johnston Forbes-Robertson, had played

323

Dogberry with Henry Irving. The character actor William Wyes died a few months after Shaw's recommendation of him, at the age of 46. Walter Melville (1874–1934) was the author of many popular melodramas at the Standard and Lyceum Theatres including *The World of Sin* (1900) and *That Wretch of a Woman* (1901).]

My dear Mrs Gunnar

I went last night to see the last of The Vikings. On the whole, the best epitaph for Hiördis is the one in Great Expectations—

> For, whatsome'er the failings on her part,
> Remember, reader, she were that good in her eart.

However, I want to tell you one or two things about it. Mr Tedward Gordon Craig is a young man of much talent; but he committed two crimes over this business, which have probably cost you a thousand pounds apiece.

Crime number one: matricide. The relation between man and mother is too serious a one for romance and mystery and color schemes. In dealing with you his faculty for stage art totally deserted him. I will explain more exactly presently.

Crime number two: treachery to the author, recoiling on your head and his own. You know the story of the doctor who could not cure measles but was death on fits; so he always gave children fits instead of curing them of measles. Well, Tedward is death on moonlight and on rows of spears borrowed from Paolo Uccello, a certain Tintoretto picture in Venice, and the Surrender at Breda, by Velasquez. Now the first act of The Vikings should be a most lovely morning scene, all rosy mists, fresh air, virgin light, and diamond dewdrops. The men should be glowing from their baths, robust, solid, with no nonsense about them. Into this cheerful and real scene there should come a woman like the shadow of death—a woman in black, with white face and snakes in her hair, so to speak, a messenger of death to every man in the play.

Instead of which, Signor Teduardo, not being able to manage full light and local color, turns the dawn into night; makes the warriors fantastic and unreal; and finally introduces comfort and color in the shape of a fine figure of a woman in a particularly cosy bearskin mantle which heaps her shoulders up to her ears and gives her an air of jollity which positively radiates goodnature in spite of the unfortunate lady's efforts to make mischief. Having ruined her shoulders, he abolishes her neck with its stately nape, by connecting her head with the small of her back with a hedge of porcupine quills which only needed a coat of yellow ochre to make Hiordis a perfect squaw on the warpath. Result:

the play drops stone dead the moment you walk on the stage. It is all over in a second. The mistake is irretrievable. Ibsen is revenged; and you are left with the pleasant certainty that the critics will all say that it is your fault. Now I consider this a very black crime indeed. If Master Teddy wants to use plays as stalking horses for his clever effects, let him write them himself. To take an author of Ibsen's importance, and deliberately alter his play to suit the limelight man, is the folly of a child, not the act of a responsible man. And it is additionally injudicious because it gives away the last act (in which the moonlight is all right) quite hopelessly. You cannot run a theatre on moonlight. If E.G.C. Esquire cannot put every hour in the day on the stage, and every season in the year, let him become an impressionist painter and paint nocturnes; for there is no career for him on the stage. You in particular want sunlight, because when all is said and done you are a comedian; and your tears are only April showers and not Arctic hailstones. Of course the young villain will say that you should not have played Hiördis; and in a way he is right; but then the difficulty could have been got round: you always had a power of suggesting strangeness which could have been turned to account, not by porcupine bonnets and bearskin rugs, but by a terrible simplicity and by loyalty to Ibsen. The matter is past praying for now; but please rub into the delinquent that he has failed; and that all the silly compliments that have been paid him for his cleverness in the wrong place dont alter that fact. You need not spare him; for he has talent enough to bear being flayed alive and being rather the better for it. In fact, that is the mischief of it: what he aimed at was so well done that he has bowled over all the critics who have any artistic perception; and they have forgotten to tell him that his business was to bring out Ibsen's qualities and not his own. If he did that to a play of mine, I would sacrifice him on the prompter's table before his mother's eyes.

Now as to Much Ado. Your advertisements are a little too perfunctory: they belittle your company. The public has a right to know who is going to play Benedick and Dogberry; and this means that Hero, Leonato, the Prince and all the rest must be announced. Remember, the public will always fear in your case that it will be Miss Terry and *quelques poupées*; and you must advertize your nobodies to the utmost so as to give importance to your productions. And be careful to have a very pretty Hero. Sarah Bernhardt's plan of always keeping her stage full of the prettiest women she can find is a very worldly-wise one. I emphasize this, because Dagny [Hutin Britton] was not winsome enough to do justice to Hiordis's good looks: you should not have

325

exhibited yourself as having been thrown over by Sigurd for a much plainer woman. Besides, the public will think that you are jealous; and I shall say so myself in the most brutal manner unless you have a very pretty Hero for me.

Further, do not copy the Lyceum production: it was a most unskilful one in many points. For instance, you had to play the scene "The prince's jester: a very dull fool &c" in the middle of a crowd of people, where it was entirely lost. The proper way to play that is the old way (at least I suppose it is the old way because I saw it done by Barry Sullivan, who never gave the audience half a dozen other things to look at when he wanted them to look at him). He had an empty scene with curtains, and the noise and music of the ball going on behind, subdued. Presently a couple of maskers stole in through the curtains, flitted mysteriously across the stage, and disappeared. More music; then another couple. Of course the final couple was Barry and Mrs Louisa Viner (or was it Vining?); and as the attention was tremendously concentrated on them, and the curiosity of the audience highly roused, the effect was very great. At the Lyceum the passage went for nothing.

Dogberry was an utter failure at the Lyceum. This was because Dogberry's first scene was omitted—the one where he calls on Leonato with Verges. Without this to prepare the audience for the Ass scene, it falls perfectly flat. With it, Dogberry is irresistible. I implore you not to trifle with Dogberry; for the play, which is a bad one, cannot do without him. You ought to get William Wyes to play him; but I suppose the part is already cast. I write this in haste, late at night, with the object of being useful and disagreeable rather than of entertaining you. This venture of yours makes me uneasy: dont, for heaven's sake, risk anything serious over it. You can always shut up & let the theatre to some desperado in the season if Much Ado is too stale to pay its way. Why dont you get Melville to write you a melodrama—The Demon Duchess or something like that?

GBS

To HARLEY GRANVILLE BARKER

Maybury Knoll. Woking
[A/3; X/168]   26th May 1903

[*The Admirable Bashville*, staged by Shaw for the Stage Society, was presented at the Imperial Theatre on 7th and 8th June 1903. Henrietta Watson

(1873–1964) had appeared in Barker's *The Marrying of Ann Leete* in 1902. She later performed at the Royal Court in Shaw's *You Never Can Tell* (1906).]

Dear Barker

I have now looked through Bashville & find him most expensive. We shall want a crowd, including policemen and chiefs, also the following props.

A rapidly portable dais & throne for Cetewayo.

Various birdwhistles, including a cuckoo.

Goblet and wine vase of gilt pasteboard on massive salver.

A large key (Lydia's door key to put down Cashel's back)

A knockout sceptre for Cetewayo, not too unwieldy for a broadsword combat with Lucian's umbrella.

Softnosed spears for the chiefs.

Four enormous boxing gloves stuffed with feathers (eider down preferred).

A property posthorn.

A mossgrown tree trunk for Lydia to sit on, not too low, and really round, so that she can get her heels well under herself when Cashel lifts her with one finger under her chin.

An umbrella for Lucian to fight with, as he cannot reasonably be asked to sacrifice his own.

And several trees, in tubs or otherwise.

   Then, as to costumes.

A white beaver hat for Mellish.

A gorgeous livery with tags, plush smalls, calves, and a heavily powdered wig for Bashville. The wig is important, as when he says O Bathos! in his great soliloquy he must strike his head & send up a cloud of powder from it.

A blue handkerchief with white spots, large enough to tie round Cashel's waist, passing under the front flap of his breeches.

A crimson or yellow handkerchief for Paradise.

One break must be made at the end of the Agricultural Hall scene. If Henrietta Watson happens to have a blue dress with white spots on it she might pay Cashel a touching compliment by changing to it hastily during the break, which need not be a long one.

I am calculating on the traverses; so that unless the stage is

like this   I shall be stumped.

I am terrified by the length of the thing, considering the need for slow delivery & the constant making of elocutionary points. If we can coach the company up to the mark they will be able to amaze the public in Shakespear for ever after: its splendid practice.

GBS

We come up to town tomorrow. Come to lunch & report progress.

To GERTRUDE ELLIOTT

10 Adelphi Terrace W C
[A/1]   8th June 1903

[The idea of a Stage Society production of Act I of *Cæsar and Cleopatra* was soon abandoned. No Shaw play was produced by the Stage Society in 1903-4.]

Dear Mrs Forbes Robertson

Now that you have actually seen the Stage Society and know the worst of it, do you think you could ever condescend to try an experiment on it with the first act of Cæsar & Cleopatra (I am afraid we couldnt afford the rest). It has been borne in upon me for a long time—ever since I met you, in fact—that Providence sent you to London for the express purpose of playing Cleopatra for me. The Stage Society wants to do a play of mine next season; and the only unperformed play besides C & C is a detestable thing called The Philanderer, which I shrink from as instinctively as I am tempted by Miss Gertrude Cleopatra. If I could hold out the faintest hope to the Society, it would make an effort to scrape together the price of a sphinx & an old pantomime wardrobe for the Egyptian & Roman soldiers.

This is my only chance of ever seeing you in a piece of mine again; for my conviction of the unfitness of the playgoing public for my work is so strong—so *increasingly* strong—that nothing will ever induce me to run the risk of ruining you by consenting to a regular business production of anything of mine. I dont mind ruining syndicates & speculators & managers who keep a theatre as they might keep a hotel or anything else in the way of business; but when Dick Dudgeon mentions even The Devil's Disciple to me I have a vision of brokers in Bedford Square, of a handsome figure with its head blown off and a pistol clenched in its white hand, and of a beautiful dark lady playing

328

a street piano with her children in baskets at each end of it. And I snatch at my excuse for getting out of it. The poor man who played Dick in Vienna the other day will never be able to shew his face there again; and he was not only a father, but a grandfather: indeed I am not sure that he was not a great grandfather, though he did not look a day over eighty, and was a solid, experienced, thoroughly popular actor of some sixtyfive years unblemished professional record.

Think over Cleopatra and let me know the result before the announcements for next season come due.

yours faithfully
G. Bernard Shaw

PS If you can think of anyone who would play Cæsar for us, please suggest him. The part is quite open.

To MAX BEERBOHM

[A/1]

Maybury Knoll. Woking
9th June 1903

[Beerbohm, in his notice of *The Admirable Bashville* in the *Saturday Review* on 13th June, commented: "The right way to act it is to take it quite seriously, reproducing in all their beauty the sonorous elocution and dignified deportment of the traditional Shakespearean mimes. Pre-eminently well by Miss Fanny Brough, that invaluable lady, this trick was performed." Ben Webster (1865–1947), who played Cashel Byron, later created the rôle of Sir Colenso Ridgeon in *The Doctor's Dilemma* (1906).]

Dear Max

I am terrified lest you were one of those too precipitate critics who left the theatre yesterday at the end of the scrimmage scene in Bashville under the impression that all was over. If you did, I implore you not to overlook the fact that Fanny Brough appeared in the second act to do about twenty lines for me. Walkley writes in today's Times that Mr Webster, Miss Watson *and others* appeared. Fancy my feelings! Fanny, the inimitable Fanny, has nearly killed herself by taking on this little part on top of the Criterion rehearsals, and has played it for ten times what it is worth—not to mention speaking the verse beautifully—all for the sake of the beaux yeux of the author of Mrs Warren, without getting even a blessed cabfare from the struggling Stage Society; and her reward is to be described as "and others."

I prithee, dearest Max, make her amends. Which is blank verse.

yrs ever
G. Bernard Shaw

P.S. Why dont you write a comedy for Webster? I had no idea that he had that Jeffersonian gift of keeping people amused in an agreeable way, even when he was not doing anything but ambling about. He held the whole tomfoolery together for me.

To GERTRUDE ELLIOTT

10 Adelphi Terrace W C

[A/1]   10th June 1903

[*Carrots* was a one-act psychological drama by Alfred Sutro, from the French of Jules Renard, which the Forbes-Robertsons had first performed as an after-piece to *The Devil's Disciple* in Dublin on 18th October 1900.]

Dear Mrs Forbes Robertson

Many, many thanks. It is fixed for next June. Hurrah!

You have been deceived about the D's D. There will never be a better Dick than F.R. It is you, and you alone, who are the impossible one. I never saw anything so absurd as Carrots after Judith—Carrots all right, Judith all wrong. Judith with her chin up and her imperious forefinger shooting magnetically at everybody on the stage, ordering everybody about, was almost as inconceivable a thing as Tree's Falstaff. The one quality that Judith must have above everything is the quality that excites pity: to wit, weakness. Mark that, madam, pity, pity, pity, pity, pity, pity, PITY. When you come on the stage the audience pities everybody else—if you are crossed in any way. When your devoted husband proposed to try The D's D after Mice & Men, I told him this, and said that you ought not to be supplanted after your success in Mice & Men, but that if he was determined to play Dick, he must play it to the pitiable Judith of Lena Ashwell. Whereupon, wounded in his deepest feelings, he glared upon me frightfully, almost embraced my wife (who adores him) under my very nose, left the house, and went straight and told you that I objected to *him*. That was chivalry. Never believe anything a chivalrous man tells you: come to me whenever you dont want your feelings spared.

330

If you want to have a really splendid benefit in New York, play the Strange Lady in my Man of Destiny to Forbes's Napoleon, and Carrots afterwards—or the other way about. It is technically by far my most difficult piece, and is absolutely out of the question for anyone who cannot hold up Hamlet from end to end. Your appearance & his in a play by me will be a great literary event which will extract columns on columns from the press; and you may buy candy with the author's fees and present them to your young family. Only, I must rehearse it before you start; for I alone know all the business of it—endless business. The Strange Lady is ten times as difficult as Judith; but that is all the better for you, as you need brainy parts. As to F.R. as the young Napoleon, America would erect an altar to him.

At all events, you can't pretend now that I dont appreciate you both. Mind, only *one* performance—$25 to all parts of the house.

yours really & truly
G. Bernard Shaw

To SIEGFRIED TREBITSCH

[A/5]

10 Adelphi Terrace W C
12th June 1903

[The policeman in *The Admirable Bashville*, C. Aubrey Smith (1863–1948), later became one of the best-known character actors in motion pictures. In 1903 he was Secretary of the Stage Society.]

Dear Trebitsch

Ouf!!! I have been nearly killed by the rehearsals of my greatest play—"The Admirable Bashville." However, I got an admirable cast (for nothing) and it went with a roar from beginning to end. The policeman made himself up like me; and my aunt [Georgina Shaw] firmly believes that I actually played the part. It was hard work; and writing letters, except to the cast, was out of the question.

Yes: Cæsar & Cleopatra is too long; but the only remedy is to omit the third act—the lighthouse act. It is a pity; but it would be a still greater pity to mutilate the rest. . . .

The new book is now *printed*—not published. As soon as I can spare a complete set of proofs I will send it to you.

In haste
ever
G. Bernard Shaw

331

To THE MACMILLAN CO.

[A/56]

10 Adelphi Terrace W C
19th June 1903

[After nearly eight months of negotiations Shaw still had not found an American publisher for *Man and Superman*. By now he had resorted to the transatlantic cable, and proof sheets of the play bounced from Harper to Macmillan to Appleton (the latter firm reporting that the book was "not suitable" for their list). The London office of McClure, Phillips & Co. informed him that Mr Phillips "is fearful that certain conventions to which as a publisher he is forced to adhere will prevent his making you an offer for the American rights . . . He regards it as one of your most brilliant achievements, and deplores the limitations that cost him the privilege of issuing this work" (Texas).

There had been equal difficulty finding a British publisher for the book. Shaw had finally determined to give it to Constable, after making one more effort to have it published by an established and respected house, sending it to John Murray for a personal opinion. Murray's response on 9th June was friendly and paternalistic, but the view it offered clearly marked the publisher as a lineal descendant of the man who had burned the manuscript of Byron's memoirs:

"From the publishers point of view the question is . . . whether he would care to give his imprint to such a book. To this question I am afraid that I personally can only answer 'no.'

"The object of the book is to cast ridicule upon—or perhaps I should say to assail—marriage and other social & religious institutions.

"Now however much a man may disapprove of these institutions it seems to me that respect for the very deep seated feelings which hundreds of thousands of educated people entertain in regard to them should induce him to make the attack in a somewhat reverent form: setting forth the arguments on both sides and stating clearly what is to be the substitute & how it is to be attained. . . .

"I daresay you will say that I am old fashioned & conventional; I am fully prepared to accept the description. However imperfectly I may express my meaning I write from a very sincere conviction for which I am sure you will make all proper allowance" (Texas).

George Herbert Thring (1859–1941) was Secretary of the Society of Authors from 1892 to 1930.]

Dear Sirs

Thank you for your cable message just received. I presume you have received the proof sheets of my book "Man & Superman" from Messrs Harper. I am sorry I have had to hurry my proposal by cabling; but I am in a difficulty with the book owing to the fact that the best time for me to publish in London is July, before the rising of parliament for the August recess; and I must either lose that season or else get my book printed at once in the United States for simultaneous (formal) publication there. In consequence of a certain exchange of courtesies between myself and Messrs Harper some time ago, I felt bound to offer them the refusal of the book; but I knew that it was not at all the sort of thing they wanted; and I asked them to cable their anticipated refusal, which they did yesterday. Mr Thring, the secretary of the Author's Society here, recommended me strongly to submit the book to you; and as your very enterprising & catholic activity had already disposed me to meet this recommendation more than half way, I cabled you forthwith.

My books have hitherto been published in America by Messrs Stone of Chicago, except the novels issued by Brentano, which are un-authorized non-copyright editions of which I know nothing except that I sometimes buy copies from a London firm which smuggles them extensively. I have not quarreled with Messrs Stone; but I do not intend to publish with them again, because they seem to me to be content to sell enough copies to see them through—which can always be done with my books without advertisement—and leave the matter there. I may be wrong in this; but at all events I shall try whether I am or not by changing.

Roughly, I think any book of mine ought to sell a thousand copies in America without much pressing, on the strength of the reviews and paragraphs, which I generally draw from the press in greater profusion than is at all personally convenient to me. Beyond that, it would be a matter of pushing; but I should probably never attain a large popular circulation. From the purely business side, I doubt if I am worth dealing with, as it seems to me that the necessary capital could always be invested in a book that would bring a larger return.

As to terms, I have given up the royalty system in England. I manufacture the book myself, and publish on commission. But I find that publishers prefer the royalty system; and in America I prefer it myself, as I cannot easily manufacture books at such a distance. I ask (and get) from America a royalty of $12\frac{1}{2}\%$ on the nominal price for the first thousand copies, and 15% for the rest. In England I get 20%. The agreement, in the form of a license, not of an assignment, to be limited to a period of five years (or to be terminable thereafter at six months notice) or to an edition of a stated number of copies. This is important to me, as my books never die completely: a dribbling demand keeps on

333

continually even when the novelty is worn off & the advertising dropped. My earliest books still sell a little.

The English edition will be published by Archibald Constable & Co.

yours faithfully
G. Bernard Shaw

PS Should you decide not to publish the book, will you be so good as to keep it until I cable a request as to its disposal; so as to save the great delay of two journeys across the Atlantic. Will you also let me have a yes or no cable message as to your decision.

To GRANT RICHARDS

[Maybury Knoll. Woking]
[H/4]   21st June 1903

[*The Perfect Wagnerite* had just been reprinted, with a brief new preface.]

Dear G.R.

A difference of a month is nothing to a dramatist. In combing my facts I aim at effectiveness, not at chronological accuracy. Besides, you may depend on it the thing happens every day.

I have at last come to terms with your rival Constable; and I now look forward to a frantic competitive struggle between the two firms as to which can sell most copies. You really owe me some reparation for the perfectly damnable trouble and disturbance you have brought upon me in my old age, when I might have reasonably hoped my publishing arrangements were settled for life in the hands of a man likely to survive me by a quarter of a century. The new edition of The Perfect Wagnerite is excellent. When I went to The Ring cycle in May I had to fight my way through crowds of men offering other Wagner books for sale; but I only saw one Perfect Wagnerite in the stalls; and I afterwards found out it was my wife's.

Have you ever considered the question of a cheap edition of my works—something on India paper at 1/- or the like?—At worst it is a way of making the books advertize one another. I do not press for a reply, as the thing will probably be done by Dent or somebody else; but dont say, when you finally drive me to desperation, that I did not appeal to you repeatedly to think over the matter.

yrs ever
G. Bernard Shaw

334

To OTTO KYLLMANN

Maybury Knoll. Woking
[A/3]   5th July 1903

[Otto Kyllmann (1860–1959) and William Maxse Meredith (1865–1937), son of George Meredith, were partners in the firm of Archibald Constable & Co., which had been founded in 1890. The agreement with Constable's, to serve as commission agent for Shaw's works, consisted of a few lines scribbled by Shaw on a sheet of letter paper: it served for 47 years. *Man and Superman* was published on 11th August 1903.]

Dear Kyllmann

Courage! the book will be ready by July 1904 at all events.

It is difficult to find out about paper. I have been looking for a machine made paper of good material; and everybody says to begin with that no such thing exists. However, I have found it at last (Dickenson's All Rag) and have instructed Clark to get it and send the dummy.

The American business is still unsettled. When it comes to hustling, the American is simply not in it. If I had time to explain their business to them, and allow them a fortnight to take in the explanation, there would be no difficulty, as the idiots all *want* the book; but I am forced to dash from one to another until I find one who is awake. I had it practically settled with the Macmillan Co; but their intelligence gave out on a minor point (for *them*) on Friday; and I have had to switch off to Appleton, who had in the meantime made overtures spontaneously.

I advise you to change your profession: it wrecks the intellect sooner or later.

I return to town on Wednesday.

yrs faithfully
G. Bernard Shaw

To GEORGE P. BRETT

10 Adelphi Terrace W C
[H/56]   10th July 1903

[George Platt Brett (1858–1936), who had served the Macmillan Co., New York, since 1874, eventually became its president and chairman. Brett had stated in his letter of 30th June that Macmillan "should have been very glad to publish the book . . . under the royalties named by you were it not for the fact that we almost never undertake the publication of any book on which a

335

time limit is placed; and we could not make an exception for a book of this character, which we should expect to be longer in finding its public than if, for instance, it were a novel.

"We should much have liked to have had the pleasure of publishing for you on this side of the water but the publication of books under a time limit is so contrary to our policy, which is the development as far as we can possibly do so of an author's interests as a whole in this country" (New York Public Library).]

Dear Sir

Your letter of the 30th June has just reached me.

It is a pity that we have not been able to conclude a perfectly straightforward piece of business, convenient for me, safe and profitable for you, and likely to lead to permanent relations between us unless you handled the book very badly indeed. But as long as you persist in treating me as a literary idiot whilst I treat you as an intelligent man of the world, nothing is likely to come of our negotiations. Anyhow, I have no time to prolong them; so I have settled the matter by sending the book to an American printer, who will set it up and effect formal publication and registration of copyright. I can then wait for the effect of the English publication and arrange for the American publication at my convenience at reasonable terms. . . .

yours faithfully
G. Bernard Shaw

To GEORGE P. BRETT

[A/56]

[Maybury Knoll. Woking]
13th July 1903

[Brett's letter of 3rd July, in answer to a cablegram from Shaw, merely reiterated the position he had taken in his earlier letter concerning a time limit.]

Dear Sir

Your letter of the 3rd July arrived yesterday. I shall send it to the Secretary of The Author's Society here, as it was he who advised me to offer you the book. He may as well know your terms for his future guidance.

I am quite aware that authors, under pressure of money difficulties, often do very unthrifty things for the sake of an advance, and that publishers are not slow to take advantage of their impecuniosity. But I

336

must confess that in a case where no advance is asked or offered, where the author is a man of established reputation and independent means, where there is practically neither a risk nor even a temporary advance of the cost of production involved (I am assuming that you can get a few months credit from your printer), and where the royalties are ordinary and reasonable, a demand that the author shall also bind himself to you for life for better for worse, takes away my breath. I shall always be interested in your success, because I am sufficient of an economist to watch with curiosity how far so spirited a commercial policy can go; but our relations must in future be purely friendly ones: my publishing will be done elsewhere.

Why on earth dont you put your cable address on your notepaper and invoices? Have you shares in one of the cable companies? Think of all the dollars you have cost me by this omission!

yours faithfully
G. Bernard Shaw

To CONSTABLE & CO.

10 Adelphi Terrace W C
15th July 1903

[A/4]

[The firm was known as Archibald Constable & Co. until 1910.]

Dear Sirs

After expending some two or three millions on cable messages, and convincing the American publishers that they could name their own terms because I was tied to time, I have at last cut the Gordian knot by printing the book myself in the United States. The University Press of Cambridge Mass. have just cabled to me that they are at work on Man & Superman, and that they will effect a formal publication for copyright purposes on the 25th instant: that is, on Saturday in next week. I have just sent a card to warn Clark. Will this suit you? All that is necessary, of course (in case the day is inconvenient) is formal publication, meaning exposure of a copy for sale, and entry at Stationers' Hall, a purely antiquarian custom which I keep up because it settles the date of publication for the benefit of the inheritor of the copyright and the enlightenment of future literary historians.

May I pass the title page for press? I have passed everything else. By the way, I wish you would change your name: it does not fit my page at all. An alteration of Archibald to Osbaldiston would just do it; and Archibald, though again at large, probably wouldnt mind. As it is, to avoid that horrible gap after the colon I have had to shorten the line by an em, and print Ltd at full length as Limited, omitting the commas, so as to close up the type. My title fits beautifully.

As to advertisements, the list you sent me might be enlarged. The Saturday Review is of more use to me than to other people because I was one of its bright particular stars for some years. And I am prepared to submit to black mail from The Academy: it must live, poor thing! What about the Queen, the Lady's Pictorial, and the Free Lance? The Outlook & the Speaker probably dont count for ordinary business; but if their charges are at all modest, their reviews are (to me) worth the bribe of an ad. To whom do you propose to send review copies?

yrs faithfully
G. Bernard Shaw

PS. The main thing to advertize is "new book by Bernard Shaw."

To G. MORRIS PHILLIPS

10 Adelphi Terrace W C
16th July 1903

[A/57]

[George Morris Phillips (1851–1920), Principal of the State Normal School, West Chester, Pa., had sent Shaw a copy of the Brentano unauthorised edition of *An Unsocial Socialist* (1901) with a request for an autograph. Shaw had written in it: "Contraband copy smuggled into the United Kingdom by an enterprising American, who sends it to the author with a request to autograph it and smuggle it out again. America is quite welcome to the book; but, really, to demand autographs into the bargain is not reasonable."]

Dear Sir

I do not object to what you call pirated editions, except when I have to autograph them; and that objection applies to all editions whatever.

I think the English people have a grievance in the matter, as they have to contribute to the support of the author whilst the American people take his work for nothing; but the author himself has not much to complain of, as the field over which he has copyright is in most cases sufficiently wide for all his reasonable requirements. For example Dickens, who had no way of obtaining American copyright, got a fair living by his pen. If he were flourishing now, he would, through the

338

new copyright law, get enormously overpaid. A book is a peculiar commodity: the one of which a million copies are sold costs no more labor than the one of which a thousand are sold; and the common arguments which claim for the author the same property rights in his books as a baker has in his loaves, will not stand a moment's examination.

What I wrote in your volume was not intended as a reproach to you personally; and it is, from the autograph collectors' point of view, quite as valuable a curiosity as an ordinary inscription.

yours faithfully
G. Bernard Shaw

To T. FISHER UNWIN

[A/5]

10 Adelphi Terrace W C
23rd July 1903

[Sir Walter Besant was the founder and first president of the Society of Authors. Shaw's article in the July issue of *The Author* was titled "Book Distribution."]

Dear Fisher Unwin

I quite understand, of course, that you have no interest in the dealings of the American publishers. Lord forbid that you ever should; for they are shocking duffers.

It seems to me that the grievance involved by the absence of copyright, as it existed formerly between England & the U.S, and as it partly exists today, is the grievance of the English public against the American public for not sharing the expense of keeping the author alive. Besant's complaints were frankly anti-social: he said that with universal copyright a successful book would be "a silver mine" for the author—that is, that the author should get paid over and over again for the same job, once for every country in which he had copyright. As soon as this is understood, copyrights will be shortened every time they are widened. Possibly also books will have to be registered in different classes with different terms of copyright; for it really is ridiculous to treat, say, Smith & Elder's Dictionary of National Biography, representing an enormous investment of capital, exactly as you treat a flashy novel representing a few pints of whisky and a couple of months of a third rate writer's time. In short, copyright is a public question, and

339

not an author's question. Can anything be more absurd than to give fortytwo years monopoly of an obscene book to a literary blackguard and only fourteen years to the inventor of the steam engine?

My new book is on the verge of appearing: I am only waiting to secure simultaneous publication. Constable is publishing it. You will find an interesting article by me in the current number of The Author on the real want of the age, which is, not more publishers but more bookshops. I can sell 1800 copies of a new 6/- book without advertising; but when I want to improve on that, I am stopped in two ways, 1st, the publisher *wont* advertize because the 1800 copies have landed him safely, and 2nd, there are no shops where people can see & buy anything except five quires of notepaper for a shilling and a Bible, with a 6d reprint or so.

yrs faithfully
G. Bernard Shaw

To HENRY S. SALT

[A/1]

Springburn. Strachur
2nd August 1903

[The Shaws had left for Scotland on 1st August. They spent two months at Strachur and a few days, early in October, in Glasgow. Dr Alexander Haig (1853–1924), a London physician and physiological researcher, was the author of *Diet and Food Considered in Relation to Strength and Power of Endurance, Training and Athletics* (1898). *The Way of All Flesh* had been published by Grant Richards in May 1903. "Thompson" is James Thomson (1834–82), the pessimist poet. Salt had published a life of Thomson in 1889.]

Dear Salt

Constable, the publishers of my new book, will send a review copy to the Humane Review. I have given the address of that publication as Henry Salt, Crockham Hill, Edenbridge, Kent; so that Kate can read it and you review it (if you like). It will not be out for a fortnight or so yet. If you have changed your address, there will be time to warn me.

The book is one of the most colossal efforts of the human mind, and contains several passages which you will find congenial, and which will make Kate blush for having gradually argued herself into a conviction that I am a lost soul.

340

As a matter of fact I go on much as I used to, except that my pecuniary circumstances are embarrassed. My wife has at last become a convinced vegetarian (Haig having cured her of rheumatism & indigestion); and she now eats nothing but birds & fish, which are not "butcher's meat." She is also converted to simplicity of life, and now, although we have both a town & country residence, we keep no horses and spend hardly £3,000 a year on our housekeeping. I have great hopes of reducing this ultimately to £2,500, especially as Charlotte is never happy except when we are staying in some grubby public house out of reach of the servants & the two residences. My own poverty is due to my Irish estate, which is revenging all my Socialism on me by demanding a fertilizing stream of money to redeem it from being the barren plague spot my ancestors left it. I am in debt at the bank to the tune of nearly all my old savings (the only money I can touch the capital of); I keep a solicitor and an agent; and on the strength of these calamities I am supposed to be fabulously rich.

Have you read Samuel Butler's posthumous "Way of All Flesh"? If not, get it instantly. It is one of the great books of the world. You will throw Shelley, Thompson, Meredith & all the rest out of the window & take Butler to your heart for ever. I do not exaggerate: it is enormous. The man loves the Church & the University even as you love them yourself. *Is* there any chance of ever seeing you again? Charlotte says you dont like the food at Adelphi Terrace. Or is it that you dont like *her*?

G.B.S.

To SIEGFRIED TREBITSCH

Springburn. Strachur
4th August 1903

[A/5]

Trebitsch, Trebitsch, du bist ganz und gar unverbesserlich. I tell you you are utterly, totally, completely and absolutely wrong about the stage directions, and I am u, t, c & a right about them. What you must do is this. Write a translator's preface; and explain all your departures from custom. Explain that one of the most important things I have done in England is to effect a reform in the printing of plays. Say that the English people had for a whole century absolutely refused to read plays, although they had been free from the ridiculous French convention of Sz 27—Die Vorige und ein Diener—two lines and then—Sz 28, Die Vorige, ohne der Diener. Mention the fact that, curiously enough,

341

in the first play I ever printed I introduced this silly fashion myself, and, in doing so, cured myself for ever of such folly. Nobody bought that play: the English people have too much imagination to tolerate these conventions. I then set to work to make plays readable. I abolished the list of characters at the beginning. I introduced them as they entered by descriptions as elaborate & far more concise than those of Tolstoy and Turgenieff. I never made any reference to the stage technically, never used the words "enter" or "exit," never shattered the reader's dream by the smell of the footlights, and yet concealed in my apparently purely poetic directions a technical specification for the stage manager far more detailed and complete than any author has ever given before.

Now *you* think me an old ass, and coolly propose to undo all my work and reduce my reformed drama to the old silly prompt book. "Not at all important" you call it. It is *all*-important. You say that every manager will alter for his stage as he likes & that you will only be present at Berlin & Vienna. Infant that you are! I tell you that managers are the most slavish copiers of the metropolis in the world. What is done at Berlin & Vienna will be reproduced without a single original idea everywhere in Germany, Austria, Poland, Switzerland & probably Russia. And of what use will your presence be in Vienna or Austria unless you have the whole stage business at your finger's ends? An author who is not thus prepared is paid a few empty compliments & pushed into a corner at rehearsal. I get the command of my rehearsals, not because I am the author, but because I stop all the compliments & introductions by rushing at the work, placing the chairs to mark the entrances &c, and leading on the actors to their right places, which they presently find to be the most effective places for themselves. I get through the first act and say "Now let's run through that act again" before the stage manager has finished staring at me. I never assert my authority, and never give an order: I simply tell them what to do; and when they see that I know my business they leave it all to me & appeal to me whenever they are in doubt. Mind! it is hard work: I have to slave at it the night before like a schoolboy until I have learnt my lesson; but the result is well worth the trouble. All this you will have to do; and unless you make the directions clear you will not be able to do it. You are young & have plenty of time for this. I am old—47—and can ill afford to waste a moment. Yet I think it important enough.—Historisches Schauspiel is the right term.—I do not object to the book giving the *cast* of the first performance, provided it is not made part of the play. See Mrs Warren z.b.

GBS

342

To SIEGFRIED TREBITSCH

Springburn. Strachur
[A/5]   10th August 1903

[*Cæsar and Cleopatra* was produced by Max Reinhardt in Berlin on 31st
March 1906.]

Dear Trebitsch

You are perfectly mad—mad as a hatter. You were as anxious as
possible about that Raimund Theater affair, at which we could do
nothing but send poor old Wiené back to his grandchildren, a ruined
man; and now that this Berlin performance, on which our whole fate
depends, is coming on, you calmly tell me "not to be too careful about
Cæsar." I am working like a slave at it; and you must not omit the
smallest detail, or neglect the most trifling precaution, to ensure a good
performance. When you have provided for every possible contingency,
and left your part of the work as good as your utmost faculty can make
it, then it will be time to trust to luck & leave the management to lose
its 20,000 marks (it should be 120,000—20,000 is not half enough) or
double them, as the gods may decree.

Now first—and this is most important and must be done within the
next ten minutes. Write to the manager to stop the designing of the
scenery &c until he has our plans & sketches. If they get the scenery
wrong—and they cannot help doing so if they work from your stage
directions, which are DISASTROUSLY inaccurate—the whole play
will be thrown into confusion, and the stage business will be found
impracticable. If the scenes are right, it will be as easy as possible; and
we shall save a month of changing and disputing & mangling the play
to suit the mistakes of the painters & machinists.

Will you find out for me *at once* what the mechanical resources of
the Neues Theater are. All I want to know is, 1. Have they an electric
turntable? 2 Have they hydraulic bridges? 3 Have they hydraulic
clutches—that is, ropes to draw up weights from above—or is everything pushed up by a piston from below? 4 What is the depth of the
stage from the footlights to the back wall & what is its width from side
to side? Promise them drawings. I cannot draw; but I can make the
painters & carpenters understand what I mean.

Tomorrow I shall telegraph to you to Munich that I posted Act II
on Aug 4. to Ischl, and Act III on Aug 7 to Bad-Gastein. Both were
sealed up in registered letters; so it must be possible to recover them.
If possible I shall send Act IV by the same post as this letter; but

343

probably it will be a day later. The postal communication here is frightfully slow. As Glasgow is 8 hours from London & this place is 5 hours from Glasgow, you must not think of coming. The distance is too great & the journey too expensive. However, we can settle that later on. For the moment the all-important thing is to stop all scene painting & designing until our plans are sent in. If you like I will write direct to the Neues Theater in my worst German.

yrs
G.B.S.

To SIEGFRIED TREBITSCH

[A/5]

Springburn. Strachur
16th August 1903

[The correct title of the poem by Charlotte Perkins Stetson (1860–1935) which Shaw quoted was "An Obstacle" (in *In This Our World*, 1895). It concerned a lady who vanquished a prejudice, after many unsuccessful attempts, by walking through it as if it weren't there. Despite Shaw's injunction, the published text of *Cæsar and Cleopatra* contained "an idiotic list of nameless characters": "Gefolge des Ptolemäus, römische Soldaten, Sklaven, Volk." Trebitsch's translation of Georges Rodenbach's play *Le Mirage*, under the title *Verkauft Lächeln* (*The Sold Smile*), was produced at the Deutsches Theater, Vienna, on 12th September 1903.]

My dear Trebitsch

Your letter arrived yesterday—Saturday evening—too late to post the IV & V acts to you. Today is Sunday; and in Scotland nothing can be done on Sunday except go to Church. So I cannot post this & register it until tomorrow. Perhaps you will get it on Wednesday.

. . . The corrections are very important, because the production in Berlin, whether successful or not—but especially if successful—will not crush Kellner: it will, on the contrary, give him a much better chance than he had before of taking your scalp. His article in the Wiener Tagblatt did not matter outside Vienna; and even in Vienna it was possible to counter it by the Zeit articles, my own, Bahr's &c &c. But a Berlin production at the Neues Theater will create a demand for magazine articles on me, just as the production of Cyrano here created a demand for magazine articles on Rostand in England & America. Kellner, who lives, I suppose, by his pen, is pretty sure to seize the

344

opportunity to earn the price of a magazine article. And if Kellner sets the fashion of saying that there are blunders in the translation, all the others will follow suit: for 99 out of a 100 of them cannot read English; but all of them will have to pretend that they speak & read it like natives. The bigger the success the more articles there will be. Therefore now is the time to give no chance to the enemy. This is why I have brought down a huge Muret-Sanders dictionary here and spent a month revising a translation in a language that I have never learnt. In future I will make the translation and you shall revise it. The dialogue seems to me to be just as good as the original and sometimes better; but still there are lots of mistakes. Mistakes dont matter: they can always be corrected, and they dont kill a play even if they are left uncorrected; but they are just what Kellner wants for a slashing review. For instance, he could write ten pages about Rufio swearing by Zeus instead of by Jove; and as to the centurion's cudgel being changed into the Dionysiac Thyrsusstab, you would never hear the end of it. You race recklessly through these things, which dont interest you. You care for nothing but the drama. That is just as it should be, as the drama is the main thing. But you give yourself away to the people who are interested in Roman history, Roman politics & Roman institutions. And indeed you ought to be interested in them. A true dramatist should be interested in everything. Kellner would write ten pages of the most erudite Roman history to shew that only the most ungebildeter Uebersetzer could possibly make Lucius Septimius call the Okkupationsarmée "rebels," or indeed mention such a delicate subject as rebellion to Cæsar at all. So be very careful to set all these little things right. I should not have sweated over them all these days if I were not convinced that they would get you into trouble.

Barbarous as my drawings of the scenery are, a great deal depends on them. Even an ordinary modern play like Es Lebe das Leben, with drawingroom scenes throughout, depends a good deal on the author writing his dialogue with a clear plan of stage action in his head; but in a play like Cæsar it is absolutely necessary: the staging is just as much a part of the play as the dialogue. It will not do to let a scenepainter & a sculptor loose on the play without a specification of the conditions with which their scenery must comply. Will you therefore tell the Neues manager that we will supply sketches. I will not inflict my own draughtsmanship on him; but I will engage a capable artist to make presentable pictures.

Now as to all this obsolete powder & pigtail—Szene VIII—Die Vorige &c &c—! There is no point in the Schlachtenlenker or in the

345

Drei Dramen at which these silly interpolations are positively insufferable; but in the 4th act of C & C. there are two places at least in which they are simply an outrage. Believe me, nobody will miss them. If their disappearance would incommode anybody I should not be so cocksure about omitting them; but I am so certain that they will die unlamented and even unnoticed that if I were you I should not even mention the matter in a preface. I only suggested that, in order to break the innovation to you as gently as possible. When you meet a foolish superstition, dont stop to remonstrate or argue or apologize: walk straight through it as if it didnt exist. As the American poetess (Charlotte Stetson) says in her poem "The Prejudice"—

"I simply walked straight through it
            As if it wasnt there."

and that is what we must do with this nonsensical pedantry. If anybody points out that we have effected an audacious reform, so much the better for us; but I am afraid the blow will be so completely in the water—in the sense that there will be no resistance to it—that we shall have to do without that useful advertisement.

As to waiting for a success, do you realize that if Cæsar fails we shall never have another chance? You must never wait for anything. We must plank everything on this production. We must do everything on the assumption that it is going to be a triumph, and that its failure will be the end of all things. As to thinking twice as to such a trumpery affair as this "Die Vorige &c" business, that would be absurd. Of course the play *may* fail. Very likely it will; for as you, being an Austrian, very well know, the Germans are as stupid as any people under the sun, and are not a bit likely to treat me better than they treated Wagner—except that they adore foreigners & despise themselves. But what then? We shall simply begin again, & treat the next production in the same way, as if it, too, were the crisis of our destiny. That is the way things are done in this world. Meanwhile be as peculiar & as affected & as conceited & as bizarre as you possibly can about the trifles whose importance exists only in the imaginations of the journalists & *flaneurs*. Reserve your seriousness for the real things of which they know nothing. If the play fails, I hope they will say that my plays are only good to read; for then the public will buy them from Fischer.

I do not object to the cast being published. You will find it in Mrs Warren. But there must not be an idiotic list of nameless characters, ending with "soldiers, citizens, boatmen, performing dogs &c &c &c."

If Hauptamme wont do, let Ftata call herself Kronamme or König-lichamme or Reichs Amme or something pretentious & prahlerisch.

Now as to Pilum. Mommsen's "Wurfspiess" is *vieux jeu*: it dates from 1871, when Bismarck & the Germans affected an extravagant Nationalism and called the telephone the Fernsprecher. Nowadays Nationalism has expanded into Imperialism; and ancient Rome is fashionable. The Kaiser will see himself as Cæsar; and when Britannus says "Only as Cæsar's slave have I found true freedom" he will give an enthusiastic Hoch & decorate you with the Iron Cross. I have carefully considered all this before recommending you to call the Pilum by its Roman name; and I am still of that opinion—more than ever, in fact.

If Bahr disagrees with me on this or any other point, it shews that he needs a holiday. The work of the season has been too much for him.

Yes, Du der Du is all right: I became resigned to it after the 6th or 7th time.

I never heard of Rodenbach. The Sold Smile suggests women & love—the most tedious subjects on earth. However, I am delighted to find that you have not been sacrificing your own work to mine. When is the Verkauft Lächeln to appear?

I forgot to say that you have not translated the notes to C & C. This is a fearful insult to me. I cherish those notes beyond all the rest of the play. You must translate them.

I see by the London papers that my new book is out; but I have not yet seen a copy. The publishers were to send me a supply; but the communications here are so bad that I may have to wait a week or more before the parcel reaches me.

You do not say how long you are going to stay at Dieppe.

And now as to your visit. It sounds inhospitable; but I seriously advise you not to come unless you make up your mind to take a Scotch holiday. It would be easier for me to go to London than to Scarborough or Cromer, because the railway journey from Glasgow to London is much faster than the cross-country journeys to intermediate places off the main line. As to meeting you in Glasgow, that would be very dismal indeed. If you come so far, you may as well take the rest of the trip by steamer from Gourock. You would, by leaving Glasgow at 8.45 a.m., go to Gourock by train (a short journey) and then go on board the Lord of the Isles (you can get a reasonably good lunch on board), go through the Kyles of Bute and up Loch Fyne, and land at Strachur at about 2 in the afternoon. Most likely it will rain—it has rained almost continuously since we came here on the 1st Aug. To do this for one day

347

would be absurd: you had better come for a week, or for as long as you can bear it. I can imagine no place more dreadful to a Viennese. There is no railway, no town, no shops, no society, no music, no entertainments, no beautiful ladies, absolutely nothing but fresh air and eternal rain. Our house is primitive; our food is primitive; we do nothing but wander about, cycle against impossible winds, or pull a heavy fisherman's boat about the loch when the weather is fair enough. If you like this sort of thing, come by all means: you can write as much as you like—indeed there is nothing else to do. But if you dont like it, let nothing induce you to come; for you can get away only once a day, and you would commit suicide in twelve hours at most.

I must now positively stop: everything is said.

yrs ever
G. Bernard Shaw

P.S. One more thing I forgot to warn you of. Wine is unknown here: whiskey is the only beverage. Charlotte says that if I tell you all these things you will think I dont want you to come; but as a matter of fact I dont: the expense & fatigue of the journey are far too great for a one-day visit. Except for this we should both be delighted to see you; and, after all, the place is very pretty.

To HENRY S. SALT

[C/5; X/164.e]

Springburn. Strachur
19th August 1903

[Clarence Darrow (1857–1938) was the noted Chicago attorney, whose most publicized case was the Scopes "monkey trial," which pitted him against William Jennings Bryan. Shaw's article on the subject, "Where Darwin is Taboo," appeared in the *New Leader*, 10th July 1925.]

Can you send me Darrow's address: I want to send him a Superman. At Euston he told me he was at the Langham Hotel; but I concluded that he would soon get out of that. For some instinctive reason I like him, perhaps because he is a genuine noble savage—with that cheekbone he wants only a few feathers and a streak of ochre to be a perfect Mohican, unlike that ultra-civilized impostor the ex-clergyman of Millthorpe [Edward Carpenter].

348

I have become an ardent sportsman here, pursuing porpoises all over Loch Fyne in a thickset fisherman's boat with a telephotographic camera at full cock. . . .

Tell Kate that Superman = Mahatma.

GBS

To FRANCIS COLLISON

[A/4]

Springburn. Strachur
20th August 1903

[Francis Collison (1850–1912) was the proprietor of a stationery and newspaper shop in Colchester, to whom Shaw had made a loan a year or two earlier. In gratitude, Collison, who raised canaries as a hobby, had decided to send one to Shaw. He had also offered to obtain a kitten for Shaw, presumably from Mrs Ricketts of Bishops Stortford.]

Now I ask you, Mr Collison, as a sensible man, what the devil you suppose I want with a canary. I am a vegetarian, and cant eat it; and it is not big enough to eat me. But you are not a sensible man: you are a "fancier"; and you believe that the height of earthly happiness is to be surrounded with pigeons & Persian cats & guinea pigs & rabbits, with a tub full of toads & newts under the counter. I once had a canary, a little green brute that flew in through the open window one day & would not go away. I hated it and it hated me. I bought it a cage—a thing I abhor—& gave it everything I could find at the seedsman's; but it was utterly miserable & did its best to make me miserable until some benevolent person stole it. I have been happy ever since until this day, when I have received from Woking the devastating news that you have inflicted another canary on me. Now if you had sent me a seagull or a nightjar (the nightjar is my favorite bird) I could have let it loose & watched it flying & stalked it with a camera—the only sort of sport I can endure—; but this unhappy little wretch would be killed if it flew about, and will do nothing but titivate itself in its absurd cage (I have telegraphed to the gardener's wife to buy the largest cage in Woking for it) and make a confounded noise which will frighten all the thrushes & blackbirds away. And now, having taken advantage of my being away on my holiday to introduce this ornithological pest into my household, you want to send me a kitten as well. Why, man, the kitten will kill the canary when it grows up. Have you no common sense?

349

Prince Sam indeed! Damn Prince Sam! I am a republican, and care nothing for your Princes. Do you suppose I want a noisome little beast to cover my house with its excrements, and bring all the cats in Woking to celebrate its debaucheries with nocturnal yowlings? You speak of it as "her"; so I conclude it is a female, which means that I shall have sixteen mongrels added to the menagerie every two months. Mrs Ricketts of Bishops Stortford ought to be ashamed of herself. What did I ever do to her or to you that you should heap these injuries on me? Did my books ever do you any harm? did they disturb you with silly whistlings at your work, or bring forth litters of little books that you had to drown? In your letter of the 5th, you said you would forward the animals "when convenient to me and mine." I said to myself, "Thank God: he will wait until I ask him for the accursed things; and in the meantime he will be happy nursing the detestable kitten & trying to teach the bird tunes." But in the excess & exuberance of your destructive benevolence you were not content to wait. You sent the bird; and for all I know, the wretched kitten may now be on its way. My only hope is in the gardener's wife. She has one canary already; and perhaps, if I make her a present of the cage, she will consent to take the other if I offer her five shillings a week for the term of its natural life. I shall then hear it only when I walk in the garden; and at every trill I shall curse the name of F. Collison.

G. Bernard Shaw

To WILLIAM ARCHER

Springburn. Strachur

[A/2]
27th August 1903

[Archer's *Morning Leader* article on 22nd August, "Mr. Shaw and Mr. Pinero," was a discussion on the "New Movement" in drama, growing out of the preface to *Man and Superman.* Audrey Lesden is a character in Henry Arthur Jones's *Michael and His Lost Angel* (1896). *Iris* was a Pinero play, produced in 1901. For "Max's excellent picture," see Shaw's letter to Max Beerbohm of 17th December 1901. Shaw had noticed *Trelawny of the "Wells"* (1898), *The Benefit of the Doubt* (1895), and the revival of *The Hobbyhorse,* all plays by Pinero, in his *Saturday Review* articles.

James Albery (1838–89) was the author of *The Two Roses* (1870) and *The Pink Dominos* (1877). Henry B. Farnie (d. 1889) was the author and/or adaptor of comic operas, including *The Mascotte* (1881) and *Les Cloches de*

Corneville (1879). Robert Reece (1838–91) wrote burlesques and comic operas, as well as domestic dramas. Cecil Raleigh (1856–1914) was best known for his Drury Lane melodramas. Henry Pettitt (1848–93) was a popular dramatist who collaborated with G.R.Sims and George Conquest. Sir James M.Barrie (1860–1937), Scottish novelist and playwright, had been writing for the theatre since 1893. He had had two dramatic successes in 1902: *Quality Street* and *The Admirable Crichton*, and his new play *Little Mary* was due to open at Wyndham's Theatre on 24th September. Robert Louis Stevenson's *Prince Otto: A Romance* was published in 1885.]

Saul, Saul: why persecutest thou me? What do you mean by this conduct in the Morning Leader? I warned you that I was going to make such a blinding brain display as has not occurred in the British drama since Shakespear's advent—and to make it for your sake, too, to give you a decent asset to put in the window of that shop which you are so heroically trying to save from its manifest intellectual bankruptcy—and yet you go and lose your head—your buffle head—because your poor nurslings cannot live up to me, and thoughtlessly force A.W.P's neat little perambulator right across my motor car when I am going 80 miles an hour. Nobody would have thought of his venerable Paula anymore than of Audrey Lesden (Jones doesnt really deserve this; but I sacrifice him to propitiate you) or the New Magdalene or the Lady of the Camellias or Iris or any other version of the old formula: I tell you that these things cease to exist on the plane to which I lift my readers.

Just think of your dates a little. You started dramatic-critic in 1876, before Pinero & Jones were born (playwrightfully) & when Grundy was complaining of a "ring." I began in 1895, when P.J. & G were absolute masters of the commercial situation. Well, we did them handsome: you, having nursed Pinero as a son & Jones as a stepson, continued the treatment; and I backed you, except that I gave J a turn as son & P. as stepson—and even that was due to the outrageous way you were spoiling him by—but see Max's excellent picture of the situation. I was unkind about Mrs Ebbsmith pulling the Holy Bible out of the stove & Alexander sitting on the drawingroom table with a paper foolscap on his head; but what would you have had me say? did I not damn myself almost by my praises of Trelawny & the Benefit of the Doubt & the revived Hobbyhorse? Did I not retire in time to save myself from absolutely killing & burying the author of Iris, who would never have done it if you had not lured him to his doom by your flatteries? But the point is that what you call the New Movement—meaning the substitution of Pinero for Robertson, Grundy for Albery, Farnie & Reece, Jones for Boucicault, & Cecil Raleigh for Pettitt, with Charles

351

Reade & Wilkie Collins still awaiting their successor in Barrie—was no more a New Movement in 1895 than the Robertson movement was new in 1889, though Clement Scott still thought it so. It did not need any bottle feeding then; and your refusal to wean it—due probably to a strain of Esquimaux blood in you—was becoming an open scandal.

In any case, what had I to do with "New Movements"? My business is to fight for the Grand School—the people who are building up the intellectual consciousness of the race. My men are Wagner, Ibsen, Tolstoy, Schopenhauer, Nietzsche, who have, as you know, nobody to fight for them, especially since you have, with pathetic self-abnegation (I am really serious) constituted yourself commercial traveller to our West End Theatre because your overgrown nursling cries for Praise, Praise, Praise. I have also to keep my good words for such neglected things as Barker's Ann Leete, by far the finest bit of literature since Stephenson's Prince Otto, and of a much more original quality of excellence too. To imply, as you do, that the dreadful leading-article clichés which serve for "literary" dialogue in Iris is the work of a master & a leader, whilst Ann Leete is not worth noticing, is to commit a crime for which you ought to be condemned to sit out a Pinero Festival. Can you not let the man sit safely on his little throne with his well filled treasury, and turn the limelight on his good deeds and not on his follies, instead of forcing him into a position which he knows he cannot hold or defend? He is a sensitive man: you can hear the nerve quiver in his plays at times if you listen; and you are just torturing him by dragging him into *my* arena.

I find this country quite native to me: my descent from Macduff was at once admitted by the cook, who belongs to the elder branch herself.

In haste.
yrs ever
G.B.S.

To WILLIAM DANA ORCUTT

[X/177]

[Springburn. Strachur]
28th August 1903

[William Dana Orcutt (1870–1953), a book designer and author, at this time associated with the University Press, Cambridge, Mass., had been requested to prepare an American copyright edition of *Man and Superman*. Shaw, who had been introduced to Orcutt in London a month or two earlier by Cobden-Sanderson of the Doves Press, sent a copy of the edition set and printed by

Clark's of Edinburgh, with instructions that Orcutt was to duplicate the volume "line for line." This, said Orcutt in *Celebrities Off Parade* (1935), "gave his American printer no opportunity to produce a page in keeping with his own typographical judgment. To complicate matters . . . the letters in American-cut type faces differ in width from those cut abroad. These physical limitations could not possibly be overcome without disregarding the author's implicit instructions, so I simply accepted the situation and did the best I could."]

I send you by book post "Man and Superman" with the necessary corrections. I have made no attempt to deal with the apostrophes you introduced in "don't," "you've," etc., etc. But my own usage was carefully considered; and the inconsistencies were only apparent. For instance, Ive, youve, lets, thats are quite unmistakeable; but Ill, hell, shell, for I'll, he'll, she'll, are impossible without a phonetic alphabet to distinguish between long and short e. In such cases I retained the apostrophe: in all others I discarded it.

Now you may ask me why I discarded it. Solely because it spoils the printing. If you print a Bible, you can make a handsome job of it, because there are no apostrophes and inverted commas to break up the letterpress with holes and dots. Until you force people to have some consideration for a book as something to look at as well as something to read, you will never get rid of these senseless disfigurements that have destroyed all the old sense of beauty in printing.

Whilst I am on this subject, let me beg you not to be offended if I tell you that whilst I am astonished at the way in which you have followed my proof sheets line by line, and grateful for the promptitude with which you have put the work through, the book, as you have produced it, is a perfectly shocking piece of printing—almost as bad as the work of the Roycroft Shop, which is the worst in the world. Dont be angry; just turn to p. 130. Look at the last ten lines. I have marked the blemishes. The enormous quads at the end of each sentence are bad enough; but when it comes to allowing two of these gaps to occur at the same point in two successive lines, it amounts to a misdemeanor. Now your compositor has actually put four of these gaps in a straight line down the page. Four! He ought to be boiled!

If you look at one of the books printed by William Morris, the greatest printer of the xix century, and one of the greatest printers of all the centuries, you will see that he occasionally puts in a little leaf ornament, like this 🌿🌿🌿, or something of the kind. Your Roycroft idiots, not understanding this, pepper such things all over their "art" books,

353

and generally manage to stick an extra large quad before each to show how little they understand about the business. Morris does not do this in his own books; he rewrites the sentence so as to make it justify without bringing a gap underneath another in the line above. But in printing other people's books, which he had no right to alter, he sometimes found it impossible to avoid this. Then, sooner than spoil the rich, even color of his block of letterpress by a big, white hole, he filled it up with a leaf.

Now that is 99% of the secret of good printing. Dont have patches of white or trickling rivers of it trailing down the page like raindrops on a window. At the top of p. 131, I have marked these rivers. Are they not horrible? *White* is the enemy of the printer. *Black*, rich, fat, even, black, without grey patches, are, or should be, his pride. Leads and quads and displays of different kinds of type should be reserved for insurance prospectuses and advertisements of lost dogs.

If your type were a genuine Caslon, like that of my Scotch printer, you might have followed him line for line without doing any worse than he has done. But your fount has narrower letters: eleven of them occupy the same space as ten of the Caslon; so that you have had to put 10% more white into every line than the Scotch printer; and that 10% is fatal. You should have saved 30 pages out of the Glasgow printer's 244. Of course he has not been able to live up to William Morris (in fact he thinks me stark mad); but then he had the great disadvantage of having to suffer all the damage to his original setting made by my corrections.

Now for the minor points. Your margins are very far from being those of the Mazarin Bible. Your top margin is a full inch—*much* too wide (perhaps your man made the mistake of measuring it from the running title up instead of from the top line of the text)—and the lower only $1\frac{1}{4}''$. The difference is only enough to make them look equal. Try $\frac{1}{2}''$ for the top margin, ignoring the title and pagination and measuring from the top line of the text, and the top and bottom margins will come about right. The inner margins are monstrous—$\frac{3}{4}''$ each, making a Broadway of $1\frac{1}{2}''$ down the middle of the book, so that it looks like two tombstones side by side. The rule here is simple: the book, when open, should look as if there were no division at all

 instead of

The best looking margin would be from $\frac{1}{4}''$ to $\frac{3}{8}''$—total Broadway $\frac{1}{2}''$ to $\frac{3}{4}''$.

On the title page you have only used two different founts of type.

For that I bless you, as most printers would have used at least sixteen. But why two when one would have been so much better? I send you my Glasgow title page, and invite you to note that there are no rivers in it (there is a Mississippi and a Missouri in yours), and that the measure of the publishers imprint has been contracted to avoid a big quad after the colon. See how nice and fat and black and solid it looks!

I am only too painfully aware that when all is done that can be done, a play, with its broken lines of dialogue, its mixture of roman and italic, and its spaced out words for emphasis, can never enable a printer to do full justice to himself. But something can be done. You can hardly imagine how atrocious you could make that play look by simply leading the page and putting large initial capitals to the names of the speakers. We can at least make the best of a bad job.

Tell the compositor that in spacing out letters for emphasizing the word, German fashion, he must be careful to make the space at the beginning and end of the word still wider than the spaces between the letters. It means more white, unhappily; but it cannot be helped.

That, I think, is all. Do not dismiss it as not being "business": I assure you I have a book [the Kelmscott Chaucer] which Morris gave me—a single copy—by selling which I could cover the whole cost of setting up the "Superman"; and its value is due *solely* to its having been manufactured in the way I advocate: there's absolutely no other secret about it; and there is no reason why you should not make yourself famous through all the ages by turning out editions of standard works on these lines whilst the Roycroft people are exhausting themselves in dirty felt end papers, sham Kelmscott capitals, leaf ornaments in quad sauce, and then wondering why nobody in Europe will pay twopence for a Roycroft book, whilst Kelmscott books and the Doves Press books of Morris's friends Walker and Cobden Sanderson fetch fancy prices before the ink is thoroughly dry.

By the way, the Roycroft people may have learnt a little since I last saw their work. They once reprinted something of mine, with literary improvements by Mr. Elbert Hubbard. He sent me a copy; and I have seldom written a more candid letter than the one in which I acknowledged it. It ought to have taught him something; but I fear he is incorrigible.

After this, I shall have to get you to print all my future books, so please have this treatise printed in letters of gold and preserved for future reference.

[yours sincerely
G. Bernard Shaw]

355

To WILLIAM ARCHER

[A/2; X/108.e]

[Springburn.] Strachur
2nd September 1903

[Archer's reply to Shaw's letter of 27th August ran to nine pages of pencilled scrawl, ending "I never got off such a sermon in my life before." He noted that "ever since I read that Nietzschean motor-car, I have had vials of remonstrance simmering within me which the possession of your address causes to boil over. . . . [I]n no way are you making the mark either upon literature or upon life, that you have it in you to make. The years are slipping away . . . and you have done nothing really big, nothing original, solid, first-rate, enduring. If you were to die tomorrow, what would happen? In the history of literature you would find a three-line mention,—like that we now give to Peacock or Beddoes—as an eccentric writer, hard to classify, whose writings a few people still remember with pleasure. I think it highly probable that for thirty years or so Shaw Societies would spring up from time to time, especially in Boston—and I can't imagine a more doleful way of going to oblivion. In political history you would be still more briefly dismissed as perhaps the most brilliant & futile of the brilliant and futile group of Fabians. If you are content with this, good & well; but I am not content for you. You are a great force wasted . . .

"You say 'your men are Wagner, Ibsen, Tolstoy, Schopenhauer, Nietzsche,'—I should reverse it & say you are *their* man. Why should this be? Why should you always be flying somebody else's banner and shouting somebody else's war-cry, with only the addition of your own Irish accent? . . . [Y]our great intellectual foible is credulity. The moment someone comes along with a nostrum, you seize upon it as the last word of human wisdom. Here is Nietzsche with his Superman, for instance—a brilliant piece of philosophic mythology, giving definiteness and tangibility, so to speak, to a more or less unformed ideal that has been hovering in the air ever since 'The Origin of Species' was published—but, after all, only a piece of transitory jargon, the catchword of a decade or a half-century, which will 'have its day & cease to be' very likely in our own time. Well, you seize upon this concept, & you rethink your whole mental system in the light of it, and produce your 'Revolutionist's Handbook' and aphorisms—a glittering jumble of untested, unweeded, unharmonized thought, devoid of perspective or proportion, the old humanitarianism cropping out every here & there through the new Nietzscheism, a good deal that is really profound in it, a great deal that is hasty & superficial, and not a little that is merely personal, crotchetty, Shawesque—in short, a philosophical treatise composed in a hopelessly unphilosophical spirit—and treating, I repeat, a new nostrum, a new piece of jargon, as though it were the 'Open Sesame' of all light & truth. . . .

"I dont mean to say that I despair of you as a dramatist; but I am bound

356

to confess that 'Man & Superman' rather dashes my hopes. I think, with all your extraordinary talent, you want a measure of mental discipline before you can produce a real work of art, which it is rather late to think of your attaining. I don't despair, but I am not sanguine" (BM).

Alfred Harmsworth (1865–1922), Viscount Northcliffe, was a newspaper proprietor and journalist. Peter Simon, Marquis de Laplace (1749–1827), was a French astronomer and mathematician. It was not the famous physicist, Dr Thomas Young (1773–1829), who described Mrs Siddons, but the actor Charles M. Young (1777–1856) in an interview by Thomas Campbell, reported in the D.N.B. Claude Lorrain (1600–82) was a French landscape painter and engraver, whose studio was in Rome.]

The weather here is gradually producing a sense of awe. Two fine days since the 1st August! . . .

Your Chronicle review [of *Man and Superman*, under the title "Mr. Shaw's Pom Pom," on 24th August] roused the greatest indignation here. Charlotte declared you a gross impostor—a man absolutely without perception of greatness. I argued feebly for your intellectual competence for the whole afternoon; but the weight of evidence against me in the Chronicle was overwhelming. Fortunately your letter has to some extent rehabilitated you. Charlotte, I regret to say, has no sense of humor: indeed she thought your toleration of the heliograph joke a most unreasonable encouragement to my vulgarest weakness; and she also objects to what you happily call my waving the banner with an Irish accent. To that extent therefore she is willing to concede your possession of a limited critical faculty.

As for me, I find you more modest than ever on my account. I feel as Harmsworth or Pierpont Morgan might feel if you wrote to exhort them to turn over a new leaf and make a little money. All that you ask for is there, not only in Man & Superman, but in my early immature scrawlings. You are asking me to begin, not seeing that I began years ago far ahead of where you expect me to leave off. Your review, apparently colossally stupid, is really blind and careless. Let me give you a single simple example. In the fougue of your theme, which is that the book is a mere rechauffée of stale Shavianized Nietzsche &c, you say that the cycle theory is Nietzschean. Now you knew Thomas Tyler. Nobody could ever have enjoyed that privilege without having it burned into his brain that Shakespear was a cyclist. Laplace and Carlyle between them rubbed the physical theory of cycles as hard as possible into us before Nietzsche was ever heard of. It is news to me that Nietzsche ever alluded to the subject—I must really read some of his stuff. The cycle theory has been one of the staples of Pessimism ever

357

since Pessimism existed. It was inevitable that my Devil should trot it out. But as far as I know, nobody before Don Juan has ever given the simple answer that the perpetual motion may be effected by a pendulum mechanism—that the notion that a clock does not go because the bob of the pendulum does not seem to get any forrader is the notion of a blackbeetle on the wall and not of a man setting his watch by Big Ben. No doubt that answer has been given; but it has been forgotten; and to describe its statement as being a mere repetition of Tyler's despairing difficulty is a most outrageous piece of carelessness. Read the book again. Read it fifty times over. If it leaves you exactly where Nietzsche & Darwin & Ibsen & Wagner & Tolstoy have left you, then I have nothing more to say, except that you have never really troubled yourself about philosophical questions and dont really believe that it matters whether Thackeray's view of life is right or Bunyan's. In that case, my work can never have any reality for you because it must appear to you passionless and therefore fundamentally undramatic. The first act of the Superman, for instance, will be to you, not a tragedy, but simply a sell, and that not in the best taste.

The odd thing about it all is that you, with this apparent amblyopia for every passion except divorce & police passion, should yet be so susceptible to philosophic poetry that you get quite upset by it. If your review were the placid utterance of a color blind man criticizing Titian —or, to take an actual case, of the famous physicist Young describing Mrs Siddons's Volumnia—there would be nothing more to say. But it is an outburst of recalcitrance, the splutterings of a protesting, incommoded, deeply stirred victim. It is the same with Ibsen. You translate Ibsen; you cry over Ibsen; you have forced Ibsen on the English stage; but when it comes to criticize or produce him you declare that he is mad, disgraceful, deplorable; and you cut his plays to pieces for representation. Compare your treatment of When We Dead Awaken to Walkley's. You first protest with all your might against such a scandal as the performance must be in any case; and then you half apologize for the play, half denounce it as an infamy. Walkley walks up to it with his boulevardier air, duly chaffs it in his manner, but finally says "Do not misunderstand me, ladies & gentlemen" and takes off his hat to genius as he retires. Whereas you kick the thing, shewing that in some way it has hurt you.

You really are a very curious character. You admit the superiority of my talent and wit. You are quite wrong. Incredible as it sometimes seems, you have just as much talent and wit as I have. You have all the tools of the trade; but you have no conscience. There are a great many men who sin against the light because they cant do without wine & cigars & a thousand a year or ten thousand. They go to hell because the train has first class carriages, whereas the train for heaven has third class ones. There are other men so fond of money that they take the hell train because the ticket costs twopence less than the other. But you are perfectly content with plain living, and care so little for money that any publisher can get the better of you in a bargain; and yet you dont think the train to heaven worth taking. There is an absolute gratuitousness about your perversity that is inexplicable unless one sees you as a sort of child in fairyland who has never learnt to live in the world and who resents the intrusion of moral problems as angrily as it joyfully welcomes the advent of the poetic glamor. Blugginess you dont object to at all—quite the contrary. Fun is quite acceptable. But conscience avaunt! you turn pettish at the first taste of it. If Tom had not a mother as well as a father he would never to the end of his days walk out of Piona.

Now that you have exhausted all that talent & wit can do for you, you are falling back on the excuse of incapacity. But you are capable enough; and your bolt is not shot yet, though mine is. To all your heartsearching questions I answer without a moments hesitation or affectation Yes. I am astonished at what I have done with so little means. I am as willing to hang up my *théâtre* beside Shakespear's— leaving everything that has been written for the stage in the interim out of account as completely negligible—as Turner was to hang his landscapes beside Claude's; and I attach no importance whatever to that or any other comparison. But you have done nothing that bears the same relation to your talent as my output does to mine. In your letter to me, you say the absolute truth about Pinero; but when you write about him for the public, and *for himself* (which is the main thing) you will lie like a Trojan about him & lure him down to further Iris abysses with a horrible childish ignorance of the fact—which can be learned only in public life, not divined by wit & talent—that flattery will ruin a man more surely & swiftly than any extremity of abuse. Walkley has done Jones no harm. I have encouraged Jones; but if you read my notice of Michael, you will see that I dealt faithfully with him. You have almost destroyed A.W.P: another Iris and, with Barrie already far outrunning him, he is lost. And all this to keep up a pretence, which imposes on nobody, that William Morris was an ignorant & foolish person who was incapable of appreciating the greatness of the British Theatre. If you want to be an advocate, put on your wig & go into the courts; but while you are a critic, be a critic.

The sun is shining. I have not half finished, but must go & bathe before lunch. More anon—on sufficient provocation.

GBS

To HARLEY GRANVILLE BARKER

[A/3; X/168]

[Springburn.] Strachur
2nd September 1903

[Clotilde Graves (1863–1932) was a popular novelist, under the pseudonym of Richard Dehan, and playwright. George S. Titheradge had toured with Henry Miller's company in *The Devil's Disciple* in America early in 1903. Barker had performed Marlowe's *Edward II* at the New Theatre, Oxford, in August. *Candida* was presented by Barker for six matinées at the Royal Court Theatre commencing 26th April 1904.]

Dear Barker

Kate Rorke's equivalent in the new generation* would certainly hit off Candida very well; but whether Kate herself would take kindly to it is another matter. I have never found a single case in which the heros & heroines of the eighties were of any use to us. The comedic geniuses, yes: the leading ladies & gentlemen, no. The more winningly natural they were in their own line, the more appallingly artificial & sub-consciously recalcitrant they are in ours. Candida is not half such a chance for Kate as Lady Cicely was for Ellen Terry; and yet you see that Ellen dared even Ibsen (the Bedford Park Ibsen) sooner, and, if that had not been forced on her by Ted [Gordon Craig], would have produced a play by Clo Graves.

As to Eugene, he cant be acted: it is a question of being the creature or at least having him in you; so that the casting of Eugene is either an insuperable difficulty or, as in your case, no difficulty at all as long as you keep your figure. But Eugene cannot save the play, though he can damn it unless the others can create the necessary environment. Burgess must be thoroughly & richly amusing (Lionel Brough at least) & Prossy must be thoroughly snappy and lively, as well as the Morells being very sympathetic. Tith could manage Morell (though I shouldnt have sup-posed it if I hadnt seen him in Beyond Human Power) but not with anything to spare.

---

* Whoever she may be; but Madge McIntosh is much more in our line. Have you thought of her?

360

Why dont you propose the play to Mrs Pat? She once asked for it; but at that time my promise to let Janet have the first bite in London was unfulfilled; and I had to excuse myself. At the same time, Mrs Pat would not be a bit Candida; but she would help you with her prestige; and her cleverness would carry her very far in it. Mrs Kendal & Kendal would be ideal if only they were of our generation; but, as in Kate's case, they would rebel against it in their hearts; and Mrs Kendal would make points to help the lame dog over the stile.

I dont want to sit on the play in the least: it is ancient history for me now. But I dont think your position would be improved unless it were an unequivocal success, because, as I have already said, not only can Eugene not save the play himself, but the part would become harsh, ridiculous, and even violently unpopular if it were wrongly supported. It is useless to be impatient, especially with your present prosperous engagement.

What did you make of Trebitsch?

I have read—or rather re-read—Edward II. Had I done so two months ago I should have advised you strongly not to wipe out Richard II by playing it. There is nothing in it—no possibility of success; and the infernal tradition that Marlowe was a great dramatic poet instead of a XVI century Henley throws all the blame of his wretched half-achievement on the actor. Marlowe had words & a turn for their music, but nothing to say—a barren amateur with a great air.

G.B.S.

To WILLIAM ARCHER

Springburn. Strachur
[L/2]   7th September 1903

[Archer's *Die Zeit* article, published as a feuilleton on 2nd September, was titled "Das moderne Drama in England." Sir Gerald du Maurier (1873–1934), actor-manager son of George du Maurier, had appeared in Tree's production of his father's novel *Trilby* (1895) and in Harris's *Mr and Mrs Daventry* (1900). Ellis Jeffreys (1873–1943) had begun her career in Gilbert and Sullivan operas at the Savoy Theatre. She had performed for several years with Charles Wyndham, and had appeared in Pinero's *The Notorious Mrs Ebbsmith* (1895) and in Louis N. Parker's *The Vagabond King* (1897). J. Farren Soutar (1871–1962) was a young actor who had played a number of romantic and comedy juvenile parts in London and New York. Re *You*

Never Can Tell, see I, 759. Rose Leclercq (1845–99) was a superb character actress, much admired by Shaw, who had appeared in 1895 in Wilde's *The Importance of Being Earnest* and in 1896 in the Forbes-Robertson revival at the Lyceum Theatre of Sheridan's *The School for Scandal*.]

(Dictated) (From Shaw—handwriting Mrs S's)

William Archer

I have just been reading an article of yours in Die Zeit which proves beyond all question my contention that you are not a nincompoop but a perfectly disinterested liar. I can only hope that neither Pinero nor Jones are familiar with the German language; for the callous brutality with which you tell the truth in German when the mere monotony of telling lies in English becomes unbearable, would lead to a straining of personal relations which would end in Pinero inviting me to dinner & Jones taking Walkley to his breast.

However, what I want you to do is to complete the picture by shewing the effects of the situation on the actors. One of the noteworthy points about my own situation is that though I get performed by the Stage Society only, I have no difficulty in getting casts quite as good as & in some respects better than Jones & Pinero can get at the regular theatres. Even in the early days, up to & including Brassbound, when there were overwhelming extraneous difficulties of one kind & another, I never had to face such hopeless misfits as the casting of Gerald Du Maurier for the old actor in Trelawney, or Ellis Jeffreys for the second woman in Mrs Ebbsmith, or the various misfortunes which make Jones declare that casting a play has become impossible, even apart from the obligation to give the actor manager the leading part. As to Mrs Warren & Bashville, I could not have got even an approach to my Stage Society casts at any regular theatre. One reason for this you have mentioned in passing: it applies to Farren Soutar as Bashville. I found that he was quite capable of first rate work; & of course the result is that he is mopped up by musical comedy. But the main point that wants bringing out is that the player with a specific acting talent has been driven off the stage by the walking toff. Although what you say in the article about my plays being kept off the stage because they are not toffish is roughly true, yet this does not apply to "You Never Can Tell," which was deliberately manufactured to admit of enough Saturday to Monday millinery & champagne to pass muster. What really shipwrecked the Haymarket production of that play was just the state of things you have described in your article. When the question of casting the play came up for settlement, the management was bent on having Allen

362

Aynesworth. I at once said that it was quite impossible; that Aynesworth was an amusing farce actor & had done very well in "The Prisoner of Zenda" & still better in "The Importance of being Ernest," but that the end of the second act of "You Never Can Tell," the failure of which must inevitably mean the failure of the whole play, was utterly beyond any power that he had ever shewn. Cyril Maude pleaded that he had never had a chance; that I ought not to refuse to let him shew what he could do; that he had never failed; & finally (& this was of course the whole secret of it) that he was a very nice fellow; that he had rooms in Bond Street; & that he was, in short, a Paffick Genlmn. Of course the onus of naming an alternative was thrown on me. I could only name, as men whom I would accept, Drew, Fred Kerr, Bourchier, or Yorke Stephens. It so happened that the first three were not available; & I was flatly met by the objection that Yorke Stephens was not a gentleman! The end of it was that I had to give Aynesworth his chance; & the result was precisely & exactly what I had predicted. He broke down at the end of the second act; & I got them all out of a very painful difficulty by withdrawing the play & promising to support any version that might be most convenient of its being dropped; for I saw that if the real reason reached the public Aynesworth would be undeservedly damaged, just as Granville Barker was the other day by Jones taking the part in "The Princess's Nose" away from him. I say undeservedly because Aynesworth rehearsed all the scenes that were in his line extremely well, & it was entirely my fault & Maude's folly that he was wrecked on a scene that was out of his line. Consequently my play was shelved; I got a reputation for impossibility at rehearsals which lasted until the Stage Society enabled me to live it down; & finally the play was performed by the Stage Society with Yorke Stephens in the part.

The next serious proposal from a West End theatre was Alexander's for Brassbound. I had to tell Alexander that if he produced the play he would have to play Brassbound; that it was just the kind of part that any secondrate young leading man in provincial melodrama could play just as well as he, if not better; that it was wholly the woman's play & not Brassbound's; that his leading lady was no use for Lady Cicely; & that, in short, I could not honestly advise him to produce the play.

Next comes Forbes Robertson. I had let him take the Devil's Disciple into the provinces at a time when he was so desperately hard up that there was clearly nothing better for him to do. He wanted to produce it in London on two occasions: first, at the Comedy, & second after "Mice & Men" & before "Othello." I refused on both occasions, solely because we could not cast the play. Of course he was very angry: they are always angry when you save them from obvious & certain ruin; but you will see by what I have put up with & made the best of in the way of scratch performances & appalling scenery in the Independent Theatre & the beginnings of the Stage Society that I am not an Impossibilist in these matters.

Now if you put all these things together; if you reflect on the fact that until "Mr & Mrs Daventry" & "Mrs Warren's Profession" were produced Fred Kerr & Fanny Brough had never got a chance of doing anything but comic relief; that Yorke Stephens & Kate Philips & others with a genuine modicum of temperament & skill languished for years without engagements whilst parts that they could have played with perfect dexterity were being amateured through by people who were simply more eligible acquaintances for socially ambitious managers; that Kate Terry could not get the succession to Rose Leclercq though she bid for it at the psychological moment; that Hermann Vezin couldnt get anything at all, then you will see that the case you have made out as to the effect of the fashionable play on dramatic authorship holds good also as to its effect on actorship; & that just as I have had to fall back on the Stage Society along with Barker & Brieux & all the rest of the author geniuses so it has come to be recognized in the Profession that the serious actor's only chance lies on the same distinguished boards.

Thus the expression used by your German translator "Halb-amateur theater" to describe the Stage Society is just the wrong word; for the half-amateurs are at the West End theatres walking through the smart plays, whilst the skilled temperamental professionals are playing for the Stage Society, ostensibly for honor & glory alone, but in some cases, I am greatly afraid, because the two guineas "expenses" are not a matter of indifference to them.

I suggest the working out of this to you because there is some truth in the current complaint that the critics care nothing about acting, & that you in particular, whilst you are never tired of watering that hardy annual the fashionable drama (upon which, in Austrian papers, you lavish a gallon of weed killer) the unfortunate actor never gets more notice from you than the few crumbs which a particularly importunate dog might coax from a man who disliked animals.

There is one other aspect of the case to be worked out; & that is the reaction of the actor's incapacity on the dramatist. It is perfectly possible, up to a certain point, to produce an illusion of acting from marionettes, & this is what the modern author has to do. I went a little into this in my notice of "The Benefit of the Doubt," where I shewed how Pinero, having ventured to keep a popular leading man & leading lady continuously in evidence on the stage for nearly half an hour, instead of cleverly bustling them about for five minutes & getting them off before the audience had found them out, practically wrecked his piece, & confirmed himself in his scepticism as to the wisdom of allowing the actor any initiative whatever.

It seems to me that if you were to add two articles on these lines to the one in Die Zeit the three would make an excellent view of the English stage during the toffification period which culminated in the knighting of Irving; & it would only be fair to shew that though dramatic literature & the art of acting were practically left out of account in this period, & although the actor in striving to make himself a gentleman has only succeeded in making himself eligible for stock-brokers' dinner parties, yet it is an open question whether the general clearing out of the old Bohemian dirt & drunkenness & slatternliness may not be worth the temporary artistic sacrifice.

I have now spent the whole morning writing to you, or rather making my wife write to you; & I decline to go on.

GBS

To WILLIAM ARCHER

[A/2]

Springburn. Strachur
8th September 1903

[Thomas Lovell Beddoes (1803–49) was a minor playwright and poet, author of *The Bride's Tragedy* (1822). Edward Bulwer Lytton (1803–73) was a popular novelist, also known for his plays *The Lady of Lyons* (1838) and *Richelieu* (1839). James Sheridan Knowles (1784–1862) was an actor and playwright, whose plays included *The Hunchback* (1832) and *The Love Chase* (1837). Sir Sidney Lee (1859–1926) was the author of the *Life of William Shakespeare* (1898).]

All right: I am quite satisfied: Archer still lives. I do not even ruefully ask why I should be pilloried in the Leader as the traitor who bit the hand of my unquestioned leader as he brought me up out of the land of Egypt. But I wish Pinero could see my private protests that I always flattered him and yours that you always exposed him.

The connexion between Pessimism & the cycles is obvious. If the theory is true, we are only squirrels in a revolving cage; and our frantic efforts to keep the thing going are purposeless. That's Shakespear. But perhaps it turns something. That's Shaw. What the deuce does it matter? That's Archer—the unconscionable.

You villain, you cut Ibsen to ribbons for the stage—first, Pillars; and then the first act of The Wild Duck. I didn't mean the books. The old man's brain is about as soft as a Brazil nut: the only effect of age is to make him utterly reckless in his stonethrowing.

As to whether the biographical dictionaries will give me a paragraph with Beddoes or ten pages with Shakespear I care not one single damn. Whatever drives me to sweat Superman & the like for the benefit of the world is certainly not driving at my personal posthumous fame. I have no doubt that a course of serious Bashville would raise me to a pinnacle higher than Lytton, Knowles or even Calmour. But the matter isnt really in my hands. I have to say the things that seem to me to want saying; and if you consider that one thing is as well worth saying as another, and that the thing is to say it (whichever it is) in such a way as to have my life written in the XXIII century by the S.L.Lee of that age, you dont understand my internal mechanism in the least. I look on at the Superman just as helplessly as you do: I could not have produced anything else. But I have great hopes that my fate may set a very beneficial example to the rising literary generation. I am, as you perfectly well know, by no means such a stupendously clever person as I seem just at present. If I lived as Pinero lives & ate what he eats, I greatly doubt whether I should ever have written a play at all. My twelve years of stump oratory, my six years of lighting & paving & dust collecting, my twenty years of Fabian agitation, on top of a childish grounding in Mozart, Beethoven, Verdi, Meyerbeer, Donizetti, Gounod &c &c &c: all that is within the reach of everybody; and when others, convinced by my example, follow it, do you really suppose I shall be anybody in particular? Not a bit of it: everybody's shop window will blaze as tawdrily as mine by the time I am 80.

G.B.S.

To OTTO KYLLMANN

[Springburn.] Strachur
9th September 1903

[A/3]

[Copyright deposit of Man and Superman in the United States was made on 12th August 1903. The book was not actually issued by Brentano until 1st

June 1904. G.K.Chesterton's review appeared in the *Daily News* on 22nd August under the heading "Man v. The Superman." It is unlikely that Kyllmann would have quoted the passage that begins: "Shaw has betrayed and embodied at last his one mistake. He has always prided himself on seeing things and men as they are. He has never really done so: as one might have guessed by his not admiring them. . . . Mr. Shaw, in the tone of this play, falls in some degree at least into the great weakness of his master, Nietzsche, which was the strange notion that the greater and stronger a man was, the more he would scorn common men." The notice in the *British Weekly*, "Superman and the New Man," on 3rd September, described Shaw as "that most modern and unfettered of thinkers."]

Dear Kyllmann

The copyright of Man & Superman in the U.S. is now secured; & no importation of sheets can affect it in any way. But the book has been set up & printed & (technically) published in America; and the electros are lying there, duly insured, at my disposal; so that on coming to an arrangement with an American publisher, I can at once order an edition to be printed on the spot. The legal position, as I understand it, is that English copies are now contraband in the United States; and even if imported with the consent of the holder of the copyright (myself) would be subject to the protective tariff, which would presumably be heavy enough to make it cheaper to manufacture in America.

My own intention, now that I have made myself master of the situation at a cost of about £70 cash, is simply to wait and let America wait. I gave the American publishers—at least a representative few of them—their chance; and they wasted my time, put me out of temper, compelled me to spend a lot of money rather than be cornered or else delay publication here, and finally landed me in perfect security as regards copyright, and in a thoroughly mulish and vindictive humor as regards publishing. Mahomet having gone to the mountain in vain, the mountain may now come to Mahomet. My bargain will depend, of course, on the success of the book here. I am in no hurry; and if anybody wants to handle it on the royalty system, he will have to begin by buying my electros from me at a satisfactory profit. Of course, having the electros, I am open to a proposal to publish on commission; but on the whole I am disposed to wait. The book will lose nothing by keeping.

Do you see all the reviews of the book? I see you quoted Chesterton in one of the advertisements; but there was a review in the British Weekly that could be quoted far more effectively in the religious papers. I will give my mind to the whole business of advertising one of these

367

days—when the rain has stopped long enough to allow me another holiday in addition to the three fine days we have had since I arrived here on the 1st August.

yrs faithfully
G. Bernard Shaw

To JOHN BURNS

[H/2; X/141]

Springburn. Strachur
11th September 1903

[This letter was dictated to Charlotte Shaw in a boat on Loch Fyne, but her pen, Shaw informed Burns, "was so joggled by the waves that I had to get it fair-copied for you by a professional typist..." A copy of this letter was sent to Sidney Webb. William Thomson (1824–1907), 1st Baron Kelvin, was an Irish-born mathematician and physicist, who was Professor at Glasgow University 1846–99. Jesse Collings (1831–1920) was a land reform leader and M.P. (1880–1908), who had taken part in Joseph Chamberlain's municipal reform efforts. Shaw had discussed Chamberlain's proposals in an essay "The Fiscal Policy of the Empire" in the *Daily Mail* on 3rd July 1903.]

Dear Burns

I'm glad you like the Superman: it has relieved me of a great deal that has been on my chest for a long time. However, it is not really pessimistic: quite the contrary. All that it says is that we shall not get any further until we get rid of property and of promiscuous breeding in that hopeless little rabbit-hutch the British home. Just consider for a moment what it is that we have found out. Not merely that the British workman is anti-catastrophic—that is rather to his credit than otherwise—but that he is anti-Socialistic; and that's rather serious, because it's as true as ever it was that nothing but Socialism can secure his industrial interests. For some reason or other Socialism doesn't interest him. It is not that the subject is a difficult one: for the matter of that, the science of backing horses is one that might tax the brain of Lord Kelvin himself (if Lord Kelvin has any brains, which I sometimes doubt); and yet the [worker] learns how to make a book and to play games at cards which are far beyond my powers of understanding. I therefore conclude that the side of the subject upon which Marx depended—that is, the demonstration that out of every pound the worker makes, 10/- is pinched by some noble sportsman or other—doesnt interest the working man. The truth is, very few people care enough about money to take any trouble to get it. This is proved by the fact that the few people who are really mad on it get such a tremendous lot without any particular ability. Dickens pointed out long ago [in *Our Mutual Friend*] that the whole secret of Fascination Fledgeby's wealth was not that he had any brains in particular, but that he never did anything else but make money, never thought about anything else, and never cared about anything else. Take your own case and mine for example. The newspaper proprietors made surplus value out of me just as the engineering firms made surplus value out of you. Well, honest Injun! did you ever care a damn? did you grudge it to the poor devils? I certainly didnt; and I'm quite certain you didnt. And yet we two went about trying to convert the workers to Socialism by appealing to this very grievance that we ourselves set no *effective* store by. I have since seen you achieve success after success by appealing to the workers pride of citizenship and pride of manhood. Very well then: I am a teachable man; and I take my money off surplus value and put it on pride of manhood. I am going to see whether I cannot sink those two rotten old ships Property and Promiscuity with pedigree dynamite. That may succeed or it may not succeed; but the attempt is not pessimism: there is more life left in the old dog than that gentlemanly fatuity.

Now as to the politics of the moment. I have done six years Borough Councilling; and I am convinced that the Borough Councils must be abolished. But the County Council is not what it was. The real Progressivism—*our* Progressivism—might have held its own against the constant tendency to relapse into Gladstonism but for the South African war and the Education Bill. The wave of feeling produced by these has sloshed us back into the position of 1885. This is an intolerable state of things. The Gladstonian rump is climbing on to your platform as if you were simply a good liberal who had sown your wild oats. On the other hand the Tory democrats are trying to drag me on to their platform because, like a Mohammedan, I would as soon give money to a Church school as to a Nonconformist one, and because, being a Socialist, I am a Protectionist right down to my boots, not to mention the fact that the knocking over of a Krugerite theocracy by a Milnerite plutocracy leaves me as cool as the extinction of the stage coach by the locomotive. Now I need hardly say that I have no more intention of becoming the successor of Jesse Collings than you have of becoming the successor of [Thomas] Burt or [Henry] Broadhurst. We

369

have both got the same job immediately before us: that is, to strike out a line for the advanced guard that is clearly neither Manchester resurrection-pie on the one hand nor Protectionist resurrection-pie on the other.

As I am so near Glasgow here, I am going to make a speech on the fiscal question on my way back. My main line is quite simple. First, to knock Free Trade into a cocked hat; to shew that the economic history of the 19th Century shews us Trade Unionism, or working class economics, coming out right all along the line, and Free Trade, or Capitalist economics, coming out wrong. I shall contend that the labor movement is both actually and rightly a Protectionist movement, and that in Birmingham, if a Free Trade candidate is put up against Chamberlain, every working man ought to vote against him and for Chamberlain, although if a labor Candidate is put up against Chamberlain every workman ought to vote for the labor Candidate and against Chamberlain. In the event of the candidate announcing himself as both a labor and a Free Trade Candidate, he should be rejected on the simple ground that he is a muddlehead who doesnt understand the situation.

So much for firstly: now for secondly. It does not at all follow from our being Protectionists that we are bound to approve of every particular import duty or to put a duty on every import which is now free. Take a case. The English manufacturer of electrical machinery cannot compete with the American or the German-Swiss manufacturer. He asks (I am taking an actual St Pancras case) thirteen thousand pounds for a converter which he obviously doesnt know how to make, and which a German Company, which obviously does know how to make it, offers to supply for eight thousand pounds. Let us suppose that in the next Parliament Chamberlain therefore proposes a protective duty of $62\frac{1}{2}\%$ on converters. What should the attitude of the Labor member be? It seems to me simple enough. If I were a Labor member I should say "Mr Speaker: everything depends on what the right honorable gentleman is going to do with the duty when he gets it—if he ever does get it. For let me point out that if the effect of the duty is to exclude the German machines, the right honorable gentleman wont get it: it will be paid by the British householder in his electric lighting bill, and will go into the pockets of the British landlord, the British capitalist, the British employer, and the British working man. As the British working man is my constituent, and is more interested in the electric light as a producer than as a consumer, I need not object to this, although I had rather see the British working man making a steam engine the right way under capable direction, than making a converter the wrong way under incapable direction. But as a matter of fact I believe that what will happen will be that even when you have put up the price of a converter to a figure that will cover the extra cost of the incapacity of our ignorant manufacturers, we shall still buy the German-Swiss machine because it will be the better article anyhow. In that case the right honorable gentleman will get the duty; and now, as I said before, I want to know what he is going to do with it before I give him my vote; for everything depends on that. If he is going to apply it to reduce the income tax, which is the only constitutional means by which the class I represent can at present get a bit of its own back, then I will see the right honorable gentleman most strenuously damned before I will vote for his proposition. If, on the other hand, he proposes to apply that duty to such a development of technical education as will finally give us an engineering trade that can turn out converters as cheaply and efficiently as the German firms, thereby saving the cost of carriage from Germany and the humiliation of standing confessed before the whole world as inferior engineers, then I will vote for the proposition. I am only too well aware that the right honorable gentleman can go no further than his plutocratic and aristocratic supporters will allow him, and that no matter what pledges he may give the labor members, the money will probably be seized by the party which has a majority in Parliament. That, however, is not the right honorable gentleman's fault: it is the fault of the working classes of this country, who have not self-respect enough to stretch out their hands and take what is easily within their grasp: namely, parliamentary representation in proportion to their stake in the country."

If you were the Labor member in question, you would have no difficulty in clothing this skeleton line of argument with all the necessary wealth of illustration and oratory. Unless all my political instinct is at fault, it would be an extremely popular line. The Liberals have [so] rubbed it into the political shepherds of labor that Free Trade is necessarily the true Progressive doctrine, that the workers think that they are bound to raise the old cry; but, as Jimmy Macdonald shrewdly says, the majority of them are instinctively on the side of Chamberlain, which really means that they are on the side of Carlyle and Ruskin, who never bowed the knee to Manchester. But how can they trust Chamberlain? What they want is a man whom they *can* trust, whom they can follow without feeling tarred by the Jingo-Tory brush, or mucked with the Manchester shop sweepings. If there is anybody answering to that description in Battersea, give him the tip with my

371

compliments, and remember me to his wife; but dont tell him that I have still got all the red ribbons she used to pin on my coat in Hyde Park.

yours ever
G. Bernard Shaw

PS I have not enlarged on the Food of the People cry, as the counter to that is obvious—a demand for an Imperial Minimum Wage. Webb has worked out the facts and economics of that in his Industrial Democracy; so that nobody need be at a loss for platform ammunition in working up the question.

To MAX BEERBOHM

[Springburn.] Strachur

[A/1]   15th September 1903

[Beerbohm's article, "Mr. Shaw's New Dialogues," in the *Saturday Review* on 12th September was a review of *Man and Superman*, in which Max stated that Shaw "cannot create living human characters," but added, "This is his masterpiece, so far. Treasure it as the most complete expression of the most distinct personality in current literature." Marie Bashkirtsev (1860–84) was a Russian painter and diarist, whose *Journal* (published in English, 1890), a remarkable document, was the subject of much interest and discussion. For Pater on style, see his *Appreciations: With an Essay on Style* (1889). Shaw's reference to Beerbohm's "Jewish genius" elicited the reply on 21st September: "I am *not* a Jew. My name was originally Beerboom. The family can be traced back through the centuries in Holland. Nor is there, so far as one can tell, any Hebraism on the distaff side. Do I *look* like a Jew? (The question is purely rhetorical.)" (BM)]

My dear Max

This wont do. Your article in the Saturday is most laborious, most conscientious: the spasms of compliment almost draw tears; but the whole thing is wrong: the *gene* of offended academicism makes it almost unreadable.

Suppose you published a collection of drawings which had to be criticized not only by "the press" in the usual sense, but by the drawing masters of England. You would find every one of them complaining that your figures, though clever, were unnatural, untrue, unlifelike. You would perhaps retort by saying contemptuously: "Of course I know perfectly well that R. L. Stevenson was not an animated candle,

372

and that William Archer is not twice & a half as tall as Pinero." But you would soon recognize that this was not what the drawingmasters meant. Again, they would point to your caricatures of yourself, and shew that beneath all your pretences of caricaturing other people the same treatment, the same trick of the hand, the same fantastic line, the same untruth to nature could be detected: in short, that all your King Edwards & Roseberys & Bernard Shaws & so on were merely thinly disguised Maxes, & that when they ceased to be so they ceased to be entertaining. And you would again exclaim impatiently: "Of course I have my style, like Velasquez or Rembrandt; and my pictures are all Maxes just as Turner's Dovers & Nottinghams & Venices & Schaff-hausens are all Turners." But you would soon find that they knew all about that too, and that this was not the real confusion in their minds. And you would at last find that what they missed in your work was not life nor truth nor any other vital quality, but "the antique," and that your works, considered in terms of this overwhelming defect, were all reduced to a common level of failure. This too, in all honesty, their belief being that every man strips to the Hermes, Laocoon or Farnese Hercules, & every woman to the Venus of Milo.

Just so have you become convinced, as all the "dramatic critics" do sooner or later (for no man can long resist either absinthe or environment), that the fantoccini of romance are real, & the tax collector & the district visitor either mere human utensils or comic relief—that Rosalind the pantomime "leading boy" is a real woman, & Isabella of Measure for Measure a failure. Years ago Stead said eloquently of Marie Bashkirtseff "A woman she was NOT." You laughed; but you are now explaining my creations away in the same fashion. In vain do I give you a whole gallery of perfectly miraculous life studies. Not even your Jewish genius enables you to recognize my two types of English-women. They are reduced, for you, to the same barren Shavian formula by the fact that they are not Italian prima donnas. The chauffeur, the Irishman & his American son are positively labelled for you as Hogarthian life studies—in vain: they are not "the antique," and so your nerves refuse to conduct them to your brain. Most astonishing of all, you have before you in Bashville the Gay & Superman the Serious two terrific displays of literary bravura—the by-product of quarter of a century of struggling for the mastery of words on top of a born capacity for them—and yet you make the usual gull's apology—you, Max, a gull on such a point!—for complimenting me on my art. You idiot, do you suppose I dont know my own powers? I tell you in this book as plainly as the thing can be told, that the reason Bunyan reached

373

such a pitch of mastery in literary art (and knew it) whilst poor Pater could never get beyond a nerveless amateur affectation which had not even the common workaday quality of vulgar journalism (and, alas! didnt know it, though he died of his own futility), was that it was life or death with the tinker to make people understand his message and see his vision, whilst Pater had neither message nor vision & only wanted to cultivate style, with the result that of the two attempts I have made to read him the first broke down at the tenth sentence & the second at the first. Pater took a genteel walk up Parnassus: Bunyan fled from the wrath to come: that explains the difference in their pace & in the length they covered.

And now, what is to be done with you? The answer is indicated by the one piece of sense in your article. You have yourself a certain command of the living word: you can make a page talk (when it's not about me); and you have found by experience that this leads to the platform, and can be developed by it so as to give a man twenty forms and appositions of phrase for every one possessed by the mere book & pen man. But your evil angel has led you to the one platform where your academicism gets confirmed & indurated—the Playgoers Club. Ten minutes on the Drainage Sub Committee of the St Pancras Borough Council, which has taken many an afternoon on days when the Superman took the morning, would shatter that academicism for ever.

As to your views of Woman, lovely Woman, you were false to them when you omitted to say a good word for Octavius. You say some women pursue men—meaning those of whom Stead says "Woman she was NOT." The truth is very simple. Walk down Piccadilly, and ask yourself at every woman that passes you, could I bear to have her as my mistress? You will be astonished at your own virtue: 99.99999999999999999 per cent of them will leave you cold—perhaps 100%. It is just so with Miss Ann Whitefield. Her behaviour with regard to 99% of the men she meets will exactly confirm your Octavian conceptions of a womanly woman and a Paffick Lidy. But what if the 1% come along? Imogen refused Iachimo & Joseph Potiphar's wife; but what if the Life Force had short-circuited them?

There will be a Borough Council election in November. *Verb. sap.* Quit the theatre & *draw* for a living. Shake the Playgoers' dust off your shoes. Abjure Academicism. Urgent. Important. Forward immediately.

yrs ever
G.B.S.

374

To SIEGFRIED TREBITSCH

10 Adelphi Terrace W C
[H/5; X/176]   7th October 1903

[Shaw had lectured in Glasgow to the local Fabians on 2nd October on "Is Free Trade Dead or Alive?" and on 4th October to the local I.L.P. on "Socialist Unity." Shaw's book *The Commonsense of Municipal Trading* was published in February 1904. Helene Odilon (1865–1939) was a popular Viennese actress; there is no evidence that she ever appeared in a Shaw play.]

Dear Trebitsch

Here I am back in London, with a mountain of dull correspondence to deal with. I shall have time for only a line or two.

My exploits as a mob orator in Glasgow were highly successful; and I have hardly yet quite recovered from the self-loathing which such triumphs produce. I am an incorrigible mountebank; but I always suffer torments of remorse when the degrading exhibition is over. However, the thing had to be done; and there was no use doing it by halves. I was in good training, and delivered two harangues of ninety minutes each, besides a roaring quarter hour oration at another meeting, where I was invited to the platform and yelled for by the intelligent Scotch proletariat. I am not at all ashamed of what I said: it was excellent sense; but the way I said it—ugh! All that prodigious expenditure of nervous energy—that assumption of stupendous earnestness—merely to drive a little common sense into a crowd, like nails into a very tough board—leaves one empty, exhausted, disgusted.

And now the worst of it is that I shall have to set to work to write a Fabian Manifesto on the subject instead of setting to at a new play— or rather at the abominable book on Municipal Trading that I have to finish first. That is the secret of the greatness of my dramatic master-pieces: I have to work like a dog at the most sordid things between every hundred lines.

My rage about the Cæsarian cuts did not hurt me much. I always get into a rage very carefully and conscientiously when it is necessary, because it saves a lot of time and makes people realize my opinion vividly and promptly; but my indignation, as you probably guess, is purely histrionic—mere mountebanking! I knew you would not find C&C cuttable. I cut everything out of it that could be spared before I published it—including, by the way, a lovely scene in which Cæsar received four ambassadors in succession and humbugged them all.

The Superman play, with a big cut in the scene between Ann and

375

Tanner in the first act, and the omission of the dream, would make an amusing comedy: perhaps I may try it at the Stage Society. But it would suffer greatly in German, because the Irishman and his American son would be much stranger and less interesting than in England.

If ever you try your hand on Brassbound, let me know before you begin, as the part of the cockney is absolutely unintelligible to anyone who has not lived twenty years in London and included several coster-mongers among his personal friends. I will have it copied out for you in normal spelling. I think you are wrong in dismissing it as an impracticable play. In some ways it is unique. Take your Austrian actress Odilon, for example. She is getting too old to stand the competition of pretty young women side by side with her on the stage. But in Brassbound she has a great part, and no other woman in the play, the want of bright costumes (usually supplied by the women's dresses) being supplied in Brassbound by the costumes of the Arabs. It is a tremendously effective part for a comedy actress of the first order, though no use at all for a second rater. Therefore, though until you find your Odilon the play is worthless, yet when you do find her it is the only one of my plays that she is likely to want—and to want very badly. Widowers' Houses, ugly as it is, is a very effective stage play, especially for Berlin audiences, who are trained not to mind a little squalor. The part of Lickcheese is one of the best for a character actor in my whole repertory: it made the reputation of James Welch here in London even at a desperately shabby performance in 1892. The Philanderer I cannot answer for, as it has never been played; but I suspect it would make money if properly handled. It is the little plays that pay for the great ones in actual theatrical business.

I am somewhat perplexed as to what I should do in view of the long arrears of my works that you propose to translate. How old are you? everything turns on that. You may easily be led into a frightful waste of your life on another man's work; and my conscience is not quite at peace on the subject. Can you not arrange to set aside only a part of your time to translate?

I have thought of Cromwell, and may perhaps do him someday. But my next play is to be an Irish one [*John Bull's Other Island*, but known at this early date as *Rule, Britannia*], not, I am afraid, of much use for Germany.

I must break off now, and go back to Free Trade, and preferential duties and exports and Chamberlain &c &c &c &c.

GBS

376

PS Are you sure that your eyes are not partly the cause of your neuralgia? Have you had them carefully tested for astigmatism? I have very slight astigmatism of my right eye; but slight as it is it has probably a great deal to do with my occasional headaches.

To BEATRICE WEBB

10 Adelphi Terrace W C
[A/14; X/217.e]   8th October 1903

[Shaw was at work on the draft of a tract (No. 116), subsequently issued on 31st March 1904 as *Fabianism and the Fiscal Question: An Alternative Policy*, which would successfully harmonize the divergent opinions of Fabian members, especially those of S. G. Hobson and Robert Dell.]

Dear Beatrice

Just a word of contrition—on your account solely—for having worried Sidney last night; but it was an inevitable preliminary to an understanding. It is always the same: first he works out a subject & convinces me; and then I have to convince him and to bear the brunt of the surprise & indignation with which he receives his own conclusions. It comes of a difference in our ways of working: he is kind to his old intellectual habits and does not like to have them disturbed: I switch off the old current & switch on the new with treacherous & disconcerting suddenness. Besides, I systematically persuade him that I am going to monstrous extremes in order that he may accept my real views with relief as a concession.

Still, we shall have to work on this subject a little; and what I propose to do is to set down a string of simple economic & political propositions and submit them to you for criticism. I do not think we can intervene in a sudden crisis of this kind without risking a mistake or two which a couple of years investigation might avert; but we can at all events make our position as sure as we can; and then take our chance, as all great commanders do. I shall rely on you to some extent to anæsthetize Sidney whilst I eradicate Mill. There is an old stump of him left in the gum which is always getting in the way. My propositions will include those of Industrial Democracy; and I fully expect that these will be received with the most furious recalcitrance; but they will prevail in the end.

GBS

377

To H. J. TOZER

10 Adelphi Terrace W C
11th December 1903

[Henry John Tozer was a member of the council of the Passmore Edwards Settlement. When Graham Wallas, in June 1903, had considered running for the London County Council from South St Pancras, Shaw had minimized his chances, and Wallas, in 1904, offered his candidacy from another district and won a seat. "I do not think I should have the ghost of a chance myself as a carpet bagger," Shaw told Wallas on 22nd June, though his five years' work on the Vestry and the Borough Council "have given me a certain hold. . . . You may consider me as out of the running for the moment . . ." (British Library of Political and Economic Science). By December, however, he had begun to have serious thoughts about contesting the Council seat.

Frank W. Galton (1867–1952), who was private secretary to the Webbs in the 1890's, later succeeded Edward Pease as Secretary of the Fabian Society (1920–39). C. Silvester Horne (1865–1914), a nonconformist minister, became Liberal M.P. for Ipswich in 1910. Joseph R. Diggle (1849–1917) was chairman of the London School Board 1885–94.

The Fabians had been proposing educational reforms since May 1899, when they passed a series of resolutions on the question. The introduction in Parliament of an Education Bill in March 1902 led to the preparation by Webb, with revisions by Shaw, of two new tracts, Nos. 114 and 117, on the Education Bill. The London Education Act, as passed in 1903, contained eleven of the thirteen amendments proposed by the Fabians. Shaw's views on education, especially his Fabian argument that "since half the children in the country were in Church schools their education must not be sacrificed to sectarian bigotry, and that the real way to obtain popular control of the Church schools was to subsidize them and make conditions of efficiency" (Shaw to Julius Bab, 5th September 1910, Hanley, Texas), won him the support of the clergy but the enmity of such publications as *Reynolds's Newspaper* and *The Echo*.]

Dear Mr Tozer

If you can do no better, I am willing to contest the seat. I said as much to Mr Graham Wallas; and I thought you would have learnt it —as perhaps you have—from Mr Galton.

I have always fought tooth and nail for the tramway, which is now, I suppose, a settled question, the opposition of the Borough Council being at an end. But if by any chance the old situation should come about again, I should strongly oppose the County Council policy of using the Hampstead Road improvement to force the hand of the

Borough Council; and I should insist that we should have the improvement at once, tramway or no tramway. It was on this point that I differed from our sitting member. All this is ancient history; but I mention it as it may possibly have given rise to a vague notion that I was unsound on the tramway question.

As to the Education Act, I take the official Progressive position. The Act establishes a state of things enormously better than the *status quo ante*; and if any candidate were to run in South St Pancras with an avowed policy of postponing or preventing its adoption by the Council, or urging its repeal by the next Liberal Government, I should oppose that candidate with all my might, and even vote Moderate to defeat him. Years ago, when Mr Diggle and Mr Athelstane Riley were supreme on the London Schoolboard, and were absolute ciphers on the Technical Education Board, I advocated the abolition of the ad hoc body and the substitution of the County Council Committee; and I have never regretted it. Long before the present Act was ever thought of, I urged that since more than half the children in the country were in voluntary schools and could not be got out of them, these voluntary schools should be fully financed by the State, and brought under its control. When this was done, the Church naturally made the best bargain it could. I am not bound by that bargain; and I shall do everything I can to alter its terms so as to complete the control by the Education authority, and secure the same recognition for the Free Churches as factors in religious education as the Establishment now enjoys. But I shall do what I can to discourage Passive Resistance; and as to the contention that each citizen's contribution to the common fund must not be spent except on his own personal requirements, I cannot, as a public man, give countenance to such a repudiation of all citizenship. I pay for the licensing authorities though I am a teetotaller; I pay for the inspection of slaughter houses and for the maintenance of the Deptford Victualling Yard though I am a vegetarian; and I pay for the education of State Church children and Free Church children, though I belong to neither myself, as conscientiously as I pay taxes which are used to punish people for selling the Bible in Khartoum, and for punishing blasphemy against Brahma and Vishnu in India. I am sorry to differ from my friend and fellow Fabian Dr Clifford on this point; but I think the Progressive party on the Council is right and Dr Clifford wrong; and I shall give effect to that conviction if I am returned.

I may add that I am not a believer in the possibility of what is called Secular Education. You must either give children religious reasons for

379

behaving themselves or else use the brute force of the cane. I object to the cane. And as to modern science and ethics, I know too much about them to imagine that they are any less superstitious than the creeds of the sects.

I learn from Mr Graham Wallas (who has just called on me) that it is still possible that he may contest Hoxton instead of South St Pancras. However, he will no doubt explain his position to you directly.

My views on the general policy of the Council may be gathered from the fact that I am a Socialist of the Fabian variety, and was a member of the Fabian Society when it drew up the Progressive program. A book of mine on Municipal Trading, strongly defending it, will be in the hands of the public before the election. I am neither a Liberal nor a Conservative, and object just as strongly to the Gladstone tradition as to the Salisbury position. And my opinions are so well known to the press and the public through my writings that there is not the least chance of passing me off at the polls as a politician of the conventional party type.

I think you now know the worst. Your committee will have to consider how far you will be able, if you select me, to get your action endorsed by Mr Sylvester Horne and the more passionate passive resisters in the constituency.

yours faithfully
G. Bernard Shaw

To H. J. TOZER

[A/4]

10 Adelphi Terrace W C
21st December 1903

Dear Mr Tozer

I think on the whole it was wise not to come to a decision on Friday. The more candidates you can give the body to choose from, the better.

It ought to be frankly admitted at once that if the Passive Resisters disapprove of your selection so much as to feel conscientiously obliged to run a third pair of candidates against you, or to split the vote in any way, they can secure your defeat; and they would be tactically justified in doing this if they felt that they would as soon have the Moderate candidates as a pair of Progressives who did not represent their views. The responsibility really rests with them finally. I have put my pro-Education Bill views very strongly so that they may not be misled by my reputation for being against everything; but as I should vote for Holmes, if he could run, without bothering about his logic, so no doubt he would vote for a good man who stopped short of passive resistance and repeal. A reasonable arrangement ought to be possible; and if it can be facilitated by setting me aside, do so by all means.

As to Belgian rails, I am an enthusiastic Protectionist in principle, and object very strongly to the cheapest market when the cheapness is founded on labor conditions which we cannot control. It is manifestly idiotic to pass an elaborate Factory Code & fair wages clause, and then allow exempt manufacturers to tender in competition with subject home manufacturers. At the same time it is impossible to make a rule, as English prices sometimes mean sheer incompetence. On the Borough Council I voted for buying our electrical converters from competent German-Swiss firms for £8,000 apiece instead of from English novices who asked £13,000. But in principle I am thoroughly hostile to Free Imports. I should keep out a whole mass of manufactures that we can produce just as well for ourselves; but the question of food is an Imperial one which will not concern the Council.

What will the Liberals think of *this*?!!!

yours faithfully
G. Bernard Shaw

To JOHNSTON FORBES-ROBERTSON

[H/1; X/167]

10 Adelphi Terrace W C
21st and 22nd December 1903

["Lights that Succeed" refers to Forbes-Robertson's production of *The Light That Failed*, adapted by George Fleming from Kipling's novel, at the Lyric Theatre on 7th February 1903, which had been one of the actor's greatest successes. George Walker (*c*.1872–1911) and Bert Williams (1876?–1922) were a Negro vaudeville team, then touring in a musical play *In Dahomey*, with music by Will Marion Cook and lyrics by Paul Laurence Dunbar, which had opened at the Shaftesbury Theatre on 16th May 1903. Williams later became a star of the *Ziegfeld Follies*.

Peter Christopher Daly (1875–1927), who assumed the stage name of Arnold Daly, was a young actor who had worked as a messenger in Charles Frohman's office, as a dresser for John Drew, and as call boy at the old Lyceum Theatre in New York. He had played minor parts for several years, with brief success in an adaptation of Mark Twain's *Pudd'nhead Wilson* in New York in 1895 (his first appearance on the New York stage), and momentary attention as a crazed lover in Clyde Fitch's *Barbara Frietchie* (1899–1900)

381

starring Julia Marlowe. In 1903, after appearing in eight consecutive failures, Daly conceived the idea of becoming his own manager and stage director, and in partnership with a friend Winchell Smith, on a bankroll of $1350, he produced a special matinée of *Candida* at the Princess Theatre, New York, on 8th December 1903. Shaw agreed to the production in consideration of 10% on the gross, "no contract or reservation of rights—only permission to give half a dozen performances" (Shaw to Elisabeth Marbury, 16th November 1903, Hanley, Texas).]

My dear Forbes Robertson

Your letter from Cincinnati finds me in a state of extreme prostration. I incautiously witnessed Tree's Richard II the night before last; and the spectacle of our friend sitting on the ground telling sad stories of the death of kings, not to mention his subsequent appearance in Westminster Hall in the character of Doré's Christ leaving the Praetorium, has been almost too much for us.

As to Caesar, it is to be produced with great splendor at the Neues Theater in Berlin in February, an event from which we may get some hints as to the Sphinx, which I have always conceived as something faked up with a clothes horse and a mangle. There is a Shaw boom on in Germany, because four of my plays have been produced in Vienna, Leipzig, Dresden and Frankfurt; and they have all failed so violently, and been hounded from the stage with such furious execrations, that the advanced critics proclaim me the choice and master spirit of the age; and no manager respects himself until he has lost at least 200 marks by me. My plays have become as Louis Parker's: they simply cannot be kept off the stage. The managers make me large advances on account of royalties: they think nothing of twelve-pound-ten apiece for myself and the translator; and they never get it back, as two nights is the record run so far. Happily everyone here thinks these productions have been immense successes; and for your sake and Caesar's I have said nothing to the contrary.

But Caesar will cost a lot of money to dress, though the cast will not cost much with the two title parts in the family. There are six scenes and a Sphinx, even without the third act, which must, I fear, be cut clean out without benefit of clergy, for want of time. You could not play the first act alone except at the Stage Society or a charitable matinee: the literary scandal would be too great. Besides, it is in the other acts that Caesar is built up: in the first he might as well be Haroun al Raschid. You would not be taken with full seriousness in it. My last book has turned the tables on the people who will not admit that I am serious: they used to laugh when I was serious; but now the fashion has changed: they take off their hats when I joke, which is still more trying.

But my position has become odder than ever; for I have been knocked out of time in a curious way by Barrie. His "Little Mary," which is a vegetarian pamphlet—a didactic lark compared to which my most wayward exploits are conventional, stagey, & old fashioned—is having as great a success as Crichton, to the intense astonishment of John Hare, who visibly wonders, as he brings the house down with line after line, what the devil they can see in such incomprehensible stuff; and Barrie is now first and the rest nowhere as a popular playwright. In fact, I have given the drama such a powerful impulse that it has jumped clean over my own head. When you went away I had not yet arrived: when you come back you will find me obsolete; and if you play me at all, it must be as a classic, and not as a modern. I have actually taken to going to the theatre to see Barrie's plays; and I not only stand them without discomfort, but enjoy them.

Have you ever thought of Richard III as a possible successor to your Hamlet? Nobody now alive has seen what can be done with Richard. The provinces have by this time forgotten Barry Sullivan; and Irving's Richard does not count. A really brilliant Nietzschean Richard would be fresh and delightful. I believe I could fill it with the most captivating business for you, and practically get rid of the old fashioned fight at the end. No actor has ever done the curious recovery by Richard of his old gaiety of heart in the excitement of the battle. It whirls him up out of his vulgar ambition to be a king (which makes the middle acts rather tedious after the fantastic superhumanity of the first) and he is again the ecstatic prince of mischief of the "Shine out, fair sun, till I have bought a glass" phase which makes the first act so rapturous. All Nietzsche is in the lines

> Conscience is but a word that cowards use,
> Devised at first to keep the strong in awe.
> Our strong arms be our conscience, swords our law!

And after all the pious twaddle of Richmond, his charging order is delicious

> Upon them! To 't pell mell,
> If not to heaven, then hand in hand to hell.

The offer of his kingdom for a horse is part of the same thing: any means of keeping up the ecstasy of the fight is worth a dozen kingdoms. In the last scene he should have a bucket of rose pink thrown in his face, and then reel on; all cut to pieces, killed already six times over, with a broken sword and his armour all in splinters, wrenching off the battered crown which is torturing his poor split head. Being hunted down just then by the Reverend Pecksniff Richmond & his choir, he is just able, after an impulse to hold on to the crown tooth & nail, to pitch it gaily to him & die like a gentleman. That would be real Shakespear too; for William's villains are all my eye: neither Iago, Edmund, Richard nor Macbeth have any real malice in them. When William did a really malicious creature, like Don John, he couldnt take any real interest in him. Now you would be a charming Richard; and though the production might or might not be a financial success in London, it would be a good investment, as it would last your life in the provinces as a repertory play. Mrs Robertson could play Edward V: she is not silly enough for Lady Ann. By all means keep up your banking account with Lights that Succeed; but build up the big repertory all the same: it provides for old age, and is the only means of becoming the undisputed head of the profession.

Caesar, of course, will be in the big repertory of the future; and you ought to create him. But you dont half believe in him; and the public might not believe in him at all. I never could get you quite up to the scratch with Richard IV [Dick Dudgeon]: you did the part; but you never did the play. Caesar would have a better chance with you because it is not only a much bigger part, but Mrs Robertson could make a hit with Cleopatra, whereas she would have had to get her brains extracted and her face soft-boiled to play the poor pitiful creature Judith. Further the D's D. requires three or four stars (Anderson and Burgoyne are more difficult to cast than Dick), whereas in Caesar the minor parts are within the scope of ordinary talent. [Still,] Caesar is not a cheap venture. Even the Neues Theater has found it necessary to spend £1000 on the production (equal to, say, £6000 in London); and I have a certain cautious stinginess in me which makes me shrink from gambling with the bread of your infants. You could do Richard III for the same money; and Richard could not fail utterly, whereas the Lord only knows what might or might not happen with Caesar. I think you had better sample it at the Stage Society before committing yourself or me any further. I should give it without remorse to a better Caesar, either in England or America, if I could find one; but where is he? The only American star who would have the cheek to touch it is Mansfield; and he refused it long ago; whereupon I said "Adieu, Pompey," and disowned him.

By far the best acting now in London is that of Walker and Williams

384

in "In Dahomey." I shall certainly ask Williams to play Ftatateeta. . . .
I see that one Arnold Daly is playing Candida in New York. If he plays anywhere within your reach, ask Mrs Robertson to go and see it and tell me what it's like. There is a sort of snivelling success possible for Candida if the right cast could be got for it.

You can read this latter as a serial, in instalments. I am so tired of writing about the Fiscal Question that I cannot help spreading myself on a genial human theme.

> yours ever
> G. Bernard Shaw

To CHARLES CHARRINGTON

Maybury Knoll. Woking
[A/4]   26th December 1903

[Thomas Corneille (1625–1709), younger brother of the celebrated Pierre Corneille, made a verse adaptation (1677) of Molière's *Le Festin de Pierre*.]

I forgot all about Candida; so your qualms were wasted. After all, if you hadnt emptied the treasury in Leeds & Bradford, you would have gone on and done it somewhere else. Ibsen must by this time owe you a good deal more than you owe him. Away with melancholy therefore, and rejoice—if you are in Naples—in the Italian sunshine.

None of the Candida enthusiasts like the Superman. It nevertheless had to be written. You are quite right about Tanner being married & settled before the play begins; but you will find that in the play itself —"the trap was laid from the beginning." As to Goethe, he really anticipated me in the final earthly scene where Mephistopheles falls in love with a male angel and lets his bargain slip through his fingers in consequence. Faust keeps doing things: Meph. keeps shewing him what a sentimental dreamer he is to bother about them instead of enjoying himself. As to your prescription of real artistic conscience & self control, the supply is already large, and the results available in the British and foreign drama of today. How would you like it if I took your advice? I foresee "The Dramatic Works of Bernard Shaw, bowdlerized by the Rev. Charles Charrington." By the way there actually is a version of Molières Festin de Pierre (the Don Juan play) invested with artistic conscience & self control by Corneille, not the great Corneille, but the other one. It is most edifying. When Don Juan is swallowed up by the flames, Sganarelle does not exclaim "My wages! my wages! Here is everybody satisfied—injured fathers, seduced virgins, outraged husbands, law defied, and God offended—except ME —my wages! my wages!" No sir: he points the moral, with great self control, exactly in the manner of an archbishop. But I prefer the original; and so do you—ass that you are to come Pecksniffing at me in this fashion. No wonder you felt a sort of gêne when you met me. I wonder you could look me in the face with such a sermon in your soul. And you explained it all to yourself on the ground that I have sold out and married for money, you old ruffian, you. That's the real gêne nowadays. And the aggravating thing about it is that I, who used to sling money about in golden showers, am now bankrupt, overdrawn at the bank, forced to spend twice my income on the crumbling shops of Carlow & other things. Well, I will let you all see that the scoundrel over forty will be just as amusing as the saint under forty.

I have a sort of dream recollection that you told me that Janet is in Naples; but that *must* be a delusion. Why the devil should she be in Naples? Or is it an elopement? Have you preached artistic conscience and self-control to *her*? If so, she is justified. Farewell, as far as letters are concerned, until next Xmas: I have not had time to write a really private & personal letter for months & months.

yrs ever

G. Bernard Shaw

PART II

1904-1905

II

(1904-5)

Shaw had written a dozen plays by 1904, most of which had achieved production somewhere—in America, in Germany, in the English and Scottish provinces, in the private theatre societies. Virtually none of them, however, had received a public professional performance in London. To the average theatregoer Shaw was still an unknown quantity as a dramatic author. Clearly, one of England's greatest needs was a theatre for the Theater of Ideas. Providentially, this was soon supplied—but it came about, as such things often do, quite by chance.

Harley Granville Barker had, in 1903, conceived the idea of presenting "a stock season of the uncommercial drama" at the intimate Royal Court Theatre in Sloane Square (far from the madding West End crowd), but the twenty-five-year-old actor was unable to obtain the financing for his idealistic venture. Later in the same year, when a wealthy amateur actor, J. H. Leigh, purchased the lease of the Royal Court to mount a series of "Shakespeare Representations" in which he and his wife, Thyrza Norman, would appear, William Archer recommended Barker as a director. The latter, seeing an excellent opportunity, agreed to stage *The Two Gentlemen of Verona* for Leigh on the condition that he be permitted to produce, on his own, six matinées of *Candida*, in which he would appear as the poet Eugene Marchbanks. Leigh not only gave his approval for the presentation of Shaw's play on 26th April 1904, but generously offered the services of his manager, John Eugene Vedrenne (1867–1930).

Flushed by the instant success of the *Candida* experiment, Barker entered into an agreement with Vedrenne to offer a series of matinées on days which did not conflict with commercial matinées in London theatres, to commence in October. They opened their season with the *Hippolytus* of Euripides, in Gilbert Murray's translation, followed on 1st November by Shaw's new play *John Bull's Other Island*, and on 26th November by additional performances of *Candida*. On 1st May 1905 *John Bull* usurped the evening bill, and Vedrenne–Barker took over the theatre.

"No theatrical enterprise of this century," as C. B. Purdom noted in his biography of Barker, "has left a deeper mark upon the theatrical history of London . . ." It had a pervasive influence out of all proportion to its brief existence, serving as the impetus for the campaign to establish a National Theatre in Britain. The Vedrenne–Barker experiment altered the public's attitude toward theatre, creating a new audience; it encouraged a new generation of dramatists to write serious plays; it inspired actors to abandon the old-style histrionics which had served them for generations in the commercial theatre and to experiment in new directions. Barker, admittedly, was the presiding genius, but Shaw's contribution was equally great. Although the management offered the public the work of such young men as John Galsworthy, St John Hankin, Laurence Housman, John Masefield, and Barker himself, and although it popularised Greek drama and brought to London the plays of Schnitzler, Hauptmann, Maeterlinck, and Ibsen, it was Shaw who dominated the Royal Court stage. Eleven of his plays were presented, for a total of 701 of the 988 performances recorded by Desmond MacCarthy in a history of the Royal Court enterprise.

Shaw and Barker worked extraordinarily well together, considering the disparity of their ages and their differences of temperament. And the relationship of both with Vedrenne was equally agreeable. Shaw, moreover, provided most of the financing for the venture. From first to last, Shaw closely supervised the production of his plays: he selected the casts, approved (and sometimes designed) the scenery, and handled most of the press relations, quietly supplying tidbits of news for drama editors to insert in their columns, and self-drafting dozens of interviews. He entrusted most of the production details to Barker, but firmly took charge of rehearsals. For three years he undertook all of his own staging, a prodigious feat considering the number of productions of his plays which were scheduled at the Royal Court. Despite the myriad commitments of his professional and personal life, Shaw found the time to rehearse not only the new productions, but the scheduled revivals, the touring productions sent out under the Vedrenne–Barker banner, the understudy rehearsals, and even the cast replacements.

His directional methods were startlingly new to most of the actors with whom he dealt, and his demands upon them were enormous. His system was based largely on musical principles. The actors had to be helped to find "the music in the piece," for much depended upon the tone in which the dialogue was delivered. Invariably Shaw would begin by reading the play in its entirety to the assembled cast, thus indicating his basic intent as to rhythms, pacing, intonation, and accent. He would annotate the actors' scripts musically: Robert Loraine's *Don Juan in Hell* script, his widow recalled, "twinkled with crotchets,

crescendoes and minims; with G clefs, F clefs, and pianissimos."
Actors embarking on long speeches were given a specific pitch on
which to begin, and were instructed at specific points to modulate to
another pitch. As Shaw told a performer on a later occasion, "[B]egin
at a low pitch and drag the time a little; then take the whole speech as
a crescendo—*p* to *ff*."

Timing was an equally important factor. Shaw demanded a delib-
erateness in his comedies which was a far remove from the frenetic pace
of stage comedy at the turn of the century. He also stressed artificiality for dramatic effect: when Kate Rorke objected to an exit speech
as "terribly stagey" Shaw blithely retorted, "You can't be too stagey
on the stage." He violated most of the directorial rules, "feeding"
readings of lines to performers, or handing them series of final instructions on changes in blocking and interpretation just hours or minutes
before an opening performance. Yet his actors loved him, for he was
patient, considerate, tactful, open to suggestion, respectful of disagreement, and tolerant of innovation. "The praise I received for my performance," Louis Calvert wrote to him immediately after the opening
of *John Bull's Other Island*, "was really due to you, who looked after
your actor with a father's care, giving him the exact emphasis &
accentuation. . . . You made us all act as if we were living breathing
human beings . . ."

The Royal Court experiment ended on 29th June 1907, when Barker
and Vedrenne, overconfidently inspirited by their success, decided the
time was right for them to invade the West End. Their grandiose
schemes initially included the formation of a syndicate for the building
of a new theatre (they went so far as to take an option on a site in
central London on "a street which already contains two successful
theatres" for an eighty-year lease). They also sought to turn Vedrenne–
Barker into a limited company, but were deterred by Shaw's refusal to
participate in such a venture, which seemed to him to have no useful
purpose and a considerable number of disadvantages. Eventually they
settled for the tenancy of the Savoy Theatre, in the Strand. They were
unable, however, to kindle sufficient audience enthusiasm in the large,
uncomfortable theatre to duplicate the success at the Royal Court,
and, hampered additionally by the censorship of Barker's new play
Waste, they were forced to end their brief season on 14th March 1908,
when their noble enterprise, like most other attempts to reconcile art
and commerce, ignominiously ended in bankruptcy. The firm survived
for a few more years as sponsor of provincial tours, mostly of Shaw's
plays, but as a London producing unit it had run its course—"dead,"

391

as Shaw stated in one of his self-interviews in 1909, "after being damned for four years by the London Press."

There were compensations, of course. Shaw's plays had vastly increased in value internationally due to the attention they received from their production at the Royal Court, and he had at last achieved domestic stature as a dramatist. Barker, at the age of twenty-nine, had won renown as a stage producer, actor, and playwright, and had also acquired a wife. And Vedrenne? "The King and Queen," he informed Shaw at Christmas 1908, "have sent me a diamond scarf pin."

To JAMES HUNEKER

[H/45; X/193.e; 186]

10 Adelphi Terrace W C
4th January 1904

[James Gibbons Huneker (1860–1921) was an American critic of music, drama and art, whose books included *Iconoclasts* (1905), *Egoists* (1909), and *Ivory, Apes, and Peacocks* (1915). In his review in the New York *Sun* on 25th October 1903, Huneker echoed Richard Mansfield's sentiments about *Candida* in his insistence that *Man and Superman* was "talk, talk, talk" and "unactable." The Cromwell quotation is a paraphrase of a statement made by Oliver Cromwell to M. de Bellièvre, reported by Cardinal de Retz in his *Mémoires* (1717).]

Dear Huneker

I was sorry not to see more of you on your visit here, as you struck me as being a likeable old ruffian. My wife, since your review of "Man and Superman," will not allow that you have a spark of intelligence, but you must come and mollify her in person when you are over next.

It always amuses me to see Candida stirring up oceans of sentiment. I think I see you wallowing in it.

Your writing always interests me; but you will never really master the English drama until you know English life and character. I speak as an Irish foreigner who has had to learn it as one learns Chinese. My first play, though performed in a crude version in 1892, was not completed as it stands at present until I had been more than twenty years in London; and a great deal of the complaints made of it and other works of mine by Scotch literary men in London (you know that the literary life is lived in a vacuum) and by Yankees like yourself, is explained by the fact that English life, as I present it with a vestryman's and politician's knowledge of it (to say nothing of my private adventures) is to them irritatingly unnatural and repugnant. When I am on the general human nature plane, they are delighted with me. When I am on the English plane, they become soreheaded at once. They love Candida: she might be an American, an Irishwoman, a Scotchwoman, any woman you please. But take my specifically English women— Blanche in Widowers' Houses (only one remove from her grandmother's washtub), Vivie Warren, Lady Cicely Waynflete in that

393

excellent Christian tract Captain Brassbound's Conversion, and, above all, Ann Whitefield and Violet Robinson in the Superman drama (Ann being my most gorgeous female creation): you can no more appreciate these from the other side of the Atlantic, clever as you are, than you could write Anthony Trollope's novels. The men annoy you in the same way: you can see the fun of Britannus in "Cæsar and Cleopatra," and perhaps of the American captain in Brassbound and young Malone in the Superman, where national types are openly made fun of; but the Hooligan in Brassbound, the chauffeur Straker in the Superman, the whole gang in Widowers' Houses, rouse your instinctive anti-English prejudice almost as if they had been done by Thackeray, who was so stupidly English that, being a man of genius, he wasted his life, for gentility's sake, on silly tittle tattle relieved by occasional maudlin drivel. I tell you you dont appreciate the vitality of the English: you see nothing but their stupidity, their moral cowardice, their utter lack of common sense, their naïve acquisitiveness, their brainless cruelty to children and criminals, their uncritical obtuseness or idolatry (as the case may be), their childish unscrupulousness, their insensibility to and disbelief in any means of persuasion except intimidation and coercion, and, at the blackest end of the scale, their flagellomania and sodomy and all the rest of it. But the truth is that these vices are either to be found abroad, or else have equivalents there. And the stupidity, peculiar to the Englishman, which prevents him from knowing what he is doing, is really a stroke of genius on his part and is far more voluntary than the bright American thinks. Cromwell said that no man goes further than the man who doesnt know where he is going; and in that you have the whole secret of English success. What is the use of being bright, subtle, witty, genial, if these qualities lead to the subjection and poverty of India and Ireland, and to the political anarchy and corruption of the United States? What says my beautiful, vital, victorious, odious-to-all-good-Americans Miss Ann Whitefield? "The only really simple thing is to go straight for what you want and grab it." How disgusting! how cynical! So say you; and so also say the Filipino and the Red Indian of you and yours.

Would you like to see what the English think of the Americans? Read "Algernon Casterton" by Lady Sykes, a recent English novel. There you will see the English conception of the American woman as a cold blooded, sexless prostitute, who sells herself without scruple and without affection to the man who can give her the best time in London society, and who makes her husband pay for her favors as if he were a stranger. This is a revolting notion to an Englishman, whose chief conception of a wife is a woman who will not only keep house for him in return for her board, but will allow him the use of her person gratuitously. Some day I will write a play shewing the good side of this American "sexlessness" of which London complains so much in private.

However, the moral for you is, study the English. There is much to be learnt from them; and I, who have been struggling for more than quarter of a century with their knavish brainlessness, lose patience often enough; but I get on very well with them personally; find them enormously interesting; have got a good deal of training from them; and, in short, intend to stay here, and be one of the glories of their literature.

What is this tomfool story about my objecting to Mansfield's Bluntschli? I never saw it—never objected to it. All these Mansfield stories are fudge. They are not exaggerations: quite the contrary. Richard's reputation is a feeble, vulgar, blundering attempt to suggest an outrageous but actual truth. But we are on excellent terms. He tells me that the American public will not stand me—that The Devil's Disciple was played by him to empty houses out of sheer devotion to art. On the other hand I call him Pompey and revile him as an obsolete barnstormer because he funked Caesar and would not even condescend to notice my alternative offer to let him play the waiter in You Never Can Tell. But these passages leave no bad blood, because I have in my desk the returns shewing that the American public spent about $150,000 to gloat over his Richard Dudgeon; and *he* considers Caesar and Cleopatra an imbecile burlesque. So we both remain, each perfectly pleased with himself, and perfectly friendly.

Who is Arnold Daly? Is he anything to the late Augustin? Talking of Augustin, Miss Marbury shewed Ada Rehan Captain Brassbound's Conversion, thinking she would jump at such a part as Lady Cicely. But alas! Ada shared your opinion that Brassbound is rot—could see no point in it at all. Does not this make you feel ashamed of yourself?

This is a Christmas holiday letter, hence its length. I spend the whole slack holiday time in a mad race to get abreast of my correspondence.

yours ever
G. Bernard Shaw

To ARNOLD DALY

[G.u/2]
[10 Adelphi Terrace W C]
[Undated: assigned to 4th January 1904]

[The critical reaction to *Candida* in New York had been quite positive. Of the major drama critics, only Alan Dale in the *New York Journal* on 13th December had serious reservations, finding Daly as Marchbanks too violent, though clever and intelligent: "Mr. Daly was a caged lion; he rampaged; he was alarming; he was even melodramatic. This was not the spirit of the role. Mr. Shaw does not dally with heroics." He concluded, however, that *Candida* was "a bright spot in a dull season." Daly instantly scheduled additional matinées at the Madison Square Theatre. In January he moved the production to the Vaudeville Theatre, then to the Carnegie Lyceum (a lecture hall), where he temporarily added *The Man of Destiny* as a curtain-raiser on 10th February, then for a single performance to a tiny room in 27th Street known as the Strollers' Club, and finally back to the Vaudeville for an extended run. The play achieved a total of 132 performances before it was withdrawn late in April. Shaw's royalties for the first matinée amounted to $19.17, but by the end of the New York season he had collected $2534. *You Never Can Tell* was produced in New York by Daly on 9th January 1905.]

Dear Mr Daly

Are you related to the late Augustin Daly?

Your success as Eugene makes you an interesting man at once; for the part, difficult as it is to cast, gives no further trouble. If you are the right man, you cannot help acting it: if you are not, it is all up with the play: no degree of professional cleverness will help you in the least.

With Morell, on the other hand, a good deal may be done by coaching. It is important that Morell should be made very sympathetic. Now you can generally trust an actor to play for all the sympathy he can get; but in my plays an actor is often as puzzled by the fact that his most earnest efforts bring him laughs—which he doesnt understand—that after the first performance he begins to play for the laughs; and then goodbye to the piece. So you must look after your Morell's & see that they do not resign themselves to being mere butts for you. Eugene scoring off a conceited fool is an ungenerous & cheap spectacle; but the apparently weak Eugene mysteriously coming in on top of a really good and able man who is doing his best according to his lights, and is really deep enough to feel, if not to understand, that there is some higher force than his own in the "little snivelling cowardly whelp," is quite another matter.

Arnold Daly as Marchbanks in *Candida*, 1903
(*Photograph by Tom Hadaway*)

At one point, however, a good deal depends on the mere stage trick of the scene. You know the passage

"I accept your sentence, Candida."

"Do you understand, Eugene?"

"Oh I am lost. He cannot bear the burden."

"Do you mean me, Candida?"

Now the whole driving in of the nail depends here on Morell. When he accepts the sentence, he stands humbly with drooping head (flattered a little, all the same). That is easy enough; but when he lifts his head incredulously, and, after a moment to take the amazing truth in, blurts out quite prosaically "Do you mean ME, Candida?", the whole strain of the situation on the audience should go off in a hearty laugh—not a ribald laugh, but a sincere, sympathetic one. Unless this is hit off to perfection, the movement where they all sit down to talk it over quietly will be quite unmanageable: it cannot be naturally done if Morell has kept the strain on by wallowing in his emotion.

This trick of getting the strain off just at the breaking point is what gets Candida through in several awkward places—for instance, the end of the scene between Morell and Candida in the second act, when Burgess brings them all down to sea level again by his exclamation—"Wot! Candy mad too!"

When you try the Man of Destiny, you will find it a series of anti-climaxes from beginning to end; but in it the laughter may be as ribald as it likes. I only compare the two as an illustration of a technical method which I use pretty largely. Any playwright or actor can manufacture an emotional crisis; but few know how to get away from it again after the magic instant—it should never be longer than an instant. That is why lots of our plays have no third acts & lots of our emotional actors live their lives on their top note, as if they were half drunk—which, by the way, they sometimes are, I regret to say.

The Man of Destiny is an extremely inconvenient play—too short to make a whole bill and too long for a curtain raiser. It also requires two people of the very first rank, as they have to hold the attention and interest of the audience for an hour without relief. If you have realized how the popularity of most of our fashionable leading ladies & gentlemen is due to the fact that modern plays are so constructed that nobody has a turn longer than five minutes or so, you will understand how very dangerous the Man of Destiny is. Unless you can get an actress as clever & fascinating as Ada Rehan used to be (I have not seen her for seven or eight years past), you had better let the Man of Destiny alone; and if you *can* get her, then dont bother about a short play but go

397

straight at Captain Brassbound, which is an excellent Christian tract, and—given the right woman and a Robsonian genius to play the cockney guttersnipe—a capital acting play.

As to Mrs Warren's Profession, you have at this moment a chance that you may never have again. Miss Fanny Brough, who created the part here, and who is an actress of genius whom we waste on farcical comedies, is in America playing with [Charles] Hawtrey for [Charles] Frohman. She has no means of giving a performance in the United States, though she has in her pocket my authorization to do so, and is very anxious to play the part where there is no Lord Chamberlain to forbid the play and confine it to a wretched little stage in a private club. You could play Frank Gardiner, an amusing young rascal, not at all like Eugene. Of course the scandal will be terrific. I send you by this post a copy of the edition I issued after the London performance, with photographs of the cast, and the preface with which I countered the attack of the newspapers. That preface will shew you what to expect. Nevertheless the production of Mrs Warren is one of those exploits which startles everyone by its apparent daring, but which is really perfectly safe. No play of mine has made me more friends; and Miss Brough, who was to have been ruined by it, has never been idle since. Think about it if Mrs Warren interests you; for if you dont do it before Miss Brough returns to England this spring, you will never do it at all. Fanny is really a great actress in her way & a great character, or she would never have ventured on Mrs Warren in the teeth of all her friends and councillors at a time when she was not personally acquainted with the author.

Do not, in the pride of your youth, be too hard on those New York managers. They were quite right according to their lights. If you were a man of business and not an artist, you would not touch Candida: you would go for thousand dollar houses plus nothing instead of two hundred dollar houses plus the feat of playing Eugene—producing Candida. I have never advised them to meddle with me. Charles Frohman once offered to shew me how to rewrite You Never Can Tell so as to make it fit for the stage; but I received the proposition with such ecstasies of delight & anticipation that he got an attack of shyness and the promised instruction never came off. You had better go ahead with "You Never Can Tell" as soon as you can: I will certainly give you all the preference I can without hanging the play up too long. There is, as you say, money in a success with it.

There is no money in Mrs Warren; and it ought not to be played for money. But there are other considerations which make it well worth playing. If you can get Candida out of the matinée phase into the evening bill, and then, when its novelty has worn off, stir up public consciousness to its depths by a few matinées of Mrs Warren, you will not be forgotten in a hurry; and your next season will begin with a rush.

All my plays are thoroughly protected; and the rights of all of them are in my own hands and at my own disposal—including Arms & the Man & The Devil's Disciple. Many people conclude that these plays are the property of my friend Mansfield; but this is not so. However, he has squeezed the last dollar out of both of them on his own circuit; so they dont count.

> yours faithfully
> [G. Bernard Shaw]

To REV. ENSOR WALTERS

[A/43]
10 Adelphi Terrace W C
8th January 1904

[Walter Hazell (d. 1919), Liberal M.P. for Leicester 1894–1900, was chairman of the printing firm of Hazell, Watson, and Viney. James Timewell (1857–1926), a master tailor who resided in Gower Street, was much involved in St Pancras municipal affairs. In 1902 he helped to found the Police and Public Vigilance Society, and served for nearly twenty years as its secretary. George E. Gladstone had succeeded Timewell as Election Committee secretary. John Russell declined to stand again for the L.C.C., of which he had been a member since 1895. During January Shaw approached Hazell, Ensor Walters, W.M. Meredith of Constable's, and the Rev. Frederick Hastings.]

Dear Ensor Walters

The finger of Providence is pointing steadily to 123 Gower St for the County Council election. On Thursday the Progressive Committee selected me & Walter Hazell as their candidates. Sylvester Horne at last undertook not to oppose (I pressed him to stand himself). Today news comes that an unexpected vacancy in East Islington, a perfectly safe seat, has occurred, & that it is being offered to Hazell, who will of course accept, all the more readily as I behaved with the most outrageous extravagance at the selection farce, gave rabid Tory answers to all their questions, and generally stood the meeting on its head, knowing that they couldnt help themselves.

So now I am left without a colleague. If you wont stand yourself— and I have now reached the infatuated stage of believing that we could

399

romp in, though I should compromise you horribly by my declarations that the Education Bill is the Magna Charta of the Free Churches & that Clifford is wrecking Progressivism—do you know any presentable Noncom (saving your presence) whom you could give the candidature to? I called at 123 today & was told that you had left town for a week. As time presses fearfully, and Timewell (much hurt by having been superseded as election committee secretary by a Passmore-Edwardite named Gladstone on the ground that he alienates the police vote)—Timewell, I say, is rushing after Sheffield—after Russell—after anybody to stuff into the vacancy.

If you can suggest any name, or will come to the rescue gloriously yourself (probably you oughtnt to; but my conscience is laid by until the 6th March) send me a wire. Address it to Shaw, Maybury, Woking, whither I go by an an afternoon train tomorrow (Saturday). Sylvester, I think, doubts the soundness of Wesleyan Methodists on the Bill: "they have schools," he says.

yrs ever
G. Bernard Shaw

To HUBERT BLAND

[A/39]

Maybury Knoll. Woking
19th January 1904

[At the Fabian Members' Meeting on 22nd January, Shaw introduced and spoke on the draft tract on the tariff question. Graham Wallas moved against it, seconded by Aylmer Maude, Isaac Mitchell, and H.D. Pearsall. After much debate the Wallas motion was defeated, and on 24th January he resigned from the Fabian Society.]

Dear Bland

We shall have to watch the proceedings on Friday carefully. An attempt will probably be made to omit every passage that could possibly hurt the feelings of a Liberal; and unless this is instantly met by a demand to leave out all the counter references, the tract will be Daily Newsified. For instance, Hobson wants me to cut out the reference to Gladstone. I have replied that if Gladstone's age comes out, Chamberlain's age must come out too and the whole opening will be spoiled.

Certain other amendments must be kept in reserve. For instance, there is the question of sweating. Webb's Industrial Democracy shews that the export trade is collared either by the most highly regulated trades, or by the sweated trades. [Percy] Ashley gives figures to shew that the sweated trades—slops, pickles, vinegar, sauces, confectionery, jam, oil & floor cloth, india rubber goods, soap, furniture, cabinet & upholstery, cordage &c—are gaining. Now we can stop this by Factory Legislation; but what about the imports? If you dont stop the import of sweated lino, or the export of capital to found lino factories on un-regulated foreign soil, you are likely to have a tremendous outcry against Factory Legislation before you get a wonderfully improved British lino process as the reward of Heaven to Free Trade.

Webb is most intensely averse to having Industrial Democracy ex-ploited in Chamberlain's interest. Naturally enough too, as that is not what he put in the work for. But the Fabians would sympathize with a proposal to open up this side of the subject in the tract. An amend-ment to recommit the tract for this purpose would very soon bring to their senses any Liberals attempting to nobble it for their own side.

Again, there is the dumping question. On this a proposal to deal fully with it would lead to a conflict between the following views. 1. That there is no such thing as dumping—the bogey view. 2. That the more dumping the better, since it gives us goods under cost price—Webb's view in his speeches to the Society on the subject. 3. That dumping enables the British *finisher* to produce goods so cheaply with dumped materials that the German finisher, undersold by his British competitor, will revolt against the dumping of German pig as a bounty to English finishing, and compel the German Government to forbid dumping—[Henry W.] Macrosty's view. 4. On my replying to 3 that it is better for us to stop dumping at once before it ruins our extractive industries first, and then unruins them & ruins the inflated finishing industries in order to stop itself by a roundabout way, Mac shifts his ground & says that the dumping would be done somewhere else where we have a market if not here; so we could not wholly stop it. By threaten-ing to recommit the tract until this muddle was unravelled you could force an opponent to give up any attempt to tamper with the tract as it stands.

Finally there is the Empire question, which we have agreed to cover up with our oceanic proposals. Suppose our railways are *not* national-ized & our shipping *not* supplied free, are we going to let things drift? Webb says he would give up general Free Trade for Free Trade within the empire. Do we agree with him or would we sacrifice the Empire to Free Trade?

You have enough stuff here to control the situation on Friday. You can say that you and those who agree with you have consented to drop all these difficult questions for the sake of getting a good Fabian pronouncement, although they positively reek with considerations that tell strongly against Free Trade. But if the Free Traders insist on trying to turn the tract into a Liberal electioneering document, or to force a declaration in favor of Free Trade, then the compact is broken, and the point at issue must be thoroughly thrashed out.

I dont anticipate much trouble; but we must be prepared.

yrs ever
G. Bernard Shaw

To FRANK W. GALTON

10 Adelphi Terrace W C
[A/5]   3rd February 1904

[James William Cleland (1874–1914), a barrister who had been a member of the L.C.C. from Lewisham since 1901, had been encouraged to stand as Shaw's running-mate, as had the Rev. Frederick Hastings (1838–1937), of Tolmers Square Church, who had considered accepting the invitation until he read the election address Shaw had already prepared for the occasion! The final choice was Sir William Nevill Geary, Bart, J.P., D.L. (1859-1945). The *St Pancras Guardian*, on 27th February, reported, "Sir William Geary is a baronet, and that is all we know about him."

Victor Lytton (1876–1947), 2nd Earl of Lytton, took an active interest in the arts throughout his life, becoming president of the Royal Society of Literature and chairman of the Old Vic Association. Sir John William Gilbert (1871–1934) was secretary of Providence Row Night Refuge and Home; he was elected to the L.C.C. in 1910.]

Dear Galton

Bad news for Cleland & the Progressive centre. Geary has done the trick: the St Pancras selection committee would not hear of Hastings & Hazell; and Geary & I are the chosen ones. Geary, if he wins, would, I believe, contest the parliamentary seat, vice Lange retired. He would be a rattling good candidate in comparison with the next best man they are likely to get. He is of course much more Liberal than I am. Will you therefore make your Northumberland Avenue reactionaries understand that they must support him. I am willing to pledge myself, if they get him in, not to assume the leadership of the party on the Council until they themselves implore me to do so.

402

At the last moment, after settling with Geary, I was offered Lord
Lytton. You had better tell Wiles & Gilbert that he is available. Now
that it is known that *I* am standing, it will be far easier to get first rate
people: next time I shall accept nothing under a marquis. My eye!
what a time the whips will have when I am on!...

I tell you this is going to be a very superior and extraordinary thing;
and I have serious thoughts of publishing a manifesto instructing the
Progressives to vote for no candidate who does not produce a letter of
recommendation signed by Webb and

> yrs ever
> G. Bernard Shaw

To GILBERT MURRAY

10 Adelphi Terrace W C
[C/36]   [Undated: assigned to 23rd February 1904]

[The postcard on which Shaw had written to Murray had a printed heading,
announcing "I am one of the Progressive candidates in South St. Pancras for
the London County Council," and concluded: "Helpers, carriages and
motor cars in unlimited numbers wanted for polling day, the 5th March."
The Hon. Rosalind Stanley, Lady Carlisle, was Murray's mother-in-law.]

Geary contested Durham as a Liberal in 1900, a fact which entitles
him clearly to the loan of all the motors the Stanley influence can command. The election will be won largely by brake horse power. He has
incorrigible Radical leanings, I am sorry to say. I am running as an
enthusiastic supporter of the London Education Act, and as the proprietor of the Fox & Pelican, Grayshott. There is a strong Nonconformist demand for atheist candidates just now, as a guarantee against
Church influence; but my halo of high Anglican mysticism is proof
against all such temptations.

> GBS

To T. P. WHITTAKER

10 Adelphi Terrace W C
[H.c.u/2]   23rd February 1904

[Sir Thomas Palmer Whittaker (1850–1919) was a Liberal M.P., active in
the temperance movement. He had seconded Shaw's nomination for the St

Pancras Borough Council in October 1900. The Shaw-Geary nomination papers were signed by Whittaker, Ensor Walters, the widow of the Rev. Hugh Price Hughes, Percy Bunting (editor of the *Contemporary Review*), A.B.Walkley, the actor H.B.Irving (son of Sir Henry), and the actress Lily Hanbury (see letter of 24th February 1904 to Walters).]

Dear Mr Whittaker

Will you do what you can for me to smooth down the more ferocious opponents of the Education Act. It is very difficult to make the denominations which have no schools take a reasonable view of the Act. To begin with, they ask recklessly that I and Sir William Geary shall declare in favor of the abolition of all religious tests, quite overlooking the curious fact that under an Act like this a religious test is the only guarantee of religious liberty. For instance, suppose the Free Churchmen sulk because the Progressives have accepted the Act! The result will be a Church majority on the Council. Now the only way of preventing that Church majority from imposing an extreme High Churchman on a Methodist School under cover of his attainments as a mathematician is just what the Free Churchmen now call a religious test: that is, a condition that the master of a Methodist School shall be himself a Methodist. All I or any person who has really studied the Act and forecast its practical bearings can say is that I shall oppose all attempts to substitute religious qualifications for educational ones.

Again, they want the Act to be repealed or postponed or at least amended. I need not tell you that repeal is all nonsense: the Act embodies an enormous reform (the endowment of secondary education) which will never be given up, as well as power to establish non-sectarian training colleges, which the Passive Resisters themselves would die in the last ditch to defend. And the ratepayer will not hear of postponement when he realises that the grant of £500 a day will be postponed too. But I personally feel quite sure that the Act will not even be amended. The Country Act will, of course: the case of the village with only one school is too bad to be left where it is now; but in London the foundation managers will have no chance of doing anything unpopular if the majority on the Council is Progressive. And unless they do something that will make London's blood boil, London will not buy them out at a cost of from two to five millions. Six months from now, the opposition to the London Act will be as dead as the old opposition to buying out the Water Companies. The ordinary Free Churchman has not enough practical political experience to see this. But he will take it from you (in judiciously diluted doses) when he will not take it from me. Of course my own natural view, so to speak, is that we should from the first have undertaken a national system of education and superseded the voluntary schools without counting the cost; but the nation, being mostly members of the Church of England, thought otherwise; and the tide of State Education never rose above the Church steps. It is useless to kick against that now: the situation must be accepted as representing, on the whole, the balance of power in the constitution. And we shall not do so badly as the Free Churchmen fear. Those who pay the piper generally call the tune in the long run.

Another difficulty is that the Gladstonian and Free Church sections in South St Pancras do not realize that the seat cannot be won for the Progressives by their votes. They allowed the Progressives to be defeated so ignominiously at the Borough Council election that they should be only too thankful that they have succeeded in finding any candidates at all for the C.C. [County Council], much less two rather exceptionally presentable ones, though I say it that should not. But they cannot complain if I have been forced to concentrate all my energy on getting the necessary makeweight of Church and Unionist and doubtful and indifferent voters, relying on the fact that the Liberals and Free Churchmen *must* vote for me or let the Conservatives and the Church triumph, and South St Pancras pass for ever into the Holborn category as a hopeless constituency. I, who am so strenuous a teetotaller that I do not even drink tea or coffee (my tap is barley water) or eat meat, have actually to court the publicans by explaining to them that the Council's Temperance policy protects them from the competition of the music hall, and mentioning the fact that I am one of the proprietors of the Fox and Pelican on Hindhead—a house which we opened on the Bishop of Chester's plan when it was a question of either doing that or allowing the license to go to the Alton brewers. I also have to force the note of the merits of the Act to the utmost. This is quite inevitable: on a stalwart Passive Resister, Teetotal platform my defeat is absolutely certain; and it is equally certain if the Passive Resisters do not poll their last man for me. You must help me to bring them to reason. I have done everything I could to secure them a candidate after their own hearts. I urged Mr Ensor Walters to stand. I urged Mr Silvester Horne to stand. I offered to withdraw in their favour. I undertook to persuade Sir William Geary to run with one of them. I urged Mr Hazell to make up his mind to run with Mr Hastings of Tolmers Square, and begged Mr Hastings to attend the final selection committee meeting and address it. When neither of them would do it, I placed the alternative of a Hazell-Hastings candidature before the Committee myself. All in vain. It was impossible for the Committee to trifle any longer with an election which was already half lost by delay. Mr Hastings had no money, Mr Horne and Mr Walters could not spare the time for the work, Mr Hazell could not make up his mind. I had to save the situation; and now they must put up with me whether they like me or not. And, as aforesaid, I want you to do what you can to rub this into them. If Sir William Geary gets in handsomely, he will probably fight [a] parliamentary seat, for which it has long been impossible to find a serious candidate. So, since Geary's Liberalism is unquestioned (he contested Durham in 1900) the irreconcileables must at least vote for him. I lured him into this contest; and if he gets in I shall not be disappointed, as I have more than enough work waiting for me in the world without piling up the County Council on top of it.

I write bluntly and in great haste; but I know you will not mind that at election time.

yours faithfully
[G. Bernard Shaw]

To REV. ENSOR WALTERS

[A/43]

10 Adelphi Terrace WC
24th February 1904

[The subject of this letter, Lily Hanbury, was a young actress who made her first important appearance in Pinero's *The Benefit of the Doubt* (1895). She died in 1908, at the age of 33.]

Dear Walters

It occurs to me that I had better tell you that this nomination business is not an inconsiderate coruscation of mine. You have no idea how gratified the lady is by finding herself treated as the possessor of an immortal soul equally with the other lady. Every act of ostracism to a woman on the stage is, so to speak, deliberately kicking her into hell, which is always open for her; and similarly every act of respect towards her makes her footing enormously more secure. It is a small thing; but one may as well get some good out of even an election when the chance offers. Mrs P.H. will be glad afterwards, when I give her a hint of the bearings of my little joke.

GBS

To SIDNEY WEBB

10 Adelphi Terrace W C
[H/14]   25th February 1904

[Rev. Alexander Connell (1866–1920) was minister of the Regent Square Church 1893–1906. The King's Cross meeting on the 24th was in St Jude's School, Britannia Street. The local Labour man was K. MacCrae. John Alfred Spender (1862–1942) was editor of the *Westminster Gazette*. The *Daily Express* interview was not published. The article Shaw mentions throughout the letter, "County Councilitis," was published in the *Daily Mail* on 27th February. Webb's recent book was *London Education*, published in January.]

First, may the curses of all the prophets of his race fall on that idiot [Max] Hecht for stealing my MS and worrying you with it. I need hardly say I had no intention of letting you have a glimpse of it until it was published.

Now I shall have to waste precious time in convincing you that you are totally and perversely wrong, and I obviously and sympathetically right.

My misdeeds go back further than that article. I got your letter from Whittaker, with your note on it not to write to him as he would vote for me. I wanted him not only to vote for me but to nominate me: accordingly I wrote him the long letter of which I enclose a copy, and sent copies of it to Holmes of the Whitfield Tabernacle and Connell of the Presbyterian Church in Regent Square, with suitable letters. Result: Whittaker has nominated me.

Last night at the meeting at Kings Cross, I obeyed your orders not to speak on the Education Act. I said I would answer questions on any subject except the E.A., and that if anybody wanted to know about that he must ask me outside privately, as I did not want my Liberal friends to hear it. The meeting chuckled; and when McCrea, a local labor man, got up and said I was quite right about the Act and he wished every workman in London could read my address, there was not a breath of dissent. And, in moving thanks to the parson, I said that if I was elected I would spend the rates of all the Nonconformists on that particular school like water, everybody chuckled again. Result: one vote promised by a prominent Moderate.

Now for the events of the week as to the press. Reynolds [News] has attacked me; the Echo has attacked me; Spender has written to me to say that he would prefer a Moderate victory to my success—he having

407

attacked me before I wrote to him. The Telegraph, the P.M.G., the St. James's, the Globe, even the Times in a way, have given me a lift. The Morning Advertiser has published an interview today ["Mr. Bernard Shaw on Compensation": self-drafted] in which I pitch into the anti-compensation nonsense of the Liberals. The Express has an interview in type in which I ridicule the Protestant League attitude. And the Daily Mail article is my reply to Spender's challenge. Poor Hecht lives in anguish. Worst of all, Bunting came into the Committee Room this evening, and Hecht was about to appeal to him against the D.M. article when he plumped down on the sofa and said "Make a personal sensation. Get talked about," and Hecht mournfully left the subject untouched.

I dont mind Hecht's panics; but you really ought to be used to me by this time. Your letter is in the handwriting of the author of London Education (which you probably recollect dimly as a brochure designed to disparage the Act and conciliate the Liberals in a very artful and Machiavellian manner); but the words are the words of Wallas. Your attempts to alter my article into accuracy, as you call it, do not include a single alteration of the sense; and if you wish the style altered so as to give color to the suggestion which would probably be made that you inspired it, I am too crafty to help you in that innocent effort. As the article stands, nobody will ever dream for a moment that it is anything but individual, irresponsible, uncontrollable Shaw. I shall revise it with a view to making it still more outrageous if possible.

You have such an unreal notion of your own position and of the dramatic effect that I produce (which is simply that of George Bernard Washington who cannot tell a lie even to get the Liberal vote) that it is very hard to manage you. My view of the Act is perfectly well known to be your view of it. You have written a book and published it on the verge of the election to affirm that view. You have forced the Progressives, bitterly against their grain, to accept it by threatening them with the vengeance of the Church. You have kicked Wallas out of the Fabian Society and trampled on Headlam ferociously for feebly suggesting that there is any flaw whatever in the Act. It is popularly believed in St Pancras that the Bishop of Stepney calls you "my son." One of my worst sins in the south division has been my cool announcement that I proposed to pitch the Liberals out of their own Association Rooms and put you, the infidel, in charge of them. And yet you are firmly persuaded that you have handled the Liberals with such tact that the least hint on my part in the Daily Mail that we two are not the foremost

Passive Resisters in London will create a ruinous scandal. How can you expect me to be impressed? There is only one relation possible henceforth between you and the Liberals or the Liberal Progressives; and that is the relation of leader and dictator. Your polite representations are just as intelligible, and less confusing, than my strident yells. Nobody is in the least in the dark as to your view of the Act; and your singular professions of Liberalism take in nobody but your simple and sedulous self. When you come down next Saturday you will not get me a single Liberal vote: you will only accentuate my heresy. You will get me hundreds of votes, probably, by simply, as at Deptford, totally ignoring the very existence of Liberalism, except perhaps occasionally to snap the head off some poor devil who bleats out some nonsense from the Daily News. And I will burn the red fire in the wings, and take care that your candidate is always making a noise somewhere in the neighborhood.

Now one thing more. The D.M. article may be taken by a few Conservatives as a lift to the Government. I hope it will. We asked them for an Education Act. They gave us as much of it as was at all politically possible under the circumstances. We are bound in honor to give them full and generous credit for it. To stint the acknowledgment in order to gratify Alfred Spender & Co. would not propitiate Alfred, and would destroy all our influence with the Conservatives. I am a vindictive beast; but I have the quality of that fault: I will make what acknowledgment I can to these poor devils who have done something for us. I know there is no gratitude in politics; but there is no ingratitude either; and there is retribution, of which gratitude is occasionally a form.

Confound you for making me write all this stuff when I have such a lot else to do. I totally disbelieve your story about Beatrice agreeing with you.

GBS

PS As Ensor Walters agrees with us perfectly about the Act, anything that will break down the prevalent nonsense on the subject will be of the greatest service to him. By next Wednesday the cry of stinking fish will be dead. Then I shall fire my last shot—a demonstration that the one flaw in the Act is a clause absolutely prohibiting the appointment of a teacher who does not belong to the denomination for which he teaches—in other words, a religious test to prevent religious persecution.

Progressive Committee Rooms
21 Gower Place W C
25/2/04

PS I reopen this letter to say, with fury, that on revising the article more carefully with your corrections, I find that you have actually been gingering it up, and that your only anxiety has been lest I should omit any of the excellences of the Act. I have therefore retained all your corrections, including one which has your signature all over it; and I am sending off the article with a reassured feeling that nothing would disappoint you more than my putting it into the fire, which you very nearly made me do with your hypocritical letter.

GBS

To SIEGFRIED TREBITSCH

[A/5]

10 Adelphi Terrace W C
14th March 1904

[In the election on 5th March, Shaw (1460 votes) and Geary (1412 votes) lost to two Moderates (1927 and 1808 votes). Rev. F. Hastings instantly announced that it was Shaw's "eccentricities" which had caused the defeat, and Beatrice Webb recorded in her diary that Shaw had showed himself "hopelessly intractable." The editor of the *St Pancras Guardian*, however, in his "Editorial Notes" on 19th March, called Shaw "the most accommodating candidate that was ever known. His policy might have been summed up in the one word 'oblige.' He was geniality itself to all who approached him, and we know very well that the people who are against the Education act were those who worked hard for Mr. Shaw and canvassed for him might and main."

Max Reinhardt (1873–1943), a German actor who had turned to theatre managing and directing in 1903, had presented *Candida*, directed by Felix Holländer, at his Neues Theater, Berlin, on 4th March 1904, starring Agnes Sorma (1865–1927), reigning star of the Deutsches Theater since 1883 and best-known actress in Germany. Of the long list of people mentioned by Shaw, Alfred Kerr and Osborn were critics. Christian Morgenstern, also a critic, was a member of Reinhardt's original "Brille" group of performers in 1900, later known as the "Schall und Rauch," as were the actors Martin Zickel and Friedrich Kayssler. Moritz Heimann (1868–1925), a playwright and critic, was Gerhart Hauptmann's brother-in-law. Eduard Stucken was a playwright, the author of a cycle of plays dealing with Arthurian legend. Arthur Kahane was Reinhardt's literary director.]

410

My dear Trebitsch

I have been defeated—wiped out—annihilated at the polls, mostly through the stupidity of my own side. Consequently I am perfectly furious. It is no use sending me congratulatory telegrams about that silly old Candida. To the devil with Candida! Agnes Sorma is an idiot, Reinhardt a duffer, Kerr an impostor, Gold an imbecile, Duesel a humbug, Heimann a bounder, Holländer a noodle, Morgenstern an ass, Osborn a dolt, Zickel a booby, [Efraim] Frisch a fool, Stucken a driveller, Kayssler an oaf, and Kahane a dunderhead. I tell you I got only 1400 votes and my opponent got 1900. And everybody is delighted —openly and indecently delighted—at my discomfiture. What is Candida to me at such a moment? Away with Candida! "Verehrung" indeed! I wanted 500 more votes. I am convinced that the performance was execrable, ridiculous, disastrous. It has been described by English correspondents in the papers here—Mill as a comic curate with misfitting clothes, Morell as a Tyrolese pastor of the XVIII century, Heaven knows what not! I have not had time to read the German notices: they are all lies. Reinhardt ought to be ashamed of himself. The theatre ought to be closed, and all the actors sent to a fortress for six months.

However, the election is over now; and time will restore my peace of mind.

Why the devil did not Sorma send me her photograph instead of a silly telegram?

I have received an application for authorization from the Freie Bühne people. They say the censorship will not allow a public performance of Mrs Warren's Profession. I have replied that I can give no authorization to translate or perform any play of mine, as I have made arrangements with you which would be contravened by such authorization. I have also referred them to you, saying that you might possibly allow them to perform the play if the press were excluded, and that I should not object in that case. The play would make a great effect among the Social-Democrats, and would start a good deal of talk about it. You can judge best whether to allow the performance or not. Did the performance of Helden do any harm? . . .

Granville Barker is going to give six matinees of Candida here in April as an experiment. Why not come over & soothe your nerves by attending the rehearsals?

yrs ever
G. Bernard Shaw

To GRANT RICHARDS

10 Adelphi Terrace W C
[A/4]
30th March 1904
My dear G.R.

Three Plays for Puritans appeared on the 15th Jan 1901. Up to June 1901 you sold 1204. Net royalty to author £80.5.4.

Man & Superman appeared in August 1903. Up to 31 Dec. Constable sold 2707, three hundred more than double. Net profit to author, £148.2.10 + 634 copies in hand completed for sale, on which I shall get about £111.

What is more important is that future editions will be printed from my plates; and then my takings per copy will considerably exceed a one & fourpenny royalty.

Consider also this frightful fact. In the 18 months ending 30 June 1902—the latest accounts to hand—you had sold only 1421 Puritans all told. At the first issue, when the reviewing acted as an advertisement, you sold 1204. In the second 6 months (no advertisement) only 137. In the third 6 months, 80!

Mind: I dont blame you in the least for not advertising. It is absolutely inevitable in the struggle for life that you should bring all your ammunition to bear on your risks & leave your certainties to take care of themselves. But it would be perfectly silly in me to continue our arrangement for ever & ever. You are now an established institution; and my books are of no real consequence to you. You sometimes fancy they are; but that is an amiable delusion. If you had made me a serious offer for the Superman I should have taken it. You virtually shifted me to Constable, and changed my system; and it is now inevitable in the course of business that I should get all my books into my own hands & work the thing myself. I am growing old & avaricious & fond of handling capital instead of being dry nursed like the ordinary author-duffer. What about my accounts? I expect an ENORMOUS cheque.

yrs ever
G. Bernard Shaw

To CLIFF KEANE

10 Adelphi Terrace W C
[A/3]
2nd April 1904
[Cliff Keane was the stage name of Clifford Deane (1855–1942) later a railway official, who was for many years secretary to the local Theosophical

412

Society at Harlesden. William Paley (1743–1805), English clergyman and philosopher, author of *Natural Theology* (1802), insisted on the relation of form to function, and argued that from the design of a watch we can surmise the existence of a watchmaker.]

Dear Mr Cliff Keane

The man who said that the rights were all the children's and the duties all the parents', was a most pestilential ass. You have no more duties to your children than you have to me, and no less. And they have no more rights against you than against me, and no less.

If I lived in your house, it would be possible for me to disregard your comfort & convenience to an extent which would justify you in taking me by the scruff of the neck & putting me out of the room, or using your fists, or the poker, or even a revolver. The situation would not be altered if I were your son, or you mine. People have to learn to consider their neighbors by the simple experience that when they dont they create social friction and incur resentment, resistance, and even retaliation. You will find that the best brought-up children, other things being equal, are those who have been brought up in a large family, where the parents have had no time to study individual children much, and where the children themselves have knocked one another into some sort of communal conscience without the least sense of duty or the least desire to impose a moral program. Next to them come the children of busy parents, who have lived their own lives frankly before their children as hard as they can, and not bothered about their characters or tried experiments in moral abortion.

Someday I will deal more fully with the question of Secularism. The god of my fathers was such an intolerable god that when I was a boy I simply bolted Darwin without chewing him because I was so very anxious to get rid of "the argument from design," Paley & the watch &c&c. I did not notice that, as Butler used to say, Darwin banished mind from the universe. It was not until "neo-Darwinism" began to apply the doctrine practically—politically, in dynamite, and socially in vivisection—that I began to see that to the ordinary man Darwinism meant simply the application of a pigeon fancier's ideals to all the social problems. Secularism is not a philosophy of life: it is only an attempt to leave life out of the question because no rationalistic, materialistic explanation of it has been found. It had its uses in making us drop many superstitions—forcing us to admit that much ground that we had romanced about as the undiscovered country had really been explored & mapped and was not at all like the descriptions given in our romance—but when it took to pretending that it had explored the

413

universe, it was time to send it packing after the other exhausted reactions.

I will send you back your papers presently.

yrs faithfully
G. Bernard Shaw

To H. G. WELLS

[C/26]

[Maybury Knoll.] Woking
5th April 1904

[Wells, who had been encouraged by the Webbs and Shaw to join the Fabian Society in 1903, submitted his resignation in March 1904 over the tariff tract, *Fabianism and the Fiscal Question.* Shaw had written to Wells on 26th March: "The tariff tract was submitted to you as well as to everybody else. It cost me months of work to fit it to the greatest common measure of all the members" [A/26]. Wells soon withdrew his resignation. Sardanapalus (7th century B.C.) was the last of a line of thirty Assyrian kings, who surpassed all his forebears in his sybaritic way of life. The Shaws gave up their rented cottage in Woking on 25th April. They subsequently leased The Old House in Harmer Green, Welwyn, which they occupied on 2nd July.]

Et tu, Sardanapale!

Luxury & indolence indeed!

Well, write the next tract yourself, and be blowed. *I* shant resign: I shall chuckle.

We are in the agonies of househunting. Now is the time to produce an eligible residence, if you have one handy.

GBS

To JAMES HUNEKER

[A/45; X/178]

10 Adelphi Terrace W C
6th April 1904

[Huneker, in reply to Shaw's request for "a decent publisher," recommended Arthur Brentano. The book which had just arrived was Huneker's *Overtones: A Book of Temperaments* (1904).]

Dear Huneker

Dont ask me conundrums about that very immoral female Candida. Observe the entry of Mr Burgess. "Youre not the lady as hused to typewrite for him." "No." "Naaaoww: *she* was younger." And therefore Candida sacked her. Prossy is a very highly selected young person indeed, devoted to Morell to the extent of helping in the kitchen, but to him the merest pet rabbit, unable to get the smallest hold on him. Candida is as unscrupulous as Siegfried: Morell himself at last sees that "no law will bind her." She seduces Eugene just exactly as far as it is worth her while to seduce him. She is a woman without "character" in the conventional sense. Without brains and strength of mind she would be a wretched slattern & voluptuary. She is straight for natural reasons, not for conventional ethical ones. Nothing can be more coldbloodedly reasonable than her farewell to Eugene. "All very well, my lad; but I dont quite see myself at 50 with a husband of 35." It is just this freedom from emotional slop, this unerring wisdom on the domestic plane, that makes her so completely mistress of the situation.

Then consider the poet. She makes a man of him finally by shewing him his own strength—that David must do without poor Uriah's wife. And then she pitches in her picture of the home, the onions & the tradesmen & the cossetting of big baby Morell. The New York Hausfrau thinks it a little paradise; but the poet rises up and says "Out, then, into the night with me"—Tristan's holy night. If this greasy fool's paradise is happiness, then I give it to you with both hands: "life is nobler than that." That is "the poet's secret." The young things in front weep to see the poor boy going out lonely & brokenhearted in the cold night to save the properties of New England Puritanism; but he is really a god going back to his heaven, proud, unspeakably contemptuous of the "happiness" he envied in the days of his blindness, clearly seeing that he has higher business on hand than Candida. She has a little quaint intuition of the completeness of his cure: she says "he has learnt to do without happiness."

As I should certainly be lynched by the infuriated Candidamaniacs if this view of the case were made known, I confide it to your discretion. I tell it to you because it is an interesting example of the way in which a scene which could be conceived & written only by transcending the ordinary notion of the relations between the persons, nevertheless stirs the ordinary emotions to a very high degree, all the more because the language of the poet, to those who have not the clue to it, is mysterious & bewildering & therefore worshipful. I divined it myself before I found out the whole truth about it.

[Benjamin] Tucker is a very decent fellow; but he persists, like most intellectuals, in dictating conditions to a world which has to organize itself in obedience to laws of life which he doesnt understand any more than you or I. Individualism is all very well as a study product; *but that is not what is happening*. Society is integrating, not individualizing; and it is better to lay hold of what it is doing & make the best of it than sit complaining that it wont do something else. Trusts are most excellent things—as superior to competitive shopkeeperism as symphonies are to cornet solos; but they need more careful scoring & longer rehearsal & better conducting. The only individualism worth looking at now is breeding the race & getting rid of the promiscuity & profligacy called marriage.

Is there such a thing in America as a decent publisher—one whom I could trust, in reason, to sell my books on commission if I manufactured them myself. I am tired of wasting time negotiating with fools who are afraid to publish the Superman, & rogues who want to get too soft a bargain over it. It is copyrighted all safely; but it lies there dead whilst McClures & Harpers & the like funk it, and others want to grab it for ever & ever.

yrs
G. Bernard Shaw

PS The book has just arrived. More about it when I have read it.

PPS I subscribe to an American press clipping agency; so dont bother to send me anything that is likely to reach me through that channel.

To MRS L. E. COMPTON

32 Via Porta Pinciana. Rome
7th May 1904

[C/5]

[Shaw and Charlotte had left for Italy on 1st May. They visited Turin, Pisa, and Rome (until 2nd June). On the return journey they visited Geneva before proceeding to London on 10th June.]

Your letter has just reached me in Rome, where I shall be for some time to come. I am not "one of the Shaws": I am actually THE Shaw, conferring, not deriving, the honor of the name. I know nothing about my ancestry except that they are said to have come to Ireland from Yorkshire in the reign of William III, and to descend from Macduff— the original Shakespearean Thane of Fife. My mother's name was

Gurly, a Carlow family of Norman (Gourlay) origin. I cannot guarantee the accuracy of any of these legends; but I can vouch for the family habit of talking about "the Shaws."

G. Bernard Shaw

To WILLIAM ARCHER

32 Via di Porta Pinciana. Rome
[A/2]   12th May 1904

[A.B. Walkley had published a very short, reportorial notice on the *Candida* matinées in *The Times* on 27th April, promising a critical review later. The promise was not kept. Trebitsch apparently was confusing the *Times* and *Observer* critics. Archer, in a notice in *The World* on 3rd May, referred to *Candida* as "the most human of Mr. Shaw's plays, and the one in which he is most successful in concealing himself behind his puppets—or rather in distributing himself among them. As a rule, he himself, almost undisguised, is the protagonist of his fables . . ." Jens Martin Borup (1880–1960), a young Dane, resident in London, was translating *Plays Pleasant and Unpleasant* (published by Gyldendal in Copenhagen, 1907).]

My dear Archer

Trebitsch's howlers are certainly mighty ones and millions, though I think I got them driven out of the dialogue of the Schlachtenlenker. But how can I reproach him when he sends me the following, which I am sending on to Walkley.

"The Observer has sent me the Times-critic about Candida. Who is that desperate impostor, who wrote all this frightful nonsense? Not even his grand-children will be able to understand this deep and poetic work. I did not finish to read that writing: it would have caused me neuralgics."

I shall send him your criticism in the hope of extracting some further blossoms from him. By the way, there is one naiveté in your notices which you always produce with ingenuous pride; and that is nothing less than the discovery that Cæsar, Napoleon &c &c are only masks through which G.B.S. speaks. The implication that Hamlet, Macbeth, Falstaff, Georges Dandin, Don Juan &c are authentic realities with which Shakspear & Molière had no more to do than a reporter has with

417

Chamberlain, is stupendous. Confound you for a romancing idiot, with your imagination always in Piona, what did you expect my people to be? Bluntschli & Napoleon are as violently differentiated as any man whose charm lies in his perfect simplicity can be from an inveterate poseur—Sidney Webb is not more distinct from Mansfield—but of course the two are the work of the same hand, stamped with the same style, getting their effects by the same stage tricks. How can that be helped, except by having every part written by a different author? Burgomaster Six, old Mrs Van Rhyn and Saskia are all Rembrandts; Peter & Paul and Christ are all Raphaels; and Napoleon, Cæsar, Dick Dudgeon, Captain Brassbound & Candida are all Shaws. There is nothing in that as you state it: it sounds as if you were announcing with a penetrating air that Sloane Square is not Victoria Park and 5 in the afternoon not 10.30 at night. You must either drop it or else carry it very much further. For my own part, I am amazed at how little a touch of emotion will carry off the most monstrous unrealities. Candida's "I give myself to the weaker of the two" is the climax of all impossibility; yet it passes. The situation is true; the characters are true; the solution is the right one; but the actual words uttered, and the state of clear intellectual consciousness of the situation which they imply, is outrageously unreal.

Now if you will only sit down and tell yourself that Shakespear & Co have never been real men to you, and that in my plays you have for the first time faced the big drama (for I assure you in all unhumility I am the greatest dramatist of the XX century) with such a personal knowledge of the man behind it that for once, in spite of Piona propensities, the author is more real to you than the play, you will get some critical advance out of it. You are behind the scenes for the first time in your life; and you are complaining that instead of a scenic illusion, you find nothing there but obvious carpentry and seamy-side-of-the-canvas rigged up by me. Just as Ben Jonson could never for the life of him see that Shakespear was such a dramatist as his idolaters made out; so you, whilst heaping encomiums on my wit &c &c &c, are always wondering that people cannot see that it is all Shaw, Shaw, Shaw, nothing but Shaw. Critically, this leads you to an abuse of your private knowledge of me. I *cannot* illude a man who knows me, just as Kate Rorke cannot persuade me that she is anybody but Kate Rorke. But she has a right to demand that I shall discount this in criticising her acting; and I claim, too, that you should either allow me the same discount in criticising my plays, or else discount your own criticism by announcing at the start that you are not at the optical point

418

of the ordinary spectator, and can hear the sound of my voice in every line I write.

This ought to furnish you with materials for at least a dozen Study & Stage articles.

Has Borup *finished* The Man of Destiny? If so, I shall get a copy typewritten by Miss Dickens & try to arrange a performance in Denmark. Mrs Weeks tells me that Gyllendal is afraid to touch my books.

yrs ever
GBS

To GEORGINA SHAW

32 Via Porta Pinciana. Rome
13th May 1904

[A/29]

My dear Georgina

I have written to London to have my tickets for the Stage Society play [R.O.Prowse's *Ina*] sent to you; but it is possible that they may already have been sent on to me, and that the letters have crossed, in which case it is too late to save the situation. I forgot about the performance, & left no instructions as to the opening of the S.S. letter and the disposal of the tickets.

As to the tea, Charlotte & I do not drink that deleterious fluid. The servants cater for themselves—probably drink China tea at 7/6 a pound: at all events I dare not ask Charlotte to go to so eminent a person as our cook & ask her to buy her tea from my aunt. She would give notice on the spot.

If we hear of any opening for the maid I will let you know; but there is not much chance of that. These tragedies are always happening. Servants after a certain time ought to inherit annuities just like relatives, and *before* any but very near relatives—children, for instance.

yrs sincerely
G.Bernard Shaw

To J. B. PINKER

[32 Via Porta Pinciana.] Rome
[S/1]   30th May 1904

[Shaw had demanded and received a high royalty because he was supplying
the *Man and Superman* plates, but he subsequently managed to obtain the
same royalty from Brentano for all of his books.]

I have closed with an offer from Brentano of 25% for five years:
that, I think, was good enough. Otherwise I should have availed myself
of your suggestion with pleasure.

G. Bernard Shaw

To ELLEN TERRY

10 Adelphi Terrace W C
[U(A)/10; X/117]   12th June 1904

My dear Ellen
    I was on my way to call on you yesterday when I suddenly bethought
me that it was Saturday and that you were matinéeing.
    As you have no doubt heard, Granville Barker & the Court people
gave half a dozen matinées of Candida, with Kate Rorke in the title
part. Result very satisfactory: heaps of press notices, all compliments
for the company, and a modest profit for Barker & the theatre, besides
some thirty pounds or so fees for the author.
    Naturally they want to try again—with Brassbound.
    Now you see what I am driving at.
    They will lose by Brassbound, because it is a *much* more expensive
play than Candida (the cheapest piece in the world). There will be
extras, and scenery, and costumes, and ten parts. The highly cultivated
audiences who came to Candida at the rate of from £60 to £80 each
matinée will not be sufficient to cover the larger expenses of Brassbound, much less give a profit. But the loss will not be great, and if
Lady Cicely hit the public at all, it might disappear altogether. The
theatre is to be redecorated in the autumn; and Brassbound would
come on in October, probably.
    Now consider. Six matinées only would be announced & given. No
failure would be possible. The press notices would be much more
voluminous and interesting than the Lyceum ones ever were. Lady

420

Cicely would get no salary, of course—£25 and "find her own gowns" is the sort of thing the Court runs to—but then she would lose nothing, and she would be promoted from Shakespear & Ibsen to Shaw. What do you think of it? Remember, I dare not ever let you do the play under your own management at your own risk; and it is only in some such way as at the Court that you will be engaged for the part, because no regular management will touch my plays—why should they? It was written for you; and unless you do it at least once, posterity will never forgive you: you will go down to all the ages as the woman who made *il gran' rifiuto*; for there never was and never will be again such a part written for any mortal: I stooped for your sake to do what Shakespear did when he manufactured Rosalind. *He* gave her away by flinging her at the public with a shout of "as *you* like it" (Pilate washing his hands); but I will gravely offer this impossible quintessence of Ellen as a real woman; and everybody will be delighted.

If you are too lazy to learn the part I will teach it to you speech by speech until you can repeat it in your sleep. Would you like to talk it over? If yes, shall I call on you or will you come here—say to lunch on Wednesday on your way to the matinée, if there is a matinée? If you will, let me have a line by return, with any instructions you may wish given to our cook.

your still faithful
GBS

To WILLIAM ARCHER

10 Adelphi Terrace W C
13th June 1904

[A/2]

[Max Meyerfeld (1875–?) was a German literary critic, whose constant sniping at Trebitsch's translations of Shaw culminated in a Trebitsch–Shaw attack on Meyerfeld and his translation of Wilde's *De Profundis* (1905), in *Die Schaubühne*, 9th April 1908. Beerbohm Tree and Ellen Terry appeared the afternoon of 13th June in Shakespeare's *The Merry Wives of Windsor* at His Majesty's Theatre in the Haymarket.]

I have written to Meyerfeldt to come at 1 instead of half past; so come along. I will do the talking; and you can spare yourself for Tree & get a comfortable lunch & have plenty of time to get to the Haymarket.

As to your letter, all I can say is—Yah! go and stereotype your own confounded article. If you keep hitting the same key you naturally get the same note. You are quite wrong about the others saying the same thing. A few who know me set up the same cliché; but they have had the sense to drop it because they cant get any further with it. As to your knowing other dramatists who dont reproduce their own views & ideas, the explanation is obvious: they havnt any to reproduce—at least none peculiar to themselves. They deal in the readymade article, which is as characteristic of the first score of men you meet in the Strand as of themselves. Their heroes are not themselves because their heroes are not heroes at all, but nobodies. My heroes are all Shaws because, like myself, they are somebodies. As to Shakespear, if you cant see the underlying identity of Iago, Richard III, Edmund, and Thersites, of Hamlet, Macbeth, the Duke in Measure for M., Ulysses and Prospero, of Timon & Jacques &c &c &c, then you are no critic, but only a beglamoured joskyn in a booth. But what is the use of arguing as if Shakespear's or my "creations" *could* be anything but impersonations? Of course one can read the police news in different voices, like Sloppy in [Dickens's] Our Mutual Friend: one can do Faust & Mephistopheles, Athos & Aramis [in Dumas' *The Three Musketeers*], Romeo & Mercutio, Morell & Eugene, Napoleon & Cæsar; but after all what is it but Goethe or Dumas or Shakespear character-acting? These men, like me, understand that men fundamentally *are* identical: they seek for their characters in themselves, and know how to say "But for the grace of God there go I." It has been said of me repeatedly of late that I do not do this; that I am an observer only & not a sympathizer; and this, though false, is further on the way to the truth than your inane formula, which only shuts the path in your own face. If you write a play with the characters all Archers, it will be a good play; and you will be astonished to find how many different people you are. As to my disappointing you, it bereaves me of breath. You infernal lazy scoundrel, which of us has had to produce works of genius for both—you or I? Who went to sleep over Widowers' Houses & has never woke up since? Disappointed! Million millions!!! You ought to be shot for such a reproach.

GBS

To LADY GREGORY

10 Adelphi Terrace W C
[C/1]   20th June 1904

[Augusta Gregory (1852–1932), an author and playwright, had joined forces with William Butler Yeats in Dublin to found an Irish National Theatre Society. They had taken a 99-year lease from 1st May 1904 on an auditorium in Abbey Street and the adjoining premises in Marlborough Street, formerly known as the Old Morgue, and had requested a grant of Letters Patent from the government for the establishment of an Irish Literary Theatre in Dublin. The request was made in the name of Annie Elizabeth Fredericka Horniman, who had been Florence Farr's anonymous backer at the Avenue Theatre, London, in 1894. The Patent eventually was granted to Lady Gregory as trustee for Miss Horniman.

Shaw had promised Yeats and Lady Gregory a new play for their theatre (Yeats had urged him as early as October 1901 to come back to Ireland to "stir up" things), and it now began to emerge as *John Bull's Other Island*. The statement that "not a word" was yet on paper was not true. Shaw had begun the draft of the play at Hindhead on 17th June; it was completed at Rosemarkie on 23rd August.]

Yes, back.
Not a word of the play yet on paper

Seething in the brain.

I have been abroad for more than a month & letters & business have accumulated frightfully. When I have cleared them, the play will start.

G.B.S.

To ADA REHAN

10 Adelphi Terrace WC
[H/4]   29th June 1904

[Ada Rehan, the Irish-born actress, whom Shaw had long admired, as he confessed in his *Saturday Review* articles, was in England on an extended visit from the United States. *The Countess Gucki*, an adaptation by Augustin Daly from the German of Franz von Schonthan, had been presented at the Comedy Theatre on 11th July 1896.]

Dear Madam

Have you ever by any chance read a play of mine called Captain Brassbound's Conversion? If not, will you allow me either to send you a copy, or to read it to you?

Captain Brassbound's Conversion is a modern repertory play for a great actress. There is only one woman in it. You could have played her when you were 25; you can play her now; and you will be able to play her when I am dead and you are 70. In spite of the scarcity of women's frocks in the play, there is color enough on the stage as the scene is laid in Morocco, with plenty of oriental costume.

You were in the author's mind when he wrote the play; and he has often wished to approach you on the subject. But that has been rather a difficult thing to do. Until within the last few months, when the success of Fräulein Agnes Sorma as Candida in Berlin was followed by an outbreak of Candidamania in New York, I had nothing to shew in the way of a successful play except one called The Devil's Disciple, in which the interest centres in a man, not in a woman. The fact that I could provide Mr Mansfield with a successful part did not prove that I could provide you with one. Besides, I had been a critic, and sometimes a very disagreeable one, pursuing the late Mr Augustin Daly with implacable and vindictive malice because, having helped you to acquire a wonderful technique, and not seeing all that I thought I could see behind that technique, he wasted your genius on man-made foolishnesses like the Countess Gucki when you had become one of the greatest actresses in the world. I hated the Countess Gucki, and did my best to slay her—not a very obliging course to take from your point of view. And then, what likelihood was there of your having ever heard of me as a dramatist, even if you had ever heard of my existence at all? My reputation, such as it was, was as bad an introduction as I could offer you. And so I had to bide my time.

Even now I feel some delicacy about intruding on you. But my hand has been forced by the demands for the rights of Captain Brassbound which the Candida business has brought on me. I cannot let the play go without asking you whether there is any chance, under any circumstances, at any time, of your playing Lady Cicely (she is the lady who converts Captain Brassbound). Do you think it possible that a part in

424

a play by me could interest you—interest you TREMENDOUSLY—
for nothing less than that will bring out all your magic?
Will you excuse my typewriter. It is sordidly ugly; but it is easier to
read than a strange handwriting.

yours faithfully
G. Bernard Shaw

To ARCHIBALD HENDERSON

10 Adelphi Terrace W C
[A/23; X/116]   30th June 1904

[Archibald Henderson (1877–1963), who was at this time an Assistant
Professor of Mathematics at the University of North Carolina, had become
a Shavian enthusiast after attending a drama-school performance of *You
Never Can Tell* in Chicago on 24th February 1903. He wrote to Shaw in
June 1904 (Shaw instantly added his name to the card list of "Disciples")
stating his intention of writing a biography of Shaw, and asking for detailed
information concerning his early uncollected writings.]

Dear Sir
    I am afraid there is no way of getting at the mass of critical articles
which I wrote between 1885 & 1898 except by coming to London &
misspending several weeks at the British Museum library. . . . Total,
over a million words, most of them about matters long since stone dead,
and many of them become absolutely unintelligible now that they can
no longer be read with the context of the events of the week in which
they appeared.
    Then there are my economic & political essays—my Socialist mani-
festoes, my defence of the value theory of Marx against that of Jevons,
ending in my own conversion and my demolition of Marx on Jevonian
lines with my own hand. All this is quite unknown to the admirers of
my plays; but my first play "Widowers' Houses" could only have been
written by a Socialistic economist; and the same thing is true of "Mrs
Warren's Profession." Indeed, in all the plays my economic studies
have played as important a part as a knowledge of anatomy does in the
works of Michael Angelo.
    I believe my career as a public speaker was also an important part
of my training. There was a period of twelve years during which I
delivered about three harangues every fortnight, many of them in the
open air at the street corners and before audiences of all sorts, from

university dons & British Association committees to demonstrations of London washerwomen, always followed by questions & discussion.

I never lived the literary life, or belonged to a literary club; and though I brought all my powers unsparingly to the criticism of the fine arts, I never frequented their social surroundings. My time was fully taken up (when I was not actually writing or attending performances) by public work, in which I was fortunate enough to be associated with a few men of exceptional ability and character. I got the committee habit, the impersonality and imperturbability of the statesman, the constant and unceremonious criticism of men who were at many points much abler & better informed than myself, a great deal of experience which cannot be acquired in conventional grooves, and that "behind the scenes" knowledge of the mechanism & nature of political illusion which seems so cynical to the spectators in front.

I advise you in anything you write to insist on this training of mine, as otherwise you will greatly exaggerate my natural capacity. It has enabled me to produce an impression of being an extraordinarily clever, original, & brilliant writer, deficient only in feeling, whereas the truth is that though I am in a way a man of genius—otherwise I suppose I would not have sought out & enjoyed my experience, and been simply bored by holidays, luxury & money—yet I am not in the least naturally "brilliant" and not at all ready or clever. If literary men generally were put through the mill I went through & kept out of their stuffy little coteries, where works of art breed in and in until the intellectual & spiritual product becomes hopelessly degenerate, I should have a thousand rivals more brilliant than myself. There is nothing more mischievous than the notion that my works are the mere play of a delightfully clever & whimsical hero of the salons: they are the result of perfectly straightforward drudgery, beginning in the ineptest novel writing juvenility, and persevered in every day for 25 years. Anybody can get my skill for the same price; and a good many people could probably get it cheaper. Man & Superman no doubt sounds as if it came from the most exquisite atmosphere of art. As a matter of fact, the mornings I gave to it were followed by afternoons & evenings spent in the committee rooms of a London Borough Council, fighting questions of drainage, paving, lighting, rates, clerk's salaries &c &c &c; and that is exactly why it is so different from the books that are conceived at musical at homes. My latest book, The Common Sense of Municipal Trading, is in its way one of the best and most important I have ever written. I beg you, if you write about my "extraordinary career," to make it clear to all young aspirants, that its extraordinariness

426

lies in its ordinariness—that, like a greengrocer & unlike a minor poet, I have lived instead of dreaming and feeding myself with artistic confectionery. With a little more courage & a little more energy I could have done much more; and I lacked these because in my boyhood I lived on my imagination instead of on my work.

Excuse all this twaddle; but it is probably what you require to help you out if you pursue the subject.

Widowers' Houses is out of print, thank Heaven, in the original edition; but the preface & appendices were probably better reading than the text of the play in its original foolishness. I do not know where a copy is to be had. . . .

It is quite true that the best authority on Shaw is Shaw. My activities have lain in so many watertight compartments that nobody has yet given anything but a sectional and inaccurate account of me except when they have tried to piece me out of my own confessions.

yours faithfully
G. Bernard Shaw

To W. T. STEAD

[G.u/2; X/179]

[The Old House. Harmer Green]
[Undated: c. July 1904]

[William Stead had published, in the July issue of the *Review of Reviews*, his "First Impressions of the Theatre"—"by one who, until his fifty-fifth year, has never witnessed any stage play other than the Passion Play of Ober Ammergau." In the article he referred to D'Annunzio's *The Flame of Life* (1900) and one of its leading characters, La Foscarina.]

My dear Stead

As a playgoer of nearly forty years' standing, a playwright, and a practised critic of the theatre, I have read your maiden effort with many chuckles.

As to your autobiographical beginning, we knew already that you were very badly brought up, and are a person of outrageously excessive temperament. All that need be said in this connexion is to point out that if you had been taken to the pantomime when you were six, & therafter regularly every year, you would have compounded for all later temptations in your childhood by a perfectly innocent adoration of the fairy queen, and would have been as proof at 21 against the leading lady's make-up as you are now against the blandishments of a lady journalist. The real danger of "cloistered virtue" is that when it is let out of the cloister (as it needs must be sooner or later) it is duped by the tawdriest wiles of vice & beglamored by attractions that no self-respecting profligate would deign to look twice at.

If you really went to the theatre for the first time expecting to see something like D'Annunzio's Foscarini, and trembling lest she should rouse your ardent nature to disreputable transports, then I offer you my sincere condolements. You must have been frightfully disappointed. If you ever do hear "the vibrating accents of passion" from the lips of a beautiful young actress, will you be so good as to send me her name at once. Dramatists do almost all their playgoing in a tedious search for her, and often die without succeeding [in finding her]. What a gorgeous thing it must have been for you to live for 55 years happily believing that there was such a treasure in every theatre.

Your question "Is the Theatre a power making for righteousness?" is as useless as the same question would be about Religion or Gravitation or Government or Music. There are theatres in England in which the entertainment on the stage is simply a device to lure people to the drinking bars which are the real sources of profit to the manager. There are theatres everywhere which deal in nothing but dramatic aphrodisiacs. And there are theatres which deal with more serious representations of life and greater achievements of literary art than any to be found in the grossly overrated bundle of Hebrew literature which you were taught to idolize to the exclusion of your natural literary birthright. Between these extremes lie every possible grade of theatre; and to lump them all as an unreal abstraction called "the theatre" will only land you in confusion. A theatre is a potent engine for working up the passions and the imagination of mankind; and like all such engines it is capable of the noblest recreations or the basest debauchery according to the spirit of its direction. So is a church. A church can do great things by precisely the same arts as those used in the theatre (there is no difference fundamentally, and very little even superficially); but every church is in a state of frightful pecuniary dependence on Pharisees who use it to whitewash the most sordid commercial scoundrelism by external observances; it organizes the sale of salvation at a reasonable figure to these same Pharisees by what it calls charity; it invariably provides occasion for envy and concupiscence by an open exhibition of millinery and personal adornment for both sexes; and it sometimes, under cover of the text that God is love, creates and maintains a pseudo-pious ecstatic communion compared to which the atmosphere of the

428

theatre is prosaically chilly. That is why many people who take their children to the theatre do not send them to church. The moral is, as "pagans like Domitian and Trajan" saw, that both churches and theatres need to be carefully looked after so as to prevent them from abusing their powers for pecuniary profit.

Finally, *dont* talk about immoral actresses. What do you mean, you foolish William Stead, by an immoral actress? I will take you into any church you like, and shew you gross women who are visibly gorged with every kind of excess, with coarse voices and bloated features, to whom money means unrestrained gluttony and marriage unrestrained sensuality, but against whose characters—whose "purity" as you call it—neither you nor their pastors dare level a rebuke. And I will take you to the theatre, and shew you women whose work requires a constant physical training, an unblunted nervous sensibility, and a fastidious refinement and self control which one week of ordinary plutocratic fat feeding and self indulgence would wreck, and who anxiously fulfil these requirements; and yet, when you learn that they do not allow their personal relations to be regulated by your gratuitously unnatural and vicious English marriage laws, you will not hesitate to call them "immoral." The truth is that if the average British matron could be made half as delicate about her sexual relations or half as abstemious in her habits as the average stage heroine, there would be an enormous improvement in our national manners & morals. When next time you sit in the stalls, think of this, and, as the curtain rises and your eyes turn from the stifling grove of fat naked shoulders around you to the decent and refined lady on the stage, humble your bumptious spirit with a new sense of the extreme perversity and wickedness of that uncharitable Philistine bringing up of yours.

Hoping that your mission will end in your own speedy & happy conversion, I am, as ever, your patient Mentor

[G. Bernard Shaw]

To ADA REHAN

The Old House. Harmer Green
[H/4]   5th July 1904

[Ada Rehan had written on 30th June to inform Shaw that she was familiar with *Captain Brassbound's Conversion*, but would be delighted to have him read it to her. She cautioned, however, that he "must understand that I am

429

in the hands of my management over whom I have little control" (Hanley, Texas). Arnold Daly's production of *You Never Can Tell* opened on 9th January 1905 at the Garrick Theatre, New York. Fanny Brough did not appear in *Mrs Warren's Profession* in New York; the rôle of Kitty Warren in the 1905 production was undertaken by Mary Shaw (no relation to GBS). Frank Curzon (1868–1927) was a former actor, now a successful theatre manager.]

Dear Miss Rehan

Your letter has had to follow me down here: that is why the answer comes so late.

We have upset Granville Barker and the poor people at the Court Theatre fearfully. They are trying to establish a repertory theatre; and the success of the matinees of Candida and Hippolytus has encouraged them to spend £6,000 on redecorating the house. They were relying on Brassbound to open their winter season with; and now their only hope is in a play I am writing for the Irish Literary Theatre—a sort of political farce, of no use to anybody but cranks—which *may* be finished in time for their opening in October.

As a rule when an author offers a play to an artist instead of to a management, his object is to get that artist's services for nothing and spend all her money on his play into the bargain (including his royalties). And this is what actually happens nine times out of ten. Even if the play is successful, its complete exploitation involves the artist in a great deal of troublesome business. She herself never visits the smaller and more out-of-the-way towns; and minor companies have to be organized and sent on tour to these places, losing money here, making it there, and always having to be financed and looked after constantly and sharply. All this is becoming every day more and more the business of theatrical trusts, which are quite inevitable modern developments, just like the other trusts. Clearly your business is to leave theatrical speculation to the speculators, and depend on your own personal monopoly of the highest order of ability. It is true that the highest order has a smaller and more select market than some of the lower ones. The speculator doesnt understand it, is afraid of it, and prefers flashy second rate talent in cheap plays backed by large advertisement and expenditure. But the public, which is frightfully capricious with the favorites of the speculator, is much more faithful to those who never make it feel that it has wasted an evening and its money. As long as first rate acting can find first rate plays, it will survive many theatrical generations of the pets of Jerusalem. All these well boomed leading ladies, clever as some of them are, can be replaced: *you* cannot—or if you can, I will give $500 cash down for the lady's address. If you retired tomorrow, Brassbound would simply go to the highest bidder; and Lady Cicely might be played by anyone of half a dozen American actresses, each vouched for by her admirers as the only possible Lady Cicely now living. But you have no competitor. Now that I have secured your approval, my position is clear. If anybody else wants Brassbound, he can have it for just as long as he can engage you! No Miss Rehan, no Brassbound! But if he accepts these terms and produces Brassbound with you as Lady Cicely, he can, during your engagement, have the play for the smaller towns as well, and let his minor companies and secondary stars do their worst with it there.

On your part, you are in a position to make the production of Brassbound a condition of your engagement if you think it wise to do so. You also can say, No Brassbound, no Miss Rehan. You can undertake not only to obtain my license to perform the play, but—provided the management pays my royalties and relieves you of all pecuniary responsibility to me—to produce it without making the usual advance payments to the author. In this way you would have a secure hold on the play without having to enter into all the undertakings that the acquirement of the rights of a play involves. The bargain between us would be something like this: I would give you an undertaking not to let anyone else play Lady Cicely in the big towns in America or England for, say, three years from the date of its successful production in New York or London provided that production takes place within the next two years. The rest would follow from this.

My royalty would be ten per cent. My asking no advance would be a solid and unusual concession to the speculator; but to you it would be no concession at all, as the play, instead of dying stone dead after its first production, would drop into your repertory and I should thus profit later on. When that happened, a ten per cent royalty would be oppressive except when business was very good, as you might tour with your own company, taking theatres on sharing terms, in which case, assuming your share for the sake of argument to be 50%, my 10% on the gross would amount to 20% on your share. Under these circumstances, since Shakespear asks no fees, you would play Katharine and Rosalind as often as possible, and Lady Cicely as seldom as possible. I should therefore in my own interest compromise on a sliding scale enabling you to reduce the 10% to 7½ and to 5 when the receipts dropped below certain amounts.

In all this I am trying to get as much out of you as I prudently can, and taking care of myself precisely as I should if I were Tubal and you were Jessica. I am a most scientific driver of bargains; and you need apprehend no chivalry on my part. I stand to gain much more than you do, because Lady Cicely can add nothing to your reputation, wheras you, by playing her, can add greatly to mine. There is, however, an advantage in my business keenness, and in the fact that I am not nearly so disagreeable personally as you would suppose from my writings. It is always useful to have a terrible and inexorable partner in the background. Most people who have never met me will believe anything unpleasant about me; so if you are forced to be disagreeable to the management, blame it on to me.

And now, as to immediate action. Do not commit yourself to an American production in October. America still follows London; and it is better to take a London success, or even a London failure, to New York, than to bring a New York success to London. The interest in my plays will be kept up by Arnold Daly's production of "You Never Can Tell," and by the frightful scandal of a production of "Mrs Warren's Profession" by Daly and Miss Fanny Brough next spring. If you could achieve a London production of Brassbound in the spring, its success in New York in the winter of next year would be as well assured as any such uncertainty can be. Therefore I suggest that you should at once try whether you can arrange anything for London next spring. If you succeed, then reserve Brassbound for 1905 in New York, and be content with the old repertory for this winter, taking advantage of the interest created by Daly's production to paragraph the announcement of your Brassbound project.

Unfortunately, as there is no London actor-manager who is a possible Brassbound, except perhaps Lewis Waller, whose co-operation would be costly in many ways, and Forbes Robertson, whose wife could not be shelved, you are thrown back on Curzon or Charles Frohman. Of the two, Frohman is greatly to be preferred, as Curzon would stray after the first comic opera that came his way. Now if Frohman would engage [John] Drew to support you in London, there would be a tremendous revival of the old enthusiasm. Of course if Drew is now so self-sufficient a star that he needs nobody worth more than 50 dollars a week in his company, the combination may be economically impossible; but I doubt if his position is so assured as to make him refuse a visit to London on reasonable terms. An occasional London season is a necessary advertisement for him. It is worth trying for at all events. The worst of it is that Brassbound would not suit him in the least.

I understand, however, that you would not care to make any overtures to Frohman. And he has no particular reason to love me. Still, a

432

rebuff will not damage me; and I do not mind feeling his pulse on this subject. Indeed let me say very seriously that a permanent quarrel with Frohman is out of the question for you. The Trust, as I said before, is a perfectly inevitable commercial development; and though it was bound to upset things at first, especially in the very few cases where it crushed really artistic managements, it is a good thing on the whole, because the huge majority of theatres were (and in England still are) in the hands of much coarser and stupider men than even the Trust magnates, bad as some of them may be. Frohman began by trying (very superfluously) to demoralize London. But London has moralized him; and now his theatre is one of our best and most advanced. I confess I should like to make him own that his omission to make a friend of you was one of his greatest mistakes.

If all the other managers fail, the Court Theatre people will be only too glad to arrange with you.

I shall be in Town from Thursday afternoon to Saturday morning.

yours sincerely
G. Bernard Shaw

To ADA REHAN

[A/4]

10 Adelphi Terrace W C
9th July 1904

[Miss Rehan replied on 8th July: "I am sorry to say that the business conditions that you propose are not possible for me to accept. I entertained the idea of your play because I gathered from our conversation that it [was] possible for me to acquire the rights entirely for myself. This would have enabled me to produce it whenever the opportunity should arise, and I thought that it might come during my tour this winter. As I have much hard work before me it would be unwise to pledge myself to any promise for the Spring. In justice to you therefore I must give up all thought of playing in Capt Brassbound. Thank you again for the honor you have done me in wishing me to be associated with your play. After long experience I am convinced that the play is the thing. The personality of the interpreter of Lady Cicely is after all a secondary matter. And 'Capt Brassbound' will live on its own merits" (Hanley, Texas).

Mark Klaw (1858–1936) and A.L. Erlanger (1860–1930) were American theatrical managers in partnership. Erlanger had helped to form (in 1896) the Theatrical Syndicate, which for years had a virtual monopoly of American theatrical business. Shubert Enterprises was a group of young brothers,

433

headed by Sam S. Shubert, who had entered the managerial scene importantly at the turn of the century, and were crowding the older managers. Shaw frequently referred to them as the Brothers Shoeblack.]

My dear Miss Rehan

Very well, very well, very well.

Now tear up my letter of the 5th and begin all over again. You shall lead this time. Make your proposal; name your terms; tell me exactly what you want. I spent a whole day thinking out the position for you and for myself. My proposals were not final: I am open to any other arrangement that will secure your interests better. You must spend a day in thinking now—or get somebody you can trust to do it for you—and then name your conditions.

Only, remember certain things. When you think of "acquiring the rights entirely for yourself," remember that I have enjoyed the absolute and complete possession of the rights "entirely to myself" for five years; and much good they have done me! The only way in which I can bring the play to life is by first giving up all my rights in the part of Lady Cicely to you, and then by giving up my commercial rights (subject to your rights) to the controllers of the business organization of the American & English theatres.

Now suppose I make you a total and unconditional present of Captain Brassbound. Will you be able to keep the rights "entirely to yourself"? Not in the least. Every concession, every farthing that the theatres can now get out of me, they will then be able to get out of you. Indeed, they will get more. They will bargain with you without scruple, without delicacy, without caring one rap for your interests, and quite possibly without even confining their own aims to business matters—for instance, they may be trying to build up a reputation for somebody else. It would be far better to leave them to fight it out with me if once you could feel sure that I would not let the part go elsewhere, as, under the arrangement I proposed, I *could* not.

Dont for one moment imagine that either you or I can be free or absolute outside our own little kingdom in which there are no laws & no sharks. We cannot set foot on the boards of a modern theatre until we have arranged to divide the spoils with the owners & controllers of that theatre. If you feel strong enough in finance and business organization to enter that sordid arena yourself—to control fifty theatres all day and act and study all night—then you can buy my play, throw me overboard, and fight Frohman & Klaw & Erdlanger & Shubert & all the rest single handed. But you know that such a thing is impossible—

434

that it would be your death as an artist and your ruin as a capitalist. Be reasonable with me, or be unreasonable if you like; but dont be impossible. Suppose I *do* cheat you, does it matter so much? has nobody else ever cheated you? I MUST have you for Lady Cicely; & I WILL, WILL, WILL. So there!

G.B.S.

To ALVIN LANGDON COBURN

The Old House. Harmer Green
[X/180]   26th July 1904

[Alvin Langdon Coburn (1882–1966) was a young American photographer, introduced to Shaw by Frederick Evans, who had established residence in England. He did the frontispieces for the 23-volume "New York Edition" of Henry James, 1905–7. Coburn and Evans visited Shaw on August Bank Holiday.]

Dear Sir

Just now I am hard at work on a new play, and so do not want to come up to town if I can help it. But if you will come down here any day you choose to appoint (except Thursday next) by the 1.15 train from King's Cross, arriving at Welwyn station at 2.2, we will wait lunch for you; and you can photograph me afterwards to your heart's content. Bring Evans with you if you can; I have not seen him for several months.

If it will save your carrying a lot of traps, I can place at your disposal some odds and ends of apparatus which are in a very incomplete condition, as I have only just moved into this house, and have not attempted to equip it completely for photography. But the bath room can be used as a makeshift dark room to change plates or develop a trial exposure. I have a 10″ × 8″ camera that will stretch to 30″ and a half-plate camera that will stretch nearly to 20″. I have an anastigmat (Dallmeyer's Stigmatic F6) that will cover a half-plate, and a Dallmeyer portrait lens F4, that will cover the side of a house with a telephoto attachment, and a half-plate without it. I have a quarter-plate hand camera, also available for telephoto work. Unluckily my 10″ × 8″ slides have no carriers for smaller plates, though I have ordered some. I have a few 10″ × 8″ Cristoid Orthochromatic films which are fresh, and a box of half-plate extra-rapid Ortho plates which I got 6 months

435

ago, and some quarter and half plate Kodoids of uncertain age. But if you will tell me what you require, I will order them. The rooms here are whitewashed and fairly lighted; but I have not yet found out what exposure they will respond to.

Let me know as soon as you can what day will suit you, and whether Evans will come. Also what plates or films you would like to have, or what I can do to facilitate your operations.

yours faithfully
G. Bernard Shaw

To ELLEN TERRY

[U(A)/10; X/117]

The Old House. Harmer Green
26th July 1904

[The play by Barrie was *Alice Sit-by-the-Fire*, presented by Charles Frohman at the Duke of York's Theatre on 5th April 1905.]

Madam

So you have got Barrie to write a new play for you. Very well. VERY well. But why, oh *why* didnt you make Frohman undertake the London production, and give you a nice salary and a percentage, with no anxiety, no risk, and nothing to do but walk to your dressing room and wait there without a care for the respectful summons of the call boy? As it is, you have all the trouble & risk, and he comes in for the certainty—America being the certainty.

As for me, when I realized that you really and finally and honestly didnt believe in Brassbound, I at last did the irrevocable thing: I read it to Ada Rehan. Now she, too, had read Brassbound; and she, too, had discovered that it wasnt a play—that it *might* be something clever to read, but was not fit for the stage—that Lady Cicely's part was a small one and didnt dominate the play, &c., &c. And when she heard the play even badly read (I was not at my best or she would have expired with amazement) she was the most astonished lady as ever you could see in all your born days, mum. I told her I'd written it for you, and that your opinion was precisely as stated above; and she owned up nobly and said she was no better herself. "You know," says she, "the truth is, we were so accustomed to beautiful poetry in those days that we did not understand a real woman like that—and besides, it's so different when you *hear* it." In short, she must have it for England and for America and for all the world. Serve Ellen right, thought I: I hope

436

she's proud of herself *now*, with her Vikings & her Beatrices & her Barries.

But alas! this stately Rehan is a most fiery, simple, sentimental, loyal, faithful soul; and now she dismisses Brassbound from her life as her bitterest disappointment because "we can never see things from the same point of view," which means that she has found me out in two brutal & cynical crimes: first, that I actually want her to make terms with the syndicate which squeezed her dear dead teacher & manager [Augustin] Daly almost into bankruptcy, and second and worst, that my opinion of the said Daly as a manager for a woman of genius when Ibsen revolutions are taking place is hardly more flattering than my opinion of Henry Irving in the same capacity. She is simpler than you and has not your literary genius; so that I am much more disagreeable and bewildering for her. Besides, your infamous treatment of me has soured my disposition; and now I see that the way to treat women is to parade the most utter disregard of their interest and their feelings.

And then I am dashing ahead with my new play and care for nothing else just at present. . . .

Will you *really* come? If so, name your day—except next Thursday. There is a 1.15 train from King's Cross in time for lunch. Charlotte says you wont; and I daresay she's right—

your turned worm
G. Bernard Shaw

[Ellen replied on 28th July: "You ought to give A.R. your play. She would do great things with it. I *do* think it a fine play, but Lady C. is not strong enough to act itself. Most of your things do. You ought to give away all your work as Tolstoy does, because you know no middle, reasonable course in your business arrangements, or so it appears to me. *I* am going to begin to be extortionate now, to try to make some money, and to keep a little for a trifle a week, and this farm [Smallhythe, Tenterden] for my old age."]

To FREDERICK H. EVANS

The Old House. Harmer Green
30th July 1904

[C/4]

[Although Evans accompanied Coburn to Welwyn on 1st August, his interest was not in cameras but in Shaw's pianola. Alfred Stieglitz (1864–1946), a well-known American photographer, was editor of *Camera Work*, in which Shaw's appreciation of Evans had been published in October 1903.]

Sensitive is not the word for my metrostyle: it is as tough as a canal barge. I have 24 library rolls here, among them Beethoven's big Hammerklavier Sonata Op 106, Bach's A minor fugue, Chromatic Fantasia & Toccata & Fugue in F, and a couple of the symphonies transcribed by Liszt. This may possibly save you the trouble of bringing any rolls.

I have just heard from Stieglitz about the photograph you sent him in Man & Superman.

G. Bernard Shaw

To ADA REHAN

[H/4]

The Old House. Harmer Green
2nd August 1904

[Milka Ternina (1864–1941), a Croatian soprano noted for Wagnerian rôles, had first sung in London in 1895. Emily Fotheringay is the beautiful but stupid actress in Thackeray's novel, *Pendennis*. Mrs Oscar Beringer, known professionally as Aimée Daniell, had presented *Pillars of Society* on 17th June 1889. "'Ostler Joe" was a recitation written by George R. Sims. The plays in Barry Sullivan's repertoire were Edward Moore's *The Gamester* (1753), August von Kotzebue's *The Stranger* (1789–90), which had been seen in England in several translations, Lord Lytton's *Richelieu* (1839), Mrs Susannah Centlivre's *The Wonder: A Woman Keeps a Secret* (1676), Dion Boucicault's adaptation of C. Delavigne's *Louis XI* (1854). Augustin Daly's *The Countess Gucki* had been performed by Ada Rehan at the Comedy Theatre on 11th July 1896.]

My dear Miss Rehan

. . . Let me now tell you something apparently quite irrelevant about my mother, who is between 70 and 80 and *much* younger than I am. My mother teaches singing. She teaches it as well as you were taught acting, though she took to it late in life to support herself and me. She taught my sister to sing and would have taught me if I had had any voice. My obligations to her, and the personal tie between us, are as strong as yours can possibly be to your teacher. But you surely will not think me unfeeling if I say that the change that was made in music, and especially in the seriousness of women's parts in dramatic music, by Wagner, put my mother out of date as a teacher and a guide for women of genius of the highest order on the lyric stage. She is a wonderful old

438

woman in her way; but if Ternina had got her ideas and training from her, Ternina would now be singing Donizetti, Rossini and Mozart in provincial towns instead of playing Brünhilde and Isolde at Covent Garden and Bayreuth. I no more blame or dislike your friend for not making you play Nora in A Doll's House in the nineties than I blame or dislike my mother for not teaching my sister the parts of Brünhilde or Sieglinde. On the contrary, I highly value my knowledge of the old school, which many Wagner enthusiasts lack, to their own serious disablement.

But that does not alter the fact that my mother's very competence and self-confidence in the old operatic school of music made it impossible for her to understand or deal with Wagner's music. Ibsen did for women in the spoken drama exactly what Wagner had done for them in music drama: that is, he lifted them from being mere doll-sweethearts, with no influence except the influence of their pretty faces, into serious and sometimes heroic figures, exercising moral influences and religious influences; responding to these influences from others; and struggling with all the currents of the thought of their day. That was why women instinctively jumped at Ibsen, and also why many men instinctively objected to him.

Now tell me this. Have you ever tried to imagine what effect The Taming of the Shrew, on the old Garrick lines, would produce on a person who, the night before, had seen Ibsen's Doll's House for the first time? I dont believe you ever did, because you never saw the Doll's House at the psychological moment, and never experienced the curious shock which it gave. For all that, your independent and original share in the instinct of the time enabled you to make the married part of The Taming of the Shrew tragic, and to win a success of the first order in a part that had never before carried a success of more than the second order. Now I *know* that this must have been done by yourself; for if you had merely Fotheringayed it under the guidance of your manager, he would have remodeled his whole version and made Drew play Shakespear's Petruchio to your Katharine, whereas Drew only played Garrick's Petruchio and cut a very poor figure beside you in consequence. The truth is that when the public changes its point of view, everything has to be altered; and the safest guides and most trusted traditions become more dangerous than the innocence of a novice. Up to a certain moment the public exult in the downfall of Shylock, the taming of Katharine, and the discomfiture of Malvolio. Then they suddenly open their eyes and become ashamed of the treatment of these three unfortunate people. The sympathy goes with instead

439

of against them. Irving's Shylock succeeds; and your Katharine succeeds. Malvolio has to be grossly clowned, because when he takes his part seriously Twelfth Night becomes a most uncomfortable play. In the same way, for a whole century Charles Surface's traditional explosions of laughter at the screen disclosure in The School for Scandal amused his audiences and enlivened the play. Then there came a moment—especially when you played Lady Teazle—when people no longer laughed: they only said "What a cad!" And from that moment the greenest amateur, left to himself, had a better chance as Charles than the most experienced repository of all the traditions.

Let me describe to you a curious scene I saw in the early Ibsen days, when Mrs Beringer got up a performance of Ibsen's Pillars of Society at the Opera Comique. As it seemed a dreadful venture then, she asked Mrs Kendal to help out the matinée by reciting something. But no help was wanted. Ibsen attracted a very special audience, and stood it on its head with his usual grim magic. We all felt very serious indeed when the curtain fell. Enter, suddenly, Mrs Kendal, newly arrived, charmingly dressed, beaming, fluttering with popularity and condescension, conscious that she was doing a kind thing to Mrs Beringer, and going to console and delight a houseful of people bored to death with gloomy Norwegian nonsense. She walked round the house at the back of the circle (that was the way the Opera Comique was built), an entrancing vision, and presently appeared on the stage and recited—oh, so cleverly —Ostler Joe! She felt, I think, that she was producing a tremendous effect; but she did not know what sort of effect, and does not, probably, to this day. It was as if some goodnatured pagan, coming into a cathedral at high mass, and seeing a number of people looking very grave, had with the best intentions tried to cheer them up with a comic song. Please remember that Mrs Kendal was then incomparably the cleverest, most highly skilled, most thoroughly trained, and most successful actress on the London stage. And yet she vanished from it in the prime of her power simply because she persisted in believing in [Pinero's] the Ironmaster and [Sardou's] A Scrap of Paper and Ostler Joe, and in asides and soliloquys, and in rooms with three doors, a French window in the flat, and an entrance through a conservatory in the corner, when people had seen plays which, however disagreeable they were, somehow made all these things seem artificial and old fashioned. It was not in the least because she was forty; for there had never been a time when women of her age were more triumphant in society, or the old-fashioned ingenue more snubbed. All the demand was for fully matured women playing women's parts; and when Mrs Kendal failed in trivial girl's

440

parts (which real girls could not play as well as she, but *could* play well enough), the objection was not to the age of Mrs Kendal but to the age of the part. Unluckily for Mrs Kendal, the drama of 1860 dealt exclusively in heroines under 25; and as Mrs Kendal had made up her mind, on the strength of thirty years successful experience, that the drama of 1860 was the right thing, she vanished into the provinces as aforesaid. Irving followed her; and even Wyndham might have kept them company had he not been modernized at the last moment by [Jones's The Case of] Rebellious Susan, which he denounced and protested against, up to the very last rehearsal, as a hopeless blunder.

Now bear with me a moment (I am going to be more appreciative than you think) whilst I say a word about Augustin Daly. You know that his view was practically that of Mrs Kendal and of Wyndham, and indeed of all the experienced, trained, competent, successful people of his day, as opposed to the cranks of whom you may take me as a modest sample. What is more, he was very largely right: that is why it was impossible to convince him that he was partly wrong. It is easy to say of Mrs Kendal that she has vanished into the provinces; but this means only that she makes so much money there, and is so popular there, that it is not worth her while to trouble about the west end of London. The Scrap of Paper actually does make more money for her than Hedda Gabler would. This would be ten times more true of anyone who could play Shakespear in the grand manner, as you can. Barry Sullivan turned his back indignantly on London about 40 years ago because he lost £800 in two months in London management! Irving must have often lost more than that in a week. Sullivan became "a provincial actor"; and Irving became the head of his profession in London. But Sullivan's whole career was a triumphal progress: he died enormously rich; and his monument and statue might be envied by Garrick. And all this he did on Shakespear and Cibber-Shakespear, on The School for Scandal, The Gamester, The Stranger, The Wonder: a Woman Keeps a Secret, and, by way of something modern, Richelieu! Irving, whose London management ended in a collapse so complete that his friends had to subscribe to send him to the seaside, is recovering himself as a provincial actor playing old plays—The Merchant of Venice, Louis XI &c &c &c. Take the case of Duse, who affects the ultra-modern, the super-intellectual. Her real financial stand-by is that ancient sensation La Dame aux Camellias, which she puts up always to recover what she loses by more modern plays. Everywhere the old school is triumphant when its exponents can act: those who despise it are generally people who, not being strong or skilful enough for it, make a merit of their

441

own weakness, and cloak their defects by the morbidity of sham problem plays and the strangeness and novelty of Ibsen and Maeterlinck. There is no mortal reason why you should not pursue your career with great gain and glory on the old lines, and have *your* statue—a much finer one than Mrs Siddons' on Paddington Green—without having ever played a single part that Ristori might not have played and Augustin Daly admired. You have therefore nothing to reproach him with: his guidance was sound; his advice was good; and even if, like Sarah Bernhardt, you keep in touch with London, and try an occasional experiment in a new direction, you will still find yourself working mostly on his lines simply because up to a certain point there are no better lines. If his spirit ever sees the tamed Brassbound kissing your hand, he may say "After all, that is what I was driving at in Gucki, though in my day it was supposed that a woman's triumphs must be triumphs of coquetry and not of character—Heaven forgive us all!". So you see the way of loyalty to his influence and gratitude for his teaching is still the way of security, prosperity, popularity and peace.

But this does not mean that you are to sacrifice yourself to his traditions. Many things that were right when he said them are now wrong. Changes took place in the public point of view in his own lifetime, when his views and sympathies and traditions had become habits that he could not change; and the consequence was that the guidance that was helpful to you before the change, hindered you and involved him in difficulties after the change. Above all, it was not possible for him to see the artist he taught as I see the artist who taught me; and you must not press me to pretend that you did not outgrow his guidance. Finally —and here I can only beg you to make some allowances for that part of my career which lies quite outside your experience and temperament (I am alluding now to Shaw the political economist)—there came an economic change by which the old system of One Manager, One Theatre had to give way to the new order of One Syndicate, Fifty Theatres. Take my word for it that with all its faults it will be an improvement on the old system, though the old system would have held its own easily if every manager had been a Daly. You know well how far that was from being so. You tell me that you never quarrel with any one; and in the next sentence you quarrel with me "finally." May we live to have many more quarrels, provided you have no disappointments! ... I am only feebly trying to take care of you, thereby reversing the natural order in which the woman always has to take care of the man. You said a woman ought to be taken care of. She ought; but she never is. It is only, I suppose, because you are such a magnificent

442

instrument for my art that I have risked wounding you for the sake of making business easier for you.

And now, on what terms may I be forgiven? Must I be your devoted friend, and treat you as a splendid lady with white hair and sacred memories, all past, and no present nor future? Must I lie and pretend and conceal, in the manner of an affectionate and devoted daughter whose mother must never have anything mentioned that could remind or wound her? If only I were strong enough, I had much rather deliver you from all stifling, ageing, sentimental ties and loyalties; tap your heart all over with an adamant hammer to convince you that it is not in the least broken; and inspire you to the conquest of a new world, with new ideas, new people, new plays, new struggles, new failures that will turn out to be triumphs, new hopes and fears, new everything. That is not the way to be nice to you; but it is the only way to be of real use to you. Hermione [in *The Winter's Tale*] has been long enough on her pedestal.

To conclude prosaically, here is George Alexander's reply to my letter. There is nothing in it: he is evidently not ripe for the project just now and only wishes to be friendly.

yours sincerely
G. Bernard Shaw

To HARLEY GRANVILLE BARKER

Alness
[C/3; X/168]   12th August 1904

[From early August until the end of September the Shaws were in Scotland, at Alness, Rosemarkie, and Edinburgh. They visited North Berwick before their return to London in October. The curtain-raiser for Arnold Daly was *How He Lied to Her Husband*, Shaw's reply to the American Candidamaniacs, which he commenced on 13th August and completed in four days.]

Our expedition has been so far a ruinous failure. The place is impossible—no place to write—no place to bathe—the inn a new tumor on an old public house in a village shed—the firth a sludgy morass except at high tide. The journey wrecked me; put me out of my stride; lost me four days work for nothing. Oh these holidays, these accursed holidays! Now Charlotte must go forth & find me a possible habitation, whilst I abandon Rule Britt. to write a curtain-raiser for Daly, who

443

writes to say that he wants to produce it at latest on the 10th Sept.!!!
There is no comfort in your list. I think, however, that I may have the
play finished early in September.

GBS

To HARLEY GRANVILLE BARKER

Firthview. Rosemarkie. Fortrose

[C/3; X/168]   24th August 1904

[Barker *did* play Keegan in the Royal Court production of *John Bull's Other
Island*. He appeared as Larry Doyle only once, in a special performance of
Act III at No. 10 Downing Street, on 30th June 1911, in the presence of
King George V, Queen Mary, and the Prime Minister, Herbert Asquith.
Charles Vernon France (1868–1949) appeared later in the year at the Royal
Court Theatre as Morell in *Candida*.]

We shall probably stay here for some time, if not for all the time. I
finished the first draft of the play yesterday, and began the revision &
staging this morning. There is no ending at all: only a transcendental
conversation which will stagger the very soul of Vedrenne & send the
audience away howling. Larry is now a very unsympathetic part, and
is not at all an actor's treasure, Keegan being the serious star & Broadbent the comic one. You may have to play Keegan after all. France
might play Larry if he is destitute enough to want the job. Rule
Britannia will not do: it is too frankly a jest; and we shall have to play
off the piece as a very advanced and earnest card in the noble game of
elevating the British theatre. I am too busy to write to Vedrenne yet:
I must cram all sail on to finishing the staging and getting the prompt
copies typed. I have little hope of reaching that haven much before the
10th Sept.

If the first performance is to be on the 18th Oct, we should not begin
rehearsing much later than the 15th at latest; and it would be better to
begin on the 3rd, which will mean a rehearsal *every day*. If the cast is
otherwise engaged & wants Wednesdays & Saturdays off &c &c, then
the production must be postponed, or else I must lose my holiday &
die; for remember that I have been working like ten galley slaves all
the time down here & I must get a lazy fortnight before I attack the
rehearsals.

GBS

J. E. Vedrenne

Granville Barker
(*Photograph by Johnson & Hoffman*)

Gilbert Murray

Archibald Henderson
(*Photograph by Lizzie Caswall Smith*)

Ellen O'Malley

Lena Ashwell

Louis Calvert
(*Mander & Mitchenson
Theatre Collection*)

Robert Loraine
(*Mander & Mitchenson
Theatre Collection*)

To J. E. VEDRENNE

Firthview. Rosemarkie

[C/40]   25th August 1904

[The first performance of *John Bull's Other Island* was at a matinée on 1st November. Shaw's self-drafted interview, "'Plays Which Irritate': Mr. Bernard Shaw Describes His New Work," appeared in the *Daily Mail* on 30th August.]

Barker writes to me that you are thinking of the 18th Oct as the date of the production of my play. That is too early: it would be throwing away money to produce it before parliament meets again. The political people will count for a great deal in the stalls; and they will not come back to town before the session opens. At all costs you must wait for them—alternate matinees of Candida & East Lynne will fill up any gap.

A Daily Mail man has written to me for a lot of information about my projects. I shall send him as much as I think good for him.

G. Bernard Shaw

To HARLEY GRANVILLE BARKER

Firthview. Rosemarkie

[A/3; X/168]   28th August 1904

[Shaw gave his personal supervision to the casting of all of his plays, even when he was not producing them. He kept extensive files of names of performers who interested him, and, as a consequence, he rapidly gained a reputation for the excellence of his casts—and for his stubbornness in refusing to accede to the casting ideas of the managers and producers of his plays.

Of the many actors named in this letter, most appeared in various productions at the Royal Court under the Vedrenne-Barker management. J.L. Shine (1854–1930), who had had a long and varied career in the theatre, gave a splendid performance as Larry Doyle, but soon relinquished the part to C.M. Hallard and never appeared thereafter in a Shaw play at the Royal Court. His brother Wilfred Shine (1862–1939) appeared as Barney Doran. The valet Hodson was played by Nigel (later Sir Nigel) Playfair (1874–1934). A.E. George (1869–1920) was Matthew Haffigan. Lillah McCarthy (1876–1960) first appeared on the stage in 1895 in A.E. Drinkwater's company. She subsequently appeared as leading lady to Wilson Barrett in London and America 1900–04. The Irish-born Ellen O'Malley (d. 1961), who was Shaw's choice for Nora, also played Gloria Clandon in *You Never*

445

Can Tell and Candida, and in 1919 appeared as Ellie Dunn in the first London production of *Heartbreak House*.

W. Kingsley Tarpey's *Windmills* had been produced by the Stage Society in June 1901. *The Death of Cromwell* was never written, although Shaw toyed with the idea as late as 1927.]

Dear Barker

Attention!

There are 12 people in the cast. I do not think any of them need be expensive people. I renounce Brandon Thomas: there is nothing worth his salary.

There are 6 male dialect Irish parts. One of them, the stage Irishman, who does not reappear after the first act, might be done by, say, Neville Doone, if he can sling the dialect.

Patsy Farrell is a young, silly, flaxen polled, mossy headed Irish lad. If you could achieve the brogue, you might play him as a variation on Speed. For him I suggest Graham Browne.

The two parts in this dialect set which will be coveted, and create jealousy as to the lead in that line, are Matt. Haffigan, an old, small, peat faced, leathery man with a very deep plaintively surly voice, and Barney Doran, a coarse, red haired reckless man of barbarous humor. Haffigan has his chance in the third act (he does not reappear); and Doran has what will be professionally considered the fattest bit—the story of the pig in the first scene of Act IV. I should give [J.D.] Beveridge [the rôle of] Doran, as he is veteran enough to be entitled to the best bit. I confess I dont quite see Shine as Haffigan: who would suit [Mark] Kinghorne better if K were an Irishman; but we shall want Shine anyhow either for that, or for Father Dempsey. He would be good as the priest; but the job is rather too small for him. Failing Beveridge, he or Wilfred Shine might play Doran. Failing Wilfred, [Ernest] Hendrie—always if he can cackle appropriately. Corney Doyle, an elderly, careworn, country town man of business, presents no difficulty & needs no big salary. I have not thought of anybody in particular for him. Query, Charrington?

Hodson stands by himself. [O.B.] Clarence, [George] Trollope, [Charles] Brookfield, Playfair, anybody who can do the conventional valet, and break out a bit in the third act. Not, observe, a butler like [Frederick] Volpe; but a valet.

Keegan is a part apart. One suggestion will surprise you. I believe Shine (J.L.) could be made do it; but this is by the way for the present. The age presents no difficulty, because Keegan is not an aged or heavy man. For instance, if you had to play Newman, or even Leo XIII, you

446

would need only the make-up. Kyrle Bellew, Harry Irving, Courtenay Thorpe(!) Forbes Robertson, could all do it with a wrinkle and a touch of powder. So you need not funk Keegan's years. I do not know whether so unsentimental a Roman as you are could possibly catch the patriotic emotion of Keegan, with his island of the saints; but if I were you I think I should try.

Now as to Broadbent & Larry. George's fitness depends on whether he is clever enough to give a new, robust, Aschelike version of his Harelike old gent in Tarpey's Windmills. There is a rather overwhelming love scene where he carries Nora of[f] her feet by mere depth of chest, so to speak. [Oscar] Asche could do it; but I know nobody else; and if it must be faked, George might fake it as well as another. It is essentially a character part. [Charles] Goodhart has the physique for it; so has [Edmund] Maurice; *but*—! What can Playfair do? Anything in that line? Is Calvert capable of character acting? Cyril Maude would do it enormously—some of it; but he could only do superlatively well the bits that George could do well enough. Broadbent's a difficulty. We certainly do want Asche for it very badly.

As to Larry, I see nobody better than France. But if France could do Broadbent (I have seen him only in Les Bienfaiteurs, which he played Larrylike—altogether without the sanguine geniality which is the soul of Broadbent) then we might chuck you into Larry and J.L. Shine into Keegan & worry through. My own feeling is that Broadbent is not in France's line.

Finally, as to the women. I cannot for the life of me recall G[ladys] Ffolliott, though I have seen her often enough. One concludes that Dolores Drummond could do it on her head. But I am quite disposed to give Freda Bramleigh a chance. My wild suggestion of Mrs Waring was based on her Gina in The Wild Duck, which was very good.

Nina Boucicault must be impossible, as Hare is touring with Little Mary; and I presume Nina is with him. Lilla is a frightful temptation: my heart cries Yes By All Means; but there will be grave risk of a scandal. She is a gorgeous creature: I could almost make another Rehan of her. By the way, would her brother [Daniel McCarthy] be of any use? Can Ellen O'Malley play an Irish part naturally? I wonder! I have no other suggestions ready.

[A. G.] Poulton seems not to be fittable. Blake Adams's name conveys nothing to me except associations with Benjamin Franklin & Washington.

I have not thought of any better title than John Bull's Other Island. But I dont mind its being announced as Vedrenne's Folly.

I anticipated the difficulty about postponement; so I have told the Daily Mail that it *will* be postponed until parliament meets. This answers your remark about the need for more paragraphs. A D.M. man wrote to me begging for particulars, Vedrenne having put him on to it. I sent an interview, nominally about Daly, but really about the Irish play.

Remember that the new piece How He Lied to Her Husband is immediately available to make up a program with The Man of Destiny.

I want to write a one act piece called The Death of Cromwell. Cromwell & Napoleon would make a splendid historical program. Also a triple bill

How He Lied

Cromwell *or* Napoleon

Bashville.

for Vedrenne's benefit, with V. as Cetewayo.

I am writing this after dinner, which is sheer suicide. The place is telling heavily on me: I am not sanguine as to the 10th; and I see no difficulty whatever about a postponement or ten postponements, except your Italian origin. When you go to Italy you will find that the waiter, though a most pleasant & social fellow, will be very unlike an English waiter in one important respect. The English waiter waits for orders; carries them out; does not anticipate them; and is neither surprised nor incommoded when you change your mind. The Italian waiter forms the strongest preconception of where you are going to sit and what you are going to have; and if you attempt to upset his expectations he knifes you. Hence your attachment to your arbitrary & totally premature dates.

Keep me advised of your changes of address.

G.B.S.

To ADA REHAN

Firthview. Rosemarkie

30th August 1904

[A/4]

[Ada Rehan informed Shaw at the end of August: "I leave . . . on the 1st for London and hope to sail the middle of September. I well understand your desire to rehearse Captain B, and think it very right. However I will not make a reappearance in London without an assured successful play, that is why I wished to produce the play this winter in America. . . . Then if the play is a success, there would be no difficulties in having it produced by Shubert or anybody else in London. This is the only possible way I can see of my being able to do your play, and that only if you succeed in getting the Shuberts to accept it."

Shaw attached to his reply a small note: "All this is dull stuff about theatrical business. It need not be read until you are quite idle: indeed it need not be read at all. Keep it for your voyage: it will help you to sleep if you have a comfortable deck chair."

Miss Rehan returned to the stage only briefly during the 1904-5 season. On 2nd May 1905 she appeared on the stage for the last time when she took part in the farewell to Helena Modjeska at the Metropolitan Opera House, New York.]

My dear Miss Rehan

I am glad to learn from your letter that Cumberland has done you good. You demand "*an assured success*" for your re-entry in London. O sovereign and auspicious lady, the thing in its absoluteness is impossible; but somewhat may be done; and I now relapse into the character of your faithful family solicitor, and proceed to advise you as best I can.

First, remember that it has happened over and over again that a London success proves an American failure, and—what is more to your point—an American success a London failure.

Now the failure of a London success in America does nobody any harm except the manager, because it is always claimed that a play good enough for London is good enough for anywhere, and that the Americans ought to be ashamed of themselves for not appreciating it.

BUT—and this is important—the failure of an American success in London is bad for everybody, because it is attributed at once to the superior taste of London.

Moral: always try London first. If you succeed, no subsequent failure can discredit your success or lower your prestige in the part. If you dont succeed, the management has a far stronger interest in keeping the piece on and nursing it as an apparent success for America & the provinces than in the case of an American production. If you fail, you can still try America far more easily and hopefully than you could try London after an American failure. And you can win in London what is called a moral victory: that is, if your venture is recognized as aiming high, you can come out of a financial failure with an enhanced reputation, whereas in America nothing succeeds but financial success.

Now in my humble opinion, you need run virtually no risk of failure if you play your cards wisely. Of course if you let yourself be put up

449

against our regulation leading ladies in Sundays & Sweet Nells and the like, you might fail most frightfully, sinking into their class in London critical estimation, and not doing their work as well as they do; for it is no use doing anything but your best: you are tied to the stake by your genius; and in the case of genius the greater does not include the less: it *excludes* it.

But in a *first rate play* by a *first rate author* at a *first rate theatre* under *first rate management*, you *cannot* [underscored four times] fail. The management may lose money, or make less than they hoped; and the piece may not have a recorded run. *But you cannot fail.* There will be great interest, a big first night, respectful notices by all the best critics on their mettle, cabled reports to America, an assumption of success and a high tone in dealing with an important occasion. That is *the least* that can happen. The most may be anything you like to imagine.

Now we are getting closer to business. Who are the first rate authors? Pinero, Jones, and Barrie. I omit for the moment Shakespere, who is played out, and Shaw, who is not yet played in. Very well.

What are the objections to Pinero? Only two. 1. Pinero's heroines might not suit you any better than Mrs Tanqueray suited Duse—but that is for you to decide. 2. Pinero would probably insist on your playing the run unbroken to the bitter end, whereas you might want to play a few of your old parts in the summer star season.

What are the objections to Jones? If you feel that he could fit you with a part, there is only one objection; and that is that you are aiming at a certainty; and Jones, though perhaps on the whole the most successful dramatist of his class, is a hit-or-miss author, sometimes succeeding tremendously, sometimes failing openly and disastrously, especially when he does his best or his worst.

What are the objections to Barrie? Absolutely none. If you can make Shubert get a play from Barrie to open with in London, written expressly for you, do so without hesitation & let Brassbound go hang for the present. Barrie is always popular; always successful; he is a Scotchman who can understand an Irishwoman; and everybody would be prepared to be delighted, which is half the battle. That is why I suggested to Frohman to get a Barrie play for you. The reasons for Shubert doing it are equally strong.

There is, however, one objection common to Pinero & Barrie. If by any chance the leading lady fails to make a brilliant success in their plays, it is she, and not the author, who is blamed. Which, speaking as an author, I consider quite as it should be.

Now I alone of all living authors can claim the advantage corresponding to this objection. If a play of mine fails, everybody says the fault is mine. Nobody ever fails in a play of mine. Nobody can ignore a play of mine. Nobody can get away from it. They write about it, fight about it, misquote scraps of it for ever after. They abuse the author sometimes; but they never abuse the cast. If Brassbound succeeds they will say that Miss Rehan's magnificent acting prevailed over the absurdity of the author. If it fails they will say that not even Miss Rehan's magnificent acting could save it. And my own party, the devout Shavians, will pester me for your autograph or a lock of your hair.

My money value as a dramatist is curious. When my first trial was made in 1894 with Arms & The Man, it drew about $100 a night with the most ridiculous regularity, and would have gone on at that for ever, apparently, if it had not cost about $450 to send up the curtain. With Mansfield in America the same play drew, on big occasions $1000, but mostly from $600 to $800. The Devil's Disciple was a success, though Mansfield now declares that it ruined him (he has read this so often in the papers that he believes it). He sent me about $12,500 royalties, which means that it drew $125,000. I calculate now that any play of mine will draw a steady $2000 a week *by itself*, without stars or a first rate production. Now if you add to this your own minimum: that is, the sum you draw whenever you appear, whether the play is successful or not, you will get the worst that will happen to a management producing Brassbound. This makes a dead loss impossible. In London it often happens that there is hardly $5 in the house—a dead frost. The loss at that is frightful. But with me that does not happen; and with you it cannot happen. We should, even at the worst, reduce the loss to a bearable point. Now this gives me a very much stronger position than outsiders imagine. Nine London productions out of ten do not pay their expenses. No experienced manager expects them to. Therefore, whilst he hopes that the one in ten—the silver mine—will come as soon as possible, he is extremely glad to get plays which will secure a certain quantity of business in any case. If he can say confidently—"Forty pounds worth of fools will always come to hear Shaw's rubbish; —ty pounds worth will always come to see Ada Rehan play, no matter what the bill is; my own clientèle is worth so much; So & So in the cast is 'a forty pound actor' and will draw ten pounds more than his salary: the total will at all events keep the losses down to such & such a figure in case of failure; and with Shaw and A.R. lots of press notices and literary & artistic credit are secure"—if he can say this he will often venture even when he does not believe complete success possible. That is where we great people come in, in spite of our being too good for the public. And you are popular as well as great.

This is too long; but you can read it at leisure; and it is sound economics, dry but useful.

I believe Shubert can be tempted to plank himself on a great Rehan season if he is properly handled. At all events, let him have the chance, whether Barrie or Brassbound is the result.

I must not turn another page.

GBS

To WILLIAM BUTLER YEATS

Firthview. Rosemarkie
[C/5]   31st August 1904

Is there any modern machinery in the I.L. Theatre? Is there, for instance, a hydraulic bridge? There is an extremely awkward change of scene in my second act, and again in my fourth; and I should like to know what I can depend on in the way of modern appliances, if any. It seems to me that as you will deal in fairy plays you may have indulged yourself with hydraulic bridges.

I am greatly touched by learning that history is repeating itself in the matter of our backer. It was revealed to me in a dream (this is literally true) that Miss Horniman backed Arms & The Man & The Land of Heart's Desire; and now I see that she is the benefactress of the I.L.T. also.

G.B.S.

I hope to have a prompt copy completed by the 10th; but I cant guarantee it. Shall I send it to you, or whither?

[By the time Shaw completed *John Bull's Other Island* it had become a play too large and too difficult for the Irish Literary Theatre to handle. W. G. Fay (1872–1949), an Irish actor who served as the company's manager, and who in 1909 toured for Vedrenne-Barker as Matt Haffigan in the play, informed Yeats that, while it was "full of good things," he was afraid "the difficulty of getting a cast for it would be considerable" (BM). Yeats too had reservations, especially about the play's length, and cautiously wrote to Shaw on 5th October:

"I was disappointed by the first act and a half. The stage Irishman who wasn't an Irishman was very amusing, but then I said to myself 'What the devil did Shaw mean by all this Union of Hearts-like conversation? What

452

Shaw's sketch for John Bull's Other Island, 1904

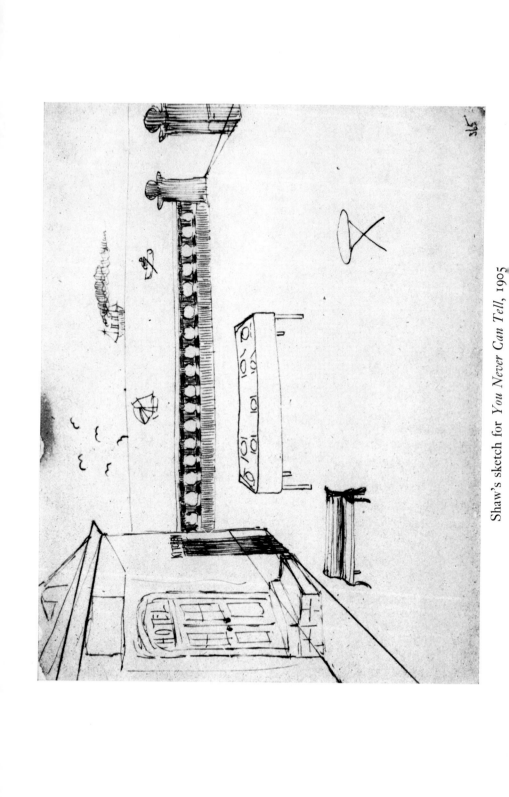

Shaw's sketch for *You Never Can Tell*, 1905

do we care here in this country . . . about the English Liberal party and the Tariff, and the difference between English and Irish character, or whatever else it was all about. Being raw people, I said, we do care about human nature in action, and that he's not giving us.' Then my interest began to awake. That young woman who persuaded that Englishman, full of the impulsiveness that comes from a good banking account, that he was drunk on nothing more serious than poteen, was altogether a delight. The motor car too, the choosing the member of Parliament, and so on right to the end, often exciting and mostly to the point. I thought in reading the first act that you had forgotten Ireland, but I found in the other acts that it is the only subject on which you are entirely serious. In fact you are so serious that sometimes your seriousness leaps upon the stage, knocks the characters over, and insists on having all the conversation to himself. However the inevitable cutting (the play is as you say immensely too long) is certain to send your seriousness back to the front row of the stalls. You have said things in this play which are entirely true about Ireland, things which nobody has ever said before, and these are the very things that are most part of the action. It astonishes me that you should have been so long in London and yet have remembered so much. . . .

"Synge who is as good an opinion as I know, thinks that 'it will hold a Dublin audience, and at times move them if even tolerably played.' He thinks however that you should cut out the Grasshopper, and a scene which I cannot recall, but which he describes as 'The Handy Andy like scene about carrying the goose' and some of the Englishman's talk about Free Trade, Tariffs &c. . . . I have no doubt you will cut in your own way . . ." (BM).

"You have laughed at the things that are ripe for laughter, and not where the ear is still green," Yeats concluded, but when he returned to Dublin the next week and discussed the play with the company, the reaction was less than enthusiastic. Negotiations dragged on for months, and finally, on 1st May 1905, Yeats agreed to drop any claims to the play and to free Louis Calvert to tour in the production in Ireland. "All right," he wrote, "give that queer elephant to Calvert. We all admire it but don't feel that we could do the English men at all. We might be able to play it but it is all uncertain and the great thing is to get it done here. Calvert will do it far better than we could" (Parke-Bernet sale catalogue, 10th April 1962).]

To H. G. WELLS

[A/26]

The Marine Hotel. North Berwick
29th September 1904

[Wells, like virtually every important fiction writer in London except Kipling, had tried his hand at playwriting, with a dramatisation of his novel

453

The Wheels of Chance under the title *Hoopdriver's Holiday*, which was never produced. In August 1904 he had drafted the first act of an original play, *The Tail of the Comet*, which was subsequently abandoned. Eventually he achieved productions of his dramatic adaptations of *Kipps* and *The Wonderful Visit*, but he never wrote a successful play. *'Op o' Me Thumb*, a one-act play by Frederick Fenn and Richard Pryce, had been produced by the Stage Society at the Royal Court Theatre on 13th March 1904.]

Dear H.G.W.

Just a word about your Haymarket suggestion, as you may easily mistake the situation.

If you imagine that you have so artfully concealed your brains that Cyril Maude (compared to whom in point of intellectual appetite [James] Welch is a Goethe) or Frederick Harrison (who is a man of reasonable culture) will accept you unsuspiciously as a disciple of Jerome K. Jerome, you err most prodigiously. In the west end theatrical world the War of the Worlds seems as abstruse as Newton's Principia; and Anticipations & Mankind [in the Making] have given away the rest of the show. And this is so much the better, because the successes of Barrie, whose mighty brain staggers the Strand, and the current suspicions that there has been some mistake about me, have now set the managers hankering after intellectual superiority and even Stage-Societyness, if only it can be combined with popularity. If you could once demonstrate that your stuff would get over the footlights, and not involve giants and Martians & suchlike games, you would not have as much trouble as the regular old stagers.

One thing that is almost beyond conception is the ignorance of the theatrical people of every world besides their own, however contiguous. When Forbes Robertson—one of our "scholarly" actors—said of R.L. Stevenson "Oh, I thought it (Macaire) was by THE Stephenson" (meaning B.C. of that ilk, who perpetrated the libretto of "Dorothy"), he *placed* himself and his whole profession exactly, as far as knowledge of current literature & its reputations goes. If you get a play produced by the Stage Society or any other enterprise that can secure the regulation notices, those notices, with their allusions to your literary fame, will be your first introduction to nine tenths of "the profession." And the superstitious awe with which they will regard you then will be a product of the dense ignorance in which they live now concerning you. The other tenth will have accidentally read your books and will know too much about you to be at the mercy of conventional inferences from an S.S. performance.

But as a matter of fact, it is waste of time to trouble about these

454

considerations. Until you actually write the play, you dont know what it will be like. The chances are that it will not be a play for 100,000 Hoopdriver's colleagues, male & female, but for a smaller number of better people. Now at the Stage Society there is one blessing: you can't fail. There is no means of ascertaining failure. Your audience is bagged beforehand; and the number of performances cannot be exceeded or fallen short of. If the audience is pleased, the play is none the worse: Op 'o my Thumb went up like a shot at the St James's; and other plays that we have done—commonplace ones enough—are now getting played on the strength of their London notices in the provinces & colonies. The suspicion that S.S. plays mean clever plays has been most effectually dissipated by poignant experiences, in spite of my masterpieces.

You must also consider that a dramatist wants rehearsal experience, a part of his apprenticeship that is worth a good deal of solid gold to him. By jumping at all my chances I have rehearsed for public performance nine of my plays, with the result that I am as much an expert behind the scenes as Pinero, and am not sent to the stalls to see my work botched by idiots who havnt read it and wouldnt know what it is about if they did. You cant trust anybody to handle your play; and yet it is only by practice that you can make the company accept your direction as a matter of course. The author is the only person who really wants everybody to be a success, and who can get rehearsals through without friction amid general devotion and hallucination as to being on the brink of a great event. And the most heaven born author-stage-manager cannot do this the first time he goes behind the curtain. Your £20,000 will be all the surer if, by the time it is rehearsed, you have learnt exactly how much of the thousand blunders of the first rehearsal will correct themselves later on without your interference, and how many of the rest you may safely correct at one rehearsal without wrecking the nerves of the company. There are heaps of things to learn even if you start with the fullest knowledge of what is to be done.

Another point for you to consider is this. A £20,000 success is all very well; but the repertory play like Hamlet is still better. The popular play blazes and dies, whilst a thing like "Everyman" goes dragging round the world for ever. I cannot say that I have made much by playwriting—less than £5,000 probably, from first to last (ten years); but only three or four of my 14 plays have been exploited, and these with two exceptions (in New York) not seriously exploited, whilst in the meantime I have had to make the running for the eternal "new" drama. If the hardy pioneer can make nearly £500 a year average in his first ten years, and still have a whole fistful of virgin plays which will

455

hereafter bring him in lots of money, the game is not such a bad one—
not bad enough to justify any first rate man in doing second rate work
on the plea of—but this is moral babble, as Comus says. The main
point is that the Stage Society game is by no means to be despised, and
that if the people who scorned the old Independent Theatre had written
for it all they could, several of them would have been expert dramatists
now.

Finally I would urge that if you are going to write plays, the 20,000
pounder will only be one of them. You can easily give another, not
necessarily to the S.S., but to the Court or some other venture of the
kind. I scribble all this to knock the thing straight in your head, as the
career of a dramatist is not to be entered on without careful consideration, and the great game in it cannot be won without an apparently
reckless preliminary expenditure of genius on all sorts of side shows.

GBS

To HARLEY GRANVILLE BARKER

[A/3; X/168]

Marine Hotel. North Berwick
3rd October 1904

[J.H.Barnes (1850–1925), who appeared in several of the Vedrenne-Barker
productions, had appeared with Irving at the Lyceum Theatre 1901–3.
Charles Daly played Father Dempsey. Arthur Chesney (1882–1949) later
appeared as Lawyer Hawkins in the 1907 production of *The Devil's Disciple*.
Compton Coutts (1850–1910) never appeared in a Shaw production. "Dot"
was Dion G. Boucicault (1859–1929), actor and stage director, who served
as manager for Charles Frohman's repertory scheme in 1910. His sister,
Nina Boucicault (1867–1950), did not appear in *John Bull's Other Island*,
having elected to create the title rôle in Barrie's *Peter Pan* at the Duke of
York's Theatre in December.]

Granville Barker

Do you wish to drive me mad? WHY do you keep on asking me
whether I "really" wish Barnes to refuse Dempsey. I suggested him
for Dempsey. I never uttered or wrote or wired a syllable to imply that
there was the faintest objection to him for Dempsey if you could afford
to have him for it. And here you are with a fixed idea that Barnes rankles
in me. Your head is addled over the job; and you want to addle mine.

I cannot understand your clinging to George as a possible Matt
Haffigan. Is he an Irishman? He seems, from all I have seen him do,

456

to be just the very utter last man alive to touch it. Blake Adams is bad enough: I dont believe he can be Irish at all except under high pressure & false vivacity; but he is more like it than George.

If Barnes does Dempsey (I do NOT object to his doing it) Daly could, I suppose, do Corney.

I have been looking through the III act & think it is as well that we retain Shine: G.B. would not be good in the candidate scene.

The cutting bothers me fearfully. There is too much in the play. I think I shall have to cut out Keegan and Matt Haffigan chock-a-block: there are five separate tragedies in the thing besides the Broadbent comedy.

Do you fully understand that I shall be quite satisfied with Barnes as Dempsey?

I protest again & again that your Chesneys & Comptons & Couttses and so on do not exist for me. Why demand my opinion of phantasms? I never saw them. I question whether *anybody* ever saw them.

On reading the IV act I am more than ever impressed with the necessity of getting Nina. That scene with Larry requires great emotional play of exactly her kind. We *must* get her & Dot. Tell them those are my *orders*. The booming of "How He Lied to Her Husband" ([Arthur] Bourchier wrote for it by return of post) ought to help us.

Barnes will do very well for Dempsey. You could not have a better man.

Our train gets to Kings †, if punctual, at 9. So if you look us up at 10, we shall probably be there.

GBS

PS I assure you I have NO grudge against Barnes.

To J. E. VEDRENNE

10 Adelphi Terrace W C
[A/40]   17th October 1904

[The Prime Minister eventually saw *John Bull's Other Island* no fewer than five times, once inviting Campbell-Bannerman to accompany him, and on another occasion playing host to Asquith.]

Dear Vedrenne

Balfour cannot come to the first performance of John Bull—worse luck. Thursday the 10th is the only day he is disengaged; but he will

457

come then. Will you reserve the Royal box for him & send the voucher
to his hostess, Mrs Sidney Webb, 41 Grosvenor Road S.W.

yrs ever
G. Bernard Shaw

To ADA REHAN

10 Adelphi Terrace W C
[H/58]   27th October 1904

My dear Miss Rehan
  This is Thursday. My play is to be produced next Tuesday. You can
imagine the state I am in with rehearsing. It is great fun; and I have
got them all to the point of believing that this is the turning point of
their careers, and that something immense is happening; but it is
pretty hard work. . . . At present [Granville Barker] is in a wretched
condition of nerves, as he has to play a magnificent part in my new
piece, and cannot get hold of it, being weak from overwork. He is a
very remarkable young man indeed, deriving his artistic genius from
an Italian grandfather, and being already, at 24, noticed considerably
as an actor and dramatic author. . . .
  That little wretch Nina Boucicault refused the leading part in my
new piece in the most old fashioned manner, and spoiled her monopoly
of Irish parts: I suppose because my poor heroine is 34, and has only forty
pounds a year. I now have a very nice clever hardworking Irish girl named
Ellen O'Malley. It is quite delightful to hear her say, when a huge
Englishman (Louis Calvert) hugs her, "Aah dont do that; I dont like
it," with the true Irish maiden peevishness. After all, Nina can hardly
be blamed for feeling doubtful about this new sort of drama; for two
such love scenes have never been seen on the stage before. This is
the first time I have tried my hand on Ireland; and of course, being an
Irishman, I get a quality into the play that is quite unlike anything in
my other plays. It is not particularly complimentary to either the Irish
or the English; but it is fascinating. There is only one stage Irishman
in it; and he has ten minutes in the first act, during which he makes an
English audience think he is a thorough, rollicking, very funny broth of
a boy. He is then convicted of being a Scotchman who has never been
in Ireland in his life.
  How soon shall I rehearse you as Lady Cicely? Probably never; for

458

I think I shall supersede it by something better (and much more terrifying) before we succeed in bringing anything off in the way of a negotiation for its production. . . .

always your devoted author
G. Bernard Shaw

To ELLEN O'MALLEY

10 Adelphi Terrace W C
[H/3]   29th October 1904

[Although Agnes Thomas had been on the stage since 1881, she made her first great successes in the Vedrenne-Barker productions of Shaw's plays, especially as Aunt Judy in *John Bull's Other Island* and as Mrs Clandon in *You Never Can Tell*.]

My dear Miss O'Malley
    We shall have to alter the business at the beginning of Act III for the sake of Miss Thomas. As Shine has taken my script I can't work it out now; but I daresay you can devise something, such as going to the gate or sitting on the bench or remaining on the doorstep and coming down behind Broadbent to tell him about the thump that woke you and getting across above the table before Haffigan enters or something of that sort. The simplest thing would be to remain above the table beside Aunt Judy instead of in front of her; but perhaps you can think of something better. I am writing in great haste; and my wits are addled: I shall lose the post if I try to solve the problem myself.
    Dont let Calvert spoil the earnestness of "Then why didnt you if you are an honorable man?"
    This is the only note that concerns you in the heap that I made today. You are certainly a jewel.

yours sincerely
G. Bernard Shaw

459

10 Adelphi Terrace W C
[H/3]   29th October 1904

Dear Shine

I was trying to make out today how to break up that long speech in the first act, so as not to make it too killing for you. To take it in one straight length from beginning to end is beyond all reason, though you seem equal to it. How would it do this way?—

BROADBENT The usual thing in the country, Larry. Just the same here.

LARRY (not too quick, and shaking his head) No, no: the climate is different. Here, (in this sanguinary England,) if the life is dull, you can be dull too, and no great harm done. (Laughter at the expense of English dulness. So far, shew no sign that there is a long speech coming; and keep your eye on Louis, or he'll immediately bung in a corruscation of some kind, probably out of the fourth act).

(Now go right into sheer poetry with) "But your wits cant thicken &c" down to "dreaming dreaming." Get back to prose in the "No debauchery" sentence by a shiver of disgust and a nervous fidget; and then turn to Broadbent and *tell* him about "An Irishman's imagination"—rub it into him, the climax being your quoting his own words "agreeable to strangers." Then add bitterly and with a sort of half tender reproach to him "like a good-for-nothing woman on the streets," meaning "A nice compliment to pay me, Tom: to tell me that I have the accomplishments of a whore—*agreeable to strangers.*"

Then comes "Its all dreaming—all imagination," which you have got all right. It brings you quite back to cool description, which you need not trouble about, as the audience will be satisfied with the political interest of what you are saying, and will perhaps laugh at Yeats's expense when you mention Kathleen ni Hoolihan.

Then you get back to work again on "It saves thinking." Go ahead angrily, contemptuously, disgustedly, but not poetically; and finish on "useless devils like yourself."

Now comes the final section. At "And all the while" you drop your voice in a sort of horrible shame, because you are no longer describing what the other people do, but remembering what you did yourself. Get the change right; and your talent will pull you through the rest without any further suggestion, the last part of the speech being purely poetic and emotional.

I think this will help you to get command of the speech, and sufficient

460

variety to save you from the feeling of holding on to it for dear life and not being able to stop yourself. But dont worry yourself by trying to carry out my suggestions exactly or hampering yourself in any way with them. Very likely when you study them over you will be able to improve on them. That's all they're for. I think I am probably nearly right as to the best changes and stopping places on the journey; but as to the way of making them, follow your own feeling and make the most of your own skill: turn the whole thing inside out if you like—in fact you wont be able to help yourself when the spirit takes possession of you at full pressure—but dont hesitate on my account to make the part entirely your own: my idea of having my play acted is not to insist on everybody rattling my particular bag of tricks. And so more power to your elbow!

I jotted down today a few of the phrases you are most apt to miss. Here they are. In the last scene you say to Keegan "In heaven, I suppose." The exact words are "Oh, in heaven, no doubt," which sounds more sceptical. In the first act "Now look here, Tom: you want to get in a speech on Free Trade; and youre not going to do it: I wont stand it." This always takes you by surprise; and you fluff it in consequence. Then there is "Yes, yes: I know that as well as you do." The "Yes, yes" gives a much better effect of nervous irritability than an improvised substitute. Today you said "undersell England in the EYES of the world" instead of "markets of the world," which is bad political economy. Act IV, page 8, "He'll tell it himself as if it were one of the most providential episodes in the history of England and Ireland." You generally forget the word providential, and in your agitation extemporize the most amazing variations on the whole sentence. In the scene with Nora you have not quite mastered the place where the neuralgia comes in. It always takes you unawares; you are unable to get as much as there is to be got out of the cross to her and the sympathetic "You seem rather out of spirits." Finally, you shew an irresistible propensity to cut in when she utters the first words of your own speech "eighteen years" (page 18) instead of waiting for her to say "though you dont seem to have much to say to me after all."

That finishes my danger signals. Even if we make a slip or two, there is enough in hand now for success. You and Calvert help one another most amazingly by the contrast of the Englishman and the Irishman. I do not know whether even God feels quite sure of what Calvert will say on Tuesday; but he will be an uncommonly good Broadbent no matter what he says or does, and he gives immense value to your individuality by making a sort of massive background to it. You will both be remembered in the parts; and nothing is rarer than a really

461

memorable performance. And of course you do him the same service. It is like sharpening two knives on one another—or rather sharpening a rapier on a millstone. On the whole, whatever happens to the play, you will score.

I am rather uneasy about Wilfred. He seemed really ill this morning. Excuse haste: I am writing against time. I hope I am intelligible.

yours faithfully
G. Bernard Shaw

To J. L. SHINE

[H/4]

10 Adelphi Terrace W C
1st November 1904

[In replying on the 30th October to Shaw's letter of instructions, Shine paid tribute to Shaw's ability as a director, as well as to his courtesy and tact: "You are a man *worth* working for, and, if your brilliant play is not efficiently rendered, we alleged actors & actresses deserve extermination, for your Godlike patience and courteous consideration, combined with your skilful and workmanlike handling of detail, has been a revelation to me" (BM).]

Dear Shine

I am sorry those confounded words of mine proved so troublesome today; and I cannot sufficiently admire the way in which you managed to get out of that muddle in the third act without disaster.

I think however that we have underrated the difficulty of following the first act now that it is so extensively cut. Some of the people who imagined they could not hear today did hear, but could not follow the moods which developed so rapidly and on such unexpected lines. A man in my box said he could not make it out—could not get the thread of the ideas; and he can hardly have missed the actual words. Try and get it less impetuous and more distinct. I heard perfectly myself; but then I am no judge; for I knew what you were going to say (at least conjecturally: you surprised me once or twice, I admit) and I cannot tell how it would have been if the whole thing had been strange to me. There was no difficulty after the first act; and now that you know what the house requires you will have no trouble when you have got comfortable with the words.

After all deductions you did it well enough to do yourself out of the part; for I have just had an offer from Alexander to play Larry and put up the play straight away. Whether this will come off or not I dont know; but he is in earnest, and the offer is a solid compliment to your playing.

I think you owe St Peter a candle or two; but your church policy was excellent at such short notice, though the martyrs got a little extra martyrdom. If you care to rehearse a bit with Calvert and can settle it with him, and if I can be of any use, let me know.

yours faithfully
G. Bernard Shaw

To ELLEN O'MALLEY

10 Adelphi Terrace W C

[H/3]   1st November 1904

My dear Miss O'Malley

I dont know whether any manager rushed round and engaged you for three years after your performance today; but if not, will you let me know before you do anything decisive during the next day or two. There seems a possibility of something further being done with John Bull in a quarter where an engagement would be useful to you; and though I greatly dislike mentioning proposals that will probably come to nothing, still I am so delighted with your Nora that I had rather risk a disappointment than even an off-chance of finding you engaged if the matter goes any further.

I have heard only one opinion about you from everybody; and I have taken care to explain, and shall always be glad to repeat the explanation, that you did not hear me read the play; got practically no assistance from me at the rehearsals; and created the part entirely yourself, not to mention your unfailing goodhumor and patience and steadiness at the rehearsals. You will excuse my saying this; but I know very well that it is often the artists who give the author least trouble who get the least acknowledgment and have their virtues taken as a matter of course. That is not so, I hope, with me: I am very sensible of how good you have been in every way, though I have had no opportunity of saying so.

yours sincerely
G. Bernard Shaw

To ARNOLD DALY

[G.u/2]

10 Adelphi Terrace W C
15th November 1904

My dear Arnold Daly

As you say, Mrs Warren's Profession ought not to be produced without a word of warning to keep the wrong people away from it. Yet it is very difficult to frame a warning that will not attract the wrong people and keep away the right people. The slightest suggestion that the play is a scandalous one, unfit for young people to witness, will attract those who like licentious entertainments. Yet those are the very people who are disappointed and disgusted by Mrs Warren's Profession, because it takes the one subject that they desire to make romantic and attractive, and makes it sordid & even horrifying. And it rouses their conscience, which they expect the theatre to keep fast asleep for them at all times.

What is worse, the same sort of suggestion will keep away the thoughtful and earnest people whose support alone makes the firm public handling of such a subject possible. The play is simply a study of prostitution; and its aim is to shew that prostitution is not the prostitute's fault but the fault of a society which pays for a poor & pretty woman's prostitution in solid gold and pays for her honesty with starvation, drudgery & pious twaddle. Now there are people with whom you can discuss such subjects, and people to whom you cannot mention them. The patrons of prostitutes form the main body of the latter class; and the women who are engaged in rescuing women from prostitution are the backbone of the former. Get the rescuers into the theatre and keep the patrons out of it; and you need have no fear about the reception of the play.

There is one point on which you were naturally anxious when we discussed the play in London; and that was, as to the presence of young people at performances. I can reassure you as to that from actual experience. Everybody old enough to understand the play will be the wiser and safer for seeing it. Their juniors will learn nothing from it prematurely. As you know, I have labelled the play unpleasant, and put a terrible couplet from Blake's "Auguries of Innocence" on the title-page of the separate edition to prevent anyone from buying the play as a present for children or a school prize or any of the other astonishing & incredible things that people often do with books which they have never read, when there is a reputable author's name on them. But those wise parents who, knowing how effectually innocence protects itself, let their children read what they please, soon assured me

464

that Mrs Warren's Profession is actually a favorite with children; that children find Mrs Warren, with her vulgar tongue and her ancestral fried fish shop, a harmlessly funny person, and the love affairs of Vivie & Frank—especially their playing at the Babes in The Wood—infinitely pretty & touching. And the point which seems so startling to grown up people, and to shirk which would have been to shirk half the problem raised by the relations of Mrs Warren with her old patrons— I mean of course the possibility of close consanguinity between their children—only adds to the charm of the story for children, in whose innocent conception of love there is no distinction between family relationship & sex relationship. As you can imagine, when I learnt this, I had my reward for making Vivie & Frank take the revelation simply & naturally instead of romantically & conventionally.

I should say, therefore, that the young people are the only people who will enjoy the play if anybody brings them to see it in ignorance of its character. Their elders will not enjoy it. It was not written to produce enjoyment, nor even the Aristotelian catharsis of pity and terror, but to make people stop knocking women down and then blaming them for being "fallen." If I have done this with a brutal hand, I do not feel in the least disposed to apologize. I neither saw nor see any reason to be gentle or pleasant with people whose enthusiasm for "purity" and "morality" stops short of paying a living wage for them.

yours faithfully
[G. Bernard Shaw]

To PAKENHAM BEATTY

10 Adelphi Terrace W C
[S/1]   23rd November 1904

[Artemus Ward was the pseudonym of Charles Farrar Browne (1834–67), an American humourist whose writings had been extremely popular in England. Shaw's reference was to "Roberto the Rover: A Tale of Sea and Shore."]

Look here, I am not altogether satisfied that you are not wasting energy in struggling along always some months behind your rents. And overwhelmed as I am by rehearsals, and by the frightful arrears of work and business which rehearsals leave after them, I haven't time to go and see you or even to write promptly when I hear from you. It seems to me that unless you were living quite madly beyond your income in the old days, the economies of the last few years ought by this time to have produced some degree of recouperation. Unluckily economies sometimes cost too much when you have to raise money at ruinous rates, or stave off creditors by practically throwing your children to the wolves.

As to work, that is all my eye. You have never been apprenticed to that trade; and if you went to the British Museum to devil for eighteen-pence an hour, you might possibly do the work better than the drunkards who have the catalogue at their fingers' ends; but you wouldn't do it as well as Mrs [Ellen] Salmon or the respectable ones. You would be like a unicorn asking for a job as a cab horse; you might be the nobler animal; but the cabman would feel more comfortable with the more familiar gee.

As to attempting serious literary work, you WON'T do that. It is one of the mysteries of life that you, being perfectly capable of writing amusingly, humorously, wittily, scholarlily, and like a gentleman in a private letter, are invincibly persuaded that real professional writing for print is a dull, artificial, precedent-limited, imitative, lamp-smelly ceremony, and that there is something indecent in a man putting his real thoughts and feelings and whims on paper for the mob to read. It is too late to hope that you will ever get out of that paralyzing belief now; and since it is clear that nature offers you as work, literature or nothing, and since some fatal *mauvaise honte* forbids you to choose literature, I think it would be far wiser for you to give up all nonsense about working, and frankly consider how you can live like a gentleman.

Now there is only one way to do this; and that is to borrow money enough to enable you to recapture your property, or at least to wait until the remnant of it gets level with your wants. It is useless to be delicate about the matter: a man who has committed the crime of lending as you have done has no right to be squeamish about the comparatively venial offence of borrowing. One disadvantage of lending is that it makes borrowing difficult, because no man likes to lend money to a man who cannot keep it, and will, as likely as not, be bled of it by the first spunge he meets. In short, you must cease lending and begin borrowing.

Now you need not borrow very much, probably. Just sit down and figure out how much you want to enable you to pay off your tradesmen, your landlord, and the rate-collector. Add to that enough to keep the house going until your December rent (or whatever the next ship home is to be), and enough to supply reasonable pocket money. Don't minimise it; and don't make discounts on what you expect to earn in the interim, because you won't earn anything. On the other hand don't

466

put down anything for debts of honour or sums due to Octavius [Beatty's brother], or to make good embezzlement by friends of the family. A new suit and hat, and the price of a champagne treat to your uncle (who will not leave you a farthing if he thinks that you want it) would be a fair item; but nothing of an altruistic nature is admissable. Then send me a note of the demd total; and you shall have it if I can spare it, which I can, if it does not outrageously exceed a hundred pounds. You may as well have it as my banker; and you will pay me someday. I simply lend it to you on your personal security which you cannot expect a stranger to do. You cannot save the situation by going to Holloway or getting sold up, as I should have to come to the rescue after instead of before and pay costs into the bargain. And unless your creditors are richer men than I am, you have no right to refuse. Besides which, as you know, delicacy of any sort is utterly wasted on me. I never objected to your paying for me when you were flush and I was stony; and there is no reason why you should be less debonair now that I have made a few hundreds out of Candida in America. And when you get your mind easy for the moment it is always possible that, as to your literary paralysis, you may presently, like Artemus Ward's Corsair, open the window and get out. [Approx. three lines of dots follow in the transcript.] Your letter has just come; and I really cannot express my feelings. You have borrowed £50 at 62½% per annum, and given your furniture as security. Are you mad? Or are all your advisers and friends sharks? I enclose a cheque for £100. Go immediately and pay off the two instalments and the principal, *at once, before another day's interest accrues* (Need I rub in the fact that your blasted delicacy about getting that £50 from me has ended in my having to pay the 62½% interest to Shylock when I could have borrowed it myself at less than 4%. This is what you call business and friendship! Get out!) and, if possible, husband the change so as to get on to the first of January in a solvent condition. Keep this dark; for if you let it be known that you have a penny in hand somebody will borrow it—Tavy or another. Better put a fiver in your pocket and give the rest to your wife.

Tell her, by the way, that I was startled to hear that Edith Livia was getting ONLY twenty-five shillings a week for work at the Record Office. Why, I had a tough fight the other day to get a young woman twenty-one shillings for a much more responsible post; and a relative of mine is getting ten shillings a week as assistant [to the] Librarian at the London School of Economics, to which my wife has given thousands —a wage which we have to supplement by fifteen to bring it up to Edith's standard. She is very lucky, the little wretch!

Tell Mrs Beatty also that I have no means of helping Bertie with the directors of his company: I don't know any of them. You must be patient for the moment. And tell him parentally that his chief has given him a really very valuable and friendly testimonial and that when he is as old as we are, he will know that though the old man naturally looks after his own people he has been more good natured than many men would be in his place.

Thanks for the tip about "silenced priest." I did not myself use the term "unfrocked": in the play the man [Peter Keegan] says they "took away his papers"; but I have been trying all round to get the right adjective.

G.B.S.

To J. E. VEDRENNE

[A/40]

10 Adelphi Terrace W C
26th November 1904

[Shaw had just attended a matinée of *Candida* at the Royal Court Theatre. This was one of two "Extra Performances" scheduled because of the strong demand for seats.]

Dear Vedrenne

Archer came into my box today because he couldnt stand the cold in the stalls. Four cases of frostbite were treated at the Chelsea infirmary —one stall & three pit. A man in the dress circle got so rhe[u]matic after the second act that he had to be lifted out by the attendants. The Morning Post has lumbago for life. The Daily Mail threatens to head his article "A Frost at The Court." The fireman caught one man attempting to set fire to the theatre. You will have to warm the theatre and to announce the fact in the advertisements, or the Christmas piece is done for.

There is not a hook or a hat peg in the boxes. You can get excellent ones for threepence apiece. The man in Box B said that if there had been a hook he would have hanged himself to draw public attention to the frightful cold. My wife was affected to tears by the play; and her tears froze so that it took me five minutes to get her eyes open with the warmth of my hands, which are now covered with chilblains. My mother

468

went to sleep; and we are still (6.15) vainly trying to wake her. I think
you have done for her. You can get coals & blankets at the Parish Hall,
I believe. Why not apply?

ever
G.B.S.

To GRANT RICHARDS

10 Adelphi Terrace W C
[D/4]   30th November 1904

My dear G.R.
   What's going to happen? I gather from the proposals I am receiving
from publishers that something is. Do not let me add to your worries:
I dont want anything but a little first hand information; but that would
be welcome as a counterweight to the mass of secondhand that is
accumulating.
   Can one see you these times—I don't mean calls at the office, but in
comparatively private life.

yrs ever
G. Bernard Shaw

To HARLEY GRANVILLE BARKER

The Old House. Harmer Green
[A/3; X/168]   6th December 1904

[Lady Mary was Gilbert Murray's wife. Miss Tita was Tita Brand (b. 1879),
daughter of the opera singer Marie Brema; she played Gloria Clandon in
the Royal Court production of *You Never Can Tell* in May 1905.]

   Your labors—heroic, I gratefully admit—are conclusive. With
regard to all that part of the play which you took part in yourself for
six performances, you find that it can't be cut except in mere desperation, to shorten the last scene.
   As to the rest, you cut it as Irving cut Lear: that is, cut wherever
you can make a skip and a clean joint. Nora fades ineffectively from the
stage with a little gasp like the last flicker of a burnt-out candle. Broadbent's laughs are cut out (obviously under the influence of Lady Mary)

469

because they encourage him in buffoonery; but I grieve to say that Keegan's solemnities are not cut out on the far more serious ground that they encourage him in slow preaching. You will be stupended at my meanness in this obvious & cheap retort; but if you send the play round to the rest of the cast and ask them to cut it, they will all do the same thing in perfectly good faith. Playfair, for instance, wont cut his reason for being a Home Ruler, one of the most quoted & penetrating passages in the play on the superficial political side. Broadbent wont cut his naturalization reductio-ad-absurdum of Gladstonian pro-Irishism. Nora wont cut her exit—perhaps the best exit in the play. But they will skip and join gaily in the passages that did not come home to themselves; and the total result will be a very brief play indeed. Irving got Lear down to one third of its length. Result: an unbearably tedious failure, because the characters became mere shells. The mechanical part of them walked & stalked: their souls & the air of ancient Britain had fled. If he had played the original from 6 to 12 word for word, or smartened his own business & played it from 7.30 to 11.30, the people would have been very weary; but they'd have been fascinated & talked about it for a week after so that everybody they talked to *must* have gone to it. Now you want to do the same thing to John Bull, partly because you want to save time at any cost, but also partly because you have as much taste for Ireland as Irving has for Shakespear, and some sound natural dislike into the bargain.

There is only one way out of the difficulty; and that is to re-write the play as a west end theatre piece. To this there are two objections: first, that I dont want to sacrifice my aim to the box office, and, second, that I could write a new play in the time. It would be much more sensible to announce a Shaw festival, and play the piece at its full original length, two acts after lunch & two after dinner.

No: there's nothing to be done but either drop the play—which, after all, has served its turn pretty well—or else play it as before from 2.30 to 6 (or whatever it was) and from 8 to 11.30 if you hamper yourself with an evening performance. But better let it go altogether; for the difficulty of getting the cast together again will be considerable—insuperable if you play at night, probably.

I am sorry to be pigheaded; but right is necessarily pigheaded. Your first act (or scene) in Cork, with Broadbent already in tweeds on Irish soil, would be about ten minutes longer than the existing first act, and would do its work worse. It's no use: you cant get round the central immovable fact that there are too many life histories in John Bull to be lived in two hours & a quarter. The theme is a huge one; and it cant be cut down to Court size. Almost all the misfires which have already occurred have been caused by the omissions: a cut play is always a long one. Bow, therefore, hardily to Fate & waste no more time over a hopeless job.

Miss Tita, quite uncrushed—nay, stimulated by being called a flouncing rhapsodist and a dozen other names; challenged also to name any *human* thing she can do; now without the smallest hint from me, asks to be allowed to study Gloria. The more I think of this, the more I feel disposed to make a virtue of Tita's difference from the leading lady type (an Italian prima donna type essentially) and try whether we cannot educate the public a little in that direction. It's rather a case of Rebecca or Rowena; and as you violently object to Rebecca, you had better give Rowena a chance. After all Tita has a personality of an ardent kind; and it is just this personality that rules her out, whereas if we had a scrap of originality it would rule her in. Mrs Theodore Wright & Tita would make Y.N.C.T. a perfectly new thing. It has always seemed merely a farce written round a waiter. It ought to be a very serious comedy, dancing gaily to a happy ending round the grim earnest of Mrs Clandon's marriage & her XIX century George-Eliotism. You are at present such an old professional that you are much more Philistine than Vedrenne; and unless you make haste to become as a little child again, you will have musical comedy on at the Court before the end of 1905. No time for more. I dont think we shall come up to Adelphi until Friday morning.

G. Bernard Shaw

To ARCHIBALD HENDERSON

The Old House. Harmer Green
[C/7; X/141.e]   6th December 1904

[Shaw's insistence upon taking an active part in the preparation of the biography, coupled with his endless involvements in other directions, resulted in long delays in the provision of information and the reading of manuscripts. As a consequence, Henderson's book was not published until 1911.]

I have had many twinges of conscience about your questions; but I have not forgotten them, and hope, now that my new play is finished and produced, that Christmas will see me through the fearful arrears of business & correspondence that have accumulated.

Do not bother about Truth & the picture articles. I can tell you all that is necessary about them. I hope my replies to the questions will help you out. Do not be in too great a hurry to dispose of the book, by the way.

G. Bernard Shaw

To GRANT RICHARDS

[H/4]

The Old House. Harmer Green
18th December 1904

Dear Grant Richards

Matters have now reached a point at which I must take action. I have lost and am daily losing considerable sums by your failure to keep the market supplied with my plays, which are just now in special demand. And my royalties are some years in arrear. I take it that as you have not answered my private letter asking how you were situated, you prefer to leave our affairs to the ordinary course of business.

You at present have the plates of the books you have published for me. I must either get those plates into my hands at once, or else have the volumes which are out of print set up again. Under our agreements your license to print them is limited to 2500 copies; and there is a proviso that this license lapses if the books are not continuously on sale, or the royalties not paid within a certain period. In short—since all the conditions have been disregarded—you have practically no license to print my books now at all. Therefore the plates are useless to you. To me they would save time and expense in getting my books on the market again. I therefore ask you at what price you would let me have them. If the price is reasonable, it can be deducted, for the benefit of your other creditors, from the royalties due to me; and I can wait for the balance until your affairs are sufficiently recovered to enable you to make some settlement.

Failing an arrangement of this kind, I shall proceed to recover my royalties, and force a definite bankruptcy; for the present position (as I understand it) in which you are neither bankrupt nor solvent, and in which booksellers are complaining that they cannot obtain copies of my books to meet a special demand for them, is intolerable. A glance at my account will remind you that I have not been an unfriendly creditor; but as you gave me no notice of the meetings which have taken place, and have not responded to a friendly inquiry, I conclude

472

that your affairs have reached a point at which you do not care what I do.

Unless I have a satisfactory reply in the course of next week I shall put the matter into my solicitor's hands, and instruct him to go ahead with all possible expedition and vigor.

I shall be in London for a part of Tuesday; but for the rest of the week I shall be here at Harmer's Green.

yours faithfully
G. Bernard Shaw

To ALMA MURRAY

The Old House. Harmer Green
[A/5; X/109]   27th December 1904

My dear Miss Alma Murray

Arms & The Man is off. As luck would have it I took to reading it one day on my way back from a Candida rehearsal, and was startled to find what flimsy, fantastic, unsafe stuff it is. I countermanded it at the Court then and there, and made them put up You Never Can Tell instead. I think we had better rest on our 1894 laurels; for unless we could get a very brilliant cast together, the result of a revival would be general disappointment. . . .

I can never think of you as even middle aged; but I confess that sometimes, when I look at my own whitening hairs, and see my latest photographs all coming out positively decrepit (and I do not yet feel grown-up), I wonder what all these infant Granville Barkers and people think of us all. But I am very good at mature heroines. My latest confessed to 34; but when Ellen O'Malley, at the dress rehearsal, asked with evident misgiving was her make-up all right (17 at the utmost) I had not the heart to ask her for a single line in her face. *You* would have looked 25; but you would not have been Irish enough.

Let me make a full confession. I *did* think for a moment that you could play the mother for me in You Never Can Tell, as she is not an old lady, but an intelligent, interesting & attractive woman of forty; but I gave up the notion because Mrs Theodore Wright has a certain private claim on the part, and has long ago gone definitely into parts of that age, whereas I felt that it would be rather difficult for you to mother two young women in a play without taking an irrevocable step in that direction, a thing not to be done lightly for the sake of such a

473

poor engagement as half a dozen Court matinées. But I should like to know would you have been angry if I *had* asked you.

I used to know Mrs Theodore in old days when she was a revolutionary beauty, and was the friend of Karl Marx & the widow of one of the Holyoakes. I owe her the part if she will play it. But suppose she wont!—she may not have forgiven me for giving Mrs Warren to Fanny Brough. What then?

I often think what an amazingly unlucky choice we two made of a day to be born on. The theatre is only just now beginning to get ready for us.

yours sincerely
G. Bernard Shaw

To JOSEPHINE PRESTON PEABODY

The Old House. Harmer Green
29th December 1904

[A/6]

[Josephine Preston Peabody (1874–1922) of Cambridge, Mass., was a poet and dramatist, whose play *The Piper* won the Stratford-upon-Avon play competition in 1909.]

My dear lady

That is a very energetic letter; and I hope you feel better now that it is off your mind. But it does not tell me anything except what I knew before: namely, that many people have a thoughtless and extremely wicked habit of calling the sexual instinct bestial. Until you get beyond that point there is no use in my writing to you or for you.

You do not seem to have quite taken in the very important passage in my preface [to *Man and Superman*] in which you yourself, as what you call (rightly) an Artist Woman, are put out of court in this matter. The ordinary woman lets you write about her, and laughs at you, having quite another purpose in life than yours. And she will not even read you unless your central theme is what you call her bestiality.

You talk of the Mother Woman as if she could be bracketed with the Artist Woman. You might as well bracket her with the mere pleasure fancier. Ann is the Mother Woman. She is not an artist aiming at the production of poems & romances like Octavius, or at the formulation of a philosophy of life, like Tanner. She is not a moralist, like Ramsden, nor a sensualist like nobody in the play. She is a breeder of men,

474

specialized by Nature to that end and endowed with enormous fascination for it; and all the twaddling little minor moralities that stand between her and her purpose—as, for instance, that she must not be a naughty girl and tell fibs, and that she must not be what you (I rub in this reproach purposely) call "bestial"—all become the merest impertinences. As she says in her transfiguration "I believe in the life to come"; and when you feel the mightiness of that belief and the vital Force of All Forces that is behind it, you will blush at having had no more to say to it than "How unladylike!" (on five sheets of paper).

You are quite right in what you say about laughter: I should probably not have answered your letter but for that flash of insight in it. You will find it, if you want to see it in print, in the preface to my Plays, Pleasant & Unpleasant.

I daresay you have been repelled somewhat by the fact that Ann, being a person in a comedy, has to have a particular as well as a universal character, and that one of her particularities is that she is an Englishwoman. As an American or an Irishwoman she would be impossible unless she surrounded her instinct with a halo of illusions and called it her Purity (the American formula) or refused to discuss it at all (the Irish practice). The Englishwoman looks her function in the face in an astonishingly businesslike manner; and the American who hastily concludes that this is an inferiority should think three times before saying so.

You must not ask me to put Candida into every play. When Ann is married she will look after Tanner exactly as Candida looks after Morell. But when Candida was capturing Morell, and had not yet become his housekeeper and his nurserymistress, she was Ann. The author of Candida is clearly the author of Ann.

Dont, I beg of you, write to me again until you have learnt to respect your sex, and to appreciate that very vital protest of Don Juan against the degradation of the sex relation into a personal & sentimental romance. And whenever you write again on the subject to a person who does not know you, will you please mention your age. It is at least as important as the number of your house, which, by the way, I see you have not given me.

yours faithfully
G. Bernard Shaw

To HAMLIN GARLAND

[H/56; X/181]

10 Adelphi Terrace W C
29th December 1904

[Hamlin Garland, as chairman of a committee in charge of a "Progress and Poverty" dinner to be held in New York on 24th January 1905 to honour the memory of Henry George, had written to Shaw to ask for a message. Garland (1860–1940), an American novelist and historian, had visited Shaw at Haslemere in 1899. For details of Shaw's first encounter with Henry George, see I, 18. John Stuart Mill's "pamphlet" was a small book, *Chapters and Speeches on the Irish Land Question* (1870).]

Dear Hamlin Garland

Henry George has one thing to answer for that has proved more serious than he thought when he was doing it—without knowing it.

One evening in the early eighties I found myself—I forget how and cannot imagine why—in the Memorial Hall, Farringdon St, London, listening to an American finishing a speech on the Land Question. I knew he was an American because he pronounced "necessarily"—a favorite word of his—with the accent on the third syllable instead of the first; because he was deliberately and intentionally oratorical, which is not customary among shy people like the English; because he spoke of Liberty, Justice, Truth, Natural Law, and other strange eighteenth century superstitions; and because he explained with great simplicity and sincerity the views of The Creator, who had gone completely out of fashion in London in the previous decade and had not been heard of there since. I noticed also that he was a born orator, and that he had small, plump, pretty hands.

Now at that time I was a young man not much past 25, of a very revolutionary and contradictory temperament, full of Darwin and Tyndall, of Shelley and De Quincey, of Michael Angelo and Beethoven, and never having in my life studied social questions from the economic point of view, except that I had once, in my boyhood, read a pamphlet by John Stuart Mill on the Irish Land Question. The result of my hearing that speech, and buying from one of the stewards of the meeting a copy of Progress & Poverty for sixpence (Heaven only knows where I got that sixpence!) was that I plunged into a course of economic study, and at a very early stage of it became a Socialist and spoke from that very platform on the same great subject, and from hundreds of others as well, sometimes addressing distinguished assemblies in a formal manner, sometimes standing on a borrowed chair at a street corner, or simply on the kerbstone. And I too, had my oratorical successes; for I can still recall with some vanity a wet afternoon (Sunday of course) on Clapham Common, when I collected as much as sixteen and sixpence in my hat after my lecture, for The Cause. And that all the work was not mere gas, let the feats and pamphlets of the Fabian Society attest!

When I was thus swept into the great Socialist revival of 1883, I found that five sixths of those who were swept in with me had been converted by Henry George. This fact would have been far more widely acknowledged had it not been that it was not possible for us to stop where Henry George stopped. America, in spite of all its horrors of rampant Capitalism and industrial oppression, was nevertheless still a place where there was hope for the Individualist and the hustler. Every American who came over to London was amazed at the apathy, the cynical acceptance of poverty and servitude as inevitable, the cunning shuffling along with as little work as possible, that seemed to the visitor to explain our poverty, and moved him to say Serve us right! If he had no money, he joyfully started hustling himself, and was only slowly starved and skinned into realizing that the net had been drawn so close in England, the opportunities so exhaustively monopolized, the crowd so dense, that his hustling was only a means of sweating himself for the benefit of the owners of England, and that the English workman, with his wonderfully cultivated art of sparing himself and extracting a bit of ransom here and a bit of charity there, had the true science of the situation. Henry George had no idea of this. He saw only the monstrous absurdity of the private appropriation of rent; and he believed that if you took that burden off the poor man's back, he could help himself out as easily as a pioneer on a pre-empted clearing. But the moment he took an Englishman to that point, the Englishman saw at once that the remedy was not so simple as that, and that the argument carried us much further, even to the point of total industrial reconstruction. Thus George actually felt bound to attack the Socialism he had himself created; and the moment the antagonism was declared, and to be a Henry Georgite meant to be an anti-Socialist, some of the Socialists whom he had converted became ashamed of their origin, and concealed it; whilst others, including myself, had to fight hard against the Single Tax propaganda.

But I am glad to say that I never denied or belittled our debt to Henry George. If we outgrew Progress & Poverty in many respects, so did he himself too; and it is perhaps just as well that he did not know too much when he made his great campaign here; for the complexity of the problem would have overwhelmed him if he had realized it, or, if it had not, it would have rendered him unintelligible. Nobody has

477

ever got away, or ever will get away, from the truths that were the centre of his propaganda: his errors anybody can get away from. Some of us regretted that he was an American, and therefore necessarily about fifty years out of date in his economics and sociology from the point of view of an older country; but only an American could have seen in a single lifetime the growth of the whole tragedy of civilization from the primitive forest clearing. An Englishman grows up to think that the ugliness of Manchester and the slums of Liverpool have existed since the beginning of the world: George knew that such things grow up like mushrooms, and can be cleared away easily enough when people come to understand what they are looking at and mean business. His genius enabled him to understand what he looked at better than most men; but he was undoubtedly helped by what had happened within his own experience in San Francisco as he could never have been helped had he been born in Lancashire.

What George did not teach you, you are being taught now by your great Trusts and Combines, as to which I need only say that if you would take them over as national property as cheerfully as you took over the copyrights of all my early books, you would find them excellent institutions, quite in the path of progressive evolution, and by no means to be discouraged or left unregulated as if they were nobody's business but their own. It is a great pity that you all take America for granted because you were born in it. I, who have never crossed the Atlantic, and have taken nothing American for granted, find I know ten times as much about your country as you do yourselves; and my ambition is to repay my debt to Henry George by coming over some day and trying to do for your young men what Henry George did nearly a quarter of a century ago for me.

yours faithfully
G. Bernard Shaw

To GRANT RICHARDS

10 Adelphi Terrace W C
[A/4]   31st December 1904

Dear Grant Richards

As I have had no reply from you to my last letter (though some infatuated person has sent me a circular meant for your trade creditors), I must join with your other author creditors on the 4th to have you

478

adjudicated a bankrupt. I am quite unable to understand why you let things come to this pass. Has the crisis paralyzed you? Our position as authors is absolutely desperate, not so much—in my case not at all—because of the arrears of royalty, but because our books are out of print and tied up, and your business in the hands of the trade creditors whose interests are quite different from ours. We must have somebody to deal with; and if you sit down and refuse to move or act or even answer a civil question—confound you!—we MUST substitute a trustee in bankruptcy.

I cant help thinking the situation might have been saved; for your business must be sound enough to go on; and it is the interest of *all* your creditors that it should go on. Yet you force us to wreck it by simply letting things slide. I conclude that on turning it over you have concluded that you had better ride for a fall than face the economies that would be needed to allow the shop to clear itself; and you may be right; but I wish I could feel sure that you have not simply lost your nerve. At least tell the Sheriff, with my compliments, that you have no power—nor can your trade creditors derive any—to sell any book of mine on any other terms than those specified in my license.

yrs as ever
G. Bernard Shaw

To ARCHIBALD HENDERSON

[A/1; X/113.e, 116.e, 141.e]

[Harmer Green.] Welwyn
3rd January 1905

[Shaw's first attempt to answer Henderson's questions ran to 54 holograph pages (he took the precaution to make a carbon copy for preservation in his files), and was not completed until 17th January. Many of the incidents mentioned in the letter will be found in Volume I, but it is interesting to see how Shaw dramatises and embroiders them, as well as to note which incidents he details and which he suppresses, and the degree of accuracy of his recollections. A large portion of the letter was subsequently revised by Shaw for inclusion in *Sixteen Self Sketches*, 1949 (see "How I became a Public Speaker").

Charles Whibley (1859–1930) was a scholarly writer, with a special interest in biography. Dr Charles Robert Drysdale (1829–1907) was the author of a biography of Thomas R. Malthus (1892) and *Medical Opinions on the Population Question* (1901). Sir Edward C. K. Gonner (1862–1922) was Professor

479

of Economic Science at the University of Liverpool, and author of *The Socialist State* (1895). Rev. John E. Symes (1847–1921), a Christian Socialist clergyman, was Principal of University College, Nottingham, 1890–1912. James Martineau (1805–1900) was a Unitarian theologian, who became principal of Manchester New College.]

Dear Henderson (no use Mistering one's biographer)

I must make a beginning at your questions.

No. 1. Article in which I "brained the critics" of Arms & The Man. I cannot lay my hand on it just now; but The New Review, June 1904 (or possibly May 1904) contains it. [July 1894: "A Dramatic Realist to His Critics"]

No 2. Reference in N.Y. Bookman to an article dealing with my youth & early manhood. It must be to an article "George Bernard Shaw" by Clarence Rook, in The Chap Book (published by H. S. Stone & Co, of Chicago) for November 1896. This is one of the best things of the kind ever done about me. (Copy enclosed).

The phrase "I made all my acquaintances think me madder than usual &c" you will find on page 16 of Fabian Tract 41, a copy of which I enclose herewith.

Another indispensable document ["Who I Am and What I Think"] is to be found in an extinct London illustrated weekly called The Candid Friend. It is in two parts, the first in No 2, Vol I, 11th May 1901, the other in the following number 3, Vol I, 18th May 1901. I will try to find a spare copy for you: if not, Drew must copy it. You might almost reprint these three documents verbatim, & call your book, "G.B.S.: Biography & Autobiography."

No 3. I do not remember any public reference to Cashel Byron by W. E. Henley. We corresponded a little; but the only conversation I can remember was a short one at the Royal Academy press view, when we were both too busy to talk much. As I gave up picture criticism in 1889, and have hardly ever been to the Academy since, our meeting was probably not later than that date. But I did one more press view— I forget when—as art critic to the Observer, a Sunday paper which had just then passed into the hands of a Jewish lady [Mrs Rachael Sassoon-Beers], who made Kinloch Cooke editor. I wrote one Academy notice; and it appeared padded out to an extraordinary length by interpolations praising the works of the Jewish lady's acquaintances—"No 2744 is a sweet head of Mrs —— – —— by that talented young artist Miss —— ——" and so on. [See I, 299] Naturally I resigned in a highly explosive manner; but the episode makes it possible that it was at this particular press view (post 1889) that Henley & I met. All I recollect about it is that poor Henley was rather embarrassed, and got away as soon as possible; for our correspondence had been of a nature to lead to strained relations with anybody other than myself; and Henley didnt quite know why they weren't strained, nor how to treat me. For a year before his death I had country quarters in Woking within three minutes walk of his house there; and I was slowly making up my mind to make his acquaintance seriously when he escaped me by dying.

I forget how we first corresponded. I know that James Runciman, now deceased, the uncle of John F.Runciman the musical critic, was a Cashel Byronite, and used to write me letters about Henley (among other subjects). He had known Henley and quarrelled with him; and what between Runciman & Cashel Byron, I got into correspondence with Henley. Henley admired Cashel Byron—I have always considered this the mark of a fool, by the way—and among the various literary and artistic Dulcineas whose championship Henley mistook for criticism was Mozart. As I also knew Mozart's value, Henley induced me to write articles on music for his paper the Scots Observer, afterwards the National Observer; and I did write some—not more than half a dozen —perhaps not so many. Henley was an impossible editor. He had no idea of criticism except to glorify the masters he liked, and pursue their rivals with spiteful jealousy. To appreciate Mozart without reviling Wagner was to Henley a black injustice to Mozart. Now he knew that I was what he called a Wagnerite, and that I thought his objections to Wagner *vieux jeu*, stupid, ignorant & common. Therefore he amused himself by interpolating abuse of Wagner into my articles over my signature. Naturally he lost his contributor; and it was highly character-istic of him that he did not understand why he could not get any more articles from me. At the same time he made the National Observer an organ, politically & socially, of the commonest sort of plutocratic & would-be aristocratic Toryism, and clamored in the usual forcible-feeble way for the strong hand to "put down" the distress which then —in the eighties—was threatening insurrection. For this sort of thing I had no mercy. I did not object to tall talk about hanging myself and my friends who were trying to get something done for the condition of the people; but what moved me to utter scorn was the association of the high republican atmosphere of Byron, Shelley & Keats, and the gallantry of Dumas *père* (another idol of ours), with the most dastardly class selfishness and political vulgarity. When Henley at last pressed me very hard for another article I wrote to him in a perfectly friendly but frankly contemptuous strain, chaffing him rather fiercely as the master of his fate, the captain of his soul, with his head bloody yet unbowed (you remember his most famous poem?) and his hat always off to the police & the upper classes.

I believe that even then Henley was simply puzzled, and thought I was only making a senseless literary display of smartness at his expense; but of course he saw that I did not want to write for him. This is why our interview at the Royal Academy was rather an embarrassed one on his side—not on mine.

I was not the only person who was revolted by the atrocious vulgarity of Henley's politics as contrasted with the pretentiousness of his literary attitude. The defence after his death was that he knew nothing of politics, and that he placed himself as to the politics of the paper in the hands of his friend Charles Whibley. Whether this was so or not I cannot say. The explanation disarmed me somehow; for I liked Whibley well enough, he being a clever fellow in literary matters, but so utter a mugwump politically that nobody would dream of holding him responsible for any opinions he might conceive himself as holding in that department.

Henley interested me as being what I call an Elizabethan, by which I mean a man with an extraordinary and imposing power of saying things, and with nothing whatever to say. The real disappointment about his much discussed article on Stevenson was not that he said spiteful things about his former friend, but that he said nothing at all about him that would not have been true of any man in all the millions then alive. The world very foolishly reproached him because he did not tell the usual epitaph monger's lies about "Franklin, my loyal friend." But the real tragedy of the business was that a man who had known Stevenson intimately, and who was either a penetrating critic or nothing, had nothing better worth saying about him than that he was occasionally stingy about money and that when he passed a looking glass he looked at it. Which Stevenson's parlormaid could have told us as well as Henley if she had been silly enough to suppose that the average man is a generous sailor in a melodrama, and totally incurious and unconscious as to his personal appearance. But it was always thus with Henley. He could appreciate literature and enjoy criticism. He could describe anything that was forced on his observation and experience, from a tomcat in an area to a hospital operation. Give him the thing to be expressed, and he could find its expression wonderfully either in prose or verse. But beyond that he could not go: the things he said—or the things he wrote (I know nothing of his conversation)—are always conventionalities, all the worse because they are selected from the worst part of the great stock of conventionalities—the conventional uncon-

482

ventionalisms. He could discover and encourage talent, and was thus half a good editor, but he could not keep friends with it; and so his papers finally fell through. This is my opinion of him for what it is worth. My only review of him—that of his poems in the old Pall Mall Gazette under Stead's editorship—was written before I had formed my view of him. I have read it through since I wrote what I have scratched out here, and find I was mistaken in supposing that it contained anything likely to shew him that I did not think him a fertile writer. [The cancelled passage, following "editorship," reads: "so perhaps it was natural that we did not overcome the very slight obstacles that existed to a close personal acquaintance between us."]

I was often accused of brutality in this matter. First, because Henley admired me, and it was ungenerous to repay him by a denial of the sort of talent he desired to excel in. Second, because it was doubly ungenerous of a man sound in wind and limb to disparage a man who was physically a wreck, fighting bravely with his crutches against infirmity and pain. This, of course, is absurd. And yet people have a strong feeling that if a man has lost his hearing or sight bravely in a noble cause, the world is thereby bound in decency to assume for ever after that he had the eye of an eagle and the ear of a hare. I have never belittled a misfortune in that way. Long ago, when [name crossed out: Philip Bourke Marston], a blind poet, (on second thoughts I scratch out his forgotten name) died, and certain maudlin speeches of his were repeated in print as expressions of the pathos of his darkened existence, I said, also in print [*Pall Mall Gazette*, 25th August 1887], that he always said these things when he was drunk, and that the fact that he was blind may have added to the pity of them, but did not give them any sort of validity. In the same way when, in the European revolutionary movement, men came with horrible experiences of prison & Siberian wandering on them, or women whose husbands had been hanged or committed suicide, I have always had to stand out against the notion that they were the better instead of the worse for these misfortunes, or that they derived any credit or authority whatever from them. Give them the indulgence due to enforced weakness or the help due to unavoidable distress; but dont make them heroes & leaders *ex officio* because they have been unlucky enough to be lamed. And so I have often conveyed to sentimental people an impression of revolting callousness simply because I know that suffering is suffering, and not merely the acquisition of a romantic halo. Henley's infirmities were to me trifles compared to those which I had encountered in other cases; and in any case I was trained to look in the face the fact that infirmities

483

disable people instead of reinforcing them. People who learn in suffering what they teach in song usually give very dangerous lessons; and I admired Henley for having no doctrine of that sort. Besides, I have always abhorred the petty disloyalties which we call sparing one another's feelings. And—to make an end of the matter—Henley, though a barren critic & poet, had enough talent and character to command plenty of consideration. A man cannot be everything. I am as fond of music as Henley was of literature; but I am the worst of players, and have a very poor voice.

No 4. The twelve years public speaking is dated in the Chap Book article. 1883 to 1895 would be about right. My first public speech was delivered late in 1879. The late James Lecky, author of the article on Temperament (Systems of tuning keyed instruments) in the first edition of Grove's Dictionary of Music & Musicians, was one of my friends at that time. He was always working at some subject connected with music or languages on the scientific side; and he insisted on dragging all his friends into them too, which was a good thing for them if they had any brains. Through him I got a grounding in Temperament (I am probably the only living musical critic who knows what it means), and, if not a knowledge of Phonetics, at least an interest in it (a permanent protection against such superficial catchpenny stuff as the reformed spellings that are invented every six months by faddists); a due appreciation of Pitman's Shorthand, which I could write myself at the rate of 20 words per minute and could not read afterwards on any terms, as probably the worst system of shorthand ever invented, yet the best pushed on its business side; and finally some acquaintance with men like the late Alexander Ellis, and one which I greatly value with Henry Sweet of Oxford, a revolutionary don who in any other place or country in the world, would be better known than I am myself. This is the explanation of the fact that the cockney dialect which so astonishes readers of "Captain Brassbound's Conversion" is so much more scientific in its analysis of London coster lingo than anything that had previously appeared in fiction.

However, to return to the public speaking. In the winter of 1879 Lecky joined a debating society called The Zetetical Society, a junior copy of the once well known Dialectical Society, which (the D.S.) had been founded to discuss Stuart Mill's essay on Liberty when that was new. Both societies were strongly Millite. In both there was complete freedom of discussion, political, religious & sexual. Women took an important part in the debates, a special feature of which was that each speaker, at the conclusion of his speech, could be cross examined on it

484

by any of the others in a series of questions. The tone was strongly individualistic, atheistic, Malthusian, evolutionary, Ingersollian, Darwinian, Herbert Spencerian. Huxley, Tyndall & George Eliot were on the shelves of all the members. Championship of the Married Women's Property Act had hardly been silenced even by the Act itself. Indignation at prosecutions for "blasphemy," at Mrs Besant's children being torn from her like Shelley's,* were *de rigueur*. Socialism was regarded as an exploded fallacy; and nobody dreamt that within five years it would revive, snatch away all the younger generation, & sweep the Dialectical & Zetetical into the blind cave of eternal night.

Well, one night in the winter of 1879, Lecky dragged me to the Zetetical, which then met weekly in the rooms of The Women's Protective & Provident League in Great Queen St, Long Acre. I knew nothing about public meetings or public order. I had an air of impudence, but was really an arrant coward, nervous & self-conscious to a heartbreaking degree. Yet I could not hold my tongue. I started up and said something in the debate, and then felt that I had made such a fool of myself (mere vanity; for I had probably done nothing in the least noteworthy) that I vowed I would join the Society; go every week; speak every week; and become a speaker or perish in the attempt. And I carried out this resolution. I suffered agonies that no one suspected. During the speech of the debater I resolved to follow, my heart used to beat as painfully as a recruit's, going under fire for the first time. I could not use notes: when I looked at the paper in my hand I could not collect myself enough to decipher a word. And of the four or five wretched points that were my pretext for this ghastly practice of mine, I invariably forgot three—the best three. And yet I must have seemed rather uppish & self possessed; for at my third meeting I was asked to take the chair. I consented as offhandedly as if I were the Speaker of the House of Commons; and the secretary probably got his first inkling of my hidden terror by seeing that my hand shook so that I could hardly sign the minutes of the previous meeting. My speeches must have been little less dreaded by the Society than they were by myself; but I noticed that they were hardly ever ignored. The speaker of the evening, in replying at the end, usually addressed himself with some vigour to

---

* Even then I was Socialist enough to defend the action of the State in both cases; for I have always been somewhat of William Morris's opinion that "There may be some doubt as to who are the best people to have charge of children; but there can be no doubt that the parents are the worst."

485

my remarks, and seldom in an appreciative vein. I was really horribly ignorant of the Society's subjects, though I had read, in my boyhood, Mill on Liberty, on Representative Government, and on the Irish Land Question, and was as full of Darwin, Tyndall, George Eliot &c as most of them. But I knew nothing of political economy, and was a foreigner & a recluse. Everything struck my mind at an angle that produced reflections quite as puzzling as at present, but not so dazzling. My one success was when the Society paid to Art, of which it was stupendously ignorant, the tribute of setting aside an evening for a paper on it by a lady in the "æsthetic" dress of the period. I wiped the floor with that meeting; and several members confessed to me afterwards that it was this performance that first made them reconsider their first impression of me as a discordant idiot.

I persevered doggedly. After about a year of the Zetetical I joined the Dialectical, and was faithful to it for years after it had dwindled into a group of five or six friends of Dr Drysdale, the apostle of Malthus. I went to a series of debates in South Place Chapel and there tried my hand for the first time in a fairly large hall on an audience counted by hundreds instead of by scores. Later on I joined another debating society, the Bedford, presided over by Stopford Brooke, who had not then as yet given up his pastorate at Bedford Chapel to devote himself exclusively to literature. I haunted public meetings like an officer afflicted with cowardice, who takes every opportunity of going under fire to get over it and learn his business.

One of the public meetings was at the Memorial Hall in Farringdon St; and the speaker of the evening was Henry George. As to this, look out for the reports of the Henry George memorial dinner on the 24th of this month (Jan 1905). I have sent them a letter containing a bit of autobiography which I need not duplicate here. Suffice it to say that George shunted me on to the economic tack. I read Progress & Poverty, and went to a meeting of the Democratic Federation at which I rose & protested against their drawing a red herring across the track opened by George. They told me I was a novice, and that I should read Karl Marx's Capital. I promptly went and did so, and then found that my advisers were awestruck, as they had not read it themselves, it being then accessible only in the French version at the British Museum Library. I immediately became a Socialist, and from that hour I was a man with some business in the world. I was so full of it at first that I dragged it in by the ears on all occasions, and presently so annoyed an audience at South Place that for the only time in my life I was met with a demonstration of impatience. I took the hint so rapidly & apprehensively that no great harm was done; but I still remember it as an unpleasant & mortifying discovery that there is a limit even to the patience of that poor helpless longsuffering animal the public, with political speakers. It had never occurred before; and it never occurred again. I now set to work to apply my dogged practice to propagating Socialism. In 1883 I accepted an invitation to address a workman's club [Invicta Working Men's Club, 4th May 1884] at Woolwich; and I thought at first of writing a lecture & even of committing it to memory; for it seemed hardly possible to speak for an hour without text when I had thitherto only spoken for ten minutes in a debate. But I saw that if I were to speak often on Socialism—as I fully meant to do—writing and learning by rote would be impossible for mere want of time. I made a few notes, being by this time cool enough to be able to use them. The lecture was called Thieves, and was a demonstration that the proprietor of an unearned income inflicted on the community exactly the same injury as a burglar does. I spoke for an hour easily, and from that time forth considered the battle won.

From 1883 [1885] to 1888 I was criticising books in the Pall Mall Gazette & pictures in The World; so that my evenings were free. I therefore did a tremendous lot of public speaking & debating. I spoke in the open air, in the streets, in the parks, at demonstrations, anywhere & everywhere. I had quiet literary offnights at the New Shakespear Society under F.J.Furnival, and breezy literary offnights at the Browning Society, to which I was elected by mistake, though I stood by the mistake willingly enough. The papers thought that the Browning Society was an assemblage of longhaired aesthetes: in truth it was a conventicle where pious ladies disputed about religion with Furnival, and Gonner and I (Gonner is now a professor of political economy in Liverpool) egged them on. When Furnival founded the Shelley Society I of course joined that; and we pulled off a great performance of The Cenci before we succumbed to our heavy printers' bills. But my main business was Socialism. It was first come first served with me: when I got an application for a lecture I gave the applicant the first date I had vacant, whether it was for a street corner, or the economic section of the British Association, or a chapel, or a drawingroom. Twice, in difficulties raised by attempts of the police to stop street meetings (which always failed because the religious people joined with us to resist them) I was within an ace of going to prison. The first time, the police capitulated on the morning of the day when I was the chosen victim. The second time, a member of a rival Socialist Society disputed the choice with me, and, on a division, defeated me by two votes, to

487

my secret relief. My longest oration was about four hours, in the open air on a Sunday morning at Trafford Bridge Manchester. One of my best speeches, about an hour and a half long, was delivered in Hyde Park in pouring rain to six policemen sent to watch me, and the secretary of the little society that had asked me to speak for them. I was determined to interest those policemen, because as they were sent there to listen to me, their ordinary course, after being once convinced that I was a reasonable and well conducted person, would be to pay no further attention. But I quite entertained them. I can still see their waterproof capes shining in the rain when I shut my eyes.

In 1888, when I became a music critic, I was restricted to lectures on Sundays, as I could not foresee whether I should have the opera or a concert to attend on weeknights. But still I did a good deal at short notice. At last the strain began to tell; and I found it impossible to deal with all the applications I received. And the repetition of the old figures & old demonstrations became tiresome: I felt the danger of becoming a windbag. By 1895 I was no longer by any means in full blast; and the collapse of my health in 1898 finished me as a systematic and indefatigable propagandist, though I was working harder than ever on the St Pancras Vestry (now the St P. Borough Council). Since then I have only lectured occasionally; and I do not know whether I shall ever undertake another platform campaign.

I return for a moment to the Zetetical Society to fill an important omission in my account of it. A few weeks after I joined it, I was much struck by a speaker who took part in one of the debates. He was a young man of about 21, rather below middle height, but with small, pretty hands & feet, and a profile that suggested an improvement on Napoleon the Third, his nose & imperial being of that sort. He had a fine forehead, a long head, eyes that were built on top of two highly developed organs of speech (according to the phrenologists), and remarkably thick, strong, dark hair. He knew all about the subject of debate; knew more than the lecturer; knew more than anybody present; had read everything that had ever been written on the subject; and remembered all the facts that bore on it. He used notes, read them, ticked them off one by one, threw them away, and finished with a coolness & clearness that, to me in my then trembling state, seemed miraculous. This young man was the ablest man in England—Sidney Webb. Quite the cleverest thing I ever did in my life was to force my friendship on him, to extort his, and to keep it. Lecky presently died and was out of the saga; but Webb fortunately survived; and from that time I became a much more effective person; for I was really a committee of

Shaw & Webb. It is impossible for me to pursue this association further at present: I can only warn you that Webb is one of the most extraordinary and capable men alive, and that the difference between Shaw with Webb's brains & knowledge at his disposal and Shaw by himself is enormous. Nobody has as yet gauged it, because as I am an incorrigible mountebank, and Webb is one of the simplest of geniuses, I have always been in the centre of the stage whilst Webb has been prompting me, invisible, from the side. I am an expert picker of other men's brains; and I have been exceptionally fortunate in my friends.

Now let me interpolate a little more history here. The Henry George episode was, I think, in 1883. A body called The Land Reform Union, which still survives as The English Land Restoration League, was formed to propagate Georgite Land Nationalization. It had a paper called, I think, the Christian Socialist, which did not last long owing to a scarcity of Christians. I joined the Land Reform Union, and met there James Leigh Joynes, an Eton master (son of a well known Eton dignitary), Sydney Olivier, and Henry Hyde Champion, besides two Christian Socialist clergymen, Stewart Headlam and Symes of Nottingham. Symes, I remember, argued that Land Nationalization would settle everything, to which I replied that if capital were still privately appropriated, Symes would remain "the chaplain of a pirate ship." I still think this a very fair description of the position of a clergyman under our present system.

Now Joynes was a vegetarian, a humanitarian, a Shelleyan. He had just been deprived of his Eton post because he had made a tour in Ireland with George, and been arrested with him under the Coercion Act by the police, who did not understand Land Nationalization, & supposed the two to be emissaries of the Clan na Gael. Joynes's sister was married to another Eton master, Henry Salt. Salt was also a vegetarian, a humanitarian, a Shelleyan, a De Quinceyite. He loathed Eton, being a born revolutionist. As soon as he had saved enough to live with a Thoreau-like simplicity in a laborer's cottage in the country (he had no children) he threw up his post and shook the dust of Eton off his feet. Instead of working at Socialism, he founded the Humanitarian League, of which he is still secretary. He and I and his wife, Kate Salt, with whom I used to play endless pianoforte duets on the noisiest grand piano that ever descended from Eton to a Surrey cottage, became very close friends. My article "A Sunday on the Surrey Hills" in the Pall Mall Gazette of (send you this date later) [25th April 1888] describes my first visit to them in [the] country (I had visited them once before at Eton with Joynes); and several scenes of my Pleasant

489

& Unpleasant plays were written in the heather on Limpsfield Common during my visits to them at Oxted (they did not stay very long at Tilford, the scene of the article). Here you have the link between me and the Humanitarians. Another intimate of the Salt household was Edward Carpenter, the author of Towards Democracy, whose works give you the man. We called him The Noble Savage. He also played duets; and we all wore sandals (in the house—though Carpenter used them out of doors too) which he had taught a workman friend of his to make at Millthorpe, a village near Sheffield at which he resided. In this circle there was no question of Henry George and Karl Marx, but a good deal of Walt Whitman & Thoreau. The worst that happened was the death of Joynes, who was slaughtered by a medical treatment so grossly and openly stupid & ruinous that I have never forgiven the medical profession for it since. He left a volume [*Songs of a Revolutionary Epoch*, 1888] of excellent translations of the revolutionary songs of the German revolutionists of 1848, Herwegh, Freiligrath &c. Salt, by the way, has published several monographs on Shelley, James Thompson, [Richard] Jefferies, De Quincey, *et hoc genus omne*.

Now go back for a moment to the Land Reform Union. As I have said, I met Sydney Olivier there. Sydney Olivier was an upper division clerk in the Colonial Office. So was Sidney Webb. At this time they were the two resident clerks there, and were very close friends. When the Fabian Society occurred, so to speak, in 1884, I chose it for my head quarters. It was nothing until I induced Webb to join. Olivier joined too, and was secretary for several years. Now Carpenter's brother, Captain Alfred Carpenter (Royal Navy) and Olivier married sisters; and in this way there was a sort of family connexion between the Socialist & Humanitarian movements.

Further, Olivier had made friends at Oxford with Graham Wallas, who afterwards joined us. In the days of the Hampstead Historic (see the Fabian Tract) Shaw, Webb, Olivier & Wallas were the Three Musketeers & D'Artagnan; and as Olivier & Wallas were men of very exceptional character and attainments, I was able to work with a four-man power—equal to a 400 ordinary-man-power—which made my feuilletons and other literary performances quite unlike anything that the ordinary literary hermit-crab could produce. In fact, the brilliant, extraordinary Shaw *was* brilliant & extraordinary; but then I had an incomparable threshing machine for my ideas—a machine which contributed heaps of ideas to my little store; and when I seemed most original and fantastic, I was often simply an amanuensis with a rather exceptional literary knack, cultivated by dogged practice. They knocked a tremendous lot of nonsense, ignorance & vulgarity out of me; for we were on quite ruthless terms with one another. There were other clever fellows and good friends; but through circumstances of time & place & marriage and what not, they could not be in such constant & intimate touch with us as we were with one another.

Including this wider circle, there was room for considerable strife of temperaments; and in the other socialist societies quarrels and splits and schisms were rather frequent. I believe that my own usefulness, apart from my knack of drafting things in literary form and arranging the other fellows' ideas for them with Irish lucidity, lay chiefly in getting rid of personal friction by a sort of tact which superficially looked like the most outrageous want of it. Whenever there was a grievance I betrayed everybody's confidence by stating it before the whole set in the most monstrously exaggerated terms. Result: everybody repudiated it; anything that was in it got immediately explained; and I was denounced as a reckless mischief maker & forgiven as a privileged lunatic. That role of privileged lunatic has been very useful to me and others during the last 25 years. Fortunately I knew the value of our friendship and combination; and I also knew that it is not sensitiveness that need be dreaded, but malice. And in our freedom from that we were, happily, picked men.

Graham Wallas's book on Francis Place is well worth reading if you want to know how politics are wirepulled in England by real reformers. Olivier began innumerable works. He has a peculiar literary gift & writes verses, essays, stories & plays (a play of his called "Mrs Maxwell's Marriage" was performed by the Stage Society); but, roughly speaking, he never finishes anything; and he is now a C.M.G. and gets Crown Colonies out of difficulties for the Colonial Office. His last job was as Acting Governor of Jamaica; and his views on the negro question are more interesting than acceptable to good Americans.

Your question about the public speaking has led me pretty far afield [of] you. To conclude, do not forget that simultaneously with my desperate attack on the platform, I was acquiring "the committee habit." Whenever I joined a society—even the Zetetical—I soon got on the committee, and learnt the habits of public life & public action simultaneously with the art of public speaking. And I also became accustomed from the first to work with women & regard their presence & participation in public affairs as a matter of course.

I never became an orator. People do not orate in England as they do in America; but the difference exists none the less between the born orator like Jaurès & Mrs Besant and the practised public speaker. All

491

that can be acquired I acquired. As all my public addresses were followed by questions & discussion I got a pretty thorough training. I was fluent & fertile; I did not leave all my literary qualities behind me when I mounted the platform; and, on the whole, I fulfilled my vow and acquired what could be acquired. I daresay I have delivered a thousand public addresses; and no doubt the best ten of them were pretty good as such things go. But I have only a very ordinary voice; and when I have to make a large audience hear me comfortably I have to be very careful with my articulation. As I have always had to try to make my audience think new things, I have never had the successes of the orator who is the mouthpiece of his audience. But I have once or twice been the most unpopular man in a meeting and yet carried a resolution against the most popular orator there by driving in its necessity. And this is all I wanted. I never practised speaking as an art or an accomplishment. The desire for that would never have nerved me to utter a word in public. I needed it as a weapon, as an instrument, as a means to the end of making people listen to what I had to say. I had no use for the transports which the popular orator raises by saying what the people want to have said. And as to the great orator's power of entrancing people and having his own way at the same time, I have never had a scrap of it.

To avoid misunderstanding I had better add that I never took payment for speaking. It often happened that provincial Sunday Societies asked me to come down for the usual ten guinea fee and give the usual sort of lecture, avoiding politics & religion. I always replied that I never lectured on anything but politics & religion, and that my fee was the price of my railway ticket third class if the place was further off than I could afford to go at my own expense. The Sunday Society would then assure me that I might, on these terms, lecture on anything I liked; and I *did*. Occasionally, to avoid embarrassing other lecturers who lived by lecturing, the thing was done by a debit & credit entry: that is, I took the usual fee & expenses, and gave it back as a donation to the society. In this way I secured perfect freedom of speech, and was armed against the accusation of being a professional agitator. At the election of 1892, I was making a speech in the Town Hall of Dover when a man rose & shouted to the audience not to let itself be talked to by a hired speaker from London. I immediately offered to sell him my emoluments for £5. He hesitated; and I came down to £4. At last I offered to take five shillings—half a crown—a shilling—sixpence—for my fees, and when he would not take them at that, claimed that he must know perfectly well that I was there at my own expense. If I had not been able to do this, the meeting, which was a difficult & hostile one (Dover being a hopeless corrupt Tory constituency) would probably have been broken up.

Once, in St James's Hall, London, at a meeting [26th April 1892] in favor of Women's Suffrage, I ventured on a curious trick with success. Just before I spoke, a hostile contingent entered the room; and I saw that we were outnumbered, and that an amendment would be carried against us. They were all Socialists of the anti-Fabian sort, led by a man [Herbert Burrows] whom I knew very well, and who was at that time worn out with public agitation and private worry; so that he was excitable almost to frenzy. It occurred to me that if they, instead of carrying an amendment, could be goaded to break up the meeting and disgrace themselves, the honors would remain with us. I made a speech that would have made a bishop swear and a sheep fight. My friend the enemy, stung beyond endurance, dashed madly to the platform to answer me then and there. His followers, thinking he was leading a charge, instantly stormed the platform; and broke up the meeting. Then the assailants reconstituted the meeting & appointed one of their number chairman. I then demanded a hearing, which was duly granted me as a matter of fair play; and I had another innings with great satisfaction to myself. No harm was done and no blow struck; but the papers next morning described a scene of violence & destruction that left nothing to be desired by the most sanguinary schoolboy.

One other point. I never challenged anyone to debate publicly with me. It seemed to me an unfair practice for a seasoned public speaker, and no test at all of the validity of his case—a sort of duel with tongues, of no more value than any other sort of duel. But I am now sorry that the debate between me and Charles Bradlaugh which the Socialist League (Morris's body) tried to arrange in the eighties did not come off. Bradlaugh was a most tremendous debater; and I should have made a very poor show with him in point of personal thunder and hypnotism; but I had tackled him in his own hall—the Hall of Science in Old St, St Luke's—and I could at least have said my say. The Socialist League challenged him to debate, and chose me as their speaker, though I was not a member. But Bradlaugh made it a condition that I should be bound by all the pamphlets and utterances of the Social-Democratic Federation, a strongly anti-Fabian body. Of course I should have let him make what conditions he pleased, and said my say without troubling about them. But I was too young for that. I proposed a simple proposition "Will Socialism benefit the English people?" with a simple

493

general definition of Socialism. He refused this; and the debate—as I think he intended—did not come off, rather to my relief; for I was very doubtful of being able to make any show against him.

Later on he debated the question of the Eight Hours Day with Hyndman—their second platform encounter. Both sides were dissatisfied, as neither of them stuck to the subject, and the result was inconclusive. It was then arranged that a debate between G.W. Foote, Bradlaugh's successor as President of The National Secular Society, and me should take place on the same question. It lasted two nights. I enclose you a copy of the verbatim report. This was my only public set debate, except one [13th March 1886] at South Place in earlier days, a smaller business, one of a series of four, in which I do not think I particularly distinguished myself. My opponent, a clergyman named [F.W.] Ford, gave me as good as I brought; and my performance was quite eclipsed by Webb, who was in the series and who annihilated his adversary. Mrs Besant, too, was much more interesting & eloquent. The fact is, I had neither memory enough for effective facts, nor presence of mind enough, to be a good debater unless I knew my subject very well and had had lots of practice in it. There came a time, of course, when my readiness in answering questions & meeting hostile arguments seemed astonishing to strange audiences. The reason was that as everybody asks the same questions and uses the same arguments I knew the most effective replies by heart. Before the questioner or debater had uttered five words I knew exactly what he was going to say, and floored him with an apparent impromptu that had done duty fifty times before. (Since writing the above I have found a copy of the bill of the South Place debates. I enclose it).

So now I think you may regard your question as to my public speaking as pretty fully answered.

No. 5. Fabian Tract No 41 [*The Fabian Society: What It Has Done and How It Has Done It*] will give you this. I was not one of the original Fabians. I knew nothing of the society until its first tract "Why Are The Many Poor?" fell into my hands. Somehow the name struck me as being an inspiration. The Social-Democratic Federation and the Socialist League aimed at being big working class organizations. I wanted something in which I could work with a few educated & clever men of Webb's type. So I joined when the Society, only a month or so old, was in the "labor notes *versus* pass books" stage (Tract 41, p 4, 9th line from foot); and Tracts 2 [*A Manifesto*] & 3 [*To Provident Landlords and Capitalists*], which are mere literary boutades and are now

494

scarce, were from my pen.* But the great impression made on me by the mass of facts quoted from bluebooks in Marx's Capital convinced me that a tract stuffed with facts & figures, with careful references to official sources, was what was wanted; but I could not produce such a tract myself, whereas I knew that Webb, who was a walking encyclopedia, and literally knew everything, could do it as well as it could be done. At last he joined, after many long discussions late at night strolling up and down Whitehall outside the Colonial office door; and Tract No 5, Facts for Socialists, was the result. It was a new departure for the Society; and a comparison between it and No 2 or No 3 will shew you what a tremendous difference Webb made. Tract No 7, Capital & Land, aimed at the Georgites, who regarded capital as sacred, was drafted by Olivier. Tract 41 will tell you the rest. By the way, the William Clarke who contributed one of the Fabian Essays was a remarkable man whom I found at the Bedford Debating Society, a Whitmanite, a man with strong religious feelings of a rationalist type well understood in America by the Ethical Society people whose position was led up to by Martineau & the Unitarians. He had lectured in America & known Whitman. He wrote several books which are accessible still. He was some years older than we, and had exhausted the interest of lecturing—which he did very well—before the Socialist boom came. He was a most unlucky man, who suffered much from poverty and the stupidity of the world until the Daily Chronicle did as described in Tract 41, p 18, line 26. In trying to get young blood, it made a bid for me; and I contrived to substitute Clarke for myself without, as far as I remember, letting him know it; for his temper was very sour, & he quarrelled with everything, even his bread & butter. He immediately began to work as a journalist with frenzied energy to secure himself against the poverty he had suffered so much from. In a few years he had saved about £1000, which he invested in the Liberator Building Society—the enterprise of the notorious Jabez Balfour. It went smash; Jabez went to prison; and Clarke was again living from hand to mouth. However, he was now in work as a journalist & author, & could easily have recovered, but for the first great influenza epidemic, which all but killed him. He got it every year in its worst form, followed by horrible depression. Finally he tried foreign travel, and died [in 1901] in Herzegovina, the first leading Fabian to drop. But we never saw very much of him. He had a

---

*I enclose a copy of No 2. The only blunder in it (corrected in Fabian Essays) is the reference to the monopoly of the Postmaster General.

495

profound moral horror of me: I was to him *monstrum horrendum*, a moral anarchist. He was an ethicist & moralist to the backbone; and the dawning of Ibsenism & Nietzscheanism & "Shavianism" seemed to him the coming of chaos. Yet the fact that I knew his value and insisted on it, and that I could sympathize even with his horror of me, kept our personal relations remorsefully cordial. The last time I called on him was in the influenza period. He was working madly, as usual. He would have certainly refused to see anyone; but he was alone in his flat, and opened the door for me. With a savage set face that would have made even Ibsen's mouth look soft by contrast, he said, through his shut teeth, "I can give you five minutes; and that is ALL." "My dear Clarke," I replied, ambling idly into his study, "I MUST leave in half an hour to keep an appointment; and I have just been thinking how I am to get away from you so soon; for I know you wont let me go." And it turned out exactly as I said. We began to discuss the Parnell divorce case & the Irish crisis; and I could not get away from him until the half hour was nearly doubled.

Another Fabian essayist, Hubert Bland, a man of fierce Norman exterior and huge physical strength, lived at Blackheath on the south side of the river. His wife, "Edith Nesbit," a very clever woman and distinguished poetess, was a remarkable figure at the Fabian meetings during the period covered by the tract. Bland is a journalist, a strong Conservative & Imperialist by temperament, very different from our Millite, Benthamite recruits. He had a circle of his own at Blackheath in the Hampstead Historic [Society] times, Hampstead being north of London & quite out of his district; but we used sometimes to descend on his evening parties; and I have a vivid recollection of Mrs Bland stopping us at the door with a needle & thread, and sewing up the sleeve of a brown velveteen jacket of Olivier's. The sleeve was all but torn out; and though Olivier looked even then like the Governor of Jamaica no matter what he wore, our reckless disregard of evening dress must have been very trying to the decorum of Blackheath. Bland, by the way, had an utter contempt for this sort of Bohemianism, and never was seen without an irreproachable frock coat, tall hat, and a single eyeglass which infuriated everybody. He was pugnacious, powerful, a skilled pugilist, and had a voice like the scream of an eagle. Nobody dared be uncivil to him. He is now much mellower; but I still avoid sitting next him at a meeting because his shoulders are so broad & massive that it is impossible for his next neighbors to sit upright. His individuality, his opposite point of view to Webb's, and his common sense, were of great value to us, and are still.

When Olivier gave up being Fabian secretary we got Edward Reynolds Pease, one of the original Fabians. He came of good Quaker
stock, and was at first a stockbroker. But finding Capel Court (our
Wall St) against his conscience, he became a carpenter, and actually
worked for years as an ordinary mechanic. Finally, when our business
became so big that we required a paid man, he returned to London from
Newcastle (the scene of his carpentering), and, having a little property
of his own, took the Fabian secretaryship, which he still holds, at a
small salary. He travelled with Webb in America in 1888 or 9 (I think),
carrying his carpenter's tools with him; and he has written a book on
the Drink Question. Another original Fabian was Frank Podmore, a
Post Office civil servant. He and Pease were great friends; and the
earliest Fabian meetings were held alternately at Pease's rooms in
Osnaburgh St and at Podmore's in Dean's Yard, Westminster. Pease
& Podmore were then much wrapped up in the Psychical Research
Society, which had its office in the Dean's Yard rooms; and we were
thus brought in touch with the exploits of the P.R. Society at its most
exciting time, when Madame Blavatsky was exposed by a countryman
of yours ([W. Earl] Hodgson, was it not?). Thus I have attended a
Fabian meeting, gone on to hear the end of a Psychical Research one,
and finished by sleeping in a haunted house with a committee of ghost
hunters. And I had a nightmare & woke up in a corner of the room
struggling with the ghost, to my own intense disgust. [See I, 187]
However, that is another story.

No 6. I must try to make a bibliography for you. It will be a heavy
job; and you must give me time. Consider this question postponed
only.

No 7. As to William Morris, that is a very big business too; and I
cannot deal with it fully just now. I wrote articles about him, when he
died, in the Daily Chronicle & Saturday Review. The Saturday article
made Burne-Jones, Morris's greatest friend, anxious to make my
acquaintance. We made several appointments; but they all fell through
by one accident or another. At last we resolved to see one another once
for all; and a firm engagement was made. But Fate was not to be defied;
for Burne Jones died suddenly of angina pectoris before our day arrived.

Morris was a much greater man than his contemporaries—including
even his own set—had any idea of. I will tell you how much I knew of
him later on.

No 8. The "delightful performances at Battersea" were nothing
particular. I used to lecture pretty often in Battersea because it was
John Burns's stronghold; and one of my orations [1st December 1895,

on "The Political Situation"] at the Washington Music Hall, with Clement Edwards in the chair, was counted one of my best displays. I proved in it that no conclusion could be drawn from a bare profession of Socialism as to what side a man would take on any concrete political issue. All I remember about it particularly is that I was completely floored by a workman who got up and said "I know quite well that Bernard Shaw is very clever at argument, and that when I sit down he will make mincemeat of everything I say. But what does that matter to me? I still have my principles." I had to admit that this was unanswerable, & thoroughly sound at bottom. I also remember hearing a workman say to his wife as I came up behind them on my way to the station "When I hear a man of intellect talk like that for a whole evening, it makes me feel like a WORM." Which made me feel horribly ashamed of myself. I felt the shabbiest of impostors, somehow, though really I gave him the best lecture I could.

No 9. No: I did not begin my career as an actor. I never was on the stage, nor ever dreamt of going on it. I once acted at some theatricals got up for the benefit of an old workman member of the International, with Edward Aveling, Eleanor Marx, May Morris & Sidney Pardon [Philip Sydney?], all amateurs. I have taken part in a copyrighting performance; and I vaguely remember impersonating a photographer at Morris's house at one of the soirées of the Socialist League. But there is not the very remotest foundation for the statement you refer to. Acting was very poor fun compared to the work I was doing in all those years.

No 10. As to my early life, that I also skip; and I doubt whether it will be possible to go into it in much detail. I will get a genealogy, perhaps, before you are ready for the press. For the moment I can only tell you hastily that my family was a Protestant one; that my father's rank—a very damnable one—was that of a poor relation of that particular grade of the *haute bourgeoisie* which makes strenuous social pretensions. His people, who were prolific and numerous, revolved round a baronetcy, and always spoke of themselves as "the Shaws" with an intense sense of their own importance. My father's father, a Dublin notary and stockbroker, died leaving a huge family unprovided for; and my father, after a couple of clerkships, got a Government appointment in the Four Courts (the Courts of Justice) in Dublin. It must have been a gross sinecure (all the Shaws considered it the first duty of a respectable government to provide them with sinecures); for it got abolished, leaving my father unoccupied with a small pension. He raised capital by selling the pension, and went into business as a wholesale dealer in corn. He had a flour mill at a place called Dolphin's Barn a few miles outside the city, a warehouse & office in the city, & so on. The name of the firm was Clibborn & Shaw; and their standing was higher than their profits. (As Mr Clibborn survived my father, and may still be carrying on the business for all I know, this last remark must remain private for the present).

At about 40 he married my mother, Lucinda Elizabeth Gurly, the daughter of a country gentleman. The estate in Carlow which I am unlucky enough to own descended to me from him through my mother's brother. I am the son of an old father (comparatively) and a young mother (she is still vigorous & young minded between 70 & 80), a fact which may have some interest eugenically. My mother's marriage was merely the shift of an absurdly inexperienced young woman, quite ignorant of the world and of the value of money (the result of an extremely severe upbringing by a formidable humpbacked aunt who intended to make her a paragon and leave her a fortune, and of course disinherited her in a rage when the paragon made a mess of her affairs by marrying my father) to—I have got this long sentence frightfully mixed up—a shift to escape from her home, which was made uncomfortable for her just then by her father's second marriage. My poor father was anything but a satisfactory husband for a clever woman; and he was far too poor to live on the scale to which she was accustomed. He was amiable, unlucky, timid, and given to furtive drinking whilst proclaiming & half believing himself to be a teetotaller. It was in music that my mother found a refuge from her domestic disappointment. She became the right hand of an energetic genius who had formed a musical society and an orchestra (all amateurs—there was no other chance in Dublin). He taught her to sing; and she sang for him; copied orchestral parts for him; scored songs &c for him (she had learnt thoroughbass from old Logier); led the chorus for him; appeared in operas that he got up (she played Azucena in Il Trovatore, Donna Anna in Don Giovanni, Margaret in Gounod's Faust, and Lucrezia Borgia in Donizetti's opera of that name; and as they were all rehearsed in our house, I whistled & sang them from the first bar to the last whilst I was a small boy, not to mention all the oratorios got up by the musical society); and, to facilitate all this, kept house for him by setting up a joint household—a sort of blameless *ménage à trois*; for she was the sort of woman who never troubled herself about gossip, and consequently might have had a dozen men in her house without more scandal than any hotel keeper would have raised. As to ordinary domestic mothering and wifing she was utterly unfitted for the sentiment of it. I was not treated as a child.

499

I was let do as I liked; and I knew everything that was going on and was present on all occasions as if I were an adult member of the family. The fact that one of the men of the house was an artist, a conductor, and a man of quite exceptional temperament and energy, must have had a considerable influence on me.

This man, by name George John Vandaleur Lee, was ambitious. He had trained himself to teach singing by repudiating the traditions of the local professors, who all loathed him, and by first working at the anatomy of the throat by actual dissection and at practical singing until he acquired sufficient knowledge to know, by watching a singer and listening to him (or her) exactly what he (or she) was doing. Then, from an Italian opera singer named Badeali, who preserved a splendid voice to a great age, he found out how people sang who did not lose their voices; and this method he taught to my mother, who gave up singing, not because her voice failed in her old age, but because her age made singing ridiculous. Nobody ever taught me music in my youth; but I sang incessantly to myself & for myself as a boy—opera & oratorio—in an absurd gibberish which was Italian picked up by ear—and Irish Italian at that. When I grew up I had no voice worth talking about. But I made my mother give me some lessons; and when she began, I could not make a *rightly produced* sound that was audible two yards off. But I acquired her secrets of breathing &c; and they have stood me in stead on the platform. My voice, which is now at least audible, and is no worse than ever it was—rather better, if anything—is a commonplace baritone of the most ordinary range—B flat to F, and French pitch preferred for the F.

However, to return to Lee's ambitions. Having made himself a good and original teacher, he wanted to conduct operas. Having achieved that, he wanted to conduct a Handel Festival in Dublin with all the greatest singers of the day—Tietjens, Agnesi &c. He did it. Then he wanted to have a house in Park Lane in London—an unheard-of address for a teacher of singing—and be a fashionable professor getting a guinea a lesson. And he did that, too, only to learn that fashionable people would not spend years learning to sing properly; did not like good singing; and got tired of everything & everybody, like children, when the novelty wore off them. He had a year or two of huge vogue, during which, by teaching the fools according to their folly, he destroyed his own artistic conscience. He died at the house in Park Lane at last, quite suddenly; and it was then found that he had exhausted his stock of health in his Dublin period, and that the days of his vanity in London were also days of progressive decay.

When he left Dublin, in 1872 or thereabouts, the joint household broke up; and all musical activity ceased. My father's affairs were as unprosperous as ever; the return to a single household on his income was almost impossible; and there was some question of my two sisters becoming professional singers. So my mother boldly went to London too, and became a professional teacher of singing. She made no concessions to fashion, stuck to her master's old method in all its rigor, behaved with complete independence of manner and speech in the manner of an Irish lady confronted with English people openly describing themselves as "middle class," and had a very bad time of it in consequence until she took to training choirs in schools, when the results she produced so pleased the inspectors & the parents at the prize distributions that the headmistresses were sensible enough to let her go her own way. She still works at the North London Collegiate School for Girls, a famous modern school. She has for some years sought to retire for the same reason that she stopped singing: namely, that it is ridiculous for a first rate school to have an old woman of between 70 & 80 waving a stick and conducting a choir; but Dr Sophia Bryant, the principal, an old friend of hers, does not yet see her way to change for the better; and she is perhaps right, as it is very difficult to get a woman in England who can take command in music, and who knows it as an artist, and not as a schoolmistress who has got up the subject for the sake of the certificates and the job. Indeed but for this, my mother's total insensibility to the petty dignities so cherished in English school life, her perfectly indiscriminate onslaughts on visiting rectors, head mistresses, local bigwigs, parents, and all and sundry who come across her path and want things done the wrong way (as everybody does in England) would have made her quite impossible, in spite of the fact that the right sort of people have supported her, and the real bigwigs understood her manners.

In 1871, I then being fifteen, and there being no money to give me a university education—which, by the way, I despised, half ignorantly, half penetratingly, because it seemed to me to turn out men who all thought alike, and who were snobs—I went into the office of an Irish land agent, and remained there until about March 1876, living all that time in lodgings with my father (who had given up drinking, by the way) in Dublin. I got £18 a year; called myself a junior clerk; and was really a genteel sort of office boy. I took not the slightest interest in landagency; but I laid up a large stock of observations for use after Henry George explained their significance to me, though at the time I simply disliked my business and did not think about it. At the end of

501

about a year, a sudden vacancy occurred in the most active post in the office, that of cashier. As this involved a sort of miniature banking business for the clients, and the daily receipt and payment of all sorts of rents, interests, insurances, private allowances &c &c &c, it was a comparatively bustling post, and a position of trust as well. The vacancy occurred so suddenly that I had to try to stop the gap pending the engagement of a new cashier of mature age and high character. But as I found no difficulty in doing the work, and actually succeeded in changing my very sloped, straggly, weakminded handwriting for a very fair imitation of the excellent script of my predecessor, and as, furthermore, I was prepared to regard the doubling of my salary (now £24) to £48, as a considerable step ahead, the engagement of the new man was first delayed and then dropped. I was a remarkably correct cashier & accountant. Though I never knew how much money I had in the pocket I reserved for my private property, and have never since gained that knowledge or taken the least trouble about personal accounts, yet, as it happened, I was never a farthing out in my accounts at the office, and would have been a model young man at a desk, but for the fact that my heart was not in the thing; and I never made a payment without a hope or even a half resolve that I should never have to make it again. In spite of which I was so wanting in enterprise & so shy and helpless in worldly matters (though I believe I had the air of being rather the reverse) that six months later I found myself making the payment again. Land agency in Ireland is a socially pretentious business; and the office was thought a very "nice" one; but this meant that it was saturated with a class feeling which I loathed. On the other hand, this secured for me the society of a set of "apprentices," who were in fact idle young gentlemen who had paid a big premium to be taught a genteel profession. Though the premium was not paid to me I taught them various operatic scenes, which were occasionally in full swing when the principal or the public would enter unexpectedly; and I remember one apprentice in particular who sang "Ah, che la morte" in his tower (standing on the wash stand with his head appearing above a tall screen) so feelingly, that, once started, he became insensible to all external events, and would go on to the bitter end with the whole office suddenly struck busy and silent by the arrival of the senior partner, Mr Charles Uniacke Townshend, who would stare, stupended, at the bleating countenance above the screen, and finally flee upstairs, completely beaten by the situation. So there was plenty of fun, and the society of educated men there; but I hated my position and my work all the same; and in 1876, I simply walked out and threw myself recklessly into London, joining my mother there immediately after the death of my sister Agnes in the Isle of Wight.

One or two things I may as well mention about this period from the winter of 1871 to the spring of 1876. A little time after I entered the office the appalling discovery was made that instead of being an extremely correct Protestant & churchgoer, as became a youth introduced by a high official in the Valuation Office (my uncle Frederick Shaw, who got me the berth) I was actually what used to be called in those days "an infidel." Arguments arose in which I, being young & untrained in dialectic, got severely battered. "What is the use," said Humphrey Lloyd (an apprentice) "of arguing when you dont know what a syllogism is?" I promptly went and found out what it was, learning, like Molière's hero, that I had been making syllogisms all my life without knowing it. On the matter coming to the ears of Mr Uniacke Townshend, who was a pillar of the Church, of the Royal Dublin Society, and of everything else that wanted pillaring, he respected my freedom of conscience so far as to make no attempt to reason with me nor interfere with my religion or irreligion; but he asked me to promise not to discuss the subject in his office. I gave him my word, and kept it, the understanding being general in the office that the subject was to be dropped. But though I was glad to be rid of it at the time, and though it was undoubtedly an indispensable condition of reasonable sociality among people who disagreed strongly on such a matter, yet I knew that I could not live under such limitations permanently; and the incident would by itself have had the effect of making me at bottom a bad employee; for it put landagency and business out of the question for me as a serious career: I was only there because it was necessary for me to do something towards earning my living; and though my principal gave me a handsome testimonial when my father asked for it (I remember I was furious that such a demand should have been made) and was probably sorry to lose me, yet I can remember that once or twice he shewed himself puzzled and annoyed when some accident lifted the veil for a moment and gave him a glimpse of the fact that his excellent and pecuniarily incorruptible young clerk's mind and interest and even intelligence were ten thousand leagues away, in a region foreign if not hostile.

I was of course by no means clearly conscious of my own position & destiny. But one day the apprentice who sang "Ah, che la morte" so passionately (he was eight or ten years my senior) happened to observe that every young fellow thinks he is going to be a great man until he is twenty. The shock that this gave me made me suddenly aware that this was my own precise intention. But a very brief consideration reassured me—why, I dont know; for I could do nothing that gave me the smallest hope of making good my calm classification of myself as one of the world to which Shelley and Mozart and Praxiteles and Michael Angelo belonged, and as totally foreign to the plane on which land agents labored.

What was wrong with me then was the want of self respect, the diffidence, the cowardice of the ignoramus & the duffer. What saved me was my consciousness that I must learn to do something—that nothing but the possession of skill, of efficiency, of mastery in short, was of any use. The sort of aplomb which my cousins seemed to derive from the consciousness that their great great grandfather had also been the great great grandfather of Sir Robert Shaw of Bushy Park was denied to me. You cannot be imposed on by remote baronets if you belong to the republic of art. I was chronically ashamed and even miserable simply because I couldnt do anything. It is true that I could keep Mr Townshend's cash, and that I never dreamt of stealing it; and riper years have made me aware that many of my artistic feats may be less highly estimated in the books of the Recording Angel than this prosaic achievement; but at the time it counted for less than nothing. It was a qualification for what I hated; and the notion of my principal actually giving me a testimonial to my efficiency as a cashier drove me, as aforesaid, to an exhibition of rage that must have seemed merely perverse to my unfortunate father.

My literary activity during this time, though I did not count it as such, was considerable. An old schoolfellow of mine named McNulty, who is the author of three very remarkable novels of Irish life entitled "Misther O'Ryan," "The Son of a Peasant" and "Maureen," was an official in the Bank of Ireland, and had been drafted to the Newry branch of that institution. We had struck up a curious friendship, being both imaginative geniuses, although circumstances separated us so effectually that after our schooldays we saw little of one another. But during these years we kept up a tremendous correspondence, writing immense letters to one another by return of post, sometimes illustrated with crude drawings & enlivened by brief dramas. It was understood that the letters were to be destroyed as soon as answered, as we did not like the possibility of our unreserved soul histories falling into strange hands.

I also made a valuable acquaintance at this time through the accident of coming to lodge in the same house with him. This was Chichester Bell, a cousin of Graham Bell, the inventor of the telephone, consequently a nephew of Melville Bell the inventor of the phonetic script known as Visible Speech, and the son of Alexander Bell (author of the Standard Elocutionist, and by far the most majestic and imposing man that ever lived on this or any other planet. He was the elocution professor in my old school, the Wesleyan Connexional, now Wesley College, attendance at which by no means implied Methodism). Chichester Bell was a qualified physician, but not caring for medical practice, he had gone to Germany and devoted himself to chemistry & physics in the school of Helmholtz. My intercourse with Bell was of great use to me. We studied Italian together; and though I did not learn Italian I learned a good deal else, mostly about physics & pathology. I read Tyndall and Trousseau's Clinical Lectures. And it was Bell who made me take Wagner seriously. I had heard nothing of his except the Tannhäuser march on a second rate military band; and my only comment was that the second theme was a weak imitation of the famous theme, made up of a chain of turns, in Weber's Freischütz overture. When I found that Bell regarded Wagner as a great composer, I bought a vocal score of Lohengrin, the only sample to be had at the Dublin music shops; and the first few bars completely converted me.

This reminds me that when our household broke up and my mother went to London I suddenly found myself deprived of music, which had been my daily food all through my life. I had never thought of this, and it took me by surprise. But the piano remained, though I had never touched it except to pick out a tune with one finger. In desperation I went out and bought a technical handbook of music, containing a diagram of the keyboard. I then got out "Don Giovanni," and tried to play the overture. It took me ten minutes to arrange my fingers on the notes of the first chord. What I suffered, what everybody in the house suffered, whilst I struggled on, laboring through arrangements of Beethoven's symphonies, of Tannhauser, and of all the operas & oratorios I knew, will never be told. In the end I learnt enough to thumb my way through anything; and there is an article of mine called "The Religion of the Pianoforte" which is worth reading in this connection; but I never mastered the instrument, although I did a good deal of accompanying at one time, and even once, in a desperate emergency, supplied the place of the absent half of the orchestra at a performance of Il Trovatore at a People's Entertainment evening at the Victoria Theatre in the Waterloo Road, and came off without disaster. Nowadays I revel in the Pianola.

I also made frightful efforts to learn languages; but for that sort of application I have no aptitude; and though I can read French as easily as English, I have only a smattering of other tongues, and cannot speak French decently. Later on I will tell you how I mastered French.

And now I must break off for a longish time & leave you to digest all this and to devise fresh questions in addition to those which I have left unanswered. That is, if you seriously intend to go ahead with this job. When you began it I knew quite well that you had no idea of what you were attempting—that a complete life of me in my public capacity would be a history of all the "movements" of the last quarter of the XIX century in London, with very little about me personally in it. I knew that you thought you were dealing simply with a "new" dramatist, whereas to myself, all the fuss about Candida was only a remote ripple from the splashes I made in the days of my warfare long ago. I do not think what you propose is important as *my* biography; but a thorough biography of any man who is up to the chin in the life of his own time as I have been is worth writing as a historical document; and therefore if you still care to face it I am willing to give you what help I can. Indeed you can force my hand to some extent; for any story that you start will pursue me to all eternity; and if there *is* to be a biography it is worth my while to make it as accurate as possible[.]

yours faithfully
G. Bernard Shaw

P.S. I have just found an old photograph, taken in 1863, of my father, my mother, Lee, & three others, taken by Richard Pigott, the famous forger of the Parnell letters. I will copy it for you if you are curious about it.

Welwyn‾17/1/05

To HILAIRE BELLOC

The Old House. Harmer Green
[C/3]   8th January 1904 [1905]

[Hilaire Belloc (1870–1953) son of a French father and an English mother, became a naturalized British subject in 1902. Belloc was a man of letters with a simplistic religious view of life, who, like his friend Gilbert K. Chesterton, looked back to the middle ages for tradition and order. Gaston Boissier (1823–1908) was a French historian, who had written several books on the age of the Cæsars.]

Decidedly you are a man of taste. I delight in Bashville. It is my only achievement in pure letters; and it wrote itself, proving, as I have always contended, that anybody can write Elizabethan mighty lines if they can write anything at all. But of course in this illiterate country nobody appreciates it.

Never heard of Boissier—must get him.

What's been the matter with you—but dont trouble to answer: the doctor's name for the thing doesnt matter.

G.B.S.

To GRANT RICHARDS

The Old House. Harmer Green
[A/4]   15th January 1905

[The firm of Grant Richards went into bankruptcy in January 1905. Field Roscoe was a firm of solicitors which handled much of Shaw's legal work.

Dear Grant Richards

Listen to me attentively if you can; for you are in the most deadly peril of spending irrecoverable years as an undischarged bankrupt through your poetic inaptitude for business.

You never proposed any agreement for Plays, Pleasant & Unpleasant. I drafted one, much against your will; and you wrote at the foot of it "approved, Grant Richards." That agreement has expired: it was for a period of 5 years from 1897.

I forced you, in your own interest, to execute an agreement for Three Plays for Puritans. Very likely you have lost your copy. Mine is in the hands of Thring or Field & Roscoe; but it does not matter, as it was for 2,500 copies only; and you have had that number printed; consequently it is only valid now as to the royalties due me.

For the other books we had no agreement, though I warned you repeatedly that the absence of an agreement left you defenceless. I did not press the matter because the Puritans agreement was there to shew the nature of our verbal understanding as to "the usual terms." You wrote me a letter as to the royalty on the separate plays.

You are therefore right when you say that I am at liberty to take the books away and stop you publishing them at any moment and to arrange with anybody else to publish them without reference to you or to the Receiver.

Unfortunately this liberty includes the liberty to pay for the setting

507

up of the books all over again, and the ruinous expenditure of time in correcting the proofs, whilst all the time you are sitting calmly on a set of plates which are of no use to you, and which would save me all this. You are the proprietor of those bits of metal; and though you may not print copies of my books from them, you may mend your saucepans with them, or melt them down, or hammer them up, or sell them at the nearest marine stores as scrap iron. Clark holds them at present because he has a lien on them for what you owe him; but that gives him no power to print from them; and meanwhile my books, just now in brisk demand through the Court performances, are out of print.

I have explained this to you very carefully some 17,000,000,000,000,000, odd times, and offered to buy the plates at a reasonable advance on their value to anyone else except myself; and I cannot get the explanation into that solid head of yours. You betray no consciousness of having ever heard of my difficulty; and you shew not the faintest intention of helping me out of it. In desperation, therefore, I have had to take steps to transfer those plates from you to somebody whom I *can* deal with, however slowly and expensively and officially: namely, a trustee in bankruptcy.

And this, mind you, whilst it is my interest as well as yours that you should *not* be made a bankrupt, and that your business should be kept up as a going concern, either for disposal to a new firm, or even in your own hands. I am doing what I can to make Thring endeavor to release the other authors from messes similar to mine, and then to avert the bankruptcy by withdrawing the petition. But you persist in frustrating my efforts. The unanswerable reply of Thring is "We must have someone with whom we can deal; and the only way of securing that in the face of Richards's airy apathy and the inertia of the Receiver, who cares for nothing but seizing what comes in from day to day for the mortgagee, is to force a bankruptcy." Your solicitor cannot help you, because you are in the absurd position of having a solicitor with whom you are not on speaking terms. Mr Adam Walker consents to do your solicitor's work, only to discover, at his first interview with me, that you have told him nothing about my position, and have probably not even read my letters, much less shewn them to him. What is to be done with you under such circumstances? I am anxious to save you from bankruptcy; Walker is anxious to save you from it; your trade creditors are strongly interested in saving you from it; it is inconceivable that you and the trade creditors and the Receiver could not in two days give Thring all the MSS, plates, rights &c that he wants, and so make it his

508

interest also to save you; but the one person who baffles all these salvage corps is Grant Richards himself (and perhaps his hostile solicitor).

Do you realize what bankruptcy means for you? You wont get your discharge easily: as far as I can ascertain there is not an extenuating circumstance connected with it. You will be stranded for years, unable, under penalty of prison, to order a pair of boots without warning the bootmaker that you are an undischarged bankrupt, unable to spend a five pound note without carefully considering whether it is not a fraud on your creditors, and impossible as a publisher or anything else that requires a clean bill of health. Dont, in the name of common sense, run yourself into all this when all the forces that are driving you to it can be so easily disarmed, and all the forces against it so easily united.

However, I write all this with the conviction that it will be utterly lost on you. *Quem Deus vult perdere &c*

yrs ever
G. Bernard Shaw

To FLORENCE FARR

10 Adelphi Terrace W C
[A/3; X/115]   8th February 1905

[The first production of *The Philanderer* was presented by the New Stage Club at the Cripplegate Institute on 20th February 1905, its cast of amateurs including the same women who had appeared in *Candida* in 1902. Shaw participated in a number of its rehearsals, but an attack of influenza prevented him from attending the performance on the 20th. The Leeds visit was for the purpose of giving his first lecture there in fifteen years, to the Leeds Arts Club on 14th February on "What is the Use of an Arts Club?" *How He Lied to Her Husband* was presented at the Royal Court Theatre at a matinée on 28th February, on a bill with Yeats's *The Pot of Broth* and Arthur Schnitzler's *In the Hospital*. It was subsequently transferred, with the same cast, to the St James's Theatre on a bill with two plays by Alfred Sutro, *A Maker of Men* and *Mollentrave on Women*.]

This Philanderer affair has knocked me endways. I thought it was an ordinary amateur business for a charity; and now it turns out to be a sort of junior Stage Society. I must try to save the situation by barring any invitations to the press. Miss Murby, who has written about it, is a very clever young woman—a Fabian, who is firmly persuaded that my views on the production of the Superman involve the forcible coercion by the State of selected women to breed with selected men;

and she, being a goodlooking & clever person, very likely to be selected under such a scheme, fears the worst. Now I protest that I never proposed anything more compulsory than offering, say £2000 for a satisfactory baby, *à prendre ou à laisser*, as the lady likes.

If you are going to stage-manage, so much the better. I will go down with you and start the affair—arrange the business &c, as I may as well learn this confounded play now. I go down to Leeds next Tuesday; but except for that I shall be in town rehearsing "How He Lied" at the Court—fairly free in the evenings, I hope.

GBS

To ARCHIBALD HENDERSON

[H/6; X/141.e]

10 Adelphi Terrace W C
10th February 1905

[John Corbin (1870–1959) was an author and dramatic critic of the New York *Sun* 1905-7, who had studied at Oxford. Later in 1905 he wrote an introduction to a separate edition of the *Mrs Warren* preface, *The Author's Apology*, rushed into print in New York by Brentano to capitalise on the scandal that ensued from Arnold Daly's production there in October. Henderson's biography, when published in 1911, contained no dedication.]

Dear Mr Henderson

Your letter of the 23rd January has crossed my big budget.

I advise you to go slowly about this book until it has grown on your hands to its full size. The truth is, you are not taking yourself seriously enough as a university professor. A theatrical biography, with portraits of actors and a preface by a theatrical journalist, will be set aside at once as a mere puff: such things are circulated by the advance agents of touring actors and musical virtuosi by the hundred; and nobody ever dreams of taking them as serious literature. Nobody buys them: they are presented to managers, who put them on a shelf, and sent to newspapers, who give them to their "dramatic editors," to be thrown straight into the waste paper basket or else cut up with scissors and paste to pad columns of "Green Room Gossip" and the like. You must be most careful to keep off the lines of these costly advertisements, and to keep on the lines of Boswell's Johnson and Lockhart's Scott, not to mention Plutarch.

Archer would no doubt write you a preface out of friendship for me, if not out of kindness to you; but the only proper person to write a

510

book's preface is the book's author. A preface by Archer or Corbin would cost you several unnecessary guineas, and would be thoroughly inappropriate; for—and I cannot impress this too strongly on you—a merely theatrical biography of me would be a most unworthy waste of your time, and an unspeakable annoyance to me. My plays speak for themselves; and the newspapers chronicle what need be chronicled about them over and above what is to be found in the prefaces. I want you to do something that will be useful to yourself and to the world; and that is, to make me a mere peg on which to hang a study of the last quarter of the XIX century, especially as to the Collectivist movement in politics, ethics, and sociology; the Ibsen-Nietzschean movement in morals; the reaction against the materialism of Marx & Darwin of which (as to Darwin) Samuel Butler was the greatest exponent (you must read the works of that man of genius); the Wagnerian movement in music, and the anti-romantic movement (including what people call realism, naturalism, and impressionism) in literature and art. I am quite aware that this is a very large order; but it is only by taking on a large order and putting a lot of work into it that a professor of twenty-seven can make his mark and get a permanent position clear above bookmaking journalism. If you shew me as a ghastly little celebrity posing in a vacuum, you will make both of us ridiculous. Unless you can shew me in the context of my time, as a member of a very interesting crowd, you will fail to produce the only thing that makes biography tolerable. Observe, I am not treating you as a smart young journalist. Clarence Rook can beat you at that probably. I am treating you as a possible Gibbon; and I urge you to treat yourself so, and play the great game all through. If it ends in your discovering that you have something much bigger on hand than a biography of Shaw, and discarding him altogether, so much the better. But no doubt I shall be as good an excuse for your communication to the public as anybody or anything else.

If you really want an introduction, better let *me* write it. But at least let it not be by anybody connected with the theatre. Let your main line about me be that my theatrical history is already on record, and that your object is not to tell an already told tale; but rather to deal with the fact that my theatrical activity has been confined to the last ten years of my life (and has played no very absorbing part even in those ten years) and to seek in the other activities of my career for the explanation of the difference between my plays and those of other playwrights, a difference obviously much greater than can be accounted for by any difference in my personal ability.

You can use my own stuff when convenient by the usual device. "The following extract from a letter written by Mr Shaw gives the picture &c" and then you quote. . . .

My advice is, Dont dedicate, unless, as in the case of my dedication of the Superman to Walkley, the dedication is a vital part of the book, or unless you want to compel a nobleman to buy fifty copies. By all means make ample acknowledgment to Archer for his help, and boom him as much as you can; but bear in mind that Archer did his utmost, when he heard the first two acts of Widowers' Houses, to dissuade me from indulging the faintest hope of becoming a playwright, and that he is violently disaffected to all my views, although he is personally anxious to do me what good he can, and is fond of Candida and Mrs Warren. You might dedicate a biography of Pinero to him appropriately enough; but if you dedicate one of me to him, he will have to write an article explaining that though he is an admirer of Shaw, he is no Shavian. Having written it, he will refrain from publishing it, and decide to say nothing in public about the book lest he should seem to be advertising himself. Better dedicate to the Superman, or to the life of the coming age. And I will try to find a photograph of Archer for you, or take one myself, to include in the illustrations & give him his due prominence in my history.

I am frightfully busy just now, and have not had time to complete my answers to your questions; but you have enough to go on with!

In haste—ever yrs
G. Bernard Shaw

To AUGUSTIN HAMON

10 Adelphi Terrace W C
[S/1]   17th February 1905

[Shaw had authorised Hamon, in the autumn of 1903, to translate his plays, after refusing to accept the services of a young man named E.M.Muraour, to whom Hamon had introduced him. Now Hamon had encouraged another young man, Dr Stéphane Epstein-Estienne (1866- ?), a Russian Jew, whose translations of Schnitzler and of Hofmannsthal's *Elektra* had been produced in Paris, to translate *Arms and the Man*, misleading him into believing Hamon controlled both translation and performing rights in Shaw's plays in France. A similar complication arose in 1907 when Siegfried

Trebitsch, without authority, contracted for operetta rights in *Arms and the Man* (see Shaw's letters to Trebitsch of 18th December 1907, 20th January and 11th April 1908). Maurice Donnay (1859–1945) and Alfred Capus (1858–1922) were popular "Boulevard" dramatists in Paris. Shaw had been elected on 6th February to the Council and Committee of Management of the Society of Authors, to replace the late Edward Rose. He served on the committee for ten years.]

My dear Hamon

Do not fear a process: the law is very foolish; but things have not yet come to such a pass that a man who offers his services as agent can thereby establish a legal claim on the stage rights of the play. Any theatrical agent will arrange with a theatre for the production of a play and collect the author's fees for 10% on what he collects. A share is unheard-of.

I will have nothing to do with this cosmopolite Hebrew either as translator, agent, or in any other way. I want no introductions to Paris theatres and will accept none. I dare say many Parisian managers have never heard of me, just as many London managers have never heard of Brieux, nor Donnay, nor Capus, nor Sardou, nor Molière, nor Victor Hugo. That does not matter to me: they will not think any the better of me because some gentleman whose name ends in "stein" goes to them and announces my existence. I am, as a matter of fact, the most talked about and written about author in Berlin, Vienna and New York, not to mention London; and until the Parisian managers are prepared to deal with me as with an author of established reputation, I shall not deal with them at all.

You must write politely to Dr Barabbas, and explain to him, with all proper regrets, that the arrangement between you and me is not a legal one, but a friendly one only, and that you have no power to make any agreement concerning the plays that would not fall through if I disapproved of it. Say also that I am a member of the English Society of Authors (I have just been elected to the committee), and that I am a very sharp and experienced man of business, and that you yourself are an innocent artist and literary man with no influence over me in such matters.

Then go on to say that you have informed me of his proposal, and that, to your surprise, it seems to have given me great offence. Say that I am indignant at the suggestion that an author of my position needs any introduction to any theatre in Europe, and that I seem to think that in any case such an introduction is part of the duty of an agent, who would be remunerated by a percentage on the tantièmes, and not by a

513

share in the rights of the play. Say too—and this is very important—that I am a rich man, quite independent of the theatre, and quite unmanageable in the usual way by pecuniary pressure. And conclude by expressing your desolation at having to announce that I have absolutely vetoed the proposed arrangement, and that it must therefore, to your extreme grief, be considered as cancelled. With, of course, every assurance of your most distinguished consideration.

If anybody else tries the same game, simply tell them that the matter is in your hands and that you will take whatever steps are necessary. If you let anybody share your fees it will no longer be worth your while to go on with the work. All these men who pretend that they have influence at the theatres are impostors. All they can do is to ask a manager to read a manuscript and talk big about my reputation, and about my successes. That you can do as well as they. For the rest, the French Authors' Society, which is a very well organized one, will protect you.

If you think I am wrong in all this, I will make new proposals to you. Meanwhile, send me one of your translations as soon as you can and remember that "Plays, Pleasant and Unpleasant" was published seven years ago; so that there is no time to lose.

I write in great haste, as I am badly overworked by arrears of business and the rehearsal of two plays simultaneously.

My compliments to Madame, and to the olive branch.

yours ever
G. Bernard Shaw

To ARCHIBALD HENDERSON

[H/6; X/116]

10 Adelphi Terrace W C
18th February 1905

Dear Henderson

My father's name was George Carr Shaw, my mother's, Lucinda Elizabeth Gurly.

Do not be too much alarmed by the large program I have suggested. It is appalling how small even the most extensive knowledge boils down when it is pithily used. A knowledge of the movements I have been in need not bulk in the pages of the book; but it will count tremendously behind them. After all, you must relate me to my time

514

somehow; and that can only be done if you know my time. As I was born to all intents and purposes in the seventeenth century in Ireland, and traversed the ages up to the twentieth and twentyfirst; and as I have been influenced mainly by works of art in my artificial culture, and have been always more *consciously* susceptible to music and painting than to literature, so that Mozart and Michelangelo count for a great deal in the making of my mind, and the English dramatists after Shakespear do not count at all, you will have to know a good deal before you know me inside-out.

What you say as to the things that attract you in me, and that make the work interesting to you are very significant. I quite understand (and chuckle a little); but I now ask you to face this question. Are you going to write a natural history, like a true Shavian, or a romance, like an incorrigible anti-Shavian? Surely the right thing to do is to begin with a vivid romantic picture of the miraculous Shaw, the wonderful personality, the brilliant, the witty, the paradoxical, the accomplished, the critic of a thousand arts, and the master of half a dozen. Having got this off your afflated chest, then get to business. Point out as a matter of common sense that the admirable creature you have just been describing clearly does not exist, and never did nor could nor will exist under the heavens—that the real George Bernard Shaw was born into the world not by parthenogenesis but in the vulgar way, and inherited all the weaknesses, follies, and limitations of his kind—that he goes about on two legs, blowing his nose and failing and fudging along as best he can in an extremely prosaic way, perceptibly short of many accomplishments which are fairly common, and in some ways an obviously ignorant, stupid and unready man. Then state your task, which should be, the explanation of how this prosaic reality produces this romantic effect, and does actually get a certain quality into his work, creative and critical, which distinguishes it from the work of men with much more remarkable natural qualifications.

In this way you will lay down the lines of a scientific biography without drily ignoring the glamor. Of course you will have to snuff out what you call my "astounding personality" and smash your idol; but you cannot possibly do yourself a greater service. Until you know me from behind the scenes, you may be my dupe, but not my biographer.

There is no use in our agreeing *now* as to what is to be written. You might as well agree with your wife as to whether you were to have a boy or a girl. You will have to labor and bring forth as best you can, and see what will come of it. When you have written careful essays on all my plays separately you can put them in the fire, or keep them for

515

magazine padding. All that you can profitably do is, not to do over again what I have done before (which is what that sort of thing mostly comes to) but to tell the story of the play briefly from the point of view of my philosophy, as I have done with Ibsen's, or with Der Ring. My books on Ibsen and Wagner are very small—much shorter than what you contemplate; yet there is everything in them that is necessary. Be as accurate as you can; but as to being just, who are you that you should be just? That is mere American childishness. Write boldly according to your bent: say what you WANT to say and not what you think you ought to say or what is right or just or any such arid nonsense. You are not God Almighty; and nobody will expect justice from you, or any other superhuman attribute. This affected, manufactured, artificial conscience of morality and justice and so on is of no use for the making of works of art: for that you must have the real conscience that gives a man courage to fulfil his will by saying what he likes. Accuracy only means discovering the relation of your will to facts instead of cooking the facts to save trouble. . . .

In haste
ever
G. Bernard Shaw

To STÉPHANE EPSTEIN-ESTIENNE

[S/1]

[10 Adelphi Terrace W C]
24th February 1905

Dear Sir

It is necessary for me to begin by saying formally that this letter and any other communication that may pass between us is without prejudice to any steps that I may have to take to defend my copyright.

Since you submit your reply to M. Hamon to me, I presume that you invite me to comment on it. I cannot of course express any opinion as to the part of the affair that lies between M. Hamon and you; but I may point out that the *ultimatum* you present to M. Hamon is impracticable, because M. Hamon, being neither the author nor the owner of my plays, and having no more power over them than I have over the plays of M. Victorien Sardou, cannot authorize you to make a translation, nor to attach your name to one, nor to touch a share of the tantièmes. No doubt he can contract with you to pay you a share of any payments he may himself receive on account of the plays: but as I shall take care that he does not receive any payment except for work done

516

by himself under his own name, such a clause would be of no value to you. I do not need two translators for each of my plays; nor do I permit any subletting of my authorizations.

What concerns me is the following phrase in your letter: "La pièce a été traduite, revue, copiée, lué et acceptée." Whoever has done this has violated my copyright, and is liable to all the consequences of that illegal act. The translation was a breach of the law; the copying was a breach of the law; the exhibition of the copy to another person was a breach of the law; and the dealing with the rights of representation was a breach of the law. If you have the slightest doubt of this, consult a lawyer or the Society of Authors.

Now I hope I may exclude the hypothesis that these breaches of the law have been committed knowingly and wilfully. I take it that you supposed that an authorization to translate was the same thing as an assignment of copyright, and that M. Hamon was, in effect, the owner of the plays in France. Any lawyer will tell you that you ought to have known better: *I* will confine myself to assuring you that you were mistaken. Further, as a moment's reflection will convince you, an authorization to translate is not transferable or assignable. The translator's personality, his professional skill, his reputation are essential parts of the arrangement. Suppose, for instance, you wrote a play and authorised and paid me to translate it on the strength of my reputation. How would you feel if I proposed to hand it over to a stranger, and have it performed with his name instead of mine as the translator?

Even if you could plead ignorance of the exact nature of M. Hamon's position, the law would not absolve you on that account. It was your business to ascertain, before you touched my plays, that M. Hamon held an assignment of the rights and could legally authorize you to translate. By omitting to do this you took your chance of what has actually happened to you. But you cannot plead ignorance. You applied to me for authorization; and I refused it and explained to you the nature of my arrangement with M. Hamon. No doubt you did not understand the legal limits of that arrangement: and M. Hamon, possibly, did not understand them either. But the law does not allow for that. It was your business to understand them, and his business to understand them; and since you both failed on this point, it is useless to talk of going to law or arbitration to decide which of you is the owner of *my* play. No court or arbitrator can order M. Hamon to give you what he does not possess; and any arrangement you may have made with him, or he with you, will be held to have been subject to the law and to such knowledge of the facts as you had either actually acquired, or might have acquired had you taken the trouble. The fact that M. Hamon did not expressly warn you that the play belonged to the author and not to himself will not be held to justify you in assuming the contrary without evidence. If you meddle with literary property without first carefully acquiring a legal right to do so, you must take the consequences, however disappointing they may be.

I am unable to suggest a friendly way out of the difficulty, because I do not, in your case, know with whom I am dealing. As I am a foreigner, unacquainted with Parisian reputations, you will not, I hope, be offended when I say that your name is not known to me. It is not a French name; and you write English so well that I can hardly believe you a Frenchman. You seem to be energetic, which is in your favour; but on the other hand your rashness in making an unauthorised translation, and your naive disregard of legal conditions and business precautions, suggest to me that you are about eighteen years of age. I wish you would so far waive ceremony as to tell me how old you are, whether you are a Jew (I am not an anti-Semite), what is your native language, whether you are a doctor of medicine or philosophy (clearly you are not a doctor of law), whether you have ever translated or written a play before: in short, whether you are at all the sort of person who might be of use to me in case I should have occasion in the future to alter my existing arrangements as to my plays in France.

I may mention that I myself am not an ambitious young playwright, but an elderly gentleman in no need of tantièmes, who very heartily wishes that the theatres would leave his plays alone, as the business which public performances bring upon him is a most unwelcome addition to the burdens of his advancing years.

yours faithfully
[G. Bernard Shaw]

To LILLAH McCARTHY

The Old House. Harmer Green
1st March 1905

[D/4; X/182]

[The first performance of Man and Superman was later postponed to 21st May.]

Dear Miss McCarthy

I want to ask you two questions "without prejudice."

1. If the Stage Society were to ask you to play for them on Sunday evening the 9th April, and on the afternoons of the 10th & 11th, in an

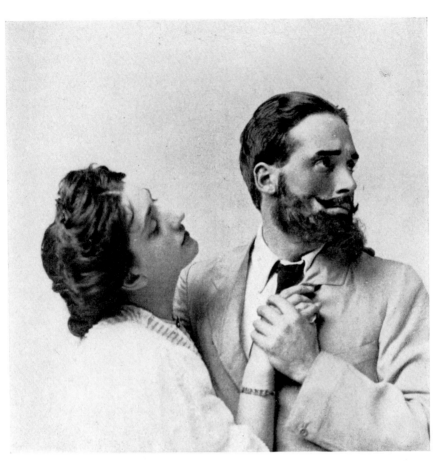

Lillah McCarthy as Ann Whitefield and Granville Barker
as John Tanner in *Man and Superman*, 1905
(*Mander & Mitchenson Theatre Collection*)

The Bystander, 5 April 1905

exceedingly difficult & possibly shockingly unpopular leading part, by which you would gain nothing but three guineas to pay for your cabs, and enough trouble & worry to take quite 50 guineas' worth of energy & temper out of you, would you say yes or no?

2. Did you ever read a play by me called Man & Superman; and, if so, can you imagine any woman playing the part of Ann Whitefield? If not, I will send you a copy.

yours faithfully
G.Bernard Shaw

To FLORENCE FARR

[A/3; X/115]

The Old House. Harmer Green
5th March 1905

[Shaw was negotiating at this moment with Sam Shubert and Charles Frohman simultaneously for rights to *Captain Brassbound's Conversion*, and there were nibbles from America for *John Bull's Other Island* the moment the news was circulated that Edward VII had requested a special performance for 11th March. This was Shubert's last trip to London prior to his violent death at the age of thirty in a train accident on 12th May 1905. Gilbert Murray's translation of *The Trojan Women* was performed at the Royal Court Theatre on 11th April 1905. His translation of *Hippolytus* had been performed at the Lyric Theatre on 28th May 1904, and at the Royal Court Theatre the following October.]

Out of town, as you see. I am getting quite maddened by the business (mostly refusing it) that my recent boom has brought on me. It is enough to make one curse the day I ever wrote a play. If I would consent, the whole 13 plays would be produced simultaneously about the middle of April.

By the way, are you arranging the choruses for the Trojan Women? If so, be very discreet about using modern fashionable discords. In the Hippolytus, towards the end, you began to ramble up and down staircases of minor thirds in a deplorable manner. I strenuously advise you not to introduce deliberate figuration of discords. For instance

The effect is modern, cheap & mechanical. Stick to the common chord, major and minor, and avoid regular sequences & figurations. I should

stick to the old lines of Cherubini's counterpoint, which grew out of unaccompanied vocal harmony & barred not only discords, but even this position of the common chord 𝄞. The moment you begin to figure diminished sevenths & the like, Euripides gives way to Liszt, & the harmony becomes *instrumental* in its suggestion. In haste, haste, oh Lord!

GBS

To J. E. VEDRENNE

[The Old House. Harmer Green]
[X/183]   7th March 1905

Dear Vedrenne
  The Stage Society is to produce Man & Superman on the 9th April (Sunday evening) and on the afternoons of the 10th & 11th.
  If I can get a good cast, this may have as much money in it as John Bull; and already the S.S. talks of speculating with it by giving extra matinees and asking the libraries to guarantee them. For various reasons I shall probably not allow this. They can get a theatre big enough to hold their members at the first two performances and then repair their exhausted finances by selling out the third house (if it will sell); but they cannot go beyond this without going into regular commercial business and paying full salaries and so on. Still, those three performances will just mop up the slack that always comes before the public catches on, and might start a round of nine matinées or a fortnight's evening shows if anybody was ready to take the job on. Why not Vedrenne-Barker? There is the Savoy eating its head off, and the Scala. I have not thought the thing out, but just mention it as it occurs to me on the spur of the S.S.'s proposal. I come up to town tomorrow afternoon.

yrs ever
G. Bernard Shaw

To ROBERT ROSS

The Old House. Harmer Green
[A/1; X/184]   13th March 1905

[Robert Ross (1869–1918), a director of the Carfax Gallery from 1900 to 1908, was the executor of Oscar Wilde's estate. Wilde's *De Profundis*,

520

edited by Ross, had just been published in England. Shaw's article on Wilde, in a translation by Siegfried Trebitsch, was published in the *Neue Freie Presse* on 23rd April 1905. Jacob Epstein (1880–1959), the American-born sculptor, had just moved to London after a brief residence in Paris.]

Dear Ross

I have written an article on Wilde for the Neue Freie Presse of Vienna! I am half tempted to cut into the Saturday Review correspondence with a letter giving the *comedic* view of De Profundis. It is really an extraordinary book, quite exhilarating and amusing as to Wilde himself, and quite disgraceful & shameful to his stupid tormentors. There is pain in it, inconvenience, annoyance, but no unhappiness, no real tragedy, all comedy. The unquenchable spirit of the man is magnificent: he maintains his position & puts society squalidly in the wrong—rubs into them every insult & humiliation he endured—comes out the same man he went in—with stupendous success. The little aside in which, after writing several pages with undisguised artistic enjoyment & detachment, he remarks that they have been feeding him satisfactorily of late, is irresistible. It annoys me to have people degrading the whole affair to the level of sentimental tragedy. There is only one moment at which he shows himself subject to the common lot of mankind unconscious of its own comedy; and that is where he calls himself "enfant de son siècle." Of course, except in his personality and his super-morality, he was thoroughly Irish & old fashioned, a Gautierist in 1875–1900 (!) a chivalrous romanticist (see the Ideal Husband &c) in the days of Strindberg & Ibsen. The British press is as completely beaten by him *de profundis* as it was *in excelsis*.

By the way there is a young American sculptor named Jacob Epstein, of 219 Stanhope St N.W (therefore poor), who has come to London with amazing drawings of human creatures like withered trees embracing. He wants to exhibit them at the Carfax, which is to him the centre of real art in London. He has a commendatory letter from Rodin; and when I advised him to get commissions for busts of railway directors, he repudiated me with such utter scorn that I relented & promised to ask you to look at his portfolio. It is a bad case of helpless genius in the first blaze of youth; and the drawings are queer and Rodinesque enough to be presentable at this particular moment. If you feel disposed to be bothered with him for ten minutes send him a card & he'll call on you. There may be something in him.

yrs always
G. Bernard Shaw

521

To VEDRENNE & BARKER

[A/1]

10 Adelphi Terrace W C
14th March 1905

Dear Sirs

I learn with regret that the Royal prerogative has been stretched—in direct contravention of the Bill of Rights—to the extent of compelling you to give an unauthorized performance of my play "John Bull's Other Island."

Were I to accept royalties I should be subject to heavy penalties for compounding a felony.

Short of organizing a revolution, for which there seems to [be] even less popular demand at present than for "How He Lied," I have no remedy.

I return your cheque, and hope you may not be held responsible hereafter for an offence committed at the behest of your sovereign.

yours faithfully
G. Bernard Shaw

To LILLAH McCARTHY

[C/4; X/182]

The Old House. Harmer Green
14th March 1905

Yes: I think that will do very well; only dont have any light blue ribbon with the white muslin: use violet or purple.

Mrs William Morris wore a black mantle with violet lining at her husband's funeral: that was what gave me the idea of the dress in the first act. Ann should not produce an impression of artless simplicity: there should be a certain pomegranate splendor lurking somewhere in the effect—just a touch even in the muslin dress. I trust your judgment in this matter: do what you like.

G.B.S.

To LILLAH McCARTHY

[A/4]

The Old House. Harmer Green
18th March 1905

Dear Miss McCarthy

The Stage Society will postpone the Superman to the 28th May (or perhaps the 21st) if this will suit you.

522

There are three reasons for regarding the postponement as a blessing in disguise. 1. We shall perform at the climax of the season. 2. We shall get a much better cast as regards the three most important men. 3. I hope to be able to induce the Vedrenne-Barker management at the Court to take up the play and give at least nine matinées of it; so that we shall all get a better return for our labor than the Stage Society could give us.

If by any chance the thing were a great success—and Heaven only knows what may happen with an incalculable person like you in an incalculable part—it would not drop after nine matinées.

Let me know whether May will suit you.

yours faithfully
G. Bernard Shaw

To E. F. SAXON

The Old House. Harmer Green
10th April 1905

[A/5]

[E.F.Saxon was general stage manager for Vedrenne-Barker at the Royal Court Theatre. *You Never Can Tell* was presented at the Royal Court in a series of nine matinées, commencing 2nd May, and was then transferred to the evening bill on 12th June for three weeks.]

Dear Saxon

Do not trouble trying to extract the scenes of Y.N.C.T. from the stage directions. Here they are

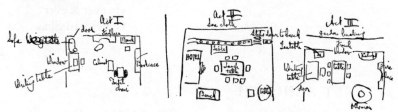

In haste
G. Bernard Shaw

To ELEANOR ROBSON

[A/38; X/129]

10 Adelphi Terrace W C
13th April 1905

[Eleanor Robson (b. 1879), a British-born actress, had returned from New York to star in Israel Zangwill's *Merely Mary Ann*, which had opened for a highly successful run at the Duke of York's Theatre on 8th September 1904. Miss Robson later became Mrs August Belmont. The new play was *Major Barbara*, which Shaw had begun on 22nd March 1905. It was completed on 15th October.]

To the Gifted, Beautiful & Beloved—Greeting.
My dear Miss Eleanor

Fate has done its work. I have put you out of my mind and settled down hard to my business since you left England. After weary months of mere commercial affairs & rehearsals, I have begun another play— half finished it, indeed; and lo! there you are in the middle of it. I said I would write a play for you; but I did not mean in the least to keep my promise. I swear I never thought of you until you came up a trap in the middle of the stage & got into my heroine's empty clothes and said Thank you: *I* am the mother of that play. Though I am not sure that you are not its father; for you simply danced in here & captivated me & then deserted me & left me with my unborn play to bring into existence. I simply dare not count the number of months. Anyhow the heroine is so like you that I see nobody in the wide world who can play her except you.

And the play is wildly impossible, of course. You are a major in the Salvation Army & you do wonderful & mystical things in the most natural & prosaic way. It would run for a week. But what a week that would be! When are you coming over?

yrs ever & ever
G. Bernard Shaw

To JANET ACHURCH

The Old House. Harmer Green

[A/4]

23rd April 1905

My dear Janet

I really dont know what to say. It is all very well to beg me not to jibe; but you have such an amazing knack of overlaying a situation

524

which, as I can well believe, is serious enough, with side splitting touches of pathos, that all hope of your doing anything rational with a hundred-pound-note dies in my breast as I read. Just consider a moment (I am going to end up with a sort of half & half offer; so dont be impatient)! You begin with a tragic announcement that you have lost all shame & have at last desperately resolved to take a new and appalling step. Which unprecedented and dark extremity, as it presently appears, is nothing less than to ask for a loan. Your entry being thus made sufficiently dramatic, you become clever in your own inimitably artful and diplomatic way, and hint that 15 per cent is a practical certainty to a real friend, though to a sordid usurer there seems to be no security for it. You then touch in a little picture of the hollow cheeks of Mr Micawber, and sketch him as devoting himself to the education of his only child with cheerful industry, but with the worm gnawing at his heart. Finally, after a passing apology for being unable, through the law's unreasonableness, to exploit Nora's little all, you suggest as a rather likely quarter for gold mining Mrs Webb!!!

What is to be done with such a woman! Can you wonder that seas of money, oceans of talent, and hosts of friends have been showered on you in vain? It is a fascinating psychological problem, this of a woman quite extraordinarily clever and subtle in all fictitious dramas, and in the real drama a baby convinced that any sort of salt is good enough to sprinkle on the tails of mere live flesh & blood acquaintances. When will you be convinced that good acting is supremely important off the stage, and of so little importance on it that marionette plays are as good as A Doll's House in point of illusion?

All this is merely to relieve my temper & nerves, just now rehearsed into rags. I am perfectly aware that I might as well try to impress the gate post by hitting it with a poker.

Now here is my offer. Will you put me into communication with that solicitor? I will pay him whatever his writing to me & perusing my letters may cost. If he can convince me that your debts as you now stand—I mean those debts which you can be sued & sold up for—can be extinguished by a payment of a hundred pounds, and the way left perfectly clear for you to get comfortably into debt again after securing for Charles a few days breathing time, then I will consider what can be done; for You Never Can Tell has captivated Noo York, and a week's royalties would clean the slate. In saying this I know that I run the risk of your instantly borrowing £20 on a promissory note for *my* £100, and therewith starting a tour with a collection of eligible Whitsun dates from impossible theatres, with Doll's House & Forget me Not

525

as the two leading novelties. But I will take the risk. Mind: I must deal with the creditors myself; for I know that if you deal between us you will sacrifice both yourself & me to them. You can't get yourself out of difficulties; so you had better let me try. Only, I wont be stage managed into it. Your mantle of shame & Charles's gnawing worm leave me a man of stone. Fifteen per cent does not rouse my cupidity. Nora learning the arts of life from her father hardly stirs even my irony. I fully expect to find the requisite amount about seven times your estimate, in which case my offer is off. I am fond of money, and grudge it extremely to your creditors. And if I *do* have to pay £100, I shall be moral and sarcastic to its full value. Reply to Adelphi Terrace.

yrs morosely
G. Bernard Shaw

To JAMES HUNEKER

10 Adelphi Terrace W C
9th May 1905

[C/45; X/186]

[Brentano published a selection by Huneker from the *Saturday Review* articles, under the title *Dramatic Opinions and Essays*, in two volumes, in 1906. Shaw's music criticism in *The World* was not collected until 1931. Huneker's article on Shaw in the April 1905 issue of *Success Magazine* had contained a sub-title caption: "His Rise From an Irish Peasant Lad." Lucy Carr Shaw, for reasons of health, resided at this time in Gotha, Germany.]

John Bull is not yet published. I am too busy rehearsing and producing to attend to any publishing business for the moment.

I proposed to Brentano that they should get you to edit a selection from my musical feuilletons in The World &c. They said it was an excellent idea to get you to edit my dramatic feuilletons & that they had bought up the old numbers of The Saturday Review accordingly. Knock the difference into their heads if you can.

My sister in Germany is furious because you have compromised her social position by describing me in "Success" (which has reached Germany) as "a peasant lad." The Shaws peasants! Good God! You know not what you say.

Why did you give me the slip last fall?

G. Bernard Shaw

To SIEGFRIED TREBITSCH

The Old House. Harmer Green

[A/5]   30th May 1905

[The Burgtheater production of *You Never Can Tell* (*Der verlorene Vater*) opened on 17th March 1906.]

My dear Trebitsch

It is no use: you *must* take it; or I will put an end to our partnership & take on Meyerfeldt. If once we begin trying to calculate on each separate job how much you have done and how much I have done, and dividing the money proportionately, life will become unbearable & dishonorable for both of us. The agreement is that we are partners, sharing half & half. I take my half when you have had a lot of trouble and I have had none. You must take your half when—as happens much seldomer—I have had more trouble than you. So take your cheque and pay me instantly my 30 kronen. You also owe me twopence-halfpenny, the postage of this letter, as you have made me send the cheque twice over.

There are no photos of You Never Can Tell, except an album of American ones weighing about 10 tons. The Court scenery is too cheap & shabby for the Burgtheater to copy. I can send you rough plans & sketches to work from as soon as the scenery seems likely to be put in hand. At present I am too hard pressed to spend a moment on them until we know that Schlenther really means business.

GBS

To EDWARD R. PEASE

The Old House. Harmer Green

[C/35]   5th June 1905

If the agenda for the next Exec. is not too crowded, will you put down "Motion by G.B.S. for a report on the results of the Society's political recommendations during the last ten years." I think a stock-taking would do us no harm; and such a report would be useful in answering the eternal "What does the Fabian Society *do*?"—that is, if the results have been satisfactory. If they havnt, the sooner we have a definite eye-opener on the subject, the better.

G. Bernard Shaw

To LILLAH McCARTHY

[A/4; X/182]

10 Adelphi Terrace W C
7th June 1905

[The Vedrenne–Barker production of *Man and Superman* at the Royal Court opened on 23rd May. Shaw had attended a matinée on 6th June. Granville Barker played John Tanner. Lewis Casson (1875–1969), who played Octavius in *Man and Superman*, appeared in several other Shaw plays for Vedrenne–Barker before joining Annie Horniman's company at the Gaiety Theatre, Manchester, in 1908. There he married Sybil Thorndike on 22nd December 1908. Dame Edith S. Lyttelton (1865–1948), a playwright and friend of Mrs Patrick Campbell, later served with Shaw on the Executive Committee of the Shakespeare Memorial National Theatre.]

My dear Miss Lillah

I was in front on Tuesday, and noticed a point or two of importance to you.

In the third act, when Malone, Ramsden & Tanner go off making a great cackle & fuss, do not begin the scene with Tavy until the noise is over and the audience's attention has quite come back to you. Just wait, looking provokingly at Tavy, until there is a dead silence & expectation & then say, without the least hurry, "Wont you go with them, Tavy?" Otherwise you will not get the new key and the slow movement.

At the end when you say "I want to make you cry for the last time" say it to Tavy alone: the others are not supposed to hear it: it is one of Anne's wicked asides.

Dont forget to say "but you nearly killed me, Jack, for all that" as if you meant it. He *has* nearly killed you. Mrs Lyttelton, close behind me, explained to her party that Ann was only pretending to faint. That is not exactly true. Ann doesnt faint exactly, but she does collapse from utter exhaustion after her "daring so frightfully."

It was one of the best performances I have seen you do.

Why did you come on on your wrong side after the wait? If it occurs again, dont hurry: go round and come on with aggravating leisureliness. I was unfeeling enough to shake with laughter at poor Barker & Casson.

yrs ever
G. Bernard Shaw

Man and Superman.

Messrs. VEDRENNE and BARKER beg leave to explain that the acting version of *Man and Superman* now presented has been prepared solely by the author. None of the omissions by which he has brought the performance within the customary limits of time have been made or suggested by the managers. They do not regard a complete performance, occupying both afternoon and evening, as impossible or unacceptable. But as Mr. BERNARD SHAW designed the play from the beginning so as to admit of the excision, for practical stage purposes, of the scene in which John Tanner's motor-car is stopped in Spain by brigands, of the philosophic episode of Don Juan in hell, and of the disquisition on the evolution of morality as a passion, they feel that they can present the rest of the play as a complete comedy in three acts without injury to the artistic integrity of the work, or violation of the author's wishes, which have been unconditionally complied with on all points.

ROYAL COURT THEATRE,
    23rd May, 1905.

Statement, drafted by Shaw, distributed with programme of first public performance.

To FLORENCE HAYDON

[A/46]

10 Adelphi Terrace W C
7th June 1905

[Florence Haydon (1838–1918), who had first appeared on the stage in 1860, came out of retirement to play Mrs Whitefield in *Man and Superman*. She became a prominent member of the Vedrenne-Barker company. Violet was played by Sarah Brooke.]

Dear Miss Haydon

I was in front on Tuesday. Do not let them get you up the stage in the last act before your exit with Violet, or you will find it miss fire. You were at the steps before you began to talk, which was fatal. Keep right down & get a long walk. Take plenty of time: there is not the least need for hurry. Dont let your effects be whittled away for the sake of getting the curtain down 20 seconds sooner: the audience doesnt want the curtain to come down whilst you are on the stage.

In haste, which please excuse,
yrs sincerely
G. Bernard Shaw

To GILBERT MURRAY

[C/36]

The Old House. Harmer Green
17th June 1905

[Forbes-Robertson's production of *Cæsar and Cleopatra* was first presented at the New Amsterdam Theatre, New York, on 30th October 1906.]

Forbes Robertson is going to produce Cæsar & Cleopatra; and a dispute has arisen as to whether Britannus should be called "Briton us" or "Brit. Annus." I do not ask you to dogmatize on the subject; but what would you call him if you met him? I mean, of course, apart from calling him an ensanguined fool or anything of that sort.

Also, can you give me a[n] adjective to denote an author with several publishers? I have used publygamous; but this suggests the "hippos a river & potamos a horse" style of derivation.

G.B.S.

[Murray replied on 18th June: "Brit. Annus without doubt, though, if I met him, I should perhaps address him in the vocative, as 'Brit. Annie.' This is the sort of question that makes me feel the real superiority of a classical education over all others. Fancy the humiliating position you would be in if you did meet him. No position for a creator.

"The other question is difficult. A publisher is Ekdotês; so that 'monecdotous' and 'polyecdotous' would seem to be correct words. (the o short; the accent on the ec.) I should avoid 'publygamous'; it would be Graecolatin for a prostitute, unless you could show by the context that it meant 'married to a poplar tree!'" (BM)]

To ADA REHAN

[A/4]

The Old House. Harmer Green
21st June 1905

My dear Miss Rehan

Yesterday I had a visit here from a man of noble sentiments and exquisite nature. His beautiful name is David Belasco—a poem in itself. David thinks—but I havnt time to write you all he thinks. Suffice it for the moment that he wants to get into partnership with Lee Shubert, and exploit Brassbound; so you will probably hear from him if you have not done so already. David is slightly too good for this wicked world: he talks of fighting the syndicate (the usual preliminary to joining it), of putting down the starring system (this is what they

all say to an author: he wont mention it to you), of Art with a large A, and generally of any sort of nonsense that he thinks good enough for a British Litter-Airy pusson. Still, David is a man to be considered: he is a bit of a stage manager, for instance. He offered to start a theatre for me in New York and devote the rest of his life to the performance of my works on the anti-star system, the author being the one person to be put in the foreground. Thus, if you made the audience laugh as Lady Cicely, I should step out and bow. If you had a curtain call, *I* should take it. And so on. This seems to me a very proper view of the matter; but we got no further than a rather plaintive remark from David that I am a very difficult man to talk to. Ever since he went, my head has been buzzing with "Lord: remember David. Teach him to know thy ways."

I leave for Ireland about the 5th July for three months. Before I go I must start the rehearsals of Cæsar & Cleopatra for Forbes Robertson, so that the production may be in shape for September, when I will perhaps run back for a week to give the finishing touches. This will keep me busy in town next week, I expect. What day could you conveniently give me a latish appointment: say about five.

I am very uneasy about your idea of trying Lady Cicely in the backwoods all by yourself. You see, you have been brought up to do all the work on the stage & have the other people simply hanging sulkily & silently on to your apron strings. That comes of having a manager who cares more for you than for the play or the author or anything else in the world & who steals other people's lines for you & is jealous if anyone else gets a chance. Now *my* plan is to make the other people do all the work. You sit quietly whilst they rage & deliver long speeches and act and work the thing up; and then you simply put away your knitting and scoop the whole deal. Lady Cicely hasnt to utter one word that can be put on anyone else: it is all built up for her to play on top of. What I am so afraid of is that you dont know this game, and would feel miserable sitting there with Brassbound doing all the hard labor for you. But you would take to it tremendously after the first shock if I were there to keep up your spirits. That is why I want to rehearse the play before you venture on it.

G.B.S.

To ELEANOR ROBSON

[A/38; X/187]

10 Adelphi Terrace W C
21st June 1905

[George Tyler (1867–1946) was an important American theatrical manager.]

My dear Miss Robson

Miss Marbury tells me that you are going straight to Paris, and are due there tomorrow. This is a shattering blow to me: I had hoped you would pass through London, as I am leaving for Ireland about the 5th July. However, there is one consolation: nothing is ready for you yet in the shape of a play. I have been overwhelmed with rehearsals and business for months past; and my retreat to Ireland is a desperate measure to get a moments rest and then finish the Salvation play, of which only an act and a half (in the rough) is on paper. And I have no idea what it will be like from the practical business point of view when it is finished.

There is much distraction as to the ultimate destination of the play. The Court Theatre management has, of course, very strong claims on me: they say that if I insist on you (to which I always reply that I adore you) they will do what they humanly can to secure you; but their house holds only $800 (£160), and they fear they cannot afford you. Tyler offers me a blank contract, a book of blank cheques, anything & everything I please. Frederick Harrison of the Haymarket Theatre says that even if there is no money in the play he will cheerfully sacrifice his little all for its sake. How it will end, heaven perhaps knows—probably in my reading you the play some day, and then our parting in tears, you to play Miss Hardcastle [in Goldsmith's *She Stoops to Conquer*] or some such nonsense, and I to coach some deserving young female at fifty dollars a week or so in the part of the Salvation major. I can do nothing but sit tight and, when they ask me what I want for the play, what I demand from them, what my ultimatum is, reply Eleanor Robson, Eleanor Robson, Eleanor Robson. And she will probably be frightfully disappointed with the part & refuse to play it when the play is complete.

Meanwhile I contemplate Eleanor's photographs in the intervals of business & domestic earthquake—for we have to leave our countryhouse in Hertfordshire at the end of this month; and the horrors of moving are added to all the other horrors.

In haste
ever devoted
G. Bernard Shaw

To JOHNSTON FORBES-ROBERTSON

The Old House. Harmer Green
[A/1; X/167]   29th June 1905

["Phelpsing along" is an allusion to Samuel Phelps (1804–78), the Shakespearean actor-manager under whom Forbes-Robertson had studied elocution. Rosina Filippi (1866?–1930) was a character actress who created the rôle of Lady Britomart in *Major Barbara* at the Royal Court Theatre later that year, and appeared as Madame Petkoff in the revival of *Arms and the Man* at the Savoy Theatre in December 1907. A. & S. Gatti were the managers of the Vaudeville Theatre. The Scala was a new theatre, which opened on 23rd September 1905 with R.E.Fyffe's *The Conqueror*, in which Forbes-Robertson appeared. Norman McKinnel (1870–1932), a Scottish actor, had played Morell in the Royal Court production of *Candida* in April 1904. He created, in June 1907, the rôle of the Devil in *Don Juan in Hell*.]

Johnston Forbes Robertson!

Patience! thou young and rose lipped cherubim! I have waited six years for you; and you ask me to be patient. No: the difficulty is all the other way: it is you who are impatient, with your six weeks holiday and your production in September. What you dont grasp is that unless I have a holiday I shall go raving mad and die. You think because I am going away for three months, I am trifling with you. But in that three months I have to write a new play and to revise half a dozen French and German translations of my old ones. I have to see an old novel [*The Irrational Knot*] through the American press and write a preface for it. I have to prepare John Bull's Other Island for publication. I have to do half a dozen articles now months in arrear. The translators are howling, pressed by the Berlin & Viennese theatres for prompt copies. The publishers are howling, because the public are red hot for Shaw books. Everybody's fame and future is staked on my attending to him before the end of the week. How much holiday do you see for me in all this? You say I am to wait until the end of July to go, and to come back early in August. Well, I'm blowed if I will! The worm turns under the steamroller. And I wont risk C & C without rehearsing it myself. You are too deadly tired of the whole business to be trusted. You would go Phelpsing along, crushing poor Ian, and taking no interest in the unfortunate crowd, who would be cast anyhow and snubbed into more than their natural dufferdom. That is all very well for a monologue like Hamlet; but it will not do for C & C. I might be content with the first week and the last at a pinch; but they must not come out of my three months. The idea of rehearsing now seems hopeless, because we havnt our cast. Rosina Filippi tells me that her husband insists on her leaving the stage at the end of her engagement to Gatti. [Frederick] Kerr has slipped through our fingers for the moment. The more I look into the play the more impressed I am with the importance of Rufio & Ftatateeta. And we have more than 20 other people to get into their places, not to mention crowds to be drilled. It looks to me much more like the 1st December than any earlier date. Can you not live on your fat until then? I quite agree that the Scala ought to open with C & C; but it had better wait, since better, it appears, may not be.

Remember, I have the strongest interest in getting C & C out of my way early; for I am threatened with productions at the Court which will need rehearsing; but there is no use heading straight for a breakdown by trying to put twelve months work into three.

Anyhow, the difficulty is no more of my making than of yours. We are under the corner stone of Necessity, as cheerful old Ibsen says [in

534

Emperor and Galilean]. If you could start rehearsing on Saturday next, and produce on the 10th October, the thing might be done; but we have not the cast. [Norman] McK[innell] is absolutely no good for Rufio; and Calvert is wanted at the Court, like all the other people who are any good to me.

Oh this cursed packing—fancy our having to change houses at this fatal moment! [The Shaws moved from Harmer Green back to London on 30th June.]

I am quite addled & barren of resource & suggestion.

Why did I ever write the confounded play? I know I can get a magnificent performance out of it if only I can get a fair chance at it. Let's put it off to next year.

GBS

To J. E. VEDRENNE

10 Adelphi Terrace W C
[X/183]   4th July 1905

[Christina Lady Barrington (1847–1937), wife of the Hon. Eric Barrington, had taken the ailing Ada Rehan into her home and corresponded at length with Shaw about Miss Rehan's health and business problems. The first public performance in London of *Captain Brassbound's Conversion* was offered by Vedrenne-Barker at the Royal Court Theatre on 20th March 1906.]

Dear Vedrenne

The doctor has positively forbidden Miss Rehan to play for a year. It is possible that eight months rest would make a new woman of her, and enable her to do half a dozen dazzling matinées of Brassbound for us next May; but this is the best we can hope for.

I have thought it over and talked it up and down (with Lady Barrington) and written you two letters and torn them up; and my conclusion is that we had better let Brassbound alone for another year. There is no use throwing it away with a Lady Cicely not up to the proper weight. Ellen Terry is the only one at all equal to it; and she does not believe in it: she would play it on the strength of my "success"; and the result would be very doubtful.

I also think it would have more chance after the new play (also a Conversion play) than before it. At all events I have been suddenly switched off it; and so let us consider it postponed for another year.

535

Forbes Robertson's scheme for the Scala has definitely broken down: the backers will not do anything but back out. You had better organize the Caesar production yourself (with someone else's money): properly handled there is a big success in it.

yrs ever
G. Bernard Shaw

To EDWARD R. PEASE

[C/35]

10 Adelphi Terrace W C
4th July 1905

[Shaw's suggestion about two reports was adopted, with Wells drafting a Special Committee report on suggested changes within the Fabian Society, and Shaw replying for the Executive Committee. The printed reports were issued to the Fabian membership in December 1906. Cecil E. Chesterton (1879–1918), brother of G. K. Chesterton, was a journalist who founded and edited the *New Witness* (1912). He was on the Fabian Executive from 1904 to 1907, when he abandoned Fabian Socialism.]

The proper thing would be two reports, pro & con. If you and Webb were to make out the best case you could for the old policy & the old gang, and Wells, Guest & Chesterton were to do all they could to explode us, we should get something that would really give us an over-hauling. Our methods are substantially what they were 15 years ago; and they and we must be getting rather stale, not to mention the slow change in the situation—for instance, in the importance & prestige of the House of Commons & the efficiency of the departments. All I want is a stir up and a stocktaking to make Fabianism interesting again. I have no far reaching design, nor any very definite intention beyond a general desire to reflect on our past life.

G.B.S.

To ARCHIBALD HENDERSON

[A.c/2; X/113.e, 116.e]

Derry [Rosscarbery. Co. Cork]
15th July 1905

[The Shaws had departed for Ireland on 6th July. They returned to London on 29th September. It was Shaw's first visit to Ireland since his departure

536

in 1876. The unpublished article on the German Socialist leaders may be an undated holograph manuscript "The Fabian Society and the German Party" in the British Museum (Add. Mss. 50689, ff. 204–209). Jacob Maris (1837–99) was a Dutch painter of landscapes.]

Dear Henderson

I must try to spare you an hour; but I wish you would put off that biography for a few years: it has come upon me at a fearfully crowded moment. However, here goes for some of your questions.

On turning up your second list, I find that some of them are already answered—at least I think I explained about the Nordau criticism in Liberty and some other things.

Question 18, b. My "championship of Wagner in England" is of no importance now. Wagner & anti-Wagner was the great controversy of the time in music until anti-Wagnerism finally became ridiculous in the face of Wagner's overwhelming popularity. In the same way Ibsen and anti-Ibsen was the great controversy in drama in London after 1889. I was on the right side in both instances: that is all. According to The Daily Telegraph, Wagner and Ibsen were offensive impostors. As a matter of fact they were the greatest living masters in their respective arts; and I knew that quite well. The critics of the XIX century had two first rate chances—Ibsen & Wagner. For the most part they missed both. Second-best they could recognize; but best was beyond them.

However, a German would laugh at the notion that Wagner required any "championing" in 1889–94, since the Bayreuth performances, which I first attended in 1888 (or 9, I forget which), began in 1876. The chief novelty in my Wagner criticisms was my attack on Bayreuth for various old fashioned absurdities in the scenery & dresses, for beer barrels of singers who did not know how to sing &c &c. . . . Up to that time Bayreuth criticism had been either worship or blasphemy. I threw off all this, and criticised performances of Wagner's works at Bayreuth precisely as I should have criticised performances of Mozart's works at Covent Garden. The effect on pious Wagnerians was as though I had brawled in Church. In much the same way, when I attended the International Socialist Congresses at Zurich in 1893 & in London in 1896 (these dates need verification, by the way) I reported them day by day in the Star [8th–14th August 1893; 27th July–1st August 1896] as unsparingly as I should report a sitting of Congress; and the Socialists, amazed and indignant at their first taste of real criticism, concluded that I was going over to the enemy. At the Zurich Congress I first became acquainted with the leaders of the movement on the continent. Chief among them was the German leader Liebknecht, a '48 veteran, who, having become completely parliamentarized, still thought it necessary to dupe his younger followers with the rhetoric of the barricade. After a division in which an attempt to secure unanimity by the primitive method of presenting the resolution before the Congress to the delegates of the different nations in their various languages in several versions adapted to their views; so that whilst they believed they were all saying Yes to the same proposition the wording was really very different in the different translations, and sometimes highly contradictory, it turned out that the stupidity of the English section had baffled the cleverness of the German-Swiss bureau, because the English voted No when they meant Yes, and upset the apple cart. Happening to be close to Liebknecht on the platform at the luncheon adjournment, I said a few words to him in explanation of the apparently senseless action of the English. He looked wearily round at me; saw a comparatively young Socialist whom he did not know, and immediately treated me to a long assurance that the German Social Democrats did not shrink from a conflict with the police on Labor Day (the 1st May); that they were as ready as ever &c &c &c &c &c. I turned away as soon and as shortly as I could without being rude; and from that time I discounted the German leaders as being 40 years out of date, and totally negligible except as very ordinary republican Radicals with a Socialist formula which was simply a convenient excuse for doing nothing new.

When the German leaders visited London in the eighties they treated the Fabian Society as a foolish joke. Later on they found their error (the story has elements of romantic tragedy, by the way, through the suicide of Karl Marx's daughter; and when I return to London in October I may hunt you out an article of mine on the subject which was never published); and Liebknecht was entertained at a great Fabian meeting; but to this day the German Socialist press does not dare to publish the very articles it asks me to write, because of my ruthless criticism of Bebel, Singer and the old tradition & the "old gang" generally. My heresy as to Marx is, of course, another horror to those Germans who got their ideas of political economy in the 48–71 period.

Question 19. My "art criticisms" written in The World from 1885 to 1889—also a few in "Our Corner"—and for one season (?1889 or 90) in Truth, consist in about half a dozen signed articles per year and (this applies only to The World) a great many paragraphs now hardly to be identified. When I took to musical criticism (? in 1888) I began to consider whether I was making enough money by the very hard

538

work of plodding through all the picture exhibitions. At last I counted my gains, and found, to my amazement, that my remuneration for paragraphs at 5ᵈ per line, worked out at—as well as I can recollect—less than £40 a year. £200 would not have been at all excessive for the work. Edmund Yates, when I resigned and told him why, was as much staggered as I was myself, and proposed a much more lucrative arrangement by which I should divide the work with Lady Colin Campbell. But the division would not have been fair to her; and Yates, recognizing this, did what I asked, which was, to hand the whole department over to Lady Colin, and confine my contributions to music alone. Then I wrote about pictures for Truth for the best part of a season until a naive proposal was made to me editorially that I should oblige certain artist-friends of the editorium by favorable notices, and was assured that I might oblige any friends of my own in the same way. This proposal was made in perfect good faith and in all innocence, it never having occurred to the editors of Truth that art criticism was a serious pursuit or that any question of morals or conduct could possibly arise over it. Of course I resigned with some vigor, though without any ill humor; and the editorium was quite sincerely[,] pathetically hurt by my eccentric, unfriendly and disobliging conduct. That was the end of my career as an art critic. I did write one more article on the Academy on my appointment as critic of a Sunday paper called The Observer. To my amazement the article appeared with profuse interpolations by a Jewish lady who had an interest in the paper. That produced another resignation; and so I vanished from the picture galleries. Truth and The Observer were both papers of some standing. They were no more guilty of corruption than a man with no notion of property can be guilty of theft; and to this day they probably have not the least idea why I threw up a reasonably well paid job and assumed an attitude vaguely implying some sort of disapproval of their right to do what they liked with their own papers.

As to my line in criticism, the only controversial question that came up in my time was raised by the Impressionists, of whom, in England, Whistler was the chief. People accustomed to see the "good north light" of a St John's Wood studio represented at exhibitions as sunlight in the open air were naturally amazed by the pictures of Manet. I backed up the Impressionists strongly; refused to call Whistler "Jimmy" instead of Mr Whistler; boomed the Dutch school vigorously and tried to persuade the public that James Maris was a great painter; stood up for Van Uhde not only in defence of his pictures of Christ

539

surrounded by people in tall hats and frock coats, but also of his excellent painting of light in a dry crisp diffused way then quite unfashionable; and, on the whole, picked out my men and supported movements with fairly good judgment as far as subsequent events enable one to say. And of course I did not fall into the Philistine trap & talk "greenery yallery" nonsense about Burne Jones & the pre-Raphaelite school.

(to be continued in my next)

G.B.S.

To JANET ACHURCH

[A/4]

Derry. Rosscarbery
18th July 1905

My dear Janet

I said so! The only use that £30 has been is to convince you that I owe you £70.

Well, I dont. The transaction was quite clear. You wrote to me and said that £100 would get you out of debt. I replied that if your solicitor could shew me that £100 would clean the slate for you I would find the £100. Thereupon you drew £30 on account; and Charrington sent me a statement of liabilities which I went through very carefully. By a striking series of discounts, such as "Smith & Jones, £24-3-6—would probably take £7; Miss Brown, an old friend, £50, say £10; Edith Craig £25—has given up the business; so this doesnt matter &c &c &c," he got the total down to something like £300. Now even if I had seen the smallest reason to believe that the creditors would have accepted this composition £300 is not £100. I should not have stood on a matter of £20 or so; but £200 is another matter. The conditions of my offer did not exist; and the offer is off.

The fact is, you are beyond human help in this matter. You have no faculty for money matters; and Charlie has no conscience in them. Your friends are not unfriendly; but you dont realize the difficulties all this business sets up. Edie Craig's £25 alone cost you more than £2,500 of debt to local seedsmen & florists. I turned aside Ellen Terry's wrath; but other and harder shelled people than Ellen had vetoes at the Stage Society and elsewhere which were conclusive. Then, as Charlie knows, when you engage a company on the chance of paying them out of the takings, you are gambling with your whole future or

540

thereabouts: forever after in casting Charlie for a part, one has to consider not only whether he can act it, but whether anyone else in the cast is a sufficiently staunch professional to regard the gamble as the one unpardonable sin—and there always is such a person, or, in the case of repertory plays like mine, the chance of having to fall back on such a person later on. The worst of it is that they are perfectly right; and we who weaken through personal friendship are entirely wrong. Charlie has many more friends than he deserves; but we are all compelled to admit that he will not play the game, and that the one drawback to his remarkable qualities—namely, that he is a most infernal scoundrel—is one which some of his victims cannot be prevented from taking seriously. Now as you know I am not a moralist (though I regret to say Charlie is), and quite see that the risks he took were perhaps worth taking from his point of view. Well, he staked and lost his commercial position, because, as events proved, he was penny foolish and pound-wise commercially, and also because his commercial integrity as a caterer for the public was upset by his being stage-struck himself, and postulating the quite irrelevant condition that you should always be in the centre of the stage. And now the loss must be stood by. Certain triumphs came of the game: instead of saying with Francis I "I have lost all save honor" he could say "I have spent my honor very profitably on doing something that my honorable censors have failed to do; and if Granville Barker can now run a repertory theatre without knocking a chip off his rigid Roman conscience, it is because that theatre is built on the ruins of my credit and character." But all this lashing of hypocrisy does not alter the facts, which are, as I said, that your present situation is beyond any help that I or any of your friends can render. Do not, by the way, imagine from the juxtaposition of "censors" & "Barker" at the top of the page, that Barker is unfriendly. But he is as hard and clearheaded as I am myself, and sees the situation in spite of his artistic sympathies.

If you were in London I should recommend a frank bankruptcy. The old excuse for avoiding it is exploded; for no bankruptcy could have produced the mountain of impossibility that has been heaped up by the shifts that have staved it off. As it is, I can suggest nothing; and I only write all this because you may as well know how useless your friends must be to you inside the theatre even when they attain the success to which your work led up.

In short, Charlie must borrow £1000 from somebody, and begin over again. I will not produce that sum; so I am of no use for the moment.

541

Barker says you ought to become a producer; and there may be something in that when you are really resigned to retire. It is extraordinarily difficult to get a play intelligently produced: I should be lost if I did not waste month after month at rehearsal.

I must now close this very disagreeable, but not wholly unprovoked letter. I shall be here until October, when I must return to take up rehearsals at the Court.

yrs ever
G. Bernard Shaw

To LOUIS CALVERT

Derry. Rosscarbery
[S/8, 38; X/189, 190, 191]   23rd July 1905

[This letter (the original of which has not been located) was published on several occasions, but there are important discrepancies in the texts, as there are in the two typed transcripts which survive. The following is an edited version of the letter, which attempts to provide the most likely reading. Shaw's choice of a brass instrument for Undershaft serves as a reminder that he himself had taken up the cornet in 1873, though he abandoned it the following year. Giovanni Matteo Mario (1810–83) was a celebrated Italian tenor.]

Dear Calvert

Can you play the trombone? If not, I beg you to acquire a smattering of the art during your holidays. I am getting on with the new play scrap by scrap; and the part of the millionaire cannon founder is becoming more and more formidable. Broadbent and Keegan rolled into one, with Mephistopheles thrown in; that is what it is like. [Sydney Grundy's] Business is Business will be cheap melodrama in comparison. Irving and Tree will fade into third class when Calvert takes the stage as Andrew Undershaft. It will be TREMENJOUS, simply. But there is a great scene at the end of the second act where he buys up the Salvation Army, and has to take part in a march to a big meeting. Barker will play the tamborine. You will have a trombone—or a bombardon if you prefer that instrument—and it would add greatly to the effect if you could play it prettily. Besides, if you took to music you could give up those confounded cigars and save your voice and your memory (both wrecks, like Mario's, from thirty-seven cigars a day) for this immense part. It is very long, speeches longer than

542

Keegan's, and dozens of them, and infinite nuances of execution. Undershaft is diabolically subtle, gentle, self-possessed, powerful, stupendous, as well as amusing and interesting. There are the makings of ten Hamlets and six Othellos in his mere leavings. Learning it will half kill you; but you can retire next day as pre-eminent and unapproachable. That penny-plain and tuppence-colored pirate Brassbound will be beneath your notice then. I have put him off for another year, as I cannot get the right Lady Cicely. Vedrenne, unluckily, has read my plays at Margate and is now full of the most insane proposals—wants Brassbound instantly with you and Kate Rorke, for one thing.

But the trombone is the urgent matter of the moment. By the way, trombone players never get cholera nor consumption—never die, in fact, until extreme old age makes them incapable of working the slide.

G. Bernard Shaw

To CHARLES CHARRINGTON

[A/5]

Derry. Rosscarbery
27th July 1905

[Edmund Maurice (1863–1928) had gained a reputation as a suave leading man in a number of West End successes.]

Dear Charrington

It is only partly for amusement that I jab you in the vitals. The only chance you have left is some approximate realization of the infamy of your past career; and it is evident from your letter that you are as far from that as ever. I tell you that you are regarded as a dangerous man; and you reply, with some indignation, that you have only murdered two persons, and that one of them got you hanged by going to the trouble & risk of appealing to the law. Waring & Maurice means the whole Green Room Club. Of course you can get actors, because they will do anything for a show; but that only makes it possible for you to ruin yourself rather oftener than you could do if the whole profession was as well organized as it ought to be. Take the case of Forbes Robertson the other day! He wanted to produce Cæsar at the Scala. He was very full of it; built very much on it; committed himself so far that it was very painful to retreat. And he had all the signatures of his syndicate except, I believe, two. These two backed out at the last moment. You would have gone on ten times over with half what he had in hand. He

543

refused to make a single engagement until he was secure against the possibility of retreating with everybody paid in the event of a failure. It was not very pleasant to give up the project and own that in his position he had been unable to command the necessary backing; but he did it. The result is that he will have his turn at Cæsar later on, and will have an unshaken position though he has lost more money than you and will lose more. The more familiar I become with theatrical business the more I see that the bogus manager—the man who spends his last penny on the production and trusts to the gate to make the ghost walk, which is exactly what you always do (how the deuce you got out of Mrs Daintry in Manchester heaven alone knows!)—is the one person against whom the actor must for dear life fight tooth & nail. It is no use having promises & hopes and prospects: you must have money in the bank. You are in the position of a bookmaker: the possibility and likelihood of welshing are so imminent that you must be twice as particular as an ordinary commercial speculator. Instead of which, you welsh.

That is the only thing you have to fear. Nobody wants to injure you: your stupendous borrowings are treated with a positively wicked indulgence: your cleverness & Janet's is exaggerated instead of demurred to. BUT, your credit as a manager is gone. If you could once see that instead of feeling injured about it, you might be in a way to get it back. But you will never see it. I tell it to you in my mechanical beast-of-burden way because you are entitled to your chance of being shewn brutally what is the matter; but you are too old to change now. Here endeth &c &c &c.

yrs
GBS

To LADY BARRINGTON

Derry. Rosscarbery
[A/4]   8th August 1905

[Despite Shaw's desire to postpone a production of *Captain Brassbound's Conversion* for a year, Vedrenne had pressed for an immediate production, and had at last obtained Ellen Terry's consent to undertake the rôle of Lady Cicely. Shaw, anxious about his commitment to Ada Rehan, wrote to Ellen Terry to plead a moral obligation. His letter elicited no response. Another letter, to Ada Rehan, urged her to undertake the play at once. This brought a reply from Lady Barrington that Miss Rehan was not physically strong enough to face the rigours of a theatrical engagement.]

Dear Lady Barrington

Very well: Ellen Terry (an undeserving and ungrateful wretch) can have the part; and now, if you wish to express *my* feelings towards your angel patient, go and knock her head against the bedpost. It is perfect nonsense her not being able to do it in March: she will be prancing through her Katharines and Lady Teazles long before that. It will be the greatest relief to her to get rid of the part and of my importunities: her regrets are pure crocodile. However, she will get well all the sooner now that the part is off her mind: mark my words, you will see an improvement tomorrow.

In future I will have nothing to do with great geniuses. I will take orphans out of institutions and teach them my parts. Better still, I will abandon the theatre to its wretched fate, and devote myself to literature.

A nice time I shall have of it with Ellen. Your Ada, though she has no respect for really first rate plays and *great* dramatists, can at all events sit still and look noble. Ellen will fidget and flounce all about the place unless I freeze her with mere terror; and then she'll forget every word of her part.

There! I have telegraphed to Vedrenne to settle with her.

I do not believe Miss Rehan is ill at all. She is a consummate actress; and depend on it, the whole thing has been got up merely to escape Brassbound.

I do not care a dump what becomes of the play now. You say Miss Rehan wants to know whether Miss Terry is to have it for America too. What is that to her? How dare she ask me such a question after the way she has treated me? It goes to the Court Theatre for 6 matinees & 12 weeks at night, and no further for the present.

As to the difficulties about my new play—well!!!!

Cæsar & Cleopatra is off. Forbes Robertson could not get his syndicate complete for it; though now he seems to have got it complete for something else.

Give up these acting people, Lady Barrington: they have no consciences.

furiously
GBS

To ELLEN TERRY

[C/1; X/192]

Derry. Rosscarbery
[Undated: assigned to 10th August 1905]

[Beneath his photograph, on the reverse of the postcard, Shaw has written: "Greyer—having waited much longer."]

If I do not hear from you before the end of the month I shall commit suicide, with a full confession in my left boot to be read at the inquest.

GBS

To LADY BARRINGTON

[A/4]

Derry. Rosscarbery
13th August 1905

[Annie Russell (1869–1936) was born in Liverpool, but established her theatrical reputation in New York with the Madison Square Theatre company. She first appeared on the London stage in June 1898 in *Sue*, by Bret Harte and T.E.Pemberton, at the Garrick Theatre. The "complications" about *Major Barbara* and Eleanor Robson involved her American manager, George Tyler, who could not come to terms with Vedrenne for Miss Robson's services or with Shaw for the American rights to the play.]

My dear Lady Barrington

You dont realize what a lot of knocking about a really thoroughbred person can stand; and you think *I* dont realize what a little thing will knock the same treasure all to pieces. You may tell Miss Rehan anything that you dare tell yourself; and you mustnt tell her lies except to save her from small bothers. There are certain risks that must be taken; and these risks include, in *her* case, risks of sleepless nights and depressions caused by the inevitable cancelling of arrangements and cold-blooded preparations to do without her.

Now the one unforgivable outrage in such a case is to smile over the preparations and inquire politely after her health and assure her it doesnt matter. It *does* matter. I am furiously disappointed. It is forty thousand times the disappointment to me that it can possibly be to her, because she has done all that can be done and has no more worlds to conquer, whereas my play has yet to begin the world. I have seen her doing great things—have learnt from her what could be done by a great actress—whereas to her it is still a new and only half-convincing idea

546

that the stuff I write is really effective on the stage or can move people's feelings and imaginations. I have had in my mind the notion of her playing Lady Cicely for 6 years very strongly & confidently: she has played with it for six minutes or thereabouts as a sort of escapade that she might—that she wondered if she dared—venture on as a very quaint experiment. The whole project on her part has been nine tenths kindness to me: on my side it has been the ferocious selfishness of the artist who wants a rare talent for a particular piece of work. I am quite sure of myself and sure of her (and should be if the play through some accident or other failed ten times over); and though I must give way to the inevitable, it is too much to expect me to do it blandly and say "Its of no consequence: some other lady will oblige and will do quite as well." *No* other lady will do quite as well, nor nearly as well.

If she had told you to say positively that she must have her years rest, but would then play Lady C. at the Court in the autumn or winter of 1906—or two years rest or a hundred years—then I should have waited unhesitatingly. But the tragedy of the thing is that she could not very well say this with Ellen in the field; and I could not very well risk smashing Vedrenne & Barker (for really Barker's career is a little at stake) and being vindictive to Ellen without a definite promise in my hand; so I had to let London go. There remains America.

There are complications, too—a similar difficulty about my new play and Eleanor Robson. But she—dear creature—after giving me an honestly favorable account of her rival (Annie Russell) ended by "BUT—she must not have MY play." Now that is what I call believing in an author, as distinguished from having a generous nature & being kind to him.

I think you had better either tell her that I am dancing mad & that my letters are unfit for publication, or else let her know the worst. Of course it *may* kill her; but *I* should take my chance of that.

yours implacably
G. Bernard Shaw

To JOHNSTON FORBES-ROBERTSON

Derry. Rosscarbery

[C/1]   [Undated: assigned to 13th August 1905]

The new [Scala] theatre should have been kept for Cæsar. Terry's would have done quite well enough for the other fellows. I consider that Cæsar has been treated with an almost profane levity in being put off with a worn-out shop-soiled stage instead of an unpolluted temple. If you dont want a holiday you could at least have fasted and prayed for a few months.

GBS

To ELEANOR ROBSON

[A/38; X/187]

Derry. Rosscarbery
21st August 1905

[Annie Russell eventually played Barbara in the Royal Court production of *Major Barbara* on 28th November 1905. There was no American production until 1915. Henry Ainley (1879–1945) had been leading man to Maude Adams in *The Little Minister* in New York, and to Eleanor Robson in *Merely Mary Ann* in London. Eric Lewis (1855–1935) was a character actor who appeared mostly in comedy. He had performed in the burlesque melodrama *Passion, Poison, and Petrifaction*, which Shaw had written for the annual Theatrical Garden Party in Regent's Park, on 14th July 1905, and in 1906 he played Sir Ralph Bloomfield Bonington in *The Doctor's Dilemma*.]

My dear Miss Robson
I really have nothing to say. What's the use?
It was my fault inasmuch as I left London and so allowed Tyler and Vedrenne to wreck the scheme to their own entire satisfaction. But Vedrenne is not to blame. He never saw you act; he was greatly interested in Miss Russell, whom, for the sake of the London opening and the Shaw part he can get much cheaper than you; he had heard the second act of the play and knew that Granville Barker (his partner) was absolutely indispensable in the cast; he had the Shaw theatre in his hands and the Shaw audience; and he had his houses guaranteed by the libraries on condition that the play was mine & the theatre the Court (the visits of the King & the Prince of Wales &c have made the theatre fashionable when Shaw plays are on). Naturally he wanted to escape your salary. But I had made your engagement a condition of his getting the play; and Barker was prepared for a ruinous salary of $1250 a week for you if necessary. If Tyler had been serious in the matter nothing could have prevented an arrangement; and a failure would have been impossible. But Tyler, secure in his monopoly of you, and probably imagining that the Court was inferior to the Haymarket in standing, patronized Vedrenne; and Vedrenne, knowing the situation

548

far better, and being only too glad to have difficulties raised for which I could not blame him, patronized Tyler; and so between them we were sacrificed.

Of course I retain the American rights still; but what am I [to] do if Miss Russell—whom I have never seen—makes a great hit in the part, and then asks me whether I am going to throw her over in America? And suppose this does not happen, what sort of unspeakable mess will be made of it for you when you have not been at or in the London performance? I foresee that either the play will fail, in which case Tyler rightly enough will not touch it, or else it will succeed, and Miss Russell will be the heroine of the success, in which case I should not deserve to have anybody act for me if I denied her the refusal of the part in America.

The part is not a specially difficult one. To me there would be all the difference between you and anyone else in it because of a certain quality of yours that is a secret between you and the choice spirits of the earth. But to the public an actress such as you describe Miss Russell to be could do all that is necessary to make a mere acting success with Barbara. Now this is not the case with Barbara's lover, an exceedingly curious & difficult part. Nobody else except Barker could touch it or make the public accept it. There is Ainley, no doubt; and he wants to play at the Court in a play by me; but he could not touch Barker in the part because he does not know the original, a remarkable man who has just been travelling in the East with Barker. Then there is Calvert, who is engaged by Vedrenne. Tyler laughs at Calvert because C. wanted $500 a week in America (he would be quite worth it); but Calvert is a good actor and a manager whose time is worth money; and there is no use in laughing at him unless you can replace him. *I* was laughed at when I cast him for John Bull; but he made a huge success in it. In "Major Barbara" he could be replaced by Eric Lewis or John Hare, just as you could be replaced by a clever Pinero heroine; but the whole play would instantly lose its freshness, and fail as if it were a bad attempt at a Pinero play. Unfortunately I cannot get Tyler to see this. His head is full of the fashionable fashions of five years ago. *My* people are "outsiders" to him. When I propose a 25 dollar actor for a part and ask 40 dollars for him, George feels as if I had asked him to buy a second hand hat and carry a pinchbeck watch: what he wants is to pay 300 dollars to somebody whom Frohman engaged last season at 250. There is no getting over this by post and cable. No doubt in five years or so, when he has seen my tactics succeed about fifty times (if they ever do), I shall be able to paralyse him into doing what I tell him. But

549

by that time you will have married and left the stage. After all, he is devoted to your interests, and thinks nothing good enough for you, which would be splendid if he only knew good from bad in London.

You may ask why I did not wait until we had time to straighten out the affair between us. The answer is that I should have ruined Vedrenne & Barker, and in doing so discredited my own authorship & destroyed the only conditions in which so unusual a play could succeed. V & B are not capitalists—not yet. They have got their position purely by an artistic success; but nothing they have done has paid except my plays. By the help of my plays & the guarantee they carry they are able to give matinees of good plays which give the theatre its standing as *the* artistic & intellectual London theatre; but these matinees barely pay expenses at best; and without my support the enterprise must collapse, and Granville Barker's career get a heavy set back at a critical moment when one more successful season would have brought him safe ashore.

I tell you all this so that you may see that the Court scheme was really a very carefully planned and eligible one—unfortunately so well planned that it was impossible to drop it or defer it. Your great blundering baby has simply made it a present to Miss Russell because his head is filled with the east wind and he thinks he can do as he likes—pick up a theatre here and a cast there, put you on the stage and succeed anyhow. He may be right, provided he picks up the play also and does the ordinary thing right through; but to try to pluck me up by the roots and transplant me when I have only just made Major Barbara possible by a very delicate combination of circumstances & chances & interests is inconsiderateness gone mad.

I have not yet finished the play; and my inspiration, as far as the heroine is concerned, is gone. I shall finish it with my brains alone; and it will not now go right up into heaven. And I solemnly curse Tyler into the uttermost generation of his descendants.

I told him to get a Joan of Arc play for you from some real poet. No doubt he is in treaty with David Belasco for it.

Perhaps I may write another that "might suit you." But this was *your* play. I hope [Frederick] Harrison will find something good for you: he was very enthusiastic about you when he urged me some months ago to let him have Major Barbara for you; and he knows a good play from a bad one better than most managers.

I feel that I shall tear up all this unless I shut it up & post it suddenly: it rattles & grits like sand in the teeth; and I am furious.

G.B.S.

To VLADIMIR TCHERTKOFF

[X/195]

[Derry. Rosscarbery]
[Undated: *c.* August 1905]

[Vladimir G. Tchertkoff (1854–1936), a Russian émigré residing in London, was the editor and translator of Tolstoy's works. Extracts from Shaw's letter were published by Tchertkoff in *Tolstoy on Shakespeare* (first published in German translation in 1906). Shaw had not seen any of the Tolstoy material at the time he wrote his letter. The proof of the preface to *The Irrational Knot* was passed for press on 26th July. Nicholas Rowe's life of Shakespeare was published in 1823. Dr Samuel Johnson's preface to his edition of Shakespeare's plays first appeared in 1765. Samuel Ireland's forgeries of Shakespeare were published in 1796. The book containing Napoleon's opinions of the drama probably was Arthur Lévy's *Napoléon Intime* (1893), translated by S. L. Simeon as *The Private Life of Napoleon* (1894).]

[My dear Tchertkoff]
As you know, I have striven hard to open English eyes to the emptiness of Shakespeare's philosophy, to the superficiality and secondhandedness of his morality, to his weakness and incoherence as a thinker, to his snobbery, his vulgar prejudices, his ignorance, his disqualifications of all sorts for the philosophic eminence claimed for him. . . .* The preface to my 'Three Plays for Puritans' contains a section headed 'Better than Shakespeare?' which is, I think, the only utterance of mine on the subject to be found in a book. There is at present in the press a new preface to an old novel of mine called 'The Irrational Knot.' In that preface I define the first order in literature as consisting of those works in which the author, instead of accepting the current morality and religion ready made without any question as to their validity, writes from an original moral standpoint of his own, thereby making his book an original contribution to morals, religion, and sociology, as well as to *belles lettres*. I place Shakespeare with Dickens, Scott, Dumas *père*, etc., in the second order, because, though they are enormously entertaining, their morality is ready made; and I point out that the one play, 'Hamlet,' in which Shakespeare made an attempt to give as a hero one who was dissatisfied with the ready made morality, is the one which has given the highest impression of his genius, although Hamlet's revolt is unskilfully and inconclusively suggested and not worked out with any philosophic competence. . . .

* The ellipses are Tchertkoff's.

551

May I suggest that you should be careful not to imply that Tolstoy's great Shakespearean heresy has no other support than mine. The preface of Nicholas Rowe to his edition of Shakespeare, and the various prefaces of Dr. Johnson, contain, on Rowe's part, an apology for him as a writer with obvious and admitted shortcomings (very ridiculously ascribed by Rowe to his working by 'a mere light of nature'), and, on Johnson's, a good deal of downright hard hitting criticism. You should also look up the history of the Ireland forgeries, unless, as is very probable, Tolstoy has anticipated you in this. Among 19th century poets Byron and William Morris saw clearly that Shakespeare was enormously overrated intellectually. A French book, which has been translated into English, has appeared within the last ten years, giving Napoleon's opinions of the drama. His insistence on the superiority of Corneille to Shakespeare on the ground of Corneille's power of grasping a political situation, and of seeing men in their relation to the State, is interesting. Of course you know about Voltaire's criticisms, which are the more noteworthy because Voltaire began with an extravagant admiration for Shakespeare, and got more and more bitter against him as he grew older, and less disposed to accept artistic merit as a cover for philosophic deficiencies.

Finally, I for one shall value Tolstoy's criticism all the more because it is the criticism of a foreigner who cannot possibly be enchanted by the mere word music which makes Shakespeare so irresistible in England.

In Tolstoy's estimation, Shakespeare must stand or fall as a thinker, in which capacity I do not think he will stand a moment's examination from so hardheadedly keen a critic and religious realist. Unfortunately, the English, being bad analysts, worship their great artists indiscriminately and abjectly, so that it is impossible to make them understand that Shakespeare's prodigious literary power, his fun, his mimicry, and the endearing qualities that earned him the title of 'the gentle Shakespeare'—all of which, whatever Tolstoy may say, are unquestionable facts—do not stand or fall with his absurd reputation as a thinker. Tolstoy will certainly treat that side of his reputation with the severity it deserves; and you will find that the English Press will instantly announce that Tolstoy considers his own works greater than Shakespeare's (which in some respects they most certainly are, by the way), and that he has attempted to stigmatise our greatest poet as a liar, a thief, a forger, a murderer, an incendiary, a drunkard, a libertine, a fool, a madman, a coward, a vagabond, and even a man of questionable gentility. You must not be surprised or indignant at this: it is what is called 'dramatic criticism' in England and America. Only a few of the best of our journalist-critics will say anything worth reading on the subject.

yours faithfully
G. Bernard Shaw

To ARCHIBALD HENDERSON

[A/4; X/113.e, 116.e]

Derry. Rosscarbery
5th September 1905

[The "one book and one play" by Strindberg which Shaw had read were *The Diary of a Madman* and *The Father*, the latter in Nellie Erichsen's 1899 translation.]

My dear Henderson
    Question 22, about Nietzsche.
    The first time I heard Nietzsche's name was from a German lady who had read The Quintessence of Ibsenism, and who told me that she knew where I had got it all. I asked where. She said from Nietzsche's "Beyond Good & Evil." I instantly understood the title, and thereafter took an interest in Nietzsche; but I could not read much of the few English translations that were attempted, except Thomas Common's book of selections [*Nietzsche as Critic, Philosopher, Poet, and Prophet*, 1901]; and I never tackled the originals. The truth is I am rather an impostor as a pundit in the philosophy of Schopenhauer & Nietzsche. Just as almost every London paper attributed "Widowers' Houses" in 1892 to the influence of Ibsen, though the play was written before I had heard of Ibsen's existence; so there is a fashion now of referring my philosophy to Schopenhauer and Nietzsche, partly because, to people without philosophy, all philosophies seem the same, and partly because I have often referred to them to remind my readers that what they called my individual eccentricities and paradoxes are part of the common European stock. In The Perfect Wagnerite I have shewn in passing that an acceptance of Schopenhauer's metaphysics (metaphysiology, you may almost call it) does not in the least involve acceptance of his philosophy. Nietzsche's notions of art, his admiration of the Romans &c, are very unlike any views of mine; and his erudition I believe to be all nonsense: I think he was academic in the sense of having a great deal of secondhand

booklearning about him, and dont care for him except when he is perfectly original—that is, when he is dealing with matters which a peasant might have dealt with if he had brains enough, and had had the run of a library. You feel how clever and imaginative he is, and how much he has divined from writers of genius and from his own humanity about men and nations; but there is a want of actual contact knowledge about him: he is always the speculative university professor or the solitary philosopher and poet, never quite the worker and man of affairs or the executive artist in solid materials. As to his view of Christianity as a slave-morality, that was put forward here by Stuart Glennie, a Scotch historical philosopher, still living and much neglected, in a far more sensible way, Stuart Glennie regarding it as the means by which the white races (the Supermen) enslaved the darker races and mean whites, whilst Nietzsche regards it (if my notions of his utterances are correct) as an imposition by the slaves themselves. Both views are obviously necessary to a grasp of the situation; but Nietzsche's is an impression, and Stuart Glennie's a piece of history. It annoys me to see English writers absolutely ignoring the work of British thinkers, and swallowing foreign celebrities—whether philosophers or opera-singers—without a grain of salt. It shews an utter want of intellectual self-respect; and the result of it is that Nietzsche's views, instead of being added soberly to the existing body of philosophy, are treated as if they were a sort of music hall performance.

Question 23. I have read one book and one play by Strindberg; but here again I was perfectly familiar with his peculiar hatred of woman-idolization through the writings and conversation of Ernest Belfort Bax, whose essays attacking bourgeois morality were published here before Strindberg or Nietzsche had been heard of. Both Stuart Glennie and Belfort Bax were (and are) Socialists and strenuous opponents of Christianity, basing their views on a philosophy of history. As I am notoriously a Socialist, the first authors whose influence might have been traced in my works by English critics are Stuart Glennie and Bax. But no. Our critics must run to Strindberg & Nietzsche, knowing nothing about them except that their opinions, like mine, are not those of the Times or Spectator.

I should not be at all surprised if Strindberg turned out to be the noblest Roman of us all in dramatic literature; but until I read the rest of his works I have no very great faith in this impression. . . .

G. Bernard Shaw

554

To ARCHIBALD HENDERSON

[A.c/2; X/116.e, 141.e]

Derry. Rosscarbery
11th September 1905

[The Shaw bibliography for Henderson had been undertaken by Robert Alec Peddie (1869–1951), a Fabian who was a professional bibliographer, associated for many years with the booksellers Grafton & Co. He had compiled a bibliography of Trade Unionism for the Webbs in 1894.]

Dear Henderson

Your question as to Morris is rather a large one, as Morris was a large man. In the early eighties he threw himself into the Socialist revival just as I did. A monthly magazine called To Day was one of the organs of the movement; and in this magazine my novel "An Unsocial Socialist" appeared as a serial (see the preface to Cashel Byron &c &c). Morris read the instalments and got curious about the author. So one evening I found myself in Gatti's big restaurant in the Strand at a table with Morris & H.M.Hyndman. Hyndman was then the head critic of London Socialism; and Morris was a member of his Society, the Democratic Federation, now the Social Democratic Federation, or, more familiarly, the S.D.F.

I remember Morris saying that he was prepared to do whatever he was told and go wherever he was led: that was all he could say; and I remember also being privately tickled by this announcement from an obviously ungovernable man who was too big to be led by any of us. And this was a personal judgment across the table; for though I had heard of Morris, and had once, years before, seen him in—of all places in the world!—the Doré Gallery, yet my notions about him were very vague. I knew he was a poet, and belonged to the Rossetti circle, and was associated with Burne Jones and with what was then called Aestheticism; but I had never read a line of his and knew nothing accurately about him. And the other Socialists were in the same predicament. Morris himself said afterwards that it was among us that he first realized that he was an elderly buffer. His old Rossettian associates called him Topsy (see Lady Burne Jones's Memorials of Burne Jones, who used to be angry when she called him Topsy before strangers), and regarded him as a young man. As he looked older than he was (60 at 50, though a magnificent 60), he was to us a patriarch.

When he died, I wrote obituary articles in the Daily Chronicle [6th October 1896] and in the Saturday Review [10th October 1896]; and when McKail's life of him appeared, I reviewed it in the Daily Chronicle [27th April 1899]. We must try to get hold of these articles:

555

perhaps I have copies in London. Burne Jones was pleased by the Saturday Review article, and wanted to meet me. We made appointment after appointment; but something always occurred—an illness, a journey, or the like—to defeat us. At last we resolved that the meeting MUST come off; and a firm arrangement was made—I think for a Sunday lunch—to be kept at all hazards. But Destiny had a card up its sleeve that we did not reckon with. Burne Jones died the day before; so I never met him as an acquaintance, and only saw him twice, once at an exhibition where I heard him say that a picture attributed to Morris had been partly painted by Madox Brown, and once at a theatre, when our seats happened to be next one another.

We none of us bothered at all about Morris's eminence: in fact, I was not myself conscious of the impression he had made on me until one evening, at a debating society organized by Stopford Brook, when Morris, in a speech on Socialism in the course of a debate, astonished me by saying that he left the economics to me—"in that respect I regard Shaw as my master." The phrase meant only that he left that side of the case to me, as he always did when we campaigned together; but though I knew this, still it gave me a shock which made me aware that I had unconsciously rated him so highly that his compliment gave me a sort of revulsion.

Although when we settled down, he into the Socialist League & subsequently into the Hammersmith Socialist Society, and I into the Fabian Society, we were at the opposite poles of the movement, we never had any personal friction. I have never liked to call myself his friend: I was too much his junior and too little necessary or serviceable to him in his private affairs to be that; but I enjoyed an unstinted and unreserved intercourse with him; and he greatly enjoyed one or two things I wrote in which I said things that he wanted to have said. After the Nordau article, for instance, he suddenly began to talk to me about Whistler and the Impressionists in a way which shewed that he knew all about them and what they were driving at, though before that I had given him up as—on that subject—an intolerant and ignorant veteran of the pre-Raphaelite movement. And this was very characteristic of him. Up to a certain point he would not agree nor discuss: he simply gave you up as walking in darkness and presented himself as impervious and prejudiced. But the moment you had worked your way through the subject and come out into the clear air on the other side, he would suddenly begin to talk like an expert and shew all sorts of knowledge—scientific, political, commercial, intellectual-as-opposed-to-artistic, &c—that you never suspected him of. He was fond

556

of quoting Robert Owen's rule "Dont argue: repeat your assertion"; and mere debating, which he knew to be an intellectual game and not an essential part of the Will-to-Socialism (so to speak) did not interest him enough to make him good at it. But he highly enjoyed hearing anyone else do it cleverly on his side, and was furious when it was done on the other side. In point of command of modern critical language he was by no means a ready man; and as I was in great practice just then, he would take a prompt from me (if it was the right one) with as much relief and simplicity as if I had found his spectacles for him.

Morris's artistic integrity was, humanly speaking, perfect. You could not turn him aside from the question of the beauty and decency of a thing by bringing up its *interest*, scientific, casuistic, novel, curious, historical, or what not. This was most extraordinary in so clever a man; for he was capable of all the interests. Compared to him Ruskin was not an artist at all: he was only a man whose interest in nature led him to study Turner, and whose insight into religion gave him a clue to the art of the really religious painters. He would not give twopence for a rarity or a curiosity or a relic; but when he saw a sanely beautiful thing, and it was for sale, he went into the shop; seized it; held it tight under his arm (it was generally a medieval book); and after the feeblest & most transparent shew of bargaining, bought it for whatever was asked. Once, when he was rebuked for paying £800 for something that a dealer would have got for £450, I said "If you *want* a thing, you always get the worst of the bargain." Morris was delighted with my wisdom, & probably spent many unnecessary pounds on the strength of that poor excuse.

This artistic integrity of his was what made him unintelligible to the Philistine public. When the Americans set to work to imitate his printing, they shewed that they regarded him as a fashionably quaint and foolish person; and the Roycroft Shop and all the rest of the culture-curiosity shops of the States poured forth abominations which missed every one of his lessons and exaggerated every one of the practices he tried to cure printers of. In the same way his houses at Hammersmith and Kelmscott were, though quite homely, as beautiful in their domestic way as St Sophias in Stamboul; but other people's "Morris houses" always went wrong, even when he started them right.

I did a good deal of speaking in public with him in the early days, most of it at the street corner. We often thought ourselves lucky if we had an audience of 20.

But I must hurry away from Morris. The subject is too big.

557

The bibliography is not yet to hand, confound it! From it you will get a list of the Marx articles. Please note—*not* "the demolition of Marx *and* his theory of value" but the demolition of his theory alone. Marx's "Capital" is as amateurish in its abstract economics as Ruskin's Munera Pulveris, or, for the matter of that, as Adam Smith's Wealth of Nations; but for all that it is one of the books that has changed the mind of the world. It knocked the moral stuffing out of the bourgeoisie, and made an end for ever of middle class self complacency and optimism. The reading of Marx had a tremendous effect on me. And the controversy about the value theory led me to make a really thorough study of political economy—to stick at it for years until I had completely mastered the theories of rent and value.

I should not call myself a "leader" of the reaction against the materialism of Darwin. But you will see by the Quintessence of Ibsenism, the Perfect Wagnerite & Man & Superman that I am not a materialist—that I am in the line of descent from the German philosophers & composers (Schopenhauer & Wagner, for instance) rather than from the materialist-natural selectionists. But on this point I feel like Morris. There is no use telling you until you know. But my part in the humanitarian campaign against vivisection, modern science generally, vaccination, "education," flogging &c &c are all part of my attitude as a "mystic." I have not escaped from a literal belief in the book of Genesis only to fall back into the gross blindness of seeing nothing in the world but the result of natural selection operating on a chapter of accidents, which is popular Darwinism. The leader of the reaction in England at present is Sir William Lodge.

John Bull, How He Lied, and Major Barbara (just finished) are still in MS. I must get them into print this winter if possible & send you proofs.

The bibliography will, I hope, come to hand soon. I suppose my bibliographer has gone for a holiday.

Have I left any questions unanswered *now*?

yours faithfully
G. Bernard Shaw

P.S. I hope these sheets are not too difficult to read. I have to spoil my handwriting in order to make a carbon duplicate to keep in case of miscarriage.

To ROBERT W. WELCH

[Derry. Rosscarbery]

[X/196]   [Undated: *c.* 22nd–23rd September 1905]

[Arthur E. Bostwick (1860–1942), an official of the New York Public Library, had issued instructions to branch librarians to remove from open shelves certain of Shaw's works, including *Man and Superman* (which opened at the Hudson Theatre, New York, on 5th September). When questioned by the press, Dr John S. Billings, director of the library, insisted there was no restricted list in the library, but that the librarians tried to make access to certain volumes difficult for "the young and inexperienced." Robert W. Welch, of the London bureau of the *New York Times*, wrote to Shaw in Ireland to obtain his opinion, and cabled it to New York. Immediately after publication of Shaw's letter, the order was quietly rescinded. "Comstockery" was a generic name coined by Shaw for the activities of men like Anthony Comstock (1844–1915), secretary and special agent of the New York Society for the Suppression of Vice. Comstock, employed as a postal inspector in New York, boasted that since 1873 he had brought about 3670 criminals to justice, and destroyed 160 tons of "obscene" literature and pictures.

The imprisoned editor was Moses Harman (1830–1910), a pioneer in eugenics, who had been prosecuted by the postal censors and imprisoned at Leavenworth in 1895. He was arrested again in 1906 on charges that his journal *Lucifer, the Light Bearer* contained "obscene, lewd, lascivious or indecent matter," and sentenced to Joliet for six months. Robert Loraine (1876–1935), actor and aviator, for whom Shaw was to develop a special affection, was appearing as Tanner in the successful New York production of *Man and Superman*.]

Dear Sir

Nobody outside of America is likely to be in the least surprised. Comstockery is the world's standing joke at the expense of the United States. Europe likes to hear of such things. It confirms the deep-seated conviction of the Old World that America is a provincial place, a second-rate country-town civilization after all.

Personally I do not take the matter so lightly. American civilization is enormously interesting and important to me, if only as a colossal social experiment, and I shall make no pretense of treating a public and official insult from the American people with indifference.

It is true I shall not suffer either in reputation or pocket. Everybody knows I know better than your public library officials what is proper for people to read, whether they are young or old. Everybody knows also that if I had the misfortune to be a citizen of the United States I

559

should probably have my property confiscated by some postal official and be myself imprisoned as a writer of 'obscene' literature.

But as I live in a comparatively free country and my word goes further than that of mere officialdom, these things do not matter. What does matter is that this incident is only a symptom of what is really a moral horror both in America and elsewhere, and that is the secret and intense resolve of the petty domesticity of the world to tolerate no criticism and suffer no invasion.

The one refuge left in the world for unbridled license is the married state. That is the shameful explanation of the fact that a journal has just been confiscated and its editor imprisoned in America for urging that a married woman should be protected from domestic molestation when childbearing. Had that man filled his paper with aphrodisiac pictures and aphrodisiac stories of duly engaged couples, he would now be a prosperous, respected citizen.

If 'Man and Superman' were a specimen of the same propaganda its 'wholesomeness' would not be questioned. But 'Man and Superman' contains an explicit attack on marriage as the most licentious of human institutions. Consequently the domestic Alsatia, which has for so long wielded the stolen thunders of morality and religion to defend its excesses, with the result that man is the most morbid of all the animals, is terrified to find the thunderbolts burning its own hands and coming back like boomerangs at its own head. Well, let it defend itself if it can, how it can, and as long as it can.

I am an artist, and, it is inevitable, a public moralist, and if everybody supposes that by going through a marriage ceremony or any other ceremony he can put himself outside the moral world on any subject whatever, he is mistaken.

I have honor and humanity on my side, wit in my head, skill in my hand, and a higher life for my aim. Let those who put me on their restricted lists so that they may read me themselves while keeping their children in the dark, acknowledge their allies, state their qualifications, and avow their aims, if they dare.

I hope the New York press will in common humanity to those who will now for the first time hasten to procure my books and witness the performances of my plays under the impression that they are Alsatian, warn them that nothing but the most extreme tedium and discomfort of conscience can be got by thoughtless people from my sermons, whether on the stage or in the library.

I hope also that the many decent and honorable citizens who are bewildered and somewhat scandalized by my utterances will allow me to choose my own methods of breaking through the very tough crusts that form on the human conscience in large modern civilizations. Indeed, a man is hardly considered thoroughly respectable until his conscience is all crust and nothing else. The more respectable you are the more you need the pickaxe.

I am extremely sorry that the insult implied in the action of the library authorities should to some extent reflect on Richard Mansfield, Arnold Daly, Robert Loraine, and the many artists who as members of their companies have been associated with my plays in America. Without for a moment pretending that the actor is committed to all the ideas of which he becomes the interpreter, I am yet convinced that the extraordinary enthusiasm with which my plays have been pushed to success on the American stage in the teeth of managerial skepticism and general incredulity has been due to moral as well as artistic enthusiasm.

Pray do not suppose I am insensible of the good intentions of the leaders of the Comstockers, however corrupt and sensual may be the bigoted connubiality which provides them with the huge following that emboldens them to meddle with matters the greatest men touch with extreme diffidence. But, as I have said in 'Man and Superman,' 'All men mean well,' and 'Hell is paved with good intentions, not bad ones.'

Before you undertake to choose between evil and good in a public library or anywhere else, it is desirable that you should first learn to distinguish one from the other. The moment you do that, say, after forty years' study of social problems, you realize that you cannot make omelettes without breaking eggs; that is, you cannot have an advance in morality until you shake the prevailing sense of right and wrong sufficiently to compel a readjustment.

Now, if you shake the sense of right and wrong you give to every rascal his opportunity and to every fool his excuse. Preaching of Christianity makes some men Doukhobors instead of better citizens. Socialism may become the plea of the Anarchist or the dynamiter, science of the vivisectionist, and Puritanism of the Comstocker; but the nation that will not take these risks will never advance morally.

I do not say that my books and plays cannot do harm to weak or dishonest people. They can, and probably do. But if the American character cannot stand that fire even at the earliest age at which it is readable or intelligible, there is no future for America.

Finally, I can promise the Comstockers that, startling as 'Man and

Superman' may appear to them, it is the merest Sunday school tract compared with my later play, 'Major Barbara,' with which they will presently be confronted.

yours faithfully
G. Bernard Shaw

To ROBERT W. WELCH

[C/3]

Derry. Rosscarbery
27th September 1905

I am sorry to say that every time I scratch an American I *do* find a Comstocker. Comstock is a thoroughly representative man. Bostwick also is not "one man": he is the representative of the citizens of New York. When the "appreciative Americans" say it is not their fault, all they mean is that they are mugwumps. You make your institutions & you must stand the blame they bring you.

GBS

To ERICA COTTERILL

[A/3]

last day but one at
Derry. Rosscarbery
28th September 1905

["I want to find a *real* passion ... I want great blazing racing feelings that flame round you like a glorious wind; I want some gorgeous thing to live for and love with every atom of my whole soul." Thus speaks Ursula Wind-ridge in Erica Cotterill's play, *A Professional Socialist*, published in 1908. Erica Cotterill (1881–1950), like her persona, was an irrepressible creature. Determined to be emancipated, yet with no idea of how to accomplish this end, Erica flitted from interest to interest, teaching cricket at a girls' school, travelling abroad, residing in London among medical students, working in a settlement, and opting for Socialism. Attending a Shaw play in 1905, Erica became hopelessly infatuated with the author, and impulsively thrust some of her impassioned writings upon him in a letter which she signed "Miss Charmer," giving her address as Poste Restante, Godalming, Surrey.

When Shaw responded, she bombarded him with letters—strange, effer-vescent, rambling effusions, often unintelligible, and generally illegible.

562

Erica Cotterill
(*The Sun, London*)

Gradually she revealed that she was the only child of Charles Clement Cotterill (1842–1917), headmaster of Combe Field Preparatory School at Godalming, a Socialist (who became a Fabian in 1908), and author of several books, including *Human Justice for Those at the Bottom* (1907). Cotterill's sister was the mother of Rupert Brooke, who through his formative years at Rugby and Cambridge maintained an intimate, babes-in-the-wood relationship with Erica. She was financially secure, petted and spoiled, and she subscribed to the philosophy of a then-current song, "I Want What I Want When I Want It."

Erica's blandishments apparently appealed to Shaw's vanity, and he impishly plied her with advice and theatre tickets, invited her to lunch, and introduced her to his friends. She rewarded him by becoming a fearful nuisance, roaring up to Ayot on a motor bicycle and disrupting his work schedule, taking charge of the household as if she were in her own home and Shaw her spouse. After a London meeting she would frequently follow him home to Adelphi Terrace in a trance-like state of adoration. When her protestations of love for him threatened to get out of hand, Shaw craftily conspired with Charlotte to curb her ardor.

Eventually Erica sublimated her physical cravings by writing and privately publishing a series of epistolary "confessions," most of which were addressed or dedicated to Shaw, in which she fantasized her relationship with "this person [who] was passionate and fierce, yet what came out of him was clear and stern, and often very cold and very hard. And what was in me bowed down to what was in him . . ." (*An Account*, 1916). She disappeared from Shaw's life as abruptly as she had entered it, settling eventually on a farm in North Devon, unmarried but calling herself Mrs Erica May Saye (her mother's maiden name), and quietly raising two adopted sons. Upon learning of her death in 1950, Shaw admitted that, though he had not seen her in forty years, he had never quite got over his dread that she would turn up again.]

Dear Madam

All this is the greatest nonsense. You will find it excellently described in the early pages of Théophile Gautier's Mademoiselle de Maupin, a reputedly improper book, but quite harmless, as no sane human being could possibly read it through.

Love is an infinite mystery, like everything else, until you have been through it, when it becomes as finite to you as anything else. Marry and have children: then you will not ask from works of art what you can get only from life.

yours faithfully
G. Bernard Shaw

To GILBERT MURRAY

[C/36; X/197]

10 Adelphi Terrace W C
1st October 1905

I find that the result of our conference is a most appallingly strong temptation *not* to delete "And dont call me mother" but to develop it to full tragic proportions with the utmost Euripidity. Fortunately there is not room in the play for this; so I hand the temptation on to you. Clearly there is a great dramatic theme here—a Woman Lear with three sons—just the sort of Aeschylean subject in modern life you want.

I am quite desperate about my last act: I think I must simply re-write it. Merely cutting the cackle—and cackle is just what it is—will be no use.

G.B.S.

To J. E. VEDRENNE

[X/183]

10 Adelphi Terrace W C
2nd October 1905

[Shaw had just attended a special memorial meeting of the Salvation Army, "to commemorate dead comrades," presided over by General William Booth, in the Albert Hall.]

Dear Vedrenne

When the roll-ll-ll is called up yon-der

* grosse caisse
ad. lib.

When the roll-ll-ll is called up yon-der

When the roll-ll-ll is called up yon-der

When the roll is called up yonder

I'LL BE THERE.

I stood in the middle of the centre grand tier box, in the front row, and sang it as it has never been sung before. The Times will announce my conversion tomorrow.

What other author would do that for his management?

The sooner we get John Bull off, the better. It has gone to pieces,

like Candida. An abominable, coarse, careless, play-for-laughs, third
class suburban performance. Tell them so,
    For the Conquering Saviour shall break every chain,
    And give us the victory again and again.

Glory Hallelujah!
GBS

P.S. I now doubt whether Major B will be ready. I read it yesterday
to Barker & Murray. The last act is a total failure: I must sit down and
write it absolutely afresh.

To GILBERT MURRAY

Edstaston. Wem. Shropshire
7th October 1905

[A/36; X/188]

[The Shaws were visiting Charlotte's sister and her husband, the Cholmondeleys. Shaw, who had drawn heavily on Gilbert Murray, his wife
Lady Mary, and her mother, the Countess of Carlisle, as models for
Adolphus Cusins, Barbara Undershaft, and Lady Britomart in *Major
Barbara*, consulted frequently with Murray during the writing of the play.
After he had read the play to Murray and Barker on 1st October, Murray
had found himself "brooding" over Act III, and on 2nd October he set
down his "accompanying thoughts," sending Shaw two typewritten pages
of suggested treatment and dialogue, with apologies for "the cheek of this
interference" (Texas).]

Dear Murray
    Thanks for the Barbara stuff. If anything further occurs to you,
send it along.
    I want to get Cusins beyond the point of wanting power. I shall use
your passage to bring out the point that Undershaft is a fly on the
wheel; but Cusins would not make the mistake of imagining that he
could be anything else. The fascination that draws him is the fascination of reality, or rather—for it is hardly a fascination—the impossibility of refusing to put his hand to Undershaft's plough, which
is at all events doing something, when the alternative is to hold aloof
in a superior attitude and beat the air with words. To use your metaphor of getting his hand on the lever, his choice lies, not between going
with Undershaft or not going with him, but between standing on the
footplate at work, and merely sitting in a first class carriage reading

Ruskin & explaining what a low dog the driver is and how steam is ruining the country.

I am writing the whole scene over again. The moisture which serves for air in Ireland spoiled it hopelessly. I will send the new version to you when it is in shape.

I have taken rather special care to make Cusins the reverse in every point of the theatrical strong man. I want him to go on his quality wholly, and not to make the smallest show of physical robustness or brute determination. His selection by Undershaft should be a puzzle to people who believe in the strong-silent-still-waters-run-deep hero of melodrama. The very name Adolphus Cusins is selected to that end.

As to the triumph of Undershaft, that is inevitable because I am in the mind that Undershaft is in the right, and that Barbara and Adolphus, with a great deal of his natural insight and cleverness, are very young, very romantic, very academic, very ignorant of the world. I think it would be unnatural if they were able to cope with him. Cusins averts discomfiture & scores off him by wit & humorous dexterity; but the facts are too much for him; and his strength lies in the fact that he, like Barbara, refuses the Impossibilist position (which their circumstances make particularly easy for them) even when the alternative is the most sensationally anti-moral department of commerce. The moral is drawn by Lomax "There is a certain amount of tosh about this notion of wickedness."

I have been writing this letter in scraps for three days—impossible to write letters here. I shall be back in London on Friday at latest.

Handsome of me not to make you a Rhodes scholar, by the way.

GBS

To SIEGFRIED TREBITSCH

10 Adelphi Terrace W C
25th October 1905

[A/5]

[Sir Henry Irving died on 13th October and was buried in Westminster Abbey. Shaw was requested by the *Neue Freie Presse* to provide an obituary article, which it published in Vienna on 20th October. Although Shaw had specified that Trebitsch was to provide the translation, the editor gave the assignment, as Shaw had feared, to a bungling hack, which resulted in serious distortions in the published article. On 24th October Stephen Coleridge published in *The Times* a letter he had sent to the editor of the

Neue Freie Presse in which he refuted, "on the authority of personal knowledge, Mr. Shaw's statement that Irving ever solicited anybody at any time or place for a knighthood." Shaw denied that he had said any such thing, and for several days a controversy raged in London and Vienna over what he actually had said and to what extent he had been misinterpreted by the translator's faulty English and Coleridge's faulty German. He had the original article typeset and distributed in galleys to all the London press, with authorisation to reproduce it in full without payment. Only the *Morning Post* took up the offer, but not until 5th December.

The meeting Shaw had attended the previous day was a public discussion sponsored by the London Shakespeare League at the Guildhall School of Music. When a member of the audience protested against Shaw being heard, the chairman of the meeting, Arthur Bourchier, put it to the meeting whether they would approve of such an interruption to the discussion. Why not take Shakespeare's own words, asked Hermann Vezin: "Why, let us hear Bernardo speak of this." There were loud cheers, and Shaw addressed the meeting without further interruption.

John Bull's Other Island, Shaw's first failure in America, presented by Daly at the Garrick Theatre on 10th October, survived only for two weeks. Alan Dale, critic of the *New York Journal*, described the audience as "sitting in fuddled bewilderment during the presentation of a thick, glutinous and impenetrable four-act tract," while Acton Davies in the New York *Sun* said it was doubtful if any play ever presented to a New York audience had proved "so insufferably dull."]

Dear Trebitsch

I send you the last act [of *Widowers' Houses* or *Mrs Warren's Profession*] & will presently send you the other copy with some notes as to the stage business.

There has been an appalling row here in consequence of the article in Die Neue Freie Presse. I wish I could get a copy of the German translation, to see whether it really corresponds to my MS. All day yesterday I was besieged by interviewers; and when I appeared at a public meeting in the afternoon an attempt was made to prevent me from speaking. Today I have a letter in The Times. I expressly told the editor of the N.F.P. to get you to translate it; and if I find that he has made a hash of it I will give him a piece of my mind on the subject. A stupid translator might easily have bungled it frightfully.

John Bull's Other Island seems to have failed in America.

GBS

To LAURENCE IRVING

[A/30]

10 Adelphi Terrace, W C
25th October 1905

[Re Shaw's business dealings with Sir Henry Irving, see I, 747–755. Chekhov was first produced in England by the Stage Society, which presented *The Cherry Orchard* in 1911 and *Uncle Vanya* in 1914. Mrs Laurence Irving was Mabel Hackney.]

Dear Irving

In case it should escape your notice, I send you a copy of my letter to The Times. You are one of the few people who will understand the extraordinary difficulty of writing about your father. If you want the public at large to accept reasonable conclusions about him, you must tell them, not the real facts, but the romances from which they are accustomed to draw those conclusions. On the other hand, if you tell them the real facts, heaven only knows what absurdity they will infer from them. And yet silence is impossible.

I did not like to bother you with an acknowledgment of my invitation to the Abbey, which I took as a matter of public routine & acknowledged to Alexander. But he tells me that this was not so. Will you therefore convey my thanks for being remembered, intercepting a due share for yourself. Suppress the fact that I did not go, partly from an overwhelming pre-occupation with my terribly belated new play, partly because all funerals inspire me with an insane desire to misconduct myself and damn everybody's hypocrisy, partly because I could not resist the temptation to pose at Alexander as the representative of slighted Literature with a large L (Alick went into hysterics & implored me to spare you this heartless revelation), partly because the ceremonial method of expressing feeling is not natural to me. Your father did not like me, partly* in consequence of an interview [on 26th September 1896] at which I demagnetized him (quite unintentionally) and made him uncomfortable; partly through an article the offence in which (also unintentional) I never understood until Harrison enlightened me by quoting a sardonically unfilial comment made on it by your brother. But I was much too conceited to be unfriendly; and if he had only had your extra inch across the forehead we should have got on excellently.

I want to fix up a lunch here some day so that we may make your wife's private acquaintance & see you again. I should have done so

---

* Excuse all these partlies. I am too tired to invent another locution.

568

before, but for an accident to Charlotte, who has damaged a nerve in her arm & had a very bad time of it—bed, disablement, & much anguish.

I hear that there are several dramas extant by Whatshisname (Tchekoff, or something like that)—the late Russian novelist who wrote The Black Monk &c. Have you any of them translated for the Stage Society, or anything of your own that would suit us? We are in a hole for the moment, as all the plays we used to get now go to Vedrenne & Barker.

yrs ever
G. Bernard Shaw

To LAURENCE IRVING

10 Adelphi Terrace W C
[A/30]   27th October 1905

My dear Irving

Will Wednesday next at 1.30 suit you? If so, my wife will have her arm in sound condition again by that time, and will be delighted to see you again & to meet Mrs Laurence.

I could have written you a really nice letter about the Coleridge incident if you had not completely upset my gravity by your very Irvingesque assurance—which I do not doubt for a moment—that your father would willingly have defrayed the expenses of my funeral at any time.

I have now at last got copies of the Neue Freie Presse, and enclose you a cutting, so that you may see for yourself what I really said. It is, I think, a fair translation. The word Fähigkeit in the passage about Romeo rather suggests want of skill than physical impossibility, which was what I meant. I have underlined in ink the passage which has been reported as "a narrow minded egoist, devoid of culture, and living on the dream of his own greatness." You will see that what I said, though too subtle, no doubt, for the Referee or the Pelican to understand, is the absolute bottom truth not only of your father but of the psychology of intense acting. Towards the end I have underlined in pencil the only really severe thing I have said; but what else could I say?

I am sincerely sorry, as to the family, that it is not, and in the nature of things never can be possible for those who were in purely personal relations with a great man to stand up without flinching to the stern

569

account to which all greatness must be called. They think of his kind-
nesses—that is, of all the qualities which he has in common with other
men. But I, standing between Westminster Abbey & Europe, have
nothing to do with things that Carnegie & Passmore Edwards beat him
at easily. Such personalities are a belittlement of the issue and of the
man. Dont try to explain this to your wounded circle; but *do* remind
them, on occasion, that the malicious lie "he *importuned* the Court for
a knighthood" was circulated, not by me, but by Coleridge, and that
there is not a shadow of justification for it. I always admired the demand for a knighthood; and those who cannot admire it may be left
to worship deprecatory shopwalkers & the like.

yrs ever

G. Bernard Shaw

To ELLEN TERRY

10 Adelphi Terrace W C

28th October 1905

[U(A)/10; X/117]

[Ellen had written on 24th October: "You never wrote the words they say
you wrote, except when Henry was well, was at work and *fighting*. Then it
was all right enough—fair. You never said it I'm sure when all his friends
were sore and smarting. *You* don't add hyssop to the wounds. That would
be *un*fair. I never knew you do an unkind action . . . I'm far away in the
North and have only just heard you were unkind. I dont believe that."]

My dear Ellen

Beyond sending you that Times letter to prevent Coleridge making
you loathe me, I did not like to intrude on you and Irving in this
matter. But now that you have accorded me the privilege of knowing
how you feel, just let me explain to you how hopeless it is to depend on
the papers when really delicate and intimate matters are in question.
In the now famous Vienna article (I believe you dont read German; so
I dont send you a copy) I said—"The truth is, Irving was interested
in nothing but himself; and the self in which he was interested was an
imaginary self in an imaginary world. He lived in a dream." Now, first
comes the German translator who gives this as "nur (only) ein imaginären Person in einer imaginären Pose." And next comes the Referee,
the Pelican, &c &c, translating from the German—not from the
original article but from descriptions of it in other German papers—
thus: "He was a narrow minded egoist, devoid of culture, and living
on the dream of his own greatness."

570

Of course I told the truth about him on such matters as concerned his claim to Westminster Abbey; and part of that truth was necessarily sterner than the polite things that are said of small men at funerals in Brompton Cemetery. But when all is said, I seem to be the only journalist in England who really remembers him as he was, or ever knew him as he was—strength & weakness together.

Laurence, who is coming to lunch with me on Wednesday, says the family regard me as a most unmitigated Yahoo, and assures me, very Irvingesquely, that his father was so truly kindhearted that he would willingly have paid my funeral expenses at any time. Such is the unquenchable heart of youth. . . .

ever, dearest Ellen,
your hardest hearted lover
G.B.S.

To REV. H. MONTAGU VILLIERS

[G/2]

[10 Adelphi Terrace W C]
3rd November 1905

[H. Montague Villiers (d. 1908) was Vicar of St Paul's, Knightsbridge. He had written to Shaw to object to one of John Tanner's statements in *Man and Superman*.]

Dear Sir

If you have never before had those words presented to you as a living truth instead of "an unspeakable solemnity" you owe your first glimpse of religion to the theatre. The shock would not have occurred if the thought had been familiar to you; & if you had ever known what you were doing when you baptized a child or churched its mother it would have been familiar to you. If you cannot see the birth of the Son of Man in the birth of *every* child—if you cannot see that the whole misery of the world is due to its want of reverence for every child's birthright, which I take to be what you call the Holy Ghost—then the laying of hands on you has been in vain, & you do not even begin to understand your profession.

My own profession is the same as yours, my inspiration the same as that of the prophets you expound, my heritage every word they have uttered, my responsibility great in proportion to the numbers of people I reach, & the subtlety & variety & fascination of the art in which I am

571

skilled. A theatre is a place where 2 or 3 are gathered together; & an actor one whose function is fundamentally priestly. In surmising that Mr Granville Barker introduced those words as a gag, you are speaking as a very ignorant actor might, if, considering an allusion to so prosaic a matter as our daily bread to be out of place in a church, he concluded that you had introduced a gag into the Lord's Prayer. If the actor did not see what you have failed to see, he would refuse to utter the words. In my play entitled "John Bull's Other Island" Mr Louis Calvert always omitted a certain sentence in a bitingly ironic description of a child's artificially inculcated notion of Heaven, because he had not so completely freed himself from that notion as to be able to make the audience laugh at it without a feeling of irreverence. I respected that feeling & did not insist, just as I respect your feeling in the matter, & earnestly beg you not to go to performances of my plays until you have learnt to respect me & the theatre & the actor. Indeed I put it to you that if there be any place in the world where in your opinion the use of serious words is "profanity," then you have no right to go there, much less to pay for the maintenance & encouragement of it.

I hope I do not convey an impression of being in any way annoyed by your letter: on the contrary, I am much obliged to you for writing it. But none the less it is insulting to me & to my profession in the pro- foundest degree—all the more so as you have evidently no suspicion that it is so. Deeply as I am horrified whenever I enter a church during service by the frightful error & even wickedness of certain passages in the ritual, I have never questioned the right of the celebrant & the preacher to speak his belief, or suggested that his hands were too un- clean & the place too infamous for holy things. You have done this to the theatre, & denied my right to the word of God. And you have finished with that most unchristian & unwise of all things, a threat.

Think it over a little. God (as you would put it) fulfils himself in many ways; & he also reveals himself in many ways; so that you can count on nothing but the way being unexpected. First it is generally a joke. Next it is a blasphemy. The third time it is a troublesome call to work. It is never solemn until its time is past & it is nothing but a formula reverberating in hollow hats, sometimes, as you have no doubt observed, of the shovel pattern.

As it is Saturday & late for the post, I send you down this by messenger, because if you are the right sort of person it will make you preach a good sermon tomorrow. If not, I offer you my very polite apologies for troubling you with a letter which must doubtless seem very strange &, as the young lady says in Man & Superman, rather in bad taste. In either case deliver your own message in your own way, & leave me to deliver mine in my way, leaving the public to choose for itself between your church & my theatre, or to go to both or neither.

yours faithfully
G. B[ernard] S[haw]

To WILLIAM ARCHER

10 Adelphi Terrace W C
7th November 1905

[D/2]

[Arnold Daly, shaken by the unexpected failure of *John Bull's Other Island* in New York, and determined to protect his newly-gained reputation as a daring exponent of the Shavian drama of ideas, hastily placed *Mrs Warren's Profession* into rehearsal. Shaw had long since warned Daly that careful groundwork would be necessary to educate the public as to the play's meaning and social value, in order to minimise the dangers of controversy and governmental interference. The contract between Shaw and Daly, dated 20th July 1904, contained a special clause requiring that "the Manager shall endeavour as far as may be practicable to apprise the public of the fact that the Play is suitable for representation before serious adult audiences only..." (Hanley, Texas).

Daly, however, plunged ahead, ignoring all of Shaw's earlier injunctions, as well as a cable, countermanding the performance, which Shaw had sent upon learning that Anthony Comstock had written a furious letter to Daly threatening to take action against the play in order to protect the American stage from the "Irish Smut Dealer." *Mrs Warren's Profession* opened at the Garrick Theatre on 30th October. Hundreds of people were turned away from the box office, while outside a black market in tickets flourished, with seats selling for as much as $30 each. The New York *World* polled the audience as to its opinion on the fitness of the play.

In your opinion is "Mrs. Warren's Profession" a play fit to be presented on the American stage?

Erase one { FIT

{ UNFIT

This card will be collected as you leave the theatre.

Sixty percent of the audience responded, 304 voting "Fit" and 272 "Unfit." The New York press the following morning was almost uniformly condemnatory, its reviewers and editorial writers castigating the play as "illuminated gangrene," "pervading poison," "the limit of stage indecency," "a play about as elevating as a post-mortem." Police Commissioner William Mc-Adoo, who had been incited to action by Comstock ("We sowed," Comstock gloated in his annual report to his Society, "and the Police reaped the harvest"), and who had personally attended the performance, immediately obtained arrest warrants, on charges of "disorderly conduct," for Daly, the leading lady Mary Shaw, the manager Winchell Smith, and various others associated with the production. He was persuaded finally to arrest only the house manager, Samuel W. Gumpertz, who was charged with maintaining a public nuisance. The others agreed to appear in Jefferson Market Court voluntarily for preliminary hearings. Daly, stunned by the turn of events, withdrew the play after its first performance, and hastily substituted *Candida* until the end of the week, when his enterprise at the Garrick collapsed.

The "spare proof" sent by Shaw to Archer was of a written statement published in the New York *Sun* on 1st November as "Shaw Proud of His Play." Archer's article in the *Morning Leader* on 4th November was on "America and 'Mrs. Warren'." A letter of reply from Shaw appeared on 7th November, defending the play, and concluding: "Mr. Comstock has declared his intention of suppressing me. He had better; for if he does not I am afraid I shall end by shocking him out of his wits."]

I send you a spare proof [of] the part of my reply which was meant for American consumption only.

Apart from the emergency created by the trial in America, I am glad to have the opportunity of making you reconsider your old explanation—that I cannot touch pitch without wallowing in it &c &c. The incestuous part of Mrs Warren is a genuine part of the original plan because it is what you call an anecdote, or rather two anecdotes. I knew of a case of a young man who, on being initiated by a modern Madame de Warens (observe the name), was rather taken aback by her reproaching him for being "not half the man his father was." I also watched the case of a man who was a friend of my mother in her young days. When my sister grew up he became infatuated about her and wanted to marry her. And there was, of course, the famous ——* case, where a young married woman was seduced (in the street from which Mrs W's name was taken) by a man who had formerly seduced her mother. A certain inevitability about these cases had struck me as being dramatic long before I wrote Mrs Warren, also a certain squalid comicality consisting partly, I think, in the fact that there was such an

---

* The dash is Shaw's.

574

utter absence of any tragic consequences when there was no exposure. These and many confirmatory observations made the solid mass of "Mrs W's P"—there is really no side issue.

Thanks for letter in today's Leader—just the thing.

G.B.S.

To WILLIAM ARCHER

[H/2]

10 Adelphi Terrace W C
15th November 1905

[*Parisina* (1833) is an opera by Donizetti, founded on Byron's poem.]

My dear Archer

You are the laziest man in London. The way you calmly leave me to do all your thinking for you is beyond words.

Now listen.

Carry your mind back to the case of Linnaeus, who first explained the fertilization of plants. His book was immediately denounced as immoral. So it was. The instructive bee, improving the shining hour to the edification of the infant mind, became an infamous go-between; and every hedgerow became a pornographic exhibition.

Now can you conceive it possible for Linnaeus to have returned to the assumption that every flower came straight from the hand of God? Suppose he had seen the whole of Europe proceed straight from the study of botany to the wildest sexual excesses, could he have withdrawn his discovery on that account? Clearly not.

Well, no more is it possible for me to give a false answer to any question raised by the human relations with which I deal merely because the consequences of the true answer may be this, that, or the other. If the avowal of Vivie and Frank that the suggestion of Crofts made no difference in their feeling towards one another—as under those circumstances it most assuredly would not—resulted in the immediate committal of incest by every brother and sister witnessing the play, I could no more alter the passage on that account than Linnaeus could alter his treatise on botany. It is useless to preach the refusal of knowledge and of the consequences of knowledge.

Now as to the family question. I have never denied the existence of family love in the sense in which you describe it. I should as soon think of denying the existence of the affection of schoolfellows or shipmates or any other of the forms of affection resulting from intimate

575

association. I do not deny, for instance, that you have a strong affection for Charles. But why you should deny him all credit for that, and insist that his being a nice fellow has nothing to do with it—that it is a mere symptom of consanguinity—I cannot understand. If you come to that, *I* like Charles, and should probably have formed a strong affection for him if we had been brought up in the same house at the same ages. Besides, you confess to a preference in the matter, though your other brothers are equally close in blood. Consanguinarily they are all equally near to you. But are they all equally dear to you? Not a bit of it. You paint the degrees with a graphic pen. For Charles, strong affection. For Jim, benevolent affability. For the others, apologetic indifference, with a perceptible vagueness as to their names and numbers. That is to say, exactly the feeling you would have towards schoolfellows of different ages and generations. A more convincing demonstration of the wisdom and scientific soundness of my refusal to accept the popular theory of family affection as a result of consanguinity could hardly be adduced.

One of the objections to that theory is this. It is obviously expedient that sexual intercourse should be ruled out as between brothers and sisters under our family system. It is equally obvious that it must be ruled out in a mixed school, the reason being the same in both cases: that is, the danger of sexual precocity. It should be a point of honor not to make love to your sister, your schoolfellow, your friend's wife, a nun &c.; and the most important case is the housemate in childhood, whether relative or stranger in blood. Young children need not be bothered about it: I find that they like Mrs Warren's Profession because to them the crowning charm of the Babes in the Wood courtship is that the babes turn out to be brother and sister. In the same way, if you ask a little boy whom he would like to marry, he is as likely as not to say his mother. But when childhood is over, and reasons have to be given, it is a hideous error to bring in the consanguinity theory and represent incest as being "wrapped in a strange cloud of sin and shame." From that you get The Cenci, Parisina, and the sharpening of Crofts's pursuit of Vivie by the morbidity of his imagination.

Note, in passing, that the incest in Die Walküre has never been felt to be incest at all, because Siegmund and Sieglinde were not brought up together.

What is the general evidence on the subject? Clearly, it is that the tables of affinity are conventional, not natural. The convention varies from country to country. Among Christians marriage between uncle and niece and between first cousins is lawful in one country and incestuous in another. So is marriage with a deceased wife's sister. The refusal of a man to marry his deceased brother's wife is in some societies the climax of unnatural horror. There are actually cases in which a widow is expected to marry her own son to provide a head for the family; and you may remember that Caesar's dream about his mother before he crossed the Rubicon was considered by him a happy omen, and is recorded without the slightest revolt by Plutarch. We are more horrified by incest between parent and child than between brother and sister, though the consanguinity between brother and sister is the closest possible—much closer than between parent and child, the reason being, obviously, that it is more inconvenient socially, and therefore more unbecoming. A union between stepmother and stepson would horrify us equally, though here there is no blood relationship at all.

Why has all this such an interest for me? I think you have sometimes suspected me of a quite unholy fancy for it. But to anybody whose main work is to fight for real morality in its continual struggle for life with the spurious morality of mere custom, it is too valuable and interesting as an illustration not to recur pretty frequently. There is no other case in which a pure convention masquerades so effectually as a human instinct. The next best is an equally unpleasant one: namely, the fact that a man who will commit the horrible wickedness of marrying when he has syphilis, will shrink with genuine repugnance from walking down Bond St in the afternoon in a frock coat and bowler hat. But in spite of the enormous irony of this, it is not so good an illustration of the force of custom and convention as incest, because after all, nobody pretends that the bowler hat is anything worse than an offence against good taste, whereas people have been burnt alive for marriages which under other codes are regarded as quite normal, and even desirable.

Whether consanguinity has a real effect in sexual relations is very doubtful. Let me explain what I mean by a real effect. When I was a small boy I once saw a jar in a chemist's shop labelled Ipecacuanha Lozenges. I thought the name fascinating; and I thought all lozenges were sweetmeats. I went in and asked for some. The chemist asked me would I have an ounce. I said I would have a pennorth, that being the utmost of my means. He gave me about a dozen; and I ate them and rather liked them. Half an hour later I was a retching, belching, spewing, agonized worm. I call that a real effect, because it occurred without suggestion, without expectation, in flat violation of my mental attitude towards the lozenges. Now imagine yourself lunching with a

577

Fijian chief. He gives you some excellent pork; and it agrees with you perfectly, as he is careful not to inform you that it is really the remains of his deceased uncle. But if somebody came in and let the cat out of the bag, you would probably be hideously sick. That is not a real effect of the uncle on your stomach, but of our customs on your imagination.

Suppose now you had committed some crime or had some adventure in your youth that caused you to leave the country and settle in America under an assumed name, concealing your action from your family. Suppose one of your sisters afterwards emigrates also and marries, thus changing her name. Suppose you meet her and, in entire ignorance of your relationship, are led to contemplate sexual intercourse with her. Do you believe you would both avoid such a thing by instinctive repugnance? I see no reason to believe that you would. But if you would, then it seems to me that the repugnance must affect all the sympathetic sentiments more or less, and that, as Tanner says, "the tables of consanguinity have a natural basis in a natural repugnance." My own belief is that the case would be the Fijian one over again: that is, that if you discovered your relationship next morning you would both be shocked, or even take a quite morbid view of the situation, according to the strength of your prejudices, but that if you were never the wiser you might marry and bring up a large family without the smallest misgiving or anybody being a penny the worse.

However, this does not mean that I consider that the ordinary laws of attraction and repulsion are altered by consanguinity. It is roughly true that liking goes by contraries; and sisters and brothers are commonly too like one another to attract one another. If you try the experiment of walking from end to end of Oxford Street and counting the women whom you would care to entertain sexually, you will probably be surprised by your own fastidiousness. Two per cent would be a quite Turkish proportion. I should expect you to find that the odds against any particular woman attracting you are about 5000 to 1. Under these circumstances the fact that our sisters do not attract us needs no consanguinity theory to explain it. I am disposed to insist on this view of the matter because I think it is the less morbid one. I think our imaginations are systematically inflamed by surrounding sex with imaginary and imputed horrors, and that a great deal of the fuss we make about such things is as absurd and mischievous as the fuss savages make about touching anything that a menstruating woman has touched. I deliberately make a point of "callousness" on the subject; and I think I am right.

My more extreme views on the sex question are to be inferred from a remarkable (and consequently unremarked) passage in Man & Super-man, where Don Juan asks Dona Ana whether the sex relation is really a personal one. "Do my sex the justice to admit, Senora, that we have always recognized that the sex relation is not a personal or friendly relation at all." ANA—Not a personal nor friendly relation! What relation can be more personal! more sacred! more holy! DON JUAN—Sacred and holy if you like, Ana, but not personally friendly. Your relation to God is sacred and holy: dare you call it personally friendly? &c &c &c. I feel quite sure that in the long run it will be seen that the arch-incest is the sexual intercourse of husband and wife, and that the intercourse from which the race will be bred will be an intercourse between people who do not know one another, and who will make it a most sacred point of honor not to associate their breeding intercourse with any further intrusion whatever. Suppose such a state of things to have taken place, then incest would no longer have anything to do with consanguinity, because there would be no necessity for people to know their parents or their relatives. Incest would then mean intercourse between housemates—an important matter if children were brought up in households of ten or so in consequence of the common obser-vation that the children of large families are the most humanized and successful.

I have not time to work this out further for you; so you must take it with a reasonable construction, and not conclude that I am a lunatic on the strength, not of what I expect, but of the many associations which people without my fine analytic mind persist in attaching to things that do not involve them in the least.

yours ever
GBS

[Archer replied at length, on 18th November, protesting that he had agreed with Shaw on every point, and had tried to say so. After again discussing the issue of incest in *Mrs Warren's Profession* and the question of family affection ("I seem to have confused you by passing from the subject of incest to that of family affection. They were entirely distinct in my mind, the two points of my letter having no more connection than if the one had been on astron-omy & the other on the tariff question."), Archer concluded: "Now make a great effort, and try to conceive that I am not an idiot: whence it will follow that when you are controverting something idiotic, the chances are you are controverting something I didn't say. On political questions I may often be practically an idiot, simply because I have never had time to give them any study. But on such elementary questions of morals & psychology, it is really no good assuming that I am a superstitious ass. The assumption is all the less reasonable as, point for point, I agree with you on the moral & psychological plane. The trouble is that when you come to translate theory into art, you are so jolly apt (in my judgment) to do it at once inartistically & illogically & thus to repel your audience while falsifying your own real conviction. So there!" (BM)]

To ANNIE RUSSELL

[A/56; X/227]

10 Adelphi Terrace W C
20th November 1905

[Although Barker was officially credited as the producer of *Major Barbara*, Shaw had been attending most of the rehearsals and, as in the case of *John Bull's Other Island*, had undertaken supervision of the staging, usurping Barker's function.]

Dear Miss Russell

I made a few notes today which I may as well give you.

When Bill says "If you want to bring a charge agen me, bring it," look puzzled, as Barbara doesnt know what on earth he means. Then, when he says "My name's Bill Walker" you are enlightened, as you think he means charging him for hitting Jenny.

When Undershaft coughs and you say "It's all right, papa: we havnt forgotten you," dont laugh. Say it in a businesslike way, and it will be more effective.

When Bill comes out with his plan of paying Jenny, Barbara should have a sort of impulse towards him, as it is really his second attempt to right himself—a sign of conscience on his part. And the smile at the earl's granddaughter should come through this feeling—not a smile of pure dry fun, but a smile on the surface of an emotion.

"Nonsense! of course its funny" might be a little more peremptory. There are one or two points, like the "Nonsense! she must do as she's told" (about Rummy) in which Barbara, with all her sweetness, shews that she is her mother's daughter, and that it comes very natural to her to order people about. There is a curious touch of aristocratic pride at the very end, where she says she does not want to die in God's debt, and will forgive him "as becomes a woman of her rank" for all the starvation & mischief he is responsible for. Barbara has great courage, great pride & a high temper at the back of her religious genius; and you need not hesitate to let them flash through at moments if any of the passages catch you that way.

From 11 to 12 tomorrow I am getting Calvert & Miss Filippi to rehearse with the understudies, as there is no reason why you should be hearing them their words, as we were all doing today. They are, unfortunately for us, very busy at other things; and we have got ahead of them for the moment. They will be very good on the 28th; but I quite understand how very hard it is on you to have the work on the words stopping the work on the play.

If I can help you in any way, let me know. But do not take any suggestion of mine as of any greater value than a suggestion. You have already shewn me more about the part than I could possibly have shewn you. If I make suggestions or offer criticisms freely it is only on the understanding that you need not give them a second thought if they do not chime in with your own feeling. Dont hamper your inspiration: do just what you want to do without stopping to think of the author. He will get more than his fair share of the credit anyhow.

yrs faithfully
G. Bernard Shaw

To ELLEN TERRY

10 Adelphi Terrace W C
[U(A)/10; X/117]   25th November 1905

[Shaw had been to the Duke of York's Theatre to see *Alice Sit-by-the-Fire*. The quotation, "old as I am, for ladies' love unfit," is from John Dryden's "Cymon and Iphigenia." The article on Ellen Terry was published, in Trebitsch's translation, in the *Neue Freie Presse* on 24th December.]

My dear Ellen

It appears now that Kerr will be available for Brassbound. Unless you contradict me I shall assume that you prefer him to the available alternatives.

You must allow me to teach you the part of Lady C. What I dread is that you will set your nurses and young ladies to read it to you, so that it will get into your head all wrong. You will then be forced to try to learn it by main force through your eyes, and ruin your nerves and wreck your happiness. You can learn it as easily as a child learns hush-a-bye-baby if only you hear it *rightly* read to you. But that can only be done by another Ellen Terry or by me.

I came to see you at the theatre because I *must* accustom myself to meet you. At present, "old as I am, for ladies' love unfit," something wild happens inside me; and I have to look on gasping for breath whilst

581

an artificial G.B.S. talks to an equally artificial Miss Terry, the two minuetting on the carpet while we stagger in the immensities. I took Barker with me to chaperone me. By the way, that young man is a genius—a cold hearted Italian devil, but a noble soul all the same.

I did not succeed in making you understand about the Irving article; but now comes my revenge. Die Neue Freie Presse, delighted with G.B.S. on Irving, now asks for G.B.S. on Ellen Terry; and as Teddy is delaying my Cæsar & Cleopatra very badly in Berlin (he is to do the scenery) I shall say yes, and immortalize you.

I think Brassbound will be better understood after Major Barbara, a frankly religious play in which the most effective scene is the conversion of a rough by a Salvation girl.

I think Alice a horrid part; and I am more than ever bent on shewing the people something nobler in you than that. I like Barrie & his work; but someday a demon in the shape of Alice will sit by the fire in hell and poke up the flames in which he is consuming.

GBS

To ANNIE RUSSELL

10 Adelphi Terrace W C
[H/56; X/227]   27th November 1905

My dear Miss Russell

I am sorry you had such a tedious, coughing, fluffing, discouraging, tiring, apparently hopeless dress rehearsal. But that is what always occurs at the Court Theatre; and it has hitherto ended in a successful first performance. Calvert is a very different man when he has the public in front to keep his liver active.

In the last act, when he says "neither reason, nor morals, nor the lives of other men," turn away; but do not leave your place. I think it would be better not to move until, on the line "It is no use running away from wicked people" you can emphasize your refusal to go with your mother by going right over to her chair, and standing behind it for a while. This avoids the risk of masking Lomax when he makes his speech. Afterwards, when he jumps up at the cue "Mr Lomax is sitting on them," keep the line of sight open for him. I feel very much to blame for not having worked out this scene for you more completely; but the fact is, Calvert distracts me so completely that I cannot see what is to be done by anybody else.

Keep your articulation distinct in "laying a snare for my soul["]: the theatre is a little dangerous in that respect.

The artistic drawingroom still seems to take you a bit by surprise; so that you attack it in too light a vein. And unfortunately I am afraid to suggest anything as to your best way of handling it, because I do not know yet exactly how you get your effects, except that it is not in my rather rhetorical, public-speaker kind of way. I may therefore quite easily set you wrong. I believe now that the long string of questions beginning "Why not! Do you know what my father is" &c. &c. is quite unsuited to your methods when it is done in my way; so please do not try to do it in my way. Get round it in your own way. I should prefer this in any case, as I shall learn something from you, whereas if you only reproduce my handling, you will only confirm me in my mannerisms, which are sometimes a great nuisance. You have much greater resources in the direction of gentleness than I have; and I assure you you will go wrong every time you try to do what *I* like instead of letting yourself do what *you* like. A part that is any good can be played fifty different ways by fifty different people; so just assume that Barbara is yourself (not that you are Barbara) and let it come just as it takes you. You need not be in the least anxious about the result. The end of the last act cannot fail as you play it; and if the middle of it should come to grief by a fluff or a letdown, the effect in front will be that the play is undramatic, not that the acting is at fault—which yours wont be in any case. So dont be anxious.

I write in haste, very tired, as I have had to write long lists of fluffy passages and good advice generally to the fluffy members of the cast; and I am now a wreck.

yours always
G.B.S.

To ANNIE RUSSELL

[A/56; X/227]   10 Adelphi Terrace W C
                                   28th [29th] November 1905

[*Major Barbara* had its first performance at a matinée on 28th November at the Royal Court Theatre. Miss Russell's husband, Oswald Yorke (1867–1943), a British-born actor who had been in America for the past ten years, played Bill Walker.]

My dear Miss Russell

I am glad to see that the half dozen papers I have read this morning are no more disappointed with you than I am. All the same, there is something wanting, and that is a few nights sound sleep and perhaps a day at the seaside. You will be twice as bright next week; and the week after you will laugh at yourself for feeling discouraged.

Besides, perhaps Calvert will collect his wits and remember his part now that he knows he is not going to be stoned for blasphemy.

Just to think that we have all been slaving to make a big success for your wretched husband. Do his hats still fit him?

yrs always
G. Bernard Shaw

To LOUIS CALVERT

[S/33; X/189, 190, 191]

10 Adelphi Terrace W C
29th November 1905

[This letter, like the one of 23rd July 1905 to Louis Calvert, and for the same reasons, has been edited slightly. Fred Cremlin, who had read the part of Burgess in the 1895 copyright performance of *Candida*, and who had appeared in *John Bull's Other Island*, was playing Peter Shirley. Clare Greet was Rummy Mitchens.]

My dear Calvert

I see with disgust that the papers all say that your Undershaft was a magnificent piece of acting, and Major Barbara a rottenly undramatic play, instead of pointing out that Major B. is a masterpiece and you the most infamous amateur that ever disgraced the boards.

Do let me put Cremlin into it. A man who could let the seven deadly sins go for nothing could sit on a hat without making an audience laugh. I have taken a box for Friday and had a hundredweight of cabbages, dead cats, eggs, and gingerbeer bottles stacked in it. Every word you fluff, every speech you unact, I will shy something at you. Before you go on the stage I will insult you until your temper gets the better of your liver. You are an impostor, a sluggard, a blockhead, a shirk, a malingerer, and the worst actor that ever lived or ever will live. I will apologize to the public for engaging you: I will tell your mother of you. Barker played you off the stage; Cremlin dwarfed you; Bill annihilated you; Clare Greet took all eyes from you. If you do not recover yourself

Annie Russell as Barbara Undershaft and Oswald Yorke
as Bill Walker in *Major Barbara*, 1905
(*The Bystander*)

next time, a thunderbolt will end you. If you are too lazy to study the lines, *I'll* coach you in them. That last act MUST be saved, or I'll withdraw the play and cut you off with a shilling.

yours
G.B.S.

To GILBERT MURRAY

[A/36; X/197]

10 Adelphi Terrace W C
29th November 1905

[Henry Noel Brailsford (1873–1958) was a Socialist writer and journalist, who became editor of the *New Leader* 1922–6. David S. Margoliouth (1858–1940) was a classical scholar of Greek, Hebrew, and Arabic literature, at New College, Oxford. He was a very close friend of Murray, and served as best man at his wedding. The correct words of Undershaft in the last act of *Major Barbara* are: "They look after their own drains, but I look after their dreams."]

My dear Murray

I have to congratulate you on a remarkable success. Your lines went immensely; and Barker surpassed himself in your spectacles.

I intended to send you the script of the last act; but I refrained, partly because I hadnt time to write, and partly because your reluctance to accept the Undershaft inheritance finally drove me to clinch the matter by a surpassingly mean reference to Brailsford, which I thought had better be exploded on you from the stage. I do not see how you can get out of it now. Barker suggested that if Stephen (the pious son) were to talk Murray-Margolouth the effect would be irresistible; but we resisted the temptation as a breach of good taste.

Barker was at his best, even as a drum virtuoso: he came out magnificently after being sticklike beyond all belief at rehearsals. Calvert suddenly realized that his part was blasphemous, and that Balfour, glaring from a box, might order him to the stake at any moment. He collapsed hopelessly and said, in the last act, "They have to find their own drains; but I look after their dreams." The last act was consequently a hideous failure.

I hear you are all coming to next Friday's performance. For your presence I do not give a damn; but the prospect of Lady Carlisle, filled with idle rumors, contemplating Miss Filippi and drawing conclusions as to my conception of her, terrifies me. Miss Filippi, though genial

585

and artistic, has not the grand manner. Her nose is seriously enlarged
by a bad cold; and she doesnt know her part. She also thinks the play
wicked. She is, on the whole, about as like the alleged original as I am
like Gladstone.

Barker has been cultivating the closest resemblance to you in private
life for a fortnight past. Everybody recognized it—Charlotte, Mrs Pat
Campbell &c &c—instantly & spontaneously the moment the spectacles went on. On the stage he obliterated it by a careful make-up.
Calvert, on the other hand, made up so exactly like a photograph of the
Turkish ambassador I supplied him with, that he could get his dinner
any day at the Embassy & give the real Turk to the police as an impostor. Yet nobody will find out Calvert; and everybody will find out
Euripides.

I am urging Barker to take a music hall engagement for a turn
entitled "Bad Taste: or My Gallery of Eminent Men."

yrs ever
G. Bernard Shaw

To WILLIAM T. STEAD

10 Adelphi Terrace W C
[X/147]   13th December 1905

Glad you liked it. But the cap & bells are necessary. Without them
people settle down into a comfortable solemn feeling that they have
done something good, and in fact dispose of the whole matter credit-
ably & sufficiently, when they have assented to the play & enjoy it. It
is just at that point that a laugh in their face disconcerts them & leaves
them without the fatal impression that *I* have solved the problem for
them.

G.B.S.

To ELEANOR ROBSON

Edstaston. Wem. Shropshire
[A/38; X/187]   24th December 1905

[The Shaws spent the holidays with the Cholmondeleys, from 16th December to 1st January. The new Rostand play was *Polichinelle*, a comedy in
verse. The "paragraph" about George Tyler appeared in the New York

586

World on 22nd October, under the heading "Shaw Calls Tyler a Baby: Dramatist Tells Why Eleanor Robson is Not to Play 'Major Barbara'." The attack on *Major Barbara* came from the critic of the *Morning Post* in his notice on 29th November: "It is bad enough when he makes one of the Major's sham converts refuse the offer of a piece of bread with the remark that he is satisfied with 'the peace which passeth all understanding.' It is worse—and it is so bad that we wonder at its escaping the notice of the censorship—when Major Barbara in her disappointment is allowed to exclaim: 'My God! My God! why has Thou forsaken me!' and to be answered by the ribald retort: 'What price salvation now?'" Shaw's letter of reply appeared in the *Morning Post* on 1st December, as did another letter in the *Morning Leader*, replying to an attack in that paper by Col. Jolliffe of the Salvation Army.]

Eleanor, Eleanor, Eleanor

At last a ray of comfort. A cutting from an American paper tells me that Tyler has at last done what I told him to do, and got you a play from Rostand. Is it Joan of Arc? For this be all his sins forgiven him!

I had to write a paragraph about him myself. The papers here sent me an interviewer with a statement from an American paper giving just the account the blasphemous rascals thought *you* would like about "Major Barbara." Mostly that my theatre was not good enough for you, and my salary not high enough for you, and it was like my impudence &c &c &c &c. I could not reply that you would have played *your* play for nothing in a barn; so I drank Tyler's blood in ten lines and then set you right as best I could by saying that you got Annie Russell the part.

That is what I must write to you about. I have had no luck since Barbara went wrong. I intended that you should play Barbara for me, and that thereafter no man in America would ever dare to misunderstand any play of mine; so that Daly could produce "Mrs Warren's Profession" with impunity. But Daly was as bad as Tyler. By disregarding my instructions as to the cast, he made an utter failure of "John Bull," and then, in desperation at his loss, rushed at "Mrs Warren's Profession," also in defiance of my warning that it was the wrong moment, with the result that I soon had reason to thank my stars that your skirts were well out of the way of the ocean of mud which was flung at me. Rostand will come to you with clean clothes and a young soul. At the same moment I had to fight a furious attack on Barbara, which was denounced as blasphemous (because Barbara says "My God: why has thou forsaken me?") and also a tremendous fuss about an article of mine on Irving in a Viennese newspaper, which got

587

stupidly misrepresented. It was a perfect Gettysburg—good for me, I dare say; but I really dont like fighting, especially with poor wretches who cannot defend themselves when I drive my pen through them.

But all this was a joke compared to the rehearsals of Barbara. I was very nice, patient, considerate, did not turn a hair externally; but I was inwardly furious, jealous, baffled, revolted at first, and then resigned and ineffective. I could only look on and do nothing. Miss Russell was all you said she would be, and very patient under very trying circumstances; for the other principals could not master their parts. At last she couldnt sleep and was panic stricken. At the first matinée (we began with six matinees) she broke down after the performance, thinking she had made a hideous failure. Happily the press next day applauded her to the skies and cursed me by its gods for inflicting on it a play that was no play at all—that had not a dramatic moment in it. It lasted from 2.30 to 5.55! Even my cleverest friends confessed that the last act beat them; that their brains simply gave way under it. We have now finished our six matinées. Every one of them has been crowded to bursting; and hundreds of people have been turned away. Poor Candida is eclipsed—a back number—people write frantic letters to me about Barbara. The audiences suffer horribly; they are pained, puzzled, bored in the last act to madness; but they sit there to the bitter end and come again, & again. Oswald Yorke has made a great success as the rough whom Barbara converts. Granville Barker was extraordinarily good in a part which nobody else could have touched. The enormously difficult and heavy part of Barbara's father beats Calvert. He admits it and is trying to get hold of it; but he has kept up appearances well enough to be enormously praised; and he may yet master it. After a few performances I cut the last act to make it easier for him and for Miss Russell. How she plays you can imagine better than I can describe. All the part that is within her range she plays excellently in a really touching intimate way, with sincere feeling, very right and sympathetic. But she is hampered by the heavier, more tragic passages. She has not a strong voice, and has no idea of making rhetorical effects in long speeches. And the whole balance of the play is strange to her. To have to struggle for supremacy with the other parts; to be scored off and have the sympathy snatched from her, and her own sympathetic attitude suddenly shown in a fiercely ironical light; to know at moments that the interest has gone away from her and that the audience is in a scare (about their own souls): all that is a bother to her. But fortunately Yorke, who makes the most obvious success in the ordinary sense, is her husband; and

588

she is apparently very fond of him. And she has had splendid notices, and feels that the occasion is an important one and a success; so I hope she is, on the whole, satisfied.

But oh! Eleanor, between ourselves, the play, especially in the last act, is a mere ghost; at least so it seems to me. This is no doubt your fault to some extent: I see you in the part; I love you in the part; I was inspired to write the part so that when the Word became Flesh (these old religious catchwords are the plainest common sense to me) the flesh should be yours. I cant let the play go to America now. When I said to Vedrenne one day that I did not see Miss Russell succeeding with Barbara in America, he replied promptly "She doesn't want to." I have strained the resources of the stage to breaking point: the acting requires three stars of the first magnitude. Once or twice at the early rehearsals I felt that I ought to kill you. You should have done it. You should have broken all your engagements—risen up in the middle of the night—come naked & hungry if no better might be. I could have waited two years, ten years, any number of years; but unless you saw the play you could not understand how impossible it was anywhere but at the Court Theatre. I don't know what is to be done now. Miss Russell cannot stay here all her life to play Barbara: it is hard enough on her that when it goes into the evening bill on New Years Day it is only for six weeks, when another Court play goes up in the course of the repertory system. Later on comes Brassbound with Ellen Terry. Barbara will not come on again until the winter of 1906-7. Some day perhaps you will be free to play it for us by way of rehearsal and then go to America with the whole Court company. All dreams!

If Rostand does less than his greatest for you, may his name perish and all his plays be revised by Tyler!

How is that immeasurable blunderer? Had you to make him go to Rostand, or had he the saving grace to see that this was the only amends he could make you?

I am just recovering from a touch of exhaustion after Barbara. It was a fearful job: I did what I never have had to do before, threw the last act away and wrote it again. Brainwork comes natural to me; but this time I knew I was working—and now nobody understands. No matter: there is the thing done: there is your baby; for it is yours, though you have left Miss Russell to nurse it.

Man & Superman seems inexhaustible: even Tyler would gape at the houses in New York & London, full every night, and apparently always the same people. And Barbara's spirit homeless in America!

I will strive to get it into print soon so that you may read it. I wonder will you be horribly disappointed with it. Oh Eleanor, Eleanor, dearest Eleanor! Oh infamous Tyler! When shall we see you again in London?

G.B.S.

To FLORENCE FARR

[A/3; X/115]

Edstaston. Wem. Shropshire
27th December 1905

[Charles Ricketts (1866–1931) was a painter, art critic, stage designer, and founder of the Vale Press (1896–1904). He, Thomas Sturge Moore, and Laurence Binyon had formed the Literary Theatre Society, which eventually mounted three productions: Moore's *Aphrodite against Artemis* (with Florence Farr as Phaedra) in April 1906; a double-bill of Wilde's *A Florentine Tragedy* and *Salome* (with Miss Farr as Herodias) in June 1906; a double-bill of Barker's *A Miracle* and Aeschylus's *The Persians* in March 1907. They abandoned the idea of doing Shelley's *The Cenci*, and Shaw eventually gave the rights to *Don Juan in Hell* to Vedrenne-Barker after first considering a Stage Society production of it. Ricketts designed the costumes.

Shaw's electioneering schedule from 4th to 11th January 1906 included speeches for S.G.Hobson at Rochdale, Stanton Coit at Wakefield, H.M. Hyndman at Burnley, Dan Irving at Accrington, John Burns at Battersea, and W.S.Sanders at Portsmouth.]

I strongly deprecate the Cenci. It is out of date, false in sentiment, and ludicrously unreal to the sort of audience you want.

As to the Superman scene, I do not say No; and of course I dont want any fees ("where there is nothing the King loses his rights"); but have you realized the size of the job? Is Ricketts taken with it; for unless there is a really artistic fantastic picture, with top lighting in the manner of Craig, and cunning costumes—a violet velvet Don Juan (horribly expensive), a crimson scarlet Mephistopheles, a masterpiece of white marble sculpture, and a radiant female (will you radiate?), the thing will be unendurable. And the stage must have a trap to work the change from the old woman to the young. And then, have you considered the appalling length of the parts? Where will you find a Don Juan willing to learn that prodigious part, and intelligent enough to make it interesting. Think of the last act of "Barbara," which is a trifle in comparison, and yet it almost drove the audience mad because Undershaft had not mastered his part sufficiently to make it interesting.

You had better ask Barker?—perhaps he will give you the Court stage for it. The Superman is licensed; and as Judith [a one-act play by Sturge Moore] is not canonical but only apochryphal, there is no reason why Redford should not license it. The boxers' hall [King's Hall, Covent Garden, where the first two L.T.S. productions were presented] is not a very delightful place; and the chairs are quite damnably uncomfortable; nothing short of a glove fight could distract the sitters from their agony.

Of course Murray did not object to "Major Barbara." Was ever man so flattered? He says it is extraordinary how very personal I can be without his seeming to mind, somehow. . . .

I dont see why you should not reblossom and have a great period now that you are about forty (*I'm* 50!). In the old days you caught on prematurely to old men and egotists—Ibsen, a grim old rascal; Todhunter, exactly like God in an illustrated family Bible, and me, an unintentional blighter of every purpose but my own. You were eaten up & preyed on: now you can have your turn with the knife and fork whilst we, whitehaired & doddering, look on at you with watering mouths.

I return to town tomorrow for a few rehearsals to get "Barbara" straight for the evening bill on the 1st. I return here on the 4th as a centre for electioneering in the north for about a week.

GBS

PART III

1906-1907

1906–1907

For years Shaw had been "acquiring the committee habit." He had served since 1885 on the Fabian Society's Executive Committee, and for almost as many years he had chaired its Publications Committee. He had participated as a member of several committees of the St Pancras Vestry and Borough Council. He was a member of the Committee of Management of the Society of Authors, and of its Dramatic Sub-Committee. He served on the Labour Representation Committee of the I.L.P., the Organising Committee of the Shakespeare Memorial National Theatre, the Body of Associates of the Academy of Dramatic Art, the Committee of Management of the Stage Society, and the General Committee of the London Shakespeare League.

He attended with regularity the meetings of all of these organisations and institutions (except when health and travel prevented this), for he never gave his name ornamentally to a committee, and he treated every meeting "as a matter of life and death." Often he found his fellow committeemen to be inflexible, lazy, and churlish—"to call them hogs would be an insult to a comparatively co-operative animal" —and had to undertake most of the work himself, harmonising divergent opinions as draftsman of tracts, treaties, constitutions and bye-laws, reports of sub-committees, letters to editors, petitions to the government, and ghosted speeches. To be a good committeeman, he insisted, required many virtues: one must be "invincibly patient," never lose one's temper, "spend precious working hours in drafting documents and then see your work wasted and spoiled without turning an outward hair . . . [and] use your wits to prevent the idle people from squabbling and then let all the bad blood pass off as being your fault . . ."

In the role of "privileged lunatic" on committees (see Shaw's letter of 3rd January 1905 to Archibald Henderson, p. 491), he wheedled, cajoled, flattered, overwhelmed, and not infrequently galvanised his fellow committeemen into action. As a result, few of them had much personal affection for him. Pinero, Shaw recalled, signed his letters "With admiration and detestation," and when in 1909 Pinero was urged, as chairman of the Dramatic Sub-Committee of the Society of Authors, to call a special meeting, he replied: "I am strongly against summoning a meeting . . . Even if I could get the fellows together, it would mean discussion, discussion, and—G.B.S.!"

Throughout crises and teapot tempests Shaw remained infuriatingly equable. "There are a few superior, happy beings," William Hazlitt pointed out, "who are born with a temper exempt from every trifling annoyance." Shaw could, as he once noted, "stand up to, and even enjoy, hammerings that drive other men to fury or reduce them to tears . . . When, as a critic or debater, I *have* to inflict pain I do it like a dentist, with great reluctance, and with all the anæsthesia I can produce. But note that as nothing is so maladroit as any show of sparing the victim's feelings I always hit as exultantly as I can, with an air of hitting as hard as I can. . . . I like my man to feel that he has had a good fight and been worthy of my steel, and not that I have been showing off my good taste at his expense . . ." Nowhere was this more evident than in the Fabian tug of war that pitted H. G. Wells against Shaw and the old guard of the Executive Committee.

Wells, encouraged by Beatrice Webb, had allowed Shaw and Graham Wallas to propose him for membership in February 1903. A month later he lectured to the Fabians on "The Question of Scientific Administrative Areas in Relation to Municipal Undertakings." Although the meeting was confined to members and to subscribers to the lecture series, Wells attracted the record audience of the year. Thereafter, however, he remained inactive, despite proddings from Shaw, until the autumn of 1905, when he suddenly offered to lecture on "Faults of the Fabian." He eventually delivered his talk on 9th February 1906, to a meeting "confined strictly to members of the Fabian Society." It was a damning indictment.

"So far from being a little band of true believers in an individualistic or quite unenlightened and hostile world," Wells argued, "we are, I hold, an extraordinarily inadequate and feeble organization in the midst of a world that teems with undeveloped possibilities of support and help for the cause we profess to further." The Fabians, he stated, were twenty years out of date; they had failed "either to organize, develop, or represent the spirit of social reconstruction that is arising all about us, in its failure to use the prestige it has accumulated, to fulfil the promises it once made to the world." It had, he noted with asperity, "an air of arrested growth . . ." He called, finally, for the appointment of a committee to "consider what means should be taken to increase the scope, influence, income and activity of the Society . . ." And he further moved that the rules be so altered as to delay new elections until after the report of this special committee could be circulated.

Rather than oppose Wells, the Executive encouraged the membership to grant him these options, and both resolutions were adopted without opposition. When Wells insisted on nominating the members of the committee, the Executive genially appointed to the committee all those members nominated by Wells who agreed to serve. It was Shaw who pressured the Executive to extend this co-operation. It would have been very easy for him to destroy Wells at this point, for as a combatant he was as seasoned as Wells was untried, and he could be devastating when he desired to be. But, although Wells complained that Shaw was playing "spring-heeled Jack, his favourite part," and informed Webb that "you two men are the most intolerable egotists, narrow, suspicious, obstructive, I have ever met," Shaw had actually been manipulating and manœuvering to *assist* Wells, for he was sympathetic to several of Wells's propositions for reform, and believed that, if properly educated and harnessed, Wells might become an energetic worker and a strong Fabian asset. He even urged Wells—at the height of the controversy—to run for the Executive, and later campaigned for his election!

Unfortunately, Wells was as impatient as he was idealistic. He yearned to reform the world overnight, and scornfully rejected the Webb–Shaw philosophy of the inevitability of gradualness. His dedication to his ideals, however, did not extend to a willingness to work co-operatively to bring about the changes he sought; he had contempt for committees, was boorish and inconsiderate ("You must study people's corns when you go clog dancing," Shaw reminded him), and showed complete ignorance of the demanding skills of administration. He was incapable of self-criticism and, unlike Shaw, could not view a thing apart from himself. Worst of all, he suffered from an inability to communicate ideas effectively in public address. "In conversation," Ivor Brown recalled, "Wells bubbled and Shaw flowed. It was the difference between a mountain beck and the river Shannon."

What was most disturbing to Shaw throughout the controversy was that he had a genuine affection for Wells. Those who see only the reckless, querulous, irresponsible side of Wells need to be reminded that his contemporaries knew him also to be, as Beatrice Webb recorded in her diary, a man of "agreeable disposition and intellectual vivacity." At his worst a spiteful, acerbic man, Wells was in his Jekyllian moments affable, effervescent, full of charm and genuine good fellowship. When, however, Wells elected, at the special Fabian meeting of 7th December 1906, to gamble on complete success or failure by attempting to force upon the members acceptance of his

Special Committee report, which Shaw argued would necessitate the resignation of the Executive and oblige its members not to stand for re-election, there was no alternative for Shaw but to destroy the monster he had been instrumental in creating. He did it, as spokesman for the Executive, at a second special meeting on 14th December, with courtesy, tact, and finesse, but hitting as hard as he could at Wells's dissentience, indolence, and intractability. It was a masterful speech, and the result was entirely predictable. Wells went down in mortifying defeat.

The saddest note of the whole affair was sounded by Wells, in a letter to Shaw, after the worst of the hubbub had subsided: "Well, I had some handsome ambitions [these] last twelve months & theyve come to nothing—nothing measured by what I wanted—and your friendship & the Webbs among the assets have gone for my gross of green spectacles. Because it's all nonsense to keep up sham amiabilities. I've said & written things that change relationships and the old attitudes are over for ever. On the whole I dont retract the things Ive said & done—bad & good together it's me. I'm damnably sorry we're all made so."

"I never met such a chap," Shaw remarked a year or two later; "I could not survive meeting such another."

To WILLIAM ARCHER

10 Adelphi Terrace W C

[A/2]   1st January 1906

[Archer had written in *The World* on 5th December 1905: "[Shaw] has determined to prove . . . that he can make a mere discussion 'as good as a play.' And he has unquestionably succeeded; *Major Barbara* is a fascinating entertainment. Its plot is a negligible figment of unconditioned fantasy, which neither Mr. Shaw nor anyone else takes seriously for a moment." *The Tribune* was a new paper, which commenced publication on 12th January. W.T.Stead's notice of *Major Barbara* appeared in the *Review of Reviews*, January 1906. Sir Oliver Lodge (1851–1940), scientist and writer, and recent president of the Psychical Society, had published a response, in *The Clarion*, 29th December 1905, to Robert Blatchford's review of the play, in which he deplored the "hideous gospel" which Shaw preached in the last act, although he favoured much of the rest of the play.]

My dear Archer

I have only just heard of your transfer from The World to The Tribune. . . .

Your article on "Major Barbara," the worst you ever wrote, delighted me. The complete success with which I wrecked your mind and left you footling—simply footling—was really the greatest proof of your fundamental sensibility to my magic. The third act is so novel and revolutionary that it will never get across the footlights—at least on top of the second—at one hearing; but the second has been completely grasped by Stead, who has written an admirable notice of it, and by Lodge (Sir Oliver of that ilk—see The Clarion). You, wretched atheist that you are, must see it again tonight. It is a MAGNIFICENT play, a summit in dramatic literature.

yrs

G.B.S.

To WILLIAM ROTHENSTEIN

[C/6; X/199.e]

10 Adelphi Terrace W C
4th January 1906

[Ever since the Boer War there had been growing enmity between Britain and Germany, much of it fostered by prejudiced reporting by the newspapers of the rival nations. Count Harry Kessler (1868–1937), an English-educated politician living in Weimar, who was a humanist and a lover of the arts, sought to allay feelings of mistrust within the two nations by calling upon the intellectuals of Germany and Britain—representatives of art, literature, and science—to issue friendly letters of mutual esteem to be published simultaneously. William Rothenstein and Emery Walker undertook the responsibility of obtaining signatures for the British letter, which they asked Shaw to draft for them. Kessler found Shaw's letter to be "quite admirable, and most amusing and interesting besides" (unpublished letter to Emery Walker, courtesy of LaFayette Butler), but several eminent men to whom it was submitted thought that two controversial passages in it were offensive, and refused to affix their signatures unless these passages were deleted. Rothenstein and Walker, to keep the project from falling apart, reluctantly obliged them, whereupon Shaw declined to sign. The German letter, with forty signatures, including those of Richard Strauss, Siegfried Wagner, Gerhart Hauptmann, and Kessler, and the emasculated British letter, with forty-one signatures, including those of Thomas Hardy, Edward Elgar, Sir George Darwin, and R.B.Cunninghame Graham, were published in *The Times* on 12th January 1906.

The Rt.Hon.Sir Frederick Pollock (1845–1937), a barrister and writer, who had taught law at University College, London, and later at Oxford, was Shaw's neighbour at Haslemere in 1898–9.]

20 names and a letter which really says something will make quite as much impression as 40 names and twaddle—which, by the way, is just what the German letter is. What IS the use of getting Pollock's signature when you know he will be waving the anti-German flag of the Navy League next day? These chaps simply dont agree: they are Jingoes. Why foist them on Europe as Internationalists? Remember Conan Doyle & the Peace people. He took the chair for them & then publicly apologized to the army. Let us be simple and TEREWTHFUL.

G.B.S.

To EMERY WALKER

[A/1]

10 Adelphi Terrace W C
10th January 1906

My dear Walker
  It is impossible for me to sign the letter as it now stands. Not that I object so much to the letter. What I *do* object to is the signatures. If it were signed only by those who would have signed it at full length, it might be taken to mean something; but now that it is going to have the Navy Leaguers to shew that it means nothing, I am off. I had much rather sign a letter to say honestly that we did our best to get forty signatures to a letter like the German one, but that we failed; and that we therefore think it better to confess that outside the ranks of Socialism in England the prevailing sentiment seems to be the usual one of entire indifference or ordinary Chauvinism. That is the truth: why not tell it or else hold our tongues?
  What is the use of faking up these things? Why should you or I lend credit to a spurious manifesto? Our one pull is that we dont do that sort of thing? Why the blankety jankety wankety hank should we throw away our reputation for (at least) sincerity, to please the Navy League?

yrs
G.B.S.

To AUGUSTIN HAMON

[S/1]

10 Adelphi Terrace W C
22nd January 1906

[Suzanne Després (1875–1951), who was married to A.-F. Lugné-Poe, performed at the Théâtre Antoine and at the Comédie Française. When Lugné-Poe presented Henri Bernstein's *La Rafale* in London in 1908, Shaw attended in order, as he told Sir Almeric Fitzroy that night, to satisfy himself that Suzanne Després "would be able to interpret 'Mrs Warren's Profession' to a Parisian audience: a very few minutes left him in no doubt as to her competence to undertake any rôle he could invent" (Fitzroy, *Memoirs*, 1925).]

601

My dear Hamon

I send you the third act [of the French translation of *Mrs Warren's Profession*].

In the conversation between Frank & his father, & also between Frank & Vivie, will you consider very carefully where they should "tutoyer" one another. The distinction does not exist in English, as we say "vous" to the smallest child, but the change from "vous" to "tu" is of great dramatic value in French. It seems to me that Frank would "tutoyer" his father all through, whilst his father would call him "Monsieur" & "vous" whenever he tries to be pompous. And I should think Frank would "tutoyer" Vivie also whenever they are alone together, though Vivie would call him "vous" whenever she wishes to snub him. Would not Mrs Warren occasionally "tutoyer" Crofts or Praed?

I find that you have seized my meaning quite correctly. Except in one or two idioms or proverbs that you could not possibly guess.

By the way, I very much doubt whether Lugné Poe will care to produce Mrs Warren after all, because Suzanne Després would hardly care to play Mrs Warren, which is the leading part.

yours ever
G. Bernard Shaw

To ARNOLD DOLMETSCH

[C/24]

10 Adelphi Terrace W C
26th January 1906

More power to your elbow.

Have you ever studied the pianola. A pianola that will play the clavichord is indispensable if the clavichord is to be a success.

I can no longer bear to hear pianists struggling with their fingers. The human hand is too mechanical for music: pneumatic suction and no trouble about fingering allows much more poetry and individuality.

G. Bernard Shaw

To M. MOUILLOT

[G.u/2; X/200]

[10 Adelphi Terrace W C]
[Undated: *c*. 1st–6th February 1906]

[Miss M. Mouillot was secretary to the Amateur Players' Association. Shaw's address in the Unitarian Hall, Plumstead Common, on 14th February, was on "The Super-Man."]

Dear Madam

I shall be unable to attend the meeting of the Amateur Players' Association on the 14th, as I have to deliver an address at Plumstead on that evening.

I have a strong grudge against clubs of amateur actors because they habitually insult the art they dabble in by assuming that it is a sin which can only be covered by charity. It is quite a common thing for organizers of amateur performances to appeal to the author to forego his fees on the ground that the proceeds are to be given to some charitable institution. That is to say, a popular dramatic author is asked to hand over some hundreds a year to amateur societies to give to their pet charities, and that, too, without the slightest guarantee that the management of the performance will be businesslike enough to realize for the charities the whole value of his contribution, or indeed any part of it at all. A more unreasonable demand can hardly be imagined within the limits of practicable human audacity. Even professional millionaire philanthropists like Mr Carnegie & Mr Passmore Edwards reserve the right to choose for themselves the objects of their endowments.

Besides, the charity is hardly ever really charitable in its motive. It is a mere coat of whitewash for an indulgence which is regarded as questionable, if not positively disreputable. It is also adulterated by a desire for the acquaintance of the titled patrons & patronesses of charities. And the economic effect of the performance, when the expenses leave any surplus, is simply to relieve the ratepayers of their social obligations by helping to keep hospitals out of public hands & in private ones. Why on earth should a playwright be expected to contribute to the rates of places he has never lived in?

What makes this additionally exasperating is that whilst there is little difficulty in raising vast sums of ransom & conscience money from the rich in the form of charitable subscriptions, it is hard to get a farthing for the starving art of the theatre either from public or private sources. If all the money that has been wasted on charities by amateur actors had been devoted to the endowment of theatrical art by building up

603

local dramatic societies with repertories, wardrobes, & even theatres of their own, not only would dramatic art be much more highly developed than it is now in England, but other arts would have grown up round the local theatres. Just think of what a playhouse would mean to a country town if it had its own dressmakers, its own tapestry weavers, its own armourers, its own embroideresses, and its own dress designers and painters and machinists. What is to be said in defence of the stage-struck stupidity and ignorance that is content with a basket of soiled second hand clothes and toy swords sent down by a London costumier and hired out for a night at about treble the price the whole parcel of rubbish would sell for in Houndsditch? Do you expect me or any dramatic author to be lenient in the matter of fees to people who keep up these nasty, vulgar, ignorant practices? Rather let us heap crushing exactions on them and starve their folly to death.

Almost all amateurs desire to imitate the theatre rather than to act a play. They actually call their performances "theatricals," and are as proud of that illiterate insult as any genuine dramatic artist would be outraged by it. They lose all their ordinary decent instincts the moment they give themselves up to what they privately think is the sin of acting. You see gentlemen who are morbidly particular about the cut & fit of their coats and trousers, walking on to the stage in ludicrously mis-fitting tunics from the costumier's amateur ragbag. You see the amateur forester carrying a tinsel topped pantomime spear, for the hire of which he has paid more than the local blacksmith would have charged him for a real spear. Women who would die rather than be dowdy in church or at a garden party face the footlights in costumes & make-ups which no selfrespecting figure in a penny waxwork would tolerate. Reach-me-down dresses, reach-me-down scenery, reach-me-down equipments are considered good enough for dramatic masterpieces—are positively preferred to decent & beautiful things because they are so much more theatrical.

As to plays, they, too, must be second hand reach-me-downs. Your amateurs dont want to bring plays to a correct and moving represen-tation for the sake of the life they represent: they want to do Hawtrey's part in this, or Ellen Terry's part in that, or Cyril Maude's part in the other, not to mention the amateur Salvinis & Duses & Bernhardts and Coquelins. The enormous & overwhelming advantage possessed by amateurs—the advantage of being free from commercial pressure and having unlimited time for rehearsal—is the last one they think of using. The commercial plays which are the despair of actors, but which they must produce or starve, are the favorites of our amateurs. They do out

of sheer folly & vulgarity what our real dramatic artists do of necessity
and give some saving grace & charm to in the doing. Richard Wagner
said that the music of the great masters is kept alive not by professional
concerts and opera speculations, but on the cottage piano of the
amateur. I wish I could say as much for the amateur theatre. As I
cannot, I shall only beg your amateur clubs to let my plays alone and to
assure them that as long as they persist in their present ways the only
part I shall play in the matter of fees is the part of Shylock.

> yours faithfully
> [G. Bernard Shaw]

To A.-F. LUGNÉ-POE

10 Adelphi Terrace W C
[G.u/13]   17th February 1906

[Lugné-Poe had written on 13th December 1905: "J'aurais voulu avec un
ami (M. Willy) jouer Mrs Warren's Profession" (British Library of Political
and Economic Science). "Willy" was the pseudonym of Henri Gauthier-
Villars (1859–1931), a prominent journalist and playwright, who had collaborated with Lugné-Poe.]

D'abord, mon cher Lugné Poe, je ne sais ni écrire ni parler votre
langue. Pour moi, le grammaire n'existe pas. Comprenez vous l'Anglais
assez de permettre que je m'en sers en vous écrivant?

Il y a peut etre trois ou quatre mois qu'un M. Boulestin m'a de-
mandé pour Willy (en ce moment[-]la. je n'avais jamais entendu parler
de Willy) ma pièce "Mrs Warren's Profession"? Il m'a expliqué très
obligeamment qu'une piece aussi pornographe était sur à réussir avec
Willy comme traducteur et Madame Suzanne Despres jouant le role
principale. C'était du tact, cela, n'est ce pas?

Naturellement je fis un réponse écrasante. Cette idée d'offrir a
Madame Despres un role dans une piece pornographe me sembla
manquer horriblement de respect pour elle comme femme et comme
artiste. D'ailleurs, je ne suis pas pornographist. "Mrs Warren's Profession" est une drama aussi serieuse que le "Ghosts" d'Ibsen.

J'ai confié la traduction de tout mon œuvre to M. Auguste Hamon,
Kerhuel-en-Camlez, par Penvenan, Cotes du Nord. Son traduction de
"Mrs Warren's Profession" est achevé; et nous ne demandons mieux—
Hamon et moi—que d'entamer notre carrière sur le scene Francais sous

605

vos auspices. Il faut deux actrices de talent pour Mrs Warren et sa fille Vivie. Vivie est l'ingenue; mais le beau role est celui de la mere—énorme!—tragédie, comédie, caractère, tout!

Mais lisez la traduction de Hamon; et puis nous verrons. Lisez le à Madame Suzanne. Je l'ai vu trois ou quatre fois en scene; et j'ai trouvé une qualité tres touchante en son talent et personalité.

Excusez moi, je vous prie, de vous avoir fait attendre cette reponse si inconsciemment. Je suis comblé d'affaires literaires et politiques. L'election m'a criblé—veritablement.

yours faithfully
[G. Bernard Shaw]

To CHARLES GANE

[X/201]

10 Adelphi Terrace W C
22nd February 1906

[Charles Gane was secretary to the National Anti-Vaccination League. Mrs Squeers was the wife of the proprietor of Dotheboys Hall in Dickens's *Nicholas Nickleby*.]

Dear Sir

I regret that I shall be unable to attend your meeting on the 27th.

I cannot help thinking that the time is not far off when the work of your League will be lightened by the co-operation of the leaders of bacteriological therapeutics. For years past the strain of countenancing a proceeding so grossly reckless, dirty, and dangerous as vaccination from the calf, has been growing unbearable to all genuine bacteriological experts. The utmost that professional pressure has been able to extort from them of late is silence; but their disgust will soon become too intense for silence. Mrs. Squeers's method of opening abscesses with an inky penknife is far less repugnant to modern surgeons than the Local Government Board's method of inoculating children with casual dirt moistened with an undefined pathogenic substance obtained from calves is to modern bacteriologists. Nothing but the natural ignorance of the public, countenanced by the inculcated erroneousness of the ordinary medical general practitioner, makes such a barbarism as vaccination possible. The question whether it is practicable to fortify

606

the blood against disease by inoculations is still an open and very interesting one. Its recent developments have shewn that an inoculation made in the usual general practitioner's light-hearted way, without a previous highly skilled examination of the state of the patient's blood, is just as likely to be a simple manslaughter as a cure or preventive. But vaccination is really nothing short of attempted murder. A skilled bacteriologist would as soon think of cutting his child's arm and rubbing the contents of the dustpan into the wound as vaccinating it in the official way. The results would be exactly the same. They *are* exactly the same.

You cannot urge too insistently that even if the modern serum treatment not only justified itself to-morrow, but could be made practicable on a large scale instead of as a laboratory experiment, the objection to vaccination as a quite infamously careless and ignorant method of inoculation would become more obvious than ever.

yours faithfully
G. Bernard Shaw

To HARLEY GRANVILLE BARKER

[A/3; X/168]

10 Adelphi Terrace W C
14th March 1906

[Rehearsals of *Captain Brassbound's Conversion* with Ellen Terry had begun in February, with the first performance being given at a matinée at the Royal Court Theatre on 20th March. After six successful matinées it went into the evening bill on 16th April, for a run of twelve weeks.]

Dear Barker

I did not do anything about the chanty. We should have a special rehearsal of extras for it if we attempt it: it is impossible to stop a rehearsal for it. Unless they pick it up very easily it wont be worth the trouble.

Do not let Ellen repeat any scene. When she gets through she always wants to do it over and over again until it is right. There are two fatal objections. 1. She always goes to pieces the second time & discourages & demoralizes herself more & more every time. 2. She has just strength enough to get through the play once without tiring herself & before lunch; and the repetition of a scene means a corresponding omission at the end. Go straight through & dont let them stop for anything. In

607

any case the policy of sticking at it until we get it is a vulgar folly. Let them take their failure & the shame of it home & they will think about it & pull it off next time.

Do not make [Lewis] Casson [Sidi el Assif] *play out.* It spoils the part completely & anticipates the Cadi [Trevor Lowe], who plays out all the time. The contrast between the immoveably dignified & self contained Sidi and the rumbustious blethering Cadi cannot be too marked. If there is the slightest self assertion in the line "Brassbound: I am in my own house and among mine own people. *I* am the Sultan here" the effect is utterly lost. It should be as the voice of God.

[C. L.] Delph [Redbrook] is hopelessly bothered & puzzled by the business of taking off Sir Howard [J. H. Barnes]; and no wonder, as the dialogue is quite wrong for the new business. Possibly it may help to have more words for Sir Howard—for instance, "You will be laid by the heels yet, my friend (they seize him). You have no right to lay your hand on me, sir. You are breaking the law. You are committing an assault. I will let you know that you cannot outrage me with impunity. Your captain is a scoundrel who is getting you and himself into trouble. I will not stand &c &c &c &c &c." Meanwhile Johnson [Edmund Gurney] can say "All right, sir, *all* right: take it easy: nobody's offering to hurt you: better leave the cap'n to himself: no offence: steady on: come along, sir." Redbrook can say Tut tut &c as in the book. I think if they all talk themselves off the stage together without bothering about Lady Cicely, it will not only be more natural, but she may quite easily be reassured by the men's talk that they will not hurt him. If we try the other Delph will botch it.

[Frederick] Kerr [Captain Brassbound] thinks the meeting too slow, as he works himself up a good deal over it. You might mention to him beforehand that the effect is more convincing when they are obviously half hearted & all the vigor is on his side. Say I watched it carefully today & came to that conclusion.

Do let us have the Court stage & the scenery on Saturday as well as on Monday. Remember how the scenery in John Bull knocked Calvert to pieces.—Blunt has no saddles worth talking about; so we must do with a couple of bales.

G.B.S.

To ELLEN TERRY

[10 Adelphi Terrace W C]
[X/117.u]   14th March 1906

[True to his promise in his letter of 25th November 1905, Shaw was teaching
Ellen her part, to the point of feeding her the very stresses in her lines.]

(*a*) Have you ever thought of the GRANDEUR of wickedness?
Grand! That's the word. Something grandly wicked.
Not very wicked, not dreadfully wicked, not shockingly wicked, but
GRANDLY WICKED.
GRANDIOSO
SOMETHING Grandly WICKED to their enemies.
(*b*) If you take a man and pay him £500 a year, and HAVE—
Ah, that's it.
Beautiful Phrase! Happy expression! "And HAVE policemen and
courts and laws and juries etc."
Just think of it!
HAVE policemen and courts and laws
and juries to DRIVE him into it. HAVE!
Ah! *Have!*
(*c*) *That's what English people are like, Captain Kearney.*
Yes, positively.
That's what English people are like.
No use your contradicting it, Captain Kearney. I tell you THAT'S
what English people are like.

To COUNTESS FEODORA GLEICHEN

Harmer Green. [Welwyn]
[A/1]   22nd March 1906

[Julia Frankau (1865–1916), a novelist writing under the name "Frank
Danby," had commissioned a monument to honour her late husband from
the highly reputed sculptor and teacher of the Royal Academy, Sir Alfred
Gilbert (1854–1934), who created the famed Eros fountain in Piccadilly
Circus. After obtaining a considerable amount of money from Mrs Frankau,
Gilbert procrastinated for eighteen months, while writing misleading letters,
until Mrs Frankau, convinced that she had been bilked, appealed to Sir

609

Edward Poynter, president of the Royal Academy, and advertised for information concerning other commissions to build a case against Gilbert. He was finally embarrassed to the point of having to resign from the Royal Academy. Gilbert's friend and admirer, Countess Feodora Gleichen (1861–1922), also a well-known sculptor, rashly sought to enlist Shaw's aid for Gilbert. The incident appears to have provided an inspiration for Shaw's next play, *The Doctor's Dilemma*, which he began to write less than five months later.

The Shaws had taken a short lease on a house in Harmer Green, which they occupied between 5th February and 13th June 1906.]

My dear Countess

I do not think a sculptor should be treated like a commercial mechanic. A commercial mechanic can be sent to Holloway on a judgment summons, or be refused his discharge in bankruptcy when he cannot meet his engagements. But a dishonest sculptor should be shot. For Gilbert, if Mrs Frankau's story be true, shooting is too honorable a death. He should be drowned in the fountain with which he disfigured Piccadilly Circus.

Pray do not suppose that I deny an artist's right to be judged by a different standard to other people. I grant that—in fact I insist on it— and as the artist's standard is more exacting and higher than the tradesman's standard I know that it not only binds the artist to accept obligations that are too severe for the tradesman, but also relieves him from obligations that the tradesman accepts. But Gilbert accepts neither the artist's obligations nor the tradesman's. He accepts a tradesman's job for a monument; takes the money for it; and then— well, would *you* do what he did? Would you write those letters and make those excuses and tell those lies? You are artist enough to know that they are lies—that the picture of the great sculptor striving vainly to do justice to the memory of Mrs Frankau's husband, and shattering his work in despair, is an ignoble, ridiculous fiction—dont you? It dishonors us all, you, me, everyone whose work is fine art. It encourages the public to believe that artists are people who claim the privilege of being worse than other people instead of the honor of being better than them.

In the course of my life I have had to support myself for many years by journalistic work which was not the highest work in my power. What would you have thought of me if I had taken the money for it and not done it instead of doing it as well as I could? I could at this moment get a considerable sum from any London manager by promising him a popular play to be ready by next October. Suppose I took it, and then

610

said I really could not control my genius and harness it to the box office of fashionable theatres! Would you not say, "then why did you take the money?"

The love of titles & dignities you mention seems to me quite of a piece with his other characteristics. The duty of the R.A. is quite plain in the matter; and Poynter's apparent want of perception seems to me to justify that attitude of the British Philistine towards artists of which you complain.

If I were you I would make a statue of Mrs Frankau for nothing, to commemorate her very proper and public spirited action. It is the best virtue of the Jew that when he (or she) makes an agreement $\left\{\begin{array}{l} he \\ she \end{array}\right\}$ means it. She paid her money honestly. That was not mean. Gilbert took it and denied her the agreed consideration. What do you call that? *I* call it Christian roguery. There!

yours faithfully
G. Bernard Shaw

To H. G. WELLS

[A/26]

10 Adelphi Terrace W C
24th March 1906

[Wells was about to leave for America. His committee was a Special Committee of Enquiry, of which he was chairman, created by the Fabian membership to consider and report on what Wells, in his address to the Society on 9th February 1906, had called "Faults of the Fabian." Charlotte Shaw was a member of the committee. Wells's basis was a "Proposed Revised Basis," to which each new member of the Society would be required to subscribe. His committee had submitted it to the Executive for joint discussion on 25th March, and Shaw had apparently received a copy by this time from Edward Pease.

Stanton Coit (see I, 235–7) was president of the West London Ethical Society. Aylmer Maude (1858–1938), writer and translator of Tolstoy, was on the Fabian Executive 1907–12. Victor Fisher and H. Isaac Mitchell were Fabian supporters of Wells. Mitchell, a leading official of the Boilermakers' Society, was an alderman on the London County Council. Rev. Charles L. Marson (1858–1914) was a crusading Socialist priest.

Samurai, a Japanese word for "military knighthood," made familiar in

Britain through newspaper reports of the recent Russo-Japanese war, was a name given by Wells, in *A Modern Utopia* (1905), to a group of "volunteer noblemen," a self-perpetuating élite order of professional men, who would serve as enlightened leaders of the nation. As Edwin E. Slosson noted in *Six Major Prophets* (1917), Wells's Utopia was "a curious conception . . . a combination of Puritanism and Bushido, of Fourier and St Francis, of Bacon's Salomon's House, Plato's philosophers ruling the republic, and Cecil Rhodes's secret order of millionaires ruling the world."

In their self-discipline through spiritual exercises, their distinctive garb, their annual retreat for complete solitude to meditate, the Samurai anticipated Shaw's Ancients in *Back to Methuselah*, and at the same time bore a distinct resemblance to Shaw's "philosophic man" as extolled by Don Juan in *Man and Superman*: "he who seeks in contemplation to discover the inner will of the world, in invention to discover the means of fulfilling that will, and in action to do that will by the so-discovered means."]

Dear H.G.W.

Do not forget to call on Brentano, Union Square, New York. They are expecting you. They have treated me very well, and are very satisfactory people to deal with, as they began, not as literary amateurs with a capacity for doing nothing and a taste for talking to authors, but as newsboys in the street. Arthur Brentano, the one who called on me here, is quite a decent human being. They write to say that they will appreciate a visit from you enormously. They also have views about your works & the American public which they will no doubt intimate with due regard to your susceptibilities—most complimentary to you and uncomplimentary to the A.P.

During your absence I will write the report of your committee, probably, and get it adopted through Charlotte. Your intellectual vivacity and sense of humor have certain disadvantages—among them an inordinate delight in pure impish cheek. Your basis is of course obviously much better than the existing basis; but as I told you, anybody who was the least bit of a literary workman could have produced a better basis any time these 20 years. But he couldnt have produced one that would have conciliated Lawson Dodd and Headlam and Webb and Pease and Macrosty and all the sections they represent. To get anything through a corporate body, you must say the same thing over again in different ways. You must stick on absurd excrescences in the nature of china eggs to make the hen lay. You must get round differences of meaning between members by saying something that neither disputant means or that means nothing. And you finally never get anything more artistic out of them than an average King's-speech.

Now it is no use imagining that the conciliations of 20 years ago are out of date. I assure you they are not. Either you have the very same men to deal with—Headlam, Pease, Webb, Bland &c, or you have *abler* successors to the departed ones—Stanton Coit, Dodd, [Cecil] Chesterton. Your one chance is to shew a perfect appreciation of and sympathy with the exigencies which imposed on us the obvious blemishes in the basis, and to appeal for an attempt to get a more attractive one through by a concentration of our prestige & authority sufficient to silence the guerilla leaders in the society—though when I think of Aylmer Maude, Victor Fisher, Isaac Mitchell, Marson &c &c &c I dare not hold out any hopes of that proving possible. But that is your best chance. Instead of which, you amuse yourself by treating us to several pages of cheek to the effect that the imperfections of the basis are the result of our own folly and literary clumsiness. This doesnt irritate me, nor Bland, nor Webb (*much*), nor any of the old birds with a spice of your own impishness in them; but it does irritate Macrosty and some of the others. None of them, old or young, enjoy a sally at their own expense as much as a sally at yours; and as the game is one which both sides can play at, it is not a helpful one. [George] Standring's lampoon, for instance, is a very harmless stuffed bludgeon compared to your thrusts; but you probably found that it did not conduce to cordial co-operation on your side with George. Your tactics would be admirable if you wanted to force a fight. But you dont; so you had better drop them. You may say that you are making superhuman efforts to be amiable. No doubt you are; but you are not amiable enough, in spite of your efforts. And you are too reckless of etiquette. You really mustnt poach on our departments. You had no more right to report that debate than you had to write our cheques; and that is just one of the things that the human animal will not stand. If, instead of making unscientific, obsolete and untenable distinctions between habits and instincts, you would *préciser* the distinction between the terms of your committee's reference and the duties of the executive, you would have none of these difficulties. Even if your report had been approximately accurate instead of a blaze of wanton mendacity from beginning to end (I go this length because I told you myself viva voce that you must not claim more than that your resolutions had been carried nem. con.; and you agreed), still the committee—*any* human committee—would have jibbed at having its account of its own action dictated to it. You must study people's corns when you go clog dancing.

Generally speaking, you must identify yourself frankly with us, and

613

not play the critical outsider and the satirist. We are all very clever; and long ago we have come to understand that we must not play our cleverness off against one another for the mere fun of it. The whole business is a ridiculous one for us. It is a case of Songs of Innocence & Experience. Your innocence is stupendous in some ways. Our experience has humbled us until we are morbidly afraid of playing off our experience against you, and willing to allow you to teach your grandmother to milk ducks to any extent on the chance of getting a workable idea here & there, and, at all events, a fresh impulse. But there are limits to our powers of enduring humiliations that are totally undeserved. You havnt told us anything yet that we dont know—havnt pointed out any error in our ways that is not the work of Natural Selection. You havnt discovered the real difficulties of democratic work; and you assume that our own folly and ill will account for their results.

If you want to persuade us to throw the basis into the melting pot, you will have either to convince us that it is excluding desirable recruits on a serious scale, or else to add something to it—say a proposal for a set of observances of the Samurai order. An expansion of the basis is always a thing to keep open for. But a change on what I called academic grounds is too risky: the more perfect your draft is when it goes in, the more grotesque it is likely to be when it comes out of the general butchery.

Give my love to Jane, that well behaved woman. Why she married you (I being single at the time) the Life Force only knows.

G.B.S.

PS   I have just had a talk with Olivier, and suggested to him a means by which we might possibly get the new basis through unaltered by adding to it a lot of Samurai order regulations which would draw all the debate and, though not surviving it themselves, secure an undisturbed passage for the rest. It would be very interesting besides: Webb & I, for instance, are far keener on pushing notions of this sort than on academic discussions about rent & interest & so forth. Olivier also is of the same mind.

[Wells replied on 26th March: "You leave my committee alone while I'm in America.

"If I'm to identify myself with 'us,' who's us? I'm not going to identify myself with your damned executive nohow, but I'm always open to a deal that will give results. . . . I've got five names now of people excluded by the Basis, & more will no doubt turn up" (BM).]

614

To HUGO VALLENTIN

10 Adelphi Terrace W C
[A/5]   4th April 1906

[Hugo Vallentin (d. 1921), a journalist and literary man, was Shaw's Swedish translator. He later became Press Officer for the Swedish Embassy in London. *Arms and the Man* (*Hjältar*) had opened on 17th March at the Svenska Theater, Stockholm, with the cast receiving twenty-three curtain calls.]

My dear Vallentin

Thanks for your cheque for £19.19.8 for performances of Arms & The Man from the 24th to the 30th ult. inclusive. . . .

Do not send me the translations. I do not know a single word of Swedish; so I could not read them. Be very careful, whenever I use a phrase repeatedly, to repeat exactly in the same words in Swedish. For instance, in The Man of Destiny, the Lieutenant several times says "the better side of my nature," and "to shew his confidence in me." The lady betrays herself to Napoleon by repeating this phrase—"You see! I shew my confidence in you." If you vary the wording, using one version in one place & a different one in the next, the stage effect will be completely spoiled. That is the chief danger in translations.

If any passage puzzles [you] send me a postcard and I will explain.

yours ever
G. Bernard Shaw

To ERICA COTTERILL

Harmer Green. Welwyn
[D/1; X/202]   5th April 1906

My dear lady

Why dont you join some Socialist Society and get some work to do? There are always envelopes to be directed and tracts to be distributed. What is the use of thinking about yourself and writing long letters (three full stops in 8 pages!) to an elderly gentleman—letters which he always tears up the moment they threaten to be of the kind that the writer wants to get back an hour after they are posted.

If you dont find some business to do that is not specially your own business you will go quite cracked.

yours faithfully
G. Bernard Shaw

PS The poems are too careless in form to be satisfactory.

To SIEGFRIED TREBITSCH

[A/5]

Harmer Green. Welwyn
13th April 1906

[*Cæsar and Cleopatra* had been produced by Max Reinhardt at the Neues Theater, Berlin, on 31st March. Theodor Mommsen (1817–1903), the German historian, was the author of the three-volume *Römische Geschichte* (1854–5), which Shaw had read in the W. P. Dickson translation. The famous French sculptor Auguste Rodin (1840–1917) had called at Adelphi Terrace on 1st March, at which time he arranged for Shaw to sit for him on 16th April. The Shaws remained in Paris until 8th May.]

My dear Trebitsch

. . . I am sorry Cæsar was not more successful in Berlin. It would have been better to omit the third act: the play is too long. Was the Cæsar able to rise to the greater moments of the part in Act IV and in the scene with Septimius in Act II? What I dread is that they played it as a comedy all through—five acts of Bluntschli in a bald pate instead of Cæsar. However, if Reinhardt is so anxious to secure Man & Superman he can hardly have had a complete disaster with Cæsar. Why on earth does he not induce the Kaiser to pay a visit. Wilhelm would see himself as Cæsar, and perhaps write an additional act or play the part himself some night. And then Reinhardt's fortune would be made. He should also set his press agents to work to emphasize the fact that the play owes its inspiration to Germany, as my Cæsar is Mommsen's Caesar dramatized.

However, it is a shame to bother you with all this on your holiday. I feel, myself, that if I write another letter or think out another sentence

616

I shall go stark mad. On Sunday I start for Paris—Hotel Palais d'Orsay. Rodin has influenza; but he thinks he can at least make a beginning. I have the greatest doubt of the bust being ever finished.

GBS

To ALVIN LANGDON COBURN

[X/180]

Hotel Palais d'Orsay. Paris
17th April 1906

[Coburn, upon receipt of this letter, responded with alacrity, arriving in Paris in time to accompany the Shaws and Sydney Cockerell to the unveiling of Rodin's sculpture "Le Penseur" outside the Panthéon (it was subsequently moved to the grounds of the Musée Rodin in St Germain). Edward Steichen (b. 1879), an American photographer (born in Luxembourg), later became director of the Department of Photography of the Museum of Modern Art, New York, 1947–62.]

Come along any time you like. Rodin, seeing that I had a camera, invited me to photograph his place if I liked. I took the opportunity to press your claims; and he said certainly. I guaranteed you a good workman. The sculpting sittings are at Meudon 25 minutes train from Paris, where he has a lot of beautiful things. No photograph yet taken has touched him: Steichen was right to give him up and silhouette him. He is by a million chalks the biggest man you ever saw; all your other sitters are only fit to make gelatin to emulsify for his negative.

G.B.S.

617

To SYDNEY COCKERELL

Hotel Palais d'Orsay. Paris

[A/3]   20th April 1906

[Rainer Maria Rilke (1875–1926), who at this time was Rodin's secretary, informed William Rothenstein on 26th April that Rodin had found Shaw to be a perfect model, "qui pose avec la même energie et sincérité qui font sa gloire d'écrivain" (Rothenstein, *Men and Memories*, 1932). Rodin is also alleged to have remarked: "M. Shaw ne parle très bien; mais il s'exprime avec une telle violence qu'il s'impose" (Robert Boothby, *I Fight to Live*, 1947).]

Dear Cockerell

Will you come & dejeuner with us here tomorrow at 12.45, and then come with us to the inauguration of Rodin's Penseur statue at the Pantheon at 2. We have tickets.

I think I must try to get Rodin & you acquainted. He is extraordinarily like Morris in some ways—the same stature & figure, the same way of looking quickly at his job when he is putting in a stroke of work, and the same atmosphere about him. You must add him to your collection of great men.

As a collector in the plastic line (he has a regular museum at his house at Meudon) he is, like Morris, never wrong—no curios, nothing but the right things, and all of them treasures. But he does not know what a book is. He has Pliny in 20 volumes, Quintilian in a lot more, autographed presentation copies of all sorts of rubbish, and a few old bindings, one of them concealing a Jensenish looking Latin book, well printed, which may be some good. He knows absolutely nothing about books—thinks they are things to be read.

He is perfectly simple and quite devilishly skilful at his work—not the smallest whiff of professionalism about him—cares about nothing but getting the thing accurate and making it live. It is my solemn opinion that he is the biggest thing at present going—or likely to be going for a long time again—nobody in the running with him but Praxiteles & Michel Angelo, and both of them beaten in some points. Morris is the only man I ever met who made anything like the same impression on me. Imagine Morris without his temper, without the spoiling of the family income, and with an astonishing gift of shaping things into intense life, and you will get something like Rodin.

There is to be no sitting tomorrow in consequence of the Pantheon affair. This is the first day off since I came; and I shall be at a loose

618

end all the morning unless Charlotte wants particularly to go somewhere. Perhaps I shall go to the Cluny or the Trocadero—Rodin
advised the Trocadero. I shall leave here any time after 9.45.

Anyhow, come between 12.45 & 1, or else send us word not to expect
you.

G.B.S.

To SIEGFRIED TREBITSCH

Hotel Palais d'Orsay. Paris

[A/5]   7th May 1906

[Granville Barker had married Lillah McCarthy on 24th April. They went
to Germany for their honeymoon, where Barker attended a performance of
the Berlin production of *Cæsar and Cleopatra* and reported to Shaw that it
had been mutilated.]

My dear Trebitsch

The secret of Cæsar's failure is out at last; and never again shall
Reinhardt have a play of mine to ruin. Barker has seen it and told me
all about it.

They have cut out the first scene of the 4th act!!! Of course that
meant utter failure. It is in that scene that the change in Cleopatra's
character is shewn, and the audience prepared for the altered atmosphere and deeper seriousness of the later scene. To omit it is such
a hopeless artistic stupidity that the man who would do it would do
anything. I will not trust him with the Superman or with anything else
after that. Write to him and tell him so. If you don't, I will write myself, not to him, but to the Berlin papers.

He has also cut out the burning of the library, which must make the
end of the second act unintelligible. In short, he has done everything
that a thoroughpaced blockhead could do to achieve a failure; and he
has achieved it accordingly. If he has advanced any money on the
Superman, send it back to him at once; and tell him that I protest
against any further performances of Cæsar with his abominable
mutilations. I told him what to do—to omit the third act. He was too
clever to do that; so he spoiled the 2nd 3rd & 4th acts instead, and
wrecked the play. May his soul perish for it!

It is always a mistake to trust to these people to alter a play. They see
the effects, but they dont see the preparation of the effects—the

gradual leading of the audience up to them. They cut the preparation out, and then are surprised because the effects miss fire.

Barker presented your introduction to Reinhardt, and sent him two letters & a telegram. Reinhardt took not the smallest notice of either your letter or Barker's. Barker naturally regards this as a Schweinerei of the first order.

Please challenge him (R) to a duel with redhot sabres at once.

I give Rodin a final sitting tomorrow (Tuesday the 8th) and leave for London by the 4 o'clock train, arriving at midnight.

GBS

PS. Barker says that the Roman army consisted of about half as many men as the crew of Captain Brassbound's ship at the little Court theatre. But that I could forgive. It is the cutting of the 4th act that rouses me to an implacable, vindictive fury. My play has been deliberately murdered.

To HARLEY GRANVILLE BARKER

[A/3; X/168]

Hotel Palais d'Orsay. Paris
7th May 1906

[Due to the illness of Rodin, which delayed the sittings, Shaw found it necessary to cancel a proposed trip to the Côte du Nord to visit the Hamons. Instead, he and Charlotte had participated on May Day in a mob demonstration which the French government had labelled a Revolution. He wrote to the *Labour Leader* on 2nd May (published 11th May): "As I spent Labor Day on the Place de la Republique, the only message that occurs to me is that it will presently be well to organise some means of protecting the public against the police and military. The Government here wishes to win the general election by suppressing a revolution. Unluckily there is no revolution to suppress. The Government therefore sends the police and the dragoons to shove and charge the lazy and law abiding Parisians until they are goaded into revolt. No use: the people simply WON'T revolt. But several respectable persons have been shoved and galloped over and even sabred. Surely it ought to be within the resources of modern democracy to find a remedy for this sort of official amateur revolution making. It is a clear interference with our business as scientific revolutionists."

Harold Bauer (1873–1951), a British virtuoso, had played the violin until Paderewski convinced him to study piano. He became one of the century's best-known concert artists. Felix Weingartner (1863–1942) was the noted German conductor of the Kaim concerts in Munich and of the Royal Orchestra in Berlin.]

My dear Barker

May the soul of Reinhardt scream through all eternity in boiling brimstone! The cut explains everything. It is that first scene of the 4th act that effects the modulation of the play into the serious key of the murder scene. I have written to Trebitsch about it. I do not see how the end of the 2nd act explains itself without the burning of the library.

We went to the Antoine the night before the revolution, and found it calmly closed—no reason alleged—got our money back. Went on with Trebitsch to the Grand Guignol and saw four out of five short plays, all fairly amusing, especially a farce with a guillotine in it. On the first of May Paris looked like London on Sunday. After breakfast I crossed the Rivoli; and as I live by bread I could see only two cabs about a mile and a mile and a half off respectively, and not twenty people between me and the horizon. In the afternoon we went to the Place de la Republique, where Charlotte clung to lamp posts to see over the people's heads, and got so furious when she saw a real crowd charged by real soldiers that she wanted to throw stones. By dignified strategy which did not at any time go to the length of absolutely running away, we left the field without wounds. In the evening we heard the Egmont overture, the choral fantasia (piano by Harold Bauer, who acted it capitally), and the 9th symphony. The chorus piffled into the sky borders rather feebly; but a few pretty nuances were achieved by the sopranos—mostly, as usual, ladies in reduced circumstances. The four principals (from the Opera—this was at the Opera) were awful. When the basso rose to plead for more harmonious sounds after Beethoven's humorous and even attractive cacophony, this creature set up—in French—an obscene and staggering uproar such as I never heard in my life, nearly splitting on the F. sharp (I wish he had). The chorus stuck to Schiller's German, and when the basso roared "Joie!" replied soberly "Freude" with rebukeful effect. So it went on, the operoarers singing "flamme prise au throne de Dieu" against the choral "Götterfunken," and the soprano indignant and bewildered because Weingartner wouldnt stop the band to let her smile and take breath in the wrong place. None of the four had ever heard of Beethoven, or could conceive that the public cared more for the band and the conductor than for them; but the tenor, after some

621

perplexed listening, rose to the occasion and was bully. Frantic demonstrations at the end.

Yesterday (Sunday), the elections, and the Canard Sauvage [Ibsen's *The Wild Duck*] at the Theatre Antoine. The garret scene was admirable; but there would not be room for it at the Court. It was played at great speed, and raced at the end of every act to get a curtain. Gregers, described by Relling as an expectorator of phrases, went full steam ahead all through. There was no character in Gina nor in old Ekdal—indeed there was no character in the acting at all as we understand it, but it was a bustling piece of work (to conceal Ibsen's deficiencies, no doubt); and Relling brought down the house at the end when he rounded on the Expectorator. Hialmar enjoyed himself enormously, and was amusing & convincing. Hedvig's voice was the voice of experienced and authoritative maturity; but she pulled off her pathos with professional efficiency. Stage management ad lib; Gregers and his father walked ten miles in the first act if they walked a foot.—I must finish.—Esmond be blowed!—I slipped and fell today in the Boul St Germain & tore my trousers scandalously in the face of all Paris.—We went to a Socialist election meeting on Saturday. It was just like any other Socialist meeting where the candidate has no chance & knows it.—Tomorrow I sit to Rodin for the last time; and we leave Paris for London by the 4 o'clock train.—All my photographs (9 dozen) are ruined by a defect in the shutter of my most expensive camera.—Love to Lillah.

G.B.S.

To ELLEN TERRY

[U(A)/10; X/117.e]

Harmer Green. Welwyn
27th May 1906

[Madge McIntosh (1873–1950), a young actress and producer, had toured America with Forbes-Robertson in 1904–5. She had just directed the Stage Society production of Brieux's *Maternité*, at the King's Hall on 8th April, in a translation by Charlotte Shaw (who had asked not to be credited in the programme). Edmund Gwenn (1877–1959), who was playing the rôle of the cockney Drinkwater, later became one of the most famous character actors in motion pictures. Charles George ("Chinese") Gordon (1833–85) was the fanatical military leader who held Khartoum against besieging forces for ten months before he was killed.]

Johnston Forbes-Robertson and Gertrude Elliott in
Cæsar and Cleopatra, London 1907
(*Photograph by Daily Mirror Studios*)

Ellen Terry as Lady Cicely Waynflete and Frederick Kerr as
Captain Brassbound in
Captain Brassbound's Conversion, 1906
(*Photograph by Foulsham & Banfield*)

My dear dearest Ellen

I should have attended to your letter ten days ago; but it would have been no use. What is wrong with Brassbound is not anything that is remediable. Drinkwater in the first act is not amusing. Brassbound in the second act is not thrilling. If it were not for the third act, in which Brassbound is very good at the end, whilst you have the beginning all in your hands, the play would be a failure. As it is, it is half a failure. It should draw £160 a night: it does draw rather less than £80. Without you, it draws £32. Roughly, you draw £40; and if you deduct from this the difference between Madge's salary and yours, there is a clear gain of from £16 to £20 a night in having you to play. Or rather the loss would be from £16 to £20 greater if you were not in the bill. I made Vedrenne ascertain this in a coldblooded way by advertising your absence on the Brighton night, so as to prove that the loss was not your fault.

Both Gwenn and Kerr are doing their best. But Kerr does not dare attempt anything beyond character acting. He is incurably *shy*. At the rehearsals I knew, when he gave up the end of the first act, and invented that slouch round and up past Barnes (character business), that the change of key into the grand style was beyond him. The sudden deep note that should prepare the second act should be the note of a bell, not of a banjo string. If that were a thing that any quantity of working at could get done, I should have worked at it. But at Kerr's age, you can either do it (in which case you *want* to do it) or you can't (in which case you daren't). The difficulty with [Laurence] Irving would have been to prevent him from doing it all through the play. Now Kerr *can* do the character business very well; so he insists on having business all through the play. In the second act there is no tiger for you to tame. There is no real danger in it for you, and so there is nothing for you to play against—at least nothing that seriously threatens you. I tried to make him feel this; but he only said that it was very hard to have the one serious part in a comic play. I have no right to complain: he does his best and does it very well. If he were discouraged he would be worse. The *fanaticism* of the part—the Gordon note—is not in his nature; and one does not like him personally any the worse for that. But he hasnt even *faith*: hence the shyness.

As to Gwenn, he plays like a steam hammer. His physical strength, his directness of character, his conscientious industry all make him more & more unlike Drinkwater the harder he works at him. The only seafaring character he could possibly play is Ham Peggotty [in Dickens's *David Copperfield*]. Unfortunately unless Drinkwater is as idiotically

623

funny as Robson or Dan Leno might perhaps have made him, he is a bore. Morally, he ought to be so obviously hopeless that it would not be a crime to laugh at him. Gwenn plays everybody off the stage, morally. Even Cremlin has no chance against him; and Kerr appears the merest heavy dragoon about town. Well, nothing that I can do can remedy that. You cannot expel Nature. We must try next time with another cast; and then I suppose the last scene will go wrong. *You* are all right. Ada Rehan is coming to see you play: she is due in England on the 2nd June.

G.B.S.

To LILLAH McCARTHY

[A/4; X/182.e]

Harmer Green. Welwyn
30th May 1906

[Barker had suddenly decided to be known professionally by his full name, Harley Granville Barker. He did not, however, hyphenate the Granville-Barker until after his second marriage. Lena Ashwell had achieved a great critical success in *The Shulamite* by Claude Askew and Edward Knoblauch at the Savoy Theatre on 12th May. *The Devil's Disciple* was revived at the Savoy Theatre on 14th October 1907, with Barker as General Burgoyne. He shifted rôles, playing Dick Dudgeon, when the production was transferred to the Queen's Theatre a month later. *Prunella, or, Love in a Garden*, by Laurence Housman and Barker, had originally been presented at the Royal Court Theatre in December 1904. It was revived on 24th April 1906.]

My dear Mrs Granville Barker (sounds imposing, doesnt it?)

You should not let Harley work after lunch. He will only muddle his morning's work & destroy his digestion. Stop it at once.

I cannot reconcile myself to his new name, which sounds harley appropriate. I wish you would call him Barker, or even B. Vulgar, but graphic & familiar.

Tell him that I am buried in Welwyn and have not seen the Shulamite. The Star system has gone up a little since Miss McIntosh drew only £32 in Brassbound.

Tell him further that the notion of engaging Esmond for Burgoyne was one of Vedrenne's Saturday to Monday sentimentalities. It was so grossly obvious that Arley would play it better and be much cheaper that VD yielded without a struggle.

I really cannot stand Harley. Let's call him Granny—Annie's Granny.

If the Shulamite is a success, it may mean that Hainley—there! this comes of calling a man Harley when his real name is Barker—that Ainley may soar into impossible terms. For I seriously think the Court Theatre must be transferred to a tent on Putney Heath. The returns for the week just to hand (I have by this time reached the 5th June—compare with the date above) are disgraceful: only £67-17-5 4/7 per performance. In short, Brassbound has been a failure; Barbara has been a failure; Candida has been a failure; You Never Can Tell has been a failure: the sole successes have been the two plays you appeared in; and now you have gone and shattered the dream by getting married. I ask you, how is the thing to go on?

I havnt even seen Prunella, and now it's over.

Tell Barley (this seems after all the best compromise) that a combination of all parties to reform the House of Lords is quite possible, as it is always a safe hare to start when Labor is too hot on the Socialist scent. Also the demand for disestablishment by the extreme Anglicans, who catch Larry Doyle's point of view as to the power of a Church independent of the Government, might serve his turn.

I have so much to say that I despair of getting it on paper before you come back; so it must wait until then. Thank you for the notes on Cleopatra.

It seems likely now that we shall build a house here (if we can get the site we want), and live meanwhile at Eyot St Laurence, a village at the other side of the Welwyn valley. We cannot get the house there until October, which leaves us three months for the seaside, possibly in Cornwall. But nothing is settled.

I am in such a hopeless mess with masses of unsettled affairs and undone work that I have grown reckless & rascally. Après moi le deluge!

Rodin writes that the bust is a success—that people divine my character from it and call me "a young Moses"!!! Justice at last—from a Frenchman, of course.

yours ever
G.B.S.

To WILLIAM ARCHER

Harmer Green. Welwyn
[L/2]   7th June 1906

[The portion of the *Major Barbara* preface which Shaw had enclosed was "First Aid to Critics." Ibsen had died on 23rd May; the *Clarion* article was an obituary notice by Shaw, published on 1st June 1906, declaring: "The greatest dramatic genius of the nineteenth century is dead, leaving most of our critics proud of having mistaken him for a criminal, an imbecile, and an ephemeral. Contemporary journalism, like democracy, is always a better judge of second-rate than of first-rate."]

(Dictated)

My dear Archer

Charlotte terrifies me by the news that you are going to let loose on the Continent a selection from the staggering hallucinations which you firmly believe to be a sound critical biography of my unfortunate self. Will you therefore read through & return to me the enclosed first draft—rather a scrawly one I am afraid—of part of the Preface to my next volume of plays. The Schopenhauer-Nietzsche stereo may not matter much in England, as it seems impossible to knock any national self-respect into English literary journalism; but when you are addressing a foreign audience you really must not talk as if England were an intellectual vacuum into which the ideas of half a dozen foreign writers rush like the east wind into the receiver of an air pump.

As to Kellner, he came to see me in 1898 on Hindhead,—played billiards with John Burns & Massingham whilst I was taken out for a walk on crutches by my nurse. Thenceforth I regarded him as having eaten my salt; so that I was not free to make a personal attack on him of any kind even if I'd wanted to, which I didnt; for Kellner struck me as being a very worthy chump. However, he wanted to translate some of my works; & I would not let him do it because it was absolutely necessary for me to find some young man who would devote himself to reproducing my entire œuvre in German, exactly as you have reproduced Ibsen in English, wheras all that Kellner wanted was to translate Candida, for which he had a snivelling affection, & perhaps to make a further selection of what he might happen to think worthy of me. I found my man in Trebitsch. Trebitsch began with Candida. He was foolish enough to rush a first edition of his translation into print before I had been through it. In his utter ignorance of London local government, & of the construction of front gardens in the Hackney road, & also of English Socialist literature, he came quite

626

indescribably to grief in Burgess's references to the Vestry, in the preliminary description of the neighborhood of Victoria Park, & in the list of books in Morell's library. Kellner, eine feste Burg of sound information on these & all other concrete points, took advantage of them to publish a slashing attack on poor Trebitsch, who was held up without mercy as an ignoramus & impostor, le dernier des derniers. Trebitsch has no power of defending himself against attacks of this kind; but he has fought 3 duels. He declared that Kellner was an infamy, & that he must give him an ear-box; & Kellner would probably have fallen beneath his avenging sabre if I had not pacified him by declaring my satisfaction with his translations.

In the meantime exactly the same thing had begun in Germany & Vienna as has been going on about your translations of Ibsen. Journalists who didnt know English tried to imply that they spoke it like natives by pooh poohing Trebitsch as impossible. Journalists who did know English & wanted to supplant him as translator did the same thing; & some of them actually wrote me private letters on the subject which might have made me very uncomfortable if I had not been warned by your experience, & known enough of German to be able to ascertain for myself that the case against Trebitsch rested on mistakes that did not matter & not on real incompetence. In short, there was Meyerfeld in Germany just as there was Gosse in England; & though I have no more reason to complain of Meyerfeld personally than you have of Gosse, everything was done that could be done to discredit Trebitsch with me. Naturally I was not going to let them play the Hedda Gabler trick on me. When they all jumped at Kellner's attack & rejoiced in it, I made it clear that I attributed a good deal of the hostility to him to the feeling of would-be rival translators. No doubt Kellner put the cap on—I shall not pretend to think it was altogether a misfit—but I of course did not attack him personally. As far as he was hit on the *ricochet*, he brought it on himself. His attack on Trebitsch was bitter & contemptuous; & the intention to damage Trebitsch to the utmost of his opportunity was unmistakeable. I went no further in my defence than loyalty to Trebitsch required: in fact Trebitsch was very rueful over the good humor with which I took his ill usage. . . .

Have you seen the enclosed Clarion article on Ibsen? As usual I have had to use up my space in contradiction of current fallacies rather than in affirmation of the old man's qualities: however, he can look after himself in that respect. Until I read the Monthly Review [June 1906: Archer's "Ibsen as I Knew Him"] I had no idea that you had seen so much of him. It throws a light on the gross secretiveness of your disposition. Apparently the only person you ever tell anything to is Charles [Archer].

G.B.S.

["Make your mind easy," Archer replied on 8th June, "I am neither addressing a foreign audience, nor am I talking about Schopenhauer and Nietzsche. Were it my cue to do so, I should not go to Meyerfeld for prompting. I am only giving, in the course of an interview on the German stage in general, some purely external data as to the performances of your plays. Of course nothing whatever is said as to rival translators or anything of that sort. I don't know how I came to mention Kellner's complaint to Mrs. Shaw, but anyway it had nothing to do with the interview. I respect your loyalty to Trebitsch, & I have no doubt he is useful; but since I read carefully about half of his version of the MAN OF DESTINY, I feel that you ought to insist on having his translations revised by some thoroughly competent German—your own German, unless it has vastly improved, is quite inadequate to cope with master T's enormities, which *must* present you in a distorted light to the German public. As he admits the fact of numerous errors, I don't see that he could reasonably object to a revision, so long as the right of ultimate decision rested with him" (BM).]

To ARCHIBALD HENDERSON

[C/7; X/141]

[Stevenage]
10th June 1906

[Henderson had sent Shaw the manuscript of a portion of the biography. The new volume of plays (*John Bull's Other Island, How He Lied to Her Husband, Major Barbara*) was delayed all through 1906, and did not appear until June 1907.]

I received the MS just as I was starting for Paris to sit to Rodin. So I sent it to the typists to be copied, and have since kept the two copies in different houses, to reduce risk of loss by fire &c. I shall presently send you back the original; but I shall work on the typed copy & correct it. It is a remarkable work; but there is no use being in a hurry about it, as it will improve in value every day. I have a bibliography, genealogy, & deuce knows what not for it. And you must come over and see me some time or other: the vision is still wildly romantic.

G.B.S.

PS I am just finishing the preface to John Bull's Other Island, which will soon, I hope, be in print.

To ELLEN TERRY

[A/34; X/183]

[Harmer Green. Welwyn]
[Undated: assigned to 11th June 1906]

[Ellen Terry celebrated her Stage Jubilee—fifty years in the theatre—on 12th June. A star matinée at Drury Lane and a public dinner afterwards, at which the Rt. Hon. Winston S. Churchill presided, realised £5783. In addition, a testimonial fund was organised by the newspaper *The Tribune* (presumably at the instigation of its new drama critic, William Archer) for public subscription. Shaw's contribution to the occasion was a personal tribute to Ellen, in verse.]

> Oh, Ellen, was it kind of Fate
> To make your youth so thrifty
> That you are young at fiftyeight
> Whilst we are old at fifty?
>
> Though for our sakes you strive to seem
> A tiny little older—
> To be the woman of our dream
> Yet leave our grandsons colder,
>
> They love you too. Change plays its part
> In every known direction
> Save your imperishable art
> And our unchanged affection.
>
> Joy be for ever by your side
> And roses all your bedding!
> Our stage could have no dearer bride
> To grace its golden wedding.

G.B.S.

To SIEGFRIED TREBITSCH

[H/5]

10 Adelphi Terrace W C
25th June 1906

[*Man and Superman* was produced by Max Reinhardt at his new Kammerspiele des Deutschen Theaters, Berlin, on 6th December 1906.]

My dear Trebitsch

If you allow Reinhardt to depart by one millimetre from the strict letter of my instructions, the Superman will [be] a disastrous failure. I

629

have been through all this clamor in London. All the wiseacres there were equally convinced that the play was unfit for the stage, especially without the third act. Nobody was such an utter idiot as to propose to play the dream with heads only visible; but they were quite sure that the play without the dream and the brigands would be uninteresting.

Tell Reinhardt that I will pay him £50, to surrender his contract and let us have the Superman back again. If he refuses, tell him that this time I will take steps to protect myself from having my work spoiled as he spoiled Cæsar. I am making the acquaintance of the German editors who are now visiting London, expressly that I may be able to use the press to appeal against any attempt to mutilate my play. My conditions are clear. The cuts will be made by me. They will include the whole third act, and a large part of the second half of the first act, just as I explained to you. Mendoza will not appear at all: his lines at the end of the fourth act will be spoken by Straker. There will be no cutting of the long speeches of Tanner: they must be spoken at full length not only on the first night but on every other night. I will not have this rascally chicanery of giving a play properly on the first night to secure good press notices, and then cheating the public with shortened and spoiled performances later on. It is no use telling me that it is always done in Germany: you might as well tell me that pockets are always being picked in Germany. If Reinhardt does not like my ideas of art and business he can write plays himself or go to other authors.

I most earnestly beg you not to put this aside as what you call a Shawish answer, and smooth over things with Reinhardt. If you do not like to deal with him in my fashion, tell me so; and I will write to him direct. I can easily get my letters translated here if he does not know English. I know that it is rather difficult for you to behave as if you were fifty, and were thoroughly practised in the way of handling managers; but it is still harder for me to throw away my advantages and let these people muddle my plays as if I were a beginner with no position and no experience of the stage. Besides, I am doing it as much for your sake as mine. You must learn to say No, and to throw money in the faces of the managers: otherwise they will go on believing that they have only to hold out and you will give in. You thought Schlenther would not give in about the agreement for Y.N.C.T. Well, he did give in. You threw away the Superman on a minor theatre because you thought—in spite of my assurances—that Schlenther would never do it at the Burg. He would have done it next year.

When you see Reinhardt, the FIRST thing to do is to offer him whatever money he advanced us on the Superman (I forget whether he advanced any) *and* £50 down to break the contract. If he accepts, I will pay the money at once. The effect of that on Reinhardt will be worth £100 to me. If he wants to know why, say that his violation of my instructions by performing the lighthouse scene in Caesar, and thereby sacrificing the fourth act and turning a success into a failure, has convinced me that he has not the necessary grasp of theatrical conditions to handle my plays, and that his monstrous proposal to do the dream with cuts and four heads has completed my disillusion. If he refuses the offer and sticks to the play, let it be clearly understood that he does so on my conditions, which are as I have stated them above. I shall also ask him to put upon the program a statement that the stage version has been made by the author; that the omission of the third act is in accordance with my instructions; and that the management placed themselves at my disposal in the matter and are not responsible for the cuts except in so far as they have had to admit that some cutting was necessary, as the play in its entirety would take nearly eight hours to perform.

You need not fear the result. I know what I am about, and the sort of people I am dealing with; and you, O Siegfried, are far too amiable to be left in the hands of these sharks. They take advantage of your inexperience. I dont want you to bully them. Be as nice as you like; but be inexorable.

I am afraid I have lost the post after all, confound it!

GBS

To EDITOR OF THE NEW YORK *WORLD*

[YY.u/9; X/198] [10 Adelphi Terrace W C]
[Undated: assigned to 6th July 1906]

[The New York Court of Special Sessions, on 6th July, acquitted Arnold Daly and the manager of the Garrick Theatre, Samuel Gumpertz, of the charge of immorality. In the opinion of the court "the complaining police officer, who was the sole witness, testified to no indecent or suggestive act on the part of any performer.

"The Court is called upon, therefore, to decide whether the language of the prompt-book, as spoken on the stage, was a public nuisance, per se, because offensive to public decency. There is nothing in the words themselves, or in any particular phrase or expression which can be said to be

631

indecent, and the Court is compelled to resort to the theme and motive of the play to find the indecency complained of.

"The theme is not a pleasant one. In fact, the play has to do with a courtesan's excuses for her calling. [The play is then summarized] . . .

"This attack on existing social conditions, particularly those which relate to the commercial employment of women, seems to be the motive which has led the playwright to present this unpleasant play-picture for public consideration. That his main idea is not the discussion of the social evil, so-called, seems to be demonstrated by the fact that not one of the characters of the play refutes the sophistical reasoning of the courtesan mother with the statement, which we judiciously know, that the woman of the street is not ordinarily driven to her choice of calling by anything other than her motive to obtain the luxuries of life without work; that the only social condition which would keep her from the life which she chooses would be one where man is not compelled to eat his bread in the sweat of his brow—where luxuries are furnished without money and without price.

"Surely the playwright is not so superficial a scholar that he is ignorant that the ordinary woman of the street is on the same plane with the common vagrant in this regard. In fact, the statute classes her with the vagrant.

"The dramatist has in this play used old and hackneyed materials, the common tools of scores of other playwrights; but he has used them more boldly—so boldly, in fact, that their tendency is to surprise and shock his audience. It must be said for him that he has in this play made vice less attractive than many other dramatists whose plays have never received the censorious attention of the police.

"While the Court may hold a decided opinion regarding the fitness of this play as a stage production, when it comes to consider the question of criminality of the acts of these defendants in publicly producing it, it must make application of the principle of law laid down by the Court of Appeals as the test of criminality.

"It appears that instead of exciting impure imagination in the mind of the spectator, that which is really excited is disgust; that the unlovely, the repellant, the disgusting in the play, are merely accessories to the main purpose of the drama, which is an attack on certain social conditions relating to the employment of women, which, the dramatist believes, as do many others with him, should be reformed" (*Wilshire's Magazine*, August 1906).

Upon learning the decision of the Court, the editor of the New York *World* cabled to Shaw: "WHATS YOUR OPINION AMERICAN MORALS NOW?"]

STRANGE COUNTRY WHERE THE PRESS IS BLIND AND THE EYES OF JUSTICE OPEN I AM PROFOUNDLY GRATEFUL

To EDITOR OF THE *NEW YORK AMERICAN*

[10 Adelphi Terrace W C]

[X/211]   [Undated: assigned to 6th July 1906]

[A similar request for a statement was made by the London representative of the *New York American*. The message, cabled to New York, was published the following day.]

I have nothing to say except to contrast my position in America. In America, every conceivable insult and outrage was heaped on me by the New York press, which forced the police to arrest Arnold Daly, and his whole company; but America has also given me my remedy.

My case has been heard and my play restored to the stage with its motives. My character and that of Mr. Daly and his company has been publicly vindicated.

Here I have no such remedy—the King's reader of plays takes the view of the New York newspaper men whose minds resemble his in most respects, and he keeps my plays from the stage without any possibility of my calling him to account. I have no redress. He is above all the courts.

I think America has the best of it this time. I certainly prefer the American system in this respect.

G. Bernard Shaw

To WILLIAM ARCHER

10 Adelphi Terrace W C

[A/2]   7th July 1906

[Archer's *Tribune* article on Gilbert and Sullivan was headed "A National Benefaction . . . Has the Time Come for a Revival?" In speaking of English translators of French comic operas, Archer had commented: "The French librettos fell into the hands of a tribe of hack adaptors congenitally deficient in metrical sense, who substituted for the graceful French lyrics abhorrent jingles equally devoid of metre and of meaning." Charles Lecocq was the composer of *La Fille de Madame Angot*, Jean-Robert Planquette of *Les Cloches de Corneville*, and Daniel-François Auber of *Fra Diavolo*. Strauss's *Salome* was first performed in London on 8th December 1910. F. Anstey's popular comedy *The Man from Blankley's* had been revived at the Haymarket Theatre on 24th March 1906.

Shaw had made his balloon ascension on 3rd July, in company with Barker, Robert Loraine, and Mary Cholmondeley. The balloon was the "Norfolk," piloted by Percival Spencer. Loraine described the adventure in his diary:

633

"Ascending from Wandsworth Gas Works we were soon floating above the clouds at about 9,000 feet, exhilarated but somewhat awed by our first experience of altitude. After about forty minutes' drifting, very pleasant and seraphic with nothing happening, except that Shaw would peer through a hole in the boarding at his feet which made him feel rather sick, we discussed landing. We wondered what our reception would be on coming down in somebody's garden. I thought the people would be rather interested to receive visitors from the air, and especially flattered when they discovered Shaw's identity. 'Don't be so certain,' said Shaw. 'They may think my works detestable.' Mr. Spencer, the aeronaut, assured us that no matter where we landed or who we might be, we should be overwhelmed by the warmth of our welcome owing to the unusual nature of our arrival.

"In due course [two and a half hours later] we came down on a field near Cobham Common, and after assisting to deflate the balloon, we turned to find ourselves surrounded by people who seemed to have appeared from nowhere. We were just going to tell them all about it, when a purple-faced individual came rushing towards us waving a shooting-stick. This he had the grace to hide when he saw Mrs. Cholmondel[e]y, but he was suffocating with fury, and the welcome he gave us was a curt direction as to the quickest way off his property" (Winifred Loraine, *Robert Loraine*, 1938).

Shaw eventually wove the incident into his play *Misalliance*, turning the balloon into an aeroplane, which crashes into the Tarletons' greenhouse.]

My dear Archer

There is an error in your Tribune article today which is of profound historical importance. Offenbach was a characteristic product of the Hohenstiehl-Schwangan empire. La Belle Helene could not possibly have been written after 1871. The genre gave a last kick in La Fille de Madame Angot, and was succeeded by Les Cloches de Corneville &c &c.

Also, you have smitten W.S.G. inadvertently in your contemptuous dismissal of the English adaptations of opera bouffe. One of the most popular of them was The Brigands; and the author of that adaptation was Gilbert.

I dont think it can be honestly said that any Gilbert-Sullivan opera touched La Grand Duchesse [de Gérolstein] or Fra Diavolo; and in my opinion a revival of Savoy opera would be resurrection pie with a good deal of ptomain in it. It is of considerable importance to have Strauss's Salome done here; but nobody will be the worse if The Pirates of Penzance &c are left on the shelf. Trial by Jury is the only really vital product of the collaboration: the rest were market pieces, with an entirely spurious air of what the Daily Telegraph calls "wholesomeness." Dont get sentimental about old times: you are much too young to play the veteran. Sullivan's operas are no more worth reviving than Robertson's plays. Call for a revival of Mrs Warren if you like.

This week I have seen The Man from Blankley's and been up in a balloon. I never saw a meaner play or felt more acutely what it would be like to stand on the tip top of the Eiffel Tower on one toe. Today I saw seven balloons from my window; and I thought I was mad until I called the parlormaid & found that she saw them too.

G.B.S.

To GILBERT MURRAY

10 Adelphi Terrace W C

[C/36]   10th July 1906

[Forbes-Robertson and Shaw were co-directing *Cæsar and Cleopatra*, which had just gone into rehearsal. Originally it was intended to send the production on a provincial tour, prior to Forbes-Robertson's visit to America, but this idea was eventually abandoned.]

At the rehearsals of Cæsar and Cleopatra there is much difference of opinion as to Mithridates of Pergamos. Mith*ridd*ities of Per*gay*mos sounds to me wrong: I incline towards Mithri*day*tes of *Perg*amos; but I have no settled convictions on the subject; and Robertson prefers Mithra*dy*tes of Per*gay*mos. How do you address the gentleman? Is P. Garmoss out of the question?

And is Clay O'Partrer admissible? Or Cleeopaytra. I say Cleeopattra, as she is usually called that in Ireland. Does Eupator rhyme to Equator or to Jupiter?

G.B.S.

To JOHNSTON FORBES-ROBERTSON

10 Adelphi Terrace W C

[A/1; X/167.e]   15th July 1906

[Shaw's concern for detail led him to prepare explicit dialogue for the extras in the crowd scenes, each receiving his own script containing speeches and stage directions. *Cæsar and Cleopatra* opened in New York at the New Amsterdam Theatre on 30th October 1906. *The Era*'s New York correspondent reported on 17th November: "The success of Mr Forbes Robertson and Miss Gertrude Elliott in this clever compound of truth, travesty, and satire, was most emphatic. Rarely has an audience shown such enthusiastic approval so early in the evening as was exhibited at the opening performance ... Mr. Shaw's paradoxical wit ... is quite *en rapport* with the American sense of humour ..."]

Address tomorrow—Pentillie, Mevagissey, Cornwall

Dear Forbes Robertson

Many thanks for your very kind letter—all the more welcome as I was afraid I had been worrying [you] too much at the rehearsals.

I enclose Gilbert Murray's reply to my inquiries. *Eu*pator is rather a surprise: I thought it rhymed to Equator.

I quite agree about the Burning of the Library: they would expect something like Nero. Alter anything that strikes you as wrong: I very seldom get a thing right at the first shot; & I corrected that program rather hastily.

The bucina will require a little management & the help of the conductor of the band or whoever does the music for the piece. The one thing to put your foot on is the use of a cornet. That easy and vulgar instrument is always at hand and always detestable except for sentimental melodies. If an ophicleide (which sounds like a bullock) can be got, it might be effective as the bucina. Or a tuba (bombardon) in E flat or B flat—the latter for preference. But probably the best thing is a tenor trombone, which is always easy to get. If only we could get some of the long trumpets which came in a few years ago as Bach trumpets, & which are often now played by music hall virtuosos, they would be just the thing for a few high ringing notes following the bellow of the bucina. Only, no cornets under any circumstances.

The Roman soldiers need have only one greave, on the right knee. That would be correct, and cheaper. The tunics in Cæsar's time came below the knee, as breeches were not worn. There is authority for the sword being either left or right. The soldiers' helmets were leather. But these things dont matter much unless they are convenient & handsome.

I enclose a bundle of papers I got Miss Dickens to do for the crowd in the 1st & 2nd acts, not having then got the 3rd & 4th. The idea is that you give one to each of the extras, & he (or she) fills in his (or her) line opposite the cue from dictation at rehearsal. Give them to Ian: they may save him the bother of copying out the cues for the first two acts at all events.

In haste, yrs ever
G. Bernard Shaw

To SIEGFRIED TREBITSCH

Pentillie. Mevagissey
19th July 1906

[The Shaws remained in Cornwall until 3rd September. Shaw had sent a letter for publication in the Socialist paper *Vorwärts*, which rejected it. He gave it instead to the *Berliner Tageblatt*, which published it on 25th July under the heading "Bernard Shaw über die deutsche Sozialdemokratie." *Vorwärts* reprinted it the following day under the heading "Heitere und ernste Missverständnisse." Max Reinhardt gave up direction of the Kleines Theater, Berlin, on 30th June 1906. The new director, Viktor Bornowsky, produced *You Never Can Tell* (known variously as *Man kann nie wissen* and *Der verlorene Vater*) on 24th September.]

My dear Trebitsch

You are giving yourself the most horrible worry and trouble for nothing at all. You are trying to fight the whole battle of my life over again, and to make it a series of surrenders instead of victories. Germany & Austria & the Viennese-Palace-Theatre-Chamberlain are all going to do just what I choose & not what they choose. Man & Superman will have the same title all over the world. Mensch und Übermensch is precisely right. Such a title as Der neue Don Juan, or Donna Juana, would mislead the public & create furious disappointment. Die Jagd nach dem Mann would belittle the play & drag it down to the level of the silliest & vulgarest of the critics. Mensch und Übermensch affirms its essentially philosophic quality & dignity. It has been so enormously successful merely as a title that the phrase has become a proverb in England & America; and so it shall in Germany.

Why, oh why, do you devote your life to translating me if you dont believe in me, and are ready to throw over my most carefully considered plans whenever some blockhead mentions the first objections that come into a fool's head in the first five minutes? You are too modest—too diffident. Well, as Drinkwater in Brassbound says, "If you want to be modest, be modest on your own account, not on mine." And when you find how successful my policy will be, you will try it on your own account too. . . .

There is a violent controversy going on about me in Berlin because I told the German editors that the Social-Democrats are too old fashioned & reactionary to dare print my articles in their papers.

637

What is the exact date of your departure from Marienbad? I am afraid of the M & S acts going astray.

yrs ever
G. Bernard Shaw

PS. The publication of the hell scene in the Rundschau is impossible: it is far too long; and it must not be mutilated. You will utterly ruin me by throwing my works in crumbs to the dogs instead of publishing them complete. And what is this Kleines Theater to which you are giving Y.N.C.T.? Why not the Grosses Theater?

To A. J. MARRIOTT

[S/1; X/126]

Pentillie. Mevagissey
1st August 1906

[The Mimram is a stream in Hertfordshire, quite close to Welwyn and Ayot St Lawrence. Harold Cox (1859–1936), a political economist and journalist, was at this time a Liberal M.P. for Preston.]

Dear Marriott

Certainly London is pretty bad; but I think it has passed its worst. The fact that it has begun to scatter is shewn by the way in which some of the schools have been emptying. Of course this scattering means the obliteration of the Welsh Harp and the filling up of such rural places as the valley of the Mimram with rows of houses; but this is better than the old congestion at the centre.

It is no use depending on the millionaires: what we have to do is to sit down and try to settle how many people should be let live on an acre of ground, and then pass a Building Act to enforce our conclusions. What maddens me is not so much to see houses cropping up over the old Sunday-outing places, but to see that they are cropping up in such a way as to form the beginnings of slums. It is our infernal improvidence and intellectual laziness that prevent us from stopping the reproduction in the country under our eyes of the evils that we have had such bitter experience of in towns.

You may remember from your reading that one of the things that infuriated the people under the old régime before the French Revolution was the furious driving of the nobles in their carriages. The motor car has shewn that the world is much the same now as it was 150 years ago. But the motor car is doing one good thing; it is reducing rents on the frontages of the main roads; and it is possible that this may help to popularize your idea of strips of public garden between the road and the houses.

But the more one thinks of it the more one is driven back to what I said before. It is no use grumbling: we must make up our minds as to exactly what we want; and then agitate for a national Building Act. Also, by the way, for a "Right to Roam" Act (as Harold Cox used to call it) putting a stop to the "Trespassers will be Prosecuted" business except in cases where mischief would be done. The worst of it is that our present city populations are so savage that they drive even the most public spirited people to put up barbed wire all over the place. They mean no harm; but if you let them near a bank of violets they leave it a mere dust heap, and are no more to be trusted with trees & animals than a baby can be trusted with a butterfly.

Excuse my being a very bad correspondent at most times. I am at the seaside now trying to get some leisure; but I have a sack of un-answered letters with me & havnt opened it yet.

yrs faithfully
G. Bernard Shaw

To ARCHIBALD HENDERSON

[H/7]
[Pentillie.] Mevagissey
11th August 1906

[The Brieux *Three Plays* consisted of *Maternity* (translated by Charlotte Shaw), *The Three Daughters of M. Dupont* (translated by St John Hankin), and *Damaged Goods* (translated by John Pollock), to which Shaw added a preface. The work, underwritten by Charlotte, was not published until May 1911. The new play was *The Doctor's Dilemma*. Shaw had begun the draft of the play (the last one he ever wrote in longhand) on that day; it was completed on 3rd September. Henderson did not come to London until June 1907. His article was "Aspects of Contemporary Fiction" published in the July issue of *The Arena*.]

My dear Henderson

I am taking what is called a holiday by the sea: that is, I am getting my work concentrated on me with an intensity impossible in London.

I am not at all insensible to the importance to you of getting the biography afloat; and I am not indifferent to it on my own account either, as its publication will save me a great deal of trouble and mis-representation. But this is a terrible year for me. Under the Berne Convention my copyrights lapse all over the continent in 1908 as far as the seven plays, pleasant and unpleasant, are concerned, unless I exercise my rights before then. This means that I must find out and enthuse and set to work deputy Bernard Shaws in every country in Europe. . . . Then John Bull and Barbara have to be provided with prefaces (just finished, thank heaven) and seen through the press. I have also to write a preface to three plays of Brieux which my wife is going to publish in English. I have been forced by events to write certain political communications to the press about current events. One of them, a letter [in] the Berliner Tagblatt about German Social-Democracy, has made a sensation which may involve me in further correspondence. Then the fortunes of the Court Theatre depend on my writing a new play this year; and not until this morning had I a notion of what it is to be about. I know now, and will probably be unable to resist working at it to the neglect of everything else. Add to all this as much ordinary business arising out of my theatrical interests in Europe and America as any merchant has to deal with, and several years arrears of correspondence hanging round my neck, and you will see that I am not neglecting you without some excuse.

What I hope to do is to wait until you send me the rest of your MS, when I will get it copied as before, and then turn myself completely on to it as if it were a book of my own. If within the next six months you can come to England for a while, so much the better, as it is not desirable that the only American now living who has not called on me should be my biographer. There are, in fact, signs here and there in your manuscript, that you still regard me as a fantastic figure in a Pantheon rather than as a human being. I cannot put you up in London, because our flat overlooking the river is too small; but you could stay with us for a while in our country retreat for week ends in Hertfordshire and get thoroughly disillusioned. By that time we might have the book in type if we decide to print it ourselves in England, and have it sold, like my own works, by my own publisher on commission. I could advance the cost of this (practically this would mean its being done by my printers and binders on my credit), and when I got the cost back, then you could come in and get the profits. I could also propose to my German translator, Siegfried Trebitsch, to translate the book and share with you half-and-half in Germany as he does with me. Brentano would be your best publisher in America. You could make your own bargain with him or you could even let him have the English rights as well (as in the case of The Irrational Knot) so that he could export the book to England ready printed and exploit it there, saving the cost of a separate setting up of the type. However, we can discuss these plans when we are ready for print. . . . The book should be an important professional one—a *debut* for you into first class literature; and there must be nothing of the smart journalistic *pièce d'occasion* about it: you have put your back into it; and you must come in on the top grade, every inch a university professor. You see, if you make yourself an ornament to the University of N.C. you will be able to make them let you spend six months of every year in some civilized place, and finally become wholly independent of teaching differentials to passmen, which ought not to be the final doom of a mathematician.

I am sorry to have to add that since I began this letter two days ago, I have begun the new play, and am already through the best part of the first act. This means a devouring and importunate job; but I think I see my way through quickly. The subject is modern serumpathy, if you know what that is. My hero will be a doctor.

And so farewell for the moment. Be patient: there is an end to everything, even to my biography.

Your article has come; but Granville Barker is reading it; so I shall not see it until I have to close & post this.

yrs ever
G. Bernard Shaw

To WILLIAM POEL

Pentillie. Mevagissey
[A/1]   14th August 1906

[William Poel (1852–1934) was an actor, manager, and scholar, who had founded the Elizabethan Stage Society. He appeared as Peter Keegan in *John Bull's Other Island* at the Royal Court Theatre on 17th September.]

My dear Poel
    I hear you are going to have a shot at Keegan.
    Do not make any attempt to *act* Keegan. Do not confuse yourself with any theory as to what John Bull's Other Island may be—comedy, tragedy, or farce. My plays are not planned for any calculation of that sort. They come right only when the actor, abandoning all idea of acting, discovers himself in the part and abounds in it for all he is

worth. This is especially true of a part like Keegan, which is poetic all through. You can do as you like in it without bothering about the rest: if only we can get Keegan, Broadbent, Larry and Ireland on the stage, the balance will be automatic. You need not make up; you need not wear a wig; you need not change your coat (provided its a longish black one): you need only steep yourself in the part & forget everything else. If anything technical needs a lift here or there, Barker can look after it.

The most difficult speech, technically, is the long one in the last scene about the liquidations. The speeches about the world being hell, and about the Hindoo, which Barker thinks difficult, are really safer: the audience always listens to them attentively, whereas the other has to [be] forced on them a little by adroit intensifications here & there— Barker knows them.

Keegan plays a very important part silently in the atrocious scene of the recital of the pig story by Doran. It is his presence that keeps the scene human. He really feels in hell. And I need not tell you that the effect is very mixed; for the audience are caught one way by the infection of Doran's barbarous fun (which they also foolishly think the proper Irish thing) and are consequently as much rebuked by Keegan's attitude as the laughers on the stage. But this is an effect that makes itself *if you know about it*, a matter as to which I have no doubt in your case.

I am curious to see what you will make of it, or what it will make of you. You are not an empty spook wandering in search of a fictitious romantic soul; and you are not a tomfool. Consequently you are very dependent on finding a part in which you can be more really yourself than you can be in actual life. I hope you will find something of the sort in Keegan.—Post hour: I must close hastily.

G. Bernard Shaw

To SIEGFRIED TREBITSCH

[Pentillie.] Mevagissey
[A/5]   18th August 1906

[Hamon's French translation of *Candida* was performed for four matinées commencing 4th February 1907 at the Théâtre Royal du Parc, Brussels, with Mlle Alice Archainbaud in the title part. *Ein Wagnerbrevier* (*The Perfect Wagnerite*) was published in 1907 with a new chapter and preface by Shaw.]

My dear Trebitsch

... The Superman dream has been very troublesome because it requires exact translation. You have in several places thought I was writing poetry when I was writing the most rigidly scientific psychology. I have just come to a place where you have translated the bob of a pendulum as a "triple bob major" rung on a peal of church bells. This makes a sort of glorious nonsense suggestive of the music of the spheres; but as I was carrying out the mechanical idea of the pendulum with the most careful exactitude, it knocks the whole argument to pieces. Again, what Don Juan says about the evolution of the brain may be a rather transcendental sort of physiology; but it *is* physiology and not poetic metaphor, and should be translated as if it were a scientific treatise. It is quite amazing how well you have succeeded; but it is still more amazing that, understanding it so well, you should have let one or two passages pass as sheer nonsense. I rub this into you because you must not underrate the importance of my corrections. I often have to go behind the popular use of a word into its etymology to get it quite right; and though you may think it mere pedantry on my part to reject "unbedeutungsvoll" as an equivalent for "irrelevant," I dont do so without good reason. I never alter anything merely because it says the thing in a different way to me: only when it alters the meaning or risks an ambiguity do I question it. And of course I may sometimes be quite wrong, owing to my ignorance of German usage. When I am, disregard my corrections.

I am sorry to say that my unfortunate French translator has become desperate, as he will lose a production at Brussels unless I immediately send him back Candida & You Never Can Tell (which I have had for months) with my corrections. Also I have begun a new play which must be ready at the Court Theatre by the end of October. I have received the Wagner Brevier safely. The copyright is safe: I wrote it in 1898; so 1892 is impossible. I hope you have the corrected English edition instead of the American one, which is a mass of errors.

Yesterday I had to stop working through a colossal headache.

ever
G. Bernard Shaw

Pentillie. Mevagissey
[A/4; X/182]   1st September 1906

[In her autobiography, *Myself and My Friends* (1933), written a number of
years after her divorce, Lillah McCarthy deleted or altered, in this and other
letters, all references to Granville Barker. In all the letters published in the
present edition the original text has been restored.]

My dear Lillah

I have instructed Archer to announce that you will play the heroine
of The Doctor's Dilemma. It will be a lucky play, as this morning,
coming up from the beach by a special act of Providence (to retrieve a
book Charlotte had lost) I found in my path a most beautiful snake,
two feet long, with an exquisite little head about the size of the tip of
your little finger, and a perfect design in lozenges on its back. It stayed
nearly two minutes (the first ten seconds of which were spent in hissing
at me) and then went away, sometimes tumbling down a precipice two
feet high into a heap of rings, sometimes gliding through the grass. It
finally vanished into a bramble; but we parted the best of friends; and
I am now convinced that The Doctor's Dilemma will be a complete
success for you, for me, for the Court & for the universe.

After all, the snake had not much of a part; but its figure produced
an extraordinary poetic effect.

However, the setting was good. It was a very fine day & the sun was
blazing on the creature's lozenges. It would not have produced any
effect at all in the Brighton Aquarium. The moral is, that a salary is
not everything. Although in view of the recent returns at the Court, I
think you may want all you can get to save H.G.B. from having to go
on tour at thirty shillings a week, yet there is no golden rule as to
taking big salaries & doing anything you are paid for; for it is no use
making yourself dear in order to make yourself cheap. Whenever they
make you an offer, say, Shew me the play. Miss Evelyn Millard did
that years ago when they offered her an engagement at the Haymarket
to play Gloria. They shewed her the play; and she said No. Now she
was wrong to say No; but she was right to insist on seeing the book &
to refuse the engagement, rather than let herself be seen to disadvantage
(as she thought).

I wish you would suggest a name for yourself in this new play. I
cannot very well call the lady Lillah. Provisionally I have called her
Andromeda; but Mrs Andromeda Dubedat is too long. Here in King
Arthur's country the name Guinevere survives as Jennifer; but that

does not hit it exactly either. I have used up such a lot of good names that I am driven back on the more artificial ones.

I have a hochnäsig letter from H.G.B. in which he will not have the new play at any price before January. But it is not clear what is going to happen to John Bull & The Superman. They may be exhausted. Six matinees of a new play may be needed to freshen the boom and avert ruin. For Heaven's sake do not sign for the run of anything until we have very carefully considered the situation. I am writing at the rate of an act a week; and I know exactly what is coming: there is no abyss to be filled up as in Barbara. It is just screaming, every line of it.

He [Barker] has, I presume, told you about the dresses. They can be done for the £100, I think, on *your* back. On anybody else's, £800.

yours ever
G.B.S.

P.S. We expect to arrive in town on Monday evening in time for dinner.

To G. K. CHESTERTON

10 Adelphi Terrace W C

[A/1; X/203.e] 6th September 1906

[Gilbert Keith Chesterton (1874–1936), novelist, essayist, biographer, and journalist, one of the most colourful figures in English letters, was the one man besides Shaw whom the public instantly recognised by his initials. Chesterton had just published a study of Dickens. Of the Dickens characters that Shaw mentions, Silas Wegg, Mr Venus, Rogue Riderhood, "Fascination" Fledgeby, and Alfred Lammle appear in *Our Mutual Friend*; Mrs Nickleby, Wackford Squeers, and Mantalini in *Nicholas Nickleby*; Flora Finching, Arthur Clennam, Edmund Sparkler, Mr F's aunt, and John Chivery in *Little Dorrit*; Capt. Jack Bunsby in *Dombey and Son*; Bill Sikes in *Oliver Twist*; Jerry Cruncher in *A Tale of Two Cities*; Trabbs's boy and Mr Wopsle in *Great Expectations*; Dick Swiveller in *The Old Curiosity Shop*; Mrs Sapsea, Bazzard, and Rev. Luke Honeythunder in *The Mystery of Edwin Drood*.

All the Year Round commenced publication in April 1859. *Household Words* was absorbed into *All the Year Round* at the end of May 1859. Shaw was right in recalling that there had been an original unhappy ending to *Great Expectations*. However, as he recorded in his preface to the Limited Editions Club edition of *Great Expectations* (1937), he had read the ending, not in *All the Year Round*, but in *The Clarion* on 16th May 1902.]

Dear G.K.C.

As I am a supersaturated Dickensite, I pounced on your book & read it, as Wegg read Gibbon & other authors, right slap through.

In view of a second edition, let me hastily note for you one or two matters.

First and chiefly, a fantastic and colossal howler in the best manner of Mrs Nickleby & Flora Finching.

There is an association in your mind (well founded) between the quarrell over Dickens's determination to explain his matrimonial difficulty to the public, and the firm of Bradbury & Evans. There is also an association (equally well founded) between B & E. & Punch. They were the publishers of Punch. But to gravely tell the XX century that Dickens wanted to publish his explanation in Punch is gas & gaiters carried to an incredible pitch of absurdity. The facts are: B & E were the publishers of Household Words. They objected to Dickens explaining in H.W. He insisted. They said that in that case they must take H.W. out of his hands. Dickens, like a lion threatened with ostracism by a louse in his tail, published his explanation, which stands to this day, and informed his readers that they were to ask in future, not for Household Words, but for All The Year Round. Household Words, left Dickensless, gasped for a few weeks & died. All The Y.R., in exactly the same format, flourished & entered largely into the diet of my youth.

Great Expectations was published in All The Year Round (I was Pip to the life when I first read it) with the unhappy ending, which will, I hope, soon be accepted as the classic one. The alteration was made later at Lytton's suggestions, and under economic pressure probably; but the original version actually got into print and on record as above[.]

Dickens's moderation in drinking must be interpreted according to the old standard for mail coach travellers. In the Staplehurst railway accident, a few years before his death, he congratulated himself on having a bottle and a half of brandy with him; and he killed several of the survivors by administering hatfulls of it as first aid. I invite you to consider the effect on the public mind if, in a railway accident today, Mr Gilbert Chesterton were reported as having been in the train with a bottle and a half of brandy on his person as normal refreshment.

There is a curious contrast between Dickens's sentimental indiscretions concerning his marriage & his sorrows & quarrels, and his impenetrable reserve about himself as displayed in his published correspondence. He writes to his family about waiters, about hotels, about screeching tumblers of hot brandy and water, and about the seasick man in the next berth, but never one really intimate word, never a real confession of his soul. David Copperfield is a failure as an autobiography because when he comes to deal with the grown-up David, you find that he has not the slightest intention of telling you the truth—or indeed anything—about himself. Even the child David is more remarkable for the reserves than for the revelations: he falls back on fiction at every turn. Clennam and Pip are the real autobiographies.

I find that Dickens is at his greatest after the social awakening which produced Hard Times. Little Dorrit is an enormous work. The change is partly the disillusion produced by the unveiling of capitalist civilization, but partly also Dickens's discovery of the gulf between himself as a man of genius & the public. That he did not realize this early is shewn by the fact that he found out his wife *before he married her* as much too small for the job, and yet plumbed the difference so inadequately that he married her thinking he could go through with it. When the situation became intolerable, he must have faced the fact that there was something more than "incompatibilities" between him and the average man & woman. Little Dorrit is written, like all the later books, frankly & somewhat sadly, *de haut en bas*. In them Dickens recognizes that quite everyday men are as grotesque as Bunsby. Sparkler, one of the most extravagant of all his gargoyles, is an untouched photograph almost. Wegg & Riderhood are sinister and terrifying because they are simply real, which Squeers & Sikes are not. And please remark that whilst Squeers & Sikes have their speeches written with anxious verisimilitude (comparatively) Wegg says, "Man shrouds and grapple, Mr Venus, or she dies" and Riderhood describes Lightwood's sherry (when retracting his confession) as, "I will not say a hocussed wine, but a wine as was far from elthy for the mind." Dickens doesnt care what he makes Wegg or Riderhood or Sparkler or Mr F's aunt say, because he knows them & has got them, and knows what matters & what doesnt. Fledgeby, Lammle, Jerry Cruncher, Trabbs's boy, Wopsle, &c &c, are human beings as seen by a master. Swiveller & Mantalini are human beings as seen by Trabbs's boy. Sometimes Trabbs's boy has the happier touch. When I am told that young John Chivery (whose epitaphs you ignore whilst quoting Mrs Sapsea's) would have gone barefoot through the prison against rules for Little Dorrit had it been paved with red hot ploughshares, I am not so affected by his chivalry as by Swiveller's exclamation when he gets the legacy—"For she [the Marchioness] shall walk in silk attire & siller hae to spare." Edwin Drood is no good, in spite of the stone throwing boy,

Bazzard & Honeythunder. Dickens was a dead man before he began it. [Wilkie] Collins corrupted him with plots. And oh! the Philistinism! the utter detachment from the great human heritage of art & philosophy! Why not a sermon on that?

G.B.S.

To H. G. WELLS

[H/26]

10 Adelphi Terrace W C
11th September 1906

["This Misery of Boots," a paper read by Wells to the Fabian Society on 12th January 1906, was published by the Society in 1907. G.K.Chesterton, in an article, "The Darkness of Virtue," in his weekly column in the *Daily News* on 28th July 1906, had written: "In my youth I had a scheme for a kind of ethical university which should achieve this end by conferring degrees upon people—all sorts and conditions of people—in accordance with their moral behaviour and the general social impression they produced upon their equals and comrades. If a man had certain letters after his name it would mean that he had created a certain favourable impression upon his circle. Thus the degree of N.B. ('Not Bad') would be taken before the degree of N.H.B. or 'Not Half Bad.' . . . [But] I am afraid that my moral [heroes], the men who really achieved the gowns and degrees, would be really quite nasty people, as nasty as Mr. H.G.Wells's Samurai or any other prigs."

Spade House was Wells's home at Sandgate, near Folkestone. The Shaws had visited there the first week in April 1905 (on which occasion they had met Gerhart Hauptmann), and Shaw had returned in November and December 1905. As the Special Committee's report was not officially presented to the Fabian Executive until October, it is obvious that Charlotte, who was Secretary of the Special Committee, had given him a copy.]

Horatio Gustavus Wells

First, my hearty curse on you for compelling me to write you a letter when I am horribly pressed with necessary business, Fabian and other.

You sit down and write to Pease telling him that the Boot tract is at the disposal of the Publishing Committee (or the Executive) to strike out any passages they think injudicious.

Some time ago Gilbert Chesterton enlivened a Daily News article by mentioning, quite gratuitously (except for the satisfaction of the boyish impulse to put out his tongue at the man on the other side of the street) "Mr Wells's prigs of Samurai." Remonstrance being made by some sane person who was shocked at this breach of good manners and good feeling, Gilbert owned up, and said he really didnt mean any harm.

Now suppose we publish something of Chesterton's in this new series of tracts. Suppose he gives us a good socialistic article to republish, which would be very good business for us. And suppose, when it is read at the publishing committee, it is found to contain an important assurance that Socialism does not mean making us all into an impossible lot of prigs called Samurai, and that on the Publishing Committee requesting him to omit that sally, he refuses to alter a line of the article on the grounds (a) that Wells would be the last man to endorse the ridiculous objection of the committee, and that (b) it is to him (Gilbert) quite vital to disavow the priggish conceptions of Socialism that have got into circulation, what would you expect us to do?

Come! indicate our line of conduct in this hypothetical case, and distinguish it, if you can, from your own. And remember, as the mantling blush oerspreads your extensive cheek, that you discussed these very passages with me personally at Spade House as ever was, and admitted—nay, chucklingly gloried in the obvious fact—that they were deliberate gibes, and would naturally come out in the permanent Fabian edition of the paper.

Remember also, that the municipalization of gas and water is Socialism in gas and water, and that the contrary belief (of which the Social-Democratic Federation is the recognized exponent) is gas and gaiters. Remember also, that there is such a thing as intellectual loyalty, and that though it is quite natural and proper for the stockbroker on the Leas to sneer instinctively at Nietzsche, it would be for the Fabian an act of unpardonable Philistinism and for you personally an act of the blackest treachery. From your Martians to your Samurai, what have you been preaching all your life but the Superman? and what have you to say of Brer Nietzsche that does not recoil on your own head?

Write to Pease by return of post—wire—take a motor car and tell him in person, with ashes on your hat.

yrs ever
G. Bernard Shaw

PS. I have read your report. It is Webbism gone mad. However, I will explain that to you later on. Meanwhile (since you never think of such things) remember that it is not etiquet to issue your report until the sub-committees have reported; so be careful to conciliate them on this score or there will be ructions.

10 Adelphi Terrace W C
[H&A/26]   [Undated: assigned to 14th September 1906]

[Wells's new novel *In the Days of the Comet* had just been published. He was elected in March 1907 to the Fabian Executive Committee, which was expanded in that year from 15 to 21 members. Prince Rupert's toy "drops" were glass bubbles, invented in Holland. Each bubble had a tail, and if the smallest part of the tail was broken off the bubble exploded. James Brudenell (1797–1868), 7th Earl of Cardigan, was the cavalry commander who led the famous charge of the Light Brigade in the Crimea (1854). Lewis Edward Nolan (1820–54) was the soldier who had insulted Lord Cardigan. The Croydon lecture, on " Socialism and the Middle Class" had been scheduled for 25th October 1906. Wells lectured to the Fabians on the same topic on 12th October. Mr Hoopdriver is the protagonist of Wells's novel *The Wheels of Chance* (1896). *Kipps: The Story of a Simple Soul* was published in October 1905.]

My dear H.G.W.

May I without indelicacy ask whether Jane has been unusually trying of late? Can it be that during your absence in America that Roman matron has formed an attachment for some man of genius nearer home—I will name no names, but, say, one whose more mature judgment, more majestic stature, more amiable disposition, and more obvious devotion to her person, has placed you at a disadvantage in her eyes? At all events, when I take the opportunity presented by a letter of my wife's which I am asked to correct (and touch up), to invite myself to Spade House for a week-end, and when the recipient of that invitation (for such it was), instead of expressing the delight with which he looks forward to my arrival, morosely declines to take the hint and compels me to go up the river with Barker, I feel justified in demanding whether he considers himself a gentleman. Surely something is due to Hospitality in the abstract if not to me in the concrete. I am the last man to thrust myself in where I am not welcome; but I cannot help suspecting that some reason beyond the mere exhaustion of my conversation is at work here. What is all this in the Comet about a *menage à quatre*? What does it mean? Why does the book break off so abruptly? Why not take some green gas and be frank? I have never concealed my affection for Jane. If the moroseness and discontent which have marked your conduct of late are the symptoms of a hidden passion for Charlotte, say so like a man. She takes a great interest in you—one which might easily ripen into a deeper feeling if ardently cultivated. It seems hardly possible that she can be tired of

Shaw and H. G. Wells, Spade House, Sandgate,
2nd November 1905
(*Photograph by Alvin Langdon Coburn*)

me: still, the first freshness is undoubtedly rubbed off our union. On the other hand Jane MUST be tired of you if you go on at her the way you have been lately going on at me. Well, a single example is worth all the fine writing and all the fictitious comets in the world. Jane is an extremely nice woman; and I doubt if you have ever appreciated her. I have always had an exceptionally open mind on these subjects. Do not let a mere legal technicality stand between us. If you would like to make it a group marriage, and can get round Charlotte, and Jane doesnt mind (if she does, I can at least be a father to her), you need apprehend no superstitious difficulties on my part.

As you say, we are a lot of rich and comfortable sentimentalists, fiddling while Rome is starving. And therein lies a peril to the poor Fabian. I have had 22 years of the Fabian. There must be an end of it someday. There are not wanting those who say that it has done its work. It hasnt; but *I* have done *my* turn. Webb has done his turn. The old gang has done its turn. Pease has burnt his boats and must stick to the ship because he cannot afford to drop his £150 a year; but you have no idea how strong the temptation is for the rest of us to unload on you. We have done enough for honor: why not let you walk over? If you really mean business; if you will steer that crazy little craft for five years to come, making the best of it no matter how ridiculously it may disappoint you, I will abdicate and the others will do the same. That is the real and hideous danger that confronts you.

You had much better come on the executive for a year or two before you commit yourself. You have no idea—nobody without actual experience can have any idea—of the instability of these little beginnings of social crystallization. They are like Prince Rupert's drops: they fly into fragments at the slightest nip. The energy that wastes itself in senseless quarrelling would reform the world three times over if it could be concentrated and brought to bear on Socialism. The whole thing is so ridiculous that if you once let your mind turn from your political object to criticism of the conduct and personality of the men round you, you are lost. Instantly you find them insufferable; they find you the same; and the problem of how to get rid of one another supersedes Socialism, to the great advantage of the capitalist. Lord Cardigan riding into the Balaclava charge with his mind wholly preoccupied with the fact that Nolan had insulted him personally is a type of the sort of human material you have to work with. Here are you, a quite exceptionally reasonable and strongminded man, already turned completely from your message to the Fabian by an irresistible impulse to expose the futility of the lot of us. You want to play the part of the Comet;

651

and you sit down to make yourself wretched by insisting on the jerki-
ness of Bland's literary style. Figure that to yourself from any point of
view remote enough from Bland to prevent his blotting out the sun
from you; and then imagine yourself with a committee of a dozen
Wellses, bound to make the most of them, forced to recognize that so
far from their being bad material, they are exceptionally good material,
and able to do nothing unless you can drive them all twelve-in-hand,
although their soft mouths and sore heads make it certain that the
first impatient word that escapes you will send them all kicking and
snorting in different directions. Then you will begin to see what you
are up against just now.

I dont myself believe that you are going to do more with the Fabian
than we have done; but you can use it, as we have done, as an instrument for increasing your own efficiency. You cannot go on spinning
comets out of your head for ever. You have done Kipps; and you have
done the Comet hero; and having done them you will dry up like
Kipling unless by a continuous activity you push your experience
further. You must get the committee habit: that is, you must learn the
habits of the human political animal as a naturalist learns the habits of
wasps, by watching them. And you must learn their possibilities by
trying to accomplish definite political ends through them. You must
acquire the personal force of the practised speaker (and not entrap a
few poor devils in Croydon into engaging a public hall, and then leave
ME to save them from ruin by taking your place on the platform).
You must, in short, learn your business as a propagandist and peripa-
tetic philosopher if you are ever to be anything more than a novelist
bombinating in vacuo except for a touch of reality gained in your early
life. We have all been throug[h] the Dickens blacking factory; and we
are all socialists by reaction against that; but the world wants from men
of genius what they have divined as well as what they have gone
through. You must end either in being nothing, or in being something
more than a man with a grievance, which is what your Comet chap
is. I was accidentally and externally a clerk like him once; but really I
was a prince. Your Kippses and people are true to nature, or rather to
modern civilization, just as David Copperfield's dread of Littimer
[confidential servant of Steerforth] and his adventures with his landlady are true to civilization; but David Copperfield is not a man at all:
Dickens has never for a moment given himself away in that book; and
your Hoopdrivers & Kippses & Comet man, though excellent as
demonstrations, are mere masks behind which you hide yourself. You
are always bragging that you have been Kipps & that you know. This is

a quintessential lie: if you had been Kipps you wouldnt know. If you said "I am God: and I know," it would be more to the point. Well, now that Kipps is demonstrated, you must learn a new trade—the Fabian trade. And the product will be, not a suite of offices & a million subscribers, but an approfounded and disillusioned and more variously effective Wells.—I am off to Ireland today & havnt time for more. Address:—Castle Haven. Castle Townshend. Skibbereen. Co. Cork.

GBS

To H. G. WELLS

[A/26]

Castle Haven [Rectory]. Castle Townshend
22nd September 1906

[The Shaws visited Ireland from 14th September to 6th October. Wells had replied to Shaw on 18th September: "You write the most gorgeous letters. I bow down. You are wonderful. The amazing thing is that just at one point the wonderfulness stops short. Why *dont* you see how entirely I am expressing *you* in all these things. . . . Fall in with my tri-umvirate. (They'll never elect me)." The letter was signed "H.G.B.Shawells" (BM). Wells's idea of a "triumvirate" leadership for the Fabian Society (Shaw frequently referred to it as a "troika") was incorporated in the Report of the Special Committee.]

My dear H.G.W.

The triumvirates will be wrecked by Democracy with a large D. A triumvirate would have no power at all, any more than the Czar has. It would be a fatal mistake for you to accept office as a triumvir; and I should refuse with a flourish, as the others would. The executive is in effect so autocratic that the society is always a little on the defensive; and when a new man gets on, he generally comes in to make a stand against the domination of the old gang. Muggeridge will tell you what happens. The new man finds that he has nothing to object to; that he has his say & is friendly entreated; and that if he finds that there is very little for him to do, it is because he is a fifth wheel to the coach, and not in the least because he is denied his place on the axle. Also he finds that the executive works well; that its smoking & joking lubricate its discussions; and that its business gets rather over- than under-debated.

Out of this comes the difficulty that it is not always easy to retain good recruits. For instance, we cannot keep capable women. Mrs

653

Besant & Mrs Stanton Blatch were the forerunners of a long string of really energetic women who have come on the executive and gone off again on discovering that they were fifth wheels—that the work was being done as well as it could be done by the old lot; that they were not being tyrannized or ignored; that there were no practical grievances; in short, that there was nothing for them to do except what was being done equally well without them. This was not quite true: once a year they made a difference; but that was not value enough for their time & trouble: they would not spend three years marking time for the sake of kicking a small stone out of the way three times or less.

It has been the same with all the men who have not found the executive atmosphere specially congenial to them. I planned for years to get the late William Clarke, for instance, on the executive; but he was a cantankerous man, and would not attend for the fun of the thing; so he really made no difference and dropped it. And here you have the real difficulty about new blood. We want a new set to unload on, and have wanted it for a long time past; but we automatically repel the capable, because the capable will not take up a burden which is being carried by somebody else in a manner which, on close examination, proves to be as efficient as is possible under the circumstances. If you came on the executive—which is a thing much to be desired by us—you would retire at the end of two years at the very outside unless you personally enjoyed it, or unless you could develop & lead a new policy (and we have tried all the new policies years ago). I think you would have a good chance of really catching on; but what is most to be feared in the event of your failing to acquire the executive habit—that is, of finding the executive, on the whole, rather amusing—is your becoming convinced that old Pease & old Shaw & old Webb & old Bland & the rest were getting all that was to be got out of the poor old Fabian, and saving your own time & energy for literature at large.

Fortunately, you are the sort of man that does not finish his education, and always wants a school. Well, the Fabian is a school for the exercise & development of certain personal powers—committee power, public speaking & debating &c—and that might hold you a little.

Now as to the democratic point. Democracy does not mean government of the Fabians by the Fabians & never can mean it; but it does mean government of the Fabians by consent of the Fabians. The Fabians put up with me because they know that they can chuck me when they please. And as I am tolerably confident that they wont please, I cling to the arrangement. My position as a triumvir would be far more precarious; and so would yours. If I supported the triumvirate scheme they would regard it (rightly) as an attempt on my part to make myself independent of them & boss them whether they liked it or not. I am already under suspicion of being a very lukewarm democrat because, as we all do, I deride the notions of crude democracy which the young revolutionist always boils with until he has ten minutes administrative experience. The more we fight against the dream of government *by* the people, the more we must stick to government by consent of the people; and that is, for the Fabian, represented by our present system of universal suffrage and direct election of the executive.

I still think that the whole strength & charm of your report lies in the group scheme, especially the Samurai groups. I believe if you developed that in the largest imaginative way, and even boldly suggested rules of life for the central Fabian, the society would be excited & interested; you would become enormously popular; and you would carry your new basis & as much as would save your face of the rest—

Here is the post. I have not time even to read this over—

GBS

To OTTO KYLLMANN

Castle Haven Rectory. Castle Townshend
[C/1]   24th September 1906

[The new play was *The Doctor's Dilemma*. The book was *Dramatic Opinions and Essays*, which Brentano issued in New York in 1906, but for which Shaw now provided a preface for a copyright-protected English edition, published in 1907.]

I have performed prodigies in my efforts to get John Bull into print; and the preface is actually set up & would be passed for press but for an addition which political events compelled me to make to it. It will be ready before Christmas anyhow. The Major Barbara preface is set up & complete. Both prefaces are epoch makers. . . .

I have a new play ready, and also a new book. Patience: the deluge will come.

G.B.S.

To SIDNEY WEBB

[A/2]

Castle Haven Rectory. Castle Townshend
29th September 1906

[George Robert Sterling Taylor (1873–1936), a prolific writer of history and biography, as well as of Socialist subjects, was a member of the Fabian Executive 1905–8. Shaw eventually drafted the Executive Committee's counter-report, which was published jointly with the Special Committee report and distributed privately to the full membership in December 1906.]

My dear Webb

I have seen a later state of the report, with notice of several amendments on almost every page. It is now much less offensive, and will probably come out finally without anything that will seem spiteful to the Society. Also, H.G.W. has cheered up & is now as friendly as ever with me. It took some patience to achieve this; for he was so out of sorts over the matter that when Taylor (his most staunch supporter) went down to see him, they all but quarrelled, and I gave him up as personally hopeless; but since that H.G.W. has buried the hatchet with which he had obscurely menaced me in several letters, and shone out again in full sunshine. This is a relief to me, as it would have been a wretched result—whether his report were carried out or not—if it had left a personal quarrel with so considerable a man.

Now as to our course. Parrallel columns are impossible. They worry the reader; and they are the weapons of quibblers & squabblers. I feel very strongly that when Wells's report is given to the Society, it must be followed, not by a vindication or a defence or an explanation or apology or counter-attack, but simply by a better report on the Society, its history, position, prospects & policy, than Wells's. With our greater knowledge & experience we ought to be able to do this. I do not want to play him off the stage: on the contrary, I want to star him for all he is worth as an addition to the strength of the company. The rank & file do not want to have to desert their old government & accept a Boulanger: what will please them is to feel what a splendid lot of fellows their leaders are & what a score it is to have such a swell as Wells taking the juvenile lead. Therefore our report must be full of ideas & vigour, quite free from any petty recriminations, throwing new & inspiring light on the old policy, and shewing a power of assimilating and giving practical shape to the new.

Now this means that we ought to accept some of Wells's proposals, and that we ought to convince the Society that we have always accepted the practicable part of most of them. The real difficulty will be—what shall we accept?

As a main concession, I think we might accept the new basis. Nine tenths of the unrest to which Wells appeals is simply want of novelty—fatigue of the retina after contemplating the same formula for 22 years. I find, myself, after having had the proposal before me for months, that I really do not care a danky dump about the old basis, any more than C.B. [Campbell Bannerman] cares about the British constitution. If the susceptibilities which its dragged-in clauses were meant to soothe no longer exist, let them go. Wells's basis reads fresher, and will make no difference whatever to our policy. And I cannot see that it will be less attractive to recruits. So, subject of course to an amendment or two if necessary, I propose that we welcome the new basis.

Then as to the group organization. We may accept that with high compliments, as it is really not new at all except for the Samurai touch, which is an improvement.

And we are of course in favor of new tracts, and of a new format if a satisfactory one can be found.

By making the most of these agreements, I think we can differ with dignity and good fellowship on the points we cannot accept. These are, to my mind,—

1. The change of name. We are not against a change of name from a worse to a better. British Socialist Society is impossible.

2. The triumvirates, on the ground that the nine worthies cannot be found to take the responsibility; and that the few whom the Wells Com^tee probably had in mind prefer to work with the support of a larger representative committee. Three is not the Fabian consultative unit.

3. The commercial Utopia of a big publishing business & a weekly paper on Wyman's bookstalls. Here we must explain the old policy of never doing anything that other people are doing in the ordinary course of commerce. This includes, of course, the palatial office.

4. The policy of refusing to look to Tory or Whig governments for instalments of Socialism. This is only the usual confusion of ideas as to Permeation, & must be brilliantly exposed as such.

— Open Questions —

These are, the enlargement of the executive to 26[,] the 7/6 fixed subscription, the alteration of the mode of election, the running of Fabian candidates at elections.

Wells will probably oppose the enlargement of the Exec. unless 9 of them are elected as triumvirs.

As to the subscription, we ought to have statistics before we decide.

As to the mode of election, I think we might abolish the two letters, and accept the signature of the basis as sufficient to cover all considerations of orthodoxy. Even the proposing & seconding & the need for attending two meetings might be dropped. I also think that exclusion by one black ball ought to be replaced by decision by a majority of the executive. But I am against automatic election on signing the basis. I think the names ought to come before the exec. as at present, and that the exec. should elect, and consequently have power to refuse to elect; and I think we might, in consideration of these concessions, and of the abolition of the proposer & seconder, ask for absolute discretion in this matter & do away with the potential appeal to the society. We have never abused the power of the blackball except once, in the very early days, when James Lecky was blackballed. Since then, I can recall only four cases—[Edward] Aveling, [Albert] Sabine, Madame de Salis & Miss Amy M****t [Morant]; but these I think are enough to justify us in retaining some sort of sieve.

As to the running of Fabian candidates, we might point out that that is, and always has been, a question of pure expediency, and that the introduction of proportional representation or second ballot might alter the whole aspect of it.

G.B.S.

This exhausts me for the present. What do you think?

PS Dont destroy this letter. It might be well to send it on to Pease & perhaps to multiply portions of it & circulate it through the exec.

[P]PS. As the report of the Wells Com^tee must go to the Society as they pass it (mere public curiosity will make this binding on us) it does not matter whether it is in galleys or not: in fact, pages will be far handier. We shall of course withold it until our own report is ready to append to it.

To ERICA COTTERILL

10 Adelphi Terrace W C
[D/3]   24th October 1906

The letter is very good. You are certainly a clever young devil; and I suppose I shall have to treat you as a friend. Only, dont expect me to write letters.

GBS

To WILLIAM ARCHER

10 Adelphi Terrace W C
[A/2]   14th November 1906

[The drama critic of the *Daily Express*, Archibald Haddon (1872–1942), had published a full synopsis of *The Doctor's Dilemma*, with bits of dialogue from the Epilogue, in the "Green-Room Gossip" column on 14th November. Shaw wrote an angry letter to the editor, demanding to know the identity of the "traitor," but Haddon refused to reveal his informant even under threat of legal action. The theatre was placed under such heavy security that even Lillah McCarthy's mother couldn't gain admission and went into hysterics.]

My dear W.A.

If Barker asks you to a rehearsal of The Doctor's Dilemma, please put him off with an apology. It is utterly impossible that a rehearsal can be a rehearsal with you present. Some of them would act frantically: others would walk through with no other thought than to make it clear that they were walking through. I should very much like to have you concealed in a box & consult with you afterwards; but that is not possible, & wouldnt be fair to the company. You cannot imagine—or rather you *can* imagine—how impossible your position as a critic makes you on such an occasion. When Barker suggested it I said "Yes, of course," as I wish you to be considered a privileged person in all my enterprises & affairs; but unless Barker will undertake to conceal you even from me (so that I shall not have to be disloyal to my company by cheating them) I depend on you to get me out of the scrape by excusing yourself.

Some wretch in the theatre has just given away the whole plot & some of the dialogue to the Express. I am hunting down the traitor.

G.B.S.

To LILLAH McCARTHY

[A.u/4; X/182.e]

[Ayot St Lawrence. Welwyn]
Bedtime, 17th November 1906

[Shaw and Charlotte had moved on 3rd November into the Rectory at Ayot, a small, undistinguished house which they purchased fourteen years later, and in which they lived until their deaths. It was eventually given the name "Shaw's Corner." On this weekend, the last before the opening of *The Doctor's Dilemma*, the Shaws were playing host to the Barkers.]

Overlooked last night [presumably added on the 18th]

Instructions have been given that you are not to be disturbed in the morning until you ring.

Lunch can be taken in bed if desired.

If Barker desires to play the Pianola before retiring, he is requested to select a quiet piece, and wedge down the soft pedal.

As there is not oil enough in the lamps to last, I am putting them out and lighting the candles.

If you want anything, search freely for it. If that fails, shout until somebody wakes and attends to you.

Goodnight—goo-oo-oo-d nahight—go-oo-oo-oo-d night &c &c &c &c.

To A.B.WALKLEY

[S/1]

Ayot St Lawrence. Welwyn
18th November 1906

[*The Doctor's Dilemma* was presented at a matinée at the Royal Court Theatre on 20th November. Sir Almroth Wright (1861–1947) was an Irish-born bacteriologist, long associated with St Mary's Hospital, Paddington.]

My dear A.B.W.

Let me hit you, in view of Tuesday afternoon, with some information that does not touch the artistic merits of my play.

The scientific side of it is correct and up to date. Sir Colenso Ridgeon, the hero, is, serum pathologically, Sir Almroth Wright, knighted last birthday (~~June~~ May) for his opsonic discovery. His description of his discovery in the first act is accurate in every detail. "St Annes" in the play is St Marys, Paddington. The situation of the doctor having more cases than he could treat, and consequently having to choose whom to cure & whom to let go, actually existed last year and does to some extent exist still. The "nuciform sac" (of which you will hear in the play) is imaginary—a *nom de theatre* for the vermiform appendix. The blunders of the court physician are founded on fact.

A vaccine is quite different from an anti-toxin. An anti-toxin is of the nature of a specific antidote. A vaccine opsinises your disease germs—to opsinize = à rendre friande—so that the white blood corpuscles (alias phagocytes) pitch into them with an appetite. My court physician makes two mistakes. He confuses anti-toxins with vaccines and imagines that vaccines stimulate the phagoctyes instead of buttering the bacilli. His cardinal error is sufficiently explained in the play.

As I have not explained this to any one else, please give the fraternity a scientific lecture during entractes if you find them volunteering erroneous views of phagocytes.

In haste
G.B.S.

To SIDNEY WEBB

Ayot St Lawrence. Welwyn
[L/14]   25th November 1906

[Sir John Lubbock (1834–1913), 1st Baron Avebury, a banker, and Leonard Courtney (Webb's brother-in-law) were radicals who had isolated themselves from their fellows by opposing Home Rule. H.G.Wells's article in the November issue of the *Independent Review* was "Modern Socialism and the Family," in which he advocated endowed motherhood.]

(Dictated)

My dear Webb

This Fabian job has compelled me to lay my mind seriously to the question of the Fabian; & I now see clearly that "das Lied ist aus." We cannot sit there any longer making a mere habit of the thing, knowing all the time that we shall have to drop it within, at the utmost, 5 years from now, & that it will then perish miserably & abortively unless we make the end of it the beginning of something else. Incidentally too, we shall have Pease & [E. J.] Howell [the office clerk] on the streets—starving.

We have also to consider that we have at last made the Labor Party.

Now that we have made it, it is quite impossible for us to belong to it; & yet whilst it is there, we cannot decently belong to any other party; nor is it any use for us to peter out as nondescripts like Lubbock & Courtenay.

It is clear to me that we must consummate the Fabian section of our lives by setting on foot a Fabian parliamentary party. This is a thing which will either catch on, in which case it will be the right climax to the whole Fabian adventure, & make the opportunity for us to claim superannuation & drop out, or else it will not catch on, in which case the attempt will be so futile that nobody will notice that we have done anything. Whether or no, I am convinced that this is the psychological moment, not only in the movement but in the old gang. Pease wants a better job; Macrosty wants an opportunity of skipping out; so do we; & by springing to the front & snatching the flag from the hands of Hobson & Taylor, we shall dish the rebellion completely.

Consequently do not bother about the demand for a new "Party." The word is quite inevitable now; & before the Labor Party has been blazing away in Parliament for another year, there will be the beginnings of a big middle class demand for an educated middle class handling of the new problems in Parliament.

Just one word more. It seems to me eminently probable that Wells, instead of embracing one go-ahead proposal, will jib at it, just as some of the other stalwarts, after clamoring for an independent Socialist Party, will quiet down considerably when we bring them right up against it. But do not underrate Wells. What you said the other day about his article in the Independent Review being a mere piece of journalism suggested to me that you did not appreciate the effect his writing produces on the imagination of the movement. You will admit that he writes much better than [L.Haden] Guest can; yet on Friday night, in a full meeting of members only, Guest was as much applauded as I was.

We must spend the next few years in educating these chaps in Committee work & public life; then throw the whole thing into their hands as a federation of Fabian Socialist Associations; formally wind up the old Fabian & make our bow, as we shall both by that time be too wise, too various, & too old to play with them any longer.

yrs ever
G.Bernard Shaw

662

To MARY HAMILTON

Ayot St Lawrence. [Welwyn]
[S/1]   29th November 1906

[Mary Hamilton (1877–1945) was a young Canadian actress (daughter of the Archbishop of Ottawa) who appeared as Violet Robinson in *Man and Superman* and Minnie Tinwell in *The Doctor's Dilemma*.]

Dear Miss Hamilton

Violet was all right: you did everything we planned to do very successfully except one line "Let us talk sense," which you perhaps thought inapplicable to my dialogue.

In Minnie you make only one little miscalculation. You have found out how to make a point; but, being still a young thing, you insist on making all the points. Now there are some points that make themselves. One of them is "*I'm* his wife, sir." You make a little pause before this to shew the audience that there is something good coming. Now that is the right thing to do when there is any chance of their being unprepared; but it is stagey when they *are* prepared. In this scene everybody is listening with all their ears; and you begin by saying "Dont believe him sir: she cant be his wife." Go straight on, quite simply and spontaneously, and you will find it comes ever so much better. Perhaps you have found that out already: if so, do not bear malice against me for telling you.

Everything else was just *peu* ee-fict (the peu is in French): you will do very well in your profession unless some millionaire snaps you up and marries you.

in great haste
yours sincerely
G. Bernard Shaw

To AUGUSTIN HAMON

10 Adelphi Terrace W C
[S/1]   4th December 1906

[Shaw had given eleven lectures between 20th October and 29th November. He had visited Manchester, Birmingham, and Reading, and had delivered three major addresses in London: "The Religion of the British Empire" at the City Temple on 22nd November; "Socialism and Art" to the Fabian Society on 23rd November; and "Some Necessary Repairs to Religion" to the Guild of St Matthew on 29th November. The "laborious development" of the Fabian Society was the H. G. Wells reform movement. The "crisis" in the Society of Authors, at its meeting on 3rd December, involved decisions as to the position to be maintained by the Society in the war that had broken out between the Publishers' Association and the Times Book Club over the Net Book Agreement (see Shaw's letters of *c.* 24th and 26th March 1907 to Otto Kyllmann and Constable's.)]

My dear Hamon

I am very sorry to have kept you so long waiting for Candida; and even now I can send you only the second act; but I will send the third tomorrow. I have been overwhelmed with work this last month: in fact I have narrowly escaped a break-down. I have had to deliver two addresses to large audiences every week; I have had to deal with a most laborious development of the Fabian Society; I have had to deal with a crisis in the affairs of the Society of Authors; and I have had to produce my new play, The Doctor's Dilemma. Each of these singly was work enough for one man: the whole together has knocked me almost to pieces. That is how you came to be so scandalously neglected.

I find you are more at home in the part of Burgess than in the serious parts of Candida. Remember that the great failing of the Frenchman is his respect for the academic. Every Frenchman is a born pedant. He thinks it is a crime to repeat a word—the crime of tautology. He wants to have in every sentence a subject, a predicate, a noun, a verb, a complete grammatical structure. Now on the stage, where the word is spoken, and so much depends on the way it is spoken, grammatical completeness does not matter at all. If a string of interjections or broken phrases will give the meaning, so much the better. So far from its being a crime to repeat words and phrases, it is the worst of crimes to vary them, since the effect is often lost by doing so. Ne cherchez pas le style: cherchez toujours la vie.

Now as to our friend Lugné. You understand of course that all this about Madame Suzanne Després is mere formality: she is his wife, and will play in anything he produces as a matter of course; in fact, he would not touch a play unless it had a good part for her in it. I know all about Madame Suzanne, and what Lugné did for Ibsen & Maeterlinck. I have written several articles about him [in the *Saturday Review*], and came over from London when he produced Peer Gynt in Paris expressly to write about it—I was the only London critic who did so. I understand his position, and know that he is not one of the regular permanent managers, but, as he says, a défricheur. And it is a testimony to the value of his services to the theatre that I am willing to entrust the piece to him. . . .

Suzanne ought to play Vivie, & Sarah Bernhardt Mrs Warren.

664

All the stories about Rodin's madness are pure mensonges. His bust of me—I have received the bronze [it was also done in marble and in terra cotta]—is a *chef d'œuvre*.

I will write to you tomorrow about the printing. I shall lose the post if I wait to write now. . . .

yours ever
G. Bernard Shaw

To HUBERT BLAND

10 Adelphi Terrace W C
10th December 1906

[A/39]

[Discussion of Wells's Special Committee Report had begun at a Fabian business meeting on 7th December and continued at subsequent meetings on 14th December, 11th and 18th January 1907, 1st February, and 8th March. Shaw's resolution called for an increase in the number of the Executive from fifteen members to twenty-one. Wells's amendment called for the Executive to make instant arrangements for the election of a new Executive, which would automatically give effect to Wells's report. This called for the abolition of the present Executive and the substitution of a Council of twenty-five, with a virtual executive of three persons, directly responsible to the Council and, through it, to the Society as a whole.

The "urgent whip" which Shaw was sending was a postcard:

May I urge you not to be absent from the adjourned meeting of the Fabian Society next Friday at Essex Hall at 7.30. I find that many members have not noticed that the amendment by Mr. H. G. Wells, on which a division will be taken, is drawn in such a manner that, if carried, it will act as an instruction to me and my colleagues on the Executive Committee (with the exception of Mr. G. R. S. Taylor) to resign AND NOT OFFER OURSELVES FOR RE-ELECTION. Nothing but an overwhelming expression of opinion in a full meeting can avert the most serious consequences to the Society, as the matter cannot be settled by a mere majority in a small meeting. I shall explain fully when I address the meeting on behalf of the Executive Committee. I beg you to attend and vote if you possibly can.

G. BERNARD SHAW.

10 ADELPHI TERRACE, W.C. 11 DEC. 1906.

665

Wells's speech, which Shaw had disliked, was hastily printed and distributed, between the meetings of 7th and 14th December, in galleys headed "Reconstruction of the Fabian Society."]

Dear Bland

No: on the whole, dont speak. Wells has said "We must have a speech from Mr Bland"; and as his method of obtaining it is one which leaves no practicable alternative to dignified silence except retorts of a nature impossible from so big a man as you to so little a man as he (except with pistols), I think you had better leave the job to me. He came here on Saturday morning quite blithe & affectionate. He said, "Shaw: I apologize. NOW!" I tried to explain that this would not get him out of his corner. He said I was an Irishman—meaning, as far as I could make out, that I was vindictive. I had to bundle off to a train then; so all I gathered was that he expected defeat, but thought it so near a thing that I might compromise.

What I propose to do is to take the weight of the debate on myself (for, as usual with the draughtsman, I am the only one whose mind has been really laid to the job), and demand an unconditional surrender—that is, a withdrawal of the amendment. I have all the points of detail noted, and can smash him to atoms on every one of them. I will play the moral game on them in an eye-opening manner. With luck, I believe we can get a smashing victory. All I dread is being in bad form; for I am overworked. I am going to the country to recruit.

Meanwhile I am sending a whip to every blessed London & contiguous member—an urgent whip. I am clear as to my plan of debate; but we must be careful not to compromise our moral superiority by saying anything unkind. His speech was AWFUL—SHOCKING.

G.B.S.

To H. G. WELLS

10 Adelphi Terrace W C
[H/26]   17th December 1906

[In his speech at the Fabian meeting on 7th December (as printed during the following week), Wells had said: "[W]e do want such members as Mr. Sydney Olivier, Mrs. [Magdalen Pember] Reeves, Dr. [Stanton] Coit and Mr. Aylmer Maude . . . to replace the more obstructive section" of the Executive.]

My dear H.G.W.

Just a few lines in great haste provisionally. There will be no executive election until the regular one, probably; nor would it be desirable for you to have one. Just now you would be at your zero electorally. But you can easily retrieve the situation if you will study your game carefully, or else do exactly what I tell you. We shall have a series of adjournments to discuss the reforms one after the other; and your Committee will no doubt move amendments to resolution 2, that the proposed 21 committee men be twentyfive councillors; that the sub-committees be triumvirates; that a fixed subscription be adopted; that the basis be altered by such and such clauses &c., keeping up a running fight with us. Now we shall no doubt score pretty well, and carry our resolutions against the amendments; but there is glory to be won in the engagements; and that glory will mean votes at the election. *Some* amendments will be carried against us, or at least accepted by us: I always make a point of accepting what I can. Your merry men will also have plenty of chances of making themselves known by speaking, which is the only way in which recruits ever get on the executive. These battles will carry us over until it is too close to the ordinary election time to make it possible to attempt a belated 1906 election.

Meanwhile, you MUST make up your mind to two things: first, that the moral superiority tack is an impossible one as against such strong and straight players as we are, and second, that you must carefully study the etiquette of public routine. You have outrageously disregarded the elementary rights of your people, and thereby driven [Rev. Stewart] Headlam to lead the attack on you instead of supporting you. Headlam had an absolute right to be summoned to all your conferences on the report, and to have a part in determining the procedure to be adopted at the meeting. Olivier had a sacred claim to move the committee resolution: the fact that he was thrust over into the five-minute ruck, and that I had to rise to claim unlimited time for him, was a horrible scandal. Your reckless mention of Coit and Mrs Reeves in your printed speech was simple madness from the point of view of the experienced parliamentarian. Now people will stand this and worse from a leader who will carry them to smashing victories, just as the Irish party submitted to unheard-of contempt from Parnell. But you havnt led your people to victory: you have delivered them helpless into our hands, so that your defeat was a mere mechanical operation. This wont do. You must win your committee back by giving up the leadership to Olivier, and contenting yourself with supporting his motions. And you must win back the Society too; for you made a mistake which is hardly exaggerable in refusing to alter that tract. You should have offered, with a noble air, to allow me to edit it exactly as I pleased: that would have won back most of your flying followers at a stroke. But you dont know these things yet; and they cant be learnt except by a very impersonal study of them.

Goodnight: I must stop.

G.B.S.

To AUGUSTIN HAMON

[S/1]
10 Adelphi Terrace W C
9th January 1907

[Hamon lectured on "Bernard Shaw et son Théâtre" at the New University, Brussels, in February in conjunction with the performances of *Candida* in that city. The text of his lecture was published in the *Revue Socialiste* in September 1907. Augustin Filon (1841–1916) was a French literary critic. Comte George de Buffon (1707–88) was the noted French naturalist, from whom Shaw derived many of the ideas incorporated in his theory of Creative Evolution.]

My dear Hamon

... In preparing your lecture, you must not depend in any way on [A.B.] Walkley, Filon &c &c. To do so would be to throw away all the advantage your special training & special knowledge of social questions gives you. I want you to come forward in this matter as an original force in literature. ...

You must, however, be careful not to go thesis hunting. All this stuff about Candida meaning the triumph of duty or the triumph of love is mere intellectual chess playing. My plays are studies in the natural history of mankind: I am simply a dramatic Buffon or St Hilaire. When you read Buffon's description of the Horse you do not begin to ask whether Buffon regarded the Horse as a triumph of speed, or a triumph of traction power, or a triumph of fidelity; you understand that he is simply trying to shew you what sort of animal a horse is. Well, in Candida I am simply trying to shew you the sort of animal the people in Candida are. I take a great interest in animals of that sort, just as Buffon did in animals in general; and I write for the gratification of people who share my interest. I have a perfectly definite, clear-cut view of the social function of the writer of fiction, whether in Dramas or Romances. I can illustrate it from your own work. You began by trying to write down the events of a year of actual life in France just as it occurred. But it occurred hap-hazard, higgledy-piggledy, without any sort of logical order. For instance, a young officer in Paris lost a million francs at the gambling table. A month later a young labourer in Lille was discharged. A fortnight later an old peasant committed suicide. Now I need not explain to you as a socialist how those three events, apparently quite disconnected, might easily stand in the closest relations of cause & effect. You have only to suppose that the officer's father, a manufacturer in Lille, had to withdraw capital from his business to pay his son's debts, and was thereby compelled to discharge some of his workmen. Also that one of these workmen had a father whom he kept alive by sending him part of his wages, & that the old man killed himself when the son could no longer send him any money. Now when you write down those events in the order in which they actually occur, with long intervals of time between them, and plenty of railway accidents, receptions at the Elysée, balloon ascents, Socialist demonstrations, deaths of eminent men &c &c &c, occurring meanwhile & distracting the reader's attention, the relation of the three events is completely concealed. Life appears a mere chaos of accidents, & your attempt to make an "Annual Register" of it necessarily as devoid of dramatic interest as a Post Office Directory. To make life intelligible & interesting, you have to select typical incidents & typical people, & shew how they act and re-act upon one another by clearing away all the accidents and irrelevancies which in actual life obscure their relations. Thus, you would write a drama in which the officer would lose his money in Act I, the workman would be discharged in Act II, and the workman's father would kill himself in Act III, arranging the incidents so as to shew their true economic, social and emotional relations to one another, & of course leaving [out] all the balloon ascents, Elysée receptions and other irrelevancies. In this way you would tell the story of the officer & the two proletarians much more truthfully than it is told in the newspapers. This, according to me, is the whole function of the dramatist. You can work out the rest for yourself; & if you have written anything about the triumph of Love you can put it all into the fire.

If you tell the world that the essential idea in my works is Determinism, I solemnly swear that I will go over to Brussels & murder you. If a man has nothing more to say in this world than "what will be will be," than "what must be must be," he had better give up literature & sweep a crossing, although it is pretty sure he will sweep it badly, & then say he couldn't help it because his inefficiency was determined beforehand by his heredity and his *milieu*. I am before all things a believer in the power of Will (Volonté). I believe that all evolution has been produced by Will, and that the reason you are Hamon the Anarchist, instead of being a blob of protoplasmic slime in a ditch, is that there was at work in the Universe a Will which required brains & hands to do its work & therefore evolved your brains & your hands. I have the most unspeakable contempt for Determinism, Rationalism, and Darwinian natural selection as explanations of the Universe. They destroy all human courage & human character; & they fail utterly to account for the most obvious facts of life—for instance, for the fact that you have spent your life in ruining yourself instead of studying your own comfort and minding your own business.

That is all I have time to tell you today about my opinions. It is enough to make you understand how far I have got away from the twopenny-halfpenny bourgeois materialism of our nineteenth century friends & indeed of all capitalistic civilization since Shakespear. . . .

yours ever
G. Bernard Shaw

To CHARLES ROWLEY

[A/4; X/159]

10 Adelphi Terrace W C
11th February 1907

[Charles Rowley (1840–1933) was a humanitarian whose Ancoats Brotherhood, founded in Manchester in 1877, anticipated the social settlement movement that sprang up with the foundation of Toynbee Hall, London, in 1884. Shaw had addressed the inaugural meeting of the Manchester Fabian Society on 20th October 1906 and the Ancoats Brotherhood the following afternoon. The Manchester *Daily Dispatch* informed its readers on the 23rd: "G.B.S. Overhauls the Ten Commandments." On that same day Bishop James E. C. Welldon (1854–1937), the new Dean of Manchester, speaking at a local meeting of the British and Foreign Bible Society, declaimed: "[W]e don't want men of letters coming down to tell us the Commandments are of no use. (Applause.) . . . Let that man of letters go home and learn the rudiments of morals and religion, and let him never come to Manchester again." The Birmingham and Midland Institute speech on 22nd October, like the Ancoats speech of the preceding day, was on "The Religion of the British Empire" (which Shaw subsequently delivered at the City Temple, London, on 22nd November.]

My dear Rowley

I am sorry my religious discourse to the Brotherhood last October was turned into something like a religious scandal by the levity of the Manchester Dispatch. That newspaper apparently does not encourage specialization in its reporters. Or, if it does, it mistook the Ancoats Brotherhood for a football team, and sent the wrong specialist.

The consequences of this misplaced expert's failure to rise to a rather serious occasion were disastrous in Yorkshire. In one of the chief seaports of that county the sitting member was called from the House of Commons to defend religion against me. His address, which would have highly edified the Dispatch, was a striking proof of the need for mine. He pleaded, in effect, that we must not hit religion when it is down. The Bible, he said, is venerable because, although nobody believes it now, it has old associations which no man of taste wishes to disturb. In short, religion is a sore subject; and every man who considers himself a gentleman instinctively avoids it.

Although I cannot accept this very parliamentary view as a deeply devout one, I think it does very correctly express the feeling of the irreligious majority today. It is a significant fact that all the protests raised by my speech to the Brotherhood, and to the three addresses which immediately followed it to the Birmingham and Midland Institute, the London City Temple, and the Guild of St Matthew, almost all came from people who had not heard them, the only doubtful cases being those of persons who either confessed themselves as having no faith and much "taste," or betrayed themselves as being in what theologians might call a very active state of damnation.

I am afraid it is quite hopeless to attempt to clear up the misunderstanding. The Manchester Dispatch trying to sort out my theology is like a blind man trying to sort out colors; and it represents the Bishop as having as little divinity as itself. You will always have to struggle with the effect that any stroke of humor or familiarity in religion produces on those whose idea of being religious is to sit in their best clothes in a condition of solemn paralysis, holding all their affection and sympathy and fun and intellect in strained and miserable abeyance, like a child who is told it will be beaten if it fidgets. Now people to whom religion is real invariably joke about it if they have any sense of humor. I should rather like to get up a performance of the old mystery of Cain & Abel for the benefit of your Bishop and the editor of the Manchester Dispatch. They could not possibly doubt that the writer believed the story with medieval devoutness, which is very different from believing it as a matter of modern good taste. But what they would

671

feel when they heard an outrageously comic Cain not only addressing his farm servants and his brother in language that would make Squire Western [in Fielding's *Tom Jones*] blush, but subsequently addressing his Creator in the same Rabelaisian terms, is beyond my imagination. I wonder, by the way, whether the Bishop ever reflects on the fact that his own Church was founded with a pun. I have a suspicion that in spite of the account given in the Bible, he conceives the charge to Peter as having been given in the style of a modern bishop laying the foundation stone of a cathedral, and listened to by the disciples with their heads bowed reverently into their best hats. At all events he would not have ventured on such a joke as the famous "super hanc petram"—"You are Mr Stone; and on this stone will I build my church." Bad taste, on so solemn an occasion, was it not?

I think, however, the bishop might have been Christian enough to back the Christian view of the Commandments taken by me against the Pharisaic view taken by the Manchester Dispatch. The Jews sought to kill Christ because he broke the Commandments without the smallest scruple whenever they conflicted with his humanity and common sense, and not only justified his action and called the Pharisees hypocrites for objecting to it, but insisted strenuously on the worthlessness of the sort of morality that consists in mere legality, or commandment observance. It is true that I do not profess myself a Christian; yet though, as I gather, the bishop does not object to me on that account, but because I am a clever man from London, I think even a clever man, no matter where he comes from, should be allowed to agree with Christ occasionally without being denounced for it by the bishop. If I had preached the higher criticism, or even passive resistance, I could understand the bishop's indignation; but why should he quarrel with me for preaching the gospel?

I have just seen myself described in an Italian paper as a "Conservatore feroce"; and the Italian paper is not so far out about me as the Manchester Dispatch. I am a Socialist because I have learnt from the history of Manchester & other places that freedom without law is impossible; and I have become a religious agitator because I have observed that men without religion have no courage. Ever since Darwin's discovery of Natural Selection obliterated the true theory of Evolution in Europe and explained the universe as a senseless chapter of cruel accidents, religion has practically ceased to exist in England, and moral cowardice has deepened to such an extent that even bishops take their cue from flippant reporters, and warn their flocks against clever men who call on them to associate religion with live beliefs and ennobling truths instead of with childish legends and abominable idolatries. How strong that call is becoming you can judge by the impression which my attempt to express it has made on my audiences, who have in no instance mistaken my addresses for bad jokes. The bishops of Manchester and London have not yet risen to the occasion, and have hindered where they should have helped, incidentally, I am sorry to say, causing many worthy people to think evil of the Ancoats Brotherhood and the Guild of St Matthew. I can only say that I think the Bishop of Manchester owes you every reparation in his power. Let him come again to the Brotherhood, and give them his view of the Ten Commandments: whether he thinks the Corporation of Manchester and the Church of England justified in spending large sums to induce artists to break the second; why he himself, like Christ, systematically breaks the fourth; whether the fifth admits of no exceptions; why he countenances the wholesale breach of the sixth by armaments and law courts; and whether he can declare on his honor that he has never met a case in which the defects of our marriage law did not make the observance of the seventh a greater crime against humanity than at least those simulated breaches which are now the only legal means of escape from ruinously mistaken unions. If he can say a word more or less than I did on the subject, I shall be very much surprised. No doubt he will be misunderstood by the Dispatch, which will take all his strokes of humor for deadly earnest, just as it took my earnest for jest; but I have no doubt he will risk that as cheerfully as I did. And he will enjoy the consciousness of righting you and the Brotherhood, even if he cannot persuade himself to apologize to

> yours faithfully
> G. Bernard Shaw

To H.G.WELLS

10 Adelphi Terrace W C
[C/26]   15th February 1907

[Nearly 80 of the Fabian membership voted in the March election. Wells, who finally agreed to stand for the Executive, received the fourth largest number of votes, after Webb, Pease, and Shaw.]

Do not forget that next Friday, the 22nd, is the last day for nominations for the new Exec. I found tonight that nobody has been nominated except by the executive committee. If you are not nominated by next Friday, I shall nominate you myself unless you refuse to stand. You have no idea how people get caught out by neglecting these formalities: hence this reminder.

GBS

To ERICA COTTERILL

Ayot St Lawrence. Welwyn

[A/3] 27th February 1907

Yes, yes, yes: I'll read it; only dont be in such a hurry. I am years behindhand with pressing work, and I can't answer letters.

I cant even read them without distraction when they are all in one sentence and in one key—E flat minor.

Why dont you get a type writer? Why dont you learn punctuation? Why dont you use paragraphs?

How would you like my books if I wrote like this?

Dear Miss Cotterill I have received your letter, & I'm rather busy & I'm not always so but I am so at times & it seems as if it would be always so & somehow I'm not really like that but partly so & I daresay it's very foolish but still it is so & yet it sometimes isnt so & Ive tried and tried not to be so but still it seems no use & perhaps it will always be so &c&c&c.

Oh, you are a dreary, DREARY young devil.

Why dont you send away the doctors & get up and stop thinking about yourself as long as your headaches will let you? They dont cure you. They dont even kill you. They *do* keep you in an appalling hypochondria.

I really cannot be bothered with you unless you get more lively and divide your sentences & smarten your style. You can do *that* at all events, if you like.

GBS

To ARCHIBALD HENDERSON

10 Adelphi Terrace WC

[H/7] 21st March 1907

[The book on religion, which Shaw was trying to develop out of the lectures he had delivered the previous autumn, was eventually abandoned under the pressures of other commitments and duties. Archibald Henderson finally arrived in England on 17th June. Shaw met him at St Pancras Station, at which time Henderson introduced him to a fellow passenger, Samuel L. Clemens (1835–1910), who was en route to Oxford for an honorary degree.]

My dear Henderson

I grieve to see that your last despairing letter is dated so far back as the 8th of January. The delay is pretty maddening no doubt; but just consider all that has to be done before you can finish the book. You were to have come over here in March to see me; but by the time this reaches you, March will be over, and we are still personally strangers. Then again you have to read my last four plays; and your book will be grievously incomplete until it also deals in a very important chapter with my views of religion, which will be embodied in a book as yet only half written and not likely to be in print until next fall at the earliest. It is only by the most desperate exertions that I have at last got "John Bull's Other Island" and "Major Barbara" into type. I have already sent nearly all the sheets to New York to be set up, and I hope to be able to place a copy in your hands very soon. All this means delay; but it also means more completeness and more authority for the book. You need not be afraid of a Shavian slump: the heathen are rejoicing in New York just now over what they call the passing of the Shaw craze but by the time your book is ready America will be crazier than ever. The sales that are influenced by my name go up steadily from year to year; and all the apparent slumps are cases of "reculer pour mieux sauter." In fact I should not hurry the book at all if it were not that I am anxious to get you well out into the limelight as the only genuine American authority on Shaw.

I presume you have not wholly abandoned the idea of coming over to see me. Remember: you must not come in July August or September. All the other Americans come then, and are disgusted to find nobody but themselves in London. Can't you get a research scholarship, and travel for a year or so on that?

yours faithfully
G. Bernard Shaw

To UNIDENTIFIED CORRESPONDENT

[G.u/4]

10 Adelphi Terrace WC
23rd March 1907

[On 24th January 1907 a young man named Horace George Rayner (1879–) entered the office of William Whiteley (1831–1907), founder and owner of the first great department store in Britain, who was known by the slogan The Universal Provider. Claiming to be the merchant's illegitimate son, Rayner demanded financial aid and, being refused, drew a gun from his pocket and threatened suicide. When the frightened Whiteley sent for police assistance, Rayner fatally wounded him. He then turned the gun to his temple, but succeeded only in facially disfiguring himself. He was sentenced to death in March 1907, but the sentence was later commuted to penal servitude for life. Shaw capitalized upon the incident in his play *Misalliance* (1910).]

Dear Sir

On what ground do you want this man reprieved? I have not read the evidence; but the main facts of the case are clear; and I see nothing in them that specially appeals to my sympathy. As a Socialist I am under no illusions as to Mr Whiteley's morals. He made his money very ably and very usefully in the only way that our social conditions allowed him to make it. His relations with women were those which society practically forced on a man of his temperament in his position. If he had shot Rayner I should have protested strongly against hanging a useful, able, energetic man for the sake of a worthless young lunatic. But when the worthless young lunatic shoots the able man merely as a theatrical demonstration of the most ignorant kind of virtuous indignation, I think that young man had better be exterminated than waste other lives in watching him and locking him up. I am sorry that it will be done barbarously and vindictively; but it will be a shorter way of taking the man's life than the alternative of penal servitude.

Sometimes a man will commit a murder which does not suggest any serious danger of his doing it again; but Rayner seems to me to be a dangerous man; and as I am vehemently [opposed] to punishment of any kind, as a thing entirely vicious and mischievous, I am an advocate of the removal of dangerous men. People who go about vindicating popular morality with revolvers on their private responsibility are not fit for London life any more than a tiger or a mad dog is fit for it. You dont punish a tiger or a mad dog; but you kill it; and on the whole, I do not see why Rayner should be left about, unless there [is] some reasonable chance of his being made to understand that he was wrong to murder Whiteley. Unfortunately all the teaching he is likely to get will only confirm him in the belief that he discharged a sacred duty in doing what he did.

[yours faithfully
G. Bernard Shaw]

676

To OTTO KYLLMANN

[A/1]

[10 Adelphi Terrace WC]
[Undated: *c.* 24th March 1907]

[The Times Book Club, founded in 1905, sought to offer its lending-library subscribers extra values, including free delivery within London, and discount purchases of recently published books and remainder stock. By 1907 its sales averaged 1300 volumes a day, but the drastic price-cuts and the publicity methods of *The Times* infuriated rival booksellers and created much hostility among publishers, most of whom withdrew their advertisements from the newspaper and refused to supply books. Although most authors backed their publishers in the quarrel, Shaw saw this as a foolish move. At the annual general meeting of the Society of Authors in March 1907 he asked: "As authors, what are we here for except to make the greatest gain we can from our efforts? . . . We, associated as an Authors' Society, have nothing to do with the higher aims of literature beyond what we have in common with *The Times* and the publishers, and the whole human race. Our special object here is to look after the business interests of authors. (Hear, hear.) The business of the publishers is to make as much money as they can in the easiest way to themselves; that is also the business of *The Times* newspaper; and it is also our business in our business capacity. We all have other objects: there is no person in this room who would deliberately produce a lower class of literature than his best for the sake of making more money; but having produced the best class of literature he can, it is his business to make as much money by doing so as he can, and it is our business here to secure that. (Hear, hear.) The line that I have taken in this matter is not in the interests of the publishers, and not in the interests of *The Times* newspaper, but in the interests of the authors . . ." (*Report of the Annual General Meeting*, 1907).

Earlier, in *The Times* on 17th November 1906, he had argued: "As to all this pious horror about throwing new books at scrap prices on the market, pray how many books do we see every year produced by publishers who, too languid to sustain their interest in them, too poor to advertise them, and too incapable to distribute them, 'remainder' them at a few pence a copy, and leave the author penniless or out of pocket whilst the bookseller sells off the stock with a very fair profit at a large reduction on the published price? Can folly go further than that of the authors who have nothing to say about this abuse, but who shriek at *The Times* when it, too, remainders a book after having benefited both author and publisher by buying every copy it remainders at full trade price?"

To prove his point that publishers were unnecessarily craven in sticking to their net book agreement because of the threat of a boycott by booksellers, Shaw arranged to issue a special edition of his new volume of plays, containing *John Bull's Other Island* and *Major Barbara*. An impression of 500 copies was printed in August 1907 with the imprint of the Times Book Club

677

replacing that of Constable on the title-page and on the binding. On 23rd
September Shaw informed readers of *The Times* that, far from boycotting
the book and thus protecting the publisher against the loss created by Shaw's
sales direct to the Times Book Club, the booksellers had ordered and sold
larger quantities of this book than of any of his earlier ones, cashing in on the
publicity created by the action and by the Book Club's advertisements, at
Constable's expense.

Despite Shaw's efforts, the members of the Society of Authors voted to
back the boycott. The publishers placed heavy restraints upon the Times
Book Club, and only after a two years' "war" did the Club and the Publishers' Association arrive at a settlement of their differences, with the Club
agreeing to a time lapse before offering secondhand or remaindered copies
for sale, and recognising limitations to its rôle as bookseller.]

Dear Kyllmann

I am desperately anxious to get John Bull & Barbara through the
press; and you may depend on it the delay is not my fault. I confess I
am less concerned about the novels; but they also will be dealt with as
soon as I can spare the time.

As to the Times Book Club, I object strongly to differential treatment
of customers; and I shall give the Times no more discount than anyone
else so long as, like anyone else, they simply buy as they go, sending
the boy round for half a dozen when they are short. But of course if
they give an order for a thousand copies, that is another matter.
Special terms for special orders is reasonable; but special terms for
normal orders is a black offence to all other buyers, who are each
clearly entitled to a "most favored nation" clause. This is so, isnt it?
It used to be, anyhow.

yrs ever
G. Bernard Shaw

To CONSTABLE & COMPANY

[10 Adelphi Terrace WC]
[H.c.u/1]   26th March 1907

My dear Constables

Your letter does not get us any further; and if we were to start
talking about the matter we should go back six months before the end
of ten minutes.

The first thing to grasp in this matter is that you are hopelessly and

678

entirely in the wrong, and that I am absolutely and solidly in the right. The booksellers and libraries want to extinguish a new and dangerous competitor. It is the interest both of the publisher and the author to have as much competition in book selling as possible. The booksellers assure you that if you sell one hundred copies of my "Dramatic Essays" to the Times Book Club, they will take as few copies of that work from you as possible. Now you know perfectly well that they are already taking as few copies from you as possible, and that they would not take one copy more or less if you supplied forty thousand million copies to the "Times Book Club" (which I presume you would heroically refuse to do if you got the order, in your existing frame of mind). By refusing to supply those copies, you are depriving me of a richly earned five pound note; you are depriving yourselves of another, Brentano of another, the "Times Book Club" of the equivalent of another; and you are doing no mortal good to any of the parties.

The great difficulty which confronts us all is that the bookselling trade in England is so absolutely incapable and insufficient. Although I, who am not a book-buyer, buy at least 30 books for every pair of boots I buy, I can find a thousand boot-shops for you more easily than a single book-shop. What is wanted is a great extension of the big general shop with a counter for books: that is to say, a bringing to bear on book-selling of large capitals and of combinations in retail trade as opposed to the old-fashioned separate shops for separate articles.

This way of doing business involves a good deal of speculative buying, and of periodical clearance sales—what you and I call remaindering. And this means the scrapping of all your net book agreements and such like reactionary rubbish. If you allow a big distributor unlimited powers of remaindering, or even of giving away your books with a pound of tea if he likes, he will order from you in hundreds or thousands. If you limit him, he will simply send round a boy to you for one copy as it is asked for; and he will not do even this until he has done his utmost to persuade the customer that the book is one which no real lady or gentleman would read, and that some other book, published by sensible people like Routledge or half a dozen others who stand outside the ring, is the proper food for a respectable mind.

Then there is the inevitable division between the publisher's interest and the author's. You make your livings out of a whole body of authors. Consequently your interest is, not to do your best for each individual author, but to get the greatest result out of the whole mass of them taken in a lump. The notion that the two interests come to the same thing—a notion much exploited by literary agents—is quite illusory. If you are ever reduced to selling umbrellas at corners of streets by auction, you will find that the way to thrive at that is not to stand out for the highest price for each umbrella, but to sell as many umbrellas as possible at a comparatively modest profit. Now if each umbrella belong to a separate owner for whom you are acting, these owners would clearly all be sacrificed to enlarge your income. I do not admit that in the Times business, this particular separation of interests comes in. I am quite convinced that in boycotting the Times you are injuring yourselves as much as you are injuring me, and limiting your future prospects very much more than you are limiting mine; but I put the point merely to show you that an author is fairly entitled to make an individual bargain as to the handling of his books, and to bar certain conditions, or to admit certain other conditions, which the publisher would not bar or admit if left a free hand.

The condition which has sprung up to meet this boycott, is quite simple and effectual. It is, that the author shall have the right to buy as many copies of his book at trade price as he chooses, to be delivered to his order at any accessible address he may give, without any question as to what he purposes to do with them. No matter what settlement may be arrived at in the "Times" case, every author who is worth his salt as a man of business will for the future always make this stipulation. I have never in all my experience heard of a publisher refusing to let an author have copies of his own book at trade price until the present difficulty arose. No doubt the publisher who wants to boycott a particular distributer at the author's expense as well as his own, would rather be able to force the author to support him in the boycott. But it is really difficult to find polite language to express one's contempt for the imbecility of an author who would allow himself to be used in that way when there was no lack of alternatives open to him.

The whole question between us then comes to this. Will you supply the Times' Book Club with my books or not. I am quite willing to save your face with the Publishers' Association, if you desire it, by taking the order from t Club myself, and giving the order as from myself. But as you will know perfectly well what the transaction means, it would be far more sensible for your Association to decide that in cases where the book is under the author's control and he disapproves of the boycott, his wishes must be fulfilled, however deeply his opinions may be deplored.

The only other sensible thing to do is to refuse to publish my books; for what can be more absurd than to boycott a hostile bookseller and at the same time act for a hostile author.

The matter of my new book is really very urgent, as I am dispatching the last corrected sheets to America today; and I want to publish here the moment the book is set up in America.

Also the question of the hundred copies of "Dramatic Opinions" presses. I asked the Book Club people to hold hard until I tried to settle the matter amicably; but their subscribers are bothering them, and, naturally, they are bothering me. If they cannot dodge you in some way (and I warn you that I will abet them in any game that they can devise for that purpose), they will have to buy their supply at full price from the nearest book-shop, whilst you and I will only get trade price subject.

Let me hear from you as soon as you can bring yourselves to face the situation.

yours faithfully
[G. Bernard Shaw]

To G.K.CHESTERTON

Ayot St Lawrence. Welwyn
[A/1]   28th March 1907

[Horace Rayner, the murderer of William Whiteley, was at St Mary's Hospital, Paddington, in a critical condition, following emergency surgery.]

My dear Chesterton

However abhorrent the ceremony (damn those silly surgeons at St Mary's!) we must get that man killed.

Just think of it! Here is a wretched woman in childbed, who has had the misfortune to saddle herself with a half-witted assassin—the worst sort of assassin—the morally pretentious assassin—the amateur judge, jury & executioner all in the person of one hopeless degenerate fool who first asks for money & then shoots. Do you want her to spend the next 20 years in celibate loneliness, with the consciousness that this creature is waiting in stultifying misery behind the bars, to come out, more useless than ever, to throw himself on her hands just as her children are beginning their adult lives? I can imagine nothing more inconsiderately cruel. He is half blind & featureless—no very welcome father & husband even if his character were respectable: in the name of vital economy let them hang him for his own sake and everyone else's. Then the cloud will fade away from the woman's life: she will be too busy with the children to remember him often: she will probably

681

marry & his name will be forgotten. Is there any more merciful solution possible? . . .

I am writing in great haste for post with a strange & unmanageable pen; so I have to throw the case at you in a heap; but you will see that if Rayner is reprieved, we shall have to cast lots which of us will visit him in gaol & kill him.

But he will not be reprieved if the Daily Mail can help it. If Whiteley is to perish unavenged, how much is Northcliff's life worth?

To turn to a matter of real importance, I hope your wife is no worse than an Easter holiday will cure. My wife is also out of sorts from the change of weather & season. So is everybody. If it is nothing specific, dont be uneasy.

yrs ever
G. Bernard Shaw

To SYDNEY C. COCKERELL

[C/3]

[Hotel d'Angleterre. Rouen]
[Undated: assigned to 3rd April 1907]

[The Shaws departed for France on 30th March, where they visited Havre, Yvetot, Caudebec, Rouen, Beauvais, Laon, Rheims, and Amiens. They returned to London on 11th April.]

Here we are in Rouen (Hotel de l'Angleterre) after three days at Caudebec on the Seine. I intended to go to Caen; but stress of weather drove me back eastward. I shall go to Beauvais probably tomorrow or next day, and shall either do the cathedral in ten minutes & hurry on Lord knows where, or stay there a day or two. The necessity of being back on the 12th makes me reckless as to what I do; but the cessation of writing & talking has done me a lot of good. Caudebec is, architecturally, piffle; but Jumièges & St Wandrille are fine.

GBS

To ERICA COTTERILL

[A/3]

10 Adelphi Terrace W C
2nd May 1907

[Erica Cotterill's play *A Professional Socialist* was published by the New Age Press in 1908.]

You had better definitely make up your mind to adopt literature as a serious profession. You will never make a decent or tolerable young lady in county society; and you will, if you work enough, succeed in literature.

I have made a note at the end of the play of what you must do to finish it so as to make a practicable play of it.

You must come to London & join the Fabian Society or some other public organization & live the life of a student & worker. . . . If you are to write for the theatre you must go to it occasionally & watch the mechanism of it. And you must worry your own way through as best you can. When you are forced to take care of yourself, you will develop plenty of common sense—or if not, you will make a mess of your life anyhow, and perhaps sooner & more completely in Godalming than elsewhere. You can get self respect only by doing something & doing it well, and self control only by having to control yourself outside the fortifications of home life, which you will never learn to value until you have to do without it for a while. At the same time, make sensible arrangements and dont suppose that you have to hurl yourself romantically into a void. You must, if you are to succeed in literature, get free from all tutelage, and be in a position to go to the gallery of a theatre or a public meeting by yourself & go about alone at all hours, dressed as you please; but remember that millions of girls have to do that—shop assistants, typists, actresses, students &c &c &c—and do it without raising the slightest question as to their respectability. It is as natural & proper in their position as it is appalling in that of the young lady who has never been out of doors without an escort, which I take (at a guess) to be your condition.

I cannot hazard any more suggestions on guesses; but I repeat you have literary faculty enough to justify you in making literature the serious business of your life.

GBS

To JAMES DOUGLAS

10 Adelphi Terrace W C
[X/205]   9th May 1907

[James Douglas (1867–1940) was a well-known London journalist and critic. The United States government had attempted to bar Maxim Gorki's entrance into the U.S. in 1905 on grounds of moral turpitude, because he and his wife were not legally wed. The intervention of liberal men of letters finally made it possible for the celebrated author of *The Lower Depths* (1903) to obtain a landing permit for his visit. Gorki (1868–1936) and Shaw corresponded during World War I and later became friends. In January 1907 Richard Strauss's *Salome*, produced at the Metropolitan Opera House, caused such a scandal that the management was obliged to withdraw it after a single performance.]

Dear Douglas

The reason I do not go to America is that I am afraid of being arrested by Mr Anthony Comstock and imprisoned like Moses Harman. After the Gorki and Strauss episodes it is clear that no European author of any distinction is safe in the United States, which is now infested by moral brigands, who have turned the Post Office into a most Unholy Inquisition, and are apparently in supreme command of the police.

How can I bring my wife to a country where she cannot obtain rooms at a hotel without producing her marriage certificate and showing it to all the other guests, and where, because she believes *Mrs. Warren's Profession* to be a righteous play, she can be dragged to the nearest police court, bullied, insulted, and told that if she does not take herself and her husband out of the city in twenty four hours, she will be charged in general terms with indecency?

If the brigands can, without any remonstrance from public opinion, seize a man of Mr Harman's advanced age, and imprison him for a year under conditions which amount to an indirect attempt to kill him, simply because he shares the opinion expressed in my *Man and Superman* that "marriage is the most licentious of human institutions," what chance shall I have of escaping?

No, thank you; no trips to America for me.

If I want adventures among brigands I shall go to Sicily or Macedonia. The brigands there are comparatively honest fellows: at least they do not, like a certain leading New York newspaper, make their living by publishing advertisements of Mrs. Warren's houses, and use their columns to destroy my reputation because I expose Mrs. Warren's traffic. America is not safe for any honourable and public-spirited man nowadays, though it is the paradise of those who traffic in prostitution. That is why educated Americans crowd into Europe, whilst educated Europeans keep carefully away from America.

G. Bernard Shaw

To WILLIAM ARCHER

[G.u/2]   [Undated: *c.* 20th–24th May 1907]

[Archer, in his article "A Talk on Technique" in *The Tribune* on 18th May, had questioned the validity of Shaw's attack on Pinero's "naïve machinery" in *The Second Mrs Tanqueray* (*Saturday Review*, 23rd February 1895, but recently reprinted in *Dramatic Opinions and Essays*, which Archer had been reading). "Richardson's Show" was a portable booth theatre in which plays and pantomimes were performed at fairs by John Richardson (*c.* 1763–1837). "Charles his friend" refers to the usual programme billing of the second juvenile part, the hero's friend, in the old light comedies. Vilhelm Foldal is the government office clerk in Ibsen's *John Gabriel Borkman. La Grande Duchesse de Gérolstein* (1867) was an *opéra bouffe* by Jacques Offenbach. Josephine Butler (1828–1906), Elizabeth C. Wolstonholme-Elmy (1834–1918), Eva MacLaren, and Gertrude M. Tuckwell (1861–1951) were active in the women's suffrage movement. Louise Creighton (1850–1936), widow of the Bishop of London, was a writer of historical studies.]

for publication if you like.
Excuse joggly writing. I am in a S.W. express

My dear W.A.

I cannot agree with the proposition laid down in your article of last Saturday: to wit, that the number of doors and windows in a man's drawingroom is proportionate to his income. I have not observed it. The fact—amazing as it is—that your own house has four doors and a French window or two per room is not evidence. As a dramatic critic you would naturally build a house that way. Or, if you did not build it, you would choose one of that sort. For all you know, your house may have been built by Mr Pinero. Just as stage morals and manners, as our police & divorce reports shew, get copied in real life; so does stage domestic architecture.

As you very rightly said in conclusion, all this does not matter *now*. But in my time it did matter very much. The stage was in process of evolution from the scenery of our boyhood, when the side walls of stage rooms were represented by open wings. In those days there were three entrances on each side even when a practicable door had to be introduced for the sake of some special bit of business; and people walked calmly off and on through the wainscotting, like ghosts. Long after the stage was really walled in as it is today, the traditions of the old plan lingered as pure superstitions. I never objected to the Criterion farces in which there were more doors than even in that wonderful house of yours, because these doors were a necessary part

685

of the machinery of the play. But when authors, managers & actors of serious plays kept on assuming, as they persistently did, that the 1st 2nd & 3rd entrances, and the practicable entrance in the centre of the flat were indispensable to the stage presentation of every proper West End play, it became necessary to laugh them out of that delusion, all the more as it interfered very seriously indeed with the naturalness of the acting. When my Arms & The Man was produced in 1894, all its alleged novelties were as old as Richardson's Show: the real novelty, which nobody off the stage noticed, was that Major Petkoff's library had only one door. The Reverend James Morell's room in "Candida" was in the same predicament; but to this day American and (I believe) German stage management has not dared to face the innovation; and St Dominic's semi-detached parsonage is provided with a door into the next house. For the matter of that I have often seen a stage room with a door into the open air on the third floor, close beside the window.

I found, in my own practice, that by accepting the ordinary conditions of life on the stage as far as possible, I greatly improved my plays. Later on Mr Granville Barker, in The Voysey Inheritance, not only presented a room with one door, but filled it up with a huge dining table, which left only a narrow strip of floor round it for the actors to squeeze themselves about in. I defy you to deny that the staging of The Voysey Inheritance produced much more illusion than the staging of The Second Mrs Tanqueray. Take another illustration. I am a rather old fashioned stage manager. I presented the second act of Man & Superman with an empty stage, save for the inevitable garden seat (for two) right centre. Mr Robert Loraine, a contemporary of Mr Granville Barker, persuaded me to pitch the garden seat into the property room & fill up the stage with a huge motor car. I was naturally furious at being taught my business by a younger man—I, the highly superior critic of Mr Pinero—but the improvement was so prodigious that I had to capitulate. Please observe that I do not offer the blocking up of the stage with dining tables & motor cars as indispensable to good stage management: I am only mentioning two convincing examples of the advantage of discarding traditions which arose from mechanical conditions long since superseded.

As to the activity of the stage postman & the stage telegraph boy, I may remind you that in Sardou's "Delia Harding," written for Mr [J. W.] Comyns Carr [who translated it in 1895] in the Tanqueray period, the postal and telegraphic system was so completely substituted for the nervous & emotional system that on the first night the gallery broke into open derision during the performance. No doubt you will now ask me why letters & telegrams should be excluded from the stage. You will assure me that you get stacks of letters every day, and that the telegraph messenger is a frequent knocker at your door. You will remind me that the Swiss captain gets a letter in the last act of Arms & The Man, and that Candida's husband actually gets a reply paid telegram. The objection to that style of argument is not that it is illogical, but that, if you get into a confirmed habit of it, your room with the four doors & the two French windows will be replaced by a room with one window (barred), one door (locked on the outside), no razors or clothes pegs, and padded walls. If you cannot see the difference between Monmouth & Macedon because there is a river in both or between Delia Harding & A Doll's House because there is a letter box in both, or between the stage craft of The Second [Mrs] Tanqueray & The Voysey Inheritance because there is a dining table in both, or between "Charles his friend" and Iago or Foldal because they are both confidants, or between the coincidence of Hamlet's arrival in Denmark just when Ophelia is being buried & the coincidence of Box & Cox taking the same lodging, then, Father William, you are no longer fit to be at large.

What is the explanation of all this affectation of an impossible addle-headedness—this burlesque argument in favor of superfluous doors and too-opportune telegrams? Is it to combat my "violent prejudice against Mr Pinero"? Bosh! I am much too deeply interested in the theatre to be prejudiced against any dramatist: I always start with a violent prejudice in favor. It is you who are openly & shamelessly prejudiced: the thing is a positive scandal. In the eighties & nineties, you said, "We must make English dramatic literature serious. We must banish the adaptation from the French. We must praise and encourage the men who are doing the best work. If we cannot have what we admire, let us at least admire what we have." Mr Pinero was your first and chief victim. When, having followed his own bent, and made the Court Theatre the leading theatre of London by writing original comedies, he suddenly relapsed into producing old fashioned trade articles like The Profligate & The Second Mrs Tanqueray, you, instead of heading him off as I tried to do, lured him on the downward path by declaring that there was a new English drama, a new literary departure, a native master arisen in London. And because we all crowded to see Miss Kate Rorke's wonderful teetotum faint and to hear Mrs Patrick Campbell play the piano, not to mention the inevitable failure of Mr Pinero's strenuous attempt to write thoroughly bad plays, circumstances seemed to favor your attempt. Fortunately I

687

came upon the scene as a critic when matters got as serious as The Notorious Mrs Ebbsmith. All the king's horses and all the king's men will not set that shocking misconception of the public women of England up again on the pinnacle where you sought to place it. Mr Pinero meant no harm: he erred in pure ignorance of public life; but you should have known better. I had no prejudice against Mr Pinero: I simply loathed and abominated The Notorious Mrs Ebbsmith, and do so still and always shall. What would you say if I accused you of a violent prejudice against Wilson Barrett because you loathed & abominated The Sign of The Cross, and were angry with me because I could not, for the life of me, take the play seriously, and saw importance & hope in the move it made towards getting the chapel & churchgoing public into the theatre.

Your policy—borrowed unconsciously from the grand duchess of Gerolstein—was in the long run an impossible one. Its generosity made it seductive and easy; and there is always an air of common sense and good humor about making the best of a bad job. And it is well established in England, where the worse our generals are the more we pretend that they are Cæsars & Hannibals, and the more helpless our diplomatists are, the more gravely do we hold them up as Cavours & Bismarcks. But political emergencies expose political humbugs, whereas in the drama there are no emergencies, and if you lower the standard you debauch the theatre. There were certain quite hideous deficiencies in the drama we criticized. Chief among them was the absence of any conception of the higher passions, moral passion, intellectual passion, philosophic passion, religious passion, poetic passion. Not a single character had any real motives except appetites: the other motives were all undisguised conventions. Contemplating these plays, one asked oneself amazedly whether the authors had ever met a decent dog, much less a decent human being. The one sign of grace about Mr Pinero in this period was that he at least knew that since his heroines saw no interest in life but love, and no tragedy in it but the tragedy of growing old and unattractive, they were harlots, dramatically tolerable only because they were so pitiable. The other authors mostly presented such women without the faintest sense that they were not everything that a woman could possibly be or desire to be. The special horror of Mrs Ebbsmith was that Pinero here deliberately took a woman of the type of George Eliot, Mrs Josephine Butler, Mrs Besant, Mrs Wolstonholme Elmy, Miss Eva Maclaren, Mrs Creighton, Miss Tuckwell, Mrs Sidney Webb (I could give you fifty convincing names) and explained to the public that these were all Mrs Tanquerays & Irises to whom the one supreme moment of their lives was that in which they threw a man into a state of erotic excitement by putting on a low necked evening dress for him. When you let that pass without reproach you practically announced that you were going to manufacture your modern school of London dramatic literature without the slightest regard to the elementary decencies of criticism. Yet Mrs Ebbsmith was not worse than the dramatisation, in the case of Quex [Pinero's *The Gay Lord Quex*], of the countryside superstition that a man can cure himself of venereal disease by ravishing a virgin.

[The draft ends here.]

To HARLEY GRANVILLE BARKER

[H/3; X/168]

10 Adelphi Terrace W C
24th May 1907

[The Barkers' country house was at Fernhurst, Surrey. *The Man of Destiny*, with Barker officially credited as producer but with Shaw really controlling the directorial reins, had its first public London performance at the Royal Court at a matinée on 4th June. The production by the Pioneer Players at the Imperial Theatre on Sunday, 26th May, was George Paston's *Clothes and the Woman*, preceded by a one-act play *A Man's Foes* by Diana Cholmondeley. Dame Adeline Genée (1878–1970), a Dane, was leading ballerina at the Empire, Leicester Square, 1897–1907. John Vedrenne's wife was Phyllis Blair. Edward Sothern and Julia Marlowe were appearing at the Waldorf Theatre, Aldwych, in Percy Mackaye's *Jeanne d'Arc*. *Man and Superman*, with Robert Loraine as Tanner, was revived at the Royal Court on 27th May. The "Don Juan in Hell" sequence was performed for the first time at a matinée on 4th June. Michael Sherbrooke (1874–1957) had performed for William Poel in the Elizabethan Stage Society productions, and was a member of Martin Harvey's company 1901–3.]

Dear Barker

I am in two minds about going down to Fernhurst on Sunday. If I have to rehearse Destiny on Monday morning, which seems possible, I should hardly be able to get up in time. I am also faintly curious to see a Pioneer performance on Sunday evening. Ordinarily I should not think of staying in town for it; but Charlotte has gone off in a motor car to hunt for a house in the river district; and the result is that I find myself going in for all manner of games which I never dream of when I am a married man. For instance, I have only been two nights by myself; and the first night I went to the Adelphi to hear Offenbach's

Contes d'Hoffmann, which was quite worth hearing; and yesterday, my vicious habits growing on me, I actually went to the Empire to see Genée dance.* I have not seen Vedrenne for some time; but before I despatch this letter I will try to get on to Mrs Phyllis through the telephone and find out how he is.

In the theatre, the state of things would break your heart. I have destroyed the very last remnants of discipline. Loraine, who always starts a Company by sacking at least three members of it after the first rehearsal to intimidate the rest, is aghast, and has impulses, which recur at intervals of ten minutes, to take the next boat back to America and leave you to play Tanner. I have assimilated all of his business that is to the good so instantaneously that he is quite unconscious of any of it having been assimilated at all, whilst I have so utterly rejected the starry part of it that he is in consternation and despair. The motor car is now—I was going to say in the middle of the stage, but as a matter of fact it is all over the stage, like your dining table in Voysey. He wanted to deliver the great speech about the tyranny of mothers enthroned in the motor car, with Lillah somewhere under the wheels with her back to the audience. I immediately saw the value of the idea, and put Lillah in the car in a fascinating attitude with her breast on the driving wheel, and Loraine ranting about on the gravel. He declares that this is utter ruin and that I might as well put on your understudy at once; but his dismay imparts an invaluable quality of earnestness to his acting. He feels that he is on the brink of a catastrophe, which is exactly what one wants from Tanner. He acts extremely well in the style of Wyndham. His vigour is apparently inexhaustible: even when he tires he presently gets a perfect tornado of second wind and goes stronger than ever. He has got all the comedy side of the part capitally, and does it quite in my old-fashioned way, with a relish and not under protest, like you. He keeps the play very tense and bright and lively whilst he is at work; but he has evidently had to carry the whole play on his own shoulders in America; and he has played it from beginning to end as comedy. He has quite missed the peculiar intimacy of the Robinson-Whitefield family circle; he has left the poetry out altogether; and he has never given Tanner away to Ann: in fact, it is pretty plain to me that he has never had an Ann to give himself away to. You can imagine that with all this readjusted for him after 500 nights of playing it the other way, he is pretty miserable. He looks gloomier and gloomier every day; but he keeps his temper admirably—not perhaps like an angel, but

* Last night, Joan of Arc, Sothern-Marlowe.

at all events like a very capable demon. I am hoping that he will begin to feel the new business before Monday night: if not, perhaps he will feel it when he has an audience to bite on it. Meanwhile Don Juan has been absolutely suspended, as Loraine is so disoriented that he wants three times as many rehearsals of the Superman as there is time for; and as I cannot let him rehearse the Hell scene on Monday (it is frightfully exhausting) we shall only have from Tuesday to Tuesday to get Hell into order. To add to the confusion [Norman] McKinnel is stage managing the Pioneer performance for Sunday next; and he seems to have got the whole Court company into it. Altogether I shall have everybody's nerves in a highly sensitive state for the first night. Whatever else there will be there will not be any staleness.

I enclose you the manuscript of an analytical programme for Don Juan. I think we ought to print it either on the programme or on a spare leaf to be distributed with the programme. There is no use in leaving the wretched critics to discredit the whole affair by their misunderstandings. Hitherto the first thing we have always had to do with a new play is to live down their confounded follies. In future we had better tell them what to say and what to think beforehand. It will save some of the mischief, if not all of it. . . .

Our minds seem to have jumped together as to McKinnel. I should not now hesitate to try him as Undershaft: in fact, I have now ticked down Barbara as a possible early revival. I found I was right about the Hell scene: both McKinnel and Sherbrooke are fitted perfectly, and would be ghastly if they exchanged parts.

When Vedrenne is well enough to bear it I want to cross him on one point. The more I think of it the more I am convinced that we must not put up The Devil's Disciple or any other play, except perhaps You Never Can Tell, for eight weeks; and I only except You Never Can Tell because it has been revived so often that no revival is now likely to be mistaken for a run. Six weeks is the limit for The Devil's Disciple; and I would almost make a stand for four weeks at first productions if it were not that it means such a devil of a lot of rehearsing and producing.

If anything comes of the American project, Loraine is a youth to be very carefully considered. He is far and away the best alternative to yourself that we have been able to find. Just at present he loathes the Court. The shabbiness of the motor car and of Ramsden's study, the absence of his beautiful trees laden with chestnuts and the grassy banks round which he used to drive the motor, above all, what he calls the amateur acting, and my deliberate smudging out of the trade

691

finish and disciplined smartness which is a point of honour with him, are all straining his devotion to myself to the very utmost. But when he gets into touch with the Court audience and begins to understand the game a little, his sufferings will be mitigated. With Lillah, he would make The Philanderer a tremendous success; and indeed I think, that if you take the linch-pin out of our London applecart by going to New York, he could keep it going better than anybody else now in sight. However, we shall see what will happen on Monday night. I hope he will have quite a considerable success, because he is going through a fearful trial, and if he does not succeed he will blame me for it, and lose faith in Der Meister.

Lillah appears to be completely re-established. When she saw what Loraine wanted in the second act, she promptly came down the stage and turned her back to the footlights like a schoolgirl; and poor Loraine was publicly informed that it was all right, as she had been many years with Wilson Barrett and quite understood. This was additionally hard on Robert, as, to do him justice, he really believed he had been doing the best for everybody, and perhaps had been if they were rather a poor lot. . . .

G.B.S.

To FELIX MOSCHELES

10 Adelphi Terrace W C
10th June 1907

[H/1]

[Moscheles was at this time the president of the International Arbitration and Peace Association. Shaw had contributed to a symposium "England und die 'Abrüstung' " in the Neues Wiener Tageblatt on 19th May.]

My dear Moscheles

I always seem to be dodging you in the most disgraceful way when you want me to do anything. This is destiny, not malice. What is the use of having a friend if you have to treat him as well as you treat strangers?

My difficulty about the Peace Association is that my views on the subject of war are far more congenial to the Jingos than to the Quakers. For instance, I am against disarmament, and have just created a scandal among the German pacificators by informing the leading Viennese newspaper that I consider disarmament quite as absurd as the cutting off of men's hands and the putting out of their eyes to prevent them punching one another's heads. I believe in making war on war—policing the world by a terrific international armament which shall destroy any national armament which attempts to begin fighting.

Also—though this does not matter—I have talked and worked myself almost dead for this season; and my wife threatens to leave me if I accept even one more engagement to speak before my holiday.

yours ever
G. Bernard Shaw

To ERICA COTTERILL

10 Adelphi Terrace WC
12th June 1907

[A/3]

Dear Miss Cotterill

If you care to come to the Court Theatre on Friday afternoon to see the very wonderful way in which Ricketts has produced the scene of Don Juan in Hell from Man & Superman, come up by the 11.40 train & come here from Waterloo as fast as you can, as the performance begins at 2.30 sharp, and we must be punctual with lunch at 1.30. You will be just in time. I am going myself with my wife to a poky little stage box where nobody can see us; but it will only hold two; so I shall get you a seat somewhere in the middle of the house. We (my wife & I) will have to rush off to a committee before the end. You must make your way to the 6.20 from Waterloo as best you can without expressing the feelings inspired by the performance.

This is the only way in which I can see you. Except at lunch, I have not a moment to spare for conversation.

By the way, you will get nothing but vegetarian food unless you give notice that you need meat.

Send me a wire on the enclosed form to say whether you will come. And send it early, as I shall not telephone to secure your seat until I hear from you.

yrs sincerely
G. Bernard Shaw

To GILBERT MURRAY

[A/36]

10 Adelphi Terrace W C
22nd June 1907

[*Medea* was presented at the Savoy Theatre on 22nd October 1907; neither Lillah McCarthy nor Janet Achurch appeared in it. *The Trojan Women* had been performed at the Royal Court Theatre on 11th April 1905.]

My dear Murray

I am rather exercised in my mind by the proposed performances of Medea & The Trojan Women; and I have a quaint suggestion to make.

You will get no good out of The T.W. unless you have a strikingly beautiful and rather magical Hecuba. She ought to touch the imagination so as to make men see a past in her—not merely a personal or historical past, but *the* tragic past of all the destinies. The experienced actress in a strong part will shatter every such possibility. Therefore I, being of sound mind &c &c, do deliberately advise you to cast Lillah McCarthy for Hecuba. She makes a curiously beautiful old woman; and her notion of conveying the dignity of age is to speak much better than she does in a young part. And her blitherings and lunacies will become Cassandrated in the Euripidean atmosphere.

I dont think she could touch Medea. Medea mustnt blither: there must be no holes in her; and Lillah is always tumbling from heights into holes and bouncing up again, like a pantomime demon with a star trap. There is only one woman on the stage who can do Medea, and that is Janet Achurch. In Little Eyolf she *was* Medea. I think we shall have to get her a new set of teeth; and she must not be left to the guidance of her own ear in delivering the verse, or she will decorate it with the most subversive caterwaulings; but Medea is a big thing that breaks through all mere prudences; and if any of her old strength remains (and I shouldnt hesitate to ask her to rehearse on approval to find that out) the next best within reach is a thousand miles behind.

I write this on the spur of the moment lest you should get committed to Lillah as Medea, and some too too solid chump of a Hecuba before you have heard me.

yrs ever
G.B.S.

To CHARLES CHARRINGTON

Ayot St Lawrence. Welwyn
[A/4]   30th June 1907

[Shaw had participated in a discussion which followed Cecil Chesterton's lecture "Socialism and the Press" at the Fabian Society meeting on 28th June.]

Dear Charrington

You may console Janet—if so vain a woman can be consoled. I did not warn her not to let anyone *see* her at the Court: on the contrary, the more they see her the better, as she is much more fairylike than she has been at any time since the Australian trip [1889–91]. What I said was that she must not *speak* to anybody until the teeth are in. When I am trying to persuade Murray & Barker that she is the woman for Medea, which requires the finest diction imaginable, what chance will I have of success if she comes and gnashes her gums at them and goo-goos and ga-gaas like a baby? When I spoke at the Fabian on Friday, I had artificial teeth in my mouth for the first time in my life: they had been there exactly four hours. It was awful: the conviction that they would fall out every time I opened my mouth and the impulse to swallow them every time I shut it, made that speech the most agonizing public effort I ever made. But I now understand why Demosthenes practised oratory by putting pebbles in his mouth. It compelled him to make a much greater effort to articulate.

GBS

To JULIO BROUTÁ

10 Adelphi Terrace W C
[A/6]   30th June 1907

[Dr Julio Broutá (d. 1932) was Shaw's authorised translator in Spain until his death. His translations, however, were not highly regarded, and very few of Shaw's plays received professional production in Spain. Shaw's Italian translator was Antonio Agresti (1866–1926). The suggested device of publishing one act of each play to obtain technical copyright did not prove necessary, as Broutá rapidly translated and published all seven of the *Plays Pleasant and Unpleasant* within the deadline. It was later employed, however, by Augustin Hamon in 1910 for French copyright protection of *Three Plays for Puritans*.]

695

Dear Sir

I am urgently in need of a Spanish translator. Hitherto I have refused all applications for my permission to translate particular plays, because what I want is a Spanish Trebitsch: that is, someone who will become the Bernard Shaw of Spain—who will translate all my works, both literary and dramatic, taking 50% of all profits and tantièmes. Trebitsch has spoken of you in such high terms that I should be very glad if I could induce you to undertake this rather arduous task.

As my plays will make their way slowly; and as it will be necessary to translate some of them long before they are likely to be performed, I should—unless you are a man of property, like Trebitsch—have to make you an advance on account of tantièmes &c to enable you to devote the necessary time to the translations. What sum would you consider sufficient for this purpose? My Italian translator asks me for an advance of £16 for each full length play.

Now comes the most pressing part of the affair, which I tell you of in strict confidence. No less than 7 of my plays were published here under the title Plays, Pleasant & Unpleasant, in April 1898. Unless they are published in Spanish before next April, the translation rights will be lost. There is not time left now for a complete translation; but a volume of selections, containing one act of each play, or at least some vital scene, would suffice to protect us. It could be cheaply printed; and the sale of a single copy, with whatever registration is customary in Spain, would be enough. I should of course bear the cost. I am instructing my publishers to send you copies of the plays in question.

yours faithfully
G. Bernard Shaw

To SAMUEL L. CLEMENS

10 Adelphi Terrace W C
[A/41]   3rd July 1907

[Clemens had lunched with the Shaws at Adelphi Terrace that day, as had Max Beerbohm. (It was a busy week for Charlotte, as her luncheon guests a day later were Auguste Rodin and Yvette Guilbert.) Clemens's *A Connecticut Yankee in King Arthur's Court* was first published in 1889. His *Personal Recollections of Joan of Arc* (1896) had originally borne the pseudonym of Sieur Louis de Conte, ostensibly Joan's page and secretary, the work being announced as "freely translated out of the ancient French into modern English from the original unpublished manuscript in the national archives of France, by Jean François Alden."]

My dear Mark Twain—not to say Dr Clemens (though I have always regarded Clemens as mere raw material—might have been your brother or your uncle)

Just a line to excuse myself for running away today. A domestic bargain was made to the effect that I should not keep you all to myself; so I cleared out to give Charlotte & Max a good turn. I had my reward at the dentist's.

I meant to ask you whether you had ever met William Morris. I wont ask you now, because it would put you to the trouble of answering this letter; so let it stand over until I look you up in America. But what put it into my head was this. Once, when I was in Morris's house, a superior anti-Dickens sort of man (sort of man that thinks Dickens no gentleman) was annoyed by Morris disparaging Thackeray. With studied gentleness he asked whether Morris could name a greater master of English. Morris promptly said "Mark Twain." This delighted me extremely, as it was my own opinion; and I then found that Morris was an incurable Huckfinomaniac. This was the more remarkable, as Morris would have regarded the Yankee at the Court of King Arthur as blasphemy, and would have blown your head off for implying that the contemporaries of Joan of Arc could touch your own contemporaries in villainy.

I am persuaded that the future historian of America will find your works as indispensable to him as a French historian finds the political tracts of Voltaire. I tell you so because I am the author of a play [*John Bull's Other Island*] in which a priest says "Telling the truth's the funniest joke in the world," a piece of wisdom which you helped to teach me.

yours ever
G. Bernard Shaw

To CHARLES RICKETTS

10 Adelphi Terrace WC
[H/2; X/206]   8th July 1907

[Shaw had spoken on the previous evening in reply to a toast by the Earl of Lytton, at a dinner in the Criterion Restaurant honouring J. E. Vedrenne and Harley Granville Barker. Ricketts (acknowledging receipt of a presentation copy of *John Bull's Other Island*, published on 19th June), had been moved by Shaw's preface to comment in a letter on 7th July: "I hate the Wellington legend, the 'no damned nonsense or damned fool' legend! Surely of all the forms of theatricality the impassive one is the most odious. . . . I have also foamed at the lips over your sixpenny fulminator! Why all this pathos over a mere mad dog? A mad dog has to be removed, however good-looking. The knife and even the revolver are excusable in an expression of opinion (the Press use them daily on distinguished persons); but think of a bomb at the Court Theatre because Barker does not give enough new plays by obscure persons" (Ricketts, *Self-Portrait*, 1939).]

My dear Ricketts

When I arose to speak last night it was five minutes past eleven and the Commendatore from Scotland Yard was knocking at the door, consequently I had to give up all idea of saying anything of any importance. I should, however, have liked very much to have brought out the artistic significance of our Don Juan experiment. It seems to me that we (I say "we" much as an organ-blower uses the plural pronoun when speaking of the organist's performance of a Bach Fugue) hit on a most valuable and fascinating stage convention. William Morris used always to say that plays should be performed by four people in conventional costumes, the villain in a red cloak, the father in a bob wig, etc., etc., etc., and I have always loved Harlequin, Columbine, Sganarelle etc., in eighteenth century Italian comedy and French champêtre painting. If only we could get a few plays with invisible backgrounds and lovely costumes like that in a suitable theatre, with fairy lights all round the proscenium, there would be no end to the delight of the thing.

As to Wellington and Nelson: don't be angry with me: I was not taking sides: I was only stating facts. My sympathies are all with Nelson: the comparison between the magnificent effect he produced with three or four trumpery naval engagements which I am convinced you or I could have won, and the uppish dulness of Wellington's much more difficult achievements, is all, to my mind, in favour of Nelson. On the other hand, there was an invaluable element of intellectual honesty in Wellington's refusal to be idolised.

As to the sixpenny fulminators I am quite impenitent. If nothing else will have any effect on you, you must be fulminated. Just consider the one fact that my Denshavian chapter [in the preface to *John Bull's Other Island*] has not elicited a single expression of concern about that unfortunate devil [Abd-el Nebi]—a young man of twenty-five—who is undergoing a sentence of imprisonment for life because he threw stones at a silly squad of British officers who had just shot his wife. What are you to do with people who have absolutely no social conscience? I throw paper bombs at them without producing the smallest effect. Can you blame the logical Southerner who prefers to throw dynamite ones? You call him a mad dog: but really—really—*is* that an adequate way of dealing with the situation? Does such a summing-up tickle your sense of humour now that I put it to you in cold blood?

It is true that Butler loved Handel; but don't forget that he hated Raphael.—By the way, do you know that he actually wrote Oratorios in the style and with the most ridiculously complete command of the Handelian manner and technique? I have got two of them.

yours ever
G.B.S.

PS Shall we do a pantomime for Christmas at the Savoy—a real pantomime?

To ERICA COTTERILL

In the Granville Express to Margate
11th July 1907

[A/3]

[The salutation suggests that Erica May Cotterill, possibly in emulation of Shaw's name, had asked to be called M. Erica Cotterill. Charlotte Shaw was a frequent customer of Mme Hayward's fashionable dress shop in Bond Street. Aline Solness is the wife of Ibsen's *Master Builder*. A Vedrenne-Barker touring company, under the management of E. Taylor Platt, was appearing at the Theatre Royal, Margate. The "new actor" was P. Clayton Greene, performing that night in *John Bull's Other Island*.]

My dear Emerica (how does that please you?)

If you dont learn to punctuate & paragraph, you will never be a writer. I get sympathetically out of breath with that unending flow of ands and horrids and I thinks, stopped only by the end of the paper, and nothing said after all.

Now listen to me. I cannot be bothered with a grown up baby. I am quite prepared to be considerate and gentle to weak people; but I have no mercy for strong people who wont face their position and shoulder its burden and bear its isolation. You have been very badly brought up; but that is nobody's fault, because you are one of those people who have to bring themselves up. You are a woman of exceptional strength, well bred, refined, and of altogether superior quality. Even your appearance is extraordinary: you are like the edge of a knife. You could make yourself a distinguished, memorable, attractive woman; and if you did, a thousand difficulties would vanish from your path—difficulties which hamper the great mass of dowdy, rowdy, painfully titivated girls who go about asking for work & opportunities, and answering every question as to what they can do by Ow now. But this requires a vigorous effort of self detachment, and a resolute training of the taste. It is quite useless for you to dress like anyone else, to do your hair like anyone else, to flop into a chair like anyone else, just as it is useless for a queen to behave like anyone else. The ordinary woman, even when she gets her dresses made by Madame Hayward, wears a reach-me-down as much as the girl who buys an avowed one at the Brixton Bon Marché. The woman who wears an eccentric costume is like an amateur in a tableau. They all buy their dresses and put them on without modification or design. They dont even really select: they only fancy something that excites their imagination; and their imagination sees it, not on themselves, but on some ideal figure.

You are not even one of those reach-me-down people. You have never yet seen yourself as a woman, any more than your mother (who ought to buy your dresses until you are prepared to dress yourself—only she would buy short ones) has. You skimp the knife edge with something black, apparently because the law & custom compel you to cover it somehow, without valuing it, respecting it, insisting on its dignity.

It is the same with your literary style. You dont want to be bothered with stops & paragraphs: let your mother & your governess put all that in. You are, in short, a naughty little girl; and everybody bullies you instinctively. *I* bullied you; but do you suppose I dare bully a responsible, dignified, grown-up woman like that—I, who am just as shy & sensitive as you are? You ought to make it absolutely impossible for anyone to treat you so, instead of making it impossible for them to treat you otherwise. Remember, nobody will spare the strong who shirk their strength &, as the Americans say, "put up the baby stunt." You must not turn for help to a world which is looking to you for leadership. You must put away childish things from you, or at least lock them up in your privatest press, where Mrs Solness locked up her dolls.

I am quite aware of the difficulty of your case. The common girl arrives at maturity soon, both in body & character. The super girl is

700

still a terrified child at 25. Nothing is more difficult than to realize a superiority which the world has always treated as an inferiority. But it has to be done. People in a false position are always extraordinarily disagreeable; but the beggar on horseback is far more endurable than the knight on foot. You will always be exasperating until you achieve something which will cause people to accept you as a woman of distinction & encourage you to discharge the duties of that position & take its proper attitude. There are other ways for untalented women— religion, which makes them realize their divinity, or bearing children, which makes them realize their humanity; but for you I suppose the safest way is to do something.

Anyhow, even if you cannot make up your mind as to what you are going to say, dont write always in the same key, the same tone, the same time. Try blank verse, for practice.

The train is joggling frightfully. I must stop.

G.B.S.

PS I am going to Wales in a day or two for three months. Margate is only for one night to see a new actor in a play of mine.

To EDWARD GARNETT

10 Adelphi Terrace W C
[A/3]   15th July 1907

[Edward Garnett (1868–1937), a writer, was married to Constance Black (see I, 421). The refusal by the Lord Chamberlain's office to license his play *The Breaking Point* (produced privately by the Stage Society at the Haymarket Theatre on 5th April 1908) and Granville Barker's *Waste* gave impetus to a resurgence of authorial rebellion against the censorship and led to the parliamentary hearings in 1909.]

Dear Garnett

I am quite in favor of a combination of authors and everybody else against the censorship. The difficulty hitherto has been that both the authors & the managers have supported it; and the critics have backed them. If the authors & managers had petitioned parliament (or the King) in the matter, something would have been done; but when it came to the point it always turned out that their opinions were, at bottom, exactly the same as Redford's.

I do not believe matters have changed much. There is Vedrenne & Barker & the Court authors as the nucleus of a new generation; but all the others are in the old groove, partly intimidated, partly aware that the censorship is their main defence against the competition of a sort of drama they cannot handle. However, the oftener we try to get a move made, the better. . . .

yrs ever
G. Bernard Shaw

To FREDERICK H. EVANS

Hafod y Bryn. Llanbedr
25th July 1907

[C/4]

[The Shaws spent their summer holiday in Merionethshire, Wales, from 15th July to 13th October, participating from 27th July to 14th September in the first annual Fabian Summer School, held at Llanbedr. Shaw lectured on education, marriage, foreign politics, and Socialism for novices. He frequently took part in debates, and gave readings from his plays.

Cristoid was a very strong film, entirely gelatin, which on development grew to a larger size, thus automatically giving an enlargement.]

Observe my address.

It is no use bothering because the parsons cant preach. What people really want them for is marriage, baptism &c. When the secular affirmations of these things are firmly established as popular superstitions, the parson will find himself superfluous to an extent that will astonish him. He may even have to preach religion; and then he will not be tolerated at all.

I am supposed to be holidaying here. Anyhow I bathe & take snaps on Cristoid films through a ×3 screen on your recommendation.

By the way, Steichen showed me some of the new Lumière color plates & took a couple of portraits of me on them—90″ exposure. They beat the three color business hollow.

G.B.S.

To J.E. VEDRENNE

Hafod y Bryn. Llanbedr
27th July 1907

[A/40; X/168.e]

[At the end of the 1907 season Vedrenne and Barker had relinquished management of the Royal Court Theatre. They now planned to invade the

West End by undertaking a season at the Savoy Theatre, and Vedrenne had written to Shaw to ask him to contribute financially to the venture. Shaw's next play, provisionally titled *Any Just Cause or Impediment?* (from the Church of England marriage ceremony) but later called *Getting Married*, was begun on 5th August; it was not completed until 14th March 1908. William Greet (1851-1914) and E.L.Engelbach (1847-1916) were West End theatre managers.]

My dear VD

I havnt any money worth talking about. All Europe now draws on my exchequer for advances on translations, printings to save copyright (the ten years limit for 7 plays expires next April), and lawsuits against pirates. £2,000 is all I can guarantee. I have barely £3000 loose at the bank; and I cannot get on with less than £1000 under my hand to produce the necessary effect of being a millionaire.

It is not at all easy to draw up the conditions.

What I propose as a basis for discussion is that we lodge £4000 to a separate a/c as a guarantee fund, I contributing £2000 & you & G.B. £1000 apiece. This will be a real proceeding on my part and a purely paper one on yours.

Interest on this sum at the rate of not less than 5% is to be a first charge on V & B's business, payable monthly or quarterly. This will be also a real proceeding as regards me and a paper one as regards you. Its effect will be that you will have an interest in getting rid of the fund as soon as possible. Considering the risk, I ought to have 30% at least; but as a Socialist and a Man of Feeling, I am willing to make you a present of 25%.

The paying off of my £2000 is to be a first charge on the profits of V & B (total profits for London + the provinces), profits to be reckoned *after* salaries of £1000 a year apiece to V & B have been charged as expenses. Barker also, of course, to draw salary & fees as author & actor at the rate of £5 per act, and fees on not more than the Shavian scale. My own salary—another thousand—to be taken out in moral superiority.

The guarantee fund shall not be drawn upon for current expenses at the Savoy (Barker would spree it on a single scene in Peer Gynt). It shall be available only for Shavian tours. BUT it shall be available in the last resort to secure the rent payable by you as lessee of the Savoy for the season ending Easter 1908.

The only question that remains is the question of what constitutes your profit. I want you to pay me off and go on your own as soon as possible; but profit can always be held back by calling it reserve fund.

Therefore, as the guarantee is itself a sort of reserve fund, I think we ought to bar a reserve fund until I am paid off, and treat the net surplus after expenses as all profit.

I also want a "most favored nation" clause as regards myself. Nobody else must be let in without my knowledge, and nobody must get a higher rate of interest. Otherwise what I spare, Greet & Engelbach will grab in return for an extra £250.

What say you to this?

I am becoming more & more convinced that my next play will not be begun this year. I have an appalling heap of mere business arrears to work through.

yours ever
G. Bernard Shaw

To ARCHIBALD HENDERSON

Hafod y Bryn. Llanbedr
[A/9]   29th July 1907

[Gertrud Käsebier (1852–1934) in the United States, Robert Demachy (d. 1937) in France, and Baron A. de Meyer (1868?–1946) in Germany all were members of the international "Linked Ring Brotherhood" of photographers.]

My dear Henderson

You must restrain your enthusiasm for photogravure, unless you propose to issue a Bernard Shaw album at $25. Each photogravure has to be separately printed on separate paper at a cost of about twopence. The three in Three Plays for Puritans knock about sixpence a copy off the profits, and probably dont increase the sales a bit.

I am glad you liked Coburn. He is a specially white youth, and, on the whole, the best photographer in the world. He is quite right in saying that he could do no better with the Rodin than he has already done. You see, that was what he meant to do; and if you dont like it (says Master Alvin) there is always the trade photographer to fall back on. He is quite an eligible subject for an article. He has carried photography clean beyond the Käsebier–Stieglitz boom. The best workman that movement produced was, perhaps, Demachy; but Demachy does not aim at making an art of photography, but at producing the effects of the painters—notably the Barbizon school and the Impressionists— by photographic methods and artistic manipulation of the print. Mrs

Käsebier's work is most charming; her lucky negatives are first rate; but though she knew what to try for, and valued it when she got it, she had to make merits of glaring deficiencies in the photographic process, and use her power of appeal to the imagination to make us swallow huge blotches of shadow which were not merely underexposed but actually not effectively photographed at all. Coburn, though even he cannot get the whole scale of natural light out of his plates (or rather his Cristoid films) any more than Turner could get it out of his paints, nevertheless never exhibits a print that does not owe much of its value to great skill in developing and printing, or that is not an artistic photograph sui generis, and not an imitation of a Corot landscape or a charcoal drawing. I consider that the only living photographer within London ken who has kept pace with him technically in certain processes is Baron de Meyer. When his work & de Meyer's appeared last in London with a miscellaneous collection of the masterpieces of the Stieglitz boom, these latter were visibly beaten hollow: some which delighted us all a few years ago now proclaimed themselves simply as Straight Prints from Spoiled Negatives. In short, Coburn is a good workman; and whenever his work does not please you, watch & pray for a while and you will find that your opinion will change.

I havnt seen any of Steichen's results except the color plate which you saw. . . .

I have not yet read your chapters for you, as I have to give all my spare time to clearing off the arrears of my translation business. When I get through them I will post them to Chapel Hill.

Do not mistake the attitude of most of us towards America. You must remember that we have all found out over here what a devil of a mess our civilization has got into. The American still has illusions about modern progress, and liberty, and God's good intentions and strong preference for the principles of the 4th July. It is rather puzzling for him at first to be accepted—as all men are accepted in a thieves' kitchen—as a thief, liar, scoundrel, and hypocrite, supporting a government which would disgrace the quarter deck of a pirate ship. It seems to him that what he is up against is a monstrous prejudice against America. He is wrong: he is only up against the exposure of all modern Capitalism and of the doctrine of Laissez Faire by modern Socialism. All we mean is that you are just as bad as we are except where you are conspicuously worse owing to your behindhandedness in Factory Legislation & public organization—that is, in public conscience & social responsibility. We do not say that the American is worse than the Englishman: we *do* point out that the unspeakable

705

horrors of the Lancashire factories of 1800–1848 are the horrors of today in South Carolina, and that you have no right to look Europe in the face until you have stopped them as we have stopped them. We have horrors enough left, no doubt; but *that* horror at least is mitigable; and until it is mitigated it is important that every American should be received in England as a criminal. Tell South Carolina so with my compliments.

Bon voyage! And au revoir!

G. Bernard Shaw

To J.E. VEDRENNE

[A/40]

Hafod y Bryn. Llanbedr
1st August 1907

[The men named by Shaw all were commercial theatre managers.]

My dear VD

You are an incorrigible spendthrift. If you let in anybody for a share in your profits, you may as well go to Greet, Engelbach, Davies, [Tom B. Davis], Curzon, Marks & Co at once. That is exactly what I want to save you from.

I am not going into partnership: I shall act simply as a usurer. I put down £2000; you pay me 5% on it; and you make no profits until you have paid it off. But when it *is* paid off, you will have a reserve fund of your own amounting to £4000; and if you are wise you will maintain and increase this when I am paid out of it.

You cannot be called upon to pay off the £2000 until there *are* profits over and above your respective thousands a year; but you will always have to pay five per cent on it until it is paid off as long as you & Barker remain in business.

There is a risk of course of my finding myself with my money gone and no V & B firm in existence; and nobody in the city would take this risk without a share. *I will*, provided that if you voluntarily dissolve partnership to better yourselves (as in the case of Barker's going to America) you pay me off.

I can draft an agreement when we are agreed. I had better let my solicitor have a look at it, not that he will alter it, but that in case I die

706

there may be somebody with some knowledge of my affairs. Besides, it is possible that my drafting might inadvertently land me in some complication with the law of partnership.

yrs ever
G.B.S.

To B. IDEN PAYNE

Hafod y Bryn. Llanbedr
4th August 1907

[A/1; X/204]

[Ben Iden Payne (b. 1880), an actor and manager, was closely associated with Annie Horniman as manager of the Midland and Gaiety Theatres, Manchester. He had been negotiating with Shaw for rights to *Mrs Warren's Profession*, with Shaw abetting him in his attempt to win from the play examiner, G.A.Redford, a reversal of his earlier decision not to license the play. The effort failed. Tolstoy's *Dominion of Darkness* is better known as *The Power of Darkness* (see Shaw's letter of 14th February 1910 to Tolstoy).]

Dear Mr Iden Payne

Mr Redford has committed one of his characteristic indiscretions in replying to you in that fashion. It is human, but not officially correct.

I enclose a draft letter which I advise you to send him. Please keep a copy carefully, with all the rest of the correspondence.

yours faithfully
G.Bernard Shaw

[Shaw's original holograph of the draft letter is in the Houghton Library, Harvard University:

Aug 4/1907

Dear Sir

In reply to my letter of the 29th July, forwarding you a copy of Mrs Warren's Profession, with your fee of £2–2–0 for reading it, I have received my letter back again with a note in your hand and over your signature as follows:

"Surely you must be aware that the Licence for Representation of this piece was refused some years ago."

I do not know what you mean me to conclude from this. I am of course aware that in the year 1902, when considerable misunderstanding existed as to Mr Bernard Shaw's position, the play had to be performed without a licence. Since then the situation has altered. The play has become part of the repertory of the ordinary reputable German and Austrian theatres. The question of its morality has been definitely raised in America and decided

707

in the author's favor by the United States Courts. It has been played throughout the past winter there by two companies. As manager of a theatre addressing itself specially to the more thoughtful and cultured classes I find that my public regards Mr Shaw as an important author, and considers "Mrs Warren's Profession" in particular one of his masterpieces, not only as a play but as a dramatic sermon aimed at a crying social evil.

Under these circumstances I have ventured to submit the play for reconsideration. The usage of your department in such cases is well established. When a license is refused for a play which is in advance of public opinion, or is the work of an author who has not yet gained a sufficient reputation to justify you in leaving the moral responsibility for this work on his own shoulders, your department holds itself open to revise its verdict later on. Cases in point are those of La Dame aux Camellias, which was ultimately licensed in deference to the reputation of Dumas fils (the subject remaining as questionable as ever) and Tolstoy's Dominion of Darkness, the licensing of which was virtually an admission that the purpose of the play had been mistaken and its author underrated.

You must be aware that there is a considerable body of public opinion which regards the cases of The Dominion of Darkness and Mrs Warren's Profession as parallel. The play will certainly be sent in to you again and again for reconsideration; and in the meantime it will probably be performed by subscription (by me among other managers, as I need hardly say I conscientiously dissent from your former view of it). I admit that a reasonable interval should elapse between the applications; but as the interval in my case is five years—very eventful years as far as the author's position is concerned—you will not, I hope, consider my action premature.

Should you, however, decide that it is within your discretion to refuse to read the play again, will you be so good as to return the reader's fee, with a reply in correct official form which I can lay before the author in proof of my inability to carry out my agreement to produce his play. I presume your note is to be taken as private and personal to myself.

yours faithfully
B. Iden Payne
Manager.]

To H.G. WELLS

[A/26]

Hafod y Bryn. Llanbedr
14th August 1907

[Irving Fisher (1867–1947), a professor of political economy at Yale University, was active in the Eugenics Research Association. Russell H. Chittenden (1856–1943) was director of the Sheffield Scientific School at Yale, 1898–1922.]

. . . The day before yesterday I had an interesting adventure. I went into a pretty rough sea; the tide suddenly turned; and when I tried to swim back I found the shore had walked away fifty feet, and was on its way to another fifty in spite of all I could do. You know what numbers 7 8 & 9 are in every 10 waves in a rough sea. I had been diving through them until I was quite tired before I got swept out. But when you are trying to swim to shore, you dont bother about them; and they come up behind & snow you under and smother your head and sluice your stomach, and, when you try to take advantage of their sweep shore-ward, drag you back with an almighty swirl just nicely for the next one. [Robert] Loraine, bathing with me & following me out, shared my fate. For five hours (probably minutes) I swam without the slightest hope of escape, solely to put off the disagreeableness of drowning as long as possible, and noting how the tide was carrying me northwards along the shore and out. I gave up struggling to get back the moment I found that I was overpowered. My reflections were of the most

THIS IS THE SEA. A = G.B.S.

prosaic kind: I utterly failed to rise to the occasion dramatically. Chiefly I damned my folly for having postponed altering my now obsolete will, which I had brought down to Llanbedr for the purpose. My affairs were not in order: Charlotte would be a widow and would never make out about my translators, whose contracts are all higgledy pigg—confound you (this to number seven) I must get my head up and get breath before number eight comes—*there* you are, you brute: now for number nine and a lull. When I think how carefully I ducked through them when we were in our depth!—and now I dont even look over my shoulder when I hear the rush and roar coming at my occiput. Where is Loraine? is he done for too? yes: there he is swirling like a tub in the suds, not gaining an inch, up against it, but not, like me, having had his fling. Can I help him? Good heavens, *I* help anybody! Number seven again, very eloquent on that point. Number eight rubs it in. Number nine half hearted—a lull. No use telling him I am pretty nearly done: it might lead to his telling me that he was worse. Preserve a calm countenance, as of one who knew the coast and did this for pleasure every day. Can the people on the shore do anything? Clearly nothing. None of them know the sea as well as I do: if I cannot save myself nobody can save me: I cannot help Loraine nor can he help me. (What an idiot I was about that will!) They are all hulking about on the stones, or talking in groups without the faintest suspicion that we are not having a delightful swim. The dabblers in the surf are quite happy. Number seven again—eight—nine—Loraine swimming in foam—streaky foam—not in water at all—probably nearly done but keeping up appearances as industriously as myself. I am bound to try to save him; but as to doing anything! oh vanity of chivalry and un-speakable rebuke to safe-between-the-sheets estimates of one's courage and strength!—number seven: thank you: I am quite convinced; but arnt you a little before your time? hello! a stone: for a moment I can stand on it—only the tenth of a second; but it rested me perceptibly—damn! my toe is doubled back by another stone or rock or something—this is that beastly spit of rocks & sand that is to the north—swirl again, swim again, why? I am in my depth (not the slightest exulta-tion, but great physical relief)—where's Loraine? gone—gone down—no use: I cant go back and fish for him: if all the kingdoms of the earth depended on my going back into that wallow I could not swim another stroke: I have reached bottom at last: I am absolutely *beaten*, BEATEN. Talk of the treasure of the humble! Beaten.

I turned to look at the sea generally; and there was Loraine, who had been carried behind me and swept past me during the last 7—8—9 (I suppose), stumbling among the rocks, hardly up to his waist. The incident being over, I switched off with my usual inhuman suddeness, and went off to fetch my shoes, which I had left opposite the place where we went in. When I came back to the bathing boxes I passed Loraine's, remarking to him casually "A bit of a shave, that." "Yes," said Loraine. We kept up appearances to the last.

Conclusions. Whenever you get a serious call at the apparent ap-proach of death, you may depend on it that your imagination is only at play, and that your organism hasnt the slightest intention of dying. The only really true fiction about death is the story of the American soldier dying at Gettysburg. "Are you saved?" said the chaplain. "Now *IS* this a time to ask coh-nundrums?" said the soldier, exas-perated. If anybody had suggested a discussion on religion or im-mortality or the ethical aspect of my past to me, I should have given him my last kick for obtruding such heartlessly unreal and irrelevant stuff on me under such circumstances. Nothing of the kind occurred to me for a moment. The business inconvenience of my death pre-occupied me completely. I was also concerned about drowning, not as death, but as a disagreeable inevitable, exactly like a dental operation. That was the sole personal aspect.

Also, though I was reduced to such a depth of utter selfishness as

I have never experienced since I was a small child (that was how it felt when I missed Loraine & left it at that) this supreme result was the effect of fatigue, not of panic, of which I had no symptom at all. The question presented itself as "Will you let Loraine drown?" but the answer was "I would rather die than face the effort of keeping myself afloat and raising a ton of lead and pulling it in." And yet I was not out of breath, not even discomposed. But my arms were deadly tired; and though the hopelessness of a rescue was also at the back of my mind, the main thing was the intense fatigue of my upper arms near the elbow and my thighs near the knees. But it passed off very rapidly: I did not feel it after I saw that Loraine was safe. It was a purely local fatigue: my heart & lungs were no more distressed than they are now.

I learnt afterwards that Loraine had a much worse time than I. Although I am not much of a swimmer (the modern swimming-bath athlete would not admit that I can swim at all) I have been accustomed to the sea since I was a small boy; and I have somewhat exceptionally capacious lungs. In the sea I keep myself afloat mechanically, wallowing about in any attitude & only swimming when I want to swim. Loraine is not at home in the water to this extent. He tried resolutely all the time to fight his way back; and the big waves not only smothered him under their forward rush, but also dragged him under in the recoil —a thing that has never happened to me. Twice he was so tempted to give up and go down that it was only by a dogged exertion of will & concentration of his purpose to get back that he resisted it. His impression about me was that I was going strong, and that though it was an unheroic thing to allow the great brain of G.B.S. to become a salt water sop, he could hardly keep going himself, & had better not say anything. Fortunately he is a young and powerful man; and his muscle and will-to-live pulled him through. He got badly cut about on the stones, though. He said he felt "grateful" when he escaped. Not a ray of any such sentiment passed through my mind. I realized the safety just as I had realized the danger, and had no sentiment about either. This shews what a brute I am in some respects, as you have no doubt discovered for yourself.

I also conclude, in the light of the experiments of Irving Fisher and Chittenden in America, that Loraine was badly handicapped as a meat eater. But that is a controversial point. Still, the extraordinary difference in favor of the vegetarians in the Irving Fisher experiment of holding out the arms for a long time, taken with the fact that this was just the sort of fatigue I felt, is suggestive. Renounce, H.G: abstain.

I have just read this carefully through, to eliminate all the dramatic

711

lies. I have found only one—the phrase "for five hours (probably five minutes)." This is a flourish of the "for a moment that seemed eternal" order. As a matter of fact I dont believe our estimate of the time was affected beyond our power of automatically adjusting to allow for the effect of anxiety. When we went into the water, the sand was covered, and the water up to the stones above high water mark. When we came out there was a strip of sand as broad as, say, two thirds the length of Spade House, uncovered. I should put the adventurous part of the bathe at over five minutes and probably under ten.

Whilst I was dressing in the bathing box the waves in which I had been swimming were vivid before my imagination. When I went out and looked at the reality, my disgust—also Loraine's—was unspeakable. Simply nothing. A little rough, no doubt; but good Lord! make a fuss about a swim in that!! Rubbish! Mere imagination—funk—folly.

Here I am dragged off to bathe again. Charlotte & her sister were not present on that occasion, fortunately. It was too cold & windy & rough for them to come down [to the beach].

yrs ever
G.B.S.

[Wells replied on 23rd August: "Wasted chances! You shouldn't have come out. There you were—lacking nothing but a little decent resolution to make a distinguished end. You should have swum to Loraine, embraced him & gone to the bottom—a noble life wasted in an insane attempt to rescue an actor-manager. ... As for me I could have sailed in with one or two first class obituary articles and put you right with America and Germany. I should have invented a series of confidential conversations & practically gutted your 'serious side.' ... But fundamentally you are a weak man. You & I know it. No advice of mine will save you from a fourth act and too much. You will probably die about 1938—obscurely."]

To C.H. NORMAN

[A/4]

Hafod y Bryn. Llanbedr
17th August 1907

[Clarence H. Norman was a journalist and shorthand writer, employed in the law courts. For many years Shaw employed him to make the verbatim reports of his public addresses. Norman was acting as secretary for a petition, drafted by Shaw, on the Denshawai incident (see letter of 8th July 1907 to

Charles Ricketts), calling for the immediate release of the Egyptian prisoners. It was published, with the signatures of 53 notables, in the *New Age* on 24th October. Shaw's motive in publishing it, he revealed to Holbrook Jackson (1874–1948), an editor of the *New Age* on 12th November, was to force Campbell-Bannerman to revise his cabinet: "I believe that by a steady singling out of Morley (for his refusal to interfere with the flogging of Indians for political offences) and Grey (for Denshawai), and some grumbling about Gladstone's reactionary free-contract attitude at the Home Office, we might make black sheep of them among the Liberals, and even compel C.B. to reconstitute his Cabinet on more popular lines" [A/4].

Sir Edward Grey (1862–1933), Viscount Grey of Fallodon, was Secretary of State for Foreign Affairs, 1905–16. Evelyn Baring (1841–1917), 1st Earl of Cromer, had for many years been Agent and Consul-General in Egypt; he resigned in 1907. The Rt. Hon. Will Thorne (1857–1946) was Labour M.P. for West Ham, 1906–45.]

Dear Mr Norman

The address is Wilfred Scawen Blunt, Newbuildings Place, Horsham, Sussex. I think you had better ask him what is being done and what can be done (if anything) on this side. There is no use in blackguarding Grey: it puts his back up; and he and the rest of the Cabinet will conclude as a matter of course that the agitation is the usual party move to blacken the Government in the interest of the Opposition. That is the view they would take of Wyndham's signature, if you can get it; but what chance is there of the front Opposition bench touching a petition that is virtually a demonstration against Lord Cromer? Cunninghame Graham's address is 28 Margaret St W.

As to Thorne, why only he? Why not get the whole Labor Party to sign? If they refused I could comment on their refusal very strongly in The Clarion. Burns ought to sign, too.

But as Grey declared virtually that he was going to give in at the first opportunity, we had better be careful not to do anything that would give him the appearance of yielding to threats or admitting that he was in the wrong. The first thing to be done is to get Abdel Nebi & Co. out of jail. After that, we can tell his jailers what we think of them.

yours faithfully
G. Bernard Shaw

To EDITH LIVIA BEATTY

10 Adelphi Terrace W C

[A/3]   20th September 1907

My dear Livia

. . . I daresay Dalkey is actually and really and prosaically a stupid little suburban seaside place; but to me it is wonderland. Though you would not suppose so from my present appearance, I was once a boy, apparently disreputable & worthless, but a prince in a world of my own imagination. I lived then in a house called Torca Cottage, half way up the hill that has a castle on top, on the Dalkey side of Killiney Hill. The front garden commanded Killiney bay: the back garden Dublin Bay. When *I* was in those gardens they commanded all the kingdoms of the earth, all the regions of the sky, and all the ages of history. I once described the place to an English lady in such terms that she went to Ireland to see it, and was unspeakably disgusted at the piffling reality that confronted her.

I gather from your letter that your Olympian host and uncle [Charles Dowling] shares my impression of the place and flourishes greatly.

yrs, rather overworked
G. Bernard Shaw

To GILBERT MURRAY

10 Adelphi Terrace W C

[A/36]   10th October 1907

[A letter attacking theatre censorship was published in *The Times* on 29th October 1907, bearing the signatures of 71 playwrights and authors who had formed themselves into a committee of protest against the censorship of the plays by Edward Garnett and Granville Barker. The signatories included Henry James, W. S. Gilbert, George Meredith, Algernon Swinburne, Joseph Conrad, Thomas Hardy, Shaw, Wells, Pinero, Barrie, Yeats, Galsworthy, Synge, and Maugham. *The Devil's Disciple* was presented at the Savoy Theatre on 14th October, with Granville Barker as Burgoyne.]

Dear Murray

Tell Barrie that he cannot disguise his thrifty Scotch desire to pay out the names in small instalments as statesmanship—at least not from me. He must pay in full, or we are lost.

We shall get in one blow, and one only; and it must be a smasher. The list of names will not be too long, unfortunately: it would not be that if we got all the decent playwrights in England. It is the length and completeness of the list that will make the impression. Nobody would read a second lot: in fact, no editor who was a good journalist would put them in except into a corner. Royal Academy—Second Notice—Third Notice—is a game now abandoned to provincial papers of special obsolescence.

It positively must not be. Stiffen your back; for I assure you your opinion is worth a round hundred of those of recluse-playwrights. They know nothing about public life, bless them.

The D's D. revolts Barker's soul: he strives earnestly to crush the cast and get a delicate galsworthy result. Then I sail in and turn the whole thing into a blatant Richardson's Show. Between us, we shall pull it through; but his loathing of the stage and of the vulgarity called acting is getting serious; so keep plenty of oxygen playing on Medea or he will mix it with hydrogen and apply it cold.

G.B.S.

To FLORENCE FARR

[H/3]

10 Adelphi Terrace WC
12th October 1907

[A gentleman named Alfred W. Southey, having read a contribution by Florence Farr on prostitution, published in the *New Age*, had written to her on 9th October to offer practical steps for wiping out prostitution, including Union: "I suggest that as Union has materially improved the position of the workers, it would also strengthen and benefit those who from their circumstances need assistance far more than the matchmakers and dock labourers." If such a Union were established "on purely *secular* lines," Southey concluded, he would be "ready to undertake all the secretarial work and pay the preliminary expenses" to further the scheme (Texas).]

If I were you, I should reply to the gentleman as follows:

Dear Sir

There is no doubt that a union among the women would be a great advantage to them and to Society, and that it would be the first step towards rescuing them from the state of outlawry which makes their condition at present so desperate.

715

But you must allow me to say that the very first condition of such an organisation must be that it shall be entirely in the hands of women. If you can induce one of the "clever, brainy women" of whom you write, to undertake the work, and if you are sufficiently skilled in the history and practice of Trade Unionism, and a sufficiently sensible man, to be able to help her with advice and guidance, then no doubt you can be of service in the matter; but in my opinion you cannot take any more direct part in it. A male secretary would be in an intolerable position from the beginning, and probably be in an improper position at the end. When you consider that the mere existence of a Union would be regarded at first as a scandal, you will see how very undesirable it would be to make the scandal worse by a feature to which even sympathisers might justly take strong exception.

yours faithfully

I think this will settle the gentleman. You cannot be too careful in dealing with male champions of this cause. Ask any theosophist who has been in the movement since the death of Madame Blavatsky, and you will probably hear something of this sort of man which is not at all to his advantage.

I believe I broached this notion of a Trade Union to Mrs Ormiston Chant years ago; and it has remained at the back of my mind as a possible development; but the difficulties are appalling. It is always difficult to get women into a trade union, because none of them regard their occupation as permanent: they all intend to stop it and get married next month at latest. When this difficulty is complicated by the fact that the Trade is not socially tolerated and that the people engaged in it are themselves the loudest denouncers of it (its protectors and rescuers being usually persons of extraordinarily good character) the project seems pretty utopian.

No doubt the thing could be done by a very energetic, muscular, and violent woman, with the devotion of a Saint, and the arbitrariness and executive power of a prize-fighter; but such women do not grow on the bushes.

Anyhow, keep clear of the Gentleman of the White Rose!

GBS

To SIDNEY WEBB

Ayot St Lawrence. Welwyn

[A/14]   21st October 1907

[The Fabian business meeting on 18th October had consisted of a discussion on "the Progress of the Society." Shaw had no hand in the Fabian manifesto on the railway workers' dispute issued by the Executive Committee in November. He did, however, publish four unsigned paragraphs on the dispute in the *New Age* on 14th November.]

Dear Webb

Wells asked Charlotte to read his stuff. I did not know this when I sent it on. Will you send it to Adelphi Terrace, and leave it to her to send it on. I should like to see your comments.

I noticed his omission of the G.B.S. factor in the Fabian; and no doubt he had a chuckle over it; but I think it is intellectually defensible. He has taken Fabian Socialism to mean Administrative Socialism exclusively; and I think he is right, as that is undoubtedly our specialty: the rest was common ground for all the societies. Now I dont believe I ever contributed an administrative solution: in all that, as in many other things, I only played Tyndall to your Helmholtz; so Wells has done substantial justice and given a welcome rest from the perpetual Shaw clatter by leaving me out. If the positive side of his account of you had been as complete as the negative side of his criticism of me, I should be more than satisfied.

What the devil does he mean by saying that you lisp?

I certainly mean my notes to go to him. I chose their language with that in view. He has stuff enough in him to stand lots of hammering.

I was amazed, like everybody else, by your onslaught on Hobson, because I *couldnt* attend to his speech. Four women in the front row were asleep. My wandering mind took not a word of it in; and the meeting was in the same predicament. When you suddenly let fly I was bewildered, and tried in vain to recollect what the dickens he had said. I dont know even now.

As to the Political Committee, all I want to do just now is to talk and push the Middle Class propaganda. I dont want to do more than talk, unless there is pressure enough to make something do itself. I find that my line of telling the middle class that they are getting badly left between Labor & Plutocracy in parliament, & that the cost of pensions & all other reforms extorted by Labor will be thrown on their rates & taxes if they dont organize, is effective; and it involves emphasizing the limitations of Labor; but it seems to me that what we

717

want is a couple of years of this sort of talk rather than any immediate attempt to organize anything or formulate anything. Still, I dont suppose anything that the committee can do can do any harm or good; so I am rather lazy about it. Laziness is apt to be mischievous; but really nothing that seriously matters is possible. A storm in a teacup will blow over: let Hobson & Mugg[eridge] have one if they like.

I think the Basis uninspiring & old fashioned; and I should like to be able to place before possible recruits Wells's generalizations, Tract 70, and a restatement of the Basis if we could get it through without excessive friction. However, it would do equally well to retain the Basis and serve it up in new commentary. There is nothing exactly wrong with the Basis; but it is like an old pastel: the color is still unaltered but it has become undefinably shabby.

I havnt a notion about the Railway Strike. What on earth am I to say, except generalize about nationalization? For God's sake write it yourself.

In haste for post—
(return to town Wednesday morning)
GBS

To LENA ASHWELL

[H/4]

10 Adelphi Terrace W C
4th November 1907

[Lena Ashwell had gone into management, leasing the Great Queen Street Theatre, which she renamed the Kingsway, opening on 9th October. Norman McKinnel was a member of her company. Edward St John Hankin (1869–1909) was one of the most promising dramatists of the "new" theatre. His play presumably was *The Last of the De Mullins*, produced by the Stage Society at the Haymarket Theatre on 6th and 7th December 1908.]

My dear Miss Lena

How can you be so very unkind as to mock me in my extremity like this? Dont you see the situation? You have suddenly destroyed us by withdrawing McKinnel (oh promise breaker, heartless promise breaker) and now we cannot give Barker's Waste. You have broken his back in the middle of his wrestle with the wretched Redford. We are doing all we can: Pinero, Barrie and the rest of us are working like Trojans to get at the Censorship from above; and there is now no doubt that we shall obtain at least some concession; but we cannot get Waste reconsidered in time for the rehearsals to go on. We are told that the managers are going to desert us in terror, and lick the boots of their tyrant. And you have deserted us in the face of the public: "Miss Ashwell has withdrawn her permission in deference to &c &c" —oh, that I should have lived to write those words! And we have taken the Imperial Theatre, the only one independent of the Censor, because it will be pulled down the next day.

What are we to do? Our one chance of stopping the gap is to rush Hankin's play into rehearsal with Lillah McCarthy. We have nothing else ready—nothing good enough to offer in the teeth of the enormous disappointment YOU (wretch!) have dealt us. And now you ask me to hold over Hankin's play just long enough to make its production impossible. You are determined to destroy us either way.

What am I to do? I cant honestly tell Hankin that he ought not to keep the play for you: it is far more to his interest to have the play produced by you than by us. I cant honestly pretend to you that it is to your interest to fight the battles of the authors and of the Stage Society when you have enough to do to take care of yourself. I can only rage helplessly. And oh! I ask you before the high heavens what harm McKinnel's appearance could do to you? True, you can demonstrate against us by forbidding him—you ARE demonstrating against us by forbidding him. If I bring Barrie and Barker and Pinero to kneel to you—if I abase my own whitening hairs in the dust of your dressing room, will that soften you?

I collect my lost manners with a sigh. Forgive me: I did not hint a word of all this in my first note, though my soul was bitter with it. Do me the justice to remember that. But when you replied asking us to wait and lose Hankin, my despair overflowed. Heaven forgive you; and farewell, farewell, farewell.

heartbroken
G.B.S.

To LENA ASHWELL

[H/4]

10 Adelphi Terrace WC
7th November 1907

[Despite the implication in this letter that Miss Ashwell had now consented to Norman McKinnel's appearance in *Waste*, he was finally replaced during rehearsals by Granville Barker, who also staged the production. It was presented at the Imperial Theatre by the Stage Society for two private performances on 24th and 26th November.]

... I am quite sure that this performance of Waste will be a good thing for you and for McKinnel, though it will be a much better thing for Barker and for the Stage Society. It is utterly impossible for your genius to develop to its last inch within the limits of the Censorship unless we can hit Mr. Redford very hard whenever he makes a thoroughly stupid mistake. If we can get rid of him altogether, it will be so much the better for you. If he beats us this time—and the withdrawal of Waste would be a signal victory for him—he would refuse to license Hankin's play, and practically condemn you to spend the rest of your life either as the guilty woman of the stage, or the conventionally innocent one in a white frock with a blue ribbon round your neck. The issue between us and the Censor is a very big one; and it is part of the dignity of the position you have won that you should act in it as an artist and a woman of genius without regard to the mere business advice which business people are bound to give you. Big people must play the big game; but they cannot expect their solicitors to advise them to do it, any more than they can expect their parents to advise them to go on the stage. So you must come, Oh divinely-gifted Lena Ashwell, and play the big game with me, even though it leads you to destruction. Noblesse oblige. And we both look best with our chins in the air and the little world miles beneath us.

Mac, by the way, will act all the better for having his feelings deeply stirred. He may be feeling deeply about you; but the public will think he is feeling deeply about Barker's play. This is how I have lured Barker into holding him to his promise.

Oh, if only that woman in Waste were not a contemptible creature who got killed off as so much worthless rubbish at the end of the second Act! Then I should have tried to make you play yourself for us. That would have been a master-stroke.

ever and ever yours
G.B.S.

P.S. By the way, do you realize that the Censor loves thoroughly nasty heroines? Now you used to have a wonderful art of going straight up to heaven for a moment (I put it into Major Barbara); and Redford would drag you down for ever into the mud if you strengthened his hand. Can you still go up into heaven?

To HUGO VALLENTIN

10 Adelphi Terrace WC
[E.u/8]   8th November 1907

[Vallentin's translation of *The Philanderer* was produced in Stockholm under the title *Kurtisören* ("Love-makers") on 14th September 1909. It was Shaw's first failure in Sweden, surviving for only five performances.]

No language that I know has an equivalent for "philanderer." A philanderer is a man who is strongly attracted by women. He flirts with them, falls half in love with them, makes them fall in love with him, but will not commit himself to any permanent relation with them, and often retreats at the last moment if his suit is successful—loves them but loves himself more—is too cautious, too fastidious, ever to give himself away.

To C.H.NORMAN

10 Adelphi Terrace WC
[H/3]   13th November 1907

[Charles R. Wynn-Carrington (1843–1928), 1st Earl Carrington, later Marquess of Lincolnshire, was a member of Campbell-Bannerman's cabinet, and chairman of the Home Counties Liberal Federation. Augustine Birrell was a Liberal M.P. for North Bristol, as well as chief secretary for Ireland. "Police and Public agitation" refers to the activity of James Timewell's Police and Public Vigilance Society.]

Dear Norman

I also see a chance of getting a rise out of the Little Englanders in the Government against the imperialism of Grey and Morley. The difficulty is that it is almost impossible to cure our side of the habit of attacking the Liberals indiscriminately. For the present purpose it is necessary to crack up Lloyd-George, Haldane, Carrington, Birrell, Burns, and C.-B. himself, as the successes of the Government, so as to contrast them with Morley and Grey as the imperialist disgracers of Liberalism, and Herbert Gladstone, who has shown himself ignorant, out-of-date, and reactionary on industrial questions, and half sentimental, half police-ridden in criminal matters like the Rayner case and the Police and Public agitation.

However, the pot is not boiling so badly, all things considered.

yours faithfully
G.B.S.

721

To SIEGFRIED TREBITSCH

[E.u/5]

10 Adelphi Terrace W C
13th November 1907

[Richard Strauss (1864–1949), who since 1904 had been general musical director of the Berlin Royal Opera, was better known at this time as a composer of symphonic works than of operas. He had composed three operas, *Guntram* (1894), *Feuersnot* (1901), and *Salome* (1905), none of which had yet been performed in England.]

Great heavens, no! Strauss wird furchtbar beleidigt sein. Bashville is far too trivial. I wish he would compose the incidental music for the Hell Scene in Superman—a Mozartian fantasia by Richard would be magnificent. But I should like enormously to do a new libretto for him.

To R.B. HALDANE

[H/18]

10 Adelphi Terrace W C
16th November 1907

[Haldane was Secretary of State for War, 1905–12. The next general election was in January 1910. Campbell-Bannerman resigned his office on 4th April 1908, and died eighteen days later. He was succeeded as Prime Minister by Herbert Asquith.]

My dear Haldane

Do you think the Cabinet really knows how much feeling there is about this abominable Denshawai affair? How can you all be so weak as to let Grey smudge out your successes by committing you all to a sensational horror. In the name of common sense, do not wreck the next General Election merely because it is good form to be loyal to a colleague who is being obstinately and grossly disloyal, not only to his party, but to every decent human sentiment and political tradition. Surely, when it comes to a Liberal Minister being fiercely defended by The Saturday Review against The Daily News, it is time to ask him which side of the House he intends to sit on.

I shall revolt you if I begin, in the manner of our public men, to discuss poor C.B.'s indisposition as if it were going to be the end of him; but there is something that you have to realize, which is not altogether unconnected with the impossibility of Grey; and that is that you are C.-B.'s only possible successor. I hope you are going to make it clear from the outset that you intend this to be the solution. Do not lie low and be modest merely because the thing is inevitable: it is really important that there should be no wobbling and rumours about other people, and all the rest of it. You must seize the crown; and when you have got it let the first acts of your reign be to give me that [Civil List] pension for Ashton Ellis (who is pawning his spare scarf-pins) and to abolish the Censorship of plays.

yours ever
G. Bernard Shaw

To JOHN BURNS

10 Adelphi Terrace WC
[H/2]   16th November 1907

My dear Burns

Can you not take Grey by the scruff of the neck at the next Cabinet meeting, and hold him out of the window over the railings until he lets out Abdel Nebi, and the rest of the surviving victims of that infernal business at Denshawai? I have refrained from bothering you about it hitherto, taking it for granted that your sympathies in the matter would be pretty much the same as mine, and know[ing] the difficulty of your position. But, as you know, I held back the publication of my last book for six months so as to be able to handle the matter with the official reports before me; and the consequence is that all the people who feel strongly about it communicate with me. Chesterton's article in The Daily News today is a symptom of the way in which the consciences of all the decent Liberals are getting sorer and sorer about it. Unless the rest of the Cabinet tells Grey flatly that he has got to release those men at once or wreck his party, there will be a violent split, partly through genuine horror at the infamy of the whole business, and partly by the readiness of the old Liberals, and your people, and Lloyd George's people, to seize the opportunity to purge the party by hoofing the Imperialists out of the Cabinet.

I know, of course, that you must make the best of the Government, and stand by the ship. But that is only possible on condition that the rest stand by it too. Grey made a most horrible mistake; and the notion that you are all to be involved in it at the next General Election because he will not acknowledge it, and because the Saturday Review encourages him in his stupid obstinacy, is silly. If a man's heart and

723

conscience and good sense have all run so completely to mere county family cellulose, that there is nothing left of him but a large nose, that nose has got to be pulled; and there can be no doubt that you are the man to pull it.

Do not trouble to answer this. Take it for what it is worth as a storm signal for the Government and give them a friendly hint accordingly.

yours ever
G. Bernard Shaw

P.S. If C.B.'s indisposition should prove permanent, I suppose it would be premature to suggest that you should succeed him. But at all events, Grey shant: that's flat. Haldane is the inevitable man. Say so from the outset; for if you cannot be King yet, you may as well be Kingmaker.

To HARLEY GRANVILLE BARKER

[A/3; X/168]

Ayot St Lawrence. Welwyn
17th November 1907

[Despite Shaw's blandishments, Lillah McCarthy appeared as Raïna in the revival of *Arms and the Man* at the Savoy Theatre on 30th December 1907. Auriol Lee (1881–1941), who played Louka, later created the rôle of Edith Bridgenorth in *Getting Married* at the Haymarket Theatre in May 1908. A projected revival of *Man and Superman* was abandoned.]

PRIVATE. Not to be communicated to Lillah on any account.

The other night at the D's D., when Arnold Lucy was having a rare beano as Swindon, Charlotte said that she had often noticed that in my plays *any* part, however apparently insignificant, could become the principal one if it got into the right hands.

I suppose, after this, you will not mind playing Octavius, vice Casson transferred to Manchester.

However, that is not the great treachery now about to be whispered. How far is it possible for Sergius & Louka to shift the centre of levity from [crossed-out word] (bother!—cant spell it)—from Blunt Chilly and Raina to themselves, or at least to make themselves a centre of gravity in contrast? Strictly between our guilty selves, if I can get Lillah into the play to walk in beauty like the night, I do not care a twopenny—or say a tenpenny—damn what she plays. She can play

Raina on her head; but so can anybody. She doesnt like playing with the ice eyed Bobby [Loraine], who will simply play off her as if she were a concrete wall at rackets; and she plays very magically with you. Edith Wynne Matthison can play Raina at 12 hours notice, with less color & blood than Lillah, but to perfection for Loraine's purposes & her own. It is in Louka that one wants color & blood. Suppose Lillah were to play Louka to your Sergius!! It is in tradition for Louka to be the manageresse's part; and Sergius is to be the manager. The question is, dare you, as a married man, propose it? To me the scenes between Sergius & Louka are so much more deeply felt than those between Bluntschli & Raina that I had myself rather play Sergius than Bluntschli, & rather have the strong woman of the cast as my Louka than as my Raina; but I know that this is not how it would strike most leading ladies. Just think over it before we commit ourselves to Auriol Lee, who will drop a little vinegar into your cup. She could play Violet, by the way, and Sylvia in The Philanderer—cant she?

G.B.S.

To ERICA COTTERILL

Ayot St Lawrence. Welwyn
[A/3]   17th November 1907

I never sent anything to the silly Express. Probably it quoted some articles I wrote [in August] in The Clarion (44 Worship St E.C.) with several passages written on purpose to shock people like your informant. It is sometimes useful to épater la bourgeoise as well as le bourgeois.

Your family relations—granted the unnatural and extraordinary conditions—are quite natural and ordinary. Take an ordinary old fashioned British home with from four to ten children and the father out all day at his business. There is no time for sentiment in that household. Even if they begin by giving one another birthday presents, the strain soon becomes intolerable, and the presents are abolished by general consent. The children fight one another for their rights; and the mother polices the warfare as best she can. She tries to "mould" the eldest child & bring it up scientifically. It usually dies unless it is hardy enough to survive until it is displaced by its successors from the focus of her sense of duty. The younger children have a roaring time comparatively: by the time they come the parents are cured of meddling & are simply on the defensive, providing food & clothes & schooling. (Have you ever seen the two old maids of a very long family —the two who got no liberty & no husbands—bitterly watching the two youngest dressing & flirting & snapping up husbands like swallows catching flies?). An old buffer called The Governor turns up at breakfast and at dinner. He is not a stranger, because he can be asked for things—for money, for a family motor car, for France or Italy instead of Bognor, for lots of things. He is mother's husband (by the way, *my* mother is Mamma: mothers were vulgar peasant commodities in my time); but the idea of any sentiment between her and the Gov. is too ridiculous to be entertained. The atmosphere is one of jolly derision. Sensitivenesses get fearfully trampled on. The children grow up hardy & thickskinned; and experienced people note that the members of large families always get on in the world. They dont suffer from shyness, nor from illusions about the other sex (except when they are in love; and they get over that without too painful a disenchantment when they are married). They have the same advantage over solitary people & only children that university men and officers on liners have over lower middle class men: they have lived the communal life for a while and in a fashion. That's ordinary, and fairly natural.

Now do you recognize the enormity—the monstrous morbidezza— of your own case. First, you are shut up in a house with two people who were adults when you were a baby, and were middle aged— perhaps elderly—when you became adolescent. How hideously unnatural! Then consider how unwholesome their own condition was even if there had been no unfortunate child to share it. Your mother had energy enough to manage a housefull of children, and depended for her real education on the experience that comes from that. The first child would be a terrible trial to her. The dread, the illness, the suspension of all the instinctive and acquired decencies as between herself & the doctor & nurse, the long months of it, and finally a troublesome little animal not a bit like a human being, and not even a man child. You may say, What about the maternal instinct? But you dont get that at your first attempt: sometimes it is not until the third or fourth, when the whole process has become familiar and normal, that the maternal instinct wakes up, and the baby gets spoiled instead of being left to servants and pitied and endured, if not positively hated, as far as an amiable woman (if she *is* amiable) can hate a helpless infant, however nasty and noisy & troublesome it may be, and however much pain and dread and disgust it may have caused. Sometimes it happens that way: sometimes the first child is idolized; but in that case, as long as it is an only child, it gets far more attention than is good for it, and its value as "the only one" creates a dread of losing it which often ends by its death from excessive solicitude.

You were either one or the other; and you will never *quite* know which; for your mother has to keep some corners of herself from you, especially as there is that ungentle cross in your blood which makes you a bit of a foreigner.

But your mother had a most unnatural care on her hands as well— a husband always devoted to her, and always in the house. Domestic love is all very well; but it is not good to be stewed in it all your life. The reason why artists & literary people come to grief domestically oftener than other people is that they live too much together. The people who have to live in one room generally beat one another—with fists, pokers, boots, even lighted parafine lamps. Dont call them brutal: if you were shut up in great discomfort in one room with one man continually, even if you began by loving him, you would end by murdering him unless he murdered you first. That happens with a laborer who is out at work all day. What must it be like when the man is in the house all day?

Your mother rescued your father, it seems, from the most de-humanizing of all professions: schoolmastering. She then, instead of driving him out to earn his bread either directly or by public work of some kind, made a nest for him with her property & gentle ways, and gradually stewed his backbone into arrowroot. And you, poor child, are kept at the fireside to watch the operation.

Can anything be more natural than that he should get on your nerves in proportion to his having any positive character at all?

It would be quite natural for you to arise & go to your father and say, "Mr Cotterill. Sir. You are an excellent man; and I have nothing to allege against you; but having been kept in violent proximity to you these twenty |——| years, having exhausted your conversation, and being of a widely different age, I am tired of you, and should prefer the society of a younger and stranger man." To which he might well reply, "My dear Erica: since you are so frank, you will not mind my saying that you cannot possibly find me more trying than I occasionally find you. You have made life so hard at times that your mother and I have almost quarrelled with one another for bringing you into the world, she asserting that you are a thorough Cotterill, and I protesting that you are every inch a Vere de Vere. However, we know it is not your fault, and have read in our Bible that you must desire to leave us and cleave to your husband. Whilst pitying that victim from the bottom

727

of my heart, I wish he would hurry along; for what you want, dearest Erica, to cure your headaches and broaden and sweeten your character & temper, is just two or three fat babies; and I only wish the conventions of our society would admit of your acquiring them without saddling yourself for life with a troublesome man. Unfortunately, they dont; so we must make the best of one another for the present. Meanwhile, dont argue, as it sets me arguing, which upsets me at the moment & causes me remorse afterwards, not to mention your mother's perpetual "Why *do* you argue with her, Sidney?" She also, I may add, blames my comparatively middle class stock for your appalling indelicacies."

There is no use bothering: it is neither his fault nor yours; and it is just as easy to make a comedy of it as a tragedy.

That is all I have time to say.

GBS

To GILBERT MURRAY

10 Adelphi Terrace W C
[A/36]   18th November 1907

[Arthur Ponsonby (1871–1946), a former diplomat, was private secretary to Campbell-Bannerman. Shaw's letter, "The Censorship of Plays," was published in *The Nation* on 16th November.]

My dear Murray

I was sorry to miss you. I wanted to see you to ask you for a nice Greek word. You know my theory of the inheritance of acquired habits, which neo-Darwinians deny. First I say that since breathing, circulating the blood, and digesting food are beyond all question acquired habits—and rather late acquirements at that—the fact that they are inherited settles for ever the position of the neo-Darwinians as hopeless idiots.

But every man who has acquired the habit of bicycling knows that he relapses between each lesson & finally acquires the faculty in an instant, miraculously, as a fulfilled aspiration which has *created* the means of fulfilling it. Now, that relapse between the lessons is repeated in a still larger relapse between father & son; so that your son will not be born a bicyclist, but only an infinitesimal fraction of one; and many generations must elapse before little Murrays are born not only able to ride,

728

but furnished with extensions of the skeleton into complete bicycles. Give me a good word for this phenomenon of relapse—something that will sound Weissmanic, like panmixia. . . .

Arthur Ponsonby, one of C.B.'s secretarys, says that the Nation letter, which was expressly intended for him, fairly knocked him. In justice to Arthur I must add that this is not his own phrase; but I know no equally exquisite equivalent.

yrs ever
G.B.S.

[Murray suggested two possible words: *Metanesis* ("an intermittent loss of hold or of strength") and *Metasphalsis* (the process of "trip[ping] or fall[ing] in between"), although he admitted the second was "rather ugly." "You might," he added, "make a plain intelligible Latin word 'interlapse,' but that is giving Weissmann an unfair advantage. I am strongly with you in the controversy. Weissmann's essay on the Origin of Death is very interesting and good, but I felt in the other essays that he was confusing two questions. He proved that for practical purposes acquired characteristics are not inherited right off, as wholes; and then argued that there was no faint modification which would need a hundred generations to be clearly visible—which does not follow at all. Your instances seem to me fair" (BM).]

To A.F. LUGNÉ-POE

[G.u/13]

[10 Adelphi Terrace W C]
[Undated: *c.* November 1907]

[Shaw's terms for *Mrs Warren's Profession* at the Théâtre des Œuvres included a stipulation that it be performed a minimum of twelve times, with receipts averaging 1000 francs per performance, or the rights revert to the author and the translator. Lugné-Poe would not accept Shaw's terms, and negotiations broke down.]

My dear Lugné Poë

Hamon has sent me your indignant letter. But what is the use of writing indignant letters to me? Writing is my métier: you can no more impress me by writing your indignation than I could impress you by acting it.

You have not yet taken in the situation. I am not a poor & obscure man of genius needing the aid of a defricheur: I am a shark eager to

729

devour French artists & French theatres as I am devouring English, American, German, Austrian & Scandinavian artists & theatres. I have plenty of money; and I want more. I have plenty of reputation; and I want more. Every night five or six performances of my plays take place: I want to have ten. Here, on the other hand, are you, with nothing but your artistic talent and that of your wife. Your theatre, L'Oeuvre, is only the name of a phantom. You cannot get plays from Capus, Bernstein &c, because you cannot compete for them with Guitry & the boulevard theatres. You are a lost soul without a body. The reputation you have gained by Ibsen & Maeterlinck condemns you for life to introduce new foreign geniuses to the Parisian public, and rejoice when you can fill a theatre (hired for the occasion) ten times. I know all this. I have deliberately calculated the weakness of your commercial position; and I have found out from your correspondence with Hamon that you do not know the strength of mine, & that, like most artists, you cannot cope with a shark-author & with the Société as a man of business. But I also think that I could exploit you with some advantage to you as well as to myself. You could play the part of Crofts well. Madame Lugné Poë might make a hit as Mrs Warren. If you failed, you would drop the play. If you succeeded, I should not spoil a success by instantly taking it from you out of mere love of mischief; for I have the constancy of a shark as well as its voracity. I have no less than thirteen plays, not one of which has failed. In London and New York, men with less prestige than you have established themselves in theatrical management by producing my plays alone. My works might make L'Oeuvre a reality instead of a name. They might make you a manager instead of a leader of forlorn hopes. They might do for Madame Lugné Poë what Phedre can never do for her. Thus chance is open to you, with the added privilege of writing me as many indignant letters as you like. Write me another; and then—think over the situation. I have conquered London, Berlin, Vienna, New York, Budapest & Stockholm; and I shall conquer Paris in due time. Would it not amuse you to take part in the campaign?

You see I have no delicacy; but you have a great deal too much; so the balance is about equal.

yours faithfully
[G. Bernard Shaw]

Ayot St Lawrence. Welwyn
[A/3]   27th November 1907

[Erica had written to Shaw that Barker "is the only person I have ever seen acting who gives you a special sort of feeling—I dont know exactly what it is, only that . . . it is somehow as if your soul was laughing for joy, even if your heart was aching & aching for sorrow, always, until everything in you & round you is full of a wonderful wonderful quivering thing, until it is as if the whole world but you is dancing for the beauty of it—and O to think of being no more, if its quite absolutely true—" Shaw had sent it to Barker with a note: "Unsolicited Testimonial . . . Quite a clever girl she is, too—has written a play. Would you like to see it?" (BM)

The "woman who got married years ago" was probably Grace Black. Shaw's account to Erica was an exaggerated and highly romanticized version of the letter sent to him by Miss Black on 31st March 1889, in which she informed him that she retained her affection for him, but at a now-diminished level: "Long ago I saw that my love for you was a waste of force, because you were so difficult to me: but it is only lately that I have been able to love anyone else. I do now, and am engaged to marry Edwin Human, a socialist" (BM)]

My dear Emerica

How very nice of you to tell me! Of course I knew it; but I did not know who was the particular idol: in fact I thought it was Barker because of your fury about the censor. I gave him your letter because it is good for him to know that people love him. He was so impressed that he said I was a brute to shew it to him, & returned it most carefully.

You are quite right about my being young. I have never yet been able to feel grown up; and now I never shall. I save appearances by a certain art of life which I have become accomplished in just as an actor becomes accomplished; but the child remains there all the time. My body, unfortunately, persists incongruously in the usual course. Every two years or so, my spectacles become too weak; and I have to get new ones. My hair gets whiter: I have gold plates and artificial teeth in my mouth: my feet seem a longer way off; and when I race down a hill or cross a stream on stepping stones I am not quite so sure that they will go exactly where I mean to place them, and go swiftly there, as I used to [do] when I never thought about them at all. I have to bear in mind the saying of Larochefoucauld, that very young persons and old people who wish to avoid being ridiculous should never speak of love as a thing that concerns them personally. And I have to cultivate the

731

acquaintance of young, interesting, & if possible goodlooking men to keep my wife amused.

Life is like the theatre in one respect. Its charm depends on the imagination of the spectators. If you ever get the chance of seeing a good marionette theatre, you will be astonished to find that dolls can produce almost as much effect as—sometimes more than—live actors & actresses. The moment a man walks on the stage, or mounts the platform or the pulpit, the imagination of the spectators goes to work at once; and so long as he does nothing to contradict it too violently, he will be an idol. The Life Force in women will play round him and bring him sometimes the most extravagant offers of devotion until he passes into the obviously fatherly stage, at which point he is made much of in an opener, less romantic way, and gets declarations of love only from quite young things, and only very sensitive & imaginative young things at that—yourself, for instance. To the normal young animal he is simply an elderly gentleman; and if he hasnt grown old inside, he has to pretend that he has.

Remember always that these adorations are very good things for the adorers when the adored is a person of reasonable sense and honor. He is not always so: I have known Socialist orators & others who, on the slightest symptom of adoration from a woman, seduced her, borrowed money from her, lied to her, and left her with her idol most horribly & shamefully shattered. You will not have to go far to find a curate whose head is so turned by the inevitable adoration that he really believes himself to be a saint, and by trying to live up to his halo & finally imposing on himself an attitudinizing habit which he cannot get rid of to the end of his life, does even more harm than the thoughtlessly selfish, common, but *natural* seducer person. As for me, I have taken declarations of love all in the day's work, as it were. They are not all illusion: there is really a divine spark in me to which the divine spark in the woman yearns: the ultimate goal of the impulse is holy. There are moments—very rare and very brief—in which I really do touch all that you can imagine, just as you yourself touch it. But woe to those who understand those moments so little as to imagine that they endure continually or that they are personal and peculiar to any individual! The man who marries a prima donna expecting her to sing her high C continually, or the woman who marries a champion athlete expecting him to live at the record point of his highest jump, would not be more completely disillusioned than the spouses who marry saints or poets expecting them to differ more from Mr Jones and Mrs Smith during $\frac{99999}{100000}$ of their lives than Mr Jones & Mrs Smith differ from Mrs

Brown and Mr Robinson. And the consequence of that for you is that if you really want to adore me *scientifically* (if you will excuse that hard word) you must marry some decent fellow whom you dont adore at all, and tell him all about your love for me, stipulating that I must always be the first & greatest (he will grin and not mind in the least) and then give your mother those grandchildren for whom she is longing.

On Monday last, at Cæsar & Cleopatra, I met a woman who got married years ago, and sent me a note to say what she was going to do, adding, by way of apology for throwing me over, that she could never marry a man she loved. She looked extraordinarily youthful; she has children; her marriage is obviously as happy as it is possible for a marriage to be; her husband no more grudges her her adorations than he grudges her a motor car; and (if she still adores me) I have not the smallest doubt that if he and I were drowning and she had only one lifebelt to throw, she would throw it to him and think it a splendid thing for me to die. There are others—most respectable married ladies, who adore me & tell me so, and are no doubt much the better for it, since I take care that they are none the worse, and should lose their adoration if I didnt. And their husbands know it, and bless me for feeding their wives' imaginations & relieving them of the strain of being the family idol. As for me, I could not get on for three months without a retinue of men to amuse my wife & exercise her imagination and adoration without worrying her. They keep her fresh and youthful. Not that I do not interest her too: I am her property, and she is very particular about me; but I am also a fearful trouble & worry, as she has to take the whole of me instead of picking out my better moments. Most of my moments are commonplace; some are much worse; some she doesnt like whether they are worse or better; and some are moments of headache.

Now it is clear that you cant marry me, because I am married already, and too old anyhow. But please do not suppose that your loving me is the smallest reason for your not marrying someone else. On the contrary, it is an additional reason for doing it as soon as you can. To begin with, a great deal of the *pain* in youthful love is purely physical. Every complete and vital person wants to fulfil the sexual function; and that is quite an impersonal matter, though the imagination attaches it to particular persons. When I call it impersonal, I do not mean indiscriminate: the impulse selects to some extent; but the selection is not confined to a single person—a small man likes a big woman, a dark woman likes a fair man & so forth; but there are lots of big women

733

& lots of fair men; and one will do as well as another for purposes of physical fulfilment. As William Morris used to say (and you will not suspect him of lack of passion & poetry) "they all taste alike." Get married and have children; and all this part of your destiny will no longer torment you: your adorations will be unadulterated & painless. Also, you will not lecture me about love; for you will know what you are talking about, which you only partly do at present. Wait until you have been through as much kissing as I: then I will value your opinion on it.

One thing you will learn, the ignorance of which prevents many sensitive women & men from marrying. That is, that marriage is mostly an acquired taste, not a readymade one. If you choose a husband with reasonable precaution just as you would choose a horse—that is, demand nothing more than that he shall have "no vices" in the horse-dealers sense, and be healthy & wealthy (in reason) & of the color you like—you will acquire a taste for him & make a pet of him with surprising certainty. Even if you dont, you will be all the less anxious about him, and will have all your energy for your own business. And you will at least have settled that side of life for yourself. My mother did not care for my father; but the result was not tragic: on the contrary, she was much less sacrificed to him & to domesticity than she would otherwise have been. Marriage is a difficult business no matter how it turns out; but you had better get married all the same: celibacy for you means morbidezza and imperfect development. If you are to teach the world and move the world—and that is what being a writer means—you must share its cardinal experiences; and you cant do that without marrying, as things are arranged at present. You will find many women who denounce marriage, and with good cause; but you will never find a woman who regrets having gone through the experience of marriage, though you will find many who regret having missed it.

Everything that I said about you & your parents is confirmed exactly by the details you append to your denial; so I need say no more about that. Do not worry about your mother's health; and in heaven's name send the doctors out of the house. They live on the fear of death. Your mother will die someday; so will I; so will you: be content with that, and give her, if you really love her, a whole lapful of grandchildren to amuse her.

I have no more time now to give you more advice. Again, thank you for telling me. I thought I was too old; for it is quite a long time since I had my last declaration. They used to come much more frequently.

GBS

PS I had some notion of asking you to meet Barker someday. Are you sure you are not polyandrist enough to love us both simultaneously? I can still manage the meeting. Of course he doesnt know that it was you who wrote the letter I shewed him.

To GERTRUDE ELLIOTT

Ayot St Lawrence. Welwyn
[D/1]   27th November 1907

[*Cæsar and Cleopatra* had opened at the Savoy Theatre on 25th November under the management of Vedrenne-Barker "by arrangement with Forbes Robertson." It ran for only forty performances. Ian Robertson was stage manager for the production. General Rt. Hon. Sir Redvers Buller (1839–1908) was an army commander during the Boer War.]

A pedant writes to say that Britannus is spelt Brittanus on the program.

Kill Ian for getting the curtain down thirty seconds too soon & spoiling your discovery of Ftatateeta slain.

Make Cæsar be much tenderer with the boy when you pull him out of the chair; & glare jealously at them for fully half an hour before you speak. Also make a much slower & statelier march down to the chair; so that your sudden assault on little Ptolly may be a surprise.

Did you ever try lying *across* the Sphinx's paws as if it was dandling you. If I had such a pretty profile and such pretty arms I would not throw them away by being propped up against the beast like a sack of apples.

Also, why all that cross swathing in black in the last act? Perpendicular draperies would be better, with the arms hanging. With your elbow energetically doubled & all that tight wrapping, you should have a megaphone & be on the bridge of a cross-channel steamer in half a gale.

F.R. is very fine; but he is very like Lorenzo di Medici. His head ought to be like a bladder of lard when you take off his wreath; but I suppose his adorers would not stand it.

Everybody was nervous on Monday; and though they were perfect in the words & business the performance was a little underdone; but that will wear off. You were much admired.

Belzanor [A.W. Tyrer] is a calamity. He should be an elderly character actor, made up like Buller.

Pothinus [John M. Troughton] rose nobly to the occasion.

Brittanus is the success of Ian's life. He was my original cast for it, & F.R. was shocked & said he must play Septimius! In haste—until I go again.

G.B.S.

To WILFRED VOYNICH

10 Adelphi Terrace W C

[H/1]   2nd December 1907

[Wilfred Voynich (1865–1930) was a bibliographer, lecturer, and antiquarian bookseller. His wife, the former Ethel Boole (1864–1960), was the author of the revolutionary novel *The Gadfly* (1897). Alexander P. Watt (d. 1914) was the first and most successful literary agent in London at this time. Curtis Brown (1866–1945) had handled the sale of Shaw's fantastic story "Aerial Football" to *Collier's Weekly*, to protect the American copyright.]

Dear Voynich

A. P. Watt and James Pinker are, I should say, the most firmly established literary agents in London. Watt is the doyen of the craft.

For my own part, I prefer a young agent. The old agents have all found out that it saves trouble to make things easy for the publisher, and that it does not pay to stand out for the highest terms. Just consider your own business for a moment. Suppose that all the books you have, belonged, not to yourself, but each to a different owner. It would be the interest of each owner to insist on your getting the very highest price you could possibly squeeze out for each separate book. But that would be very bad business for you. It would pay you much better to sell a hundred books in a day and get a commission of 5/- on each of them, than to sell three books at a much higher price and get a commission of a pound. In exactly the same way, a literary agent like Watt or Pinker knows that it does not pay him to stand out for the highest obtainable price for each manuscript. What does pay him is to dispose of a great many manuscripts on terms easy enough to make them go off his hands quickly. Thus he becomes rich; but the authors remain poor, and often find themselves given away most scandalously on vital points to save trouble. I should say therefore that an author who writes only one book a year or less, and whose works keep on selling steadily, should never employ an agent at all.

However, there is another side to the question. Most books are as dead as mutton eighteen months after they are born; consequently it does not matter a rap how much the agent gives the author away providing he secures him for that short period. Further, when authors are continually producing short stories and have to sell the serial rights of them, they must either keep a secretary to do their business or else employ an agent. If Mrs Voynich decides to employ an agent, she had better select a fairly young one who is still anxious to show his prowess and to make his name, and will be therefore glad to get so well-known a writer on his list. Curtis Brown, 5 Henrietta St., Covent Garden, W.C., did a stroke of business for me very well the other day. If I wanted anything else of the sort done I should try him.

However, you can now judge the situation for yourself and advise Mrs Voynich accordingly.

yours faithfully
G. Bernard Shaw

To GERTRUDE ELLIOTT

10 Adelphi Terrace W C
[H/1] 4th December 1907

[Seymour Hicks (1871–1949) was a well-known actor-manager and author of many popular farces and musical comedies. In the six weeks of the run of *The Devil's Disciple* at the Savoy Theatre Shaw's total royalties had amounted to £275 for 42 performances. The final 33 performances, after the play was transferred to the Queen's Theatre, netted him an additional £143.]

My dear Mrs Forbes Robertson

Who said I was in front on Monday? I was not. I have been intending to see you ever since you came back to town; but I never seem to be able now to do anything that I want to do. I shall certainly go and see the play again soon; but the theatre is so close to me that I keep putting it off till the last moment and then there is something that must be done, and I wait until another night. . . .

It requires a deliberate and conscious effort of reason not to be furiously disgusted with the Public and the Press over Caesar. They have not seen acting like that for Lord knows how many years—indeed most of them have never seen anything like it at all. And instead of appreciating it, they positively grumble at it. They complain that it is all very graceful, and eloquent, and noble; but still it is not Seymour Hicks. There are people who know better; and they are the best people; but one is lucky when there is as much as eighty pounds worth of them going to the theatre on any particular night. I am sorry now that it was not possible to produce the play anonymously; for it is plain that the critics let their preconceived ideas of me get between themselves and the acting. It is quite remarkable how exactly they have gone back in their notices of Caesar, to what they said of Arms and the Man in 1894. They talk about the barley water exactly as they talked then about the chocolate. They are still utterly unable to understand or to like manly virtue as distinguished from stage heroism. And those who saw the play in Berlin tell me that the Cleopatra there [Gertrud Eysoldt] was wonderful, which on enquiry, I find to mean that she had next to nothing on, that she sat on Caesar's knee the whole time, and that she took care not to disappoint those members of the audience who, when they pay for Egypt, will not accept the abstemious State of Maine instead. But in the long run, that will be all to the good. The State of Maine is very strongly represented in England; and in the Provinces it actually goes to the theatre, especially when the company plays Shakespear. In London it boycotts the theatre to some extent; and what is worse, the people who do go to the theatre in London are a rather specialized set—specialized mostly in the wrong direction. What we are doing is to build up a new play-going public, consisting for the most part of people who never troubled about the theatre at all before, and who are still very far from having formed a solid habit of play-going. The critics do not belong to this new set at all: they always hated the new stuff, even when they were trying their hardest to rise intellectually to the occasion. The consequence has been that every play of mine has had to begin by facing a unanimous and staggering attack from the Press, and has not become really successful until its revival.

I am sorry to say that if you could see the returns from The Devil's Disciple over the way, you would begin to regard Caesar as an enormous success. Unless we can retrieve the situation with Arms and the Man, Vedrenne-Barker and Shaw will have to go round with a street-piano.

By the way, why does Master Ptolemy mispronounce Ftatateeta? As an Egyptian, he would pronounce it quite glibly; and the joke is worked for as much as it is worth without him.

738

I will tell you more about it when I see the play again: meanwhile, I feel confident that Cleopatra's virtue will be forgiven for the sake of her beauty.

yours sincerely
G. Bernard Shaw

To ARNOLD DALY

[10 Adelphi Terrace WC]
[F/2]   [Undated: December 1907]

[*The Devil's Disciple* had moved to the Queen's Theatre on 23rd November. James Kilduff (1860–1912), a banker who invested in theatrical enterprises, presumably was the backer of Daly's ill-fated New York season (15th October–10th December) of one-act plays. The revival of *Arms and the Man* achieved a run of 56 performances. James Hearn (1873–1913) had worked with Irving and Tree before joining Vedrenne-Barker.]

Dear Daly

I cannot make up my mind to send you The Doctor's Dilemma. You would spoil it for me as you spoilt John Bull. There is an enormous part for a comedian in it. Eric Lewis played it here. He was the star of the piece. But there is another star, the young artist who dies on the stage in the arms of his lovely wife. And there is the doctor who is in the dilemma, and who kills the young artist for the sake of the lovely wife—the young artist being one of the worst. You havnt a lovely wife (on the stage, I mean); and you would want to play all the parts. Also, even if you imported Lewis and another pair of stars, the Berkeley would not stand the salaries. On the whole, I must keep it for Barker.

The Devil's Disciple is no good for a small theatre: we never could produce it at the Court. Now we have produced it at the Savoy and moved it to the Queens (a new theatre), we wish we hadnt; for business here has been disastrous: with the bank rate up on the [discount?], and society out of town during the parliamentary recess, theatre stalls have been empty. The cheap seats have been faithful; but London rents depend on the $2\frac{1}{2}$ people, not on the widow's mite. I am sorry for James Kilduffer; but you have fared no worse than we.

I cannot imagine why you did not stick to poor old Mrs Warren. She is bound to win in the long run. As to 5%, I cannot cut prices. But I long ago offered to take 5% when the takings were not above $250. When they exceed $250 but do not exceed $500 I am content with a modest $7\frac{1}{2}\%$ on the gross. Above that the 10% comes in. As your theatre holds only $40 or so, and there is never anybody in it, that ought to bring you out at 5% most nights. But on the other hand I cannot let my Barbaras and Dilemmas, or even Arms and The Man go to so small a house. You must do the best you can with Candida and with Napoleon [*The Man of Destiny*] and How He Lied.

On the 30th I play my last card in the Savoy game—a revival of Arms and The Man, the first since 1894, with a very strong cast—Loraine, Barker, his wife, Sherbrook, Auriol Lee and Hearn. This is the charge of the old guard at Waterloo; and it may prove that I am making the same mistake as Napoleon, not knowing when I am beaten and advancing when I should retreat. Loraine has given up a New York season to lead this forlorn hope for me. Take that excellent young man as your model in future, Arnold. He made my fortune with Man & Superman, and is profoundly grateful to me for it. You ruin me with John Bull and Mrs Warren; and you expect me to be grateful to you for it. Shame!

yours ever
[G. Bernard Shaw]

To ERICA COTTERILL

Ayot St Lawrence. Welwyn
Saturday to Monday, 14th–16th
[A/1; X/202]   December 1907
[Charles Cotterill was the author of *Suggested Reforms in Public Schools* (1885).]

Oh, you are young, Miss Merriker, very VERY young.

You duffer, why didnt you tell your father & mother that you are in love with me, and that you write to me whenever you have nothing better to do, and that what you couldnt stand was to have your father's trash set up as superior to my inspired scriptures? How can you expect to get on with your parents if you never tell them anything about yourself? That would explain everything in a perfectly inoffensive and highly amusing way. Instead of which you go on nagging at the poor man and pretending to criticise, when you are really in a condition of delightful infatuation & furious jealousy. He wouldnt mind the truth: it is human, natural, sympathetic. But this arguing—this saying things—this—yah!

Do stop talking about whether this is wrong or that right. Have you read my works in vain that you are still irritating yourself & everybody else with this artificial academic illnatured stuff about guilt & innocence? You talk of your father and mother and of yourself as if you were three clocks always arguing about the correct time & accusing each other of being slow or fast. Can't you take your parents as they are, and let them know you as you are instead of stalking them from a perpetual ambush & shooting little arrows at them.

Your priest seems to be a sensible man. But why not marry somebody with a short temper and a heavy fist, who would knock you down the moment you began to say that much of what he said was true but that some of it was wrong?

Oh, you want work, regular work. And babies. You are at present living on yourself, consuming your own spirit. You are consequently a nagging prig. My blood runs cold when I think of those poor parents of yours. And Mr Cotterill's works on Education!! "How to Keep in Perfect Health," by a Doctor with a Sick Family.

It's no use: nothing that I can say will be of any use to you. You must fight your own way out. Only, try a little courage, as you did in telling me. Take people—even your parents—as they are, not as they ought to be on some academic system of yours. But also, carry out your side of the bargain. Plank yourself down as what you are, and not as what you ought to be. What's the use of telling me that you are in love with me & then hiding that dominant factor in your sentiments from everybody else. How are they to understand you otherwise.

I must break off—post hour

GBS

To SIEGFRIED TREBITSCH

10 Adelphi Terrace W C
[H/5]   18th December 1907

[Trebitsch and Antoinette ("Tina") Keindl had just returned from their honeymoon. The librettists Rudolf Bernauer (1880–1953) and Leopold Jacobson (1878–?) had approached Trebitsch to obtain operetta rights to his translation of *Arms and the Man*. Their adaptation, with music by Oscar Straus, emerged as *Der tapfere Soldat*, receiving its first performance in Vienna on 15th November 1908. As *The Chocolate Soldier* it became one of the greatest musical successes of the decade in New York and London, although the Viennese production survived only for 62 performances.]

My dear Trebitsch

I have written you dozens of letters; but you have been so absorbed in your honeymoon that you either have not read them, or have forgotten all about them.

Can you tell me what are the exact terms on which you accepted that money from Oscar Strauss's librettists? As I understood it, they said they only wanted to use the situation from the First Act. But paragraphs are now appearing in the English papers to the effect that Strauss is setting the play to music, and that his opera will be practically a musical setting of the play. This would never do. Such a musical version would simply drive the play off the boards. Let me know, if you can, the exact wording of the authorization you gave them. . . .

yours ever
G. Bernard Shaw

To J.E. VEDRENNE

10 Adelphi Terrace W C
19th December 1907

[D/3]

[Shaw enclosed £500. It was his third loan to Vedrenne-Barker.]

My dear VD

I am stony. The enclosed is all I can scrape up. It leaves just enough at the bank to pay my Income Tax & my mother's quarter on the 25th. Will it take you over the new production? If not—the brokers!

yrs ever
G.B.S.

To HENRYK SIENKIEWICZ

10 Adelphi Terrace W C
30th December 1907

[H.c.u/2]

[Henryk Sienkiewicz (1846–1916) was a Polish novelist, best known for his novel *Quo Vadis?* (1896). He was awarded the Nobel Prize for Literature in 1905. Sienkiewicz had sent Shaw a multigraphed letter, dated Paris, 14th December, concerning a bill of "Compulsory Dispossession" which had been proposed to the Prussian parliament to deprive Poles of their estates and to implant Germans in their stead. He requested opinions about the bill to serve as public censure, promising to publish them. "We do not suppose of course that your opinion may be anything else than an utterance of indignation and reprobation," he concluded, "but a public censure coming from

a man of your eminent merit, will be the condemnation of the greatest
iniquity and infamy in the history of the twentieth century; your answer will
fill the Polish nation with sanguine hope . . ." Sienkiewicz edited a volume,
Prusse et Pologne (1909), out of the replies; Shaw's letter was not included.]

Dear Sir

Although I, as an Irishman, can fully understand the folly and
stupidity of any attempt of the German Government to suppress
Polish nationality, I do not feel the slightest indignation at the proposal to buy out Polish landlords and to colonize Prussian Poland with
cultivators deliberately selected by the Government as the fittest
people for the purpose. Such a proceeding is entirely correct in Social
principle; and its adoption in every country in the world would be an
enormous advance in social organization. What you are entitled to
protest against is any attempt to force a foreign industrial or agricultural garrison on the soil of Poland. By all means let the Government
buy up the land of Poland, and pay for it by a tax levied on the landlords of Poland. I applaud and encourage such a piece of practical
Socialism with all my soul; and I am delighted to find that the German
Social Democrats have educated the Kaiser and his Ministers up to so
desirable a point. But the land must be bought for the people of Poland
and not for an army of Prussian immigrants. Unless you keep these
two halves of the proposal quite distinct, and reserve all your powers of
resistance for the objectionable half, you will be defeated, because the
Government will use your mistaken opposition to what is good in their
proposal to discredit your opposition to what is bad in it; and Prussian
Poland will be plunged into an unofficial civil war for years in consequence.

Even to the question of the schools there are two sides. Nothing can
be stupider and more ignorant than the prohibition of the use of the
Polish language. England tried to do the same thing in Wales a hundred
years ago. The attempt failed; but the effect of it is felt powerfully in
English politics to this day in the implacable hostility of the Welsh
voters to the established church and to all measures, good or bad, of an
imperialist tendency. The result will be the same in Prussian Poland
if the Government is foolish enough to persist. But none the less it
must be kept in mind that a knowledge of the German language is an
enormous advantage to a Pole. The children will of course learn Polish
at home in spite of Prussia's teeth; and the child who grows up with
the knowledge of two languages will be better off than the child with
only one. If it were necessary to choose between the two a wise child
would choose German. Take my own case as an example. I am an

743

Irishman but I do not know a word of Irish. I speak and write English; and this gives me the power of influencing public opinion wherever English is spoken not only with my voice from the platform but with my pen. All the leaders of the Irish Nationalists have been in the same position. If the Prussian Government succeeded in extinguishing the Polish language tomorrow and substituting the German, the only effect would be that the Poles would begin to propagate Polish nationalism in German instead of in Polish; their arguments and eloquence would resound not only in Poland, but through the whole German and Austrian Empires, through much of Switzerland, and through that considerable part of the new world which speaks German. The Prussian Government would then probably curse its own folly, and strain every nerve to restore the Polish language and make the knowledge of German a punishable offence in Poland.

You tell me in the letter which you have addressed to me that Prussian Poland "has never kindled revolutionary flames; she behaves peacefully, and strictly fulfils the hard duties that events impose upon her. She pays the taxes and yields a military contingent whose courage was more than once admired by Bismarck." The only comment that I can make on this is that a country which has in the past valued the admiration of Bismarck more than its own freedom must not be surprised if the Prussian Government treats it very much as it would a regiment of mutinous soldiers. In my country we have always been kindling revolutionary flames. We have never behaved peacefully, and we have never fulfilled any hard duty imposed on us when we could possibly help it. And we also yielded a military contingent whose courage was admired by George II; but on that occasion it was victoriously charging his troops at Fontenoy instead of supporting them. The result is that though we have a bad name in England, and are not admired by our second-hand Bismarcks, we have forced the English Government to buy out the English landlords and give their land to Irish cultivators; and there is a considerable movement on foot for reviving the Irish language without any opposition from the Government. On the whole then I should strongly support the Land Bill of the Prussian Government provided it were amended so as to secure that the first offer of the expropriated land should be made to Polish cultivators, and that these cultivators should under no circumstances be allowed to become absolute proprietors of the soil, but should pay rent for their privilege to the entire nation.

yours faithfully
[G. Bernard Shaw]

PART IV

1908–1910

PART IV

1908-1910

IV
(1908–1910)

The English stage had languished under the shadow of an official censorship since the creation of a statute in 1737 by the Prime Minister, Robert Walpole, designed to gag the controversial dramatist Henry Fielding, whose contempt for Walpole's administration was frequently reflected in his plays. The statute was reconstituted in the Theatre Act of 1843 for the protection of public morality, bringing public amusements under the control of the Lord Chamberlain, and making him official licenser of theatres.

Ironically, as Bernard Shaw was quick to point out, the censorship was a well-intentioned institution which actually debauched the stage by fostering immorality at the expense of serious drama. It did not forbid vice: paradoxically it insisted, rather, that vice be made to appear attractive. Plays dealing frivolously and even lecherously with seduction, promiscuity, adultery, and prostitution were granted licences so long as these subjects were presented "agreeably," or so long as their practitioners received retributive justice in the final act. Earnest dramas, written by "stern, public-spirited and intellectually honest writers," were inexorably suppressed.

The serious plays, said Shaw, were condemned because the censor was afraid of what they had to say. The pornographer, on the other hand, had no trouble with the censor: "It is quite possible to conduct a theatre in such a fashion as to make the stage a mere shop-window for the brothel." Ever since the censor had licensed Pinero's *The Notorious Mrs Ebbsmith*, Shaw contended, "the stage has been given over openly to teaching that there is only one passion, the appetite of sex, and that intellectual, moral, social passion is revolting, unnatural, and hopelessly undramatic." His own play *Mrs Warren's Profession*, he indicated, was not proscribed by the censor because Kitty Warren was a procuress, but because her explanation of the method by which society manufactures procuresses was forbidden.

The public, he admitted, was largely unconcerned. Britain, said Shaw, was a nation of moral cowards, who preferred to be protected by the censor from unpleasant realities. "The Englishman," he noted in a symposium in 1900, "forms in his childhood the habit of having a nurse to keep him out of mischief; and he never loses it. His sole

747

concern is that the nurse shall be respectable. If she turns to drink or runs away with a soldier, he never dreams of taking care of himself; he whimpers until another nurse comes to take care of him." Nor did the theatrical manager object to the strictures of the censor, for the Lord Chamberlain's certificate guaranteed him immunity from further interference or prosecution for obscenity, sedition, blasphemy, or libel.

A wise control of the stage by the community, Shaw argued, was very much to be desired, "and the mischief of the present situation lies, not in the existence of such a control, but in its utter defeat by the false and silly pretence that the censorship of the Lord Chamberlain supplies it." Public taste, he believed, would be more fitted to produce decorum than any bungling censor. Not that Shaw sought impunity for the artist: "I only claim the same freedom, as a playwright, that I already enjoy as author. If I produce a pernicious play let me be prosecuted for it." His sole objection to the Theatre Act was that a dramatist was forced to submit to the caprice of an irresponsible individual, that an artist could be stifled by a despot from whose decision there was no possible appeal. He called for freedom of the stage on the same terms as those enjoyed by the press.

When members of the Playgoers' Club in March 1892 debated the issue of theatre censorship, Shaw suggested to them that the only con- stitutional means of getting rid of the Examiner of Plays was to abolish the monarchy! The failure, in that same year, of a Select Committee of members of both houses of Parliament to recommend reformation of the Theatre Act served to underscore and bolster Shaw's cynical argument. A further Parliamentary hearing in 1906 brought no better results. In 1909, after sustained agitation most of the previous year against the existing system of licensing—including publication of a protest in *The Times* signed by seventy well-known playwrights (ranging from W. S. Gilbert, George Meredith, Thomas Hardy, and Henry James to Barrie, Pinero, Galsworthy, and Shaw) and a deputation of dramatic authors to the Prime Minister (represented on the occasion, due to his illness, by Herbert Gladstone)—a new Joint Select Committe was established by Parliament to re-examine the whole troubling question. And this time Shaw, as chief protagonist, undertook to run the whole show!

He was determined to be the star witness, and to this end he set to work on a written statement which would eclipse anything submitted as evidence in 1892, particularly the published evidence of Henry Irving. He printed 250 copies at his own expense for distribution to committee members, colleagues, and the press. Being chief actor and author was

748

not sufficient, however. Shaw also appointed himself director, stage manager, puppet master, and fencing instructor! He conferred endlessly with Herbert Samuel, who had been appointed to chair the committee. He drafted letters to fellow dramatists, which he had multigraphed and distributed through the Society of Authors. He sent appeals to his translators to gather and send all available information on censorship in their own countries. What, he asked Augustin Hamon, was the truth about censorship in France? "Was its abolition a failure? Has it been restored? What was it? Who exercised it? . . . Was there any appeal from its decision? What was the penalty for defying it?" He drew up a manifesto for managers, and pressed all those managers of his personal acquaintance to submit requests to the committee for a hearing: "All the regular Managers," he told Herbert Trench, "will support the censor; and you would be useful on the other side." He prepared a series of "Model Proofs" of testimony for co-operating peers, churchmen, and titled ladies, to suggest the lines that statements from each of them to the committee might follow. He supplied informational circulars to scheduled witnesses, and planted unsigned articles and news notes in the publications of co-operating editors.

Eventually, however, he was rebuffed by the Select Committee, which declined to accept his printed statement in evidence, and although Shaw had indicated to Samuel that he "should like to be on again in the 2nd act," it refused to recall him for further examination after his first appearance. In November 1909, after fifteen meetings, the committee published its report, together with a full transcript of the proceedings, as a mammoth blue book. It did not recommend abolition of the Examiner of Plays, but the report, which the Dramatic Sub-Committee of the Society of Authors called "a notable advance on anything of the kind that has appeared before," incorporated many of the dramatic authors' suggestions "for preventing the abuse as an instrument of censorship of the power of licensing theatres."

Among the committee's important recommendations were suggestions that licensing be optional; that unlicensed plays be permitted to be performed, subject to prosecution; that subsequent control of licensed plays be placed in the hands of the public prosecutor; and that the present legal differentiation between theatres and music halls be abolished. Another significant recommendation was the institution of a Privy Council standing committee to be final arbiter of unlicensed plays in doubtful cases. This suggestion was not adopted, but in 1910 an Advisory Committee, which included representatives of the theatre, was appointed to assist and advise the censor.

749

Shaw, needless to say, was not satisfied. He had one additional suggestion to make, which he communicated through a letter to *The Times*: "If the nation still clings madly to the ideal censor clamoured for by so many witnesses—the man of the world, the man of culture, of brains, of public experience, of sympathy with literature and art, of some knowledge of the French and German drama—why not make me Censor?"

To JOHN MARTIN HARVEY

[C/6]

Edstaston. Wem
3rd January 1908

[John Martin Harvey (1863–1944) was an actor-manager who toured the provinces extensively. His great success was *The Only Way* (1899), Freeman Wills's melodrama adapted from Dickens's *A Tale of Two Cities*. Martin Harvey later produced *The Shewing-up of Blanco Posnet* in variety (1926) and *The Devil's Disciple* in the West End (1930). Charles A. McEvoy (1879–1929), a dramatist whose *David Ballard* had been presented by the Stage Society in June 1907, founded and managed the Aldbourne Village Theatre in 1910.]

I am getting too old now for melodrama—even Shavian melodrama. All my recent plays have been long & preachy: the next one will probably be quite unplayable. Why dont you get something out of the new men—the young men—Charles McEvoy, & all the other Stage Society discoveries? I have done something to break the hedges for them; and now it is time for them to take up the running & let the veteran retire.

G.B.S.

To CHARLES RICKETTS

[C/2; X/207]

Edstaston. Wem
7th January 1908

[Ricketts had written in December, inviting Shaw to become an honorary member of the International Society, and to attend a reception for which "Rodin has sent some remarkable exhibits, and there are, of course, my bronzes" (Ricketts, *Self-Portrait*, 1939).]

Am I to understand that as a Member of the International I shall have the right to exhibit drawings & models when I please? Vedrenne has several highly finished paintings of scenery which should see the light. I am not the man to be content with a purely ornamental position.

My ambition as a boy was to be a great artist: I am a writer only by
force of circumstances. For instance:

This
leg
is wrong I think.
What I mean it for is
Don Juan sitting
down & playing the mandoline. I omit the chair, as I cannot draw a
chair in correct perspective.

G.B.S.

1 Don Juan
2 The Devil
3 The statue (your crinoline notion left no room for the horse; so I
   had to bend him down).

To SIEGFRIED TREBITSCH

[H/5]

10 Adelphi Terrace WC
20th January 1908

[Samuel Fischer (1859–1934) was Shaw's Berlin publisher. The authorised
Hungarian translator was Dr Sándor (Alexandre) Hevesi (1873–1939),
who in 1923 became the director of the National Theatre, Budapest.]

My dear Trebitsch

. . . The agreement you signed about Arms and the Man is perfectly
appalling. The only thing in it that saves us from utter ruin is the word

operetta. I think we can prevent them from going beyond one act by that blessed word. But what a reckless ruffian you are to go and sign an agreement for all countries and all languages and all time! Do you realize that there are seven other translators in Europe with whom I am under solemn contract that they shall have the exclusive rights to deal with my works in their country and in their language? I am happy to say that the Hungarian affair seems to be settled satisfactorily. I had a long correspondence with poor Fischer, who complained bitterly of the wounding expressions in my letters. He pointed out to me that if I took proceedings against the Hungarian with whom he had made the contract, the Hungarian would proceed against him. I said the Hungarian was quite welcome to proceed against him as much as he liked, but that I must defend my translator. I am greatly afraid that poor Fischer got the contract cancelled at last only by paying through the nose. It serves him right; for the contract he made was a most monstrous one.

When do you expect to arrive in London? You must see the present production of Helden [*Arms and the Man*] at the Savoy Theatre: the cast is extraordinarily good, and you will be able to see how it comes out under my stage management.

yours ever
G. Bernard Shaw

To AUGUSTE RODIN

Ayot St Lawrence. Welwyn
26th January 1908

[G/2]

[Rodin had finished Shaw's bust in bronze, in marble, and in terra cotta. He had also, in 1906, done sculptures of Jean-Claude Georges Leygues (1857–1933), a French politician who became Premier of France in 1920; Mme N. de Goloubeff, wife of an archæologist friend of Rodin; and Mrs Charles Hunter (1851–1931), a famous British hostess, recommended to Rodin by John Singer Sargent, who painted several portraits of her. Paul Troubetskoy (1866–1938), Italian-born sculptor, later did a life-size sculpture of Shaw which stands at present before the entrance to the National Gallery of Ireland. Jules Dalou (1838–1902) was a French sculptor who had long been a teacher in London. Paul-Albert Bartholomé (1848–1928), another French sculptor, created the monument to Rousseau in the Panthéon. Henri Farman (1874–1958) was a French pioneer aviator, who on 13th January 1908 had excited the world by being the first man to make a sustained flight in public, in what was to become known as a biplane.]

Cher Maitre

J'ai vu le buste; mais ce diable d'homme qui marche foule toute l'exposition sous ses pieds. On m'a beau donné la place d'honneur au centre de la salle: je ne suis qu'un petit caillon que le marcheur va flanquer de son chemin. Tous les marbres, les platres, les bronzes ont l'air de filer au son du cor d'automobile. Georges Leygues, blotti contre le mur, proteste en vain qu'il est aussi de Rodin. On a peur de regarder Madame Goloubeff et Madame Hunter, parceque ce n'est pas possible sans tourner le dos au marcheur au risque d'etre écrasé. La Madame Hunter de Troubetskoy, quatre pas du terrible piéton, appelle les agents. Dalou, tout décontenancé, veut grimper les murs pour atteigner sa propre place, le plafond. Bartholomé offre un monument pour Père-Lachaise; mais le marcheur offre d'en fournir les cadavres; et personne ne fait plus d'attention au pauvre Barth. Inutile de me poser près du buste et d'inviter les comparaisons: les yeux de tout le monde ne regardent que le chemineau divin. On entend une voix qui crie "Place, tetes-mortes, place pour le sans-tête vive!" Jamais de la vie n'ai je vu un tour pareil joué par un maitre géant à ses pygmes contemporains. Moi, je suis désolé. Sans ces deux jambes satanées, je serais le roi de l'exposition—la Goulouboff et la Hunter mes odalisques —Leygues mon valet. Et me voila rien, absolument rien! Au diable votre colosse! Qu'il soit désormais exposée au plain d'Issy avec l'aeroplane de Henry Farman, là on peut au moins s'esquiver à son approche. Autrefois j'ai dit que la seule sculpture vive qui nous restent, c'est les bras d'or avec marteau saillant des boutiques des batteurs d'or. Maintenant je prévois une exposition de membres—forgerons sans jambes, penseurs sans corps, bouches-volontés sans visage, yeux de voyant sans nez, l'ensemble entitué "La part est plus que le tout." C'est franc concurrence avec Dieu—le crime de Promethée, mais Promethée réussi. À Paris vous manquez votre carrière: Paris ne demande que les objets d'art (pas trop d'art); mais l'Orient demandent les idoles—idoles qui sauraient dompter les incredules avec leur regard seulement. Voila votre métier!

Saisez votre prochain moment de simple humanité de penser amicalement de nous et de nous rappeler à la pensée de Madame.

J'ajoute quelques esquisses—

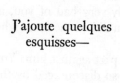

"Anch'io son pittore."

toujours à vous, Maitre
G. Bernard Shaw

PS S.Jean a marché un peu aussi, mais pas sur mon visage.

PPS. Charlotte m'implore de la laisser corriger mon style Français; mais vous ne tenez pas trop à l'academique, je crois.

To LILLAH McCARTHY

[A/4; X/182.e]

Ayot St Lawrence. Welwyn
6th February 1908

My dear Lillah

Raina has gone to bits. I do not mean as to the drying up: that I understand. But it is clear that you have never gone back to the beginning of the play since you said "How did you find me out?" on the first night. You now play the part unstilted all through; and the effect is disastrous. Loraine is ten times as good as he was; and Auriol Lee is as solid as a rock and has been advancing too; but Raina has gone back; and the result is that Robert plays you off the stage now. What is worse, in his desperation at your failure to feed him properly, he has found out how to drive the play through without you. Since you

755

will not let him get his effects by walking over him & making the anti-climax possible, he gets them by walking over you. If he didnt there would be no effect at all; and as it is, a great deal is lost, and what is saved goes altogether to his credit. This is really very bad of you, as there is nothing to prevent you from doing as you did on the first night, when you were very fine.

What is wrong is that you do not hold your part against him. You take his tone; you take his speed; and you are so discouraged by the failure of the effects to come off that you plunge on harder than ever and make things worse. Raina is never in a hurry, never frightened after her first pop into bed after the shots, always disdainful, patronising, superior, queening it, until her collapse. Until then it never occurs to her for a moment to doubt her enormous moral superiority to Blunt-schli, or Sergius's superiority. She likes him as she would like a pet dog. Her exclamation, "Oh, it is useless to make YOU understand," has no sense, no effect, unless she has been on her high horse all through. Well, you have got down off the high horse. You have become Blunt-schli's little pet, and Petkoff's little darling, and Katharine's naughty little girl; and the audience see what is meant only by a strained attention to the author's words, & are confused and disappointed because what they have read does not come over the footlights except when Loraine is driving it over. You never pay the slightest attention to him; and when he looks at you, and finds you dreaming about something else—when you give him his cue in his own tone & ruin his reply—his jaw sets visibly in despair and he becomes a man of iron. If I were he, I would give a yell of rage; seize you by the ankles and swing you round my head and let you fly into the pit; and rush screaming from the theatre.

What Raina wants is the extremity of style—style—Comedie Française, Queen of Spain style. Do you hear, worthless wretch that you are?—

STYLE.

The infamy of Barker's performance I do not mind. His farcical ecstasies & imitations of the exploded king of Portugal appeal to my sense of humor, though they ruin the play. There is not a human note in his voice from end to end; but after all, his performance is a criticism—a frightfully unsympathetic criticism, but still a criticism—of the

756

unfortunate Sergius. *Your* abandonment of the part is mere want of interest in it and susceptibility to what is suggested to you at the moment by what is going on on the stage. A shot excites you, Loraine's voice hurries you, Rosina [Filippi]'s comedy amuses you, and immediately off you go miles away from the character—the sport of every accident and impression—and the receipts go down to £59.

Vedrenne was quite right: you were born to be Barker's ruin, my ruin, the ruin of the English stage. Oh, give me that nice good Auriol Lee, who gets her teeth into her part and holds on, biting deeper and holding tighter every night.

Thank heaven it is post hour & I shall get this sent off before there is time to relent or flatter or give way to my wretched weakness of character.

Demon—demon—demon!

GBS

To H.W.MASSINGHAM

[C/1]

Ayot St Lawrence. Welwyn
9th February 1908

[Massingham had asked Shaw to review for *The Nation* Thomas Hardy's "Epic-Drama of the War with Napoleon," *The Dynasts*, the third part of which was to be published on 11th February.]

I am afraid—simply afraid. I tried the first volume; and the proof that it really did not interest me (beyond sampling) is that I have not looked at the second & third. Of all literary genres the one I am most down on is le faux, perhaps because I drop into it so often myself; and this mixture of Shelley's Prometheus style, Shakespear & Wessex torments me. I am afraid I should tear it to pieces; and as I know the author a very little personally & like the kernel of his work, I had rather not run any risks of being uselessly unsympathetic. Besides, I should delay too long: I am frightfully pressed just now.

G.B.S.

To NORMAN HAPGOOD

[X/208]
[10 Adelphi Terrace W C]
[Undated: *c*. 25th–29th February 1908]

[Shaw's short story "Aerial Football: The New Game" had been published in *Collier's Weekly* on 23rd November 1907, and, as Shaw's letter to the editor indicates, had been chosen for a $1000 prize bonus.]

Sir:

What do you mean by this unspeakable outrage? You send me a cheque for a thousand dollars, and inform me that it is a bonus offered by Messrs. P.F. Collier and Son for the best story received during the quarter in which my contribution appeared. May I ask what Messrs. P.F. Collier and Son expected my story to be?

If it were not the best they could get for the price they were prepared to pay, they had no right to insert it at all. If it was the best, what right have they to stamp their own contributors publicly as inferior when they have taken steps to secure the result beforehand by paying a special price to a special writer?

And what right have they to assume that I want to be paid twice over for my work, or that I am in the habit of accepting bonuses and competing for prizes?

Waiving all these questions for a moment, I have another one to put to you. How do Messrs. P.F. Collier and Son know that my story was the best they received during the quarter? Are they posterity? Are they the verdict of history? Have they even the very doubtful qualification of being professional critics?

I had better break this letter off lest I should be betrayed into expressing myself as strongly as I feel. I return the cheque. If you should see fit to use it for the purpose of erecting a tombstone to Messrs. P.F. Collier and Son, I shall be happy to contribute the epitaph, in which I shall do my best to do justice to their monstrous presumption.

G. Bernard Shaw

[Archibald Henderson's biography recorded the editor's response: "In quite good humour the editor of *Collier's Weekly* assured Mr. Shaw that the award was a mistake. The 'responsible' readers were out of town, and the sporting editor, who was a devotee of football, a vegetarian, a Socialist, a misanthrope, a misogynist—in short, a true disciple of G.B.S.—made the award. Of course, on receipt of Mr. Shaw's letter the sporting editor was summarily discharged!"]

To G.K.CHESTERTON

[A/1; X/203]   1st March 1908

[Shaw had been badgering Chesterton for several years to write a play, and continued to do so until Chesterton, at last, in 1913 took up the challenge and created the critically acclaimed comedy, *Magic*, which ran for more than one hundred performances. The *New Age* article, published on 29th February, was "The Last of the Rationalists," which Chesterton had written as a rebuttal to Shaw's "Belloc and Chesterton" (containing the now-famous reference to Chesterton and Hilaire Belloc as a pantomime beast, "The Chesterbelloc") in the *New Age* on 15th February. The lecture information provided by Shaw indicates that Chesterton had begun work on his critical study of Shaw, which was published in August 1909.]

My dear G.K.C.

What about that play? It is no use trying to answer me in The New Age: the real answer to my article is the play. I have tried fair means: the New Age article was the inauguration of an assault below the belt. I shall deliberately destroy your credit as an essayist, as a journalist, as a critic, as a Liberal, as everything that offers your laziness a refuge, until starvation & shame drive you to serious dramatic parturition. I shall repeat my public challenge to you; vaunt my superiority; insult your corpulence; torture Belloc; if necessary, call on you and steal your wife's affections by intellectual and athletic displays, until you contribute something to the British drama. You are played out as an essayist: your ardor is soddened, your intellectual substance crumbled, by the attempt to keep up the work of your twenties in your thirties. Another five years of this, and you will be the apologist of every infamy that wears a Liberal or Catholic mask. You, too, will speak of the portraits of Vecelli & the Assumption of Allegri, and declare that Democracy refuses to lackey-label these honest citizens as Titian & Correggio. Even that colossal fragment of your ruined honesty that still stupendously dismisses Beethoven as "some rubbish about a piano" will give way to remarks about "a graceful second subject in the relative minor." Nothing can save you now except a rebirth as a dramatist. I have done my turn; and I now call on you to take yours & do a man's work.

It is my solemn belief that it was my Quintessence of Ibsenism that rescued you and all your ungrateful generation from Materialism & Rationalism. You were all tired young atheists turning to Kipling and Ruskinian Anglicanism whilst I, with the angel's wings beating in my ears from Beethoven's 9th symphony (oh blasphemous walker in deafness), gave you in 1880 & 1881 two novels in which you had your Rationalist-Secularist hero immediately followed by my Beethovenian hero. True, nobody read them; but was that my fault? They are read now, it seems, mostly in pirated reprints, in spite of their appalling puerility & classical perfection of style (you are right as to my being a born pedant, like all great artists); and are at least useful as documentary evidence that I was no more a materialist when I wrote Love Among the Artists at 24 than when I wrote Candida at 39.

(Turn over—if a human whale *can* turn over

My appearances on the platform of the Hall of Science were three in number. Once for a few minutes in a discussion, in opposition to Bradlaugh, who was defending property against Socialism. Bradlaugh died after that, though I do not claim to have killed him. The Socialist League challenged him to debate with me at St James's Hall; but we could not or would not agree as to the proposition to be debated, he insisting on my being bound by all the publications of the Democratic Federation (to which I did not belong) and I refusing to be bound by anything on earth or in heaven except the proposition that Socialism would benefit the English people. And so the debate never came off.

Now in those days they were throwing Bradlaugh out of the House of Commons with bodily violence; and all one could do was to call oneself an atheist all over the place, which I accordingly did. At the first public meeting [10th March 1886] of the Shelley Society at University College, addressed by Stopford Brooke, I made my then famous (among 100 people) declaration, "I am a Socialist, an Atheist and a Vegetarian" (ergo, a true Shelleyan), whereupon two ladies who had been palpitating with enthusiasm for Shelley under the impression that he was a devout Anglican, resigned on the spot.

My second Hall of Science appearance was after the last of the Bradlaugh-Hyndman debates at St James's Hall, where the two champions never touched the ostensible subject of their difference— the Eight Hours Day—at all, but simply talked Socialism or Anti-Socialism with a hearty dislike and contempt for one another. G.W. Foote was then in his prime as the successor of Bradlaugh; and as neither the Secularists nor the Socialists were satisfied with the result of the debate, it was renewed for two nights [14th and 15th January 1891] at the Hall of Science between me and Foote. A verbatim report was published for sixpence and is now a treasure of collectors. Having the last word on the second night, I had to make a handsome wind-up; and the Secularists were much pleased by my declaring that I was altogether on Foote's side in his struggle with the established religion of the country.

When Bradlaugh died, the Secularists wanted a new leader, because B.'s enormous and magnetic personality left a void that nobody was big enough to fill—it was really like the death of Napoleon in that world. There was J.M.Robertson, Foote, and Charles Watts. But Bradlaugh liked Foote as little as most autocrats like their successors; and when he, before his death, surrendered the gavel (the hammer for thumping the table to secure order at a meeting) which was the presidential sceptre of the National Secular Society, he did so with an ill will which he did not attempt to conceal; and so though Foote was the nearest size to Bradlaugh's shoes then available, he succeeded him at the disadvantage of inheriting the distrust of the old chief. J.M. Robertson you know: he was not a mob orator. Watts was not sufficient: he had neither Foote's weight (being old) nor Robertson's scholarship.

So whilst the survivors of Bradlaugh were trying to keep up the Hall of Science and to establish a memorial library, &c, there, they cast round for new blood. What more natural than that they should think of me as a man not afraid to call himself an atheist and able to hold his own on the platform? Accordingly, they invited me to address them; and one memorable night [22nd February 1891] I held forth on Progress in Freethought. I was received with affectionate hope; and when the chairman announced that I was giving my share of the gate to the memorial library (I have never taken money for lecturing) the enthusiasm was quite touching. The anti-climax was super-Shavian. I proceeded to smash materialism, rationalism, and all the philosophy of Tyndall, Helmholtz, Darwin and the rest of the 1860 people into smithereens. I ridiculed and exposed every inference of science, and justified every dogma of religion, especially shewing that the Trinity and the Immaculate Conception were the merest common sense. That finished me up as a possible leader of the N.S.S. Robertson came on the platform, white with honest Scotch Rationalist rage and denounced me with a fury of conviction that startled his own followers. Never did I grace that platform again. I repeated the address once to a branch of the N.S.S. on the south side of the Thames—Kennington, I think [Camberwell, 26th April 1891]—and was interrupted by yells of rage from the veterans of the society. The Leicester Secularists [1st November 1891], a pious folk, rich and independent of the N.S.S., were kinder to me; but they were no more real atheists than the congregation of St Paul's is made wholly of real Christians.

Foote is still bewildered about me, imagining that I am a pervert. But anybody who reads my stuff from the beginning (a Shelleyan beginning, as far as it could be labelled at all) will find implicit, and sometimes explicit, the views which, in their more matured form, will appear in that remarkable forthcoming masterpiece, Shavianism: a Religion.

By the way, I have omitted one more appearance at the Hall of Science. At a four nights' debate on Socialism between Foote and Mrs Besant, I took the chair on one of the nights [16th February 1887].

I take advantage of a snowy Sunday afternoon to scribble all this down for you because you are in the same difficulty that beset me formerly: namely, the absolute blank in the history of the immediate past that confronts every man when he first takes to public life. Written history stops several decades back; and the bridge of personal recollection on which older men stand does not exist for the recruit. Nothing is more natural than that you should reconstruct me as the last of the Rationalists (his real name is Blatchford); and nothing could be more erroneous. It would be much nearer the truth to call me, in that world, the first of the mystics.

If you can imagine the result of trying to write your spiritual history in complete ignorance of painting, you will get a notion of trying to write mine in ignorance of music. Bradlaugh was a tremendous platform heavyweight; but he had never in his life, as far as I could make out, seen anything, heard anything or read anything in the artistic sense. He was almost beyond belief incapable of intercourse in private conversation. He could tell you his adventures provided you didnt interrupt him (which you were mostly afraid to do, as the man was a mesmeric terror); but as to exchanging ideas, or expressing the universal part of his soul, you might as well have been reading the letters of Charles Dickens to his family—those tragic monuments of dumbness of soul and noisiness of pen. Lord help you if you ever lose your gift of speech, G.K.C.! Dont forget that the race is only struggling out of its dumbness, and that it is only in moments of inspiration that we get out a sentence. All the rest is padding.

yours ever
G. Bernard Shaw

To H.G.WELLS

[C/26]

10 Adelphi Terrace WC
2nd March 1908

[*"My* balloon" refers to the ascension described in the headnote to Shaw's letter of 7th July 1906 to William Archer.]

Book [*The War in the Air*] just arrived. Will look through it presently.

Why didnt you consult an experienced aeronaut (me, for example) before you romanced about balloons? The great rip saw trick was done a few years ago by an aeronaut who came out of a cloud & found himself just crossing a beach on his way out to sea. He took his chance & ripped. The lower part of the balloon folded up into the top & the balloon became a parachute. He & his party got down safely. It was not so desperate a stroke either, because balloons often come down pretty nearly empty. *My* balloon went up to 4000ft, came down to 400; & then went up to 9000 with a rush through expansion in the sun. When we cooled after that we dropped half empty.

G.B.S.

To H.G.WELLS

[A/26]

Ayot St Lawrence. Welwyn
22nd March 1908

[Wells's "confounded book" was *New Worlds for Old*, published that month. Selwyn Image (1849–1930) was an ordained minister, turned artist, who became Slade Professor of Fine Art at Oxford. Shaw lectured on "Socialism" at a Fabian Society public meeting in the Queen's Hall on 24th March. Alfred Shaw (1842–1907) was a famous English cricketer.]

My dear H.G.W.

There are various things that you are forgetting.

Imprimis, you have chucked Women's Suffrage out of the basis as well as all the other democratic implications of Socialism; and this would make it absolutely impossible from the start to get it through without amendments.

Further, you are forgetting your committee manners—if a man can be said to forget what he never knew. Just consider what you have done. When the committee was formed, Webb & I got to work at once; and within a fortnight we had spent a day together down here at Ayot over the job & sent you down a draft for discussion. This remarkable document you absolutely ignored, saying you were too busy to be bothered about it & would do a proper basis yourself later on when you had finished your book, we to await your convenience in the meantime. The meantime proved to be just a year, during which we had to read through your confounded book for you & neglect our own immortal works for your sake. Then you send us a new basis with the proposal, not that we shall consider it, but that we shall immediately send it out to the Fabian groups in order, as you naïvely tell us, that they may override the committee by an overwhelming rally to the side of your popular pen.

Now *I* dont mind this. But if I were an opponent desiring to thwart you, and at all hostile to you personally, I might seize the opportunity to take serious offence, and put you hopelessly in the wrong before the society. You will remember (or rather forget; for you never remember anything) that one of the reasons why I gobbled you up so easily at the great Special Committee corobbery was that you insanely accused us of deliberately and maliciously delaying the report when as a matter of fact we had done in six weeks what you had dawdled over for seven months. This time the proportion is more glaring still—Shaw & Webb, less than a fortnight, and the strictest consideration for you as our committee colleague: Wells, over eleven months, and the gross insult to his colleagues of absolutely ignoring their work & proposing to send on his draft to the groups & the society without meeting them or discussing with them.

Now I tell you you mustnt do these things. You can treat me privately without the least ceremony; and though you annoy Webb extremely by your unruliness and by your occasionally *cold* incivilities, he has to put up with you. But in public work we must proceed on publishable lines. I cant get up at Fabian meetings & put the matter to them as a series of private larks between us. We must proceed in proper form. You may call us all the fools, liars, egotists & nincompoops you can lay your tongue or pen to; but you must be careful all the time not to take liberties of a technical kind. You may draw caricatures of us; but you must not copy our signatures at the foot of cheques. There is an art of public life which you have not mastered, expert as you are in the art of private life. The fine art of private life consists almost wholly in taking liberties: the art of public life consists fundamentally in respecting political rights. Intimate as I am with Webb, I should no more dream of treating him as you have treated him than of walking into the House of Lords & pulling the Lord Chancellor's nose. It was your duty—

your DUTY, Herbert George—to send that draft of yours in with the intimation that you were now ready for a meeting to collate it with my draft & discuss it; and when we asked you to let it stand over until we were through with some pressing work, you should have cordially awaited our convenience as we did yours.

Also, though this does not touch our committee, when you address a public meeting, you must do so according to the forms of public meeting, and not publicly insult the chairman by not only assuming his duties & privileges, but actually thrusting him bodily out of his place. You may do that with impunity with worms who know no more about "order" than you do. But have you any idea of what would happen to you if you tried it on with, say, Lord Courtney, or with the Speaker of the House of Commons? Learn, rash egotist, that if you were a thousand H. G. Wellses, there is one sacrosanct person who is greater than you all, and that is the chairman of a public meeting. To be ignorant of this, to fail in respect for The Chair, is the lowest depth of misdemeanor to which a public man can fall.

I have yet another technical lesson to give you. When you first spoke at a Fabian meeting, I told you to hold up your head & speak to the bracketed bust of Selwyn Image on the back wall. To shew that you were not going to be taught by me, you made the commonest blunder of the tyro: you insisted on having a table; leaning over it on your knuckles; and addressing the contents of your contracted chest to the tablecloth. I will now, having tried to cure you of that by fair means in vain, cure you of it by a blow beneath the belt. Where did you get that attitude? In the shop. IN THE SHOP. At the New Reform Club, when your knuckles touched the cloth, you said unconsciously, by reflex action "Anything else today, madam," and later on "What's the next article?" Fortunately, you were inaudible, thanks to the attitude. Now I swear that the next time you take that attitude in my presence I will ask you for a farthing paper of pins. I will make a decent public man of you yet, and an effective public speaker, if I have to break your heart in the process.

And this brings me to a matter of immediate importance. As I, thank Heaven, am an ORATOR, and not a mulish draper's assistant, the announcement that I am to speak at the Queen's Hall on Tuesday has sold the whole house out like a shot, without a single advertisement. Clear profit, at unnecessarily low prices, over £100. I think it possible that if you were to undertake another such oration, and stand on your heels instead of on your knuckles, you might do the same. Remember, there is a good deal to be made as a professional lecturer if you prefer to emancipate yourself from Fabian auspices & simply let the Lecture Agency take you on as a speculation. They implore me at brief intervals to let them make my fortune & their own. But if you prefer to do as I do, there is still the fact that you can become a platform athlete in propaganda if you choose to. When there is no table handy you are already a very tolerable speaker; and the rest is only a matter of practice and of a little daily exercise over the alphabet. What is more, when you become a rhetorician, you will have acquired a new literary power. Why is it that you cant write a play, and I can? You think it is because you dont choose. Yah!

That reminds me that I have just finished a dramatic masterpiece [*Getting Married*]—unities so perfectly preserved that I have got two & a half hours drama into a single act & a single scene. I should like to read it to you & Jane. Jane could not but be impressed by the contrast between my splendid skill in the most difficult of all the literary arts and your wretched texts for sensational illustrations in sixpenny magazines. Jane is a woman of spirit: she will not long be content with a Second Best. The real motive of your attempts to pick Fabian quarrels with me, and to put a stop to the intercourse which previously existed between our families, cannot be hidden from so shrewd a woman. Some comparisons make themselves, ignore them how we will. I say nothing of the facts that I am three feet taller than you; that the greatest living sculptor spent a month enthusiastically modelling my features; that my father's second cousin was a Baronet (no professional cricketers in *my* family, thank Heaven: Alfred Shaw was an impostor); that Jane, an exquisitely small woman, naturally admires big men; that, in short, Jane and I were made for one another. But I *do* say that I can write a play and you cant; that I can make the back row of 4000 people hear every word I say whilst you dare not look your customer straight in the eye—only look *up* at him (her) with a propitiatory smile; and whilst women are women such contrasts will not be lost on them.

It is up to you to cancel your natural disadvantages by a strenuous effort of genius & by years of perseverance. Otherwise I will not answer for the second chair at the Spade House fireside retaining its occupant for long. I say no more. You are warned. The path is pointed out to you. Follow it or perish. And we will consider the basis when Webb is a little less rushed.

GBS

To A.J.MARRIOTT

[S/1]

10 Adelphi Terrace WC
25th March 1908

[Marriott had written to Shaw immediately after attending the Fabian public meeting in the Queen's Hall the previous evening.]

Dear Marriott

It is no use promising the British middle classes what you and I want; we must shew them how to get what they want themselves. As a matter of fact, I myself should not like to sail into Socialism without a powerful Army and Navy and a highly susceptible patriotic sense of nationality. It was only by a tremendous outburst of militant national feeling that the French Revolution was saved from the allied sovereigns of Europe. I am very keen on rescuing the soldier and sailor from his present condition of abject outlawry and making him a citizen with full civic rights, so that he can punch a Field Marshall's or Admiral's head for two pounds or fourteen days; but I am calculating on his being a much more formidable fighting man after his emancipation than before it.

I should never make any headway as a propagandist of Socialism if I insisted on tacking on my personal views to it. The nation is more a peace-at-any-price nation than it is a vegetarian nation; and I might as well attach the one thing to Socialism as the other. If we can only get hold of the money we are now wasting, we can then settle the question of how we are to spend it. It is a matter of the greatest astonishment to me how any sane man can adopt a naval career. As a matter of fact sane men do not adopt it: they have to be kidnapped when they are young, and by the time they have found out what a mistake they have made, they are too old to throw up their job and their pension on the off-chance of bettering themselves. Still, there they are; and the nation dare not do without them. I can understand a proposal to have no navy at all: what I cannot understand is the notion of having a little one.

I daresay the dose of Socialism I gave the five shilling seats seemed very small in comparison to the quantities you and I have seen offered and swallowed in our time; but it was quite as much as they could hold; and when they have digested it, they can have as much more as they like at the same shop.

yours ever
G. Bernard Shaw

767

To SIEGFRIED TREBITSCH

[A/5]

10 Adelphi Terrace WC
11th April 1908

[Sir Edward Elgar (1857–1934), today one of Britain's most celebrated composers, was championed by Shaw from the start of his career to the end of his life. Shaw's tract *The Impossibilities of Anarchism* appeared under the title "Die Unmöglichkeiten des Anarchismus" in *Morgen* on 10th April, presumably in Trebitsch's translation. It was revised for publication in *Essays von Bernard Shaw* later in the same year. Gustav Landauer and his wife Hedwig Lachmann made a speciality of translating non-copyrighted works by modern British writers, including Shaw and Wilde.]

My dear Trebitsch

I have read Mr Jacobsen's letter. The difficulty is that he does not know the law and is not in possession of the facts. The agreement should have been made with me, not with you. I never saw it until quite lately; and then, as you know, I at once protested against it. It was represented to me that you had had an offer of 1000 crowns for permission to use "the idea" of the first act of Arms & The Man for an operetta: that is an opera in one act. I was very doubtful about it at the time, not being able to see what they were paying for; but I did not like to deprive you of 500 crowns; so I let the thing pass on the understanding that the bargain was to be limited as above. My receipt, drawn by my secretary, was a mere matter between you and me: it was not a receipt to Mr Slivinski, and cannot imply any contract with him.

However, it is no use wrangling as to the facts. The question is, how to get out of the difficulty we are in. The first thing to do is to return the 1000 crowns. You obtained them by going beyond your legal powers; and since I refuse to confirm the contract (to do so would be to violate my own contracts in other quarters) you cannot honorably keep the money. I enclose a cheque for the amount, as it is really my fault— or rather the fault of the heavy pressure of business which compels me to let so many matters pass without sufficient attention—and there is no reason why you should suffer for my negligence. When the money is returned and the contract torn up, then the position will be as follows.

The opera, as performed, must not be called Helden, nor announced as a musical setting of it. None of the names of my characters must be used. None of my dialogue must be used. There must be no possibility of a foreign manager attempting to stop performances of my play on the ground that they violate his rights in the opera. Further, there must be no possibility of an attempt to stop a performance of a real attempt to

768

set Arms & The Man to music, if I should at any future time authorize a composer to do it. This is not likely to happen; but it is possible that if Elgar or Richard Strauss were to propose to set the play—not paraphrased into a string of waltzes, but just as it stands—I might not refuse. This would not interfere with the Oscar Straus—Jacobsen paraphrase. You will note that these conditions are just as important to Herr Straus as to me: more so, in fact, as he could not claim an infringement against me without admitting the identity of his libretto with my play. If the similarity went beyond the limits of a general similarity of subject, he would be liable to an appeal to the courts to stop the performance in every copyright country in Europe. In France, where my translator is a member of the powerful Société des Auteurs, which under its *traité générale* with the theatres, can stop a performance at will, a contract signed *ultra vires* by a German in violation of a Frenchman's rights would not be of much use to him. I should have to publish the warning I have already sent privately to Herr Straus in all the countries; and immediately a cloud of difficulties would arise, costly and troublesome to Herr Straus, costly and troublesome to me, very unfavorable to Herr Slivinski's international reputation as a careful man of business, and profitable to nobody but the lawyers.

On the other hand, if the libretto complies with my conditions, or is altered so as to comply with them, Herr Jacobsen is quite welcome to any suggestions or ideas he has taken from our play. If he or Herr Oscar Straus had applied directly to me (as I applied directly to Herr Strauss) without relying on these men of business who are regarded as men of business only by artists and as artists by real men of business, there would have been no trouble: I should have pointed out at once the limits within which my work could be used. I have no right to be generous at your expense; but now that I return the 1000 crowns, Herr Jacobsen gets his borrowed ideas for nothing. It may be that the borrowing is so obvious that the critics will accuse him of plagiarism, especially if he has done nothing very brilliant before. In that case he can put a note in the program as follows:— "One of the scenes in this operetta has been suggested by Herr Siegfried Trebitsch's translation of one of Bernard Shaw's best known plays." But it would be much better to say nothing, as it is hard to devise a formula that is legally unobjectionable. At all events, any such statement must be submitted to us and agreed upon before publication. It must not convey the impression that the operetta is an authorized musical version of Helden or that I have disposed of any rights.

The next step is to get from them a copy of their libretto. Until I see that, I can give no undertaking in the matter. Any suggestions I may have to make about it are far more likely to be in the nature of improvements than otherwise. I am probably as clever a dramatist as Herr Jacobsen; and I know a good deal about music, and of the situations that musicians can handle effectively.

I consider that Herren Straus & Jacobsen will now have no reason to suspect me of any intention to act unreasonably or to make money out of them. I shall get nothing whatever out of the business except the loss of a good deal of time in which I might have been earning money with my pen. I have made no attempt to make them the butt of my wit. The difficulty has not been of my making. It would have been obvious to anyone in the world except a theatrical agent that your powers did not extend beyond the German language, and that an agreement for international rights should be made with the author.

I write this letter with great difficulty, as I have had a severe attack of influenza—in fact, I am in the middle of it, and am unfit for any sort of business.

Please lose no time in returning the money & getting a copy of the libretto. Impress on Herr Jacobsen that the matter is of great importance, as even if he could make his case good against me in Germany, he would still have to deal with seven translators throughout Europe who have exclusive rights of unquestionable validity in the text of Helden in their respective languages.

yours ever

G. Bernard Shaw

P.S. Morgen has just arrived, like a bombshell. Oh Siegfried, Siegfried, what have you done? Here is my best and most useful piece of economic analysis mutilated so as to appear like a strong defence of Anarchism & revival of Bakunin, and presented to the German public as an authentic work of mine. What on earth am I to do? You have utterly ruined me. Llandauer would have translated the whole thing. Have you gone stark mad? Or has the influenza given me hallucinations? Is the Morgen affair a piracy, or is it yours? It reads like yours. But to—oh Lord! oh Lord! This is the VERY WORST thing that has ever happened since the world was created. Do you realize that Anarchism is a serious thing? Heaven forgive you!

To J.E.VEDRENNE

[X/183]

Ayot St Lawrence. Welwyn
15th April 1908

[Shaw was preparing for the production of *Getting Married*, rehearsals for which commenced on 21st April. The play opened at the Haymarket Theatre on 12th May. Barker was in the United States, following the collapse of the Savoy Theatre enterprise, unsuccessfully negotiating for the directorship of the New Theatre, New York, still under construction. The post eventually went to Winthrop Ames. Malcolm Watson (1853–1929), Scottish journalist and playwright, was the drama critic of the *Daily Telegraph*.]

My dear VD

Here is the sketch for the scene: I think it is intelligible. Style—Tower of London, Norwich Cathedral, Durham Cathedral, Choir of St Albans, etc. The glimpse of the garden should be pretty.

Yes: I suppose we must begin on Tuesday; but I feel utterly unable to face it. Charlotte has been in bed for some days at 103 in the shade—temperature down now, fortunately, and will be up tomorrow. As for me, after a regular tearing bout of influenza, I recuperated and immediately bicycled off to St Albans and rode 7 miles back against a hurricane. Result: collapse, senile decay, childish impotence, ruin. This happened yesterday; and I still feel as if any possibility of rehearsal were 3 months off. However no doubt I shall be ready on Tuesday.

No word from Barker. The press must wait now [for press releases] until about a week before the performance. I have promised Watson first bite.

G.B.S.

To SIEGFRIED TREBITSCH

[A/5]

Ayot St Lawrence. Welwyn
20th April 1908

[Trebitsch had suggested publication of *The Doctor's Dilemma* with the fifth act (epilogue) omitted.]

My dear Trebitsch

... It is not the 5th act of the Doctor's D. that kills the play: it is the 4th. Everything will depend on whether Dubedat can make an acting success of this. Barker made it ghastly: people used to go out & faint

771

& ask for brandy at the Court Theatre: he missed the peculiar softness & prettiness that gives pathos to the death, and made it hard & frightful. Of course the critics did not know what was wrong: they never do. Lots of people thought the 5th act the gem of the play: others thought it spoiled everything.

G.B.S.

To ERICA COTTERILL

10 Adelphi Terrace WC
22nd April 1908

[A/1; X/202]

... Now that I have taught you some respect for business and the law, let me assure you that marriage is more sacred than either, and that unless you are prepared to treat my wife with absolute loyalty, you will be hurled into outer darkness for ever. The privilege of pawing me, such as it is, is hers exclusively. She has to tolerate worshipping females whose efforts to conceal the fact that they take no interest in her are perfunctory, and who bore her to distraction with their adoration of me; but it is my business to see that her patience is not abused. You are a luxurious young devil, with the ethics, and something of the figure, of an anteater; and I have no doubt you can coax your mother & your Rupert [Brooke] by crawling all over them; but if you dare to try those tactics with me in my wife's house, you will be very startlingly awakened to the iron laws of domestic honor. Also, it is not sensible nor decent to write about such demonstrations except to men of your own time of life, and with some assurance that they are equally infatuated, and will read it all as touching poetry.

Whenever I get anything in the nature of a loveletter, I hand it straight to Charlotte; and I am not at all sure that this may not be the explanation of the fact that the lunch here & the meeting with Mr G.B. did not come off.

Remember that your best behaviour will not be too good for me, as you hardly yet know how to behave yourself at all, being the very worst brought-up young woman I have ever met in the course of my half century of "taking notice."

GBS

772

To J.E.VEDRENNE

[X/183]

Ayot St Lawrence. Welwyn
26th April 1908

[Frederick Harrison, manager of the Haymarket Theatre, was co-presenter of *Getting Married*, the billing reading: "Mr Frederick Harrison and Messrs Vedrenne and Barker's series of Vedrenne-Barker Matinées." The play was scheduled for six matinées, and subsequently went into the evening bill on 1st June. Edward A. Baughan (1865–1938) was drama and music critic of the *Daily News*, but also contributed to *The Nation*. William Lee-Matthews (d. 1931), a business executive, was Arnold Bennett's drama agent for several years. He had succeeded Shaw in 1905 as chairman of the Stage Society producing committee.]

My dear VD

May I urge the enormous importance of selling the house to the public for the first performance of G.M.—barring the inevitable press only. If we get the usual invited 1st nighters, we shall have an atmosphere of ill will and failure. Remember the first night of Caesar & Cleopatra and the first matinée of The Doctor's Dilemma. Caesar went at half its value, The Doctor at twice its value. We must convert Harrison on the question of deadheads. I shall pay for my two dress circle seats; and I protest against the admission of a single soul without payment apart from the press and our own immediate belongings. Remember that the west end routine is fatal to us: the deadheads are our worst enemies: our real friends all pay.

As to the press, see that The Nation is taken care of. Massingham, the editor, backed us up nobly at the Savoy, writing the notices himself instead of Baughan.

By the way, the Beadle's costume must not be a comic one out of sketches by Boz. A modern Borough Council Beadle is rather like a fashionable music hall chucker-out. The cocked hat still exists; and there is a short caped Inverness with gold braid; but the rest is an immaculate frock coat and trousers with gold braid and stripe down the leg; and the man is not a fat red-nosed guy, but an imposing person like Lee-Mathews and George Edwards rolled into one. The mace may be ad lib.

G.B.S.

773

To ERICA COTTERILL

[A/1; X/202]

10 Adelphi Terrace W C
27th April 1908

My dear Emerica

I am so hard pressed for time by my rehearsals that I can write only in the curtest & baldest fashion.

I do not accuse you of proposing to act "wrongly & indecently": I tell you that your proposal was unlawful.

It is entirely natural for a hungry man to take a loaf of bread & eat it. It is entirely natural for an adult woman to kiss a man she likes. People who do these natural things are socially impossible.

There is no more intolerable nuisance than the man who makes love to other men's wives and the woman who makes love to other women's husbands. Unless when you walk into the house of a married woman you accept the obligation (a highly unnatural one) to consider her husband's person as sacred, you break the covenant of bread & salt, and are a thief, a libertine, & a betrayer.

If you say that you mean no harm, you are a fool as well. The reason is very simple. When an adult woman and an adult man caress one another, the result is entirely different from the result of your kissing your mother. The whole creative force of the universe suddenly leaps into activity in their bodies. They lose all power of acting otherwise than instinctively. They act instinctively; and the consequence is that the adult man wakes from his dream exceedingly ashamed of himself; and the adult woman has a baby. That is what will happen to you the very first time you act in that perfectly natural and beautiful and happy and innocent way which you imagine you can trifle with as a woman because you have trifled with it as a child. And until you understand this danger, you will be a mischievous & silly girl, quite unfit to be trusted by yourself in London or anywhere else. You have a box of matches & you propose to go about striking them and throwing them into barrels of gunpowder, because you are quite sure you dont mean anything to happen. When it does happen, the Life Force will make very short work of your intentions.

In brief, if you enter my wife's house, you enter it on the understanding that you dont make love to her husband. If I introduce you to Mrs Barker, I shall do so on the understanding that you dont make love to *her* husband. You may admire & dream & worship & adore until you are black in the face; but you are not to sit and hold their hands, nor kiss them, nor cuddle them, nor nestle in their manly bosoms—oh, so

774

sweetly, so innocently, so heavenlikely—because if you do the Life Force will suddenly leap out and gobble you up. All these exquisite visions & reveries are only the bait in the trap the Life Force is setting for you.

The reason everybody tells you to get married & have children is that they thoroughly understand the wiles of the Life Force, and wish heartily that you would come to understand it too, & become a reasonable and sympathetic human being through that experience.

That is all I have time to say. That it should have been left to me to say it shews the utter uselessness of parents in this matter.

Remember, in entering the world now as an adult woman you must take on yourself the Laws of Honor.

GBS

To ERICA COTTERILL

[A/1; X/202]
10 Adelphi Terrace WC
29th April 1908

My dear Erica

It is all very terrible and agonizing and glorious and tragic and unbearable, isnt it? You are certainly enjoying it enormously and rising to it with great literary power. Only, you might let your poor mother alone. *I* dont matter: writing letters to me is like giving tracts to a missionary: I just cock my eye at all this beautiful, eloquent, childlike-sincere-selfish squirming, and bang it goes into the fire lest it should fall into somebody else's hands; and if you suppose you need explain things to me that I understand better than you, then you are very youthfully mistaken.

It is, I suppose, rather brutal of me to tell you things that few people can bear to be told until they are forty. But just as I have to take care of you in literary & dramatic copyright business, I have to take care of you in more personal matters; and some of these matters are so delicate that delicacy in dealing with them is intolerable. Jupiter could not help shrivelling up Semele: if you dare to fall in love with a god, you must be prepared for thunderbolts.

Now, once for all and finally, when you come to London to begin the world there, you must do so as an adult woman, and accept all the obligations & limitations I have so bluntly described to you. I am speaking quite impersonally, as I—an old gentleman of 52—would

775

speak to any young woman who innocently proposed to behave like a child & expect the privileges of a child. Stop thinking about yourself, and read my last letter as if it were a letter you had found from an old man you did not know to a young woman you did not know, and consider whether any other course of conduct is possible. Anyhow, that is my ultimatum: those are my *orders*, if you have not sense enough to take them in any other way. And now you must fight it out with yourself to the end. It is exceedingly difficult for me to educate you in this matter—impossible, in fact. I beg you to spare me as much as you can. Would you mind not writing again until you have taken a few weeks to think over it.

G.B.S.

To AUGUSTIN HAMON

[H/1]

10 Adelphi Terrace W C
1st May 1908

[Vicomte Robert d'Humières (1868–1915), dramatist and translator of Conrad and Kipling, was a stage director of the Théâtre des Arts, where *Candida* was presented on 7th May for a run of 28 performances. Shaw had written to him on 3rd May to thank him for his list of suggested corrections in the translation, adding his own candid views on the proposed alterations, and informing him that final decision on use of the revisions would rest with Hamon. The Vicomte was quoted later as saying that Shaw was "attached" to his translator "like a criminal is attached to the rope which hanged him." The attachment, he added, was "a defiant and heroic act," but in the end it could only prove to be "suicide on the threshold of our admiration" (Archibald Henderson, *George Bernard Shaw: Man of the Century*, 1956).]

My dear Hamon

The Marquis is decidedly a man of talent. He has sent me a list of twenty-two corrections; and the great majority of them we may embrace with enthusiasm, as they are decided improvements. You have not yet fathomed the utter illiteracy of the playgoing public. You are so accustomed to write and to read that you do not realize that methods of literary expression which are instantaneously intelligible to you are Chinese to the parterre. The Marquis knows better. Besides, he is not so conscientious about the translation; neither am I. He has got one enormous advantage over you. In making the translation, you were working from an English original; and you produced a version under the direct influence of that original. The Marquis, unobsessed by this original, starts perfectly fresh on your French version and instantly sees how it can be made more French and more clear. You have occasionally made an obscure translation because, as the meaning was not quite clearly into your head by the original, you could not become conscious of the obscurity in the translation. The Marquis, starting completely in the dark, detects your obscurity at once and clears it up. The truth is, we are lucky to have so intelligent a critic; and you had better encourage him to tear the whole thing to pieces as much as he likes.

It is not merely in the case of translations that this happens. I myself, in writing the original, have my own meaning so clearly in my head that I occasionally express it in a way that is quite unintelligible to readers who have no clue to it. I correct an actor at rehearsal for emphasizing the wrong word, and find, to my astonishment, that he has quite misunderstood the meaning, and that the fault is mine. You will soon get accustomed to eye-openers of this kind. Molière's plan of reading his plays to his cook was a very good one. I am always reading my plays to cooks, so to speak; and the discoveries I have made in this way have long ago left me without a rag of amour propre. In 1894, when I was rehearsing Arms and the Man, one of the business officials of the theatre happened to be passing through the house. He loitered for a moment to hear a few words of the rehearsal; and presently, at a most serious passage, he burst into a roar of laughter, to our great indignation. We asked him what he meant by behaving in such an unseemly fashion. He said he was laughing at the joke made by the Swiss soldier. I then found that he had completely mistaken the meaning of the speech; and the construction he put on it became obvious the moment he pointed it out. And yet, though we had rehearsed it for nearly three weeks, neither I nor any of the actors had seen it. I of course altered the passage; and nowadays, if I saw a stage-carpenter smile in the wrong place, I would stop the rehearsal and find out what he was laughing at, and would very probably find out that he had detected some double meaning or other which I had overlooked.

The Marquis is very much afraid of you, because he thinks you are very touchy, and I have told him that you are the responsible party and must have your own way—also that you are as obstinate as twenty thousand devils. But in the theatre it is no use being touchy. The whole business of rehearsal from one end to the other consists in altering, correcting, improving. It is actually advisable for an author to pretend to make mistakes and to revile himself before the company as an imbecile even when he has made no mistakes at all, rather than pretend

777

to infallibility. One moment, you may be puzzled because a speech sounds awkward and call on the Marquis to improve it on the ground that he knows English and that you do not. The next moment you may have to tell him that his corrections are all wrong, because you know French and he does not. Frankness and good humor will save any situation: delicacy, sparing one another's susceptibilities, doing the right thing, will spoil any situation. You must, however, make this agreement with the Marquis. Tell him that you are under contract not to accept any collaboration of any kind, and that therefore, though you intend to take advantage of all his corrections, you will steal them and never give him the smallest public credit for them. Also that he must produce all the Shaw plays for you as you find it very useful to get your translations improved for nothing.

By the way, is he really a Marquis? I always begin my letters to him My dear Marquis; but I address the envelope to him M. Robert D'Humières. Is that correct? In England we have a curious usage in directing envelopes. A letter to a gentleman is directed to John Smith, Esq.; but if John Smith has no social pretensions he is addressed as Mr. John Smith. Many Englishmen would be furiously angry if you used Mr in directing an envelope to them. I never quite know how to address an envelope to a Frenchman. In my childhood I was taught that you should begin by writing À Mons., and then on the line beneath, M Augustin Hamon; but nobody seems to do that nowadays. What *is* the correct method? I submit the question to you and the Marquis jointly.

yours faithfully
G. Bernard Shaw

To A.B. WALKLEY

[X/209]

[10 Adelphi Terrace WC]
11th May 1908

My dear A.B.W.

The few typed copies of Getting Married that exist have all been heavily overworked; and it has been difficult for me to cling to my own copy throughout the rehearsals. I shall not be done with it until the curtain rises tomorrow, as there is still a passage or two to be arranged at the last moment. Also I cannot without scandal give it to you in the theatre; but if you will send me a line to say where you will write your notice, or telephone me to 14615 Central (not in the book) I will contrive to send it thither for you. I shall be here until 2 o'clock, probably.

In haste, much exhausted by "producing"—

yrs ever
G.B.S.

PS The French Press on Candida is immense. The Debats particularly nice. The bewilderment almost worse than English. No duel! No adultery! Continence of poet très malsaine.

To REV. JOHN OLIVER

10 Adelphi Terrace WC
[H/1]   12th May 1908

[John Oliver was Minister of Mayhill, Glasgow.]

Dear Sir

I do not know of any section of the Socialist Party in which it is maintained that free love is better than marriage. I do not know what free love means; and I am pretty sure that most of the people who are using the expression so freely at present are equally ignorant.

Nor do I know what you mean by your phrase "looseness of opinion on the marriage question." Marriage is a term applied indiscriminately to a great variety of contracts. The contracts vary from country to country in Europe and from state to state in America. I am legally a married man; but no Roman Catholic or high Anglican would recognize my marriage. A few months ago, people who were married to their deceased wife's sisters in Jersey or in the Colonies were not married in Scotland: today their relations are legal. All the people who really know what they are talking about—a very small number, by the way—admit that a marriage contract is a social necessity; but some of them are advocates of indissoluble Roman Catholic marriage without the possibility of divorce, whilst others prefer the marriage laws of South Dakota. Hardly anyone, as far as I know, is in favour of the English marriage law as it stands at present. For instance, the fact that a woman can get a divorce if her husband boxes her ears and seduces the housemaid, whereas if he commits murder or becomes an atheist, she remains tied to him for life, is not on the face of it a desirable or defensible one.

779

There is another objection to marriage—quite the most formidable of all—which has not yet been grasped; and that is its appalling licentiousness. It is usually assumed by people who have not studied the question that the revolt against marriage has arisen amongst people who wish to live looser lives than our marriage institutions permit. As a matter of fact, such people never dare to give expression to their designs, and are invariably the loudest defenders of what they call domestic purity. But the horror of marriage which was so strong among the early Christians exists with undiminished force today. For example, I hardly know any thoughtful Minister of religion who is not troubled by the fact that sexual intemperance among professed libertines is negligible in comparison with its prevalence among married people.

Finally, as bearing on your reference to The Irrational Knot, you must remember that lawlessness always has a demoralizing effect to some extent no matter how bad the violated law may be. A high-minded Russian may conceive it to be his duty to rebel against the Russian Government. Dr Clifford may feel it to be his duty to refuse to pay the education rate. But rebellion and refusal to pay taxes are not at all likely to have a good effect on those who carry them into practice. That is why it is of such enormous social importance that bad institutions should be reformed or got rid of. The marriage of men with their deceased wife's sisters probably had not at all a good effect on the people who did it when it was illegal; but the remedy was, not that they should stop doing it, but that marriage with a deceased wife's sister should be legalized, which at once made it no more demoralizing than any other variety of marriage.

yours faithfully
G. Bernard Shaw

P.S. As I wrote The Irrational Knot when I was twenty-four, and I am now fifty-two, it has rather a remote interest for me. I have often wondered where the title came from. I did not invent it; and it has been stated that it was first used as the title of a club to which Doctor Johnson belonged; but I have never found any confirmation of this. I must have heard it somewhere.

To LILLAH McCARTHY

[H/14]

10 Adelphi Terrace WC
13th May 1908

[The opening sentence echoes a comic speech in *Getting Married*.]

My dear Lillah

You must eat your rice pudding with a spoon. If I had wanted what you want, I should not have had to go as far as Fanny Brough for my Mrs George. It was just the touch of Oxford Street that was so absolutely indispensable to the sermon. The play, though it is so largely a discussion on Marriage, is really a sermon on Equality. There could have been no rebuke whatever to the snobbery of Hotchkiss if Mrs George had been what you call an uncommon woman: that is why you would have ruined the play if you had appeared in it. The part is one for a sublime low comedian. With all your qualities, you are not a low comedian, are you? Perhaps you will end by becoming one when you have been battered for about ten years by my ideas and Barker's and shocked by our endless treacheries.

yours ever
G. Bernard Shaw

To AUGUSTIN HAMON

[H.ss/1]

10 Adelphi Terrace WC
15th May 1908

[Ty an Diaoul was Hamon's home in Port Blanc, Penvénan, Côtes du Nord, for which Shaw had lent him 30,000 francs on the mortgage.]

My dear Hamon

. . . My new play was produced on Tuesday last. There was a splendid audience; and the excitement was immense. At the end the curtain had to be raised six times; and the audience would not disperse until one of the actors stepped forward and assured them that I had left the house. Next day, the daily papers almost without exception, in articles of great length, assured the public that the play had been an unexampled failure; that it was intolerable and monstrously dull; that it was not a play at all; that it was silly, foolish, verbose, wearisome, and unintelligible; and that it was received at first with faint applause and

781

finally with hisses. I wonder what you would say if that happened to you. Would anything persuade you that these notices were perfectly sincere; that these poor devils of critics did really and honestly believe that the whole audience was bored and bewildered because they themselves were bored and bewildered; that the people who were applauding were really hissing? Why, you would tear your hair with fury, and write to everyone of the papers denouncing the critics as liars, hypocrites, and conspirators.

You see, when I recommend impassibility to you, I only recommend what I have to practise myself.

Believe me, you have done very well indeed over Candida. You have not had a perfect performance, because a perfect performance of a play is an utter impossibility. The reason that I consider D'Humière's tenue perfect is that, by sheer savoir vivre, he contrived to carry off his helpless position as if it were a victorious one. You and I have had all the advertisement and the éclat: he has had very little, considering that it is he who has done the job for us. You can think of nothing but his spoiling Burgess and what you call his hypocrisy and his desinvolture. *I* find that he has been extremely useful to us; and I do not care two-pence about his attempts "de toutes facons a faire disparaitre Hamon," because it is quite impossible for him to move you an inch. Why should you blame him for wanting to be my translator; and do you seriously think that he is any worse than other people? I have to deal with men who tell me half a dozen lies a day; and who try in the most childish way to take advantage of me. I have not only to look after my own interests but to look after theirs as well. This does not in the least prevent me from being on the most friendly terms with them and even really liking them personally a good deal. All these moral categories of liar, hypocrite, thief, putain hysterique, and so forth, may be useful as excuses for punishing children in Sunday schools, but they are of no use in dealing seriously in real affairs with men and women. Every actress in France—for the matter of that, every woman in the world— is a putain hysterique if you choose to call her so. Every man of sense and good manners is a liar and a hypocrite, if you choose to take that view of his sense and good manners. D'Humières, though evidently by no means a man of very strong character, knows this; and that is why he is able to give you the impression of having got the better of you even when you have humiliated and smashed him by the mere brute force of your authority as my translator. In writing to me, he has never once played off the moral categories against you.

However, it is waste of time preaching to you. After all, you must have been enjoying yourself enormously. I myself am hugely pleased by your behaviour, because it proves that my inspiration about you was right: you are a born homme de théâtre. Only remember this. The day may come when you will want to write an original play instead of merely translating my plays. You will never be able to do this as long as you are the slave of moral categories. Suppose, for instance, you were to attempt to write a play about D'Humières. In your present temper, you would simply write a savage attack on him, like a Socialist editor writing about an employer during a strike. Until you are prepared to accept men from their own point of view, and to take an interest in them from that point of view, and even to make a good cause for them and to fight their battles for them, recognizing that their nature is a part of your own nature, you will never have the least idea of what being a dramatist means. At present, you will be inclined to retort that this means having no conscience. Well, it does mean exactly that as far as other people are concerned. You can be as conscientious as you like about your own conduct; but you must allow D'Humières to act according to his own conscience, and not according to yours. His conscience is just as valid as yours. And he is quite entitled to despise you if he feels inclined that way. Why shouldnt he? To begin with, he is a Vicomte with very good manners; and you are a bourgeois with no manners at all—nothing but moral categories.

Free your soul from the moral categories and get rid of all this fictitious anger and resentment (mere instinctive anger and resentment, *without moral pretensions*, is quite a different thing and may be forgiven to anybody), and your Vicomte will respect you at once. But as long as you keep trumping up a moral case against him, and making it an excuse for malice towards him, you will be in a state of hopeless inferiority.

The most naive thing in your letter—it is exactly what an Englishman would say—is your protest about having to remain silent when the critics complain of faults which you have not committed. But any man can remain silent when no injustice is done him. In the same way you say it is unreasonable to expect you to be amiable to D'Humières because you despise him. But there would be no difficulty in being amiable to him if you loved him. He cannot be very fond of you; but he manages to be polite to you. You say "dire a un acteur qui a mal joue, qu'il joue bien, est au dessus de mes forces." But to tell a bad actor that he has acted badly is cruel, discouraging, and useless. It is much better to say something consolatory and helpful. You may depend on it he has not acted badly on purpose. If you can shew him how to do better, by all means do it; but do not break the unfortunate creature's heart by simply expressing contempt and dislike for his performance.

In short, and this is the central point of my preaching, do try to realize that you are a man of strong character in an unassailable position of authority amongst a lot of people of comparatively weak character who are not sure of their livelihood or their success for six weeks ahead. When the theatrical world is no longer strange to you, and you have learnt the practical applications of your instinct for the theatre, you will look back with a blush at the barbarity of your recent proceedings.

Now, as to Man and Superman. I have no intention of exploding it on Paris immediately without consulting you; but I have not the slightest doubt that the real objection to my doing it is not the danger of its failing, but, on the contrary, the danger of its making such a success that the earlier plays would seem vieux jeu after it. In London, all my friends, including some very clever dramatists, thought as you think about Man and Superman. In America, the young actor [Robert Loraine] who ventured on it strove vainly for a couple of years to induce anyone to finance its production. In both cases it had a brilliant success. In America, which can hardly be considered a more enlightened country than France, its success was colossal: among other things, it built Ty an Diaoul. The only place where it has failed is Berlin. This one instance shews that it *can* fail—at least comparatively —unless it is well cast, with a really brilliant actor as Tanner and an actress of exceptional[ly] fascinating and uncommon personality as Ann Whitefield. But given such a cast, it is irresistible.

However, we need not argue the matter as our different views lead to the same conclusion. We had better exploit the earlier plays first, because, when once Paris has tasted Man and Superman, it will not go back to such comparatively childish stuff as Non Olet without disappointment.

Lugné and Suzanne are coming again this afternoon. I find that Suzanne has a great dread of you. She says, naturally enough, that life is so hard for her that she cannot do anything unless she is working with people who are kind and human. She says you have a frightful pride, a despotic obstinacy, that would crush all artistic life in her. Nevertheless, I think we shall have to try to get hold of Suzanne for Mrs Warren. She is a very remarkable actress: nobody else that I have seen seems to give the sense of simplicity and reality. But we shall never do anything with her if you do not treat her as carefully as if she were one of your own daughters recovering from a bad illness. She is

784

timid and sensitive like all geniuses—like yourself, for instance—and if we have any dealings with her, you must be prepared to tell her at least ten times a day that she is the only great actress in the world; that she may say anything she likes; that neither you nor I can refuse her anything: in short, to put it as you would if you were speaking of D'Humières, you must lie and be a hypocrite until you are black in the face.

And here, as Eugene says in Candida, endeth the thousand and first lesson.

yours ever
G. Bernard Shaw,
pp. G. Gillmore
Secretary

P.S. I am so overworked and exhausted just now that I cannot face the fatigue and effort of a journey to Paris; but it is just barely possible that after a few days comparative rest, I might [have] energy enough to run over. Still, I do not think I will. Anyhow, I will give you notice if I change my mind.

To MAUD CHURTON BRABY

10 Adelphi Terrace WC
[H/1; X/210.e]   18th May 1908

[Mrs Braby (1875–1932) was a popular novelist and journalist, active in the women's suffrage movement. She had just sent a copy of her new novel, *Downward*, to Shaw. Laurence Housman and Joseph Moorat's *The Chinese Lantern* was presented on 16th June for a series of eight matinées. *Getting Married* was not withdrawn until 11th July, when it had achieved a run of 54 performances (including the trial matinées).]

Dear Mrs Braby

... The play is going into the evening bill on the 1st of June for four weeks. I made it a condition that somebody else should get a chance on the back of my play; so Laurence Housman's Chinese Lantern will probably take the place of Getting Married at the end of that time. I did not know that the Haymarket management sets its face against advertisements. Are you sure of this?

As to the proceedings of the people in the last act, I am not really responsible for them. I am merely a conduit for the Life Force in the matter; and that act is pure inspiration. But you may not have noticed that the play, besides being a disquisition on the marriage problem, is also a sermon on equality. You must learn to come down to earth without a shock, or else get the earth up to you. Still, I am a good deal to blame in the matter. Love costs a man so little, and brings him so much, that his lightheartedness on the subject degenerates into comic mischievousness. I cannot escape altogether from the vulgarity of my sex in that matter, though I make an effort now and then to shew that I know better. In order to do this in Getting Married, I was forced to resort to the device of clairvoyance, in order that I might for the moment obliterate Mrs George as a comedic personality, and substitute the entire female sex crying to the ages from her lips. The moment she became Mrs George again it was all over: Anthony had to be tempted.

When I read your book I will tell you what I think of it if I think anything worth telling.

yours sincerely
G.B.S.

To J. E. VEDRENNE

[X/183]

10 Adelphi Terrace WC
22nd [early A.M. 23rd] May 1908

[Robert Loraine was playing St John Hotchkiss in *Getting Married*. John Masefield's *Nan* was given a private performance by the Pioneer Players at the New Royalty Theatre on 24th May and its first public performance at a matinée at the Haymarket Theatre on 2nd June. Lillah McCarthy appeared in the title rôle. The Pinero play to which Shaw refers is *The Thunderbolt*, which had opened at the St James's Theatre on 9th May.]

Dear VD

I saw most of G.M. today: the audience simply hung on every word of the contract scene and were furious when it was interrupted by the beadle. The cast finds out more every time of what it is all about; and so, consequently, does the audience. It just wants to be made an hour longer and played every day for the next ten years, like Madame Tussaud's. The gallery actually spotted the allusion to the Education Act, and began to cheer it, to the amazement of Loraine. All that play wants is £10,000 to nurse it into a full grown institution.

Barker says you want to put it up for a fortnight only, as you are terrified by the booking. But the booking is nothing to me: I want four weeks. There is no reason to suppose that you will do better with anything else. But if you will start real repertory, I am quite game for that. I should not mind being cut down to a fortnight provided I then went into repertory with The Chinese Lantern. If Nan succeeds tomorrow, Hankin has two short plays [*The Constant Lover* and *The Burglar Who Failed*] either or both of which would make up a program with it. Voysey would get a good press in the form of favorable comparisons with G.M.: but it would be a fearful job to produce it; and three plays with a family round a big table getting buried and married (mine, Pinero's, and G.B.'s) would be a large dose: I think something more fantastic—Masefield and Housman—would be safer. . . .

G.B.S.

PS. I go down to Ayot after breakfast. Up on Sunday afternoon by motor (Barker up) to see Nan. Shall be in town on Monday.

To RUTLAND BOUGHTON

[H/2; X/212.e] 10 Adelphi Terrace WC
27th May 1908

[Rutland Boughton (1878–1960), a musician best known as a composer of operas, was the founder of the Glastonbury Festival and its School of Music Drama in 1914.]

Dear Sir

I tried over the Bashville music. It is no good: I could compose Waldweben of that sort by the yard myself. Besides, it spoils *my* music. What musicians seldom understand is that all artistic literature is itself music—word music. The Admirable Bashville is written from end to end in the music of blank verse; and the whole comic effect of it depends on its burlesque of the music of the Elizabethans. To smother this up with orchestral tremolandos and six-eight tunes is a piece of philistinism. I do not say that it would be impossible to find a sort of music that would really incorporate with the word music; but the man who could do this would not waste his time on The Admirable Bashville; and his style would not be the tremolandish sugary-modulatory style that has been compounded out of Gounod and Wagner.

For the present there is nothing to be got out of the Shakespear Memorial. The project is still in a fluid condition, and is practically without funds. I greatly mistrust your project of a series of Arthurian music dramas. You will simply produce a second-hand Ring. The Ring itself would never have existed if it had not been to Wagner an expression of his strongest religious and social convictions; and unless you have equally strong convictions and an equally deep penetration into the social life that surrounds you, you will only waste a good deal of scoring paper which you might employ far better by trying to deal, as Strauss does, (not to mention Elgar) with the modern world in a crisp and powerful style, making a clean sweep of the tremolandos and the sentimental and grandiose modulations of the nineteenth century.

I shall be in London on Friday; but I am sorry to say that I cannot find a spare half hour in which I could ask you to call: I am overwhelmed with work and engagements of one sort and another at this moment.

yours faithfully
G. Bernard Shaw

To JOHN LANE

10 Adelphi Terrace W C
[H/1]   2nd June 1908

[Lane had undertaken to publish a uniform edition of the works of the celebrated French author, Anatole France (1844–1924). France's preface appeared in Emile Combes's *Une campagne laïque* (*1902–1903*), published in Paris in 1904.]

Dear John Lane

This notion of yours about a preface by me or by Walkley or by [Edmund] Gosse or by any other Englishman is a mistake. Such a preface can be nothing but an impertinence. A solemn impertinence would be insufferable; and a vivacious impertinence would be like flat ginger ale compared with Anatole's champagne.

You will observe that I, who say this, am a great writer of prefaces —that I have in fact revived the preface for the first time since Dryden made it classical. But this does not mean that there were not in the meantime plenty of prefaces which nobody ever read. What it does mean is that Dryden wrote his own prefaces and that I do the same. What you want is a preface to the English edition by Anatole France himself—a preface which must be an entirely frank statement of his impressions of the English and of his attitude towards them. There must be no standing on ceremony, no playing to the entente cordiale, any more than there is in my preface to John Bull's Other Island. Tell Anatole France that such a preface is expected from him in England and that the substitution of a sort of literary chairman's speech for it would be an insufferable banality.

He will not need much explanation. His preface to a pamphlet by Combes first sold up an enormous edition of the pamphlet and was then reprinted without the pamphlet. Such a preface as I suggest, if there were enough Anatolian pepper and salt in it, would give your edition such a send off both in the way of reviews and sales, that you could afford to pay Anatole France handsomely for his trouble.

Anyhow, *I* wont write the preface; and in my opinion anybody else who does will thereby shew himself very highly qualified to do it unsuccessfully.

yours faithfully
G. Bernard Shaw

To MAURICE BARING

10 Adelphi Terrace WC
26th June 1908

[H/3]

[Maurice Baring (1874–1945), poet and man of letters, served in the diplomatic corps 1898–1904 and was special correspondent in Manchuria, Russia, and the Balkans 1904–12.]

My dear Baring

Will you ask your man to search in the débris of last night for a blue cloth cap which formerly contained my head and now probably contains a much worn pair of buttonless slaty-colored reindeer gloves, and to send them to me if he finds them.

I had to walk home bareheaded last night, because one of your guests who was very drunk, and H. G. Wells, who was laboriously trying to persuade himself and everybody else that he was as drunk as a lord, were trying to make a disturbance about my going, and would have done so if I had gone back through the tent.

yours ever
G. Bernard Shaw

To MATTHEW EDWARD McNULTY

10

10 Adelphi Terrace WC

[H/4]   29th June 1908

[Arthur Schnitzler's *In the Hospital* had been performed at the Royal Court
Theatre on 28th February 1905, as part of a triple bill with Shaw's *How He
Lied to Her Husband* and Yeats's *The Pot of Broth*. Shaw, in 1873 or 1874,
had spent his holidays in Newry, where McNulty was employed by the
Bank of Ireland. McNulty later recalled, in an unpublished memoir (transcript courtesy of the late Ivo Currall), that they jointly produced a
manuscript collection of their individual writings under the title *The Newry
Nights' Entertainment*, and drew up a declaration of "Eternal Friendship,"
which declared, among other things, that "we would always share one
another's prosperity or adversity . . . We pricked our respective arms with
a pin and signed this agreement in our blood."]

My dear Mac

Lucy has just sent me a letter of yours—the first news I have had of
you for years. I had no idea that you were still in the bank. It is nearly
forty years since you entered it. I thought that thirty years at most
would qualify you for a pension, and that since you had always refused
to take banking seriously, you would retire at the first possible moment
and devote yourself to journalism and literature. I pictured you as a
Dublin musical critic, dramatic critic, what not. I hasten to add that I
think you are wise to prefer a settled safe income and a routine to the
precarious vagabondage of journalism, which is a very poor business
for a man over forty.

Also I had of course no knowledge of your wife's illness. That is
downright bad luck: one of those things there is nothing to be said
about.

I note that you think that I could have held out a helping hand to you
in literature, and that I didnt. But literature is one of those things in
which no man can help another. I talked about Misther O'Ryan and
The Son of a Peasant for all I was worth, and wrote about them when I
had the opportunity. My wife liked them and was much interested in
you; so she also talked. I did succeed to some extent in spreading a
notion among the Irish Literary Theatre people that you were a sort of
Irish Dickens; and I tried to persuade you to follow up my chatter
with a play—you published the letter afterwards, confound you,
without the least regard to my relations with Yeats! But you did nothing
fresh; and I had to drop the subject. Have you any stuff unpublished?
On your known record it is a case of thirty years, three children, and
three books. It is now clear that you are not going to stun the world by

mere brute bulk of work. Think of my five novels, my sixteen plays, my million words of journalism, my thousand lectures! Do you wonder that you cannot open a newspaper without finding some silly lie about me in it, the cumulative effect of all the lies being what you call my reputation. There is still however a way of catching me up. Three men, Cervantes, Bunyan and Swift, have conquered the world with a single book at your age. You are still a young man. You should see me! Indeed you shall see me: I enclose a couple of photographs taken last year. Add five years to their age and you have me as I am now, though after my holiday, I hope to get back to their age.

Now please observe that you have all the fun of this and and I have all the drudgery. You are much better off than most of the public in the quantity of emotional luxury and dramatic situation-imagining you get out of the great Shavian idol. "He, my ancient friend, rich, famous, successful: I poor, obscure, starving (in a manner of speaking). He growing colder, more distant, dropping me: I proud, silent, sitting with an iron face by the side of my sick wife and the three beings I have brought into the world—but enough of this weakness etc., etc, etc." You get a whole days romance out of saying all this to Lucy; but what do I get out of it? Just this, that on Saturday next I am going to let my wife drag me by main force across the North Sea in belching misery to Sweden, a country which I do not particularly want to see, and of the language of which I cannot speak a word, simply because there I shall be out of reach of the post and telegraph, the platform and committee room, the theatre with its endless rehearsals, and the paralysing arrears of literary work that I cannot keep my hands off at home. Every year the same struggle arises two or three times—the eternal "you must come away" and "oh, let me alone: I havent time: you know how I loathe travelling." I am actually buying a motor car, the very mention of which brings out a cold sweat of terror on me, so as to be able to substitute a common mechanical worry for the subtler worries of my work. I can at least choose my time to drive the thing, whereas the emergencies with which I have to deal (my life is one long string of emergencies) always come as a last straw that breaks the camel's back. Of course I make the best of it; enjoy it; am vain about it; say that it is better to wear out than rust out; argue that life is nothing but action and that the idle man does not live etc., etc. (for I, too, must dramatize myself for my Lucies); but there is reason in everything; and at such moments as the present, at the end of the season, the only effect of the gospel of the strenuous life on me is to make me feel inclined to brain the man who preaches it.

There is a little play by Schnitzler, the Austrian dramatist, called The Hospital. An unsuccessful man is dying there. He sends a message to a successful friend whom he has not seen for a long time to come and see him on his deathbed. He means to tell him that he (the failure) was the lover of his (the success's) wife, and to take it out of him generally. The successful one comes in due course, and after a few perfunctory expressions of sympathy, begins to talk about himself—his overwork, his health, his ungrateful children, his money troubles, the injustice of the world to him, and so on. At last he says he is sorry but he really must go; and what did the failure wish to say to him? "Nothing" says the failure; and dies with his little scene unplayed. That is true to life! As between you and me there is obviously a grotesquely inequitable distribution of money: that is why I am a Socialist. But the rest is all imagination.

As to money, by the way, I am often spoken of as the millionaire Socialist. I havent the least idea what our exact income is: when I married my wife put her income roughly at £4000. I had made that year between £2000 and £3000 through the success of The Devil's Disciple in America in 1897. Since then I have touched as much as £13,000 in one year, mostly through the blazing success of Man and Superman in America. But these are only spurts: they do not last. At one moment I get £300 a week: then I get nothing, and even have to disgorge thousands to bolster up the drama here. For instance, Getting Married at the Haymarket is apparently a success; and it certainly has been a tremendous victory over the press. But I refused to let it be produced unless the management produced at least two plays by young men [Housman and Masefield]—plays without the faintest chance of paying their way or even avoiding heavy loss. Result: I shall be out of pocket by the job, not to mention the quantity of work both at rehearsals and in the way of business it has cost me. I am lucky in having only two foreign lawsuits on just now to defend myself against piracy. That is what I call luck. I mention these two things as stray samples of the reality that is behind my apparently triumphant career. I might pile the agony almost indefinitely; but the upshot of it all is that I am neither a rich man nor a successful man as riches and success are imagined, but simply a Great Man—a man of genius—still playing the game on the old Newry lines. And how small and timid a thing the reality behind the Great Man is, you very well know.

And now, having behaved like the man in Schnitzler's Hospital, I bid you farewell for another spell. You will not answer this letter probably; and after a while you will persuade yourself that I have not answered a letter of yours, and that I am steadily growing more and more cold and distant. If I can be of use at any time, let me know. There is one way in which you might make use of my spare money. At present publishers have you at their mercy because they know you cannot do without their capital. But if a publisher really wants a book and will not give decent terms for it you can generally bring him to reason by proposing to manufacture it yourself and giving it to him to sell on commission. This of course is only a bluff if you have not £150 at hand. You could, however, raise that from me on the security of the book, which would be just as safe a speculation for me as for the publisher.

Take reasonable care of this letter. You have no idea of the trade that goes on in autographs containing private information. The other day I was confronted with an old copy of The Academy, dated 1898, with some shorthand notes on the margin of a lot of doggrel verses I sent to Ellen Terry with a copy of Plays, Pleasant and Unpleasant. Read without any clue to their subject, they seemed to be about a man instead of a book; and as Ellen has a habit of reading in bed, and the book was poetically exhorted to nestle in her blankets, you can imagine how the honest Pitmanite who was asked to decipher it by a second-hand bookseller, and who was generous enough to return it to me, believed that he had saved me from a fearful scandal. But the real point is that I have not the least idea how the paper got into the hands of the bookseller, or how he knew that the shorthand notes were by me. Therefore I exhort you to be careful, as the figures mentioned above as to Getting Married must not reach the public.

yours ever
G. Bernard Shaw

To SIEGFRIED TREBITSCH

[H/5]

10 Adelphi Terrace WC
29th June 1908

[Julius Bab (1880–1955), a German theatre scholar and critic, wrote one of the earliest critical studies of Shaw (Berlin, 1910; rewritten 1926). Their Scandinavian trip took the Shaws to Gothenburg and Stockholm, with Hugo Vallentin as guide. They then proceeded to Germany, where they visited Hamburg, Hanover, Bayreuth (for the Festival), Munich, Heidelberg, Darmstadt, Bremen, and a dozen other cities, returning from Bremerhaven on 1st September in the Krönprinz Wilhelm. *The Doctor's Dilemma* (*Der Arzt am Scheideweg*) was produced on 21st November 1908 at the Kammerspiele des Deutchen Theaters, Berlin.]

My dear Trebitsch

I have ordered the books you mentioned to be sent to Julius Bab. As to the enormously comprehensive question as to what literature he ought to read about Irish civilization, it is quite unanswerable. My advice to him is to read the preface to John Bull's Other Island and be content with that. The alternative is to spend the next twenty years in a Public Library reading everything he can find there on the subject of Ireland.

On Saturday next, the 4th, I start for Stockholm by sea, via Gotenburg and the Gotha Canal. As my wife has never been to Bayreuth, we shall go there at the end of July. Our present intention is to hire a motor car and do our travelling in that way. This might conceivably take us even as far as Vienna; but I am not quite sure as to that. However, I must break away from my work and have a good holiday, as I am pretty nearly at the end of my tether. You can judge of the extent to which I have been pressed by the impossibility of getting a letter out of me.

As to the title of the Doctor's Dilemma, tell Reinhardt that if he wants a play called Der Arzt und der Tod he had better write it himself: I simply wont have it. Der Arzt am Scheideweg exactly expresses my title; and unless Reinhardt can find an alternative which is equally correct as well as more effective, I shall vote for the Scheideweg.

Bad as the press notices of The Doctor's Dilemma were, they were nothing to the torrent of denunciation that burst over Getting Married. The effect is of course very bad in Germany; but here the reaction produced by the fact that the play has not been a failure after all, has been rather useful to me. Many of the notices declared that though the first act was tolerably well received, the play was received at the end with hisses. As a matter of fact, I heard a solitary hiss at the end of the first act; but at the end of the play there were six curtain calls, although the great length of the play must have made it most exhausting to the audience. I believe it will prove a money making play. . . .

Meyerfeld is in London; but he has made no attempt to see me this time, though he has been stuffing Archer, and I presume everybody else, with stories of your horrible incapacity as translator.

Now as to Jacobson. First, will you tell him that if he wishes to make any impression on me by his letters, he must write in Latin script. I cannot decipher those infernal German characters. I have read his libretto. With the exception of certain passages which can easily be altered or removed, and which are simply translations of my dialogue and therefore violations of the rights of my translators in other countries, there is nothing I need object to, provided it is not implied in any way that I am responsible for the operetta, and provided especially that a stop be put to the statements in the press that the managers who have acquired the rights of the operetta have acquired also the rights of Arms and the Man. The libretto should be announced frankly as parodierte von Bernard Shaw's Helden. The first act is an allowable and amusing parody. The second and third acts may succeed if the music and the actresses are pretty enough. Of the passages to which I object, the principal one begins on page 24 of Act 3 with the words "Wie viel Pferde haben Sie?" This is not a parody of the situation in my play, but a literal translation of it. Again, on page 40 of the second Act, the first eight speeches, about the pawning of the coat, must be left out, because they also are practically translated straight out of the original. A good deal of the act, especially the passages about the chocolate, the cavalry charge, and the portrait, are really open to the same objection; but we can let them pass, partly because we should make the whole libretto impossible if we objected, and partly because the first Act is a genuine parody, and genuine parody is quite allowable.

My conditions then are as follows. The passages I have marked with blue pencil . . . must be omitted. I have made the cuts in each case so that it will not spoil the scene: it will only shorten it and make it play closer. The operetta may be announced as parodierte nach Bernard Shaw's Helden von Rudolf Bernauer and Leopold Jacobson. The title used in England and America must be The Chocolate Cream Soldier, a musical parody of Arms and the Man (with apologies to Mr Bernard Shaw). Further, the English version must be a bona fide translation of the German of Messrs Bernauer and Jacobson, and must not reproduce verbatim any sentence in Arms and the Man. There must, in short, be no greater use made of my play in England and America than in Germany. Now as to the advance of a thousand kronen. The return of this sum must be accepted. The entire sum must be returned by you, and returned on the express ground that you find, on referring to the exact terms of your agreement with me, that you went beyond your powers in signing the letter dated 13th October 1907. That letter must be returned to you in exchange for the thousand kronen and for a letter setting forth the conditions I am now making. (If they refuse this—if they persist on standing on this agreement and maintaining its validity, then all negotiations are at an end; and I hold myself free to take legal action in England and America the moment a performance is

795

announced.) There is, however, no reason why you should not accept any payment they choose to make you for your trouble in the matter. Only, it must be clear that I get none of it.

If these conditions are accepted, I shall take no steps to hinder the production either in English or German. Also, I will not suggest any hostile proceedings in other countries; but it must be distinctly understood that my translators, under my agreement with them, have the right, not only to take proceedings themselves, but to make me a party to those proceedings if they choose, and that in the event of their doing so, I am bound to stand by them. The purchaser of the rights can, however, guard himself by employing my translators to translate the libretto. Still, I repeat that I cannot guarantee their consent.

yrs ever
G. Bernard Shaw

To AUGUSTIN HAMON

[H/1]

10 Adelphi Terrace W C
2nd July 1908

[None of Shaw's grandiose schemes for French production came to fruition. Coquelin died on 27th March 1909; Lugné-Poe and Suzanne Després produced neither *L'Homme et le surhomme* nor *La Profession de Madame Warren* at the Théâtre de l'Oeuvre; and although the French comedian and *chanteuse* Yvette Guilbert (1869?–1944), before her return to France, sent Shaw a farewell injunction, "I hope you will not forget your promise to make a play for me!" (BM), the play was never written. Ethel Grenfell (1867–1952), Lady Desborough, was a famous hostess who entertained lavishly at two country houses. Hamon's article on Shaw in the July 1908 issue of *Nineteenth Century* was "Un nouveau Molière."]

My dear Hamon

I have no fresh news; but this is the last chance I shall have to write to you, as I sail for Sweden the day after tomorrow. I cannot sufficiently urge you not to build Spanish castles on such incidents as the letter from Brieux about Antoine and my meeting with Coquelin. In order to meet Coquelin, I had to depart from my usual habits so far as to "go into Society." I arrived before Coquelin, and when he came I was in a discussion with the Swiss Ambassador . . . When Coquelin came in, there was only time to exchange three or four sentences with him when we had to go down to lunch. Our hostess, Lady Stanley, appropriated Coquelin; and I was planted between the Prime Minister's wife and a duchess. By the time we got back to the drawingroom, Coquelin was gone, as he had a rehearsal to attend. However, all the women had been jabbering at him that he must act this, that, or the other play of mine—whatever their favourite play happened to be, without the least regard whether it was suitable to him (Candida was the favourite!)—and Charlotte sent him a copy of Arms and the Man the same evening with a letter in the best French that this household can produce. This, as it turned out, was quite unnecessary: I learn from the people at His Majesty's Theatre that Coquelin speaks English very well. I have not heard from him since. In order to meet him again, I have actually consented to go to the Prime Minister's garden party this evening where he is to recite. More than this I cannot do. . . .

Brieux said nothing about the translation of Candida. Possibly he thought that that would not interest me; but most probably he accepted it as part of the general impression the play made on him. The fact that it did not occur to him to criticize the translation is to me the most satisfactory proof that it did not jar on him in any way. . . .

I have had a letter from Suzanne Despres demanding whether I will *give* her L'Homme et le Surhomme. I have not had time to reply. I have a very strong impression, with which I know you will not agree, that our next Parisian move will be either Mrs Warren's Profession or the Surhomme; but I have grave doubts as to whether Antoine will be of much use to us for either. Antoine, I suspect, is at the wrong theatre for us. However, we must wait and see how things will develop. Yvette Guilbert is here with her husband; and we duly arranged a luncheon party for them last week; but Yvette got a bad attack of lumbago and could not come; so now it seems doubtful whether we shall see them at all this time. She is at her old business of singing songs at the Palace Theatre; and I am told she is enormously successful, all of which looks as if it would be more and more difficult for her to break loose from the variety stage. Still, as she is no doubt getting an enormous salary— much more than she can possibly spend—she must be accumulating a good deal of money. As likely as not, she will take a theatre; and mourira sur la paille.

3rd July

After writing the above yesterday, I went to the garden party. Coquelin was there. He recited a thing by Daudet. He then discovered me and began explaining to me with great cordiality that he had

797

received from Charlotte a truly charming letter and a brochure, but that he had been unable to acknowledge them. He then added "You know what my life is—" when Lady Desborough swept into the conversation by asking him did he remember a most amusing recitation that he had given at the Spanish Ambassador's—an imitation of an Englishman speaking French. Coquelin said he did, and proceeded to give us the recitation there and then. It was excessively funny; but I was the only person who enjoyed it, because I was the only person present who knew the difference between our English dipthongs and French vowels. The others were pleased because they understood what he was saying when he was imitating the Englishman much better than when he was talking real French. But when he pronounced très as treille and beaucoup as boh-ou-cou-ou, they were perfectly satisfied with his pronunciation and could not understand what on earth I was laughing at. However, the net result is that Coquelin has not read the play and probably has not the slightest intention of reading it, which was precisely what I anticipated. On the other hand, any idea that he may have had that I am an eccentric and ill-mannered bohemian has been effectually done away with. He has met me in the most distinguished circles, and does not know that I went into them for the express purpose of meeting him. And the few words we had together were quite cordial and unembarrassed, whilst my wife, who is a fearfully ladylike person, and dresses herself with perfect taste, would reassure the greatest sceptic as to my perfect correctness. Coquelin is a man who understands these things: his manners are altogether admirable from the best human point of view.

I have not yet read your article in the Nineteenth Century; but it is being quoted in all directions in the press and will positively add considerably to my reputation. The English never know what to admire until some foreigner tells them; but when they are at last told what to do, it is astonishing how obediently and zealously they do it. It now only remains for me to write an article in a French magazine to say that you are the greatest author and statesman of the age, and you will get the next vacant fauteuil at the Academy. I will read your article tomorrow on the North Sea. . . .

yours ever
G. Bernard Shaw

To WILLIAM ARCHER

[H/2]

10 Adelphi Terrace W C
3rd July 1908

[At the Annual General Meeting of the Society of Authors, on 20th March 1908, several members led a rebellion against the Dramatic Sub-Committee and the Society's secretary, G. Herbert Thring, informing the meeting that forty members of the Society had quietly held a meeting to discuss the formation of an independent Dramatic Authors' Society, with Pinero serving as acting chairman of the organising committee. The Committee of Management of the Society of Authors, in an effort to forestall the defection, ordered the reconstitution of its twelve-man sub-committee in June, a task which was not completed until early in 1909. Although Pinero complained violently to Archer (for whom he had manœuvred an election to the sub-committee in June) that the Society was scheming "to burke the movement" and admitted that he sympathised with the members who had "no special fondness for Mr. Thring and the gentlemen [especially Shaw] who help him to pull the strings" (letter, 30 June 1908, BM), he remained on the sub-committee and in 1909 became its chairman. But he also continued to nourish the idea of "a little exclusive society for our own amusement and, perhaps, benefit," and on 3rd March 1909 the dream became a reality with the founding of the Dramatists' Club.

Anthony Hope Hawkins (1863–1933), noted for his novel *The Prisoner of Zenda* (1894), Alfred Sutro (1863–1933), and Capt. Robert Marshall (1863–1910) were fellow dramatists on the sub-committee, of which Shaw had been a member since March 1906. The Savage Club at this time had a tradition of heavy drinking, foul-mouthedness, and generally rather free-and-easy, raffish bohemianism. The meeting on 30th June at the home of Robert George Windsor-Clive (1857–1923), 1st Earl of Plymouth, was to formulate plans growing out of the union, which had been effected on 19th May 1908, of the committees to establish a National Repertory Theatre and to erect a Memorial to Shakespeare in connection with his approaching Tercentenary in 1916. Shaw pursued the subject of Pinero's knighthood throughout 1908, and with the assistance of Lord Esher and Margot Asquith (1864–1945), wife of the new prime minister, he obtained the honour for Pinero in the Birthday Honours of 1909.]

My dear W.A.

. . . In steering this Authors' Society business, you must bear steadily in mind that the thing we have got to do is to educate our men, and that all these reports and draft agreements and so forth have that as their first function—possibly also their last. They have to be educated, not only in the economic and practical business they have to face, and in public procedure, of which, as you can see for yourself, they are all

799

childishly ignorant, but above all in the impersonal habit of mind—the committee habit—without which every attempt to face and deal with the simplest hard fact leads to wounded feelings, squabbling, resignations, and, generally, the sort of baby stunt that Sutro treated us to the other day. Also, we must keep a perfectly open mind as to which body finally captures the position. I am at present applying all my driving force (which, you will observe, consists simply in sitting down and doing the work that nobody else will do) to make the Authors' Society Committee out-do, out-think, and out-goodmanner the other Committee. The effect has already been to straighten up the new Committee tremendously, and to set them at work at the agency scheme of which Marshall spoke yesterday, and of which, a month ago, they were as incapable as a litter of kittens. I shall continue at every opportunity to goad them with insults to further exertions. I have already done my best, by kindly and patronizing insolence, to make them feel that they will be simply like infants in my hands and those of the Authors' Society unless they really put their backs into the affair. The effect of this will be altogether good, because neither side can conceal its operations from the other. In a rash moment the new body invited me to attend one of their meetings; and five minutes after I had entered the room I had in an innocent manner raised the question of preliminary expenses and sent the hat round with a sovereign of my own in it. With that sovereign I purchased their souls: they can no more keep me out of their councils now than the Society of Authors can keep them out. Each side will benefit by all the work the other does; and whether the result is a new Society or a complete regeneration of the dramatic committee of the old Society, all the intermediate work will be to the good. On the whole I lean towards the side of literary solidarity, not only for financial and general human reasons, but also because I rather mistrust the tendency of the old gang of dramatic authors towards the traditions of the Savage Club. Do what you can while I am away to keep things wholesome; and remember that nothing whatever can be done as long as the authors are inactive. In the Authors Society in the old days (meaning in fact yesterday) we really did all we could to galvanise the dramatic committee into life; but the authors simply would not take any interest in it. When Pinero found that nothing was being done, instead of saying that something must be done and doing it, he acquiesced in the situation with a relief which was human and natural enough in the circumstances. Edward Rose and Grundy, like Jones, were driven to the same fatalistic acceptance of the uselessness of getting the dramatic authors to assemble and put in any work. At last, Hawkins and myself made the Executive Committee add us to the Dramatic Sub-Committee; and we did what we could until the censorship agitation gave us our chance. But we should collapse again tomorrow if the old apathy set in again.

Now for a bit of diplomacy in which you might help me. I have made up my mind to make Pinero a knight. In this National Theatre scheme we have a lot of knight-actors; but we have no knight-dramatist except Gilbert, who is too old and not really representative. Pinero is the man. The other day, when Pinero, Hare, Lytton and myself met at Lord Plymouth's, I sounded Pinero as to whether he would accept a knighthood if it came his way. His position, like Irving's, is strong enough to save him from any suspicion of wanting a knighthood on personal grounds; and the accolade would undoubtedly strengthen the theatre movement. He said that it had never occurred to him, and that he would rather have something nice in the way of a little red ribbon; but he is prepared to suffer knighthood on public grounds. So yesterday I made the heroic sacrifice of going into Society. I went to Mrs Asquith's garden party, and told her flatly that A.W.P. must be made a knight. She said she could not do it until next November. I said next November would do. Finally the whole assembly of duchesses and other social daisies began discussing it; and though of course the whole thing was wildly irresponsible, I think it quite possible that something may come of it, because Mrs Asquith quite understood that I was in earnest about it, and quite agreed that it would be a very proper birthday honour. Will you take any opportunity you may have of propagating the idea, in print or in private. But take due care not to let anybody compromise A.W.P. or make him ridiculous. It is rather desirable that he should know what is going on; but I cannot tell him because I cannot make him an accomplice in my wire-pulling. All the more reason why you should tell him if you get the chance.

I am now going off into the wilds, leaving no address; but any letters addressed here will be forwarded at such moments as I am discoverable. This also, by the way, is rather queer English; but 'twill serve.

yrs ever
G.B.S.

To WILLIAM ARCHER

[C/2; X/108]

[Stockholm]
[Undated: assigned to 16th July 1908]

[August Strindberg (1849–1912), famed Swedish playwright and novelist, had never been produced professionally on the English stage. J.T. Grein had announced a production of Justin Huntly M'Carthy's translation of *The Father* by the Independent Theatre in 1891, but it was not presented.]

I achieved the impossible—a meeting with Strindberg—today. He said "Archer is not in sympathy with me." I said "Archer wasnt in sympathy with Ibsen either; but he couldnt help translating him all the same, being accessible to poetry, though otherwise totally impenetrable." After some further conversation, consisting mainly of embarrassed silence & a pale smile or two by A.S. & floods of energetic eloquence in a fearful lingo, half French, half German, by G.B.S., A.S. took out his watch & said, in German, "At two o'clock I am going to be sick." The visitors accepted this delicate intimation & withdrew.

GBS

To SYDNEY C. COCKERELL

[C/3]

On the Baltic from Stockholm to Lubeck
18th July 1908

Stockholm is a very jolly town to look at & the people very superior within certain limits of high mediocrity. All the art they understand is ornamental XVII–XVIII century—grand ducal—Louis Quatorze &c; but there is a Codex Aurens in the Library (quite unknown to the inhabitants) and some very nice Icelandish MSS.

G.B.S.

To ARCHIBALD HENDERSON

[X/213]

[Bayreuth]
[Undated: c. 27th–31st July 1908]

Courage! Think of how long HE [Wagner] waited. Besides, I want to get this biography off my mind. I am going to hurry up. A year or two more; and THEN we shall go gaily to the printer.

802

To MAUD CHURTON BRABY

[C/1]

[Bayreuth]

[Undated: assigned to 31st July 1908]

[In a review of Mrs Braby's book *Modern Marriage, and How to Bear It*, the anonymous reviewer in the *Pall Mall Gazette* had said on 10th July: "She starts with the assumption that there is 'a growing dread of the conjugal bond, especially among men,' the fact being that there is a small increase in the marriage rate. She has mistaken the cultured Bohemia of the Fabians for the country at large, while the fact probably is that it is only in that limited society and wheresoever the New Woman, shrieking and suffragetic, is found, that the male's reluctance to wed is specially noticeable." Mrs Braby, in a letter of reply published on 16th July, corrected the reviewer about the Fabian Society: "Among those of its members who are over thirty, married people predominate, and of the fifteen male members of the executive committee, only one is a bachelor!"]

I was in Stockholm when your letter was posted; and it did not overtake me until I arrived here (Bayreuth), too late for a rejoinder to the P.M.G. As a matter of fact the F.S. has for 24 years been recognized as a well stocked preserve for husband hunters. It used to be a perfect scandal the way women would join & resign the moment they had bagged their bird.

G.B.S.

To J. E. VEDRENNE

[A/4; X/183]

Just leaving Bayreuth

2nd August 1908

I shall arrive in Munich—Hotel Vier Jahreszeiten, Maximilianstr 4 —on Thursday next (the 6th) if nothing upsets my program. After that I shall be beyond reach for some time. I shall work round to Bremen with the car & come to Southampton by a Norddeutscher Lloyd at the end of the month: that is, any time after the 20th or thereabouts. If there is anything very pressing, better nail me at Munich.

Did I send you a picture of the inside of the Festspielhaus?

GBS

[Accompanying the letter to Vedrenne were four programmes of the Bayreuth Festival, annotated by Shaw.]

25 July   Das Rheingold.

conducted by Richter

The second scene was quite spoiled by the heavy dark brown foreground. One would think Turner had never painted, and that Gaspar[d]

803

Poussin and the tradition of the yellow sun & brown tree had never been exploded. Great pity; for the castle was fine.

Wotan [Walter Soomer] magnificent voice—man under 30.

Loge [Dr Otto Briesemeister] style of Barker

The three Rhinedaughters [Frieda Hempel, Bella Alten, Adr. v. Kraus-Osborne], not being able to sing like salmon, sang like pheasants instead, with amazing realism. First scene consequently ugly beyond words—Alberich [Max Dawison] jolly well out of it.

27 July   Siegfried

I forgot to get bills of the Walküre & Die Gotterdämmerung. The casts were not changed. Richter conducted the last three performances magnificently. He is too old to care much about the Walkürenritt & that sort of thing; but all the rest was masterly: not a stroke wrong and the broadest & grandest parts the best.

The Rheingold was not so good: the singers drowned the orchestra. I told Richter he would have to write additional accompaniments presently.

There were some very clever tricks of stage lighting in the second act of Siegfried, especially getting the sun behind the tree & casting a strong shadow *towards* the footlights with the bare sun glittering at you through the leaves.

Soomer ought to be captured for London (from a business point of view). His singing at the end of Die Walküre produced a wild demonstration from the audience. He talks to Brynhild on ♪ as easily as a basso profundo, and gets pianos on ♪ as easily as a tenor. Very rich voice & sings in tune. Too young for the 3rd act of Siegfried, but splendid in the first act with Mime & in the Walküre farewell. Talk to Schulz-Curtius or the opera people about it.

Siegfried [Alois Burgstaller] very good—couldnt have believed it was the same man I saw at his debut on my last visit [1894].

Mime [Hans Breuer] excellent—really sings now.

Alberich [a] stick—also vibrato

Brünnhilde [Ellen Gulbranson] sings in tune. Most matronly

31 July   Lohengrin

Wonderful stage pictures, very well composed. But I missed a certain manœuvre by which, when Lohengrin was first produced in Bayreuth, the women (in the finale to the first act) suddenly swept forward & changed the whole color of the stage at the exact moment when the key changed.

Musically the performance was a little muzzy: the later Wagnerian style blots out something of the sharpness & brilliancy of the age of Spontini.

Heinrich der Vogler, deutscher König [Allen C. Hinckley] & Vibrato.

Elsa [Kath. Fleischer-Edel], in a flaxen wig, exactly like the doll in the second act of the Contes d'Hoffmann.

Ortrud [Edith Walker], looking very Irish in the 1st act.

1 August   Parsifal

This was the most perfectly managed performance I ever saw (and I had seen 6 before at Bayreuth). The only sort of curtain call allowed by tradition there is a tableau curtain at the end of Parsifal; and this time the impression was so perfect that there was a shocked protest—quite a lot of hissing—when the curtain was taken up again.

To EDITOR OF UNIDENTIFIED MUNICH NEWSPAPER

[G/2]

[Munich]

[Undated: assigned to *c*. 6th August 1908, but may be of 11th–14th August 1911]

[This draft presumably was never completed.]

May I venture through your columns to call attention to the scandalously careless treatment of some of the most precious of the many treasures of art possessed by Munich. On visiting the Royal Library today I was astonished to find books which in England or France would be handled with the most anxious care; classed with the masterpieces of painting and sculpture; and exhibited so as to shew them to the greatest advantage, actually worse displayed & less cared for than the contents of a railway book stall. I gasped when I saw the Fouquet Boccaccio with another heavy book lumped on top of its open page. The 1483 German Bible was dog-eared: nobody had taken the trouble to unfold the corners and put the book straight. Book after book was opened in such a way as to help it to break its back by its own weight; and the process was helped in several cases by piling another book on it. But even worse than this carelessness was the utter insensibility to the beauty of the books as works of art shewn by the way in which they were thrust into the shabby, rickety cases in which they were exhibited. As all connoisseurs in printing know [Text ends here]

[B/3; X/168]   [Undated: assigned to 6th August 1908]

Hotel Vier Jahreszeiten, München

Telegramm-Adresse: **Jahreszeiten**   Telephon: 4323 & 4024

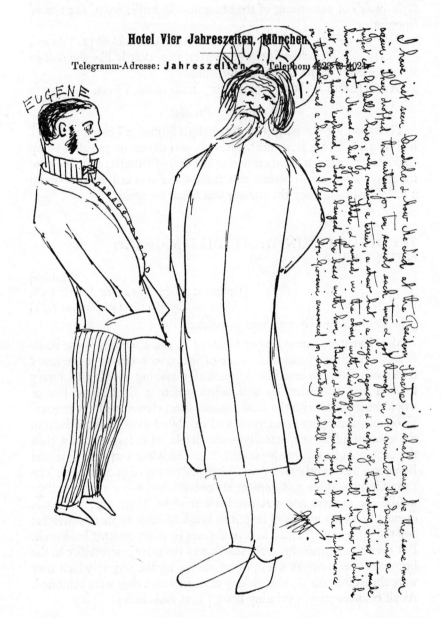

I have just seen Laudisia & show she did at the Residenz Theater. I shall never be the same man again. They dropped the curtain for ten seconds each time & got bumps in 90 minutes. La Duse was a fake. I shall hire only making a tour; a show hat, a bright agony, & a copy of the starting tired to make him smile. She was a big of an attitude, & gazed in the chair with her long curved neck. She show she did at no place beyond & softly banged the bed with him. Thighs & troubles was good; but the inference. One [...] answered. [...] Saturday I shall wait for it.

EUGENE

To HARLEY GRANVILLE BARKER

[X/168]

Rothenburg
12th August 1908

The motor having backjumped & sent Charlotte like a rocket to the roof of the car (a limousine, unluckily) she is now uncertain whether her neck is broken or not. She leans to the belief that it is. Anyhow we shall stay here tomorrow to give her a rest.

G.B.S.

To MESSRS VEDRENNE & BARKER

[A/40]

Schloss-Hotel. Heidelberg
19th August 1908

[*Getting Married* was not produced in the United States until 1916. The phrase "their names sweet symphonies" is a variation of a line in Rossetti's poem "The Blessed Damozel." The Shakespeare quotation is a variant of Sonnet 116.]

Sirs

I reluctantly enclose £350. £100 of it is, I am told, for Superman scenery. Since the opening of the Haymarket season I have paid for Superman scenery over and over again. The sums disbursed under this head since May would equip all my plays & cover a few Shakespearean revivals into the bargain. My last contribution settled all outstanding debts; provided a final set of scenes for Superman; and left £50 over & above for petty cash. And now the last act of Superman is sceneless. I believe that Vedrenne pawns the scenery and spends the proceeds in unbridled personal extravagance. There is no other way of accounting for the fact that however often I extricate the firm from debt, it is as insolvent as ever within a week.

Suppose this tour is a financial failure, where is the deficit to come from? I am getting no money in at present to repair my ruinous losses; and I have refused to let G.M. be produced in America before the presidential election. Consequently the purse of Fortunatus is empty.

The question of Barker's salary is simple enough. If he dies before the tour starts, what will it cost to replace him? That is his value as leading man. Add it to his old salary as manager and you get the final figure. Vedrenne acts better & more frequently; but he does not charge for admission (except to the author, at an average of £300 per performance); so he must submit to the annoyance of getting less than

Barker. At £5 an act for six acts—three of Arms & three of Superman (the cumulative method being introduced to compensate for provincial expenses) Barker's minimum for acting would be £30. His draw as partner would be £20. Total £50, and his share of the profits. Vedrenne would draw £20, plus the same golden prospect. I would get my author's fees on the usual scale, and my share of the profits until I am paid off.

The alternative is to engage Loraine, who would want £80, and would not get rid of Barker as producer & partner; so that producer + partner + Bluntschli + Tanner would cost £100 as against £50, or whatever sum between £50 & £100 Barker will take—for £30 is not by any means handsome from the Italian point of view regarded as a simple actor's salary. Still, £50 a week is enough for a young man with a lucrative wife.

The arrangement is unjust and anti-Socialistic, because the notion of one man drawing for two professions is absurd: Barker has no more hours in the day to give than Vedrenne; and Vedrenne has a child & an equally beautiful wife. On the other hand Mrs Vedrenne might be earning as much as Mrs Barker but for Vedrenne himself. I have repeatedly offered her parts which he has prevented her from accepting. Still, that is beside the point; and the point (the Socialist one) is beside the way of the world, according to which Barker is actually worth so much solid cash as an actor, especially in the provinces, where they have not yet seen him.

Now as to the profit sharing. That ought to take place in proportion to the cash we have advanced. Since the Court business was closed, I have put down so much, Vedrenne so much, Barker so much. The original understanding was that the proportions were to be—Shaw 50, Vedrenne 25, Barker 25. The actual proportions are, roughly, Shaw 1000,000,000,000,0000 Vedrenne $\frac{9}{10}$ Barker $\frac{7}{8}$, there or thereabouts. Well, let the net profit on the tour be divided among us in like proportion. I think we had better count only the actual hard cash put down by each contributor since the first levy was made on me—that is, since the institution of the guarantee fund made me a theatrical speculator instead of a respectable author. I do not think that the pact should be retrospective.

Even on that basis the transaction is getting complicated. There is a lot of scenery, some dresses (hell scene, for instance), some sketches of scenery of enormous value as autographs, prompt books, log books &c &c. To whom do they belong? As to the Superman scenery, I have already expressed an opinion. Suppose we all three died—we are mortal, after all—how would our widows settle it? Could we count on a sisterly affection, intensified by a common grief, making all difficulties easy? Phyllis, Lillah, Charlotte—"their names sweet symphonies"—would they quite hit it off? Would their solicitors hit it off? What would they hit off? One another's heads, perhaps.

It is to be observed, anyhow, that Vedrenne & Barker as individuals have created a Frankenstein's Monster (the firm of Vedrenne & Barker with a Goodwill for a soul) that they cannot easily slay, however much they may loathe it. They cannot take each what is his & go his several way any more than Solomon's litigants could take each her half of the child. "Let me not to the marriage of true souls admit impediment" said Shakespear....

I had intended to leave this place today; but I shall stay now until Friday morning probably. I shall probably strike the Hotel Pfeiffer, Marburg, on my way north to Bremen, where I shall take a Norddeutscher Lloyd to Southampton, with a view to the west of Ireland, where rooms are engaged from the 1st Sept. Unless I order a motor to transport me from Southampton to Fishguard, I shall pass through London; but you had better have everything settled before then.

G.B.S.

To C. H. NORMAN

Belmullet

[A/4]   24th September 1908

[The Shaws reached Ireland on 7th September, and did not return to London until 4th October. Norman had sought Shaw's co-operation in the formation of a new political party (which he advocated calling the Collectivist Party), to be developed through the creation of a society or club. Shaw had suggested alternatively the title "the New Police," meaning a police force to protect Society, but his letter had not been encouraging enough to satisfy Norman. Alfred Richard Orage (1873–1934), an ex-schoolteacher who propagated Guild Socialism, became publisher and editor of the *New Age* in May 1907, financed by £500 each from Shaw and Lewis A. R. Wallace, a banker. When the journal and the New Age Press were formed into a company in November 1908, Norman became chairman. The Rev. Reginald John Campbell (1867–1956), who from 1903 to 1915 was Minister of City Temple, finally resigned from the Fabian Executive because of his inability to attend meetings. Mrs Wells, despite her husband's resignation, remained on the Executive until March 1910].

Dear Norman

When you have come to my age in the movement you will sympathize with me. You abuse me because, at 52, I do not throw over the Fabian Society on receipt of a brief and vague intimation from you that you have a new society that needs all my devotion. Orage abuses me because, having given the New Age £500 to keep it going for six months, and contributed a thousand pounds worth of copy to it for nothing, I intimate that I am not prepared to repeat the effort. So he tells me that Webb and I are no Fabians because we do not devote ourselves to writing articles in his paper. Have you any sort of notion of the limits set by Nature to our time, energy and means? What the dickens do we lend you young men a hand for at all except to shift our surplus work on to you and your generation? And instead of taking it up, you calmly ask us to begin life over again in your societies and papers for your amusement. When will you realize that you have nothing more to hope for from us—that we are only fit to be pensioned after 30 years work—that though we still have plenty to do in our old age, it is old men's work and not young men's work? Our reputation is built on what we were doing at your ages: at present as far as propaganda is concerned, we are merely living on it. Your business is to supersede us. You say you are disgusted and discouraged after 25 minutes. What do you suppose *we* are after 25 years? Make your new society a success as we made the Fabian; and then you can depend on us to come along and take all the credit of it.

I am much more concerned at present about the vacancies on the Fabian Executive Committee created by Wells's resignation, Campbell's absolutely blank attendance sheet, and the probable withdrawal of Mrs Wells (three vacancies) than with the newest Society or the newest paper. Also I am in Belmullet, held up by the rain; and if you dont know what that means you know nothing of life's tragedy.

yours ever
G.B.S.

To HUGH LANE

[H.c.u/2; X/214]

10 Adelphi Terrace W C
5th October 1908

[Sir Hugh Lane (1875–1915), art collector and leader in the revival of Irish art, later became Director of the National Gallery of Art in Dublin; he died in the sinking of the Lusitania. Lane, encouraged by his aunt Lady Gregory, had asked Shaw to sit to the young Irish-born artist William Orpen (1878–

1931) for a portrait for "my series of Irishmen." He also urged Shaw to contribute the marble bust of himself by Rodin to the new Municipal Gallery which he had founded, in 1906, to house modern art.]

Dear Mr. Lane

I have so little sense of my own private property in the bust, and so strong a sense of Rodin's human rights in the matter, that I had rather not dispose of it without consulting him. Would it be too much to ask you to write to him saying that you believe the only obstacle to your acquiring the bust for the Gallery is some delicacy on my part in disposing of it without his sanction. While it is in my hands it is always at his command, in case he should desire to exhibit it. I do not know what powers you may have under your constitution of lending works for exhibition elsewhere; but my last scruple in the matter would be removed if you could assure Rodin that during his lifetime the bust would be practically as much at his disposal as if it were still in my house. You may tell him that if that condition were complied with, I had much rather the bust were under your care in the quite extraordinarily good collection you have founded in my native city, than hidden in a private house which already possesses an even more cherished masterpiece in the bronze cast taken from the original plaster.

Has any provision been made for the time when your modern pictures will be no longer modern? The obvious course would be to transfer the works to the National Gallery, keeping the M.A.G. continually replenished with modern work. Even as it is, it is impossible to go through your gallery without remembering that the painters of some of the pictures are as dead—in the sense of being im-modern—as the XIXth century. I have a very great affection for the National Gallery, in which I spent many of the happiest hours of my boyhood; and if in the long run the Rodins should find their way there ... I should have no desire unfulfilled in the matter.

I am afraid the portrait by Orpen is out of the question until I am superannuated. Even if I were to consent to sit, I should have to give two or three quite distinguished artists their turn first in redemption of old half promises and even some whole ones.

When you have settled matters with Rodin, let me know about the packing.

[yours faithfully
G. Bernard Shaw]

[Rodin's reply, reported the *Dublin Express* on 8th October, was a two-word telegram: "Yes; enchanted." Shaw shipped the bust to Dublin in November.]

To COL. DAVID LAMB

[10 Adelphi Terrace W C]

[X/215]   5th October 1908

[David C. Lamb (1866–1951), a Colonel in the Salvation Army, was a leading authority on problems of emigration.]

Dear Colonel Lamb

Your letter of the 17th July has only just reached me on my return to London. I would rather not say anything on the subject of emigration. Emigration is inevitable at present; and its organization is therefore a necessary and useful work, which comes well under that general heading of doing good which is the business of the Salvation Army. But to me the necessity for emigration is like the necessity of a surgical operation; it would not exist if the patient were in decent health; and as I could not honestly say anything on the subject without making it clear that I regard it as a national disgrace, and one that could be perfectly well wiped out by economic reforms at home, my utterances, however friendly in their references to the Salvation Army, would inevitably discourage subscriptions and turn the interest away from your Department.

yours faithfully

G. Bernard Shaw

To FRANK HARRIS

10 Adelphi Terrace W C

[H/4]   7th October 1908

[The "Chicago business" was the Haymarket Square riot, on 4th May 1886, a disturbance during which several policemen were killed by a bomb. Eight anarchist leaders were convicted of inciting violence; four of them were hanged. Lucy E. Parsons was the widow of the labour agitator Albert R. Parsons, one of the executed anarchists. She visited England in November 1888, sponsored by the Socialist League, to stir up and exploit sympathy for the executed men. Shaw attended a meeting of anarchists in Hyde Park on 11th November 1888 and provided an unsigned report for *The Star* the next day. Gov. John Peter Altgeld (1847–1902), a champion of human rights, eventually pardoned three of the imprisoned anarchists.]

My dear Harris

I have just found your letter here on my return to London. I am confronted by such a monstrous heap of arrears of work, both professional and friendly, that I know perfectly well that if you send me a manuscript, it will lie on my hands and on my conscience for two years if I am really to give my mind to it and read it with the horrible responsibility of having to give an opinion for serious business use afterwards. So be warned; and dont press me with it, though if I saw it advertized as actually published I should certainly order it and read it at once.

I have forgotten the details of the Chicago business of 1886. At the time I was so much interested in it that I tried to get signatures to a petition for the reprieve of the men. Outside the Socialist League and other circles in which it was signed as a matter of course, the only name I got was that of Oscar Wilde. It was really a very handsome thing of him to do, because all the associations of the thing were vulgar and squalid, and Oscar, as you know, was a snob to the marrow of his bones, having been brought up in Merrion Square, Dublin. I do not know whether you saw anything of Mrs Parsons when she came to this country to exploit our sympathy with the men who were executed: if not, your book may lack an element of comedy which she was eminently qualified to supply. If I recollect aright, Governor Altgeld some years afterwards published a book [*The Reasons for Pardoning Fielden, Neebe and Schwab*, 1893] which I did not read, but which was reviewed in the Socialist press as a vindication of the hanged anarchists and a blighting exposure of their prosecutors.

By the way, on looking at your letter again to see whether I have left anything unanswered, I see that you have actually sent me the book [*The Bomb*]. Heaven only knows where it is: I have not yet got through half the sackful that was waiting for me. When I reach it, I will communicate further.

yours ever
G. Bernard Shaw

P.S. I have routed out the book, and find myself unable to part with it until I have read it.

To LUCY CARR SHAW

Ayot St Lawrence. Welwyn
26th October 1908

[A/2]

[Lucy Carr Shaw, attending a performance of *Man and Superman* at the Coronet Theatre, Notting Hill Gate, about ten days earlier, had been intercepted in the lobby by Eade Montefiore (1866–1944), the manager of the theatre, with whom she had been associated in Cellier's *Dorothy* in 1886–87. Montefiore proceeded to impart to the startled Lucy the information that her husband Charles Butterfield and Montefiore's wife, known professionally as Constance Barclay, had lived together adulterously during all of the ten years of Lucy's absence in Germany. He further offered to provide evidence that would satisfy her as to the validity of his accusation.

Shaw, in *Sixteen Self Sketches* (1949), published a letter which he had written, *circa* 1938, to his Australian cousin Charles Shaw, informing him that "in a burst of fury [Lucy] came to see me and said she must have a divorce. As she had already practically divorced him I suggested that the operation was superfluous; but she was determined to be legally rid of him . . ." This version of the story (published, ironically, under the caption "Biographers' Blunders Corrected") was largely a fabrication. As the letter of 26th October 1908 to Lucy attests, Shaw had completely altered the truth. It was he, as much as his sister, who had determined upon the divorce with Lucy carrying out his explicit instructions without demur. Messrs Lewis & Lewis obtained a decree *nisi* for her on 13th January 1909, with costs in the amount of £91. 13. 8, which Shaw undertook to pay as the price of keeping Butterfield from contesting the action. The decree became absolute on 19th July 1909.

"Frau Major," the mother of Lucy's friend and nurse-companion, Eva Maria Schneider (1874–1957), had maintained a *pension* in Gotha. Lucy had resided with the kindly Schneiders from 1904 until her return to England. Douglas Butterfield (1854–1923), a younger brother of Charles, remained one of Lucy's closest friends until her death.]

My dear Lucy

I dont see any reason for maintaining the marriage that can weigh for a moment against the reasons for dissolving it. The tie is onerous enough even in the case of people whose marriages have been successful; who are living comfortably together and bringing up a family. But in your case the marriage does nothing but mischief. It compels your husband to live an immoral life; to seduce women who he might otherwise honorably marry; to have no children except illegitimate ones; and, generally, to be rated as a man of loose character—and such strong rating generally produces the reality sooner or later. It exposes you to the imputation of being either a spiteful woman who will not divorce her husband lest he should marry the other woman, or a woman of bad character whose hands are not clean enough for the divorce court. At any moment your husband—possibly a paralyzed & broken man—may dump himself on your doorstep and compel you to maintain him. It is just this kind of chicken that always does finally come home to roost. You have all the disadvantages of a married woman and none of

Lucy Carr Shaw, Gotha, 1907

(*Photograph by Eva Schneider; Burgunder Collection, Cornell University Library*)

Georgina Gillmore and Lucy Carr Shaw, De Crespigny Park,
Denmark Hill, London, 1910

the advantages. You cannot marry if you want to. You cannot form any sort of friendship with a man without exposing him to the risk of being threatened with a divorce petition in which he would be the co-respondent—and all sensible men are keenly alive to this danger. It makes it much more difficult to provide for you: a will in your favor is a will in your husband's favor, as you would probably soon find out if you were no longer protected by the poverty that is not worth black-mailing. Your husband has the most precarious of occupations: age will soon disqualify him as an acting manager, and as an actor he may be out of an engagement for a long period at any time. There is every likelihood of his finding himself confronted with the alternative of very disagreeable personal privation or appealing to you for help. He can molest you to an intolerable extent if you drive him to extremity (that is, if you dont buy him off): the formula "This woman is my wife" will paralyse every hand that is raised to protect you.

The cost of an undefended suit, screwed down to the lowest possible figure, is £30; but you will not get off so cheaply. Still, there is no likelihood of the costs going beyond what I am willing to find for you. It is of the utmost importance that you should act instantly upon Montefiore's communication, because if you wait you will be held to have condoned the adultery. Write at once to Messrs Lewis & Lewis, Ely Place, Holborn E.C, asking them will they act for you in a petition for divorce. Make out a businesslike statement for them under such headings as your own name, maiden & married; your age; the respon-dent's name and status (wife of—— Montefiore of — —); the date of your marriage; the date of your separation; the exact nature of the understanding on which you separated (was it desertion on his part or on yours?); whether you have seen him or cohabited with him since, & if so when; the date of your discovery through Montefiore of the adultery; whether you ever condoned adultery on his part by, for instance, refusing intercourse with him & telling him to go to other women & not bother you; whether he ever accused you of relations with other men, and on what evidence; and whether you can prove that since you lived with him you have always lived either with your mother, your mother-in-law, or with the incontestibly respectable Frau Major. You had better also mention that you have no intention of marrying again and that there is no man in the case on your side. They will want to know why you did not move before: the answer is that until Monte-fiore spoke to you you had no knowledge of an actual case of adultery.

Say also that you have taken no other step in the matter, thinking it better to place yourself in Messrs Lewis & Lewis's hands & only act by their advice. Add that if they can estimate the cost of the petition in round figures you can give them satisfactory security or make any advances they may require. And, finally, "As I have no introduction to you, perhaps I had better give you, as a personal reference, my brother Mr Bernard Shaw, of 10 Adelphi Terrace W.C., by whose advice I am writing to you."

GBS

PS Your letter to Douglas is not very tactful. The passage I have marked will be taken to express a sense of degradation by your connexion with the Butterfield family. If you really have no feeling about them except a desire to be rid of them all, you have expressed it very effectively. But it would have been rather nicer to assure them that you do not associate them with their bad boy in your sense of injury.

Also, you should not have raised *their* objection. Leave them to raise it themselves if they choose. Probably they will see that they cannot reasonably stand in the way of your release; and in that case any reference to their private feelings would be very embarrassing to them. You are apt to be callous where English conventional family feeling has to be considered.

To FRANCES DILLON

[H/1]

10 Adelphi Terrace W C
21st November 1908

[Frances Dillon (1872–1947) was an actress whom Shaw personally selected to appear in the Vedrenne-Barker summer and autumn tour of *Man and Superman* and *Arms and the Man*: "I saw Frances Dillon this morning, and collapsed at the first glance. Simply heaven-sent for our tour. A superb Ann . . . I have told V.D. to secure her at once. Cannot understand why you did not send her to me before: she is the best discovery since Lillah" (letter to Barker, 17th June 1908, in *Bernard Shaw's Letters to Granville Barker*, 1957). He was less ecstatic after seeing a performance of the production on 14th October at the Coronet Theatre, Notting Hill Gate: "I should like some days to elapse," he wrote to Vedrenne the next day, "before trusting myself to express a calm opinion of that infamy. . . . [M]ost of the characters are hopelessly wrong . . . Ann Whitefield looks like a dowdy Brixton widow of forty in the first Act and does not even pretend to think her part worth a tinker's oath until the love scene in the last act, for which she puts on a new

A. J. Kilsby and the De Dietrich, 1910

(Photograph by Bernard Shaw; Burgunder Collection, Cornell University Library)

make up . . . It is perfectly awful to think that the Vedrenne-Barker Man and Superman has been introduced to the provinces so villainously" [H/40].

Detmar Blow (1867–1939), a well-known architect, designed the Lord Kitchener Memorial Chapel and the rebuilding of Grosvenor Square.]

Dear Miss Dillon

. . . I strongly advise you to read the letters of Queen Victoria through from beginning to end. Then try to imagine yourself Queen Victoria every night in the 1st Act. You will notice that Queen Victoria, even when she was most infatuatedly in love with Prince Albert, always addressed him exactly as if he were a little boy of three and she his governess. That is the particular kind of English ladylikeness in which you are deplorably deficient. An English lady in mourning is a majestic and awful spectacle. No matter how improperly she may behave, an English lady never admits she is behaving improperly. Just as there are lots of women who are good-hearted and honest and innocent in an outrageously rowdy way, so are there ladies who do the most shocking things with a dignity and gentility which a bishop might envy. Ann is one of the latter sort; and this is what you have not got in Ann. Ann's dignity, her self-control, her beautifully measured speed, her impressive grief for her father, which absolutely forbids her to smile until she is out of mourning, a sort of rich, chaste, noble self-respect about her which makes you feel that she belongs to carriage folk and is probably very highly connected, must be splendidly and very firmly handled on the stage in order to give effect to her audacity. In this you fail most hideously. From the moment of your entrance, you give Ann away as an easy-going, not very particular sort of person. You smiled freely; and when you threw your boa round Tanner's neck, there was nothing in it, because it was just exactly what one would have expected you to do. I was perfectly shocked at your second-rate behaviour when I should have been thrilled and stupended by the lifting of the goddess's veil only to disclose a syren. Your view of yourself was simply "With these pretty teeth, and this pretty smile, and these little ways, I can get round any man," whereas your view should have been "I am Miss Ann Whitefield, of Whitefield Court, Richmond, Surrey. I belong to a distinguished intellectual set; and although I do things that vulgar people might misunderstand because they are vulgar, the fact that I do them hallmarks them as eternally correct and right. Therefore be good enough not to shew your ignorance by sniggering." What gave me a final blow was your going off the stage in the last act and coming back with a new make-up on and a general air of saying "Now I am going to shew you something. Now I'm going to get my teeth into the only scene that makes this rotten part worth playing." You play it very well; but nobody on earth could play that scene badly if once they could play it at all. It is the 1st Act of Man and Superman that tests an actress; and I solemnly declare that your performance of the 1st Act would have been dear at fifteen shillings a week. I believe this was the effect of uncertainty as to how to take Ann. Try whether you can get any more out of it on the lines I have sketched above.

I also think you have been rather shabbily treated in the matter of the first act dress. Mourning is cheap; but it expressly says in the book that Ann does not wear ordinary mourning—that she has dressed herself handsomely not only in black but in violet. Ann's set is not a conventional set. What exasperates Ramsden so much in Tanner is that Tanner will not accept him as a highly intellectual artistic and advanced character. The late Whitefield's will is not a conventional will. Octavius Robinson is not at all a conventional johnny. Ann herself insists that she is quite used to Tanner's unconventional opinions, and to unconventional opinions generally; and she is the last woman in the world to turn conventional and commonplace in the matter of dress when she had plenty of precedents in the most distinguished and intellectual and artistic society for being original and artistic. In another play of mine, The Doctor's Dilemma, I have returned to this subject of the repudiation of the ugliness of conventional mourning by artistic people. The question was brought home to me by the death of William Morris. Mrs Morris wore a very beautiful and splendid mourning; and the poet's body was carried to the grave not in a hearse, but in a great harvest waggon, driven by Detmar Blow the architect, in a waggoner's smock. This is precisely the sort of thing that the Whitefields would know about, and that Ann would copy as the most distinguished thing to do, not to mention that it was the most becoming to herself. So the next time you accept an engagement for Ann, bargain for an eighty-guinea dress to begin with.

I do not think you will find the part difficult when you once get hold of Ann's character and circumstances. Once you have found out what to do, you will have no difficulty in doing it. You have quite talent enough and quite personality enough for the part.

yours sincerely
G. Bernard Shaw

To J. E. VEDRENNE

10 Adelphi Terrace WC
22nd November 1908

[A/4; X/183]

[While on tour, in Dublin in November, Barker had been stricken with what a local homœopathist had diagnosed as influenza, but which subsequently proved to be typhoid fever. He was being nursed by Allan Wade (1881–1955), a young actor and stage manager who had been one of the original members of the Vedrenne-Barker company at the Royal Court, and who was active for many years with the Stage Society. Dr Charles Edwin Wheeler (1868–1947), a famous homœopathic physician, was active also in the theatre, as a member of the managing committee of the Stage Society in its earlier years and as translator with Janet Achurch of Hauptmann's *The Coming of Peace* (1900). Lillah McCarthy had been appearing at the Royal Court in Murray's translation of Euripides' *The Bacchae*, but withdrew to join her husband in Dublin when apprised by Lady Gregory of the gravity of the situation.]

My dear VD

Let me confirm my telephone message. I gathered in the course of the week that the withdrawal of Wade might become a grievance. On Saturday Charlotte saw Wheeler; and he said in the course of the conversation that he thought it a pity that Wade could not stay with G.B. Also that he was going to see Mrs G.B. That settled it. I promptly rushed to the telephone.

I am not anxious about G.B.: he has the tenacity of ten cats. But I am old enough to realize that people really do die—even people one knows—people who never died before. And women (not to mention men) never blame nature or microbes: they always blame an individual. I foresaw that if Wade left and anything happened, you would be the villain of the piece in no time. So I took care not to understate the case.

Already you are the hero of a screaming story, which I cannot resist telling with fresh embellishments every time. Lillah tossing on her couch after two performances, longing for sleep. You, as the Voice of Conscience, waking her up at half hour intervals through the night to thunder through the telephone "Woman: your place is at the bedside of your dying husband" &c &c &c. *Did* you?

G.B.S.

P.S. I come up to town on Tuesday afternoon & pass on to Edinburgh to orate. Back on Thursday morning.

Ayot St Lawrence. Welwyn
[A/1]   24th November 1908

[Shaw's friend was J.S.Stuart-Glennie, who had deserted Henry Thomas Buckle in Damascus in 1862.]

My dear Wade

I am afraid I have done you an ill turn by getting permission for you to stay by Barker, and thereby making it practically impossible for you to refuse. However, I did not do so inconsiderately. I have been quite conscious all along that you were having a very unpleasant time, and running some risk into the bargain. My reasons for becoming an accomplice in the sacrifice were as follows.

Did you ever read Buckle's History of Civilization? If not, *do*. Well, Buckle was travelling in Syria when he died; and it happened that a friend of mine (another philosophic historian) came across him there a little before. The two men naturally caught on to one another and travelled a bit together. Presently Buckle got out of sorts and did not want to push on as fast as my friend, who was a hardy Highlander. So my friend pushed on alone, leaving Buckle to recuperate. Buckle didnt recuperate: he died. When my friend returned to civilization he found himself in the appalling position of having left his friend—a famous man—to die deserted in the desert. That took a lot of living down. Protestations were no use: the facts were the facts: he *had* left Buckle dying in a strange place; and he found that to do a thing that requires explanation is as bad as to do a thing that cant be explained.

You will see the application of this true story to your own position. All I need point out is its application to Vedrenne. When Dr Wheeler came back, he said it was a pity you had to leave, as you were a great comfort to Barker, not to mention all Barker's friends. He mentioned this to my wife, & also to Mrs Barker, who is, as you know, on somewhat strained terms with VD. It was plain to me that if VD insisted on your leaving, and anything happened to Barker, Vedrenne would be reproached for having refused a favor to his dying partner—said partner having reputation enough to ensure wide publicity for all details. When I warned him of this, he at once yielded, and left you in the cleft stick. But as you were in it already, it was useless to hold back. Until the doctors say definitely "Out of danger" you must hold on anyhow, as your name would figure largely in the obituaries if he died.

It is very good of you to stick to him; but it is jolly hard luck to have to be good in this way; and I hope you will soon get loose, and exercise your amiability on more reasonable terms. However, one must put up with these things as best one can. I write this only because I feared it might seem to you that I did not appreciate the extent and risk of the services thrown upon you, or how completely outside your contract and inside your own goodwill they are.

yours ever

G. Bernard Shaw

To EDWARD R. PEASE

Carlton Hotel. Edinburgh

[A/4]   25th [early A.M. 26th] November 1908

[Shaw had addressed the Edinburgh Fabians on 25th November on "Socialist Politics."]

I came down here last night in a sleeping car, and shall go back tonight the same way. I have made up my mind to take advantage of the occasion to plank down an unauthorized program. I shall point out that the Labor Party is a cipher because it has no program, and that such items as Nationalization of Railways &c need no new party, as they can obviously be tacked on to the Liberal or Unionist program. Same as regards Old Age Pensions, Poor Law, Health, Education &c &c. My program must therefore break away emphatically from the possibilities of Liberal & Unionist legislation. It is as follows:—

1 Communization of Bread.
2. Municipalization of Building
[No. 3 omitted by Shaw]
4. Heavy Tariff on Unearned Imports.
5. Webb's Unemployed Scheme.

That is enough to begin with. Every item in it is specifically Socialistic; and number one, which I believe to be the easiest to attain has the necessary shock in it—the necessary excitement of an apparently new departure (its really nothing but a common sense application of the Act of Elizabeth). I am seriously thinking of proposing that the Fabian Parliamentary Fund shall be given only to candidates who adopt this program, even if I withdraw it (as Portsmouth perhaps wouldnt stand it) before going to a division. Anyhow, I am tired of talking *round*

821

parliamentary Socialism and, when it comes to the point, finding that
J.R. Macdonald will die in the last ditch sooner than accept the
principle of National Minimum, like the thoroughgoing Scotch
Individualist he is.

Tonight I shall see how a Scotch audience will take my program.

yrs ever
G.B.S.

To HARLEY GRANVILLE BARKER

[C/4; X/168]

Ayot St Lawrence. Welwyn
31st December 1908

[Barker was at Spade House, Sandgate, visiting the H. G. Wellses. The After
Noon Theatre, founded by Beerbohm Tree and managed for him by Frederick Whelen and Henry Dana (1855–1921), had been inaugurated at His
Majesty's Theatre on 8th December with a performance of Hauptmann's
Hannele, translated by William Archer. *The Admirable Bashville* was first
presented publicly in London at His Majesty's Theatre on 26th January
1909 for six performances.

Shaw had just purchased his first automobile, a 28–30 h.p. De Dietrich,
built by Todd & Wright Ltd. of London to the specifications of Mervyn
O'Gorman and E. H. Cozens-Hardy, consulting engineers, delivered on 22nd
December. "It is a double cabriolet, with detachable hind part," reported
The Autocar on 5th December. "When the back seats are removed another
hind part replaces them which is so constructed as to carry spare tyres inside
and luggage outside, the top being covered with a thick cork carpet and brass
bound. . . . [T]here is a small hood for use with the car in its two-seated trim.
The lines of the car are uncommon and graceful . . . [The] rear doors have
invisible locks, which are so constructed as to form a tie to the body as well
as to lock the doors. . . . Rudge-Whitworth detachable wheels are employed,
the curved step box being cut away to allow for the carriage of the spare
wheel on the right-hand side."

Charlotte had taken driving lessons in November from H. E. M. Studdy,
who had earlier taught Shaw to drive. The gardener, Harry Higgs (1875–
1961), had been sent to the Royal Automobile Club in London for instruction
in July, so that he might double as chauffeur, but Shaw soon found it
necessary to hire a full-time chauffeur who was a better driver than Charlotte
or Higgs (or G.B.S. himself, he being a shockingly careless driver, though he
never admitted to the fact).]

Charlotte is in Shropshire [visiting the Cholmondeleys for Christ-
mas]. I am here in Ayot St Lawrence, snowed up and slushed up in the

822

filthiest manner. I shall have to get up to town tomorrow somehow to attend the [Shakespeare Memorial National Theatre] committee. I shouldnt come if I were you: you cant get any grip at this eleventh hour, and I daresay the prelude will pass with all suggestion of the confounded poor man cut out. We should get £5 notes instead of thousands if we began in that key. First get your theatre out of the rich: then capture it for the million if you like—though *I* want it for about a dozen righteous men.

The Afternoon Theatre has had to fall back on Bashville for the 26th. Such is the end of the first attempt at a Shawless theatre. Letter just to hand from Lillah about Frohman. It shall be attended to.

The car is here—at least the steel part of it. The splashboards &c are mostly lying about in the lanes. Charlotte wrecked it the first day. The professional kept her in countenance by knocking off the paddle-box against the gate. Higgs & I took up the game then.—No room left to insult old Tono Bungay; but you may give my love to Jane.

G.B.S.

To SIEGFRIED TREBITSCH

10 Adelphi Terrace WC
15th January 1909

[T/5]

[Wilhelm II (1859–1941), the German head of state, had produced a sensation in England and created an internal crisis in Germany by impetuously giving an interview to an unidentified "ex-diplomatist" for publication in the London *Daily Telegraph* on 28th October 1908. The Kaiser's controversial and extraordinarily candid comments on the Boer War, North African politics, and the armaments race (defending Germany's right to build as many ships as she wished without dictation by Britain or any other power) stimulated Shaw to write a commentary on the interview which, in Trebitsch's translation, appeared in the *Neue Freie Presse*, Vienna, on 19th November.

"I have never before felt any very strong impulse to congratulate an Emperor," Shaw had written. "I am a republican by instinct, and a Socialist by conviction; so congratulation of kings is not in my line. But the present occasion is irresistible. For the first time in history a solidly established German emperor has succeeded in throwing the whole of Germany, absolutely without the exception of a single individual or class, into a paroxysm of lèse majesté. His own Minister [Prince Bernhard von Bülow] has thrown him over; apologised for him; and made a compliment of not resigning. All Europe agrees. Wilhelm II is alone contra mundum.

"The explanation is very simply, he has committed the one unpardonable sin. He has done the right thing in the most effective way. And he has told the exact truth. Never before has he been completely master of the situation; but he is now at last. All his people are against him; and it is patent to Heaven and earth that his people are in the wrong and that he is in the right.

"It is to be observed that nobody seriously disputes the truth of the statements communicated to The Daily Telegraph. The contention is that it is quite intolerable that an Emperor should be allowed to go about telling the truth. From the modern Liberal point of view, a monarch is simply a mouth-piece of whatever lies his Ministers regard as expedient, ostensibly for the good of the country, but really for the quietness of their own lives. Second-rate men make an enormous use of lies. Third-rate men hardly use anything else. First-rate men make a very large use of truth. Diplomacy is a game which a fool plays with his cards up his sleeve, and which a great man plays with his cards on the table. Bismarck was in some respects a ridiculously over-rated man who has since his death become a mischievous national idol. His images, as at Hamburg for instance, are visibly monstrous stone Dagons and Baals; but German statesmen might at least have learnt from him to be a little more economical in the matter of lying. He did not waste his time in fumbling at the Gordian knot of diplomacy with lies when it was so easy to cut it with a single well-directed truth. That is precisely what the German Emperor has done in the present instance. Anti-English feeling in Germany was supposed to be an unnatural phenomenon fomented by court intrigues, and contrary to the instincts of the solid honest genuine German nation. It was assumed that the building of the German fleet could have no other object than an insane war of conquest against England the moment there were German Dreadnoughts enough to cope with the English Fleet. It was assumed that during the South African War the sympathies of the Emperor and of the most highly organised Imperial Government in Europe were enthusiastically on the side of the most reactionary little republic in the world. Now notions such as these are always essentially popular notions; that is to say, they are the romantic notions of ignorant men. The Emperor saw that the time had come for knocking them on the head. He chose his moment with perfect judgment; and he chose his means of communication with remarkable shrewdness. The success of the stroke is proved, first, by the enormous reverberation of his message throughout the world, and second, the completeness with which it has altered and rectified the popular conception of the real distribution of Anglophobia in German society.

"On one point, unfortunately, English public opinion is unalterable; but on that point it is also childish. It is perfectly true that the English nation assumes that the very first condition on which England can condescend to allow the rest of the universe to exist is that no other power must presume to build a fleet which is more than half as strong as the English fleet. In the face of so monstrous and cowardly a pretension, it seems to me to be the bounden

824

duty of every self-respecting German, from the Emperor to the poorest Berlin bootblack, to insist that Germany shall not be content with one gun, one ship, or one man less in her fleet than England. If England cannot fight Germany unless Germany ties one of her own hands behind her, then England cannot fight Germany at all, and had better sell herself to Germany as it sold Heligoland. England's want of respect for Germany is the measure of its want of respect for itself. One bold word on this subject from a really brave German to a really brave Englishman (if such persons exist) would put an end to this ignoble controversy for ever; and I hope that such a word will be the subject of the Emperor's next 'indiscretion'" (BM).

The Doctor's Dilemma, remained in the repertory of Reinhardt's Kammerspiele Theatre until 1913. It proved to be one of Shaw's most successful plays in Germany, achieving a total of 245 performances. Max O'Rell was the pseudonym of Léon Paul Blouët (1848–1903). In later years many of Shaw's plays were produced abroad before they were seen in London: *Pygmalion* in Vienna, Prague, and Budapest; *Androcles* in Hamburg; *Heartbreak House* in New York, Vienna, and Stockholm; *The Apple Cart* in Warsaw.]

My dear Trebitsch

... I return you the cheque for two pounds ten (£2:10:0). If you had been paid anything for the translation [of "Das Interview der Kaisers Wilhelm"], I should have dunned you for half of it. It is not a question of exactly how much you do or I do: there is hardly a single transaction which involves exactly equal work for you and me. The sensible thing to do is to share the proceeds of the business equally. Sometimes you will get a windfall; sometimes I will: the thing will average itself out in the long run.

I quite understand that the reason there was such a fuss in Germany about the Kaiser's communication to the Daily Telegraph was that the Germans are thorough-going Pro-Boers, and were infuriated to find that the Kaiser sympathised with Roberts and not with Kruger. They think I misunderstood because I did not say the thing they wanted to have said, but the thing that it was good for them to hear. As that happened to be also what the Kaiser himself probably wanted to have said, I think the Kaiser ought to have come to the Doctor's Dilemma in state, and crowned my bust with laurels. But kings are ever ungrateful.

Of course I never read that confounded contract. Why should I? It is much easier to assume that it is all wrong, and complain to you about it. Then you read it yourself for the first time, and are able to correct me, besides learning something about it yourself.

John Bull's Zweite Insel seems to me as good a title as you can find. The English title grew out of a book written by a Frenchman who called himself Max O'Rell (since dead), which was much spoken of here some years ago. It was called John Bull and his Island: so I called my play John Bull's Other Island. I was afraid that you would have had to find a new title altogether, as I did not know that the Germans were familiar with the name John Bull.

I do not think it likely that Fischer took any steps to secure the American copyright of the Doctor's Dilemma. Unless he were expressly warned to the contrary he would have assumed that publication had already taken place in England. However, I am not very anxious about it, as no American publisher of any standing is likely to bring out a hack translation from the German as my original work. I am rehearsing The Admirable Bashville for His Majesty's Theatre just now, and have no time to do anything; so the corrections for the Doctor's Dilemma must wait a little longer. You evidently don't understand my explanations about the error in the medical theory. It is my solemn belief that you don't know what the circulation of the blood means. You can, however, find out by a very simple experiment. At dinner this evening take the carving knife and give yourself a good deep slash across the wrist, or ask your wife to drive it into your neck just under your ear. You will then discover that your heart acts as a force-pump and drives your blood to the tips of your toes and sucks it back again about 60 times a minute when you are in a condition of calm, and about 135 times immediately after you have received a letter from me.

This is the circulation of the blood; and it has nothing whatever to do with the positive and negative phases. Nevertheless, you have applied the word circulation—Blutkreislauf—to this alteration of the positive and negative phases in the secretion of opsonin.

Are the performances still going on?

What the deuce is the good of making your will if you have not insured your life? The will is no use unless you have something to leave.

I have several times considered very seriously the question of having my next play produced for the first time in Germany. It would be quite useful to the pioneers of the dramatic movement here to be able to point to an English author driven to Berlin by the attacks of the English Press. Besides, now that the Vedrenne and Barker enterprise is suspended, my plays are no longer wanted for immediate use in London.

I have several remittances from you which are still unacknowledged. My secretary [Georgina Gillmore] has gone to bed for a month; and

826

my new secretary [Mabel W. McConnell] does not yet know how to spell your name; but you will have all due acknowledgments in the course of a year or so.

yours ever
G. Bernard Shaw

To HENRY JAMES

Ayot St Lawrence. Welwyn

[A/6; X/216]   17th January 1909

[Henry James (1843–1916), like almost every successful novelist of his time, harboured a desire to create a successful stage drama. A few of his plays had reached the stage (and several had been published), but all had been failures. Now, under the encouragement of St John Hankin, James had submitted a play *The Saloon* (dramatised from his tale "Owen Wingrave") to the Stage Society. The Reading Committee had rejected it on 12th January, and Shaw had undertaken to impart the news to James. *The Saloon* eventually was produced by Gertrude Kingston in 1911. Henry James Sr (1811–82), a well-known philosopher and theological writer, was a disciple of Swedenborg. Dr Samuel Johnson's "ghost" remark may be found in the entry for 15th August 1773 in James Boswell's *The Journal of a Tour to the Hebrides* (1786).]

My dear Henry James

   Shaw's writing—Bernard Shaw

   There is a play of yours called The Saloon in the hands of the Stage Society. My wife made me read it some time ago, and it has been sticking in my gizzard ever since.

   What that play wants is a third act by your father. What do you want to break men's spirits for? Surely George Eliot did as much of that as is needed. Do you seriously think that you would have been beaten by that ghost? Are you more superstitious than Dr Johnson, who said, "I, sir, should have frightened the ghost." In the name of human vitality WHERE is the charm in that useless, dispiriting, discouraging fatalism which broke out so horribly in the eighteen-sixties at the word of Darwin, and persuaded people in spite of their own teeth and claws that Man is the will-less slave and victim of his environment? What is the use of writing plays?—what is the use of anything?—if there is not a Will that finally moulds chaos itself into a race of gods with heaven for an environment, and if that Will is not incarnated in man, and if the hero (of a novel or play or epoch or what you please) does not by the strength of his portion in that Will exorcise ghosts, sweep fathers into

827

the chimney corner, and burn up all the rubbish within his reach with his torch before he hands it on to the next hero?

It is really a damnable sin to draw with such consummate art a houseful of rubbish, and a dead incubus of a father waiting to be scrapped; to bring on for us the hero with his torch and his scrapping shovel; and, then, when the audience is saturated with interest and elate[d] with hope, waiting for the triumph and the victory, calmly announce that the rubbish has choked the hero, and that the incubus is the really strong master of all our souls. WHY have you done this? If it were true to nature—if it were scientific—if it were common sense, I should say let us face it, let us say Amen. But it isn't. Every man who really wants his latchkey gets it. No man who doesnt believe in ghosts ever sees one. Families like these are smashed every day and their members delivered from bondage, not by heroic young men, but by one girl who goes out and earns her living or takes a degree somewhere. Why do you preach cowardice to an army which has victory always and easily within its reach?

I, as a Socialist, have had to preach, as much as anyone, the enormous power of the environment. But I never idolized environment as a dead destiny. We can change it: we must change it: there is absolutely no other sense in life than the work of changing it; and every young man who lays a ghost and puts his father in his proper place in the second fighting line—not obstructive across the vanguard's path—is doing his bit of the job, and is delighted in (however secretly) by youth and the crowd.

You must write that third act, even if you have to lay your own ghost first. There is a fine play there; but it is like a king with his head cut off. As the thing stands now, it is very talented; but is it any better than Turgenief? People dont want works of art from you: they want help: they want, above all, encouragement, encouragement, encouragement, encouragement, encouragement, and again encouragement until there is no more room on the paper.

yrs ever
G. Bernard Shaw

[Although his response was suffused with cordiality, James must have been infuriated to have his artistic genius assaulted by a man whose own work, in his opinion, contained neither point nor form, art nor sense. "I do not think highly of [Shaw]," James confessed to an American friend in 1910; "Wilde wrote a better play, I think, 'Lady Windermere's Fan.' It is a distinctly good play, better than anything Shaw has written. Shaw has the sort of success that consists in being talked about, but I do not think him great" (New York *Sun*, 12th March 1916). To James, who told Wells that "it is art that *makes* life," and for whom the "*grasping* imagination" and "psychological reason" were vital elements for the creative artist, Shaw's insensitive "socialistic" view of *The Saloon* was intolerable. In a lengthy reply on 20th January he passionately defended his art:

"I do such things because I happen to be a man of imagination and taste, extremely interested in life, and because the imagination, thus, from the moment direction and motive play upon it from all sides, absolutely enjoys and insists on and incurably leads a life of its own, for which just this vivacity itself is its warrant. . . . Half the beautiful things that the benefactors of the human species have produced would surely be wiped out if you don't allow this adventurous and speculative imagination its rights. You simplify too much, by the same token, when you limit the field of interest to what you call the scientific . . . In the one sense in which The Saloon *could* be scientific—that is by being done with all the knowledge and intelligence relevant to its motive, I really think it quite supremely so. That is the only sense in which a work of art can be scientific—though in that sense, I admit, it may be so to the point of becoming an everlasting blessing to man. And if you waylay me here . . . on the ground that we 'don't want works of art,' ah then, my dear Bernard Shaw, I think I take such issue with you that—if we didn't both *like* to talk—there would be scarce use in your talking at all. I think . . . we scarce want anything else at all. They are capable of saying more things to man about himself than any other 'works' whatever are capable of doing—and its only by thus saying as much to him as possible, by saying, as nearly as we can, all there is, and in as many ways and on as many sides, and with a vividness of presentation that 'art,' and art alone, is an adequate mistress of, that we enable him to pick and choose and compare and know, enable him to arrive at any sort of synthesis that isn't, through all its superficialities and vacancies, a base and illusive humbug. On which statement I rest my sense that all *direct* 'encouragement'—the thing you enjoin on me—encouragement of the short-cut and say 'artless' order, is really more likely than not to be shallow and misleading, and to make him turn on you with a vengeance for offering him some scheme that takes account but of a tenth of his attributes. In fact I view with suspicion the 'encouraging' *representational* work, altogether, and think even the question not an *a priori* one at all; that is save under this peril of too superficial a view of what it is we have to be encouraged or discouraged *about*. The artist helps us to know this—if he have a due intelligence—better than anyone going, because he undertakes to represent the world to us; so that, certainly, if *a posteriori*, we can on the whole feel encouraged, so much the better for us all round. But I can imagine no scanter source of exhilaration than to find the brute undertake that presentation without the most consummate 'art' he can muster!" (Henry James, *Complete Plays*, ed. Leon Edel, 1949)]

829

To HENRY JAMES

[H/6; X/216]

10 Adelphi Terrace WC
21st January 1909

My dear Henry James

You cannot evade me thus. The question whether the man is to get the better of the ghost or the ghost of the man is not an artistic question: you can give victory to one side just as artistically as to the other.

And your interest in life is just the very reverse of a good reason for condemning your hero to death. You have given victory to death and obsolescence: I want you to give it to life and regeneration. Therefore, to oblige me, write that third act at once.

Nothing is commoner than for a man to begin amusing himself with a trifle, and presently discover that the trifle is the biggest thing he has ever tackled. Almost all my greatest ideas have occurred to me first as jokes. It is quite in keeping that your biggest play should be begun as a curtain-raiser.

In haste—I am in the thick of rehearsals [of *The Admirable Bashville*]—

yours ever
G. Bernard Shaw

[James's letter of 23rd January ended the correspondence. In it he said: "No, I am not 'evading' . . . I inveterately hold any quarrel with the subject of an achievable or achieved thing the most futile and profitless of demonstrations. Criticism begins, surely, with one's seeing and judging what the work has made of it—to which end there is nothing we *can* do but accept it. . . . I seem not to understand, further, what you mean by the greater representational interest of the 'man's getting the better of the ghost,' than of the 'ghost's getting the better of the man'; for it wasn't in those 'getting the better' terms on one side or the other that I saw my situation at all. There was only one question to me, that is, that of my hero's within my narrow compass, and on the lines of my very difficult scheme of compression and concentration, getting the *best of everything*, simply; which his death makes him do by, in the first place, purging the house of the beastly legend, and in the second place by his creating for us . . . such an intensity of impression and emotion about him as must promote his romantic glory and edifying example for ever. I don't know what you could have more. He wins the victory—that is he clears the air, and he pays with his life. The whole point of the little piece is that he, while protesting against the tradition of his 'race,' proceeds and pays exactly like the soldier that he declares he'll never be. . . . Danger there must be [for Owen Wingrave] . . . and I had but one way to prove dramatically, strikingly, touchingly, that in the case before us there *had* been; which was to exhibit the peril incurred. . . . You look at the little piece, I hold, with a luxurious perversity . . ." (Henry James, *Complete Plays*, ed. Leon Edel, 1949)]

To MISS POGÁNY

10 Adelphi Terrace WC
[H/56]   1st February 1909

[Fräulein Pogány, who had invited Shaw to lecture in Budapest, has not been identified; she does not appear to be the "Mlle Pogány" sculpted by Brancusi.]

Dear Madam

Your letter and that of Fraulein Wilma Glücklich found me, unfortunately, suffering from a painful illness, which forced me to cease working for a couple of weeks. Short as that period is, I have so much work in hand that the delay makes it quite impossible for me to find time for a visit to Hungary.

Besides, I am compelled to reply to you as I have so often to reply to the Women's Suffrage Societies here, that the vote will never be won by speeches made by men on behalf of women. Every time you ask a man to appear on your platform, you confess the insufficiency of women to plead their own cause. I have taken every means in my power to make public my strong conviction of the enormous social importance of not only giving women the vote, but of enabling them to sit on all representative public authorities including Imperial Parliaments as well as local bodies. Therefore, if my support is of any value, it can be claimed without fear of contradiction by the speakers in your movement.

But the speaking must be done by the women themselves. A speech made by me may prove *my* political competence; but it cannot possibly prove that of women. In fact, many of the men who are most excited in their advocacy of the Feminist cause, are actuated by sentimental infatuation; and all of them without exception are suspected of it by the public. I strongly advise you to keep the movement altogether in the hands of women. Having recommended you to make this rule you can hardly expect me to set the example of breaking it.

yours faithfully
G. Bernard Shaw

831

To ARTHUR W. PINERO

A/4]

Queens Hotel. Southsea (until Friday morning)
3rd February 1909

[William John Locke (1863–1930), who had written several popular novels
and plays, was a member of the Dramatic Sub-Committee of the Society of
Authors, as were Richard Claude Carton (1853?–1928), a successful writer of
comedies who had had more than twenty plays produced in the West End;
Cicely Hamilton (1872–1952), playwright and actress, who in 1911 appeared
as Mrs Knox in Shaw's comedy *Fanny's First Play*; and Jerome K. Jerome
(1859–1927), novelist and dramatist, whose play *The Passing of the Third
Floor Back* had won plaudits in 1908. Philip Carr (1874–1958) was at this
time the London drama critic for the *Manchester Guardian*. He had served as
secretary since 1908 to the newly organised Shakespeare Memorial National
Theatre committee. Paul A. Rubens (1876–1917), who had been dropped
from the reorganised sub-committee, was a librettist and composer who had
contributed some of the songs to *Floradora* (1899) and had composed the
score of the popular *Miss Hook of Holland* (1907).]

My dear Pinero

At last we have got this business of the new Dramatic Sub-Committee
promisingly settled.

First let me explain the delay. I have had a comic illness—a sort of
pathological harlequinade. Figure me with all my celebrated brilliancy
undimmed, my observation unclouded, my sense of humor & character
sharpened and fed by the contrast between a cheerily encouraging
doctor and a tenderly sympathetic one, writhing in hideous, lancinating,
grinding agonies of a demoniacal & unnatural maternity, bringing forth
a stone from my kidney to my bladder, grunting, groaning, yowling,
invoking all the saints, and being violently sick at every climax of the
torture! Imagine this beginning in the middle of a rehearsal! Picture
me just keeping up appearances whilst I got out of sight into a passage
& collapsing in a box lobby, where a cleaner presently found me &
discreetly passed on, deeming me drunk! Conceive me wallowing in a
taxicab punctuating my groans with wild instructions as to stage
business! Follow me to my bed, where, after 2½ hours of it, the sympathetic doctor could stand it no longer & stopped it with morphia.
Shudder at its coming on again—the stone resuming its checked
journey—at midnight, and racking me (without an audience, too:
think of *that*, Master Ford, think of *that*!) all the night with intervals
of dead sleep induced by exhaustion for moments only, until at

832

breakfast time, with two final and excruciating paroxysms, the stone at last got through the pit door into a comfortable seat in the front row.

And this is the reward of 28 years of the diet of Pythagoras!

Still, it was effective as a grotesque knockabout turn. And it enabled me to play for sympathy for a week—all through the Labor Conference down here.

I came down the moment the Xrays shewed that my confounded kidney had given up all its stones; and I am staying to recruit until Friday, as the mere endurance—though I was careful not to intensify it with any vain theatrical display of fortitude—pulled me down a good deal. However, I got through the Conference, orated in good form on Sunday, & went up to London for the Society of Authors business on Monday, returning yesterday.

It is a melancholy fact that at the meeting which I missed when I lay howling like the cemetery parson in Hamlet, *nobody turned up except Jones & Barker.* Yesterday was not quite so bad . . . but the absences were sufficient to shew that all the work will have to be done by four or five of us.

The result was that I was asked to get your consent to the following list of 12—it being felt that it was useless to ask the Committee of Management to appoint a sub-committee larger by four than itself. Barker, Barrie, Carton, Cicely Hamilton, Jerome, Jones, Locke, Marshall, Pinero, Raleigh, Shaw, Sutro.

This, I think, is a better list from the point of view of Raleigh, Carton & Sutro than I could reasonably have hoped to get through. You will observe that we have dropped Rubens because he has neither attended meetings nor responded to our applications for information on his special subject. Carr is dropped at his own request.

We must still keep our eyes open for recruits. In the course of the year it will become apparent that some of the list wont attend. Mrs Bland has resigned handsomely, though she did not pledge herself; but you must warn Sutro that I have promised to make a vacancy for her presently by provoking him to resign—a superfluous undertaking, as he is sure to resign with loud imprecations at the end of the first ten minutes without any provocation at all.

In the bliss of the cessation of my pain I read The Thunderbolt, which my bookseller sent in just then on an old standing order. It got me through the evening most blessedly. But why dont you write prefaces? You have done everything except the one final thing: you have not given yourself away. Remember the words [in *The Pilgrim's*

833

Progress] of my pet John Bunyan:-
   There was a man—though some did think him mad—
   The more he gave away, the more he had.

yrs ever

G. Bernard Shaw

To MATTHEW EDWARD McNULTY

10 Adelphi Terrace W C

22nd February 1909

[H/4]

[Jonathan Swift in 1724 wrote a series of "letters," purporting to have been written by M.B.Drapier, concerning the brass halfpence coined by William Woods, an ironmaster. Re McNulty's plays, see I, 7. Tom Taylor (1817–80), a Victorian writer of comedies and farces, became editor of *Punch*.]

My dear Mac
   It is useless to kick against the pricks. The successful plays of which you are thinking have the advantage of being written by donkeys; and of being absolutely the dead-best that the donkeys could do. They have misled many clever men into attempting to compete with them by a process of deliberate self-stultification. It is never any good: the clever man trying to play down to a foolish public never succeeds. There have been cases, like Swift's popular tracts on Wood's Hapence, in which a man of first-rate literary power has ingeniously and dramatically worked on the minds of illiterate people by using the idioms and making the jokes that they understand; but Swift was nerved to this by an entirely unselfish public purpose, and was doing his blood best just as much as in Gulliver's Travels or A Tale of a Tub. The thing can't be done cynically or mercenarily by a man of your sort: you are not built that way. The fashionable men who have succumbed to writing for the market, and who flatter themselves that but for the tyranny of the public they could produce great Art, never do succeed in producing it when they get the chance.
   The fashionable stuff is their best, though they are ashamed of it. There are no Royalties to be got out of The Love Artist. In writing with deliberate venality you have not taken the trouble even to study your market. There are no good parts in it. There are bushels of asides and other tricks that are as dead as Tom Taylor. I repeat, it is no use: you will have to do all the things that you say you won't—to aim at revolutionizing the Stage and all the rest of it—to do absolutely the

834

best and most disinterested work you can; and then you will be jolly lucky if you produce a reasonably decent play.

The brazen head has spoken.

yours ever
G. Bernard Shaw

To ARCHIBALD HENDERSON

[S/52]

10 Adelphi Terrace W C
15th March 1909

My dear Henderson

I write to you on the eve of my departure for Algeria, whence I propose to motor to Tunis and back. . . .

I had one go at the Biography. I read the chapter in which you gave an account of our table-talk. A more monstrous string of inventions never was put on paper. You are just as far as ever from realizing that I am a human being like yourself. My prudent counsels, my careful prosaic conscientious views, have been totally lost on you. It would take me months to unravel the extraordinary knots into which you have managed to tie up the golden threads of my discourse. You evidently never thought of what I was talking about: you only thought about me. If I talked about the cat on Tuesday and about Shakespear on Thursday, you came out of it with a notion that I objected to Shakespear because he stole milk. My first impulse after reading the chapter was to sit down and take you at your word by writing the Preface there and then. Had I done so, the world would now be one shriek of laughter at the great Biography. On reflection I concluded that I had better wait as you are pretty sure to write it all over again . . . Chesterton says that he is actually quite really and seriously writing that long promised Stars of the Stage biography; but that need not interfere with you as there will be no facts in it. For the matter of that, there wont be any in yours either; but there will be pseudo facts. . . .

I have just finished a crude melodrama in one act [*The Shewing-up of Blanco Posnet*]—the crudity and melodrama both intentional—which I should say will be played by Tree if it were not that my plays have such an extraordinary power of getting played by anybody in the world rather than by the people for whom they were originally intended. . . .

yours ever
G. Bernard Shaw

835

To LILLAH McCARTHY

Norddeutscher Lloyd Dampfer "Derfflinger"

[A/4]   19th March 1909

[The Shaws and Mary Cholmondeley had departed from Southampton on
16th March, bringing the new automobile with them. They travelled through
Algeria and Tunisia for five weeks, sailed back in the Bremen, and returned
to London on 3rd May. The first two lines of Shaw's letter are a misquotation
from a song by Martyn Parker (d. 1656). John M. Rodwell's translation of
the Koran was first published in 1861. George Sale's translation appeared in
1734. Shaw never wrote a play about Mahomet, but depicted him as "the
Arab" in his religious fable, *The Adventures of the Black Girl in Her Search
for God* (1932).]

You gentlemen of England
That sit at home at ease

you should have seen the Atlantic yesterday. It was simply a dance of
mountains. What unspeakable equinoctial typhoon was raging in the
middle of it, Heaven only knows: the squalls that hit us were not rain
but solid water—a sea above the sea; but the mountain dance was in
full sunshine, blue & beautiful. As I staggered up and down the deck
in a desperate effort not to lie in my berth prostrate all day, I was
positively exhilarated, though I would not have joined the dance if I
could have helped it. An absurd old song which Archer used to imitate
[W.S.] Penley singing before the days of Charley's Aunt, with the
refrain

"I was in it
Fairly in it"

suddenly burst into my head out of the past; and I reeled from end to
end of the deck, grinning through my nausea, and insanely proclaiming
in music, aside to myself that,

We were in it
Fai-awly in it

again & again & again, whilst the few who had got as far as deck chairs
looked at me with pale loathing, thinking perhaps that I was not
seasick, and was glorying in it.

Today the waves were only 24 feet high; and now we have turned St
Vincent and are making east for Gibraltar, where I shall post this when
the mail closes at 10.30 tomorrow morning. It is now 10 at night; and
I have had lunch & dinner in the saloon & am bumptious in consequence.

Our first day, across the Bay, was smooth. We looked forward to getting the scent of the myrtles & the southern warmth when we passed Finisterre, instead of which, dance of mountains as aforesaid, and we

In it

F'yAWly in it.

The weatherwise promised us a following wind and the shelter of Europe. Whereupon it shifted to the west, and went for us with all the rushing air in the world.

My last news from Vedrenne was that Calvert has renounced him with oaths, and that Playfair remains the classic provincial exponent of Broadbent.

I am reading the Koran daily. At last, after years of urging, I have got Rodwell's translation (Sale being utterly unreadable) included in Everyman's Library. Rodwell has the Suras in their order as Mahomet produced them (they are higgledy-piggledy in the authorized version & in Sale), and has put them into readable English. Mahomet's turn is coming: I shall write a play about him as a companion to Cæsar, I think.

I am afraid to give addresses in Algeria, as the trains are so slow that automobiles overtake them; but I shall have to call at the Tunisia Palace Hotel, Tunis, and at the Hotel Bertrand, El Kantara, Algeria. Dont send anything important though.

G.B.S.

To HUGH CHOLMONDELEY

Alexandra Hôtel. Algiers

[T/1]
23rd March 1909

My dear Cholmondeley

I have just been making a list of communication possibilities for my secretary in case of emergency; and I may as well send it to you as well, with my independent testimony as to Sissy's health. She is now apparently in firstrate condition. On the voyage there was a most tumultuous sea from Finisterre to near Lisbon. We were probably not in the middle of the gale; but it must have been a regular typhoon, as the sea was tremendous & we were 7 hours late at Gibraltar. That laid us all low for 24 hours; and I think Sissy got a touch of that *maladie du pays* which sometimes follows a change to the southern climate (I got it myself) immediately afterwards. But she pulled round promptly, and this morning refrained with difficulty from hiring an Arab & careering over the hills here.

837

This morning I got letters posted to me in England on the 18th & 19th. This is Algiers—six days! The Algerian railways go 15 miles an hour; and as there is a railway strike here to complicate the postal strike; and as our route is uncertain, depending on what roads are passable, I have for the moment given up the idea of getting letters before we get to the Tunisia Palace Hotel, Tunis, which will not be before the 7th April.

I have therefore told my secretary to wire anything very urgent to the Hotel Bertrand, El Kantara, Algeria, until the 29th; to the Hotel Mille, Timgad, Algeria, until the 31st; to the Grand Hotel, Constantine, Algeria, until the 1st April; and to the Tunisia Palace Hotel, Tunis (*not* in Algeria) as aforesaid until the 7th. Probably all these dates will be upset by the female travellers insisting on staying some days at the places they like. In that case I can wire to you "Advance two days" or three days or whatever it may be, and you can alter the list accordingly.

In haste, packing for tomorrow's start

G. Bernard Shaw

P.S. Conversation just occurred as follows:—

Sissy. Oh I *am* so anxious for news of Hugh

G.B.S. (reassuringly). Depend on it, he's quite well. No news is good news &c &c &c

Sissy - Oh it's not that. I want to know how he got on in the point to point.

(Curtain)

To JOSEPH FELS

Alexandra Hôtel. Algiers
[A/51]   23rd March 1909

[Joseph Fels (1854–1914), an American millionaire soap manufacturer, was a Socialist and single-tax propagandist who contributed generously to the British Back-to-the-Land Movement. Webb and Shaw had spoken on "The Remedy for Unemployment" at a Fabian Society public meeting in St James's Hall on 5th March. Voltaire's tract is read by the Empress in the last act of Shaw's *Great Catherine* (1919).]

My dear Fels

I was much shocked that evening when Webb told me that it was you who had called out at the end of the meeting. I thought it was one of the profane.

838

It would never do for me to take the chair at your meeting. I am violently opposed to the notion that the social question is now a land question except in the sense that every question is a land question. I have always wanted to have Voltaire's Homme aux Quarante Ecus— the tract in which he smashed up old Mirabeau's Single Tax panacea (*l'impôt unique*)—translated & reprinted as a Fabian tract. We had trouble enough in the old days to get rid of Henry George's impossible distinction between land & capital, between industry & agriculture, without reviving it again. All attempts to distinguish between income derived from rent of land & interest on capital are futile. All notions that you can solve the social problem for men by giving every one of them access to land are as impossible as giving them all access to a city office or an electrical workshop. Until you organize men's industry for them in their own interests and attack unearned incomes as such, regardless of their source (thereby getting such a mass of capital into the hands of the State that it *must* be used immediately *as* capital for the support of those thrown out of parasitic private employment) you will not achieve the purposes of Socialism.

Webb's remedy *is* a remedy *for unemployment*; and it incidentally lays the foundation of the machinery of Socialism. I know of no trick that you can play with the land outside his scheme that will be of any use except to make small masters, or large ones, out of monsters with a depraved taste for the revolting pursuit of agriculture, against which Nature herself protests by immediately striking down with fever the man who first strikes pick or spade into her virgin bosom. How you, who have prospered by the blessed & beneficent work of making men's clothes clean (men with clean clothes need no washing—would that Mahomet had understood this instead of preaching ablutions!) how you, I say, can deliberately set to work to make their clothes dirty as agriculture alone can do, passes my understanding. But it is always the same: the lunacy of country life always attacks the manufacturer first.

Algiers in spring is not the place for economic treatises; and I write at random in great haste, as I am packing for my departure to Tunis via Biskra. But I have said enough to shew you that I am not the man for the chair at your meeting. If you want more, come out & let us argue it to a finish in the desert.

yours ever
G. Bernard Shaw

To HARLEY GRANVILLE BARKER

Biskra

[X/168] [Undated: assigned to 1st April 1909]

I have this day ridden for two hours on a camel; and my tail is sore in consequence; but my seat on this most difficult of mounts was admitted to be superb. I have also seen, but not touched, the improper woman of the Outlet Nail, and seen a star artist disguised as a Mahometan Zealot licking red hot iron; sticking himself full of skewers; and holding a blazing branch under his vest. In short I am at Biskra, my southernest point.

G.B.S.

To MATTHEW EDWARD McNULTY

[Mila Constantine]

[C(three cards)/4] [Undated: assigned to 20th April 1909]

[The recently acquired chauffeur was Albert J. Kilsby (1876–?), who was employed by Shaw until he emigrated to Brisbane, Australia, in 1917. Maurice Hewlett (1861–1923), novelist and poet, was active in the Society of Authors as a member of the Committee of Management.]

Here in this little town in the mountains of Algeria I have just met a man who reminded me of Maurice Hewlett. That reminded me of how I told Hewlett lately, when he sent me a very charming & clever play, just what I told you: that is, that he did not put his best into his plays as he did into his novels, whereupon M.H. though a most proud & sensitive grandee, as you may imagine from his books, said it was perfectly true. This, again, reminded me of you, and set me chuckling over the drama of the rich man in the motor car (cost of car, about £1000: expenses of trip, about £5 a day) and the poor man in the bank. Also of my chauffeur, who gets 50/- a week, a first rate car to drive & shew off, an eminent man of letters to act as courier for him, and an Algerian holiday with all his expenses paid & not a care in the world. I even do half his driving for him: today he did 45 miles & I did 55. I am also courier to two rich ladies: my wife & her sister, as well as to the chauffeur. I plan the journeys; I provide the money; I select the hotels; I pay the bills & tips; I concentrate all the energies of my celebrated mind on organizing the tour; and the world envies me.

840

However, this is by the way. My chuckling ended suddenly in the discovery that here was an uproarious subject for a comedy. The two friends: their destiny. Sit down & write it at once: it may end in *your* having a motor car and becoming a courier too; and then, ha! ha! you will learn much. At La Calle the other night I was benighted in a hotel where the sanitary arrangements were so horrible that everybody used the staircase instead. I slept, shuddering, in my motor coat & gloves, fully dressed, and rose at daybreak to bathe in the Mediterranean. Enviable, eh?

GBS

To ARTHUR W. PINERO

10 Adelphi Terrace WC

[A/4]   4th May 1909

[Charles Frohman had begun to make grandiose plans to establish a repertory theatre. After nearly a year of preparation, he opened his season at the Duke of York's Theatre on 21st February 1910 with John Galsworthy's *Justice*. This was followed by a triple-bill consisting of two short Barrie plays, *Old Friends* and *The Twelve-Pound Look*, and *The Sentimentalists* by the late George Meredith; Granville Barker's *The Madras House* and a revival of the Barker-Housman *Prunella*; Shaw's *Misalliance*; Elizabeth Baker's *Chains*; and Anthony Hope and Cosmo Lennox's *Helena's Path*. In the preliminary announcement a play by Somerset Maugham and Henry James's *The Outcry* were listed, as well as Euripides' *Iphigenia in Tauris* in Murray's translation, and revivals of Barrie's *The Admirable Crichton*, Shaw's *Man and Superman* and *Major Barbara*, and Galsworthy's *Strife*, none of which attained production. Pinero would not contribute a new play to the repertory, but eventually allowed Frohman to revive *Trelawny of the 'Wells,'* which ironically was to prove so successful that it crowded all the new plays out of the bill. Charles Marlowe's *When Knights Were Bold* had been produced at Wyndham's Theatre on 29th January 1907.]

My dear Pinero

This letter is going to be an impertinence. However, you will forgive me since I am aware of it.

I have only just learnt that you said No to Barrie when he asked you to contribute a play to the Frohman repertory enterprise. I wish you would turn it over again in your mind, because it seems to me that this new game will involve a sorting-out of authors that has not hitherto been effected. At present you cannot compromise yourself by a success,

841

as you have so often done, without being thrown into the same category with the Charley's Aunters & Knights-Were-Bolders & so forth. I myself have just received an enthusiastic provincial notice of 'that roaring farce, "TOM Never Can Tell."' The repertory plan will draw a line nearer the top; and I shall take care to ticket myself for the top compartment. I think Frohman has succeeded in persuading the public that the present address of that compartment is the Duke of York's Theatre; and though of course your accession would help this pretension more than it could help you at present, yet in the long run his batches of authors will be stronger than any of us can be individually; and the repertory men will get classed as the intellectuals as against the fashionable long-runners. Therefore, if you can spare the time for a play like a Royal Academician's diploma picture, it might be good policy to let Frohman have it. I know that there are other and deeper considerations involved; but these are for each man his own sacred business, whereas a friend may without indelicacy offer a suggestion on a point of policy: which I accordingly do. Dont bother to answer.

yours ever
G.B.S.

To REGINALD BRETT

[A/26]

10 Adelphi Terrace W C
4th May 1909

[Reginald Baliol Brett (1852–1930), 2nd Viscount Esher, former Liberal M.P. and government official, was active in the Shakespeare Memorial project. Sir Israel Gollancz (1864–1930), professor of English language and literature at King's College, London, was Honorary Secretary of the Shakespeare Memorial committee.]

Dear Lord Esher

Here I am again.

I shall be at the committee on Thursday. As to that body, whenever I try to think of it, my head begins to seethe with the chorus in The Frogs of Aristophanes:—

Brek-ek-ek-ex, Gollancz, Gollancz,
Brek-ek-ek-ex, Gollancz.

If you leave us with any sort of public emphasis, you will break our backs. If you continue to attend the committee as it now is, and to preside over its babblings & chatterings, you will lose your reason. We must try to avert both catastrophes, though at this moment, writing in great haste, I dont know how. There is much to be escaped by simply staying away until another phase of real business is reached. . . .

What about Pinero's knighthood? Barrie wouldnt dress it; Jones wouldnt look it; Pin would do both to perfection; and the national aspiration towards a higher drama would receive a thrilling impulse. Could it be managed for June?

yours ever

G. Bernard Shaw

To BERTHA NEWCOMBE

10 Adelphi Terrace W C

14th May 1909

[H/4]

[Shaw and Bertha Newcombe (1870–1939) had not met since before his marriage; she had remained a spinster. Now, as Honorary Secretary of the Civic and Dramatic Guild, she was in charge of arrangements for the production of Shaw's *Press Cuttings*, a topical sketch on suffragism which he had begun in North Africa in March and completed on 2nd May, to be presented for two matinées in aid of the London Society for Women's Suffrage. On 24th June the Lord Chamberlain's reader informed Barker that the play could not be licensed, and the performances on 9th and 12th July were held privately by invitation only.]

My dear Bertha

The sketch is not yet available. I shall have to correct the draft made from my shorthand notes and reduce it to proper acting dimensions and coherence. Then I will get prompt copies typed and the parts copied for you. Until these prompt copies are ready, there is no use in my attempting to read it, as it would only delay the proceedings. Perhaps the best plan would be to read it to you and Forbes Robertson —though really the thing is such a ghastly absurdity, that a reading is hardly bearable.

I do not think the pretty part would suit Mrs Forbes Robertson, because it is not a sympathetic one. The only really sympathetic woman in it is a charwoman. This is the part I want Agnes Thomas for. The other is a Gertrude Kingston sort of part.

As soon as everything is ready I will tell Forbes Robertson.

yours ever

G. Bernard Shaw

To CHARLES T. McCOTTER

[C/4]

Ayot St Lawrence. [Welwyn]
23rd May 1909

[McCotter was the manager of the Ball Publishing Co., Boston, which had just published an edition of the *Fabian Essays in Socialism* with a new preface by Shaw. The article on socialism by Theodore Roosevelt (1858–1919) had appeared in *The Outlook* on 20th and 27th March. In June of the following year, when Shaw reported the ex-president's London Guildhall speech to readers of Hearst's *New York American,* he described it as "one of the most remarkable performances in his new character of the Innocent Abroad."]

A serious reply to Mr Roosevelt's article on Socialism in The Outlook cannot be written in this country. In England the article is only The Noodle's Oration up to date. Its sentiments would be very proper and suitable for the sheriff of a district on the pioneering edge of a territory of the United States [the setting for Shaw's recently completed play *The Shewing-up of Blanco Posnet*]; but coming as it does from the pen of one who has been President for nearly 8 years it is a staggering revelation of how little an American President may know about his own business. He might almost as well be a King.

Are you quite sure that Theodore is not just pulling your legs in the first flush of high spirits following his release from the White House?

G. Bernard Shaw

To CONSTABLE & CO.

[H/52]

10 Adelphi Terrace W C
7th June 1909

My dear Constables

When are you going to send me my money? I have just sent in my income tax return, the preparation of which has revealed the most alarming facts as to my financial condition. My income is considerably less than half what it was in the previous year; and yet I have had to set up a motor car solely to keep up the credit of your list of authors.

Just consider a moment. I have had to pay in the course of the year £557.17.5 hard cash out of pocket to supply you with books to sell. On the 31st December last you owed me in round figures £1600. Had you paid me I could have invested it with complete security at 4%; and I should by this time have had £32. No doubt you have been able to employ it at about 300% at a considerable risk (to *me*) of the entire loss of it; but you do not propose to give me any of that money, nor am I getting any interest on my £557. Add to this that your printers probably give you six years credit sooner than risk losing your custom and leaving their plant unemployed. You will tell me that you cannot get the money in yourselves from the booksellers; that Kyllman is now married and has to be very careful; that Meredith is an orphan; and that you lose so much by my books that if it were not for the County Guides, you would have to give them up altogether. I reply that I also am married; I also am an orphan; and my creditors very often do not pay me at all, whilst the market value of the time that I spend in advertizing for your benefit by my public activity would be under-estimated at £10,000 a year. Under these circumstances, would it be too much to ask you to let me have a couple of pounds to go on with until you are thoroughly solvent again? I do not wish to be too hard on you; but a man must live. And if when you have fully consolidated your position, you could guarantee me a reasonably prompt annual settlement, it will make matters much easier for you when I die, and you suddenly find your-selves in the hands of some shark without a ray of personal affection for you and with some elementary knowledge of business.

yours, almost destitute
G. Bernard Shaw

To BERTHA NEWCOMBE

10 Adelphi Terrace WC
[D/4]   9th June 1909

[Arthur Bourchier (1864–1927) was an actor who had for fifteen years been in management with his wife Violet Vanbrugh at the Royalty and, later, the Garrick Theatre.]

Cyril Maude wont give us the Playhouse. He is terrified by the prospect of women getting into parliament (of which I gather that his wife is strongly in favor). He implored me to ask him for the theatre for any other mortal purpose to prove that he would do anything that was not positively against his conscience. So that's no good. Also, Bourchier wont. We must not ask Harrison for the Haymarket without consulting Forbes Robertson. They were once partners; and I dont know on what terms they stand. Lena Ashwell will do nothing for *me*: perhaps she would for the cause. Altogether, the prospect is not bright at present.

I did not notice any embarrassment; nor did I expect it after such a barefaced assignation. I expected to find a broken hearted, prematurely aged woman: I found an exceedingly smart lady, not an hour older, noting with a triumphant gleam in her eye my white hairs and lined face.

When I think that I allowed those brutal letters to hurt me—ME—Bernard Shaw!!

Are you not ashamed?

GBS

To LADY GREGORY

10 Adelphi Terrace WC
[H/1]   12th June 1909

Dear Lady Gregory

... [N]ever give people books: I never read books that people give me; but when I buy them I feel I have thrown my money away unless I read them. Let this sordid truth be your golden rule through life. The real superiority of the English to the Irish lies in the fact that an Englishman will do anything for money and an Irishman will do nothing for it.

yours sincerely
G. Bernard Shaw

To ERICA COTTERILL

Ayot St Lawrence. Welwyn
[A/1; X/202]   22nd June 1909

My dear Emerica

It is no use calling on me: I am engaged up to the last minute every afternoon this week after my return to town; and I am rehearsing in the mornings.

Do write a separate short letter or postcard when you make any practical proposal of this kind. I never now dream of attempting to

846

read your long letters when they come. They have to be left for spare moments; and they often dont get read at all. You write them to relieve yourself, without the slightest consideration for me; and as they are all the same, they meet the fate they deserve.

I have read the play. It shews, of course, remarkable literary power and dramatic talent; but it is made impossible by your nymphomania. There are two men in it (so-called), one a satyromaniac, the other a mere imaginary male figment to focus the nymphomania of all the women. The thing has a certain value as a document, and would no doubt interest young people. It bores old people, and rather disgusts them. I am an old person; and you have got nearly to the end of my patience. I am not preaching or striking moral attitudes for your good: I am telling you quite frankly as one unaffected human being to another that if you can write & think about nothing but your adolescence I will neither read your letters or meet you if I can possibly help it. These letters contain perhaps one single sentence which mentions an amusing or interesting fact: all the rest is a slovenly muddle of oh dears and oh please and sort of and you know which is quite maddening and which generally ends in a proposal to come to London and paw me which simply curdles my blood. I would not stand it from Cleopatra herself. All this is transfigured by your adolescence into something very touching & beautiful; but I am not adolescing but senescing, and it is intolerably disagreeable to me. So drop it or you will drop me. Keep it for young people who idealize you. To me you are only a quite disgustingly ill behaved young devil, grossly abusing the privilege of my acquaintance.

GBS

To ALFRED SUTRO

[Ayot St Lawrence. Welwyn]
23rd June 1909

[X/167]

[St John Hankin, obsessed following a surgical operation by the belief that he was suffering from a disease which had wrecked his father's life, had prepared a suicide note and, on 15th June, had quietly jumped into a river, wearing a pair of metal barbells tied round his neck for ballast. Three days later Shaw issued a multigraphed statement to the press, saying: "Hankin's death is a public calamity. He was a most gifted writer of high comedy of the kind that is a stirring and important criticism of life. . . . He suffered a good deal, as we all have to suffer, from stupid and ignorant criticism; but even the critics who were not stupid quarrelled with his style, which was thought thin, because it was not their own style. As a matter of fact the thinness was a quality, not a defect.

"In his recent letters to me there was nothing that prepared me in the very least for the shock of his death . . . [H]e was the last man whom I should have expected to come to such an end. I very deeply regret it, not only on personal grounds but on public ones" (BM).

The Dramatists' Club had held its foundation meeting at the Criterion Restaurant on 17th March. Among the founders were Barrie, R. C. Carton, W. J. Locke, Maugham, Pinero, Cecil Raleigh, Sutro, and H. M. Paull (Honorary Secretary). Shaw had accepted an offer of membership on 4th May. The Club began, Shaw told Hesketh Pearson, "as a clique of old stagers who insisted on excluding everyone who was not 'a dramatist of established reputation' which was their definition of one of themselves. They invited me to join in the sure and certain hope that I would refuse; but as I was for years trying to get them to organise the profession—any sort of organisation being better than none—I joined and made a duty of attending their lunches for quite a long time. They hated me . . . But all they could do was to blackmail every candidate I proposed. I soon gave up my attempts to declique the place" (Pearson, *Bernard Shaw: His Life and Personality*, 1942). Hankin, proposed for membership by Shaw, had been rejected.

Enoch Arnold Bennett (1867–1931), who had recently published his best novel, *The Old Wives Tale* (1908), had begun to write for the theatre. His *Cupid and Common Sense* was produced by the Stage Society in January 1908 and *What the Public Wants* in May 1909. Sir Francis Burnand (1836–1917), playwright and journalist, was the editor of *Punch* 1880–1906.]

I feel pretty sure that Hankin knew nothing of what passed at the Club. There was nobody to tell him; and, anyhow, it would have been a breach of confidence and a damned ill-natured thing into the bargain.

It was a frightful waste of a good man; and one feels that if any of us had been able to talk to him for half an hour it would not have happened. There must have been something Japanese in his character as well as in his appearance; for the suicide was Japanese all over except perhaps for the charming touches of comedy in his letter. I am really very sorry, which is quite an extraordinary thing; for I do not usually fuss about death, having every intention of dying myself presently.

To return for a moment to the incident at the Club, I think, on turning it over in my mind, that we must amnesty all the young men who attack us, as otherwise we shall never get recruits worth having. Ever since I can remember, the younger generation's particular method of knocking at the door has been to denounce what they always call 'the dramatic ring,' meaning the older men who have fully arrived. I can remember Grundy's onslaught before the dramatic ring became Pinero, Jones, Carton and Grundy, perhaps the smallest and closest that has ever existed. You were really the man who broke that ring; and although I cannot bring any documents against you, I feel quite convinced that in the days when you translated Maeterlinck, and were a remarkably handsome young man with apparently a million in each pocket, you must have out-Hankined Hankin in contempt for the man in possession. The latest assailant is Arnold Bennett, who has published his *Cupid and Commonsense* with a preface which is a very capital preface in all respects except that it ends with a perfectly gratuitous insult to Pinero and to the older-than-Bennett school generally. Now Bennett is one of the men I want to get in, because, although he sedulously keeps up an air of being a fourth-rate clerk from the potteries, and out of a job at that, he has some knowledge of the world and of business, and is not afraid of the managers, as his preface very abundantly demonstrates. At all events, a rule which would have the effect of excluding two such clever chaps as Hankin and Bennett, and that would, if it were made retrospective, exclude Grundy, myself, Barker, yourself, and probably every other blessed member of the Club, is clearly one that will not work. At the same time I want to stop these silly attacks; and the best way to do it is to get the young lions into the Club as soon as they have given sufficiently unmistakable proof of their ability. Recruiting Burnand is all very well; but it is recruiting at the wrong end: it is, now that Hankin has brought us right up against it, absurd that we elected Burnand and refused to elect him. Of course we were technically right: Hankin, like Bennett, should not have done what he did; but one has to admit that all the clever young men do it whilst they are outsiders. If we get them in, they will promptly discover that Pinero is their fellow-creature. After all, the amnesty will probably not be altogether one-sided. The older hands have a certain advantage in not having been journalists or preface-writers, so that their utterances do not stand recorded against them; but they have all probably said things they would not have said if we had all known one another better. After all, that is the English way. I have spent a considerable part of my life in trying to prevent Englishmen from quarrelling and insulting one another in Societies and on Committees and the like; and I assure you it cannot be done at all without letting bygones be bygones. Hankin himself was a perfect fiend on a committee; and yet he was an exceptionally amiable man. You must always remember that an Englishman, because he has no logic and no memory, and never expects anybody else to have them either, allows himself a degree of license that would be impossible in a society where these two faculties were not practically ruled out. Do not, I implore you, attempt to introduce them at the Club, or you will split it all to pieces.

To GILBERT MURRAY

[H/36]

10 Adelphi Terrace W C
17th July 1909

[The sustained agitation against the Lord Chamberlain's censorship powers had led at last to the appointment of a committee of inquiry, under the chairmanship of the Rt. Hon. Herbert Samuel. It held its first meeting on 29th July, and continued to meet until 2nd November, when it issued its Blue Book report. Forty-nine witnesses were examined, including the Speaker of the House of Commons, the examiner of plays, George Alexander Redford, and numerous government officials, plus a large number of managers, dramatists, actors, and critics. As soon as Shaw heard of the formation of the Joint Select Committee of the House of Lords and the House of Commons, he began to draft a statement to present in evidence to the committee. The completed text, published at his own expense, ran to more than 11,000 words, and was designed, as Shaw jocularly noted, to rival John Milton's plea to the Parliament of England "for the liberty of unlicenc'd printing" known as *Areopagitica* (1644).]

My dear Murray
  ... I am almost killed by the sudden addition to my work of the preparation of a huge proof that will supersede Milton. I will send you a copy of it as soon as I get it into print; for I think you are the man to back up my special line. I am hammering at the absolute necessity to the life of a nation of tolerance of immoral and heretical doctrines on the practical grounds that though the arguments used to justify the powers of the Censor are precisely those which justify the powers of any civil magistrate, there is a momentous difference between the two, founded, not on sentiment nor on any moral abstract theory of rights, but on the unquestionable historical fact that whereas nations prosper in direct proportion to their intolerance of theft and murder, they decay (witness Spain and the Inquisition) in direct proportion to their intolerance of immoral and heretical doctrines, the reason being, of course, that all doctrines are necessarily immoral and heretical at their first propounding (immorality and heresy being involved by novelty);

850

but theft and murder are neither novel nor in any sense questionable, but are simply familiar and tried pieces of mischief.

Now it seems to me that if you would write one of your finest essays to shew that some of the masterpieces of Greek drama were censored in their time, and that they are actually being censored again now when after many centuries we are at last rising again to the point of being able to enjoy them, pointing out at the same time what a power they must have been in raising Greece from the Homeric level to the Euripidean, your scholarship would make a great impression; and your talent for making an essay on Greek civilization a vivid piece of contemporary social criticism, have a rare chance.

The other fellows can do the drudgery of Old Baileying Redford and exposing the absurdity of the present system. Barker can deal with the loss and hardship to the author. Raleigh can deal with the music-hall side of the question. But you must ride the high horse. I want the Bluebook containing the evidence of the Select Committee to be a classic instead of the wretched piffling things the former bluebooks are.

yours ever
G. Bernard Shaw

To MEMBERS OF THE DRAMATISTS' CLUB

10 Adelphi Terrace W C
28th July 1909

[H/6]

[The following is a multigraphed letter, distributed to Shaw's colleagues in the Dramatists' Club. Enclosed with it was a copy of Shaw's *Statement of the Evidence in chief of Bernard Shaw before the Joint-Committee on Stage Plays*. The Rt. Hon. Sir Cuthbert Headlam (1876–1964) was a novelist, political author, and editor of the House of Lords Manuscripts. The Rt. Hon. Sir Henry Slesser (b. 1883), a lawyer who later became a Lord Justice of Appeal, was a Fabian, known at this time as Henry Schloesser.]

Dear Colleague

I enclose a copy of the evidence I propose to give to the Select Committee on Stage Plays on Friday next, the 30th. On page 39 you will find the objections to the proposal of an appeal to arbitration. At our last lunch I had to be rather dogmatic on this subject, because, though I felt sure that the proposal would break down on the point of constitutional law, I had not then consulted a lawyer about it. I have since done so, and he has confirmed my view that the proposal is one that no parliamentary committee would entertain for a moment.

In 1892, when the last Select Committee was appointed, there was no organization on our side. The authors were not represented; and the managers, who had then, as now, no thought of anything but escape from the County Council, and were therefore clinging to the Lord Chamberlain without an attempt to make conditions of any sort, had it all their own way. This time the authors will be well represented; and we are doing our best to secure some eminent witnesses representing the highest class of public opinion.

Any author who wishes to give evidence should write at once to the Secretary of the Committee, Mr Cuthbert Headlam, Joint Committee on Stage Plays, House of Lords, expressing his desire and asking that it be communicated to the Chairman. After this week it may be too late, as the Committee will have to decide at once what evidence it will take.

An unofficial organizer of evidence is needed on these occasions by every interest that is represented. Those of us who have been busy in the matter have asked Mr. Henry Schloesser, 2 Plowden Buildings, Temple, E.C., to act for us. Please let him know if you propose to take any action. He will give you any information or assistance in his power; or, what is equally important, he will receive any useful information or suggestions you may have to give him.

In any opportunities you may have of influencing opinion in private discussion, the main points to be remembered are:

1. That the managers are mistaken in assuming that local licensing necessarily involves censorship.

2. That we must support the managers in their contention that a play which passes unchallenged in London on its first production must not be reconsidered and perhaps prohibited in every town it comes to on tour.

3. That this can be secured in practice, by (a) restraining the local authorities from taking into consideration the character of any play that has not been successfully prosecuted; and (b) by confining the initiative in prosecutions to the Attorney General, who could not decently let a play run in London and then attack it in the provinces.

4. That the Variety Theatre managers ought to jump at this opportunity of getting rid of County Council censorship under cover of protecting the regular theatres from it.

As you have doubtless, like myself, received enough requests for sketches lately to convince you that much of our most lucrative work in future will be done in the variety theatres, you will see the great importance of our making a stand against allowing the licensing authorities to use their powers for the purpose of establishing local censorships. We must fight censorship in every form, or a change in the law—which we are fairly likely to get—may leave some of us worse off than we are at present.

yours faithfully
G. Bernard Shaw

To HERBERT SAMUEL

[H/53; X/218.e]

10 Adelphi Terrace W C
31st July 1909

[Copies of Shaw's *Statement* were distributed to the members of the Joint Select Committee in advance of his appearance on 30th July (Archer and Shaw were the first non-official witnesses to be called). The Committee informed him, however, that it could not accept the printed statement as evidence since it would be going against precedent. To its chagrin Shaw was able to cite precedent in the 1892 parliamentary hearings on censorship in no fewer than three instances—Henry Irving, John Hare, and Clement Scott—all three statements being testimony in favour of censorship! The committee's acting chairman (Samuel was absent on other business) abruptly closed the meeting until the committee could discuss the matter in secret session. When the committee reconvened, Shaw was informed, without explanation, that his statement would not be received. His letters on the untoward behaviour of the committee appeared in *The Times* on 2nd and 6th August and in *The Clarion* on 20th August. In 1911 he incorporated the full text of "The Rejected Statement" in the preface to *The Shewing-up of Blanco Posnet*.

Sir William Fladgate (1853–1937), solicitor to the West End Managers' Association in 1909, was examined at length by the committee on 5th August. Maud Allan (1879–1956) revived the lost art of the classic dance, creating a sensation with her performance of the "Vision of Salome" at the Palace Theatre, London, in March 1908, and afterwards touring the provinces. When the Sabbatarians prosecuted the Brighton Aquarium as a disorderly house for presenting Sunday concerts, an act was hastily legislated to restrict the initiative in such cases to the Attorney General.]

Private

My dear Samuel

On reflection I think the refusal of the Committee to publish my statement [*i.e.*, enter it into the official record] is a grievance, which is

853

always a valuable property in an agitation like this. I went into the precedents very carefully; and if you look at the 1892 bluebook . . . I think you will see that the Committee discriminated against me. In the morning, whilst you were away, they decided to stick to precedent, being then (poor lambs!) under the impression that precedent was against me. The sudden volte face when I cited precedent, the dramatic secret conclave, the point blank refusal without reason given, are too good to be thrown away. Also I want to get into the papers that the room had to be cleared when one of the licensed plays was discussed [by G.A.Redford], as it was too indecent to be mentioned in public. I shall fly to the last refuge of the oppressed: a letter to The Times.

The serious part of the business is that all my plans for making the report a classical bluebook instead of the wretched business the 1892 bluebook was, are upset. I had got Lord Esher to promise to come after August 8th and fire off a statement. I am at present in correspondence with the Bishop of Birmingham with the same object. I want you to ask the Chief Rabbi to weigh in. I have some hopes of getting Mrs Lyttelton, who is only holding back because she says she has nothing positive to suggest. Surrounded with such a galaxy, your report would be one of your greatest successes. I thought it would all come off, because you are a spoilt child of fortune (quite unspoilt, I hasten to admit). But by barring statements, the Committee has knocked all this on the head. None of the people I mention will come to answer questions merely.

Do you think there is any chance of the decision being rescinded? Later on, when you get the managers, you will find it fearfully inconvenient asking questions. You have tried it with Redford, only to find that he does not understand the simplest question. The managers and actors will be as bad. You will have to let them read statements (composed by Fladgate mostly); and then your treatment of me will be utterly indefensible.

As it is, I cannot think for the life of me why you let them spoil your bluebook by cutting me out of it. You have no idea how much work that statement cost, nor how completely you will find yourself driven back to it finally. Redford must go. The County Councils must license. The managers must be protected against having to face a fresh Censor in every town they come to. Their proposal of a new Government Department *ad hoc* is tosh: what Liberal Government would recommend it with the obvious alternative of County Council control ready to hand? The only solution on the cards (unless you have another up your sleeve) is local licensing, censoring only on prosecution, and prosecution only by the Attorney General, as in the Brighton Aquarium Act. There you get your local control and central censorship combined, because the Attorney General could not decently prosecute Maud Allen in the provinces after letting her dance unhindered in London. And any local body could pass a resolution calling on the Attorney General to prosecute if anything flagrant had to be dealt with.

yrs ever
G. Bernard Shaw

PS Oh, if parliaments & committees would only do just what I tell them!

To WILLIAM ARCHER

[C/2]

Ayot St Lawrence. Welwyn
11th August 1909

[Through all the censorship turmoil of July and August, the Shaws were house-hunting.]

... I liked the Chipperfield Sheeny & will be specially civil to him; and I liked the house; but Charlotte would have none of it. She wants a park; & I daren't tell her we can't afford it. So we are waiting until Blenheim or Haddon Hall is to let.

G.B.S.

To LADY GREGORY

[A/5]

10 Adelphi Terrace WC
12th August 1909

[*The Shewing-up of Blanco Posnet*, a melodrama in one act, was written between 16th February and 8th March 1909 for Beerbohm Tree, to enable him to "appear with éclat at the Afternoon Theatre, and generally to show that there is life in the old dog yet" (Shaw to Vedrenne, 5th March [H/1]). Rehearsals had begun on 13th May under Shaw's direction, for a 4th June opening at His Majesty's Theatre, when the management was notified that the Lord Chamberlain's reader had denied the play a licence on grounds that it was blasphemous. Revision was out of the question, Shaw told a *Daily Chronicle* reporter on 21st May: "I am not obstinate," he insisted,

855

"But what Mr Redford demands is, practically, that I should cut out the play. So I am afraid there will be nothing for it but to abandon the production."

There was, however, a way in which the play could be produced publicly and yet evade the censor's jurisdiction. As the Lord Chamberlain had no powers over production in Ireland, Shaw offered his play to Lady Gregory to produce at the Abbey Theatre. At once the British government sought to exert pressures upon the Lord Lieutenant of Ireland, John Campbell Gordon (1847–1934), Earl of Aberdeen. In the absence of the Viceroy, his undersecretary Sir James Dougherty (1844–1934) reacted by sending a letter from Dublin Castle to the Abbey Theatre in which he committed, in the Viceroy's name, the impropriety of threatening to revoke the patent of the Abbey Theatre if Shaw's play were produced. Lady Gregory and William Butler Yeats, the theatre's directors, responded to the attempt at intimidation by issuing a public manifesto in which they obdurately refused to withdraw the play: "[T]he Lord Lieutenant is about to revive, on what we consider a frivolous pretext, a right not exercised for 150 years, to forbid, at the Lord Chamberlain's pleasure, any play produced in any Dublin theatre, all these theatres holding their patents from him. . . . [W]e must not, by accepting the English Censor's ruling, give away anything of the liberty of the Irish theatre of the future. Neither can we accept, without protest, the revival of the Lord Lieutenant's claim at the bidding of the Censor or otherwise. The Lord Lieutenant is definitely a political personage holding office from the party in power, and what would sooner or later grow into a political censorship cannot be lightly accepted" (*The Observer*, 22nd August).

The statement also indicated, however, that the directors had made a few significant alterations in the text, and this fact, plus an announcement by Shaw the next day that in deference to the Lord Lieutenant he had made a deletion or two, may have convinced Lord Aberdeen that it would be inexpedient to provoke the situation by further interference. Dublin Castle remained silent, and Shaw's play was performed on 25th August without further incident. Charlotte Shaw and her sister Mrs Cholmondeley were in the audience, but the author remained in seclusion in Parknasilla.]

My dear Lady Gregory

Your news is almost too good to be true. If the Lord Lieutenant would only forbid an Irish play, without reading it, and after it had been declared entirely guiltless and admirable by the leading high class journal on the side of his own party (The Nation)—forbid it at the command of an official of the King's household in London, then the green flag would indeed wave over Abbey St, and we should have questions in parliament and all manner of reverberating advertisement and nationalist sympathy for the theatre.

I gather from your second telegram that the play has perhaps been

[Great] Southern Hotel. Parknasilla
19th August 1909

[A/5]

[The Shaws had departed by automobile from Ayot on 14th August, driving to Fishguard, whence they crossed to Waterford on the 17th, then completed the journey to Parknasilla. There Shaw settled down to his "holiday" by dipping into a bag containing huge arrears of correspondence, drafting a long preface for an edition of plays by Brieux, and beginning work on a new play, which was to be a sequel to *Getting Married*. Agnes Lady Grove (1864–1926), a writer active in the women's suffrage movement and other socio-political activities, had crossed pens with Shaw in letters to *The Academy* in June 1907, over his lecture "The New Theology," delivered on 16th May. Shaw's quotation is from the anonymous ballad "The Wearing of the Green."]

Dear Lady Gregory

I have just arrived and found all your letters waiting for me.

I am naturally much entertained by your encounters & Yeats', with the Castle. I leave that building cheerfully in your hands.

But observe the final irony of the situation. The English censorship being too stupid to see the real blasphemy, makes a fool of itself. But you, being clever enough to put your finger on it at once, immediately proceed to delete what Redford's blindness spared.

To me, of course, the whole purpose of the play lies in the problem "What about the croup?" When Lady Grove, in her most superior manner, told me "He is the God of Love," I said "He is also the God of Cancer & Epilepsy." That does not present any difficulty to me. All this problem of the origin of evil, the mystery of pain, and so forth, does not puzzle me. My doctrine is that God proceeds by the method of "trial and error," just like a workman perfecting an aeroplane. He has to make hands for himself & brains for himself in order that his will may be done. He has tried lots of machines—the diptheria bacillus, the tiger, the cockroach; and he cannot extirpate them except by making something that can shoot them or walk on them, or, cleverer still, devise vaccines & anti toxins to prey on them. To me the sole hope of human salvation lies in teaching Man to regard himself as an experiment in the realization of God, to regard his hands as God's hand, his brain as God's brain, his purpose as God's purpose. He must regard God as a helpless Longing, which *longed* him into existence by its desperate need for an executive organ. You will find it all in Man & Superman, as you will find it all behind Blanco Posnet. Take it o[ut]

The Shewing-up of Blanco Posnet, Dublin, 1909
(Mander & Mitchenson Theatre Collection)

submitted for approval. If so, that will be the wo
can then say they forbade it on its demerits
reference to the Lord Chamberlain.

In any case, do not threaten them with a cor
Threaten that we shall be suppressed; that we ɜ
of; that we shall suffer as much and as publicly
that they can depend on me to burn with a brig
yells than all Fox's martyrs.

On Saturday I start on a motoring tour. I expec
on Tuesday morning, and to reach Parknasilla Hot
a couple of days later.

y
G

To LADY GREGORY

[Y/5]

W

[H. W. Massingham, in an unsigned article "The Inco
The Nation on 25th May, had enumerated the censor's su
the *Blanco Posnet* text.]

THE NATION ARTICLE GIVES PARTICUL
DEMANDED WHICH I REFUSED AS THEY
DESTROYED THE RELIGIOUS SIGNIFICA
PLAY THE LINE ABOUT IMMORAL RELAT
PENSABLE AS THEY ARE MENTIONED
OTHER PLACES SO IT CAN BE CUT IF TE
SILLY ENOUGH TO OBJECT TO SUCH RELA
CALLED IMMORAL BUT I WILL CUT NC
IT IS AN INSULT TO THE LORD LIEUTENAN
HIM AND REFER ME TO THE REQUIREM
SUBORDINATE ENGLISH OFFICIAL I W
PARTY TO ANY SUCH INDELICACY PLEASE
SO IF NECESSARY BERNARD SHAW

my play, and the play becomes nothing but the old cry of despair—Shakespear's "As flies to wanton boys so we are to the gods: they kill us for their sport" [*King Lear*]—the most frightful blasphemy ever uttered, and the one from which it is my mission to deliver the world.

Frankly, I dont think the excision will save the play. If the actor cannot take the audience by storm with his desperate perplexity of soul, they will probably stop him long before he reaches that line. If he does reach it they will either miss its meaning or swallow it with a gasp. However, the matter is in your hands. Only, I must play fair with Redford. If it be really true that the play is less possible in Ireland than in England, you must not ask me to conceal the fact.

But the practical moral of all this is that we had better ride for a fall. Between the last two sentences your telegram of today (Thursday) arrived. If we can only fix the suppression of the play on the King, then "if the color we must wear be England's cruel red" we perish gloriously. You say it is necessary to see me; but it really isnt. I can say nothing in Dublin that I cannot say here; and spoil the second half of my holiday for Redford as I have already spoilt the first, I flatly will not. I must close this hastily on the chance of catching tonight's post, if there is such a thing here.

yours sincerely
G. Bernard Shaw

PS I hope to see you at Coole Park later on, when all this is over.

To WILLIAM BUTLER YEATS

Great Southern Hotel. Parknasilla
22nd August 1909

[A/5; X/219.e]

[Shaw had suffered from recurrent migraine since the early 1890's. For several years, commencing in 1906, he maintained an index file of headaches, noting the date on which each occurred, its effect upon his system, and the degree of effectiveness of the medications to which he resorted in his desperation.

The portion of the Abbey Directors' statement on the 21st to which Shaw refers was: "We have ourselves, considering the special circumstances of Ireland, cut out some passages which we thought might give offence at a hasty hearing, but these are not the passages because of which the English censor refused his license." Yeats carried out Shaw's instructions by issuing to the press the relevant portions of Shaw's letter (see *Daily Telegraph*, 24th

August). *Blanco Posnet* was the first Shaw play for which he prepared a printed, paper-wrapped "rehearsal copy." These copies were, in a sense, page proofs; after corrections had been made, the published book was printed from the standing type.]

My dear Yeats

I was prevented from writing yesterday by a blazing headache—a periodical affliction which knocks me to pieces for 24 hours or so about once a month.

Today the papers have arrived; and now this poor worm turns. The statement that you have bowdlerized the play practically confesses that it is not fit for representation. Also, the bowdlerized version is to me nothing but a message of despair & death.

Now there are only two courses which are tolerable to me.

Course 1. Withdraw the play, you announcing simply that I did so the moment I saw the statement that passages were to be omitted.

Course 2. Make the following alterations.

On page 31, line 5 from foot, omit the words "Either He killed the child a purpose or else He was beat by the croup."

On page 32, lines 15–23, substitute for the printed text, the enclosed version on green paper.

And make a further statement to the press that since the last statement Lady Gregory has written to me pointing out that a certain speech was open to misconstruction, and that I immediately rewrote it much more strongly and clearly; consequently the play will now be given exactly as written by the author without concessions of any kind to the attacks that have been made upon it, except that to oblige the Lord Lieutenant I have consented to withdraw the word "immoral" as applied to the relations between a woman of bad character and her accomplices. In doing so I wish it to be stated that I still regard those relations as not only immoral but vicious; nevertheless, as the English Censorship apparently regards them as delightful and exemplary, and the Lord Lieutenant does not wish to be understood as contradicting the English Censorship, I am quite content to leave the relations to the unprompted judgment of the Irish people. Also, I have consented to withdraw the words "Dearly beloved brethren," as the Castle fears that they may shock the nation. For the rest, I can assure the Lord Lieutenant that there is nothing in the other passages objected to by the English Censorship that might not have been written by the Catholic Archbishop of Dublin, and that in point of consideration for the religious beliefs of the Irish people the play compares very favorably

860

indeed with the Coronation Oath. (All this you can put into the third person without otherwise altering it).

As to the actor of Blanco [Fred O'Donovan] having learnt his part, he must rise to the occasion, and get that new speech in. And he must not funk it, as the Playboy people funked when they first played in London [at the Great Queen St. Theatre, 10th June 1907]. The speech, as now written, will carry any audience if it is rammed down their throats with conviction & energy. If there is a row it will be the actor's fault; but there wont be a row. And he MUST study it & master it: there is plenty of time. Tell him the play will be withdrawn if he doesnt.

I must break off to catch the post.

G. Bernard Shaw

To LADY GREGORY

[S/2; X/220]

[Great Southern Hotel.] Parknasilla
27th August 1909

[This statement was intended for publication but was delayed in reaching Lady Gregory; she published it in her book *Our Irish Theatre* (1913). "My chief reason for writing it," Shaw told Lady Gregory on 29th August [A/5], "is that I think we ought to divide the Castle, and make the officials thoroughly afraid of meddling again without instructions from the L.L. What I have tried to convey all through is that they made fools of themselves; that the subordinates acted ignorantly, insolently, improperly, and without authority; and that when the really important people came back the sub-ordinates were thoroughly snubbed & the matter set right. This will save the face of the L.L., and establish the notion that he is on the side of the theatre in his capacity of cultured & liberal minded patron of the arts. . . . You and W.B.Y. handled the campaign nobly. You have made the Abbey Theatre the real centre of capacity & character in the Irish movement: let Sinn Fein and the rest look to it."

Sir Harry Poland (1829–1928) was a noted criminal lawyer who, after his retirement in 1895, became a leading advocate of law reform. The "licensed" play Shaw had offered to the Abbey as an alternative to *Blanco Posnet* was *Press Cuttings*, which had been licensed by the censor on 17th August after Shaw had consented to alter the suggestive names of two leading characters, Mitchener and Balsquith, to the minstrel-inspired Bones and Johnson.]

Now that the production of Blanco Posnet has revealed the character of the play to the public, it may be as well to clear up some of the points raised by the action of the Castle in the matter.

By the Castle, I do not mean the Lord Lieutenant. He was in

Scotland when the trouble began. Nor do I mean the higher officials and law advisers. I conclude that they also were either in Scotland, or preoccupied by the Horse Show, or taking their August holiday in some form. As a matter of fact the friction ceased when the Lord Lieutenant returned. But in the meantime the deputies left to attend to the business of the Castle found themselves confronted with a matter which required tactful handling and careful going. They did their best; but they broke down rather badly in point of law, in point of diplomatic etiquette, and in point of common knowledge.

First, they committed the indiscretion of practically conspiring with an English official who has no jurisdiction in Ireland in an attempt to intimidate an Irish theatre.

Second, they assumed that this official acts as the agent of the King, whereas, as Sir Harry Poland established in a recent public controversy on the subject, his powers are given him absolutely by Act of Parliament (1843). If the King were to write a play, this official could forbid its performance, and probably would if it were a serious play and were submitted without the author's name, or with mine.

Third, they assumed that the Lord Lieutenant is the servant of the King. He is nothing of the sort. He is the Viceroy: that is, he *is* the King in the absence of Edward VII. To suggest that he is bound to adopt the views of a St. James's Palace official as to what is proper to be performed in an Irish theatre is as gross a solecism as it would be to inform the King that he must not visit Marienbad because some Castle official does not consider Austria a sufficiently Protestant country to be a fit residence for an English monarch.

Fourth, they referred to the Select Committee which is now investigating the Censorship in London whilst neglecting to inform themselves of its purpose. The Committee was appointed because the operation of the Censorship had become so scandalous that the Government could not resist the demand for an inquiry. At its very first sitting it had to turn the public and press out of the room and close its doors to discuss the story of a play licensed by the official who barred Blanco Posnet; and after this experience it actually ruled out all particulars of licensed plays as unfit for public discussion. With the significant exception of Mr George Edwards, no witness yet examined, even among those who have most strongly supported the Censorship as an institution, has defended the way in which it is now exercised. The case which brought the whole matter to a head was the barring of this very play of mine, The Shewing up of Blanco Posnet. All this is common knowledge. Yet the Castle, assuming that I, and not the Censorship, am the defendant in the trial now proceeding in London, treated me, until the Lord Lieutenant's return, as if I were a notoriously convicted offender. This, I must say, is not like old times in Ireland. Had I been a Catholic, a Sinn Feiner, a Land Leaguer, a tenant farmer, a labourer, or anything that from the Castle point of view is congenitally wicked and coercible, I should have been prepared for it; but if the Protestant landed gentry, of which I claim to be a perfectly correct member, even to the final grace of absenteeism, is to be treated in this way by the Castle, then English rule must indeed be going to the dogs. Of my position of a representative of literature I am far too modest a man to speak; but it was the business of the Castle to know it and respect it; and the Castle did neither.

Fifth, they reported that my publishers had refused to supply a copy of the play for the use of the Lord Lieutenant, leaving it to be inferred that this was done by my instructions as a deliberate act of discourtesy. Now no doubt my publishers were unable to supply a copy, because, as it happened, the book was not published, and could not be published until the day of the performance without forfeiting my American copyright, which is of considerable value. Private copies only were available; but if the holiday deputies of the Castle think that the Lord Lieutenant found the slightest difficulty in obtaining such copies, I can only pity their total failure to appreciate either his private influence or his public importance.

Sixth, they claimed that Sir Herbert Beerbohm Tree, who highly values a good understanding with the Dublin public, had condemned the play. What are the facts? Sir Herbert, being asked by the Select Committee whether he did not think that my play would shock religious feeling, replied point-blank, "No, it would heighten religious feeling." He announced the play for production at his theatre; the Censorship forced him to withdraw it; and the King instantly shewed his opinion of the Censorship by making Sir Herbert a Knight. But it also happened that Sir Herbert, who is a wit, and knows the weight of the Censor's brain to half a scruple, said with a chuckle, when he came upon the phrase "immoral relations" in the play, "They won't pass that." And they did not pass it. That the deputy officials should have overlooked Sir Herbert's serious testimony to the religious propriety of the play, and harped on his little jest at the Censor's expense as if it were at my expense, is a fresh proof of the danger of transacting important business at the Castle when all the responsible officials are away bathing.

On one point, however, the Castle followed the established Castle tradition. It interpreted the patent (erroneously) as limiting the theatre to Irish plays. Now the public is at last in possession of the fact that the real protagonist in my play, who does not appear in person on the stage at all, is God. In my youth the Castle view was that God is essentially Protestant and English; and as the Castle never changes its views, it is bound to regard the divine protagonist as anti-Irish and consequently outside the terms of the patent. Whether it will succeed in persuading the Lord Lieutenant to withdraw the patent on that ground will probably depend not only on His Excellency's theological views, but on his private opinion of the wisdom with which the Castle behaves in his absence. The Theatre thought the risk worth while taking; and I agreed with them. At all events Miss Horniman will have no difficulty in insuring the patent at an extremely reasonable rate.

In conclusion, may I say that from the moment when the Castle made its first blunder I never had any doubt of the result, and that I kept away from Dublin in order that our national theatre might have the entire credit of handling and producing a new play without assistance from the author or from any other person trained in the English theatres. Nobody who has not lived, as I have to live, in London, can possibly understand the impression the Irish players made there [in June, at the Royal Court Theatre] this year, or appreciate the artistic value of their performances, their spirit and their methods. It has been suggested that I placed Blanco Posnet at their disposal only because it was, as an unlicensed play, the refuse of the English market. As a matter of fact there was no such Hobson's choice in the matter. I offered a licensed play as an alternative, and am all the more indebted to Lady Gregory and Mr Yeats for not choosing it. Besides, Ireland is really not so negligible from the commercial-theatrical point of view as some of our more despondent patriots seem to suppose. Of the fifteen countries outside Britain in which my plays are performed, my own is by no means the least lucrative; and even if it were, I should not accept its money value as a measure of its importance.

G. Bernard Shaw

To GILBERT MURRAY

[Great] Southern Hotel. Parknasilla

[A/36]   29th August 1909

[Kathleen Lyttelton (1860–1943) was the wife of Gen. the Honourable Sir Neville Lyttelton (1845–1931), commander-in-chief of British forces in

864

Ireland. Maeterlinck's *Monna Vanna*, proscribed by the censor, had been performed in London in the original French by Lugné-Poe's company, under the auspices of the Stage Society, privately in June 1902. Hall Caine's novel *The White Prophet*, published on 12th August, had been severely slated by the press. Shaw, in a reply written at Parknasilla on 6th September and intended to be a preface to the second edition, but published by Heinemann in October as a pamphlet *To the Critics of The White Prophet*, argued that the savage reception was an emotional response to the home truths about Britain's policies in Egypt contained in the novel, and to the fact that its hero, an Arab, "has a 'creeping' resemblance to Jesus ... [Caine] has suggested that Jesus was a reality instead of a picture by Holman Hunt." Caine's dramatic version of the novel had been announced for production several months earlier by Tree, but had been cancelled without public explanation. The "Aspects of the East" series in the *Daily Telegraph* consisted of eight articles published between 4th and 20th August.]

My dear Murray

You have contributed very materially to the Dublin victory.

The real point at issue was not the liberty of the stage or the merits of Blanco, but whether Lady Lyttelton, the wife of the Generalissimo, would come with her party. The fate of the Castle hung on that; and Lady L. at first said she could not possibly bring her young people to a wicked play or bring a blush to the cheek of the military. An unscrupulous use of your letter and Lady Mary's verdict [that the play was not immoral] decided the struggle. I sent the letter to Lady Gregory; Lady Gregory planked it down confidentially on Lady L's dressing table; and Lady L. took her Bible & hymnbook and brought her whole flock to the play with military honors. Down came the Castle flag; Charlotte was overwhelmed with invitations to the Vice Regal Lodge, and, on her regretting that her immediate return to her post by her palpitating husband would prevent &c &c &c, received through the Vice Regal telephone from the private secretary a long and agitated mixture of apology and hope that no further statements would be sent to the press in view of the good behaviour of the authorities. The rest you have seen in the papers, though I havnt, as this is within hail of the remotest tail-ends of Ireland. Really, it was Lady Mary who was the Woman of Destiny in the affair. ...

There is a case which interests me personally much more than any of our Monna Vannas & other stock grievances; and that is the case of Hall Caine's White Prophet. I think H.C. should be backed up. Egypt is a leading case on which we shall have to fight the whole question of coercive Imperialism versus federated commonwealths. The stock abuse of H.C. is nine tenths envy of a novelist who is supposed to make more money than anyone else except Marie Corelli, and one tenth superciliousness because H.C. goes in industriously for matter and doesnt practise style. I have read half through The White Prophet & seen some of the Aspects of The East articles in the Daily Telegraph; and I have no doubt that H.C. is in earnest and on the right tack. I hear Heinemann is getting up some sort of testimonial preface or manifesto as a counterblast to the Imperialist attacks on the book and to the snobbish shame that prevents the men who privately sympathize with H.C. from letting him use their names. I am quite game to contribute (much good that will do him, I fear!); and I also want him to go before the Select Committee & tell the story of how the censorship stopped The White Prophet at His Majestys—that is, if it was really the Censor, and not Tree, who stopped it.

yrs ever
G.B.S.

To B.IDEN PAYNE

[Great Southern Hotel.] Parknasilla
[A/4]   12th September 1909

[Shaw had suggested to Annie Horniman that she apply for a license for *Blanco Posnet* in Manchester. Her manager Iden Payne wrote at once to the censor to ask for his reconsideration. Redford replied on 8th September: "I have read the copy of 'The Shewing up of Blanco Posnet' proposed to be produced at your Theatre, which purports to have been revised and altered since the piece was submitted by the Manager of His Majestys Theatre, London. I have no means of comparing the two copies, but I observe that this print copy contains the passages originally objected to . . . in fact I should say that the copy now before me is practically identical. Under these circumstances it would clearly be impossible for the Examiner of Plays to recommend the issue of the Lord Chamberlain's Licence for Representation, *in its present form*. At present there is no ground on which I could ask the Lord Chamberlain to reconsider his decision. If you are prepared to comply with the Lord Chamberlain's requirements, which it appears to me would be very easy, I shall be most happy to place the revised copy before him" (Hanley, Texas).]

Dear Iden Payne

I have read Mr Redford's letter; and I doubt whether it will be possible to make him understand the situation.

866

Our contention is not, as he seems to think, that the play has been altered so as to meet his objections to it. It *has* been altered—altered in one passage of such importance that the change could hardly have been missed by anyone who had taken in the religious point of the play; and this alteration would have enabled Mr Redford to recommend license of a "revised version." But the change was made without the slightest reference to his objections.

What we do contend is that Mr Redford made a grave error of judgment, which has been brought to light by the Dublin performance. He probably does not know that the Lord Lieutenant, who at first naturally assumed that Mr Redford's opinion of the play was correct, was not "defied" in the matter, but was made acquainted with the indignant dissent of persons of influence (to whom I shall ask the Lord Chamberlain to refer the question if it becomes necessary to do so), and consequently withdrew his opposition. But what Mr Redford ought to know is that critics of every complexion and authority, from the Rector of Westport (in the Spectator & the Manchester Guardian) to Mr Walkley in The Times & Lord Dunsany in The Saturday Review, have borne such overwhelming testimony against the action of The Lord Chamberlain, and the gross libel upon me implied by it, that I am clearly entitled to an immediate and careful reconsideration of his verdict.

I do not, however, advise you to press for it—at least through Mr Redford. Mr Redford has a fixed delusion that I am a dangerous and disreputable person, a blasphemer and a blackguard. Just consider his conduct in the present case. He has publicly assured the Select Committee on Stage Plays that a play can always be sent in again and reconsidered. He was specially questioned on the point because it was known to the Committee that he had refused to reconsider a play of mine [*Mrs Warren's Profession*] even after some years had elapsed, and a public trial had resulted in a judicial decision that the play was not improper and might even lead to desirable reforms. The Committee naturally concluded that he had changed his practice and is now prepared to reconsider plays. Yet he now refuses to submit my play to the Lord Chamberlain: that is to say, he assumes the powers of the Lord Chamberlain, and takes upon himself the authority given by the Act of 1843 to his principal. Of course he does not mean his letter to be taken in this way: his intention to you is friendly. What he means is, "If your blasphemous blackguard of an author will only be reasonable, and turn his play into a coarse and worthless melodrama, and thereby confess that I was right about him, he can have his license without any trouble." It is useless to reason with a man who is in this state of mind; and it is brutal to argue with him about a play which he simply does not understand, and concerning which his attitude to you is quite considerate and kindly. He even means to be kind to me in the way in which a police court missionary is kind to a pickpocket; and the only difficulty in the matter is that, as it happens, I am not a pickpocket.

Will you therefore write Mr Redford an entirely polite and friendly letter to say that the play was sent in for reconsideration on the strength of his statement to the Select Committee, and that all we want is the Lord Chamberlain's license or his definite refusal to license, as the case may be. If he refuses, then I shall know what to do. If he grants the license, then the business is at an end. But this position in which there is neither a grant nor a refusal is intolerable; and I feel sure Mr Redford will not persist in it when you make him aware that it is— however considerate in intention—extremely inconvenient in practice.

yours faithfully
G. Bernard Shaw

To BEATRICE WEBB

[Great Southern Hotel.] Parknasilla

[A/14]   30th September 1909

[H. G. Wells had scandalised the Fabians by his attempted seduction of the not unwilling Rosamund Bland (1886–1950), illegitimate daughter of the Fabian treasurer. In October 1909 Miss Bland, who was secretary to the Fabian Nursery (a department created for the education of young Fabians), married Clifford Sharp (1883–1935), a protégé of the Webbs, who was appointed first editor of the *New Statesman* in 1913. Wells had subsequently entered into a liaison with the headstrong young treasurer of the Cambridge University Fabian Society, Amber Reeves, whose father was director of the London School of Economics and whose mother was a member of the Fabian Executive. Discovering that she was pregnant, Amber entered into a marriage of convenience in July 1909 with a young barrister, George R. Blanco White (1883–1966); she gave birth to Wells's daughter in December. Wells fictionalised the episode in *Ann Veronica*, published in October 1909. Shaw had attempted to remonstrate with Wells about his behaviour; the resultant "torrent of abuse" that descended upon him (not without some justification) was climaxed by Wells vituperatively labelling him "an unmitigated middle-Victorian ass."

868

W. Arthur Colegate (1884–1956), a young civil servant who later became a business director and Conservative M.P., and who was knighted in 1955, was secretary in 1909 to the newly organised National Committee for the Break-Up of the Poor Law, founded by Beatrice Webb in May.]

My dear Beatrice

Yes: the real difficulty seems to be that Amber brags of her exploit. However, I hope I have made it clear to W. that this must not be done.

I have had a long letter from Mrs Reeves giving me the whole history of the affair, the most astonishing part of which is the length of time it has been going on, and the fact that W. held out against his determined assailant for a whole year.

Since you have already shut up Colegate as far as you can, the only other thing I think you can do—if you get a chance—is to prevent Reeves from advertising the affair by betraying his feelings about it. I still think that the situation can be saved by letting it alone. Amber has a very strong hand if she plays it well and resists the temptation to boast. Nobody knows from the outside who pays for the cottage; nor would it greatly matter if they did. Why should not W., who, if not 70, is old enough to be Amber's father, pay for the young couple's cottage? If H.S. [Herbert Spencer] had paid for a cottage for you & Sidney when you were 20 and he was 50, would any mortal have seen anything wrong in it? Suppose I pay a years rent of a cottage for Rosamund Bland & Sharpe & furnish it & go down to see them often, will there be the faintest impropriety in it? Not a scrap. I stick to my Spencerian proposition. Taking that old relationship as probably the most obviously & unsuspectably innocent thing of the kind available for citation, I say that from the outside the Woldingham menage looks just as innocent, and can only be blown up from within. And the consequences of a blow-up are far too serious to be faced if we can possibly avert them. Wells of course threatens: it is the right card for him to play against an enemy. He ought to know better than to play it against you; but I am not altogether sorry that he is doing it. I have told him flatly that if you asked my advice in the matter I should urge you most strongly not to commit yourself to a word of anything but the sternest disapproval of the whole affair; that you must not be made an accomplice in questionable social experiments; that the Nat[1] Committee & all you stand for must not be played with to amuse Amber. If you are on bad terms with him on account of the affair—if you have nothing to say to him but "Drop it"—why, so much the better if anything happens. Leave the friendly part of the business to me.

Remember, there is no practical question now of disapproval or approval. The question is not what the parties ought to do except in so far as there is a possibility that they *will* do it. Perhaps Sidney ought to join the Unionist party. But he wont; and there's an end to it. Perhaps Wells & Amber ought to recognize that they have behaved badly & part; but as they finally and certainly WONT, I am not going to waste my time either giving advice that wont be taken or suggesting action on the basis of what will not occur. The only sane course is to calculate on what *will* occur, & make the best of it. What will occur, then, is that W. will stand by Amber until the "ripping child" (who, alas! may not be a ripping child) is born. That much is certain. After that, we shall see. I have told W. that there is no apparent element of permanence in the relation—that in the course of nature he will go back to Jane, and she will pass on to fresh adventures (finishing probably with Blanco)—that he cannot be fonder of her than he must have been of Jane when he left his first wife [Isabel Williams] with her—that he can hardly, with such a record, ask Amber to regard him as a constant lover. I think it very likely that the compact originally made with Blanco, and now repudiated by Amber, will keep itself no matter how much they may repudiate it. At all events we must give it a chance: there is nothing else to be done.

Do not be distressed about our difference of opinion. You always differ from me; but as I never differ from you, nothing happens except your invariable surprise at things happening exactly as if we agreed perfectly. As you know, the only way to understand a subject is to write a book about it. You have never written a book about psychology and conduct: I have never written a book about anything else. You have never written a book about me: I have written lots of books about you. You have never quite found yourself out: I have very nearly found myself out. I dont want to sympathize with you over this case: I want to clear your mind about it. When W. dragged me into it (by a torrent of abuse) nobody, as far as I could ascertain, saw the real possibilities & probabilities of it at all. They were making straight for a smash. I havnt bothered about the right & wrong of the affair, which is clearly one of those in which the right & wrong are very largely conventional, but simply about the best way of avoiding the smash. Such unnatural detachment from the ethical interest of the problem is aggravating; but it has its value. Also, there is something exasperating in the fact that the person who will suffer least by an explosion is H.G.W., and that therefore he will not say thank you to us for warding it off, if we *do* ward it off. But dont confuse the fact with the man who sees it. I aim at the minimum of mischief; and if everybody agrees that the minimum is all my own fault, all the better. I have broad shoulders & a bad character & shant suffer as others would.

G.B.S.

To J.E.VEDRENNE

[A/1]
[Great] Southern Hotel. Parknasilla
3rd October 1909

[Shaw had begun the composition of *Misalliance* on 8th September; originally titled *Just Exactly Nothing*, it was completed on 4th November.]

. . . I object to any definite arrangement about V & B. I have been dodging it, in spite of Barker's businesslike & prudent scruples, ever since we retired from the West End. A definite arrangement would have meant a winding-up; and what I want is a hanging-up until you realize that your only real stand-by for your old ages is beating the provinces with the old Court Repertory.

The play for Frohman is already longer than Getting Married & it hasnt got to business yet. Nothing but endless patter: my bolt as a real playwright is shot.

See you when I return.

GBS

To ERICA COTTERILL

[A/1; X/202]
Ayot St Lawrence. Welwyn
13th October 1909

[Erica, who had known Amber Reeves from the Fabian Nursery, had apparently indicated that she intended to write to Wells about the affair, for Shaw on 6th September had written a hurried note of admonishment from Parknasilla: "Do not write to W. This is important. I will tell you why presently" [C/4]. That Erica continued to dwell on the subject may be adduced from Shaw's inscription on a postcard photo of himself posted to her on 11th January 1910 [C/4]: "There! Isnt he nice? Why dont you take an interest in the elections, or in anything except that tiresome girl who is as mad as a hatter?"]

My dear Emerica

The reason I asked you not to meddle in that affair was that I was having a great deal of trouble over it because it had been too much meddled in already. People had lost their heads and were treating a catastrophe as inevitable. I was doing what I could to bring them all to their senses; and I hope I have succeeded.

I am greatly indebted to you for typewriting your letters; but I cant answer them, partly because I havn't time, and also because they never tell me anything. It is just as if a strange girl stopped me on the road and said "Oh please you mustnt think I really meant to go there and oh dear if you would only not take that view of my wanting to get there because of what the doctor said; for I really meant the other whenever I meant anything &c &c &c &c." Imagine me replying "Madam: what the devil is the matter?" and the answer coming "They have told me this time that it is impossible for me to go on much longer like this." Like *what? Who* told you?

But dont answer me: I am too busy to want to know. As you have nothing to do, and are accordingly in an appalling state of hypochondriasis, you are a little insane; and insane people, Emerica, are frightful *bores* [underscored 4 times]. They write to me reams & reams about their symptoms. I get letters from other women which are almost word for word *your* letters. I glance at them; recognize the old song; and away they go—five or six sheets of tears and blood and confessions—into the waste paper basket. I used to bear a great deal of it from you because you occasionally got some little thing worth saying, or some definite bit of amusing news into it; but the strain was too great: you have no idea when you are writing what is worth reading, and when you are going on like the telephone girls & typists & school teachers who write endless & absurd letters (poor things!) to public men who have struck their imagination. They all want to make the victim their priest; and when he takes pity on them & hears their confessions & helps them, they promptly abuse the relationship, which is horribly dishonorable & indelicate. I allow one page, typed, in answer, & no more; and I shall not answer the answer if it is not healthy and amusing.

G.B.S.

To JULIE MOORE

10 Adelphi Terrace WC

[H.c.u/3] 15th October 1909

[Miss Moore was a young Fabian, who had been one of Shaw's campaign assistants in the 1904 London County Council election. G.W.Foote (see I, 324), the successor to Charles Bradlaugh, was president of the National Secular Society 1890–1915.]

Dear Madam

It is really not possible for me to put my theology into so small a parcel as you demand. Of course if a man to whom Jehovah is a mere tribal idol like Baal or Moloch or Dagon is an atheist, then I am an atheist, and practically all the educated people in Europe are atheists. When I was a young man the word God was so generally used to denote either Jehovah or some cognate idol, that really the most convenient way of expressing one's attitude towards the worship of such idols was to call oneself an atheist. Besides, at that time, the persecution of Charles Bradlaugh for avowing himself an atheist made it a point of honor with all intellectually honest men to confirm in the most striking and unmistakeable way that they were entirely on his side as against his persecutors. But the matter is not quite so easy nowadays. On the one hand, Jehovah is now pretty effectually classed with the idols of the Sandwich Islands; and the most earnestly religious people, when they speak of God, do not mean Jehovah or anything like Jehovah: they really mean the purpose behind evolution. On the other hand, Atheism, in spite of the protests of the most intelligent atheists, has come to mean a denial of any purpose behind evolution, and the explanation of the whole evolutionary process by the chapter of accidents called Natural Selection. Consequently, the term atheist, which had always the disadvantage of being a mere negation, has now the additional disadvantage to me personally of being a misleading one, as I am very strongly on the side of the late Samuel Butler as against the Darwinians.

When, in addressing an ordinary religious audience, I have occasion to speak of the force which they call the Will of God, and which I myself have called the Life Force, I use the term which is familiar and intelligible to them. The force in question is as obvious a reality to me as magnetism or gravitation; and I had very much rather be misunderstood as accepting some of its legendary associations than as denying a reckoning without its existence. But as a matter of fact, my references to it are always accompanied by other observations which could not possibly be taken as proceeding from an ordinary Evangelical. I hope to define my views on this subject more precisely in a book entirely devoted to them[;] but should anything prevent me from accomplishing this design, the 3rd Act of Man and Superman will remain on record as a statement of my creed. If you care to read it, you will see that it belongs to a stage of thought at which the term atheist is as useless and obsolete as any of the sectarian terms to which it is usually opposed.

Like all great preachers, Mr Foote has had the disadvantage of being considerably ahead of his congregation. The denominational atheist is exactly like the denominational christian: his atheism is often a crude and rather spiteful superstition which would revolt the Fathers of his Church if he could explain it to them. But the denomination has to be kept together for the sake of organization; and since Mr Foote is the head of it in England, his freedom is no greater than that of an English Bishop. He is hampered by the "old folk," exactly as the Commissioners of the Salvation Army are hampered. In the Salvation Army the superstitious element which the leaders are forced to humor is Evangelicalism and fetish worship of The Bible. In the Secularist movement it is materialism and the theory that all religious people are men of Belial. Mr Foote has to do the best he can in his struggle with obsolescence and stupidity. Personally, I think it a pity that so able, humane and independent a thinker should be tied to a "Connexion" of any sort; and I should rejoice to see him gain a direct relation with the general culture and though[t] of his time, which has got far beyond the point at which Mr Foote had to take over the Secularist organization from Charles Bradlaugh.

You need not treat this letter as confidential. Everybody is welcome to the fullest knowledge of my opinions.

yours faithfully
[G. Bernard Shaw]

To G. K. CHESTERTON

[H/1; X/203]

10 Adelphi Terrace WC
30th October 1909

[The Chesterton critical study of Shaw had been reviewed by Shaw in *The Nation* on 28th August.]

CHESTERTON.
SHAW SPEAKS.
ATTENTION! . . .

I still think that you could write a useful sort of play if you were started. When I was in Kerry last month I had occasionally a few moments to spare; and it seemed to me quite unendurable that you should be wasting your time writing books about me. I liked the book very much, especially as it was so completely free from my own influence, being evidently founded on a very hazy recollection of a five-year-old perusal of Man and Superman; but a lot of it was fearful nonsense. There was one good thing about the scientific superstition which you came a little too late for. It taught a man to respect facts. You have no conscience in this respect; and your punishment is that you substitute such dull inferences as my "narrow puritan home" for delightful and fantastic realities which you might very easily have ascertained if you had taken greater advantage of what is really the only thing to be said in favour of Battersea: namely, that it is within easy reach of Adelphi Terrace. However, I have no doubt that when Wilkins Micawber junior grew up and became eminent in Australia, references were made to *his* narrow puritan home; so I [do] not complain. If you had told the truth, nobody would have believed it.

Now to business. When one breathes Irish air, one becomes a practical man. In England I used to say what a pity it was you did not write a play. In Ireland I sat down and began writing a scenario for you. But before I could finish it I had come back to London; and now it is all up with the scenario: in England I can do nothing but talk. I therefore now send you the thing as far as I scribbled it; and I leave you to invent what escapades you please for the hero, and to devise some sensational means of getting him back to heaven again, unless you prefer to end with the millennium in full swing.

But experience has made me very doubtful of the efficacy of help as the means of getting work out of the right sort of man. When I was young I struck out one invaluable rule for myself, which was, Whenever you meet an important man, contradict him. If possible, insult him. But such a rule is one of the privileges of youth. I no longer live by rules. Yet there is one way in which you may possibly be insultable. It can be plausibly held that you are a venal ruffian, pouring forth great quantities of immediately saleable stuff, but altogether declining to lay up for yourself treasures in heaven. It may be that you cannot afford to do otherwise. Therefore I am quite ready to make a deal with you.

A full length play should contain about 18,000 words (mine frequently contain two or three times that number). I do not know what your price per thousand is. I used to be considered grossly extortionate by Massingham and others for insisting on £3. 18,000 words at £3 per thousand is £54. I need make no extra allowance for the republication in book form, because even if the play aborted as far as the theatre is concerned, you could make a book of it all the same. Let us assume that your work is worth twice as much as mine: this would make £108. I have had two shockingly bad years of it pecuniarily speaking, and am therefore in that phase of extravagance which straitened means have always produced in me. Knock off 8% as a sort of agent's commission to me for starting you on the job and finding you a theme. This leaves £100. I will pay you £100 down on your contracting to supply me within three months with a mechanically possible, i.e. stageable drama dealing with the experiences of St Augustine after re-visiting England. The literary copyright to be yours, except that you are not to prevent me making as many copies as I may require for stage use. The stage right to be mine; but you are to have the right to buy it back from me for £250 whenever you like.* The play, if performed, to be announced as your work and not as a collaboration. All rights which I may have in a scenario to go with the stage right and literary copyright as prescribed as far as you may make use of it. What do you say? There is a lot of spending in £100.

One condition more. If it should prove impossible to achieve a performance otherwise than through the Stage Society (which does not pay anything), a resort to that body is not to be deemed a breach of the spirit of our agreement.

Do you think it would be possible to make Belloc write a comedy? If he could only be induced to believe in some sort of God instead of in that wretched little conspiracy against religion which the pious Romans have locked up in the Vatican, one could get some drive into him. As it is, he is wasting prodigious gifts in the service of King Leopold and the Pope and other ghastly scarecrows. If he must have a Pope, there is quite a possible one at Adelphi Terrace.

For the next few days I shall be at my country quarters, Ayot St. Lawrence, Welwyn, Herts. I have a motor car which could carry me on sufficient provocation as far as Beaconsfield; but I do not know how much time you spend there and how much in Fleet Street. Are you only a week-ender; or has your wise wife taken you properly in hand and committed you to a pastoral life.

yours ever
G. Bernard Shaw

P.S. Remember that the play is to be practical (in the common managerial sense) only in respect of its being mechanically possible as a stage representation. It is to be neither a likely-to-be-successful play nor a literary lark: it is to be written for the good of all souls.

* [Shaw's footnote in Maisie Ward's *Gilbert Keith Chesterton* (1944)]: "I could not very well offer him £100 as a present."

[Shaw's scenario, dated October 1909, was never used. It is reproduced here from the original holograph manuscript in the British Museum. Lord Carmelite is a caricature of the newspaper proprietor Lord Northcliffe, who acquired and reorganised the *Evening News* in 1894 and founded the halfpenny morning newspaper, the *Daily Mail*, in 1896. Roger L'Estrange (1616–1704) was an English journalist who, after the Restoration, became licenser of the press. Jemappes is a town in Belgium, where the French defeated the Austrians in one of the first major battles of the French Revolutionary Wars (1792). Lepanto, presumably mentioned because of Chesterton's poem glorifying the victory, was a naval battle off the coast of Greece, in which the fleet of the Holy League destroyed the Turkish fleet (1571). The joke of placing Belloc on the scene is enhanced by one's knowledge that one of the crusaders actually present was Cervantes. The Council of Trent was an ecumenical council which, between 1545 and 1563, clarified Catholic doctrine and brought about major reforms in the Roman Catholic Church. Christabel Pankhurst (1880–1958) was a barrister active in the women's suffrage movement with her famous mother Mrs Emmeline Pankhurst and her sister Sylvia. C.F.G.Masterman (1874–1927) was a Liberal M.P. and journalist, who had recently published a book *The Condition of England*. Mary Baker Eddy (1821–1910) was the American founder of the Christian Science Church.]

SCENARIO
Prologue.
Scene. The Holy Mountain. Rocks, Trees, Hermits' Cells.
St Augustine in ecstasy at the entrance to his cell.
At the conclusion of his adoration, which may be in verse
The Devil comes by.

—Dialogue of the Devil & St Augustine—

The Devil asks Augustine who he is, and what he has done, anyhow. On Augustine innocently replying that he has converted England to Christianity, the Devil, overcome by the stupendousness of the joke, roars with laughter. The offended saint asks the unseemly stranger who he is. The Devil, who is not at all ashamed of himself, introduces himself. The Saint intolerantly resorts to ostracism, to the tongs of St Dunstan, to holy water &c &c, and concludes in despair, as they produce no effect, that he has fallen into sin. The Devil points out that the Saint has contracted the English habit of treating a simple question of fact as a question of the respectability of the person who states it. All he wished to convey was that as a matter of fact the English are not Christians—not even Catholics. The Saint is incredulous—recalls martyrs—eminent men—bishops & the like. The Devil seems to recall certain bishops burnt by a Christian queen for idolatry of the Bible & defence of the Church, but cannot recollect anything of the sort lately except a few atheists in the lower classes. The Saint, conscience stricken, admits that since he took to adoring in verse, he has been so taken up with the literary art of the thing that he has not kept much of an eye on England, but is positive that it was all right in the XII–XIII century. The Devil remarks that it is now the XX century. "God bless my soul: you dont say so" says the Saint, & deplores the absence of clocks & calendars in Eternity.

Finally the Devil, who is spending his annual fortnight in Heaven (for which overhaul your Job), & is, as usual, getting confoundedly bored, suggests a trip to London. "The question is," says Augustine, "are you tempting me?" "The question is," says Satan, "does it matter whether I'm tempting you or not, if there's work for you to do." "True," says the Saint: "anyhow, London is worth a Black Mass"; & off they go, by magic cloak, flying carpet, fiery chariot, or anything that will work on the stage.

End of Prologue.

—Act I, following Prologue—

Westminster Hall. The Devil, & St Augustine, about to proceed to the Lobby, are stopped by a Policeman.

They explain who they are & what they want, which is to find a Bishop who will lend St Augustine his body for a while, & take his place in heaven until the saint has investigated England.

The policeman is incredulous, & resents the supposed disrespect to his function & insult to his intelligence. The Devil suggests convincing him by a miracle. The policeman grimly remarks that the most useful miracle to the saint would be to turn his truncheon into a cucumber. He draws his truncheon & discovers that it *is* a cucumber. He then becomes very respectful; apologizes; and regrets that, as a Protestant, he does not hold with saints, offering however to fetch an Irish police-man who is a Catholic. The Saint, who does not know what a Protestant is, endeavors to elicit particulars—especially doctrinal particulars—as to the Reformation. The policeman consults his book of instructions, but can find nothing nearer than "Respiration—Artificial."

The Bishop of Blackfriars enters on his way to the House of Lords. The policeman appeals to him & explains the situation. The Bishop is incredulous, & threatens to report the policeman (on account of the cucumber) for behaving like a policeman in a harlequinade. Another miracle being evidently needed, the saint changes all the half crowns in the bishop's pocket into pennies. This infuriates the bishop, who denounces it as a most ungentlemanly trick. The saint, in all humility, apologizes, & turns all the bishop's sixpences into half sovereigns. This, the bishop says, is most interesting, though he must reserve his judgment. The saint then proposes a fortnight in heaven to the bishop, in order to use his body on earth. The bishop is not at all enthusiastic & begins to ask questions about heaven. The saint has to confess that most of the things the bishop likes are not to be found there. Finally the bishop considers that it would be wrong to desert his flock—a sort of temporary suicide—and declines the bargain with a great show of self sacrifice. The saint, discouraged, asks him whether he knows anybody in the building who would oblige. The bishop doesnt, & implies that if it were the other gentleman, it might be easier to oblige him. The policeman remarks that Lord Carmelite often says he wishes he was in heaven—thinks he's so rich that he's tired of everything on earth, & might venture it. The bishop thinks the idea a good one, and the policeman goes off to fetch Lord Carmelite.

Whilst the policeman is away, the bishop describes lovingly the enormous enterprise of Lord Carmelite, the newspaper king. He piously regrets that his newspapers are not always accurate nor scrupulous, but cannot deny that they are enormously smart, sensational, readable & exciting.

The policeman returns with the melancholy Carmelite. The bishop introduces him; congratulates him on having something really startling to report in tomorrow's Daily Mail & Evening News; and hurries off to a fashionable appointment, saying to the Saint, "Happy to have made your acquaintance," & to the Devil "I hope to have the pleasure of seeing you again," to which the Devil, with a sigh, replies that he supposes it cant be helped.

Carmelite then explains that he is a disappointed man—that he established two cheap & good newspapers & spared no money to make them of the brightest & the best—that they failed & failed & failed until he was reduced to paying his editors eighteen shillings a week & getting his news & his articles from clerks discharged for incompetence. In the hands of these illiterates, all merit vanished from his papers. News was discontinued; nothing of importance was mentioned; silly little scraps of ignorant gossip about mean events—a larceny in Fulham—a bicycle stolen at Croydon—filled the columns. Suddenly the circulation went up: the papers began to catch on. He reduced wages all round in disgust at their dullness & made them absolutely unreadable by any intelligent man. Result: a circulation of six millions & a torrent of gold into his pockets. Also settled melancholia induced by contempt for his papers, his public, and himself. He will sell his body to the saint & his soul to the devil if only they will stand up before the British public & say "These papers are not smart, they are dull. They do not contain the latest news: they never contain any news at all. They are not written by unscrupulous but brilliant young lions: they are written by honest parochial illiterates. They are not up-to-date: they would seem obsolete to Roger Lestrange. They are not the highest organs of civilization: they are the rudimentary organs, the unstriped muscles, which enable us to connect Shakespear with an ancestor who was little better than a group of slime cells newly risen from the ditch."

The saint promises to read the papers & see whether he can conscientiously make the required declaration. Carmelite says this is tantamount to a refusal, as no person so advanced as a saint of the ——th century can possibly read such trash. The devil then says he once tried to read a copy of the Evening News, & is quite prepared to carry out the bargain. This clinches the matter. The saint & Lord Carmelite exchange bodies in view of the audience. This can be done either by a double Faust transformation, or, more logically, by simply swopping dialogue, the Carmelite actor taking up the character of St Augustine & the impersonator of the saint the character of Carmelite.

Carmelite, transfigured, begins to ascend to heaven. When he is a little way up he comes down again & remarks "Oh, by the way, I forgot to warn you that I am engaged to a young person of quality, who despises me, but wants my money. You will have to keep up the courtship. Ta ta," and up he goes, leaving the saint in the greatest perturbation. He explains to the Devil & the Policeman that his vows make it absolutely impossible for him to carry out this part of Lord Carmelite's destiny. The Policeman says he has been thinking over the Reformation & rather thinks that it got over that difficulty. Is quite certain that Father Martin Luther, who was every inch an Englishman, married a nun. Would not go that far himself, but makes allowances for uncivilized times. The Devil confirms this historical aperçu; and the Saint is reassured.

An angel now arrives hastily in a remonstrant mood to say that Carmelite is no use—that he turned to dust the moment the air of heaven touched him, and that the whole economy of the spheres is upset by the saint's escapade. The Saint does not know what to do. The Policeman suggests that Scotland Yard should be applied to to send him (the P.) on fixed point duty to heaven. Both the saint & the devil agree that this would be an excellent solution, as the policeman appears to be the real ruler of parliament & to be privileged to go everywhere and order everybody about. The Policeman thinks if the Prime Minister or the Leader of the Opposition were to mention it to the Superintendent (who is lying low to avoid having his face slapped by Suffragets), it could be managed.

At this moment the Prime Minister & the Opposition Leader enter arm in arm, very affectionately. The Policeman introduces them. The Saint is horrified at their cynical conduct. Why are they not sword in hand, hacking at one another's helmets, hurling execrations at one another. They try to snub him by explaining the views of English gentlemen. He treats them to a splendid burst of eloquence; and they are quite at a loss until the Policeman remarks that the saint seems to be fairly friendly with the Devil, and propounds the view that a man can't always be on duty—that policeman & prisoner must sometimes be simply Man & Man, or perhaps Man & Superman. He then explains the situation. Asquith is unimpressed, incredulous, contemptuous, and insists on the angel getting proper clothes & having his wings cut. Balfour is interested, curious, but philosophically doubtful. The saint threatens to exchange their heads and throw the House of Commons into utter confusion unless they get serious & attend to him. The Angel flies up to the rafters and begins to sing. This makes Asquith very angry: he says it will embarrass the Government, the one unpardonable crime. Balfour, delighted, encourages the angel, and tries to sing a second to him (? it). At last Asquith, with a very bad grace, consents to settle with Scotland Yard if the Saint will call the angel down. The angel flies down, alighting on Asquith's head as a stepping stone. Asquith angrily examines the damage to his hat. The Angel, apologizing, takes it out of his hands, brushes it carefully with his elbow, takes a feather out of his wing & sticks it in it, and returns it. Asquith throws the feather away & says "Dont be silly." The policeman is the only man with sense enough to pick it up & ask whether he may be allowed to take it home for his children.

The Saint now asks that some Christian may be told off to shew him through parliament. Balfour is puzzled—admits that he does not know any M.P. or peer who would quite like to be called a Christian. This remark is overheard by Mr Bellairs Hilloc on his way to the Lobby. He claims to be a Christian, to the astonishment of the policeman, who says "Fancy you a Christian, Mr Hilloc. We never thought you was anything." Hilloc dazzles the Saint with his conversation, & with tales of his pilgrimages & of his exploits as a French gunner in the 1870–1 war, also at Waterloo, Jemappes, Lepanto & the Council of Trent. He sings rounds with the Angel—"Frère Jacques" &c—in the middle of which the division bells ring; and Balfour, Asquith & Hilloc rush precipitately from the Hall. The Saint complains that Hilloc has given him congestion of the brain & sits down on the top step with his head in his hands. Carmelite's betrothed, in gorgeous dinner toilet & opera cloak, enters & sees him. She rushes to console him. The angel, a charming but childish creature, begins to cry because the earth is so unhappy & ugly.

The rest of the play will consist of whatever these people do when you once start them in your imagination. They are all to have fair play & to be taken from their own point of view. With a saint, an angel (really a fairy) & a devil, you can always keep poesy & philosophy on hand, and for realism you can introduce Massingham, [Clement] Shorter, Christabel Pankhurst, Dilke, Max Beerbohm, Masterman, Burns, Whiteley, Mrs Eddy, Roosevelt, tramps, prostitutes, soldiers &c &c. You can change the scene (alternating fronts & full sets) every ten minutes or you can write in the Greek style in Westminster Hall with all the unities observed. The best way to end a play is to ring down the curtain.

And so good luck.   October 1909

To C. A. VANDERVELL & CO.

                                                [Ayot St Lawrence. Welwyn]
[A.c/9]   4th November 1909

[The Vandervell system of electric lighting, by a variable speed dynamo, adapted for use in automobiles, was displayed in November at the Motor Car Exhibition in London. Shaw, as a member of the Royal Automobile Club, wrote occasional reports for it on the quality of motor cars and equipment, the conditions of foreign roads and hotels, and suggested scenic routes. At least one of these was published anonymously in the Club's journal.]

Dear Sirs

I have now carried my trial of your electric lighting system on my car as far as you can reasonably expect; and the report I have to make of it is as follows.

With all the lamps alight—2 headlights, 2 carriage lamps, 1 tail light & 1 dashboard light—the illumination can be depended on for about 25 minutes.

With all the lamps cut out except 1 headlight, about 40 minutes can be obtained, followed by perhaps an hour of very dim light, enabling the car to be driven at less than 10 miles an hour, at the risk of being driven into from behind or prosecuted by the police for the absence of a tail light.

By taking the car to the C.A.V. works and having the battery charged from their supply—not from the dynamo—the lamps can be used successfully that night and until the battery runs down, which it does rapidly.

There is no conclusive evidence that the dynamo really produces any current at all, in spite of the indicator. Driving the car for hundreds of miles with the dynamos working all the time does not appear to charge the battery or to check its exhaustion.

The return of the car to the works, and the replacement of broken wires & "putting in order" makes no difference: the lighting fails at the end of half an hour as before.

The charge made for labor in installing the system on the car is about 4 times what might be expected from the nature of the operations & from comparison with the time given by the Bleriot Company for the instalment of their dynamo.

On every occasion on which the system has been relied on for night driving as distinguished from returning home for the end of an afternoon drive (say 10 to 15 minutes lighting), it has broken down, with extremely inconvenient & dangerous consequences for the owner.

All that can be said for the system is that during the 25 minutes during which it operates efficiently, it is in every way superior to acetylene. But the consequences of its failure are so serious, and its failure is so inevitable, that nobody but a lunatic would continue its use after putting it to trial in actual touring.

I am therefore obliged to discard it, and to advise my fellow members of the R.A.C. that the system is not yet a practical one, at least in the form used by the C.A.V. company.

Before I commit myself finally to these conclusions (there can be no question as to the *facts*), I should like you to have an opportunity of commenting on my experience. If you wish, I can send the car again to you; but as I have done that twice already without any substantial improvement I cannot say that I feel very sanguine as to the result....

yours faithfully
G. Bernard Shaw

883

To ARTHUR W. PINERO

[H/4]

10 Adelphi Terrace WC
29th November 1909

[Harry M. Paull (1854–1934), a retired civil servant who became a dramatic author of no particular note, was for many years the secretary of the Dramatists' Club. Pinero's *Mid-Channel*, a problem play, had been running at the St James's Theatre since 2nd September. Charles M. Lowne (1863–1941), one of the leading performers in *Mid-Channel*, created the rôle of Tarleton in *Misalliance* in 1910. "Alick" was George Alexander, Actor-manager of the St James's Theatre. Rev. William Booth (1829–1912) was General and commander-in-chief of the Salvation Army. Baron Croodle is a character in Pinero's first successful play, *The Money-Spinner* (1880).]

My dear Pinero

I have to go to Oxford next Wednesday afternoon [1st December] to beat the big drum for the National Theatre; so I shall not be at the Club lunch.

I have a notion that some such resolution as you propose was brought up at a recent lunch; but for the life of me I cannot remember what happened to it. I am quite in favor of it, not only for the sake of its positive side, but because it emphasizes the sacredness of the confidence in which our proceedings are to be held in the absence of a special authorization to make them public. Nobody but the waiter should be allowed to hear a word we say.

The truth is, our chaps want some screwing up as to their manners. At the last lunch I attended I raised the question as to whether Hall Caine should be invited to be a member. There was a shriek of "Good God! No!" which astounded the head waiter into betraying by his face that he had hitherto regarded Hall Caine as being an author so much more eminent than any of us that it would be the height of presumption on our part to hope for his presence. However, after some discussion it was admitted that Hall Caine was a man whom we could not very well ignore; and the end was unanimous consent to his being invited. I now hear from Paull that at the last lunch—at which I was not present— there were such threats of blackballing that the entry regarding the previous proceedings had to be expunged. Now it so happens, by God's mercy, that nobody appears to have met Hall Caine in the interim or sounded him as to whether he would accept the invitation. If that had happened, we should simply have had to compel the Club to stand by their decision by threats of resignation and the like. I think I shall bring the matter up in some artless way so as to make them feel they must not

884

play games of this sort. Fancy our feelings if we sounded a man as to whether he would accept an invitation, giving him the usual undertaking that he would be an acceptable member, and then found him blackballed by some chap who had not turned up at the lunch at which the affair was settled. We must rub it into them that the men who stay away must stand by what the members who attend have decided.

Thring frantically sent word to me that all was lost when he heard that you had made alterations in the manifesto. I reassured him, and rejoice to find that the case was exactly as I had told him it would turn out to be. I had a suspicion that the hash we produced at that stormy meeting would not do credit to our syntax.

On reflection, I am not sure that the Hall Caine incident does not shew the need of a rule that no proposal of a new member should be discussed, or minuted, or mentioned-outside-the-Club unless and until notice has been sent to all the members. Without this precaution, a Scratch lunch might commit us to an Undesirable. I think that would be a necessary condition of an understanding that the decisions at the lunches must not be gone back upon in the matter of inviting a recruit.

I have suggested a discussion of the claims of Gilbert Murray. Murray would be a very desirable member; and his position as Regius Professor of Greek at Oxford, and the social influence he has through his marriage with Lady Mary, a daughter of the Earl of Carlisle, would attach us to that big nerve system of the general social world from which our over-professionalized rank-and-file are a bit too much cut off. Nearly all of them suffer more or less from living by taking in one another's washing in the matter of ideas. Murray is one of those very rare men who combine the genuine artistic anarchic character and sympathies with academic distinction and political and social attachments in the big outside world. The technical objection to him is that his great stage achievements have been his translations of Euripides. As far as I know, the two original plays of his which have been produced, Carlyon Sahib and the Andromache play, are not what Carton calls works of established reputation. But I think we may accept really great translations—and his are jolly good—as enough for us.

I hear that Alexander and Bourchier threaten to denounce the National Theatre scheme because there are no actors on the Committee. An exquisite flavor is given to this situation by the fact that they have apparently appealed to Tree (who is on the Committee) for sympathy. More delightful still, Tree is said to be more than half inclined to agree with them. They totally forget Hare and Forbes Robertson. If you get a conversational chance of reminding them of the existence of these two obscure mummers, it might save them from making goats of themselves.

I saw Mid-Channel at the St James's, and discovered a new stage effect which you did not contemplate. Lowne pretended to play the piano with so successful an assumption of musical sentiment, that when the pianola outside totally failed to hit off the right moment at which his fingers came down on the keyboard, the audience went into shrieks of laughter for two minutes, during which the back of Lowne's neck, which at the best of times does not resemble a lily, looked like a beet-root. Between ourselves, I greatly dislike the audience at the St. James's Theatre. I think it has gradually got specialized for a certain kind of staylace drama, and in a furtive sort of way is quite determined to have that and nothing else. They are the very people you are getting at in the play. They do not enjoy that scene where the young man has to put up with familiarities from the maid. The women do not want to be told that they are not wives in any real sense, but only kept women. The husbands, who have brought their wives to the theatre because they are afraid of quarrelling if they stay at home, do not want to have the quarrel thrown in their faces across the footlights. And as you have no sort of mercy on them and no sort of hope for them, and simply rub their own misery and disgrace into them with the skill and ruthlessness of a scientific torturer, they stay away, and give Alick thereby a broad hint that they are not taking it kindly. I remember when a little play of mine called How He Lied to Her Husband was stuck up at the St. James's for a few weeks to prop up a failing bill (which it promptly brought down with a crash), Barker told me that the stalls received it with dull resentment because the vulgar South Kensington woman in it was one of themselves. When I went to The Thunderbolt, Alexander told me between the acts that the cheaper parts of the house were all right, but that the stalls would not come. That was not resentment but simply absence of sexual interest—the only sort of interest of which they are capable. There was a time when we were all cynical ruffians and could give these lost souls what they wanted, because we had no positive side ourselves—nothing but a humorous, critical, sceptical, anti-puritan side which left us nothing to drive the action of our plays with but the animal appetites, exaggerated and glorified for the purpose in an entirely hypocritical way, as we were not ourselves in the least voluptuaries with bulging cerebellums. But now something has got hold of us that spoils that game. Nowadays when I contemplate your remarkable nose, I think of that other remarkable nose, the nose of General Booth—both noses out for soul saving—*led* out—by the nose.

886

Why do you still struggle against it and *construct* plays? I never construct a play: I let myself rip. I give myself away. That is why I give everybody else away, which after all, is the whole purpose of comedy. You are like Ananias: you keep something back. There is not enough fun in Mid-Channel: you bite hard; but you do not let yourself wag your tail. The fun is in you: it is the divine secret of the light hand and the merry and charitable heart; but you seem to me to have begun to mistrust it in these later times: I miss Baron Croodle among all these dull, scared, vulgar people who are so fiercely true to their own life, and so very false to yours. Hang it all, a man of genius—and you are that or nothing—is a wild man; and there should be wild people in every play. What is the beadle, the doctor, the hangman without Punch?

This letter is about long enough even for a man with influenza. My wife, by the way, is down with it; so I shall probably have a turn myself in the course of a week.

Remind the Club, when they talk sceptically about our influence, that the blue-book containing the evidence of the Select Committee is now out; and that the report does not contain a single idea that we did not put into their heads. Absolutely not one.

Here endeth etc., etc.
G. Bernard Shaw

To ARTHUR W. PINERO

10 Adelphi Terrace WC
2nd December 1909

[H/4]

[The phrase "according to Cocker," popularised by Arthur Murphy in his farce *The Apprentice* (1756), refers to an arithmetic book written by Edward Crocker (1631–77), and means "according to established rules." Shaw told Hesketh Pearson that the Dramatists' Club members "were on the point of blackballing Gilbert Murray when Pinero, of whom they were mortally afraid, appeared and sternly ordered them to elect him" (*Bernard Shaw: His Life and Personality*, 1942).]

My dear Pinero

I know about the rule; and as far as the rule was concerned, everything was according to Cocker. But I gathered from Paull's letter—perhaps erroneously—that the objection to Hall Caine came from so many members that it must have included some of those who had consented on the previous occasion. The difficulty is not in the printed rule, but in that unwritten law which forbids a white man to nominate another unless he has previously sounded the elective body and made sure that his nominee will not suffer the rebuff of a blackball. No matter what our rules may be, there will always be an informal discussion of a proposed new member before his name goes down in black and white. The Club seems to have had a guilty conscience about H.C., because they actually ordered the nomination to be expunged from the minutes—a proceeding, by the way, which is not authorized by any rule and which would be questionable practice in a club which was less of a family party than ours. The truth is, I am not sure that all our chaps quite know the rules of the game; and the way to complete their education is by raising little difficulties and making little complaints of this sort just to make an opportunity of mentioning something that is being overlooked. Of course I may be completely in the wrong: it is possible that the objection to H.C. was confined to the members who had not been present when I sounded the Club about it. I shall try and find that out from Paull. But anyhow we had better make the Club clearly conscious that no matter what rule we make as to formal nomination, there must always be a preliminary ascertainment of how cold the water is; and that the results of that sounding must be considered as binding on the parties to it as the subsequent formal nomination and election.

We can apply the sounding process to Gilbert Murray at the next lunch . . .

When my wife is out of quarantine you must come along and see her. I will fix up an occasion. People never believe that I am real until they see me at home.

yours ever
G. Bernard Shaw

To ARCHIBALD HENDERSON

[A/4; X/116.e]

10 Adelphi Terrace W C
15th December 1909

[Henderson had been negotiating with the Boston publishing firm of Houghton, Mifflin, for publication of the Shaw biography. Eventually it was published in Cincinnati by Stewart & Kidd, and in London by Hurst & Blackett. Eugène Brieux (1858–1932) was a French journalist who, influenced by Ibsen, turned to the theatre as an effective medium for airing his controversial views on contemporary social problems. Publication of the volume containing *The Doctor's Dilemma* and *Getting Married* was delayed until 1911.

Since 18th November, Shaw had given eight lectures and political addresses, speaking at Llandudno, Shrewsbury, North Kensington, Portsmouth, Oxford, Manchester, and Huddersfield. Alvin Langdon Coburn's photographs of Edinburgh, ranging from 1905 to 1954, were published as illustrations to an edition of Robert Louis Stevenson's *Edinburgh: Picturesque Notes* (1954).]

My dear Henderson

Go to those Piffling Mifflings & demand your MSS. Tell them that as they refuse to set it up, and I cannot write a preface until it is set up, and the proofsheets in my hands, you must change your method of publishing, and manufacture the book yourself, subsequently finding a publisher to undertake it on commission.

Then we shall see what we shall see.

My secretary sent you my statement of evidence & a copy of Blanco Posnet & Press Cuttings and all the latest works. If the United States chooses to place its postal arrangements in the hands of its leading public criminals, I cannot help it. The mails are systematically robbed of all interesting books on the ground that they are immoral. Probably the Postmaster passes them on to the President when he has read them. Get a search warrant and rootle out the White House.

I have finished a new play & now have to stage it. I have finished a monumental preface to three plays by Brieux which my wife is publishing. I have yet to finish my own prefaces (the medical one involving stupendous labor) for my long delayed volume containing The Doctor's Dilemma & Getting Married. My oratorical flights at the election would exhaust six average Presidents.

I should think Göttingen the very place to finish the great biography. After a year or so there you will be another man. You can run up to Berlin & see all my plays there. You can become a Good European instead of a ringtailed pioneer. And you can write the book all over again in your new lights, with the new chapters which I shall keep adding til I die.

If Hookey Miffling has any doubts as to the bona fides of your offer to procure a preface, why doesn't he write to me and satisfy himself? I will settle his doubts with my well known lucidity.

I approve of research in Germany much more than of vain belles lettres.

Forgive my want of conscience. It failed at 40; and the last relics passed away three years ago.

yours ever
G. Bernard Shaw

PS Charlotte desires me to say all sorts of nice things, and to acknowledge the Coburn Edinburgh, the German Mark Twain & lots more.

PPS By the way, what did you tell me about Coburn photographing the houses I was born in? I was born in one only; and I photographed that myself in Dublin last year—an awful little kennel, like this

lots
more
like it

a row of
similar
ones.

To LOUIS WILKINSON

[D/3; X/226.E]

[Ayot St Lawrence. Welwyn]
20th December 1909

[Louis Wilkinson (1887–1966), who wrote under the pseudonym Louis Marlow, had circulated a manifesto among distinguished writers, artists, and scientists, for their signature, condemning the laws which made homosexuality a crime. "E.C." was Edward Carpenter.]

No movement could survive association with such a propaganda. I can sympathize with E.C's efforts to make people understand that the curious reversal in question is a natural accident, and that it is absurd to persecute it or connect any general moral deficiency with it. But to attempt to induce it in normal people as a social safety valve would be ruinous, and could seem feasible only to abnormal people who are unable to conceive how frightfully disagreeable—how abominable, in fact—it is to the normal, even to the normal who are abnormally susceptible to natural impulses.

G.B.S.

To ELIZABETH DUTCHER

[X/221]

[Bentley's Central Hotel. Merthyr Tydfil]
[Undated: c. 4th January 1910]

[Shaw was in Wales, electioneering for Keir Hardie. Elizabeth Dutcher, a representative of the Women's Trade Union League in New York, had

cabled him: MAGISTRATE TELLS SHIRTWAIST MAKER HERE HE
IS ON STRIKE AGAINST GOD, WHOSE PRIME LAW IS MAN
SHOULD EARN BREAD IN SWEAT OF BROW. PLEASE CHARAC-
TERIZE. REPLY, CHARGES PAID.]

DELIGHTFUL, MEDIAEVAL AMERICA—ALWAYS IN THE
INTIMATE PERSONAL CONFIDENCE OF THE ALMIGHTY.

[SHAW]

To A.B.KERSHAW

Queen's Hotel. Southsea (until Sunday morning)
[A/9]   7th January 1910

[Shaw's chauffeur had accidentally killed the pet dog of an eight-year-old
child, Gladys Kershaw, while driving Shaw through Accrington, Lancashire,
on his way to a lecture meeting at Burnley on 31st December.]

Dear Sir

Your letter has only just overtaken me, as I have been on the road
ever since the accident.

I am very sorry for the mishap to the poor doggie, and still more for
the distress it caused your daughter. I know quite well how completely a
pet dog becomes one of the family. Your daughter is too young to know
how shortlived they are even when no accidents happen, and how
unhappy they are when their old age comes on. She would have lost
Jess in any case only too soon. If she can find another pet, and will let
me know the price, I think you may promise her that she shall have it.

She must not imagine that she was in any way to blame for the accident. Nothing, I am sorry to say, could have saved Jess. There were
two other dogs in the road; and poor Jess was attending to them instead of the traffic. I was not driving myself at the time. We were passing
another vehicle and just coming to a cross road, and were therefore
pretty busy at the moment. My driver avoided two dogs, swerving a
little to the left to do so. Suddenly a little brown dog, quite unconscious of us, and intent on the other dogs, stepped from the middle of
the road right under us. It was so close that my driver did not see it. I
warned him; but before he could get his clutch out we were over it.
As it did not cry out, and we felt no shock or blow, we concluded that
it had escaped either by crouching between the wheels or slipping out
just in time; so we went on until I heard a shout, when I told my

891

driver to stop, and looked back. The poor little creature died almost as I did so. It had been making a few convulsive movements, which must have been very heartbreaking to its young mistress; but it is very unlikely indeed that it suffered at all. My car weighs nearly two tons; and after the tremendous shock of being crushed by such a weight, it would be a long time before any living creature could feel anything. A hurt dog cries out piteously; but Jess only tried to get up; found that she could not; and died probably without feeling anything. I have had a violent accident myself, and can assure you that the pain does not begin until long after the smash.

Perhaps you had better not remind your daughter of the scene by repeating these details; but you may assure her that Jess never felt anything but a most bewildering shock, & died without knowing what was the matter; that she could have been protected only by keeping her on a string continually, which would have made her unhappy and unhealthy; and that I will buy another Jess for her if one can be found.

By the way, what I was looking for and could not find was my card, and not, of course, another dog.

yours faithfully
G. Bernard Shaw

To AUGUSTIN HAMON

10 Adelphi Terrace WC
24th January 1910

[H.u/1]

[A portion of Hamon's translation of the Brieux preface was published, under the title "De Molière à Brieux," in *L'Illustration* on 7th May 1910. Jean Finot (1858–1922) was the editor of the *Revue des Revues* and author of several books on philosophy and race prejudice. Munier, a Paris publisher, had printed a special edition of one hundred copies each of Hamon's translations of the seven *Plays Pleasant and Unpleasant* in 1908, at Shaw's expense. Hamon was considering the possibility of campaigning for election to the French Chamber as Deputy for Nantes. Dorbon was a Parisian printer with whom Hamon and Shaw had been negotiating for publication of *Three Plays for Puritans*.]

My dear Hamon

I enclose the Brieux Preface. Will you translate it, and send it to Brieux, asking him to fill in the blanks in the last paragraph. Will you also ask him to deal with it quite freely in the way of modifying or altering or omitting anything that may be for any reason disagreeable or inconvenient to him. Say that as I read French quite easily, he need have no hesitation in writing to me direct; but that I hesitate to inflict letters of my own on him, as my French is extremely Brittannic, and must be positively painful to a man of his literary sensibility. Tell him that you propose to have the Preface published in France as a magazine article if he does not object. You had better explain that although we are submitting it to his approval, no public allusion will be made to this; so that he will not be in any way responsible for my views. . . . [The] plays, with my preface and the portrait, will make a decent volume, and will attract plenty of attention, and be turned out in a style worthy of Brieux's importance. Some time will have to lapse before the publication is effected, because the simultaneous American publication has to be arranged for, and until I get back the preface with Brieux's private sanction to its publication, I cannot send it over to America. To shorten this inevitable delay, will you beg him to let you have it back as soon as possible. I do not know whether he knows English or not; but you had better send him the English pages along with your translation, in case he would care to compare them at any point. . . .

The fact that Finot is a Polish Jew is a strong point in his favor. Always do business with a Jew when you can. You will usually get rather better terms out of him than out of a Christian, because his businesss ability enables him to make more. If you treat him as an honorable man, he appreciates your consideration, whereas a Frenchman either accepts it as a matter of course or demands it as a right. Furthermore, he never makes a bargain without fully understanding its terms, and meaning to carry it out; whereas an Englishman (I cannot answer for a Frenchman) never understands any document, and never means to carry it out unless it turns out exactly as he expected. My German translator is a Jew; and he sends me £500 a year from Germany and makes £500 a year for himself. My Swedish translator is a Jew; and he does even better for me than my German translator in proportion to the importance of the two countries. My American publisher is a Jew; and he not only pays me himself, but has made my previous publisher, who is a Christian and a swindler, disgorge his plunder to the uttermost farthing. If you were a Jew, you would not only be drawing a comfortable income from my plays at this moment, but probably have built half a dozen Ty an Diaouls and let them all on the most advantageous terms. Therefore, let us embrace the brave Finkelstein. Even if we do not deal with him, part with him on friendly terms.

I see that I have been guilty of a colossal stupidity in overlooking the fact that France and Belgium are two independent countries, and neglecting to secure publication of the Munier edition in Brussels as well as in Paris. How could we have been so stupid as not to think of this? Is there by any chance a convention existing between France and Belgium by which French books are copyright in Belgium and Belgian books copyright in France? If not, I see nothing to prevent the Brussels theatres seizing on Plays Pleasant and Unpleasant the moment they make any sort of success in Paris. I am at present taking Counsel's opinion as to whether there is any way of recovering fees for the Antwerp performances of Mrs Warren. I know that both in Italy and Hungary the Courts have held that the lapse of right of translation after ten years does not involve the lapse of the performing rights. If I could get a Belgian Court to pronounce in the same sense, the situation would be saved. But the danger of raising the question is that the decision might be the other way; and that would be very bad for us indeed. Can you obtain any guidance on the subject from any of the Societies to which we belong?

I think it is a mistake to offer John Bulls Other Island for publication. It is the one play of mine that is too local in its interest to cross the frontier successfully. It may possibly be published later on, if my works obtain such a vogue in France that editors will take anything, however unsuitable, provided they can advertize it as a play by me; but under existing circumstances, it can only create an impression that my plays are too foreign to be of any use in France. I therefore strongly urge you to keep it locked up.

What you call the "manière noire et sanglante" of the Grand Guignol applies only to one side of it, and that the stupidest and least popular side. They depend very largely on amusing plays and surprising plays. Except that Blanco Posnet is perhaps a little too long, it is exactly the sort of thing they want.

I will ask my American publisher (the Jew aforesaid) to send you copies of An Unsocial Socialist and Love Among the Artists, as they are both out of print here, and the American pirate editions are the only ones available; but do not neglect my later plays for these silly novels. Try in particular to get The Doctor's Dilemma ready for action. I will send you presently a copy of my play Misalliance just finished. I read it to the Company today and shall start rehearsing tomorrow. I must try to make some money. I am sorry to say that the warning I gave you as to the state of my finances has proved only too well-founded. I have sailed round the end of the year very close to the wind indeed; and unless I can reap some new harvests in London and America I shall have hardly any spare money until the income from my ordinary investments begins to accumulate a little again.

I have made a note of the translations and other documents that I am to return to you. I shall do my best; but until the 23rd February, which is the date fixed for the production of my play, my time will be almost completely taken up with rehearsals and the rest of the business connected with a theatrical production.

How does the question of the candidature progress? I strongly advise you not to gamble on a seat in the Chamber. Your chance of being elected is not strong enough to justify you in risking future burdens on your income. Naturally, the chance of 12,000 fr. a year is more than Henriette or any woman could resist; so do not be guided wholly by domestic embobinations.

yours ever
[unsigned]

P.S. 25.1.10 Since writing the above, two things have happened: I have sent you the preface to the Unpleasant Plays and I have received your letter containing the Dorbon agreement. . . . If the negotiation with Dorbon falls through, we shall have to wait until my finances begin to mend. Just at present I cannot afford to undertake publication at my own expense, either of the plays or of The Quintessence. Later on, I hope to be in funds again; but for the moment economy is the order of the day. . . .

Le Vrai Blanco Posnet does not strike me as quite the right title. You want something like Blanco Posnet Demasqué, or Dieu et Blanco Posnet.

That reminds me to warn you that in the Brieux Preface in the section on venereal disease where I use some such phrase as "to the third and fourth generation of them that buy her" I am quoting from the 2nd Commandment, which you will find in the 5th verse of the 20th Chapter of Exodus—"qui punis l'iniquité des pères sur les enfants, en la troisième et quatrième génération de ceux que me haïssent."

To ROBERT BRIDGES

10 Adelphi Terrace W C
[H/1]   4th February 1910

[Robert Bridges (1844–1930), who became Poet Laureate in 1913, had a life-long interest in philology and spelling reform. He and Shaw served together in later years on the Committee of English (1921), created by the Academic Committee of the Royal Society of Literature, and on the Advisory Committee on Spoken English formed by the B.B.C. in April 1926. William Archer, since September 1908, had been Secretary to the English Simplified Spelling Society, with an office in Great Russell Street underwritten by the Simplified Spelling Board, New York, with Carnegie funds.]

Dear Mr Bridges

It is very hard to say that there is a psychological moment for reforming spelling, or the calendar, or for adding those two digits to our numbers which would combine the advantages of the decimal and duodecimal methods of computation. It may be, however, that we have at last succeeded in making the anti-phonetic stupidity unfashionable. But I confess I am not very sanguine about it. The only people who have got any money in the business are those silly Simplified Spelling Americans, who have provided my friend William Archer with an office and a secretaryship in London. As far as I know, they are doing what in them lies to make the reform thoroughly unpopular and ridiculous.

I have been for a long time convinced that the two most important points to get into people's heads are, first, that unless phonetic spelling is carried out with sufficient boldness and thoroughness to make it quite unlike ordinary spelling and so avoid that ludicrous effect of being simply illiterate mis-spelling which was so comic in the works of Artemus Ward, the reform will die of ridicule; and, second, that if we do not spell words as they are pronounced, our readers will pronounce words as they are spelt; so that in the end we shall have a change in the English spoken language which is in no way desirable. On this second point in particular I blame the phoneticians for the lack of debating instinct which has prevented them from carrying the war into the enemy's country. The modern pronunciation of such words as 'oblige' proves that in the long run scholarly pronunciation cannot stand out against spelling. This has been especially forced on my attention by my intercourse, in labor and Socialist movements, with working men who read a great deal, but have no opportunity in their own class of hearing the words they read actually spoken. They therefore have to resort to such pronunciation as the spelling may suggest to them: for instance, semi-conscious becomes see-my-conscious. If this only led to their being laughed at, it would be painful and unjust; but it would not hurt the language. Unfortunately, it becomes accepted as the standard pronunciation with quite appalling rapidity, because if you and I persist in the orthodox pronunciation, we are simply not understood; just

896

as if you tell a London cabman to drive to A'rundel Street, he does not understand you, whereas if you tell him to drive to a Rundle Street, he understands you at once. Perhaps he is right: I really do not know what the proper pronunciation of Arundel is; but the illustration is none the worse.

An insistence on these points has been practically my only contribution to the movement. I do not know whether I was the first to urge them; but certainly in the old days of Alexander J. Ellis, and James Lecky, none of the men on our side made any use of them.

The man of that time I had most hopes of was Henry Sweet; but Sweet's utter want of any sort of social tact—sometimes even of common humanity—seems to make him hopeless except as a writer of books which are only read by specialists. At the time when Imperialism was booming, I induced the editor of one of the leading reviews to invite Sweet to write an article on the importance of phonetics as a means of not only making the English language easy to learn, but of preventing it from finally splitting up into dialects which would make American and Australian and South African and Eurasian practically foreign languages. Sweet jumped at the opportunity to make a terrific attack on an Oxford professor whom he regarded as an impostor from the phonetic point of view, on the University for giving the professor the appointment, and on the Universe generally for tolerating the University. The editor of course refused to print the article (which would probably have involved him in a libel action); and if Sweet ever writes another magazine article he will probably devote it to a similar denunciation of that editor, of that magazine, and, by extension, of the entire press of the world. I then tried to get a sort of Chair of Languages established at the London School of Economics; and if Sweet had been capable of following this up, and had been willing to shift his quarters to London, I believe I might have pulled it off. But Sweet has now got the Oxford habit of life in his antagonistic way just as hopelessly as any Don has got it in the conformist way; so nothing came of it.

What we want now is a phonetic institute of some kind or another, either independent, or as a branch of one of our great educational institutions. I believe the British Museum has already taken steps to procure and store for future reference phonographic records of contemporary speech. As a definite project which might strike the imagination of the country a little, I suggest a fund for the purpose of printing a phonetic Shakespear. It so happens that at this moment we have one actor, Forbes Robertson, who, being Scotch by extraction, speaks a

897

dignified, handsome, and what I should call correct English, and not the dialect of the motor car and the week-end hotel. If we could get some good gramophone records of speeches from Robertson's Shakespearian parts, and agree upon a method of recording his pronunciation in ordinary type, so as to make the book available for the use of actors and the public generally, we could employ some young man—say one of Sweet's pupils—to prepare a complete phonetic Shakespear. This, of course, would be a considerable job; but it has the advantage that if it were found too large an undertaking, it could be cut down to a selected number of plays, or even to one play: say Hamlet. I have sometimes thought of getting a gramophone record made of Robertson's delivery of the Sphinx speech in my own Caesar and Cleopatra, and proceeding as above to issue a phonetic edition of the play as a sort of document in the history of the language. But I have only time to imagine these things: when it comes to action, I find myself always with two years arrears of pressing literary work on my hands; and so nothing gets done. I daresay you are pretty much in the same predicament yourself. Until by some means we can get a little group of trained phoneticians who will put all their time into the work for a modest salary, nothing but talk will come of it.

I need hardly say that it would be very useful to make gramophone records of some of your poems, as spoken by yourself. The advantage of this sort of thing is that it gets rid of the entirely impossible and insoluble question as to whether your pronunciation is ideally correct, which is the rock that splits all the phonetic enterprises. If we could leave in the British Museum—failing a public institution specialized for phonetics—a record of your pronunciation, with a simple statement of your birthplace, and education, and class, and, if necessary, a string of testimonials from your contemporaries to say that your speech was that customary among educated Englishmen of your time, with any criticisms they liked to add, as, for instance, that you pronounced such and such words like a Kentish man, or that you had an Oxford drawl, or had inherited some locution from an Irish grandmother, or anything else that might strike them, the phoneticians of the 25th century would at any rate have something to go on that we have not got with regard to Shakespear or Chaucer. In the same way, all questions as to whether Robertson's pronunciation is correct could be set aside: the record would go down as Robertson's pronunciation for what it is worth, with of course the information that Robertson was accepted as the finest speaker on the English stage. If we had such a record of Garrick's pronunciation we should never dream of questioning its value simply because no twenty scholars of Garrick's time could have been induced to agree that his pronunciation was ideally correct.

I throw out these suggestions more or less at random. I do not exactly know what you propose that we should do, though I am tolerably certain that I shall not have time to do anything of it. But if you can plan a campaign with any sort of promise in it, I am game to give it my blessing and subscribe a few pounds towards paying for the executive part of the business.

Are you ever in London? Until the 23rd., when a play of mine is to be produced, I shall be in town rehearsing; and although this work makes my hours rather uncertain, I daresay we could manage to meet if you happen to come within reach of me within that time.

> yours faithfully
> G. Bernard Shaw

To VEDRENNE & BARKER

[H/4]

10 Adelphi Terrace WC
9th February 1910

Dear Sirs

With reference to the sum now standing to the credit of Messrs Vedrenne & Barker, as to the disposal of which you have consulted me, I am of opinion, as one of the firm's creditors, that it should be applied in the first instance to repaying the loans made by Mr. Granville Barker. I have been informed by Mr. Granville Barker that this arrangement would be convenient to him just now; and you may regard me as a consenting party to his immediate repayment.

> yours faithfully
> G. Bernard Shaw

To LEO TOLSTOY

[X/222.e; 223]

10 Adelphi Terrace WC
14th February 1910

[Count Leo Tolstoy (1828–1910), the great Russian writer and humanitarian, had first corresponded with Shaw in August 1908, after receiving Shaw's gift of an inscribed copy of *Man and Superman*. Tolstoy's letter of acknowledgment reflected an earnest, humourless view of life. "I particularly appreciate Don Juan's speeches in the Interlude," he told Shaw, and in *The Revolutionist's Handbook* "I am pleased by your attitude toward civilization and progress . . ." He chided Shaw, however, for his constant jesting, reminding him that "life is a great and serious affair," and that one "should not speak jestingly of such a subject as the purpose of human life, the causes of its perversion, and the evil that fills the life of humanity today." The questions raised in the play were of such importance, he insisted, that people like Shaw, who understand the evils of life so well and possess such brilliant literary talent, do more harm than good by treating the problems merely as "the subject of satire" (Archibald Henderson, *Bernard Shaw: Playboy and Prophet*, 1932).

Tolstoy's play *The Power of Darkness* (1889), in a translation by Louise and Aylmer Maude, had been produced by the Stage Society at the Royalty Theatre on 18th December 1904. In the preface to *Heartbreak House* (1919), Shaw acknowledged that he had been influenced also by Tolstoy's *The Fruits of Enlightenment* (1891).]

My dear Count Tolstoy

I send you herewith, through our friend Aylmer Maude, a copy of a little play called "The Shewing Up of Blanco Posnet." "Shewing up" is American slang for unmasking a hypocrite. In form it is a very crude melodrama, which might be played in a mining camp to the roughest audience.

It is, if I may say so, the sort of play that you do extraordinarily well. I remember nothing in the whole range of drama that fascinated me more than the old soldier in your "Powers of Darkness" (I do not know the Russian title: that is what we call it in England).

One of the things that struck me in that play was that the preaching of the pious old father, right as he was, could never be of any use—that it could only anger his son and rub the last grains of self-respect out of him. But what the pious and good father could not do the old rascal of a soldier did as if he was the voice of God. To me that scene where the two drunkards are wallowing in the straw, and the older rascal lifts the younger one above his cowardice and his selfishness, has an intensity of effect that no merely romantic scene could possibly attain; and in Blanco Posnet I have exploited in my own fashion this mine of dramatic material which you were the first to open up to modern playwrights.

I will not pretend that its mere theatrical effectiveness was the beginning and end of its attraction for me. I am not an "Art for Art's sake" man, and would not lift my finger to produce a work of art if I thought there was nothing more than that in it. But it has always been clear to me that the ordinary methods of inculcating honourable conduct are not merely failures, but—still worse—they actually drive all generous and imaginative persons into a dare-devil defiance of them. We are ashamed to be good boys at school, ashamed to be gentle and sympathetic instead of violent and revengeful, ashamed to confess that we are very timid animals instead of reckless idiots: in short, ashamed of everything that ought to be the basis of our self-respect.

All this is the fault of our way of teaching. We tell men to be good without giving them any better reason for it than the opinion of other men who are neither attractive to them nor respectful to them, and who, being much older, are to a great extent not only incomprehensible to them, but ridiculous.

Elder Daniels will never convert Blanco Posnet: on the contrary, he perverts him, because Blanco does not want to be like his brother; and I think the root reason why we do not do as our fathers advise us to do is that we none of us want to be like our fathers, the intention of the universe being that we shall be like God.

You will also see that my theology and my explanation of the existence of evil is expressed roughly by Blanco. To me God does not yet exist; but there is a creative force constantly struggling to evolve an executive organ of godlike knowledge and power: that is, to achieve omnipotence and omniscience; and every man and woman born is a fresh attempt to achieve this object.

The current theory that God already exists in perfection involves the belief that God deliberately created something lower than Himself when He might just as easily have created something equally perfect. That is a horrible belief: it could only have arisen among people whose notion of greatness is to be surrounded by inferior beings—like a Russian nobleman—and to enjoy the sense of superiority to them.

To my mind, unless we conceive God as engaged in a continual struggle to surpass Himself—as striving at every birth to make a better man than before, we are conceiving nothing better than an omnipotent snob.

Also we are compelled by the theory of God's already achieved perfection to make Him a devil as well as a god, because of the existence of evil. The god of love, if omnipotent and omniscient, must be the god of cancer and epilepsy as well. The great English poet William Blake concludes his poem "The Tiger" with the question:

Did He who made the lamb make thee?

Whoever admits that anything living is evil must either believe that

God is malignantly capable of creating evil, or else believe that God has made many mistakes in His attempts to make a perfect being. But if you believe, as I do, and as Blanco Posnet finally guesses, that the croup bacillus was an early attempt to create a higher being than anything achieved before that time, and that the only way to remedy the mistake was to create a still higher being, part of whose work must be the destruction of that bacillus, the existence of evil ceases to present any problem; and we come to understand that we are here to help God, to do His work, to remedy His old errors, to strive towards Godhead ourselves.

I put all this very roughly and hastily; but you will have no trouble in making out my meaning. It is all in Man and Superman; but expressed in another way—not in the way that an uneducated man can understand. You said that my manner in that book was not serious enough—that I made people laugh in my most earnest moments. But why should I not? Why should humour and laughter be excommunicated? Suppose the world were only one of God's jokes, would you work any the less to make it a good joke instead of a bad one?

yours sincerely
G. Bernard Shaw

[Tolstoy recorded the receipt of the letter in his diary on 15th April. Across the envelope he scribbled "Intelligent stupidities from Shaw" (*Last Diaries*, ed. Leon Stillman, 1960). On 9th May he replied to Shaw from his estate at Yasnaya Poliana:

"My dear Mr Bernard Shaw,

"I have received your play and your witty letter. I have read your play with pleasure. I am in full sympathy with its subject.

"Your remark that the preaching of righteousness has generally little influence on people and that young men regard as laudable that which is contrary to righteousness is quite correct. It does not however follow that such preaching is unnecessary. The reason of the failure is that those who preach do not fulfill what they preach, i.e. hypocrisy.

"I also cannot agree with what you call your theology. You enter into controversy with that in which no thinking person of our time believe[s] or can believe: with a God-creator. And yet you seem yourself to recognise a God who has got definite aims comprehensible to you . . .

"Concerning the rest of what you say about God and about evil I will repeat the words I said, as you write, about your 'Man and Superman,' namely that the problem about God and evil is too important to be spoken of in jest. And therefore I will tell you frankly that I received a very painful impression from the concluding words of your letter . . ." (Texas)]

902

To LENA ASHWELL

[C(two cards).u/4]

[10 Adelphi Terrace W C]

[Undated: assigned to 24th February 1910]

[Lena Ashwell had appeared in the bravura rôle of Lina Szczepanowska, the Polish aviatrix and acrobat, in *Misalliance*, which opened the previous evening at the Duke of York's Theatre. Her laconic comment in her autobiography (*Myself A Player*, 1927) concerning the rôle was: "The part in 'Misalliance' was small and hardly in my line . . ."]

The final blow was missing you last night after the performance. I wanted to see you again in the beautiful dress, and waited at the photographic affair until you had time to change. I waited too long: you were gone. I exclaimed bitterly "I have waited ten years for this; and she has not waited ten minutes." I hope you now understand the mystic meaning of all your lines, especially "the wicked lie of pretending to be somebody else." That is what you have been doing until this evening, when at last you could achieve the real miracle of our art and be yourself instead of that accidental fiction of christening & circumstances, Lena Ashwell. That is the secret of all my parts. . . .

To ARCHIBALD HENDERSON

[S/52]

[10 Adelphi Terrace W C]

8th March 1910

[Renée M. Deacon had just published a small book, *Bernard Shaw as Artist-Philosopher*, for which Charlotte Shaw had underwritten the costs.]

My dear Henderson

. . . Why are you in such a confounded hurry? You admit that it is only six years since you began the book: I told you it would take twenty-five. All the disappointment you have suffered has arisen from your rooted conviction that I always mean exactly the opposite of what I say. You cannot now publish the book until you have dealt with my last year's plays: indeed you will have to wait for some forthcoming publications of mine which are of great importance. You will also have to read the studies of Shaw by Chesterton, by Julius Bab, and by Miss Deacon. And you will have to get older and wiser; so that the book will be improving every year.

We can discuss the matter further when we meet. Meanwhile, do not be discouraged, and do not inflate yourself with delusions concerning the Celtic temperament and tosh of that sort. You must remember that if you have to write the life, I have to live it; and whilst time persists in going sixty minutes to the hour, it is not physically possible to hurry me up.

yours ever

G. Bernard Shaw

To LUCY CARR SHAW

[FF/2]

[10 Adelphi Terrace WC]
9th March 1910

[Lucy had asked Shaw to give further assistance to a cousin J.C. Shaw (known as "Kaffir"), to whom he had already lent £1200 to buy a house in Dublin.]

. . . [A]part from the merits of the case, I must wash my hands of Kaffir. I cannot afford the time for these philanthropic affairs. If it were a mere question of giving money, it would be bad enough; but the letters and the interviews and the interruptions that these things involve waste my time and energy to an intolerable extent; and now that I have got over those first stages of an enlarged income in which one has money to spare simply because one has not yet had time to bring the whole income into effective employment, I am compelled to be quite ruthless in pushing off all the human wreckage which daily tries to attach itself to me.

I can find money for you as soon as you want it; so you need not trouble about that. I was speaking of *spare* money, which is another matter.

As to the women's societies, I have explained to them all, over and over and over again, that I am not going to speak for them. My views on the subject are perfectly well known, and at all my lectures, when I dont myself introduce the subject, it is always possible to extract an utterance from me by means of a question. The Fabian Society gives me as much work on the platform as I can possibly do; and if I were to listen for a moment to the demands of the Institute of Financiers, the Institute of Phoneticians, the vegetarians, the suffragists and all the other people who imagine I have nothing else to do [but] to campaign for them, I should be a dead man in three months. The thing to grasp about me is that I am full up, and that to my life's end I shall be throwing things overboard to lighten the ship instead of taking on fresh

904

cargo. This also applies to my income. When people try to get at me through you, you must try and impress this on them; for the plague of my life is having to write letters to say that I cannot do things.

[GBS]

To LENA ASHWELL

10 Adelphi Terrace W C

[H/4] 11th March 1910

Dear Lena Ashwell

I indulged in the luxury of a peep at you at the matinée yesterday. I had in my box W.B. Yeats who, being a poet, occasionally says the right thing. At the end of the 2nd Act he said "That is what is so extremely rare: *beautiful gaiety*." So you see it is not quite completely a secret between you and me. There is something pathetic about the bewilderment of the audience at that point. They have had it so hammered into them for years that a scene like that and a dress like that mean coarse gaiety ... that they hardly know where they are when they find something lovely has passed by them. But we will clean up their minds after a while; and you shall spend the rest of your life in beautiful gaiety, and hear no more of Mrs Dane and all those other dreadful Mrs'es which foolish people classify as Lena Ashwell parts....

yours ever

G. Bernard Shaw

To ARTHUR W. PINERO

10 Adelphi Terrace W C

[H/4] 14th March 1910

[During the seventeen-week existence of the Frohman repertory season, John Galsworthy's *Justice* received 26 performances, as against 11 for *Misalliance* and 10 for Barker's *The Madras House*. However, Barrie's short play *The Twelve-Pound Look*, on three different bills, accumulated 25 performances, and Pinero's *Trelawny of the 'Wells,'* added to the bill on 5th April, topped all the rest with 42 performances.]

My dear Pinero

A word of warning. At the Duke of York's, Galsworthy's play, Justice, has caught on, and is driving everything else out of the bill. In

those three weeks Barrie and I between us are having only five performances to its eleven; and presently we shall be out of the bill altogether until Justice is exhausted. Better hold back Trelawney until
Justice, which is now drawing over £200 a night, drops to about half
that figure. You need not hesitate to face the competition of Misalliance,
which has now, after its first gathering in of the devotees, settled down
to a steady £80 or thereabouts; and I gather that Barrie is in an even
more deplorable condition. Barker will be in the same fix presently. If
Trelawney is as successful as Justice, you and Galsworthy can divide
the Repertory Theatre between you, with no greater disadvantage than
the spreading of your fees over double the time that exclusive possession
would require; but suppose you only draw, say, £150 a night, then
Frohman would lose £50 every time he put Trelawney in the bill
instead of Justice; and this would put a strain on him which he is not
bound to bear. Therefore it would be well for you to consider the
advisability of stipulating for a certain number of performances within
a certain time, with perhaps a loop-hole for Frohman in the event of
your average of seats dropping to [a] figure at which you could not
reasonably exact the entire pound of flesh. However, you know how to
take care of yourself: I interfere only to let you know about Justice.

I am asking Frohman to lunch here on Thursday. Would you care to
come with Lady Pinero and meet him. If not, what about Friday? Is
there anybody I know whom you would like to meet? Our establishment is modest; but the parlormaid can tackle an extra guest or two on
occasion.

yours ever

G. Bernard Shaw

To AUGUST STRINDBERG

[H/54]
10 Adelphi Terrace W C
16th March 1910

[Frederic Herbert Trench (1865–1923), a poet and dramatist, had entered
into management at the Haymarket Theatre in September 1909. W.
Graham Robertson's *Pinkie and the Fairies*, with music by Frederick Norton,
was presented at His Majesty's Theatre on 19th December 1908. Maeterlinck's *The Blue Bird* was first presented at the Haymarket Theatre on 8th
December 1909; it was revived in December 1910. *Lycko-Pers resa* (*Lucky
Peter's Travels*), written in 1882, was not produced by Tree. *Fröken Julie*

(*Miss Julie*), written in 1888, was first presented in London in 1912 by the Adelphi Play Society, in a translation by Maurice Elvey and Lucy Carr Shaw. Strindberg had founded the Intima Teatern, Stockholm, in 1907 for the production of his plays. Frederick Whelen's efforts to produce Strauss's *Salome* were unsuccessful.]

My dear Strindberg

Since we met in Stockholm in 1909 a few things have happened which may have the effect of rescuing England from its present condition of darkness concerning your works. 1. Vallentin has come to live in London; and Vallentin is the perfect modern Jew, devoted, intelligent, friendly, loyal, with no fault except excessive sentimentality—in short, everything that a Jew, according to Christian tradition, cannot and should not be. At all events, that is what Vallentin is to me—no doubt because he likes me and likes Charlotte (Charlotte is my wife, whom you may remember); and since you were kind to him in connection with our visit to you, he now includes us all in his circle of sympathy. You may trust Vallentin.

In the theatre things have also altered for the better. Last year Herbert Trench, a poet who had made a considerable reputation by a really remarkable poem called Apollo and the Seaman, was entrusted with a large sum of money by two rich patrons of the arts to found a theatre for the production of plays of literary excellence. As he knew nothing of the traditions of the theatre, he was expected to fail ignominiously. You will not be surprised to hear that what actually happened was that he was exceptionally successful. His greatest commercial triumph has been his production of Maeterlinck's Blue Bird. He was more envied for this than for any other of his exploits, for reasons which concern you.

Let me explain. A few years ago, one of our most popular authors, J. M. Barrie, wrote a sort of fairy play for children called Peter Pan, which had such an enormous success that it has since been revived every Christmas, ostensibly as a holiday entertainment for children, but really as a play for grown-up people; for, as you know, when we buy toys for children, we take care to select the ones which amuse ourselves. Ever since this happened it has been the dream of every London manager to find another Peter Pan. Sir Herbert Beerbohm Tree, the manager of His Majesty's Theatre, had one manufactured for him. It was called Pinkie and the Fairies, and was successful at its first production; but an attempt to revive it on the following Christmas shewed that its attractions were exhausted. Then came the success of the Blue Bird, which Herbert Trench now expects to revive every

Christmas as successfully as Peter Pan. Meanwhile Tree with Pinkie and the Fairies languishing on his hands is desperately anxious to find another piece like The Blue Bird.

Now you will begin to see what I am driving at. Tree knows that among your early plays is one called Lycko Per; and he also knows that there is only one name that strikes the European imagination more than Maeterlinck, and that is Strindberg. Why not let him have the play? Your later pieces are quite impossible at his theatre; not because it is a very big one (for I still contend, in spite of all you say, that your Intimes Teater is far too small even for Fröken Julie, and that nothing smaller than the Opera House is big enough for you); but because his theatre is a favorite with the innocent bourgeoisie and their daughters, who would fly horror-stricken at the very first [moment] of Julie. There is, however, attached to His Majesty's Theatre an enterprise called the Afternoon Theatre, appealing to the sort of people who come to your Intimes Teater; and this Afternoon Theatre might very well handle one of your later works. In any case, the man who directs this Afternoon Theatre for Tree is a certain Frederick Whelen, who is also Chairman of the Stage Society (which has produced Ibsen, Brieux, Tolstoi etc.), and who is now organizing a Society for the performance of Strauss's Salome, forbidden here by the Censor. It is really Whelen who has worked Tree up to the pitch of believing that he must have Lycko Per or die. Apart from the fact that the production of Lycko Per might be pecuniarily useful to you, it would bring you into relations with Whelen, who would go to Stockholm by the next train if he thought you would entertain Tree's proposal.

Unfortunately, there are the usual impossible reports. It is said that you absolutely refuse to discuss Lycko Per because it is an early play—that you would fall on Whelen with fire and sword—in short, all the old Strindberg legends which circulate here just as they do in Stockholm, in spite of my wife's assurances to everybody that you are a most friendly man, with memorable dark blue eyes and an appealing smile. As a matter of fact, it is necessary to keep a touch of brimstone for some people; and there are circumstances under which I should resent a proposal to begin a Strindberg campaign with Lycko Per as a declaration of cowardice to start with. But this consideration does not arise in Tree's case. He really does specifically need a play like Lycko Per for the purposes of his theatre; and nobody expects him to handle your later works there. It would be thoroughly understood that Lycko Per was your Midsummer Night's Dream and not your Hamlet; and the mere discussion and reiteration of this fact would create a good deal of

908

curiosity to see your Hamlet in London. I therefore venture to advise
you to consider the matter carefully and, if possible, favorably. I think
it would be worth your while to enter into pourparlers on the subject—
even if nothing came of it—for the sake of getting into communication
with Whelen, who is at present much more likely to bring about a
production of your later work than any other man in London; for the
recently established Repertory Theatre of Charles Frohman has decided,
for the present at least, to confine itself to works by English writers;
and Herbert Trench, though as a poet and man of letters he understands your position and the importance of your work, is just at present
too busy making money and enjoying the novelty of having proved
himself a successful man of affairs, to attempt anything more than a
comparatively mild sort of pioneering.

Excuse the length of this letter. If I had time I would pay another
visit to Stockholm and tell you all this by word of mouth; but as it is, I
must content myself this Easter with a modest trip in France.

yours ever
G. Bernard Shaw

To ARTHUR W. PINERO

10 Adelphi Terrace WC
17th March 1910

[H/4]

[Gilbert Cannan (1884–1955), who was parodied as Gunn in *Fanny's First
Play* (1911), was at this time the drama critic for *The Star*. He had
recently run off with Barrie's wife.]

My dear Pinero

Right oh! That is the situation to a T. So long as you know that we
are all throwing our plays into the dust destructor to stoke up the
Repertory Theatre idea which finally means a National Theatre in
which they will not perform any of our plays, there is nothing more to
be said except grin and bear it. I do think, however, that you are being
half a trifle more reckless than we are, because Trelawney is quite likely
to be a real money maker. . . .

I made a disgraceful scene at the Club yesterday. They drank the
health of the institution with melting pathos; and I promptly cut in
and said that in the course of the year I had never blackballed a single
candidate who had been proposed; and that every candidate whom I

had proposed had been blackballed; that therefore I had quite given up the idea of proposing any further candidates; and that I did not consider this a healthy state of mind for any member of the Club to be in. This produced the desired effect with appalling promptitude. Wild recriminations arose on all sides; and I fomented the excitement by citing the cases of Hankin, Hall Caine, and Gilbert Murray. All sorts of reasons why these candidates should not have been elected were presently hurtling through the air. Hall Caine was a self-advertiser; Conan Doyle had written a pamphlet against him fifteen years ago and would not come to lunches if he came; he was unclubbable; he would go about declaring that he belonged to the Dramatists' Club and speaking in its name &c, &c. Gilbert Murray was not a dramatist; he had never written anything; he was no doubt a most desirable and excellent man in his proper place; but that proper place was not a club of dramatists with established reputations. Sutro, in a transport of friendly self-control, first tried to reason with me, and finally declared that he did not regret anything that he had done and would continue to blackball everybody and everything that could possibly be suggested by anybody in the universe. I insinuated that members of the Club simply blackballed everybody except their own pals on purely private, personal, and sentimental grounds; and I demanded that if sentiment was to be the rule, I should have my share of it, and that members should reflect that if they blackball any of my nominees or refuse to do anything that I want they are placing a personal affront and outrage on myself. Grundy then rushed into the fray and declared that I was making the most monstrous claims to have my personal feelings set up above the best interests of the Club. In the end I got more than I bargained for, as thus. Barrie was not present at the lunch; and I had carefully noted this fact. When the discussion was at its hottest and was turning on the point of how far members were justified in letting themselves be influenced by personal motives in blackballing, I said, by way of illustration, that if Gilbert Cannan were proposed as a member I should certainly blackball him unless he were proposed by Barrie himself. Having fired this off with some more soothing rhetoric of the same description, I happened to look round, and found that Barrie had just come in and had heard everything I had said. Of course it really did not matter, as Barrie and I are good friends, and he knew that I had not seen him come in; but it gave me a ghastly shock for the moment. I then had to go off to the annual meeting of the Society of Authors with Hawkins, leaving the turmoil to assuage itself as best it could. On the whole, I was pretty well satisfied. It has been evident for some time that our process of recruiting was coming to be a declaration by Raleigh or somebody else that So and So was a good chap and one of his friends and did we object to his being invited to become a member, to which we have always assented. On the other hand, whenever we have proposed a man on purely public grounds, the other chaps have demurred quite obviously from no other reason than that they did not know him and felt uncomfortable with strangers. Another year of that, and the Club would be a mere clique of cronies; and we should have to secede and form a Superdramatists' Club with strenuous rites of initiation.

Tell Lady Pinero that I refuse to sympathize with her cold until she comes to see me; but with that in view, I recognize the importance of her taking care of herself.

In haste,
yours ever
G.B.S.

PS. Today I was in the hands of Dr Anders Ryman, a Swede who works the Swedish massage system in his practice with more success, apparently, than anybody else. I pumped him on the question of pleurisy. He says he is at loggerheads with his profession as to its treatment, but that he has done so well with his patients that he is sure he is right. He says he cant support the orthodox treatment because it doesnt get rid of the pleurisy. As you know, I have no delusions about the medical priesthood; but Anders Ryman really does things— mostly with his thumbs. . . .

To ARTHUR W. PINERO

10 Adelphi Terrace W C
21st March 1910

[H/4]

[Ashley Dukes (1885–1959), a dramatic critic on various journals 1909–14, became a successful playwright and translator, best known for *The Man with a Load of Mischief* (1924). Shaw's "shocking attack" on Hall Caine was a review of Wilson Barrett's stage adaptation of Caine's *The Manxman*, in the *Saturday Review* on 23rd November 1895.]

My dear Pinero

The despatch was not explicit enough: my feelings were not wounded, as you rightly divine; but I am prepared to put up that game without a blush if the other side refuses to take public ground.

Apparently Murray's case was the worst; but I do not attach any real importance to it except for debating purposes, because it was the effect of sheer ignorance; and they will presently find this out.

To me the serious case was that of Hankin, because all the young men whom we must enlist in the future are doing exactly what Hankin did. I speak feelingly, for I have superseded you of late as the whipping boy of the youthful educator of the public in the higher drama. Hankin swore by me and went for you. Arnold Bennett went for you but did not exactly swear by me. But now the still younger generation knocking at the door knocks on my nose. Gilbert Cannan (who, when he heard that I opposed the performance of his first play [*Dull Monotony*, 1909] by the Stage Society, exclaimed "Christ betraying Judas!"), Ashley Dukes and Co now damn me beneath Tom Taylor. It is the latest note. Some of them swear by Barker: others hint that he is my natural son; but most of them reject this hypothesis on the ground that I am physically incapable of parentage. Even Max [Beerbohm], always with the youngest, proclaims that he can no longer support me. Now it is no use saying that there is a way of doing these things nicely. No young man worth his salt ever gives any quarter in his fight for a higher life, as he conceives it. They all see themselves as Wagner, and see the man who has arrived as Meyerbeer. The defence is as savage as the attack. Ever since Clement Scott, in the Ibsen campaign, called Archer and myself "muck ferretting dogs," the best criticism has accounted for what it does not like by alleging infamous deficiencies in character on the part of the playwright. And as the playwright of today begins as a journalist, and often as a pamphleteer and agitator (I set that fashion—after Wagner) he has opportunities of letting out which were not so common in the previous generation.

The moral is that if we blackball for conduct like Hankin's, we shall blackball all the men of the rising generation who have any ginger in them, and become a hopeless old gang.

My policy is to pick up my recruits on the battle field, carefully choosing those who have hit me hardest. We shall have plenty of fighting to do; and our dear good fellows whom nobody objects to are no good for that.

Besides, half the dislike that leads to blackballing comes from men not knowing one another. Hankin was far too conceited a man—far too colossal and avowed a snob—to have envied anybody. He was quite a good fellow, and was sincerely concerned when his bad manners were pointed out to him. His death was taken straight out of Ibsen's Ghosts. His father had gone wrong in his health and become a useless and wretched burden to everybody. Hankin got his father's symptoms and found his power to work failing. He was so afraid that if he did not act at once he would lose the nerve to do it and come on his wife's hands as an incurable invalid that he made a hole in the water. Nobody but a very nice man could have written the charming letter he left her.

Hall Caine takes himself and his work, and consequently takes us and our work, very seriously; but that is why I rather want to have him. You and I and Carton are at the mercy of a good joke, or even a bad one. Our dignity is a laborious assumption: our pockets are stuffed with sausages and we have red hot pokers always in the fire; but H.C. is the real thing: he can keep a joke in its place when he recognizes it at all. As to his clubability, all I can say is that years ago I wrote a shocking attack on him, beginning "Who is Hall Caine?" which is quoted, to my great shame and grief, to this day. He wrote me a quite nice and human remonstrance; and I replied with infernal brutality. But when we met afterwards, he never betrayed the slightest feeling about it: he treated me with the frankest friendliness; and I was jolly glad to make amends later on by writing a preface for him when everybody attacked him for standing up for the Egyptians. How many of our colleagues in the Club would be so clubbable as that?

However, as I said before, the case to moralize on is the Hankin case. If we boycott the young chaps who attack us, we shall find that we have boycotted the choice and master spirits of the age; for they all begin like that.

Do not answer. It encourages me to write, which is bad for both of us ...

yours ever
G.B.S.

To AUGUSTIN HAMON

[H/1]

10 Adelphi Terrace WC
21st March 1910

[Vicomte François de Curel (1854–1928) was a French playwright, known best at this time for *La Fille sauvage* (1902). Jean-Louis Janvier, a well-known character actor, played Crofts in the Paris production of *Mrs Warren's Profession* in 1912. Antonio Agresti's translation of *Arms and the Man* (*L'Eroe*) was presented at the Argentine Theatre, Rome, in March 1909. It proved to be a poor choice, for in Italy it was interpreted as a political manifesto of sympathy with Austria.]

My dear Hamon

When Brieux returns, please make it clear to him that he need not have the slightest delicacy about doing exactly what he likes with that preface of mine. There must be some things in it which are not quite right as matters of fact; and there may possibly be some expressions of opinion which may jar on him. At all events, beg him to treat me as a friend to the extent of making as free with my preface as he would with one of his own. He need not take my susceptibilities into account; for I have not got any.

The discovery of a new version of Maternité was a fearful blow to my wife, as her version is already set up and stereotyped; however, there is nothing to be done but make the alterations and have the type reset. . . .

You will find that I am right as to Brieux's position in French literature. De Curel and the other men you mention are all very well in their way; but if you consider a moment, you will recognize two facts: 1, that what you call their superiority to Brieux can be exactly parallelled by the superiority of about a dozen novelists of the seventies and eighties to Zola, and, 2, by the superiority of our friend M. le Vicomte D'Humières to yourself. Zola was vulgar; Zola had no humor; Zola had no style. Yet he was head and shoulders above contemporaries of his who had refinement, wit, and style to a quite exquisite degree. The truth is that what determines a writer's greatness is neither his accomplishments nor the number of things he knows by learning or observation; but solely his power of perceiving the relative importance of things. The men who do not possess this power are always protesting against the reputation of the men who have it. Take Karl Marx as an example familiar to both of us. Anybody could demonstrate that Karl Marx was wrong in his theory of value; that his mathematical knowledge was a pretence; that he made an enormous parade of references to a great mass of books and pamphlets, some of which he had read and others grossly misunderstood; that he had no idea of what a workman was actually like or what a capitalist was actually like; that the erudition which he paraded only imposed on uneducated people; that he could not bear to admit the slightest merit in any of his rivals: in short, that he had a mass of failings of which any commonplace Sorbonne professor would have been ashamed. All that, though perfectly true, does not alter the fact that Marx was by far the greatest economist of his time, because he saw the importance of the industrial revolution, and stated in the Communist Manifesto a string of great generalizations which the ordinary Sorbonne professor not only did not see the importance of, but did not see at all. What is more, when the Sorbonne professor read them he still did not see that they were of any importance; and consequently he could not understand why he and his immaculate little treatises should die obscure while Marx should become a sort of European portent. Now, if you apply this to Brieux, or to yourself, you will begin to understand things. You inherited from your father a sense of the importance of block-tin piping. Other people could not see that it was any better than lead piping. Later on, you perceived the importance of the psychology of militarism and of my plays, and certain other important matters. M. le Vicomte D'Humières thereupon observes that you are no gentleman. It is not necessary to dispute the fact: geniuses cannot be confined within the limits of the gentlemanly. But when you hear people cackling about the deficiencies of Brieux, remember D'Humières and remember Karl Marx and Proudhon and all the other people whose reputations so puzzled the academic and elegant world. Brieux knows what is important and what is not: the other fellows do not; and that is what finally settles the matter.

Next week I shall go for a tour in France. My present intention is to make for the Pyrenees. How long do you remain in Paris? I shall carefully avoid passing through Paris on my way south; but I might pass near Ty an Diaoul on my way back and have a look at it and you if you are not still in Paris.

If anything is likely to come of Janvier's proposal, tell Antoine about it. However much he may dislike Janvier he cannot reasonably object unless he makes an alternative proposal to you himself; but I think we owe it to him to give him the chance of doing so. I do not much believe in beginning with Arms and the Man. Of all my plays, it is the one that most fatally encourages all sorts of wrong ideas about me, and that is most difficult to cast satisfactorily. Its production in Italy, where it was positively hissed off the stage, was partly due to the gross stupidity of the management in producing it at the moment when Italian feeling was excited on the Balkan question; but the fiasco was also to some extent due to the fact that the actors did not understand it and that it was not a suitable play to begin with.

yours ever
G. Bernard Shaw

To ROBERT BRIDGES

[H/1]

10 Adelphi Terrace WC
24th March 1910

[When Miriam Lewes withdrew from *Misalliance* to replace the ailing Julia Neilson in William Devereux's *Henry of Navarre*, the rôle of Hypatia was undertaken by Mona Limerick. Bridges had sent Shaw a copy of his essay "On the Present State of English Pronunciation," which was published later in the year in *Essays and Studies by Members of the English Association*. Helen Taylor (1831–1907) was a social reformer and advocate of women's rights.]

Dear Mr Bridges

I am sorry to say that I did not get my play off my hands as soon as I expected. After my production, when I thought I was through with the thing for good, Miss Julia Neilson got ill; and though she was not in my cast, the only lady who could take her place was; so I had to change and undertake a fresh set of rehearsals. What with that and other things, correspondence has been out of the question; and I am now off to the south of France for a month's holiday to set me up again after a winter into which I have had to crowd a year's work.

I think the new script very promising. It is extremely difficult to persuade the average inartistic person that the most important thing about a script is that it should look well. It is the last thing that ordinary spelling reformers ever think of; and the fact that you begin with it impresses me considerably. I have not time to study it critically. The only two things that I feel inclined to protest against are the apostrophe in the word Heaven and the spelling of the word Father with the ordinary th, which gives no clue to the pronunciation.

The apostrophes I object to because they are so horribly ugly. Why not spell heaven frankly hevn. I always spell hav'nt havnt without any apostrophe.

As to father, my own father had a habit of jocularly pronouncing father fat her and Stephen step hen and so on; and, as you know, it is quite hopeless to expect the proper pronunciation of Lewis-ham, Elt-ham, and Cars-halton to be preserved in spite of the spelling. It therefore seems to me that any phonetic script which does not provide special characters for sh, th, etc., fails in the most obvious instance for the need for it.

I should like to let you persuade me that I am nice enough in my speech to pronounce the i in nation, attention, Russian, etc; but the flat truth is that I say nayshun. The late Helen Taylor went so far as to say Russy-an, Prussy-an; so I suppose I ought at least to say Rushy-an and Prusshy-an; but I am prevented by vivid recollections of the difficulty with which I prevented myself from throwing things at Helen when she talked like this. Still, there is no reason why, if we can get phonetics fairly started, we should not use them to improve pronunciation, not, of course, on any academic grounds as to this or that pronunciation being right or wrong, but solely on artistic grounds. If you are justified in redesigning a script so as to make a word look better, you are equally justified in redesigning the pronunciation so as to make it sound better.

Avoid accents if you can: they are just as bad as apostrophes. You simply cannot make a page of type look decent if it is peppered over with them.

I retain the printed slips and return the MS., which looks very nice.

yours faithfully
G. Bernard Shaw

To AUGUST STRINDBERG

10 Adelphi Terrace WC
29th March 1910

[H/54]

[Since virtually none of Strindberg's plays had yet been translated into English, they were known to Shaw only through their German translations. *Svarta handsken* (*The Black Glove*), a verse fantasy, was published in 1909. The other plays mentioned by Shaw are *Totentanz* (*The Dance of Death*), from *Dödsdansen* (1901); *Die Kronbraut* (*The Bridal Crown*), from *Kronbruden* (1902); and *Vater* (*The Father*), from *Fadren* (1887).]

My dear Strindberg

If Lycko Per is what you describe it to be, you must have been inspired directly by heaven to write it for the satisfaction and delight of the British public. It will suit Sir Herbert Tree exactly, as his theatre is so big and expensive that he must give the public what it wants or perish.

It seems to me that the best thing you can do is to let Tree have Lycko Per on condition that it is not to be produced until he has performed Svarta Handsken, or whatever other play you may select, at the Afternoon Theatre, the position of which I explained to you in my last letter.

Unfortunately I cannot read Swedish; but I see that a good deal of

Svarta Handsken is in verse. This is a terrible difficulty. We have only one English writer for the stage who can turn foreign poetry into English poetry; and that is Gilbert Murray, who cares for nobody but Euripides. If Totentanz and Kronenbraut are in prose, perhaps it might be better to suggest them. I purposely leave out Vater, because somehow or other that nurse with the strait-waistcoat got on the nerves of London about twenty years ago; and ever since that people persist in talking as if you had written but one play, The Father Eternal. That, by the way, is another reason for letting them see Lycko Per in the fulness of time. It will help them to realize that you are not a man with only one plane.

I am just starting for the South of France for a month; but I shall send a copy of your letter and of this letter to Frederick Whelen, asking him to communicate with you if he can offer you a combined contract for Lycko Per with a prior production of a play to be chosen by yourself.

William Archer, the translator of Ibsen, might be persuaded to tackle Svarta Handsken. He would make a better job of the verse than most other translators.

yours sincerely
G. Bernard Shaw

To HARLEY GRANVILLE BARKER

Hotel du Palais. [Bordeaux]

[C(four cards)/3]   1st April 1910

[The Shaws and Mary Cholmondeley departed for France by automobile on 30th March, their itinerary including Boulogne, Bordeaux, Rouen, Bayonne, Biarritz, Perpignon, Toulouse (where Charlotte and her sister abandoned the tour), Carcassone, Tulle, Chartres, Beauvais, and Amiens. Shaw and his chauffeur returned to London on 2nd May. Lillah McCarthy did not perform in any of the plays in the Frohman repertory season.]

Charlotte's longing for warmth & sunshine has produced the usual results. We have only had two snowstorms so far; but such a devil of an east wind has never blown as has raged today. At Le Mans (where the cathedral is a whopper) we were only 3 degrees above freezing in the sunshine. The roads present straight switchbacks right away to the horizon; and slow & solid as our respectable car is I have rushed her up to 44 miles an hour. But the wind makes the waggoners wrap their heads in hoods & hide under tents; so that in spite of the grunts of the horn & opening the cut-out with volleys of shattering explosions, they hear nothing & check the car almost every time.

Charlotte requests that some of these cards be placed to her credit: she will send some herself (that is: addressed by herself) presently.

In spite of furious driving & couriering, I am already twice the man I was when I left.

How is Lillah getting on? Will she have made her first appearance at the Repertory before I return? Or will there be any Repertory left then?

Do not utterly neglect the Dramatists Club during my absence. It needs nursing.

The only address I can give you ahead is Grand Hotel & Hotel du Commerce (the two are one) Bayonne, 21 Rue Thiers. We shall probably stay a couple of days there, arriving on Monday evening the 4th.

GBS

To HARLEY GRANVILLE BARKER

[C/3]

Bayonne
5th April 1910. Wet day

... We have carried out our program & done 660 miles in 5½ days in snow, sleet, east wind, and rain. These splendid French roads are all very well; but I am rather fed up with tearing along keeping her nose in the centre of the stage & going for all she is worth, not to mention the appalling wear & tear of the tyres. There is something to be said for the Hertfordshire lanes after all.

We shall stay here for a day or two to get our clothes washed.

G.B.S.

To HARLEY GRANVILLE BARKER

[C(three cards)/1]

Hotel Marnau. Tarbes
Sunday. 10th April 1910

[Charlotte had become ill several days earlier at the Hotel Grand, Bayonne. Before leaving London, Shaw had gone to the Palace Theatre to see Mlle Emilie Polaire (1880–1939), a French dancer and singer in variety, who billed herself as "the ugliest woman in the world."]

919

On Friday Charlotte's temperature was so unyielding and her condition so moribund that I had to take serious measures, as Mrs Chumly was anxious to call in a doctor and the landlady was becoming suspicious. So I fell on Charlotte with my fists in the most violent Swedish manner, and in spite of her protests that she could not bear to be touched, pummeled her and thumped her and banged her and kneaded her and wobbled her and rolled her about from head to foot with such miraculous effect that her temperature fell half a degree in ten minutes and Mrs C came back to find her remonstrating in a voice of thunder though she had left her moaning & hopeless quarter of an hour before. Next morning she was normal; so I put her into the car & rattled her off to St Jean de Luz & Biarritz to see how she could stand it. The result was quite satisfactory; so we struck camp this morning & left Bayonne for ever. I shall go to St Girons tomorrow, Perpignan next day, and Ax les Thermes (Hotel de France) on the 13th; Hotel de la Post, Bagnères de Luchon on the 14th; Hotel des Voyageurs, Gavarnie, on the 15th; Hotel de France, Auch, on the 16th; & Hotel du Grand St Antoine, Albi, on the 17th are safe dates: that is, I shall certainly not be there earlier, though I may later if we decide to stay for more than a day at any of them for rest or laundry or the like. The weather cleared up today; and it looks as if the tour was going to be good for a week or so.

Before we left London we went to the Palace & saw La Whatshername, who was only a catchpenny; but one La Pia tried some interesting experiments by pretending to swim in cinematographed waves & using lantern slides for scenery *and dresses*. Technically quite worth seeing.

G.B.S.

To HARLEY GRANVILLE BARKER

[C(two cards)/1]

[Bourg Madame]
[Undated: assigned to 14th April 1910]

[*Prunella* was revived by Charles Frohman at the Duke of York's Theatre on 13th April.]

We had a rebuff yesterday—travelled all day, and at nightfall were stopped by the snow on the Col Puymorens within 20 miles of our destination. We had to turn back, & immediately went over a big stone in the dusk & smashed our tray. The edges of the fracture caught the flywheel; and we went back down the valley making a most horrible clanking. We had to put up at a little inn at Bourg Madame, a frontier village, with France on this side of the bridge & Spain on the other. It is primitive; but almost painfully clean. Today it rains; & Kilsby is banging the tray into shape. We shall get away at one, perhaps, and try another pass, which a carter claims to have got over. Failing that, we shall have to go back almost to the Mediterranean. The scenery here is magnificent, stupendous valleys & gorges, with snowy summits on the back cloth; but we are quite light headed with the perpetual journeying. When we at last get to Ax—if we ever do—there will be a general strike against further motoring. I drive half the day; lie deliriously awake half the night; and am visibly waning towards my grave.

Possibly I shall hear from you at Ax. I have seen no papers, and havnt a notion of what is happening. Are Madras & Miss Alliance ever played now? Is Prunella out? and, if so, has she revived well? What about Trelawny.

G.B.S.

To HARLEY GRANVILLE BARKER

[Quillan]

[C/1]   [Undated: assigned to 16th April 1910]

Two more assaults on Ax have failed at the final peak. As my spirits rise at each rebuff, and the tempers of the ladies are affected in the same way, the situation becomes very strained at moments. There is a tendency to attribute to me the acts of God—as if *I* made the snow expressly to baffle & annoy my fellow travellers. Further excitement is provided by the institution of *vin compris* at meals. Kilsby partakes of the wine of the country at lunch; and when he starts immediately afterwards on mountain roads rushing corners on his wrong side & explaining cheerfully that he feels as if he could drive through anything, the effect is all that could be desired. For three days we have led the lives of lost dogs; and our behaviour to one another shews it.

G.B.S.

To HARLEY GRANVILLE BARKER

[C(two cards)/3]

Massat
17th April 1910

Picture this scene [a stable built of stone at Col de Port (1249m) in the Pyrénées Ariégeoises] snowclad, with real hailstorms, at the summit of a stupendous mountain; and you will faintly imagine what we have just climbed over. When I say "we," I mean Kilsby & myself. Last night we at last achieved Ax. It was very cold, the hotel was hardly open, the baths closed, the season not yet begun, & the place second rate. Charlotte abandoned all semblance of good humor; tried to make herself ill (fortunately in vain); abused me; snubbed the landlady; worried the servants; refused the food; repudiated her room & got another with a cheminé (which smoked); declared that all her life she had hated & loathed being shut in by mountains; made it clear that she also hated & loathed me; and finally went to bed resolved to wake up with a raging temperature, the victim of a deliberate conspiracy to kill her. On waking up in obviously rude health she was so infuriated that she went off by train to Toulouse, carrying off Mrs Chum (who has really had a rather bad time with her asthma) leaving me to complete my Pyrenean program with Kilsby & the car. Her last act was—on being requested to pay a few sous for the registration of her luggage—to put down a 20 franc piece & to insist on change (absorbing the whole currency of the town) which the wretched official in his nervousness was wholly unable to count. No letters from you at Ax.

G.B.S.

To LENA ASHWELL

[C(three cards)/4]

Tulle (which I find is a place, not a material)
24th April 1910

[Mona Limerick (c. 1882–1968), the wife of B. Iden Payne, also appeared as Mary Fitton in Shaw's play *The Dark Lady of the Sonnets* in December 1910. Sir Henry J. F. Simson (1872–1932), a Scottish surgeon, was Lena Ashwell's second husband (the first was Arthur Playfair). "Dot" was Dion Boucicault, who since 1901 had been producer of plays for Charles Frohman. He appeared in *Justice* and *Trelawny of the 'Wells'*.]

A letter from Miss Limerick mentioning that she is out of engagement is my first intimation of the outrageous fact that poor Miss

Alliance has been jilted by Charles Frohman. Blood will flow for this when I return. Barker writes that The Madras House has also had its shutters put up. This is not to be borne. He and I will take the Court Theatre & run it with our own plays exclusively. Come and be our leading lady, £5 a week will be guaranteed: small but regular. If you cannot live down to it, Henry must work. Lillah McCarthy can take a tour of The Sign of The Cross to the provinces and maintain Barker with the spoils. Thus only, as far as I can see, can Lina Shch be preserved, and women with pasts averted. Why did I go away? Here is your true career nipped in the very bud; for you never existed before in your real quintessence: Lina was the coming-to-life: the other things were only acting; and anybody can act. Next time we shall do it in spangles: I saw quite a nice acrobat at a travelling circus in Bayonne, also a boneless dear who stood on two end-up bricks & then picked up her handkerchief in her teeth from the floor behind her; and they had a plastic charm which our critics couldnt have resisted. I hear that Trelawny is carrying everything before it for the moment & that crinoline is the only wear; but they will run it to death instead of nursing it. They dont know how to play this repertory game. I shouldnt have gone away. But I told Dot that nothing of mine—nothing *else* of mine would go on at the Repertory Theatre until after the 50th performance of Miss A.; and the wretch hastened to get rid of me by taking Miss A. off at once. Well, well: a time will come. I will see you again as Lina—or rather see Lina again as you—if I die for it. I shall be back again in London on the 2nd May. No illuminations, by request.

G.B.S.

To N.F.W.FISHER

10 Adelphi Terrace WC
[H.c.u/1; X/224]   5th May 1910

[Shaw had received an official demand from the Office of the Special Commissioners of Income Tax to make "a return of your total income from all sources" for the purpose of determining the new supertax assessment, which had just come into effect. Shaw's reply was addressed to N.F.W. (later Sir Norman) Fisher (1879–1948), clerk to the Special Commissioners, a civil servant who later became permanent secretary of the treasury and official head of the civil service. David Lloyd George (1863–1945), 1st Earl Lloyd George of Dwyfor, was chancellor of the exchequer 1908–15. He became Prime Minister in 1916.]

Dear Sir

In reply to your letter dated 4th May, which concludes with an invitation to apply to you for further information, I beg to submit the following points to you.

1. In the third explanatory note, I am directed to make a return for supertaxation of what is called my gross income, meaning, apparently my gross dividends without deduction of income tax. Let me put an extreme case to you. A large number of Socialists, representing a political force which is growing with remarkable rapidity in all the countries of Europe, advocate a tax of 20/- in the pound on incomes derived from rent and interest. The supertax is avowedly an advance in this direction. Let us suppose for the sake of illustration that Mr. Lloyd George next year introduces an income tax of 20/- in the pound on unearned incomes. Am I to understand that in that case not only will incomes derived from rent and interest be entirely confiscated, but that the recipients of such incomes, though left entirely destitute, will be called on to pay a Supertax on the income they have not received. No doubt this extreme event is not likely to occur; but you will see that long before the point of 20/- in the pound is reached a rate of taxation may be imposed which will raise this question in a very serious form. My contention is that the Special Commissioners must sooner or later adopt in their practice the principle that a man cannot be taxed on income that he has not actually received. Even under Schedule D., it is already a hardship that we should be taxed on our gross incomes; but in that case we at least enjoy the possession of the income for a year or a fraction of a year. In the case of rent and interest, the gross amount never reaches us at all; and you have only to conceive the taxation getting to a certain figure to foresee a situation in which you will be taxing a poor man on the scale of a rich man, and finally taxing a destitute man on the assumption that he is enjoying £20,000 a year.

2. Direction (e) page 2, reads as follows. "The income of a married woman living with her husband is deemed by the Income Tax Acts to be his income, and full particulars thereof must be included in any statement of income rendered by him for the purpose of the Supertax." Now I have absolutely no means of ascertaining my wife's income except by asking her for the information. Her property is a separate property. She keeps a separate banking account at a separate bank. Her solicitor is not my solicitor. I can make a guess at her means from her style of living, exactly as the Surveyor of Income Tax does when he makes a shot at an assessment in the absence of exact information; but beyond that I have no more knowledge of her income than I have of

yours. I have therefore asked her to give me a statement. She refuses, on principle. As far as I know, I have no legal means of compelling her to make any such disclosure; and if I had, it does not follow that I am bound to incur law costs to obtain information which is required not by myself but by the State. Clearly, however, it is in the power of the Commissioners to compel my wife to make a full disclosure of her income for the purposes of taxation; but equally clearly they must not communicate that disclosure to me or to any other person. It seems to me under these circumstances that all I can do for you is to tell you who my wife is and leave it to you to ascertain her income and make me pay the tax on it. Even this you cannot do without a violation of secrecy as it will be possible for me by a simple calculation to ascertain my wife's income from your demand. I need not dwell on the further obvious objection that as my wife enjoys a fixed income derived from property whereas a large part of my own is a fluctuating income derived from the precarious profession of play-writing, my income may in any year be much smaller than my wife's, in which case I shall have to pay on a larger income than I enjoy, without, as far as I know, having any legal power of recovering from my wife the amount I have paid on her income.

I shall be very glad to hear from you on both these points. The 2nd is perhaps the more important, because you can compel me, whilst the rate of taxation remains as low as it is at present, to pay on my gross instead of my net income, if you can obtain the support of the law for that unreasonable course; but by no possible process, legal or illegal, can you extract from me information which I do not possess, and to which I have no means of access.

yours faithfully
G. Bernard Shaw

To SIEGFRIED TREBITSCH

Ayot St Lawrence. Welwyn
[C/5]   17th May 1910

[Julius Bab's interpretation of *The Doctor's Dilemma* apparently was communicated to Trebitsch through correspondence, for it does not appear in his study of Shaw published in 1908. Bab's book was never published in an English translation.]

Bab is right. Walpole is not subtle enough for that; and it would be a frightfully brutal thing for him to say in Jennifer's presence as a mere

925

guess. Dubedat is in full possession of all his faculties until he dies. His mind is active; his hearing is so sharp that he overhears Ridgeon's remark about the dying actor; but he is too weak to turn his head to look at anything. He is quite conscious of the fact that he is dying splendidly as an artistic spectacle (note how thoroughly he understands Ridgeon's allusion to "the dying actor & his audience"), and he wants the world to hear about it. The newspaper man is the world: it is the presence of that spectator which has nerved him to the scene. His last anxiety is to be assured that he is still present.

I am writing to Constable about Bab. That book must be published somehow.

Our love to your very nice lady.

G.B.S.

To N.F.W.FISHER

[A.c/1; X/224]

[10 Adelphi Terrace WC]
31st May 1910

[Fisher had replied to Shaw on 27th May, informing him that under the Income Tax Acts "the 'total income' of a taxpayer is the amount of the income before the liability to income-tax has been satisfied. Moreover, the income of a married woman living with her husband is deemed to be the husband's income, and he is made accountable to the Revenue for the liability arising in respect of that income. While the Special Commissioners are happy to furnish any information as to the basis on which returns should be made, their functions do not extend so far as to admit of their advising as to the means to be adopted in a particular case to enable the taxpayer to acquire the information necessary to put him in a position to make the return required by the Acts" (*The Times*, 10th June 1910).]

Dear Sir

Your letter . . . does not meet my second point.

You say "the income of a married woman living with her husband is deemed to be the husband's income, and he is made accountable to the Revenue for the liability arising in respect of that income." To which I reply "By all means. I am quite willing to have my wife's income deemed to be my income, and to pay the tax on it; but you have gone beyond this: you have required me to ascertain the amount of my wife's income, which I have no means of doing.

The Income Tax Acts give you power to obtain from my wife a

926

return of her income. Do they give me that power? If so, can you refer me to the particular clause?

Observe that I claim neither exemption nor abatement, and am ready to pay when you assess me.

yours faithfully
G. Bernard Shaw

[Shaw informed the editor of *The Times*, in a letter published on 10th June, that his second letter to Fisher "led to a personal interview, in which I was able to satisfy the Commissioners that the difficulty was in no sense a personal one, and that we were both up against two obstacles—first, an oversight in the Income Tax Acts; and, second, the suffragist movement. Beyond that the solution of the problem has not advanced."]

To EDITH NESBIT BLAND

[C/4]

Ayot St Lawrence. Welwyn
5th June 1910

[Shaw and Mrs Bland had corresponded in May about the then-current theory that Bacon had written Shakespeare's plays. In this postcard communication Shaw is mocking all the arguments of the Baconians. John Dickens (1785?–1851) was Charles Dickens's impecunious father, whose financial irresponsibilities had landed him in a debtors' prison.]

Have you ever considered (this is a belated reply to yours of the 8th May) how utterly impossible it is that Shaw of Dublin could have written his wonderful plays. Is it not clear that they were really written by Sidney Webb, L.L.B. Shaw was an utterly ignorant man. His father was an unsuccessful business man always on the verge of bankruptcy, just like old Shakespear or John Dickens. Shaw had a very narrow escape from the police for setting fire to a common [in Dalkey, at the age of 12]. He was a disgrace to his school, where he acquired little Latin & less Greek. He got no secondary education & came to London an unknown & obscure provincial. And this is the man to whom people attribute the omniscience, the knowledge of public affairs, of law, of medicine, of navigation &c&c&c which informs the plays & prefaces of G.B.S. Absurd! Webb, the L.L.B, the man who carried all before him in examinations in his boyhood, the upper division civil servant of the Foreign & Colonial Offices, the author of Industrial Democracy &c, was clearly the man. I could pile the case much higher if there was room.

G.B.S.

To THE BETTER CITIZENSHIP ASSOCIATION

[I/2]

Ayot St Lawrence. Welwyn
6th July 1910

[The Better Citizenship Association of Portland, Oregon, had requested a message to be read at its First Anniversary meeting. Its credo included the statement, "The Better Citizenship Association believes in the goodness of man. It believes that Nature never designed a bad man. It believes that the Creator of all things would not and did not create anything that was bad, but that badness is the product of unjust conditions, brought about by man's ignorance."]

The underlined passages prove that the Better Citizenship Association is a goose. Nature has designed plenty of bad men; and some of the worst are Americans. The Creator has created everything that is bad as well as everything that is good. The Creator makes mistakes just as American citizens do. In trying to make a successful world he has had to proceed by the method of Trial and Error, just like his creatures. The Creator created the American people, as he created all the other peoples, to do his work for him; and from what I can make out, they are doing it so badly, that he will presently have to scrap them and try some more efficient tools. He has tried a good many different sorts of agents, including the cancer germ, the tetanus germ, the typhoid germ, the shark, the crocodile, the cobra, the tiger, the eagle, the black man, the yellow man, the red man, the white man, the Lincoln sort of President, the Roosevelt sort of President, the fighting man from Joshua and St Louis to [the prizefighters] Jeffries and Johnson, the pious man from Enoch to Anthony Comstock, the rich preachers from Solomon to Rockefeller, the poor ones from John the Baptist to Moses Harman, and so on through all sorts and conditions, including Shakespear and myself; and we seem to be all one worse than the other. But He is not going to stop. He will try again, and next time, if we are not careful, it will be a Superman who will wipe us out as carefully as we wipe out the typhoid bacillus when we can catch him.

You have no more right to be cruel to a bad man than to a tiger. But you can scrap him, in a lethal chamber, if you can once make up your mind that he is more trouble than he is worth. You cant educate him: he does not want to be educated except for purposes of forgery and fraud. You might as well try to educate a good man to be bad. America is doing all she knows in that direction; and yet there are a few honest Americans left though we [have] never heard of them in England. What your Association should advocate is the formation of a Committee of Public

928

Safety for the purpose of eliminating all Americans who cannot justify their existence by proving that they are every year producing what they consume in addition to a sinking fund to pay off the cost of their schooling and up-bringing and an insurance premium for their old age, and FIVE DOLLARS OVER.

If they cant, you may take it from me that the Creator wants them scrapped, and that he relies on you to do it. That's the reality of Citizenship Betterment.

To JOSEPH FELS

10 Adelphi Terrace W C
[H/51; X/230]   8th July 1910

[Upton Sinclair (1878–1968), American Socialist crusader and politician, whose books Shaw greatly admired, had been encouraging the endowment of young writers. Fels solicited Shaw's opinion for a symposium. Re readers' reports on Shaw's novels, see I. The report to Macmillan on *Immaturity* appears to have been written by George Meredith.]

My dear Fels

Everything that Upton Sinclair says in the circular is true enough; but it is not conceivable that any fund such as he proposes would get into the hands of those for whom it was intended. An original writer of genius always raises hostility and inspires terror and dislike. Committees always select the second-best man. Now I do not say that the endowment of second-best men might not be better than no endowment at all; but it is not what Upton Sinclair is driving at. Great men of the type he wishes to encourage are not really helpable in their beginnings. But it too often happens that the poverty through which they have to fight in their youth either dogs them unremittingly through life, or returns in their old age, especially if in their latest utterances they get further and further estranged from contemporary taste, as in the case of [J.M.W.] Turner and Beethoven. In this phase they might have just a chance of being selected by a committee for an old age pension. But that, again, is not what Upton Sinclair wants.

There is only one serious and effective way of helping young men of the kind in view; and that is by providing everybody with enough leisure in the intervals of well-paid and not excessive work to enable them to write books in their spare time and pay for the printing of

929

them. Nothing else seems to me to be really hopeful. I myself seem an example of a man who achieved literary eminence without assistance; but as a matter of fact certain remnants of family property made all the difference. For fully nine years I had to sponge shamelessly on my father and mother; but even at that we only squeezed through because my mother's grandfather had been a rich man. In fact I was just the man for whom Upton wants to establish his fund. Yet for the life of me I cannot see how any committee in the world could have given me a farthing. All I had to shew was five big novels which nobody would publish; and as the publishers' readers by whose advice they were rejected included Lord Morley and George Meredith, it cannot be said that I was in any worse hands than those of any committee likely to be appointed. Of course Sinclair may say to this that if Morley and Meredith, instead of having to advise a publisher as to the prospects of a business speculation, had only had to consider how to help a struggling talent without reference to commercial considerations, they might have come to my rescue. Unfortunately, I have seen both their verdicts; and I can assure Sinclair that I produced on both of them exactly the impression that is inevitably produced in every such case: that is, that I was a young man with more cleverness than was good for me and that what I needed was snubbing and not encouraging. No doubt there are talents which are not aggressive and do not smell of brimstone; but these are precisely the talents which are marketable, except, of course, in the case of the highest poetry, which, however, is out of the question anyhow as a means of livelihood. William Morris, when he was at the height of his fame as a poet, long after the publication of his most popular poem The Earthly Paradise, told me that his income from his poems was about a hundred a year; and I happen to know that Robert Browning threatened to leave the country because the Income Tax Commissioners assessed him with a modest but wholly imaginary income on the strength of his reputation. Poetry is thus frankly a matter for endowment; but for the rest I think a writer's chance of being helped by the fund would be in inverse ratio to his qualifications as conceived by Upton Sinclair.

yours ever
G. Bernard Shaw

To LILLAH McCARTHY

[H/4; X/182]

10 Adelphi Terrace WC
8th July 1910

[Shaw's "interlude" was *The Dark Lady of the Sonnets*, which he had written in June, at the suggestion of Edith Lyttelton, for the National Theatre movement. Its performance was postponed until 24th November, when it was presented, with Barrie's *A Slice of Life* and two short plays by George Paston, for two charity matinées. Lillah McCarthy did not appear. Elizabeth was played by Suzanne Sheldon and Shakespeare by Granville Barker. As mentioned earlier, Mona Limerick was the "Dark Lady," Mary Fitton. Dame Geneviève Ward (1838–1922), an American-born singer, had become a *grande dame* of the dramatic stage. Strauss's one-act opera *Feuersnot* (1901) received its first London performance, conducted by Thomas Beecham, at His Majesty's Theatre on 9th July.]

My dear Lillah

It seems to be decided that there is to be a performance on the 21st consisting of Barrie's little play followed by my interlude and the masque: the two last possibly jumbled up into a single piece. But your fancy for the part of Elizabeth is most distracting. Here you are, a ready made dark lady; and you want to build up your nose into a hook, stick on a frizzy red wig and ferret's eyebrows, and prance about as Queen Elizabeth, whom you do not in the least resemble. Also, the Dark Lady has to supply a little storm of sincere emotion which needs some real acting power, whereas all the rest is artificial rhetoric, and can be put on by anybody. My notion is to condemn you to the Dark Lady and Tragedy in the Masque, and to get Gertrude Kingston to do Elizabeth. I do not at all agree that you should give up your entry in the Masque: it is far too splendid to be thrown away, and just what is wanted to show that your recent inactivity did not mean a loss of your figure or good looks. Nobody thinks of Queen Elizabeth as a young woman; but the Dark Lady may be eighteen. The first suggestion for Elizabeth was Genevieve Ward: I want Gertrude Kingston because she will be neither too old nor too young, and can give the unsympathetic side of Elizabeth without being undignified.

Of course, if I cannot get this—if all historical verisimilitude is to [be] thrown over and Elizabeth is to be simply a handsome leading lady, then you might as well commit that outrage as anybody else; but I see no necessity for this.

As the hour is drawing nigh Phil Carr is rather in a state about getting the cast settled. Is Harley going to play Shakespear or is he not? May

931

Gertrude Kingston be asked to play Elizabeth without driving you to wash your hands of the whole business? I think you had better send Phil Carr a line direct.

We shall probably stay in London until Sunday morning, as I shall go and see Strauss's Feuersnot if we can get seats. On Sunday morning I shall go down to Oxford to lunch with Robert Bridges, and return to Ayot in the evening. Then I shall probably die. On Wednesday I got a sort of lightening before death under the influence of which I did about a week's work in sixteen hours; and now the lamp of life burns extremely low. I am therefore incapable of resisting any ultimatum which you may plank down; so do not abuse your advantage.

You and Harley as Shakespear and old Elizabeth would be a wretched spectacle; besides, as Mary you would have the satisfaction of clouting the other woman's head.

yours ever
G. Bernard Shaw

To ARCHIBALD HENDERSON

London
13th July 1910

[YY/52]

[Henderson was still worrying about the publication of his biography.]

MANUSCRIPT SAFE   KEPT IT TO READ MORE CHAPTERS

SHAW

To ARNOLD BENNETT

10 Adelphi Terrace WC
16th July 1910

[H/3]

[Bennett wrote a weekly column in the *New Age* from 1908 to 1911, under the pseudonym of Jacob Tonson.]

Dear Arnold Bennett

I gather from some of your Tonsonic utterances that you know something about the publishing business in Paris. I am just now very much at a loss for any sort of dependable guidance in that quarter. My translator, Augustin Hamon, infamous as an anarchist and author of the Psychologie Militaire Professionelle and other subversive works, is like all anarchists, as innocent as a lamb and as poor as a church mouse. All his literary experience is that of a desperado—an editor of impossible reviews and the author of such desperate pamphlets as these reviews live on. He had about as much notion of becoming a translator of plays as of becoming a banker or a bishop; but for reasons that I need not trouble you with, I beguiled him into it. As he has no sense of humor— or at least as that sort of thing had never occurred to him in his life—he finds it a very trying job, though, strangely enough, he translates the funny bits rather better than the serious bits. A performance of Candida in Brussels made an epoch in his life. He began by preparing the Belgian public for it by delivering lectures on my philosophy at those strange universities where they seem to allow anybody to lecture provided he will do it for nothing. He went to the first performance in a very serious frame of mind. The first act had not proceeded very far when the audience shewed signs of hilarity. He turned frantically to his wife and exclaimed "Mon Dieu, on rit. Tout est perdu." The epoch occurred when he went into the foyer at the end of the act and was congratulated on the laughter. It was such a revelation to him that he straightway plunged into the opposite extreme and now regards me as an author of harlequinades. So much for Hamon personally. Now comes my difficulty.

In order to save the translation right of my first seven plays from lapsing at the expiration of the ten years prescribed by the Convention, I had to get them printed in France at my own expense and put a little edition of 100 copies on the market. This left me with the plates. Since then, France, even Paris, always half a century behind Cork or Waterford, has been acquiring some sort of dim knowledge of me as an English reputation; and it is now possible to get offers from publishers to undertake the publication of my works. But the proposals made are monstrous. The printers are just as bad as the publishers. They ask for an edition, printed from my ready-made plates on paper that no self-respecting man would use for a pawnbroker's handbill, more than double[—]in fact, all but triple[—]what I pay my Edinburgh printer for the same book printed on extravagantly and unnecessarily good linen rag paper. When I ask a publisher to sell on commission for 15% on the net as Constable is glad to do for me in England, he asks 20% on the gross, and tries on every worn out swindle that the Society of Authors has knocked out of the English publishers, plus, of course, all those which it has not knocked out.

933

What would you do if you were in my place? Hamon, like all anarchists, has an exaggerated opinion of the invincibility of the capitalist system; and he is too hard up to have his heart in the standing out process which is a necessary part of bargaining. You mentioned the other day some Parisian publisher as a man with a future. All those I have hitherto come across are men with pasts, mostly extending apparently into the days of Montaigne and Rabelais. I should be very glad of any tips you can give me, not only for my own sake but partly for that of the Society of Authors. For my sins I slave on the Managing Committee and the Dramatic Committee of that body; and we are very much hampered by want of knowledge. In France particularly matters are complicated by the Society of Men of Letters and the Society of Dramatic Authors, which are, on paper, the most complete and magnificent organizations of literary interests in existence, but in fact are obstructive and unmanageable bodies, hopelessly enfeebled by amateur constitutions and bye-laws which are made inoperative and impossible by penalties far too terrible to be practicable. Thus, if the Théatre Français infringes my rights in some trumpery particular, the remedy is to shut up the theatre by withdrawing all the authorizations to perform given by the Society. That is to say, there is no remedy at all, as, if it came to that, the Théatre Français could shut up the Society much more easily than the Society could shut it up. However, that is merely by the way. I mention it as an example of the difference between the ideal and real literary and dramatic France.

yours ever

G. Bernard Shaw

To J.E. VEDRENNE

10 Adelphi Terrace WC

[H/40]   19th July 1910

[Vedrenne had sent to Shaw a copy of the translated libretto of *The Chocolate Soldier*, with a covering letter: "Here is the script of 'A Chocolate Soldier' left with me by Whitney for the purpose of your going through it and pointing out to him whether there is anything in the script which you object to." Frederick C. Whitney (1855–1930), an American manager active in the West End, presented the operetta at the Lyric Theatre on 10th September. Shaw finally saw a performance of the work on 10th November, standing at the back of the pit, as there were no seats available.]

This libretto infringes my copyright, and in several places violates the conditions on which I promised Mr. Jacobsohn to raise no obstacle to the performance of the original libretto in Germany. One of the names—Louka—is borrowed from my play; and several passages of dialogue are not merely burlesqued but lifted from my book verbatim.

If this is the libretto which was used in America, then my agent should have stopped the performances. It is not a translation of the German book: it is a rehash of it, made without the slightest regard to the understanding to which I was a party.

An even more important matter than the libretto is the description of the work in the program. If it be stated, or even remotely implied, that the work is a musical setting of Arms and The Man or that I am in any way a party to it, I shall at once take proceedings. [When] Mr. Jacobsohn pleaded that if he did not acknowledge some indebtedness to me, he would be denounced as a plagiarist, I made matters as easy for Mr. Jacobsohn and Mr. Oscar Strauss as I could by allowing them to sail very close to the wind in the dialogue, and countenancing some such phrase in the program as "Suggested by one of Mr. Bernard Shaw's comedies," or "with apologies to Mr. Bernard Shaw for an unauthorized parody"; and beyond this I shall not go.

In this copy I have struck out all the dialogue to which I object as being simply quoted from my play. I have replaced it with a few phrases which preserve the sense and continuity of the scenes (such as they are). I have struck out the name Louka, which can be replaced by Katinka or any Bulgarian name *not* taken from my play. I stipulate that the title Arms and the Man shall not be used on the program or in any announcement or communication to the press, and that if any reference whatever is made to me, it shall be worded as above "with apologies to Mr. Bernard Shaw for an unauthorized parody."

Why did not Mr. Whitney approach me directly on this matter before he produced this work in America? Why does he not approach me directly now?

Without prejudice
G. Bernard Shaw

To GILBERT MURRAY

The Giant's Causeway
[A/36]   24th July 1910
[The Shaws left London on 23rd July on a motoring tour of Ireland, via Liverpool and Belfast, returning to London on 7th October. During their

visit they spent twelve days at Coole Park with Lady Gregory. The Royal Society of Literature had instituted an Academic Committee, with the selection of members to be made by the Society of Authors. The public announcement of the formation of the Committee, with a list of the first 26 members (out of an ultimate 40), had been made on 20th July. The members ranged from Henry James, Hardy, Conrad, Yeats, and Murray, to the classical scholars S.H.Butcher and A.W.Verrall (translator of Aeschylus and Euripides), R.B.Haldane, Robert Bridges, and Alfred Austin. Maurice Hewlett was chairman of the Society of Authors' Committee of Management.]

Dear Gilbert Murray

Just this much: that I am a member of the Committee of the Society of Authors, and missed Hewlett's statement of the conspiracy to jump up an Academy by the Royal Society of Literature offering to elect a gang from the S. of A. if the S. of A. would return the compliment, and the nucleus thus secured electing anybody they were not too much afraid of.

I dont think it will do as it is. You are only on it because they little know your real character: they think you are only a Regius Professor. They have no right to form the thing yet. The final consent should take the form of "I, Blank Blank, am willing to associate myself with the undermentioned 39 authors as an Academy of Letters." There should be no *election:* the thing is ridiculous: we must boldly elect ourselves. The existing lot should consider themselves only the necessary organizing committee. A list which omits Barker, Belloc, Chesterton, Herbert Trench, Barrie, Kipling, and myself, not to mention Galsworthy, and which includes a choice collection of old-age-pensioners, and recognizes the translations of classics into unreadable English by—you know who, whilst ignoring Archer's translation of Ibsen, is intolerable. I think Massingham should be on for his editorial services to literature. I think you could do a great deal by threatening to nominate Frank Harris. Margoliouth is worth six of some of the chaps they have put on. Two of them I positively never heard of.

Anyhow, I am not prepared to tackle Lady Mary without a better case than Les Quarant Gosses have supplied. (Gosse, by the way, is, I believe, rather sound on the subject).

I have written to my secretary to send you a Misalliance if she can find one.

G.B.S.

To MRS HUMPHRY WARD

[A/1; X/210.e]

Parknasilla Hotel. Sneem
10th September 1910

[Mrs Ward had indicated to Shaw that at the next semi-annual Council meeting of the Society of Authors on 22nd November she proposed to offer a resolution, for which she requested his support: "That this meeting of Council protests against the manner of appointment of those representatives of the Society of Authors who acted on the so-called 'Joint Committee' which nominated the Academic Committee recently formed by the Royal Society of Literature; that it desires to draw the attention of the Society to the inadequacy of the authority under which action was taken; to the ignorance of members of Council on the subject; and to the exclusion of women from the Joint Committee." In 1911 Lady Ritchie (1837–1919), a novelist who was the eldest daughter of W.M.Thackeray, was elected to the Academic Committee, as was Shaw in June. Marie Belloc Lowndes (1868–1947), sister of Hilaire Belloc, was a journalist and novelist, whose best-known work is *The Lodger* (1913).]

Dear Mrs Humphry Ward

We are all in a mess about this Academy business; and if we begin recriminating, none of us will come out of it well. At all events, *I* am in that apparently unhappy, but really perhaps chastening position. I am a member of the Managing Committee, and ought to know all about it; but unluckily I was so horribly pressed for time when the matter was under discussion that I was late on the day it was explained by Maurice Hewlett; and I never overtook it afterwards. I was quite taken aback by the announcement in The Times, as I had no notion that anything public would be done until everybody had been consulted—not to say squared—as to the names, constitution, method of announcement &c. But that seems past praying for now: the joint committee jumped the claim, and fell as flat as might have been expected from the idiotic omissions in their list—two of which, by the way (Barrie & Kipling) seem to have been refusals of nomination. I am in a very poor position. I was late when I should have been punctual; and I cannot now go back on the men who *were* punctual. Consequently I cannot back you unless you direct your attack on the soi-disant Academy, and treat us of the Committee as fellow victims & not as conspirators.

Do not be furious with me if I say that you are in even a worse position than I. However intelligible and pardonable the abstention of members of the Council from the Annual Meeting may appear between ourselves, the Councillors abstain at their peril and must take the consequences. Sir Alfred Lyall came, and one or two others. You

937

trusted us not to take advantage of your absence, and stayed away. We betrayed you, if you like; but you took your chance of that, and cannot *publicly* reproach us. So far, you are in my position. BUT—worse remains behind. When, on the announcement of the list, one or two Academicians communicated with me in some bewilderment as to what they ought to do, I at once said that, among other conditions which I set forth, a certain number of the fauteuils must be reserved for women. It was immediately objected by an ardent Suffragist (male) that if such a thing were done *you* would be the first person to be elected. I agreed, & said Why not? Of course the reply was that you yourself had proclaimed the unfitness of women for &c &c &c &c &c. Now that is a good debating point, though quite irrelevant as an argument. Saul among the prophets always amuses an audience; and the more unfair the gibe the more it tickles. I suggest therefore that you ask Mrs Belloc-Lowndes to raise the point about the exclusion of women. At least that is a way out of the difficulty. You may, however, turn the difficulty into an advantage if you wish to use the opportunity to show that your opinions about the Suffrage must not be taken to imply any general exclusion of women from representative institutions. I simply point out the situation as an old platform hand; so that you may not be taken by surprise.

The Committee is in a weak position because, as you say, the Council should have specific notice (I suppose you are quite sure there was nothing on the agenda paper: I cant remember myself); and the justification of its omission can be at best only a technical one, though I will say, both for myself and my sorely tried colleagues, that since the Council never takes the smallest interest in us nor gives us any help, it has itself to thank if we find it hard in the press of business always to remember its existence. Still, that is only human nature: it is not business; and Heaven forbid that the Council should wake up and worry us more than we are already worried.

So there it is. I knew, and did nothing. You did not know; but you ought to have known. The Committee took the matter too easily and got let in. The moral is that we must work together without attacking one another to remedy all the mistakes if we can. In particular, the Committee, having left Maurice Hewlett to make the best of it without help, must not now go back on him.

What then are we to do, exactly?

Speaking here as the improvist, so to speak, without anyone to take counsel with, I think we should have a Council Meeting in October (not too early for autumn holidayers), and give notice of certain

938

resolutions, in none of which need the conduct of the Society be called into question; for I repeat, if once we begin recriminating, we shall do nothing but squabble. We can, however, criticize the Academy to our hearts' content. We might affirm the following propositions in whatever form may seem convenient:-

A—That the proceedings of the Academy so far must be regarded as provisional only; and that the Constitution and the election of the first forty members must be submitted to the Society of Authors and other constituent bodies before the final inauguration of the Academy.

B—That the first Academy shall contain a sufficient number of women of letters to make it clear that no sex disqualifications are to be allowed to become traditional in the body.

C. That at least ten of the Academicians shall always be under 50 years of age, and that the retirement of the older (but not necessarily the oldest) members to maintain this regulation be compulsory; but that retired Academicians shall retain their privilege of attending meetings and addressing them, though not of voting. (This last clause is a softener & is not essential).

D. That a clear majority of the Academy shall always consist of members having as their main occupation the production of permanent works of art as distinguished from ephemeral criticism.

E. That as the first Academy must necessarily be virtually self-elected, it is desirable that the organizing body should, with the help of its constituents, draw up a list of forty persons, and invite each of these persons to form an Academy in concert with the other thirtynine, whose names should be given, on the lines of a stated constitutional basis, and that the existing members be invited to resign and submit themselves for invitation in this manner.

F. That the Academy be open to all men and women of letters who are British subjects without reference to color, race, nationality, sect, party, or opinion.

This is all I can think of just at present. The most important clause, after the sex clause, is the age clause. It secures fairly young blood, and avoids the otherwise inevitable senile decay of the Academy by squeezing off the old people without the brutality of direct superannuation.

Some of the members already elected will have to come off to make room for the women and for at least half a dozen omitted names without which the affair is ridiculous.

I think you are entirely wrong in saying that you will not accept an invitation to become a member yourself. If you think the institution a good one, you ought to support it in what is, for you, the only really sincere and effective way: that is, by joining it. If you think it a blunder and an absurdity (and there is no middle opinion apparent) then you have no locus standi in an attempt to reform it. Besides, everybody hates a self-sacrificing woman; and you will look like a bad case of that. Not that you are in any way bound to take office if you prefer retirement

939

or have other fish to fry. But you must not say beforehand that you will not join. It is like getting a proposal of marriage by promising not to accept it. And how do you know that when this controversy has taken hold of you and interested you in the affair, you will not change your mind and be rather keen on becoming an Academician?

yours sincerely
G. Bernard Shaw

P.S. I write without ceremony, after my manner; but I am much obliged to you for writing to me about it, and my intentions are altogether friendly.

To HARLEY GRANVILLE BARKER

[Londonderry]
26th July 1910

[C(five cards)/3; X/168]

MY 54th BIRTHDAY

["Tarletonian" refers to the underwear manufacturer John Tarleton in *Misalliance*.]

Charlotte has just reminded me very unnecessarily of the above ghastly fact. After all, it has been a fine day, which is something, considering that from our landing at Belfast on Sunday morning it rained hard for 36 hours, causing a steady rise in Charlotte's temper. In that downpour we drove round the Antrim coast to the Giants Causeway. In that downpour I sat under my umbrella in my aquascutum, like a putrid mushroom, whilst a drenched mariner rowed me round the cliffs and told me lies about them. In that downpour we drove back next day to Lough Bay, only to find the hotel too revolting to pass the night in. In that downpour we pushed on to Antrim, only to find two hotels there so loathsome that we simply turned tail and returned to Belfast where the hotel we didnt go to (Charlotte at the last moment consented to stay at the Grand Central after heaping insults on the manager and ordering the instant repacking of all the luggage) was burnt to the ground with some slaughter and much concussion of the brain through the people who jumped out casting themselves from the third floor head foremost. Today the sun reappeared; and we came across the mountains—mountains I had never heard of: the Sperrins— to Londonderry, where Charlotte, as aforesaid, reminded me that I am 54. Here men still chalk up on the walls "No surrender" and "No

Popery," with XVII century dates attached. And here they preserve the old walls; and you mount them to look out at the place where the besieged Protestant heroes once watched the relief ships breaking the boom across the Foyle, and discover, as you may see by this card, that nothing whatever can be seen from the walls now except the hideous houses that have been built outside them. The ugliness of these towns, and the slightness of the provocation on which the inhabitants raise up their voices and call one another sanguinary liars is quite astonishing. Yet, like Larry Doyle [in *John Bull's Other Island*], they are civil to strangers. In this Northern Counties Hotel there is an apparently young & lovely spaniel. I have just discovered that it is blind and 18 years old.

Possibly I shall find a letter from you at Rosapenna tomorrow.

Fiftyfour is a devil of an age. I cannot feel it—cannot believe it; and yet there is the Tarletonian repulsive mask. Fifty four! *Fifty* four! Well!

GBS

To FREDERICK JACKSON

Parknasilla Hotel. Sneem

[H.c.u/2; X/141]   18th September 1910

[George Meredith lived at Box Hill, Surrey, until his death in 1909.]

My dear Jackson

We are both here—in the only place in the world that makes Tarn Moor a mere dust heap.

Yesterday I left the Kerry coast in an open boat 33 feet long, propelled by ten men at 5 oars. These men started at 49 strokes a minute, a rate which I did not believe they could keep up for five minutes. They kept it without slackening half a second for two hours, at the end of which they landed me on the most fantastic and impossible rock in the world: Skellig Michael, or the Great Skellig, where, in south west gales, the spray knocks stones out of the lighthouse keeper's house, 160 feet above calm sea level. There is a little Skellig covered with gannets— white with them (and their guano)—covered with screaming crowds of them. The Bass rock is a mere lump in comparison: both the Skelligs are pinnacled, crocketed, spired, arched, caverned, minaretted; and these Gothic extravagances are not curiosities of the islands: they *are* the islands: there is nothing else. The rest of the cathedral may be under the sea for all I know: there are 90 fathoms by the chart, out of which the Great Skellig rushes up 700 feet so suddenly that you have to go straight upstairs to the top—over 600 steps. And at the top amazing beehives of flat rubble stones, each overlapping the one below until the circles meet in a dome—cells, oratories, churches, and outside them cemeteries, wells, crosses, all clustering like shells on a prodigious rock pinnacle, with precipices sheer down on every hand, and, lodged on the projecting stones overhanging the deep, huge stone coffins made apparently by giants, and dropped there, God knows how. An incredible, impossible, mad place, which still tempts devotees to make "stations" of every stair landing, and to creep through "needle's eyes" at impossible altitudes, and kiss "stones of pain" jutting out 700 feet above the Atlantic. Most incredible of all, the lighthouse keeper will not take a tip, but sits proud, melancholy and haunted in his kitchen after placing all his pantry at your disposal—will also accompany you down to the desperate little harbor to squeeze the last word out of you before you abandon him, and gives you letters to post like the Flying Dutchman—also his strange address to send newspapers and literature to; for these he will accept.

I tell you the thing does not belong to any world that you and I have ever lived and worked in: it is part of our dream world.

And you talk of your Hindhead! Skellig Michael, sir, is the Forehead.

Then back in the dark, without compass, and the moon invisible in the mist, 49 strokes to the minute striking patines of white fire from the Atlantic, spurting across threatening currents and furious tideraces, pursued by terrors, ghosts from Michael, possibilities of the sea rising making every fresh breeze a fresh fright, impossibilities of being quite sure whither we were heading, two hours and a half before us at best, all the rowers wildly imaginative, superstitious, excitable, and apparently superhuman in energy and endurance, two women sitting with the impenetrable dignity and quiet comeliness of Italian saints and Irish peasant women silent in their shawls with their hands on the quietest part of the oars (next the gunwale) like spirit rappers, keeping the pride of the men at the utmost tension, so that every interval of dogged exhaustion and drooping into sleep (the stroke never slackening, though) would be broken by an explosion of "Up-up-up-keep her up!" "Up Kerry!"; and the captain of the stroke oar—a stranger imported by ourselves, and possessed by ten devils each with a formidable second wind, would respond with a spurt in which he would, with short yelps of "Double it—double it—double it" almost succeed in doubling it, and send the boat charging through the swell.

Three pound ten, my dear Jackson—six shillings a man—including interest on the price of the boat and wear and tear of ten oars, was what they demanded. They had thrown down their farming implements (they dont fish on Saturdays) to take to the sea for us at that figure.

I hardly feel real again yet.

Hindhead! Pooh! I repeat it in your teeth. POOH!!!

Celt and Saxon—you and me—I mean me and you—or is it you and I? Meredith and Anatole France! Is Box Hill a beehive cell 700 feet up? What does any Parisian know of Skellig Michael? Get out!

To ERICA COTTERILL

[10 Adelphi Terrace W C]

[G.u/4; X/151]   [Undated: assigned to 11th October 1910]

[Erica Cotterill's incursions at Ayot and her unmannerly behaviour had impelled Shaw to apply restraint by drafting a letter for Charlotte to send to her. Mrs Shaw made a few revisions in the letter; the variant text was published by Hesketh Pearson in *Horizon*, January 1958. Her restoration of a cancelled passage has been inserted in square brackets.]

[My dear Miss Cotterill]

I think I had better write to you to explain exactly why I intentionally shewed you that I strongly disapproved of your presence in my house, and that I did not—and do not—intend that your visit should be repeated. You might easily think that I was merely annoyed by your coming at an inconsiderate and unusual hour—as indeed I was—or that I disliked you. That was not it at all. I should object to your coming at teatime just as much and I do not particularly dislike you. On the contrary, it is because you are in some ways rather fine and sensitive, so that it is very difficult to be unkind to you, that I am determined to put a stop at once and for ever to any personal intimacy between us.

The matter is a very simple one. You have made a declaration of your feelings to my husband, and you have followed that up by coming to live near us with the avowed object of gratifying those feelings by seeing as much as possible of him. If you were an older & more experienced woman I should characterize that in terms which would make any further acquaintance between us impossible. As you are young & entirely taken up with your own feelings, I can only tell you that when a

943

woman once makes such a declaration to a married man, or a man to a married woman, there is an end of all honorable question of their meeting one another again—intentionally at least. You do not understand this, perhaps; but you will later on, when you are married and know what loyalty men and women owe to one another in that very delicate and difficult relation. The present case is a specially dangerous one; for my husband is not a common man: if you become at all intimate with him he would become a necessity of life to you; and then the inevitable parting would cost you much more suffering than it can now. [I could not trust him to keep you at a distance:] He is quite friendly & sympathetic with everybody, from dogs & cats to dukes & duchesses; and none of them can imagine that his universal friendliness is not a special regard for them. He has already allowed you to become far more attracted to him then he should; and I do not intend to let you drift any further into an impossible position.

If I must end by saying that this letter does not admit of any argument or reply, and that I do not mean it to lead to any correspondence between us, do not conclude that I am writing in an unfriendly spirit. It would be no use to discuss the matter now; and later on, when you are married and as old as I am, it will not be necessary. Meanwhile, please believe that my decision is quite inevitable & irrevocable.

yours sincerely
[Charlotte F. Shaw]

To AUGUSTIN HAMON

[H/1]

10 Adelphi Terrace W C
15th October 1910

[Hamon, in translating *Captain Brassbound's Conversion*, was encountering difficulty in translating the speeches of the cockney Drinkwater, whom he called Boisdeleau.]

My dear Hamon

In Brassbound, Drinkwater does not talk much slang. In the Socialist movement I met a costermonger who was quite an effective public speaker. He was very fluent, and had a copious vocabulary, as he was fond of reading. But he spoke with the strongest Whitechapel accent; and the contrast between his comparatively literary style and his appalling pronunciation was very quaint. Now you will remark that in the last act of Brassbound it comes out that Drinkwater is a devoted reader of cheap romance. That is why he is not only able to express himself without slang, but even fond of doing so. Therefore if you want to get Boisdeleau right, you must not use the slang of Blanco Posnet, but rather the literary clichés of the proletarian orator with the lowest possible Parisian pronunciation. If he spoke slang, he would not be understood by Lady Cicely and Rankin and the rest.

945

As to the notes at the end about cockney pronunciation, they must of course be dropped, as they have no sense in a French translation. As to replacing them by an essay of your own on the faubourien pronunciation of Paris, that will be excellent if you are quite sure of yourself as a phonetician. Otherwise, let it alone, unless you know some professed phonetician to whom you could submit your notes. The subject is a very difficult one, and without some special training and a practised ear, it is impossible to avoid mistakes. . . .

I greatly regret the frightful delays; but you can have no conception of the pressure on my time just now.

yours ever
G. Bernard Shaw

To AUGUSTIN HAMON

10 Adelphi Terrace WC
[H/1]   24th October 1910

[Aristide Briand (1862–1932), French statesman, was Président du Conseil et Ministre de l'Intérieur 1909–11. He won the Nobel Peace Prize in 1926. Alexandre Millerand (1859–1943) was minister of public works 1909–10. In 1920 he became president of France. John Lilburne (1614?–57), leader of the Levelers, attacked Cromwell's commonwealth as too aristocratic. Hamon was attempting to publish a new journal, in partnership with Sidney Parry. The project never got beyond the planning stage.]

My dear Hamon

. . . I am much alarmed by what you say about Briand. In heaven's name why should not Briand be a mouchard if he likes? You know very well that if you took all the intransigeants who are now denouncing Briand and Millerand and the rest as traitors, and put them into a Cabinet with a country to govern instead of their principles to talk about, they would do exactly as Briand has had to do, as John Burns has had to do, and as Bebel and the old gang of the German Social-Democrats have reduced themselves to nonentities by not doing. What would you yourself do if you were Prime Minister? The General Strike can never succeed, because, like all strikes, it is nothing but the old eastern plan of starving on your enemy's doorstep until he surrenders. You catch your oppressor round the waist and jump into the water with him, hoping that he will yield rather than drown; but when he is a capitalist and you a workman, he can live longer under water

946

than you. Besides, you are dragging all the other workers under water with you, and the moment they find, to their surprise, that they are suffocating as well as the capitalist, and suffocating much faster, they break loose from you and beg the capitalist's pardon. If the workers had character enough and determination enough to carry a general strike through, they would have more sense than to begin so silly a thing, and there would be no need of it either, as the capitalists would not be able to oppress them. All that a strike can do is to remind the public that labor is as indispensable to their daily bread as capital; but even that reminder cannot be given without making the workers suffer much more than the capitalists or the public.

On the other hand, had the workers been intelligent, they would have received the mobilization order with shouts of joy. "We have no wages; and the government comes forward to feed us, house us, clothe us. The capitalists have failed to work the railways: the State steps in and works them. Hurrah!" The real moment to resist would be when it was proposed to hand the railways back to the capitalists.

If you denounced Briand years ago, this would be an excellent moment to apologize for that absurdity. France is a democratic country; Briand must govern, on the whole, very much as the French people think it right that he should govern. Your business is to rub it into the French people that they have taken a man who was on the side of the people and shewn him that the people were not on his side—that in order to have a career as a statesman it is necessary in France to be on the side of capital and property and against labor. Any baby can trump up a moral indictment against any practical statesman: Lilburne denounced Cromwell; Tom Paine denounced Washington; Victor Hugo denounced Napoleon III. All waste of breath: it is just such recriminations that make labor politics impossible. Read Machiavelli; and then read his critics; and you will see that the criticism is all what Milton called "moral babble." The new Review must make an end of such sermonizing. Do not start it as Briand's schoolmaster. Smash him—dissolve him in vitriol if you want to thrust him out of office (that is, if you think that the man who will succeed him will be any better) but do not lecture him for being a bad boy. On the contrary, seize the moment to shew that the new review is going to break away from that sort of moralizing, and has no illusions as to the workman being the hero and the capitalist the villain of the world drama.

yours ever
G. Bernard Shaw

To BEATRICE WEBB

[H/14]

10 Adelphi Terrace W C
24th October 1910

[In Edinburgh on 26th October Shaw addressed the University Fabians in the late afternoon on "University Socialism"; in the evening he and Beatrice Webb spoke on unemployment and the Poor Law, at a meeting sponsored by the Scottish National Committee for the Prevention of Destitution. In Glasgow on the 27th Shaw lectured on "Public Enterprise and Dramatic Art" at an afternoon meeting in the Royalty Theatre sponsored by the Glasgow Repertory Theatre; in the evening he and Sidney Webb spoke on the Minority Report of the Royal Commission on the Poor Law (which had been written by the Webbs and published in February 1909), at a meeting sponsored by the New Crusade against Unemployment and Destitution.

Webb had addressed the Amalgamated Society of Railway Servants at Paddington on 17th September (and again on 18th October) on the Poor Law Minority Report. The Rt. Hon. Lord Claud J. Hamilton (1843–1925), chairman of the Great Eastern Railway Co. and a governor of the London School of Economics, headed a group of railway magnates in calling for Webb's resignation of the chairmanship of the L.S.E. The leader writer of *The Times* chimed in on 19th October, charging that, since the Webbs had started "on what they themselves call their 'Crusade' on behalf of the Minority Report on the Poor Law, the chairman of the School of Economics has preferred agitation to science." W. A. S. Hewins and H. J. Mackinder (1861–1947), former directors of the School, wrote rejoinders to *The Times*, published on 22nd and 24th October. The governors of the L.S.E., at their meeting early in November, "passed a unanimous resolution of confidence" in Webb.

Shaw's letter, "Mr Mallock's Ideals," appeared in *The Times* on 5th February 1909; it was reprinted in *Socialism and Superior Brains*, Fabian Tract No. 146, in November 1909.]

My dear Beatrice

I shall put up at the North British Station Hotel. Very likely I shall arrive there on Tuesday night, unless the horrors of an all-day railway journey make me funk it at the last moment, and travel on Tuesday night instead. But as I generally lie awake in sleeping cars I think I had better have my night's rest in peace in the hotel. The Fabians, confound them, have put my meeting at five, which lands me closer to the evening meeting than I like. I take it for granted that the meeting begins at 8: if not, send me a note to the hotel to say when. Do not bother further about me: I shall turn up at the Music Hall five minutes before the appointed hour; and I will talk for half an hour, since you wish me to, if the audience will stand putting off your speech so long.

I do not know where Webb is, and have not the least idea of what is going to happen at Glasgow. Something was said about my taking the Chair for him; but it would be far better to get some local celebrity to take the Chair, and let the two visitors be mere speechifyers, especially if Sidney wishes to speak first. Of course, even if I were in the Chair, I could reserve my speech until after he had finished; but when I want to run a bit free I never feel quite comfortable in the Chair. At Edinburgh it does not matter, as I shall have to behave myself.

I have just been reading the noble tributes of Hewins and Mackinder in The Times; but all that is poppycock: the enemy has declared war at last. It is a fact worth noting that when The Times started a sort of Capital and Labor discussion in the silly season, and I intervened with a destructive letter, The Times sent me back my letter with polite regrets and shut up the correspondence. I think it quite possible that it may have been brought home to them that in allowing me to smash up Mallock merely because my letters are good copy, they were not playing the game. Anyhow, it looks as if the days of sullen peace were over. I am not sure that Lord Claude's bomb-shell will not do the London School more good than harm; but if it comes as a signal for everybody who has any sort of pull against us anywhere to do their little worst it may possibly make matters livelier for us than they have been hitherto. Certainly it will have an effect on Sidney, who has only preserved his reputation for being a prudent and moderate man because he has never yet met with a really embittered opposition. The moment they really begin to blacken his eyes, he will retort not only with argument but with furious invective. He never suffered fools with any real gladness; and when the fools begin to injure him and hurt his feelings as well as bore him there will be wigs on the green. Already one or two people have remarked to me with some surprise that the Paddington speech was "not like Webb," to which I could only reply "You do not know Webb."

The moral of all this is that you must not let this campaign overwork him. He requires a certain amount of fat not so much on his body as on his temper; and if you let him get too much overwrought he will make the air ring with more liars and scoundrels and thieves than Hyndman in his wildest moments ever ventured on.

I have to lecture at the Royalty Theatre in Glasgow on Friday afternoon on Private Enterprise and Dramatic Art. I have not quite made up my mind whether to return to London that night or wait until the morning. Since I have taken to motoring my loathing of railway journeys has become unbounded; but even if the car were not in hospital, which it is, 400 miles is too long a journey to attempt by car except as part of a regular tour.

yours ever
G. Bernard Shaw

To AUGUSTIN HAMON

[H/1]

10 Adelphi Terrace WC
29th October 1910

Dear Hamon

. . . Your pen portrait of Briand is excellent; but the moral judgment you pass on him is that of an old Huguenot or a Plymouth Brother. Why on earth should you call Briand base because he loves Wein, Weib und Gesang, and is particular about the quality of them? Dont you recognize it as a frightful defect in yourself that you are indifferent to money and care for nothing but abstractions? If Millerand likes power and organization, surely these are vigorous and virile tastes. You must shake off this ridiculous censoriousness of the working-class movement. You are not Briand's governess; and, if you were, you ought to praise him for refusing to be a futile martyr and for fulfilling his ambition, such as it is.

I return Sheet 4 of The Devil's Disciple. Are you sure that you are not making the translation too literal? I have marked some places where I am in doubt—where the phrase seems to me to be a simple transliteration, and where the people address one another as vous where I should have expected them to tutoyer one another.

In great haste,

yours ever
G.B.S.

To ERICA COTTERILL

[A/3]

Ayot St Lawrence. Welwyn
30th October 1910

[Having chastised Erica for her egregious deportment, Shaw now apparently was making amends by praising her artistry. Many years later, when Erica's "novel," Form of Diary (1939), was published anonymously, this letter was quoted as a blurb on a paper band surrounding the volume.]

950

I had forgotten all about this MS, and in fact read it for the first time last night. It is a literary masterpiece—quite out-of-the-way extraordinary—shewing a talent as irresistible as Shelley's & Tolstoy's rolled into one. You will either die a lunatic before you are 33 or be the greatest English woman writer—indeed one of the greatest of English writers—before you are 40.

You must therefore accustom yourself to the superior position, which needs a lot of common sense & sacrifice of the immunities of the weak.

GBS

To H.G.WELLS

[D/26]

10 Adelphi Terrace WC
18th November 1910

[*The New Machiavelli*, which satirised the Fabian Society and contained devastating portraits of the Webbs, appeared serially in the *English Review* from May to November.]

My dear Wells

I have just come across a passage in William Blake—in Vala, alias The Four Zoas [in "Night the Second," spoken by the Voice of Enion].

"What is the price of Experience? Do men buy it for a song? / Or wisdom for a dance in the street? No: it is bought with the price / of all that a man hath—his house, his wife, his children."

This would be a good motto for The New Machiavelli, which, by the way, is a frightfully unfinished masterpiece; for the truth appears to be that the parties will live happily ever after.

GBS

To CHARLES RICKETTS

[H/2; X/207]

10 Adelphi Terrace WC
21st November 1910

[Ricketts designed the costumes and setting for *The Dark Lady of the Sonnets*. Charles La Trobe (1879–1967), stage director and producer, was stage manager at the Haymarket Theatre 1908–15. The music for the production was provided by Norman O'Neill, musical director at the Haymarket.]

My dear Ricketts

Our matinée is naturally upsetting the arrangements at the Haymarket in a most frightful manner; and poor La Trobe sent a furious letter yesterday to declare that we could not have a dress rehearsal at all except at a time totally impossible for Barker and myself. He seems to have been worried by the other pieces. However, he has been very nice about our show; and he promises us a rehearsal with the scene and the lights tomorrow morning at half-past ten—absolutely our only chance, he says. It now appears that we cannot have the dresses, which is exasperating, but must be faced with what resignation we can muster. Perhaps we shall be able to get at least a couple of cloaks and a farthingale. Could you possibly come down?

Music seems to me to be called for at three points—perhaps four. 1. A prelude to take up the curtain and exhibit the sky and the warder. My notion is simply a long sustained mysterious note on the bassoon and the Westminster chimes presently played in single notes by the harp, which will finally strike the hour on its lowest E (I think Big Ben is in E). The music stops when the Warder challenges Shakespear. 2. A shimmering from the fiddles when the light heralds Elizabeth, continuing more or less until she wakes, when it stops abruptly. 3. I am not quite sure about this; but there might be some music when the Dark Lady enters, rising rapidly to a climax and breaking off when she boxes their ears. 4. The Westminster chimes again as at first at the end, as Shakespear is led off by the Warder. This will puzzle you until I explain that as we have omitted the dance, Elizabeth, instead of saying "And now, Sir, I see my Court approach" etc. will say "And now, Sir, tis time for the Queen to go to bed; but I hold it not safe to do so until my warder hath conducted you off these premises and seen you safely home," or something of that kind. Anyhow, I shall get the Warder on to lead Shakespear off whilst Elizabeth retires in to her original ray of light. In short, a very quiet "Exeunt severally"—stealing off to mysterious music.

> yours ever
> G. Bernard Shaw

To JOSEPH TELEKI

[F/2; X/225]   [10 Adelphi Terrace W C]
                                   22nd November 1910
[Joseph Teleki, a Hungarian literary agent, resided in London. It was he who had introduced Shaw to Sándor Hevesi in July 1907. Hevesi's trans-

lation of *Mrs Warren's Profession* had been produced at the Hungarian Theatre, Budapest, on 22nd October 1909; his translation of *Captain Brassbound's Conversion* at the National Theatre, Budapest, on 14th January 1910; and his translation of *The Doctor's Dilemma* at the Hungarian Theatre on 24th September 1910. All had brief runs, but the strong critical reception and the interest they engendered led to Shaw's greater popularity in Hungary in later years. Teleki, who had been ailing for some time, died suddenly at Arad, Hungary, on 25th July 1911.

Baroness Emmuska Orczy (1865–1947), an English novelist and playwright born in Hungary, was the author of *The Scarlet Pimpernel* (1905) and other historical adventure tales, set mostly in the French Revolution. Dr Heinrich Lahmann was chief medical officer of a sanatorium bearing his name, in Dresden. He treated Siegfried Trebitsch there for migraine headache.]

My dear Teleki

Why on earth should you waste your time and damage the great European firm of Bernard Shaw Unlimited by convicting Trebitsch of mistakes in his translations? It is useless to trouble about his old versions; the edition he declares to be perfect is a new one not yet published, for which I am writing a preface. No matter whether it is correct or not, you must swear that he is the greatest translator now living, except Hevesi; and I will instruct Trebitsch to return the compliment and swear that Hevesi's versions are models of everything that a translation should be. Naturally being a Hungarian, you loathe all Austrians; but do not let the battles of Hungary and Austria be fought over my body. Literature has enemies enough without its unfortunate votaries making war on one another.

If you carry out the test of the Hungarian translations by having them translated back again by the Baroness Orczy, I shall conclude, if the translation is word for word, that she has my books on her shelf, and has copied them out instead of really translating. But if they are merely accurate paraphrases, I shall immediately conclude that Hevesi is a schoolmaster. I do not want a walking dictionary; I want a living dramatist. If he knows a little English, so much the better; but it is not essential. Trebitsch knows quite as much as is necessary. His version of Mrs Warren's Profession has been a success; his Brassbound was played by Sorma. Hevesi's versions have been failures. That is what comes of making correct translations. Beg Hevesi to make inaccurate ones that the Hungarians will like. . . .

I have been a vegetarian since 1880 and am quite satisfied that it is a good diet to live and work on. At the same time, it is a mistake to

953

suppose that it will cure all sorts of diseases. Some people are extraordinarily the better for it—especially gouty, rheumatic, neuralgic people. It improves the temper and nerves of irritable people. It is a change; and changes are often beneficial merely as changes, no matter what you change to. Also, when people take to vegetarianism, it generally means that they are taking to studying their food a little, and to be much more careful and intelligent as to selection and quantity than when they were merely pursuing the old habits they accepted as children without thinking. Consequently a good many of the successes which the vegetarians point to are probably incidental rather than direct. But you need not have the slightest fear as to the sufficiency of a vegetarian diet. For athletic purposes it seems to be positively superior to a meat diet; indeed, its one disadvantage (if it be a disadvantage) is that a vegetarian requires more exercise to digest his food. Only you must not suppose that vegetarianism means simply omitting the meat from your ordinary dietary. I will not go so far as to say that the first rule for the vegetarian is never to eat vegetables; but it is very important that he should not allow vegetables to form any larger part of his list than they do in the diet of a meat eater. What you have to do is to replace the meat with the staple vegetarian foods, such as macaroni, nut foods, egg foods, cereals, and so forth, and to be particularly careful not to eat too much, as people often do under the impression that as vegetarian diet is less sustaining than meat diet they ought to eat much more of it. This is a dangerous mistake. If you try to eat the same bulk of dates or brown lentils as of beefsteak, you will find yourself extremely uncomfortable afterwards through having over-eaten yourself.

Dr Lahmann's Anstalt may be all very well as an excuse for a holiday; but there is not the slightest need for you to go there to try vegetarianism. You can go to Eustace Miles' Restaurant or the St George's Restaurant opposite the Duke of York's theatre, and try experiments in the way of meals. But I am rather doubtful as to whether the change of diet will be of much use to your bronchial tubes. . . .

yours ever
G. Bernard Shaw

To HARLEY GRANVILLE BARKER

[C/3]

[10 Adelphi Terrace WC]
[Undated: assigned to 25th November 1910]

[Shaw had viewed the charity matinée of *The Dark Lady of the Sonnets* on the 24th, sharing the author's box with Mr and Mrs Frank Harris, and was anticipating the second and final performance on the 25th.]

Forgot to warn you that you made an astonishing XIX century start by saying "on the contrary" instead of "Far from it." Remember "endless naughtinesses to a gentleman as lewd as herself" and "high nature and fruitful industry" (or whatever it is: my last copy has gone). The costume was killing: there has been a great rally of the old adoration.

G.B.S.

To C.C.FAGG

[H/1]

10 Adelphi Terrace WC
15th December 1910

[Christopher C. Fagg, a fellow of the Geological Society, had a special interest in regional surveying.]

Dear Mr Fagg

Your paper, which is quite new to me, naturally interests me. There are just one or two points on which you will have to be careful. What we must come to is not equal wages but equal incomes. You have said on your last page that "People who would not work would not get a house to live in, or anything to eat." In this one sentence you have reintroduced the essence of the error you are trying to dispel. You are making a man's income depend on his industry. If you once do that, you let in the whole system of inequality over again. If a man will not work, you may punish him, or force him to work, or kill him; but the one thing you clearly must not do is to throw him into the streets to die of starvation. Nor, if he is merely lazy, and only does half as much work as other people, must you attempt to meet that case by only giving him half as much. By doing so, you immediately create a class of lazy men with only half the income of the normally energetic men.

I am afraid I have unintentionally cut you out as far as the Fabian Society is concerned [in 9th December speech on Equality]; but I hope

955

you will pursue the subject. Like yourself, I have become more and more convinced that this doctrine of Equality, instead of being an absurdity which no-one will stand, is really the only form in which Socialism is interesting and intelligible—I might say that it is the only form in which it is convincing.

A point which I omitted the other evening, but which you will find it interesting to illustrate, is that the notion of trying to make the distribution of wealth reflect differences in individual merit is quite a recent one, and that it has been a total failure in practice. Until the XIX century, for example, no officer in the army would have dreamt of asking for promotion on the strength of his services: he always based it on his family connections: that is, on his class. The idea was universal that a man of higher class than another should have more money; but class was a hereditary matter; and a man who acquired it by his own hand was looked on as an upstart and an adventurer. Within the limits of each class, Equality was the rule; and in spite of the enormous commercial propaganda of the XIX century and the Manchester School, that equality is the rule still. What we have to fight for, therefore, is not equality of income between individuals, for this is and always has been the rule. What we have to break down is inequality between classes, for this, too, exists and always has existed in highly civilized societies.

I return the paper with many thanks.

yours faithfully
G. Bernard Shaw

To SIEGFRIED TREBITSCH

[H/5]

10 Adelphi Terrace W C
21st December 1910

[Shaw had hastily written a preface "What I Owe to German Culture" for Vol. I of his *Dramatische Werke*, published in Berlin in March 1911. The new German edition of the plays contained a number of textual refinements and the alteration of one or two play titles. The allusion to Sudermann in the preface is a contrast between Du Maurier's *Trilby* and Sudermann's *The Song of Songs* (which Shaw had just read: see his letter to John Lane on the threatened suppression of the novel, in the preface to Lane's edition of the novel issued in 1913). In the preface to the Trebitsch edition, Shaw said: "No Puritan ever penned such an attack on Bohemianism. Sudermann's doctrine is, in effect, 'Respectability may be hypocrisy, but Bohemianism is damnation.'"

The December general election (the second in 1910) had just ended. Shaw had spoken on behalf of the candidacy of R. C. Phillimore on several occasions early in December: "I have bellowed all over the place," he wrote to Beatrice Webb on 9th December [A/13]. "On Wednesday [7th December, at Radlett] I 'kept the meeting together for him': that is, in a hall crammed with a howling opposition, I spent an hour and a half shouting, bullying, chaffing, challenging, thundering & reparteeing until I was as one in a Turkish bath. Tonight I had another ninety minutes reading to the Fabians."]

My dear Trebitsch

I enclose the Preface, such as it is. The General Election has been a frightful misfortune for me. I had to speak in public for ten nights running; and the physical effort, coming on top of the work of getting my new volume through the press, not to mention half a dozen other things, has left me good for nothing. I am therefore starting on a voyage to Jamaica next Friday. I shall stay there about a week, and come back, arriving in England on the 25th January.

This has forced me to finish the Preface by a violent effort as best I can. As you will see, it all goes to pieces at the end; but I must send it as it is, as it will be too late when I come back.

I have not had time to look at the proofs, except for a hasty glance here and there. I fully expect that there are ten mistakes in it for every one that occurred in the old version; for I do not believe a bit in your schoolmasters and professors and people. I notice that they do not know that when an Englishman names an hour with a "the" before it, he always means a train. Thus, when Frank Warren says that his mother has gone up to town by the 11.15, he means that she has gone to catch the 11.15 train. However, it does not matter. I sampled the dialogue in one or two places; and it seemed to me to have a distinct style, and to be not only accurate in the schoolmaster's way, but artistically expressive.

We leave on Friday evening. If you get this on Friday morning, there will be just time for you to wire to me in case I have forgotten anything of importance.

Do not be infuriated by the allusion to Sudermann. We must not give ourselves the airs of a superior coterie. Sudermann has a good substantial talent; and we should be on friendly terms with him.

yours ever
G. Bernard Shaw

To ERNEST PARKE

[C/8]

10 Adelphi Terrace WC
23rd December 1910

[The Shaws were preparing to visit Sydney Olivier, who had been appointed Governor General of Jamaica, B.W.I., in 1907.]

I am off to Jamaica—sail early tomorrow morning from Bristol by the S.S. Port Antonio. England can breathe peacefully for a whole month; and [the Morning] Leader interviewers can join the unemployed. I return on the 25th Jan.—if I ever return.

Anything to avoid Christmas in England!

G. Bernard Shaw

Corrections and additions for
Collected Letters 1874–1897

The first numeral refers to page, the second to line. There are separate line counts for headnote and text. Recipient is indicated when more than one letter appears on a page. H indicates Headnote, T text, and C the bracketed code of sources and descriptions of correspondence.

xii: 14	For "Musters" read "Gillmore"
4: 26	Alter to read "Theatre Royal"
17: 9	For "prodigy" read "protégé"
36: H, 5	Alter to read "Lalage Virtue"
71: H, 17	For "woman's hand" read "woman's mind"
80: H, 2	For "secretary" read "member"
155: H, 4	(Murray) For "*on the 'Scutcheon*" read "*in the 'Scutcheon*"
175: H, 1	For "*Rheingold*" read "*Rhinegold*"
184: T, 20	Alter to read "panem and circenses"
187: H, 9	For "*on the 'Scutcheon*" read "*in the 'Scutcheon*"; for "Blanche" read "Mildred"
188: H, 2	(Murray) for "Blanche" read "Mildred"
235: T, 3	(Reid) Alter to read "Goschen & Hartington [or]"
242	Unidentified correspondent is Pharall Smith, author of *Wanted a Messiah* (1890)
244: T, 24–5	Alter to read "[where a by-election had been completed on 11th February]?"
244: H, 4	For "Liberal Unionist" read "Liberal"
272: H, 13	For "*The Master Builder*" read "*Hedda Gabler*"
288: T, 12	For "not" read "now"
291: C	For "A/33" read "A/4"
296: H, 8–9	Alter to read "I was horribly tired & shocked & upset; but I kept patience & did not behave badly nor ungently. Did not get to bed until 4, and had but a disturbed night of it."
296: H, 11	Alter to read "This was to send"
297: T, 16	For "then" read "than"
313: H, 6–7	(Robins) Alter to read "was presented, in French, at Her Majesty's Theatre, on 11th June 1886."

324: T, 8	For "[Frank]" read "[Augustus]"
346: C	For "H/1" read "H/3"
355: C	(Guinandeau) For "G.u/1" read "G.u/3"
364: H, 3 and 5	For "Labour" read "Liberal"
378: H, 9–10	Alter to read: "Leonard Hall of Manchester was the organiser of the Navvies."
383: H, 3	For "Conservative" read "Liberal"
383: H, 5–6	Alter to read: "Sir George Livesey (1834–1908), director of the South Metropolitan Gas Company, was a promoter of labour co-partnership."
393	Alter recipient from ELIZABETH ROBINS to WILLIAM ARCHER
408	(Richards) Alter date to "30th November"
412: H, 4	For "June" read "January"
420: C	(Jones) For "S/2" read "B/4"
429: C	For "S/2" read "A/4"
443: C	For "S/2" read "H/4"
454: H, 3	For "1895" read "1894"
459: C	Alter to read "B/4; X/124"
461: C	For "S/2" read "A/4"; alter date to "24th December"
515: H, 5	Alter to read "4th April"
607: C	Alter to read "C/4; X/124"
611: T, 20	For "normally" read "morally"
674: H, 1	(Magny) For "6th" read "9th"
697: H, 7	(Newcombe) For "1898" read "1897"
708: T, 5	(Robins) Alter to read "Asta is too atrociously ladylike"
731: C	For "A/1" read "A/3"
731: H, 4	For "mother" read "grandmother"
749: H, 5	Alter to read "Janet and Charrington"
778: H, 1	Alter to read "(1829–1915)"
812: C	Alter to read "A/4; X/124"
877 (Index)	For "Yates, E.D." read "Yates, C.D."

Index of Recipients

GENERAL INDEX

COMPILED BY A. C. WARD

Dark, Sidney, 270
Darnley, J. H.: *Facing the Music*, 165
Darrow, Clarence, 348
Darwin, Charles, 133, 186, 358, 413, 476, 485, 486, 511, 558, 670, 672, 761, 827, 873
   The Origin of Species, 356
Darwin, Sir George, 600
Das Kapital: *see* Marx, Karl
Daudet, Alphonse, 797
David Ballard: *see* McEvoy, Charles
David Copperfield: *see* Dickens, Charles
Davies: *see* Davis, Tom B.
Davies, Acton, 567
Davis, Tom B., 706
Day, Thomas: *Sandford and Merton*, 93
De Curel, Vicomte François, 914
   La Fille sauvage, 913
Deacon, Renée M.: *Bernard Shaw as Artist-Philosopher*, 903
Deane, Clifford: *see* Keane, Cliff
Dearmer, Canon Percy, 83
Death, 129, 729
Death of Cromwell, The: *see* Shaw—Unwritten Plays
Delaroche, Hippolyte (Paul), 167
Delavigne, Casimir: *Louis XI*, 438
Delia Harding: *see* Sardou, V.
Dell, Robert E., 118, 158, 377
Delph, C. L., 608
Demachy, Robert, 704
Democracy, 89, 235, *and passim*
Democratic Federation, 486, 760
Denshawai affair, 722, 723
Dent, J. M., 334
De Profundis: *see* Wilde, Oscar
De Quincey, Thomas, 476, 489, 490
Desborough, Lady (*née* Ethel Grenfell), 796, 798
Després, Suzanne (Madame Lugné-Poe), 601–2, 605–6, 664, 730, 784, 796, 797
Determinism, 669–70
Deutcher Theater: *see* Berlin
Deutsches Volkstheater, Vienna, 282, 300
Devereux, William: *Henry of Navarre*, 916
Devil's Disciple, The: *see* Shaw—Plays
Dialectical Society, 484, 485, 486

Diary of a Madman, The: *see* Strindberg, August
Dickens, Charles, 35, 338, 551, 652, 697
   All the Year Round, 645, 646
   Bleak House, 221, 222
   David Copperfield, 69, 525, 623, 647, 652, 857
   Dombey and Son, 645
   Great Expectations, 34, 155, 324, 645, 646
   Household Words, 645, 646
   Letters, 762
   Little Dorrit, 34, 645, 647
   Martin Chuzzlewit, 118
   The Mystery of Edwin Drood, 645, 647–8
   Nicholas Nickleby, 606, 645
   The Old Curiosity Shop, 645
   Oliver Twist, 645
   Our Mutual Friend, 134, 179, 180, 208, 210, 369, 422, 645
   A Tale of Two Cities, 136, 751
Dickens, Ethel (typing services), 92, 419, 636
Dickens, John, 927
Dictionary of National Biography, 65, 339, 357
Diet and Food Considered in Relation to Strength and Power of Endurance, Training and Athletics: *see* Haig, Dr Alexander
Diggle, Joseph R., 378, 379
Dilke, Sir Charles W., 40, 186–7, 277, 882
Dillon, Frances, 816–18
Disarmament Conference, 4, 73
"Disciples" of Shaw, 203
Divorce, 61, 81, 813–16
Dixon, J. W., 38
Dobbs, Arthur C., 244–5
Doctor's Dilemma, The: *see* Shaw—Plays
Dodd, Dr Frederick Lawson, 118, 154, 157, 612, 613
Dodd, Richard Jefferson, 14, 15
Dodgson, C. L.: *see* Carroll, Lewis
Doll's House, A: *see* Ibsen, Henrik
Dolmetsch, Arnold, 104, 148, 248, 602
   Shaw offers help with surgical expenses, 55–6

Granville Barker, Harley, 204, 264, 321, 360–1, 363, 364, 389–92, 411, 430, 443–4, 445–8, 456–7, 469–471, 548–50, 580, 620–2, 641, 642, 644–5, 689–92, 698, 724–5, 731, 806, 807, 822–3, 833, 840, 849, 851, 912, 936, 940
first contact with Shaw, 169–70
success in *Candida*, 175
in *Captain Brassbound's Conversion*, 208
in *The Man of Destiny*, 221, 227
in *Mrs Warren's Profession*, 243, 249–250
in Heijerman's *The Good Hope*, 317, 318
in *The Admirable Bashville*, 326–8
Candida matinées, 420
"a very remarkable young man," 458, 582
in *Man and Superman*, 528
"hard and clearheaded," 541
in *Major Barbara*, 584, 585–6, 588
marries Lillah McCarthy, 619
decides on professional name, 624
balloon ascent with Shaw and others, 633
and *The Devil's Disciple*, 659, 714–15
in *Arms and the Man*, 756–7
in *The Doctor's Dilemma*, 771–2
visits U.S.A., 771
his salary, 807–8
Shaw on Frances Dillon in *Man and Superman* to, 816
contracts typhoid, 819
his loans to Vedrenne-Barker repaid, 899
Shaw's letters from France to, 918–22
in *The Dark Lady of the Sonnets*, 931, 932, 955
The Madras House, 841, 905, 921, 923
The Marrying of Ann Leete, 249–50, 352
A Miracle, 590
The Voysey Inheritance, 686, 687, 690, 787
Waste, 391, 701, 714, 718, 719, 720
Granville Barker, Mrs: *see* McCarthy, Lillah

Graves, Clotilde, 360
Grayshott and District Refreshment Association, 255–7; *and see* Fox and Pelican
Grayshott Men's Club, 255
Great Catherine: *see* Shaw—Plays
Great Expectations: *see* Dickens, Charles
Great Queen Street Theatre, 718, 861
Green, Alice (Mrs J. R. Green), 230
Green, J. Frederick, 116, 126, 127, 154
Green Room Club, 543
Greene, P. Clayton, 699
Greet, Clare, 584
Greet, William, 703, 704, 706
Gregory, Augusta, Lady, 423, 810, 846, 855–9, 861–4, 936
Our Irish Theatre, 861
Grein, J. T., 221, 300, 802
Grenfell, Edith: *see* Desborough, Lady
Grey, Sir Edward (later Viscount Grey of Fallodon), 713, 721, 722, 723–724
Gribble, Francis Henry: *Sunlight and Limelight*, 38
Grillparzer, Franz, 300
Grin: birth name of "Louis de Rougemont"
Grove, Agnes, Lady, 858
Grove, F. C.: *see* *Forget-me-not*
Grove, Florence, 80, 81
Grove's Dictionary of Music and Musicians, 484
Grundy, Sydney, 303, 351, 800, 849, 910
Guardians, Board of, 285–6
Guesde, Jules, 145
Guest, Emily, 285–6
Guest, Haden: *see* Haden-Guest
Guilbert, Yvette, 796, 797
Guild of St Matthew, 84, 671, 673
Guild Socialism, 809
Guildhall, City of London, 844
Guildhall School of Music, 567
Guitry, Sacha, 730
Gulliver's Travels: *see* Swift, Jonathan
Gumpertz, Samuel W., 574, 631
Guntram: *see* Strauss, Richard
Gurly, Kate, 60
Gurly, Lucinda Elizabeth: *see* Shaw, Mrs G. C.

982

986

989

993

Rationalism, 84, 670, 759–62
Rayner, Horace George, 675–6, 681–2, 721
Reade, Charles, 352
 Nance Oldfield, 192
Record Office, 467
Records of Personal Chastisement (with pirated Shaw lecture), 19
Redford, George Alexander (Lord Chamberlain's Reader of Plays), 13–14, 15, 30, 102, 241, 242, 591, 633, 701, 707–8, 718, 720, 843, 850, 851, 854, 856, 858, 859, 866–8
Reece, Robert, 351
Reed, Edward Tennyson, 248
Reeves, Amber (Mrs George R. Blanco White), 868, 869, 870, 871
Reeves, William Pember, 28, 93, 100, 868
Reeves, Mrs William Pember (née Magdalen Stuart Robison), 666, 667, 869
Referee, The, 569, 570
Reform Bill of 1832, 252, 254
Rehan, Ada, 101, 193, 302, 309, 395, 397, 423–5, 429–35, 436, 437, 438–43, 447, 448–52, 458–9, 531–2, 535, 544–5, 546–7, 624
Reid, G. Archdall: Alcoholism, 244, 246
Reinhardt, Max, 343, 410, 411, 616, 619–20, 621, 629–31, 637, 794
Réjane, Gabrielle, 131
"Religion of the Pianoforte, The": see Shaw—Other Works
Rembrandt, Harmensz van Rijn, 305, 373, 418
Renard, Jules, 330
Repertory Theatre: see Frohman, C.
Retz, Cardinal de: Mémoires, 393
Reuter, 313
Review of Reviews, 427, 599
"Revolutionist's Handbook, The" (appended to Shaw's Man and Superman), 356
Revue Socialiste, 668
Reynolds's Newspaper, 40, 184, 378, 407
Rhodes, Cecil, 122, 124, 126, 161, 169, 182, 612

Rhodesia, 122
Richard II: see Shakespeare, W.
Richard III: see Shakespeare, W.
Richards, Grant, 23, 25, 41, 44, 48, 58–59, 63, 90–1, 163–4, 184–6, 202–203, 224–5, 226, 283–5, 321, 334, 340, 412, 469, 472–3
 his bankruptcy, 478–9, 507–9
Richardson, John: "Richardson's Show," 685, 686, 715
Richelieu: see Lytton, Lord
Richter, Hans, 803, 804
Ricketts, Charles, 590, 693, 697–9, 751–2, 951–2
 Self-Portrait, 698, 751
Ricketts, Mrs, 349, 350
Riley, John Athelstan Lawrie, 232, 235, 379
Rilke, Rainer Maria, 618
Ring of the Nibelungs, The: see Wagner, R.
Ristori, Adelaide, 212
Ritchie, Lady (née Anne Isabella Thackeray), 937
Roberto the Rover: see Ward, Artemus
Roberts, Arthur, 29, 30
Roberts, Field Marshal Frederick Sleigh (1st Earl Roberts), 232, 235
Roberts, R. Ellis, 145–6
Robertson, Ian, 137–8, 166–8, 534, 636, 735, 736
Robertson, Mrs Ian: see Knight, Gertrude
Robertson, John M., 8, 155, 156, 761
Robertson, Johnston Forbes: see Forbes-Robertson
Robertson, T. W., 194, 351, 352, 635
 Caste, 308
Robertson, W. Graham: Pinkie and the Fairies, 906, 907, 908
Robespierre, Maximilien Marie Isidore, 106
Robins, Elizabeth, 20, 76–8, 136–7, 139, 141, 143
 "Miss Robins was a lie," 77
Robson, Eleanor (Mrs August Belmont), 524, 532–3, 546, 547, 548–50, 586–90
Robson, Frederick, 96, 97, 398, 624

1005

1009

1013

Women and war, 259–61
Women's Liberal Federation, 235
Women's Protective and Property League, 485
Women's Suffrage, London Society for, 843
Women's Trade Union League, New York, 890
Wonder, The: *see* Centlivre, Susannah
Wonderful Visit, The: *see* Wells, H. G.
Wood, Charles Lindley: *see* Halifax, 2nd Viscount
Woods, William, 834
Wood's Ha'pence: *see* Swift, Jonathan
Workman's Times, 121
Workmen's Compensation Act, 68
World, The, 39, 417, 487, 526, 538, 599
World of Sin, The: *see* Melville, Walter
World War I, 89, 684
Wright, Sir Almroth, 660
Wright, Mrs Theodore, 240, 471, 473–4
Wrong Box, The: *see* Stevenson (R. L.) and Osbourne (Lloyd)
Wyndham, (Sir) Charles, 74, 90, 142, 361, 441
Wyndham, George, 713

Wynn-Carrington, Charles R. (1st Earl Carrington, later Marquess of Lincolnshire), 721

Yates, Edmund, 539
Yeats, William Butler, 274–5, 423, 452–453, 714, 790, 859–61, 864, 905, 936
The Land of Heart's Desire, 452
The Pot of Broth, 509, 790
Yorke, Oswald, 583, 588–9
Yorke, Mrs Oswald: *see* Russell, Annie
You Never Can Tell: *see* Shaw—Plays
Young, Arthur, 133
Young, Charles M., 357, 358
Young, Dr Thomas, 357

Zangwill, Israel: *Merely Mary Ann*, 524, 548
Zaza: *see* Belasco, David
Zeit, Die, 312, 313, 319, 361–5
Zetetical Society, 484, 485, 486, 488, 491
Zickel, Martin, 410, 411
Ziegfeld, Florenz, 264
Ziegfeld Follies, 381
Zola, Émile, 113, 139, 914
La Fécondité, 136, 138

Table of Critical Values of t	df	$t_{.100}$	$t_{.050}$	$t_{.025}$	$t_{.010}$	$t_{.005}$	df
	1	3.078	6.314	12.706	31.821	63.657	1
	2	1.886	2.920	4.303	6.965	9.925	2
	3	1.638	2.353	3.182	4.541	5.841	3
	4	1.533	2.132	2.776	3.747	4.604	4
	5	1.476	2.015	2.571	3.365	4.032	5
	6	1.440	1.943	2.447	3.143	3.707	6
	7	1.415	1.895	2.365	2.998	3.499	7
	8	1.397	1.860	2.306	2.896	3.355	8
	9	1.383	1.833	2.262	2.821	3.250	9
	10	1.372	1.812	2.228	2.764	3.169	10
	11	1.363	1.796	2.201	2.718	3.106	11
	12	1.356	1.782	2.179	2.681	3.055	12
	13	1.350	1.771	2.160	2.650	3.012	13
	14	1.345	1.761	2.145	2.624	2.977	14
	15	1.341	1.753	2.131	2.602	2.947	15
	16	1.337	1.746	2.120	2.583	2.921	16
	17	1.333	1.740	2.110	2.567	2.898	17
	18	1.330	1.734	2.101	2.552	2.878	18
	19	1.328	1.729	2.093	2.539	2.861	19
	20	1.325	1.725	2.086	2.528	2.845	20
	21	1.323	1.721	2.080	2.518	2.831	21
	22	1.321	1.717	2.074	2.508	2.819	22
	23	1.319	1.714	2.069	2.500	2.807	23
	24	1.318	1.711	2.064	2.492	2.797	24
	25	1.316	1.708	2.060	2.485	2.787	25
	26	1.315	1.706	2.056	2.479	2.779	26
	27	1.314	1.703	2.052	2.473	2.771	27
	28	1.313	1.701	2.048	2.467	2.763	28
	29	1.311	1.699	2.045	2.462	2.756	29
	∞	1.282	1.645	1.960	2.326	2.576	∞

Source: From "Table of Percentage Points of the t-Distribution," *Biometrika* 32 (1941):300. Reproduced by permission of the *Biometrika* Trustees.

Introduction to Probability and Statistics

Eleventh Edition

William Mendenhall
University of Florida, Emeritus

Robert J. Beaver
University of California, Riverside

Barbara M. Beaver
University of California, Riverside

THOMSON

BROOKS/COLE

Australia • Canada • Mexico • Singapore • Spain
United Kingdom • United States

THOMSON

BROOKS/COLE

Sponsoring Editor: Carolyn Crockett
Assistant Editor: Ann Day
Editorial Assistant: Julie Bliss
Marketing Manager: Joe Rogove
Marketing Assistant: Marina Salinas
Project Manager, Editorial Production: Janet Hill
Print/Media Buyer: Vena Dyer
Permissions Editor: Mary Kay Polesmen

Production Service: Hearthside Publishing Services
Text Designer: Roy Neuhaus
Illustrator: Better Graphics, Inc.
Cover Designer: Cloyce Wall
Cover Image: Steve Taylor/Getty Images
Cover Printer: Lehigh Press, NJ
Compositor: Better Graphics, Inc.
Printer: Quebecor World, Taunton

Printed in the United States of America

1 2 3 4 5 6 7 06 05 04 03 02

For more information about our products, contact us at:
Thomson Learning Academic Resource Center
1-800-423-0563

For permission to use material from this text, contact us by:
Phone: 1-800-730-2214
Fax: 1-800-730-2215
Web: http://www.thomsonrights.com

Library of Congress Control Number 2002104701

ISBN: 0-534-39519-8

1 00 3 2 3 4 5 2 1

Brooks/Cole–Thomson Learning
511 Forest Lodge Road
Pacific Grove, CA 93950
USA

Asia
Thomson Learning
5 Shenton Way #01-01
UIC Building
Singapore 068808

Australia
Nelson Thomson Learning
102 Dodds Street
South Melbourne, Victoria 3205
Australia

Canada
Nelson Thomson Learning
1120 Birchmount Road
Toronto, Ontario M1K 5G4
Canada

Europe/Middle East/Africa
Thomson Learning
High Holborn House
50/51 Bedford Row
London WC1R 4LR
United Kingdom

Latin America
Thomson Learning
Seneca, 53
Colonia Polanco
11560 Mexico D.F.
Mexico

Spain
Paraninfo Thomson Learning
Calle/Magallanes, 25
28015 Madrid, Spain

Preface

Every time you pick up a newspaper or a magazine, when you watch TV or surf the internet, you encounter statistics. Every time you fill out a questionnaire, register at an online website, or pass your grocery rewards card through an electronic scanner, your personal information becomes part of a database containing your personal statistical information. You cannot avoid the fact that in this information age, data collection and analysis are an integral part of our day-to-day activities. In order to be an educated consumer and citizen, you need to understand how statistics are used and misused in our daily lives.

The Secret to Our Success

The first college course in introductory statistics that we ever took used *Introduction to Probability and Statistics* by William Mendenhall. Since that time, this text, currently in the eleventh edition, has helped several generations of students understand what statistics is all about, and how it can be used as a tool in their particular area of application. The secret to the success of *Introduction to Probability and Statistics* is in its ability to blend the old with the new. With each revision, we try to build on the strong points of previous editions, while always looking for new ways to motivate, encourage, and interest students using new technological tools.

Hallmark Features of the Eleventh Edition

The eleventh edition retains the traditional outline for the coverage of descriptive and inferential statistics. In fact, in this revision, we have made a purposeful decision to maintain the straightforward presentation of the tenth edition. In the spirit of the tenth edition, we have continued to simplify and clarify the language, and to make the language and style more readable and "user friendly"—without sacrificing the statistical integrity of the presentation. Great effort has been taken to explain not only how to apply statistical procedures, but also to explain

- how to meaningfully describe real sets of data
- what the results of statistical tests mean in terms of their practical applications
- how to evaluate the validity of the assumptions behind statistical tests
- what to do when statistical assumptions have been violated

Exercises

In the tradition of all previous editions, the variety and number of real applications in the exercise sets is a major strength of this edition. We have revised the exercise sets to provide new and interesting real-world situations and real data sets, many of which are drawn from current periodicals and journals. The eleventh edition contains over 1000 exercises, many of which are new. Any exercises from previous editions that have been deleted will be available to the instructor as *Classic Exercises* on the Instructor's Suite CD and on a text-specific website. Exercises are graduated in level of difficulty; some, involving only basic techniques, can be solved by almost all students, while others, involving practical applications and interpretation of results, will challenge students to use more sophisticated statistical reasoning and understanding.

Organization and Coverage

Chapters 1–3 present descriptive data analysis for both one and two variables, using state-of-the-art *MINITAB* graphics. We believe that Chapters 1 through 10—with the possible exception of Chapter 3—should be covered in the order presented. The remaining chapters can be covered in any order. The analysis of variance chapter precedes the regression chapter, so that the instructor can present the analysis of variance as part of a regression analysis. Thus, the most effective presentation would order these three chapters as well.

Chapter 4 includes a full presentation of probability and probability distributions. Three optional sections—Counting Rules, the Total Law of Probability, and Bayes' Rule—are placed into the general flow of the text, and instructors will have the option of complete or partial coverage. The two sections that present event relations, independence and conditional probability, and the Additive and Multiplicative Rules have been rewritten in an attempt to clarify concepts that often are difficult for students to grasp. As in the tenth edition, the chapters on analysis of variance and linear regression include both calculational formulas and computer printouts in the basic text presentation. These chapters can now be used with equal ease by instructors who wish to use the "hands-on" computational approach to linear regression and ANOVA and by those who choose to focus on the interpretation of computer-generated statistical printouts.

One important change implemented in the tenth and eleventh editions involves the emphasis on p-values and their use in judging statistical significance. With the advent of computer-generated p-values, these probabilities have become essential components in reporting the results of a statistical analysis. As such, the observed value of the test statistic and its p-value are presented together at the outset of our discussion of statistical hypothesis testing as equivalent tools for decision-making. Statistical significance is defined in terms of preassigned values of α, and the *p-value approach* is presented as an alternative to the *critical value approach* for testing a statistical hypothesis. Examples are presented using both the *p-value* and *critical value* approaches to hypothesis testing. Discussion of the practical interpretation of statistical results, along with the difference between statistical significance and practical significance, is emphasized in the practical examples in the text.

Do It Yourself!—New to the Eleventh Edition

Easy access to the internet has made it possible for students to visualize statistical concepts using an interactive webtool called an **applet**. These applets were written by Gary McClelland, author of *Seeing Statistics*™, and have been customized specifically to match the presentation and notation used in this edition. Found on the CD-ROM that accompanies the text and accessed using a browser such as Internet Explorer or

Netscape Navigator, they provide visual reinforcement of the concepts presented in the text. Applets allow the user to perform a statistical experiment, to interact with a statistical graph to change its form, or to access an interactive "statistical table." At appropriate points in the text, a screen capture of each applet is displayed and explained, and each student is encouraged to "Do It Yourself" using newly written exercises at the end of each chapter. We are excited to see these applets integrated into statistical pedagogy and hope that you will take advantage of their visual appeal to your students.

DO IT YOURSELF!

Example 7.4 can be solved using the **Normal Probabilities for Means** applet. If you enter the values for $\bar{x}$, σ, μ, and n (press "Enter" to record each change) and adjust the dropdown list at the bottom of the applet, you can calculate a tail area, a cumulative area, or the area between $-z_0$ and z_0. Conversely, if you need to find the value of $\bar{x}$ that cuts off a certain area under the curve, enter the area in the box marked "prob:" at the bottom of the applet, and the applet will provide the value of $\bar{x}$. The applet in Figure 7.10 is set to calculate $P(7 < \bar{x} < 9) = .829$, correct to three decimal places. You will use this applet for the *Do It Yourself Exercises* at the end of the chapter.

FIGURE 7.10
**Normal
Probabilities for
Means** applet

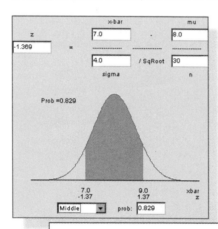

Do It Yourself! text
and exercises from
pages 250 and 271.

Exercises   DO IT YOURSELF!

7.66 Refer to the die-tossing experiment with $n = 1$ in Section 7.4 in which x is the number on the upper face of a single balanced die.

   a. Use the formulas in Section 4.8 to verify that $\mu = 3.5$ and $\sigma = 1.71$ for this population.

   b. Use the **Central Limit Theorem** applet to toss a single die at least 2000 times. (Your simulation can be done quickly by using the [Roll 100 Sets] button.) What are the mean and standard deviation of these 2000 observations? What is the shape of the histogram?

   c. Compare the results of part b to the actual probability distribution shown in Figure 7.3 and the actual mean and standard deviation in part a. They should be similar!

7.67 Two balanced dice are thrown, and the average number on the two upper faces is recorded.

   a. Use the values $\mu = 3.5$ and $\sigma = 1.71$ from Exercise 7.66. What are the theoretical mean and standard deviation of the sampling distribution for $\bar{x}$?

   b. Use the **Central Limit Theorem** applet to toss a single die at least 2000 times. (Your simulation can be done quickly by using the [Roll 100 Sets] button.) What are the mean and standard deviation of these 2000 observations? What is the shape of the histogram?

   c. Compare the results of part b to the actual probability distribution shown in Figure 7.4 and the actual mean and standard deviation in part a.

7.68 Repeat the instructions in Exercise 7.67 when three dice are tossed.

7.69 Repeat the instructions in Exercise 7.67 when four dice are tossed.

7.70 Suppose a random sample of $n = 5$ observations is selected from a population that is normally distributed, with mean equal to 1 and standard deviation equal to .36.

   a. Give the mean and the standard deviation of the sampling distribution of $\bar{x}$.

   b. Find the probability that $\bar{x}$ exceeds 1.3, using the **Normal Probabilities for Means** applet.

   c. Find the probability that the sample mean $\bar{x}$ is less than .5.

   d. Find the probability that the sample mean deviates from the population mean $\mu = 1$ by more than .4.

Other Features New to the Eleventh Edition

- Graphical and numerical data description includes both traditional and EDA methods, using computer graphics generated by *MINITAB 13* for Windows.

Graphical and numerical data description using computer graphics generated by *MINITAB 13* from page 25.

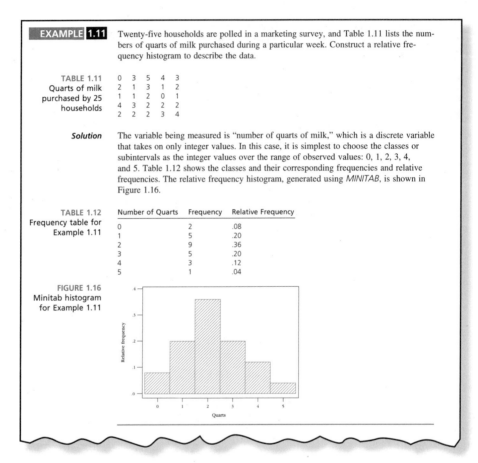

EXAMPLE 1.11   Twenty-five households are polled in a marketing survey, and Table 1.11 lists the numbers of quarts of milk purchased during a particular week. Construct a relative frequency histogram to describe the data.

TABLE 1.11
Quarts of milk purchased by 25 households

0	3	5	4	3
2	1	3	1	2
1	1	2	0	1
4	3	2	2	2
2	2	2	3	4

Solution   The variable being measured is "number of quarts of milk," which is a discrete variable that takes on only integer values. In this case, it is simplest to choose the classes or subintervals as the integer values over the range of observed values: 0, 1, 2, 3, 4, and 5. Table 1.12 shows the classes and their corresponding frequencies and relative frequencies. The relative frequency histogram, generated using *MINITAB*, is shown in Figure 1.16.

TABLE 1.12
Frequency table for Example 1.11

Number of Quarts	Frequency	Relative Frequency
0	2	.08
1	5	.20
2	9	.36
3	5	.20
4	3	.12
5	1	.04

FIGURE 1.16
Minitab histogram for Example 1.11

■ Presentation of the box plot is now preceded by the introduction of the five-number summary. The box plot has been simplified to include only one lower and upper fence for detecting outliers. This is in keeping with the procedure now implemented in *MINITAB 13*.

The five-number summary and box plot descriptions from page 77.

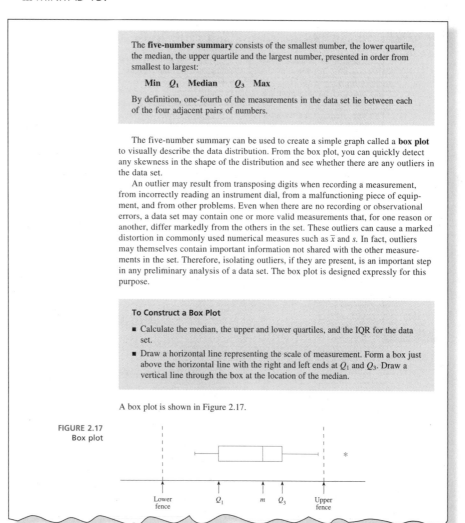

The **five-number summary** consists of the smallest number, the lower quartile, the median, the upper quartile and the largest number, presented in order from smallest to largest:

Min Q_1 Median Q_3 Max

By definition, one-fourth of the measurements in the data set lie between each of the four adjacent pairs of numbers.

The five-number summary can be used to create a simple graph called a **box plot** to visually describe the data distribution. From the box plot, you can quickly detect any skewness in the shape of the distribution and see whether there are any outliers in the data set.

An outlier may result from transposing digits when recording a measurement, from incorrectly reading an instrument dial, from a malfunctioning piece of equipment, and from other problems. Even when there are no recording or observational errors, a data set may contain one or more valid measurements that, for one reason or another, differ markedly from the others in the set. These outliers can cause a marked distortion in commonly used numerical measures such as $\bar{x}$ and s. In fact, outliers may themselves contain important information not shared with the other measurements in the set. Therefore, isolating outliers, if they are present, is an important step in any preliminary analysis of a data set. The box plot is designed expressly for this purpose.

To Construct a Box Plot

■ Calculate the median, the upper and lower quartiles, and the IQR for the data set.

■ Draw a horizontal line representing the scale of measurement. Form a box just above the horizontal line with the right and left ends at Q_1 and Q_3. Draw a vertical line through the box at the location of the median.

A box plot is shown in Figure 2.17.

FIGURE 2.17
Box plot

Lower fence Q_1 m Q_3 Upper fence

■ The presentation in Chapter 4 has been rearranged and rewritten to clarify the concepts of event relations, independence and conditional probabilities, and the Additive and Multiplicative Rules of Probability.

■ The table of standard normal curve areas (Table 3 in Appendix I) has been changed to show cumulative probabilities—that is, $P(z \leq z_0)$. The table gives cumulative probabilities, correct to four decimal places, for values of z from -3.49 to 3.49. This change makes the table consistent with the format of the binomial and Poisson tables, and should be easier for students to use.

■ All examples and exercises in the text contain new printouts based on *MINITAB 13*. *MINITAB* printouts are provided for some exercises, while other exercises require the student to obtain solutions without using the computer.

Small-Sample Testing and Estimation

The tests and confidence intervals for population means based on the Student's *t* distribution are found in a *MINITAB* submenu by choosing **Stat → Basic Statistics.** You will see choices for **1-Sample t, 2-Sample t,** and **Paired t,** which will generate Dialog boxes for the procedures in Sections 10.3, 10.4, and 10.5, respectively. You must choose the columns in which the data are stored and the null and alternative hypotheses to be tested (or the confidence coefficient for a confidence interval). In the case of the two-sample *t* test, you must indicate whether the population variances are assumed equal or unequal, so that *MINITAB* can perform the correct test. We will display some of the Dialog boxes and Session window outputs for the examples in this chapter, beginning with the one-sample *t* test of Example 10.3.

First, enter the six recorded weights—.46, .61, .52, .48, .57, .54—in column C1 and name th...

alog box...
to select...
enter **.5**...
native" t...
Notice t...
populati...
the **Opti**...
dotplot c...

Data...
workshe...

■ Enter...
(1 or 2...
comes...
■ Enter...

An About MINITAB section from pages 411–413.

FIGURE 10.22

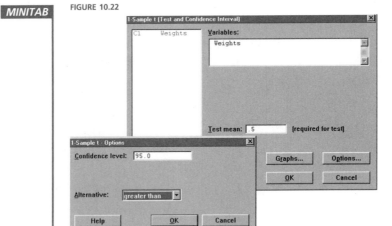

FIGURE 10.23

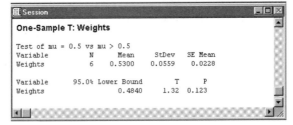

Use the second method and enter the data from Example 10.5 into columns C2 and C3. Then use **Stat → Basic Statistics → 2-Sample t** to generate the Dialog box in Figure 10.24. Check "Samples in different columns," selecting C2 and C3 from the box on the left. Select the proper alternative hypothesis in the Options box, and check the "Assume equal variances" box. (Otherwise, *MINITAB* will perform Satterthwaite's approximation for unequal variances.) The two-sample output when you click **OK** twice automatically contains a 95% one- or two-sided confidence interval as well as the test statistic and *p*-value (you can change the confidence coefficient if you like). The output for Example 10.5 is shown in Figure 10.13 on page 382.

For a paired-difference test, the two samples are entered into separate columns, which we did with the tire wear data in Table 10.3. Use **Stat → Basic Statistics → Paired t** to generate the Dialog box in Figure 10.25. Select C4 and C5 from the box on the left, and use **Options** to pick the proper alternative hypothesis. You may change the

FIGURE 10.24

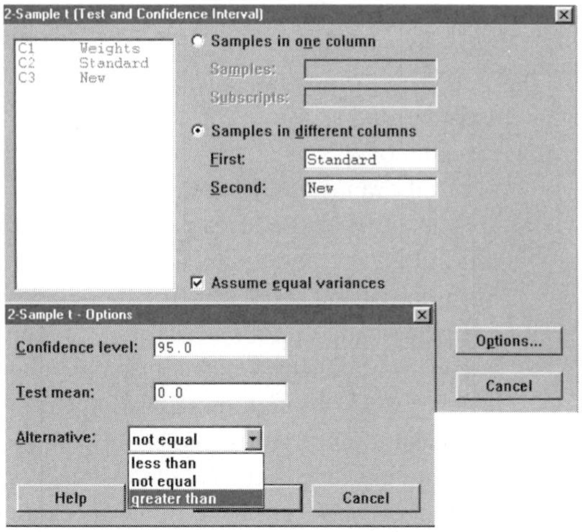

FIGURE 10.25

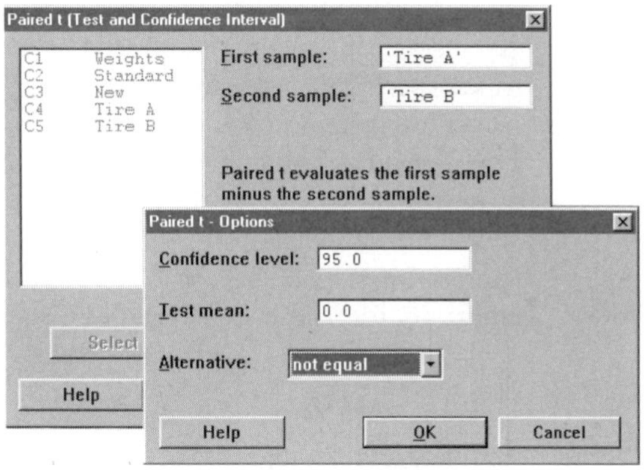

confidence coefficient or the test value (the default value is zero). When you click **OK** twice, you will obtain the output shown in Figure 10.15 on page 390.

Finally, although you cannot use *MINITAB* to perform either the χ^2 or the F test in this chapter, you can use **Calc → Probability Distributions → Chi-square (or F),** selecting "Cumulative probability" to calculate the appropriate p-value.

■ The presentation of linear regression in Chapter 12 has been rearranged and rewritten, so that the discussion of diagnostic tests and residual plots precedes the section on estimation and testing.

The Role of the Computer in the Eleventh Edition

Computers are now a common tool for college students in all disciplines. Most students are accomplished users of word-processors, spreadsheets, and databases, and they have no trouble navigating through software packages in the Windows environment. We believe, however, that advances in computer technology should not turn statistical analyses into a "black box." Rather, we choose to use the computational shortcuts and interactive visual tools that modern technology provides to give us more time to emphasize statistical reasoning as well as the understanding and interpretation of statistical results.

In this edition, students will be able to use the computer both for standard statistical analyses and as a tool for reinforcing and visualizing statistical concepts. *MINITAB 13* for Windows is used exclusively as the computer package for statistical analysis. Almost all graphs and figures, as well as all computer printout, are generated using this version of *MINITAB*. However, we have chosen to isolate the instructions for generating this output into individual sections called "About *MINITAB*" at the end of each chapter. Each discussion used numerical examples to guide the student through the *MINITAB* commands and options necessary for the procedures presented in that chapter. We have included references to visual screen captures from *MINITAB 13*, so that the student can actually work through these sections as "mini-labs."

If you do not need "hands-on" knowledge of *MINITAB*, or if you are using another software package, you may choose to skip these sections and simply use the *MINITAB* printouts as guides for the basic understanding of computer printouts.

Any student who has access to a computer with a browser such as Internet Explorer or Netscape Navigator can use the applets found on the CD-ROM that accompanies the text to visualize a variety of statistical concepts. In addition, some of the applets can be used instead of computer software to perform simple statistical analyses. Exercises written specifically for use with these applets appear in a section at the end of each chapter. Students can use the applets at home or in a computer lab. They can use them as they read through the text material, once they have finished reading the entire chapter, or as a tool for exam review. Instructors can assign applet exercises to the students, use the applets as a tool in a lab setting, or use them for visual demonstrations during lectures. We believe that these applets will be a powerful tool that will increase student enthusiasm for, and understanding of, statistical concepts and procedures.

Study Aids

The many and varied exercises in the text provide the best learning tool for students embarking on a first course in statistics. An exercise number printed in color indicates that a detailed solution appears in the *Study Guide and Student Solutions Manual*, which is available as a supplement for students.

Icons to the left of the exercise numbers are used to identify areas of application such as quality control, engineering, education, social sciences, biological sciences, psychology, entertainment, and so on. The coding used to indicate the area of application is shown below and is also reproduced on the inside left of the back cover.

Icons used in the exercise sections to identify applications.

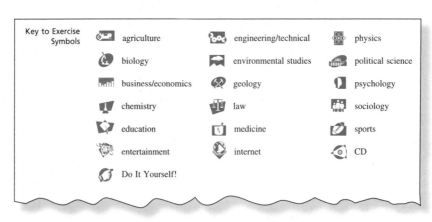

Key to Exercise Symbols			
agriculture	engineering/technical	physics
biology	environmental studies	political science
business/economics	geology	psychology
chemistry	law	sociology
education	medicine	sports
entertainment	internet	CD
Do It Yourself!		

The CD-ROM that accompanies each new copy of the text provides students with an array of study resources, including the complete set of *Do It Yourself!* applets, data sets for many of the text exercises saved in a variety of formats, and a set of interactive tutorial files. Students will also have access to a section of the text-specific website containing PowerPoint slides, the data sets and a set of web quizzes.

Sections called *Key Concepts and Formulas* appear in each chapter as a review in outline form of the material covered in that chapter.

Key Concepts and Formulas from page 410.

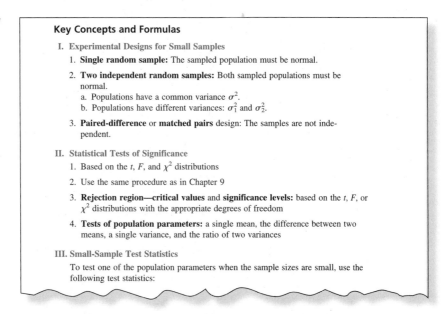

Key Concepts and Formulas

I. **Experimental Designs for Small Samples**
   1. **Single random sample:** The sampled population must be normal.
   2. **Two independent random samples:** Both sampled populations must be normal.
      a. Populations have a common variance σ^2.
      b. Populations have different variances: σ_1^2 and σ_2^2.
   3. **Paired-difference** or **matched pairs** design: The samples are not independent.

II. **Statistical Tests of Significance**
   1. Based on the t, F, and χ^2 distributions
   2. Use the same procedure as in Chapter 9
   3. **Rejection region—critical values** and **significance levels:** based on the t, F, or χ^2 distributions with the appropriate degrees of freedom
   4. **Tests of population parameters:** a single mean, the difference between two means, a single variance, and the ratio of two variances

III. **Small-Sample Test Statistics**
   To test one of the population parameters when the sample sizes are small, use the following test statistics:

The *Do It Yourself!* sections appear within the body of the text, explaining the use of a particular Java applet. Boxed and shaded definitions are again included, along with step-by-step hints for problem solving in displays called *How Do I . . . ?*

How Do I display from page 180.

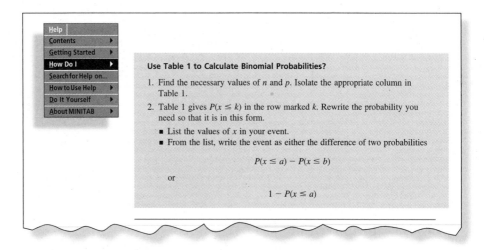

Help	
Contents	▶
Getting Started	▶
How Do I	▶
Search for Help on...	
How to Use Help	▶
Do It Yourself	▶
About MINITAB	▶

Use Table 1 to Calculate Binomial Probabilities?

1. Find the necessary values of n and p. Isolate the appropriate column in Table 1.
2. Table 1 gives $P(x \le k)$ in the row marked k. Rewrite the probability you need so that it is in this form.
   - List the values of x in your event.
   - From the list, write the event as either the difference of two probabilities

$$P(x \le a) - P(x \le b)$$

or

$$1 - P(x \le a)$$

In addition, a TI-83 Manual that shows students how to perform the techniques in the text using the TI-83 graphing calculator is available.

Instructor Resources

The Instructor's Suite CD supplied to adopters of the eleventh edition contains a variety of teaching aids, including:

- The Complete Solutions Manual in pdf format
- Test bank files in Microsoft Word
- Animated PowerPoint presentations
- The complete set of Do It Yourself! applets
- Data sets in a variety of formats

The PowerPoint presentations and data sets will also be available in the instructor's section of a text-specific website. The website will also contain the *Classic Exercises* with solutions in pdf format, and three real data sets, along with *Exercises using the Large Data Sets,* which can be used throughout the course. A file named "Fortune" contains the revenues (in millions) for the *Fortune* 500 largest U.S. industrial corporations in 2002; a file named "Batting" contains the batting averages for the National and American baseball league batting champions from 1876 to 2001; and a file named "BldPress" contains the age and diastolic and systolic blood pressures for 965 men and 945 women compiled by the National Institutes of Health.

Acknowledgments

The authors are grateful to Carolyn Crockett and the editorial staff of Duxbury for their patience, assistance, and cooperation in the preparation of this edition. A special thanks to Gary McClelland for his careful customization of the *Do It Yourself!* applets used in the text, and for his patient and even enthusiastic responses to our constant emails! Thanks are also due to Francis P. Mathur, California Polytechnic University, Pomona; George Montopoli, Arizona Western College; Keith Williams, University of Arkansas for Medical Sciences; and S. T. Ziliak, Georgia Institute of Technology, for their helpful reviews of the manuscript. We wish to thank authors and organizations for allowing us to reprint selected material; acknowledgments are made wherever such material appears in the text.

Robert J. Beaver
Barbara M. Beaver
William Mendenhall

Contents

2   Describing Data with Numerical Measures   50

3   Describing Bivariate Data   93

4   Probability and Probability Distributions   119

5 Several Useful Discrete Distributions   174

6 The Normal Probability Distribution   205

11   The Analysis of Variance   426

12 Linear Regression and Correlation 483

13 Multiple Regression Analysis 532

14 Analysis of Categorical Data 575

15 Nonparametric Statistics 610

Introduction

An Invitation to Statistics

What is statistics? Have you ever met a statistician? Do you know what a statistician does? Perhaps you are thinking of the person who sits in the broadcast booth at the Rose Bowl, recording the number of pass completions, yards rushing, or interceptions thrown on New Year's Day. Or perhaps the mere mention of the word *statistics* sends a shiver of fear through you. You may think you know nothing about statistics; however, it is almost inevitable that you encounter statistics in one form or another every time you pick up a daily newspaper. Here is an example:

A Dead Heat

PRINCETON, NJ—The latest CNN/USA Today/Gallup tracking poll shows that the margin between George W. Bush and Al Gore has narrowed, and is now—at a 46% to 44% Bush lead—within the poll's margin of error. As was the case after the first debate, the third debate on October 17th was followed by an increase in support for Bush, but—as also happened after the first debate—the race has tightened. About a quarter of the likely voters indicate they could change their minds by Election Day and vote for someone other than their currently preferred candidate, underscoring the closeness and volatility of this year's race. The poll also shows that on several other measures, except for honesty (where Bush fares considerably better than Gore) the electorate sees only slight differences between the two candidates.

—Gallup News Service[1]

Articles similar to this one are commonplace in our newspapers and magazines. In fact, in the period just prior to a presidential election, a new poll is reported almost every day. The language of this article is very familiar to us; however, it leaves the inquisitive reader with some unanswered questions. How were the people in the poll selected? Will these people give the same response tomorrow? Will they give the same response on election day? Will they even vote? Are these people representative of all those who will vote on election day? It is the job of a statistician to ask these questions and to find answers for them in the language of the poll.

Great Xpectations

Who would have thought the kids would start taking over so soon? . . . Slapped with the label Generation X, they've turned the tag into a badge of honor. They are X-citing, X-igent, X-pansive. They're the next big thing. Boomers, beware!

A recent University of Michigan study found that 25-to-34-year-olds are trying to start businesses at three times the rate of 35-to-55-year-olds. . . .

"I prefer working on my own to working for someone else."
AGREE: 87% of GenXers
79% of Boomers
77% of Matures

"If I just work hard enough, I will eventually achieve what I want."
AGREE: 91% of GenXers
84% of Boomers
82% of Matures

—Time magazine[2]

When you see an article like this one in a magazine, do you simply read the title and the first paragraph, or do you read further and try to understand the meaning of the numbers? What does "three times the rate" really mean? How did the authors get these numbers? Did they really interview every American in a particular age category? It is the job of the statistician to interpret the language of this study.

Hot News: 98.6 Not Normal

After believing for more than a century that 98.6 was the normal body temperature for humans, researchers now say normal is not normal anymore.

For some people at some hours of the day, 99.9 degrees could be fine. And readings as low as 96 turn out to be highly human.

The 98.6 standard was derived by a German doctor in 1868. Some physicians have always been suspicious of the good doctor's research. His claim: 1 million readings—in an epoch without computers.

So Mackowiak & Co. took temperature readings from 148 healthy people over a three-day period and found that the mean temperature was 98.2 degrees. Only 8 percent of the readings were 98.6.

—The Press-Enterprise[3]

What questions come to your mind when you read this article? How did the researcher select the 148 people, and how can we be sure that the results based on these 148 people are accurate when applied to the general population? How did the researcher arrive at the normal "high" and "low" temperatures given in the article? How did the German doctor record 1 million temperatures in 1868? Again, we encounter a statistical problem with an application to everyday life.

Statistics is a branch of mathematics that has applications in almost every facet of our daily life. It is a new and unfamiliar language for most people, however, and, like any new language, statistics can seem overwhelming at first glance. We invite you to learn this new language *one step at a time*. Once the language of statistics is learned and understood, it provides a powerful data analytic tool in many different fields of application.

The Population and the Sample

In the language of statistics, one of the most basic concepts is **sampling.** In most statistical problems, a specified number of measurements or data—a **sample**—is drawn from a much larger body of measurements, called the **population.**

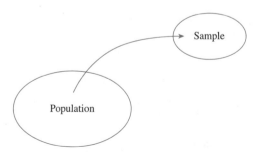

For the body-temperature experiment, the sample is the set of body-temperature measurements for the 148 healthy people chosen by the experimenter. We hope that the sample is representative of a much larger body of measurements—the population—the body temperatures of all healthy people in the world!

Which is of primary interest, the sample or the population? In most cases, we are interested primarily in the population, but the population may be difficult or impossible to enumerate. Imagine trying to record the body temperature of every healthy person on earth or the presidential preference of every registered voter in the United States! Instead, **we try to describe or predict the behavior of the population on the basis of information obtained from a representative sample from that population.**

The words *sample* and *population* have two meanings for most people. For example, you read in the newspapers that a Gallup poll conducted in the United States was based on a sample of 1823 people. Presumably, each person interviewed is asked a particular question, and that person's response represents a single measurement in the sample. Is the sample the set of 1823 people, or is it the 1823 responses that they give?

When we use statistical language, we distinguish between the set of objects on which the measurements are taken and the measurements themselves. To experimenters, the objects on which measurements are taken are called **experimental units.** The sample survey statistician calls them **elements of the sample.**

Descriptive and Inferential Statistics

When first presented with a set of measurements—whether a sample or a population—you need to find a way to organize and summarize it. The branch of statistics that presents techniques for describing sets of measurements is called **descriptive statistics.** You have seen descriptive statistics in many forms: bar charts, pie charts, and line charts presented by a political candidate; numerical tables in the newspaper; or the average rainfall amounts reported by the local television weather forecaster. Computer-generated graphics and numerical summaries are commonplace in our everyday communication.

Definition   **Descriptive statistics** consists of procedures used to summarize and describe the important characteristics of a set of measurements.

If the set of measurements is the entire population, you need only to draw conclusions based on the descriptive statistics. However, it might be too expensive or too time consuming to enumerate the entire population. Perhaps enumerating the population would destroy it, as in the case of "time to failure" testing. For these or other reasons, you may have only a sample from the population. By looking at the sample, you want to answer questions about the population as a whole. The branch of statistics that deals with this problem is called **inferential statistics.**

Definition   **Inferential statistics** consists of procedures used to make inferences about population characteristics from information contained in a sample drawn from this population.

The **objective of inferential statistics** is to make inferences (that is, draw conclusions, make predictions, make decisions) about the characteristics of a population from information contained in a sample.

Achieving the Objective of Inferential Statistics: The Necessary Steps

How can you make inferences about a population using information contained in a sample? The task becomes simpler if you organize the problem into a series of logical steps.

1. **Specify the questions to be answered and identify the population of interest.** In the presidential election poll, the objective is to determine who will get the most votes on election day. Hence, the population of interest is the set of all votes in the presidential election. When you select a sample, it is important that the sample be representative of *this* population, not the population of voter preferences on July 5 or on some other day prior to the election.

2. **Decide how to select the sample.** This is called the *design of the experiment* or the *sampling procedure.* Is the sample representative of the population of interest? For example, if a sample of registered voters is selected from the state of Arkansas, will this sample be representative of all voters in the United States? Will it be the same as a sample of "likely voters"—those who are likely to actually vote in the election? Is the sample large enough to answer the questions posed in step 1 without wasting time and money on additional information? A good sampling design will answer the questions posed with minimal cost to the experimenter.

3. **Select the sample and analyze the sample information.** No matter how much information the sample contains, you must use an appropriate method of analysis to extract it. Many of these methods, which depend on the sampling procedure in step 2, are explained in the text.

4. **Use the information from step 3 to make an inference about the population.** Many different procedures can be used to make this inference, and some are better than others. For example, ten different methods might be available to estimate human response to an experimental drug, but one procedure might be more accurate than others. You should use the best inference-making procedure available (many of these are explained in the text).

5. **Determine the reliability of the inference.** Since you are using only a fraction of the population in drawing the conclusions described in step 4, you might be wrong! How can this be? If an agency conducts a statistical survey for you and estimates that your company's product will gain 34% of the market this year, how much confidence can you place in this estimate? Is this estimate accurate to within 1, 5, or 20 percentage points? Is it reliable enough to be used in setting production goals? Every statistical inference should include a measure of reliability that tells you how much confidence you have in the inference.

Now that you have learned some of the basic terms and concepts in the language of statistics, we again pose the question asked at the beginning of this discussion: Do you know what a statistician does? It is the job of the statistician to implement all of the preceding steps. This may involve questioning the experimenter to make sure that the population of interest is clearly defined, developing an appropriate sampling plan or experimental design to provide maximum information at minimum cost, correctly analyzing and drawing conclusions using the sample information, and finally measuring the reliability of the conclusions based on the experimental results.

As you proceed through the book, you will learn more and more words, phrases, and concepts from this new language of statistics. Statistical procedures, for the most part, consist of commonsense steps that, given enough time, you would most likely have discovered for yourself. Since statistics is an applied branch of mathematics, many of these basic concepts are mathematical—developed and based on results from calculus or higher mathematics. However, you do not have to be able to derive results in order to apply them in a logical way. In this text, we use numerical examples and intuitive arguments to explain statistical concepts, rather than more complicated mathematical arguments.

In recent years, computers and microcomputers have become readily available to many students and provide them with an invaluable tool. In the study of statistics, even the beginning student can use packaged programs to perform statistical analyses with a high degree of speed and accuracy. Some of the more common statistical packages available at computer facilities are *MINITAB*™, SAS (Statistical Analysis System), and SPSS (Statistical Package for the Social Sciences); personal computers will support packages such as *MINITAB*, MS Excel, and others. There are even online statistical programs and interactive "applets" on the Internet.

These programs, called **statistical software,** differ in the types of analyses available, the options within the programs, and the forms of printed results (called **output**). However, they are all similar. In this book, we primarily use *MINITAB* as a statistical tool; understanding the basic output of this package will help you interpret the output from other software systems.

At the end of most chapters, you will find a section called "About *MINITAB*." These sections present numerical examples to guide you through the *MINITAB* commands and options that are used for the procedures in that chapter. If you are using *MINITAB* in a lab or home setting, you may want to work through this section at your own computer so that you become familiar with the hands-on methods in *MINITAB* analysis. If you do not need hands-on knowledge of *MINITAB*, you may choose to skip this section and simply use the *MINITAB* printouts for analysis as they appear in the text.

You will also find a section called "Do It Yourself" in many of the chapters. These sections provide a useful introduction to the statistical **applets** available using the CD-ROM that accompanies new copies of this book. You can use these applets to visualize many of the chapter concepts and to find solutions to exercises in a new section called "Do It Yourself Exercises."

Most important, using statistics successfully requires common sense and logical thinking. For example, if we want to find the average height of all students at a particular university, would we select our entire sample from the members of the basketball team? In the body-temperature example, the logical thinker would question an 1868 average based on 1 million measurements—when computers had not yet been invented.

As you learn new statistical terms, concepts, and techniques, remember to view every problem with a critical eye and be sure that the rule of common sense applies. Throughout the text, we will remind you of the pitfalls and dangers in the use or misuse of statistics. Benjamin Disraeli once said that there are three kinds of lies: *lies, damn lies,* and *statistics*! Our purpose is to dispel this claim—to show you how to make statistics *work* for you and not *lie* for you!

As you continue through the book, refer back to this "Invitation to Statistics" periodically. Each chapter will increase your knowledge of the language of statistics and should, in some way, help you achieve one of the steps described here. Each of these steps is essential in attaining the overall objective of inferential statistics: to make inferences about a population using information contained in a sample drawn from that population.

Data Sources

1. David W. Moore and Frank Newport, "As Race Narrows, Voters See Little Difference between Bush and Gore on Leadership Qualities and Effectiveness of their Policies," Gallup News Service (http://www.gallup.com/poll/releases/pr001024.asp), 24 October 2000.

2. Margaret Hornblower, "Great Xpectations," *Time,* 9 June 1997, p. 58.

3. "Hot News: 98.6 Not Normal," *The Press-Enterprise* (Riverside, CA), 23 September 1992.

1

Describing Data with Graphs

Case Study

Is your blood pressure normal, or is it too high or too low? The case study at the end of this chapter examines a large set of blood pressure data. You will use graphs to describe these data and compare your blood pressure with that of others of your same age and gender.

General Objectives

Many sets of measurements are samples selected from larger populations. Other sets constitute the entire population, as in a national census. In this chapter, you will learn what a *variable* is, how to classify variables into several types, and how measurements or data are generated. You will then learn how to use graphs to describe data sets.

Specific Topics

1. Variables, experimental units, samples and populations, data (1.1)
2. Univariate and bivariate data (1.1)
3. Qualitative and quantitative variables—discrete and continuous (1.2)
4. Data distributions and their shapes (1.1, 1.4)
5. Pie charts, bar charts, line charts (1.3, 1.4)
6. Dotplots (1.4)
7. Stem and leaf plots (1.4)
8. Relative frequency histograms (1.5)

1.1 Variables and Data

In Chapters 1 and 2, we will present some basic techniques in *descriptive statistics*—the branch of statistics concerned with describing sets of measurements, both *samples* and *populations*. Once you have collected a set of measurements, how can you display this set in a clear, understandable, and readable form? First, you must be able to define what is meant by measurements or "data" and to categorize the types of data that you are likely to encounter in real life. We begin by introducing some definitions—new terms in the statistical language that you need to know.

Definition   A **variable** is a characteristic that changes or varies over time and/or for different individuals or objects under consideration.

For example, body temperature is a variable that changes over time within a single individual; it also varies from person to person. Religious affiliation, ethnic origin, income, height, age, and number of offspring are all variables—characteristics that vary depending on the individual chosen.

In the Introduction, we defined an *experimental unit* or an *element of the sample* as the object on which a measurement is taken. Equivalently, we could define an experimental unit as the object on which a variable is measured. When a variable is actually measured on a set of experimental units, a set of measurements or **data** result.

Definition   An **experimental unit** is the individual or object on which a variable is measured. A single **measurement** or data value results when a variable is actually measured on an experimental unit.

If a measurement is generated for every experimental unit in the entire collection, the resulting data set constitutes the *population* of interest. Any smaller subset of measurements is a *sample*.

Definition   A **population** is the set of all measurements of interest to the investigator.

Definition   A **sample** is a subset of measurements selected from the population of interest.

EXAMPLE 1.1   A set of five students is selected from all undergraduates at a large university, and measurements are entered into a spreadsheet as shown in Figure 1.1. Identify the various elements involved in generating this set of measurements.

Solution   There are several *variables* in this example. The *experimental unit* on which the variables are measured is a particular undergraduate student on the campus. Five variables are measured for each student: grade point average (GPA), gender, year in college, major, and current number of units enrolled. Each of these characteristics varies from student to student. If we consider the GPAs of all students at this university to be the population of interest, the five GPAs represent a *sample* from this population. If the GPA of each undergraduate student at the university had been measured, we would have generated the entire *population* of measurements for this variable.

FIGURE 1.1
Measurements on
five undergraduate
students

⊞ Worksheet 1 ***					
↓	**C1**	**C2**	**C3-T**	**C4-T**	**C5-T**	**C6**
	Student	**GPA**	**Gender**	**Year**	**Major**	**Number of Units**
1	1	2.0	F	Fr	Psychology	16
2	2	2.3	F	So	Mathematics	15
3	3	2.9	M	So	English	17
4	4	2.7	M	Fr	English	15
5	5	2.6	F	Jr	Business	14

The second variable measured on the students is gender, which can fall into one of two categories—male or female. It is not a numerically valued variable and hence is somewhat different from GPA. The population, if it could be enumerated, would consist of a set of Ms and Fs, one for each student at the university. Similarly, the third and fourth variables, year and major, generate nonnumerical data. Year has four categories (Fr, So, Jr, Sr), and major has one category for each undergraduate major on campus. The last variable, current number of units enrolled, is numerically valued, generating a set of numbers rather than a set of qualities or characteristics.

Although we have discussed each variable individually, remember that we have measured each of these five variables on a single experimental unit: the student. Therefore, in this example, a "measurement" really consists of five observations, one for each of the five measured variables. For example, the measurement taken on student 2 produces this observation:

(2.3, F, So, Mathematics, 15)

You can see that there is a difference between a *single* variable measured on a single experimental unit and *multiple* variables measured on a single experimental unit as in Example 1.1.

Definition

Univariate data result when a single variable is measured on a single experimental unit.

Definition

Bivariate data result when two variables are measured on a single experimental unit. **Multivariate data** result when more than two variables are measured.

If you measure the body temperatures of 148 people, the resulting data are *univariate*. In Example 1.1, five variables were measured on each student, resulting in *multivariate data*.

1.2 Types of Variables

Variables can be classified into one of two categories: **qualitative** or **quantitative**.

Definition	**Qualitative variables** measure a quality or characteristic on each experimental unit. **Quantitative variables** measure a numerical quantity or amount on each experimental unit.

Qualitative variables produce data that can be categorized according to similarities or differences in kind; hence, they are often called **categorical data**. The variables gender, year, and major in Example 1.1 are qualitative variables that produce categorical data. Here are some other examples:

- Political affiliation: Republican, Democrat, Independent
- Taste ranking: excellent, good, fair, poor
- Color of an M&M® candy: brown, yellow, red, orange, green, blue

Quantitative variables, often represented by the letter x, produce numerical data, such as those listed here:

- x = Prime interest rate
- x = Number of unregistered taxicabs in a city
- x = Weight of a package ready to be shipped
- x = Volume of orange juice in a glass

Notice that there is a difference in the types of numerical values that these quantitative variables can assume. The number of unregistered taxicabs, for example, can take on only the values $x = 0, 1, 2, \ldots$, whereas the weight of a package can take on any value greater than zero, or $0 < x < \infty$. To describe this difference, we define two types of quantitative variables: **discrete** and **continuous**.

Definition	A **discrete variable** can assume only a finite or countable number of values. A **continuous variable** can assume the infinitely many values corresponding to the points on a line interval.

The name *discrete* relates to the discrete gaps between the possible values that the variable can assume. Variables such as number of family members, number of new car sales, and number of defective tires returned for replacement are all examples of discrete variables. On the other hand, variables such as height, weight, time, distance, and volume are *continuous* because they can assume values at any point along a line interval. For any two values you pick, a third value can always be found between them!

EXAMPLE 1.2 Identify each of the following variables as qualitative or quantitative:

1. The most frequent use of your microwave oven (reheating, defrosting, warming, other)
2. The number of consumers who refuse to answer a telephone survey
3. The door chosen by a mouse in a maze experiment (A, B, or C)
4. The winning time for a horse running in the Kentucky Derby
5. The number of children in a fifth-grade class who are reading at or above grade level

Solution Variables 1 and 3 are both *qualitative* because only a quality or characteristic is measured for each individual. The categories for these two variables are shown in parentheses. The other three variables are *quantitative*. Variable 2, the number of consumers, is a *discrete* variable that can take on any of the values $x = 0, 1, 2, \ldots$, with a maximum value depending on the number of consumers called. Similarly, variable 5, the number of children reading at or above grade level, can take on any of the values $x = 0, 1, 2, \ldots$, with a maximum value depending on the number of children in the class. Variable 4, the winning time for a Kentucky Derby horse, is the only *continuous* variable in the list. The winning time, if it could be measured with sufficient accuracy, could be 121 seconds, 121.5 seconds, 121.25 seconds, or any values between any two times we have listed.

Figure 1.2 depicts the types of data we have defined. Why should you be concerned about different kinds of variables and the data that they generate? The reason is that the methods used to describe data sets depend on the type of data you have collected. For each set of data that you collect, the key will be to determine what type of data you have and how you can present them most clearly and understandably to your audience!

FIGURE 1.2
Types of data

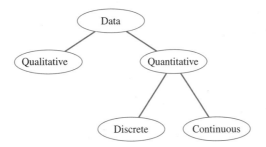

1.3   Graphs for Categorical Data

After the data have been collected, they can be consolidated and summarized to show the following information:

- What values of the variable have been measured
- How often each value has occurred

For this purpose, you can construct a *statistical table* that can be used to display the data graphically as a data distribution. The type of graph you choose depends on the type of variable you have measured.

When the variable of interest is *qualitative,* the statistical table is a list of the categories being considered along with a measure of how often each value occurred. You can measure "how often" in three different ways:

- The **frequency,** or number of measurements in each category
- The **relative frequency,** or proportion of measurements in each category
- The **percentage** of measurements in each category

For example, if you let n be the total number of measurements in the set, you can find the relative frequency and percentage using these relationships:

$$\text{Relative frequency} = \frac{\text{Frequency}}{n}$$

$$\text{Percent} = 100 \times \text{Relative frequency}$$

You will find that the sum of the frequencies is always *n*, the sum of the relative frequencies is 1, and the sum of the percentages is 100%.

The categories for a qualitative variable should be chosen so that

- a measurement will belong to one and only one category
- each measurement has a category to which it can be assigned

For example, if you categorize meat products according to the type of meat used, you might use these categories: beef, chicken, seafood, pork, turkey, other. To categorize ranks of college faculty, you might use these categories: professor, associate professor, assistant professor, instructor, lecturer, other. The "other" category is included in both cases to allow for the possibility that a measurement cannot be assigned to one of the earlier categories.

Once the measurements have been categorized and summarized in a *statistical table*, you can use either a pie chart or a bar chart to display the distribution of the data. A **pie chart** is the familiar circular graph that shows how the measurements are distributed among the categories. A **bar chart** shows the same distribution of measurements in categories, with the height of the bar measuring how often a particular category was observed.

EXAMPLE 1.3

In a survey concerning public education, 400 school administrators were asked to rate the quality of education in the United States. Their responses are summarized in Table 1.1. Construct a pie chart and a bar chart for this set of data.

Solution To construct a pie chart, assign one sector of a circle to each category. The angle of each sector should be proportional to the proportion of measurements (or *relative frequency*) in that category. Since a circle contains 360°, you can use this equation to find the angle:

$$\text{Angle} = \text{Relative frequency} \times 360°$$

TABLE 1.1
U.S. education rating by 400 educators

Rating	Frequency
A	35
B	260
C	93
D	12
Total	400

Table 1.2 shows the ratings along with the frequencies, relative frequencies, percentages, and sector angles necessary to construct the pie chart. Figure 1.3 shows the pie chart constructed from the values in the table. While pie charts use percentages to determine the relative sizes of the "pie slices," bar charts usually plot frequency against the categories. A bar chart for these data is shown in Figure 1.4.

The visual impact of these two graphs is somewhat different. The pie chart is used to display the relationship of the parts to the whole; the bar chart is used to emphasize the actual quantity or frequency for each category. Since the categories in this example are

TABLE 1.2
Calculations for the pie chart in Example 1.3

Rating	Frequency	Relative Frequency	Percent	Angle
A	35	35/400 = .09	9%	.09 × 360 = 32.4°
B	260	260/400 = .65	65%	234.0°
C	93	93/400 = .23	23%	82.8°
D	12	12/400 = .03	3%	10.8°
Total	400	1.00	100%	360°

ordered "grades" (A, B, C, D), we would not want to rearrange the bars in the chart to change its *shape*. In a pie chart, the order of presentation is irrelevant.

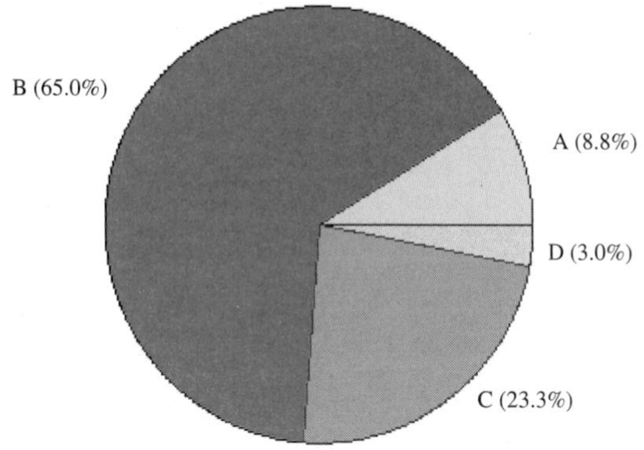

FIGURE 1.3 Pie chart for Example 1.3

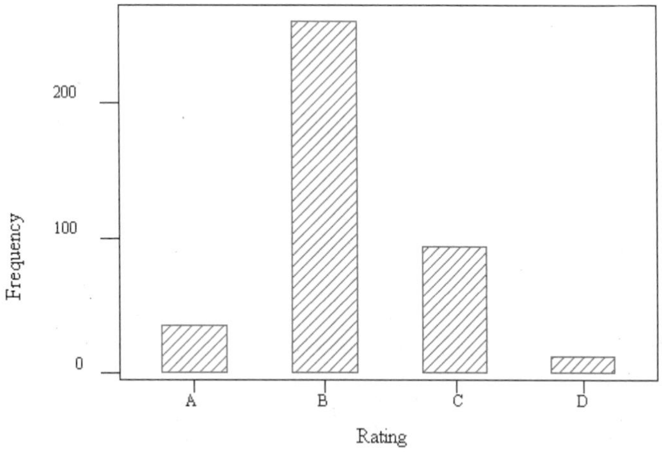

FIGURE 1.4 Bar chart for Example 1.3

EXAMPLE 1.4

A snack size bag of peanut M&M® candies contains 21 candies with the colors listed in Table 1.3. The variable "color" is *qualitative,* so Table 1.4 lists the six categories along with a tally of the number of candies of each color. The last three columns of Table 1.4 give the three different measures of how often each category occurred. Since the categories are colors and have no particular order, you could construct bar charts with many different *shapes* just by reordering the bars. To emphasize that brown is the most frequent color, followed by blue, green, and orange, we order the bars from largest to smallest and generate the bar chart using *MINITAB* in Figure 1.5. A bar chart in which the bars are ordered from largest to smallest is called a **Pareto chart.**

TABLE 1.3 Colors of 21 candies

Brown	Green	Brown	Blue
Red	Red	Green	Brown
Yellow	Orange	Green	Blue
Brown	Blue	Blue	Brown
Orange	Blue	Brown	Orange
Yellow			

TABLE 1.4 M&M data for Example 1.4

Category	Tally	Frequency	Relative Frequency	Percent
Brown	~~||||~~ |	6	6/21	28%
Green	|||	3	3/21	14
Orange	|||	3	3/21	14
Yellow	||	2	2/21	10
Red	||	2	2/21	10
Blue	~~||||~~	5	5/21	24
Total		21	1	100%

FIGURE 1.5
MINITAB bar chart
for Example 1.4

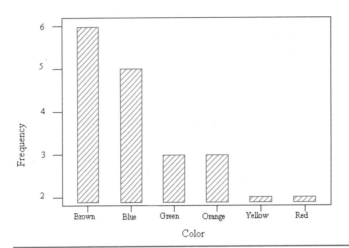

Exercises

Understanding the Concepts

1.1 Identify the experimental units on which the following variables are measured:

a. Gender of a student

b. Number of errors on a midterm exam

c. Age of a cancer patient

d. Number of flowers on an azalea plant

e. Color of a car entering the parking lot

1.2 Identify each variable as quantitative or qualitative:

a. Amount of time it takes to assemble a simple puzzle

b. Number of students in a first-grade classroom

c. Rating of a newly elected politician (excellent, good, fair, poor)

d. State in which a person lives

1.3 Identify the following quantitative variables as discrete or continuous:

a. Population in a particular area of the United States

b. Weight of newspapers recovered for recycling on a single day

c. Time to complete a sociology exam

d. Number of consumers in a poll of 1000 who consider nutritional labeling on food products to be important

 1.4 A data set consists of the ages at death for each of the 41 past presidents of the United States.

a. Is this set of measurements a population or a sample?

b. What is the variable being measured?

c. Is the variable in part b quantitative or qualitative?

 1.5 You are a candidate for your state legislature, and you want to survey voter attitudes regarding your chances of winning. Identify the population that is of interest to you and from which you would like to select your sample. How is this population dependent on time?

 1.6 A medical researcher wants to estimate the survival time of a patient after the onset of a particular type of cancer and after a particular regimen of radiotherapy.

a. What is the variable of interest to the medical researcher?

b. Is the variable in part a qualitative, quantitative discrete, or quantitative continuous?

c. Identify the population of interest to the medical researcher.

d. Describe how the researcher could select a sample from the population.

e. What problems might arise in sampling from this population?

1.7 An educational researcher wants to evaluate the effectiveness of a new method for teaching reading to deaf students. Achievement at the end of a period of teaching is measured by a student's score on a reading test.

a. What is the variable to be measured? What type of variable is it?

b. What is the experimental unit?

c. Identify the population of interest to the experimenter.

Basic Techniques

1.8 Fifty people are grouped into four categories—A, B, C, and D—and the number of people who fall into each category is shown in the table:

Category	Frequency
A	11
B	14
C	20
D	5

a. What is the experimental unit?

b. What is the variable being measured? Is it qualitative or quantitative?

c. Construct a pie chart to describe the data.

d. Construct a bar chart to describe the data.

e. Does the shape of the bar chart in part d change depending on the order of presentation of the four categories? Is the order of presentation important?

f. What *proportion* of the people are in category B, C, or D?

g. What *percentage* of the people are *not* in category B?

1.9 A manufacturer of jeans has plants in California, Arizona, and Texas. A group of 25 pairs of jeans is randomly selected from the computerized database, and the state in which each is produced is recorded:

CA	AZ	AZ	TX	CA
CA	CA	TX	TX	TX
AZ	AZ	CA	AZ	TX
CA	AZ	TX	TX	TX
CA	AZ	AZ	CA	CA

a. What is the experimental unit?

b. What is the variable being measured? Is it qualitative or quantitative?

c. Construct a pie chart to describe the data.

d. Construct a bar chart to describe the data.

e. What *proportion* of the jeans are made in Texas?

f. What state produced the most jeans in the group?

g. If you want to find out whether the three plants produced equal numbers of jeans, or whether one produced more jeans than the others, how can you use the charts from parts c and d to help you? What conclusions can *you* draw from these data?

Applications

1.10 During the presidential election of 2000, the news media regularly presented opinion polls that tracked the fortunes of the four major candidates. One such poll, taken for CNN/TIME, showed the following results[1]:

Suppose the election for President were being held today, and you had to choose from Al Gore and Joseph Lieberman, the Democrats; George W. Bush and Dick Cheney, the Republicans; Ralph Nader and Winona LaDuke, the Green Party candidates; and Pat Buchanan, the Reform Party candidate. For whom would you vote—Gore, Bush, Buchanan, or Nader?

Bush	47%
Gore	45%
Nader	4%
Buchanan	1%

The results were based on a sample taken October 4 and 5, 2000, of 1244 adult Americans, including 636 likely voters—those most likey to cast ballots in November.

a. If the pollsters were planning to use these results to predict the outcome of the 2000 election, describe the population of interest to them.

b. Describe the actual population from which the sample was drawn.

c. What is the difference between "registered voters" and "likely voters"? Why is this important?

d. Is the sample selected by the pollsters representative of the population described in part a? Explain.

1.11 "For all the speeches given, the commercials aired, the mud splattered in any election, a hefty percentage of people decide whom they will vote for only at the last minute."[2] Suppose that a sample of people were asked, "When did you finally decide whom to vote for in the presidential election?" These answers were given:

Answer	Percent
Only in the past 3 days	17%
In the past week	8
In the past 2 weeks (after the debates)	18
In early fall (after the convention)	24
Earlier than that	33

a. Would you use a pie chart or a bar chart to graphically describe the data? Why?

b. Draw the chart you chose in part a.

c. What does the chart tell you about the reliability of election polls taken early in the election campaign?

1.12 The 1960s generation was never as radical as it was portrayed. According to an opinion poll in *The American Enterprise*,[3] when a group of 30–40-year-olds were asked to describe their political views in the 1960s and early 1970s, they gave these responses:

Conservative:	28%
Moderate:	35%
Liberal:	31%
Radical:	6%

a. Define the variable that has been measured in this survey.

b. Is the variable qualitative or quantitative?

c. What do the numbers represent?

d. Define the sample and the population of interest to the researchers.

e. Construct a pie chart to describe the data.

f. What percentage of 30–40-year-olds described themselves as either moderate or conservative during the 1960s and early 1970s?

g. What other types of questions might you want to investigate, based on the results of part f?

1.13   How long does it take you to adjust to your normal work routine after coming back from vacation? A bar graph with data from the Snapshots section of *USA Today* is shown below[4]:

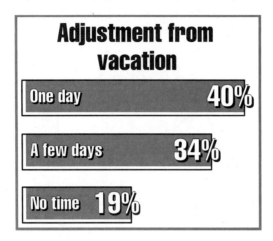

a. Are all of the opinions accounted for in the table? Add another category if necessary.

b. Use a pie chart to describe the opinions. Which graph is more interesting to look at?

1.4   Graphs for Quantitative Data

Quantitative variables measure an amount or quantity on each experimental unit. If the variable can take only a finite or countable number of values, it is a *discrete* variable. A variable that can assume an infinite number of values corresponding to points on a line interval is called *continuous*.

Pie Charts and Bar Charts

Sometimes information is collected for a quantitative variable measured on different segments of the population, or for different categories of classification. For example, you might measure the average incomes for people of different age groups, different genders, or living in different geographic areas of the country. In such cases, you can use pie charts or bar charts to describe the data, using the amount measured in each category rather than the frequency of occurrence of each category. The *pie chart* displays how the total quantity is distributed among the categories, and the *bar chart* uses the height of the bar to display the amount in a particular category.

EXAMPLE 1.5   The amount of money expended in fiscal year 2000 by the U.S. Department of Defense in various categories is shown in Table 1.5.[5] Construct both a pie chart and a bar chart to describe the data. Compare the two forms of presentation.

TABLE 1.5
Expenses by
category

Category	Amount (in billions)
Military personnel	$ 76.0
Operation and maintenance	105.9
Procurement	51.6
Research and development	37.6
Military construction	5.1
Total	$276.2

Solution   Two variables are being measured: the category of expenditure (*qualitative*) and the amount of the expenditure (*quantitative*). The bar chart in Figure 1.6 displays the categories on the horizontal axis and the amounts on the vertical axis. For the pie chart in

FIGURE 1.6
Bar chart for
Example 1.5

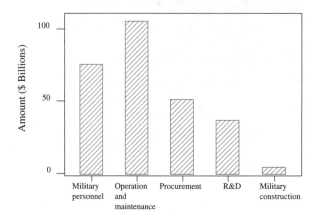

Figure 1.7, each "pie slice" represents the proportion of the total expenditures ($276.2 billion) corresponding to its particular category. For example, for the research and development category, the angle of the sector is

$$\frac{37.6}{276.2} \times 360° = 49.0°$$

FIGURE 1.7
Pie chart for
Example 1.5

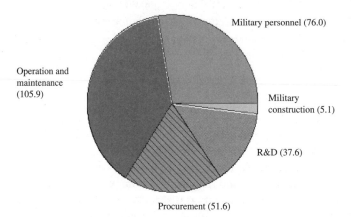

Both graphs show that the largest amounts of money were spent on personnel and operations; however, the pie chart does not allow you to redetermine the actual dollar amounts spent. Since there is no inherent order to the categories, you are free to rearrange the bars or sectors of the graphs in any way you like. The *shape* of the bar chart has no bearing on its interpretation.

Line Charts

When a quantitative variable is recorded over time at equally spaced intervals (such as daily, weekly, monthly, quarterly, or yearly), the data set forms a **time series**. Time series data are most effectively presented on a **line chart** with time as the horizontal axis. The idea is to try to discern a pattern or **trend** that will likely continue into the future, and then to use that pattern to make accurate predictions for the immediate future.

EXAMPLE 1.6

As "baby boomers" (born in 1946–1964) are aging, the U.S. government is becoming more concerned about the stability of the Social Security system. The actual and projected percentages of disability-insured workers for the years 1985–2005 are listed in Table 1.6.[6] Construct a line chart to illustrate the data. What is the effect of stretching and shrinking the vertical axis on the line chart?

TABLE 1.6
Percentages of
insured workers

Year	1985	1990	1995	2000	2005
Percent	2.9	3.0	3.8	4.3	4.9

Solution

The quantitative variable "percent" is measured over five time intervals, creating a *time series* that you can graph with a line chart. The time intervals are marked on the horizontal axis and the percentages on the vertical axis. The data points are then connected by line segments to form the line charts in Figure 1.8. Notice the marked difference in the vertical scales of the two graphs. *Shrinking* the scale on the vertical axis causes large changes to appear small, and vice versa. To avoid misleading conclusions, you must look carefully at the scales of the vertical and horizontal axes. However, from both graphs you get a clear picture of the steadily increasing percentages as we enter the new millennium.

FIGURE 1.8 Line charts for Example 1.6

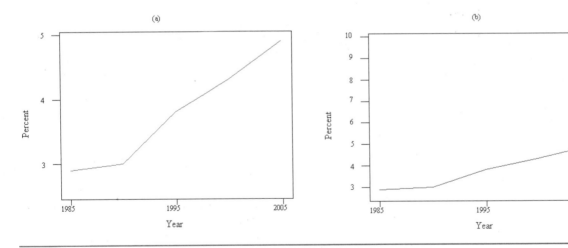

Dotplots

Many sets of quantitative data consist of numbers that cannot easily be separated into categories or intervals of time. You need a different way to graph this type of data!

The simplest graph for quantitative data is the **dotplot**. For a small set of measurements—for example, the set 2, 6, 9, 3, 7, 6—you can simply plot the measurements as points on a horizontal axis. This dotplot, generated by *MINITAB*, is shown in Figure 1.9(a). For a large data set, however, such as the one in Figure 1.9(b), the dotplot can be uninformative and tedious to interpret.

FIGURE 1.9
Dotplots for large
and small data sets

Character Dotplots

(a)

```
         .        .               :        .                .
    +---------+---------+---------+-------Small Set
    2.0       4.0       6.0       8.0
```

(b)

```
              .              : :   .          .                   :
    :        :.  ..  ...  :: :: ::.  .:  ..  :.   .:      .:     .  . ....
    -----+---------+---------+---------+---------+---------+---------+-Large Set
        21.0      28.0      35.0      42.0      49.0      56.0
```

Stem and Leaf Plots

Another simple way to display the distribution of a quantitative data set is the **stem and leaf plot**. This plot presents a graphical display of the data using the actual numerical values of each data point.

Construct a Stem and Leaf Plot?

1. Divide each measurement into two parts: the **stem** and the **leaf**.
2. List the stems in a column, with a vertical line to their right.
3. For each measurement, record the leaf portion in the same row as its corresponding stem.
4. Order the leaves from lowest to highest in each stem.
5. Provide a key to your stem and leaf coding so that the reader can re-create the actual measurements if necessary.

EXAMPLE 1.7

Table 1.7 lists the prices (in dollars) of 19 different brands of walking shoes. Construct a stem and leaf plot to display the distribution of the data.

TABLE 1.7
Prices of walking
shoes

90	70	70	70	75	70
65	68	60	74	70	95
75	70	68	65	40	65
70					

Solution

To create the stem and leaf, you could divide each observation between the ones and the tens place. The number to the left is the stem; the number to the right is the leaf. Thus, for the shoes that cost $65, the stem is 6 and the leaf is 5. The stems, ranging from 4 to 9, are listed in Figure 1.10, along with the leaves for each of the 19 measure-

FIGURE 1.10
Stem and leaf plot
for the data in
Table 1.8

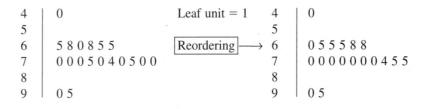

ments. If you indicate that the leaf unit is 1, the reader will realize that the stem and leaf 6 and 8, for example, represent the number 68, recorded to the nearest dollar.

Sometimes the available stem choices result in a plot that contains too few stems and a large number of leaves within each stem. In this situation, you can stretch the stems by dividing each one into several lines, depending on the leaf values assigned to them. Stems are usually divided in one of two ways:

- Into two lines, with leaves 0–4 in the first line and leaves 5–9 in the second line
- Into five lines, with leaves 0–1, 2–3, 4–5, 6–7, and 8–9 in the five lines, respectively

EXAMPLE 1.8   The data in Table 1.8 are the GPAs of 30 Bucknell University freshmen, recorded at the end of the freshman year. Construct a stem and leaf plot to display the distribution of the data.

TABLE 1.8
Grade point averages of 30 Bucknell University freshmen

2.0	3.1	1.9	2.5	1.9
2.3	2.6	3.1	2.5	2.1
2.9	3.0	2.7	2.5	2.4
2.7	2.5	2.4	3.0	3.4
2.6	2.8	2.5	2.7	2.9
2.7	2.8	2.2	2.7	2.1

Solution   The data, though recorded to an accuracy of only one decimal place, are measurements of the continuous variable x = GPA, which can take on values in the interval 0–4.0. By examining Table 1.8, you can quickly see that the highest and lowest GPAs are 3.4 and 1.9, respectively. But how are the remaining GPAs distributed? If you use the decimal point as the dividing line between the stem and the leaf, you have only three stems, which does not produce a very good picture. Even if you divide each stem into two lines, there are only four stems, since the first line of stem 1 and the second line of stem 4 are empty! Dividing each stem into five lines produces the most descriptive plot, as shown in Figure 1.11. For these data, the leaf unit is .1, and the reader can infer that the stem and leaf 2 and 6, for example, represent the measurement $x = 2.6$.

FIGURE 1.11
Stem and leaf plot for the data in Table 1.8

1	9 9		1	9 9	
2	0 1 1		2	0 1 1	
2	3 2		2	2 3	
2	5 4 5 5 5 5 4	Reordering →	2	4 4 5 5 5 5 5	
2	7 6 7 6 7 7 7		2	6 6 7 7 7 7 7	
2	9 8 8 9		2	8 8 9 9	
3	1 0 1 0		3	0 0 1 1	
3			3		
3	4	Leaf unit = .1	3	4	

If you turn the stem and leaf plot sideways, so that the vertical line is now a horizontal axis, you can see that the data have "piled up" or been "distributed" along the axis in a pattern that can be described as "mound-shaped"—much like a pile of sand on the beach. One GPA was somewhat higher than the rest ($x = 3.4$), and the gap in the distribution shows that no GPAs were between 3.1 and 3.4.

Interpreting Graphs with a Critical Eye

Once you have created a graph or graphs for a set of data, what should you look for as you attempt to describe the data?

- First, check the horizontal and vertical **scales,** so that you are clear about what is being measured.
- Examine the **location** of the data distribution. Where on the horizontal axis is the center of the distribution? If you are comparing two distributions, are they both centered in the same place?
- Examine the **shape** of the distribution. Does the distribution have one "peak," a point that is higher than any other? If so, this is the most frequently occurring measurement or category. Is there more than one peak? Are there an approximately equal number of measurements to the left and right of the peak?
- Look for any unusual measurements or **outliers.** That is, are any measurements much bigger or smaller than all of the others? These outliers may not be representative of the other values in the set.

Distributions are often described according to their **shapes**.

Definition A distribution is **symmetric** if the left and right sides of the distribution, when divided at the middle value, form mirror images.

A distribution is **skewed to the right** if a greater proportion of the measurements lie to the right of the peak value. Distributions that are **skewed right** contain a few unusually large measurements.

A distribution is **skewed to the left** if a greater proportion of the measurements lie to the left of the peak value. Distributions that are **skewed left** contain a few unusually small measurements.

A distribution is **unimodal** if it has one peak; a **bimodal** distribution has two peaks. Bimodal distributions often represent a mixture of two different populations in the data set.

EXAMPLE 1.9 Examine the three dotplots generated by *MINITAB* and shown in Figure 1.12. Describe these distributions in terms of their locations and shapes.

FIGURE 1.12
Shapes of data distributions for Example 1.9

Character Dotplots

```
          :                      :                                :
        : :                    : : :                            : : :
    : : : : :                : : : : .              . : : : : :
  : : : : : :              : : : : : .   . .        . . . : : : : : : :
  ----+--------          -----+---------+--         ----+---------+--
  1 2 3 4 5 6 7          1 2 3 4 5 6 7 8 9          1 2 3 4 5 6 7 8 9
```

Solution The first dotplot shows a *relatively symmetric* distribution with a single peak located at $x = 4$. If you were to fold the page at this peak, the left and right halves would *almost* be mirror images. The second dotplot, however, is far from symmetric. It has a long "right tail," meaning that there are a few unusually large observations. If you were to fold the page at the peak, a larger proportion of measurements would be on the right side than on the left. This distribution is *skewed to the right*. Similarly, the third dotplot with the long "left tail" is *skewed to the left*.

EXAMPLE 1.10 A quality control analyst is interested in monitoring the weights of a particular style of walking sneaker. She enters the weights (in ounces) of eight randomly selected shoes into the database but accidentally misplaces the decimal point in the last entry:

9.72   9.74   9.70   9.71   9.71   9.73   9.72   .972

Use a dotplot to describe the data and uncover the analyst's mistake.

Solution The dotplot of this small data set is shown in Figure 1.13(a). You can clearly see the *outlier* or unusual observation caused by the analyst's data entry error. Once the error has been corrected, as in Figure 1.13(b), you can see the correct distribution of the data set. Since this is a very small set, it is difficult to describe the shape of the distribution, although it seems to have a peak value around 9.72 and it appears to be relatively symmetric.

FIGURE 1.13
Distributions of weights for Example 1.10

Character Dotplots

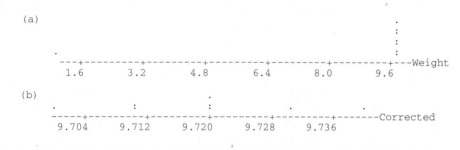

When comparing graphs created for two data sets, you should compare their *scales of measurement, locations,* and *shapes,* and look for unusual measurements or outliers. Remember that outliers are not always caused by errors or incorrect data entry. Sometimes they provide very valuable information that should not be ignored. You may need additional information to decide whether an outlier is a valid measurement that is simply unusually large or small, or whether there has been some sort of mistake in the data collection. If the scales differ widely, be careful about making comparisons or drawing conclusions that might be inaccurate!

1.5 Relative Frequency Histograms

A relative frequency histogram resembles a bar chart, but it is used to graph quantitative rather than qualitative data. The data in Table 1.9 are the GPAs of 30 Bucknell University freshmen, reproduced from Example 1.8 and shown as a dotplot in Figure 1.14(a). First, divide the interval from the smallest to the largest measurements into subintervals or *classes of equal length.* If you stack up the dots in each subinterval (Figure 1.14(b)), and draw a bar over each stack, you will have created a **frequency histogram** or a **relative frequency histogram,** depending on the scale of the vertical axis.

TABLE 1.9
Grade point averages of 30 Bucknell University freshmen

2.0	3.1	1.9	2.5	1.9
2.3	2.6	3.1	2.5	2.1
2.9	3.0	2.7	2.5	2.4
2.7	2.5	2.4	3.0	3.4
2.6	2.8	2.5	2.7	2.9
2.7	2.8	2.2	2.7	2.1

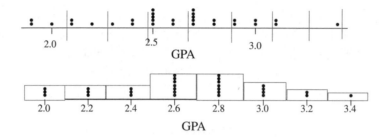

FIGURE 1.14
How to construct a
histogram

Definition | A **relative frequency histogram** for a quantitative data set is a bar graph in which the height of the bar shows "how often" (measured as a proportion or relative frequency) measurements fall in a particular class or subinterval. The classes or subintervals are plotted along the horizontal axis.

As a rule of thumb, the number of classes should range from 5 to 12; the more data available, the more classes you need.[†] The classes must be chosen so that each measurement falls into *one and only one* class. For the GPAs in Table 1.9, we decided to use *eight* intervals of equal length. Since the total span of the GPAs is

$$3.4 - 1.9 = 1.5$$

the approximate class width is $(1.5 \div 8) = .1875$. For convenience, we round this approximate width up to .2. Beginning the first interval at the lowest value, 1.9, we form subintervals from 1.9 up to *but not including* 2.1, 2.1 up to *but not including* 2.3, and so on. By using the **method of left inclusion**, and including the left class boundary point but not the right boundary point in the class, we eliminate any confusion about where to place a measurement that happens to fall on a class boundary point.

Table 1.10 shows the eight classes, labeled from 1 to 8 for identification. The boundaries for the eight classes, along with a tally of the number of measurements that fall in each class, are also listed in the table. As with the charts in Section 1.3, you can now measure *how often* each class occurs using *frequency* or *relative frequency*.

To construct the relative frequency histogram, plot the class boundaries along the horizontal axis. Draw a bar over each class interval, with height equal to the relative frequency for that class. The relative frequency histogram for the GPA data, Figure 1.15, shows at a glance how GPAs are distributed over the interval 1.9 to 3.4.

TABLE 1.10
Relative
frequencies for
data of Table 1.9

Class	Class Boundaries	Tally	Class Frequency	Class Relative Frequency
1	1.9 to <2.1	|||	3	3/30
2	2.1 to <2.3	|||	3	3/30
3	2.3 to <2.5	|||	3	3/30
4	2.5 to <2.7	⩗||	7	7/30
5	2.7 to <2.9	⩗||	7	7/30
6	2.9 to <3.1	||||	4	4/30
7	3.1 to <3.3	||	2	2/30
8	3.3 to <3.5			1	1/30

[†]You can use this table as a guide for selecting an appropriate number of classes. Remember that this is only a guide; you may use more or fewer classes than the table recommends if it makes the graph more descriptive.

Sample Size	25	50	100	200	500
Number of Classes	6	7	8	9	10

FIGURE 1.15
Relative frequency
histogram

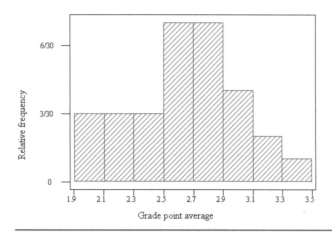

EXAMPLE 1.11 Twenty-five households are polled in a marketing survey, and Table 1.11 lists the numbers of quarts of milk purchased during a particular week. Construct a relative frequency histogram to describe the data.

TABLE 1.11
Quarts of milk
purchased by 25
households

0	3	5	4	3
2	1	3	1	2
1	1	2	0	1
4	3	2	2	2
2	2	2	3	4

Solution The variable being measured is "number of quarts of milk," which is a discrete variable that takes on only integer values. In this case, it is simplest to choose the classes or subintervals as the integer values over the range of observed values: 0, 1, 2, 3, 4, and 5. Table 1.12 shows the classes and their corresponding frequencies and relative frequencies. The relative frequency histogram, generated using *MINITAB*, is shown in Figure 1.16.

TABLE 1.12
Frequency table for
Example 1.11

Number of Quarts	Frequency	Relative Frequency
0	2	.08
1	5	.20
2	9	.36
3	5	.20
4	3	.12
5	1	.04

FIGURE 1.16
Minitab histogram
for Example 1.11

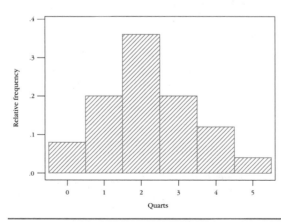

A relative frequency histogram can be used to describe the distribution of a set of data in terms of its *location* and *shape*, and to check for *outliers* as you did with other graphs. For example, both the GPA and the "milk" data were relatively symmetric, with no unusual measurements. Since the bar constructed above each class represents the *relative frequency* or proportion of the measurements in that class, these heights can be used to give us further information:

- The proportion of the measurements that fall in a particular class or group of classes
- The probability that a measurement drawn at random from the set will fall in a particular class or group of classes

Consider the relative frequency histogram for the GPA data in Figure 1.15. What proportion of the students had GPAs of 2.7 or higher? This involves all classes beyond 2.7 in Table 1.10. Because there are 14 students in those classes, the proportion who have GPAs of 2.7 or higher is 14/30, or approximately 47%. This is also the percentage of the total area under the histogram in Figure 1.15 that lies to the right of 2.7.

Suppose you wrote each of the 30 GPAs on a piece of paper, put them in a hat, and drew one at random. What is the chance that this piece of paper contains a GPA of 2.7 or higher? Since 14 of the 30 pieces of paper fall in this category, you have 14 chances out of 30; that is, the probability is 14/30. The word *probability* is not unfamiliar to you; we will discuss it in more detail in Chapter 4.

Although we are interested in describing the set of $n = 30$ measurements, we might also be interested in the population from which the sample was drawn, which is the set of GPAs of all freshmen currently in attendance at Bucknell University. Or, if we are interested in the academic achievement of college freshmen in general, we might consider our sample as representative of the population of GPAs for freshmen attending Bucknell or colleges *similar* to Bucknell. A sample histogram provides valuable information about the population histogram—the graph that describes the distribution of the entire population. Remember, though, that different samples from the same population will produce *different* histograms, even if you use the same class boundaries. However, you can expect that the sample and population histograms will be similar. As you add more and more data to the sample, the two histograms become more and more alike. If you enlarge the sample to include the entire population, the two histograms are identical!

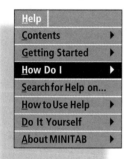

Construct a Relative Frequency Histogram?

1. Choose the number of classes, usually between 5 and 12. The more data you have, the more classes you should use.
2. Calculate the approximate class width by dividing the difference between the largest and smallest values by the number of classes.
3. Round the approximate class width up to a convenient number.
4. If the data are discrete, you might assign one class for each integer value taken on by the data. For a large number of integer values, you may need to group them into classes.
5. Locate the class boundaries. The lowest class must include the smallest measurement. Then add the remaining classes using the left inclusion method.
6. Construct a statistical table containing the classes, their frequencies, and their relative frequencies.
7. Construct the histogram like a bar graph, plotting class intervals on the horizontal axis and relative frequencies as the heights of the bars.

Exercises

Basic Techniques

EX0114

1.14 Construct a stem and leaf plot for these 50 measurements:

3.1	4.9	2.8	3.6	2.5	4.5	3.5	3.7	4.1	4.9
2.9	2.1	3.5	4.0	3.7	2.7	4.0	4.4	3.7	4.2
3.8	6.2	2.5	2.9	2.8	5.1	1.8	5.6	2.2	3.4
2.5	3.6	5.1	4.8	1.6	3.6	6.1	4.7	3.9	3.9
4.3	5.7	3.7	4.6	4.0	5.6	4.9	4.2	3.1	3.9

a. Describe the shape of the data distribution. Do you see any outliers?

b. Use the stem and leaf plot to find the smallest observation.

c. Find the eighth and ninth largest observations.

1.15 Refer to Exercise 1.14. Construct a relative frequency histogram for the data.

a. Approximately how many class intervals should you use?

b. Suppose you decide to use classes starting at 1.6 with a class width of .5 (i.e., 1.6 to <2.1, 2.1 to <2.6). Construct the relative frequency histogram for the data.

c. What fraction of the measurements are less than 5.1?

d. What fraction of the measurements are larger than 3.6?

e. Compare the relative frequency histogram with the stem and leaf plot in Exercise 1.14. Are the shapes similar?

1.16 Consider this set of data:

4.5	3.2	3.5	3.9	3.5	3.9
4.3	4.8	3.6	3.3	4.3	4.2
3.9	3.7	4.3	4.4	3.4	4.2
4.4	4.0	3.6	3.5	3.9	4.0

a. Construct a stem and leaf plot by using the leading digit as the stem.

b. Construct a stem and leaf plot by using each leading digit twice. Does this technique improve the presentation of the data? Explain.

1.17 A discrete variable can take on only the values 0, 1, or 2. A set of 20 measurements on this variable is shown here:

1	2	1	0	2
2	1	1	0	0
2	2	1	1	0
0	1	2	1	1

a. Construct a relative frequency histogram for the data.

b. What proportion of the measurements are greater than 1?

c. What proportion of the measurements are less than 2?

d. If a measurement is selected at random from the 20 measurements shown, what is the probability that it is a 2?

e. Describe the shape of the distribution. Do you see any outliers?

1.18 Refer to Exercise 1.17.

a. Draw a dotplot to describe the data.

b. How could you define the stem and the leaf for this data set?

c. Draw the stem and leaf plot using your decision from part b.

d. Compare the dotplot, the stem and leaf plot, and the relative frequency histogram (Exercise 1.17). Do they all convey roughly the same information?

1.19   An experimental psychologist measured the length of time it took for a rat to successfully navigate a maze on each of five days. The results are shown in the table. Create a line chart to describe the data. Do you think that any learning is taking place?

Day	1	2	3	4	5
Time (sec.)	45	43	46	32	25

1.20   The value of a quantitative variable is measured once a year for a 10-year period. Here are the data:

Year	Measurement	Year	Measurement
1	61.5	6	58.2
2	62.3	7	57.5
3	60.7	8	57.5
4	59.8	9	56.1
5	58.0	10	56.0

a. Create a line chart to describe the variable as it changes over time.

b. Describe the measurements using the chart constructed in part a.

1.21   The test scores on a 100-point test were recorded for 20 students:

61	93	91	86	55	63	86	82	76	57
94	89	67	62	72	87	68	65	75	84

a. Use an appropriate graph to describe the data.

b. Describe the shape and location of the scores.

c. Is the shape of the distribution unusual? Can you think of any reason the distribution of the scores would have such a shape?

Applications

1.22   The length of time (in months) between the onset of a particular illness and its recurrence was recorded for $n = 50$ patients:

2.1	4.4	2.7	32.3	9.9	9.0	2.0	6.6	3.9	1.6
14.7	9.6	16.7	7.4	8.2	19.2	6.9	4.3	3.3	1.2
4.1	18.4	.2	6.1	13.5	7.4	.2	8.3	.3	1.3
14.1	1.0	2.4	2.4	18.0	8.7	24.0	1.4	8.2	5.8
1.6	3.5	11.4	18.0	26.7	3.7	12.6	23.1	5.6	.4

a. Construct a relative frequency histogram for the data.

b. Would you describe the shape as roughly symmetric, skewed right, or skewed left?

c. Give the fraction of recurrence times less than or equal to 10 months.

1.23   The American population over the past 50 years has been grouped by nicknames that try to describe their common traits. According to a recent magazine article, the numbers of Americans in each of four age categories are as shown in the table:[7]

Generation	Number of Americans (in millions)
Matures (born before 1946)	68.3
Baby boomers (born 1946–1964)	77.6
GenXers (born 1965–1976)	44.6
Others (born after 1976)	72.4

a. What graphical methods could you use to describe the data?

b. Select the method from part a that you think best describes the data.

c. Why are there fewer Americans in the GenX group than in the other three groups?

EX0124

1.24 To decide on the number of service counters needed for stores to be built in the future, a supermarket chain wanted to obtain information on the length of time (in minutes) required to service customers. To find the distribution of customer service times, a sample of 1000 customers' service times was recorded. Sixty of these are shown here:

3.6	1.9	2.1	.3	.8	.2	1.0	1.4	1.8	1.6
1.1	1.8	.3	1.1	.5	1.2	.6	1.1	.8	1.7
1.4	.2	1.3	3.1	.4	2.3	1.8	4.5	.9	.7
.6	2.8	2.5	1.1	.4	1.2	.4	1.3	.8	1.3
1.1	1.2	.8	1.0	.9	.7	3.1	1.7	1.1	2.2
1.6	1.9	5.2	.5	1.8	.3	1.1	.6	.7	.6

a. Construct a stem and leaf plot for the data.

b. What fraction of the service times are less than or equal to 1 minute?

c. What is the smallest of the 60 measurements?

1.25 Refer to Exercise 1.24. Construct a relative frequency histogram for the supermarket service times.

a. Describe the shape of the distribution. Do you see any outliers?

b. Assuming that the outliers in this data set are valid observations, how would you explain them to the management of the supermarket chain?

c. Compare the relative frequency histogram with the stem and leaf plot in Exercise 1.24. Do the two graphs convey the same information?

EX0126

1.26 The calcium (Ca) content of a powdered mineral substance was analyzed ten times with the following percent compositions recorded:

.0271	.0282	.0279	.0281	.0268
.0271	.0281	.0269	.0275	.0276

a. Draw a dotplot to describe the data. (HINT: The scale of the horizontal axis should range from .0260 to .0290.)

b. Draw a stem and leaf plot for the data. Use the numbers in the hundredths and thousandths places as the stem.

c. Are any of the measurements inconsistent with the other measurements, indicating that the technician may have made an error in the analysis?

EX0127

1.27 Listed below are the ages at the time of death for the 37 American presidents from George Washington to Richard Nixon[5]:

Washington	67	Polk	53	Garfield	49	Harding	57
J. Adams	90	Taylor	65	Arthur	56	Coolidge	60
Jefferson	83	Fillmore	74	Cleveland	71	Hoover	90
Madison	85	Pierce	64	B. Harrison	67	F. D. Roosevelt	63
Monroe	73	Buchanan	77	Cleveland	71	Truman	88
J. Q. Adams	80	Lincoln	56	McKinley	58	Eisenhower	78
Jackson	78	A. Johnson	66	T. Roosevelt	60	Kennedy	46
Van Buren	79	Grant	63	Taft	72	L. Johnson	64
W. H. Harrison	68	Hayes	70	Wilson	67	Nixon	81
Tyler	71						

a. Before you graph the data, try to visualize the distribution of the ages at death for the presidents. What shape do you think it will have?

b. Construct a stem and leaf plot for the data. Describe the shape. Does it surprise you?

c. The five youngest presidents at the time of death appear in the lower "tail" of the distribution. Three of the five youngest have one common trait. Identify the five youngest presidents at death. What common trait explains these measurements?

EX0128

1.28 The red blood cell count of a healthy person was measured on each of 15 days. The number recorded is measured in 10^6 cells per microliter (μL).

5.4	5.2	5.0	5.2	5.5
5.3	5.4	5.2	5.1	5.3
5.3	4.9	5.4	5.2	5.2

a. Use an appropriate graph to describe the data.

b. Describe the shape and location of the red blood cell counts.

c. If the person's red blood cell count is measured today as $5.7 \times 10^6/\mu$L, would you consider this unusual? What conclusions might you draw?

EX0129

1.28 The officials of major league baseball have crowned a batting champion in the National League each year since 1876. A sample of winning batting averages is listed in the table[5]:

Year	Name	Average	Year	Name	Average
1876	Roscoe Barnes	.403	1954	Willie Mays	.345
1893	Hugh Duffy	.378	1975	Bill Madlock	.354
1915	Larry Doyle	.320	1958	Richie Ashburn	.350
1917	Edd Roush	.341	1942	Ernie Lombardi	.330
1934	Paul Waner	.362	1948	Stan Musial	.376
1911	Honus Wagner	.334	1971	Joe Torre	.363
1898	Willie Keeler	.379	1996	Tony Gwynn	.353
1924	Roger Hornsby	.424	1961	Roberto Clemente	.351
1963	Tommy Davis	.326	1968	Pete Rose	.335
1992	Gary Sheffield	.330	1885	Roger Connor	.371

a. Construct a relative frequency histogram to describe the batting averages for these 20 champions.

b. If you were to randomly choose one of the 20 names, what is the chance that you would choose a player whose average was above .400 for his championship year?

EX0130

1.30 The table shows the average ticket prices for the top 20 Broadway shows during the week of July 30–August 5, 2001[8]:

Show	Average Ticket Price	Show	Average Ticket Price
1. *The Producers*	$78	11. *Annie Get Your Gun*	$53
2. *The Lion King*	71	12. *Chicago*	53
3. *Aida*	67	13. *Kiss Me Kate*	55
4. *42nd Street*	68	14. *Rent*	49
5. *Beauty and the Beast*	62	15. *Cabaret*	64
6. *The Phantom of the Opera*	61	16. *Contact*	62
7. *The Music Man*	60	17. *Proof*	58
8. *Riverdance*	48	18. *Fosse*	53
9. *The Full Monty*	71	19. *Blast!*	41
10. *Les Miserables*	50	20. *The Tale of the Allergist's Wife*	48

a. Draw a stem and leaf plot for the data. Describe the shape of the distribution. Are there any outliers?

b. Construct a dotplot for the data. Which of the two graphs is more informative? Explain.

EX0131

1.31 How safe is your neighborhood? Are there any hazardous waste sites nearby? The table shows the number of hazardous waste sites in each of the 50 states and the District of Columbia in the year 2001:[5]

AL	15	HI	3	MA	33	NM	13	SD	2
AK	7	ID	10	MI	69	NY	92	TN	14
AZ	10	IL	45	MN	24	NC	27	TX	41
AR	12	IN	29	MS	4	ND	0	UT	21
CA	99	IA	16	MO	26	OH	34	VT	9
CO	17	KS	12	MT	14	OK	12	VA	31
CT	16	KY	15	NE	10	OR	12	WA	48
DE	17	LA	15	NV	1	PA	99	WV	9
DC	1	ME	13	NH	19	RI	12	WI	40
FL	52	MD	19	NJ	116	SC	25	WY	2
GA	15								

a. What variable is being measured? Is the variable discrete or continuous?

b. A stem and leaf plot generated by *MINITAB* is shown here. Describe the shape of the data distribution. Identify the unusually large measurements marked "HI" by state.

Stem-and-Leaf Display: HazWaste

```
Stem-and-leaf of HazWaste   N  = 51
Leaf Unit = 1.0

    7   0 0112234
   10   0 799
   22   1 000222223344
  (10)  1 5555667799
   19   2 14
   17   2 5679
   13   3 134
   10   3
   10   4 01
    8   4 58
    6   5 2

       HI    69,   92,   99,   99,  116,
```

c. Can you think of any reason these five states would have a large number of hazardous waste sites? What other variable might you measure to help explain why the data behave as they do?

As you continue to work through the exercises in this chapter, you will become more experienced in recognizing different types of data and in determining the most appropriate graphical method to use. Remember that the type of graphic you use is not as important as the interpretation that accompanies the picture. Look for these important characteristics:

- Location of the center of the data
- Shape of the distribution of data
- Unusual observations in the data set

Using these characteristics as a guide, you can interpret and compare sets of data using graphical methods, which are only the first of many statistical tools that you will soon have at your disposal.

Key Concepts

I. **How Data Are Generated**
   1. Experimental units, variables, measurements
   2. Samples and populations
   3. Univariate, bivariate, and multivariate data

II. **Types of Variables**
   1. Qualitative or categorical
   2. Quantitative
      a. Discrete
      b. Continuous

III. **Graphs for Univariate Data Distributions**
   1. Qualitative or categorical data
      a. Pie charts
      b. Bar charts
   2. Quantitative data
      a. Pie and bar charts
      b. Line charts
      c. Dotplots
      d. Stem and leaf plots
      e. Relative frequency histograms
   3. Describing data distributions
      a. Shapes—symmetric, skewed left, skewed right, unimodal, bimodal
      b. Proportion of measurements in certain intervals
      c. Outliers

DO IT YOURSELF!

Easy Access to the Web has made it possible for you to understand statistical concepts using an interactive Web tool called an **applet.** These applets provide visual reinforcement for the concepts that have been presented in the chapter. Sometimes you will be able to perform statistical experiments, sometimes you will be able to interact with a statistical graph to change its form, and sometimes you will be able to use the applet as an interactive "statistical table." At the end of each chapter, you will find exercises designed specifically for use with a particular applet. We want you to "Do it yourself!"

Rather than having to access these applets online, they have been included on the CD-ROM that accompanies each new copy of the text. When you insert the CD-ROM into the appropriate drive of your computer, the main menu will appear. Click on "Do It Yourself!–Applets". If necessary, follow the instructions to download the latest web browser, or just click the button to launch the Do It Yourself! applets. Your web browser will open the index of applets, organized by chapter and name. When you click a particular applet title, the applet will appear in your browser. To return to the index of applets, simply click the link at the bottom of the page.

Dotplots

Click the Chapter 1 applet called **Building a Dotplot.** If you move your cursor over the applet marked **Dotplot Demo** you will see a green line with a value that changes as you move along the horizontal axis. When you left-click your mouse, a dot will appear at that point on the dotplot. If two measurements are identical, the dots will pile up on top of each other (Figure 1.17). Follow the directions in the **Dotplot Demo,** using the sample data given there. If you make a mistake, the applet will tell you. The second applet, marked **Do It Yourself,** will not correct your mistakes; you can add as many dots as you want!

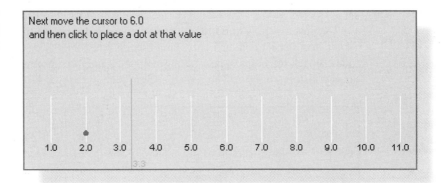

Histograms

Click the Chapter 1 applet called **Building a Histogram.** If you scroll down to the applet marked **Histogram Demo,** you will see the interval boundaries (or interval midpoints) for the histogram along the horizontal axis. As you move the mouse across the graph, a light gray box will show you where the measurement will be added at your next mouse click. When you release the mouse, the box turns blue. The distribution in Figure 1.18 contains two 0s, one 1, three 2s, and one 3. Follow the directions in the **Histogram Demo** using the sample data given there. Click the link to compare your results to the correct histogram. The second applet, marked **Do It Yourself,** will be used for some of the *Do It Yourself Exercises.*

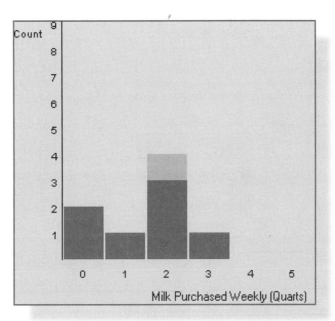

Click the applet called **Flipping Fair Coins,** and scroll down to the applet marked **sample size = 3.** The computer will collect some data by "virtually" tossing 3 coins and recording the quantitative discrete variable

$$x = \text{number of heads observed}$$

Click on "New Coin Flip." You will see the result of your three tosses in the upper-left-hand corner, along with the value of x. For the experiment in Figure 1.19 we observed $x = 2$.

The applet begins to build a relative frequency histogram to describe the data set, which at this point contains only one observation. Click "New Coin Flip" a few more times. Watch the coins appear, along with the value of x, and watch the relative frequency histogram grow. The red area (light blue in Figures 1.19 and 1.20) represents

FIGURE 1.19
Flipping Fair coins applet

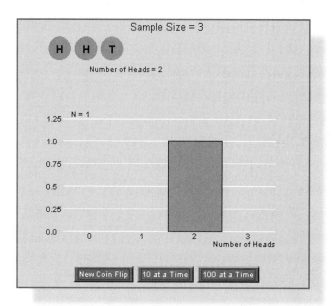

FIGURE 1.20
Flipping Fair Coins applet

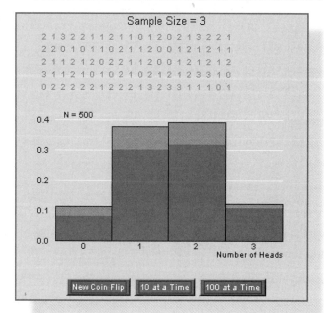

the current data added to the histogram, and the dark blue area in Figure 1.20 is contributed from the previous coin flips. You can flip the three coins 10 at a time or 100 at a time to generate data more quickly.

Figure 1.20 shows the relative frequency histogram for 500 observations in our data set. Your data set will look a little different. However, it should have the same approximate shape—it should be relatively symmetric. For our histogram, we can say that the values $x = 0$ and $x = 3$ occurred about 12–13% of the time, while the values $x = 1$ and $x = 2$ occurred between 38% and 40% of the time. Does your histogram produce similar results?

Help
Contents ▶
Getting Started ▶
How Do I ▶
Search for Help on...
How to Use Help ▶
Do It Yourself ▶
About MINITAB ▶

Introduction to *MINITAB*™

MINITAB is a computer software package that is available in many forms for different computer environments. The current version of *MINITAB* at the time of this printing is *MINITAb 13*, which is used in the Windows environment. We will assume that you are familiar with Windows. If not, perhaps a lab or teaching assistant can help you to master the basics.

Once you have started Windows, there are two ways to start *MINITAB*:

- If there is a *MINITAB* shortcut icon on the desktop, double-click on the icon.
- Click the Start button on the taskbar. Follow the menus, highlighting
  Programs → *MINITAB* 13 for Windows → *MINITAB*. Click on *MINITAB* to start the program.

When *MINITAB* is opened, the main *MINITAB* screen will be displayed (see Figure 1.21). It contains two windows: the Data window and the Session window. Clicking anywhere on the window will make that window active so that you can either enter data or type commands. Although it is possible to manually type *MINITAB* commands

FIGURE 1.21

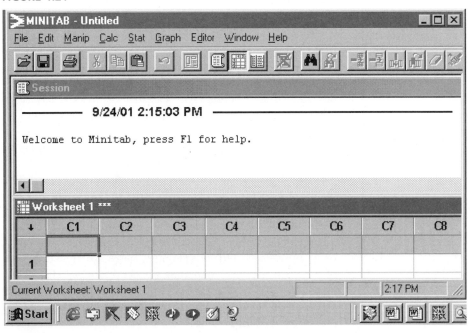

MINITAB

in the Session window, we choose to use the Windows approach, which will be familiar to most of you. If you prefer to use the typed commands, consult the *MINITAB* manual for detailed instructions.

At the top of the Session window, you will see a Menu bar. Highlighting and clicking on any command on the Menu bar will cause a menu to drop down, from which you may then select the necessary command. We will use the standard notation to indicate a sequence of commands from the drop-down menus. For example, **File → Open Worksheet** will allow you to retrieve a "worksheet"—a set of data from the Data window—which you have previously saved. To close the program, the command sequence is **File → Exit**.

MINITAB 13 allows multiple worksheets to be saved as "projects." When you are working on a project, you can add new worksheets or open worksheets from other projects to add to your current project. As you become more familiar with *MINITAB*, you will be able to organize your information into either "worksheets" or "projects," depending on the complexity of your task. If you are using an earlier version of *MINITAB*, you only need to open, use, and save stand-alone worksheets.

Graphing with *MINITAB*

The first data set to be graphed consists of qualitative data whose frequencies have already been recorded. The class status of 105 students in an introductory statistics class are listed in Table 1.13. Before you enter the data into the Minitab Data window, start a project called "Chapter 1" by highlighting **File → New.** A Dialog box called "New" will appear. Highlight **New project** and click **OK.** Before you continue, let's save this project as "Chapter 1" using the series of commands **File → Save Project.** Type **Chapter 1** in the File Name box and click on **Save.** In the Data window at the top of the screen, you will see your new project name, "Chapter 1.MPJ".

TABLE 1.13 Status of students in statistics class

Status	Freshman	Sophomore	Junior	Senior	Grad Student
Frequency	5	23	32	35	10

To enter the data into the worksheet, click on the gray cell just below the name C1 in the Data window. You can enter your own descriptive name for the categories—possibly "Status." Now use the down arrow ↓ or your mouse to continue down column C1, entering the five status descriptions. Notice that the name **C1** has changed to **C1-T** because you are entering text rather than numbers. Continue by naming column 2 (C2) "Frequency," and enter the five numerical frequencies into C2. The Data window will appear as in Figure 1.22.

To construct a pie chart for these data, click on **Graph → Pie Chart,** and a Dialog box will appear (see Figure 1.23). In this box, you must specify how you want to create the chart. Click on **Chart table → Categories in.** Either highlight and select C1 from the list at the left of the box, or type C1 in the "Categories in" box. Click on **Select.** Similarly, place the cursor in the box marked "Frequencies" and select C2. When you click **OK,** *MINITAB* will create the pie chart in Figure 1.24.

As you become more proficient at using the pie chart command, you may want to take advantage of some of the options available. You can change the colors and format of the chart, "explode" important sectors of the pie, change the order of the categories, or change labeling or color options using the **Options** command. Once the chart is created, you can also *manually edit* the chart—moving, adding, or deleting text using the **Editor → Edit** command.

MINITAB

FIGURE 1.22

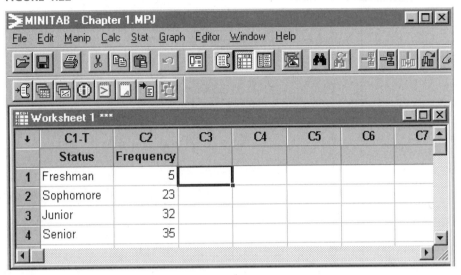

FIGURE 1.23

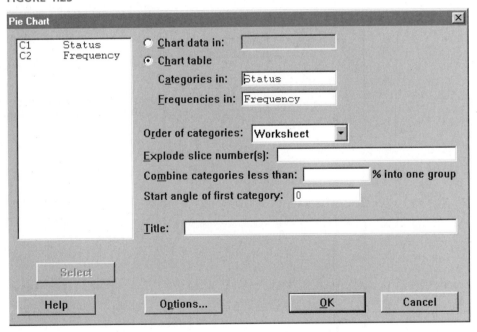

If you would rather construct a bar chart, use the command **Graph → Chart.** When the Dialog box appears, **select** C2 for the Y-axis and C1 for the X-axis. You can choose colors and fill for the chart using **Edit Attributes.** Other options are also available for changing the look of the graph. Click **Help** if you need it! The bar chart for this example is shown in Figure 1.25.[†] Again, you can *manually edit* the chart using the **Editor → Edit** command.

[†]To keep the bars in order from "freshman" to "grad student," use **Editor → Column → Value Order** after highlighting C1-T. Choose "Order of occurrence in worksheet."

MINITAB

FIGURE 1.24

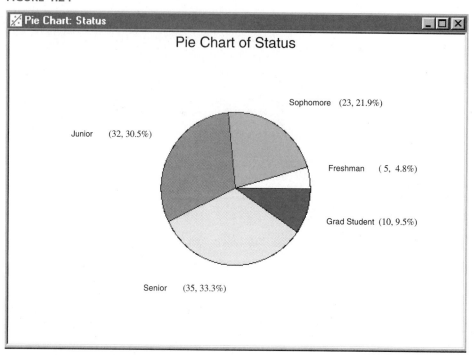

FIGURE 1.25

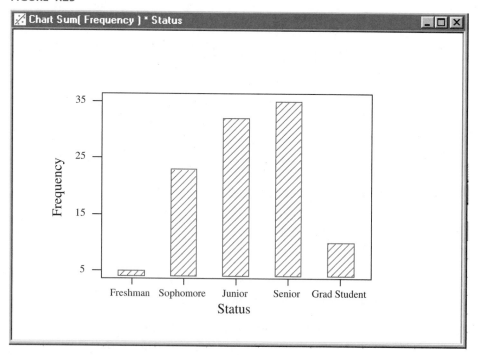

MINITAB can create dotplots, stem and leaf plots, and histograms for quantitative data. The top 40 stocks on the over-the-counter (OTC) market, ranked by percentage of outstanding shares traded on a particular day, are listed in Table 1.14. Although we

MINITAB

TABLE **1.14**   Percentage of OTC stocks traded

11.88	6.27	5.49	4.81	4.40	3.78	3.44	3.11	2.88	2.68
7.99	6.07	5.26	4.79	4.05	3.69	3.36	3.03	2.74	2.63
7.15	5.98	5.07	4.55	3.94	3.62	3.26	2.99	2.74	2.62
7.13	5.91	4.94	4.43	3.93	3.48	3.20	2.89	2.69	2.61

could simply enter these data into the third column (C3) of Worksheet 1 in the "Chapter 1" project, let's start a new worksheet within "Chapter 1" using **File → New,** highlighting *MINITAB* **Worksheet,** and clicking **OK.** Worksheet 2 will appear on the screen. Enter the data into column C1 and name them "Stocks" in the gray cell just below the C1.

To create a dotplot or a stem and leaf plot, use the command **Graph → Dotplot** or **Graph → Stem-and-Leaf,** respectively.† In the "Variables" box, select "Stocks" from the list to the left (see Figure 1.26).

You can choose from a variety of grouping options before clicking **OK.** The dotplot appears as a graph, while the stem and leaf plot appears in the Session window. To print either a Graph window or the Session window, click on the window to make it active and use **File → Print Graph** (or **Print Session Window**).

To create a histogram, use **Graph → Histogram,** selecting "Stocks" for the "Graph variables" box. Using the **Options** command, choose "Frequency" for the type of histogram. (You can edit the histogram later to display relative frequencies.) Choose "Cut Point" or "Midpoint" for the type of boundaries, depending on your preference. You can specify your own class boundaries or let *MINITAB* do it for you! Click **OK.** The **Edit**

FIGURE **1.26**

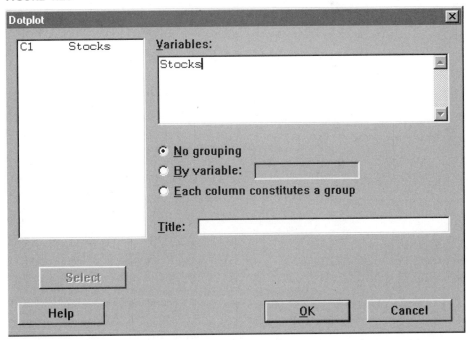

---

†You can also use the command sequence **Graphs → Character Graphs → Dotplot** (or **Stem-and-Leaf**). The dotplot appears as a character graph in the Session window.

MINITAB

Attributes command will let you change the color and style of the graph before you click **OK** to generate the histogram shown in Figure 1.27.

As you become more familiar with *MINITAB* for Windows, you can explore the various options available for each type of graph. It is possible to plot more than one variable at a time, to change the axes, to choose the colors, and to modify graphs in many ways. However, even with the basic default commands, it is clear that the distribution of OTC stocks is highly skewed to the right.

Make sure to save your work using the **File → Save Project** command before you exit *MINITAB*!

FIGURE 1.27

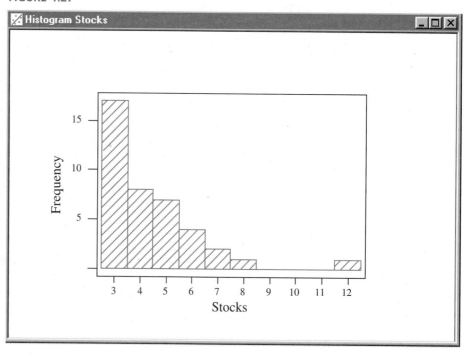

Supplementary Exercises

1.32 Identify each variable as quantitative or qualitative:

a. Ethnic origin of a candidate for public office

b. Score (0–100) on a placement examination

c. Fast-food establishment preferred by a student (McDonald's, Burger King, or Carl's Jr.)

d. Mercury concentration in a sample of tuna

1.33 Do you expect the distributions of the following variables to be symmetric or skewed? Explain.

a. Size in dollars of nonsecured loans

b. Size in dollars of secured loans

c. Price of an 8-ounce can of peas

d. Height in inches of freshman women at your university

e. Number of broken taco shells in a package of 100 shells

f. Number of ticks found on each of 50 trapped cottontail rabbits

1.34   Identify each variable as continuous or discrete:

a. Number of homicides in Detroit during a one-month period

b. Length of time between arrivals at an outpatient clinic

c. Number of typing errors on a page of manuscript

d. Number of defective lightbulbs in a package containing four bulbs

e. Time required to finish an examination

1.35   Identify each variable as continuous or discrete:

a. Weight of two dozen shrimp

b. A person's body temperature

c. Number of people waiting for treatment at a hospital emergency room

d. Number of properties for sale by a real estate agency

e. Number of claims received by an insurance company during one day

1.36   Identify each variable as continuous or discrete:

a. Number of people in line at a supermarket checkout counter

b. Depth of a snowfall

c. Length of time for a driver to respond when faced with an impending collision

d. Number of aircraft arriving at the Atlanta airport in a given hour

EX0137

1.37   Aqua running has been suggested as a method of cardiovascular conditioning for injured athletes and others who want a low-impact aerobics program. In a study to investigate the relationship between exercise cadence and heart rate, the heart rates of 20 healthy volunteers were measured at a cadence of 48 cycles per minute (a cycle consisted of two steps).[9] The data are listed here:

87	109	79	80	96	95	90	92	96	98
101	91	78	112	94	98	94	107	81	96

Construct a stem and leaf plot to describe the data. Discuss the characteristics of the data distribution.

1.38   An advertising flyer for the *Princeton Review,* a review course designed for high school students taking the SAT tests, presents the accompanying bar graph to show the average score improvements for students using various study methods.[10]

a. What graphical techniques did the *Princeton Review* use to make their average improvement figures look as dramatic as possible?

b. If you were in charge of promoting a review course at your high school, how would you modify the graph to make the average improvement for students using a school review course look more impressive?

Graph for Exercise
1.38

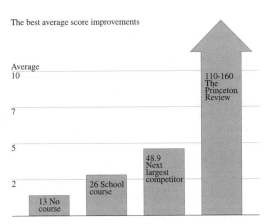

The best average score improvements

1.39 The average per-site gross weekend revenue (in dollars) for the top 20 movies were measured for two consecutive weekends in August 2001.[11]

August 3–5, 2001		August 10–12, 2001	
$21,619	$1,042	$14,730	$1,781
7,800	1,315	10,621	941
9,012	902	5,254	871
3,545	1,062	8,397	1,130
2,670	1,196	3,911	1,021
2,918	5,129	2,370	974
2,307	758	2,287	2,935
2,200	882	1,640	3,313
1,352	941	1,858	20,202
3,211	14,895	1,402	630

a. Draw a relative frequency histogram to describe the distribution of the average per-site revenues for these movies. How would you describe the shape of the distribution?

b. Construct two stem and leaf plots to compare the average per-site revenues for the two weekends.

c. Write a short paragraph summarizing the results of parts a and b.

1.40 Refer to Exercise 1.39 and data set EX0139. The *MINITAB* stem and leaf output is shown here for the two weekends. Compare the output with the stem and leaf plots constructed in Exercise 1.39. Explain the similarities and differences in the computer- and hand-generated plots.

Stem-and-Leaf Display: Aug3–5

Stem-and-leaf of Aug 3-5   N = 20
Leaf Unit = 100

```
   4     0  7899
   9     1  00133
  (4)    2  2369
   7     3  25
   5     4
   5     5  1
   4     6
   4     7  8
   3     8
   3     9  0

  HI   148, 216,
```

Stem-and-Leaf Display: Aug10-12

Stem-and-leaf of Aug 10-12   N = 20
Leaf Unit = 100

```
   4     0  6899
  10     1  014678
  10     2  239
   7     3  39
   5     4
   5     5  2
   4     6
   4     7
   4     8  3

  HI   106, 147, 202,
```

1.41 Here is a list of the 42 presidents of the United States along with the number of vetoes used by each[5]:

Washington	2	J. Adams	0	Jefferson	0	Madison	5
Monroe	1	J. Q. Adams	0	Jackson	5	Van Buren	0
W. Harrison	0	Tyler	6	Polk	2	Taylor	0
Fillmore	0	Pierce	9	Buchanan	4	Lincoln	2
A. Johnson	21	Grant	45	Hayes	12	Garfield	0
Arthur	4	Cleveland	304	B. Harrison	19	Cleveland	42
McKinley	6	T. Roosevelt	42	Taft	30	Wilson	33
Harding	5	Coolidge	20	Hoover	21	F. Roosevelt	372
Truman	180	Eisenhower	73	Kennedy	12	L. Johnson	16
Nixon	26	Ford	48	Carter	13	Reagan	39
Bush	29	Clinton	36				

Use an appropriate graph to describe the number of vetoes cast by the 42 presidents. Write a summary paragraph describing this set of data.

EX0142

1.42 Are some cities more windy than others? Does Chicago deserve to be nicknamed "The Windy City"? These data are the average wind speeds (in miles per hour) for 48 selected cities in the United States[5]:

8.9	7.1	9.1	8.9	10.2	12.4	11.8	10.9	12.8	10.4
10.5	10.7	8.6	10.7	10.3	8.4	7.7	11.3	7.7	9.6
7.9	10.6	9.3	9.1	7.8	6.0	8.3	8.8	9.2	11.5
10.5	8.8	35.2	8.2	9.3	10.5	9.5	6.2	9.0	7.9
9.6	9.7	8.8	7.0	8.7	8.9	8.9	9.4		

a. Construct a relative frequency histogram for the data. (HINT: Choose the class boundaries without including the value $x = 35.2$ in the range of values.)

b. The value $x = 35.2$ was recorded at Mt. Washington, New Hampshire. Does the geography of that city explain the observation?

c. The average wind speed in Chicago is recorded as 10.4 miles per hour. Do you consider this unusually windy?

EX0143

1.43 The following data set shows the winning times (in seconds) for the Kentucky Derby races from 1950 to 2001.[12]

(1950)	121.3	122.3	121.3	122.0	123.0	121.4	123.2	122.1
(1958)	125.0	122.1	122.2	124.0	120.2	121.4	120.0	121.1
(1966)	122.0	120.3	122.1	121.4	123.2	123.1	121.4	119.2†
(1974)	124.0	122.0	121.3	122.1	121.1	122.2	122.0	122.0
(1982)	122.2	122.1	122.2	120.1	122.4	123.2	122.2	125.0
(1990)	122.0	123.0	123.0	122.2	123.3	121.1	121.0	122.4
(1998)	122.2	123.2	121.0	119.97				

†Record time set by Secretariat in 1973

a. Do you think there will be a trend in the winning times over the years? Draw a line chart to verify your answer.

b. Describe the distribution of winning times using an appropriate graph. Comment on the shape of the distribution and look for any unusual observations.

1.44 In July of 2000, 22.4 million teenagers and young adults worked, a substantial number more than in April, when school is still in session. Many of these young people worked in amusement and theme parks, whose average number of employees jumps dramatically during the summer months. Here are the most common injuries suffered on the job by kids under 18[13]:

Most Common Injury	Percentage
Bruises and contusions	14%
Cuts and lacerations	13%
Fractures	8%
Heat burns	9%
Sprains and strains	33%

a. Are all possible injuries accounted for in the table? Add another category if necessary.

b. Create a pie chart to describe the data.

c. Rearrange the bars in part c so that the categories are ranked from the largest percentage to the smallest.

e. Which of the three methods of presentation—part b, c, or d—is the most effective?

EX0145

1.45 The 2000 election was a close race, in which George W. Bush defeated Al Gore, Ralph Nader, and Pat Buchanan by the closest of margins. The popular vote (in thousands) for George W. Bush in each of the 50 states is listed below[5]:

AL	940	HI	138	MA	876	NM	245	SD	191
AK	135	ID	336	MI	1936	NY	2219	TN	1056
AZ	674	IL	2012	MN	1110	NC	1607	TX	3796
AR	470	IN	1232	MS	549	ND	176	UT	512
CA	4055	IA	629	MO	1190	OH	2294	VT	119
CO	870	KS	614	MT	240	OK	744	VA	1427
CT	545	KY	870	NE	409	OR	586	WA	795
DE	137	LA	925	NV	302	PA	2264	WV	330
FL	2909	ME	284	NH	273	RI	132	WI	1236
GA	1404	MD	771	NJ	1248	SC	805	WY	148

a. By just looking at the table, what shape do you think the data distribution for the popular vote by state will have?

b. Draw a relative frequency histogram to describe the distribution of the popular vote for President Bush in the 50 states.

c. Did the histogram in part b confirm your guess in part a? Are there any outliers? How can you explain them?

EX0146

1.46 Refer to Exercise 1.45. Listed here is the *percentage* of the popular vote received by President Bush in each of the 50 states[5]:

AL	57	HI	38	MA	33	NM	47	SD	61
AK	60	ID	70	MI	47	NY	36	TN	51
AZ	50	IL	43	MN	46	NC	56	TX	60
AR	52	IN	58	MS	57	ND	61	UT	67
CA	42	IA	48	MO	51	OH	50	VT	41
CO	51	KS	59	MT	59	OK	61	VA	53
CT	39	KY	57	NE	63	OR	49	WA	45
DE	42	LA	53	NV	50	PA	47	WV	52
FL	49	ME	44	NH	48	RI	32	WI	48
GA	56	MD	40	NJ	41	SC	57	WY	70

a. By just looking at the table, what shape do you think the data distribution for the *percentage* of the popular vote by state will have?

b. Draw a relative frequency histogram to describe the distribution. Describe the shape of the distribution and look for outliers. Did the graph confirm your answer to part a?

1.47 Refer to Exercises 1.45 and 1.46. The accompanying stem and leaf plots were generated using *MINITAB* for the variables named "Pop-vote" and "Pct-vote."

Stem-and-Leaf Display: Pop-vote, Pct-vote

Stem-and-leaf of Pop-vote N = 50
Leaf Unit = 100

```
   8    0 11111111
  15    0 2222333
  21    0 445555
  (6)   0 666777
  23    0 888899
  17    1 011
  14    1 222
  11    1 44
   9    1 6
   8    1 9
   7    2 0
   6    2 222
        HI  29, 37, 40,
```

Stem-and-leaf of Pct-vote N = 50
Leaf Unit = 1.0

```
   2    3 23
   5    3 689
  12    4 0112234
  22    4 5677788899
  (10)  5 0001112233
  18    5 667777899
   9    6 001113
   2    7 00
```

a. Describe the shapes of the two distributions. Are there any outliers?

b. Do the stem and leaf plots resemble the relative frequency histograms constructed in Exercises 1.45 and 1.46?

c. Explain why the distribution of the popular vote for President Bush by state is skewed while the percentage of popular votes by state is mound-shaped.

EX0148

1.48   The self-reported heights of 105 students in a biostatistics class are described in the relative frequency histogram below.

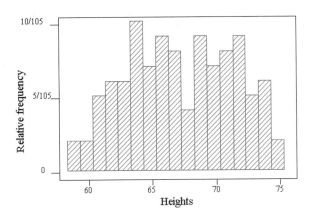

a. Describe the shape of the distribution.

b. Do you see any unusual feature in this histogram?

c. Can you think of an explanation for the two peaks in the histogram? Is there some other factor that is causing the heights to mound up in two separate peaks? What is it?

EX0149

1.49   One week after the terrorist attack on the World Trade Center on September 11, 2001, the Gallup poll presented a summary of various polls that had asked the question: "How worried are you that you or someone in your family will become a victim of a terrorist attack?" The data are shown in the table below[14]:

Date	Very/Somewhat Worried (%)	Not Too/Not at All Worried (%)
April 1995	41	57
April 1996	35	65
July 1996	39	61
August 1998	32	67
April 2000	24	75
September 11, 2001	58	40
September 14–15, 2001	51	48

a. Draw a line chart to describe the percentages that are very/somewhat worried. Use time as the horizontal axis.

b. Superimpose another line chart on the one drawn in part b to describe the percentages that are not too/not at all worried.

c. Use your line chart to summarize the changes in the polls during the period just after the attack on the World Trade Center.

d. The following line chart was presented on the www.gallup.com Web page. How does it differ from the graph that you drew? What characteristic of the Gallup line chart might cause distortion when the graph is interpreted?

**Worried That You or a
Family Member Will Become
A Victim of a Terrorist Attack?**

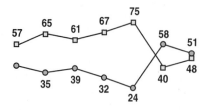

─□─ % Very / Somewhat worried
─□─ % Not too / Not at all worried

| | Apr.
21 - 23,
1995 | Apr.
9 - 10,
1996 | Jul.
20 - 21,
1996 | Aug.
20,
1998 | Apr.
7 - 9,
2000 | Sep.
11,
2001 | Sep.
14 - 15,
2001 |

EX0150

1.50 A group of 50 biomedical students recorded their pulse rates by counting the number of beats for 30 seconds and multiplying by 2.

80	70	88	70	84	66	84	82	66	42
52	72	90	70	96	84	96	86	62	78
60	82	88	54	66	66	80	88	56	104
84	84	60	84	88	58	72	84	68	74
84	72	62	90	72	84	72	110	100	58

a. Why are all of the measurements even numbers?

b. Draw a stem and leaf plot to describe the data, splitting each stem in to two lines.

c. Construct a relative frequency histogram for the data.

d. Write a short paragraph describing the distribution of the student pulse rates.

1.51 There is an increasing demand among consumers for broadband Internet access, which will increase the speed at which they can access the Internet. Cable currently leads the broadband market over DSL and up-and-coming satellite access, and it is predicted that cable will continue to dominate the U.S. residential broadband market over the next 4 years.[15]

Broadband Access in 2005
(U.S.—Year end 2005)

Technology	Subscribers
Cable	15.7 Million
DSL	10.5 Million
Satellite	4.5 Million
Fixed Wireless	359,000

Source: The Yankee Group

a. Use a pie chart to describe the predicted broadband market in 2005.

b. Use a bar chart to describe the predicted broadband market in 2005.

c. Which of the two graphical methods is less susceptible to distortion by the presenter?

Exercises

DO IT YOURSELF!

1.52 If you have not yet done so, use the first applet in **Building a Dotplot** to create a dotplot for the following data set: 2, 3, 9, 6, 7, 6.

1.53 Use the second applet in **Building a Dotplot** to create a dotplot for the number of cheeseburgers consumed in a given week by 10 college students:

```
4   5   4   2   1
3   3   4   2   7
```

a. How would you describe the shape of the distribution?

b. What proportion of the students ate more than 4 cheeseburgers that week?

1.54 A group of 70 students were asked to record the last digit of their social security number.

EX0154

```
1   6   9   1   5   9   0   2   8   4
0   7   3   4   2   3   5   8   4   2
3   2   0   0   2   1   2   7   7   4
0   0   9   9   5   3   8   4   7   4
6   6   9   0   2   6   2   9   5   8
5   1   7   7   7   8   7   5   1   8
3   4   1   9   3   8   6   6   6   6
```

a. Before graphing the data, use your common sense to guess the shape of the data distribution. Explain your reasoning.

b. Use the second applet in **Building a Dotplot** to create a dotplot to describe the data. Was your intuition correct in part a?

1.55 If you have not yet done so, use the first applet in **Building a Histogram** to create a histogram for the data in Example 1.11, the number of quarts of milk purchased during a particular week.

1.56 The following data set records the yearly charitable contributions (in dollars) to the United Fund for a group of employees at a public university.

EX0156

```
41    81    80    65    47    56    80    69    79    63
28    51   112    71    83    84    82   103    80    70
77    75    59    63    63    80   101   115    99    67
42    78    81    90   103   125    92    79    24    93
```

Use the second applet in **Building a Histogram** to construct a relative frequency histogram for the data. What is the shape of the distribution? Can you see any obvious outliers?

1.57 The most visited site on the Internet is AOL Time Warner Network, which averaged 1240.7 minutes per month per unique visitor. The average minutes spent at the next most visited sites are shown in the table below.[16]

EX0157

Site	Avg Minutes per Month	Site	Avg Minutes per Month
Yahoo!	135.5	Infospace Infrastructure	8.7
Microsoft	150.3	Walt Disney Internet	36.4
X10.com	1.4	Viacom Online	20.1
Terra Lycos	19.3	Google Sites	23.7
Excite	37.7	eUniverse Network	15.7
About/Primedia	17.1	Ask Jeeves	15.3
EBay	98.0	iVillage	23.5
Vivendi-Universal	25.2	Real.com Network	5.6
Amazon	16.0	AT&T Web Sites	29.8
CNET	17.9	NBC Internet Sites	12.6

a. Look at the data. Can you guess the approximate shape of the data distribution?

b. Use the second applet in **Building a Histogram** to construct a relative frequency histogram for the data. What is the shape of the distribution?

c. Are there any outliers in the set? If so, at what sites do people spend a large amount of time, on average?

Case Study

BLD PRESS

How Is Your Blood Pressure?

Blood pressure is the pressure that the blood exerts against the walls of the arteries. When physicians or nurses measure your blood pressure, they take two readings. The systolic blood pressure is the pressure when the heart is contracting and therefore pumping. The diastolic blood pressure is the pressure in the arteries when the heart is relaxing. The diastolic blood pressure is always the lower of the two readings. Blood pressure varies from one person to another. It will also vary for a single individual from day to day and even within a given day.

If your blood pressure is too high, it can lead to a stroke or a heart attack. If it is too low, blood will not get to your extremities and you may feel dizzy. Low blood pressure is usually not serious.

So, what should *your* blood pressure be? A systolic blood pressure of 120 would be considered normal. One of 150 would be high. But since blood pressure varies with gender and increases with age, a better gauge of the relative standing of your blood pressure would be obtained by comparing it with the population of blood pressures of all persons of your gender and age in the United States. Of course, we cannot supply you with that data set, but we can show you a very large sample selected from it. The CD-ROM provides blood pressure data on 1910 persons, 965 men and 945 women between the ages of 15 and 20. The data are part of a health survey conducted by the National Institutes of Health (NIH). Entries for each person include that person's age and systolic and diastolic blood pressures at the time the blood pressure was recorded.

1. Describe the variables that have been measured in this survey. Are the variables quantitative or qualitative? Discrete or continuous? Are the data univariate, bivariate, or multivariate?

2. What types of graphical methods are available for describing this data set? What types of questions could be answered using various types of graphical techniques?

3. Using the systolic blood pressure data set, construct a relative frequency histogram for the 965 men and another for the 945 women. Use a statistical software package if you have access to one. Compare the two histograms.

4. Consider the 965 men and 945 women as the entire population of interest. Choose a sample of $n = 50$ men and $n = 50$ women, recording their systolic blood pressures and their ages. Draw two relative frequency histograms to graphically display the systolic blood pressures for your two samples. Do the shapes of the histograms resemble the population histograms from part 3?

5. How does your blood pressure compare with that of others of your same gender? Check your systolic blood pressure against the appropriate histogram in part 3 or 4 to determine whether your blood pressure is "normal" or whether it is unusually high or low.

Data Sources

1. Keating Holland, "Poll: Presidential race a dead heat: Two point Bush lead within margin of error," CNN/TIME POLL (http:www.cnn.com/2000/ALLPOLITICS/stories/10/06/cnn.poll/index.html), 6 October 2000.

2. "Electoral Hope Springs Eternal," *Time,* 4 November 1996, p. 16.

3. Karlyn Bowman, ed., "Opinion Pulse: '60s Kids: The Way They Were," *The American Enterprise,* May/June 1997, p. 91.

4. "Getting Back to Work," http://www.usatoday.com/snapshot/news/2001-07-17-back-towork.htm, 2 October 2001.

5. William A. McGeveran, Jr., ed., *The World Almanac and Book of Facts 2002* (Mahwah, NJ: St. Martin's Press, 2002.

6. "Tomorrow's Markets: Short-Term Security," *American Demographics,* April 1997, p. 4.

7. Margaret Hornblower, "Great Xpectations," *Time,* 9 June 1997, p. 58.

8. "'Tale' and Farewell," *Entertainment Weekly,* #610/611, 24/31 August 2001, p. 127.

9. Robert P. Wilder, D. Brennan, and D. E. Schotte, "A Standard Measure for Exercise Prescription for Aqua Running," *American Journal of Sports Medicine* 21, no. 1 (1993):45.

10. *Princeton Review,* Irvine, CA, 1993.

11. "The Slice Is Right" and "Funny Money," *Entertainment Weekly,* #609/610/611, 17 August 2001 and 24/31 August 2001, p. 49 and p. 107.

12. "Derby Statistics," http://www.churchilldowns.com/kderby/history/racestats/, 24 September 2001.

13. Sandra Yin, Pamela Paul, and David Whelan, "What Summer Break?" *American Demographics,* July 2001, p. 64.

14. "Gallup Glance," http://www.gallup.com/, 18 September 2001.

15. "Quest for Broadband Usually Ends at Cable", (http://cyberatlas.internet.com/markets/broadband/article/0,,10099_879101,00.html#table) 18 September 2001.

16. "Top 50 Digital Media/Web Properties of July 2001," http://cyberatlas.internet.com/big_picture/traffic_patterns/article/0,,5931_865681,00.html, 28 September 2001.

Describing Data with Numerical Measures

Case Study

Are the baseball champions of today better than those of "yesteryear"? Do players in the National League hit better than players in the American League? The case study at the end of this chapter involves the batting averages of major league batting champions. Numerical descriptive measures can be used to answer these and similar questions.

General Objectives

Graphs are extremely useful for the visual description of a data set. However, they are not always the best tool when you want to make inferences about a population from the information contained in a sample. For this purpose, it is better to use numerical measures to construct a mental picture of the data.

Specific Topics

1. Measures of center: mean, median, and mode (2.2)
2. Measures of variability: range, variance, and standard deviation (2.3)
3. Tchebysheff's Theorem and the Empirical Rule (2.4)
4. Measures of relative standing: z-scores, percentiles, quartiles, and the interquartile range (2.6)
5. Box plots (2.7)

2.1 Describing a Set of Data with Numerical Measures

Graphs can help you describe the basic shape of a data distribution; "a picture is worth a thousand words." There are limitations, however, to the use of graphs. Suppose you need to display your data to a group of people and the bulb on the overhead projector blows out! Or you might need to describe your data over the telephone—no way to display the graphs! You need to find another way to convey a mental picture of the data to your audience.

A second limitation is that graphs are somewhat imprecise for use in statistical inference. For example, suppose you want to use a sample histogram to make inferences about a population histogram. How can you measure the similarities and differences between the two histograms in some concrete way? If they were identical, you could say "They are the same!" But, if they are different, it is difficult to describe the "degree of difference."

One way to overcome these problems is to use **numerical measures**, which can be calculated for either a sample or a population of measurements. You can use the data to calculate a set of *numbers* that will convey a good mental picture of the frequency distribution. These measures are called **parameters** when associated with the population, and they are called **statistics** when calculated from sample measurements.

Definition   Numerical descriptive measures associated with a population of measurements are called **parameters**; those computed from sample measurements are called **statistics.**

2.2 Measures of Center

In Chapter 1, we introduced dotplots, stem and leaf plots, and histograms to describe the distribution of a set of measurements on a quantitative variable x. The horizontal axis displays the values of x, and the data are "distributed" along this horizontal line. One of the first important numerical measures is a **measure of center**—a measure along the horizontal axis that locates the center of the distribution.

The GPA data presented in Table 1.9 ranged from a low of 1.9 to a high of 3.4, with the center of the histogram located in the vicinity of 2.6 (see Figure 2.1). Let's consider some rules for locating the center of a distribution of measurements.

The arithmetic average of a set of measurements is a very common and useful measure of center. This measure is often referred to as the **arithmetic mean,** or simply the **mean,** of a set of measurements. To distinguish between the mean for the sample and the mean for the population, we will use the symbol $\bar{x}$ (x-bar) for a sample mean and the symbol μ (Greek lowercase mu) for the mean of a population.

Definition   The **arithmetic mean** or **average** of a set of n measurements is equal to the sum of the measurements divided by n.

Since statistical formulas often involve adding or "summing" numbers, we use a shorthand symbol to indicate the process of summing. Suppose there are n measure-

FIGURE 2.1
Center of the GPA
data

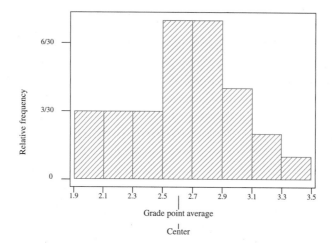

ments on the variable x—call them $x_1, x_2, \ldots, x_n$. To add the n measurements together, we use this shorthand notation:

$$\sum_{i=1}^{n} x_i \quad \text{which means } x_1 + x_2 + x_3 + \cdots + x_n$$

The Greek capital sigma (Σ) tells you to add the items that appear to its right, beginning with the number below the sigma ($i = 1$) and ending with the number above ($i = n$). However, since the typical sums in statistical calculations are almost always made on the total set of n measurements, you can use a simpler notation:

$$\Sigma x_i \quad \text{which means "the sum of all the } x \text{ measurements"}$$

Using this notation, we write the formula for the sample mean:

Notation

Sample mean: $\quad \bar{x} = \dfrac{\Sigma x_i}{n}$

Population mean: $\quad \mu$

EXAMPLE 2.1 Draw a dotplot for the $n = 5$ measurements 2, 9, 11, 5, 6. Find the sample mean and compare its value with what you might consider the "center" of these observations on the dotplot.

Solution The dotplot in Figure 2.2 seems to be centered between 6 and 8. To find the sample mean, calculate

$$\bar{x} = \frac{\Sigma x_i}{n} = \frac{2 + 9 + 11 + 5 + 6}{5} = 6.6$$

FIGURE 2.2
Dotplot for
Example 2.1

Character Dotplot

The statistic $\bar{x} = 6.6$ is the balancing point or fulcrum shown on the dotplot. It does seem to mark the center of the data.

Remember that samples are measurements drawn from a larger population that is usually unknown. An important use of the sample mean $\bar{x}$ is as an estimator of the unknown population mean μ. The GPA data in Table 1.9 are a sample from a larger population of GPAs, and the distribution is shown in Figure 2.1. The mean of the 30 GPAs is

$$\bar{x} = \frac{\Sigma x_i}{30} = \frac{77.5}{30} = 2.58$$

shown in Figure 2.1; it marks the balancing point of the distribution. The mean of the entire population of GPAs is unknown, but if you had to guess its value, your best estimate would be 2.58. Although the sample mean $\bar{x}$ changes from sample to sample, the population mean μ stays the same.

A second measure of central tendency is the **median**, which is the value in the middle position in the set of measurements ordered from smallest to largest.

Definition   The **median** m of a set of n measurements is the value of x that falls in the middle position when the measurements are ordered from smallest to largest.

EXAMPLE 2.2   Find the median for the set of measurements 2, 9, 11, 5, 6.

Solution   Rank the $n = 5$ measurements from smallest to largest:

$$2 \quad 5 \quad 6 \quad 9 \quad 11$$
$$\uparrow$$

The middle observation, marked with an arrow, is in the center of the set, or $m = 6$.

EXAMPLE 2.3   Find the median for the set of measurements 2, 9, 11, 5, 6, 27.

Solution   Rank the measurements from smallest to largest:

$$2 \quad 5 \quad \boxed{6 \quad 9} \quad 11 \quad 27$$
$$\uparrow$$

Now there are two "middle" observations, shown in the box. To find the median, choose a value halfway between the two middle observations:

$$m = \frac{6 + 9}{2} = 7.5$$

The value $.5(n + 1)$ indicates the **position of the median** in the ordered data set. If the position of the median is a number that ends in the value **.5**, you need to average the two adjacent values.

EXAMPLE 2.4   For the $n = 5$ ordered measurements from Example 2.2, the position of the median is $.5(n + 1) = .5(6) = 3$, and the median is the *3rd ordered observation*, or $m = 6$. For the $n = 6$ ordered measurements from Example 2.3, the position of the median is $.5(n + 1) = .5(7) = 3.5$, and the median is the *average of the 3rd and 4th ordered observations,* or $m = (6 + 9)/2 = 7.5$.

Although both the mean and the median are good measures of the center of a distribution, the median is less sensitive to extreme values or *outliers.* For example, the value $x = 27$ in Example 2.3 is much larger than the other five measurements. The median, $m = 7.5$, is not affected by the outlier, whereas the sample average,

$$\bar{x} = \frac{\Sigma x_i}{n} = \frac{60}{6} = 10$$

is affected; its value is not representative of the remaining five observations.

When a data set has extremely small or extremely large observations, the sample mean is drawn toward the direction of the extreme measurements (see Figure 2.3).

FIGURE 2.3 Relative frequency distributions showing the effect of extreme values on the mean and median

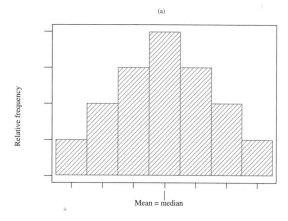
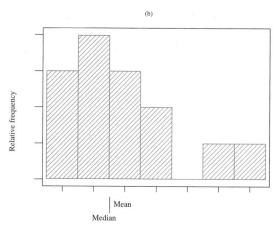

If a distribution is skewed to the right, the mean shifts to the right; if a distribution is skewed to the left, the mean shifts to the left. The median is not affected by these extreme values because the numerical values of the measurements are not used in its calculation. When a distribution is symmetric, the mean and the median are equal. If a distribution is strongly skewed by one or more extreme values, you should use the median rather than the mean as a measure of center.

DO IT YOURSELF!

You can see the effect of extreme values on both the mean and the median using the **How Extreme Values Affect the Mean and Median** applet. The first of three applets (Figure 2.4) shows a dotplot of the data in Example 2.2. Use your mouse to move the largest observation ($x = 11$) even further to the right. How does this larger observation affect the mean? How does it affect the median? We will use this applet again for the *Do It Yourself Exercises* at the end of the chapter.

FIGURE 2.4
**How Extreme
Values Affect the
Mean and Median**
applet

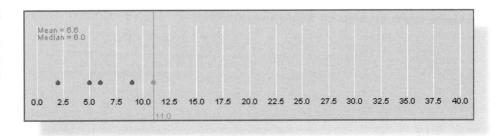

Another way to locate the center of a distribution is to look for the value of *x* that occurs with the highest frequency. This measure of the center is called the **mode.**

Definition   The **mode** is the category that occurs most frequently, or the most frequently occurring value of *x*. When measurements on a continuous variable have been grouped as a frequency or relative frequency histogram, the class with the highest peak or frequency is called the **modal class**, and the midpoint of that class is taken to be the mode.

The mode is generally used to describe large data sets, whereas the mean and median are used for both large and small data sets. From the data in Example 1.11, the mode of the distribution of the number of quarts of milk purchased during one particular week is 2. The modal class and the value of *x* occurring with the highest frequency are the same, as shown in Figure 2.5(a).

For the data in Table 1.9, a GPA of 2.5 occurs five times, and therefore the mode for the distribution of GPAs is 2.5. Using the histogram to find the modal class, you find two classes that occur with equal frequency. Fortunately, these classes are side by side in the tabulation, and the choice for the value of the mode is thus 2.7, the value centered between the fourth and fifth classes. See Figure 2.5(b).

It is possible for a distribution of measurements to have more than one mode. These modes would appear as "local peaks" in the relative frequency distribution. For example, if we were to tabulate the length of fish taken from a lake during one season, we might get a *bimodal distribution,* possibly reflecting a mixture of young and old fish in the population. Sometimes bimodal distributions of sizes or weights reflect a mixture of measurements taken on males and females. In any case, a set or distribution of measurements may have more than one mode.

FIGURE 2.5   Relative frequency histograms for the milk and GPA data

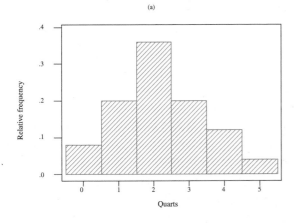

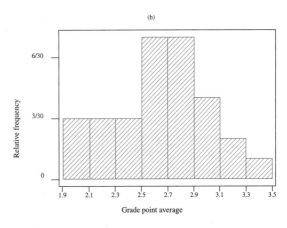

Exercises

Basic Techniques

2.1 You are given $n = 5$ measurements: 0, 5, 1, 1, 3.

a. Draw a dotplot for the data. (HINT: If two measurements are the same, place one dot above the other.) Guess the approximate "center."

b. Find the mean, median, and mode.

c. Locate the three measures of center on the dotplot in part a. Based on the relative positions of the mean and median, are the measurements symmetric or skewed?

2.2 You are given $n = 8$ measurements: 3, 2, 5, 6, 4, 4, 3, 5.

a. Find $\bar{x}$.

b. Find m.

c. Based on the results of parts a and b, are the measurements symmetric or skewed? Draw a dotplot to confirm your answer.

2.3 You are given $n = 10$ measurements: 3, 5, 4, 6, 10, 5, 6, 9, 2, 8.

a. Calculate $\bar{x}$.

b. Find m.

c. Find the mode.

Applications

2.4 The cost of automobile insurance has become a sore subject in California because insurance rates are dependent on so many different variables, such as the city in which you live, the number of cars you insure, and the company with which you are insured. Here are the 6-month premiums in 2001 for a married male, licensed for 6–8 years, who drives about 15,000 miles per year and has no violations or accidents[1]:

City	Allstate	21st Century
Long Beach	$1,050	$682
Pomona	984	638
San Bernardino	900	578
Moreno Valley	964	524

a. What is the average premium for Allstate Insurance?

b. What is the average premium for 21st Century Insurance?

c. If you were a consumer, would you be interested in the average premium cost? If not, what would you be interested in?

2.5 The VCR (videocassette recorder) is a common fixture in most American households. In fact, most American households have VCRs, and many have more than one. A sample of 25 households produced the following measurements on x, the number of VCRs in the household:

EX0205

```
1   0   2   1   1
1   0   2   1   0
0   1   2   3   2
1   1   1   0   1
3   1   0   1   1
```

a. Is the distribution of x, the number of VCRs in a household, symmetric or skewed? Explain.

b. Guess the value of the mode, the value of x that occurs most frequently.

c. Calculate the mean, median, and mode for these measurements.

d. Draw a relative frequency histogram for the data set. Locate the mean, median, and mode along the horizontal axis. Are your answers to parts a and b correct?

EX0206

2.6 Ten of the largest corporations in the United States, randomly selected from the *Fortune* 500, are listed below along with their revenues (in millions of dollars)[2]:

State Farm Insurance Company	$48,069.0	Litton Industries	$5588.2
American Express	23,675.0	BB&T Corp	5338.2
American General	11,063.0	Arvin Meritor	5153.0
Guardian Life Insurance Company	8967.6	USG	3781.0
Genuine Parts	8369.9	Owens & Minor	3503.6

a. Draw a stem and leaf plot for the data. Are the data skewed?

b. Calculate the mean revenue for these 10 corporations. Calculate the median revenue.

c. Which of the two measures in part b best describes the center of the data? Explain.

2.7 Does birth order have any effect on a person's personality? A report on a study by an MIT researcher indicates that later-born children are more likely to challenge the establishment, more open to new ideas, and more accepting of change.[3] In fact, the number of later-born children is increasing. During the Depression years of the 1930s, families averaged 2.5 children (59% later born), whereas the parents of baby boomers averaged 3 to 4 children (68% later born). What does the author mean by an average of 2.5 children?

EX0208

2.8 The following data show the price—an estimated average for a 6-ounce can or a 7.06-ounce pouch—for 14 different brands of water-packed light tuna, based on prices paid nationally in supermarkets[4]:

.99	1.92	1.23	.85	.65	.53	1.41
1.12	.63	.67	.69	.60	.60	.66

a. Find the average price for the 14 different brands of tuna.

b. Find the median price for the 14 different brands of tuna.

c. Based on your findings in parts a and b, do you think that the distribution of prices is skewed? Explain.

2.9 As professional sports teams become a more and more lucrative business for their owners, the salaries paid to the players have also increased. In fact, sports superstars are paid astronomical salaries for their talents. If you were asked by a sports management firm to describe the distribution of players' salaries in several different categories of professional sports, what measure of center would you choose? Why?

2.10 In a psychological experiment, the time on task was recorded for 10 subjects under a 5-minute time constraint. These measurements are in seconds:

175	190	250	230	240
200	185	190	225	265

a. Find the average time on task.

b. Find the median time on task.

c. If you were writing a report to describe these data, which measure of central tendency would you use? Explain.

2.3 Measures of Variability

Data sets may have the same center but look different because of the way the numbers *spread out* from the center. Consider the two distributions shown in Figure 2.6. Both distributions are centered at $x = 4$, but there is a big difference in the way the measure-

FIGURE 2.6   Variability or dispersion of data

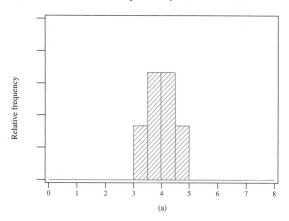

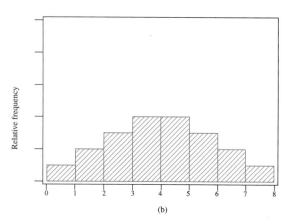

ments spread out, or *vary.* The measurements in Figure 2.6(a) vary from 3 to 5; in Figure 2.6(b) the measurements vary from 0 to 8.

Variability or **dispersion** is a very important characteristic of data. For example, if you were manufacturing bolts, extreme variation in the bolt diameters would cause a high percentage of defective products. On the other hand, if you were trying to discriminate between good and poor accountants, you would have trouble if the examination always produced test grades with little variation, making discrimination very difficult.

Measures of variability can help you create a mental picture of the spread of the data. We will present some of the more important ones. The simplest measure of variation is the **range.**

Definition | The **range, R,** of a set of *n* measurements is defined as the difference between the largest and smallest measurements.

For the GPA data in Table 1.9, the measurements vary from 1.9 to 3.4. Hence, the range is (3.4 − 1.9) = 1.5. The range is easy to calculate, easy to interpret, and is an adequate measure of variation for small sets of data. But, for large data sets, the range is not an adequate measure of variability. For example, the two relative frequency distributions in Figure 2.7 have the same range but very different shapes and variability.

FIGURE 2.7   Distributions with equal range and unequal variability

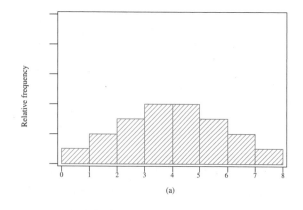

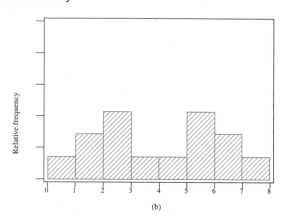

Is there a measure of variability that is more sensitive than the range? Consider, as an example, the sample measurements 5, 7, 1, 2, 4, displayed as a dotplot in Figure 2.8. The mean of these five measurements is

$$\bar{x} = \frac{\Sigma x_i}{n} = \frac{19}{5} = 3.8$$

FIGURE 2.8
Dotplot showing the deviations of points from the mean

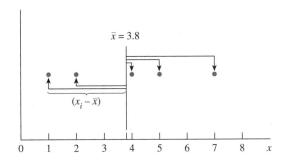

as indicated on the dotplot. The horizontal distances between each dot (measurement) and the mean $\bar{x}$ will help you to measure the variability. If the distances are large, the data are more spread out or *variable* than if the distances are small. If x_i is a particular dot (measurement), then the **deviation** of that measurement from the mean is $(x_i - \bar{x})$. Measurements to the right of the mean produce positive deviations, and those to the left produce negative deviations. The values of x and the deviations for our example are listed in the first and second columns of Table 2.1.

TABLE 2.1
Computation of $\Sigma(x_i - \bar{x})^2$

x	$(x_i - \bar{x})$	$(x_i - \bar{x})^2$
5	1.2	1.44
7	3.2	10.24
1	−2.8	7.84
2	−1.8	3.24
4	.2	.04
19	0.0	22.80

Because the deviations in the second column of the table contain information on variability, one way to combine the five deviations into one numerical measure is to average them. Unfortunately, the average will not work because some of the deviations are positive, some are negative, and the sum is always zero (unless round-off errors have been introduced into the calculations). Note that the deviations in the second column of Table 2.1 sum to zero.

Another possibility might be to disregard the signs of the deviations and calculate the average of their absolute values.[†] This method has been used as a measure of variability in exploratory data analysis and in the analysis of time series data. We prefer, however, to overcome the difficulty caused by the signs of the deviations by working with their sum of squares. From the sum of squared deviations, a single measure called the **variance** is calculated. To distinguish between the variance of a *sample* and the variance of a *population,* we use the symbol s^2 for a sample variance and σ^2 (Greek lowercase sigma) for a population variance. *The variance will be relatively large for highly variable data and relatively small for less variable data.*

[†]The absolute value of a number is its magnitude, ignoring its sign. For example, the absolute value of −2, represented by the symbol | −2 |, is 2. The absolute value of 2—that is, | 2 |—is 2.

Definition

The **variance of a population** of N measurements is the average of the squares of the deviations of the measurements about their mean μ. The population variance is denoted by σ^2 and is given by the formula

$$\sigma^2 = \frac{\Sigma(x_i - \mu)^2}{N}$$

Most often, you will not have all the population measurements available but will need to calculate the *variance of a sample* of n measurements.

Definition

The **variance of a sample** of n measurements is the sum of the squared deviations of the measurements about their mean $\bar{x}$ divided by $(n - 1)$. The sample variance is denoted by s^2 and is given by the formula

$$s^2 = \frac{\Sigma(x_i - \bar{x})^2}{n - 1}$$

For the set of $n = 5$ sample measurements presented in Table 2.1, the square of the deviation of each measurement is recorded in the third column. Adding, we obtain

$$\Sigma(x_i - \bar{x})^2 = 22.80$$

and the sample variance is

$$s^2 = \frac{\Sigma(x_i - \bar{x})^2}{n - 1} = \frac{22.80}{4} = 5.70$$

The variance is measured in terms of the square of the original units of measurement. If the original measurements are in inches, the variance is expressed in square inches. Taking the square root of the variance, we obtain the **standard deviation,** which returns the measure of variability to the original units of measurement.

Definition

The **standard deviation** of a set of measurements is equal to the positive square root of the variance.

Notation

n: number of measurements in the sample

s^2: sample variance

$s = \sqrt{s^2}$: sample standard deviation

N: number of measurements in the population

σ^2: population variance

$\sigma = \sqrt{\sigma^2}$: population standard deviation

For the set of $n = 5$ sample measurements in Table 2.1, the sample variance is $s^2 = 5.70$, so the sample standard deviation is $s = \sqrt{s^2} = \sqrt{5.70} = 2.39$. The more variable the data set is, the larger the value of s.

For the small set of measurements we used, the calculation of the variance is not too difficult. However, for a larger set, the calculations can become very tedious. Most scientific calculators have built-in programs that will calculate $\bar{x}$ and s or μ and σ, so that your computational work will be minimized. The sample or population mean key is usually marked with $\bar{x}$. The sample standard deviation key is usually marked with s, s_x, or σ_{xn-1}, and the population standard deviation key with σ, σ_x, or σ_{xn}. In using any calculator with these built-in function keys, be sure you know which calculation is being carried out by each key!

If you need to calculate s^2 and s by hand, it is much easier to use the alternative computing formula given next. This computational form is sometimes called the **shortcut method for calculating s^2.**

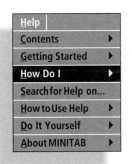

Use the Computing Formula to Calculate s^2?

$$s^2 = \frac{\Sigma x_i^2 - \dfrac{(\Sigma x_i)^2}{n}}{n - 1}$$

The symbols $(\Sigma x_i)^2$ and Σx_i^2 in the computing formula are shortcut ways to indicate the arithmetic operation you need to perform. You know from the formula for the sample mean that Σx_i is the sum of all the measurements. To find Σx_i^2, you square each individual measurement and then add them together.

$\Sigma x_i^2 =$ Sum of the squares of the individual measurements

$(\Sigma x_i)^2 =$ Square of the sum of the individual measurements

The *sample standard deviation, s,* is the positive square root of s^2.

EXAMPLE 2.5 Calculate the variance and standard deviation for the five measurements in Table 2.2, which are 5, 7, 1, 2, 4. Use the computing formula for s^2 and compare your results with those obtained using the original definition of s^2.

TABLE 2.2
Table for simplified
calculation of
s^2 and s

x_i	x_i^2
5	25
7	49
1	1
2	4
4	16
19	95

Solution The entries in Table 2.2 are the individual measurements, x_i, and their squares, x_i^2, together with their sums. Using the computing formula for s^2, you have

$$s^2 = \frac{\Sigma x_i^2 - \dfrac{(\Sigma x_i)^2}{n}}{n - 1}$$

$$= \frac{95 - \dfrac{(19)^2}{5}}{4} = \frac{22.80}{4} = 5.70$$

and $s = \sqrt{s^2} = \sqrt{5.70} = 2.39$, as before.

You may wonder why you need to divide by $(n - 1)$ rather than n when computing the sample variance. Just as we used the sample mean $\bar{x}$ to estimate the population mean μ, you may want to use the sample variance s^2 to estimate the population variance σ^2. It turns out that the sample variance s^2 with $(n - 1)$ in the denominator provides better estimates of σ^2 than would an estimator calculated with n in the denominator. **For this reason, we always divide by $(n - 1)$ when computing the sample variance s^2 and the sample standard deviation s.**

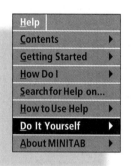

DO IT YOURSELF!

You can compare the accuracy of estimators of the population variance σ^2 using the **Why Divide by $n - 1$?** applet. The applet selects samples from a population with standard deviation $\sigma = 29.2$. It then calculates the standard deviation s using $(n - 1)$ in the denominator as well as a standard deviation calculated using n in the denominator. You can choose to compare the estimators for a single new sample, for 10 samples, or for 100 samples. Notice that each of the 10 samples shown in Figure 2.9 has a different sample standard deviation. However, when the 10 standard deviations are averaged at the bottom of the applet, one of the two estimators is closer to the population standard deviation, $\sigma = 29.2$. Which one is it? We will use this applet again for the *Do It Yourself Exercises* at the end of the chapter.

FIGURE 2.9
Why Divide by $n - 1$? applet

> Results displayed for last 10 samples of size3
> St. Dev. when dividing by n-1
>   38.6 42.8 33.7 13.5 26.0 14.2 9.0 23.3 9.3 32.7
> St. Dev. when dividing by n
>   31.5 34.9 27.5 11.0 21.2 11.6 7.4 19.0 7.6 26.7
> Averages of St. Dev. from all 10 samples:
> when dividing by n-1 : 27.0
> when dividing by n   : 22.0
>
> [New Sample] [10 Samples] [100 Samples]

At this point, you have learned how to compute the variance and standard deviation of a set of measurements. Remember these points:

- The value of s is always greater than or equal to zero.
- The larger the value of s^2 or s, the greater the variability of the data set.
- If s^2 or s is equal to zero, all the measurements must have the same value.
- In order to measure the variability in the same units as the original observations, we compute the standard deviation $s = \sqrt{s^2}$.

This information allows you to compare several sets of data with respect to their locations and their variability. How can you use these measures to say something more specific about a single set of data? The theorem and rule presented in the next section will help answer this question.

Exercises

Basic Techniques

2.11   You are given $n = 5$ measurements: 2, 1, 1, 3, 5.

   a. Calculate the sample mean, $\bar{x}$.

   b. Calculate the sample variance, s^2, using the formula given by the definition.

   c. Find the sample standard deviation, s.

   d. Find s^2 and s using the computing formula. Compare the results with those found in parts b and c.

2.12   Refer to Exercise 2.11.

   a. Use the data entry method in your scientific calculator to enter the five measurements. Recall the proper memories to find the sample mean and standard deviation.

   b. Verify that the calculator provides the same values for $\bar{x}$ and s as in Exercise 2.11, parts a and c.

2.13   You are given $n = 8$ measurements: 4, 1, 3, 1, 3, 1, 2, 2.

   a. Find the range.

   b. Calculate $\bar{x}$.

   c. Calculate s^2 and s using the computing formula.

   d. Use the data entry method in your calculator to find $\bar{x}$, s, and s^2. Verify that your answers are the same as those in parts b and c.

2.14   You are given $n = 8$ measurements: 3, 1, 5, 6, 4, 4, 3, 5.

   a. Calculate the range.

   b. Calculate the sample mean.

   c. Calculate the sample variance and standard deviation.

   d. Compare the range and the standard deviation. The range is approximately how many standard deviations?

2.4   On the Practical Significance of the Standard Deviation

We now introduce a useful theorem developed by the Russian mathematician Tchebysheff. Proof of the theorem is not difficult, but we are more interested in its application than its proof.

| Tchebysheff's Theorem | Given a number k greater than or equal to 1 and a set of n measurements, at least $[1 - (1/k^2)]$ of the measurements will lie within k standard deviations of their mean. |

Tchebysheff's Theorem applies to *any set of measurements* and can be used to describe either a sample or a population. We will use the notation appropriate for populations, but you should realize that we could just as easily use the mean and the standard deviation for the sample.

The idea involved in Tchebysheff's Theorem is illustrated in Figure 2.10. An interval is constructed by measuring a distance $k\sigma$ on either side of the mean μ. The number k can be any number as long as it is greater than or equal to 1. Then Tchebysheff's Theorem states that at least $1 - (1/k^2)$ of the total number n measurements lies in the constructed interval.

FIGURE 2.10
Illustrating
Tchebysheff's
Theorem

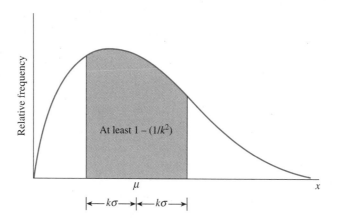

In Table 2.3, we choose a few numerical values for k and compute $[1 - (1/k^2)]$.

TABLE 2.3
Illustrative values
of $[1 - (1/k^2)]$

k	$1 - (1/k^2)$
1	$1 - 1 = 0$
2	$1 - 1/4 = 3/4$
3	$1 - 1/9 = 8/9$

From the calculations in Table 2.3, the theorem states:

- At least none of the measurements lie in the interval $\mu - \sigma$ to $\mu + \sigma$.
- At least 3/4 of the measurements lie in the interval $\mu - 2\sigma$ to $\mu + 2\sigma$.
- At least 8/9 of the measurements lie in the interval $\mu - 3\sigma$ to $\mu + 3\sigma$.

Although the first statement is not at all helpful, the other two values of k provide valuable information about the proportion of measurements that fall in certain intervals. The values $k = 2$ and $k = 3$ are not the only values of k you can use; for example, the proportion of measurements that fall within $k = 2.5$ standard deviations of the mean is at least $1 - [1/(2.5)^2] = .84$.

EXAMPLE 2.6

The mean and variance of a sample of $n = 25$ measurements are 75 and 100, respectively. Use Tchebysheff's Theorem to describe the distribution of measurements.

Solution

You are given $\bar{x} = 75$ and $s^2 = 100$. The standard deviation is $s = \sqrt{100} = 10$. The distribution of measurements is centered about $\bar{x} = 75$, and Tchebysheff's Theorem states:

- *At least* 3/4 of the 25 measurements lie in the interval $\bar{x} \pm 2s = 75 \pm 2(10)$—that is, 55 to 95.
- *At least* 8/9 of the measurements lie in the interval $\bar{x} \pm 3s = 75 \pm 3(10)$—that is, 45 to 105.

Since Tchebysheff's Theorem applies to *any* distribution, it is very conservative. This is why we emphasize "at least $1 - (1/k^2)$" in this theorem.

Another rule for describing the variability of a data set does not work for *all* data sets, but it does work very well for data that "pile up" in the familiar mound shape shown in Figure 2.11. The closer your data distribution is to the mound-shaped curve in Figure 2.11, the more accurate the rule will be. Since mound-shaped data distributions occur quite frequently in nature, the rule can often be used in practical applications. For this reason, we call it the **Empirical Rule.**

FIGURE 2.11
Mound-shaped
distribution

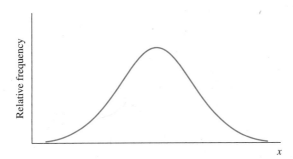

Empirical Rule

Given a distribution of measurements that is approximately mound-shaped:

The interval $(\mu \pm \sigma)$ contains approximately 68% of the measurements.

The interval $(\mu \pm 2\sigma)$ contains approximately 95% of the measurements.

The interval $(\mu \pm 3\sigma)$ contains approximately 99.7% of the measurements.

The mound-shaped distribution shown in Figure 2.11 is commonly known as the **normal distribution** and will be discussed in detail in Chapter 6.

EXAMPLE 2.7

In a time study conducted at a manufacturing plant, the length of time to complete a specified operation is measured for each of $n = 40$ workers. The mean and standard deviation are found to be 12.8 and 1.7, respectively. Describe the sample data using the Empirical Rule.

Solution

To describe the data, calculate these intervals:

$$(\bar{x} \pm s) = 12.8 \pm 1.7 \quad \text{or} \quad 11.1 \text{ to } 14.5$$
$$(\bar{x} \pm 2s) = 12.8 \pm 2(1.7) \quad \text{or} \quad 9.4 \text{ to } 16.2$$
$$(\bar{x} \pm 3s) = 12.8 \pm 3(1.7) \quad \text{or} \quad 7.7 \text{ to } 17.9$$

According to the Empirical Rule, you expect approximately 68% of the measurements to fall into the interval from 11.1 to 14.5, approximately 95% to fall into the interval from 9.4 to 16.2, and approximately 99.7% to fall into the interval from 7.7 to 17.9.

If you doubt that the distribution of measurements is mound-shaped, or if you wish for some other reason to be conservative, you can apply Tchebysheff's Theorem and be absolutely certain of your statements. Tchebysheff's Theorem tells you that at least 3/4 of the measurements fall into the interval from 9.4 to 16.2 and at least 8/9 into the interval from 7.7 to 17.9.

EXAMPLE 2.8

Student teachers are trained to develop lesson plans, on the assumption that the written plan will help them to perform successfully in the classroom. In a study to assess the relationship between written lesson plans and their implementation in the classroom, 25 lesson plans were scored on a scale of 0 to 34 according to a Lesson Plan Assessment Checklist. The 25 scores are shown in Table 2.4. Use Tchebysheff's Theorem and the Empirical Rule (if applicable) to describe the distribution of these assessment scores.

TABLE 2.4
Lesson plan assessment scores

26.1	26.0	14.5	29.3	19.7
22.1	21.2	26.6	31.9	25.0
15.9	20.8	20.2	17.8	13.3
25.6	26.5	15.7	22.1	13.8
29.0	21.3	23.5	22.1	10.2

Solution

Use your calculator or the computing formulas to verify that $\bar{x} = 21.6$ and $s = 5.5$. The appropriate intervals are calculated and listed in Table 2.5. We have also referred back to the original 25 measurements and counted the actual number of measurements that fall into each of these intervals. These frequencies and relative frequencies are shown in Table 2.5.

TABLE 2.5
Intervals $\bar{x} \pm ks$ for the data of Table 2.4

k	Interval $\bar{x} \pm ks$	Frequency in Interval	Relative Frequency
1	16.1–27.1	16	.64
2	10.6–32.6	24	.96
3	5.1–38.1	25	1.00

Is Tchebysheff's Theorem applicable? Yes, because it can be used for any set of data. According to Tchebysheff's Theorem,

- at least 3/4 of the measurements will fall between 10.6 and 32.6.
- at least 8/9 of the measurements will fall between 5.1 and 38.1.

You can see in Table 2.5 that Tchebysheff's Theorem is true for these data. In fact, the proportions of measurements that fall into the specified intervals exceed the lower bound given by this theorem.

Is the Empirical Rule applicable? You can check for yourself by drawing a graph—either a stem and leaf plot or a histogram. The *MINITAB* histogram in Figure 2.12 shows that the distribution is *relatively* mound-shaped, so the Empirical Rule should work *relatively well.* That is,

- approximately 68% of the measurements will fall between 16.1 and 27.1.
- approximately 95% of the measurements will fall between 10.6 and 32.6.
- approximately 99.7% of the measurements will fall between 5.1 and 38.1.

The relative frequencies in Table 2.5 closely approximate those specified by the Empirical Rule.

FIGURE 2.12
MINITAB histogram
for Example 2.8

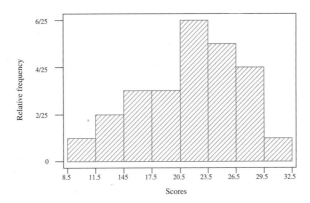

Using Tchebysheff's Theorem and the Empirical Rule

Tchebysheff's Theorem can be proven mathematically. It applies to any set of measurements—sample or population, large or small, mound-shaped or skewed.

Tchebysheff's Theorem gives a *lower bound* to the fraction of measurements to be found in an interval constructed as $\bar{x} \pm ks$. *At least* $1 - (1/k^2)$ of the measurements will fall into this interval, and probably more!

The Empirical Rule is a "rule of thumb" that can be used as a descriptive tool only when the data tend to be roughly mound-shaped (the data tend to pile up near the center of the distribution).

When you use these two tools for describing a set of measurements, Tchebysheff's Theorem will always be satisfied, but it is a very conservative estimate of the fraction of measurements that fall into a particular interval. If it is appropriate to use the Empirical Rule (mound-shaped data), this rule will give you a more accurate estimate of the fraction of measurements that fall into the interval.

2.5 A Check on the Calculation of *s*

Tchebysheff's Theorem and the Empirical Rule can be used to detect gross errors in the calculation of *s*. Roughly speaking, these two tools tell you that *most of the time,* measurements lie within *two* standard deviations of their mean. This interval is marked off in Figure 2.13, and it implies that the total range of the measurements, from smallest to largest, should be somewhere around four standard deviations. This is, of course, a very rough approximation, but it can be very useful in checking for large errors in your calculation of *s*. If the range, *R,* is about four standard deviations, or 4*s,* you can write

$$R \approx 4s \quad \text{or} \quad s \approx \frac{R}{4}$$

The computed value of *s* using the shortcut formula should be of roughly the same order as the approximation.

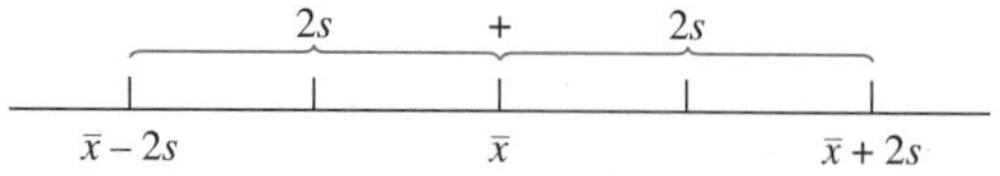

FIGURE 2.13
Range
approximation to s

EXAMPLE 2.9

Use the range approximation to check the calculation of s for Table 2.2.

Solution   The range of the five measurements—5, 7, 1, 2, 4—is

$$R = 7 - 1 = 6$$

Then

$$s \approx \frac{R}{4} = \frac{6}{4} = 1.5$$

This is the same order as the calculated value $s = 2.4$.

The range approximation is *not* intended to provide an accurate value for s. Rather, its purpose is to detect gross errors in calculating, such as the failure to divide the sum of squares of deviations by $(n - 1)$ or the failure to take the square root of s^2. If you make one of these mistakes, your answer will be many times larger than the range approximation of s.

EXAMPLE 2.10

Use the range approximation to determine an approximate value for the standard deviation for the data in Table 2.4.

Solution   The range $R = 31.9 - 10.2 = 21.7$. Then

$$s \approx \frac{R}{4} = \frac{21.7}{4} = 5.4$$

Since the exact value of s is 5.5 for the data in Table 2.4, the approximation is very close.

The range for a sample of n measurements will depend on the sample size, n. For larger values of n, a larger range of the x values is expected. The range for large samples (say, $n = 50$ or more observations) may be as large as $6s$, whereas the range for small samples (say, $n = 5$ or less) may be as small as or smaller than $2.5s$.

The range approximation for s can be improved if it is known that the sample is drawn from a mound-shaped distribution of data. Thus, the calculated s should not differ substantially from the range divided by the appropriate ratio given in Table 2.6.

TABLE 2.6
Divisor for
the range
approximation of s

Number of Measurements	Expected Ratio of Range to s
5	2.5
10	3
25	4

Exercises   **Basic Techniques**

2.15   A set of $n = 10$ measurements consists of the values 5, 2, 3, 6, 1, 2, 4, 5, 1, 3.

a. Use the range approximation to estimate the value of s for this set. (HINT: Use the table at the end of Section 2.5.)

b. Use your calculator to find the actual value of s. Is the actual value close to your estimate in part a?

c. Draw a dotplot of this data set. Are the data mound-shaped?

d. Can you use Tchebysheff's Theorem to describe this data set? Why or why not?

e. Can you use the Empirical Rule to describe this data set? Why or why not?

2.16   Suppose you want to create a mental picture of the relative frequency histogram for a large data set consisting of 1000 observations, and you know that the mean and standard deviation of the data set are 36 and 3, respectively.

a. If you are fairly certain that the relative frequency distribution of the data is mound-shaped, how might you picture the relative frequency distribution? (HINT: Use the Empirical Rule.)

b. If you have no prior information concerning the shape of the relative frequency distribution, what can you say about the relative frequency histogram? (HINT: Construct intervals $\bar{x} \pm ks$ for several choices of k.)

2.17   A distribution of measurements is relatively mound-shaped with mean 50 and standard deviation 10.

a. What proportion of the measurements will fall between 40 and 60?

b. What proportion of the measurements will fall between 30 and 70?

c. What proportion of the measurements will fall between 30 and 60?

d. If a measurement is chosen at random from this distribution, what is the probability that it will be greater than 60?

2.18   A set of data has a mean of 75 and a standard deviation of 5. You know nothing else about the size of the data set or the shape of the data distribution.

a. What can you say about the proportion of measurements that fall between 60 and 90?

b. What can you say about the proportion of measurements that fall between 65 and 85?

c. What can you say about the proportion of measurements that are less than 65?

Applications

2.19   The length of time required for an automobile driver to respond to a particular emergency situation was recorded for $n = 10$ drivers. The times (in seconds) were .5, .8, 1.1, .7, .6, .9, .7, .8, .7, .8.

a. Scan the data and use the procedure in Section 2.5 to find an approximate value for s. Use this value to check your calculations in part b.

b. Calculate the sample mean $\bar{x}$ and the standard deviation s. Compare with part a.

2.20   The data listed here are the weights (in pounds) of 27 packages of ground beef in a supermarket meat display:

EX0220

1.08	.99	.97	1.18	1.41	1.28	.83
1.06	1.14	1.38	.75	.96	1.08	.87
.89	.89	.96	1.12	1.12	.93	1.24
.89	.98	1.14	.92	1.18	1.17	

a. Construct a stem and leaf plot or a relative frequency histogram to display the distribution of weights. Is the distribution relatively mound-shaped?

b. Find the mean and standard deviation of the data set.

c. Find the percentage of measurements in the intervals $\bar{x} \pm s$, $\bar{x} \pm 2s$, and $\bar{x} \pm 3s$.

d. How do the percentages obtained in part c compare with those given by the Empirical Rule? Explain.

e. How many of the packages weigh exactly 1 pound? Can you think of any explanation for this?

2.21   Is your breathing rate normal? Actually, there is no standard breathing rate for humans. It can vary from as low as 4 breaths per minute to as high as 70 or 75 for a person engaged in strenuous exercise. Suppose that the resting breathing rates for college-age students have a relative frequency distribution that is mound-shaped, with a mean equal to 12 and a standard deviation of 2.3 breaths per minute. What fraction of all students would have breathing rates in the following intervals?

a. 9.7 to 14.3 breaths per minute

b. 7.4 to 16.6 breaths per minute

c. More than 18.9 or less than 5.1 breaths per minute

EX0222

2.22 A geologist collected 20 different ore samples, all the same weight, and randomly divided them into two groups. She measured the titanium (Ti) content of the samples using two different methods.

Method 1					Method 2				
.011	.013	.013	.015	.014	.011	.016	.013	.012	.015
.013	.010	.013	.011	.012	.012	.017	.013	.014	.015

a. Construct stem and leaf plots for the two data sets. Visually compare their centers and their ranges.

b. Calculate the sample means and standard deviations for the two sets. Do the calculated values confirm your visual conclusions from part a?

2.23 The data from Exercise 1.54 (see data set EX0154), reproduced below, show the last digit of the social security number for a group of 70 students.

1	6	9	1	5	9	0	2	8	4
0	7	3	4	2	3	5	8	4	2
3	2	0	0	2	1	2	7	7	4
0	0	9	9	5	3	8	4	7	4
6	6	9	0	2	6	2	9	5	8
5	1	7	7	7	8	7	5	1	8
3	4	1	9	3	8	6	6	6	6

a. You found in Exercise 1.54 that the distribution of this data was relatively "flat," with each different value from 0 to 9 occurring with nearly equal frequency. Using this fact, what would be your best estimate for the mean of the data set?

b. Use the range approximation to guess the value of s for this set.

c. Use your calculator to find the actual values of $\bar{x}$ and s. Compare with your estimates in parts a and b.

2.24 Refer to the data set in Exercise 2.23.

a. Find the percentage of measurements in the intervals $\bar{x} \pm s$, $\bar{x} \pm 2s$, and $\bar{x} \pm 3s$.

b. How do the percentages obtained in part a compare with those given by the Empirical Rule? Should they be approximately the same? Explain.

2.25 A group of experimental animals are infected with a particular form of bacteria, and their survival time is found to average 32 days, with a standard deviation of 36 days.

a. Visualize the distribution of survival times. Do you think that the distribution is relatively mound-shaped, skewed right, or skewed left? Explain.

b. Within what limits would you expect at least 3/4 of the measurements to lie?

2.26 Refer to Exercise 2.25. You can use the Empirical Rule to see why the distribution of survival times could not be mound-shaped.

a. Find the value of x that is exactly one standard deviation below the mean.

b. If the distribution is in fact mound-shaped, approximately what percentage of the measurements should be less than the value of x found in part a?

c. Since the variable being measured is time, is it possible to find any measurements that are more than one standard deviation below the mean?

d. Use your answers to part b and c to explain why the data distribution cannot be mound-shaped.

EX0227

2.27 To estimate the amount of lumber in a tract of timber, an owner decided to count the number of trees with diameters exceeding 12 inches in randomly selected 50-by-50-foot squares. Seventy 50-by-50-foot squares were chosen, and the selected trees were counted in each tract. The data are listed here:

7	8	7	10	4	8	6	8	9	10
9	6	4	9	10	9	8	8	7	9
3	9	5	9	9	8	7	5	8	8
10	2	7	4	8	5	10	7	7	7
9	6	8	8	8	7	8	9	6	8
6	11	9	11	7	7	11	7	9	13
10	8	8	5	9	9	8	5	9	8

a. Construct a relative frequency histogram to describe the data.

b. Calculate the sample mean $\bar{x}$ as an estimate of μ, the mean number of timber trees for all 50-by-50-foot squares in the tract.

c. Calculate s for the data. Construct the intervals $\bar{x} \pm s$, $\bar{x} \pm 2s$, and $\bar{x} \pm 3s$. Calculate the percentage of squares falling into each of the three intervals, and compare with the corresponding percentages given by the Empirical Rule and Tchebysheff's Theorem.

2.28 Refer to Exercise 2.8 and data set EX0208. The prices of a 6-ounce can or a 7.06 pouch for 14 different brands of water-packed light tuna, based on prices paid nationally in supermarkets are reproduced here.[4]

.99	1.92	1.23	.85	.65	.53	1.41
1.12	.63	.67	.69	.60	.60	.66

a. Use the range approximation to find an estimate of s.

b. How does it compare to the computed value of s?

Calculating the Mean and Standard Deviation for Grouped Data (Optional)

2.29 Suppose that some measurements occur more than once and that the data $x_1, x_2, \ldots, x_k$ are arranged in a frequency table as shown here:

Observations	Frequency f_i
x_1	f_1
x_2	f_2
$\vdots$	$\vdots$
x_k	f_k

The formulas for the mean and variance for grouped data are

$$\bar{x} = \frac{\Sigma x_i f_i}{n}, \qquad \text{where } n = \Sigma f_i$$

and

$$s^2 = \frac{\Sigma x_i^2 f_i - \dfrac{(\Sigma x_i f_i)^2}{n}}{n-1}$$

Notice that if each value occurs once, these formulas reduce to those given in the text. Although these formulas for grouped data are primarily of value when you have a large number of measurements, demonstrate their use for the sample 1, 0, 0, 1, 3, 1, 3, 2, 3, 0, 0, 1, 1, 3, 2.

a. Calculate $\bar{x}$ and s^2 directly, using the formulas for ungrouped data.

b. The frequency table for the $n = 15$ measurements is as follows:

x	f
0	4
1	5
2	2
3	4

Calculate $\bar{x}$ and s^2 using the formulas for grouped data. Compare with your answers to part a.

 2.30 The International Baccalaureate (IB) program is an accelerated academic program offered at a growing number of high schools throughout the country. Students enrolled in this program are placed in accelerated or advanced courses and must take IB examinations in each of six subject areas at the end of their junior or senior year. Students are scored on a scale of 1–7, with 1–2 being poor, 3 mediocre, 4 average, and 5–7 excellent. During its first year of operation at John W. North High School in Riverside, California, 17 juniors attempted the IB economics exam, with these results:

Exam Grade	Number of Students
7	1
6	4
5	4
4	4
3	4

Calculate the mean and standard deviation for these scores.

2.31 To illustrate the utility of the Empirical Rule, consider a distribution that is heavily skewed to the right, as shown in the accompanying figure.

a. Calculate $\bar{x}$ and s for the data shown. (NOTE: There are 10 zeros, 5 ones, and so on.)

b. Construct the intervals $\bar{x} \pm s$, $\bar{x} \pm 2s$, and $\bar{x} \pm 3s$ and locate them on the frequency distribution.

c. Calculate the proportion of the $n = 25$ measurements that fall into each of the three intervals. Compare with Tchebysheff's Theorem and the Empirical Rule. Note that, although the proportion that falls into the interval $\bar{x} \pm s$ does not agree closely with the Empirical Rule, the proportions that fall into the intervals $\bar{x} \pm 2s$ and $\bar{x} \pm 3s$ agree very well. Many times this is true, even for non-mound-shaped distributions of data.

Distribution for
Exercise 2.31

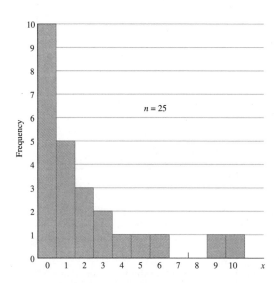

2.6 Measures of Relative Standing

Sometimes you need to know the position of one observation relative to others in a set of data. For example, if you took an examination with a total of 35 points, you might want to know how your score of 30 compared to the scores of the other students in the class. The mean and standard deviation of the scores can be used to calculate a *z*-**score,** which measures the relative standing of a measurement in a data set.

Definition   The **sample** *z*-**score** is a measure of relative standing defined by

$$z\text{-score} = \frac{x - \bar{x}}{s}$$

A *z*-**score measures the distance between an observation and the mean, measured in units of standard deviation.** For example, suppose that the mean and standard deviation of the test scores (based on a total of 35 points) are 25 and 4, respectively. The *z*-score for your score of 30 is calculated as follows:

$$z\text{-score} = \frac{x - \bar{x}}{s} = \frac{30 - 25}{4} = 1.25$$

Your score of 30 lies 1.25 standard deviations above the mean ($30 = \bar{x} + 1.25s$).

The *z*-score is a valuable tool for determining whether a particular observation is likely to occur quite frequently or whether it is unlikely and might be considered an **outlier.** According to Tchebysheff's Theorem and the Empirical Rule,

- at least 75% and more likely 95% of the observations lie within two standard deviations of their mean: their *z*-scores are between −2 and +2. *Observations with z-scores exceeding 2 in absolute value happen less than 5% of the time and are considered somewhat unlikely.*
- at least 89% and more likely 99.7% of the observations lie within three standard deviations of their mean: their *z*-scores are between −3 and +3. *Observations with z-scores exceeding 3 in absolute value happen less than 1% of the time and are considered very unlikely.*

You should look carefully at any observation that has a *z*-score exceeding 3 in absolute value. Perhaps the measurement was recorded incorrectly or does not belong to the population being sampled. Perhaps it is just a highly unlikely observation, but a valid one nonetheless!

EXAMPLE 2.11   Consider this sample of $n = 10$ measurements:

1, 1, 0, 15, 2, 3, 4, 0, 1, 3

The measurement $x = 15$ appears to be unusually large. Calculate the *z*-score for this observation and state your conclusions.

Solution   Calculate $\bar{x} = 3.0$ and $s = 4.42$ for the $n = 10$ measurements. Then the *z*-score for the suspected outlier, $x = 15$, is calculated as

$$z\text{-score} = \frac{x - \bar{x}}{s} = \frac{15 - 3}{4.42} = 2.71$$

Hence, the measurement $x = 15$ lies 2.71 standard deviations above the sample mean, $\bar{x} = 3.0$. Although the *z*-score does not exceed 3, it is close enough so that you might suspect that $x = 15$ is an outlier. You should examine the sampling procedure to see whether $x = 15$ is a faulty observation.

A **percentile** is another measure of relative standing and is most often used for large data sets. (Percentiles are not very useful for small data sets.)

Definition A set of n measurements on the variable x has been arranged in order of magnitude. The p**th percentile** is the value of x that exceeds p% of the measurements and is less than the remaining $(100 - p)$%.

EXAMPLE 2.12 Suppose you have been notified that your score of 610 on the Verbal Graduate Record Examination placed you at the 60th percentile in the distribution of scores. Where does your score of 610 stand in relation to the scores of others who took the examination?

Solution Scoring at the 60th percentile means that 60% of all the examination scores were lower than your score and 40% were higher.

In general, the 60th percentile for the variable x is a point on the *horizontal axis* of the data distribution that is greater than 60% of the measurements and less than the others. That is, 60% of the measurements are less than the 60th percentile and 40% are greater (see Figure 2.14). Since the total area under the distribution is 100%, 60% of the area is to the left and 40% of the area is to the right of the 60th percentile. Remember that the median, m, of a set of data is the middle measurement; that is, 50% of the measurements are smaller and 50% are larger than the median. Thus, the *median is the same as the 50th percentile!*

FIGURE 2.14
The 60th percentile shown on the relative frequency histogram for a data set

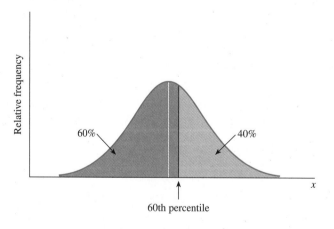

The 25th and 75th percentiles, called the **lower** and **upper quartiles,** along with the median (the 50th percentile), locate points that divide the data into four sets, each containing an equal number of measurements. Twenty-five percent of the measurements will be less than the lower (first) quartile, 50% will be less than the median (the second quartile), and 75% will be less than the upper (third) quartile. Thus, the median and the lower and upper quartiles are located at points on the x-axis so that the area under the relative frequency histogram for the data is partitioned into four equal areas, as shown in Figure 2.15.

FIGURE 2.15
Location of
quartiles

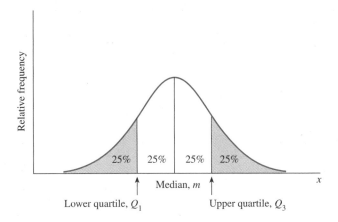

Definition

A set of n measurements on the variable x has been arranged in order of magnitude. The **lower quartile (first quartile), Q_1,** is the value of x that exceeds one-fourth of the measurements and is less than the remaining three-fourths. The **second quartile** is the median. The **upper quartile (third quartile), Q_3,** is the value of x that exceeds three-fourths of the measurements and is less than one-fourth.

For small sets of data, a quartile may fall between two observations, in which case many numbers may satisfy the preceding definition. To avoid this ambiguity, we use the following rule to locate the sample quartiles.

Calculate Sample Quartiles?

■ When the measurements are arranged in order of magnitude, the **lower quartile, Q_1,** is the value of x in position $.25(n + 1)$, and the **upper quartile, Q_3,** is the value of x in position $.75(n + 1)$.

■ When $.25(n + 1)$ and $.75(n + 1)$ are not integers, the quartiles are found by interpolation, using the values in the two adjacent positions.[†]

EXAMPLE 2.13

Find the lower and upper quartiles for this set of measurements:

16, 25, 4, 18, 11, 13, 20, 8, 11, 9

Solution

Rank the $n = 10$ measurements from smallest to largest:

4, 8, 9, 11, 11, 13, 16, 18, 20, 25

Calculate

Position of $Q_1 = .25(n + 1) = .25(10 + 1) = 2.75$
Position of $Q_3 = .75(n + 1) = .75(10 + 1) = 8.25$

[†]This definition of quartiles is consistent with the one used in the *MINITAB* package. Some textbooks use ordinary rounding when finding quartile positions, whereas others compute sample quartiles as the medians of the upper and lower halves of the data set.

Since these positions are not integers, the lower quartile is taken to be the value 3/4 of the distance between the second and third ordered measurements, and the upper quartile is taken to be the value 1/4 of the distance between the eighth and ninth ordered measurements. Therefore,

$$Q_1 = 8 + .75(9 - 8) = 8 + .75 = 8.75$$

and

$$Q_3 = 18 + .25(20 - 18) = 18 + .5 = 18.5$$

Because the median and the quartiles divide the data distribution into four parts, each containing approximately 25% of the measurements, Q_1 and Q_3 are the upper and lower boundaries for the middle 50% of the distribution. We can measure the range of this "middle 50%" of the distribution using a numerical measure called the **interquartile range.**

Definition   The **interquartile range (IQR)** for a set of measurements is the difference between the upper and lower quartiles; that is, IQR $= Q_3 - Q_1$.

For the data in Example 2.13, IQR $= Q_3 - Q_1 = 18.50 - 8.75 = 9.75$. We will use the IQR along with the quartiles and the median in the next section to construct another graph for describing data sets.

Many of the numerical measures that you have learned are easily found using computer programs or even graphics calculators. The *MINITAB* command **Stat → Basic Statistics → Display Descriptive Statistics** (see the section "About *MINITAB*" at the end of this chapter) produces output containing the mean, the standard deviation, the median, and the lower and upper quartiles, as well as the values of some other statistics that we have not discussed. The **trimmed mean** (given as TrMean) is the mean of the middle 90% of the measurements after excluding the smallest 5% and the largest 5%. Unlike the ordinary arithmetic mean, the trimmed mean is not sensitive to extremely large or extremely small values in the data set. The data from Example 2.13 produced the *MINITAB* output shown in Figure 2.16. Notice that the quartiles are identical to the hand-calculated values in that example.

FIGURE 2.16
MINITAB output
for the data in
Example 2.13

Descriptive Statistics: x

Variable	N	Mean	Median	TrMean	StDev	SE Mean
x	10	13.50	12.00	13.25	6.28	1.98

Variable	Min	Max	Q1	Q3
x	4.00	25.00	8.75	18.50

2.7   The Five-Number Summary and the Box Plot

The median and the upper and lower quartiles shown in Figure 2.15 divide the data into four sets, each containing an equal number of measurements. If we add the largest number (Max) and the smallest number (Min) in the data set to this group, we will have a set of numbers that provide a quick and rough summary of the data distribution.

The **five-number summary** consists of the smallest number, the lower quartile, the median, the upper quartile and the largest number, presented in order from smallest to largest:

Min Q_1 **Median** Q_3 **Max**

By definition, one-fourth of the measurements in the data set lie between each of the four adjacent pairs of numbers.

The five-number summary can be used to create a simple graph called a **box plot** to visually describe the data distribution. From the box plot, you can quickly detect any skewness in the shape of the distribution and see whether there are any outliers in the data set.

An outlier may result from transposing digits when recording a measurement, from incorrectly reading an instrument dial, from a malfunctioning piece of equipment, and from other problems. Even when there are no recording or observational errors, a data set may contain one or more valid measurements that, for one reason or another, differ markedly from the others in the set. These outliers can cause a marked distortion in commonly used numerical measures such as $\bar{x}$ and s. In fact, outliers may themselves contain important information not shared with the other measurements in the set. Therefore, isolating outliers, if they are present, is an important step in any preliminary analysis of a data set. The box plot is designed expressly for this purpose.

To Construct a Box Plot

- Calculate the median, the upper and lower quartiles, and the IQR for the data set.
- Draw a horizontal line representing the scale of measurement. Form a box just above the horizontal line with the right and left ends at Q_1 and Q_3. Draw a vertical line through the box at the location of the median.

A box plot is shown in Figure 2.17.

FIGURE 2.17
Box plot

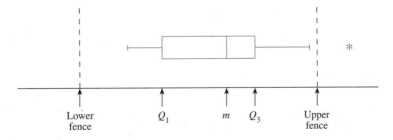

In Section 2.6, the z-score provided boundaries for finding unusually large or small measurements. You looked for z-scores greater than 2 or 3 in absolute value. The box plot uses the IQR to create imaginary "fences" to separate outliers from the rest of the data set:

Detecting Outliers—observations that are beyond:

- Lower fence: $Q_1 - 1.5(\text{IQR})$
- Upper fence: $Q_3 + 1.5(\text{IQR})$

The upper and lower fences are shown with broken lines in Figure 2.17, but they are not usually drawn on the box plot. Any measurement beyond the upper or lower fence is an **outlier**; the rest of the measurements, inside the fences, are not unusual. Finally, the box plot marks the range of the data set using "whiskers" to connect the smallest and largest measurements (*excluding outliers*) to the box.

To Finish the Box Plot

- Mark any **outliers** with an asterisk (*) on the graph.
- Extend horizontal lines called "whiskers" from the ends of the box to the smallest and largest observations that are *not* outliers.

EXAMPLE 2.14

As American consumers become more careful about the foods they eat, food processors try to stay competitive by avoiding excessive amounts of fat, cholesterol, and sodium in the foods they sell. The following data are the amounts of sodium per slice (in milligrams) for each of eight brands of regular American cheese. Construct a box plot for the data and look for outliers.

$$340, \quad 300, \quad 520, \quad 340, \quad 320, \quad 290, \quad 260, \quad 330$$

Solution The $n = 8$ measurements are first ranked from smallest to largest:

$$260, \quad 290, \quad 300, \quad 320, \quad 330, \quad 340, \quad 340, \quad 520$$

The positions of the median, Q_1, and Q_3 are:

$$.5(n + 1) = .5(9) = 4.5$$
$$.25(n + 1) = .25(9) = 2.25$$
$$.75(n + 1) = .75(9) = 6.75$$

so that $m = (320 + 330)/2 = 325$, $Q_1 = 290 + .25(10) = 292.5$, and $Q_3 = 340$. The interquartile range is calculated as

$$\text{IQR} = Q_3 - Q_1 = 340 - 292.5 = 47.5$$

Calculate the upper and lower fences:

$$\text{Lower fence: } 292.5 - 1.5(47.5) = 221.25$$
$$\text{Upper fence: } 340 + 1.5(47.5) = 411.25$$

The value $x = 520$, a brand of cheese containing 520 milligrams of sodium, is the only *outlier*, lying beyond the upper fence.

The box plot for the data is shown in Figure 2.18. The outlier is marked with an asterisk (*). Once the outlier is excluded, we find (from the ranked data set) that the smallest and largest measurements are $x = 260$ and $x = 340$. These are the two values that form the whiskers. Since the value $x = 340$ is the same as Q_3, there is no whisker on the right side of the box.

FIGURE 2.18
Box plot for
Example 2.14

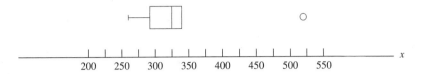

DO IT YOURSELF!

Now would be a good time to try the **Building a Box Plot** applet. The applet in Figure 2.19 shows a dotplot of the data in Example 2.14. Using the [Next Step] button, you will see a step-by-step description explaining how the box plot is constructed. We will use this applet again for the *Do It Yourself Exercises* at the end of the chapter.

FIGURE 2.19
**Building a
Box Plot** applet

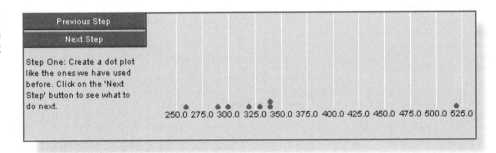

You can use the box plot to describe the shape of a data distribution by looking at the position of the median line compared to Q_1 and Q_3, the left and right ends of the box. If the median is close to the middle of the box, the distribution is fairly symmetric, providing equal-sized intervals to contain the two middle quarters of the data. If the median line is to the left of center, the distribution is skewed to the right; if the median is to the right of center, the distribution is skewed to the left. Also, for most skewed distributions, the whisker on the skewed side of the box tends to be longer than the whisker on the other side.

We used the *MINITAB* command **Graph → Boxplot** to draw two box plots, one for the sodium contents of the eight brands of cheese in Example 2.14, and another for five brands of fat-free cheese with these sodium contents:

$$300, \quad 300, \quad 320, \quad 290, \quad 180$$

The two box plots are shown together in Figure 2.20. Look at the long whisker on the left side of both box plots and the position of the median lines. Both distributions are skewed to the left; that is, there are a few unusually small measurements. The regular cheese data, however, also show one brand ($x = 520$) with an unusually large amount of sodium. In general, it appears that the sodium content of the fat-free brands is lower than that of the regular brands, but the variability of the sodium content for regular cheese (excluding the outlier) is less than that of the fat-free brands.

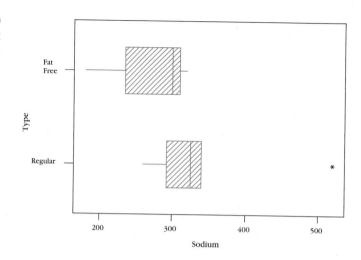

FIGURE 2.20
MINITAB output
for regular and
fat-free cheese

Exercises

Basic Techniques

2.32 Given the following data set: 8, 7, 1, 4, 6, 6, 4, 5, 7, 6, 3, 0

a. Find the five-number summary and the IQR.

b. Calculate $\bar{x}$ and s.

c. Calculate the z-score for the smallest and largest observations. Is either of these observations unusually large or unusually small?

2.33 Find the five-number summary and the IQR for these data:

$$19, 12, 16, 0, 14, 9, 6, 1, 12, 13, 10, 19, 7, 5, 8$$

2.34 Construct a box plot for these data and identify any outliers:

$$25, 22, 26, 23, 27, 26, 28, 18, 25, 24, 12$$

2.35 Construct a box plot for these data and identify any outliers:

$$3, 9, 10, 2, 6, 7, 5, 8, 6, 6, 4, 9, 22$$

Applications

2.36 If you scored at the 69th percentile on a placement test, how does your score compare with others?

EX0237

2.37 Environmental scientists are increasingly concerned with the accumulation of toxic elements in marine mammals and the transfer of such elements to the animals' offspring. The striped dolphin (*Stenella coeruleoalba*), considered to be the top predator in the marine food chain, was the subject of one such study. The mercury concentrations (micrograms/gram) in the livers of 28 male striped dolphins were as follows:

1.70	183.00	221.00	286.00
1.72	168.00	406.00	315.00
8.80	218.00	252.00	241.00
5.90	180.00	329.00	397.00
101.00	264.00	316.00	209.00
85.40	481.00	445.00	314.00
118.00	485.00	278.00	318.00

a. Calculate the five-number summary for the data.

b. Construct a box plot for the data.

c. Are there any outliers?

d. If you knew that the first four dolphins were all less than 3 years old, while all the others were more than 8 years old, would this information help explain the difference in the magnitude of those four observations? Explain.

2.38 The weights (in pounds) of the 27 packages of ground beef from Exercise 2.20 (see data set EX0220) are listed here in order from smallest to largest:

.75	.83	.87	.89	.89	.89	.92
.93	.96	.96	.97	.98	.99	1.06
1.08	1.08	1.12	1.12	1.14	1.14	1.17
1.18	1.18	1.24	1.28	1.38	1.41	

a. Confirm the values of the mean and standard deviation, calculated in Exercise 2.20 as $\bar{x} = 1.05$ and $s = .17$.

b. The two largest packages of meat weigh 1.38 and 1.41 pounds. Are these two packages unusually heavy? Explain.

c. Construct a box plot for the package weights. What does the position of the median line and the length of the whiskers tell you about the shape of the distribution?

2.39 *American Demographics* is a magazine that investigates various aspects of life in the United States using all sorts of descriptive statistics. These facts were noted in a recent issue:[5]

- 26% of all U.S. adults between the ages of 18 and 24 own five or more pairs of wearable sneakers.

- 61% of U.S. households have two or more television sets.

Identify any percentiles that can be determined from this information.

2.40 The set of presidential vetoes in Exercise 1.41 and data set EX0141 is listed here, along with a box plot generated by *MINITAB*. Use the box plot to describe the shape of the distribution and identify any outliers.

Washington	2	J. Adams	0	Jefferson	0	Madison	5
Monroe	1	J. Q. Adams	0	Jackson	5	Van Buren	0
W. Harrison	0	Tyler	6	Polk	2	Taylor	0
Fillmore	0	Pierce	9	Buchanan	4	Lincoln	2
A. Johnson	21	Grant	45	Hayes	12	Garfield	0
Arthur	4	Cleveland	304	B. Harrison	19	Cleveland	42
McKinley	6	T. Roosevelt	42	Taft	30	Wilson	33
Harding	5	Coolidge	20	Hoover	21	F. Roosevelt	372
Truman	180	Eisenhower	73	Kennedy	12	L. Johnson	16
Nixon	26	Ford	48	Carter	13	Reagan	39
Bush	29	Clinton	36				

Box plot for Exercise 2.40

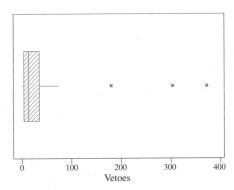

EX0241

2.41 The top 20 movies and their gross revenues (in millions of dollars) from Labor Day weekend (August 31–September 3, 2001) are shown below[7]:

Movie	Weekend Gross	Movie	Weekend Gross
Jeepers Creepers	$15.8	Planet of the Apes	$3.8
Rush Hour 2	11.7	Jurassic Park III	2.3
American Pie 2	11.0	John Carpenter's Ghosts of Mars	2.1
The Others	10.2	The Curse of the Jade Scorpion	2.0
Rat Race	9.2	The Deep End	1.8
The Princess Diaries	7.6	Legally Blonde	1.7
O	6.9	America's Sweethearts	1.3
Jay and Silent Bob Strike Back	6.5	American Outlaws	1.3
Summer Catch	4.9	Bubble Boy	1.3
Captain Corelli's Mandolin	3.9	Pearl Harbor	1.2

a. Can you tell by looking at the data whether it is roughly symmetric? Or is it skewed?

b. Calculate the mean and the median. Use these measures to decide whether or not the data are symmetric or skewed.

c. Draw a box plot to describe the data. Explain why the box plot confirms your conclusions in part b.

Key Concepts and Formulas

I. Measures of the Center of a Data Distribution

   1. Arithmetic mean (mean) or average
      a. Population: μ
      b. Sample of n measurements: $\bar{x} = \dfrac{\Sigma x_i}{n}$
   2. Median; **position** of the median $= .5(n + 1)$
   3. Mode
   4. The median may be preferred to the mean if the data are highly skewed.

II. Measures of Variability

   1. Range: $R =$ largest $-$ smallest
   2. Variance
      a. Population of N measurements: $\sigma^2 = \dfrac{\Sigma(x_i - \mu)^2}{N}$
      b. Sample of n measurements:

      $$s^2 = \frac{\Sigma(x_i - \bar{x})^2}{n - 1} = \frac{\Sigma x_i^2 - \dfrac{(\Sigma x_i)^2}{n}}{n - 1}$$

   3. Standard deviation
      a. Population: $\sigma = \sqrt{\sigma^2}$
      b. Sample: $s = \sqrt{s^2}$
   4. A rough approximation for s can be calculated as $s \approx R/4$. The divisor can be adjusted depending on the sample size.

III. Tchebysheff's Theorem and the Empirical Rule

   1. Use Tchebysheff's Theorem for any data set, regardless of its shape or size.
      a. At least $1 - (1/k^2)$ of the measurements lie within k standard deviations of the mean.

      b. This is only a lower bound; there may be more measurements in the interval.
2. The Empirical Rule can be used only for relatively mound-shaped data sets. Approximately 68%, 95%, and 99.7% of the measurements are within one, two, and three standard deviations of the mean, respectively.

IV. **Measures of Relative Standing**

    1. Sample z-score: $z = \dfrac{x - \bar{x}}{s}$

    2. pth percentile; $p\%$ of the measurements are smaller, and $(100 - p)\%$ are larger.
    3. Lower quartile, Q_1; **position** of $Q_1 = .25(n + 1)$
    4. Upper quartile, Q_3; **position** of $Q_3 = .75(n + 1)$
    5. Interquartile range: IQR $= Q_3 - Q_1$

V. **The Five-Number Summary and Box Plots**

    1. The **five-number summary:**

$$\textbf{Min} \quad \textbf{\textit{Q}}_1 \quad \textbf{Median} \quad \textbf{\textit{Q}}_3 \quad \textbf{Max}$$

One-fourth of the measurements in the data set lie between each of the four adjacent pairs of numbers.

    2. Box plots are used for detecting outliers and shapes of distributions.
    3. Q_1 and Q_3 form the ends of the box. The median line is in the interior of the box.
    4. Upper and lower fences are used to find outliers, observations that lie outside these fences.
        a. **Lower fence:** $Q_1 - 1.5$(IQR)
        b. **Upper fence:** $Q_3 + 1.5$(IQR)
    5. **Outliers** are marked on the box plot with an asterisk (*).
    6. **Whiskers** are connected to the box from the smallest and largest observations that are *not* outliers.
    7. Skewed distributions usually have a long whisker *in the direction of the skewness*, and the median line is drawn *away from the direction of the skewness*.

Help	
Contents	▶
Getting Started	▶
How Do I	▶
Search for Help on...	
How to Use Help	▶
Do It Yourself	▶
About MINITAB	▶

Numerical Descriptive Measures

MINITAB provides most of the basic descriptive statistics presented in Chapter 2 using a single command in the drop-down menus. Once you are on the Windows desktop, double-click on the *MINITAB* icon or use the Start button to start *MINITAB*.

    Practice entering some data into the Data window, naming the columns appropriately in the gray cell just below the column number. When you have finished entering your data, you will have created a *MINITAB* **worksheet,** which can be saved either singly or as a *MINITAB* **project** for future use. Click on **File → Save Current Worksheet** or **File → Save Project.** You will need to name the worksheet (or project)—perhaps "test data"—so that you can retrieve it later.

    The following data are the floor lengths (in inches) behind the second and third seats in nine different minivans[8]:

        Second seat: 62.0, 62.0, 64.5, 48.5, 57.5, 61.0, 45.5, 47.0, 33.0

        Third seat: 27.0, 27.0, 24.0, 16.5, 25.0, 27.5, 14.0, 18.5, 17.0

Since the data involve two variables, we enter the two rows of numbers into columns C1 and C2 in the *MINITAB* worksheet and name them "2nd Seat" and "3rd Seat," respectively. Using the drop-down menus, click on **Stat → Basic Statistics → Display Descriptive Statistics.** The Dialog box is shown in Figure 2.21.

MINITAB

MINITAB

Now click on the Variables box and **select** both columns from the list on the left. (You can click on the **Graphs** option and choose one of several graphs if you like.) Click **OK.** A display of descriptive statistics for both columns will appear in the Session window (see Figure 2.22). You may print this output using **File → Print Session Window** if you choose.

To examine the distribution of the two variables and look for outliers, you can create box plots using the command **Graph → Boxplot.** Select the appropriate column as Y (measurements) in the Dialog box (see Figure 2.23). You may change the style with **Edit Attributes** and orient the box plot horizontally using **Options → Transpose X and Y.** The box plot for the third seat lengths is shown in Figure 2.24.

FIGURE 2.21

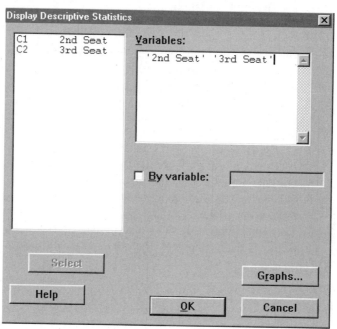

FIGURE 2.22

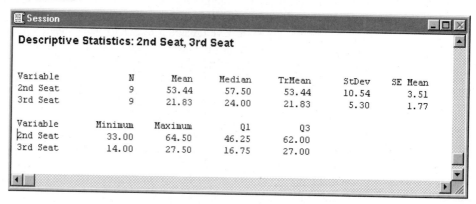

MINITAB

You can use the *MINITAB* commands from Chapter 1 to display stem and leaf plots or histograms for the two variables. How would you describe the similarities and differences in the two data sets? Save this worksheet in a file called "Minivans" before exiting *MINITAB*. We will use it again in Chapter 3.

FIGURE 2.23

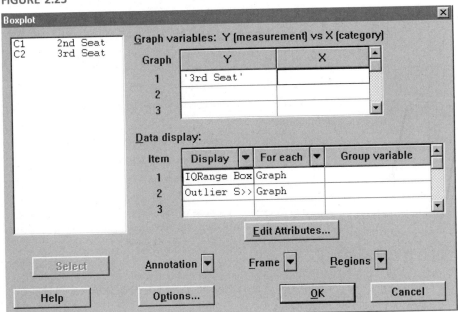

FIGURE 2.24

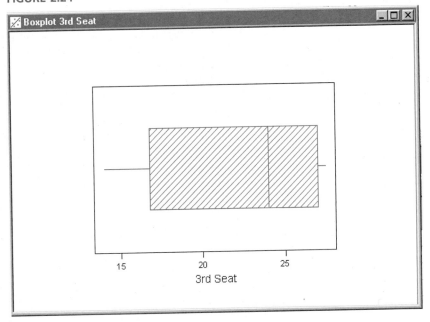

Supplementary Exercises

EX0242

2.42 The number of raisins in each of 14 miniboxes (1/2-ounce size) was counted for a generic brand and for Sunmaid brand raisins. The two data sets are shown here:

Generic Brand				Sunmaid			
25	26	25	28	25	29	24	24
26	28	28	27	28	24	28	22
26	27	24	25	25	28	30	27
26	26			28	24		

a. What are the mean and standard deviation for the generic brand?

b. What are the mean and standard deviation for the Sunmaid brand?

c. Compare the centers and variabilities of the two brands using the results of parts a and b.

2.43 Refer to Exercise 2.42.

a. Find the median, the upper and lower quartiles, and the IQR for each of the two data sets.

b. Construct two box plots on the same horizontal scale to compare the two sets of data.

c. Draw two stem and leaf plots to depict the shapes of the two data sets. Do the box plots in part b verify these results?

d. If we can assume that none of the boxes of raisins are being underfilled (that is, they all weigh approximately 1/2 ounce), what do your results say about the average number of raisins for the two brands?

2.44 The number of television viewing hours per household and the prime viewing times are two factors that affect television advertising income. A random sample of 25 households in a particular viewing area produced the following estimates of viewing hours per household:

EX0244

3.0	6.0	7.5	15.0	12.0
6.5	8.0	4.0	5.5	6.0
5.0	12.0	1.0	3.5	3.0
7.5	5.0	10.0	8.0	3.5
9.0	2.0	6.5	1.0	5.0

a. Scan the data and use the range to find an approximate value for s. Use this value to check your calculations in part b.

b. Calculate the sample mean $\bar{x}$ and the sample standard deviation s. Compare s with the approximate value obtained in part a.

c. Find the percentage of the viewing hours per household that falls into the interval $\bar{x} \pm 2s$. Compare with the corresponding percentage given by the Empirical Rule.

2.45 Refer to Exercise 1.22. The lengths of time (in months) between the onset of a particular illness and its recurrence were recorded:

2.1	4.4	2.7	32.3	9.9
9.0	2.0	6.6	3.9	1.6
14.7	9.6	16.7	7.4	8.2
19.2	6.9	4.3	3.3	1.2
4.1	18.4	.2	6.1	13.5
7.4	.2	8.3	.3	1.3
14.1	1.0	2.4	2.4	18.0
8.7	24.0	1.4	8.2	5.8
1.6	3.5	11.4	18.0	26.7
3.7	12.6	23.1	5.6	.4

a. Find the range.

b. Use the range approximation to find an approximate value for s.

c. Compute s for the data and compare it with your approximation from part b.

2.46   Refer to Exercise 2.45.

  a. Examine the data and count the number of observations that fall into the intervals $\bar{x} \pm s$, $\bar{x} \pm 2s$, and $\bar{x} \pm 3s$.

  b. Do the percentages that fall into these intervals agree with Tchebysheff's Theorem? With the Empirical Rule?

  c. Why might the Empirical Rule be unsuitable for describing these data?

2.47   Find the median and the lower and upper quartiles for the data on times until recurrence of an illness in Exercise 2.45. Use these descriptive measures to construct a box plot for the data. Use the box plot to describe the data distribution.

2.48   Refer to Exercise 2.8. The prices of a 6-ounce can or a 7.06-ounce pouch for 14 different brands of water-packed light tuna, based on prices paid nationally in supermarkets are reproduced here.[4]

.99	1.92	1.23	.85	.65	.53	1.41
1.12	.63	.67	.69	.60	.60	.66

  a. Calculate the five-number summary.

  b. Construct a box plot for the data. Are there any outliers?

  c. The value $x = 1.92$ looks large in comparison to the other prices. Use a z-score to decide whether this is an unusually expensive brand of tuna.

2.49   An analytical chemist wanted to use electrolysis to determine the number of moles of cupric ions in a given volume of solution. The solution was partitioned into $n = 30$ portions of .2 milliliter each. Each of the $n = 30$ unknown portions was tested. The average number of moles of cupric ions for the $n = 30$ portions was found to be .17 mole; the standard deviation was .01 mole.

  a. Describe the distribution of the measurements for the $n = 30$ portions of the solution using Tchebysheff's Theorem.

  b. Describe the distribution of the measurements for the $n = 30$ portions of the solution using the Empirical Rule. (Do you expect the Empirical Rule to be suitable for describing these data?)

  c. Suppose the chemist had used only $n = 4$ portions of the solution for the experiment and obtained the readings .15, .19, .17, and .15. Would the Empirical Rule be suitable for describing the $n = 4$ measurements? Why?

2.50   According to the EPA, chloroform, which in its gaseous form is suspected of being a cancer-causing agent, is present in small quantities in all of the country's 240,000 public water sources. If the mean and standard deviation of the amounts of chloroform present in the water sources are 34 and 53 micrograms per liter, respectively, describe the distribution for the population of all public water sources.

2.51   In contrast to aptitude tests, which are predictive measures of what one can accomplish with training, achievement tests tell what an individual can do at the time of the test. Mathematics achievement test scores for 400 students were found to have a mean and a variance equal to 600 and 4900, respectively. If the distribution of test scores was mound-shaped, approximately how many of the scores would fall into the interval 530 to 670? Approximately how many scores would be expected to fall into the interval 460 to 740?

2.52   The gross revenue (in millions of dollars) for the top 20 movies over the 2001 Labor Day weekend (Exercise 2.41 and data set EX0241) are reproduced below[7]:

15.8	11.7	11.0	10.2	9.2	7.6	6.9	6.5	4.9	3.9
3.8	2.3	2.1	2.0	1.8	1.7	1.3	1.3	1.3	1.2

  a. Calculate the mean and standard deviation for these 20 observations.

  b. Calculate the z-score for the largest and smallest observations ($x = 15.8$ and $x = 1.2$). Should either movie, *Jeepers Creepers* or *Pearl Harbor*, be considered unusual?

c. Construct a box plot for the data, or refer to the box plot drawn in Exercise 2.41. Does the box plot confirm your results in part b? [HINT: Since the z-score and the box plots are two unrelated methods for detecting outliers, and use different types of statistics, they do not necessarily have to (but usually do) produce the same results.]

2.53 Petroleum pollution in seas and oceans stimulates the growth of some types of bacteria. A count of petroleumlytic micro-organisms (bacteria per 100 milliliters) in ten portions of seawater gave these readings:

$$49, 70, 54, 67, 59, 40, 61, 69, 71, 52$$

a. Guess the value for s using the range approximation.

b. Calculate $\bar{x}$ and s and compare with the range approximation of part a.

c. Construct a box plot for the data and use it to describe the data distribution.

2.54 Attendances at a high school's basketball games were recorded and found to have a sample mean and variance of 420 and 25, respectively. Calculate $\bar{x} \pm s$, $\bar{x} \pm 2s$, and $\bar{x} \pm 3s$ and then state the approximate fractions of measurements you would expect to fall into these intervals according to the Empirical Rule.

2.55 The College Board's verbal and mathematics scholastic aptitude tests are scored on a scale of 200 to 800. Although the tests were originally designed to produce mean scores of approximately 500, the mean verbal and math scores in recent years have been as low as 463 and 493, respectively, and have been trending downward. It seems reasonable to assume that a distribution of all test scores, either verbal or math, is mound-shaped. If σ is the standard deviation of one of these distributions, what is the largest value (approximately) that σ might assume? Explain.

2.56 A favorite summer pastime for many Americans is camping. In fact, camping has become so popular at the California beaches that reservations must sometimes be made months in advance! Data from a *USA Today* Snapshot is shown below.[9]

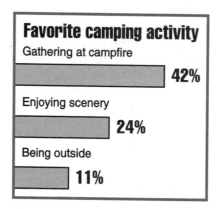

The Snapshot also reports that men go camping 2.9 times a year, women go 1.7 times a year; and men are more likely than women to want to camp more often. What does the magazine mean when they talk about 2.9 or 1.7 times a year?

2.57 The mean duration of television commercials on a given network is 75 seconds, with a standard deviation of 20 seconds. Assume that durations are approximately normally distributed.

a. What is the approximate probability that a commercial will last less than 35 seconds?

b. What is the approximate probability that a commercial will last longer than 55 seconds?

2.58 A random sample of 100 foxes was examined by a team of veterinarians to determine the prevalence of a particular type of parasite. Counting the number of parasites per fox, the veterinarians found that 69 foxes had no parasites, 17 had one parasite, and so on. A frequency tabulation of the data is given here:

Number of Parasites, x	0	1	2	3	4	5	6	7	8
Number of Foxes, f	69	17	6	3	1	2	1	0	1

a. Construct a relative frequency histogram for x, the number of parasites per fox.

b. Calculate $\bar{x}$ and s for the sample.

c. What fraction of the parasite counts fall within two standard deviations of the mean? Within three standard deviations? Do these results agree with Tchebysheff's Theorem? With the Empirical Rule?

2.59 Consider a population consisting of the number of teachers per college at small 2-year colleges. Suppose that the number of teachers per college has an average $\mu = 175$ and a standard deviation $\sigma = 15$.

a. Use Tchebysheff's Theorem to make a statement about the percentage of colleges that have between 145 and 205 teachers.

b. Assume that the population is normally distributed. What fraction of colleges have more than 190 teachers?

2.60 From the following data, a student calculated s to be .263. On what grounds might we doubt his accuracy? What is the correct value (to the nearest hundredth)?

EX0260

| 17.2 | 17.1 | 17.0 | 17.1 | 16.9 | 17.0 | 17.1 | 17.0 | 17.3 | 17.2 |
| 17.1 | 17.0 | 17.1 | 16.9 | 17.0 | 17.1 | 17.3 | 17.2 | 17.4 | 17.1 |

2.61 In the summer of 2001, Barry Bonds began his quest to break Mark McGwire's record of 70 home runs hit in a single season. At the end of the major league baseball season, the number of home runs hit by each of four major league superstars in their careers were recorded and shown in the box plots below[10]:

EX0261

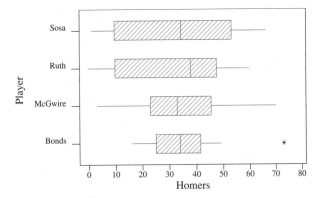

Write a short paragraph comparing the home run hitting patterns of these four players.

2.62 Here are a few facts reported as snapshots in *USA Today*.

■ Fifty-two percent of Americans believe that the ideal family size is 2 or fewer children.[11]

■ Seventy percent of Americans reheat leftovers in their microwave at least two times a week.[12]

■ Fifty percent of Americans typically wait 15 minutes or less to have a prescription filled.[13]

Identify the variable x being measured, and any percentiles you can determine from this information.

2.63 Research psychologists are interested in finding out whether a person's breathing patterns are affected by a particular experimental treatment. To determine the general respiratory patterns of the $n = 30$ people in the study, the researchers collected some baseline measurements—the total ventilation in liters of air per minute adjusted for body size—for each person before the treatment. The data are shown here, along with some descriptive tools generated by *MINITAB*.

EX0263

```
5.23   4.79   5.83   5.37   4.35   5.54   6.04   5.48   6.58   4.82
5.92   5.38   6.34   5.12   5.14   4.72   5.17   4.99   4.51   5.70
4.67   5.77   5.84   6.19   5.58   5.72   5.16   5.32   4.96   5.63
```

Descriptive Statistics: Liters

Variable	N	Mean	Median	TrMean	StDev	SE Mean
Liters	30	5.3953	5.3750	5.3877	0.5462	0.0997

Variable	Minimum	Maximum	Q1	Q3
Liters	4.3500	6.5800	4.9825	5.7850

Stem-and-Leaf Display: Liters

```
Stem-and-leaf of Liters   N  = 30
Leaf Unit = 0.10

    1     4 3
    2     4 5
    5     4 677
    8     4 899
   12     5 1111
   (4)    5 2333
   14     5 455
   11     5 6777
    7     5 889
    4     6 01
    2     6 3
    1     6 5
```

a. Summarize the characteristics of the data distribution using the *MINITAB* output.

b. Does the Empirical Rule provide a good description of the proportion of measurements that fall within two or three standard deviations of the mean? Explain.

c. How large or small does a ventilation measurement have to be before it is considered unusual?

Exercises   DO IT YOURSELF!

2.64 Refer to Data Set #1 in the **How Extreme Values Affect the Mean and Median** applet. This applet loads with a dotplot for the following $n = 5$ observations: 2, 5, 6, 9, 11.

a. What are the mean and median for this data set?

b. Use your mouse to change the value $x = 11$ (the moveable green dot) to $x = 13$. What are the mean and median for the new data set?

c. Use your mouse to move the green dot to $x = 33$. When the largest value is extremely large compared to the other observations, which is larger, the mean or the median?

d. What effect does an extremely large value have on the mean? What effect does it have on the median?

2.65 Refer to Data Set #2 in the **How Extreme Values Affect the Mean and Median** applet. This applet loads with a dotplot for the following $n = 5$ observations: 2, 5, 10, 11, 12.

a. Use your mouse to move the value $x = 12$ to the left until it is smaller than the value $x = 11$.

b. As the value of x gets smaller, what happens to the sample mean?

c. As the value of x gets smaller, at what point does the value of the median finally change?

d. As you move the green dot, what are the largest and smallest possible values for the median?

2.66 Refer to Data Set #3 in the **How Extreme Values Affect the Mean and Median** applet. This applet loads with a dotplot for the following $n = 5$ observations: 27, 28, 32, 34, 37.

a. What are the mean and median for this data set?

b. Use your mouse to change the value $x = 27$ (the moveable green dot) to $x = 25$. What are the mean and median for the new data set?

c. Use your mouse to move the green dot to $x = 5$. When the smallest value is extremely small compared to the other observations, which is larger, the mean or the median?

d. At what value of x does the mean equal the median?

e. What are the smallest and largest possible values for the median?

f. What effect does an extremely small value have on the mean? What effect does it have on the median?

2.67 Refer to the **Why Divide by $n - 1$** applet. The first applet on the page randomly selects sample of $n = 3$ from a population in which the standard deviation is $\sigma = 29.2$.

a. Click [New Sample]. A sample consisting of $n = 3$ observations will appear. Use your calculator to verify the values of the standard deviation when dividing by $n - 1$ and n as shown in the applet.

b. Click [New Sample] again. Calculate the average of the two standard deviations (dividing by $n - 1$) from parts a and b. Repeat the process for the two standard deviations (dividing by n). Compare your results to those shown in red on the applet.

c. You can look at how the two estimators in part a behave "in the long run by clicking [10 Samples] or [100 Samples] a number of times, until the average of all the standard deviations begins to stabilize. Which of the two methods gives a standard deviation closer to $\sigma = 29.2$?

d. In the long run, how far off is the standard deviation when dividing by n?

2.68 Refer to **Why Divide by $n - 1$** applet. The second applet on the page randomly selects sample of $n = 10$ from the same population in which the standard deviation is $\sigma = 29.2$.

a. Repeat the instructions in part c and d of Exercise 2.67.

b. Based on your simulation, when the sample size is larger, does it make as much difference whether you divide by n or $n - 1$ when computing the sample standard deviation?

2.69 If you have not yet done so, use the first **Building a Box Plot** applet to construct a box plot for the data in Example 2.14.

a. Compare the finished box plot to the plot shown in Figure 2.18.

b. How would you describe the shape of the data distribution?

c. Are there any outliers? If so, what is the value of the unusual observation?

2.70 Use the second **Building a Box Plot** applet to construct a box plot for the data in Example 2.13.

a. How would you describe the shape of the data distribution?

b. Use the box plot to approximate the values of the median, the lower quartile and the upper quartile. Compare your results to the actual values calculated in Example 2.13.

Case Study   The Boys of Summer

BATTING

Which baseball league has had the best hitters? Many of us have heard of baseball greats like Stan Musial, Hank Aaron, Roberto Clemente, and Pete Rose of the National League and Ty Cobb, Babe Ruth, Ted Williams, Rod Carew, and Wade Boggs of the American League. But have you ever heard of Willie Keeler, who batted .432 for the Baltimore Orioles, or Nap Lajoie, who batted .422 for the Philadelphia A's? The batting averages for the batting champions of the National and American Leagues are given on the CD-ROM. The batting averages for the National League begin in 1876 with Roscoe Barnes, whose batting average was .403 when he played with the Chicago Cubs.

The last entry for the National League is for the year 2001, when Larry Walker of the Colorado Rockies averaged .350. The American League records begin in 1901 with Nap Lajoie of the Philadelphia A's, who batted .422, and end in 2001 with Ichiro Suzuki of the Seattle Mariners, who batted .350.[6] How can we summarize the information in this data set?

1. Use *MINITAB* or another statistical software package to describe the batting averages for the American and National League batting champions. Generate any graphics that may help you in interpreting these data sets.
2. Does one league appear to have a higher percentage of hits than the other? Do the batting averages of one league appear to be more variable than the other?
3. Are there any outliers in either league?
4. Summarize your comparison of the two baseball leagues.

Data Sources

1. "2000 Automobile Insurance," California Department of Insurance, http://www.insurance.ca.gov/docs/FS-Surveys.htm.
2. "Fortune 500: America's Largest Corporation," 14 April 2001, http://www.fortune.com/indexw.jhtml?channel=list.jhtml&list_frag=list_3column_fortune500_list.jhtml&list=15&_requestid=124360.
3. "Birth Order and the Baby Boom," *American Demographics* (Trend Cop), March 1997, p. 10.
4. "Tuna Goes Upscale," *Consumer Reports*, June 2001, p. 19.
5. *American Demographics*, May 1997, p. 32.
6. William A. McGeveran, Jr., ed., *The World Almanac and Book of Facts 2002*. (Mahwah, NJ: St. Martin's Press).
7. "Cheap Hit," *Entertainment Weekly*, #614, 14 September 2001, p. 69.
8. "Four People Movers," *Consumer Reports*, July 1997, p. 57.
9. "Favorite Camping Activity," http://www.usatoday.com/snapshot/news/2001-05-22-camping.htm, 26 September 2001 (*Source:* Wirthlin Worldwide for Coleman Company).
10. www.mlb.com 8 October 2001.
11. "Ideal Family Size," http://www/usatoday.com/snapshot/news/2001-07-06-familysize.htm, 26 September 2001 (*Source:* Gallup).
12. "Microwaving Leftovers," http://www.usatoday.com/snapshot/life/2001-09-06-microwaving-leftovers.htm, 26 September 2001 (*Source:* Opinion Research for Tupperware).
13. "Waiting for a Prescription," http://www.usatoday.com/snapshot/life/2001-06-10-drug wait.htm, 26 September 2001 (*Source:* Opinion Research for AmeriSource Health).

3

Describing Bivariate Data

Case Study

Does the price of an appliance, such as a dishwasher, convey something about its quality? In the case study at the end of this chapter, we rank 20 different brands of dishwashers according to their prices, and then we rate them on various character- istics, such as how the dishwasher performs, how much noise it makes, its cost for either gas or electricity, its cycle time, and its water use. The techniques presented in this chapter will help to answer our question.

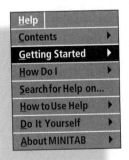

General Objectives

Sometimes the data that are collected consist of observations for two variables on the same experimental unit. Special techniques that can be used in describing these variables will help you identify possible relationships between them.

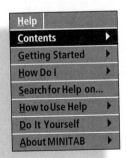

Specific Topics

1. Bivariate data (3.1)
2. Side-by-side pie charts, comparative line charts (3.2)
3. Side-by-side bar charts, stacked bar charts (3.2)
4. Scatterplots for two quantitative variables (3.3)
5. Covariance and the correlation coefficient (3.4)
6. The best-fitting line (3.4)

3.1 Bivariate Data

Very often researchers are interested in more than just one variable that can be measured during their investigation. For example, an auto insurance company might be interested in the number of vehicles owned by a policyholder as well as the number of drivers in the household. An economist might need to measure the amount spent per week on groceries in a household and also the number of people in that household. A real estate agent might measure the selling price of a residential property and the square footage of the living area.

When two variables are measured on a single experimental unit, the resulting data are called **bivariate data.** How should you display these data? Not only are both variables important when studied separately, but you also may want to explore the *relationship between the two variables*. Methods for graphing bivariate data, whether the variables are qualitative or quantitative, allow you to study the two variables together. As with *univariate data*, you use different graphs depending on the type of variables you are measuring.

3.2 Graphs for Qualitative Variables

When at least one of the two variables is *qualitative*, you can use either simple or more intricate pie charts, line charts, and bar charts to display and describe the data. Sometimes you will have one qualitative and one quantitative variable that have been measured in two different populations or groups. In this case, you can use two **side-by-side pie charts** or a bar chart in which the bars for the two populations are placed side by side. Another option is to use a **stacked bar chart,** in which the bars for each category are stacked on top of each other.

EXAMPLE 3.1

Are professors in private colleges paid more than professors at public colleges? The data in Table 3.1 were collected from a sample of 400 college professors whose rank, type of college, and salary were recorded. The number in each cell is the average salary (in thousands of dollars) for all professors who fell into that category. Use a graph to answer the question posed for this sample.

TABLE 3.1
Salaries of professors by rank and type of college

	Full Professor	Associate Professor	Assistant Professor
Public	55.8	42.2	35.2
Private	61.6	43.3	35.5

Solution To display the average salaries of these 400 professors, you can use a side-by-side bar chart, as shown in Figure 3.1. The height of the bars is the average salary, with each pair of bars along the horizontal axis representing a different professorial rank. Salaries are substantially higher for full professors in private colleges, but there is very little difference at the lower two ranks.

FIGURE 3.1
Comparative bar charts for Example 3.1

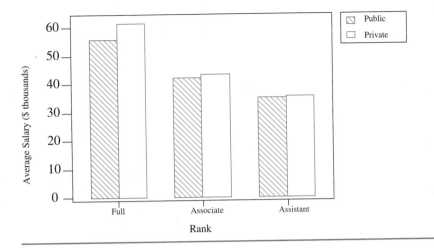

EXAMPLE 3.2   Along with the salaries for the 400 college professors in Example 3.1, the researcher recorded two qualitative variables for each professor: rank and type of college. Table 3.2 shows the number of professors in each of the $2 \times 3 = 6$ categories. Use comparative charts to describe the data. Do the private colleges employ as many high-ranking professors as the public colleges do?

TABLE 3.2
Number of professors by rank and type of college

	Full Professor	Associate Professor	Assistant Professor	Total
Public	24	57	69	150
Private	60	78	112	250

Solution   The numbers in the table are not quantitative measurements on a single experimental unit (the professor). They are *frequencies,* or counts of the number of professors who fall into each category. To compare the numbers of professors at public and private colleges, you might draw two pie charts and display them side by side, as in Figure 3.2.

FIGURE 3.2
Comparative pie charts for Example 3.2

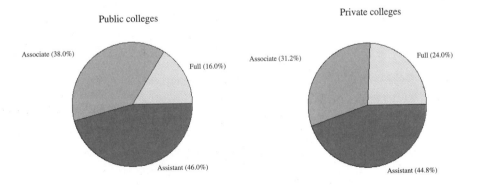

Alternatively, you could draw either a stacked or a side-by-side bar chart. The stacked bar chart is shown in Figure 3.3.

Although the graphs are not strikingly different, you can see that public colleges have fewer full professors and more associate professors than private colleges. The reason for these differences is not clear, but you might speculate that private colleges, with

FIGURE 3.3
Stacked bar chart
for Example 3.2

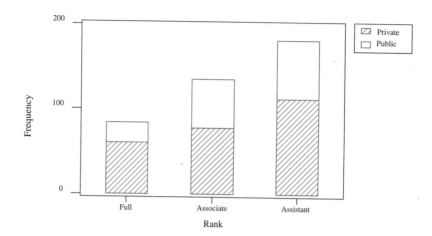

their higher salaries, are able to attract more full professors. Or perhaps public colleges are not as willing to promote professors to the higher-paying ranks. In any case, the graphs provide a means for comparing the two sets of data.

You can also compare the distributions for public versus private colleges by creating *conditional data distributions*. These conditional distributions are shown in Table 3.3. One distribution shows the proportion of professors in each of the three ranks under the *condition* that the college is public, and the other shows the proportions under the *condition* that the college is private. These *relative frequencies* are easier to compare than the *actual frequencies* and lead to the same conclusions:

- That the proportion of assistant professors is roughly the same for both public and private colleges
- That public colleges have a smaller proportion of full professors and a larger proportion of associate professors.

TABLE 3.3
Proportions of
professors by rank
for public and
private colleges

	Full Professor	Associate Professor	Assistant Professor	Total
Public	$\dfrac{24}{150} = .16$	$\dfrac{57}{150} = .38$	$\dfrac{69}{150} = .46$	1.00
Private	$\dfrac{60}{250} = .24$	$\dfrac{78}{250} = .31$	$\dfrac{112}{250} = .45$	1.00

Exercises

Basic Techniques

3.1   Male and female respondents to a questionnaire about gender differences are categorized into three groups according to their answers on the first question:

	Group 1	Group 2	Group 3
Men	37	49	72
Women	7	50	31

a. Create side-by-side pie charts to describe these data.

b. Create a side-by-side bar chart to describe these data.

c. Draw a stacked bar chart to describe these data.

d. Which of the three charts best depicts the difference or similarity of the responses of men and women?

3.2 A group of items are categorized according to a certain attribute—X, Y, Z—and according to the state in which they are produced:

	X	Y	Z
New York	20	5	5
California	10	10	5

a. Create a comparative (side-by-side) bar chart to compare the numbers of items of each type made in California and New York.

b. Create a stacked bar chart to compare the numbers of items of each type made in the two states.

c. Which of the two types of presentation in parts a and b is more easily understood? Explain.

d. What other graphical methods could you use to describe the data?

3.3 The table below shows the average amounts spent per week by men and women in each of four spending categories:

	A	B	C	D
Men	$54	$27	$105	$22
Women	21	85	100	75

a. What possible graphical methods could you use to compare the spending patterns of women and men?

b. Choose two different methods of graphing and display the data in graphical form.

c. What can you say about the similarities or differences in the spending patterns for men and women?

d. Which of the two methods used in part b provides a better descriptive graph?

Applications

3.4 The color distributions for two snack-size bags of M&M® candies, one plain and one peanut, are displayed in the table. Choose an appropriate graphical method and compare the distributions.

	Brown	Yellow	Red	Orange	Green	Blue
Plain	15	14	12	4	5	6
Peanut	6	2	2	3	3	5

3.5 When you were growing up, did you feel that you did not have enough free time? Parents and children have differing opinions on this subject. A research group surveyed 198 parents and 200 children and recorded their responses to the question, "How much free time does your child have?" or "How much free time do you have?" The responses are shown in the table below[1]:

	Just the right amount	Not enough	Too much	Don't know
Parents	138	14	40	6
Children	130	48	16	6

a. Define the sample and the population of interest to the researchers.

b. Describe the variables that have been measured in this survey. Are the variables qualitative or quantitative? Are the data univariate or bivariate?

c. What do the entries in the cells represent?

d. Use comparative pie charts to compare the responses for men and women.

e. What other graphical techniques could be used to describe the data? Would any of these techniques be more informative than the pie charts constructed in part d?

3.6 The price of transportation in the United States has increased dramatically in the past decade, as demonstrated by the consumer price indexes (CPIs) for both private and public transportation. These CPIs are listed in the table for the years 1985, 1990, 1995, and 2000[2]:

	Public	Private
1985	110.5	106.2
1990	142.6	118.8
1995	175.9	136.3
2000	209.6	149.1

a. Create side-by-side comparative bar charts to describe the CPIs over time.

b. Draw two line charts on the same set of axes to describe the CPIs over time.

c. What conclusions can you draw using the two graphs in parts a and b? Which is the most effective?

3.3 Scatterplots for Two Quantitative Variables

When both variables to be displayed on a graph are *quantitative,* one variable is plotted along the horizontal axis and the second along the vertical axis. The first variable is often called x and the second is called y, so that the graph takes the form of a plot on the (x, y) axes, which is familiar to most of you. Each pair of data values is plotted as a point on this two-dimensional graph, called a **scatterplot.** It is the two-dimensional extension of the dotplot we used to graph one quantitative variable in Section 1.4.

You can describe the relationship between two variables, x and y, using the patterns shown in the scatterplot.

- **What type of pattern do you see?** Is there a constant upward or downward trend that follows a straight-line pattern? Is there a curved pattern? Is there no pattern at all, but just a random scattering of points?
- **How strong is the pattern?** Do all of the points follow the pattern exactly, or is the relationship only weakly visible?
- **Are there any unusual observations?** An outlier is a point that is far from the cluster of the remaining points. Do the points cluster into groups? If so, is there an explanation for the observed groupings?

EXAMPLE 3.3 The number of household members, x, and the amount spent on groceries per week, y, are measured for six households in a local area. Draw a scatterplot of these six data points.

x	2	2	3	4	1	5
y	$45.75	$60.19	$68.33	$100.92	$35.86	$130.62

Solution Label the horizontal axis x and the vertical axis y. Plot the points using the coordinates (x, y) for each of the six pairs. The scatterplot in Figure 3.4 shows the six pairs marked as dots. You can see a pattern even with only six data pairs. The cost of weekly groceries increases with the number of household members in an apparent straight-line relationship.

Suppose you found that a seventh household with two members spent $115 on groceries. This observation is shown as an X in Figure 3.4. It does not fit the linear pattern of the other six observations and is classified as an outlier. Possibly these two people were having a party the week of the survey!

FIGURE 3.4
Scatterplot for
Example 3.3

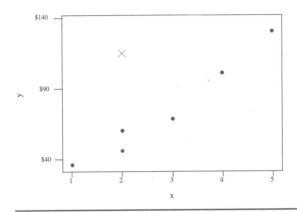

EXAMPLE 3.4

A distributor of table wines conducted a study of the relationship between price and demand using a type of wine that ordinarily sells for $10.00 per bottle. He sold this wine in 10 different marketing areas over a 12-month period, using five different price levels—from $10 to $14. The data are given in Table 3.4. Construct a scatterplot for the data, and use the graph to describe the relationship between price and demand.

TABLE 3.4
Cases of wine sold
at five price levels

Cases Sold per 10,000 Population	Price per Bottle
23, 21	$10
19, 18	11
15, 17	12
19, 20	13
25, 24	14

Solution   The 10 data points are plotted in Figure 3.5. As the price increases from $10 to $12 the demand decreases. However, as the price continues to increase, from $12 to $14, the demand begins to *increase*. The data show a curved pattern, with the relationship changing as the price changes. How do you explain this relationship? Possibly, the increased price is a signal of increased quality for the consumer, which causes the increase in demand once the cost exceeds $12. You might be able to think of other reasons, or perhaps some other variable, such as the income of people in the marketing areas, that may be causing the change.

FIGURE 3.5
Scatterplot for
Example 3.4

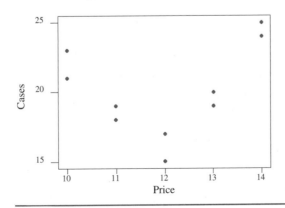

Help

Contents ▶

Getting Started ▶

How Do I ▶

Search for Help on...

How to Use Help ▶

Do It Yourself ▶

About MINITAB ▶

DO IT YOURSELF!

Now would be a good time for you to try creating a scatterplot on your own. Use the applets in **Building a Scatterplot** to create the scatterplots that you see in Figure 3.5 and 3.7. You will find step-by-step instructions on the left-hand side of the applet, and you will be corrected if you make a mistake!

FIGURE 3.6
Building a Scatterplot applet

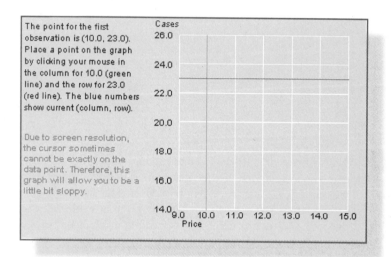

The point for the first observation is (10.0, 23.0). Place a point on the graph by clicking your mouse in the column for 10.0 (green line) and the row for 23.0 (red line). The blue numbers show current (column, row).

Due to screen resolution, the cursor sometimes cannot be exactly on the data point. Therefore, this graph will allow you to be a little bit sloppy.

3.4 Numerical Measures for Quantitative Bivariate Data

A constant rate of increase or decrease is perhaps the most common pattern found in bivariate scatterplots. The scatterplot in Figure 3.4 exhibits this *linear* pattern—that is, a straight line with the data points lying both above and below the line and within a fixed distance from the line. When this is the case, we say that the two variables exhibit a *linear relationship*.

EXAMPLE 3.5

The data in Table 3.5 are the size of the living area (in square feet), x, and the selling price, y, of 12 residential properties. The *MINITAB* scatterplot in Figure 3.7 shows a linear pattern in the data.

TABLE 3.5
Living area and selling price of 12 properties

Residence	x (sq. ft.)	y (in thousands)
1	1360	$178.5
2	1940	275.7
3	1750	239.5
4	1550	229.8
5	1790	195.6
6	1750	210.3
7	2230	360.5
8	1600	205.2
9	1450	188.6
10	1870	265.7
11	2210	325.3
12	1480	168.8

FIGURE 3.7
Scatterplot of *x* versus *y* for Example 3.5

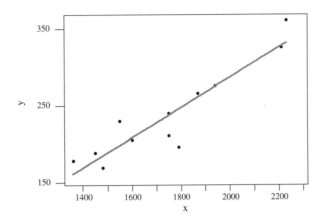

For the data in Example 3.5, you could describe each variable, *x* and *y*, individually using descriptive measures such as the means ($\bar{x}$ and $\bar{y}$) or the standard deviations (s_x and s_y). However, these measures do not describe the relationship between *x* and *y* for a particular residence—that is, how the size of the living space affects the selling price of the home. A simple measure that serves this purpose is called the **correlation coefficient,** denoted by *r*, and is defined as

$$r = \frac{s_{xy}}{s_x s_y}$$

The quantities s_x and s_y are the standard deviations for the variables *x* and *y*, respectively, which can be found by using the statistics function on your calculator or the computing formula in Section 2.3. The new quantity s_{xy} is called the **covariance** between *x* and *y* and is defined as

$$s_{xy} = \frac{\Sigma(x_i - \bar{x})(y_i - \bar{y})}{n - 1}$$

There is also a computing formula for the covariance:

$$s_{xy} = \frac{\Sigma x_i y_i - \dfrac{(\Sigma x_i)(\Sigma y_i)}{n}}{n - 1}$$

where $\Sigma x_i y_i$ is the sum of the products $x_i y_i$ for each of the *n* pairs of measurements. How does this quantity detect and measure a linear pattern in the data?

Look at the signs of the cross-products $(x_i - \bar{x})(y_i - \bar{y})$ in the numerator of *r*, or s_{xy}. When a data point (*x*, *y*) is in either area I or III in the scatterplot shown in Figure 3.8,

FIGURE 3.8
The signs of the cross-products $(x_i - \bar{x})(y_i - \bar{y})$ in the covariance formula

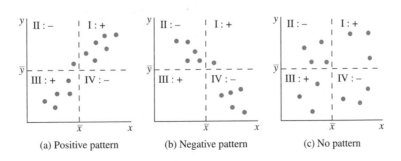

the cross-product will be positive; when a data point is in area II or IV, the cross-product will be negative. We can draw these conclusions:

- If most of the points are in areas I and III (forming a positive pattern), s_{xy} and r will be positive.
- If most of the points are in areas II and IV (forming a negative pattern), s_{xy} and r will be negative.
- If the points are scattered across all four areas (forming *no* pattern), s_{xy} and r will be close to 0.

DO IT YOURSELF!

The applet called **Exploring Correlation** will help you to visualize how the pattern of points affects the correlation coefficient. Use your mouse to move the slider at the bottom of the scatterplot (Figure 3.9). You will see the value of r change as the pattern of the points changes. Notice that a positive pattern (a) results in a positive value of r; no pattern (c) gives a value of r close to zero; and a negative pattern (b) results in a negative value of r. What pattern do you see when $r = 1$? When $r = -1$? You will use this applet again for the *Do It Yourself Exercises* section at the end of the chapter.

FIGURE 3.9
**Exploring
Correlation** applet

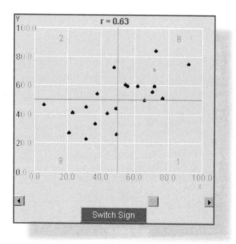

Most scientific and graphics calculators can compute the correlation coefficient, r, when the data are entered in the proper way. Check your calculator manual for the proper sequence of entry commands. Computer programs such as *MINITAB* are also programmed to perform these calculations. The *MINITAB* output in Figure 3.10 shows the covariance and correlation coefficient for x and y in Example 3.5. In the covariance table, you will find these values:

$$s_{xy} = 15{,}545.20 \qquad s_x^2 = 79{,}233.33 \qquad s_y^2 = 3571.16$$

and in the correlation output, you find $r = .924$.

However you decide to calculate the correlation coefficient, it can be shown that the value of r always lies between -1 and 1. When r is positive, x increases when y increases, and vice versa. When r is negative, x decreases when y increases, or

FIGURE 3.10
MINITAB output of covariance and correlation for Example 3.5

Covariances: x, y

```
            x          y
x   79233.33
y   15545.20   3571.16
```

Correlations: x, y

```
Pearson correlation of x and y = 0.924
P-Value = 0.000
```

x increases when y decreases. When r takes the value 1 or -1, all the points lie exactly on a straight line. If $r = 0$, then there is no apparent linear relationship between the two variables. The closer the value of r is to 1 or -1, the stronger the linear relationship between the two variables.

EXAMPLE 3.6

Find the correlation coefficient for the number of square feet of living area and the selling price of a home for the data in Example 3.5.

Solution

Three quantities are needed to calculate the correlation coefficient. The standard deviations of the x and y variables are found using a calculator with a statistical function. You can verify that $s_x = 281.4842$ and $s_y = 59.7592$. Finally,

$$s_{xy} = \frac{\Sigma x_i y_i - \dfrac{(\Sigma x_i)(\Sigma y_i)}{n}}{n - 1}$$

$$= \frac{5{,}142{,}383 - \dfrac{(20{,}980)(2843.5)}{12}}{11} = 15{,}545.19697$$

This agrees with the value given in the *MINITAB* printout in Figure 3.10. Then

$$r = \frac{s_{xy}}{s_x s_y} = \frac{15{,}545.19697}{(281.4842)(59.7592)} = .9241$$

which also agrees with the value of the correlation coefficient given in Figure 3.10. (You may wish to verify the value of r using your calculator.) This value of r is fairly close to 1, which indicates that the linear relationship between these two variables is very strong. Additional information about the correlation coefficient and its role in analyzing linear relationships, along with alternative calculation formulas, can be found in Chapter 12.

Sometimes the two variables, x and y, are related in a particular way. It may be that the value of y depends on the value of x; that is, the value of x in some way explains the value of y. For example, the cost of a home (y) may *depend* on its amount of floor space (x); a student's grade point average (x) may *explain* her score on an achievement test (y). In these situations, we call y the **dependent variable,** while x is called the **independent variable.**

If one of the two variables can be classified as the dependent variable y and the other as x, and if the data exhibit a straight-line pattern, it is possible to describe the relationship relating y to x using a straight line given by the equation

$$y = a + bx$$

as shown in Figure 3.11.

FIGURE 3.11
The graph of a
straight line

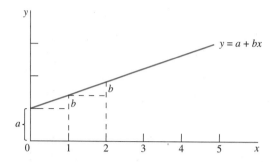

As you can see, *a* is where the line crosses or intersects the *y*-axis: *a* is called the *y-intercept*. You can also see that for every one-unit increase in *x, y* increases by an amount *b*. The quantity *b* determines whether the line is increasing ($b > 0$), decreasing ($b < 0$), or horizontal ($b = 0$) and is appropriately called the **slope** of the line.

DO IT YOURSELF!

You can see the effect of changing the slope and the *y*-intercept of a line using the applet called **How a Line Works**. Use your mouse to move the slider on the right side of the scatterplot. As you move the slider, the slope of the line, shown as the vertical side of the green triangle (light gray in Figure 3.12), will change. Moving the slider on the left side of the applet causes the *y*-intercept, shown in red (light blue in Figure 3.12), to change. What is the slope and *y*-intercept for the line shown in the applet in Figure 3.12? You will use this applet again for the *Do It Yourself Exercises* section at the end of the chapter.

FIGURE 3.12
**How a Line
Works** applet

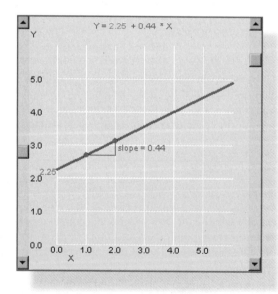

Our points (*x, y*) do not all fall on a straight line, but they do show a trend that could be described as a linear pattern. We can describe this trend by fitting a line as best we can through the points. This best-fitting line relating *y* to *x*, often called the

regression or **least-squares line,** is found by minimizing the sum of the squared differences between the data points and the line itself, as shown in Figure 3.13. The formulas for computing b and a, which are derived mathematically, are

$$b = r\left(\frac{s_y}{s_x}\right) \quad \text{and} \quad a = \bar{y} - b\bar{x}$$

FIGURE 3.13
The best-fitting line

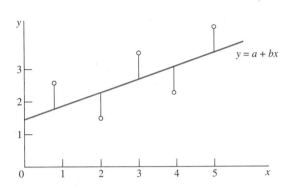

Since s_x and s_y are both positive, b and r have the same sign, so that:

- When r is positive, so is b, and the line is increasing with x.
- When r is negative, so is b, and the line is decreasing with x.
- When r is close to 0, then b is close to 0.

EXAMPLE 3.7

Find the best-fitting line relating y to x for the following data. Plot the line and the data points on the same graph.

x	2	3	4	5	6	7
y	3.0	5.0	5.5	6.0	8.0	9.5

Solution

Use the data entry method for your calculator to find these descriptive statistics for the bivariate data set:

$$\bar{x} = 4.5 \qquad \bar{y} = 6.167 \qquad s_x = 1.871 \qquad s_y = 2.295 \qquad r = .978$$

Then

$$b = r\left(\frac{s_y}{s_x}\right) = .978\left(\frac{2.295}{1.871}\right) = 1.1996311 \cong 1.200$$

and

$$a = \bar{y} - b\bar{x} = 6.167 - 1.200(4.5) = 6.167 - 5.4 = .767$$

Therefore, the best-fitting line is $y = .767 + 1.200x$. The plot of the regression line and the actual data points are shown in Figure 3.14.

The best-fitting line can be used to estimate or predict the value of the variable y when the value of x is known. For example, if the value $x = 3$ was observed at some time in the future, what would you predict for the value of y? From the best-fitting line in Figure 3.14, the best estimate would be

$$y = a + bx = .767 + 1.200(3) = 4.367$$

FIGURE 3.14
Fitted line and data points for Example 3.7

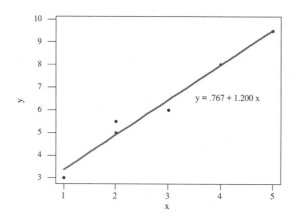

When should you describe the linear relationship between x and y using the correlation coefficient r, and when should you use the regression line $y = a + bx$? The regression approach is used when the values of x are set in advance and then the corresponding value of y is measured. The correlation approach is used when an experimental unit is selected at random and then measurements are made on both variables x and y. This technical point will be taken up in Chapter 12 on regression analysis.

Most data analysts begin any data-based investigation by examining plots of the variables involved. If the relationship between two variables is of interest, bivariate plots are also explored in conjunction with numerical measures of location, dispersion, and correlation. Graphs and numerical descriptive measures are only the first of many statistical tools you will soon have at your disposal.

Exercises

Basic Techniques

3.7 A set of bivariate data consists of these measurements on two variables, x and y:

EX0307

$$(3, 6) \quad (5, 8) \quad (2, 6) \quad (1, 4) \quad (4, 7) \quad (4, 6)$$

a. Draw a scatterplot to describe the data.

b. Does there appear to be a relationship between x and y? If so, how do you describe it?

c. Calculate the correlation coefficient, r, using the computing formula given in this section.

d. Find the best-fitting line using the computing formulas. Graph the line on the scatterplot from part a. Does the line pass through the middle of the points?

3.8 Refer to Exercise 3.7.

a. Use the data entry method in your scientific calculator to enter the six pairs of measurements. Recall the proper memories to find the correlation coefficient, r, the y-intercept, a, and the slope, b, of the line.

b. Verify that the calculator provides the same values for r, a, and b as in Exercise 3.7.

3.9 Consider this set of bivariate data:

EX0309

x	1	2	3	4	5	6
y	5.6	4.6	4.5	3.7	3.2	2.7

a. Draw a scatterplot to describe the data.

b. Does there appear to be a relationship between x and y? If so, how do you describe it?

c. Calculate the correlation coefficient, r. Does the value of r confirm your conclusions in part b? Explain.

3.10 The value of a quantitative variable is measured once a year for a 10-year period:

EX0310

Year	Measurement	Year	Measurement
1	61.5	6	58.2
2	62.3	7	57.5
3	60.7	8	57.5
4	59.8	9	56.1
5	58.0	10	56.0

a. Draw a scatterplot to describe the variable as it changes over time.

b. Describe the measurements using the graph constructed in part a.

c. Use this *MINITAB* output to calculate the correlation coefficient, r:

MINITAB output
for Exercise 3.10

Covariances

```
              x         y
x        9.16667
y       -6.42222    4.84933
```

d. Find the best-fitting line using the results of part c. Verify your answer using the data entry method in your calculator.

e. Plot the best-fitting line on your scatterplot from part a. Describe the fit of the line.

Applications

3.11 These data relating the amount spent on groceries per week and the number of household members are from Example 3.3:

EX0311

x	2	2	3	4	1	5
y	$45.75	$60.19	$68.33	$100.92	$35.86	$130.62

a. Find the best-fitting line for these data.

b. Plot the points and the best-fitting line on the same graph. Does the line summarize the information in the data points?

c. What would you estimate a household of six to spend on groceries per week? Should you use the fitted line to estimate this amount? Why or why not?

3.12 The data relating the square feet of living space and the selling price of 12 residential properties given in Example 3.5 are reproduced here. First find the best-fitting line that describes these data, and then plot the line and the data points on the same graph. Comment on the goodness of the fitted line in describing the selling price of a residential property as a linear function of the square feet of living area.

EX0312

x (sq. ft.)	y (in thousands)
1360	$178.5
1940	275.7
1750	239.5
1550	229.8
1790	195.6
1750	210.3
2230	360.5
1600	205.2
1450	188.6
1870	265.7
2210	325.3
1480	168.8

EX0313

3.13 A social skills training program was implemented for seven students with mild handicaps in a study to determine whether the program caused improvement in pre/post measures and behavior ratings.[3] For one such test, these are the pretest and posttest scores for the seven students:

Student	Pretest	Posttest
Earl	101	113
Ned	89	89
Jasper	112	121
Charlie	105	99
Tom	90	104
Susie	91	94
Lori	89	99

a. Draw a scatterplot relating the posttest score to the pretest score.

b. Describe the relationship between pretest and posttest scores using the graph in part a. Do you see any trend?

c. Calculate the correlation coefficient and interpret its value. Does it reinforce any relationship that was apparent from the scatterplot? Explain.

EX0314

3.14 Investors are becoming more and more concerned about securities fraud, especially involving initial public offerings (IPOs).[4] During a 6-year period, the number of federal securities-fraud class action suits has continued to increase:

Year	1996	1997	1998	1999	2000	2001
Suits	110	178	236	205	211	282

a. Plot the data using a scatterplot. How would you describe the relationship between year and number of class action suits?

b. Find the least squares regression line relating the number of class action suits to the year being measured.

c. If you were to predict the number of class action suits in the year 2002, what problems might arise with your predictions?

Key Concepts

I. Bivariate Data

    1. Both qualitative and quantitative variables

    2. Describing each variable separately

    3. Describing the relationship between the two variables

II. Describing Two Qualitative Variables

    1. Side-by-side pie charts

    2. Comparative line charts

    3. Comparative bar charts

        a. Side-by-side

        b. Stacked

    4. Relative frequencies to describe the relationship between the two variables

III. Describing Two Quantitative Variables

    1. Scatterplots

        a. Linear or nonlinear pattern

        b. Strength of relationship

        c. Unusual observations: clusters and outliers

2. Covariance and correlation coefficient
3. The best-fitting regression line
    a. Calculating the slope and *y*-intercept
    b. Graphing the line
    c. Using the line for prediction

Help	
_Contents	▶
_Getting Started	▶
How Do I	▶
Search for Help on...	
How to Use Help	▶
Do It Yourself	▶
About MINITAB	▶

Describing Bivariate Data

MINITAB provides different graphical techniques for *qualitative* and *quantitative* bivariate data, as well as commands for obtaining bivariate descriptive measures when the data are quantitative. To explore both types of bivariate procedures, you need to enter two different sets of bivariate data into a *MINITAB* worksheet. Once you are on the Windows desktop, double-click on the *MINITAB* icon or use the Start button to start *MINITAB*.

Start a new project using **File → New → *MINITAB* Project.** Then open the existing project called "Chapter 1." We will use the college student data, which should be in Worksheet 1. Suppose that the 105 students already tabulated were from the University of California, Riverside, and that another 100 students from an introductory statistics class at UC Berkeley were also interviewed. Table 3.6 shows the status distribution for both sets of students. Create another variable in C3 of the worksheet called "College" and enter UCR for the first five rows. Now enter the UCB data in columns C1–C3. You can use the familiar Windows cut-and-paste icons if you like.

TABLE 3.6

	Freshman	Sophomore	Junior	Senior	Grad Student
Frequency (UCR)	5	23	32	35	10
Frequency (UCB)	10	35	24	25	6

The other worksheet in "Chapter 1" is not needed and can be deleted by clicking on the X in the top right corner of the worksheet. We *will* use the worksheet called "Minivans" from Chapter 2, which you should open using **File → Open Worksheet** and selecting "Minivans.mtw." Now **save** this new **project** as "Chapter 3."

To graphically describe the UCR/UCB student data, you can use comparative pie charts—one for each school (see Chapter 1). Alternatively, you can use either stacked or side-by-side bar charts. Use **Graph → Chart,** selecting "Frequency" for **Y** and "Status" for **X,** and displaying a bar for each **Group,** with the groups selected as "College" (see Figure 3.15). Click on **Options** and choose either **Stack** or **Cluster** within "College." Finally, use the Edit Attributes box to choose colors and patterns for the bars. The resulting bar chart, shown in Figure 3.16, was edited so that the vertical axis reads "Frequency" and the categories stay in the order presented in C1.

Turn to Worksheet 2, in which the bivariate minivan data from Chapter 2 are located. To examine the relationship between the second and third car seat lengths, you can plot the data and numerically describe the relationship with the correlation coefficient and the best-fitting line. Use **Stat → Regression → Fitted Line Plot,** and select

MINITAB

MINITAB

FIGURE 3.15

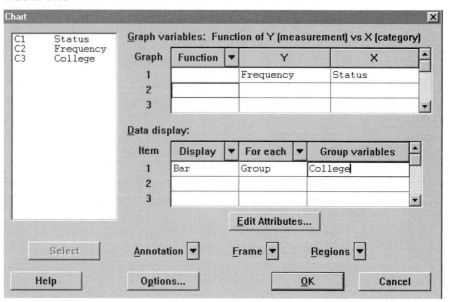

FIGURE 3.16

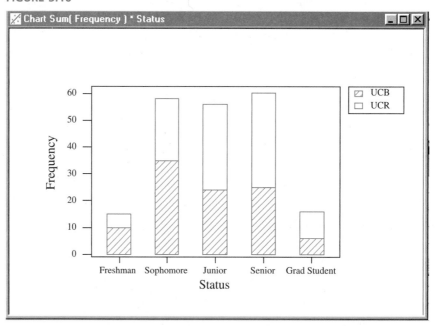

"2nd Seat" and "3rd Seat" for **Y** and **X,** respectively (see Figure 3.17). Make sure that the dot next to **Linear** is selected, and click **OK.** The plot of the nine data points and the best-fitting line will be generated as in Figure 3.18.

To calculate the correlation coefficient, use **Stat → Basic Statistics → Correlation,** selecting "2nd Seat" and "3rd Seat" for the Variables box. To select both variables at once, hold the **Shift** key down as you highlight the variables and then click **Select.** Click **OK,** and the correlation coefficient will appear in the Session window (see Figure 3.19). Notice the relatively strong positive correlation and the positive slope

MINITAB

of the regression line, indicating that a minivan with a long floor length behind the second seat will also tend to have a long floor length behind the third seat.

Save "Chapter 3" before you exit *MINITAB*!

FIGURE 3.17

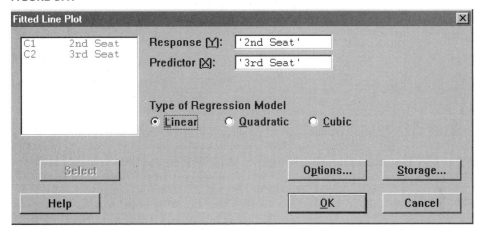

FIGURE 3.18

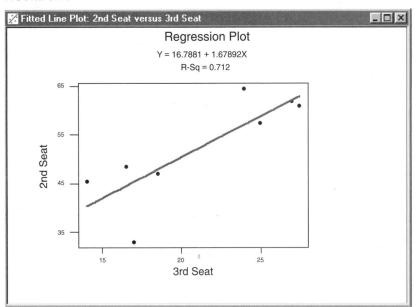

FIGURE 3.19

Supplementary Exercises

3.15 Professor Isaac Asimov was one of the most prolific writers of all time. He wrote nearly 500 books during a 40-year career prior to his death in 1992. In fact, as his career progressed, he became even more productive in terms of the number of books written within a given period of time.[5] These data are the times (in months) required to write his books, in increments of 100:

Number of Books	100	200	300	400	490
Time (in months)	237	350	419	465	507

a. Plot the accumulated number of books as a function of time using a scatterplot.

b. Describe the productivity of Professor Asimov in light of the data set graphed in part a. Does the relationship between the two variables seem to be linear?

3.16 Health-conscious Americans often consult the nutritional information on food packages in an attempt to avoid foods with large amounts of fat, sodium, or cholesterol. The following information was taken from eight different brands of American cheese slices:

Brand	Fat (g)	Saturated Fat (g)	Cholesterol (mg)	Sodium (mg)	Calories
Kraft Deluxe American	7	4.5	20	340	80
Kraft Velveeta Slices	5	3.5	15	300	70
Private Selection	8	5.0	25	520	100
Ralphs Singles	4	2.5	15	340	60
Kraft 2% Milk Singles	3	2.0	10	320	50
Kraft Singles American	5	3.5	15	290	70
Borden Singles	5	3.0	15	260	60
Lake to Lake American	5	3.5	15	330	70

a. Which pairs of variables do you expect to be strongly related?

b. Draw a scatterplot for fat and saturated fat. Describe the relationship.

c. Draw a scatterplot for fat and calories. Compare the pattern to that found in part b.

d. Draw a scatterplot for fat versus sodium and another for cholesterol versus sodium. Compare the patterns. Are there any clusters or outliers?

e. For the pairs of variables that appear to be linearly related, calculate the correlation coefficients.

f. Write a paragraph to summarize the relationships you can see in these data. Use the correlations and the patterns in the four scatterplots to verify your conclusions.

3.17 Is it harder for single parents to make ends meet than it is for two working parents? The monthly expenses for families with two children in Riverside, San Bernardino, Orange, and Ventura, California, are displayed in the side-by-side bar chart.[6]

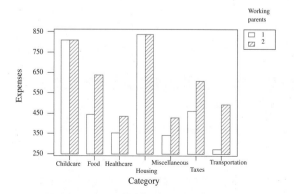

a. What variables have been measured in this study? Are the variables qualitative or quantitative?

b. Describe the population of interest. Do these data represent a population or a sample drawn from the population?

c. What type of graphical presentation has been used? What other type could have been used?

d. If you wanted to make the increase in the expenses for families with two working parents look as dramatic as possible, what changes would you make in the graphical presentation?

3.18   The demand for healthy foods that are low in fats and calories has resulted in a large number of "low-fat" and "fat-free" products at the supermarket. The table shows the numbers of calories and the amounts of sodium (in milligrams) per slice for five different brands of fat-free American cheese.

Brand	Sodium (mg)	Calories
Kraft Fat Free Singles	300	30
Ralphs Fat Free Singles	300	30
Borden Fat Free	320	30
Healthy Choice Fat Free	290	30
Smart Beat American	180	25

a. Draw a scatterplot to describe the relationship between the amount of sodium and the number of calories.

b. Describe the plot in part a. Do you see any outliers? Do the rest of the points seem to form a pattern?

c. Based *only* on the relationship between sodium and calories, can you make a clear decision about which of the five brands to buy? Is it reasonable to base your choice on only these two variables? What other variables should you consider?

3.19   Using a chemical procedure called *differential pulse polarography,* a chemist measured the peak current generated (in microamperes) when a solution containing a given amount of nickel (in parts per billion) is added to a buffer. The data are shown here:

EX0319

x = Ni (ppb)	y = Peak Current (μA)
19.1	.095
38.2	.174
57.3	.256
76.2	.348
95	.429
114	.500
131	.580
150	.651
170	.722

Use a graph to describe the relationship between x and y. Add any numerical descriptive measures that are appropriate. Write a paragraph summarizing your results.

3.20   Does the opening weekend adequately predict the success or failure of a new movie? In the summer of 2001, 36 movies were investigated, and the following variables were recorded.[7]

EX0320

■ The movie's first weekend's gross earnings (in millions)

■ The movie's total gross earnings in the United States

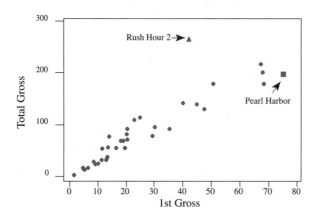

a. How would you describe the relationship between the first weekend's gross and the total gross?

b. Are there any outliers? If so, explain how they do not fit the pattern of the other movies.

c. Which dot represents the movie with the best opening weekend? Did it also have the highest total gross?

d. The film *Pearl Harbor* opened on a 3-day weekend (Memorial Day, 2001). Does that help to explain its position in relation to the other data points?

 3.21   The data from Exercise 3.20 were entered into a *MINITAB* worksheet, and the following output was obtained.

Covariances: 1st Gross, Total Gross

	1st Gross	Total Gross
1st Gross	412.528	
Total Gross	1232.231	4437.109

a. Use the *MINITAB* output or the original data to find the correlation between first weekend and total gross.

b. Which of the two variables would you classify as the independent variable? The dependent variable?

c. If the average first weekend gross is 25.66 million dollars and the average total gross is 86.71 million dollars, find the regression line for predicting total gross as a function of the first weekend's gross.

d. If another film was released and grossed $30 million on the first weekend, what would you predict that its total gross earnings will be?

3.22   Refer to Exercise 1.48. When the heights of these 105 students were recorded, their gender was also recorded.

a. What variables have been measured in this experiment? Are they qualitative or quantitative?

b. Look at the histogram from Exercise 1.48 along with the comparative box plots shown below. Do the box plots help to explain the two local peaks in the histogram? Explain.

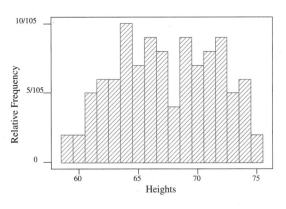

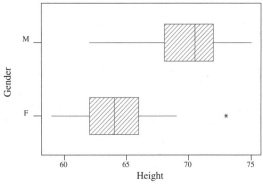

EX0323

3.23 The data in Exercise 1.31 gave the number of hazardous waste sites in each of the 50 states and the District of Columbia in 2001.[2] Suspecting that there might be a relationship between the number of waste sites and the size of the state (in thousands of square miles), researchers recorded both variables and generated a scatterplot with *MINITAB*.

State	Sites	Area	State	Sites	Area	State	Sites	Area
AL	15	52	KY	15	40	ND	0	71
AK	7	663	LA	15	52	OH	34	45
AZ	10	114	ME	13	35	OK	12	70
AR	12	53	MD	19	12	OR	12	98
CA	99	164	MA	33	11	PA	99	46
CO	17	104	MI	69	97	RI	12	2
CT	16	6	MN	24	87	SC	25	32
DE	17	2	MS	4	48	SD	2	77
DC	1	0	MO	26	70	TN	14	42
FL	52	66	MT	14	147	TX	41	269
GA	15	59	NE	10	77	UT	21	85
HI	3	11	NV	1	111	VT	9	10
ID	10	84	NH	19	9	VA	31	43
IL	45	58	NJ	116	9	WA	48	71
IN	29	36	NM	13	122	WV	9	24
IA	16	56	NY	92	55	WI	40	65
KS	12	82	NC	27	54	WY	2	98

MINITAB printout for Exercise 3.23

Covariances: Sites, Area

```
            Sites       Area
Sites     708.290
Area      -92.633   9346.603
```

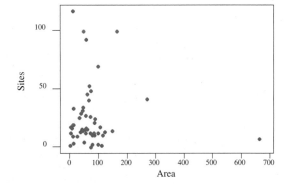

a. Is there any clear pattern in the scatterplot? Describe the relationship between number of waste sites and the size of the state.

b. Use the *MINITAB* output to calculate the correlation coefficient. Does this confirm your answer to part a?

c. Are there any outliers or clusters in the data? If so, can you explain them?

d. What other variables could you consider in trying to understand the distribution of hazardous waste sites in the United States?

Exercises   DO IT YOURSELF!

3.24 If you have not yet done so, use the first applet in **Building a Scatterplot** to create a scatterplot for the data in Example 3.4.

3.25 If you have not yet done so, use the second applet in **Building a Scatterplot** to create a scatterplot for the data in Example 3.5.

EX0326

3.26 The table below shows the prices of eight portable CD players along with their overall score (on a scale of 0–100) in a consumer rating survey.[8]

Brand and Model	Price	Overall Score
Sony D-EJ611	$80	70
Panasonic SL-SX280	50	66
Aiwa XP-V713	70	60
Aiwa XP-SP911	80	65
Panasonic SL-CT470	100	59
Phillips AZ9213	80	60
GPX C3948B1	60	47
RCA RP-2360FM	65	42

a. Calculate the correlation coefficient r between price and overall score. How would you describe the relationship between price and overall score?

b. Use the applet called **Correlation and the Scatterplot** to plot the eight data points. What is the correlation coefficient shown on the applet? Compare with the value you calculated in part a.

c. Describe the pattern that you see in the scatterplot. Are there any clusters or outliers? If so, how would you explain them?

EX0327

3.27 Is there a correlation between Math and Verbal SAT test scores? That is, do students who do well on the Math portion typically do well on the Verbal portion of the test? The data below (score − 400) show the average scores on standardized math and verbal tests for seven high schools in Southern California.[9]

School	Verbal	Math
Centennial	64	84
Norco	74	95
Moreno Valley	27	45
Valley View	75	71
Ramona	20	50
San Bernardino	38	27
Canyon Springs	68	85
North	85	98

a. Calculate the correlation coefficient r between verbal and math scores. How would you describe the relationship between verbal and math scores?

b. Use the applet called **Correlation and the Scatterplot** to plot the eight data points. What is the correlation coefficient shown on the applet? Compare with the value you calculated in part a.

c. Describe the pattern that you see in the scatterplot. Are there any clusters or outliers? If so, how would you explain them?

3.28   Acess the applet called **Exploring Correlation.**

a. Move the slider in the first applet so that $r \approx .75$. Now switch the sign using the [Switch Sign] button at the bottom of the applet. Describe the change in the pattern of the points.

b. Move the slider in the first applet so that $r \approx 0$. Describe the pattern of points on the scatterplot.

c. Refer to part b. In the second applet labeled "Correlation and the Quadrants," with $r \approx 0$, count the number of points falling in each of the four quadrants of the scatterplot. Is the distribution of points in the quadrants relatively uniform, or do more points fall into certain quadrants than others?

d. Use the second applet labeled "Correlation and the Quadrants" and change the correlation coefficient to $r \approx -0.9$. Is the distribution of points in the quadrants relatively uniform, or do more points fall into certain quadrants than others? What happens if $r \approx 0.9$?

e. Use the third applet labeled "Correlation and the Regression Line." Move the slider to see the relationship between the correlation coefficient r, the slope of the regression line and the direction of the relationship between x and y. Describe the relationship.

3.29   Suppose that the relationship between two variables x and y can be described by the regression line $y = 2.0 + 0.5x$. Use the applet in **How a Line Works** to answer the following questions:

a. What is the change in y for a one-unit change in x?

b. Do the values of y increase or decrease as x increases?

c. At what point does the line cross the y-axis? What is the name given to this value?

d. If $x = 2.5$, use the least squares equation to predict the value of y. What value would you predict for y if $x = 4.0$?

3.30   Access the applet in **How a Line Works.**

a. Use the slider to change the y-intercept of the line, but do not change the slope. Describe the changes that you see in the line.

b. Use the slider to change the slope of the line, but do not change the y-intercept. Describe the changes that you see in the line.

Case Study

DISHWASHERS

Do You *Think* Your Dishes Are *Really* Clean?

Does the price of an appliance convey something about its quality? Twenty different dishwashers, beginning with a Kenmore model 16941 that sold for $565 and ranging down to another Kenmore, this time model 16541 that sold for $319, were ranked on characteristics including an overall satisfaction score, the yearly cost of gas or electricity, the cycle time (in minutes), and the water used per wash (in gallons).[10] The information shown in the table can also be found on the CD-ROM. Use a statistical computer package to explore the relationships between various pairs of variables in the table.

Brand and Model	Price ($)	Overall Score	Electricity Cost/Year ($)	Gas Cost/Year ($)	Time (minutes)	Water Used (gallons)
Kenmore (Sears) 16941	565	84	61	38	85	7.5
Kenmore (Sears) 16779 A BEST BUY	400	83	66	43	95	7.5
KitchenAid KUDA23SBWH0	840	78	56	32	80	7.5
Kenmore (Sears) 16649 A BEST BUY	369	77	69	47	100	7.5
Maytag DWU9921AAE	550	76	66	35	90	9.5

Brand	Price ($)	Overall Score	Electricity Cost/Year ($)	Gas Cost/Year ($)	Time (minutes)	Water Used (gallons)
KitchenAid KUDP230B0	510	75	58	35	75	7.5
Maytag DWU9200AAX	460	74	65	35	95	9.5
Magic Chef DU5JV	330	73	60	30	90	9.5
Maytag DWU7400AAE	400	71	66	35	95	9.5
Jenn-Air DW960W	470	70	57	30	95	9.0
General Electric GSD1230TWW	400	66	71	42	110	9.0
KitchenAid KUDB230BO	380	64	59	35	80	7.5
White-Westinghouse WDB632RS0	350	61	56	32	70	7.5
Caloric CDU600CWW	375	60	70	40	105	9.5
General Electric GSD1930TWW	450	60	69	41	110	9.0
Hotpoint HDA430VWW	290	56	70	40	110	9.5
Tappan TDB668RBS0	379	55	71	45	95	8.0
Frigidaire FDB878RS0	280	54	73	45	95	9.0
Frigidaire FDB663RBS0	320	53	70	45	95	8.0
Kenmore (Sears) 16541	319	52	70	40	105	9.5

1. Look at each variable individually. What can you say about symmetry? About outliers?
2. Look at the variables in pairs. Which pairs of variables are positively correlated? Which are negatively correlated? Do any pairs exhibit little or no correlation? Are some of these results counterintuitive? Can you offer an explanation for these cases?
3. Answer the questions: Does the price of an appliance, specifically a dishwasher, convey something about its quality? Which variables did you use in arriving at your answer?

Data Sources

1. Adapted from Michael J. Weiss, "The New Summer Break," *American Demographics,* August 2001, p. 55.
2. William A. McGeveran, Jr., ed., *The World Almanac and Book of Facts 2002* (New York: World Almanac Books, 2002).
3. Gregory K. Torrey, S.F. Vasa, J.W. Maag, and J.J. Kramer, "Social Skills Interventions Across School Settings: Case Study Reviews of Students with Mild Disabilities," *Psychology in the Schools* 29 (July 1992):248.
4. Sharon Epperson, "Getting to the Bottom of Things," *Time,* 3 September 2001, p. 93.
5. Stellan Ohlsson, "The Learning Curve for Writing Books: Evidence from Professor Asimov," *Psychological Science* 3, no. 6 (1992):380–382.
6. "Making a Living," *The Press Enterprise* (Riverside, CA), 25 September 2001, p. A-1.
7. "Summery Scoreboard," *Entertainment Weekly* #614, 14 September 2001, p. 13.
8. "Music on the Move," *Consumer Reports,* July 2001, p. 41.
9. "College-Entry Scores Show Little Change in California," *The Press Enterprise* (Riverside, CA), 29 August 2001, p. A-10.
10. "Dishwashers," *Consumer Reports* 60, no. 8 (August 1995):536.

4

Probability and Probability Distributions

Case Study

In his exciting novel *Congo,* author Michael Crichton describes an expedition racing to find boron-coated blue diamonds in the rain forests of eastern Zaire. Can probability help the heroine Karen Ross in her search for the Lost City of Zinj? The case study at the end of this chapter involves Ross's use of probability in decision-making situations.

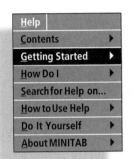

General Objectives

Now that you have learned to describe a data set, how can you use sample data to draw conclusions about the sampled populations? The technique involves a statistical tool called *probability.* To use this tool correctly, you must first understand how it works. The first part of this chapter will teach you the new language of probability, presenting the basic concepts with simple examples.

The variables that we measured in Chapters 1 and 2 can now be redefined as random variables, whose values depend on the chance selection of the elements in the sample. Using probability as a tool, you can create probability distributions that serve as models for discrete random variables, and you can describe these random variables using a mean and standard deviation similar to those in Chapter 2.

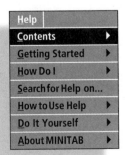

Specific Topics

1. Experiments and events (4.2)
2. Relative frequency definition of probability (4.3)
3. Counting rules (Optional) (4.4)
4. Intersections, unions, and complements (4.5)
5. Conditional probability and independence (4.6)
6. Additive and Multiplicative Rules of Probability (4.6)
7. Bayes' Rule and the Law of Total Probability (Optional) (4.7)
8. Random variables (4.8)
9. Probability distributions for discrete random variables (4.8)
10. The mean and standard deviation for a discrete random variable (4.8)

4.1 The Role of Probability in Statistics

Probability and statistics are related in an important way. Probability is used as a *tool*; it allows you to evaluate the reliability of your conclusions about the population when you have only sample information. Consider these situations:

- When you toss a single coin, you will see either a head (H) or a tail (T). If you toss the coin repeatedly, you will generate an infinitely large number of Hs and Ts—the entire population. What does this population look like? If the coin is fair, then the population should contain 50% Hs and 50% Ts. Now toss the coin one more time. What is the chance of getting a head? Most people would say that the "probability" or chance is 1/2.
- Now suppose you are not sure whether the coin is fair; that is, you are not sure whether the makeup of the population is 50–50. You decide to perform a simple experiment. You toss the coin $n = 10$ times and observe 10 heads in a row. Can you conclude that the coin is fair? Probably not, because if the coin were fair, observing 10 heads in a row would be very *unlikely*; that is, the "probability" would be very small. It is more *likely* that the coin is biased.

As in the coin-tossing example, statisticians use probability in two ways. When the population is *known*, probability is used to describe the likelihood of observing a particular sample outcome. When the population is *unknown* and only a sample from that population is available, probability is used in making statements about the makeup of the population—that is, in making statistical inferences.

In Chapters 4–7, you will learn many different ways to calculate probabilities. You will assume that the population is *known* and calculate the probability of observing various sample outcomes. Once you begin to use probability for statistical inference in Chapter 8, the population will be *unknown* and you will use your knowledge of probability to make reliable inferences from sample information. We begin with some simple examples to help you grasp the basic concepts of probability.

4.2 Events and the Sample Space

Data are obtained by observing either uncontrolled events in nature or controlled situations in a laboratory. We use the term **experiment** to describe either method of data collection.

Definition An **experiment** is the process by which an observation (or measurement) is obtained.

The observation or measurement generated by an experiment may or may not produce a numerical value. Here are some examples of experiments:

- Recording a test grade
- Measuring daily rainfall
- Interviewing a householder to obtain his or her opinion on a greenbelt zoning ordinance
- Testing a printed circuit board to determine whether it is a defective product or an acceptable product
- Tossing a coin and observing the face that appears

Each experiment may result in one or more outcomes, which we call **events** and denote by capital letters.

| Definition | An **event** is an outcome of an experiment. |

EXAMPLE 4.1

Experiment: Toss a die and observe the number that appears on the upper face. Here are some events:

Event A: Observe an odd number
Event B: Observe a number less than 4
Event E_1: Observe a 1
Event E_2: Observe a 2
Event E_3: Observe a 3
Event E_4: Observe a 4
Event E_5: Observe a 5
Event E_6: Observe a 6

Sometimes when one event occurs, it means that another event cannot.

| Definition | Two events are **mutually exclusive** if, when one event occurs, the other cannot, and vice versa. |

There is a distinct difference between events A and B and events $E_1, E_2, \ldots, E_6$ in Example 4.1. Events A and B are not mutually exclusive because both events occur when the number on the upper face of the die is a 1 or a 3. Since event A occurs when the upper face is 1, 3, or 5, A can be decomposed into a collection of simpler events—namely, E_1, E_3, and E_5—which *are* mutually exclusive. Likewise, event B occurs when E_1, E_2, or E_3 occurs and can be viewed as a collection of these mutually exclusive simpler events. In contrast, the six events $E_1, E_2, \ldots, E_6$ form a set of all mutually exclusive outcomes of the experiment. These events are called **simple events** and are denoted by the capital E with a subscript.

| Definition | An event that cannot be decomposed is called a **simple event**. |

| Definition | The set of all simple events is called the **sample space**. |

Now we can redefine the outcome of an experiment in terms of simple events.

| Definition | An **event** is a collection of one or more simple events. |

Sometimes it helps to visualize an experiment using a **Venn diagram,** shown in Figure 4.1. The outer box represents the *sample space,* which contains all of the *simple events,* represented by points and labeled $E_1, E_2, \ldots, E_6$. Since an event A is a collection of simple events, the appropriate points are circled and labeled with the letter A. For the die-tossing example, the event A consists of E_1, E_3, and E_5; these simple events are circled in Figure 4.1.

FIGURE 4.1
Venn diagram for
die tossing

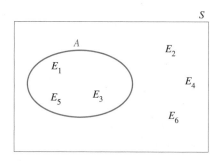

EXAMPLE 4.2   Experiment: Toss a single coin and observe the result. These are the simple events:

E_1: Observe a head (H)
E_2: Observe a tail (T)

The sample space is $S = \{E_1, E_2\}$.

EXAMPLE 4.3   Experiment: Record a person's blood type. The four mutually exclusive possible outcomes are these simple events:

E_1: Blood type A
E_2: Blood type B
E_3: Blood type AB
E_4: Blood type O

The sample space is $S = \{E_1, E_2, E_3, E_4\}$.

Some experiments can be generated in stages, and the sample space can be displayed in a **tree diagram.** Each successive level of branching on the tree corresponds to a step required to generate the final outcome.

EXAMPLE 4.4   A medical technician records a person's blood type and Rh factor. List the simple events in the experiment.

Solution   For each person, a two-stage procedure is needed to record the two variables of interest. The tree diagram is shown in Figure 4.2. The eight simple events in the tree diagram form the sample space, $S = \{A+, A-, B+, B-, AB+, AB-, O+, O-\}$.

An alternative way to display the simple events is to use a **probability table,** as shown in Table 4.1. The rows and columns show the possible outcomes at the first and second stages, respectively, and the simple events are shown in the cells of the table.

FIGURE 4.2
Tree diagram for
Example 4.4

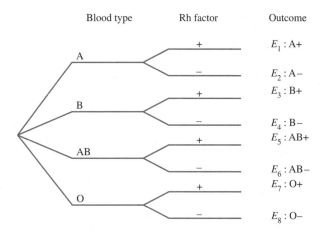

TABLE 4.1
Probability table
for Example 4.4

Rh Factor	Blood Type			
	A	B	AB	O
Negative	A−	B−	AB−	O−
Positive	A+	B+	AB+	O+

4.3 Calculating Probabilities Using Simple Events

The probability of an event A is a measure of our belief that the event A will occur. One practical way to interpret this measure is with the concept of *relative frequency*. Recall from Chapter 1 that if an experiment is performed n times, then the relative frequency of a particular occurrence—say, A—is

$$\text{Relative frequency} = \frac{\text{Frequency}}{n}$$

where the frequency is the number of times the event A occurred. If you let n, the number of repetitions of the experiment, become larger and larger ($n \to \infty$), you will eventually generate the entire population. In this population, the relative frequency of the event A is defined as the **probability of event A**; that is,

$$P(A) = \lim_{n \to \infty} \frac{\text{Frequency}}{n}$$

Since $P(A)$ behaves like a relative frequency, $P(A)$ must be a proportion lying between 0 and 1; $P(A) = 0$ if the event A never occurs, and $P(A) = 1$ if the event A always occurs. The closer $P(A)$ is to 1, the more likely it is that A will occur.

For example, if you tossed a balanced, six-sided die an infinite number of times, you would expect the relative frequency for any of the six values, $x = 1, 2, 3, 4, 5, 6$, to be 1/6. Needless to say, it would be very time-consuming, if not impossible, to repeat an experiment an infinite number of times. For this reason, there are alternative methods for calculating probabilities that make use of the relative frequency concept.

An important consequence of the relative frequency definition of probability involves the simple events. Since the simple events are mutually exclusive, their probabilities must satisfy two conditions.

Requirements for Simple-Event Probabilities

■ Each probability must lie between 0 and 1.
■ The sum of the probabilities for all simple events in S equals 1.

When it is possible to write down the simple events associated with an experiment and to determine their respective probabilities, we can find the probability of an event A by summing the probabilities for all the simple events contained in the event A.

Definition   The **probability of an event A** is equal to the sum of the probabilities of the simple events contained in A.

EXAMPLE 4.5   Toss two fair coins and record the outcome. Find the probability of observing exactly one head in the two tosses.

Solution   To list the simple events in the sample space, you can use a tree diagram as shown in Figure 4.3. The letters H and T mean that you observed a head or a tail, respectively, on a particular toss. To assign probabilities to each of the four simple events, you need to remember that the coins are fair. Therefore, any of the four simple events is as likely as any other. Since the sum of the four simple events must be 1, each must have probability $P(E_i) = 1/4$. The simple events in the sample space are shown in Table 4.2, along with their *equally likely probabilities*. To find $P(A) = P$ (observe exactly one head), you need to find all the simple events that result in event A—namely, E_2 and E_3:

$$P(A) = P(E_2) + P(E_3)$$
$$= \frac{1}{4} + \frac{1}{4} = \frac{1}{2}$$

FIGURE 4.3
Tree diagram for
Example 4.5

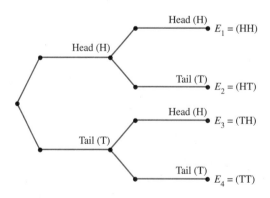

| First coin | Second coin | Outcome |

TABLE 4.2
Simple events and
their probabilities

Event	First Coin	Second Coin	$P(E_i)$
E_1	H	H	1/4
E_2	H	T	1/4
E_3	T	H	1/4
E_4	T	T	1/4

EXAMPLE 4.6

The proportions of blood phenotypes A, B, AB, and O in the population of all Caucasians in the United States are reported as .41, .10, .04, and .45, respectively.[1] If a single Caucasian is chosen randomly from the population, what is the probability that he or she will have either type A or type AB blood?

Solution

The four simple events, A, B, AB, and O, do *not* have equally likely probabilities. Their probabilities are found using the relative frequency concept as

$$P(A) = .41 \qquad P(B) = .10 \qquad P(AB) = .04 \qquad P(O) = .45$$

The event of interest consists of two simple events, so

$$P(\text{person is either type A or type AB}) = P(A) + P(AB)$$
$$= .41 + .04 = .45$$

EXAMPLE 4.7

A candy dish contains one yellow and two red candies. You close your eyes, choose two candies one at a time from the dish, and record their colors. What is the probability that both candies are red?

Solution

Since no probabilities are given, you must list the simple events in the sample space. The two-stage selection of the candies suggests a tree diagram, shown in Figure 4.4. There are two red candies in the dish, so you can use the letters R_1, R_2, and Y to indicate that you have selected the first red, the second red, or the yellow candy, respectively. Since you closed your eyes when you chose the candies, all six choices should be *equally likely* and are assigned probability 1/6. If A is the event that both candies are red, then

$$A = \{R_1R_2, R_2R_1\}$$

Thus,

$$P(A) = P(R_1R_2) + P(R_2R_1)$$
$$= \frac{1}{6} + \frac{1}{6} = \frac{1}{3}$$

FIGURE 4.4
Tree diagram for
Example 4.7

First choice	Second choice	Simple event	Probability
R_1	R_2	$R_1 R_2$	1/6
	Y	$R_1 Y$	1/6
R_2	R_1	$R_2 R_1$	1/6
	Y	$R_2 Y$	1/6
Y	R_1	$Y R_1$	1/6
	R_2	$Y R_2$	1/6

Help
Contents ▶
Getting Started ▶
How Do I ▶
Search for Help on...
How to Use Help ▶
Do It Yourself ▶
About MINITAB ▶

Calculate the Probability of an Event?

1. List all the simple events in the sample space.
2. Assign an appropriate probability to each simple event.
3. Determine which simple events result in the event of interest.
4. Sum the probabilities of the simple events that result in the event of interest.

In your calculation, you must always be careful that you satisfy these two conditions:

- Include all simple events in the sample space.
- Assign realistic probabilities to the simple events.

When the sample space is large, it is easy to unintentionally omit some of the simple events. If this happens, or if your assigned probabilities are wrong, your answers will not be useful in practice.

One way to determine the required number of simple events is to use the counting rules presented in the next optional section. These rules can be used to solve more complex problems, which generally involve a large number of simple events. If you need to master only the basic concepts of probability, you may choose to skip the next section.

Exercises Basic Techniques

4.1 An experiment involves tossing a single die. These are some events:

A: Observe a 2
B: Observe an even number
C: Observe a number greater than 2
D: Observe both A and B
E: Observe A or B or both
F: Observe both A and C

a. List the simple events in the sample space.

b. List the simple events in each of the events A through F.

c. What probabilities should you assign to the simple events?

d. Calculate the probabilities of the six events A through F by adding the appropriate simple-event probabilities.

4.2 A sample space S consists of five simple events with these probabilities:

$$P(E_1) = P(E_2) = .15 \qquad P(E_3) = .4 \qquad P(E_4) = 2P(E_5)$$

a. Find the probabilities for simple events E_4 and E_5.

b. Find the probabilities for these two events:

A: E_1, E_3, E_4
B: E_2, E_3

c. List the simple events that are either in event A or event B or both.

d. List the simple events that are in both event A and event B.

4.3 A sample space contains 10 simple events: $E_1, E_2, \ldots, E_{10}$. If $P(E_1) = 3P(E_2) = .45$ and the remaining simple events are equiprobable, find the probabilities of these remaining simple events.

4.4 A particular basketball player hits 70% of her free throws. When she tosses a pair of free throws, the four possible simple events and three of their associated probabilities are as given in the table:

Simple Event	Outcome of First Free Throw	Outcome of Second Free Throw	Probability
1	Hit	Hit	.49
2	Hit	Miss	?
3	Miss	Hit	.21
4	Miss	Miss	.09

a. Find the probability that the player will hit on the first throw and miss on the second.

b. Find the probability that the player will hit on at least one of the two free throws.

4.5   A jar contains four coins: a nickel, a dime, a quarter, and a half-dollar. Three coins are randomly selected from the jar.

a. List the simple events in *S*.

b. What is the probability that the selection will contain the half-dollar?

c. What is the probability that the total amount drawn will equal 60¢ or more?

4.6   On the first day of kindergarten, the teacher randomly selects 1 of his 25 students and records the student's gender, as well as whether or not that student had gone to preschool.

a. How would you describe the experiment?

b. Construct a tree diagram for this experiment. How many simple events are there?

c. The table below shows the distribution of the 25 students according to gender and preschool experience. Use the table to assign probabilities to the simple events in part b.

	Male	Female
Preschool	8	9
No preschool	6	2

d. What is the probability that the randomly selected student is male? What is the probability that the student is a female and did not go to preschool?

4.7   A bowl contains three red and two yellow balls. Two balls are randomly selected and their colors recorded. Use a tree diagram to list the 20 simple events in the experiment, keeping in mind the order in which the balls are drawn.

4.8   Refer to Exercise 4.7. A ball is randomly selected from the bowl containing three red and two yellow balls. Its color is noted, and the ball is returned to the bowl before a second ball is selected. List the additional five simple events that must be added to the sample space in Exercise 4.7.

Applications

4.9   A survey classified a large number of adults according to whether they were judged to need eyeglasses to correct their reading vision and whether they used eyeglasses when reading. The proportions falling into the four categories are shown in the table. (Note that a small proportion, .02, of adults used eyeglasses when in fact they were judged not to need them.)

Judged to Need Eyeglasses	Used Eyeglasses for Reading	
	Yes	No
Yes	.44	.14
No	.02	.40

If a single adult is selected from this large group, find the probability of each event:

a. The adult is judged to need eyeglasses.

b. The adult needs eyeglasses for reading but does not use them.

c. The adult uses eyeglasses for reading whether he or she needs them or not.

4.10 The game of roulette uses a wheel containing 38 pockets. Thirty-six pockets are numbered 1, 2, . . . , 36, and the remaining two are marked 0 and 00. The wheel is spun, and a pocket is identified as the "winner." Assume that the observance of any one pocket is just as likely as any other.

a. Identify the simple events in a single spin of the roulette wheel.

b. Assign probabilities to the simple events.

c. Let A be the event that you observe either a 0 or a 00. List the simple events in the event A and find $P(A)$.

d. Suppose you placed bets on the numbers 1 through 18. What is the probability that one of your numbers is the winner?

4.11 Three people are randomly selected from voter registration and driving records to report for jury duty. The gender of each person is noted by the county clerk.

a. Define the experiment.

b. List the simple events in S.

c. If each person is just as likely to be a man as a woman, what probability do you assign to each simple event?

d. What is the probability that only one of the three is a man?

e. What is the probability that all three are women?

4.12 Refer to Exercise 4.11. Suppose that there are six prospective jurors, four men and two women, who might be impaneled to sit on the jury in a criminal case. Two jurors are randomly selected from these six to fill the two remaining jury seats.

a. List the simple events in the experiment (HINT: There are 15 simple events if you ignore the order of selection of the two jurors.)

b. What is the probability that both impaneled jurors are women?

4.13 A food company plans to conduct an experiment to compare its brand of tea with that of two competitors. A single person is hired to taste and rank each of three brands of tea, which are unmarked except for identifying symbols A, B, and C.

a. Define the experiment.

b. List the simple events in S.

c. If the taster has no ability to distinguish difference in taste among teas, what is the probability that the taster will rank tea type A as the most desirable? As the least desirable?

4.14 Four equally qualified runners, John, Bill, Ed, and Dave, run a 100-meter sprint, and the order of finish is recorded.

a. How many simple events are in the sample space?

b. If the runners are equally qualified, what probability should you assign to each simple event?

c. What is the probability that Dave wins the race?

d. What is the probability that Dave wins and John places second?

e. What is the probability that Ed finishes last?

4.15 In a genetics experiment, the researcher mated two *Drosophila* fruit flies and observed the traits of 300 offspring. The results are shown in the table.

	Wing Size	
Eye Color	Normal	Miniature
Normal	140	6
Vermillion	3	151

One of these offspring is randomly selected and observed for the two genetic traits.

a. What is the probability that the fly has normal eye color and normal wing size?

b. What is the probability that the fly has vermillion eyes?

c. What is the probability that the fly has either vermillion eyes or miniature wings, or both?

 4.16 Americans can be quite suspicious, especially when it comes to government conspiracies. On the question of whether the U.S. Air Force is withholding proof of the existence of intelligent life on other planets, the proportions of Americans with varying opinions are approximately as shown in the table[2]:

Opinion	Proportion
Very likely	.24
Somewhat likely	.24
Unlikely	.40
Other	.12

Suppose that one person is randomly selected and his or her opinion on this question is recorded.

a. What are the simple events in the experiment?

b. Are the simple events in part a equally likely? If not, what are the probabilities?

c. What is the probability that the person finds it at least somewhat likely that the Air Force is withholding information about aliens?

d. What is the probability that the person finds it unlikely that the Air Force is withholding information?

4.4 Useful Counting Rules (Optional)

Suppose that an experiment involves a large number N of simple events and you know that all the simple events are *equally likely*. Then each simple event has probability $1/N$, and the probability of an event A can be calculated as

$$P(A) = \frac{n_A}{N}$$

where n_A is the number of simple events that result in the event A. In this section, we present three simple rules that can be used to count either N, the number of simple events in the sample space, or n_A, the number of simple events in event A. Once you have obtained these counts, you can find $P(A)$ without actually listing all the simple events.

> **The *mn* Rule**
>
> Consider an experiment that is performed in two stages. If the first stage can be accomplished in m ways and for each of these ways, the second stage can be accomplished in n ways, then there are mn ways to accomplish the experiment.

For example, suppose that you can order a car in one of three styles and in one of four paint colors. To find out how many options are available, you can think of first picking one of the $m = 3$ styles and then selecting one of the $n = 4$ paint colors. Using the *mn* Rule, as shown in Figure 4.5, you have $mn = (3)(4) = 12$ possible options.

FIGURE 4.5
Style–color
combinations

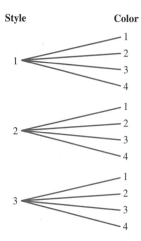

EXAMPLE 4.8

Two dice are tossed. How many simple events are in the sample space S?

Solution

The first die can fall in one of $m = 6$ ways, and the second die can fall in one of $n = 6$ ways. Since the experiment involves two stages, forming the pairs of numbers shown on the two faces, the total number of simple events in S is

$$mn = (6)(6) = 36$$

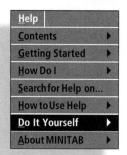

DO IT YOURSELF

The Java applet called **Tossing Dice** gives a visual display of the 36 simple events described in Example 4.8. You can use this applet to find probabilities for any event involving the tossing of two fair dice. By clicking on the appropriate dice combinations, we have found the probability of observing a sum of 3 on the upper faces to be $2/36 = .056$. What is the probability that the sum equals 4? You will use this applet for the *Do It Yourself Exercises* at the end of the chapter.

FIGURE 4.6
Tossing Dice
applet

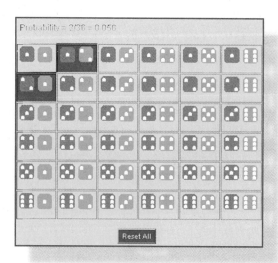

EXAMPLE 4.9

A candy dish contains one yellow and two red candies. Two candies are selected one at a time from the dish, and their color is recorded. How many simple events are in the sample space S?

Solution

The first candy can be chosen in $m = 3$ ways. Since one candy is now gone, the second candy can be chosen in $n = 2$ ways. The total number of simple events is

$$mn = (3)(2) = 6$$

These six simple events were listed in Example 4.7.

We can extend the mn Rule for an experiment that is performed in more than two stages.

> **The Extended mn Rule**
>
> If an experiment is performed in k stages, with n_1 ways to accomplish the first stage, n_2 ways to accomplish the second stage, ..., and n_k ways to accomplish the kth stage, then the number of ways to accomplish the experiment is
>
> $$n_1 n_2 n_3 \cdots n_k$$

EXAMPLE 4.10

How many simple events are in the sample space when three coins are tossed?

Solution

Each coin can land in one of two ways. Hence, the number of simple events is

$$(2)(2)(2) = 8$$

EXAMPLE 4.11

A truck driver can take three routes from city A to city B, four from city B to city C, and three from city C to city D. If, when traveling from A to D, the driver must drive from A to B to C to D, how many possible A-to-D routes are available?

Solution

Let

$n_1 =$ Number of routes from A to $B = 3$
$n_2 =$ Number of routes from B to $C = 4$
$n_3 =$ Number of routes from C to $D = 3$

Then the total number of ways to construct a complete route, taking one subroute from each of the three groups, (A to B), (B to C), and (C to D), is

$$n_1 n_2 n_3 = (3)(4)(3) = 36$$

A second useful counting rule follows from the mn Rule and involves **orderings** or **permutations.** For example, suppose you have three books, A, B, and C, but you have room for only two on your bookshelf. In how many ways can you select and arrange the two books? There are three choices for the two books—A and B, A and C, or B and C—but each of the pairs can be arranged in two ways on the shelf. All the permutations of the two books, chosen from three, are listed in Table 4.3. The mn Rule implies that there are 6 ways, because the first book can be chosen in $m = 3$ ways and the second in $n = 2$ ways, so the result is $mn = 6$.

TABLE 4.3	Combinations of Two	Reordering of Combinations
Permutations of	AB	BA
two books chosen	AC	CA
from three	BC	CB

In how many ways can you arrange all three books on your bookshelf? These are the six permutations:

$$ABC \quad ACB \quad BAC$$
$$BCA \quad CAB \quad CBA$$

Since the first book can be chosen in $n_1 = 3$ ways, the second in $n_2 = 2$ ways, and the third in $n_3 = 1$ way, the total number of orderings is $n_1 n_2 n_3 = (3)(2)(1) = 6$.

Rather than applying the *mn* Rule each time, you can find the number of orderings using a general formula involving *factorial notation*.

A Counting Rule for Permutations

The number of ways we can arrange n distinct objects, taking them r at a time, is

$$P_r^n = \frac{n!}{(n-r)!}$$

where $n! = n(n-1)(n-2)\cdots(3)(2)(1)$ and $0! = 1$.

Since r objects are chosen, this is an *r-stage* experiment. The first object can be chosen in n ways, the second in $(n-1)$ ways, the third in $(n-2)$ ways, and the rth in $(n-r+1)$ ways. We can simplify this awkward notation using the counting rule for permutations because

$$\frac{n!}{(n-r)!} = \frac{n(n-1)(n-2)\cdots(n-r+1)(n-r)\cdots(2)(1)}{(n-r)\cdots(2)(1)} = n(n-1)\cdots(n-r+1)$$

EXAMPLE 4.12 Three lottery tickets are drawn from a total of 50. If the tickets will be distributed to each of three employees in the order in which they are drawn, the order will be important. How many simple events are associated with the experiment?

Solution The total number of simple events is

$$P_3^{50} = \frac{50!}{47!} = 50(49)(48) = 117,600$$

EXAMPLE 4.13 A piece of equipment is composed of five parts that can be assembled in any order. A test is to be conducted to determine the time necessary for each order of assembly. If each order is to be tested once, how many tests must be conducted?

Solution The total number of tests equals

$$P_5^5 = \frac{5!}{0!} = 5(4)(3)(2)(1) = 120$$

When we counted the number of permutations of the two books chosen for your bookshelf, we used a systematic approach:

- First we counted the number of *combinations* or pairs of books to be chosen.
- Then we counted the number of ways to arrange the two chosen books on the shelf.

Sometimes the ordering or arrangement of the objects is not important, but only the objects that are chosen. In this case, you can use a counting rule for **combinations.** For example, you may not care in what order the books are placed on the shelf, but only which books you are able to shelve. When a five-person committee is chosen from a group of 12 students, the order of choice is unimportant because all five students will be equal members of the committee.

A Counting Rule for Combinations

The number of distinct combinations of n distinct objects that can be formed, taking them r at a time, is

$$C_r^n = \frac{n!}{r!(n-r)!}$$

The number of *combinations* and the number of *permutations* are related:

$$C_r^n = \frac{P_r^n}{r!}$$

You can see that C_r^n results when you divide the number of permutations by $r!$, the number of ways of rearranging each distinct group of r objects chosen from the total n.

EXAMPLE 4.14   A printed circuit board may be purchased from five suppliers. In how many ways can three suppliers be chosen from the five?

Solution   Since it is important to know only which three have been chosen, not the order of selection, the number of ways is

$$C_3^5 = \frac{5!}{3!2!} = \frac{(5)(4)}{2} = 10$$

The next example illustrates the use of counting rules to solve a probability problem.

EXAMPLE 4.15   Five manufacturers produce a certain electronic device, whose quality varies from manufacturer to manufacturer. If you were to select three manufacturers at random, what is the chance that the selection would contain exactly two of the best three?

Solution   The simple events in this experiment consist of all possible combinations of three manufacturers, chosen from a group of five. Of these five, three have been designated as "best" and two as "not best." You can think of a candy dish containing three red and two yellow candies, from which you will select three, as illustrated in Figure 4.7. The total number of simple events N can be counted as the number of ways to choose three of the five manufacturers, or

$$N = C_3^5 = \frac{5!}{3!2!} = 10$$

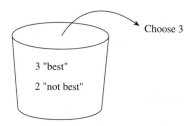

Since the manufacturers are selected at random, any of these 10 simple events will be *equally likely*, with probability 1/10. But how many of these simple events result in the event

A: Exactly two of the "best" three

You can count n_A, the number of events in A, in two steps because event A will occur when you select two of the "best" three and one of the two "not best." There are

$$C_2^3 = \frac{3!}{2!1!} = 3$$

ways to accomplish the first stage and

$$C_1^2 = \frac{2!}{1!1!} = 2$$

ways to accomplish the second stage. Applying the *mn* Rule, we find there are $n_A = (3)(2) = 6$ of the 10 simple events in event A and $P(A) = n_A/N = 6/10$.

Many other counting rules are available in addition to the three presented in this section. If you are interested in this topic, you should consult one of the many textbooks on combinatorial mathematics.

Exercises   Basic Techniques

4.17   You have *two* groups of distinctly different items, 10 in the first group and 8 in the second. If you select one item from each group, how many different pairs can you form?

4.18   You have *three* groups of distinctly different items, four in the first group, seven in the second, and three in the third. If you select one item from each group, how many different triplets can you form?

4.19   Evaluate the following *permutations*. (HINT: Your scientific calculator may have a function that allows you to calculate permutations and combinations quite easily.)

  a. P_3^5 **b.** P_9^{10} **c.** P_6^6 **d.** P_1^{20}

4.20   Evaluate these *combinations*:

  a. C_3^5 **b.** C_9^{10} **c.** C_6^6 **d.** C_1^{20}

4.21   In how many ways can you select five people from a group of eight if the order of selection is important?

4.22   In how many ways can you select two people from a group of 20 if the order of selection is not important?

4.23   Three dice are tossed. How many simple events are in the sample space?

4.24   Four coins are tossed. How many simple events are in the sample space?

4.25   Three balls are selected from a box containing 10 balls. The order of selection is not important. How many simple events are in the sample space?

Applications

4.26   You own 4 pairs of jeans, 12 clean T-shirts, and 4 wearable pairs of sneakers. How many outfits (jeans, T-shirt, and sneakers) can you create?

4.27   A businessman in New York is preparing an itinerary for a visit to six major cities. The distance traveled, and hence the cost of the trip, will depend on the order in which he plans his route. How many different itineraries (and trip costs) are possible?

4.28   Your family vacation involves a cross-country air flight, a rental car, and a hotel stay in Boston. If you can choose from four major air carriers, five car rental agencies, and three major hotel chains, how many options are available for your vacation accommodations?

4.29   Three students are playing a card game. They decide to choose the first person to play by each selecting a card from the 52-card deck and looking for the highest card in value and suit. They rank the suits from lowest to highest: clubs, diamonds, hearts, and spades.

  a. If the card is replaced in the deck after each student chooses, how many possible configurations of the three choices are possible?

  b. How many configurations are there in which each student picks a different card?

  c. What is the probability that all three students pick exactly the same card?

  d. What is the probability that all three students pick different cards?

4.30   A French restaurant in Riverside, California, offers a special summer menu in which, for a fixed dinner cost, you can choose from one of two salads, one of two entrees, and one of two desserts. How many different dinners are available?

4.31   Five cards are selected from a 52-card deck for a poker hand.

  a. How many simple events are in the sample space?

  b. A *royal flush* is a hand that contains the A, K, Q, J, and 10, all in the same suit. How many ways are there to get a royal flush?

  c. What is the probability of being dealt a royal flush?

4.32   Refer to Exercise 4.31. You have a poker hand containing four of a kind.

  a. How many possible poker hands can be dealt?

  b. In how many ways can you receive four cards of the same face value *and* one card from the other 48 available cards?

  c. What is the probability of being dealt four of a kind?

4.33   A study is to be conducted in a hospital to determine the attitudes of nurses toward various administrative procedures. If a sample of 10 nurses is to be selected from a total of 90, how many different samples can be selected? (HINT: Is order important in determining the makeup of the sample to be selected for the survey?)

4.34   Two city council members are to be selected from a total of five to form a subcommittee to study the city's traffic problems.

  a. How many different subcommittees are possible?

  b. If all possible council members have an equal chance of being selected, what is the probability that members Smith and Jones are both selected?

4.35   Professional basketball is now a reality for women basketball players in the United States. There are two conferences in the WNBA, each with eight teams, as shown in the table:

Western Conference	Eastern Conference
Houston Comets	Indiana Fever
Portland Fire	New York Liberty
Minnesota Lynx	Orlando Miracle
Phoenix Mercury	Washington Mystics
Sacramento Monarchs	Cleveland Rockers
Los Angeles Sparks	Detroit Shock
Seattle Storm	Miami Sol
Utah Starzz	Charlotte Sting

Two teams, one from each conference, are randomly selected to play an exhibition game.

a. How many pairs of teams can be chosen?

b. What is the probability that the two teams are Los Angeles and New York?

c. What is the probability that the Western Conference team is from California?

4.36 Refer to Exercise 4.14, in which a 100-meter sprint is run by John, Bill, Ed, and Dave. Assume that all of the runners are equally qualified, so that any order of finish is equally likely. Use the *mn* Rule or permutations to answer these questions:

a. How many orders of finish are possible?

b. What is the probability that Dave wins the sprint?

c. What is the probability that Dave wins and John places second?

d. What is the probability that Ed finishes last?

4.37 The following case occurred in Gainesville, Florida. The eight-member Human Relations Advisory Board considered the complaint of a woman who claimed discrimination, based on her gender, on the part of a local surveying company. The board, composed of five women and three men, voted 5–3 in favor of the plaintiff, the five women voting for the plaintiff and the three men against. The attorney representing the company appealed the board's decision by claiming gender bias on the part of the board members. If the vote in favor of the plaintiff was 5–3 and the board members were not biased by gender, what is the probability that the vote would split along gender lines (five women for, three men against)?

4.38 A student prepares for an exam by studying a list of 10 problems. She can solve 6 of them. For the exam, the instructor selects 5 questions at random from the list of 10. What is the probability that the student can solve all 5 problems on the exam?

4.39 A monkey is given 12 blocks: 3 shaped like squares, 3 like rectangles, 3 like triangles, and 3 like circles. If it draws three of each kind in order—say, 3 triangles, then 3 squares, and so on—would you suspect that the monkey associates identically shaped figures? Calculate the probability of this event.

4.5 Event Relations and Probability Rules

Sometimes the event of interest can be formed as a combination of several other events. Let *A* and *B* be two events defined on the sample space *S*. Here are three important relationships between events.

Definition | The **union** of events *A* and *B*, denoted by $A \cup B$, is the event that either *A* or *B* or both occur.

Definition | The **intersection** of events *A* and *B*, denoted by $A \cap B$, is the event that both *A* and *B* occur.[†]

[†]Some authors use the notation *AB*.

Definition	The **complement** of an event A, denoted by A^c, is the event that A *does not* occur.

Figures 4.8, 4.9 and 4.10 show Venn diagram representations of $A \cup B$, $A \cap B$, and A^c, respectively. Any simple event in the shaded area is a possible outcome resulting in the appropriate event. One way to find the probabilities of the union, the intersection, or the complement is to sum the probabilities of all the associated simple events.

FIGURE 4.8 Venn diagram of $A \cup B$ **FIGURE 4.9** Venn diagram $A \cap B$

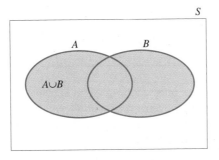 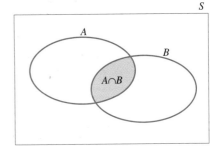

FIGURE 4.10 The complement of an event

EXAMPLE **4.16** Two fair coins are tossed, and the outcome is recorded. These are the events of interest:

A: Observe at least one head
B: Observe at least one tail

Define the events A, B, $A \cap B$, $A \cup B$, and A^c as collections of simple events, and find their probabilities.

Solution Recall from Example 4.5 that the simple events for this experiment are:

E_1: HH (head on first coin, head on second)
E_2: HT
E_3: TH
E_4: TT

and that each simple event has probability 1/4. Event A, at least one head, occurs if E_1, E_2, or E_3 occurs, so that

$$A = \{E_1, E_2, E_3\} \qquad P(A) = \frac{3}{4}$$

and

$$A^c = \{E_4\} \qquad P(A^c) = \frac{1}{4}$$

Similarly,

$$B = \{E_2, E_3, E_4\} \qquad\qquad P(B) = \frac{3}{4}$$

$$A \cap B = \{E_2, E_3\} \qquad\qquad P(A \cap B) = \frac{1}{2}$$

$$A \cup B = \{E_1, E_2, E_3, E_4\} \qquad P(A \cup B) = \frac{4}{4} = 1$$

Note that $(A \cup B) = S$, the sample space, and is thus certain to occur.

The concept of unions and intersections can be extended to more than two events. For example, the union of three events A, B, and C, which is written as $A \cup B \cup C$, is the set of simple events that are in A or B or C or in any combination of those events. Similarly, the intersection of three events A, B, and C, which is written as $A \cap B \cap C$, is the collection of simple events that are common to the three events A, B, and C.

Calculating Probabilities for Unions and Complements

When we can write the event of interest in the form of a union, a complement, or an intersection, there are special probability rules that can simplify our calculations. The first rule deals with *unions* of events.

Additive Rule of Probability

Given two events, A and B, the probability of their union, $A \cup B$, is equal to

$$P(A \cup B) = P(A) + P(B) - P(A \cap B)$$

Notice in the Venn diagram in Figure 4.11 that the sum $P(A) + P(B)$ double counts the simple events that are common to both A and B. Subtracting $P(A \cap B)$ gives the correct result.

FIGURE 4.11
The Additive Rule
of Probability

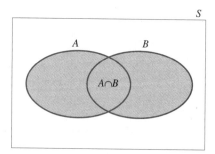

When two events A and B are **mutually exclusive** or **disjoint,** it means that when A occurs, B cannot, and vice versa. This means that the probability that they both occur,

$P(A \cap B)$, must be zero. Figure 4.12 is a Venn diagram representation of two such events with no simple events in common.

FIGURE 4.12
Two disjoint events

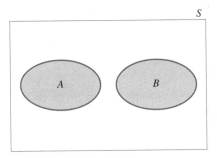

When two events A and B are **mutually exclusive,** then $P(A \cap B) = 0$ and the Additive Rule simplifies to

$$P(A \cup B) = P(A) + P(B)$$

The second rule deals with *complements* of events. You can see from the Venn diagram in Figure 4.10 that A and A^c are mutually exclusive and that $A \cup A^c = S$, the entire sample space. It follows that

$$P(A) + P(A^c) = 1 \quad \text{and} \quad P(A^c) = 1 - P(A)$$

Rule for Complements

$$P(A^c) = 1 - P(A)$$

EXAMPLE 4.17   An oil-prospecting firm plans to drill two exploratory wells. Past evidence is used to assess the possible outcomes listed in Table 4.4.

TABLE 4.4
Outcomes for oil-drilling experiment

Event	Description	Probability
A	Neither well produces oil or gas	.80
B	Exactly one well produces oil or gas	.18
C	Both wells produce oil or gas	.02

Find $P(A \cup B)$ and $P(B \cup C)$.

Solution   By their definition, events A, B, and C are jointly mutually exclusive because the occurrence of one event precludes the occurrence of either of the other two. Therefore,

$$P(A \cup B) = P(A) + P(B) = .80 + .18 = .98$$

and

$$P(B \cup C) = P(B) + P(C) = .18 + .02 = .20$$

The event $A \cup B$ can be described as the event that *at most* one well produces oil or gas, and $B \cup C$ describes the event that *at least* one well produces gas or oil.

EXAMPLE 4.18   In a telephone survey of 1000 adults, respondents were asked about the expense of a college education and the relative necessity of some form of financial assistance.[3] The respondents were classified according to whether they currently had a child in college and whether they thought the loan burden for most college students is too high, the right amount, or too little. The proportions responding in each category are shown in the **probability table** in Table 4.5. Suppose one respondent is chosen at random from this group.

TABLE 4.5
Probability table

	Too High (A)	Right Amount (B)	Too Little (C)
Child in College (D)	.35	.08	.01
No Child in College (E)	.25	.20	.11

1. What is the probability that the respondent has a child in college?
2. What is the probability that the respondent does not have a child in college?
3. What is the probability that the respondent has a child in college or thinks that the loan burden is too high?

Solution   Table 4.5 gives the probabilities for the six simple events in the cells of the table. For example, the entry in the top left corner of the table is the probability that a respondent has a child in college *and* thinks the loan burden is too high ($A \cap D$).

1. The event that a respondent has a child in college will occur regardless of his or her response to the question about loan burden. That is, event D consists of the simple events in the first row:

$$P(D) = .35 + .08 + .01 = .44$$

In general, the probabilities of *marginal* events such as D and A are found by summing the probabilities in the appropriate row or column.

2. The event that the respondent does not have a child in college is the complement of the event D denoted by D^c. The probability of D^c is found as

$$P(D^c) = 1 - P(D)$$

Using the result of part 1, we have

$$P(D^c) = 1 - .44 = .56$$

3. The event of interest is $P(A \cup D)$. Using the additive rule

$$P(A \cup D) = P(A) + P(D) - P(A \cap D)$$
$$= .60 + .44 - .35$$
$$= .69$$

4.6   Conditional Probability, Independence, and the Multiplicative Rule

There is a probability rule that can be used to calculate the probability of the intersection of several events. However, this rule depends on the important statistical concept of **independent** or **dependent events.**

Definition   Two events, A and B, are said to be **independent** if and only if the probability of event B is not influenced or changed by the occurrence of event A.

Suppose a researcher notes a person's gender and whether or not the person is color-blind to red and green. Does the probability that a person is colorblind change depending on whether the person is a male or a female? In this case, since colorblindness is a male sex-linked characteristic, the probability that a man is colorblind will be greater than the probability that a person chosen from the general popoulation will be color-blind. The event A, that a person is colorblind, is dependent on the event B, that the person is a man.

The probability of an event A, given that the event B has occurred, is called the **conditional probability of A, given that B has occurred,** denoted by $P(A|B)$. The vertical bar is read "given" and the events appearing to the right of the bar are those that you know have occurred.

Definition   The **conditional probability of A,** given that B has occurred, is

$$P(A|B) = \frac{P(A \cap B)}{P(B)} \quad \text{if } P(B) \neq 0$$

The **conditional probability of B,** given that A has occurred, is

$$P(B|A) = \frac{P(A \cap B)}{P(A)} \quad \text{if } P(A) \neq 0$$

Let's continue with the example of gender and colorblindness. Assume that there are 50% men and 50% women in the population, so that $P(B) = .5$. Suppose also that 4% of the population are colorblind men; that is, $P(A \cap B) = .04$. Figure 4.13 displays this information in a Venn diagram. The sample space S is divided into two areas (men and women) and the event A (colorblindness) is the oval in the center. The area shaded in blue is the proportion of men (event B) who are colorblind. The conditional probability $P(A|B)$ is the proportion of the "B area" that results in event A or $P(A|B) = .04/.50 = .08$. This agrees with the definition:

$$P(A|B) = \frac{P(A \cap B)}{P(B)} = \frac{.04}{.50} = .08$$

If you had the additional information that the proportion of colorblind women, $P(A \cap B^c)$, is .002, then you could calculate the conditional probability that

FIGURE 4.13
Venn diagram for
conditional
probabilities

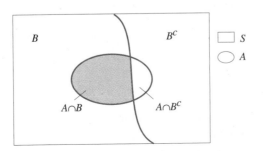

an individual is colorblind, given that the person is a woman, $P(A|B^c)$, using

$$P(A|B^c) = \frac{P(A \cap B^c)}{P(B)^c} = \frac{.002}{.500} = .004$$

You can see that these two conditional probabilities are not the same. The probability that a person is colorblind, given that the person is a man, is much greater than the probability that a person is colorblind, given that the person is a woman. You could say that the probability of being colorblind *depends* on whether you are a man or a woman.

We can now redefine **independence** in terms of conditional probabilities.

Definition   Two events A and B are said to be **independent** if and only if either

$$P(A|B) = P(A)$$

or

$$P(B|A) = P(B)$$

Otherwise, the events are said to be **dependent.**

EXAMPLE 4.19   Toss two coins and observe the outcome. Define these events:

A: Head on the first coin
B: Tail on the second coin

Are events A and B independent?

Solution   From previous examples, you know that $S = \{HH, HT, TH, TT\}$. Then

$$P(A) = \frac{1}{2}$$

and

$$P(A|B) = \frac{P(A \cap B)}{P(B)} = \frac{P(HT)}{P(T)} = \frac{1/4}{1/2} = \frac{1}{2}$$

Since the two probabilities are equal, the two events must be independent. This makes sense because the outcome of one coin toss should not affect the outcome of the second coin toss.

EXAMPLE 4.20   Refer to the probability table in Example 4.18, which is reproduced below.

	Too High (A)	Right Amount (B)	Too Little (C)
Child in College (D)	.35	.08	.01
No Child in College (E)	.25	.20	.11

1. Given that the respondent has a child in college, what is the probability that he or she ranks the loan burden as "too high"?
2. Are events D and A independent? Explain.

Solution   1. To find the probability of A given D, we use the definition of conditional probability:

$$P(A|D) = \frac{P(A \cap D)}{P(D)} = \frac{.35}{.44} = .80$$

2. Since $P(A|D) = .80$ and $P(A) = .35 + .25 = .60$, events A and D must *not* be independent.

Calculating Probabilities for Intersections

Once you have determined whether or not events are independent or dependent, you can use the following rule to calculate the *intersection* of several events.

Multiplicative Rule of Probability

The probability that both of two events, A and B, occur is

$$P(A \cap B) = P(A)P(B|A)$$
$$= P(B)P(A|B)$$

If A and B are independent,

$$P(A \cap B) = P(A)P(B)$$

Similarly, if A, B, and C are mutually independent events, then the probability that A, B, *and* C occur is

$$P(A \cap B \cap C) = P(A)P(B)P(C)$$

EXAMPLE 4.21   In a color preference experiment, eight toys are placed in a container. The toys are identical except for color—two are red, and six are green. A child is asked to choose two toys *at random*. What is the probability that the child chooses the two red toys?

Solution   You can visualize the experiment using a tree diagram as shown in Figure 4.14. Define the following events:

R: Red toy is chosen
G: Green toy is chosen

The event A (both toys are red) can be constructed as the intersection of two events:

$$A = (\text{R on first choice}) \cap (\text{R on second choice})$$

Since there are only two red toys in the container, the probability of choosing red on the first choice is 2/8. However, once this red toy has been chosen, the probability of red on the second choice is *dependent* on the outcome of the first choice (see Figure 4.14). If the first choice was red, the probability of choosing a second red toy is only 1/7 because there is only one red toy among the seven remaining. If the first choice was green, the probability of choosing red on the second choice is 2/7 because

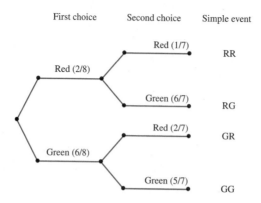

FIGURE 4.14
Tree diagram for
Example 4.21

there are two red toys among the seven remaining. Using this information and the Multiplicative Rule, you can find the probability of event A:

$$P(A) = P(\text{R on first choice} \cap \text{R on second choice})$$

$$= P(\text{R on first choice}) \, P(\text{R on second} \mid \text{R on first})$$

$$= \left(\frac{2}{8}\right)\left(\frac{1}{7}\right) = \frac{2}{56} = \frac{1}{28}$$

Using probability rules to calculate the probability of a compound event requires some experience and ingenuity. You need to express the event of interest as a union or intersection (or the combination of both) of two or more events whose probabilities are known or easily calculated. Often you can do this in different ways; the key is to find the right combination. If the event of interest is the union of mutually exclusive events, then the probabilities of the intersections will be zero and the probability of the union will be the sum of the probabilities of each event. If the events are independent, then the probability of an intersection is simply the product of the unconditional probabilities. The next example illustrates the use of the probability rules.

EXAMPLE 4.22   Two cards are drawn from a deck of 52 cards. Calculate the probability that the draw includes an ace and a ten.

Solution   Consider the event of interest:

$$A\text{: Draw an ace and a ten}$$

Then $A = B \cup C$, where

        B: Draw the ace on the first draw and the ten on the second
        C: Draw the ten on the first draw and the ace on the second

Events B and C were chosen to be mutually exclusive and also to be intersections of events with known probabilities; that is,

$$B = B_1 \cap B_2 \quad \text{and} \quad C = C_1 \cap C_2$$

where

B_1: Draw an ace on the first draw
B_2: Draw a ten on the second draw
C_1: Draw a ten on the first draw
C_2: Draw an ace on the second draw

Applying the Multiplicative Rule, you get

$$P(B_1 \cap B_2) = P(B_1)P(B_2|B_1)$$
$$= \left(\frac{4}{52}\right)\left(\frac{4}{51}\right)$$

and

$$P(C_1 \cap C_2) = \left(\frac{4}{52}\right)\left(\frac{4}{51}\right)$$

Then, applying the Additive Rule,

$$P(A) = P(B) + P(C)$$
$$= \left(\frac{4}{52}\right)\left(\frac{4}{51}\right) + \left(\frac{4}{52}\right)\left(\frac{4}{51}\right) = \frac{8}{663}$$

Check each composition carefully to be certain that it is actually equal to the event of interest.

Exercises Basic Techniques

4.40 An experiment can result in one of five equally likely simple events, $E_1, E_2, \ldots, E_5$. Events A, B, and C are defined as follows:

A: E_1, E_3 $P(A) = .4$
B: E_1, E_2, E_4, E_5 $P(B) = .8$
C: E_3, E_4 $P(C) = .4$

Find the probabilities associated with these compound events by listing the simple events in each.

a. A^c **b.** $A \cap B$ **c.** $B \cap C$
d. $A \cup B$ **e.** $B|C$ **f.** $A|B$
g. $A \cup B \cup C$ **h.** $(A \cap B)^c$

4.41 Refer to Exercise 4.40. Use the definition of a complementary event to find these probabilities:

a. $P(A^c)$ **b.** $P((A \cap B)^c)$

Do the results agree with those obtained in Exercise 4.40?

4.42 Refer to Exercise 4.40. Use the definition of conditional probability to find these probabilities:

a. $P(A|B)$ **b.** $P(B|C)$

Do the results agree with those obtained in Exercise 4.40?

4.43 Refer to Exercise 4.40. Use the Additive and Multiplicative Rules of Probability to find these probabilities:

a. $P(A \cup B)$ **b.** $P(A \cap B)$ **c.** $P(B \cap C)$

Do the results agree with those obtained in Exercise 4.40?

4.44 Refer to Exercise 4.40.

a. Are events A and B independent?   **b.** Are events A and B mutually exclusive?

4.45 An experiment consists of tossing a single die and observing the number of dots that show on the upper face. Events A, B, and C are defined as follows:

A: Observe a number less than 4
B: Observe a number less than or equal to 2
C: Observe a number greater than 3

Find the probabilities associated with these compound events using either the simple event approach or the rules and definitions from this section.

a. S **b.** $A|B$ **c.** B

d. $A \cap B \cap C$ **e.** $A \cap B$ **f.** $A \cap C$

g. $B \cap C$ **h.** $A \cup C$ **i.** $B \cup C$

4.46   Refer to Exercise 4.45.

a. Are events A and B independent? Mutually exclusive?

b. Are events A and C independent? Mutually exclusive?

4.47   Suppose that $P(A) = .4$ and $P(B) = .2$. If events A and B are independent, find these probabilities:

a. $P(A \cap B)$ **b.** $P(A \cup B)$

4.48   Suppose that $P(A) = .3$ and $P(B) = .5$. If events A and B are mutually exclusive, find these probabilities:

a. $P(A \cap B)$ **b.** $P(A \cup B)$

4.49   Suppose that $P(A) = .4$ and $P(A \cap B) = .12$.

a. Find $P(B|A)$.

b. Are events A and B mutually exclusive?

c. If $P(B) = .3$, are events A and B independent?

4.50   An experiment can result in one or both of events A and B with the probabilities shown in this probability table:

	A	A^c
B	.34	.46
B^c	.15	.05

Find the following probabilities:

a. $P(A)$ **b.** $P(B)$ **c.** $P(A \cap B)$

d. $P(A \cup B)$ **e.** $P(A|B)$ **f.** $P(B|A)$

4.51   Refer to Exercise 4.50.

a. Are events A and B mutually exclusive? Explain.

b. Are events A and B independent? Explain.

Applications

4.52   Many companies are testing prospective employees for drug use, with the intent of improving efficiency and reducing absenteeism, accidents, and theft. Opponents claim that this procedure is creating a class of unhirables and that some persons may be placed in this class because the tests themselves are not 100% reliable. Suppose a company uses a test that is 98% accurate—that is, it correctly identifies a person as a drug user or nonuser with probability .98—and to reduce the chance of error, each job applicant is required to take two tests. If the outcomes of the two tests on the same person are independent events, what are the probabilities of these events?

a. A nonuser fails both tests.

b. A drug user is detected (i.e., he or she fails at least one test).

c. A drug user passes both tests.

4.53   Whether a grant proposal is funded quite often depends on the reviewers. Suppose a group of research proposals was evaluated by a group of experts as to whether the proposals were worthy of funding. When these same proposals were submitted to a second independent group of experts, the decision to fund was reversed in 30% of the cases. If the probability that a proposal is judged worthy of funding by the first peer review group is .2, what are the probabilities of these events?

a. A worthy proposal is approved by both groups.

b. A worthy proposal is disapproved by both groups.

c. A worthy proposal is approved by one group.

4.54 A study of the behavior of a large number of drug offenders after treatment for drug abuse suggests that the likelihood of conviction within a 2-year period after treatment may depend on the offender's education. The proportions of the total number of cases that fall into four education/conviction categories are shown in the table below:

	Status Within 2 Years After Treatment		
Education	Convicted	Not Convicted	Totals
10 Years or More	.10	.30	.40
9 Years or Less	.27	.33	.60
Totals	.37	.63	1.00

Suppose a single offender is selected from the treatment program. Here are the events of interest:

A: The offender has 10 or more years of education

B: The offender is convicted within 2 years after completion of treatment

Find the appropriate probabilities for these events:

a. A **b.** B **c.** $A \cap B$

d. $A \cup B$ **e.** A^c **f.** $(A \cup B)^c$

g. $(A \cap B)^c$ **h.** A given that B has occurred   **i.** B given that A has occurred

4.55 Use the probabilities of Exercise 4.54 to show that these equalities are true:

a. $P(A \cap B) = P(A)P(B|A)$ **b.** $P(A \cap B) = P(B)P(A|B)$

c. $P(A \cup B) = P(A) + P(B) - P(A \cap B)$

4.56 Two people enter a room and their birthdays (ignoring years) are recorded.

a. Identify the nature of the simple events in S.

b. What is the probability that the two people have a specific pair of birthdates?

c. Identify the simple events in event A: Both people have the same birthday.

d. Find $P(A)$.   **e.** Find $P(A^c)$.

4.57 If n people enter a room, find these probabilities:

A: None of the people have the same birthday

B: At least two of the people have the same birthday

Solve for

a. $n = 3$ **b.** $n = 4$

[NOTE: Surprisingly, $P(B)$ increases rapidly as n increases. For example, for $n = 20$, $P(B) = .411$; for $n = 40$, $P(B) = .891$.]

4.58 A college student frequents one of two coffee houses on campus, choosing Starbucks 70% of the time and Peetes 30% of the time. Regardless of where she goes, she buys a cafe mocha on 60% of her visits.

a. The next time she goes into a coffee house on campus, what is the probability that she goes to Starbucks and orders a cafe mocha?

b. Are the two events in part a independent? Explain.

c. If she goes into a coffee house and orders a cafe mocha, what is the probability that she is at Peetes?

d. What is the probability that she goes to Starbucks or orders a cafe mocha or both?

4.59 A certain manufactured item is visually inspected by two different inspectors. When a defective item comes through the line, the probability that it gets by the first inspector is .1. Of those that get past the first inspector, the second inspector will "miss" 5 out of 10. What fraction of the defective items get by both inspectors?

4.60 A survey of people in a given region showed that 20% were smokers. The probability of death due to lung cancer, given that a person smoked, was roughly 10 times the probability of death due to lung cancer, given that a person did not smoke. If the probability of death due to lung cancer in the region is .006, what is the probability of death due to lung cancer given that a person is a smoker?

4.61 A smoke-detector system uses two devices, A and B. If smoke is present, the probability that it will be detected by device A is .95; by device B, .98; and by both devices, .94.

    a. If smoke is present, find the probability that the smoke will be detected by device A or device B or both devices.

    b. Find the probability that the smoke will not be detected.

4.62 Gregor Mendel was a monk who suggested in 1865 a theory of inheritance based on the science of genetics. He identified heterozygous individuals for flower color that had two alleles (one r = recessive white color allele and one R = dominant red color allele). When these individuals were mated, 3/4 of the offspring were observed to have red flowers and 1/4 had white flowers. The table summarizes this mating; each parent gives one of its alleles to form the gene of the offspring.

	Parent 2	
Parent 1	r	R
r	rr	rR
R	Rr	RR

We assume that each parent is equally likely to give either of the two alleles and that, if either one or two of the alleles in a pair is dominant (R), the offspring will have red flowers.

    a. What is the probability that an offspring in this mating has at least one dominant allele?

    b. What is the probability that an offspring has at least one recessive allele?

    c. What is the probability that an offspring has one recessive allele, given that the offspring has red flowers?

4.63 During the inaugural season of Major League Soccer in the United States, the medical teams documented 256 injuries that caused a loss of participation time to the player. The results of this investigation is shown in the table.[3]

Severity	Practice (P)	Game (G)	Total
Minor (A)	66	88	154
Moderate (B)	23	44	67
Major (C)	12	23	35
Total	101	155	256

If one individual is drawn at random from this group of 256 soccer players, find the following probabilities:

    a. $P(A)$ **b.** $P(G)$ **c.** $P(A \cap G)$

    d. $P(G|A)$ **e.** $P(G|B)$ **f.** $P(G|C)$

    g. $P(C|P)$ **h.** $P(B^c)$

4.64 Men and women often disagree on how they think about selecting a mate. Suppose that a poll of 1000 individuals in their twenties gave the following responses to the question of whether it is more important for their future mate to be able to communicate their feelings (F) than it is for that person to make a good living (G).

	Feelings (F)	Good Living (G)	Totals
Men (M)	.35	.20	.55
Women (W)	.36	.09	.45
Totals	.71	.29	1.00

If an individual is selected at random from this group of 1000 individuals, calculate the following probabilities

a. $P(F)$ **b.** $P(G)$ **c.** $P(F|M)$ **d.** $P(F|W)$

e. $P(M|F)$ **f.** $P(W|G)$

4.7 Bayes' Rule (Optional)

Let us reconsider the experiment involving red and green colorblindness from Section 4.6. Notice in Figure 4.13 that the two events

B: The person selected is a man
B^c: The person selected is a woman

taken together make up the sample space consisting of both men and women. You can also see that the event A consists of both those simple events that are in A and B and those simple events that are in A and B^c. Since these two *intersections* are *mutually exclusive,* you can write the event A as

$$A = (A \cap B) \cup (A \cap B^c)$$

and

$$
\begin{aligned}
P(A) &= P(A \cap B) + P(A \cap B^c) \\
&= .04 + .002 = .042
\end{aligned}
$$

Suppose now that the sample space can be partitioned into k subpopulations, S_1, S_2, S_3, ..., S_k, that, as in the colorblindness example, are **mutually exclusive and exhaustive;** that is, taken together they make up the entire sample space. In a similar way, you can express an event A as

$$A = (A \cap S_1) \cup (A \cap S_2) \cup (A \cap S_3) \cup \cdots \cup (A \cap S_k)$$

Then

$$P(A) = P(A \cap S_1) + P(A \cap S_2) + P(A \cap S_3) + \cdots + P(A \cap S_k)$$

This is illustrated for $k = 3$ in Figure 4.15.

FIGURE 4.15
Decomposition of event A

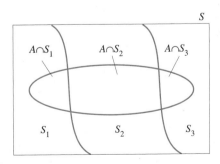

You can go one step further and use the Multiplicative Rule to write $P(A \cap S_i)$ as $P(S_i)P(A|S_i)$, for $i = 1, 2, \ldots, k$. The result is known as the **Law of Total Probability.**

Law of Total Probability

Given a set of events $S_1, S_2, S_3, \ldots, S_k$ that are mutually exclusive and exhaustive and an event A, the probability of the event A can be expressed as

$$P(A) = P(S_1)P(A|S_1) + P(S_2)P(A|S_2) + P(S_3)P(A|S_3) + \cdots + P(S_k)P(A|S_k)$$

EXAMPLE 4.23

Sneakers are no longer just for the young. In a recent issue of *American Demographics,* an article gave the fraction of U.S. adults 18 years of age and older who own five or more pairs of wearable sneakers. Table 4.6 lists that information along with the fraction of the U.S. adult population 18 years of age and older in each of five age groups.[4] Use the Law of Total Probability to determine the unconditional probability of an adult 18 years and older owning five or more pairs of wearable sneakers.

TABLE 4.6
Probability table

	Groups and Ages				
	G_1 18–24	G_2 25–34	G_3 35–49	G_4 50–64	G_5 ≥65
Fraction with ≥5 Pairs	.26	.20	.13	.18	.14
Fraction of U.S. Adults 18 and Older	.19	.22	.29	.17	.13

Solution Let A be the event that a person chosen at random from the U.S. adult population 18 years of age and older owns five or more pairs of wearable sneakers. Let $G_1, G_2, \ldots, G_5$ represent the event that the person selected belongs to each of the five age groups, respectively. Since the five groups are *exhaustive,* you can write the event A as

$$A = (A \cap G_1) \cup (A \cap G_2) \cup (A \cap G_3) \cup (A \cap G_4) \cup (A \cap G_5)$$

Using the Law of Total Probability, you can find the probability of A as

$$P(A) = P(A \cap G_1) + P(A \cap G_2) + P(A \cap G_3) + P(A \cap G_4) + P(A \cap G_5)$$
$$= P(G_1)P(A|G_1) + P(G_2)P(A|G_2) + P(G_3)P(A|G_3)$$
$$+ P(G_4)P(A|G_4) + P(G_5)P(A|G_5)$$

From the probabilities in Table 4.6,

$$P(A) = (.19)(.26) + (.22)(.20) + (.29)(.13) + (.17)(.18) + (.13)(.14)$$
$$= .0494 + .0440 + .0377 + .0306 + .0182 = .1799$$

The *unconditional probability* that a person selected at random from the population of U.S. adults 18 years of age and older owns at least five pairs of wearable sneakers is about .18. Notice that the Law of Total Probability is a weighted average of the probabilities within each group, with weights .19, .22, .29, .17, and .13, which reflect the relative sizes of the groups.

Often you need to find the conditional probability of an event B, given that an event A has occurred. One such situation occurs in screening tests, which used to be associated primarily with medical diagnostic tests but are now finding applications in a variety of fields. Automatic test equipment is routinely used to inspect parts in high-volume production processes. Steroid testing of athletes, home pregnancy tests, and AIDS testing are some other applications. Screening tests are evaluated on the probability of a false negative or a false positive, and both of these are *conditional probabilities.*

A **false positive** is the event that the test is positive for a given condition, given that the person does not have the condition. A **false negative** is the event that the test is negative for a given condition, given that the person has the condition. You can evaluate these conditional probabilities using a formula derived by the probabilist Thomas Bayes.

The experiment involves selecting a sample from one of k subpopulations that are mutually exclusive and exhaustive. Each of these subpopulations, denoted by $S_1, S_2, \ldots, S_k$, has a selection probability $P(S_1), P(S_2), P(S_3), \ldots, P(S_k)$, called *prior probabilities*. An event A is observed in the selection. What is the probability that the sample came from subpopulation S_i, given that A has occurred?

You know from Section 4.6 that $P(S_i|A) = [P(A \cap S_i)]/P(A)$, which can be rewritten as $P(S_i|A) = [P(S_i)P(A|S_i)]/P(A)$. Using the Law of Total Probability to rewrite $P(A)$, you have

$$P(S_i|A) = \frac{P(S_i)P(A|S_i)}{P(S_1)P(A|S_1) + P(S_2)P(A|S_2) + P(S_3)P(A|S_3) + \cdots + P(S_k)P(A|S_k)}$$

These new probabilities are often referred to as *posterior probabilities*—that is, probabilities of the subpopulations (also called *states of nature*) that have been updated after observing the sample information contained in the event A. Bayes suggested that if the prior probabilities are unknown, they can be taken to be $1/k$, which implies that each of the events S_1 through S_k is equally likely.

Bayes' Rule

Let $S_1, S_2, \ldots, S_k$ represent k mutually exclusive and exhaustive subpopulations with prior probabilities $P(S_1), P(S_2), \ldots, P(S_k)$. If an event A occurs, the posterior probability of S_i given A is the conditional probability

$$P(S_i|A) = \frac{P(S_i)P(A|S_i)}{\sum_{j=1}^{k} P(S_j)P(A|S_j)}$$

for $i = 1, 2, \ldots, k$.

EXAMPLE 4.24   Refer to Example 4.23. Find the probability that the person selected was 65 years of age or older, given that the person owned at least five pairs of wearable sneakers.

Solution   You need to find the conditional probability given by

$$P(G_5|A) = \frac{P(A \cap G_5)}{P(A)}$$

You have already calculated $P(A) = .1799$ using the Law of Total Probability. Therefore,

$P(G_5|A) =$

$$\frac{P(G_5)P(A|G_5)}{P(G_1)P(A|G_1) + P(G_2)P(A|G_2) + P(G_3)P(A|G_3) + P(G_4)P(A|G_4) + P(G_5)P(A|G_5)}$$

$$= \frac{(.13)(.14)}{(.19)(.26) + (.22)(.20) + (.29)(.13) + (.17)(.18) + (.13)(.14)}$$

$$= \frac{.0182}{.1799} = .1012$$

In this case, the posterior probability of .10 is somewhat less than the prior probability of .13 (from Table 4.6). This group *a priori* was the smallest, and only a small proportion of this segment had five or more pairs of wearable sneakers.

What is the posterior probability for those aged 35 to 49? For this group of adults, we have

$$P(G_3|A) = \frac{(.29)(.13)}{(.19)(.26) + (.22)(.20) + (.29)(.13) + (.17)(.18) + (.13)(.14)} = .2096$$

This posterior probability of .21 is substantially less than the prior probability of .29. In effect, this group was *a priori* the largest segment of the population sampled, but at the same time, the proportion of individuals in this group who had at least five pairs of wearable sneakers was the smallest of any of the groups. These two facts taken together cause a downward adjustment of almost a third in the *a priori* probability of .29.

Exercises

Basic Techniques

4.65 A sample is selected from one of two populations, S_1 and S_2, with probabilities $P(S_1) = .7$ and $P(S_2) = .3$. If the sample has been selected from S_1, the probability of observing an event A is $P(A|S_1) = .2$. Similarly, if the sample has been selected from S_2, the probability of observing A is $P(A|S_2) = .3$.

a. If a sample is randomly selected from one of the two populations, what is the probability that event A occurs?

b. If the sample is randomly selected and event A is observed, what is the probability that the sample was selected from population S_1? From population S_2?

4.66 If an experiment is conducted, one and only one of three mutually exclusive events S_1, S_2, and S_3 can occur, with these probabilities:

$$P(S_1) = .2 \qquad P(S_2) = .5 \qquad P(S_3) = .3$$

The probabilities of a fourth event A occurring, given that event S_1, S_2, or S_3 occurs, are

$$P(A|S_1) = .2 \qquad P(A|S_2) = .1 \qquad P(A|S_3) = .3$$

If event A is observed, find $P(S_1|A)$, $P(S_2|A)$, and $P(S_3|A)$.

4.67 A population can be divided into two subgroups that occur with probabilities 60% and 40%, respectively. An event A occurs 30% of the time in the first subgroup and 50% of the time in the second subgroup. What is the unconditional probability of the event A, regardless of which subgroup it comes from?

Applications

4.68 City crime records show that 20% of all crimes are violent and 80% are nonviolent, involving theft, forgery, and so on. Ninety percent of violent crimes are reported versus 70% of nonviolent crimes.

a. What is the overall reporting rate for crimes in the city?

b. If a crime in progress is reported to the police, what is the probability that the crime is violent? What is the probability that it is nonviolent?

c. Refer to part b. If a crime in progress is reported to the police, why is it more likely that it is a nonviolent crime? Wouldn't violent crimes be more likely to be reported? Can you explain these results?

4.69 A worker-operated machine produces a defective item with probability .01 if the worker follows the machine's operating instructions exactly, and with probability .03 if he does not. If the worker follows the instructions 90% of the time, what proportion of all items produced by the machine will be defective?

4.70 Suppose that, in a particular city, airport A handles 50% of all airline traffic, and airports B and C handle 30% and 20%, respectively. The detection rates for weapons at the three airports are .9, .5, and .4, respectively. If a passenger at one of the airports is found to be carrying a weapon through the boarding gate, what is the probability that the passenger is using airport A? Airport C?

4.71 A particular football team is known to run 30% of its plays to the left and 70% to the right. A linebacker on an opposing team notes that the right guard shifts his stance most of the time (80%) when plays go to the right and that he uses a balanced stance the remainder of the time. When plays go to the left, the guard takes a balanced stance 90% of the time and the shift stance the remaining 10%. On a particular play, the linebacker notes that the guard takes a balanced stance.

a. What is the probability that the play will go to the left?

b. What is the probability that the play will go to the right?

c. If you were the linebacker, which direction would you prepare to defend if you saw the balanced stance?

4.72 Many public schools are implementing a "no pass, no play" rule for athletes. Under this system, a student who fails a course is disqualified from participating in extracurricular activities during the next grading period. Suppose the probability that an athlete who has not previously been disqualified will be disqualified is .15 and the probability that an athlete who has been disqualified will be disqualified again in the next time period is .5. If 30% of the athletes have been disqualified before, what is the unconditional probability that an athlete will be disqualified during the next grading period?

4.73 Medical case histories indicate that different illnesses may produce identical symptoms. Suppose a particular set of symptoms, which we will denote as event H, occurs only when any one of three illnesses—A, B, or C—occurs. (For the sake of simplicity, we will assume that illnesses A, B, and C are mutually exclusive.) Studies show these probabilities of getting the three illnesses:

$$P(A) = .01$$
$$P(B) = .005$$
$$P(C) = .02$$

The probabilities of developing the symptoms H, given a specific illness, are

$$P(H|A) = .90$$
$$P(H|B) = .95$$
$$P(H|C) = .75$$

Assuming that an ill person shows the symptoms H, what is the probability that the person has illness A?

4.74 Suppose 5% of all people filing the long income tax form seek deductions that they know are illegal, and an additional 2% incorrectly list deductions because they are unfamiliar with income tax regulations. Of the 5% who are guilty of cheating, 80% will deny knowledge of the error if confronted by an investigator. If the filer of the long form is confronted with an unwarranted deduction and he or she denies the knowledge of the error, what is the probability that he or she is guilty?

4.75 Suppose that a certain disease is present in 10% of the population, and that there is a screening test designed to detect this disease if present. The test does not always work perfectly. Sometimes the test is negative when the disease is present, and sometimes it is positive when the disease is absent. The table below shows the proportion of times that the test produces various results:

	Test is Positive (P)	Test is Negative (N)
Disease present (D)	.08	.02
Disease absent (D^c)	.05	.85

a. Find the following probabilities from the table: $P(D)$, $P(D^c)$, $P(N|D^c)$, $P(N|D)$.

b. Use Bayes' Rule and the results of part a to find $P(D|N)$.

c. Use the definition of conditional probability to find $P(D|N)$. (Your answer should be the same as the answer to part b.)

d. Find the probability of a false positive, that the test is positive, given that the person is disease-free.

e. Find the probability of a false negative, that the test is negative, given that the person has the disease.

f. Are either of the probabilities in parts d or e large enough that you would be concerned about the reliability of this screening method? Explain.

4.8 Discrete Random Variables and Their Probability Distributions

In Chapter 1, *variables* were defined as characteristics that change or vary over time and/or for different individuals or objects under consideration. *Quantitative variables* generate numerical data, whereas *qualitative variables* generate categorical data. However, even qualitative variables can generate numerical data if the categories are numerically coded to form a scale. For example, if you toss a single coin, the qualitative outcome could be recorded as "0" if a head and "1" if a tail.

Random Variables

A numerically valued variable x will vary or change depending on the particular outcome of the experiment being measured. For example, suppose you toss a die and measure x, the number observed on the upper face. The variable x can take on any of six values—1, 2, 3, 4, 5, 6—depending on the *random* outcome of the experiment. For this reason, we refer to the variable x as a **random variable.**

Definition | A variable x is a **random variable** if the value that it assumes, corresponding to the outcome of an experiment, is a chance or random event.

You can think of many examples of random variables:

- x = Number of defects on a *randomly selected* piece of furniture
- x = SAT score for a *randomly selected* college applicant
- x = Number of telephone calls received by a crisis intervention hotline during a *randomly selected* time period

As in Chapter 1, quantitative random variables are classified as either *discrete* or *continuous*, according to the values that x can assume. It is important to distinguish between discrete and continuous random variables because different techniques are used to describe their distributions. We focus on discrete random variables in the remainder of this chapter; continuous random variables are the subject of Chapter 6.

Probability Distributions

In Chapters 1 and 2, you learned how to construct the *relative frequency distribution* for a set of numerical measurements on a variable x. The distribution gave this information about x:

- What values of x occurred
- How often each value of x occurred

You also learned how to use the mean and standard deviation to measure the center and variability of this data set.

In this chapter, we defined *probability* as the limiting value of the relative frequency as the experiment is repeated over and over again. Now we define the **probability distribution** for a random variable x as the *relative frequency distribution* constructed for the entire population of measurements.

Definition The **probability distribution** for a discrete random variable is a formula, table, or graph that gives the possible values of x, and the probability $p(x)$ associated with each value of x.

The values of x represent mutually exclusive numerical events. Summing $p(x)$ over all values of x is equivalent to adding the probabilities of all simple events and therefore equals 1.

> **Requirements for a Discrete Probability Distribution**
> - $0 \le p(x) \le 1$
> - $\Sigma \, p(x) = 1$

EXAMPLE 4.25 Toss two fair coins and let x equal the number of heads observed. Find the probability distribution for x.

Solution The simple events for this experiment with their respective probabilities are listed in Table 4.7. Since $E_1 = $ HH results in two heads, this simple event results in the value

TABLE 4.7
Simple events and probabilities in tossing two coins

Simple Event	Coin 1	Coin 2	$P(E_i)$	x
E_1	H	H	1/4	2
E_2	H	T	1/4	1
E_3	T	H	1/4	1
E_4	T	T	1/4	0

$x = 2$. Similarly, the value $x = 1$ is assigned to E_2, and so on. For each value of x, you can calculate $p(x)$ by adding the probabilities of the simple events in that event. For example, when $x = 0$,

$$p(0) = P(E_4) = \frac{1}{4}$$

and when $x = 1$,

$$p(1) = P(E_2) + P(E_3) = \frac{1}{2}$$

The values of x and their respective probabilities, $p(x)$, are listed in Table 4.8. Notice that the probabilities add to 1.

TABLE 4.8		Simple Events	
Probability	x	in x	$p(x)$
distribution for x	0	E_4	1/4
(x = number of	1	E_2, E_3	1/2
heads)	2	E_1	1/4

$$\Sigma\, p(x) = 1$$

The probability distribution in Table 4.8 can be graphed using the methods of Section 1.5 to form the **probability histogram** in Figure 4.16.[†] The three values of the random variable x are located on the horizontal axis, and the probabilities $p(x)$ are located on the vertical axis (replacing the relative frequencies used in Chapter 1). Since the width of each bar is 1, the area under the bar is the probability of observing the particular value of x and the total area equals 1.

FIGURE 4.16
Probability
histogram for
Example 4.25

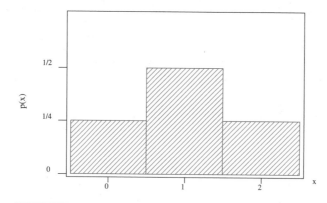

DO IT YOURSELF!

There are two Java applets that will allow you to approximate discrete probability distributions using *simulation methods*. That is, even though the probabilities ($p(x)$ can only be found as the long-run relative frequencies when the experiment is repeated an *infinite* number of times, we can get close to these probabilities if we repeat the experiment a *large* number of times. The applets called **Flipping Fair Coins** and **Flipping Weighted Coins** are two such simulations. The fastest way to generate the approximate probability distribution for x, the number of heads in n tosses of the coin is to repeat the experiment "100 at a Time," using the `100 at a Time` button at the bottom of the applet. The probability distribution will build up rather quickly. You can approximate the values of $p(x)$ and compare to the actual values calculated using probability rules. We will use these applets for the *Do It Yourself Exercises* at the end of the chapter.

[†]The probability distribution in Table 4.8 can also be presented using a formula, which is given in Section 5.2.

FIGURE 4.17 **Flipping Fair Coins** applet

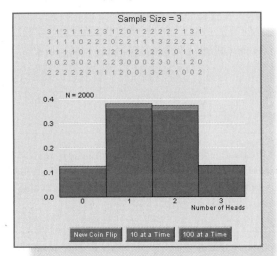

FIGURE 4.18 **Flipping Weighted Coins** applet

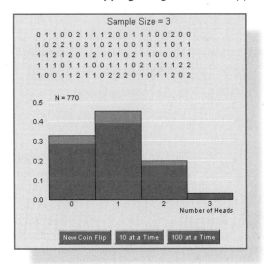

The Mean and Standard Deviation for a Discrete Random Variable

The probability distribution for a discrete random variable looks very similar to the relative frequency distribution discussed in Chapter 1. The difference is that the relative frequency distribution describes a *sample* of n measurements, whereas the probability distribution is constructed as a model for the *entire population* of measurements. Just as the mean $\bar{x}$ and the standard deviation s measured the center and spread of the sample data, you can calculate similar measures to describe the center and spread of the population.

The population mean, which measures the average value of x in the population, is also called the **expected value** of the random variable x. It is the value that you would *expect* to observe on *average* if the experiment is repeated over and over again. The formula for calculating the population mean is easier to understand by example. Toss those two fair coins again, and let x be the number of heads observed. We constructed this probability distribution for x:

x	0	1	2
$p(x)$	1/4	1/2	1/4

Suppose the experiment is repeated a large number of times—say, $n = 4,000,000$ times. Intuitively, you would expect to observe approximately 1 million zeros, 2 million ones, and 1 million twos. Then the average value of x would equal

$$\frac{\text{Sum of measurements}}{n} = \frac{1,000,000(0) + 2,000,000(1) + 1,000,000(2)}{4,000,000}$$

$$= \left(\frac{1}{4}\right)(0) + \left(\frac{1}{2}\right)(1) + \left(\frac{1}{4}\right)(2)$$

Note that the first term in this sum is $(0)p(0)$, the second is equal to $(1)p(1)$, and the third is $(2)p(2)$. The average value of x, then, is

$$\Sigma xp(x) = 0 + \frac{1}{2} + \frac{2}{4} = 1$$

This result provides some intuitive justification for the definition of the expected value of a discrete random variable x.

Definition

Let x be a discrete random variable with probability distribution $p(x)$. The mean or **expected value of x** is given as

$$\mu = E(x) = \Sigma\, xp(x)$$

where the elements are summed over all values of the random variable x.

We could use a similar argument to justify the formulas for the **population variance** σ^2 and the **population standard deviation** σ. These numerical measures describe the spread or variability of the random variable using the "average" or "expected value" of the squared deviations of the x-values from their mean μ.

Definition

Let x be a discrete random variable with probability distribution $p(x)$ and mean μ. The **variance of x** is

$$\sigma^2 = E[(x - \mu)^2] = \Sigma(x - \mu)^2 p(x)$$

where the summation is over all values of the random variable x.[†]

Definition

The **standard deviation σ of a random variable x** is equal to the square root of its variance.

EXAMPLE 4.26

An electronics store sells a particular model of computer notebook. There are only four notebooks in stock, and the manager wonders what today's demand for this particular model will be. She learns from the marketing department that the probability distribution for x, the daily demand for the laptop, is as shown in the table. Find the mean, variance, and standard deviation of x. Is it likely that five or more customers will want to buy a laptop today?

x	0	1	2	3	4	5
$p(x)$	.10	.40	.20	.15	.10	.05

Solution

Table 4.9 shows the values of x and $p(x)$, along with the individual terms used in the formulas for μ and σ^2. The sum of the values in the third column is

$$\mu = \Sigma\, xp(x) = (0)(.10) + (1)(.40) + \cdots + (5)(.05) = 1.90$$

while the sum of the values in the fifth column is

$$\sigma^2 = \Sigma(x - \mu)^2 p(x) = (0 - 1.9)^2(.10) + (1 - 1.9)^2(.40) + \cdots + (5 - 1.9)^2(.05) = 1.79$$

and

$$\sigma = \sqrt{\sigma^2} = \sqrt{1.79} = 1.34$$

[†]It can be shown (proof omitted) that

$$\sigma^2 = \Sigma(x - \mu)^2 p(x) = \Sigma\, x^2 p(x) - \mu^2$$

This result is analogous to the computing formula for the sum of squares of deviations given in Chapter 2.

TABLE 4.9	x	$p(x)$	$xp(x)$	$(x - \mu)^2$	$(x - \mu)^2 p(x)$
Calculations for	0	.10	.00	3.61	.361
Example 4.26	1	.40	.40	.81	.324
	2	.20	.40	.01	.002
	3	.15	.45	1.21	.1815
	4	.10	.40	4.41	.441
	5	.05	.25	9.61	.4805
	Totals	**1.00**	$\mu = 1.90$		$\sigma^2 = 1.79$

The graph of the probability distribution is shown in Figure 4.19. Since the distribution is approximately mound-shaped, approximately 95% of all measurements should lie within *two* standard deviations of the mean—that is,

$$\mu \pm 2\sigma \Rightarrow 1.90 \pm 2(1.34) \qquad \text{or} \quad -.78 \text{ to } 4.58$$

Since $x = 5$ lies outside this interval, you can say it is unlikely that five or more customers will want to buy a laptop today. In fact, $P(x \geq 5)$ is exactly .05, or 1 time in 20.

FIGURE 4.19
Probability
distribution for
Example 4.26

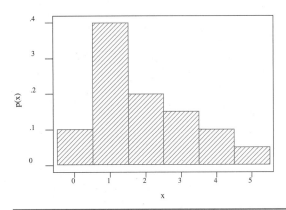

EXAMPLE 4.27   In a lottery conducted to benefit the local fire company, 8000 tickets are to be sold at $5 each. The prize is a $12,000 automobile. If you purchase two tickets, what is your expected gain?

Solution   Your gain x may take one of two values. You will either lose $10 (i.e., your "gain" will be $-$10) or win $11,990, with probabilities 7998/8000 and 2/8000, respectively. The probability distribution for the gain x is shown in the table:

x	$p(x)$
$-$10	7998/8000
$11,990	2/8000

The expected gain will be

$$\mu = E(x) = \Sigma \, xp(x)$$
$$= (-\$10)\left(\frac{7998}{8000}\right) + (\$11,900)\left(\frac{2}{8000}\right) = -\$7$$

Recall that the expected value of x is the average of the theoretical population that would result if the lottery were repeated an infinitely large number of times. If this were done, your average or expected gain per lottery ticket would be a loss of $7.

EXAMPLE 4.28   Determine the yearly premium for a $1000 insurance policy covering an event that, over a long period of time, has occurred at the rate of 2 times in 100. Let x equal the yearly financial gain to the insurance company resulting from the sale of the policy, and let C equal the unknown yearly premium. Calculate the value of C such that the expected gain $E(x)$ will equal zero. Then C is the premium required to break even. To this, the company would add administrative costs and profit.

Solution   The first step in the solution is to determine the values that the gain x may take and then to determine $p(x)$. If the event does not occur during the year, the insurance company will gain the premium of $x = C$ dollars. If the event does occur, the gain will be negative; that is, the company will lose $1000 less the premium of C dollars already collected. Then $x = -(1000 - C)$ dollars. The probabilities associated with these two values of x are 98/100 and 2/100, respectively. The probability distribution for the gain is shown in the table:

x = Gain	$p(x)$
C	98/100
$-(1000 - C)$	2/100

Since the company wants the insurance premium C such that, in the long run (for many similar policies), the mean gain will equal zero, you can set the expected value of x equal to zero and solve for C. Then

$$\mu = E(x) = \Sigma x p(x)$$
$$= C\left(\frac{98}{100}\right) + [-(1000 - C)]\left(\frac{2}{100}\right) = 0$$

or

$$\frac{98}{100}C + \frac{2}{100}C - 20 = 0$$

Solving this equation for C, you obtain $C = \$20$. Therefore, if the insurance company charged a yearly premium of $20, the average gain calculated for a large number of similar policies would equal zero. The actual premium would equal $20 plus administrative costs and profit.

The method for calculating the expected value of x for a continuous random variable is similar to what you have done, but in practice it involves the use of calculus. Nevertheless, the basic results concerning expectations are the same for continuous and discrete random variables. For example, regardless of whether x is continuous or discrete, $\mu = E(x)$ and $\sigma^2 = E[(x - \mu)^2]$.

Exercises   Basic Techniques

4.76   Identify the following as discrete or continuous random variables:

a. Total number of points scored in a football game

b. Shelf life of a particular drug

c. Height of the ocean's tide at a given location

d. Length of a 2-year-old black bass

e. Number of aircraft near-collisions in a year

4.77 Identify the following as discrete or continuous random variables:

a. Increase in length of life attained by a cancer patient as a result of surgery

b. Tensile breaking strength (in pounds per square inch) of 1-inch-diameter steel cable

c. Number of deer killed per year in a state wildlife preserve

d. Number of overdue accounts in a department store at a particular time

e. Your blood pressure

4.78 A random variable x has this probability distribution:

x	0	1	2	3	4	5
$p(x)$	.1	.3	.4	.1	?	.05

a. Find $p(4)$.

b. Construct a probability histogram to describe $p(x)$.

c. Find μ, σ^2, and σ.

d. Locate the interval $\mu \pm 2\sigma$ on the x-axis of the histogram. What is the probability that x will fall into this interval?

e. If you were to select a very large number of values of x from the population, would most fall into the interval $\mu \pm 2\sigma$? Explain.

4.79 A random variable x can assume five values: 0, 1, 2, 3, 4. A portion of the probability distribution is shown here:

x	0	1	2	3	4
$p(x)$	.1	.3	.3	?	.1

a. Find $p(3)$.

b. Construct a probability histogram for $p(x)$.

c. Calculate the population mean, variance, and standard deviation.

d. What is the probability that x is greater than 2?

e. What is the probability that x is 3 or less?

4.80 Let x equal the number observed on the throw of a single balanced die.

a. Find and graph the probability distribution for x.

b. What is the average or expected value of x?

c. What is the standard deviation of x?

d. Locate the interval $\mu \pm 2\sigma$ on the x-axis of the graph in part a. What proportion of all the measurements would fall into this range?

4.81 Let x represent the number of times a customer visits a grocery store in a 1-week period. Assume this is the probability distribution of x:

x	0	1	2	3
$p(x)$	.1	.4	.4	.1

Find the expected value of x, the average number of times a customer visits the store.

Applications

4.82 Who is the king of late night TV? An Internet survey estimates that, when given a choice between David Letterman and Jay Leno, 52% of the population prefers to watch Jay Leno. Suppose that you randomly select three late night TV watchers and ask them which of the two talk show hosts they prefer.

a. Find the probability distribution for x, the number of people in the sample of three who would prefer Jay Leno.

b. Construct the probability histogram for $p(x,)$

c. What is the probability that exactly one of the three would prefer Jay Leno?

d. What are the population mean and standard deviation for the random variable x?

4.83 A key ring contains four office keys that are identical in appearance, but only one will open your office door. Suppose you randomly select one key and try it. If it does not fit, you randomly select one of the three remaining keys. If it does not fit, you randomly select one of the last two. Each different sequence that could occur in selecting the keys represents one of a set of equiprobable simple events.

a. List the simple events in S and assign probabilities to the simple events.

b. Let x equal the number of keys that you try before you find the one that opens the door $(x = 1, 2, 3, 4)$. Then assign the appropriate value of x to each simple event.

c. Calculate the values of $p(x)$ and display them in a table.

d. Construct a probability histogram for $p(x)$.

4.84 Exercise 4.10 described the game of roulette. Suppose you bet $5 on a single number—say, the number 18. The payoff on this type of bet is usually 35 to 1. What is your expected gain?

4.85 A company has five applicants for two positions: two women and three men. Suppose that the five applicants are equally qualified and that no preference is given for choosing either gender. Let x equal the number of women chosen to fill the two positions.

a. Find $p(x)$.

b. Construct a probability histogram for x.

4.86 A piece of electronic equipment contains six computer chips, two of which are defective. Three chips are selected at random, removed from the piece of equipment, and inspected. Let x equal the number of defectives observed, where $x = 0, 1,$ or 2. Find the probability distribution for x. Express the results graphically as a probability histogram.

4.87 Past experience has shown that, on the average, only 1 in 10 wells drilled hits oil. Let x be the number of drillings until the first success (oil is struck). Assume that the drillings represent independent events.

a. Find $p(1)$, $p(2)$, and $p(3)$.

b. Give a formula for $p(x)$.

c. Graph $p(x)$.

4.88 Two tennis professionals, A and B, are scheduled to play a match; the winner is the first player to win three sets in a total that cannot exceed five sets. The event that A wins any one set is independent of the event that A wins any other, and the probability that A wins any one set is equal to .6. Let x equal the total number of sets in the match; that is, $x = 3, 4,$ or 5. Find $p(x)$.

4.89 The probability that a tennis player A can win a set from tennis player B is one measure of the comparative abilities of the two players. In Exercise 4.88 you found the probability distribution for x, the number of sets required to play a best-of-five-sets match, given that the probability that A wins any one set—call this $P(A)$—is .6.

a. Find the expected number of sets required to complete the match for $P(A) = .6$.

b. Find the expected number of sets required to complete the match when the players are of equal ability—that is, $P(A) = .5$.

c. Find the expected number of sets required to complete the match when the players differ greatly in ability—that is, say, $P(A) = .9$.

4.90 One professional golfer plays best on short-distance holes. Experience has shown that the numbers *x* of shots required for 3-, 4-, and 5-par holes have the probability distributions shown in the table:

Par-3 Holes		Par-4 Holes		Par-5 Holes	
x	p(x)	x	p(x)	x	p(x)
2	.12	3	.14	4	.04
3	.80	4	.80	5	.80
4	.06	5	.04	6	.12
5	.02	6	.02	7	.04

What is the golfer's expected score on these holes?

a. A par-3 hole

b. A par-4 hole

c. A par-5 hole

4.91 You can insure a $50,000 diamond for its total value by paying a premium of *D* dollars. If the probability of theft in a given year is estimated to be .01, what premium should the insurance company charge if it wants the expected gain to equal $1000?

4.92 The maximum patent life for a new drug is 17 years. Subtracting the length of time required by the FDA for testing and approval of the drug provides the actual patent life of the drug—that is, the length of time that a company has to recover research and development costs and make a profit. Suppose the distribution of the lengths of patent life for new drugs is as shown here:

Years, x	3	4	5	6	7	8	9	10	11	12	13
p(x)	.03	.05	.07	.10	.14	.20	.18	.12	.07	.03	.01

a. Find the expected number of years of patent life for a new drug.

b. Find the standard deviation of *x*.

c. Find the probability that *x* falls into the interval $\mu \pm 2\sigma$.

4.93 Do you believe in heaven? In a survey conducted for *Time* magazine, 81% of the adult Americans surveyed expressed a belief in "heaven, where people live forever with God after they die."[5] Suppose you had conducted your own telephone survey at the same time. You randomly called people and asked them whether they believe in heaven. Assume that the percentage given in the *Time* survey can be taken to approximate the percentage of all adult Americans who believe in heaven.

a. Find the probability distribution for *x*, the number of calls until you find the first person who *does not* believe in heaven.

b. What problems might arise as you randomly call people and ask them to take part in your survey? How would this affect the reliability of the probabilities calculated in part a?

4.94 From experience, a shipping company knows that the cost of delivering a small package within 24 hours is $14.80. The company charges $15.50 for shipment but guarantees to refund the charge if delivery is not made within 24 hours. If the company fails to deliver only 2% of its packages within the 24-hour period, what is the expected gain per package?

4.95 A manufacturing representative is considering taking out an insurance policy to cover possible losses incurred by marketing a new product. If the product is a complete failure, the representative feels that a loss of $80,000 would be incurred; if it is only moderately successful, a loss of $25,000 would be incurred. Insurance actuaries have determined from market surveys and other available information that the probabilities that the product will be a failure or only moderately successful are .01 and .05, respectively. Assuming that the manufacturing representative is willing to ignore all other possible losses, what premium should the insurance company charge for a policy in order to break even?

Key Concepts and Formulas

I. **Experiments and the Sample Space**

1. Experiments, events, mutually exclusive events, simple events
2. The sample space
3. Venn diagrams, tree diagrams, probability tables

II. **Probabilities**

1. Relative frequency definition of probability
2. Properties of probabilities
   a. Each probability lies between 0 and 1.
   b. Sum of all simple-event probabilities equals 1.
3. $P(A)$, the sum of the probabilities for all simple events in A

III. **Counting Rules**

1. *mn* Rule; extended *mn* Rule
2. Permutations: $P_r^n = \dfrac{n!}{(n-r)!}$
3. Combinations: $C_r^n = \dfrac{n!}{r!(n-r)!}$

IV. **Event Relations**

1. Unions and intersections
2. Events
   a. Disjoint or mutually exclusive: $P(A \cap B) = 0$
   b. Complementary: $P(A) = 1 - P(A^c)$
3. Conditional probability: $P(A|B) = \dfrac{P(A \cap B)}{P(B)}$
4. Independent and dependent events
5. Additive Rule of Probability: $P(A \cup B) = P(A) + P(B) - P(A \cap B)$
6. Multiplicative Rule of Probability: $P(A \cap B) = P(A)P(B|A)$
7. Law of Total Probability
8. Bayes' Rule

V. **Discrete Random Variables and Probability Distributions**

1. Random variables, discrete and continuous
2. Properties of probability distributions
   a. $0 \leq p(x) \leq 1$
   b. $\Sigma p(x) = 1$
3. Mean or expected value of a discrete random variable: $\mu = \Sigma x p(x)$
4. Variance and standard deviation of a discrete random variable: $\sigma^2 = \Sigma (x - \mu)^2 p(x)$ and $\sigma = \sqrt{\sigma^2}$

Discrete Probability Distributions

Although *MINITAB* cannot help you solve the types of general probability problems presented in this chapter, it is useful for graphing the probability distribution $p(x)$ for a general discrete random variable x when the probabilities are known, and for calculating the mean, variance, and standard deviation of the random variable x. In Chapters 5 and 6, we will use *MINITAB* to calculate exact probabilities for three special cases: the binomial, the Poisson, and the normal random variables.

MINITAB

Suppose you have this general probability distribution:

x	0	1	3	5
p(x)	.25	.35	.25	.15

Enter the values of x and $p(x)$ into columns C1 and C2 of a new *MINITAB* worksheet. You can now use the **Calc → Calculator** command to calculate μ, σ^2, and σ and to store the results in columns C3–C5 (named "Mean," "Variance," and "Std Dev") of the worksheet. Use the same approach for the three parameters. In the Calculator dialog box, **select** "Mean" as the column in which to store μ. In the Expression box, use the Functions box, the calculator keys, and the variables list on the left to highlight, **select,** and create the expression for the mean (see Figure 4.20):

SUM('x'*'p(x)')

FIGURE 4.20

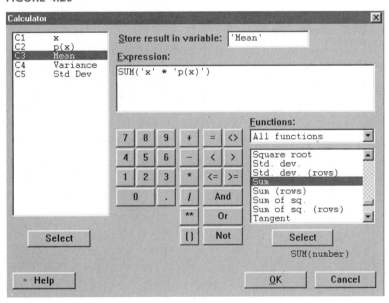

MINITAB will multiply each row element in C1 times the corresponding row element in C2, sum the resulting products, and store the result in C3! You can check the result by hand if you like. The formulas for the variance and standard deviation are selected in a similar way:

Variance: SUM(('x' − 'Mean')**2*'p(x)')
Std Dev: Sqrt('Variance')

To see the tabular form of the probability distribution and the three parameters, use **Manip → Display Data** and select all five columns. Click **OK** and the results will be displayed in the Session window, as shown in Figure 4.21.

The probability histogram can be plotted using the *MINITAB* command **Graph → Plot.** In the Plot dialog box, select 'p(x)' for Y and 'x' for X. To display the discrete probability bars, select **Project** in the Data display options (see Figure 4.22) and use **Edit Attributes** to change the **Line Size** to 50 rather than 1 (which would project a single straight line at each point). Finally, click on **Frame → Min and Max** and

MINITAB

select $-.5$ and 5.5 for the X Scale Extremes. The probability histogram is shown in Figure 4.23.

Locate the mean on the graph. Is it at the center of the distribution? If you mark off two standard deviations on either side of the mean, do most of the possible values of x fall into this interval?

FIGURE 4.21

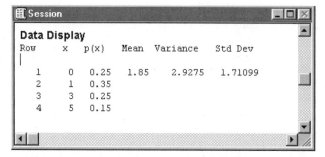

FIGURE 4.22

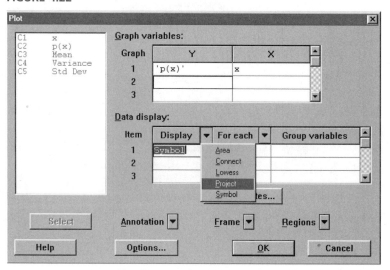

FIGURE 4.23

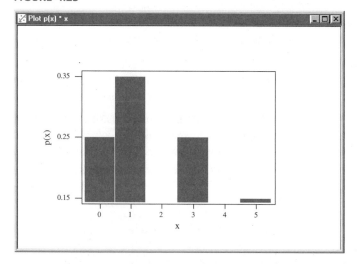

Supplementary Exercises

Starred (*) exercises are optional.

4.96   A slot machine has three slots; each will show a cherry, a lemon, a star, or a bar when spun. The player wins if all three slots show the same three items. If each of the four items is equally likely to appear on a given spin, what is your probability of winning?

4.97   "Whistle blowers" is the name given to employees who report corporate fraud, theft, and other unethical and perhaps criminal activities by fellow employees or by their employer. Although there is legal protection for whistle blowers, it has been reported that approximately 23% of those who reported fraud suffered reprisals such as demotion or poor performance ratings. Suppose the probability that an employee will fail to report a case of fraud is .69. Find the probability that a worker who observes a case of fraud will report it and will subsequently suffer some form of reprisal.

4.98   Two cold tablets are accidentally placed in a box containing two aspirin tablets. The four tablets are identical in appearance. One tablet is selected at random from the box and is swallowed by the first patient. A tablet is then selected at random from the three remaining tablets and is swallowed by the second patient. Define the following events as specific collections of simple events:

a. The sample space S

b. The event A that the first patient obtained a cold tablet

c. The event B that exactly one of the two patients obtained a cold tablet

d. The event C that neither patient obtained a cold tablet

4.99   Refer to Exercise 4.98. By summing the probabilities of simple events, find $P(A)$, $P(B)$, $P(A \cap B)$, $P(A \cup B)$, $P(C)$, $P(A \cap C)$, and $P(A \cup C)$.

4.100   A retailer sells two styles of high-priced compact disc players that experience indicates are in equal demand. (Fifty percent of all potential customers prefer style 1, and 50% favor style 2.) If the retailer stocks four of each, what is the probability that the first four customers seeking a CD player all purchase the same style?

4.101   A boxcar contains seven complex electronic systems. Unknown to the purchaser, three are defective. Two of the seven are selected for thorough testing and are then classified as defective or nondefective. What is the probability that no defectives are found?

4.102   A heavy-equipment salesman can contact either one or two customers per day with probability 1/3 and 2/3, respectively. Each contact will result in either no sale or a $50,000 sale with probability 9/10 and 1/10, respectively. What is the expected value of his daily sales?

4.103   A county containing a large number of rural homes is thought to have 60% of those homes insured against fire. Four rural homeowners are chosen at random from the entire population, and x are found to be insured against fire. Find the probability distribution for x. What is the probability that at least three of the four will be insured?

4.104   A fire-detection device uses three temperature-sensitive cells acting independently of one another in such a manner that any one or more can activate the alarm. Each cell has a probability $p = .8$ of activating the alarm when the temperature reaches 100°F or higher. Let x equal the number of cells activating the alarm when the temperature reaches 100°F.

a. Find the probability distribution of x.

b. Find the probability that the alarm will function when the temperature reaches 100°F.

c. Find the expected value and the variance for the random variable x.

4.105   Is your chance of getting a cold influenced by the number of social contacts you have? A study by Sheldon Cohen, a psychology professor at Carnegie Mellon University, seems to show that the more social relationships you have, the *less susceptible* you are to colds. A group of 276 healthy men and women were grouped according to their number of relationships (such as parent, friend, church member, neighbor). They were then exposed to a virus that causes colds. An adaptation of the results is shown in the table[6]:

	Number of Relationships		
	Three or Fewer	Four or Five	Six or More
Cold	49	43	34
No Cold	31	57	62
Total	80	100	96

a. If one person is selected at random from the 276 people in the study, what is the probability that the person got a cold?

b. If two people are randomly selected, what is the probability that one has four or five relationships and the other has six or more relationships?

c. If a single person is randomly selected and has a cold, what is the probability that he or she has three or fewer relationships?

4.106 Refer to the experiment conducted by Gregor Mendel in Exercise 4.62. Suppose you are interested in following two independent traits in snap peas—seed texture (S = smooth, s = wrinkled) and seed color (Y = yellow, y = green)—in a second-generation cross of heterozygous parents. Remember that the capital letter represents the dominant trait. Complete the table with the gene pairs for both traits. All possible pairings are equally likely.

	Seed Color			
Seed Texture	yy	yY	Yy	YY
ss	(ss yy)	(ss yY)		
sS				
Ss				
SS				

a. What proportion of the offspring from this cross will have smooth yellow peas?

b. What proportion of the offspring will have smooth green peas?

c. What proportion of the offspring will have wrinkled yellow peas?

d. What proportion of the offspring will have wrinkled green peas?

e. Given that an offspring has smooth yellow peas, what is the probability that this offspring carries one s allele? One s allele *and* one y allele?

4.107 An investor has the option of investing in three of five recommended stocks. Unknown to her, only two will show a substantial profit within the next 5 years. If she selects the three stocks at random (giving every combination of three stocks an equal chance of selection), what is the probability that she selects the two profitable stocks? What is the probability that she selects only one of the two profitable stocks?

4.108 Four union men, two from a minority group, are assigned to four distinctly different one-man jobs, which can be ranked in order of desirability.

a. Define the experiment.

b. List the simple events in *S*.

c. If the assignment to the jobs is unbiased—that is, if any one ordering of assignments is as probable as any other—what is the probability that the two men from the minority group are assigned to the least desirable jobs?

4.109 A salesperson figures that the probability of her consummating a sale during the first contact with a client is .4 but improves to .55 on the second contact if the client did not buy during the first contact. Suppose this salesperson makes one and only one callback to any client. If she contacts a client, calculate the probabilities for these events:

a. The client will buy.

b. The client will not buy.

4.110   A man takes either a bus or the subway to work with probabilities .3 and .7, respectively. When he takes the bus, he is late 30% of the days. When he takes the subway, he is late 20% of the days. If the man is late for work on a particular day, what is the probability that he took the bus?

 4.111   The failure rate for a guided missile control system is 1 in 1000. Suppose that a duplicate, but completely independent, control system is installed in each missile so that, if the first fails, the second can take over. The reliability of a missile is the probability that it does not fail. What is the reliability of the modified missile?

4.112   A rental truck agency services its vehicles on a regular basis, routinely checking for mechanical problems. Suppose that the agency has six moving vans, two of which need to have new brakes. During a routine check, the vans are tested one at a time.

a. What is the probability that the last van with brake problems is the fourth van tested?

b. What is the probability that no more than four vans need to be tested before both brake problems are detected?

c. Given that one van with bad brakes is detected in the first two tests, what is the probability that the remaining van is found on the third or fourth test?

4.113   Probability played a role in the rigging of the April 24, 1980, Pennsylvania state lottery. To determine each digit of the three-digit winning number, each of the numbers 0, 1, 2, . . . , 9 is written on a Ping-Pong ball, the ten balls are blown into a compartment, and the number selected for the digit is the one on the ball that floats to the top of the machine. To alter the odds, the conspirators injected a liquid into all balls used in the game except those numbered 4 and 6, making it almost certain that the lighter balls would be selected and determine the digits in the winning number. They then proceeded to buy lottery tickets bearing the potential winning numbers. How many potential winning numbers were there (666 was the eventual winner)?

*4.114   Refer to Exercise 4.113. Hours after the rigging of the Pennsylvania state lottery was announced on September 19, 1980, Connecticut state lottery officials were stunned to learn that *their* winning number for the day was 666.

a. All evidence indicates that the Connecticut selection of 666 was pure chance. What is the probability that a 666 would be drawn in Connecticut, given that a 666 had been selected in the April 24, 1980, Pennsylvania lottery?

b. What is the probability of drawing a 666 in the April 24, 1980, Pennsylvania lottery (remember, this drawing was rigged) *and* a 666 on the September 19, 1980, Connecticut lottery?

*4.115   In a study of 810 women collegiate rugby players who have a history of knee injuries, the two common knee injuries investigated were medial cruciate ligament (MCL) sprains and anterior cruciate ligament (ACL) tears.[7] For backfield players, it was found that 39% had MCL sprains and 61% had ACL tears. For forwards, it was found that 33% had MCL sprains and 67% had ACL tears. Since a rugby team consists of eight forwards and seven backs, you can assume that 47% of the players with knee injuries are backs and 53% are forwards.

a. Find the unconditional probability that a rugby player selected at random from this group of players has experienced an MCL sprain.

b. Given that you have selected a player who has an MCL sprain, what is the probability that the player is a forward?

c. Given that you have selected a player who has an ACL tear, what is the probability that the player is a back?

4.116   Magnetic resonance imaging (MRI) is an accepted noninvasive test to evaluate changes in the cartilage in joints. In a study to compare the results of MRI evaluation with arthroscopic surgical evaluation of cartilage tears at two sites in the knees of 35 patients, the following classifications of the $2 \times 35 = 70$ examinations resulted.[8] Actual tears were confirmed by arthroscopic surgical examination.

	Tears	No Tears	Total
MRI Positive	27	0	27
MRI Negative	4	39	43
Total	31	39	70

a. What is the probability that a site selected at random has a tear and has been identified as a tear by MRI?

b. What is the probability that a site selected at random has no tear and has been identified as having a tear?

c. What is the probability that a site selected at random has a tear and has not been identified by MRI?

d. What is the probability of a positive MRI, given that there is a tear?

e. What is the probability of a false negative—that is, a negative MRI, given that there is a tear?

4.117 Two men each toss a coin. They obtain a "match" if either both coins are heads or both are tails. Suppose the tossing is repeated three times.

a. What is the probability of three matches?

b. What is the probability that all six tosses (three for each man) result in tails?

c. Coin tossing provides a model for many practical experiments. Suppose that the coin tosses represent the answers given by two students for three specific true–false questions on an examination. If the two students gave three matches for answers, would the low probability found in part a suggest collusion?

4.118 Experience has shown that, 50% of the time, a particular union–management contract negotiation led to a contract settlement within a 2-week period, 60% of the time the union strike fund was adequate to support a strike, and 30% of the time both conditions were satisfied. What is the probability of a contract settlement given that the union strike fund is adequate to support a strike? Is settlement of a contract within a 2-week period dependent on whether the union strike fund is adequate to support a strike?

4.119 Suppose the probability of remaining with a particular company 10 years or longer is 1/6. A man and a woman start work at the company on the same day.

a. What is the probability that the man will work there less than 10 years?

b. What is the probability that both the man and the woman will work there less than 10 years? (Assume they are unrelated and their lengths of service are independent of each other.)

c. What is the probability that one or the other or both will work 10 years or longer?

4.120 Accident records collected by an automobile insurance company give the following information: The probability that an insured driver has an automobile accident is .15; if an accident has occurred, the damage to the vehicle amounts to 20% of its market value with probability .80, 60% of its market value with probability .12, and a total loss with probability .08. What premium should the company charge on a $22,000 car so that the expected gain by the company is zero?

4.121 Suppose that at a particular supermarket the probability of waiting 5 minutes or longer for checkout at the cashier's counter is .2. On a given day, a man and his wife decide to shop individually at the market, each checking out at different cashier counters. They both reach cashier counters at the same time.

a. What is the probability that the man will wait less than 5 minutes for checkout?

b. What is probability that both the man and his wife will be checked out in less than 5 minutes? (Assume that the checkout times for the two are independent events.)

c. What is the probability that one or the other or both will wait 5 minutes or longer?

4.122 A quality-control plan calls for accepting a large lot of crankshaft bearings if a sample of seven is drawn and none are defective. What is the probability of accepting the lot if none in the lot are defective? If 1/10 are defective? If 1/2 are defective?

4.123 Only 40% of all people in a community favor the development of a mass transit system. If four citizens are selected at random from the community, what is the probability that all four favor the mass transit system? That none favors the mass transit system?

4.124 A research physician compared the effectiveness of two blood pressure drugs A and B by administering the two drugs to each of four pairs of identical twins. Drug A was given to one member of a pair; drug B to the other. If, in fact, there is no difference in the effects of the drugs, what is the probability that the drop in the blood pressure reading for drug A exceeds the corresponding drop in the reading for drug B for all four pairs of twins? Suppose drug B created a greater drop in blood pressure than drug A for each of the four pairs of twins. Do you think this provides sufficient evidence to indicate that drug B is more effective in lowering blood pressure than drug A?

4.125 To reduce the cost of detecting a disease, blood tests are conducted on a pooled sample of blood collected from a group of n people. If no indication of the disease is present in the pooled blood sample (as is usually the case), none have the disease. If analysis of the pooled blood sample indicates that the disease is present, each individual must submit to a blood test. The individual tests are conducted in sequence. If, among a group of five people, one person has the disease, what is the probability that six blood tests (including the pooled test) are required to detect the single diseased person? If two people have the disease, what is the probability that six tests are required to locate both diseased people?

4.126 How many times should a coin be tossed to obtain a probability equal to or greater than .9 of observing at least one head?

4.127 The number of companies offering flexible work schedules has increased as companies try to help employees cope with the demands of home and work. One flextime schedule is to work four 10-hour shifts. However, a big obstacle to flextime schedules for workers paid hourly is state legislation on overtime. A survey provided the following information for 220 firms located in two cities in California.

| | Flextime Schedule | | |
City	Available	Not Available	Total
A	39	75	114
B	25	81	106
Totals	64	156	220

A company is selected at random from this pool of 220 companies.

a. What is the probability that the company is located in city A?

b. What is the probability that the company is located in city B and offers flextime work schedules?

c. What is the probability that the company does not have flextime schedules?

d. What is the probability that the company is located in city B, given that the company has flextime schedules available?

Exercises DO IT YOURSELF!

4.128 Two fair dice are tossed. Use the **Tossing Dice** applet to answer the following questions.

a. What is the probability that the sum of the number of dots shown on the upper faces is equal to 7? To 11?

b. What is the probability that you roll "doubles"—that is, both dice have the same number on the upper face?

c. What is the probability that both dice show an odd number?

4.129 If you toss a pair of dice, the sum T of the number of dots appearing on the upper faces of the dice can assume the value of an integer in the interval $2 \leq T \leq 12$.

a. Use the **Tossing Dice** applet to find the probability distribution for *T*. Display this probability distribution in a table.

b. Construct a probability histogram for *p(T)*. How would you describe the shape of this distribution?

4.130   Access the **Flipping Fair Coins** applet. The experiment consists of tossing three fair coins and recording *x*, the number of heads.

a. Use the laws of probability to write down the simple events in this experiment.

b. Find the probability distribution for *x*. Display the distribution in a table and in a probability histogram.

c. Use the **Flipping Fair Coins** applet to simulate the probability distribution—that is, repeat the coin-tossing experiment a large number of times until the relative frequency histogram is very close to the actual probability distribution. Start by performing the experiment once (click [New Coin Flip]) to see what is happening. Then speed up the process by clicking [100 at a Time]. Generate at least 2000 values of *x*. Sketch the histogram that you have generated.

d. Compare the histograms in parts b and c. Does the simulation confirm your answer from part b?

4.131   Refer to Exercise 4.130.

a. If you were to toss only one coin, what would the probability distribution for *x* look like?

b. Perform a simulation using the **Flipping Fair Coins** applet with *n* = 1, and compare your results with part a.

4.132   Refer to Exercise 4.130. Access the **Flipping Weighted Coins** applet. The experiment consists of tossing three coins that are *not fair*, and recording *x*, the number of heads.

a. Perform a simulation of the experiment using the **Flipping Weighted Coins** applet. Is the distribution symmetric or skewed? Which is more likely, heads or tails?

b. Suppose that we do not know the probability of getting a head, *P*(H). Write a formula for calculating the probability of no heads in three tosses.

c. Use the approximate probability *P*(*x* = 0) from your simulation and the results of part b to approximate the value of *P*(T). What is the probability of getting a head?

Case Study   Probability and Decision Making in the Congo

In his exciting novel *Congo*, Michael Crichton describes a search by Earth Resources Technology Service (ERTS), a geological survey company, for deposits of boron-coated blue diamonds, diamonds that ERTS believes to be the key to a new generation of optical computers.[9] In the novel, ERTS is racing against an international consortium to find the Lost City of Zinj, a city that thrived on diamond mining and existed several thousand years ago (according to African fable), deep in the rain forests of eastern Zaire.

After the mysterious destruction of its first expedition, ERTS launches a second expedition under the leadership of Karen Ross, a 24-year-old computer genius who is accompanied by Professor Peter Elliot, an anthropologist; Amy, a talking gorilla; and the famed mercenary and expedition leader, "Captain" Charles Munro. Ross's efforts to find the city are blocked by the consortium's offensive actions, by the deadly rain forest, and by hordes of "talking" killer gorillas whose perceived mission is to defend the diamond mines. Ross overcomes these obstacles by using space-age computers to evaluate the probabilities of success for all possible circumstances and all possible actions that the expedition might take. At each stage of the expedition, she is able to quickly evaluate the chances of success.

At one stage in the expedition, Ross is informed by her Houston headquarters that their computers estimate that she is 18 hours and 20 minutes behind the competing Euro-Japanese team, instead of 40 hours ahead. She changes plans and decides to have the 12 members of her team—Ross, Elliot, Munro, Amy, and eight native porters—parachute into a volcanic region near the estimated location of Zinj. As Crichton relates, "Ross had double-checked outcome probabilities from the Houston computer, and the results were unequivocal. The probability of a successful jump was .7980, meaning that there was approximately one chance in five that someone would be badly hurt. However, given a successful jump, the probability of expedition success was .9943, making it virtually certain that they would beat the consortium to the site."

Keeping in mind that this is an excerpt from a novel, let us examine the probability, .7980, of a successful jump. If you were one of the 12-member team, what is the probability that you would successfully complete your jump? In other words, if the probability of a successful jump by all 12 team members is .7980, what is the probability that a single member could successfully complete the jump?

Data Sources

1. C. Salmon, J.-P. Cartron, and P. Rouger, *The Human Blood Groups* (New York: Masson Publishing, 1984).

2. Thomas Hargrove and G.H. Stempel III, "Poll's Message to Pentagon: Denials Will Not Work," *The Press-Enterprise* (Riverside, CA), 5 July 1997, p. A-13.

3. Bruce E. Morgan, and Michael A. Oberlander, "An Examination of Injuries in Major League Soccer," *The American Journal of Sports Medicine,* 29(4), 2001, pp. 426–429.

4. Data adapted from "Demo Memo," *American Demographics,* May 1997, p. 32.

5. David Van Biema, "Does Heaven Exist?" *Time,* 24 March 1997, p. 73.

6. Adapted from David L. Wheeler, "More Social Roles Means Fewer Colds," *Chronicle of Higher Education* XLIII, no. 44 (July 11, 1997):A13.

7. Andrew S. Levy, M.J. Wetzler, M. Lewars, and W. Laughlin, "Knee Injuries in Women Collegiate Rugby Players," *The American Journal of Sports Medicine* 25, no. 3 (1997):360.

8. P.D. Frankin, R.A. Lemon, and H.S. Barden, "Accuracy of Imaging the Menisci on an In-Office, Dedicated, Magnetic Resonance Imaging Extremity System," *The American Journal of Sports Medicine* 25, no. 3 (1997):382.

9. Michael Crichton, *Congo* (New York: Knopf, 1980).

5

Several Useful Discrete Distributions

Case Study

Is the Pilgrim I nuclear reactor responsible for an increase in cancer cases in the surrounding area? A political controversy was set off when the Massachusetts Department of Public Health found an unusually large number of cases in a 4-mile-wide coastal strip just north of the nuclear reactor in Plymouth, Massachusetts. The case study at the end of this chapter examines how this question can be answered using one of the discrete probability distributions presented here.

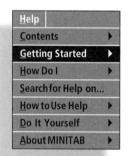

General Objectives

Discrete random variables are used in many practical applications. Three important discrete random variables—the binomial, the Poisson, and the hypergeometric—are presented in this chapter. These random variables are often used to describe the number of occurrences of a specified event in a fixed number of trials or a fixed unit of time or space.

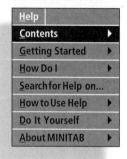

Specific Topics

1. The binomial probability distribution (5.2)
2. The mean and variance for the binomial random variable (5.2)
3. The Poisson probability distribution (5.3)
4. The hypergeometric probability distribution (5.4)

5.1   Introduction

Examples of *discrete random variables* can be found in a variety of everyday situations and across most academic disciplines. However, there are three discrete probability distributions that serve as *models* for a large number of these applications. In this chapter we study the binomial, the Poisson, and the hypergeometric probability distributions and discuss their usefulness in different physical situations.

5.2   The Binomial Probability Distribution

A coin-tossing experiment is a simple example of an important discrete random variable called the **binomial random variable.** Many practical experiments result in data similar to the head or tail outcomes of the coin toss. For example, consider the political polls used to predict voter preferences in elections. Each sampled voter can be compared to a coin because the voter may be in favor of our candidate—a "head"—or not—a "tail." In most cases, the proportion of voters who favor our candidate does not equal 1/2; that is, the coin is not fair. In fact, the proportion of voters who favor our candidate is exactly what the poll is designed to measure!

Here are some other situations that are similar to the coin-tossing experiment:

- A sociologist is interested in the proportion of elementary school teachers who are men.
- A soft-drink marketer is interested in the proportion of cola drinkers who prefer her brand.
- A geneticist is interested in the proportion of the population who possess a gene linked to Alzheimer's disease.

Each sampled person is analogous to tossing a coin, but the probability of a "head" is not necessarily equal to 1/2. Although these situations have different practical objectives, they all exhibit the common characteristics of the **binomial experiment.**

Definition   A **binomial experiment** is one that has these five characteristics:

1. The experiment consists of n identical trials.
2. Each trial results in one of two outcomes. For lack of a better name, the one outcome is called a success, S, and the other a failure, F.
3. The probability of success on a single trial is equal to p and remains the same from trial to trial. The probability of failure is equal to $(1 - p) = q$.
4. The trials are independent.
5. We are interested in x, the number of successes observed during the n trials, for $x = 0, 1, 2, \ldots, n$.

EXAMPLE 5.1   Suppose there are approximately 1,000,000 adults in a county and an unknown proportion p favor term limits for politicians. A sample of 1000 adults will be chosen in such a way that every one of the 1,000,000 adults has an equal chance of being selected, and each adult is asked whether he or she favors term limits. (The ultimate objective of this survey is to estimate the unknown proportion p, a problem that we will discuss in Chapter 8.) Is this a binomial experiment?

Solution   Does the experiment have the five binomial characteristics?

1. A "trial" is the choice of a single adult from the 1,000,000 adults in the county. This sample consists of $n = 1000$ identical trials.
2. Since each adult will either favor or not favor term limits, there are two outcomes that represent the "successes" and "failures" in the binomial experiment.[†]
3. The probability of success, p, is the probability that an adult favors term limits. Does this probability remain the same for each adult in the sample? For all practical purposes, the answer is *yes*. For example, if 500,000 adults in the population favor term limits, then the probability of a "success" when the first adult is chosen is 500,000/1,000,000 = 1/2. When the second adult is chosen, the probability p changes slightly, depending on the first choice. That is, there will be either 499,999 or 500,000 successes left among the 999,999 adults. In either case, p is still approximately equal to 1/2.
4. The independence of the trials is guaranteed because of the large group of adults from which the sample is chosen. The probability of an adult favoring term limits does not change depending on the responses of previously chosen people.
5. The random variable x is the number of adults in the sample who favor term limits.

Because the survey satisfies the five characteristics reasonably well, for all practical purposes it can be viewed as a binomial experiment.

EXAMPLE 5.2

A purchaser who has received a shipment containing 20 personal computers (PCs) wants to sample three of the PCs to see whether they are in working order before accepting the shipment. The nearest three PCs are selected for testing and, afterward, are declared either defective or nondefective. Unknown to the purchaser, two of the PCs in the shipment of 20 are defective. Is this a binomial experiment?

Solution   Again, check the sampling procedure for the characteristics of a binomial experiment.

1. A "trial" is the selecting and testing of one PC from the total of 20. This experiment consists of $n = 3$ identical trials.
2. Each trial results in one of two outcomes. Either a PC is defective (call this a "success") or it is not (a "failure").
3. Suppose the PCs were randomly loaded into a boxcar so that any one of the 20 PCs could have been placed near the boxcar door. Then the unconditional probability of drawing a defective PC on a given trial would be 2/20.
4. The condition of independence between trials is *not* satisfied because the probability of drawing a defective PC on the second and third trials is dependent on the outcome of the first trial. For example, if the first trial results in a defective PC, then there is only one defective left among the remaining 19 in the shipment. Therefore,

$$P(\text{defective on trial 2}|\text{defective on trial 1}) = 1/19$$

If the first trial *does not* result in a defective, then there are still two defective PCs in the shipment and the probability of a "success" (a defective) changes to

$$P(\text{defective on trial 2}|\text{nondefective on trial 1}) = 2/19$$

Therefore, the trials are dependent and the sampling does not represent a binomial experiment.

[†]Although it is traditional to call the two possible outcomes of a trial "success" and "failure," they could have been called "head" and "tail," "red" and "white," or any other pair of words. Consequently, the outcome called a "success" does not need to be viewed as a success in the ordinary use of the word.

Think about the difference between these two examples. When the sample (the n identical trials) came from a large population, the probability of success p stayed about the same from trial to trial. When the population size N was small, the probability of success p changed quite dramatically from trial to trial, and the experiment *was not* binomial.

Rule of Thumb

If the sample size is large relative to the population size—in particular, if $n/N \geq .05$—then the resulting experiment is not binomial.

In Chapter 4, we tossed two fair coins and constructed the probability distribution for x, the number of heads—a binomial experiment with $n = 2$ and $p = .5$. The general binomial probability distribution is constructed in the same way, but the procedure gets complicated as n gets large. Fortunately, the probabilities $p(x)$ follow a general pattern. This allows us to use a single formula to find $p(x)$ for any given value of x.

The Binomial Probability Distribution

A binomial experiment consists of n identical trials with probability of success p on each trial. The probability of k successes in n trials is

$$P(x = k) = C_k^n p^k q^{n-k} = \frac{n!}{k!(n-k)!} \, p^k q^{n-k}$$

for values of $k = 0, 1, 2, \ldots, n$. The symbol

$$C_k^n = \frac{n!}{k!(n-k)!} \qquad \text{where } n! = n(n-1)(n-2) \cdots (2)(1) \text{ and } 0! \equiv 1$$

The general formulas for μ, σ^2, and σ given in Chapter 4 can be used to derive the following simpler formulas for the binomial mean and standard deviation.

Mean and Standard Deviation for the Binomial Random Variable

The random variable x, the number of successes in n trials, has a probability distribution with this center and spread:

$$\text{Mean:} \quad \mu = np$$
$$\text{Variance:} \quad \sigma^2 = npq$$
$$\text{Standard deviation:} \quad \sigma = \sqrt{npq}$$

EXAMPLE 5.3 Find $P(x = 2)$ for a binomial random variable with $n = 10$ and $p = .1$.

Solution $P(x = 2)$ is the probability of observing two successes and eight failures in a sequence of 10 trials. You might observe the 2 successes first, followed by 8 consecutive failures:

S, S, F, F, F, F, F, F, F, F

Since p is the probability of success and q is the probability of failure, this particular sequence has probability

$$ppqqqqqqqq = p^2q^8$$

However, many *other* sequences also result in $x = 2$ successes. The binomial formula uses C_2^{10} to count the number of sequences and gives the exact probability when you use the binomial formula with $k = 2$:

$$P(x = 2) = C_2^{10}(.1)^2(.9)^{10-2}$$

$$= \frac{10!}{2!(10 - 2)!}(.1)^2(.9)^8 = \frac{10(9)}{2(1)}(.01)(.430467) = .1937$$

You could repeat the procedure in Example 5.3 for each value of x—0, 1, 2, . . . , 10—and find all the values of $p(x)$ necessary to construct a probability histogram for x. This would be a long and tedious job, but the resulting graph would look like Figure 5.1(a). You can check the height of the bar for $x = 2$ and find $p(2) = P(x = 2) = .1937$. The graph is skewed right; that is, most of the time you will observe small values of x. The mean or "balancing point" is around $x = 1$; in fact, you can use the formula to find the exact mean:

$$\mu = np = 10(.1) = 1$$

Figures 5.1(b) and 5.1(c) show two other binomial distributions with $n = 10$ but with different values of p. Look at the shapes of these distributions. When $p = .5$, the distribution is exactly symmetric about the mean, $\mu = np = 10(.5) = 5$. When $p = .9$, the distribution is the "mirror image" of the distribution for $p = .1$ and is skewed to the left.

FIGURE 5.1 Binomial probability distributions

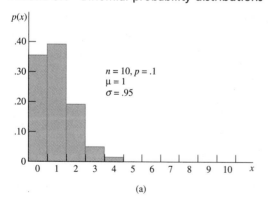

(a)

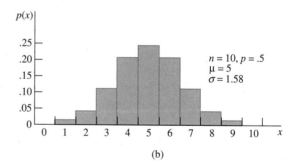

(b)

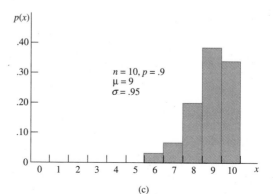

(c)

EXAMPLE 5.4

Over a long period of time it has been observed that a given marksman can hit a target on a single trial with probability equal to .8. Suppose he fires four shots at the target.

1. What is the probability that he will hit the target exactly two times?
2. What is the probability that he will hit the target at least once?

Solution

A "trial" is a single shot at the target, and you can define a "success" as a hit and a "failure" as a miss, so that $n = 4$ and $p = .8$. If you assume that the marksman's chance of hitting the target does not change from shot to shot, then the number x of times he hits the target is a *binomial random variable*.

1. $P(x = 2) = p(2) = C_2^4(.8)^2(.2)^{4-2}$

$$= \frac{4!}{2!2!}(.64)(.04) = \frac{4(3)(2)(1)}{2(1)(2)(1)}(.64)(.04) = .1536$$

The probability is .1536 that he will hit the target exactly two times.

2. $P(\text{at least once}) = P(x \geq 1) = p(1) + p(2) + p(3) + p(4)$
$$= 1 - p(0)$$
$$= 1 - C_0^4(.8)^0(.2)^4$$
$$= 1 - .0016 = .9984$$

Although you could calculate $P(x = 1)$, $P(x = 2)$, $P(x = 3)$, and $P(x = 4)$ to find this probability, using the complement of the event makes your job easier; that is,

$$P(x \geq 1) = 1 - P(x < 1) = 1 - P(x = 0)$$

Can you think of any reason your assumption of independent trials might be wrong? If the marksman learns from his previous shots (that is, he notices the location of his previous shot and adjusts his aim), then his probability p of hitting the target may increase from shot to shot. The trials would *not* be independent, and the experiment would *not* be binomial.

Calculating binomial probabilities can become tedious even for relatively small values of n. As n gets larger, it becomes almost impossible without the help of a calculator or computer. Fortunately, both of these tools are available to us. Computer-generated tables of **cumulative binomial probabilities** are given in Table 1 of Appendix I for values of n ranging from 2 to 25 and for selected values of p. These probabilities can also be generated using *MINITAB* or the Java applets on your CD-Rom.

Cumulative binomial probabilities differ from the *individual* binomial probabilities that you calculated with the binomial formula. Once you find the column of probabilities for the correct values of n and p in Table 1, the row marked k gives the sum of all the binomial probabilities from $x = 0$ to $x = k$. Table 5.1 shows part of Table 1 for $n = 5$ and $p = .6$. If you look in the row marked $k = 3$, you will find

$$P(x \leq 3) = p(0) + p(1) + p(2) + p(3) = .663$$

TABLE 5.1
Portion of Table 1 in Appendix I for $n = 5$

k	.01	.05	.10	.20	.30	.40	.50	.60	.70	.80	.90	.95	.99	k
								p						
0	—	—	—	—	—	—	—	.010	—	—	—	—	—	0
1	—	—	—	—	—	—	—	.087	—	—	—	—	—	1
2	—	—	—	—	—	—	—	.317	—	—	—	—	—	2
3	—	—	—	—	—	—	—	.663	—	—	—	—	—	3
4	▲	—	—	—	—	—	—	.922	—	—	—	—	—	4
5	—	—	—	—	—	—	—	1.000	—	—	—	—	—	5

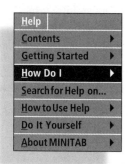

If the probability you need to calculate is not in this form, you will need to think of a way to rewrite your probability to make use of the tables!

Use Table 1 to Calculate Binomial Probabilities?

1. Find the necessary values of n and p. Isolate the appropriate column in Table 1.
2. Table 1 gives $P(x \leq k)$ in the row marked k. Rewrite the probability you need so that it is in this form.
   - List the values of x in your event.
   - From the list, write the event as either the difference of two probabilities

   $$P(x \leq a) - P(x \leq b)$$

   or

   $$1 - P(x \leq a)$$

EXAMPLE 5.5

Use the cumulative binomial table for $n = 5$ and $p = .6$ to find the probabilities of these events:

1. Exactly three successes
2. Three or more successes

Solution

1. If you find $k = 3$ in Table 5.1, the tabled value is

   $$P(x \leq 3) = p(0) + p(1) + p(2) + p(3)$$

   Since you want only $P(x = 3) = p(3)$, you must subtract out the unwanted probability:

   $$P(x \leq 2) = p(0) + p(1) + p(2)$$

   which is found in Table 5.1 with $k = 2$. Then

   $$P(x = 3) = P(x \leq 3) - P(x \leq 2)$$
   $$= .663 - .317 = .346$$

2. To find $P(\text{three or more successes}) = P(x \geq 3)$ using Table 5.1, you must use the complement of the event of interest. Write

   $$P(x \geq 3) = 1 - P(x < 3) = 1 - P(x \leq 2)$$

   You can find $P(x \leq 2)$ in Table 5.1 with $k = 2$. Then

   $$P(x \geq 3) = 1 - P(x \leq 2)$$
   $$= 1 - .317 = .683$$

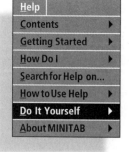

DO IT YOURSELF!

The Java applet called **Calculating Binomial Probabilities** gives a visual display of the binomial distribution for values of $n \leq 100$ and any p that you choose. You can use this applet to calculate binomial probabilities for any value of x or for any interval $a \leq x \leq b$. To reproduce the results of Example 5.5, enter **5** in the box labeled "n:"

and **0.6** in the box labeled "p," pressing the "Enter" key after each entry. Next enter the beginning and ending values for x (if you need to calculate an individual probability, both entries will be the same). The probability will be calculated and shaded in red on your monitor (light blue in Figure 5.2) when you press "Enter." What is the probability of three or more successes from Figure 5.2? Does this confirm our answer in Example 5.5? You will use this applet again for the *Do It Yourself Exercises* section at the end of the chapter.

FIGURE 5.2
Calculating
Binomial
Probabilities
applet

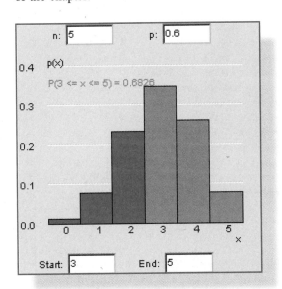

EXAMPLE 5.6   A regimen consisting of a daily dose of vitamin C was tested to determine its effectiveness in preventing the common cold. Ten people who were following the prescribed regimen were observed for a period of 1 year. Eight survived the winter without a cold. Suppose the probability of surviving the winter without a cold is .5 when the vitamin C regimen is not followed. What is the probability of observing eight or more survivors, given that the regimen is ineffective in increasing resistance to colds?

Solution   If you assume that the vitamin C regimen is ineffective, then the probability p of surviving the winter without a cold is .5. The probability distribution for x, the number of survivors, is

$$p(x) = C_x^{10}(.5)^x(.5)^{10-x}$$

You have learned four ways to find $P(8 \text{ or more survivors}) = P(x \geq 8)$. You will get the same results with any of the four; choose the most convenient method for your particular problem.

1. *The binomial formula:*

$$
\begin{aligned}
P(8 \text{ or more}) &= p(8) + p(9) + p(10) \\
&= C_8^{10}(.5)^{10} + C_9^{10}(.5)^{10} + C_{10}^{10}(.5)^{10} \\
&= .055
\end{aligned}
$$

2. *The cumulative binomial tables:* Find the column corresponding to $p = .5$ in the table for $n = 10$:

$$
\begin{aligned}
P(8 \text{ or more}) &= P(x \geq 8) = 1 - P(x \leq 7) \\
&= 1 - .945 = .055
\end{aligned}
$$

3. *The Calculating Binomial Probabilities applet:* Enter $n = 10$, $p = .5$ and calculate the probability that x is between 8 and 10. The probability, $P(x \geq 8) = .0547$, is shaded in red on your monitor (light blue in Figure 5.3).

FIGURE 5.3
Java applet for
Example 5.6

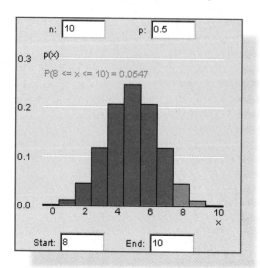

4. *Output from MINITAB:* The output shown in Figure 5.4 gives the **cumulative distribution function,** which gives the same probabilities you found in the cumulative binomial tables. The **probability density function** gives the individual binomial probabilities, which you found using the binomial formula.

FIGURE 5.4
MINITAB output
for Example 5.6

Cumulative Distribution Function

Binomial with n = 10 and p = 0.500000

x	P(X <= x)
0.00	0.0010
1.00	0.0107
2.00	0.0547
3.00	0.1719
4.00	0.3770
5.00	0.6230
6.00	0.8281
7.00	0.9453
8.00	0.9893
9.00	0.9990
10.00	1.0000

Probability Density Function

Binomial with n = 10 and p = 0.500000

x	P(X = x)
0.00	0.0010
1.00	0.0098
2.00	0.0439
3.00	0.1172
4.00	0.2051
5.00	0.2461
6.00	0.2051
7.00	0.1172
8.00	0.0439
9.00	0.0098
10.00	0.0010

Using the cumulative distribution function, calculate

$$P(x \geq 8) = 1 - P(x \leq 7)$$
$$= 1 - .9453 = .0547$$

Or, using the probability density function, calculate

$$P(x \geq 8) = p(8) + p(9) + p(10)$$
$$= .0439 + .0098 + .0010 = .0547$$

EXAMPLE 5.7

Would you rather take a multiple-choice or a full recall test? If you have absolutely no knowledge of the material, you will score zero on a full recall test. However, if you are given five choices for each question, you have at least one chance in five of guessing correctly! If a multiple-choice exam contains 100 questions, each with five possible answers, what is the expected score for a student who is guessing on each question? Within what limits will the "no-knowledge" scores fall?

Solution If x is the number of correct answers on the 100-question exam, the probability of a correct answer, p, is one in five, so that $p = .2$. Since the student is randomly selecting answers, the $n = 100$ answers are independent, and the expected score for this binomial random variable is

$$\mu = np = 100(.2) = 20 \quad \text{correct answers}$$

To evaluate the spread or variability of the scores, you can calculate

$$\sigma = \sqrt{npq} = \sqrt{100(.2)(.8)} = 4$$

Then, using your knowledge of variation from Tchebysheff's Theorem and the Empirical Rule, you can make these statements:

- A large proportion of the scores will lie within two standard deviations of the mean, or from $20 - 8 = 12$ to $20 + 8 = 28$.
- Almost all the scores will lie within three standard deviations of the mean, or from $20 - 12 = 8$ to $20 + 12 = 32$.

The "guessing" option gives the student a better score than the zero score on the full recall test, but the student still will not pass the exam. What other options does the student have?

Exercises   Basic Techniques

5.1 A jar contains five balls: three red and two white. Two balls are randomly selected without replacement from the jar, and the number x of red balls is recorded. Explain why x is or is not a binomial random variable. (HINT: Compare the characteristics of this experiment with the characteristics of a binomial experiment given in this section.) If the experiment is binomial, give the values of n and p.

5.2 Refer to Exercise 5.1. Assume that the sampling was conducted with replacement. That is, assume that the first ball was selected from the jar, observed, and then replaced, and that the balls were then mixed before the second ball was selected. Explain why x, the number of red balls observed, is or is not a binomial random variable. If the experiment is binomial, give the values of n and p.

5.3 Evaluate these binomial probabilities:
  a. $C_2^8(.3)^2(.7)^6$ **b.** $C_0^4(.05)^0(.95)^4$ **c.** $C_3^{10}(.5)^3(.5)^7$ **d.** $C_1^7(.2)^1(.8)^6$

5.4 Use the formula for the binomial probability distribution to calculate the values of $p(x)$, and construct the probability histogram for x when $n = 6$ and $p = .2$. [HINT: Calculate $P(x = k)$ for seven different values of k.]

5.5 Refer to Exercise 5.4. Construct the probability histogram for a binomial random variable x with $n = 6$ and $p = .8$. Use the results of Exercise 5.4; do not recalculate all the probabilities.

5.6 If x has a binomial distribution with $p = .5$, will the shape of the probability distribution be symmetric, skewed to the left, or skewed to the right?

5.7 Let x be a binomial random variable with $n = 10$ and $p = .4$. Find these values:
  a. $P(x = 4)$ **b.** $P(x \geq 4)$ **c.** $P(x > 4)$
  d. $P(x \leq 4)$ **e.** $\mu = np$ **f.** $\sigma = \sqrt{npq}$

5.8 Use Table 1 in Appendix I to find the sum of the binomial probabilities from $x = 0$ to $x = k$ for these cases:
  a. $n = 10, p = .1, k = 3$ **b.** $n = 15, p = .6, k = 7$ **c.** $n = 25, p = .5, k = 14$

5.9 Use Table 1 in Appendix I to evaluate the following probabilities for $n = 6$ and $p = .8$:

    a. $P(x \geq 4)$ **b.** $P(x = 2)$ **c.** $P(x < 2)$ **d.** $P(x > 1)$

Verify these answers using the values of $p(x)$ calculated in Exercise 5.5.

5.10 Find $P(x \leq k)$ in each case:

    a. $n = 20, p = .05, k = 2$ **b.** $n = 15, p = .7, k = 8$ **c.** $n = 10, p = .9, k = 9$

5.11 Use Table 1 in Appendix I to find the following:

    a. $P(x < 12)$ for $n = 20, p = .5$ **b.** $P(x \leq 6)$ for $n = 15, p = .4$

    c. $P(x > 4)$ for $n = 10, p = .4$ **d.** $P(x \geq 6)$ for $n = 15, p = .6$

    e. $P(3 < x < 7)$ for $n = 10, p = .5$

5.12 Find the mean and standard deviation for a binomial distribution with these values:

    a. $n = 1000, p = .3$ **b.** $n = 400, p = .01$

    c. $n = 500, p = .5$ **d.** $n = 1600, p = .8$

5.13 Find the mean and standard deviation for a binomial distribution with $n = 100$ and these values of p:

    a. $p = .01$ **b.** $p = .9$ **c.** $p = .3$

    d. $p = .7$ **e.** $p = .5$

5.14 In Exercise 5.13, the mean and standard deviation for a binomial random variable were calculated for a fixed sample size, $n = 100$, and for different values of p. Graph the values of the standard deviation for the five values of p given in Exercise 5.13. For what value of p does the standard deviation seem to be a maximum?

5.15 Let x be a binomial random variable with $n = 20$ and $p = .1$.

    a. Calculate $P(x \leq 4)$ using the binomial formula.

    b. Calculate $P(x \leq 4)$ using Table 1 in Appendix I.

    c. Use the Minitab output on page 184 to calculate $P(x \leq 4)$. Compare the results of parts a, b, and c.

    d. Calculate the mean and standard deviation of the random variable x.

    e. Use the results of part d to calculate the intervals $\mu \pm \sigma$, $\mu \pm 2\sigma$, and $\mu \pm 3\sigma$. Find the probability that an observation will fall into each of these intervals.

    f. Are the results of part e consistent with Tchebysheff's Theorem? With the Empirical Rule? Why or why not?

MINITAB output for Exercise 5.15

Probability Density Function

Binomial with n = 20 and p = 0.100000

x	P(X = x)
0.00	0.1216
1.00	0.2702
2.00	0.2852
3.00	0.1901
4.00	0.0898
5.00	0.0319
6.00	0.0089
7.00	0.0020
8.00	0.0004
9.00	0.0001
10.00	0.0000
11.00	0.0000
12.00	0.0000
13.00	0.0000
14.00	0.0000
15.00	0.0000
16.00	0.0000
17.00	0.0000
18.00	0.0000
19.00	0.0000
20.00	0.0000

Applications

5.16 A meteorologist in Chicago recorded the number of days of rain during a 30-day period. If the random variable x is defined as the number of days of rain, does x have a binomial distribution? If not, why not? If so, are both values of n and p known?

5.17 A market research firm hires operators to conduct telephone surveys. The computer randomly dials a telephone number, and the operator asks the respondent whether or not he has time to answer some questions. Let x be the number of telephone calls made until the first respondent is willing to answer the operator's questions. Is this a binomial experiment? Explain.

5.18 In 2001 the average combined SAT score (math + verbal) for students in the United States was 1020, and 45% of all high school graduates took this test.[1] Suppose that 100 students are randomly selected from throughout the United States. Which of the following random variables has an approximate binomial distribution? If possible, give the values for n and p.

   a. The number of students who took the SAT

   b. The scores of the 100 students on the SAT

   c. The number of students who scored above average on the SAT

   d. The amount of time it took each student to complete the SAT

5.19 A home security system is designed to have a 99% reliability rate. Suppose that nine homes equipped with this system experience an attempted burglary. Find the probabilities of these events:

   a. At least one of the alarms is triggered.

   b. More than seven of the alarms are triggered.

   c. Eight or fewer alarms are triggered.

5.20 In a certain population, 85% of the people have Rh-positive blood. Suppose that two people from this population get married. What is the probability that they are both Rh-negative, thus making it inevitable that their children will be Rh-negative?

5.21 Car color preferences change over the years and according to the particular model that the customer selects. In a recent year, 10% of all luxury cars sold were black. If 25 cars of that year and type are randomly selected, find the following probabilities:

   a. At least five cars are black.   **b.** At most six cars are black.

   c. More than four cars are black.   **d.** Exactly four cars are black.

   e. Between three and five cars (inclusive) are black.

   f. More than 20 cars are not black.

5.22 Of all the Harry Potter books purchased last year, about 60% were purchased for readers 14 or older.[2] If 12 Harry Potter fans who bought books last year are surveyed, find the following probabilities.

   a. At least five of them are 14 or older.

   b. Exactly nine of them are 14 or older.

   c. Less than three of them are 14 or older.

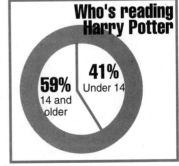

5.23 Records show that 30% of all patients admitted to a medical clinic fail to pay their bills and that eventually the bills are forgiven. Suppose $n = 4$ new patients represent a random selection from the large set of prospective patients served by the clinic. Find these probabilities:

a. All the patients' bills will eventually have to be forgiven.

b. One will have to be forgiven.

c. None will have to be forgiven.

5.24 Consider the medical payment problem in Exercise 5.23 in a more realistic setting. Of all patients admitted to a medical clinic, 30% fail to pay their bills and the debts are eventually forgiven. If the clinic treats 2000 different patients over a period of 1 year, what is the mean (expected) number of debts that have to be forgiven? If x is the number of forgiven debts in the group of 2000 patients, find the variance and standard deviation of x. What can you say about the probability that x will exceed 700? (HINT: Use the values of μ and σ, along with Tchebysheff's Theorem, to answer this question.)

5.25 Suppose that 10% of the fields in a given agricultural area are infested with the sweet potato whitefly. One hundred fields in this area are randomly selected and checked for whitefly.

a. What is the average number of fields sampled that are infested with whitefly?

b. Within what limits would you expect to find the number of infested fields, with probability approximately 95%?

c. What might you conclude if you found that $x = 25$ fields were infested? Is it possible that one of the characteristics of a binomial experiment is not satisfied in this experiment? Explain.

5.26 In a psychology experiment, the researcher plans to test the color preference of mice under certain experimental conditions. She designs a maze in which the mouse must choose one of two paths, colored either red or blue, at each of 10 intersections. At the end of the maze, the mouse is given a food reward. The researcher counts the number of times the mouse chooses the red path. If you were the researcher, how would you use this count to decide whether the mouse has any preference for color?

5.27 Across the board, 22% of car leisure travelers rank "traffic and other drivers" as their pet peeve while traveling. Of car leisure travelers in the densely populated Northeast, 33% list this as their pet peeve.[3] A random sample of $n = 8$ such travelers in the Northeast were asked to state their pet peeve while traveling. The *MINITAB* printout shows the *cumulative* and *individual* probabilities.

MINITAB output for Exercise 5.27

Cumulative Distribution Function

Binomial with n = 8 and p = 0.330000

x	P(X <= x)
0.00	0.0406
1.00	0.2006
2.00	0.4764
3.00	0.7481
4.00	0.9154
5.00	0.9813
6.00	0.9976
7.00	0.9999
8.00	1.0000

Probability Density Function

Binomial with n = 8 and p = 0.330000

x	P(X = x)
0.00	0.0406
1.00	0.1600
2.00	0.2758
3.00	0.2717
4.00	0.1673
5.00	0.0659
6.00	0.0162
7.00	0.0023
8.00	0.0001

a. Use the binomial formula to find the probability that all eight give "traffic and other drivers" as their pet peeve.

b. Confirm the results of part a using the *MINITAB* printout.

c. What is the probability that at most seven give "traffic and other drivers" as their pet peeve?

5.28 Forty percent of all Americans who travel by car look for gas and food outlets that are close to or visible from the highway. Suppose a random sample of $n = 25$ Americans who travel by car are asked how they determine where to stop for food and gas. Let x be the number in the sample who respond that they look for gas and food outlets that are close to or visible from the highway.

a. What are the mean and variance of x?

b. Calculate the interval $\mu \pm 2\sigma$. What values of the binomial random variable x fall into this interval?

c. Find $P(4 \le x \le 16)$. How does this compare with the fraction in the interval $\mu \pm 2\sigma$ for any distribution? For mound-shaped distributions?

5.3 The Poisson Probability Distribution

Another discrete random variable that has numerous practical applications is the **Poisson random variable.** Its probability distribution provides a good model for data that represent the number of occurrences of a specified event in a given unit of time or space. Here are some examples of experiments for which the random variable x can be modeled by the Poisson random variable:

- The number of calls received by a switchboard during a given period of time
- The number of bacteria per small volume of fluid
- The number of customer arrivals at a checkout counter during a given minute
- The number of machine breakdowns during a given day
- The number of traffic accidents at a given intersection during a given time period

In each example, **x represents the number of events that occur in a period of time or space during which an average of μ such events can be expected to occur.** The only assumptions needed when one uses the Poisson distribution to model experiments such as these are that the counts or events occur **randomly and independently** of one another. The formula for the Poisson probability distribution, as well as its mean and variance, are given next.

> **The Poisson Probability Distribution**
> Let μ be the average number of times that an event occurs in a certain period of time or space. The probability of k occurrences of this event is
>
> $$P(x = k) = \frac{\mu^k e^{-\mu}}{k!}$$
>
> for values of $k = 0, 1, 2, 3, \ldots$. The mean and standard deviation of the Poisson random variable x are
>
> $$\text{Mean:} \quad \mu$$
> $$\text{Standard deviation:} \quad \sigma = \sqrt{\mu}$$

The symbol $e = 2.71828 \ldots$ is evaluated using your scientific calculator, which should have a function such as e^x. For each value of k, you can obtain the individual probabilities for the Poisson random variable, just as you did for the binomial random variable.

Alternatively, you can use **cumulative Poisson tables** (Table 2 in Appendix I) or the cumulative or individual probabilities generated by *MINITAB*. Both of these options are usually more convenient than hand calculation. The procedures are similar to those used for the binomial random variable.

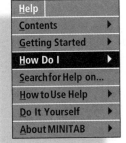

> **Use Table 2 to Calculate Poisson Probabilities?**
> - Find the necessary values of μ. Isolate the appropriate column in Table 2.
> - Table 2 gives $P(x \le k)$ in the line marked k. Rewrite the probability you need so that it is in this form.
>   List the values of x in your event.
>   From the list, write the event as either the difference of two probabilities
>
> $$P(x \le a) - P(x \le b) \qquad \text{or} \qquad 1 - P(x \le a)$$

Graphs of the Poisson probability distribution for $\mu = .5$, 1, and 4 are shown in Figure 5.5.

FIGURE 5.5
Poisson probability distributions for $\mu = .5$, 1, and 4

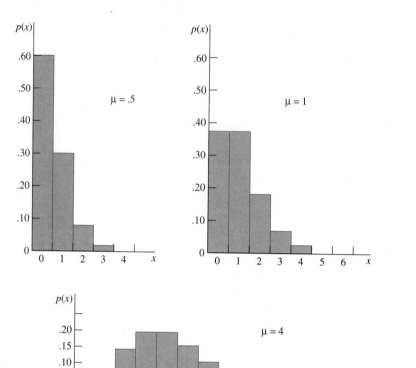

EXAMPLE 5.8

The average number of traffic accidents on a certain section of highway is two per week. Assume that the number of accidents follows a Poisson distribution with $\mu = 2$.

1. Find the probability of no accidents on this section of highway during a 1-week period.
2. Find the probability of at most three accidents on this section of highway during a 2-week period.

Solution

1. The average number of accidents per week is $\mu = 2$. Therefore, the probability of no accidents on this section of highway during a given week is

$$P(x = 0) = p(0) = \frac{2^0 e^{-2}}{0!} = e^{-2} = .135335$$

2. During a 2-week period, the average number of accidents on this section of highway is $2(2) = 4$. The probability of at most three accidents during a 2-week period is

$$P(x \le 3) = p(0) + p(1) + p(2) + p(3)$$

where

$$p(0) = \frac{4^0 e^{-4}}{0!} = .018316 \qquad p(2) = \frac{4^2 e^{-4}}{2!} = .146525$$

$$p(1) = \frac{4^1 e^{-4}}{1!} = .073263 \qquad p(3) = \frac{4^3 e^{-4}}{3!} = .195367$$

Therefore,

$$P(x \le 3) = .018316 + .073263 + .146525 + .195367 = .433471$$

This value could be read directly from Table 2 in Appendix I, indexing $\mu = 4$ and $k = 3$, as $P(x \le 3) = .433$.

In Section 5.2, we used the cumulative binomial tables to simplify the calculation of binomial probabilities. Unfortunately, in practical situations, n is often large and no tables are available.

> The Poisson probability distribution provides a simple, easy-to-compute, and accurate approximation to binomial probabilities when n is large and $\mu = np$ is small, preferably with $np < 7$. An approximation suitable for larger values of $\mu = np$ will be given in Chapter 6.

EXAMPLE 5.9   Suppose a life insurance company insures the lives of 5000 men aged 42. If actuarial studies show the probability that any 42-year-old man will die in a given year to be .001, find the exact probability that the company will have to pay $x = 4$ claims during a given year.

Solution   The exact probability is given by the binomial distribution as

$$P(x = 4) = p(4) = \frac{5000!}{4!4996!}(.001)^4(.999)^{4996}$$

for which binomial tables are not available. To compute $P(x = 4)$ without the aid of a computer would be very time-consuming, but the Poisson distribution can be used to provide a good approximation to $P(x = 4)$. Computing $\mu = np = (5000)(.001) = 5$ and substituting into the formula for the Poisson probability distribution, we have

$$p(4) \approx \frac{\mu^4 e^{-\mu}}{4!} = \frac{5^4 e^{-5}}{4!} = \frac{(625)(.006738)}{24} = .175$$

The value of $p(4)$ could also be obtained using Table 2 in Appendix I with $\mu = 5$ as

$$p(4) = P(x \le 4) - P(x \le 3) = .440 - .265 = .175$$

EXAMPLE 5.10   A manufacturer of power lawn mowers buys 1-horsepower, two-cycle engines in lots of 1000 from a supplier. She then equips each of the mowers produced by her plant with one of the engines. History shows that the probability of any one engine from that supplier proving unsatisfactory is .001. In a shipment of 1000 engines, what is the probability that none is defective? Three are? Four are?

Solution   This is a binomial experiment with $n = 1000$ and $p = .001$. The expected number of defectives in a shipment of $n = 1000$ engines is $\mu = np = (1000)(.001) = 1$. Since this is a binomial experiment with $np < 7$, the probability of x defective engines in the shipment may be approximated by

$$P(x = k) = p(k) = \frac{\mu^k e^{-\mu}}{k!} = \frac{1^k e^{-1}}{k!} = \frac{e^{-1}}{k!}$$

Therefore,

$$p(0) \approx \frac{e^{-1}}{0!} = \frac{.368}{1} = .368$$

$$p(3) \approx \frac{e^{-1}}{3!} = \frac{.368}{6} = .061$$

$$p(4) \approx \frac{e^{-1}}{4!} = \frac{.368}{24} = .015$$

The individual Poisson probabilities for $\mu = 1$ along with the individual binomial probabilities for $n = 1000$ and $p = .001$ were generated by *MINITAB* and are shown in Figure 5.6. The individual probabilities, even though they are computed with totally different formulas, are almost the same. The exact binomial probabilities are in the left section of Figure 5.6, and the Poisson approximations are on the right. Notice that *MINITAB* stops computing probabilities once the value is equal to zero within a preassigned accuracy level.

FIGURE 5.6

MINITAB output of binomial and Poisson probabilities

Probability Density Function

Binomial with n = 1000 and p = 0.00100000

x	P(X = x)
0.00	0.3677
1.00	0.3681
2.00	0.1840
3.00	0.0613
4.00	0.0153
5.00	0.0030
6.00	0.0005
7.00	0.0001
8.00	0.0000

Probability Density Function

Poisson with mu = 1.00000

x	P(X = x)
0.00	0.3679
1.00	0.3679
2.00	0.1839
3.00	0.0613
4.00	0.0153
5.00	0.0031
6.00	0.0005
7.00	0.0001
8.00	0.0000

Exercises

Basic Techniques

5.29 Let x be a Poisson random variable with mean $\mu = 2$. Calculate these probabilities:

a. $P(x = 0)$ **b.** $P(x = 1)$ **c.** $P(x > 1)$ **d.** $P(x = 5)$

5.30 Let x be a Poisson random variable with mean $\mu = 2.5$. Use Table 2 in Appendix I to calculate these probabilities:

a. $P(x \geq 5)$ **b.** $P(x < 6)$ **c.** $P(x = 2)$ **d.** $P(1 \leq x \leq 4)$

5.31 Let x be a binomial random variable with $n = 20$ and $p = .1$.

a. Calculate $P(x \leq 2)$ using Table 1 in Appendix I to obtain the exact binomial probability.

b. Use the Poisson approximation to calculate $P(x \leq 2)$.

c. Compare the results of parts a and b. Is the approximation accurate?

5.32 To illustrate how well the Poisson probability distribution approximates the binomial probability distribution, calculate the Poisson approximate values for $p(0)$ and $p(1)$ for a binomial probability distribution with $n = 25$ and $p = .05$. Compare the answers with the exact values obtained from Table 1 in Appendix I.

Applications

5.33 The increased number of small commuter planes in major airports has heightened concern over air safety. An eastern airport has recorded a monthly average of five near-misses on landings and takeoffs in the past 5 years.

      a. Find the probability that during a given month there are no near-misses on landings and take-offs at the airport.

      b. Find the probability that during a given month there are five near-misses.

      c. Find the probability that there are at least five near-misses during a particular month.

5.34 The number x of people entering the intensive care unit at a particular hospital on any one day has a Poisson probability distribution with mean equal to five persons per day.

      a. What is the probability that the number of people entering the intensive care unit on a particular day is two? Less than or equal to two?

      b. Is it likely that x will exceed 10? Explain.

5.35 Parents who are concerned that their children are "accident prone" can be reassured, according to a study conducted by the Department of Pediatrics at the University of California, San Francisco. Children who are injured two or more times tend to sustain these injuries during a relatively limited time, usually 1 year or less. If the average number of injuries per year for school-age children is two, what are the probabilities of these events?

      a. A child will sustain two injuries during the year.

      b. A child will sustain two or more injuries during the year.

      c. A child will sustain at most one injury during the year.

5.36 Refer to Exercise 5.35.

      a. Calculate the mean and standard deviation for x, the number of injuries per year sustained by a school-age child.

      b. Within what limits would you expect the number of injuries per year to fall?

5.37 If a drop of water is placed on a slide and examined under a microscope, the number x of a particular type of bacteria present has been found to have a Poisson probability distribution. Suppose the maximum permissible count per water specimen for this type of bacteria is five. If the mean count for your water supply is two and you test a single specimen, is it likely that the count will exceed the maximum permissible count? Explain.

5.38 Increased research and discussion have focused on the number of illnesses involving the organism *Escherichia coli* (01257:H7), which causes a breakdown of red blood cells and intestinal hemorrhages in its victims.[4] Sporadic outbreaks of *E. coli* have occurred in Colorado at a rate of 2.5 per 100,000 for a period of 2 years. Let us suppose that this rate has not changed.

      a. What is the probability that at most five cases of *E. coli* per 100,000 are reported in Colorado in a given year?

      b. What is the probability that more than five cases of *E. coli* per 100,000 are reported in a given year?

      c. Approximately 95% of occurrences of *E. coli* involve at most how many cases?

5.4 The Hypergeometric Probability Distribution

Suppose you are selecting a sample of elements from a population and you record whether or not each element possesses a certain characteristic. You are recording the typical "success" or "failure" data found in the binomial experiment. The sample survey of Example 5.1 and the sampling for defectives of Example 5.2 are practical illustrations of these sampling situations.

    If the number of elements in the population is large relative to the number in the sample (as in Example 5.1), the probability of selecting a success on a single trial is equal to the proportion p of successes in the population. Because the population is large in relation to the sample size, this probability will remain constant (for all practical purposes) from trial to trial, and the number x of successes in the sample will follow a binomial probability distribution. However, if the number of elements in the population is small in relation to the sample size ($n/N \geq .05$), the probability of a success for a given trial is dependent on the outcomes of preceding trials. Then the number x of successes follows what is known as a **hypergeometric probability distribution.**

It is easy to visualize the **hypergeometric random variable** x by thinking of a bowl containing M red balls and $N - M$ white balls, for *a total of N* balls in the bowl. You select n balls from the bowl and record x, the number of red balls that you see. If you now define a "success" to be a red ball, you have an example of the hypergeometric random variable x.

The formula for calculating the probability of exactly k successes in n trials is given next.

The Hypergeometric Probability Distribution

A population contains M successes and $N - M$ failures. The probability of exactly k successes in a random sample of size n is

$$P(x = k) = \frac{C_k^M C_{n-k}^{N-M}}{C_n^N}$$

for values of k that depend on N, M, and n with

$$C_n^N = \frac{N!}{n!(N-n)!}$$

The mean and variance of a hypergeometric random variable are very similar to those of a binomial random variable with a correction for the finite population size:

$$\mu = n\left(\frac{M}{N}\right)$$

$$\sigma^2 = n\left(\frac{M}{N}\right)\left(\frac{N-M}{N}\right)\left(\frac{N-n}{N-1}\right)$$

EXAMPLE 5.11 A case of wine has 12 bottles, 3 of which contain spoiled wine. A sample of 4 bottles is randomly selected from the case.

1. Find the probability distribution for x, the number of bottles of spoiled wine in the sample.
2. What are the mean and variance of x?

Solution For this example, $N = 12$, $n = 4$, $M = 3$, and $(N - M) = 9$. Then

$$p(x) = \frac{C_x^3 C_{4-x}^9}{C_4^{12}}$$

1. The possible values for x are 0, 1, 2, and 3, with probabilities

$$p(0) = \frac{C_0^3 C_4^9}{C_4^{12}} = \frac{1(126)}{495} = .25$$

$$p(1) = \frac{C_1^3 C_3^9}{C_4^{12}} = \frac{3(84)}{495} = .51$$

$$p(2) = \frac{C_2^3 C_2^9}{C_4^{12}} = \frac{3(36)}{495} = .22$$

$$p(3) = \frac{C_3^3 C_1^9}{C_4^{12}} = \frac{1(9)}{495} = .02$$

2. The mean is given by

$$\mu = 4\left(\frac{3}{12}\right) = 1$$

and the variance is

$$\sigma^2 = 4\left(\frac{3}{12}\right)\left(\frac{9}{12}\right)\left(\frac{12-4}{11}\right) = .5455$$

EXAMPLE 5.12

A particular industrial product is shipped in lots of 20. Testing to determine whether an item is defective is costly; hence, the manufacturer samples production rather than using a 100% inspection plan. A sampling plan constructed to minimize the number of defectives shipped to customers calls for sampling five items from each lot and rejecting the lot if more than one defective is observed. (If the lot is rejected, each item in the lot is then tested.) If a lot contains four defectives, what is the probability that it will be accepted?

Solution

Let x be the number of defectives in the sample. Then $N = 20$, $M = 4$, $(N - M) = 16$, and $n = 5$. The lot will be rejected if $x = 2$, 3, or 4. Then

$$P(\text{accept the lot}) = P(x \le 1) = p(0) + p(1) = \frac{C_0^4 C_5^{16}}{C_5^{20}} + \frac{C_1^4 C_4^{16}}{C_5^{20}}$$

$$= \frac{\left(\frac{4!}{0!4!}\right)\left(\frac{16!}{5!11!}\right)}{\frac{20!}{5!15!}} + \frac{\left(\frac{4!}{1!3!}\right)\left(\frac{16!}{4!12!}\right)}{\frac{20!}{5!15!}}$$

$$= \frac{91}{323} + \frac{455}{969} = .2817 + .4696 = .7513$$

Exercises

Basic Techniques

5.39   Evaluate these probabilities:

a. $\dfrac{C_1^3 C_1^2}{C_2^5}$ **b.** $\dfrac{C_2^4 C_1^3}{C_3^7}$ **c.** $\dfrac{C_4^5 C_0^3}{C_4^8}$

5.40   Let x be the number of successes observed in a sample of $n = 5$ items selected from $N = 10$. Suppose that, of the $N = 10$ items, 6 are considered "successes."

a. Find the probability of observing no successes.

b. Find the probability of observing at least two successes.

c. Find the probability of observing exactly two successes.

5.41   Let x be a hypergeometric random variable with $N = 15$, $n = 3$, and $M = 4$.

a. Calculate $p(0)$, $p(1)$, $p(2)$, and $p(3)$.

b. Construct the probability histogram for x.

c. Use the formulas given in Section 5.4 to calculate $\mu = E(x)$ and σ^2.

d. What proportion of the population of measurements fall into the interval $(\mu \pm 2\sigma)$? Into the interval $(\mu \pm 3\sigma)$? Do these results agree with those given by Tchebysheff's Theorem?

5.42 A candy dish contains five blue and three red candies. A child reaches up and selects three candies without looking.

a. What is the probability that there are two blue and one red candies in the selection?

b. What is the probability that the candies are all red?

c. What is the probability that the candies are all blue?

Applications

5.43 A piece of electronic equipment contains six computer chips, two of which are defective. Three computer chips are randomly chosen for inspection, and the number of defective chips is recorded. Find the probability distribution for x, the number of defective computer chips. Compare your results with the answers obtained in Exercise 4.86.

5.44 A company has five applicants for two positions: two women and three men. Suppose that the five applicants are equally qualified and that no preference is given for choosing either gender. Let x equal the number of women chosen to fill the two positions.

a. Write the formula for $p(x)$, the probability distribution of x.

b. What are the mean and variance of this distribution?

c. Construct a probability histogram for x.

5.45 In southern California, a growing number of persons pursuing a teaching credential are choosing paid internships over traditional student teaching programs. A group of eight candidates for three local teaching positions consisted of five candidates who had enrolled in paid internships and three candidates who had enrolled in traditional student teaching programs. Let us assume that all eight candidates are equally qualified for the positions. Let x represent the number of internship-trained candidates who are hired for these three positions.

a. Does x have a binomial distribution or a hypergeometric distribution? Support your answer.

b. Find the probability that three internship-trained candidates are hired for these positions.

c. What is the probability that none of the three hired was internship-trained?

d. Find $P(x \leq 1)$.

5.46 Seeds are often treated with a fungicide for protection in poor-draining, wet environments. In a small-scale trial prior to a large-scale experiment to determine what dilution of the fungicide to apply, five treated seeds and five untreated seeds were planted in clay soil and the number of plants emerging from the treated and untreated seeds were recorded. Suppose the dilution was not effective and only four plants emerged. Let x represent the number of plants that emerged from treated seeds.

a. Find the probability that $x = 4$.

b. Find $P(x \leq 3)$.

c. Find $P(2 \leq x \leq 3)$.

Key Concepts and Formulas

I. The Binomial Random Variable

1. **Five characteristics:** n identical independent trials, each resulting in either *success S* or *failure F*; probability of success is p and remains constant from trial to trial; and x is the number of successes in n trials

2. **Calculating binomial probabilities**
   a. Formula: $P(x = k) = C_k^n p^k q^{n-k}$

b. Cumulative binomial tables

c. Individual and cumulative probabilities using *MINITAB*

3. Mean of the binomial random variable: $\mu = np$

4. Variance and standard deviation: $\sigma^2 = npq$ and $\sigma = \sqrt{npq}$

II. The Poisson Random Variable

1. The number of events that occur in a period of time or space, during which an average of μ such events are expected to occur

2. **Calculating Poisson probabilities**

   a. Formula: $P(x = k) = \dfrac{\mu^k e^{-\mu}}{k!}$

   b. Cumulative Poisson tables

   c. Individual and cumulative probabilities using *MINITAB*

3. Mean of the Poisson random variable: $E(x) = \mu$

4. Variance and standard deviation: $\sigma^2 = \mu$ and $\sigma = \sqrt{\mu}$

5. Binomial probabilities can be approximated with Poisson probabilities when $np < 7$, using $\mu = np$.

III. The Hypergeometric Random Variable

1. The number of successes in a sample of size n from a finite population containing M successes and $N - M$ failures

2. Formula for the probability of k successes in n trials:

$$P(x = k) = \frac{C_k^M C_{n-k}^{N-M}}{C_n^N}$$

3. Mean of the hypergeometric random variable: $\mu = n\left(\dfrac{M}{N}\right)$

4. Variance and standard deviation:

$$\sigma^2 = n\left(\frac{M}{N}\right)\left(\frac{N - M}{N}\right)\left(\frac{N - n}{N - 1}\right) \quad \text{and} \quad \sigma = \sqrt{\sigma^2}$$

Binomial and Poisson Probabilities

For a random variable that has either a binomial or a Poisson probability distribution, *MINITAB* has been programmed to calculate either exact probabilities—$P(x = k)$—for a given value of k or the cumulative probabilities—$P(x \le k)$—for a given value of k. You must specify which distribution you are using and the necessary parameters: n and p for the binomial distribution and μ for the Poisson distribution. Also, you have the option of specifying only one single value of k or several values of k, which should be stored in a column (say, C1) of the *MINITAB* worksheet.

Consider a binomial distribution with $n = 16$ and $p = .25$. Neither n nor p appears in the tables in Appendix I. Since the possible values of x for this binomial random variable range from 0 to 16, we can generate the entire probability distribution as well as the cumulative probabilities by entering the numbers 0 to 16 in C1. One way to quickly enter a set of consecutive integers in a column is to use **Calc → Make Patterned Data → Simple Set of Numbers.** In the resulting Dialog box (see Figure 5.7), we select numbers from **0** to **16** to be stored in C1 (named "x"). You may change the default settings so that integers are entered more than one time, and so on. Click on **OK.**

Once the necessary values of x have been entered, use **Calc→ Probability Distributions → Binomial** to generate the Dialog box shown in Figure 5.8. Type the number

MINITAB

FIGURE 5.7

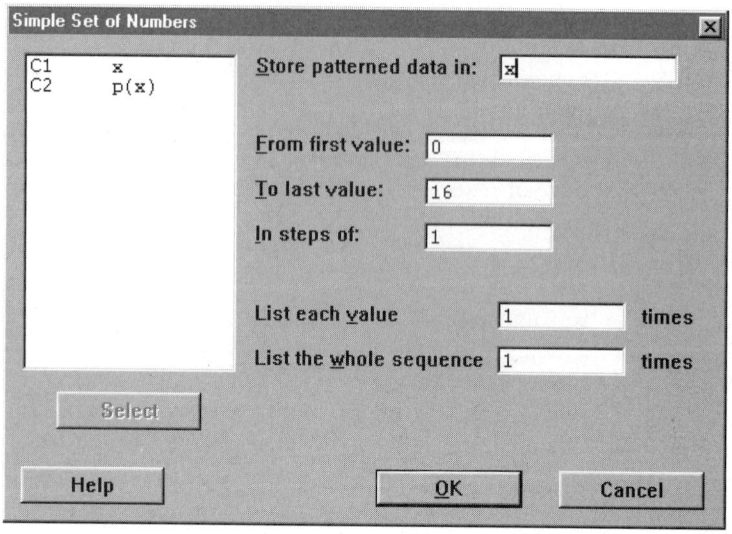

Simple Set of Numbers   ☒

| C1   x |
| C2   p(x) |

<u>S</u>tore patterned data in: [x]

<u>F</u>rom first value: [0]

<u>T</u>o last value: [16]

<u>I</u>n steps of: [1]

List each <u>v</u>alue   [1]   times

List the <u>w</u>hole sequence   [1]   times

[Select]

[Help]   [<u>O</u>K]   [Cancel]

FIGURE 5.8

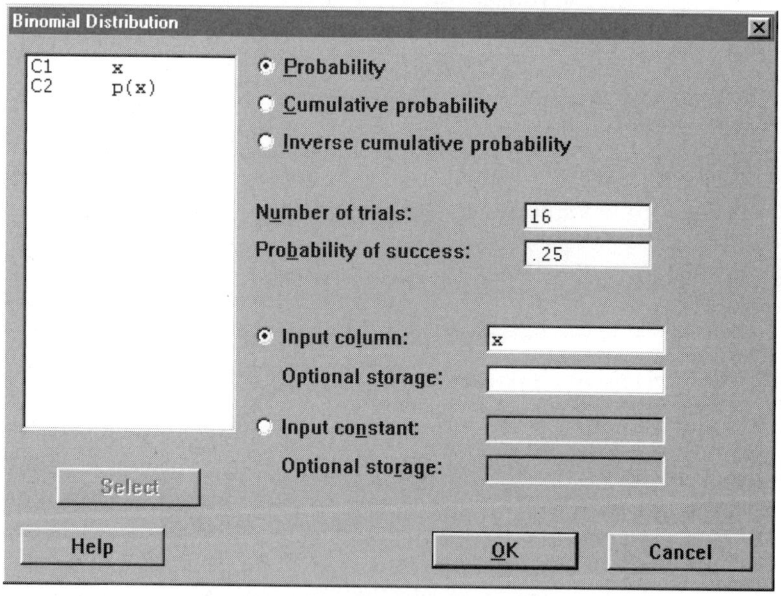

Binomial Distribution   ☒

| C1   x |
| C2   p(x) |

◉ <u>P</u>robability

○ <u>C</u>umulative probability

○ <u>I</u>nverse cumulative probability

N<u>u</u>mber of trials: [16]

Pro<u>b</u>ability of success: [.25]

◉ Input col<u>u</u>mn: [x]

   Optional st<u>o</u>rage: [   ]

○ Input co<u>n</u>stant: [   ]

   Optional sto<u>r</u>age: [   ]

[Select]

[Help]   [<u>O</u>K]   [Cancel]

of trials and the value of p in the appropriate boxes, and select "x" for the input column. (If you do not type a column number for storage, *MINITAB* will display the results in the Session window.) Make sure that the dot marked "Probability" is selected. The probability density function appears in the Session window when you click **OK** (a portion is shown in Figure 5.9). What is the probability that x equals 4? That x is either 3 or 4?

To calculate cumulative probabilities, make sure that the dot marked "Cumulative probability" is selected, and enter the appropriate values of x in C1. If you have only one value of x, it is simpler to select the Input constant box and enter the appropriate value. For example, for a Poisson random variable with $\mu = 5$, use **Calc → Probability Distributions → Poisson** and enter a mean of 5. If the number 6 is entered into the Input constant box, the probability that x is less than or equal to 6 appears in the Session window (see Figure 5.10).

MINITAB

What value k is such that only 5% of the values of x exceed this value (and 95% are less than or equal to k)? If you enter the probability .95 into the Input constant box and select the option marked "Inverse cumulative probability" (see Figure 5.11), then

FIGURE 5.9

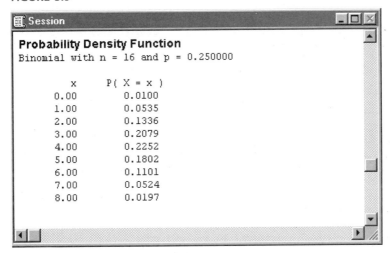

FIGURE 5.10

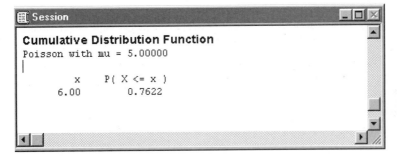

FIGURE 5.11

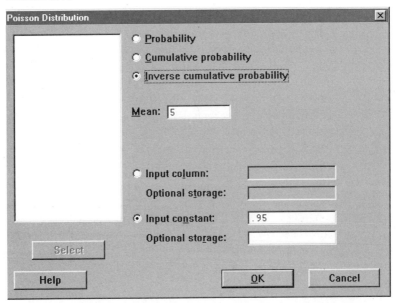

MINITAB

the values of x on either side of the ".95 mark" are shown in the Session window as in Figure 5.12. Hence, if you observed a value of $x = 10$, this would be an unusual observation because $P(x > 9) = 1 - .9682 = .0318$.

FIGURE 5.12

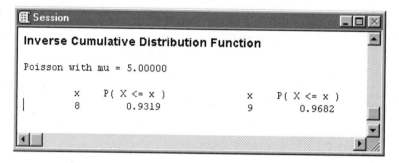

Supplementary Exercises

5.47 List the five identifying characteristics of the binomial experiment.

5.48 Under what conditions can the Poisson random variable be used to approximate the probabilities associated with the binomial random variable? What application does the Poisson distribution have other than to estimate certain binomial probabilities?

5.49 Under what conditions would you use the hypergeometric probability distribution to evaluate the probability of x successes in n trials?

5.50 A balanced coin is tossed three times. Let x equal the number of heads observed.

    a. Use the formula for the binomial probability distribution to calculate the probabilities associated with $x = 0, 1, 2,$ and 3.

    b. Construct the probability distribution.

    c. Find the mean and standard deviation of x, using these formulas:

$$\mu = np$$
$$\sigma = \sqrt{npq}$$

    d. Using the probability distribution in part b, find the fraction of the population measurements lying within one standard deviation of the mean. Repeat for two standard deviations. How do your results agree with Tchebysheff's Theorem and the Empirical Rule?

5.51 Refer to Exercise 5.50. Suppose the coin is definitely unbalanced and the probability of a head is equal to $p = .1$. Follow the instructions in parts a, b, c, and d. Note that the probability distribution loses its symmetry and becomes skewed when p is not equal to 1/2.

5.52 The 10-year survival rate for bladder cancer is approximately 50%. If 20 people who have bladder cancer are properly treated for the disease, what is the probability that:

    a. At least 1 will survive for 10 years?

    b. At least 10 will survive for 10 years?

    c. At least 15 will survive for 10 years?

5.53 A city commissioner claims that 80% of all people in the city favor garbage collection by contract to a private concern (in contrast to collection by city employees). To check the theory that the proportion of people in the city favoring private collection is .8, you randomly sample 25 people and find that x, the number of people who support the commissioner's claim, is 22.

    a. What is the probability of observing at least 22 who support the commissioner's claim if, in fact, $p = .8$?

b. What is the probability that x is exactly equal to 22?

c. Based on the results of part a, what would you conclude about the claim that 80% of all people in the city favor private collection? Explain.

5.54 If a person is given the choice of an integer from 0 to 9, is it more likely that he or she will choose an integer near the middle of the sequence than one at either end?

a. If the integers are equally likely to be chosen, find the probability distribution for x, the number chosen.

b. What is the probability that a person will choose a 4, 5, or 6?

c. What is the probability that a person will not choose a 4, 5, or 6?

5.55 Refer to Exercise 5.54. Twenty people are asked to select a number from 0 to 9. Eight of them choose a 4, 5, or 6.

a. If the choice of any one number is as likely as any other, what is the probability of observing eight or more choices of the numbers 4, 5, or 6?

b. What conclusions would you draw from the results of part a?

5.56 It has been reported that approximately 60% of U.S. households have two or more television sets and that at least half of Americans watch television by themselves.[5] Suppose that $n = 15$ U.S. households are sampled and x is the number of households that have two or more television sets.

a. What is the probability distribution for x?

b. Find $P(x \le 8)$.

c. What is the probability that x exceeds eight?

d. What is the largest value of c for which $P(x \le c) \le .10$?

5.57 As Americans start the 21st century, the number one status symbol is no longer being a top executive. Approximately 60% of Americans rank "owning a vacation home nestled on a beach or near a mountain resort" number one as a status symbol. A sample of $n = 400$ Americans is randomly selected.

a. What is the average number in the sample who would rank owning a vacation home number one?

b. What is the standard deviation of the number in the sample who would rank owning a vacation home number one?

c. Within what range would you expect to find the number in the sample who would rank having a vacation home as the number one status symbol?

d. If only 200 in a sample of 400 people ranked owning a vacation home as the top status symbol, would you consider this unusual? Explain. What conclusions might you draw from this sample information?

5.58 Reality TV (*Survivor, Big Brother*, etc.) is a new phenomenon in television programming, with contestants escaping to remote locations, taking dares, breaking world records, or racing across the country. Of those who watch reality TV, 50% say that their favorite reality show involves escaping to remote locations.[5] If 20 reality-TV fans are randomly selected, find the following probabilities:

a. Exactly 16 say that their favorite reality show involves escaping to remote locations.

b. From 15 to 18 say that their favorite reality show involves escaping to remote locations.

c. Five or fewer say that their favorite reality show involves escaping to remote locations. Would this be an unlikely occurrence?

5.59 A psychiatrist believes that 80% of all people who visit doctors have problems of a psychosomatic nature. She decides to select 25 patients at random to test her theory.

a. Assuming that the psychiatrist's theory is true, what is the expected value of x, the number of the 25 patients who have psychosomatic problems?

b. What is the variance of x, assuming that the theory is true?

c. Find $P(x \le 14)$. (Use tables and assume that the theory is true.)

d. Based on the probability in part c, if only 14 of the 25 sampled had psychosomatic problems, what conclusions would you make about the psychiatrist's theory? Explain.

 5.60 A student government states that 80% of all students favor an increase in student fees to subsidize a new recreational area. A random sample of $n = 25$ students produced 15 in favor of increased fees. What is the probability that 15 or fewer in the sample would favor the issue if student government is correct? Do the data support the student government's assertion, or does it appear that the percentage favoring an increase in fees is less than 80%?

5.61 College campuses are graying! According to a recent article, one in four college students is aged 30 or older. Many of these students are women updating their job skills. Assume that the 25% figure is accurate, that your college is representative of colleges at large, and that you sample $n = 200$ students, recording x, the number of students age 30 or older.

a. What are the mean and standard deviation of x?

b. If there are 35 students in your sample who are age 30 or older, would you be willing to assume that the 25% figure is representative of your campus? Explain.

5.62 Most weather forecasters protect themselves very well by attaching probabilities to their forecasts, such as "The probability of rain today is 40%." Then, if a particular forecast is incorrect, you are expected to attribute the error to the random behavior of the weather rather than to the inaccuracy of the forecaster. To check the accuracy of a particular forecaster, records were checked only for those days when the forecaster predicted rain "with 30% probability." A check of 25 of those days indicated that it rained on 10 of the 25.

a. If the forecaster is accurate, what is the appropriate value of p, the probability of rain on one of the 25 days?

b. What are the mean and standard deviation of x, the number of days on which it rained, assuming that the forecaster is accurate?

c. Calculate the z-score for the observed value, $x = 10$. [HINT: Recall from Section 2.6 that z-score $= (x - \mu)/\sigma$.]

d. Do these data disagree with the forecast of a "30% probability of rain"? Explain.

5.63 A packaging experiment is conducted by placing two different package designs for a breakfast food side by side on a supermarket shelf. The objective of the experiment is to see whether buyers indicate a preference for one of the two package designs. On a given day, 25 customers purchased a package from the supermarket. Let x equal the number of buyers who choose the second package design.

a. If there is no preference for either of the two designs, what is the value of p, the probability that a buyer chooses the second package design?

b. If there is no preference, use the results of part a to calculate the mean and standard deviation of x.

c. If 5 of the 25 customers choose the first package design and 20 choose the second design, what do you conclude about the customers' preference for the second package design?

5.64 One model for plant competition assumes that there is a zone of resource depletion around each plant seedling. Depending on the size of the zones and the density of the plants, the zones of resource depletion may overlap with those of other seedlings in the vicinity. When the seeds are randomly dispersed over a wide area, the number of neighbors that a seedling may have usually follows a Poisson distribution with a mean equal to the density of seedlings per unit area. Suppose that the density of seedlings is four per square meter (m^2).

a. What is the probability that a given seedling has no neighbors within 1 m^2?

b. What is the probability that a seedling has at most three neighbors per m^2?

c. What is the probability that a seedling has five or more neighbors per m^2?

d. Use the fact that the mean and variance of a Poisson random variable are equal to find the proportion of neighbors that would fall into the interval $\mu \pm 2\sigma$. Comment on this result.

5.65 A peony plant with red petals was crossed with another plant having streaky petals. The probability that an offspring from this cross has red flowers is .75. Let x be the number of plants with red petals resulting from ten seeds from this cross that were collected and germinated.

   a. Does the random variable x have a binomial distribution? If not, why not? If so, what are the values of n and p?

   b. Find $P(x \geq 9)$.

   c. Find $P(x \leq 1)$.

   d. Would it be unusual to observe one plant with red petals and the remaining nine plants with streaky petals? If these experimental results actually occurred, what conclusions could you draw?

5.66 The alleles for black (B) and white (b) feather color in chickens show incomplete dominance; individuals with the gene pair Bb have "blue" feathers. When one individual that is homozygous dominant (BB) for this trait is mated with an individual that is homozygous recessive (bb) for this trait, 1/4 of the offspring will carry the gene pair BB, 1/2 will carry the gene pair Bb, and 1/4 will carry the gene pair bb. Let x be the number of chicks with "blue" feathers in a sample of $n = 20$ chicks resulting from crosses involving homozygous dominant chickens (BB) with homozygous recessive chickens (bb).

   a. Does the random variable x have a binomial distribution? If not, why not? If so, what are the values of n and p?

   b. What is the mean number of chicks with "blue" feathers in the sample?

   c. What is the probability of observing fewer than five chicks with "blue" feathers?

   d. What is the probability that the number of chicks with "blue" feathers is greater than or equal to 10 but less than or equal to 12?

5.67 During the 1992 football season, the Los Angeles Rams (now the St. Louis Rams) had a bizarre streak of coin-toss losses. In fact, they lost the call 11 weeks in a row.[7]

   a. The Rams' computer system manager said that the odds against losing 11 straight tosses are 2047 to 1. Is he correct?

   b. After these results were published, the Rams lost the call for the next two games, for a total of 13 straight losses. What is the probability of this happening if, in fact, the coin was fair?

5.68 Insulin-dependent diabetes (IDD) is a common chronic disorder of children. This disease occurs most frequently in persons of northern European descent, but the incidence ranges from a low of 1–2 cases per 100,000 per year to a high of more than 40 per 100,000 in parts of Finland.[8] Let us assume that an area in Europe has an incidence of 5 cases per 100,000 per year.

   a. Can the distribution of the number of cases of IDD in this area be approximated by a Poisson distribution? If so, what is the mean?

   b. What is the probability that the number of cases of IDD in this area is less than or equal to 3 per 100,000?

   c. What is the probability that the number of cases is greater than or equal to 3 but less than or equal to 7 per 100,000?

   d. Would you expect to observe 10 or more cases of IDD per 100,000 in this area in a given year? Why or why not?

5.69 A manufacturer of videotapes ships them in lots of 1200 tapes per lot. Before shipment, 20 tapes are randomly selected from each lot and tested. If none is defective, the lot is shipped. If one or more are defective, every tape in the lot is tested.

   a. What is the probability distribution for x, the number of defective tapes in the sample of 20?

   b. What distribution can be used to approximate probabilities for the random variable x in part a?

   c. What is the probability that a lot will be shipped if it contains 10 defectives? 20 defectives? 30 defectives?

5.70 California residents love to complain about smog, freeway traffic, crime, and earthquakes, and although the quality of life in California may not be what it once was, roughly 75% of Californi-ans think that it is "one of the best places to live" or "nice, but not outstanding."[9] Suppose that five randomly selected California residents are interviewed.

a. Find the probability that all five residents think that California is a nice or very nice place to live.

b. What is the probability that at least one resident does not think that California is a nice or very nice place to live?

c. What is the probability that exactly one resident does not think that California is a nice or very nice place to live?

5.71 Tay–Sachs disease is a genetic disorder that is usually fatal in young children. If both parents are carriers of the disease, the probability that their offspring will develop the disease is approximately .25. Suppose a husband and wife are both carriers of the disease and the wife is pregnant on three different occasions. If the occurrence of Tay–Sachs in any one offspring is independent of the occurrence in any other, what are the probabilities of these events?

a. All three children will develop Tay–Sachs disease.

b. Only one child will develop Tay–Sachs disease.

c. The third child will develop Tay–Sachs disease, given that the first two did not.

Exercises DO IT YOURSELF!

Use the **Calculating Binomial Probabilities** applet for the following set of exercises.

5.72 Refer to Exercise 5.4 and 5.5.

a. Use the applet to construct the probability histogram for a binomial random variable x with $n = 6$ and $p = .2$.

b. Use the applet to construct the probability histogram for a binomial random variable x with $n = 6$ and $p = .8$. How would you describe the shapes of the distributions in parts a and b?

c. Use the applet to construct the probability histogram for a binomial random variable x with $n = 6$ and $p = .5$. How would you describe the shape of this distribution?

5.73 Use the applet to find the following:

a. $P(x < 6)$ for $n = 22$, $p = .65$

b. $P(x = 8)$ for $n = 12$, $p = .4$

c. $P(x) > 14)$ for $n = 20$, $p = .5$

d. $P(2 < x < 6)$ for $n = 15$, $p = .3$

e. $P(x \geq 6)$ for $n = 50$, $p = .7$

5.74 A new surgical procedure is said to be successful 80% of the time. Suppose the operation is per-formed five times and the results are assumed to be independent of one another. What are the probabilities of these events?

a. All five operations are successful.

b. Exactly four are successful.

c. Less than two are successful.

5.75 Refer to Exercise 5.74. If less than two operations were successful, how would you feel about the performance of the surgical team?

5.76 Suppose the four engines of a commercial aircraft are arranged to operate independently and that the probability of in-flight failure of a single engine is .01. What is the probability of these events on a given flight?

a. No failures are observed.

b. No more than one failure is observed.

5.77 Suppose that 50% of all young adults prefer McDonald's to Burger King when asked to state a preference. A group of 100 young adults were randomly selected and their preferences recorded.

a. What is the probability that more than 60 preferred McDonald's?

b. What is the probability that between 40 and 60 (inclusive) preferred McDonald's?

c. What is the probability that between 40 and 60 (inclusive) preferred Burger King?

5.78 Most of today's college seniors want to start earning money as soon as they graduate from college. In fact, only 14% of college seniors say that they are likely to take some time off to travel and relax after graduation.[10] Suppose that 50 college seniors were randomly selected.

a. What is the average value of x, the number of college seniors in the group who say they will take some time off after graduation? What is the standard deviation of x?

b. Would it be unlikely to find 15 or more in the group who say they will take some time off after graduation? Use the applet to find the probability of this event.

c. How many standard deviations from the mean is the value $x = 15$? Does this confirm your answer in part b?

Case Study   A Mystery: Cancers Near a Reactor

How safe is it to live near a nuclear reactor? Men who lived in a coastal strip that extends 20 miles north from a nuclear reactor in Plymouth, Massachusetts, developed some forms of cancer at a rate 50% higher than the statewide rate, according to a study endorsed by the Massachusetts Department of Public Health and reported in the May 21, 1987, edition of the *New York Times*.[11]

The cause of the cancers is a mystery, but it was suggested that the cancer was linked to the Pilgrim I reactor, which had been shut down for 13 months because of management problems. Boston Edison, the owner of the reactor, acknowledged radiation releases in the mid-1970s that were just above permissible levels. If the reactor was in fact responsible for the excessive cancer rate, then the currently acknowledged level of radiation required to cause cancer would have to change. However, confounding the mystery was the fact that women in this same area were seemingly unaffected.

In his report, Dr. Sidney Cobb, an epidemiologist, noted the connection between the radiation releases at the Pilgrim I reactor and 52 cases of hematopoietic cancers. The report indicated that this unexpectedly large number might be attributable to airborne radioactive effluents from Pilgrim I, concentrated along the coast by wind patterns and not dissipated, as assumed by government regulators. How unusual was this number of cancer cases? That is, statistically speaking, is 52 a highly improbable number of cases? If the answer is yes, then either some external factor (possibly radiation) caused this unusually large number, or we have observed a very rare event!

The Poisson probability distribution provides a good approximation to the distributions of variables such as the number of deaths in a region due to a rare disease, the number of accidents in a manufacturing plant per month, or the number of airline crashes per month. Therefore, it is reasonable to assume that the Poisson distribution provides an appropriate model for the number of cancer cases in this instance.

1. If the 52 reported cases represented a rate 50% higher than the statewide rate, what is a reasonable estimate of μ, the average number of such cancer cases statewide?
2. Based on your estimate of μ, what is the estimated standard deviation of the number of cancer cases statewide?
3. What is the z-score for the $x = 52$ observed cases of cancer? How do you interpret this z-score in light of the concern about an elevated rate of hematopoietic cancers in this area?

Data Sources

1. "College-Entry Scores Show Little Change in California," *The Press Enterprise* (Riverside, CA), 29 August 2001, p. A-10.

2. http://usatoday.com/snapshot/life/2001-06-11-potter.htm. *Source:* Ipsos-NPD Book Trends 9 October 2001.

3. Christy Fisher, "The Not-So-Great American Road Trip," *American Demographics,* May 1997, p. 47.

4. L.D. Williams, P.S. Hamilton, B.W. Wilson, and M.D. Estock, "An Outbreak of *Escherichia coli 01257:H7* involving Long Term Shedding and Person-to-Person Transmission in a Child Care Center," *Environmental Health,* May 1997, p. 9.

5. Data adapted from *American Demographics,* May 1997, p. 32.

6. http://www.usatoday.com/snapshot/life/2001-08-09-reality-tv.htm. *Source:* E-Poll, July 2001, 9 October 2001.

7. "Call It in the Air," *The Press-Enterprise* (Riverside, CA), 19 October 1992.

8. Mark A. Atkinson, "Diet, Genetics, and Diabetes," *Food Technology* 51, no. 3 (March 1997), p. 77.

9. Sam Delson, "State Rated Best Despite Negative Feelings," *The Press-Enterprise* (Riverside, CA), 30 June 1997, p. A-3.

10. Sandra Yin, Pamela Paul, and David Whelan, "What Summer Break?" *American Demographics,* July 2001, p. 64.

11. Matthew L. Wald, "Cancers Near a Reactor: A Mystery and a Debate," *New York Times,* 21 May 1987, p. A-22.

6

The Normal Probability Distribution

Case Study

If you were the boss, would height play a role in your selection of a successor for your job? Would you purposely choose a successor who was shorter than you? The case study at the end of this chapter examines how the normal curve can be used to investigate the height distribution of Chinese men eligible for a very prestigious job.

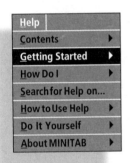

General Objectives

In Chapters 4 and 5, you learned about discrete random variables and their probability distributions. In this chapter, you will learn about continuous random variables and their probability distributions and about one very important continuous random variable—the normal. You will learn how to calculate normal probabilities and, under certain conditions, how to use the normal probability distribution to approximate the binomial probability distribution. Then, in Chapter 7 and in the chapters that follow, you will see how the normal probability distribution plays a central role in statistical inference.

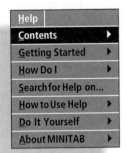

Specific Topics

1. Probability distributions for continuous random variables (6.1)
2. The normal probability distribution (6.2)
3. Calculation of areas associated with the normal probability distribution (6.3)
4. The normal approximation to the binomial probability distribution (6.4)

6.1 Probability Distributions for Continuous Random Variables

When a random variable x is discrete, you can assign a positive probability to each value that x can take and get the probability distribution for x. The sum of all the probabilities associated with the different values of x is 1. However, not all experiments result in random variables that are discrete. **Continuous random variables,** such as heights and weights, length of life of a particular product, or experimental laboratory error, can assume the infinitely many values corresponding to points on a line interval. If you try to assign a positive probability to each of these uncountable values, the probabilities will no longer sum to 1, as with discrete random variables. Therefore, you must use a different approach to generate the probability distribution for a continuous random variable.

Suppose you have a set of measurements on a continuous random variable, and you create a relative frequency histogram to describe their distribution. For a small number of measurements, you could use a small number of classes; then as more and more measurements are collected, you can use more classes and reduce the class width. The outline of the histogram will change slightly, for the most part becoming less and less irregular, as shown in Figure 6.1. As the number of measurements becomes very large

FIGURE 6.1 Relative frequency histograms for increasingly large sample sizes

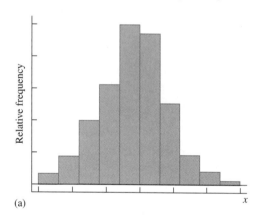

(a)

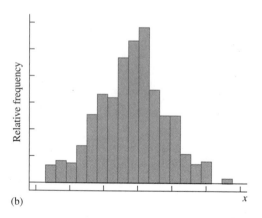

(b)

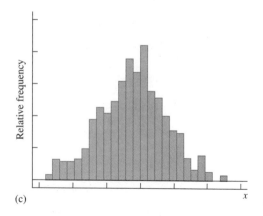

(c)

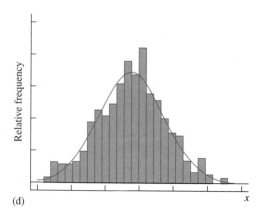

(d)

and the class widths become very narrow, the relative frequency histogram appears more and more like the smooth curve shown in Figure 6.1(d). This smooth curve describes the **probability distribution of the continuous random variable.**

How can you create a model for this probability distribution? A continuous random variable can take on any of an infinite number of values on the real line, much like the infinite number of grains of sand on a beach. The probability distribution is created by distributing one unit of probability along the line, much as you might distribute a handful of sand. The probability—grains of sand or measurements—will pile up in certain places, and the result is the probability distribution shown in Figure 6.2. The depth or **density** of the probability, which varies with x, may be described by a mathematical formula $f(x)$, called the **probability distribution** or **probability density function** for the random variable x.

FIGURE 6.2
The probability distribution $f(x)$; $P(a < x < b)$ is equal to the shaded area under the curve

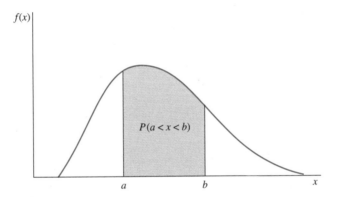

Several important properties of continuous probability distributions parallel their discrete counterparts. Just as the sum of discrete probabilities (or the sum of the relative frequencies) is equal to 1, and the probability that x falls into a certain interval can be found by summing the probabilities in that interval, continuous probability distributions have the characteristics listed next.

- The area under a continuous probability distribution is equal to 1.
- The probability that x will fall into a particular interval—say, from a to b—is equal to the area under the curve between the two points a and b. This is the shaded area in Figure 6.2.

There is also one important difference between discrete and continuous random variables. Consider the probability that x equals some particular value—say, a. Since there is no area above a single point—say, $x = a$—in the probability distribution for a continuous random variable, our definition implies that the probability is 0.

- $P(x = a) = 0$ for continuous random variables.
- This implies that $P(x \geq a) = P(x > a)$ and $P(x \leq a) = P(x < a)$.
- This is *not* true in general for discrete random variables.

How do you choose the model—that is, the probability distribution $f(x)$—appropriate for a given experiment? Many types of continuous curves are available for modeling. Some are mound-shaped, like the one in Figure 6.1(d), but others are not. In general, try to pick a model that meets these criteria:

- It fits the accumulated body of data.
- It allows you to make the best possible inferences using the data.

Your model may not always fit the experimental situation perfectly, but you should try to choose a model that *best fits* the population relative frequency histogram. The better the model approximates reality, the better your inferences will be. Fortunately, many continuous random variables have mound-shaped frequency distributions, such as the data in Figure 6.1(d). The **normal probability distribution** provides a good model for describing this type of data.

6.2 The Normal Probability Distribution

Continuous probability distributions can assume a variety of shapes. However, a large number of random variables observed in nature possess a frequency distribution that is approximately mound-shaped or, as the statistician would say, is approximately a normal probability distribution. The formula that generates this distribution is shown next.

Normal Probability Distribution

$$f(x) = \frac{1}{\sigma\sqrt{2\pi}}\, e^{-(x-\mu)^2/(2\sigma^2)} \qquad -\infty \leq x \leq \infty$$

The symbols e and π are mathematical constants given approximately by 2.7183 and 3.1416, respectively; μ and σ ($\sigma > 0$) are parameters that represent the population mean and standard deviation.

The graph of a normal probability distribution with mean μ and standard deviation σ is shown in Figure 6.3. The mean μ locates the *center* of the distribution, and the distribution is *symmetric* about its mean μ. Since the total area under the normal probability distribution is equal to 1, the symmetry implies that the area to the right of μ is .5 and the area to the left of μ is also .5. The *shape* of the distribution is determined by σ, the population standard deviation. As you can see in Figure 6.4, large values of σ reduce the height of the curve and increase the spread; small values of σ increase the

FIGURE 6.3
Normal probability distribution

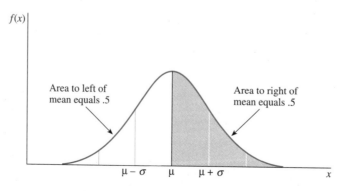

FIGURE 6.4
Normal probability
distributions with
differing values of
μ and σ

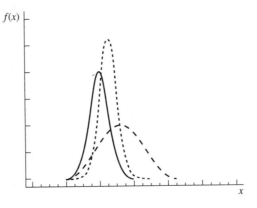

height of the curve and reduce the spread. Figure 6.4 shows three normal probability distributions with different means and standard deviations. Notice the differences in shape and location.

DO IT YOURSELF!

The Java applet called **Visualizing Normal Curves** gives a visual display of the normal distribution for values of μ between -10 and $+8$ and for values of σ between 0.5 and 1.8. The dark blue curve is the standard normal z with mean 0 and standard deviation 1. You can use this applet to compare its shape to the shape of other normal curves (the red curve on your monitor, light blue in Figure 6.5) by moving the sliders to change the mean and standard deviation. What happens when you change the mean? When you change the standard deviation?

FIGURE 6.5
**Visualizing Normal
Curves** applet

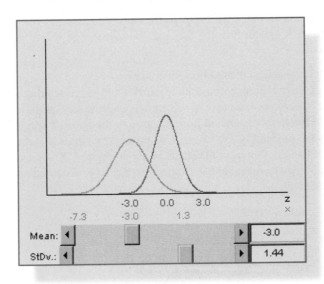

You rarely find a variable with values that are infinitely small $(-\infty)$ or infinitely large $(+\infty)$. Even so, many *positive* random variables (such as heights, weights, and times) have distributions that are well approximated by a normal distribution. According to the Empirical Rule, almost all values of a normal random variable lie in the interval $\mu \pm 3\sigma$. As long as these values are *positive*, the normal distribution provides a good model to describe the data.

6.3 Tabulated Areas of the Normal Probability Distribution

To find the probability that a normal random variable x lies in the interval from a to b, we need to find the area under the normal curve between the points a and b (see Figure 6.2). However (see Figure 6.4), there are an infinitely large number of normal distributions—one for each different mean and standard deviation. A separate table of areas for each of these curves is obviously impractical. Instead, we use a standardization procedure that allows us to use the same table for all normal distributions.

The Standard Normal Random Variable

A normal random variable x is **standardized** by expressing its value as the number of standard deviations (σ) it lies to the left or right of its mean μ. This is really just a change in the units of measure that we use, as if we were measuring in inches rather than in feet! The standardized normal random variable, z, is defined as

$$z = \frac{x - \mu}{\sigma}$$

or equivalently,

$$x = \mu + z\sigma$$

From the formula for z, we can draw these conclusions:

- When x is less than the mean μ, the value of z is negative.
- When x is greater than the mean μ, the value of z is positive.
- When $x = \mu$, the value of $z = 0$.

The probability distribution for z, shown in Figure 6.6, is called the **standardized normal distribution** because its mean is 0 and its standard deviation is 1. Values of z on the left side of the curve are negative, while values on the right side are positive. The area under the standard normal curve to the left of a specified value of z—say, z_0—is the probability $P(z \le z_0)$. This **cumulative area** is recorded in Table 3 of Appendix I and is shown as the shaded area in Figure 6.6. An abbreviated version of Table 3 is given in Table 6.1. Notice that the table contains both positive and negative

FIGURE 6.6
Standardized
normal distribution

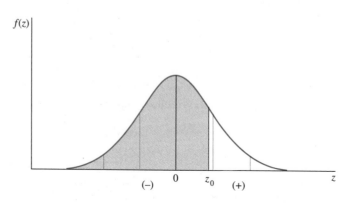

values of z. The left-hand column of the table gives the value of z correct to the tenth place; the second decimal place for z, corresponding to hundredths, is given across the top row.

TABLE 6.1 Abbreviated version of Table 3 in Appendix 1

Table 3. Areas under the Normal Curve

z	.00	.01	.02	.03	...	.09
−3.4	.0003	.0003	.0003	.0003		
−3.3	.0005	.0005	.0005	.0004		
−3.2	.0007	.0007	.0006	.0006		
−3.1	.0010	.0009	.0009	.0009		
−3.0	.0013	.0013	.0013	.0012	...	.0010
−2.9	.0019	·	·	·		
−2.8	.0026	·	·	·		
−2.7	.0035	·	·	·		
−2.6	.0047					
−2.5	.0062					
·	·					
·	·					
−2.0	.0228					

Table 3. Areas under the Normal Curve (*continued*)

z	.00	.01	.02	.03	.04	...	.09
0.0	.5000	.5040	.5080	.5120	.5160		
0.1	.5398	.5438	.5478	.5517	.5557		
0.2	.5793	.5832	.5871	.5910	.5948		
0.3	.6179	.6217	.6255	.6293	.6331		
0.4	.6554	.6591	.6628	.6664	.6700	...	.6879
0.5	.6915	·	·	·			
0.6	.7257	·	·	·			
0.7	.7580	·	·	·			
0.8	.7881						
0.9	.8159						
·	·						
·	·						
2.0	.9772						

EXAMPLE 6.1 Find $P(z \leq 1.63)$. This probability corresponds to the area to the left of a point $z = 1.63$ standard deviations to the right of the mean (see Figure 6.7).

FIGURE 6.7
Area under the standard normal curve for Example 6.1

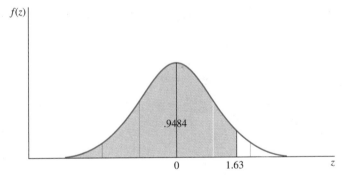

Solution The area is shaded in Figure 6.7. Since Table 3 in Appendix I gives areas under the normal curve to the left of a specified value of z, you simply need to find the tabled value for $z = 1.63$. Proceed down the left-hand column of the table to $z = 1.6$ and across the top of the table to the column marked .03. The intersection of this row and column combination gives the area .9484, which is $P(z \leq 1.63)$.

Areas to the left of $z = 0$ are found using negative values of z.

EXAMPLE 6.2 Find $P(z \geq -0.5)$. This probability corresponds to the area to the *right* of a point $z = -0.5$ standard deviation to the left of the mean (see Figure 6.8).

FIGURE 6.8
Area under the
standard normal
curve for
Example 6.2

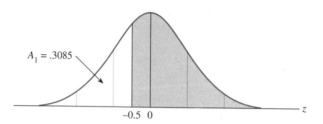

Solution The area given in Table 3 is the area to the left of a specified value of z. Indexing $z = -0.5$ in Table 3, we can find the area A_1 to the *left* of -0.5 to be .3085.

Since the area under the curve is 1, we find $P(z \geq -0.5) = 1 - A_1 = 1 - .3085 = .6915$.

EXAMPLE 6.3 Find $P(-.5 \leq z \leq 1.0)$. This probability is the area between $z = -0.5$ and $z = 1.0$, as shown in Figure 6.9.

FIGURE 6.9
Area under the
standard normal
curve for
Example 6.3

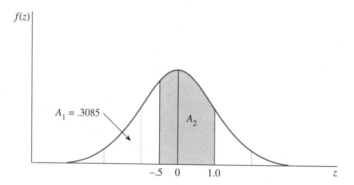

Solution The area required is the shaded area A_2 in Figure 6.9. From Table 3 in Appendix I, you can find the area to the left of $z = -0.5$ ($A_1 = .3085$) and the area to the left of $z = 1.0$ ($A_1 + A_2 = .8413$). To find the area marked A_2, we subtract the two entries:

$$A_2 = (A_1 + A_2) - A_1 = .8413 - .3085 = .5328$$

That is, $P(-.5 \leq z \leq 1.0) = .5328$.

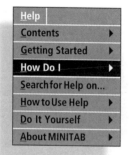

Use Table 3 to Calculate Probabilities under the Standard Normal Curve?

- To calculate the area to the left of a z-value, find the area directly from Table 3.
- To calculate the area to the right of a z-value, find the area in Table 3, and subtract from 1.
- To calculate the area between two values of z, find the two areas in Table 3, and subtract one area from the other.

EXAMPLE 6.4   Find the probability that a normally distributed random variable will fall within these ranges:

1. One standard deviation of its mean
2. Two standard deviations of its mean

Solution   1. Since the standard normal random variable z measures the distance from the mean in units of standard deviations, you need to find

$$P(-1 \leq z \leq 1) = .8413 - .1587 = .6826$$

Remember that you calculate the area between two z-values by subtracting the tabled entries for the two values.

2. As in part 1, $P(-2 \leq z \leq 2) = .9772 - .0228 = .9544$.

These probabilities agree with the approximate values of 68% and 95% in the Empirical Rule from Chapter 2.

EXAMPLE 6.5   Find the value of z—say z_0—such that .95 of the area is within $\pm z_0$ standard deviations of the mean.

Solution   The shaded area in Figure 6.10 is the area within $\pm z_0$ standard deviations of the mean, which needs to be equal to .95. The "tail areas" under the curve are not shaded, and have a combined area of $1 - .95 = .05$. Because of the symmetry of the normal curve, these two tail areas have the same area, so that $A_1 = .05/2 = .025$ in Figure 6.10. Thus, the entire *cumulative area* to the left of z_0 to equal $A_1 + A_2 = .95 + .025 = .9750$. This area is found in the interior of Table 3 in Appendix I in the row corresponding to $z = 1.9$ and the .06 column. Hence, $z_0 = 1.96$. Note that this result is very close to the approximate value, $z = 2$, used in the Empirical Rule.

FIGURE 6.10
Area under the
standard normal
curve for
Example 6.5

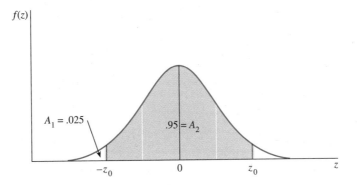

Calculating Probabilities for a General Normal Random Variable

Most of the time, the probabilities you are interested in will involve x, a normal random variable with mean μ and standard deviation σ. You must then *standardize* the interval of interest, writing it as the equivalent interval in terms of z, the standard normal random variable. Once this is done, the probability of interest is the area that you find using the *standard normal probability distribution*.

EXAMPLE 6.6   Let x be a normally distributed random variable with a mean of 10 and a standard deviation of 2. Find the probability that x lies between 11 and 13.6.

Solution   The interval from $x = 11$ to $x = 13.6$ must be standardized using the formula for z. When $x = 11$,

$$z = \frac{x - \mu}{\sigma} = \frac{11 - 10}{2} = .5$$

and when $x = 13.6$,

$$z = \frac{x - \mu}{\sigma} = \frac{13.6 - 10}{2} = 1.8$$

The desired probability is therefore $P(.5 \leq z \leq 1.8)$, the area lying between $z = .5$ and $z = 1.8$, as shown in Figure 6.11. From Table 3 in Appendix I, you find that the area to the left of $z = .5$ is .6915, and the area to the left of $z = 1.8$ is .9641. The desired probability is the difference between these two probabilities, or

$$P(.5 \leq z \leq 1.8) = .9641 - .6915 = .2726$$

FIGURE 6.11
Area under the standard normal curve for Example 6.6

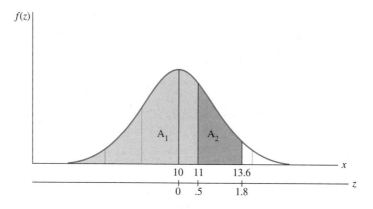

DO IT YOURSELF!

The Java applet called **Normal Distribution Probabilities** allows you to calculate areas under a normal distribution for any values of μ and σ you select. Simply type the appropriate mean and standard deviation into the boxes at the top of the applet, type the interval of interest into the boxes at the bottom of the applet, and press "Enter" at each step to record your changes. (The "Tab" key will move your cursor from box to box.) The necessary area will be shaded in red on your monitor (blue in Figure 6.12) and the probability is given to the left of the curve.

- If you need an area under the standard normal distribution, use $\mu = 0$ and $\sigma = 1$.
- In Example 6.6, we need an area under a normal distribution with $\mu = 10$ and $\sigma = 2$. Notice the values of x and z located along the horizontal axis. Find the probability, $P(11 \leq x \leq 13.6) = P(0.5 \leq z \leq 1.8) = .2726$, in Figure 6.12.

FIGURE 6.12
**Normal
Distribution
Probabilities**
applet

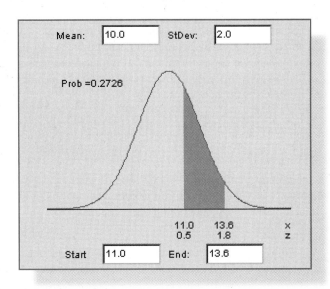

EXAMPLE 6.7

Studies show that gasoline use for compact cars sold in the United States is normally distributed, with a mean of 25.5 miles per gallon (mpg) and a standard deviation of 4.5 mpg. What percentage of compacts get 30 mpg or more?

Solution

The proportion of compacts that get 30 mpg or more is given by the shaded area in Figure 6.13. To solve this problem, you must first find the z-value corresponding to $x = 30$. Substituting into the formula for z, you get

$$z = \frac{x - \mu}{\sigma} = \frac{30 - 25.5}{4.5} = 1.0$$

The area A_1 to the left of $z = 1.0$, is .8413 (from Table 3 in Appendix I). Then the proportion of compacts that get 30 mpg or more is equal to:

$$P(x \geq 30) = 1 - P(z < 1) = 1 - .8413 = .1587$$

The percentage exceeding 30 mpg is

$$100(.1587) = 15.87\%$$

FIGURE 6.13
Area under the
standard normal
curve for
Example 6.7

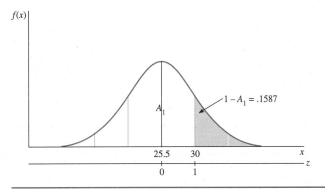

EXAMPLE 6.8

Refer to Example 6.7. In times of scarce energy resources, a competitive advantage is given to an automobile manufacturer who can produce a car that has substantially better fuel economy than the competitors' cars. If a manufacturer wishes to develop a compact car that outperforms 95% of the current compacts in fuel economy, what must the gasoline use rate for the new car be?

Solution   The gasoline use rate x has a normal distribution with a mean of 25.5 mpg and a standard deviation of 4.5 mpg. You need to find a particular value—say, x_0—such that

$$P(x \leq x_0) = .95$$

This is the 95th percentile of the distribution of gasoline use rate x. Since the only information you have about normal probabilities is in terms of the standard normal random variable z, start by standardizing the value of x_0:

$$z_0 = \frac{x_0 - 25.5}{4.5}$$

Since the value of z_0 corresponds to x_0, it must *also* have area .95 to its left, as shown in Figure 6.14. If you look in the interior of Table 3 in Appendix I, you will find that the area .9500 is exactly halfway between the areas for $z = 1.64$ and $z = 1.65$. Thus, z_0 must be exactly halfway between 1.64 and 1.65, or

$$z_0 = \frac{x_0 - 25.5}{4.5} = 1.645$$

Solving for x_0, you obtain

$$x_0 = \mu + z_0\sigma = 25.5 + (1.645)(4.5) = 32.9$$

FIGURE 6.14
Area under the
standard normal
curve for
Example 6.8

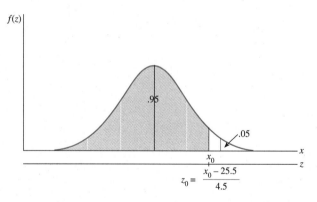

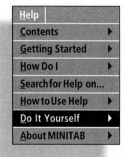

The manufacturer's new compact car must therefore get 32.9 mpg to outperform 95% of the compact cars currently available on the U.S. market.

DO IT YOURSELF!

The Java applet called **Normal Probabilities and z-scores** allows you to calculate areas under a normal distribution for any values of μ and σ you select. Once you specify one value for x, the applet calculates the value of z, and one of four types of areas, which you can select from the dropdown list at the bottom of the applet:

■ Cumulative ⟹ area to the left of z
■ One-tailed ⟹ area to the right of z

■ Two-tailed ⟹ area in two tails cut off by $-z$ and z
■ Middle ⟹ area between $-z$ and z

You can also work backward as we did to solve the problem in Example 6.8. We entered the mean and standard deviation, and then selected "Cumulative" with a probability of **.95**. If the boxes for x and z are left blank, pressing "Enter" will solve for these values, as shown in Figure 6.15. What is the value of x, correct to 6 decimal places?

FIGURE 6.15
Normal Probabilities and z-scores applet

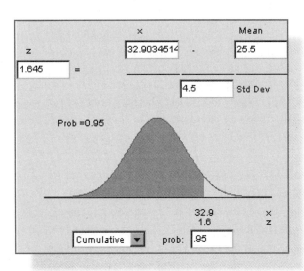

Exercises

Basic Techniques

6.1   Calculate the area under the standard normal curve to the left of these values:
  a. $z = 1.6$ **b.** $z = 1.83$
  c. $z = .90$ **d.** $z = 4.18$

6.2   Calculate the area under the standard normal curve between these values:
  a. $z = -1.4$ and $z = 1.4$ **b.** $z = -3.0$ and $z = 3.0$

6.3   Find the following probabilities for the standard normal random variable z:
  a. $P(-1.43 < z < .68)$ **b.** $P(.58 < z < 1.74)$
  c. $P(-1.55 < z < -.44)$ **d.** $P(z > 1.34)$ **e.** $P(z < -4.32)$

6.4   Find these probabilities for the standard normal random variable z:
  a. $P(z < 2.33)$ **b.** $P(z < 1.645)$
  c. $P(z > 1.96)$ **d.** $P(-2.58 < z < 2.58)$

6.5   **a.** Find a z_0 such that $P(z > z_0) = .025$.   **b.** Find a z_0 such that $P(z < z_0) = .9251$.

6.6   Find a z_0 such that $P(-z_0 < z < z_0) = .8262$.

6.7   **a.** Find a z_0 that has area .9505 to its left.
  b. Find a z_0 that has area .05 to its left.

6.8   **a.** Find a z_0 such that $P(-z_0 < z < z_0) = .90$.
  b. Find a z_0 such that $P(-z_0 < z < z_0) = .99$.

6.9   Find the following *percentiles* for the standard normal random variable z:
  a. 90th percentile   **b.** 95th percentile
  c. 98th percentile   **d.** 99th percentile

6.10 A normal random variable x has mean $\mu = 10$ and standard deviation $\sigma = 2$. Find the probabilities of these x-values:

a. $x > 13.5$ **b.** $x < 8.2$ **c.** $9.4 < x < 10.6$

6.11 A normal random variable x has mean $\mu = 1.20$ and standard deviation $\sigma = .15$. Find the probabilities of these x-values:

a. $1.00 < x < 1.10$ **b.** $x > 1.38$ **c.** $1.35 < x < 1.50$

6.12 A normal random variable x has an unknown mean μ and standard deviation $\sigma = 2$. If the probability that x exceeds 7.5 is .8023, find μ.

6.13 A normal random variable x has mean 35 and standard deviation 10. Find a value of x that has area .01 to its right. This is the *99th percentile* of this normal distribution.

6.14 A normal random variable x has mean 50 and standard deviation 15. Would it be unusual to observe the value $x = 0$? Explain your answer.

6.15 A normal random variable x has an unknown mean and standard deviation. The probability that x exceeds 4 is .9772, and the probability that x exceeds 5 is .9332. Find μ and σ.

Applications

6.16 The meat department at a local supermarket specifically prepares its "1-pound" packages of ground beef so that there will be a variety of weights, some slightly more and some slightly less than 1 pound. Suppose that the weights of these "1-pound" packages are normally distributed with a mean of 1.00 pound and a standard deviation of .15 pound.

a. What proportion of the packages will weigh more than 1 pound?

b. What proportion of the packages will weigh between .95 and 1.05 pounds?

c. What is the probability that a randomly selected package of ground beef will weigh less than .80 pound?

d. Would it be unusual to find a package of ground beef that weighs 1.45 pounds? How would you explain such a large package?

6.17 Human heights are one of many biological random variables that can be modeled by the normal distribution. Assume the heights of men have a mean of 69 inches with a standard deviation of 3.5 inches.

a. What proportion of all men will be taller than 6'0"? (HINT: Convert the measurements to inches.)

b. What is the probability that a randomly selected man will be between 5'8" and 6'1" tall?

c. President Bush is 6'0" tall. Is this an unusual height?

d. Of the 36 elected presidents from 1856 to the present, 17 were 6'0" or taller.[1] Would you consider this to be unusual, given the proportion found in part a?

6.18 The diameters of Douglas firs grown at a Christmas tree farm are normally distributed with a mean of 4 inches and a standard deviation of 1.5 inches.

a. What proportion of the trees will have diameters between 3 and 5 inches?

b. What proportion of the trees will have diameters less than 3 inches?

c. Your Christmas tree stand will expand to a diameter of 6 inches. What proportion of the trees will not fit in your Christmas tree stand?

6.19 Cerebral blood flow (CBF) in the brains of healthy people is normally distributed with a mean of 74 and a standard deviation of 16.

a. What proportion of healthy people will have CBF readings between 60 and 80?

b. What proportion of healthy people will have CBF readings above 100?

c. If a person has a CBF reading below 40, he is classified as at risk for a stroke. What proportion of healthy people will mistakenly be diagnosed as "at risk"?

6.20 For a car traveling 30 miles per hour (mph), the distance required to brake to a stop is normally distributed with a mean of 50 feet and a standard deviation of 8 feet. Suppose you are traveling 30 mph in a residential area and a car moves abruptly into your path at a distance of 60 feet.

   a. If you apply your brakes, what is the probability that you will brake to a stop within 40 feet or less? Within 50 feet or less?

   b. If the only way to avoid a collision is to brake to a stop, what is the probability that you will avoid the collision?

6.21 Suppose you must establish regulations concerning the maximum number of people who can occupy an elevator. A study of elevator occupancies indicates that, if eight people occupy the elevator, the probability distribution of the total weight of the eight people has a mean equal to 1200 pounds and a variance equal to 9800 lbs^2. What is the probability that the total weight of eight people exceeds 1300 pounds? 1500 pounds? (Assume that the probability distribution is approximately normal.)

6.22 The discharge of suspended solids from a phosphate mine is normally distributed, with a mean daily discharge of 27 milligrams per liter (mg/l) and a standard deviation of 14 mg/l. What proportion of days will the daily discharge exceed 50 mg/l?

6.23 An experimenter wondered if the stem diameters of the dicot sunflower would change depending on whether the plant was left to sway freely in the wind or was artificially supported.[2] Suppose that the unsupported stem diameters at the base of a particular species of sunflower plant have a normal distribution with an average diameter of 35 millimeters (mm) and a standard deviation of 3 mm.

   a. What is the probability that a sunflower plant will have a basal diameter of more than 40 mm?

   b. If two sunflower plants are randomly selected, what is the probability that both plants will have a basal diameter of more than 40 mm?

   c. Within what limits would you expect the basal diameters to lie, with probability .95?

   d. What diameter represents the 90th percentile of the distribution of diameters?

6.24 The number of times x an adult human breathes per minute when at rest depends on the age of the human and varies greatly from person to person. Suppose the probability distribution for x is approximately normal, with the mean equal to 16 and the standard deviation equal to 4. If a person is selected at random and the number x of breaths per minute while at rest is recorded, what is the probability that x will exceed 22?

6.25 One method of arriving at economic forecasts is to use a consensus approach. A forecast is obtained from each of a large number of analysts, and the average of these individual forecasts is the consensus forecast. Suppose the individual 2003 January prime interest rate forecasts of all economic analysts are approximately normally distributed, with the mean equal to 7.5% and the standard deviation equal to 1.3%. If a single analyst is randomly selected from among this group, what is the probability that the analyst's forecast of the prime interest rate will take on these values?

   a. Exceed 10%

   b. Be less than 7%

6.26 How does the IRS decide on the percentage of income tax returns to audit for each state? Suppose they do it by randomly selecting 50 values from a normal distribution with a mean equal to 1.55% and a standard deviation equal to .45%. (Computer programs are available for this type of sampling.)

   a. What is the probability that a particular state will have more than 2.5% of its income tax returns audited?

   b. What is the probability that a state will have less than 1% of its income tax returns audited?

6.27 Suppose the numbers of a particular type of bacteria in samples of 1 milliliter (ml) of drinking water tend to be approximately normally distributed, with a mean of 85 and a standard deviation of 9. What is the probability that a given 1-ml sample will contain more than 100 bacteria?

6.28 A grain loader can be set to discharge grain in amounts that are normally distributed, with mean μ bushels and standard deviation equal to 25.7 bushels. If a company wishes to use the loader to fill containers that hold 2000 bushels of grain and wants to overfill only one container in 100, at what value of μ should the company set the loader?

6.29 A publisher has discovered that the numbers of words contained in a new manuscript are normally distributed, with a mean equal to 20,000 words in excess of that specified in the author's contract and a standard deviation of 10,000 words. If the publisher wants to be almost certain (say, with a probability of .95) that the manuscript will have less than 100,000 words, what number of words should the publisher specify in the contract?

6.30 A stringer of tennis rackets has found that the actual string tension achieved for any individual racket stringing will vary as much as 6 pounds per square inch from the desired tension set on the stringing machine. If the stringer wishes to string at a tension lower than that specified by a customer only 5% of the time, how much above or below the customer's specified tension should the stringer set the stringing machine? (NOTE: Assume that the distribution of string tensions produced by the stringing machine is normally distributed, with a mean equal to the tension set on the machine and a standard deviation equal to 2 pounds per square inch.)

6.4 The Normal Approximation to the Binomial Probability Distribution (Optional)

In Chapter 5, you learned three ways to calculate probabilities for the binomial random variable x:

- Using the binomial formula, $P(x = k) = C_k^n p^k q^{n-k}$
- Using the cumulative binomial tables
- Using the Java applets

The binomial formula produces lengthy calculations, and the tables are available for only certain values of n and p. There is another option available when $np < 7$; the Poisson probabilities can be used to approximate $P(x = k)$. When this approximation *does not work* and n is large, the normal probability distribution provides another approximation for binomial probabilities.

The Normal Approximation to the Binomial Probability Distribution
Let x be a binomial random variable with n trials and probability p of success. The probability distribution of x is approximated using a normal curve with

$$\mu = np \quad \text{and} \quad \sigma = \sqrt{npq}$$

This approximation is adequate as long as n is large and p is not too close to 0 or 1.

Since the normal distribution is continuous, the area under the curve at any single point is equal to 0. Keep in mind that this result applies only to continuous random variables. Because the binomial random variable x is a discrete random variable, the probability that x takes some specific value—say, $x = 11$—will not necessarily equal 0.

Figures 6.16 and 6.17 show the binomial probability histograms for $n = 25$ with $p = .5$ and $p = .1$, respectively. The distribution in Figure 6.16 is exactly symmetric. If you superimpose a normal curve with the same mean, $\mu = np$, and the same standard deviation, $\sigma = \sqrt{npq}$, over the top of the bars, it "fits" quite well; that is, the areas under the curve are almost the same as the areas under the bars. However, when the probability of success, p, gets small and the distribution is skewed, as in Figure 6.17, the symmetric normal curve no longer fits very well. If you try to use the normal curve areas to approximate the area under the bars, your approximation will not be very good.

FIGURE 6.16
The binomial probability distribution for $n = 25$ and $p = .5$ and the approximating normal distribution with $\mu = 12.5$ and $\sigma = 2.5$

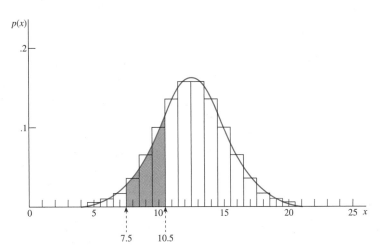

FIGURE 6.17
The binomial probability distribution and the approximating normal distribution for $n = 25$ and $p = .1$

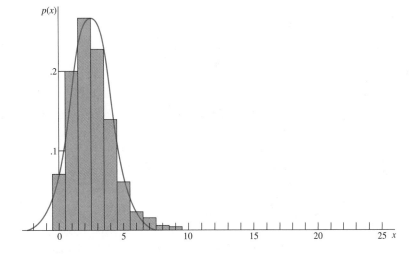

EXAMPLE 6.9
Use the normal curve to approximate the probability that $x = 8$, 9, or 10 for a binomial random variable with $n = 25$ and $p = .5$. Compare this approximation to the exact binomial probability.

Solution
You can find the exact binomial probability for this example because there are cumulative binomial tables for $n = 25$. From Table 1 in Appendix I,

$$P(x = 8, 9, \text{ or } 10) = P(x \le 10) - P(x \le 7) = .212 - .022 = .190$$

To use the normal approximation, first find the appropriate mean and standard deviation for the normal curve:

$$\mu = np = 25(.5) = 12.5$$
$$\sigma = \sqrt{npq} = \sqrt{25(.5)(.5)} = 2.5$$

The probability that you need corresponds to the area of the three rectangles lying over $x = 8$, 9, and 10. The equivalent area under the normal curve lies between $x = 7.5$ (the lower edge of the rectangle for $x = 8$) and $x = 10.5$ (the upper edge of the rectangle for $x = 10$). This area is shaded in Figure 6.16.

To find the normal probability, follow the procedures of Section 6.3. First you standardize each interval endpoint:

$$z = \frac{x - \mu}{\sigma} = \frac{7.5 - 12.5}{2.5} = -2.0$$

$$z = \frac{x - \mu}{\sigma} = \frac{10.5 - 12.5}{2.5} = -.8$$

Then the approximate probability (shaded in Figure 6.18) is found from Table 3 in Appendix I:

$$P(-2.0 < z < -.8) = .2119 - .0228 = .1891$$

You can compare the approximation, .1891, to the actual probability, .190. They are quite close!

FIGURE 6.18
Area under the normal curve for Example 6.9

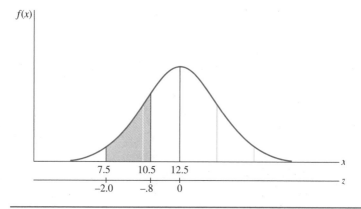

DO IT YOURSELF!

You can use the Java applet called **Normal Approximation to Binomial Probabilities** shown in Figure 6.19 to compare the actual and approximate probabilities for the binomial distribution in Example 6.9. Enter the appropriate values of n and p in the boxes at the top left corner of the applet, and press "Enter" to record each entry. The exact binomial distribution on the left of the applet will change depending on the value of n you have entered. Now change the value of k in the box at the bottom left corner of the applet, and press "Enter." The applet will calculate the exact binomial probability $P(x \le k)$ in the box marked "Prob:" It will also calculate the approximate probability using the area under the normal curve. The z-value, with the continuity correction is shown at the top right, and the approximate probability is shown to the left of the normal curve. For Example 6.9, the applet calculates the normal approximation as $P(x \le 10) \approx .2119$. What is the exact value of $P(x \le 10)$? If you change k to 7 and press "Enter," what is the approximate value for $P(x \le 7)$? Now calculate $P(8 \le x \le 10)$. Does it match the answer we got in Example 6.9? You will use this applet again for the *Do It Yourself Exercises* section at the end of the chapter.

FIGURE 6.19
**Normal
Approximation to
Binomial
Probabilities** applet

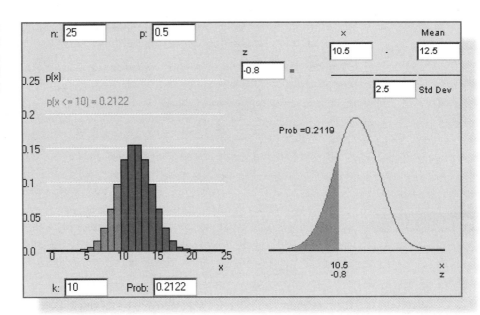

You must be careful not to exclude half of the two extreme probability rectangles when you use the normal approximation to the binomial probability distribution. This adjustment, called the **continuity correction,** helps account for the fact that you are approximating a *discrete random variable* with a *continuous* one. If you forget the correction, your approximation will not be very good! Use this correction only for *binomial probabilities;* do not try to use it when the random variable is already continuous, such as a height or weight.

How can you tell when it is appropriate to use the normal approximation to binomial probabilities? The normal approximation works well when the binomial histogram is roughly symmetric. This happens when the binomial distribution is not "bunched up" near 0 or *n*—that is, when it can spread out at least two standard deviations from its mean without exceeding its limits, 0 and *n*. Using this criterion, you can derive this simple rule of thumb:

Rule of Thumb
The normal approximation to the binomial probabilities will be adequate if both

$$np > 5 \quad \text{and} \quad nq > 5$$

Calculate Binomial Probabilities Using the Normal Approximation?

- Find the necessary values of n and p. Calculate $\mu = np$ and $\sigma = \sqrt{npq}$.
- Write the probability you need in terms of x and locate the appropriate area on the curve.

(continued)

> **Calculate Binomial Probabilities Using the Normal Approximation?** *(continued)*
>
> - Correct the value of x by $\pm.5$ to include the entire block of probability for that value. This is the *continuity correction*.
> - Convert the necessary x-values to z-values using
>
> $$z = \frac{x \pm .5 - np}{\sqrt{npq}}$$
>
> - Use Table 3 in Appendix I to calculate the approximate probability.

EXAMPLE 6.10

The reliability of an electrical fuse is the probability that a fuse, chosen at random from production, will function under its designed conditions. A random sample of 1000 fuses was tested and $x = 27$ defectives were observed. Calculate the approximate probability of observing 27 or more defectives, assuming that the fuse reliability is .98.

Solution   The probability of observing a defective when a single fuse is tested is $p = .02$, given that the fuse reliability is .98. Then

$$\mu = np = 1000(.02) = 20$$
$$\sigma = \sqrt{npq} = \sqrt{1000(.02)(.98)} = 4.43$$

The probability of 27 or more defective fuses, given $n = 1000$, is

$$P(x \geq 27) = p(27) + p(28) + p(29) + \cdots + p(999) + p(1000)$$

It is appropriate to use the normal approximation to the binomial probability because

$$np = 1000(.02) = 20 \quad \text{and} \quad nq = 1000(.98) = 980$$

are both greater than 5. The normal area used to approximate $P(x \geq 27)$ is the area under the normal curve to the right of 26.5, so that the entire rectangle for $x = 27$ is included. Then, the z-value corresponding to $x = 26.5$ is

$$z = \frac{x - \mu}{\sigma} = \frac{26.5 - 20}{4.43} = \frac{6.5}{4.43} = 1.47$$

and the area to the left of $z = 1.47$ is equal to .9292, as shown in Figure 6.20. Since the total area under the curve is 1, you have

$$P(x \geq 27) \approx P(z \geq 1.47) = 1 - .9292 = .0708$$

FIGURE 6.20
Normal approximation to the binomial for Example 6.10

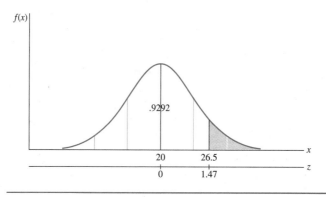

EXAMPLE 6.11   A producer of soft drinks was fairly certain that her brand had a 10% share of the soft drink market. In a market survey involving 2500 consumers of soft drinks, $x = 211$ expressed a preference for her brand. If the 10% figure is correct, find the probability of observing 211 or fewer consumers who prefer her brand of soft drink.

Solution   If the producer is correct, then the probability that a consumer prefers her brand of soft drink is $p = .10$. Then

$$\mu = np = 2500(.10) = 250$$
$$\sigma = \sqrt{npq} = \sqrt{2500(.10)(.90)} = 15$$

The probability of observing 211 or fewer who prefer her brand is

$$P(x \leq 211) = p(0) + p(1) + \cdots + p(210) + p(211)$$

The normal approximation to this probability is the area to the left of 211.5 under a normal curve with a mean of 250 and a standard deviation of 15. First calculate

$$z = \frac{x - \mu}{\sigma} = \frac{211.5 - 250}{15} = -2.57$$

Then

$$P(x \leq 211) \approx P(z < -2.57) = .0051$$

The probability of observing a sample value of 211 or less when $p = .10$ is so small that you can conclude that one of two things has occurred: Either you have observed an unusual sample even though really $p = .10$, *or* the sample reflects that the actual value of p is less than .10 and perhaps closer to the observed sample proportion, $211/2500 = .08$.

Exercises

Basic Techniques

6.31   Let x be a binomial random variable with $n = 25$ and $p = .3$.

a. Is the normal approximation appropriate for this binomial random variable?

b. Find the mean and standard deviation for x.

c. Use the normal approximation to find $P(6 \leq x \leq 9)$.

d. Use Table 1 in Appendix I to find the exact probability $P(6 \leq x \leq 9)$. Compare the results of parts c and d. How close was your approximation?

6.32   Let x be a binomial random variable with $n = 15$ and $p = .5$.

a. Is the normal approximation appropriate?

b. Find $P(x \geq 6)$ using the normal approximation.

c. Find $P(x > 6)$ using the normal approximation.

d. Find the exact probabilities for parts b and c, and compare these with your approximations.

6.33   Let x be a binomial random variable with $n = 100$ and $p = .2$. Find approximations to these probabilities:

a. $P(x > 22)$ b. $P(x \geq 22)$

c. $P(20 < x < 25)$ d. $P(x \leq 25)$

6.34   Let x be a binomial random variable for $n = 25$, $p = .2$.

a. Use Table 1 in Appendix I to calculate $P(4 \leq x \leq 6)$.

b. Find μ and σ for the binomial probability distribution, and use the normal distribution to approximate the probability $P(4 \leq x \leq 6)$. Note that this value is a good approximation to the exact value of $P(4 \leq x \leq 6)$ even though $np = 5$.

6.35 Suppose the random variable x has a binomial distribution corresponding to $n = 20$ and $p = .30$. Use Table 1 of Appendix I to calculate these probabilities:

a. $P(x = 5)$ **b.** $P(x \geq 7)$

6.36 Refer to Exercise 6.35. Use the normal approximation to calculate $P(x = 5)$ and $P(x \geq 7)$. Compare with the exact values obtained from Table 1 in Appendix I.

6.37 Consider a binomial experiment with $n = 20$ and $p = .4$. Calculate $P(x \geq 10)$ using each of these methods:

a. Table 1 in Appendix I

b. The normal approximation to the binomial probability distribution

6.38 Find the normal approximation to $P(355 \leq x \leq 360)$ for a binomial probability distribution with $n = 400$ and $p = .9$.

Applications

6.39 What is your favorite LifeSaver flavor? The data from a *USA Today* Snapshot claims that 32% of Americans prefer cherry LifeSavers.[4]

Does this hold true for you and your statistics classmates? Assume that it does and that your class contains 50 students. What are the approximate probabilities for these events?

a. More than 20 students prefer cherry LifeSavers.

b. Fewer than 15 students prefer cherry LifeSavers.

c. Fewer than 28 students *do not* prefer cherry LifeSavers.

d. Are you willing to assume that you and your classmates are a representative sample of all Americans when it comes to this question? How does your answer affect the probabilities in parts a to c?

6.40 Data collected over a long period of time show that a particular genetic defect occurs in 1 of every 1000 children. The records of a medical clinic show $x = 60$ children with the defect in a total of 50,000 examined. If the 50,000 children were a random sample from the population of children represented by past records, what is the probability of observing a value of x equal to 60 or more? Would you say that the observation of $x = 60$ children with genetic defects represents a rare event?

6.41 Airlines and hotels often grant reservations in excess of capacity to minimize losses due to no-shows. Suppose the records of a hotel show that, on the average, 10% of their prospective guests will not claim their reservation. If the hotel accepts 215 reservations and there are only 200 rooms in the hotel, what is the probability that all guests who arrive to claim a room will receive one?

6.42   Compilation of large masses of data on lung cancer shows that approximately 1 of every 40 adults acquires the disease. Workers in a certain occupation are known to work in an air-polluted environment that may cause an increased rate of lung cancer. A random sample of $n = 400$ workers shows 19 with identifiable cases of lung cancer. Do the data provide sufficient evidence to indicate a higher rate of lung cancer for these workers than for the national average?

6.43   Is a tall president better than a short one? Do Americans tend to vote for the taller of the two candidates in a presidential election? In 31 of our presidential elections since 1856, 17 of the winners were taller than their opponents.[1] Assume that Americans are not biased by a candidate's height and that the winner is just as likely to be taller or shorter than his opponent. Is the observed number of taller winners in the U.S. presidential elections unusual?

   a. Find the approximate probability of finding 17 or more of the 31 pairs in which the taller candidate wins.

   b. Based on your answer to part a, can you conclude that Americans might consider a candidate's height when casting their ballot?

6.44   In a certain population, 15% of the people have Rh-negative blood. A blood bank serving this population receives 92 blood donors on a particular day.

   a. What is the probability that 10 or fewer are Rh-negative?

   b. What is the probability that 15 to 20 (inclusive) of the donors are Rh-negative?

   c. What is the probability that more than 80 of the donors are Rh-positive?

6.45   Two of the biggest soft drink rivals, Pepsi and Coke, are very concerned about their market share. The following pie chart, which appeared on the company website (http://www.pepsico.com) in October 2001, claims that Pepsi-Cola's market share is 32%.[5] Assume that this proportion will be *close to* the probability that a person selected at random indicates a preference for a Pepsi product when choosing a soft drink.

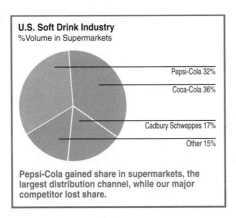

A test group of 500 consumers is randomly selected. Use the normal curve to approximate the following binomial probabilities:

   a. Exactly 160 consumers prefer a Pepsi product.

   b. Between 100 and 150 consumers (inclusive) prefer a Pepsi product.

   c. Fewer than 150 consumers prefer a Pepsi product.

   d. Would it be unusual to find that 232 of the 500 consumers preferred a Pepsi product?

   If this were to occur, what conclusions would you draw?

Key Concepts and Formulas

I. **Continuous Probability Distributions**
 1. Continuous random variables
 2. Probability distributions or probability density functions
  a. Curves are smooth.
  b. The area under the curve between a and b represents the probability that x falls between a and b.
  c. $P(x = a) = 0$ for continuous random variables.

II. **The Normal Probability Distribution**
 1. Symmetric about its mean μ
 2. Shape determined by its standard deviation σ

III. **The Standard Normal Distribution**
 1. The normal random variable z has mean 0 and standard deviation 1.
 2. Any normal random variable x can be transformed to a standard normal random variable using

$$z = \frac{x - \mu}{\sigma}$$

 3. Convert necessary values of x to z.
 4. Use Table 3 in Appendix I to compute standard normal probabilities.
 5. Several important z-values have tail areas as follows:

Tail Area	.005	.01	.025	.05	.10
z-Value	2.58	2.33	1.96	1.645	1.28

Normal Probabilities

When the random variable of interest has a normal probability distribution, you can generate either of these probabilities:

- Cumulative probabilities—$P(x \le k)$—for a given value of k
- Inverse cumulative probabilities—the value of k such that the area to its left under the normal probability distribution is equal to a

You must specify which normal distribution you are using and the necessary parameters: the mean μ and the standard deviation σ. As in Chapter 5, you have the option of specifying only one single value of k (or a) or several values of k (or a), which should be stored in a column (say, C1) of the *MINITAB* worksheet.

 Suppose that the average birth weights of babies born at hospitals owned by a major health maintenance organization (HMO) are approximately normal with mean 6.75 pounds and standard deviation .54 pound. What proportion of babies born at these hospitals weigh between 6 and 7 pounds? To use *MINITAB* to find $P(6 < x < 7)$, enter the critical values $x = 6$ and $x = 7$ into a column (say, C1) of a *MINITAB* worksheet. Use **Calc → Probability Distributions → Normal** to generate the Dialog box, as shown in Figure 6.21.
 Type the values for μ and σ in the appropriate boxes (the default values generate probabilities for the standard normal z distribution), and select C1 for the input column. (If you do not type a column number for storage, *MINITAB* will display the results in

MINITAB

FIGURE 6.21

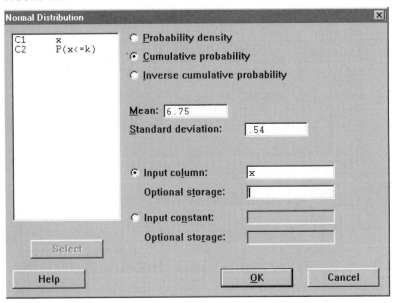

FIGURE 6.22

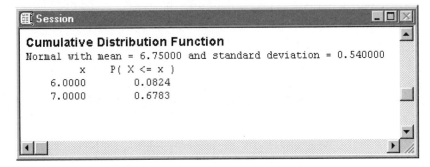

the Session window.) Make sure that the radio button marked "Cumulative probability" is selected. The cumulative distribution function for $x = 6$ and $x = 7$ appears in the Session window when you click **OK** (see Figure 6.22). To find $P(6 < x < 7)$, remember that the cumulative probability is the area to the left of the given value of x. Hence,

$$P(6 < x < 7) = P(x < 7) - P(x < 6) = .6783 - .0824 = .5959$$

You can check this calculation using Table 3 in Appendix I if you wish!

To calculate inverse cumulative probabilities, make sure that the radio button marked "Inverse cumulative probability" is selected. Then enter the appropriate values of a in C1, or if you have only a single value, enter the value in the Input constant box. For example, to find the 95th percentile of the birth weights, you look for a value k such that only 5% of the values of x exceed this value (and 95% are less than or equal to k). If you enter the probability **.95** into the Input constant box and select the option marked "Inverse cumulative probability," the 95th percentile will appear in the Session window, as in Figure 6.23. That is, 95% of all babies born at these hospitals weigh 7.6382 pounds or less. Would you consider a baby who weighs 9 pounds to be unusually large?

MINITAB

FIGURE 6.23

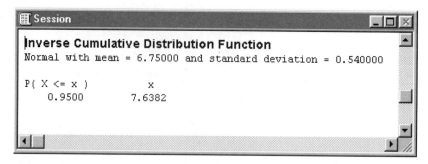

Supplementary Exercises

6.46   Using Table 3 in Appendix I, calculate the area under the standard normal curve to the left of:

    a. $z = 1.2$ **b.** $z = -.9$

    c. $z = 1.46$ **d.** $z = -.42$

6.47   Find the following probabilities for the standard normal random variable:

    a. $P(.3 < z < 1.56)$ **b.** $P(-.2 < z < .2)$

6.48   **a.** Find the probability that z is greater than $-.75$.

    b. Find the probability that z is less than 1.35.

6.49   Find z_0 such that $P(z > z_0) = .5$.

6.50   Find the probability that z lies between $z = -1.48$ and $z = 1.48$.

6.51   Find z_0 such that $P(-z_0 < z < z_0) = .5$. What percentiles do $-z_0$ and z_0 represent?

6.52   The life span of oil-drilling bits depends on the types of rock and soil that the drill encounters, but it is estimated that the mean length of life is 75 hours. Suppose an oil exploration company purchases drill bits that have a life span that is approximately normally distributed, with a mean equal to 75 hours and a standard deviation equal to 12 hours.

    a. What proportion of the company's drill bits will fail before 60 hours of use?

    b. What proportion will last at least 60 hours?

    c. What proportion will have to be replaced after more than 90 hours of use?

6.53   The influx of new ideas into a college or university, introduced primarily by new young faculty, is becoming a matter of concern because of the increasing ages of faculty members; that is, the distribution of faculty ages is shifting upward due most likely to a shortage of vacant positions and an oversupply of PhDs. Thus, faculty members are reluctant to move and give up a secure position. If the retirement age at most universities is 65, would you expect the distribution of faculty ages to be normal?

6.54   A machine operation produces bearings whose diameters are normally distributed, with mean and standard deviation equal to .498 and .002, respectively. If specifications require that the bearing diameter equal .500 inch ± .004 inch, what fraction of the production will be unacceptable?

6.55   A used-car dealership has found that the length of time before a major repair is required on the cars it sells is normally distributed, with a mean equal to 10 months and a standard deviation of 3 months. If the dealer wants only 5% of the cars to fail before the end of the guarantee period, for how many months should the cars be guaranteed?

6.56   The daily sales total (excepting Saturday) at a small restaurant has a probability distribution that is approximately normal, with a mean μ equal to $530 per day and a standard deviation σ equal to $120.

    a. What is the probability that the sales will exceed $700 for a given day?

b. The restaurant must have at least $300 in sales per day to break even. What is the probability that on a given day the restaurant will not break even?

6.57 The life span of a type of automatic washer is approximately normally distributed, with mean and standard deviation equal to 3.1 and 1.2 years, respectively. If this type of washer is guaranteed for 1 year, what fraction of original sales will require replacement?

6.58 Most users of automatic garage door openers activate their openers at distances that are normally distributed, with a mean of 30 feet and a standard deviation of 11 feet. To minimize interference with other remote-controlled devices, the manufacturer is required to limit the operating distance to 50 feet. What percentage of the time will users attempt to operate the opener outside its operating limit?

6.59 The average length of time required to complete a college achievement test was found to equal 70 minutes, with a standard deviation of 12 minutes. When should the test be terminated if you wish to allow sufficient time for 90% of the students to complete the test? (Assume that the time required to complete the test is normally distributed.)

6.60 The length of time required for the periodic maintenance of an automobile will usually have a probability distribution that is mound-shaped and, because some long service times will occur occasionally, is skewed to the right. The length of time required to run a 5000-mile check and to service an automobile has a mean equal to 1.4 hours and a standard deviation of .7 hour. Suppose that the service department plans to service 50 automobiles per 8-hour day and that, in order to do so, it must spend no more than an average of 1.6 hours per automobile. What proportion of all days will the service department have to work overtime?

6.61 An advertising agency has stated that 20% of all television viewers watch a particular program. In a random sample of 1000 viewers, $x = 184$ viewers were watching the program. Do these data present sufficient evidence to contradict the advertiser's claim?

6.62 A researcher notes that senior corporation executives are not very accurate forecasters of their own annual earnings. He states that his studies of a large number of company executive forecasts "showed that the average estimate missed the mark by 15%."

a. Suppose the distribution of these forecast errors has a mean of 15% and a standard deviation of 10%. Is it likely that the distribution of forecast errors is approximately normal?

b. Suppose the probability is .5 that a corporate executive's forecast error exceeds 15%. If you were to sample the forecasts of 100 corporate executives, what is the probability that more than 60 would be in error by more than 15%?

6.63 A soft drink machine can be regulated to discharge an average of μ ounces per cup. If the ounces of fill are normally distributed, with standard deviation equal to .3 ounce, give the setting for μ so that 8-ounce cups will overflow only 1% of the time.

6.64 A manufacturing plant uses 3000 electric light bulbs whose life spans are normally distributed, with mean and standard deviation equal to 500 and 50 hours, respectively. In order to minimize the number of bulbs that burn out during operating hours, all the bulbs are replaced after a given period of operation. How often should the bulbs be replaced if we wish no more than 1% of the bulbs to burn out between replacement periods?

6.65 The admissions office of a small college is asked to accept deposits from a number of qualified prospective freshmen so that, with probability about .95, the size of the freshman class will be less than or equal to 120. Suppose the applicants constitute a random sample from a population of applicants, 80% of whom would actually enter the freshman class if accepted.

a. How many deposits should the admissions counselor accept?

b. If applicants in the number determined in part a are accepted, what is the probability that the freshman class size will be less than 105?

6.66 An airline finds that 5% of the persons making reservations on a certain flight will not show up for the flight. If the airline sells 160 tickets for a flight that has only 155 seats, what is the probability that a seat will be available for every person holding a reservation and planning to fly?

6.67 It is known that 30% of all calls coming into a telephone exchange are long-distance calls. If 200 calls come into the exchange, what is the probability that at least 50 will be long-distance calls?

6.68 In Exercise 5.65, a cross between two peony plants—one with red petals and one with streaky petals—produced offspring plants with red petals 75% of the time. Suppose that 100 seeds from this cross were collected and germinated, and x, the number of plants with red petals, was recorded.

   a. What is the exact probability distribution for x?

   b. Is it appropriate to approximate the distribution in part a using the normal distribution? Explain.

   c. Use an appropriate method to find the approximate probability that between 70 and 80 (inclusive) offspring plants have red flowers.

   d. What is the probability that 53 or fewer offspring plants had red flowers? Is this an unusual occurrence?

   e. If you actually observed 53 of 100 offspring plants with red flowers, and if you were certain that the genetic ratio 3:1 was correct, what other explanation could you give for this unusual occurrence?

6.69 A purchaser of electric relays buys from two suppliers, A and B. Supplier A supplies two of every three relays used by the company. If 75 relays are selected at random from those in use by the company, find the probability that at most 48 of these relays come from supplier A. Assume that the company uses a large number of relays.

6.70 Is television dangerous to your diet? Psychologists believe that excessive eating may be associated with emotional states (being upset or bored) and environmental cues (watching television, reading, and so on). To test this theory, suppose you randomly selected 60 overweight persons and matched them by weight and gender in pairs. For a period of 2 weeks, one of each pair is required to spend evenings reading novels of interest to him or her. The other member of each pair spends each evening watching television. The calorie count for all snack and drink intake for the evenings is recorded for each person, and you record $x = 19$, the number of pairs for which the television watchers' calorie intake exceeded the intake of the readers. If there is no difference in the effects of television and reading on calorie intake, the probability p that the calorie intake of one member of a pair exceeds that of the other member is .5. Do these data provide sufficient evidence to indicate a difference between the effects of television watching and reading on calorie intake? (HINT: Calculate the z-score for the observed value, $x = 19$.)

6.71 The gestation time for human babies is approximately normally distributed with an average of 278 days and a standard deviation of 12.[6]

   a. Find the upper and lower quartiles for the gestation times.

   b. Would it be unusual to deliver a baby after only 6 months of gestation? Explain.

6.72 In Exercise 6.26 we suggested that the IRS assign auditing rates per state by randomly selecting 50 auditing percentages from a normal distribution with a mean equal to 1.55% and a standard deviation of .45%.

   a. What is the probability that a particular state would have more than 2% of its tax returns audited?

   b. What is the expected value of x, the number of states that will have more than 2% of their income tax returns audited?

   c. Is it likely that as many as 15 of the 50 states will have more than 2% of their income tax returns audited?

6.73 There is a difference in sports preferences between men and women, according to a recent survey. Among the 10 most popular sports, men include competition-type sports—pool and billiards, basketball, and softball—whereas women include aerobics, running, hiking, and calisthenics. However, the top recreational activity for men was still the relaxing sport of fishing, with 41% of those surveyed indicating that they had fished during the year. Suppose 180 randomly selected men are asked whether they had fished in the past year.

a. What is the probability that fewer than 50 had fished?

b. What is the probability that between 50 and 75 had fished?

c. If the 180 men selected for the interview were selected by the marketing department of a sporting-goods company based on information obtained from their mailing lists, what would you conclude about the reliability of their survey results?

Exercises DO IT YOURSELF!

Use one of the three applets (**Normal Distribution Probabilities, Normal Probabilities and z-scores,** or **Normal Approximation to Binomial Probabilities**) described in this chapter to solve the following exercises.

6.74 Calculate the area under the standard normal curve to the left of these values:

a. $z = -.90$ **b.** $z = 2.34$ **c.** $z = 5.4$

6.75 Calculate the area under the standard normal curve between these values:

a. $z = -2.0$ and $z = 2.0$ **b.** $z = -2.3$ and -1.5

6.76 Find the following probabilities for the standard normal random variable z:

a. $P(-1.96 \leq z \leq 1.96)$ **b.** $P(z > 1.96)$ **c.** $P(z < -1.96)$

6.77 **a.** Find a z_0 such that $P(z > z_0) = .9750$ **b.** Find a z_0 such that $P(z > z_0) = .3594$

6.78 **a.** Find a z_0 such that $P(-z_0 \leq z \leq z_0) = .95$.

b. Find a z_0 such that $P(-z_0 \leq z \leq z_0) = .98$.

6.79 A normal random variable x has mean $\mu = 5$ and $\sigma = 2$. Find the following probabilities of these x-values:

a. $1.2 < x < 10$ **b.** $x > 7.5$ **c.** $x \leq 0$

6.80 Let x be a binomial random variable with $n = 36$ and $p = .54$. Use the normal approximation to find:

a. $P(x \leq 25)$ **b.** $P(15 \leq x \leq 20)$ **c.** $P(x > 30)$

6.81 Forty-nine percent of adult Americans say that money issues are the top cause of stress for them in their daily lives.[7] Suppose that 100 adult Americans are randomly selected.

a. Use the **Calculating Binomial Probabilities** applet from Chapter 5 to find the exact probability that 60 or more adults would give money reasons as the top cause of stress.

b. Use the **Normal Approximation to Binomial Probabilities** applet to approximate the probability in part a. Compare your answers.

6.82 Philatelists (stamp collectors) often buy stamps at or near retail prices, but, when they sell, the price is considerably lower. For example, it may be reasonable to assume that (depending on the mix of a collection, condition, demand, economic conditions, etc.) a collection will sell at x% of the retail price, where x is normally distributed with a mean equal to 45% and a standard deviation of 4.5%. If a philatelist has a collection to sell that has a retail value of $30,000, what is the probability that the philatelist receives these amounts for the collection?

a. More than $15,000

b. Less than $15,000

c. Less than $12,000

6.83 The scores on a national achievement test were approximately normally distributed, with a mean of 540 and a standard deviation of 110.

a. If you achieved a score of 680, how far, in standard deviations, did your score depart from the mean?

b. What percentage of those who took the examination scored higher than you?

6.84   Although faculty salaries at colleges and universities in the United States continue to rise, they do not always keep pace with the cost of living. During the 2000–2001 academic year, female assistant professors earned an average of $49,707 per year.[3] Suppose that these salaries are normally distributed, with a standard deviation of $4000.

a. What proportion of female assistant professors will have salaries less than $40,000?

b. What proportion of female assistant professors will have salaries between $45,000 and $50,000?

6.85   Briggs and King developed the technique of nuclear transplantation, in which the nucleus of a cell from one of the later stages of the development of an embryo is transplanted into a zygote (a single-cell fertilized egg) to see whether the nucleus can support normal development. If the probability that a single transplant from the early gastrula stage will be successful is .65, what is the probability that more than 70 transplants out of 100 will be successful?

Case Study   The Long and the Short of It

If you were the boss, would height play a role in your selection of a successor for your job? In his *Fortune* column, Daniel Seligman discussed his ideas concerning height as a factor in Deng Xiaoping's choice of Hu Yaobang as his replacement as Chairman of the Chinese Communist Party.[8] As Seligman notes, the facts surrounding the case arouse suspicions when examined in the light of statistics.

Deng, it seemed, was only 5 feet tall, a height that is short even in China. Therefore, the choice of Hu Yaobang, who was also 5 feet tall, raised (or lowered) some eyebrows because, as Seligman notes, "the odds against a 'height-blind' decision producing a chairman as short as Deng are about 40 to 1." In other words, if we had the relative frequency distribution of the heights of all Chinese men, only 1 in 41 (i.e., 2.4%) would be 5 feet tall or shorter. To calculate these odds, Seligman notes that the Chinese equivalent of the U.S. Health Service does not exist and hence that health statistics on the current population of China are difficult to acquire. He says, however, that "it is generally held that a boy's length at birth represents 28.6% of his final height" and that, in prerevolutionary China, the average length of a Chinese boy at birth was 18.9 inches. From this, Seligman deduces that the mean height of mature Chinese men is

$$\frac{18.9}{.286} = 66.08 \text{ inches, or 5 feet 6.08 inches}$$

He then assumes that the distribution of the heights of men in China follows a normal distribution ("as it does in the U.S."), with a mean of 66 inches and a standard deviation equal to 2.7 inches, "a figure that looks about right for that mean."

1. Using Seligman's assumptions, calculate the probability that a single adult Chinese man, chosen at random, will be less than or equal to 5 feet tall, or equivalently, 60 inches tall.

2. Do the results in part 1 agree with Seligman's odds?

3. Comment on the validity of Seligman's assumptions. Are there any basic flaws in his reasoning?

4. Based on the results of parts 1 and 3, do you think that Deng Xiaoping took height into account in selecting his successor?

Data Sources

1. Paul M. Sommers, "Presidential Candidates Who Measure Up," *Chance* 9, no. 3 (Summer 1996):30, and http://www.whitehouse.gov/news/releases/2001/20010804-2.html.

2. Adapted from A.M. Goodman and A.R. Ennos, "The Response of Field-grown Sunflower and Maize to Mechanical Support," *Annals of Botany* 79 (1997):703.

3. "Average Salary for Men and Women Faculty," Academe: Bulletin of the American Association of University Professors, March–April 2001, p. 43.

4. "Favorite Flavors," *Source:* International Consumer Research for LifeSavers, http://www.usatoday.com/snapshot/life/2001-08-07-lifesaver.htm, 11 October 2001.

5. http://www.pepsico.com, Home page for Pepsico, Inc., 11 October 2001.

6. Philip A. Altman and D.S. Dittmer, *The Biology Data Book,* 2nd ed., Vol I. (Bethesda, MD: Federation of American Societies for Experimental Biology, 1964), p. 137.

7. "What Stresses Us Out," http://www.usatoday.com/snapshot/life/2001-05-23-stress.htm. *Source:* CyberPulse for Wrigley Healthcare's Surpass, 11 October 2001.

8. Daniel Seligman, "Keeping Up," *Fortune,* 27 July 1981.

7

Sampling Distributions

Case Study

How would you like to try your hand at gambling without the risk of losing? You could do it by simulating the gambling process, making imaginary bets, and observing the results. This technique, called a Monte Carlo procedure, is the topic of the case study at the end of this chapter.

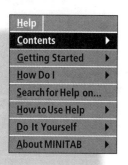

General Objectives

In the past several chapters, we studied *populations* and the *parameters* that describe them. These populations were either discrete or continuous, and we used *probability* as a tool for determining how likely certain sample outcomes might be. In this chapter, our focus changes as we begin to study *samples* and the *statistics* that describe them. These sample statistics are used to make inferences about the corresponding population parameters. This chapter involves sampling and sampling distributions, which describe the behavior of sample statistics in repeated sampling.

Specific Topics

1. Random samples (7.2)
2. Sampling plans and experimental designs (7.2)
3. Statistics and sampling distributions (7.3)
4. The Central Limit Theorem (7.4)
5. The sampling distribution of the sample mean, $\bar{x}$ (7.5)
6. The sampling distribution of the sample proportion, $\hat{p}$ (7.6)
7. Statistical process control: $\bar{x}$ and p charts (7.7)

7.1 Introduction

In the previous three chapters, you have learned a lot about probability distributions, such as the binomial and normal distributions. The shape of the normal distribution is determined by its mean μ and its standard deviation σ, whereas the shape of the binomial distribution is determined by p. These numerical descriptive measures—called **parameters**—are needed to calculate the probability of observing sample results.

In practical situations, you may be able to decide which *type* of probability distribution to use as a model, but the values of the *parameters* that specify its *exact form* are unknown. Here are two examples:

- A pollster is sure that the responses to his "agree/disagree" questions will follow a binomial distribution, but p, the proportion of those who "agree" in the population, is unknown.
- An agronomist believes that the yield per acre of a variety of wheat is approximately normally distributed, but the mean μ and standard deviation σ of the yields are unknown.

In these cases, you must rely on the *sample* to learn about these parameters. The proportion of those who "agree" in the pollster's sample provides information about the actual value of p. The mean and standard deviation of the agronomist's sample approximate the actual values of μ and σ. If you want the sample to provide *reliable information* about the population, however, you must select your sample in a certain way!

7.2 Sampling Plans and Experimental Designs

The way a sample is selected is called the **sampling plan** or **experimental design** and determines the quantity of information in the sample. Knowing the sampling plan used in a particular situation will often allow you to measure the reliability or goodness of your inference.

Simple random sampling is a commonly used sampling plan in which every sample of size n has the same chance of being selected. For example, suppose you want to select a sample of size $n = 2$ from a population containing $N = 4$ objects. If the four objects are identified by the symbols x_1, x_2, x_3, and x_4, there are six distinct pairs that could be selected, as listed in Table 7.1. If the sample of $n = 2$ observations is selected so that each of these six samples has the same chance of selection, given by 1/6, then the resulting sample is called a **simple random sample,** or just a **random sample.**

TABLE 7.1
Ways of selecting a sample of size 2 from 4 objects

Sample	Observations in Sample
1	x_1, x_2
2	x_1, x_3
3	x_1, x_4
4	x_2, x_3
5	x_2, x_4
6	x_3, x_4

Definition   If a sample of n elements is selected from a population of N elements using a sampling plan in which each of the possible samples has the same chance of selection, then the sampling is said to be **random** and the resulting sample is a **simple random sample**.

Perfect random sampling is difficult to achieve in practice. If the size of the population N is small, you might write each of N numbers on a poker chip, mix the chips, and select a sample of n chips. The numbers that you select correspond to the n measurements that appear in the sample. Since this method is not always very practical, a simpler and more reliable method uses **random numbers**—digits generated so that the values 0 to 9 occur randomly and with equal frequency. These numbers can be generated by computer or may even be available on your scientific calculator. Alternatively, Table 10 in Appendix I is a table of random numbers that you can use to select a *random sample.*

EXAMPLE 7.1

A computer database at a downtown law firm contains files for $N = 1000$ clients. The firm wants to select $n = 5$ files for review. Select a simple random sample of 5 files from this database.

Solution

You must first label each file with a number from 1 to 1000. Perhaps the files are stored alphabetically, and the computer has already assigned a number to each. Then generate a sequence of ten three-digit random numbers. If you are using Table 10 of Appendix I, select a random starting point and use a portion of the table similar to the one shown in Table 7.2. The random starting point ensures that you will not use the same sequence over and over again. The first three digits of Table 7.2 indicate the number of the first file to be reviewed. The random number 001 corresponds to file #1, and the last file, #1000, corresponds to the random number 000. Using Table 7.2, you would choose the five files numbered 155, 450, 32, 882, and 350 for review.

TABLE 7.2			
Portion of a table	15574	35026	98924
of random	45045	36933	28630
numbers	03225	78812	50856
	88292	26053	21121

The situation described in Example 7.1 is called an **observational study** because the data already existed before you decided to *observe* or describe their characteristics. Most sample surveys, in which information is gathered with a questionnaire, fall into this category. Computer databases make it possible to assign identification numbers to each element even when the population is large and to select a simple random sample. You must be careful when conducting a *sample survey,* however, to watch for these frequently occurring problems:

■ **Nonresponse:** You have carefully selected your random sample and sent out your questionnaires, but only 50% of those surveyed return their questionnaires. Are the responses you received still representative of the entire population, or are they **biased** because only those people who were particularly opinionated about the subject chose to respond?

■ **Undercoverage:** You have selected your random sample using telephone records as a database. Does the database you used systematically exclude certain segments of the population—perhaps those who do not have telephones?

■ **Wording bias:** Your questionnaire may have questions that are too complicated or tend to confuse the reader. Possibly the questions are sensitive in nature—for example, "Have you ever used drugs?" or "Have you ever cheated on your income tax?"—and the respondents will not answer truthfully.

Methods have been devised to solve some of these problems, but only if you know that they exist. If your survey is *biased* by any of these problems, then your conclusions will not be very reliable, even though you did select a random sample!

Some research involves **experimentation,** in which an experimental condition or *treatment* is imposed on the *experimental units.* Selecting a simple random sample is more difficult in this situation.

EXAMPLE 7.2

A research chemist is testing a new method for measuring the amount of titanium (Ti) in ore samples. She chooses 10 ore samples of the same weight for her experiment. Five of the samples will be measured using a standard method, and the other 5 using the new method. Use random numbers to assign the 10 ore samples to the new and standard groups. Do these data represent a simple random sample from the population?

Solution   There are really two populations in this experiment. They consist of titanium measurements, using either the new or standard method, for *all possible* ore samples of this weight. These populations do not exist in fact; they are **hypothetical populations,** envisioned in the mind of the researcher. Thus, it is impossible to select a simple random sample using the methods of Example 7.1. Instead, the researcher selects what she believes are 10 *representative* ore samples and hopes that these samples will *behave as if* they had been randomly selected from the two populations.

The researcher can, however, randomly select the five samples to be measured with each method. Number the samples from 1 to 10. The five samples selected for the new method may correspond to five one-digit random numbers. Use this sequence of random digits generated on a scientific calculator:

948247817184610

Since you cannot select the same ore sample twice, you must skip any digit that has already been chosen. Ore samples 9, 4, 8, 2, and 7 will be measured using the new method. The other samples—1, 3, 5, 6, and 10—will be measured using the standard method.

In addition to *simple random sampling,* there are other sampling plans that involve randomization and therefore provide a probabilistic basis for inference making. Three such plans are based on *stratified, cluster,* and *systematic sampling.*

When the population consists of two or more subpopulations, called **strata,** a sampling plan that ensures that each subpopulation is represented in the sample is called a **stratified random sample.**

Definition   **Stratified random sampling** involves selecting a simple random sample from each of a given number of subpopulations, or **strata.**

Citizens' opinions about the construction of a performing arts center could be collected using a stratified random sample with city voting wards as strata. National polls usually involve some form of stratified random sampling with states as strata.

Another form of random sampling is used when the available sampling units are groups of elements, called **clusters.** For example, a household is a *cluster* of individuals living together. A city block or a neighborhood might be a convenient sampling unit and might be considered a *cluster* for a given sampling plan.

Definition   A **cluster sample** is a simple random sample of clusters from the available clusters in the population.

When a particular cluster is included in the sample, a census of every element in the cluster is taken.

Sometimes the population to be sampled is ordered, such as an alphabetized list of people with driver's licenses, a list of utility users arranged by service addresses, or a list of customers by account numbers. In these and other situations, one element is chosen at random from the first k elements, and then every kth element thereafter is included in the sample.

Definition   A **1-in-k systematic random sample** involves the random selection of one of the first k elements in an ordered population, and then the systematic selection of every kth element thereafter.

Not all sampling plans, however, involve random selection. You have probably heard of the nonrandom telephone polls in which those people who wish to express support for a question call one "900 number" and those opposed call a second "900 number." Each person must pay for his or her call. It is obvious that those people who call do not represent the population at large. This type of sampling plan is one form of a **convenience sample**—a sample that can be easily and simply obtained without random selection. Advertising for subjects who will be paid a fee for participating in an experiment produces a convenience sample. **Judgment sampling** allows the sampler to decide who will or will not be included in the sample. **Quota sampling,** in which the makeup of the sample must reflect the makeup of the population on some preselected characteristic, often has a nonrandom component in the selection process. **Remember that nonrandom samples can be described but cannot be used for making inferences!**

Exercises   Basic Techniques

7.1   A population consists of $N = 500$ experimental units. Use a random number table to select a random sample of $n = 20$ experimental units. (HINT: Since you need to use three-digit numbers, you can assign two three-digit numbers to each of the sampling units in the manner shown in the table.) What is the probability that each experimental unit is selected for inclusion in the sample?

Experimental Units	Random Numbers
1	001, 501
2	002, 502
3	003, 503
4	004, 504
⋮	⋮
499	499, 999
500	500, 000

 7.2   A political analyst wishes to select a sample of $n = 20$ people from a population of 2000. Use the random number table to identify the people to be included in the sample.

 7.3   A population contains 50,000 voters. Use the random number table to identify the voters to be included in a random sample of $n = 15$.

 7.4   A small city contains 20,000 voters. Use the random number table to identify the voters to be included in a random sample of $n = 15$.

 7.5   A random sample of public opinion in a small town was obtained by selecting every 10th person who passed by the busiest corner in the downtown area. Will this sample have the characteristics of a random sample selected from the town's citizens? Explain.

7.6 A questionnaire was mailed to 1000 registered municipal voters selected at random. Only 500 questionnaires were returned, and of the 500 returned, 360 respondents were strongly opposed to a surcharge proposed to support the city Parks and Recreation Department. Are you willing to accept the 72% figure as a valid estimate of the percentage in the city who are opposed to the surcharge? Why or why not?

7.7 In many states, lists of possible jurors are assembled from voter registration lists and Department of Motor Vehicles records of licensed drivers and car owners. In what ways might this list not cover certain sectors of the population adequately?

7.8 One question on a survey questionnaire is phrased as follows: "Don't you agree that there is too much sex and violence during prime TV viewing hours?" Comment on possible problems with the responses to this question. Suggest a better way to pose the question.

Applications

7.9 A byproduct of chlorination called MX has been linked to cancer in rats.[1] A scientist wants to conduct a validation study using 25 rats in the experimental group, each to receive a fixed dose of MX, and 25 rats in a control group that will receive no MX. Determine a randomization scheme to assign the 50 individual rats to the two groups.

7.10 Does the race of an interviewer matter? This question was investigated by Chris Gilberg and colleagues and reported in an issue of *Chance* magazine.[2] The interviewer asked, "Do you feel that affirmative action should be used as an occupation selection criteria?" with possible answers of yes or no.

a. What problems might you expect with responses to this question when asked by interviewers of different ethnic origins?

b. When people were interviewed by an African-American, the response was about 70% in favor of affirmative action, approximately 35% when interviewed by an Asian, and approximately 25% when interviewed by a Caucasian. Do these results support your answer in part a?

7.11 In a study described in the *American Journal of Sports Medicine,* Peter D. Franklin and colleagues reported on the accuracy of using magnetic resonance imaging (MRI) to evaluate ligament sprains and tears on 35 patients.[3] Consecutive patients with acute or chronic knee pain were selected from the clinical practice of one of the authors and agreed to participate in the study.

a. Describe the sampling plan used to select study participants.

b. What chance mechanism was used to select this sample of 35 individuals with knee pain?

c. Can valid inferences be made using the results of this study? Why or why not?

d. Devise an alternative sampling plan. What would you change?

7.12 A study of an experimental blood thinner was conducted to determine whether it works better than the simple aspirin tablet in warding off heart attacks and strokes.[4] The study involved 19,185 people who had suffered heart attacks, strokes, or pain from clogged arteries. Each person was randomly assigned to take either aspirin or the experimental drug for 1 to 3 years. Assume that each person was equally likely to be assigned one of the two medications.

a. Devise a randomization plan to assign the medications to the patients.

b. Will there be an equal number of patients in each treatment group? Explain.

7.3 Statistics and Sampling Distributions

When you select a random sample from a population, the numerical descriptive measures you calculate from the sample are called **statistics.** These statistics vary or change for each different random sample you select; that is, they are *random variables.* The probability distributions for statistics are called **sampling distributions** because, in repeated sampling, they provide this information:

- What values of the statistic can occur
- How often each value occurs

Definition

The **sampling distribution of a statistic** is the probability distribution for the possible values of the statistic that results when random samples of size n are repeatedly drawn from the population.

There are three ways to find the sampling distribution of a statistic:

1. Derive the distribution *mathematically* using the laws of probability.
2. Use a *simulation* to approximate the distribution. That is, draw a large number of samples of size n, calculating the value of the statistic for each sample, and tabulate the results in a relative frequency histogram. When the number of samples is large, the histogram will be very close to the theoretical sampling distribution.
3. Use *statistical theorems* to derive exact or approximate sampling distributions.

The next example demonstrates how to derive the sampling distributions of two statistics for a very small population.

EXAMPLE 7.3

A population consists of $N = 5$ numbers: 3, 6, 9, 12, 15. If a random sample of size $n = 3$ is selected without replacement, find the sampling distributions for the sample mean $\bar{x}$ and the sample median m.

Solution

You are sampling from the population shown in Figure 7.1. It contains five distinct numbers and each is equally likely, with probability $p(x) = 1/5$. You can easily find the population mean and median as

$$\mu = \frac{3 + 6 + 9 + 12 + 15}{5} = 9 \quad \text{and} \quad M = 9$$

FIGURE 7.1
Probability histogram for the $N = 5$ population values in Example 7.3

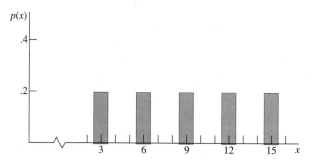

There are 10 possible random samples of size $n = 3$ and each is equally likely, with probability 1/10. These samples, along with the calculated values of $\bar{x}$ and m for each, are listed in Table 7.3. You will notice that some values of $\bar{x}$ are more likely than others because they occur in more than one sample. For example,

$$P(\bar{x} = 8) = \frac{2}{10} = .2 \quad \text{and} \quad P(m = 6) = \frac{3}{10} = .3$$

The values in Table 7.3 are tabulated, and the sampling distributions for $\bar{x}$ and m are shown in Table 7.4 and Figure 7.2.

Since the population of $N = 5$ values is symmetric about the value $x = 9$, both the *population mean* and the *median* equal 9. It would seem reasonable, therefore, to consider using either $\bar{x}$ or m as a possible estimator of $M = \mu = 9$. Which estimator

TABLE 7.3
Values of $\bar{x}$ and m for simple random sampling when $n = 3$ and $N = 5$

Sample	Sample Values	$\bar{x}$	m
1	3, 6, 9	6	6
2	3, 6, 12	7	6
3	3, 6, 15	8	6
4	3, 9, 12	8	9
5	3, 9, 15	9	9
6	3, 12, 15	10	12
7	6, 9, 12	9	9
8	6, 9, 15	10	9
9	6, 12, 15	11	12
10	9, 12, 15	12	12

TABLE 7.4
Sampling distributions for (a) the sample mean and (b) the sample median

(a) $\bar{x}$	$p(\bar{x})$	(b) m	$p(m)$
6	.1	6	.3
7	.1	9	.4
8	.2	12	.3
9	.2		
10	.2		
11	.1		
12	.1		

would you choose? From Table 7.3, you see that, in using m as an estimator, you would be in error by $9 - 6 = 3$ with probability .3 or by $9 - 12 = -3$ with probability .3. That is, the error in estimation using m would be 3 with probability .6. In using $\bar{x}$, however, an error of 3 would occur with probability only .2. On these grounds alone, you may wish to use $\bar{x}$ as an estimator in preference to m.

FIGURE 7.2
Probability histograms for the sampling distributions of the sample mean, $\bar{x}$, and the sample median, m, in Example 7.3

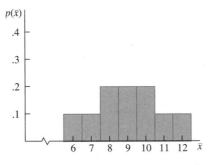
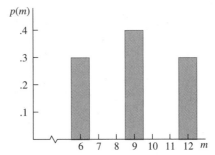

It was not too difficult to derive these sampling distributions in Example 7.3 because the number of elements in the population was very small. When this is not the case, you may need to use one of these methods:

- Use a simulation to approximate the sampling distribution empirically.
- Rely on statistical theorems and theoretical results.

One important statistical theorem that describes the sampling distribution of statistics that are sums or averages is presented in the next section.

7.4 The Central Limit Theorem

The **Central Limit Theorem** states that, under rather general conditions, sums and means of random samples of measurements drawn from a population tend to have an approximately normal distribution. Suppose you toss a balanced die $n = 1$ time. The random variable x is the number observed on the upper face. This familiar random variable can take six values, each with probability 1/6, and its probability distribution is shown in Figure 7.3. The shape of the distribution is *flat* or *uniform* and symmetric about the mean $\mu = 3.5$.

FIGURE 7.3
Probability
distribution for *x,*
the number
appearing on a
single toss of a die

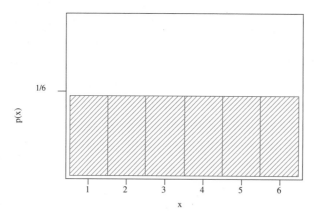

Now, take a sample of size $n = 2$ from this population; that is, toss two dice and record the sum of the numbers on the two upper faces, $\Sigma x_i = x_1 + x_2$. Table 7.5 shows the 36 possible outcomes, each with probability 1/36. The sums are tabulated, and each of the possible sums is divided by $n = 2$ to obtain an average. The result is the **sampling distribution** of $\bar{x} = \Sigma x_i/n$, shown in Figure 7.4. You should notice the dramatic difference in the shape of the sampling distribution. It is now roughly mound-shaped but still symmetric about the mean $\mu = 3.5$.

TABLE 7.5
Sums of the upper
faces of two dice

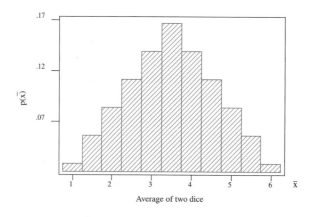

		First Die					
Second Die		1	2	3	4	5	6
1		2	3	4	5	6	7
2		3	4	5	6	7	8
3		4	5	6	7	8	9
4		5	6	7	8	9	10
5		6	7	8	9	10	11
6		7	8	9	10	11	12

FIGURE 7.4
Sampling
distribution of $\bar{x}$
for $n = 2$ dice

Using *MINITAB*, we generated the sampling distributions of $\bar{x}$ when $n = 3$ and $n = 4$. For $n = 3$, the sampling distribution in Figure 7.5 clearly shows the mound shape of the normal probability distribution, still centered at $\mu = 3.5$. Figure 7.6 dramatically shows that the distribution of $\bar{x}$ is approximately normally distributed based on a sample as small as $n = 4$. This phenomenon is the result of an important statistical theorem called the **Central Limit Theorem.**

FIGURE 7.5 *MINITAB* sampling distribution of $\bar{x}$ for $n = 3$ dice

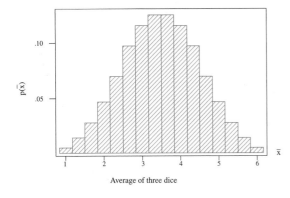

Average of three dice

FIGURE 7.6 *MINITAB* sampling distribution of $\bar{x}$ for $n = 4$ dice

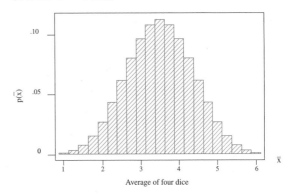

Average of four dice

Central Limit Theorem

If random samples of n observations are drawn from a nonnormal population with finite mean μ and standard deviation σ, then, when n is large, the sampling distribution of the sample mean $\bar{x}$ is approximately normally distributed, with mean μ and standard deviation

$$\frac{\sigma}{\sqrt{n}}$$

The approximation becomes more accurate as n becomes large.

Regardless of its shape, the sampling distribution of $\bar{x}$ always has a mean identical to the mean of the sampled population and a standard deviation equal to the population standard deviation σ divided by $\sqrt{n}$. Consequently, *the spread of the distribution of sample means is considerably less than the spread of the sampled population.*

The Central Limit Theorem can be restated to apply to the **sum of the sample measurements** Σx_i, which, as n becomes large, also has an approximately normal distribution with mean $n\mu$ and standard deviation $\sigma\sqrt{n}$.

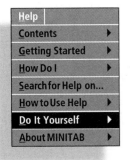

DO IT YOURSELF!

The Java applet called **The Central Limit Theorem** can be used to perform a *simulation* for the sampling distributions of the average of one, two, three or four dice. Figure 7.7 shows the applet after the pair of dice ($n = 2$) has been tossed 2500 times. This is not as hard as it seems, since you need only press the Roll 100 Sets button 25 times. The simulation shows the possible values for $\bar{x} = \Sigma x_i/10$ and also shows the mean and standard deviation for these 2500 measurements. The mean, 3.55, is not exactly equal to $\mu = 3.5$, but it is very close. What is the standard deviation for these 2500 measurements? Is it close to the theoretical value, $\sigma/\sqrt{n}$? You will use this applet again for the *Do It Yourself Exercises* at the end of the chapter.

FIGURE 7.7
**Central Limit
Theorem** applet

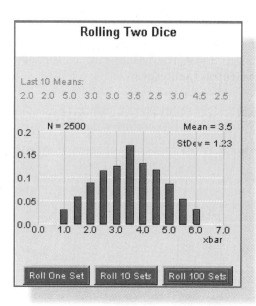

The important contribution of the Central Limit Theorem is in statistical inference. Many estimators that are used to make inferences about population parameters are sums or averages of the sample measurements. When the sample size is sufficiently large, you can expect these estimators to have sampling distributions that are approximately normal. You can then use the normal distribution to describe the behavior of these estimators in repeated sampling and evaluate the probability of observing certain sample results. As in Chapter 6, these probabilities are calculated using the standard normal random variable

$$z = \frac{\text{Estimator} - \text{Mean}}{\text{Standard deviation}}$$

As you reread the Central Limit Theorem, you may notice that the approximation is valid as long as the sample size n is "large"—but how large is "large"? Unfortunately, there is no clear answer to this question. The appropriate value of n depends on the shape of the population from which you sample as well as on how you want to use the approximation. However, these guidelines will help:

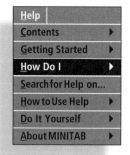

Decide when the Sample Size Is Large Enough?

- If the sampled population is **normal,** then the sampling distribution of $\bar{x}$ will also be normal, no matter what sample size you choose. This result can be proven theoretically, but it should not be too difficult for you to accept without proof.
- When the sampled population is approximately **symmetric,** the sampling distribution of $\bar{x}$ becomes approximately normal for relatively small values of n. Remember how rapidly ($n = 3$) the "flat" distribution in the dice example became mound-shaped.
- When the sampled population is **skewed,** the sample size n must be larger, with n at least 30 before the sampling distribution of $\bar{x}$ becomes approximately normal.

These guidelines suggest that, for many populations, the sampling distribution of $\bar{x}$ will be approximately normal for moderate sample sizes; an exception to this rule occurs in sampling a binomial population when either p or $q = (1 - p)$ is very small. As specific applications of the Central Limit Theorem arise, we will give you the appropriate sample size n.

7.5 The Sampling Distribution of the Sample Mean

If the population mean μ is unknown, you might choose several *statistics* as an estimator; the sample mean $\bar{x}$ and the sample median m are two that readily come to mind. Which should you use? Consider these criteria in choosing the estimator for μ:

- Is it easy or hard to calculate?
- Does it produce estimates that are consistently too high or too low?
- Is it more or less variable than other possible estimators?

The sampling distributions for $\bar{x}$ and m with $n = 3$ for the small population in Example 7.3 showed that, in terms of these criteria, the sample mean performed better than the sample median as an estimator of μ. In many situations, the sample mean $\bar{x}$ has desirable properties as an estimator that are not shared by other competing estimators; therefore, it is more widely used.

The Sampling Distribution of the Sample Mean, $\bar{x}$

- If a random sample of n measurements is selected from a population with mean μ and standard deviation σ, the sampling distribution of the sample mean $\bar{x}$ will have mean μ and standard deviation[†]

$$\frac{\sigma}{\sqrt{n}}$$

- If the population has a *normal* distribution, the sampling distribution of $\bar{x}$ will be *exactly* normally distributed, *regardless of the sample size, n.*
- If the population distribution is *nonnormal*, the sampling distribution of $\bar{x}$ will be *approximately* normally distributed for large samples (by the Central Limit Theorem).

[†]When repeated samples of size n are randomly selected from a *finite* population with N elements whose mean is μ and whose variance is σ^2, the standard deviation of $\bar{x}$ is

$$\frac{\sigma}{\sqrt{n}} \sqrt{\frac{N - n}{N - 1}}$$

where σ^2 is the population variance. When N is large relative to the sample size n, $\sqrt{(N - n)/(N - 1)}$ is approximately equal to 1, and the standard deviation of $\bar{x}$ is

$$\frac{\sigma}{\sqrt{n}}$$

Standard Error

Definition

The standard deviation of a statistic used as an estimator of a population parameter is also called the **standard error of the estimator** (abbreviated **SE**) because it refers to the precision of the estimator. Therefore, the standard deviation of $\bar{x}$—given by $\sigma/\sqrt{n}$—is referred to as the **standard error of the mean** (abbreviated as $SE(\bar{x})$ or just SE).

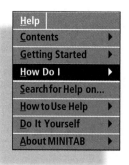

Calculate Probabilities for the Sample Mean $\bar{x}$?

If you know that the sampling distribution of $\bar{x}$ is *normal* or *approximately normal,* you can describe the behavior of the sample mean $\bar{x}$ by calculating the probability of observing certain values of $\bar{x}$ in repeated sampling.

1. Find μ and calculate SE $(\bar{x}) = \sigma/\sqrt{n}$.
2. Write down the event of interest in terms of $\bar{x}$, and locate the appropriate area on the normal curve.
3. Convert the necessary values of $\bar{x}$ to z-values using

$$z = \frac{\bar{x} - \mu}{\sigma/\sqrt{n}}$$

4. Use Table 3 in Appendix I to calculate the probability.

EXAMPLE 7.4

The duration of Alzheimer's disease from the onset of symptoms until death ranges from 3 to 20 years; the average is 8 years with a standard deviation of 4 years. The administrator of a large medical center randomly selects the medical records of 30 deceased Alzheimer's patients from the medical center's database and records the average duration. Find the approximate probabilities for these events:

1. The average duration is less than 7 years.
2. The average duration exceeds 7 years.
3. The average duration lies within 1 year of the population mean $\mu = 8$.

Solution

Since the administrator has selected a random sample from the database at this medical center, he can draw conclusions about only past, present, or future patients with Alzheimer's disease at this medical center. If, on the other hand, this medical center can be considered representative of other medical centers in the country, it may be possible to draw more far-reaching conclusions.

What can you say about the shape of the sampled population? It is not symmetric because the mean $\mu = 8$ does not lie halfway between the maximum and minimum values. Since the mean is closer to the minimum value, the distribution is skewed to the right, with a few patients living a long time after the onset of the disease. Regardless of the shape of the population distribution, however, the sampling distribution of $\bar{x}$ has a mean $\mu = 8$ and standard deviation $\sigma/\sqrt{n} = 4/\sqrt{30} = .73$. In addition, because the sample size is $n = 30$, the Central Limit Theorem ensures the approximate normality of the sampling distribution of $\bar{x}$.

1. The probability that $\bar{x}$ is less than 7 is given by the shaded area in Figure 7.8. To find this area, you need to calculate the value of z corresponding to $\bar{x} = 7$:

$$z = \frac{\bar{x} - \mu}{\sigma/\sqrt{n}} = \frac{7 - 8}{.73} = -1.37$$

From Table 3 in Appendix I, you can find the cumulative area corresponding to $z = -1.37$ and

$$P(\bar{x} < 7) = P(z < -1.37) = .0853$$

FIGURE 7.8
The probability that $\bar{x}$ is less than 7 for Example 7.4

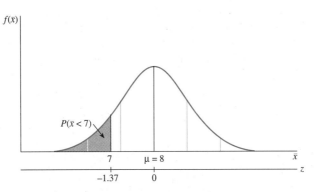

[NOTE: You must use $\sigma/\sqrt{n}$ (not σ) in the formula for z because you are finding an area under the sampling distribution for $\bar{x}$, not under the probability distribution for x.]

2. The event that $\bar{x}$ exceeds 7 is the complement of the event that $\bar{x}$ is less than 7. Thus, the probability that $\bar{x}$ exceeds 7 is

$$P(\bar{x} > 7) = 1 - P(\bar{x} \leq 7)$$
$$= 1 - .0853 = .9147$$

3. The probability that $\bar{x}$ lies within 1 year of $\mu = 8$ is the shaded area in Figure 7.9. The z-value corresponding to $\bar{x} = 7$ is $z = -1.37$, from part 1, and the z-value for $\bar{x} = 9$ is

$$z = \frac{\bar{x} - \mu}{\sigma/\sqrt{n}} = \frac{9 - 8}{.73} = 1.37$$

The probability of interest is

$$P(7 < \bar{x} < 9) = P(-1.37 < z < 1.37)$$
$$= .9147 - .0853 = .8294$$

FIGURE 7.9
The probability that $\bar{x}$ lies within 1 year of $\mu = 8$ for Example 7.4

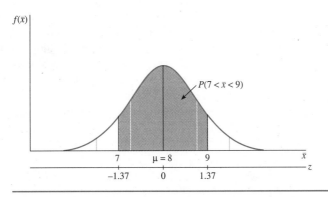

DO IT YOURSELF!

Example 7.4 can be solved using the **Normal Probabilities for Means** applet. If you enter the values for $\bar{x}$, σ, μ, and n (press "Enter" to record each change) and adjust the dropdown list at the bottom of the applet, you can calculate a tail area, a cumulative area, or the area between $-z_0$ and z_0. Conversely, if you need to find the value of $\bar{x}$ that cuts off a certain area under the curve, enter the area in the box marked "prob:" at the bottom of the applet, and the applet will provide the value of $\bar{x}$. The applet in Figure 7.10 is set to calculate $P(7 < \bar{x} < 9) = .829$, correct to three decimal places. You will use this applet for the *Do It Yourself Exercises* at the end of the chapter.

FIGURE 7.10
Normal Probabilities for Means applet

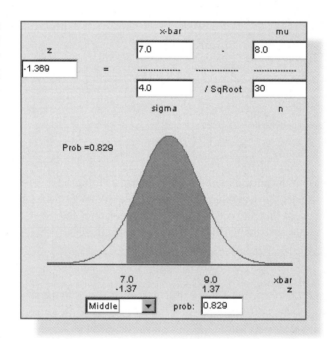

EXAMPLE **7.5**

To avoid difficulties with the Federal Trade Commission or state and local consumer protection agencies, a beverage bottler must make reasonably certain that 12-ounce bottles actually contain 12 ounces of beverage. To determine whether a bottling machine is working satisfactorily, one bottler randomly samples 10 bottles per hour and measures the amount of beverage in each bottle. The mean $\bar{x}$ of the 10 fill measurements is used to decide whether to readjust the amount of beverage delivered per bottle by the filling machine. If records show that the amount of fill per bottle is normally distributed, with a standard deviation of .2 ounce, and if the bottling machine is set to produce a mean fill per bottle of 12.1 ounces, what is the approximate probability that the sample mean $\bar{x}$ of the 10 test bottles is less than 12 ounces?

Solution

The mean of the sampling distribution of the sample mean $\bar{x}$ is identical to the mean of the population of bottle fills—namely, $\mu = 12.1$ ounces—and the standard error of $\bar{x}$ is

$$SE = \frac{\sigma}{\sqrt{n}} = \frac{.2}{\sqrt{10}} = .063$$

(NOTE: σ is the standard deviation of the population of bottle fills, and n is the number of bottles in the sample.) Since the amount of fill is normally distributed, $\bar{x}$ is also normally distributed, as shown in Figure 7.11.

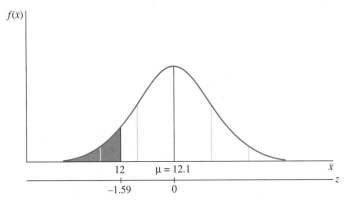

FIGURE 7.11
Probability distribution of $\bar{x}$, the mean of the $n = 10$ bottle fills, for Example 7.5

To find the probability that $\bar{x}$ is less than 12 ounces, express the value $\bar{x} = 12$ in units of standard deviations:

$$z = \frac{\bar{x} - \mu}{\sigma/\sqrt{n}} = \frac{12 - 12.1}{.063} = -1.59$$

Then

$$P(\bar{x} < 12) = P(z < -1.59) = .0559 \approx .056$$

Thus, if the machine is set to deliver an average fill of 12.1 ounces, the mean fill $\bar{x}$ of a sample of 10 bottles will be less than 12 ounces with a probability equal to .056. When this danger signal occurs ($\bar{x}$ is less than 12), the bottler takes a larger sample to recheck the setting of the filling machine.

Exercises   Basic Techniques

7.13   Random samples of size n were selected from populations with the means and variances given here. Find the mean and standard deviation of the sampling distribution of the sample mean in each case:

a. $n = 36$, $\mu = 10$, $\sigma^2 = 9$

b. $n = 100$, $\mu = 5$, $\sigma^2 = 4$

c. $n = 8$, $\mu = 120$, $\sigma^2 = 1$

7.14   Refer to Exercise 7.13.

a. If the sampled populations are normal, what is the sampling distribution of $\bar{x}$ for parts a, b, and c?

b. According to the Central Limit Theorem, if the sampled populations are *not* normal, what can be said about the sampling distribution of $\bar{x}$ for parts a, b, and c?

7.15   Refer to Exercise 7.13, part b.

a. Sketch the sampling distribution for the sample mean and locate the mean and the interval $\mu \pm 2\sigma/\sqrt{n}$ along the $\bar{x}$-axis.

b. Shade the area under the curve that corresponds to the probability that $\bar{x}$ lies within .15 unit of the population mean μ.

c. Find the probability described in part b.

7.16 A random sample of n observations is selected from a population with standard deviation $\sigma = 1$. Calculate the standard error of the mean (SE) for these values of n:

    a. $n = 1$ **b.** $n = 2$ **c.** $n = 4$ **d.** $n = 9$

    e. $n = 16$ **f.** $n = 25$ **g.** $n = 100$

7.17 Refer to Exercise 7.16. Plot the standard error of the mean (SE) versus the sample size n and connect the points with a smooth curve. What is the effect of increasing the sample size on the standard error?

7.18 Suppose a random sample of $n = 25$ observations is selected from a population that is normally distributed, with mean equal to 106 and standard deviation equal to 12.

    a. Give the mean and the standard deviation of the sampling distribution of the sample mean $\bar{x}$.

    b. Find the probability that $\bar{x}$ exceeds 110.

    c. Find the probability that the sample mean deviates from the population mean $\mu = 106$ by no more than 4.

Applications

7.19 When research chemists perform experiments, they may obtain slightly different results on different replications, even when the experiment is performed identically each time. These differences are due to a phenomenon called "measurement error."

    a. List some variables in a chemical experiment that might cause some small changes in the final response measurement.

    b. If you want to make sure that your measurement error is small, you can replicate the experiment and take the sample average of all the measurements. To decrease the amount of variability in your average measurement, should you use a large or a small number of replications? Explain.

7.20 Explain why the weight of a package of one dozen tomatoes should be approximately normally distributed if the dozen tomatoes represent a random sample.

7.21 Use the Central Limit Theorem to explain why a Poisson random variable—say, the number of a particular type of bacteria in a cubic foot of water—has a distribution that can be approximated by a normal distribution when the mean μ is large. (HINT: One cubic foot of water contains 1728 cubic inches of water.)

7.22 Suppose that college faculty with the rank of professor at 2-year institutions earn an average of $57,785 per year[5] with a standard deviation of $4000. In an attempt to verify this salary level, a random sample of 60 professors was selected from a personnel database for all 2-year institutions in the United States.

    a. Describe the sampling distribution of the sample mean $\bar{x}$.

    b. Within what limits would you expect the sample average to lie, with probability .95?

    c. Calculate the probability that the sample mean $\bar{x}$ is greater than $60,000.

    d. If your random sample actually produced a sample mean of $60,000, would you consider this unusual? What conclusion might you draw?

7.23 An important expectation of a federal income tax reduction is that consumers will reap a substantial portion of the tax savings. Suppose estimates of the portion of total tax saved, based on a random sampling of 35 economists, have a mean of 26% and a standard deviation of 12%.

    a. What is the approximate probability that a sample mean, based on a random sample of $n = 35$ economists, will lie within 1% of the mean of the population of the estimates of all economists?

    b. Is it necessarily true that the mean of the population of estimates of all economists is equal to the percentage of tax savings that will actually be achieved? Why?

7.24 A manufacturer of paper used for packaging requires a minimum strength of 20 pounds per square inch. To check on the quality of the paper, a random sample of 10 pieces of paper is selected each hour from the previous hour's production and a strength measurement is recorded for each. The standard deviation σ of the strength measurements, computed by pooling the sum of squares of deviations of many samples, is known to equal 2 pounds per square inch, and the strength measurements are normally distributed.

a. What is the approximate sampling distribution of the sample mean of $n = 10$ test pieces of paper?

b. If the mean of the population of strength measurements is 21 pounds per square inch, what is the approximate probability that, for a random sample of $n = 10$ test pieces of paper, $\bar{x} < 20$?

c. What value would you select for the mean paper strength μ in order that $P(\bar{x} < 20)$ be equal to .001?

7.25 The normal daily human potassium requirement is in the range of 2000 to 6000 milligrams (mg), with larger amounts required during hot summer weather. The amount of potassium in food varies, depending on the food. For example, there are approximately 7 mg in a cola drink, 46 mg in a beer, 630 mg in a banana, 300 mg in a carrot, and 440 mg in a glass of orange juice. Suppose the distribution of potassium in a banana is normally distributed, with mean equal to 630 mg and standard deviation equal to 40 mg per banana. You eat $n = 3$ bananas per day, and T is the total number of milligrams of potassium you receive from them.

a. Find the mean and standard deviation of T.

b. Find the probability that your total daily intake of potassium from the three bananas will exceed 2000 mg. (HINT: Note that T is the sum of three random variables, x_1, x_2, and x_3, where x_1 is the amount of potassium in banana number 1, etc.)

7.26 The total daily sales, x, in the deli section of a local market is the sum of the sales generated by a fixed number of customers who make purchases on a given day.

a. What kind of probability distribution do you expect the total daily sales to have? Explain.

b. For this particular market, the average sale per customer in the deli section is $8.50 with $\sigma = \$2.50$. If 30 customers make deli purchases on a given day, give the mean and standard deviation of the probability distribution of the total daily sales, x.

7.6 The Sampling Distribution of the Sample Proportion

There are many practical examples of the binomial random variable x. One common application involves consumer preference or opinion polls, in which we use a random sample of n people to estimate the proportion p of people in the population who have a specified characteristic. If x of the sampled people have this characteristic, then the sample proportion

$$\hat{p} = \frac{x}{n}$$

can be used to estimate the population proportion p (Figure 7.12).[†]

The binomial random variable x has a probability distribution $p(x)$, described in Chapter 5, with mean np and standard deviation $\sqrt{npq}$. Since $\hat{p}$ is simply the value of x, expressed as a proportion $\left(\hat{p} = \dfrac{x}{n}\right)$, the sampling distribution of $\hat{p}$ is identical to the probability distribution of x, except that it has a new scale along the horizontal axis.

[†]A "hat" placed over the symbol of a population parameter denotes a statistic used to estimate the population parameter. For example, the symbol $\hat{p}$ denotes the sample proportion.

FIGURE 7.12
Sampling
distribution of the
binomial random
variable x and
the sample
proportion $\hat{p}$.

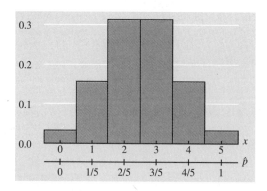

Because of this change of scale, the mean and standard deviation of $\hat{p}$ are also rescaled, so that the mean of the sampling distribution of $\hat{p}$ is p, and its standard error is

$$SE(\hat{p}) = \sqrt{\frac{pq}{n}} \qquad \text{where } q = 1 - p$$

Finally, just as we can approximate the probability distribution of x with a normal distribution when the sample size n is large, we can do the same with the sampling distribution of $\hat{p}$.

Properties of the Sampling Distribution of the Sample Proportion, $\hat{p}$

- If a random sample of n observations is selected from a binomial population with parameter p, then the sampling distribution of the sample proportion

$$\hat{p} = \frac{x}{n}$$

will have a mean

$$p$$

and a standard deviation

$$SE(\hat{p}) = \sqrt{\frac{pq}{n}} \qquad \text{where } q = 1 - p$$

- When the sample size n is large, the sampling distribution of $\hat{p}$ can be approximated by a normal distribution. The approximation will be adequate if $np > 5$ and $nq > 5$.

EXAMPLE 7.6

In a survey, 500 mothers and fathers were asked about the importance of sports for boys and girls. Of the parents interviewed, 60% agreed that the genders are equal and should have equal opportunities to participate in sports. Describe the sampling distribution of the sample proportion $\hat{p}$ of parents who agree that the genders are equal and should have equal opportunities.

Solution   You can assume that the 500 parents represent a random sample of the parents of all boys and girls in the United States and that the true proportion in the population is equal to some unknown value that you can call p. The sampling distribution of $\hat{p}$ can be approximated by a normal distribution,[†] with mean equal to p (see Figure 7.13) and standard error

$$SE(\hat{p}) = \sqrt{\frac{pq}{n}}$$

FIGURE 7.13
The sampling distribution for $\hat{p}$ based on a sample of $n = 500$ parents for Example 7.6

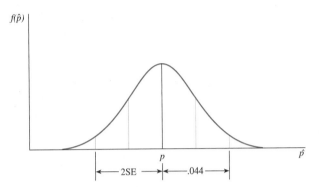

You can see from Figure 7.13 that the sampling distribution of $\hat{p}$ is centered over its mean p. Even though you do not know the exact value of p (the sample proportion $\hat{p} = .60$ may be larger or smaller than p), an approximate value for the standard deviation of the sampling distribution can be found using the sample proportion $\hat{p} = .60$ to approximate the unknown value of p. Thus,

$$SE = \sqrt{\frac{pq}{n}} \approx \sqrt{\frac{\hat{p}\hat{q}}{n}}$$

$$= \sqrt{\frac{(.60)(.40)}{500}} = .022$$

Therefore, approximately 95% of the time, $\hat{p}$ will fall within $2SE \approx .044$ of the (unknown) value of p.

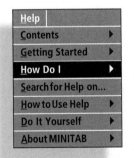

Calculate Probabilities for the Sample Proportion $\hat{p}$?

1. Find the necessary values of n and p.

2. Check whether the normal approximation to the binomial distribution is appropriate ($np > 5$ and $nq > 5$).

3. Write down the event of interest in terms of $\hat{p}$, and locate the appropriate area on the normal curve.

4. Convert the necessary values of $\hat{p}$ to z-values using

$$z = \frac{\hat{p} - p}{\sqrt{\frac{pq}{n}}}$$

5. Use Table 3 in Appendix I to calculate the probability.

[†]Checking the conditions that allow the normal approximation to the distribution of $\hat{p}$, you can see that $n = 500$ is adequate for values of p near .60 because $n\hat{p} = 300$ and $n\hat{q} = 200$ are both greater than 5.

EXAMPLE 7.7

Refer to Example 7.6. Suppose the proportion p of parents in the population is actually equal to .55. What is the probability of observing a sample proportion as large as or larger than the observed value $\hat{p} = .60$?

Solution

Figure 7.14 shows the sampling distribution of $\hat{p}$ when $p = .55$, with the observed value $\hat{p} = .60$ located on the horizontal axis. The probability of observing a sample proportion $\hat{p}$ equal to or larger than .60 is approximated by the shaded area in the upper tail of this normal distribution with

$$p = .55$$

and

$$SE = \sqrt{\frac{pq}{n}} = \sqrt{\frac{(.55)(.45)}{500}} = .0222$$

FIGURE 7.14
The sampling distribution of $\hat{p}$ for $n = 500$ and $p = .55$ for Example 7.7

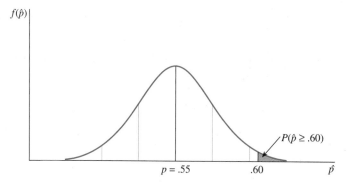

To find this shaded area, first calculate the z-value corresponding to $\hat{p} = .60$:

$$z = \frac{\hat{p} - p}{\sqrt{pq/n}} = \frac{.60 - .55}{.0222} = 2.25$$

Using Table 3 in Appendix I, you find

$$P(\hat{p} > .60) \approx P(z > 2.25) = 1 - .9878 = .0122$$

That is, if you were to select a random sample of $n = 500$ observations from a population with proportion p equal to .55, the probability that the sample proportion $\hat{p}$ would be as large as or larger than .60 is only .0122.

When the normal distribution was used in Chapter 6 to approximate the binomial probabilities associated with x, a correction of $\pm.5$ was applied to improve the approximation. The equivalent correction here is $\pm(.5/n)$. For example, for $\hat{p} = .60$ the value of z with the correction is

$$z_1 = \frac{(.60 - .001) - .55}{\sqrt{\dfrac{(.55)(.45)}{500}}} = 2.20$$

with $P(\hat{p} > .60) \approx .0139$. To two-decimal-place accuracy, this value agrees with the earlier result. When n is large, the effect of using the correction is generally negligible. You should solve problems in this and the remaining chapters *without* the correction factor unless you are specifically instructed to use it.

Exercises

Basic Techniques

7.27   Random samples of size n were selected from binomial populations with population parameters p given here. Find the mean and the standard deviation of the sampling distribution of the sample proportion $\hat{p}$ in each case:

   a. $n = 100$, $p = .3$

   b. $n = 400$, $p = .1$

   c. $n = 250$, $p = .6$

7.28   Sketch each of the sampling distributions in Exercise 7.27. For each, locate the mean p and the interval $p \pm 2$ SE along the $\hat{p}$-axis of the graph.

7.29   Refer to the sampling distribution in Exercise 7.27, part a.

   a. Sketch the sampling distribution for the sample proportion and shade the area under the curve that corresponds to the probability that $\hat{p}$ lies within .08 of the population proportion p.

   b. Find the probability described in part a.

7.30   Random samples of size $n = 500$ were selected from a binomial population with $p = .1$.

   a. Is it appropriate to use the normal distribution to approximate the sampling distribution of $\hat{p}$? Check to make sure the necessary conditions are met.

   Using the results of part a, find these probabilities:

   b. $\hat{p} > .12$

   c. $\hat{p} < .10$

   d. $\hat{p}$ lies within .02 of p

7.31   Calculate SE($\hat{p}$) for $n = 100$ and these values of p:

   a. $p = .01$ **b.** $p = .10$ **c.** $p = .30$ **d.** $p = .50$

   e. $p = .70$ **f.** $p = .90$ **g.** $p = .99$

   h. Plot SE($\hat{p}$) versus p on graph paper and sketch a smooth curve through the points. For what value of p is the standard deviation of the sampling distribution of $\hat{p}$ a maximum? What happens to the standard error when p is near 0 or near 1.0?

7.32   **a.** Is the normal approximation to the sampling distribution of $\hat{p}$ appropriate when $n = 400$ and $p = .8$?

   b. Use the results of part a to find the probability that $\hat{p}$ is greater than .83.

   c. Use the results of part a to find the probability that $\hat{p}$ lies between .76 and .84.

Applications

7.33   One of the ways most Americans relieve stress is to reward themselves with sweets. According to one study, 46% admit to overeating sweet foods when stressed.[6] Suppose that the 46% figure is correct and that a random sample of $n = 100$ Americans is selected.

   a. Does the distribution of $\hat{p}$, the sample proportion of Americans who relieve stress by overeating sweet foods, have an approximately normal distribution? If so, what are its mean and standard deviation?

   b. What is the probability that the sample proportion, $\hat{p}$, exceeds .5?

   c. What is the probability that $\hat{p}$ lies within the interval .35 to .55?

   d. What might you conclude if the sample proportion were as small as 30%?

7.34   Do you use the Internet to gather information for a project? The percentage of students who used the Internet as their major resource for a school project in the past year was 66%.[7] Suppose that you take a sample of $n = 1000$ students, and record the number of students who used the Internet as their major resource for their school project during the past year. Let $\hat{p}$ be the proportion of students surveyed who used the Internet as a major resource in the past year.

a. What is the exact distribution of $\hat{p}$? How can you approximate the distribution of $\hat{p}$?

b. What is the probability that the sample proportion $\hat{p}$ exceeds 68%?

c. What is the probability that the sample proportion lies between 64% and 68%?

d. Would a sample proportion of 70% contradict the reported value of 66%?

7.35 According to *Chance* magazine, the average percentage of brown M&M® candies in a package of plain M&Ms is 30%.[8] (This percentage varies, however, among the different types of packaged M&Ms.) Suppose you randomly select a package of plain M&Ms that contains 55 candies and determine the proportion of brown candies in the package.

a. What is the approximate distribution of the sample proportion of brown candies in a package that contains 55 candies?

b. What is the probability that the sample proportion of brown candies is less than 20%?

c. What is the probability that the sample proportion exceeds 35%?

d. Within what range would you expect the sample proportion to lie about 95% of the time?

7.7 A Sampling Application: Statistical Process Control (Optional)

Statistical process control (SPC) methodology was developed to monitor, control, and improve products and services. Steel bearings must conform to size and hardness specifications, industrial chemicals must have a low prespecified level of impurities, and accounting firms must minimize and ultimately eliminate incorrect bookkeeping entries. It is often said that statistical process control consists of 10% statistics, 90% engineering and common sense. We can statistically monitor a process mean and tell when the mean falls outside preassigned limits, but we cannot tell *why* it is out of control. Answering this last question requires knowledge of the process and problem-solving ability—the other 90%!

Product quality is usually monitored using statistical control charts. Measurements on a process variable to be monitored change over time. The cause of a change in the variable is said to be *assignable* if it can be found and corrected. Other variation—small haphazard changes due to alteration in the production environment—that is not controllable is regarded as *random variation*. If the variation in a process variable is solely random, the process is said to be *in control*. The first objective in statistical process control is to eliminate assignable causes of variation in the process variable and then get the process in control. The next step is to reduce variation and get the measurements on the process variable within *specification limits,* the limits within which the measurements on usable items or services must fall.

Once a process is in control and is producing a satisfactory product, the process variables are monitored with **control charts.** Samples of n items are drawn from the process at specified intervals of time, and a sample statistic is computed. These statistics are plotted on the control chart, so that the process can be checked for shifts in the process variable that might indicate control problems.

A Control Chart for the Process Mean: The $\bar{x}$ Chart

Assume that n items are randomly selected from the production process at equal intervals and that measurements are recorded on the process variable. If the process is in control, the sample means should vary about the population mean μ in a random manner. Moreover, according to the Central Limit Theorem, the sampling distribution of $\bar{x}$ should be approximately normal, so that almost all of the values of $\bar{x}$ fall into the interval $(\mu \pm 3\text{ SE}) = \mu \pm 3(\sigma/\sqrt{n})$. Although the exact values of μ and σ are unknown, you can obtain accurate estimates by using the sample measurements.

Every control chart has a *centerline* and *control limits*. The centerline for the $\bar{x}$ **chart** is the estimate of μ, the grand average of all the sample statistics calculated from the measurements on the process variable. The upper and lower *control limits* are placed three standard deviations above and below the centerline. If you monitor the process mean based on k samples of size n taken at regular intervals, the centerline is $\bar{\bar{x}}$, the average of the sample means, and the control limits are at $\bar{\bar{x}} \pm 3(\sigma/\sqrt{n})$, with σ estimated by s, the standard deviation of the nk measurements.

EXAMPLE 7.8

A statistical process control monitoring system samples the inside diameters of $n = 4$ bearings each hour. Table 7.6 provides the data for $k = 25$ hourly samples. Construct an $\bar{x}$ chart for monitoring the process mean.

Solution

The sample mean was calculated for each of the $k = 25$ samples. For example, the mean for sample 1 is

$$\bar{x} = \frac{.992 + 1.007 + 1.016 + .991}{4} = 1.0015$$

TABLE 7.6
25 hourly samples of bearing diameters, $n = 4$ bearings per sample

Sample	Sample Measurements				Sample Mean, $\bar{x}$
1	.992	1.007	1.016	.991	1.00150
2	1.015	.984	.976	1.000	.99375
3	.988	.993	1.011	.981	.99325
4	.996	1.020	1.004	.999	1.00475
5	1.015	1.006	1.002	1.001	1.00600
6	1.000	.982	1.005	.989	.99400
7	.989	1.009	1.019	.994	1.00275
8	.994	1.010	1.009	.990	1.00075
9	1.018	1.016	.990	1.011	1.00875
10	.997	1.005	.989	1.001	.99800
11	1.020	.986	1.002	.989	.99925
12	1.007	.986	.981	.995	.99225
13	1.016	1.002	1.010	.999	1.00675
14	.982	.995	1.011	.987	.99375
15	1.001	1.000	.983	1.002	.99650
16	.992	1.008	1.001	.996	.99925
17	1.020	.988	1.015	.986	1.00225
18	.993	.987	1.006	1.001	.99675
19	.978	1.006	1.002	.982	.99200
20	.984	1.009	.983	.986	.99050
21	.990	1.012	1.010	1.007	1.00475
22	1.015	.983	1.003	.989	.99750
23	.983	.990	.997	1.002	.99300
24	1.011	1.012	.991	1.008	1.00550
25	.987	.987	1.007	.995	.99400

The sample means are shown in the last column of Table 7.6. The centerline is located at the average of the sample means, or

$$\bar{\bar{x}} = \frac{24.9675}{25} = .9987$$

The calculated value of s, the sample standard deviation of all $nk = 4(25) = 100$ observations, is $s = .011458$, and the estimated standard error of the mean of $n = 4$ observations is

$$\frac{s}{\sqrt{n}} = \frac{.011458}{\sqrt{4}} = .005729$$

The upper and lower control limits are found as

$$\text{UCL} = \bar{\bar{x}} + 3\frac{s}{\sqrt{n}} = .9987 + 3(.005729) = 1.015887$$

and

$$\text{LCL} = \bar{\bar{x}} - 3\frac{s}{\sqrt{n}} = .9987 - 3(.005729) = .981513$$

Figure 7.15 shows a *MINITAB* printout of the $\bar{x}$ chart constructed from the data. If you assume that the samples used to construct the $\bar{x}$ chart were collected when the process was in control, the chart can now be used to detect changes in the process mean. Sample means are plotted periodically, and if a sample mean falls outside the control limits, a warning should be conveyed. The process should be checked to locate the cause of the unusually large or small mean.

FIGURE 7.15
MINITAB $\bar{x}$ chart
for Example 7.8

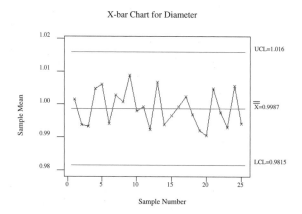

A Control Chart for the Proportion Defective: The p Chart

Sometimes the observation made on an item is simply whether or not it meets specifications; thus, it is judged to be defective or nondefective. If the fraction defective produced by the process is p, then x, the number of defectives in a sample of n items, has a binomial distribution.

To monitor a process for defective items, samples of size n are selected at periodic intervals and the sample proportion $\hat{p}$ is calculated. When the process is in control, $\hat{p}$ should fall into the interval $p \pm 3\text{SE}$, where p is the proportion of defectives in the population (or the process fraction defective) with standard error

$$\text{SE} = \sqrt{\frac{pq}{n}} = \sqrt{\frac{p(1-p)}{n}}$$

The process fraction defective is unknown but can be estimated by the average of the k sample proportions:

$$\bar{p} = \frac{\Sigma \hat{p}_i}{k}$$

and the standard error is estimated by

$$\text{SE} = \sqrt{\frac{\bar{p}(1 - \bar{p})}{n}}$$

The centerline for the **p chart** is located at $\bar{p}$, and the upper and lower control limits are

$$\text{UCL} = \bar{p} + 3\sqrt{\frac{\bar{p}(1 - \bar{p})}{n}}$$

and

$$\text{LCL} = \bar{p} - 3\sqrt{\frac{\bar{p}(1 - \bar{p})}{n}}$$

EXAMPLE 7.9   A manufacturer of ballpoint pens randomly samples 400 pens per day and tests each to see whether the ink flow is acceptable. The proportions of pens judged defective each day over a 40-day period are listed in Table 7.7. Construct a control chart for the proportion $\hat{p}$ defective in samples of $n = 400$ pens selected from the process.

TABLE 7.7
Proportions of defectives in samples of $n = 400$ pens

Day	Proportion	Day	Proportion	Day	Proportion	Day	Proportion
1	.0200	11	.0100	21	.0300	31	.0225
2	.0125	12	.0175	22	.0200	32	.0175
3	.0225	13	.0250	23	.0125	33	.0225
4	.0100	14	.0175	24	.0175	34	.0100
5	.0150	15	.0275	25	.0225	35	.0125
6	.0200	16	.0200	26	.0150	36	.0300
7	.0275	17	.0225	27	.0200	37	.0200
8	.0175	18	.0100	28	.0250	38	.0150
9	.0200	19	.0175	29	.0150	39	.0150
10	.0250	20	.0200	30	.0175	40	.0225

Solution   The estimate of the process proportion defective is the average of the $k = 40$ sample proportions in Table 7.7. Therefore, the centerline of the control chart is located at

$$\bar{p} = \frac{\Sigma \hat{p}_i}{k} = \frac{.0200 + .0125 + \cdots + .0225}{40} = \frac{.7600}{40} = .019$$

An estimate of SE, the standard error of the sample proportions, is

$$\sqrt{\frac{\bar{p}(1 - \bar{p})}{n}} = \sqrt{\frac{(.019)(.981)}{400}} = .00683$$

and $3\,\text{SE} = (3)(.00683) = .0205$. Therefore, the upper and lower control limits for the p chart are located at

$$\text{UCL} = \bar{p} + 3\,\text{SE} = .0190 + .0205 = .0395$$

and

$$\text{LCL} = \bar{p} - 3\,\text{SE} = .0190 - .0205 = -.0015$$

Or, since p cannot be negative, LCL = 0.

The p control chart is shown in Figure 7.16. Note that all 40 sample proportions fall within the control limits. If a sample proportion collected at some time in the future falls outside the control limits, the manufacturer should be concerned about an increase in the defective rate. He should take steps to look for the possible causes of this increase.

FIGURE 7.16
MINITAB p chart
for Example 7.9

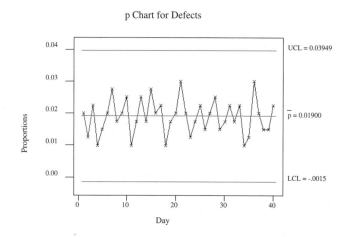

Other commonly used control charts are the *R chart,* which is used to monitor variation in the process variable by using the sample range, and the *c chart,* which is used to monitor the number of defects per item.

Exercises

Basic Techniques

7.36 The sample means were calculated for 30 samples of size $n = 10$ for a process that was judged to be in control. The means of the 30 $\bar{x}$-values and the standard deviation of the combined 300 measurements were $\bar{\bar{x}} = 20.74$ and $s = .87$, respectively.

   a. Use the data to determine the upper and lower control limits for an $\bar{x}$ chart.

   b. What is the purpose of an $\bar{x}$ chart?

   c. Construct an $\bar{x}$ chart for the process and explain how it can be used.

7.37 The sample means were calculated for 40 samples of size $n = 5$ for a process that was judged to be in control. The means of the 40 values and the standard deviation of the combined 200 measurements were $\bar{\bar{x}} = 155.9$ and $s = 4.3$, respectively.

   a. Use the data to determine the upper and lower control limits for an $\bar{x}$ chart.

   b. Construct an $\bar{x}$ chart for the process and explain how it can be used.

7.38 Explain the difference between an $\bar{x}$ chart and a p chart.

7.39 Samples of $n = 100$ items were selected hourly over a 100-hour period, and the sample proportion of defectives was calculated each hour. The mean of the 100 sample proportions was .035.

   a. Use the data to find the upper and lower control limits for a p chart.

   b. Construct a p chart for the process and explain how it can be used.

7.40 Samples of $n = 200$ items were selected hourly over a 100-hour period, and the sample proportion of defectives was calculated each hour. The mean of the 100 sample proportions was .041.

   a. Use the data to find the upper and lower control limits for a p chart.

   b. Construct a p chart for the process and explain how it can be used.

Applications

7.41   A gambling casino records and plots the mean daily gain or loss from five blackjack tables on an $\bar{x}$ chart. The overall mean of the sample means and the standard deviation of the combined data over 40 weeks were $\bar{\bar{x}} = \$10,752$ and $s = \$1605$, respectively.

a. Construct an $\bar{x}$ chart for the mean daily gain per blackjack table.

b. How can this $\bar{x}$ chart be of value to the manager of the casino?

7.42   A producer of brass rivets randomly samples 400 rivets each hour and calculates the proportion of defectives in the sample. The mean sample proportion calculated from 200 samples was equal to .021. Construct a control chart for the proportion of defectives in samples of 400 rivets. Explain how the control chart can be of value to a manager.

EX0743

7.43   The manager of a building-supplies company randomly samples incoming lumber to see whether it meets quality specifications. From each shipment, 100 pieces of 2 × 4 lumber are inspected and judged according to whether they are first (acceptable) or second (defective) grade. The proportions of second-grade 2 × 4s recorded for 30 shipments were as follows:

.14   .21   .19   .18   .23   .20   .25   .19   .22   .17   .21   .15   .23   .12   .19
.22   .15   .26   .22   .21   .14   .20   .18   .22   .21   .13   .20   .23   .19   .26

Construct a control chart for the proportion of second-grade 2 × 4s in samples of 100 pieces of lumber. Explain how the control chart can be of use to the manager of the building-supplies company.

7.44   A coal-burning power plant tests and measures three specimens of coal each day to monitor the percentage of ash in the coal. The overall mean of 30 daily sample means and the combined standard deviation of all the data were $\bar{\bar{x}} = 7.24$ and $s = .07$, respectively. Construct an $\bar{x}$ chart for the process and explain how it can be of value to the manager of the power plant.

EX0745

7.45   The data in the table are measures of the radiation in air particulates at a nuclear power plant. Four measurements were recorded at weekly intervals over a 26-week period. Use the data to construct an $\bar{x}$ chart and plot the 26 values of $\bar{x}$. Explain how the chart can be used.

Week	Radiation				Week	Radiation			
1	.031	.032	.030	.031	14	.029	.028	.029	.029
2	.025	.026	.025	.025	15	.031	.029	.030	.031
3	.029	.029	.031	.030	16	.014	.016	.016	.017
4	.035	.037	.034	.035	17	.019	.019	.021	.020
5	.022	.024	.022	.023	18	.024	.024	.024	.025
6	.030	.029	.030	.030	19	.029	.027	.028	.028
7	.019	.019	.018	.019	20	.032	.030	.031	.030
8	.027	.028	.028	.028	21	.041	.042	.038	.039
9	.034	.032	.033	.033	22	.034	.036	.036	.035
10	.017	.016	.018	.018	23	.021	.022	.024	.022
11	.022	.020	.020	.021	24	.029	.029	.030	.029
12	.016	.018	.017	.017	25	.016	.017	.017	.016
13	.015	.017	.018	.017	26	.020	.021	.020	.022

Key Concepts and Formulas

I. Sampling Plans and Experimental Designs

    1. Simple random sampling

        a. Each possible sample is equally likely to occur.

        b. Use a computer or a table of random numbers.

        c. Problems are nonresponse, undercoverage, and wording bias.

    2. Other sampling plans involving randomization

        a. Stratified random sampling

    b. Cluster sampling

    c. Systematic 1-in-k sampling

  3. Nonrandom sampling

    a. Convenience sampling

    b. Judgment sampling

    c. Quota sampling

II. Statistics and Sampling Distributions

1. Sampling distributions describe the possible values of a statistic and how often they occur in repeated sampling.

2. Sampling distributions can be derived mathematically, approximated empirically, or found using statistical theorems.

3. The Central Limit Theorem states that sums and averages of measurements from a nonnormal population with finite mean μ and standard deviation σ have approximately normal distributions for large samples of size n.

III. Sampling Distribution of the Sample Mean

1. When samples of size n are randomly drawn from a normal population with mean μ and variance σ^2, the sample mean $\bar{x}$ has a normal distribution with mean μ and standard deviation $\sigma/\sqrt{n}$.

2. When samples of size n are randomly drawn from a nonnormal population with mean μ and variance σ^2, the Central Limit Theorem ensures that the sample mean $\bar{x}$ will have an approximately normal distribution with mean μ and standard deviation $\sigma/\sqrt{n}$ when n is large ($n \geq 30$).

3. Probabilities involving the sample mean can be calculated by standardizing the value of $\bar{x}$ using z:

$$z = \frac{\bar{x} - \mu}{\sigma/\sqrt{n}}$$

IV. Sampling Distribution of the Sample Proportion

1. When samples of size n are drawn from a binomial population with parameter p, the sample proportion $\hat{p}$ will have an approximately normal distribution with mean p and standard deviation $\sqrt{pq/n}$ as long as $np > 5$ and $nq > 5$.

2. Probabilities involving the sample proportion can be calculated by standardizing the value $\hat{p}$ using z:

$$z = \frac{\hat{p} - p}{\sqrt{\dfrac{pq}{n}}}$$

V. Statistical Process Control

1. To monitor a quantitative process, use an $\bar{x}$ chart. Select k samples of size n and calculate the overall mean $\bar{\bar{x}}$ and the standard deviation s of all nk measurements. Create upper and lower control limits as

$$\bar{\bar{x}} \pm 3 \frac{s}{\sqrt{n}}$$

If a sample mean exceeds these limits, the process is out of control.

2. To monitor a *binomial* process, use a p chart. Select k samples of size n and calculate the average of the sample proportions as

$$\bar{p} = \frac{\Sigma \hat{p}_i}{k}$$

Create upper and lower control limits as

$$\bar{p} \pm 3 \sqrt{\frac{\bar{p}(1 - \bar{p})}{n}}$$

If a sample proportion exceeds these limits, the process is out of control.

The Central Limit Theorem at Work

MINITAB provides a perfect tool for exploring the way the Central Limit Theorem works in practice. Remember that, according to the Central Limit Theorem, if random samples of size n are drawn from a nonnormal population with mean μ and standard deviation σ, then when n is large, the sampling distribution of the sample mean $\bar{x}$ will be approximately normal with the same mean μ and with standard error $\sigma/\sqrt{n}$. Let's try sampling from a nonnormal population with the help of *MINITAB*.

In a new *MINITAB* worksheet, generate 100 samples of size $n = 30$ from a nonnormal distribution called the exponential distribution. Use **Calc → Random Data → Exponential.** Type **100** for the number of rows of data, and store the results in C1–C30 (see Figure 7.17). Leave the mean at the default of 1.0, and click **OK.** The data are generated and stored in the worksheet. Use **Graph → Histogram** to look at the distribution of some of the data—say, C1 (as in Figure 7.18). Notice that the distribution is not mound-shaped; it is highly skewed to the right.

For the exponential distribution that we have used, the mean and standard deviation are $\mu = 1$ and $\sigma = 1$, respectively. Check the descriptive statistics for one of the columns (use **Stat → Basic Statistics → Display Descriptive Statistics**), and you will find that the 100 observations have a sample mean and standard deviation that

FIGURE 7.17

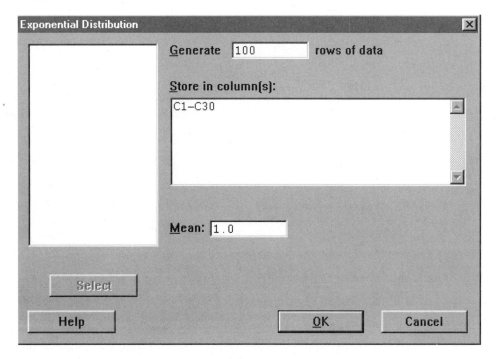

MINITAB

FIGURE 7.18

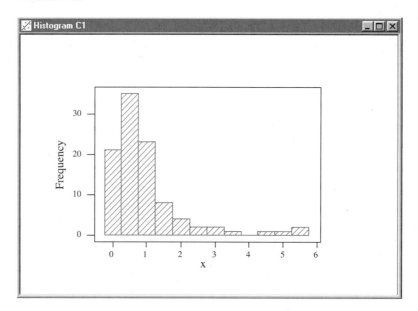

are both *close to* but not exactly equal to 1. Now, generate 100 values of $\bar{x}$ based on samples of size $n = 30$ by creating a column of means for the 100 rows. Use **Calc → Row Statistics,** and select **Mean.** To average the entries in all 30 columns, select or type **C1–C30** in the Input variables box, and store the results in **C31** (see Figure 7.19). You can now look at the distribution of the sample means using **Graph → Histogram** and selecting **C31.** The distribution of the 100 sample means generated for our example is shown in Figure 7.20.

FIGURE 7.19

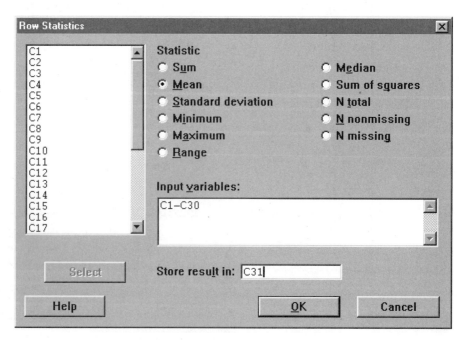

MINITAB

FIGURE 7.20

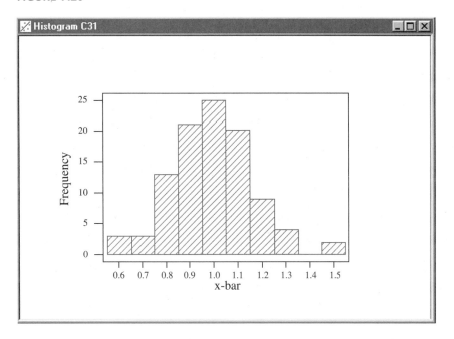

Notice the distinct mound shape of the distribution in Figure 7.20 compared to the original distribution in Figure 7.18. Also, if you check the descriptive statistics for C31, you will find that the mean and standard deviation of our 100 sample means are not too different from the theoretical values, $\mu = 1$ and $\sigma/\sqrt{n} = 1/\sqrt{30} = .18$. (For our data, the sample mean is .9955 and the standard deviation is .1695.) Since we had only 100 samples, our results are not *exactly* equal to the theoretical values. If we had generated an *infinite* number of samples, we would have gotten an exact match. This is the Central Limit Theorem at work!

Supplementary Exercises

7.46   A finite population consists of four elements: 6, 1, 3, 2.

    a. How many different samples of size $n = 2$ can be selected from this population if you sample *without replacement*? (Sampling is said to be *without replacement* if an element cannot be selected twice for the same sample.)

    b. List the possible samples of size $n = 2$.

    c. Compute the sample mean for each of the samples given in part b.

    d. Find the sampling distribution of $\bar{x}$. Use a probability histogram to graph the sampling distribution of $\bar{x}$.

    e. If all four population values are equally likely, calculate the value of the population mean μ. Do any of the samples listed in part b produce a value of $\bar{x}$ exactly equal to μ?

7.47   Refer to Exercise 7.46. Find the sampling distribution for $\bar{x}$ if random samples of size $n = 3$ are selected *without replacement*. Graph the sampling distribution of $\bar{x}$.

7.48   Studies indicate that drinking water supplied by some old lead-lined city piping systems may contain harmful levels of lead. An important study of the Boston water supply system showed that the distribution of lead content readings for individual water specimens had a mean and standard deviation of approximately .033 milligrams per liter (mg/l) and .10 mg/l, respectively.[9]

    a. Explain why you believe this distribution is or is not normally distributed.

b. Because the researchers were concerned about the shape of the distribution in part a, they calculated the average daily lead levels at 40 different locations on each of 23 randomly selected days. What can you say about the shape of the distribution of the average daily lead levels from which the sample of 23 days was taken?

c. What are the mean and standard deviation of the distribution of average lead levels in part b?

7.49 The total amount of vegetation held by the earth's forests is important to both ecologists and politicians because green plants absorb carbon dioxide. An underestimate of the earth's vegetative mass, or biomass, means that much of the carbon dioxide emitted by human activities (primarily fossil-burning fuels) will not be absorbed, and a climate-altering buildup of carbon dioxide will occur. Studies[10] indicate that the biomass for tropical woodlands, thought to be about 35 kilograms per square meter (kg/m^2), may in fact be too high and that tropical biomass values vary regionally—from about 5 to 55 kg/m^2. Suppose you measure the tropical biomass in 400 randomly selected square-meter plots.

a. Approximate σ, the standard deviation of the biomass measurements.

b. What is the probability that your sample average is within two units of the true average tropical biomass?

c. If your sample average is $\bar{x} = 31.75$, what would you conclude about the overestimation that concerns the scientists?

7.50 The safety requirements for hard hats worn by construction workers and others, established by the American National Standards Institute (ANSI), specify that each of three hats pass the following test. A hat is mounted on an aluminum head form. An 8-pound steel ball is dropped on the hat from a height of 5 feet, and the resulting force is measured at the bottom of the head form. The force exerted on the head form by each of the three hats must be less than 1000 pounds, and the average of the three must be less than 850 pounds. (The relationship between this test and actual human head damage is unknown.) Suppose the exerted force is normally distributed, and hence a sample mean of three force measurements is normally distributed. If a random sample of three hats is selected from a shipment with a mean equal to 900 and $\sigma = 100$, what is the probability that the sample mean will satisfy the ANSI standard?

7.51 A research psychologist is planning an experiment to determine whether the use of imagery—picturing a word in your mind—affects people's ability to memorize. He wants to use two groups of subjects: a group that memorizes a set of 20 words using the imagery technique, and a control group that does not use imagery.

a. Use a randomization technique to divide a group of 20 subjects into two groups of equal size.

b. How can the researcher randomly select the group of 20 subjects?

c. Suppose the researcher offers to pay subjects $50 each to participate in the experiment and uses the first 20 students who apply. Would this group behave as if it were a simple random sample of size $n = 20$?

7.52 A study of nearly 2000 women included questions dealing with child abuse and its effect on the women's adult life.[11] The study reported on the likelihood that a woman who was abused as a child would suffer either physical abuse or physical problems arising from depression, anxiety, low self-esteem, and drug abuse as an adult.

a. Is this an observational study or a designed experiment?

b. What problems might arise because of the sensitive nature of this study? What kinds of biases might occur?

7.53 A biology experiment was designed to determine whether sprouting radish seeds inhibit the germination of lettuce seeds.[12] Three 10-centimeter petri dishes were used. The first contained 26 lettuce seeds, the second contained 26 radish seeds, and the third contained 13 lettuce seeds and 13 radish seeds.

a. Assume that the experimenter had a package of 50 radish seeds and another of 50 lettuce seeds. Devise a plan for randomly assigning the radish and lettuce seeds to the three treatment groups.

b. What assumptions must the experimenter make about the packages of 50 seeds in order to assure randomness in the experiment?

7.54 A study of about $n = 1000$ individuals in the United States during September 21–22, 2001, revealed that 43% of the respondents indicated that they were less willing to fly following the events of September 11, 2001.[13]

a. Is this an observational study or a designed experiment?

b. What problems might or could have occurred because of the sensitive nature of the subject? What kinds of biases might have occurred?

7.55 Suppose a telephone company executive wishes to select a random sample of $n = 20$ (a small number is used to simplify the exercise) out of 7000 customers for a survey of customer attitudes concerning service. If the customers are numbered for identification purposes, indicate the customers whom you will include in your sample. Use the random number table and explain how you selected your sample.

7.56 The proportion of individuals with an Rh-positive blood type is 85%. You have a random sample of $n = 500$ individuals.

a. What are the mean and standard deviation of $\hat{p}$, the sample proportion with Rh-positive blood type?

b. Is the distribution of $\hat{p}$ approximately normal? Justify your answer.

c. What is the probability that the sample proportion $\hat{p}$ exceeds 82%?

d. What is the probability that the sample proportion lies between 83% and 88%?

e. 99% of the time, the sample proportion would lie between what two limits?

7.57 What survey design is used in each of these situations?

a. A random sample of $n = 50$ city blocks is selected, and a census is done for each single-family dwelling on each block.

b. The highway patrol stops every tenth vehicle on a given city artery between 9:00 A.M. and 3:00 P.M. to perform a routine traffic safety check.

c. One hundred households in each of four city wards are surveyed concerning a pending city tax relief referendum.

d. Every 10th tree in a managed slash pine plantation is checked for pine needle borer infestation.

e. A random sample of $n = 1000$ taxpayers from the city of San Bernardino is selected by the Internal Revenue Service and their tax returns are audited.

7.58 The maximum load (with a generous safety factor) for the elevator in an office building is 2000 pounds. The relative frequency distribution of the weights of all men and women using the elevator is mound-shaped (slightly skewed to the heavy weights), with mean μ equal to 150 pounds and standard deviation σ equal to 35 pounds. What is the largest number of people you can allow on the elevator if you want their total weight to exceed the maximum weight with a small probability (say, near .01)? (HINT: If $x_1, x_2, \ldots, x_n$ are independent observations made on a random variable x, and if x has mean μ and variance σ^2, then the mean and variance of Σx_i are $n\mu$ and $n\sigma^2$, respectively. This result was given in Section 7.4.)

7.59 The number of wiring packages that can be assembled by a company's employees has a normal distribution, with a mean equal to 16.4 per hour and a standard deviation of 1.3 per hour.

a. What are the mean and standard deviation of the number x of packages produced per worker in an 8-hour day?

b. Do you expect the probability distribution for x to be mound-shaped and approximately normal? Explain.

c. What is the probability that a worker will produce at least 135 packages per 8-hour day?

7.60 Refer to Exercise 7.59. Suppose the company employs 10 assemblers of wiring packages.

a. Find the mean and standard deviation of the company's daily (8-hour day) production of wiring packages.

b. What is the probability that the company's daily production is less than 1280 wiring packages per day?

7.61 The table lists the number of defective 60-watt lightbulbs found in samples of 100 bulbs selected over 25 days from a manufacturing process. Assume that during these 25 days the manufacturing process was not producing an excessively large fraction of defectives.

Day	1	2	3	4	5	6	7	8	9	10	11	12	13
Defectives	4	2	5	8	3	4	4	5	6	1	2	4	3

Day	14	15	16	17	18	19	20	21	22	23	24	25
Defectives	4	0	2	3	1	4	0	2	2	3	5	3

a. Construct a p chart to monitor the manufacturing process, and plot the data.

b. How large must the fraction of defective items be in a sample selected from the manufacturing process before the process is assumed to be out of control?

c. During a given day, suppose a sample of 100 items is selected from the manufacturing process and 15 defective bulbs are found. If a decision is made to shut down the manufacturing process in an attempt to locate the source of the implied controllable variation, explain how this decision might lead to erroneous conclusions.

7.62 A hardware store chain purchases large shipments of lightbulbs from the manufacturer described in Exercise 7.61 and specifies that each shipment must contain no more than 4% defectives. When the manufacturing process is in control, what is the probability that the hardware store's specifications are met?

7.63 Refer to Exercise 7.61. During a given week the number of defective bulbs in each of five samples of 100 were found to be 2, 4, 9, 7, and 11. Is there reason to believe that the production process has been producing an excessive proportion of defectives at any time during the week?

7.64 During long production runs of canned tomatoes, the average weights (in ounces) of samples of five cans of standard-grade tomatoes in puree form were taken at 30 control points during an 11-day period. These results are shown in the table.[14] When the machine is performing normally, the average weight per can is 21 ounces with a standard deviation of 1.20 ounces.

a. Compute the upper and lower control limits and the centerline for the $\bar{x}$ chart.

b. Plot the sample data on the $\bar{x}$ chart and determine whether the performance of the machine is in control.

Sample Number	Average Weight	Sample Number	Average Weight
1	23.1	16	21.4
2	21.3	17	20.4
3	22.0	18	22.8
4	21.4	19	21.1
5	21.8	20	20.7
6	20.6	21	21.6
7	20.1	22	22.4
8	21.4	23	21.3
9	21.5	24	21.1
10	20.2	25	20.1
11	20.3	26	21.2
12	20.1	27	19.9
13	21.7	28	21.1
14	21.0	29	21.6
15	21.6	30	21.3

7.65 The battle for consumer preference continues between Pepsi and Coke. How can you make your preferences known? There is a webpage where you can vote for one of these colas if you click on the link that says PAY CASH for your opinion. Explain why the respondents do not represent a random sample of the opinions of purchasers or drinkers of these drinks. Explain the types of distortions tht could creep into a call-in opinion poll.

Exercises   DO IT YOURSELF!

7.66 Refer to the die-tossing experiment with $n = 1$ in Section 7.4 in which x is the number on the upper face of a single balanced die.

    a. Use the formulas in Section 4.8 to verify that $\mu = 3.5$ and $\sigma = 1.71$ for this population.

    b. Use the **Central Limit Theorem** applet to toss a single die at least 2000 times. (Your simulation can be done quickly by using the ⟨Roll 100 Sets⟩ button.) What are the mean and standard deviation of these 2000 observations? What is the shape of the histogram?

    c. Compare the results of part b to the actual probability distribution shown in Figure 7.3 and the actual mean and standard deviation in part a. They should be similar!

7.67 Two balanced dice are thrown, and the average number on the two upper faces is recorded.

    a. Use the values $\mu = 3.5$ and $\sigma = 1.71$ from Exercise 7.66. What are the theoretical mean and standard deviation of the sampling distribution for $\bar{x}$?

    b. Use the **Central Limit Theorem** applet to toss a single die at least 2000 times. (Your simulation can be done quickly by using the ⟨Roll 100 Sets⟩ button.) What are the mean and standard deviation of these 2000 observations? What is the shape of the histogram?

    c. Compare the results of part b to the actual probability distribution shown in Figure 7.4 and the actual mean and standard deviation in part a.

7.68 Repeat the instructions in Exercise 7.67 when three dice are tossed.

7.69 Repeat the instructions in Exercise 7.67 when four dice are tossed.

7.70 Suppose a random sample of $n = 5$ observations is selected from a population that is normally distributed, with mean equal to 1 and standard deviation equal to .36.

    a. Give the mean and the standard deviation of the sampling distribution of $\bar{x}$.

    b. Find the probability that $\bar{x}$ exceeds 1.3, using the **Normal Probabilities for Means** applet.

    c. Find the probability that the sample mean $\bar{x}$ is less than .5.

    d. Find the probability that the sample mean deviates from the population mean $\mu = 1$ by more than .4.

7.71 A certain type of automobile battery is known to last an average of 1110 days with a standard deviation of 80 days. If 400 of these batteries are selected, use the **Normal Probabilities for Means** applet to find the following probabilities for the average length of life of the selected batteries:

    a. The average is between 1100 and 1110.

    b. The average is greater than 1120.

    c. The average is less than 900.

Case Study   Sampling the Roulette at Monte Carlo

The technique of simulating a process that contains random elements and repeating the process over and over to see how it behaves is called a **Monte Carlo procedure.** It is widely used in business and other fields to investigate the properties of an operation that is subject to random effects, such as weather, human behavior, and so on. For example, you could model the behavior of a manufacturing company's inventory by creating, on paper, daily arrivals and departures of manufactured products from the company's warehouse. Each day a random number of items produced by the company would be received into inventory. Similarly, each day a random number of orders of varying random sizes would be shipped. Based on the input and output of items, you could calculate the inventory—that is, the number of items on hand at the end of each day. The values of the random variables, the number of items produced, the number of orders, and the number of items per order needed for each day's simulation would be obtained from theoretical distributions of observations that closely model the corresponding distributions of the variables that have been observed over time in the manufacturing operation. By repeating the simulation of the supply, the shipping, and the calculation of daily inventory for a large number of days (a sampling of what might really happen), you can observe the behavior of the plant's daily inventory. The Monte Carlo procedure is particularly valuable because it enables the manufacturer to see how the daily inventory would behave when certain changes are made in the supply pattern or in some other aspect of the operation that could be controlled.

In an article entitled "The Road to Monte Carlo," Daniel Seligman comments on the Monte Carlo method, noting that, although the technique is widely used in business schools to study capital budgeting, inventory planning, and cash flow management, no one seems to have used the procedure to study how well we might do if we were to gamble at Monte Carlo.[15]

To follow up on this thought, Seligman programmed his personal computer to simulate the game of roulette. Roulette involves a wheel with its rim divided into 38 pockets. Thirty-six of the pockets are numbered 1 to 36 and are alternately colored red and black. The two remaining pockets are colored green and are marked 0 and 00. To play the game, you bet a certain amount of money on one or more pockets. The wheel is spun and turns until it stops. A ball falls into a slot on the wheel to indicate the winning number. If you have money on that number, you win a specified amount. For example, if you were to play the number 20, the payoff is 35 to 1. If the wheel does not stop at that number, you lose your bet. Seligman decided to see how his nightly gains (or losses) would fare if he were to bet $5 on each turn of the wheel and repeat the process 200 times each night. He did this 365 times, thereby simulating the outcomes of 365 nights at the casino. Not surprisingly, the mean "gain" per $1000 evening for the 365 nights was a *loss* of $55, the average of the winnings retained by the gambling house. The surprise, according to Seligman, was the extreme variability of the nightly "winnings." Seven times out of the 365 evenings, the fictitious gambler lost the $1000 stake, and only once did he win a maximum of $1160. On 141 nights, the loss exceeded $250.

1. To evaluate the results of Seligman's Monte Carlo experiment, first find the probability distribution of the gain x on a single $5 bet.
2. Find the expected value and variance of the gain x from part 1.
3. Find the expected value and variance for the evening's gain, the sum of the gains or losses for the 200 bets of $5 each.
4. Use the results of part 2 to evaluate the probability of 7 out of 365 evenings resulting in a loss of the total $1000 stake.
5. Use the results of part 3 to evaluate the probability that the largest evening's winnings were as great as $1160.

Data Sources

1. "Chlorinated Water Byproduct, Rat Cancer Linked," *The Press-Enterprise* (Riverside, CA), 18 June 1997, p. A-6.

2. Chris Gilberg, J.L. Cos, H. Kashima, and K. Eberle, "Survey Biases: When Does the Interviewer's Race Matter?" *Chance,* Fall 1996, p. 23.

3. P.D. Franklin, R.A. Lemon, and H.S. Barden, "Accuracy of Imaging the Menisci on an In-Office, Dedicated, Magnetic Resonance Imaging Extremity System," *The American Journal of Sports Medicine* 25, no. 3 (1997):382.

4. "New Drug a Bit Better Than Aspirin," *The Press-Enterprise* (Riverside, CA), 14 November 1996, p. A-14.

5. "Average Salary and Average Compensation Levels," *Academe: Bulletin of the American Association of University Professors,* March–April 2001, p. 38.

6. A. Elizabeth Sloan, "How Sweet It Is," *Food Technology* 51, no. 3 (March 1997):26.

7. "Views Mixed on Role of Internet in Education," *The Press-Enterprise* (Riverside, CA) 21 August 2001, p. A-7.

8. Ronald D. Fricker, Jr., "The Mysterious Case of the Blue M&Ms®," *Chance* 9, no. 4 (Fall 1996):19.

9. P.C. Karalekas, Jr., C.R. Ryan, and F.B. Taylor, "Control of Lead, Copper, and Iron Pipe Corrosion in Boston," *American Water Works Journal,* February, 1983.

10. *Science News* 136 (19 August 1989):124.

11. "Half in Study Were Abused As Adults," *The Press-Enterprise* (Riverside, CA), 15 July 1997, p. D-4.

12. Catherine M. Santaniello and R.E. Koning, "Are Radishes Really Allelopathic to Lettuce?" *The American Biology Teacher* 58, no. 2 (February 1996):102.

13. http://www.gallup.com/poll/indicators/indairlines.asp#RelatedAnalyses. Gallup Poll News Service, 16 October 2001.

14. J. Hackl, *Journal of Quality Technology,* April 1991.

15. Daniel Seligman, "The Road to Monte Carlo," *Fortune,* 15 April 1985.

Large-Sample Estimation

Case Study

Do the national polls conducted by the Gallup and Harris organizations, the news media, and others provide accurate estimates of the percentages of people in the United States who favor various propositions? The case study at the end of this chapter examines the reliability of a poll conducted by the Gallup organization using the theory of large-sample estimation.

General Objective

In previous chapters, you learned about the probability distributions of random variables and the sampling distributions of several statistics that, for large sample sizes, can be approximated by a normal distribution according to the Central Limit Theorem. This chapter presents a method for estimating population parameters and illustrates the concept with practical examples. The Central Limit Theorem and the sampling distributions presented in Chapter 7 play a key role in evaluating the reliability of the estimates.

Specific Topics

1. Types of estimators (8.3)
2. Picking the best point estimator (8.4)
3. Point estimation for a population mean or proportion (8.4)
4. Interval estimation (8.5)
5. Large-sample confidence intervals for a population mean or proportion (8.5)
6. Estimating the difference between two population means (8.6)
7. Estimating the difference between two binomial proportions (8.7)
8. One-sided confidence bounds (8.8)
9. Choosing the sample size (8.9)

8.1 Where We've Been

The first seven chapters of this book have given you the building blocks you will need to understand statistical inference and how it can be applied in practical situations. The first three chapters were concerned with using descriptive statistics, both graphical and numerical, to describe and interpret sets of measurements. In the next three chapters, you learned about probability and probability distributions—the basic tools used to describe *populations* of measurements. The binomial and the normal distributions were emphasized as important for practical applications. The seventh chapter provided the link between probability and statistical inference. Many statistics are either sums or averages calculated from sample measurements. The Central Limit Theorem states that, even if the sampled populations are not normal, the sampling distributions of these *statistics* will be approximately normal when the sample size n is large. These statistics are the tools you use for *inferential statistics*—making inferences about a population using information contained in a sample.

8.2 Where We're Going—Statistical Inference

Inference—specifically, decision making and prediction—is centuries old and plays a very important role in most peoples' lives. Here are some applications:

- The government needs to predict short- and long-term interest rates.
- A broker wants to forecast the behavior of the stock market.
- A metallurgist wants to decide whether a new type of steel is more resistant to high temperatures than the old type.
- A consumer wants to estimate the selling price of her house before putting it on the market.

There are many ways to make these decisions or predictions, some subjective and some more objective in nature. How good will your predictions or decisions be? Although you may feel that your own built-in decision-making ability is quite good, experience suggests that this may not be the case. It is the job of the mathematical statistician to provide methods of statistical inference making that are better and more reliable than just subjective guesses.

Statistical inference is concerned with making decisions or predictions about **parameters**—the numerical descriptive measures that characterize a population. Three parameters you encountered in earlier chapters are the population mean μ, the population standard deviation σ, and the binomial proportion p. In statistical inference, a practical problem is restated in the framework of a population with a specific parameter of interest. For example, the metallurgist could measure the *average* coefficients of expansion for both types of steel and then compare their values.

Methods for making inferences about population parameters fall into one of two categories:

- **Estimation**: Estimating or predicting the value of the parameter
- **Hypothesis testing**: Making a decision about the value of a parameter based on some preconceived idea about what its value might be

EXAMPLE 8.1

The circuits in computers and other electronics equipment consist of one or more printed circuit boards (PCB), and computers are often repaired by simply replacing one or more defective PCBs. In an attempt to find the proper setting of a plating process applied to one side of a PCB, a production supervisor might *estimate* the average thickness of copper plating on PCBs using samples from several days of operation. Since he has no knowledge of the average thickness μ before observing the production process, his is an *estimation* problem.

EXAMPLE 8.2

The supervisor in Example 8.1 is told by the plant owner that the thickness of the copper plating must not be less than .001 inch in order for the process to be in control. To decide whether or not the process is in control, the supervisor might formulate a test. He could *hypothesize* that the process is in control—that is, assume that the average thickness of the copper plating is .001 or greater—and use samples from several days of operation to decide whether or not his hypothesis is correct. The supervisor's decision-making approach is called a *test of hypothesis.*

Which method of inference should be used? That is, should the parameter be estimated, or should you test a hypothesis concerning its value? The answer is dictated by the practical question posed and is often determined by personal preference. Since both estimation and tests of hypotheses are used frequently in scientific literature, we include both methods in this and the next chapter.

A statistical problem, which involves planning, analysis, and inference making, is incomplete without a measure of the **goodness of the inference.** That is, how accurate or reliable is the method you have used? If a stockbroker predicts that the price of a stock will be $80 next Monday, will you be willing to take action to buy or sell your stock without knowing how reliable her prediction is? Will the prediction be within $1, $2, or $10 of the actual price next Monday? Statistical procedures are important because they provide two types of information:

- Methods for making the inference
- A numerical measure of the goodness or reliability of the inference

8.3 Types of Estimators

To estimate the value of a population parameter, you can use information from the sample in the form of an **estimator.** Estimators are calculated using information from the sample observations, and hence, by definition they are also *statistics.*

Definition An **estimator** is a rule, usually expressed as a formula, that tells us how to calculate an estimate based on information in the sample.

Estimators are used in two different ways.

- **Point estimation**: Based on sample data, a single number is calculated to estimate the population parameter. The rule or formula that describes this calculation is called the **point estimator,** and the resulting number is called a **point estimate.**
- **Interval estimation**: Based on sample data, two numbers are calculated to form an interval within which the parameter is expected to lie. The rule or formula that describes this calculation is called the **interval estimator,** and the resulting pair of numbers is called an **interval estimate** or **confidence interval.**

EXAMPLE 8.3

A veterinarian wants to estimate the average weight gain per month of 4-month-old golden retriever pups that have been placed on a lamb and rice diet. The *population* consists of the weight gains per month of all 4-month-old golden retriever pups that are given this particular diet. The veterinarian wants to estimate the unknown parameter μ, the average monthly weight gain for this *hypothetical* population. One possible *estimator* based on sample data is the sample mean, $\bar{x} = \Sigma x_i/n$. It could be used in the form of a single number or *point estimate*—for instance, 3.8 pounds—or you could use an *interval estimate* and estimate that the average weight gain will be between 2.7 and 4.9 pounds.

Both point and interval estimation procedures use information provided by the sampling distribution of the specific estimator you have chosen to use. We will begin by discussing *point estimation* and its use in estimating population means and proportions.

8.4 Point Estimation

In a practical situation, there may be several statistics that could be used as point estimators for a population parameter. To decide which of several choices is best, you need to know how the estimator behaves in repeated sampling, described by its *sampling distribution.*

By way of analogy, think of firing a revolver at a target. The parameter of interest is the bull's-eye, at which you are firing bullets. Each bullet represents a single sample estimate, fired by the revolver, which represents the estimator. Suppose your friend fires a single shot and hits the bull's-eye. Can you conclude that he is an excellent shot? Would you stand next to the target while he fires a second shot? Probably not, because you have no measure of how well he performs in repeated trials. Does he always hit the bull's-eye, or is he consistently too high or too low? Do his shots cluster closely around the target, or do they consistently miss the target by a wide margin? Figure 8.1 shows several target configurations. Which target would you pick as belonging to the best shot?

FIGURE 8.1
Which marksman is best?

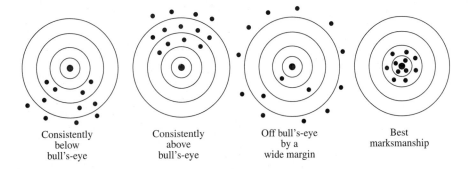

| Consistently below bull's-eye | Consistently above bull's-eye | Off bull's-eye by a wide margin | Best marksmanship |

Sampling distributions provide information that can be used to select the **best estimator.** What characteristics would be valuable? First, the **sampling distribution of the point estimator should be centered over the true value of the parameter to be estimated.** That is, the estimator should not consistently underestimate or overestimate the parameter of interest. Such an estimator is said to be **unbiased.**

Definition

An estimator of a parameter is said to be **unbiased** if the mean of its distribution is equal to the true value of the parameter. Otherwise, the estimator is said to be **biased**.

The sampling distributions for an unbiased estimator and a biased estimator are shown in Figure 8.2. The sampling distribution for the biased estimator is shifted to the right of the true value of the parameter. This biased estimator is more likely than an unbiased one to overestimate the value of the parameter.

FIGURE 8.2
Distributions for
biased and
unbiased
estimators

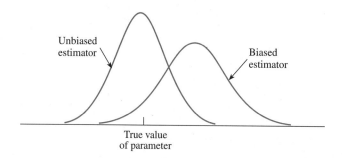

The second desirable characteristic of an estimator is that **the spread (as measured by the variance) of the sampling distribution should be as small as possible.** This ensures that, with a high probability, an individual estimate will fall close to the true value of the parameter. The sampling distributions for two unbiased estimators, one with a small variance[†] and the other with a larger variance, are shown in Figure 8.3. Naturally, you would prefer the estimator with the smaller variance because the estimates tend to lie closer to the true value of the parameter than in the distribution with the larger variance.

FIGURE 8.3
Comparison of
estimator
variability

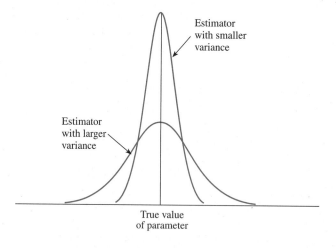

In real-life sampling situations, you may know that the sampling distribution of an estimator centers about the parameter that you are attempting to estimate, but all you have is the estimate computed from the n measurements contained in the sample. How

---

[†]Statisticians usually use the term *variance of an estimator* when in fact they mean the variance of the sampling distribution of the estimator. This contractive expression is used almost universally.

far from the true value of the parameter will your estimate lie? How close is the marksman's bullet to the bull's-eye? The distance between the estimate and the true value of the parameter is called the **error of estimation.**

Definition	The distance between an estimate and the estimated parameter is called the **error of estimation**.

In this chapter, you may assume that the sample sizes are always large and, therefore, that the *unbiased* estimators you will study have sampling distributions that can be approximated by a normal distribution (because of the Central Limit Theorem). Remember that, for any point estimator with a normal distribution, the Empirical Rule states that approximately 95% of all the point estimates will lie within two (or more exactly, 1.96) standard deviations of the mean of that distribution. For *unbiased* estimators, this implies that the difference between the point estimator and the true value of the parameter will be less than 1.96 standard deviations or 1.96 standard errors (SE), and this quantity, called the **margin of error,** provides a practical upper bound for the error of estimation (see Figure 8.4). It is possible that the error of estimation will exceed this margin of error, but that is very unlikely.

FIGURE 8.4
Sampling distribution of an unbiased estimator

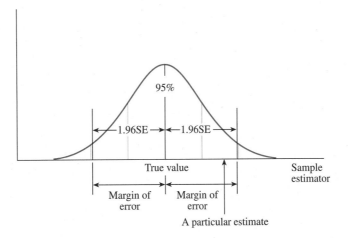

Point Estimation of a Population Parameter

Point estimator: a statistic calculated using sample measurements
Margin of error: $1.96 \times$ Standard error of the estimator

The sampling distributions for two *unbiased* point estimators were discussed in Chapter 7. It can be shown that both of these point estimators have the *minimum variability* of all unbiased estimators and are thus the *best estimators* you can find in each situation.

The variability of the estimator is measured using its standard error. However, you might have noticed that the standard error usually depends on unknown parameters such as σ or p. These parameters must be estimated using sample statistics such as s and $\hat{p}$. Although not exactly correct, experimenters generally refer to the estimated standard error as *the standard error*.

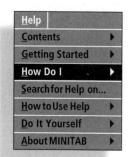

Help

Contents ▶

Getting Started ▶

How Do I ▶

Search for Help on…

How to Use Help ▶

Do It Yourself ▶

About MINITAB ▶

Estimate a Population Mean or Proportion?

■ To estimate the population mean μ for a quantitative population, the point estimator $\bar{x}$ is *unbiased* with standard error estimated as

$$SE = \frac{s}{\sqrt{n}} \,^{\dagger}$$

The margin of error when $n \geq 30$ is estimated as

$$\pm 1.96\left(\frac{s}{\sqrt{n}}\right)$$

■ To estimate the population proportion p for a binomial population, the point estimator $\hat{p} = x/n$ is *unbiased,* with standard error estimated as

$$SE = \sqrt{\frac{\hat{p}\hat{q}}{n}}$$

The margin of error is estimated as

$$\pm 1.96 \sqrt{\frac{\hat{p}\hat{q}}{n}}$$

Assumptions: $n\hat{p} > 5$ and $n\hat{q} > 5$.

EXAMPLE 8.4

An investigator is interested in the possibility of merging the capabilities of television and the Internet. A random sample of $n = 50$ Internet users who were polled about the time they spend watching television produced an average of 11.5 hours per week, with a standard deviation of 3.5 hours. Use this information to estimate the population mean time Internet users spend watching television.

Solution

The random variable measured is the time spent watching television per week. This is a quantitative random variable best described by its mean μ. The point estimate of μ, the average time Internet users spend watching television, is $\bar{x} = 11.5$ hours. The margin of error is estimated as

$$1.96 \; SE = 1.96\left(\frac{s}{\sqrt{n}}\right) = 1.96\left(\frac{3.5}{\sqrt{50}}\right) = .97 \approx 1$$

You can feel fairly confident that the sample estimate of 11.5 hours of television watching for Internet users is within ± 1 hour of the population mean.

In reporting research results, investigators often attach either the sample standard deviation s (sometimes called SD) or the standard error $s/\sqrt{n}$ (usually called SE or SEM) to the estimates of population means. You should always look for an explanation somewhere in the text of the report that tells you whether the investigator is reporting $\bar{x} \pm$ SD or $\bar{x} \pm$ SE. In addition, the sample means and standard deviations or standard errors are often presented as "error bars" using the graphical format shown in Figure 8.5.

---

†When you sample from a normal distribution, the statistic $(\bar{x} - \mu)/(s/\sqrt{n})$ has a t distribution, which will be discussed in Chapter 10. When the sample is *large,* this statistic is approximately normally distributed whether the sampled population is normal or nonnormal.

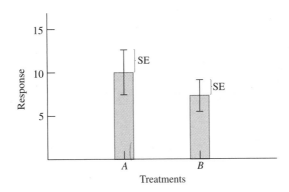

FIGURE 8.5
Plot of treatment
means and their
standard errors

EXAMPLE 8.5   In addition to the average time Internet users spend watching television, the researcher from Example 8.4 is interested in estimating the proportion of individuals in the population at large who want to purchase a television that also acts as a computer. In a random sample of $n = 100$ adults, 45% in the sample indicated that they might buy one. Estimate the true population proportion of adults who are interested in buying a television that also acts as a computer, and find the margin of error for the estimate.

Solution   The parameter of interest is now p, the proportion of individuals in the population who want to purchase a television that also acts as a computer. The best estimator of p is the sample proportion, $\hat{p}$, which for this sample is $\hat{p} = .45$. In order to find the margin of error, you can approximate the value of p with its estimate $\hat{p} = .45$:

$$1.96 \text{ SE} = 1.96 \sqrt{\frac{\hat{p}\hat{q}}{n}} = 1.96 \sqrt{\frac{.45(.55)}{100}} = .10$$

With this margin of error, you can be fairly confident that the estimate of .45 is within $\pm .10$ of the true value of p. Hence, you can conclude that the true value of p could be as small as .35 or as large as .55. This margin of error is quite large when compared to the estimate itself and reflects the fact that large samples are required to achieve a small margin of error when estimating p.

TABLE 8.1
Some calculated
values of $\sqrt{pq}$

p	pq	$\sqrt{pq}$	p	pq	$\sqrt{pq}$
.1	.09	.30	.6	.24	.49
.2	.16	.40	.7	.21	.46
.3	.21	.46	.8	.16	.40
.4	.24	.49	.9	.09	.30
.5	.25	.50			

Table 8.1 shows how the numerator of the standard error of $\hat{p}$ changes for various values of p. Notice that, for most values of p—especially when p is between .3 and .7—there is very little change in $\sqrt{pq}$, the numerator of SE, reaching its maximum value when $p = .5$. This means that the margin of error using the estimator $\hat{p}$ will also be a maximum when $p = .5$. Some pollsters routinely use the maximum margin of error when esimating p, in which case they calculate

$$1.96 \text{ SE} = 1.96 \sqrt{\frac{.5(.5)}{n}} \quad \text{or sometimes} \quad 2 \text{ SE} = 2 \sqrt{\frac{.5(.5)}{n}}$$

Gallup, Harris, and Roper polls generally use sample sizes of approximately 1000, so their margin of error is

$$1.96\sqrt{\frac{.5(.5)}{1000}} = .031 \qquad \text{or approximately } 3\%$$

In this case, the estimate is said to be within ± 3 percentage points of the true population proportion.

Exercises

Basic Techniques

8.1 Explain what is meant by "margin of error" in point estimation.

8.2 What are two characteristics of the best point estimator for a population parameter?

8.3 Calculate the margin of error in estimating a population mean μ for these values:

a. $n = 30$, $\sigma^2 = .2$ **b.** $n = 30$, $\sigma^2 = .9$ **c.** $n = 30$, $\sigma^2 = 1.5$

8.4 Refer to Exercise 8.3. What effect does a larger population variance have on the margin of error?

8.5 Calculate the margin of error in estimating a population mean μ for these values:

a. $n = 50$, $s^2 = 4$ **b.** $n = 500$, $s^2 = 4$ **c.** $n = 5000$, $s^2 = 4$

8.6 Refer to Exercise 8.5. What effect does an increased sample size have on the margin of error?

8.7 Calculate the margin of error in estimating a binomial proportion for each of the following values of n. Use $p = .5$ to calculate the standard error of the estimator.

a. $n = 30$ **b.** $n = 100$

c. $n = 400$ **d.** $n = 1000$

8.8 Refer to Exercise 8.7. What effect does increasing the sample size have on the margin of error?

8.9 Calculate the margin of error in estimating a binomial proportion p using samples of size $n = 100$ and the following estimated values for p:

a. $p = .1$ **b.** $p = .3$ **c.** $p = .5$

d. $p = .7$ **e.** $p = .9$

f. Which of the estimated values of p produces the largest margin of error?

8.10 Suppose you are writing a questionnaire for a sample survey involving $n = 100$ individuals. The questionnaire will generate estimates for several different binomial proportions. If you want to report a single margin of error for the survey, which margin of error from Exercise 8.9 is the correct one to use?

8.11 A random sample of $n = 900$ observations from a binomial population produced $x = 655$ successes. Estimate the binomial proportion p and calculate the margin of error.

8.12 A random sample of $n = 50$ observations from a quantitative population produced $\bar{x} = 56.4$ and $s^2 = 2.6$. Give the best point estimate for the population mean μ, and calculate the margin of error.

Applications

8.13 Geologists are interested in shifts and movements of the earth's surface indicated by fractures (cracks) in the earth's crust. One of the most famous large fractures is the San Andreas fault in California. A geologist attempting to study the movement of the relative shifts in the earth's crust at a particular location found many fractures in the local rock structure. In an attempt to determine the mean angle of the breaks, she sampled $n = 50$ fractures and found the sample mean and standard deviation to be 39.8° and 17.2°, respectively. Estimate the mean angular direction of the fractures and find the margin of error for your estimate.

8.14 Estimates of the earth's biomass, the total amount of vegetation held by the earth's forests, are important in determining the amount of unabsorbed carbon dioxide that is expected to remain in the earth's atmosphere.[1] Suppose a sample of 75 1-square-meter plots, randomly chosen in North America's boreal (northern) forests, produced a mean biomass of 4.2 kilograms per square meter (kg/m^2), with a standard deviation of 1.5 kg/m^2. Estimate the average biomass for the boreal forests of North America and find the margin of error for your estimate.

8.15 An increase in the rate of consumer savings is frequently tied to a lack of confidence in the economy and is said to be an indicator of a recessional tendency in the economy. A random sampling of $n = 200$ savings accounts in a local community showed a mean increase in savings account values of 7.2% over the past 12 months, with a standard deviation of 5.6%. Estimate the mean percent increase in savings account values over the past 12 months for depositors in the community. Find the margin of error for your estimate.

8.16 Although most school districts do not specifically recruit men to be elementary school teachers, those men who do choose a career in elementary education are highly valued and find the career very rewarding.[2] If there were 40 men in a random sample of 250 elementary school teachers, estimate the proportion of male elementary school teachers in the entire population. Give the margin of error for your estimate.

8.17 Are you "sports crazy"? Most Americans love participating in or at least watching a multitude of sporting events, but many feel that sports have more than just an entertainment value. In a survey of 1000 adults conducted by KRC Research & Consulting, 78% feel that spectator sports have a positive effect on society.[3]

a. Find a point estimate for the proportion of American adults who feel that spectator sports have a positive effect on society. Calculate the margin of error.

b. The poll reports a margin of error of "plus or minus 3.1%." Does this agree with your results in part a? If not, what value of p produces the margin of error given in the poll?

8.18 One of the major costs involved in planning a summer vacation is the cost of lodging. Even within a particular chain of hotels, costs can vary substantially depending on the type of room and the amenities offered.[4] Suppose that we randomly select 50 billing statements from the computer databases of the Marriott, Radisson, and Wyndham hotel chains, and record the nightly room rates.

	Marriott	Radisson	Wyndham
Sample average	$120	$95	$110
Sample standard deviation	17.5	10	16.5

a. Describe the sampled population(s).

b. Find point estimate for the average room rate for the Marriott hotel chain. Calculate the margin of error.

c. Find a point estimate for the average room rate for the Radisson hotel chain. Calculate the margin of error.

d. Find a point estimate for the average room rate for the Wyndham hotel chain. Calculate the margin of error.

e. Display the results of parts b, c, and d graphically, using the form shown in Figure 8.5. Use this display to compare the average room rates for the three hotel chains.

8.19 Radio and television stations often air controversial issues during broadcast time and ask viewers to indicate their agreement or disagreement with a given stand on the issue. A poll is conducted by asking those viewers who *agree* to call a certain 900 telephone number and those who *disagree* to call a second 900 telephone number. All respondents pay a fee for their calls.

a. Does this polling technique result in a random sample?

b. What can be said about the validity of the results of such a survey? Do you need to worry about a margin of error in this case?

8.5 Interval Estimation

An *interval estimator* is a rule for calculating two numbers—say, *a* and *b*—to create an interval that you are fairly certain contains the parameter of interest. The concept of "fairly certain" means "with high probability." We measure this probability using the **confidence coefficient,** designated by $1 - \alpha$.

Definition   The probability that a confidence interval will contain the estimated parameter is called the **confidence coefficient.**

For example, experimenters often construct 95% confidence intervals. This means that the confidence coefficient, or the probability that the interval will contain the estimated parameter, is .95. You can increase or decrease your amount of certainty by changing the confidence coefficient. Some values typically used by experimenters are .90, .95, .98, and .99.

Consider an analogy—this time, throwing a lariat at a fence post. The fence post represents the parameter that you wish to estimate, and the loop formed by the lariat represents the confidence interval. Each time you throw your lariat, you hope to rope the fence post; however, sometimes your lariat misses. In the same way, each time you draw a sample and construct a confidence interval for a parameter, you hope to include the parameter in your interval, but, just like the lariat, sometimes you miss. Your "success rate"—the proportion of intervals that "rope the post" in repeated sampling—is the confidence coefficient.

Constructing a Confidence Interval

When the sampling distribution of a point estimator is approximately normal, an interval estimator or **confidence interval** can be constructed using the following reasoning. For simplicity, assume that the confidence coefficient is .95 and refer to Figure 8.6.

FIGURE 8.6
Parameter
±1.96 SE

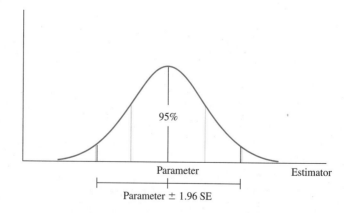

- We know that, of all possible values of the estimator that we might select, 95% of them will be in the interval

    Parameter $\pm$ 1.96SE

shown in Figure 8.6.

■ Since the value of the parameter is unknown, consider constructing the interval

   estimator $\pm$ 1.96 SE

which has the same width as the first interval, but has a variable center.

■ How often will this interval work properly and enclose the parameter of interest? Refer to Figure 8.7.

FIGURE 8.7
Some 95% confidence intervals

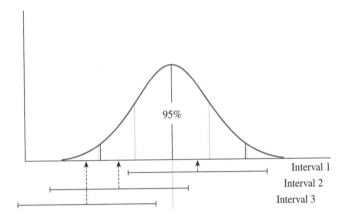

The first two intervals work properly—the parameter (marked with a dotted line) is contained within both intervals. The third interval does not work, since it fails to enclose the parameter. This happened because the value of the estimator at the center of the interval was too far away from the parameter. Fortunately, values of the estimator only fall this far away 5% of the time—our procedure will work properly 95% of the time!

You may want to change the *confidence coefficient* from $(1 - \alpha) = .95$ to another confidence level $(1 - \alpha)$. To accomplish this, you need to change the value $z = 1.96$, which locates an area .95 in the center of the standard normal curve, to a value of z that locates the area $(1 - \alpha)$ in the center of the curve, as shown in Figure 8.8. Since the total area under the curve is 1, the remaining area in the two tails is α, and each tail contains area $\alpha/2$. The value of z that has "tail area" $\alpha/2$ to its right is called $z_{\alpha/2}$, and the area between $-z_{\alpha/2}$ and $z_{\alpha/2}$ is the confidence coefficient $(1 - \alpha)$. Values of $z_{\alpha/2}$ that are typically used by experimenters will become familiar to you as you begin to construct confidence intervals for different practical situations. Some of these values are given in Table 8.2.

FIGURE 8.8
Location of $z_{\alpha/2}$

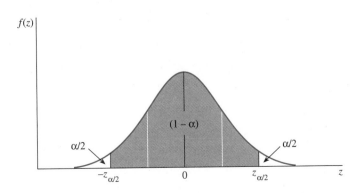

A (1 − α)100% Large-Sample Confidence Interval

(Point estimator) $\pm z_{\alpha/2} \times$ (Standard error of the estimator)

where $z_{\alpha/2}$ is the z-value with an area $\alpha/2$ in the right tail of a standard normal distribution. This formula generates two values; the **lower confidence limit (LCL)** and the **upper confidence limit (UCL).**

TABLE 8.2
Values of z
commonly used

Confidence coefficient, $(1 − \alpha)$	α	$\alpha/2$	$z_{\alpha/2}$
.90	.10	.05	1.645
.95	.05	.025	1.96
.98	.02	.01	2.33
.99	.01	.005	2.58

Large-Sample Confidence Interval for a Population Mean μ

Practical problems very often lead to the estimation of μ, the mean of a population of quantitative measurements. Here are some examples:

- The average achievement of college students at a particular university
- The average strength of a new type of steel
- The average number of deaths per age category
- The average demand for a new cosmetics product

When the sample size n is large, the sample mean $\bar{x}$ is the best point estimator for the population mean μ. Since its sampling distribution is approximately normal, it can be used to construct a confidence interval according to the general approach given earlier.

A (1 − α)100% Large-Sample Confidence Interval for a Population Mean μ

$$\bar{x} \pm z_{\alpha/2}\frac{\sigma}{\sqrt{n}}$$

where $z_{\alpha/2}$ is the z-value corresponding to an area $\alpha/2$ in the upper tail of a standard normal z distribution, and

n = Sample size

σ = Standard deviation of the sampled population

If σ is unknown, it can be approximated by the sample standard deviation s when the sample size is large ($n \geqslant 30$) and the approximate confidence interval is

$$\bar{x} \pm z_{\alpha/2}\frac{s}{\sqrt{n}}$$

Another way to find the large-sample confidence interval for a population mean μ is to begin with the statistic

$$z = \frac{\bar{x} - \mu}{\sigma/\sqrt{n}}$$

which has a standard normal distribution. If you write $z_{\alpha/2}$ as the value of z with area $\alpha/2$ to its right, then you can write

$$P\left(-z_{\alpha/2} < \frac{\bar{x} - \mu}{\sigma/\sqrt{n}} < z_{\alpha/2}\right) = 1 - \alpha$$

You can rewrite this inequality as

$$-z_{\alpha/2}\frac{\sigma}{\sqrt{n}} < \bar{x} - \mu < z_{\alpha/2}\frac{\sigma}{\sqrt{n}}$$

$$-\bar{x} - z_{\alpha/2}\frac{\sigma}{\sqrt{n}} < -\mu < -\bar{x} + z_{\alpha/2}\frac{\sigma}{\sqrt{n}}$$

so that

$$P\left(\bar{x} - z_{\alpha/2}\frac{\sigma}{\sqrt{n}} < \mu < \bar{x} + z_{\alpha/2}\frac{\sigma}{\sqrt{n}}\right) = 1 - \alpha$$

Both $\bar{x} - z_{\alpha/2}(\sigma/\sqrt{n})$ and $\bar{x} + z_{\alpha/2}(\sigma/\sqrt{n})$, the lower and upper confidence limits, are actually random quantities that depend on the sample mean $\bar{x}$. Therefore, in repeated sampling, the random interval, $\bar{x} \pm z_{\alpha/2}(\sigma/\sqrt{n})$, will contain the population mean μ with probability $(1 - \alpha)$.

EXAMPLE 8.6   A scientist interested in monitoring chemical contaminants in food, and thereby the accumulation of contaminants in human diets, selected a random sample of $n = 50$ male adults. It was found that the average daily intake of dairy products was $\bar{x} = 756$ grams per day with a standard deviation of $s = 35$ grams per day. Use this sample information to construct a 95% confidence interval for the mean daily intake of dairy products for men.

Solution   Since the sample size of $n = 50$ is large, the distribution of the sample mean $\bar{x}$ is approximately normally distributed with mean μ and standard error estimated by $s/\sqrt{n}$. The approximate 95% confidence interval is

$$\bar{x} \pm 1.96\left(\frac{s}{\sqrt{n}}\right)$$

$$756 \pm 1.96\left(\frac{35}{\sqrt{50}}\right)$$

$$756 \pm 9.70$$

Hence, the 95% confidence interval for μ is from 746.30 to 765.70 grams per day.

Interpreting the Confidence Interval

What does it mean to say you are "95% confident" that the true value of the population mean μ is within a given interval? If you were to construct 20 such intervals, each using different sample information, your intervals might look like those shown in Figure 8.9. Of the 20 intervals, you might expect that 95% of them, or 19 out of 20, will perform as planned and contain μ within their upper and lower bounds. Remember that you cannot be absolutely sure that any one particular interval contains the mean μ. You will never know whether your particular interval is one of the 19 that "worked," or whether it is the one interval that "missed." Your confidence in the estimated interval follows from the fact that when repeated intervals are calculated, 95% of these intervals will contain μ.

FIGURE 8.9
Twenty confidence intervals for the mean for Example 8.6

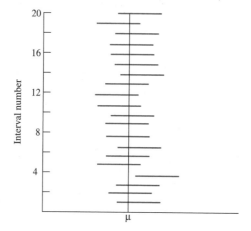

DO IT YOURSELF!

You can try this experiment on your own using the Java applet called **Interpreting Confidence Intervals.** The applet shown in Figure 8.10(a) shows the calculation of a 95% confidence interval for μ when $n = 50$ and $\sigma = 35$. For this particular confidence interval, we used the *One Sample* button. You can see the value of μ shown as a vertical green line on your monitor (gray in Figure 8.10). Notice that this confidence interval worked properly and enclosed the vertical line between its upper and lower limits. Figure 8.10(b) shows the calculation of 100 such intervals, using the *100 Samples* button. The intervals that fail to work properly are shown in red on your monitor (black in Figure 8.10). How many intervals fail to work? Is it close to the 95% confidence that we claim to have? You will use this applet again for the *Do It Yourself Exercises* section at the end of the chapter.

FIGURE 8.10
Interpreting Confidence Intervals applet

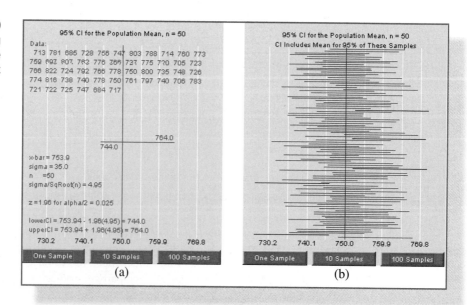

A good confidence interval has two desirable characteristics:

- It is as narrow as possible. The narrower the interval, the more exactly you have located the estimated parameter.
- It has a large confidence coefficient, near 1. The larger the confidence coefficient, the more likely it is that the interval will contain the estimated parameter.

EXAMPLE 8.7

Construct a 99% confidence interval for the mean daily intake of dairy products for adult men in Example 8.6.

Solution

To change the confidence level to .99, you must find the appropriate value of the standard normal z that puts area $(1 - \alpha) = .99$ in the center of the curve. This value, with tail area $\alpha/2 = .005$ to its right, is found from Table 8.2 to be $z = 2.58$ (see Figure 8.11). The 99% confidence interval is then

$$\bar{x} \pm 2.58\left(\frac{s}{\sqrt{n}}\right)$$

$$756 \pm 2.58(4.95)$$

$$756 \pm 12.77$$

FIGURE 8.11
Standard normal values for a 99% confidence interval

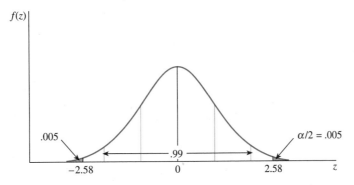

or 743.23 to 768.77 grams per day. This confidence interval is *wider* than the 95% confidence interval in Example 8.6. The increased width is necessary to increase the confidence, just as you might want a wider loop on your lariat to ensure roping the fence post! The only way to *increase the confidence* without increasing the width of the interval is to *increase the sample size, n.*

The standard error of $\bar{x}$,

$$SE = \frac{\sigma}{\sqrt{n}}$$

measures the variability or spread of the values of $\bar{x}$. The more variable the population data, measured by σ, the more variable will be $\bar{x}$, and the standard error will be larger. On the other hand, if you increase the sample size n, more information is available for estimating μ. The estimates should fall closer to μ and the standard error will be smaller. You can use the **Exploring Confidence Intervals** applet, shown in Figure 8.12, to see the effect of changing the sample size n, the standard deviation σ, and the confidence coefficient $1 - \alpha$ on the width of the confidence interval.

The confidence intervals of Examples 8.6 and 8.7 are approximate because you substituted s as an approximation for σ. That is, instead of the confidence coefficient being .95, the value specified in the example, the true value of the coefficient may be .92,

FIGURE 8.12
Exploring
Confidence
Intervals applet

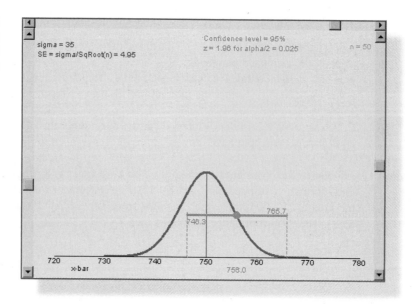

.94, or .97. But this discrepancy is of little concern from a practical point of view; as far as your "confidence" is concerned, there is little difference among these confidence coefficients. Most interval estimators used in statistics yield approximate confidence intervals because the assumptions upon which they are based are not satisfied exactly. Having made this point, we will not continue to refer to confidence intervals as "approximate." It is of little practical concern as long as the actual confidence coefficient is near the value specified.

Large-Sample Confidence Interval for a Population Proportion p

Many research experiments or sample surveys have as their objective the estimation of the proportion of people or objects in a large group that possess a certain characteristic. Here are some examples:

- The proportion of sales that can be expected in a large number of customer contacts
- The proportion of seeds that germinate
- The proportion of "likely" voters who plan to vote for a particular political candidate

Each is a practical example of the binomial experiment, and the parameter to be estimated is the binomial proportion p.

When the sample size is large, the sample proportion,

$$\hat{p} = \frac{x}{n} = \frac{\text{Total number of successes}}{\text{Total number of trials}}$$

is the best point estimator for the population proportion p. Since its sampling distribution is approximately normal, with mean p and standard error $\text{SE} = \sqrt{pq/n}$, $\hat{p}$ can be used to construct a confidence interval according to the general approach given in this section.

> **A $(1 - \alpha)100\%$ Large-Sample Confidence Interval for a Population Proportion p**
>
> $$\hat{p} \pm z_{\alpha/2} \sqrt{\frac{pq}{n}}$$
>
> where $z_{\alpha/2}$ is the z-value corresponding to an area $\alpha/2$ in the right tail of a standard normal z distribution. Since p and q are unknown, they are estimated using the best point estimators: $\hat{p}$ and $\hat{q}$. The sample size is considered large when the normal approximation to the binomial distribution is adequate—namely, when $n\hat{p} > 5$ and $n\hat{q} > 5$.

EXAMPLE 8.8   A random sample of 985 "likely" voters—those who are likely to vote in the upcoming election—were polled during a phone-athon conducted by the Republican party. Of those surveyed, 592 indicated that they intended to vote for the Republican candidate in the upcoming election. Construct a 90% confidence interval for p, the proportion of likely voters in the population who intend to vote for the Republican candidate. Based on this information, can you conclude that the candidate will win the election?

Solution   The point estimate for p is

$$\hat{p} = \frac{x}{n} = \frac{592}{985} = .601$$

and the standard error is

$$\sqrt{\frac{\hat{p}\hat{q}}{n}} = \sqrt{\frac{(.601)(.399)}{985}} = .016$$

The z-value for a 90% confidence interval is the value that has area $\alpha/2 = .05$ in the upper tail of the z distribution, or $z_{.05} = 1.645$ from Table 8.2. The 90% confidence interval for p is thus

$$\hat{p} \pm 1.645 \sqrt{\frac{\hat{p}\hat{q}}{n}}$$

$$.601 \pm .026$$

or $.575 < p < .627$. You estimate that the percentage of likely voters who intend to vote for the Republican candidate is between 57.5% and 62.7%. Will the candidate win the election? Assuming that she needs more than 50% of the vote to win, and since both the upper and lower confidence limits exceed this minimum value, you can say with 90% confidence that the candidate will win.

There are some problems, however, with this type of sample survey. What if the voters who consider themselves "likely to vote" do not actually go to the polls? What if a voter changes his or her mind between now and election day? What if a surveyed voter does not respond truthfully when questioned by the campaign worker? The 90% confidence interval you have constructed gives you 90% confidence only if you have selected *a random sample from the population of interest*. You can no longer be assured of "90% confidence" if your sample is biased, or if the population of voter responses changes before the day of the election!

You may have noticed that the point estimator with its margin of error looks very similar to a 95% confidence interval for the same parameter. This close relationship exists for most of the parameters estimated in this book, but it is not true in general. Sometimes the best point estimator for a parameter *does not* fall in the middle of the best confidence interval; the best confidence interval may not even be a function of the best point estimator. Although this is a theoretical distinction, you should remember that there is a difference between point and interval estimation, and that the choice between the two depends on the preference of the experimenter.

Exercises

Basic Techniques

8.20 Find and interpret a 95% confidence interval for a population mean μ for these values:

a. $n = 36, \bar{x} = 13.1, s^2 = 3.42$ b. $n = 64, \bar{x} = 2.73, s^2 = .1047$

8.21 Find a 90% confidence interval for a population mean μ for these values:

a. $n = 125, \bar{x} = .84, s^2 = .086$ b. $n = 50, \bar{x} = 21.9, s^2 = 3.44$

c. Interpret the intervals found in parts a and b.

8.22 Find a $(1 - \alpha)100\%$ confidence interval for a population mean μ for these values:

a. $\alpha = .01, n = 38, \bar{x} = 34, s^2 = 12$ b. $\alpha = .10, n = 65, \bar{x} = 1049, s^2 = 51$

c. $\alpha = .05, n = 89, \bar{x} = 66.3, s^2 = 2.48$

8.23 A random sample of $n = 300$ observations from a binomial population produced $x = 263$ successes. Find a 90% confidence interval for p and interpret the interval.

8.24 Suppose the number of successes observed in $n = 500$ trials of a binomial experiment is 27. Find a 95% confidence interval for p. Why is the confidence interval narrower than the confidence interval in Exercise 8.23?

8.25 A random sample of n measurements is selected from a population with unknown mean μ and known standard deviation $\sigma = 10$. Calculate the width of a 95% confidence interval for μ for these values of n:

a. $n = 100$ b. $n = 200$ c. $n = 400$

8.26 Compare the confidence intervals in Exercise 8.25. What effect does each of these actions have on the width of a confidence interval?

a. Double the sample size

b. Quadruple the sample size

8.27 Refer to Exercise 8.26.

a. Calculate the width of a 90% confidence interval for μ when $n = 100$.

b. Calculate the width of a 99% confidence interval for μ when $n = 100$.

c. Compare the widths of 90%, 95%, and 99% confidence intervals for μ. What effect does increasing the confidence coefficient have on the width of the confidence interval?

Applications

8.28 Due to a variation in laboratory techniques, impurities in materials, and other unknown factors, the results of an experiment in a chemistry laboratory will not always yield the same numerical answer. In an electrolysis experiment, a class measured the amount of copper precipitated from a saturated solution of copper sulfate over a 30-minute period. The $n = 30$ students calculated a sample mean and standard deviation equal to .145 and .0051 mole, respectively. Find a 90% confidence interval for the mean amount of copper precipitated from the solution over a 30-minute period.

8.29 Acid rain, caused by the reaction of certain air pollutants with rainwater, appears to be a growing problem in the northeastern United States. (Acid rain affects the soil and causes corrosion on exposed metal surfaces.) Pure rain falling through clean air registers a pH value of 5.7 (pH is a measure of acidity: 0 is acid; 14 is alkaline). Suppose water samples from 40 rainfalls are analyzed for pH, and $\bar{x}$ and s are equal to 3.7 and .5, respectively. Find a 99% confidence interval for the mean pH in rainfall and interpret the interval. What assumption must be made for the confidence interval to be valid?

8.30 When it comes to advertising, "'tweens" (kids aged 10 to 13) are not ready for the hardline messages that advertisers often use to reach teenagers. The Geppetto Group study found that 78% of 'tweens understand and enjoy ads that are silly in nature. Unlike teenagers, 'tweens would much rather see dancing (69%) and "boyfriends and girlfriends" (63%) than "sexy looking people" or "kissing."[5] Suppose that these results are based on a sample of size $n = 1030$ 'tweens.

   a. Construct a 95% confidence interval estimate of the proportion of 'tweens who understand and enjoy ads that are silly in nature.

   b. Construct a 95% confidence interval for the proportion of 'tweens who would rather see dancing.

8.31 The meat department of a local supermarket chain packages ground beef using meat trays of two sizes: one designed to hold approximately 1 pound of meat, and one that holds approximately 3 pounds. A random sample of 35 packages in the smaller meat trays produced weight measurements with an average of 1.01 pounds and a standard deviation of .18 pound.

   a. Construct a 99% confidence interval for the average weight of all packages sold in the smaller meat trays by this supermarket chain.

   b. What does the phrase "99% confident" mean?

   c. Suppose that the quality control department of this supermarket chain intends that the amount of ground beef in the smaller trays should be 1 pound on average. Should the confidence interval in part a concern the quality control department? Explain.

8.32 Is America's romance with movies on the wane? In a poll of $n = 800$ randomly chosen adults, 45% indicated that movies were getting better, while 43% indicated that movies were getting worse.[6] However, these results vary by age: 69% of the 18-to-29-year-olds say that movies are getting better, 39% of 50-to-64-year-olds and just 15% of those over 60 agree. Construct a 90% confidence interval for the overall proportion of adults who say that movies are getting better.

8.33 A sample survey is designed to estimate the proportion of sports utility vehicles being driven in the state of California. A random sample of 500 registrations are selected from a Department of Motor Vehicles database, and 68 are classified as sports utility vehicles.

   a. Use a 95% confidence interval to estimate the proportion of sports utility vehicles in California.

   b. How can you estimate the proportion of sports utility vehicles in California with a higher degree of accuracy? (HINT: There are two answers.)

8.34 In a report of why e-shoppers abandon their online sales transactions, Alison Stein Wellner[7] found that "pages took too long to load" and "site was so confusing that I couldn't find the product" were the two complaints heard most often. Based on customers' responses, the average time to complete an online order form will take 4.5 minutes. Suppose that $n = 50$ customers responded and that the standard deviation of the time to complete an online order is 2.7 minutes.

   a. Do you think that x, the time to complete the online order form, has a mound-shaped distribution? If not, what shape would you expect?

   b. If the distribution of the completion times is not normal, you can still use the standard normal distribution to construct a confidence interval for μ, the mean completion time for online shoppers. Why?

   c. Construct a 95% confidence interval for μ, the mean completion time for online orders.

8.6 Estimating the Difference between Two Population Means

A problem equally as important as the estimation of a single population mean μ for a quantitative population is the comparison of two population means. You may want to make comparisons like these:

- The average scores on the Medical College Admission Test (MCAT) for students whose major was biochemistry and those whose major was biology
- The average yields in a chemical plant using raw materials furnished by two different suppliers
- The average stem diameters of plants grown on two different types of nutrients

For each of these examples, there are two populations: the first with mean and variance μ_1 and σ_1^2 and the second with mean and variance μ_2 and σ_2^2. A random sample of n_1 measurements is drawn from population 1 and a second random sample of size n_2 is independently drawn from population 2. Finally, the estimates of the population parameters are calculated from the sample data using the estimators $\bar{x}_1$, s_1^2, $\bar{x}_2$, and s_2^2 as shown in Table 8.3.

TABLE 8.3

Samples from two quantitative populations

	Population 1	Population 2
Mean	μ_1	μ_2
Variance	σ_1^2	σ_2^2

	Sample 1	Sample 2
Mean	$\bar{x}_1$	$\bar{x}_2$
Variance	s_1^2	s_2^2
Sample size	n_1	n_2

Intuitively, the difference between two sample means would provide the maximum information about the actual difference between two population means, and this is in fact the case. The best point estimator of the difference $(\mu_1 - \mu_2)$ between the population means is $(\bar{x}_1 - \bar{x}_2)$. The sampling distribution of this estimator is not difficult to derive, but we state it here without proof.

Properties of the Sampling Distribution of $(\bar{x}_1 - \bar{x}_2)$, the Difference between Two Sample Means

When independent random samples of n_1 and n_2 observations have been selected from populations with means μ_1 and μ_2 and variances σ_1^2 and σ_2^2, respectively, the sampling distribution of the difference $(\bar{x}_1 - \bar{x}_2)$ has the following properties:

1. The mean of $(\bar{x}_1 - \bar{x}_2)$ is

$$\mu_1 - \mu_2$$

and the standard error is

$$SE = \sqrt{\frac{\sigma_1^2}{n_1} + \frac{\sigma_2^2}{n_2}}$$

which is estimated as

$$SE = \sqrt{\frac{s_1^2}{n_1} + \frac{s_2^2}{n_2}}$$

2. **If the sampled populations are normally distributed,** then the sampling distribution of $(\bar{x}_1 - \bar{x}_2)$ is **exactly** normally distributed, regardless of the sample size.

3. **If the sampled populations are not normally distributed,** then the sampling distribution of $(\bar{x}_1 - \bar{x}_2)$ is **approximately** normally distributed when n_1 and n_2 are both 30 or more, due to the Central Limit Theorem.

Since $(\mu_1 - \mu_2)$ is the mean of the sampling distribution, it follows that $(\bar{x}_1 - \bar{x}_2)$ is an unbiased estimator of $(\mu_1 - \mu_2)$ with an approximately normal distribution when n_1 and n_2 are large. That is, the statistic

$$z = \frac{(\bar{x}_1 - \bar{x}_2) - (\mu_1 - \mu_2)}{\sqrt{\frac{s_1^2}{n_1} + \frac{s_2^2}{n_2}}}$$

has an approximately standard normal z distribution, and the general procedures of Section 8.5 can be used to construct point and interval estimates. Although the choice between point and interval estimation depends on your personal preference, most experimenters choose to construct confidence intervals for two-sample problems. The appropriate formulas for both methods are given next.

Large-Sample Point Estimation of $(\mu_1 - \mu_2)$

Point estimator: $(\bar{x}_1 - \bar{x}_2)$

Margin of error: $\pm 1.96 \ SE = \pm 1.96 \sqrt{\frac{s_1^2}{n_1} + \frac{s_2^2}{n_2}}$

A $(1 - \alpha)100\%$ Large-Sample Confidence Interval for $(\mu_1 - \mu_2)$

$$(\bar{x}_1 - \bar{x}_2) \pm z_{\alpha/2} \sqrt{\frac{s_1^2}{n_1} + \frac{s_2^2}{n_2}}$$

EXAMPLE 8.9   The wearing qualities of two types of automobile tires were compared by road-testing samples of $n_1 = n_2 = 100$ tires for each type. The number of miles until wearout was defined as a specific amount of tire wear. The test results are given in Table 8.4. Estimate $(\mu_1 - \mu_2)$, the difference in mean miles to wearout, using a 99% confidence interval. Is there a difference in the average wearing quality for the two types of tires?

TABLE 8.4
Sample data summary for two types of tires

Tire 1	Tire 2
$\bar{x}_1 = 26{,}400$ miles	$\bar{x}_2 = 25{,}100$ miles
$s_1^2 = 1{,}440{,}000$	$s_2^2 = 1{,}960{,}000$

Solution The point estimate of $(\mu_1 - \mu_2)$ is

$$(\bar{x}_1 - \bar{x}_2) = 26,400 - 25,100 = 1300 \text{ miles}$$

and the standard error of $(\bar{x}_1 - \bar{x}_2)$ is estimated as

$$SE = \sqrt{\frac{s_1^2}{n_1} + \frac{s_2^2}{n_2}} = \sqrt{\frac{1,440,000}{100} + \frac{1,960,000}{100}} = 184.4 \text{ miles}$$

The 99% confidence interval is calculated as

$$(\bar{x}_1 - \bar{x}_2) \pm 2.58 \sqrt{\frac{s_1^2}{n_1} + \frac{s_2^2}{n_2}}$$
$$1300 \pm 2.58(184.4)$$
$$1300 \pm 475.8$$

or $824.2 < (\mu_1 - \mu_2) < 1775.8$. The difference in the average miles to wearout for the two types of tires is estimated to lie between LCL = 824.2 and UCL = 1775.8 miles of wear.

Based on this confidence interval, can you conclude that there is a difference in the average miles to wearout for the two types of tires? If there were no difference in the two population means, then μ_1 and μ_2 would be equal and $(\mu_1 - \mu_2) = 0$. If you look at the confidence interval you constructed, you will see that 0 is not one of the possible values for $(\mu_1 - \mu_2)$. Therefore, it is not likely that the means are the same; you can conclude that there is a difference in the average miles to wearout for the two types of tires. The confidence interval has allowed you to *make a decision* about the equality of the two population means.

EXAMPLE 8.10 The scientist in Example 8.6 wondered whether there was a difference in the average daily intakes of dairy products between men and women. He took a sample of $n = 50$ adult women and recorded their daily intakes of dairy products in grams per day. He did the same for adult men. A summary of his sample results is listed in Table 8.5. Construct a 95% confidence interval for the difference in the average daily intakes of dairy products for men and women. Can you conclude that there is a difference in the average daily intakes for men and women?

TABLE 8.5
Sample values for
daily intakes of
dairy products

	Men	Women
Sample size	50	50
Sample mean	756	762
Sample standard deviation	35	30

Solution The confidence interval is constructed using a value of z with tail area $\alpha/2 = .025$ to its right; that is, $z_{.025} = 1.96$. Using the sample standard deviations to approximate the unknown population standard deviations, the 95% confidence interval is

$$(\bar{x}_1 - \bar{x}_2) \pm 1.96 \sqrt{\frac{s_1^2}{n_1} + \frac{s_2^2}{n_2}}$$
$$(756 - 762) \pm 1.96 \sqrt{\frac{35^2}{50} + \frac{30^2}{50}}$$
$$-6 \pm 12.78$$

or $-18.78 < (\mu_1 - \mu_2) < 6.78$. Look at the possible values for $(\mu_1 - \mu_2)$ in the confidence interval. It is possible that the difference $(\mu_1 - \mu_2)$ could be negative (indicating that the average for women exceeds the average for men), it could be positive (indicating that men have the higher average), or it could be 0 (indicating no difference between the averages). Based on this information, you *should not be willing to conclude* that there is a difference in the average daily intakes of dairy products for men and women.

Examples 8.9 and 8.10 deserve further comment with regard to using sample estimates in place of unknown parameters. The sampling distribution of

$$\frac{(\bar{x}_1 - \bar{x}_2) - (\mu_1 - \mu_2)}{\sqrt{\dfrac{\sigma_1^2}{n_1} + \dfrac{\sigma_2^2}{n_2}}}$$

has a standard normal distribution for all sample sizes when both sampled populations are normal and an *approximate* standard normal distribution when the sampled populations are not normal but the sample sizes are large (≥ 30). When σ_1^2 and σ_2^2 are not known and are estimated by the sample estimates s_1^2 and s_2^2, the resulting statistic will still have an approximate standard normal distribution when the sample sizes are large. The behavior of this statistic when the population variances are unknown and the sample sizes are small will be discussed in Chapter 10.

Exercises Basic Techniques

8.35 Independent random samples were selected from populations 1 and 2. The sample sizes, means, and variances are as follows:

	Population	
	1	2
Sample size	35	49
Sample mean	12.7	7.4
Sample variance	1.38	4.14

a. Find a 95% confidence interval for estimating the difference in the population means $(\mu_1 - \mu_2)$.

b. Based on the confidence interval in part a, can you conclude that there is a difference in the means for the two populations? Explain.

8.36 Independent random samples were selected from populations 1 and 2. The sample sizes, means, and variances are as follows:

	Population	
	1	2
Sample size	64	64
Sample mean	2.9	5.1
Sample variance	0.83	1.67

a. Find a 90% confidence interval for the difference in the population means. What does the phrase "90% confident" mean?

b. Find a 99% confidence interval for the difference in the population means. Can you conclude that there is a difference in the two population means? Explain.

Applications

8.37 A small amount of the trace element selenium, 50–200 micrograms (μg) per day, is considered essential to good health. Suppose that random samples of $n_1 = n_2 = 30$ adults were selected from two regions of the United States and that a day's intake of selenium, from both liquids and solids, was recorded for each person. The mean and standard deviation of the selenium daily intakes for the 30 adults from region 1 were $\bar{x}_1 = 167.1$ and $s_1 = 24.3$ μg, respectively. The corresponding statistics for the 30 adults from region 2 were $\bar{x}_2 = 140.9$ and $s_2 = 17.6$. Find a 95% confidence interval for the difference in the mean selenium intakes for the two regions. Interpret this interval.

8.38 A study was conducted to compare the mean numbers of police emergency calls per 8-hour shift in two districts of a large city. Samples of 100 8-hour shifts were randomly selected from the police records for each of the two regions, and the number of emergency calls was recorded for each shift. The sample statistics are listed here:

	Region	
	1	2
Sample size	100	100
Sample mean	2.4	3.1
Sample variance	1.44	2.64

Find a 90% confidence interval for the difference in the mean numbers of police emergency calls per shift between the two districts of the city. Interpret the interval.

8.39 In developing a standard for assessing the teaching of precollege sciences in the United States, an experiment was conducted to evaluate a teacher-developed curriculum, "Biology: A Community Context" (BACC) that was standards-based, activity-oriented, and inquiry-centered. This approach was compared to the historical presentation through lecture, vocabulary, and memorized facts. Students were tested on biology concepts that featured biological knowledge and process skills in the traditional sense. The perhaps not-so-startling results from a test on biology concepts are shown in the following table.[8]

Biology Concepts	Mean	Sample Size	Standard Deviation
Pretest: All BACC Classes	13.38	372	5.59
Pretest: All Traditional	14.06	368	5.45
Posttest: All BACC Classes	18.5	365	8.03
Posttest: All Traditional	16.5	298	6.96

a. Find a 95% confidence interval for the mean score for the posttest for all BACC classes.

b. Find a 95% confidence interval for the mean score for the posttest for all traditional classes.

c. Find a 95% confidence interval for the difference in mean scores for the posttest BACC classes and the posttest traditional classes.

d. Does the confidence interval in c provide evidence that there is a real difference in the posttest BACC and traditional class scores? Explain.

8.40 An experiment was conducted to compare two diets A and B designed for weight reduction. Two groups of 30 overweight dieters each were randomly selected. One group was placed on diet A and the other on diet B, and their weight losses were recorded over a 30-day period. The means and standard deviations of the weight-loss measurements for the two groups are shown in the table. Find a 95% confidence interval for the difference in mean weight loss for the two diets. Interpret your confidence interval.

Diet A	Diet B
$\bar{x}_A = 21.3$	$\bar{x}_B = 13.4$
$s_A = 2.6$	$s_B = 1.9$

8.41   In an attempt to compare the starting salaries of college graduates majoring in education and social sciences, random samples of 50 recent college graduates in each major were selected and the following information was obtained:

Major	Mean	SD
Education	35,554	2225
Social science	33,348	2375

a. Find a point estimate for the difference in the average starting salaries of college students majoring in education and the social sciences. What is the margin of error for your estimate?

b. Based on the results of part a, do you think that there is a significant difference in the means for the two groups in the general population? Explain.

8.42   Refer to Exercise 8.39. In addition to tests involving biology concepts, students were also tested on process skills. The results of prettest and posttest scores are given below.[8]

Process Skills	Mean	Sample Size	Standard Deviation
Pretest: All BACC Classes	10.52	395	4.79
Pretest: All Traditional	11.97	379	5.39
Posttest: All BACC Classes	14.06	376	5.65
Posttest: All Traditional	12.96	308	5.93

a. Find a 95% confidence interval for the mean score on process skills for the posttest for all BACC classes.

b. Find a 95% confidence interval for the mean score on process skills for the posttest for all traditional classes.

c. Find a 95% confidence interval for the difference in mean scores on process skills for the posttest BACC classes and the posttest traditional classes.

d. Does the confidence interval in c provide evidence that there is a real difference in the mean process skills scores between posttest BACC and traditional class scores? Explain.

8.43   Refer to Exercise 8.18. The means and standard deviations for 50 billing statements from the computer databases of each of the three hotel chains are given in the table[4]:

	Marriott	Radisson	Wyndham
Sample average	$120	$95	$110
Sample standard deviation	17.5	10	16.5

a. Find a 95% confidence interval for the difference in the average room rates for the Marriott and the Wyndham hotel chains.

b. Find a 99% confidence interval for the difference in the average room rates for the Radisson and the Wyndham hotel chains.

c. Do the intervals in parts a and b contain the value $(\mu_1 - \mu_2) = 0$? Why is this of interest to the researcher?

d. Do the data indicate a difference in the average room rates between the Marriott and the Wyndham chains? Between the Radisson and the Wyndham chains?

8.7   Estimating the Difference between Two Binomial Proportions

A simple extension of the estimation of a binomial proportion p is the estimation of the difference between two binomial proportions. You may wish to make comparisons like these:

- The proportion of defective items manufactured in two production lines
- The proportion of female voters and the proportion of male voters who favor an equal rights amendment
- The germination rates of untreated seeds and seeds treated with a fungicide

These comparisons can be made using the difference $(p_1 - p_2)$ between two binomial proportions, p_1 and p_2. Independent random samples consisting of n_1 and n_2 trials are drawn from populations 1 and 2, respectively, and the sample estimates $\hat{p}_1$ and $\hat{p}_2$ are calculated. The unbiased estimator of the difference $(p_1 - p_2)$ is the sample difference $(\hat{p}_1 - \hat{p}_2)$.

Properties of the Sampling Distribution of the Difference $(\hat{p}_1 - \hat{p}_2)$ between Two Sample Proportions

Assume that independent random samples of n_1 and n_2 observations have been selected from binomial populations with parameters p_1 and p_2, respectively. The sampling distribution of the difference between sample proportions

$$(\hat{p}_1 - \hat{p}_2) = \left(\frac{x_1}{n_1} - \frac{x_2}{n_2} \right)$$

has these properties:

1. The mean of $(\hat{p}_1 - \hat{p}_2)$ is

   $$p_1 - p_2$$

   and the standard error is

   $$SE = \sqrt{\frac{p_1 q_1}{n_1} + \frac{p_2 q_2}{n_2}}$$

   which is estimated as

   $$SE = \sqrt{\frac{\hat{p}_1 \hat{q}_1}{n_1} + \frac{\hat{p}_2 \hat{q}_2}{n_2}}$$

2. The sampling distribution of $(\hat{p}_1 - \hat{p}_2)$ can be approximated by a normal distribution when n_1 and n_2 are large, due to the Central Limit Theorem.

Although the range of a single proportion is from 0 to 1, the difference between two proportions ranges from -1 to 1. To use a normal distribution to approximate the distribution of $(\hat{p}_1 - \hat{p}_2)$, both $\hat{p}_1$ and $\hat{p}_2$ should be approximately normal; that is, $n_1 \hat{p}_1 > 5$, $n_1 \hat{q}_1 > 5$, and $n_2 \hat{p}_2 > 5$, $n_2 \hat{q}_2 > 5$.

The appropriate formulas for point and interval estimation are given next.

Large-Sample Point Estimation of $(p_1 - p_2)$

Point estimator: $(\hat{p}_1 - \hat{p}_2)$

Margin of error: $\pm 1.96 \, SE = \pm 1.96 \sqrt{\frac{\hat{p}_1 \hat{q}_1}{n_1} + \frac{\hat{p}_2 \hat{q}_2}{n_2}}$

A $(1 - \alpha)100\%$ Large-Sample Confidence Interval for $(p_1 - p_2)$

$$(\hat{p}_1 - \hat{p}_2) \pm z_{\alpha/2} \sqrt{\frac{\hat{p}_1\hat{q}_1}{n_1} + \frac{\hat{p}_2\hat{q}_2}{n_2}}$$

Assumption: n_1 and n_2 must be sufficiently large so that the sampling distribution of $(\hat{p}_1 - \hat{p}_2)$ can be approximated by a normal distribution—namely, if $n_1\hat{p}_1$, $n_1\hat{q}_1$, $n_2\hat{p}_2$, and $n_2\hat{q}_2$ are all greater than 5.

EXAMPLE 8.11   A bond proposal for school construction will be submitted to the voters at the next municipal election. A major portion of the money derived from this bond issue will be used to build schools in a rapidly developing section of the city, and the remainder will be used to renovate and update school buildings in the rest of the city. To assess the viability of the bond proposal, a random sample of $n_1 = 50$ residents in the developing section and $n_2 = 100$ residents from the other parts of the city were asked whether they plan to vote for the proposal. The results are tabulated in Table 8.6.

TABLE 8.6
Sample values for opinion on bond proposal

	Developing Section	Rest of the City
Sample size	50	100
Number favoring proposal	38	65
Proportion favoring proposal	.76	.65

1. Estimate the difference in the true proportions favoring the bond proposal with a 99% confidence interval.
2. If both samples were pooled into one sample of size $n = 150$, with 103 in favor of the proposal, provide a point estimate of the proportion of city residents who will vote for the bond proposal. What is the margin of error?

Solution   1. The best point estimate of the difference $(p_1 - p_2)$ is given by

$$(\hat{p}_1 - \hat{p}_2) = .76 - .65 = .11$$

and the standard error of $(\hat{p}_1 - \hat{p}_2)$ is estimated as

$$\sqrt{\frac{\hat{p}_1\hat{q}_1}{n_1} + \frac{\hat{p}_2\hat{q}_2}{n_2}} = \sqrt{\frac{(.76)(.24)}{50} + \frac{(.65)(.35)}{100}} = .0770$$

For a 99% confidence interval, $z_{.005} = 2.58$, and the approximate 99% confidence interval is found as

$$(\hat{p}_1 - \hat{p}_2) \pm z_{.005} \sqrt{\frac{\hat{p}_1\hat{q}_1}{n_1} + \frac{\hat{p}_2\hat{q}_2}{n_2}}$$

$$.11 \pm (2.58)(.0770)$$

$$.11 \pm .199$$

or $(-.089, .309)$. Since this interval contains the value $(p_1 - p_2) = 0$, it is possible that $p_1 = p_2$, which implies that there may be no difference in the proportions favoring the bond issue in the two sections of the city.

2. If there is no difference in the two proportions, then the two samples are not really different and might well be combined to obtain an overall estimate of the proportion

of the city residents who will vote for the bond issue. If both samples are pooled, then $n = 150$ and

$$\hat{p} = \frac{103}{150} = .69$$

Therefore, the point estimate of the overall value of p is .69, with a margin of error given by

$$\pm 1.96 \sqrt{\frac{(.69)(.31)}{150}} = \pm 1.96(.0378) = \pm .074$$

Notice that $.69 \pm .074$ produces the interval .62 to .76, which includes only proportions greater than .5. Therefore, if voter attitudes do not change adversely prior to the election, the bond proposal should pass by a reasonable majority.

Exercises   Basic Techniques

8.44   Independent random samples of $n_1 = 500$ and $n_2 = 500$ observations were selected from binomial populations 1 and 2, and $x_1 = 120$ and $x_2 = 147$ successes were observed.

a. What is the best point estimator for the difference $(p_1 - p_2)$ in the two binomial proportions?

b. Calculate the approximate standard error for the statistic used in part a.

c. What is the margin of error for this point estimate?

8.45   Independent random samples of $n_1 = 800$ and $n_2 = 640$ observations were selected from binomial populations 1 and 2, and $x_1 = 337$ and $x_2 = 374$ successes were observed.

a. Find a 90% confidence interval for the difference $(p_1 - p_2)$ in the two population proportions. Interpret the interval.

b. What assumptions must you make for the confidence interval to be valid? Are these assumptions met?

8.46   Independent random samples of $n_1 = 1265$ and $n_2 = 1688$ observations were selected from binomial populations 1 and 2, and $x_1 = 849$ and $x_2 = 910$ successes were observed.

a. Find a 99% confidence interval for the difference $(p_1 - p_2)$ in the two population proportions. What does "99% confidence" mean?

b. Based on the confidence interval in part a, can you conclude that there is a difference in the two binomial proportions? Explain.

Applications

8.47   Does the M&M®/Mars corporation use the same proportion of red candies in its plain and peanut varieties? A random sample of 56 plain M&Ms contained 12 red candies, and another random sample of 32 peanut M&Ms contained 8 red candies.

a. Construct a 95% confidence interval for the difference in the proportions of red candies for the plain and peanut varieties.

b. Based on the confidence interval in part a, can you conclude that there is a difference in the proportions of red candies for the plain and peanut varieties? Explain.

8.48   Instead of paying to support welfare recipients, many Californians want them to find jobs; if necessary, they want the state to create public service jobs for those who cannot find jobs in private industry.[9] In a survey of 500 registered voters—250 Republicans and 250 Democrats—70% of the Republicans and 86% of the Democrats favored the creation of public service jobs. Use a large-sample estimation procedure to compare the proportions of Republicans and Democrats in the population of registered voters in California who favor creating public service jobs. Explain your conclusions.

8.49 Do well-rounded people get fewer colds? A study conducted by scientists at Carnegie Mellon University, the University of Pittsburgh, and the University of Virginia found that people who have only a few social outlets get more colds than those who are involved in a variety of social activities.[10] Suppose that of the 276 healthy men and women tested, $n_1 = 96$ had only a few social outlets and $n_2 = 105$ were busy with six or more activities. When these people were exposed to a cold virus, the following results were observed:

	Few Social Outlets	Many Social Outlets
Sample size	96	105
Percent with colds	62%	35%

a. Construct a 99% confidence interval for the difference in the two population proportions.

b. Does there appear to be a difference in the population proportions for the two groups?

c. You might think that coming into contact with more people would lead to more colds, but the data show the opposite effect. How can you explain this unexpected finding?

8.50 A sampling of political candidates—200 randomly chosen from the West and 200 from the East—was classified according to whether the candidate received backing by a national labor union and whether the candidate won. In the West, 120 winners had union backing, and in the East, 142 winners were backed by a national union. Find a 95% confidence interval for the difference between the proportions of union-backed winners in the West versus the East. Interpret this interval.

8.51 In a study of the relationship between birth order and college success, an investigator found that 126 in a sample of 180 college graduates were firstborn or only children. In a sample of 100 nongraduates of comparable age and socioeconomic background, the number of firstborn or only children was 54. Estimate the difference between the proportions of firstborn or only children in the two populations from which these samples were drawn. Use a 90% confidence interval and interpret your results.

8.52 Do you think that we should let Radio Shack film a commercial in outer space? The commercialism of our space program is a topic of great interest since Dennis Tito paid $20 million dollars to ride along with the Russians on the space shuttle.[11] In a survey of 500 men and 500 women, 20% of the men and 26% of the women responded that space should remain commercial-free.

a. Construct a 98% confidence interval for the difference in the proportions of men and women who think that space should remain commercial-free.

b. What does it mean to say that you are "98% confident"?

c. Based on the confidence interval in part a, can you conclude that there is a difference in the proportions of men and women who think space should remain commercial-free?

8.8 One-Sided Confidence Bounds

The confidence intervals discussed in Sections 8.5–8.7 are sometimes called **two-sided confidence intervals** because they produce both an upper (UCL) and a lower (LCL) bound for the parameter of interest. Sometimes, however, an experimenter is interested in only one of these limits; that is, he needs only an upper bound (or possibly a lower bound) for the parameter of interest. In this case, you can construct a **one-sided confidence bound** for the parameter of interest, such as μ, p, $\mu_1 - \mu_2$ or $p_1 - p_2$.

When the sampling distribution of a point estimator is approximately normal, an argument similar to the one in Section 8.5 can be used to show that one-sided confidence bounds, constructed using the following equations *when the sample size is large,* will contain the true value of the parameter of interest $(1 - \alpha)100\%$ of the time in repeated sampling.

A $(1 - \alpha)100\%$ Lower Confidence Bound (LCB)

(Point estimator) $- z_\alpha \times$ (Standard error of the estimator)

A $(1 - \alpha)100\%$ Upper Confidence Bound (UCB)

(Point estimator) $+ z_\alpha \times$ (Standard error of the estimator)

The z-value used for a $(1 - \alpha)100\%$ one-sided confidence bound, z_α, locates an area α in a single tail of the normal distribution as shown in Figure 8.13.

FIGURE 8.13
z-value for a
one-sided
confidence bound

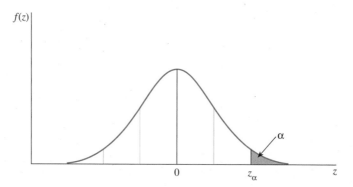

EXAMPLE 8.12 A corporation plans to issue some short-term notes and is hoping that the interest it will have to pay will not exceed 11.5%. To obtain some information about this problem, the corporation marketed 40 notes, one through each of 40 brokerage firms. The mean and standard deviation for the 40 interest rates were 10.3% and .31%, respectively. Since the corporation is interested in only an upper limit on the interest rates, find a 95% upper confidence bound for the mean interest rate that the corporation will have to pay for the notes.

Solution Since the parameter of interest is μ, the point estimator is $\bar{x}$ with standard error $\text{SE} \approx \dfrac{s}{\sqrt{n}}$. The confidence coefficient is .95, so that $\alpha = .05$ and $z_{.05} = 1.645$. Therefore, the 95% upper confidence bound is

$$\text{UCB} = \bar{x} + 1.645\left(\frac{s}{\sqrt{n}}\right) = 10.3 + 1.645\left(\frac{.31}{\sqrt{40}}\right) = 10.3 + .0806 = 10.3806$$

Thus, you can estimate that the mean interest rate that the corporation will have to pay on its notes will be less than 10.3806%. The corporation should not be concerned about its interest rates exceeding 11.5%. How confident are you of this conclusion? Fairly confident, because intervals constructed in this manner contain μ 95% of the time.

8.9 Choosing the Sample Size

Designing an experiment is essentially a plan for buying a certain amount of information. Just as the price you pay for a video game varies depending on where and when you buy it, the price of statistical information varies depending on how and where the information is collected. As when you buy any product, you should buy as much statistical information as you can for the minimum possible cost.

The total amount of relevant information in a sample is controlled by two factors:

- The **sampling plan** or **experimental design**: the procedure for collecting the information
- The **sample size** n: the amount of information you collect

You can increase the amount of information you collect by *increasing* the sample size, or perhaps by *changing* the type of sampling plan or experimental design you are using. We will discuss the simplest sampling plan—random sampling from a relatively large population—and focus on ways to choose the sample size n needed to purchase a given amount of information.

A researcher makes little progress in planning an experiment before encountering the problem of sample size. **How many measurements should be included in the sample?** How much information does the researcher want to buy? The total amount of information in the sample will affect the reliability or goodness of the inferences made by the researcher, and it is this reliability that the researcher must specify. In a statistical estimation problem, the accuracy of the estimate is measured by the *margin of error* or the *width of the confidence interval*. Since both of these measures are a function of the sample size, specifying the accuracy determines the necessary sample size.

For instance, suppose you want to estimate the average daily yield μ of a chemical process and you need the margin of error to be less than 4 tons. This means that, approximately 95% of the time in repeated sampling, the distance between the sample mean $\bar{x}$ and the population mean μ will be less than 1.96 SE. You want this quantity to be less than 4. That is,

$$1.96\ \text{SE} < 4 \quad \text{or} \quad 1.96\left(\frac{\sigma}{\sqrt{n}}\right) < 4$$

Solving for n, you obtain

$$n > \left(\frac{1.96}{4}\right)^2 \sigma^2 \quad \text{or} \quad n > .24\sigma^2$$

If you know σ, the population standard deviation, you can substitute its value into the formula and solve for n. If σ is unknown—which is usually the case—you can use the best approximation available:

- An estimate s obtained from a previous sample
- A range estimate based on knowledge of the largest and smallest possible measurements: $\sigma \approx \text{Range}/4$

For this example, suppose that a prior study of the chemical process produced a sample standard deviation of $s = 21$ tons. Then

$$n > .24\sigma^2 = .24(21)^2 = 105.8$$

Using a sample of size $n = 106$ or larger, you could be reasonably certain (with probability approximately equal to .95) that your estimate of the average yield will be within ± 4 tons of the actual average yield.

The solution $n = 106$ is only approximate because you had to use an approximate value for σ to calculate the standard error of the mean. Although this may bother you, it is the best method available for selecting the sample size, and it is certainly better than guessing!

Sometimes researchers request a different confidence level than the 95% confidence specified by the margin of error. In this case, the half-width of the confidence interval provides the accuracy measure for your estimate; that is, the bound B on the error of your estimate is

$$z_{\alpha/2}\left(\frac{\sigma}{\sqrt{n}}\right) < B$$

This method for choosing the sample size can be used for all four estimation procedures presented in this chapter. The general procedure is described next.

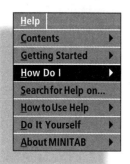

Choose the Sample Size?

Determine the parameter to be estimated and the standard error of its point estimator. Then proceed as follows:

1. Choose B, the bound on the error of your estimate, and a confidence coefficient $(1 - \alpha)$.

2. For a one-sample problem, solve this equation for the sample size n:

   $$z_{\alpha/2} \times (\text{Standard error of the estimator}) = B$$

   where $z_{\alpha/2}$ is the value of z having area $\alpha/2$ to its right.

3. For a two-sample problem, set $n_1 = n_2 = n$ and solve the equation in step 2.

[NOTE: For most estimators (all presented in this textbook), the standard error is a function of the sample size n.]

EXAMPLE 8.13

Producers of polyvinyl plastic pipe want to have a supply of pipes sufficient to meet marketing needs. They wish to survey wholesalers who buy polyvinyl pipe in order to estimate the proportion who plan to increase their purchases next year. What sample size is required if they want their estimate to be within .04 of the actual proportion with probability equal to .90?

Solution

For this particular example, the bound B on the error of the estimate is .04. Since the confidence coefficient is $(1 - \alpha) = .90$, α must equal .10 and $\alpha/2$ is .05. The z-value corresponding to an area equal to .05 in the upper tail of the z distribution is $z_{.05} = 1.645$. You then require

$$1.645\ \text{SE} = 1.645\sqrt{\frac{pq}{n}} = .04$$

In order to solve this equation for n, you must substitute an approximate value of p into the equation. If you want to be certain that the sample is large enough, you should use

$p = .5$ (substituting $p = .5$ will yield the largest possible solution for n because the maximum value of pq occurs when $p = q = .5$). Then

$$1.645\sqrt{\frac{(.5)(.5)}{n}} = .04$$

or

$$\sqrt{n} = \frac{(1.645)(.5)}{.04} = 20.56$$

$$n = (20.56)^2 = 422.7$$

Therefore, the producers must include approximately 423 wholesalers in its survey if it wants to estimate the proportion p correct to within .04.

EXAMPLE 8.14

A personnel director wishes to compare the effectiveness of two methods of training industrial employees to perform a certain assembly operation. A number of employees are to be divided into two equal groups: the first receiving training method 1 and the second training method 2. Each will perform the assembly operation, and the length of assembly time will be recorded. It is expected that the measurements for both groups will have a range of approximately 8 minutes. For the estimate of the difference in mean times to assemble to be correct to within 1 minute with a probability equal to .95, how many workers must be included in each training group?

Solution

Equating 1.96 SE to $B = 1$ minute, you get

$$1.96\sqrt{\frac{\sigma_1^2}{n_1} + \frac{\sigma_2^2}{n_2}} = 1$$

Since you wish n_1 to equal n_2, you can let $n_1 = n_2 = n$ and obtain the equation

$$1.96\sqrt{\frac{\sigma_1^2}{n} + \frac{\sigma_2^2}{n}} = 1$$

As noted above, the variability (range) of each method of assembly is approximately the same, and hence $\sigma_1^2 = \sigma_2^2 = \sigma^2$. Since the range, equal to 8 minutes, is approximately equal to 4σ, you have

$$4\sigma \approx 8 \quad \text{or} \quad \sigma \approx 2$$

Substituting this value for σ_1 and σ_2 in the earlier equation, you get

$$1.96\sqrt{\frac{(2)^2}{n} + \frac{(2)^2}{n}} = 1$$

$$1.96\sqrt{\frac{8}{n}} = 1$$

$$\sqrt{n} = 1.96\sqrt{8}$$

Solving, you have $n = 31$. Thus, each group should contain approximately $n = 31$ workers.

Table 8.7 provides a summary of the formulas used to determine the sample sizes required for estimation with a given bound on the error of the estimate or confidence interval width W ($W = 2B$). Notice that to estimate p, the sample size formula uses $\sigma^2 = pq$, whereas to estimate ($p_1 - p_2$), the sample size formula uses $\sigma_1^2 = p_1q_1$ and $\sigma_2^2 = p_2q_2$.

TABLE 8.7
Sample size formulas

Parameter	Estimator	Sample Size	Assumptions
μ	$\bar{x}$	$n \geq \dfrac{z_{\alpha/2}^2 \sigma^2}{B^2}$	
$\mu_1 - \mu_2$	$\bar{x}_1 - \bar{x}_2$	$n \geq \dfrac{z_{\alpha/2}^2 (\sigma_1^2 + \sigma_2^2)}{B^2}$	$n_1 = n_2 = n$
p	$\hat{p}$	$\begin{cases} n \geq \dfrac{z_{\alpha/2}^2 pq}{B^2} \\ \text{or} \\ n \geq \dfrac{(.25)z_{\alpha/2}^2}{B^2} \quad p = .5 \end{cases}$	
$p_1 - p_2$	$\hat{p}_1 - \hat{p}_2$	$\begin{cases} n \geq \dfrac{z_{\alpha/2}^2 (p_1q_1 + p_2q_2)}{B^2} \quad n_1 = n_2 = n \\ \text{or} \\ n \geq \dfrac{2(.25)z_{\alpha/2}^2}{B^2} \quad n_1 = n_2 = n \text{ and } p_1 = p_2 = .5 \end{cases}$	

Exercises

Basic Techniques

8.53 Find a 90% one-sided upper confidence bound for the population mean μ for these values:

a. $n = 40$, $s^2 = 65$, $\bar{x} = 75$ **b.** $n = 100$, $s = 2.3$, $\bar{x} = 1.6$

8.54 Find a 99% lower confidence bound for the binomial proportion p when a random sample of $n = 400$ trials produced $x = 196$ successes.

8.55 Independent random samples of size 50 are drawn from two quantitative populations, producing the sample information in the table. Find a 95% upper confidence bound for the difference in the two population means.

	Sample 1	Sample 2
Sample size	50	50
Sample mean	12	10
Sample standard deviation	5	7

8.56 Suppose you wish to estimate a population mean based on a random sample of n observations, and prior experience suggests that $\sigma = 12.7$. If you wish to estimate μ correct to within 1.6, with probability equal to .95, how many observations should be included in your sample?

8.57 Suppose you wish to estimate a binomial parameter p correct to within .04, with probability equal to .95. If you suspect that p is equal to some value between .1 and .3 and you want to be certain that your sample is large enough, how large should n be? (HINT: When calculating the standard error, use the value of p in the interval $.1 < p < .3$ that will give the largest sample size.)

8.58 Independent random samples of $n_1 = n_2 = n$ observations are to be selected from each of two populations 1 and 2. If you wish to estimate the difference between the two population means correct to within .17, with probability equal to .90, how large should n_1 and n_2 be? Assume that you know $\sigma_1^2 \approx \sigma_2^2 \approx 27.8$.

8.59   Independent random samples of $n_1 = n_2 = n$ observations are to be selected from each of two binomial populations 1 and 2. If you wish to estimate the difference in the two population proportions correct to within .05, with probability equal to .98, how large should n be? Assume that you have no prior information on the values of p_1 and p_2, but you want to make certain that you have an adequate number of observations in the samples.

Applications

8.60   A random sampling of a company's monthly operating expenses for $n = 36$ months produced a sample mean of \$5474 and a standard deviation of \$764. Find a 90% upper confidence bound for the company's mean monthly expenses.

8.61   Exercise 8.17 discussed a research poll conducted for *U.S. News & World Report* to determine the public's attitudes concerning the effect of spectator sports on society.[3] Suppose you were designing a poll of this type.

   a. Explain how you would select your sample. What problems might you encounter in this process?

   b. If you wanted to estimate the percentage of the population who agree with a particular statement in your survey questionnaire correct to within 1%, with probability .95, approximately how many people would have to be polled?

8.62   A questionnaire is designed to investigate attitudes about political corruption in government. The experimenter would like to survey two different groups—Republicans and Democrats—and compare the responses to various "yes–no" questions for the two groups. The experimenter requires that the sampling error for the difference in the proportion of yes responses for the two groups is no more than ± 3 percentage points. If the two samples are the same size, how large should the samples be?

8.63   Americans are becoming more conscious of the importance of good nutrition, and some researchers believe that we may be altering our diets to include less red meat and more fruits and vegetables. To test this theory, a researcher decides to select hospital nutritional records for subjects surveyed 10 years ago and to compare the average amount of beef consumed per year to the amounts consumed by an equal number of subjects she will interview this year. She knows that the amount of beef consumed annually by Americans ranges from 0 to approximately 104 pounds. How many subjects should the researcher select for each group if she wishes to estimate the difference in the average annual per-capita beef consumption correct to within 5 pounds with 99% confidence?

8.64   Refer to Exercise 8.63. The researcher selects two groups of 400 subjects each and collects the following sample information on the annual beef consumption now and 10 years ago:

	Ten Years Ago	This Year
Sample mean	73	63
Sample standard deviation	25	28

   a. The researcher would like to show that per-capita beef consumption has decreased in the last 10 years, so she needs to show that the difference in the averages is greater than 0. Find a 99% lower confidence bound for the difference in the average per-capita beef consumptions for the two groups.

   b. What conclusions can the researcher draw using the confidence bound from part a?

8.65   If a wildlife service wishes to estimate the mean number of days of hunting per hunter for all hunters licensed in the state during a given season, with a bound on the error of estimation equal to 2 hunting days, how many hunters must be included in the survey? Assume that data collected in earlier surveys have shown σ to be approximately equal to 10.

8.66   Suppose you wish to estimate the mean pH of rainfalls in an area that suffers heavy pollution due to the discharge of smoke from a power plant. You know that σ is in the neighborhood of .5 pH, and you wish your estimate to lie within .1 of μ, with a probability near .95. Approximately how many rainfalls must be included in your sample (one pH reading per rainfall)? Would it be valid to select all of your water specimens from a single rainfall? Explain.

8.67 Refer to Exercise 8.66. Suppose you wish to estimate the difference between the mean acidity for rainfalls at two different locations, one in a relatively unpolluted area along the ocean and the other in an area subject to heavy air pollution. If you wish your estimate to be correct to the nearest .1 pH, with probability near .90, approximately how many rainfalls (pH values) would have to be included in each sample? (Assume that the variance of the pH measurements is approximately .25 at both locations and that the samples will be of equal size.)

8.68 You want to estimate the difference in grade point averages between two groups of college students accurate to within .2 grade point, with probability approximately equal to .95. If the standard deviation of the grade point measurements is approximately equal to .6, how many students must be included in each group? (Assume that the groups will be of equal size.)

8.69 Refer to the comparison of the daily adult intake of selenium in two different regions of the United States in Exercise 8.37. Suppose you wish to estimate the difference in the mean daily intakes between the two regions correct to within 5 micrograms, with probability equal to .90. If you plan to select an equal number of adults from the two regions (i.e., $n_1 = n_2$), how large should n_1 and n_2 be?

Key Concepts and Formulas

I. Types of Estimators

1. Point estimator: a single number is calculated to estimate the population parameter.
2. Interval estimator: two numbers are calculated to form an interval that contains the parameter.

II. Properties of Good Estimators

1. Unbiased: the average value of the estimator equals the parameter to be estimated.
2. Minimum variance: of all the unbiased estimators, the best estimator has a sampling distribution with the smallest standard error.
3. The margin of error measures the maximum distance between the estimator and the true value of the parameter.

III. Large-Sample Point Estimators

To estimate one of four population parameters when the sample sizes are large, use the following point estimators with the appropriate margins of error.

Parameter	Point Estimator	Margin of Error
μ	$\bar{x}$	$\pm 1.96\left(\dfrac{s}{\sqrt{n}}\right)$
p	$\hat{p} = \dfrac{x}{n}$	$\pm 1.96\sqrt{\dfrac{\hat{p}\hat{q}}{n}}$
$\mu_1 - \mu_2$	$\bar{x}_1 - \bar{x}_2$	$\pm 1.96\sqrt{\dfrac{s_1^2}{n_1} + \dfrac{s_2^2}{n_2}}$
$p_1 - p_2$	$(\hat{p}_1 - \hat{p}_2) = \left(\dfrac{x_1}{n_1} - \dfrac{x_2}{n_2}\right)$	$\pm 1.96\sqrt{\dfrac{\hat{p}_1\hat{q}_1}{n_1} + \dfrac{\hat{p}_2\hat{q}_2}{n_2}}$

IV. Large-Sample Interval Estimators

To estimate one of four population parameters when the sample sizes are large, use the following interval estimators.

Parameter	$(1 - \alpha)100\%$ Confidence Interval
μ	$\bar{x} \pm z_{\alpha/2}\left(\dfrac{s}{\sqrt{n}}\right)$
p	$\hat{p} \pm z_{\alpha/2}\sqrt{\dfrac{\hat{p}\hat{q}}{n}}$
$\mu_1 - \mu_2$	$(\bar{x}_1 - \bar{x}_2) \pm z_{\alpha/2}\sqrt{\dfrac{s_1^2}{n_1} + \dfrac{s_2^2}{n_2}}$
$p_1 - p_2$	$(\hat{p}_1 - \hat{p}_2) \pm z_{\alpha/2}\sqrt{\dfrac{\hat{p}_1\hat{q}_1}{n_1} + \dfrac{\hat{p}_2\hat{q}_2}{n_2}}$

1. All values in the interval are possible values for the unknown population parameter.
2. Any values outside the interval are unlikely to be the value of the unknown parameter.
3. To compare two population means or proportions, look for the value 0 in the confidence interval. If 0 is in the interval, it is possible that the two population means or proportions are equal, and you should not declare a difference. If 0 is not in the interval, it is unlikely that the two means or proportions are equal, and you can confidently declare a difference.

V. One-Sided Confidence Bounds

Use either the upper ($+$) or lower ($-$) two-sided bound, with the critical value of z changed from $z_{\alpha/2}$ to z_α.

VI. Choosing the Sample Size

1. Determine the size of the margin of error, B, that you are willing to tolerate.
2. Choose the sample size by solving for n or $n = n_1 = n_2$ in the inequality: $z_{\alpha/2} \le B$, where SE is a function of the sample size n.
3. For quantitative populations, estimate the population standard deviation using a previously calculated value of s or the range approximation $\sigma \approx$ Range/4.
4. For binomial populations, use the conservative approach and approximate p using the value $p = .5$.

Supplementary Exercises

8.70 State the Central Limit Theorem. Of what value is the Central Limit Theorem in large-sample statistical estimation?

8.71 A random sample of $n = 64$ observations has a mean $\bar{x} = 29.1$ and a standard deviation $s = 3.9$.

    a. Give the point estimate of the population mean μ and find the margin of error for your estimate.

    b. Find a 90% confidence interval for μ. What does "90% confident" mean?

    c. Find a 90% lower confidence bound for the population mean μ. Why is this bound different from the lower confidence limit in part b?

    d. How many observations do you need to estimate μ to within .5, with probability equal to .95?

8.72 Independent random samples of $n_1 = 50$ and $n_2 = 60$ observations were selected from populations 1 and 2, respectively. The sample sizes and computed sample statistics are given in the table:

	Population	
	1	2
Sample size	5	60.
Sample mean	100.4	96.2
Sample standard deviation	.8	1.3

Find a 90% confidence interval for the difference in population means and interpret the interval.

8.73 Refer to Exercise 8.72. Suppose you wish to estimate $(\mu_1 - \mu_2)$ correct to within .2, with probability equal to .95. If you plan to use equal sample sizes, how large should n_1 and n_2 be?

8.74 A random sample of $n = 500$ observations from a binomial population produced $x = 240$ successes.

  a. Find a point estimate for p, and find the margin of error for your estimator.

  b. Find a 90% confidence interval for p. Interpret this interval.

8.75 Refer to Exercise 8.74. How large a sample is required if you wish to estimate p correct to within .025, with probability equal to .90?

8.76 Independent random samples of $n_1 = 40$ and $n_2 = 80$ observations were selected from binomial populations 1 and 2, respectively. The number of successes in the two samples were $x_1 = 17$ and $x_2 = 23$. Find a 99% confidence interval for the difference between the two binomial population proportions. Interpret this interval.

8.77 Refer to Exercise 8.76. Suppose you wish to estimate $(p_1 - p_2)$ correct to within .06, with probability equal to .99, and you plan to use equal sample sizes—that is, $n_1 = n_2$. How large should n_1 and n_2 be?

8.78 Ethnic groups in America buy differing amounts of various food products because of their ethnic cuisine. Asians buy fewer canned vegetables than do other groups, and Hispanics purchase more cooking oil. A researcher interested in market segmentation for these two groups would like to estimate the proportion of households that select certain brands for various products. If the researcher wishes these estimates to be within .03 with probability .95, how many households should she include in the samples?

8.79 Women on Wall Street ean earn large salaries, but may need to make sacrifices in their personal lives. In fact, many women in the securities industry have to make significant personal sacrifices. A survey of 482 women and 356 men found that only half of the women have children, compared to three-quarters of the men surveyed.[12]

  a. What are the values of $\hat{p}_1$ and $\hat{p}_2$ for the women and men in this survey?

  b. Find a 95% confidence interval for the difference in the proportion of women and men on Wall Street who have children.

  c. What conclusions can you draw regarding the groups compared in part b?

8.80 An experiment was conducted to estimate the effect of smoking on the blood pressure of a group of 35 college-age cigarette smokers. The difference for each participant was obtained by taking the difference in the blood pressure readings at the time of graduation and again 5 years later. The sample mean increase, measured in millimeters of mercury, was $\bar{x} = 9.7$. The sample standard deviation was $s = 5.8$. Estimate the mean increase in blood pressure that one would expect for cigarette smokers over the time span indicated by the experiment. Find the margin of error. Describe the population associated with the mean that you have estimated.

8.81 Using a confidence coefficient equal to .90, place a confidence interval on the mean increase in blood pressure for Exercise 8.80.

8.82 Based on repeated measurements of the iodine concentration in a solution, a chemist reports the concentration as 4.614, with an "error margin of .006."

a. How would you interpret the chemist's "error margin"?

b. If the reported concentration is based on a random sample of $n = 30$ measurements, with a sample standard deviation $s = .017$, would you agree that the chemist's "error margin" is .006?

8.83 If it is assumed that the heights of men are normally distributed, with a standard deviation of 2.5 inches, how large a sample should be taken to be fairly sure (probability .95) that the sample mean does not differ from the true mean (population mean) by more than .50 in absolute value?

8.84 An experimenter fed different rations, A and B, to two groups of 100 chicks each. Assume that all factors other than rations are the same for both groups. Of the chicks fed ration A, 13 died, and of the chicks fed ration B, 6 died.

a. Construct a 98% confidence interval for the true difference in mortality rates for the two rations.

b. Can you conclude that there is a difference in the mortality rates for the two rations?

8.85 You want to estimate the mean hourly yield for a process that manufactures an antibiotic. You observe the process for 100 hourly periods chosen at random, with the results $\bar{x} = 34$ ounces per hour and $s = 3$. Estimate the mean hourly yield for the process using a 95% confidence interval.

8.86 The average American has become accustomed to eating away from home, especially at fast-food restaurants. Partly as a result of this fast-food habit, the per-capita consumption of cheese (the main ingredient in pizza) and nondiet soft drinks has risen dramatically from a decade ago. A study in *American Demographics* reports that the average American consumes 25.7 pounds of cheese and drinks 40 gallons (or approximately 645 8-ounce servings) of nondiet soft drinks per year.[13] To test the accuracy of these reported averages, a random sample of 40 consumers is selected, and these summary statistics are recorded:

	Cheese (lb/yr)	Soft Drinks (gal/yr)
Sample mean	28.1	39.2
Sample standard deviation	3.8	4.5

Use your knowledge of statistical estimation to estimate the average per-capita annual consumption for these two products. Does this sample cause you to support or to question the accuracy of the reported averages? Explain.

8.87 Don't Americans know that eating pizza and french fries leads to being overweight? In the same *American Demographics* article referenced in Exercise 8.86, a survey of women who are the main meal preparers in their households reported these results:

■ 90% know that obesity causes health problems.

■ 80% know that high fat intake may lead to health problems.

■ 86% know that cholesterol is a health problem.

■ 88% know that sodium may have negative effects on health.

a. Suppose that this survey was based on a random sample of 750 women. How accurate do you expect the percentages given above to be in estimating the actual population percentages? (HINT: If these are the only four percentages for which you need a margin of error, a conservative estimate for p is $p \approx .80$.)

b. If you want to decrease your sampling error to $\pm 1\%$, how large a sample should you take?

8.88 In an article in the *Annals of Botany,* a researcher reported the basal stem diameters of two groups of dicot sunflowers: those that were left to sway freely in the wind and those that were artificially supported.[14] A similar experiment was conducted for monocot maize plants. Although the authors measured other variables in a more complicated experimental design, assume that each group consisted of 64 plants (a total of 128 sunflower and 128 maize plants). The values shown in the table are the sample means plus or minus the standard error.

	Sunflower	Maize
Free-standing	$35.3 \pm .72$	$16.2 \pm .41$
Supported	$32.1 \pm .72$	$14.6 \pm .40$

Use your knowledge of statistical estimation to compare the free-standing and supported basal diameters for the two plants. Write a paragraph describing your conclusions, making sure to include a measure of the accuracy of your inference.

8.89 In a survey involving $n = 1000$ American citizens who were asked how the term "patriotic" described them, the following summary was obtained[15]:

	All	18–34	60+
Very Well	53%	35%	77%
Somewhat well	31%	41%	17%
Not very well	10%	16%	4%
Not well at all	6%	8%	2%

a. Construct a 95% confidence interval for the proportion of all American citizens who agreed that the term described them "very well."

b. If the 60+ age group consisted of $n = 150$ individuals, find a 95% confidence interval for the proportion of American citizens 60+ years of age who agreed that the term described them "somewhat well."

c. If the 18–34 age group consisted of $n = 340$ individuals, find a 98% confidence interval for the true difference in proportions of those aged 60+ and those 18–34 years of age who agreed that the term described them "very well."

8.90 A dean of men wishes to estimate the average cost of the freshman year at a particular college correct to within $500, with a probability of .95. If a random sample of freshmen is to be selected and each asked to keep financial data, how many must be included in the sample? Assume that the dean knows only that the range of expenditures will vary from approximately $4800 to $13,000.

8.91 A quality-control engineer wants to estimate the fraction of defectives in a large lot of film cartridges. From previous experience, he feels that the actual fraction of defectives should be somewhere around .05. How large a sample should he take if he wants to estimate the true fraction to within .01, using a 95% confidence interval?

8.92 Samples of 400 printed circuit boards were selected from each of two production lines A and B. Line A produced 40 defectives, and line B produced 80 defectives. Estimate the difference in the actual fractions of defectives for the two lines with a confidence coefficient of .90.

8.93 Refer to Exercise 8.92. Suppose 10 samples of $n = 400$ printed circuit boards were tested and a confidence interval was constructed for p for each of the ten samples. What is the probability that exactly one of the intervals will not contain the true value of p? That at least one interval will not contain the true value of p?

8.94 The ability to accelerate rapidly is an important attribute for an ice hockey player. G. Wayne Marino investigated some of the variables related to the acceleration and speed of a hockey player from a stopped position.[17] Sixty-nine hockey players, varsity and intramural, from the University of Illinois were included in the experiment. Each player was required to move as rapidly as possible from a stopped position to cover a distance of 6 meters. The means and standard deviations of some of the variables recorded for each of the 69 skaters are shown in the table:

	Mean	SD
Weight (kilograms)	75.270	9.470
Stride length (meters)	1.110	.205
Stride rate (strides/second)	3.310	.390
Average acceleration (meters/second^2)	2.962	.529
Instantaneous velocity (meters/second)	5.753	.892
Time to skate (seconds)	1.953	.131

    a. Give the formula that you would use to construct a 95% confidence interval for one of the population means (e.g., mean time to skate the 6-meter distance).

    b. Construct a 95% confidence interval for the mean time to skate. Interpret this interval.

8.95 Exercise 8.94 presented statistics from a study of fast starts by ice hockey skaters. The mean and standard deviation of the 69 individual average acceleration measurements over the 6-meter distance were 2.962 and .529 meters per second, respectively.

    a. Find a 95% confidence interval for this population mean. Interpret the interval.

    b. Suppose you were dissatisfied with the width of this confidence interval and wanted to cut the interval in half by increasing the sample size. How many skaters (total) would have to be included in the study?

8.96 The mean and standard deviation of the speeds of the sample of 69 skaters at the end of the 6-meter distance in Exercise 8.94 were 5.753 and .892 meters per second, respectively.

    a. Find a 95% confidence interval for the mean velocity at the 6-meter mark. Interpret the interval.

    b. Suppose you wanted to repeat the experiment and you wanted to estimate this mean velocity correct to within .1 second, with probability .99. How many skaters would have to be included in your sample?

8.97 Summer school break adds more than 20 million teenagers to the American workforce, and in fact, July is the peak time for summer jobs for teenagers.[16] It is reported that amusement and theme parks average 100 full-time employees, but at peak season average 665 workers per site. A group of $n = 40$ amusement and theme parks are randomly selected at peak season, and the average number of full-time workers is found to be 652 with a standard deviation of 32. Find a 99% confidence interval estimate for the true mean number of full-time workers at amusement and theme parks at peak season. Does this contradict the reported average of 665 workers per site?

Exercises   DO IT YOURSELF!

8.98 Refer to the **Interpreting Confidence Intervals** applet.

    a. Suppose that you have a random sample of size $n = 50$ from a population with unknown mean μ and known standard deviation $\sigma = 35$. Calculate the half width of a 95% confidence interval for μ. What would the width of this interval be?

    b. Use the | One Sample | button to create a single confidence interval for μ. What is the width of this interval? Compare your results to the calculation you did in part a.

8.99 Refer to the **Interpreting Confidence Intervals** applet.

    a. Use the | 10 Samples | button to create ten confidence intervals for μ.

    b. What do you notice about the widths of these intervals?

    c. How many of the intervals work properly and enclose the true value of μ?

    d. Try this simulation again by clicking the | 10 Samples | button a few more times and counting the number of intervals that work correctly. It is close to our 95% confidence level?

8.100 Refer to the **Interpreting Confidence Intervals** applet.

    a. Use the | 100 Samples | button to create one hundred confidence intervals for μ.

b. What do you notice about the widths of these intervals?

c. How many of the intervals work properly and enclose the true value of μ?

d. Try this simulation again by clicking the [100 Samples] button a few more times and counting the number of intervals that work correctly. It is close to our 95% confidence level?

8.101 Suppose that a random sample of size n is selected from a population with mean $\mu = 750$ and standard deviation σ. The **Exploring Confidence Intervals** applet shows the sampling distribution of $\bar{x}$ and a representative confidence interval, calculated as

$$\bar{x} \pm z_{\alpha/2} \frac{\sigma}{\sqrt{n}}$$

a. The applet loads with $n = 50$, $\sigma = 35$ and $\bar{x} = 756$. Calculate the half-width of a 95% confidence interval for μ.

b. Calculate the upper and lower confidence limits and compare these limits to the endpoints of the interval shown in the applet.

c. Does the confidence interval work properly? That is, does it enclose the true value of $\mu = 750$?

8.102 Refer to the **Exploring Confidence Intervals** applet.

a. Use the applet to find the values of $z_{\alpha/2}$ for a 99% confidence interval. For a 95% confidence interval? For a 90% confidence interval?

b. What effect does reducing the confidence level have on the width of the confidence interval?

c. A narrower interval indicates a more precise estimate of μ, consisting of a smaller range of values. To obtain a more precise estimate by using a smaller z-value, what has been sacrificed?

8.103 Refer to the **Exploring Confidence Intervals** applet.

a. Move the slider marked "n" from bottom to top.

b. What is the effect of increasing the sample size on the standard error of $\bar{x}$? On the width of the confidence interval?

c. Can you think of a practical explanation for the phenomena you observe in part b?

8.104 Refer to the **Exploring Confidence Intervals** applet.

a. Move the slider marked "sigma" from bottom to top.

b. What is the effect of increasing the variability on the standard error of $\bar{x}$? On the width of the confidence interval?

c. Can you think of a practical explanation for the phenomena you observe in part b?

Case Study   How Reliable Is That Poll?

In the days and weeks following any important or controversial events, opinion polls saturate the media. This was especially evident following the terrorist attacks in the United States in the fall of 2001, and after the unprecedented outcome of the 2000 presidential election. In that election, Al Gore won the popular vote, but was defeated in the Electoral College by George W. Bush. The results of the election were subject to a number of legal and political challenges, finally ending up with the Supreme Court.

It is almost impossible to read a daily newspaper, listen to the radio, surf the Internet, or watch television without hearing or seeing some opinion poll or economic survey. How reliable are the percentages derived from these samples of public opinion? Do national polls conducted by the Gallup and Harris organizations, the news media, and so on really provide accurate estimates of the percentages of people in the United States who favor various propositions?

A report of the results of a Gallup Organization poll provides a clue to these answers.[18] The poll was conducted November 11–12, 2000, and consisted of a series of 15 questions about the presidential election, at a time when the outcome was not yet confirmed. A portion of the survey results are shown here:

CNN/USA Today/Gallup Poll—Presidential Election Reaction Poll

1. Which of these statements do you think best describes the situation that has occurred since Tuesday's election for president—[ROTATED: it is a constitutional crisis, it is a major problem for the country, it is a minor problem for the country, (or) it is not a problem for the country at all]?

	Constitutional Crisis	Major problem	Minor problem	Not a problem	No opinion
National adults	15	49	25	9	2
Gore voters	17	49	23	9	2
Bush voters	14	50	27	8	1

2. [ROTATED w/Q.3] If Al Gore is declared the winner and inaugurated next January, would you accept him as the legitimate president, or not?

	Yes, accept	No, not accept	No opinion
National adults	82	16	2
Gore voters	97	1	2
Bush voters	66	31	3

3. [ROTATED w/Q.2] If George W. Bush is declared the winner and inaugurated next January, would you accept him as the legitimate president, or not?

	Yes, accept	No, not accept	No opinion
National adults	79	19	2
Gore voters	61	36	3
Bush voters	97	1	2

At the top of this report, which appeared on the Gallup Organization website (www.gallup.com) is a paragraph summarizing the poll:

Results are based on telephone interviews with—1,014—National Adults, aged 18+, conducted November 11–12, 2000. For results based on the total sample of National Adults, one can say with 95% confidence that the margin of sampling error is +/−3 percentage points.

Results based on the subsample of—395—Gore voters have a margin of sampling error of $+/-5$ percentage points.

Results based on the subsample of—340—Bush voters have a margin of sampling error of $+/-6$ percentage points.

1. Verify the three margins of error given by the Gallup Organization. Why must the pollster use different margins of error for the two subsamples (Gore voters and Bush voters)?
2. Do the numbers reported in the three tables represent the number of people who fell into that category? If not, what do those numbers represent?
3. When Question 1 was asked, the pollster rotated the order of options given to the respondent. Why do you suppose this technique was used?
4. When Questions 2 and 3 were asked, the pollster rotated the order of the questions. Why do you suppose this was done?
5. Refer to Question 1. Construct a 95% confidence interval to compare the proportion of Gore and Bush voters who think that the outcome of the election poses a constitutional crisis. Is there a significant difference in these two proportions?
6. Refer to Question 2. Construct a 95% confidence interval to compare the proportion of Gore and Bush voters who think that, if Al Gore is declared the winner, he should be accepted as the legitimate president. Is there a significant difference in these two proportions?
7. What do you notice when you compare the percentages reported in Questions 2 and 3? Does this surprise you?
8. Would the percentage of people who thought that the outcome of the election posed a constitutional crisis change if the poll were taken at a different date, perhaps in the fall of the year 2001?

Data Sources

1. *Science News* 136 (19 August 1989): 124.
2. Laurie Lucas, "It's Elementary, Mister," *The Press-Enterprise* (Riverside, CA), 28 May 1997, p. D-1.
3. Mike Tharp, "Ready, Set, Go. Why We Love Our Games—Sports Crazy," *U.S. News & World Report,* 15 July 1997, p.31.
4. Adapted from "Suite Dreams," *Consumer Reports,* July 2001, p. 12–16.
5. "Caught in the Middle," *American Demographics,* July 2001, p. 14–15.
6. "Movie Mania Ebbing?" Gallup Poll of 800 adults March 16–18, 2001. Web site: http://www.usatoday.com/snapshot/news/2001-06-14-moviemania.htm.
7. Alison Stein Wellner, "A New Cure for Shoppus Interuptus," *The Marketing Tool Directory,* 2002.
8. William Leonard, Barbara Speziale, and John Pernick. (2001) "Performance Assessment of a Standards-Based High School Biology Curriculum," *The American Biology Teacher,* 63(5)310–316.
9. "Voters Want Welfare Recipients Put to Work, Statewide Poll Finds," *The Press-Enterprise* (Riverside, CA), 30 May 1997.
10. David L. Wheeler, "More Social Roles Means Fewer Colds," *Chronicle of Higher Education* XLIII, no. 44 (11 July 1997):A13.
11. Adapted from "Toplines: To the Moon?" Rebecca Gardyn, ed., *American Demographics,* August 2001, p. 9.

12. Reed Abelson, "A Survey of Wall St. Finds Women Disheartened," *The New York Times on the Web,* www.nytimes.com, July 26, 2001.

13. Shannon Dortch, "America Weighs In," *American Demographics,* June 1997, p. 39.

14. Adapted from A.M. Goodman and A.R. Ennos, "The Responses of Field-grown Sunflower and Maize to Mechanical Support," *Annals of Botany* 79 (1997):703.

15. Adapted from "I'm a Yankee Doodle Dandy," Knowledge Networks: 2000, *American Demographics,* July 2001, p. 9.

16. Sandra Yin, Pamela Paul, and David Whelan, "What Summer Break?" *American Demographics,* July 2001, p. 64.

17. G. Wayne Marino, "Selected Mechanical Factors Associated with Acceleration in Ice Skating," *Research Quarterly for Exercise and Sport* 54, no. 3 (1983).

18. "CNN/USA Today/ Gallup Poll—Presidential Election Reaction Poll," http://gallup.com/poll/surveys/2000/Topline001111/index.asp, 18 October 2001.

9

Large-Sample Tests of Hypotheses

Case Study

Will an aspirin a day reduce the risk of heart attack? A very large study of U.S. physicians showed that a single aspirin taken every other day reduced the risk of heart attack in men by one-half. However, 3 days later, a British study reported a completely opposite conclusion. How could this be? The case study at the end of this chapter looks at how the studies were conducted, and you will analyze the data using large-sample techniques.

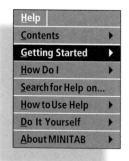

General Objective

In this chapter, the concept of a statistical test of hypothesis is formally introduced. The sampling distributions of statistics presented in Chapters 7 and 8 are used to construct large-sample tests concerning the values of population parameters of interest to the experimenter.

Specific Topics

1. A statistical test of hypothesis (9.2)
2. Large-sample test about a population mean μ (9.3)
3. Large-sample test about $(\mu_1 - \mu_2)$ (9.4)
4. Testing a hypothesis about a population proportion p (9.5)
5. Testing a hypothesis about $(p_1 - p_2)$ (9.6)

9.1 Testing Hypotheses about Population Parameters

In practical situations, statistical inference can involve either estimating a population parameter or making decisions about the value of the parameter. For example, if a pharmaceutical company is fermenting a vat of antibiotic, samples from the vat can be used to *estimate* the mean potency μ for all of the antibiotic in the vat. In contrast, suppose that the company is not concerned about the exact mean potency of the antibiotic, but is concerned only that it meet the minimum government potency standards. Then the company can use samples from the vat to decide between these two possibilities:

- The mean potency μ does not exceed the minimum allowable potency.
- The mean potency μ exceeds the minimum allowable potency.

The pharmaceutical company's problem illustrates a **statistical test of hypothesis.**

The reasoning used in a statistical test of hypothesis is similar to the process in a court trial. In trying a person for theft, the court must decide between innocence and guilt. As the trial begins, the accused person is assumed to be *innocent.* The prosecution collects and presents all available evidence in an attempt to contradict the innocent hypothesis and hence obtain a conviction. If there is enough evidence against innocence, the court will reject the innocence hypothesis and declare the defendant *guilty.* If the prosecution does not present enough evidence to prove the defendant guilty, the court will find him *not guilty.* Notice that this does not prove that the defendant is innocent, but merely that there was not enough evidence to conclude that the defendant was guilty.

We use this same type of reasoning to explain the basic concepts of hypothesis testing. These concepts are used to test the four population parameters discussed in Chapter 8: a single population mean or proportion (μ or p) and the difference between two population means or proportions ($\mu_1 - \mu_2$ or $p_1 - p_2$). When the sample sizes are large, the point estimators for each of these four parameters have normal sampling distributions, so that all four large-sample statistical tests follow the same general pattern.

9.2 A Statistical Test of Hypothesis

A statistical test of hypothesis consists of five parts:

1. The null hypothesis, denoted by H_0
2. The alternative hypothesis, denoted by H_a
3. The test statistic and its *p*-value
4. The rejection region
5. The conclusion

When you specify these five elements, you define a particular test; changing one or more of the parts creates a new test. Let's look at each part of the statistical test of hypothesis in more detail.

Definition   The two competing hypotheses are the **alternative hypothesis** H_a, generally the hypothesis that the researcher wishes to support, and the **null hypothesis** H_0, a contradiction of the alternative hypothesis.

As you will soon see, it is easier to show support for the alternative hypothesis by proving that the null hypothesis is false. Hence, the statistical researcher always begins by assuming that the null hypothesis H_0 is true. The researcher then uses the sample data to decide whether the evidence favors H_a rather than H_0 and draws one of these two **conclusions**:

- Reject H_0 and conclude that H_a is true.
- Accept (do not reject) H_0 as true.

EXAMPLE 9.1   You wish to show that the average hourly wage of construction workers in the state of California is different from \$14, which is the national average. This is the alternative hypothesis, written as

$$H_a : \mu \neq 14$$

The null hypothesis is

$$H_0 : \mu = 14$$

You would like to reject the null hypothesis, thus concluding that the California mean is not equal to \$14.

EXAMPLE 9.2   A milling process currently produces an average of 3% defectives. You are interested in showing that a simple adjustment on a machine will decrease p, the proportion of defectives produced in the milling process. Thus, the alternative hypothesis is

$$H_a : p < .03$$

and the null hypothesis is

$$H_0 : p = .03$$

If you can reject H_0, you can conclude that the adjusted process produces fewer than 3% defectives.

There is a difference in the forms of the alternative hypotheses given in Examples 9.1 and 9.2. In Example 9.1, no directional difference is suggested for the value of μ; that is, μ might be either larger or smaller than \$14 if H_a is true. This type of test is called a **two-tailed test of hypothesis**. In Example 9.2, however, you are specifically interested in detecting a directional difference in the value of p; that is, if H_a is true, the value of p is less than .03. This type of test is called a **one-tailed test of hypothesis.**

The decision to reject or accept the null hypothesis is based on information contained in a sample drawn from the population of interest. This information takes these forms:

- **Test statistic**: a single number calculated from the sample data
- **p-value**: a probability calculated using the test statistic

Either or both of these measures act as decision makers for the researcher in deciding whether to reject or accept H_0.

EXAMPLE 9.3   For the test of hypothesis in Example 9.1, the average hourly wage $\bar{x}$ for a random sample of 100 California construction workers might provide a good *test statistic* for testing

$$H_0 : \mu = 14 \quad \text{versus} \quad H_a : \mu \neq 14$$

If the null hypothesis H_0 is true, then the sample mean should not be too far from the population mean $\mu = 14$. Suppose that this sample produces a sample mean $\bar{x} = 15$ with standard deviation $s = 2$. Is this sample evidence likely or unlikely to occur, if in fact H_0 is true? You can use two measures to find out. Since the sample size is large, the sampling distribution of $\bar{x}$ is approximately normal with mean $\mu = 14$ and standard error $\sigma/\sqrt{n}$, estimated as

$$\text{SE} = \frac{s}{\sqrt{n}} = \frac{2}{\sqrt{100}} = .2$$

- The **test statistic** $\bar{x} = 15$ lies

$$z = \frac{\bar{x} - \mu}{\sigma/\sqrt{n}} \approx \frac{15 - 14}{.2} = 5$$

standard deviations from the population mean μ.

- The **p-value** is the probability of observing a test statistic that is five or more standard deviations from the mean. Since z measures the number of standard deviations a normal random variable lies from its mean, you have

$$p\text{-value} = P(z > 5) + P(z < -5) \approx 0$$

The *large value of the test statistic* and the *small p-value* mean that you have observed a very unlikely event, if indeed H_0 is true and $\mu = 14$.

How do you decide whether to reject or accept H_0? The entire set of values that the test statistic may assume is divided into two sets, or regions. One set, consisting of values that support the alternative hypothesis and lead to rejecting H_0, is called the **rejection region.** The other, consisting of values that support the null hypothesis, is called the **acceptance region.**

For example, in Example 9.1, you would be inclined to believe that California's average hourly wage was different from \$14 if the sample mean is either much less than \$14 or much greater than \$14. The two-tailed rejection region consists of very small and very large values of $\bar{x}$, as shown in Figure 9.1. In Example 9.2, since you want to prove that the percentage of defectives has *decreased,* you would be inclined to reject H_0 for values of $\hat{p}$ that are much smaller than .03. Only *small* values of $\hat{p}$ belong in the left-tailed rejection region shown in Figure 9.2. When the rejection region is in the left tail of the distribution, the test is called a **left-tailed test.** A test with its rejection region in the right tail is called a **right-tailed test.**

FIGURE 9.1
Rejection and acceptance regions for Example 9.1

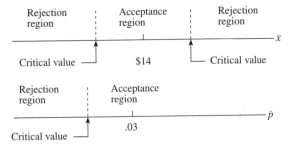

FIGURE 9.2
Rejection and acceptance regions for Example 9.2

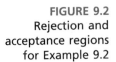

If the test statistic falls into the rejection region, then the null hypothesis is rejected. If the test statistic falls into the acceptance region, then either the null hypothesis is accepted or the test is judged to be inconclusive. We will clarify the different types of conclusions that are appropriate as we consider several practical examples of hypothesis tests.

Finally, how do you decide on the **critical values** that separate the acceptance and rejection regions? That is, how do you decide how much statistical evidence you need before you can reject H_0? This depends on the amount of confidence that you, the researcher, want to attach to the test conclusions and the **significance level α**, the risk you are willing to take of making an incorrect decision.

Definition   A **Type I error** for a statistical test is the error of rejecting the null hypothesis when it is true. The **level of significance (significance level)** for a statistical test of hypothesis is

$$\alpha = P(\text{Type I error}) = P(\text{falsely rejecting } H_0) = P(\text{rejecting } H_0 \text{ when it is true})$$

This value α represents the *maximum tolerable risk* of incorrectly rejecting H_0. Once this significance level is fixed, the rejection region can be set to allow the researcher to reject H_0 with a fixed degree of confidence in the decision.

In the next section, we will show you how to use a test of hypothesis to test the value of a population mean μ. As we continue, we will clarify some of the computational details and add some additional concepts to complete your understanding of hypothesis testing.

9.3 A Large-Sample Test about a Population Mean

Consider a random sample of n measurements drawn from a population that has mean μ and standard deviation σ. You want to test a hypothesis of the form[†]

$$H_0 : \mu = \mu_0$$

where μ_0 is some hypothesized value for μ, versus a one-tailed alternative hypothesis:

$$H_a : \mu > \mu_0$$

The subscript zero indicates the value of the parameter specified by H_0. Notice that H_0 provides an exact value for the parameter to be tested, whereas H_a gives a range of possible values for μ.

The Essentials of the Test

The sample mean $\bar{x}$ is the best estimate of the actual value of μ, which is presently in question. What values of $\bar{x}$ would lead you to believe that H_0 is false and μ is, in fact, greater than the hypothesized value? The values of $\bar{x}$ that are extremely *large* would imply that μ is larger than hypothesized. Hence, you should reject H_0 if $\bar{x}$ is too large.

The next problem is to define what is meant by "too large." Values of $\bar{x}$ that lie too many standard deviations to the right of the mean are not very likely to occur. Those values have very little area to their right. Hence, you can define "too large" as being

---

[†]Note that if the test rejects the null hypothesis $\mu = \mu_0$ in favor of the alternative hypothesis $\mu > \mu_0$, then it will certainly reject a null hypothesis that includes $\mu < \mu_0$, since this is even more contradictory to the alternative hypothesis. For this reason, in this text we state the null hypothesis for a one-tailed test as $\mu = \mu_0$ rather than $\mu \leq \mu_0$.

too many standard deviations away from μ_0. But what is "too many"? This question can be answered using the *significance level* α, the probability of rejecting H_0 when H_0 is *true*.

Remember that the standard error of $\bar{x}$ is estimated as

$$SE = \frac{s}{\sqrt{n}}$$

Since the sampling distribution of the sample mean $\bar{x}$ is approximately normal when n **is large,** the number of standard deviations that $\bar{x}$ lies from μ_0 can be measured using the **standardized test statistic:**

$$z = \frac{\bar{x} - \mu_0}{s/\sqrt{n}}$$

which has an approximate standard normal distribution when H_0 is true and $\mu = \mu_0$. The significance level α is equal to the area under the normal curve lying above the rejection region. Thus, if you want $\alpha = .01$, you will reject H_0 when $\bar{x}$ is more than 2.33 standard deviations to the right of μ_0. Equivalently, you will reject H_0 if the standardized test statistic z is greater than 2.33 (see Figure 9.3).

FIGURE 9.3
The rejection region for a right-tailed test with $\alpha = .01$

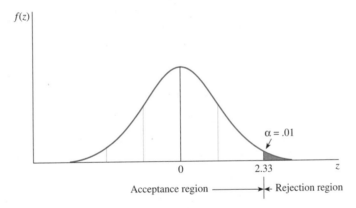

Acceptance region ──────────→|← Rejection region

EXAMPLE 9.4

The average weekly earnings for women in managerial and professional positions is $670. Do men in the same positions have average weekly earnings that are higher than those for women? A random sample of $n = 40$ men in managerial and professional positions showed $\bar{x} = \$725$ and $s = \$102$. Test the appropriate hypothesis using $\alpha = .01$.

Solution

You would like to show that the average weekly earnings for men are higher than $670, the women's average. Hence, if μ is the average weekly earnings in managerial and professional positions for men, the hypotheses to be tested are

$$H_0 : \mu = 670 \quad \text{versus} \quad H_a : \mu > 670$$

The rejection region for this one-tailed test consists of large values of $\bar{x}$ or, equivalently, values of the *standardized test statistic z* in the right tail of the standard normal distribution, with $\alpha = .01$. This value is found in Table 3 of Appendix I to be $z = 2.33$, as shown in Figure 9.3. The observed value of the test statistic, using s as an estimate of the population standard deviation, is

$$z \approx \frac{\bar{x} - 670}{s/\sqrt{n}} = \frac{725 - 670}{102/\sqrt{40}} = 3.41$$

Since the observed value of the test statistic falls in the rejection region, you can reject H_0 and conclude that the average weekly earnings for men in managerial and professional positions are significantly higher than those for women. The probability that you have made an incorrect decision is $\alpha = .01$.

If you wish to detect departures either greater or less than μ_0, then the alternative hypothesis is *two-tailed,* written as

$$H_a : \mu \neq \mu_0$$

which implies either $\mu > \mu_0$ or $\mu < \mu_0$. Values of $\bar{x}$ that are either "too large" or "too small" in terms of their distance from μ_0 are placed in the rejection region. If you choose $\alpha = .01$, the area in the rejection region is equally divided between the two tails of the normal distribution, as shown in Figure 9.4. Using the standardized test statistic z, you can reject H_0 if $z > 2.58$ or $z < -2.58$. For different values of α, the critical values of z that separate the rejection and acceptance regions will change accordingly.

FIGURE 9.4
The rejection region for a two-tailed test with $\alpha = .01$

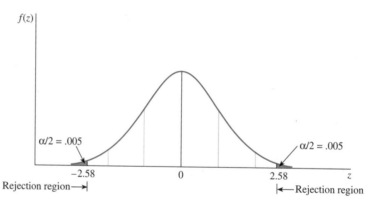

EXAMPLE 9.5

The daily yield for a local chemical plant has averaged 880 tons for the last several years. The quality control manager would like to know whether this average has changed in recent months. She randomly selects 50 days from the computer database and computes the average and standard deviation of the $n = 50$ yields as $\bar{x} = 871$ tons and $s = 21$ tons, respectively. Test the appropriate hypothesis using $\alpha = .05$.

Solution

The null and alternative hypotheses are

$$H_0 : \mu = 880 \quad \text{versus} \quad H_a : \mu \neq 880$$

The point estimate for μ is $\bar{x}$. Therefore, the test statistic is

$$z \approx \frac{\bar{x} - \mu_0}{s/\sqrt{n}} = \frac{871 - 880}{21/\sqrt{50}} = -3.03$$

Using $\alpha = .05$, the rejection region consists of values of $z > 1.96$ and values of $z < -1.96$. Since -3.03, the calculated value of z, falls in the rejection region, the manager can reject the hypothesis that $\mu = 880$ tons and conclude that it has changed. The probability of rejecting H_0 when H_0 is true is $\alpha = .05$. Hence, she is reasonably confident that the decision is correct.

Large-Sample Statistical Test for μ

1. Null hypothesis: $H_0 : \mu = \mu_0$
2. Alternative hypothesis:

      One-Tailed Test   **Two-Tailed Test**

        $H_a : \mu > \mu_0$ $H_a : \mu \neq \mu_0$
     (or, $H_a : \mu < \mu_0$)

3. Test statistic: $z = \dfrac{\bar{x} - \mu_0}{\sigma\sqrt{n}}$ estimated as $z = \dfrac{\bar{x} - \mu_0}{s\sqrt{n}}$

4. Rejection region: Reject H_0 when

      One-Tailed Test   **Two-Tailed Test**

        $z > z_\alpha$ $z > z_{\alpha/2}$ or $z < -z_{\alpha/2}$
   (or $z < -z_\alpha$ when the
  alternative hypothesis is
       $H_a : \mu < \mu_0$)

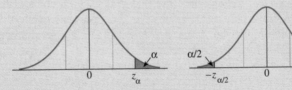

Assumptions: The n observations in the sample are randomly selected from the population and n is large—say, $n \geq 30$.

Calculating the *p*-Value

In the previous examples, the decision to reject or accept H_0 was made by comparing the calculated value of the test statistic with a critical value of z based on the significance level α of the test. However, different significance levels may lead to different conclusions. For example, if in a right-tailed test, the test statistic is $z = 2.03$, you can reject H_0 at the 5% level of significance because the test statistic exceeds $z = 1.645$. However, you cannot reject H_0 at the 1% level of significance because the test statistic is less than $z = 2.33$ (see Figure 9.5). To avoid any ambiguity in their conclusions, some experimenters prefer to use a variable level of significance called the **p-value** for the test.

Definition   The **p-value** or observed significance level of a statistical test is the smallest value of α for which H_0 can be rejected. It is the *actual risk* of committing a Type I error, if H_0 is rejected based on the observed value of the test statistic. The *p*-value measures the strength of the evidence against H_0.

In the right-tailed test with observed test statistic $z = 2.03$, the smallest critical value you can use and still reject H_0 is $z = 2.03$. For this critical value, the risk of an incorrect decision is

$$P(z \geq 2.03) = 1 - .9788 = .0212$$

This probability is the *p-value* for the test. *Notice that it is actually the area to the right of the calculated value of the test statistic.*

FIGURE 9.5
Variable rejection
regions

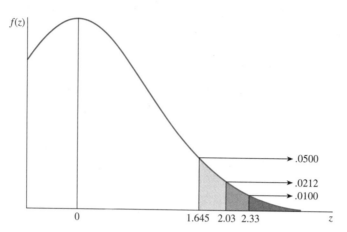

A *small p-value* indicates that the observed value of the test statistic lies far away from the hypothesized value of μ. This presents strong evidence that H_0 is false and should be rejected. *Large p-values* indicate that the observed test statistic is not far from the hypothesized mean and does not support rejection of H_0. How small does the *p*-value need to be before H_0 can be rejected?

Definition   If the *p*-value is less than a preassigned significance level α, then the null hypothesis can be rejected, and you can report that the results are **statistically significant** at level α.

In the previous instance, if you choose $\alpha = .05$ as your significance level, H_0 can be rejected because the *p*-value is less than .05. However, if you choose $\alpha = .01$ as your significance level, the *p*-value (.0212) is not small enough to allow rejection of H_0. The results are significant at the 5% level, but not at the 1% level. You might see these results reported in professional journals as *significant* $(p < .05)$.[†]

EXAMPLE 9.6   Calculate the *p*-value for the two-tailed test of hypothesis in Example 9.5. Use the *p*-value to draw conclusions regarding the statistical test.

Solution   The rejection region for this two-tailed test of hypothesis is found in both tails of the normal probability distribution. Since the observed value of the test statistic is $z = -3.03$, the smallest rejection region that you can use and still reject H_0 is $|z| > 3.03$. For this rejection region, the value of α is the *p*-value:

$$p\text{-value} = P(z > 3.03) + P(z < -3.03) = (1 - .9988) + .0012 = .0024$$

Notice that the two-tailed p-value is actually twice the tail area corresponding to the calculated value of the test statistic. If this *p*-value $= .0024$ is less than the preassigned level of significance α, H_0 can be rejected. For this test, you can reject H_0 at either the 1% or the 5% level of significance.

[†]In reporting statistical significance, many researchers write $(p < .05)$ or $(P < .05)$ to mean that the *p*-value of the test was smaller than .05, making the results significant at the 5% level. The symbol *p* or *P* in the expression has no connection with our notation for probability or with the binomial parameter *p*.

If you are reading a research report, how small should the *p*-value be before you decide to reject H_0? Many researchers use a "sliding scale" to classify their results.

- If the *p*-value is less than .01, H_0 is rejected. The results are **highly significant.**
- If the *p*-value is between .01 and .05, H_0 is rejected. The results are **statistically significant.**
- If the *p*-value is between .05 and .10, H_0 is usually not rejected. The results are only **tending toward statistical significance.**
- If the *p*-value is greater than .10, H_0 is not rejected. The results are **not statistically significant.**

EXAMPLE 9.7

Standards set by government agencies indicate that Americans should not exceed an average daily sodium intake of 3300 milligrams (mg). To find out whether Americans are exceeding this limit, a sample of 100 Americans is selected, and the mean and standard deviation of daily sodium intake are found to be 3400 mg and 1100 mg, respectively. Use $\alpha = .05$ to conduct a test of hypothesis.

Solution The hypotheses to be tested are

$$H_0 : \mu = 3300 \quad \text{versus} \quad H_a : \mu > 3300$$

and the test statistic is

$$z \approx \frac{\bar{x} - \mu_0}{s/\sqrt{n}} = \frac{3400 - 3300}{1100/\sqrt{100}} = .91$$

The two approaches developed in this section yield the same conclusions.

- **The critical value approach:** Since the significance level is $\alpha = .05$ and the test is one-tailed, the rejection region is determined by a critical value with tail area equal to $\alpha = .05$; that is, H_0 can be rejected if $z > 1.645$. Since $z = .91$ is not greater than the critical value, H_0 is not rejected (see Figure 9.6).
- **The *p*-value approach:** Calculate the *p*-value, the probability that z is greater than or equal to $z = .91$:

$$p\text{-value} = P(z > .91) = 1 - .8186 = .1814$$

The null hypothesis can be rejected only if the *p-value is less than the specified 5% significance level.* Therefore, H_0 is not rejected and the results are *not statistically significant* (see Figure 9.6). There is not enough evidence to indicate that the average daily sodium intake exceeds 3300 mg.

FIGURE 9.6
Rejection region and *p*-value for Example 9.7

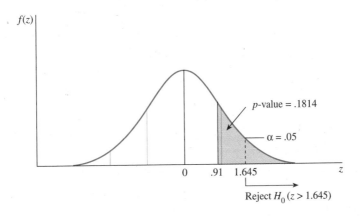

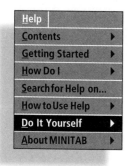

DO IT YOURSELF!

You can use the **Large Sample Test of a Population Mean** applet to visualize the *p*-values for either one- or two-tailed tests of the population mean μ (Figure 9.7). Remember, however, that these large sample *z*-tests are restricted to samples of size $n \geq 30$. The applet does not prohibit you from entering a value of $n < 30$; you'll have to be careful to check the sample size before you start! The procedure follows the same pattern as with previous applets. You enter the values of $\bar{x}$, n, and s—remember to press "Enter" after each entry to record the changes. The applet will calculate z (using full accuracy) and give you the option of choosing one- or two-tailed *p*-values (as well as a *cumulative* and a *middle* area that you will not need.)

FIGURE 9.7
Large Sample Test of a Population Mean applet

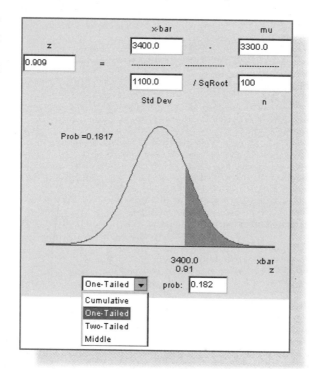

For the data of Example 9.7, the *p*-value is the one-tailed area to the right of $z = .909$. Do the results shown in the applet confirm our conclusions in Example 9.7? Remember that the applet uses full accuracy for the calculation of z and its corresponding probability. This means that the probability we calculate using Table 3 may be slightly different from the probability shown in the applet.

Notice that these two approaches are actually the same, as shown in Figure 9.6. As soon as the calculated value of the test statistic z becomes *larger than* the critical value, z_α, the *p*-value becomes *smaller than* the significance level α. You can use the most convenient of the two methods; the conclusions you reach will always be the same! The *p*-value approach does have two advantages, however:

- Statistical output from packages such as *MINITAB* usually reports the *p*-value of the test.

- Based on the *p*-value, your test results can be evaluated using any significance level you wish to use. Many researchers report the smallest possible significance level for which their results are *statistically significant.*

Sometimes it is easy to confuse the significance level α with the *p*-value (or observed significance level). They are both probabilities calculated as areas in the tails of the sampling distribution of the test statistic. However, the significance level α is preset by the experimenter before collecting the data. The *p*-value is linked directly to the data and actually describes how likely or unlikely the sample results are, assuming that H_0 is true. *The smaller the p-value, the more unlikely it is that H_0 is true!*

Two Types of Errors

You might wonder why, when H_0 was not rejected in the previous example, we did not say that H_0 was definitely true and $\mu = 3300$. This is because, if we choose to *accept* H_0, we must have a measure of the probability of error associated with this decision.

Since there are two choices in a statistical test, there are also two types of errors that can be made. In the courtroom trial, a defendant could be judged not guilty when he's really guilty, or vice versa—the same is true in a statistical test. In fact, the null hypothesis may be either true or false, regardless of the decision the experimenter makes. These two possibilities, along with the two decisions that can be made by the researcher, are shown in Table 9.1.

TABLE 9.1
Decision table

	Null Hypothesis	
Decision	True	False
Reject H_0	Type I error	Correct decision
Accept H_0	Correct decision	Type II error

In addition to the Type I error with probability defined earlier in this section, it is possible to commit a second error, called a **Type II error**, which has probability β.

Definition

A **Type I error** for a statistical test is the error of rejecting the null hypothesis when it is true. The probability of making a Type I error is denoted by the symbol α.

A **Type II error** for a statistical test is the error of accepting the null hypothesis when it is false and some alternative hypothesis is true. The probability of making a Type II error is denoted by the symbol β.

Notice that the probability of a Type I error is exactly the same as the **level of significance α** and is therefore controlled by the researcher. When H_0 is rejected, you have an accurate measure of the reliability of your inference; the probability of an incorrect decision is α. However, the probability β of a Type II error is not always controlled by the experimenter. In fact, when H_0 is false and H_a is true, you may not be able to specify an exact value for μ but only a range of values. This makes it difficult, if not impossible, to calculate β. Without a measure of reliability, it is not wise to conclude that H_0 is true. Rather than risk an incorrect decision, you should withhold judgment, concluding that you *do not have enough evidence to reject H_0.* Instead of *accepting H_0,* you should *not reject* or *fail to reject H_0.*

Keep in mind that *"accepting" a particular hypothesis means deciding in its favor. Regardless of the outcome of a test, you are never *certain* that the hypothesis you "accept" is true. *There is always a risk of being wrong (measured by α or β).* Consequently, you never "accept" H_0 if $β$ is unknown or its value is unacceptable to you. When this situation occurs, you should withhold judgment and collect more data.

The Power of a Statistical Test

The goodness of a statistical test is measured by the size of the two error rates: $α$, the probability of rejecting H_0 when it is true, and $β$, the probability of accepting H_0 when H_0 is false and H_a is true. A "good" test is one for which both of these error rates are small. The experimenter begins by selecting $α$, the probability of a Type I error. If he or she also decides to control the value of $β$, the probability of accepting H_0 when H_a is true, then an appropriate sample size is chosen.

Another way of evaluating a test is to look at the complement of a Type II error—that is, rejecting H_0 when H_a is true—which has probability

$$1 - β = P(\text{reject } H_0 \text{ when } H_a \text{ is true})$$

The quantity $(1 - β)$ is called the **power** of the test because it measures the probability of taking the action that we wish to have occur—that is, rejecting the null hypothesis when it is false and H_a is true.

Definition

The **power of a statistical test,** given as

$$1 - β = P(\text{reject } H_0 \text{ when } H_a \text{ is true})$$

measures the ability of the test to perform as required.

A graph of $(1 - β)$, the probability of rejecting H_0 when in fact H_0 is false, as a function of the true value of the parameter of interest is called the **power curve** for the statistical test. Ideally, you would like $α$ to be small and the *power* $(1 - β)$ to be large.

EXAMPLE 9.8   Refer to Example 9.5. Calculate $β$ and the power of the test $(1 - β)$ when $μ$ is actually equal to 870 tons.

Solution   The acceptance region for the test of Example 9.5 is located in the interval $[μ_0 \pm 1.96(s/\sqrt{n})]$. Substituting numerical values, you get

$$880 \pm 1.96\left(\frac{21}{\sqrt{50}}\right) \quad \text{or} \quad 874.18 \text{ to } 885.82$$

The probability of accepting H_0, given $μ = 870$, is equal to the area under the sampling distribution for the test statistic $\bar{x}$ in the interval from 874.18 to 885.82. Since $\bar{x}$ is normally distributed with a mean of 870 and SE $= 21/\sqrt{50} = 2.97$, $β$ is equal to the area under the normal curve with $μ = 870$ located between 874.18 and 885.82 (see Figure 9.8). Calculating the z-values corresponding to 874.18 and 885.82, you get

$$z_1 \approx \frac{\bar{x} - μ}{s/\sqrt{n}} = \frac{874.18 - 870}{21/\sqrt{50}} = 1.41$$

$$z_2 \approx \frac{\bar{x} - μ}{s/\sqrt{n}} = \frac{885.82 - 870}{21/\sqrt{50}} = 5.33$$

Then

$$\beta = P(\text{accept } H_0 \text{ when } \mu = 870) = P(874.18 < \bar{x} < 885.82 \text{ when } \mu = 870)$$
$$= P(1.41 < z < 5.33)$$

You can see from Figure 9.8 that the area under the normal curve with $\mu = 870$ above $\bar{x} = 885.82$ (or $z = 5.33$) is negligible. Therefore,

$$\beta = P(z > 1.41)$$

FIGURE 9.8
Calculating β in Example 9.8

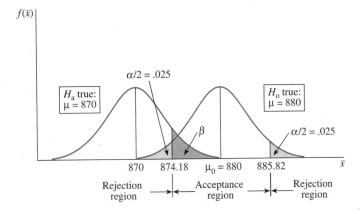

From Table 3 in Appendix I you can find

$$\beta = 1 - .9207 = .0793$$

Hence, the power of the test is

$$1 - \beta = 1 - .0793 = .9207$$

The probability of correctly rejecting H_0, given that μ is really equal to 870, is .9207, or approximately 92 chances in 100.

DO IT YOURSELF!

You can use the **Power of a z-Test** applet to calculate the power for the hypothesis test in Example 9.8, and also for the same test when the sample size is changed. Refer to Figure 9.9. The applet in Figure 9.9 shows a sample size of $n = 50$. The slider at the bottom of the applet allows you to change the true value of μ; the power is recalculated as the mean changes. What is the true value of μ and the power of the test shown in the applet? Compare this to the value found in Table 9.2. The slider on the left side of the applet allows you to change α, and the slider on the right allows you to change the sample size n. Remember that *n must be > 30* for the z-test to be appropriate. You will use these applets to explore power using the *Do It Yourself Exercises* at the end of the chapter.

FIGURE 9.9
Power of a *z*-Test
applet

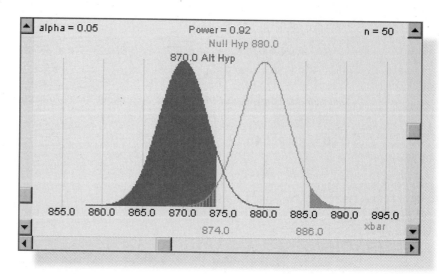

Values of $(1 - \beta)$ can be calculated for various values of μ_a different from $\mu_0 = 880$ to measure the power of the test. For example, if $\mu_a = 885$,

$$\beta = P(874.18 < \overline{x} < 885.82 \text{ when } \mu = 885)$$
$$= P(-3.64 < z < .28)$$
$$= .6103 - 0 = .6103$$

and the power is $(1 - \beta) = .3897$. Table 9.2 shows the power of the test for various values of μ_a, and a power curve is graphed in Figure 9.10. Note that the power of the test increases as the distance between μ_a and μ_0 increases. The result is a U-shaped curve for this two-tailed test.

TABLE 9.2
Value of $(1 - \beta)$
for various values
of μ_a for
Example 9.8

μ_a	$(1 - \beta)$	μ_a	$(1 - \beta)$
865	.9990	883	.1726
870	.9207	885	.3897
872	.7673	888	.7673
875	.3897	890	.9207
877	.1726	895	.9990
880	.0500		

FIGURE 9.10
Power curve for
Example 9.8

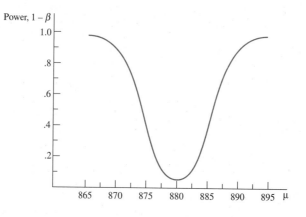

There are many important links among the two error rates, α and β, the power, $(1 - \beta)$, and the sample size, n. Look at the two curves shown in Figure 9.8.

- If α (the sum of the two tail areas in the curve on the right) is increased, the shaded area corresponding to β decreases, and vice versa.
- The only way to decrease β for a fixed α is to "buy" more information—that is, increase the sample size n.

What would happen to the area β as the curve on the left is moved closer to the curve on the right ($\mu = 880$)? With the rejection region in the right curve fixed, the value of β will *increase*. What effect does this have on the power of the test? Look at Figure 9.10.

You may also want to use the **Power of a z-Test** applet to help you visualize the following statements:

- As the distance between the true (μ_a) and hypothesized (μ_0) values of the mean increases, the power $(1 - \beta)$ increases. The test is better at detecting *differences* when the distance is *large*.
- The closer the true value (μ_a) gets to the hypothesized value (μ_0), the less power $(1 - \beta)$ the test has to detect the difference.
- The only way to increase the power $(1 - \beta)$ for a fixed α is to "buy" more information—that is, increase the sample size, n.

The experimenter must decide on the values of α and β—measuring the risks of the possible errors he or she can tolerate. He or she also must decide how much power is needed to detect differences that are practically important in the experiment. Once these decisions are made, the sample size can be chosen by consulting the power curves corresponding to various sample sizes for the chosen test.

Calculate β?

1. Find the critical value or values of $\bar{x}$ used to separate the acceptance and rejection regions.
2. Using one or more values for μ consistent with the alternative hypothesis H_a, calculate the probability that the sample mean $\bar{x}$ falls in the *acceptance region*. This produces the value $\beta = P(\text{accept } H_a \text{ when } \mu = \mu_a)$.
3. Remember that the **power** of the test is $(1 - \beta)$.

Exercises

Basic Techniques

9.1 Find the appropriate rejection regions for the large-sample test statistic z in these cases:

a. A right-tailed test with $\alpha = .01$

b. A two-tailed test at the 5% significance level

c. A left-tailed test at the 1% significance level

d. A two-tailed test with $\alpha = .01$

9.2 Find the p-value for the following large-sample z tests:

a. A right-tailed test with observed $z = 1.15$

b. A two-tailed test with observed $z = -2.78$

c. A left-tailed test with observed $z = -1.81$

9.3 For the three tests given in Exercise 9.2, use the p-value to determine the significance of the results. Explain what "statistically significant" means in terms of rejecting or accepting H_0 and H_a.

9.4 A random sample of $n = 35$ observations from a quantitative population produced a mean $\bar{x} = 2.4$ and a standard deviation $s = .29$. Suppose your research objective is to show that the population mean μ exceeds 2.3.

a. Give the null and alternative hypotheses for the test.

b. Locate the rejection region for the test using a 5% significance level.

c. Find the standard error of the mean.

d. Before you conduct the test, use your intuition to decide whether the sample mean $\bar{x} = 2.4$ is likely or unlikely, assuming that $\mu = 2.3$. Now conduct the test. Do the data provide sufficient evidence to indicate that $\mu > 2.3$?

9.5 Refer to Exercise 9.4.

a. Calculate the p-value for the test statistic in part d.

b. Use the p-value to draw a conclusion at the 5% significance level.

c. Compare the conclusion in part b with the conclusion reached in part d of Exercise 9.4. Are they the same?

9.6 Refer to Exercise 9.4. You want to test $H_0 : \mu = 2.3$ against $H_a : \mu > 2.3$.

a. Find the critical value of $\bar{x}$ used for rejecting H_0.

b. Calculate $\beta = P(\text{accept } H_0 \text{ when } \mu = 2.4)$.

c. Repeat the calculation of β for $\mu = 2.3, 2.5,$ and 2.6.

d. Use the values of β from parts b and c to graph the power curve for the test.

9.7 A random sample of 100 observations from a quantitative population produced a sample mean of 26.8 and a sample standard deviation of 6.5. Use the p-value approach to determine whether the population mean is different from 28. Explain your conclusions.

Applications

9.8 High airline occupancy rates on scheduled flights are essential to corporate profitability. Suppose a scheduled flight must average at least 60% occupancy in order to be profitable, and an examination of the occupancy rate for 120 10:00 A.M. flights from Atlanta to Dallas showed a mean occupancy per flight of 58% and a standard deviation of 11%.

a. If μ is the mean occupancy per flight and if the company wishes to determine whether or not this scheduled flight is unprofitable, give the alternative and the null hypotheses for the test.

b. Does the alternative hypothesis in part a imply a one- or two-tailed test? Explain.

c. Do the occupancy data for the 120 flights suggest that this scheduled flight is unprofitable? Test using $\alpha = .05$.

9.9 Exercise 8.31 involved the meat department of a local supermarket chain that packages ground beef in trays of two sizes. The smaller tray is intended to hold 1 pound of meat. A random sample of 35 packages in the smaller meat tray produced weight measurements with an average of 1.01 pounds and a standard deviation of .18 pound.

a. If you were the quality control manager and wanted to make sure that the average amount of ground beef was indeed 1 pound, what hypotheses would you test?

b. Find the p-value for the test and use it to perform the test in part a.

c. How would you, as the quality control manager, report the results of your study to a consumer interest group?

9.10 "Welcome to the new movie pre-show!" Before you can see the newly released movie you have just paid to see, you must sit through a variety of trivia slides, snack bar ads, paid product advertising, and movie trailers. Although the total barrage of advertising may last up to 20 minutes or more, a particular theater chain claims that the average length of any one advertisement is no more than 3 minutes.[1] To test this claim, 50 theater advertisements were randomly selected and found to have an average duration of 3 minutes 15 seconds with a standard deviation of 30 seconds. Do the data provide sufficient evidence to indicate that the average duration of theater ads is more than that claimed by the theater? Test at the 1% level of significance. (HINT: Change "seconds" to fractions of a "minute.")

9.11 A drug manufacturer claimed that the mean potency of one of its antibiotics was 80%. A random sample of $n = 100$ capsules were tested and produced a sample mean of $\bar{x} = 79.7\%$, with a standard deviation of $s = .8\%$. Do the data present sufficient evidence to refute the manufacturer's claim? Let $\alpha = .05$.

a. State the null hypothesis to be tested.

b. State the alternative hypothesis.

c. Conduct a statistical test of the null hypothesis and state your conclusion.

9.12 Many companies are becoming involved in *flextime,* in which a worker schedules his or her own work hours or compresses work weeks. A company that was contemplating the installation of a flextime schedule estimated that it needed a minimum mean of 7 hours per day per assembly worker in order to operate effectively. Each of a random sample of 80 of the company's assemblers was asked to submit a tentative flextime schedule. If the mean number of hours per day for Monday was 6.7 hours and the standard deviation was 2.7 hours, do the data provide sufficient evidence to indicate that the mean number of hours worked per day on Mondays, for all of the company's assemblers, will be less than 7 hours? Test using $\alpha = .05$.

9.13 In Exercise 1.39, we examined an advertising flyer for the *Princeton Review,* a review course designed for high school students taking the SAT tests.[2] The flyer claimed that the average score improvements for students who have taken the *Princeton Review* course is between 110 and 160 points. Are the claims made by the *Princeton Review* advertisers exaggerated? That is, is the average score improvement less than 110, the minimum claimed in the advertising flyer? A random sample of 100 students who took the *Princeton Review* course achieved an average score improvement of 107 points with a standard deviation of 13 points.

a. Use the *p*-value approach to test the *Princeton Review* claim. At which significance levels can you reject H_0?

b. If you were a competitor of the *Princeton Review,* how would you state your conclusions to put your company in the best possible light?

c. If you worked for the *Princeton Review,* how would you state your conclusions to protect your company's reputation?

9.4 A Large-Sample Test of Hypothesis for the Difference between Two Population Means

In many situations, the statistical question to be answered involves a comparison of two population means. For example, the U.S. Postal Service is interested in reducing its massive 350 million gallons/year gasoline bill by replacing gasoline-powered trucks with electric-powered trucks. To determine whether significant savings in operating costs are achieved by changing to electric-powered trucks, a pilot study should be undertaken using, say, 100 conventional gasoline-powered mail trucks and 100 electric-powered mail trucks operated under similar conditions.

The statistic that summarizes the sample information regarding the difference in population means ($\mu_1 - \mu_2$) is the difference in sample means ($\bar{x}_1 - \bar{x}_2$). Therefore, in testing whether the difference in sample means indicates that the true difference in population means differs from a specified value, $(\mu_1 - \mu_2) = D_0$, you can use the standard error of $(\bar{x}_1 - \bar{x}_2)$:

$$\sqrt{\frac{\sigma_1^2}{n_1} + \frac{\sigma_2^2}{n_2}} \quad \text{estimated by} \quad SE = \sqrt{\frac{s_1^2}{n_1} + \frac{s_2^2}{n_2}}$$

in the form of a z-statistic to measure how many standard deviations the difference $(\bar{x}_1 - \bar{x}_2)$ lies from the hypothesized difference D_0. The formal testing procedure is described next.

Large-Sample Statistical Test for $(\mu_1 - \mu_2)$

1. **Null hypothesis:** $H_0 : (\mu_1 - \mu_2) = D_0$, where D_0 is some specified difference that you wish to test. For many tests, you will hypothesize that there is no difference between μ_1 and μ_2; that is, $D_0 = 0$.

2. Alternative hypothesis:

One-Tailed Test	Two-Tailed Test
$H_a : (\mu_1 - \mu_2) > D_0$	$H_a : (\mu_1 - \mu_2) \neq D_0$
[or $H_a : (\mu_1 - \mu_2) < D_0$]	

3. Test statistic: $z \approx \dfrac{(\bar{x}_1 - \bar{x}_2) - D_0}{SE} = \dfrac{(\bar{x}_1 - \bar{x}_2) - D_0}{\sqrt{\dfrac{s_1^2}{n_1} + \dfrac{s_2^2}{n_2}}}$

4. **Rejection region:** Reject H_0 when

One-Tailed Test	Two-Tailed Test
$z > z_\alpha$	$z > z_{\alpha/2}$ or $z < -z_{\alpha/2}$
[or $z < -z_\alpha$ when the alternative hypothesis is $H_a : (\mu_1 - \mu_2) < D_0$]	

or when p-value $< \alpha$

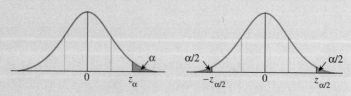

Assumptions: The samples are randomly and independently selected from the two populations and $n_1 \geq 30$ and $n_2 \geq 30$.

EXAMPLE 9.9

To determine whether car ownership affects a student's academic achievement, two random samples of 100 male students were each drawn from the student body. The grade point average for the $n_1 = 100$ non-owners of cars had an average and variance equal to $\bar{x}_1 = 2.70$ and $s_1^2 = .36$, while $\bar{x}_2 = 2.54$ and $s_2^2 = .40$ for the $n_2 = 100$ car owners. Do the data present sufficient evidence to indicate a difference in the mean achievements between car owners and nonowners of cars? Test using $\alpha = .05$.

Solution   To detect a difference, if it exists, between the mean academic achievements for non-owners of cars μ_1 and car owners μ_2, you will test the null hypothesis that there is no difference between the means against the alternative hypothesis that $(\mu_1 - \mu_2) \neq 0$; that is,

$$H_0 : (\mu_1 - \mu_2) = D_0 = 0 \quad \text{versus} \quad H_a : (\mu_1 - \mu_2) \neq 0$$

Substituting into the formula for the test statistic, you get

$$z \approx \frac{(\bar{x}_1 - \bar{x}_2) - D_0}{\sqrt{\dfrac{s_1^2}{n_1} + \dfrac{s_2^2}{n_2}}} = \frac{2.70 - 2.54}{\sqrt{\dfrac{.36}{100} + \dfrac{.40}{100}}} = 1.84$$

- **The critical value approach**: Using a two-tailed test with significance level $\alpha = .05$, you place $\alpha/2 = .025$ in each tail of the z distribution and reject H_0 if $z > 1.96$ or $z < -1.96$. Since $z = 1.84$ does not exceed 1.96 and is not less than -1.96, H_0 cannot be rejected (see Figure 9.11). That is, there is insufficient evidence to declare a difference in the average academic achievements for the two groups. Remember that you should not be willing to *accept* H_0—declare the two means to be the same—until β is evaluated for some meaningful values of $(\mu_1 - \mu_2)$.

FIGURE 9.11
Rejection region
and *p*-value for
Example 9.9

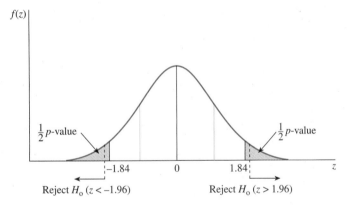

- **The *p*-value approach**: Calculate the *p*-value, the probability that z is greater than $z = 1.84$ plus the probability that z is less than $z = -1.84$, as shown in Figure 9.11:

$$p\text{-value} = P(z > 1.84) + P(z < -1.84) = (1 - .9671) + .0329 = .0658$$

The *p*-value lies between .10 and .05, so you can reject H_0 at the .10 level but not at the .05 level of significance. Since the *p*-value of .0658 exceeds the specified significance level $\alpha = .05$, H_0 cannot be rejected. Again, you should not be willing to *accept* H_0 until β is evaluated for some meaningful values of $(\mu_1 - \mu_2)$.

Hypothesis Testing and Confidence Intervals

Whether you use the critical value or the *p*-value approach for testing hypotheses about $(\mu_1 - \mu_2)$, you will always reach the same conclusion because the calculated value of the test statistic and the critical value are related *exactly* in the same way that the *p*-value and the significance level α are related. You might remember that the confidence intervals constructed in Chapter 8 could also be used to answer questions about the difference between two population means. In fact, for a two-tailed test, the $(1 - \alpha)100\%$

confidence interval for the parameter of interest can be used to test its value, just as you did informally in Chapter 8. The value of α indicated by the confidence coefficient in the confidence interval is equivalent to the significance level α in the statistical test. For a one-tailed test, the equivalent confidence interval approach would use the one-sided confidence bounds in Section 8.8 with confidence coefficient α. In addition, by using the confidence interval approach, you gain a range of possible values for the parameter of interest, regardless of the outcome of the test of hypothesis.

- If the confidence interval you construct *contains* the value of the parameter specified by H_0, then that value is one of the likely or possible values of the parameter and H_0 should not be rejected.
- If the hypothesized value *lies outside* of the confidence limits, the null hypothesis is rejected at the α level of significance.

EXAMPLE 9.10　Construct a 95% confidence interval for the difference in average academic achievements between car owners and non-owners. Using the confidence interval, can you conclude that there is a difference in the population means for the two groups of students?

Solution　For the large-sample statistics discussed in Chapter 8, the 95% confidence interval is given as

Point estimator $\pm$ 1.96 $\times$ (Standard error of the estimator)

For the difference in two population means, the confidence interval is approximated as

$$(\bar{x}_1 - \bar{x}_2) \pm 1.96\sqrt{\frac{s_1^2}{n_1} + \frac{s_2^2}{n_2}}$$

$$(2.70 - 2.54) \pm 1.96\sqrt{\frac{.36}{100} + \frac{.40}{100}}$$

$$.16 \pm .17$$

or $-.01 < (\mu_1 - \mu_2) < .33$. This interval gives you a range of possible values for the difference in the population means. Since the hypothesized difference, $(\mu_1 - \mu_2) = 0$, is contained in the confidence interval, you should not reject H_0. Look at the signs of the possible values in the confidence interval. You cannot tell from the interval whether the difference in the means is negative $(-)$, positive $(+)$, or zero (0)—the latter of the three would indicate that the two means are the same. Hence, you can really reach no conclusion in terms of the question posed. There is not enough evidence to indicate that there is a difference in the average achievements for car owners versus non-owners. The conclusion is the same one reached in Example 9.9.

Exercises

Basic Techniques

9.14　Independent random samples of 80 measurements were drawn from two quantitative populations, 1 and 2. Here is a summary of the sample data:

	Sample 1	Sample 2
Sample size	80	80
Sample mean	11.6	9.7
Sample variance	27.9	38.4

a. If your research objective is to show that μ_1 is larger than μ_2, state the alternative and the null hypotheses that you would choose for a statistical test.

b. Is the test in part a one- or two-tailed?

c. Calculate the test statistic that you would use for the test in part a. Based on your knowledge of the standard normal distribution, is this a likely or unlikely observation, assuming that H_0 is true and the two population means are the same?

d. *p-value approach:* Find the *p*-value for the test. Test for a significant difference in the population means at the 1% significance level.

e. *Critical value approach:* Find the rejection region when $\alpha = .01$. Do the data provide sufficient evidence to indicate a difference in the population means?

9.15 Independent random samples of 36 and 45 observations are drawn from two quantitative populations, 1 and 2, respectively. The sample data summary is shown here:

	Sample 1	Sample 2
Sample size	36	45
Sample mean	1.24	1.31
Sample variance	.0560	.0540

Do the data present sufficient evidence to indicate that the mean for population 1 is smaller than the mean for population 2? Use one of the two methods of testing presented in this section, and explain your conclusions.

9.16 Suppose you wish to detect a difference between μ_1 and μ_2 (either $\mu_1 > \mu_2$ or $\mu_1 < \mu_2$) and, instead of running a two-tailed test using $\alpha = .05$, you use the following test procedure. You wait until you have collected the sample data and have calculated $\bar{x}_1$ and $\bar{x}_2$. If $\bar{x}_1$ is larger than $\bar{x}_2$, you choose the alternative hypothesis $H_a : \mu_1 > \mu_2$ and run a one-tailed test placing $\alpha_1 = .05$ in the upper tail of the z distribution. If, on the other hand, $\bar{x}_2$ is larger than $\bar{x}_1$, you reverse the procedure and run a one-tailed test, placing $\alpha_2 = .05$ in the lower tail of the z distribution. If you use this procedure and if μ_1 actually equals μ_2, what is the probability α that you will conclude that μ_1 is not equal to μ_2 (i.e., what is the probability α that you will incorrectly reject H_0 when H_0 is true)? This exercise demonstrates why statistical tests should be formulated *prior* to observing the data.

Applications

9.17 An experiment was planned to compare the mean time (in days) required to recover from a common cold for persons given a daily dose of 4 milligrams (mg) of vitamin C versus those who were not given a vitamin supplement. Suppose that 35 adults were randomly selected for each treatment category and that the mean recovery times and standard deviations for the two groups were as follows:

	No Vitamin Supplement	4 mg Vitamin C
Sample size	35	35
Sample mean	6.9	5.8
Sample standard deviation	2.9	1.2

a. Suppose your research objective is to show that the use of vitamin C reduces the mean time required to recover from a common cold and its complications. Give the null and alternative hypotheses for the test. Is this a one- or a two-tailed test?

b. Conduct the statistical test of the null hypothesis in part a and state your conclusion. Test using $\alpha = .05$.

9.18 Americans are becoming more conscious about the importance of good nutrition, and some researchers believe we may be altering our diets to include less red meat and more fruits and vegetables. To test the theory that the consumption of red meat has decreased over the last 10 years, a researcher decides to select hospital nutrition records for 400 subjects surveyed 10 years ago and to compare their average amount of beef consumed per year to amounts consumed by an equal number of subjects interviewed this year. The data are given in the table.

	Ten Years Ago	This Year
Sample mean	73	63
Sample standard deviation	25	28

a. Do the data present sufficient evidence to indicate that per-capita beef consumption has decreased in the last 10 years? Test at the 1% level of significance.

b. Find a 99% lower confidence bound for the difference in the average per-capita beef consumptions for the two groups. (This calculation was done as part of Exercise 8.64.) Does your confidence bound confirm your conclusions in part a? Explain. What additional information does the confidence bound give you?

9.19 Analyses of drinking water samples for 100 homes in each of two different sections of a city gave the following means and standard deviations of lead levels (in parts per million):

	Section 1	Section 2
Sample size	100	100
Mean	34.1	36.0
Standard deviation	5.9	6.0

a. Calculate the test statistic and its p-value (observed significance level) to test for a difference in the two population means. Use the p-value to evaluate the statistical significance of the results at the 5% level.

b. Use a 95% confidence interval to estimate the difference in the mean lead levels for the two sections of the city.

c. Suppose that the city environmental engineers will be concerned only if they detect a difference of more than 5 parts per million in the two sections of the city. Based on your confidence interval in part b, is the statistical significance in part a of *practical significance* to the city engineers? Explain.

9.20 In an attempt to compare the starting salaries for college graduates who majored in education and the social sciences (see Exercise 8.41), random samples of 50 recent college graduates in each major were selected and the following information was obtained:

Major	Mean	SD
Education	35,554	2225
Social science	33,348	2375

a. Do the data provide sufficient evidence to indicate a difference in average starting salaries for college graduates who majored in education and the social sciences? Test using $\alpha = .05$.

b. Compare your conclusions in part a with the results of part b in Exercise 8.41. Are they the same? Explain.

9.21 In Exercise 8.18, we explored the average cost of lodging at three different hotel chains.[3] We randomly select 50 billing statements from the computer databases of the Marriott, Radisson, and Wyndham hotel chains, and record the nightly room rates. A portion of the sample data is shown in the table.

	Marriott	Radisson
Sample average	$120	$95
Sample standard deviation	17.5	10

a. Before looking at the data, would you have any preconceived idea about the direction of the difference between the average room rates for these two hotels? If not, what null and alternative hypotheses should you test?

b. Use the *critical value* approach to determine if there is a significant difference in the average room rates for the Marriott and the Radisson hotel chains. Use $\alpha = .01$.

c. Find the *p*-value for this test. Does this *p*-value confirm the results of part b?

9.22 Refer to Exercise 9.21. The table below shows the sample data collected to compare the average room rates at the Wyndham and Radisson hotel chains.[3]

	Wyndham	Radisson
Sample average	$110	$95
Sample standard deviation	16.5	10

a. Do the data provide sufficient evidence to indicate a difference in the average room rates for the Wyndham and the Radisson hotel chains? Use $\alpha = .05$.

b. Construct a 95% confidence interval for the difference in the average room rates for the two chains. Does this interval confirm your conclusions in part a?

9.23 The addition of MMT, a compound containing manganese (Mn), to gasoline as an octane enhancer has caused concern about human exposure to Mn because high intakes have been linked to serious health effects. In a study of ambient air concentrations of fine Mn, Wallace and Slonecker presented the accompanying summary information about the amounts of fine Mn (in nanograms per cubic meter) in mostly rural national park sites and in mostly urban California sites.[4]

	National Parks	California
Mean	.94	2.8
Standard deviation	1.2	2.8
Number of sites	36	26

a. Is there sufficient evidence to indicate that the mean concentrations differ for these two types of sites at the $\alpha = .05$ level of significance? Use the large-sample z-test. What is the *p*-value of this test?

b. Construct a 95% confidence interval for $(\mu_1 - \mu_2)$. Does this interval confirm your conclusions in part a?

9.5 A Large-Sample Test of Hypothesis for a Binomial Proportion

When a random sample of n identical trials is drawn from a binomial population, the sample proportion $\hat{p}$ has an approximately normal distribution when n is large, with mean p and standard error

$$SE = \sqrt{\frac{pq}{n}}$$

When you test a hypothesis about p, the proportion in the population possessing a certain attribute, the test follows the same general form as the large-sample tests in Sections 9.3 and 9.4. To test a hypothesis of the form

$$H_0 : p = p_0$$

versus a one- or two-tailed alternative

$$H_a : p > p_0 \quad \text{or} \quad H_a : p < p_0 \quad \text{or} \quad H_a : p \neq p_0$$

the test statistic is constructed using $\hat{p}$, the best estimator of the true population proportion p. The sample proportion $\hat{p}$ is standardized, using the hypothesized mean and standard error, to form a test statistic z, which has a standard normal distribution if H_0 is true. This large-sample test is summarized next.

Large-Sample Statistical Test for p

1. Null hypothesis: $H_0 : p = p_0$
2. Alternative hypothesis:

One-Tailed Test	Two-Tailed Test
$H_a : p > p_0$	$H_a : p \neq p_0$
(or $H_a : p < p_0$)	

3. Test statistic: $z = \dfrac{\hat{p} - p_0}{\text{SE}} = \dfrac{\hat{p} - p_0}{\sqrt{\dfrac{p_0 q_0}{n}}}$ with $\hat{p} = \dfrac{x}{n}$

   where x is the number of successes in n binomial trials.[†]
4. Rejection region: Reject H_0 when

One-Tailed Test	Two-Tailed Test
$z > z_\alpha$	$z > z_{\alpha/2}$ or $z < -z_{\alpha/2}$
(or $z < -z_\alpha$ when the alternative hypothesis is $H_a : p < p_0$)	

   or when p-value $< \alpha$

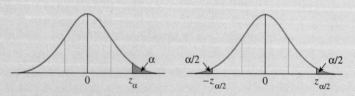

Assumption: The sampling satisfies the assumptions of a binomial experiment (see Section 5.2), and n is large enough so that the sampling distribution of $\hat{p}$ can be approximated by a normal distribution ($np_0 > 5$ and $nq_0 > 5$).

[†]An equivalent test statistic can be found by multiplying the numerator and denominator by z by n to obtain

$$z = \frac{x - np_0}{\sqrt{np_0 q_0}}$$

EXAMPLE 9.11 Regardless of age, about 20% of American adults participate in fitness activities at least twice a week. However, these fitness activities change as the people get older, and occasionally participants become nonparticipants as they age. In a local survey of $n = 100$ adults over 40 years old, a total of 15 people indicated that they participated in a fitness activity at least twice a week. Do these data indicate that the participation rate for adults over 40 years of age is significantly less than the 20% figure? Calculate the p-value and use it to draw the appropriate conclusions.

Solution Assuming that the sampling procedure satisfies the requirements of a binomial experiment, you can answer the question posed using a one-tailed test of hypothesis:

$$H_0 : p = .2 \quad \text{versus} \quad H_a : p < .2$$

Begin by assuming that H_0 is true—that is, the true value of p is $p_0 = .2$. Then $\hat{p} = x/n$ will have an approximate normal distribution with mean p_0 and standard error $\sqrt{p_0 q_0/n}$. [This is different from the estimation procedure in which the unknown standard error is estimated by $\sqrt{\hat{p}\hat{q}/n}$.] The observed value of $\hat{p}$ is $15/100 = .15$ and the test statistic is

$$z = \frac{\hat{p} - p_0}{\sqrt{\dfrac{p_0 q_0}{n}}} = \frac{.15 - .20}{\sqrt{\dfrac{(.20)(.80)}{100}}} = -1.25$$

The p-value associated with this test is found as the area under the standard normal curve to the left of $z = -1.25$ as shown in Figure 9.12. Therefore,

$$p\text{-value} = P(z < -1.25) = .1056$$

FIGURE 9.12
p-value for
Example 9.11

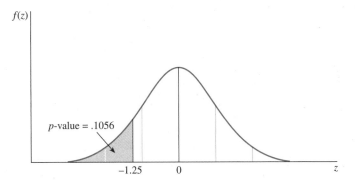

If you use the guidelines for evaluating p-values, then .1056 is greater than .10, and you would not reject H_0. There is insufficient evidence to conclude that the percentage of adults over age 40 who participate in fitness activities twice a week is less than 20%.

Statistical Significance and Practical Importance

It is important to understand the difference between results that are "significant" and results that are practically "important." In statistical language, the word *significant* does not necessarily mean "important," but only that the results could not have occurred by chance. For example, suppose that in Example 9.11, the researcher had used $n = 400$

adults in her experiment and had observed the same sample proportion. The test statistic is now

$$z = \frac{\hat{p} - p_0}{\sqrt{\dfrac{p_0 q_0}{n}}} = \frac{.15 - .20}{\sqrt{\dfrac{(.20)(.80)}{400}}} = -2.50$$

with

$$p\text{-value} = P(z < -2.50) = .0062$$

Now the results are *highly significant:* H_0 is rejected, and there is sufficient evidence to indicate that the percentage of adults over age 40 who participate in physical fitness activities is less than 20%. However, is this drop in activity really *important*? Suppose that physicians would be concerned only about a drop in physical activity of more than 10%. Within what limits does the true value of p actually lie? Using a 95% confidence interval, you have

$$\hat{p} \pm 1.96 \sqrt{\frac{\hat{p}\hat{q}}{n}}$$

$$.15 \pm 1.96 \sqrt{\frac{(.15)(.85)}{400}}$$

$$.15 \pm .035$$

or $.115 < p < .185$. The physical activity for adults aged 40 and older has dropped from 20% but not below 10%, so the results, though *statistically significant,* are not *practically important.*

In this book, you will learn how to determine whether results are statistically significant. When you use these procedures in a practical situation, however, you must also make sure the results are practically important.

Exercises   Basic Techniques

9.24   A random sample of $n = 1000$ observations from a binomial population produced $x = 279$.

   a. If your research hypothesis is that p is less than .3, what should you choose for your alternative hypothesis? Your null hypothesis?

   b. What is the critical value that determines the rejection region for your test with $\alpha = .05$?

   c. Do the data provide sufficient evidence to indicate that p is less than .3? Use a 5% significance level.

9.25   A random sample of $n = 1400$ observations from a binomial population produced $x = 529$.

   a. If your research hypothesis is that p differs from .4, what hypotheses should you test?

   b. Calculate the test statistic and its p-value. Use the p-value to evaluate the statistical significance of the results at the 1% level.

   c. Do the data provide sufficient evidence to indicate that p is different from .4?

9.26   A random sample of 120 observations was selected from a binomial population, and 72 successes were observed. Do the data provide sufficient evidence to indicate that p is greater than .5? Use one of the two methods of testing presented in this section, and explain your conclusions.

Applications

9.27   It has been reported that approximately 60% of U.S. households have two or more television sets and that at least half of Americans sometimes watch television alone.[5] Suppose that $n = 75$ U.S.

households are sampled, and of those sampled, 49 had two or more television sets and 35 respondents sometimes watch television alone.

a. Two claims can be tested using the sample information. What are the two sets of hypotheses to be tested?

b. Do the data present sufficient evidence to contradict the claim that at least half of Americans sometimes watch television alone?

c. Do the data present sufficient evidence to show that the 60% figure claimed in the magazine article is incorrect?

9.28 A peony plant with red petals was crossed with another plant having streaky petals. A geneticist states that 75% of the offspring resulting from this cross will have red flowers. To test this claim, 100 seeds from this cross were collected and germinated and 58 plants had red petals.

a. What hypothesis should you use to test the geneticist's claim?

b. Calculate the test statistic and its p-value. Use the p-value to evaluate the statistical significance of the results at the 1% level.

9.29 Of those women who are diagnosed to have early-stage breast cancer, one-third eventually die of the disease. Suppose a community public health department instituted a screening program to provide for the early detection of breast cancer and to increase the survival rate p of those diagnosed to have the disease. A random sample of 200 women was selected from among those who were periodically screened by the program and who were diagnosed to have the disease. Let x represent the number of those in the sample who survive the disease.

a. If you wish to detect whether the community screening program has been effective, state the null hypothesis that should be tested.

b. State the alternative hypothesis.

c. If 164 women in the sample of 200 survive the disease, can you conclude that the community screening program was effective? Test using $\alpha = .05$ and explain the practical conclusions from your test.

d. Find the p-value for the test and interpret it.

9.30 Suppose that 10% of the fields in a given agricultural area are infested with the sweet potato whitefly. One hundred fields in this area are randomly selected, and 25 are found to be infested with whitefly.

a. Assuming that the experiment satisfies the conditions of the binomial experiment, do the data indicate that the proportion of infested fields is greater than expected? Use the p-value approach, and test using a 5% significance level.

b. If the proportion of infested fields is found to be significantly greater than .10, why is this of practical significance to the agronomist? What practical conclusions might she draw from the results?

9.31 An article in the *Washington Post* stated that nearly 45% of the U.S. population is born with brown eyes, although they don't necessarily stay that way.[6] To test the newspaper's claim, a random sample of 80 people was selected, and 32 had brown eyes. Is there sufficient evidence to dispute the newspaper's claim regarding the proportion of brown-eyed people in the United States? Use $\alpha = .01$.

9.32 Refer to Exercise 9.31. Contact lenses, worn by about 26 million Americans, come in many styles and colors. Most Americans wear soft lenses, with the most popular colors being the blue varieties (25%), followed by greens (24%), and then hazel or brown. A random sample of 80 tinted contact lens wearers was checked for the color of their lenses. Of these people, 22 wore blue lenses and only 15 wore green lenses.[6]

a. Do the sample data provide sufficient evidence to indicate that the proportion of tinted contact lens wearers who wear blue lenses is different from 25%? Use $\alpha = .05$.

b. Do the sample data provide sufficient evidence to indicate that the proportion of tinted contact lens wearers who wear green lenses is different from 24%? Use $\alpha = .05$.

c. Is there any reason to conduct a one-tailed test for either part a or b? Explain.

9.33 According to the National Center for Education Statistics in Washington, DC, approximately 16% of all elementary school teachers are men.[7] A researcher randomly selected 1000 elementary school teachers in California from a statewide computer database and found that 142 were men. Does this sample provide sufficient evidence that the percentage of male elementary school teachers in California is different from the national percentage?

9.6 A Large-Sample Test of Hypothesis for the Difference between Two Binomial Proportions

When random and independent samples are selected from two *binomial* populations, the focus of the experiment may be the difference $(p_1 - p_2)$ in the proportions of individuals or items possessing a specified characteristic in the two populations. In this situation, you can use the difference in the sample proportions $(\hat{p}_1 - \hat{p}_2)$ along with its standard error,

$$\text{SE} = \sqrt{\frac{p_1 q_1}{n_1} + \frac{p_2 q_2}{n_2}}$$

in the form of a z-statistic to test for a significant difference in the two population proportions. The null hypothesis to be tested is usually of the form

$$H_0 : p_1 = p_2 \quad \text{or} \quad H_0 : (p_1 - p_2) = 0$$

versus either a one- or two-tailed alternative hypothesis. The formal test of hypothesis is summarized in the next display. In estimating the standard error for the z-statistic, you should use the fact that when H_0 is true, the two population proportions are equal to some common value—say, p. To obtain the best estimate of this common value, the sample data are "pooled" and the estimate of p is

$$\hat{p} = \frac{\text{Total number of successes}}{\text{Total number of trials}} = \frac{x_1 + x_2}{n_1 + n_2}$$

Remember that, in order for the difference in the sample proportions to have an approximately normal distribution, the sample sizes must be large and the proportions should not be too close to 0 or 1.

Large-Sample Statistical Test for $(p_1 - p_2)$

1. Null hypothesis: $H_0 : (p_1 - p_2) = 0$ or equivalently $H_0 : p_1 = p_2$

2. Alternative hypothesis:

One-Tailed Test	Two-Tailed Test
$H_a : (p_1 - p_2) > 0$	$H_a : (p_1 - p_2) \neq 0$
[or $H_a : (p_1 - p_2) < 0$]	

3. Test statistic: $z = \dfrac{(\hat{p}_1 - \hat{p}_2) - 0}{\text{SE}} = \dfrac{\hat{p}_1 - \hat{p}_2}{\sqrt{\dfrac{p_1 q_1}{n_1} + \dfrac{p_2 q_2}{n_2}}} = \dfrac{\hat{p}_1 - \hat{p}_2}{\sqrt{\dfrac{pq}{n_1} + \dfrac{pq}{n_2}}}$

(continued)

Large-Sample Statistical Test for ($p_1 - p_2$) *(continued)*

where $\hat{p}_1 = x_1/n_1$ and $\hat{p}_2 = x_2/n_2$. Since the common value of $p_1 = p_2 = p$ (used in the standard error) is unknown, it is estimated by

$$\hat{p} = \frac{x_1 + x_2}{n_1 + n_2}$$

and the test statistic is

$$z = \frac{(\hat{p}_1 - \hat{p}_2) - 0}{\sqrt{\dfrac{\hat{p}\hat{q}}{n_1} + \dfrac{\hat{p}\hat{q}}{n_2}}} \quad \text{or} \quad z = \frac{\hat{p}_1 - \hat{p}_2}{\sqrt{\hat{p}\hat{q}\left(\dfrac{1}{n_1} + \dfrac{1}{n_2}\right)}}$$

4. Rejection region: Reject H_0 when

One-Tailed Test

$z > z_\alpha$
[or $z < -z_\alpha$ when the alternative hypothesis is $H_a : (p_1 - p_2) < 0$]

Two-Tailed Test

$z > z_{\alpha/2}$ or $z < -z_{\alpha/2}$

or when p-value $< \alpha$

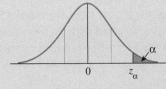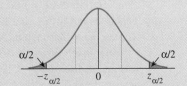

Assumptions: Samples are selected in a random and independent manner from two binomial populations, and n_1 and n_2 are large enough so that the sampling distribution of ($\hat{p}_1 - \hat{p}_2$) can be approximated by a normal distribution. That is, $n_1\hat{p}_1$, $n_1\hat{q}_1$, $n_2\hat{p}_2$, and $n_2\hat{q}_2$ should all be greater than 5.

EXAMPLE 9.12   The records of a hospital show that 52 men in a sample of 1000 men versus 23 women in a sample of 1000 women were admitted because of heart disease. Do these data present sufficient evidence to indicate a higher rate of heart disease among men admitted to the hospital? Use $\alpha = .05$.

Solution   Assume that the number of patients admitted for heart disease has an approximate binomial probability distribution for both men and women with parameters p_1 and p_2, respectively. Then, since you wish to determine whether $p_1 > p_2$, you will test the null hypothesis $p_1 = p_2$—that is, $H_0 : (p_1 - p_2) = 0$—against the alternative hypothesis $H_a : p_1 > p_2$ or, equivalently, $H_a : (p_1 - p_2) > 0$. To conduct this test, use the z-test statistic and approximate the standard error using the pooled estimate of p. Since H_a implies a one-tailed test, you can reject H_0 only for large values of z. Thus, for $\alpha = .05$, you can reject H_0 if $z > 1.645$ (see Figure 9.13).

The pooled estimate of p required for the standard error is

$$\hat{p} = \frac{x_1 + x_2}{n_1 + n_2} = \frac{52 + 23}{1000 + 1000} = .0375$$

FIGURE 9.13
Location of the rejection region in Example 9.12

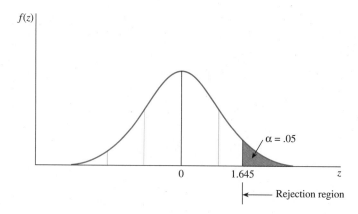

and the test statistic is

$$z = \frac{\hat{p}_1 - \hat{p}_2}{\sqrt{\hat{p}\,\hat{q}\left(\dfrac{1}{n_1} + \dfrac{1}{n_2}\right)}} = \frac{.052 - .023}{\sqrt{(.0375)(.9625)\left(\dfrac{1}{1000} + \dfrac{1}{1000}\right)}} = 3.41$$

Since the computed value of z falls in the rejection region, you can reject the hypothesis that $p_1 = p_2$. The data present sufficient evidence to indicate that the percentage of men entering the hospital because of heart disease is higher than that of women. (NOTE: This does not imply that the *incidence* of heart disease is higher in men. Perhaps fewer women enter the hospital when afflicted with the disease!)

How *much* different are the proportions of men and women entering the hospital with heart disease? A 95% confidence interval will help you find a range of likely values for the difference:

$$(\hat{p}_1 - \hat{p}_2) \pm 1.96\sqrt{\frac{\hat{p}_1\hat{q}_1}{n_1} + \frac{\hat{p}_2\hat{q}_2}{n_2}}$$

$$(.052 - .023) \pm 1.96\sqrt{\frac{.052(.948)}{1000} + \frac{.023(.977)}{1000}}$$

$$.029 \pm .017$$

or $.012 < (p_1 - p_2) < .046$. The difference in the proportions is roughly 1% to 5% higher for men. Is this of *practical importance*? This is a question for the researcher to answer.

In some situations, you may need to test for a difference D_0 (other than 0) between two binomial proportions. If this is the case, the test statistic is modified for testing $H_0 : (p_1 - p_2) = D_0$, and a pooled estimate for a common p is no longer used in the standard error. The modified test statistic is

$$z = \frac{(\hat{p}_1 - \hat{p}_2) - D_0}{\sqrt{\dfrac{\hat{p}_1\hat{q}_1}{n_1} + \dfrac{\hat{p}_2\hat{q}_2}{n_2}}}$$

Although this test statistic is not used often, the procedure is no different from other large-sample tests you have already mastered!

Exercises   Basic Techniques

9.34   Independent random samples of $n_1 = 140$ and $n_2 = 140$ observations were randomly selected from binomial populations 1 and 2, respectively. Sample 1 had 74 successes, and sample 2 had 81 successes.

a. Suppose you have no preconceived idea as to which parameter, p_1 or p_2, is the larger, but you want to detect only a difference between the two parameters if one exists. What should you choose as the alternative hypothesis for a statistical test? The null hypothesis?

b. Calculate the standard error of the difference in the two sample proportions, $(\hat{p}_1 - \hat{p}_2)$. Make sure to use the pooled estimate for the common value of p.

c. Calculate the test statistic that you would use for the test in part a. Based on your knowledge of the standard normal distribution, is this a likely or unlikely observation, assuming that H_0 is true and the two population proportions are the same?

d. *p-value approach:* Find the p-value for the test. Test for a significant difference in the population proportions at the 1% significance level.

e. *Critical value approach:* Find the rejection region when $\alpha = .01$. Do the data provide sufficient evidence to indicate a difference in the population proportions?

9.35   Refer to Exercise 9.34. Suppose, for practical reasons, you know that p_1 cannot be larger than p_2.

a. Given this knowledge, what should you choose as the alternative hypothesis for your statistical test? The null hypothesis?

b. Does your alternative hypothesis in part a imply a one- or two-tailed test? Explain.

c. Conduct the test and state your conclusions. Test using $\alpha = .05$.

9.36   Independent random samples of 280 and 350 observations were selected from binomial populations 1 and 2, respectively. Sample 1 had 132 successes, and sample 2 had 178 successes. Do the data present sufficient evidence to indicate that the proportion of successes in population 1 is smaller than the proportion in population 2? Use one of the two methods of testing presented in this section, and explain your conclusions.

Applications

9.37   An experiment was conducted to test the effect of a new drug on a viral infection. The infection was induced in 100 mice, and the mice were randomly split into two groups of 50. The first group, the *control group,* received no treatment for the infection. The second group received the drug. After a 30-day period, the proportions of survivors, $\hat{p}_1$ and $\hat{p}_2$, in the two groups were found to be .36 and .60, respectively.

a. Is there sufficient evidence to indicate that the drug is effective in treating the viral infection? Use $\alpha = .05$.

b. Use a 95% confidence interval to estimate the actual difference in the cure rates for the treated versus the control groups.

9.38   Marketing to targeted age groups has become a standard method of advertising, even in movie theater advertising. Advertisers use computer software to track the demographics of moviegoers and then decide on the type of products to advertise before a particular movie.[1] One statistic that might be of interest is how frequently adults with children under 18 attend movies as compared to those without children. Suppose that a theater database is used to randomly select 1000 adult ticket purchasers. These adults are then surveyed and asked whether they were frequent moviegoers—that is, do they attend movies 12 or more times a year? The results are shown in the table:

	With Children under 18	Without Children
Sample size	440	560
Number who attend 12^+ times per year	123	145

a. Is there a significant difference in the population proportions of frequent moviegoers in these two demographic groups? Use $\alpha = .01$.

b. Why would a statistically significant difference in these population proportions be of *practical importance* to the advertiser?

9.39 In Exercise 8.47, you investigated whether Mars, Inc., uses the same proportion of red M&Ms® in its plain and peanut varieties. Random samples of plain and peanut M&Ms provide the following sample data for the experiment:

	Plain	Peanut
Sample size	56	32
Number of red M&Ms	12	8

Use a test of hypothesis to determine whether there is a significant difference in the proportions of red candies for the two types of M&Ms. Let $\alpha = .05$ and compare your results with those of Exercise 8.47.

9.40 American teenagers are very excited about technology and the impact it will have on their lives. In fact, most have regular access to computers and the Internet. A survey of 508 teenagers, aged 12–17, was conducted for *Newsweek* with the following sample results.[8] Assume that the sample consisted of 272 girls and 236 boys.

	Boys	Girls
Have online experience	66%	56%
Think technology makes a positive difference in their lives	57%	46%

a. Is there a difference in the proportions of boys and girls who "surf the net"? Calculate the test statistic and its *p*-value. Use the *p*-value to evaluate the statistical significance of the results.

b. Do boys and girls differ in the proportions who think that technology makes a positive difference in their lives? Use one of the two methods of testing presented in this section, and explain your conclusions.

c. Are the two tests in parts a and b independent? Explain how this might affect the reliability of your conclusions.

9.41 Refer to Exercise 9.40. The survey conducted by *Newsweek* found that 89% of teens use computers several times a week, and that there is no significant difference in this percentage between teens from lower-income homes and teens from wealthier families. Does this surprise you? What would make this statistically significant result of *practical importance*? (HINT: Where do teens have access to computers?)

9.42 A large study was conducted to test the effectiveness of an experimental blood thinner, clopidogrel, in warding off heart attacks and strokes.[9] The study involved 19,185 patients who had suffered heart attacks, strokes, or pain from clogged arteries. They were each randomly assigned to take either aspirin or clopidogrel for a period of 1 to 3 years. Of the patients taking aspirin, 5.3% suffered heart attacks, strokes, or death from cardiovascular disease; the corresponding percentage in the clopidogrel patients was 5.8%.

a. The article states that each patient was randomly assigned to one of the two medications. Explain how you could use the random number table to make these assignments.

b. Although the article does not give the sample sizes, assume that the randomization in part a results in 9925 aspirin and 9260 clopidogrel assignments. Are the results of the study statistically significant? Use the appropriate test of hypothesis.

c. What do the results of the study mean in terms of their *practical importance*?

9.43 Does a baby's sleeping position affect the development of motor skills? In one study, 343 full-term infants were examined at their 4-month checkups for various developmental milestones, such as rolling over, grasping a rattle, reaching for an object, and so on.[10] The baby's predominant sleep position—either prone (on the stomach) or supine (on the back) or side—was determined by a telephone interview with the parent. The sample results for 320 of the 343 infants for whom information was received are shown here:

	Prone	Supine or Side
Number of infants	121	199
Number that roll over	93	119

The researcher reported that infants who slept in the side or supine position were less likely to roll over at the 4-month checkup than infants who slept primarily in the prone position ($P < .001$). Use a large-sample test of hypothesis to confirm or refute the researcher's conclusion.

9.7 Some Comments on Testing Hypotheses

A statistical test of hypothesis is a fairly clear-cut procedure that enables an experimenter to either reject or accept the null hypothesis H_0, with measured risks α and β. The experimenter can control the risk of falsely rejecting H_0 by selecting an appropriate value of α. On the other hand, the value of β depends on the sample size and the values of the parameter under test that are of practical importance to the experimenter. When this information is not available, an experimenter may decide to select an affordable sample size, in the hope that the sample will contain sufficient information to reject the null hypothesis. The chance that this decision is in error is given by α, whose value has been set in advance. If the sample does not provide sufficient evidence to reject H_0, the experimenter may wish to state the results of the test as "The data do not support the rejection of H_0" rather than accepting H_0 without knowing the chance of error β.

Some experimenters prefer to use the observed p-value of the test to evaluate the strength of the sample information in deciding to reject H_0. These values can usually be generated by computer and are often used in reports of statistical results:

- If the p-value is greater than .05, the results are reported as NS—not significant at the 5% level.
- If the p-value lies between .05 and .01, the results are reported as $P < .05$—significant at the 5% level.
- If the p-value lies between .01 and .001, the results are reported as $P < .01$—"highly significant" or significant at the 1% level.
- If the p-value is less than .001, the results are reported as $P < .001$—"very highly significant" or significant at the .1% level.

Still other researchers prefer to construct a confidence interval for a parameter and perform a test informally. If the value of the parameter specified by H_0 is included within the upper and lower limits of the confidence interval, then "H_0 is not rejected." If the value of the parameter specified by H_0 is not contained within the interval, then "H_0 is rejected." These results will agree with a two-tailed test; one-sided confidence bounds are used for one-tailed alternatives.

Finally, consider the choice between a one- and two-tailed test. In general, experimenters wish to know whether a treatment causes what could be a beneficial increase in a parameter or what might be a harmful decrease in a parameter. Therefore, most tests are two-tailed unless a one-tailed test is strongly dictated by practical considerations. For example, assume you will sustain a large financial loss if the mean μ is greater than μ_0 but not if it is less. You will then want to detect values larger than μ_0 with a high probability and thereby use a right-tailed test. In the same vein, if pollution levels higher than μ_0 cause critical health risks, then you will certainly wish to detect levels higher than μ_0 with a right-tailed test of hypothesis. In any case, the choice of a one- or two-tailed test should be dictated by the practical consequences that result from a decision to reject or not reject H_0 in favor of the alternative.

Key Concepts and Formulas

I. Parts of a Statistical Test

1. **Null hypothesis:** a contradiction of the alternative hypothesis
2. **Alternative hypothesis:** the hypothesis the researcher wants to support
3. **Test statistic** and its **p-value:** sample evidence calculated from the sample data
4. **Rejection region—critical values** and **significance levels:** values that separate rejection and nonrejection of the null hypothesis
5. **Conclusion:** Reject or do not reject the null hypothesis, stating the practical significance of your conclusion

II. Errors and Statistical Significance

1. The **significance level** α is the probability of rejecting H_0 when it is in fact true.
2. The **p-value** is the probability of observing a test statistic as extreme as or more extreme than the one observed; also, the smallest value of α for which H_0 can be rejected.
3. When the **p-value** is less than the **significance level** α, the null hypothesis is rejected. This happens when the **test statistic** exceeds the **critical value.**
4. In a **Type II error,** β is the probability of accepting H_0 when it is in fact false. The **power of the test** is $(1 - \beta)$, the probability of rejecting H_0 when it is false.

III. Large-Sample Test Statistics Using the z Distribution

To test one of the four population parameters when the sample sizes are large, use the following test statistics:

Parameter	Test Statistic
μ	$z = \dfrac{\bar{x} - \mu_0}{s/\sqrt{n}}$
p	$z = \dfrac{\hat{p} - p_0}{\sqrt{\dfrac{p_0 q_0}{n}}}$
$\mu_1 - \mu_2$	$z = \dfrac{(\bar{x}_1 - \bar{x}_2) - D_0}{\sqrt{\dfrac{s_1^2}{n_1} + \dfrac{s_2^2}{n_2}}}$
$p_1 - p_2$	$z = \dfrac{\hat{p}_1 - \hat{p}_2}{\sqrt{\hat{p}\hat{q}\left(\dfrac{1}{n_1} + \dfrac{1}{n_2}\right)}}$ or $z = \dfrac{(\hat{p}_1 - \hat{p}_2) - D_0}{\sqrt{\dfrac{\hat{p}_1\hat{q}_1}{n_1} + \dfrac{\hat{p}_2\hat{q}_2}{n_2}}}$

Supplementary Exercises

Starred (*) exercises are optional.

9.44   **a.** Define α and β for a statistical test of hypothesis.

      b. For a fixed sample size n, if the value of α is decreased, what is the effect on β?

      c. In order to decrease both α and β for a particular alternative value of μ, how must the sample size change?

9.45   What is the p-value for a test of hypothesis? How is it calculated for a large-sample test?

9.46   What conditions must be met so that the z test can be used to test a hypothesis concerning a population mean μ?

9.47   Define the power of a statistical test. As the alternative value of μ gets farther from μ_0, how is the power affected?

9.48   Refer to Exercise 8.29 and the collection of water samples to estimate the mean acidity (in pH) of rainfalls in the northeastern United States. As noted, the pH for pure rain falling through clean air is approximately 5.7. The sample of $n = 40$ rainfalls produced pH readings with $\bar{x} = 3.7$ and $s = .5$. Do the data provide sufficient evidence to indicate that the mean pH for rainfalls is more acidic ($H_a : \mu < 5.7$ pH) than pure rainwater? Test using $\alpha = .05$. Note that this inference is appropriate only for the area in which the rainwater specimens were collected.

9.49   A manufacturer of automatic washers provides a particular model in one of three colors. Of the first 1000 washers sold, it is noted that 400 were of the first color. Can you conclude that more than one-third of all customers have a preference for the first color?

      a. Find the p-value for the test.

      b. If you plan to conduct your test using $\alpha = .05$, what will be your test conclusions?

9.50   The commercialism of our space program[11] was the topic of Exercise 8.52. In a survey of 500 men and 500 women, 20% of the men and 26% of the women responded that space should remain commercial-free.

      a. Is there a significant difference in the population proportions of men and women who think that space should remain commercial-free? Use $\alpha = .01$.

      b. Can you think of any reason why a statistically significant difference in these population proportions might be of *practical importance* to the administrators of the space program? To the advertisers? To the politicians?

9.51   The pH factor is a measure of the acidity or alkalinity of water. A reading of 7.0 is neutral; values in excess of 7.0 indicate alkalinity; those below 7.0 imply acidity. Loren Hill states that the best chance of catching bass occurs when the pH of the water is in the range 7.5 to 7.9.[12] Suppose you suspect that acid rain is lowering the pH of your favorite fishing spot and you wish to determine whether the pH is less than 7.5.

      a. State the alternative and null hypotheses that you would choose for a statistical test.

      b. Does the alternative hypothesis in part a imply a one- or a two-tailed test? Explain.

      c. Suppose that a random sample of 30 water specimens gave pH readings with $\bar{x} = 7.3$ and $s = .2$. Just glancing at the data, do you think that the difference $\bar{x} - 7.5 = -.2$ is large enough to indicate that the mean pH of the water samples is less than 7.5? (Do *not* conduct the test.)

      d. Now conduct a statistical test of the hypotheses in part a and state your conclusions. Test using $\alpha = .05$. Compare your statistically based decision with your intuitive decision in part c.

9.52   A central Pennsylvania attorney reported that the Northumberland County district attorney's (DA) office trial record showed only 6 convictions in 27 trials from January to mid-July 1997. Four central Pennsylvania county DAs responded, "Don't judge us by statistics!"[13]

      a. If the attorney's information is correct, would you reject a claim by the DA of a 50% or greater conviction rate?

b. The *actual* records show that there have been 455 guilty pleas and 48 cases that have gone to trial. Even assuming that the 455 guilty pleas are the *only* convictions of the 503 cases reported, what is the 95% confidence interval for p, the true proportion of convictions by this district attorney?

c. Using the results of part b, are you willing to reject a figure of 50% or greater for the true conviction rate? Explain.

9.53 In an article entitled "A Strategy for Big Bucks," Charles Dickey discusses studies of the habits of white-tailed deer that indicate that they live and feed within very limited ranges—approximately 150 to 205 acres.[14] To determine whether there was a difference between the ranges of deer located in two different geographic areas, 40 deer were caught, tagged, and fitted with small radio transmitters. Several months later, the deer were tracked and identified, and the distance x from the release point was recorded. The mean and standard deviation of the distances from the release point were as follows:

	Location 1	Location 2
Sample size	40	40
Sample mean	2980 ft	3205 ft
Sample standard deviation	1140 ft	963 ft

a. If you have no preconceived reason for believing one population mean is larger than another, what would you choose for your alternative hypothesis? Your null hypothesis?

b. Does your alternative hypothesis in part a imply a one- or a two-tailed test? Explain.

c. Do the data provide sufficient evidence to indicate that the mean distances differ for the two geographic locations? Test using $\alpha = .05$.

9.54 In a study to assess various effects of using a female model in automobile advertising, 100 men were shown photographs of two automobiles matched for price, color, and size, but of different makes. One of the automobiles was shown with a female model to 50 of the men (group A), and both automobiles were shown without the model to the other 50 men (group B). In group A, the automobile shown with the model was judged as more expensive by 37 men; in group B, the same automobile was judged as the more expensive by 23 men. Do these results indicate that using a female model influences the perceived cost of an automobile? Use a one-tailed test with $\alpha = .05$.

9.55 Random samples of 200 bolts manufactured by a type A machine and 200 bolts manufactured by a type B machine showed 16 and 8 defective bolts, respectively. Do these data present sufficient evidence to suggest a difference in the performance of the machine types? Use $\alpha = .05$.

9.56 Exercise 7.49 reported that the biomass for tropical woodlands, thought to be about 35 kilograms per square meter (kg/m^2), may in fact be too high and that tropical biomass values vary regionally—from about 5 to 55 kg/m^2.[15] Suppose you measure the tropical biomass in 400 randomly selected square-meter plots and obtain $\bar{x} = 31.75$ and $s = 10.5$. Do the data present sufficient evidence to indicate that scientists are overestimating the mean biomass for tropical woodlands and that the mean is in fact lower than estimated?

a. State the null and alternative hypotheses to be tested.

b. Locate the rejection region for the test with $\alpha = .01$.

c. Conduct the test and state your conclusions.

9.57 A researcher believes that the fraction p_1 of Republicans in favor of the death penalty is greater than the fraction p_2 of Democrats in favor of the death penalty. She acquired independent random samples of 200 Republicans and 200 Democrats and found 46 Republicans and 34 Democrats favoring the death penalty. Do these data support the researcher's belief?

a. Find the p-value for the test.

b. If you plan to conduct your test using $\alpha = .05$, what will be your test conclusions?

9.58* Refer to Exercise 9.57. Some thought should have been given to designing a test for which β is tolerably low when p_1 exceeds p_2 by an important amount. For example, find a common sample size n for a test with $\alpha = .05$ and $\beta \le .20$, when in fact p_1 exceeds p_2 by .1. [HINT: The maximum value of $p(1 - p)$ is .25.]

9.59 In a comparison of the mean 1-month weight losses for women aged 20–30 years, these sample data were obtained for each of two diets:

	Diet I	Diet II
Sample size n	40	40
Sample mean $\bar{x}$	10 lb	8 lb
Sample variance s^2	4.3	5.7

Do the data provide sufficient evidence to indicate that diet I produces a greater mean weight loss than diet II? Use $\alpha = .05$.

9.60 An agronomist has shown experimentally that a new irrigation/fertilization regimen produces an increase of 2 bushels per quadrat (significant at the 1% level) when compared with the regimen currently in use. The cost of implementing and using the new regimen will not be a factor if the increase in yield exceeds 3 bushels per quadrat. Is statistical significance the same as practical importance in this situation? Explain.

9.61 A test of the breaking strengths of two different types of cables was conducted using samples of $n_1 = n_2 = 100$ pieces of each type of cable.

Cable I	Cable II
$\bar{x}_1 = 1925$	$\bar{x}_2 = 1905$
$s_1 = 40$	$s_2 = 30$

Do the data provide sufficient evidence to indicate a difference between the mean breaking strengths of the two cables? Use $\alpha = .05$.

9.62 The braking ability was compared for two 2002 automobile models. Random samples of 64 automobiles were tested for each type. The recorded measurement was the distance (in feet) required to stop when the brakes were applied at 40 miles per hour. These are the computed sample means and variances:

$$\bar{x}_1 = 118 \qquad \bar{x}_2 = 109$$
$$s_1^2 = 102 \qquad s_2^2 = 87$$

Do the data provide sufficient evidence to indicate a difference between the mean stopping distances for the two models?

9.63 A fruit grower wants to test a new spray that a manufacturer claims will *reduce* the loss due to insect damage. To test the claim, the grower sprays 200 trees with the new spray and 200 other trees with the standard spray. The following data were recorded:

	New Spray	Standard Spray
Mean yield per tree $\bar{x}$ (lb)	240	227
Variance s^2	980	820

a. Do the data provide sufficient evidence to conclude that the mean yield per tree treated with the new spray exceeds that for trees treated with the standard spray? Use $\alpha = .05$.

b. Construct a 95% confidence interval for the difference between the mean yields for the two sprays.

9.64 A biologist hypothesizes that high concentrations of actinomycin D inhibit RNA synthesis in cells and hence the production of proteins as well. An experiment conducted to test this theory compared the RNA synthesis in cells treated with two concentrations of actinomycin D: .6 and .7 microgram per milliliter. Cells treated with the lower concentration (.6) of actinomycin D showed that 55 out of 70 developed normally, whereas only 23 out of 70 appeared to develop normally for the higher concentration (.7). Do these data provide sufficient evidence to indicate a difference between the rates of normal RNA synthesis for cells exposed to the two different concentrations of actinomycin D?

a. Find the p-value for the test.

b. If you plan to conduct your test using $\alpha = .05$, what will be your test conclusions?

9.65 How do California high school students compare to students nationwide in their college readiness, as measured by their SAT scores? The national average scores for the class of 2001 were 506 on the verbal portion and 514 on the math portion.[16] Suppose that 100 California students from the class of 2001 were randomly selected and their SAT scores recorded in the following table:

	Verbal	Math
Sample average	499	516
Sample standard deviation	21	20

a. Do the data provide sufficient evidence to indicate that the average verbal score for all California students in the class of 2001 is different from the national average? Test using $\alpha = .05$.

b. Do the data provide sufficient evidence to indicate that the average math score for all California students in the class of 2001 is different from the national average? Test using $\alpha = .05$.

c. Could you use this data to determine if there is a difference between the average math and verbal scores for all California students in the class of 2001? Explain your answer.

Exercises DO IT YOURSELF!

9.66 In Exercise 8.97, it was reported that amusement and theme parks average 100 full-time employees, but at peak season average 665 workers per site.[17] If $n = 40$ amusement and theme parks are sampled at peak season and the average number of full-time workers is found to be 652 with a standard deviation of 32, does this contradict the reported average of 665 workers per site?

a. What are the null and alternative hypotheses to be tested?

b. Use the **Large-Sample Test of a Population Mean** applet to find the observed value of the test statistic.

c. Use the **Large-Sample Test of a Population Mean** applet to find the p-value for this test.

d. Based on your results from part c, what conclusions can you draw about the average of 665 workers reported in Exercise 8.97?

9.67 The daily wages in a particular industry are normally distributed with a mean of $54 and a standard deviation of $11.88. Suppose a company in this industry employs 40 workers and pays them $51.50 per week on the average. Can these workers be viewed as a random sample from among all workers in the industry?

a. What are the null and alternative hypotheses to be tested?

b. Use the **Large-Sample Test of a Population Mean** applet to find the observed value of the test statistic.

c. Use the **Large-Sample Test of a Population Mean** applet to find the *p*-value for this test.

d. If you planned to conduct your test using $\alpha = .01$, what would be your test conclusions?

e. Was it necessary to know that the daily wages are normally distributed? Explain your answer.

9.68   Refer to Example 9.8. Use the **Power of a z-Test** applet to verify the power of the test of

$$H_0: \mu = 880 \quad \text{versus} \quad H_a: \mu \neq 880$$

for values of μ equal to 870, 875, 880, 885 and 890. Check your answers against the values shown in Table 9.2.

9.69   Refer to Example 9.8.

a. Use the method given in Example 9.8 to calculate the power of the test of

$$H_0: \mu = 880 \quad \text{versus} \quad H_a: \mu \neq 880$$

when $n = 30$ and the true value of μ is 870 tons.

b. Repeat part a using $n = 70$ and $\mu = 870$ tons.

c. Use the **Power of a z-Test** applet to verify your hand-calculated results in parts a and b.

d. What is the effect of increasing the sample size on the power of the test?

9.70   Use the appropriate slider on the **Power of a z-Test** applet to answer the following questions. Write a sentence for each part, describing what you see using the applet.

a. What effect does increasing the sample size have on the power of the test?

b. What effect does increasing the distance between the true value of μ and the hypothesized value, $\mu = 880$, have on the power of the test?

c. What effect does decreasing the significance level α have on the power of the test?

Case Study   An Aspirin A Day . . . ?

On Wednesday, January 27, 1988, the front page of the *New York Times* read "Heart attack risk found to be cut by taking aspirin: Lifesaving effects seen." A very large study of U.S. physicians showed that a single aspirin tablet taken every other day reduced by one-half the risk of heart attack in men.[18] Three days later, a headline in the *Times* read "Value of daily aspirin disputed in British study of heart attacks." How could two seemingly similar studies, both involving doctors as participants, reach such opposite conclusions?

The U.S. physicians' health study consisted of two randomized clinical trials in one. The first tested the hypothesis that 325 milligrams (mg) of aspirin taken every other day reduces mortality from cardiovascular disease. The second tested whether 50 mg of β-carotene taken on alternate days decreases the incidence of cancer. From names on an American Medical Association computer tape, 261,248 male physicians between the ages of 40 and 84 were invited to participate in the trial. Of those who responded, 59,285 were willing to participate. After the exclusion of those physicians who had a history of medical disorders, or who were currently taking aspirin or had negative reactions to aspirin, 22,071 physicians were randomized into one of four treatment groups: (1) buffered aspirin and β-carotene, (2) buffered aspirin and a β-carotene placebo, (3) aspirin placebo and β-carotene, and (4) aspirin placebo and β-carotene placebo. Thus, half were assigned to receive aspirin and half to receive β-carotene.

The study was conducted as a double-blind study, in which neither the participants nor the investigators responsible for following the participants knew to which group a participant belonged. The results of the American study concerning myocardial infarctions (the technical name for heart attacks) are given in the following table:

American Study

	Aspirin ($n = 11{,}037$)	Placebo ($n = 11{,}034$)
Myocardial infarction		
Fatal	5	18
Nonfatal	99	171
Total	104	189

The objective of the British study was to determine whether 500 mg of aspirin taken daily would reduce the incidence of and mortality from cardiovascular disease. In 1978 all male physicians in the United Kingdom were invited to participate. After the usual exclusions, 5139 doctors were randomly allocated to take aspirin, unless some problem developed, and one-third were randomly allocated to *avoid* aspirin. Placebo tablets were not used, so the study was not blind! The results of the British study are given here:

British Study

	Aspirin ($n = 3429$)	Control ($n = 1710$)
Myocardial infarction		
Fatal	89 (47.3)	47 (49.6)
Nonfatal	80 (42.5)	41 (43.3)
Total	169 (89.8)	88 (92.9)

To account for unequal sample sizes, the British study reported rates per 10,000 subject-years alive (given in parentheses).

1. Test whether the American study does in fact indicate that the rate of heart attacks for physicians taking 325 mg of aspirin every other day is significantly different from the rate for those on the placebo. Is the American claim justified?
2. Repeat the analysis using the data from the British study in which one group took 500 mg of aspirin every day and the control group took none. Based on their data, is the British claim justified?
3. Can you think of some possible reasons the results of these two studies, which were alike in some respects, produced such different conclusions?

Data Sources

1. Adapted from Paul, Pamela, "Coming Soon: More Ads Tailored to Your Tastes," *American Demographics,* August 2001, p. 28.
2. *The Princeton Review* (Irvine, CA, 1993).
3. Adapted from "Suite Dreams," *Consumer Reports,* July 2001, pp. 12–16.
4. Lance Wallace and Terrence Slonecker, "Ambient Air Concentrations of Fine ($PM_{2.5}$) Manganese in the U.S. National Parks and in California and Canadian Cities: The Possible Impact of Adding MMT to Unleaded Gasoline," *Journal of the Air and Waste Management Association* 47 (June 1997):642–651.
5. Diane Crispell, "TV Soloists," *American Demographics,* May 1997, p. 32.
6. "Seeing the World Through Tinted Lenses," *Washington Post,* 16 March 1993, p. 5.

7. Laurie Lucas, "It's Elementary, Mister," *The Press-Enterprise* (Riverside, CA), 28 May 1997, p. D-1.

8. "Teenagers and Technology," (Focus on Technology) *Newsweek,* 28 April 1997, Vol. 129, No. 17, p. 86.

9. "New Drug a Bit Better Than Aspirin," *The Press-Enterprise* (Riverside, CA), 14 November 1996, p. A-14.

10. Jonathan W. Jantz, C.D. Blosser, and L.A. Fruechting, "A Motor Milestone Change Noted with a Change in Sleep Position," *Archives of Pediatric Adolescent Medicine* 151 (June 1997):565.

11. Adapted from "Toplines: To the Moon?" Rebecca Gardyn, ed., *American Demographics,* August 2001, p. 9.

12. Loren Hill, *Bassmaster,* September/October 1980.

13. Joe Sylvester, "Area District Attorneys: Don't Judge Us by Statistics," *The Daily Item* (Sunbury, PA), 17 August 1997, p. A-1.

14. Charles Dickey, "A Strategy for Big Bucks," *Field and Stream,* October 1990.

15. *Science News* 136 (19 August 1989):124.

16. "College-Entry Scores Show Little Change in California, *The Press-Enterprise* (Riverside, CA), Wednesday, August 29, 2001, p. A-10.

17. Sandra Yin, Pamela Paul, and David Whelan, "What Summer Break?" *American Demographics,* July 2001, p. 64.

18. Joel B. Greenhouse and Samuel W. Greenhouse, "An Aspirin a Day . . . ?" *Chance: New Directions for Statistics and Computing* 1, no. 4 (1988):24–31.

10

Inference from Small Samples

Case Study

Will a flexible work-week schedule result in positive benefits for both employer and employee? Four obvious benefits are (1) less time traveling from field positions to the office, (2) fewer employees parked in the parking lot, (3) reduced travel expenses, and (4) allowance for employees to have another day off. But does the flexible work week make employees more efficient and cause them to take fewer sick and personal days? The answers to some of these questions are posed in the case study at the end of this chapter.

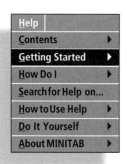

General Objective

The basic concepts of large-sample statistical estimation and hypothesis testing for practical situations involving population means and proportions were introduced in Chapters 8 and 9. Because all of these techniques rely on the Central Limit Theorem to justify the normality of the estimators and test statistics, they apply only when the samples are large. This chapter supplements the large-sample techniques by presenting small-sample tests and confidence intervals for population means and variances. Unlike their large-sample counterparts, these small-sample techniques require the sampled populations to be normal, or approximately so.

Specific Topics

1. Student's t distribution (10.2)
2. Small-sample inferences concerning a population mean (10.3)
3. Small-sample inferences concerning the difference in two means: Independent random samples (10.4)
4. Paired-difference test: Dependent samples (10.5)
5. Inferences concerning a population variance (10.6)
6. Comparing two population variances (10.7)
7. Small-sample assumptions (10.8)

10.1 Introduction

Suppose you need to run an experiment to estimate a population mean or the difference between two means. The process of collecting the data may be very expensive or very time-consuming. If you cannot collect a *large sample,* the estimation and test procedures of Chapters 8 and 9 are of no use to you.

This chapter introduces some equivalent statistical procedures that can be used when the *sample size is small.* The estimation and testing procedures involve these familiar parameters:

- A single population mean, μ
- The difference between two population means, $(\mu_1 - \mu_2)$
- A single population variance, σ^2
- The comparison of two population variances, σ_1^2 and σ_2^2

Small-sample tests and confidence intervals for binomial proportions will be omitted from our discussion.[†]

10.2 Student's *t* Distribution

In conducting an experiment to evaluate a new but very costly process for producing synthetic diamonds, you are able to study only six diamonds generated by the process. How can you use these six measurements to make inferences about the average weight μ of diamonds from this process?

In discussing the sampling distribution of $\bar{x}$ in Chapter 7, we made these points:

- When the original sampled population is normal, $\bar{x}$ and $z = (\bar{x} - \mu)/(\sigma/\sqrt{n})$ both have normal distributions, *for any sample size.*
- When the original sampled population is *not* normal, $\bar{x}$, $z = (\bar{x} - \mu)/(\sigma/\sqrt{n})$, and $z \approx (\bar{x} - \mu)/(s/\sqrt{n})$ all have approximately normal distributions, if the sample size is *large.*

Unfortunately, when the sample size n is small, the statistic $(\bar{x} - \mu)/(s/\sqrt{n})$ *does not* have a normal distribution. Therefore, all the critical values of z that you used in Chapters 8 and 9 are no longer correct. For example, you *cannot say* that $\bar{x}$ will lie within 1.96 standard errors of μ 95% of the time.

This problem is not new; it was studied by statisticians and experimenters in the early 1900s. To find the sampling distribution of this statistic, there are two ways to proceed:

- Use an empirical approach. Draw repeated samples and compute $(\bar{x} - \mu)/(s/\sqrt{n})$ for each sample. The relative frequency distribution that you construct using these values will approximate the shape and location of the sampling distribution.
- Use a mathematical approach to derive the actual density function or curve that describes the sampling distribution.

This second approach was used by an Englishman named W.S. Gosset in 1908. He derived a complicated formula for the density function of

$$t = \frac{\bar{x} - \mu}{s/\sqrt{n}}$$

[†]A small-sample test for the binomial parameter *p* will be presented in Chapter 15.

for random samples of size n from a normal population, and he published his results under the pen name "Student." Ever since, the statistic has been known as **Student's t.** It has the following characteristics:

- It is mound-shaped and symmetric about $t = 0$, just like z.
- It is more variable than z, with "heavier tails"; that is, the t curve does not approach the horizontal axis as quickly as z does. This is because the t statistic involves two random quantities, $\bar{x}$ and s, whereas the z statistic involves only the sample mean, $\bar{x}$. You can see this phenomenon in Figure 10.1.
- The shape of the t distribution depends on the sample size n. As n increases, the variability of t decreases because the estimate s of σ is based on more and more information. Eventually, when n is infinitely large, the t and z distributions are identical!

FIGURE 10.1
Standard normal
z and the t
distribution with
5 degrees of
freedom

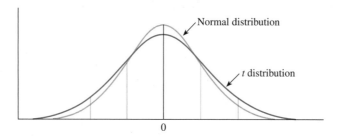

The divisor $(n - 1)$ in the formula for the sample variance s^2 is called the **number of degrees of freedom (df) associated with s^2.** It determines the *shape* of the t distribution. The origin of the term *degrees of freedom* is theoretical and refers to the number of independent squared deviations in s^2 that are available for estimating σ^2. These degrees of freedom may change for different applications and, since they specify the correct t distribution to use, you need to remember to calculate the correct degrees of freedom for each application.

The table of probabilities for the standard normal z distribution is no longer useful in calculating critical values or p-values for the t statistic. Instead, you will use Table 4 in Appendix I, which is partially reproduced in Table 10.1. When you index a particular number of degrees of freedom, the table records t_a, a value of t that has tail area a to its right, as shown in Figure 10.2.

TABLE 10.1
Format of the
Student's t table
from Table 4 in
Appendix I

df	$t_{.100}$	$t_{.050}$	$t_{.025}$	$t_{.010}$	$t_{.005}$	df
1	3.078	6.314	12.706	31.821	63.657	1
2	1.886	2.920	4.303	6.965	9.925	2
3	1.638	2.353	3.182	4.541	5.841	3
4	1.533	2.132	2.776	3.747	4.604	4
5	1.476	2.015	2.571	3.365	4.032	5
6	1.440	1.943	2.447	3.143	3.707	6
7	1.415	1.895	2.365	2.998	3.499	7
8	1.397	1.860	2.306	2.896	3.355	8
9	1.383	1.833	2.262	2.821	3.250	9
.	.	.	.	.	.	.
.	.	.	.	.	.	.
.	.	.	.	.	.	.
26	1.315	1.706	2.056	2.479	2.779	26
27	1.314	1.703	2.052	2.473	2.771	27
28	1.313	1.701	2.048	2.467	2.763	28
29	1.311	1.699	2.045	2.462	2.756	29
inf.	1.282	1.645	1.960	2.326	2.576	inf.

FIGURE 10.2
Tabulated values of
Student's *t*

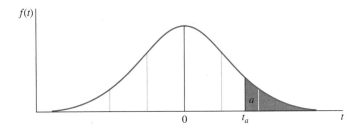

EXAMPLE 10.1

For a *t* distribution with 5 degrees of freedom, the value of *t* that has area .05 to its right is found in row 5 in the column marked $t_{.050}$. For this particular *t* distribution, the area to the right of *t* = 2.015 is .05; only 5% of all values of the *t* statistic will exceed this value.

Help
Contents ▶
Getting Started ▶
How Do I ▶
Search for Help on...
How to Use Help ▶
Do It Yourself ▶
About MINITAB ▶

DO IT YOURSELF!

You can use the **Student's *t* Probabilities** applet to find the *t*-value described in Example 10.1. The first applet, shown in Figure 10.3, provides *t*-values and their two-tailed probabilities, while the second applet provides *t*-values and one-tailed probabilities. Use the slider on the right side of the applet to select the proper degrees of freedom. For Example 10.1, you should choose *df* = 5 and type .10 in the box marked "prob:" at the bottom of the first applet. The applet will provide the value of *t* that puts .05 in one tail of the *t* distribution. The second applet will show the identical *t* for a one-tailed area of .05. The applet in Figure 10.3 shows *t* = 2.02 which is correct to two decimal places. We will use this applet for the *Do It Yourself Exercises* at the end of the chapter.

FIGURE 10.3
**Student's *t*
Probabilities** applet

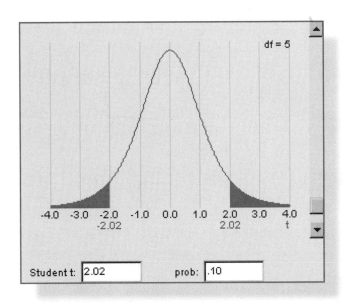

EXAMPLE 10.2   Suppose you have a sample of size $n = 10$ from a normal distribution. Find a value of t such that only 1% of all values of t will be smaller.

Solution   The degrees of freedom that specify the correct t distribution are $df = n - 1 = 9$, and the necessary t-value must be in the lower portion of the distribution, with area .01 to its left, as shown in Figure 10.4. Since the t distribution is symmetric about 0, this value is simply the negative of the value on the right-hand side with area .01 to its right, or $-t_{.01} = -2.821$.

FIGURE 10.4
t Distribution for
Example 10.2

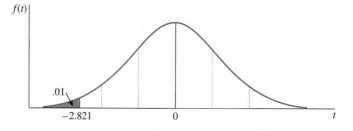

DO IT YOURSELF!

Comparing the *t* and *z* Distributions

Look at one of the columns in Table 10.1. As the degrees of freedom increase, the critical value of t decreases until, when $df = $ inf., the critical t-value is the same as the critical z-value for the same tail area. You can use the **Comparing *t* and *z*** applet to visualize this concept. Look at the three applets in Figure 10.5, which show the critical

FIGURE 10.5   Comparing *t* and *z* applet

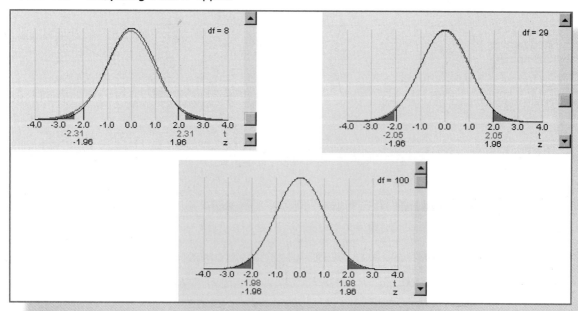

values for $t_{.025}$ compared with $z_{.025}$ for $df = 8$, 29 and 100. (The slider on the right side of the applet allows you to change the df.) The red curve (black in Fig. 10.5) is the standard normal distribution, with $z_{.025} = 1.96$.

The blue curve is the t distribution. With 8 df, you can clearly see a difference in the t and z curves, especially in the critical values that cut off an area of .025 in the tails. As the degrees of freedom increase, the difference in the shapes of t and z becomes very similar, as do their critical values, until at $df = 100$, there is almost no difference. This helps to explain why we use $n = 30$ as the somewhat arbitrary dividing line between large and small samples. When $n = 30$ ($df = 29$), the critical values of t are quite close to their normal counterparts. Rather than produce a t table with rows for many more degrees of freedom, the critical values of z are sufficient when the sample size reaches $n = 30$.

Assumptions behind Student's t Distribution

The critical values of t allow you to make reliable inferences *only if* you follow all the rules; that is, your sample must meet these requirements specified by the t distribution:

- The sample must be randomly selected.
- The population from which you are sampling must be normally distributed.

These requirements may seem quite restrictive. How can you possibly know the shape of the probability distribution for the entire population if you have only a sample? If this were a serious problem, however, the t statistic could be used in only very limited situations. Fortunately, the shape of the t distribution is not affected very much as long as the sampled population has an *approximately mound-shaped* distribution. Statisticians say that the t statistic is **robust,** meaning that the distribution of the statistic does not change significantly when the normality assumptions are violated.

How can you tell whether your sample is from a normal population? Although there are statistical procedures designed for this purpose, the easiest and quickest way to check for normality is to use the graphical techniques of Chapter 2: Draw a dotplot or construct a stem and leaf plot. As long as your plot tends to "mound up" in the center, you can be fairly safe in using the t statistic for making inferences.

The random sampling requirement, on the other hand, is quite critical if you want to produce reliable inferences. If the sample is not random, or if it does not at least *behave as* a random sample, then your sample results may be affected by some unknown factor and your conclusions may be incorrect. When you design an experiment or read about experiments conducted by others, look critically at the way the data have been collected!

10.3 Small-Sample Inferences Concerning a Population Mean

As with large-sample inference, small-sample inference can involve either **estimation** or **hypothesis testing,** depending on the preference of the experimenter. We explained the basics of these two types of inference in the earlier chapters, and we use them again now, with a different sample statistic, $t = (\bar{x} - \mu)/(s/\sqrt{n})$, and a different sampling distribution, the Student's t, with $(n - 1)$ degrees of freedom.

Small-Sample Hypothesis Test for μ

1. Null hypothesis: $H_0 : \mu = \mu_0$
2. Alternative hypothesis:

One-Tailed Test	Two-Tailed Test
$H_a : \mu > \mu_0$	$H_a : \mu \neq \mu_0$
(or $H_a : \mu < \mu_0$)	

3. Test statistic: $t = \dfrac{\bar{x} - \mu_0}{s/\sqrt{n}}$

4. Rejection region: Reject H_0 when

One-Tailed Test	Two-Tailed Test
$t > t_\alpha$	$t > t_{\alpha/2}$ or $t < -t_{\alpha/2}$
(or $t < -t_\alpha$ when the alternative hypothesis is $H_a : \mu < \mu_0$)	

or when p-value $< \alpha$

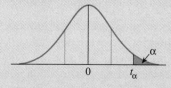 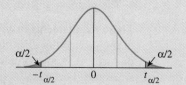

The critical values of t, t_α, and $t_{\alpha/2}$ are based on $(n - 1)$ degrees of freedom. These tabulated values can be found using Table 4 of Appendix I or the **Student's t Probabilities** applet.
Assumption: The sample is randomly selected from a normally distributed population.

Small-Sample $(1 - \alpha)100\%$ Confidence Interval for μ

$$\bar{x} \pm t_{\alpha/2} \frac{s}{\sqrt{n}}$$

where $s/\sqrt{n}$ is the estimated standard error of $\bar{x}$, often referred to as the **standard error of the mean.**

EXAMPLE 10.3   A new process for producing synthetic diamonds can be operated at a profitable level only if the average weight of the diamonds is greater than .5 karat. To evaluate the profitability of the process, six diamonds are generated, with recorded weights .46, .61, .52, .48, .57, and .54 karat. Do the six measurements present sufficient evidence to indicate that the average weight of the diamonds produced by the process is in excess of .5 karat?

Solution   The population of diamond weights produced by this new process has mean μ, and the hypotheses to be tested are

$$H_0 : \mu = .5 \quad \text{versus} \quad H_a : \mu > .5$$

You can use your calculator to verify that the mean and standard deviation for the six diamond weights are .53 and .0559, respectively. The test statistic is a t statistic, calculated as

$$t = \frac{\bar{x} - \mu_0}{s/\sqrt{n}} = \frac{.53 - .5}{.0559/\sqrt{6}} = 1.32$$

As with the large-sample tests, the test statistic provides evidence for either rejecting or accepting H_0 depending on how far from the center of the t distribution it lies. If you choose a 5% level of significance ($\alpha = .05$), the right-tailed rejection region is found using the critical values of t from Table 4 in Appendix I. With $df = n - 1 = 5$, you can reject H_0 if $t > t_{.05} = 2.015$, as shown in Figure 10.6. Since the calculated value of the test statistic, 1.32, does not fall into the rejection region, you cannot reject H_0. The data do not present sufficient evidence to indicate that the mean diamond weight exceeds .5 karat.

FIGURE 10.6
Rejection region for Example 10.3

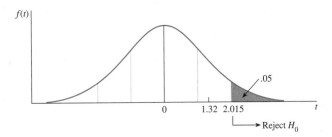

As in Chapter 9, the conclusion to *accept* H_0 would require the difficult calculation of β, the probability of a Type II error. To avoid this problem, we choose to *not reject* H_0. We can then calculate a range of possible values for μ using a small sample confidence interval. This interval is similar to the large sample confidence interval, except that the critical $z_{\alpha/2}$ is replaced by a critical $t_{\alpha/2}$ from Table 4. For this example, a 95% confidence interval for μ is:

$$\bar{x} \pm t_{\alpha/2}\left(\frac{s}{\sqrt{n}}\right)$$

$$.53 \pm 2.571\left(\frac{.0559}{\sqrt{6}}\right)$$

$$.53 \pm .059$$

The 95% interval estimate for μ is .471 to .589. The range of possible values includes mean diamond weights both smaller and greater than .5; this confirms the failure of our test to show that μ exceeds .5.

Remember from Chapter 9 that there are two ways to conduct a test of hypothesis:

- **The critical value approach:** Set up a rejection region based on the critical values of the statistic's sampling distribution. If the test statistic falls in the rejection region, you can reject H_0.

■ **The p-value approach:** Calculate the p-value based on the observed value of the test statistic. If the p-value is smaller than the significance level, α, you can reject H_0. If there is no *preset* significance level, use the guidelines in Section 9.3 to judge the statistical significance of your sample results.

We used the first approach in the solution to Example 10.3. We use the second approach to solve Example 10.4.

EXAMPLE 10.4

Labels on 1-gallon cans of paint usually indicate the drying time and the area that can be covered in one coat. Most brands of paint indicate that, in one coat, a gallon will cover between 250 and 500 square feet, depending on the texture of the surface to be painted. One manufacturer, however, claims that a gallon of its paint will cover 400 square feet of surface area. To test this claim, a random sample of ten 1-gallon cans of white paint were used to paint ten identical areas using the same kind of equipment. The actual areas (in square feet) covered by these 10 gallons of paint are given here:

310   311   412   368   447
376   303   410   365   350

Do the data present sufficient evidence to indicate that the average coverage differs from 400 square feet? Find the p-value for the test, and use it to evaluate the statistical significance of the results.

Solution

To test the claim, the hypotheses to be tested are

$$H_0 : \mu = 400 \quad \text{versus} \quad H_a : \mu \neq 400$$

The sample mean and standard deviation for the recorded data are

$$\bar{x} = 365.2 \qquad s = 48.417$$

and the test statistic is

$$t = \frac{\bar{x} - \mu_0}{s/\sqrt{n}} = \frac{365.2 - 400}{48.417/\sqrt{10}} = -2.27$$

The p-value for this test is the probability of observing a value of the t statistic as contradictory to the null hypothesis as the one observed for this set of data—namely, $t = -2.27$. Since this is a two-tailed test, the p-value is the probability that either $t \leq -2.27$ or $t \geq 2.27$.

Unlike the z-table, the table for t gives the values of t corresponding to upper-tail areas equal to .100, .050, .025, .010, and .005. Consequently, you can only approximate the upper-tail area that corresponds to the probability that $t > 2.27$. Since the t statistic for this test is based on 9 df, we refer to the row corresponding to $df = 9$ in Table 4. The five critical values for various tail areas are shown in Figure 10.7, an enlargement of the

FIGURE 10.7
Calculating the p-value for Example 10.4 (shaded area $= \frac{1}{2}$ p-value)

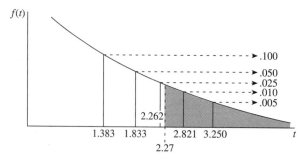

tail of the t distribution with 9 degrees of freedom. The value $t = 2.27$ falls between $t_{.025} = 2.262$ and $t_{.010} = 2.821$. Therefore, the right-tail area corresponding to the probability that $t > 2.27$ lies between .01 and .025. Since this area represents only half of the p-value, you can write

$$.01 < \frac{1}{2}(p\text{-value}) < .025 \quad \text{or} \quad .02 < p\text{-value} < .05$$

What does this tell you about the significance of the statistical results? For you to reject H_0, the p-value must be less than the specified significance level, α. Hence, you could reject H_0 at the 5% level, but not at the 2% or 1% level. Therefore, the p-value for this test would typically be reported by the experimenter as

$$p\text{-value} < .05 \quad \text{(or sometimes } P < .05)$$

For this test of hypothesis, H_0 is rejected at the 5% significance level. There is sufficient evidence to indicate that the average coverage differs from 400 square feet.

Within what limits does this average coverage *really* fall? A 95% confidence interval gives the upper and lower limits for μ as:

$$\bar{x} \pm t_{\alpha/2}\left(\frac{s}{\sqrt{n}}\right)$$

$$365.2 \pm 2.262\left(\frac{48.417}{\sqrt{10}}\right)$$

$$365.2 \pm 34.63$$

Thus, you can estimate that the average area covered by 1 gallon of this brand of paint lies in the interval 330.6 to 399.8. A more precise interval estimate (a shorter interval) can generally be obtained by increasing the sample size. Notice that the upper limit of this interval is very close to the value of 400 square feet, the coverage claimed on the label. This coincides with the fact that the observed value of $t = -2.27$ is just slightly less than the left-tail critical value of $t_{.025} = -2.262$, making the p-value just slightly less than .05.

Most statistical computing packages contain programs that will implement the Student's t test or construct a confidence interval for μ when the data are properly entered into the computer's database. Most of these programs will calculate and report the *exact p-value* of the test, allowing you to quickly and accurately draw conclusions about the statistical significance of the results. The results of the *MINITAB* one-sample t test and confidence interval procedures are given in Figure 10.8. Besides the observed value of $t = -2.27$ and the confidence interval (330.6, 399.8), the output gives the sample mean, the sample standard deviation, the standard error of the mean (SE Mean $= s/\sqrt{n}$), and the exact p-value of the test ($P = .049$). This is consistent with the range for the p-value that we found using Table 4 in Appendix I:

$$.02 < p\text{-value} < .05$$

FIGURE 10.8
MINITAB output for
Example 10.4

One-Sample T: Area
```
Test of mu = 400 vs mu not = 400

Variable       N       Mean     StDev    SE Mean
Area          10      365.2      48.4      15.3

Variable            95.0% CI             T       P
Area        (   330.6,    399.8)      -2.27   0.049
```

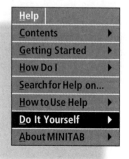

Help

Contents ▶
Getting Started ▶
How Do I ▶
Search for Help on...
How to Use Help ▶
Do It Yourself ▶
About MINITAB ▶

DO IT YOURSELF!

You can use the **Small Sample Test of a Population Mean** applet to visualize the p-values for either one- or two-tailed tests of the population mean μ. The procedure follows the same pattern as with previous applets. You enter the values of $\bar{x}$, n, and s and press "Enter" after each entry; the applet will calculate t and give you the option of choosing one- or two-tailed p-values (as well as a *cumulative* and a *middle* area that you will not need.)

FIGURE 10.9
Small Sample Test of a Population Mean applet

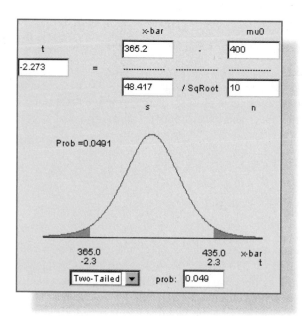

For the data of Example 10.4, the p-value is the two-tailed area to the right of $t = 2.273$ and to the left of $t = -2.273$. Can you find this same p-value in the *MINITAB* printout shown in Figure 10.8?

You can see the value of using the computer output or the Java applet to evaluate statistical results:

- The exact p-value eliminates the need for tables and critical values.
- All of the numerical calculations are done for you.

The most important job—which is left for the experimenter—is to *interpret* the results in terms of their practical significance!

Exercises

Basic Techniques

10.1 Find the following t-values in Table 4 of Appendix I:

a. $t_{.05}$ for 5 df **b.** $t_{.025}$ for 8 df

c. $t_{.10}$ for 18 df **d.** $t_{.025}$ for 30 df

10.2 Find the critical value(s) of t that specify the rejection region in these situations:

    a. A two-tailed test with $\alpha = .01$ and 12 df

    b. A right-tailed test with $\alpha = .05$ and 16 df

    c. A two-tailed test with $\alpha = .05$ and 25 df

    d. A left-tailed test with $\alpha = .01$ and 7 df

10.3 Use Table 4 in Appendix I to approximate the p-value for the t statistic in each situation:

    a. A two-tailed test with $t = 2.43$ and 12 df

    b. A right-tailed test with $t = 3.21$ and 16 df

    c. A two-tailed test with $t = -1.19$ and 25 df

    d. A left-tailed test with $t = -8.77$ and 7 df

EX1004

10.4 The test scores on a 100-point test were recorded for 20 students:

71	93	91	86	75
73	86	82	76	57
84	89	67	62	72
77	68	65	75	84

    a. Can you reasonably assume that these test scores have been selected from a normal population? Use a stem and leaf plot to justify your answer.

    b. Calculate the mean and standard deviation of the scores.

    c. If these students can be considered a random sample from the population of all students, find a 95% confidence interval for the average test score in the population.

10.5 The following $n = 10$ observations are a sample from a normal population:

7.4	7.1	6.5	7.5	7.6	6.3	6.9	7.7	6.5	7.0

    a. Find the mean and standard deviation of these data.

    b. Find a 99% confidence interval for the population mean μ.

    c. Test $H_0 : \mu = 7.5$ versus $H_a : \mu < 7.5$. Use $\alpha = .01$.

    d. Do the results of part b support your conclusion in part c?

Applications

EX1006

10.6 Is there a difference in the prices of tuna, depending on the method of packaging? *Consumer Reports* gives the estimated average price for a 6-ounce can or a 7.06-ounce pouch of tuna, based on prices paid nationally in supermarkets.[1] These prices are recorded for a variety of different brands of tuna.

Light Tuna in Water			White Tuna in Oil	White Tuna in Water	Light Tuna in Oil	
.99	.53	1.27		1.49	2.56	.62
1.92	1.41	1.22		1.29	1.92	.66
1.23	1.12	1.19		1.27	1.30	.62
.85	.63	1.22		1.35	1.79	.65
.65	.67			1.29	1.23	.60
.69	.60			1.00		.67
.60	.66			1.27		
				1.28		

Assume that the tuna brands included in this survey represent a random sample of all tuna brands available in the United States.

a. Find a 95% confidence interval for the average price for light tuna in water. Interpret this interval. That is, what does the "95%" refer to?

b. Find a 95% confidence interval for the average price for white tuna in oil. How does the width of this interval compare to the width of the interval in part a? Can you explain why?

c. Find 95% confidence intervals for the other two samples (white tuna in water and light tuna in oil.) Plot the four treatment means and their standard errors in a two-dimensional plot similar to Figure 8.5. What kind of broad comparisons can you make about the four treatments? (We will discuss the procedure for comparing more than two population means in Chapter 11.)

10.7 Industrial wastes and sewage dumped into our rivers and streams absorb oxygen and thereby reduce the amount of dissolved oxygen available for fish and other forms of aquatic life. One state agency requires a minimum of 5 parts per million (ppm) of dissolved oxygen in order for the oxygen content to be sufficient to support aquatic life. Six water specimens taken from a river at a specific location during the low-water season (July) gave readings of 4.9, 5.1, 4.9, 5.0, 5.0, and 4.7 ppm of dissolved oxygen. Do the data provide sufficient evidence to indicate that the dissolved oxygen content is less than 5 ppm? Test using $\alpha = .05$.

10.8 In a study of the infestation of the *Thenus orientalis* lobster by two types of barnacles, *Octolasmis tridens* and *O. lowei,* the carapace lengths (in millimeters) of 10 randomly selected lobsters caught in the seas near Singapore are measured[2]:

78 66 65 63 60 60 58 56 52 50

Find a 95% confidence interval for the mean carapace length of the *T. orientalis* lobsters.

EX1009

10.9 It is recognized that cigarette smoking has a deleterious effect on lung function. In a study of the effect of cigarette smoking on the carbon monoxide diffusing capacity (DL) of the lung, researchers found that current smokers had DL readings significantly lower than those of either exsmokers or nonsmokers. The carbon monoxide diffusing capacities for a random sample of $n = 20$ current smokers are listed here:

103.768	88.602	73.003	123.086	91.052
92.295	61.675	90.677	84.023	76.014
100.615	88.017	71.210	82.115	89.222
102.754	108.579	73.154	106.755	90.479

Do these data indicate that the mean DL reading for current smokers is significantly lower than 100 DL, the average for nonsmokers? Use $\alpha = .01$.

10.10 Refer to Exercise 10.9 and data set EX1009 and find a 95% confidence interval estimate for the mean DL reading for current smokers.

10.11 Organic chemists often purify organic compounds by a method known as fractional crystallization. An experimenter wanted to prepare and purify 4.85 grams (g) of aniline. Ten 4.85-g quantities of aniline were individually prepared and purified to acetanilide. The following dry yields were recorded:

3.85 3.80 3.88 3.85 3.90
3.36 3.62 4.01 3.72 3.82

Estimate the mean grams of acetanilide that can be recovered from an initial amount of 4.85 g of aniline. Use a 95% confidence interval.

10.12 Refer to Exercise 10.11. Approximately how many 4.85-g specimens of aniline are required if you wish to estimate the mean number of grams of acetanilide correct to within .06 g with probability equal to .95?

10.13 Although there are many treatments for bulimia nervosa, some subjects fail to benefit from treatment. In a study to determine which factors predict who will benefit from treatment, Wendy Baell and E.H. Wertheim found that self-esteem was one of these important predictors.[3] The table gives the mean and standard deviation of self-esteem scores prior to treatment, at posttreatment, and during a follow-up:

	Pretreatment	Posttreatment	Follow-up
Sample mean $\bar{x}$	20.3	26.6	27.7
Standard deviation s	5.0	7.4	8.2
Sample size n	21	21	20

a. Use a test of hypothesis to determine whether there is sufficient evidence to conclude that the true pretreatment mean is less than 25.

b. Find a 95% confidence interval estimate for the true posttreatment mean.

c. In Section 10.4, we will introduce small-sample techniques for making inferences about the difference between two population means. Without the formality of a statistical test, what are you willing to conclude about the differences among the three sampled population means represented by the results in the table?

EX1014

10.14 Here are the red blood cell counts (in 10^6 cells per microliter) of a healthy person measured on each of 15 days:

```
5.4   5.2   5.0   5.2   5.5
5.3   5.4   5.2   5.1   5.3
5.3   4.9   5.4   5.2   5.2
```

Find a 95% confidence interval estimate of μ, the true mean red blood cell count for this person during the period of testing.

EX1015

10.15 These data are the weights (in pounds) of 27 packages of ground beef in a supermarket meat display:

```
1.08    .99    .97   1.18   1.41   1.28    .83
1.06   1.14   1.38    .75    .96   1.08    .87
 .89    .89    .96   1.12   1.12    .93   1.24
 .89    .98   1.14    .92   1.18   1.17
```

a. Interpret the accompanying *MINITAB* printouts for the one-sample test and estimation procedures.

MINITAB output for
Exercise 10.15

```
One-Sample T: Weights
Test of mu = 1 vs mu not = 1

Variable        N      Mean     StDev    SE Mean
Weights        27    1.0522    0.1657     0.0319

Variable              95.0% CI               T       P
Weights        (  0.9867,   1.1178)      1.64   0.113
```

b. Verify the calculated values of t and the upper and lower confidence limits.

10.4 Small-Sample Inferences for the Difference between Two Population Means: Independent Random Samples

The physical setting for the problem considered in this section is the same as the one in Section 8.6, except that the sample sizes are no longer large. Independent random samples of n_1 and n_2 measurements are drawn from two populations, with means and variances μ_1, σ_1^2, μ_2, and σ_2^2, and your objective is to make inferences about $(\mu_1 - \mu_2)$, the difference between the two population means.

When the sample sizes are small, you can no longer rely on the Central Limit Theorem to ensure that the sample means will be normal. If the original populations *are* *normal*, however, then the sampling distribution of the difference in the sample means, $(\bar{x}_1 - \bar{x}_2)$, will be normal (even for small samples) with mean $(\mu_1 - \mu_2)$ and standard error

$$\sqrt{\frac{\sigma_1^2}{n_1} + \frac{\sigma_2^2}{n_2}}$$

In Chapters 7 and 8, you used the sample variances, s_1^2 and s_2^2, to calculate an *estimate* of the standard error, which was then used to form a large-sample confidence interval or a test of hypothesis based on the large-sample z statistic:

$$z \approx \frac{(\bar{x}_1 - \bar{x}_2) - (\mu_1 - \mu_2)}{\sqrt{\frac{s_1^2}{n_1} + \frac{s_2^2}{n_2}}}$$

Unfortunately, when the sample sizes are small, this statistic does not have an approximately normal distribution—nor does it have a Student's t distribution. In order to form a statistic with a sampling distribution that can be derived theoretically, you must make one more assumption.

Suppose that the variability of the measurements in the two normal populations is the same and can be measured by a common variance σ^2. That is, *both populations have exactly the same shape,* and $\sigma_1^2 = \sigma_2^2 = \sigma^2$. Then the standard error of the difference in the two sample means is

$$\sqrt{\frac{\sigma_1^2}{n_1} + \frac{\sigma_2^2}{n_2}} = \sqrt{\sigma^2\left(\frac{1}{n_1} + \frac{1}{n_2}\right)}$$

It can be proven mathematically that, if you use the appropriate sample estimate s^2 for the population variance σ^2, then the resulting test statistic,

$$t = \frac{(\bar{x}_1 - \bar{x}_2) - (\mu_1 - \mu_2)}{\sqrt{s^2\left(\frac{1}{n_1} + \frac{1}{n_2}\right)}}$$

has a *Student's t distribution.* The only remaining problem is to find the sample estimate s^2 and the appropriate number of *degrees of freedom* for the t statistic.

Remember that the population variance σ^2 describes the shape of the normal distributions from which your samples come, so that either s_1^2 or s_2^2 would give you an estimate of σ^2. But why use just one when information is provided by both? A better procedure is to combine the information in both sample variances using a *weighted average,* in which the weights are determined by the relative amount of information (the number of measurements) in each sample. For example, if the first sample contained twice as many measurements as the second, you might consider giving the first sample variance twice as much weight. To achieve this result, use this formula:

$$s^2 = \frac{(n_1 - 1)s_1^2 + (n_2 - 1)s_2^2}{n_1 + n_2 - 2}$$

Remember from Section 10.3 that the degrees of freedom for the one-sample t statistic are $(n - 1)$, the denominator of the sample estimate s^2. Since s_1^2 has $(n_1 - 1)$ df and s_2^2 has $(n_2 - 1)$ df, the total number of degrees of freedom is the sum:

$$(n_1 - 1) + (n_2 - 1) = n_1 + n_2 - 2$$

shown in the denominator of the formula for s^2.

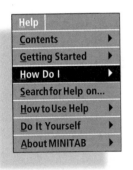

Calculate s^2?

- If you have a scientific calculator, calculate each of the two sample standard deviations s_1 and s_2 separately, using the data entry procedure for your particular calculator. These values are squared and used in this formula:

$$s^2 = \frac{(n_1 - 1)s_1^2 + (n_2 - 1)s_2^2}{n_1 + n_2 - 2}$$

It can be shown that s^2 is an unbiased estimator of the common population variance σ^2. If s^2 is used to estimate σ^2 and if the samples have been randomly and independently drawn from normal populations with a common variance, then the statistic

$$t = \frac{(\bar{x}_1 - \bar{x}_2) - (\mu_1 - \mu_2)}{\sqrt{s^2 \left(\dfrac{1}{n_1} + \dfrac{1}{n_2} \right)}}$$

has a Student's t distribution with $(n_1 + n_2 - 2)$ degrees of freedom. The small-sample estimation and test procedures for the difference between two means are given next.

Test of Hypothesis Concerning the Difference between Two Means: Independent Random Samples

1. Null hypothesis: $H_0 : (\mu_1 - \mu_2) = D_0$, where D_0 is some specified difference that you wish to test. For many tests, you will hypothesize that there is no difference between μ_1 and μ_2; that is, $D_0 = 0$.

2. Alternative hypothesis:

One-Tailed Test	Two-Tailed Test
$H_a : (\mu_1 - \mu_2) > D_0$	$H_a : (\mu_1 - \mu_2) \neq D_0$
[or $H_a: (\mu_1 - \mu_2) < D_0$]	

3. Test statistic: $t = \dfrac{(\bar{x}_1 - \bar{x}_2) - D_0}{\sqrt{s^2 \left(\dfrac{1}{n_1} + \dfrac{1}{n_2} \right)}}$ where

$$s^2 = \frac{(n_1 - 1)s_1^2 + (n_2 - 1)s_2^2}{n_1 + n_2 - 2}$$

(continued)

Test of Hypothesis Concerning the Difference between Two Means: Independent Random Samples (continued)

4. Rejection region: Reject H_0 when

One-Tailed Test	Two-Tailed Test
$t > t_\alpha$	$t > t_{\alpha/2}$ or $t < -t_{\alpha/2}$
[or $t < -t_\alpha$ when the	
alternative hypothesis is	
$H_a : (\mu_1 - \mu_2) < D_0$]	

or when p-value $< \alpha$

The critical values of t, t_α, and $t_{\alpha/2}$ are based on $(n_1 + n_2 - 2)$ df. The tabulated values can be found using Table 4 of Appendix I or the **Student's t Probabilities** applet.

Assumptions: The samples are randomly and independently selected from normally distributed populations. The variances of the populations σ_1^2 and σ_2^2 are equal.

Small-Sample $(1 - \alpha)100\%$ Confidence Interval for $(\mu_1 - \mu_2)$ Based on Independent Random Samples

$$(\bar{x}_1 - \bar{x}_2) \pm t_{\alpha/2}\sqrt{s^2\left(\frac{1}{n_1} + \frac{1}{n_2}\right)}$$

where s^2 is the pooled estimate of σ^2.

EXAMPLE 10.5 An assembly operation in a manufacturing plant requires approximately a 1-month training period for a new employee to reach maximum efficiency in assembling a device. A new method of training was suggested, and a test was conducted to compare the new method with the standard procedure. Two groups of nine new employees were trained for a period of 3 weeks, one group using the new method and the other following the standard training procedure. The length of time (in minutes) required for each employee to assemble the device was recorded at the end of the 3-week period. These measurements appear in Table 10.2. Do the data present sufficient evidence to indicate that the mean time to assemble at the end of a 3-week training period is less for the new training procedure?

TABLE 10.2
Assembly times after two training procedures

Standard Procedure	New Procedure
32	35
37	31
35	29
28	25
41	34
44	40
35	27
31	32
34	31

Solution   Let μ_1 and μ_2 be the mean time to assemble after the standard and the new training procedures, respectively. Then, since you seek evidence to support the theory that $\mu_1 > \mu_2$, you can test the null hypothesis

$$H_0 : \mu_1 = \mu_2 \qquad [\text{or } H_0 : (\mu_1 - \mu_2) = 0]$$

versus the alternative hypothesis

$$H_a : \mu_1 > \mu_2 \qquad [\text{or } H_a : (\mu_1 - \mu_2) > 0]$$

To conduct the t test for these two independent samples, you must assume that the sampled populations are both normal and have the same variance σ^2. Is this reasonable? Stem and leaf plots of the data in Figure 10.10 show at least a "mounding" pattern, so that the assumption of normality is not unreasonable.

FIGURE 10.10
Stem and leaf plots
for Example 10.5

Standard		New	
2	8	2	579
3	124	3	1124
3	557	3	5
4	14	4	0

Furthermore, the standard deviations of the two samples, calculated as

$$s_1 = 4.9441 \quad \text{and} \quad s_2 = 4.4752$$

are not different enough for us to doubt that the two distributions may have the same shape. If you make these two assumptions and calculate (using full accuracy) the pooled estimate of the common variance as

$$s^2 = \frac{(n_1 - 1)s_1^2 + (n_2 - 1)s_2^2}{n_1 + n_2 - 2} = \frac{8(4.9441)^2 + 8(4.4752)^2}{9 + 9 - 2} = 22.2361$$

you can then calculate the test statistic,

$$t = \frac{\bar{x}_1 - \bar{x}_2}{\sqrt{s^2\left(\dfrac{1}{n_1} + \dfrac{1}{n_2}\right)}} = \frac{35.22 - 31.56}{\sqrt{22.2361\left(\dfrac{1}{9} + \dfrac{1}{9}\right)}} = 1.65$$

The alternative hypothesis $H_a : \mu_1 > \mu_2$ or, equivalently, $H_a : (\mu_1 - \mu_2) > 0$ implies that you should use a one-tailed test in the upper tail of the t distribution with $(n_1 + n_2 - 2) = 16$ degrees of freedom. You can find the appropriate critical value for a rejection region with $\alpha = .05$ in Table 4 of Appendix I, and H_0 will be rejected if $t > 1.746$. Comparing the observed value of the test statistic $t = 1.65$ with the critical value $t_{.05} = 1.746$, you cannot reject the null hypothesis (see Figure 10.11). There is insufficient evidence to indicate that the new training procedure is superior at the 5% level of significance.

FIGURE 10.11
Rejection region
for Example 10.5

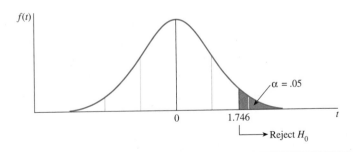

EXAMPLE 10.6 Find the *p*-value that would be reported for the statistical test in Example 10.5.

Solution The observed value of *t* for this one-tailed test is $t = 1.65$. Therefore,

$$p\text{-value} = P(t > 1.65)$$

for a *t* statistic with 16 degrees of freedom. Remember that you cannot obtain this probability directly from Table 4 in Appendix I; you can only *bound* the *p*-value using the critical values in the table. Since the observed value, $t = 1.65$, lies between $t_{.100} = 1.337$ and $t_{.050} = 1.746$, the tail area to the right of 1.65 is between .05 and .10. The *p*-value for this test would be reported as

$$.05 < p\text{-value} < .10$$

Because the *p*-value is greater than .05, most researchers would report the results as *not significant*.

Help	
Contents	▶
Getting Started	▶
How Do I	▶
Search for Help on...	
How to Use Help	▶
Do It Yourself	▶
About MINITAB	▶

DO IT YOURSELF!

You can use the **Two-Sample *t* Test: Independent Samples** applet to visualize the *p*-values for either one- or two-tailed tests of the difference between two population means. The procedure follows the same pattern as with previous applets. You need to enter summary statistics—the values of $\bar{x}_1$, $\bar{x}_2$, n_1, n_2, s_1, and s_2 and press "Enter" after each entry; the applet will calculate *t* (assuming equal variances) and give you the option of choosing one- or two-tailed *p*-values, (as well as a *cumulative* and a *middle* area that you will not need.)

FIGURE 10.12
Two-Sample
***t* Test: Independent**
Samples applet

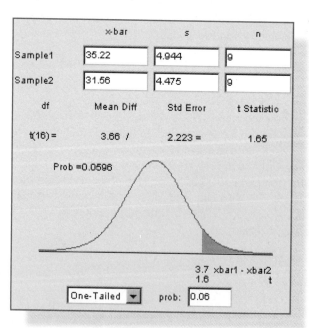

For the data of Example 10.5, the *p*-value is the one-tailed area to the right of $t = 1.65$. Does the *p*-value confirm the conclusions for the test in Example 10.5?

EXAMPLE 10.7 Use a 95% confidence interval to estimate the difference $(\mu_1 - \mu_2)$ in Example 10.5. Does the confidence interval indicate that there is a significant difference in the means?

Solution The confidence interval formula takes a familiar form—the point estimator $(\bar{x}_1 - \bar{x}_2)$ plus or minus an amount equal to $t_{\alpha/2}$ times the standard error of the estimator. Substituting into the formula, you can calculate the 95% confidence interval:

$$(\bar{x}_1 - \bar{x}_2) \pm t_{\alpha/2} \sqrt{s^2\left(\frac{1}{n_1} + \frac{1}{n_2}\right)}$$

$$(35.22 - 31.56) \pm 2.120 \sqrt{22.2361\left(\frac{1}{9} + \frac{1}{9}\right)}$$

$$3.66 \pm 4.71$$

or $-1.05 < (\mu_1 - \mu_2) < 8.37$. Since the value $(\mu_1 - \mu_2) = 0$ is included in the confidence interval, it is possible that the two means are equal. There is insufficient evidence to indicate a significant difference in the means.

Notice that the confidence interval is quite wide; if this width is not acceptable to you, you might choose to increase the size of the samples and reestimate the difference in the means using this additional information.

The two-sample procedure that uses a pooled estimate of the common variance σ^2 relies on four important assumptions:

- The samples must be *randomly selected*. Samples not randomly selected may introduce bias into the experiment and thus alter the significance levels you are reporting.
- The samples must be *independent*. If not, this is not the appropriate statistical procedure. We discuss another procedure for dependent samples in Section 10.5.
- The populations from which you sample must be *normal*. However, moderate departures from normality do not seriously affect the distribution of the test statistic, especially if the sample sizes are nearly the same.
- The population *variances should be equal* or nearly equal to ensure that the procedures are valid.

If the population variances are far from equal, there is an alternative procedure for estimation and testing that has an *approximate t* distribution in repeated sampling. As a rule of thumb, you should use this procedure if the ratio of the two sample variances,

$$\frac{\text{Larger } s^2}{\text{Smaller } s^2} > 3$$

Since the population variances are not equal, the pooled estimator s^2 is no longer appropriate, and each population variance must be estimated by its corresponding sample variance. The resulting test statistic is

$$\frac{(\bar{x}_1 - \bar{x}_2) - D_0}{\sqrt{\dfrac{s_1^2}{n_1} + \dfrac{s_2^2}{n_2}}}$$

When the sample sizes are *small*, critical values for this statistic are found using degrees of freedom approximated by the formula

$$df \approx \frac{\left(\dfrac{s_1^2}{n_1} + \dfrac{s_2^2}{n_2}\right)^2}{\dfrac{(s_1^2/n_1)^2}{(n_1 - 1)} + \dfrac{(s_2^2/n_2)^2}{(n_2 - 1)}}$$

The degrees of freedom are taken to be the integer part of this result.

Computer packages such as *MINITAB* can be used to implement this procedure, sometimes called *Satterthwaite's approximation,* as well as the *pooled method* described earlier. In fact, some experimenters choose to analyze their data using *both* methods. As long as both analyses lead to the same conclusions, you need not concern yourself with the equality or inequality of variances.

The *MINITAB* output resulting from the pooled method of analysis for the data of Example 10.5 is shown in Figure 10.13. Notice that the ratio of the two sample variances, $(4.94/4.48)^2 = 1.22$, is less than 3, which makes the pooled method appropriate. The calculated value of $t = 1.65$ and the exact *p*-value $= .059$ with 16 degrees of freedom are shown in the last line of the output. The exact *p*-value makes it quite easy for you to determine the significance or nonsignificance of the sample results. You will find instructions for generating this *MINITAB* output in the section "About *MINITAB*" at the end of this chapter.

FIGURE 10.13
MINITAB output for Example 10.5

Two-Sample T-Test and CI: Standard, New

```
Two-sample T for Standard vs New
                N     Mean     StDev    SE Mean
Standard   9      35.22     4.94       1.6
New        9      31.56     4.48       1.5

Difference = mu Standard - mu New
Estimate for difference:  3.67
95% lower bound for difference: -0.21
T-Test of difference = 0 (vs >): T-Value = 1.65   P-Value = 0.059   DF = 16
Both use Pooled StDev = 4.72
```

If there is reason to believe that the normality assumptions have been violated, you can test for a shift in location of two population distributions using the nonparametric Wilcoxon rank sum test of Chapter 15. This test procedure, which requires fewer assumptions concerning the nature of the population probability distributions, is almost as sensitive in detecting a difference in population means when the conditions necessary for the *t* test are satisfied. It may be more sensitive when the normality assumption is not satisfied.

Exercises

Basic Techniques

10.16 Give the number of degrees of freedom for s^2, the pooled estimator of σ^2, in these cases:

a. $n_1 = 16, n_2 = 8$

b. $n_1 = 10, n_2 = 12$

c. $n_1 = 15, n_2 = 3$

10.17 Calculate s^2, the pooled estimator for σ^2, in these cases:

a. $n_1 = 10, n_2 = 4, s_1^2 = 3.4, s_2^2 = 4.9$

b. $n_1 = 12, n_2 = 21, s_1^2 = 18, s_2^2 = 23$

10.18 Two independent random samples of sizes $n_1 = 4$ and $n_2 = 5$ are selected from each of two normal populations:

Population 1	12	3	8	5	
Population 2	14	7	7	9	6

a. Calculate s^2, the pooled estimator of σ^2.

b. Find a 90% confidence interval for $(\mu_1 - \mu_2)$, the difference between the two population means.

c. Test $H_0 : (\mu_1 - \mu_2) = 0$ against $H_a : (\mu_1 - \mu_2) < 0$ for $\alpha = .05$. State your conclusions.

10.19 Independent random samples of $n_1 = 16$ and $n_2 = 13$ observations were selected from two normal populations with equal variances:

	Population	
	1	2
Sample size	16	13
Sample mean	34.6	32.2
Sample variance	4.8	5.9

a. Suppose you wish to detect a difference between the population means. State the null and alternative hypotheses for the test.

b. Find the rejection region for the test in part a for $\alpha = .01$.

c. Find the value of the test statistic.

d. Find the approximate p-value for the test.

e. Conduct the test and state your conclusions.

10.20 Refer to Exercise 10.19. Find a 99% confidence interval for $(\mu_1 - \mu_2)$.

10.21 The *MINITAB* printout shows a test for the difference in two population means.

MINITAB output for Example 10.21

Two-Sample T-Test and CI: Sample 1, Sample 2

```
Two-sample T for Sample 1 vs Sample 2
            N      Mean    StDev   SE Mean
Sample 1    6     29.00     4.00       1.6
Sample 2    7     28.86     4.67       1.8

Difference = mu Sample 1 - mu Sample 2
Estimate for difference:  0.14
95% CI for difference: (-5.2, 5.5)
T-Test of difference = 0 (vs not =): T-Value = 0.06   P-Value = 0.95   DF = 11
Both use Pooled StDev = 4.38
```

a. Do the two sample standard deviations indicate that the assumption of a common population variance is reasonable?

b. What is the observed value of the test statistic? What is the p-value associated with this test?

c. What is the pooled estimate s^2 of the population variance?

d. Use the answers to part b to draw conclusions about the difference in the two population means.

e. Find the 95% confidence interval for the difference in the population means. Does this interval confirm your conclusions in part d?

Applications

10.22 Jan Lindhe conducted a study on the effect of an oral antiplaque rinse on plaque buildup on teeth.[4] Fourteen people whose teeth were thoroughly cleaned and polished were randomly assigned to two groups of seven subjects each. Both groups were assigned to use oral rinses (no brushing) for a 2-week period. Group 1 used a rinse that contained an antiplaque agent. Group 2, the control group, received a similar rinse except that, unknown to the subjects, the rinse contained no antiplaque agent. A plaque index x, a measure of plaque buildup, was recorded at 4, 7, and 14 days. The mean and standard deviation for the 14-day plaque measurements are shown in the table for the two groups.

	Control Group	Antiplaque Group
Sample size	7	7
Mean	1.26	.78
Standard deviation	.32	.32

a. State the null and alternative hypotheses that should be used to test the effectiveness of the antiplaque oral rinse.

b. Do the data provide sufficient evidence to indicate that the oral antiplaque rinse is effective? Test using $\alpha = .05$.

c. Find the approximate p-value for the test.

EX1023

10.23 In Exercise 10.6 we presented data on the estimated average price for a 6-ounce can or a 7.06-ounce pouch of tuna, based on prices paid nationally in supermarkets. A portion of the data is reproduced in the table below. Use the *MINITAB* printout to answer the questions.

Light Tuna in Water		Light Tuna in Oil	
.99	.53	2.56	.62
1.92	1.41	1.92	.66
1.23	1.12	1.30	.62
.85	.63	1.79	.65
.65	.67	1.23	.60
.69	.60		.67
.60	.66		

MINITAB output for Exercise 10.23

Two-Sample T-Test and CI: Water, Oil

```
Two-sample T for Water vs Oil
          N     Mean    StDev    SE Mean
Water    14    0.896    0.400     0.11
Oil      11    1.147    0.679     0.20

Difference = mu Water - mu Oil
Estimate for difference:  -0.251
95% CI for difference: (-0.700, 0.198)
T-Test of difference = 0 (vs not =): T-Value = -1.16   P-Value = 0.260   DF = 23
Both use Pooled StDev = 0.539
```

a. Do the data in the table present sufficient evidence to indicate a difference in the average prices of light tuna in water versus oil? Test using $\alpha = .05$.

b. What is the p-value for the test?

c. The *MINITAB* analysis uses the pooled estimate of σ^2. Is the assumption of equal variances reasonable? Why or why not?

10.24 Chronic anterior compartment syndrome is a condition characterized by exercise-induced pain in the lower leg. Swelling and impaired nerve and muscle function also accompany this pain, which is relieved by rest. Susan Beckham and colleagues conducted an experiment involving ten healthy runners and ten healthy cyclists to determine whether there are significant differences in pressure measurements within the anterior muscle compartment for runners and cyclists.[5] The data summary—compartment pressure in millimeters of mercury (Hg)—is as follows:

Condition	Runners		Cyclists	
	Mean	Standard Deviation	Mean	Standard Deviation
Rest	14.5	3.92	11.1	3.98
80% maximal O_2 consumption	12.2	3.49	11.5	4.95
Maximal O_2 consumption	19.1	16.9	12.2	4.47

a. Test for a significant difference in compartment pressure between runners and cyclists under the resting condition. Use $\alpha = .05$.

b. Construct a 95% confidence interval estimate of the difference in means for runners and cyclists under the condition of exercising at 80% of maximal oxygen consumption.

c. To test for a significant difference in compartment pressure at maximal oxygen consumption, should you use the pooled or unpooled t test? Explain.

 10.25 An experiment to determine the efficacy of using 95% ethanol or 20% bleach as a disinfectant in removing bacterial and fungal contamination when culturing plant tissues was repeated 15 times with each disinfectant.[6] The plant tissue being cultured was sweet potato. Five cuttings per plant were placed on a petri dish for each disinfectant and stored at 25°C for 4 weeks. The observation reported was the number of uncontaminated eggplant cuttings after the 4-week storage.

Disinfectant	95% Ethanol	20% Bleach
Mean	3.73	4.80
Variance	2.78095	.17143
n	15	15
	Pooled variance 1.47619	

a. Are you willing to assume that the underlying variances are equal?

b. Using the information from part a, are you willing to conclude that there is a significant difference in the mean numbers of uncontaminated eggplants for the two disinfectants tested?

 10.26 A geologist collected 20 different ore samples, all of the same weight, and randomly divided them into two groups. The titanium contents of the samples, found using two different methods, are listed in the table:

EX1026

Method 1					Method 2				
.011	.013	.013	.015	.014	.011	.016	.013	.012	.015
.013	.010	.013	.011	.012	.012	.017	.013	.014	.015

a. Use an appropriate method to test for a significant difference in the average titanium contents using the two different methods.

b. Determine a 95% confidence interval estimate for $(\mu_1 - \mu_2)$. Does your interval estimate substantiate your conclusion in part a? Explain.

 10.27 The numbers of raisins in each of 14 miniboxes (1/2-ounce size) were counted for a generic brand and for Sunmaid brand raisins:

EX1027

Generic Brand				Sunmaid			
25	26	25	28	25	29	24	24
26	28	28	27	28	24	28	22
26	27	24	25	25	28	30	27
26	26			28	24		

a. Although counts cannot have a normal distribution, do these data have approximately normal distributions? (HINT: Use a histogram or stem and leaf plot.)

b. Are you willing to assume that the underlying population variances are equal? Why?

c. Use the *p*-value approach to determine whether there is a significant difference in the mean numbers of raisins per minibox. What are the implications of your conclusion?

 10.28 Refer to Exercise 10.7, in which we measured the dissolved oxygen content in river water to determine whether a stream had sufficient oxygen to support aquatic life. A pollution control inspector suspected that a river community was releasing amounts of semitreated sewage into a river. To check his theory, he drew five randomly selected specimens of river water at a location above the town, and another five below. The dissolved oxygen readings (in parts per million) are as follows:

Above Town	4.8	5.2	5.0	4.9	5.1
Below Town	5.0	4.7	4.9	4.8	4.9

a. Do the data provide sufficient evidence to indicate that the mean oxygen content below the town is less than the mean oxygen content above? Test using $\alpha = .05$.

b. Suppose you prefer estimation as a method of inference. Estimate the difference in the mean dissolved oxygen contents for locations above and below the town. Use a 95% confidence interval.

10.5 Small-Sample Inferences for the Difference between Two Means: A Paired-Difference Test

To compare the wearing qualities of two types of automobile tires, A and B, a tire of type A and one of type B are randomly assigned and mounted on the rear wheels of each of five automobiles. The automobiles are then operated for a specified number of miles, and the amount of wear is recorded for each tire. These measurements appear in Table 10.3. Do the data present sufficient evidence to indicate a difference in the average wear for the two tire types?

TABLE 10.3
Average wear for two types of tires

Automobile	Tire A	Tire B
1	10.6	10.2
2	9.8	9.4
3	12.3	11.8
4	9.7	9.1
5	8.8	8.3
	$\bar{x}_1 = 10.24$	$\bar{x}_2 = 9.76$
	$s_1 = 1.316$	$s_2 = 1.328$

Table 10.3 shows a difference of $(\bar{x}_1 - \bar{x}_2) = (10.24 - 9.76) = .48$ between the two sample means, while the standard deviations of both samples are approximately 1.3. Given the variability of the data and the small number of measurements, this is a rather small difference, and you would probably not suspect a difference in the average wear for the two types of tires. Let's check your suspicions using the methods of Section 10.4.

Look at the *MINITAB* analysis in Figure 10.14. The two-sample *pooled* t test is used for testing the difference in the means based on two independent random samples. The calculated value of *t* used to test the null hypothesis $H_0 : \mu_1 = \mu_2$ is $t = .57$ with *p*-value $= .582$, a value that is not nearly small enough to indicate a significant difference in the two population means. The corresponding 95% confidence interval, given as

$$-1.448 < (\mu_1 - \mu_2) < 2.408$$

is quite wide and also does not indicate a significant difference in the population means.

FIGURE 10.14
MINITAB output
using *t* test for
independent
samples for the
tire data

Two-Sample T-Test and CI: Tire A, Tire B

```
Two-sample T for Tire A vs Tire B
         N    Mean   StDev   SE Mean
Tire A   5   10.24    1.32    0.59
Tire B   5    9.76    1.33    0.59

Difference = mu Tire A - mu Tire B
Estimate for difference:  0.480
95% CI for difference: (-1.448, 2.408)
T-Test of difference = 0 (vs not =): T-Value = 0.57  P-Value = 0.582  DF = 8
Both use Pooled StDev = 1.32
```

Take a second look at the data and you will notice that the wear measurement for type A is greater than the corresponding value for type B for *each* of the five automobiles. Wouldn't this be unlikely, if there's really no difference between the two tire types?

Consider a simple intuitive test, based on the binomial distribution of Chapter 5. If there is no difference in the mean tire wear for the two types of tires, then it is just as likely as not that tire A shows more wear than tire B. The five automobiles then correspond to five binomial trials with $p = P$(tire A shows more wear than tire B) = .5. Is the observed value of $x = 5$ positive differences unusual? The probability of observing $x = 5$ or the equally unlikely value $x = 0$ can be found in Table 1 in Appendix I to be $2(.031) = .062$, which is quite small compared to the likelihood of the more powerful t-test, which had a p-value of .58. Isn't it peculiar that the t test, which uses more information (the actual sample measurements) than the binomial test, fails to supply sufficient information for rejecting the null hypothesis?

TABLE 10.4
Differences in tire
wear, using the
data of Table 10.3

Automobile	A	B	$d = A - B$
1	10.6	10.2	.4
2	9.8	9.4	.4
3	12.3	11.8	.5
4	9.7	9.1	.6
5	8.8	8.3	.5
			$\bar{d} = .48$

There is an explanation for this inconsistency. The *t* test described in Section 10.4 is *not* the proper statistical test to be used for our example. The statistical test procedure of Section 10.4 requires that the two samples be *independent and random*. Certainly, the independence requirement is violated by the manner in which the experiment was conducted. The (pair of) measurements, an A and a B tire, for a particular automobile are definitely related. A glance at the data shows that the readings have approximately the same magnitude for a particular automobile but vary markedly from one automobile to another. This, of course, is exactly what you might expect. Tire wear is largely determined by driver habits, the balance of the wheels, and the road surface. Since each automobile has a different driver, you would expect a large amount of variability in the data from one automobile to another.

In designing the tire wear experiment, the experimenter realized that the measurements would vary greatly from automobile to automobile. If the tires (five of type A and five of type B) were randomly assigned to the ten wheels, resulting in *independent* random samples, this variability would result in a large standard error and make it difficult to detect a difference in the means. Instead, he chose to "pair" the measurements, comparing the wear for type A and type B tires on each of the five automobiles. This experimental design, sometimes called a **paired-difference** or **matched pairs** design, allows us to eliminate the car-to-car variability by looking at only the five difference measurements shown in Table 10.4. These five differences form a single random sample of size $n = 5$.

Notice that in Table 10.4 the sample mean of the differences, $d = A - B$, is calculated as

$$\bar{d} = \frac{\Sigma \, d_i}{n} = .48$$

and is exactly the same as the difference of the sample means: $(\bar{x}_1 - \bar{x}_2) = (10.24 - 9.76) = .48$. It should not surprise you that this can be proven to be true in general, and also that the same relationship holds for the population means. That is, the average of the population differences is

$$\mu_d = (\mu_1 - \mu_2)$$

Because of this fact, you can use the sample differences to test for a significant difference in the two population means, $(\mu_1 - \mu_2) = \mu_d$. The test is a single-sample t test of the difference measurements to test the null hypothesis

$$H_0 : \mu_d = 0 \qquad [\text{or } H_0 : (\mu_1 - \mu_2) = 0]$$

versus the alternative hypothesis

$$H_a : \mu_d \neq 0 \qquad [\text{or } H_a : (\mu_1 - \mu_2) \neq 0]$$

The test procedures take the same form as the procedures used in Section 10.3 and are described next.

Paired-Difference Test of Hypothesis for $(\mu_1 - \mu_2) = \mu_d$: Dependent Samples

1. Null hypothesis: $H_0 : \mu_d = 0$
2. Alternative hypothesis:

One-Tailed Test	Two-Tailed Test
$H_a : \mu_d > 0$	$H_a : \mu_d \neq 0$
(or $H_a : \mu_d < 0$)	

3. Test statistic: $t = \dfrac{\bar{d} - 0}{s_d/\sqrt{n}} = \dfrac{\bar{d}}{s_d/\sqrt{n}}$

   where n = Number of paired differences
   $\bar{d}$ = Mean of the sample differences
   s_d = Standard deviation of the sample differences

4. Rejection region: Reject H_0 when

One-Tailed Test	Two-Tailed Test
$t > t_\alpha$	$t > t_{\alpha/2} \quad \text{or} \quad t < -t_{\alpha/2}$
(or $t < -t_\alpha$ when the alternative hypothesis is $H_a : \mu_d < 0$)	

   or when p-value $< \alpha$

The critical values of t, t_α, and $t_{\alpha/2}$ are based on $(n - 1)$ df. These tabulated values can be found using Table 4 or the **Student's t Probabilities** applet.

> **$(1 - \alpha)$100% Small-Sample Confidence Interval for $(\mu_1 - \mu_2) = \mu_d$,**
> **Based on a Paired-Difference Experiment**
>
> $$\bar{d} \pm t_{\alpha/2}\left(\frac{s_d}{\sqrt{n}}\right)$$
>
> **Assumptions**: The experiment is designed as a paired-difference test so that the n differences represent a random sample from a normal population.

EXAMPLE 10.8   Do the data in Table 10.3 provide sufficient evidence to indicate a difference in the mean wear for tire types A and B? Test using $\alpha = .05$.

Solution   You can verify using your calculator that the average and standard deviation of the five difference measurements are

$$\bar{d} = .48 \quad \text{and} \quad s_d = .0837$$

Then

$$H_0 : \mu_d = 0 \quad \text{and} \quad H_a : \mu_d \neq 0$$

and

$$t = \frac{\bar{d} - 0}{s_d/\sqrt{n}} = \frac{.48}{.0837/\sqrt{5}} = 12.8$$

The critical value of t for a two-tailed statistical test, $\alpha = .05$ and 4 df, is 2.776. Certainly, the observed value of $t = 12.8$ is extremely large and highly significant. Hence, you can conclude that there is a difference in the mean wear for tire types A and B.

EXAMPLE 10.9   Find a 95% confidence interval for $(\mu_1 - \mu_2) = \mu_d$ using the data in Table 10.3.

Solution   A 95% confidence interval for the difference between the mean wears is

$$\bar{d} \pm t_{\alpha/2}\left(\frac{s_d}{\sqrt{n}}\right)$$

$$.48 \pm 2.776\left(\frac{.0837}{\sqrt{5}}\right)$$

$$.48 \pm .10$$

or $.38 < (\mu_1 - \mu_2) < .58$. How does the width of this interval compare with the width of an interval you might have constructed *if* you had designed the experiment in an unpaired manner? It probably would have been of the same magnitude as the interval calculated in Figure 10.14, where the observed data were *incorrectly* analyzed using the unpaired analysis. This interval, $-1.45 < (\mu_1 - \mu_2) < 2.41$, is much wider than the paired interval, which indicates that the paired difference design increased the accuracy of our estimate, and we have gained valuable information by using this design.

The *paired-difference test* or *matched pairs design* used in the tire wear experiment is a simple example of an experimental design called a **randomized block design.** When there is a great deal of variability among the experimental units, even before any experimental procedures are implemented, the effect of this variability can be minimized by **blocking**—that is, comparing the different procedures within groups of relatively similar experimental units called **blocks.** In this way, the "noise" caused by the large variability does not mask the true differences between the procedures. We will discuss randomized block designs in more detail in Chapter 11.

It is important for you to remember that the *pairing* or *blocking* occurs when the experiment is planned, and not after the data are collected. An experimenter may choose to use pairs of identical twins to compare two learning methods. A physician may record a patient's blood pressure before and after a particular medication is given. Once you have used a paired design for an experiment, you no longer have the option of using the unpaired analysis of Section 10.4. The independence assumption has been purposely violated, and your only choice is to use the paired analysis described here!

Although pairing was very beneficial in the tire wear experiment, this may not always be the case. In the paired analysis, the degrees of freedom for the t test are cut in half—from $(n + n - 2) = 2(n - 1)$ to $(n - 1)$. This reduction *increases* the critical value of t for rejecting H_0 and also increases the width of the confidence interval for the difference in the two means. If pairing is not effective, this increase is not offset by a *decrease* in the variability, and you may in fact lose rather than gain information by pairing. This, of course, did not happen in the tire experiment—the large reduction in the standard error more than compensated for the loss in degrees of freedom.

Except for notation, the paired-difference analysis is the same as the single-sample analysis presented in Section 10.3. However, *MINITAB* provides a single procedure called **Paired t** to analyze the differences, as shown in Figure 10.15. The p-value for the paired analysis, .000, indicates a *highly significant* difference in the means. You will find instructions for generating this *MINITAB* output in the section "About *MINITAB*" at the end of this chapter.

FIGURE 10.15
MINITAB output for paired-difference analysis of tire wear data

Paired T-Test and CI: Tire A, Tire B

```
Paired T for Tire A - Tire B
                 N      Mean    StDev   SE Mean
Tire A           5    10.240    1.316     0.589
Tire B           5     9.760    1.328     0.594
Difference       5    0.4800   0.0837    0.0374

95% CI for mean difference: (0.3761, 0.5839)
T-Test of mean difference = 0 (vs not = 0): T-Value = 12.83   P-Value = 0.000
```

Exercises

Basic Techniques

10.29 A paired-difference experiment was conducted using $n = 10$ pairs of observations. Test the null hypothesis $H_0 : (\mu_1 - \mu_2) = 0$ against $H_a : (\mu_1 - \mu_2) \neq 0$ for $\alpha = .05$, $\bar{d} = .3$, and $s_d^2 = .16$. Give the approximate p-value for the test.

10.30 Find a 95% confidence interval for $(\mu_1 - \mu_2)$ in Exercise 10.29.

10.31 How many pairs of observations do you need if you want to estimate $(\mu_1 - \mu_2)$ in Exercise 10.29 correct to within .1 with probability equal to .95?

10.32 A paired-difference experiment consists of $n = 18$ pairs, $\bar{d} = 5.7$, and $s_d^2 = 256$. Suppose you wish to detect $\mu_d > 0$.

a. Give the null and alternative hypotheses for the test.

b. Conduct the test and state your conclusions.

10.33 A paired-difference experiment was conducted to compare the means of two populations:

	Pairs				
Population	1	2	3	4	5
1	1.3	1.6	1.1	1.4	1.7
2	1.2	1.5	1.1	1.2	1.8

a. Do the data provide sufficient evidence to indicate that μ_1 differs from μ_2? Test using $\alpha = .05$.

b. Find the approximate p-value for the test and interpret its value.

c. Find a 95% confidence interval for $(\mu_1 - \mu_2)$. Compare your interpretation of the confidence interval with your test results in part a.

d. What assumptions must you make for your inferences to be valid?

Applications

EX1034

10.34 The cost of automobile insurance has become a sore subject in California because the rates are dependent on so many variables, such as the city in which you live, the number of cars you insure, and the company with which you are insured. Here are the 6-month premiums in 2001 for a married male, licensed for 6–8 years, who drives about 15,000 miles per year, and who has no violations or accidents[7]:

City	Allstate	21st Century
Long Beach	$1050	$682
Pomona	984	638
San Bernardino	900	578
Moreno Valley	964	524

a. Why would you expect these pairs of observations to be dependent?

b. Do the data provide sufficient evidence to indicate that there is a difference in the average 6-month premiums between Allstate and 21st Century insurance? Test using $\alpha = .01$.

c. Find the approximate p-value for the test and interpret its value.

d. Find a 99% confidence interval for the difference in the average 6-month premiums for Allstate and 21st Century insurance.

e. Can we use the information in the table to make valid comparisons between Allstate and 21st Century insurance throughout the United States? Why or why not?

10.35 Refer to Exercise 10.24. In addition to the compartment pressures, the level of creatine phosphokinase (CPK) in blood samples, a measure of muscle damage, was determined for each of 10 runners and 10 cyclists before and after exercise.[5] The data summary—CPK values in units/liter—is as follows:

	Runners		Cyclists	
Condition	Mean	Standard Deviation	Mean	Standard Deviation
Before exercise	255.63	115.48	173.8	60.69
After exercise	284.75	132.64	177.1	64.53
Difference	29.13	21.01	3.3	6.85

a. Test for a significant difference in mean CPK values for runners and cyclists before exercise under the assumption that $\sigma_1^2 \neq \sigma_2^2$; use $\alpha = .05$. Find a 95% confidence interval estimate for the corresponding difference in means.

b. Test for a significant difference in mean CPK values for runners and cyclists after exercise under the assumption that $\sigma_1^2 \neq \sigma_2^2$; use $\alpha = .05$. Find a 95% confidence interval estimate for the corresponding difference in means.

c. Test for a significant difference in mean CPK values for runners before and after exercise.

d. Find a 95% confidence interval estimate for the difference in mean CPK values for cyclists before and after exercise. Does your estimate indicate that there is no significant difference in mean CPK levels for cyclists before and after exercise?

EX1036

10.36 An advertisement for Albertsons, a supermarket chain in the western United States, claims that Albertsons has had consistently lower prices than four other full-service supermarkets. As part of a survey conducted by an "independent market basket price-checking company," the average weekly total, based on the prices of approximately 95 items, is given for two different supermarket chains recorded during 4 consecutive weeks in a particular month.

Week	Albertsons	Ralphs
1	254.26	256.03
2	240.62	255.65
3	231.90	255.12
4	234.13	261.18

a. Is there a significant difference in the average prices for these two different supermarket chains?

b. What is the approximate p-value for the test conducted in part a?

c. Construct a 99% confidence interval for the difference in the average prices for the two supermarket chains. Interpret this interval.

EX1037

10.37 An experiment was conducted to compare the mean reaction times to two types of traffic signs: prohibitive (No Left Turn) and permissive (Left Turn Only). Ten drivers were included in the experiment. Each driver was presented with 40 traffic signs, 20 prohibitive and 20 permissive, in random order. The mean time to reaction and the number of correct actions were recorded for each driver. The mean reaction times (in milliseconds) to the 20 prohibitive and 20 permissive traffic signs are shown here for each of the ten drivers:

Driver	Prohibitive	Permissive
1	824	702
2	866	725
3	841	744
4	770	663
5	829	792
6	764	708
7	857	747
8	831	685
9	846	742
10	759	610

a. Explain why this is a paired-difference experiment and give reasons why the pairing should be useful in increasing information on the difference between the mean reaction times to prohibitive and permissive traffic signs.

b. Do the data present sufficient evidence to indicate a difference in mean reaction times to prohibitive and permissive traffic signs? Use the p-value approach.

c. Find a 95% confidence interval for the difference in mean reaction times to prohibitive and permissive traffic signs.

10.38 Exercise 10.22 describes a dental experiment conducted to investigate the effectiveness of an oral rinse used to inhibit the growth of plaque on teeth. Subjects were divided into two groups: One group used a rinse with an antiplaque ingredient, and the control group used a rinse containing inactive ingredients. Suppose that the plaque growth on each person's teeth was measured after using the rinse after 4 hours and then again after 8 hours. If you wish to estimate the difference in plaque growth from 4 to 8 hours, should you use a confidence interval based on a paired or an unpaired analysis? Explain.

10.39   The earth's temperature (which affects seed germination, crop survival in bad weather, and many other aspects of agricultural production) can be measured using either ground-based sensors or infrared-sensing devices mounted in aircraft or space satellites. Ground-based sensoring is tedious, requiring many replications to obtain an accurate estimate of ground temperature. On the other hand, airplane or satellite sensoring of infrared waves appears to introduce a bias in the temperature readings. To determine the bias, readings were obtained at six different locations using both ground- and air-based temperature sensors. The readings (in degrees Celsius) are listed here:

Location	Ground	Air
1	46.9	47.3
2	45.4	48.1
3	36.3	37.9
4	31.0	32.7
5	24.7	26.2

a. Do the data present sufficient evidence to indicate a bias in the air-based temperature readings? Explain.

b. Estimate the difference in mean temperatures between ground- and air-based sensors using a 95% confidence interval.

10.40   Refer to Exercise 10.39. How many paired observations are required to estimate the difference between mean temperatures for ground- versus air-based sensors correct to within .2°C, with probability approximately equal to .95?

10.41   In response to a complaint that a particular tax assessor (A) was biased, an experiment was conducted to compare the assessor named in the complaint with another tax assessor (B) from the same office. Eight properties were selected, and each was assessed by both assessors. The assessments (in thousands of dollars) are shown in the table:

EX1041

Property	Assessor A	Assessor B
1	76.3	75.1
2	88.4	86.8
3	80.2	77.3
4	94.7	90.6
5	68.7	69.1
6	82.8	81.0
7	76.1	75.3
8	79.0	79.1

Use the *MINITAB* printout to answer the questions.

MINITAB output for
Exercise 10.41

Paired T-Test and CI: A, B

```
Paired T for A - B
                  N      Mean     StDev    SE Mean
A                 8     80.77      7.99       2.83
B                 8     79.29      6.85       2.42
Difference        8     1.487     1.491      0.527

95% lower bound for mean difference: 0.489
T-Test of mean difference = 0 (vs > 0): T-Value = 2.82   P-Value = 0.013
```

a. Do the data provide sufficient evidence to indicate that assessor A tends to give higher assessments than assessor B?

b. Estimate the difference in mean assessments for the two assessors.

c. What assumptions must you make in order for the inferences in parts a and b to be valid?

    d. Suppose that assessor A had been compared with a more stable standard—say, the average $\bar{x}$ of the assessments given by four assessors selected from the tax office. Thus, each property would be assessed by A and also by each of the four other assessors and $(x_A - \bar{x})$ would be calculated. If the test in part a is valid, can you use the paired-difference t test to test the hypothesis that the bias, the mean difference between A's assessments and the mean of the assessments of the four assessors, is equal to 0? Explain.

EX1042

10.42 A psychology class performed an experiment to compare whether a recall score in which instructions to form images of 25 words were given is better than an initial recall score for which no imagery instructions were given. Twenty students participated in the experiment with the following results:

Student	With Imagery	Without Imagery	Student	With Imagery	Without Imagery
1	20	5	11	17	8
2	24	9	12	20	16
3	20	5	13	20	10
4	18	9	14	16	12
5	22	6	15	24	7
6	19	11	16	22	9
7	20	8	17	25	21
8	19	11	18	21	14
9	17	7	19	19	12
10	21	9	20	23	13

Does it appear that the average recall score is higher when imagery is used?

EX1043

10.43 These data are the price per square foot for existing homes in 13 different areas of Southern California[8]:

Area	June–Aug. 2001	June–Aug. 2000
1	$83.89	$72.47
2	88.72	72.94
3	94.94	88.86
4	72.92	54.65
5	81.21	72.06
6	83.69	71.08
7	146.89	136.20
8	84.80	75.54
9	87.81	73.43
10	90.08	80.06
11	92.09	83.13
12	82.80	72.05
13	80.73	63.67

    a. Explain why a paired-difference design is appropriate to determine whether there has been a significant change in the average cost per square foot of existing homes.

    b. Can you conclude that the average cost per square foot of existing homes has changed significantly over this 1-year period?

10.6   Inferences Concerning a Population Variance

You have seen in the preceding sections that an estimate of the population variance σ^2 is usually needed before you can make inferences about population means. Sometimes, however, the population variance σ^2 is the primary objective in an experimental investigation. It may be *more* important to the experimenter than the population mean! Consider these examples:

- Scientific measuring instruments must provide unbiased readings with a very small error of measurement. An aircraft altimeter that measures the correct altitude on the *average* is fairly useless if the measurements are in error by as much as 1000 feet above or below the correct altitude.
- Machined parts in a manufacturing process must be produced with minimum variability in order to reduce out-of-size and hence defective parts.
- Aptitude tests must be designed so that scores *will* exhibit a reasonable amount of variability. For example, an 800-point test is not very discriminatory if all students score between 601 and 605.

In previous chapters, you have used

$$s^2 = \frac{\Sigma(x_i - \overline{x})^2}{n - 1}$$

as an unbiased estimator of the population variance σ^2. This means that, in repeated sampling, the average of all your sample estimates will equal the target parameter, σ^2. But how close or far from the target is your estimator s^2 likely to be? To answer this question, we use the sampling distribution of s^2, which describes its behavior in repeated sampling.

Consider the distribution of s^2 based on repeated *random* sampling from a *normal* distribution with a specified mean and variance. We can show theoretically that the distribution begins at $s^2 = 0$ (since the variance cannot be negative) with a mean equal to σ^2. Its shape is *nonsymmetric* and changes with each different sample size and each different value of σ^2. Finding critical values for the sampling distribution of s^2 would be quite difficult and would require separate tables for each population variance. Fortunately, we can simplify the problem by *standardizing*, as we did with the z distribution.

Definition   The standardized statistic

$$\chi^2 = \frac{(n - 1)s^2}{\sigma^2}$$

is called a **chi-square variable** and has a sampling distribution called the **chi-square probability distribution.**

The equation of the density function for this statistic is quite complicated to look at, but it traces the curve shown in Figure 10.16.

FIGURE 10.16
A chi-square distribution

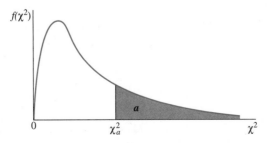

Certain critical values of the chi-square statistic, which are used for making inferences about the population variance, have been tabulated by statisticians and appear in Table 5 of Appendix I. Since the shape of the distribution varies with the sample size n

or, more precisely, the degrees of freedom associated with s^2, Table 5, partially reproduced in Table 10.5, is constructed in exactly the same way as the t table, with the degrees of freedom in the first and last columns. The symbol χ_a^2 indicates that the tabulated χ^2-value has an area a to its right (see Figure 10.16).

TABLE 10.5
Format of the chi-square table from Table 5 in Appendix I

df	$\chi^2_{.995}$	$\cdots$	$\chi^2_{.950}$	$\chi^2_{.900}$	$\chi^2_{.100}$	$\chi^2_{.050}$	$\cdots$	$\chi^2_{.005}$	df
1	.0000393		.0039321	.0157908	2.70554	3.84146		7.87944	1
2	.0100251		.102587	.210720	4.60517	5.99147		10.5966	2
3	.0717212		.351846	.584375	6.25139	7.81473		12.8381	3
4	.206990		.710721	1.063623	7.77944	9.48773		14.8602	4
5	.411740		1.145476	1.610310	9.23635	11.0705		16.7496	5
6	.0675727		1.63539	2.204130	10.6446	12.5916		18.5476	6
$\vdots$	$\vdots$		$\vdots$	$\vdots$	$\vdots$	$\vdots$		$\vdots$	$\vdots$
15	4.60094		7.26094	8.54675	22.3072	24.9958		32.8013	15
16	5.14224		7.96164	9.31223	23.5418	26.2962		34.2672	16
17	5.69724		8.67176	10.0852	24.7690	27.5871		35.7185	17
18	6.26481		9.39046	10.8649	25.9894	28.8693		37.1564	18
19	6.84398		10.1170	11.6509	27.2036	30.1435		38.5822	19
$\vdots$	$\vdots$		$\vdots$	$\vdots$	$\vdots$	$\vdots$		$\vdots$	$\vdots$

You can see in Table 10.5 that, because the distribution is nonsymmetric and starts at 0, both upper and lower tail areas must be tabulated for the chi-square statistic. For example, the value $\chi^2_{.95}$ is the value that has 95% of the area under the curve to its right and 5% of the area to its left. This value cuts off an area equal to .05 in the lower tail of the chi-square distribution.

EXAMPLE 10.10   Check your ability to use Table 5 in Appendix I by verifying the following statements:

1. The probability that χ^2, based on $n = 16$ measurements ($df = 15$), exceeds 24.9958 is .05.
2. For a sample of $n = 6$ measurements, 95% of the area under the χ^2 distribution lies to the right of 1.145476.

These values are shaded in Table 10.5.

DO IT YOURSELF!

You can use the **Chi-Square Probabilities** applet to find the χ^2-value described in Example 10.10. Since the applet provides χ^2-values and their one-tailed probabilities for the degrees of freedom that you select using the slider on the right side of the applet, you should choose $df = 5$ and type .95 in the box marked "prob:" at the bottom of the applet. The applet will provide the value of that puts .95 in the right tail of the χ^2 distribution and hence .05 in the left tail. The applet in Figure 10.17 shows $\chi^2 = 1.14$, which differs only slightly from the value in Example 10.10. We will use this applet for the *Do It Yourself Exercises* at the end of the chapter.

FIGURE 10.17
Chi-Square Probabilities applet

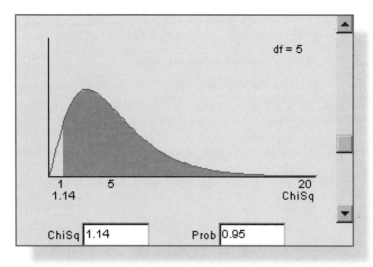

The statistical test of a null hypothesis concerning a population variance

$$H_0 : \sigma^2 = \sigma_0^2$$

uses the test statistic

$$\chi^2 = \frac{(n-1)s^2}{\sigma_0^2}$$

Notice that when H_0 is true, s^2/σ_0^2 should be near 1, so χ^2 should be close to $(n-1)$, the degrees of freedom. If σ^2 is really greater than the hypothesized value σ_0^2, the test statistic will tend to be larger than $(n-1)$ and will probably fall toward the upper tail of the distribution. If $\sigma^2 < \sigma_0^2$, the test statistic will tend to be smaller than $(n-1)$ and will probably fall toward the lower tail of the chi-square distribution. As in other testing situations, you may use either a one- or a two-tailed statistical test, depending on the alternative hypothesis. This test of hypothesis and the $(1 - \alpha)100\%$ confidence interval for σ^2 are both based on the chi-square distribution and are described next.

Test of Hypothesis Concerning a Population Variance

1. Null hypothesis: $H_0 : \sigma^2 = \sigma_0^2$

2. Alternative hypothesis:

One-Tailed Test	Two-Tailed Test
$H_a : \sigma^2 > \sigma_0^2$	$H_a : \sigma^2 \neq \sigma_0^2$
(or $H_a : \sigma^2 < \sigma_0^2$)	

3. Test statistic: $\chi^2 = \dfrac{(n-1)s^2}{\sigma_0^2}$

(continued)

Test of Hypothesis Concerning a Population Variance *(continued)*

4. Rejection region: Reject H_0 when

One-Tailed Test	**Two-Tailed Test**
$\chi^2 > \chi^2_\alpha$ (or $\chi^2 < \chi^2_{(1-\alpha)}$ when the alternative hypothesis is $H_a : \sigma^2 < \sigma^2_0$), where χ^2_α and $\chi^2_{(1-\alpha)}$ are, respectively, the upper- and lower-tail values of χ^2 that place α in the tail areas	$\chi^2 > \chi^2_{\alpha/2}$ or $\chi^2 < \chi^2_{(1-\alpha/2)}$, where $\chi^2_{\alpha/2}$ and $\chi^2_{(1-\alpha/2)}$ are, respectively, the upper- and lower-tail values of χ^2 that place $\alpha/2$ in the tail areas

or when p-value $< \alpha$

The critical values of χ^2 are based on $(n - 1)$ *df*. These tabulated values can be found using Table 5 of Appendix I or the **Chi-Square Probabilities** applet.

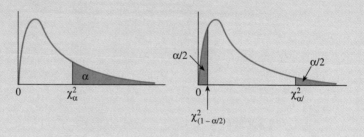

$(1 - \alpha)100\%$ Confidence Interval for σ^2

$$\frac{(n - 1)s^2}{\chi^2_{\alpha/2}} < \sigma^2 < \frac{(n - 1)s^2}{\chi^2_{(1-\alpha/2)}}$$

where $\chi^2_{\alpha/2}$ and $\chi^2_{(1-\alpha/2)}$ are the upper and lower χ^2-values, which locate one-half of α in each tail of the chi-square distribution.
Assumption: The sample is randomly selected from a normal population.

EXAMPLE 10.11 A cement manufacturer claims that concrete prepared from his product has a relatively stable compressive strength and that the strength measured in kilograms per square centimeter (kg/cm^2) lies within a range of 40 kg/cm^2. A sample of $n = 10$ measurements produced a mean and variance equal to, respectively,

$$\bar{x} = 312 \quad \text{and} \quad s^2 = 195$$

Do these data present sufficient evidence to reject the manufacturer's claim?

Solution In Section 2.5, you learned that the range of a set of measurements should be approximately four standard deviations. The manufacturer's claim that the range of the strength measurements is within 40 kg/cm^2 must mean that the standard deviation of the measurements is roughly 10 kg/cm^2 or less. To test his claim, the appropriate hypotheses are

$$H_0 : \sigma^2 = 10^2 = 100 \quad \text{versus} \quad H_a : \sigma^2 > 100$$

If the sample variance is much larger than the hypothesized value of 100, then the test statistic

$$\chi^2 = \frac{(n-1)s^2}{\sigma_0^2} = \frac{1755}{100} = 17.55$$

will be unusually large, favoring rejection of H_0 and acceptance of H_a. There are two ways to use the test statistic to make a decision for this test.

- **The critical value approach:** The appropriate test requires a one-tailed rejection region in the right tail of the χ^2 distribution. The critical value for $\alpha = .05$ and $(n-1) = 9$ df is $\chi^2_{.05} = 16.9190$ from Table 5 in Appendix I. Figure 10.18 shows the rejection region; you can reject H_0 if the test statistic exceeds 16.9190. Since the observed value of the test statistic is $\chi^2 = 17.55$, you can conclude that the null hypothesis is false and that the range of concrete strength measurements exceeds the manufacturer's claim.

FIGURE 10.18
Rejection region and p-value (shaded) for Example 10.11

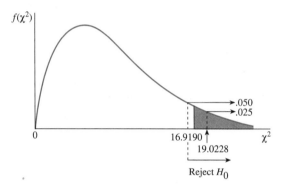

- **The p-value approach:** The p-value for a statistical test is the smallest value of α for which H_0 can be rejected. It is calculated, as in other one-tailed tests, as the area in the tail of the χ^2 distribution to the right of the observed value, $\chi^2 = 17.55$. Although computer packages allow you to calculate this area exactly, Table 5 in Appendix I allows you only to bound the p-value. Since the value 17.55 lies between $\chi^2_{.050} = 16.9190$ and $\chi^2_{.025} = 19.0228$, the p-value lies between .025 and .05. Most researchers would reject H_0 and report these results as significant at the 5% level, or $P < .05$. Again, you can reject H_0 and conclude that the range of measurements exceeds the manufacturer's claim.

EXAMPLE 10.12 An experimenter is convinced that her measuring instrument had a variability measured by standard deviation $\sigma = 2$. During an experiment, she recorded the measurements 4.1, 5.2, and 10.2. Do these data confirm or disprove her assertion? Test the appropriate hypothesis, and construct a 90% confidence interval to estimate the true value of the population variance.

Solution Since there is no preset level of significance, you should choose to use the p-value approach in testing these hypotheses:

$$H_0 : \sigma^2 = 4 \quad \text{versus} \quad H_a : \sigma^2 \neq 4$$

Use your scientific calculator to verify that the sample variance is $s^2 = 10.57$ and the test statistic is

$$\chi^2 = \frac{(n-1)s^2}{\sigma_0^2} = \frac{2(10.57)}{4} = 5.29$$

Since this is a two-tailed test, the rejection region is divided into two parts, half in each tail of the χ^2 distribution. If you approximate the area to the right of the observed test statistic, $\chi^2 = 5.29$, you will have only *half* of the p-value for the test. Since an equally unlikely value of χ^2 might occur in the lower tail of the distribution, with equal probability, you must *double* the upper area to obtain the p-value. With 2 *df*, the observed value, 5.29, falls between $\chi^2_{.10}$ and $\chi^2_{.05}$ so that

$$.05 < \frac{1}{2} \, (p\text{-value}) < .10 \quad \text{or} \quad .10 < p\text{-value} < .20$$

Since the p-value is greater than .10, the results are not statistically significant. There is insufficient evidence to reject the null hypothesis $H_0 : \sigma^2 = 4$.

The corresponding 90% confidence interval is

$$\frac{(n-1)s^2}{\chi^2_{\alpha/2}} < \sigma^2 < \frac{(n-1)s^2}{\chi^2_{(1-\alpha/2)}}$$

The values of $\chi^2_{(1-\alpha/2)}$ and $\chi^2_{\alpha/2}$ are

$$\chi^2_{(1-\alpha/2)} = \chi^2_{.95} = .102587$$
$$\chi^2_{\alpha/2} = \chi^2_{.05} = 5.99147$$

Substituting these values into the formula for the interval estimate, you get

$$\frac{2(10.57)}{5.99147} < \sigma^2 < \frac{2(10.57)}{.102587} \quad \text{or} \quad 3.53 < \sigma^2 < 206.07$$

Thus, you can estimate the population variance to fall into the interval 3.53 to 206.07. This very wide confidence interval indicates how little information on the population variance is obtained from a sample of only three measurements. Consequently, it is not surprising that there is insufficient evidence to reject the null hypothesis $\sigma^2 = 4$. To obtain more information on σ^2, the experimenter needs to increase the sample size.

Exercises

Basic Techniques

10.44 A random sample of $n = 25$ observations from a normal population produced a sample variance equal to 21.4. Do these data provide sufficient evidence to indicate that $\sigma^2 > 15$? Test using $\alpha = .05$.

10.45 A random sample of $n = 15$ observations was selected from a normal population. The sample mean and variance were $\bar{x} = 3.91$ and $s^2 = .3214$. Find a 90% confidence interval for the population variance σ^2.

10.46 A random sample of size $n = 7$ from a normal population produced these measurements: 1.4, 3.6, 1.7, 2.0, 3.3, 2.8, 2.9.

a. Calculate the sample variance, s^2.

b. Construct a 95% confidence interval for the population variance, σ^2.

c. Test $H_0 : \sigma^2 = .8$ versus $H_a : \sigma^2 \neq .8$ using $\alpha = .05$. State your conclusions.

d. What is the approximate p-value for the test in part c?

Applications

10.47 A precision instrument is guaranteed to read accurately to within 2 units. A sample of four instrument readings on the same object yielded the measurements 353, 351, 351, and 355. Test the null hypothesis that $\sigma = .7$ against the alternative $\sigma > .7$. Use $\alpha = .05$.

10.48 Find a 90% confidence interval for the population variance in Exercise 10.47.

10.49 To properly treat patients, drugs prescribed by physicians must have a potency that is accurately defined. Consequently, not only must the distribution of potency values for shipments of a drug have a mean value as specified on the drug's container, but also the variation in potency must be small. Otherwise, pharmacists would be distributing drug prescriptions that could be harmfully potent or have a low potency and be ineffective. A drug manufacturer claims that his drug is marketed with a potency of $5 \pm .1$ milligram per cubic centimeter (mg/cc). A random sample of four containers gave potency readings equal to 4.94, 5.09, 5.03, and 4.90 mg/cc.

  a. Do the data present sufficient evidence to indicate that the mean potency differs from 5 mg/cc?

  b. Do the data present sufficient evidence to indicate that the variation in potency differs from the error limits specified by the manufacturer? [HINT: It is sometimes difficult to determine exactly what is meant by limits on potency as specified by a manufacturer. Since he implies that the potency values will fall into the interval $5.0 \pm .1$ mg/cc with very high probability— the implication is *always*—let us assume that the range .2; or (4.9 to 5.1), represents 6σ, as suggested by the Empirical Rule. Note that letting the range equal 6σ rather than 4σ places a stringent interpretation on the manufacturer's claim. We want the potency to fall into the interval $5.0 \pm .1$ with very high probability.]

10.50 Refer to Exercise 10.49. Testing of 60 additional randomly selected containers of the drug gave a sample mean and variance equal to 5.04 and .0063 (for the total of $n = 64$ containers). Using a 95% confidence interval, estimate the variance of the manufacturer's potency measurements.

10.51 A manufacturer of hard safety hats for construction workers is concerned about the mean and the variation of the forces helmets transmit to wearers when subjected to a standard external force. The manufacturer desires the mean force transmitted by helmets to be 800 pounds (or less), well under the legal 1000-pound limit, and σ to be less than 40. A random sample of $n = 40$ helmets was tested, and the sample mean and variance were found to be equal to 825 pounds and 2350 pounds^2, respectively.

  a. If $\mu = 800$ and $\sigma = 40$, is it likely that any helmet, subjected to the standard external force, will transmit a force to a wearer in excess of 1000 pounds? Explain.

  b. Do the data provide sufficient evidence to indicate that when the helmets are subjected to the standard external force, the mean force transmitted by the helmets exceeds 800 pounds?

10.52 Refer to Exercise 10.51. Do the data provide sufficient evidence to indicate that σ exceeds 40?

10.53 A manufacturer of industrial light bulbs likes its bulbs to have a mean life that is acceptable to its customers and a variation in life that is relatively small. If some bulbs fail too early in their life, customers become annoyed and shift to competitive products. Large variations above the mean reduce replacement sales, and variation in general disrupts customers' replacement schedules. A sample of 20 bulbs tested produced the following lengths of life (in hours):

EX1053

| 2100 | 2302 | 1951 | 2067 | 2415 | 1883 | 2101 | 2146 | 2278 | 2019 |
| 1924 | 2183 | 2077 | 2392 | 2286 | 2501 | 1946 | 2161 | 2253 | 1827 |

The manufacturer wishes to control the variability in length of life so that σ is less than 150 hours. Do the data provide sufficient evidence to indicate that the manufacturer is achieving this goal? Test using $\alpha = .01$.

10.7 Comparing Two Population Variances

Just as a single population variance is sometimes important to an experimenter, you might also need to compare two population variances. You might need to compare the precision of one measuring device with that of another, the stability of one manufacturing process with that of another, or even the variability in the grading procedure of one college professor with that of another.

One way to compare two population variances, σ_1^2 and σ_2^2, is to use the ratio of the sample variances, s_1^2/s_2^2. If s_1^2/s_2^2 is nearly equal to 1, you will find little evidence to indicate that σ_1^2 and σ_2^2 are unequal. On the other hand, a very large or very small value for s_1^2/s_2^2 provides evidence of a difference in the population variances.

How large or small must s_1^2/s_2^2 be for sufficient evidence to exist to reject the following null hypothesis?

$$H_0 : \sigma_1^2 = \sigma_2^2$$

The answer to this question may be found by studying the distribution of s_1^2/s_2^2 in repeated sampling.

When independent random samples are drawn from two *normal* populations with *equal variances*—that is, $\sigma_1^2 = \sigma_2^2$—then s_1^2/s_2^2 has a probability distribution in repeated sampling that is known to statisticians as an **F distribution**, shown in Figure 10.19.

FIGURE 10.19
An *F* distribution
with $df_1 = 10$ and
$df_2 = 10$

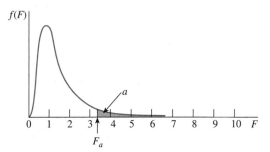

Assumptions for s_1^2/s_2^2 to Have an F Distribution

- Random and independent samples are drawn from each of two normal populations.
- The variability of the measurements in the two populations is the same and can be measured by a common variance, σ^2; that is, $\sigma_1^2 = \sigma_2^2 = \sigma^2$.

It is not important for you to know the complex equation of the density function for F. For your purposes, you need only to use the well-tabulated critical values of F given in Table 6 in Appendix I.

Critical values of F and p-values for significance tests can also be found using the **F Probabilities** applet shown in Figure 10.20.

Like the χ^2 distribution, the shape of the F distribution is nonsymmetric and depends on the number of degrees of freedom associated with s_1^2 and s_2^2, represented as $df_1 = (n_1 - 1)$ and $df_2 = (n_2 - 1)$, respectively. This complicates the tabulation of critical values of the F distribution because a table is needed for each different combination of df_1, df_2, and a.

In Table 6 in Appendix I, critical values of F for right-tailed areas corresponding to $a = .100, .050, .025, .010,$ and $.005$ are tabulated for various combinations of df_1 numerator degrees of freedom and df_2 denominator degrees of freedom. A portion of Table 6 is reproduced in Table 10.6. The numerator degrees of freedom df_1 are listed across the top margin, and the denominator degrees of freedom df_2 are listed along the side margin. The values of a are listed in the second column. For a fixed combination of df_1 and df_2, the appropriate critical values of F are found in the line indexed by the value of a required.

FIGURE 10.20
F Probabilities
applet

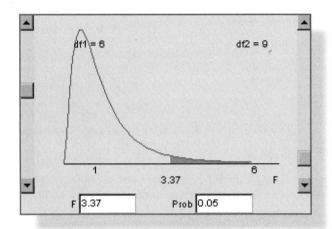

EXAMPLE 10.13   Check your ability to use Table 6 in Appendix I by verifying the following statements:

1. The value of F with area .05 to its right for $df_1 = 6$ and $df_2 = 9$ is 3.37.
2. The value of F with area .05 to its right for $df_1 = 5$ and $df_2 = 10$ is 3.33.
3. The value of F with area .01 to its right for $df_1 = 6$ and $df_2 = 9$ is 5.80.

These values are shaded in Table 10.6.

TABLE 10.6
Format of the *F*
table from Table 6
in Appendix I

		df_1					
df_2	a	1	2	3	4	5	6
1	.100	39.86	49.50	53.59	55.83	57.24	58.20
	.050	161.4	199.5	215.7	224.6	230.2	234.0
	.025	647.8	799.5	864.2	899.6	921.8	937.1
	.010	4052	4999.5	5403	5625	5764	5859
	.005	16211	20000	21615	22500	23056	23437
2	.100	8.53	9.00	9.16	9.24	9.29	9.33
	.050	18.51	19.00	19.16	19.25	19.30	19.33
	.025	38.51	39.00	39.17	39.25	39.30	39.33
	.010	98.50	99.00	99.17	99.25	99.30	99.33
	.005	198.5	199.0	199.2	199.2	199.3	199.3
3	.100	5.54	5.46	5.39	5.34	5.31	5.28
	.050	10.13	9.55	9.28	9.12	9.01	8.94
	.025	17.44	16.04	15.44	15.10	14.88	14.73
	.010	34.12	30.82	29.46	28.71	28.24	27.91
	.005	55.55	49.80	47.47	46.19	45.39	44.84
.	.			.			.
.	.			.			.
.	.			.			.
9	.100	3.36	3.01	2.81	2.69	2.61	2.55
	.050	5.12	4.26	3.86	3.63	3.48	3.37
	.025	7.21	5.71	5.08	4.72	4.48	4.32
	.010	10.56	8.02	6.99	6.42	6.06	5.80
	.005	13.61	10.11	8.72	7.96	7.47	7.13
10	.100	3.29	2.92	2.73	2.61	2.52	2.46
	.050	4.96	4.10	3.71	3.48	3.33	3.22
	.025	6.94	5.46	4.83	4.47	4.24	4.07
	.010	10.04	7.56	6.55	5.99	5.64	5.39
	.005	12.83	9.43	8.08	7.34	6.87	6.54

The statistical test of the null hypothesis

$$H_0 : \sigma_1^2 = \sigma_2^2$$

uses the test statistic

$$F = \frac{s_1^2}{s_2^2}$$

When the alternative hypothesis implies a one-tailed test—that is,

$$H_a : \sigma_1^2 > \sigma_2^2$$

you can find the right-tailed critical value for rejecting H_0 directly from Table 6 in Appendix I. However, when the alternative hypothesis requires a two-tailed test—that is,

$$H_0 : \sigma_1^2 \neq \sigma_2^2$$

the rejection region is divided between the upper and lower tails of the F distribution. These left-tailed critical values are *not given* in Table 6 for the following reason: You are free to decide which of the two populations you want to call "Population 1." If you always choose to call the population with the *larger* sample variance "Population 1," then the observed value of your test statistic will always be in the right tail of the F distribution. Even though half of the rejection region, the area $\alpha/2$ to its left, will be in the lower tail of the distribution, you will never need to use it! Remember these points, though, for a two-tailed test:

- The area in the right tail of the rejection region is only $\alpha/2$.
- The area to the right of the observed test statistic is only $1/2(p$-value$)$.

The formal procedures for a test of hypothesis and a $(1 - \alpha)100\%$ confidence interval for two population variances are shown next.

Test of Hypothesis Concerning the Equality of Two Population Variances

1. Null hypothesis: $H_0 : \sigma_1^2 = \sigma_2^2$
2. Alternative hypothesis:

One-Tailed Test	Two-Tailed Test
$H_a : \sigma_1^2 > \sigma_2^2$	$H_a : \sigma_1^2 \neq \sigma_2^2$
(or $H_a : \sigma_1^2 < \sigma_2^2$)	

3. Test statistic:

One-Tailed Test	Two-Tailed Test
$F = \dfrac{s_1^2}{s_2^2}$	$F = \dfrac{s_1^2}{s_2^2}$

where s_1^2 is the larger sample variance

4. Rejection region: Reject H_0 when

One-Tailed Test	Two-Tailed Test
$F > F_\alpha$	$F > F_{\alpha/2}$

or when p-value $< \alpha$

The critical values of F_α and $F_{\alpha/2}$ are based on $df_1 = (n_1 - 1)$ and $df_2 = (n_2 - 1)$. These tabulated values, for $a = .100, .050, .025, .010,$ and $.005,$ can be found using Table 6 in Appendix I, or the **F Probabilities** applet.

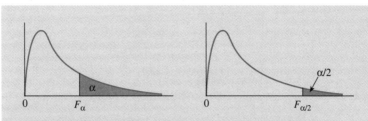

Assumptions: The samples are randomly and independently selected from normally distributed populations.

Confidence Interval for σ_1^2/σ_2^2

$$\left(\frac{s_1^2}{s_2^2}\right)\frac{1}{F_{df_1,df_2}} < \frac{\sigma_1^2}{\sigma_2^2} < \left(\frac{s_1^2}{s_2^2}\right)F_{df_2,df_1}$$

where $df_1 = (n_1 - 1)$ and $df_2 = (n_2 - 1)$. F_{df_1,df_2} is the tabulated critical value of F corresponding to df_1 and df_2 degrees of freedom in the numerator and denominator of F, respectively, with area $\alpha/2$ to its right.
Assumptions: The samples are randomly and independently selected from normally distributed populations.

EXAMPLE 10.14 An experimenter is concerned that the variability of responses using two different experimental procedures may not be the same. Before conducting his research, he conducts a prestudy with random samples of 10 and 8 responses and gets $s_1^2 = 7.14$ and $s_2^2 = 3.21$, respectively. Do the sample variances present sufficient evidence to indicate that the population variances are unequal?

Solution Assume that the populations have probability distributions that are reasonably mound-shaped and hence satisfy, for all practical purposes, the assumption that the populations are normal. You wish to test these hypotheses:

$$H_0 : \sigma_1^2 = \sigma_2^2 \quad \text{versus} \quad H_a : \sigma_1^2 \neq \sigma_2^2$$

Using Table 6 in Appendix I for $\alpha/2 = .025$, you can reject H_0 when $F > 4.82$ with $\alpha = .05$. The calculated value of the test statistic is

$$F = \frac{s_1^2}{s_2^2} = \frac{7.14}{3.21} = 2.22$$

Because the test statistic does not fall into the rejection region, you cannot reject $H_0 : \sigma_1^2 = \sigma_2^2$. Thus, there is insufficient evidence to indicate a difference in the population variances.

EXAMPLE 10.15 Refer to Example 10.14 and find a 90% confidence interval for σ_1^2/σ_2^2.

Solution The 90% confidence interval for σ_1^2/σ_2^2 is

$$\left(\frac{s_1^2}{s_2^2}\right)\frac{1}{F_{df_1,df_2}} < \frac{\sigma_1^2}{\sigma_2^2} < \left(\frac{s_1^2}{s_2^2}\right)F_{df_2,df_1}$$

where

$$s_1^2 = 7.14 \qquad\qquad s_2^2 = 3.21$$
$$df_1 = (n_1 - 1) = 9 \qquad df_2 = (n_2 - 1) = 7$$
$$F_{9,7} = 3.68 \qquad\qquad F_{7,9} = 3.29$$

Substituting these values into the formula for the confidence interval, you get

$$\left(\frac{7.14}{3.21}\right)\frac{1}{3.68} < \frac{\sigma_1^2}{\sigma_2^2} < \left(\frac{7.14}{3.21}\right)3.29 \quad \text{or} \quad .60 < \frac{\sigma_1^2}{\sigma_2^2} < 7.32$$

The calculated interval estimate .60 to 7.32 includes 1.0, the value hypothesized in H_0. This indicates that it is quite possible that $\sigma_1^2 = \sigma_2^2$ and therefore agrees with the test conclusions. Do not reject $H_0 : \sigma_1^2 = \sigma_2^2$.

EXAMPLE 10.16 The variability in the amount of impurities present in a batch of chemical used for a particular process depends on the length of time the process is in operation. A manufacturer using two production lines 1 and 2 has made a slight adjustment to line 2, hoping to reduce the variability as well as the average amount of impurities in the chemical. Samples of $n_1 = 25$ and $n_2 = 25$ measurements from the two batches yield these means and variances:

$$\bar{x}_1 = 3.2 \qquad s_1^2 = 1.04$$
$$\bar{x}_2 = 3.0 \qquad s_2^2 = .51$$

Do the data present sufficient evidence to indicate that the process variability is less for line 2?

Solution The experimenter believes that the average levels of impurities are the same for the two production lines but that her adjustment may have decreased the variability of the levels for line 2, as illustrated in Figure 10.21. This adjustment would be good for the company because it would decrease the probability of producing shipments of the chemical with unacceptably high levels of impurities.

FIGURE 10.21
Distributions
of impurity
measurements
for two
production lines

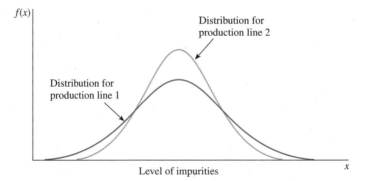

To test for a decrease in variability, the test of hypothesis is

$$H_0 : \sigma_1^2 = \sigma_2^2 \quad \text{versus} \quad H_a : \sigma_1^2 > \sigma_2^2$$

and the observed value of the test statistic is

$$F = \frac{s_1^2}{s_2^2} = \frac{1.04}{.51} = 2.04$$

Using the p-value approach, you can bound the one-tailed p-value using Table 6 in Appendix I with $df_1 = df_2 = (25 - 1) = 24$. The observed value of F falls between $F_{.050} = 1.98$ and $F_{.025} = 2.27$, so that $.025 < p\text{-value} < .05$. The results are judged significant at the 5% level, and H_0 is rejected. You can conclude that the variability of line 2 is less than that of line 1.

The F test for the difference in two population variances completes the battery of tests you have learned in this chapter for making inferences about population parameters under these conditions:

■ The sample sizes are small.
■ The sample or samples are drawn from normal populations.

You will find that the F and χ^2 distributions, as well as the Student's t distribution, are very important in other applications in the chapters that follow. They will be used for different estimators designed to answer different types of inferential questions, but the basic techniques for making inferences remain the same.

In the next section, we review the assumptions required for all of these inference tools, and discuss options that are available when the assumptions do not seem to be reasonably correct.

Exercises

Basic Techniques

10.54 Independent random samples from two normal populations produced the variances listed here:

Sample Size	Sample Variance
16	55.7
20	31.4

a. Do the data provide sufficient evidence to indicate that σ_1^2 differs from σ_2^2? Test using $\alpha = .05$.

b. Find the approximate p-value for the test and interpret its value.

10.55 Refer to Exercise 10.54 and find a 95% confidence interval for σ_1^2/σ_2^2.

10.56 Independent random samples from two normal populations produced the given variances:

Sample Size	Sample Variance
13	18.3
13	7.9

a. Do the data provide sufficient evidence to indicate that $\sigma_1^2 > \sigma_2^2$? Test using $\alpha = .05$.

b. Find the approximate p-value for the test and interpret its value.

Applications

10.57 The average total SAT scores (verbal plus math) were recorded for two groups of students: one group planning to major in engineering and one group planning to major in language/literature.

Engineering	Language/Literature
$\bar{x} = 994$	$\bar{x} = 1051$
$s = 71$	$s = 69$
$n = 15$	$n = 15$

To use the two-sample t test with a pooled estimate of σ^2, you must assume that the two population variances are equal. Test this assumption using the F test for equality of variances. What is the approximate p-value for the test?

10.58 The stability of measurements on a manufactured product is important in maintaining product quality. In fact, it is sometimes better to have small variation in the measured value of some important characteristic of a product and have the process mean be slightly off target than to suffer wide variation with a mean value that perfectly fits requirements. The latter situation may produce a higher percentage of defective products than the former. A manufacturer of light bulbs suspected that one of her production lines was producing bulbs with a wide variation in length of life. To test this theory, she compared the lengths of life for $n = 50$ bulbs randomly sampled from the suspect line and $n = 50$ from a line that seemed to be "in control." The sample means and variances for the two samples were as follows:

"Suspect Line"	Line "in Control"
$\bar{x}_1 = 1520$	$\bar{x}_2 = 1476$
$s_1^2 = 92,000$	$s_2^2 = 37,000$

a. Do the data provide sufficient evidence to indicate that bulbs produced by the "suspect line" have a larger variance in length of life than those produced by the line that is assumed to be in control? Test using $\alpha = .05$.

b. Find the approximate p-value for the test and interpret its value.

10.59 Construct a 90% confidence interval for the variance ratio in Exercise 10.58.

10.60 In Exercise 10.23 and dataset EX1023, you conducted a test to detect a difference in the average prices of light tuna in water versus light tuna in oil.

a. What assumption had to be made concerning the population variances so that the test would be valid?

b. Do the data present sufficient evidence to indicate that the variances violate the assumption in part a? Test using $\alpha = .05$.

10.61 Refer to Exercise 10.24. Susan Beckham and colleagues conducted an experiment involving 10 healthy runners and 10 healthy cyclists to determine if there are significant differences in pressure measurements within the anterior muscle compartment for runners and cyclists.[5] The data—compartment pressure, in millimeters of mercury (Hg)—are reproduced here:

	Runners		Cyclists	
Condition	Mean	Standard Deviation	Mean	Standard Deviation
Rest	14.5	3.92	11.1	3.98
80% maximal O_2 consumption	12.2	3.49	11.5	4.95
Maximal O_2 consumption	19.1	16.9	12.2	4.47

For each of the three variables measured in this experiment, test to see whether there is a significant difference in the variances for runners versus cyclists. Find the approximate p-values for each of these tests. Will a two-sample t test with a pooled estimate of σ^2 be appropriate for all three of these variables? Explain.

10.62 A pharmaceutical manufacturer purchases a particular material from two different suppliers. The mean level of impurities in the raw material is approximately the same for both suppliers, but the manufacturer is concerned about the variability of the impurities from shipment to shipment. If the level of impurities tends to vary excessively for one source of supply, it could affect the quality of the pharmaceutical product. To compare the variation in percentage impurities for the two suppliers, the manufacturer selects 10 shipments from each of the two suppliers and measures the percentage of impurities in the raw material for each shipment. The sample means and variances are shown in the table:

Supplier A	Supplier B
$\bar{x}_1 = 1.89$	$\bar{x}_2 = 1.85$
$s_1^2 = .273$	$s_2^2 = .094$
$n_1 = 10$	$n_2 = 10$

a. Do the data provide sufficient evidence to indicate a difference in the variability of the shipment impurity levels for the two suppliers? Test using $\alpha = .01$. Based on the results of your test, what recommendation would you make to the pharmaceutical manufacturer?

b. Find a 99% confidence interval for σ_2^2 and interpret your results.

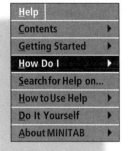

Decide Which Test to Use?

Are you interested in testing means? If the design involves:

a. One random sample, use the one-sample t statistic.

b. Two independent random samples, are the population variances equal?

    i. If equal, use the two-sample t statistic with pooled s^2.

    ii. If unequal, use the unpooled t with estimated df.

c. Two paired samples with random pairs, use a one-sample t for analyzing differences.

Are you interested in testing variances? If the design involves:

a. One random sample, use the χ^2 test for a single variance.

b. Two independent random samples, use the F test to compare two variances.

10.8 Revisiting the Small-Sample Assumptions

All of the tests and estimation procedures discussed in this chapter require that the data satisfy certain conditions in order that the error probabilities (for the tests) and the confidence coefficients (for the confidence intervals) be equal to the values you have specified. For example, if you construct what you believe to be a 95% confidence interval, you want to be certain that, in repeated sampling, 95% (and not 85% or 75% or less) of all such intervals will contain the parameter of interest. These conditions are summarized in these assumptions:

Assumptions

1. For all tests and confidence intervals described in this chapter, it is assumed that **samples are randomly selected from normally distributed populations.**

2. When two samples are selected, it is assumed that they are **selected in an independent manner** except in the case of the paired-difference experiment.

3. For tests or confidence intervals concerning the difference between two population means μ_1 and μ_2 based on independent random samples, it is assumed that $\sigma_1^2 = \sigma_2^2$.

In reality, you will never know everything about the sampled population. If you did, there would be no need for sampling or statistics. It is also highly unlikely that a population will *exactly* satisfy the assumptions given in the box. Fortunately, the procedures presented in this chapter give good inferences even when the data exhibit moderate departures from the necessary conditions.

A statistical procedure that is not sensitive to departures from the conditions on which it is based is said to be **robust.** The Student's *t* tests are quite robust for moderate departures from normality. Also, as long as the sample sizes are nearly equal, there is not much difference between the pooled and unpooled *t* statistics for the difference in two population means. However, if the sample sizes are not clearly equal, and if the population variances are unequal, the pooled *t* statistic provides inaccurate conclusions.

If you are concerned that your data do not satisfy the assumptions, other options are available:

- If you can select relatively large samples, you can use one of the large-sample procedures of Chapters 8 and 9, which do not rely on the normality or equal variance assumptions.

- You may be able to use a *nonparametric test* to answer your inferential questions. These tests have been developed specifically so that few or no distributional assumptions are required for their use. Tests that can be used to compare the locations or variability of two populations are presented in Chapter 15.

Key Concepts and Formulas

I. Experimental Designs for Small Samples

1. **Single random sample:** The sampled population must be normal.

2. **Two independent random samples:** Both sampled populations must be normal.
   a. Populations have a common variance σ^2.
   b. Populations have different variances: σ_1^2 and σ_2^2.

3. **Paired-difference** or **matched pairs** design: The samples are not independent.

II. Statistical Tests of Significance

1. Based on the *t*, *F*, and χ^2 distributions

2. Use the same procedure as in Chapter 9

3. **Rejection region—critical values** and **significance levels:** based on the *t*, *F*, or χ^2 distributions with the appropriate degrees of freedom

4. **Tests of population parameters:** a single mean, the difference between two means, a single variance, and the ratio of two variances

III. Small-Sample Test Statistics

To test one of the population parameters when the sample sizes are small, use the following test statistics:

Parameter	Test Statistic	Degrees of Freedom
μ	$t = \dfrac{\bar{x} - \mu_0}{s/\sqrt{n}}$	$n - 1$
$\mu_1 - \mu_2$ (equal variances)	$t = \dfrac{(\bar{x}_1 - \bar{x}_2) - (\mu_1 - \mu_2)}{\sqrt{s^2\left(\dfrac{1}{n_1} + \dfrac{1}{n_2}\right)}}$	$n_1 + n_2 - 2$
$\mu_1 - \mu_2$ (unequal variances)	$t \approx \dfrac{(\bar{x}_1 - \bar{x}_2) - (\mu_1 - \mu_2)}{\sqrt{\dfrac{s_1^2}{n_1} + \dfrac{s_2^2}{n_2}}}$	Satterthwaite's approximation
$\mu_1 - \mu_2$ (paired samples)	$t = \dfrac{\bar{d} - \mu_d}{s_d/\sqrt{n}}$	$n - 1$
σ^2	$\chi^2 = \dfrac{(n-1)s^2}{\sigma_0^2}$	$n - 1$
σ_1^2/σ_2^2	$F = s_1^2/s_2^2$	$n_1 - 1$ and $n_2 - 1$

Help

Contents ▶
Getting Started ▶
How Do I ▶
Search for Help on... ▶
How to Use Help ▶
Do It Yourself ▶
About MINITAB ▶

Small-Sample Testing and Estimation

The tests and confidence intervals for population means based on the Student's t distribution are found in a *MINITAB* submenu by choosing **Stat → Basic Statistics.** You will see choices for **1-Sample t, 2-Sample t,** and **Paired t,** which will generate Dialog boxes for the procedures in Sections 10.3, 10.4, and 10.5, respectively. You must choose the columns in which the data are stored and the null and alternative hypotheses to be tested (or the confidence coefficient for a confidence interval). In the case of the two-sample t test, you must indicate whether the population variances are assumed equal or unequal, so that *MINITAB* can perform the correct test. We will display some of the Dialog boxes and Session window outputs for the examples in this chapter, beginning with the one-sample t test of Example 10.3.

First, enter the six recorded weights—.46, .61, .52, .48, .57, .54—in column C1 and name them "Weights." Use **Stat → Basic Statistics → 1-Sample t** to generate the Dialog box in Figure 10.22. To test $H_0 : \mu = .5$ versus $H_a : \mu > .5$, use the list on the left to select "Weights" for the Variables box. Check the box marked "Test mean:" and enter **.5** as the test value. Finally, use **Options** and the drop-down menu marked "Alternative" to select "greater than." Click **OK** twice to obtain the output in Figure 10.23. Notice that *MINITAB* produces a one- or a two-sided confidence interval for the single population mean; you can change the confidence coefficient from the default of **.95** in the **Options** box. Also, the **Graphs** option will produce a histogram, a box plot, or a dotplot of the data in column C1.

Data for a two-sample t test with independent samples can be entered into the worksheet in one of two ways:

■ Enter measurements from both samples into a single column and enter numbers (1 or 2) in a second column to identify the sample from which the measurement comes.

■ Enter the samples in two separate columns.

MINITAB

MINITAB

FIGURE 10.22

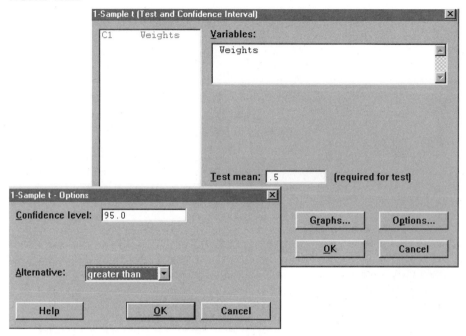

FIGURE 10.23

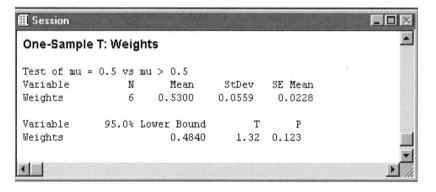

Use the second method and enter the data from Example 10.5 into columns C2 and C3. Then use **Stat → Basic Statistics → 2-Sample t** to generate the Dialog box in Figure 10.24. Check "Samples in different columns," selecting C2 and C3 from the box on the left. Select the proper alternative hypothesis in the Options box, and check the "Assume equal variances" box. (Otherwise, *MINITAB* will perform Satterthwaite's approximation for unequal variances.) The two-sample output when you click **OK** twice automatically contains a 95% one- or two-sided confidence interval as well as the test statistic and *p*-value (you can change the confidence coefficient if you like). The output for Example 10.5 is shown in Figure 10.13 on page 382.

For a paired-difference test, the two samples are entered into separate columns, which we did with the tire wear data in Table 10.3. Use **Stat → Basic Statistics → Paired t** to generate the Dialog box in Figure 10.25. Select C4 and C5 from the box on the left, and use **Options** to pick the proper alternative hypothesis. You may change the

MINITAB

FIGURE 10.24

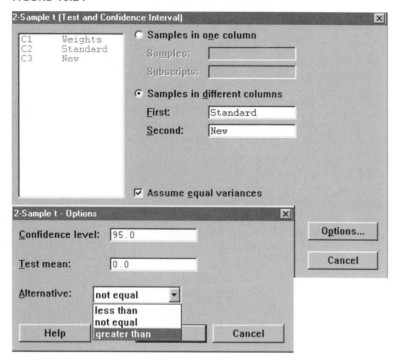

FIGURE 10.25

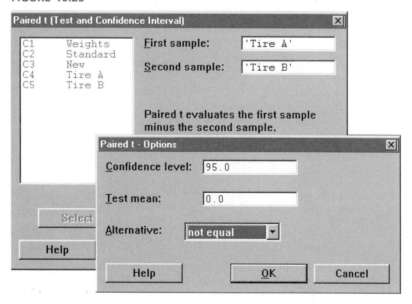

confidence coefficient or the test value (the default value is zero). When you click **OK** twice, you will obtain the output shown in Figure 10.15 on page 390.

Finally, although you cannot use *MINITAB* to perform either the χ^2 or the F test in this chapter, you can use **Calc → Probability Distributions → Chi-square (or F)**, selecting "Cumulative probability" to calculate the appropriate *p*-value.

Supplementary Exercises

10.63 What assumptions are made when Student's t test is used to test a hypothesis concerning a population mean?

10.64 What assumptions are made about the populations from which random samples are obtained when the t distribution is used in making small-sample inferences concerning the difference in population means?

10.65 Why use paired observations to estimate the difference between two population means rather than estimation based on independent random samples selected from the two populations? Is a paired experiment always preferable? Explain.

10.66 A manufacturer can tolerate a small amount [.05 milligrams per liter (mg/l)] of impurities in a raw material needed for manufacturing its product. Because the laboratory test for the impurities is subject to experimental error, the manufacturer tests each batch ten times. Assume that the mean value of the experimental error is 0 and hence that the mean value of the ten test readings is an unbiased estimate of the true amount of the impurities in the batch. For a particular batch of the raw material, the mean of the ten test readings is .058 mg/l, with a standard deviation of .012 mg/l. Do the data provide sufficient evidence to indicate that the amount of impurities in the batch exceeds .05 mg/l? Find the p-value for the test and interpret its value.

10.67 The main stem growth measured for a sample of seventeen 4-year-old red pine trees produced a mean and standard deviation equal to 11.3 and 3.4 inches, respectively. Find a 90% confidence interval for the mean growth of a population of 4-year-old red pine trees subjected to similar environmental conditions.

10.68 The object of a general chemistry experiment is to determine the amount (in milliliters) of sodium hydroxide (NaOH) solution needed to neutralize 1 gram of a specified acid. This will be an exact amount, but when the experiment is run in the laboratory, variation will occur as the result of experimental error. Three titrations are made using phenolphthalein as an indicator of the neutrality of the solution (pH equals 7 for a neutral solution). The three volumes of NaOH required to attain a pH of 7 in each of the three titrations are as follows: 82.10, 75.75, and 75.44 milliliters. Use a 99% confidence interval to estimate the mean number of milliliters required to neutralize 1 gram of the acid.

10.69 Measurements of water intake, obtained from a sample of 17 rats that had been injected with a sodium chloride solution, produced a mean and standard deviation of 31.0 and 6.2 cubic centimeters (cm^3), respectively. Given that the average water intake for noninjected rats observed over a comparable period of time is 22.0 cm^3, do the data indicate that injected rats drink more water than noninjected rats? Test at the 5% level of significance. Find a 90% confidence interval for the mean water intake for injected rats.

10.70 An experimenter was interested in determining the mean thickness of the cortex of the sea urchin egg. The thickness was measured for $n = 10$ sea urchin eggs. These measurements were obtained:

4.5 6.1 3.2 3.9 4.7
5.2 2.6 3.7 4.6 4.1

Estimate the mean thickness of the cortex using a 95% confidence interval.

10.71 A production plant has two extremely complex fabricating systems; one system is twice as old as the other. Both systems are checked, lubricated, and maintained once every 2 weeks. The number of finished products fabricated daily by each of the systems is recorded for 30 working days. The results are given in the table. Do these data present sufficient evidence to conclude that the variability in daily production warrants increased maintenance of the older fabricating system? Use the p-value approach.

New System	Old System
$\bar{x}_1 = 246$	$x_2 = 240$
$s_1 = 15.6$	$s_2 = 28.2$

EX1072

10.72 The data in the table are the diameters and heights of ten fossil specimens of a species of small shellfish, *Rotularia (Annelida) fallax*, that were unearthed in a mapping expedition near the Antarctic Peninsula.[9] The table gives an identification symbol for the fossil specimen, the fossil's diameter and height in millimeters, and the ratio of diameter to height.

Specimen	Diameter	Height	D/H
OSU 36651	185	78	2.37
OSU 36652	194	65	2.98
OSU 36653	173	77	2.25
OSU 36654	200	76	2.63
OSU 36655	179	72	2.49
OSU 36656	213	76	2.80
OSU 36657	134	75	1.79
OSU 36658	191	77	2.48
OSU 36659	177	69	2.57
OSU 36660	199	65	3.06
$\bar{x}$:	184.5	73	2.54
s:	21.5	5	.37

a. Find a 95% confidence interval for the mean diameter of the species.

b. Find a 95% confidence interval for the mean height of the species.

c. Find a 95% confidence interval for the mean ratio of diameter to height.

d. Compare the three intervals constructed in parts a, b, and c. Is the average of the ratios the same as the ratio of the average diameter to average height?

10.73 Refer to Exercise 10.72 and data set EX1072. Suppose you want to estimate the mean diameter of the fossil specimens correct to within 5 millimeters with probability equal to .95. How many fossils do you have to include in your sample?

EX1074

10.74 In behavior analysis, self-control is most often defined as the choice of a large, delayed reinforcer over a small, immediate reinforcer. In an experiment by Stephen Flora and fellow researchers to determine the effects of noise on human self-control, subjects pressed two buttons for points that were exchangeable for money.[10] Pressing one of the buttons produced 2 points over 4 seconds; pressing the other button, the self-control choice, produced 10 points over 4 seconds after a delay of 16 seconds. Seven subjects were asked to make 30 choices in the presence of aversive noise and in the absence of noise. Another six subjects were asked to make 30 choices, first in the absence of noise and then in the presence of aversive noise. The number of correct choices for each subject for both conditions is given here:

Subject	Noise	Quiet	Subject	Quiet	Noise
1	17	11	8	26	30
2	24	27	9	26	30
3	11	13	10	10	25
4	16	30	11	19	24
5	25	27	12	20	26
6	12	17	13	26	30
7	17	12			
Means	17.43	19.57		21.17	27.5

a. Test for a significant difference in the mean numbers of self-control choices made by the first seven subjects and the second six subjects under the *quiet* condition at the $\alpha = .05$ level of significance.

b. Test for a significant difference in the mean numbers of self-control choices made by the first seven subjects and the second six subjects under the *noise* condition at the $\alpha = .05$ level of significance.

c. Since each subject was tested under both conditions (either *noise* followed by *quiet* or *quiet* followed by *noise*), these within-subject observations are, in fact, paired. Using the data for the first seven subjects, test for a significant difference in the average number of self-control choices between the *noise* and *quiet* conditions, with $\alpha = .05$.

d. Using the data for the six subjects numbered 8–13, use a paired *t* test to determine whether there is a significant mean difference between the *quiet* and *noise* conditions. Use $\alpha = .05$.

e. Calculate the differences *Quiet − Noise* for the two groups representing different orders of noise conditions (*noise* first or *quiet* first). Does there appear to be a significant difference in the average difference in self-control choices for the two orders? What conclusions can you draw from this experiment?

EX1075

10.75 Here are the prices per ounce of $n = 13$ different brands of individually wrapped cheese slices:

29.0 24.1 23.7 19.6 27.5
28.7 28.0 23.8 18.9 23.9
21.6 25.9 27.4

Construct a 95% confidence interval estimate of the underlying average price per ounce of individually wrapped cheese slices.

10.76 An experiment was conducted to compare the mean lengths of time required for the bodily absorption of two drugs A and B. Ten people were randomly selected and assigned to receive one of the drugs. The length of time (in minutes) for the drug to reach a specified level in the blood was recorded, and the data summary is given in the table:

Drug A	Drug B
$\bar{x}_1 = 27.2$	$\bar{x}_2 = 33.5$
$s_1^2 = 16.36$	$s_2^2 = 18.92$

a. Do the data provide sufficient evidence to indicate a difference in mean times to absorption for the two drugs? Test using $\alpha = .05$.

b. Find the approximate *p*-value for the test. Does this value confirm your conclusions?

10.77 Refer to Exercise 10.76. Find a 95% confidence interval for the difference in mean times to absorption. Does the interval confirm your conclusions in Exercise 10.76?

10.78 Refer to Exercise 10.76. Suppose you wish to estimate the difference in mean times to absorption correct to within 1 minute with probability approximately equal to .95.

a. Approximately how large a sample is required for each drug (assume that the sample sizes are equal)?

b. If conducting the experiment using the sample sizes of part a will require a large amount of time and money, can anything be done to reduce the sample sizes and still achieve the 1-minute margin of error for estimation?

EX1079

10.79 Insects hovering in flight expend enormous amounts of energy for their size and weight. The data shown here were taken from a much larger body of data collected by T. M. Casey and colleagues.[11] They show the wing stroke frequencies (in hertz) for two different species of bees, $n_1 = 4$ *Euglossa mandibularis* Friese and $n_2 = 6$ *Euglossa imperialis* Cockerell.

E. mandibularis Friese	*E. imperialis* Cockerell
235	180
225	169
190	180
188	185
	178
	182

a. Based on the observed ranges, do you think that a difference exists between the two population variances?

b. Use an appropriate test to determine whether a difference exists.

c. Explain why a Student's t test with a pooled estimator s^2 is unsuitable for comparing the mean wing stroke frequencies for the two species of bees.

EX1080

10.80 The calcium (Ca) content of a powdered mineral substance was analyzed 10 times with the following percent compositions recorded:

.0271 .0282 .0279 .0281 .0268
.0271 .0281 .0269 .0275 .0276

a. Find a 99% confidence interval for the true calcium content of this substance.

b. What does the phrase "99% confident" mean?

c. What assumptions must you make about the sampling procedure so that this confidence interval will be valid? What does this mean to the chemist who is performing the analysis?

10.81 Karl Niklas and T.G. Owens examined the differences in a particular plant, *Plantago Major L.*, when grown in full sunlight versus shade conditions.[12] In this study, shaded plants received direct sunlight for less than 2 hours each day, whereas full-sun plants were never shaded. A partial summary of the data based on $n_1 = 16$ full-sun plants and $n_2 = 15$ shade plants is shown here:

	Full Sun		Shade	
	$\bar{x}$	s	$\bar{x}$	s
Leaf area (cm²)	128.00	43.00	78.70	41.70
Overlap area (cm²)	46.80	2.21	8.10	1.26
Leaf number	9.75	2.27	6.93	1.49
Thickness (mm)	.90	.03	.50	.02
Length (cm)	8.70	1.64	8.91	1.23
Width (cm)	5.24	.98	3.41	.61

a. What assumptions are required in order to use the small-sample procedures given in this chapter to compare full-sun versus shade plants? From the summary presented, do you think that any of these assumptions have been violated?

b. Do the data present sufficient evidence to indicate a difference in mean leaf area for full-sun versus shade plants?

c. Do the data present sufficient evidence to indicate a difference in mean overlap area for full-sun versus shade plants?

10.82 Refer to Exercise 10.81.

a. Find a 95% confidence interval for the difference in mean leaf thickness for full-sun versus shade plants.

b. Find a 95% confidence interval for the difference in mean leaf width for full-sun versus shade plants.

c. Use the confidence intervals from parts a and b to determine whether there is a significant difference in mean leaf thickness and width for the two populations.

10.83 Four sets of identical twins (pairs A, B, C, and D) were selected at random from a computer database of identical twins. One child was selected at random from each pair to form an "experimental group." These four children were sent to school. The other four children were kept at home as a control group. At the end of the school year, the following IQ scores were obtained:

Pair	Experimental Group	Control Group
A	110	111
B	125	120
C	139	128
D	142	135

Does this evidence justify the conclusion that lack of school experience has a depressing effect on IQ scores? Use the p-value approach.

EX1084

10.84 Eight obese persons were placed on a diet for 1 month, and their weights, at the beginning and at the end of the month, were recorded:

	Weights	
Subjects	Initial	Final
1	310	263
2	295	251
3	287	249
4	305	259
5	270	233
6	323	267
7	277	242
8	299	265

Estimate the mean weight loss for obese persons when placed on the diet for a 1-month period. Use a 95% confidence interval and interpret your results. What assumptions must you make so that your inference is valid?

EX1085

10.85 Car manufacturers try to design the bumpers of their automobiles to prevent costly damage in parking-lot type accidents. To compare two models of automobiles, the cars were purposely subject to a series of four front and rear impacts at 5 mph, and the repair costs were recorded.[13]

Impact Type	Honda Civic	Hyundai Elantra
Front into barrier	$403	$247
Rear into barrier	447	0
Front into angle barrier	404	407
Rear into pole	227	185

Do the data provide sufficient evidence to indicate a difference in the average cost of repair for the Honda Civic and the Hyundai Elantra? Test using $\alpha = .05$.

EX1086

10.86 Research psychologists measured the baseline breathing patterns—the total ventilation (in liters of air per minute) adjusted for body size—for each of $n = 30$ patients, so that they could estimate the average total ventilation for patients before any experimentation was done. The data, along with some *MINITAB* output, are presented here:

5.23	5.72	5.77	4.99	5.12	4.82
5.54	4.79	5.16	5.84	4.51	5.14
5.92	6.04	5.83	5.32	6.19	5.70
4.72	5.38	5.48	5.37	4.96	5.58
4.67	5.17	6.34	6.58	4.35	5.63

MINITAB output for Exercise 10.86

Stem-and-Leaf Display: Ltrs/min
```
Stem-and-leaf of Ltrs/min  N = 30
Leaf Unit = 0.10

     1   4 3
     2   4 5
     5   4 677
     8   4 899
    12   5 1111
    (4)   5 2333
    14   5 455
    11   5 6777
     7   5 889
     4   6 01
     2   6 3
     1   6 5
```

Descriptive Statistics: Ltrs/min
```
Variable        N       Mean     Median     TrMean      StDev    SE Mean
Ltrs/min       30     5.3953     5.3750     5.3877     0.5462     0.0997

Variable  Minimum    Maximum         Q1         Q3
Ltrs/min   4.3500     6.5800     4.9825     5.7850
```

a. What information does the stem and leaf plot give you about the data? Why is this important?

b. Use the *MINITAB* output to construct a 99% confidence interval for the average total ventilation for patients.

10.87 A comparison of reaction times (in seconds) for two different stimuli in a psychological word-association experiment produced the following results when applied to a random sample of 16 people:

Stimulus 1	1	3	2	1	2	1	3	2
Stimulus 2	4	2	3	3	1	2	3	3

Do the data present sufficient evidence to indicate a difference in mean reaction times for the two stimuli? Test using $\alpha = .05$.

10.88 Refer to Exercise 10.87. Suppose that the word-association experiment is conducted using eight people as blocks and making a comparison of reaction times within each person; that is, each person is subjected to both stimuli in a random order. The reaction times (in seconds) for the experiment are as follows:

Person	Stimulus 1	Stimulus 2
1	3	4
2	1	2
3	1	3
4	2	1
5	1	2
6	2	3
7	3	3
8	2	3

Do the data present sufficient evidence to indicate a difference in mean reaction times for the two stimuli? Test using $\alpha = .05$.

10.89 Refer to Exercises 10.87 and 10.88. Calculate a 95% confidence interval for the difference in the two population means for each of these experimental designs. Does it appear that blocking increased the amount of information available in the experiment?

EX1090

10.90 The following data are readings (in foot-pounds) of the impact strengths of two kinds of packaging material:

A	B
1.25	.89
1.16	1.01
1.33	.97
1.15	.95
1.23	.94
1.20	1.02
1.32	.98
1.28	1.06
1.21	.98

MINITAB output for
Exercise 10.90

Two-Sample T-Test and CI: A, B

```
Two-sample T for A vs B
      N    Mean    StDev   SE Mean
A    9    1.2367   0.0644    0.021
B    9    0.9778   0.0494    0.016

Difference = mu A - mu B
Estimate for difference:  0.2589
95% CI for difference: (0.2015, 0.3163)
T-Test of difference = 0 (vs not =): T-Value = 9.56   P-Value = 0.000   DF = 16
Both use Pooled StDev = 0.0574
```

a. Use the *MINITAB* printout to determine whether there is evidence of a difference in the mean strengths for the two kinds of material.

b. Are there practical implications to your results?

10.91   Would the amount of information extracted from the data in Exercise 10.90 be increased by pairing successive observations and analyzing the differences? Assume that the observations are paired in the order given Exercise 10.90.

a. Calculate 90% confidence intervals for $(\mu_1 - \mu_2)$ for the two methods of analysis (paired and unpaired) and compare the widths of the intervals.

b. Is it correct to perform two different types of analysis (paired and unpaired) using the same data, and then use the analysis that gives you the most information? Explain.

10.92   When should one use a paired-difference analysis in making inferences concerning the difference between two means?

10.93   An experiment was conducted to compare the densities (in ounces per cubic inch) of cakes prepared from two different cake mixes. Six cake pans were filled with batter A, and six were filled with batter B. Expecting a variation in oven temperature, the experimenter placed a pan filled with batter A and another with batter B *side by side* at six different locations in the oven. The six paired observations of densities are as follows:

Batter A	.135	.102	.098	.141	.131	.144
Batter B	.129	.120	.112	.152	.135	.163

a. Do the data present sufficient evidence to indicate a difference between the average densities of cakes prepared using the two types of batter?

b. Place a 95% confidence interval on the difference between the average densities for the two mixes.

10.94   Under what assumptions can the F distribution be used in making inferences about the ratio of population variances?

10.95   A dairy is in the market for a new container-filling machine and is considering two models, manufactured by company A and company B. Ruggedness, cost, and convenience are comparable in the two models, so the deciding factor is the variability of fills. The model that produces fills with the smaller variance is preferred. If you obtain samples of fills for each of the two models, an F test can be used to test for the equality of population variances. Which type of rejection region would be most favored by each of these individuals?

a. The manager of the dairy—Why?

b. A sales representative for company A—Why?

c. A sales representative for company B—Why?

10.96   Refer to Exercise 10.95. Wishing to demonstrate that the variability of fills is less for her model than for her competitor's, a sales representative for company A acquired a sample of 30 fills from her company's model and a sample of 10 fills from her competitor's model. The sample variances were $s_A^2 = .027$ and $s_B^2 = .065$, respectively. Does this result provide statistical support at the .05 level of significance for the sales representative's claim?

10.97   A chemical manufacturer claims that the purity of his product never varies by more than 2%. Five batches were tested and given purity readings of 98.2, 97.1, 98.9, 97.7, and 97.9%.

a. Do the data provide sufficient evidence to contradict the manufacturer's claim? (HINT: To be generous, let a range of 2% equal 4σ.)

b. Find a 90% confidence interval for σ^2.

10.98   A cannery prints "weight 16 ounces" on its label. The quality control supervisor selects nine cans at random and weighs them. She finds $\bar{x} = 15.7$ and $s = .5$. Do the data present sufficient evidence to indicate that the mean weight is less than that claimed on the label?

10.99 A psychologist wishes to verify that a certain drug increases the reaction time to a given stimulus. The following reaction times (in tenths of a second) were recorded before and after injection of the drug for each of four subjects:

	Reaction Time	
Subject	Before	After
1	7	13
2	2	3
3	12	18
4	12	13

Test at the 5% level of significance to determine whether the drug significantly increases reaction time.

EX10100

10.100 At a time when energy conservation is so important, some scientists think closer scrutiny should be given to the cost (in energy) of producing various forms of food. Suppose you wish to compare the mean amount of oil required to produce 1 acre of corn versus 1 acre of cauliflower. The readings (in barrels of oil per acre), based on 20-acre plots, seven for each crop, are shown in the table. Use these data to find a 90% confidence interval for the difference between the mean amounts of oil required to produce these two crops.

Corn	Cauliflower
5.6	15.9
7.1	13.4
4.5	17.6
6.0	16.8
7.9	15.8
4.8	16.3
5.7	17.1

10.101 The effect of alcohol consumption on the body appears to be much greater at high altitudes than at sea level. To test this theory, a scientist randomly selects 12 subjects and randomly divides them into two groups of six each. One group is put into a chamber that simulates conditions at an altitude of 12,000 feet, and each subject ingests a drink containing 100 cubic centimeters (cc) of alcohol. The second group receives the same drink in a chamber that simulates conditions at sea level. After 2 hours, the amount of alcohol in the blood (grams per 100 cc) for each subject is measured. The data are shown in the table. Do the data provide sufficient evidence to support the theory that retention of alcohol in the blood is greater at high altitudes?

Sea Level	12,000 Feet
.07	.13
.10	.17
.09	.15
.12	.14
.09	.10
.13	.14

10.102 The closing prices of two common stocks were recorded for a period of 15 days. The means and variances are

$$\bar{x}_1 = 40.33 \quad \bar{x}_2 = 42.54$$
$$s_1^2 = 1.54 \quad s_2^2 = 2.96$$

a. Do these data present sufficient evidence to indicate a difference between the variabilities of the closing prices of the two stocks for the populations associated with the two samples? Give the p-value for the test and interpret its value.

b. Place a 99% confidence interval on the ratio of the two population variances.

10.103 An experiment is conducted to compare two new automobile designs. Twenty people are randomly selected, and each person is asked to rate each design on a scale of 1 (poor) to 10 (excellent). The resulting ratings will be used to test the null hypothesis that the mean level of approval is the same for both designs against the alternative hypothesis that one of the automobile designs is preferred. Do these data satisfy the assumptions required for the Student's t test of Section 10.4? Explain.

10.104 The data shown here were collected on lost-time accidents (the figures given are mean work-hours lost per month over a period of 1 year) before and after an industrial safety program was put into effect. Data were recorded for six industrial plants. Do the data provide sufficient evidence to indicate whether the safety program was effective in reducing lost-time accidents? Test using $\alpha = .01$.

	Plant Number					
	1	2	3	4	5	6
Before program	38	64	42	70	58	30
After program	31	58	43	65	52	29

EX10105

10.105 To compare the demand for two different entrees, the manager of a cafeteria recorded the number of purchases of each entree on seven consecutive days. The data are shown in the table. Do the data provide sufficient evidence to indicate a greater mean demand for one of the entrees? Use the *MINITAB* printout.

Day	A	B
Monday	420	391
Tuesday	374	343
Wednesday	434	469
Thursday	395	412
Friday	637	538
Saturday	594	521
Sunday	679	625

MINITAB output for Exercise 10.105

Paired T-Test and CI: Entree A, Entree B

```
Paired T for Entree A vs Entree B
                 N      Mean    StDev   SE Mean
Entree A         7     504.7    127.2      48.1
Entree B         7     471.3     97.4      36.8
Difference       7      33.4     47.5      18.0

95% CI for mean difference: (-10.5, 77.4)
T-Test of mean difference = 0 (vs not = 0): T-Value = 1.86   P-Value = 0.112
```

10.106 The EPA limit on the allowable discharge of suspended solids into rivers and streams is 60 milligrams per liter (mg/l) per day. A study of water samples selected from the discharge at a phosphate mine shows that over a long period, the mean daily discharge of suspended solids is 48 mg/l, but day-to-day discharge readings are variable. State inspectors measured the discharge rates of suspended solids for $n = 20$ days and found $s^2 = 39$ (mg/l)^2. Find a 90% confidence interval for σ^2. Interpret your results.

10.107 Two methods were used to measure the specific activity (in units of enzyme activity per milligram of protein) of an enzyme. One unit of enzyme activity is the amount that catalyzes the formation of 1 micromole of product per minute under specified conditions. Use an appropriate test or estimation procedure to compare the two methods of measurement. Comment on the validity of any assumptions you need to make.

Method 1	125	137	130	151	142
Method 2	137	143	151	156	149

Exercises   DO IT YOURSELF!

10.108   Use the **Student's *t* Probabilities** applet to find the following probabilities:

a. $P(t > 1.2)$ with 5 *df*

c. $P(t < -3.3)$ with 8 *df*

b. $P(t > 2) + P(t < -2)$ with 10 *df*

d. $P(t > .6)$ with 12 *df*

10.109   Use the **Student's *t* Probabilities** applet to find the following critical values:

a. an upper one-tailed rejection region with $\alpha = .05$ and 11 *df*

b. a two-tailed rejection region with $\alpha = .05$ and 7 *df*

c. a lower one-tailed rejection region with $\alpha = .01$ and 15 *df*

10.110   Refer to the **Interpreting Confidence Intervals** applet.

a. Suppose that you have a random sample of size $n = 10$ from a population with unknown mean μ. What formula would you use to construct a 95% confidence interval for the unknown population mean?

b. Use the ┌─────────┐ One Sample └─────────┘ button in the first applet to create a single 95% confidence interval for μ. Use the formula in part a and the information given in the applet to verify the confidence limits provided. (The applet rounds to the nearest integer.) Did this confidence interval enclose the true value, $\mu = 100$?

10.111   Refer to the **Interpreting Confidence Intervals** applet.

a. Use the ┌─────────┐ 10 Samples └─────────┘ button in the first applet to create ten 95% confidence intervals for μ.

b. Are the widths of these intervals all the same? Explain why or why not.

c. How many of the intervals work properly and enclose the true value of μ?

d. Try this simulation again by clicking the ┌─────────┐ 10 Samples └─────────┘ button a few more times and counting the number of intervals that work correctly. Is it close to our 95% confidence level?

e. Use the ┌─────────┐ 10 Samples └─────────┘ button in the second applet to create ten 99% confidence intervals for μ. How many of these intervals work properly?

10.112   Refer to the **Interpreting Confidence Intervals** applet.

a. Use the ┌─────────┐ 100 Samples └─────────┘ button to create one hundred 95% confidence intervals for μ. How many of the intervals work properly and enclose the true value of μ?

b. Repeat the instructions of part a to construct 99% confidence intervals. How many of the intervals work properly and enclose the true value of μ?

c. Try this simulation again by clicking the ┌─────────┐ 100 Samples └─────────┘ button a few more times and counting the number of intervals that work correctly. Use both the 95% and 99% confidence intervals. Do the percentage of intervals that work come close to our 95% and 99% confidence levels?

10.113   A random sample of $n = 12$ observations from a normal population produced $\bar{x} = 47.1$ and $s^2 = 4.7$. Test the hypothesis $H_0: \mu = 48$ against $H_a: \mu \neq 48$. Use the **Small Test of a Population Mean** applet and a 5% significance level.

10.114   In Exercise 9.65, we reported that the national average SAT scores for the class of 2001 were 506 on the verbal portion and 514 on the math portion. Suppose that we only have a small random sample of 15 California students from the class of 2001; their SAT scores are recorded in the following table.

	Verbal	Math
Sample average	499	516
Sample standard deviation	21	20

a. Use the **Small Sample Test of a Population Mean** applet. Do the data provide sufficient evidence to indicate that the average verbal score for all California students in the class of 2001 is different from the national average? Test using $\alpha = .05$.

b. Use the **Small Sample Test of a Population Mean** applet. Do the data provide sufficient evidence to indicate that the average math score for all California students in the class of 2001 is different from the national average? Test using $\alpha = .05$.

10.115 The length of time to recovery was recorded for patients randomly assigned and subjected to two different surgical procedures. The data (recorded in days) are as follows:

	Procedure I	Procedure II
Sample average	7.3	8.9
Sample variance	1.23	1.49
Sample size	11	13

Do the data present sufficient evidence to indicate a difference between the mean recovery times for the two surgical procedures? Perform the test of hypothesis, calculating the test statistic and the approximate p-value by hand. Then check your results using the **Two Sample t test: Independent Samples** applet.

10.116 Refer to Exercise 10.102 in which we reported the closing prices of two common stocks, recorded over a period of 15 days.

$$\bar{x}_1 = 40.33 \quad \bar{x}_2 = 42.54$$
$$s_1^2 = 1.54 \quad s_2^2 = 2.96$$

Use the **Two Sample t test: Independent Samples** applet. Do the data provide sufficient evidence to indicate that the average prices of the two common stocks are different? Use the p-value to access the significance of the test.

Case Study

FLEXTIME

How Would You Like a Four-Day Work Week?

Will a flexible work-week schedule result in positive benefits for both employer and employee? Is a more rested employee, who spends less time commuting to and from work, likely to be more efficient and take less time off for sick leave and personal leave? A report on the benefits of flexible work schedules that appeared in *Environmental Health* looked at the records of $n = 11$ employees who worked in a satellite office in a county health department in Illinois under a 4-day work-week schedule.[14] Employees worked a conventional work week in year 1 and a 4-day work week in year 2. Some statistics for these employees are shown in the following table:

Employee	Personal Leave		Sick Leave	
	Year 2	Year 1	Year 2	Year 1
1	26	33	30	37
2	18	37	61	45
3	24	20	59	56
4	19	26	2	9
5	17	1	79	92
6	34	2	63	65
7	19	13	71	21
8	18	22	83	62
9	9	22	35	26
10	36	13	81	73
11	26	18	79	21

1. A 4-day work week ensures that employees will have one more day that need not be spent at work. One possible result is a reduction in the average number of personal-leave days taken by employees on a 4-day work schedule. Do the data indicate that this is the case? Use the *p*-value approach to testing to reach your conclusion.

2. A 4-day work-week schedule might also have an effect on the average number of sick-leave days an employee takes. Should a directional alternative be used in this case? Why or why not?

3. Construct a 95% confidence interval to estimate the average difference in days taken for sick leave between these 2 years. What do you conclude about the difference between the average number of sick-leave days for these two work schedules?

4. Based on the analysis of these two variables, what can you conclude about the advantages of a 4-day work-week schedule?

Data Sources

1. "Tuna Goes Upscale," *Consumer Reports,* June 2001, p. 19.

2. W.B. Jeffries, H.K. Voris, and C.M. Yang, "Diversity ad Distribution of the Pedunculate Barnacles *Octolasmis* Gray, 1825 Epizoic on the Scyllarid Lobster *Thenus orientalis* (Lund, 1793)," *Crustaceana* 46, no. 3 (1984).

3. Wendy K. Baell and E.H. Wertheim, "Predictors of Outcome in the Treatment of Bulimia Nervosa," *British Journal of Clinical Psychology* 31 (1992):330–332.

4. Jan D. Lindhe, "Clinical Assessment of Antiplaque Agents," *Compendium of Continuing Education in Dentistry,* Suppl. 5 (1984).

5. Susan J. Beckham, W.A. Grana, P. Buckley, J.E. Breasile and P.L. Claypool, "A Comparison of Anterior Compartment Pressures in Competitive Runners and Cyclists," *American Journal of Sports Medicine* 21, no. 1 (1992):36.

6. Michael A. Brehm, J.S. Buguliskis, D.K. Hawkins, E.S. Lee, D. Sabapathi, and R.A. Smith, "Determining Differences in Efficacy of Two Disinfectants Using *t*-tests," *The American Biology Teacher* 58, no. 2 (February 1996):111.

7. "2000 Automobile Insurance," www4.insurance.ca.gov, 29 August 2001.

8. Adapted from "Market Snapshot: Central Riverside County," *The Press-Enterprise* (Riverside, CA), 28 October 2001, p. G3.

9. Carlos E. Macellari, "Revision of Serpulids of the Genus *Rotularia (Annelida)* at Seymour Island (Antarctic Peninsula) and Their Value in Stratigraphy," *Journal of Paleontology* 58, no. 4 (1984).

10. Stephen Flora, T.R. Schieferecke, and H.G. Bremenkamp III, "Effects of Aversive Noise on Human Self-Control for Positive Reinforcement." *Psychological Record* 42 (1992):505–517.

11. T.M. Casey, M.L. May, and K.R. Morgan, "Flight Energetics of Euglossine Bees in Relation to Morphology and Wing Stroke Frequency," *Journal of Experimental Biology* 116 (1985).

12. Karl J. Niklas and T.G. Owens, "Physiological and Morphological Modifications of *Plantago Major (Plantaginaceae)* in Response to Light Conditions," *American Journal of Botany* 76, no. 3 (1989):370–382.

13. "Expensive Bumper Repair: Latest Crash Tests," *Consumers' Research,* April 2001, pp. 20–21.

14. Charles S. Catlin, "Four-day Work Week Improves Environment," *Environmental Health,* March 1997, p. 12.

11

The Analysis of Variance

Case Study

Do you risk a fine by parking your car in red zones or next to fire hydrants? Do you fail to put enough money in a parking meter? If so, you are among the thousands of drivers who receive parking tickets every day in almost every city in the United States. Depending on the city in which you receive a ticket, your fine can be as little as $8 for overtime parking in San Luis Obispo, California, or as high as $340 for illegal parking in a handicapped space in San Diego, California. The case study at the end of this chapter statistically analyzes the variation in parking fines in southern California cities.

General Objective

The quantity of information contained in a sample is affected by various factors that the experimenter may or may not be able to control. This chapter introduces three different *experimental designs,* two of which are direct extensions of the unpaired and paired designs of Chapter 10. A new technique called the *analysis of variance* is used to determine how the different experimental factors affect the average response.

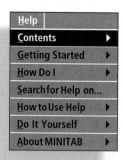

Specific Topics

1. The analysis of variance (11.2)
2. The completely randomized design (11.4, 11.5)
3. Tukey's method of paired comparisons (11.6)
4. The randomized block design (11.7, 11.8)
5. Factorial experiments (11.9, 11.10)

11.1   The Design of an Experiment

The way that a sample is selected is called the *sampling plan* or *experimental design* and determines the amount of information in the sample. Some research involves an **observational study,** in which the researcher does not actually produce the data but only *observes* the characteristics of data that already exist. Most sample surveys, in which information is gathered with a questionnaire, fall into this category. The researcher forms a plan for collecting the data—called the *sampling plan*—and then uses the appropriate statistical procedures to draw conclusions about the population or populations from which the sample comes.

Other research involves **experimentation.** The researcher may deliberately impose one or more experimental conditions on the experimental units in order to determine their effect on the response. Here are some new terms we will use to discuss the design of a statistical experiment.

Definition   An **experimental unit** is the object on which a measurement (or measurements) is taken.

A **factor** is an independent variable whose values are controlled and varied by the experimenter.

A **level** is the intensity setting of a factor.

A **treatment** is a specific combination of factor levels.

The **response** is the variable being measured by the experimenter.

EXAMPLE 11.1   A group of people is randomly divided into an experimental and a control group. The control group is given an aptitude test after having eaten a full breakfast. The experimental group is given the same test without having eaten any breakfast. What are the factors, levels, and treatments in this experiment?

Solution   The *experimental units* are the people on which the *response* (test score) is measured. The *factor* of interest could be described as "meal" and has two *levels:* "breakfast" and "no breakfast." Since this is the only factor controlled by the experimenter, the two levels—"breakfast" and "no breakfast"—also represent the *treatments* of interest in the experiment.

EXAMPLE 11.2   Suppose that the experimenter in Example 11.1 began by randomly selecting 20 men and 20 women for the experiment. These two groups were then randomly divided into 10 each for the experimental and control groups. What are the factors, levels, and treatments in this experiment?

Solution   Now there are two *factors* of interest to the experimenter, and each factor has two *levels:*

- "Gender" at two levels: men and women
- "Meal" at two levels: breakfast and no breakfast

In this more complex experiment, there are four *treatments,* one for each specific combination of factor levels: men without breakfast, men with breakfast, women without breakfast, and women with breakfast.

In this chapter, we will concentrate on experiments that have been designed in three different ways, and we will use a technique called the *analysis of variance* to judge the effects of various factors on the experimental response. Two of these *experimental designs* are extensions of the unpaired and paired designs from Chapter 10.

11.2 What Is an Analysis of Variance?

The responses that are generated in an experimental situation always exhibit a certain amount of *variability*. In an **analysis of variance,** you divide the total variation in the response measurements into portions that may be attributed to various *factors* of interest to the experimenter. If the experiment has been properly designed, these portions can then be used to answer questions about the effects of the various factors on the response of interest.

You can better understand the logic underlying an analysis of variance by looking at a simple experiment. Consider two sets of samples randomly selected from populations 1 (◆) and 2 (○), each with identical pairs of means, $\bar{x}_1$ and $\bar{x}_2$. The two sets are shown in Figure 11.1. Is it easier to detect the difference in the two means when you look at set A or set B? You will probably agree that set A shows the difference much more clearly. In set A, the variability of the measurements *within* the groups (◆s and ○s) is much smaller than the variability *between* the two groups. In set B, there is more variability *within* the groups (◆s and ○s), causing the two groups to "mix" together and making it more difficult to see the *identical* difference in the means.

FIGURE 11.1
Two sets of samples with the same means

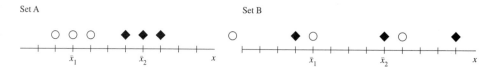

The comparison you have just done intuitively is formalized by the analysis of variance. Moreover, the analysis of variance can be used not only to compare two means but also to make comparisons of *more than two* population means and to determine the effects of various factors in more complex experimental designs. The analysis of variance relies on statistics with sampling distributions that are modeled by the *F* distribution of Section 10.7.

11.3 The Assumptions for an Analysis of Variance

The assumptions required for an analysis of variance are similar to those required for the Student's *t* and *F* statistics of Chapter 10. Regardless of the experimental design used to generate the data, you must assume that the observations within each treatment group are **normally distributed** with a **common variance** σ^2. As in Chapter 10, the analysis of variance procedures are fairly **robust** when the sample sizes are equal and when the data are fairly mound-shaped. Violating the assumption of a common variance is more serious, especially when the sample sizes are not nearly equal.

Assumptions for Analysis of Variance Test and Estimation Procedures

- The observations within each population are normally distributed with a common variance σ^2.
- Assumptions regarding the sampling procedure are specified for each design in the sections that follow.

This chapter describes the analysis of variance for three different experimental designs. The first design is based on independent random sampling from several populations and is an extension of the *unpaired t test* of Chapter 10. The second is an extension of the *paired-difference* or *matched pairs* design and involves a random assignment of treatments within matched sets of observations. The third is a design that allows you to judge the effect of two experimental factors on the response. The sampling procedures necessary for each design are restated in their respective sections.

11.4 The Completely Randomized Design: A One-Way Classification

One of the simplest experimental designs is the **completely randomized design,** in which random samples are selected independently from each of k populations. This design involves only one *factor,* the population from which the measurement comes—hence the designation as a **one-way classification.** There are k different *levels* corresponding to the k populations, which are also the *treatments* for this one-way classification. Are the k population means all the same, or is at least one mean different from the others?

Why do you need a new procedure, the *analysis of variance,* to compare the population means when you already have the Student's t test available? In comparing $k = 3$ means, you could test each of three pairs of hypotheses:

$$H_0 : \mu_1 = \mu_2 \qquad H_0 : \mu_1 = \mu_3 \qquad H_0 : \mu_2 = \mu_3$$

to find out where the differences lie. However, you must remember that each test you perform is subject to the possibility of error. To compare $k = 4$ means, you would need six tests, and you would need 10 tests to compare $k = 5$ means. The more tests you perform on a set of measurements, the more likely it is that at least one of your conclusions will be incorrect. The analysis of variance procedure provides one overall test to judge the equality of the k population means. Once you have determined whether there is *actually* a difference in the means, you can use another procedure to find out where the differences lie.

How can you select these k random samples? Sometimes the populations actually exist in fact, and you can use a computerized random number generator or a random number table to randomly select the samples. For example, in a study to compare the average sizes of health insurance claims in four different states, you could use a computer database provided by the health insurance companies to select random samples from the four states. In other situations, the populations may be *hypothetical,* and responses can be generated only after the experimental treatments have been applied.

EXAMPLE 11.3

A researcher is interested in the effects of five types of insecticides for use in controlling the boll weevil in cotton fields. Explain how to implement a completely randomized design to investigate the effects of the five insecticides on crop yield.

Solution

The only way to generate the equivalent of five random samples from the hypothetical populations corresponding to the five insecticides is to use a method called a **randomized assignment.** A fixed number of cotton plants are chosen for treatment, and each is assigned a random number. Suppose that each sample is to have an equal number of measurements. Using a randomization device, you can assign the first n plants chosen to receive insecticide 1, the second n plants to receive insecticide 2, and so on, until all five treatments have been assigned.

Whether by *random selection* or *random assignment,* both of these examples result in a completely randomized design, or one-way classification, for which the analysis of variance is used.

11.5 The Analysis of Variance for a Completely Randomized Design

Suppose you want to compare k population means, $\mu_1, \mu_2, \ldots, \mu_k$, based on independent random samples of size $n_1, n_2, \ldots, n_k$ from normal populations with a common variance σ^2. That is, each of the normal populations has the same shape, but their locations might be different, as shown in Figure 11.2.

FIGURE 11.2
Normal
populations with a
common variance
but different
means

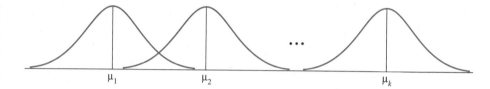

Partitioning the Total Variation in an Experiment

Let x_{ij} be the jth measurement ($j = 1, 2, \ldots, n_i$) in the ith sample. The analysis of variance procedure begins by considering the total variation in the experiment, which is measured by a quantity called the **total sum of squares**:

$$\text{Total SS} = \Sigma(x_{ij} - \overline{x})^2 = \Sigma x_{ij}^2 - \frac{(\Sigma x_{ij})^2}{n}$$

This is the familiar numerator in the formula for the sample variance for the entire set of $n = n_1 + n_2 + \cdots + n_k$ measurements. The second part of the calculational formula is sometimes called the **correction for the mean.** If we let G represent the *grand total* of all n observations, then

$$\text{CM} = \frac{(\Sigma x_{ij})^2}{n} = \frac{G^2}{n}$$

This Total SS is partitioned into two components. The first component, called the **sum of squares for treatments (SST),** measures the variation among the k sample means:

$$\text{SST} = \Sigma n_i(\overline{x}_i - \overline{x})^2 = \Sigma \frac{T_i^2}{n_i} - \text{CM}$$

where T_i is the total of the observations for treatment i. The second component, called the **sum of squares for error (SSE),** is used to measure the pooled variation within the k samples:

$$\text{SSE} = (n_1 - 1)s_1^2 + (n_2 - 1)s_2^2 + \cdots + (n_k - 1)s_k^2$$

This formula is a direct extension of the numerator in the formula for the pooled estimate of σ^2 from Chapter 10. We can show algebraically that, in the analysis of variance,

$$\text{Total SS} = \text{SST} + \text{SSE}$$

Therefore, you need to calculate only two of the three sums of squares—Total SS, SST, and SSE—and the third can be found by subtraction.

Each of the sources of variation, when divided by its appropriate **degrees of freedom,** provides an estimate of the variation in the experiment. Since Total SS involves n squared observations, its degrees of freedom are $df = (n - 1)$. Similarly, the sum of squares for treatments involves k squared observations, and its degrees of freedom are $df = (k - 1)$. Finally, the sum of squares for error, a direct extension of the pooled estimate in Chapter 10, has

$$df = (n_1 - 1) + (n_2 - 1) + \cdots + (n_k - 1) = n - k$$

Notice that the degrees of freedom for treatments and error are additive—that is,

$$df(\text{total}) = df(\text{treatments}) + df(\text{error})$$

These two sources of variation and their respective degrees of freedom are combined to form the **mean squares** as MS = SS/df. The total variation in the experiment is then displayed in an **analysis of variance** (or **ANOVA**) **table.**

ANOVA Table for k Independent Random Samples: Completely Randomized Design

Source	df	SS	MS	F
Treatments	$k - 1$	SST	MST = SST/($k - 1$)	MST/MSE
Error	$n - k$	SSE	MSE = SSE/($n - k$)	
Total	$n - 1$	Total SS		

where

$$\text{Total SS} = \Sigma x_{ij}^2 - \text{CM}$$
$$= (\text{Sum of squares of all } x\text{-values}) - \text{CM}$$

with

$$\text{CM} = \frac{(\Sigma x_{ij})^2}{n} = \frac{G^2}{n}$$

$$\text{SST} = \Sigma \frac{T_i^2}{n_i} - \text{CM} \qquad \text{MST} = \frac{\text{SST}}{k - 1}$$

$$\text{SSE} = \text{Total SS} - \text{SST} \qquad \text{MSE} = \frac{\text{SSE}}{n - k}$$

and

G = Grand total of all n observations

T_i = Total of all observations in sample i

n_i = Number of observations in sample i

$n = n_1 + n_2 + \cdots + n_k$

EXAMPLE 11.4   In an experiment to determine the effect of nutrition on the attention spans of elementary school students, a group of 15 students were randomly assigned to each of three meal plans: no breakfast, light breakfast, and full breakfast.

Their attention spans (in minutes) were recorded during a morning reading period and are shown in Table 11.1. Construct the analysis of variance table for this experiment.

TABLE 11.1

Attention spans of students after three meal plans

No Breakfast	Light Breakfast	Full Breakfast
8	14	10
7	16	12
9	12	16
13	17	15
10	11	12
$T_1 = 47$	$T_2 = 70$	$T_3 = 65$

Solution

To use the calculational formulas, you need the $k = 3$ treatment totals together with $n_1 = n_2 = n_3 = 5$, $n = 15$, and $\Sigma x_{ij} = 182$. Then

$$CM = \frac{(182)^2}{15} = 2208.2667$$

$$\text{Total SS} = (8^2 + 7^2 + \cdots + 12^2) - CM = 2338 - 2208.2667 = 129.7333$$

with $(n - 1) = (15 - 1) = 14$ degrees of freedom,

$$SST = \frac{47^2 + 70^2 + 65^2}{5} - CM = 2266.8 - 2208.2667 = 58.5333$$

with $(k - 1) = (3 - 1) = 2$ degrees of freedom, and by subtraction,

$$SSE = \text{Total SS} - SST = 129.7333 - 58.5333 = 71.2$$

with $(n - k) = (15 - 3) = 12$ degrees of freedom. These three sources of variation, their degrees of freedom, sums of squares, and mean squares are shown in the shaded area of the ANOVA table generated by *MINITAB* and given in Figure 11.3. You will find instructions for generating this output in the section "About *MINITAB*" at the end of this chapter.

FIGURE 11.3

MINITAB output for Example 11.4

One-way ANOVA: Attn Span versus Meal

```
Analysis of Variance for Attn Span
Source     DF        SS        MS        F        P
Meal        2     58.53     29.27     4.93    0.027
Error      12     71.20      5.93
Total      14    129.73

                                  Individual 95% CIs For Mean
                                  Based on Pooled StDev
Level     N      Mean    StDev  -------+---------+---------+---------+---------
1         5     9.400    2.302  (-------*-------)
2         5    14.000    2.550                     (-------*-------)
3         5    13.000    2.449              (-------*------)
                                  -------+---------+---------+---------+---------
Pooled StDev =    2.436            9.0      12.0      15.0
```

The *MINITAB* output gives some additional information about the variation in the experiment. The second section shows the means and standard deviations for the three meal plans. More important, you can see in the first section of the printout two columns marked "F" and "P." We can use these values to test a hypothesis concerning the equality of the three treatment means.

Testing the Equality of the Treatment Means

The *mean squares* in the analysis of variance table can be used to test the null hypothesis

$$H_0 : \mu_1 = \mu_2 = \cdots = \mu_k$$

versus the alternative hypothesis

$$H_a : \text{At least one of the means is different from the others}$$

using the following theoretical argument:

- Remember that σ^2 is the common variance for all k populations. The quantity

$$MSE = \frac{SSE}{n - k}$$

is a pooled estimate of σ^2, a weighted average of all k sample variances, whether or not H_0 is true.

- If H_0 is true, then the variation in the sample means, measured by MST = [SST/(k − 1)], also provides an unbiased estimate of σ^2. However, if H_0 is false and the population means are different, then MST—which measures the variation in the sample means—is unusually *large*, as shown in Figure 11.4.

FIGURE 11.4
Sample means drawn from identical versus different populations

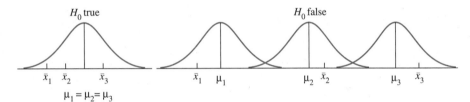

- The test statistic

$$F = \frac{MST}{MSE}$$

tends to be larger than usual if H_0 is false. Hence, you can reject H_0 for large values of F, using a *right-tailed* statistical test. When H_0 is true, this test statistic has an F distribution with $df_1 = (k − 1)$ and $df_2 = (n − k)$ degrees of freedom, and *right-tailed* critical values of the F distribution (from Table 6 in Appendix I) or computer-generated p-values can be used to draw statistical conclusions about the equality of the population means.

F Test for Comparing *k* Population Means

1. Null hypothesis: $H_0 : \mu_1 = \mu_2 = \cdots = \mu_k$
2. Alternative hypothesis: $H_a :$ One or more pairs of population means differ
3. Test statistic: $F = MST/MSE$, where F is based on $df_1 = (k − 1)$ and $df_2 = (n − k)$
4. Rejection region: Reject H_0 if $F > F_\alpha$, where F_α lies in the upper tail of the F distribution (with $df_1 = k − 1$ and $df_2 = n − k$) or if the p-value $< \alpha$.

(continued)

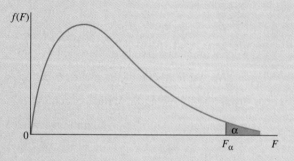

F Test for Comparing k Population Means (continued)

Assumptions

- The samples are randomly and independently selected from their respective populations.
- The populations are normally distributed with means $\mu_1, \mu_2, \ldots, \mu_k$ and equal variances, $\sigma_1^2 = \sigma_2^2 = \cdots = \sigma_k^2 = \sigma^2$.

EXAMPLE 11.5

Do the data in Example 11.4 provide sufficient evidence to indicate a difference in the average attention spans depending on the type of breakfast eaten by the student?

Solution To test $H_0 : \mu_1 = \mu_2 = \mu_3$ versus the alternative hypothesis that the average attention span is different for at least one of the three treatments, you use the analysis of variance F statistic, calculated as

$$F = \frac{\text{MST}}{\text{MSE}} = \frac{29.2667}{5.9333} = 4.93$$

and shown in the column marked "F" in Figure 11.3. It will not surprise you to know that the value in the column marked "P" in Figure 11.3 is the exact p-value for this statistical test.

The test statistic MST/MSE calculated above has an F distribution with $df_1 = 2$ and $df_2 = 12$ degrees of freedom. Using the critical value approach with $\alpha = .05$, you can reject H_0 if $F > F_{.05} = 3.89$ from Table 6 in Appendix I (see Figure 11.5). Since the observed value, $F = 4.93$, exceeds the critical value, you reject H_0. There is sufficient evidence to indicate that at least one of the three average attention spans is different from at least one of the others.

FIGURE 11.5
Rejection region
for Example 11.5

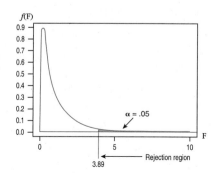

You could have reached this same conclusion using the exact p-value, $P = .027$, given in Figure 11.3. Since the p-value is less than $\alpha = .05$, the results are statistically significant at the 5% level. You still conclude that at least one of the three average attention spans is different from at least one of the others.

DO IT YOURSELF!

You can use the **F Probabilities** applet to find critical values of F or p-values for the analysis of variance F test. Look at the two applets in Figure 11.6. Use the sliders on the left and right of the applets to select the appropriate degrees of freedom (df_1 and df_2). To find the critical value for rejection of H_0, enter the significance level α in the box marked "Prob" and press Enter. To find the p-value, enter the observed value of the test statistic in the box marked "F" and press Enter. Can you identify the critical value for rejection and the p-value for Example 11.5?

FIGURE 11.6
F Probabilities
applet

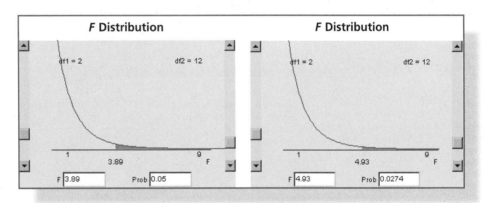

Estimating Differences in the Treatment Means

The next obvious question you might ask involves the nature of the differences in the population means. Which means are different from the others? How can you estimate the difference, or possibly the individual means for each of the three treatments? In Section 11.6, we will present a procedure that you can use to compare all possible pairs of treatment means simultaneously. However, if you have a special interest in a particular mean or pair of means, you can construct confidence intervals using the small-sample procedures of Chapter 10, based on the Student's t distribution. For a single population mean, μ_i, the confidence interval is

$$\bar{x}_i \pm t_{\alpha/2}\left(\frac{s}{\sqrt{n_i}}\right)$$

where $\bar{x}_i$ is the sample mean for the ith treatment. Similarly, for a comparison of two population means—say, μ_i and μ_j—the confidence interval is

$$(\bar{x}_i - \bar{x}_j) \pm t_{\alpha/2}\sqrt{s^2\left(\frac{1}{n_i} + \frac{1}{n_j}\right)}$$

Before you can use these confidence intervals, however, two questions remain:

- How do you calculate s or s^2, the best estimate of the common variance σ^2?
- How many degrees of freedom are used for the critical value of t?

To answer these questions, remember that in an analysis of variance, the mean square for error, MSE, always provides an unbiased estimator of σ^2 and uses information from the entire set of measurements. Hence, it is the best available estimator of σ^2, regardless of what test or estimation procedure you are using. You should *always* use

$$s^2 = \text{MSE} \qquad \text{with } df = (n - k)$$

to estimate σ^2! You can find the positive square root of this estimator, $s = \sqrt{\text{MSE}}$, on the last line of Figure 11.3 labeled "Pooled StDev."

Completely Randomized Design: $(1 - \alpha)100\%$ Confidence Intervals for a Single Treatment Mean and the Difference between Two Treatment Means

Single treatment mean:

$$\bar{x}_i \pm t_{\alpha/2}\left(\frac{s}{\sqrt{n_i}}\right)$$

Difference between two treatment means:

$$(\bar{x}_i - \bar{x}_j) \pm t_{\alpha/2}\sqrt{s^2\left(\frac{1}{n_i} + \frac{1}{n_j}\right)}$$

with

$$s = \sqrt{s^2} = \sqrt{\text{MSE}} = \frac{\text{SSE}}{n - k}$$

where $n = n_1 + n_2 + \cdots + n_k$ and $t_{\alpha/2}$ is based on $(n - k)\ df$.

EXAMPLE 11.6

The researcher in Example 11.4 believes that students who have no breakfast will have significantly shorter attention spans but that there may be no difference between those who eat a light or a full breakfast. Find a 95% confidence interval for the average attention span for students who eat no breakfast, as well as a 95% confidence interval for the difference in the average attention spans for light versus full breakfast eaters.

Solution With $s^2 = \text{MSE} = 5.9333$ so that $s = \sqrt{5.9333} = 2.436$ with $df = (n - k) = 12$, you can calculate the two confidence intervals:

- For no breakfast:

$$\bar{x}_1 \pm t_{\alpha/2}\left(\frac{s}{\sqrt{n_1}}\right)$$

$$9.4 \pm 2.179\left(\frac{2.436}{\sqrt{5}}\right)$$

$$9.4 \pm 2.37$$

or between 7.03 and 11.77 minutes.

■ For light versus full breakfast:

$$(\bar{x}_2 - \bar{x}_3) \pm t_{\alpha/2} \sqrt{s^2 \left(\frac{1}{n_2} + \frac{1}{n_3} \right)}$$

$$(14 - 13) \pm 2.179 \sqrt{5.9333 \left(\frac{1}{5} + \frac{1}{5} \right)}$$

$$1 \pm 3.36$$

a difference of between -2.36 and 4.36 minutes.

You can see that the second confidence interval does not indicate a difference in the average attention spans for students who ate light versus full breakfasts, as the researcher suspected. If the researcher, because of prior beliefs, wishes to test the other two possible pairs of means—none versus light breakfast, and none versus full breakfast—the methods given in Section 11.6 should be used for testing all three pairs.

Some computer programs have graphics options that provide a powerful visual description of data and the k treatment means. One such option in the *MINITAB* program is shown in Figure 11.7. Notice that the "no breakfast" mean appears to be somewhat different from the other two means, as the researcher suspected, although there is a bit of overlap in the boxplots. In the next section, we present a formal procedure for testing the significance of the differences between all pairs of treatment means.

FIGURE 11.7
Boxplots for
Example 11.6

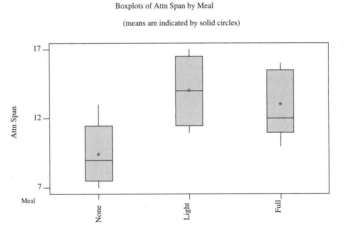

Know Whether My Calculations Are Accurate?

The following suggestions apply to all the analyses of variance in this chapter:

1. When calculating sums of squares, be certain to carry at least six significant figures before performing subtractions.

2. Remember, sums of squares can never be negative. If you obtain a negative sum of squares, you have made a mistake in arithmetic.

3. Always check your analysis of variance table to make certain that the degrees of freedom sum to the total degrees of freedom $(n - 1)$ and that the sums of squares sum to Total SS.

Exercises   Basic Techniques

11.1 Suppose you wish to compare the means of six populations based on independent random samples, each of which contains 10 observations. Insert, in an ANOVA table, the sources of variation and their respective degrees of freedom.

11.2 The values of Total SS and SSE for the experiment in Exercise 11.1 are Total SS $= 21.4$ and SSE $= 16.2$.

a. Complete the ANOVA table for Exercise 11.1.

b. How many degrees of freedom are associated with the F statistic for testing
$$H_0: \mu_1 = \mu_2 = \cdots = \mu_6?$$

c. Give the rejection region for the test in part b for $\alpha = .05$.

d. Do the data provide sufficient evidence to indicate differences among the population means?

e. Estimate the p-value for the test. Does this value confirm your conclusions in part d?

11.3 The sample means corresponding to populations 1 and 2 in Exercise 11.1 are $\bar{x}_1 = 3.07$ and $\bar{x}_2 = 2.52$.

a. Find a 95% confidence interval for μ_1.

b. Find a 95% confidence interval for the difference $(\mu_1 - \mu_2)$.

11.4 Suppose you wish to compare the means of four populations based on independent random samples, each of which contains six observations. Insert, in an ANOVA table, the sources of variation and their respective degrees of freedom.

11.5 The values of Total SS and SST for the experiment in Exercise 11.4 are Total SS $= 473.2$ and SST $= 339.8$.

a. Complete the ANOVA table for Exercise 11.4.

b. How many degrees of freedom are associated with the F statistic for testing $H_0: \mu_1 = \mu_2 = \mu_3 = \mu_4$?

c. Give the rejection region for the test in part b for $\alpha = .05$.

d. Do the data provide sufficient evidence to indicate differences among the population means?

e. Approximate the p-value for the test. Does this confirm your conclusions in part d?

11.6 The sample means corresponding to populations 1 and 2 in Exercise 11.4 are $\bar{x}_1 = 88.0$ and $\bar{x}_2 = 83.9$.

a. Find a 90% confidence interval for μ_1.

b. Find a 90% confidence interval for the difference $(\mu_1 - \mu_2)$.

11.7 These data are observations collected using a completely randomized design:

EX1107

Sample 1	Sample 2	Sample 3
3	4	2
2	3	0
4	5	2
3	2	1
2	5	

a. Calculate CM and Total SS.

b. Calculate SST and MST.

c. Calculate SSE and MSE.

d. Construct an ANOVA table for the data.

e. State the null and alternative hypotheses for an analysis of variance F test.

f. Use the p-value approach to determine whether there is a difference in the three population means.

11.8 Refer to Exercise 11.7 and data set EX1107. Do the data provide sufficient evidence to indicate a difference between μ_2 and μ_3? Test using the t test of Section 10.4 with $\alpha = .05$.

11.9 Refer to Exercise 11.7 and data set EX1107.

    a. Find a 90% confidence interval for μ_1.

    b. Find a 90% confidence interval for the difference $(\mu_1 - \mu_3)$.

Applications

11.10 A clinical psychologist wished to compare three methods for reducing hostility levels in university students using a certain psychological test (HLT). High scores on this test were taken to indicate great hostility. Eleven students who got high and nearly equal scores were used in the experiment. Five were selected at random from among the 11 problem cases and treated by method A, three were taken at random from the remaining six students and treated by method B, and the other three students were treated by method C. All treatments continued throughout a semester, when the HLT test was given again. The results are shown in the table.

Method	Scores on the HLT Test				
A	73	83	76	68	80
B	54	74	71		
C	79	95	87		

    a. Perform an analysis of variance for this experiment.

    b. Do the data provide sufficient evidence to indicate a difference in mean student response to the three methods after treatment?

11.11 Refer to Exercise 11.10. Let μ_A and μ_B, respectively, denote the mean scores at the end of the semester for the populations of extremely hostile students who were treated throughout that semester by method A and method B.

    a. Find a 95% confidence interval for μ_A.

    b. Find a 95% confidence interval for μ_B.

    c. Find a 95% confidence interval for $(\mu_A - \mu_B)$.

    d. Is it correct to claim that the confidence intervals found in parts a, b, and c are jointly valid?

EX1112

11.12 An experiment was conducted to compare the effectiveness of three training programs, A, B, and C, in training assemblers of a piece of electronic equipment. Fifteen employees were randomly assigned, five each, to the three programs. After completion of the courses, each person was required to assemble four pieces of the equipment, and the average length of time required to complete the assembly was recorded. Several of the employees resigned during the course of the program; the remainder were evaluated, producing the data shown in the accompanying table. Use the *MINITAB* printout to answer the questions.

Training Program	Average Assembly Time (min)				
A	59	64	57	62	
B	52	58	54		
C	58	65	71	63	64

    a. Do the data provide sufficient evidence to indicate a difference in mean assembly times for people trained by the three programs? Give the p-value for the test and interpret its value.

    b. Find a 99% confidence interval for the difference in mean assembly times between persons trained by programs A and B.

    c. Find a 99% confidence interval for the mean assembly times for persons trained in program A.

    d. Do you think the data will satisfy (approximately) the assumption that they have been selected from normal populations? Why?

MINITAB output for
Exercise 11.12

One-way ANOVA: Time versus Program

```
Analysis of Variance for Time
Source     DF       SS       MS       F        P
Program     2    170.5     85.2     5.70    0.025
Error       9    134.5     14.9
Total      11    304.9

                               Individual 95% CIs For Mean
                               Based on Pooled StDev
Level    N      Mean    StDev   -+---------+---------+---------+-----
A        4    60.500    3.109                  (--------*--------)
B        3    54.667    3.055    (---------*---------)
C        5    64.200    4.658                        (------*-------)
                                -+---------+---------+---------+-----
Pooled StDev =   3.865          50.0      55.0      60.0      65.0
```

EX1113

11.13   An ecological study was conducted to compare the rates of growth of vegetation at four swampy undeveloped sites and to determine the cause of any differences that might be observed. Part of the study involved measuring the leaf lengths of a particular plant species on a preselected date in May. Six plants were randomly selected at each of the four sites to be used in the comparison. The data in the table are the mean leaf length per plant (in centimeters) for a random sample of ten leaves per plant. The *MINITAB* analysis of variance computer printout for these data is also provided.

Location	Mean Leaf Length (cm)					
1	5.7	6.3	6.1	6.0	5.8	6.2
2	6.2	5.3	5.7	6.0	5.2	5.5
3	5.4	5.0	6.0	5.6	4.9	5.2
4	3.7	3.2	3.9	4.0	3.5	3.6

MINITAB output for
Exercise 11.13

One-way ANOVA: Length versus Location

```
Analysis of Variance for Length
Source     DF       SS       MS       F        P
Location    3    19.740    6.580    57.38    0.000
Error      20     2.293    0.115
Total      23    22.033              Individual 95% CIs For Mean
                                     Based on Pooled StDev
Level    N      Mean    StDev   --------+---------+---------+---------
1        6    6.0167   0.2317                            (--*---)
2        6    5.6500   0.3937                        (---*--)
3        6    5.3500   0.4087                     (---*--)
4        6    3.6500   0.2881   (---*--)
                                --------+---------+---------+---------
Pooled StDev =   0.3386          4.00      4.80      5.60
```

a. You will recall that the test and estimation procedures for an analysis of variance require that the observations be selected from normally distributed (at least, roughly so) populations. Why might you feel reasonably confident that your data satisfy this assumption?

b. Do the data provide sufficient evidence to indicate a difference in mean leaf length among the four locations? What is the *p*-value for the test?

c. Suppose, prior to seeing the data, you decided to compare the mean leaf lengths of locations 1 and 4. Test the null hypothesis $\mu_1 = \mu_4$ against the alternative $\mu_1 \neq \mu_4$.

d. Refer to part c. Construct a 99% confidence interval for $(\mu_1 - \mu_4)$.

e. Rather than use an analysis of variance *F* test, it would seem simpler to examine one's data, select the two locations that have the smallest and largest sample mean lengths, and then compare these two means using a Student's *t* test. If there is evidence to indicate a difference in these means, there is clearly evidence of a difference among the four. (If you were to use this logic, there would be no need for the analysis of variance *F* test.) Explain why this procedure is invalid.

EX1114

11.14 Water samples were taken at four different locations in a river to determine whether the quantity of dissolved oxygen, a measure of water pollution, varied from one location to another. Locations 1 and 2 were selected above an industrial plant, one near the shore and the other in midstream; location 3 was adjacent to the industrial water discharge for the plant; and location 4 was slightly downriver in midstream. Five water specimens were randomly selected at each location, but one specimen, corresponding to location 4, was lost in the laboratory. The data and a *MINITAB* analysis of variance computer printout are provided here (the greater the pollution, the lower the dissolved oxygen readings).

Location	Mean Dissolved Oxygen Content				
1	5.9	6.1	6.3	6.1	6.0
2	6.3	6.6	6.4	6.4	6.5
3	4.8	4.3	5.0	4.7	5.1
4	6.0	6.2	6.1	5.8	

MINITAB output for
Exercise 11.11

One-way ANOVA: Oxygen versus Location

```
Analysis of Variance for Oxygen
Source     DF        SS        MS        F        P
Location    3    7.8361    2.6120    63.66    0.000
Error      15    0.6115    0.0410
Total      18    8.4516                 Individual 95% CIs For Mean
                                        Based on Pooled StDev
Level       N      Mean     StDev    ----+---------+---------+---------+--
1           5    6.0800    0.1483                         (--*---)
2           5    6.4400    0.1140                              (--*---)
3           5    4.7800    0.3114    (---*--)
4           4    6.0250    0.1708                      (--*---)
                                     ----+---------+---------+---------+--
Pooled StDev =    0.2026              4.80      5.40      6.00      6.60
```

a. Do the data provide sufficient evidence to indicate a difference in the mean dissolved oxygen contents for the four locations?

b. Compare the mean dissolved oxygen content in midstream above the plant with the mean content adjacent to the plant (location 2 versus location 3). Use a 95% confidence interval.

EX1115

11.15 The calcium content of a powdered mineral substance was analyzed five times by each of three methods, with similar standard deviations:

Method	Percent Calcium				
1	.0279	.0276	.0270	.0275	.0281
2	.0268	.0274	.0267	.0263	.0267
3	.0280	.0279	.0282	.0278	.0283

Use an appropriate test to compare the three methods of measurement. Comment on the validity of any assumptions you need to make.

EX1116

11.16 In Exercise 10.6, we reported the estimated average prices for a 6-ounce can or a 7.06-ounce pouch of tuna fish, based on prices paid nationally for a variety of different brands of tuna.[1]

Light Tuna in Water		White Tuna in Oil	White Tuna in Water	Light Tuna in Oil	
.99	.53	1.27	1.49	2.56	.62
1.92	1.41	1.22	1.29	1.92	.66
1.23	1.12	1.19	1.27	1.30	.62
.85	.63	1.22	1.35	1.79	.65
.65	.67		1.29	1.23	.60
.69	.60		1.00		.67
.60	.66		1.27		
			1.28		

a. Use an analysis of variance for a completely randomized design to determine if there are significant differences in the prices of tuna packaged in these four different ways. Can you reject the hypothesis of no difference in average price for these packages at the $\alpha = .05$ level of significance? At the $\alpha = .01$ level of significance?

b. Find a 95% confidence interval estimate of the difference in price between light tuna in water and light tuna in oil. Does there appear to be a significant difference in the price of these two kinds of packaged tuna?

c. Find a 95% confidence interval estimate of the difference in price between white tuna in water and white tuna in oil. Does there appear to be a significant difference in the price of these two kinds of packaged tuna?

d. What other confidence intervals might be of interest to the researcher who conducted this experiment?

11.6 Ranking Population Means

Many experiments are exploratory in nature. You have no preconceived notions about the results and have not decided (before conducting the experiment) to make specific treatment comparisons. Rather, you want to rank the treatment means, determine which means differ, and identify sets of means for which no evidence of difference exists.

One option might be to order the sample means from the smallest to the largest and then to conduct t tests for adjacent means in the ordering. If two means differ by more than

$$ t_{\alpha/2} \sqrt{s^2 \left(\frac{1}{n_1} + \frac{1}{n_2} \right)} $$

you conclude that the pair of population means differ. The problem with this procedure is that the probability of making a Type I error—that is, concluding that two means differ when, in fact, they are equal—is α for each test. If you compare a large number of pairs of means, the probability of detecting at least one difference in means, when in fact none exists, is quite large.

A simple way to avoid the high risk of declaring differences when they do not exist is to use the **studentized range,** the difference between the smallest and the largest in a set of k sample means, as the yardstick for determining whether there is a difference in a pair of population means. This method, often called **Tukey's method for paired comparisons,** makes the probability of declaring that a difference exists between at least one pair in a set of k treatment means, when no difference exists, equal to α.

Tukey's method for making paired comparisons is based on the usual analysis of variance assumptions. **In addition, it assumes that the sample means are independent and based on samples of equal size.** The yardstick that determines whether a difference exists between a pair of treatment means is the quantity ω (Greek letter omega), which is presented next.

Yardstick for Making Paired Comparisons

$$ \omega = q_\alpha(k, df) \left(\frac{s}{\sqrt{n_t}} \right) $$

(continued)

> **Yardstick for Making Paired Comparisons** (continued)
>
> where
>
> $$k = \text{Number of treatments}$$
> $$s^2 = \text{MSE} = \text{Estimator of the common variance } \sigma^2 \text{ and } s = \sqrt{s^2}$$
> $$df = \text{Number of degrees of freedom for } s^2$$
> $$n_t = \text{Common sample size—that is, the number of observations in each of the } k \text{ treatment means}$$
> $$q_\alpha(k, df) = \text{Tabulated value from Tables 11(a) and 11(b) in Appendix I, for } \alpha = .05 \text{ and } .01, \text{ respectively, and for various combinations of } k \text{ and } df$$
>
> **Rule:** Two population means are judged to differ if the corresponding sample means differ by ω or more.

Table 11(a) and 11(b) in Appendix I list the values of $q_\alpha(k, df)$ for $\alpha = .05$ and .01, respectively. To illustrate the use of the tables, refer to the portion of Table 11(a) reproduced in Table 11.2. Suppose you want to make pairwise comparisons of $k = 5$ means with $\alpha = .05$ for an analysis of variance, where s^2 possesses 9 df. The tabulated value for $k = 5$, $df = 9$, and $\alpha = .05$, shaded in Table 11.2, is $q_{.05}(5, 9) = 4.76$.

TABLE 11.2
A partial reproduction of Table 11(a) in Appendix I; upper 5% points

df	2	3	4	5	6	7	8	9	10	11	12
1	17.97	26.98	32.82	37.08	40.41	43.12	45.40	47.36	49.07	50.59	51.96
2	6.08	8.33	9.80	10.88	11.74	12.44	13.03	13.54	13.99	14.39	14.75
3	4.50	5.91	6.82	7.50	8.04	8.48	8.85	9.18	9.46	9.72	9.95
4	3.93	5.04	5.76	6.29	6.71	7.05	7.35	7.60	7.83	8.03	8.21
5	3.64	4.60	5.22	5.67	6.03	6.33	6.58	6.80	6.99	7.17	7.32
6	3.46	4.34	4.90	5.30	5.63	5.90	6.12	6.32	6.49	6.65	6.79
7	3.34	4.16	4.68	5.06	5.36	5.61	5.82	6.00	6.16	6.30	6.43
8	3.26	4.04	4.53	4.89	5.17	5.40	5.60	5.77	5.92	6.05	6.18
9	3.20	3.95	4.41	4.76	5.02	5.24	5.43	5.59	5.74	5.87	5.98
10	3.15	3.88	4.33	4.65	4.91	5.12	5.30	5.46	5.60	5.72	5.83
11	3.11	3.82	4.26	4.57	4.82	5.03	5.20	5.35	5.49	5.61	5.71
12	3.08	3.77	4.20	4.51	4.75	4.95	5.12	5.27	5.39	5.51	5.61

EXAMPLE 11.7

Refer to Example 11.4, in which you compared the average attention spans for students given three different "meal" treatments in the morning: no breakfast, a light breakfast, or a full breakfast. The ANOVA F test in Example 11.5 indicated a significant difference in the population means. Use Tukey's method for paired comparisons to determine which of the three population means differ from the others.

Solution

For this example, there are $k = 3$ treatment means, with $s = \sqrt{\text{MSE}} = 2.436$. Tukey's method can be used, with each of the three samples containing $n_t = 5$ measurements and $(n - k) = 12$ degrees of freedom. Consult Table 11 in Appendix I to find $q_{.05}(k, df) = q_{.05}(3, 12) = 3.77$ and calculate the "yardstick" as

$$\omega = q_{.05}(3, 12)\left(\frac{s}{\sqrt{n_t}}\right) = 3.77\left(\frac{2.436}{\sqrt{5}}\right) = 4.11$$

The three treatment means are arranged in order from the smallest, 9.4, to the largest, 14.0, in Figure 11.8. The next step is to check the difference between every pair of means. The only difference that exceeds $\omega = 4.11$ is the difference between no breakfast and a light breakfast. These two treatments are thus declared significantly different. You cannot declare a difference between the other two pairs of treatments. To indicate this fact visually, Figure 11.8 shows a line under those pairs of means that are not significantly different.

FIGURE 11.8
Ranked means for
Example 11.7

None	Full	Light
9.4	13.0	14.0

The results here may seem confusing. However, it usually helps to think of ranking the means and interpreting nonsignificant differences as our inability to distinctly rank those means underlined by the same line. For this example, the light breakfast definitely ranked higher than no breakfast, but the full breakfast could not be ranked higher than no breakfast, or lower than the light breakfast. The probability that we make at least one error among the three comparisons is at most $\alpha = .05$.

Most computer programs provide an option to perform **paired comparisons,** including Tukey's method. The *MINITAB* output in Figure 11.9 shows its form of Tukey's test, which differs slightly from the method we have presented. The three intervals that you see in the printout represent the difference in the two sample means plus or minus the yardstick ω. If the interval contains the value 0, the two means are judged to be not significantly different. You can see that only means 1 and 2 (none versus light) show a significant difference.

FIGURE 11.9
MINITAB **output for**
Example 11.7

```
Tukey's pairwise comparisons
    Family error rate = 0.0500
Individual error rate = 0.0206
Critical value = 3.77

Intervals for (column level mean) - (row level mean)
              1             2
    2      -8.707
           -0.493

    3      -7.707        -3.107
            0.507         5.107
```

As you study two more experimental designs in the next sections of this chapter, remember that, once you have found a factor to be significant, you should use Tukey's method or another method of paired comparisons to find out exactly where the differences lie!

Exercises

Basic Techniques

11.17 Suppose you wish to use Tukey's method of paired comparisons to rank a set of population means. In addition to the analysis of variance assumptions, what other property must the treatment means satisfy?

11.18 Consult Tables 11(a) and 11(b) in Appendix I and find the values of $q_\alpha(k, df)$ for these cases:

    a. $\alpha = .05$, $k = 5$, $df = 7$ **b.** $\alpha = .05$, $k = 3$, $df = 10$

    c. $\alpha = .01$, $k = 4$, $df = 8$ **d.** $\alpha = .01$, $k = 7$, $df = 5$

11.19 If the sample size for each treatment is n_t and if s^2 is based on 12 df, find ω in these cases:

    a. $\alpha = .05$, $k = 4$, $n_t = 5$ **b.** $\alpha = .01$, $k = 6$, $n_t = 8$

11.20 An independent random sampling design was used to compare the means of six treatments based on samples of four observations per treatment. The pooled estimator of σ^2 is 9.12, and the sample means follow:

$$\bar{x}_1 = 101.6 \qquad \bar{x}_2 = 98.4 \qquad \bar{x}_3 = 112.3$$
$$\bar{x}_4 = 92.9 \qquad \bar{x}_5 = 104.2 \qquad \bar{x}_6 = 113.8$$

a. Give the value of ω that you would use to make pairwise comparisons of the treatment means for $\alpha = .05$.

b. Rank the treatment means using pairwise comparisons.

Applications

11.21 Refer to Exercise 11.13 and data set EX1113. Rank the mean leaf growth for the four locations. Use $\alpha = .01$.

11.22 Refer to Exercise 11.15 and data set EX1115. The paired comparisons option in *MINITAB* generated the output provided here. What do these results tell you about the differences in the population means? Does this confirm your conclusions in Exercise 11.15?

MINITAB output for Exercise 11.22

```
Tukey's pairwise comparisons
      Family error rate = 0.0500
Individual error rate = 0.0206
Critical value = 3.77

Intervals for (column level mean) - (row level mean)
              1              2

     2    0.0002423
          0.0014377

     3   -0.0010177     -0.0018577
          0.0001777     -0.0006623
```

EX1123

11.23 Physicians depend on laboratory test results when managing medical problems such as diabetes or epilepsy. In a uniformity test for glucose tolerance, three different laboratories were each sent $n_t = 5$ identical blood samples from a person who had drunk 50 milligrams (mg) of glucose dissolved in water. The laboratory results (in mg/dl) are listed here:

Lab 1	Lab 2	Lab 3
120.1	98.3	103.0
110.7	112.1	108.5
108.9	107.7	101.1
104.2	107.9	110.0
100.4	99.2	105.4

a. Do the data indicate a difference in the average readings for the three laboratories?

b. Use Tukey's method for paired comparisons to rank the three treatment means. Use $\alpha = .05$.

11.7 The Randomized Block Design: A Two-Way Classification

The *completely randomized design* introduced in Section 11.4 is a generalization of the *two independent samples* design presented in Section 10.4. It is meant to be used when the experimental units are quite similar or *homogeneous* in their makeup and when there is only one factor—the *treatment*—that might influence the response. Any other variation in the response is due to random variation or *experimental error*. Sometimes it is clear to the researcher that the experimental units are *not homogeneous*. Experimental subjects or animals, agricultural fields, days of the week, and other experimental units often add their own variability to the response. Although the researcher is not really interested in this source of variation, but rather in some *treatment* he chooses to apply, he may be able to increase the information by isolating this source of variation using the **randomized block design**—a direct extension of the *matched pairs* or *paired-difference design* in Section 10.5.

In a randomized block design, the experimenter is interested in comparing *k* treatment means. The design uses *blocks* of *k* experimental units that are relatively similar, or *homogeneous*, with one unit within each block *randomly* assigned to each treatment. If the randomized block design involves *k* treatments within each of *b* blocks, then the total number of observations in the experiment is $n = bk$.

A production supervisor wants to compare the mean times for assembly-line operators to assemble an item using one of three methods: A, B, or C. Expecting variation in assembly times from operator to operator, the supervisor uses a randomized block design to compare the three methods. Five assembly-line operators are selected to serve as blocks, and each is assigned to assemble the item three times, once for each of the three methods. Since the sequence in which the operator uses the three methods may be important (fatigue or increasing dexterity may be factors affecting the response), each operator should be assigned a random sequencing of the three methods. For example, operator 1 might be assigned to perform method C first, followed by A and B. Operator 2 might perform method A first, then C and B.

To compare four different teaching methods, a group of students might be divided into blocks of size 4, so that the groups are most nearly *matched* according to academic achievement. To compare the average costs for three different cellular phone companies, costs might be compared at each of three usage levels: low, medium, and high. To compare the average yields for three species of fruit trees when a variation in yield is expected because of the field in which the trees are planted, a researcher uses five fields. She divides each field into three *plots* on which the three species of fruit trees are planted.

Matching or *blocking* can take place in many different ways. Comparisons of treatments are often made within blocks of time, within blocks of people, or within similar external environments. The purpose of blocking is to remove or isolate the *block-to-block* variability that might otherwise hide the effect of the treatments. You will find more examples of the use of the randomized block design in the exercises at the end of this section.

11.8 The Analysis of Variance for a Randomized Block Design

The randomized block design identifies two factors: **treatments** and **blocks**—both of which affect the response.

Partitioning the Total Variation in the Experiment

Let x_{ij} be the response when the *i*th treatment ($i = 1, 2, \ldots, k$) is applied in the *j*th block ($j = 1, 2, \ldots, b$). The total variation in the $n = bk$ observations is

$$\text{Total SS} = \Sigma(x_{ij} - \overline{x})^2 = \Sigma x_{ij}^2 - \frac{(\Sigma x_{ij})^2}{n}$$

This is partitioned into *three* (rather than two) parts in such a way that

Total SS = SSB + SST + SSE

where

- SSB (sum of squares for blocks) measures the variation among the block means.
- SST (sum of squares for treatments) measures the variation among the treatment means.
- SSE (sum of squares for error) measures the variation of the differences among the treatment observations *within* blocks, which measures the experimental error.

The calculational formulas for the four sums of squares are similar in form to those you used for the completely randomized design in Section 11.5. Although you can simplify your work by using a computer program to calculate these sums of squares, the formulas are given next.

Calculating the Sums of Squares for a Randomized Block Design, k Treatments in b Blocks

$$CM = \frac{G^2}{n}$$

where

$$G = \Sigma x_{ij} = \text{Total of all } n = bk \text{ observations}$$

$$\text{Total SS} = \Sigma x_{ij}^2 - CM$$

$$= (\text{Sum of squares of all } x\text{-values}) - CM$$

$$SST = \Sigma \frac{T_i^2}{b} - CM$$

$$SSB = \Sigma \frac{B_j^2}{k} - CM$$

$$SSE = \text{Total SS} - SST - SSB$$

with

$$T_i = \text{Total of all observations receiving treatment } i, \, i = 1, 2, \ldots, k$$

$$B_j = \text{Total of all observations in block } j, \, j = 1, 2, \ldots, b$$

Each of the three **sources of variation,** when divided by the appropriate **degrees of freedom,** provides an estimate of the variation in the experiment. Since Total SS involves $n = bk$ squared observations, its degrees of freedom are $df = (n - 1)$. Similarly, SST involves k squared totals, and its degrees of freedom are $df = (k - 1)$, while SSB involves b squared totals and has $(b - 1)$ degrees of freedom. Finally, since the degrees of freedom are additive, the remaining degrees of freedom associated with SSE can be shown algebraically to be $df = (b - 1)(k - 1)$.

These three sources of variation and their respective degrees of freedom are combined to form the **mean squares** as MS = SS/df, and the total variation in the experiment is then displayed in an **analysis of variance** (or **ANOVA**) **table** as shown here:

ANOVA Table for a Randomized Block Design, k Treatments and b Blocks

Source	df	SS	MS	F
Treatments	$k - 1$	SST	MST = SST/$(k - 1)$	MST/MSE
Blocks	$b - 1$	SSB	MSB = SSB/$(b - 1)$	MSB/MSE
Error	$(b - 1)(k - 1)$	SSE	MSE = SSE/$(b - 1)(k - 1)$	
Total	$n - 1 = bk - 1$			

EXAMPLE 11.8 The cellular phone industry is involved in a fierce battle for customers, with each company devising its own complex pricing plan to lure customers. Since the cost of a cell phone minute varies drastically depending on the number of minutes per month used by the customer, a consumer watchdog group decided to compare the average costs for four cellular phone companies using three different usage levels as blocks. The monthly costs (in dollars) computed by the cell phone companies for peak-time callers at low (20 minutes per month), middle (150 minutes per month), and high (1000 minutes per month) usage levels are given in Table 11.3. Construct the analysis of variance table for this experiment.

TABLE 11.3
Monthly phone costs of four companies at three usage levels

	Company				
Usage Level	A	B	C	D	Totals
Low	27	24	31	23	$B_1 = 105$
Middle	68	76	65	67	$B_2 = 276$
High	308	326	312	300	$B_3 = 1246$
Totals	$T_1 = 403$	$T_2 = 426$	$T_3 = 408$	$T_4 = 390$	$G = 1627$

Solution The experiment is designed as a *randomized block design* with $b = 3$ usage levels (blocks) and $k = 4$ companies (treatments), so there are $n = bk = 12$ observations and $G = 1627$. Then

$$\text{CM} = \frac{G^2}{n} = \frac{1627^2}{12} = 220{,}594.0833$$

$$\text{Total SS} = (27^2 + 24^2 + \cdots + 300^2) - \text{CM} = 189{,}798.9167$$

$$\text{SST} = \frac{403^2 + \cdots + 390^2}{3} - \text{CM} = 222.25$$

$$\text{SSB} = \frac{105^2 + 276^2 + 1246^2}{4} - \text{CM} = 189{,}335.1667$$

and by subtraction,

$$\text{SSE} = \text{Total SS} - \text{SST} - \text{SSB} = 241.5$$

These four sources of variation, their degrees of freedom, sums of squares, and mean squares are shown in the shaded area of the analysis of variance table, generated by

MINITAB and given in Figure 11.10. You will find instructions for generating this output in the section "About *MINITAB*" at the end of this chapter.

FIGURE 11.10
MINITAB output for
Example 11.8

Two-way ANOVA: Dollars versus Usage, Company

```
Analysis of Variance for Dollars
Source      DF        SS        MS        F        P
Usage        2   189335.2   94667.6   2351.99   0.000
Company      3     222.3      74.1      1.84    0.240
Error        6     241.5      40.3
Total       11   189798.9
```

Notice that the *MINITAB* ANOVA table shows two different F statistics and p-values. It will not surprise you to know that these statistics are used to test hypotheses concerning the equality of both the *treatment* and *block* means.

Testing the Equality of the Treatment and Block Means

The *mean squares* in the analysis of variance table can be used to test the null hypotheses

H_0 : No difference among the k treatment means

or

H_0 : No difference among the b block means

versus the alternative hypothesis

H_a : At least one of the means is different from at least one other

using a theoretical argument similar to the one we used for the completely randomized design.

- Remember that σ^2 is the common variance for the observations in all bk block–treatment combinations. The quantity

$$\text{MSE} = \frac{\text{SSE}}{(b-1)(k-1)}$$

is an unbiased estimate of σ^2, whether or not H_0 is true.

- The two mean squares, MST and MSB, estimate σ^2 only if H_0 is true and tend to be unusually *large* if H_0 is false and either the treatment or block means are different.
- The test statistics

$$F = \frac{\text{MST}}{\text{MSE}} \quad \text{and} \quad F = \frac{\text{MSB}}{\text{MSE}}$$

are used to test the equality of treatment and block means, respectively. Both statistics tend to be larger than usual if H_0 is false. Hence, you can reject H_0 for large values of F, using *right-tailed* critical values of the F distribution with the appropriate degrees of freedom (see Table 6 in Appendix I) or computer-generated p-values to draw statistical conclusions about the equality of the population means. As an alternative, you can use the **F Probabilities** applet to find either critical values of F or p-values.

Tests for a Randomized Block Design

For comparing treatment means:

1. Null hypothesis: H_0 : The treatment means are equal
2. Alternative hypothesis: H_a : At least two of the treatment means differ
3. Test statistic: $F = MST/MSE$, where F is based on $df_1 = (k - 1)$ and $df_2 = (b - 1)(k - 1)$
4. Rejection region: Reject if $F > F_\alpha$, where F_α lies in the upper tail of the F distribution (see the figure), or when the p-value $< \alpha$

For comparing block means:

1. Null hypothesis: H_0 : The block means are equal
2. Alternative hypothesis: H_a : At least two of the block means differ
3. Test statistic: $F = MSB/MSE$, where F is based on $df_1 = (b - 1)$ and $df_2 = (b - 1)(k - 1)$
4. Rejection region: Reject if $F > F_\alpha$, where F_α lies in the upper tail of the F distribution (see the figure), or when the p-value $< \alpha$

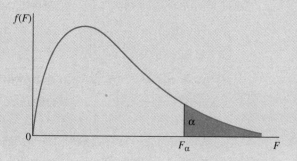

EXAMPLE 11.9   Do the data in Example 11.8 provide sufficient evidence to indicate a difference in the average monthly cell phone cost depending on the company the customer uses?

Solution   The cell phone companies represent the *treatments* in this randomized block design, and the differences in their average monthly costs are of primary interest to the researcher. To test

H_0 : No difference in the average cost among companies

versus the alternative that the average cost is different for at least one of the four companies, you use the analysis of variance F statistic, calculated as

$$F = \frac{MST}{MSE} = \frac{74.1}{40.3} = 1.84$$

and shown in the column marked "F" and the row marked "Company" in Figure 11.10. The exact p-value for this statistical test is also given in Figure 11.10 as .240, which is too large to allow rejection of H_0. The results do not show a significant difference in the treatment means. That is, there is insufficient evidence to indicate a difference in the average monthly costs for the four companies.

The researcher in Example 11.9 was fairly certain in using a *randomized block design* that there would be a significant difference in the block means—that is, a significant difference in the average monthly costs depending on the usage level. This suspicion is justified by looking at the test of equality of block means. Notice that the observed test statistic is $F = 2351.99$ with $P = .000$, showing a highly significant difference, as expected, in the block means.

Identifying Differences in the Treatment and Block Means

Once the overall F test for equality of the treatment or block means has been performed, what more can you do to identify the nature of any differences you have found? As in Section 11.5, you can use Tukey's method of paired comparisons to determine which pairs of treatment or block means are significantly different from one another. However, if the F test does not indicate a significant difference in the means, there is no reason to use Tukey's procedure. If you have a special interest in a particular *pair* of treatment or block means, you can estimate the difference using a $(1 - \alpha)100\%$ confidence interval.[†] The formulas for these procedures, shown next, follow a pattern similar to the formulas for the completely randomized design. Remember that MSE always provides an unbiased estimator of σ^2 and uses information from the entire set of measurements. Hence, it is the best available estimator of σ^2, regardless of what test or estimation procedure you are using. You will again use

$$s^2 = \text{MSE} \qquad \text{with } df = (b - 1)(k - 1)$$

to estimate σ^2 in comparing the treatment and block means.

Comparing Treatment and Block Means

Tukey's yardstick for comparing block means:

$$\omega = q_\alpha(b, df)\left(\frac{s}{\sqrt{k}}\right)$$

Tukey's yardstick for comparing treatment means:

$$\omega = q_\alpha(k, df)\left(\frac{s}{\sqrt{b}}\right)$$

$(1 - \alpha)100\%$ confidence interval for the difference in two block means:

$$(\overline{B}_i - \overline{B}_j) \pm t_{\alpha/2}\sqrt{s^2\left(\frac{1}{k} + \frac{1}{k}\right)}$$

where $\overline{B}_i$ is the average of all observations in block i

$(1 - \alpha)100\%$ confidence interval for the difference in two treatment means:

$$(\overline{T}_i - \overline{T}_j) \pm t_{\alpha/2}\sqrt{s^2\left(\frac{1}{b} + \frac{1}{b}\right)}$$

where $\overline{T}_i$ is the average of all observations in treatment i.

(continued)

[†]You cannot construct a confidence interval for a single mean unless the blocks have been randomly selected from among the population of all blocks. The procedure for constructing intervals for single means is beyond the scope of this book.

> **Comparing Treatment and Block Means** (continued)
>
> **Note:** The values $q_\alpha(*, df)$ from Table 11 in Appendix I, $t_{\alpha/2}$ from Table 4 in Appendix I, and $s^2 = \text{MSE}$ all depend on $df = (b - 1)(k - 1)$ degrees of freedom.

EXAMPLE 11.10 Identify the nature of any differences you found in the average monthly cell phone costs from Example 11.8.

Solution Since the F test did not show any significant differences in the average costs for the four companies, there is no reason to use Tukey's method of paired comparisons. Suppose, however, that you are an executive for company B and your major competitor is company C. Can you claim a significant difference in the two average costs? Using a 95% confidence interval, you can calculate

$$(\bar{T}_2 - \bar{T}_3) \pm t_{.025}\sqrt{\text{MSE}\left(\frac{2}{b}\right)}$$

$$\left(\frac{426}{3} - \frac{408}{3}\right) \pm 2.447\sqrt{40.3\left(\frac{2}{3}\right)}$$

$$6 \pm 12.68$$

so the difference between the two average costs is estimated as between $-\$6.68$ and $\$18.68$. Since 0 is contained in the interval, you do not have evidence to indicate a significant difference in your average costs. Sorry!

Some Cautionary Comments on Blocking

Here are some important points to remember:

- A randomized block design should not be used when treatments and blocks both correspond to **experimental** factors of interest to the researcher. In designating one factor as a *block,* you may assume that the effect of the treatment will be the same, regardless of which block you are using. If this is *not* the case, the two factors—blocks and treatments—are said to **interact,** and your analysis could lead to incorrect conclusions regarding the relationship between the treatments and the response. When an *interaction* is suspected between two factors, you should analyze the data as a **factorial experiment,** which is introduced in the next section.

- Remember that blocking may not always be beneficial. When SSB is removed from SSE, the number of degrees of freedom associated with SSE gets smaller. For blocking to be beneficial, the information gained by isolating the block variation must outweigh the loss of degrees of freedom for error. Usually, though, if you suspect that the experimental units are not homogeneous and you can group the units into blocks, it pays to use the *randomized block design!*

- Finally, remember that you cannot construct confidence intervals for individual treatment means unless it is reasonable to assume that the b blocks have been randomly selected from a population of blocks. If you construct such an interval, the sample treatment mean will be biased by the positive and negative effects that the blocks have on the response.

Exercises   ## Basic Techniques

11.24 A randomized block design was used to compare the means of three treatments within six blocks. Construct an ANOVA table showing the sources of variation and their respective degrees of freedom.

11.25 Suppose that the analysis of variance calculations for Exercise 11.24 are SST = 11.4, SSB = 17.1, and Total SS = 42.7. Complete the ANOVA table, showing all sums of squares, mean squares, and pertinent F-values.

11.26 Do the data of Exercise 11.24 provide sufficient evidence to indicate differences among the treatment means? Test using $\alpha = .05$.

11.27 Refer to Exercise 11.24. Find a 95% confidence interval for the difference between a pair of treatment means A and B if $\bar{x}_A = 21.9$ and $\bar{x}_B = 24.2$.

11.28 Do the data of Exercise 11.24 provide sufficient evidence to indicate that blocking increased the amount of information in the experiment about the treatment means? Justify your answer.

11.29 The data that follow are observations collected from an experiment that compared four treatments, A, B, C, and D, within each of three blocks, using a randomized block design.

EX1129

	Treatment				
Block	A	B	C	D	Total
1	6	10	8	9	33
2	4	9	5	7	25
3	12	15	14	14	55
Total	22	34	27	30	113

a. Do the data present sufficient evidence to indicate differences among the treatment means? Test using $\alpha = .05$.

b. Do the data present sufficient evidence to indicate differences among the block means? Test using $\alpha = .05$.

c. Rank the four treatment means using Tukey's method of paired comparisons with $\alpha = .01$.

d. Find a 95% confidence interval for the difference in means for treatments A and B.

e. Does it appear that the use of a randomized block design for this experiment was justified? Explain.

11.30 The data shown here are observations collected from an experiment that compared three treatments, A, B, and C, within each of five blocks, using a randomized block design:

EX1130

	Block					
Treatment	1	2	3	4	5	Total
A	2.1	2.6	1.9	3.2	2.7	12.5
B	3.4	3.8	3.6	4.1	3.9	18.8
C	3.0	3.6	3.2	3.9	3.9	17.6
Total	8.5	10.0	8.7	11.2	10.5	48.9

MINITAB output for Example 11.30

Two-way ANOVA: Response versus Trts, Blocks

```
Analysis of Variance for Response
Source      DF       SS       MS       F       P
Trts         2   4.4760   2.2380   79.93   0.000
Blocks       4   1.7960   0.4490   16.04   0.001
Error        8   0.2240   0.0280
Total       14   6.4960
```

Use the *MINITAB* ouput to analyze the experiment. Investigate possible differences in the block and/or treatment means and, if any differences exist, use an appropriate method to specifically identify where the differences lie. Has blocking been effective in this experiment? Present your results in the form of a report.

11.31 The partially completed ANOVA table for a randomized block design is presented here:

Source	df	SS	MS	F
Treatments	4	14.2		
Blocks		18.9		
Error	24			
Total	34	41.9		

a. How many blocks are involved in the design?

b. How many observations are in each treatment total?

c. How many observations are in each block total?

d. Fill in the blanks in the ANOVA table.

e. Do the data present sufficient evidence to indicate differences among the treatment means? Test using $\alpha = .05$.

f. Do the data present sufficient evidence to indicate differences among the block means? Test using $\alpha = .05$.

Applications

EX1132

11.32 A study was conducted to compare automobile gasoline mileage for three brands of gasoline, A, B, and C. Four automobiles, all of the same make and model, were used in the experiment, and each gasoline brand was tested in each automobile. Using each brand in the same automobile has the effect of eliminating (blocking out) automobile-to-automobile variability. The data (in miles per gallon) are as follows:

Gasoline Brand	Automobile			
	1	2	3	4
A	15.7	17.0	17.3	16.1
B	17.2	18.1	17.9	17.7
C	16.1	17.5	16.8	17.8

a. Do the data provide sufficient evidence to indicate a difference in mean mileage per gallon for the three brands of gasoline?

b. Is there evidence of a difference in mean mileage for the four automobiles?

c. Suppose that *prior to looking at the data,* you had decided to compare the mean mileage per gallon for gasoline brands A and B. Find a 90% confidence interval for this difference.

d. Use an appropriate method to identify the pairwise differences, if any, in the average mileages for the three brands of gasoline.

EX1133

11.33 An experiment was conducted to compare the effects of four different chemicals, A, B, C, and D, in producing water resistance in textiles. A strip of material, randomly selected from a bolt, was cut into four pieces, and the four pieces were randomly assigned to receive one of the four chemicals, A, B, C, or D. This process was replicated three times, thus producing a randomized block design. The design, with moisture-resistance measurements, is as shown in the figure (low readings indicate low moisture penetration). Analyze the experiment using a method appropriate for this randomized block design. Identify the blocks and treatments, and investigate any possible differences in treatment means. If any differences exist, use an appropriate method to specifically identify where the differences lie. What are the practical implications for the chemical producers?

Has blocking been effective in this experiment? Present your results in the form of a report.

Illustration for
Exercise 11.33

Blocks (bolt samples)

1	2	3
C 9.9	D 13.4	B 12.7
A 10.1	B 12.9	D 12.9
B 11.4	A 12.2	C 11.4
D 12.1	C 12.3	A 11.9

11.34 An experiment was conducted to compare the glare characteristics of four types of automobile rearview mirrors. Forty drivers were randomly selected to participate in the experiment. Each driver was exposed to the glare produced by a headlight located 30 feet behind the rear window of the experimental automobile. The driver then rated the glare produced by the rearview mirror on a scale of 1 (low) to 10 (high). Each of the four mirrors was tested by each driver; the mirrors were assigned to a driver in random order. An analysis of variance of the data produced this ANOVA table:

Source	df	SS	MS	F
Mirrors		46.98		
Drivers			8.42	
Error				
Total		638.61		

a. Fill in the blanks in the ANOVA table.

b. Do the data present sufficient evidence to indicate differences in the mean glare ratings of the four rearview mirrors? Calculate the approximate p-value and use it to make your decision.

c. Do the data present sufficient evidence to indicate that the level of glare perceived by the drivers varied from driver to driver? Use the p-value approach.

d. Based on the results of part b, what are the practical implications of this experiment for the manufacturers of the rearview mirrors?

EX1135

11.35 An experiment was conducted to determine the effects of three methods of soil preparation on the first-year growth of slash pine seedlings. Four locations (state forest lands) were selected, and each location was divided into three plots. Since it was felt that soil fertility within a location was more homogeneous than between locations, a randomized block design was employed using locations as blocks. The methods of soil preparation were A (no preparation), B (light fertilization), and C (burning). Each soil preparation was randomly applied to a plot within each location. On each plot, the same number of seedlings were planted and the average first-year growth of the seedlings was recorded on each plot. Use the *MINITAB* printout to answer the questions.

Soil Preparation	Location			
	1	2	3	4
A	11	13	16	10
B	15	17	20	12
C	10	15	13	10

a. Conduct an analysis of variance. Do the data provide evidence to indicate a difference in the mean growths for the three soil preparations?

b. Is there evidence to indicate a difference in mean rates of growth for the four locations?

c. Use Tukey's method of paired comparisons to rank the mean growths for the three soil preparations. Use $\alpha = .01$.

d. Use a 95% confidence interval to estimate the difference in mean growths for methods A
and B.

MINITAB output for
Exercise 11.35

Two-way ANOVA: Growth versus Soil Prep, Location

```
Analysis of Variance for Growth
Source       DF        SS        MS       F       P
Soil Prep     2     38.00     19.00   10.06   0.012
Location      3     61.67     20.56   10.88   0.008
Error         6     11.33      1.89
Total        11    111.00

                         Individual 95% CI
Soil Prep      Mean    ---------+---------+---------+---------+--
A             12.50        (--------*-------)
B             16.00                          (-------*-------)
C             12.00    (-------*-------)
                       ---------+---------+---------+---------+--
                          12.00     14.00     16.00     18.00

                         Individual 95% CI
Location       Mean    ------+---------+---------+---------+-----
1             12.00            (-------*-------)
2             15.00                     (-------*-------)
3             16.33                        (------*-------)
4             10.67      (-------*------)
                       ------+---------+---------+---------+-----
                          10.00     12.50     15.00     17.50
```

11.36 A study was conducted to compare the effects of three levels of digitalis on the levels of calcium
in the heart muscles of dogs. Because general level of calcium uptake varies from one animal to
another, the tissue for a heart muscle was regarded as a block, and comparisons of the three
digitalis levels (treatments) were made within a given animal. The calcium uptakes for the three
levels of digitalis, A, B, and C, were compared based on the heart muscles of four dogs and the
results are given in the table. Use the MINITAB printout to answer the questions.

EX1136

	Dogs		
1	2	3	4
A	C	B	A
1342	1698	1296	1150
B	B	A	C
1608	1387	1029	1579
C	A	C	B
1881	1140	1549	1319

a. How many degrees of freedom are associated with SSE?

b. Do the data present sufficient evidence to indicate a difference in the mean uptakes of calcium
for the three levels of digitalis?

c. Use Tukey's method of paired comparisons with $\alpha = .01$ to rank the mean calcium uptakes
for the three levels of digitalis.

d. Do the data indicate a difference in the mean uptakes of calcium for the four heart muscles?

e. Use Tukey's method of paired comparisons with $\alpha = .01$ to rank the mean calcium uptakes
for the heart muscles of the four dogs used in the experiment. Are these results of any practical value to the researcher?

f. Give the standard error of the difference between the mean calcium uptakes for two levels of
digitalis.

g. Find a 95% confidence interval for the difference in mean responses between treatments A
and B.

MINITAB output for
Exercise 11.36

Two-way ANOVA: Uptake versus Digitalis, Dog

```
Analysis of Variance for Uptake
Source      DF       SS        MS       F        P
Digitalis    2    542177    262089   258.24    0.000
Dog          3    173415     57805    56.96    0.000
Error        6      6089      1015
Total       11    703682
```

```
                        Individual 95% CI
Digitalis    Mean    -----+---------+---------+---------+------
A            1165    (--*-)
B            1403                       (--*-)
C            1677                                        (--*-)
                     -----+---------+---------+---------+------
                        1200      1350      1500      1650
```

```
                        Individual 95% CI
Dog          Mean    ------+---------+---------+---------+-----
1            1610                                   (---*----)
2            1408                     (----*---)
3            1291      (---*----)
4            1349          (----*---)
                     ------+---------+---------+---------+-----
                        1300      1400      1500      1600
```

11.37 A building contractor employs three construction engineers, A, B, and C, to estimate and bid on jobs. To determine whether one tends to be a more conservative (or liberal) estimator than the others, the contractor selects four projected construction jobs and has each estimator independently estimate the cost (in dollars per square foot) of each job. The data are shown in the table:

EX1137

Estimator	Construction Job 1	2	3	4	Total
A	35.10	34.50	29.25	31.60	130.45
B	37.45	34.60	33.10	34.40	139.55
C	36.30	35.10	32.45	32.90	136.75
Total	108.85	104.20	94.80	98.90	406.75

Analyze the experiment using the appropriate methods. Identify the blocks and treatments, and investigate any possible differences in treatment means. If any differences exist, use an appropriate method to specifically identify where the differences lie. Has blocking been effective in this experiment? What are the practical implications of the experiment? Present your results in the form of a report.

11.38 The cost of automobile insurance varies by location, ages of the drivers and type of coverage. The following are estimates for a 6-month policy for basic liability coverage for a married male who has been licensed for 6–8 years with no violations or accidents, and who drives between 12,600 and 15,000 miles per year provided by the California Department of Insurance for the year 2001 on the Web site (///http:www4.insurance.ca.gov).[2]

EX1138

Location	21st Century	Allstate	AAA	Firemans Fund	State Farm
Riverside	$524	$964	$586	$813	$665
San Bernardino	578	900	465	813	665
Los Angeles	638	984	559	1229	657
Long Beach	682	1050	617	1481	705

a. What type of design was used in collecting these data?

b. Is there sufficient evidence to indicate that insurance premiums for the same type of coverage differs from company to company?

c. Is there sufficient evidence to indicate that insurance premiums vary from location to location?

d. Use Tukey's procedure to determine which insurance companies listed here differ from others in the premiums they charge for this typical client. Use $\alpha = .05$.

e. Summarize your findings.

11.9 The $a \times b$ Factorial Experiment: A Two-Way Classification

Suppose the manager of a manufacturing plant suspects that the output (in number of units produced per shift) of a production line depends on two factors:

- Which of two supervisors is in charge of the line
- Which of three shifts—day, swing, or night—is being measured

That is, the manager is interested in two *factors:* "supervisor" at two levels and "shift" at three levels. Can you use a randomized block design, designating one of the two factors as a block factor? In order to do this, you would need to assume that the effect of the two supervisors is the same, regardless of which shift you are considering. This may not be the case; maybe the first supervisor is most effective in the morning, and the second is more effective at night. You cannot generalize and say that one supervisor is better than the other or that the output of one particular shift is best. You need to investigate not only the average output for the two supervisors and the average output for the three shifts, but also the **interaction** or relationship between the two factors. Consider two different examples that show the effect of *interaction* on the responses in this situation.

EXAMPLE 11.11   Suppose that the two supervisors are each observed on three randomly selected days for each of the three different shifts. The average outputs for the three shifts are shown in Table 11.4 for each of the supervisors. Look at the relationship between the two factors in the line chart for these means, shown in Figure 11.11. Notice that supervisor 2 always produces a higher output, regardless of the shift. The two factors behave *independently;* that is, the output is always about 100 units higher for supervisor 2, no matter which shift you look at.

TABLE 11.4 Average outputs for two supervisors on three shifts

	Shift		
Supervisor	Day	Swing	Night
1	487	498	550
2	602	602	637

FIGURE 11.11 Interaction plot for means in Table 11.4

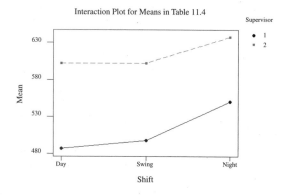

Now consider another set of data for the same situation, shown in Table 11.5. There is a definite difference in the results, depending on which shift you look at, and the *interaction* can be seen in the crossed lines of the chart in Figure 11.11.

TABLE 11.5 Average outputs for two supervisors on three shifts

Supervisor	Shift		
	Day	Swing	Night
1	602	498	450
2	487	602	657

FIGURE 11.12 Interaction plot for means in Table 11.5

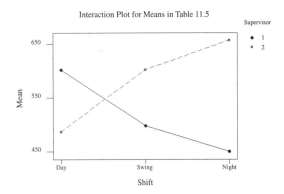

This situation is an example of a **factorial experiment** in which there are a total of 2×3 possible combinations of the levels for the two factors. These $2 \times 3 = 6$ combinations form the *treatments*, and the experiment is called a **2 × 3 factorial experiment.** This type of experiment can actually be used to investigate the effects of three or more factors on a response and to explore the interactions between the factors. However, we confine our discussion to two factors and their interaction.

When you compare treatment means for a factorial experiment (or for any other experiment), you will need more than one observation per treatment. For example, if you obtain two observations for each of the factor combinations of a complete factorial experiment, you have two **replications** of the experiment. In the next section on the analysis of variance for a factorial experiment, you can assume that each treatment or combination of factor levels is replicated the same number of times r.

11.10 The Analysis of Variance for an $a \times b$ Factorial Experiment

An analysis of variance for a two-factor factorial experiment replicated r times follows the same pattern as the previous designs. If the letters A and B are used to identify the two factors, the total variation in the experiment

$$\text{Total SS} = \Sigma(x - \overline{x})^2 = \Sigma x^2 - \text{CM}$$

is partitioned into *four* parts in such a way that

$$\text{Total SS} = \text{SSA} + \text{SSB} + \text{SS(AB)} + \text{SSE}$$

where

- SSA (sum of squares for factor A) measures the variation among the factor A means.
- SSB (sum of squares for factor B) measures the variation among the factor B means.
- SS(AB) (sum of squares for interaction) measures the variation *among* the different combinations of factor levels.
- SSE (sum of squares for error) measures the variation of the differences among the observations *within* each combination of factor levels—the experimental error.

Sums of squares SSA and SSB are often called the **main effect** sums of squares, to distinguish them from the **interaction** sum of squares. Although you can simplify your work by using a computer program to calculate these sums of squares, the calculational formulas are given next. You can assume that there are:

- a levels of factor A
- b levels of factor B
- r replications of each of the ab factor combinations
- A total of $n = abr$ observations

Calculating the Sums of Squares for a Two-Factor Factorial Experiment

$$CM = \frac{G^2}{n} \qquad \text{Total SS} = \Sigma x^2 - CM$$

$$SSA = \Sigma \frac{A_i^2}{br} - CM \qquad SSB = \Sigma \frac{B_j^2}{ar} - CM$$

$$SS(AB) = \Sigma \frac{(AB)_{ij}^2}{r} - CM - SSA - SSB$$

where

$G = $ Sum of all $n = abr$ observations

$A_i = $ Total of all observations at the ith level of factor A, $i = 1, 2, \ldots, a$

$B_j = $ Total of all observations at the jth level of factor B, $j = 1, 2, \ldots, b$

$(AB)_{ij} = $ Total of the r observations at the ith level of factor A and the jth level of factor B

Each of the five **sources of variation,** when divided by the appropriate **degrees of freedom,** provides an estimate of the variation in the experiment. These estimates are called **mean squares**—MS = SS/df—and are displayed along with their respective sums of squares and df in the **analysis of variance** (or **ANOVA**) **table.**

ANOVA Table for r Replications of a Two-Factor Factorial Experiment: Factor A at a Levels and Factor B at b Levels

Source	df	SS	MS	F
A	$a - 1$	SSA	$MSA = \dfrac{SSA}{a-1}$	$\dfrac{MSA}{MSE}$
B	$b - 1$	SSB	$MSB = \dfrac{SSB}{b-1}$	$\dfrac{MSB}{MSE}$
AB	$(a-1)(b-1)$	SS(AB)	$MS(AB) = \dfrac{SS(AB)}{(a-1)(b-1)}$	$\dfrac{MS(AB)}{MSE}$
Error	$ab(r-1)$	SSE	$MSE = \dfrac{SSE}{ab(r-1)}$	
Total	$abr - 1$	Total SS		

Finally, the equality of means for various levels of the factor combinations (the interaction effect) and for the levels of both main effects, A and B, can be tested using the ANOVA F tests, as shown next.

Tests for a Factorial Experiment

■ **For interaction:**

1. Null hypothesis: H_0 : Factors A and B do not interact

2. Alternative hypothesis: H_a : Factors A and B interact

3. Test statistic: $F = \text{MS(AB)/MSE}$, where F is based on $df_1 = (a - 1)(b - 1)$ and $df_2 = ab(r - 1)$

4. Rejection region: Reject H_0 when $F > F_\alpha$, where F_α lies in the upper tail of the F distribution (see the figure), or when the p-value $< \alpha$

■ **For main effects, factor A:**

1. Null hypothesis: H_0 : There are no differences among the factor A means

2. Alternative hypothesis: H_a : At least two of the factor A means differ

3. Test statistic: $F = \text{MSA/MSE}$, where F is based on $df_1 = (a - 1)$ and $df_2 = ab(r - 1)$

4. Rejection region: Reject H_0 when $F > F_\alpha$ (see the figure) or when the p-value $< \alpha$

■ **For main effects, factor B:**

1. Null hypothesis: H_0 : There are no differences among the factor B means

2. Alternative hypothesis: H_a : At least two of the factor B means differ

3. Test statistic: $F = \text{MSB/MSE}$, where F is based on $df_1 = (b - 1)$ and $df_2 = ab(r - 1)$

4. Rejection region: Reject H_0 when $F > F_\alpha$ (see the figure) or when the p-value $< \alpha$

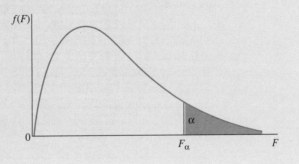

EXAMPLE 11.12 Table 11.6 shows the original data used to generate Table 11.5 in Example 11.11. That is, the two supervisors were each observed on three randomly selected days for each of the three different shifts, and the production outputs were recorded. Analyze these data using the appropriate analysis of variance procedure.

TABLE 11.6
Outputs for two
supervisors on
three shifts

Supervisor	Shift		
	Day	Swing	Night
1	571	480	470
	610	474	430
	625	540	450
2	480	625	630
	516	600	680
	465	581	661

Solution The computer output in Figure 11.13 was generated using the two-way analysis of variance procedure in the *MINITAB* software package. You can verify the quantities in the ANOVA table using the calculational formulas presented earlier, or you may choose just to use the results and interpret their meaning.

FIGURE 11.13
MINITAB output for
Example 11.12

Two-way ANOVA: Output versus Supervisor, Shift

```
Analysis of Variance for Output
Source        DF      SS       MS       F       P
Supervisor     1    19208    19208    26.68   0.000
Shift          2      247      124     0.17   0.844
Interaction    2    81127    40564    56.34   0.000
Error         12     8640      720
Total         17   109222

                       Individual 95% CI
Supervisor    Mean    --+---------+---------+---------+---------
1            516.7    (-------*------)
2            582.0                              (-------*-------)
                      --+---------+---------+---------+---------
                     500.0     525.0     550.0     575.0

                       Individual 95% CI
Shift         Mean    ---+---------+---------+---------+---------
1             545    (---------------*---------------)
2             550       (---------------*---------------)
3             554          (---------------*---------------)
                      ---+---------+---------+---------+---------
                        525       540       555       570
```

At this point, you have undoubtedly discovered the familiar pattern in testing the significance of the various experimental factors with the *F* statistic and its *p*-value. The small *p*-value ($P = .000$) in the row marked "Supervisor" means that there is sufficient evidence to declare a difference in the mean levels for factor A—that is, a difference in mean outputs per supervisor. This fact is visually apparent in the nonoverlapping confidence intervals for the supervisor means shown in the printout. But this is overshadowed by the fact that there is strong evidence ($P = .000$) of an *interaction* between factors A and B. This means that the average output for a given shift depends on the supervisor on duty. You saw this effect clearly in Figure 11.11. The three largest mean outputs occur when supervisor 1 is on the day shift and when supervisor 2 is on either the swing or night shift. As a practical result, the manager should schedule supervisor 1 for the day shift and supervisor 2 for the night shift.

If the interaction effect *is* significant, the differences in the treatment means can be further studied, *not* by comparing the means for factor A or B individually but rather by looking at comparisons for the 2×3 (AB) factor–level combinations. If the interaction effect is *not significant,* then the significance of the main effect means should be investigated, first with the overall *F* test and next with Tukey's method for paired comparisons and/or specific confidence intervals. Remember that these analysis of variance procedures always use $s^2 = \text{MSE}$ as the best estimator of σ^2 with degrees of freedom equal to $df = ab(r - 1)$.

For example, using Tukey's yardstick to compare the average outputs for the two supervisors on each of the three shifts, you could calculate

$$\omega = q_{.05}(6, 12)\left(\frac{s}{\sqrt{r}}\right) = 4.75\left(\frac{\sqrt{720}}{\sqrt{3}}\right) = 73.59$$

Since all three pairs of means—602 and 487 on the day shift, 498 and 602 on the swing shift, and 450 and 657 on the night shift—differ by more than ω, our practical conclusions have been confirmed statistically.

Exercises

Basic Techniques

11.39 Suppose you were to conduct a two-factor factorial experiment, factor A at four levels and factor B at five levels, with three replications per treatment.

a. How many treatments are involved in the experiment?

b. How many observations are involved?

c. List the sources of variation and their respective degrees of freedom.

11.40 The analysis of variance table for a 3×4 factorial experiment, with factor A at three levels and factor B at four levels, and with two observations per treatment, is shown here:

Source	df	SS	MS	F
	2	5.3		
	3	9.1		
	6			
	12	24.5		
Total	23	43.7		

a. Fill in the missing items in the table.

b. Do the data provide sufficient evidence to indicate that factors A and B interact? Test using $\alpha = .05$. What are the practical implications of your answer?

c. Do the data provide sufficient evidence to indicate that factors A and B affect the response variable x? Explain.

11.41 Refer to Exercise 11.40. The means of two of the factor–level combinations—say, A_1B_1 and A_2B_1—are $\bar{x}_1 = 8.3$ and $\bar{x}_2 = 6.3$, respectively. Find a 95% confidence interval for the difference between the two corresponding population means.

11.42 The table gives data for a 3×3 factorial experiment, with two replications per treatment:

	Levels of Factor A		
Levels of Factor B	1	2	3
1	5, 7	9, 7	4, 6
2	8, 7	12, 13	7, 10
3	14, 11	8, 9	12, 15

a. Perform an analysis of variance for the data, and present the results in an analysis of variance table.

b. What do we mean when we say that factors A and B interact?

c. Do the data provide sufficient evidence to indicate interaction between factors A and B? Test using $\alpha = .05$.

d. Find the approximate p-value for the test in part c.

e. What are the practical implications of your results in part c? Explain your results using a line graph similar to the one in Figure 11.11.

11.43

EX1143

The table gives data for a 2×2 factorial experiment, with four replications per treatment:

	Levels of Factor A	
Levels of Factor B	1	2
1	2.1, 2.7, 2.4, 2.5	3.7, 3.2, 3.0, 3.5
2	3.1, 3.6, 3.4, 3.9	2.9, 2.7, 2.2, 2.5

a. The accompanying graph was generated by *MINITAB*. Verify that the four points that connect the two lines are the means of the four observations within each factor–level combination. What does the graph tell you about the interaction between factors A and B?

MINITAB interaction plot for Exercise 11.43

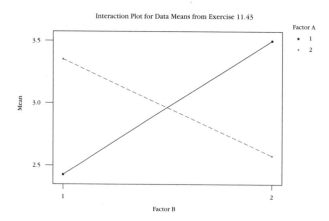

b. Use the *MINITAB* output to test for a significant interaction between A and B. Does this confirm your conclusions in part a?

MINITAB output for Exercise 11.43

Two-way ANOVA: Response versus Factor A, Factor B

```
Analysis of Variance for Response
Source        DF      SS        MS       F       P
Factor A       1   0.0000    0.0000    0.00   1.000
Factor B       1   0.0900    0.0900    1.00   0.338
Interaction    1   3.4225    3.4225   37.85   0.000
Error         12   1.0850    0.0904
Total         15   4.5975
```

c. Considering your results in part b, how can you explain the fact that neither of the main effects is significant?

d. If a significant interaction is found, is it necessary to test for significant main effect differences? Explain.

e. Write a short paragraph summarizing the results of this experiment.

Applications

11.44 A chain of jewelry stores conducted an experiment to investigate the effect of price and location on the demand for its diamonds. Six small-town stores were selected for the study, as well as six stores located in large suburban malls. Two stores in each of these locations were assigned to each of three item percentage markups. The percentage gain (or loss) in sales for each store was recorded at the end of 1 month. The data are shown in the accompanying table.

Location	Markup 1	2	3
Small towns	10	−3	−10
	4	7	−24
Suburban malls	14	8	−4
	18	3	3

a. Do the data provide sufficient evidence to indicate an interaction between markup and location? Test using $\alpha = .05$.

b. What are the practical implications of your test in part a?

c. Draw a line graph similar to Figure 11.11 to help visualize the results of this experiment. Summarize the results.

d. Find a 95% confidence interval for the difference in mean change in sales for stores in small towns versus those in suburban malls if the stores are using price markup 3.

 11.45 A study was conducted to determine the effect of two factors on terrain visualization training for soldiers.[3] During the training programs, participants viewed contour maps of various terrains and then were permitted to view a computer reconstruction of the terrain as it would appear from a specified angle. The two factors investigated in the experiment were the participants' spatial abilities (abilities to visualize in three dimensions) and the viewing procedures (active or passive). Active participation permitted participants to view the computer-generated reconstructions of the terrain from any and all angles. Passive participation gave the participants a set of preselected reconstructions of the terrain. Participants were tested according to spatial ability, and from the test scores 20 were categorized as possessing high spatial ability, 20 medium, and 20 low. Then 10 participants within each of these groups were assigned to each of the two training modes, active or passive. The accompanying tables are the ANOVA table computed the researchers and the table of the treatment means.

Source	df	MS	Error df	F	p
Main effects:					
Training condition	1	103.7009	54	3.66	.0610
Ability	2	760.5889	54	26.87	.0005
Interaction:					
Training condition × Ability	2	124.9905	54	4.42	.0167
Within cells	54	28.3015			

Spatial Ability	Training Condition Active	Passive
High	17.895	9.508
Medium	5.031	5.648
Low	1.728	1.610

Note: Maximum score = 36.

a. Explain how the authors arrived at the degrees of freedom shown in the ANOVA table.

b. Are the F-values correct?

c. Interpret the test results. What are their practical implications?

d. Use Table 6 in Appendix I to approximate the p-values for the F statistics shown in the ANOVA table.

EX1146

11.46 In an attempt to determine what factors affect airfares, a researcher recorded a weighted average of the costs per mile for two airports in each of three major U.S. cities for each of four different travel distances.[2] The results are shown in the table.

	City		
Distance	New York	Houston	Chicago
< 300 miles	40, 48	20, 26	19, 40
301–750 miles	19, 26	15, 17	14, 24
751–1500 miles	10, 14	10, 13	9, 15
> 1500 miles	9, 10	8, 11	7, 12

Use the *MINITAB* output to analyze the experiment with the appropriate method. Identify the two factors, and investigate any possible effect due to their interaction or the main effects. What are the practical implications of this experiment? Explain your conclusions in the form of a report.

MINITAB output for Exercise 11.46

Two-way ANOVA: Cost versus City, Distance

```
Analysis of Variance for Cost
Source        DF       SS       MS       F       P
City           2    201.3    100.7    3.06   0.084
Distance       3   1873.3    624.4   18.97   0.000
Interaction    6    303.7     50.6    1.54   0.247
Error         12    395.0     32.9
Total         23   2773.3

                         Individual 95% CI
Distance     Mean    -----+---------+---------+---------+------
1            32.2                                 (-----+------)
2            19.2                     (-----+-----)
3            11.8         (------+-----)
4             9.5    (------+-----)
                     -----+---------+---------+---------+------
                        8.0      16.0      24.0      32.0
```

MINITAB plots for Exercise 11.46

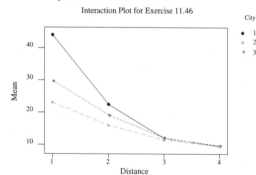

Interaction Plot for Exercise 11.46

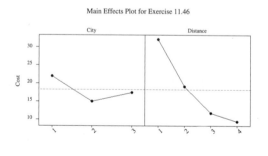

Main Effects Plot for Exercise 11.46

EX1147

11.47   A local school board was interested in comparing test scores on a standarized reading test for fourth-grade students in their district. They selected a random sample of five male and five female fourth grade students at each of four different elementary schools in the district and recorded the test scores. The results are shown in the table below.

Gender	School 1	School 2	School 3	School 4
Male	631	642	651	350
	566	710	611	565
	620	649	755	543
	542	596	693	509
	560	660	620	494
Female	669	722	709	505
	644	769	545	498
	600	723	657	474
	610	649	722	470
	559	766	711	463

a. What type of experimental design is this? What are the experimental units? What are the factors and levels of interest to the school board?

b. Perform the appropriate analysis of variance for this experiment.

c. Do the data indicate that effect of gender on the average test score is different depending on the student's school? Test the appropriate hypothesis using $\alpha = .05$.

d. Plot the average scores using an interaction plot. How would you describe the effect of gender and school on the average test scores?

e. Do the data indicate that either of the main effects is significant? If the main effect is significant, use Tukey's method of paired comparisons to examine the differences in detail. Use $\alpha = .01$.

11.11 Revisiting the Analysis of Variance Assumptions

In Section 11.3, you learned that the assumptions and test procedures for the analysis of variance are similar to those required for the t and F tests in Chapter 10—namely, that observations within a treatment group must be normally distributed with common variance σ^2. You also learned that the analysis of variance procedures are fairly robust when the sample sizes are equal and the data are fairly mound-shaped. If this is the case, one way to protect yourself from inaccurate conclusions is to try when possible to select samples of equal sizes!

There are some quick and simple ways to check the data for violation of assumptions. Look first at the type of response variable you are measuring. You might immediately see a problem with either the normality or common variance assumption. It may be that the data you have collected cannot be measured *quantitatively*. For example, many responses, such as product preferences, can be ranked only as "A is better than B" or "C is the least preferable." Data that are *qualitative* cannot have a normal distribution. If the response variable is *discrete* and can assume only three values—say, 0, 1, or 2—then it is again unreasonable to assume that the response variable is normally distributed.

Suppose that the response variable is binomial—say, the proportion p of people who favor a particular type of investment. Although binomial data can be approximately mound-shaped under certain conditions, they violate the equal variance assumption. The variance of a sample proportion is

$$\sigma^2 = \frac{pq}{n} = \frac{p(1-p)}{n}$$

so that the variance changes depending on the value of p. As the treatment means change, the value of p changes and so does the variance σ^2. A similar situation occurs when the response variable is a Poisson random variable—say, the number of industrial accidents per month in a manufacturing plant. Since the variance of a Poisson random variable is $\sigma^2 = \mu$, the variance changes exactly as the treatment mean changes.

If you cannot see any flagrant violations in the type of data being measured, look at the range of the data within each treatment group. If these ranges are nearly the same, then the common variance assumption is probably reasonable. To check for normality, you might make a quick dotplot or stem and leaf plot for a particular treatment group. However, quite often you do not have enough measurements to obtain a reasonable plot.

If you are using a computer program to analyze your experiment, there are some valuable **diagnostic tools** you can use. These procedures are too complicated to be performed using hand calculations, but they are easy to use when the computer does all the work!

Residual Plots

In the analysis of variance, the total variation in the data is partitioned into several parts, depending on the factors identified as important to the researcher. Once the effects of these sources of variation have been removed, the "leftover" variability in each observation is called the **residual** for that data point. These residuals represent **experimental error,** the basic variability in the experiment, and should have an approximately *normal distribution* with a mean of 0 and the *same variation* for each treatment group. Most computer packages will provide options for plotting these residuals:

- The **normal probability plot of residuals** is a graph that plots the residuals for each observation against the expected value of that residual *had it come from a normal distribution*. If the residuals are approximately normal, the plot will closely resemble a *straight line,* sloping upward to the right.
- The **plot of residuals versus fit** or **residuals versus variables** is a graph that plots the residuals against the expected value of that observation *using the experimental design we have used*. If no assumptions have been violated and there are no "leftover" sources of variation other than experimental error, this plot should show a *random scatter* of points around the horizontal "zero error line" for each treatment group, with approximately the same vertical spread.

EXAMPLE 11.13 The data from Example 11.4 involving the attention spans of three groups of elementary students were analyzed using *MINITAB*. The graphs in Figure 11.14, generated by *MINITAB*, are the normal probability plot and the residuals versus fit plot for this experiment. Look at the straight-line pattern in the normal probability plot, which indicates a normal distribution in the residuals. In the other plot, the residuals are plotted against the estimated expected values, which are the sample averages for each of the three treatments in the completely randomized design. The random scatter around the horizontal "zero error line" and the constant spread indicate *no violations* in the constant variance assumption.

FIGURE 11.14 *MINITAB* diagnostic plots for Example 11.13

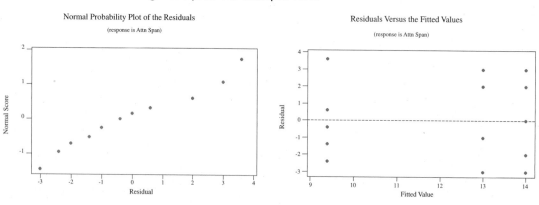

EXAMPLE 11.14 A company plans to promote a new product by using one of three advertising campaigns. To investigate the extent of product recognition from these three campaigns,

15 market areas were selected and five were randomly assigned to each advertising plan. At the end of the ad campaigns, random samples of 400 adults were selected in each area and the proportions who were familiar with the new product were recorded, as in Table 11.7. Have any of the analysis of variance assumptions been violated in this experiment?

TABLE 11.7
Proportions of product recognition for three advertising campaigns

Campaign 1	Campaign 2	Campaign 3
.33	.28	.21
.29	.41	.30
.21	.34	.26
.32	.39	.33
.25	.27	.31

Solution   The experiment is designed as a *completely randomized design,* but the response variable is a binomial sample proportion. This indicates that both the normality and the common variance assumptions might be invalid. Look at the normal probability plot of the residuals and the plot of residuals versus fit generated as an option in the *MINITAB* analysis of variance procedure and shown in Figure 11.15. The curved pattern in the normal probability plot indicates that the residuals *do not have a normal distribution.* In the residual versus fit plot, you can see three vertical lines of residuals, one for each of the three ad campaigns. Notice that two of the lines (campaigns 1 and 3) are close together and have similar spread. However, the third line (campaign 2) is farther to the right, which indicates a larger sample proportion and consequently a *larger variance* in this group. Both analysis of variance assumptions are suspect in this experiment.

FIGURE 11.15
MINITAB diagnostic plots for Example 11.14

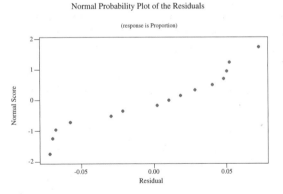

Normal Probability Plot of the Residuals

(response is Proportion)

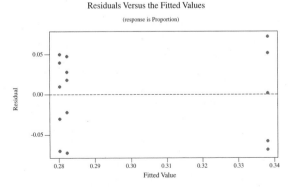

Residuals Versus the Fitted Values

(response is Proportion)

What can you do when the ANOVA assumptions are not satisfied? The *constant variance* assumption can often be remedied by **transforming** the response measurements. That is, instead of using the original measurements, you might use their square roots, logarithms, or some other function of the response. Transformations that tend to stabilize the variance of the response also tend to make their distributions more nearly normal.

When nothing can be done to *even approximately* satisfy the ANOVA assumptions or if the data are rankings, you should use **nonparametric** testing and estimation procedures, presented in Chapter 15. We have mentioned these procedures before; they are almost as powerful in detecting treatment differences as the tests presented in this chapter when the data are normally distributed. When the parametric ANOVA assumptions are violated, the nonparametric tests are generally more powerful.

11.12 A Brief Summary

We presented three different experimental designs in this chapter, each of which can be analyzed using the analysis of variance procedure. The objective of the analysis of variance is to detect differences in the mean responses for experimental units that have received different treatments—that is, different combinations of the experimental factor levels. Once an overall test of the differences is performed, the nature of these differences (if any exist) can be explored using methods of paired comparisons and/or interval estimation procedures.

The three designs presented in this chapter represent only a brief introduction to the subject of analyzing designed experiments. Designs are available for experiments that involve several design variables, as well as more than two treatment factors and other more complex designs. Remember that **design variables** are factors whose effect you want to control and hence remove from experimental error, whereas **treatment variables** are factors whose effect you want to investigate. If your experiment is properly designed, you will be able to analyze it using the analysis of variance. Experiments in which the levels of a variable are *measured experimentally* rather than *controlled* or *preselected* ahead of time may be analyzed using **linear** or **multiple regression analysis**—the subject of Chapters 12 and 13.

Key Concepts and Formulas

I. **Experimental Designs**

1. Experimental units, factors, levels, treatments, response variables.
2. Assumptions: Observations within each treatment group must be normally distributed with a common variance σ^2.
3. One-way classification—completely randomized design: Independent random samples are selected from each of k populations.
4. Two-way classification—randomized block design: k treatments are compared within b relatively homogeneous groups of experimental units called *blocks*.
5. Two-way classification—$a \times b$ factorial experiment: Two factors, A and B, are compared at several levels. Each factor–level combination is replicated r times to allow for the investigation of an interaction between the two factors.

II. **Analysis of Variance**

1. The total variation in the experiment is divided into variation (sums of squares) explained by the various experimental factors and variation due to experimental error (unexplained).

2. If there is an effect due to a particular factor, its mean square (MS = SS/df) is usually large and F = MS(factor)/MSE is large.

3. Test statistics for the various experimental factors are based on F statistics, with appropriate degrees of freedom (df_2 = Error degrees of freedom).

III. Interpreting an Analysis of Variance

1. For the completely randomized and randomized block design, each factor is tested for significance.

2. For the factorial experiment, first test for a significant interaction. If the interaction is significant, main effects need not be tested. The nature of the differences in the factor–level combinations should be further examined.

3. If a significant difference in the population means is found, Tukey's method of pairwise comparisons or a similar method can be used to further identify the nature of the differences.

4. If you have a special interest in one population mean or the difference between two population means, you can use a confidence interval estimate. (For a randomized block design, confidence intervals do not provide unbiased estimates for single population means.)

IV. Checking the Analysis of Variance Assumptions

1. To check for normality, use the normal probability plot for the residuals. The residuals should exhibit a straight-line pattern, increasing upwards toward the right.

2. To check for equality of variance, use the residuals versus fit plot. The plot should exhibit a random scatter, with the same vertical spread around the horizontal "zero error line."

Analysis of Variance Procedures

The statistical procedures used to perform the analysis of variance for the three different experimental designs in this chapter are found in a *MINITAB* submenu by choosing **Stat → ANOVA.** You will see choices for **One-way, One-way (unstacked),** and **Two-way** that will generate Dialog boxes used for the completely randomized, randomized block, and factorial designs, respectively. You must properly store the data and then choose the columns corresponding to the necessary factors in the experiment. We will display some of the Dialog boxes and Session window outputs for the examples in this chapter, beginning with a one-way classification—the completely randomized breakfast study in Example 11.4.

First, enter the 15 recorded attention spans in column C1 of a *MINITAB* worksheet and name them "Span." Next, enter the integers 1, 2, and 3 into a second column C2 to identify the meal assignment (*treatment*) for each observation. You can let *MINITAB* set this pattern for you using **Calc → Make Patterned Data → Simple Set of Numbers,** as shown in Figure 11.16. Then use **Stat → ANOVA → One-way** to generate the Dialog box in Figure 11.17.[†] You must select the column of observations for the "Response" box and the column of treatment indicators for the "Factor" box. Then you have several options. Under **Comparisons,** you can select "Tukey's family error rate" (which has a default level of 5%) to obtain paired comparisons output. Under **Graphs,** you can select dotplots and/or box plots to compare the three meal assignments, and

---

[†]If you had entered each of the three samples into separate columns, the proper command would have been **Stat → ANOVA → One-way (Unstacked).**

MINITAB

FIGURE 11.16

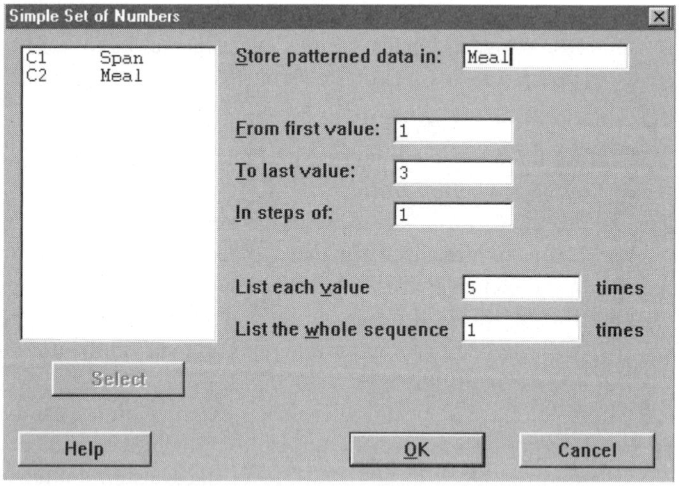

Simple Set of Numbers

| C1 | Span |
| C2 | Meal |

Store patterned data in: Meal

From first value: 1

To last value: 3

In steps of: 1

List each value 5 times

List the whole sequence 1 times

Select

Help   OK   Cancel

FIGURE 11.17

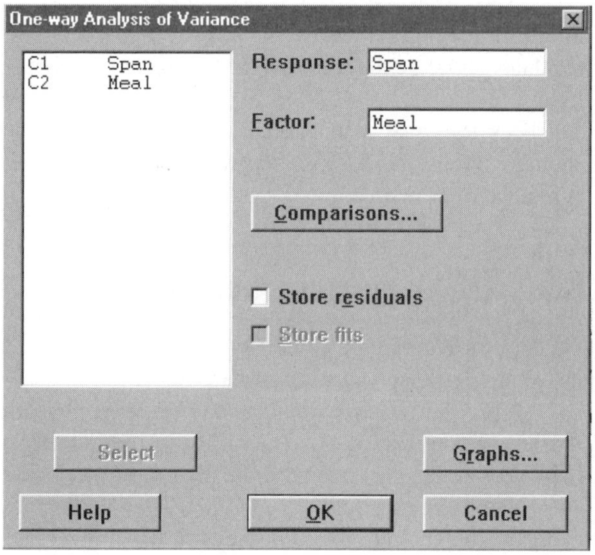

One-way Analysis of Variance

| C1 | Span |
| C2 | Meal |

Response: Span

Factor: Meal

Comparisons...

☐ Store residuals
☐ Store fits

Select   Graphs...

Help   OK   Cancel

you can generate residual plots (use "Normal plot of residuals" and/or "Residuals versus fits") to verify the validity of the ANOVA assumptions. Click **OK** to obtain the output in Figure 11.3 in the text.

The **Stat → ANOVA → Two-way** command can be used for both the randomized block and the factorial designs. You must first enter all of the observations into a single column and then integers to indicate either of these cases:

■ The *block* and *treatment* for each of the measurements in a randomized block design
■ The levels of *factors A and B* for the factorial experiment.

MINITAB will recognize a number of replications within each factor–level combination in the factorial experiment and will break out the sum of squares for interaction (as long as you do not check the box "Fit additive model"). Since these two designs involve the same sequence of commands, we will use the data from Example 11.12 to

MINITAB

generate the analysis of variance for the factorial experiment. The data are entered into the worksheet in Figure 11.18. See if you can use the **Calc → Make Patterned Data → Simple Set of Numbers** to enter the data into columns C2–C3. Once the data have been entered, use **Stat → ANOVA → Two-way** to generate the Dialog box in Figure 11.19. Choose "Output" for the "Response" box, and "Supervisor" and "Shift" for the "Row factor" and "Column factor," respectively. You may choose to display the main effect means along with 95% confidence intervals by checking "Display means," and you may select residual plots if you wish. Click **OK** to obtain the ANOVA printout in Figure 11.13.

Since the interaction between supervisors and shifts is highly significant, you may want to explore the nature of this interaction by plotting the average output for each supervisor at each of the three shifts. Use **Stat → ANOVA → Interactions plot** and choose the appropriate response and factor variables. The plot is generated by *MINITAB* and shown in Figure 11.20. You can see the strong difference in the behaviors of the mean outputs for the two supervisors, indicating a strong interaction between the two factors.

FIGURE 11.18

```
Data Display
Row   Output   Supervisor   Shift
  1      571            1       1
  2      610            1       1
  3      625            1       1
  4      480            2       1
  5      516            2       1
  6      465            2       1
  7      480            1       2
  8      474            1       2
  9      540            1       2
 10      625            2       2
 11      600            2       2
 12      581            2       2
 13      470            1       3
 14      430            1       3
 15      450            1       3
 16      630            2       3
 17      680            2       3
 18      661            2       3
```

FIGURE 11.19

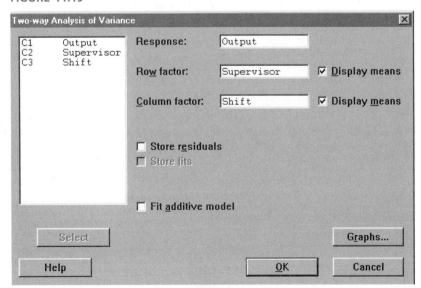

MINITAB

FIGURE 11.20

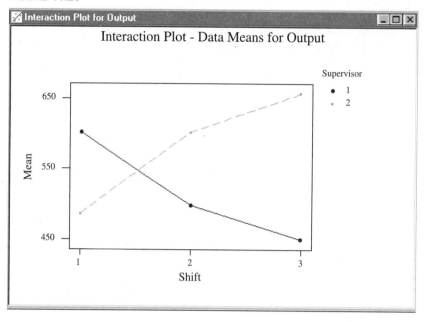

Supplementary Exercises

11.48 Twenty-seven people participated in an experiment to compare the effects of five different stimuli on reaction time. The experiment was run using a completely randomized design, and, regardless of the results of the analysis of variance, the experimenters wanted to compare stimuli A and D. The results of the experiment are given here. Use the *MINITAB* printout to complete the exercise.

EX1148

Stimulus	Reaction Time (sec)							Total	Mean
A	.8	.6	.6	.5				2.5	.625
B	.7	.8	.5	.5	.6	.9	.7	4.7	.671
C	1.2	1.0	.9	1.2	1.3	.8		6.4	1.067
D	1.0	.9	.9	1.1	.7			4.6	.920
E	.6	.4	.4	.7	.3			2.4	.480

MINITAB output for
Exercise 11.48

One-way ANOVA: Time versus Stimulus

```
Analysis of Variance for Time
Source      DF       SS       MS       F        P
Stimulus     2   1.2118   0.3030   11.67    0.000
Error       22   0.5711   0.0260
Total       26   1.7830

                                  Individual 95% CIs for Mean
                                  Based on Pooled StDev
Level    N     Mean    StDev  -------+---------+---------+---------
A        4   0.6250   0.1258        (------*------)
B        7   0.6714   0.1496          (----*----)
C        6   1.0667   0.1966                         (-----*----)
D        5   0.9200   0.1483                    (-----*-----)
E        5   0.4800   0.1643  (-----*-----)
                              -------+---------+---------+---------
Pooled StDev =   0.1611             0.50      0.75      1.0
```

a. Conduct an analysis of variance and test for a difference in the mean reaction times due to the five stimuli.

b. Compare stimuli A and D to see if there is a difference in mean reaction times.

11.49 Refer to Exercise 11.48. Use this *MINITAB* output to identify the differences in the treatment means.

MINITAB **output for Exercise 11.49**

```
Tukey's pairwise comparisons
    Family error rate = 0.0500
Individual error rate = 0.00707
Critical value = 4.20

Intervals for (column level mean) - (row level mean)
                 A               B               C               D
      B      -0.3463
              0.2535

      C      -0.7505         -0.6615
             -0.1328         -0.1290

      D      -0.6160         -0.5288         -0.1431
              0.0260          0.0316          0.4364

      E      -0.1760         -0.0888          0.2969          0.1374
              0.4660          0.4716          0.8764          0.7426
```

11.50 Refer to Exercise 11.48. What do the normal probability plot and the residuals versus fit plot tell you about the validity of your analysis of variance results?

MINITAB **diagnostic plots for Exercise 11.50**

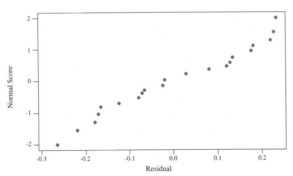

Normal Probability Plot of the Residuals
(response is Time)

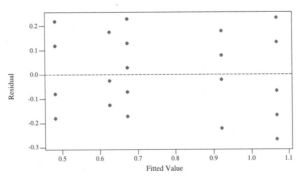

Residuals Versus the Fitted Values
(response is Time)

EX1151

11.51 The experiment in Exercise 11.48 might have been conducted more effectively using a randomized block design with people as blocks, since you would expect mean reaction time to vary from one person to another. Hence, four people were used in a new experiment, and each person was subjected to each of the five stimuli in a random order. The reaction times (in seconds) are listed here:

			Stimulus		
Subject	A	B	C	D	E
1	.7	.8	1.0	1.0	.5
2	.6	.6	1.1	1.0	.6
3	.9	1.0	1.2	1.1	.6
4	.6	.8	.9	1.0	.4

MINITAB output for
Exercise 11.51

Two-way ANOVA: Time versus Subject, Stimulus

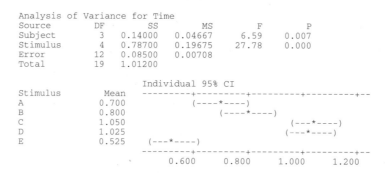

```
Analysis of Variance for Time
Source       DF       SS         MS         F         P
Subject       3    0.14000    0.04667     6.59     0.007
Stimulus      4    0.78700    0.19675    27.78     0.000
Error        12    0.08500    0.00708
Total        19    1.01200

                            Individual 95% CI
Stimulus        Mean     ---------+---------+---------+---------+--
A              0.700             (----*----)
B              0.800                  (----*----)
C              1.050                            (---*----)
D              1.025                            (---*----)
E              0.525       (---*----)
                         ---------+---------+---------+---------+--
                          0.600     0.800     1.000     1.200
```

a. Use the *MINITAB* printout to analyze the data and test for differences in treatment means.

b. Use Tukey's method of paired comparisons to identify the significant pairwise differences in the stimuli.

c. Does it appear that blocking was effective in this experiment?

EX1152

11.52 An experiment was conducted to examine the effect of age on heart rate when a person is subjected to a specific amount of exercise. Ten men were randomly selected from four age groups: 10–19, 20–39, 40–59, and 60–69. Each man walked on a treadmill at a fixed grade for a period of 12 minutes, and the increase in heart rate, the difference before and after exercise, was recorded (in beats per minute):

	10–19	20–39	40–59	60–69
	29	24	37	28
	33	27	25	29
	26	33	22	34
	27	31	33	36
	39	21	28	21
	35	28	26	20
	33	24	30	25
	29	34	34	24
	36	21	27	33
	22	32	33	32
Total	309	275	295	282

Use an appropriate computer program to answer these questions:

a. Do the data provide sufficient evidence to indicate a difference in mean increase in heart rate among the four age groups? Test by using $\alpha = .05$.

b. Find a 90% confidence interval for the difference in mean increase in heart rate between age groups 10–19 and 60–69.

c. Find a 90% confidence interval for the mean increase in heart rate for the age group 20–39.

d. Approximately how many people would you need in each group if you wanted to be able to estimate a group mean correct to within two beats per minute with probability equal to .95?

EX1153

11.53 A company wished to study the effects of four training programs on the sales abilities of their sales personnel. Thirty-two people were randomly divided into four groups of equal size, and each group was then subjected to one of the different sales training programs. Because there were some dropouts during the training programs due to illness, vacations, and so on, the number of trainees completing the programs varied from group to group. At the end of the training programs, each salesperson was randomly assigned a sales area from a group of sales areas that were judged to have equivalent sales potentials. The sales made by each of the four groups of salespeople during the first week after completing the training program are listed in the table:

	Training Program			
	1	2	3	4
	78	99	74	81
	84	86	87	63
	86	90	80	71
	92	93	83	65
	69	94	78	86
	73	85		79
		97		73
		91		70
Total	482	735	402	588

Analyze the experiment using the appropriate method. Identify the treatments or factors of interest to the researcher and investigate any significant effects. What are the practical implications of this experiment? Write a paragraph explaining the results of your analysis.

11.54 Suppose you were to conduct a two-factor factorial experiment, factor A at four levels and factor B at two levels, with r replications per treatment.

a. How many treatments are involved in the experiment?

b. How many observations are involved?

c. List the sources of variation and their respective degrees of freedom.

11.55 The analysis of variance table for a 2×3 factorial experiment, factor A at two levels and factor B at three levels, with five observations per treatment, is shown in the table.

Source	df	SS	MS	F
A		1.14		
B		2.58		
AB		.49		
Error				
Total		8.41		

a. Do the data provide sufficient evidence to indicate an interaction between factors A and B? Test using $\alpha = .05$. What are the practical implications of your answer?

b. Give the approximate p-value for the test in part a.

c. Do the data provide sufficient evidence to indicate that factor A affects the response? Test using $\alpha = .05$.

d. Do the data provide sufficient evidence to indicate that factor B affects the response? Test using $\alpha = .05$.

11.56 Refer to Exercise 11.55. The means of all observations at the factor A levels A_1 and A_2 are $\bar{x}_1 = 3.7$ and $\bar{x}_2 = 1.4$, respectively. Find a 95% confidence interval for the difference in mean response for factor levels A_1 and A_2.

EX1157

11.57 The whitefly, which causes defoliation of shrubs and trees and a reduction in salable crop yields, has emerged as a pest in southern California. In a study to determine factors that affect the life cycle of the whitefly, an experiment was conducted in which whiteflies were placed on two different types of plants at three different temperatures. The observation of interest was the total number of eggs laid by caged females under one of the six possible treatment combinations. Each treatment combination was run using five cages.

Plant	Temperature		
	70°F	77°F	82°F
Cotton	37	34	46
	21	54	32
	36	40	41
	43	42	36
	31	16	38
Cucumber	50	59	43
	53	53	62
	25	31	71
	37	69	49
	48	51	59

MINITAB output for Exercise 11.57

Two-way ANOVA: Eggs versus Temperature, Plant

```
Analysis of Variance for Eggs
Source         DF        SS        MS       F        P
Temperature     2       487       244    1.98    0.160
Plant           1      1512      1512   12.29    0.002
Interaction     2       111        56    0.45    0.642
Error          24      2952       123
Total          29      5063
```

a. What type of experimental design has been used?

b. Do the data provide sufficient evidence to indicate that the effect of temperature on the number of eggs laid is different depending on the type of plant? Use the *MINITAB* printout to test the appropriate hypothesis.

c. Plot the treatment means for cotton as a function of temperature. Plot the treatment means for cucumber as a function of temperature. Comment on the similarity or difference in these two plots.

d. Find the mean number of eggs laid on cotton and cucumber based on 15 observations each. Calculate a 95% confidence interval for the difference in the underlying population means.

EX1158

11.58 Four chemical plants, producing the same product and owned by the same company, discharge effluents into streams in the vicinity of their locations. To check on the extent of the pollution created by the effluents and to determine whether this varies from plant to plant, the company collected random samples of liquid waste, five specimens for each of the four plants. The data are shown in the table:

Plant	Polluting Effluents (lb/gal of waste)				
A	1.65	1.72	1.50	1.37	1.60
B	1.70	1.85	1.46	2.05	1.80
C	1.40	1.75	1.38	1.65	1.55
D	2.10	1.95	1.65	1.88	2.00

a. Do the data provide sufficient evidence to indicate a difference in the mean amounts of effluents discharged by the four plants?

b. If the maximum mean discharge of effluents is 1.5 lb/gal, do the data provide sufficient evidence to indicate that the limit is exceeded at plant A?

c. Estimate the difference in the mean discharge of effluents between plants A and D, using a 95% confidence interval.

11.59 Exercise 10.36 examined an advertisement for Albertsons, a supermarket chain in the western United States. The advertiser claims that Albertsons has consistently had lower prices than four other full-service supermarkets. As part of a survey conducted by an "independent market basket price-checking company," the average weekly total based on the prices of approximately 95 items is given for five different supermarket chains recorded during 4 consecutive weeks.[5]

EX1159

Week	Albertsons	Ralphs	Vons	Alpha Beta	Lucky
1	$254.26	$256.03	$267.92	$260.71	$258.84
2	240.62	255.65	251.55	251.80	242.14
3	231.90	255.12	245.89	246.77	246.80
4	234.13	261.18	254.12	249.45	248.99

a. What type of design has been used in this experiment?

b. Conduct an analysis of variance for the data.

c. Is there sufficient evidence to indicate that there is a difference in the average weekly totals for the five supermarkets? Use $\alpha = .05$.

d. Use Tukey's method for paired comparisons to determine which of the means are significantly different from each other. Use $\alpha = .05$.

11.60 The yields of wheat (in bushels per acre) were compared for five different varieties, A, B, C, D, and E, at six different locations. Each variety was randomly assigned to a plot at each location. The results of the experiment are shown in the accompanying table, along with a *MINITAB* printout of the analysis of variance. Analyze the experiment using the appropriate method. Identify the treatments or factors of interest to the researcher and investigate any effects that exist. Use the diagnostic plots to comment on the validity of the analysis of variance assumptions. What are the practical implications of this experiment? Write a paragraph explaining the results of your analysis.

EX1160

	Location					
Variety	1	2	3	4	5	6
A	35.3	31.0	32.7	36.8	37.2	33.1
B	30.7	32.2	31.4	31.7	35.0	32.7
C	38.2	33.4	33.6	37.1	37.3	38.2
D	34.9	36.1	35.2	38.3	40.2	36.0
E	32.4	28.9	29.2	30.7	33.9	32.1

MINITAB output for Exercise 11.60

Two-way ANOVA: Yield versus Varieties, Location

```
Analysis of Variance for Yield
Source        DF        SS        MS        F        P
Varieties      4    142.67     35.67    18.61    0.000
Locations      5     68.14     13.63     7.11    0.001
Error         20     38.33      1.92
Total         29    249.14

                       Individual 95% CI
Varieties     Mean   ----------+---------+---------+---------+-
A            34.35                  (-----*-----)
B            34.28            (----*-----)
C            36.30                            (-----*----)
D            36.78                             (-----*-----)
E            31.20    (-----*-----)
                      ----------+---------+---------+---------+-
                        32.00     34.00     36.00     38.00
```

MINITAB diagnostic
plots for
Exercise 11.60

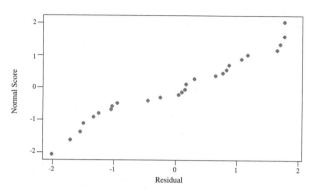

Normal Probability Plot of the Residuals
(response is Yield)

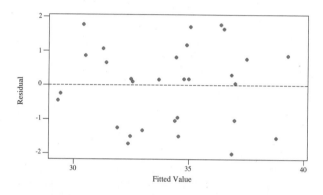

Residuals Versus the Fitted Values
(response is Yield)

11.61 The latest information on average crash tests conducted by the Insurance Institute for Highway Safety regarding bumper repair costs for damage sustained in front and rear crashes of 2000 and 2001 vehicles into barriers/pole at 5 mph are given in the following table. These types of crash tests evaluate how well the bumpers prevent costly damage to vehicles in parking lot–type impacts.[6]

EX1161

| | Types of Crash | | | |
Autos	Front into Barrier	Rear into Barrier	Front into Angle Barrier	Rear into Pole
Hyundai Elantra	$ 247	$ 0	$ 407	$ 185
Ford Focus	31	1,137	507	939
Honda Civic	403	447	404	227
Dodge Stratus Chrysler Cirrus	278	174	626	1473
Lexus LS 30	75	395	1,526	765
Dodge Grand Caravan	329	822	703	2,268
Isuzu Rodeo	1,769	924	1,932	552
Mitsubishi Montero	1,210	2,495	2,525	2,831

a. What is the type of design was used in these crash tests? If the design used is a randomized block design, what are the blocks and what are the treatments?

b. Are there significant differences in the cost of crashes for the vehicles considered here?

c. Are there significant differences among the four types of crashes?

d. Use Tukey's pairwise procedure to investigate the differences in average repair costs for the eight vehicles. Comment on the results found using this procedure. Use $\alpha = .05$.

EX1162

11.62 In a study of starting salaries of assistant professors,[7] five male assistant professors and five female assistant professors at each of three types of institutions granting doctoral degrees were polled and their initial starting salaries were recorded under the condition of anonymity. The results of the survey in $1,000 are given in the following table.

Gender	Public Universities	Private-Independent	Church-Related
	58.5	62.1	52.7
	54.3	59.7	54.0
Males	55.9	63.2	57.4
	51.4	62.6	57.6
	50.0	62.1	55.0
	45.2	56.0	54.9
	45.1	61.2	50.4
Females	48.3	60.3	44.2
	50.0	52.8	54.3
	48.1	58.0	47.1

a. What type of design was used in collecting these data?

b. Use an analysis of variance to test if there are significant differences in gender, in type of institution, and to test for a significant interaction of gender $\times$ type of institution.

c. Find a 95% confidence interval estimate for the difference in starting salaries for male assistant professors and female assistant professors. Interpret this interval in terms of a gender difference in starting salaries.

d. Use Tukey's procedure to investigate differences in assistant professor salaries for the three types of institutions. Use $\alpha = .01$.

e. Summarize the results of your analysis.

Case Study   "A Fine Mess"

TICKETS

Do you risk a parking ticket by parking where you shouldn't or forgetting how much time you have left on the parking meter? Do the fines associated with various parking infractions vary depending on the city in which you receive a parking ticket? To look at this issue, the fines imposed for overtime parking, parking in a red zone, and parking next to a fire hydrant were recorded for 13 cities in southern California.[8]

City	Overtime Parking	Red Zone	Fire Hydrant
Long Beach	$17	$30	$30
Bakersfield	17	33	33
Orange	22	30	32
San Bernardino	20	30	78
Riverside	21	30	30
San Luis Obispo	8	20	75
Beverly Hills	23	38	30
Palm Springs	22	28	46
Laguna Beach	22	22	32
Del Mar	25	40	55
Los Angeles	20	55	30
San Diego	35	60	60
Newport Beach	32	42	30

1. Identify the design used for the data collection in this case study.
2. Analyze the data using the appropriate analysis. What can you say about the variation among the cities in this study? Among fines for the three types of violations? Can Tukey's procedure be of use in further delineating any significant differences you may find? Would confidence interval estimates be useful in your analysis?
3. Summarize the results of your analysis of these data.

Data Sources

1. "Tuna Goes Upscale," *Consumer Reports,* June 2001, p. 19.
2. "2000 Automobile Insurance," www4.insurance.ca.gov, 29 August 2001.
3. H.F. Barsam and Z.M. Simutis, "Computer-Based Graphics for Terrain Visualisation Training," *Human Factors,* no. 26, 1984. Copyright 1984 by the Human Factors Society, Inc. Reproduced by permission.
4. "How Fares Differ by Airport and Airline," *Consumer Reports,* July 1997, p. 24.
5. *The Press-Enterprise* (Riverside, CA), 11 February 1993.
6. "Expensive Bumper Repair: Latest Crash Tests," *Consumers Research,* April 2001, pp. 20–22.
7. "Average Salary for Men and Women Faculty, by Category, Affiliation, and Academic Rank 2000–2001," *Academe,* March–April 2001, p. 39.
8. Robert McGarvey, "A Fine Mess," *Avenues,* July/August 1994, pp. 19–25.

Linear Regression and Correlation

Case Study

The phrase "made in the U.S.A." has become a battle cry in the past few years as American workers try to protect their jobs from overseas competition. In the case study at the end of this chapter, we explore the changing attitudes of American consumers toward automobiles made outside the United States, using a simple linear regression analysis.

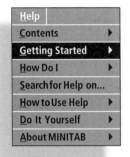

General Objectives

In this chapter, we consider the situation in which the mean value of a random variable y is related to another variable x. By measuring both y and x for each experimental unit, thereby generating bivariate data, you can use the information provided by x to estimate the average value of y and to predict values of y for pre-assigned values of x.

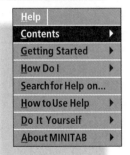

Specific Topics

1. A simple linear probabilistic model (12.2)
2. The method of least squares (12.3)
3. Analysis of variance for linear regression (12.4)
4. Testing the usefulness of the linear regression model: inferences about β, the ANOVA F test, and r^2 (12.5)
5. Diagnostic tools for checking the regression assumptions (12.6)
6. Estimation and prediction using the fitted line (12.7)
7. Correlation analysis (12.8)

12.1 Introduction

High school seniors, freshmen entering college, their parents, and a university administration are concerned about the academic achievement of a student after he or she has enrolled in a university. Can you estimate or predict a student's grade point average (GPA) at the end of the freshman year before the student enrolls in the university? At first glance this might seem like a difficult problem. However, you would expect highly motivated students who have graduated with a high class rank from a high school with superior academic standards to achieve a high GPA at the end of the college freshman year. On the other hand, students who lack motivation or who have achieved only moderate success in high school are not expected to do so well. You would expect the college achievement of a student to be a function of several variables:

- Rank in high school class
- High school's overall rating
- High school GPA
- SAT scores

This problem is of a fairly general nature. You are interested in a random variable y (college GPA) that is related to a number of independent variables. The objective is to create a *prediction equation* that expresses y as a function of these independent variables. Then, if you can measure the independent variables, you can substitute these values into the prediction equation and obtain the prediction for y—the student's college GPA in our example. But which variables should you use as predictors? How strong is their relationship to y? How do you construct a good prediction equation for y as a function of the selected predictor variables? We will answer these questions in the next two chapters.

In this chapter, we restrict our attention to the simple problem of predicting y as a linear function of a single predictor variable x. This problem was originally addressed in Chapter 3 in the discussion of *bivariate data.* Remember that we used the equation of a straight line to describe the relationship between x and y and we described the strength of the relationship using the correlation coefficient r. We rely on some of these results as we revisit the subject of linear regression and correlation.

12.2 A Simple Linear Probabilistic Model

Consider the problem of trying to predict the value of a response y based on the value of an independent variable x. The best-fitting line of Chapter 3,

$$y = a + bx$$

was based on a *sample* of n bivariate observations drawn from a larger *population* of measurements. The line that describes the relationship between y and x in the *population* is similar to, but not the same as, the best-fitting line from the *sample.* How can you construct a **population model** to describe the relationship between a random variable y and a related independent variable x?

You begin by assuming that the variable of interest, y, is *linearly* related to an independent variable x. To describe the linear relationship, you can use the **deterministic model**

$$y = \alpha + \beta x$$

where α is the y-intercept—the value of y when $x = 0$—and β is the slope of the line, defined as the change in y for a one-unit change in x, as shown in Figure 12.1. This model describes a deterministic relationship between the variable of interest y, sometimes called the **response variable,** and the independent variable x, often called the **predictor variable.** That is, the linear equation determines an exact value of y when the value of x is given. Is this a realistic model for an experimental situation? Consider the following example.

FIGURE 12.1
The y-intercept and slope for a line

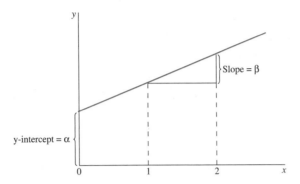

Table 12.1 displays the mathematics achievement test scores for a random sample of $n = 10$ college freshmen, along with their final calculus grades. A bivariate plot of these scores and grades is given in Figure 12.2. You can use the **Building a Scatterplot** applet to refresh your memory as to how this plot is drawn. Notice that the points *do not lie exactly on a line* but rather seem to be deviations about an underlying line. A simple way to modify the deterministic model is to add a **random error component** to explain the deviations of the points about the line. A particular response y is described using the **probabilistic model**

$$y = \alpha + \beta x + \epsilon$$

TABLE 12.1
Mathematics achievement test scores and final calculus grades for college freshmen

Student	Mathematics Achievement Test Score	Final Calculus Grade
1	39	65
2	43	78
3	21	52
4	64	82
5	57	92
6	47	89
7	28	73
8	75	98
9	34	56
10	52	75

FIGURE 12.2
Scatterplot of the data in Table 12.1

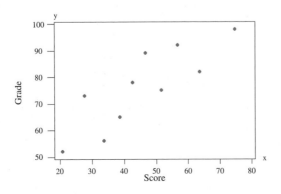

The first part of the equation, $\alpha + \beta x$—called the **line of means**—describes the average value of y for a given value of x. The error component ϵ allows each individual response y to deviate from the line of means by a small amount.

In order to use this *probabilistic model* for making inferences, you need to be more specific about this "small amount," ϵ.

Assumptions About the Random Error ϵ

Assume that the values of ϵ satisfy these conditions:

- Are independent in the probabilistic sense
- Have a mean of 0 and a common variance equal to σ^2
- Have a normal probability distribution

These assumptions about the random error ϵ are shown in Figure 12.3 for three fixed values of x—say, x_1, x_2, and x_3. Notice the similarity between these assumptions and the assumptions necessary for the tests in Chapters 10 and 11. We will revisit these assumptions later in this chapter and provide some diagnostic tools for you to use in checking their validity.

FIGURE 12.3
Linear probabilistic model

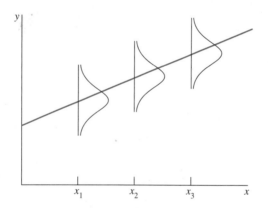

Remember that this model is created for a population of measurements that is generally unknown to you. However, you can use sample information to estimate the values of α and β, which are the coefficients of the line of means, $E(y) = \alpha + \beta x$. These estimates are used to form the best-fitting line for a given set of data, called the **least squares line** or **regression line.** We review how to calculate the intercept and the slope of this line in the next section.

12.3 The Method of Least Squares

The statistical procedure for finding the best-fitting line for a set of bivariate data does mathematically what you do visually when you move a ruler until you think you have minimized the vertical distances, or deviations, from the ruler to a set of points. The formula for the best-fitting line is

$$\hat{y} = a + bx$$

where a and b are the estimates of the intercept and slope parameters α and β, respectively. The fitted line for the data in Table 12.1 is shown in the **Method of Least Squares** applet, Figure 12.4. The red vertical lines (light blue in Figure 12.4) drawn from the prediction line to each point (x_i, y_i) represent the deviations of the points from the line.

FIGURE 12.4
Method of Least Squares applet

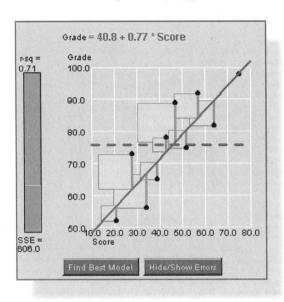

To minimize the distances from the points to the fitted line, you can use the **principle of least squares.**

> **Principle of Least Squares**
>
> The line that minimizes the sum of squares of the deviations of the observed values of y from those predicted is the **best-fitting line.** The sum of squared deviations is commonly called the **sum of squares for error** (SSE) and defined as
>
> $$SSE = \Sigma(y_i - \hat{y}_i)^2 = \Sigma(y_i - a - bx_i)^2$$

Look at the regression line and the data points in Figure 12.4. SSE is the sum of the squared distances represented by the area of the yellow squares (light blue in Figure 12.4).

Finding the values of a and b, the estimates of α and β, uses differential calculus, which is beyond the scope of this text. Rather than derive their values, we will simply present formulas for calculating the values of a and b—called the **least-squares estimators** of α and β. We will use notation that is based on the **sums of squares** for the variables in the regression problem, which are similar in form to the sums of squares used in Chapter 11. These formulas look different from the formulas presented in Chapter 3, but they are in fact algebraically identical!

You should use the data entry method for your scientific calculator to enter the sample data.

■ If your calculator has only a one-variable statistics function, you can still save some time in finding the necessary sums and sums of squares.

- If your calculator has a two-variable statistics function, or if you have a graphing calculator, the calculator will automatically store all of the sums and sums of squares as well as the values of a, b, and the correlation coefficient r.
- Make sure you consult your calculator manual to find the easiest way to obtain the least squares estimators.

Least-Squares Estimators of α and β

$$b = \frac{S_{xy}}{S_{xx}} \quad \text{and} \quad a = \bar{y} - b\bar{x}$$

where the quantities S_{xy} and S_{xx} are defined as

$$S_{xy} = \Sigma(x_i - \bar{x})(y_i - \bar{y}) = \Sigma x_i y_i - \frac{(\Sigma x_i)(\Sigma y_i)}{n}$$

and

$$S_{xx} = \Sigma(x_i - \bar{x})^2 = \Sigma x_i^2 - \frac{(\Sigma x_i)^2}{n}$$

Notice that the sum of squares of the x-values is found using the computing formula given in Section 2.3 and the sum of the cross-products is the numerator of the *covariance* defined in Section 3.4.

EXAMPLE 12.1 Find the least-squares prediction line for the calculus grade data in Table 12.1.

Solution Use the data in Table 12.2 and the data entry method in your scientific calculator to find the following sums of squares:

TABLE 12.2
Calculations for the data in Table 12.1

y_i	x_i	x_i^2	$x_i y_i$	y_i^2
65	39	1521	2535	4225
78	43	1849	3354	6084
52	21	441	1092	2704
82	64	4096	5248	6724
92	57	3249	5244	8464
89	47	2209	4183	7921
73	28	784	2044	5329
98	75	5625	7350	9604
56	34	1156	1904	3136
75	52	2704	3900	5625
Sum 760	460	23,634	36,854	59,816

$$S_{xx} = \Sigma x_i^2 - \frac{(\Sigma x_i)^2}{n} = 23,634 - \frac{(460)^2}{10} = 2474$$

$$S_{xy} = \Sigma x_i y_i - \frac{(\Sigma x_i)(\Sigma y_i)}{n} = 36,854 - \frac{(460)(760)}{10} = 1894$$

$$\bar{y} = \frac{\Sigma y_i}{n} = \frac{760}{10} = 76 \qquad \bar{x} = \frac{\Sigma x_i}{n} = \frac{460}{10} = 46$$

Then

$$b = \frac{S_{xy}}{S_{xx}} = \frac{1894}{2474} = .76556 \quad \text{and} \quad a = \bar{y} - b\bar{x} = 76 - (.76556)(46) = 40.78424$$

The least-squares regression line is then

$$\hat{y} = a + bx = 40.78424 + .76556x$$

The graph of this line is shown in Figure 12.4. It can now be used to predict y for a given value of x—either by referring to Figure 12.4 or by substituting the proper value of x into the equation. For example, if a freshman scored $x = 50$ on the achievement test, the student's predicted calculus grade is (using full decimal accuracy)

$$\hat{y} = a + b(50) = 40.78424 + (.76556)(50) = 79.06$$

Make Sure That My Calculations Are Correct?

- Be careful of rounding errors. Carry at least six significant figures, and round off only in reporting the end result.
- Use a scientific or graphing calculator to do all the work for you. Most of these calculators will calculate the values for a and b if you enter the data properly.
- Use a computer software program if you have access to one.
- Always plot the data and graph the line. If the line does not fit through the points, you have probably made a mistake!

DO IT YOURSELF!

You can use the **Method of Least Squares** applet to find the values of a and b that determine the *best fitting line*, $\hat{y} = a + bx$. The horizontal line that you see is the line $y = \bar{y}$. Use your mouse to drag the line and watch the yellow squares change size. The object is to make SSE—the total area of the yellow squares—as small as possible. The value of SSE is the red portion of the bar on the left of the applet (blue in Figure 12.4) marked SSE = _____. When you think that you have minimized SSE, click the Find Best Model button and see how well you did!

12.4   An Analysis of Variance for Linear Regression

In Chapter 11, you used the analysis of variance procedures to divide the total variation in the experiment into portions attributed to various factors of interest to the experimenter. In a regression analysis, the response y is related to the independent variable x. Hence, the total variation in the response variable y, given by

$$\text{Total SS} = S_{yy} = \Sigma(y_i - \bar{y})^2 = \Sigma y_i^2 - \frac{(\Sigma y_i)^2}{n}$$

is divided into two portions:

- SSR (sum of squares for regression) measures the amount of variation explained by using the regression line with one independent variable x
- SSE (sum of squares for error) measures the "residual" variation in the data that is not explained by the independent variable x

so that

Total SS = SSR + SSE

For a particular value of the response y_i, you can visualize this breakdown in the variation using the vertical distances illustrated in Figure 12.5. You can see that SSR is the sum of the squared deviations of the differences between the estimated response without using x ($\bar{y}$) and the estimated response using x (the regression line, $\hat{y}$); SSE is the sum of the squared differences between the regression line ($\hat{y}$) and the point y.

FIGURE 12.5
Deviations from
the fitted line

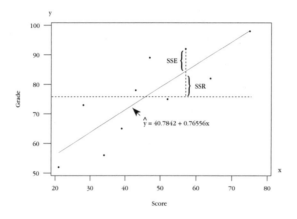

It is not too hard to show algebraically that

$$\text{SSR} = \Sigma(\hat{y}_i - \bar{y}_i)^2 = \Sigma(a + bx_i - \bar{y})^2 = \Sigma(\bar{y} - b\bar{x} + bx_i - \bar{y})^2 = b^2\Sigma(x_i - \bar{x})^2$$

$$= \left(\frac{S_{xy}}{S_{xx}}\right)^2 S_{xx} = \frac{(S_{xy})^2}{S_{xx}}$$

Since Total SS = SSR + SSE, you can complete the partition by calculating

$$\text{SSE} = \text{Total SS} - \text{SSR} = S_{yy} - \frac{(S_{xy})^2}{S_{xx}}$$

Remember from Chapter 11 that each of the various sources of variation, when divided by the appropriate **degrees of freedom,** provides an estimate of the variation in the experiment. These estimates are called **mean squares**—MS = SS/df—and are displayed in an ANOVA table.

In examining the degrees of freedom associated with each of these sums of squares, notice that the total degrees of freedom for n measurements is $(n - 1)$. Since estimating the regression line, $\hat{y} = a + bx_i = \bar{y} - b\bar{x} + bx_i$, involves estimating *one additional* parameter β, there is *one* degree of freedom associated with SSR, leaving $(n - 2)$ degrees of freedom with SSE.

As with all ANOVA tables we have discussed, the mean square for error,

$$\text{MSE} = s^2 = \frac{\text{SSE}}{n - 2}$$

is an unbiased estimator of the underlying variance σ^2. The analysis of variance table is shown in Table 12.3.

TABLE 12.3
Analysis of variance
for linear
regression

Source	df	SS	MS
Regression	1	$\dfrac{(S_{xy})^2}{S_{xx}}$	MSR
Error	$n - 2$	$S_{yy} - \dfrac{(S_{xy})^2}{S_{xx}}$	MSE
Total	$n - 1$	S_{yy}	

For the data in Table 12.1, you can calculate

$$\text{Total SS} = S_{yy} = \Sigma y_i^2 - \frac{(\Sigma y_i)^2}{n} = 59{,}816 - \frac{(760)^2}{10} = 2056$$

$$\text{SSR} = \frac{(S_{xy})^2}{S_{xx}} = \frac{(1894)^2}{2474} = 1449.9741$$

so that

$$\text{SSE} = \text{Total SS} - \text{SSR} = 2056 - 1449.9741 = 606.0259$$

and

$$\text{MSE} = \frac{\text{SSE}}{n - 2} = \frac{606.0259}{8} = 75.7532$$

The analysis of variance table, part of the *linear regression output* generated by *MINITAB*, is the lower shaded section in the printout in Figure 12.6. The first two lines give the equation of the least-squares line, $\hat{y} = 40.8 + .766x$. The least-squares estimates a and b are given with greater accuracy in the column labeled "Coef." You can find instructions for generating this output in the section "About *MINITAB*" at the end of this chapter.

FIGURE 12.6
MINITAB output for
the data of Table
12.1

Regression Analysis: y versus x

```
The regression equation is
y = 40.8 + 0.766 x

Predictor        Coef      SE Coef         T        P
Constant       40.784        8.507      4.79    0.001
x              0.7656       0.1750      4.38    0.002

S = 8.704      R-Sq = 70.5%      R-Sq(adj) = 66.8%

Analysis of Variance
Source            DF           SS          MS         F        P
Regression         1       1450.0      1450.0     19.14    0.002
Residual Error     8        606.0        75.8
Total              9       2056.0
```

The *MINITAB* output also gives some information about the variation in the experiment. Each of the least-squares estimates, a and b, has an associated standard error, labeled "SE Coef" in Figure 12.6. In the middle of the printout, you will find the best unbiased estimate of σ—$S = \sqrt{\text{MSE}} = \sqrt{75.7532} = 8.704$, which measures the **residual error**, the unexplained or "leftover" variation in the experiment. It will not surprise you to know that the t and F statistics and their p-values found in the printout are used to test statistical hypotheses. We explain these entries in the next section.

Exercises

Basic Techniques

12.1 Graph the line corresponding to the equation $y = 2x + 1$ by graphing the points corresponding to $x = 0, 1,$ and 2. Give the y-intercept and slope for the line.

12.2 Graph the line corresponding to the equation $y = -2x + 1$ by graphing the points corresponding to $x = 0, 1,$ and 2. Give the y-intercept and slope for the line. How is this line related to the line $y = 2x + 1$ of Exercise 12.1?

12.3 Give the equation and graph for a line with y-intercept equal to 3 and slope equal to -1.

12.4 Give the equation and graph for a line with y-intercept equal to -3 and slope equal to 1.

12.5 What is the difference between deterministic and probabilistic mathematical models?

12.6 You are given five points with these coordinates:

x	-2	-1	0	1	2
y	1	1	3	5	5

a. Use the data entry method on your scientific or graphing calculator to enter the $n = 5$ observations. Find the sums of squares and cross-products, $S_{xx}, S_{xy},$ and S_{yy}.

b. Find the least-squares line for the data.

c. Plot the five points and graph the line in part b. Does the line appear to provide a good fit to the data points?

d. Construct the ANOVA table for the linear regression.

12.7 Six points have these coordinates:

x	1	2	3	4	5	6
y	5.6	4.6	4.5	3.7	3.2	2.7

a. Find the least-squares line for the data.

b. Plot the six points and graph the line. Does the line appear to provide a good fit to the data points?

c. Use the least-squares line to predict the value of y when $x = 3.5$.

d. Fill in the missing entries in the *MINITAB* analysis of variance table.

MINITAB **ANOVA table for Exercise 12.7**

```
Analysis of Variance

Source           DF        SS         MS
Regression        *       ***      5.4321
Residual Error    *    0.1429       ***
Total             *    5.5750
```

Applications

12.8 Professor Isaac Asimov was one of the most prolific writers of all time. Prior to his death, he wrote nearly 500 books during a 40-year career. In fact, as his career progressed, he became even more productive in terms of the number of books written within a given period of time.[1] The data give the time in months required to write his books in increments of 100:

Number of Books, x	100	200	300	400	490
Time in Months, y	237	350	419	465	507

a. Assume that the number of books x and the time in months y are linearly related. Find the least-squares line relating y to x.

b. Plot the time as a function of the number of books written using a scatterplot, and graph the least-squares line on the same paper. Does it seem to provide a good fit to the data points?

c. Construct the ANOVA table for the linear regression.

12.9 Using a chemical procedure called *differential pulse polarography,* a chemist measured the peak current generated (in microamperes) when a solution containing a given amount of nickel (in parts per billion) is added to a buffer[2]:

EX1209

x = Ni (ppb)	y = Peak Current (mA)
19.1	.095
38.2	.174
57.3	.256
76.2	.348
95	.429
114	.500
131	.580
150	.651
170	.722

a. Use the data entry method for your calculator to calculate the preliminary sums of squares and cross-products, S_{xx}, S_{yy}, and S_{xy}.

b. Calculate the least-squares regression line.

c. Plot the points and the fitted line. Does the assumption of a linear relationship appear to be reasonable?

d. Use the regression line to predict the peak current generated when a solution containing 100 ppb of nickel is added to the buffer.

e. Construct the ANOVA table for the linear regression.

12.10 A study was conducted to determine the effects of sleep deprivation on people's ability to solve problems without sleep. A total of 10 subjects participated in the study, two at each of five sleep deprivation levels—8, 12, 16, 20, and 24 hours. After his or her specified sleep deprivation period, each subject was administered a set of simple addition problems, and the number of errors was recorded. These results were obtained:

Number of Errors, y	8, 6	6, 10	8, 14	14, 12	16, 12
Number of Hours without Sleep, x	8	12	16	20	24

a. How many pairs of observations are in the experiment?

b. What are the total number of degrees of freedom?

c. Complete the *MINITAB* printout.

MINITAB output for Exercise 12.10

Regression Analysis: y versus x

```
The regression equation is
y = 3.00 + 0.475 x

Predictor       Coef     SE Coef        T         P
Constant       3.000       2.127     1.41     0.196
x               ***      0.1253     3.79     0.005

S = 2.242     R-Sq = 64.2%     R-Sq(adj) = 59.8%

Analysis of Variance
Source           DF          SS         MS        F        P
Regression       **      72.200     72.200    14.37    0.005
Residual Error   **         ***      5.025
Total            **         ***
```

d. What is the least-squares prediction equation?

e. Use the prediction equation to predict the number of errors for a person who has not slept for 10 hours.

EX1211

12.11 The Academic Performance Index (API) is a measure of school achievement based on the results of the Stanford 9 Achievement test. Scores range from 200 to 1000, with 800 considered a long-range goal for schools. The following table shows the 2001 API for eight elementary schools in Riverside County, California, along with the percent of students at that school who are considered English Lanugage Learners.[3]

School	1	2	3	4	5	6	7	8
API	588	659	710	657	669	641	557	743
ELL	58	22	14	30	11	26	39	6

a. Which of the two variables is the independent variable and which is the dependent variable? Explain your choice.

b. Use a scatterplot to plot the data. Is the assumption of a linear relationship between x and y reasonable?

c. Assuming that x and y are linearly related, calculate the least-squares regression line.

d. Plot the line on the scatterplot in part b. Does the line fit through the data points?

EX1212

12.12 How good are you at estimating? To test a subject's ability to estimate sizes, he was shown 10 different objects and asked to estimate their length or diameter. The object was then measured, and the results were recorded in the table below.

Object	Estimated (inches)	Actual (inches)
Pencil	7.00	6.00
Dinner plate	9.50	10.25
Book 1	7.50	6.75
Cell phone	4.00	4.25
Photograph	14.50	15.75
Toy	3.75	5.00
Belt	42.00	41.50
Clothespin	2.75	3.75
Book 2	10.00	9.25
Calculator	3.50	4.75

a. Find the least-squares regression line for predicting the actual measurement as a function of the estimated measurement.

b. Plot the points and the fitted line. Does the assumption of a linear relationship appear to be reasonable?

12.5 Testing the Usefulness of the Linear Regression Model

In considering linear regression, you may ask two questions:

- Is the independent variable x useful in predicting the response variable y?

- If so, how well does it work?

This section examines several statistical tests and measures that will help you reach some answers. Once you have determined that the model is working, you can then use the model for predicting the response y for a given value of x.

Inferences Concerning β, the Slope of the Line of Means

Is the least-squares regression line useful? That is, is the regression equation that uses information provided by x substantially better than the simple predictor $\bar{y}$ that does not rely on x? If the independent variable x is *not useful* in the population model $y = \alpha + \beta x + \epsilon$, then the value of y does not change for different values of x. The only way that this happens for all values of x is when the slope β of the line of means equals 0. This would indicate that the relationship between y and x is not linear, so that the initial question about the usefulness of the independent variable x can be restated as: Is there a linear relationship between x and y?

You can answer this question by using either a test of hypothesis or a confidence interval for β. Both of these procedures are based on the sampling distribution of b, the sample estimator of the slope β. It can be shown that, if the assumptions about the random error ϵ are valid, then the estimator b has a normal distribution in repeated sampling with mean

$$E(b) = \beta$$

and standard error given by

$$SE = \sqrt{\frac{\sigma^2}{S_{xx}}}$$

where σ^2 is the variance of the random error ϵ. Since the value of σ^2 is estimated with $s^2 = MSE$, you can base inferences on the statistic given by

$$t = \frac{b - \beta}{\sqrt{MSE/S_{xx}}}$$

which has a t distribution with $df = (n - 2)$, the degrees of freedom associated with MSE.

Test of Hypothesis Concerning the Slope of a Line

1. Null hypothesis: $H_0 : \beta = \beta_0$

2. Alternative hypothesis:

One-Tailed Test	Two-Tailed Test
$H_a : \beta > \beta_0$	$H_a : \beta \neq \beta_0$
(or $\beta < \beta_0$)	

3. Test statistic: $t = \dfrac{b - \beta_0}{\sqrt{MSE/S_{xx}}}$

When the assumptions given in Section 12.2 are satisfied, the test statistic will have a Student's t distribution with $(n - 2)$ degrees of freedom.

4. Rejection region: Reject H_0 when

One-Tailed Test	Two-Tailed Test
$t > t_\alpha$	$t > t_{\alpha/2}$ or $t < -t_{\alpha/2}$
(or $t < -t_\alpha$ when the alternative hypothesis is $H_a : \beta < \beta_0$)	

or when p-value $< \alpha$

(continued)

Test of Hypothesis Concerning the Slope of a Line *(continued)*

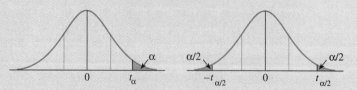

The values of t_α and $t_{\alpha/2}$ can be found using Table 4 in Appendix I or the
t Probabilities applet. Use the values of t corresponding to $(n - 2)$ degrees of
freedom.

EXAMPLE 12.2

Determine whether there is a significant linear relationship between the calculus grades
and test scores listed in Table 12.1. Test at the 5% level of significance.

Solution

The hypotheses to be tested are

$$H_0 : \beta = 0 \quad \text{versus} \quad H_a : \beta \neq 0$$

and the observed value of the test statistic is calculated as

$$t = \frac{b - 0}{\sqrt{\text{MSE}/S_{xx}}} = \frac{.7656 - 0}{\sqrt{75.7532/2474}} = 4.38$$

with $(n - 2) = 8$ degrees of freedom. With $\alpha = .05$, you can reject H_0 when
$t > 2.306$ or $t < -2.306$. Since the observed value of the test statistic falls into the rejection region, H_0 is rejected and you can conclude that there is a significant linear
relationship between the calculus grades and the test scores for the population of college freshmen.

DO IT YOURSELF!

You can use the **t Test for the Slope** applet shown in Figure 12.7 to find p-values
or rejection regions for this test. You must first calculate the standard error,
$\text{SE} = \sqrt{\text{MSE}/S_{xx}}$, type its value into the box marked "Std Error," and press "Enter."

FIGURE 12.7
t Test for the
Slope applet

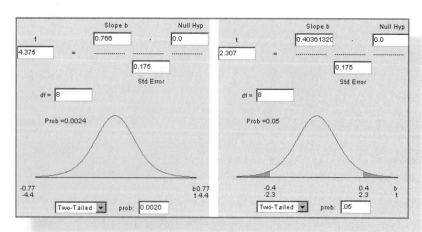

- If you enter the value of b into the formula at the top of the applet and press "Enter," the applet will calculate the test statistic and its one- or two-tailed p-value.
- If you enter the significance level α in the box marked "prob:" and select the "One-Tailed" or "Two-Tailed" option in the drop-down list, the applet will calculate the positive value of t necessary for rejecting H_0. (You could also use the **Student's t Probabilities** applet to find the critical values.)

What is the p-value for the test performed in Example 12.2? Does this p-value confirm our conclusions?

Another way to make inferences about the value of β is to construct a confidence interval for β and examine the range of possible values for β.

A $(1 - \alpha)100\%$ Confidence Interval for β

$$b \pm t_{\alpha/2}(\text{SE})$$

where $t_{\alpha/2}$ is based on $(n - 2)$ degrees of freedom and

$$\text{SE} = \sqrt{\frac{s^2}{S_{xx}}} = \sqrt{\frac{\text{MSE}}{S_{xx}}}$$

EXAMPLE 12.3 Find a 95% confidence interval estimate of the slope β for the calculus grade data in Table 12.1.

Solution Substituting previously calculated values into

$$b \pm t_{.025}\sqrt{\frac{\text{MSE}}{S_{xx}}}$$

you have

$$.766 \pm 2.306\sqrt{\frac{75.7532}{2474}}$$

$$.766 \pm .404$$

The resulting 95% confidence interval is .362 to 1.170. Since the interval does not contain 0, you can conclude that the true value of β is not 0, and you can reject the null hypothesis $H_0 : \beta = 0$ in favor of $H_a : \beta \neq 0$, a conclusion that agrees with the findings in Example 12.2. Furthermore, the confidence interval estimate indicates that there is an increase from as little as .4 to as much as 1.2 points in a calculus test score for each 1-point increase in the achievement test score.

If you are using computer software to perform the regression analysis, you will find the t statistic and its p-value on the printout. Look at the *MINITAB* regression analysis printout reproduced in Figure 12.8. In the second portion of the printout, you will find the least-squares estimates a ("Constant") and b ("x") in the column marked "Coef," their standard errors ("SE Coef"), the calculated value of the t statistic ("T") used for testing the hypothesis that the parameter equals 0, and its p-value ("P"). The t test for significant regression, $H_0 : \beta = 0$, has a p-value of $P = .002$, and the null hypothesis is rejected, as in Example 12.2. Does this agree with the p-value found using the **t Test**

for the Slope applet in Figure 12.7? In any event, there is a significant linear relationship between x and y.

FIGURE 12.8
MINITAB output for
the calculus grade
data

Regression Analysis: y versus x

```
The regression equation is
y = 40.8 + 0.766 x

Predictor        Coef      SE Coef          T        P
Constant       40.784        8.507       4.79    0.001
x              0.7656       0.1750       4.38    0.002

S = 8.704      R-Sq = 70.5%     R-Sq(adj) = 66.8%

Analysis of Variance
Source           DF           SS          MS        F        P
Regression        1       1450.0      1450.0    19.14    0.002
Residual Error    8        606.0        75.8
Total             9       2056.0
```

The Analysis of Variance F Test

The analysis of variance portion of the printout in Figure 12.8 shows an F statistic given by

$$F = \frac{MSR}{MSE} = 19.14$$

with 1 numerator degree of freedom and $(n - 2) = 8$ denominator degrees of freedom. This is an *equivalent test statistic* that can also be used for testing the hypothesis $H_0 : \beta = 0$. Notice that, within rounding error, the value of F is equal to t^2 with the identical p-value. In this case, if you use five-decimal-place accuracy prior to rounding, you find that $t^2 = (.76556/.17498)^2 = (4.37513)^2 = 19.14175 \approx 19.14 = F$ as given in the printout. This is no accident and results from the fact that the square of a t statistic with df degrees of freedom has the same distribution as an F statistic with 1 numerator and df denominator degrees of freedom. The F test is a more general test of the usefulness of the model and can be used when the model has more than one independent variable.

Measuring the Strength of the Relationship: The Coefficient of Determination

How well does the regression model fit? To answer this question, you can use a measure related to the *correlation coefficient r,* introduced in Chapter 3. Remember that

$$r = \frac{s_{xy}}{s_x s_y} = \frac{S_{xy}}{\sqrt{S_{xx}S_{yy}}} \qquad \text{for } -1 \leq r \leq 1$$

where s_{xy}, s_x, and s_y were defined in Chapter 3 and the various sums of squares were defined in Section 12.4.

The sum of squares for regression, SSR, in the analysis of variance measures the portion of the total variation, Total SS $= S_{yy}$, that can be explained by the regression of y on x. The remaining portion, SSE, is the "unexplained" variation attributed to random error. One way to measure the strength of the relationship between the response variable y and the predictor variable x is to calculate the **coefficient of determination**—the proportion of the total variation that is explained by the linear regression of y on x. For the calculus grade data, this proportion is equal to

$$\frac{\text{SSR}}{\text{Total SS}} = \frac{1450}{2056} = .705 \quad \text{or} \quad 70.5\%$$

Since Total SS $= S_{yy}$ and SSR $= \dfrac{(S_{xy})^2}{S_{xx}}$, you can write

$$\frac{\text{SSR}}{\text{Total SS}} = \frac{(S_{xy})^2}{S_{xx}S_{yy}} = \left(\frac{S_{xy}}{\sqrt{S_{xx}S_{yy}}}\right)^2 = r^2$$

Therefore, the coefficient of determination, which was calculated as SSR/Total SS, is simply the square of the correlation coefficient r. It is the entry labeled "R-Sq" in Figure 12.8.

Remember that the analysis of variance table isolates the variation due to regression (SSR) from the total variation in the experiment. Doing so reduces the amount of *random variation* in the experiment, now measured by SSE rather than Total SS. In this context, the **coefficient of determination, r^2,** can be defined as follows:

Definition   The **coefficient of determination** r^2 can be interpreted as the percent reduction in the total variation in the experiment obtained by using the regression line $\hat{y} = a + bx$, instead of ignoring x and using the sample mean $\bar{y}$ to predict the response variable y.

For the calculus grade data, a reduction of $r^2 = .705$ or 70.5% is substantial. The regression model is working very well!

Interpreting the Results of a Significant Regression

Once you have performed the t or F test to determine the significance of the linear regression, you must interpret your results carefully. The slope β of the line of means is estimated based on data from only a particular region of observation. Even if you do not reject the null hypothesis that the slope of the line equals 0, it does not necessarily mean that y and x are unrelated. It may be that you have committed a Type II error—falsely declaring that the slope is 0 and that x and y are unrelated.

Fitting the Wrong Model

It may happen that y and x are perfectly related in a nonlinear way, as shown in Figure 12.9. Here are three possibilities:

FIGURE 12.9
Curvilinear relationship

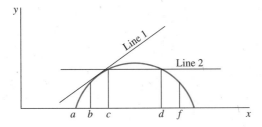

- If observations were taken only within the interval $b < x < c$, the relationship would appear to be linear with a positive slope.
- If observations were taken only within the interval $d < x < f$, the relationship would appear to be linear with a negative slope.
- If the observations were taken over the interval $c < x < d$, the line would be fitted with a slope close to 0, indicating no linear relationship between y and x.

For the example shown in Figure 12.9, no straight line accurately describes the true relationship between x and y, which is really a *curvilinear relationship*. In this case, we have chosen the *wrong model* to describe the relationship. Sometimes this type of mistake can be detected using residual plots, the subject of Section 12.7.

Extrapolation

One serious problem is to apply the results of a linear regression analysis to values of x that are *not included* within the range of the fitted data. This is called **extrapolation** and can lead to serious errors in prediction, as shown for line 1 in Figure 12.9. Prediction results would be good over the interval $b < x < c$ but would seriously overestimate the values of y for $x > c$.

Causality

When there is a significant regression of y and x, it is tempting to conclude that x *causes* y. However, it is possible that one or more unknown variables that you have not even measured and that are not included in the analysis may be causing the observed relationship. In general, the statistician reports the results of an analysis but leaves conclusions concerning causality to scientists and investigators who are experts in these areas. These experts are better prepared to make such decisions!

Exercises   Basic Techniques

12.13   Refer to Exercise 12.6. The data are reproduced below.

x	-2	-1	0	1	2
y	1	1	3	5	5

a. Do the data present sufficient evidence to indicate that y and x are linearly related? Test the hypothesis that $\beta = 0$ at the 5% level of significance.

b. Use the ANOVA table from Exercise 12.6 to calculate $F = MSR/MSE$. Verify that the square of the t statistic used in part a is equal to F.

c. Compare the two-tailed critical value for the t test in part a with the critical value for F with $\alpha = .05$. What is the relationship between the critical values?

12.14   Refer to Exercise 12.13. Find a 95% confidence interval for the slope of the line. What does the phrase "95% confident" mean?

12.15   Refer to Exercise 12.7. The data, along with the *MINITAB* analysis of variance table are reproduced below.

x	1	2	3	4	5	6
y	5.6	4.6	4.5	3.7	3.2	2.7

MINITAB ANOVA table for Exercise 12.15

Regression Analysis: y versus x

Source	DF	SS	MS	F	P
Regression	1	5.4321	5.4321	152.10	0.000
Residual Error	4	0.1429	0.0357		
Total	5	5.5750			

a. Do the data provide sufficient evidence to indicate that y and x are linearly related? Use the information in the *MINITAB* printout to answer this question at the 1% level of significance.

b. Calculate the coefficient of determination r^2. What information does this value give about the usefulness of the linear model?

Applications

EX1216

12.16 An experiment was designed to compare several different types of air pollution monitors.[4] The monitor was set up, and then exposed to different concentrations of ozone, ranging between 15 and 230 parts per million (ppm) for periods of 8–72 hours. Filters on the monitor were then analyzed, and the amount (in micrograms) of sodium nitrate (NO_3) recorded by the monitor was measured. The results for one type of monitor are given in the table.

Ozone, x (ppm/hr)	.8	1.3	1.7	2.2	2.7	2.9
NO_3, y (μg)	2.44	5.21	6.07	8.98	10.82	12.16

a. Find the least-squares regression line relating the monitor's response to the ozone concentration.

b. Do the data provide sufficient evidence to indicate that there is a linear relationship between the ozone concentration and the amount of sodium nitrate detected?

c. Calculate r^2. What does this value tell you about the effectiveness of the linear regression analysis?

EX1217

12.17 How is the cost of a plane flight related to the length of the trip? The table shows the average round-trip coach airfare paid by customers of American Airlines on each of 18 heavily traveled U.S. air routes.[5]

Route	Distance (miles)	Cost	Route	Distance (miles)	Cost
Dallas–Austin	178	$125	Chicago–Denver	901	$256
Houston–Dallas	232	123	Dallas–Salt Lake	1005	365
Chicago–Detroit	238	148	New York–Dallas	1374	459
Chicago–St. Louis	262	136	Chicago–Seattle	1736	424
Chicago–Cleveland	301	129	Los Angeles–Chicago	1757	361
Chicago–Atlanta	593	162	Los Angeles–Atlanta	1946	309
New York–Miami	1092	224	New York–Los Angeles	2463	444
New York–San Juan	1608	264	Los Angeles–Honolulu	2556	323
New York–Chicago	714	287	New York–San Francisco	2574	513

a. If you want to estimate the cost of a flight based on the distance traveled, which variable is the response variable and which is the independent predictor variable?

b. Assume that there is a linear relationship between cost and distance. Calculate the least-squares regression line describing cost as a linear function of distance.

c. Plot the data points and the regression line. Does it appear that the line fits the data?

d. Use the appropriate statistical tests and measures to explain the usefulness of the regression model for predicting cost.

12.18 Refer to the data in Exercise 12.8, relating x, the number of books written by Professor Isaac Asimov, to y, the number of months he took to write his books (in increments of 100). The data are reproduced below.

Number of books, x	100	200	300	400	490
Time in months, y	237	350	419	465	507

a. Do the data support the hypothesis that $\beta = 0$? Use the p-value approach, bounding the p-value using Table 4 of Appendix I or finding the exact p-value using the t **Test for the Slope** applet. Explain your conclusions in practical terms.

b. Use the ANOVA table in Exercise 12.8, part c, to calculate the coefficient of determination r^2. What percentage reduction in the total variation is achieved by using the linear regression model?

c. Plot the data or refer to the plot in Exercise 12.8, part b. Do the results of parts a and b indicate that the model provides a good fit for the data? Are there any assumptions that may have been violated in fitting the linear model?

12.19 Refer to the sleep deprivation experiment described in Exercise 12.10. The data and the *MINITAB* printout are reproduced here.

Number of errors, y	8, 6	6, 10	8, 14	14, 12	16, 12
Number of hours without sleep, x	8	12	16	20	24

MINITAB output for Exercise 12.19

Regression Analysis: y versus x

```
The regression equation is
y = 3.00 + 0.475 x

Predictor        Coef      SE Coef          T          P
Constant        3.000        2.127       1.41      0.196
x              0.4750       0.1253       3.79      0.005

S = 2.242      R-Sq = 64.2%      R-Sq(adj) = 59.8%

Analysis of Variance

Source             DF           SS          MS          F          P
Regression          1       72.200      72.200      14.37      0.005
Residual Error      8       40.200       5.025
Total               9      112.400
```

a. Do the data present sufficient evidence to indicate that the number of errors is linearly related to the number of hours without sleep? Identify the two test statistics in the printout that can be used to answer this question.

b. Would you expect the relationship between y and x to be linear if x varied over a wider range (say, $x = 4$ to $x = 48$)?

c. How do you describe the strength of the relationship between y and x?

d. What is the best estimate of the common population variance σ^2?

e. Find a 95% confidence interval for the slope of the line.

12.6 Diagnostic Tools for Checking the Regression Assumptions

Even though you have determined using the t-test for the slope (or the ANOVA F-test) and the value of r^2, that x is useful in predicting the value of y, the results of a regression analysis are valid only when the data satisfy the necessary regression assumptions.

Regression Assumptions

■ The relationship between y and x must be linear, given by the model

$$y = \alpha + \beta x + \epsilon$$

■ The values of the random error term ϵ (1) are independent, (2) have a mean of 0 and a common variance σ^2, independent of x, and (3) are normally distributed.

Since these assumptions are quite similar to those presented in Chapter 11 for an analysis of variance, it should not surprise you to find that the **diagnostic tools** for checking these assumptions are the same as those we used in that chapter. These tools involve the analysis of the **residual error,** the unexplained variation in each observation once the variation explained by the regression model has been removed.

Dependent Error Terms

The error terms are often dependent when the observations are collected at regular time intervals. When this is the case, the observations make up a **time series** whose error terms are correlated. This in turn causes bias in the estimates of model parameters. Time series data should be analyzed using time series methods. You will find a discussion of time-series analysis in the text *Statistics for Management and Economics,* 7th edition, by Mendenhall, Beaver and Beaver.

Residual Plots

The other regression assumptions can be checked using **residual plots,** which are fairly complicated to construct by hand but easy to use once a computer has graphed them for you!

In simple linear regression, you can use the **plot of residuals versus fit** to check for a constant variance as well as to make sure that the linear model is in fact adequate. This plot should be free of any patterns. It should appear as a random scatter of points about 0 on the vertical axis with approximately the same vertical spread for all values of $\hat{y}$. One property of the residuals is that they sum to 0 and therefore have a sample mean of 0. The plot of the residuals versus fit for the calculus grade example is shown in Figure 12.10. There are no apparent patterns in this residual plot, which indicates that the model is adequate for these data.

FIGURE 12.10
Plot of the residuals versus $\hat{y}$ for Example 12.1

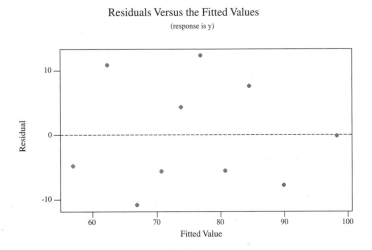

Residuals Versus the Fitted Values
(response is y)

Recall from Chapter 11 that the **normal probability plot** is a graph that plots the residuals against the expected value of that residual if it had come from a normal distribution. When the residuals are normally distributed or approximately so, the plot should appear as a straight line, sloping upward. If the residuals have a standard normal distribution, then the line slopes upward at a 45° angle. The normal probability plot for the residuals in Example 12.1 is given in Figure 12.11. With the exception of the fourth and fifth plotted points, the remaining points appear to lie approximately on a straight line. This plot is not unusual and does not indicate underlying nonnormality. The most serious violations of the normality assumption usually appear in the tails of the distribution because this is where the normal distribution differs most from other types of distributions with a similar mean and measure of spread. Hence, curvature in either or both of the two ends of the normal probability plot is indicative of nonnormality.

FIGURE 12.11
Normal probability
plot of residuals
for Example 12.1

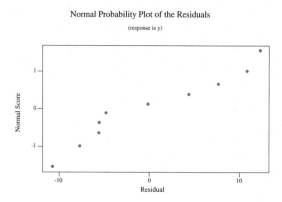

Exercises

Basic Techniques

12.20 What diagnostic plot can you use to determine whether the data satisfy the normality assumption? What should the plot look like for normal residuals?

12.21 What diagnostic plot can you use to determine whether the incorrect model has been used? What should the plot look like if the correct model has been used?

12.22 What diagnostic plot can you use to determine whether the assumption of equal variance has been violated? What should the plot look like when the variances are equal for all values of x?

12.23 Refer to the data in Exercise 12.7. The normal probability plot and the residuals versus fitted values plots generated by *MINITAB* are shown here. Does it appear that any regression assumptions have been violated? Explain.

MINITAB output for Exercise 12.23

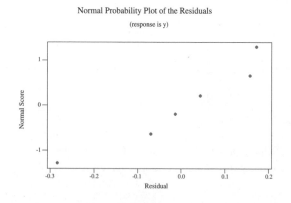

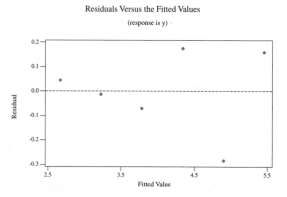

Applications

12.24 Refer to Exercise 12.16, in which an air pollution monitor's response to ozone was recorded for several different concentrations of ozone. Use the *MINITAB* residual plots to comment on the validity of the regression assumptions.

MINITAB output for Exercise 12.24

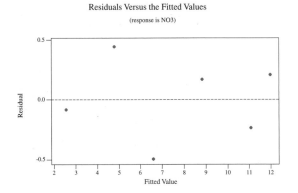

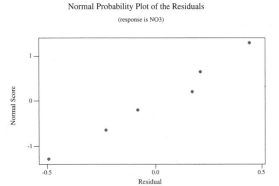

12.25 Refer to Exercise 12.8, in which the number of books x written by Isaac Asimov are related to the number of months y he took to write them. A plot of the data is shown.

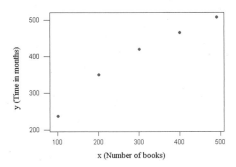

a. Can you see any pattern other than a linear relationship in the original plot?

b. The value of r^2 for these data is .959. What does this tell you about the fit of the regression line?

c. Look at the accompanying diagnostic plots for these data. Do you see any pattern in the residuals? Does this suggest that the relationship between number of months and number of books written is something other than linear?

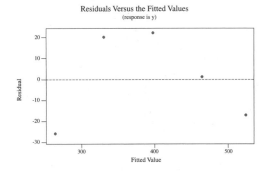

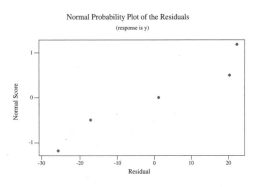

12.7   Estimation and Prediction Using the Fitted Line

Now that you have

- tested fitted regression line, $\hat{y} = a + bx$, to make sure that it is useful for prediction and
- used the diagnostic tools to make sure that none of the regression assumptions have been violated

you are ready to use the line for one of its two purposes:

- Estimating the average value of y for a given value of x
- Predicting a particular value of y for a given value of x

The sample of n pairs of observations have been chosen from a population in which the *average* value of y is related to the value of the predictor variable x by the **line of means,**

$$E(y) = \alpha + \beta x$$

an unknown line, shown as a broken line in Figure 12.12. Remember that for a fixed value of x—say, x_0—the *particular* values of y deviate from the line of means. These values of y have a normal distribution with mean equal to $\alpha + \beta x_0$ and variance σ^2, as shown in Figure 12.12.

FIGURE 12.12
Distribution of y
for $x = x_0$

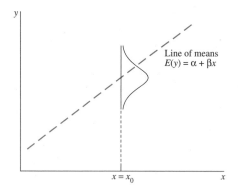

Since the computed values of a and b vary from sample to sample, each new sample produces a different regression line $\hat{y} = a + bx$, which can be used either to estimate the line of means or to predict a particular value of y. Figure 12.13 shows one of the possible configurations of the fitted line (blue), the unknown line of means (gray), and a particular value of y (the blue dot).

FIGURE 12.13
Error in estimating
$E(y)$ and in
predicting y

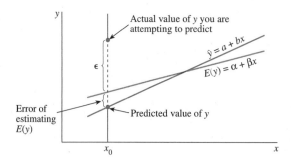

How far will our estimator $\hat{y} = a + bx_0$ be from the quantity to be estimated or predicted? This depends, as always, on the variability in our estimator, measured by its **standard error.** It can be shown that

$$\hat{y} = a + bx_0$$

the estimated value of y when $x = x_0$, is an unbiased estimator of the line of means, $\alpha + \beta x_0$, and that $\hat{y}$ is normally distributed with the standard error of $\hat{y}$ estimated by

$$SE(\hat{y}) = \sqrt{MSE\left(\frac{1}{n} + \frac{(x_0 - \bar{x})^2}{S_{xx}}\right)}$$

Estimation and testing are based on the statistic

$$t = \frac{\hat{y} - E(y)}{SE(\hat{y})}$$

which has a t distribution with $(n - 2)$ degrees of freedom.

To form a $(1 - \alpha)100\%$ confidence interval for the average value of y when $x = x_0$, measured by the line of means, $\alpha + \beta x_0$, you can use the usual form for a confidence interval based on the t distribution:

$$\hat{y} \pm t_{\alpha/2}SE(\hat{y})$$

If you choose to predict a *particular* value of y when $x = x_0$, however, there is some additional error in the prediction because of the deviation of y from the line of means. If you examine Figure 12.13, you can see that the error in prediction has two components:

- The error in using the fitted line to estimate the line of means
- The error caused by the deviation of y from the line of means, measured by σ^2

The variance of the difference between y and $\hat{y}$ is the sum of these two variances and forms the basis for the standard error of $(y - \hat{y})$ used for prediction:

$$SE(y - \hat{y}) = \sqrt{MSE\left[1 + \frac{1}{n} + \frac{(x_0 - \bar{x})^2}{S_{xx}}\right]}$$

and the $(1 - \alpha)100\%$ prediction interval is formed as

$$\hat{y} \pm t_{\alpha/2}SE(y - \hat{y})$$

$(1 - \alpha)100\%$ Confidence and Prediction Intervals

- For estimating the average value of y when $x = x_0$:

$$\hat{y} \pm t_{\alpha/2}\sqrt{MSE\left[\frac{1}{n} + \frac{(x_0 - \bar{x})^2}{S_{xx}}\right]}$$

- For predicting a particular value of y when $x = x_0$:

$$\hat{y} \pm t_{\alpha/2}\sqrt{MSE\left[1 + \frac{1}{n} + \frac{(x_0 - \bar{x})^2}{S_{xx}}\right]}$$

where $t_{\alpha/2}$ is the value of t with $(n - 2)$ degrees of freedom and area $\alpha/2$ to its right.

EXAMPLE 12.4   Use the information in Example 12.1 to estimate the average calculus grade for students whose achievement score is 50, with a 95% confidence interval.

Solution The point estimate of $E(y|x_0 = 50)$, the average calculus grade for students whose achievement score is 50, is

$$\hat{y} = 40.78424 + .76556(50) = 79.06$$

The standard error of $\hat{y}$ is

$$\sqrt{MSE\left[\frac{1}{n} + \frac{(x_0 - \bar{x})^2}{S_{xx}}\right]} = \sqrt{75.7532\left[\frac{1}{10} + \frac{(50 - 46)^2}{2474}\right]} = 2.840$$

and the 95% confidence interval is

$$79.06 \pm 2.306(2.840)$$
$$79.06 \pm 6.55$$

Our results indicate that the average calculus grade for students who scores 50 on the achievement test will lie between 72.51 and 85.61.

EXAMPLE 12.5 A student took the achievement test and scored 50 but has not yet taken the calculus test. Using the information in Example 12.1, predict the calculus grade for this student with a 95% prediction interval.

Solution The predicted value of y is $\hat{y} = 79.06$, as in Example 12.4. However, the error in prediction is measured by $SE(y - \hat{y})$, and the 95% prediction interval is

$$79.06 \pm 2.306\sqrt{75.7532\left[1 + \frac{1}{10} + \frac{(50 - 46)^2}{2474}\right]}$$
$$79.06 \pm 2.306(9.155)$$
$$79.06 \pm 21.11$$

or from 57.95 to 100.17. The prediction interval is *wider* than the confidence interval in Example 12.4 because of the extra variability in predicting the actual value of the response y.

One particular point on the line of means is often of interest to experimenters, the **y-intercept α**—the average value of y when $x_0 = 0$.

EXAMPLE 12.6 Prior to fitting a line to the calculus grade–achievement score data, you may have thought that a score of 0 on the achievement test would predict a grade of 0 on the calculus test. This implies that we should fit a model with α equal to 0. Do the data support the hypothesis of a 0 intercept?

Solution You can answer this question by constructing a 95% confidence interval for the y-intercept α, which is the average value of y when $x = 0$. The estimate of α is

$$\hat{y} = 40.784 + .76556(0) = 40.784 = a$$

and the 95% confidence interval is

$$\hat{y} \pm t_{\alpha/2}\sqrt{MSE\left[\frac{1}{n} + \frac{(x_0 - \bar{x})^2}{S_{xx}}\right]}$$

$$40.784 \pm 2.306\sqrt{75.7532\left[\frac{1}{10} + \frac{(0 - 46)^2}{2474}\right]}$$

$$40.784 \pm 19.617$$

or from 21.167 to 60.401, an interval that does not contain the value $\alpha = 0$. Hence, it is unlikely that the y-intercept is 0. You should include a nonzero intercept in the model $y = \alpha + \beta x + \epsilon$.

For this special situation in which you are interested in testing or estimating the y-intercept α for the line of means, the inferences involve the sample estimate a. The test for a 0 intercept is given in Figure 12.14 in the shaded line labeled "Constant." The coefficient given as 40.784 is a, with standard error given in the column labeled "SE Coef" as 8.507, which agrees with the value calculated in Example 12.6. The value of $t = 4.79$ is found by dividing a by its standard error with p-value $= .001$.

FIGURE 12.14
Portion of the
MINITAB output
for Example 12.6

Predictor	Coef	SE Coef	T	P
Constant	40.784	8.507	4.79	0.001
x	0.7656	0.1750	4.38	0.002

You can see that it is quite time-consuming to calculate these estimation and prediction intervals by hand. Moreover, it is difficult to maintain accuracy in your calculations. Fortunately, computer programs can perform these calculations for you. The *MINITAB* regression command provides an option for either estimation or prediction when you specify the necessary value(s) of x. The printout in Figure 12.15 gives the values of $\hat{y} = 79.06$ labeled "Fit," the standard error of $\hat{y}$, SE($\hat{y}$), labeled "SE Fit," the *confidence interval* for the average value of y when $x = 50$, labeled "95.0% CI," and the prediction interval for y when $x = 50$, labeled "95.0% PI."

FIGURE 12.15
MINITAB option for
estimation and
prediction

```
Predicted Values for New Observations
New Obs    Fit    SE Fit       95.0% CI          95.0% PI
1        79.06      2.84   (  72.51,   85.61)  (  57.95,  100.17)

Values of Predictors for New Observations
New Obs      x
1         50.0
```

The confidence bands and prediction bands generated by *MINITAB* for the calculus grades data are shown in Figure 12.16. Notice that in general the confidence bands are narrower than the prediction bands for every value of the achievement test score x. Certainly you would expect predictions for an individual value to be much more variable than estimates of the average value. Also notice that the bands seem to get wider as the value of x_0 gets farther from the mean $\bar{x}$. This is because the standard errors used in the confidence and

FIGURE 12.16
Confidence and
prediction intervals
for the data in
Table 12.1

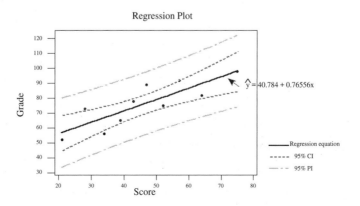

prediction intervals contain the term $(x_0 - \bar{x})^2$, which gets larger as the two values diverge. In practice, this means that estimation and prediction are more accurate when x_0 is near the center of the range of the x-values. You can locate the calculated confidence and prediction intervals when $x = 50$ in Figure 12.16.

Exercises   Basic Techniques

12.26   Refer to Exercise 12.6.

a. Estimate the average value of y when $x = 1$, using a 90% confidence interval.

b. Find a 90% prediction interval for some value of y to be observed in the future when $x = 1$.

12.27   Refer to Exercise 12.7. Portions of the *MINITAB* printout are shown here.

MINITAB output for Exercise 12.27

Regression Analysis: y versus x

```
The regression equation is
y = 6.00 - 0.557 x

Predictor        Coef      SE Coef        T         P
Constant       6.0000       0.1759    34.10     0.000
x             -0.55714      0.04518   -12.33     0.000

Predicted Values for New Observations
New Obs     Fit     SE Fit        95.0% CI              95.0% PI
1        4.8857    0.1027  ( 4.6006,  5.1708)   ( 4.2886,  5.4829)
2        1.5429    0.2174  ( 0.9391,  2.1466)   ( 0.7430,  2.3427) X
X   denotes a row with X values away from the center

Values of Predictors for New Observations
New Obs        x
1           2.00
2           8.00
```

a. Find a 95% confidence interval for the average value of y when $x = 2$.

b. Find a 95% prediction interval for some value of y to be observed in the future when $x = 2$.

c. The last line in the third section of the printout indicates a problem with one of the fitted values. What value of x corresponds to the fitted value $\hat{y} = 1.5429$? What problem has the *MINITAB* program detected?

Applications

12.28   A marketing research experiment was conducted to study the relationship between the length of time necessary for a buyer to reach a decision and the number of alternative package designs of a product presented. Brand names were eliminated from the packages to reduce the effects of brand preferences. The buyers made their selections using the manufacturer's product descriptions on the packages as the only buying guide. The length of time necessary to reach a decision was recorded for 15 participants in the marketing research study.

Length of Decision Time, y (sec)	5, 8, 8, 7, 9	7, 9, 8, 9, 10	10, 11, 10, 12, 9
Number of Alternatives, x	2	3	4

a. Find the least-squares line appropriate for these data.

b. Plot the points and graph the line as a check on your calculations.

c. Calculate s^2.

d. Do the data present sufficient evidence to indicate that the length of decision time is linearly related to the number of alternative package designs? (Test at the $\alpha = .05$ level of significance.)

e. Find the approximate p-value for the test and interpret its value.

f. If they are available, examine the diagnostic plots to check the validity of the regression assumptions.

g. Estimate the average length of time necessary to reach a decision when three alternatives are presented, using a 95% confidence interval.

12.29 If you try to rent an apartment or buy a house, you find that real estate representatives establish apartment rents and house prices on the basis of square footage of heated floor space. The data in the table give the square footages and sales prices of $n = 12$ houses randomly selected from those sold in a small city. Use the *MINITAB* printout to answer the questions.

Square Feet, x	Price, y
1,460	$ 88,700
2,108	109,300
1,743	101,400
1,499	91,100
1,864	102,400
2,391	114,900
1,977	105,400
1,610	97,000
1,530	92,400
1,759	98,200
1,821	104,300
2,216	111,700

Plot of data for Exercise 12.29

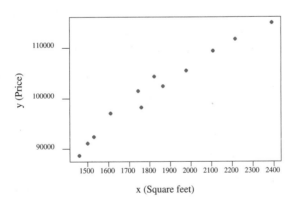

MINITAB output for Exercise 12.29

Regression Analysis: y versus x

```
The regression equation is
y = 51206 + 27.4 x

Predictor        Coef      SE Coef         T        P
Constant        51206         3389     15.11    0.000
x              27.406        1.828     14.99    0.000

Predicted Values for New Observations
New Obs      Fit     SE Fit        95.0% CI              95.0% PI
1          99989        526  (  98817,  101161)  (  4.2886,  104151)
2         106018        602  ( 104676,  107360)  ( 101804,  110232)

Values of Predictors for New Observations
New Obs        x
1           1780
2           2000
```

a. Can you see any pattern other than a linear relationship in the original plot?

b. The value of r^2 for these data is .957. What does this tell you about the fit of the regression line?

c. Look at the accompanying diagnostic plots for these data. Do you see any pattern in the residuals? Does this suggest that the relationship between price and square feet is something other than linear?

MINITAB output
for Exercise 12.29

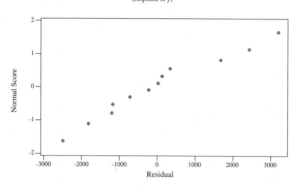

Normal Probability of the Residuals
(response is y)

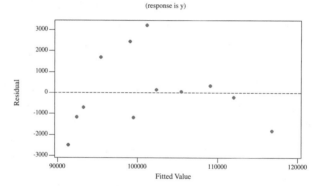

Residuals Versus the Fitted Values
(response is y)

12.30 Refer to Exercise 12.29 and data set EX1229.

a. Estimate the average increase in the price for an increase of 1 square foot for houses sold in the city. Use a 99% confidence interval. Interpret your estimate.

b. A real estate salesperson needs to estimate the average sales price of houses with a total of 2,000 square feet of heated space. Use a 95% confidence interval and interpret your estimate.

c. Calculate the price per square foot for each house and then calculate the sample mean. Why is this estimate of the average cost per square foot not equal to the answer in part a? Should it be? Explain.

d. Suppose that a house with 1780 square feet of heated floor space is offered for sale. Construct a 95% prediction interval for the price at which the house will sell.

12.31 Shareholders have filed a record number of class actions suits this year, with half of these suits alleging IPO (initial public offering) foul play. The numbers of federal securities-fraud class action suits, *y*, filed from 1996 through 2001 are given in the following table.[6] The years are coded as Year − 1995.

y	110	178	236	205	211	282
Time	1	2	3	4	5	6

Use the *MINITAB* printout to answer the questions that follow.

*MINITAB output
for Exercise 12.31*

Regression Analysis: y versus Time

```
The regression equation is
y = 111 + 26.5 Time

Predictor          Coef       SE Coef          T         P
Constant         110.87         30.76       3.60     0.023
Time             26.541          7.898       3.36     0.028

S = 33.04      R-Sq = 73.8%      R-Sq(adj) = 67.3%

Analysis of Variance
Source             DF           SS          MS         F         P
Regression          1        12303       12303     11.27     0.028
Residual Error      4         4367        1092
Total               5        16669

Predicted Values for New Observations
New Obs      Fit       SE Fit          95.0% CI                95.0% PI
1          296.5        30.8   (   211.1,   381.9)  (   171.1,   421.80

Values of Predictors for New Observations
New Obs      Time
1            7.00
```

a. What is the least-squares line relating the number of class action suits and time?

b. Are the number of class action suits linearly related to time over the period 1996 to 2001? Using a regression analysis, test the hypothesis $H_0: \beta = 0$, that there is no linear relationship between y and time.

c. What proportion of the total variation is explained by the regression of y on time?

d. What is the expected number of fraud actions for 2002? Are there any limitations on your estimate?

12.8 Correlation Analysis

In Chapter 3, we introduced the *correlation coefficient* as a measure of the strength of the linear relationship between two variables. The correlation coefficient, r—formally called the **Pearson product moment sample coefficient of correlation**—is defined next.

Pearson Product Moment Coefficient of Correlation

$$r = \frac{s_{xy}}{s_x s_y} = \frac{S_{xy}}{\sqrt{S_{xx}S_{yy}}} \qquad \text{for } -1 \le r \le 1$$

The variances and covariance can be found by direct calculation, by using a calculator with a two-variable statistics capacity, or by using a statistical package such as *MINITAB*. The variances and covariance are calculated as

$$s_{xy} = \frac{S_{xy}}{n-1} \qquad s_x^2 = \frac{S_{xx}}{n-1} \qquad s_y^2 = \frac{S_{yy}}{n-1}$$

and use S_{xy}, S_{xx}, and S_{yy}, the same quantities used in regression analysis earlier in this chapter. In general, when a sample of n individuals or experimental units is selected and two variables are measured on each individual or unit so that *both variables are random*, the correlation coefficient r is the appropriate measure of linearity for use in this situation.

EXAMPLE 12.7 The heights and weights of $n = 10$ offensive backfield football players are randomly selected from a county's football all-stars. Calculate the correlation coefficient for the heights (in inches) and weights (in pounds) given in Table 12.4.

TABLE 12.4
Heights and weights of $n = 10$ backfield all-stars

Player	Height, x	Weight, y
1	73	185
2	71	175
3	75	200
4	72	210
5	72	190
6	75	195
7	67	150
8	69	170
9	71	180
10	69	175

Solution You should use the appropriate data entry method of your scientific calculator to verify the calculations for the sums of squares and cross-products:

$$S_{xy} = 328 \qquad S_{xx} = 60.4 \qquad S_{yy} = 2610$$

using the calculational formulas given earlier in this chapter. Then

$$r = \frac{328}{\sqrt{(60.4)(2610)}} = .8261$$

or $r = .83$. This value of r is fairly close to 1, the largest possible value of r, which indicates a fairly strong positive linear relationship between height and weight.

There is a direct relationship between the calculational formulas for the correlation coefficient r and the slope of the regression line b. Since the numerator of both quantities is S_{xy}, both r and b have the same sign. Therefore, the correlation coefficient has these general properties:

■ When $r = 0$, the slope is 0, and there is no linear relationship between x and y.
■ When r is positive, so is b, and there is a positive linear relationship between x and y.
■ When r is negative, so is b, and there is a negative linear relationship between x and y.

In Section 12.5, we showed that

$$r^2 = \frac{\text{SSR}}{\text{Total SS}} = \frac{\text{Total SS} - \text{SSE}}{\text{Total SS}}$$

In this form, you can see that r^2 can never be greater than 1, so that $-1 \leq r \leq 1$. Moreover, you can see the relationship between the random variation (measured by SSE) and r^2.

■ If there is no random variation and all the points fall on the regression line, then SSE = 0 and $r^2 = 1$.
■ If the points are randomly scattered and there is no variation explained by regression, then SSR = 0 and $r^2 = 0$.

DO IT YOURSELF!

You can use the **Exploring Correlation** applet to visualize the connection between the value of r and the pattern of points shown in the scatterplot. Use your mouse to move the slider at the bottom of the scatterplot. You will see the value of r change as the pattern of the points changes. Try to reproduce the patterns described above for $r^2 = 1$ and $r^2 = 0$.

FIGURE 12.17
Exploring Correlation applet

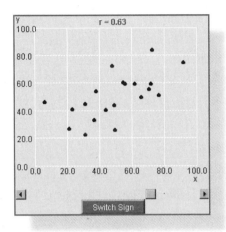

Figure 12.18 shows four typical scatterplots and their associated correlation coefficients. Notice that in scatterplot (d) there appears to be a curvilinear relationship between x and y, but r is approximately 0, which reinforces the fact that r is a measure of a *linear* (not *curvilinear*) relationship between two variables.

FIGURE 12.18
Some typical scatterplots with approximate values of r

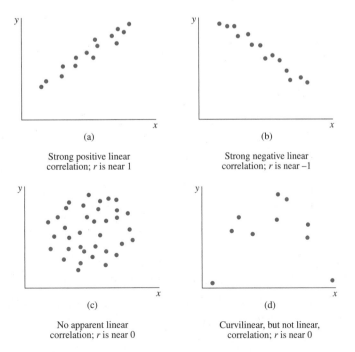

Consider a population generated by measuring two random variables on each experimental unit. In this *bivariate* population, the **population correlation coefficient** ρ (Greek letter rho) is calculated and interpreted as it is in the sample. In this situation, the experimenter can test the hypothesis that there is no correlation between the variables x and y using a test statistic that is *exactly equivalent* to the test of the slope β in Section 12.5. The test procedure is shown next.

Test of Hypothesis Concerning the Correlation Coefficient ρ

1. Null hypothesis: $H_0 : \rho = 0$

2. Alternative hypothesis:

One-Tailed Test	Two-Tailed Test
$H_a : \rho > 0$	$H_a : \rho \neq 0$
(or $\rho < 0$)	

3. Test statistic: $t = r\sqrt{\dfrac{n-2}{1-r^2}}$

When the assumptions given in Section 12.2 are satisfied, the test statistic will have a Student's t distribution with $(n-2)$ degrees of freedom.

4. Rejection region: Reject H_0 when

One-Tailed Test	Two-Tailed Test
$t > t_\alpha$	$t > t_{\alpha/2}$ or $t < -t_{\alpha/2}$
(or $t < -t_\alpha$ when the alternative hypothesis is $H_a : \rho < 0$)	

or p-value $< \alpha$

The values of t_α and $t_{\alpha/2}$ can be found using Table 4 in Appendix I or the **t-Probabilities** applet. Use the values of t corresponding to $(n-2)$ degrees of freedom.

EXAMPLE 12.8

Refer to the height and weight data in Example 12.7. The correlation of height and weight was calculated to be $r = .8261$. Is this correlation significantly different from 0?

Solution   To test the hypotheses

$$H_0 : \rho = 0 \quad \text{versus} \quad H_a : \rho \neq 0$$

the value of the test statistic is

$$t = r\sqrt{\frac{n-2}{1-r^2}} = .8261\sqrt{\frac{10-2}{1-(.8261)^2}} = 4.15$$

which for $n = 10$ has a t distribution with 8 degrees of freedom. Since this value is greater than $t_{.005} = 3.355$, the two-tailed p-value is less than $2(.005) = .01$, and the correlation is declared significant at the 1% level ($P < .01$). The value $r^2 = .8261^2 = .6824$ means that about 68% of the variation in one of the variables is explained by the other. The *MINITAB* printout in Figure 12.19 displays the correlation r and the exact p-value for testing its significance.

Correlations: x, y

```
Pearson correlation of x and y = 0.826
P-Value = 0.003
```

If the linear coefficients of correlation between y and each of two variables x_1 and x_2 are calculated to be .4 and .5, respectively, it does not follow that a predictor using both variables will account for $[(.4)^2 + (.5)^2] = .41$, or a 41% reduction in the sum of squares of deviations. Actually, x_1 and x_2 might be highly correlated and therefore contribute virtually the same information for the prediction of y.

Finally, remember that r is a measure of **linear correlation** and that x and y could be perfectly related by some **curvilinear** function when the observed value of r is equal to 0. The problem of estimating or predicting y using information given by several independent variables, $x_1, x_2, \ldots, x_k$, is the subject of Chapter 13.

Exercises

Basic Techniques

12.32 How does the coefficient of correlation measure the strength of the linear relationship between two variables y and x?

12.33 Describe the significance of the algebraic sign and the magnitude of r.

12.34 What value does r assume if all the data points fall on the same straight line in these cases?

a. The line has positive slope.

b. The line has negative slope.

12.35 You are given these data:

x	−2	−1	0	1	2
y	2	2	3	4	4

a. Plot the data points. Based on your graph, what will be the sign of the sample correlation coefficient?

b. Calculate r and r^2 and interpret their values.

12.36 You are given these data:

x	1	2	3	4	5	6
y	7	5	5	3	2	0

a. Plot the six points on graph paper.

b. Calculate the sample coefficient of correlation r and interpret.

c. By what percentage was the sum of squares of deviations reduced by using the least-squares predictor $\hat{y} = a + bx$ rather than $\bar{y}$ as a predictor of y?

12.37 Reverse the slope of the line in Exercise 12.36 by reordering the y observations, as follows:

x	1	2	3	4	5	6
y	0	2	3	5	5	7

Repeat the steps of Exercise 12.36. Notice the change in the sign of r and the relationship between the values of r^2 of Exercise 12.36 and this exercise.

EX1238

Applications

12.38 The table gives the numbers of *Octolasmis tridens* and *O. lowei* barnacles on each of 10 lobsters.[7] Does it appear that the barnacles compete for space on the surface of a lobster?

Lobster Field Number	O. tridens	O. lowei
AO61	645	6
AO62	320	23
AO66	401	40
AO70	364	9
AO67	327	24
AO69	73	5
AO64	20	86
AO68	221	0
AO65	3	109
AO63	5	350

a. If they do compete, do you expect the number x of *O. tridens* and the number y of *O. lowei* barnacles to be positively or negatively correlated? Explain.

b. If you want to test the theory that the two types of barnacles compete for space by conducting a test of the null hypothesis "the population correlation coefficient ρ equals 0," what is your alternative hypothesis?

c. Conduct the test in part b and state your conclusions.

12.39 A social skills training program was implemented with seven mildly handicapped students in a study to determine whether the program caused improvement in pre/post measures and behavior ratings. For one such test, the pre- and posttest scores for the seven students are given in the table.[8]

Subject	Pretest	Posttest
Earl	101	113
Ned	89	89
Jasper	112	121
Charlie	105	99
Tom	90	104
Susie	91	94
Lori	89	99

a. What type of correlation, if any, do you expect to see between the pre- and posttest scores? Plot the data. Does the correlation appear to be positive or negative?

b. Calculate the correlation coefficient, r. Is there a significant positive correlation?

12.40 G. W. Marino investigated the variables related to a hockey player's ability to make a fast start from a stopped position.[9] In the experiment, each skater started from a stopped position and attempted to move as rapidly as possible over a 6-meter distance. The correlation coefficient r between a skater's stride rate (number of strides per second) and the length of time to cover the 6-meter distance for the sample of 69 skaters was $-.37$.

a. Do the data provide sufficient evidence to indicate a correlation between stride rate and time to cover the distance? Test using $\alpha = .05$.

b. Find the approximate p-value for the test.

c. What are the practical implications of the test in part a?

12.41 Refer to Exercise 12.40. Marino calculated the sample correlation coefficient r for the stride rate and the average acceleration rate for the 69 skaters to be .36. Do the data provide sufficient evidence to indicate a correlation between stride rate and average acceleration for the skaters? Use the p-value approach.

12.42 Geothermal power is an important source of energy. Since the amount of energy contained in 1 pound of water is a function of its temperature, you might wonder whether water obtained from deeper wells contains more energy per pound. The data in the table are reproduced from an article on geothermal systems by A.J. Ellis.[10]

EX1242

Location of Well	Average (max.) Drill Hole Depth (m)	Average (max.) Temperature (°C)
El Tateo, Chile	650	230
Ahuachapan, El Salvador	1,000	230
Namafjall, Iceland	1,000	250
Larderello (region), Italy	600	200
Matsukawa, Japan	1,000	220
Cerro Prieto, Mexico	800	300
Wairakei, New Zealand	800	230
Kizildere, Turkey	700	190
The Geysers, United States	1,500	250

Is there a significant positive correlation between average maximum drill hole depth and average maximum temperature?

12.43 The demand for healthy foods that are low in fat and calories has resulted in a large number of "low-fat" or "fat-free" products. The table shows the number of calories and the amount of sodium (in milligrams) per slice for five different brands of fat-free American cheese.

Brand	Sodium (mg)	Calories
Kraft Fat Free Singles	300	30
Ralphs Fat Free Singles	300	30
Borden Fat Free	320	30
Healthy Choice Fat Free	290	30
Smart Beat American	180	25

a. Should you use the methods of linear regression analysis or correlation analysis to analyze the data? Explain.

b. Analyze the data to determine the nature of the relationship between sodium and calories in fat-free American cheese. Use any statistical tests that are appropriate.

Key Concepts and Formulas

I. A Linear Probabilistic Model

1. When the data exhibit a linear relationship, the appropriate model is
$y = \alpha + \beta x + \epsilon$.
2. The random error ϵ has a normal distribution with mean 0 and variance σ^2.

II. Method of Least Squares

1. Estimates a and b, for α and β, are chosen to minimize SSE, the sum of squared deviations about the regression line, $\hat{y} = a + bx$.
2. The least-squares estimates are $b = S_{xy}/S_{xx}$ and $a = \bar{y} - b\bar{x}$.

III. Analysis of Variance

1. Total SS = SSR + SSE, where Total SS = S_{yy} and SSR = $(S_{xy})^2/S_{xx}$.
2. The best estimate of σ^2 is MSE = SSE/$(n - 2)$.

IV. Testing, Estimation, and Prediction

1. A test for the significance of the linear regression—$H_0 : \beta = 0$—can be implemented using one of two test statistics:

$$t = \frac{b}{\sqrt{\text{MSE}/S_{xx}}} \quad \text{or} \quad F = \frac{\text{MSR}}{\text{MSE}}$$

2. The strength of the relationship between x and y can be measured using

$$r^2 = \frac{\text{SSR}}{\text{Total SS}}$$

which gets closer to 1 as the relationship gets stronger.

3. Use residual plots to check for nonnormality, inequality of variances, or an incorrectly fit model.

4. Confidence intervals can be constructed to estimate the intercept α and slope β of the regression line and to estimate the average value of y, $E(y)$, for a given value of x.

5. Prediction intervals can be constructed to predict a particular observation, y, for a given value of x. For a given x, prediction intervals are always wider than confidence intervals.

V. **Correlation Analysis**

1. Use the correlation coefficient to measure the relationship between x and y when both variables are random:

$$r = \frac{S_{xy}}{\sqrt{S_{xx}S_{yy}}}$$

2. The sign of r indicates the direction of the relationship; r near 0 indicates no linear relationship, and r near 1 or -1 indicates a strong linear relationship.

3. A test of the significance of the correlation coefficient uses the statistic

$$t = r\sqrt{\frac{n-2}{1-r^2}}$$

and is identical to the test of the slope β.

Linear Regression Procedures

In Chapter 3, we used some of the linear regression procedures available in *MINITAB* to obtain a graph of the best-fitting least-squares regression line and to calculate the correlation coefficient r for a bivariate data set. Now that you have studied the testing and estimation techniques for a simple linear regression analysis, more *MINITAB* options are available to you.

Consider the relationship between $x =$ mathematics achievement test score and $y =$ final calculus grade, which was used as an example throughout this chapter. Enter the data into the first two columns of a *MINITAB* worksheet. If you use **Graph → Plot,** you can generate the scatterplot for the data, as shown in Figure 12.2. However, the main inferential tools for linear regression analysis are generated using **Stat → Regression → Regression.** (You will use this same sequence of commands in Chapter 13 when you study *multiple regression analysis.*) The Dialog box for the Regression command is shown in Figure 12.20.

Select **y** for the "Response" variable and **x** for the "Predictor" variable. You may now choose to generate some residual plots to check the validity of your regression assumptions before you use the model for estimation or prediction. Choose **Graphs** to display the Dialog box in Figure 12.21.

We have used **Regular** residual plots, checking the boxes for "Normal plot of residuals" and "Residuals versus fits." Click **OK** to return to the main Dialog box. If you

MINITAB

MINITAB

FIGURE 12.20

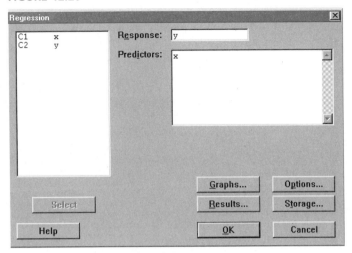

FIGURE 12.21

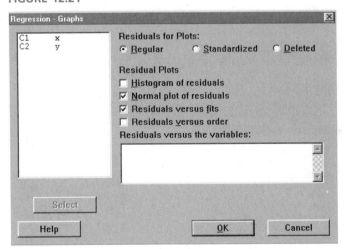

now choose **Options,** you can obtain confidence and prediction intervals for either of these cases:

- A single value of x (typed in the box marked "Prediction intervals for new observations")
- Several values of x stored in a column (say, C3) of the worksheet

Enter the value $x = 50$ in Figure 12.22 to match the output given in Figure 12.15. When you click **OK** twice, the regression output is generated as shown in Figure 12.23.

If you wish, you can now plot the data points, the regression line, and the upper and lower confidence and prediction limits (see Figure 12.16) using **Stat → Regression → Fitted line plot.** Select y and x for the response and predictor variables and click "Display confidence bands" and "Display prediction bands" in the **Options** Dialog box. Make sure that **Linear** is selected as the "Type of Regression Model," so that you will obtain a linear fit to the data.

Recall that in Chapter 3, we used the command **Stat → Basic Statistics → Correlation** to obtain the value of the correlation coefficient r. Make sure that the box marked "Display p-values" is checked. The output for this command (using the test/grade data) is shown in Figure 12.24. Notice that the p-value for the test of $H_0 : \rho = 0$ is identical to the p-value for the test of $H_0 : \beta = 0$ because the tests are exactly equivalent!

FIGURE 12.22

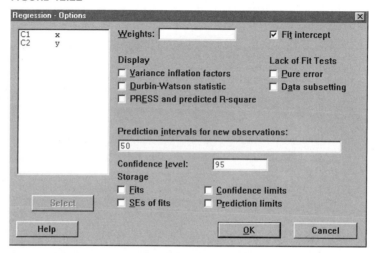

FIGURE 12.23

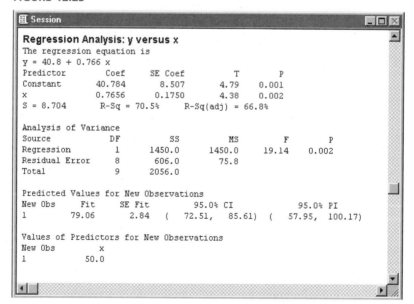

FIGURE 12.24

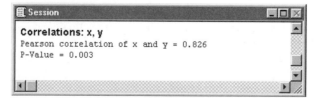

Supplementary Exercises

EX1244

12.44   An experiment was conducted to observe the effect of an increase in temperature on the potency of an antibiotic. Three 1-ounce portions of the antibiotic were stored for equal lengths of time at each of these temperatures: 30°, 50°, 70°, and 90°. The potency readings observed at each temperature of the experimental period are listed here:

Potency Readings, y	38, 43, 29	32, 26, 33	19, 27, 23	14, 19, 21
Temperature, x	30°	50°	70°	90°

Use an appropriate computer program to answer these questions:

a. Find the least-squares line appropriate for these data.

b. Plot the points and graph the line as a check on your calculations.

c. Construct the ANOVA table for linear regression.

d. If they are available, examine the diagnostic plots to check the validity of the regression assumptions.

e. Estimate the change in potency for a 1-unit change in temperature. Use a 95% confidence interval.

f. Estimate the average potency corresponding to a temperature of 50°. Use a 95% confidence interval.

g. Suppose that a batch of the antibiotic was stored at 50° for the same length of time as the experimental period. Predict the potency of the batch at the end of the storage period. Use a 95% prediction interval.

EX1245

12.45   An experiment was conducted to determine the effect of soil applications of various levels of phosphorus on the inorganic phosphorus levels in a particular plant. The data in the table represent the levels of inorganic phosphorus in micromoles (μmol) per gram dry weight of sudan grass roots grown in the greenhouse for 28 days, in the absence of zinc. Use the *MINITAB* output to answer the questions.

Phosphorus Applied, x	Phosphorus in Plant, y
.5 μmol	204
	195
	247
	245
.25 μmol	159
	127
	95
	144
.10 μmol	128
	192
	84
	71

a. Plot the data. Do the data appear to exhibit a linear relationship?

b. Find the least-squares line relating the plant phosphorus levels y to the amount of phosphorus applied to the soil x. Graph the least-squares line as a check on your answer.

c. Do the data provide sufficient evidence to indicate that the amount of phosphorus present in the plant is linearly related to the amount of phosphorus applied to the soil?

d. Estimate the mean amount of phosphorus in the plant if .20 μmol of phosphorus is applied to the soil, in the absence of zinc. Use a 90% confidence interval.

MINITAB output for
Example 12.45

Regression Analysis: y versus x

```
The regression equation is
y = 80.9 + 271 x

Predictor          Coef      SE Coef          T         P
Constant          80.85        22.40       3.61     0.005
x                270.82        68.31       3.96     0.003

S = 39.04      R-Sq = 61.1%      R-Sq(adj) = 57.2%

Predicted Values for New Observations
New Obs     Fit      SE Fit          95.0% CI              95.0% PI
1         135.0       12.6   (   112.1,   157.9)  (   60.6,    209.4)

Values of Predictors for New Observations
New Obs         x
1           0.200
```

12.46 An experiment was conducted to investigate the effect of a training program on the length of time for a typical male college student to complete the 100-yard dash. Nine students were placed in the program. The reduction *y* in time to complete the 100-yard dash was measured for three students at the end of 2 weeks, for three at the end of 4 weeks, and for three at the end of 6 weeks of training. The data are given in the table.

Reduction in Time, *y* (sec)	1.6, .8, 1.0	2.1, 1.6, 2.5	3.8, 2.7, 3.1
Length of Training, *x* (wk)	2	4	6

Use an appropriate computer software package to analyze these data. State any conclusions you can draw.

EX1247

12.47 Some varieties of nematodes, roundworms that live in the soil and frequently are so small as to be invisible to the naked eye, feed on the roots of lawn grasses and other plants. This pest, which is particularly troublesome in warm climates, can be treated by the application of nematicides. Data collected on the percent kill of nematodes for various rates of application (dosages given in pounds per acre of active ingredient) are as follows:

Rate of Application, *x*	2	3	4	5
Percent Kill, *y*	50, 56, 48	63, 69, 71	86, 82, 76	94, 99, 97

MINITAB diagnostic plots for Exercise 12.47

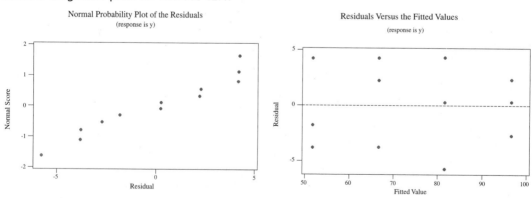

Use an appropriate computer printout to answer these questions:

a. Calculate the coefficient of correlation *r* between rates of application *x* and percent kill *y*.

b. Calculate the coefficient of determination r^2 and interpret.

c. Fit a least-squares line to the data.

d. Suppose you wish to estimate the mean percent kill for an application of 4 pounds of the nematicide per acre. What do the diagnostic plots generated by *MINITAB* tell you about the validity of the regression assumptions? Which assumptions may have been violated? Can you explain why?

12.48 Athletes and others suffering the same type of injury to the knee often require anterior and posterior ligament reconstruction. In order to determine the proper length of bone–patellar tendon–bone grafts, experiments were done using three imaging techniques to determine the required length of the grafts, and these results were compared to the actual length required. A summary of the results of a simple linear regression analysis for each of these three methods is given in the following table.[11]

Imaging Technique	Coefficient of Determination, r^2	Intercept	Slope	*p*-value
Radiographs	0.80	−3.75	1.031	<0.0001
Standard MRI	0.43	20.29	0.497	0.011
3-Dimensional MRI	0.65	1.80	0.977	<0.0001

a. What can you say about the significance of each of the three regression analyses?

b. How would you rank the effectiveness of the three regression analyses? What is the basis of your decision?

c. How do the values of r^2 and the *p*-values compare in determining the best predictor of actual graft lengths of ligament required?

12.49 Refer to Exercise 12.11 and data set EX1211 regarding the relationship between the Academic Performance Index (API), a measure of school achievement based on the results of the Stanford 9 Achievement test, and the percent of students who are considered English Language Learners. The following table shows the 2001 API for eight elementary schools in Riverside County, California, along with the percent of students at that school who are considered English Language Learners.[3]

School	1	2	3	4	5	6	7	8
API	588	659	710	657	669	641	557	743
ELL	58	22	14	30	11	26	39	6

a. Use an appropriate program to analyze the relationship between API and ELL.

b. Explain all pertinent details of your analysis.

12.50 Refer to Exercise 12.12 and data set EX1212 regarding a subject's ability to estimate sizes. The table that follows gives the actual and estimated lengths of the specified objects.

Object	Estimated (inches)	Actual (inches)
Pencil	7.00	6.00
Dinner plate	9.50	10.25
Book 1	7.50	6.75
Cell phone	4.00	4.25
Photograph	14.50	15.75
Toy	3.75	5.00
Belt	42.00	41.50
Clothespin	2.75	3.75
Book 2	10.00	9.25
Calculator	3.50	4.75

a. Use an appropriate program to analyze the relationship between the actual and estimated lengths of the listed objects.

b. Explain all pertinent details of your analysis.

12.51

EX1251

If you play tennis, you know that tennis racquets vary in their physical characteristics. The data in the accompanying table give measures of bending stiffness and twisting stiffness as measured by engineering tests for 12 tennis racquets:

Racquet	Bending Stiffness, x	Twisting Stiffness, y	Racquet	Bending Stiffness, x	Twisting Stiffness, y
1	419	227	7	424	384
2	407	231	8	359	194
3	363	200	9	346	158
4	360	211	10	556	225
5	257	182	11	474	305
6	622	304	12	441	235

a. If a racquet has bending stiffness, is it also likely to have twisting stiffness? Do the data provide evidence that x and y are positively correlated?

b. Calculate the coefficient of determination r^2 and interpret its value.

12.52

EX1252

Movement of avocados into the United States from certain areas is prohibited because of the possibility of bringing fruit flies into the country with the avocado shipments. However, certain avocado varieties supposedly are resistant to fruit fly infestation before they soften as a result of ripening. The data in the table resulted from an experiment in which avocados ranging from 1 to 9 days after harvest were exposed to Mediterranean fruit flies. Penetrability of the avocados was measured on the day of exposure, and the percentage of the avocado fruit infested was assessed.

Days after Harvest	Penetrability	Percentage Infected
1	.91	30
2	.81	40
4	.95	45
5	1.04	57
6	1.22	60
7	1.38	75
9	1.77	100

Use the *MINITAB* printout of the regression of percentage infected (y) on days after harvest (x) to analyze the relationship between these two variables. Explain all pertinent parts of the printout and interpret the results of any tests.

MINITAB output for Example 12.52

Regression Analysis: Percent versus x

```
The regression equation is
y = 18.4 + 8.18 x

Predictor       Coef      SE Coef          T          P
Constant      18.427        5.110       3.61      0.015
x             8.1768       0.9285       8.81      0.000

S = 6.356      R-Sq = 93.9%      R-Sq(adj) = 92.7%

Analysis of Variance
Source           DF           SS          MS          F          P
Regression        1       3132.9      3132.9      77.56      0.000
Residual Error    5        202.0        40.4
Total             6       3334.9
```

12.53

Refer to Exercise 12.52. Suppose the experimenter wants to examine the relationship between the penetrability and the number of days after harvest. Does the method of linear regression discussed in this chapter provide an appropriate method of analysis? If not, what assumptions have been violated? Use the *MINITAB* diagnostic plots provided.

MINITAB **diagnostic plots for Exercise 12.53**

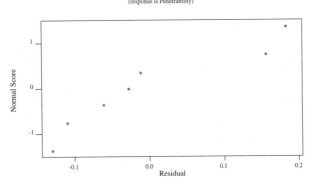

Normal Probability Plot of the Residuals
(response is Penetrability)

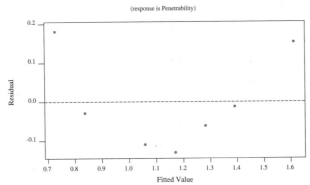

Residuals Versus the Fitted Values
(response is Penetrability)

EX1254

12.54 Why is it that one person may tend to gain weight, even if he eats no more and exercises no less than a slim friend? Recent studies suggest that the factors that control metabolism may depend on your genetic makeup. One study involved 11 pairs of identical twins fed about 1000 calories per day more than needed to maintain initial weight. Activities were kept constant, and exercise was minimal. At the end of 100 days, the changes in body weight (in kilograms) were recorded for the 22 twins.[12] Is there a significant positive correlation between the changes in body weight for the twins? Can you conclude that this similarity is caused by genetic similarities? Explain.

Pair	Twin A	Twin B
1	4.2	7.3
2	5.5	6.5
3	7.1	5.7
4	7.0	7.2
5	7.8	7.9
6	8.2	6.4
7	8.2	6.5
8	9.1	8.2
9	11.5	6.0
10	11.2	13.7
11	13.0	11.0

EX1255

12.55 How many weeks can a movie run and still make a reasonable profit? The data that follow show the number of weeks in release (x) and the average per-site gross (y) for the top 19 movies during the first weekend in September 2001.[13]

Movie	Per-site Average	Weeks in Release
Jeepers Creepers	$5,378	1
Rush Hour 2	4,146	5
American Pie 2	3,536	4
The Others	3,742	4
Rat Race	3,589	3
The Princess Diaries	2,822	5
O	4,823	1
Jay and Silent Bob Strike Back	2,357	2
Summer Catch	2,104	2
Captain Corelli's Mandolin	2,440	3
Planet of the Apes	2,557	6
Jurassic Park III	2,030	7
John Carpenter's Ghosts of Mars	1,028	2
The Curse of the Jade Scorpion	2,191	2
The Deep End	5,394	4
Legally Blonde	1,971	8
America's Sweethearts	835	7
American Outlaws	1,294	3
Bubble Boy	804	2

a. Plot the points in a scatterplot. Does it appear that the relationship between x and y is linear? How would you describe the direction and strength of the relationship?

b. Calculate the value of r^2. What percentage of the overall variation is explained by using the linear model rather than $\bar{y}$ to predict the response variable y?

c. What is the regression equation? Do the data provide evidence to indicate that x and y are linearly related? Test using a 5% significance level.

d. Given the results of parts b an c, is it appropriate to use the regression line for estimation and prediction? Explain your answer.

Exercises

DO IT YOURSELF!

You can refresh your memory about regression lines and the correlation coefficient by doing the *Do It Yourself Exercises* at the end of Chapter 3.

12.56 **a.** Graph the line corresponding to the equation $y = 0.5x + 3$ by graphing the points corresponding to $x = 0$, 1, and 2. Give the y-intercept and slope for the line.

b. Check your graph using the **How a Line Works** applet.

12.57 **a.** Graph the line corresponding to the equation $y = -0.5x + 3$ by graphing the points corresponding to $x = 0$, 1, and 2. Give the y-intercept and slope for the line.

b. Check your graph using the **How a Line Works** applet.

c. How is this line related to the line $y = 0.5x + 3$ of Exercise 12.56?

12.58 The *MINITAB* printout for the data in Table 12.1 is shown below.

MINITAB output for Example 12.58

Regression Analysis: y versus x

```
The regression equation is
y = 40.8 + 0.766 x

Predictor      Coef      SE Coef          T        P
Constant     40.784        8.507       4.79    0.001
x            0.7656       0.1750       4.38    0.002

S = 8.704       R-Sq = 70.5%      R-Sq(adj) = 66.8%

Analysis of Variance
Source          DF          SS         MS         F        P
Regression       1      1450.0     1450.0     19.14    0.002
Residual Error   8       606.0       75.8
Total            9      2056.0
```

a. Use the **Method of Least Squares** applet to find the values of a and b that determine the *best fitting line*, $\hat{y} = a + bx$. When you think that you have minimized SSE, click the `Find Best Model` button and see how well you did. What is the equation of the line? Does it match the regression equation given in the *MINITAB* printout?

b. Find the values of SSE and r^2 on the **Method of Least Squares** applet. Find these values on the *MINITAB* printout and confirm that they are the same.

c. Use the values of b and its standard error SE(b) from the *MINITAB* printout along with the t **Test for the Slope** applet to verify the value of the t statistic and its p-value, given in the printout.

 **12.59**   Use the first applet in **Building a Scatterplot** to create a scatterplot for the data in Table 12.1. Verify your plot using Figure 12.2.

EX1260   **12.60**   Is your overall satisfaction with a hotel room correlated with the cost of the room? Satisfaction scores and median room prices were recorded for nine "budget" hotels with the following results[14]:

Hotel	Median Rate	Score
Sleep Inn	55	80
Microtel	50	75
Super 8 Motel	50	70
Red Roof Inn	50	69
Motel 6	40	68
Days Inn	55	64
Econo Lodge	50	63
Travelodge	55	62
Knights Inn	45	57

a. Calculate the correlation coefficient r between price and overall score. How would you describe the relationship between price and overall score?

b. Use the applet called **Correlation and the Scatterplot** to plot the nine data points. What is the correlation coefficient shown on the applet? Compare with the value you calculated in part a.

c. Describe the pattern that you see in the scatterplot. Are there any outliers? If so, how would you explain them?

Case Study

FOREIGNCARS

Is Your Car "Made in the U.S.A."?

The phrase "made in the U.S.A." has become a battle cry in the past few years as U.S. workers try to protect their jobs from overseas competition. For the past few decades, a major trade imbalance in the United States has been caused by a flood of imported goods that enter the country and are sold at lower cost than comparable American-made goods. One prime concern is the automotive industry, in which the number of imported cars steadily increased during the 1970s and 1980s. The U.S. automobile industry has been besieged with complaints about product quality, worker layoffs, and high prices and has spent billions in advertising and research to produce an American-made car that will satisfy consumer demands. Have they been successful in stopping the flood of imported cars purchased by American consumers? The data in the table represent the numbers of imported cars y sold in the United States (in millions) for the years 1969–2000.[15] To simplify the analysis, we have coded the year using the coded variable $x = \text{Year} - 1969$.

Year	(Year − 1969), x	Number of Imported Cars, y	Year	(Year − 1969), x	Number of Imported Cars, y
1969	0	1.1	1985	16	2.8
1970	1	1.3	1986	17	3.2
1971	2	1.6	1987	18	3.1
1972	3	1.6	1988	19	3.1
1973	4	1.8	1989	20	2.8
1974	5	1.4	1990	21	2.5
1975	6	1.6	1991	22	2.1
1976	7	1.5	1992	23	2.0
1977	8	2.1	1993	24	1.8
1978	9	2.0	1994	25	1.8
1979	10	2.3	1995	26	1.6
1980	11	2.4	1996	27	1.4
1981	12	2.3	1997	28	1.4
1982	13	2.2	1998	29	1.4
1983	14	2.4	1999	30	1.8
1984	15	2.4	2000	31	2.1

1. Using a scatterplot, plot the data for the years 1969–1988. Does there appear to be a linear relationship between the number of imported cars and the year?

2. Use a computer software package to find the least-squares line for predicting the number of imported cars as a function of year for the years 1969–1988.

3. Is there a significant linear relationship between the number of imported cars and the year?

4. Use the computer program to predict the number of cars that will be imported using 95% prediction intervals for each of the years 1998, 1999, and 2000.

5. Now look at the actual data points for the years 1998–2000. Do the predictions obtained in step 4 provide accurate estimates of the *actual* values observed in these years? Explain.

6. Add the data for 1989–2000 to your database, and recalculate the regression line. What effect have the new data points had on the slope? What is the effect on SSE?

7. Given the form of the scatterplot for the years 1969–2000, does it appear that a straight line provides an accurate model for the data? What other type of model might be more appropriate? (Use residual plots to help answer this question.)

Data Sources

1. Stellan Ohlsson, "The Learning Curve for Writing Books: Evidence from Professor Asimov," *Psychological Science* 3, no. 6 (1992):380–382.

2. Daniel C. Harris, *Quantitative Chemical Analysis,* 3rd ed. (New York: Freeman, 1991).

3. "2001 Academic Performance Index (API) Report," *The Press-Enterprise* (Riverside, CA), 16 October 2001, p. A8.

4. Adapted from J. Zhou and S. Smith, "Measurement of Ozone Concentrations in Ambient Air Using a Badge-Type Passive Monitor," *Journal of the Air & Waste Management Association* 47 (June 1997):697.

5. "Round-Trip Fares on America's Most Popular Routes," *Consumer Reports,* July 1997, p. 25.

6. Julie Rawe, "In Brief: IPO Revenge," *Time,* 3 September 2001, p. 93.

7. W.B. Jeffries, H.K. Voris, and C.M. Yang, "Diversity and Distribution of the Pedunculate Barnacles *Octolasmis* Gray, 1825 Epizoic on the Scyllarid Lobster, *Thenus orientalis* (Lund, 1793)," *Crustaceana* 46, no. 3 (1984).

8. Gregory K. Torrey, S.F. Vasa, J.W. Maag, and J.J. Kramer, "Social Skills Interventions Across School Settings: Cast Study Reviews of Students with Mild Disabilities," *Psychology in the Schools* 29 (July 1992):248.

9. G. Wayne Marino, "Selected Mechanical Factors Associated with Acceleration in Ice Skating," *Research Quarterly for Exercise and Sport* 54, no. 3 (1983).

10. A.J. Ellis, "Geothermal Systems," *American Scientist,* September/October 1975.

11. David R. McAllister et al., "A Comparison of Preoperative Imaging Techniques for Predicting Patellar Tendon Graft Length before Cruciate Ligament Reconstruction," *The American Journal of Sports Medicine,* 20(4):461–465.

12. Henry Gleitman, *Basic Psychology,* 4th ed. (New York: Norton, 1996).

13. "Cheap Hit," *Entertainment Weekly,* 614:14 September 2001, p. 69.

14. "Suite Dreams," *Consumer Reports*, July 2001, p. 12.

15. *Automotive News: 1997 Market Data Book,* 28 May 1997, p 50; and *2001 Market Data Book* (online), www.autonews.com/datacenter.cms, 20 September 2001.

13

Multiple Regression Analysis

Case Study

In Chapter 12, we used simple linear regression analysis to try to predict the number of cars imported into the United States over a period of years. Unfortunately, the number of imported cars does not really follow a linear trend pattern, and our predictions were far from accurate. We reexamine the same data at the end of this chapter, using the methods of multiple regression analysis.

General Objectives

In this chapter, we extend the concepts of linear regression and correlation to a situation where the average value of a random variable y is related to several independent variables—$x_1, x_2, \ldots, x_k$—in models that are more flexible than the straight-line model of Chapter 12. With *multiple regression analysis,* we can use the information provided by the independent variables to fit various types of models to the sample data, to evaluate the usefulness of these models, and finally to estimate the average value of y or predict the actual value of y for given values of $x_1, x_2, \ldots, x_k$.

Specific Topics

1. The General Linear Model and Assumptions (13.2)
2. The Method of Least Squares (13.3)
3. Analysis of Variance for Multiple Regression (13.3)
4. Sequential Sums of Squares (13.3)
5. The Analysis of Variance F Test (13.3)
6. The Coefficient of Determination, R^2 (13.3)
7. Testing the Partial Regression Coefficients (13.3)
8. Adjusted R^2 (13.3)
9. Residual Plots (13.3)
10. Estimation and Prediction Using the Regression Model (13.3)
11. Polynomial Regression Model (13.4)
12. Qualitative Variables in a Regression Model (13.5)
13. Testing Sets of Regression Coefficients (13.6)
14. Stepwise Regression Analysis (13.8)
15. Causality and Multicollinearity (13.9)

13.1 Introduction

Multiple linear regression is an extension of simple linear regression to allow for more than one independent variable. That is, instead of using only a single independent variable x to explain the variation in y, you can simultaneously use several independent (or predictor) variables. By using more than one independent variable, you should do a better job of explaining the variation in y and hence be able to make more accurate predictions.

For example, a company's regional sales y of a product might be related to three factors:

- x_1—the amount spent on television advertising
- x_2—the amount spent on newspaper advertising
- x_3—the number of sales representatives assigned to the region

A researcher would collect data measuring the variables y, x_1, x_2, and x_3 and then use these sample data to construct a prediction equation relating y to the three predictor variables. Of course, several questions arise, just as they did with simple linear regression:

- How well does the model fit?
- How strong is the relationship between y and the predictor variables?
- Have any important assumptions been violated?
- How good are estimates and predictions?

The methods of **multiple regression analysis**—which are almost always done with a computer software program—can be used to answer these questions. This chapter provides a brief introduction to multiple regression analysis and the difficult task of model building—that is, choosing the correct model for a practical application.

13.2 The Multiple Regression Model

The **general linear model** for a multiple regression analysis describes a particular response y using the model given next.

General Linear Model and Assumptions

$$y = \beta_0 + \beta_1 x_1 + \beta_2 x_2 + \cdots + \beta_k x_k + \epsilon$$

where

- y is the **response variable** that you want to predict.
- $\beta_0, \beta_1, \beta_2, \ldots, \beta_k$ are unknown constants.
- $x_1, x_2, \ldots, x_k$ are independent **predictor variables** that are measured without error.
- ϵ is the random error, which allows each response to deviate from the average value of y by the amount ϵ. You must assume that the values of ϵ (1) are independent; (2) have a mean of 0 and a common variance σ^2 for any set $x_1, x_2, \ldots, x_k$; and (3) are normally distributed.

When these assumptions about ϵ are met, the *average* value of y for a given set of values $x_1, x_2, \ldots, x_k$ is equal to the *deterministic* part of the model:

$$E(y) = \beta_0 + \beta_1 x_1 + \beta_2 x_2 + \cdots + \beta_k x_k$$

You will notice that the multiple regression model and assumptions are *very similar* to the model and assumptions used for linear regression. It will probably not surprise you that the testing and estimation procedures are also extensions of those used in Chapter 12.

Multiple regression models are very flexible and can take many forms, depending on the way in which the independent variables $x_1, x_2, \ldots, x_k$ are entered into the model. We begin with a simple multiple regression model, explaining the basic concepts and procedures with an example. As you become more familiar with the multiple regression procedures, we increase the complexity of the examples, and you will see that the same procedures can be used for models of different forms, depending on the particular application.

EXAMPLE 13.1

Suppose you want to relate a random variable y to two independent variables x_1 and x_2. The multiple regression model is

$$y = \beta_0 + \beta_1 x_1 + \beta_2 x_2 + \epsilon$$

with the mean value of y given as

$$E(y) = \beta_0 + \beta_1 x_1 + \beta_2 x_2$$

This equation is a three-dimensional extension of the **line of means** from Chapter 12 and traces a **plane** in three-dimensional space (see Figure 13.1). The constant β_0 is called the **intercept**—the average value of y when x_1 and x_2 are both 0. The coefficients β_1 and β_2 are called the **partial slopes** or **partial regression coefficients.** The partial slope β_i (for $i = 1$ or 2) measures the change in y for a one-unit change in x_i when *all other independent variables are held constant.* The value of the partial regression coefficient—say, β_1—with x_1 and x_2 in the model is generally *not* the same as the slope when you fit a line with x_1 alone. These coefficients are the unknown constants, which must be estimated using sample data to obtain the prediction equation.

FIGURE 13.1
Plane of means for
Example 13.1

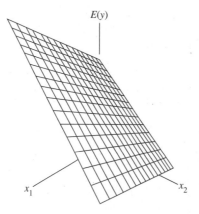

13.3 A Multiple Regression Analysis

A multiple regression analysis involves estimation, testing, and diagnostic procedures designed to fit the multiple regression model

$$E(y) = \beta_0 + \beta_1 x_1 + \beta_2 x_2 + \cdots + \beta_k x_k$$

to a set of data. Because of the complexity of the calculations involved, these procedures are almost always implemented with a regression program from one of several computer software packages. All give similar output in slightly different forms. We follow the basic patterns set in simple linear regression, beginning with an outline of the general procedures and illustrated with an example.

The Method of Least Squares

The prediction equation

$$\hat{y} = b_0 + b_1 x_1 + b_2 x_2 + \cdots + b_k x_k$$

is the line that minimizes SSE, the sum of squares of the deviations of the observed values y from the predicted values $\hat{y}$. These values are calculated using a regression program.

EXAMPLE 13.2   How do real estate agents decide on the asking price for a newly listed home? A computer database in a small community contains the listed selling price y (in thousands of dollars), the amount of living area x_1 (in hundreds of square feet), and the numbers of floors x_2, bedrooms x_3, and bathrooms x_4, for $n = 15$ randomly selected residences currently on the market. The data are shown in Table 13.1.

TABLE 13.1
Data on 15 residential properties

Observation	List Price, y	Living Area, x_1	Floors, x_2	Bedrooms, x_3	Baths, x_4
1	69.0	6	1	2	1
2	118.5	10	1	2	2
3	116.5	10	1	3	2
4	125.0	11	1	3	2
5	129.9	13	1	3	1.7
6	135.0	13	2	3	2.5
7	139.9	13	1	3	2
8	147.9	17	2	3	2.5
9	160.0	19	2	3	2
10	169.9	18	1	3	2
11	134.9	13	1	4	2
12	155.0	18	1	4	2
13	169.9	17	2	4	3
14	194.5	20	2	4	3
15	209.9	21	2	4	3

The multiple regression model is

$$E(y) = \beta_0 + \beta_1 x_1 + \beta_2 x_2 + \beta_3 x_3 + \beta_4 x_4$$

which is fit using the *MINITAB* software package. You can find instructions for generating this output in the section "About *MINITAB*" at the end of this chapter. The first portion of the regression output is shown in Figure 13.2. You will find the fitted regression equation in the first two lines of the printout:

$$\hat{y} = 18.8 + 6.27 x_1 - 16.2 x_2 - 2.67 x_3 + 30.3 x_4$$

The partial regression coefficients are shown with slightly more accuracy in the second section. The columns list the name given to each independent predictor variable, its estimated regression coefficient, its standard error, and the t- and p-values that are used to test its significance *in the presence of all the other predictor variables.* We explain these tests in more detail in a later section.

FIGURE 13.2
A portion of the
MINITAB printout
for Example 13.2

Regression Analysis: ListPrice versus SqFeet, NumFlrs, Bdrms, Baths

```
The regression equation is
ListPrice = 18.8 + 6.27 SqFeet - 16.2 Numflrs - 2.67 Bdrms + 30.3 Baths

Predictor        Coef     SE Coef         T        P
Constant       18.763       9.207      2.04    0.069
SqFeet         6.2698      0.7252      8.65    0.000
Numflrs       -16.203       6.212     -2.61    0.026
Bdrms          -2.673       4.494     -0.59    0.565
Baths          30.271       6.849      4.42    0.001
```

The Analysis of Variance for Multiple Regression

The analysis of variance divides the total variation in the response variable y,

$$\text{Total SS} = \Sigma y_i^2 - \frac{(\Sigma y_i)^2}{n}$$

into two portions:

- SSR (sum of squares for regression) measures the amount of variation explained by using the regression equation.
- SSE (sum of squares for error) measures the residual variation in the data that is not explained by the independent variables.

so that

$$\text{Total SS} = \text{SSR} + \text{SSE}$$

The **degrees of freedom** for these sums of squares are found using the following argument. There are $(n - 1)$ total degrees of freedom. Estimating the regression line requires estimating k unknown coefficients; the constant b_0 is a function of $\bar{y}$ and the other estimates. Hence, there are k regression degrees of freedom, leaving $(n - 1) - k$ degrees of freedom for error. As in previous chapters, the mean squares are calculated as $\text{MS} = \text{SS}/df$.

The ANOVA table for the real estate data in Table 13.1 is shown in the second portion of the *MINITAB* printout in Figure 13.3. There are $n = 15$ observations and $k = 4$ independent predictor variables. You can verify that the total degrees of freedom, $(n - 1) = 14$, is divided into $k = 4$ for regression and $(n - k - 1) = 10$ for error.

FIGURE 13.3
A portion of the
MINITAB printout
for Example 13.2

```
S = 6.849       R-Sq = 97.1%     R-Sq(adj) = 96.0%

Analysis of Variance
Source            DF          SS         MS        F        P
Regression         4     15913.0     3978.3    84.80    0.000
Residual Error    10       469.1       46.9
Total             14     16382.2

Source      DF      Seq SS
SqFeet       1     14829.3
Numflrs      1         0.9
Bdrms        1       166.4
Baths        1       916.5
```

The best estimate of the random variation σ^2 in the experiment—the variation that is unexplained by the predictor variables—is as usual given by

$$s^2 = \text{MSE} = \frac{\text{SSE}}{n - k - 1} = 46.9$$

from the ANOVA table. The first line of Figure 13.3 also shows $s = \sqrt{s^2} = 6.849$ using computer accuracy. The computer uses these values internally to produce test statistics, confidence intervals, and prediction intervals, which we discuss in subsequent sections.

The last section of Figure 13.3 shows a decomposition of SSR = 15,913.0 in which the conditional contribution of each predictor variable *given the variables already entered into the model* is shown for the order of entry that you specify in your regression program. For the real estate example, the *MINITAB* program entered the variables in this order: square feet, then numbers of floors, bedrooms, and baths. These conditional or **sequential sums of squares** each account for one of the $k = 4$ regression degrees of freedom. It is interesting to notice that the predictor variable x_1 alone accounts for 14,829.3/15,913.0 = .932 or 93.2% of the total variation explained by the regression model. However, if you change the order of entry, another variable may account for the major part of the regression sum of squares!

Testing the Usefulness of the Regression Model

Recall in Chapter 12 that you tested to see whether y and x were linearly related by testing $H_0 : \beta = 0$ with either a t test or an equivalent F test. In multiple regression, there is more than one *partial slope*—the *partial regression coefficients*. The t and F tests are no longer equivalent.

The Analysis of Variance *F* Test

Is the regression equation that uses information provided by the predictor variables $x_1, x_2, \ldots, x_k$ substantially better than the simple predictor $\bar{y}$ that does not rely on any of the x-values? This question is answered using an overall F test with the hypotheses:

$$H_0 : \beta_1 = \beta_2 = \cdots = \beta_k = 0$$

versus

$$H_a : \text{At least one of } \beta_1, \beta_2, \ldots, \beta_k \text{ is not } 0$$

The test statistic is found in the ANOVA table (Figure 13.3) as

$$F = \frac{\text{MSR}}{\text{MSE}} = \frac{3978.3}{46.9} = 84.80$$

which has an F distribution with $df_1 = k = 4$ and $df_2 = (n - k - 1) = 10$. Since the exact p-value, $P = .000$, is given in the printout, you can declare the regression to be highly significant. That is, at least one of the predictor variables is contributing significant information for the prediction of the response variable y.

The Coefficient of Determination, R^2

How well does the regression model fit? The regression printout provides a statistical measure of the strength of the model in the **coefficient of determination, R^2**—the proportion of the total variation that is explained by the regression of y on $x_1, x_2, \ldots, x_k$—defined as

$$R^2 = \frac{\text{SSR}}{\text{Total SS}} = \frac{15,913.0}{16,382.2} = .971 \quad \text{or } 97.1\%$$

The coefficient of determination is sometimes called **multiple R^2** and is found in the first line of Figure 13.3, labeled "R-Sq." Hence, for the real estate example, 97.1% of the total variation has been explained by the regression model. The model fits very well!

It may be helpful to know that the value of the F statistic is related to R^2 by the formula

$$F = \frac{R^2/k}{(1 - R^2)/(n - k - 1)}$$

so that when R^2 is large, F is large, and vice versa.

Interpreting the Results of a Significant Regression

Testing the Significance of the Partial Regression Coefficients

Once you have determined that the model is useful for predicting y, you should explore the nature of the "usefulness" in more detail. Do all of the predictor variables add important information for prediction *in the presence of other predictors already in the model?* The individual t tests in the first section of the regression printout are designed to test the hypotheses

$$H_0 : \beta_i = 0 \quad \text{versus} \quad H_a : \beta_i \neq 0$$

for each of the partial regression coefficients, *given that the other predictor variables are already in the model.* These tests are based on the Student's t statistic given by

$$t = \frac{b_i - \beta_i}{\text{SE}(b_i)}$$

which has $df = (n - k - 1)$ degrees of freedom. The procedure is identical to the one used to test a hypothesis about the slope β in the simple linear regression model.[†]

Figure 13.4 shows the t tests and p-values from the upper portion of the *MINITAB* printout. By examining the p-values in the last column, you can see that all the variables *except* x_3, the number of bedrooms, add very significant information for predicting y, **even with all the other independent variables already in the model.** Could the model be any better? It may be that x_3 is an unnecessary predictor variable. One option is to remove this variable and refit the model with a new set of data!

FIGURE 13.4
A portion of the
MINITAB printout
for Example 13.2

Predictor	Coef	StDev	T	P
Constant	18.763	9.207	2.04	0.069
SqFeet	6.2698	0.7252	8.65	0.000
Numflrs	-16.203	6.212	-2.61	0.026
Bdrms	-2.673	4.494	-0.59	0.565
Baths	30.271	6.849	4.42	0.001

The Adjusted Value of R^2

Notice from the definition of $R^2 = $ SSR/Total SS that its value can never decrease with the addition of more variables into the regression model. Hence, R^2 can be artificially inflated by the inclusion of more and more predictor variables.

[†]Some packages use the t statistic just described, whereas others use the equivalent F statistic ($F = t^2$), since the square of a t statistic with v degrees of freedom is equal to an F statistic with 1 df in the numerator and v degrees of freedom in the denominator.

An alternative measure of the strength of the regression model is adjusted for degrees of freedom by using mean squares rather than sums of squares:

$$R^2(\text{adj}) = \left(1 - \frac{\text{MSE}}{\text{Total SS}/(n-1)}\right)100\%$$

For the real estate data in Figure 13.3,

$$R^2(\text{adj}) = \left(1 - \frac{46.9}{16{,}382.2/14}\right)100\% = 96.0\%.$$

is found in the first line of the printout. The value "R-Sq(adj) = 96.0%" represents the percentage of variation in the response y explained by the independent variables, corrected for degrees of freedom. The adjusted value of R^2 is mainly used to compare two or more regression models that use different numbers of independent predictor variables.

Checking the Regression Assumptions

Before using the regression model for its main purpose—estimation and prediction of y—you should look at computer-generated **residual plots** to make sure that all the regression assumptions are valid. The *normal probability plot* and the *plot of residuals versus fit* are shown in Figure 13.5 for the real estate data. There appear to be three observations that do not fit the general pattern. You can see them as outliers in both

FIGURE 13.5
MINITAB diagnostic plots

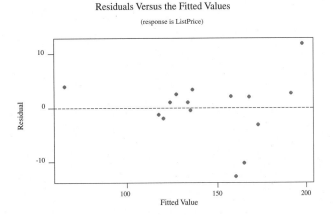

Residuals Versus the Fitted Values
(response is ListPrice)

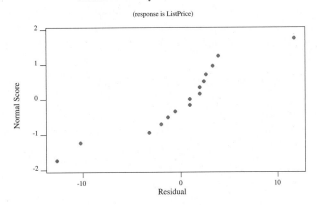

Normal Probability Plot of the Residuals
(response is ListPrice)

graphs. These three observations should probably be investigated; however, they do not provide strong evidence that the assumptions are violated.

Using the Regression Model for Estimation and Prediction

Finally, once you have determined that the model is effective in describing the relationship between y and the predictor variables $x_1, x_2, \ldots, x_k$, the model can be used for these purposes:

- Estimating the average value of y—$E(y)$—for given values of $x_1, x_2, \ldots, x_k$
- Predicting a particular value of y for given values of $x_1, x_2, \ldots, x_k$

The values of $x_1, x_2, \ldots, x_k$ are entered into the computer, and the computer generates the fitted value $\hat{y}$ together with its estimated standard error and the confidence and prediction intervals. Remember that the prediction interval is *always* wider than the confidence interval.

Let's see how well our prediction works for the real estate data, using another house from the computer database—a house with 1000 square feet of living area, one floor, three bedrooms, and two baths, which was listed at $121,500. The printout in Figure 13.6 shows the confidence and prediction intervals for these values. The actual value falls within both intervals, which indicates that the model is working very well!

FIGURE 13.6
Confidence and prediction intervals for Example 13.2

```
Predicted Values for New Observations
New Obs     Fit     SE Fit        95.0% CI              95.0% PI
1         117.78      3.11   ( 110.86, 124.70)   ( 101.02, 134.54)

Values of Predictors for New Observations
New Obs    SqFeet   NumFlrs     Bdrms     Baths
1            10.0      1.00      3.00      2.00
```

13.4 A Polynomial Regression Model

In Section 13.3, we explained in detail the various portions of the multiple regression printout. When you perform a multiple regression analysis, you should use a step-by-step approach:

1. Obtain the fitted prediction model.
2. Use the analysis of variance F test and R^2 to determine how well the model fits the data.
3. Check the t tests for the partial regression coefficients to see which ones are contributing significant information in the presence of the others.
4. If you choose to compare several different models, use R^2(adj) to compare their effectiveness.
5. Use computer-generated residual plots to check for violation of the regression assumptions.

Once all of these steps have been taken, you are ready to use your model for estimation and prediction.

The predictor variables $x_1, x_2, \ldots, x_k$ used in the general linear model do not have to represent *different* predictor variables. For example, if you suspect that one independent variable x affects the response y, but that the relationship is *curvilinear* rather than *linear*, then you might choose to fit a **quadratic model**:

$$y = \beta_0 + \beta_1 x + \beta_2 x^2 + \epsilon$$

The quadratic model is an example of a **second-order model** because it involves a term whose exponents sum to 2 (in this case, x^2).[†] It is also an example of a **polynomial model**—a model that takes the form

$$y = a + bx + cx^2 + dx^3 + \cdots$$

To fit this type of model using the multiple regression program, observed values of y, x, and x^2 are entered into the computer, and the printout can be generated as in Section 13.3.

EXAMPLE 13.3 In a study of variables that affect productivity in the retail grocery trade, W.S. Good uses value added per work-hour to measure the productivity of retail grocery outlets.[1] He defines "value added" as "the surplus [money generated by the business] available to pay for labor, furniture and fixtures, and equipment." Data consistent with the relationship between value added per work-hour y and the size x of a grocery outlet described in Good's article are shown in Table 13.2 for 10 fictitious grocery outlets. Choose a model to relate y to x.

TABLE 13.2
Data on store size and value added

Store	Value Added Per Work-Hour, y	Size of Store (thousand square feet), x
1	$4.08	21.0
2	3.40	12.0
3	3.51	25.2
4	3.09	10.4
5	2.92	30.9
6	1.94	6.8
7	4.11	19.6
8	3.16	14.5
9	3.75	25.0
10	3.60	19.1

Solution You can investigate the relationship between y and x by looking at the plot of the data points in Figure 13.7. The graph suggests that productivity, y, increases as the size of the grocery outlet, x, increases until an optimal size is reached. Above that size, productivity tends to decrease. The relationship appears to be *curvilinear,* and a quadratic model,

$$E(y) = \beta_0 + \beta_1 x + \beta_2 x^2$$

FIGURE 13.7
Plot of store size x and value added y for Example 13.5

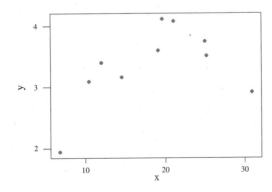

[†]The *order* of a term is determined by the sum of the exponents of variables making up that term. Terms involving x_1 or x_2 are first-order. Terms involving x_1^2, x_2^2, or $x_1 x_2$ are second-order.

may be appropriate. Remember that, in choosing to use this model, we are not saying that the true relationship is quadratic, but only that it may provide more accurate estimations and predictions than, say, a linear model.

EXAMPLE 13.4

Refer to the data on grocery retail outlet productivity and outlet size in Example 13.3. *MINITAB* was used to fit a quadratic model to the data and to graph the quadratic prediction curve, along with the plotted data points. Discuss the adequacy of the fitted model.

Solution

From the printout in Figure 13.8, you can see that the regression equation is

$$\hat{y} = -.159 + .392x - .00949x^2$$

The graph of this quadratic equation together with the data points is shown in Figure 13.9.

FIGURE 13.8
MINITAB printout for Example 13.4

Regression Analysis: y versus x, x-sq

```
The regression equation is
y = - 0.159 + 0.392 x - 0.00949 x-sq
Predictor          Coef      St Coef           T          P
Constant        -0.1594       0.5006       -0.32      0.760
x                0.39193      0.05801        6.76      0.000
x-sq           -0.009495     0.001535       -6.19      0.000

S = 0.2503      R-Sq = 87.9%      R-Sq(adj) = 84.5%

Analysis of Variance
Source             DF          SS          MS         F        P
Regression          2      3.1989      1.5994     25.53    0.001
Residual Error      7      0.4385      0.0626
Total               9      3.6374

Source       DF      Seq SS
x             1      0.8003
x-sq          1      2.3986
```

FIGURE 13.9
Fitted quadratic regression line for Example 13.4

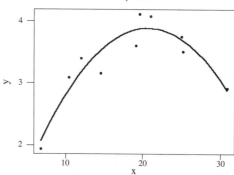

Regression Plot
y = -0.159 + 0.392 x -0.00949x-sq
R-Sq = 87.9%

To assess the adequacy of the quadratic model, the test of

$$H_0 : \beta_1 = \beta_2 = 0$$

versus

$$H_a : \text{Either } \beta_1 \text{ or } \beta_2 \text{ is not } 0$$

is given in the printout as

$$F = \frac{\text{MSR}}{\text{MSE}} = 25.53$$

with p-value = .001. Hence, the overall fit of the model is highly significant. Quadratic regression accounts for $R^2 = 87.9\%$ of the variation in y $[R^2(\text{adj}) = 84.5\%]$.

From the t tests for the individual variables in the model, you can see that both b_1 and b_2 are highly significant with p-values equal to .000. Notice from the sequential sum of squares section that the sum of squares for linear regression is .8003, with an additional sum of squares of 2.3986 when the quadratic term is added. It is apparent that the simple linear regression model is inadequate in describing the data.

One last look at the residual plots generated by *MINITAB* in Figure 13.10 ensures that the regression assumptions are valid. Notice the relatively linear appearance of the normal plot and the relative scatter of the residuals versus fits. The quadratic model provides accurate predictions for values of x that lie *within the range of the sampled values of x*.

FIGURE 13.10
MINITAB **diagnostic plots for Example 13.4**

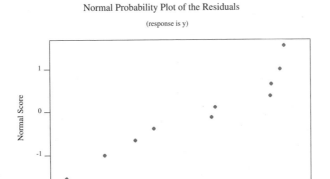

Normal Probability Plot of the Residuals
(response is y)

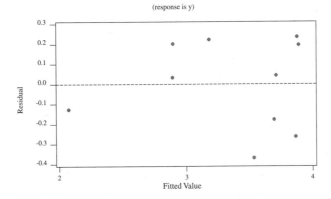

Residuals Versus the Fitted Values
(response is y)

Exercises

Basic Techniques

13.1 Suppose that $E(y)$ is related to two predictor variables, x_1 and x_2, by the equation

$$E(y) = 3 + x_1 - 2x_2$$

a. Graph the relationship between $E(y)$ and x_1 when $x_2 = 2$. Repeat for $x_2 = 1$ and for $x_2 = 0$.

b. What relationship do the lines in part a have to one another?

13.2 Refer to Exercise 13.1.

a. Graph the relationship between $E(y)$ and x_2 when $x_1 = 0$. Repeat for $x_1 = 1$ and for $x_1 = 2$.

b. What relationship do the lines in part a have to one another?

c. Suppose, in a practical situation, you want to model the relationship between $E(y)$ and two predictor variables x_1 and x_2. What is the implication of using the first-order model $E(y) = \beta_0 + \beta_1 x_1 + \beta_2 x_2$?

13.3 Suppose that you fit the model

$$E(y) = \beta_0 + \beta_1 x_1 + \beta_2 x_2 + \beta_3 x_3$$

to 15 data points and found F equal to 57.44.

a. Do the data provide sufficient evidence to indicate that the model contributes information for the prediction of y? Test using a 5% level of significance.

b. Use the value of F to calculate R^2. Interpret its value.

13.4 The computer output for the multiple regression analysis for Exercise 13.3 provides this information:

$$b_0 = 1.04 \qquad b_1 = 1.29 \qquad b_2 = 2.72 \qquad b_3 = .41$$
$$\qquad\qquad SE(b_1) = .42 \qquad SE(b_2) = .65 \qquad SE(b_3) = .17$$

a. Which, if any, of the independent variables x_1, x_2, and x_3 contribute information for the prediction of y?

b. Give the least-squares prediction equation.

c. On the same sheet of graph paper, graph y versus x_1 when $x_2 = 1$ and $x_3 = 0$ and when $x_2 = 1$ and $x_3 = .5$. What relationship do the two lines have to each other?

d. What is the practical interpretation of the parameter β_1?

13.5 Suppose that you fit the model

$$E(y) = \beta_0 + \beta_1 x + \beta_2 x^2$$

to 20 data points and obtained the accompanying *MINITAB* printout.

MINITAB output for Exercise 13.5

Regression Analysis: y versus x, x-sq

```
The regression equation is
y = 10.6 + 4.44 x - 0.648 x-sq

Predictor        Coef      SE Coef         T        P
Constant      10.5638       0.6951     15.20    0.000
x              4.4366       0.5150      8.61    0.000
x-sq         -0.64754       0.07988    -8.11    0.000

S = 1.191      R-Sq = 81.5%      R-Sq(adj) = 79.3%

Analysis of Variance
Source           DF          SS        MS        F        P
Regression        2     106.072    53.036    37.37    0.000
Residual Error   17      24.128     1.419
Total            19     130.200
```

a. What type of model have you chosen to fit the data?

b. How well does the model fit the data? Explain.

c. Do the data provide sufficient evidence to indicate that the model contributes information for the prediction of y? Use the p-value approach.

13.6 Refer to Exercise 13.5.

a. What is the prediction equation?

b. Graph the prediction equation over the interval $0 \le x \le 6$.

13.7 Refer to Exercise 13.5.

a. What is your estimate of the average value of y when $x = 0$?

b. Do the data provide sufficient evidence to indicate that the average value of y differs from 0 when $x = 0$?

13.8 Refer to Exercise 13.5.

a. Suppose that the relationship between $E(y)$ and x is a straight line. What would you know about the value of β_2?

b. Do the data provide sufficient evidence to indicate curvature in the relationship between y and x?

13.9 Refer to Exercise 13.5. Suppose that y is the profit for some business and x is the amount of capital invested, and you know that the rate of increase in profit for a unit increase in capital invested can only decrease as x increases. You want to know whether the data provide sufficient evidence to indicate a decreasing rate of increase in profit as the amount of capital invested increases.

a. The circumstances described imply a one-tailed statistical test. Why?

b. Conduct the test at the 1% level of significance. State your conclusions.

Applications

13.10 A publisher of college textbooks conducted a study to relate profit per text y to cost of sales x over a 6-year period when its sales force (and sales costs) were growing rapidly. These inflation-adjusted data (in thousands of dollars) were collected:

EX1310

Profit per Text, y	16.5	22.4	24.9	28.8	31.5	35.8
Sales Cost per Text, x	5.0	5.6	6.1	6.8	7.4	8.6

Expecting profit per book to rise and then plateau, the publisher fitted the model $E(y) = \beta_0 + \beta_1 x + \beta_2 x^2$ to the data.

MINITAB output for Exercise 13.10

Regression Analysis: y versus x, x-sq

```
The regression equation is
y = - 44.2 + 16.3 x - 0.820 x-sq

Predictor        Coef      SE Coef         T        P
Constant      -44.192        8.287     -5.33    0.013
x              16.334        2.490      6.56    0.007
x-sq          -0.8198       0.1824     -4.49    0.021

S = 0.5944      R-Sq = 99.6%      R-Sq(adj) = 99.3%

Analysis of Variance
Source            DF          SS         MS         F        P
Regression         2      234.96     117.48    332.53    0.000
Residual Error     3        1.06       0.35
Total              5      236.02

Source       DF      Seq SS
x             1      227.82
x-sq          1        7.14
```

a. Plot the data points. Does it look as though the quadratic model is necessary?

b. Find s on the printout. Confirm that

$$s = \sqrt{\frac{SSE}{n - k - 1}}$$

c. Do the data provide sufficient evidence to indicate that the model contributes information for the prediction of y? What is the p-value for this test, and what does it mean?

d. How much of the regression sum of squares is accounted for by the quadratic term? The linear term?

e. What sign would you expect the actual value of β_2 to have? Find the value of b_2 in the printout. Does this value confirm your expectation?

f. Do the data indicate a significant curvature in the relationship between y and x? Test at the 5% level of significance.

g. What conclusions can you draw from the accompanying residual plots?

MINITAB plots for Exercise 13.10

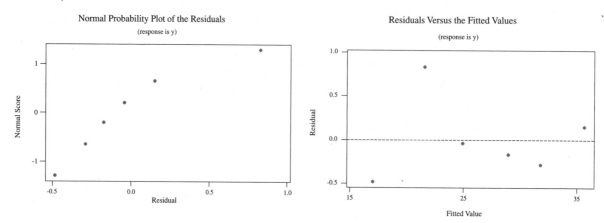

13.11 Refer to Exercise 13.10.

a. Use the values of SSR and Total SS to calculate R^2. Compare this value with the value given in the printout.

b. Calculate R^2(adj). When would it be appropriate to use this value rather than R^2 to assess the fit of the model?

c. The value of R^2(adj) was 95.7% when a simple linear model was fit to the data. Does the linear or the quadratic model fit better?

EX1312

13.12 You have a hot grill and an empty hamburger bun, but you have sworn off greasy hamburgers. Would a meatless hamburger do? The data in the table record a flavor and texture score (between 0 and 100) for 12 brands of meatless hamburgers along with the price, number of calories, amount of fat, and amount of sodium per burger.[2] Some of these brands try to mimic the taste of meat, while others do not. The *MINITAB* printout shows the regression of the taste score y on the four predictor variables: price, calories, fat, and sodium.

Brand	Score, y	Price, $x1$	Calories, $x2$	Fat, $x3$	Sodium, $x4$
1	70	91	110	4	310
2	45	68	90	0	420
3	43	92	80	1	280
4	41	75	120	5	370
5	39	88	90	0	410
6	30	67	140	4	440
7	68	73	120	4	430
8	56	92	170	6	520
9	40	71	130	4	180
10	34	67	110	2	180
11	30	92	100	1	330
12	26	95	130	2	340

MINITAB output for Exercise 13.12

Regression Analysis: y versus x1, x2, x3, x4

```
The regression equation is
y = 59.8 + 0.129 x1 - 0.580 x2 + 8.50 x3 + 0.0488 x4

Predictor         Coef      SE Coef          T         P
Constant         59.85        35.68       1.68     0.137
x1              0.1287       0.3391       0.38     0.716
x2             -0.5805       0.2888      -2.01     0.084
x3               8.498        3.472       2.45     0.044
x4             0.04876      0.04062       1.20     0.269

S = 12.72      R-Sq = 49.9%      R-Sq(adj) = 21.3%
```

(continued)

MINITAB **output for**
Exercise 13.12
(continued)

```
Analysis of Variance

Source          DF        SS        MS        F        P
Regression       4     1128.4     282.1     1.74     0.244
Residual Error   7     1132.6     161.8
Total           11     2261.0

Source     DF     Seq SS
x1          1      11.2
x2          1      19.6
x3          1     864.5
x4          1     233.2
```

a. Comment on the fit of the model using the statistical test for the overall fit and the coefficient of determination, R^2.

b. If you wanted to refit the model by eliminating one of the independent variables, which one would you eliminate? Why?

13.13 Refer to Exercise 13.12. A command in the *MINITAB* regression menu provides output in which R^2 and R^2(adj) are calculated for all possible subsets of the four independent variables. The printout is provided here.

MINITAB **output for**
Exercise 13.13

Best Subsets Regression: y versus x1, x2, x3, x4
```
Response is y
                                        x x x x
Vars   R-Sq   R-Sq(adj)    C-p       s  1 2 3 4

 1     17.0      8.7        3.6    13.697   X
 1      6.9      0.0        5.0    14.506        X
 2     37.2     23.3        2.8    12.556   X X
 2     20.3      2.5        5.1    14.153     X X
 3     48.9     29.7        3.1    12.020   X X X
 3     39.6     16.9        4.4    13.066   X X X
 4     49.9     21.3        5.0    12.720   X X X X
```

a. If you had to compare these models and choose the best one, which model would you choose? Explain.

b. Comment on the usefulness of the model you chose in part a. Is your model valuable in predicting a taste score based on the chosen predictor variables?

EX1314

13.14 An experiment was designed to compare several different types of air pollution monitors.[3] Each monitor was set up and then exposed to different concentrations of ozone, ranging between 15 and 230 parts per million (ppm), for periods of 8–72 hours. Filters on the monitor were then analyzed, and the response of the monitor was measured. The results for one type of monitor showed a linear pattern (see Exercise 12.14). The results for another type of monitor are listed in the table.

Ozone (ppm/hr), x	.06	.12	.18	.31	.57	.65	.68	1.29
Relative Fluorescence Density, y	8	18	27	33	42	47	52	61

a. Plot the data. What model would you expect to provide the best fit to the data? Write the equation of that model.

b. Use a computer software package to fit the model from part a.

c. Find the least-squares regression line relating the monitor's response to the ozone concentration.

d. Does the model contribute significant information for the prediction of the monitor's response based on ozone exposure? Use the appropriate *p*-value to make your decision.

e. Find R^2 on the printout. What does this value tell you about the effectiveness of the multiple regression analysis?

13.5 Using Quantitative and Qualitative Predictor Variables in a Regression Model

One reason multiple regression models are very flexible is that they allow for the use of both *qualitative* and *quantitative* predictor variables. For the multiple regression methods used in this chapter, the response variable *y must be quantitative,* measuring a numerical random variable that has a normal distribution (according to the assumptions of Section 13.2). However, each independent predictor variable can be either a quantitative variable *or* a qualitative variable, whose levels represent qualities or characteristics and can only be categorized.

Quantitative and qualitative variables enter the regression model in different ways. To make things more complicated, we can allow a combination of different types of variables in the model, *and* we can allow the variables to *interact,* a concept that may be familiar to you from the *factorial experiment* of Chapter 11. We consider these options one at a time.

A **quantitative variable** x can be entered as a linear term, x, or to some higher power such as x^2 or x^3, as in the quadratic model in Example 13.3. When more than one quantitative variable is necessary, the interpretation of the possible models becomes more complicated. For example, with two quantitative variables x_1 and x_2, you could use a **first-order model** such as

$$E(y) = \beta_0 + \beta_1 x_1 + \beta_2 x_2$$

which traces a plane in two-dimensional space (see Figure 13.1). However, it may be that one of the variables—say, x_2—is not related to y in the same way when $x_1 = 1$ as it is when $x_1 = 2$. To allow x_2 to behave differently depending on the value of x_1, we add an **interaction term,** $x_1 x_2$, and allow the two-dimensional plane to *twist.* The model is now a **second-order model**:

$$E(y) = \beta_0 + \beta_1 x_1 + \beta_2 x_2 + \beta_3 x_1 x_2$$

The models become complicated quickly when you allow curvilinear relationships *and* interaction for the two variables. One way to decide on the type of model you need is to plot some of the data—perhaps y versus x_1, y versus x_2, and y versus x_2 for various values of x_1.

In contrast to quantitative predictor variables, **qualitative predictor variables** are entered into a regression model through **dummy** or **indicator variables.** For example, in a model that relates the mean salary of a group of employees to a number of predictor variables, you may want to include the employee's ethnic background. If each employee included in your study belongs to one of three ethnic groups—say, A, B, or C—you can enter the qualitative variable "ethnicity" into your model using two *dummy variables:*

$$x_1 = \begin{cases} 1 & \text{if group B} \\ 0 & \text{if not} \end{cases} \qquad x_2 = \begin{cases} 1 & \text{if group C} \\ 0 & \text{if not} \end{cases}$$

Look at the effect these two variables have on the model $E(y) = \beta_0 + \beta_1 x_1 + \beta_2 x_2$: For employees in group A,

$$E(y) = \beta_0 + \beta_1(0) + \beta_2(0) = \beta_0$$

for employees in group B,

$$E(y) = \beta_0 + \beta_1(1) + \beta_2(0) = \beta_0 + \beta_1$$

and for those in group C,

$$E(y) = \beta_0 + \beta_1(0) + \beta_2(1) = \beta_0 + \beta_2$$

The model allows a different average response for each group. β_1 measures the difference in the average responses between groups B and A, while β_2 measures the difference between groups C and A.

When a qualitative variable involves k categories or levels, $(k - 1)$ dummy variables should be added to the regression model. This model may contain other predictor variables—quantitative or qualitative—as well as cross-products (**interactions**) of the dummy variables with other variables that appear in the model. As you can see, the process of model building—deciding on the appropriate terms to enter into the regression model—can be quite complicated. However, you can become more proficient at model building, gaining experience with the chapter exercises. The next example involves one quantitative and one qualitative variable that interact.

EXAMPLE 13.5 A study was conducted to examine the relationship between university salary y, the number of years of experience of the faculty member, and the gender of the faculty member. If you expect a straight-line relationship between mean salary and years of experience for both men and women, write the model that relates mean salary to the two predictor variables: years of experience (quantitative) and gender of the professor (qualitative).

Solution Since you may suspect the mean salary lines for women and men to be different, your model for mean salary $E(y)$ may appear as shown in Figure 13.11. A straight-line relationship between $E(y)$ and years of experience x_1 implies the model

$$E(y) = \beta_0 + \beta_1 x_1 \qquad \textbf{(graphs as a straight line)}$$

FIGURE 13.11
Hypothetical
relationship for
mean salary
$E(y)$, years of
experience (x_1),
and gender (x_2) for
Example 13.5

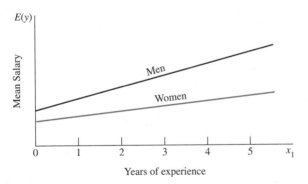

The qualitative variable "gender" involves $k = 2$ categories, men and women. Therefore, you need $(k - 1) = 1$ dummy variable, x_2, defined as

$$x_2 = \begin{cases} 1 & \text{if a man} \\ 0 & \text{if a woman} \end{cases}$$

and the model is expanded to become

$$E(y) = \beta_0 + \beta_1 x_1 + \beta_2 x_2 \qquad \textbf{(graphs as two parallel lines)}$$

The fact that the slopes of the two lines may differ means that the two predictor variables **interact**; that is, the change in $E(y)$ corresponding to a change in x_1 depends on whether the professor is a man or a woman. To allow for this interaction (difference in slopes), the interaction term x_1x_2 is introduced into the model. The complete model that characterizes the graph in Figure 13.11 is

$$E(y) = \beta_0 + \beta_1 x_1 + \beta_2 x_2 + \beta_3 x_1 x_2$$

where the labels indicate: **dummy variable for gender** points to $\beta_2 x_2$, **years of experience** points to $\beta_1 x_1$, and **interaction** points to $\beta_3 x_1 x_2$.

where

$$x_1 = \text{Years of experience}$$
$$x_2 = \begin{cases} 1 & \text{if a man} \\ 0 & \text{if a woman} \end{cases}$$

You can see how the model works by assigning values to the dummy variable x_2. When the faculty member is a woman, the model is

$$E(y) = \beta_0 + \beta_1 x_1 + \beta_2(0) + \beta_3 x_1(0) = \beta_0 + \beta_1 x_1$$

which is a straight line with slope β_1 and intercept β_0. When the faculty member is a man, the model is

$$E(y) = \beta_0 + \beta_1 x_1 + \beta_2(1) + \beta_3 x_1(1) = (\beta_0 + \beta_2) + (\beta_1 + \beta_3)x_1$$

which is a straight line with slope $(\beta_1 + \beta_3)$ and intercept $(\beta_0 + \beta_2)$. The two lines have *different slopes and different intercepts,* which allows the relationship between salary y and years of experience x_1 to behave differently for men and women.

EXAMPLE 13.6

Random samples of six female and six male assistant professors were selected from among the assistant professors in a college of arts and sciences. The data on salary and years of experience are shown in Table 13.3. Note that both samples contained two professors with 3 years of experience, but no male professor had 2 years of experience. Interpret the output of the *MINITAB* regression printout and graph the predicted salary lines.

TABLE 13.3
Salary versus gender and years of experience

Years of Experience, x_1	Salary for Men, y	Salary for Women, y
1	$50,710	$49,510
2	—	50,440
3	53,160	51,340
	53,210	51,760
4	54,140	52,750
5	55,760	53,200
	55,590	

Solution

The *MINITAB* regression printout for the data in Table 13.3 is shown in Figure 13.12. You can use a step-by-step approach to interpret this regression analysis, beginning with the fitted prediction equation, $\hat{y} = 48{,}593 + 969x_1 + 867x_2 + 260x_1x_2$. By substituting $x_2 = 0$ or 1 into this equation, you get two straight lines—one for women and one for men—to predict the value of y for a given x_1. These lines are

Women: $\hat{y} = 48{,}593 + 969x_1$
Men: $\hat{y} = 49{,}460 + 1229x_1$

and are graphed in Figure 13.13.

FIGURE 13.12

MINITAB output for Example 13.6

Regression Analysis: y versus x1, x2, x1x2

```
The regression equation is
y = 48593 + 969 x1 + 867 x2 + 260 x1x2

Predictor         Coef      SE Coef          T        P
Constant       48593.0        207.9     233.68    0.000
x1              969.00         63.67      15.22    0.000
x2               866.7         305.3       2.84    0.022
x1x2            260.13         87.06       2.99    0.017

S = 201.3      R-Sq = 99.2%      R-Sq(adj) = 98.9%

Analysis of Variance
Source           DF           SS         MS        F        P
Regression        3     42108777   14036259   346.24    0.000
Residual Error    8       324315      40539
Total            11     42433092

Source      DF       Seq SS
x1           1     33294036
x2           1      8452797
x3           1       361944
```

Next, consider the overall fit of the model using the analysis of variance F test. Since the observed test statistic in the ANOVA portion of the printout is $F = 346.24$ with $P = .000$, you can conclude that at least one of the predictor variables is contributing information for the prediction of y. The strength of this model is further measured by the *coefficient of determination*, $R^2 = 99.2\%$. You can see that the model appears to fit very well.

FIGURE 13.13

A graph of the faculty salary prediction lines for Example 13.6

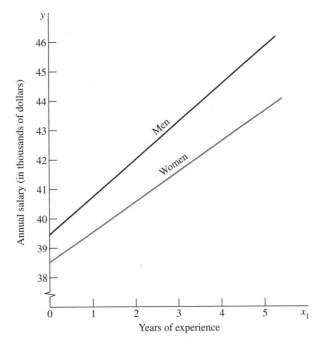

To explore the effect of the predictor variables in more detail, look at the individual t tests for the three predictor variables. The *p*-values for these tests—.000, .022, and .017, respectively—are all significant, which means that all of the predictor variables add significant information to the prediction *with the other two variables already in the model*. Finally, check the residual plots to make sure that there are no strong violations of the regression assumptions. These plots, which behave as expected for a properly fit model, are shown in Figure 13.14.

FIGURE 13.14
MINITAB residual
plots for
Example 13.6

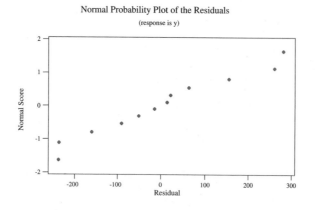

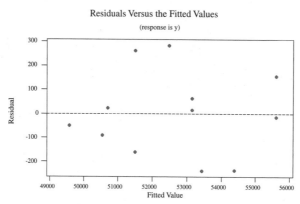

EXAMPLE 13.7

Refer to Example 13.6. Do the data provide sufficient evidence to indicate that the annual rate of increase in male junior faculty salaries exceeds the annual rate of increase in female junior faculty salaries? That is, do the data provide sufficient evidence to indicate that the slope of the men's faculty salary line is greater than the slope of the women's faculty salary line?

Solution

Since β_3 measures the difference in slopes, the slopes of the two lines will be identical if $\beta_3 = 0$. Therefore, you want to test the null hypothesis

$$H_0 : \beta_3 = 0$$

—that is, the slopes of the two lines are identical—versus the alternative hypothesis

$$H_a : \beta_3 > 0$$

—that is, the slope of the men's faculty salary line is greater than the slope of the women's faculty salary line.

The calculated value of t corresponding to β_3, shown in the row labeled "x1x2" in Figure 13.12, is 2.99. Since the *MINITAB* regression output provides p-values for two-tailed significance tests, the p-value in the printout, .017, is *twice* what it would be for a one-tailed test. For this one-tailed test, the p-value is .017/2 = .0085, and the null hypothesis is rejected. There is sufficient evidence to indicate that the annual rate of increase in men's faculty salaries exceeds the rate for women.[†]

[†]If you want to determine whether the data provide sufficient evidence to indicate that male faculty members start at higher salaries, you would test $H_0 : \beta_2 = 0$ versus the alternative hypothesis $H_a : \beta_2 > 0$.

Exercises

Basic Techniques

13.15 Suppose you wish to predict production yield y as a function of several independent predictor variables. Indicate whether each of the following independent variables is qualitative or quantitative. If qualitative, define the appropriate dummy variable(s).

a. The prevailing interest rate in the area

b. The price per pound of one item used in the production process

c. The plant (A, B, or C) at which the production yield is measured

d. The length of time that the production machine has been in operation

e. The shift (night or day) in which the yield is measured

13.16 Suppose $E(y)$ is related to two predictor variables x_1 and x_2 by the equation

$$E(y) = 3 + x_1 - 2x_2 + x_1 x_2$$

a. Graph the relationship between $E(y)$ and x_1 when $x_2 = 0$. Repeat for $x_2 = 2$ and for $x_2 = -2$.

b. Repeat the instructions of part a for the model

$$E(y) = 3 + x_1 - 2x_2$$

c. Note that the equation for part a is exactly the same as the equation in part b except that we have added the term $x_1 x_2$. How does the addition of the $x_1 x_2$ term affect the graphs of the three lines?

d. What flexibility is added to the first-order model $E(y) = \beta_0 + \beta_1 x_1 + \beta_2 x_2$ by the addition of the term $\beta_3 x_1 x_2$, using the model $E(y) = \beta_0 + \beta_1 x_1 + \beta_2 x_2 + \beta_3 x_1 x_2$?

13.17 A multiple linear regression model involving one qualitative and one quantitative independent variable produced this prediction equation:

$$\hat{y} = 12.6 + .54x_1 - 1.2x_1 x_2 + 3.9x_2^2$$

a. Which of the two variables is the quantitative variable? Explain.

b. If x_1 can take only the values 0 or 1, find the two possible prediction equations for this experiment.

c. Graph the two equations found in part b. Compare the shapes of the two curves.

Applications

EX1318

13.18 Americans are very vocal about their attempts to improve personal well-being by "eating right and exercising more." One desirable dietary change is to reduce the intake of red meat and to substitute poultry or fish. Researchers tracked beef and chicken consumption, y (in annual pounds per person) and found the consumption of beef declining and the consumption of chicken increasing over a period of seven years. A summary of their data is shown in the table.

Year	Beef	Chicken
1	85	37
2	89	36
3	76	47
4	76	47
5	68	62
6	67	74
7	60	79

Consider fitting the following model, which allows for simultaneously fitting two simple linear regression lines:

$$E(y) = \beta_0 + \beta_1 x_1 + \beta_2 x_2 + \beta_3 x_1 x_2$$

where y is the annual meat (either beef or chicken) consumption per person per year,

$$x_1 = \begin{cases} 1 & \text{if beef} \\ 0 & \text{if chicken} \end{cases} \quad \text{and} \quad x_2 = \text{Year}$$

MINITAB output for
Exercise 13.18

Regression Analysis: y versus x1, x2, x1x2

```
The regression equation is
y = 23.6 + 69.0 x1 + 7.75 x2 - 12.3 x1x2

Predictor          Coef      SE Coef           T        P
Constant         23.571        3.522        6.69    0.000
x1               69.000        4.981       13.85    0.000
x2               7.7500       0.7875        9.84    0.000
x1x2            -12.286        1.114      -11.03    0.000

S = 4.167      R-Sq = 95.4%      R-Sq(adj) = 94.1%

Analysis of Variance
Source           DF           SS          MS        F        P
Regression        3       3637.9      1212.6    69.83    0.000
Residual Error   10        173.6        17.4
Total            13       3811.5

Source      DF      Seq SS
x1           1      1380.1
x2           1       144.6
x1x2         1      2113.1

Predicted Values for New Observations
New Obs     Fit    SE Fit         95.0% CI              95.0% PI
1         56.29      3.52    ( 48.44,  64.13)    ( 44.13,  68.44)

Values of Predictors for New Observations
New Obs       x1        x2      x1x2
1           1.00      8.00      8.00
```

MINITAB diagnostic
plots for
Exercise 13.18

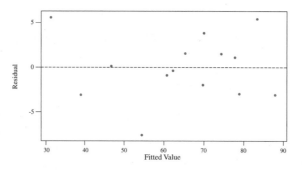

Normal Probability Plot of the Residuals
(response is y)

Residuals Versus the Fitted Values
(response is y)

a. How well does the model fit? Use any relevant statistics and diagnostic tools from the printout to answer this question.

b. Write the equations of the two straight lines that describe the trend in consumption over the period of 7 years for beef and for chicken.

c. Use the prediction equation to find a point estimate of the average per-person beef consumption in year 8. Compare this value with the value labeled "Fit" in the printout.

d. Use the printout to find a 95% confidence interval for the average per-person beef consumption in year 8. What is the 95% prediction interval for the per-person beef consumption in year 8? Is there any problem with the validity of the 95% confidence level for these intervals?

13.19 In Exercise 11.57, you used the analysis of variance procedure to analyze a 2 × 3 factorial experiment in which each factor–level combination was replicated five times. The experiment involved the number of eggs laid by caged female whiteflies on two different plants at three different temperature levels. Suppose that several of the whiteflies died before the experiment was completed, so that the number of replications was no longer the same for each treatment. The analysis of variance formulas of Chapter 11 can no longer be used, but the experiment *can* be analyzed using a multiple regression analysis. The results of this **2 × 3 factorial experiment with unequal replications** are shown in the table.

Cotton			Cucumber		
70°	77°	82°	70°	77°	82°
37	34	46	50	59	43
21	54	32	53	53	62
36	40	41	25	31	71
43	42		37	69	49
31			48	51	

a. Write a model to analyze this experiment. Make sure to include a term for the interaction between plant and temperature.

b. Use a computer software package to perform the multiple regression analysis.

c. Do the data provide sufficient evidence to indicate that the effect of temperature on the number of eggs laid is *different* depending on the type of plant?

d. Based on the results of part c, do you suggest refitting a different model? If so, rerun the regression analysis using the new model and analyze the printout.

e. Write a paragraph summarizing the results of your analyses.

13.20 The Academic Performance Index (API), described in Exercise 12.11, is a measure of school achievement based on the results of the Stanford 9 Achievement Test. The 2001 API scores for eight elementary schools in Riverside County, California are shown below, along with several other independent variables.[4]

School	API Score y	Awards x_1	% Meals x_2	% ELL x_3	% Emergency x_4	2000 API x_5
1	588	Yes	58	34	16	533
2	659	No	62	22	5	655
3	710	Yes	66	14	19	695
4	657	No	36	30	14	680
5	669	No	40	11	13	670
6	641	No	51	26	2	636
7	557	No	73	39	14	532
8	743	Yes	22	6	4	705

The variables are defined as

x_1 = 1 if the school was given a financial award for meeting growth goals, 0 if not.

x_2 = % of students who qualify for free or reduced price meals

x_3 = % of students who are English Language Learners

x_4 = % of teachers on emergency credentials

x_5 = API score in 2000

The *MINITAB* printout for a first-order regression model is given below.

Regression Analysis

```
The regression equation is
y = 269 + 33.2 x1 - 0.003 x2 - 1.02 x3 - 1.00 x4 + 0.636 x5
```

Predictor	Coef	STDev	T	P
Constant	269.03	41.55	6.48	0.023
x1	33.227	4.373	7.60	0.017
x2	-0.0027	0.1396	-0.02	0.987
x3	-1.0159	0.3237	-3.14	0.088
x4	-1.0032	0.3391	-2.96	0.098
x5	0.63560	0.05209	12.20	0.007

```
S = 4.734      R-Sq = 99.8%     R-Sq(adj) = 99.4%
```

Analysis of Variance

Source	DF	SS	MS	F	P
Regression	5	25197.2	5039.4	224.87	0.004
Residual Error	2	44.8	22.4		
Total	7	25242.0			

a. What is the model that has been fit to this data? What is the least-squares prediction equation?

b. How well does the model fit? Use any relevant statistics from the printout to answer this question.

c. Which, if any, of the independent variables are useful in predicting the 2001 API, given the other independent variables already in the model? Explain.

d. Use the values of R^2 and R^2(adj) in the printout below to choose the best model for prediction. Would you be confident in using the chosen model for predicting the 2002 API score based on a model containing similar variables? Explain.

Best Subsets regression

Response is y

Vars	R-Sq	Adj. R-Sq	C-p	s	x1	x2	x3	x4	x5
1	87.9	85.8	132.7	22.596					X
1	84.5	81.9	170.7	25.544		X			
2	97.4	96.4	27.1	11.423	X				X
2	94.6	92.4	58.8	16.512			X		X
3	99.0	98.2	11.8	8.1361	X		X		X
3	98.9	98.2	11.9	8.1654	X			X	X
4	99.8	99.6	4.0	3.8656	X		X	X	X
4	99.0	97.8	12.8	8.9626	X	X	X		X
5	99.8	99.4	6.0	4.7339	X	X	X	X	X

13.6 Testing Sets of Regression Coefficients

In the preceding sections, you have tested the complete set of partial regression coefficients using the F test for the overall fit of the model, and you have tested the partial regression coefficients individually using the Student's t test. Besides these two important tests, you might want to test hypotheses about some subsets of these regression coefficients.

For example, suppose a company suspects that the demand y for some product could be related to as many as five independent variables, x_1, x_2, x_3, x_4, and x_5. The cost of obtaining measurements on the variables x_3, x_4, and x_5 is very high. If, in a small pilot study, the company could show that these three variables contribute little or no information for the prediction of y, they can be eliminated from the study at great savings to the company.

If all five variables, x_1, x_2, x_3, x_4, and x_5, are used to predict y, the regression model would be written as

$$y = \beta_0 + \beta_1 x_1 + \beta_2 x_2 + \beta_3 x_3 + \beta_4 x_4 + \beta_5 x_5 + \epsilon$$

However, if x_3, x_4, and x_5 contribute no information for the prediction of y, then they would not appear in the model—that is, $\beta_3 = \beta_4 = \beta_5 = 0$—and the reduced model would be

$$y = \beta_0 + \beta_1 x_1 + \beta_2 x_2 + \epsilon$$

Hence, you want to test the null hypothesis

$$H_0 : \beta_3 = \beta_4 = \beta_5 = 0$$

—that is, the independent variables x_3, x_4, and x_5 contribute no information for the prediction of y—versus the alternative hypothesis

$$H_a : \text{At least one of the parameters } \beta_3, \beta_4, \text{ or } \beta_5 \text{ differs from 0}$$

—that is, at least one of the variables x_3, x_4, or x_5 contributes information for the prediction of y. Thus, in deciding whether the complete model is preferable to the reduced model in predicting demand, you are led to a test of hypothesis about a set of three parameters, β_3, β_4, and β_5.

A test of hypothesis concerning a set of model parameters involves two models:

Model 1 (reduced model)

$$E(y) = \beta_0 + \beta_1 x_1 + \beta_2 x_2 + \cdots + \beta_r x_r$$

Model 2 (complete model)

$$E(y) = \underbrace{\beta_0 + \beta_1 x_1 + \beta_2 x_2 + \cdots + \beta_r x_r}_{\text{terms in model 1}} + \underbrace{\beta_{r+1} x_{r+1} + \beta_{r+2} x_{r+2} + \cdots + \beta_k x_k}_{\text{additional terms in model 2}}$$

Suppose you fit both models to the data set and calculated the sum of squares for error for both regression analyses. If model 2 contributes more information for the prediction of y than model 1, then the errors of prediction for model 2 should be smaller than the corresponding errors for model 1, and SSE_2 should be smaller than SSE_1. In fact, the greater the difference between SSE_1 and SSE_2, the greater is the evidence to indicate that model 2 contributes more information for the prediction of y than model 1.

The test of the null hypothesis

$$H_0 : \beta_{r+1} = \beta_{r+2} = \cdots = \beta_k = 0$$

versus the alternative hypothesis

$$H_a : \text{At least one of the parameters } \beta_{r+1}, \beta_{r+2}, \ldots, \beta_k \text{ differs from 0}$$

uses the test statistic

$$F = \frac{(\text{SSE}_1 - \text{SSE}_2)/(k - r)}{\text{MSE}_2}$$

where F is based on $df_1 = (k - r)$ and $df_2 = n - (k + 1)$. Note that the $(k - r)$ parameters involved in H_0 are those added to model 1 to obtain model 2. The numerator degrees of freedom df_1 always equals $(k - r)$, the number of parameters involved in H_0. The denominator degrees of freedom df_2 is the number of degrees of freedom associated with the sum of squares for error, SSE_2, for the complete model.

The rejection region for the test is identical to the rejection region for all of the analysis of variance F tests—namely,

$$F > F_\alpha$$

EXAMPLE 13.8 Refer to the real estate data of Example 13.2 that relate the listed selling price y to the square feet of living area x_1, the number of floors x_2, the number of bedrooms x_3, and the number of bathrooms, x_4. The realtor suspects that the square footage of living area is the most important predictor variable and that the other variables might be eliminated from the model without loss of much prediction information. Test this claim with $\alpha = .05$.

Solution The hypothesis to be tested is

$$H_0 : \beta_2 = \beta_3 = \beta_4 = 0$$

versus the alternative hypothesis that at least one of β_2, β_3, or β_4 is different from 0. The **complete model 2,** given as

$$y = \beta_0 + \beta_1 x_1 + \beta_2 x_2 + \beta_3 x_3 + \beta_4 x_4 + \epsilon$$

was fitted in Example 13.2. A portion of the *MINITAB* printout from Figure 13.3 is reproduced in Figure 13.15 along with a portion of the *MINITAB* printout for the simple linear regression analysis of the **reduced model 1,** given as

$$y = \beta_0 + \beta_1 x_1 + \epsilon$$

FIGURE 13.15
Portions of the
MINITAB regression
printouts for
(a) complete and
(b) reduced models
for Example 13.8

Regression Analysis: (a) ListPrice versus SqFeet, NumFlrs, Bdrms, Baths
```
Analysis of Variance
Source           DF          SS        MS        F        P
Regression        4     15913.0    3978.3    84.80    0.000
Residual Error   10       469.1      46.9
Total            14     16382.2
```

Regression Analysis: (b) ListPrice versus SqFeet
```
Analysis of Variance
Source           DF          SS        MS        F        P
Regression        1       14829     14829   124.14    0.000
Residual Error   13        1553       119
Total            14       16382
```

Then $SSE_1 = 1553$ from Figure 13.15(b) and $SSE_2 = 469.1$ and $MSE_2 = 46.9$ from Figure 13.15(a). The test statistic is

$$F = \frac{(SSE_1 - SSE_2)/(k - r)}{MSE_2}$$

$$= \frac{(1553 - 469.1)/(4 - 1)}{46.9} = 7.70$$

The critical value of F with $\alpha = .05$, $df_1 = 3$, and $df_2 = n - (k + 1) = 15 - (4 + 1) = 10$ is $F_{.05} = 3.71$. Hence, H_0 is rejected. There is evidence to indicate that at least one of the three variables, number of floors, bedrooms, or bathrooms, is contributing significant information for predicting the listed selling price.

13.7 **Interpreting Residual Plots**

Once again, you can use residual plots to discover possible violations in the assumptions required for a regression analysis. There are several common patterns you should recognize because they occur frequently in practical applications.

The variance of some types of data changes as the mean changes:

- Poisson data exhibit variation that *increases* with the mean.
- Binomial data exhibit variation that *increases* for values of p from .0 to .5, and then *decreases* for values of p from .5 to 1.0.

Residual plots for these types of data have a pattern similar to that shown in Figure 13.16.

FIGURE 13.16
Plots of residuals against $\hat{y}$

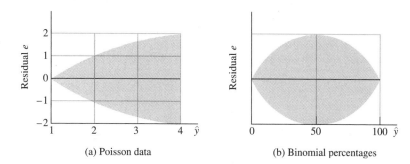

(a) Poisson data   (b) Binomial percentages

If the range of the residuals increases as $\hat{y}$ increases and you know that the data are measurements on Poisson variables, you can stabilize the variance of the response by running the regression analysis on $y^* = \sqrt{y}$. Or if the percentages are calculated from binomial data, you can use the arcsin transformation, $y^* = \sin^{-1}\sqrt{y}$.[†]

Even if you are not sure why the range of the residuals increases as $\hat{y}$ increases, you can still use a transformation of y that affects larger values of y more than smaller values—say, $y^* = \sqrt{y}$ or $y^* = \ln y$. These transformations have a tendency both to stabilize the variance of y^* and to make the distribution of y^* more nearly normal when the distribution of y is highly skewed.

Plots of the residuals versus the fits $\hat{y}$ or versus the individual predictor variables often show a pattern that indicates you have chosen an incorrect model. For example, if $E(y)$ and a single independent variable x are linearly related—that is,

$$E(y) = \beta_0 + \beta_1 x$$

and you fit a straight line to the data, then the observed y-values should vary in a random manner about $\hat{y}$, and a plot of the residuals against x will appear as shown in Figure 13.17.

FIGURE 13.17
Residual plot when the model provides a good approximation to reality

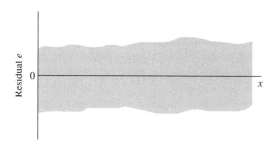

[†]In Chapter 11 and earlier chapters, we represented the response variable by the symbol x. In the chapters on regression analysis, Chapters 12 and 13, the response variable is represented by the symbol y.

In Example 13.3, you fit a quadratic model relating productivity y to store size x. If you had incorrectly used a linear model to fit these data, the residual plot in Figure 13.18 would show that the unexplained variation exhibits a curved pattern, which suggests that there is a quadratic effect that has not been included in the model.

FIGURE 13.18
Residual plot for
linear fit of
store size and
productivity data in
Example 13.3

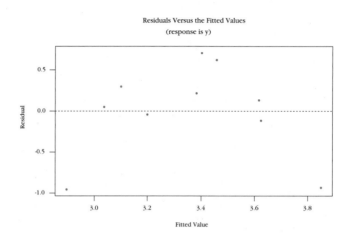

For the data in Example 13.6, the residuals of a linear regression of salary with years of experience x_1 without including gender, x_2, would show one distinct set of positive residuals corresponding to the men and a set of negative residuals corresponding to the women (see Figure 13.19). This pattern signals that the "gender" variable was not included in the model.

FIGURE 13.19
Residual plot for
linear fit of
salary data in
Example 13.6

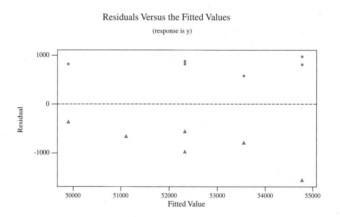

Unfortunately, not all residual plots give such a clear indication of the problem. You should examine the residual plots carefully, looking for nonrandomness in the pattern of residuals. If you can find an explanation for the behavior of the residuals, you may be able to modify your model to eliminate the problem.

13.8 Stepwise Regression Analysis

Sometimes there are a large number of independent predictor variables that *might* have an effect on the response variable y. For example, try to list all the variables that might affect a college freshman's GPA:

- Grades in high school courses, high school GPA, SAT score, ACT score
- Major, number of units carried, number of courses taken
- Work schedule, marital status, commute or live on campus

Which of this large number of independent variables should be included in the model? Since the number of terms could quickly get unmanageable, you might choose to use a procedure called a **stepwise regression analysis,** which is implemented by computer and is available in most statistical packages.

Suppose you have data available on y and a number of possible independent variables, $x_1, x_2, \ldots, x_k$. A stepwise regression analysis fits a variety of models to the data, adding and deleting variables as their significance in the presence of the other variables is either *significant* or *nonsignificant,* respectively. Once the program has performed a sufficient number of iterations and no more variables are significant when added to the model, and none of the variables in the model are nonsignificant when removed, the procedure stops.

A stepwise regression analysis is an easy way to locate some variables that contribute information for predicting y, but it is not foolproof. Since these programs always fit first-order models of the form

$$E(y) = \beta_0 + \beta_1 x_1 + \beta_2 x_2 + \cdots + \beta_k x_k$$

they are not helpful in detecting *curvature* or *interaction* in the data. The stepwise regression analysis is best used as a preliminary tool for identifying which of a large number of variables should be considered in your model. You must then decide how to enter these variables into the actual model you will use for prediction.

13.9 Misinterpreting a Regression Analysis

Several misinterpretations of the output of a regression analysis are common. We have already mentioned the importance of model selection. If a model does not fit a set of data, it does not mean that the variables included in the model contribute little or no information for the prediction of y. The variables may be very important contributors of information, but you may have entered the variables into the model in the wrong way. For example, a second-order model in the variables might provide a very good fit to the data when a first-order model appears to be completely useless in describing the response variable y.

Causality

You must be careful not to conclude that changes in x *cause* changes in y. This type of **causal relationship** can be detected only with a *carefully designed experiment.* For example, if you randomly assign experimental units to each of two levels of a variable x—say, $x = 5$ and $x = 10$—and the data show that the mean value of y is larger when $x = 10$, then you can say that the change in the level of x caused a change in the mean value of y. But in most regression analyses, in which the experiments are not designed, there is no guarantee that an important predictor variable—say, x_1—caused y to change. It is quite possible that some variable that is not even in the model causes *both* y and x_1 to change.

Multicollinearity

Neither the size of a regression coefficient nor its t-value indicates the importance of the variable as a contributor of information. For example, suppose you intend to predict

y, a college student's calculus grade, based on x_1 = high school mathematics average and x_2 = score on mathematics aptitude test. Since these two variables contain much of the same or **shared information,** it will not surprise you to learn that, once one of the variables is entered into the model, the other contributes very little additional information. The individual t-value is small. If the variables were entered in the reverse order, however, you would see the size of the t-values reversed.

The situation described above is called **multicollinearity,** and occurs when two or more of the predictor variables are highly correlated with one another. When multicollinearity is present in a regression problem, it can have these effects on the analysis:

- The estimated regression coefficients will have large standard errors, causing imprecision in confidence and prediction intervals.
- Adding or deleting a predictor variable may cause significant changes in the values of the other regression coefficients.

How can you tell whether a regression analysis exhibits multicollinearity? Look for these clues:

- The value of R^2 is large, indicating a good fit, but the individual t-tests are nonsignificant.
- The signs of the regression coefficients are contrary to what you would intuitively expect the contributions of those variables to be.
- A matrix of correlations, generated by computer, shows you which predictor variables are highly correlated with each other and with the response y.

Figure 13.20 displays the matrix of correlations generated for the real estate data from Example 13.2. The first column of the matrix shows the correlations of each predictor variable with the response variable y. They are all significantly nonzero, but the first variable, x_1 = living area, is the most highly correlated. The last three columns of the matrix show significant correlations between all but one pair of predictor variables. This is a strong indication of multicollinearity. If you try to eliminate one of the variables in the model, it may drastically change the effects of the other three! Another clue can be found by examining the coefficients of the prediction line,

```
ListPrice = 18.8 + 6.27 SqFeet − 16.2 Numflrs − 2.67 Bdrms + 30.3 Baths
```

FIGURE 13.20
Correlation matrix for the real estate data in Example 13.2

Correlations: ListPrice, SqFeet, NumFlrs, Bdrms, Baths

	ListPrice	SqFeet	Numflrs	Bdrms
SqFeet	0.951			
	0.000			
Numflrs	0.605	0.630		
	0.017	0.012		
Bdrms	0.746	0.711	0.375	
	0.001	0.003	0.168	
Baths	0.834	0.720	0.760	0.675
	0.000	0.002	0.001	0.006

Cell Contents: Pearson Correlation
                P-Value

You would expect more floors and bedrooms to increase the list price, but their coefficients are negative.

Since multicollinearity exists to some extent in all regression problems, you should think of the individual terms as *information contributors,* rather than try to measure the practical importance of each term. The primary decision to be made is whether a term contributes sufficient information to justify its inclusion in the model.

13.10 Steps to Follow When Building a Multiple Regression Model

The ultimate objective of a multiple regression analysis is to develop a model that will accurately predict y as a function of a set of predictor variables $x_1, x_2, \ldots, x_k$. The step-by-step procedure for developing this model was presented in Section 13.4 and is restated next with some additional detail. If you use this approach, what may appear to be a complicated problem can be made simpler. As with any statistical procedure, your confidence will grow as you gain experience with multiple regression analysis in a variety of practical situations.

1. Select the predictor variables to be included in the model. Since some of these variables may contain shared information, you can reduce the list by running a stepwise regression analysis (see Section 13.8). Keep the number of predictors small enough to be effective yet manageable. Be aware that the number of observations in your data set must exceed the number of terms in your model; the greater the excess, the better!
2. Write a model using the selected predictor variables. If the variables are qualitative, it is best to begin by including interaction terms. If the variables are quantitative, it is best to start with a second-order model. Unnecessary terms can be deleted later. Obtain the fitted prediction model.
3. Use the analysis of variance F test and R^2 to determine how well the model fits the data.
4. Check the t tests for the partial regression coefficients to see which ones are contributing significant information in the presence of the others. If some terms appear to be nonsignificant, consider deleting them. If you choose to compare several different models, use R^2(adj) to compare their effectiveness.
5. Use computer-generated residual plots to check for violation of the regression assumptions.

Key Concepts and Formulas

I. The General Linear Model

1. $y = \beta_0 + \beta_1 x_1 + \beta_2 x_2 + \cdots + \beta_k x_k + \epsilon$
2. The random error ϵ has a normal distribution with mean 0 and variance σ^2.

II. Method of Least Squares

1. Estimates $b_0, b_1, \ldots, b_k$, for $\beta_0, \beta_1, \ldots, \beta_k$, are chosen to minimize SSE, the sum of squared deviations about the regression line, $\hat{y} = b_0 + b_1 x_1 + b_2 x_2 + \cdots + b_k x_k$.
2. Least-squares estimates are produced by computer.

III. Analysis of Variance

1. Total SS = SSR + SSE, where Total SS = S_{yy}. The ANOVA table is produced by computer.
2. Best estimate of σ^2 is

$$\text{MSE} = \frac{\text{SSE}}{n - k - 1}$$

IV. **Testing, Estimation, and Prediction**

1. A test for the significance of the regression, $H_0 : \beta_1 = \beta_2 = \cdots = \beta_k = 0$, can be implemented using the analysis of variance F test:

$$F = \frac{\text{MSR}}{\text{MSE}}$$

2. The strength of the relationship between x and y can be measured using

$$R^2 = \frac{\text{SSR}}{\text{Total SS}}$$

which gets closer to 1 as the relationship gets stronger.

3. Use residual plots to check for nonnormality, inequality of variances, and an incorrectly fit model.

4. Significance tests for the partial regression coefficients can be performed using the Student's t test:

$$t = \frac{b_i - \beta_i}{\text{SE}(b_i)} \qquad \text{with error } df = n - k - 1$$

5. Confidence intervals can be generated by computer to estimate the average value of y, $E(y)$, for given values of $x_1, x_2, \ldots, x_k$. Computer-generated prediction intervals can be used to predict a particular observation y for given values of $x_1, x_2, \ldots, x_k$. For given $x_1, x_2, \ldots, x_k$, prediction intervals are always wider than confidence intervals.

V. **Model Building**

1. The number of terms in a regression model cannot exceed the number of observations in the data set and should be considerably less!

2. To account for a curvilinear effect in a *quantitative* variable, use a second-order polynomial model. For a cubic effect, use a third-order polynomial model.

3. To add a *qualitative* variable with k categories, use $(k - 1)$ dummy or indicator variables.

4. There may be interactions between two quantitative variables or between a quantitative and qualitative variable. Interaction terms are entered as $\beta x_i x_j$.

5. Compare models using $R^2(\text{adj})$.

Multiple Regression Procedures

In Chapter 12, you used the linear regression procedures available in *MINITAB* to perform estimation and testing for a simple linear regression analysis. You obtained a graph of the best-fitting least-squares regression line and calculated the correlation coefficient r and the coefficient of determination r^2. The testing and estimation techniques for a multiple regression analysis are also available with *MINITAB* and involve almost the same set of commands. You might want to review the section "About *MINITAB*" at the end of Chapter 12 before continuing this section.

For a response variable y that is related to several predictor variables, $x_1, x_2, \ldots, x_k$, the observed values of y and each of the k predictor variables must be entered into the first $(k + 1)$ columns of the *MINITAB* worksheet. Once this is done, the main inferential tools for linear regression analysis are generated using **Stat → Regression → Regression.** The Dialog box for the **Regression** command is shown in Figure 13.21.

MINITAB

FIGURE 13.21

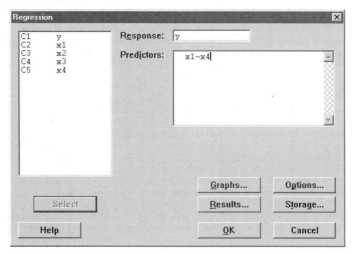

Select **y** for the Response variable and $x_1, x_2, \ldots, x_k$ for the Predictor variables. You may now choose to generate some residual plots to check the validity of your regression assumptions before you use the model for estimation or prediction. Choose **Graphs** to display the Dialog box for residual plots, and choose the appropriate diagnostic plot.

Once you have verified the appropriateness of your multiple regression model, you can choose **Options** and obtain confidence and prediction intervals for either of these cases:

- A single set of values $x_1, x_2, \ldots, x_k$ (typed in the box marked "Prediction intervals for new observations").
- Several sets of values $x_1, x_2, \ldots, x_k$ stored in k columns of the worksheet. When you click **OK** twice, the regression output is generated.

The only difficulty in performing the multiple regression analysis using *MINITAB* might be properly entering the data for your particular model. If the model involves polynomial terms or interaction terms, the **Calc → Calculator** command will help you. For example, suppose you want to fit the model

$$E(y) = \beta_0 + \beta_1 x_1 + \beta_2 x_2 + \beta_3 x_1^2 + \beta_4 x_1 x_2$$

You will need to enter the observed values of y, x_1, and x_2 into the first three columns of the *MINITAB* worksheet. Name column C4 "x1-sq" and name C5 "x1x2." You can now use the calculator Dialog box shown in Figure 13.22 to generate these two columns. In the **Expression** box, select **x1 * x1** or **x1 ** 2** and store the results in **C4** (x1-sq). Click **OK.** Similarly, to obtain the data for C5, select **x1 * x2** and store the results in **C5** (x1x2). Click **OK.** You are now ready to perform the multiple regression analysis.

If you are fitting either a quadratic or a cubic model in one variable x, you can now plot the data points, the polynomial regression curve, and the upper and lower confidence and prediction limits using **Stat → Regression → Fitted line Plot.** Select y and x for the Response and Predictor variables, and click "Display confidence bands" and "Display prediction bands" in the **Options** Dialog box. Make sure that **Quadratic** or **Cubic** is selected as the "Type of Regression Model," so that you will get the proper fit to the data.

MINITAB

FIGURE 13.22

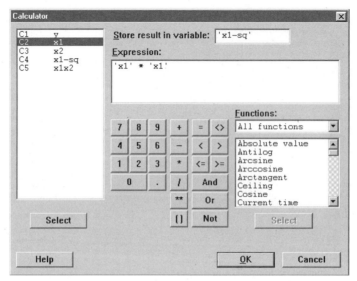

Recall that in Chapter 12, you used **Stat → Basic Statistics → Correlation** to obtain the value of the correlation coefficient r. In multiple regression analysis, the same command will generate a matrix of correlations, one for each pair of variables in the set $y, x_1, x_2, \ldots, x_k$. Make sure that the box marked "Display p-values" is checked. The p-values will provide information on the significant correlation between a particular pair, in the presence of all the other variables in the model, and they are identical to the p-values for the individual t tests of the regression coefficients.

Supplementary Exercises

EX1321

13.21 Groups of 10-day-old chicks were randomly assigned to seven treatment groups in which a basal diet was supplemented with 0, 50, 100, 150, 200, 250, or 300 micrograms/kilogram (μg/kg) of biotin. The table gives the average biotin intake (x) in micrograms per day and the average weight gain (y) in grams per day.[5]

Added Biotin	Biotin Intake, x	Weight Gain, y
0	.14	8.0
50	2.01	17.1
100	6.06	22.3
150	6.34	24.4
200	7.15	26.5
250	9.65	23.4
300	12.50	23.3

In the *MINITAB* printout, the second-order polynomial model

$$E(y) = \beta_0 + \beta_1 x + \beta_2 x^2$$

is fitted to the data. Use the printout to answer the questions.

a. What is the fitted least-squares line?

b. Find R^2 and interpret its value.

c. Do the data provide sufficient evidence to conclude that the model contributes significant information for predicting y?

d. Find the results of the test of $H_0 : \beta_2 = 0$. Is there sufficient evidence to indicate that the quadratic model provides a better fit to the data than a simple linear model does?

e. Do the residual plots indicate that any of the regression assumptions have been violated? Explain.

MINITAB output for Exercise 13.21

Regression Analysis:y versus x, x-sq

```
The regression equation is
y = 8.59 + 3.82 x - 0.217 x-sq

Predictor        Coef      SE Coef           T        P
Constant        8.585        1.641        5.23    0.006
x              3.8208       0.5683        6.72    0.003
x-sq         -0.21663      0.04390       -4.93    0.008

S = 1.833      R-Sq = 94.4%     R-Sq(adj) = 91.5%

Analysis of Variance
Source          DF           SS           MS          F          P
Regression       2       224.75       112.37      33.44      0.003
Residual Error   4        13.44         3.36
Total            6       238.19

Source          DF       Seq SS
x                1       142.92
x-sq             1        81.83
```

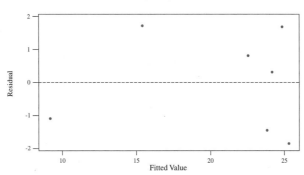

Residuals Versus the Fitted Values
(response is y)

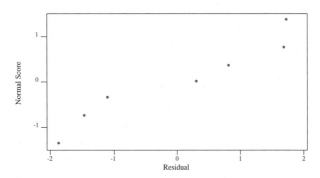

Normal Probability Plot of the Residuals
(response is y)

EX1322

13.22 A department store conducted an experiment to investigate the effects of advertising expenditures on the weekly sales for its men's wear, children's wear, and women's wear departments. Five weeks for observation were randomly selected from each department, and an advertising budget x_1 (in hundreds of dollars) was assigned for each. The weekly sales (in thousands of dollars) are shown in the accompanying table for each of the 15 1-week sales periods. If we expect weekly sales $E(y)$ to be linearly related to advertising expenditure x_1, and if we expect the slopes of the lines corresponding to the three departments to differ, then an appropriate model for $E(y)$ is

$$E(y) = \beta_0 + \underbrace{\beta_1 x_1}_{} + \underbrace{\beta_2 x_2 + \beta_3 x_3}_{} + \underbrace{\beta_4 x_1 x_2 + \beta_5 x_1 x_3}_{}$$

quantitative variable "advertising expenditure"	dummy variables used to introduce the qualitative variable "department" into the model	interaction terms that introduce differences in slopes

where

x_1 = Advertising expenditure

$$x_2 = \begin{cases} 1 & \text{if children's wear department B} \\ 0 & \text{if not} \end{cases}$$

$$x_3 = \begin{cases} 1 & \text{if women's wear department C} \\ 0 & \text{if not} \end{cases}$$

	Advertising Expenditure (hundreds of dollars)				
Department	1	2	3	4	5
Men's wear A	$5.2	$5.9	$7.7	$7.9	$9.4
Children's wear B	8.2	9.0	9.1	10.5	10.5
Women's wear C	10.0	10.3	12.1	12.7	13.6

a. Find the equation of the line relating $E(y)$ to advertising expenditure x_1 for the men's wear department A. [HINT: According to the coding used for the dummy variables, the model represents mean sales $E(y)$ for the men's wear department A when $x_2 = x_3 = 0$. Substitute $x_2 = x_3 = 0$ into the equation for $E(y)$ to find the equation of this line.]

b. Find the equation of the line relating $E(y)$ to x_1 for the children's wear department B. [HINT: According to the coding, the model represents $E(y)$ for the children's wear department when $x_2 = 1$ and $x_3 = 0$.]

c. Find the equation of the line relating $E(y)$ to x_1 for the women's wear department C.

d. Find the difference between the intercepts of the $E(y)$ lines corresponding to the children's wear B and men's wear A departments.

e. Find the difference in slopes between $E(y)$ lines corresponding to the women's wear C and men's wear A departments.

f. Refer to part e. Suppose you want to test the null hypothesis that the slopes of the lines corresponding to the three departments are equal. Express this as a test of hypothesis about one or more of the model parameters.

13.23 Refer to Exercise 13.22. Use a computer software package to perform the multiple regression analysis and obtain diagnostic plots if possible.

a. Comment on the fit of the model, using the analysis of variance F test, R^2, and the diagnostic plots to check the regression assumptions.

b. Find the prediction equation, and graph the three department sales lines.

c. Examine the graphs in part b. Do the slopes of the lines corresponding to the children's wear B and men's wear A departments appear to differ? Test the null hypothesis that the slopes do not differ ($H_0 : \beta_4 = 0$) versus the alternative hypothesis that the slopes are different.

d. Are the interaction terms in the model significant? Use the methods described in Section 13.5 to test $H_0 : \beta_4 = \beta_5 = 0$. Do the results of this test suggest that the fitted model should be modified?

e. Write a short explanation of the practical implications of this regression analysis.

13.24 Utility companies, which must plan the operation and expansion of electricity generation, are vitally interested in predicting customer demand over both short and long periods of time. A short-term study was conducted to investigate the effect of mean monthly daily temperature x_1 and cost per kilowatt-hour x_2 on the mean daily consumption (in kilowatt-hours, kWh) per household. The company expected the demand for electricity to rise in cold weather (due to heating), fall when the weather was moderate, and rise again when the temperature rose and there was need for air-conditioning. They expected demand to decrease as the cost per kilowatt-hour increased, reflecting greater attention to conservation. Data were available for 2 years, a period in which the cost per kilowatt-hour x_2 increased owing to the increasing cost of fuel. The company fitted the model

$$E(y) = \beta_0 + \beta_1 x_1 + \beta_2 x_1^2 + \beta_3 x_2 + \beta_4 x_1 x_2 + \beta_5 x_1^2 x_2$$

to the data shown in the table. The *MINITAB* printout for this multiple regression problem is also provided.

Price per kWh, x_2	Daily Temperature and Consumption	Mean Daily Consumption (kWh) Per Household											
8¢	Mean daily temperature (°F), x_1	31	34	39	42	47	56	62	66	68	71	75	78
	Mean daily consumption, y	55	49	46	47	40	43	41	46	44	51	62	73
10¢	Mean daily temperature, x_1	32	36	39	42	48	56	62	66	68	72	75	79
	Mean daily consumption, y	50	44	42	42	38	40	39	44	40	44	50	55

MINITAB output for Exercise 13.24

Regression Analysis: y versus x1, x1-sq, x2, x1x2, x1sqx2

```
The regression equation is
y = 326 - 11.4 x1 + 0.113 x1-sq - 21.7 x2 + 0.873 x1x2 - 0.00887 x1sqx2

Predictor         Coef       StDev          T        P
Constant        325.61       83.06       3.92    0.001
x1             -11.383        3.239      -3.51    0.002
x1-sq           0.11350      0.02945     3.85    0.001
x2             -21.699        9.224      -2.35    0.030
x1x2            0.8730        0.3589      2.43    0.026
x1sqx2         -0.008869      0.003257   -2.72    0.014

S = 2.908       R-Sq = 89.8%      R-Sq(adj) = 87.0%

Analysis of Variance
Source           DF          SS         MS         F        P
Regression        5     1346.45     269.29     31.85    0.000
Residual Error   18      152.18       8.45
Total            23     1498.63

Source          DF      Seq SS
x1               1      140.71
x1-sq            1      892.78
x2               1      192.44
x1x2             1       57.84
x1sqx2           1       62.68

Unusual Observations
Obs        x1          y        Fit    StDev Fit    Residual    St Resid
  9      68.0     44.000     49.640        1.104      -5.640       -2.10R
 12      78.0     73.000     67.767        2.012       5.233        2.49R

R denotes an observation with a large standardized residual
```

a. Do the data provide sufficient evidence to indicate that the model contributes information for the prediction of mean daily kilowatt-hour consumption per household? Test at the 5% level of significance.

b. Graph the curve depicting $\hat{y}$ as a function of temperature x_1 when the cost per kilowatt-hour is $x_2 = 8¢$. Construct a similar graph for the case when $x_2 = 10¢$ per kilowatt-hour. Are the consumption curves different?

c. If cost per kilowatt-hour is unimportant in predicting use, then you do not need the terms involving x_2 in the model. Therefore, the null hypothesis

$$H_0 : x_2 \text{ does not contribute information for the prediction of } y$$

is equivalent to the null hypothesis $H_0 : \beta_3 = \beta_4 = \beta_5 = 0$ (if $\beta_3 = \beta_4 = \beta_5 = 0$, the terms involving x_2 disappear from the model). The *MINITAB* printout, obtained by fitting the reduced model

$$E(y) = \beta_0 + \beta_1 x_1 + \beta_2 x_1^2$$

to the data, is shown here. Use the methods of Section 13.5 to determine whether price per kilowatt-hour x_2 contributes significant information for the prediction of y.

MINITAB output for Exercise 13.24

Regression Analysis: y versus x1, x1-sq

```
The regression equation is
y = 130 - 3.50 x1 + 0.0334 x1-sq

Predictor        Coef     SE Coef          T        P
Constant       130.01       14.88       8.74    0.000
x1            -3.5017      0.5789      -6.05    0.000
x1-sq        0.033371    0.005256       6.35    0.000

S = 4.706      R-Sq = 69.0%      R-Sq(adj) = 66.0%

Analysis of Variance
Source             DF          SS          MS        F        P
Regression          2     1033.49      516.75    23.33    0.000
Residual Error     21      465.13       22.15
Total              23     1498.63

Source        DF      Seq SS
x1             1      140.71
x1-sq          1      892.78

Unusual Observations
Obs        x1           y         Fit      SE Fit     Residual    St Resid
 12      78.0      73.000      59.906       2.243       13.094       3.16R

R denotes an observation with a large standardized residual
```

d. Compare the values of $R^2(\text{adj})$ for the two models fit in this exercise. Which of the two models would you recommend?

EX1325

13.25 Because dolphins (and other large marine mammals) are considered to be the top predators in the marine food chain, the heavy metal concentrations in striped dolphins were measured as part of a marine pollution study. The concentration of mercury, the heavy metal reported in this study, is expected to differ in males and females because the mercury in a female is apparently transferred to her offspring during gestation and nursing. This study involved 28 males between the ages of .21 and 39.5 years, and 17 females between the ages of .80 and 34.5 years. For the data in the table,

$x_1 = $ Age of the dolphin (in years)

$x_2 = \begin{cases} 0 & \text{if female} \\ 1 & \text{if male} \end{cases}$

$y = $ Mercury concentration (in micrograms/gram) in the liver

y	x_1	x_2	y	x_1	x_2	y	x_1	x_2	y	x_1	x_2
1.70	.21	1	481.00	22.50	1	241.00	31.50	1	142.00	17.50	0
1.72	0.33	1	485.00	24.50	1	397.00	31.50	1	180.00	17.50	0
8.80	2.00	1	221.00	24.50	1	209.00	36.50	1	174.00	18.50	0
5.90	2.20	1	406.00	25.50	1	314.00	37.50	1	247.00	19.50	0
101.00	8.50	1	252.00	26.50	1	318.00	39.50	1	223.00	21.50	0
85.40	11.50	1	329.00	26.50	1	2.50	.80	0	167.00	21.50	0
118.00	11.50	1	316.00	26.50	1	9.35	1.58	0	157.00	25.50	0
183.00	13.50	1	445.00	26.50	1	4.01	1.75	0	177.00	25.50	0
168.00	16.50	1	278.00	27.50	1	29.80	5.50	0	475.00	32.50	0
218.00	16.50	1	286.00	28.50	1	45.30	7.50	0	342.00	34.50	0
180.00	17.50	1	315.00	29.50	1	101.00	8.05	0			
264.00	20.50	1				135.00	11.50	0			

a. Write a second-order model relating y to x_1 and x_2. Allow for curvature in the relationship between age and mercury concentration, and allow for an interaction between gender and age.

Use a computer software package to perform the multiple regression analysis. Refer to the printout to answer these questions.

b. Comment on the fit of the model, using relevant statistics from the printout.

c. What is the prediction equation for predicting the mercury concentration in a female dolphin as a function of her age?

d. What is the prediction equation for predicting the mercury concentration in a male dolphin as a function of his age?

e. Does the quadratic term in the prediction equation for females contribute significantly to the prediction of the mercury concentration in a female dolphin?

f. Are there any other important conclusions that you feel were not considered regarding the fitted prediction equation?

EX1326

13.26 Does the cost of a plane flight depend on the airline as well as the distance traveled? In Exercise 12.15, you explored the first part of this problem. The data shown in this table compare the average cost and distance traveled for two different airlines, measured for 11 heavily traveled air routes in the United States.[6]

Route	Distance	Cost	Airline
Chicago–Detroit	238	148	American
		164	United
Chicago–Denver	901	256	American
		312	United
Chicago–St. Louis	262	136	American
		152	United
Chicago–Seattle	1736	424	American
		520	United
Chicago–Cleveland	301	129	American
		139	United
Los Angeles–Chicago	1757	361	American
		473	United
Chicago–Atlanta	593	162	American
		183	United
New York–Los Angeles	2463	444	American
		525	United
New York–Chicago	714	287	American
		334	United
Los Angeles–Honolulu	2556	323	American
		333	United
New York–San Francisco	2574	513	American
		672	United

Use a computer package to analyze the data with a multiple regression analysis. Comment on the fit of the model, the significant variables, any interactions that exist, and any regression assumptions that may have been violated. Summarize your results in a report, including printouts and graphs if possible.

13.27 Digital video recorders (DVR) are fairly new to the television-viewing public, but they allow you to record and view programs at whatever time you request. Programs can be paused while you go to the kitchen for a snack, and commercials can be eliminated. Once the DVR functions become integrated with satellite and cable television setups, marketers predict that sales will skyrocket, as projected in the following table.[7]

Year	2000	2001	2002	2003	2004	2005
DVRs (millions)	.35	.88	2.50	5.70	11.50	20.20

a. Plot the predicted number of DVRs (y) as a function of the year (x) using a scatterplot. Describe the nature of the relationship.

b. What model would you use to predict y as a function of x? Explain.

c. Using the model from part b and a computer software package, find the least-squares regression equation for predicting the DVR market penetration—that is, the number of DVRs installed in U.S. homes—as a function of year.

d. Does the model contribute information for the prediction of y? Test using $\alpha = .01$.

e. What is the value of R^2? What does this tell you about the fit of the model?

f. If they are available, examine the residual plots for the analysis. What conclusions can you draw?

13.28 The tuna fish data from Exercise 11.16 were analyzed as a completely randomized design with four treatments. However, we could also view the experimental design as a 2×2 factorial experiment with unequal replications. The data are shown below.[8]

EX1328

	Oil		Water	
Light tuna	2.56	.62	.99	1.12
	1.92	.66	1.92	.63
	1.30	.62	1.23	.67
	1.79	.65	.85	.69
	1.23	.60	.65	.60
		.67	.53	.60
			1.41	.66
White tuna	1.27		1.49	1.29
	1.22		1.29	1.00
	1.19		1.27	1.27
	1.22		1.35	1.28

The data can be analyzed using the model

$$y = \beta_0 + \beta_1 x_1 + \beta_2 x_2 + \beta_3 x_1 x_2 + \epsilon$$

where

$x_1 = 0$ if oil, 1 if water

$x_2 = 0$ if light tuna, 1 if white tuna

a. Show how you would enter the data into a computer spreadsheet, entering the data into columns for y, x_1, x_2, and $x_1 x_2$.

b. The printout generated by *MINITAB* is shown below. What is the least-squares prediction equation?

MINITAB output for
Exercise 13.28

Regression Analysis
```
The regression equation is
y = 1.15 - 0.251 x1 + 0.078 x2 + 0.306 x1x2

Predictor        Coef        StDev           T         P
Constant       1.1473       0.1370        8.38     0.000
x1            -0.2508       0.1830       -1.37     0.180
x2             0.0777       0.2652        0.29     0.771
x1x2           0.3058       0.3330        0.92     0.365

S = 0.4543      R-Sq = 11.9%       R-Sq(adj) = 3.9%

Analysis of Variance

Source            DF           SS          MS        F         P
Regression         3       0.9223      0.3074     1.49     0.235
Residual Error    33       6.8104      0.2064
Total             36       7.7328
```

c. Is there an interaction between type of tuna and type of packing liquid?

d. Which, if any, of the main effects (type of tuna and type of packing liquid) contribute significant information for the prediction of y?

e. How well does the model fit the data? Explain.

13.29 Refer to Execise 13.28. The hypothesis tested in Chapter 11—that the average prices for the four types of tuna are the same—is equivalent to saying that $E(y)$ will not change as x_1 and x_2 change. This can only happen when $\beta_1 = \beta_2 = \beta_3 = 0$. Use the *MINITAB* printout for the one-way ANOVA shown below to perform the test for equality of treatment means. Verify that this test is identical to the test for significant regression in Exercise 13.28.

MINITAB output for
Exercise 13.29

One-Way Analysis of Variance
```
Analysis of Variance for y
Source      DF          SS          MS         F         P
trt          3       0.922       0.307      1.49     0.235
Error       33       6.810       0.206
Total       36       7.733
```

Case Study

FOREIGNCARS

"Made in the U.S.A."—Another Look

The case study in Chapter 12 examined the effect of foreign competition in the automotive industry as the number of imported cars steadily increased during the 1970s and 1980s.[9] The U.S. automobile industry has been besieged with complaints about product quality, worker layoffs, and high prices and has spent billions in advertising and research to produce an American-made car that will satisfy consumer demands. Have they been successful in stopping the flood of imported cars purchased by American consumers? The data shown in the table give the number of imported cars (y) sold in the United States (in millions) for the years 1969–2000. To simplify the analysis, we have coded the year using the coded variable $x = $ Year $- $ 1969.

Year	Year − 1969, x	Number of Imported Cars, y	Year	Year − 1969, x	Number of Imported Cars, y
1969	0	1.1	1977	8	2.1
1970	1	1.3	1978	9	2.0
1971	2	1.6	1979	10	2.3
1972	3	1.6	1980	11	2.4
1973	4	1.8	1981	12	2.3
1974	5	1.4	1982	13	2.2
1975	6	1.6	1983	14	2.4
1976	7	1.5	1984	15	2.4

(continued)

Year	Year − 1969, x	Number of Imported Cars, y	Year	Year − 1969, x	Number of Imported Cars, y
1985	16	2.8	1993	24	1.8
1986	17	3.2	1994	25	1.8
1987	18	3.1	1995	26	1.6
1988	19	3.1	1996	27	1.4
1989	20	2.8	1997	28	1.4
1990	21	2.5	1998	29	1.4
1991	22	2.1	1999	30	1.8
1992	23	2.0	2000	31	2.1

By examining a scatterplot of these data, you will find that the number of imported cars does not appear to follow a linear relationship over time, but rather exhibits a curvilinear response. The question, then, is to decide whether a second-, third-, or higher-order model adequately describes the data.

1. Plot the data and sketch what you consider to be the best-fitting linear, quadratic, and cubic models.
2. Find the residuals using the fitted linear regression model. Does there appear to be any pattern in the residuals when plotted against x? What model do the residuals indicate would produce a better fit?
3. What is the increase in R^2 when you fit a quadratic rather than a linear model? Is the coefficient of the quadratic term significant? Is the fitted quadratic model significantly better than the fitted linear model? Plot the residuals from the fitted quadratic model. Does there seem to be any apparent pattern in the residuals when plotted against x?
4. What is the increase in R^2 when you compare the fitted cubic with the fitted quadratic model? Is the fitted cubic model significantly better than the fitted quadratic? Are there any patterns in a plot of the residuals versus x? What proportion of the variation in the response y is not accounted for by fitting a cubic model? Should any higher-order polynomial model be considered? Why or why not?

Data Sources

1. W.S. Good, "Productivity in the Retail Grocery Trade," *Journal of Retailing* 60, no. 3 (1984).
2. "Burgers from the Garden," *Consumer Reports,* July 1997, p. 36.
3. Adapted from J. Zhou and S. Smith, "Measurement of Ozone Concentrations in Ambient Air Using a Badge-Type Passive Monitor," *Journal of the Air & Waste Management Association* (June 1997):697.
4. "2001 Academic Performance Index (API) report," *The Press-Enterprise* (Riverside, CA), 16 October 2001, p. A8.
5. R. Blair and R. Miser, "Biotin Bioavailability from Protein Supplements and Cereal Grains for Growing Broiler Chickens," *International Journal of Vitamin and Nutrition Research* 59 (1989):55–58.
6. "Round-Trip Fares on America's Most Popular Routes," *Consumer Reports,* July 1997, p. 25.
7. Jeff Howe, "Total Control," *American Demographics,* July 2001, p. 30.
8. "Tuna Goes Upscale," *Consumer Reports,* June 2001, p. 19.
9. *Automotive News: 1997 Market Data Book,* 28 May 1997, p. 50; and 2001 Market Data Book (online), www.autonews.com/datacenter.cms, 20 September 2001.

14

Analysis of Categorical Data

Case Study

How do you rate your library? Is the atmosphere friendly, dull, or too quiet? Is the library staff helpful? Are the signs clear and unambiguous? The modern consumer-led approach to marketing, in general, involves the systematic study by organizations of their customers' wants and needs in order to improve their services or products. In the case study at the end of this chapter, we examine the results of a study to explore the attitudes of young adults toward the services provided by libraries.

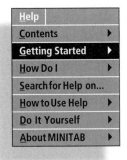

General Objectives

Many types of surveys and experiments result in qualitative rather than quantitative response variables, so that the responses can be classified but not quantified. Data from these experiments consist of the count or number of observations that fall into each of the response categories included in the experiment. In this chapter, we are concerned with methods for analyzing categorical data.

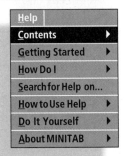

Specific Topics

1. The multinomial experiment (14.1)
2. Pearson's chi-square statistic (14.2)
3. A test of specified cell probabilities (14.3)
4. Contingency tables (14.4)
5. Comparing several multinomial populations (14.5)
6. Other applications (14.7)
7. Assumptions for chi-square tests (14.7)

14.1   A Description of the Experiment

Many experiments result in measurements that are *qualitative* or *categorical* rather than *quantitative*; that is, a *quality* or *characteristic* (rather than a numerical value) is measured for each experimental unit. You can summarize this type of data by creating a list of the categories or characteristics and reporting a **count** of the number of measurements that fall into each category. Here are a few examples:

- People can be classified into five income brackets.

- A mouse can respond in one of three ways to a stimulus.

- An M&M can have one of six colors.

- An industrial process manufactures items that can be classified as "acceptable," "second quality," or "defective."

These are some of the many situations in which the data set has characteristics appropriate for the **multinomial experiment.**

The Multinomial Experiment

- The experiment consists of n identical trials.
- The outcome of each trial falls into one of k categories.
- The probability that the outcome of a single trial falls into a particular category—say, category i—is p_i and remains constant from trial to trial. This probability must be between 0 and 1, for each of the k categories, and the sum of all k probabilities is $\Sigma p_i = 1$.
- The trials are independent.
- The experimenter counts the *observed* number of outcomes in each category, written as $O_1, O_2, \ldots, O_k$, with $O_1 + O_2 + \cdots + O_k = n$.

You can visualize the multinomial experiment by thinking of k boxes or **cells** into which n balls are tossed. The n tosses are independent, and on each toss the chance of hitting the ith box is the same. However, this chance can vary from box to box; it might be easier to hit box 1 than box 3 on each toss. Once all n balls have been tossed, the number in each box or **cell**—$O_1, O_2, \ldots, O_k$—is counted.

You have probably noticed the similarity between the *multinomial experiment* and the *binomial experiment* introduced in Chapter 5. In fact, when there are $k = 2$ categories, the two experiments are identical, except for notation. Instead of p and q, we write p_1 and p_2 to represent the probabilities for the two categories, "success" and "failure." Instead of x and $(n - x)$, we write O_1 and O_2 to represent the observed number of "successes" and "failures."

When we presented the binomial random variable, we made inferences about the binomial parameter p (and by default, $q = 1 - p$) using large-sample methods based on the z statistic. In this chapter, we extend this idea to make inferences about the *multinomial parameters*, $p_1, p_2, \ldots, p_k$, using a different type of statistic. This statistic, whose approximate sampling distribution was derived by a British statistician named Karl Pearson in 1900, is called the **chi-square** (or sometimes **Pearson's chi-square**) **statistic.**

14.2 Pearson's Chi-Square Statistic

Suppose that $n = 100$ balls are tossed at the cells (boxes) and you know that the probability of a ball falling into the first box is $p_1 = .1$. How many balls would you *expect* to fall into the first box? Intuitively, you would expect to see $100(.1) = 10$ balls in the first box. This should remind you of the average or expected number of successes, $\mu = np$, in the binomial experiment. In general, the expected number of balls that fall into cell i—written as E_i—can be calculated using the formula

$$E_i = np_i$$

for any of the cells $i = 1, 2, \ldots, k$.

Now suppose that you *hypothesize* values for each of the probabilities $p_1, p_2, \ldots, p_k$ and calculate the expected number for each category or cell. If your hypothesis is correct, the actual *observed cell counts*, O_i, should not be too different from the *expected cell counts*, $E_i = np_i$. The larger the differences, the more likely it is that the hypothesis is incorrect. The *Pearson chi-square statistic* uses the differences $(O_i - E_i)$ by first squaring these differences to eliminate negative contributions, and then forming a *weighted* average of the squared differences.

Pearson's Chi-Square Test Statistic

$$X^2 = \Sigma \frac{(O_i - E_i)^2}{E_i}$$

summed over all k cells, with $E_i = np_i$.

Although the mathematical proof is beyond the scope of this book, it can be shown that when n is large, X^2 has an approximate **chi-square probability distribution** in repeated sampling. If the hypothesized expected cell counts are correct, the differences $(O_i - E_i)$ are small and X^2 is close to 0. But, if the hypothesized probabilities are incorrect, large differences $(O_i - E_i)$ result in a *large* value of X^2. You should use a **right-tailed statistical test** and look for an unusually large value of the test statistic.

The chi-square distribution was used in Chapter 10 to make inferences about a single population variance σ^2. Like the F distribution, its shape is not symmetric and depends on a specific number of **degrees of freedom.** Once these degrees of freedom are specified, you can use Table 5 in Appendix I to find critical values or to bound the p-value for a particular chi-square statistic. As an alternative, you can use the **Chi-Square Probabilities** applet to find critical values or exact p-values for the test.

The appropriate degrees of freedom for the chi-square statistic vary depending on the particular application you are using. Although we will specify the appropriate degrees of freedom for the applications presented in this chapter, you should use the general rule given next for determining degrees of freedom for the chi-square statistic.

Help
Contents ▶
Getting Started ▶
How Do I ▶
Search for Help on...
How to Use Help ▶
Do It Yourself ▶
About MINITAB ▶

Determine the Appropriate Number of Degrees of Freedom?

1. Start with the number of *categories* or cells in the experiment.
2. Subtract one degree of freedom for each linear restriction on the cell probabilities. You will always lose one *df* because $p_1 + p_2 + \cdots + p_k = 1$.

(continued)

Determine the Appropriate Number of Degrees of Freedom? *(continued)*

3. Sometimes the expected cell counts cannot be calculated directly but must be estimated using the sample data. Subtract one degree of freedom for every independent population parameter that must be estimated to obtain the estimated values of E_i.

We begin with the simplest applications of the chi-square test statistic—the **goodness-of-fit** test.

14.3 Testing Specified Cell Probabilities: The Goodness-of-Fit Test

The simplest hypothesis concerning the cell probabilities specifies a numerical value for each cell. The expected cell counts are easily calculated using the hypothesized probabilities, $E_i = np_i$, and are used to calculate the observed value of the X^2 test statistic. For a multinomial experiment consisting of k categories or cells, the test statistic has an approximate χ^2 statistic with $df = (k - 1)$.

EXAMPLE 14.1   A researcher designs an experiment in which a rat is attracted to the end of a ramp that divides, leading to doors of three different colors. The researcher sends the rat down the ramp $n = 90$ times and observes the choices listed in Table 14.1. Does the rat have (or acquire) a preference for one of the three doors?

TABLE 14.1
Rat's Door Choices

	Door		
	Green	Red	Blue
Observed Count (O_i)	20	39	31

Solution   If the rat has no preference in the choice of a door, you would expect in the long run that the rat would choose each door an equal number of times. That is, the null hypothesis is

$$H_0 : p_1 = p_2 = p_3 = \frac{1}{3}$$

versus the alternative hypothesis

$$H_a : \text{At least one } p_i \text{ is different from } \frac{1}{3}$$

where p_i is the probability that the rat chooses door i, for $i = 1, 2,$ and 3. The expected cell counts are the same for each of the three categories—namely, $np_i = 90(1/3) = 30$. The chi-square test statistic can now be calculated as

$$X^2 = \Sigma \frac{(O_i - E_i)^2}{E_i}$$

$$= \frac{(20 - 30)^2}{30} + \frac{(39 - 30)^2}{30} + \frac{(31 - 30)^2}{30} = 6.067$$

For this example, the test statistic has $(k - 1) = 2$ degrees of freedom because the only linear restriction on the cell probabilities is that they must sum to 1. Hence, you can use Table 5 in Appendix I to find bounds for the right-tailed p-value. Since the observed value, $X^2 = 6.067$, lies between $\chi^2_{.050} = 5.99$ and $\chi^2_{.025} = 7.38$, the p-value is between .025 and .050. The researcher would report the results as significant at the 5% level ($P < .05$), meaning that the null hypothesis of no preference is rejected. There is sufficient evidence to indicate that the rat has a preference for one of the three doors.

What more can you say about the experiment once you have determined statistically that the rat has a preference? Look at the data to see where the differences lie. **The Goodness-of-Fit Test** applet, shown in Figure 14.1, will help.

FIGURE 14.1
Goodness-of-Fit applet

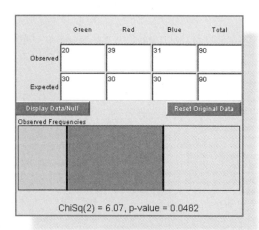

You can see the value of X^2 and its exact p-value (.0482) at the bottom of the applet. Just above them, the shaded bar shows the distribution of the observed frequencies. The blue bars represent categories that have an excess of observations relative to expected and red cells (gray in Figure 14.1) indicate a deficit of observations relative to expected. The intensity of the color reflects the magnitude of the discrepancy. For this example, that rat chose the red and blue doors more often than expected, and the green door less often. The blue door was chosen only a little more than one-third of the time:

$$\frac{31}{90} = .344$$

However, the sample proportions for the other two doors are quite different from one-third. The rat chooses the green door least often—only 22% of the time:

$$\frac{20}{90} = .222$$

The rat chooses the red door most often—43% of the time:

$$\frac{39}{90} = .433$$

You would summarize the results of the experiment by saying that the rat has a preference for the red door. Can you conclude that the preference is *caused* by the door color? The answer is no—the cause could be some other physiological or psychological factor that you have not yet explored. Avoid declaring a *causal* relationship between color and preference!

EXAMPLE 14.2   The proportions of blood phenotypes A, B, AB, and O in the population of all Caucasians in the United States are .41, .10, .04, and .45, respectively. To determine whether or not the actual population proportions fit this set of reported probabilities, a random sample of 200 Americans were selected and their blood phenotypes were recorded. The observed and expected cell counts are shown in Table 14.2. The expected cell counts are calculated as $E_i = 200p_i$. Test the goodness of fit of these blood phenotype proportions.

TABLE 14.2
Counts of blood phenotypes

	A	B	AB	O
Observed (O_i)	89	18	12	81
Expected (E_i)	82	20	8	90

Solution
The hypothesis to be tested is determined by the model probabilities:

$$H_0 : p_1 = .41; p_2 = .10; p_3 = .04; p_4 = .45$$

versus

$$H_a : \text{At least one of the four probabilities is different from the specified value}$$

Then

$$X^2 = \Sigma \frac{(O_i - E_i)^2}{E_i}$$
$$= \frac{(89 - 82)^2}{82} + \cdots + \frac{(81 - 90)^2}{90} = 3.70$$

From Table 5 in Appendix I, indexing $df = (k - 1) = 3$, you can find that the observed value of the test statistic is less than $\chi^2_{.100} = 6.25$, so that the p-value is greater than .10. You do not have sufficient evidence to reject H_0; that is, you cannot declare that the blood phenotypes for American Caucasians are *different* from those reported earlier. The results are nonsignificant (NS).

The second of the **Goodness-of-Fit** applet gives a visual display of the similarities and differences between observed and expected cell counts.

Notice the difference in the goodness-of-fit hypothesis compared to other hypotheses that you have tested. In the goodness-of-fit test, the researcher uses the null hypothesis to specify the model he believes to be *true,* rather than a model he hopes to prove false! When you could not reject H_0 in the blood type example, the results were as expected. Be careful, however, when you report your results for goodness-of-fit tests. You cannot declare with confidence that the model is absolutely correct without reporting the value of β for some practical alternatives.

Exercises

Basic Techniques

14.1 List the characteristics of a multinomial experiment.

14.2 Use Table 5 in Appendix I to find the value of χ^2 with the following area α to its right:

a. $\alpha = .05$, $df = 3$ **b.** $\alpha = .01$, $df = 8$

14.3 Give the rejection region for a chi-square test of specified probabilities if the experiment involves k categories in these cases:

a. $k = 7$, $\alpha = .05$ **b.** $k = 10$, $\alpha = .01$

14.4 Use Table 5 in Appendix I to bound the p-value for a chi-square test:

a. $X^2 = 4.29$, $df = 5$ **b.** $X^2 = 20.62$, $df = 6$

14.5   Suppose that a response can fall into one of $k = 5$ categories with probabilities $p_1, p_2, \ldots, p_5$ and that $n = 300$ responses produced these category counts:

Category	1	2	3	4	5
Observed Count	47	63	74	51	65

    a. Are the five categories equally likely to occur? How would you test this hypothesis?

    b. If you were to test this hypothesis using the chi-square statistic, how many degrees of freedom would the test have?

    c. Find the critical value of χ^2 that defines the rejection region with $\alpha = .05$.

    d. Calculate the observed value of the test statistic.

    e. Conduct the test and state your conclusions.

14.6   Suppose that a response can fall into one of $k = 3$ categories with probabilities $p_1 = .4$, $p_2 = .3$, and $p_3 = .3$, and $n = 300$ responses produce these category counts:

Category	1	2	3
Observed Count	130	98	72

Do the data provide sufficient evidence to indicate that the cell probabilities are different from those specified for the three categories? Find the approximate p-value and use it to make your decision.

Applications

14.7   A city expressway with four lanes in each direction was studied to see whether drivers prefer to drive on the inside lanes. A total of 1000 automobiles were observed during heavy early-morning traffic, and the number of cars in each lane was recorded:

Lane	1	2	3	4
Observed Count	294	276	238	192

Do the data present sufficient evidence to indicate that some lanes are preferred over others? Test using $\alpha = .05$. If there are any differences, discuss the nature of the differences.

14.8   A peony plant with red petals was crossed with another plant having streaky petals. A geneticist states that 75% of the offspring from this cross will have red flowers. To test this claim, 100 seeds from this cross were collected and germinated, and 58 plants had red petals. Use the chi-square goodness-of-fit test to determine whether the sample data confirm the geneticist's prediction.

14.9   Do you hate Mondays? Researchers from Germany have provided another reason for you: They concluded that the risk of a heart attack for a working person may be as much as 50% greater on Monday than on any other day.[1] The researchers kept track of heart attacks and coronary arrests over a period of 5 years among 330,000 people who lived near Augsburg, Germany. In an attempt to verify their claim, they surveyed 200 working people who had recently had heart attacks and recorded the day on which their heart attacks occurred:

Day	Sunday	Monday	Tuesday	Wednesday	Thursday	Friday	Saturday
Observed Count	24	36	27	26	32	26	29

Do the data present sufficient evidence to indicate that there is a difference in the incidence of heart attacks depending on the day of the week? Test using $\alpha = .05$.

14.10   Medical statistics show that deaths due to four major diseases—call them A, B, C, and D—account for 15%, 21%, 18%, and 14%, respectively, of all nonaccidental deaths. A study of the causes of 308 nonaccidental deaths at a hospital gave the following counts:

Disease	A	B	C	D	Other
Deaths	43	76	85	21	83

Do these data provide sufficient evidence to indicate that the proportions of people dying of diseases A, B, C, and D at this hospital differ from the proportions accumulated for the population at large?

14.11   Research has suggested a link between the prevalence of schizophrenia and birth during particular months of the year in which viral infections are prevalent. Suppose you are working on a similar problem and you suspect a linkage between a disease observed in later life and month of birth. You have records of 400 cases of the disease, and you classify them according to month of birth. The data appear in the table. Do the data present sufficient evidence to indicate that the proportion of cases of the disease per month varies from month to month? Test with $\alpha = .05$.

Month	Jan	Feb	Mar	Apr	May	June	July	Aug	Sept	Oct	Nov	Dec
Births	38	31	42	46	28	31	24	29	33	36	27	35

14.12   Suppose you are interested in following two independent traits in snap peas—seed texture (S = smooth, s = wrinkled) and seed color (Y = yellow, y = green)—in a second-generation cross of heterozygous parents. Mendelian theory states that the number of peas classified as smooth and yellow, wrinkled and yellow, smooth and green, and wrinkled and green should be in the ratio 9:3:3:1. Suppose that 100 randomly selected snap peas have 56, 19, 17, and 8 in these respective categories. Do these data indicate that the 9:3:3:1 model is correct? Test using $\alpha = .01$.

14.13   The Mars Company website reports the following percentages of the various colors of its M&M® candies for the "plain" variety[2]:

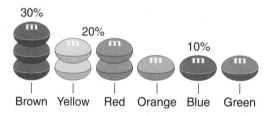

A 1-pound bag of plain M&Ms is randomly selected and contains 176 brown, 135 yellow, 79 red, 41 orange, 36 green, and 38 blue candies. Do the data substantiate the percentages reported by the Mars Company? Use the appropriate test and describe the nature of the differences, if there are any.

14.4   Contingency Tables: A Two-Way Classification

In some situations, the researcher classifies an experimental unit according to *two qualitative variables* to generate *bivariate data,* which we discussed in Chapter 3.

- A defective piece of furniture is classified according to the type of defect and the production shift during which it was made.
- A professor is classified by professional rank and the type of university (public or private) at which she works.

- A patient is classified according to the type of preventive flu treatment he received and whether or not he contracted the flu during the winter.

When two *categorical variables* are recorded, you can summarize the data by counting the observed number of units that fall into each of the various intersections of category levels. The resulting counts are displayed in an array called a **contingency table.**

EXAMPLE 14.3

A total of $n = 309$ furniture defects were recorded and the defects were classified into four types: A, B, C, or D. At the same time, each piece of furniture was identified by the production shift in which it was manufactured. These counts are presented in a contingency table in Table 14.3.

TABLE 14.3
Contingency Table

Type of Defects	Shift 1	2	3	Total
A	15	26	33	74
B	21	31	17	69
C	45	34	49	128
D	13	5	20	38
Total	94	96	119	309

When you study data that involves two variables, one important consideration is the *relationship between the two variables*. Does the proportion of measurements in the various categories for factor 1 depend on which category of factor 2 is being observed? For the furniture example, do the proportions of the various defects vary from shift to shift, or are these proportions the same, independently of which shift is observed? You may remember a similar phenomenon called *interaction* in the $a \times b$ factorial experiment from Chapter 11. In the analysis of a contingency table, the objective is to determine whether or not one method of classification is **contingent** or **dependent** on the other method of classification. If not, the two methods of classification are said to be **independent.**

The Chi-Square Test of Independence

The question of independence of the two methods of classification can be investigated using a test of hypothesis based on the chi-square statistic. These are the hypotheses:

$$H_0 : \text{The two methods of classification are independent}$$
$$H_a : \text{The two methods of classification are dependent}$$

Suppose we denote the observed cell count in row i and column j of the contingency table as O_{ij}. If you knew the expected cell counts ($E_{ij} = np_{ij}$) under the null hypothesis of independence, then you could use the chi-square statistic to compare the observed and expected counts. However, the expected values are not specified in H_0, as they were in previous examples.

To explain how to estimate these expected cell counts, we must revisit the concept of *independent events* from Chapter 4. Consider p_{ij}, the probability that an observation falls into row i and column j of the contingency table. If the rows and columns are independent, then

$$p_{ij} = P(\text{observation falls in row } i \text{ and column } j)$$
$$= P(\text{observation falls in row } i) \times P(\text{observation falls in column } j)$$
$$= p_i p_j$$

where p_i and p_j are the **unconditional** or **marginal probabilities** of falling into row i or column j, respectively. If you could obtain proper estimates of these marginal probabilities, you could use them in place of p_{ij} in the formula for the expected cell count.

Fortunately, these estimates do exist. In fact, they are exactly what you would intuitively choose:

- To estimate a row probability, use $\hat{p}_i = \dfrac{\text{Total observations in row } i}{\text{Total number of observations}} = \dfrac{r_i}{n}$.

- To estimate a column probability, use $\hat{p}_j = \dfrac{\text{Total observations in column } j}{\text{Total number of observations}} = \dfrac{c_j}{n}$.

The estimate of the expected cell count for row i and column j follows from the independence assumption.

Estimated Expected Cell Count

$$\hat{E}_{ij} = n\left(\frac{r_i}{n}\right)\left(\frac{c_j}{n}\right) = \frac{r_i c_j}{n}$$

where r_i is the total for row i and c_j is the total for column j.

The chi-square test statistic for a contingency table with r rows and c columns is calculated as

$$X^2 = \Sigma \frac{(O_{ij} - \hat{E}_{ij})^2}{\hat{E}_{ij}}$$

and can be shown to have an approximate chi-square distribution with

$$df = (r - 1)(c - 1)$$

If the observed value of X^2 is too large, then the null hypothesis of independence is rejected.

EXAMPLE 14.4   Refer to Example 14.3. Do the data present sufficient evidence to indicate that the type of furniture defect varies with the shift during which the piece of furniture is produced?

Solution   The estimated expected cell counts are shown in parentheses in Table 14.4. For example, the estimated expected count for a type C defect produced during the second shift is

$$\hat{E}_{32} = \frac{r_3 c_2}{n} = \frac{(128)(96)}{309} = 39.77$$

TABLE 14.4
Observed and estimated expected cell counts

| Type of Defects | Shift | | | |
	1	2	3	Total
A	15 (22.51)	26 (22.99)	33 (28.50)	74
B	21 (20.99)	31 (21.44)	17 (26.57)	69
C	45 (38.94)	34 (39.77)	49 (49.29)	128
D	13 (11.56)	5 (11.81)	20 (14.63)	38
Total	94	96	119	309

You can now use the values shown in Table 14.4 to calculate the test statistic as

$$X^2 = \Sigma \frac{(O_{ij} - \hat{E}_{ij})^2}{\hat{E}_{ij}}$$

$$= \frac{(15 - 22.51)^2}{22.51} + \frac{(26 - 22.99)^2}{22.99} + \cdots + \frac{(20 - 14.63)^2}{14.63}$$

$$= 19.18$$

When you index the chi-square distribution in Table 5 of Appendix I with

$$df = (r - 1)(c - 1) = (4 - 1)(3 - 1) = 6$$

the observed test statistic is greater than $\chi^2_{.005} = 18.5476$, which indicates that the *p*-value is less than .005. You can reject H_0 and declare the results to be highly significant ($P < .005$). There is sufficient evidence to indicate that the proportions of defect types vary from shift to shift.

The next obvious question you should ask involves the nature of the relationship between the two classifications. Which shift produces more of which type of defect? As with the factorial experiment in Chapter 11, once a dependence (or interaction) is found, you must look within the table at the relative or *conditional* proportions for each level of classification. For example, consider shift 1, which produced a total of 94 defects. These defects can be divided into types using the *conditional proportions* for this sample shown in the first column of Table 14.5. If you follow the same procedure for the other two shifts, you can then compare the distributions of defect types for the three shifts, as shown in Table 14.5.

TABLE 14.5
Conditional probabilities for types of defect within three shifts

	Shift		
Types of Defects	1	2	3
A	$\frac{15}{94} = .16$	$\frac{26}{96} = .27$	$\frac{33}{119} = .28$
B	$\frac{21}{94} = .22$	$\frac{31}{96} = .32$	$\frac{17}{119} = .14$
C	$\frac{45}{94} = .48$	$\frac{34}{96} = .35$	$\frac{49}{119} = .41$
D	$\frac{13}{94} = .14$	$\frac{5}{96} = .05$	$\frac{20}{119} = .17$
Total	1.00	1.00	1.00

Now compare the three sets of proportions (each sums to 1). It appears that shifts 1 and 2 produce defects in the same general order—types C, B, A, and D from most to least—though in differing proportions. Shift 3 shows a different pattern—the most type C defects again but followed by types A, D, and B in that order. Depending on which type of defect is the most important to the manufacturer, each shift should be cautioned separately about the reasons for producing too many defects.

Help

Contents ▶

Getting Started ▶

How Do I ▶

Search for Help on...

How to Use Help ▶

Do It Yourself ▶

About MINITAB ▶

DO IT YOURSELF!

The **Chi-Square Test of Independence** applet can help you visualize the distribution of the observed frequencies. In Figure 14.2(a), the blue bars represent categories that have an excess of defectives relative to expected and red cells (gray in Figure 14.2) indicate a deficit of defectives relative to expected. The intensity of the color reflects the magnitude of the discrepancy. In Figure 14.2(b), we used the [Data/Null] button to view the expected distribution of defectives if the null hypothesis is true. The relative heights of the rectangles in each of the three columns correspond to the conditional distribution of defectives per shift given in Table 14.5. We will use this applet for the *Do It Yourself Exercises* at the end of the chapter.

FIGURE 14.2
Chi-Square Test of Independence applet

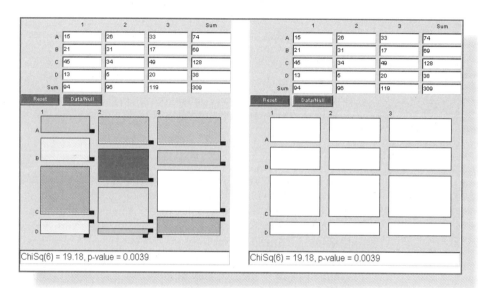

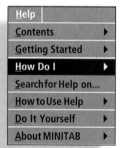

Determine the Appropriate Number of Degrees of Freedom?

Remember the general procedure for determining degrees of freedom:

1. Start with $k = rc$ categories or cells in the contingency table.
2. Subtract one degree of freedom because all of the rc cell probabilities must sum to 1.
3. You had to estimate $(r - 1)$ row probabilities and $(c - 1)$ column probabilities to calculate the estimated expected cell counts. (The last one of the row and column probabilities is determined because the *marginal* row and column probabilities must also sum to 1.) Subtract $(r - 1)$ and $(c - 1)$ *df*.

The total degrees of freedom for the $r \times c$ contingency table are

$$df = rc - 1 - (r - 1) - (c - 1) = rc - r - c + 1 = (r - 1)(c - 1)$$

EXAMPLE 14.5 A survey was conducted to evaluate the effectiveness of a new flu vaccine that had been administered in a small community. The vaccine was provided free of charge in a two-shot sequence over a period of 2 weeks. Some people received the two-shot sequence, some appeared for only the first shot, and others received neither. A survey of 1000 local residents the following spring provided the information shown in Table 14.6. Do the data present sufficient evidence to indicate that the vaccine was successful in reducing the number of flu cases in the community?

TABLE 14.6
2 × 3 contingency table

	No Vaccine	One Shot	Two Shots	Total
Flu	24	9	13	46
No Flu	289	100	565	954
Total	313	109	578	1000

Solution   The success of the vaccine in reducing the number of flu cases can be assessed in two parts:

- If the vaccine is successful, the proportions of people who get the flu should vary, depending on which of the three treatments they received.
- Not only must this dependence exist, but the proportion of people who get the flu should decrease as the amount of flu prevention treatment increases—from zero to one to two shots.

The first part can be tested using the chi-square test with these hypotheses:

H_0 : No relationship between treatment and incidence of flu

H_a : Incidence of flu depends on amount of flu treatment

As usual, computer software packages can eliminate all of the tedious calculations and, if the data are entered correctly, provide the correct output containing the observed value of the test statistic and its *p*-value. Such a printout, generated by *MINITAB*, is shown in Figure 14.3. You can find instructions for generating this printout in the section "About *MINITAB*" at the end of this chapter. The observed value of the test statistic, $X^2 = 17.313$, has a *p*-value of .000 and the results are declared highly significant. That is, the null hypothesis is rejected. There is sufficient evidence to indicate a relationship between treatment and incidence of flu.

FIGURE 14.3
MINITAB output for Example 14.5

Chi-Square Test: No Vaccine, One Shot, Two Shots

```
Expected counts are printed below observed counts

          No Vaccine One Shot Two Shots    Total
      1       24          9        13        46
            14.40       5.01     26.59

      2      289        100       565       954
           298.60     103.99    551.41

  Total      313        109       578      1000

Chi-Sq =   6.404 +   3.169 +   6.944 +
           0.309 +   0.153 +   0.335 = 17.313
DF = 2, P-Value = 0.000
```

What is the nature of this relationship? To answer this question, look at Table 14.7 and Figure 14.4, which give the *incidence* of flu in the sample for each of the three treatment groups. The answer is obvious. The group that received two shots was less susceptible to the flu; only one flu shot does not seem to decrease the susceptibility!

TABLE 14.7
Incidence of flu for three treatments

No Vaccine	One Shot	Two Shots
$\dfrac{24}{313} = .08$	$\dfrac{9}{109} = .08$	$\dfrac{13}{578} = .02$

FIGURE 14.4
Chi-Square Test of Independence applet

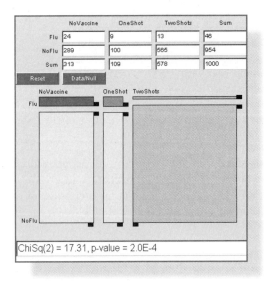

Exercises

Basic Techniques

14.14 Calculate the value and give the number of degrees of freedom for X^2 for these contingency tables:

a.
	Columns			
Rows	1	2	3	4
1	120	70	55	16
2	79	108	95	43
3	31	49	81	140

b.
	Columns		
Rows	1	2	3
1	35	16	84
2	120	92	206

14.15 Suppose that a consumer survey summarizes the responses of $n = 307$ people in a contingency table that contains three rows and five columns. How many degrees of freedom are associated with the chi-square test statistic?

14.16 A survey of 400 respondents produced these cell counts in a 2×3 contingency table:

	Columns			
Rows	1	2	3	Total
1	37	34	93	164
2	66	57	113	236
Total	103	91	206	400

a. If you wish to test the null hypothesis of "independence"—that the probability that a response falls in any one row is independent of the column it falls in—and you plan to use a chi-square test, how many degrees of freedom will be associated with the χ^2 statistic?

b. Find the value of the test statistic.

c. Find the rejection region for $\alpha = .01$.

d. Conduct the test and state your conclusions.

e. Find the approximate p-value for the test and interpret its value.

14.17   Male and female respondents to a questionnaire on gender differences were categorized into three groups according to their answers on the first question:

	Group 1	Group 2	Group 3
Men	37	49	72
Women	7	50	31

Use the *MINITAB* printout to determine whether there is a difference in the responses according to gender. Explain the nature of the differences, if any exist.

MINITAB output for Exercise 14.17

Chi-Square Test: Group 1, Group 2, Group 3

```
Chi-Sq =  2.703 +  3.346 +  0.517 +
          4.853 +  6.007 +  0.927 = 18.352
DF = 2, P-Value = 0.000
```

Applications

14.18   Is there a generation gap? A sample of adult Americans of three different generations were asked to agree or disagree with this statement: If I had the chance to start over in life, I would do things differently.[3] The results are given in the table. Do the data indicate a generation gap for this particular question? That is, does a person's opinion change depending on the generation group from which he or she comes? If so, describe the nature of the differences. Use $\alpha = .05$.

	GenXers (born 1965–1976)	Boomers (born 1946–1964)	Matures (born before 1946)
Agree	118	213	88
Disagree	80	87	61

14.19   A study was conducted by Joseph Jacobson and Diane Wille to determine the effect of early child care on infant–mother attachment patterns.[4] In the study, 93 infants were classified as either "secure" or "anxious" using the Ainsworth strange situation paradigm. In addition, the infants were classified according to the average number of hours per week that they spent in child care. The data are presented in the table:

	Low (0–3 hours)	Moderate (4–19 hours)	High (20–54 hours)
Secure	24	35	5
Anxious	11	10	8

a. Do the data provide sufficient evidence to indicate that there is a difference in attachment pattern for the infants depending on the amount of time spent in child care? Test using $\alpha = .05$.

b. What is the approximate p-value for the test in part a?

14.20   Is there a difference in the spending patterns of high school seniors depending on their gender? A study to investigate this question focused on 196 employed high school seniors. Students were asked to classify the amount of their earnings that they spent on their car during a given month:

	None or Only a Little	Some	About Half	Most	All or Almost All
Male	73	12	6	4	3
Female	57	15	11	9	6

A portion of the *MINITAB* printout is given here. Use the printout to analyze the relationship between spending patterns and gender. Write a short paragraph explaining your statistical conclusions and their practical implications.

MINITAB output for Exercise 14.20

Chi-Square Test: None, Some, Half, Most, All

```
Chi-Sq =  0.985 +  0.167 +  0.735 +  0.962 +  0.500 +
          0.985 +  0.167 +  0.735 +  0.962 +  0.500 = 6.696
DF = 4, P-Value = 0.153
2 cells with expected counts less than 5.0
```

14.21 How long do you wait to have your prescriptions filled? "About 3 in 10 Americans wait more than 20 minutes to have a prescription filled."[5] Supppose a comparison of waiting times for pharmacies in HMOs and pharmacies in drugstores produced the following results.

Waiting Time	HMO	Drugstores
≤ 15 minutes	75	119
16–20 minutes	44	21
> 20 minutes	21	37
Don't know	10	23

a. Is there sufficient evidence to indicate that there is a difference in waiting times for pharmacies in HMOs and pharmacies in drugstores? Use $\alpha = .01$.

b. If we consider only if the waiting time is more than 20 minutes, is there a significant difference in waiting times between pharmacies in HMOs and pharmacies in drugstores at the 1% level of significance?

14.22 Title IX programs mandated that colleges should have equal opportunities for men and women to participate in college sports programs.[6] The table that follows shows the number of colleges that support women's teams in these sports.

EX1422

	Women's Sports					
Years	Basketball	Track	Golf	Soccer	Lacrosse	Rowing
1986–87	275	215	99	54	34	27
1999–00	317	276	192	260	75	71

a. Do these data provide sufficient evidence to conclude that there is a difference in the distribution of women participating in these sports for the years indicated?

b. If there is a significant difference in part a, describe the nature of these differences.

14.5 ## Comparing Several Multinomial Populations: A Two-Way Classification with Fixed Row or Column Totals

An $r \times c$ contingency table results when each of n experimental units is counted as falling into one of the rc cells of a multinomial experiment. Each cell represents a pair of category levels—row level i and column level j. Sometimes, however, it is not advisable to use this type of experimental design—that is, to let the n observations fall where they may. For example, suppose you want to study the opinions of American families about their income levels—say, low, medium, and high. If you randomly select $n = 1200$ families for your survey, you may not find any who classify themselves as low-income families! It might be better to decide ahead of time to survey 400 families in each income level. The resulting data will still appear as a two-way classification, but the column totals are fixed in advance.

EXAMPLE 14.6 In another flu prevention experiment like Example 14.5, the experimenter decides to search the clinic records for 300 patients in each of the three treatment categories: no vaccine, one shot, and two shots. The $n = 900$ patients will then be surveyed regarding their winter flu history. The experiment results in a 2×3 table with the column totals fixed at 300, shown in Table 14.8. By fixing the column totals, the experimenter no longer has a multinomial experiment with $2 \times 3 = 6$ cells. Instead, there are three separate binomial experiments—call them 1, 2, and 3—each with a given probability p_j of contracting the flu and q_j of not contracting the flu. (Remember that for a binomial population, $p_j + q_j = 1$.)

TABLE 14.8
Cases of flu for three treatments

	No Vaccine	One Shot	Two Shots	Total
Flu				r_1
No Flu				r_2
Total	300	300	300	n

Suppose you used the chi-square test to test for the independence of row and column classifications. If a particular treatment (column level) does not affect the incidence of flu, then each of the three binomial populations should have the same incidence of flu so that $p_1 = p_2 = p_3$ and $q_1 = q_2 = q_3$.

The 2×3 classification in Example 14.6 describes a situation in which the chi-square test of independence is equivalent to a test of the equality of $c = 3$ binomial proportions. Tests of this type are called **tests of homogeneity** and are used to compare several binomial populations. If there are *more than two* row categories with fixed column totals, then the test of independence is equivalent to a test of the equality of c sets of multinomial proportions.

You do not need to be concerned about the theoretical equivalence of the chi-square tests for these two experimental designs. Whether the columns (or rows) are fixed or not, the test statistic is calculated as

$$X^2 = \Sigma \frac{(O_{ij} - \hat{E}_{ij})^2}{\hat{E}_{ij}} \qquad \text{where } \hat{E}_{ij} = \frac{r_i c_j}{n}$$

which has an approximate chi-square distribution in repeated sampling with $df = (r - 1)(c - 1)$.

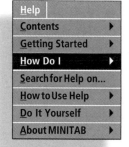

Determine the Appropriate Number of Degrees of Freedom?

Remember the general procedure for determining degrees of freedom:

1. Start with the rc cells in the two-way table.
2. Subtract one degree of freedom for each of the c multinomial populations, whose column probabilities must add to one—a total of c df.
3. You had to estimate $(r - 1)$ row probabilities, but the column probabilities are fixed in advance and did not need to be estimated. Subtract $(r - 1)$ df.

The total degrees of freedom for the $r \times c$ (fixed-column) table are

$$rc - c - (r - 1) = rc - c - r + 1 = (r - 1)(c - 1)$$

EXAMPLE **14.7**

A survey of voter sentiment was conducted in four midcity political wards to compare the fractions of voters who favor candidate A. Random samples of 200 voters were polled in each of the four wards with the results shown in Table 14.9. The values in parentheses in the table are the expected cell counts. Do the data present sufficient evidence to indicate that the fractions of voters who favor candidate A differ in the four wards?

TABLE 14.9
Voter opinions in four wards

| | Ward | | | | |
	1	2	3	4	Total
Favor A	76 (59)	53 (59)	59 (59)	48 (59)	236
Do not favor A	124 (141)	147 (141)	141 (141)	152 (141)	564
Total	200	200	200	200	800

Solution Since the column totals are fixed at 200, the design involves four binomial experiments, each containing the responses of 200 voters from each of the four wards. To test the equality of the proportions who favor candidate A in all four wards, the null hypothesis

$$H_0 : p_1 = p_2 = p_3 = p_4$$

is equivalent to the null hypothesis

H_0 : Proportion favoring candidate A is independent of ward

and will be rejected if the test statistic X^2 is too large. The observed value of the test statistic, $X^2 = 10.722$, and its associated p-value, .013, are shown in Figure 14.5. The results are significant ($P < .025$); that is, H_0 is rejected and you can conclude that there is a difference in the proportions of voters who favor candidate A among the four wards.

FIGURE 14.5
MINITAB output for Example 14.7

Chi-Square Test: Ward 1, Ward 2, Ward 3, Ward 4,

```
Expected counts are printed below observed counts

           Ward 1    Ward 2    Ward 3    Ward 4     Total
      1        76        53        59        48       236
             59.00     59.00     59.00     59.00

      2       124       147       141       152       564
            141.00    141.00    141.00    141.00

   Total      200       200       200       200       800

Chi-Sq =   4.898 +   0.610 +   0.000 +   2.051 +
           2.050 +   0.255 +   0.000 +   0.858 = 10.722
DF = 3, P-Value = 0.013
```

What is the nature of the differences discovered by the chi-square test? To answer this question, look at Table 14.10, which shows the sample proportions who favor candidate A in each of the four wards. It appears that candidate A is doing best in the first ward and worst in the fourth ward. Is this of any *practical significance* to the candidate? Possibly a more important observation is that the candidate does not have a plurality of voters in any of the four wards. If this is a two-candidate race, candidate A needs to increase his campaigning!

TABLE 14.10
Proportions in favor of candidate A in four wards

Ward 1	Ward 2	Ward 3	Ward 4
76/200 = .38	53/200 = .27	59/200 = .30	48/200 = .24

Exercises

Basic Techniques

14.23   Random samples of 200 observations were selected from each of three populations, and each observation was classified according to whether it fell into one of three mutually exclusive categories:

	Category			
Population	1	2	3	Total
1	108	52	40	200
2	87	51	62	200
3	112	39	49	200

You want to know whether the data provide sufficient evidence to indicate that the proportions of observations in the three categories depend on the population from which they were drawn.

a. Give the value of X^2 for the test.

b. Give the rejection region for the test for $\alpha = .01$.

c. State your conclusions.

d. Find the approximate p-value for the test and interpret its value.

14.24   Suppose you wish to test the null hypothesis that three binomial parameters p_A, p_B, and p_C are equal versus the alternative hypothesis that at least two of the parameters differ. Independent random samples of 100 observations were selected from each of the populations. The data are shown in the table:

	Population			
	A	B	C	Total
Successes	24	19	33	76
Failures	76	81	67	224
Total	100	100	100	300

a. Write the null and alternative hypotheses for testing the equality of the three binomial proportions.

b. Calculate the test statistic and find the approximate p-value for the test in part a.

c. Use the approximate p-value to determine the statistical significance of your results. If the results are statistically significant, explore the nature of the differences in the three binomial proportions.

Applications

14.25   How do Americans in the "sandwich generation" balance the demands of caring for older and younger relatives? In a telephone poll of Americans aged 45 to 55 years, the number providing financial support for their parents is listed in the next display?

Provide Financial Support	Yes	No
White Americans	40	160
African Americans	56	144
Hispanic Americans	68	132
Asian Americans	84	116

Is there a significant difference in the proportion of individuals providing financial support for their parents for these subpopulations of Americans? Use $\alpha = .01$.

14.26 A particular poultry disease is thought to be noncommunicable. To test this theory, 30,000 chickens were randomly partitioned into three groups of 10,000. One group had no contact with diseased chickens, one had moderate contact, and the third had heavy contact. After a 6-month period, data were collected on the number of diseased chickens in each group of 10,000. Do the data provide sufficient evidence to indicate a dependence between the amount of contact between diseased and nondiseased fowl and the incidence of the disease? Use $\alpha = .05$.

	No Contact	Moderate Contact	Heavy Contact
Disease	87	89	124
No disease	9,913	9,911	9,876
Total	10,000	10,000	10,000

EX1427

14.27 Does education really make a difference in how much money you will earn? Researchers randomly selected 100 people from each of three income categories—"marginally rich," "comfortably rich," and "super rich"—and then recorded their educational attainment, as in the table.[8]

	Marginally Rich ($70–99 K)	Comfortably Rich ($100–249 K)	Super Rich ($250 K or more)
No college	32	20	23
Some college	13	16	1
At least an undergraduate degree	43	51	60
Postgraduate study/degree	12	13	16

a. Describe the multinomial experiments whose proportions are being compared in this experiment.

b. Do these data indicate that the level of wealth is affected by educational attainment? Test at the 1% level of significance.

c. Based on the results of part b, describe the practical nature of the relationship between level of wealth and educational attainment.

14.28 W.W. Menard has conducted research involving manganese nodules, a mineral-rich concoction found abundantly on the deep-sea floor.[9] In one portion of his report, Menard provides data relating the magnetic age of the earth's crust to the "probability of finding manganese nodules." The table gives the number of samples of the earth's core and the percentage of those that contain manganese nodules for each of a set of magnetic-crust ages. Do the data provide sufficient evidence to indicate that the probability of finding manganese nodules in the deep-sea earth's crust is dependent on the magnetic-age classification?

Age	Number of Samples	Percentage with Nodules
Miocene—recent	389	5.9
Oligocene	140	17.9
Eocene	214	16.4
Paleocene	84	21.4
Late Cretaceous	247	21.1
Early and Middle Cretaceous	1120	14.2
Jurassic	99	11.0

14.6 The Equivalence of Statistical Tests

Remember that when there are only $k = 2$ categories in a multinomial experiment, the experiment reduces to a *binomial experiment* where you record the number of successes x (or O_1) in n (or $O_1 + O_2$) trials. Similarly, the data that result from *two binomial experiments* can be displayed as a two-way classification with $r = 2$ and $c = 2$, so that the chi-square test of *homogeneity* can be used to compare the two binomial proportions, p_1 and p_2. For these two situations, we have presented statistical tests for the binomial proportions based on the z-statistic of Chapter 9:

- **One sample:** $z = \dfrac{\hat{p} - p_0}{\sqrt{\dfrac{p_0 q_0}{n}}}$

$k = 2$	
Successes	Failures

- **Two samples:** $z = \dfrac{\hat{p}_1 - \hat{p}_2}{\sqrt{\hat{p}\hat{q}\left(\dfrac{1}{n_1} + \dfrac{1}{n_2}\right)}}$

$r = c = 2$	
Sample 1	**Sample 2**
Successes	Successes
Failures	Failures

Why are there two different tests for the same statistical hypothesis? Which one should you use? For these two situations, you can use *either* the z test *or* the chi-square test, and you will obtain identical results. For either the one- or two-sample test, we can prove algebraically that

$$z^2 = X^2$$

so that the test statistic z will be the square root (either positive or negative, depending on the data) of the chi-square statistic. Furthermore, we can show theoretically that the same relationship holds for the critical values in the z and χ^2 tables in Appendix I, which produces *identical p-values* for the two equivalent tests. To test a one-tailed alternative hypothesis such as $H_0: p_1 > p_2$, first determine whether $\hat{p}_1 - \hat{p}_2 > 0$, that is, if the difference in sample proportions has the appropriate sign. If so, the appropriate critical value of χ^2 from Table 5 will have one degree of freedom a right-tail area of 2α. For example, the critical χ^2 value with 1 *df* and $\alpha = .05$ will be $\chi^2_{.10} = 2.70554 = 1.645^2$.

In summary, you are free to choose the test (z or X^2) that is most convenient. Since most computer packages include the chi-square test, and most do not include the large-sample z tests, the chi-square test may be preferable to you!

14.7 Other Applications of the Chi-Square Test

The application of the chi-square test for analyzing count data is only one of many classification problems that result in multinomial data. Some of these applications are quite complex, requiring complicated or calculationally difficult procedures for estimating the expected cell counts. However, several applications are used often enough to make them worth mentioning.

- **Goodness-of-fit tests:** You can design a goodness-of-fit test to determine whether data are consistent with data drawn from a particular probability distribution—possibly the normal, binomial, Poisson, or other distributions. The cells of a sample frequency histogram correspond to the k cells of a multinomial experiment. Expected cell counts are calculated using the probabilities associated with the hypothesized probability distribution.
- **Time-dependent multinomials:** You can use the chi-square statistic to investigate the rate of change of multinomial (or binomial) proportions over time. For example, suppose that the proportion of correct answers on a 100-question exam is recorded for a student, who then repeats the exam in each of the next 4 weeks. Does the pro-

portion of correct responses increase over time? Is learning taking place? In a process monitored by a quality control plan, is there a positive trend in the proportion of defective items as a function of time?

- **Multidimensional contingency tables:** Instead of only two methods of classification, you can investigate a dependence among three or more classifications. The two-way contingency table is extended to a table in more than two dimensions. The methodology is similar to that used for the $r \times c$ contingency table, but the analysis is a bit more complex.
- **Log-linear models:** Complex models can be created in which the logarithm of the cell probability ($\ln p_{ij}$) is some linear function of the row and column probabilities.

Most of these applications are rather complex and might require that you consult a professional statistician for advice before you conduct your experiment.

In all statistical applications that use *Pearson's chi-square statistic,* assumptions must be satisfied in order that the test statistic have an approximate chi-square probability distribution.

Assumptions

- The cell counts $O_1, O_2, \ldots, O_k$ must satisfy the conditions of a multinomial experiment, or a set of multinomial experiments created by fixing either the row or column totals.
- The expected cell counts $E_1, E_2, \ldots, E_k$ should equal or exceed five.

You can usually be fairly certain that you have satisfied the first assumption by carefully preparing and designing your experiment or sample survey. When you calculate the expected cell counts, if you find that one or more is less than five, these options are available to you:

- Choose a larger sample size n. The larger the sample size, the closer the chi-square distribution will approximate the distribution of your test statistic X^2.
- It may be possible to combine one or more of the cells with small expected cell counts, thereby satisfying the assumption.

Finally, make sure that you are calculating the *degrees of freedom* correctly and that you carefully evaluate the statistical and practical conclusions that can be drawn from your test.

Key Concepts and Formulas

I. **The Multinomial Experiment**
   1. There are n identical trials, and each outcome falls into one of k categories.
   2. The probability of falling into category i is p_i and remains constant from trial to trial.
   3. The trials are independent, $\Sigma p_i = 1$, and we measure O_i, the number of observations that fall into each of the k categories.

II. **Pearson's Chi-Square Statistic**

$$X^2 = \Sigma \frac{(O_i - E_i)^2}{E_i} \qquad \text{where } E_i = np_i$$

which has an approximate chi-square distribution with *degrees of freedom* determined by the application.

III. The Goodness-of-Fit Test

1. This is a one-way classification with cell probabilities specified in H_0.
2. Use the chi-square statistic with $E_i = np_i$ calculated with the hypothesized probabilities.
3. $df = k - 1 -$ (Number of parameters estimated in order to find E_i)
4. If H_0 is rejected, investigate the nature of the differences using the sample proportions.

IV. Contingency Tables

1. A two-way classification with n observations categorized into $r \times c$ cells of a two-way table using two different methods of classification is called a *contingency table*.
2. The test for independence of classification methods uses the chi-square statistic

$$X^2 = \Sigma \frac{(O_{ij} - \hat{E}_{ij})^2}{\hat{E}_{ij}} \quad \text{with } \hat{E}_{ij} = \frac{r_i c_j}{n} \quad \text{and} \quad df = (r - 1)(c - 1)$$

3. If the null hypothesis of independence of classifications is rejected, investigate the nature of the dependence using conditional proportions within either the rows or columns of the contingency table.

V. Fixing Row or Column Totals

1. When either the row or column totals are fixed, the test of independence of classifications becomes a test of the homogeneity of cell probabilities for several multinomial experiments.
2. Use the same chi-square statistic as for contingency tables.
3. The large-sample z tests for one and two binomial proportions are special cases of the chi-square statistic.

VI. Assumptions

1. The cell counts satisfy the conditions of a multinomial experiment, or a set of multinomial experiments with fixed sample sizes.
2. All expected cell counts must equal or exceed five in order that the chi-square approximation is valid.

The Chi-Square Test

Several procedures are available in the *MINITAB* package for analyzing categorical data. The appropriate procedure depends on whether the data represent a one-way classification (a single multinomial experiment) or a two-way classification or contingency table. If the *raw categorical data* have been stored in the *MINITAB* worksheet rather than the *observed cell counts,* you may need to tally or cross-classify the data to obtain the cell counts before continuing.

For example, suppose you have recorded the gender (M or F) and the college status (Fr, So, Jr, Sr, G) for 100 statistics students. The *MINITAB* worksheet would contain two columns of 100 observations each. Each row would contain an individual's gender in column 1 and college status in column 2. To obtain the observed cell counts (O_{ij}) for the 2×5 contingency table, use **Stat → Tables → Cross Tabulation** to generate the Dialog box shown in Figure 14.6.

MINITAB

MINITAB

Select "Gender" and "Status" for the classification variables, and select **Chi-square analysis** with **Above and expected count.** This sequence of commands not only tabulates the contingency table, but also performs the chi-square test of independence and displays the results in the Session window shown in Figure 14.7. For the gender/college status data, the large p-value ($P = .153$) indicates a nonsignificant result. There is insufficient evidence to indicate that a student's gender is dependent on class status.

If the observed cell counts in the contingency table have already been tabulated, simply enter the counts into c columns of the *MINITAB* worksheet, use **Stat → Tables → Chi-Square Test,** and select the appropriate columns before clicking **OK.** For the gender/college status data, you can enter the counts into columns C3–C7 as shown in Figure 14.8. The resulting output will be labeled differently but will look exactly like the output in Figure 14.7.

A simple test of a single multinomial experiment can be set up by considering whether the proportions of male and female statistics students are the same—that is, $p_1 = .5$ and $p_2 = .5$. To obtain the observed cell counts (O_i) for the $k = 2$ cells, use **Stat → Tables → Cross Tabulation** and select *only* "gender" as the classification variable. Do not select "Chi-square analysis"; you will have to use the **Calculator**

FIGURE 14.6

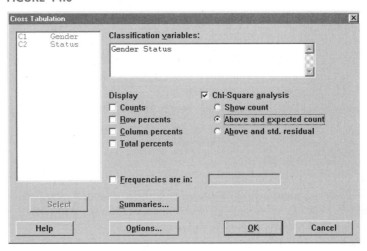

FIGURE 14.7

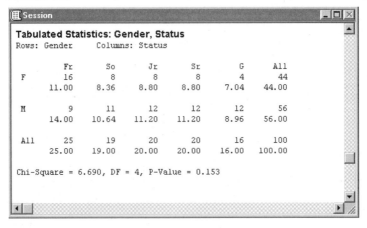

MINITAB

FIGURE 14.8

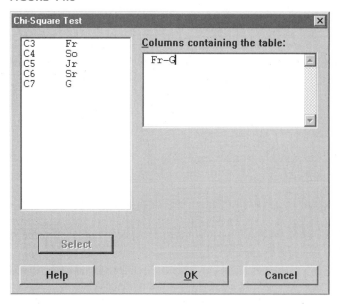

command to obtain the test statistic. Once you have determined that there are $O_1 = 44$ women and $O_2 = 56$ men in the sample, enter the observed cell counts into one column (C8) of the worksheet, and the expected cell counts, $E_1 = E_2 = 50$, into a second column (C9). Use **Calc → Calculator** and select columns and operators to form the test statistic, as shown in Figure 14.9. Store the results in some convenient location, perhaps C10. This is the observed value of the test statistic, $X^2 = 1.44$, which is not significant. There is insufficient evidence to indicate a difference in the proportion of male and female statistics students.

FIGURE 14.9

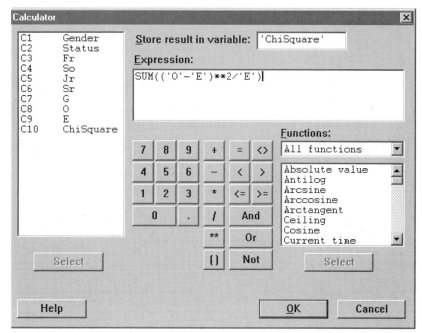

Supplementary Exercises

Starred (*) exercises are optional.

14.29 A manufacturer of floor polish conducted a consumer preference experiment to see whether a new floor polish A was superior to those produced by four competitors, B, C, D, and E. A sample of 100 housekeepers viewed five patches of flooring that had received the five polishes, and each indicated the patch that he or she considered superior in appearance. The lighting, background, and so on were approximately the same for all five patches. The results of the survey are listed here:

Polish	A	B	C	D	E
Frequency	27	17	15	22	19

Do these data present sufficient evidence to indicate a preference for one or more of the polished patches of floor over the others? If one were to reject the hypothesis of no preference for this experiment, would this imply that polish A is superior to the others? Can you suggest a better way of conducting the experiment?

14.30 A survey was conducted to investigate the interest of middle-aged adults in physical fitness programs in Rhode Island, Colorado, California, and Florida. The objective of the investigation was to determine whether adult participation in physical fitness programs varies from one region of the United States to another. A random sample of people were interviewed in each state and these data were recorded:

	Rhode Island	Colorado	California	Florida
Participate	46	63	108	121
Do not participate	149	178	192	179

Do the data indicate a difference in adult participation in physical fitness programs from one state to another? If so, describe the nature of the differences.

14.31 Accident data were analyzed to determine the numbers of fatal accidents for automobiles of three sizes. The data for 346 accidents are as follows:

	Small	Medium	Large
Fatal	67	26	16
Not fatal	128	63	46

Do the data indicate that the frequency of fatal accidents is dependent on the size of automobiles? Write a short paragraph describing your statistical results and their practical implications.

14.32 An experiment was conducted to investigate the effect of general hospital experience on the attitudes of physicians toward Medicare patients. A random sample of 50 physicians who had just completed 4 weeks of service in a general hospital and 50 physicians who had not were categorized according to their concern for Medicare patients. The data are shown in the table. Do the data provide sufficient evidence to indicate a change in "concern" after the general hospital experience? If so, describe the nature of the change.

No	Hospital Service		
Hospital Service	High	Low	Total
Low	27	5	32
High	9	9	18

MINITAB output for Exercise 14.32

Chi-Square Test: High, Low

```
Chi-Sq =  0.681 +  1.750
          1.210 +  3.111 = 6.752
DF = 1, P-Value = 0.009
```

14.33 In a telephone poll of $n = 1,262$ New York voters 795 or 63% of voters surveyed said the Port Authority of NY and NJ should rebuild the World Trade Center in some form.[10] Do these data provide sufficient evidence to indicate that a majority of New York voters would like to see the New York World Trade Center rebuilt?

a. Use a test of hypothesis based on the z-statistic to answer this question.

b. Use a χ^2-test to answer this same question.

c. How do your answers compare? Check to see that $z^2 = \chi^2$.

14.34 Does a baby's sleeping position affect the development of motor skills? In one study, 343 full-term infants were examined at their 4-month checkup for various developmental milestones, such as rolling over, grasping a rattle, and reaching for an object.[11] The baby's predominant sleep position—either prone (on the stomach) or supine (on the back) or side—was determined by a telephone interview with the parent. The sample results for 320 of the 343 infants for whom information was received are shown in the table. The researcher reported that infants who slept in the side or supine position were less likely to roll over at the 4-month checkup than infants who slept primarily in the prone position ($P < .001$).

	Prone	Supine or Side
Number of infants	121	199
Number who roll over	93	119

a. Use a large-sample z test to confirm or refute the researcher's conclusion.

b. Rewrite the sample data as a 2×2 contingency table. Use the chi-square test for homogeneity to confirm or refute the researcher's conclusion.

c. Compare the results of parts a and b. Confirm that the two test statistics are related as $z^2 = X^2$ and that the critical values for rejecting H_0 have the same relationship.

14.35 Refer to Exercise 14.34. Find the p-value for the large-sample z test in part a. Compare this p-value with the p-value for the chi-square test, shown in the *MINITAB* printout.

MINITAB output for Exercise 14.35

Chi-Square Test: Prone, Side

```
Chi-Sq =   2.056 +   1.250 +
           4.036 +   2.454 = 9.795
DF = 1,  P-Value = 0.002
```

14.36 The researchers in Exercise 14.34 also measured several other developmental milestones and their relationship to the infant's predominant sleep position.[11] The results of their research are presented in the table for the 320 infants at their 4-month checkup.

Milestone	Score	Prone	Supine or Side	P
Pulls to sit with no head lag	Pass	79	144	
	Fail	6	20	<.21
Grasps rattle	Pass	102	167	
	Fail	3	1	<.13
Reaches for object	Pass	107	183	
	Fail	3	5	<.97

Use your knowledge of the analysis of categorical data to explain the experimental design(s) used by the researchers. What hypotheses were of interest to the researchers, and what statistical test would the researchers have used? Explain the conclusions that can be drawn from the three p-values in the last column of the table and the practical implications that can be drawn from the statistical results. Have any statistical assumptions been violated?

14.37 The number of American workers who have Internet access continues to grow as recorded in the following table.[12] Two independent random samples were taken in two consecutive years.

	Had Access	Did Not Have Access	Sample Size
Last year	224	276	500
This year	328	172	500

Is there a significant difference in the proportion of workers who have access to the Internet last year compared to this year? Use $\alpha = .05$.

14.38 Is your holiday turkey safe? A "new federal survey found that 13% of turkeys are contaminated with the salmonella bacteria responsible for 1.3 million illnesses and about 500 deaths in a year in the US."[12] Use the table that follows to determine if there is a significant difference in the contamination rate at three processing plants. One hundred turkeys were randomly selected from each of the processing lines at these three plants.

Plant	Salmonella Present	Sample Size
1	42	100
2	23	100
3	22	100

Is there a significant difference in the rate of salmonella contamination among these three processing plants? If there is a significant difference, describe the nature of these differences. Use $\alpha = .01$.

14.39 A study to determine the effectiveness of a drug (serum) for arthritis resulted in the comparison of two groups, each consisting of 200 arthritic patients. One group was inoculated with the serum; the other received a placebo (an inoculation that appears to contain serum but actually is nonactive). After a period of time, each person in the study was asked to state whether his or her arthritic condition had improved. These are the results:

	Treated	Untreated
Improved	117	74
Not improved	83	126

You want to know whether these data present sufficient evidence to indicate that the serum was effective in improving the condition of arthritic patients.

a. Use the chi-square test of homogeneity to compare the proportions improved in the populations of treated and untreated subjects. Test at the 5% level of significance.

b. Test the equality of the two binomial proportions using the two-sample z test of Section 9.6. Verify that the squared value of the test statistic $z^2 = X^2$ from part a. Are your conclusions the same as in part a?

14.40 A survey was conducted to determine student, faculty, and administration attitudes about a new university parking policy. The distribution of those favoring or opposing the policy is shown in the table. Do the data provide sufficient evidence to indicate that attitudes about the parking policy are independent of student, faculty, or administration status?

	Student	Faculty	Administration
Favor	252	107	43
Oppose	139	81	40

14.41* The chi-square test used in Exercise 14.39 is equivalent to the two-tailed z test of Section 9.6 provided α is the same for the two tests. Show algebraically that the chi-square test statistic X^2 is the square of the test statistic z for the equivalent test.

14.42 You can use a goodness-of-fit test to determine whether all of the criteria for a binomial experiment have actually been met in a given application. Suppose that an experiment consisting of four trials was repeated 100 times. The number of repetitions on which a given number of successes was obtained is recorded in the table:

Possible Results (number of successes)	Number of Times Obtained
0	11
1	17
2	42
3	21
4	9

Estimate p (assuming that the experiment was binomial), obtain estimates of the expected cell frequencies, and test for goodness of fit. To determine the appropriate number of degrees of freedom for X^2, note that p was estimated by a linear combination of the observed frequencies.

14.43 Infections sometimes occur when blood transfusions are given during surgical operations. An experiment was conducted to determine whether the injection of antibodies reduced the probability of infection. An examination of the records of 138 patients produced the data shown in the table. Do the data provide sufficient evidence to indicate that injections of antibodies affect the likelihood of transfusional infections? Test by using $\alpha = .05$.

	Infection	No Infection
Antibody	4	78
No antibody	11	45

14.44 U.S. labor unions have traditionally been content to leave the management of the company to managers and corporate executives. But in Europe, worker participation in management decision making is an accepted idea that is continually spreading. To study the effect of worker participation in managerial decision making, 100 workers were interviewed in each of two separate German manufacturing plants. One plant had active worker participation in managerial decision making; the other did not. Each selected worker was asked whether he or she generally approved of the managerial decisions made within the firm. The results of the interviews are shown in the table:

	Participation	No Participation
Generally approve	73	51
Do not approve	27	49

a. Do the data provide sufficient evidence to indicate that approval or disapproval of management's decisions depends on whether workers participate in decision making? Test by using the X^2 test statistic. Use $\alpha = .05$.

b. Do these data support the hypothesis that workers in a firm with participative decision making more generally approve of the firm's managerial decisions than those employed by firms without participative decision making? Test by using the z test presented in Section 9.6. This problem requires a one-tailed test. Why?

14.45 An occupant-traffic study was conducted to aid in the remodeling of an office building that contains three entrances. The choice of entrance was recorded for a sample of 200 persons who entered the building. Do the data in the table indicate that there is a difference in preference for the three entrances? Find a 95% confidence interval for the proportion of persons favoring entrance 1.

Entrance	1	2	3
Number Entering	83	61	56

14.46 In the academic world, students and their faculty advisors often collaborate on research papers, producing works in which publication credit can take several forms. In theory, the first authorship of a student's paper should be given to the student unless the input from the faculty advisor was substantial. In an attempt to see whether this is, in fact, the case, authorship credit was studied for different levels of faculty input and two objectives (dissertation versus nondegree research). The frequency of author assignment decisions for published dissertations is shown in the table as assigned by 60 faculty members and 161 students.[14]

Faculty Respondents

Authorship Assignment	High Input	Medium Input	Low Input
Faculty first author, student mandatory second author	4	0	0
Student first author, faculty mandatory second author	15	12	3
Student first author, faculty courtesy second author	2	7	7
Student sole author	2	3	5

Student Respondents

Authorship Assignment	High Input	Medium Input	Low Input
Faculty first author, student mandatory second author	19	6	2
Student first author, faculty mandatory second author	19	41	27
Student first author, faculty courtesy second author	3	7	31
Student sole author	0	3	3

a. Is there sufficient evidence to indicate a dependence between the authorship assignment and the input of the faculty advisor as judged by faculty members? Test using $\alpha = .01$.

b. Is there sufficient evidence to indicate a dependence between the authorship assignment and the input of the faculty advisor as judged by students? Test using $\alpha = .01$.

c. If there is a dependence in the two classifications from parts a and b, does it appear from looking at the data that students are more likely to assign a higher authorship to their faculty advisors than the advisors themselves?

d. Have any of the assumptions necessary for the analysis used in parts a and b been violated? What affect might this have on the validity of your conclusions?

14.47 How would you rate yourself as a driver? According to a survey conducted by the Field Institute, most Californians think they are good drivers but have little respect for others' driving ability. The data show the distribution of opinions according to gender for two different questions, the first rating themselves as drivers and the second rating others as drivers.[15] Although not stated in the source, we assume that there were 100 men and 100 women in the surveyed group.

Rating Self as a Driver

Gender	Excellent	Good	Fair
Male	43	48	9
Female	44	53	3

	Rating Others As Drivers			
Gender	Excellent	Good	Fair	Poor/Very Poor
Male	4	42	41	13
Female	3	48	35	14

a. Is there sufficient evidence to indicate that there is a difference in the self-ratings between male and female drivers? Find the approximate p-value for the test.

b. Is there sufficient evidence to indicate that there is a difference in the ratings of other drivers between male and female drivers? Find the approximate p-value for the test.

c. Have any of the assumptions necessary for the analysis used in parts a and b been violated? What affect might this have on the validity of your conclusions?

14.48 Although white has long been the most popular car color, trends in fashion and home design have signaled the emergence of green as the color of choice in recent years. The growth in the popularity of green hues stems partially from an increased interest in the environment and increased feelings of uncertainty. According to an article in *The Press-Enterprise,* "green symbolizes harmony and counteracts emotional stress."[16] The article cites the top five colors and the percentage of the market share for four different classes of cars. These data are for the truck–van category.

Color	White	Burgundy	Green	Red	Black
Percent	29.72	11.00	9.24	9.08	9.01

In an attempt to verify the accuracy of these figures, we take a random sample of 250 trucks and vans and record their color. Suppose that the number of vehicles that fall into each of the five categories are 82, 22, 27, 21, and 20, respectively.

a. Is any category missing in the classification? How many cars and trucks fell into that category?

b. Is there sufficient evidence to indicate that our percentages of trucks and vans differ from those given? Find the approximate p-value for the test.

14.49 When you choose a greeting card, do you always look for a humorous card, or does it depend on the occasion? A comparison sponsored by two of the nation's leading manufacturers of greeting cards indicated a slight difference in the proportions of humorous designs made for three different occasions: Father's Day, Mother's Day, and Valentine's Day.[17] To test the accuracy of their comparison, random samples of 500 greeting cards purchased at a local card store in the week prior to each holiday were entered into a computer database, and the results in the table were obtained. Do the data indicate that the proportions of humorous greeting cards vary for these three holidays? (HINT: Remember to include a tabulation for all 1500 greeting cards.)

Holiday	Father's Day	Mother's Day	Valentine's Day
Percent Humorous	20	25	24

14.50 Pfizer Canada Inc is a pharmaceutical company that makes azithromycin, an antibiotic in a cherry-flavored suspension used to treat bacterial infections in children. To compare the taste of their product with three competing medications, Pfizer tested 50 healthy children and 20 healthy adults. Among other taste-testing measures, they recorded the number of tasters who rated each of the four antibiotic suspensions as the best tasting.[18] The results are shown in the table. Is there a difference in the perception of the best taste between adults and children? If so, what is the nature of the difference, and why is it of practical importance to the pharmaceutical company?

	Flavor of Antibiotic			
	Banana	Cherry*	Wild Fruit	Strawberry-Banana
Children	14	20	7	9
Adults	4	14	0	2

*Azithromycin produced by Pfizer Canada Inc

  14.51 Knee injuries are a major problem for athletes in many contact sports. However, athletes who play certain positions are more prone to get knee injuries than other players, and their injuries tend to be more severe. The prevalence and patterns of knee injuries among women collegiate rugby players were investigated using a sample questionnaire, to which 42 rugby clubs responded.[19] A total of 76 knee injuries were classified by type as well as the position (forward or back) of the player.

	Type of Knee Injury				
Position	Meniscal Tear	MCL Tear	ACL Tear	Patella Dislocation	PCL Tear
Forward	13	14	7	3	1
Back	12	9	14	2	1

MINITAB output for
Exercise 14.51

Chi-Square Test: Men, MCL, ACL, Patella, PCL
Expected counts are printed below observed counts

```
        Men Tear MCL Tear ACL Tear  Patella PCL Tear    Total
    1         13       14        7        3        1       38
           12.50    11.50    10.50     2.50     1.00

    2         12        9       14        2        1       38
           12.50    11.50    10.50     2.50     1.00

Total         25       23       21        5        2       76

Chi-Sq =  0.020 +  0.543 +  1.167 +  0.100 +  0.000 +
          0.020 +  0.543 +  1.167 +  0.100 +  0.000 = 3.660
DF = 4, P-Value = 0.454
4 cells with expected counts less than 5.0
```

a. Use the *MINITAB* printout to determine whether there is a difference in the distribution of injury types for rugby backs and fowards. Have any of the assumptions necessary for the chi-square test been violated? What effect will this have on the magnitude of the test statistic?

b. The investigators report a significant difference in the proportion of MCL tears for the two positions ($P < .05$) and a significant difference in the proportion of ACL tears ($P < .05$), but indicate that all other injuries occur with equal frequency for the two positions. Do you agree with those conclusions? Explain.

14.52 The number of Americans who visit fast-food restaurants regularly has grown steadily over the past decade. For this reason, marketing experts are interested in the *demographics* of fast-food customers. Is a customer's preference for a fast-food chain affected by the age of the customer? If so, advertising might need to target a particular age group. Suppose a random sample of 500 fast-food customers aged 16 and older was selected, and their favorite fast-food restaurants along with their age groups were recorded, as shown in the table:

EX1452

Age Group	McDonald's	Burger King	Wendy's	Other
16–21	75	34	10	6
21–30	89	42	19	10
30–49	54	52	28	18
50+	21	25	7	10

Use an appropriate method to determine whether or not a customer's fast-food preference is dependent on age. Write a short paragraph presenting your statistical conclusions and their practical implications for marketing experts.

14.53 Is your chance of getting a cold influenced by the number of social contacts you have? A recent study by Sheldon Cohen, a psychology professor at Carnegie Mellon University, seems to show that the more social relationships you have, the *less susceptible* you are to colds.[20] A group of 276 healthy men and women were grouped according to their number of relationships (such as parent, friend, church member, neighbor). They were then exposed to a virus that causes colds. An adaptation of the results is shown in the table:

	Number of Relationships		
	Three or Fewer	Four or Five	Six or More
Cold	49	43	34
No Cold	31	57	62
Total	80	100	96

a. Do the data provide sufficient evidence to indicate that susceptibility to colds is affected by the number of relationships you have? Test at the 5% significance level.

b. Based on the results of part a, describe the nature of the relationship between the two categorical variables: cold incidence and number of social relationships. Do your observations agree with the author's conclusions?

Exercises   DO IT YOURSELF!

14.54 Use the **Chi-Square Probabilities** applet to find the value of χ^2 with the following area α to its right:

a. $\alpha = .05$, $df = 15$ **b.** $\alpha = .01$, $df = 11$

14.55 Use the **Chi-Square Probabilities** applet to find the rejection region for a chi-square test of specified probabilities for a goodness-of-fit test involving k categories for the following cases:

a. $k = 14$, $\alpha = .005$ **b.** $k = 3$, $\alpha = .05$

14.56 Use the **Chi-Square Probabilities** applet to calculate the p-value for the following chi-square tests:

a. $X^2 = .81$, $df = 3$ **b.** $X^2 = 25.40$, $df = 13$

14.57 Three hundred people were surveyed, and were asked to select their preferred brand of laptop computer, given that the prices were equivalent. The results are shown in the table.

Brand I	Brand II	Brand III
115	120	65

Use the first **Goodness-of-Fit** applet to determine if consumers have a preference for one of the three brands. If a significant difference exists, describe the difference in practical terms. Use $\alpha = .01$.

14.58 In Exercise 14.13, the color distribution M&M plain candies was given. Use the third **Goodness-of-Fit** applet to verify the results of Exercise 14.13. Do the data substantiate the percentages reported by the Mars Company? Describe the nature of the differences, if there are any.

14.59 Refer to the color distribution given in Exercise 14.13. Using an individual-sized bag of plain M&Ms, count the number of M&Ms in each of the six colors. Use the third **Goodness-of-Fit** applet to determine if the percentages reported by the Mars Company can be substantiated. Describe the nature of the differences, if there are any.

14.60 Repeat the instructions in Exercise 14.59 with another individual bag of M&Ms. Are your conclusions the same?

14.61 A group of 306 people were interviewed to determine their opinion concerning a particular current U.S. foreign policy issue. At the same time, their political affiliation was recorded. Do the data in the table present sufficient evidence to indicate a dependence between party affiliation and the opinion expressed for the sampled population? Use the third **Chi-Square Test of Independence** applet.

	Approve	Do Not Approve	No Opinion
Republicans	114	53	17
Democrats	87	27	8

14.62   A study of the purchase decisions of three stock portfolio managers, A, B, and C, was conducted to compare the numbers of stock purchases that resulted in profits over a time period less than or equal to 1 year. One hundred randomly selected purchases were examined for each of the managers. Do the data provide evidence of differences among the rates of successful purchases for the three managers? Use the third **Chi-Square Test of Independence** applet.

	A	B	C
Profit	63	71	55
No profit	37	29	45

Case Study

LIBRARIES

Can a Marketing Approach Improve Library Services?

Carole Day and Del Lowenthal studied the responses of young adults in their evaluation of library services.[21] Of the $n = 200$ young adults involved in the study, $n_1 = 152$ were students and $n_2 = 48$ were nonstudents. The table presents the percents and numbers of favorable responses for each group to seven questions in which the atmosphere, staff, and design of the library were examined.

Question		Student Favorable	$n_1 = 152$	Nonstudent Favorable	$n_2 = 48$	$P(\chi^2)$
3	Libraries are friendly	79.6%	121	56.2%	27	<.01
4	Libraries are dull	77	117	58.3	28	<.05
5	Library staff are helpful	91.4	139	87.5	42	NS
6	Library staff are less helpful to teenagers	60.5	92	45.8	22	<.01
7	Libraries are so quiet they feel uncomfortable	75.6	115	52.05	25	<.01
11	Libraries should be more brightly decorated	29	44	18.8	9	NS
13	Libraries are badly signposted	45.4	69	43.8	21	NS

The entry in the last column labeled $P(\chi^2)$ is the p-value for testing the hypothesis of no difference in the proportion of students and nonstudents who answer each question favorably. Hence, each question gives rise to a 2×2 contingency table.

1. Perform a test of homogeneity for each question and verify the reported p-value of the test.
2. Questions 3, 4, and 7 are concerned with the atmosphere of the library; questions 5 and 6 are concerned with the library staff; and questions 11 and 13 are concerned

with the library design. How would you summarize the results of your analyses regarding these seven questions concerning the image of the library?
3. With the information given, is it possible to do any further testing concerning the proportion of favorable versus unfavorable responses for two or more questions simultaneously?

Data Sources

1. Daniel Q. Haney, "Mondays May Be Hazardous," *The Press-Enterprise* (Riverside, CA), 17 November 1992, p. A16.
2. http://www.m-ms.com/us/about/products/milkchocolate.jsp 29 November 2001.
3. Adapted from Margaret Hornblower, "Great Xpectations," *Time*, 9 June 1997, p. 58.
4. Adapted from Linda Schmittroth, ed., *Statistical Record of Women Worldwide* (Detroit and London: Gale Research, 1991).
5. Adapted from: http://www.USATODAY.com/snapshot/life/2001-06-10-drugwiat.htm. 26 September 2001.
6. Welch Suggs, "Left Behind," *The Chronicle of Higher Education*, 30 November 2001, A-3.
7. Adapted from Tamar Lewin, "Report Looks at a Generation, and Caring for Young and Old," *The New York Times on the Web*, 11 July 2001.
8. Adapted from Rebecca Piirto Heath, "Life on Easy Street," *American Demographics*, April 1997, p. 33.
9. W.W. Menard, "Time, Chance and the Origin of Manganese Nodules," *American Scientist*, September/October, 1976.
10. "Poll: Rebuild Trade Center," *The Press Enterprise*, (Riverside, CA) 4 October 2001.
11. Jonathan W. Jantz, C.D. Blosser, and L.A. Fruechting, "A Motor Milestone Change Noted with a Change in Sleep Position," *Archives of Pediatric Adolescent Medicine* 151 (June 1997):565.
12. Adapted from: CyberAtlas staff: "Number of American Workers Online Increases." http://cyberatlas.internet.com/big.picture.html, 29 August 2001.
13. Adapted from: "Salmonella May Taint Many Holiday Turkeys," *The Press Enterprise* (Riverside, CA) 20 November 2001, p. A3.
14. M. Martin Costa and M. Gatz, "Determination of Authorship Credit in Published Dissertations," *Psychological Science* 3, no. 6 (1992):54.
15. Dan Smith, "Motorists Have Little Respect for Others' Skills," *The Press-Enterprise* (Riverside, CA), 15 May 1991.
16. "White Cars Still Favored, but Green Fast Approaching," *The Press-Enterprise* (Riverside, CA), 19 April 1993.
17. "Every Dad Has His Day," *Time*, 16 June 1997, p. 16.
18. Doreen Matsui, R. Lim, T. Tschen, and M.J. Rieder, "Assessment of the Palatability of β-Lactamase-Resistant Antibiotics in Children," *Archives of Pediatric Adolescent Medicine* 151 (June 1997):599.
19. Andrew S. Levy, M.J. Wetzler, M. Lewars, and W. Laughlin, "Knee Injuries in Women Collegiate Rugby Players," *The American Journal of Sports Medicine* 25, no. 3 (1997):360.
20. Adapted from David L. Wheeler, "More Social Roles Means Fewer Colds," *Chronicle of Higher Education* XLIII, no. 44 (July 11, 1997):A13.
21. Carole Day and Del Lowenthal, "The Use of Open Group Discussions in Marketing Library Services to Young Adults," *British Journal of Educational Psychology* 62 (1992):324–340.

15

Nonparametric Statistics

Case Study

What is your cholesterol level? Many of us have become more health conscious in the last few years as we read the nutritional labels on the food products we buy and choose foods that are low in fat and cholesterol and high in fiber. The case study at the end of this chapter involves a taste-testing experiment to compare three types of egg substitutes, using nonparametric techniques.

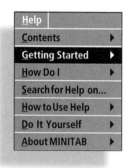

General Objective

In Chapters 8–10, we presented statistical techniques for comparing two populations by comparing their respective population parameters (usually their population means). The techniques in Chapters 8 and 9 are applicable to data that are at least quantitative, and the techniques in Chapter 10 are applicable to data that have normal distributions. The purpose of this chapter is to present several statistical tests for comparing populations for the many types of data that do not satisfy the assumptions specified in Chapters 8–10.

Specific Topics

1. Parametric versus nonparametric tests (15.1)
2. The Wilcoxon rank sum test: Independent random samples (15.2)
3. The sign test for a paired experiment (15.3)
4. The Wilcoxon signed-rank test for a paired experiment (15.5)
5. The Kruskal–Wallis H test (15.6)
6. The Friedman F_r test (15.7)
7. The rank correlation coefficient (15.8)

15.1 Introduction

Some experiments generate responses that can be ordered or ranked, but the actual value of the response cannot be measured numerically except with an arbitrary scale that you might create. It may be that you are able to tell only whether one observation is larger than another. Perhaps you can rank a whole set of observations without actually knowing the exact numerical values of the measurements. Here are a few examples:

- The sales abilities of four sales representatives are ranked from best to worst
- The edibility and taste characteristics of five brands of raisin bran are rated on an arbitrary scale of 1 to 5
- Five automobile designs are ranked from most appealing to least appealing

How can you analyze these types of data? The small-sample statistical methods presented in Chapters 10–13 are valid only when the sampled population(s) are normal or approximately so. Data that consist of ranks or arbitrary scales from 1 to 5 *do not satisfy the normality assumption,* even to a reasonable degree. In some applications, the techniques are valid if the samples are randomly drawn from populations whose variances are equal.

When data do not appear to satisfy these and similar assumptions, an alternative method of analysis can be used—**nonparametric statistical methods.** Nonparametric methods generally specify hypotheses in terms of population distributions rather than parameters such as means and standard deviations. Parametric assumptions are often replaced by more general assumptions about the population distributions, and the ranks of the observations are often used in place of the actual measurements.

Research has shown that nonparametric statistical tests are almost as capable of detecting differences among populations as the parametric methods of preceding chapters when normality and other assumptions are satisfied. They may be, and often are, *more* powerful in detecting population differences when these assumptions are not satisfied. For this reason, some statisticians advocate the use of nonparametric procedures in preference to their parametric counterparts.

We will present nonparametric methods appropriate for comparing two or more populations using either independent or paired samples. We will also present a measure of association that is useful in determining whether one variable increases as the other increases or whether one variable decreases as the other increases.

15.2 The Wilcoxon Rank Sum Test: Independent Random Samples

In comparing the means of two populations based on independent samples, the pivotal statistic was the difference in the sample means. If you are not certain that the assumptions required for a two-sample *t* test are satisfied, one alternative is to replace the values of the observations by their ranks and proceed as though the ranks were the actual observations. Two different nonparametric tests use a test statistic based on these sample ranks:

- Wilcoxon rank sum test
- Mann-Whitney *U* test

They are *equivalent* in that they use the same sample information. The procedure that we will present is the Wilcoxon rank sum test, which is based on the sum of the ranks of the sample that has the smaller sample size.

Assume that you have n_1 observations from population 1 and n_2 observations from population 2. The null hypothesis to be tested is that the two population distributions are identical versus the alternative hypothesis that the population distributions are different. These are the possibilities for the two populations:

- If H_0 is true and the observations have come from the same or identical populations, then the observations from both samples should be randomly mixed when jointly ranked from small to large. The sum of the ranks of the observations from sample 1 should be similar to the sum of the ranks from sample 2.

- If, on the other hand, the observations from population 1 tend to be smaller than those from population 2, then these observations would have the smaller ranks because most of these observations would be smaller than those from population 2. The sum of the ranks of these observations would be "small."

- If the observations from population 1 tend to be larger than those in population 2, these observations would be assigned larger ranks. The sum of the ranks of these observations would tend to be "large."

For example, suppose you have $n_1 = 3$ observations from population 1—2, 4, and 6—and $n_2 = 4$ observations from population 2—3, 5, 8, and 9. Table 15.1 shows seven observations ordered from small to large.

TABLE 15.1

Seven observations in order

Observation	x_1	y_1	x_2	y_2	x_3	y_3	y_4
Data	2	3	4	5	6	8	9
Rank	1	2	3	4	5	6	7

The smallest observation, $x_1 = 2$, is assigned rank 1; the next smallest observation, $y_1 = 3$, is assigned rank 2; and so on. The *sum of the ranks* of the observations from sample 1 is $1 + 3 + 5 = 9$, and the **rank sum** from sample 2 is $2 + 4 + 6 + 7 = 19$. How do you determine whether the rank sum of the observations from sample 1 is significantly small or significantly large? This depends on the probability distribution of the sum of the ranks of one of the samples. Since the ranks for $n_1 + n_2 = N$ observations are the first N integers, the sum of these ranks can be shown to be $N(N + 1)/2$. In this simple example, the sum of the $N = 7$ ranks is $1 + 2 + 3 + 4 + 5 + 6 + 7 = 7(8)/2$ or 28. Hence, if you know the rank sum for one of the samples, you can find the other by subtraction. In our example, notice that the rank sum for sample 1 is 9, whereas the second rank sum is $(28 - 9) = 19$. This means that only one of the two rank sums is needed for the test. To simplify the tabulation of critical values for this test, you should use the rank sum from the smaller sample as the test statistic. What happens if two or more observations are equal? Tied observations are assigned the average of the ranks that the observations would have had if they had been slightly different in value.

To implement the Wilcoxon rank sum test, suppose that independent random samples of size n_1 and n_2 are selected from populations 1 and 2, respectively. Let n_1 represent the *smaller* of the two sample sizes, and let T_1 represent the sum of the ranks of the observations in sample 1. If population 1 lies to the left of population 2, T_1 will be "small." T_1 will be "large" if population 1 lies to the right of population 2.

Formulas for the Wilcoxon Rank Sum Statistic (for Independent Samples)

Let

$$T_1 = \text{Sum of the ranks for the first sample}$$
$$T_1^* = n_1(n_1 + n_2 + 1) - T_1$$

T_1^* is the value of the rank sum for n_1 if the observations had been ranked from *large to small*. (It is *not* the rank sum for the second sample.) Depending on the nature of the alternative hypothesis, one of these two values will be chosen as the test statistic, T.

Table 7 in Appendix I can be used to locate *critical values* for the test statistic for four different values of one-tailed tests with $\alpha = .05, .025, .01,$ and $.005$. To use Table 7 for a two-tailed test, the values of α are doubled—that is, $\alpha = .10, .05, .02,$ and $.01$. The tabled entry gives the value of a such that $P(T \le a) \le \alpha$. To see how to locate a critical value for the Wilcoxon rank sum test, suppose that $n_1 = 8$ and $n_2 = 10$ for a one-tailed test with $\alpha = .05$. You can use Table 7(a), a portion of which is reproduced in Table 15.2. Notice that the table is constructed assuming that $n_1 \le n_2$. It is for this reason that we designate the population with the smaller sample size as population 1. Values of n_1 are shown across the top of the table, and values of n_2 are shown down the left side. The entry—$a = 56$, shaded—is the critical value for rejection of H_0. The null hypothesis of equality of the two distributions should be rejected if the observed value of the test statistic T is less than or equal to 56.

TABLE 15.2

A portion of the 5% left-tailed critical values, Table 7 in Appendix 1

				n_1			
n_2	2	3	4	5	6	7	8
3	—	6					
4	—	6	11				
5	3	7	12	19			
6	3	8	13	20	28		
7	3	8	14	21	29	39	
8	4	9	15	23	31	41	51
9	4	10	16	24	33	43	54
10	4	10	17	26	35	45	56

The Wilcoxon Rank Sum Test

Let n_1 denote the smaller of the two sample sizes. This sample comes from population 1. The hypotheses to be tested are

H_0 : The distributions for populations 1 and 2 are identical

versus one of three alternative hypotheses:

H_a : The distributions for populations 1 and 2 are different (a two-tailed test)

H_a : The distribution for population 1 lies to the left of that for population 2 (a left-tailed test)

H_a : The distribution for population 1 lies to the right of that for population 2 (a right-tailed test)

(continued)

The Wilcoxon Rank Sum Test *(continued)*

1. Rank all $n_1 + n_2$ observations from small to large.
2. Find T_1, the rank sum for the observations in sample 1. This is the test statistic for a left-tailed test.
3. Find $T_1^* = n_1(n_1 + n_2 + 1) - T_1$, the sum of the ranks of the observations from population 1 if the assigned ranks had been reversed from large to small. (The value of T_1^* is not the sum of the ranks of the observations in sample 2.) This is the test statistic for a right-tailed test.
4. The test statistic for a two-tailed test is T, the *minimum* of T_1 and T_1^*.
5. H_0 is rejected if the observed test statistic is less than or equal to the critical value found using Table 7 in Appendix I.

We illustrate the use of Table 7 with the next example.

EXAMPLE 15.1 The wing stroke frequencies of two species of Euglossine bees were recorded for a sample of $n_1 = 4$ *Euglossa mandibularis* Friese (species 1) and $n_2 = 6$ *Euglossa imperialis* Cockerell (species 2).[1] The frequencies are listed in Table 15.3. Can you conclude that the distributions of wing strokes differ for these two species? Test using $\alpha = .05$.

TABLE 15.3
Wing stroke frequencies for two species of bees

Species 1	Species 2
235	180
225	169
190	180
188	185
	178
	182

Solution You first need to rank the observations from small to large, as shown in Table 15.4.

TABLE 15.4
Wing stroke frequencies ranked from small to large

Data	Species	Rank
169	2	1
178	2	2
180	2	3
180	2	4
182	2	5
185	2	6
188	1	7
190	1	8
225	1	9
235	1	10

The hypotheses to be tested are

H_0 : The distributions of the wing stroke frequencies are the same for the two species

versus

H_a : The distributions of the wing stroke frequencies differ for the two species

Since the sample size for individuals from species 1, $n_1 = 4$, is the smaller of the two sample sizes, you have

$$T_1 = 7 + 8 + 9 + 10 = 34$$

and

$$T_1^* = n_1(n_1 + n_2 + 1) - T_1 = 4(4 + 6 + 1) - 34 = 10$$

For a two-tailed test, the test statistic is $T = 10$, the smaller of $T_1 = 34$ and $T_1^* = 10$.

For this two-tailed test with $\alpha = .05$, you can use Table 7(b) in Appendix I with $n_1 = 4$ and $n_2 = 6$. The critical value of T such that $P(T \leq a) \leq \alpha/2 = .025$ is 12, and you should reject the null hypothesis if the observed value of T is 12 or less. Since the observed value of the test statistic—$T = 10$—is less than 12, you can reject the hypothesis of equal distributions of wing stroke frequencies at the 5% level of significance.

A *MINITAB* printout of the Wilcoxon rank sum test (called Mann–Whitney by *MINITAB*) for these data is given in Figure 15.1. You will find instructions for generating this output in the section "About *MINITAB*" at the end of this chapter. Notice that the rank sum of the first sample is given as W = 34.0, which agrees with our calculations. With a reported p-value of .0142 calculated by *MINITAB*, you can reject the null hypothesis at the 5% level.

FIGURE 15.1
Printout for
Example 15.1

Mann-Whitney Test and CI: Species1, Species2

```
Species1  N =    4       Median =      207.50
Species2  N =    6       Median =      180.00
Point estimate for ETA1-ETA2 is       30.50
95.7 Percent CI for ETA1-ETA2 is (5.99,56.01)
W = 34.0
Test of ETA1 = ETA2  vs  ETA1 not = ETA2 is significant at 0.0142
The test is significant at 0.0139 (adjusted for ties)
```

Normal Approximation for the Wilcoxon Rank Sum Test

Table 7 in Appendix I contains critical values for sample sizes of $n_1 \leq n_2 = 3$, $4, \ldots, 15$. Provided n_1 is not too small,[†] approximations to the probabilities for the Wilcoxon rank sum statistic T can be found using a normal approximation to the distribution of T. It can be shown that the mean and variance of T are

$$\mu_T = \frac{n_1(n_1 + n_2 + 1)}{2} \quad \text{and} \quad \sigma_T^2 = \frac{n_1 n_2 (n_1 + n_2 + 1)}{12}$$

The distribution of

$$z = \frac{T - \mu_T}{\sigma_T}$$

is approximately normal with mean 0 and standard deviation 1 for values of n_1 and n_2 as small as 10.

If you try this approximation for Example 15.1, you get

$$\mu_T = \frac{n_1(n_1 + n_2 + 1)}{2} = \frac{4(4 + 6 + 1)}{2} = 22$$

[†]Some researchers indicate that the normal approximation is adequate for samples as small as $n_1 = n_2^* = 4$.

and

$$\sigma_T^2 = \frac{n_1 n_2(n_1 + n_2 + 1)}{12} = \frac{4(6)(4 + 6 + 1)}{12} = 22$$

The p-value for this test is $2P(T \geq 34)$. If you use a .5 correction for continuity in calculating the value of z because n_1 and n_2 are both small,[†] you have

$$z = \frac{T - \mu_T}{\sigma_T} = \frac{(34 - .5) - 22}{\sqrt{22}} = 2.45$$

The p-value for this test is

$$2P(T \geq 34) \approx 2P(z \geq 2.45) = 2(.0071) = .0142$$

the value reported on the *MINITAB* printout in Figure 15.1.

The Wilcoxon Rank Sum Test for Large Samples: $n_1 \geq 10$ and $n_2 \geq 10$

1. Null hypothesis: H_0 : The population distributions are identical
2. Alternative hypothesis: H_a : The two population distributions are not identical (a two-tailed test). Or H_a : The distribution of population 1 is shifted to the right (or left) of the distribution of population 2 (a one-tailed test).

3. Test statistic: $z = \dfrac{T - n_1(n_1 + n_2 + 1)/2}{\sqrt{n_1 n_2(n_1 + n_2 + 1)/12}}$

4. Rejection region:
   a. For a two-tailed test, reject H_0 if $z > z_{\alpha/2}$ or $z < -z_{\alpha/2}$.
   b. For a one-tailed test in the right tail, reject H_0 if $z > z_\alpha$.
   c. For a one-tailed test in the left tail, reject H_0 if $z < -z_\alpha$.

Or reject H_0 if p-value $< \alpha$.

Tabulated values of z are found in Table 3 of Appendix I.

EXAMPLE 15.2

An experiment was conducted to compare the strengths of two types of kraft papers: one a standard kraft paper of a specified weight and the other the same standard kraft paper treated with a chemical substance. Ten pieces of each type of paper, randomly selected from production, produced the strength measurements shown in Table 15.5. Test the null hypothesis of no difference in the distributions of strengths for the two types of paper versus the alternative hypothesis that the treated paper tends to be stronger (i.e., its distribution of strength measurements is shifted to the right of the corresponding distribution for the untreated paper).

[†]Since the value of $T = 34$ lies to the right of the mean 22, the subtraction of .5 in using the normal approximation takes into account the lower limit of the bar above the value 34 in the probability distribution of T.

	Standard 1	Treated 2
TABLE 15.5 Strength measurements (and their ranks) for two types of paper	1.21 (2) 1.43 (12) 1.35 (6) 1.51 (17) 1.39 (9) 1.17 (1) 1.48 (14) 1.42 (11) 1.29 (3.5) 1.40 (10)	1.49 (15) 1.37 (7.5) 1.67 (20) 1.50 (16) 1.31 (5) 1.29 (3.5) 1.52 (18) 1.37 (7.5) 1.44 (13) 1.53 (19)
Rank sum	$T_1 = 85.5$ $T_1^* = n_1(n_1 + n_2 + 1) - T_1 = 210 - 85.5 = 124.5$	

Solution Since the sample sizes are equal, you are at liberty to decide which of the two samples should be sample 1. Choosing the standard treatment as the first sample, you can rank the 20 strength measurements, and the values of T_1 and T_1^* are shown at the bottom of the table. Since you want to detect a shift in the standard (1) measurements to the left of the treated (2) measurements, you conduct a left-tailed test:

H_0 : No difference in the strength distributions

H_a : Standard distribution lies to the left of the treated distribution

and use $T = T_1$ as the test statistic, looking for an unusually small value of T.

To find the critical value for a one-tailed test with $\alpha = .05$, index Table 7(a) in Appendix I with $n_1 = n_2 = 10$. Using the tabled entry, you can reject H_0 when $T \leq 82$. Since the observed value of the test statistic is $T = 85.5$, you are not able to reject H_0. There is insufficient evidence to conclude that the treated kraft paper is stronger than the standard paper.

To use the normal approximation to the distribution of T, you can calculate

$$\mu_T = \frac{n_1(n_1 + n_2 + 1)}{2} = \frac{10(21)}{2} = 105$$

and

$$\sigma_T^2 = \frac{n_1 n_2(n_1 + n_2 + 1)}{12} = \frac{10(10)(21)}{12} = 175$$

with $\sigma_T = \sqrt{175} = 13.23$. Then

$$z = \frac{T - \mu_T}{\sigma_T} = \frac{85.5 - 105}{13.23} = -1.47$$

The one-tailed p-value corresponding to $z = -1.47$ is

$$p\text{-value} = P(z \leq -1.47) = .5 - .4292 = .0708$$

which is larger than $\alpha = .05$. The conclusion is the same. You cannot conclude that the treated kraft paper is stronger than the standard paper.

When should the Wilcoxon rank sum test be used in preference to the two-sample unpaired t test? The two-sample t test performs well if the data are normally distributed with equal variances. If there is doubt concerning these assumptions, a normal probability plot could be used to assess the degree of nonnormality, and a two-sample F test of sample variances could be used to check the equality of variances. If these procedures indicate either nonnormality or inequality of variance, then the Wilcoxon rank sum test is appropriate.

Exercises

Basic Techniques

15.1 Suppose you want to use the Wilcoxon rank sum test to detect a shift in distribution 1 to the right of distribution 2 based on samples of size $n_1 = 6$ and $n_2 = 8$.

  a. Should you use T_1 or T_1^* as the test statistic?

  b. What is the rejection region for the test if $\alpha = .05$?

  c. What is the rejection region for the test if $\alpha = .01$?

15.2 Refer to Exercise 15.1. Suppose the alternative hypothesis is that distribution 1 is shifted either to the left or to the right of distribution 2.

  a. Should you use T_1 or T_1^* as the test statistic?

  b. What is the rejection region for the test if $\alpha = .05$?

  c. What is the rejection region for the test if $\alpha = .01$?

15.3 Observations from two random and independent samples, drawn from populations 1 and 2, are given here. Use the Wilcoxon rank sum test to determine whether population 1 is shifted to the left of population 2.

Sample 1	1	3	2	3	5
Sample 2	4	7	6	8	6

  a. State the null and alternative hypotheses to be tested.

  b. Rank the combined sample from smallest to largest. Calculate T_1 and T_1^*.

  c. What is the rejection region for $\alpha = .05$?

  d. Do the data provide sufficient evidence to indicate that population 1 is shifted to the left of population 2?

15.4 Independent random samples of size $n_1 = 20$ and $n_2 = 25$ are drawn from nonnormal populations 1 and 2. The combined sample is ranked and $T_1 = 252$. Use the large-sample approximation to the Wilcoxon rank sum test to determine whether there is a difference in the two population distributions. Calculate the p-value for the test.

15.5 Suppose you wish to detect a shift in distribution 1 to the right of distribution 2 based on sample sizes $n_1 = 12$ and $n_2 = 14$. If $T_1 = 193$, what do you conclude? Use $\alpha = .05$.

Applications

15.6 In some tests of healthy, elderly men, a new drug has restored their memory almost to that of young people. It will soon be tested on patients with Alzheimer's disease, the fatal brain disorder that destroys the mind. According to Dr. Gary Lynch of the University of California, Irvine, the drug, called ampakine CX-516, accelerates signals between brain cells and appears to significantly sharpen memory.[2] In a preliminary test on students in their early 20s and on men aged 65–70, the results were particularly striking. After being given mild doses of this drug, the 65–70-year-old men scored nearly as high as the young people. The accompanying data are the numbers of nonsense syllables recalled after 5 minutes for 10 men in their 20s and 10 men aged 65–70. Use the Wilcoxon rank sum test to determine whether the distributions for the number of nonsense syllables recalled are the same for these two groups.

20s	3	6	4	8	7	1	1	2	7	8
65–70s	1	0	4	1	2	5	0	2	2	3

15.7 Refer to Exercise 15.6. Suppose that two more groups of 10 men each are tested on the number of nonsense syllables they can remember after 5 minutes. However, this time the 65–70-year-olds are given a mild dose of ampakine CX-516. Do the data provide sufficient evidence to conclude that this drug improves memory in men aged 65–70 compared with that of 20-year-olds? Use an appropriate level of α.

20s	11	7	6	8	6	9	2	10	3	6
65–70s	1	9	6	8	7	8	5	7	10	3

15.8 The observations in the table are dissolved oxygen contents in water. The higher the dissolved oxygen content, the greater the ability of a river, lake, or stream to support aquatic life. In this experiment, a pollution-control inspector suspected that a river community was releasing semitreated sewage into a river. To check this theory, five randomly selected specimens of river water were selected at a location above the town and another five below. These are the dissolved oxygen readings (in parts per million):

Above Town	4.8	5.2	5.0	4.9	5.1
Below Town	5.0	4.7	4.9	4.8	4.9

a. Use a one-tailed Wilcoxon rank sum test with $\alpha = .05$ to confirm or refute the theory.

b. Use a Student's t test (with $\alpha = .05$) to analyze the data. Compare the conclusion reached in part a.

EX1509

15.9 In an investigation of the visual scanning behavior of deaf children, measurements of eye movement were taken on nine deaf and nine hearing children. The table gives the eye-movement rates and their ranks (in parentheses). Does it appear that the distributions of eye-movement rates for deaf children and hearing children differ?

Deaf Children	Hearing Children
2.75 (15)	.89 (1)
2.14 (11)	1.43 (7)
3.23 (18)	1.06 (4)
2.07 (10)	1.01 (3)
2.49 (14)	.94 (2)
2.18 (12)	1.79 (8)
3.16 (17)	1.12 (5.5)
2.93 (16)	2.01 (9)
2.20 (13)	1.12 (5.5)
Rank sum 126	45

15.10 The table lists the life (in months) of service before failure of a color television circuit board for 8 television sets manufactured by firm A and 10 sets manufactured by firm B. Use the Wilcoxon rank sum test to analyze the data, and test to see whether the life of service before failure of the circuit boards differs for the circuit boards produced by the two manufacturers.

Firm	Life of Circuit Board (months)									
A	32	25	40	31	35	29	37	39		
B	41	39	36	47	45	34	48	44	43	33

EX1511

15.11 The weights of turtles caught in two different lakes were measured to compare the effects of the two lake environments on turtle growth. All the turtles were the same age and were tagged before being released into the lakes. The weights for $n_1 = 10$ tagged turtles caught in lake 1 and $n_2 = 8$ caught in lake 2 are listed here:

Lake	Weight (oz)									
1	14.1	15.2	13.9	14.5	14.7	13.8	14.0	16.1	12.7	15.3
2	12.2	13.0	14.1	13.6	12.4	11.9	12.5	13.8		

Do the data provide sufficient evidence to indicate a difference in the distributions of weights for the tagged turtles exposed to the two lake environments? Use the Wilcoxon rank sum test with $\alpha = .05$ to answer the question.

EX1512

15.12 Cancer treatment by means of chemicals—chemotherapy—kills both cancerous and normal cells. In some instances, the toxicity of the cancer drug—that is, its effect on normal cells—can be reduced by the simultaneous injection of a second drug. A study was conducted to determine whether a particular drug injection reduced the harmful effects of a chemotherapy treatment on the survival time for rats. Two randomly selected groups of 12 rats were used in an experiment in which both groups, call them A and B, received the toxic drug in a dose large enough to cause death, but in addition, group B received the antitoxin, which was to reduce the toxic effect of the chemotherapy on normal cells. The test was terminated at the end of 20 days, or 480 hours. The survival times for the two groups of rats, to the nearest 4 hours, are shown in the table. Do the data provide sufficient evidence to indicate that rats receiving the antitoxin tend to survive longer after chemotherapy than those not receiving the antitoxin? Use the Wilcoxon rank sum test with $\alpha = .05$.

Chemotherapy Only A	Chemotherapy plus Drug B
84	140
128	184
168	368
92	96
184	480
92	188
76	480
104	244
72	440
180	380
144	480
120	196

15.3 The Sign Test for a Paired Experiment

The sign test is a fairly simple procedure that can be used to compare two populations when the samples consist of paired observations. This type of experimental design is called the **paired-difference** or **matched pairs** design, which you used to compare the average wear for two types of tires in Section 10.5. In general, for each pair, you measure whether the first response—say, A—exceeds the second response—say, B. The test statistic is x, the number of times that A exceeds B in the n pairs of observations.

When the two population distributions are identical, the probability that A exceeds B equals $p = .5$, and x, the number of times that A exceeds B, has a *binomial* distribution. Only pairs without ties are included in the test. Hence, you can test the hypothesis of identical population distributions by testing $H_0 : p = .5$ versus either a one- or two-tailed alternative. Critical values for the rejection region or exact p-values can be found using the cumulative binomial tables in Appendix I.

> **The Sign Test for Comparing Two Populations**
>
> **1.** Null hypothesis: H_0 : The two population distributions are identical and $P(\text{A exceeds B}) = p = .5$
>
> **2.** Alternative hypothesis:
>   **a.** H_a : The population distributions are not identical and $p \neq .5$
>
> *(continued)*

> **The Sign Test for Comparing Two Populations** (continued)
>
> **b.** H_a : The population of A measurements is shifted to the right of the population of B measurements and $p > .5$
>
> **c.** H_a : The population of A measurements is shifted to the left of the population of B measurements and $p < .5$
>
> **3.** Test statistic: For n, the number of pairs with no ties, use x, the number of times that $(A - B)$ is positive.
>
> **4.** Rejection region:
>
> **a.** For the two-tailed test $H_a : p \neq .5$, reject H_0 if $x \leq x_L$ or $x \geq x_U$, where $P(x \leq x_L) \leq \alpha/2$ and $P(x \geq x_U) \leq \alpha/2$ for x having a binomial distribution with $p = .5$.
>
> **b.** For $H_a : p > .5$, reject H_0 if $x \geq x_U$ with $P(x \geq x_U) \leq \alpha$.
>
> **c.** For $H_a : p < .5$, reject H_0 if $x \leq x_L$ with $P(x \leq x_L) \leq \alpha$.
>
> Or calculate the p-value and reject H_0 if the p-value $< \alpha$.

One problem that may occur when you are conducting a sign test is that the measurements associated with one or more pairs may be equal and therefore result in **tied observations.** When this happens, delete the tied pairs and reduce n, the total number of pairs. The following example will help you understand how the sign test is constructed and used.

EXAMPLE 15.3   The numbers of defective electrical fuses produced by two production lines, A and B, were recorded daily for a period of 10 days, with the results shown in Table 15.6. The response variable, the number of defective fuses, has an exact binomial distribution with a large number of fuses produced per day. Although this variable will have an approximately normal distribution, the plant supervisor would prefer a quick-and-easy statistical test to determine whether one production line tends to produce more defectives than the other. Use the sign test to test the appropriate hypothesis.

TABLE 15.6
Defective fuses
from two
production lines

Day	Line A	Line B	Sign of Difference
1	170	201	−
2	164	179	−
3	140	159	−
4	184	195	−
5	174	177	−
6	142	170	−
7	191	183	+
8	169	179	−
9	161	170	−
10	200	212	−

Solution   For this *paired-difference* experiment, x is the number of times that the observation for line A exceeds that for line B in a given day. If there is no difference in the distributions of defectives for the two production lines, then p, the proportion of days on which A exceeds B, is .5, which is the hypothesized value in a test of the binomial parameter p. Very small or very large values of x, the number of times that A exceeds B, are contrary to the null hypothesis.

Since $n = 10$ and the hypothesized value of p is .5, Table 1 of Appendix I can be used to find the exact p-value for the test of

$$H_0 : p = .5 \quad \text{versus} \quad H_a : p \neq .5$$

The observed value of the test statistic—which is the number of "plus" signs in the table—is $x = 1$, and the p-value is calculated as

$$p\text{-value} = 2P(x \leq 1) = 2(.011) = .022$$

The fairly small p-value $= .022$ allows you to reject H_0 at the 5% level. There is significant evidence to indicate that the number of defective fuses is not the same for the two production lines; in fact, line B produces more defectives than line A. In this example, the sign test is an easy-to-calculate rough tool for detecting faulty production lines and works perfectly well to detect a significant difference using only a minimum amount of information.

Normal Approximation for the Sign Test

When the number of pairs n is large, the critical values for rejection of H_0 and the approximate p-values can be found using a normal approximation to the distribution of x, which was discussed in Section 6.4. Because the binomial distribution is perfectly symmetric when $p = .5$, this approximation works very well, even for n as small as 10.

For $n \geq 25$, you can conduct the sign test by using the z-statistic,

$$z = \frac{x - np}{\sqrt{npq}} = \frac{x - .5n}{.5\sqrt{n}}$$

as the test statistic. In using z, you are testing the null hypothesis $p = .5$ versus the alternative $p \neq .5$ for a two-tailed test or versus the alternative $p > .5$ (or $p < .5$) for a one-tailed test. The tests use the familiar rejection regions of Chapter 9.

Sign Test for Large Samples: n 25

1. Null hypothesis: $H_0 : p = .5$ (one treatment is not preferred to a second treatment)

2. Alternative hypothesis: $H_a : p \neq .5$, for a two-tailed test

   (NOTE: We use the two-tailed test as an example. Many analyses might require a one-tailed test.)

3. Test statistic: $z = \dfrac{x - .5n}{.5\sqrt{n}}$

4. Rejection region: Reject H_0 if $z \geq z_{\alpha/2}$ or $z \leq -z_{\alpha/2}$, where $z_{\alpha/2}$ is the z-value from Table 3 in Appendix I corresponding to an area of $\alpha/2$ in the upper tail of the normal distribution.

EXAMPLE 15.4

A production superintendent claims that there is no difference between the employee accident rates for the day versus the evening shifts in a large manufacturing plant. The number of accidents per day is recorded for both the day and evening shifts for $n = 100$ days. It is found that the number of accidents per day for the evening shift

x_E exceeded the corresponding number of accidents on the day shift x_D on 63 of the 100 days. Do these results provide sufficient evidence to indicate that more accidents tend to occur on one shift than on the other or, equivalently, that $P(x_E > x_D) \neq 1/2$?

Solution   This study is a paired-difference experiment, with $n = 100$ pairs of observations corresponding to the 100 days. To test the null hypothesis that the two distributions of accidents are identical, you can use the test statistic

$$z = \frac{x - .5n}{.5\sqrt{n}}$$

where x is the number of days in which the number of accidents on the evening shift exceeded the number of accidents on the day shift. Then for $\alpha = .05$, you can reject the null hypothesis if $z \geq 1.96$ or $z \leq -1.96$. Substituting into the formula for z, you get

$$z = \frac{x - .5n}{.5\sqrt{n}} = \frac{63 - (.5)(100)}{.5\sqrt{100}} = \frac{13}{5} = 2.60$$

Since the calculated value of z exceeds $z_{\alpha/2} = 1.96$, you can reject the null hypothesis. The data provide sufficient evidence to indicate a difference in the accident rate distributions for the day versus evening shifts.

When should the sign test be used in preference to the paired t test? When only the *direction* of the difference in the measurement is given, *only* the sign test can be used. On the other hand, when the data are quantitative and satisfy the normality and constant variance assumptions, the paired t test should be used. A normal probability plot can be used to assess normality, while a plot of the residuals $(d_i - \bar{d})$ can reveal large deviations that might indicate a variance that varies from pair to pair. When there are doubts about the validity of the assumptions, statisticians often recommend that both tests be performed. If both tests reach the same conclusions, then the parametric test results can be considered to be valid.

Exercises   Basic Techniques

15.13   Suppose you wish to use the sign test to test $H_a : p > .5$ for a paired-difference experiment with $n = 25$ pairs.

   a. State the practical situation that dictates the alternative hypothesis given.

   b. Use Table 1 in Appendix I to find values of α ($\alpha < .15$) available for the test.

15.14   Repeat the instructions of Exercise 15.13 for $H_a : p \neq .5$.

15.15   Repeat the instructions of Exercises 15.13 and 15.14 for $n = 10$, 15, and 20.

15.16   A paired-difference experiment was conducted to compare two populations. The data are shown in the table. Use a sign test to determine whether the population distributions are different.

	Pairs						
Population	1	2	3	4	5	6	7
1	8.9	8.1	9.3	7.7	10.4	8.3	7.4
2	8.8	7.4	9.0	7.8	9.9	8.1	6.9

   a. State the null and alternative hypotheses for the test.

   b. Determine an appropriate rejection region with $\alpha \approx .01$.

c. Calculate the observed value of the test statistic.

d. Do the data present sufficient evidence to indicate that populations 1 and 2 are different?

Applications

15.17 In Exercise 10.41, you compared the property evaluations of two tax assessors, A and B. Their assessments for eight properties are shown in the table:

Property	Assessor A	Assessor B
1	76.3	75.1
2	88.4	86.8
3	80.2	77.3
4	94.7	90.6
5	68.7	69.1
6	82.8	81.0
7	76.1	75.3
8	79.0	79.1

a. Use the sign test to determine whether the data present sufficient evidence to indicate that one of the assessors tends to be consistently more conservative than the other; that is, $P(x_A > x_B) \neq 1/2$. Test by using a value of α near .05. Find the p-value for the test and interpret its value.

b. Exercise 10.41 uses the t statistic to test the null hypothesis that there is no difference in the mean property assessments between assessors A and B. Check the answer (in the answer section) for Exercise 10.41 and compare it with your answer to part a. Do the test results agree? Explain why the answers are (or are not) consistent.

EX1518

15.18 Two gourmets, A and B, rated 22 meals on a scale of 1 to 10. The data are shown in the table. Do the data provide sufficient evidence to indicate that one of the gourmets tends to give higher ratings than the other? Test by using the sign test with a value of α near .05.

Meal	A	B	Meal	A	B
1	6	8	12	8	5
2	4	5	13	4	2
3	7	4	14	3	3
4	8	7	15	6	8
5	2	3	16	9	10
6	7	4	17	9	8
7	9	9	18	4	6
8	7	8	19	4	3
9	2	5	20	5	4
10	4	3	21	3	2
11	6	9	22	5	3

a. Use the binomial tables in Appendix I to find the exact rejection region for the test.

b. Use the large-sample z-statistic. (NOTE: Although the large-sample approximation is suggested for $n \geq 25$, it works fairly well for values of n as small as 15.)

c. Compare the results of parts a and b.

15.19 A study reported in the *American Journal of Public Health (Science News)*—the first to follow blood lead levels in law-abiding handgun hobbyists using indoor firing ranges—documents a significant risk of lead poisoning.[3] Lead exposure measurements were made on 17 members of a law enforcement trainee class before, during, and after a 3-month period of firearm instruction at a state-owned indoor firing range. No trainee had elevated blood lead levels before the training, but 15 of the 17 ended their training with blood lead levels deemed "elevated" by the Occupational Safety and Health Administration (OSHA). If the use of an indoor firing range causes no increase in blood lead levels, then p, the probability that a person's blood lead level increases, is less than or equal to .5. If, however, use of the indoor firing range causes an increase in a person's blood lead levels, then $p > .5$. Use the sign test to determine whether using an indoor firing range has the effect of increasing a person's blood lead level with $\alpha = .05$. (HINT: The normal approximation to binomial probabilities is fairly accurate for $n = 17$.)

EX1520

15.20 Clinical data concerning the effectiveness of two drugs in treating a particular disease were collected from ten hospitals. The numbers of patients treated with the drugs varied from one hospital to another. You want to know whether the data present sufficient evidence to indicate a higher recovery rate for one of the two drugs.

	Drug A			Drug B		
Hospital	Number in Group	Number Recovered	Percentage Recovered	Number in Group	Number Recovered	Percentage Recovered
1	84	63	75.0	96	82	85.4
2	63	44	69.8	83	69	83.1
3	56	48	85.7	91	73	80.2
4	77	57	74.0	47	35	74.5
5	29	20	69.0	60	42	70.0
6	48	40	83.3	27	22	81.5
7	61	42	68.9	69	52	75.4
8	45	35	77.8	72	57	79.2
9	79	57	72.2	89	76	85.4
10	62	48	77.4	46	37	80.4

a. Test using the sign test. Choose your rejection region so that α is near .05.

b. Why might it be inappropriate to use the Student's t test in analyzing the data?

15.4 A Comparison of Statistical Tests

The experiment in Example 15.3 is designed as a paired-difference experiment. If the assumptions of normality and constant variance, σ_d^2, for the differences were met, would the sign test detect a shift in location for the two populations as efficiently as the paired t test? Probably not, since the t test uses much more information than the sign test. It uses not only the sign of the difference, but also the actual values of the differences. In this case, we would say that the sign test is not as *efficient* as the paired t test. However, the sign test might be more efficient if the usual assumptions were not met.

When two different statistical tests can *both* be used to test a hypothesis based on the same data, it is natural to ask, Which is better? One way to answer this question would be to hold the sample size n and α constant for both procedures and compare β, the probability of a Type II error. Statisticians, however, prefer to examine the **power** of a test.

Definition Power $= 1 - \beta = P(\text{reject } H_0 \text{ when } H_a \text{ is true})$

Since β is the probability of failing to reject the null hypothesis when it is false, the **power** of the test is the probability of rejecting the null hypothesis when it is false and some specified alternative is true. It is the probability that the test will do what it was designed to do—that is, detect a departure from the null hypothesis when a departure exists.

Probably the most common method of comparing two test procedures is in terms of the relative efficiency of a pair of tests. **Relative efficiency** is the ratio of the sample sizes for the two test procedures required to achieve the same α and β for a given alternative to the null hypothesis.

In some situations, you may not be too concerned whether you are using the most powerful test. For example, you might choose to use the sign test over a more powerful competitor because of its ease of application. Thus, you might view tests as microscopes that are used to detect departures from an hypothesized theory. One need not know the exact power of a microscope to use it in a biological investigation, and the same applies to statistical tests. If the test procedure detects a departure from the null hypothesis, you are delighted. If not, you can reanalyze the data by using a more powerful microscope (test), or you can increase the power of the microscope (test) by increasing the sample size.

15.5 The Wilcoxon Signed-Rank Test for a Paired Experiment

A signed-rank test proposed by F. Wilcoxon can be used to analyze the paired-difference experiment of Section 10.5 by considering the paired differences of two treatments, 1 and 2. Under the null hypothesis of no differences in the distributions for 1 and 2, you would expect (on the average) half of the differences in pairs to be negative and half to be positive; that is, the expected number of negative differences between pairs would be $n/2$ (where n is the number of pairs). Furthermore, it follows that positive and negative differences of equal absolute magnitude should occur with equal probability. If one were to order the differences according to their absolute values and rank them from smallest to largest, the expected rank sums for the negative and positive differences would be equal. Sizable differences in the sums of the ranks assigned to the positive and negative differences would provide evidence to indicate a shift in location between the distributions of responses for the two treatments, 1 and 2.

If distribution 1 is shifted to the right of distribution 2, then more of the differences are expected to be positive, and this results in a small number of negative differences. Therefore, to detect this one-sided alternative, use the rank sum T^-—the sum of the ranks of the negative differences—and reject the null hypothesis for significantly small values of T^-. Along these same lines, if distribution 1 is shifted to the left of distribution 2, then more of the differences are expected to be negative, and the number of positive differences is small. Hence, to detect this one-sided alternative, use T^+—the sum of the ranks of the positive differences—and reject the null hypothesis if T^+ is significantly small.

Calculating the Test Statistic for the Wilcoxon Signed-Rank Test

1. Calculate the differences $(x_1 - x_2)$ for each of the n pairs. Differences equal to 0 are eliminated, and the number of pairs, n, is reduced accordingly.

2. Rank the **absolute values** of the differences by assigning 1 to the smallest, 2 to the second smallest, and so on. Tied observations are assigned the average of the ranks that would have been assigned with no ties.

3. Calculate the **rank sum** for the **negative** differences and label this value T^-. Similarly, calculate T^+, the **rank sum** for the **positive** differences.

For a **two-tailed test,** use the **smaller of these two quantities T as a test statistic** to test the null hypothesis that the two population relative frequency histograms are identical. The smaller the value of T, the greater is the weight of evidence favoring rejection of the null hypothesis. **Therefore, you will reject the null hypothesis if T is less than or equal to some value—say, T_0.**

To detect the **one-sided alternative,** that **distribution 1 is shifted to the right of distribution 2, use the rank sum T^-** of the negative differences and reject the null hypothesis for small values of T^-—say, $T^- \le T_0$. If you wish to detect a **shift of distribution 2 to the right of distribution 1, use the rank sum T^+** of the positive differences as a test statistic and reject the null hypothesis for small values of T^+—say, $T^+ \le T_0$.

The probability that T is less than or equal to some value T_0 has been calculated for a combination of sample sizes and values of T_0. These probabilities, given in Table 8 in Appendix I, can be used to find the rejection region for the T test.

An abbreviated version of Table 8 is shown in Table 15.7. Across the top of the table you see the number of differences (the number of pairs) n. Values of α for a one-tailed test appear in the first column of the table. The second column gives values of α for a two-tailed test. Table entries are the critical values of T. You will recall that the critical value of a test statistic is the value that locates the boundary of the rejection region.

For example, suppose you have $n = 7$ pairs and you are conducting a two-tailed test of the null hypothesis that the two population relative frequency distributions are identical. Checking the $n = 7$ column of Table 15.7 and using the second row (corresponding to $\alpha = .05$ for a two-tailed test), you see the entry 2 (shaded). This value is T_0, the critical value of T. As noted earlier, the smaller the value of T, the greater is the evidence to reject the null hypothesis. Therefore, you will reject the null hypothesis for all values of T less than or equal to 2. The rejection region for the Wilcoxon signed-rank test for a paired experiment is always of the form: Reject H_0 if $T \le T_0$, where T_0 is the critical value of T. The rejection region is shown symbolically in Figure 15.2.

TABLE 15.7
An abbreviated version of Table 8 in Appendix I; critical values of T

One-Sided	Two-Sided	$n = 5$	$n = 6$	$n = 7$	$n = 8$	$n = 9$	$n = 10$	$n = 11$
$\alpha = .050$	$\alpha = .10$	1	2	4	6	8	11	14
$\alpha = .025$	$\alpha = .05$		1	2	4	6	8	11
$\alpha = .010$	$\alpha = .02$			0	2	3	5	7
$\alpha = .005$	$\alpha = .01$				0	2	3	5

One-Sided	Two-Sided	$n = 12$	$n = 13$	$n = 14$	$n = 15$	$n = 16$	$n = 17$
$\alpha = .050$	$\alpha = .10$	17	21	26	30	36	41
$\alpha = .025$	$\alpha = .05$	14	17	21	25	30	35
$\alpha = .010$	$\alpha = .02$	10	13	16	20	24	28
$\alpha = .005$	$\alpha = .01$	7	10	13	16	19	23

FIGURE 15.2
Rejection region for the Wilcoxon signed-rank test for a paired experiment (reject H_0 if $T \le T_0$)

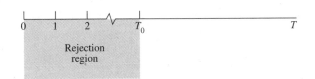

Wilcoxon Signed-Rank Test for a Paired Experiment

1. Null hypothesis: H_0 : The two population relative frequency distributions are identical

2. Alternative hypothesis: H_a : The two population relative frequency distributions differ in location (a two-tailed test). Or H_a : The population 1 relative frequency distribution is shifted to the right of the relative frequency distribution for population 2 (a one-tailed test).

3. Test statistic
   a. For a two-tailed test, use T, the smaller of the rank sum for positive and the rank sum for negative differences.
   b. For a one-tailed test (to detect the alternative hypothesis described above), use the rank sum T^- of the negative differences.

4. Rejection region
   a. For a two-tailed test, reject H_0 if $T \le T_0$, where T_0 is the critical value given in Table 8 in Appendix I.
   b. For a one-tailed test (to detect the alternative hypothesis described above), use the rank sum T^- of the negative differences. Reject H_0 if $T^- \le T_0$.[†]

$$\left[\text{NOTE: It can be shown that } T^+ + T^- = \frac{n(n+1)}{2}. \right]$$

EXAMPLE 15.5

An experiment was conducted to compare the densities of cakes prepared from two different cake mixes, A and B. Six cake pans received batter A, and six received batter B. Expecting a variation in oven temperature, the experimenter placed an A and a B cake side by side at six different locations in the oven. Test the hypothesis of no difference in the population distributions of cake densities for two different cake batters.

Solution

The data (density in ounces per cubic inch) and differences in density for six pairs of cakes are given in Table 15.8. The boxplot of the differences in Figure 15.3 shows fairly strong skewing and a very large difference in the right tail, which indicates that the data may not satisfy the normality assumption. The sample of differences is too small to make valid decisions about normality and constant variance. In this situation, Wilcoxon's signed-rank test may be the prudent test to use.

As with other nonparametric tests, the null hypothesis to be tested is that the two population frequency distributions of cake densities are identical. The alternative

TABLE 15.8
Densities of six pairs of cakes

x_A	x_B	Difference $(x_A - x_B)$	Rank
.135	.129	.006	2
.102	.120	−.018	5
.098	.112	−.014	4
.141	.152	−.011	3
.131	.135	−.004	1
.144	.163	−.019	6

[†]To detect a shift of distribution 2 to the right of the distribution 1, use the rank sum T^+ of the positive differences as the test statistic and reject H_0 if $T^+ \le T_0$.

FIGURE 15.3
Boxplot of
differences for
Example 15.5

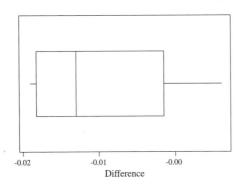

hypothesis, which implies a two-tailed test, is that the distributions are different. Because the amount of data is small, you can conduct the test using $\alpha = .10$. From Table 8 in Appendix I, the critical value of T for a two-tailed test, $\alpha = .10$, is $T_0 = 2$. Hence, you can reject H_0 if $T \leq 2$.

The differences $(x_1 - x_2)$ are calculated and ranked according to their absolute values in Table 15.8. The sum of the positive ranks is $T^+ = 2$, and the sum of the negative ranks is $T^- = 19$. The test statistic is the smaller of these two rank sums, or $T = 2$. Since $T = 2$ falls in the rejection region, you can reject H_0 and conclude that the two population frequency distributions of cake densities differ.

A *MINITAB* printout of the Wilcoxon signed-rank test for these data is given in Figure 15.4. You will find instructions for generating this output in the section "About *MINITAB*" at the end of this chapter. You can see that the value of the test statistic agrees with the other calculations, and the *p*-value indicates that you can reject H_0 at the 10% level of significance.

FIGURE 15.4
MINITAB printout
for Example 15.5

Wilcoxon Signed Rank Test: Difference

```
Test of median = 0.000000 versus median not = 0.000000

                  N for   Wilcoxon            Estimated
             N    Test   Statistic      P      Median
Difference   6     6        2.0      0.093    -0.01150
```

Normal Approximation for the Wilcoxon Signed-Rank Test

Although Table 8 in Appendix I has critical values for n as large as 50, T^+, like the Wilcoxon signed-rank test, will be approximately normally distributed when the null hypothesis is true and n is large—say, 25 or more. This enables you to construct a large-sample z test, where

$$E(T) = \frac{n(n + 1)}{4}$$

$$\sigma_T^2 = \frac{n(n + 1)(2n + 1)}{24}$$

Then the z-statistic

$$z = \frac{T^+ - E(T^+)}{\sigma_{T^+}} = \frac{T^+ - \dfrac{n(n + 1)}{4}}{\sqrt{\dfrac{n(n + 1)(2n + 1)}{24}}}$$

can be used as a test statistic. Thus, for a two-tailed test and $\alpha = .05$, you can reject the hypothesis of identical population distributions when $|z| \geq 1.96$.

A Large-Sample Wilcoxon Signed-Rank Test for a Paired Experiment: n 25

1. Null hypothesis: H_0 : The population relative frequency distributions 1 and 2 are identical.

2. Alternative hypothesis: H_a : The two population relative frequency distributions differ in location (a two-tailed test). Or H_a : The population 1 relative frequency distribution is shifted to the right (or left) of the relative frequency distribution for population 2 (a one-tailed test).

3. Test statistic: $z = \dfrac{T^+ - [n(n+1)/4]}{\sqrt{[n(n+1)(2n+1)]/24}}$

4. Rejection region: Reject H_0 if $z > z_{\alpha/2}$ or $z < -z_{\alpha/2}$ for a two-tailed test. For a one-tailed test, place all of α in one tail of the z distribution. To detect a shift in distribution 1 to the right of distribution 2, reject H_0 when $z > z_\alpha$. To detect a shift in the opposite direction, reject H_0 if $z < -z_\alpha$.

Tabulated values of z are given in Table 3 in Appendix I.

Exercises

Basic Techniques

15.21 Suppose you wish to detect a difference in the locations of two population distributions based on a paired-difference experiment consisting of $n = 30$ pairs.

a. Give the null and alternative hypotheses for the Wilcoxon signed-rank test.

b. Give the test statistic.

c. Give the rejection region for the test for $\alpha = .05$.

d. If $T^+ = 249$, what are your conclusions? [NOTE: $T^+ + T^- = n(n+1)/2$.]

15.22 Refer to Exercise 15.21. Suppose you wish to detect only a shift in distribution 1 to the right of distribution 2.

a. Give the null and alternative hypotheses for the Wilcoxon signed-rank test.

b. Give the test statistic.

c. Give the rejection region for the test for $\alpha = .05$.

d. If $T^+ = 249$, what are your conclusions? [NOTE: $T^+ + T^- = n(n+1)/2$.]

15.23 Refer to Exercise 15.21. Conduct the test using the large-sample z test. Compare your results with the nonparametric test results in Exercise 15.22, part d.

15.24 Refer to Exercise 15.22. Conduct the test using the large-sample z test. Compare your results with the nonparametric test results in Exercise 15.21, part d.

15.25 Refer to Exercise 15.16. The data in this table are from a paired-difference experiment with $n = 7$ pairs of observations.

Population	Pairs						
	1	2	3	4	5	6	7
1	8.9	8.1	9.3	7.7	10.4	8.3	7.4
2	8.8	7.4	9.0	7.8	9.9	8.1	6.9

a. Use Wilcoxon's signed-rank test to determine whether there is a significant difference between the two populations.

b. Compare the results of part a with the result you got in Exercise 15.16. Are they the same? Explain.

Applications

15.26 In Exercise 15.17, you used the sign test to determine whether the data provided sufficient evidence to indicate a difference in the distributions of property assessments for assessors A and B.

a. Use the Wilcoxon signed-rank test for a paired experiment to test the null hypothesis that there is no difference in the distributions of property assessments between assessors A and B. Test by using a value of α near .05.

b. Compare the conclusion of the test in part a with the conclusions derived from the t test in Exercise 10.43 and the sign test in Exercise 15.17. Explain why these test conclusions are (or are not) consistent.

15.27 The number of machine breakdowns per month was recorded for 9 months on two identical machines, A and B, used to make wire rope:

Month	A	B
1	3	7
2	14	12
3	7	9
4	10	15
5	9	12
6	6	6
7	13	12
8	6	5
9	7	13

a. Do the data provide sufficient evidence to indicate a difference in the monthly breakdown rates for the two machines? Test by using a value of α near .05.

b. Can you think of a reason the breakdown rates for the two machines might vary from month to month?

15.28 Refer to the comparison of gourmet meal ratings in Exercise 15.18, and use the Wilcoxon signed-rank test to determine whether the data provide sufficient evidence to indicate a difference in the ratings of the two gourmets. Test by using a value of α near .05. Compare the results of this test with the results of the sign test in Exercise 15.18. Are the test conclusions consistent?

15.29 Two methods for controlling traffic, A and B, were used at each of $n = 12$ intersections for a period of 1 week, and the numbers of accidents that occurred during this time period were recorded. The order of use (which method would be employed for the first week) was selected in a random manner. You want to know whether the data provide sufficient evidence to indicate a difference in the distributions of accident rates for traffic control methods A and B.

Intersection	Method A	Method B	Intersection	Method A	Method B
1	5	4	7	2	3
2	6	4	8	4	1
3	8	9	9	7	9
4	3	2	10	5	2
5	6	3	11	6	5
6	1	0	12	1	1

a. Analyze using a sign test.

b. Analyze using the Wilcoxon signed-rank test for a paired experiment.

15.30 Eight people were asked to perform a simple puzzle-assembly task under normal conditions and under stressful conditions. During the stressful time, a mild shock was delivered to subjects 3 minutes after the start of the experiment and every 30 seconds thereafter until the task was completed. Blood pressure readings were taken under both conditions. The data in the table are the highest readings during the experiment. Do the data present sufficient evidence to indicate higher blood pressure readings under stressful conditions? Analyze the data using the Wilcoxon signed-rank test for a paired experiment.

Subject	Normal	Stressful
1	126	130
2	117	118
3	115	125
4	118	120
5	118	121
6	128	125
7	125	130
8	120	120

EX1531

15.31 A psychology class performed an experiment to determine whether a recall score in which instructions to form images of 25 words were given differs from an initial recall score for which no imagery instructions were given. Twenty students participated in the experiment with the results listed in the table.

Student	With Imagery	Without Imagery	Student	With Imagery	Without Imagery
1	20	5	11	17	8
2	24	9	12	20	16
3	20	5	13	20	10
4	18	9	14	16	12
5	22	6	15	24	7
6	19	11	16	22	9
7	20	8	17	25	21
8	19	11	18	21	14
9	17	7	19	19	12
10	21	9	20	23	13

a. What three testing procedures can be used to test for differences in the distribution of recall scores with and without imagery? What assumptions are required for the parametric procedure? Do these data satisfy these assumptions?

b. Use both the sign test and the Wilcoxon signed-rank test to test for differences in the distributions of recall scores under these two conditions.

c. Compare the results of the tests in part b. Are the conclusions the same? If not, why not?

15.6 The Kruskal–Wallis *H* Test for Completely Randomized Designs

Just as the Wilcoxon rank sum test is the nonparametric alternative to Student's *t* test for a comparison of population means, the Kruskal–Wallis *H* test is the nonparametric alternative to the analysis of variance *F* test for a completely randomized design. It is used to detect differences in locations among more than two population distributions based on independent random sampling.

The procedure for conducting the Kruskal–Wallis *H* test is similar to that used for the Wilcoxon rank sum test. Suppose you are comparing *k* populations based on independent random samples n_1 from population 1, n_2 from population 2, . . . , n_k from population k, where

$$n_1 + n_2 + \cdots + n_k = n$$

The first step is to rank all n observations from the smallest (rank 1) to the largest (rank n). Tied observations are assigned a rank equal to the average of the ranks they would have received if they had been nearly equal but not tied. You then calculate the rank sums $T_1, T_2, \ldots, T_k$ for the k samples and calculate the test statistic

$$H = \frac{12}{n(n+1)} \Sigma \frac{T_i^2}{n_i} - 3(n+1)$$

which is proportional to $\Sigma\, n_i(\overline{T}_i - \overline{T})^2$, the sum of squared deviations of the rank means about the grand mean $\overline{T} = n(n+1)/2n = (n+1)/2$. The greater the differences in locations among the k population distributions, the larger is the value of the H statistic. Thus, you can reject the null hypothesis that the k population distributions are identical for large values of H.

How large is large? It can be shown (proof omitted) that when the sample sizes are moderate to large—say, each sample size is equal to five or larger—and when H_0 is true, the H statistic will have approximately a chi-square distribution with $(k - 1)$ degrees of freedom. Therefore, for a given value of α, you can reject H_0 when the H statistic exceeds χ_α^2 (see Figure 15.5).

FIGURE 15.5
Approximate distribution of the *H* statistic when H_0 is true

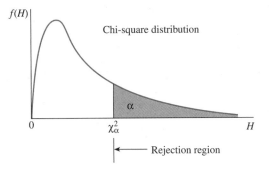

EXAMPLE 15.6 The data in Table 15.9 were collected using a completely randomized design. They are the achievement test scores for four different groups of students, each group taught by a different teaching technique. The objective of the experiment is to test the hypothesis of no difference in the population distributions of achievement test scores versus the alternative that they differ in location; that is, at least one of the distributions is shifted above the others. Conduct the test using the Kruskal–Wallis H test with $\alpha = .05$.

TABLE 15.9
Test scores (and ranks) from four teaching techniques

	1	2	3	4
	65 (3)	75 (9)	59 (1)	94 (23)
	87 (19)	69 (5.5)	78 (11)	89 (21)
	73 (8)	83 (17.5)	67 (4)	80 (14)
	79 (12.5)	81 (15.5)	62 (2)	88 (20)
	81 (15.5)	72 (7)	83 (17.5)	
	69 (5.5)	79 (12.5)	76 (10)	
		90 (22)		
Rank sum	$T_1 = 63.5$	$T_2 = 89$	$T_3 = 45.5$	$T_4 = 78$

Solution   Before you perform a nonparametric analysis on these data, you can use a one-way analysis of variance to provide the two plots in Figure 15.6. It appears that technique 4 has a smaller variance than the other three and that there is a marked deviation in the right tail of the normal probability plot. These deviations could be considered minor and either a parametric or nonparametric analysis could be used.

FIGURE 15.6
A normal probability plot and a residual plot following a one-way analysis of variance for Example 15.6

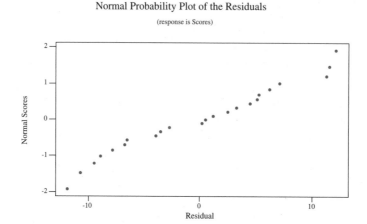

Normal Probability Plot of the Residuals
(response is Scores)

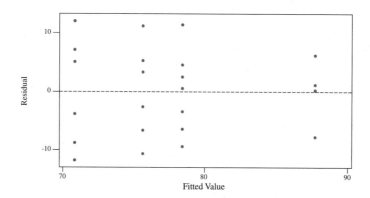

Residuals Versus the Fitted Values
(response is Scores)

In the Kruskal–Wallis H test procedure, the first step is to rank the $n = 23$ observations from the smallest (rank 1) to the largest (rank 23). These ranks are shown in parentheses in Table 15.9. Notice how the ties are handled. For example, two observations at 69 are tied for rank 5. Therefore, they are assigned the average 5.5 of the two ranks (5 and 6) that they would have occupied if they had been slightly different. The rank sums T_1, T_2, T_3, and T_4 for the four samples are shown in the bottom row of the table. Substituting rank sums and sample sizes into the formula for the H statistic, you get

$$H = \frac{12}{n(n+1)} \Sigma \frac{T_i^2}{n_i} - 3(n+1)$$

$$= \frac{12}{23(24)} \left[\frac{(63.5)^2}{6} + \frac{(89)^2}{7} + \frac{(45.5)^2}{6} + \frac{(78)^2}{4} \right] - 3(24)$$

$$= 79.775102 - 72 = 7.775102$$

The rejection region for the *H* statistic for $\alpha = .05$ includes values of $H \geq \chi_{.05}^2$, where $\chi_{.05}^2$ is based on $(k - 1) = (4 - 1) = 3$ *df*. The value of χ^2 given in Table 5 in Appendix I is $\chi_{.05}^2 = 7.81473$. The observed value of the *H* statistic, $H = 7.775102$, does not fall into the rejection region for the test. Therefore, there is insufficient evidence to indicate differences in the distributions of achievement test scores for the four teaching techniques.

A *MINITAB* printout of the Kruskal–Wallis *H* test for these data is given in Figure 15.7. Notice that the *p*-value, .051, is only slightly greater than the 5% level necessary to declare statistical significance.

FIGURE 15.7
MINITAB printout for the Kruskal–Wallis test for Example 15.6

Kruskal-Wallis Test: Scores versus Technique

```
Kruskal-Wallis Test on Scores

Technique   N     Median   Ave Rank         Z
1           6      76.00       10.6     -0.60
2           7      79.00       12.7      0.33
3           6      71.50        7.6     -1.86
4           4      88.50       19.5      2.43
Overall    23                  12.0

H = 7.78  DF = 3  P = 0.051
H = 7.79  DF = 3  P = 0.051 (adjusted for ties)

* NOTE * One or more small samples
```

EXAMPLE 15.7

Compare the results of the analysis of variance *F* test and the Kruskal–Wallis *H* test for testing for differences in the distributions of achievement test scores for the four teaching techniques in Example 15.6.

Solution

The *MINITAB* printout for a one-way analysis of variance for the data in Table 15.9 is given in Figure 15.8. The analysis of variance shows that the *F* test for testing for differences among the means for the four techniques is significant at the .028 level. The Kruskal–Wallis *H* test did not detect a shift in population distributions at the .05 level of significance. Although these conclusions seem to be far apart, the test results do not differ strongly. The *p*-value = .028 corresponding to $F = 3.77$, with $df_1 = 3$ and $df_2 = 19$, is slightly less than .05, in contrast to the *p*-value = .051 for $H = 7.78$, $df = 3$, which is slightly greater than .05. Someone viewing the *p*-values for the two tests would see little difference in the results of the *F* and *H* tests. However, if you adhere to the choice of $\alpha = .05$, you cannot reject H_0 using the *H* test.

FIGURE 15.8
MINITAB printout for Example 15.7

One-way ANOVA: Scores versus Technique

```
Analysis of Variance for Scores
Source       DF        SS        MS       F        P
Technique     3     712.6     237.5    3.77    0.028
Error        19    1196.6      63.0
Total        22    1909.2
```

The Kruskal–Wallis *H* Test for Comparing More Than Two Populations: Completely Randomized Design (Independent Random Samples).

1. Null hypothesis: H_0 : The *k* population distributions are identical.

(continued)

The Kruskal–Wallis H Test for Comparing More Than Two Populations: Completely Randomized Design (Independent Random Samples) *(continued)*

2. Alternative hypothesis: H_a: At least two of the k population distributions differ in location.

3. Test statistic: $H = \dfrac{12}{n(n+1)} \Sigma \dfrac{T_i^2}{n_i} - 3(n+1)$

where

n_i = Sample size for population i

T_i = Rank sum for population i

n = Total number of observations

$= n_1 + n_2 + \cdots + n_k$

4. Rejection region for a given α: $H > \chi_\alpha^2$ with $(k-1)$ *df*

Assumptions

- All sample sizes are greater than or equal to five.
- Ties take on the average of the ranks that they would have occupied if they had not been tied.

The Kruskal–Wallis H test is a valuable alternative to a one-way analysis of variance when the normality and equality of variance assumptions are violated. Again, normal probability plots of residuals and plots of residuals per treatment group are helpful in determining whether these assumptions have been violated. Remember that a normal probability plot should appear as a straight line with a positive slope; residual plots per treatment groups should exhibit the same spread above and below the 0 line.

Exercises

Basic Techniques

15.32

EX1532

Three treatments were compared using a completely randomized design. The data are shown in the table.

Treatment		
1	2	3
26	27	25
29	31	24
23	30	27
24	28	22
28	29	24
26	32	20
	30	21
	33	

Do the data provide sufficient evidence to indicate a difference in location for at least two of the population distributions? Test using the Kruskal–Wallis H statistic with α = .05.

15.33

EX1533

Four treatments were compared using a completely randomized design. The data are shown here:

Treatment			
1	2	3	4
124	147	141	117
167	121	144	128
135	136	139	102
160	114	162	119
159	129	155	128
144	117	150	123
133	109		

Do the data provide sufficient evidence to indicate a difference in location for at least two of the population distributions? Test using the Kruskal–Wallis H statistic with $\alpha = .05$.

Applications

15.34 Exercise 11.13 presents data (see data set EX1113) on the rates of growth of vegetation at four swampy underdeveloped sites. Six plants were randomly selected at each of the four sites to be used in the comparison. The data are the mean leaf length per plant (in centimeters) for a random sample of ten leaves per plant.

Location	Mean Leaf Length (cm)					
1	5.7	6.3	6.1	6.0	5.8	6.2
2	6.2	5.3	5.7	6.0	5.2	5.5
3	5.4	5.0	6.0	5.6	4.9	5.2
4	3.7	3.2	3.9	4.0	3.5	3.6

a. Do the data present sufficient evidence to indicate differences in location for at least two of the distributions of mean leaf length corresponding to the four locations? Test using the Kruskal–Wallis H test with $\alpha = .05$.

b. Find the approximate p-value for the test.

c. You analyzed this same set of data in Exercise 11.13 using an analysis of variance. Find the p-value for the F test used to compare the four location means in Exercise 11.13.

d. Compare the p-values in parts b and c and explain the implications of the comparison.

15.35 Exercise 11.52 presented data (data set EX1152) on the heart rates for samples of ten men randomly selected from each of four age groups. Each man walked a treadmill at a fixed grade for a period of 12 minutes, and the increase in heart rate (the difference before and after exercise) was recorded (in beats per minute). The data are shown in the table.

10–19	20–39	40–59	60–69
29	24	37	28
33	27	25	29
26	33	22	34
27	31	33	36
39	21	28	21
35	28	26	20
33	24	30	25
29	34	34	24
36	21	27	33
22	32	33	32
Total 309	275	295	282

a. Do the data present sufficient evidence to indicate differences in location for at least two of the four age groups? Test using the Kruskal–Wallis H test with $\alpha = .01$.

b. Find the approximate p-value for the test in part a.

c. Since the F test in Exercise 11.49 and the H test in part a are both tests to detect differences in location of the four heart-rate populations, how do the test results compare? Compare the p-values for the two tests and explain the implications of the comparison.

EX1536

15.36   A sampling of the acidity of rain for ten randomly selected rainfalls was recorded at three different locations in the United States: the Northeast, the Middle Atlantic region, and the Southeast. The pH readings for these 30 rainfalls are shown in the table. (NOTE: pH readings range from 0 to 14; 0 is acid, 14 is alkaline. Pure water falling through clean air has a pH reading of 5.7.)

Northeast	Middle Atlantic	Southeast
4.45	4.60	4.55
4.02	4.27	4.31
4.13	4.31	4.84
3.51	3.88	4.67
4.42	4.49	4.28
3.89	4.22	4.95
4.18	4.54	4.72
3.95	4.76	4.63
4.07	4.36	4.36
4.29	4.21	4.47

a. Do the data present sufficient evidence to indicate differences in the levels of acidity in rainfalls in the three different locations? Test using the Kruskal–Wallis H test.

b. Find the approximate p-value for the test in part a and interpret it.

15.37   The results of an experiment to investigate product recognition for three advertising campaigns were reported in Example 11.14. The responses were the percentage of 400 adults who were familiar with the newly advertised product. The normal probability plot indicated that the data were not approximately normal and another method of analysis should be used. Is there a significant difference among the three population distributions from which these samples came? Use an appropriate nonparametric method to answer this question.

	Campaign	
1	2	3
.33	.28	.21
.29	.41	.30
.21	.34	.26
.32	.39	.33
.25	.27	.31

15.7 The Friedman F_r Test for Randomized Block Designs

The Friedman F_r test, proposed by Nobel Prize–winning economist Milton Friedman, is a nonparametric test for comparing the distributions of measurements for k treatments laid out in b blocks using a randomized block design. The procedure for conducting the test is very similar to that used for the Kruskal–Wallis H test. The first step in the procedure is to rank the k treatment observations within each block. Ties are treated in the usual way; that is, they receive an average of the ranks occupied by the tied observations. The rank sums $T_1, T_2, \ldots, T_k$ are then obtained and the test statistic

$$F_r = \frac{12}{bk(k+1)} \Sigma T_i^2 - 3b(k+1)$$

is calculated. The value of the F_r statistic is at a minimum when the rank sums are equal—that is, $T_1 = T_2 = \cdots = T_k$—and increases in value as the differences among the rank sums increase. When either the number k of treatments or the number b of blocks is larger than five, the sampling distribution of F_r can be approximated by a chi-square distribution with $(k - 1)$ df. Therefore, as for the Kruskal–Wallis H test, the rejection region for the F_r test consists of values of F_r for which

$$F_r > \chi_\alpha^2$$

EXAMPLE 15.8 Suppose you wish to compare the reaction times of people exposed to six different stimuli. A reaction time measurement is obtained by subjecting a person to a stimulus and then measuring the time until the person presents some specified reaction. The objective of the experiment is to determine whether differences exist in the reaction times for the stimuli used in the experiment. To eliminate the person-to-person variation in reaction time, four persons participated in the experiment and each person's reaction time (in seconds) was measured for each of the six stimuli. The data are given in Table 15.10 (ranks of the observations are shown in parentheses). Use the Friedman F_r test to determine whether the data present sufficient evidence to indicate differences in the distributions of reaction times for the six stimuli. Test using $\alpha = .05$.

TABLE 15.10
Reaction times to six stimuli

Subject	Stimulus					
	A	B	C	D	E	F
1	.6 (2.5)	.9 (6)	.8 (5)	.7 (4)	.5 (1)	.6 (2.5)
2	.7 (3.5)	1.1 (6)	.7 (3.5)	.8 (5)	.5 (1.5)	.5 (1.5)
3	.9 (3)	1.3 (6)	1.0 (4.5)	1.0 (4.5)	.7 (1)	.8 (2)
4	.5 (2)	.7 (5)	.8 (6)	.6 (3.5)	.4 (1)	.6 (3.5)
Rank sum	$T_1 = 11$	$T_2 = 23$	$T_3 = 19$	$T_4 = 17$	$T_5 = 4.5$	$T_6 = 9.5$

Solution In Figure 15.9, the plot of the residuals for each of the six stimuli reveals that stimuli 1, 4, and 5 have variances somewhat smaller than the other stimuli. Furthermore, the normal probability plot of the residuals reveals a change in the slope of the line following the first three residuals, as well as curvature in the upper portion of the plot. It appears that a nonparametric analysis is appropriate for these data.

FIGURE 15.9 A plot of treatments versus residuals and a normal probability plot of residuals for Example 15.8

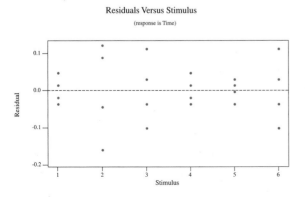
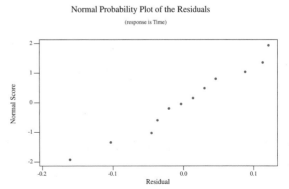

You wish to test

H_0 : The distributions of reaction times for the six stimuli are identical

versus the alternative hypothesis

H_a : At least two of the distributions of reaction times for the six stimuli differ in location

Table 15.10 shows the ranks (in parentheses) of the observations within each block and the rank sums for each of the six stimuli (the treatments). The value of the F_r statistic for these data is

$$F_r = \frac{12}{bk(k+1)} \Sigma\, T_i^2 - 3b(k+1)$$

$$= \frac{12}{(4)(6)(7)} [(11)^2 + (23)^2 + (19)^2 + \cdots + (9.5)^2] - 3(4)(7)$$

$$= 100.75 - 84 = 16.75$$

Since the number $k = 6$ of treatments exceeds five, the sampling distribution of F_r can be approximated by a chi-square distribution with $(k - 1) = (6 - 1) = 5$ df. Therefore, for $\alpha = .05$, you can reject H_0 if

$$F_r > \chi_{.05}^2 \quad \text{where} \quad \chi_{.05}^2 = 11.0705$$

This rejection region is shown in Figure 15.10. Since the observed value $F_r = 16.75$ exceeds $\chi_{.05}^2 = 11.0705$, it falls in the rejection region. You can therefore reject H_0 and conclude that the distributions of reaction times differ in location for at least two stimuli. The *MINITAB* printout of the Friedman F_r test for the data is given in Figure 15.11.

FIGURE 15.10
Rejection region
for Example 15.8

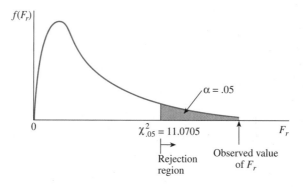

FIGURE 15.11
MINITAB printout
for Example 15.8

Friedman Test: Time versus Stimulus, Subject

```
Friedman test for Time by Stimulus blocked by Subject

S = 16.75   DF = 5   P = 0.005
S = 17.37   DF = 5   P = 0.004 (adjusted for ties)

                      Est      Sum of
Stimulus    N      Median      Ranks
1           4      0.6500       11.0
2           4      1.0000       23.0
3           4      0.8000       19.0
4           4      0.7500       17.0
5           4      0.5000        4.5
6           4      0.6000        9.5

Grand median  =    0.7167
```

EXAMPLE 15.9 Find the approximate p-value for the test in Example 15.8.

Solution Consulting Table 5 in Appendix I with 5 df, you find that the observed value of $F_r =$ 16.75 exceeds the table value $\chi^2_{.005} = 16.7496$. Hence, the p-value is very close to, but slightly less than, .005.

> **The Friedman F_r Test for a Randomized Block Design**
>
> **1.** Null hypothesis: H_0 : The k population distributions are identical.
> **2.** Alternative hypothesis: H_a : At least two of the k population distributions differ in location.
> **3.** Test statistic: $F_r = \dfrac{12}{bk(k+1)} \Sigma T_i^2 - 3b(k+1)$
>
> where
>
> $b =$ Number of blocks
>
> $k =$ Number of treatments
>
> $T_i =$ Rank sum for treatment i, $i = 1, 2, \ldots, k$
>
> **4.** Rejection region: $F_r > \chi^2_\alpha$, where χ^2_α is based on $(k-1)$ df
>
> **Assumption**: Either the number k of treatments or the number b of blocks is greater than five.

Exercises

Basic Techniques

15.38 A randomized block design is used to compare three treatments in six blocks.

	Treatment		
Block	1	2	3
1	3.2	3.1	2.4
2	2.8	3.0	1.7
3	4.5	5.0	3.9
4	2.5	2.7	2.6
5	3.7	4.1	3.5
6	2.4	2.4	2.0

a. Use the Friedman F_r test to detect differences in location among the three treatment distributions. Test using $\alpha = .05$.

b. Find the approximate p-value for the test in part a.

c. Perform an analysis of variance and give the ANOVA table for the analysis.

d. Give the value of the F statistic for testing the equality of the three treatment means.

e. Give the approximate p-value for the F statistic in part d.

f. Compare the p-values for the tests in parts a and d, and explain the practical implications of the comparison.

15.39 A randomized block design is used to compare four treatments in eight blocks.

EX1539

	Treatment			
Block	1	2	3	4
1	89	81	84	85
2	93	86	86	88
3	91	85	87	86
4	85	79	80	82
5	90	84	85	85
6	86	78	83	84
7	87	80	83	82
8	93	86	88	90

a. Use the Friedman F_r test to detect differences in location among the four treatment distributions. Test using $\alpha = .05$.

b. Find the approximate p-value for the test in part a.

c. Perform an analysis of variance and give the ANOVA table for the analysis.

d. Give the value of the F statistic for testing the equality of the four treatment means.

e. Give the approximate p-value for the F statistic in part d.

f. Compare the p-values for the tests in parts a and d, and explain the practical implications of the comparison.

Applications

EX1540

15.40 In a comparison of the prices of items at five supermarkets, six items were randomly selected and the price of each was recorded for each of the five supermarkets. The objective of the study was to see whether the data indicated differences in the levels of prices among the five supermarkets. The prices are listed in the table.

Item	Kash n' Karry	Publix	Winn-Dixie	Albertsons	Food 4 Less
Celery	.33	.34	.69	.59	.58
Colgate toothpaste	1.28	1.49	1.44	1.37	1.28
Campbell's beef soup	1.05	1.19	1.23	1.19	1.10
Crushed pineapple	.83	.95	.95	.87	.84
Mueller's spaghetti	.68	.79	.83	.69	.69
Heinz ketchup	1.41	1.69	1.79	1.65	1.49

a. Does the distribution of the prices differ from one supermarket to another? Test using the Friedman F_r test with $\alpha = .05$.

b. Find the approximate p-value for the test and interpret it.

15.41 An experiment was conducted to compare the effects of three toxic chemicals, A, B, and C, on the skin of rats. One-inch squares of skin were treated with the chemicals and then scored from 0 to 10 depending on the degree of irritation. Three adjacent 1-inch squares were marked on the backs of eight rats, and each of the three chemicals was applied to each rat. Thus, the experiment was blocked on rats to eliminate the variation in skin sensitivity from rat to rat.

	Rats							
	1	2	3	4	5	6	7	8
	B	A	A	C	B	C	C	B
	5	9	6	6	8	5	5	7
	A	C	B	B	C	A	B	A
	6	4	9	8	8	5	7	6
	C	B	C	A	A	B	A	C
	3	9	3	5	7	7	6	7

a. Do the data provide sufficient evidence to indicate a difference in the toxic effects of the three chemicals? Test using the Friedman F_r test with $\alpha = .05$.

b. Find the approximate p-value for the test and interpret it.

15.42 In a study of the palatability of antibiotics in children, Dr. Doreen Matsui and colleagues used a voluntary sample of healthy children to assess their reactions to the taste of four antibiotics.[4] The children's response was measured on a 10-centimeter (cm) visual analog scale incorporating the use of faces, from sad (low score) to happy (high score). The minimum score was 0 and the maximum was 10. For the accompanying data (simulated from the results of Matsui's report), each of five children was asked to taste each of four antibiotics and rate them using the visual (faces) analog scale from 0 to 10 cm.

Child	Antibiotic			
	1	2	3	4
1	4.8	2.2	6.8	6.2
2	8.1	9.2	6.6	9.6
3	5.0	2.6	3.6	6.5
4	7.9	9.4	5.3	8.5
5	3.9	7.4	2.1	2.0

a. What design is used in collecting these data?

b. Using an appropriate statistical package for a two-way classification, produce a normal probability plot of the residuals as well as a plot of residuals versus antibiotics. Do the usual analysis of variance assumptions appear to be satisfied?

c. Use the appropriate nonparametric test to test for differences in the distributions of responses to the tastes of the four antibiotics.

d. Comment on the results of the analysis of variance in part b compared with the nonparametric test in part c.

15.8 Rank Correlation Coefficient

In the preceding sections, we used ranks to indicate the relative magnitude of observations in nonparametric tests for the comparison of treatments. We will now use the same technique in testing for a relationship between two ranked variables. Two common rank correlation coefficients are the **Spearman** r_s and the **Kendall** τ. We will present the Spearman r_s because its computation is identical to that for the sample correlation coefficient r of Chapters 3 and 12.

Suppose eight elementary school science teachers have been ranked by a judge according to their teaching ability and all have taken a "national teachers' examination." The data are listed in Table 15.11. Do the data suggest an agreement between the judge's ranking and the examination score? That is, is there a correlation between ranks and test scores?

TABLE 15.11

Ranks and test scores for eight teachers

Teacher	Judge's Rank	Examination Score
1	7	44
2	4	72
3	2	69
4	6	70
5	1	93
6	3	82
7	8	67
8	5	80

The two variables of interest are rank and test score. The former is already in rank form, and the test scores can be ranked similarly, as shown in Table 15.12. The ranks for tied observations are obtained by averaging the ranks that the tied observations would have had if no ties had been observed. The Spearman rank correlation coefficient r_s is calculated by using the ranks of the paired measurements on the two variables x and y in the formula for r (see Chapter 12).

TABLE 15.12
Ranks of data in
Table 15.11

Teacher	Judge's Rank, x_i	Test Rank, y_i
1	7	1
2	4	5
3	2	3
4	6	4
5	1	8
6	3	7
7	8	2
8	5	6

Spearman's Rank Correlation Coefficient

$$r_s = \frac{S_{xy}}{\sqrt{S_{xx}S_{yy}}}$$

where x_i and y_i represent the ranks of the ith pair of observations and

$$S_{xy} = \Sigma\,(x_i - \bar{x})(y_i - \bar{y}) = \Sigma\, x_i y_i - \frac{(\Sigma\, x_i)\,(\Sigma\, y_i)}{n}$$

$$S_{xx} = \Sigma\,(x_i - \bar{x})^2 = \Sigma\, x_i^2 - \frac{(\Sigma\, x_i)^2}{n}$$

$$S_{yy} = \Sigma\,(y_i - \bar{y})^2 = \Sigma\, y_i^2 - \frac{(\Sigma\, y_i)^2}{n}$$

When there are no ties in either the x observations or the y observations, the expression for r_s algebraically reduces to the simpler expression

$$r_s = 1 - \frac{6\,\Sigma\, d_i^2}{n(n^2 - 1)} \qquad \text{where } d_i = (x_i - y_i)$$

If the number of ties is small in comparison with the number of data pairs, little error results in using this shortcut formula.

EXAMPLE 15.10 Calculate r_s for the data in Table 15.12.

Solution The differences and squares of differences between the two rankings are provided in Table 15.13. Substituting values into the formula for r_s, you have

$$r_s = 1 - \frac{6\,\Sigma\, d_i^2}{n(n^2 - 1)}$$

$$= 1 - \frac{6(144)}{8(64 - 1)} = -.714$$

Teacher	x_i	y_i	d_i	d_i^2
1	7	1	6	36
2	4	5	−1	1
3	2	3	−1	1
4	6	4	2	4
5	1	8	−7	49
6	3	7	−4	16
7	8	2	6	36
8	5	6	−1	1
Total				144

TABLE 15.13 Differences and squares of differences for the teacher ranks

The Spearman rank correlation coefficient can be used as a test statistic to test the hypothesis of no association between two populations. You can assume that the n pairs of observations (x_i, y_i) have been randomly selected and, therefore, no association between the populations implies a random assignment of the n ranks within each sample. Each random assignment (for the two samples) represents a simple event associated with the experiment, and a value of r_s can be calculated for each. Thus, it is possible to calculate the probability that r_s assumes a large absolute value due solely to chance and thereby suggests an association between populations when none exists.

The rejection region for a two-tailed test is shown in Figure 15.12. If the alternative hypothesis is that the correlation between x and y is negative, you would reject H_0 for negative values of r_s that are close to -1 (in the lower tail of Figure 15.12). Similarly, if the alternative hypothesis is that the correlation between x and y is positive, you would reject H_0 for large positive values of r_s (in the upper tail of Figure 15.12).

FIGURE 15.12 Rejection region for a two-tailed test of the null hypothesis of no association, using Spearman's rank correlation test

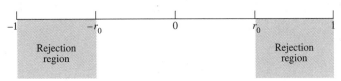

r_s = Spearman's rank correlation coefficient

The critical values of r_s are given in Table 9 in Appendix I. An abbreviated version is shown in Table 15.14. Across the top of Table 15.14 (and Table 9 in Appendix I) are the recorded values of α that you might wish to use for a one-tailed test of the null hypothesis of no association between x and y. The number of rank pairs n appears at the left side of the table. The table entries give the critical value r_0 for a one-tailed test. Thus, $P(r_s \geq r_0) = \alpha$.

For example, suppose you have $n = 8$ rank pairs and the alternative hypothesis is that the correlation between the ranks is positive. You would want to reject the null hypothesis of no association for only large positive values of r_s, and you would use a one-tailed test. Referring to Table 15.14 and using the row corresponding to $n = 8$ and the column for $\alpha = .05$, you read $r_0 = .643$. Therefore, you can reject H_0 for all values of r_s greater than or equal to .643.

The test is conducted in exactly the same manner if you wish to test only the alternative hypothesis that the ranks are negatively correlated. The only difference is that you would reject the null hypothesis if $r_s \leq -.643$. That is, you use the negative of the tabulated value of r_0 to get the lower-tail critical value.

TABLE 15.14	n	$\alpha = .05$	$\alpha = .025$	$\alpha = .01$	$\alpha = .005$
An abbreviated	5	.900	—	—	—
version of Table 9	6	.829	.886	.943	—
in Appendix 1; for	7	.714	.786	.893	—
Spearman's rank	8	.643	.738	.833	.881
correlation test	9	.600	.683	.783	.833
	10	.564	.648	.745	.794
	11	.523	.623	.736	.818
	12	.497	.591	.703	.780
	13	.475	.566	.673	.745
	14	.457	.545		
	15	.441	.525		
	16	.425			
	17	.412			
	18	.399			
	19	.388			
	20	.377			

To conduct a two-tailed test, you reject the null hypothesis if $r_s \geq r_0$ or $r_s \leq -r_0$. The value of α for the test is double the value shown at the top of the table. For example, if $n = 8$ and you choose the .025 column, you will reject H_0 if $r_s \geq .738$ or $r_s \leq -.738$. The α-value for the test is $2(.025) = .05$.

Spearman's Rank Correlation Test

1. Null hypothesis: H_0 : There is no association between the rank pairs.

2. Alternative hypothesis: H_a : There is an association between the rank pairs (a two-tailed test). Or H_a : The correlation between the rank pairs is positive or negative (a one-tailed test).

3. Test statistic: $r_s = \dfrac{S_{xy}}{\sqrt{S_{xx}S_{yy}}}$

   where x_i and y_i represent the ranks of the ith pair of observations.

4. Rejection region: For a two-tailed test, reject H_0 if $r_s \geq r_0$ or $r_s \leq -r_0$, where r_0 is given in Table 9 in Appendix I. Double the tabulated probability to obtain the value of α for the two-tailed test. For a one-tailed test, reject H_0 if $r_s \geq r_0$ (for an upper-tailed test) or $r_s \leq -r_0$ (for a lower-tailed test). The α-value for a one-tailed test is the value shown in Table 9 in Appendix I.

EXAMPLE 15.11 Test the hypothesis of no association between the populations for Example 15.10.

Solution The critical value of r_s for a one-tailed test with $\alpha = .05$ and $n = 8$ is .643. You may assume that a correlation between the judge's rank and the teachers' test scores could not possibly be positive. (A low rank means good teaching and should be associated with a high test score if the judge and the test measure teaching ability.) The alternative hypothesis is that the **population rank correlation coefficient** ρ_s is less than 0, and you are concerned with a one-tailed statistical test. Thus, α for the test is the tabulated value for .05, and you can reject the null hypothesis if $r_s \leq -.643$.

The calculated value of the test statistic, $r_s = -.714$, is less than the critical value for $\alpha = .05$. Hence, the null hypothesis is rejected at the $\alpha = .05$ level of significance. It appears that some agreement does exist between the judge's rankings and the test scores. However, it should be noted that this agreement could exist when *neither* provides an adequate yardstick for measuring teaching ability. For example, the association could exist if both the judge and those who constructed the teachers' examination had a completely erroneous, but similar, concept of the characteristics of good teaching.

What exactly does r_s measure? Spearman's correlation coefficient detects not only a linear relationship between two variables but also any other monotonic relationship (either y increases as x increases or y decreases as x increases). For example, if you calculated r_s for the two data sets in Table 15.13, both would produce a value of $r_s = 1$ because the assigned ranks for x and y in both cases agree for all pairs (x, y). It is important to remember that a significant value of r_s indicates a relationship between x and y that is either increasing or decreasing, but is not necessarily linear.

TABLE 15.15
Twin data sets with $r_s = 1$

x	$y = x^2$	x	$y = \log 10(x)$
1	1	10	1
2	4	100	2
3	9	1000	3
4	16	10,000	4
5	25	100,000	5
6	36	1,000,000	6

Exercises

Basic Techniques

15.43   Give the rejection region for a test to detect positive rank correlation if the number of pairs of ranks is 16 and you have these α-values:

    a. $\alpha = .05$ **b.** $\alpha = .01$

15.44   Give the rejection region for a test to detect negative rank correlation if the number of pairs of ranks is 12 and you have these α-values:

    a. $\alpha = .05$ **b.** $\alpha = .01$

15.45   Give the rejection region for a test to detect rank correlation if the number of pairs of ranks is 25 and you have these α-values:

    a. $\alpha = .05$ **b.** $\alpha = .01$

15.46   The following paired observations were obtained on two variables x and y:

x	1.2	.8	2.1	3.5	2.7	1.5
y	1.0	1.3	.1	$-.8$	$-.2$	.6

    a. Calculate Spearman's rank correlation coefficient r_s.

    b. Do the data present sufficient evidence to indicate a correlation between x and y? Test using $\alpha = .05$.

Applications

EX1547

15.47   A political scientist wished to examine the relationship between the voter image of a conservative political candidate and the distance (in miles) between the residences of the voter and the candidate. Each of 12 voters rated the candidate on a scale of 1 to 20.

Voter	Rating	Distance	Voter	Rating	Distance
1	12	75	7	9	120
2	7	165	8	18	60
3	5	300	9	3	230
4	19	15	10	8	200
5	17	180	11	15	130
6	12	240	12	4	130

a. Calculate Spearman's rank correlation coefficient r_s.

b. Do these data provide sufficient evidence to indicate a negative correlation between rating and distance?

EX1548

15.48 Is the number of years of competitive running experience related to a runner's distance running performance? The data on nine runners, obtained from the study by Scott Powers and colleagues, are shown in the table:[5]

Runner	Years of Competitive Running	10-Kilometer Finish Time (min)
1	9	33.15
2	13	33.33
3	5	33.50
4	7	33.55
5	12	33.73
6	6	33.86
7	4	33.90
8	5	34.15
9	3	34.90

a. Calculate the rank correlation coefficient between years of competitive running x and a runner's finish time y in the 10-kilometer race.

b. Do the data provide sufficient evidence to indicate a rank correlation between y and x? Test using $\alpha = .05$.

EX1549

15.49 The data shown in the accompanying table give measures of bending stiffness and twisting stiffness as determined by engineering tests on 12 tennis racquets.

Racquet	Bending Stiffness	Twisting Stiffness
1	419	227
2	407	231
3	363	200
4	360	211
5	257	182
6	622	304
7	424	384
8	359	194
9	346	158
10	556	225
11	474	305
12	441	235

a. Calculate the rank correlation coefficient r_s between bending stiffness and twisting stiffness.

b. If a racquet has bending stiffness, is it also likely to have twisting stiffness? Use the rank correlation coefficient to determine whether there is a significant positive relationship between bending stiffness and twisting stiffness. Use $\alpha = .05$.

15.50 A school principal suspected that a teacher's attitude toward a first-grader depended on his original judgment of the child's ability. The principal also suspected that much of that judgment was based on the first-grader's IQ score, which was usually known to the teacher. After three weeks of teaching, a teacher was asked to rank the nine children in his class from 1 (highest) to 9 (lowest) as to his opinion of their ability. Calculate r_s for these teacher–IQ ranks:

Teacher	1	2	3	4	5	6	7	8	9
IQ	3	1	2	4	5	7	9	6	8

15.51 Refer to Exercise 15.50. Do the data provide sufficient evidence to indicate a positive correlation between the teacher's ranks and the ranks of the IQs? Use $\alpha = .05$.

15.52 Two art critics each ranked ten paintings by contemporary (but anonymous) artists in accordance with their appeal to the respective critics. The ratings are shown in the table. Do the critics seem to agree on their ratings of contemporary art? That is, do the data provide sufficient evidence to indicate a positive correlation between critics A and B? Test by using a value of α near .05.

Paintings	Critic A	Critic B
1	6	5
2	4	6
3	9	10
4	1	2
5	2	3
6	7	8
7	3	1
8	8	7
9	5	4
10	10	9

EX1553

15.53 An experiment was conducted to study the relationship between the ratings of a tobacco leaf grader and the moisture content of the tobacco leaves. Twelve leaves were rated by the grader on a scale of 1 to 10, and corresponding readings of moisture content were made.

Leaf	Grader's Rating	Moisture Content
1	9	.22
2	6	.16
3	7	.17
4	7	.14
5	5	.12
6	8	.19
7	2	.10
8	6	.12
9	1	.05
10	10	.20
11	9	.16
12	3	.09

Calculate r_s. Do the data provide sufficient evidence to indicate an association between the grader's ratings and the moisture contents of the leaves?

15.54 A social skills training program was implemented with seven mildly handicapped students in a study to determine whether the program caused improvements in pre/post measures and behavior ratings. For one such test, the pre- and posttest scores for the seven students are given in the table:

Student	Pretest	Posttest
Earl	101	113
Ned	89	89
Jasper	112	121
Charlie	105	99
Tom	90	104
Susie	91	94
Lori	89	99

a. Use a nonparametric test to determine whether there is a significant positive relationship between the pre- and posttest scores.

b. Do these results agree with the results of the parametric test in Exercise 12.39?

15.9 Summary

The nonparametric tests presented in this chapter are only a few of the many nonparametric tests available to experimenters. The tests presented here are those for which tables of critical values are readily available.

Nonparametric statistical methods are especially useful when the observations can be rank ordered but cannot be located exactly on a measurement scale. Also, nonparametric methods are the only methods that can be used when the sampling designs have been correctly adhered to, but the data are not or cannot be assumed to follow the prescribed one or more distributional assumptions.

We have presented a wide array of nonparametric techniques that can be used when either the data are not normally distributed or the other required assumptions are not met. One-sample procedures are available in the literature; however, we have concentrated on analyzing two or more samples that have been properly selected using random and independent sampling as required by the design involved. The nonparametric analogues of the parametric procedures presented in Chapters 10–14 are straightforward and fairly simple to implement:

- The Wilcoxon rank sum test is the nonparametric analogue of the two-sample t test.
- The sign test and the Wilcoxon signed-rank tests are the nonparametric analogues of the paired-sample t test.
- The Kruskal–Wallis H test is the rank equivalent of the one-way analysis of variance F test.
- The Friedman F_r test is the rank equivalent of the randomized block design two-way analysis of variance F test.
- Spearman's rank correlation r_s is the rank equivalent of Pearson's correlation coefficient.

These and many more nonparametric procedures are available as alternatives to the parametric tests presented earlier. It is important to keep in mind that when the assumptions required of the sampled populations are relaxed, our ability to detect significant differences in one or more population characteristics is decreased.

Key Concepts and Formulas

I. Nonparametric Methods

1. These methods can be used when the data cannot be measured on a quantitative scale, or when

2. The numerical scale of measurement is arbitrarily set by the researcher, or when
3. The parametric assumptions such as normality or constant variance are seriously violated.

II. Wilcoxon Rank Sum Test: Independent Random Samples

1. Jointly rank the two samples. Designate the smaller sample as sample 1. Then

$$T_1 = \text{Rank sum of sample 1} \qquad T_1^* = n_1(n_1 + n_2 + 1) - T_1$$

2. Use T_1 to test for population 1 to the left of population 2. Use T_1^* to test for population 1 to the right of population 2. Use the smaller of T_1 and T_1^* to test for a difference in the locations of the two populations.
3. Table 7 of Appendix I has critical values for the rejection of H_0.
4. When the sample sizes are large, use the normal approximation:

$$\mu_T = \frac{n_1(n_1 + n_2 + 1)}{2} \qquad \sigma_T^2 = \frac{n_1 n_2(n_1 + n_2 + 1)}{12} \qquad z = \frac{T - \mu_T}{\sigma_T}$$

III. Sign Test for a Paired Experiment

1. Find x, the number of times that observation A exceeds observation B for a given pair.
2. To test for a difference in two populations, test $H_0 : p = .5$ versus a one- or two-tailed alternative.
3. Use Table 1 of Appendix I to calculate the p-value for the test.
4. When the sample sizes are large, use the normal approximation:

$$z = \frac{x - .5n}{.5\sqrt{n}}$$

IV. Wilcoxon Signed-Rank Test: Paired Experiment

1. Calculate the differences in the paired observations. Rank the *absolute values* of the differences. Calculate the rank sums T^+ and T^- for the positive and negative differences, respectively. The test statistic T is the smaller of the two rank sums.
2. Table 8 in Appendix I has critical values for the rejection of H_0 for both one- and two-tailed tests.
3. When the sample sizes are large, use the normal approximation:

$$z = \frac{T^+ - [n(n + 1)/4]}{\sqrt{[n(n + 1)(2n + 1)]/24}}$$

V. Kruskal–Wallis H Test: Completely Randomized Design

1. Jointly rank the n observations in the k samples. Calculate the rank sums, $T_i = $ rank sum of sample i, and the test statistic

$$H = \frac{12}{n(n + 1)} \Sigma \frac{T_i^2}{n_i} - 3(n + 1)$$

2. If the null hypothesis of equality of distributions is false, H will be unusually large, resulting in a one-tailed test.
3. For sample sizes of five or greater, the rejection region for H is based on the chi-square distribution with $(k - 1)$ degrees of freedom.

VI. **The Friedman F_r Test: Randomized Block Design**
1. Rank the responses within each block from 1 to k. Calculate the rank sums, T_1, T_2, . . . , T_k, and the test statistic

$$F_r = \frac{12}{bk(k+1)} \Sigma T_i^2 - 3b(k+1)$$

2. If the null hypothesis of equality of treatment distributions is false, F_r will be unusually large, resulting in a one-tailed test.
3. For block sizes of five or greater, the rejection region for F_r is based on the chi-square distribution with $(k-1)$ degrees of freedom.

VII. **Spearman's Rank Correlation Coefficient**
1. Rank the responses for the two variables from smallest to largest.
2. Calculate the correlation coefficient for the ranked observations:

$$r_s = \frac{S_{xy}}{\sqrt{S_{xx}S_{yy}}} \quad \text{or} \quad r_s = 1 - \frac{6 \Sigma d_i^2}{n(n^2-1)} \text{ if there are no ties}$$

3. Table 9 in Appendix I gives critical values for rank correlations significantly different from 0.
4. The rank correlation coefficient detects not only significant linear correlation but also any other monotonic relationship between the two variables.

Nonparametric Procedures

Many nonparametric procedures are available in the *MINITAB* package, including most of the tests discussed in this chapter. The Dialog boxes are all familiar to you by now, and we will discuss the tests in the order presented in the chapter.

To implement the Wilcoxon rank sum test for two independent random samples, enter the two sets of sample data into two columns (say, C1 and C2) of the Minitab worksheet. The Dialog box in Figure 15.13 is generated using **Stat → Nonparametrics →**

FIGURE 15.13

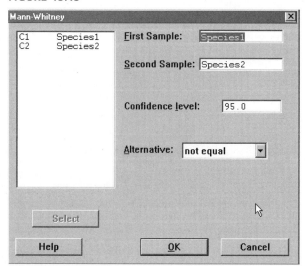

MINITAB

MINITAB

Mann-Whitney. Select C1 and C2 for the **First** and **Second Samples,** and indicate the appropriate confidence coefficient (for a confidence interval) and alternative hypothesis. Clicking **OK** will generate the output in Figure 15.1.

The sign test *and* the Wilcoxon signed-rank test for paired samples are performed in exactly the same way, with a change only in the last command of the sequence. Even the Dialog boxes are identical! Enter the data into two columns of the *MINITAB* worksheet (we used the cake mix data in Section 15.5). Before you can implement either test, you must generate a column of differences using **Calc → Calculator,** as shown in Figure 15.14. Use **Stat → Nonparametrics → 1-Sample Sign** or **Stat → Nonparametrics → 1-Sample Wilcoxon** to generate the appropriate Dialog box shown in Figure 15.15. Remember that the median is the value of a variable such that 50% of the values

FIGURE 15.14

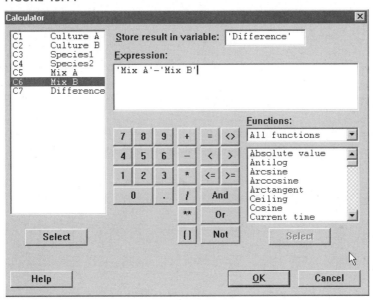

FIGURE 15.15

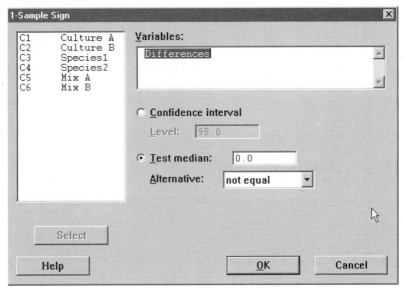

are smaller and 50% are larger. Hence, if the two population distributions are the same, the median of the differences will be 0. This is equivalent to the null hypothesis

$$H_0 : P(\text{positive difference}) = P(\text{negative difference}) = .5$$

used for the sign test. Select the column of differences for the Variables box, and select the test of the median equals 0 with the appropriate alternative. Click **OK** to obtain the printout for either of the two tests. The Session window printout for the sign test, shown in Figure 15.16, indicates a nonsignificant difference in the distributions of densities for the two cake mixes. Notice that the *p*-value (.2188) is not the same as the *p*-value for the Wilcoxon signed-rank test (.093 from Figure 15.4). However, if you are testing at the 5% level, both tests produce nonsignificant differences.

The procedures for implementing the Kruskal–Wallis *H* test for *k* independent samples and Friedman's F_r test for a randomized block design are identical to the procedures used for their parametric equivalents. Review the methods described in the section "About *MINITAB*" in Chapter 11. Once you have entered the data as explained in that section, the commands **Stat → Nonparametrics → Kruskal–Wallis** or **Stat → Nonparametrics → Friedman** will generate a Dialog box in which you specify the Response column, the Factor column, and the Block column. Click **OK** to obtain the outputs for these nonparametric tests.

FIGURE 15.16

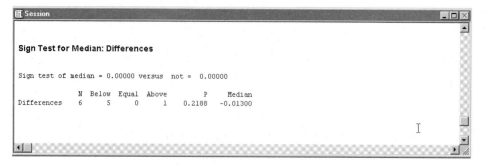

FIGURE 15.17

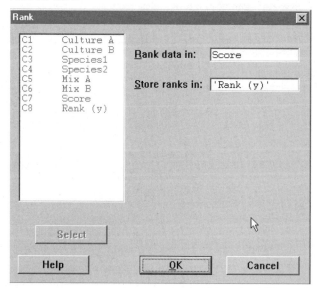

MINITAB

Finally, you can generate the nonparametric rank correlation coefficient r_s if you enter the data into two columns and rank the data using **Manip → Rank.** For example, the data on judge's rank and test scores were entered into columns C6 and C7 of our *MINITAB* worksheet. Since the judge's ranks are already in rank order, we need only to rank C7 by selecting "Score" and storing the ranks in C8 [see "Rank (y)" in Figure 15.17]. The commands **Stat → Basic Statistics → Correlation** will now produce the rank correlation coefficient when C6 and C8 are selected. However, the *p*-value that you see in the *output does not* produce exactly the same test as the critical values in Table 15.14. You should compare your value of r_s with the tabled value to check for a significant association between the two variables.

Supplementary Exercises

EX1555

15.55 An experiment was conducted to compare the response times for two different stimuli. To remove natural person-to-person variability in the responses, both stimuli were presented to each of nine subjects, thus permitting an analysis of the differences between stimuli *within* each person. The table lists the response times (in seconds):

Subject	Stimulus 1	Stimulus 2
1	9.4	10.3
2	7.8	8.9
3	5.6	4.1
4	12.1	14.7
5	6.9	8.7
6	4.2	7.1
7	8.8	11.3
8	7.7	5.2
9	6.4	7.8

a. Use the sign test to determine whether sufficient evidence exists to indicate a difference in the mean response times for the two stimuli. Use a rejection region for which $\alpha \leq .05$.

b. Test the hypothesis of no difference in mean response times using Student's *t* test.

15.56 Refer to Exercise 15.55. Test the hypothesis that no difference exists in the distributions of response times for the two stimuli, using the Wilcoxon signed-rank test. Use a rejection region for which α is as near as possible to the α achieved in Exercise 15.55, part a.

15.57 To compare two junior high schools, A and B, in academic effectiveness, an experiment was designed requiring the use of ten sets of identical twins, each twin having just completed the sixth grade. In each case, the twins in the same set had obtained their schooling in the same classrooms at each grade level. One child was selected at random from each pair of twins and assigned to school A. The remaining children were sent to school B. Near the end of the ninth grade, a certain achievement test was given to each child in the experiment. The test scores are shown in the table:

Twin Pair	School A	School B
1	67	39
2	80	75
3	65	69
4	70	55
5	86	74
6	50	52
7	63	56
8	81	72
9	86	89
10	60	47

a. Test (using the sign test) the hypothesis that the two schools are the same in academic effectiveness, as measured by scores on the achievement test, versus the alternative that the schools are not equally effective.

b. Suppose it was known that junior high school A had a superior faculty and better learning facilities. Test the hypothesis of equal academic effectiveness versus the alternative that school A is superior.

15.58 Refer to Exercise 15.57. What answers are obtained if Wilcoxon's signed-rank test is used in analyzing the data? Compare with your earlier answers.

15.59 The coded values for a measure of brightness in paper (light reflectivity), prepared by two different processes, are given in the table for samples of nine observations drawn randomly from each of the two processes. Do the data present sufficient evidence to indicate a difference in the brightness measurements for the two processes? Use both a parametric and a nonparametric test and compare your results.

Process	Brightness								
A	6.1	9.2	8.7	8.9	7.6	7.1	9.5	8.3	9.0
B	9.1	8.2	8.6	6.9	7.5	7.9	8.3	7.8	8.9

15.60 Assume (as in the case of measurements produced by two well-calibrated measuring instruments) the means of two populations are equal. Use the Wilcoxon rank sum statistic for testing hypotheses concerning the population variances as follows:

a. Rank the combined sample.

b. Number the ranked observations "from the outside in"; that is, number the smallest observation 1, the largest 2, the next-to-smallest 3, the next-to-largest 4, and so on. This sequence of numbers induces an ordering on the symbols A (population A items) and B (population B items). If $\sigma_A^2 > \sigma_B^2$, one would expect to find a preponderance of A's near the first of the sequences, and thus a relatively small "sum of ranks" for the A observations.

c. Given the measurements in the table produced by well-calibrated precision instruments A and B, test at near the $\alpha = .05$ level to determine whether the more expensive instrument B is more precise than A. (Note that this implies a one-tailed test.) Use the Wilcoxon rank sum test statistic.

Instrument A	Instrument B
1060.21	1060.24
1060.34	1060.28
1060.27	1060.32
1060.36	1060.30
1060.40	

d. Test using the equality of variance F test.

15.61 An experiment was conducted to compare the tenderness of meat cuts treated with two different meat tenderizers, A and B. To reduce the effect of extraneous variables, the data were paired by the specific meat cut, by applying the tenderizers to two cuts taken from the same steer, by cooking paired cuts together, and by using a single judge for each pair. After cooking, each cut was rated by a judge on a scale of 1 to 10, with 10 corresponding to the most tender meat. The data are shown for a single judge. Do the data provide sufficient evidence to indicate that one of the two tenderizers tends to receive higher ratings than the other? Would a Student's t test be appropriate for analyzing these data? Explain.

	Tenderizer	
Cut	A	B
Shoulder roast	5	7
Chuck roast	6	5
Rib steak	8	9
Brisket	4	5
Club steak	9	9
Round steak	3	5
Rump roast	7	6
Sirloin steak	8	8
Sirloin tip steak	8	9
T-bone steak	9	10

15.62 A large corporation selects college graduates for employment using both interviews and a psychological achievement test. Interviews conducted at the home office of the company are far more expensive than the tests that can be conducted on campus. Consequently, the personnel office was interested in determining whether the test scores were correlated with interview ratings and whether tests could be substituted for interviews. The idea was not to eliminate interviews but to reduce their number. To determine whether the measures were correlated, ten prospects were ranked during interviews and tested. The paired scores are as listed here:

Subject	Interview Rank	Test Score
1	8	74
2	5	81
3	10	66
4	3	83
5	6	66
6	1	94
7	4	96
8	7	70
9	9	61
10	2	86

Calculate the Spearman rank correlation coefficient r_s. Rank 1 is assigned to the candidate judged to be the best.

15.63 Refer to Exercise 15.62. Do the data present sufficient evidence to indicate that the correlation between interview rankings and test scores is less than 0? If this evidence does exist, can you say that tests can be used to reduce the number of interviews?

15.64 A comparison of reaction times for two different stimuli in a psychological word-association experiment produced the accompanying results when applied to a random sample of 16 people:

Stimulus	Reaction Time (sec)							
1	1	3	2	1	2	1	3	2
2	4	2	3	3	1	2	3	3

Do the data present sufficient evidence to indicate a difference in mean reaction times ~~ie two~~ stimuli? Use an appropriate nonparametric test and explain your conclusions.

~~on's~~

EX1565

15.65 The table gives the scores of a group of 15 students in mathematics and art. Use ~~icantly for~~ signed-rank test to determine whether the median scores for these students diffe the two subjects.

Student	Math	Art	Student	Math	Art
1	22	53	9	62	55
2	37	68	10	65	74
3	36	42	11	66	68
4	38	49	12	56	64
5	42	51	13	66	67
6	58	65	14	67	73
7	58	51	15	62	65
8	60	71			

15.66 Refer to Exercise 15.65. Compute Spearman's rank correlation coefficient for these data and test H_0 : no association between the rank pairs at the 10% level of significance.

15.67 Exercise 11.60 presented an analysis of variance of the yields of five different varieties of wheat, observed on one plot each at each of six different locations (see data set EX1160). The data from this randomized block design are listed here:

	Location					
Varieties	1	2	3	4	5	6
A	35.3	31.0	32.7	36.8	37.2	33.1
B	30.7	32.2	31.4	31.7	35.0	32.7
C	38.2	33.4	33.6	37.1	37.3	38.2
D	34.9	36.1	35.2	38.3	40.2	36.0
E	32.4	28.9	29.2	30.7	33.9	32.1

a. Use the appropriate nonparametric test to determine whether the data provide sufficient evidence to indicate a difference in the yields for the five different varieties of wheat. Test using $\alpha = .05$.

b. Exercise 11.60 presented a computer printout of the analysis of variance for comparing the mean yields for the five varieties of wheat. How do the results of the analysis of variance F test compare with the test in part a? Explain.

15.68 In Exercise 11.53, you compared the numbers of sales per trainee after completion of one of four different sales training programs (see data set EX1153). Six trainees completed training program 1, eight completed 2, and so on. The numbers of sales per trainee are shown in the table:

	Training Program			
	1	2	3	4
	78	99	74	81
	84	86	87	63
	86	90	80	71
	92	93	83	65
	69	94	78	86
	73	85		79
		97		73
		91		70
Total	482	735	402	588

a. Do the data present sufficient evidence to indicate that the distribution of number of sales per trainee differs from one training program to another? Test using the appropriate nonparametric test.

b. How do the test results in part a compare with the results of the analysis of variance F test in Exercise 11.48?

In Exercise 11.58, you performed an analysis of variance to compare the mean levels of effluents in water at four different industrial plants (see data set EX1158). Five samples of liquid waste were taken at the output of each of four industrial plants. The data are shown in the table:

Plant	Polluting Effluents (lb/gal of waste)				
A	1.65	1.72	1.50	1.37	1.60
B	1.70	1.85	1.46	2.05	1.80
C	1.40	1.75	1.38	1.65	1.55
D	2.10	1.95	1.65	1.88	2.00

a. Do the data present sufficient evidence to indicate a difference in the levels of pollutants for the four different industrial plants? Test using the appropriate nonparametric test.

b. Find the approximate p-value for the test and interpret its value.

c. Compare the test results in part a with the analysis of variance test in Exercise 11.55. Do the results agree? Explain.

15.70 Scientists have shown that a newly developed vaccine can shield rhesus monkeys from infection by a virus closely related to the AIDS-causing human immunodeficiency virus (HIV). In their work, Ronald C. Resrosiers and his colleagues at the New England Regional Primate Research Center gave each of $n = 6$ rhesus monkeys five inoculations with the simian immunodeficiency virus (SIV) vaccine. One week after the last vaccination, each monkey received an injection of live SIV. Two of the six vaccinated monkeys showed no evidence of SIV infection for as long as a year and a half after the SIV injection.[6] Scientists were able to isolate the SIV virus from the other four vaccinated monkeys, although these animals showed no sign of the disease. Does this information contain sufficient evidence to indicate that the vaccine is effective in protecting monkeys from SIV? Use $\alpha = .10$.

EX1571

15.71 An experiment was performed to determine whether there is an accumulation of heavy metals in plants that were grown in soils amended with sludge and whether there is an accumulation of heavy metals in insects feeding on those plants.[7] The data in the table are cadmium concentrations (in μg/kg) in plants grown under six different rates of application of sludge for three different harvests. The rates of application are the treatments. The three harvests represent time blocks in the two-way design.

	Harvest		
Rate	1	2	3
Control	162.1	153.7	200.4
1	199.8	199.6	278.2
2	220.0	210.7	294.8
3	194.4	179.0	341.1
4	204.3	203.7	330.2
5	218.9	236.1	344.2

a. Based on the *MINITAB* normal probability plot and the plot of residuals versus rates, are you willing to assume that the normality and constant variance assumptions are satisfied?

MINITAB residual plots for Exercise 15.71

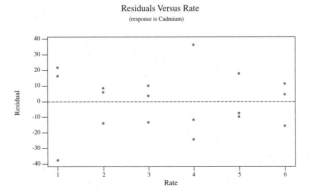

MINITAB residual plots for Exercise 15.71 (continued)

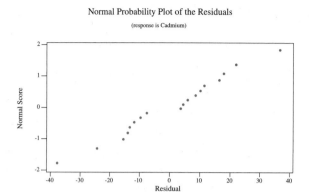

Normal Probability Plot of the Residuals
(response is Cadmium)

b. Using an appropriate method of analysis, analyze the data to determine whether there are significant differences among the responses due to rates of application.

15.72 Refer to Exercise 15.71. The data in this table are the cadmium concentrations found in aphids that fed on the plants grown in soil amended with sludge.

EX1572

Rate	Harvest		
	1	2	3
Control	16.2	55.8	65.8
1	16.9	119.4	181.1
2	12.7	171.9	184.6
3	31.3	128.4	196.4
4	38.5	182.0	163.7
5	20.6	191.3	242.8

a. Use the *MINITAB* normal probability plot of the residuals and the plot of residuals versus rates of application to assess whether the assumptions of normality and constant variance are reasonable in this case.

b. Based on your conclusions in part a, use an appropriate statistical method to test for significant differences in cadmium concentrations for the six rates of application.

MINITAB residual plots for Exercise 15.72

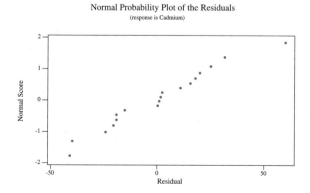

Residuals Versus Rate
(response is Cadmium)

Normal Probability Plot of the Residuals
(response is Cadmium)

Case Study

EGGS

How's Your Cholesterol Level?

As consumers become more and more interested in eating healthy foods, many "light," "fat-free," and "cholesterol-free" products are appearing in the marketplace. One such product is the frozen egg substitute, a cholesterol-free product that can be used in cooking and baking in many of the same ways that regular eggs can—though not all. Some consumers even use egg substitutes for Caesar salad dressings and other recipes calling for raw eggs because these products are pasteurized and thus eliminate worries about bacterial contamination.

Unfortunately, the products currently on the market exhibit strong differences in both flavor and texture when tasted in their primary preparation as scrambled eggs. Five panelists, all experts in nutrition and food preparation, were asked to rate each of three egg substitutes on the basis of taste, appearance, texture, and whether they would buy the product.[8] The judges tasted the three egg substitutes and rated them on a scale of 0 to 20. The results, shown in the table, indicate that the highest rating, by 23 points, went to ConAgra's Healthy Choice Egg Product, which the tasters unanimously agreed most closely resembled eggs as they come from the hen. The second-place product, Morningstar Farms' Scramblers, struck several tasters as having an "oddly sweet flavor . . . similar to carrots." Finally, none of the tasters indicated that they would be willing to buy Fleishmann's Egg Beaters, which was described by the testers as "watery," "slippery," and "unpleasant." Oddly enough, these results are contrary to a similar taste test done 4 years earlier, in which Egg Beaters were considered better than competing egg substitutes.

Taster	Healthy Choice	Scramblers	Egg Beaters
Dan Bowe	16	9	7
John Carroll	16	7	8
Donna Katzl	14	8	4
Rick O'Connell	15	16	9
Roland Passot	13	11	2
Totals	74	51	30

1. What type of design has been used in this taste-testing experiment?
2. Do the data satisfy the assumptions required for a parametric analysis of variance? Explain.
3. Use the appropriate nonparametric technique to determine whether there is a significant difference between the average scores for the three brands of egg substitutes.

Data Sources

1. T. M. Casey, M.L. May, and K.R. Morgan, "Flight Energetics of Euglossine Bees in Relation to Morphology and Wing Stroke Frequency," *Journal of Experimental Biology* 116 (1985).
2. "Alzheimer's Test Set for New Memory Drug," *The Press-Enterprise* (Riverside, CA), 18 November 1997, p. A-4.
3. *Science News* 136 (August 1989):126.
4. D. Matsui et al., "Assessment of the Palatability of β-Lactamase-Resistant Antibiotics in Children," *Archives of Pediatric Adolescent Medicine* 151 (1997):559–601.
5. Scott K. Powers and M.B. Walker, "Physiological and Anatomical Characteristics of Outstanding Female Junior Tennis Players," *Research Quarterly for Exercise and Sport* 53, no. 2 (1983).

6. *Science News,* 1989, p. 116.

7. G. Merrington, L. Winder, and I. Green, "The Uptake of Cadmium and Zinc by the Bird-cherry Oat Aphid *Rhopalosiphum Padi (Homoptera:Aphididae)* Feeding on Wheat Grown on Sewage Sludge Amended Agricultural Soil," *Environmental Pollution* 96, no. 1 (1997):111–114.

8. Karola Sakekel, "Egg Substitutes Range in Quality," *San Francisco Chronicle,* 10 February 1993, p. 8.

Appendix I

Tables

Contents

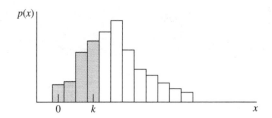

TABLE 1 Cumulative Binomial Probabilities
Tabulated values are $P(x \le k) = p(0) + p(1) + \cdots + p(k)$
(Computations are rounded at the third decimal place.)

$n = 2$

k	.01	.05	.10	.20	.30	.40	.50	.60	.70	.80	.90	.95	.99	k
0	.980	.902	.810	.640	.490	.360	.250	.160	.090	.040	.010	.002	.000	0
1	1.000	.998	.990	.960	.910	.840	.750	.640	.510	.360	.190	.098	.020	1
2	1.000	1.000	1.000	1.000	1.000	1.000	1.000	1.000	1.000	1.000	1.000	1.000	1.000	2

$n = 3$

k	.01	.05	.10	.20	.30	.40	.50	.60	.70	.80	.90	.95	99	k
0	.970	.857	.729	.512	.343	.216	.125	.064	.027	.008	.001	.000	.000	0
1	1.000	.993	.972	.896	.784	.648	.500	.352	.216	.104	.028	.007	.000	1
2	1.000	1.000	.999	.992	.973	.936	.875	.784	.657	.488	.271	.143	.030	2
3	1.000	1.000	1.000	1.000	1.000	1.000	1.000	1.000	1.000	1.000	1.000	1.000	1.000	3

$n = 4$

k	.01	.05	.10	.20	.30	.40	.50	.60	.70	.80	.90	.95	.99	k
0	.961	.815	.656	.410	.240	.130	.062	.026	.008	.002	.000	.000	.000	0
1	.999	.986	.948	.819	.652	.475	.312	.179	.084	.027	.004	.000	.000	1
2	1.000	1.000	.996	.973	.916	.821	.688	.525	.348	.181	.052	.014	.001	2
3	1.000	1.000	1.000	.998	.992	.974	.938	.870	.760	.590	.344	.185	.039	3
4	1.000	1.000	1.000	1.000	1.000	1.000	1.000	1.000	1.000	1.000	1.000	1.000	1.000	4

TABLE 1 *(continued)*

$n = 5$

k							p							k
	.01	.05	.10	.20	.30	.40	.50	.60	.70	.80	.90	.95	.99	
0	.951	.774	.590	.328	.168	.078	.031	.010	.002	.000	.000	.000	.000	0
1	.999	.977	.919	.737	.528	.337	.188	.087	.031	.007	.000	.000	.000	1
2	1.000	.999	.991	.942	.837	.683	.500	.317	.163	.058	.009	.001	.000	2
3	1.000	1.000	1.000	.993	.969	.913	.812	.663	.472	.263	.081	.023	.001	3
4	1.000	1.000	1.000	1.000	.998	.990	.969	.922	.832	.672	.410	.226	.049	4
5	1.000	1.000	1.000	1.000	1.000	1.000	1.000	1.000	1.000	1.000	1.000	1.000	1.000	5

$n = 6$

k							p							k
	.01	.05	.10	.20	.30	.40	.50	.60	.70	.80	.90	.95	.99	
0	.941	.735	.531	.262	.118	.047	.016	.004	.001	.000	.000	.000	.000	0
1	.999	.967	.886	.655	.420	.233	.109	.041	.011	.002	.000	.000	.000	1
2	1.000	.998	.984	.901	.744	.544	.344	.179	.070	.017	.001	.000	.000	2
3	1.000	1.000	.999	.983	.930	.821	.656	.456	.256	.099	.016	.002	.000	3
4	1.000	1.000	1.000	.998	.989	.959	.891	.767	.580	.345	.114	.033	.001	4
5	1.000	1.000	1.000	1.000	.999	.996	.984	.953	.882	.738	.469	.265	.059	5
6	1.000	1.000	1.000	1.000	1.000	1.000	1.000	1.000	1.000	1.000	1.000	1.000	1.000	6

$n = 7$

k							p							k
	.01	.05	.10	.20	.30	.40	.50	.60	.70	.80	.90	.95	.99	
0	.932	.698	.478	.210	.082	.028	.008	.002	.000	.000	.000	.000	.000	0
1	.998	.956	.850	.577	.329	.159	.062	.019	.004	.000	.000	.000	.000	1
2	1.000	.996	.974	.852	.647	.420	.227	.096	.029	.005	.000	.000	.000	2
3	1.000	1.000	.997	.967	.874	.710	.500	.290	.126	.033	.003	.000	.000	3
4	1.000	1.000	1.000	.995	.971	.904	.773	.580	.353	.148	.026	.004	.000	4
5	1.000	1.000	1.000	1.000	.996	.981	.938	.841	.671	.423	.150	.044	.002	5
6	1.000	1.000	1.000	1.000	1.000	.998	.992	.972	.918	.790	.522	.302	.068	6
7	1.000	1.000	1.000	1.000	1.000	1.000	1.000	1.000	1.000	1.000	1.000	1.000	1.000	7

$n = 8$

k							p							k
	.01	.05	.10	.20	.30	.40	.50	.60	.70	.80	.90	.95	.99	
0	.923	.663	.430	.168	.058	.017	.004	.001	.000	.000	.000	.000	.000	0
1	.997	.943	.813	.503	.255	.106	.035	.009	.001	.000	.000	.000	.000	1
2	1.000	.994	.962	.797	.552	.315	.145	.050	.011	.001	.000	.000	.000	2
3	1.000	1.000	.995	.944	.806	.594	.363	.174	.058	.010	.000	.000	.000	3
4	1.000	1.000	1.000	.990	.942	.826	.637	.406	.194	.056	.005	.000	.000	4
5	1.000	1.000	1.000	.999	.989	.950	.855	.685	.448	.203	.038	.006	.000	5
6	1.000	1.000	1.000	1.000	.999	.991	.965	.894	.745	.497	.187	.057	.003	6
7	1.000	1.000	1.000	1.000	1.000	.999	.996	.983	.942	.832	.570	.337	.077	7
8	1.000	1.000	1.000	1.000	1.000	1.000	1.000	1.000	1.000	1.000	1.000	1.000	1.000	8

TABLE 1 *(continued)*

n = 9

k	.01	.05	.10	.20	.30	.40	.50	.60	.70	.80	.90	.95	.99	k
0	.914	.630	.387	.134	.040	.010	.002	.000	.000	.000	.000	.000	.000	0
1	.997	.929	.775	.436	.196	.071	.020	.004	.000	.000	.000	.000	.000	1
2	1.000	.992	.947	.738	.463	.232	.090	.025	.004	.000	.000	.000	.000	2
3	1.000	.999	.992	.914	.730	.483	.254	.099	.025	.003	.000	.000	.000	3
4	1.000	1.000	.999	.980	.901	.733	.500	.267	.099	.020	.001	.000	.000	4
5	1.000	1.000	1.000	.997	.975	.901	.746	.517	.270	.086	.008	.001	.000	5
6	1.000	1.000	1.000	1.000	.996	.975	.910	.768	.537	.262	.053	.008	.000	6
7	1.000	1.000	1.000	1.000	1.000	.996	.980	.929	.804	.564	.225	.071	.003	7
8	1.000	1.000	1.000	1.000	1.000	1.000	.998	.990	.960	.866	.613	.370	.086	8
9	1.000	1.000	1.000	1.000	1.000	1.000	1.000	1.000	1.000	1.000	1.000	1.000	1.000	9

n = 10

k	.01	.05	.10	.20	.30	.40	.50	.60	.70	.80	.90	.95	.99	k
0	.904	.599	.349	.107	.028	.006	.001	.000	.000	.000	.000	.000	.000	0
1	.996	.914	.736	.376	.149	.046	.011	.002	.000	.000	.000	.000	.000	1
2	1.000	.988	.930	.678	.383	.167	.055	.012	.002	.000	.000	.000	.000	2
3	1.000	.999	.987	.879	.650	.382	.172	.055	.011	.001	.000	.000	.000	3
4	1.000	1.000	.998	.967	.850	.633	.377	.166	.047	.006	.000	.000	.000	4
5	1.000	1.000	1.000	.994	.953	.834	.623	.367	.150	.033	.002	.000	.000	5
6	1.000	1.000	1.000	.999	.989	.945	.828	.618	.350	.121	.013	.001	.000	6
7	1.000	1.000	1.000	1.000	.998	.988	.945	.833	.617	.322	.070	.012	.000	7
8	1.000	1.000	1.000	1.000	1.000	.998	.989	.954	.851	.624	.264	.086	.004	8
9	1.000	1.000	1.000	1.000	1.000	1.000	.999	.994	.972	.893	.651	.401	.096	9
10	1.000	1.000	1.000	1.000	1.000	1.000	1.000	1.000	1.000	1.000	1.000	1.000	1.000	10

n = 11

k	.01	.05	.10	.20	.30	.40	.50	.60	.70	.80	.90	.95	.99	k
0	.895	.569	.314	.086	.020	.004	.000	.000	.000	.000	.000	.000	.000	0
1	.995	.898	.697	.322	.113	.030	.006	.001	.000	.000	.000	.000	.000	1
2	1.000	.985	.910	.617	.313	.119	.033	.006	.001	.000	.000	.000	.000	2
3	1.000	.998	.981	.839	.570	.296	.113	.029	.004	.000	.000	.000	.000	3
4	1.000	1.000	.997	.950	.790	.533	.274	.099	.022	.002	.000	.000	.000	4
5	1.000	1.000	1.000	.988	.922	.754	.500	.246	.078	.012	.000	.000	.000	5
6	1.000	1.000	1.000	.998	.978	.901	.726	.467	.210	.050	.003	.000	.000	6
7	1.000	1.000	1.000	1.000	.996	.971	.887	.704	.430	.161	.019	.002	.000	7
8	1.000	1.000	1.000	1.000	.999	.994	.967	.881	.687	.383	.090	.015	.000	8
9	1.000	1.000	1.000	1.000	1.000	.999	.994	.970	.887	.678	.303	.102	.005	9
10	1.000	1.000	1.000	1.000	1.000	1.000	1.000	.996	.980	.914	.686	.431	.105	10
11	1.000	1.000	1.000	1.000	1.000	1.000	1.000	1.000	1.000	1.000	1.000	1.000	1.000	11

TABLE 1   *(continued)*

n = 12

							p							
k	.01	.05	.10	.20	.30	.40	.50	.60	.70	.80	.90	.95	.99	*k*
0	.886	.540	.282	.069	.014	.002	.000	.000	.000	.000	.000	.000	.000	0
1	.994	.882	.659	.275	.085	.020	.003	.000	.000	.000	.000	.000	.000	1
2	1.000	.980	.889	.558	.253	.083	.019	.003	.000	.000	.000	.000	.000	2
3	1.000	.998	.974	.795	.493	.225	.073	.015	.002	.000	.000	.000	.000	3
4	1.000	1.000	.996	.927	.724	.438	.194	.057	.009	.001	.000	.000	.000	4
5	1.000	1.000	.999	.981	.882	.665	.387	.158	.039	.004	.000	.000	.000	5
6	1.000	1.000	1.000	.996	.961	.842	.613	.335	.118	.019	.001	.000	.000	6
7	1.000	1.000	1.000	.999	.991	.943	.806	.562	.276	.073	.004	.000	.000	7
8	1.000	1.000	1.000	1.000	.998	.985	.927	.775	.507	.205	.026	.002	.000	8
9	1.000	1.000	1.000	1.000	1.000	.997	.981	.917	.747	.442	.111	.020	.000	9
10	1.000	1.000	1.000	1.000	1.000	1.000	.997	.980	.915	.725	.341	.118	.006	10
11	1.000	1.000	1.000	1.000	1.000	1.000	1.000	.998	.986	.931	.718	.460	.114	11
12	1.000	1.000	1.000	1.000	1.000	1.000	1.000	1.000	1.000	1.000	1.000	1.000	1.000	12

n = 15

							p							
k	.01	.05	.10	.20	.30	.40	.50	.60	.70	.80	.90	.95	.99	*k*
0	.860	.463	.206	.035	.005	.000	.000	.000	.000	.000	.000	.000	.000	0
1	.990	.829	.549	.167	.035	.005	.000	.000	.000	.000	.000	.000	.000	1
2	1.000	.964	.816	.398	.127	.027	.004	.000	.000	.000	.000	.000	.000	2
3	1.000	.995	.944	.648	.297	.091	.018	.002	.000	.000	.000	.000	.000	3
4	1.000	.999	.987	.836	.515	.217	.059	.009	.001	.000	.000	.000	.000	4
5	1.000	1.000	.998	.939	.722	.403	.151	.034	.004	.000	.000	.000	.000	5
6	1.000	1.000	1.000	.982	.869	.610	.304	.095	.015	.001	.000	.000	.000	6
7	1.000	1.000	1.000	.996	.950	.787	.500	.213	.050	.004	.000	.000	.000	7
8	1.000	1.000	1.000	.999	.985	.905	.696	.390	.131	.018	.000	.000	.000	8
9	1.000	1.000	1.000	1.000	.996	.966	.849	.597	.278	.061	.002	.000	.000	9
10	1.000	1.000	1.000	1.000	.999	.991	.941	.783	.485	.164	.013	.001	.000	10
11	1.000	1.000	1.000	1.000	1.000	.998	.982	.909	.703	.352	.056	.005	.000	11
12	1.000	1.000	1.000	1.000	1.000	1.000	.996	.973	.873	.602	.184	.036	.000	12
13	1.000	1.000	1.000	1.000	1.000	1.000	1.000	.995	.965	.833	.451	.171	.010	13
14	1.000	1.000	1.000	1.000	1.000	1.000	1.000	1.000	.995	.965	.794	.537	.140	14
15	1.000	1.000	1.000	1.000	1.000	1.000	1.000	1.000	1.000	1.000	1.000	1.000	1.000	15

TABLE 1 *(continued)*

n = 20

k	.01	.05	.10	.20	.30	.40	.50	.60	.70	.80	.90	.95	.99	*k*
0	.818	.358	.122	.012	.001	.000	.000	.000	.000	.000	.000	.000	.000	0
1	.983	.736	.392	.069	.008	.001	.000	.000	.000	.000	.000	.000	.000	1
2	.999	.925	.677	.206	.035	.004	.000	.000	.000	.000	.000	.000	.000	2
3	1.000	.984	.867	.411	.107	.016	.001	.000	.000	.000	.000	.000	.000	3
4	1.000	.997	.957	.630	.238	.051	.006	.000	.000	.000	.000	.000	.000	4
5	1.000	1.000	.989	.804	.416	.126	.021	.002	.000	.000	.000	.000	.000	5
6	1.000	1.000	.998	.913	.608	.250	.058	.006	.000	.000	.000	.000	.000	6
7	1.000	1.000	1.000	.968	.772	.416	.132	.021	.001	.000	.000	.000	.000	7
8	1.000	1.000	1.000	.990	.887	.596	.252	.057	.005	.000	.000	.000	.000	8
9	1.000	1.000	1.000	.997	.952	.755	.412	.128	.017	.001	.000	.000	.000	9
10	1.000	1.000	1.000	.999	.983	.872	.588	.245	.048	.003	.000	.000	.000	10
11	1.000	1.000	1.000	1.000	.995	.943	.748	.404	.113	.010	.000	.000	.000	11
12	1.000	1.000	1.000	1.000	.999	.979	.868	.584	.228	.032	.000	.000	.000	12
13	1.000	1.000	1.000	1.000	1.000	.994	.942	.750	.392	.087	.002	.000	.000	13
14	1.000	1.000	1.000	1.000	1.000	.998	.979	.874	.584	.196	.011	.000	.000	14
15	1.000	1.000	1.000	1.000	1.000	1.000	.994	.949	.762	.370	.043	.003	.000	15
16	1.000	1.000	1.000	1.000	1.000	1.000	.999	.984	.893	.589	.133	.016	.000	16
17	1.000	1.000	1.000	1.000	1.000	1.000	1.000	.996	.965	.794	.323	.075	.001	17
18	1.000	1.000	1.000	1.000	1.000	1.000	1.000	.999	.992	.931	.608	.264	.017	18
19	1.000	1.000	1.000	1.000	1.000	1.000	1.000	1.000	.999	.988	.878	.642	.182	19
20	1.000	1.000	1.000	1.000	1.000	1.000	1.000	1.000	1.000	1.000	1.000	1.000	1.000	20

TABLE 1 *(continued)*

$n = 25$

k							p							k
	.01	.05	.10	.20	.30	.40	.50	.60	.70	.80	.90	.95	.99	
0	.778	.277	.072	.004	.000	.000	.000	.000	.000	.000	.000	.000	.000	0
1	.974	.642	.271	.027	.002	.000	.000	.000	.000	.000	.000	.000	.000	1
2	.998	.873	.537	.098	.009	.000	.000	.000	.000	.000	.000	.000	.000	2
3	1.000	.966	.764	.234	.033	.002	.000	.000	.000	.000	.000	.000	.000	3
4	1.000	.993	.902	.421	.090	.009	.000	.000	.000	.000	.000	.000	.000	4
5	1.000	.999	.967	.617	.193	.029	.002	.000	.000	.000	.000	.000	.000	5
6	1.000	1.000	.991	.780	.341	.074	.007	.000	.000	.000	.000	.000	.000	6
7	1.000	1.000	.998	.891	.512	.154	.022	.001	.000	.000	.000	.000	.000	7
8	1.000	1.000	1.000	.953	.677	.274	.054	.004	.000	.000	.000	.000	.000	8
9	1.000	1.000	1.000	.983	.811	.425	.115	.013	.000	.000	.000	.000	.000	9
10	1.000	1.000	1.000	.994	.902	.586	.212	.034	.002	.000	.000	.000	.000	10
11	1.000	1.000	1.000	.998	.956	.732	.345	.078	.006	.000	.000	.000	.000	11
12	1.000	1.000	1.000	1.000	.983	.846	.500	.154	.017	.000	.000	.000	.000	12
13	1.000	1.000	1.000	1.000	.994	.922	.655	.268	.044	.002	.000	.000	.000	13
14	1.000	1.000	1.000	1.000	.998	.966	.788	.414	.098	.006	.000	.000	.000	14
15	1.000	1.000	1.000	1.000	1.000	.987	.885	.575	.189	.017	.000	.000	.000	15
16	1.000	1.000	1.000	1.000	1.000	.996	.946	.726	.323	.047	.000	.000	.000	16
17	1.000	1.000	1.000	1.000	1.000	.999	.978	.846	.488	.109	.002	.000	.000	17
18	1.000	1.000	1.000	1.000	1.000	1.000	.993	.926	.659	.220	.009	.000	.000	18
19	1.000	1.000	1.000	1.000	1.000	1.000	.998	.971	.807	.383	.033	.001	.000	19
20	1.000	1.000	1.000	1.000	1.000	1.000	1.000	.991	.910	.579	.098	.007	.000	20
21	1.000	1.000	1.000	1.000	1.000	1.000	1.000	.998	.967	.766	.236	.034	.000	21
22	1.000	1.000	1.000	1.000	1.000	1.000	1.000	1.000	.991	.902	.463	.127	.002	22
23	1.000	1.000	1.000	1.000	1.000	1.000	1.000	1.000	.998	.973	.729	.358	.026	23
24	1.000	1.000	1.000	1.000	1.000	1.000	1.000	1.000	1.000	.996	.928	.723	.222	24
25	1.000	1.000	1.000	1.000	1.000	1.000	1.000	1.000	1.000	1.000	1.000	1.000	1.000	25

TABLE 2 Cumulative Poisson Probabilities
Tabulated values are $P(x \leq k) = p(0) + p(1) + \quad + p(k)$
(Computations are rounded at the third decimal place.)

						μ						
k	.1	.2	.3	.4	.5	.6	.7	.8	.9	1.0	1.5
0	.905	.819	.741	.670	.607	.549	.497	.449	.407	.368	.223
1	.995	.982	.963	.938	.910	.878	.844	.809	.772	.736	.558
2	1.000	.999	.996	.992	.986	.977	.966	.953	.937	.920	.809
3		1.000	1.000	.999	.998	.997	.994	.991	.987	.981	.934
4				1.000	1.000	1.000	.999	.999	.998	.996	.981
5							1.000	1.000	1.000	.999	.996
6										1.000	.999
7											1.000

						μ						
k	2.0	2.5	3.0	3.5	4.0	4.5	5.0	5.5	6.0	6.5	7.0
0	.135	.082	.055	.033	.018	.011	.007	.004	.003	.002	.001
1	.406	.287	.199	.136	.092	.061	.040	.027	.017	.011	.007
2	.677	.544	.423	.321	.238	.174	.125	.088	.062	.043	.030
3	.857	.758	.647	.537	.433	.342	.265	.202	.151	.112	.082
4	.947	.891	.815	.725	.629	.532	.440	.358	.285	.224	.173
5	.983	.958	.916	.858	.785	.703	.616	.529	.446	.369	.301
6	.995	.986	.966	.935	.889	.831	.762	.686	.606	.563	.450
7	.999	.996	.988	.973	.949	.913	.867	.809	.744	.673	.599
8	1.000	.999	.996	.990	.979	.960	.932	.894	.847	.792	.729
9		1.000	.999	.997	.992	.983	.968	.946	.916	.877	.830
10			1.000	.999	.997	.993	.986	.975	.957	.933	.901
11				1.000	.999	.998	.995	.989	.980	.966	.947
12					1.000	.999	.998	.996	.991	.984	.973
13						1.000	.999	.998	.996	.993	.987
14							1.000	.999	.999	.997	.994
15								1.000	.999	.999	.998
16									1.000	1.000	.999
17											1.000

TABLE 2 *(continued)*

					μ				
k	7.5	8.0	8.5	9.0	9.5	10.0	12.0	15.0	20.0
0	.001	.000	.000	.000	.000	.000	.000	.000	.000
1	.005	.003	.002	.001	.001	.000	.000	.000	.000
2	.020	.014	.009	.006	.004	.003	.001	.000	.000
3	.059	.042	.030	.021	.015	.010	.002	.000	.000
4	.132	.100	.074	.055	.040	.029	.008	.001	.000
5	.241	.191	.150	.116	.089	.067	.020	.003	.000
6	.378	.313	.256	.207	.165	.130	.046	.008	.000
7	.525	.453	.386	.324	.269	.220	.090	.018	.001
8	.662	.593	.523	.456	.392	.333	.155	.037	.002
9	.776	.717	.653	.587	.522	.458	.242	.070	.005
10	.862	.816	.763	.706	.645	.583	.347	.118	.011
11	.921	.888	.849	.803	.752	.697	.462	.185	.021
12	.957	.936	.909	.876	.836	.792	.576	.268	.039
13	.978	.966	.949	.926	.898	.864	.682	.363	.066
14	.990	.983	.973	.959	.940	.917	.772	.466	.105
15	.995	.992	.986	.978	.967	.951	.844	.568	.157
16	.998	.996	.993	.989	.982	.973	.899	.664	.221
17	.999	.998	.997	.995	.991	.986	.937	.749	.297
18	1.000	.999	.999	.998	.996	.993	.963	.819	.381
19		1.000	.999	.999	.998	.997	.979	.875	.470
20			1.000	1.000	.999	.998	.988	.917	.559
21					1.000	.999	.994	.947	.644
22						1.000	.997	.967	.721
23							.999	.981	.787
24							.999	.989	.843
25							1.000	.994	.888
26								.997	.922
27								.998	.948
28								.999	.966
29								1.000	.978
30									.987
31									.992
32									.995
33									.997
34									.999
35									.999
36									1.000

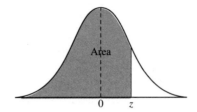

TABLE 3 Areas under the Normal Curve

z	.00	.01	.02	.03	.04	.05	.06	.07	.08	.09
−3.4	.0003	.0003	.0003	.0003	.0003	.0003	.0003	.0003	.0003	.0002
−3.3	.0005	.0005	.0005	.0004	.0004	.0004	.0004	.0004	.0004	.0003
−3.2	.0007	.0007	.0006	.0006	.0006	.0006	.0006	.0005	.0005	.0005
−3.1	.0010	.0009	.0009	.0009	.0008	.0008	.0008	.0008	.0007	.0007
−3.0	.0013	.0013	.0013	.0012	.0012	.0011	.0011	.0011	.0010	.0010
−2.9	.0019	.0018	.0017	.0017	.0016	.0016	.0015	.0015	.0014	.0014
−2.8	.0026	.0025	.0024	.0023	.0023	.0022	.0021	.0021	.0020	.0019
−2.7	.0035	.0034	.0033	.0032	.0031	.0030	.0029	.0028	.0027	.0026
−2.6	.0047	.0045	.0044	.0043	.0041	.0040	.0039	.0038	.0037	.0036
−2.5	.0062	.0060	.0059	.0057	.0055	.0054	.0052	.0051	.0049	.0048
−2.4	.0082	.0080	.0078	.0075	.0073	.0071	.0069	.0068	.0066	.0064
−2.3	.0107	.0104	.0102	.0099	.0096	.0094	.0091	.0089	.0087	.0084
−2.2	.0139	.0136	.0132	.0129	.0125	.0122	.0119	.0116	.0113	.0110
−2.1	.0179	.0174	.0170	.0166	.0162	.0158	.0154	.0150	.0146	.0143
−2.0	.0228	.0222	.0217	.0212	.0207	.0202	.0197	.0192	.0188	.0183
−1.9	.0287	.0281	.0274	.0268	.0262	.0256	.0250	.0244	.0239	.0233
−1.8	.0359	.0351	.0344	.0336	.0329	.0322	.0314	.0307	.0301	.0294
−1.7	.0446	.0436	.0427	.0418	.0409	.0401	.0392	.0384	.0375	.0367
−1.6	.0548	.0537	.0526	.0516	.0505	.0495	.0485	.0475	.0465	.0455
−1.5	.0668	.0655	.0643	.0630	.0618	.0606	.0594	.0582	.0571	.0559
−1.4	.0808	.0793	.0778	.0764	.0749	.0735	.0722	.0708	.0694	.0681
−1.3	.0968	.0951	.0934	.0918	.0901	.0885	.0869	.0853	.0838	.0823
−1.2	.1151	.1131	.1112	.1093	.1075	.0156	.1038	.1020	.1003	.0985
−1.1	.1357	.1335	.1314	.1292	.1271	.1251	.1230	.1210	.1190	.1170
−1.0	.1587	.1562	.1539	.1515	.1492	.1469	.1446	.1423	.1401	.1379
−0.9	.1841	.1814	.1788	.1762	.1736	.1711	.1685	.1660	.1635	.1611
−0.8	.2119	.2090	.2061	.2033	.2005	.1977	.1949	.1922	.1894	.1867
−0.7	.2420	.2389	.2358	.2327	.2296	.2266	.2236	.2206	.2177	.2148
−0.6	.2743	.2709	.2676	.2643	.2611	.2578	.2546	.2514	.2483	.2451
−0.5	.3085	.3050	.3015	.2981	.2946	.2912	.2877	.2843	.2810	.2776
−0.4	.3446	.3409	.3372	.3336	.3300	.3264	.3228	.3192	.3156	.3121
−0.3	.3821	.3783	.3745	.3707	.3669	.3632	.3594	.3557	.3520	.3483
−0.2	.4207	.4168	.4129	.4090	.4052	.4013	.3974	.3936	.3897	.3859
−0.1	.4602	.4562	.4522	.4483	.4443	.4404	.4364	.4325	.4286	.4247
−0.0	.5000	.4960	.4920	.4880	.4840	.4801	.4761	.4721	.4681	.4641

TABLE 3   *(continued)*

z	.00	.01	.02	.03	.04	.05	.06	.07	.08	.09
0.0	.5000	.5040	.5080	.5120	.5160	.5199	.5239	.5279	.5319	.5359
0.1	.5398	.5438	.5478	.5517	.5557	.5596	.5636	.5675	.5714	.5753
0.2	.5793	.5832	.5871	.5910	.5948	.5987	.6026	.6064	.6103	.6141
0.3	.6179	.6217	.6255	.6293	.6331	.6368	.6406	.6443	.6480	.6517
0.4	.6554	.6591	.6628	.6664	.6700	.6736	.6772	.6808	.6844	.6879
0.5	.6915	.6950	.6985	.7019	.7054	.7088	.7123	.7157	.7190	.7224
0.6	.7257	.7291	.7324	.7357	.7389	.7422	.7454	.7486	.7517	.7549
0.7	.7580	.7611	.7642	.7673	.7704	.7734	.7764	.7794	.7823	.7852
0.8	.7881	.7910	.7939	.7967	.7995	.8023	.8051	.8078	.8106	.8133
0.9	.8159	.8186	.8212	.8328	.8264	.8289	.8315	.8340	.8365	.8389
1.0	.8413	.8438	.8461	.8485	.8508	.8531	.8554	.8577	.8599	.8621
1.1	.8643	.8665	.8686	.8708	.8729	.8749	.8770	.8790	.8810	.8830
1.2	.8849	.8869	.8888	.8907	.8925	.8944	.8962	.8980	.8997	.9015
1.3	.9032	.9049	.9066	.9082	.9099	.9115	.9131	.9147	.9162	.9177
1.4	.9192	.9207	.9222	.9236	.9251	.9265	.9278	.9292	.9306	.9319
1.5	.9332	.9345	.9357	.9370	.9382	.9394	.9406	.9418	.9429	.9441
1.6	.9452	.9463	.9474	.9484	.9495	.9505	.9515	.9525	.9535	.9545
1.7	.9554	.9564	.9573	.9582	.9591	.9599	.9608	.9616	.9625	.9633
1.8	.9641	.9649	.9656	.9664	.9671	.9678	.9686	.9693	.9699	.9706
1.9	.9713	.9719	.9726	.9732	.9738	.9744	.9750	.9756	.9761	.9767
2.0	.9772	.9778	.9783	.9788	.9793	.9798	.9803	.0808	.9812	.9817
2.1	.9821	.9826	.9830	.9834	.9838	.9842	.9846	.9850	.9854	.9857
2.2	.9861	.9864	.9868	.9871	.9875	.9878	.9881	.9884	.9887	.9890
2.3	.9893	.9896	.9898	.9901	.9904	.9906	.9909	.9911	.9913	.9916
2.4	.9918	.9920	.9922	.9925	.9927	.9929	.9931	.9932	.9934	.9936
2.5	.9938	.9940	.9941	.9943	.9945	.9946	.9948	.9949	.9951	.9952
2.6	.9953	.9955	.9956	.9957	.9959	.9960	.9961	.9962	.9963	.9964
2.7	.9965	.9966	.9967	.9968	.9969	.9970	.9971	.9972	.9973	.9974
2.8	.9974	.9975	.9976	.9977	.9977	.9978	.9979	.9979	.9980	.9981
2.9	.9981	.9982	.9982	.9983	.9984	.9984	.9985	.9985	.9986	.9986
3.0	.9987	.9987	.9987	.9988	.9988	.9989	.9989	.9989	.9990	.9990
3.1	.9990	.9991	.9991	.9991	.9992	.9992	.9992	.9992	.9993	.9993
3.2	.9993	.9993	.9994	.9994	.9994	.9994	.9994	.9995	.9995	.9995
3.3	.9995	.9995	.9995	.9996	.9996	.9996	.9996	.9996	.9996	.9997
3.4	.9997	.9997	.9997	.9997	.9997	.9997	.9997	.9997	.9997	.9998

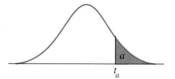

t_a

TABLE 4
Critical Values of *t*

df	$t_{.100}$	$t_{.050}$	$t_{.025}$	$t_{.010}$	$t_{.005}$	df
1	3.078	6.314	12.706	31.821	63.657	1
2	1.886	2.920	4.303	6.965	9.925	2
3	1.638	2.353	3.182	4.541	5.841	3
4	1.533	2.132	2.776	3.747	4.604	4
5	1.476	2.015	2.571	3.365	4.032	5
6	1.440	1.943	2.447	3.143	3.707	6
7	1.415	1.895	2.365	2.998	3.499	7
8	1.397	1.860	2.306	2.896	3.355	8
9	1.383	1.833	2.262	2.821	3.250	9
10	1.372	1.812	2.228	2.764	3.169	10
11	1.363	1.796	2.201	2.718	3.106	11
12	1.356	1.782	2.179	2.681	3.055	12
13	1.350	1.771	2.160	2.650	3.012	13
14	1.345	1.761	2.145	2.624	2.977	14
15	1.341	1.753	2.131	2.602	2.947	15
16	1.337	1.746	2.120	2.583	2.921	16
17	1.333	1.740	2.110	2.567	2.898	17
18	1.330	1.734	2.101	2.552	2.878	18
19	1.328	1.729	2.093	2.539	2.861	19
20	1.325	1.725	2.086	2.528	2.845	20
21	1.323	1.721	2.080	2.518	2.831	21
22	1.321	1.717	2.074	2.508	2.819	22
23	1.319	1.714	2.069	2.500	2.807	23
24	1.318	1.711	2.064	2.492	2.797	24
25	1.316	1.708	2.060	2.485	2.787	25
26	1.315	1.706	2.056	2.479	2.779	26
27	1.314	1.703	2.052	2.473	2.771	27
28	1.313	1.701	2.048	2.467	2.763	28
29	1.311	1.699	2.045	2.462	2.756	29
∞	1.282	1.645	1.960	2.326	2.576	∞

SOURCE: From "Table of Percentage Points of the *t*-Distribution," *Biometrika* 32 (1941):300. Reproduced by permission of the *Biometrika* Trustees.

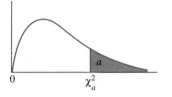

df	$\chi^2_{.995}$	$\chi^2_{.990}$	$\chi^2_{.975}$	$\chi^2_{.950}$	$\chi^2_{.900}$
1	.0000393	.0001571	.0009821	.0039321	.0157908
2	.0100251	.0201007	.0506356	.102587	.210720
3	.0717212	.114832	.215795	.351846	.584375
4	.206990	.297110	.484419	.710721	1.063623
5	.411740	.554300	.831211	1.145476	1.61031
6	.675727	.872085	1.237347	1.63539	2.20413
7	.989265	1.239043	1.68987	2.16735	2.83311
8	1.344419	1.646482	2.17973	2.73264	3.48954
9	1.734926	2.087912	2.70039	3.32511	4.16816
10	2.15585	2.55821	3.24697	3.94030	4.86518
11	2.60321	3.05347	3.81575	4.57481	5.57779
12	3.07382	3.57056	4.40379	5.22603	6.30380
13	3.56503	4.10691	5.00874	5.89186	7.04150
14	4.07468	4.66043	5.62872	6.57063	7.78953
15	4.60094	5.22935	6.26214	7.26094	8.54675
16	5.14224	5.81221	6.90766	7.96164	9.31223
17	5.69724	6.40776	7.56418	8.67176	10.0852
18	6.26481	7.01491	8.23075	9.39046	10.8649
19	6.84398	7.63273	8.90655	10.1170	11.6509
20	7.43386	8.26040	9.59083	10.8508	12.4426
21	8.03366	8.89720	10.28293	11.5913	13.2396
22	8.64272	9.54249	10.9823	12.3380	14.0415
23	9.26042	10.19567	11.6885	13.0905	14.8479
24	9.88623	10.8564	12.4011	13.8484	15.6587
25	10.5197	11.5240	13.1197	14.6114	16.4734
26	11.1603	12.1981	13.8439	15.3791	17.2919
27	11.8076	12.8786	14.5733	16.1513	18.1138
28	12.4613	13.5648	15.3079	16.9279	18.9392
29	13.1211	14.2565	16.0471	17.7083	19.7677
30	13.7867	14.9535	16.7908	18.4926	20.5992
40	20.7065	22.1643	24.4331	26.5093	29.0505
50	27.9907	29.7067	32.3574	34.7642	37.6886
60	35.5346	37.4848	40.4817	43.1879	46.4589
70	43.2752	45.4418	48.7576	51.7393	55.3290
80	51.1720	53.5400	57.1532	60.3915	64.2778
90	59.1963	61.7541	65.6466	69.1260	73.2912
100	67.3276	70.0648	74.2219	77.9295	82.3581

TABLE 5
Critical Values of Chi-Square

SOURCE: From "Tables of the Percentage Points of the χ^2-Distribution," *Biometrika Tables for Statisticians* 1, 3d ed. (1966). Reproduced by permission of the *Biometrika* Trustees.

TABLE 5
(continued)

$\chi^2_{.100}$	$\chi^2_{.050}$	$\chi^2_{.025}$	$\chi^2_{.010}$	$\chi^2_{.005}$	df
2.70554	3.84146	5.02389	6.63490	7.87944	1
4.60517	5.99147	7.37776	9.21034	10.5966	2
6.25139	7.81473	9.34840	11.3449	12.8381	3
7.77944	9.48773	11.1433	13.2767	14.8602	4
9.23635	11.0705	12.8325	15.0863	16.7496	5
10.6446	12.5916	14.4494	16.8119	18.5476	6
12.0170	14.0671	16.0128	18.4753	20.2777	7
13.3616	15.5073	17.5346	20.0902	21.9550	8
14.6837	16.9190	19.0228	21.6660	23.5893	9
15.9871	18.3070	20.4831	23.2093	25.1882	10
17.2750	19.6751	21.9200	24.7250	26.7569	11
18.5494	21.0261	23.3367	26.2170	28.2995	12
19.8119	22.3621	24.7356	27.6883	29.8194	13
21.0642	23.6848	26.1190	29.1413	31.3193	14
22.3072	24.9958	27.4884	30.5779	32.8013	15
23.5418	26.2962	28.8485	31.9999	34.2672	16
24.7690	27.8571	30.1910	33.4087	35.7185	17
25.9894	28.8693	31.5264	34.8053	37.1564	18
27.2036	30.1435	32.8523	36.1908	38.5822	19
28.4120	31.4104	34.1696	37.5662	39.9968	20
29.6151	32.6705	35.4789	38.9321	41.4010	21
30.8133	33.9244	36.7807	40.2894	42.7956	22
32.0069	35.1725	38.0757	41.6384	44.1813	23
33.1963	36.4151	39.3641	42.9798	45.5585	24
34.3816	37.6525	40.6465	44.3141	46.9278	25
35.5631	38.8852	41.9232	45.6417	48.2899	26
36.7412	40.1133	43.1944	46.9630	49.6449	27
37.9159	41.3372	44.4607	48.2782	50.9933	28
39.0875	42.5569	45.7222	49.5879	52.3356	29
40.2560	43.7729	46.9792	50.8922	53.6720	30
51.8050	55.7585	59.3417	63.6907	66.7659	40
63.1671	67.5048	71.4202	76.1539	79.4900	50
74.3970	79.0819	83.2976	88.3794	91.9517	60
85.5271	90.5312	95.0231	100.425	104.215	70
96.5782	101.879	106.629	112.329	116.321	80
107.565	113.145	118.136	124.116	128.299	90
118.498	124.342	129.561	135.807	140.169	100

TABLE 6 Percentage Points of the *F* Distribution

df_2	*a*	1	2	3	4	5	6	7	8	9
						df_1				
1	.100	39.86	49.50	53.59	55.83	57.24	58.20	58.91	59.44	59.86
	.050	161.4	199.5	215.7	224.6	230.2	234.0	236.8	238.9	240.5
	.025	647.8	799.5	864.2	899.6	921.8	937.1	948.2	956.7	963.3
	.010	4052	4999.5	5403	5625	5764	5859	5928	5982	6022
	.005	16211	20000	21615	22500	23056	23437	23715	23925	24091
2	.100	8.53	9.00	9.16	9.24	9.29	9.33	9.35	9.37	9.38
	.050	18.51	19.00	19.16	19.25	19.30	19.33	19.35	19.37	19.38
	.025	38.51	39.00	39.17	39.25	39.30	39.33	39.36	39.37	39.39
	.010	98.50	99.00	99.17	99.25	99.30	99.33	99.36	99.37	99.39
	.005	198.5	199.0	199.2	199.2	199.3	199.3	199.4	199.4	199.4
3	.100	5.54	5.46	5.39	5.34	5.31	5.28	5.27	5.25	5.24
	.050	10.13	9.55	9.28	9.12	9.01	8.94	8.89	8.85	8.81
	.025	17.44	16.04	15.44	15.10	14.88	14.73	14.62	14.54	14.47
	.010	34.12	30.82	29.46	28.71	28.24	27.91	27.64	27.49	27.35
	.005	55.55	49.80	47.47	46.19	45.39	44.84	44.43	44.13	43.88
4	.100	4.54	4.32	4.19	4.11	4.05	4.01	3.98	3.95	3.94
	.050	7.71	6.94	6.59	6.39	6.26	6.16	6.09	6.04	6.00
	.025	12.22	10.65	9.98	9.60	9.36	9.20	9.07	8.98	8.90
	.010	21.20	18.00	16.69	15.98	15.52	15.21	14.98	14.80	14.66
	.005	31.33	26.28	24.26	23.15	22.46	21.97	21.62	21.35	21.14
5	.100	4.06	3.78	3.62	3.52	3.45	3.40	3.37	3.34	3.32
	.050	6.61	5.79	5.41	5.19	5.05	4.95	4.88	4.82	4.77
	.025	10.01	8.43	7.76	7.39	7.15	6.98	6.85	6.76	6.68
	.010	16.26	13.27	12.06	11.39	10.97	10.67	10.46	10.29	10.16
	.005	22.78	18.31	16.53	15.56	14.94	14.51	14.20	13.96	13.77
6	.100	3.78	3.46	3.29	3.18	3.11	3.05	3.01	2.98	2.96
	.050	5.99	5.14	4.76	4.53	4.39	4.28	4.21	4.15	4.10
	.025	8.81	7.26	6.60	6.23	5.99	5.82	5.70	5.60	5.52
	.010	13.75	10.92	9.78	9.15	8.75	8.47	8.26	8.10	7.98
	.005	18.63	14.54	12.92	12.03	11.46	11.07	10.79	10.57	10.39
7	.100	3.59	3.26	3.07	2.96	2.88	2.83	2.78	2.75	2.72
	.050	5.59	4.74	4.35	4.12	3.97	3.87	3.79	3.73	3.68
	.025	8.07	6.54	5.89	5.52	5.29	5.12	4.99	4.90	4.82
	.010	12.25	9.55	8.45	7.85	7.46	7.19	6.99	6.84	6.72
	.005	16.24	12.40	10.88	10.05	9.52	9.16	8.89	8.68	8.51
8	.100	3.46	3.11	2.92	2.81	2.73	2.67	2.62	2.59	2.56
	.050	5.32	4.46	4.07	3.84	3.69	3.58	3.50	3.44	3.39
	.025	7.57	6.06	5.42	5.05	4.82	4.65	4.53	4.43	4.36
	.010	11.26	8.65	7.59	7.01	6.63	6.37	6.18	6.03	5.91
	.005	14.69	11.04	9.60	8.81	8.30	7.95	7.69	7.50	7.34
9	.100	3.36	3.01	2.81	2.69	2.61	2.55	2.51	2.47	2.44
	.050	5.12	4.26	3.86	3.63	3.48	3.37	3.29	3.23	3.18
	.025	7.21	5.71	5.08	4.72	4.48	4.32	4.20	4.10	4.03
	.010	10.56	8.02	6.99	6.42	6.06	5.80	5.61	5.47	5.35
	.005	13.61	10.11	8.72	7.96	7.47	7.13	6.88	6.69	6.54

Source: A portion of "Tables of percentage points of the inverted beta (*E*) distribution," *Biometrika*, vol. 33 (1943) by M. Merrington and C.M. Thompson and from Table 18 of *Biometrika Tables for Statisticians,* vol. 1, Cambridge University Press, 1954, edited by E.S. Pearson and H.O. Hartley. Reproduced with permission of the authors, editors, and *Biometrika* trustees.

TABLE 6 *(continued)*

| | | | | | df_1 | | | | | | | |
10	12	5	20	24	30	40	60	120	∞	*a*	df_2
60.19	60.71	60.22	61.74	62.00	62.26	62.53	62.79	63.06	63.33	.100	1
241.9	243.9	245.9	248.0	249.1	250.1	251.2	252.2	253.3	254.3	.050	
968.6	976.7	984.9	993.1	997.2	1001	1006	1010	1014	1018	.025	
6056	6106	6157	6209	6235	6261	6287	6313	6339	6366	.010	
24224	24426	24630	24836	24940	25044	25148	25253	25359	25465	.005	
9.39	9.41	9.42	9.44	9.45	9.46	9.47	9.47	9.48	9.49	.100	2
19.40	19.41	19.43	19.45	19.45	19.46	19.47	19.48	19.49	19.50	.050	
39.40	39.41	39.43	39.45	39.46	39.46	39.47	39.48	39.49	39.50	.025	
99.40	99.42	99.43	99.45	99.46	99.47	99.47	99.48	99.49	99.50	.010	
199.4	199.4	199.4	199.4	199.5	199.5	199.5	199.5	199.5	199.5	.005	
5.23	5.22	5.20	5.18	5.18	5.17	5.16	5.15	5.14	5.13	.100	3
8.79	8.74	8.70	8.66	8.64	8.62	8.59	8.57	8.55	8.53	.050	
14.42	14.34	14.25	14.17	14.12	14.08	14.04	13.99	13.95	13.90	.025	
27.23	27.05	26.87	26.69	26.60	26.50	26.41	26.32	26.22	26.13	.010	
43.69	43.39	43.08	42.78	42.62	42.47	42.31	42.15	41.99	41.83	.005	
3.92	3.90	3.87	3.84	3.83	3.82	3.80	3.79	3.78	3.76	.100	4
5.96	5.91	5.86	5.80	5.77	5.75	5.72	5.69	5.66	5.63	.050	
8.84	8.75	8.66	8.56	8.51	8.46	8.41	8.36	8.31	8.26	.025	
14.55	14.37	14.20	14.02	13.93	13.84	13.75	13.65	13.56	13.46	.010	
20.97	20.70	20.44	20.17	20.03	19.89	19.75	19.61	19.47	19.32	.005	
3.30	3.27	3.24	3.21	3.19	3.17	3.16	3.14	3.12	3.10	.100	5
4.74	4.68	4.62	4.56	4.53	4.50	4.46	4.43	4.40	4.36	.050	
6.62	6.52	6.43	6.33	6.28	6.23	6.18	6.12	6.07	6.02	.025	
10.05	9.89	9.72	9.55	9.47	9.38	9.29	9.20	9.11	9.02	.010	
13.62	13.38	13.15	12.90	12.78	12.66	12.53	12.40	12.27	12.14	.005	
2.94	2.90	2.87	2.84	2.82	2.80	2.78	2.76	2.74	2.72	.100	6
4.06	4.00	3.94	3.87	3.84	3.81	3.77	3.74	3.70	3.67	.050	
5.46	5.37	5.27	5.17	5.12	5.07	5.01	4.96	4.90	4.85	.025	
7.87	7.72	7.56	7.40	7.31	7.23	7.14	7.06	6.97	6.88	.010	
10.25	10.03	9.81	9.59	9.47	9.36	9.24	9.12	9.00	8.88	.005	
2.70	2.67	2.63	2.59	2.58	2.56	2.54	2.51	2.49	2.47	.100	7
3.64	3.57	3.51	3.44	3.41	3.38	3.34	3.30	3.27	3.23	.050	
4.76	4.67	4.57	4.47	4.42	4.36	4.31	4.25	4.20	4.14	.025	
6.62	6.47	6.31	6.16	6.07	5.99	5.91	5.82	5.74	5.65	.010	
8.38	8.18	7.97	7.75	7.65	7.53	7.42	7.31	7.19	7.08	.005	
2.54	2.50	2.46	2.42	2.40	2.38	2.36	2.34	2.32	2.29	.100	8
3.35	3.28	3.22	3.15	3.12	3.08	3.04	3.01	2.97	2.93	.050	
4.30	4.20	4.10	4.00	3.95	3.89	3.84	3.78	3.73	3.67	.025	
5.81	5.67	5.52	5.36	5.28	5.20	5.12	5.03	4.95	4.86	.010	
7.21	7.01	6.81	6.61	6.50	6.40	6.29	6.18	6.06	5.95	.005	
2.42	2.38	2.34	2.30	2.28	2.25	2.23	2.21	2.18	2.16	.100	9
3.14	3.07	3.01	2.94	2.90	2.86	2.83	2.79	2.75	2.71	.050	
3.96	3.87	3.77	3.67	3.61	3.56	3.51	3.45	3.39	3.33	.025	
5.26	5.11	4.96	4.81	4.73	4.65	4.57	4.48	4.40	4.31	.010	
6.42	6.23	6.03	5.83	5.73	5.62	5.52	5.41	5.30	5.19	.005	

TABLE 6 *(continued)*

df_2	a	df_1 1	2	3	4	5	6	7	8	9
10	.100	3.29	2.92	2.73	2.61	2.52	2.46	2.41	2.38	2.35
	.050	4.96	4.10	3.71	3.48	3.33	3.22	3.14	3.07	3.02
	.025	6.94	5.46	4.83	4.47	4.24	4.07	3.95	3.85	3.78
	.010	10.04	7.56	6.55	5.99	5.64	5.39	5.20	5.06	4.94
	.005	12.83	9.43	8.08	7.34	6.87	6.54	6.30	6.12	5.97
11	.100	3.23	2.86	2.66	2.54	2.45	2.39	2.34	2.30	2.27
	.050	4.84	3.98	3.59	3.36	3.20	3.09	3.01	2.95	2.90
	.025	6.72	5.26	4.63	4.28	4.04	3.88	3.76	3.66	3.59
	.010	9.65	7.21	6.22	5.67	5.32	5.07	4.89	4.74	4.63
	.005	12.23	8.91	7.60	6.88	6.42	6.10	5.86	5.68	5.54
12	.100	3.18	2.81	2.61	2.48	2.39	2.33	2.28	2.24	2.21
	.050	4.75	3.89	3.49	3.26	3.11	3.00	2.91	2.85	2.80
	.025	6.55	5.10	4.47	4.12	3.89	3.73	3.61	3.51	3.44
	.010	9.33	6.93	5.95	5.41	5.06	4.82	4.64	4.50	4.39
	.005	11.75	8.51	7.23	6.52	6.07	5.76	5.52	5.35	5.20
13	.100	3.14	2.76	2.56	2.43	2.35	2.28	2.23	2.20	2.16
	.050	4.67	3.81	3.41	3.18	3.03	2.92	2.83	2.77	2.71
	.025	6.41	4.97	4.35	4.00	3.77	3.60	3.48	3.39	3.31
	.010	9.07	6.70	5.74	5.21	4.86	4.62	4.44	4.30	4.19
	.005	11.37	8.19	6.93	6.23	5.79	5.48	5.25	5.08	4.94
14	.100	3.10	2.73	2.52	2.39	2.31	2.24	2.19	2.15	2.12
	.050	4.60	3.74	3.34	3.11	2.96	2.85	2.76	2.70	2.65
	.025	6.30	4.86	4.24	3.89	3.66	3.50	3.38	3.29	3.21
	.010	8.86	6.51	5.56	5.04	4.69	4.46	4.28	4.14	4.03
	.005	11.06	7.92	6.68	6.00	5.56	5.26	5.03	4.86	4.72
15	.100	3.07	2.70	2.49	2.36	2.27	2.21	2.16	2.12	2.09
	.050	4.54	3.68	3.29	3.06	2.90	2.79	2.71	2.64	2.59
	.025	6.20	4.77	4.15	3.80	3.58	3.41	3.29	3.20	3.12
	.010	8.68	6.36	5.42	4.89	4.56	4.32	4.14	4.00	3.89
	.005	10.80	7.70	6.48	5.80	5.37	5.07	4.85	4.67	4.54
16	.100	3.05	2.67	2.46	2.33	2.24	2.18	2.13	2.09	2.06
	.050	4.49	3.63	3.24	3.01	2.85	2.74	2.66	2.59	2.54
	.025	6.12	4.69	4.08	3.73	3.50	3.34	3.22	3.12	3.05
	.010	8.53	6.23	5.29	4.77	4.44	4.20	4.03	3.89	3.78
	.005	10.58	7.51	6.30	5.64	5.21	4.91	4.69	4.52	4.38
17	.100	3.03	2.64	2.44	2.31	2.22	2.15	2.10	2.06	2.03
	.050	4.45	3.59	3.20	2.96	2.81	2.70	2.61	2.55	2.49
	.025	6.04	4.62	4.01	3.66	3.44	3.28	3.16	3.06	2.98
	.010	8.40	6.11	5.18	4.67	4.34	4.10	3.93	3.79	3.68
	.005	10.38	7.35	6.16	5.50	5.07	4.78	4.56	4.39	4.25
18	.100	3.01	2.62	2.42	2.29	2.20	2.13	2.08	2.04	2.00
	.050	4.41	3.55	3.16	2.93	2.77	2.66	2.58	2.51	2.46
	.025	5.98	4.56	3.95	3.61	3.38	3.22	3.10	3.01	2.93
	.010	8.29	6.01	5.09	4.58	4.25	4.01	3.84	3.71	3.60
	.005	10.22	7.21	6.03	5.37	4.96	4.66	4.44	4.28	4.14
19	.100	2.99	2.61	2.40	2.27	2.18	2.11	2.06	2.02	1.98
	.050	4.38	3.52	3.13	2.90	2.74	2.63	2.54	2.48	2.42
	.025	5.92	4.51	3.90	3.56	3.33	3.17	3.05	2.96	2.88
	.010	8.18	5.93	5.01	4.50	4.17	3.94	3.77	3.63	3.52
	.005	10.07	7.09	5.92	5.27	4.85	4.56	4.34	4.18	4.04
20	.100	2.97	2.59	2.38	2.25	2.16	2.09	2.04	2.00	1.96
	.050	4.35	3.49	3.10	2.87	2.71	2.60	2.51	2.45	2.39
	.025	5.87	4.46	3.86	3.51	3.29	3.13	3.01	2.91	2.84
	.010	8.10	5.85	4.94	4.43	4.10	3.87	3.70	3.56	3.46
	.005	9.94	6.99	5.82	5.17	4.76	4.47	4.26	4.09	3.96

TABLE 6 *(continued)*

				df_1							
10	12	5	20	24	30	40	60	120	∞	a	df_2
2.32	2.28	2.24	2.20	2.18	2.16	2.13	2.11	2.08	2.06	.100	10
2.98	2.91	2.85	2.77	2.74	2.70	2.66	2.62	2.58	2.54	.050	
3.72	3.62	3.52	3.42	3.37	3.31	3.26	3.20	3.14	3.08	.025	
4.85	4.71	4.56	4.41	4.33	4.25	4.17	4.08	4.00	3.91	.010	
5.85	5.66	5.47	5.27	5.17	5.07	4.97	4.86	4.75	4.64	.005	
2.25	2.21	2.17	2.12	2.10	2.08	2.05	2.03	2.00	1.97	.100	11
2.85	2.79	2.72	2.65	2.61	2.57	2.53	2.49	2.45	2.40	.050	
3.53	3.43	3.33	3.23	3.17	3.12	3.06	3.00	2.94	2.88	.025	
4.54	4.40	4.25	4.10	4.02	3.94	3.86	3.78	3.69	3.60	.010	
5.42	5.24	5.05	4.86	4.76	4.65	4.55	4.44	4.34	4.23	.005	
2.19	2.15	2.10	2.06	2.04	2.01	1.99	1.96	1.93	1.90	.100	12
2.75	2.69	2.62	2.54	2.51	2.47	2.43	2.38	2.34	2.30	.050	
3.37	3.28	3.18	3.07	3.02	2.96	2.91	2.85	2.79	2.72	.025	
4.30	4.16	4.01	3.86	3.78	3.70	3.62	3.54	3.45	3.36	.010	
5.09	4.91	4.72	4.53	4.43	4.33	4.23	4.12	4.01	3.90	.005	
2.14	2.10	2.05	2.01	1.98	1.96	1.93	1.90	1.88	1.85	.100	13
2.67	2.60	2.53	2.46	2.42	2.38	2.34	2.30	2.25	2.21	.050	
3.25	3.15	3.05	2.95	2.89	2.84	2.78	2.72	2.66	2.60	.025	
4.10	3.96	3.82	3.66	3.59	3.51	3.43	3.34	3.25	3.17	.010	
4.82	4.64	4.46	4.27	4.17	4.07	3.97	3.87	3.76	3.65	.005	
2.10	2.05	2.01	1.96	1.94	1.91	1.89	1.86	1.83	1.80	.100	14
2.60	2.53	2.46	2.39	2.35	2.31	2.27	2.22	2.18	2.13	.050	
3.15	3.05	2.95	2.84	2.79	2.73	2.67	2.61	2.55	2.49	.025	
3.94	3.80	3.66	3.51	3.43	3.35	3.27	3.18	3.09	3.00	.010	
4.60	4.43	4.25	4.06	3.96	3.86	3.76	3.66	3.55	3.44	.005	
2.06	2.02	1.97	1.92	1.90	1.87	1.85	1.82	1.79	1.76	.100	15
2.54	2.48	2.40	2.33	2.29	2.25	2.20	2.16	2.11	2.07	.050	
3.06	2.96	2.86	2.76	2.70	2.64	2.59	2.52	2.46	2.40	.025	
3.80	3.67	3.52	3.37	3.29	3.21	3.13	3.05	2.96	2.87	.010	
4.42	4.25	4.07	3.88	3.79	3.69	3.58	3.48	3.37	3.26	.005	
2.03	1.99	1.94	1.89	1.87	1.84	1.81	1.78	1.75	1.72	.100	16
2.49	2.42	2.35	2.28	2.24	2.19	2.15	2.11	2.06	2.01	.050	
2.99	2.89	2.79	2.68	2.63	2.57	2.51	2.45	2.38	2.32	.025	
3.69	3.55	3.41	3.26	3.18	3.10	3.02	2.93	2.84	2.75	.010	
4.27	4.10	3.92	3.73	3.64	3.54	3.44	3.33	3.22	3.11	.005	
2.00	1.96	1.91	1.86	1.84	1.81	1.78	1.75	1.72	1.69	.100	17
2.45	2.38	2.31	2.23	2.19	2.15	2.10	2.06	2.01	1.96	.050	
2.92	2.82	2.72	2.62	2.56	2.50	2.44	2.38	2.32	2.25	.025	
3.59	3.46	3.31	3.16	3.08	3.00	2.92	2.83	2.75	2.65	.010	
4.14	3.97	3.79	3.61	3.51	3.41	3.31	3.21	3.10	2.98	.005	
1.98	1.93	1.89	1.84	1.81	1.78	1.75	1.72	1.69	1.66	.100	18
2.41	2.34	2.27	2.19	2.15	2.11	2.06	2.02	1.97	1.92	.050	
2.87	2.77	2.67	2.56	2.50	2.44	2.38	2.32	2.26	2.19	.025	
3.51	3.37	3.23	3.08	3.00	2.92	2.84	2.75	2.66	2.57	.010	
4.03	3.86	3.68	3.50	3.40	3.30	3.20	3.10	2.99	2.87	.005	
1.96	1.91	1.86	1.81	1.79	1.76	1.73	1.70	1.67	1.63	.100	19
2.38	2.31	2.23	2.16	2.11	2.07	2.03	1.98	1.93	1.88	.050	
2.82	2.72	2.62	2.51	2.45	2.39	2.33	2.27	2.20	2.13	.025	
3.43	3.30	3.15	3.00	2.92	2.84	2.76	2.67	2.58	2.49	.010	
3.93	3.76	3.59	3.40	3.31	3.21	3.11	3.00	2.89	2.78	.005	
1.94	1.89	1.84	1.79	1.77	1.74	1.71	1.68	1.64	1.61	.100	20
2.35	2.28	2.20	2.12	2.08	2.04	1.99	1.95	1.90	1.84	.050	
2.77	2.68	2.57	2.46	2.41	2.35	2.29	2.22	2.16	2.09	.025	
3.37	3.23	3.09	2.94	2.86	2.78	2.69	2.61	2.52	2.42	.010	
3.85	3.68	3.50	3.32	3.22	3.12	3.02	2.92	2.81	2.69	.005	

TABLE 6 *(continued)*

df_2	a	1	2	3	4	5	6	7	8	9
						df_1				
21	.100	2.96	2.57	2.36	2.23	2.14	2.08	2.02	1.98	1.95
	.050	4.32	3.47	3.07	2.84	2.68	2.57	2.49	2.42	2.37
	.025	5.83	4.42	3.82	3.48	3.25	3.09	2.97	2.87	2.80
	.010	8.02	5.78	4.87	4.37	4.04	3.81	3.64	3.51	3.40
	.005	9.83	6.89	5.73	5.09	4.68	4.39	4.18	4.01	3.88
22	.100	2.95	2.56	2.35	2.22	2.13	2.06	2.01	1.97	1.93
	.050	4.30	3.44	3.05	2.82	2.66	2.55	2.46	2.40	2.34
	.025	5.79	4.38	3.78	3.44	3.22	3.05	2.93	2.84	2.76
	.010	7.95	5.72	4.82	4.31	3.99	3.76	3.59	3.45	3.35
	.005	9.73	6.81	5.65	5.02	4.61	4.32	4.11	3.94	3.81
23	.100	2.94	2.55	2.34	2.21	2.11	2.05	1.99	1.95	1.92
	.050	4.28	3.42	3.03	2.80	2.64	2.53	2.44	2.37	2.32
	.025	5.75	4.35	3.75	3.41	3.18	3.02	2.90	2.81	2.73
	.010	7.88	5.66	4.76	4.26	3.94	3.71	3.54	3.41	3.30
	.005	9.63	6.73	5.58	4.95	4.54	4.26	4.05	3.88	3.75
24	.100	2.93	2.54	2.33	2.19	2.10	2.04	1.98	1.94	1.91
	.050	4.26	3.40	3.01	2.78	2.62	2.51	2.42	2.36	2.30
	.025	5.72	4.32	3.72	3.38	3.15	2.99	2.87	2.78	2.70
	.010	7.82	5.61	4.72	4.22	3.90	3.67	3.50	3.36	3.26
	.005	9.55	6.66	5.52	4.89	4.49	4.20	3.99	3.83	3.69
25	.100	2.92	2.53	2.32	2.18	2.09	2.02	1.97	1.93	1.89
	.050	4.24	3.39	2.99	2.76	2.60	2.49	2.40	2.34	2.28
	.025	5.69	4.29	3.69	3.35	3.13	2.97	2.85	2.75	2.68
	.010	7.77	5.57	4.68	4.18	3.85	3.63	3.46	3.32	3.22
	.005	9.48	6.60	5.46	4.84	4.43	4.15	3.94	3.78	3.64
26	.100	2.91	2.52	2.31	2.17	2.08	2.01	1.96	1.92	1.88
	.050	4.23	3.37	2.98	2.74	2.59	2.47	2.39	2.32	2.27
	.025	5.66	4.27	3.67	3.33	3.10	2.94	2.82	2.73	2.65
	.010	7.72	5.53	4.64	4.14	3.82	3.59	3.42	3.29	3.18
	.005	9.41	6.54	5.41	4.79	4.38	4.10	3.89	3.73	3.60
27	.100	2.90	2.51	2.30	2.17	2.07	2.00	1.95	1.91	1.87
	.050	4.21	3.35	2.96	2.73	2.57	2.46	2.37	2.31	2.25
	.025	5.63	4.24	3.65	3.31	3.08	2.92	2.80	2.71	2.63
	.010	7.68	5.49	4.60	4.11	3.78	3.56	3.39	3.26	3.15
	.005	9.34	6.49	5.36	4.74	4.34	4.06	3.85	3.69	3.56
28	.100	2.89	2.50	2.29	2.16	2.06	2.00	1.94	1.90	1.87
	.050	4.20	3.34	2.95	2.71	2.56	2.45	2.36	2.29	2.24
	.025	5.61	4.22	3.63	3.29	3.06	2.90	2.78	2.69	2.61
	.010	7.64	5.45	4.57	4.07	3.75	3.53	3.36	3.23	3.12
	.005	9.28	6.44	5.32	4.70	4.30	4.02	3.81	3.65	3.52
29	.100	2.89	2.50	2.28	2.15	2.06	1.99	1.93	1.89	1.86
	.050	4.18	3.33	2.93	2.70	2.55	2.43	2.35	2.28	2.22
	.025	5.59	4.20	3.61	3.27	3.04	2.88	2.76	2.67	2.59
	.010	7.60	5.42	4.54	4.04	3.73	3.50	3.33	3.20	3.09
	.005	9.23	6.40	5.28	4.66	4.26	3.98	3.77	3.61	3.48
30	.100	2.88	2.49	2.28	2.14	2.05	1.98	1.93	1.88	1.85
	.050	4.17	3.32	2.92	2.69	2.53	2.42	2.33	2.27	2.21
	.025	5.57	4.18	3.59	3.25	3.03	2.87	2.75	2.65	2.57
	.010	7.56	5.39	4.51	4.02	3.70	3.47	3.30	3.17	3.07
	.005	9.18	6.35	5.24	4.62	4.23	3.95	3.74	3.58	3.45

TABLE 6 *(continued)*

10	12	15	20	24	30	40	60	120	∞	*a*	df_2
							df_1				
1.92	1.87	1.83	1.78	1.75	1.72	1.69	1.66	1.62	1.59	.100	21
2.32	2.25	2.18	2.10	2.05	2.01	1.96	1.92	1.87	1.81	.050	
2.73	2.64	2.53	2.42	2.37	2.31	2.25	2.18	2.11	2.04	.025	
3.31	3.17	3.03	2.88	2.80	2.72	2.64	2.55	2.46	2.36	.010	
3.77	3.60	3.43	3.24	3.15	3.05	2.95	2.84	2.73	2.61	.005	
1.90	1.86	1.81	1.76	1.73	1.70	1.67	1.64	1.60	1.57	.100	22
2.30	2.23	2.15	2.07	2.03	1.98	1.94	1.89	1.84	1.78	.050	
2.70	2.60	2.50	2.39	2.33	2.27	2.21	2.14	2.08	2.00	.025	
3.26	3.12	2.98	2.83	2.75	2.67	2.58	2.50	2.40	2.31	.010	
3.70	3.54	3.36	3.18	3.08	2.98	2.88	2.77	2.66	2.55	.005	
1.89	1.84	1.80	1.74	1.72	1.69	1.66	1.62	1.59	1.55	.100	23
2.27	2.20	2.13	2.05	2.01	1.96	1.91	1.86	1.81	1.76	.050	
2.67	2.57	2.47	2.36	2.30	2.24	2.18	2.11	2.04	1.97	.025	
3.21	3.07	2.93	2.78	2.70	2.62	2.54	2.45	2.35	2.26	.010	
3.64	3.47	3.30	3.12	3.02	2.92	2.82	2.71	2.60	2.48	.005	
1.88	1.83	1.78	1.73	1.70	1.67	1.64	1.61	1.57	1.53	.100	24
2.25	2.18	2.11	2.03	1.98	1.94	1.89	1.84	1.79	1.73	.050	
2.64	2.54	2.44	2.33	2.27	2.21	2.15	2.08	2.01	1.94	.025	
3.17	3.03	2.89	2.74	2.66	2.58	2.49	2.40	2.31	2.21	.010	
3.59	3.42	3.25	3.06	2.97	2.87	2.77	2.66	2.55	2.43	.005	
1.87	1.82	1.77	1.72	1.69	1.66	1.63	1.59	1.56	1.52	.100	25
2.24	2.16	2.09	2.01	1.96	1.92	1.87	1.82	1.77	1.71	.050	
2.61	2.51	2.41	2.30	2.24	2.18	2.12	2.05	1.98	1.91	.025	
3.13	2.99	2.85	2.70	2.62	2.54	2.45	2.36	2.27	2.17	.010	
3.54	3.37	3.20	3.01	2.92	2.82	2.72	2.61	2.50	2.38	.005	
1.86	1.81	1.76	1.71	1.68	1.65	1.61	1.58	1.54	1.50	.100	26
2.22	2.15	2.07	1.99	1.95	1.90	1.85	1.80	1.75	1.69	.050	
2.59	2.49	2.39	2.28	2.22	2.16	2.09	2.03	1.95	1.88	.025	
3.09	2.96	2.81	2.66	2.58	2.50	2.42	2.33	2.23	2.13	.010	
3.49	3.33	3.15	2.97	2.87	2.77	2.67	2.56	2.45	2.33	.005	
1.85	1.80	1.75	1.70	1.67	1.64	1.60	1.57	1.53	1.49	.100	27
2.20	2.13	2.06	1.97	1.93	1.88	1.84	1.79	1.73	1.67	.050	
2.57	2.47	2.36	2.25	2.19	2.13	2.07	2.00	1.93	1.85	.025	
3.06	2.93	2.78	2.63	2.55	2.47	2.38	2.29	2.20	2.10	.010	
3.45	3.28	3.11	2.93	2.83	2.73	2.63	2.52	2.41	2.29	.005	
1.84	1.79	1.74	1.69	1.66	1.63	1.59	1.56	1.52	1.48	.100	28
2.19	2.12	2.04	1.96	1.91	1.87	1.82	1.77	1.71	1.65	.050	
2.55	2.45	2.34	2.23	2.17	2.11	2.05	1.98	1.91	1.83	.025	
3.03	2.90	2.75	2.60	2.52	2.44	2.35	2.26	2.17	2.06	.010	
3.41	3.25	3.07	2.89	2.79	2.69	2.59	2.48	2.37	2.25	.005	
1.83	1.78	1.73	1.68	1.65	1.62	1.58	1.55	l.51	1.47	.100	29
2.18	2.10	2.03	1.94	1.90	1.85	1.81	1.75	1.70	1.64	.050	
2.53	2.43	2.32	2.21	2.15	2.09	2.03	1.96	1.89	1.81	.025	
3.00	2.87	2.73	2.57	2.49	2.41	2.33	2.23	2.14	2.03	.010	
3.38	3.21	3.04	2.86	2.76	2.66	2.56	2.45	2.33	2.21	.005	
1.82	1.77	1.72	1.67	1.64	1.61	1.57	1.54	1.50	1.46	.100	30
2.16	2.09	2.01	1.93	1.89	1.84	1.79	1.74	1.68	1.62	.050	
2.51	2.41	2.31	2.20	2.14	2.07	2.01	1.94	1.87	1.79	.025	
2.98	2.84	2.70	2.55	2.47	2.39	2.30	2.21	2.11	2.01	.010	
3.34	3.18	3.01	2.82	2.73	2.63	2.52	2.42	2.30	2.18	.005	

TABLE 6 *(continued)*

df_2	a	df_1 1	2	3	4	5	6	7	8	9
40	.100	2.84	2.44	2.23	2.09	2.00	1.93	1.87	1.83	1.79
	.050	4.08	3.23	2.84	2.61	2.45	2.34	2.25	2.18	2.12
	.025	5.42	4.05	3.46	3.13	2.90	2.74	2.62	2.53	2.45
	.010	7.31	5.18	4.31	3.83	3.51	3.29	3.12	2.99	2.89
	.005	8.83	6.07	4.98	4.37	3.99	3.71	3.51	3.35	3.22
60	.100	2.79	2.39	2.18	2.04	1.95	1.87	1.82	1.77	1.74
	.050	4.00	3.15	2.76	2.53	2.37	2.25	2.17	2.10	2.04
	.025	5.29	3.93	3.34	3.01	2.79	2.63	2.51	2.41	2.33
	.010	7.08	4.98	4.13	3.65	3.34	3.12	2.95	2.82	2.72
	.005	8.49	5.79	4.73	4.14	3.76	3.49	3.29	3.13	3.01
120	.100	2.75	2.35	2.13	1.99	1.90	1.82	1.77	1.72	1.68
	.050	3.92	3.07	2.68	2.45	2.29	2.17	2.09	2.02	1.96
	.025	5.15	3.80	3.23	2.89	2.67	2.52	2.39	2.30	2.22
	.010	6.85	4.79	3.95	3.48	3.17	2.96	2.79	2.66	2.56
	.005	8.18	5.54	4.50	3.92	3.55	3.28	3.09	2.93	2.81
∞	.100	2.71	2.30	2.08	1.94	1.85	1.77	1.72	1.67	1.63
	.050	3.84	3.00	2.60	2.37	2.21	2.10	2.01	1.94	1.63
	.025	5.02	3.69	3.12	2.79	2.57	2.41	2.29	2.19	2.11
	.010	6.63	4.61	3.78	3.32	3.02	2.80	2.64	2.51	2.41
	.005	7.88	5.30	4.28	3.72	3.35	3.09	2.90	2.74	2.62

TABLE 6   *(continued)*

					df_1						
10	12	15	20	24	30	40	60	120	∞	a	df_2
1.76	1.71	1.66	1.61	1.57	1.54	1.51	1.47	1.42	1.38	.100	40
2.08	2.00	1.92	1.84	1.79	1.74	1.69	1.64	1.58	1.51	.050	
2.39	2.29	2.18	2.07	2.01	1.94	1.88	1.80	1.72	1.64	.025	
2.80	2.66	2.52	2.37	2.29	2.20	2.11	2.02	1.92	1.80	.010	
3.12	2.95	2.78	2.60	2.50	2.40	2.30	2.18	2.06	1.93	.005	
1.71	1.66	1.60	1.54	1.51	1.48	1.44	1.40	1.35	1.29	.100	60
1.99	1.92	1.84	1.75	1.70	1.65	1.59	1.53	1.47	1.39	.050	
2.27	2.17	2.06	1.94	1.88	1.82	1.74	1.67	1.58	1.48	.025	
2.63	2.50	2.35	2.20	2.12	2.03	1.94	1.84	1.73	1.60	.010	
2.90	2.74	2.57	2.39	2.29	2.19	2.08	1.96	1.83	1.69	.005	
1.65	1.60	1.55	1.48	1.45	1.41	1.37	1.32	1.26	1.19	.100	120
1.91	1.83	1.75	1.66	1.61	1.55	1.50	1.43	1.35	1.25	.050	
2.16	2.05	1.94	1.82	1.76	1.69	1.61	1.53	1.43	1.31	.025	
2.47	2.34	2.19	2.03	1.95	1.86	1.76	1.66	1.53	1.38	.010	
2.71	2.54	2.37	2.19	2.09	1.98	1.87	1.75	1.61	1.43	.005	
1.60	1.55	1.49	1.42	1.38	1.34	1.30	1.24	1.17	1.00	.100	∞
1.83	1.75	1.67	1.57	1.52	1.46	1.39	1.32	1.22	1.00	.050	
2.05	1.94	1.83	1.71	1.64	1.57	1.48	1.39	1.27	1.00	.025	
2.32	2.18	2.04	1.88	1.79	1.70	1.59	1.47	1.32	1.00	.010	
2.52	2.36	2.19	2.00	1.90	1.79	1.67	1.53	1.36	1.00	.005	

TABLE 7 Critical Values of T for the Wilcoxon Rank Sum Test, $n_1 \leq n_2$

TABLE 7(a)
5% Left-Tailed
Critical Values

							n_1							
n_2	2	3	4	5	6	7	8	9	10	11	12	13	14	15
3	—	6												
4	—	6	11											
5	3	7	12	19										
6	3	8	13	20	28									
7	3	8	14	21	29	39								
8	4	9	15	23	31	41	51							
9	4	10	16	24	33	43	54	66						
10	4	10	17	26	35	45	56	69	82					
11	4	11	18	27	37	47	59	72	86	100				
12	5	11	19	28	38	49	62	75	89	104	120			
13	5	12	20	30	40	52	64	78	92	108	125	142		
14	6	13	21	31	42	54	67	81	96	112	129	147	166	
15	6	13	22	33	44	56	69	84	99	116	133	152	171	192

TABLE 7(b)
2.5% Left-Tailed
Critical Values

							n_1							
n_2	2	3	4	5	6	7	8	9	10	11	12	13	14	15
4	—	—	10											
5	—	6	11	17										
6	—	7	12	18	26									
7	—	7	13	20	27	36								
8	3	8	14	21	29	38	49							
9	3	8	14	22	31	40	51	62						
10	3	9	15	23	32	42	53	65	78					
11	3	9	16	24	34	44	55	68	81	96				
12	4	10	17	26	35	46	58	71	84	99	115			
13	4	10	18	27	37	48	60	73	88	103	119	136		
14	4	11	19	28	38	50	62	76	91	106	123	141	160	
15	4	11	20	29	40	52	65	79	94	110	127	145	164	184

SOURCE: Adapted from "An Extended Table of Critical Values for the Mann-Whitney (Wilcoxon) Two-Sample Statistics" by Roy C. Milton, *Journal of the American Statistical Association,* Volume 59, Number 307 (September 1964). Reproduced with the permission of the Editor, *Journal of the American Statistical Association.*

TABLE 7(c)
1% Left-Tailed
Critical Values

							n_1							
n_2	2	3	4	5	6	7	8	9	10	11	12	13	14	15
3	—	—												
4	—	—	—											
5	—	—	10	16										
6	—	—	11	17	24									
7	—	6	11	18	25	34								
8	—	6	12	19	27	35	45							
9	—	7	13	20	28	37	47	59						
10	—	7	13	21	29	39	49	61	74					
11	—	7	14	22	30	40	51	63	77	91				
12	—	8	15	23	32	42	53	66	79	94	109			
13	3	8	15	24	33	44	56	68	82	97	113	130		
14	3	8	16	25	34	45	58	71	85	100	116	134	152	
15	3	9	17	26	36	47	60	73	88	103	120	138	156	176

TABLE 7(d)
.5% Left-Tailed
Critical Values

							n_1						
n_2	3	4	5	6	7	8	9	10	11	12	13	14	15
3	—												
4	—	—											
5	—	—	15										
6	—	10	16	23									
7	—	10	16	24	32								
8	—	11	17	25	34	42							
9	6	11	18	26	35	45	56						
10	6	12	19	27	37	47	58	71					
11	6	12	20	28	38	49	61	73	87				
12	7	13	21	30	40	51	63	76	90	105			
13	7	13	22	31	41	53	65	79	93	109	125		
14	7	14	22	32	43	54	67	81	96	112	129	147	
15	8	15	23	33	44	56	69	84	99	115	133	151	171

TABLE 8
Critical Values of T
in the Wilcoxon
Signed-Rank Test,
$n = 5(1)50$

One-Sided	Two-Sided	$n = 5$	$n = 6$	$n = 7$	$n = 8$	$n = 9$	$n = 10$
$\alpha = .050$	$\alpha = .10$	1	2	4	6	8	11
$\alpha = .025$	$\alpha = .05$		1	2	4	6	8
$\alpha = .010$	$\alpha = .02$			0	2	3	5
$\alpha = .005$	$\alpha = .01$				0	2	3

One-Sided	Two-Sided	$n = 11$	$n = 12$	$n = 13$	$n = 14$	$n = 15$	$n = 16$
$\alpha = .050$	$\alpha = .10$	14	17	21	26	30	36
$\alpha = .025$	$\alpha = .05$	11	14	17	21	25	30
$\alpha = .010$	$\alpha = .02$	7	10	13	16	20	24
$\alpha = .005$	$\alpha = .01$	5	7	10	13	16	19

One-Sided	Two-Sided	$n = 17$	$n = 18$	$n = 19$	$n = 20$	$n = 21$	$n = 22$
$\alpha = .050$	$\alpha = .10$	41	47	54	60	68	75
$\alpha = .025$	$\alpha = .05$	35	40	46	52	59	66
$\alpha = .010$	$\alpha = .02$	28	33	38	43	49	56
$\alpha = .005$	$\alpha = .01$	23	28	32	37	43	49

One-Sided	Two-Sided	$n = 23$	$n = 24$	$n = 25$	$n = 26$	$n = 27$	$n = 28$
$\alpha = .050$	$\alpha = .10$	83	92	101	110	120	130
$\alpha = .025$	$\alpha = .05$	73	81	90	98	107	117
$\alpha = .010$	$\alpha = .02$	62	69	77	85	93	102
$\alpha = .005$	$\alpha = .01$	55	68	68	76	84	92

One-Sided	Two-Sided	$n = 29$	$n = 30$	$n = 31$	$n = 32$	$n = 33$	$n = 34$
$\alpha = .050$	$\alpha = .10$	141	152	163	175	188	201
$\alpha = .025$	$\alpha = .05$	127	137	148	159	171	183
$\alpha = .010$	$\alpha = .02$	111	120	130	141	151	162
$\alpha = .005$	$\alpha = .01$	100	109	118	128	138	149

One-Sided	Two-Sided	$n = 35$	$n = 36$	$n = 37$	$n = 38$	$n = 39$	
$\alpha = .050$	$\alpha = .10$	214	228	242	256	271	
$\alpha = .025$	$\alpha = .05$	195	208	222	235	250	
$\alpha = .010$	$\alpha = .02$	174	186	198	211	224	
$\alpha = .005$	$\alpha = .01$	160	171	183	195	208	

One-Sided	Two-Sided	$n = 40$	$n = 41$	$n = 42$	$n = 43$	$n = 44$	$n = 45$
$\alpha = .050$	$\alpha = .10$	287	303	319	336	353	371
$\alpha = .025$	$\alpha = .05$	264	279	295	311	327	344
$\alpha = .010$	$\alpha = .02$	238	252	267	281	297	313
$\alpha = .005$	$\alpha = .01$	221	234	248	262	277	292

One-Sided	Two-Sided	$n = 46$	$n = 47$	$n = 48$	$n = 49$	$n = 50$	
$\alpha = .050$	$\alpha = .10$	389	408	427	446	466	
$\alpha = .025$	$\alpha = .05$	361	379	397	415	434	
$\alpha = .010$	$\alpha = .02$	329	345	362	380	398	
$\alpha = .005$	$\alpha = .01$	307	323	339	356	373	

Source: From "Some Rapid Approximate Statistical Procedures" (1964) 28, by F. Wilcoxon and R.A. Wilcox. Reproduced with the kind permission of Lederle Laboratories, a division of American Cyanamid Company.

TABLE 9
Critical Values of
Spearman's Rank
Correlation
Coefficient for a
One-Tailed Test

n	α = .05	α = .025	α = .01	α = .005
5	.900	—	—	—
6	.829	.886	.943	—
7	.714	.786	.893	—
8	.643	.738	.833	.881
9	.600	.683	.783	.833
10	.564	.648	.745	.794
11	.523	.623	.736	.818
12	.497	.591	.703	.780
13	.475	.566	.673	.745
14	.457	.545	.646	.716
15	.441	.525	.623	.689
16	.425	.507	.601	.666
17	.412	.490	.582	.645
18	.399	.476	.564	.625
19	.388	.462	.549	.608
20	.377	.450	.534	.591
21	.368	.438	.521	.576
22	.359	.428	.508	.562
23	.351	.418	.496	.549
24	.343	.409	.485	.537
25	.336	.400	.475	.526
26	.329	.392	.465	.515
27	.323	.385	.456	.505
28	.317	.377	.448	.496
29	.311	.370	.440	.487
30	.305	.364	.432	.478

SOURCE: From "Distribution of Sums of Squares of Rank Differences for Small Samples" by E.G. Olds, *Annals of Mathematical Statistics* 9 (1938). Reproduced with the permission of the editor, *Annals of Mathematical Statistics.*

TABLE 10 Random Numbers

Line	1	2	3	4	5	6	7	8	9	10	11	12	13	14
										Column				
1	10480	15011	01536	02011	81647	91646	69179	14194	62590	36207	20969	99570	91291	90700
2	22368	46573	25595	85393	30995	89198	27982	53402	93965	34095	52666	19174	39615	99505
3	24130	48360	22527	97265	76393	64809	15179	24830	49340	32081	30680	19655	63348	58629
4	42167	93093	06243	61680	07856	16376	39440	53537	71341	57004	00849	74917	97758	16379
5	37570	39975	81837	16656	06121	91782	60468	81305	49684	60672	14110	06927	01263	54613
6	77921	06907	11008	42751	27756	53498	18602	70659	90655	15053	21916	81825	44394	42880
7	99562	72905	56420	69994	98872	31016	71194	18738	44013	48840	63213	21069	10634	12952
8	96301	91977	05463	07972	18876	20922	94595	56869	69014	60045	18425	84903	42508	32307
9	89579	14342	63661	10281	17453	18103	57740	84378	25331	12566	58678	44947	05585	56941
10	84575	36857	53342	53988	53060	59533	38867	62300	08158	17983	16439	11458	18593	64952
11	28918	69578	88231	33276	70997	79936	56865	05859	90106	31595	01547	85590	91610	78188
12	63553	40961	48235	03427	49626	69445	18663	72695	52180	20847	12234	90511	33703	90322
13	09429	93969	52636	92737	88974	33488	36320	17617	30015	08272	84115	27156	30613	74952
14	10365	61129	87529	85689	48237	52267	67689	93394	01511	26358	85104	20285	29975	89868
15	07119	97336	71048	08178	77233	13916	47564	81056	97735	85977	29372	74461	28551	90707
16	51085	12765	51821	51259	77452	16308	60756	92144	49442	53900	70960	63990	75601	40719
17	02368	21382	52404	60268	89368	19885	55322	44819	01188	65255	64835	44919	05944	55157
18	01011	54092	33362	94904	31273	04146	18594	29852	71585	85030	51132	01915	92747	64951
19	52162	53916	46369	58586	23216	14513	83149	98736	23495	64350	94738	17752	35156	35749
20	07056	97628	33787	09998	42698	06691	76988	13602	51851	46104	88916	19509	25625	58104
21	48663	91245	85828	14346	09172	30168	90229	04734	59193	22178	30421	61666	99904	32812
22	54164	58492	22421	74103	47070	25306	76468	26384	58151	06646	21524	15227	96909	44592
23	32639	32363	05597	24200	13363	38005	94342	28728	35806	06912	17012	64161	18296	22851
24	29334	27001	87637	87308	58731	00256	45834	15398	46557	41135	10367	07684	36188	18510
25	02488	33062	28834	07351	19731	92420	60952	61280	50001	67658	32586	86679	50720	94953
26	81525	72295	04839	96423	24878	82651	66566	14778	76797	14780	13300	87074	79666	95725
27	29676	20591	68086	26432	46901	20849	89768	81536	86645	12659	92259	57102	80428	25280
28	00742	57392	39064	66432	84673	40027	32832	61362	98947	96067	64760	64585	96096	98253
29	05366	04213	25669	26422	44407	44048	37937	63904	45766	66134	75470	66520	34693	90449
30	91921	26418	64117	94305	26766	25940	39972	22209	71500	64568	91402	42416	07844	69618
31	00582	04711	87917	77341	42206	35126	74087	99547	81817	42607	43808	76655	62028	76630
32	00725	69884	62797	56170	86324	88072	76222	36086	84637	93161	76038	65855	77919	88006
33	69011	65795	95876	55293	18988	27354	26575	08625	40801	59920	29841	80150	12777	48501
34	25976	57948	29888	88604	67917	48708	18912	82271	65424	69774	33611	54262	85963	03547
35	09763	83473	73577	12908	30883	18317	28290	35797	05998	41688	34952	37888	38917	88050
36	91567	42595	27958	30134	04024	86385	29880	99730	55536	84855	29080	09250	79656	73211
37	17955	56349	90999	49127	20044	59931	06115	20542	18059	02008	73708	83517	36103	42791
38	46503	18584	18845	49618	02304	51038	20655	58727	28168	15475	56942	53389	20562	87338
39	92157	89634	94824	78171	84610	82834	09922	25417	44137	48413	25555	21246	35509	20468
40	14577	62765	35605	81263	39667	47358	56873	56307	61607	49518	89656	20103	77490	18062
41	98427	07523	33362	64270	01638	92477	66969	98420	04880	45585	46565	04102	46880	45709
42	34914	63976	88720	82765	34476	17032	87589	40836	32427	70002	70663	88863	77775	69348
43	70060	28277	39475	46473	23219	53416	94970	25832	69975	94884	19661	72828	00102	66794
44	53976	54914	06990	67245	68350	82948	11398	42878	80287	88267	47363	46634	06541	97809
45	76072	29515	40980	07391	58745	25774	22987	80059	39911	96189	41151	14222	60697	59583
46	90725	52210	83974	29992	65831	38857	50490	83765	55657	14361	31720	57375	56228	41546
47	64364	67412	33339	31926	14883	24413	59744	92351	97473	89286	35931	04110	23726	51900
48	08962	00358	31662	25388	61642	34072	81249	35648	56891	69352	48373	45578	78547	81788
49	95012	68379	93526	70765	10592	04542	76463	54328	02349	17247	28865	14777	62730	92277
50	15664	10493	20492	38391	91132	21999	59516	81652	27195	48223	46751	22923	32261	85653

Source: Abridged from *Handbook of Tables for Probability and Statistics,* 2d ed. Edited by William H. Beyer (Cleveland: The Chemical Rubber Company, 1968). Reproduced by permission of CRC Press, Inc.

TABLE 10 *(continued)*

Line	Column													
	1	2	3	4	5	6	7	8	9	10	11	12	13	14
51	16408	81899	04153	53381	79401	21438	83035	92350	36693	31238	59649	91754	72772	02338
52	18629	81953	05520	91962	04739	13092	97662	24822	94730	06496	35090	04822	86774	98289
53	73115	35101	47498	87637	99016	71060	88824	71013	18735	20286	23153	72924	35165	43040
54	57491	16703	23167	49323	45021	33132	12544	41035	80780	45393	44812	12515	98931	91202
55	30405	83946	23792	14422	15059	45799	22716	19792	09983	74353	68668	30429	70735	25499
56	16631	35006	85900	98275	32388	52390	16815	69298	82732	38480	73817	32523	41961	44437
57	96773	20206	42559	78985	05300	22164	24369	54224	35033	19687	11052	91491	60383	19746
58	38935	64202	14349	82674	66523	44133	00697	35552	35970	19124	63318	29686	03387	59846
59	31624	76384	17403	53363	44167	64486	64758	75366	76554	31601	12614	33072	60332	92325
60	78919	19474	23632	27889	47914	02584	37680	20801	72152	39339	34806	08930	85001	87820
61	03931	33309	57047	74211	63445	17361	62825	39908	05607	91284	68833	25570	38818	46920
62	74426	33278	43972	10119	89917	15665	52872	73823	73144	88662	88970	74492	51805	99378
63	09066	00903	20795	95452	92648	45454	09552	88815	16553	51125	79375	97596	16296	66092
64	42238	12426	87025	14267	20979	04508	64535	31355	86064	29472	47689	05974	52468	16834
65	16153	08002	26504	41744	81959	65642	74240	56302	00033	67107	77510	70625	28725	34191
66	21457	40742	29820	96783	29400	21840	15035	34537	33310	06116	95240	15957	16572	06004
67	21581	57802	02050	89728	17937	37621	47075	42080	97403	48626	68995	43805	33386	21597
68	55612	78095	83197	33732	05810	24813	86902	60397	16489	03264	88525	42786	05269	92532
69	44657	66999	99324	51281	84463	60563	79312	93454	68876	25471	93911	25650	12682	73572
70	91340	84979	46949	81973	37949	61023	43997	15263	80644	43942	89203	71795	99533	50501
71	91227	21199	31935	27022	84067	05462	35216	14486	29891	68607	41867	14951	91696	85065
72	50001	38140	66321	19924	72163	09538	12151	06878	91903	18749	34405	56087	82790	70925
73	65390	05224	72958	28609	81406	39147	25549	48542	42627	45233	57202	94617	23772	07896
74	27504	96131	83944	41575	10573	08619	64482	73923	36152	05184	94142	25299	84387	34925
75	37169	94851	39117	89632	00959	16487	65536	49071	39782	17095	02330	74301	00275	48280
76	11508	70225	51111	38351	19444	66499	71945	05422	13442	78675	84081	66938	93654	59894
77	37449	30362	06694	54690	04052	53115	62757	95348	78662	11163	81651	50245	34971	52924
78	46515	70331	85922	38329	57015	15765	97161	17869	45349	61796	66345	81073	49106	79860
79	30986	81223	42416	58353	21532	30502	32305	86482	05174	07901	54339	58861	74818	46942
80	63798	64995	46583	09785	44160	78128	83991	42865	92520	83531	80377	35909	81250	54238
81	82486	84846	99254	67632	43218	50076	21361	64816	51202	88124	41870	52689	51275	83556
82	21885	32906	92431	09060	64297	51674	64126	62570	26123	05155	59194	52799	28225	85762
83	60336	98782	07408	53458	13564	59089	26445	29789	85205	41001	12535	12133	14645	23541
84	43937	46891	24010	25560	86355	33941	25786	54990	71899	15475	95434	98227	21824	19585
85	97656	63175	89303	16275	07100	92063	21942	18611	47348	20203	18534	03862	78095	50136
86	03299	01221	05418	38982	55758	92237	26759	86367	21216	98442	08303	56613	91511	75928
87	79626	06486	03574	17668	07785	76020	79924	25651	83325	88428	85076	72811	22717	50585
88	85636	68335	47539	03129	65651	11977	02510	26113	99447	68645	34327	15152	55230	93448
89	18039	14367	61337	06177	12143	46609	32989	74014	64708	00533	35398	58408	13261	47908
90	08362	15656	60627	36478	65648	16764	53412	09013	07832	41574	17639	82163	60859	75567
91	79556	29068	04142	16268	15387	12856	66227	38358	22478	73373	88732	09443	82558	05250
92	92608	82674	27072	32534	17075	27698	98204	63863	11951	34648	88022	56148	34925	57031
93	23982	25835	40055	67006	12293	02753	14827	23235	35071	99704	37543	11601	35503	85171
94	09915	96306	05908	97901	28395	14186	00821	80703	70426	75647	76310	88717	37890	40129
95	59037	33300	26695	62247	69927	76123	50842	43834	86654	70959	79725	93872	28117	19233
96	42488	78077	69882	61657	34136	79180	97526	43092	04098	73571	80799	76536	71255	64239
97	46764	86273	63003	93017	31204	36692	40202	35275	57306	55543	53203	18098	47625	88684
98	03237	45430	55417	63282	90816	17349	88298	90183	36600	78406	06216	95787	42579	90730
99	86591	81482	52667	61582	14972	90053	89534	76036	49199	43716	97548	04379	46370	28672
100	38534	01715	94964	87288	65680	43772	39560	12918	86737	62738	19636	51132	25739	56947

TABLE 11(a)
Percentage Points
of the Studentized
Range, $q_{.05}(k, df)$;
Upper 5% Points

						k					
df	2	3	4	5	6	7	8	9	10	11
1	17.97	26.98	32.82	37.08	40.41	43.12	45.40	47.36	49.07	50.59
2	6.08	8.33	9.80	10.88	11.74	12.44	13.03	13.54	13.99	14.39
3	4.50	5.91	6.82	7.50	8.04	8.48	8.85	9.18	9.46	9.72
4	3.93	5.04	5.76	6.29	6.71	7.05	7.35	7.60	7.83	8.03
5	3.64	4.60	5.22	5.67	6.03	6.33	6.58	6.80	6.99	7.17
6	3.46	4.34	4.90	5.30	5.63	5.90	6.12	6.32	6.49	6.65
7	3.34	4.16	4.68	5.06	5.36	5.61	5.82	6.00	6.16	6.30
8	3.26	4.04	4.53	4.89	5.17	5.40	5.60	5.77	5.92	6.05
9	3.20	3.95	4.41	4.76	5.02	5.24	5.43	5.59	5.74	5.87
10	3.15	3.88	4.33	4.65	4.91	5.12	5.30	5.46	5.60	5.72
11	3.11	3.82	4.26	4.57	4.82	5.03	5.20	5.35	5.49	5.61
12	3.08	3.77	4.20	4.51	4.75	4.95	5.12	5.27	5.39	5.51
13	3.06	3.73	4.15	4.45	4.69	4.88	5.05	5.19	5.32	5.43
14	3.03	3.70	4.11	4.41	4.64	4.83	4.99	5.13	5.25	5.36
15	3.01	3.67	4.08	4.37	4.60	4.78	4.94	5.08	5.20	5.31
16	3.00	3.65	4.05	4.33	4.56	4.74	4.90	5.03	5.15	5.26
17	2.98	3.63	4.02	4.30	4.52	4.70	4.86	4.99	5.11	5.21
18	2.97	3.61	4.00	4.28	4.49	4.67	4.82	4.96	5.07	5.17
19	2.96	3.59	3.98	4.25	4.47	4.65	4.79	4.92	5.04	5.14
20	2.95	3.58	3.96	4.23	4.45	4.62	4.77	4.90	5.01	5.11
24	2.92	3.53	3.90	4.17	4.37	4.54	4.68	4.81	4.92	5.01
30	2.89	3.49	3.85	4.10	4.30	4.46	4.60	4.72	4.82	4.92
40	2.86	3.44	3.79	4.04	4.23	4.39	4.52	4.63	4.73	4.82
60	2.83	3.40	3.74	3.98	4.16	4.31	4.44	4.55	4.65	4.73
120	2.80	3.36	3.68	3.92	4.10	4.24	4.36	4.47	4.56	4.64
∞	2.77	3.31	3.63	3.86	4.03	4.17	4.29	4.39	4.47	4.55

TABLE 11(a)
(continued)

				k						
12	13	14	15	16	17	18	19	20	df
51.96	53.20	54.33	55.36	56.32	57.22	58.04	58.83	59.56	1
14.75	15.08	15.38	15.65	15.91	16.14	16.37	16.57	16.77	2
9.95	10.15	10.35	10.52	10.69	10.84	10.98	11.11	11.24	3
8.21	8.37	8.52	8.66	8.79	8.91	9.03	9.13	9.23	4
7.32	7.47	7.60	7.72	7.83	7.93	8.03	8.12	8.21	5
6.79	6.92	7.03	7.14	7.24	7.34	7.43	7.51	7.59	6
6.43	6.55	6.66	6.76	6.85	6.94	7.02	7.10	7.17	7
6.18	6.29	6.39	6.48	6.57	6.65	6.73	6.80	6.87	8
5.98	6.09	6.19	6.28	6.36	6.44	6.51	6.58	6.64	9
5.83	5.93	6.03	6.11	6.19	6.27	6.34	6.40	6.47	10
5.71	5.81	5.90	5.98	6.06	6.13	6.20	6.27	6.33	11
5.61	5.71	5.80	5.88	5.95	6.02	6.09	6.15	6.21	12
5.53	5.63	5.71	5.79	5.86	5.93	5.99	6.05	6.11	13
5.46	5.55	5.64	5.71	5.79	5.85	5.91	5.97	6.03	14
5.40	5.49	5.57	5.65	5.72	5.78	5.85	5.90	5.96	15
5.35	5.44	5.52	5.59	5.66	5.73	5.79	5.84	5.90	16
5.31	5.39	5.47	5.54	5.61	5.67	5.73	5.79	5.84	17
5.27	5.35	5.43	5.50	5.57	5.63	5.69	5.74	5.79	18
5.23	5.31	5.39	5.46	5.53	5.59	5.65	5.70	5.75	19
5.20	5.28	5.36	5.43	5.49	5.55	5.61	5.66	5.71	20
5.10	5.18	5.25	5.32	5.38	5.44	5.49	5.55	5.59	24
5.00	5.08	5.15	5.21	5.27	5.33	5.38	5.43	5.47	30
4.90	4.98	5.04	5.11	5.16	5.22	5.27	5.31	5.36	40
4.81	4.88	4.94	5.00	5.06	5.11	5.15	5.20	5.24	60
4.71	4.78	4.84	4.90	4.95	5.00	5.04	5.09	5.13	120
4.62	4.68	4.74	4.80	4.85	4.89	4.93	4.97	5.01	∞

Source: From *Biometrika Tables for Statisticians,* Vol. 1, 3rd ed., edited by E.S. Pearson and H.O. Hartley (Cambridge University Press, 1966). Reproduced by permission of the Biometrika Trustees.

TABLE 11(b)
Percentage Points
of the Studentized
Range, $q(k, df)$;
Upper 1% Points

df						k				
	2	3	4	5	6	7	8	9	10	11
1	90.03	135.0	164.3	185.6	202.2	215.8	227.2	237.0	245.6	253.2
2	14.04	19.02	22.29	24.72	26.63	28.20	29.53	30.68	31.69	32.59
3	8.26	10.62	12.17	13.33	14.24	15.00	15.64	16.20	16.69	17.13
4	6.51	8.12	9.17	9.96	10.58	11.10	11.55	11.93	12.27	12.57
5	5.70	6.98	7.80	8.42	8.91	9.32	9.67	9.97	10.24	10.48
6	5.24	6.33	7.03	7.56	7.97	8.32	8.61	8.87	9.10	9.30
7	4.95	5.92	6.54	7.01	7.37	7.68	7.94	8.17	8.37	8.55
8	4.75	5.64	6.20	6.62	6.96	7.24	7.47	7.68	7.86	8.03
9	4.60	5.43	5.96	6.35	6.66	6.91	7.13	7.33	7.49	7.65
10	4.48	5.27	5.77	6.14	6.43	6.67	6.87	7.05	7.21	7.36
11	4.39	5.15	5.62	5.97	6.25	6.48	6.67	6.84	6.99	7.13
12	4.32	5.05	5.50	5.84	6.10	6.32	6.51	6.67	6.81	6.94
13	4.26	4.96	5.40	5.73	5.98	6.19	6.37	6.53	6.67	6.79
14	4.21	4.89	5.32	5.63	5.88	6.08	6.26	6.41	6.54	6.66
15	4.17	4.84	5.25	5.56	5.80	5.99	6.16	6.31	6.44	6.55
16	4.13	4.79	5.19	5.49	5.72	5.92	6.08	6.22	6.35	6.46
17	4.10	4.74	5.14	5.43	5.66	5.85	6.01	6.15	6.27	6.38
18	4.07	4.70	5.09	5.38	5.60	5.79	5.94	6.08	6.20	6.31
19	4.05	4.67	5.05	5.33	5.55	5.73	5.89	6.02	6.14	6.25
20	4.02	4.64	5.02	5.29	5.51	5.69	5.84	5.97	6.09	6.19
24	3.96	4.55	4.91	5.17	5.37	5.54	5.69	5.81	5.92	6.02
30	3.89	4.45	4.80	5.05	5.24	5.40	5.54	5.65	5.76	5.85
40	3.82	4.37	4.70	4.93	5.11	5.26	5.39	5.50	5.60	5.69
60	3.76	4.28	4.59	4.82	4.99	5.13	5.25	5.36	5.45	5.53
120	3.70	4.20	4.50	4.71	4.87	5.01	5.12	5.21	5.30	5.37
∞	3.64	4.12	4.40	4.60	4.76	4.88	4.99	5.08	5.16	5.23

TABLE 11(b)
(continued)

12	13	14	15	16	17	18	19	20	df
				k					
260.0	266.2	271.8	277.0	281.8	286.3	290.0	294.3	298.0	1
33.40	34.13	34.81	35.43	36.00	36.53	37.03	37.50	37.95	2
17.53	17.89	18.22	18.52	18.81	19.07	19.32	19.55	19.77	3
12.84	13.09	13.32	13.53	13.73	13.91	14.08	14.24	14.40	4
10.70	10.89	11.08	11.24	11.40	11.55	11.68	11.81	11.93	5
9.48	9.65	9.81	9.95	10.08	10.21	10.32	10.43	10.54	6
8.71	8.86	9.00	9.12	9.24	9.35	9.46	9.55	9.65	7
8.18	8.31	8.44	8.55	8.66	8.76	8.85	8.94	9.03	8
7.78	7.91	8.03	8.13	8.23	8.33	8.41	8.49	8.57	9
7.49	7.60	7.71	7.81	7.91	7.99	8.08	8.15	8.23	10
7.25	7.36	7.46	7.56	7.65	7.73	7.81	7.88	7.95	11
7.06	7.17	7.26	7.36	7.44	7.52	7.59	7.66	7.73	12
6.90	7.01	7.10	7.19	7.27	7.35	7.42	7.48	7.55	13
6.77	6.87	6.96	7.05	7.13	7.20	7.27	7.33	7.39	14
6.66	6.76	6.84	6.93	7.00	7.07	7.14	7.20	7.26	15
6.56	6.66	6.74	6.82	6.90	6.97	7.03	7.09	7.15	16
6.48	6.57	6.66	6.73	6.81	6.87	6.94	7.00	7.05	17
6.41	6.50	6.58	6.65	6.72	6.79	6.85	6.91	6.97	18
6.34	6.43	6.51	6.58	6.65	6.72	6.78	6.84	6.89	19
6.28	6.37	6.45	6.52	6.59	6.65	6.71	6.77	6.82	20
6.11	6.19	6.26	6.33	6.39	6.45	6.51	6.56	6.61	24
5.93	6.01	6.08	6.14	6.20	6.26	6.31	6.36	6.41	30
5.76	5.83	5.90	5.96	6.02	6.07	6.12	6.16	6.21	40
5.60	5.67	5.73	5.78	5.84	5.89	5.93	5.97	6.01	60
5.44	5.50	5.56	5.61	5.66	5.71	5.75	5.79	5.83	120
5.29	5.35	5.40	5.45	5.49	5.54	5.57	5.61	5.65	∞

Answers

to Selected Exercises

Chapter 1

1.1   **a.** the student   **b.** the exam   **c.** the patient   **d.** the plant   **e.** the car

1.3   **a.** discrete   **b.** continuous   **c.** continuous   **d.** discrete

1.5   The population is the set of voter preferences for all voters in the state. Voter preferences may change over time.

1.7   **a.** score on the reading test; quantitative   **b.** the student
     c. the set of scores for all deaf students who hypothetically might take the test

1.9   **a.** a pair of jeans   **b.** the state in which the jeans are produced; qualitative
     e. 8/25   **f.** California
     g. The three states produce roughly the same numbers of jeans.

1.11   **c.** Early information is not very representative of election-day results.

1.13   **a.** no   **b.** the bar chart

1.15   **a.** eight to ten class intervals   **c.** 43/50   **d.** 33/50   **e.** yes

1.17   **b.** .30   **c.** .70   **d.** .30   **e.** relatively symmetric; no

1.21   **b.** centered at 75; two peaks (bimodal)   **c.** Scores are divided into two groups according to student abilities.

1.23   **a.** pie chart, bar chart

1.25   **a.** skewed right; several outliers

1.27   **b.**
```
Stem-and-leaf of Ages     N = 37
  Leaf Unit = 1.0
      2      4 69
      3      5 3
      7      5 6678
     13      6 003344
    (6)      6 567778
     18      7 0111234
     11      7 7889
      7      8 013
      4      8 58
      2      9 00
```
     relatively symmetric   **c.** Kennedy, Garfield, and Lincoln were assassinated.

1.29   **b.** 0.1

1.31   **a.** number of hazardous waste sites (discrete)   **b.** skewed right
     c. size of the state; amount of industrial activity

1.33   **a.** skewed   **b.** symmetric   **c.** symmetric   **d.** symmetric   **e.** skewed   **f.** skewed

1.35   **a.** continuous   **b.** continuous   **c.** discrete   **d.** discrete   **e.** discrete

1.37

```
 7 | 8  9
 8 | 0  1  7
 9 | 0  1  2  4  4  5  6  6  6  8  8
10 | 1  7  9
11 | 2
```

1.39   **a.** skewed right

1.43   **a.** no   **b.** roughly mound-shaped

1.45   **a.** skewed right   **b. c.** yes; large states

1.47   **a.** Pop-vote is skewed right; Pct-vote is relatively symmetric.   **b.** yes
c. Once the size of the state is removed, each state will be measured on an equal basis.

1.49   **d.** horizontal axis is not a true time line

1.51   **c.** the pie chart

1.53   **a.** somewhat mound-shaped   **b.** .2

1.57   **a–b.** skewed right   **c.** Yahoo!, Microsoft, eBay

Chapter 2

2.1   **b.** $\bar{x} = 2$; $m = 1$; mode $= 1$ **c.** skewed

2.3   **a.** 5.8   **b.** 5.5   **c.** 5 and 6

2.5   **a.** slightly skewed right   **c.** $\bar{x} = 1.08$; $m = 1$; mode $= 1$

2.7   2.5 is an average number calculated (or estimated) for all families in a particular category.

2.9   The median, because the distribution is highly skewed to the right.

2.11   **a.** 2.4   **b.** 2.8   **c.** 1.673

2.13   **a.** 3   **b.** 2.125   **c.** $s^2 = 1.2679$; $s = 1.126$

2.15   **a.** $s \approx 1.67$ **b.** $s = 1.75$ **c.** no   **d.** yes   **e.** no

2.17   **a.** approximately .68   **b.** approximately .95
c. approximately .815   **d.** approximately .16

2.19   **a.** $s \approx .20$ **b.** $\bar{x} = .76$; $s = .165$

2.21   **a.** approximately .68   **b.** approximately .95   **c.** approximately .003

2.23   **a.** ≈ 4.5 **b.** ≈ 2.25 **c.** $\bar{x} = 4.586$; $s = 2.892$

2.25   **a.** skewed right   **b.** 0 to 104 days

2.27   **b.** $\bar{x} = 7.729$ **c.** $s = 1.985$

k	$\bar{x} \pm ks$	Actual	Tchebysheff	Empirical Rule
1	(5.744, 9.714)	.71	At least 0	Approx. .68
2	(3.759, 11.699)	.96	At least 3/4	Approx. .95
3	(1.774, 13.684)	1.00	At least 8/9	Approx. .997

2.29   **a–b.** $\bar{x} = 1.4$; $s^2 = 1.4$

2.31   **a.** $\bar{x} = 2.04$; $s = 2.806$

b–c.

k	$\bar{x} \pm ks$	Actual	Tchebysheff	Empirical Rule
1	$(-.766, 4.846)$	.84	At least 0	Approx. .68
2	$(-3.572, 7.652)$	.92	At least 3/4	Approx. .95
3	$(-6.378, 10.458)$	1.00	At least 8/9	Approx. .997

2.33 min $= 0$, $Q_1 = 6$, $m = 10$, $Q_3 = 14$, max $= 19$; IQR $= 8$

2.35 lower and upper fences: -2.25 and 15.25; $x = 22$ is an outlier

2.37 **a.** min $= 1.70$, $Q_1 = 130.5$, $m = 246.5$, $Q_3 = 317.5$, max $= 485$
b. lower and upper fences: -150 and 598
c–d. No, but there are 4 extremely small observations, not identified by the box plot as outliers.

2.39 5 is the 74th percentile for number of pairs of wearable sneakers; 2 is the 39th percentile for number of television sets.

2.41 **a.** skewed right   **b.** $\bar{x} = 5.325$; $m = 3.85$; mean > median implies skewed right
c. lower and upper fences: -8.89 and 19.41; no outliers

2.43 **a.** *Generic:* $m = 26$, $Q_1 = 25$, $Q_3 = 27.25$, IQR $= 2.25$; *Sunmaid:* $m = 26$, $Q_1 = 24$, $Q_3 = 28$, IQR $= 4$
b. *Generic:* lower and upper fences: 21.625 and 30.625; *Sunmaid:* lower and upper fences: 18 and 34
c. yes   **d.** The average size is nearly the same; individual raisin sizes are more variable for Sunmaid raisins.

2.45 **a.** R $= 32.1$ **b.** $s \approx 8.025$ **c.** $s = 7.671$

2.47 $m = 6.35$, $Q_1 = 2.325$, $Q_3 = 12.825$; lower and upper fences: -13.425 and 28.575; one outlier ($x = 32.3$).

2.49 **a, b.**

k	$\bar{x} \pm ks$	Tchebysheff	Empirical Rule
1	$(.16, .18)$	At least 0	Approx. .68
2	$(.15, .19)$	At least 3/4	Approx. .95
3	$(.14, .20)$	At least 8/9	Approx. .997

c. No, distribution of $n = 4$ measurements cannot be mound-shaped.

2.51 68%; 95%

2.53 **a.** $s \approx 7.75$ **b.** $\bar{x} = 59.2$; $s = 10.369$ **c.** $m = 60$, $Q_1 = 51.25$, $Q_3 = 69.75$; lower and upper fences: 23.5 and 97.5; no outliers.

2.55 $\sigma \approx 100$

2.57 **a.** .025   **b.** .84

2.59 **a.** At least 3/4 have between 145 and 205 teachers.   **b.** .16

2.63 **b.** yes   **c.** more than 2 or 3 standard deviations from the mean

2.65 **b.** the sample mean gets smaller   **d.** $5 \le m \le 10$

2.67 **c.** the standard deviation when dividing by $n - 1$ is closer to σ

2.69 **b–c.** skewed left with one outlier to the right of the other observations ($x = 520$)

Chapter 3

3.3 **a.** comparative pie charts; side-by-side or stacked bar charts
c. Proportions spent in all four categories are substantially different for men and women.

3.5   **a.** *Population:* responses to free time question for all parents and children in the United States. *Sample:* responses for the 398 people in the survey.
    b. bivariate data, measuring relationship (qualitative) and response (qualitative)
    c. the number of people who fall into that relationship-opinion category
    d. stacked or side-by-side bar charts

3.7   **b.** As x increases, y increases   **c.** .903   **d.** $y = 3.58 + .815x$; yes

3.9   **b.** As x increases, y decreases   **c.** $-.987$

3.11   **a.** $y = 6.11 + 23.83x$ **c.** \$149.06; no

3.13   **b.** slight positive trend   **c.** $r = .760$

3.15   **b.** The professor's productivity appears to increase, with less time required to write later books; no.

3.17   **a.** the number of working parents (quantitative), the monthly expense for a particular type of expense (quantitative) and the category of expense being recorded (qualitative)
    b. the population of responses for families with two children in Riverside, San Bernardino, Orange and Ventura, California; population
    c. side-by-side bar charts; comparative pie charts
    d. stretch the vertical scale

3.21   **a.** .9108   **b.** $x =$ first weekend gross; $y =$ total gross
    c. $y = 10.06 + 2.987x$ **d.** 99.67 million dollars

3.23   **a.** no   **b.** $r = -.036$; yes
    c. Large cluster in lower left corner shows no apparent relationship; seven to ten states form a cluster with a negative linear trend   **d.** local environmental regulations; population per square mile; geographic region

3.27   **a.** .8544

3.29   **a.** 0.5   **b.** increase   **c.** 2.0; the y-intercept   **d.** 3.25; 4

Chapter 4

4.1   **a.** $\{1, 2, 3, 4, 5, 6\}$ **c.** 1/6
    e. $P(A) = 1/6$; $P(B) = 1/2$; $P(C) = 2/3$: $P(D) = 1/6$; $P(E) = 1/2$; $P(F) = 0$

4.3 $P(E_1) = .45$; $P(E_2) = .15$; $P(E_i) = .05$ for $i = 3, 4, \ldots , 10$

4.5   **a.** $\{NDQ, NDH, NQH, DQH\}$ **b.** 3/4   **c.** 3/4

4.9   **a.** .58   **b.** .14   **c.** .46

4.11   **a.** randomly selecting three people and recording their gender
    b. $\{FFF, FMM, MFM, MMF, MFF, FMF, FFM, MMM\}$
    c. 1/8   **d.** 3/8   **e.** 1/8

4.13   **a.** rank A, B, C   **b.** $\{ABC, ACB, BAC, BCA, CAB, CBA\}$ **d.** 1/3, 1/3

4.15   **a.** .467   **b.** .513   **c.** .533

4.17   80

4.19   **a.** 60   **b.** 3,628,800   **c.** 720   **d.** 20

4.21   6720

4.23   216

4.25   120

4.27   720

4.29   **a.** 140,608   **b.** 132,600   **c.** .00037   **d.** .943

4.31   **a.** 2,598,960   **b.** 4   **c.** .000001539

4.33 $5.720645 \times (10^{12})$

4.35   **a.** 64   **b.** 1/64   **c.** 1/4

4.37   1/56

4.39 $\dfrac{4!(3!)^4}{12!}$

4.41   **a.** 3/5   **b.** 4/5

4.43   **a.** 1   **b.** 1/5   **c.** 1/5

4.45   **a.** 1   **b.** 1   **c.** 1/3   **d.** 0   **e.** 1/3
       f. 0   **g.** 0   **h.** 1   **i.** 5/6

4.47   **a.** .08   **b.** .52

4.49   **a.** .3   **b.** no   **c.** yes

4.51   **a.** no, since $P(A \cap B) \neq 0$ **b.** no, since $P(A) \neq P(A|B)$

4.53   **a.** .14   **b.** .56   **c.** .30

4.57   **a.** P(A) = .9918; P(B) = .0082   **b.** P(A) = .9836; P(B) = .0164

4.59   .05

4.61   **a.** .99   **b.** .01

4.63   **a.** 154/256   **b.** 155/256   **c.** 88/256   **d.** 88/154   **e.** 44/67
       f. 23/35   **g.** 12/101   **h.** 189/256

4.65   **a.** .23   **b.** .6087; .3913

4.67   .38

4.69   .012

4.71   **a.** .6585   **b.** .3415   **c.** left

4.73   .3130

4.75   **a.** $P(D) = .10$; $P(D^C) = .90$; $P(N \mid D^C) = .94$; $P(N \mid D) = .20$
       b. .023   **c.** .023   **d.** .056   **e.** .20
       f. false negative

4.77   **a.** continuous   **b.** continuous   **c.** discrete   **d.** discrete   **e.** continuous

4.79   **a.** .2   **c.** $\mu = 1.9$; $\sigma^2 = 1.29$; $\sigma = 1.136$ **d.** .3   **e.** .9

4.81   1.5

4.83   **a.** {S, FS, FFS, FFFS}   **b.** $p(1) = p(2) = p(3) = p(4) = 1/4$

4.85   **a.** $p(0) = 3/10$; $p(1) = 6/10$; $p(2) = 1/10$

4.87   **a.** .1; .09; .081   **b.** $p(x) = (.9)^{x-1}(.1)$

4.89   **a.** 4.0656   **b.** 4.125   **c.** 3.3186

4.91 $1500

4.93   **a.** $p(x) = (.81)^{x-1}(.19)$ **b.** nonresponse; truthfulness on a sensitive subject

4.95 $2050

4.97   .0713

4.99 $P(A) = 1/2$; $P(B) = 2/3$; $P(A \cap B) = 1/3$; $P(A \cup B) = 5/6$; $P(C) = 1/6$;
       $P(A \cap C) = 0$; $P(A \cup C) = 2/3$

4.101   2/7

4.103 $p(0) = .0256$; $p(1) = .1536$; $p(2) = .3456$; $p(3) = .3456$; $p(4) = .1296$; .4752

4.105   **a.** .4565   **b.** .2530   **c.** .3889

4.107   3/10; 6/10

4.109   **a.** .73   **b.** .27

4.111   .999999

4.113   8

4.115   **a.** .3582   **b.** .4883   **c.** .4467

4.117   **a.** 1/8   **b.** 1/64   **c.** Not necessarily; they could have studied together, and so on.

4.119   **a.** 5/6   **b.** 25/36   **c.** 11/36

4.121   **a.** .8   **b.** .64   **c.** .36

4.123   .0256; .1296

4.125   .2; .1

4.127   **a.** .5182   **b.** .1136   **c.** .7091   **d.** .3906

4.129   **a.** $p(2) = p(12) = 1/36, p(3) = p(11) = 2/36, p(4) = p(10) = 3/36,$
$p(5) = p(9) = 4/36, p(6) = p(8) = 5/36, p(7) = 6/36$

4.131   **a.** $p(0) = .5, p(1) = .5$

Chapter 5

5.1   not binomial; dependent trials; p varies from trial to trial

5.3   **a.** .2965   **b.** .8145   **c.** .1172   **d.** .3670

5.5 $p(0) = .000; p(1) = .002; p(2) = .015; p(3) = .082; p(4) = .246; p(5) = .393;$
$p(6) = .262$

5.7   **a.** .251   **b.** .618   **c.** .367   **d.** .633   **e.** 4   **f.** 1.549

5.9   **a.** .901   **b.** .015   **c.** .002   **d.** .998

5.11   **a.** .748   **b.** .610   **c.** .367   **d.** .966   **e.** .656

5.13   **a.** 1; .99   **b.** 90; 3   **c.** 30; 4.58   **d.** 70; 4.58   **e.** 50; 5

5.15   **a.** .9568   **b.** .957   **c.** .9569   **d.** $\mu = 2; \sigma = 1.342$
e. .7455; .9569; .9977   **f.** yes; yes

5.17   No; the variable is not the number of successes in n trials. Instead, the number of trials
n is variable.

5.19   **a.** 1.000   **b.** .997   **c.** .086

5.21   **a.** .098   **b.** .991   **c.** .098   **d.** .138   **e.** .430   **f.** .902

5.23   **a.** .0081   **b.** .4116   **c.** .2401

5.25   **a.** $\mu = 10$ **b.** 4 to 16
c. If this unlikely value were actually observed, it might be possible that the trials
(fields) are not independent.

5.27   **a.** .0001406   **b.** .0001   **c.** .9999

5.29   **a.** .135335   **b.** .27067   **c.** .593994   **d.** .036089

5.31   **a.** .677   **b.** .6767   **c.** yes

5.33   **a.** .0067   **b.** .1755   **c.** .560

5.35   **a.** .271   **b.** .594   **c.** .406

5.37 $P(x > 5) = .017$; unlikely.

5.39   **a.** .6   **b.** .5143   **c.** .0714

5.41   **a.** $p(0) = .36; p(1) = .48; p(2) = .15; p(3) = .01$ **c.** $\mu = .8, \sigma^2 = .50286$
   d. .99; .99; yes

5.43 $p(0) = .2; p(1) = .6; p(2) = .2$

5.45   **a.** hypergeometric   **b.** .1786   **c.** .01786   **d.** .2857

5.51   **a.** $p(0) = .729; p(1) = .243; p(2) = .027; p(3) = .001$
   c. .3; .520   **d.** .729; .972

5.53   **a.** .234   **b.** .136   **c.** Claim is not unlikely.

5.55   **a.** .228   **b.** no indication that people are more likely to choose middle numbers

5.57   **d.** Either the sample is not random or the 60% figure is too high.

5.59   **a.** 20   **b.** 4   **c.** .006   **d.** Psychiatrist is incorrect.

5.61   **a.** $\mu = 50; \sigma = 6.124$
   b. The value $x = 35$ lies 2.45 standard deviations below the mean. It is somewhat unlikely that the 25% figure is representative of this campus.

5.63   **a.** .5   **b.** $\mu = 12.5; \sigma = 2.5$ **c.** There is a preference for the second design.

5.65   **a.** yes; $n = 10; p = .25$ **b.** .2440   **c.** .0000296
   d. Yes; genetic model is not behaving as expected.

5.67   **a.** yes   **b.** $1/8192 = .00012$

5.69   **a.** hypergeometric, or approximately binomial
   b. Poisson
   c. approximately .85; .72; .61

5.71   **a.** .015625   **b.** .421875   **c.** .25

5.73   **a.** .00006   **b.** .042   **c.** .0207   **d.** .5948   **e.** 1

5.77   **a.** .0176   **b.** .9648   **c.** .9648

Chapter 6

6.1   **a.** .9452   **b.** .9664   **c.** .8159   **d.** 1.0000

6.3   **a.** .6753   **b.** .2401   **c.** .2694   **d.** .0901   **e.** ≈ 0

6.5   **a.** 1.96   **b.** 1.44

6.7   **a.** 1.65   **b.** -1.645

6.9   **a.** 1.28   **b.** 1.645   **c.** 2.05   **d.** 2.33

6.11   **a.** .1596   **b.** .1151   **c.** .1359

6.13   58.3

6.15 $\mu = 8; \sigma = 2$

6.17   **a.** .1949   **b.** .4870   **c.** no
   d. yes; $y = 17$ lies 4.19 standard deviations above the mean

6.19   **a.** .4586   **b.** .0526   **c.** .0170

6.21   .1562; .0012

6.23   **a.** .0475   **b.** .00226   **c.** 29.12 to 40.88   **d.** 38.84

6.25   **a.** .0274   **b.** .3520

6.27   .0475

6.29   63,550

6.31   **a.** yes   **b.** $\mu = 7.5; \sigma = 2.291$ **c.** .6156   **d.** .618

6.33   **a.** .2676   **b.** .3520   **c.** .3208   **d.** .9162

6.35   **a.** .178   **b.** .392

6.37   **a.** .245   **b.** .2483

6.39   **a.** .0869   **b.** .3264   **c.** .0244

6.41   .9441

6.43   **a.** .3594   **b.** They do not consider height when casting their ballot.

6.45   **a.** .0318   **b.** .1814   **c.** .1562
          d. yes; *Pepsi's* market share is higher than claimed.

6.47   **a.** .3227   **b.** .1586

6.49 $z_0 = 0$

6.51 $z_0 = .67$; the 25th and 75th percentiles

6.53   no

6.55   5.065 months

6.57   .0401

6.59   85.36 minutes

6.61   no; $x = 184$ lies only 1.26 standard deviations below the mean.

6.63   7.301 ounces

6.65   **a.** 141   **b.** .0401

6.67   .9474

6.69   .3557

6.71   **a.** $Q_1 = 269.96$; $Q_3 = 286.04$
          b. Yes; $x = 180$ lies 8.17 standard deviations below the mean

6.73   **a.** ≈ 0 **b.** .6026   **c.** Sample is not random; results will be biased.

6.75   **a.** .9544   **b.** .0561

6.77   **a.** $z_0 = -1.96$ **b.** $z_0 = .36$

6.79   **a.** .9651   **b.** .1056   **c.** .0062

6.81   **a.** .0177   **b.** .0178

6.83   **a.** 1.273   **b.** .1016

6.85   .1244 (exact probability = .1236)

Chapter 7

7.1   1/500

7.11   **a.** convenience sample   **b.** Yes, but only if his patients behave like a random sample from the general population.

7.13   **a.** $\mu = 10$; $\sigma/\sqrt{n} = 1.5$
          b. $\mu = 5$; $\sigma/\sqrt{n} = .2$
          c. $\mu = 120$; $\sigma/\sqrt{n} = .3536$

7.15   **c.** .5468

7.17   Increasing the sample size decreases the standard error.

7.19   **b.** a large number of replications

7.23   **a.** .3758   **b.** no

7.25   **a.** 1890; 69.282   **b.** .0559

7.27 **a.** $p = .3$; $SE = .0458$ **b.** $p = .1$; $SE = .015$ **c.** $p = .6$; $SE = .0310$

7.29 **b.** .9198

7.31 **a.** .0099   **b.** .03   **c.** .0458   **d.** .05
e. .0458   **f.** .03   **g.** .0099

7.33 **a.** yes; $p = .46$; $SE = .0498$ **b.** .2119
c. .9513   **d.** The value is unusual because $\hat{p} = .30$ lies 3.21 standard deviations below the mean $p = .46$.

7.35 **a.** normal with mean $p = .3$ and standard deviation .06179
b. .0526   **c.** .2090   **d.** .18 to .42

7.37 **a.** LCL = 150.13; UCL = 161.67

7.39 **a.** LCL = 0; UCL = .090

7.41 **a.** LCL = 8598.7; UCL = 12,905.3

7.43 LCL = .078; UCL = .316

7.45 LCL = .0155; UCL = .0357

7.49 **a.** ≈ 12.5 **b.** .9986   **c.** They are probably correct.

7.51 **c.** no

7.57 **a.** cluster sample   **b.** 1-in-10 systematic sample   **c.** stratified sample
d. 1-in-10 systematic sample   **e.** simple random sample

7.59 **a.** 131.2; 3.677   **b.** yes   **c.** .1515

7.61 **a.** LCL = 0; UCL = .0848   **b.** $\hat{p} > .0848$

7.63 yes

7.67 **a.** 3.5; 1.208

7.69 **a.** 3.5; .854

7.71 **a.** .4938   **b.** .0062   **c.** .0000

Chapter 8

8.3 **a.** .160   **b.** .339   **c.** .438

8.5 **a.** .554   **b.** .175   **c.** .055

8.7 **a.** .179   **b.** .098   **c.** .049   **d.** .031

8.9 **a.** .0588   **b.** .0898   **c.** .098   **d.** .0898   **e.** .0588

8.11 $\hat{p} = .728$; margin of error (MOE) = .029

8.13 $\bar{x} = 39.8$; MOE = 4.768

8.15 $\bar{x} = 7.2\%$; MOE = .776

8.17 **a.** $\hat{p} = .78$; MOE = .026   **b.** no; $p = .5$

8.19 **a.** no   **b.** nothing; no

8.21 **a.** (.797, .883)   **b.** (21.469, 22.331)
c. Intervals constructed in this way enclose the true value of μ 90% of the time in repeated sampling.

8.23 (.846, .908)

8.25 **a.** 3.92   **b.** 2.772   **c.** 1.96

8.27 **a.** 3.29   **b.** 5.16   **c.** The width increases.

8.29 (3.496, 3.904); random sample

8.31   **a.** (.932, 1.088)   **c.** no; $\mu = 1$ is a possible value for the population mean

8.33   **a.** (.106, .166)   **b.** Increase the sample size and/or decrease the confidence level.

8.35   **a.** (4.61, 5.99)   **b.** yes

8.37   (15.463, 36.937)

8.39   **a.** (17.676, 19.324)   **b.** (15.710, 17.290)   **c.** (.858, 3.142)   **d.** yes

8.41   **a.** $\bar{x}_1 - \bar{x}_2 = 2206$; MOE $= 902.08$ **b.** yes

8.43   **a.** (3.333, 16.667)   **b.** (−22.040, −7.960)   **c.** no   **d.** yes; yes

8.45   **a.** (−.203, −.117)   **b.** random and independent samples from binomial distributions

8.47   **a.** (−.221, .149)   **b.** no

8.49   **a.** (.095, .445)   **b.** yes

8.51   (.061, .259)

8.53   **a.** $\mu < 76.63$ **b.** $\mu < 1.89$

8.55 $\mu_1 - \mu_2 < 4$

8.57   505

8.59 $n_1 = n_2 = 1086$

8.61   9604

8.63 $n_1 = n_2 = 360$

8.65   97

8.67 $n_1 = n_2 = 136$

8.69 $n_1 = n_2 = 98$

8.71   **a.** $\bar{x} = 29.1$; MOE $= .9555$ **b.** (28.298, 29.902)   **c.** $\mu > 28.48$ **d.** 234

8.73 $n_1 = n_2 = 224$

8.75   1083

8.77 $n_1 = n_2 = 925$

8.79   **a.** $\hat{p}_W = .5$; $\hat{p}_M = .75$ **b.** $-.313 < \hat{p}_W - \hat{p}_M < -.187$
c. There is a difference in the two proportions.

8.81   (8.087, 11.313)

8.83   97

8.85   (33.41, 34.59)

8.87   **a.** MOE $= .029$ **b.** 6147

8.89   **a.** (.499, .561)   **b.** (.110, .230)   **c.** (.320, .520)

8.91   at least 1825

8.93   .3874; .651

8.95   **a.** (2.837, 3.087)   **b.** 276

8.97   (638.946, 665.054); no

8.99   **b.** widths are the same

8.101   **a.** 9.702   **b.** (746.298, 765.702)   **c.** yes

8.103   **b.** The standard error and the width of the interval decrease.

Chapter 9

9.1   **a.** $z > 2.33$ **b.** $|z| > 1.96$ **c.** $z < -2.33$ **d.** $|z| > 2.58$

9.3   **a.** Do not reject H_0; results are not statistically significant.
      b. Reject H_0; results are highly significant.
      c. Reject H_0; results are statistically significant.

9.5   **a.** .0207   **b.** Reject H_0; results are statistically significant.   **c.** yes

9.7 p-value $= .0644$; do not reject H_0; results are not statistically significant.

9.9   **a.** H_0: $\mu = 1$; H_a: $\mu \neq 1$ **b.** p-value $= .7414$; do not reject H_0
      c. There is no evidence to indicate that the average weight is different from 1 pound.

9.11   **a.** H_0: $\mu = 80$ **b.** H_a: $\mu \neq 80$ **c.** $z = -3.75$; reject H_0

9.13   **a.** $z = -2.31$; p-value $= .0104$; reject H_0 at the 5% level of significance
      b. Average score improvement is less than 110 at the 5% level of significance.
      c. There is no evidence to indicate that the average score improvement is less than 110 at the 1% level of significance.

9.15   no; $z = -1.334$ with p-value $= .0918$; do not reject H_0

9.17   **a.** H_0: $\mu_1 - \mu_2 = 0$; H_a: $\mu_1 - \mu_2 > 0$; one-tailed   **b.** $z = 2.074$; reject H_0

9.19   **a.** $z = -2.26$; p-value $= .0238$; reject H_0 **b.** $(-3.55, -.25)$ **c.** no

9.21   **a.** H_0: $\mu_1 - \mu_2 = 0$; H_a: $\mu_1 - \mu_2 \neq 0$ **b.** yes; $z = 8.77$ **c.** p-value ≈ 0

9.23   **a.** yes; $z = -3.18$; p-value $= .0014$ **b.** $(-3.01, -.71)$; yes

9.25   **a.** H_0: $p = .4$; H_a: $p \neq .4$ **b.** p-value $= .093$; not statistically significant   **c.** no

9.27   **a.** H_0: $p = .6$; H_a: $p \neq .6$ and H_0: $p = .5$; H_a: $p < .5$
      b. no; $z = -.58$ **c.** no; $z = .94$

9.29   **a.** H_0: $p = 2/3$ **b.** H_a: $p > 2/3$ **c.** yes; $z = 4.6$ **d.** p-value $< .0002$

9.31   no; $z = -.90$

9.33   no; $z = -1.55$ with p-value $= .1212$

9.35   **a.** H_0: $p_1 - p_2 = 0$; H_a: $p_1 - p_2 < 0$ **b.** one-tailed
      c. do not reject H_0; $z = -.84$

9.37   **a.** yes; $z = -2.40$ **b.** $(-.43, -.05)$

9.39   Do not reject H_0; $z = -.39$; there is insufficient evidence to indicate a difference in the two population proportions.

9.43   Reject H_0; $z = 3.14$ with p-value $= .0008$; researcher's conclusions are confirmed.

9.47   The power increases.

9.49   **a.** p-value $< .0002$ **b.** Reject H_0; $z = 4.47$

9.51   **a.** H_0: $\mu = 7.5$; H_a: $\mu < 7.5$ **b.** one-tailed   **d.** $z = -5.477$; reject H_0

9.53   **a.** H_0: $\mu_1 - \mu_2 = 0$; H_a: $\mu_1 - \mu_2 \neq 0$ **b.** two-tailed   **c.** no; $z = -.954$

9.55   no; do not reject H_0; $z = 1.684$

9.57   **a.** p-value $= .0668$ **b.** do not reject H_0

9.59   yes; $z = 4$; reject H_0

9.61   yes; $z = 4.00$

9.63   **a.** yes; $z = 4.33$ **b.** $(7.12, 18.88)$

9.65   **a.** yes; $z = -3.33$ **b.** no; $z = 1$ **c.** no

9.67   **a.** H_0: $\mu = 54$; H_a: $\mu \neq 54$ **b.** $z = -1.331$ **c.** .1832
      d. do not reject H_0 **e.** no

9.69   **a.** .7422   **b.** .9783   **c.** power increases

Chapter 10

10.1   **a.** 2.015   **b.** 2.306   **c.** 1.330   **d.** 1.96

10.3   **a.** $.02 < p\text{-value} < .05$ **b.** $p\text{-value} < .005$
          c. $p\text{-value} > .20$ **d.** $p\text{-value} < .005$

10.5   **a.** $\bar{x} = 7.05$; $s = .4994$ **b.** (6.537, 7.563)   **c.** Reject H_0; $t = -2.849$
          d. No, because the hypothesis test was one-tailed.

10.7   no; $t = -1.195$

10.9   yes; $t = -3.044$

10.11 (3.652, 3.912)

10.13 **a.** Reject H_0; $t = -4.31$ **b.** (23.23, 29.97)
          c. The pretreatment mean looks smaller than the other two means.

10.17 **a.** 3.775   **b.** 21.2258

10.19 **a.** H_0: $\mu_1 - \mu_2 = 0$; H_a: $\mu_1 - \mu_2 \neq 0$ **b.** $|t| > 2.771$ **c.** $t = 2.795$
          d. $p\text{-value} < .01$ **e.** Reject H_0

10.21 **a.** Yes; larger s^2/smaller $s^2 = 1.36$ **b.** $t = .06$ with $p\text{-value} = .95$
          c. 19.1844   **d.** Do not reject H_0 **e.** $(-5.223, 5.503)$; yes

10.23 **a.** No; $t = -1.16$ **b.** $p\text{-value} = .26$ **c.** yes; larger s^2/smaller $s^2 = 2.88$

10.25 **a.** No; larger s^2/smaller $s^2 = 16.22$ **b.** Yes; $t = -2.412$; $.02 < p\text{-value} < .05$

10.27 **a.** yes   **b.** no; larger s^2/smaller $s^2 = 3.72$
          c. Do not reject H_0; $t = .10$ with $p\text{-value} > .20$

10.29 Reject H_0; $t = 2.372$ with $.02 < p\text{-value} < .05$

10.31 62 pairs

10.33 **a.** Do not reject H_0; $t = 1.177$ **b.** $p\text{-value} > .20$ **c.** $(-.082, .202)$
          d. random sample from normal distribution

10.35 **a.** Do not reject H_0; $t = 1.984$; $(-7.28, 170.94)$
          b. Reject H_0; $t = 2.307$; (6.867, 208.433)
          c. Reject H_0; $t = 4.38$ **d.** $(-1.6, 8.2)$; yes

10.37 **b.** Yes; $t = 9.150$ with $p\text{-value} < .01$ **c.** (80.472, 133.328)

10.39 **a.** yes; $t = -4.326$; reject H_0 **b.** $(-2.594, -.566)$

10.41 **a.** yes; $t = 2.82$; reject H_0 **b.** 1.488   **d.** yes

10.43 **b.** $t = 12.014$; yes

10.45 (.190, .685)

10.47 reject H_0; $\chi^2 = 22.449$

10.49 **a.** no; $t = -.232$ **b.** yes; $\chi^2 = 20.18$

10.51 **a.** no   **b.** yes; $z = 3.262$

10.53 no; $\chi^2 = 29.433$

10.55 (.667, 4.896)

10.57 $F = 1.059$ with $p\text{-value} > .20$; do not reject H_0: $\sigma_1^2 = \sigma_2^2$

10.59 (1.544, 4.003)

10.61 Rest: $F = 1.03$ with $p\text{-value} > .20$; 80% maximal O_2: $F = 2.01$ with $p\text{-value} > .20$;
          maximal O_2: $F = 14.29$ with $p\text{-value} < .01$; use the unpooled t test for maximal O_2.

10.67 (9.860, 12.740)

10.69 yes, $t = 5.985$; reject H_0; (28.375, 33.625)

10.71 yes, $F = 3.268$

10.73 72

10.75 (22.578, 26.796)

10.77 $(-10.246, -2.354)$; yes

10.79 **a.** yes **b.** $F = 19.516$; there is a difference in the population variances.

10.81 **a.** random independent samples from normal distributions with equal variances; no **b.** yes; $t = 3.237$ with p-value $< .01$ **c.** yes; $t = 60.36$ with p-value $< .01$

10.83 no; $t = 2.2$ with p-value $> .10$

10.85 no; $t = 1.586$ with p-value $> .10$

10.87 no, $t = -1.712$

10.89 Unpaired: $(-1.69, .19)$; paired: $(-1.49, -.01)$; paired interval is slightly narrower

10.91 **a.** Unpaired: (.212, .306); paired: (.209, .309) **b.** no

10.93 **a.** no, $t = 2.571$ **b.** (.000, .020)

10.95 **a.** two-tailed; $H_a: \sigma_1^2 \neq \sigma_2^2$ **b.** lower-tailed; $H_a: \sigma_1^2 < \sigma_2^2$
c. upper-tailed; $H_a: \sigma_1^2 > \sigma_2^2$

10.97 **a.** no, $\chi^2 = 7.008$ **b.** (.185, 2.465)

10.99 reject H_0; $t = 2.425$; drug increases average reaction time

10.101 yes, $t = -2.945$

10.103 no

10.105 no, $t = 1.86$ with p-value $= .112$

10.107 Use pooled t test; $t = -1.82$ with p-value $> .10$; results are nonsignificant.

10.109 **a.** $t > 1.8$ **b.** $|t| > 2.37$ **c.** $t < -2.6$

10.113 Do not reject H_0; $t = -1.438$ with p-value $= .1782$

10.115 yes; $t = -3.33$ with p-value $= .0030$

Chapter 11

11.1

Source	df
Treatments	5
Error	54
Total	59

11.3 **a.** (2.731, 3.409) **b.** (.07, 1.03)

11.5 **a.**

Source	df	SS	MS	F
Treatments	3	339.8	113.267	16.98
Error	20	133.4	6.67	
Total	23			

b. $\mathrm{df}_1 = 3$ and $\mathrm{df}_2 = 20$ **c.** $F > 3.10$ **d.** yes, $F = 16.98$
e. p-value $< .005$; yes

11.7 **a.** CM $= 103.142857$; Total SS $= 26.8571$
b. SST $= 14.5071$; MST $= 7.2536$
c. SSE $= 12.3500$; MSE $= 1.1227$

d. Analysis of Variance

```
Source  DF     SS    MS     F     P
Trts     2  14.51  7.25  6.46  0.014
Error   11  12.35  1.12
Total   13  26.86
```

f. $F = 6.46$; reject H_0 with $.01 < p\text{-value} < .025$

11.9 **a.** (1.95, 3.65)   **b.** (.27, 2.83)

11.11 **a.** (67.86, 84.14)   **b.** (55.82, 76.84)

c. $(-3.629, 22.963)$ **d.** no, they are not independent

11.13 **a.** Each observation is the mean length of ten leaves.
b. yes, $F = 57.38$ with $p\text{-value} = .000$ **c.** reject H_0; $t = 12.09$ **d.** (1.810, 2.924)

11.15
```
Analysis of Variance for Percent
Source  DF        SS          MS        F      P
Method   2  0.0000041  0.0000021  16.38  0.000
Error   12  0.0000015  0.0000001
Total   14  0.0000056
```

11.17 sample means must be independent; equal sample sizes

11.19 **a.** $1.878s$ **b.** $2.1567s$

11.21 $\bar{x}_1$ $\bar{x}_2$ $\bar{x}_3$ $\bar{x}_4$

11.23 **a.** no; $F = .60$ with $p\text{-value} = .562$ **b.** no differences

11.25

Source	df	SS	MS	F
Treatments	2	11.4	5.70	4.01
Blocks	5	17.1	3.42	2.41
Error	10	14.2	1.42	
Total	17	42.7		

11.27 $(-3.833, -.767)$

11.29 **a.** yes; $F = 19.19$ **b.** yes; $F = 135.75$ **c.** $\bar{x}_1$ $\bar{x}_3$ $\bar{x}_4$ $\bar{x}_2$
d. $(-5.332, -2.668)$ **e.** yes

11.31 **a.** 7   **b.** 7   **c.** 5   **e.** yes; $F = 9.68$ **f.** yes; $F = 8.59$

11.33 **Two-way ANOVA: y versus Blocks, Chemicals**
```
Analysis of Variance for y
Source    DF      SS       MS       F       P
Blocks     2  7.1717  3.5858  40.21  0.000
Chemical   3  5.2000  1.7333  19.44  0.002
Error      6  0.5350  0.0892
Total     11 12.9067
```

11.35 **a.** yes; $F = 10.06$ **b.** yes; $F = 10.88$ **c.** $\omega = 4.35$ **d.** (1.12, 5.88)

11.37 **Two-way ANOVA: Cost versus Estimator, Job**
```
Analysis of Variance for Cost
Source      DF      SS       MS       F       P
Estimator    2  10.862   5.431   7.20  0.025
Job          3  37.607  12.536  16.61  0.003
Error        6   4.528   0.755
Total       11  52.997
```

11.39 **a.** 20   **b.** 60   **c.**

Source	df
A	3
B	4
AB	12
Error	40
Total	59

11.41 $(-1.11, 5.11)$

11.43 **a.** strong interaction present   **b.** $F = 37.85$ with p-value $= .000$; yes   **d.** no

11.45 **b.** yes   **c.** Since the interaction is significant, attention should be focused on means for the individual factor-level combinations.
d. Training: $.05 < p$-value $< .10$; ability: p-value $< .005$; interaction: $.01 < p$-value $< .025$

11.47 **a.** 2×4 factorial; students; gender at two levels, schools at four levels
c. no; $F = 1.19$
e. main effect for schools is significant; $F = 27.75$; Tukey's $\omega = 82.63$

11.49 significant differences between treatments A and C, B and C, C and E and D and E

11.51 **a.** significant difference in treatment means; $F = 27.78$ **b.** Tukey's $\omega = .190$
c. yes; $F = 6.59$

11.53 **One-way ANOVA: Sales versus Program**
Analysis of Variance for Sales

Source	DF	SS	MS	F	P
Program	3	1385.8	461.9	9.84	0.000
Error	23	1079.4	46.9		
Total	26	2465.2			

11.55 **a.** no; $F = 1.40$ **b.** p-value $> .10$ **c.** yes; $F = 6.51$ **d.** yes; $F = 7.37$

11.57 **a.** 2×3 factorial experiment   **b.** no; $F = .45$ with p-value $= .642$
d. $(-22.56, -5.84)$

11.59 **a.** randomized block design

b. **Two-way ANOVA: Total versus Week, Store**
Analysis of Variance for Total

Source	DF	SS	MS	F	P
Week	3	571.7	190.6	8.27	0.003
Store	4	684.6	171.2	7.43	0.003
Error	12	276.4	23.0		
Total	19	1532.7			

c. yes; $F = 7.43$ **d.** $\omega = 10.81$

11.61 **a.** randomized block; blocks are types of crash, treatments are cars.
b. yes; $F = 5.72$ **c.** no; $F = 2.11$ **d.** $\omega = 1298.12$

Chapter 12

12.1 y-intercept $= 1$, slope $= 2$

12.3 $y = 3 - x$

12.7 **a.** $\hat{y} = 6.00 - .557x$ **c.** 4.05
d. Analysis of Variance

Source	DF	SS	MS
Regression	1	5.4321	5.4321
Residual Error	4	0.1429	0.0357
Total	5	5.5750	

12.9 **a.** $S_{xx} = 21066.82$; $S_{yy} = .374798$; $S_{xy} = 88.80003$
b. $\hat{y} = .0187 + .00422x$ **d.** $.44$

e. Analysis of Variance

Source	DF	SS	MS
Regression	1	0.37431	0.37431
Residual Error	7	0.00049	0.00007
Total	8	0.37480	

12.11   **a.** y = API; x = ELL   **b.** yes   **c.** $\hat{y}$ = 731.277 − 3.040x **d.** yes

12.13   **a.** yes, t = 5.20   **b.** F = 27.00   **c.** $t_{.025}$ = 3.182; $F_{.05}$ = 10.13

12.15   **a.** yes, F = 152.10 with p-value = .000   **b.** r^2 = .974

12.17   **a.** y = cost, x = distance   **b.** $\hat{y}$ = 128.58 + .12715x **d.** t = 6.09; r^2 = .699

12.19   **a.** yes; t = 3.79 and F = 14.37 with p-value = .005   **b.** no
c. r^2 = .642   **d.** MSE = 5.025   **e.** (.186, .764)

12.21   plot residuals versus fit; random scatter of points, free of patterns

12.23   no

12.25   **a.** slight curve   **b.** 95.9% of overall variation explained by the straight-line model
c. strong curvilinear pattern indicates relationship may be curvilinear

12.27   **a.** (4.6006, 5.1708)   **b.** (4.2886, 5.4829)   **c.** x = 8; extrapolation

12.29   **a.** slight curve   **b.** 95.7% of overall variation explained by the straight-line model
c. pattern indicates relationship may be curvilinear

12.31   **a.** $\hat{y}$ = 110.87 + 26.514x **b.** yes; t = 3.36 with p-value = .028   **c.** .738
d. (211.1, 381.9); prediction outside the experimental region

12.35   **a.** positive   **b.** r = .9487; r^2 = .9000

12.37   **b.** r = .982   **c.** 96.5%

12.39   **a.** positive   **b.** r = .760; yes, t = 2.615

12.41   yes; t = 3.158 with p-value < .01

12.43   **a.** correlation analysis   **b.** r = .981

12.45   **a.** yes   **b.** $\hat{y}$ = 80.85 + 270.82x **c.** yes; t = 3.96 with p-value = .003
d. (112.1, 157.9)

12.47   **a.** r = .980   **b.** r^2 = .961   **c.** $\hat{y}$ = 21.9 + 15.0x
d. variance is not constant for all x

12.49   **Regression Analysis: API versus ELL**
The regression equation is
API = 731 − 3.04 ELL

Predictor	Coef	StDev	T	P
Constant	731.28	22.81	32.06	0.000
ELL	−3.0399	0.7551	−4.03	0.007

S = 33.72   R-Sq = 73.0%   R-Sq(adj) = 68.5%

Analysis of Variance

Source	DF	SS	MS	F	P
Regression	1	18422	18422	16.21	0.007
Residual Error	6	6820	1137		
Total	7	25242			

12.51   **a.** no; t = 2.066 with p-value > .05   **b.** r^2 = .299

12.53   No; variance is not constant for all x.

12.55   **a.** weak negative relationship   **b.** r^2 = .052
c. $\hat{y}$ = 3372.0 − 155.3x; no, t = −.96   **d.** no

12.57   **a.** y-intercept = 3; slope = −0.5

Chapter 13

13.1   **b.** parallel lines

13.3   **a.** yes, F = 57.44 with p-value < .005   **b.** R^2 = .94

13.5   **a.** quadratic   **b.** $R^2 = .815$; relatively good fit
c. yes, $F = 37.37$ with p-value $= .000$

13.7   **a.** $b_0 = 10.5638$ **b.** yes, $t = 15.20$ with p-value $= .000$

13.9   **b.** $t = -8.11$ with p-value $= .000$; reject H_0: $\beta_2 = 0$ in favor of H_a: $\beta_2 < 0$

13.11   **a.** $R^2 = .9955$ **b.** R^2(adj) $= 99.3\%$ **c.** The quadratic model fits slightly better.

13.13   **a.** Use variables x_2, x_3, and x_4 **b.** no

13.15   **a.** quantitative   **b.** quantitative   **c.** qualitative; $x_1 = 1$ if plant B, 0 otherwise; $x_2 = 1$ if plant C, 0 otherwise   **d.** quantitative
e. qualitative; $x_1 = 1$ if day shift, 0 if night shift

13.17   **a.** x_2 **b.** $\hat{y} = 12.6 + 3.9x_2^2$ or $\hat{y} = 13.14 - 1.2x_2 + 3.9x_2^2$

13.19   **a.** $y = \beta_0 + \beta_1 x_1 + \beta_2 x_2 + \beta_3 x_1 x_2 + \epsilon$ with $x_2 = 1$ if cucumber, 0 if cotton
c. No, the test for interaction yields $t = .63$ with p-value $= .533$.   **d.** yes

13.21   **a.** $\hat{y} = 8.585 + 3.8208x - 0.21663x^2$ **b.** $R^2 = .944$ **c.** yes; $F = 33.44$
d. yes; $t = -4.93$ with p-value $= .008$ **e.** no

13.23   **b.** $\hat{y} = 4.10 + 1.04x_1 + 3.53x_2 + 4.76x_3 - 0.43x_1 x_2 - 0.08x_1 x_3$
c. yes; $t = -2.61$ with p-value $= .028$
d. no; $F = 3.86$; consider eliminating the interaction terms.

13.25   **a.** $y = \beta_0 + \beta_1 x_1 + \beta_2 x_2 + \beta_3 x_1^2 + \beta_4 x_1 x_2 + \beta_5 x_1^2 x_2 + \epsilon$
b. $F = 25.85$; $R^2 = .768$ **c.** $\hat{y} = 4.51 + 6.394x_1 + .1318x_1^2$
d. $\hat{y} = -46.34 + 23.458x_1 - .3707x_1^2$ **e.** no; $t = .78$ with p-value $= .439$

13.27   **a.** curvilinear relationship   **b.** $y = \beta_0 + \beta_1 x + \beta_2 x^2 + \epsilon$
c. $\hat{y} = 4114749 - 4113.4x + 1.02804x^2$ **d.** yes; $F = 542.11$ with p-value $= .000$
e. $R^2 = .997$; very good fit

Chapter 14

14.3   **a.** $X^2 > 12.59$ **b.** $X^2 > 21.666$ **c.** $X^2 > 29.8194$ **d.** $X^2 > 5.99$

14.5   **a.** H_0: $p_1 = p_2 = p_3 = p_4 = p_5 = 1/5$ **b.** 4   **c.** 9.4877
d. $X^2 = 8.00$ **e.** Do not reject H_0.

14.7   yes, $X^2 = 24.48$; drivers tend to prefer the inside lanes.

14.9   no, $X^2 = 3.63$

14.11   no, $X^2 = 13.58$

14.13 $X^2 = 29.24$; it appears that there are more brown and yellow and fewer of the other colors than reported by the Mars Company.

14.15   8

14.17   reject H_0, $X^2 = 18.352$ with p-value $= .000$

14.19   **a.** yes; $X^2 = 7.267$ **b.** $.025 < p$-value $< .05$

14.21   **a.** yes; reject H_0; $X^2 = 20.937$ **b.** no; $X^2 = 1.255$

14.23   **a.** $X^2 = 10.597$ **b.** $X^2 > 13.2767$ **c.** Do not reject H_0.
d. $.025 < p$-value $< .05$

14.25   yes; $X^2 = 24.31$

14.27   **a.** Each income category represents a multinomial population in which we measure education levels   **b.** yes; $X^2 = 19.172$

14.29   no, $X^2 = 4.4$ with p-value $> .10$

14.31   no, $X^2 = 1.89$ with p-value $> .10$

14.33   **a.** yes; $z = 9.233$ **b.** yes; $X^2 = 85.2488$

14.37   yes; $X^2 = 43.737$

14.39   **a.** reject H_0; $X^2 = 18.527$ **b.** reject H_0; $z = 4.304$; yes

14.43   yes, $X^2 = 7.488$ with $.005 < p\text{-value} < .01$

14.45   yes, $X^2 = 6.190$ with $.025 < p\text{-value} < .05$; (.347, .483)

14.47   **a.** no; $X^2 = 3.259$ with $p\text{-value} = .196$ **b.** no; $X^2 = 1.054$ with $p\text{-value} = .788$
c. yes

14.49   no, $X^2 = 3.953$ with $p\text{-value} = .139$

14.51   **a.** do not reject H_0; $X^2 = 3.660$ with $p\text{-value} = .454$; yes

14.53   **a.** yes; $X^2 = 11.690$ with $p\text{-value} = .003$ **b.** The susceptibility to a cold seems to
decrease as the number of relationships increases.

14.55   **a.** 27.69   **b.** 5.99

14.57   consumers have a preference; $X^2 = 18.5$ with $p\text{-value} = .0001$

14.61   no; $X^2 = 2.87$ with $p\text{-value} = .2378$

Chapter 15

15.1   **a.** T_1^* **b.** $T \le 31$ **c.** $T \le 27$

15.3   **a.** H_0: population distributions are identical; H_a: population 1 shifted to the left of
population 2.
b. $T_1 = 16$; $T_1^* = 39$ **c.** $T \le 19$ **d.** yes; reject H_0

15.5   do not reject H_0; $z = -1.59$

15.7   do not reject H_0; $T = 102$

15.9   yes; reject H_0; $T = 45$

15.11   yes; reject H_0; $T = 44$

15.13   **b.** $\alpha = .002, .007, .022, .054, .115$

15.15   One-tailed: **n = 10:** $\alpha = .001, .011, .055$; **n = 15:** $\alpha = .004, .018, .059$;
n = 20: $\alpha = .001, .006, .021, .058, .132$; two-tailed: **n = 10:** $\alpha = .002, .022, .110$;
n = 15: $\alpha = .008, .036, .118$; **n = 20:** $\alpha = .002, .012, .042, .116$

15.17   **a.** H_0: $p = \frac{1}{2}$; H_a: $p \ne \frac{1}{2}$; rejection region: $\{0, 1, 7, 8\}$; $x = 6$;
do not reject H_0 at $\alpha = .07$; $p\text{-value} = .290$

15.19 $z = 3.15$; reject H_0

15.21   **b.** $T = \min\{T^+, T^-\}$ **c.** $T \le 137$ **d.** Do not reject H_0.

15.23   Do not reject H_0; $z = -.34$.

15.25   **a.** Reject H_0; $T = 1.5$ **b.** Results do not agree.

15.27   **a.** no; $T = 6.5$

15.29   **a.** Do not reject H_0; $x = 8$ **b.** Do not reject H_0; $T = 14.5$.

15.31   **a.** paired difference test, sign test, Wilcoxon signed-rank test
b. reject H_0 with both tests; $x = 0$ and $T = 0$

15.33   yes, $H = 13.90$

15.35   **a.** no; $H = 2.63$ **b.** $p\text{-value} > .10$ **c.** $p\text{-value} > .10$

15.37   no; $H = 2.54$ with $p\text{-value} > .10$

15.39   **a.** Reject H_0; $F_r = 21.19$.   **b.** $p\text{-value} < .005$

d. $F = 75.43$ **e.** p-value $< .005$ **f.** Results are identical.

15.41 **a.** Do not reject H_0; $F_r = 5.81$. **b.** $.05 < p$-value $< .10$

15.43 **a.** $r_s \geq .425$ **b.** $r_s \geq .601$

15.45 **a.** $|r_s| \geq .400$ **b.** $|r_s| \geq .526$

15.47 **a.** $-.593$ **b.** yes

15.49 **a.** $r_s = .811$ **b.** yes

15.51 yes

15.53 yes, $r_s = .9118$

15.55 **a.** Do not reject H_0; $x = 2$ **b.** Do not reject H_0; $t = -1.646$

15.57 **a.** Do not reject H_0; $x = 7$ **b.** Do not reject H_0; $x = 7$

15.59 Do not reject H_0 with the Wilcoxon rank sum test ($T = 77$) or the paired difference test ($t = .30$).

15.61 Do not reject H_0 using the sign test ($x = 2$); no

15.63 yes; $r_s = -.845$

15.65 reject H_0; $T = 14$

15.67 **a.** Reject H_0; $F_r = 20.13$ **b.** The results are the same.

15.69 **a.** Reject H_0; $H = 9.08$ **b.** $.025 < p$-value $< .05$ **c.** The results are the same.

15.71 **a.** no **b.** significant differences among the responses to the three rates of application; $F_r = 10.33$ with p-value $= .006$.

Index

Credits

This page constitutes an extension of the copyright page. We have made every effort to trace the ownership of all copyrighted material and to secure permission from copyright holders. In the event of any question arising as to the use of any material, we will be pleased to make the necessary corrections in future printings. Thanks are due to the following authors, publishers, and agents for permission to use the material indicated.

Introduction: 1: Excerpt from "As Race Narrows, Voters See Little Difference between Bush and Gore on Leadership Qualities and Effectiveness of their Policies," by D. W. Moore and F. Newport, Gallup Poll, November 24, 2000. Copyright © 2000 Gallup Organization. Reprinted by permission. 1–2: Excerpt from "Great Xpectations," by M. Hornblower, Time, June 9, 1997. Copyright © 1997 Time, Inc. Reprinted by permission.

Chapter 1. 29, 30, 31, 43, 44, 45: Exercises 1.27, 1.29, 1.31, 1.41, 1.42, 1.45 & 1.46 From *The World Almanac and Book of Facts 2002*, by W. A. McGeveran, Jr., ed. Copyright © 2002 St. Martin's Press. Reprinted by permission. 46: Exercise 1.49 from September 18, 2001. Copyright © 2001 Gallup. Reprinted by permission of the Gallup Organization. 48: Exercise 1.57 from "Top 50 Digital Media/Web Properties of July 2001." Copyright © 2001 Jupiter Media Metrix. Reprinted by permission.

Chapter 3. 117–118: Case Study "Dishwashers" Copyright 1995 by Consumers Union of U.S., Inc., Yonkers, NY 10703-1057. Adapted with permission from Consumer Reports, August 1995. Although this material originally appeared in Consumer Reports, the selective adaptation and resulting conclusions presented are those of the author(s) and are not sanctioned or endorsed in any way by Consumers Union, the publisher of Consumer Reports.

ter 6. 227: Exercise 6.45 Reprinted by permission of PepsiCo., Inc.

ter 7. 270: Exercise 7.64 adapted from J. Hackl, *Journal of Quality Technology*, , 1991. Reprinted by permission.

ter 8. 283: Exercise 8.14 reprinted with permission from Science News, the ly newsmagazine of Science, copyright 1989 by Science Service, Inc. 298, 299: cises 8.39, 8.42 from "Performance Assessment of a Standards-Based High School gy Curriculum," by W. Leonard, B. Speziale, and J. Pernick, *The American Biol- Teacher*, 2001, 63(5), 310–316. Reprinted by permission of National Association of